P9-DBS-716

SOMATOFORM DISORDERS

Somatization Disorder
Conversion Disorder
Hypochondriasis
Body Dysmorphic Disorder
Pain Disorder

FACTITIOUS DISORDERS

Factitious Disorder

DISSOCIATIVE DISORDERS

Dissociative Amnesia
Dissociative Fugue
Dissociative Identity Disorder (Multiple Personality Disorder)
Depersonalization Disorder

SEXUAL AND GENDER IDENTITY DISORDERS

Sexual Dysfunctions
Sexual Desire Disorders: Hypoactive Sexual Desire Disorder; Sexual Aversion Disorder / Sexual Arousal Disorders: Female Sexual Arousal Disorder; Male Erectile Disorder / Orgasmic Disorders: Female Orgasmic Disorder (Inhibited Female Orgasm); Male Orgasmic Disorder (Inhibited Male Orgasm); Premature Ejaculation / Sexual Pain Disorders: Dyspareunia; Vaginismus / Sexual Dysfunction Due to a General Medical Condition / Substance-induced Sexual Dysfunction

Paraphilias
Exhibitionism / Fetishism / Frotteurism / Pedophilia / Sexual Masochism / Sexual Sadism / Voyeurism / Transvestic Fetishism

Gender Identity Disorders
Gender Identity Disorder: in Children; in Adolescents or Adults (Transsexualism)

EATING DISORDERS

Anorexia Nervosa
Bulimia Nervosa

SLEEP DISORDERS

Primary Sleep Disorders
Dyssomnias: Primary Insomnia; Primary Hypersomnia; Narcolepsy; Breathing-related Sleep Disorder; Circadian Rhythym Sleep Disorder (Sleep-Wake Schedule Disorder) / Parasomnias; Nightmare Disorder (Dream Anxiety Disorder); Sleep Terror Disorder; Sleepwalking Disorder / Sleep Disorders Related to Another Mental Disorder

Sleep Disorder Due to a General Medical Condition
Substance-induced Sleep Disorder

IMPULSE CONTROL DISORDERS NOT ELSEWHERE CLASSIFIED

Intermittent Explosive Disorder
Kleptomania
Pyromania
Pathological Gambling
Trichotillomania

ADJUSTMENT DISORDERS

Adjustment Disorder
With Anxiety / with Depressed Mood / with Disturbance of Conduct / with Mixed Disturbance of Emotions and Conduct / with Mixed Anxiety and Depressed Mood

Axis II

Mental Retardation
Mild Mental Retardation / Moderate Mental Retardation / Severe Mental Retardation / Profound Mental Retardation

PERSONALITY DISORDERS

Paranoid Personality Disorder
Schizoid Personality Disorder
Schizotypal Personality Disorder
Antisocial Personality Disorder
Borderline Personality Disorder
Histrionic Personality Disorder
Narcissistic Personality Disorder
Avoidant Personality Disorder
Dependent Personality Disorder
Obsessive-Compulsive Personality Disorder

OTHER CONDITIONS THAT MAY BE A FOCUS OF CLINICAL ATTENTION

Psychological Factors Affecting Medical Condition
Medication-induced Movement Disorders
Relational Problems
Relational Problem Related to a Mental Disorder or General Medical Condition / Parent-Child Relational Problem / Partner Relational Problem / Sibling Relational Problem

Problems Related to Abuse or Neglect
Physical Abuse of Child / Sexual Abuse of Child / Neglect of Child / Physical Abuse of Adult / Sexual Abuse of Adult

Additional Conditions That May Be a Focus of Clincal Attention
Bereavement / Borderline Intellectual Functioning / Academic Problem / Occupational Problem / Child or Adolescent Antisocial Behavior / Adult Antisocial Behavior / Malingering / Phase of Life Problem / Noncompliance with Treatment / Identity Problem / Religious or Spiritual Problem / Acculturation Problem / Age-related Cognitive Decline

ABNORMAL PSYCHOLOGY

SECOND CANADIAN EDITION

GERALD C. DAVISON
University of Southern California

JOHN M. NEALE
State University of New York at Stony Brook

KIRK R. BLANKSTEIN
University of Toronto

GORDON L. FLETT
York University

JOHN WILEY & SONS CANADA, LTD.

Copyright © 2005 by John Wiley & Sons Canada, Ltd
Copyright 2001 by John Wiley & Sons Inc. All rights reserved. No part of this work covered by the copyrights herein may be reproduced or used in any form or by any means—graphic, electronic, or mechanical—without the prior written permission of the publisher.

Any request for photocopying, recording, taping or inclusion in information storage and retrieval systems of any part of this book shall be directed to The Canadian Copyright Licensing Agency (Access Copyright). For an Access Copyright licence, visit www.accesscopyright.ca or call toll-free, 1-800-893-5777.

Care has been taken to trace ownership of copyright material contained in this text. The publishers will gladly receive any information that will enable them to rectify any erroneous reference or credit line in subsequent editions.

National Library of Canada Cataloguing in Publication Data
Abnormal psychology / Gerald C. Davison ... [et al.]. -- 2nd Canadian ed.
Includes bibliographical references and index.
ISBN 0-470-83388-2
1. Psychology, Pathological--Textbooks. I. Davison, Gerald C.
RC454.A255 2004 616.89 C2004-900063-2

Author Photo Credits
v: Photo of Gerald Davison courtesy Irene Fertik
v: Photo of John Neale courtesy John Neale
v: Photo of Kirk Blankstein courtesy Kirk Blankstein
vi: Photo of Gordon Flett courtesy Hayley Flett

Production Credits
Acquisitions Editor: Michael Valerio
Editorial Manager: Karen Staudinger
Publishing Services Director: Karen Bryan
Publishing Services Manager: Ian Koo
Marketing Manager: Isabelle Moreau
New Media Editor: Elsa Passera
Developmental Editor: Amanjeet Chauhan
Design: Interrobang Graphic Design Inc.
Cover Image: Marian Dale Scott, Canadian 1906-1993, Tenants c. 1939/40, Oil on board 63.6 x 42.0 cm, Art Gallery of Ontario, Toronto, Gift from J.S. McLean Collection, by Canada Packers Inc., 1990
Printing & Binding: Tri-Graphic Printing Limited

Printed and bound in Canada
10 9 8 7 6 5 4 3 2 1

John Wiley & Sons Canada, Ltd.
6045 Freemont Blvd.
Mississauga, Ontario L5R 4J3
Visit our website at: www.wiley.com/canada

Dedicated To

Mary, Karen, Andrea, Brett, P. P., M. E. J., and Diesel
(K.B)

Kathy, Hayley, and Alison
(G.F.)

About the Authors

Gerald C. Davison (B.A., Harvard, 1961; Fulbright Scholar, University of Freiburg, West Germany, 1961–1962; Ph.D., Stanford, 1965) is Professor of Psychology and Chair of the Department of Psychology at the University of Southern California. He is a Fellow of the American Psychological Association and has served on the Executive Committee of the Division of Clinical Psychology, on the Board of Scientific Affairs, on the Committee on Scientific Awards, and on the Council of Representatives. He is also a Charter Fellow of the American Psychological Society, on the Advisory Board of the Society for the Exploration of Psychotherapy Integration, a past president of the Association for Advancement of Behavior Therapy, and served as Publications Coordinator of that organization. He served two terms on the National Academy of Sciences/National Research Council Committee on Techniques for the Enhancement of Human Performance. He will serve from 2005 to 2007 as President of the Society of Clinical Psychology, which represents APA Division 12.

In 1988 Dr. Davison received an outstanding achievement award from APA's Board of Social and Ethical Responsibility; in 1989 he was the recipient of the Albert S. Raubenheimer Distinguished Faculty Award from USC's College of Letters, Arts, and Sciences; in 1993 he won the Associates Award for Excellence in Teaching, a university-wide prize; in 1995 he received the Distinguished Psychologist Award from the Los Angeles County Psychological Association; and in 1997 he given the Outstanding Educator Award of the Association for Advancement of Behavior Therapy (AABT). More recently, in 2003, AABT awarded him the prestigious Lifetime Achievement Award.

John M. Neale is Professor Emeritus of Psychology at the State University of New York at Stony Brook, where he regularly taught the undergraduate course in abnormal psychology. He received his B.A. from the University of Toronto and his M.A. and Ph.D. from Vanderbilt University. His internship in clinical psychology was as a Fellow in Medical Psychology at the Langley Porter Neuropsychiatric Institute. In 1975 he was a Visiting Fellow at the Institute of Psychiatry, London, England. In 1974 he won the American Psychological Association's Early Career Award for his research on cognitive processes in schizophrenia. In 1991 he won a Distinguished Scientist Award from the American Psychological Association's Society for a Science of Clinical Psychology.

Kirk R. Blankstein is a Professor of Psychology at the University of Toronto at Mississauga (UTM). He received his Honours B.A. in Psychology from McMaster University and his M.A. and Ph.D. in Clinical Psychology from the University of Waterloo. He completed his internship at Duke University Medical Center in 1970. His passion is teaching undergraduate students and training future psychologists. He began his teaching career as an Introductory Psychology instructor and although he has taught over 20 different undergraduate and graduate courses, he is primarily responsible for the abnormal psychology part of the program. He currently teaches introduction to abnormal psychology, courses on adult disorders and disorders of children, and a fourth-year special topics in abnormal psychology course. He is cross-appointed to the Forensic Science Program where he teaches students about psychopaths and serial killers. He is a recipient of the UTM Teaching Excellence Award.

Professor Blankstein enjoys enlivening his lectures with tongue-in-cheek references to himself and his family, using their names in association with illustrative cases and examples, and in test and exam questions. Students quickly determined that the famous, infamous, Mr., Mrs., Dr., Prof., etc. Barkley was actually his beloved Miniature Schnauzer—Barkley Blankstein! He is currently "breaking in" a new special teaching assistant, a Cockapoo named Professor Diesel. Professor Blankstein is a recipient of the UTM Teaching Excellence Award and in 2003 was recognized as an "Exceptional Teacher" in celebration of "175 Years of Great Teaching" at the University of Toronto.

Dr. Blankstein combines his research interests with his interest in teaching. He initiated the undergraduate Thesis Course at UTM (celebrating its 25th year in 2002), and has served as its Coordinator for many years. Almost 50 of his publications are with undergraduate students, many of whom have gone on to distinguished careers as professional psychologists, physicians, social workers, lawyers, criminologists, one High Commissioner, and an Ontario Court Judge. Dr. Blankstein's research focuses on the psychological problems of young people, especially anxiety, depression, and somatic distress. He has conducted research in diverse areas, including early work on the applications of biofeedback, the assessment and treatment of test anxiety. More recently, he has conducted research on moderators and mediators (such as stress, coping, and social support) of the link between cognitive-personality vulnerability factors (such as perfectionism) and negative adaptational outcomes. Besides his numerous articles in professional journals and many invited book chapters, Professor Blankstein co-edited a series of volumes on communication and affect, and serves as a regular reviewer for numerous professional journals.

Gordon L. Flett is a Professor of Psychology at York University in Toronto. He has served as Director of Undergraduate Studies in the Department of Psychology at York University, and he received the Outstanding Teaching Award from the Faculty of Arts at York University in 1993 and again in 1997. Dr. Flett has taught courses in abnormal psychology, introduction to personality, and personality theory and behavioural disorders at the undergraduate level, as well as courses in personality theory and research and in the self-concept at the graduate level. He received his B.Sc., M.A., and Ph.D. from the University of Toronto, and he began his appointment at York University in 1987.

In 2004, Dr. Flett was awarded a Tier I Canada Research Chair in Personality and Health. In 1999, Dr. Flett received the Dean's Award for Outstanding Research from the Faculty of Arts at York University and in 1996, he was recognized by the American Psychological Society as one of the top 25 scholars in psychology, based on the number of publications over a five-year period.

His research interests include the role of personality factors in depression, as well as the continuity of depression, and the interpersonal aspects of anxiety. One current research focus is the role of personality factors in postpartum adjustment among new mothers and fathers. He also investigates depression and suicide in various age groups, including adolescents and the elderly.

Dr. Flett is perhaps most recognized for his seminal contributions to research and theory on the role of perfectionism in psychopathology. His collaborative work with Dr. Paul Hewitt (UBC) has helped establish that perfectionism is multidimensional with salient interpersonal components that contribute to personal and interpersonal maladjustment. Their work on perfectionism has received widespread national and international attention and has been the subject of numerous media stories, including coverage on CTV, CNN, and the BBC.

Dr. Flett has published over 100 journal articles and chapters as well as collaborating on the first academic book on perfectionism, published in 2002. His work with Dr. Hewitt on perfectionism has led to the creation of the Multidimensional Perfectionism Scale, the Child-Adolescent Perfectionism Scale, the Perfectionism Cognitions Inventory, and the Perfectionistic Self-Presentation Scale. Dr. Flett is also the co-creator of the newly developed Endler Multidimensional Anxiety Scales (EMAS) – Social Anxiety Scales.

In addition to his academic interests, Dr. Flett has been involved actively in the school system. Dr. Flett served for many years as the chair of the school council at Middlebury Public School in Mississauga, Ontario, and he was the spokesperson for the Parents of Peel, an advocacy group for parents interested in improving and protecting public education. In 1999, his civic contributions were acknowledged when Dr. Flett was awarded the City of Mississauga Certificate of Recognition for "Outstanding Commitment to the Community."

Preface

It is remarkable that more than one million students thus far have learned about the field of abnormal psychology using various editions of Davison and Neale's *Abnormal Psychology*. This classic text has gone through many changes during the last 30 years, but it has always maintained its balance and blend of the clinical and the empirical/experimental, its use of paradigms as an organizing principle, and its effort to engage the reader in the problem-solving done by clinicians and scientists. The publication in 2002 of the first edition of Davison, Neale, Blankstein & Flett, *Abnormal Psychology*, Canadian Edition meant that Canadian students could now benefit from the structure and principles of the classic text but within the context of extensive Canadian content that highlighted the unique aspects of the people of Canada.

This blend of the Davison and Neale approach with material pertinent to Canadians has met with critical acclaim and has been widely appreciated by instructors and their students. This same approach has been retained in the second edition. However, in response to feedback from instructors, the content has been thoroughly updated and revised from the first edition to make this text even more relevant and engaging for today's student.

GOALS OF THE BOOK

Our main goal in writing *Abnormal Psychology*, Second Canadian Edition was to build upon the strengths of a classic text and present abnormal psychology from a Canadian perspective. They are as follows:

A Scientific, Clinical Approach We share Davison and Neale's strong commitment to a scientific approach and their desire to encourage readers to think critically and consider the merits of our own and others' points of view. We believe we have maintained a fair and comprehensive presentation of the major alternative conceptualizations in contemporary psychopathology.

Paradigms as an Organizing Principle One of the reasons we have used the Davison text over many years and sought to use it as a base for our Canadian text is that it has always been consistent with our orientation toward abnormal psychology and with our teaching philosophy. A recurrent theme in the book is the importance of major points of view or, to use Kuhn's (1962) phrase, "paradigms." Our experience in teaching undergraduates has made us very much aware of the importance of making explicit the unspoken assumptions underlying any quest for knowledge. In our handling of the paradigms, we have tried to make their premises clear. Long after specific facts are forgotten, the student should retain a grasp of the basic problems in the field of psychopathology and understand that the answers one arrives at are constrained by the questions one poses and the methods employed to ask those questions. Throughout the book we discuss four major paradigms: psychoanalytic, learning (behavioural), cognitive, and biological (neuroscientific). When therapy is discussed, we also describe the humanistic and existential paradigm.

An Authoritative, Contemporary Approach We hope that *Abnormal Psychology*, Second Canadian Edition maintains its reputation as one of the most current, authoritative overviews of the theories and research in psychopathology and intervention. It maintains the widely praised scientific clinical approach that blends the clinical and empirical/experimental, as the authors examine each disorder from multiple perspectives. New findings in various fields have been incorporated to ensure that this text is an accurate source of contemporary information.

We have tried to present glimpses of possible answers to two primary questions: What causes psychopathology? Which treatments are most effective in preventing or reducing psychological suffering? We tried to not only present theories and research in psychopathology and intervention, but also to convey some of the intellectual excitement that is associated with the search for answers to some of life's most puzzling questions.

NEW TO THIS EDITION

Preparation for the new edition began by conducting a comprehensive survey of current users of the text. We have been responsive to their insightful feedback without diverging from the approach and framework used historically by Davison and Neale. The main suggestions were to re-organize some textual material to increase readability and to update content to take into account new research and developments since the publication of the first edition. Also, consistent with requests made by some of the reviewers, new instructor resources have been created to further assist in the teaching of this dynamic and challenging subject. Thus, extensive revisions and improvements have been made to current resources. Key additions and changes to the book are as follows.

CONTEMPORARY FOCUS

- Over 250 new Canadian references from 2002–2004 have been integrated throughout the text, as well as many other new, international references. This helps ensure that novel findings of importance are clearly reflected in the book.
- Extensive chapter changes based on research have improved topic coverage in chapters, such as in Chapter 7 "Somatoform and Dissociative Disorders," Chapter 11 "Schizophrenia" and Chapter 15 "Disorders of Childhood."
- New description and illustration of the biopsychosocial paradigm in general, along with applications to conduct disorder and depression in children in Chapter 15.

CONTENT REVISION

- Chapters 1 and 2 have been restructured and reformatted to improve readability.
- Content areas have been strengthened. The biological perspective has been updated and expanded, including an expanded focus on neuropsychological assessment and research.
- Revision of Chapter 18 material on legal issues was guided by a thorough review and expert input from the Honourable Justice Richard Schneider of Ontario. Additions include an analysis of the Bill C-30 provisions for dealing with mentally disordered accused persons, and an updated list of landmark legal cases in Canada involving mental health issues.

CANADIAN PERSPECTIVES

- New Canadian Perspectives box in Chapter 4 on cognitive event-related potentials in neuropsychological assessment.
- Updated Canadian Perspectives 3.1 to include new Canadian research on gambling and Canadian Perspectives 12.1 to include new statistics on drinking in Canadian students.
- New Canadian Perspectives box in Chapter 18 entitled "A Beautiful Mind in Canada?" on the Scott Starson case.

FOCUS ON DISCOVERY

- Focus on Discovery 3.2 updated to include new Canadian clinical vignette case studies and Kirmayer's analysis of DSM-IV-TR, "Outline For Cultural Formulation."
- New research added to Focus on Discovery Box 9.1 "To Diet or Not to Diet."
- Updated Focus on Discovery 14.1 about John/Joan from Winnipeg.
- New Focus on Discovery 17.1 entitled "Consensus beliefs about researcher's psychotherapy beliefs."

CANADIAN CONTRIBUTIONS

- Updated Canadian Contributions 12.1 on G. Alan Marlatt and Harm Reduction Therapy.
- New Canadian Contributions 15.5 on Richard Tremblay and the GRIP Unit.
- New Canadian Contributions 16.1 on Charles Morin and the Treatment of Insomnia in Older Adults.
- New Canadian Psychotherapy Case Study by Greenberg opens Chapter 17.

SUPPLEMENTARY MATERIALS

- New CBC videos have been compiled to accompany *Abnormal Psychology*, Second Canadian Edition.
- The *Handbook of Selected DSM-IV-TR Criteria* will be packaged at no additional cost with every *Abnormal Psychology*, Second Canadian Edition textbook. This handy guide lists 30 selected DSM-IV-TR criteria to help as a reference to some of the disorders mentioned in the text. Further, there are two case studies at the end of the booklet that help show the reader how the DSM criteria are used in real-life situations.
- Existing supplements (Instructor's Manual, PowerPoint Slides, Study Guide) have been thoroughly revised. Most notably, the test bank accompanying the book has been significantly enhanced by a comprehensive review of the suitability of existing questions and the addition of hundreds of new questions.
- An updated Glossary has been integrated into this text.

ORGANIZATION OF THE TEXT

In Part 1 (Chapters 1–5), we place the field in historical context, present the concept of paradigms in science, describe the major paradigms in psychopathology and intervention, discuss the role of cultural factors in a Canadian setting, introduce our readers to Canada's mental health care system, review the fourth edition of the Diagnostic and Statistical Manual of Mental Disorders (DSM-IV), discuss critically its validity and reliability, provide an overview of major approaches and techniques in clinical assessment, and then describe the major research methods of the field.

Specific disorders and their treatment are discussed in Parts 2 and 3 (Chapters 6–16). Chapter 16 on aging provides comprehensive coverage of this important topic from a uniquely Canadian perspective.

The final section, Part 4, consists of Chapters 17 and 18. Chapter 17 discusses process and outcome research on treatment and controversial issues surrounding the therapy enterprise. In Chapter 18, legal and ethical issues are discussed and extensive "Canadian content" is provided. This closing chapter is devoted to an in-depth study of the complex interplay between scientific findings and theories, on the one hand, and the role of ethics and the law, on the other. A core issue in this regard is the dialectical tension between what science can tell us and the proper use of science in controlling the everyday lives of people.

Throughout the book we have included considerable material on cultural factors in the study of psychopathology and intervention, as well as discussion of the different ways abnormal behaviour is conceptualized in cultures other than our own. For example, we examine in-depth the ways that DSM-IV sensitizes clinicians and researchers to the role of culture in shaping abnormal behaviour, as well as the ways psychological abnormality is manifested in different parts of the world. However, a unique feature of this Canadian adaptation is our focus on how cultural factors are reflected in our Canadian setting, and we address content and issues that are uniquely Canadian. For example, we present a portrait of Canada as a multicultural country (including French Canadians, Canada's Aboriginal peoples, and those born whose first language is neither English nor French), and discuss the social policy and mental health implications of our cultural diversity. We also summarize the origins of mental health problems among Canada's Aboriginal people and discuss the issue of a possible bias in the assessment of intelligence in Aboriginal children. Consistent with this focus on our Native Canadians, we also examine the high rates of suicide and inhalant abuse among Aboriginal children. Other examples of the role of the Canadian cultural mosaic can be found throughout the book. For example, in Chapter 4 on assessment we address issues related to Canadian standardization and validation of psychological tests, including tests for use with French Canadians.

FEATURES OF THIS BOOK

In addition to the content and organization, a variety of pedagogical features support the approach of this text. These features were introduced in the first edition and are designed to make it easier for students to master and enjoy the material.

Canadian Focus Boxes

There are three types of boxes that focus solely on placing the material in a Canadian context and on highlighting past and current practices in the treatment of abnormal psychology in Canada and the research contributions Canadians have made in the field. They are: Canadian Perspectives, Canadian Clinic Focus, and Canadian Contributions.

Focus on Discovery Boxes

There are many in-depth discussions of selected topics encased in Focus boxes throughout the book. This feature allows us to involve the reader in topics that are sometimes very specialized, in a way that does not detract from the flow of the regular text. Sometimes a Focus box expands on a point in the text; sometimes it deals with an entirely separate but relevant issue, often a controversial one; often it presents material of particular interest to the Canadian student. Reading these boxes with care will deepen understanding of the subject matter.

Chapter-Opening Cases

The syndrome chapters, 6 through 16, open with extended case illustrations. These accounts provide a clinical context for the theories and research that occupy most of our attention in the chapter and help make vivid the real-life implications of the empirical work of psychopathologists and clinicians.

In-Text Cases

Many more case examples are provided throughout the chapters in order to further illustrate some of the concepts. Many of the chapter-opening and in-text cases are actual Canadian cases, and excerpts of several new cases have been added, including the case of David Adams Richards in Chapter 12 and new Canadian case examples of sexual disorders in Chapter 14. Also included are Canadian case examples of people with obsessions and compulsions (see Chapter 6) and hypochondriasis (Chapter 7).

Chapter Summaries

A summary appears at the end of each chapter. We suggest that the student read it before beginning the chapter itself in order to get a good sense of what lies ahead. Rereading the summary after completing the chapter itself will enhance the student's understanding and provide an immediate sense of what has been learned in just one reading of the chapter.

Key Terms

When an important term is introduced, it is boldfaced and defined or discussed immediately. Most such terms appear again later in the book, in which case they will not be highlighted in this way. All of these terms are listed after each chapter summary as key terms. The page number on which the term is defined appears in this list.

DSM-IV Table

The endpapers of the book contain a summary of the current psychiatric nomenclature found in the fourth edition of the *Diagnostic and Statistical Manual of Mental Disorders*, known as DSM-IV. This provides a handy guide to where particular disorders appear in the "official" taxonomy or classification. We make considerable use of DSM-IV, though in a selective and sometimes critical vein.

Sometimes we find it more effective to discuss theory and research on a particular problem in a way that is different from DSM's conceptualization.

REFERENCES

Our commitment to current and forward-looking scholarship is reflected in the inclusion of more than 4600 references, with over 250 published since the first edition. We have also included many important Canadian references. Recent Canadian references (since 1997) are highlighted with the authors' names appearing in bold.

ACKNOWLEDGMENTS

It is a pleasure to acknowledge the contributions of a number of colleagues who helped with their valuable comments and feedback in the writing of the first and second Canadian editions. We would like to acknowledge a number of our colleagues whose thoughtful comments and expert feedback helped us in writing the second Canadian edition. They are:

Paul Avery—Capilano College

Monica Baehr—Mount Royal College

Kimberley A. Clow—University of Western Ontario

John Conklin—Camosun College

Teresa DiCicco—Trent University

David J.A. Dozois—University of Western Ontario

Dawn McBride—Zayed University

Traci McFarlane—University of Toronto

Arthur Perlini—Algoma University College

Stephen Porter—Dalhousie University

Neil Rector—University of Toronto

Lorne Sexton—University of Manitoba

Tracy Vaillancourt—McMaster University

Anne Vernon—Mount Royal College

Margo C. Watt—St. Francis Xavier University

Many thanks to the staff at John Wiley and Sons Canada, Ltd. for their ongoing enthusiastic support of this project. Members of our "team" at Wiley who we would like to thank include John Horne, Publisher, and Karen Staudinger, Editorial Manager, both of whom have shown their continuing faith in this project over the years. We extend a special thank you to our Acquisitions Editor, Michael Valerio for overseeing all aspects of this project from start to finish. We particularly appreciate Michael's patience, professionalism, and determination to produce the best possible book and supplementary materials. We also thank Amanjeet Chauhan, our Developmental Editor, for her tireless efforts and superb ability to decipher and eloquently rephrase what we were trying to say. We also offer our gratitude to Karen Bryan, Publishing Services Director, for all of her efforts; Elsa Passera, New Media Editor, for her work on the website; Isabelle Moreau, Marketing Manager; and of course all the sales representatives who brought the text to you. The editorial contributions of Jane Affleck, Jennifer Howse, and Judith Turnbull were also appreciated.

Special thanks to John Conklin (Camosun College), Marnin Heisel (University of Rochester), Traci McFarlane (University of Toronto), Tracy Vaillancourt (McMaster University), and Monica Baehr (Mount Royal College) who contributed to the related supplements.

We would also like to thank the many authors who graciously provided us with preprints that described their research; this was a great help to us as we wrote the manuscript. These people are too numerous to name, but you know who you are! We would also like to thank a number of scholars who provided us with valuable assistance and advice, including Martin Antony, Marnin Heisel, Gail McVey, Patricia Pliner, Zindel Segal, Mary Lou Smith, Anne-Marie Wall, Mark Watson, and Konstantine Zakzanis. A very special thanks is owed to the Honourable Justice Richard Schneider for his willingness to thoroughly review the material in Chapter 18 and point out the required revisions. We would also like to thank the students in Kirk Blankstein's abnormal psychology courses for their feedback and suggestions for revisions. We would also like to express our continuing gratitude to Hal Harder, who served as Developmental Editor for the first edition. Both his suggestions as well as some of his photos are still reflected clearly in the second edition.

We would be remiss if we did not thank our respective families for their endless support and encouragement, even when we started to get overly absorbed in this text. This book has been a "labour of love," but, as always, we recognize that love begins and ends at home. Thank you Karen and Kathy, for your patience and understanding, and for reminding us that there is much more to life than writing books.

Finally, as was the case with the first edition, suggestions and comments from users of this book are appreciated. We have striven to produce an error-free text, but if anything has slipped through the variety of checks undertaken, please let us know so that corrections can be made to subsequent printings.

Kirk Blankstein
Gordon Flett

September, 2004

Brief Table of Contents

Contents

Canadian Perspectives, Canadian Clinic Focus, Canadian Contributions and Focus on Discovery Boxes

chapter 1

Introduction: Definitional and Historical Considerations and Canada's Mental Health System

We are all born mad. Some remain so.
— Samuel Beckett, *Waiting for Godot, II*

All of us are mad. If it weren't for the fact every one of us is slightly abnormal,
there wouldn't be any point of giving each person a separate name.
— Uggo Betti, *The Fugitive 2*

Progressive destigmatization of mental illness may be reflected by public funding for care, research, and education which is proportionate to the prevalence and the morbidity engendered by mental illnesses—a day we are nowhere near. This change will require a concerted partnership between the profession and the public—to reduce fear and ignorance, and to promote hope, compassion, and understanding.
— Paul E. Garfinkel, president and CEO, and David S. Goldbloom, physician-in-chief, of the Centre for Addiction and Mental Health, Toronto (2000, pp. 164–165).

Emily Carr 1871-1945, *Western Forest*, c.1931
oil on canvas, 128.3 x 91.8 cm, ART GALLERY OF ONTARIO, TORONTO
Purchase, 1939

BRETT'S CHILDHOOD

SLUMPING in a comfortable leather chair, J. Brett Barkley (not his real name), a 35-year-old police officer, looked skeptically at his therapist as he struggled to relate a series of problems. His recent inability to maintain an erection when making love to his wife was the immediate reason for his seeking therapy, but Brett recounted a host of other difficulties, some dating from his childhood but most originating during the previous several years.

Brett did not have a happy childhood. His mother died suddenly when he was only 6, and for the next 10 years he lived either with his father or with a maternal aunt. His father drank heavily and the man's moods were extremely variable; he had even been hospitalized with a diagnosis of manic-depressive psychosis. His father's income was so irregular that he seldom paid bills on time and could only afford to live in run-down neighbourhoods. At times Brett's father was totally incapable of caring for himself, let alone for his son. Brett would then spend weeks with his aunt in a nearby suburb.

Despite these apparent handicaps, Brett completed high school, qualified for a student loan, and entered the university near his home. He was able to support himself by waiting tables at a small restaurant. His psychological problems began to concern him at this time. He often became profoundly depressed for no apparent reason, and these bouts of sadness were sometimes followed by periods of manic elation. He was greatly troubled by his lack of control over these mood swings, for he had observed this same pattern in his alcoholic father. He also felt an acute self-consciousness with people who he felt had authority over him—his boss, his professors, and even some of his classmates. Brett was especially sensitive about his clothes, which were old and worn compared with those of his peers.

Brett first saw his future wife on the opening day of classes in his junior year. When the slender young woman moved to her seat with grace and self-assurance, his were not the only eyes that followed her. Brett spent the rest of that semester watching her from afar. Then one day, as they and the other students were leaving class, they bumped into each other quite by accident, and her warmth and charm emboldened him to ask her to join him for some coffee. When she said yes, he almost wished she had not.

Amazingly enough, as he saw it, they fell in love and were married before the end of his senior year. Brett could never quite believe that his charming wife really cared for him. As the years wore on, his doubts about himself and about her feelings toward him continued to grow.

He had hoped to enter law school—both his grades and his scores on the law-school boards made these plans a possibility—but decided instead to enter the police academy. As he later told his therapist, he had doubts about his intellectual abilities and felt increasing uneasiness in situations in which he felt himself being evaluated. College seminars had become unbearable for him in his last year in college, and he had hopes that the badge and uniform of a police officer would give him the instant respect that he seemed incapable of earning on his own.

To help him get through the academy, his wife quit college after her junior year, despite Brett's pleas, and sought a secretarial job. He felt she was far brighter than he and saw no reason why she should sacrifice her potential to help him make his way in life. But he recognized the fiscal realities and grudgingly accepted her financial support.

The police academy proved to be even more stressful than college. Brett's mood swings, though less frequent, still troubled him. And like his father, now confined to a state mental hospital, he drank to ease his psychological pain. He felt that his instructors considered him a fool when he had difficulty speaking up in front of the class, but he made it through the rigours of the academy and was assigned to foot patrol in one of the wealthier sections of the city.

Several years later, he found himself in even greater turmoil. Now 32 years old, with a fairly secure job that paid reasonably well, he began to think of starting a family. His wife wanted this as well, and it was at this time that his problems with erectile dysfunction began. He thought at first it was the alcohol—he was drinking at least six ounces of bourbon most nights—but soon he wondered whether he was actually avoiding the responsibility of having a child. Later he began to doubt that his wife found him attractive and desirable. The more understanding and patient she was about his sometimes frantic efforts to consummate sex with her, the less manly he felt. The problems in bed spread to other areas of their lives. The less often they made love, the more suspicious he was of his wife, for she had become even more beautiful and vibrant as she entered her thirties. She had also been promoted to the position of administrative assistant at the law firm where she worked and she would mention long, martini-filled lunches with her boss.

The impetus for contacting the therapist was an ugly argument with his wife one evening when she came home late from work. Brett had been agitated for several days, nightly consuming almost a bottle of bourbon to combat his fear that he was losing control. Already very drunk by the time his wife walked in the door on that final evening, he attacked her both verbally and physically about her alleged infidelity. In her own anger and fear, she questioned his masculinity in striking a woman and taunted him about their unsatisfying lovemaking. Brett stormed out, spent the night at a local bar, and the next day pulled himself together enough to seek professional help.

Every day of our lives we try to understand other people. Acquiring insight into what we consider normal, expected behaviour is difficult enough; understanding human behaviour that is beyond the normal range, such as the behaviour of the police officer just described, is even more difficult.

This book deals with the whole range of abnormalities, their description, causes, and treatment. As you will see, the human mind remains elusive; we know with certainty much less about our field than we would like. As we approach the study of psychopathology, the field concerned with the nature and development of abnormal behaviour, thoughts, and feelings, we do well to keep in mind that the subject offers few hard and fast answers. Even so, the study of psychopathology is no less worthwhile because of its ambiguities. The kinds of questions asked, rather than the specific answers to those questions, constitute the essence of the field.

Another challenge we face in studying abnormal psychology is the need to remain objective. Our subject matter, human behaviour, is personal and powerfully affecting, making objectivity difficult but no less necessary. The disturbing effects of abnormal behaviour intrude on our own lives. Who has not experienced irrational thoughts, fantasies, and feelings? Who has not felt profound sadness, even depression, that is more extreme than circumstances can explain? Many of you will have known someone, a friend or perhaps a relative, whose behaviour was upsetting and impossible to fathom, and realize how frustrating and frightening it is to try to help a person suffering psychological difficulties. Even if you have had no personal experience with the extremes of abnormal behaviour, you have probably been affected by reports in the news of the terrifying actions of individuals with a history of mental instability.

This feeling of familiarity with the subject matter adds to its intrinsic fascination—undergraduate courses in abnormal psychology are among the most popular in psychology departments and indeed in the entire college curriculum—but it has one distinct disadvantage. All of us bring to our study preconceived notions of what the subject matter is. We have developed certain ways of thinking and talking about behaviour, certain words and concepts that somehow seem to fit. For example, we may believe that a useful way to study fear is to focus on the immediate experience of fear; this is known as the phenomenological approach. It may be one way of viewing fear, but it is not the only way.

As behavioural scientists, we have to grapple with the difference between what we may feel is the appropriate way to talk about human behaviour and experience and what may be a more productive way of defining it in order to study and learn about it. For example, while most people would speak of a "feeling of terror," we might be more inclined to use a phrase such as "fear response of great magnitude." In doing so we would not be playing verbal games; the concepts and verbal labels we use in the scientific study of abnormal behaviour must be free of the subjective feelings of appropriateness ordinarily attached to certain human phenomena. As you read this book and try to understand the mental disorders it discusses, you will be asked to adopt frames of reference different from those to which you are accustomed, and indeed different from those we ourselves use when we are not wearing our professional hats.

The case study at the beginning of this chapter is open to a wide range of interpretations. No doubt you have some ideas about how J. Brett Barkley's problems developed, what his primary difficulties are, and perhaps even how you might try to help him. We know of no greater intellectual or emotional challenge than deciding both how to conceptualize the life of a person with psychological problems and how best to treat him or her. In Chapter 2, we will refer again to the case of J. Brett Barkley to illustrate how clinicians from different theoretical orientations might describe him and try to help him.

Now we will turn to a discussion of what we mean by the term *abnormal behaviour*. Then we will look briefly at how our view of abnormality has evolved through history to the more scientific perspectives of today.

What Is Abnormal Behaviour?

One of the more difficult challenges facing those in the field of abnormal psychology is how to define abnormal behaviour. Here we will consider several characteristics that have been proposed as components of abnormal behaviour. We will see that no single one is adequate, although each has merit and captures some part of what might be the full definition. Consequently, abnormality is usually determined by the presence of several characteristics at one time. Our best definition of abnormal behaviour includes such characteristics as statistical infrequency, violation of norms, personal distress, disability or dysfunction, and unexpectedness.

Statistical Infrequency

One aspect of abnormal behaviour is that it is *infrequent*. For example, alternating episodes of depression and mania such as those J. Brett Barkley experienced occur in only about 1 percent of the population. The normal curve, or bell-shaped curve, places the majority of people in the middle as far as any particular characteristic is concerned; very few people fall at either extreme. An assertion that a person is normal implies that he or she does not deviate much from the average in a particular trait or behaviour pattern.

Statistical infrequency is used explicitly in diagnosing mental retardation. Figure 1.1 shows the normal distribution of intelligence quotient (IQ) measures in the population. Though a number of criteria are used to diagnose mental retardation, low intelligence is a principal one. When an individual's IQ is below 70, his or her intellectual functioning is considered sufficiently subnormal to be designated as mental retardation. Although some infrequent behaviours or characteristics of people do strike us as abnormal, in some instances the relationship breaks down. Having great athletic ability is infrequent, but few would regard it as part of the field of abnormal psychology. Only certain infrequent behaviours, such as experiencing hallucinations or deep depression, fall into the domain considered in this book. Unfortunately, the statistical component gives us little guidance in determining which infrequent behaviours psychopathologists should study.

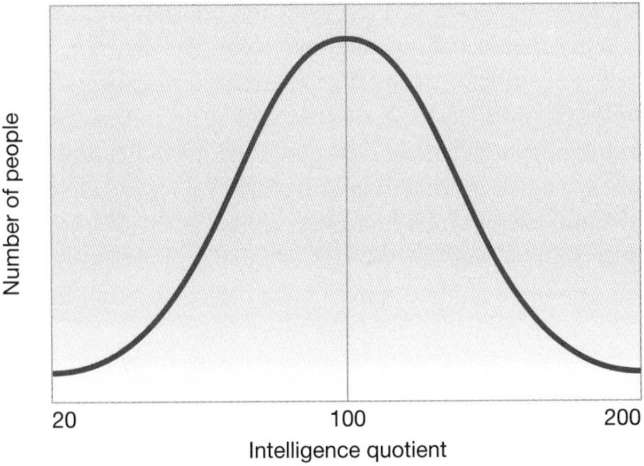

Figure 1.1 The distribution of intelligence among adults, illustrating a normal, or bell-shaped curve.

Violation of Norms

Another characteristic to consider is whether the behaviour *violates social norms* or threatens or makes anxious those observing it. J. Brett Barkley's verbal and physical attacks on his wife illustrate this criterion. This characteristic also rings true, at least partially. The antisocial behaviour of the psychopath fits the definition, as do the obsessive-compulsive person's complex rituals and the psychotic patient's conversation with imaginary voices. Violation of norms explicitly makes abnormality a relative concept; various forms of unusual behaviour can be tolerated, depending on the prevailing cultural norms. Yet violation of norms is at once too broad and too narrow. Criminals and prostitutes, for example, violate social norms but are not usually studied within the domain of abnormal psychology, and the highly anxious person, who is generally regarded as a central character in the field of abnormal psychology, typically does not violate social norms and would not be bothersome to many lay observers.

In addition, cultural diversity can affect how people view social norms-what is the norm in one culture may be abnormal in another. This subtle issue is addressed throughout the book (see especially Chapter 2 and Chapter 4).

Personal Distress

Another characteristic is *personal suffering*; that is, behaviour is abnormal if it creates great distress and torment in the person experiencing it. J. Brett Barkley's self-consciousness and distress about being evaluated illustrate this criterion. Personal distress clearly fits many of the forms of abnormality considered in this book—people experiencing anxiety disorders and depression truly suffer greatly—but some disorders do not necessarily involve distress. The psychopath, for example, treats others coldheartedly and may continually violate the law without experiencing any guilt, remorse, or anxiety whatsoever. And not all forms of distress—for example, hunger or the pain of childbirth—belong to the field.

Although abnormal behaviour is infrequent, so, too, is great athletic talent, such as that of proud Canadian Hayley Wickenheiser, Geraldine Heaney, and Colleen Sostorics. Canada won the gold medal at the 2002 Winter Olympics. Therefore, infrequency is not a sufficient definition of abnormal behaviour.

Disability or Dysfunction

Disability—that is, impairment in some important area of life (e.g., work or personal relationships) because of an abnormality—can also be a component of abnormal behaviour. The disruption of J. Brett Barkley's marital relationship fits this criterion. Substance-use disorders are also defined in part by the social or occupational disability (e.g., poor work performance, serious arguments with one's spouse) created by substance abuse. Similarly, a phobia can produce both distress and disability; for example, a severe fear of flying may prevent someone from taking a job promotion. Like suffering, disability applies to some, but not all, disorders. Transvestism (cross-dressing for sexual pleasure), for example, which is currently diagnosed as a mental disorder if it distresses the person, is not necessarily a disability. Most transvestites are married, lead conventional lives, and usually cross-dress in private. Other characteristics that might in some circumstances be considered disabilities—such as being short if you want to be a professional basketball player—do not fall within the domain of abnormal psychology. As with distress, we do not have a rule that tells us which disabilities belong and which do not.

Abnormal behaviour frequently produces disability or dysfunction, but some diagnoses, such as transvestism, are not clearly disabilities.

UNEXPECTEDNESS

We have just described how not all distress or disability falls into the domain of abnormal psychology. Distress and disability are considered abnormal when they are *unexpected* responses to environmental stressors (Wakefield, 1992). For example, an anxiety disorder is diagnosed when the anxiety is unexpected and out of proportion to the situation, as when a person who is well off worries constantly about his or her financial situation. Hunger, on the other hand, is an expected response to not eating and thus would be excluded as a state of distress that is relevant to abnormal behaviour. J. Brett Barkley was experiencing some life stress, but many people do so without developing psychological problems.

We have considered here several key characteristics of a definition of abnormal behaviour. Again, none by itself yields a fully satisfactory definition, but together they offer a useful framework for beginning to define abnormality.

In this volume we will study a list of human problems that are currently considered abnormal. The disorders in the list will undoubtedly change with time, for the field is continually evolving, and it is not possible to offer a simple definition of abnormality that captures it in its entirety. The characteristics presented constitute a partial definition, but they are not equally applicable to every diagnosis.

Focus on Discovery 1.1 describes the education and training of professionals who study and treat mental disorders. Recently, in Canada, it was estimated that approximately 3,600 practising psychiatrists, about 13,000 psychologists and psychological associates, and about 11,000 nurses specialize in the mental health area (Goering, Wasylenki, & Durbin, 2000). Thousands of social workers also work in the mental health field. Non-medical practitioners in Canada usually work within hospital or agency settings on a salary or in private practice. Medicare reimbursement of fees-for-service is limited to medical doctors. In fact, according to Goering et al. (2000, p. 350), "The major proportion of primary mental health care in Canada is delivered by general practitioners (GPs)."

Analyses of the results of the National Population Health Survey (NPHS: Statistics Canada, 1995) indicated that approximately 2.15 percent of respondents had consulted with a psychologist one or more times in the preceding 12 months (Hunsley, Lee, & Aubry, 1999). Hunsley et al. pointed out that this is equivalent to almost 515,000 people in the Canadian population aged 12 years and older. They concluded on the basis of several findings that psychological services in Canada are vastly underutilized. They also determined that psychological services are more available in urban areas than in rural areas and that psychiatrists tend to practise in major urban centres. Thus, many areas of Canada are underserviced (Goering et al., 2000) by two important mental health professions.

focus on discovery/1.1

The Mental Health Professions

The training of **clinicians**, the various professionals authorized to provide psychological services, takes different forms. Here, we discuss several types of clinicians, the training they receive, and a few related issues.

To be a **clinical psychologist** typically requires a Ph.D. or Psy.D. degree, which entails four to seven years of graduate study. However, in Canada, professional regulation of the psychology profession is within the jurisdiction of the provinces and territories and, depending upon regulatory statutes, a psychologist may have either a doctoral- or a master's-level degree (Hunsley & Johnston, 2000). In some jurisdictions the title "psychologist" is reserved for doctoral-level registrants whereas master's-level registrants are referred to as "psychological associates." As of 1998 (Ritchie & Edwards, 1998), two provinces (Quebec and Alberta) and the Northwest Territories require a master's degree; four provinces (New Brunswick, Newfoundland, Nova Scotia, and Prince Edward Island) specify the doctoral degree but allow registration with a master's degree subject to certain conditions and/or for a limited period of time; the remaining provinces (British Columbia, Manitoba, Ontario, and Saskatchewan) require the doctorate. Specific curriculum requirements vary across jurisdictions. Gauthier (2002) summarized the overall situation by concluding that there was effectively no consensus among the provinces on the minimal academic requirements, the required length of supervised practice, and the timing of such practice (i.e., before or after the degree is achieved).

In 1995 the Agreement on Internal Trade (AIT) was enacted. This agreement reduces territorial barriers that keep workers, capital, and goods and services from moving freely from one province to another. The AIT meant that a framework for mobility had to be developed so that the credentials of professional psychologists from one part of Canada would be recognized in other parts of Canada. The Mutual Recognition Agreement was signed in June 2001. According to Gauthier (2002), this is a competency-based agreement that involves five core competencies that a person has to have obtained (via his or her curriculum, practica, internships, and other experience) in order to become registered as a psychologist. The five competency areas are: (1) interpersonal relationships; (2) assessment and evaluation (including diagnosis); (3) intervention and consultation; (4) research; and (5) ethics and standards.

Training for a Ph.D. in clinical psychology is similar to that in other psychological specialties, such as developmental or physiological psychology. It requires a heavy emphasis on laboratory work, research design, statistics, and the empirically based study of human and animal behaviour. As with other fields of psychology, the Ph.D. is basically a research degree, and candidates are required to research and write a dissertation on a specialized topic. But candidates in clinical psychology learn skills in two additional areas, which distinguishes them from other Ph.D. candidates in psychology. First, they learn techniques of assessment and **diagnosis** of mental disorders; that is, they learn the skills necessary to determine that a patient's symptoms or problems indicate a particular disorder. Second, they learn how to practise **psychotherapy**, a primarily verbal means of helping troubled individuals change their thoughts, feelings, and behaviour to reduce distress and to achieve greater life satisfaction. Students take courses in which they master specific techniques under close professional supervision; then, during an intensive internship or postdoctoral training, they gradually assume increasing responsibility for the care of patients.

Other clinical graduate programs are more focused on practice than are the traditional Ph.D. programs. These programs offer the relatively new degree of Psy.D. (doctor of psychology). The curriculum is similar to that required of Ph.D. students, but with less emphasis on research and more on clinical training. The Ph.D. approach is based on the scientist-practitioner model, while the Psy.D. approach is based on the scholar-practitioner model. The Canadian Psychological Association Psy.D. Task Force (1998) described a scholar-practitioner as a "flexible, socially responsible, thinking practitioner who derives his/her skills from core knowledge in scientific psychology. This comprehensively trained professional is capable of performing in a number of roles, and would not be trained simply to be a technician in specific areas" (p. 13). The thinking behind the Psy.D. approach is that clinical psychology has advanced to a level of knowledge and certainty that justifies—even requires—intensive training in specific techniques of assessment and therapeutic intervention rather than combining practice with research. Psy.D. programs are just being introduced to certain Canadian universities, with three programs being approved in Quebec and other programs being proposed in Alberta, Ontario, New Brunswick, and Newfoundland (see Gauthier, 2002).

A **psychiatrist** holds an M.D. degree and has had postgraduate training, called a residency, in which he or she has received supervision in the practice of diagnosis and psychotherapy. By virtue of the medical degree, and in contrast with psychologists, psychiatrists can also continue functioning as physicians—giving physical examinations, diagnosing medical problems, and the like. Most often, however, the only aspect of medical practice in which psychiatrists engage is prescribing **psychoactive drugs**, chemical compounds that can influence how people feel and think.

There has recently been a lively and sometimes acrimonious debate in Canada and the United States concerning the merits of allowing clinical psychologists with suitable training to prescribe psychoactive drugs. Predictably, such a move is opposed by psychiatrists, for it would represent a clear invasion of their professional turf. It is also opposed by many psychologists, who view it as an ill-advised dilution of the behavioural science focus of psychology. Profits are an issue, but so is the question of whether a non-M.D. can learn enough about biochemistry and physiology to monitor the effects of drugs and protect patients from adverse side effects and drug interactions. This debate will undoubtedly continue for some time before any resolution is reached.

A **psychoanalyst** has received specialized training at a psychoanalytic institute. The program usually involves several years of clinical training as well as the in-depth psychoanalysis of the trainee. Although Sigmund Freud held that psychoanalysts do not need medical training, until recently most U.S. psychoanalytic institutes required of their graduates an M.D. and a psychiatric residency. It can take up to 10 years of graduate work to become a psychoanalyst.

A **social worker** obtains an M.S.W. (master of social work) degree. Master's and doctoral programs for **counselling psychologists** are somewhat similar to graduate training in clinical psychology but usually have less emphasis on research and the more severe forms of psychopathology. A **psychiatric nurse** specializes in working in the mental health field.

History of Psychopathology

"Those who cannot remember the past are condemned to repeat it."

—George Santayana, *The Life of Reason*

The search for the causes of deviant behaviour has gone on for a long time. Before the age of scientific inquiry, all good and bad manifestations of power beyond the control of humankind—eclipses, earthquakes, storms, fire, serious and disabling diseases, the passing of the seasons—were regarded as supernatural. Behaviour seemingly outside individual control was subject to similar interpretation. Many early philosophers, theologians, and physicians who studied the troubled mind believed that deviancy reflected the displeasure of the gods or possession by demons.

EARLY DEMONOLOGY

The doctrine that an evil being, such as the devil, may dwell within a person and control his or her mind and body is called demonology. Examples of demonological thinking are found in the records of the early Chinese, Egyptians, Babylonians, and Greeks. Among the Hebrews, deviancy was attributed to possession of the person by bad spirits, after God in his wrath had withdrawn protection. Christ is reported to have cured a man with an unclean spirit by casting out the devils from within him and hurling them onto a herd of swine (Mark 5:8–13).

Following from the belief that abnormal behaviour was caused by possession, its treatment often involved exorcism, the casting out of evil spirits by ritualistic chanting or torture. Exorcism typically took the form of elaborate rites of prayer, noisemaking, forcing the afflicted to drink terrible-tasting brews, and on occasion more extreme measures, such as flogging and starvation, to render the body uninhabitable to devils.

Trepanning of skulls (the making of a surgical opening in a living skull by some instrument) by Stone Age or Neolithic cave dwellers was quite widespread among the peoples of the world (Kidd, 1946). One popular theory is that it was a way of treating or relieving conditions such as epilepsy, headaches, and psychological disorders attributed to demons within the cranium. It was presumed that the individual would return to a normal state by creating an opening through which evil spirits could escape.

The assumption is that trepanning was introduced into the Americas from Siberia. Although the practice was most common in Peru and Bolivia, three aboriginal specimens have been found in Canada, all on the Pacific coast in British Columbia. One skull is that of a young male believed to be of high rank, since he received a "copper burial" (forehead and chest covered by thin sheets of native copper). The openings were located in the same area in all three specimens, the upper central occipital; the operations were performed using the same techniques and instruments; and in two cases the aboriginal survived long enough for healing to occur (Kidd, 1946). The widely accepted interpretation of the historical data has been disputed despite the extensive focus in aboriginal cultures on possession by spirits, and it has been suggested that the trepannings "were done to relieve pressure resulting from depressed fractures caused by war clubs" (Kidd, 1946, p. 515).

SOMATOGENESIS

In the fifth century B.C, Hippocrates (460?–377? B.C.), often regarded as the father of modern medicine, separated medicine from religion, magic, and superstition. He rejected the prevailing Greek belief that the gods sent serious physical diseases and mental disturbances as punishment and insisted instead that such illnesses had natural causes and hence should be treated like other, more common maladies, such as colds and constipation. Hippocrates regarded the brain as the organ of consciousness, of intellectual life and emotion; thus, he thought that deviant thinking and behaviour were indications of some kind of brain pathology. Hippocrates is often considered one of the very earliest proponents of somatogenesis—the notion that something wrong with the soma, or physical body, disturbs thought and action. Psychogenesis, in contrast, is the belief that a disturbance has psychological origins.

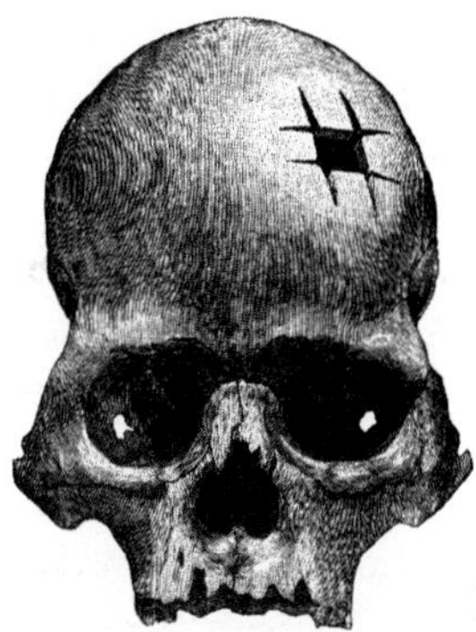

Was trepanning by the aboriginals of British Columbia performed to allow evil spirits to escape the body?

Hippocrates classified mental disorders into three categories: mania; melancholia; and phrenitis, or brain fever. Through his teachings, the phenomena of abnormal behaviour became more clearly the province of physicians than of priests. The treatments Hippocrates suggested were quite different from exorcistic tortures. For melancholia he prescribed tranquillity, sobriety, care in choosing food and drink, and abstinence from sexual activity. Such a regimen was assumed to have a healthful effect on the brain and the body. Because Hippocrates believed in natural rather than supernatural causes, he depended on his own keen observations and made a valuable contribution as a clinician. He also left behind remarkably detailed records describing many of the symptoms now recognized in epilepsy, alcoholic delusion, stroke, and paranoia.

Hippocrates's physiology was rather crude, however, for he conceived of normal brain functioning, and therefore of mental health, as dependent on a delicate balance among four humours, or fluids of the body, namely, blood, black bile, yellow bile, and phlegm. An imbalance produced disorders. If a person was sluggish and dull, for example, the body supposedly contained a preponderance of phlegm. A preponderance of black bile was the explanation for melancholia; too much yellow bile explained irritability and anxiousness; and too much blood, changeable temperament.

Hippocrates's humoral physiology did not withstand later scientific scrutiny. His basic premise, that human behaviour is markedly affected by bodily structures or substances and that abnormal behaviour is produced by some kind of physical imbalance or even damage, did foreshadow aspects of contemporary thought. In the next seven centuries, Hippocrates's naturalistic approach to disorder was generally accepted by other Greeks as well as by the Romans, who adopted the medicine of the Greeks after their city became the seat of power in the ancient European world.

The Dark Ages and Demonology

In a massive generalization, historians have often suggested that the death of Galen (A.D. 130-200), the second-century Greek who is regarded as the last major physician of the classical era, marked the beginning of the Dark Ages for western European medicine and for the treatment and investigation of abnormal behaviour. Over several centuries of decay, Greek and Roman civilization ceased to be. The churches gained in influence, and the papacy was declared independent of the state. Christian monasteries, through their missionary and educational work, replaced physicians as healers and as authorities on mental disorder.

The monasteries cared for and nursed the sick; a few were repositories for the classic Greek medical manuscripts, even though they may not have made use of the knowledge within these works. When monks cared for the mentally disordered, they prayed over them and touched them with relics or they concocted fantastic potions for them to drink in the waning phase of the moon. The families of the deranged might take them to shrines. Many of the mentally ill roamed the countryside, becoming more and more bedraggled and losing more and more of their faculties.

The Greek physician Hippocrates held a somatogenic view of abnormal behaviour, considering psychopathology a disease of the brain.

The Persecution of Witches During the 13th and the following few centuries, a populace that was already suffering from social unrest and recurrent famines and plagues again turned to demonology to explain these disasters. People in Europe become obsessed with the devil. Witchcraft, now viewed as instigated by Satan, was seen as a heresy and a denial of God. Faced with inexplicable and frightening occurrences, people tended to seize on whatever explanation was available. The times conspired to heap enormous blame on those regarded as witches, and these unfortunates were persecuted with great zeal.

Illumination from a 15th-century manuscript showing Christ exorcising a demon from a possessed youth.

In 1484 Pope Innocent VIII exhorted the clergy of Europe to leave no stone unturned in the search for witches. He sent two Dominican monks to northern Germany as inquisitors. Two years later they issued a comprehensive and explicit manual, *Malleus Maleficarum* ("the witches' hammer"), to guide the witch hunts. This legal and theological document came to be regarded by Catholics and Protestants alike as a textbook on witchcraft. Those accused of witchcraft were to be tortured if they did not confess; those convicted and penitent were to be imprisoned for life; and those convicted and unrepentant were to be handed over to the law for execution. The manual specified that a person's sudden loss of reason was a symptom of demonic possession and that burning was the usual method of driving out the supposed demon. Although records of the period are not reliable, it is thought that over the next several centuries hundreds of thousands of women, men, and children were accused, tortured, and put to death.

Witchcraft and Mental Illness For some time, the prevailing interpretation was that it was generally the mentally ill of the later Middle Ages who were considered witches (Zilboorg & Henry, 1941). In their confessions the accused sometimes reported having had intercourse with the devil and having flown to sabbats, the secret meetings of their cults. These reports have been interpreted by some writers as delusions or hallucinations and thus are taken to indicate that some of the so-called witches were psychotic.

More detailed examination of this historical period, however, indicates that most of the accused were not mentally ill. Careful analyses of the witch hunts reveal that although some accused witches were mentally disturbed, many more sane than insane people were tried. The delusion-like confessions were typically obtained during brutal torture; words were put on the tongues of the tortured by their accusers and by the beliefs of the times. Indeed, in England, where torture was not allowed, the confessions did not usually contain descriptions indicative of delusions or hallucinations (Schoeneman, 1977).

In the dunking test, if the woman did not drown, she was thought to be in league with the devil, the ultimate no-win situation.

Other information, moreover, indicates that witchcraft was not the primary interpretation of mental illness. From the 13th century on, as the cities of Europe grew larger, hospitals began to come under secular jurisdiction. Municipal authorities, gaining in power, tended to supplement or take over some of the activities of the church, one of these being the care of the ill. The foundation deed for the Holy Trinity Hospital in Salisbury, England, dating from the mid-14th century, specified the purposes of the hospital, among them that the "mad are kept safe until they are restored of reason." English laws during this period allowed both the dangerously insane and the incompetent to be confined in a hospital. Notably, the people who were confined were not described as being possessed (Allderidge, 1979).

Beginning in the 13th century, lunacy trials to determine a person's sanity were held in England. The trials were conducted under the Crown's right to protect the mentally impaired, and a judgment of insanity allowed the Crown to become guardian of the lunatic's estate (Neugebauer, 1979). The defendant's orientation, memory, intellect, daily life, and habits were at issue in the trial. Strange behaviour was typically linked to physical illness or injury or to some emotional shock. In all the cases that Neugebauer examined, only one referred to demonological possession. The preponderance of evidence thus indicates that this explanation of mental disturbance was not as dominant during the Middle Ages as was once thought.

DEVELOPMENT OF ASYLUMS

Until the end of the Crusades in the 15th century, there were very few mental hospitals in Europe, although there were thousands of hospitals for lepers. In the 12th century, England and Scotland had 220 leprosy hospitals for a population of a million and a half. After the principal Crusades had been waged, leprosy gradually disappeared from Europe, probably because with the end of the wars came a break with the eastern sources of the infection. With leprosy no longer of such great social concern, attention seems to have turned to the mad.

Confinement of the mentally ill began in earnest in the 15th and 16th centuries. Leprosariums were converted to **asylums**, refuges established for the confinement and care of the mentally ill. Many of these asylums took in a mixed lot of disturbed people and beggars. Beggars were regarded as a great social problem at the time; in 16th-century Paris the population of fewer than 100,000 included 30,000 beggars (Foucault, 1965). These asylums had no specific regimen for their inmates other than to get them to work, but during the same period hospitals geared more specifically for the confinement of the mentally ill also emerged.

Bethlehem and Other Early Asylums The Priory of St. Mary of Bethlehem was founded in 1243. By 1403 it housed six mentally ill men, and in 1547 Henry VIII handed it over to the city of London, thereafter to be a hospital devoted solely to the confinement of the mentally ill. The conditions in Bethlehem were deplorable. Over the years the word **bedlam**, a contraction and popular name for this hospital, became a descriptive term for a place or scene of wild uproar and confusion. Bethlehem eventually became one of London's great tourist attractions, by the 18th century rivalling both Westminster Abbey and the Tower of London. Even as late as the 19th century, viewing the violent patients and their antics was considered entertainment, and tickets of admission to Bedlam were sold. Similarly, in the Lunatic's Tower constructed in Vienna in 1784, patients were confined in the spaces between inner square rooms and the outer walls, where they could be viewed by passersby. The first mental hospital in what would become the United States was founded in Williamsburg, Virginia, in 1773.

A tour of St. Mary's of Bethlehem (Bedlam) provides amusement for these two upper-class women in Hogarth's 18th-century painting.

It should not be assumed that the inclusion of abnormal behaviour within the domain of hospitals and medicine necessarily led to more humane and effective treatment. Medical treatments were often crude and painful. Benjamin Rush (1745–1813), who began practising medicine in Philadelphia in 1769 and was deeply involved in his country's struggle for independence, is considered the father of American psychiatry. He believed that mental disorder was caused by an excess of blood in the brain. Consequently, his favoured treatment was to draw from "the insane" great quantities of blood (Farina, 1976)!

Rush entertained another hypothesis, that many "lunatics" could be cured by being frightened. In one recommended procedure, the physician was to convince the patient of his or her impending death. A New England doctor of the 19th century implemented this prescription in an ingenious manner: "On his premises stood a tank of water, into which a patient, packed into a coffin-like box pierced with holes, was lowered. He was kept under water until the bubbles of air ceased to rise, after which he was taken out, rubbed, and revived—if he had not already passed beyond reviving!" (Deutsch, 1949, p. 82).

Moral Treatment Philippe Pinel (1745–1826) is considered a primary figure in the movement for humanitarian treatment of the mentally ill in asylums. In 1793, while the French Revolution raged, he was put in charge of a large asylum in Paris known as La Bicêtre. A historian described the conditions at this particular hospital:

> [The patients were] shackled to the walls of their cells, by iron collars which held them flat against the wall and permitted little movement....They could not lie down at night, as a rule....Oftentimes there was a hoop of iron around the waist of the patient and in addition...chains on both the hands and the feet....These chains [were] sufficiently long so that the patient could feed himself out of a bowl, the food usually being a mushy gruel—bread soaked in a weak soup. Since little was known about dietetics, [no attention] was paid to the type of diet given the patients. They were presumed to be animals...and not to care whether the food was good or bad. (Selling, 1940, p. 54)

Pinel removed the chains of the people imprisoned in La Bicêtre and began to treat them as sick human beings rather than as beasts. Many who had been completely unmanageable became calm and much easier to handle. Formerly considered dangerous, they strolled through the hospital and grounds with no inclination to create disturbances or to harm anyone. Light and airy rooms replaced dungeons. Some patients who had been incarcerated for years were restored to health and eventually discharged from the hospital.

Freeing the patients of their restraints was not the only humanitarian reform advocated by Pinel. Consistent with the egalitarianism of the new French republic, he believed that the mental patients in his care were essentially normal people who should be approached with compassion and understanding and treated with dignity as individual human beings. He surmised that if their reason had left them because of severe personal and social problems, it might be restored to them through comforting counsel and purposeful activity. For all the good Pinel did for people with mental illness, however, he was not a complete paragon of enlightenment and egalitarianism. The more humanitarian treatment he reserved for the upper classes; patients of the lower classes were still subjected to terror and coercion as a means of control.

Pinel's freeing of the patients at La Bicêtre is often considered to mark the beginning of more humanitarian treatment of people with mental illness.

In the wake of Pinel's revolutionary work in La Bicêtre, the hospitals established in Europe and the United States were for a time relatively small and privately supported. A prominent merchant and Quaker, William Tuke (1732–1822), shocked by the conditions at York Asylum in England, proposed to the Society of Friends that it found its own institution. In 1796 the York Retreat was established on a country estate, providing mentally ill patients with a quiet and religious atmosphere in which to live, work, and rest. Patients discussed their difficulties with attendants, worked in the garden, and took walks through the countryside.

In the United States the Friends' Asylum, founded in 1817 in Pennsylvania, and the Hartford Retreat, established in 1824 in Connecticut, were patterned after the York

Retreat. Other U.S. hospitals were influenced by the sympathetic and attentive treatment provided by Pinel and Tuke. In accordance with this approach, which became known as **moral treatment**, patients had close contact with the attendants, who talked and read to them and encouraged them to engage in purposeful activity; residents led as normal lives as possible and in general took responsibility for themselves within the constraints of their disorders.

Despite the emphasis on moral treatment in the early 19th century, drugs were also used frequently used in mental hospitals. Two findings emerged from a review of detailed case records of the York Retreat from 1880 to 1884 (Renvoise & Beveridge, 1989). First, drugs were the most common treatment and included alcohol, cannabis, opium, and chloral hydrate (knockout drops). Second, the outcomes were not very favourable; fewer than one-third of the patients were discharged as improved or recovered.

Moral treatment was abandoned in the latter part of the 19th century. Ironically, the efforts of Dorothea Dix (1802–1877), a crusader for improved conditions for people with mental illness helped effect this change. Dix, a Boston schoolteacher, taught a Sunday-school class at the local prison and was shocked at the deplorable conditions in which the inmates lived. Her interest spread to the conditions of patients in private mental hospitals and to the mentally ill people of the time who had nowhere to go for treatment. Dix campaigned vigorously to improve the lot of people with mental illness; she personally helped see that 32 state hospitals were built to take in the many patients whom the private ones could not accommodate. Unfortunately, the staff in the state hospitals were unable to provide the individual attention that was a hallmark of moral treatment (Bockhoven, 1963). Moreover, these hospitals came to be administered by physicians who were interested in the biological aspects of illness and in the physical, rather than the psychological, well-being of mental patients. The money that once paid the salaries of personal attendants now paid for equipment and laboratories.

For a limited time, there were attempts to apply moral treatment in certain regions of Canada, but these were undermined by the political and economic decisions of those in power. LaJeunesse (2002) documented how attempts at moral treatment in Alberta were undercut by Premier Sifton's decision to focus on larger institutions, where patients were crowded into buildings with inadequate space. Previously, in 1846, Dr. Henry Hunt Stabb had made heroic efforts to institute moral treatment and non-restraint at the Lunatic Asylum in St. John's, Newfoundland (see Baker, 1981; O'Brien, 1989). He presided at this site (now known as the Waterford Hospital) until his death in 1892, but his efforts to provide moral treatment were hindered by inadequate financial resources and more patients than the hospital could reasonably accommodate. Also, beginning in the late 1870s, the hospital often played a custodial role, as Stabb was made to take in low-functioning patients deemed untreatable (see O'Brien, 1989).

ASYLUMS IN CANADA

In the 19th century, Dorothea Dix was a tireless social reformer who lobbied for improvement of the deplorable treatment of mentally ill people

> "This, you must remember, that patients here within,
> Are here, because we all were born into a world of sin...
> Now come inside the building, and enter into the halls,
> You will see many patients, whose sorrows for pity calls.
> But pay no attention, to what might be said of you,
> Some of them had fine intellects 'fore trouble their minds o'erthrew..."
>
> —Graeme L., 1907, patient at the Toronto Hospital for the Insane (Rheaume, 2000)

Although Dorothea Dix played a limited role in the establishment of asylums for the treatment of the mentally ill in Canada, a network of such facilities was eventually established. The history of the development of this network is a history of the institutionalization of people with serious psychological disorders. However, as pointed out by Sussman (1998, p. 260), the process "began with humane intentions as part of a progressive and reformist movement, which attempted to overcome neglect and suffering in the community, jails, penitentiaries, almshouses, poorhouses, and hospitals." Dix described poignant and shameful examples of this neglectful community care and human suffering in her eloquent 1850 memorial to the Nova Scotia Legislative Assembly (see Canadian Perspective 1.1).

Around this time, J.F. Lehman (1840) wrote the first textbook published in Canada with a focus on the care and control of mentally ill people. In contrast to the compassionate, humane views of reformers such as Dorothea Dix and Henry Hunt Stabb, both strong proponents of moral therapy, Lehman recommended stringent discipline and harsh treatments, including flogging. Although his views failed to stimulate much popular or medical support, as we will see, many strategies employed in Canada during the 20th century were just as harsh and a few were much more severe and had tragic consequences.

Sussman (1998) argued that the development of services for the mentally ill in Canada and British North America (BNA) was largely ad hoc, with little cross-fertilization of ideas from province to province (although the Dominion government finally ordered all provinces to remove "lunatics" from jails in 1884). The provinces were, however, strongly influenced by Great Britain, the "mother country." During the 1840s through to the 1880s, when most of the formal asylums were first established, all of the jurisdictions could be characterized as having a need to develop separate facilities with better conditions for the mentally ill. As pointed out by Sussman (1998, p. 261), "This segregated form of care, the psychiatric institution known as the asylum, was the very beginning of state provisions for mentally ill people in a vast and sparsely populated country."

The earliest precursor to the 19th-century asylums built in what was to become Canada was the Hotel Dieux, established in Quebec in 1714 by the Duchess d'Aiguillon, niece of Cardinal Richelieu, the effective ruler of New France. However, the facility cared for indigents and crippled people in addition to "idiots." Similar "hospitals" were built in other parts of Quebec, using a contracting-out system whereby the King of France paid religious orders of the French Roman Catholic Church to care for the mentally ill. However, following the 1763 Treaty of Paris, the English assumed power over the area, and although the contracting-out practice and the influence of the Catholic Church continued, "the British influence on care practices, daily asylum management, and funding moderated the differences between Quebec and the rest of Canada" (Sussman, 1998, p. 261). The reform movement was led primarily by pioneers from Great Britain (e.g., the Tukes) who fostered a zeal to develop asylums "worthy of a British province" (Colonial Record Office, April 15, 1847) and influenced the design and construction of asylums. Although New Brunswick and Nova Scotia erected asylums in 1847 and 1857, respectively, according to Sussman (1998), Prince Edward Island did not build an asylum until 1877 because neither the social movement nor colonial funding existed. In 1914, Alberta was the last province to open an asylum for the insane, which meant that mentally ill people no longer had to be transported from Alberta to Manitoba by the Royal North-West Mounted Police.

Table 1.1 presents a summary of the first asylums in Canada and British North America, built during the institution-building period prior to the World War I. Typically, the superintendents were British trained physicians who emigrated to Canada from England or Scotland and modelled the asylums after British forms of structure, treatment, and administration, although Bartlett (2000), in a comparative analysis of structures in Ontario and England, concluded that they functioned differently and reflected very different norms of social governance. In Upper Canada, power rested with the asylum doctor. A few years before Confederation, the Annual Report of the Board of Inspectors of Asylums, Prisons, &c., for the Year 1864 (1865, p. iii) included a memorandum "on the necessity of providing additional accommodation for lunatics in Upper and Lower Canada." The inspectors gave a glowing report on behalf of the medical superintendent of the Provincial Lunatic Asylum, Toronto, the principal asylum in Upper Canada. However, the superintendent reported that both the Chief Asylum and the University Branch were "dangerously overcrowded" and lamented the fact that this overcrowding was responsible for a striking increase in the death list (composed mostly of females) and for the impaired general health of the inmates. Further, the majority of the patients remaining in the Chief Asylum at the end of the year were "the noisy, the unruly, and the violent." Most of the women inmates were sent to the University Branch. Dr. Workman, the medical superintendent, argued that "under a system of management which will, from an inability to give prompt admission to every new case of insanity, convert every case into incurable, death will become the sole creator of vacancies" (p. 11). The average cost of each patient to the province in 1864 was $152.88! Over the years since the asylum was opened in 1841, the superintendent calculated the discharge rate to be 52 percent. Almost 20 percent of the inmates died while in the institution, a large number due to "general paresis of the insane" and to a condition called "phthisis."

In this new century, we hear much about the possibility that Canada is developing a two-tier medical system in which the wealthy will have more opportunity for, and quick access to, superior quality care (e.g., Adams & Laghi, 2000). Such a system had the force of law in the era of institution building, at least in Upper Canada. In 1853 the legislature passed the Private Lunatic Asylums Act to accommodate the wealthy in alternatives to the public asylums. The inspectors' report of 1885 noted that "as regards the insane persons of the wealthy class, it is manifest that our public Asylums...cannot afford such persons the partial seclusion and special personal attention which they desire and are prepared to pay for" (cited in Warsh, 1989, p. 9). As a consequence of the preferential legislation, the Homewood Retreat was established in 1883 at Guelph, Ontario, a profit-oriented, independent, private asylum. Homewood was able to employ the latest treatment approaches administered by practitioners dedicated to working closely with a small number of patients. As Marshall and Firestone (1999, p. 15) observed, "the history of Homewood reflects the changes throughout the English-speaking world in the perceived exemplary approach to managing and treating insane people." As you will learn, a "perceived exemplary approach" does not necessarily produce a desired outcome and in some instances has tragic consequences. In fact, Dr. Lett, the first medical superintendent of Homewood, believed in the humane care of patients. Despite his resistance to the "cult of curability" ascribed to by practitioners of moral therapy, Dr. Lett encouraged his staff to employ the principles of moral therapy in order to provide symptomatic relief to his wealthy charges (Warsh, 1989).

The history of the development of institutions for the mentally disordered in Canada can be characterized in terms of two distinctive trends: (1) with the advent of the asylums, provisions for the mentally ill were separate from provisions for the physically ill, indigents, and criminals; and (2) the process was segregated from the wider community—"The institution and the community were two separate and distinct solitudes" (Sussman, 1998, p. 262).

See Canadian Perspectives 1.2 for an examination of mental institutions in Canada in the latter part of the 20th century and the beginning of the new millennium.

Table 1.1

Asylums in Canada and BNA Built during the Insitution-Building Era

Jurisdiction	Name and Place	Date
Alberta	Insane Asylum, Ponoka	1911
British Columbia	Public Hospital for the Insane, New Westminster (moved from smaller building in Victoria, opened 1872)	1878
	British Columbia Mental Hospital, Coquitlam	1913
Manitoba	Selkirk Asylum, Selkirk	1886
	Home for Incurables, Portage la Prairie	1890
	Brandon Asylum, Brandon	1891
New Brunswick	Provincial Hospital, Saint John (temporary pioneer Canadian institution in converted cholera hospital)	1835
	Provincial Lunatic Asylum	1848
Nova Scotia	Nova Scotia Hospital for Insane, Halifax	1857
Ontario	The Provincial Lunatic Asylum, Toronto (Old York Jail made into a temporary asylum in 1841; renamed the Asylum for Insane, in 1871)	1850
	Kingston Asylum (Rockwood), Kingston	1856
	London Asylum, London	1859
	Orillia Asylum for Idiots, Orillia	1861
	Hamilton Asylum, Hamilton	1876
	Mimico Branch Asylum, Mimico	1890
	Hospital for Insane, Brockville	1894
	Cobourg Asylum	1902
	Penetanguishene Asylum, Penetanguishene	1904
	Whitby Hospital, Whitby	1914
Prince Edward Island	The Prince Edward Island Hospital for the Insane	1877
Quebec	Quebec Lunatic Asylum (Beauport), Beauport	1845
	Provincial Lunatic Asylum, St. John's	1861
	L'Hospice St. Jean de Dieu (Longue Point)	1856
	L'Hospice St. Julien, St. Ferdinand d'Halifax	1873
	L'Hospice Ste Anne, Baie St. Paul	1890
	Protestant Hospital for the Insane (Verdun), Verdun	1890
	St. Benedict Joseph Asylum, near City of Montreal	1885
Saskatchewan	The Saskatchewan Provincial Hospital, Battleford	1914
Newfoundland (crown colony)	Asylum for the Insane, St. John's	1855
Yukon	Taken to Westminster by Royal North-West Mounted Police	
Northwest Territory	Taken to asylums of Alberta and Saskatchewan	

Source: Hurd (19161), Volume IV.

Canadian Perspectives/1.1

Dorothea Dix and the Development of the Asylums in Canada: Light into the Darkness?

"One lost mind whose star is quenched
Has lessons for mankind."

Although she did her original work in the United States, Dorothea Dix made trips around the world in an attempt to improve conditions for the mentally ill. She visited "the Canadas" in 1843 and 1844, discovered the appalling conditions suffered by the "insane" who were incarcerated in the Toronto jail and the Quebec Lunatic Asylum, and lent her support to the construction of a hospital for the insane in St. John's, Newfoundland, (Hurd, Volume I, 1916).

On January 21, 1850, Dix presented a lengthy "memorial prayer" on behalf of the mentally ill to the Nova Scotia Legislature and asked for the construction of a public mental hospital. As part of her compelling address, Dix stated that "[t]hroughout the province, in short, I found cases incurable through long neglect, doomed to a life-long burden to themselves through suffering, and a life-long charge either upon their friends or the public for care and maintenance" (p. 485).

Dix also suggested treatment strategies based on what she knew of moral treatment approaches in Europe and the United States, and she commented on the outcomes of interventions and the consequences of a failure to obtain help at an early point. This emphasis on early detection and treatment, noted over 150 years ago, is consistent with current views (e.g., see the discussion of early risk detection and intervention for the schizophrenias in Chapter 11).

Dix appealed to the members of the Nova Scotia Legislature to consider what it was like to be mentally ill in Canada during the era prior to the building of the asylums:

> In imagination, for a short hour, place yourselves in their stead; enter the horrid, noisome cell, invest yourselves with the foul, tattered garments which scantily serve the purposes of decent protection; cast yourselves upon the loathsome pile of filthy straw; find companionship in your own cries and groans, or in the wailings and gibberings of wretches miserable like yourselves; call for help and release, for blessed words or soothing and kind offices of care, till the dull walls are weary in sending back the echo of your moans; then, if self-possession is not overwhelmed under the imaginary miseries of what are the actual distresses of the insane, return to the consciousness of your sound intellectual health, and answer if you will longer refuse or delay to make adequate appropriations for the establishment of a provincial hospital for those who are deprived of reason, and thereby of all that gladdens life or makes existence a blessing. (p. 493)

This appears to be Dorothea Dix's only *public* appeal to a Canadian province. She went on to take an active part in selecting the site for the Nova Scotia hospital, which opened on December 26, 1858. In addition, from 1853 to 1855 she helped Henry Hunt Stabb raise funds for the St. John's asylum (see O'Brien, 1989).

Source: Hurd, Volume I (1916)

THE FINLAY ASYLUM, QUEBEC, CANADA, EAST.—MESSRS. STENT & LAVERS, ARCHITECTS.

Drawing of the Finlay Asylum, Quebec, 1800s

Thinking Critically

1. Can you imagine yourself back in 1850 Nova Scotia, suffering with a major psychiatric disorder such as schizophrenia (described in detail in Chapter 11), living under conditions similar to those described by Dorothea Dix in her memorial prayer? What would it be like for you? Given the knowledge about mental disorders during that era, what could realistically be done to help you cope with your life circumstances and your psychological problems?
2. Given the establishment of a public "asylum" like that proposed by Dorothea Dix, what model of care would you propose? How should the "inmates" be "treated"?
3. Assuming that people in the general community treated you with humanity and compassion, cared for and supported you, do you think that it would be possible for you to live among them if you were mentally ill?

The Beginning of Contemporary Thought

Recall that in the West the death of Galen and the decline of Greco-Roman civilization temporarily ended inquiries into the nature of both physical and mental illness. Not until the late Middle Ages did any new facts begin to emerge. These facts were discovered thanks to an emerging empirical approach to medical science that gathered knowledge by direct observation. One development that fostered progress was the discovery by the Flemish anatomist and physician Vesalius (1514–1564) that Galen's presentation of human anatomy was incorrect. Galen had presumed that human physiology mirrored that of the apes he studied. It took more than a thousand years for autopsy studies of humans—not allowed during his time—to begin to prove that he was wrong. Further progress came from the efforts of the English physician Thomas Sydenham (1624–1689). Sydenham was particularly successful in advocating an empirical approach to classification and diagnosis, one that subsequently influenced those interested in mental disorders.

An Early System of Classification One of those impressed by Sydenham's approach was the German physician Wilhelm Griesinger, who insisted that any diagnosis of mental disorder specify a biological cause—a clear return to the somatogenic views first espoused by Hippocrates. A textbook of psychiatry, written by Griesinger's well-known follower Emil Kraepelin (1856-1926) and first published in 1883, furnished a classification system in order to establish the biological nature of mental illnesses.

Kraepelin discerned among mental disorders a tendency for a certain group of symptoms, called a syndrome, to appear together regularly enough to be regarded as having an underlying physical cause, much as a particular medical disease and its syndrome may be attributed to a biological dysfunction. He regarded each mental illness as distinct from all others, having its own genesis, symptoms, course, and outcome. Even though cures had not been worked out, at least the course of the disease could be predicted.

Kraepelin proposed two major groups of severe mental diseases: dementia praecox, an early term for schizophrenia, and manic-depressive psychosis. He postulated a chemical imbalance as the cause of schizophrenia and an irregularity in metabolism as the explanation of manic-depressive psychosis. Kraepelin's scheme for classifying these and other mental illnesses became the basis for the present diagnostic categories, which are described more fully in Chapter 3.

An Illustrative Case: General Paresis and Syphilis Although the workings of the nervous system were understood somewhat by the mid-1800s, not enough was known to reveal all the expected abnormalities in structure that might underlie various mental disorders. Degenerative changes in the brain cells associated with senile and presenile psychoses and some structural pathologies that accompany mental retardation were identified, however. Perhaps the most striking medical success was the discovery of the full nature and origin of syphilis, a venereal disease that had been recognized for several centuries.

The story of this discovery provides a wonderful picture of how the empirical approach, the basis for contemporary science, works. Since 1798 it was known that a number of mental patients manifested a syndrome characterized by a steady deterioration of both physical and mental abilities and that these patients suffered multiple impairments, including delusions of grandeur and progressive paralysis. Soon after these symptoms were recognized, it was observed that these patients never recovered. In 1825 this deterioration in mental and physical health was designated a disease, general paresis. Although it was established in 1857 that some patients with paresis had earlier had syphilis, there were many competing theories for the origin of paresis. For example, in attempting to account for the high rate of the disorder among sailors, some supposed that seawater might be the cause. And Griesinger, in trying to explain the higher incidence among men, speculated that liquor, tobacco, and coffee might be implicated.

In the 1860s and 1870s, Louis Pasteur established the germ theory of disease, which set forth the view that disease is caused by infection of the body by minute organisms. This theory laid the groundwork for demonstrating the relation between syphilis and general paresis. In 1897, after Richard von Krafft-Ebing inoculated paretic patients with matter from syphilitic sores, the patients did not develop syphilis, indicating that they had been infected earlier. Finally, in 1905, the specific micro-organism that causes syphilis was discovered. A causal link had been established between infection, destruction of certain areas of the brain, and a form of psychopathology. If one type of psychopathology had a biological cause, so could others. Somatogenesis gained credibility, and the search for more biological causes was off and running.

Psychogenesis The search for somatogenic causes dominated the field of abnormal psychology until well into the 20th century, no doubt partly because of the stunning discoveries made about general paresis. But in the late 18th and throughout the 19th century, some investigators considered mental illnesses to have an entirely different origin. Various psychogenic points of view, which attributed mental disorders to psychological malfunctions, were fashionable in France and Austria.

Mesmer and Charcot Many people in western Europe were at that time subject to hysterical states; they suffered from physical incapacities, such as blindness or paralysis, for which no physical cause could be found. Franz Anton Mesmer (1734–1815), an Austrian physician practising in

Mesmer's procedure for transmitting animal magnetism was generally considered a form of hypnosis.

Vienna and Paris in the late 18th century, believed that hysterical disorders were caused by a particular distribution of a universal magnetic fluid in the body. Moreover, he felt that one person could influence the fluid of another to bring about a change in the other's behaviour.

Mesmer conducted meetings cloaked in mystery and mysticism at which afflicted patients sat around a covered *baquet*, or tub. Iron rods protruded through the cover of the baquet from bottles underneath that contained various chemicals. Mesmer would enter a room, take various rods from the tub, and touch afflicted parts of his patients' bodies. The rods were believed to transmit animal magnetism and adjust the distribution of the universal magnetic fluid, thereby removing the hysterical disorder. Whatever we may think of what seems today to be a questionable theoretical explanation and procedure, Mesmer apparently helped many people overcome their hysterical problems.

The French psychiatrist Jean Charcot lectures on hysteria in this famous painting. Charcot was an important figure in reviving interest in psychogenesis.

You may wonder about our discussing Mesmer's work under the rubric of psychogenic causes, since Mesmer regarded hysterical disorders as strictly physical. Because of the setting in which Mesmer worked with his patients, however, he is generally considered one of the earlier practitioners of modern-day hypnosis. The word mesmerize is an older term for "hypnotize." (The phenomenon itself, however, was known to the ancients of probably every culture and was part of the sorcery and magic of conjurers, fakirs, and faith healers.)

Although Mesmer was regarded as a quack by his contemporaries, the study of hypnosis gradually became respectable. A great Parisian neurologist, Jean Martin Charcot (1825–1893), also studied hysterical states, including anesthesia (loss of sensation), paralysis, blindness, deafness, convulsive attacks, and gaps in memory. Charcot initially espoused a somatogenic point of view. One day, however, some of his enterprising students hypnotized a normal woman and prompted her to display certain hysterical symptoms. Charcot was deceived into believing that she was an actual hysterical patient. When the students showed him how readily they could remove the woman's symptoms by waking her, Charcot changed his mind about hysteria and became interested in non-physiological interpretations of these very puzzling phenomena.

Breuer and the Cathartic Method At about this time, in Vienna, a physician named Josef Breuer (1842–1925) treated a young woman who had become bedridden with a number of hysterical symptoms. Her legs and right arm and side were paralyzed, her sight and hearing were impaired, and she often had difficulty speaking. She also sometimes went into a dreamlike state, or "absence," during which she mumbled to herself, seemingly preoccupied with troubling thoughts. During one treatment session, Breuer hypnotized Anna O. and repeated some of her mumbled words. He succeeded in getting her to talk more freely—ultimately, with considerable emotion—about some very upsetting past events. Frequently, on awakening from these hypnotic sessions, she felt much better. With Anna O. and other hysterical patients, Breuer found that the relief and cure of symptoms seemed to last longer if, under hypnosis, they were able to recall the precipitating event for the symptom and if their original emotion was expressed. The experience of reliving an earlier emotional catastrophe and releasing the emotional tension caused by suppressed thoughts about the event was called *catharsis*. Breuer's method became known as the cathartic method. In 1895 one of his colleagues joined him in the publication of *Studies in Hysteria*, a book considered a milestone in abnormal psychology. In the next chapter we examine the thinking of Breuer's collaborator, Sigmund Freud.

Canadian Perspectives/1.2

The Mental Hospital in Canada: The Twentieth Century and into the New Millennium

"There can be no question though that where the insane are concerned the public are not only indifferent, but terror stricken and very often heartless."

—C. K. Clarke, Canada's first professor of psychiatry (Greenland, 1996)

Despite the very humane motives that were the stimulus for the institution-building period in Canada, the results during the 20th century were not very positive, especially from a patient's perspective. The provincial mental hospitals became extremely overcrowded, and in too many instances individual treatment was unavailable with the exception of some of the radical treatments described in the next chapter and, of course, whatever psychoactive drugs were available in different eras. Drugs became the central means of treatment, especially after the introduction of the antipsychotic phenothiazines in the 1950s. As Sussman (1998, p. 262) noted, "Eventually, institutionalization in Canada became a synonym for an inhumane response to mentally ill people, often because of a scarcity of resources."

In the 1970s, concerns about the restrictive nature of confinement in a mental hospital led to the deinstitutionalization of a large number of mental-hospital patients. The goal in Canada was to shift care into the psychiatric units associated with general hospitals and into the community. As Wasylenki, Goering, and MacNaughton (1994) reported, the result of this changed philosophy was a drop in the bed capacity of Canadian mental hospitals from almost 50,000 beds to about 15,000 beds between 1960 and 1976. At the same time, beds in general-hospital psychiatric units increased from fewer than 1,000 to almost 6,000 beds. Budget cuts in the 1980s and 1990s caused the trend of deinstitutionalization to continue. However, as we will discuss in Chapter 18, the enthusiasm for deinstitutionalization has been tempered by the fact that, as has been the case in the United States, many discharged patients in Canada lead lives of poverty in the community, with a significant number of them included among the homeless and the prison population. Although the official position of all of the provincial and territorial governments is an increased focus on community support systems, community mental health programs were allocated only about 3 percent of provincial mental health budgets as recently as 1990 (Freeman, 1994). Most of the mental health money still goes to the hospitals via global budgets and to physicians via fee-for-service (Goering, Wasylenki, & Durbin, 2000). For example, in Ontario in 1992 more than half of the $1.28 billion total cost for mental health went to the provincial psychiatric and general hospitals, about a third was paid to the doctors, and only 10 percent went to community mental health programs (Goering & Lin, 1996).

But the problems of chronic patients, many of whom cannot easily be deinstitutionalized at this point in the development of community-based services, have yet to be handled adequately (as we will discuss in more detail in Chapter 18). Mental hospitals in Canada today are run by the provinces and territories as part of our national universal health insurance program—Medicare—the cornerstone of the health care system. Although Medicare is administered by the provincial and territorial governments, it is regulated and in part financed by the federal government. In contrast to the situation in the United States, in Canada Medicare pays basic medical and hospital costs for all Canadians. As noted by Goering et al. (2000, p. 345), "The federal government sets standards in order to maintain common values and elements within distinct province-sponsored health insurance plans, which are responsible for delivery of services and regulation of services and professionals." Although the situation in Canada has been considerably better than in the United States, treatment of chronic patients in our provincial mental institutions can still be considered primarily custodial in nature. Patients are kept alive in a protected environment, but they receive little *individual* psychosocial treatment; their existence is monotonous and sedentary for the most part. Despite their staggering costs and significant improvements in physical amenities and patient care, many of our provincial psychiatric hospitals remain old, grim, and somewhat removed from major metropolitan centres. Nonetheless, they are far superior to the vast majority of state mental hospitals in the United States.

In contrast to the current situation in Canada, there are many private mental hospitals in the United States. Sheppard and Enoch Pratt near Baltimore, Maryland, and McLean Hospital, in Belmont, Massachusetts, are two of the most famous. The physical facilities and professional care in private hospitals tend to be superior to those of state hospitals for one reason: the private hospitals have more money. The costs to patients in these private institutions can exceed $1,000 per day and yet may not include individual therapy sessions with a member of the professional staff. Such hospitals are clearly beyond the means of most American citizens. For better or worse, public mental hospitals in Canada are more comparable to U.S. private hospitals than to the state hospitals.

A somewhat specialized mental hospital, sometimes called a *prison or forensic hospital*, is reserved for people who have been arrested and judged unable to stand trial and for those who have been acquitted of a crime because they are "not criminally responsible on account of mental disorder." Although these patients have not been sent to prison, their lives are controlled by guards and tight security. Treatment of some kind is supposed to take place during their incarceration. In Canada there are currently three maximum-security forensic hospitals, in

Ontario, Quebec, and British Columbia. The past, present, and future plans at Ontario's maximum-security hospital at Penetanguishine, Ontario, were described by Rice and Harris (1993). Also, in Ontario, forensic services are provided through the operation of small, medium-secure regional forensic units based in the provincial psychiatric hospitals (e.g., METFORS—Metropolitan Toronto Forensic Service). In Chapter 13, we will examine "Oak Ridge" in the context of our discussion of antisocial personality disorder.

Even in the best hospitals in Canada and the United States patients usually have precious little contact with psychiatrists or clinical psychologists, a situation confirmed (at least in the United States) by the careful observations of Gordon Paul and his co-workers. These investigators found that most patients had no contact with staff for 80 to 90 percent of their waking hours and that the clinical staff spent less than one-fourth of their working time in contact with patients (Paul, 1987, 1988). Patients spend most of their days and evenings either alone, in the company of other patients, or with aides, individuals who sometimes have little more than a high school education. As with imprisonment, the overwhelming feeling is of helplessness and depersonalization. Patients sit for endless hours in hallways waiting for dining halls to open, for medication to be dispensed, and for consultations with psychologists, social workers, and vocational counselors to begin. Except for the most severely disturbed, patients do have access to the various facilities of a hospital, ranging from woodworking shops to swimming pools, from gymnasiums to basket-weaving shops. Most hospitals require patients to attend group therapy—here, a general term indicating only that at least two patients attempt to relate to each other and to a group leader in a room for a specific period of time. Some patients have a few sessions alone with a professional therapist. For the most part, however, traditional hospital treatment over the past 40 years has been oriented toward dispensing drugs rather than toward offering psychotherapy. The institutional setting itself is used as a way to provide supportive care, to try to ensure that patients take their medication, and to protect and look after patients whose conditions make it impossible for them to care for themselves or render them an unreasonable burden or threat to others (Paul & Menditto, 1992).

One nagging problem is that an institutionalized mindset is difficult to reverse once people have resided in mental hospitals for more than a year. One of the authors recalls asking a patient who had improved markedly over the previous several months why he was reluctant to be discharged. "Doc," he said earnestly, "it's a jungle out there." Although we cannot entirely disagree with his view, there are at least a few advantages to living on the outside; yet this man—a veteran and chronic patient with a clinical folder more than two feet thick—had become so accustomed to the protected environment of various hospitals that the prospect of leaving was as frightening to him as the prospect of entering a mental hospital is to those who have never lived in one.

A treatment that offers some promise is **milieu therapy**, in which the entire hospital becomes a "therapeutic community" (e.g., M. Jones, 1953). All its ongoing activities and all its personnel become part of the treatment program. Milieu therapy appears to be a return to the moral practices of the 19th century. Social interaction and group activities are encouraged in the hope that through group pressure the patients are directed toward normal functioning. Patients are treated as responsible human beings rather than as custodial cases (Paul, 1969). They are expected to participate in their own readjustment as well as in the readjustment of fellow patients. Open wards allow them considerable freedom. There is some evidence for the efficacy of milieu therapy (e.g., Fairweather, 1964; Greenblatt et al., 1965), the most convincing from a milestone project by Paul and Lentz (1977).

However, in Canada the current emphasis is on psychiatric-hospital bed reduction and closure. According to Goering et al. (2000), the total bed complement in provincial psychiatric hospitals has been reduced to 11,000 beds in the remaining 41 hospitals. Most provinces plan further bed reductions. For example, in Ontario, the Health Services Restructuring Commission recommended closing half the remaining 10 provincial psychiatric hospitals. The commission set a target of 35 beds per 100,000 population for mental health services by 2003. Further, only 14 of the 35 beds should be used for longer-term care. Wasylenki et al. (2000) suggested that these beds could be reduced to as few as 7 per 100,000 people contingent on the availability of specialized outreach and alternative residential settings.

Regarding inpatient care, the role of the provincial psychiatric hospital in Canada in the new millennium will be "tertiary"; that is, they will "provide specialized treatment and rehabilitation services for individuals whose needs for care are too complex to be managed in the community" (Goering et al., 2000, p. 349). We will explore the implications of this policy change in Chapter 18. However, it is clear that as provincial governments move to develop portable and community-based tertiary care and "delink" delivery from particular settings (Goering et al., 2000), the provincial psychiatric hospitals will play a minimal role.

An ongoing concern in this context is the need to balance the rights of mentally ill individuals and the rights of the community to be protected from them. Across Canada "stakeholders" are debating the value of **community treatment orders** (CTOs). A CTO is a legal tool that is issued by a medical practitioner and establishes the conditions under which a mentally ill person may live in the community, including compliance with treatment (Goering et al., 2000). The consequence for a patient of failing to follow the CTO is being returned to a psychiatric facility for assessment. We examine this emotionally charged, contentious issue in detail in Chapter 18.

One thing is certain. The "asylums" as we have known them over the past 150 years will no doubt all but disappear in the new millennium.

Sources: Ban, Healy, and Shorter (1998); Frayn (1996); Freeman (1994); Goering, Waslenki, and Durbin (2000); Greenblatt, Solomon, Evans, and Brooks (1965); Greenland (1996); J. Marshall (1982); W. Marshall and Firestone (1999); Paul (1969, 1987, 1988); Paul and Lentz (1977); Paul and Mendito (1992); Rice and Harris (1993); Shorter (1996); Sussman (1998); Warsh, (1989); Wasylenki, Goering, and MacNaughton (1994); Wasylenki, Goering, Cochrane, Durban, Rogers, and Prendergast (2000).

Thinking Critically

1. How do you think the chronic patients currently in our psychiatric hospitals in Canada should be managed and treated so that their dignity is respected but society is protected? Think about this issue in the context of government plans to close the majority of the remaining psychiatric hospitals.
2. In 1988 the federal government published a paper entitled *Mental Health for Canadians: Striking a Balance*. It claimed that closure of psychiatric hospitals has not been offset by "strengthening community resources" for the mentally ill. It claimed further that psychiatric patients "face a life of deprivation, danger and neglect. Some are homeless, or live in social isolation and squalor. Many are forced to rely on family caregivers who themselves have little or no access to respite or other kinds of support." Do you believe that there is still a huge gap between deinstitutionalization, outpatient care, and community care? Do you believe that society has a responsibility for the treatment of the vulnerable mentally ill?
3. If there is a major gap, how would you close it? Do you agree that a major restructuring of our Canadian mental health system is necessary and justified? How would you restructure the system? How would you design a comprehensive and integrated mental health system for Canada that would be responsive to and accessible to all Canadians?
4. Would Community Treatment Orders be a part of your system? If so, how would you define the scope of CTO legislation?

Many people go about the study of abnormal psychology without considering the nature of the perspective, conceptual framework, or paradigm (see Chapter 2) they have adopted. The choice of a paradigm, however, has some important consequences for the way in which abnormal behaviour is defined, investigated, and treated. Canadian Perspectives 1.3 examines, from an historical perspective, some of the "treatment" strategies that developed as a result of adopting a particular paradigm. This material also raises a number of ethical issues and concerns that we will address in detail in Chapter 18, and it leads us to a consideration of the "lesson" of history.

Canadian Perspectives/1.3

The Lesson of History: A View from the Twenty-first Century

"CIA brainwash settlement 'a flea': Spy agency escaped lightly in lawsuit, Winnipegger says"
—Headline, *The Toronto Star*, October 6, 1988

The above excerpt from a Canadian Press report describes the settlement of a lawsuit resulting from what is probably the greatest abuse of psychiatric power in Canadian history. Similar abuses, of course, occurred in the United States and elsewhere during the same era. Tragically, such examples are all too common in some parts of the world even today. However, before proceeding, we should also point out that a majority of psychiatric patients in Canada were treated with decency and humanity within the constraints of scientific knowledge and accepted clinical practice at the time.

Dr. Ewen Cameron, a world-renowned Montreal psychiatrist, was head of the Allan Memorial Institute at McGill University in the 1950s and early 1960s. At one point in his career, he was president of the Quebec, Canadian, American, and World Psychiatric Associations. In 1955 Dr. Cameron initiated a series of experiments on unsuspecting psychiatric patients that continued for a nine-year period, apparently in a misguided attempt to discover breakthrough treatments or a "cure" for mental illness. None of the patients or their families were ever asked for their consent, nor were they informed that the patients were being administered experimental treatments that were beyond the limits of acceptable medical treatments for the era. Dr. Cameron's quest led to a bizarre theory of "beneficial brainwashing" that had tragic consequences for hundreds of Canadians, some of whom had only relatively mild problems, such as leg pain or fatigue, when they first came to the institute. Many years later, it was determined that Dr. Cameron's shocking mind-control experiments were funded secretly by the U.S. Central Intelligence Agency (through a front called the Society for the Investigation of Human Ecology) and, subsequently, by the federal government of Canada. The CIA believed that these brainwashing strategies might be used on "enemies" of the United States during the Cold War.

What did Dr. Cameron—and his staff—do to these unfortunate patients that was of such great interest to the CIA? He administered massive doses of hallucinogenic drugs, such as LSD. He administered intensive, repeated courses of electroconvulsive therapy (ECT), or "shock treatment," often three times each day, while patients were kept in a drug-induced coma for as long as three months. He also administered so-called psychic driving, in which subliminal messages, such as "You killed your mother," were repeated over and over while the patient was in the drug-induced state. The alleged purpose of these "treatments" was to "wipe away" the troubled past of his patients. The treatment was "successful"! Linda Macdonald, who initiated a lawsuit against the federal government, claimed that the experiments erased her memory for the first 26 years of her life. She received over 100 electroshock treatments and was kept in the drug-induced sleep for 86 days. Theoretically, Dr. Cameron would bestow a "new," healthy personality on her. Ms. Macdonald claimed, however, that there was no subsequent care directed at the psychological difficulties that brought her to the institute in the first place, or for the effects of Dr. Cameron's experiments on her. The many victims claimed that they suffered permanent damage, and the majority of those still alive (several committed suicide) remain in psychiatric hospitals or attempt to live in the community but require extensive support.

The role of the CIA was not discovered until 1977. In 1988 the U.S. government settled out of court for a total of $750,000 with a group of nine former patients who had initiated a lawsuit in 1980. In 1992 the Canadian government finally agreed to a settlement that would pay up to $100,000 per person. Neither the CIA nor the Canadian government has apologized to the 150 surviving patients who lost their identities and their dignity, or to the families of approximately 150 former patients who have died. In 1998, following an exposé on the investigative news program *The Fifth Estate*, CBC Television aired a miniseries dramatizing the work of Dr. Cameron and the occurrences in his "Sleep Room."

Several radical approaches for the treatment of serious mental disorders were introduced during the 20th century. At the time, they were considered to be breakthrough developments within mainstream medicine, but many are now considered just as controversial, just as inappropriate, and, in the view of some professionals and many psychiatric consumers, just as damaging as Dr. Cameron's de-patterning techniques. We can include here the various "shock" treatments, starting with metrazol shock treatment, progressing to insulin coma treatment, and culminating with Cerletti and Bini's (1938) introduction of ECT (which became a component of Dr. Cameron's experimental approach). The latter is still used today, albeit in a very different and safer form (see the discussion of modern ECT in Chapter 10). Its use is no longer as widespread, and it is typically employed as a treatment of last resort, to be carried out under stringent guidelines and with full informed consent. Nonetheless, it remains a controversial intervention.

Not without controversy today is the issue of "lobotomy" or "psychosurgery" (also discussed in Chapter 11). In this surgical procedure, the tracts connecting the frontal lobes to lower centres of the brain are destroyed. Egas Moniz of Lisbon introduced prefrontal lobotomy into psychiatry in 1935 on the strength of hearing at a medical conference about the experimental use of the procedure on two cats. Twenty years later, he was awarded the Nobel Prize for Physiology and Medicine for his use of the procedure in the treatment of schizophrenia. Psychosurgery was used and abused in Canada into the 1970s, when legislation and a general acknowledgement within the mental health professions of its ineffectiveness with, and harmful effects on, psychiatric patients led to its demise. In Canada the first lobotomies were performed in the province of Ontario in 1944 on 19 female patients from various mental hospitals (Simmons, 1987). In a careful review of archival evidence, Simmons (1987) demonstrated that psychosurgery was used in Ontario for several reasons, including to ease staffing problems and, out of curiosity, to observe the consequences to patients.

Did patients or their families give informed consent as the law required? According to Simmons (1987, p. 544), "given the superintendent's belief that lack of consent should not prevent them from giving treatment, it is probable that legal niceties did not constitute a major obstacle to the lobotomy program." Initially, media reports of a high success rate actually led to public pressure to increase the frequency of psychosurgical procedures! Simmons (1987) concluded, however, that the public's belief that psychiatrists abused their authority was responsible for the subsequent imposition of restrictions on psychosurgical operations. The evidence suggests that three operations conducted in 1981 were the last lobotomies performed in Ontario (Simmons, 1987). Lobotomies were effectively banned in all public psychiatric hospitals.

What is the lesson of history with respect to society's "treatment" of the mentally ill? The examples presented here, together with examples from the more distant past and knowledge of circumstances surrounding events, suggest the following:

1 Periods in which people exhibiting psychologically disordered behaviour were persecuted and treated cruelly (e.g., witch hunts, bloodletting, asylums) have often alternated with periods of humanitarian reform and care for suffering people (e.g., Hippocrates's humanitarian treatments, Pinel's reform of the asylums).
2 Cycles of persecution, neglect, and humanitarianism in the treatment of the mentally ill have occurred irrespective of the helping agency, whether religious, medical, or psychological.
3 Just as we now look back with revulsion on what were once accepted treatments (e.g., bloodletting), future generations may regard some of our more recent and current practices as cruel and inhumane (e.g., lobotomy, earlier versions of ECT).
4 Recent reforms may easily be reversed (as they have been throughout history) during adverse economic, political, and social conditions.

Sources: Canadian Press, October 6, 1988; Collins, 1988; Cruickshank, 1987; Gilmor, 1987; Simmons, 1987; Weinstein, 1990.

Thinking Critically

1. Do you agree with Santayana's famous dictum that "Those who forget the past are condemned to repeat it"? What specific examples are you aware of involving the "treatment" of people with psychological disorders that illustrate the wisdom of paying attention to Santayana's dictum? Is continued progress in the treatment of the mentally ill in Canada inevitable? What economic, political, and social circumstances throughout Canada or in your own region could potentially contribute to a lack of progress?
2. What steps would you take to ensure that tragic incidents, such as the "treatments" employed by Dr. Cameron, never occur again in Canada?
3. Given the knowledge base in the era of its use, do you think that lobotomy was ever justified? (After you think critically about this issue, refer to the discussion of ethical dilemmas of research and therapy in Chapter 18.)

CURRENT ATTITUDES TOWARD PEOPLE WITH PSYCHOLOGICAL DISORDERS

"Changing attitudes to mental illness continues to be our biggest challenge. Discrimination, ignorance and fear remain the enemies that we have to conquer."
—Canadian Mental Health Association National President Bill Gaudette, May 2001

Many Canadians are suspicious of people with psychological disorders. Their concerns have been reinforced by incidents involving threats, subway pushings, and other examples of frightening behaviour on the part of seriously mentally ill people, many of whom had refused to take or were no longer taking their prescribed medications. Consistent with other minority groups in Canada, people with psychological disorders are often faced with negative stereotyping and stigmatization (e.g., Herman & Smith, 1989; Kearns & Taylor, 1989; Page & Day, 1990). For example, according to the Centre for Addiction and Mental Health (CAMH, 2000), the social stigma surrounding depression is the primary reason why only one-third of the three million people in Canada who suffer from depression seek help.

Mental illness can occur regardless of fame, fortune, or power, and there are many examples of well-known Canadians, or their loved ones, who have experienced a diagnosable psychological disorder (see Crozier & Lane, 2001; Nunes & Simmie, 2002). One example is Margot Kidder, the Canadian actress from Yellowknife, Northwest Territories, who is famous for her role as Superman's girlfriend. Kidder is now also known for her publicized psychological problems, which drew extensive media coverage several years ago. Her problems with bipolar depression led to her temporary retention in a psychiatric facility. She has been critical of the "treatment" she received, especially drug treatments (CBC Radio, 1999; Moore, 1999).

Ron Ellis, a former star of the Toronto Maple Leafs hockey team, also admitted that he has suffered from depression for many years (CAMH, 2000). Michael Wilson, a former minister of finance, lost a young son to depression and suicide (see Yohemas-Hayes, 1999). A tireless crusader in his attempts to help reduce the stigma associated with depression, Mr. Wilson encourages people to seek help for themselves or for loved ones and friends. He serves as chair of a multi-year public education campaign launched by the CAMH and various individual and corporate partners, including the Canadian Mental Health Association (CMHA). The primary goal is to remove barriers that impede people from seeking treatment for mental health and addiction problems.

Many of the common misconceptions or myths of mental illness can easily be dispelled. For example, it is a common belief that people with psychological disorders are unstable and dangerous. We will revisit this issue in Chapter 18 but at this point we can state that available research (e.g., Rabkin, 1974) does not confirm this widespread idea. Using vignette data from the Mental Health Module of the General Social Survey, Phelan, Link, Stueve, and Pescosolido (2000) demonstrated that the public conception of mental illness broadened between 1950 and 1996 to include a greater proportion of non-psychotic disorders; however, perceptions that mentally ill people are frightening or violent actually *increased* (by nearly 2.5 times) among respondents who viewed mental illness in terms of psychotic behaviour. Phelan et al. (2000, p. 188) concluded that it is possible that "there has been a real move toward acceptance of many forms of mental illness as something that can happen to one of 'us,' but that people with psychosis remain a 'them' who are more feared than they were half a century ago."

In a companion paper, Martin, Pescosolido, and Tuch (2000) determined that the perception of a person's degree of dangerousness accounts for or explains many of the negative effects due to labelling someone mentally ill. This same study found that respondents want to maintain social distance from the mentally ill; they have the greatest desire to avoid alcohol or drug abusers but are also quite unwilling (as high as 50 percent) to interact with people diagnosed with schizophrenia or depression. The authors cite other findings consistent with the hypothesis that educational efforts directed at changing the public's perception of people with psychological problems have not been particularly successful at minimizing social rejection: respondents were unwilling to have people with psychological problems marry into their family, rejected them as possible coworkers, were unwilling to entertain them in their homes, and did not want them as neighbours, friends, or residents in a group home in their neighbourhood. On a more positive note, lower levels of social rejection occurred when stress was perceived as playing a major role in the development of psychological problems. In another analysis of the same survey data, Schnittker (2000) reported that people appear more willing to interact with females than with males with the same psychological problem, perhaps because females were perceived as less dangerous to others.

The reduction of the stigma of schizophrenia (see Chapter 11) is the focus of a worldwide campaign by the World Psychiatric Association. The initial results of a recent anti-stigma initiative in Alberta suggest that citizens have a higher level of acceptance of people with schizophrenia and more knowledge about the condition than expected (see Thompson et al., 2002). Nevertheless, 40 percent of the general public continue to endorse the belief that people with schizophrenia have the potential to be dangerous.

Another insidious myth (described by Rabkin, 1974) is the belief that people with psychological disorders can never be "cured" and can never contribute meaningfully to society again. Readers of the research findings presented in this text will readily conclude that such a belief is a major misconception. Further, students will no doubt be able to cite many examples of people who, though, were never "cured" of their psychological problems, nevertheless went on to make significant contributions to humanity. One such individual was Clarence Hincks, who suffered from serious and chronic psychological problems but was able to devote his life to helping the mentally ill and to trying to change the public's attitudes toward them. Hincks was a founder and long-term medical director of the Canadian Mental Health Association. See Canadian Perspective 1.4 for further information about Hincks, the CMHA, and the issue of misconceptions about the mentally ill.

A much publicized example of the issue of stereotyping and stigmatizing of the mentally ill involves the 2000 movie starring Canadian actor Jim Carrey entitled *Me, Myself & Irene*. In the movie, the character played by Mr. Carrey develops a "split personality" and fights against himself. A coalition of Canadian health organizations and advocacy groups, including the CMHA, wanted disclaimers attached to the film because it reinforces negative stereotypes of people suffering from psychiatric disorders, in particular the schizophrenias. Carrey's character is misidentified as having **schizophrenia** rather than **dissociative identity disorder**.

Another disturbing example of misguided attitudes occurred during an improvised Grey Cup parade at military barracks in Winnipeg in November 2002. The "parade" included a float with a train locomotive that pulled a jail cell containing a male soldier wearing women's underwear. The float was intended to portray a "Crazy Train" (taken from the Ozzy Osbourne song) that was taking soldiers suffering from posttraumatic stress disorder for treatment. Canada's military ombudsman was critical of the demeaning display of stressed soldiers and the minimal investigation conducted by the military. Posttraumatic stress disorder (see Chapter 6) is a debilitating disorder that can only be made worse by such insensitive treatment.

A survey commissioned by CMHA and released in time for the 50th Anniversary of Mental Health Week in Canada, in May 2001 (<http://www.pressi.com/pressi-html>), found that the majority of a representative, national sample of Canadians indicated that maintaining mental health is "very important" (95 percent of women and 88 percent of men). However, relative to a similar 1997 survey, fewer Canadians are willing to tell their bosses (only 42 percent) or friends (only 50 percent) if they are receiving treatment or counselling for depression. As is typically found in similar surveys, women were more willing to admit to receiving treatment than men. CMHA's current national public awareness initiative, launched on May 2, 2003, is designed to force Canadians to question their attitudes about who becomes mentally ill and to combat the shame associated with having a psychiatric disorder (see <http://www.cmha.ca/english/info_centre/media_release.htm>).

It is our hope and expectation that our readers will treat all people, including those with psychiatric disorders, whether real or imagined, with decency and dignity. We further hope that many of our students will take an active role in advocating for, or helping, people with psychological problems.

Canadian Perspectives/1.4

Clarence M. Hincks and the Canadian Mental Health Association

"$20,000 Secured for Institute: Canadian National Committee for Mental Hygiene Started in Mrs. Dunlap's Home"

—Headline, *The Globe and Mail*, January 26, 1918

Thus began the Canadian National Committee for Mental Hygiene (CNCMH), precursor to the Canadian Mental Health Association (CMHA), one of the oldest continuing voluntary health organizations in Canada. Clarence Meredith Hincks (1885–1964) was a co-founder who devoted his life to crusading on behalf of the mentally ill in Canada and throughout the world. Born in the town of St. Mary's, Ontario, he graduated in medicine from the University of Toronto and became involved in working with children who were experiencing difficulties in the Toronto school system. In the pejorative jargon of the era, many of these children were labelled "feebleminded" or "idiots." Hincks, however, had a less pessimistic view of them thanks to his own experiences. As a university student, Hincks had experienced a bout of what we would now refer to as major depression; he recovered (although he would experience further episodes) and was imbued with a sense of optimism about the impermanence and treatability of mental illness. He became familiar with the similar experiences and work of the American Clifford W. Beers (*A Mind That Found Itself*, 1908), a founder of the mental hygiene movement in the United States. Hincks was inspired to do something similar in Canada. The purposes and objectives of the CNCMH were initially fivefold: (1) psychiatric examination and care of war recruits and returning soldiers suffering from "shell shock"; (2) post-war psychiatric screening of immigrants; (3) adequate facilities for diagnosis and treatment of "mental disease"; (4) adequate care of the "mentally deficient"; and (5) prevention.

Hincks's first major activity was to tour mental institutions in Manitoba in the company of C.K. Clarke, dean of medicine and professor of psychiatry at the University of Toronto. They found disturbing conditions: overcrowding in the institutions, people who should not have been patients at all, and appalling custodial care. Roland (1990) included in his book excerpts from the confidential report for the Manitoba government:

> The most painful and distressing survey undertaken while we were in Manitoba was at the so-called Home for Incurables at Portage La Prairie. Two visits were made, the first on October 8, 1918, the second on October 15, 1918, as we did not wish to labour under any misapprehension in regard to what was seen there. The name, Home for Incurables, is misleading, and the institution has become a recuperation house for every kind of ailment,—as one of our party expressed it, "from eczema to dementia." Apparently, any family in Manitoba which had a troublesome member, either old or young, sent them here, until this institution possessed an unhappy conglomeration of idiots, imbeciles, epileptics, insane, seniles, and mentally normal people suffering from incurable diseases...That insane people should be housed in this institution is astonishing, as it is devoid of any equipment for caring for cases of insanity. (Roland, 1990, p. 47)

A description of one of the most astonishing cases at the Home for Incurables is contained in an excerpt from Hincks's unpublished autobiography (in Griffin, 1989):

> At the end of a long dark ward a cupboard was found containing a naked woman with deathly pale skin. There was no furniture, no bed, not even a mattress. The woman had a small piece of shawl which she placed over her eyes when the door was opened. Apparently she was unaccustomed to the light. When the Superintendent was asked how long this woman had been left in the cupboard, he replied, "two years." Hincks asked how often she had been permitted out during that period. "Once, and then only for ten minutes in a cage. She was restless, so we returned her to the cupboard." (pp. 20-21)

The Government of Manitoba responded in a positive manner to the confidential report and implemented many of its recommendations. Over the next 10 years, other provinces (except Ontario and Quebec) requested similar surveys. Numerous "horror stories" came to light and indicated that the situation was unsatisfactory throughout Canada. Roland (1990, p. 55) noted:

> ...many shocking conditions were discovered. In the asylum at Saint John, New Brunswick, a certain group of patients on the upper floor were put to bed in coffin-

like boxes with hay in the bottom and slats on the top. All boxes except two were locked at night, the two being occupied by patients who had been designated "trustees," with the responsibility of dealing with noisy patients. This they accomplished by urinating through the slats on the patients' faces. In Edmonton, Alberta, a novel method of caring for low-grade, mentally defective children was observed. At bedtime, the children were rolled in long strips of cotton with their arms and legs bound, and piled on a shelf.

Hincks and the CNCMH conducted surveys of schoolchildren in Ontario and Quebec that resulted in the establishment of over 150 special classes for retarded children. In addition to serving as medical director of the CNCMH from 1924 and for CMHA until his retirement in 1952, Hincks also helped organize the International Committee for Mental Hygiene, which eventually became the consultative mental health agency for the World Health Organization. When he received an honourary doctor of laws degree from the University of British Columbia in 1955, Hincks was recognized for "his modesty, deep humanity and his constructive sympathy. In a world where mental illness has long been, and alas, has not yet ceased to be, a target for superstitious fear, for prejudice, and even callous derision, he has continually reminded us of the claim that the mentally ill and those threatened with mental illness have upon their more fortunate fellows." The C.M. Hincks Treatment Centre in Toronto was named after him (now the Hincks-Dellcrest Centre as the result of a 1998 merger). In 1962 Hincks announced courageously on CBC cross-Canada radio that he suffered from manic depression (bipolar disorder) in a further attempt to dispel public fears and myths about mental illness.

Because of its increasingly direct focus on enhancing its contact with the Canadian public, the committee changed its name in 1950 to the Canadian Mental Health Association. CMHA continues its dedication to improving quality of life and available care for people suffering from psychological disorders. It is committed to helping "consumers," as well as their families and friends, through direct service each year to more than 100,000 Canadians via the efforts of over 10,000 volunteers and staff in locally run organizations and 135 branches throughout Canada. Programs include assistance with employment, housing, and early psychosis intervention for youth, peer support and recreation services, stress-reduction workshops, and community education campaigns. Advocacy, research, and information services are important parts of their mandate to promote the mental health of all Canadians. The association has a long, productive history of forging partnerships with individuals and organizations. For example, in 1999 CMHA "partnered" with over 350 organizations "to increase public awareness of the negative effects of stress and to promote stress management techniques for the home and workplace."

From the perspective of history, unfortunately, we cannot regard all of the efforts and contributions of C.M. Hincks in a positive light. For example, Dowbiggin (1997) described Hincks's role in the sexual sterilization of mental patients (discussed in Chapter 15). The Alberta Legislature passed the Sexual Sterilization Act on March 7, 1928. The act allowed the sterilization of "mental defectives" based on the recommendation of a four-person board and the consent of a parent or guardian. According to Dowbiggin, Hincks played a substantial role in getting the bill passed. In addition to indicating his personal support, he enlisted the aid of a prominent American authority on the subject in an attempt to convince the legislature. Hincks pledged organizational support by stating that "[o]ur National Committee will co-operate with governments in making sterilization laws that are enacted effective. We will attempt to carry the main body of public opinion with us through educational campaigns" (Dowbiggin, 1997, p. 180). Subsequently, in 1946, Hincks wrote a brief article for Maclean's magazine titled "Sterilize the Unfit." His views on sterilization reflected his belief that "mental defectiveness" has a substantial genetic component and reflects hereditary weakness.

Sources: CMHA website <http://www.cmha.ca>; Dowbiggin (1997); Griffin (1989); Roland (1990).

Thinking Critically

1. C.M. Hincks was a tireless crusader on behalf of the downtrodden and psychologically disturbed. Given this commitment, how could he come to support a eugenics movement that was so wrong and is so reviled today?
2. Very much because of the contributions of Clarence Hincks and CMHA in Canada, public perception of mental illness has improved somewhat. Do you believe that public perception is now largely positive and supportive of the mentally ill? Do you believe that some segments or groups of people within contemporary Canadian society (e.g., women) are more compassionate and supportive than others, while other groups or segments are more prone to various "myths" of mental illness? How would you test out your hypotheses?
3. What would you recommend that CMHA and its partners (including federal, provincial and territorial, and municipal governments) do to further reduce the stigma of mental illness?
4. How would you recognize attitudes and behaviours that support the stigma of mental illness? Assume that you encounter something in the media that could contribute to public misunderstanding about mental disorders. What could you do about it?

CANADA'S MENTAL HEALTH CARE SYSTEM

In Canadian Perspective 1.2 we introduced the reader to Medicare and to our current mental health care system in the context of our discussion of the mental hospital. We now continue that discussion with a focus on additional aspects of our health care system, the mental health of Canadians, issues associated with treatment and prevention of psychological disorders in Canada, the cost of mental health problems in Canada, and a look into the future, especially in view of the November 28, 2002, publication of the "Romanow Report" on the future of Canada's health care system.

Every society or culture has its own ideas and expectations with regard to health care practices, including mental health. A cultural difference between Canada and many other countries, including the United States, concerns the value placed on a health care system that is readily available to everyone. In a sense, we are a culture that, at least in this area, values collectivism—self-sacrifice and sharing of responsibility for the good of our country (see Triandis, 1994, for a discussion of collectivism versus individualism). In Canada, mental health services are tied closely to the health care system. Thus, we can place the mental health of Canadians within the context of health in general.

According to Bowman (2000), Canadians are better off than Americans across virtually all major health indicators (e.g., infant mortality rate, life expectancy, years free of disability, five-year survival rates for cancer and heart disease). Some research suggests that in Canada there is a lower prevalence of psychiatric disorders (e.g., Kessler et al., 1997) and less use of illicit drugs (e.g., Single, MacLennan, & MacNeil, 1994). Further, these health indicators are less strongly associated with income inequalities in Canada than in the United States (Bowman, 2000).

Kessler et al. (1997) concluded that the "match" between psychiatric needs and outpatient services is better in Canada (actually, in the province of Ontario) than in the United States. Thus, while a smaller percentage of Canadians receive mental health services (8 percent), their needs are significant and are directly met (Bowman, 2000); conversely, while more people (13.3 percent) in the United States receive mental health services, their disorders are less severe—a reflection of the lack of access for the poor (primarily minorities).

MEDICARE

Why is the health of Canadians better than the health of Americans? There is one critical national difference. In Canada, taxes are employed for universal health care, including care for people with psychological disorders. The Canadian **Medicare** system has been in effect since 1970. The Canada Health Act (CHA), the last major piece of legislation in this area (Ritchie & Edwards, 1998), was passed in 1984 and is the legislative cornerstone of our national health care system. Whereas in the United States health care is rationed by individual income (40 percent of families have no health insurance), in Canada it is rationed by medical judgments and the level of funding to the system (Bowman, 2000). Poor Canadians actually make greater use of the system than rich Canadians! Bowman also notes that incarcerated criminals in Canada who suffer from major psychological disorders are more likely to be sent to hospitals within the corrections system. In the United States, care of offenders with psychological disorders varies widely across the different states.

Governments in Canada are currently involved in a massive restructuring of the health care system, including mental health care, and concerns have been expressed about the possibility of a two-tier system. Nevertheless, according to Ritchie and Edwards (1998),

> Canadians remain strongly committed to the five core principles on which Medicare is based (accessibility, comprehensiveness, portability, public administration, universality) but are increasingly open-minded about the possibility of changing health service delivery mechanisms in view of economic and other realities, provided that the core principles are respected. (p. 387)

Canadians value Medicare not only because it is needed but also because it brings Canadians together as a national community.

MENTAL HEALTH OF CANADIANS: FIRST VIEW

What Factors Are Associated with Mental Health in Canada? We can get a first indication from a recent national study. Stephens, Dulberg, and Joubert (1999) analyzed data from the National Population Health Survey (NPHS), a comprehensive study of the people living in Canada's 10 provinces (excluding the territories). Stephens et al. reported that current stress, social support, life events, education, and childhood trauma were strongly and independently associated with multiple indicators of both positive (e.g., self-esteem, mastery, and happiness) and negative (e.g., level of distress, cognitive impairment) **mental health status**. Amount of current stress was the strongest correlate of mental health status, since it was consistently positively associated with all positive indicators (e.g., mastery) and negatively associated with all negative measures (e.g., distress). Second only to current stress in importance, social support was similarly associated with a majority of the indicators. Number of childhood traumas was strongly associated with several negative indicators, including depression. Amount of formal education was strongly related to positive indicators of mental health. Stephens et al. (1999) concluded that mental health is relatively poor among young people but tends to improve with age. This association runs counter to some older studies. The authors pointed out, however, that the social and economic circumstances for older people have improved markedly in Canada, whereas the lot of young people has declined. Sex differences existed on a number of measures. Women, for example, were more likely to be depressed, whereas men were more likely to report a higher sense of mastery. Nonetheless, Stephens et al. concluded that past studies might have given an impression that sex differences are more widespread than they actually are. Throughout the book, we will address these issues and many others as we describe the current status of the mental health of people in Canada.

What Is the Extent of Mental Health Problems in the People of Canada? A more in-depth examination of the extent of psychological disorders is presented in Chapter 3 (Canadian Perspective 3.2) and in the context of our discussions of specific disorders. However, to anticipate this discussion, one community study (Ontario Ministry of Health, 1994) found that about 20 percent of people in Ontario have one or more mental disorders (during a one-year period). Further, many of these people have difficulty performing their main activity (e.g., job); have difficulty conducting the typical activities of daily living; and have troubled relationships, marital problems, and difficulties relating to children. They are dissatisfied with life, income, main activity, leisure activity, and housing. It was concluded that about 2 percent of Ontarians can be considered severely mentally ill. A majority of these people (72 percent) fall in the age range from 25 to 44 years old and are separated, divorced, or widowed.

Regional Differences Does the mental health of the Canadian population differ from one region of the country to another? Do the provinces and territories differ from one another in terms of mental health? These questions are difficult to answer, especially with respect to the territories. There are, of course, some obvious differences in certain parts of Canada. In Chapter 2, for example, we will mention the high level of mental health problems among some of Canada's Aboriginal people, especially those living in remote areas. Nonetheless, the available research suggests that there are few major differences between the provinces. Returning to the NPHS study, Stephens et al. (1999) did not find any major independent relationship between mental health and a respondent's province of residence. There are, however, a few consistent differences. One of these is the good mental health in both Newfoundland and Prince Edward Island. People in these two provinces reported the most happiness and the least distress. Quebec is noteworthy because it reported very high levels of self-esteem and mastery but the least happiness and most distress. It will be important for future research to determine the reasons for these unusual findings. Unfortunately, the role of language was not reported. Stephens et al. reported that "strategies that promote resilience and other psychological resources will . . . contribute to problem reduction or even prevention" (1999, p. 10). We should not take this study as the final word on the extent of regional differences in mental health, particularly because it is difficult to determine the pervasiveness of psychological problems among people in remote areas.

Treatment and Prevention

How do the Canadian Medicare system and other initiatives affect the treatment and prevention of psychological disorders in Canada? We have already discussed the fact that direct Medicare reimbursement is limited to physicians and that psychological services are underutilized, and we discussed the role of Medicare in the mental hospital and some of the negative effects of deinstitutionalization for the chronically mentally ill. The current focus on the restructuring of the health care system has major implications for service delivery, including for the way we deal with the consequences of deinstitutionalization and community alternatives to the mental hospital, as well as with delivery of psychotherapy. It should also be noted that, in terms of service delivery, there are clearly practical constraints associated with being a small population in a geographically very large country (Hunsley & Johnston, 2000); this situation can lead to underserving and/or insufficient support of people's needs, especially in rural and remote areas (e.g., Goering et al., 2000; Kirmayer et al., 2000; Stuart, 2000). There is a need in Canada to place greater emphasis on community psychology and prevention. On a positive note, in 9 of the 10 provinces, much of the health care decision-making has devolved to local authorities so as to contain costs and improve the integration of services (Lomas, 1997; Lomas, Woods, & Veenstra, 1997). As stated previously, Medicare is regulated and in part financed by the Government of Canada; however, it is the responsibility of the provinces and territories to implement Medicare. Although provincial health ministries are primarily responsible for mental health matters, other ministries can play a significant role. For example, in Ontario, in addition to the Ministry of Health and Long-Term Care, the following ministries have at least some involvement with mental health: Community, Family, and Children's Services; Attorney General; Women's Directorate; Senior's Secretariat; Labour; Native Affairs Secretariat; Education; Training, Colleges, and Universities; Culture; Public Safety and Security; and Francophone Affairs.

Deinstitutionalization and Other Challenges to Service Delivery As stated previously, there is an emphasis in Canada on psychiatric bed reduction and closure. The consequences of **deinstitutionalization** are multiple and include homelessness and a lack of supported housing, the jailing of the mentally ill, the failure to achieve an ideal of community-focused care for people with mental disorders, a lack of home care, insufficient intensive case management, too few community-based crisis response systems, concerns about community treatment orders, and so forth. Although deinstitutionalization was a well-intended attempt to reintegrate the mentally ill with the rest of Canadian society and to prevent involuntary hospitalization and treatment, to this point many professionals and "psychiatric survivors" would consider it a failure. We will revisit some of these issues in Chapter 18.

Treatment of psychological problems in the North and other remote areas is usually carried out at a community level or people are "exported" to major centres, often a long way away. Hospitalization is not as common as it is in urban areas, except for serious conditions, such as psychosis or high risk of suicide. Nonetheless, there are innovative programs. For example, in 1999 Yukon's Whitehorse General Hospital launched an innovative Native "healing" building (CMAJ, 1999) as an addition to a very successful Aboriginal healing program. Aboriginal people account for approximately half the admissions at the 49-bed hospital. The program is staffed by First Nations professionals, many of whom are fluent in the seven Aboriginal languages spoken in the Yukon. This program should serve as a template for similar programs in the North. It is consistent with the recommendation of Kirmayer et al. (2000) that community development and local control of the health care system be extended to Canada's Aboriginal people in order (1) to make services responsive to the needs of Aboriginal people and (2) to promote the sense of individual and collective efficacy and pride that contributes to positive mental health. Conventional programs, such as those that help people with substance abuse, are also needed in many regions (e.g., Kirmayer et al., 2000).

Our universal health care system will face many challenges in the future. Much is said in the media and popular books (e.g., Foot, 1996), for example, about the consequences to the health care system of an aging "baby boom" population. Meeting the mental health needs of elderly people will involve multidisciplinary teams to provide community outreach, in-home assessment and treatment, caregiver support, and so forth (Canadian Association on Gerontology, 2000a). We will discuss community-based care of the elderly in Chapter 16. In addition to destigmatization and compassion, people with the most serious mental disorders (e.g., schizophrenia and bipolar disorder) will also need comprehensive, integrated, coordinated, and multidisciplinary services and support (Denton, 2000; Goering et al., 2000). People with cognitive disabilities (e.g., mental retardation) live longer than previously but some are prone to develop Alzheimer's-like dementia and will require expanded or additional home services (Canadian Association on Gerontology, 2000b). As noted by Goering et al. (2000), until quite recently provision of mental health services was fragmented, lacked mechanisms to coordinate or integrate services, and was not accountable.

There are now approximately 370 general-hospital psychiatric units in Canada, providing about 10,000 inpatient beds with provincially mandated services that include inpatient care, outpatient care, daycare, emergency care, and consultation (Goering et al., 2000). However, as noted by Goering et al. (2000), the preferred mental health service model is one that emphasizes intensive local community supports and services, along with the general-hospital psychiatric units and regional tertiary care centres (the provincial psychiatric hospitals or their replacements). Garfinkel and Goldbloom (2000, p. 164) predicted that there will be enhanced home care (see the discussion of the Romanow Report below) and the further development of innovative models for service delivery, both within and outside institutions. Just as there is currently an emphasis on evidence-based treatment (see below), there is currently a focus on **best practice models** of service delivery (e.g., "Best Practices in Mental Health Reform"; Health Canada, 1998). Goering et al. (2000) provided two examples, the first ensuring that newer antipsychotic and other medications are available to those who can benefit from them (see Chapter 11) and the second ensuring that new and effective rehabilitation approaches, such as community treatment teams (see Chapter 11 and Chapter 18), are widely available.

Delivery of Psychotherapy The restructuring has implications for people treated with psychotherapy or a combination of psychological and biological interventions. Evaluation of the effectiveness of psychotherapy has become a significant issue because of the increasing demands placed on psychotherapists by both the universal health care system and third-party insurance companies (Hunsley & Johnston, 2000). Psychotherapists are being asked to restrict themselves to the most effective and efficient treatments. Professional organizations are becoming involved as well. For example, the Section on Clinical Psychology of the Canadian Psychological Association (CPA) has been spearheading efforts to reach consensus on which treatments are supported by enough controlled data to be regarded as "**evidence-based" treatment** or psychological practice (Hunsley, Dobson, Johnston, & Mikail, 1999). Since time-limited psychotherapy is available as an alternative to classic psychodynamic treatment, which sometimes requires many years, provincial governments concerned about cost-effectiveness are limiting or attempting to limit the use of classical analysis and other forms of long-term psychotherapy within the Medicare system. We will revisit this issue in Chapter 17.

According to Goering et al. (2000), over a recent five-year period, use of mental health services (offered by psychiatrists and general practitioners) in British Columbia and Ontario increased faster than use of services for other health problems.

Help-Seeking As we will see in the next chapter, some people from minority groups have difficulty asking for help for psychological problems. What is the situation for the Canadian population in general? A large community study in Ontario—the Ontario Health Survey (Mental Health Supplement) (described in detail in Canadian Perspective 3.2)—determined that 7.8 percent of respondents used mental health services in the past year (Lin, Goering, Offord, Campbell, & Boyle, 1996). About half of those seeking help had a concurrent psychiatric diagnosis. The vast majority (32 to 61 percent) sought help from outpatient service providers, a majority of whom went to the general medical sector (Lin et al., 1996). Over 75 percent of those with a diagnosed disorder (see Chapter 3) in the past year did not seek help; however, 27.1 percent of those who sought help did not qualify for a diagnosis. Lin et al. (1996) concluded that there is a "mismatch" between people's needs and the care received. Although the strongest predictor of help-seeking was psychiatric diagnosis, help-seeking was also associated with marital disruption and poverty.

Another recent study confirms that professional services are underutilized. The Women's Health Study conducted in Ontario found that only about 5 of 10 women with at least one lifetime psychiatric disorder sought out mental health services (Frise et al., 2002). The presence of three or more comorbid disorders was associated with increased likelihood of seeking help, but it was still the case that 35 percent of women with three or more disorders did not seek help.

This problem of underutilization may be underestimated because women are actually more willing to seek help than men. A recent analysis of data from the Mental Health Supplement to the Ontario Health Survey confirmed the existence of gender differences in the use of outpatient mental health services for mood disorders, anxiety disorders, substance-use disorders, and antisocial behaviours (Rhodes, Goering, To, & Williams, 2002). Moreover, these gender differences remain evident after controlling for differences in type of mental disorder and associated differences in social and economic factors.

Community Psychology and Prevention Much of our discussion of therapy and interventions has focused on situations in which professionals make themselves available to clients in offices, clinics, or hospitals. This type of service delivery, long referred to as "the waiting mode" (Rappaport & Chinsky, 1974), is characteristic of traditional therapy, whether inpatient or outpatient. Community psychology (see Chapter 18 for further discussion), in contrast, operates in "the seeking mode." Rather than waiting for people to initiate contact, community psychologists seek out problems, or even potential problems. In addition, they often focus on prevention, in contrast to the more usual situation of trying to reduce the severity or duration of an already existing problem. It is generally recognized that we must focus on preventive measures if we are ever going to solve the problem of mental illness in Canada. In particular, there is a need for primary prevention programs that promote the psychological, social, and physical well-being of all people in Canada. Although we have had some success, we have a long way to go. For example, despite a proclamation by governments in Canada that child poverty would be eliminated by the year 2000, it has actually increased in the past decade (Denton, 2000). Nonetheless, there are ongoing programs that promise the fulfillment of prevention goals in the future. Here is just one example. In 1995 the Canadian federal government established "Aboriginal Head Start" to facilitate the development and school readiness of Aboriginal children by meeting their psychological, emotional, social, health, and nutritional needs. The initiative is intended to "encourage the development of locally controlled projects in First Nations communities that strive to instil a sense of pride, a desire to learn, provide parenting skills, foster emotional and social development, increase confidence, and improve family relationships" (Health Canada: <http://www.hc-sc.gc.ca/msb/fnihp/ahs_e.htr>). The program was expanded in 1998 as part of a commitment made in "Gathering Strength: Canada's Aboriginal Action Plan," with approximately $25 million annual funding to continue indefinitely beyond 2002. We will examine prevention programs throughout this book.

COST OF MENTAL HEALTH PROBLEMS

What is the cost of mental health problems in Canada? The cost in misery and human suffering among both the people who experience psychological problems and those they touch, their family, friends, and even strangers, is incalculable. We address the issue of the emotional cost of psychological disorders throughout this book. Suffice it to say at this point that an Ontario Ministry of Health study (1994) reported that disability costs to society, which often go unrecognized owing to the stigma attached to symptoms of mental disorders and their treatment, include (1) personal misery, (2) disruption of family life, (3) lower quality of life, and (4) loss of productivity. Regarding the last point, in Ontario the monthly total number of days lost by people with mental disorders was estimated at 1,828,200 in 1990. The financial burden in terms of direct costs (e.g., charges to Medicare) and indirect costs (e.g., loss of productivity) is staggering. One study estimated that these costs are at least $14.4 billion each year (Stephens & Joubert, 2001).

According to Bland (1998), schizophrenia is the fifth leading cause of disability throughout the world and its financial costs are enormous. The Schizophrenia Society of Canada (<http://www.schizophrenia.ca/>) estimates that each year more than $4 billion is spent on treatment, welfare costs, family benefits, and community services connected with the disorder. Goeree et al. (1999) calculated the costs to be a more conservative but still extremely high $2.35 billion. In 1989–1990, schizophrenia accounted for

3.6 million hospital days in Canada, or 30.2 percent of hospital days for all mental disorders (Health Canada, 1993). In the first complete cost-of-suicide analysis performed in Canada, Clayton and Barcelo (1996) estimated the economic impact of suicide deaths that occurred in New Brunswick. For the 94 deaths reported that year, direct costs for health care services, autopsies, funerals, and police investigations were over half a million dollars. Indirect costs, which estimate the value of lost productivity through premature deaths, were almost $80 million. Although the real impact is the tragic loss of human life, the total dollar cost estimate for each suicide was about $850,000. As noted previously, those who seek to provide needed services at the community level must compete with traditional institutional services for funding.

THE FUTURE

"Medicare is sustainable if we want it to be."
—Roy Romanow, Ottawa, November 28, 2002

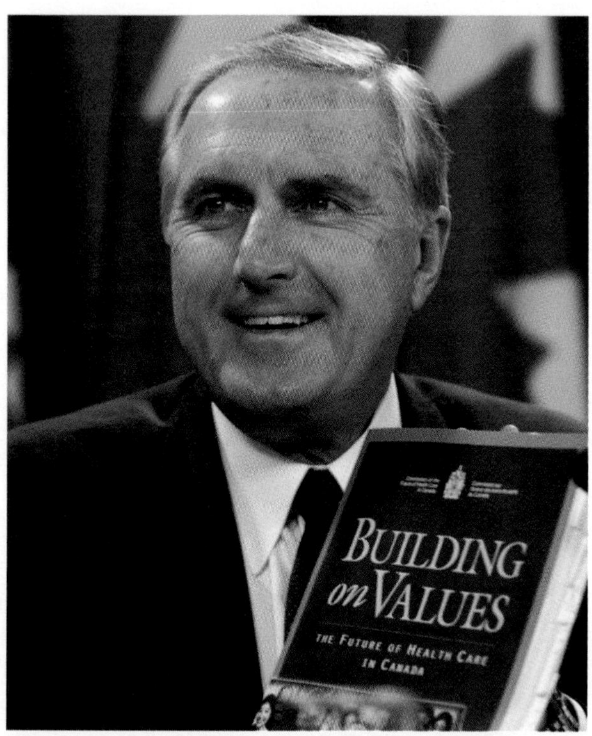

Health care commissioner Roy Romanow recommended crucial changes to Canada's system.

The Romanow Report The Government of Canada established the Royal Commission on the Future of Health Care in Canada in April 2001 (CMAJ, 2001) and appointed the former premier of Saskatchewan, Mr. Roy Romanow, as commissioner. The commission's mandate was to engage Canadians in a national dialogue and to assess various options for a long-term, sustainable universally accessible, publicly funded health care system. Although the commission intended to examine mental health issues, various "stakeholders" formed an alliance (the Canadian Alliance on Mental Illness and Mental Health or CAMIMH) to address what they saw as two key policy weaknesses in the mental health area in Canada (see <http://www.cpa-apc.org/Public/Questions.asp>): (1) a fragmented constituency and (2) the lack of a comprehensive national plan. CAMIMH is an alliance of five national organizations representing major consumer, family, community, and medical constituencies: the Canadian Mental Health Association, the Mood Disorders Association of Canada, the Schizophrenia Society of Canada, the National Network of Mental Health, and the Canadian Psychiatric Association. The accord reached among the groups meant that for the first time these diverse interests could speak in a unified way about policies in Canada that affect the mentally ill. Among other things, the organization called for a national, coordinated action plan on mental illness and mental health. Other stakeholders in the mental health field, such as the Canadian Psychological Association, as well as private citizens, made presentations and submissions to Mr. Romanow at public hearings as he criss-crossed the country.

Mr. Romanow released his final report on November 28, 2002 (see <http://finalreport.healthcarecommission.ca>). A comprehensive template for the development of health care in Canada, it reaffirmed and expanded upon the five principles of the Canada Health Act. It also proposed sweeping changes to Medicare and made 47 specific recommendations. Perhaps the central element of the report was the proposal to expand Medicare coverage beyond just physicians and hospitals. We focus here on the mental health implications. Calling mental health the "orphan child of Medicare," Mr. Romanow recommended that it be made a priority within the system. Of particular relevance, he recommended broadening Medicare to include a limited number of home care services and, eventually, some drug treatments and a national drug agency.

The proposed expansion of the Canada Health Act would specifically include home care coverage for mental health case management and intervention services (over $500 million of new funding) as part of a $1-billion home care transfer. Mr. Romanow also proposed the establishment of a new program to provide direct support to informal caregivers (e.g., family and friends) to allow them to be away from work to provide necessary home care assistance at critical times. Although he stopped short of full pharmacare, he recommended a $1-billion "catastrophic drug transfer" to cover 50 percent of the cost of drug insurance plans in excess of $1,500 per person a year, a strategy that would improve access to necessary medications for people with severe, chronic psychiatric disorders such as schizophrenia and bipolar disorder. The report also called for an improvement in services to rural and remote communities, including Aboriginal communities. Consistent with our previous discussion of best practice models and evidence-based treatment, the report stated that the principle of accountability must be added to the Canada Health Act.

Numerous mental health professional and advocacy groups (e.g., CAIMH) endorsed these and other key recommendations and urged the minister of health to ensure inclusion of them in any proposed implementation plans, since they "will offer hope to those with serious mental illnesses" (see <http://www.cpa apc.org/Press_Releases /PR_Nov28_2002.asp>). Further, the proposed transformation strategies (such as for primary care and services to remote areas) were presumed to offer a chance to improve integration of primary care and mental health reforms. However, 10 months after the report was released, Mr. Romanow expressed frustration because he perceived that his recommendations had been "stalled by either federal inaction or provincial obstinacy" (Walkom, September 20, 2003).

The Future Role of Psychology What will be psychology's role in a restructured Canadian mental health system? In their review of the use of psychological services in Canada, Hunsley et al. (1999) cite evidence that psychological interventions are effective in treating a wide range of disorders and are cost-effective for the health care system. Ritchie and Edwards (1998) anticipated that the upcoming changes would provide a tailor-made opportunity for psychologists in Canada "whose knowledge and skills are well suited for the planning, implementation, and evaluation of action-oriented programs with targeted outcomes" (p. 387). Although the Canadian Psychological Association endorsed many of the Romanow Report recommendations (CPA, December 2002) in a "Psychology Specific Analysis," (also see Romanow & Marchildon, 2003) it eschewed the "physical medicine vision" and expressed disappointment that psychology's "vision was not embraced or even referenced" (p. 4). For example, the report did not mention psychological services not covered by Medicare plans, nor did it discuss ways of linking these services to the public system. Further, the report did not address research on the efficacy of medication combined with psychological interventions or findings about the superiority of psychological treatments. With respect to the report's emphasis on strengthening the role of prevention, the CPA observed that the "physical health focus is disappointing considering the well-documented role of psychology in prevention, the plethora of health issues involving psychological factors and the central role of mental health and mental illness" (p. 11). On a positive note and consistent with the vision of Ritchie and Edwards (1998), the CPA saw the possibility of the meaningful involvement of psychology in the proposed Centres for Health Innovation because of the research skills and knowledge base of psychology.

The bottom line is that it is unlikely that psychologists will be invited to participate directly in Medicare in the future. However, when thinking about the costs of psychological disorders, we should remind ourselves of the other side of the equation. As Hunsley et al. (1999) concluded, "It is essential that policy-makers recognize the long-term costs of failing to invest in psychological services" (p. 237).

SUMMARY

- The study of psychopathology is a search for why people behave, think, and feel in unexpected, sometimes bizarre, and typically self-defeating ways. Much less is known than we would like.
- This book will focus on the ways in which psychopathologists have been trying to determine the causes of abnormal behaviour and what they know about preventing and alleviating it.
- Several characteristics are considered in evaluating whether a behaviour is abnormal: statistical infrequency, violation of societal norms, personal distress, disability or dysfunction, and unexpectedness. Each characteristic tells us something about what can be considered abnormal, but none by itself provides a fully satisfactory definition. It is impossible to offer a simple definition that captures abnormality in its entirety.
- The field of abnormal psychology has its origins in ancient demonology and crude medical theorizing. Since the beginning of scientific inquiry into abnormal behaviour, two major points of view have vied for attention: the somatogenic, which assumes that every mental aberration is caused by a physical malfunction; and the psychogenic, which assumes that the person's body is intact and that difficulties are to be explained in psychological terms.
- The somatogenic viewpoint originated in the writings of Hippocrates. After the fall of the Greco-Roman civilization, it became less prominent, but then re-emerged in the 18th and 19th centuries through the writings of such people as Kraepelin.
- The psychogenic viewpoint is akin to early demonology. Its more modern version emerged in the 19th century from the work of Charcot and the seminal writings of Breuer and Freud.
- We examined a number of issues and events that are of historical and current relevance to students in a Canadian setting or to students who are particularly interested in developments in Canada. For example, we described the role of Dorothea Dix and the confluence of factors that led to the development of the first asylums and ushered in the institution-building era in Canada. Despite humane motives, the long-term results were not very positive, as we learned from our discussion of provincial psychiatric hospitals in the latter part of the 20th centu-

ry. In Canada the current emphasis is on psychiatric-hospital bed reduction and closure.

- Public perception of the mentally ill can be negative at times. If people's attitudes are currently more favourable than in the past, it is in part due to the efforts of Clarence Hincks and the Canadian Mental Health Association.
- The mental health system in Canada is closely tied to Medicare, the universal health care system. The system will face many challenges in the future. There is a need for an increased focus on and funding for community-based interventions and prevention programs.
- The Commission on the Future of Health Care in Canada recommended that mental health be made a priority within the system. Specific recommendations included broadening Medicare to include a limited number of home care services and some drug treatments.

KEY TERMS

abnormal behaviour (p. 3)
accountability (p. 29)
asylums (p. 9)
bedlam (p. 9)
best practice models (p. 27)
Canadian Mental Health Association (p. 21)
cathartic method (p. 16)
clinical psychologist (p. 5)
clinicians (p. 5)
community psychology (p. 28)
community treatment orders (p. 18)
counselling psychologists (p. 6)
deinstitutionalization (p. 26)
demonology (p. 7)
diagnosis (p. 6)
dissociative identity disorder (p. 22)
evidence-based treatment (p. 27)
exorcism (p. 7)
general paresis (p. 15)
germ theory (of disease) (p. 15)
Medicare (p. 25)
mental health status (p. 25)
milieu therapy (p. 18)
moral treatment (p. 11)
normal curve (p. 3)
prevention (p. 28)
provincial psychiatric hospitals (p. 17)
psychiatric nurse (p. 6)
psychiatrist (p. 6)
psychoactive drugs (p. 6)
psychoanalyst (p. 6)
psychogenesis (p. 7)
psychopathology (p. 3)
psychotherapy (p. 6)
schizophrenia (p. 22)
social worker (p. 6)
somatogenesis (p. 7)
stereotyping (p. 21)
stigmatization (p. 21)
syndrome (p. 15)
trepanning (p. 7)

Reflections: Past, Present, and Future

- In your opinion, based on your reading and thinking about the material presented in this first chapter, what is the meaning or significance of each of the quotations presented at the beginning of the chapter? Do you agree with the theme of each quotation?
- Although it is very difficult to arrive at a simple or completely satisfactory definition of abnormality, you should think about the material presented in this chapter and develop your own comprehensive definition. When you have finished the exercise, turn to Chapter 3 and think about the definition accepted by the American (and Canadian) Psychiatric Association in the current version of the *Diagnostic and Statistical Manual of Mental Disorders* or DSM-IV-TR (American Psychiatric Association, 2000).
- Think of someone you have heard about (or possibly someone you know) who appears to suffer from a psychological disorder or to behave abnormally at times. How would you conceptualize that person's disorder or behaviour in terms of the somatogenic and psychogenic hypotheses? We will examine modern scientific perspectives in the next chapter. You should know that current views typically integrate several perspectives or "paradigms."
- How should we try to help the person who has a psychological disorder or problem? Are you in favour of biological interventions, psychological treatments, self-help, or social change? Do our views about the causes of psychological disorders affect our beliefs about how they should be treated?

2 chapter

Current Paradigms and the Role of Cultural Factors

"Luke, you're going to find that many of the truths we cling to depend greatly on our own point of view."
— Ben (Obi-Wan) Kenobi, *Return of the Jedi* (1983)

"We are too much accustomed to attribute to a single cause that which is the product of several, and the majority of our controversies come from that."
— Baron Justus von Liebig (1803–1873)

"Culture is the whole complex of relationships, knowledge, languages, social institutions, beliefs, values and ethical rules that bind people together and give a collective and its individual members a sense of who they are and where they belong."
— Canadian Royal Commission on Aboriginal Peoples (1996, p. 25)

Tom Thomson, *The West Wind*, 1917
oil on canvas, 120.7 x 137.2 cm,
ART GALLERY OF ONTARIO, TORONTO
Gift of the Canadian Club of Toronto, 1926

The subject of Chapter 1 was the nature of abnormality—its history and how it has been defined by characteristics such as personal distress and the violation of norms. We ended the chapter with a summary of current issues related to Canada's mental health system. In this chapter, we consider current paradigms of abnormal behaviour and treatment. A paradigm is a set of basic assumptions, a general perspective, that defines how to conceptualize and study a subject, how to gather and interpret relevant data, even how to think about a particular subject. Our discussion of paradigms lays the groundwork for the examination of the major categories of disorders and intervention. Following our discussion of paradigms, we will examine the role of cultural factors in psychopathology from a Canadian perspective.

THE ROLE OF PARADIGMS

Science is bound by the limitations imposed on scientific inquiry by the current state of knowledge. It is also bound by the scientist's own limitations. How do we handle the challenge of remaining objective when trying to understand and study abnormal behaviour? Every effort should be made to study abnormal behaviour according to scientific principles but science is not a completely objective and certain enterprise. Rather, as suggested by philosopher of science Thomas Kuhn (1962), subjective factors as well as limitations in our perspective on the universe enter into the conduct of scientific inquiry.

Central to any application of scientific principles, in Kuhn's view, is the notion of paradigm, the conceptual framework or approach within which the scientist works. A paradigm is a set of basic assumptions that outline the particular universe of scientific inquiry. It has profound implications for how scientists operate, for "[people] whose research is based on shared paradigms are committed to the same rules and standards for scientific practice" (Kuhn, 1962, p. 11). Paradigms specify what problems scientists will investigate and how they will go about the investigation. Paradigms are an intrinsic part of a science, serving the vital function of indicating the rules to be followed.

A paradigm injects inevitable biases into the definition and collection of data and may also affect the interpretation of facts. In other words, the meaning or import given to data may depend to a considerable extent on a paradigm. In this chapter, we will describe the major paradigms of abnormal psychology and provide an idea of how they operate. We present five paradigms: biological, psychoanalytic, humanistic and existential, learning, and cognitive.

Current thinking about abnormal behaviour tends to be multi-faceted. The work of clinicians and researchers is informed by an awareness of the strengths and limitations of the various paradigms. For this reason, current views of abnormal behaviour and its treatment tend to integrate several paradigms. Later in this chapter, we will describe other paradigms—the diathesis-stress and biopsychosocial—that provide the basis for an integrative approach.

THE BIOLOGICAL PARADIGM

The biological paradigm of abnormal behaviour is a continuation of the somatogenic hypothesis. This broad perspective holds that mental disorders are caused by aberrant biological processes. This paradigm has often been referred to as the medical model or disease model.

The study of abnormal behaviour is linked historically to medicine. Early and contemporary workers have used the model of physical illness as the basis for understanding deviant behaviour. Within the field of abnormal behaviour, the terminology of medicine is pervasive. As we described earlier, when Louis Pasteur discovered the relationship between bacteria and disease and soon thereafter postulated viruses, the germ theory of disease provided a new explanation for pathology. External symptoms were assumed to be produced through infection of the body by minute organisms and viruses. For a time, the germ theory was the paradigm of medicine, but it soon became apparent that this theory could not account for all diseases. Diabetes, for example, a malfunction of the insulin-secreting cells of the pancreas, cannot be attributed to infection. Nor does it have a single cause. Heart disease is another example. Many factors—genetic makeup, smoking, obesity, life stress, and perhaps even a person's personality—are causes of heart disease. Medical illnesses can differ widely from one another in their causes. However, they all share one characteristic: in all of them, some biological process is disrupted or not functioning normally. That is why we call this the biological paradigm.

The biological paradigm was the dominant paradigm in Canada and elsewhere from the late 1800s until at least the middle of the 20th century. An extreme example of its influence is provided by Hall's (1900) use of gynecological procedures to treat "insanity" in women from British Columbia. He maintained that "insanity exists when the Ego is dominated and controlled by the influence from a diseased periphery nerve tract or center...the removal of a small part of the physical disease might result in the restoration of the balance of power to such an organism and diminish if not remove the abnormal psychic phenomena." Removal of ovarian cysts or complete removal of the ovaries was employed as treatment for melancholia, mania, and delusions. In one such example, Mrs. D was reported to have delusions that her husband was trying to poison her, and she would frequently wander away from home. Her behaviour was attributed to a cyst "the size of a walnut," and both her ovaries were removed as the form of treatment.

Contemporary Approaches to the Biological Paradigm

More sophisticated approaches are used today. There is considerable literature, both research and theory based, dealing with biological factors relevant to psychopathology. Heredity probably predisposes a person to have an increased risk of developing schizophrenia (see Chapter 11), depression may result from chemical imbalances within the brain (Chapter 10), anxiety disorders may stem from a defect within the autonomic nervous system that causes a person to be too easily aroused (Chapter 6), and dementia can be traced to impairments in structures of the brain (Chapter 16). In each case, the psychopathology is viewed as caused by the disturbance of some biological process. Those working with the biological paradigm assume that answers to puzzles of psychopathology will be found within the body. In this section, we will look at two areas of research within this paradigm in which the data are particularly interesting-behaviour genetics and biochemistry.

Behaviour Genetics When the ovum, the female reproductive cell, is joined by the male's spermatozoon, a zygote, or fertilized egg, is produced. It has 46 chromosomes, the number characteristic of a human being. Each chromosome is made up of thousands of genes, the carriers of the genetic information (DNA) passed from parents to child.

Behaviour genetics is the study of individual differences in behaviour that are attributable in part to differences in genetic makeup. The total genetic makeup of an individual, consisting of inherited genes, is referred to as the genotype. An individual's genotype is his or her unobservable genetic constitution; in contrast, an individual's phenotype is the totality of his or her observable, behavioural characteristics, such as level of anxiety. The genotype is fixed at birth, but it should not be viewed as a static entity. Genes controlling various features of development switch off and on at specific times to control aspects of physical development.

The phenotype changes over time and is viewed as the product of an interaction between the genotype and the environment. For example, an individual may be born with the capacity for high intellectual achievement, but whether he or she develops this genetically given potential depends on such environmental factors as upbringing and education. Hence, any measure of intelligence is best viewed as an index of the phenotype.

It is critical to recognize that various clinical syndromes are disorders of the phenotype, not of the genotype. Thus, it is not correct to speak of the direct inheritance of schizophrenia or anxiety disorders; at most, only the genotypes for these disorders can be inherited. Whether these genotypes will eventually engender the phenotypic behaviour disorder will depend on environment and experience. A predisposition, also known as a *diathesis*, may be inherited, but not the disorder itself.

The study of behaviour genetics has relied on four basic methods to uncover whether a predisposition for psychopathology is inherited—comparison of members of a family, comparison of pairs of twins, the investigation of adoptees, and linkage analysis. The family method can be used to study a genetic predisposition among members of a family because the average number of genes shared by two blood relatives is known. Children receive a random sample of half their genes from one parent and half from the other; therefore, on average, siblings as well as parents and their children are identical in 50 percent of their genetic background. People who share 50 percent of their genes with a given individual are called *first-degree relatives* of that person. Relatives not as closely related share fewer genes. Nephews and nieces share 25 percent of the genetic makeup of an uncle and are called *second-degree relatives*. If a predisposition for a mental disorder can be inherited, a study of the family should reveal a relationship between the number of shared genes and the prevalence of the disorder in relatives.

Behaviour genetics studies the degree to which characteristics such as physical resemblance or psychopathology are shared by family members because of shared genes. The University of British Columbia twin study led by Kerry Jang (shown here) and John Livesley is a long-term investigation of the contribution of shared genes to personality factors and behavioural disorders.

The starting point in such investigations is the collection of a sample of individuals who bear the diagnosis in question. These people are referred to as index cases, or probands. Then, relatives are studied to determine the frequency with which the same diagnosis might be applied to them. If a genetic predisposition to the disorder being studied is present, first-degree relatives of the index cases should have the disorder at a rate higher than that found in the general population. For example, about 10 percent of the first-degree relatives of index cases with schizophrenia can be diagnosed as having schizophrenia, compared with about 1 percent of the general population.

In the twin method, both monozygotic (MZ) twins and dizygotic (DZ) twins are compared. MZ, or identical, twins develop from a single fertilized egg and are genetically the same. DZ, or fraternal, pairs develop from separate eggs and are on average only 50 percent alike genetically, no more alike than any other two siblings. MZ twins are always the same sex, but DZ twins can be either the same or the opposite sex. Twin studies begin with diagnosed cases and then search for the presence of the disorder in the other twin. When the twins are similar diagnostically, they are said to be concordant. To the extent that a predisposition for a mental disorder can be inherited, concordance for the disorder should be greater in genetically identical MZ pairs than in DZ pairs. When the MZ concordance rate is higher than the DZ rate, the characteristic being studied is said to be heritable. We will see in later chapters that the concordance for many forms of psychopathology is higher in MZ twins than in DZ twins.

Although the methodology of the family and twin studies is clear, the data they yield are not always easy to interpret. Let us assume that children of parents with panic disorder (see Chapter 6) are themselves more likely than average to have panic disorder. Does this mean that a predisposition for this anxiety disorder is genetically transmitted? Not necessarily. The greater number of children with panic disorder could reflect the child-rearing practices of the panic disorder parents as well as the children's imitation of adult behaviour. In other words, the data show that panic disorder runs in families, but that a genetic predisposition is not necessarily involved.

The ability to offer a genetic interpretation of data from twin studies hinges on what is called the *equal environment assumption*. Because psychopathology is a phenotypic characteristic, concordance among twins for psychopathology is a result of the operation of both genetic and environmental factors. For any diagnosis being studied, the equal environment assumption is that the environmental factors that are partial causes of concordance are equally influential for MZ pairs and DZ pairs. This does not mean that the environments of MZ and DZ twins are equal in all respects. The assumption of equality applies only to factors that are plausible environmental causes of psychopathology. The equal environment assumption would assert that MZ pairs and DZ pairs have equivalent numbers of stressful life experiences. In general, the equal environment assumption seems to be reasonable, although it is clearly in need of further study (Kendler, 1993).

Other factors can also complicate the results of twin research. In their recent study of genetic and environmental influences on posttraumatic stress disorder (an anxiety disorder discussed in Chapter 6) in community residents, Stein, Jang, Taylor, Vernon, and Livesley (2002) identified three factors as biasing heritability estimates: violation of the equal environments assumption, the sex of the participant, and his or her age when the assessment took place. When they controlled statistically for the effects of age and sex differences, they found that genetic and nonshared environmental factors contributed to symptoms of posttraumatic stress disorder. Analyses of the role of these factors in a person's exposure to traumatic events revealed that only environmental factors contributed to exposure to events involving non-assaultive traumas (e.g., motor vehicle accidents, natural disasters) but both genetic and environmental factors contributed to exposure to assaultive traumas (e.g., sexual assaults). Thus, genetic factors may determine, in part, the extent to which a person is likely to experience posttraumatic stress after an assaultive trauma. This study is illuminating because it is the first to examine this issue in a nonmilitary sample and the first to include women. Unfortunately, it is limited because the researchers had to rely on self-report measures.

Researchers using the adoptees method study children who were adopted and reared apart from their abnormal parents. Though infrequent, this situation has the benefit of eliminating the effects of being raised by disordered parents. If a high frequency of panic disorder were found in children reared apart from parents who also had panic disorder, we would have support for the theory that a genetic predisposition figures in the disorder. (The study of MZ twins reared apart would also be valuable, but this situation occurs so rarely that there is virtually no research using this method to study psychopathology. Research involving separated twins does, however, exist in the study of the inheritance of personality traits, as we will see in Chapter 13.)

A fourth method in behaviour genetics, linkage analysis, goes beyond mere attempts to show whether a disorder has a genetic component; it tries to specify the particular gene involved. Researchers using this method typically study families in which a disorder is heavily concentrated. They collect diagnostic information and blood samples from affected individuals and their relatives and use the blood samples to study the inheritance pattern of characteristics whose genetics are fully understood (referred to as genetic markers). Eye colour, for example, is known to be controlled by a gene in a specific location on a specific chromosome. If the occurrence of a form of psychopathology among relatives goes along with the occurrence of another characteristic whose genetics are known (the genetic marker), it is concluded that the gene predisposing individuals to the psychopathology is on the same chromosome and in a similar location on that chromosome (i.e., it is linked) as the gene controlling the other characteristic. We will see several examples of linkage analysis in subsequent chapters, especially when we discuss mood disorders (Chapter 10) and schizophrenia (Chapter 11). The greatest success of the method thus far has been in identifying specific genes on several chromosomes that are extremely important in Alzheimer's disease (see Chapter 16).

Biochemistry in the Nervous System The nervous system is comprised of billions of neurons. Although neurons differ in some respects, each neuron has four major parts: (1) the cell body; (2) several dendrites (the short and thick extensions); (3) one or more axons of varying lengths (usually only one long and thin axon extending a considerable distance from the cell body); and (4) terminal buttons on the many end branches of the axon (Figure 2.1). When a neuron is appropriately stimulated at its cell body or through its dendrites, a nerve impulse, which is a change in the electric potential of the cell, travels down the axon to the terminal endings. Between the terminal endings of the sending axon and the cell membrane of the receiving neuron, there is a small gap, the synapse (see Figure 2.2).

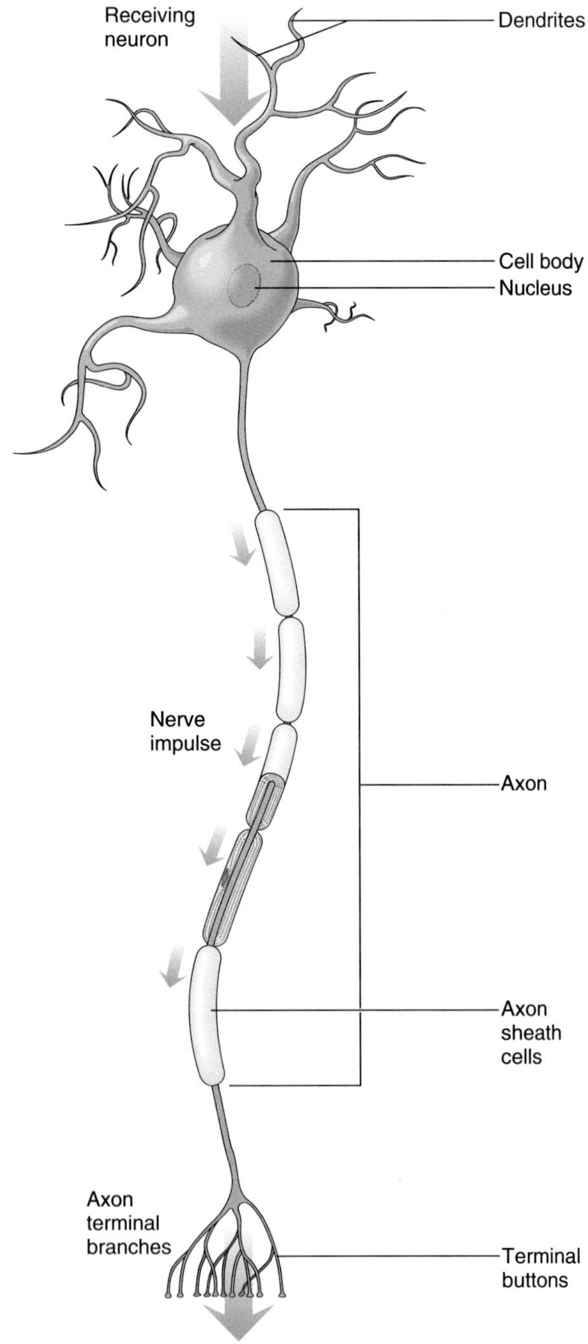

Figure 2.1 The neuron, the basic unit of the nervous system.

For a nerve impulse to pass from one neuron to another and for communication to occur, the impulse must have a way of bridging the synaptic gap. The terminal buttons of each axon contain synaptic vesicles, small structures that are filled with neurotransmitters, chemical substances that allow a nerve impulse to cross the synapse. Nerve impulses cause the synaptic vesicles to release molecules of their transmitter substances, and these molecules flood the synapse and diffuse toward the receiving, or postsynaptic, neuron. The cell membrane of the postsynaptic cell contains proteins, called receptor sites, that are configured so that specific neurotransmitters can fit into them. When a neurotransmitter fits into a receptor site, a message can be sent to the postsynaptic cell. What actually happens to the postsynaptic neuron depends on its integrating thousands of similar messages. Sometimes these messages are excitatory, leading to the creation of a nerve impulse in the postsynaptic cell; at other times, the messages can be inhibitory, making the postsynaptic cell less likely to fire.

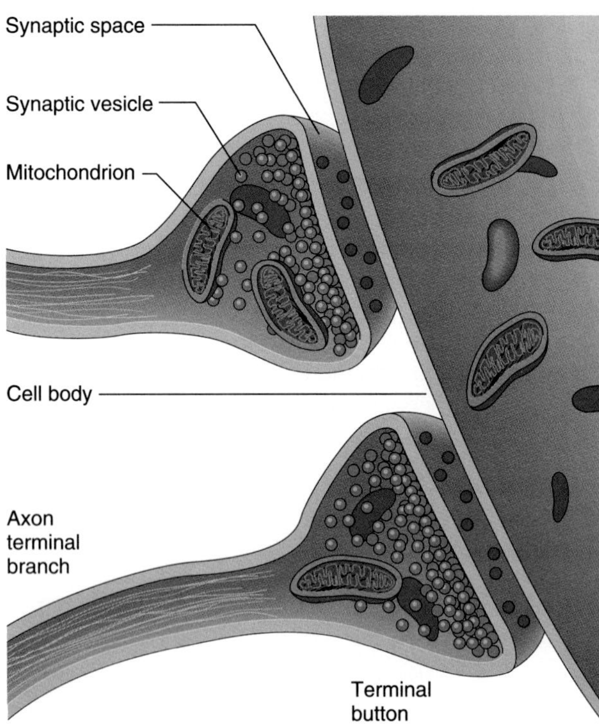

Figure 2.2 A. synapse, showing the terminal buttons of two axon branches in close contact with a very small portion of the cell body of another neuron.

Once a presynaptic neuron (the sending neuron) has released its neurotransmitter, the last step is for the synapse to be returned to its normal state. Not all of the released neurotransmitter has found its way to postsynaptic receptors. Some of what remains in the synapse is broken down by enzymes, and some is pumped back into the presynaptic cell through a process called reuptake.

Several key neurotransmitters have been implicated in psychopathology. Norepinephrine, a neurotransmitter of the peripheral sympathetic nervous system, is involved in producing states of high arousal and thus may be involved in the anxiety disorders. Both serotonin and dopamine are neurotransmitters in the brain. Serotonin may be involved in depression and dopamine in schizophrenia. Another important brain transmitter is gamma-aminobutyric acid (GABA), which inhibits some nerve impulses and may be involved in the anxiety disorders.

Some of the theories linking neurotransmitters to psychopathology have proposed that a given disorder is caused by either too much or too little of a particular transmitter (e.g., mania results from too much norepinephrine, and anxiety disorders from too little GABA). Neurotransmitters are synthesized in the neuron through a series of metabolic steps, beginning with an amino acid. Each reaction along the way to producing an actual transmitter is catalyzed by an enzyme, speeding up the metabolic process. Too much or too little of a particular transmitter could result from an error in these metabolic pathways. Similar disturbances in the amounts of specific transmitters could result from alterations in the usual processes by which transmitters are deactivated after being released into the synapse. For example, a failure to pump leftover neurotransmitter molecules back into the presynaptic cell (reuptake) would leave excess transmitter molecules in the synapse. Then, when a new nerve impulse caused further neurotransmitter substances to be released into the synapse, the postsynaptic neuron would, in a sense, get a double dose of neurotransmitter, making it more likely for a new nerve impulse to be created.

Finally, contemporary research has focused to a large extent on the possibility that the receptors are at fault in some psychopathologies. If the receptors on the postsynaptic neuron were too numerous or too easily excited, the result would be akin to having too much transmitter released. There would simply be more sites available with which the neurotransmitter could interact, increasing the chances that the postsynaptic neuron would be stimulated. The delusions and hallucinations of schizophrenia may result from an overabundance of dopamine receptors.

For many years, researchers and clinicians have attempted to observe directly or make inferences about the functioning of the brain and other parts of the nervous system in their efforts to understand both normal and abnormal psychological functioning (see Focus on Discovery 2.1 and Focus on Discovery 2.2).

focus on discovery/2.1

Structure and Function of the Human Brain

Inside the skull, the brain is enveloped within three layers of non-neural tissue, membranes referred to as meninges. Viewed from the top, the brain is divided by a midline fissure into two mirror-image cerebral hemispheres, together constituting most of the cerebrum. The cerebrum is the "thinking" centre of the brain, which includes the cortex and subcortical structures such as the basal ganglia and limbic system. The major connection between the two hemispheres is a band of nerve fibres called the corpus callosum. Figure 2.3 shows the surface of one of the cerebral hemispheres. The upper, side, and some of the lower surfaces of the hemispheres form the cerebral cortex. The cortex consists of six layers of tightly packed neuron cell bodies with many short, unsheathed interconnecting processes. These neurons, estimated to number 10 to 15 billion, make up a thin outer covering, the so-called grey matter of the brain. The cortex is vastly convoluted; the ridges are called gyri, and the depressions between them sulci, or fissures. Deep fissures divide the cerebral hemispheres into several distinct areas called lobes. The frontal lobe lies in front of the central sulcus; the parietal lobe is behind it and above the lateral sulcus; the temporal lobe is located below the lateral sulcus; and the occipital lobe lies behind the parietal and temporal lobes. Different functions tend to be localized in particular areas of the lobes: vision in the occipital; discrimination of sounds in the temporal; reasoning and other higher mental processes, as well as the regulation of fine voluntary movement, in the frontal; initiation of movements of the skeletal musculature in a band in front of the central sulcus; and receipt of sensations of touch, pressure, pain, temperature, and body position from skin, muscles, tendons, and joints in a band behind the central sulcus.

The two hemispheres of the brain have different functions. The left hemisphere, which generally controls the right half of the body because of the crossing over of motor and sensory fibres, is responsible for speech and, according to some neuropsychologists, for analytical thinking in right-handed people and in a fair number of left-handed people as well. The right hemisphere controls the left side of the body, discerns spatial relations and patterns, and is involved in emotion and intuition. But analytical thinking cannot be located exclusively in the left hemisphere, or intuitive and even creative thinking exclusively in the right; the two hemispheres communicate with each other constantly via the corpus callosum. Localization of apparently different modes of thought is probably not as clear-cut as some people would believe.

If the brain is sliced in half, separating the two cerebral hemispheres (see Figure 2.4), additional important features can be seen. The grey matter of the cerebral cortex does not extend throughout the interior of the brain. Much of the interior is white matter, made up of large tracts or bundles of myelinated (sheathed) fibres that connect cell bodies in the cortex with those

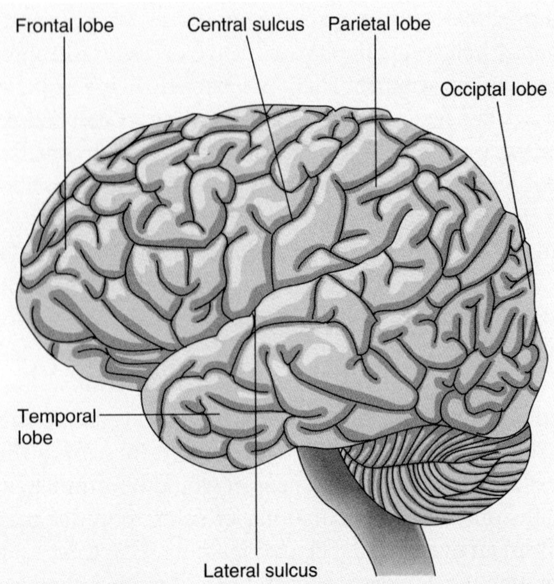

Figure 2.3 Surface of the left cerebral hemisphere, indicating the lobes and the two principal fissures of the cortex.

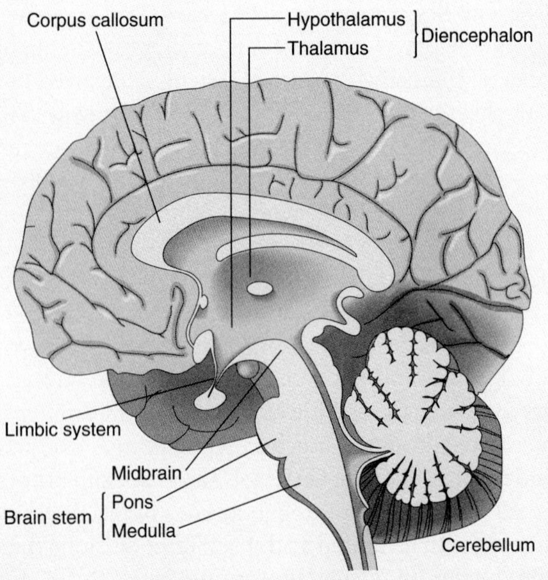

Figure 2.4 Slice of brain through the medial plane, showing the internal structures.

in the spinal cord and in other centres lower in the brain. These centres are pockets of grey matter, referred to as **nuclei**. The nuclei serve both as way stations, connecting tracts from the cortex with other ascending and descending tracts, and as integrating motor and sensory control centres. Some cortical cells project their long fibres or axons to motor neurons in the spinal cord, but others project them only as far as these clusters of interconnecting neuron cell bodies. Four masses are deep within each hemisphere, called collectively the ***basal ganglia***. Also deep within the brain are cavities called **ventricles**; these are continuous with the central canal of the spinal cord and are filled with cerebrospinal fluid.

Figure 2.4 depicts four important functional areas or structures:

1. The **diencephalon**, connected in the front with the hemispheres and behind with the midbrain, contains the **thalamus** and the **hypothalamus**, both consisting of groups of nuclei. The thalamus is a relay station for all sensory pathways except the olfactory. The nuclei making up the thalamus receive nearly all the impulses arriving from the different sensory areas of the body and then pass them on to the cerebrum, where they are interpreted as conscious sensations. The hypothalamus is the highest centre of integration for many visceral processes, regulating metabolism, temperature, perspiration, blood pressure, sleeping, and appetite.
2. The **midbrain** is a mass of nerve-fibre tracts connecting the cerebral cortex with the pons, the medulla oblongata, the cerebellum, and the spinal cord.
3. The **brain stem** comprises the pons and the medulla oblongata and functions primarily as a neural relay station. The **pons** contains tracts that connect the cerebellum with the spinal cord and with motor areas of the cerebrum. The **medulla oblongata** serves as the main line of traffic for tracts ascending from the spinal cord and descending from the higher centres of the brain. At the bottom of the medulla, many of the motor fibres cross to the opposite side. The medulla also contains nuclei that maintain the regular life rhythms of the heartbeat, of the rising and falling diaphragm, and of the constricting and dilating blood vessels. In the core of the brain stem is the **reticular formation**, sometimes called the *reticular activating system* because of the important role it plays in arousal and alertness. The tracts of the pons and medulla send in fibres to connect with the profusely interconnected cells of the reticular formation, which in turn sends fibres to the cortex, the basal ganglia, the hypothalamus, the septal area, and the cerebellum.
4. The **cerebellum**, like the cerebrum, consists primarily of two deeply convoluted hemispheres with an exterior cortex of grey matter and an interior of white tracts. The cerebellum receives sensory information from the inner ear and from muscles, tendons, and joints. The information received and integrated relates to balance, posture, equilibrium, and to the smooth coordination of the body when in motion.
5. A fifth important part of the brain, the **limbic system**, comprises structures that are continuous with one another in the lower cerebrum and that developed earlier than the mammalian cerebral cortex. The limbic system controls the visceral and physical expressions of emotion—quickened heartbeat and respiration, trembling, sweating, and alterations in facial expressions—as well as appetite and other primary drives, namely, hunger, thirst, mating, defence, attack, and flight. Important structures in the limbic system are the cingulate gyrus, stretching about the corpus callosum; the septal area, which is anterior to the thalamus; the long, tubelike hippocampus, which stretches from the septal area into the temporal lobe; and the amygdala (one of the basal ganglia), which is embedded in the tip of the temporal lobe.

BIOLOGICAL APPROACHES TO TREATMENT

An important implication of the biological paradigm is that prevention or treatment of mental disorders should be possible by altering bodily functioning. Certainly, if a deficiency in a particular biochemical substance is found to underlie or contribute to some problem, it makes sense to attempt to correct the imbalance by providing appropriate doses of the deficient chemical. In such cases, a clear connection exists between the cause of a disorder (a biological defect) and its treatment (a biological intervention).

Most biological interventions in common use, however, have not been derived from knowledge of what causes a given disorder. Nonetheless, the use of psychoactive drugs has been increasing. In 1985 psychoactive drugs were prescribed in the United States at about 33 million physician visits, and in 1994, at almost 46 million (Pincus et al., 1998). Tranquillizers such as Valium can be effective in reducing the tension associated with some anxiety disorders, perhaps by stimulating GABA neurons to inhibit other neural systems that create the physical symptoms of anxiety. Antidepressants such as Prozac, now the most widely prescribed psychoactive drugs, increase neural transmission in neurons that use serotonin as a neurotransmitter by inhibiting the reuptake of serotonin. Antipsychotic drugs such as Thorazine, used in the treatment of schizophrenia, reduce the activity of neurons that use dopamine as a neurotransmitter by blocking their receptors. Stimulants are often employed in treating children with attention-deficit/hyperactivity disorder. Stimulants increase the levels of several neurotransmitters that help children pay attention.

It should be noted that a person can believe in a biological basis for a mental problem yet recommend psychological intervention. Recall that Hippocrates proposed non-somatic therapies, such as rest for melancholia, to deal with mental disorders that he considered somatic in origin. Contemporary workers also appreciate that non-biological interventions can have beneficial effects on the soma. For example, simply preventing a person from performing a compulsive ritual is an effective and behavioural treatment for obsessive-compulsive disorder, for it has measurable effects on brain activity.

Contemporary approaches to biological assessment are discussed in detail in Chapter 4. These approaches involve attempts to make inferences about the functioning of the nervous system (e.g., neuropsychological assessment) or to "see" the actual structure and functioning of the brain and other parts of the nervous system (e.g., magnetic resonance imaging).

EVALUATING THE BIOLOGICAL PARADIGM

Our discussion of each paradigm will conclude with an evaluation section. For the most part, these sections will focus on the paradigm itself rather than on treatment. Treatments will be evaluated in the chapters dealing with specific disorders as well as in Chapter 17.

Over the past two decades, biological researchers have made great progress in elucidating brain-behaviour relationships. Biologically based research on both causes and treatment of psychopathology is proceeding at a rapid rate. Although we view these developments in a positive light, we also want to caution against reductionism. **Reductionism** refers to the view that whatever is being studied can and should be reduced to its most basic elements or

focus on discovery/2.2

The Autonomic Nervous System

The mammalian nervous system can be divided into two relatively separate functional parts: the **somatic** (or voluntary) **nervous system** and the **autonomic** (or involuntary) **nervous system (ANS)**. Because the autonomic nervous system is especially important in the study of emotional behaviour, it is useful to review its principal characteristics.

Skeletal muscles, such as those that move our limbs, are stimulated by the voluntary nervous system. Much of our behaviour, however, is dependent on a nervous system that generally operates without our awareness and has traditionally been viewed as beyond voluntary control—hence the term *autonomic*. However, research on biofeedback has shown that the ANS is under greater voluntary control than previously believed.

The autonomic nervous system stimulates the endocrine glands, the heart, and the smooth muscles found in the walls of the blood vessels, stomach, intestines, kidneys, and other organs. This nervous system is itself divided into two parts, the **sympathetic nervous system** and the **parasympathetic nervous system** (Figure 2.5), which work sometimes in opposition to each other, sometimes in unison. The sympathetic portion of the ANS, when energized, accelerates the heartbeat, dilates the pupils, inhibits intestinal activity, increases electrodermal activity, and initiates other smooth-muscle and glandular responses that prepare the organism for sudden activity and stress. Some physiologists view the sympathetic nervous system as primarily excitatory and view the other division, the parasympathetic, as responsible for maintenance functions and more quiescent behaviour, such as deceleration of the heartbeat, constriction of the pupils, and acceleration of intestinal contractions. Division of activities is not quite so clear-cut, however, for it is the parasympathetic system that increases blood flow to the genitals during sexual excitement.

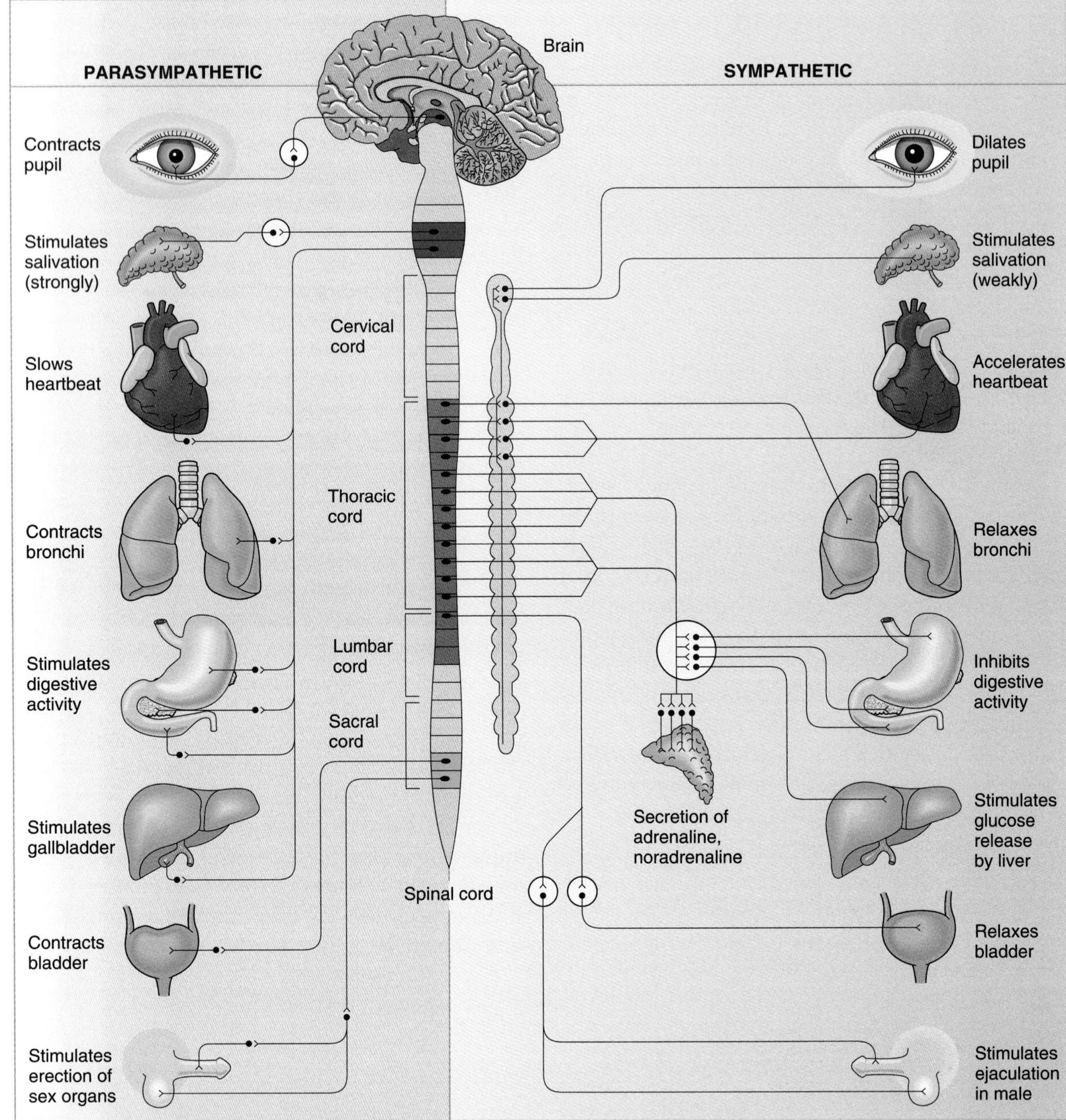

Figure 2.5 The autonomic nervous system.

constituents. In the case of mental disorders, the position proposes reducing complex mental and emotional responses to simple biology. Using this logic, the argument could be taken even further to propose that biology be reduced to atomic physics. In its extreme form, reductionism asserts that psychology and psychopathology will ultimately be nothing more than biology.

Although reductionism is an influential viewpoint among biological psychiatrists, in philosophical circles, it has been severely criticized. Once basic elements, such as individual nerve cells, are organized into more complex structures or systems, such as neural pathways or circuits, the properties of these systems cannot be deduced from the properties of the constituents. The whole is often greater than the sum of its parts. As for the field of abnormal psychology, problems such as delusional beliefs and dysfunctional attitudes may well be impossible to explain biologically, even with a detailed understanding of the behaviour of individual neurons (Turkheimer, 1998).

The Psychoanalytic Paradigm

The central assumption of the psychoanalytic or psychodynamic paradigm, originally developed by Sigmund Freud (1856–1939), is that psychopathology results from unconscious conflicts in the individual. We will look at the significant impact of Freud in the development of this paradigm, but we will also examine the ways in which the focus of this paradigm has shifted.

CLASSICAL PSYCHOANALYTIC THEORY

Classical psychoanalytic theory refers to the original views of Freud. His theories encompassed both the structure of the mind itself and the development and dynamics of personality.

Sigmund Freud was the founder of the psychoanalytic paradigm, both proposing a theory of the causes of mental disorder and devising a new method of therapy.

Structure of the Mind Freud divided the mind, or the psyche, into three principal parts: id, ego, and superego. These are metaphors for specific functions or energies. According to Freud, the id is present at birth and is the part of the mind that accounts for all the energy needed to run the psyche. It comprises the basic urges for food, water, elimination, warmth, affection, and sex. Trained as a neurologist, Freud saw the source of all the id's energy as biological. Only later, as the infant develops, is this energy, which Freud called libido, converted into psychic energy, all of it unconscious, below the level of awareness.

The id seeks immediate gratification and operates according to the pleasure principle. When the id is not satisfied, tension is produced, and the id strives to eliminate this tension. For example, the infant feels hunger, an aversive drive, and is impelled to move about, sucking, to reduce the tension. Another means of obtaining gratification is primary process thinking, generating images—in essence, fantasies—of what is desired. The infant who wants the mother's milk imagines sucking at the mother's breast and thereby obtains some short-term satisfaction.

The ego is the next aspect of the psyche to develop. Unlike the id, the ego is primarily conscious and begins to develop from the id during the second six months of life. Its task is to deal with reality. Through its planning and decision-making functions, called secondary process thinking, the ego realizes that operating on the pleasure principle at all times is not the most effective way of maintaining life. The ego thus operates on the reality principle as it mediates between the demands of reality and the immediate gratification desired by the id.

The final part of the psyche to emerge is the superego, which operates roughly as the conscience and develops throughout childhood. Freud believed that the superego developed from the ego much as the ego developed from the id. As children discover that many of their impulses, such as biting or bedwetting, are not acceptable to their parents, they begin to incorporate, or introject, parental values as their own to enjoy parental approval and avoid disapproval.

The behaviour of the human being, as conceptualized by Freud, is thus a complex interplay of these three parts of the psyche. The interplay of these forces is referred to as the psychodynamics of the personality.

Freud was drawn into studying the mind by his work with Breuer on hypnosis and hysteria. The apparently powerful role played by factors of which patients seemed unaware led Freud to postulate that much of human behaviour is determined by forces inaccessible to awareness. The id's instincts as well as many of the superego's activities are not known to the conscious mind. While the ego is primarily conscious and is involved in thinking and planning, it, too, has important unconscious aspects (the defence mechanisms) that protect it from anxiety. Freud considered most of the important determinants of behaviour to be unconscious.

Stages of Psychosexual Development Freud conceived of the personality as developing through a series of four distinct psychosexual stages. At each stage, a different part of the body is the most sensitive to sexual excitation and therefore the most capable of providing libidinal satisfaction to the id. The oral stage is the first stage of psychosexual development. From birth to about 18 months, the demands of the infant's id are satisfied primarily by feeding and the sucking and biting associated with it. As a result, the body parts involved with this stage are the lips, mouth, and tongue. From about 18 months to 3 years of age, the child's enjoyment shifts to the anus. During this anal stage, the child's main source of libidinous pleasure comes from passing and retaining faeces. The phallic stage extends from age 3 to age 5 or 6, and maximum gratification of the id now occurs through genital stimulation. Between the ages of 6 and 12, the child is in a latency period. The final and adult stage is the genital stage, during which heterosexual interests predominate.

The growing person must resolve the conflicts between what the id wants and what the environment will provide during each stage. How this is accomplished determines basic personality traits that last throughout the person's life. For example, if a person in the anal stage experiences either excessive or deficient amounts of gratification, depending on the toilet-training regimen, he or she may develop a **fixation** and is likely to regress to this stage when stressed. Such a person might develop obsessive-compulsive disorder, become stingy or be obsessed with cleanliness.

Perhaps the most important crisis of development occurs during the phallic stage, around age 4. Then, Freud asserted, the child is overcome with sexual desire for the parent of the opposite sex. At the same time, the child views the parent of the same sex as a rival and fears retaliation. The threat of punishment from the parent of the same sex may cause the child to repress the entire conflict, pushing these sexual and aggressive urges into the unconscious. This desire and repression are referred to as the **Oedipus complex** for the male and the **Electra complex** for the female. The dilemma is usually resolved through increased identification with the parent of the same sex and through the adoption of society's moral values, which forbid the child to desire the parent. Through the learning of these moral values the superego develops. According to Freud, resolving the Oedipus or the Electra complex is extremely important to the child's sexual development. Failure to do so may lead the child to feel guilty about sexual desires, to fear intimacy, or to develop other difficulties in romantic relationships.

Too much or too little gratification during one of the psychosexual stages may lead to regression to this stage during stress.

Neurotic Anxiety When one's life is in jeopardy, one feels **objective (realistic) anxiety**, the ego's reaction, according to Freud, to danger in the external world. The person whose personality has not developed fully, perhaps because he or she is fixated at one or another stage, may experience **neurotic anxiety**, a feeling of fear that is not connected to reality or to any real threat. **Moral anxiety** arises when the impulses of the superego punish an individual for not meeting expectations and thereby satisfying the principle that drives the superego—namely, the perfection principle.

Defence Mechanisms: Coping with Anxiety According to Freud and elaborated by his daughter Anna (A. Freud, 1966), the discomfort experienced by the anxious ego can be reduced in several ways. Objective anxiety, rooted in reality, can often be handled by removing or avoiding the danger in the external world or by dealing with it in a rational way. Neurotic anxiety can be handled by means of a defence mechanism. A **defence mechanism** is a strategy, unconsciously utilized, to protect the ego from anxiety. Perhaps the most important is **repression**, which pushes unacceptable impulses and thoughts into the unconscious. By remaining repressed, these infantile memories and desires cannot be corrected by adult experience and therefore retain their original intensity and immaturity. **Denial**, another important defence mechanism, entails disavowing a traumatic experience, such as being raped, and pushing it into the unconscious. **Projection** attributes to external agents characteristics or desires that an individual possesses but cannot accept in his or her conscious awareness. For example, a woman who unconsciously is averse to regarding herself as angry at others may instead see others as angry with her. Other defence mechanisms are **displacement**, redirecting emotional responses from a perhaps dangerous object to a substitute (e.g., yelling at one's spouse instead of at one's boss); **reaction formation**, converting one feeling (e.g., hate) into its opposite (in this case, love); **regression**, retreating to the behavioural patterns of an earlier age; **rationalization**, inventing a reason for an unreasonable action or attitude; and **sublimation**, converting sexual or aggressive impulses into socially valued behaviours, especially creative activity.

All these defence mechanisms allow the ego to discharge some id energy while not facing frankly the true nature of the motivation. Because defence mechanisms are more readily observed than other symptoms of a disordered personality, they often make people aware of their troubled natures and provide the impetus for consulting a therapist. It should be noted that contemporary psychoanalytic theorists consider some use of defence mechanisms to be adaptive and healthy. A period of denial after the death of a loved one, for example, can help in adjusting to the loss. For the most part, however, defence mechanisms are maladaptive.

Relationship of Psychoanalytic Concepts to Psychopathology Freud believed that the various forms of psychopathology resulted from the presence of strong drives or id instincts that set the stage for the development of unconscious conflicts linked to a particular psychosexual stage. For example, he proposed that phobias—irrational fears and avoidances of harmless objects or situations—were caused by an unresolved Oedipal conflict, with the fear of the father displaced onto some other object or situation. Similarly, obsessive-compulsive disorder was traced to the anal stage, with the urge to soil or to be aggressive transformed by reaction formation into compulsive cleanliness.

In his early work, Freud postulated that the cause of his patients' hysterical problems was sexual abuse in childhood, typically rape by the father. His views elicited outrage from his colleagues, yet he persisted until 1897, when in a letter to his colleague Wilhelm Fleiss he indicated that he had come to believe that many of his patients' accounts were fantasies. Freud struggled later with these competing theories of the origin of hysteria, sometimes favouring one, sometimes the other. But by 1905 the fantasy theory had clearly won out (Masson, 1984).

This change had a profound impact on the development of psychoanalysis, for it directed the search for the causes of psychopathology away from the environment and toward the patient and his or her fantasies. Furthermore, the emphasis on fantasy was crucial to the discovery of the Oedipal and Electra conflicts, cornerstones of psychoanalytic thought.

NEO-FREUDIAN PSYCHODYNAMIC PERSPECTIVES

The significance of Freud's theories and clinical work was widely recognized by his contemporaries, including Carl Jung and Alfred Adler. Disagreements arose, however, about many general issues, such as the relative importance of id versus ego; the significance of the earliest years of life in contrast with adult experiences; and the reflex-like nature of id impulses versus the purposive behaviour governed primarily by the ego.

If there were so many disagreements, why are neo-Freudians still associated with Freud? All have continued to embrace his emphasis on human behaviour as the product of dynamics within the psyche. For this reason, they share with Freud a psychodynamic perspective on mental disorders.

PSYCHOANALYTIC THERAPY

Since Freud's time, the body of psychoanalytic thinking has changed in important ways, but all treatments purporting to be psychoanalytic have some basic tenets in common. (See Focus on Discovery 2.3 for a discussion about psychotherapy.) Classical psychoanalysis is based on Freud's second theory of neurotic anxiety, that neurotic anxiety is the reaction of the ego when a previously punished and repressed id impulse presses for expression. The unconscious part of the ego, encountering a situation that reminds it of a repressed conflict from childhood—one usually having to do with sexual or aggressive impulses—is overcome by debilitating tension. Psychoanalytic therapy is an insight therapy. It attempts to remove the earlier repression and help the patient face the childhood conflict, gain insight into it, and resolve it in the light of adult reality. The repression, occurring so long ago, has prevented the ego from growing in an adult fashion; the lifting of the repression is supposed to enable this relearning to take place.

focus on discovery/2.3

What is Psychotherapy?

Shorn of its theoretical complexities, any **psychotherapy** is a social interaction in which a trained professional tries to help another person, the client or patient, behave and feel differently. The therapist follows procedures that are to a greater or lesser extent prescribed by a certain theory or school of thought. The basic assumption is that particular kinds of verbal and nonverbal exchanges in a trusting relationship can achieve goals, such as reducing anxiety and eliminating self-defeating or dangerous behaviour.

Basic as this definition may seem, there is little general agreement about what really constitutes psychotherapy. A person's next-door neighbour might utter the same words of comfort as a clinical psychologist, but should we regard this as psychotherapy? In what way is psychotherapy different from such nonprofessional reassurance? Is the distinction made on the straightforward basis of whether the dispenser of reassurance has a particular academic degree? Does it relate to whether the giver of information has a theory that dictates what he or she says? These are difficult questions.

Generally, people who seek or are sent for professional help have first tried nonprofessional avenues to feeling better. They have confided in friends or a spouse, perhaps spoken to the family doctor or a member of the clergy, and maybe tried several of the many self-help books and programs that are so popular. For most people in psychological distress, one or more of these options provide enough relief, and they seek no further help. But for others, these attempts fall short. These are the people who go to mental health clinics, university counselling centres, and the private offices of independent practitioners.

London (1964, 1986) categorized psychotherapies as **insight therapies** or **action** (behavioural) **therapies**. Insight therapies, such as psychoanalysis, assume that behaviour, emotions, and thoughts become disordered because people do not understand what motivates them, especially when their needs and drives conflict. Insight therapies try to help people discover why they behave, feel, and think as they do. The premise is that greater awareness of motivations will yield greater control over and subsequent improvement in thought, emotion, and behaviour.

Of course, insight is not exclusive to the insight therapies. The action, or behavioural, therapies bring insight to the individual as well, and the newer cognitive therapies can be seen as a blend of insight and behavioural therapies. It is a matter of emphasis, of focus. In the behavioural therapies, the focus is on changing behaviour; insight is often a peripheral benefit. In the insight therapies, the focus is less on changing people's behaviour directly than on enhancing their understanding of their motives, fears, and conflicts. To facilitate such insights, therapists of different theoretical persuasions employ a variety of techniques.

There are scores of theories and psychotherapies, each with its enthusiastic supporters. We present in this chapter a detailed description of the more prominent theories and methods of intervention. We hope to provide the reader with the means to evaluate critically new therapies that arise or, at the very least, to know what questions to ask in order to evaluate them effectively.

Analysts employ a number of techniques in their efforts to lift repressions. Perhaps the best known is free association. The patient reclines on a couch, facing away from the analyst, and is encouraged to give free rein to his or her thoughts, verbalizing whatever comes to mind without the censoring done in everyday life. It is assumed that the patient can learn this skill, gradually overcoming defences built up over many years, but blocks to free association often arise. The patient may suddenly become silent or change the topic. These resistances are noted by the analyst as they are assumed to signal a sensitive, or ego-threatening, area. These sensitive areas are precisely what the analyst will want to probe further.

Dream analysis is another analytic technique. Psychoanalytic theory holds that, in sleep, ego defences are relaxed, allowing normally repressed material to enter the sleeper's consciousness. Since this material is extremely threatening, it is rarely allowed into consciousness in its actual form; rather, the repressed material is disguised and dreams take on heavily symbolic content (referred to as the latent content of the dream). For example, a woman who fears sexual advances from men may dream of being attacked by warriors with spears; the spears are considered phallic symbols, substituting for an explicit sexual advance.

Another key component of psychoanalytic therapy is transference. Here, the patient's responses to the analyst are not in keeping with the analyst-patient relationship but seem instead to reflect relationships with important people in the patient's past. For example, a patient may feel that the analyst is bored by what he or she is saying (as a parent might have seemed) and, as a result, might struggle to be entertaining (as he or she had done in the past to gain parental attention). Analysts encourage the development of transference by intentionally remaining shadowy figures, sitting behind their patients and divulging little of their personal lives or feelings during a session. Through careful observation of these transferred attitudes, analysts can gain insight into the childhood origin of repressed conflicts. It is precisely when analysts notice transference developing that they take hope that an important repressed conflict is getting closer to the surface.

Countertransference refers to the analyst's feelings toward the patient. Analysts must be aware of their own feelings so that they can see the patient clearly. Thus, a training analysis, involving psychoanalysis is typically part of their training.

As previously repressed material begins to appear in therapy, interpretation comes into play. The analyst points out to the patient the meaning of certain behaviours. Defence mechanisms, the ego's unconscious tools for warding off anxiety, are a principal focus of interpretation. For instance, a man might change the subject whenever anything touches on closeness during the course of a session. The analyst will at some point interpret the patient's behaviour, pointing out its defensive nature in the hope of stimulating the patient to acknowledge that he has trouble with intimacy.

Modifications in PsychoanalyticTherapy As happens with all paradigms, psychoanalytic therapy has evolved over time. One innovation was to apply it to groups of people rather than only to individuals. Some therapists focus on the psychodynamics of individuals in the group, using typical techniques, such as free association, interpretation, and dream analysis (Wolf & Kutash, 1990). Others conceive of the group itself as having a collective set of psychodynamics, manifested by such things as group transference to the therapist. Within psychoanalytic circles, there has been controversy about the value of a group approach. The key issue is whether the group format dilutes the transference to the therapist and thus makes the therapy ineffective.

Other current analytic therapies include ego analysis, brief psychodynamic therapy, and interpersonal psychodynamic therapy.

Ego Analysis After Freud's death, a group of practitioners, generally referred to as ego analysts, introduced important modifications to psychoanalytic therapy. Their approach is sometimes described as psychodynamic rather than psychoanalytic. The major figures in this loosely formed movement include Karen Horney (1942), Anna Freud (1946), Erik Erikson (1950), David Rapaport (1951), and Heinz Hartmann (1958). Although Freud did not ignore people's interactions with the environment, he essentially believed that they are driven by intrapsychic urges. Those who subscribe to ego analysis place greater emphasis on a person's ability to control the environment and to select the time and the means for satisfying instinctual drives, contending that the individual is as much ego as id. In addition, they focus more on the person's current living conditions than did Freud, although they sometimes advocate unearthing the historical causes of a behaviour. Generally, they employ most of the psychoanalytic techniques we have described.

Ego analysts believe in a set of ego functions that are primarily conscious, capable of controlling both id instincts and the external environment, and that, significantly, do not depend on the id for their energy. They assume that these ego functions and capabilities are present at birth and develop through experience. Underemphasized by Freud, ego functions have energies and gratifications of their own, usually separate from id impulses. And, whereas Freud viewed society as essentially inhibiting—negatively—the unfettered gratification of libidinal impulses, the ego analysts hold that an individual's social interactions can provide their own special kind of gratification.

Brief Psychodynamic Therapy Freud originally conceived of psychoanalysis as a relatively short-term process. He thought that the analyst should focus on specific problems, make it clear to the patient that therapy would not exceed a certain number of sessions, and structure sessions in a directive fashion. Freud thus envisioned a more active and briefer psychoanalysis than what eventually developed.

Doidge and associates investigated the nature of psychodynamic therapy in an Ontario survey (see Doidge, 1999; Doidge, Simon, Gillies, & Ruskin, 1994). They found that 59 percent of those receiving psychoanalysis were women and that the mean number of current diagnoses was four. On average, each patient had one diagnosable personality disorder. Overall, 82 percent of the patients had tried other forms of therapy, including drug treatment. Most patients had received psychoanalytic treatment for many years. A follow-up study found that the average length of time in treatment was 4.8 years (see Doidge et al., 2002). Doidge et al. (2002) conducted a comparative analysis of patients from Canada, the United States, and Australia and found many similarities across countries. The most common diagnoses were mood disorders, anxiety disorders, sexual dysfunctions, and personality disorders.

Time-limited psychotherapy is available as an alternative to the many years sometimes required for classic psychodynamic treatment. The early pioneers in time-limited psychotherapy, called **brief therapy**, were the psychoanalysts Ferenczi (1952) and Alexander and French (1946). This shorter form was developed to meet the expectations of the many patients who prefer therapy to be fairly short term and targeted to specific problems in their everyday lives.

The growth of brief therapy also evolved from the need to respond to psychological emergencies (Koss & Shiang, 1994). Cases of shell shock during World War II led to Grinker and Spiegel's (1944) classic short-term analytic treatment of what is now called posttraumatic stress disorder. A related contribution came from Lindemann's (1944) crisis intervention with the survivors of Boston's famous Cocoanut Grove nightclub fire in 1942.

Insurance companies and government health plans have played a role in shortening the duration of treatment by encouraging therapists to adapt their ideas to brief therapy. They have become increasingly reluctant to cover more than a limited number of psychotherapy sessions in a given calendar year and have set limits on reimbursement amounts.

All these factors, combined with the growing acceptability of psychotherapy in the population at large, have set the stage for a stronger focus on time-limited psychodynamic therapy. Brief therapies share several common elements (Koss & Shiang, 1994):

- Assessment tends to be rapid and early.
- It is made clear right away that therapy will be limited and that improvement is expected within a small number of sessions (from 6 to 25).
- Goals are concrete and focused on the amelioration of the patient's worst symptoms, on helping the patient understand what is going on in his or her life, and on enabling the patient to cope better in the future.
- Interpretations are directed more toward present life circumstances and patient behaviour than on the historical significance of feelings.
- Development of transference is not encouraged, but some positive transference to the therapist is fostered to encourage the patient to follow the therapist's suggestions and advice.
- There is a general understanding that psychotherapy does not cure, but that it can help troubled individuals learn to deal better with life's inevitable stressors.

Over 400 lives were lost in the fire at the Cocoanut Grove nightclub in 1942. The crisis intervention work that followed influenced the development of brief psychodynamic therapy.

Interpersonal Psychodynamic Therapy A variant of brief psychodynamic therapy, often referred to as *interpersonal therapy*, emphasizes the interactions between a patient and his or her social environment. The American psychiatrist Harry Stack Sullivan pioneered this approach. According to Sullivan, our needs are interpersonal in that whether they are met depends on the complementary needs of other people. A key turning point for the infant is when he or she realizes that survival depends on the mother's co-operation in satisfying the infant's basic needs. Sometimes called a neo-Freudian, Sullivan held that a patient's basic difficulty is a misperception of reality stemming from disorganization in the interpersonal relationships of childhood, primarily the relationship between child and parents. He conceived of the analyst as a "participant observer" in the therapy process (not as a blank screen for transference), arguing that the therapist, like the scientist, is a part of the process that he or she is studying—an analyst does not see patients without at the same time affecting them.

A contemporary example of a brief psychodynamic therapy is the Interpersonal Therapy (IPT) of Klerman and Weissman (Klerman et al., 1984). The IPT therapist concentrates on the patient's current interpersonal difficulties and discusses with the patient better ways of relating to others. Although IPT incorporates some psychodynamic ideas, it is distinct in several ways from traditional forms of psychoanalysis. In *Mastering Depression: The Patient's Guide to Therapy*, this section appears in the description of IPT:

> The IPT therapist will not: 1) Interpret your dreams; 2) Have treatment go on indefinitely; 3) Delve into your early childhood; 4) Encourage you to free associate; 5) Make you feel very dependent on the treatment or the therapist. (Weissman, 1995, pp. 11-12)

IPT's techniques combine empathic listening and suggestions for behavioural changes as well as how to implement them. The IPT therapist might explore with the patient the complexities of present-day problems, with an emphasis on the patient's relationships with others. The therapist might then encourage the patient to make specific behavioural changes, sometimes facilitating these shifts by having the patient practice new behaviours in the consulting room (role-playing). The potential benefits of IPT were demonstrated in a study led by Queen's University researcher Kate Harkness (Harkness et al., 2002). They found that the usual link between stressful events and bouts of depression is weakened considerably among women who received IPT and then two years of maintenance IPT.

Evaluating the Psychoanalytic Paradigm

Perhaps no investigator of human behaviour has been so honoured and so criticized as Freud. When he proposed his theory of infantile sexuality, he was vilified. In turn-of-the-century Vienna, sexuality was little discussed. How scandalous, then, to assert that infants and children were motivated by sexual drives! One of the criticisms levelled against Freud's theory applies to other psychoanalytic theories as well: theories based on anecdotal evidence gathered during therapy sessions are not grounded in objectivity and therefore are not scientific. Unlike those who work within the biological paradigm or within the learning and cognitive paradigms (which entail conducting formal research on the causes and treatments of abnormal behaviour), Freud believed that the information obtained from therapy sessions was enough to validate his theory and demonstrate the effectiveness of the therapy. His patients, however, were not merely a small sample. They were also atypical, being largely affluent, educated, and Viennese. In Chapter 5, we will discuss the severe limitations of such data.

The case reports used by Freud (and his followers) can also be assailed on the grounds of the reliability of Freud's perceptions and recollections of those therapy sessions, for he did not take careful notes. Further, Freud's own interest in certain topics, such as early sexual experiences, might have affected his patients' accounts, causing them to focus on certain experiences and overlook others.

It is also important to keep in mind that psychodynamic concepts, such as id, ego, and the unconscious, though meant to be used as metaphors to describe psychic functions, sometimes were described as though they had an existence of their own, with the power to act and think. Freud spoke of "immediate and unheeding satisfaction of the instincts, such as the id demands...The id knows no solicitude about ensuring survival" (1937).

Even with these substantial criticisms, however, Freud's contribution to the field of abnormal psychology remains enormous. His ongoing influence is most evident in the following three commonly held assumptions:

1. *Childhood experiences help shape adult personality.* Contemporary clinicians and researchers still view childhood experiences as crucial. They seldom focus on the psychosexual stages about which Freud wrote, but emphasize problematic parent-child relationships and how they can influence later adult relationships in negative ways.
2. *There are unconscious influences on behaviour.* In Focus on Discovery 7.1, we review research showing that people can be unaware of the causes of their behaviour. However, most current workers neither believe in an actual unconscious nor view it as a repository of id instincts.
3. *People use defence mechanisms to control anxiety or stress.* There is a great deal of research on coping with stress (see Chapter 8), and defence mechanisms are included in an appendix of the DSM-IV-TR (the catalogue of mental disorders published by the American Psychiatric Association and reviewed in the next chapter). Contemporary research focuses on consciously adopted coping strategies (e.g., deliberately trying not to think

about some traumatic event). It has yet to be demonstrated whether any unconscious method of coping (even repression) actually plays an important role in controlling anxiety.

Although there are many legitimate concerns about the validity and usefulness of Freud's work, it is impossible to acquire a good grasp of the field of abnormal psychology without some familiarity with his writings.

Humanistic and Existential Paradigms

Humanistic and existential therapies, like psychoanalytic therapies, are insight-focused, based on the assumption that disordered behaviour results from a lack of insight, and can best be treated by increasing the individual's awareness of motivations and needs. There are, however, useful contrasts between psychoanalysis and its offshoots on the one hand and humanistic and existential approaches on the other. The psychoanalytic paradigm assumes that human nature, the id, is something in need of restraint, that effective socialization requires the ego to mediate between the environment and the basically antisocial, at best asocial, impulses stemming from biological urges. Humanistic and existential paradigms place greater emphasis on the person's freedom of choice, regarding free will as the person's most important characteristic. Yet, free will is a double-edged sword, for it can bring not only fulfillment and pleasure, but also acute pain and suffering. It's exercise, therefore, requires special courage. Not everyone can meet this challenge. Those who cannot are regarded as candidates for client-centred, existential, and Gestalt therapies. Humanistic and existential paradigms, also referred to as experiential or phenomenological, seldom focus on how psychological problems develop. Their main influence is on intervention, and so our discussion deals primarily with therapy.

Carl Rogers's Client-Centred Therapy

Carl Rogers was an American psychologist whose theorizing about psychotherapy grew slowly out of years of intensive clinical experience. After teaching at the university level in the 1940s and 1950s, he helped organize the Center for Studies of the Person in La Jolla, California. Rogers's client-centred therapy (also referred to as person-centred therapy) is based on several assumptions about human nature and the way we can try to understand it (Ford & Urban, 1963; Rogers, 1951, 1961):

- People can be understood only from the vantage point of their own perceptions and feelings, that is, from their phenomenological world. We must look at the way they experience events rather than at the events themselves, for each person's phenomenological world is the major determinant of behaviour and makes that person unique.
- Healthy people are aware of their behaviour. In this sense, Rogers's system is similar to psychoanalysis and ego analysis, for it emphasizes the desirability of being aware of motives. People with a high level of self-awareness and a sense of personal agency are said to be thoughtful, and this is a primary goal of counselling (Rennie, 1998).
- Healthy people are innately good and effective. They become ineffective and disturbed only when faulty learning intervenes.
- Healthy people are purposive and goal directed. They do not respond passively to the influence of their environment or to their inner drives. They are self-directed. In this assumption, Rogers is closer to ego analysis than to orthodox Freudian psychoanalysis.
- Therapists should not attempt to manipulate events for the individual. Rather, they should create conditions that will facilitate independent decision-making by the client. When people are not concerned with the evaluations, demands, and preferences of others, their lives are guided by an innate tendency toward self-actualization.

Carl Rogers, a humanistic therapist, proposed that the key ingredient in therapy is the attitude and style of the therapist rather than specific techniques.

Rogers's Therapeutic Intervention Consistent with his view of human nature, Rogers avoided imposing goals on the client during therapy. The client is to take the lead and direct the course of the conversation and the session. The therapist's job is to create the conditions that, during the session, help the client return to his or her basic nature and judge which course of life is intrinsically gratifying. Because of his positive view of people, Rogers assumed that their decisions would not only make them happy with themselves but also turn them into good, civilized people. The road to these good decisions is not easy, however.

According to Rogers and other humanistic and existential therapists, people must take responsibility for themselves, even when they are troubled. It is often difficult for a therapist to refrain from giving advice, from taking charge of a client's life, especially when the client appears incapable of making decisions. But Rogerians hold steadfastly to the rule that a person's innate capacity for growth and self-direction will assert itself if the therapeutic atmosphere is warm, attentive, and receptive, and especially if the therapist accepts the person for who he or she is, providing what he called unconditional positive regard.

Other people set what Rogers called "conditions of worth"—"I will love you if..." In contrast, unconditional positive regard is reflected in the client-centred therapist's valuing clients as they are, whatever their behaviour. People have value merely for being people, and the therapist must care deeply for and respect a client for the simple reason that he or she is another human being engaged in the struggle of growing and being alive.

Although client-centred therapy is not technique oriented, one strategy is central to this approach—namely, empathy. Because empathy is so important in Rogerian therapy and important as well in all other kinds of therapy (not to mention ordinary social intercourse), let us examine it more closely.

Empathy It is useful to distinguish two types of empathy, following Egan (1975):

- *Primary empathy* refers to the therapist's understanding, accepting, and communicating to the client what the client is thinking or feeling. The therapist conveys primary empathy by restating the client's thoughts and feelings, pretty much in the client's own words.
- *Advanced empathy* entails an inference by the therapist of the thoughts and feelings that lie behind what the client is saying, and of which the client may only be dimly, if at all, aware. Advanced empathy essentially involves an interpretation by the therapist of the meaning of what the client is thinking and feeling.

Bear in mind that therapists operating within the client-centred framework assume that the client views things in an unproductive way, as evidenced by the psychological distress that has brought the client into therapy. At the primary empathic level, the therapist accepts the client's view, understands it, and communicates to the client that it is appreciated. At the advanced or interpretive level, however, the therapist offers something new, a perspective that he or she hopes is better, more productive, and that implies new modes of action. Advanced empathizing builds on the information provided over a number of sessions in which the therapist concentrates on making primary-level empathic statements.

The client-centred therapist, operating within a phenomenological philosophy, must have as the goal the movement of a client from his or her present phenomenological world to another one—hence the importance of the advanced-empathy stage. Since people's emotions and actions are determined by how they construe themselves and their surroundings—by their phenomenology—those who are dysfunctional or otherwise dissatisfied with their present mode of living are in need of a new phenomenology. From the very outset then, client-centred therapy—and all other phenomenological therapies—concentrates on clients adopting frameworks different from those they had upon beginning treatment. Merely reflecting back to clients their current phenomenology cannot in itself bring therapeutic change. A new phenomenology must be acquired.

In our view, advanced empathy represents theory building on the part of the therapist. After considering over a number of sessions what the client has been saying and how he or she has been saying it, the therapist generates a hypothesis about what may be the true source of distress hidden from the client.

Exposure to an empathetic therapist can have a powerful, positive, effect as shown in studies conducted by Coons and associates with patients diagnosed with schizophrenia from Ontario psychiatric hospitals (see Coons, 1957, 1967; Coons & Peacock, 1970). Participation in groups led by an empathetic therapist led to substantial improvements in personality and intellectual functioning, improvements greater than those that followed from insight-based psychotherapy. As noted by Rice and Quinsey (1986), this result ran counter to the prevailing view at the time that these patients would benefit only from drug therapy or psychoanalytic treatment.

Existential Therapy

Humanism and existentialism have much in common, but the humanistic work of North Americans, such as Rogers, can be contrasted with the more European existential approach that derives from the writings of philosophers (e.g., Sartre and Kierkegaard) and psychiatrists (e.g., Binswanger and Frankl).

The existential and humanist points of view both emphasize personal growth. Yet, there are important distinctions between the two. Humanism stresses the goodness of human nature. It holds that if unfettered by groundless fears and societal restrictions, human beings will develop normally, even exceptionally. Existentialism is gloomier. Although it embraces free will and responsibility, it stresses the anxiety that is inevitable in making important choices, the existential choices on which existence depends, such as staying or not staying with a spouse, with a job, or even with this world. Avoiding choices may protect people from anxiety, but it also deprives them of living a life with meaning and is at the core of psychopathology.

The Goals of Existential Therapy Therapists operating within an existential framework encourage clients to confront their anxieties concerning choices about how they will live, what they will value, and how they will relate to others. They support their clients in examining what is really meaningful in life. Sometimes a choice will occasion extreme discomfort. Life is not easy for those who would be true to themselves.

At some point during therapy, the client must begin to behave differently, toward both the therapist and the outside world, to change his or her own existential condition. Hence, although the existential view is highly subjective, it entails relating to others in an open, spontaneous, and loving manner. Yet, paradoxically, each of us is essentially alone. We came into the world alone, and we must create our own existence in the world alone.

In the existential view, people create their existence anew at each moment. The potential for disorder as well as for growth is ever-present. Individuals must be encouraged to accept the responsibility for their own existence and to realize that, within certain limits, they can redefine themselves at any moment and behave and feel differently within their own social environment.

The existential writers are vague about what therapeutic techniques will help the client grow. A reliance on technique may even be seen as an objectifying process in which the therapist acts on the client as though he or she were a thing to be manipulated (Prochaska, 1984). The existential approach is best understood as a general attitude taken by certain therapists toward human nature rather than as a set of therapeutic techniques.

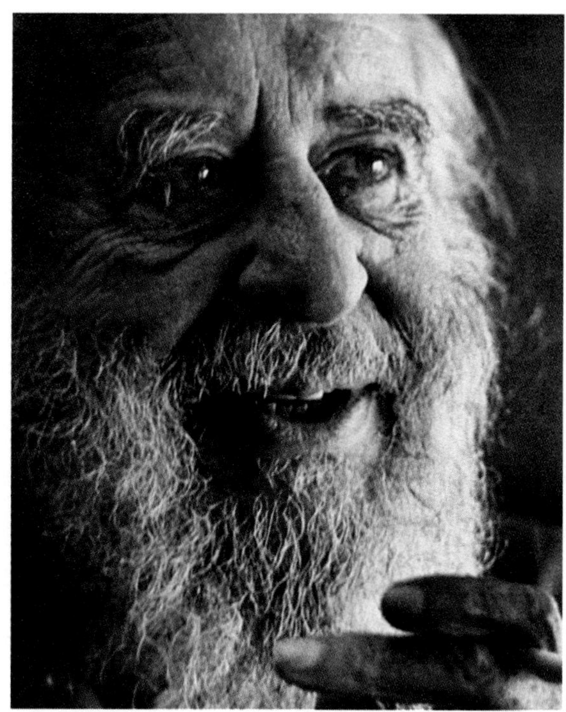

Frederich (Fritz) Perls (1893-1970) was the colourful founder of Gestalt therapy.

GESTALT THERAPY

A therapy that has both humanistic and existential elements, Gestalt therapy derives from the work of Frederich S. (Fritz) Perls. Like Rogers, Perls held that people have an innate goodness and that this basic nature should be allowed to express itself. Psychological problems originate in frustrations and denials of this inborn virtue. Gestalt therapists, along with other humanistic therapists, emphasize the creative and expressive aspects of people rather than the problematic features on which psychoanalysts seem to concentrate.

A central goal of Gestalt therapy is to help patients understand and accept their needs, desires, and fears and to enhance their awareness of how they block themselves from reaching their goals and satisfying their needs. A basic assumption is that all of us bring our needs and wants to any situation. We do not merely perceive situations as they are; instead, we project our needs, fears, or desires onto what is out there. Thus, if I am talking to a stranger, I do not merely react to the person as that person exists. I react to the stranger in the context of my needs. Unfinished business with a significant person from the past, for example, can affect how I deal with someone in the present.

Gestalt Therapy Techniques Gestalt therapists focus on what a client is doing in the consulting room here and now, without delving into the past. If the past is bothersome, it is brought into the present. Searching after causes in the past is considered an attempt to escape responsibility for making choices in the present. Clients are exhorted, cajoled, and sometimes even coerced into awareness of what is happening now.

Gestalt therapy, unlike the humanistic and existential therapies discussed so far, is noted for its emphasis on techniques, such as the following:

- *I-language*. To help patients bear responsibility for their present and future lives, the therapist instructs them to change "it" language into "I" language:

  Therapist: What do you hear in your voice?
  Patient: My voice sounds like it is crying.
  Therapist: Can you take responsibility for that by saying, I am crying? (Levitsky & Perls, 1970, p. 142)

  This simple change in language encourages patients to assume responsibility for feelings and behaviour, reduces their sense of being alienated from aspects of their very being, and helps them see the self as active rather than passive, as a searching and open person, rather than as someone whose behaviour is determined entirely by external events.
- *The empty chair*. In the empty-chair technique, a client projects and then talks to the projection (the projection could represent a feeling, a person, object, or situation). This technique is described in more detail in Chapter 17.
- *Projection of feelings*. Gestalt therapists working with groups sometimes have people pair off, close their eyes, and imagine the face of an individual to whom they have a strong emotional attachment. They are encouraged to

concentrate on the feelings they have about that person. Then, all open their eyes and look at their partner. After a few moments, they are instructed to close their eyes again and think of something neutral, such as an arithmetic problem. They then open their eyes again and look a second time at their partner. Finally, they are asked whether there was an important difference in the way they felt about their partner in the two situations. This exercise is designed to exaggerate what is assumed to be inevitable in all our social interactions—namely, the intrusion of our feelings into whatever is happening at any particular moment.

- *Attending to nonverbal cues*. All therapists pay attention to nonverbal and paralinguistic cues given by the client. Nonverbal cues are body movements, facial expressions, gestures, and the like. Paralinguistic cues are tone of voice, speed with which words are spoken, and other audible components of speech beyond its content. People can negate with their hands or their eyes what they are saying with the larynx. According to Perls (1969), "What we say is mostly lies or bullshit. But the voice is there, the gesture, the posture, the facial expression, the psychosomatic language" (p. 54).
- *The use of metaphor*. During the therapy session, Gestalt therapists often create unusual scenarios to externalize, making more vivid and understandable, a problem a client is having. The following is an example:

A HUSBAND AND WIFE sat together on a sofa, bickering about the woman's mother. The husband seemed very angry with his mother-in-law, and the therapist surmised that she was getting in the way of his relationship with his wife. The therapist wanted to demonstrate how frustrating this must be for both of them and how they could do something about it. Without warning, he rose from his chair and wedged himself between the couple. Not a word was said. The husband looked puzzled, then hurt, and gradually became angry at the therapist. He asked him to move so that he could sit next to his wife again. The therapist shook his head. When the husband repeated his request, the therapist removed his jacket and placed it over the wife's head. A long silence followed, during which the husband grew more agitated. The wife sat quietly under the therapist's coat. Suddenly, the husband stood up, walked past the therapist, and angrily removed the coat. Then he pushed the therapist off the sofa! The therapist exploded in laughter. "I wondered how long it would take you to do something!" he roared.

This staged scene drove several points home in a way that mere words might not have. The husband reported that he had felt cut off from his wife by the therapist, in much the same way that he felt alienated from her by her mother. The mother was intruding, and he was not doing anything about it. The fact that he was able to remove both the coat and the therapist made him wonder whether he might not behave similarly toward his mother-in-law. As he spoke, his wife began to sob; she confided to her husband that all along she had been wanting him to take charge of the problem with her mother. So far so good. But then the therapist turned to the woman and asked her why she had not removed the coat herself. The husband grinned as the therapist gently chided the wife for being unduly passive about her marital problems. By the end of the session, the clients felt in better contact with each other and expressed their resolve to work together actively to alter their relationship with her mother.

Metaphors are not used exclusively in Gestalt approaches; they can also be useful in other approaches, such as the psychodynamic approach (see Rasmussen & Angus, 1996). Extensive Canadian research has been conducted on the role of metaphors in the therapy process, including ongoing research by Linda McMullen at the University of Saskatchewan (McMullen, 1999) and by Lynne Angus and associates at York University (Angus, Levitt, & Hardtke, 1999; Levitt, Korman, & Angus, 2000). Metaphors often reveal how people have come to experience themselves and their mood states (McMullen, 1999). For instance, a study by Levitt et al. (2000) showed that those individuals who recovered from depression used the metaphor of feeling burdened while depressed, but a key metaphor during recovery involved a sense of "unloading the burden." As we will see in Chapter 16, perceptions of burden contribute to the distress experienced by caregivers.

Through the use of metaphors and other techniques, Gestalt therapy forcefully conveys the existential message that a person is not a prisoner of the past, that he or she can at any time make the existential choice to be different, and that the therapist will not tolerate stagnation. Perls's emphasis on responsibility is not to be confused with commitment or obligation to others. The individual has the responsibility to take care of himself or herself, to meet needs as they arise. This apparent egocentrism may trouble people who have a strong social conscience or who have made commitments to others. Perls believed that such commitments should never be made (Prochaska, 1984).

A comparison of the three humanistic and existential therapies we have discussed is presented in Table 2.1.

Table 2.1

Comparison of Humanistic and Existential Therapies

Common to All	Rogerian	Existential	Gestalt
Insight-focused Emphasize free will and responsibility Take a phenomenological approach Emphasize personal growth	People are innately good and effective and become disturbed only when faulty learning intervenes. In therapy, goals are not imposed and the therapist totally accepts the client (unconditional positive regard). Empathy is the main therapeutic strategy, both primary empathy (restating the client's thoughts and feelings) and advanced empathy (an interpretation of what lies behind what the client has been saying)	The patient is encouraged to face the anxiety that making choices entails. Therapy techniques are avoided. There is a focus on relating to others genuinely.	People are innately good and effective but can lose awareness of their needs and desires. Therapy focuses on the here and now, not on the past. Many techniques (e.g., I-language, empty chair) are used to make patients more aware of needs, desires, and fears so that they can incorporate them into their personality

EVALUATING THE HUMANISTIC AND EXISTENTIAL PARADIGMS

Rogers and the existential therapists focus on the client's phenomenology, but how can the therapist ever know that he or she is truly understanding a patient's world as it appears to the patient? The validity of the inferences made by therapists about the client's phenomenology is an important and unsolved issue. That people are innately good and, if faulty learning does not interfere, will make choices that are personally fulfilling is also an assumption that can be questioned. Other social philosophers (e.g., Thomas Hobbes) have taken a decidedly less optimistic view of human nature. Gestalt therapy conveys the message that people are not prisoners of their past, that change is possible. But if the person does not know how to behave differently, considerable damage could be done. For example, if a socially inhibited person has not learned to talk assertively to others, it may do little good to make him or her more aware of this non-assertiveness and encourage greater assertiveness. Lacking the necessary skills, the person may be doomed to fail.

Rogers should be credited with originating the field of psychotherapy research. He insisted that therapy outcomes be empirically evaluated, and he pioneered the use of tape recordings so that therapists' behaviour could be related to therapeutic outcomes. The major prediction of Rogerian therapy, of course, is that therapists' empathy should relate to outcomes. The data are inconsistent (Greenberg, Elliott, & Lietaer, 1994). However, it probably makes sense to continue to emphasize empathy in the training of therapists, as this quality is likely to make it easier for clients to reveal highly personal and sometimes unpleasant facts about themselves.

LEARNING PARADIGMS

Psychologists operating in the **learning (behavioural) paradigm** view abnormal behaviour as responses learned in the same ways other human behaviour is learned. Very early in the 20th century, psychology was dominated by structuralism, which held that the proper subject of study was mental functioning. The goal of psychology, then a very new discipline, was to learn more about what went on in the mind by analyzing its elementary constituents. Through painstaking **introspection**, self-observation, and reporting about mental processes, psychologists hoped to discover the structure of consciousness.

THE RISE OF BEHAVIOURISM

After some years, many in the field began to lose faith in the structuralist approach. The problem was that different laboratories were yielding conflicting data. This dissatisfaction was brought to a head by John B. Watson (1878–1958), who in 1913 revolutionized psychology with his views.

> Psychology as the behaviourist views it is a purely objective experimental branch of natural science. Its theoretical goal is the prediction and control of behaviour. Introspection forms no essential part of its methods, nor is the scientific value of its data dependent upon the readiness with which they lend themselves to interpretation in terms of consciousness. (p. 158)

To replace introspection, Watson looked to the psychologists who were investigating learning in animals. Because of his efforts, the dominant focus of psychology switched from thinking to learning. Behaviourism can be defined as an approach that focuses on observable behaviour rather than on consciousness. Three types of learning have attracted the research efforts of psychologists.

Classical Conditioning One type of learning, classical conditioning, was discovered by the Russian physiologist and Nobel laureate Ivan Pavlov (1849–1936) at the turn of the century. In Pavlov's studies of the digestive system, a dog was given meat powder to make it salivate. Before long, Pavlov's laboratory assistants became aware that the dog began salivating when it saw the person who fed it. As the experiment continued, the dog began to salivate even earlier, when it heard the footsteps of its feeder. Intrigued by these findings, Pavlov decided to study the dog's reactions systematically. In the first of many experiments, a bell was rung behind the dog, and then the meat powder was placed in its mouth. After this procedure had been repeated a number of times, the dog began salivating as soon as it heard the bell.

Ivan P. Pavlov, Russian physiologist and Nobel laureate, was responsible for extensive research and theory in classical conditioning.

In this experiment, because the meat powder automatically elicits salivation with no prior learning, the powder is termed an unconditioned stimulus (UCS) and the response to it, salivation, an unconditioned response (UCR). When the offering of meat powder is preceded several times by the ringing of a bell, a neutral stimulus, the sound of the bell alone (the conditioned stimulus, CS) is able to elicit the salivary response (the conditioned response, CR) (see Figure 2.6). The CR usually differs somewhat from the UCR (Rescorla, 1988), but these subtleties are beyond the needs of this book. As the number of paired presentations of the bell and the meat powder increases, the number of salivations elicited by the bell alone increases. Extinction refers to what happens to the CR when the repeated soundings of the bell are later not followed by meat powder; fewer and fewer salivations are elicited, and the CR gradually disappears.

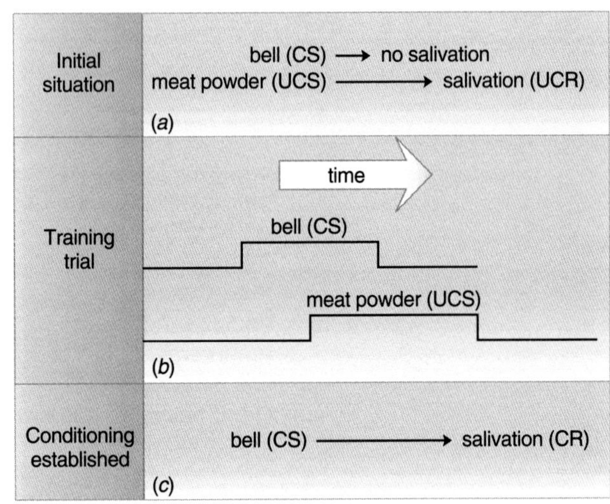

Figure 2.6 The process of classical conditioning. (a) Before learning, the meat powder (UCS) elicits salivation (UCR), but the bell (CS) does not. (b) A training or learning trial consists of presentations of the CS, followed closely by the UCS. (c) Classical conditioning has been accomplished when the previously neutral bell elicits salivation (CR).

A famous experiment, conducted by John Watson and Rosalie Rayner (1920), discovered that classical conditioning could instill pathological fear. They introduced a white rat to an 11-month-old boy, Little Albert, who indicated no fear of the animal. Whenever the boy reached for the rat, the experimenter made a loud noise (the UCS) by striking a steel bar behind Albert's head, causing him great fright (the UCR). After five such experiences, Albert became very frightened (the CR) by the sight of the white rat, even when the steel bar was not struck. The fear initially associated with the loud noise had come to be elicited by the previously neutral stimulus, the white rat (now the CS). This study suggests the possible relationship between classical conditioning and the development of certain emotional disorders, including phobias.

Operant Conditioning A second type of learning derives primarily from the work of Edward Thorndike (1874–1949), begun in the 1890s. Thorndike was interested in the effect of consequences on behaviour. He had observed that caged alley cats, in their efforts to escape, would accidentally hit the latch that freed them. Recaged again and again, they would soon come to touch the latch immediately and purposely. Thorndike formulated what would be a very important principle, the law of effect: behaviour that is followed by satisfying consequences will be repeated, and behaviour that is followed by unpleasant consequences will be discouraged. Thus, the behaviour or response that has consequences serves as an instrument, encouraging or discouraging its own repetition. Learning that focuses on consequences was first called instrumental learning.

Over 60 years ago, B.F. Skinner (1904–1990) introduced operant conditioning, so named because it applied to behaviour that operates on the environment. He reformulated the law of effect by shifting the focus from the linking of stimuli and responses (S-R connections) to the relationships between responses and their consequences or contingencies. This subtle distinction reflects Skinner's contention that stimuli do not so much get connected to responses as they become the occasions for responses to occur, if in the past they have been reinforced. Skinner introduced the concept of discriminative stimulus to refer to external events that in effect tell an organism that if it performs a certain behaviour, a certain consequence will follow.

Renaming the "law of effect" the "principle of reinforcement," Skinner distinguished two types of reinforcement. Positive reinforcement refers to the strengthening of a tendency to respond by virtue of the presentation of a pleasant event, called a *positive reinforcer*. For example, a water-deprived pigeon will tend to repeat behaviours (operants) that are followed by the availability of water. Negative reinforcement also strengthens a response, but it does so via the removal of an aversive event, such as the cessation of electric shock. Skinner called such consequences *negative reinforcers*. Extrapolating his work with pigeons to human behaviour, Skinner argued that freedom of choice is a myth and that all behaviour is determined by the reinforcers provided by the environment. The goal of the Skinnerians (Skinner, 1953), like that of their mentor, Watson, is the prediction and control of behaviour. These experimenters hope that by analyzing behaviour in terms of observable responses and

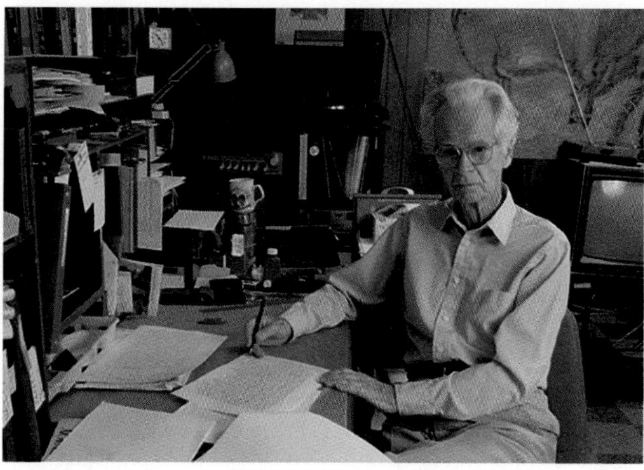

B.F. Skinner was responsible for the study of operant behaviour and the extension of this approach to education, psychotherapy, and society as a whole.

Aggressive responses in children are often rewarded, which makes such behaviour more likely to occur in the future.

reinforcement, they will be able to determine when certain behaviour will occur. The information gathered should help indicate how behaviour is acquired, maintained, changed, and eliminated.

The Skinnerian approach avoids abstract terms and concepts. Skinner believed that psychology must restrict its attention to directly observable stimuli and responses and to the effects of reinforcement.

In a prototypical operant-conditioning experiment, a hungry rat might be placed in a box, known as a Skinner box, that has a lever located at one end. The rat will explore its new environment and by chance come close to the lever. The experimenter may then drop a food pellet into the receptacle located near the lever. After a few such rewards, the animal will come to spend more and more time in the area around the lever. But now, the experimenter may drop a pellet into the receptacle only when the rat happens to touch the lever. After capitalizing on a few chance touches, the rat begins to touch the lever frequently. With lever touching well established, the experimenter can make the criterion for reward more stringent—the animal must now actually press the lever. Thus, the desired operant behaviour, lever pressing, is gradually achieved by shaping, by rewarding a series of responses that are successive approximations of the desired response.

Operant conditioning can produce abnormal behaviour. Consider a key feature of conduct disorder, a high frequency of aggressive behaviour. Aggression is often rewarded, as when one child hits another to get a toy (getting the toy is the reinforcer).

Modelling In real life, learning often goes on even in the absence of reinforcers. We all learn by watching and imitating others, a process called modelling. Experimental work by Bandura and others (see Canadian Contributions 2.1) has demonstrated that witnessing someone perform certain activities can increase or decrease diverse kinds of behaviour. Bandura and Menlove (1968) used a modelling treatment to reduce fear of dogs in children. After witnessing a

Canadian Contributions/2.1

Albert Bandura

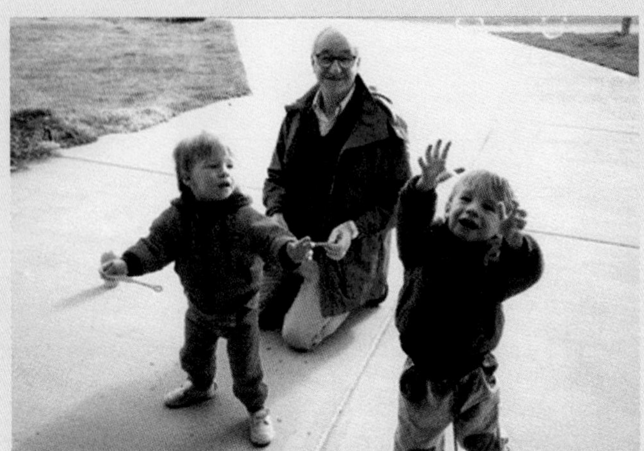

Albert Bandura developed social learning and cognitive self-regulation theories that influenced the development of both learning and cognitive paradigms.

According to Haggbloom et al. (2002), Albert Bandura is the world's greatest living psychologist—fourth in the 20th century in terms of his impact (behind Skinner, Piaget, and Freud). Born in Mundare, Alberta, in 1925, he obtained his early education in a one-room schoolhouse in this northern Alberta farming community. He received his B.A. degree in 1949 from the University of British Columbia and his Ph.D. from the University of Iowa in 1952. He joined the faculty at Stanford University in 1953, where he remains to this day. Albert Bandura has received many awards for his scientific contributions, including awards from the American Psychological Association, American Psychological Society, and Canadian Psychological Association. He has served as president of the American Psychological Association and honourary president of the Canadian Psychological Association.

Bandura's work is based on the premise that it is important to be able to study clinical phenomena in experimental situations. His initial work focused on social learning theory and on the idea that much of what we learn is through the process of imitation. Other people provide us with a range of behaviours that can be imitated. His initial observations were published in books co-authored with his first graduate student, Canadian Richard Walters (Bandura & Walters, 1959, 1963). Their classic 1963 book (*Social Learning and Personality Development*) was critical of the psychodynamic approach and offered an empirically based alternative.

In many respects, research on social learning theory is synonymous with the famous Bobo doll study conducted by Bandura, Ross, and Ross (1961). In this study, children who witnessed an adult being aggressive with a plastic Bobo doll were observed imitating this aggression while playing with other children. Bandura and associates conducted several other classic studies designed to test how situational factors contributed to observational learning (e.g., witnessing a model who is rewarded for aggressing). These variations led Bandura to conclude that there are four key processes in observational learning: (1) attention (noticing the model's behaviour), (2) retention (remembering the model's behaviour), (3) reproduction (personally exhibiting the behaviour), and (4) motivation (repeating imitated behaviours if they received positive consequences).

Bandura's more recent work is a cognitive self-regulation theory that focuses on the concept of human agency and self-efficacy, an individual's perceived sense of being capable (see Bandura, 1982, 1986, 2001). Self-regulation is a multi-stage process that involves self-observation, self-judgment by comparing personal achievements and behaviours with standards and goals, and self-response in the form of self-reinforcement and praise or self-punishment and criticism. In a wide variety of contexts, self-control therapies have been applied that focus on improving an individual's sense of personal efficacy in order to lessen distress and promote adaptive behaviours.

Bandura's focus on both social learning and self-regulation underscores the close interplay between external forces (models in our environment to be imitated) and internal forces (personal beliefs about the self) in adaptive and maladaptive behaviours.

---

fearless model engage in various activities with a dog, initially fearful children became more willing to approach and handle a dog. Modelling may explain the acquisition of abnormal behaviour. Children of parents with phobias or substance-abuse problems may acquire similar behaviour patterns, in part through modelling.

Mediational Learning Paradigms

Among the learning paradigms, modelling illustrates an important issue—namely, the role of mediators in learning and behaviour. Consider what happens in the typical modelling experiment. A person watches another do something and immediately shows a change in behaviour. No overt responding is necessary for the learning to take place, nor does the observer need to be reinforced. Something is learned before the person makes any observable response. Similar outcomes led learning theorists of the 1930s and 1940s to infer mediators of various kinds to explain overt behaviour.

A mediational theory of learning holds that an environmental stimulus does not initiate an overt response directly; rather, it does so through some intervening process, or mediator, such as fear or thinking. The mediator is conceptualized as an internal response. Without divorcing themselves from behaviourism, mediational learning theorists adopt the paradigmatic position that, under certain conditions, it is both legitimate and important to go beyond observables.

Consider the mediational learning analysis of anxiety developed by O. Hobart Mowrer (1939) and Neal Miller (1948). In a typical experiment, rats were shocked repeatedly in the presence of a neutral stimulus, such as the sound of a buzzer. The shock (UCS) produced a UCR of pain, fear, and flight. After several pairings, the fear that was naturally produced by the shock came to be produced by the buzzer. The shock could eventually be omitted, and the animal would continue to react fearfully to the previously neutral stimulus (CS). In addition, it was shown that the rat could learn new responses to avoid the CS (e.g., Miller, 1948). The question became how to conceptualize the finding that animals would learn to avoid a harmless event. Mowrer (1947) and others suggested that, in a typical avoidance conditioning experiment, two bits of learning were taking place (1) the animal, by means of classical conditioning, learned to fear the CS; and (2) the animal, by means of operant conditioning, learned an overt behaviour to remove itself from the CS and thus reduce the mediating fear response (see Figure 2.7). This came to be known as the two-factor theory.

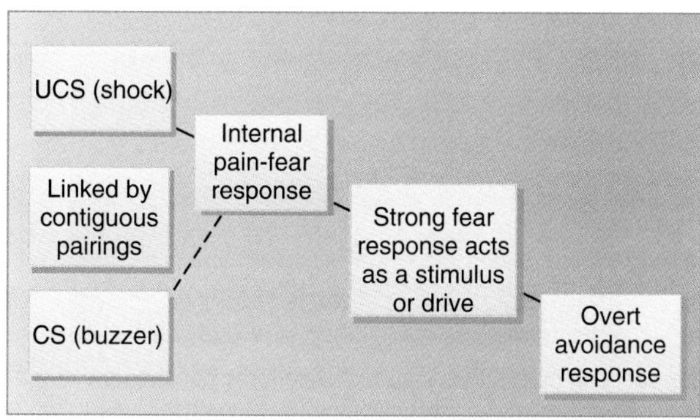

Figure 2.7 Schematic representation of Mowrer's account of avoidance learning. The dashed line indicates that the subject is learning to fear the buzzer, and the solid line that the subject is learning to avoid the shock.

The essential features of this theorizing are that fear or anxiety can be conceived of both as an internal response, which can be learned just as observable responses are learned, and as an internal drive, which can motivate avoidance behaviour. Anxiety then becomes amenable to the same kind of experimental analysis employed in the investigation of observable behaviour. For instance, if we know that repetition of an overt response without reinforcement leads to the extinction of the response, we can predict that repeated evocation of a fear response while withholding the expected pain or punishment will reduce the fear. This is no trivial prediction, since treatments based on such reasoning do help to reduce irrational fears.

BEHAVIOUR THERAPY

A new way of treating psychopathology, called behaviour therapy, emerged in the 1950s. In its initial form, this therapy applied procedures based on classical and operant conditioning to alter clinical problems. Sometimes the term behaviour modification is used as well, particularly by therapists who employ operant conditioning as a means of treatment. Although there has been debate over how to define the field (e.g., Fishman, Rodgers, & Franks, 1988; Mahoney, 1993), behaviour therapy today is characterized more by its epistemological stance—its search for rigorous standards of proof—than by allegiance to any particular set of concepts. Behaviour therapy is an attempt to change abnormal behaviour, thoughts, and feelings by applying in a clinical context the methods used and the discoveries made by experimental psychologists in their study of both normal and abnormal behaviour.

While the precise origins of behaviour therapy are unknown it did not begin with a social scientist waking up one morning and proclaiming that people with psychological problems should henceforth be treated with techniques suggested by experimental findings. Rather, over a number of years, people in the clinical field began to formulate a new set of assumptions about dealing with the problems they were encountering. It is helpful to distinguish three theoretical approaches in behaviour therapy: counterconditioning and exposure, operant conditioning, and modelling. Cognitive behaviour therapy is often considered a fourth aspect of behaviour therapy, but we will discuss it separately in the section on the cognitive paradigm because of its focus on thought processes.

Counterconditioning and Exposure Because learning paradigms assume that behaviour is the result of learning, treatment often involves relearning a new, more adaptive response. Counterconditioning is relearning achieved by eliciting a new response in the presence of a particular stimulus. A response (R_1) to a given stimulus (S) can be eliminated by eliciting a new response (R_2) in the presence of that stimulus, as diagrammed in Figure 2.8. For example, in an early and now famous demonstration, Mary Cover Jones successfully treated a young boy's fear of rabbits by feeding him in the presence of a rabbit. The animal was at first kept several feet away and then gradually moved closer on successive occasions. In this way, the fear (R_1) produced by the rabbit (S) was replaced by the stronger positive feelings evoked by eating (R_2).

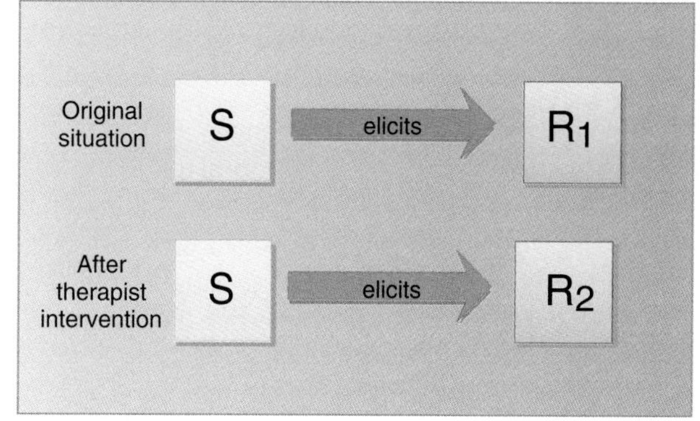

Figure 2.8 Schematic diagram of counterconditioning, whereby an original response (R_1) to a given stimulus (S) is eliminated by evoking a new response (R_2) to the same stimulus.

The counterconditioning principle is behind an important behaviour therapy technique, systematic desensitization, developed by Joseph Wolpe (1958). A person who suffers from anxiety works with the therapist to compile a list of feared situations, starting with those that arouse minimal anxiety and progressing to the most frightening. The person is also taught to relax deeply. Step-by-step, while relaxed, the person imagines the graded series of anxiety-provoking situations. The relaxation tends to inhibit any anxiety that might otherwise be elicited by the imagined scenes. The fearful person becomes able to tolerate increasingly more difficult imagined situations as he or she climbs the hierarchy over a number of therapy sessions. Wolpe hypothesized that counterconditioning underlies the efficacy of desensitization; a state or response antagonistic to anxiety is substituted for anxiety as the person is exposed gradually to stronger and stronger doses of what he or she fears. Some experiments (e.g., Davison, 1968b) suggest Wolpe's hypothesis, but other explanations are possible. Most contemporary theorists believe that exposure per se to what the person fears is important. Relaxation is then considered merely a useful way to encourage a frightened individual to confront what he or she fears (Wilson & Davison, 1971). This technique is useful in reducing a wide variety of fears.

Joseph Wolpe, one of the pioneers in behaviour therapy, is known particularly for systematic desensitization, a widely applied behavioural technique.

Another type of counterconditioning, aversive conditioning, also played an important historical role in the development of behaviour therapy. In aversive conditioning, a stimulus attractive to the patient is paired with an unpleasant event, such as a drug that produces nausea, in the hope of endowing it with negative properties. For example, a problem drinker who wishes to stop drinking might be asked to smell alcohol while he or she is being made nauseous by a drug. Aversive techniques have been employed to reduce smoking, drug use, and socially inappropriate desires, such as those of pedophiles.

Aversion therapy has been controversial for ethical reasons. A great outcry has been raised about inflicting pain and discomfort on people, even when they ask for it. In its early days, for example, aversion therapy was used in attempts to change the sexual orientation of homosexuals. Gay liberation organizations accused behaviour therapists of impeding the acceptance of homosexuality as a legitimate lifestyle. Currently, aversion therapy is rarely used in Canada or the United States as the only treatment for a particular problem. In treating a problem drinker, say, the aversion treatment may be used temporarily to reduce the problem behaviour while the client is taught new ways of coping with stress.

Time-out is an operant procedure wherein the consequence for misbehaviour is removal to an environment with no positive reinforcers.

Operant Conditioning Several behavioural procedures derive from operant conditioning. Much of this work has been done with children. Problem behaviour is analyzed to determine its function (in other words, what is reinforcing it). Generally, problem behaviour is thought to have four possible consequences: attention seeking, escape from tasks, the generation of sensory reinforcement (e.g., results from the hand flapping often seen in children with autistic disorder), and accessing tangible items or other reinforcers (Carr, 1994). Treatment typically consists of altering the consequences of the problem behaviour. For example, if the problem was motivated by attention seeking, the treatment might be to ignore it. Alternatively, the problem could be followed by time-out, where the person is banished for a period of time to a dreary location with no positive reinforcers.

Making positive reinforcers contingent on behaviour is used to increase the frequency of desirable behaviour. For example, a socially withdrawn child could be reinforced for playing with others. Problems treated with this method include autism, learning disabilities, mental retardation, bedwetting, aggression, hyperactivity, tantrums, and social withdrawal (Kazdin, 1994).

The Token Economy An early example of work within the operant tradition is the token economy, a procedure in which tokens (e.g., poker chips or stickers) are given for desired behaviour and can later be exchanged for desirable items and activities. If we could transport ourselves back in time about 45 years to Saskatchewan Hospital, a mental hospital in Weyburn, Saskatchewan, and visit Teodor Ayllon's 1957 behaviour modification ward, we would be witness to an intellectually exciting "experiment"—applied behavioural analysis in an institutional setting. In 1959 Ayllon and Michael published a classic paper on this work ("The Psychiatric Nurse as a Behavioral Engineer"), which ushered in the token economy strategy. This work has been described elsewhere (e.g., Rice & Quinsey, 1986; Sherwood & Gray, 1974) as the first behaviour modification unit in a psychiatric hospital. Subsequently, and in a different setting, Ayllon and Azrin (1968) published a book in which they described and evaluated a comprehensive token economy program with psychiatric patients. They had set aside an entire ward of a mental hospital for a series of experiments. The 45 female patients were systematically rewarded for ward work and self-care with plastic tokens that could later be exchanged for privileges, such as going to the movies, renting a private room, or enjoying extra visits to the canteen. These tokens were not given when behaviour was withdrawn or bizarre. The life of each patient was as much as possible controlled by this regime.

The rules of a token economy—the medium of exchange, the activities rewarded and by what number of tokens, the items and privileges that can be purchased and for how many tokens—are carefully established and usually posted. Ayllon, Azrin, and others demonstrated the effect of reinforcement contingencies on the behaviour of their ward patients (see Figure 2.9). The original research and subsequent studies, including work by Steffy and colleagues at the Lakeshore Psychiatric Hospital in Toronto (Steffy, Hart, Craw, Torney, & Marlett, 1969), attest to the positive impact of token-economy programs in directing staff attention to rewarding improvements in self-care and the acquisition of social skills, in contrast to the more typical situation in which patients are more likely to get attention more when they act maladaptively or dangerously (Menditto, Valdes, & Beck, 1994; Kopelowicz & Liberman, 1998). An expansion of the token economy conducted by Gordon Paul and his associates is described in more detail in Focus on Discovery 11.3.

Modelling Modelling has also been used in behaviour therapy. Bandura, Blanchard, and Ritter (1969) were able to help people reduce their fear of nonpoisonous snakes by having them view both live and filmed encounters in which people gradually approached and successfully handled snakes. Fears of surgery and dental work have been treated in a similar manner (Melamed & Siegel, 1975). Films have been used to help sexually inhibited people overcome their discomfort with sexuality (McMullen & Rosen, 1979).

In an analogous fashion, some behaviour therapists use role-playing in the consulting room. They demonstrate to patients patterns of behaviour that might prove more effective than those the patients usually engage in, and then have the patients practise them. Lazarus (1971), in his behaviour rehearsal procedures, demonstrates exemplary ways of handling a situation and then encourages patients to imitate them during the therapy session. For example, a student who feels awkward asking for an extension on a term paper might watch the therapist portray an effective way of making the request and then be helped to practise the new skill in a role-playing situation. Similar procedures have helped patients with schizophrenia acquire skills to deal more effectively with social situations (Marder et al., 1996).

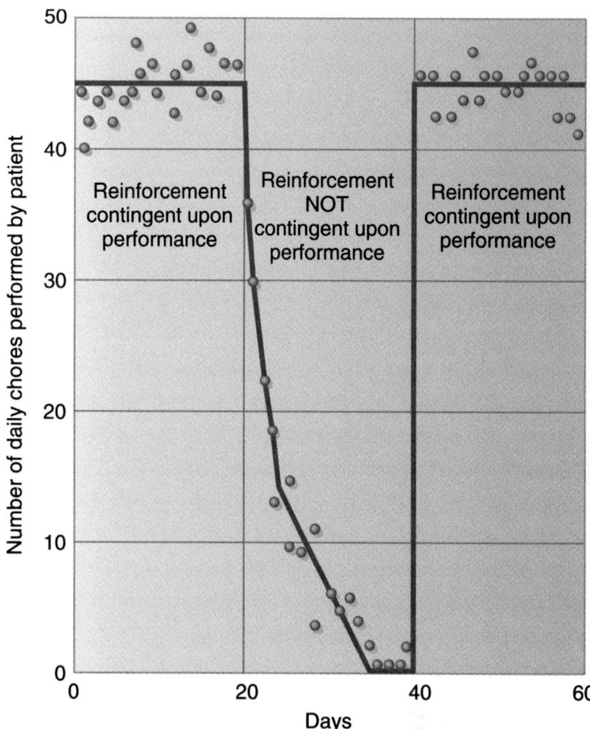

Figure 2.9 Patients on a ward spent more time grooming and doing chores when they received tokens than they did when they were given no reward. Adapted from Ayllon and Azrin (1965).

Modelling is often used to encourage assertiveness. Our society does not generally value the open expression of beliefs and feelings, and yet people often pay an emotional price for concealing their thoughts and suppressing their feelings. If patients have trouble expressing their feelings and wishes to others, assertion training may help them. Andrew Salter (1949) was the first behaviour therapist to set assertiveness as a positive goal for people. He encouraged socially inhibited people to express their feelings to others in an open, spontaneous way, without necessarily being aggressive. Assertion training is a set of techniques with the common goal of enhancing assertiveness, or what Lazarus (1971) calls "emotional freedom." The specific therapy procedures used depend on the reasons believed to be causing the individual's unassertiveness (Goldfried & Davison, 1994).

Behaviour rehearsal is a useful technique in assertion training. The therapist discusses and models appropriate assertiveness and then has the patient roleplay situations. Improvement is rewarded by praise from the therapist or from other members of an assertion-training group. Graded homework assignments, such as asking the mechanic to explain the latest bill for repairs, are given as soon as the client has acquired some degree of assertiveness through session work.

Evaluating Learning Paradigms

The learning view minimizes the importance of biological factors and focuses instead on determining the learning processes that may make behaviour maladaptive. The learning paradigm of abnormal behaviour is in much the same state of development as the biological paradigm. Just as many pertinent biological malfunctions have not been uncovered, particular learning experiences have not yet been convincingly linked to abnormality. Consider how difficult it would be to show that depression results from a particular reinforcement history. A person would have to be observed continually over a period of years while his or her behaviour and occurrences of reinforcement were noted. If identical twins reared by their natural parents became schizophrenic later in life, the clinician holding a learning view might assert that they had similar reinforcement histories. If fraternal twins were raised at home and only one became schizophrenic, the learning explanation would be that their reinforcement histories were different. Such explanations are as circular and as unsatisfactory as some psychoanalytic inferences of unconscious processes, a practice deplored by behaviourists.

While the learning explanation of abnormal behaviour has led to many treatment innovations, the fact that a treatment based on learning principles is effective in changing behaviour does not mean that the behaviour was itself learned in a similar way. For example, while the mood of depressed persons may be elevated by rewards for increased activity, this cannot be considered evidence that the depression was initially produced by an absence of rewards (Rimland, 1964).

How does a person's observation of a model lead to changes in his or her overt behaviour? As mentioned in Canadian Contribution 2.1, Bandura and Walters (1963) asserted that an observer could somehow learn new behaviour by watching others. However, in order for imitation to occur, cognitive processes must become engaged, including the ability to remember later on what had happened. Findings of research on social learning led some behavioural researchers and clinicians to include cognitive variables in their analyses of psychopathology and therapy.

The Cognitive Paradigm

"The mind is its own place, and in itself
Can make a Heav'n of Hell, a hell of Heav'n."

—Paradise Lost.

Cognition is a term that groups together the mental processes of perceiving, recognizing, conceiving, judging, and reasoning. The **cognitive paradigm** focuses on how people (and animals as well) structure their experiences, how they make sense of them, and how they relate their current experiences to past ones that have been stored in memory.

The Basics of Cognitive Theory

At any given moment, we are bombarded by far more stimuli than we can possibly respond to. How do we filter this overwhelming input, put it into words or images, form hypotheses, and arrive at a perception of what is out there? Cognitive psychologists consider the learning process much more complex than the passive formation of new stimulus-response associations. Even classical conditioning is viewed by cognitive psychologists as an active process by which organisms learn about relationships among events rather than as an automatic stamping in of associations between stimuli (Rescorla, 1988). Moreover, cognitive psychologists regard the learner as an active interpreter of a situation, with the learner's past knowledge imposing a perceptual funnel on the experience. The learner fits new information into an organized network of already accumulated knowledge, often referred to as a **schema**, or cognitive set (Neisser, 1976). New information may fit the schema, but if it does not, the learner reorganizes the schema to fit the information or construes the information in such a way as to fit the schema. The cognitive approach may remind you of our earlier discussions of paradigms; scientific paradigms are similar in function to a cognitive schema, for they act as filters to our experience of the world.

Although learning paradigms initially avoided cognitive concepts, contemporary experimental psychology is very much concerned with cognition. The following situation illustrates how a schema may alter the way in which information is processed and remembered:

> The man stood before the mirror and combed his hair. He checked his face carefully for any places he might have missed shaving and then put on the conservative tie he had decided to wear. At breakfast, he studied the newspaper carefully and, over coffee, discussed the possibility of buying a new washing machine with his wife. Then he made several phone calls. As he was leaving the house he thought about the fact that his children would probably want to go to that private camp again this summer. When the car didn't start, he got out, slammed the door and walked down to the bus stop in a very angry mood. Now he would be late. (Bransford & Johnson, 1973, p. 415)

Now read the excerpt again, but add the word "unemployed" before the word "man." Now read it a third time, substituting "stockbroker" for "man." Notice how differently you understand the passage. Ask yourself what parts of the newspaper these men read. If this query had been posed on a questionnaire, you might have answered "the want ads" for the unemployed man and "the financial pages" for the stockbroker. Since the passage does not specify which part of the paper was read, your answers might have been wrong but, in each instance, the error would have been a meaningful, predictable one.

Cognitive psychologists have until recently paid little systematic attention to how their research findings might bear on psychopathology or help generate effective therapies. Now cognitive explanations appear more and more often in the search for the causes of abnormality and for new methods of intervention. A widely held view of depression, for example, places the blame on a particular cognitive set, namely, the individual's overriding sense of hopelessness. Many people who are depressed believe that they have no important effect on their surroundings regardless of what they do. Their destiny seems to them to be out of their hands, and they expect their future to be negative. If depression does develop from a sense of hopelessness, this fact could have implications for how clinicians treat the disorder. Cognitive theorizing will be included in discussions of most of the disorders described in this book.

COGNITIVE BEHAVIOUR THERAPY

The behavioural therapies discussed earlier emphasize the direct manipulation of overt behaviour and occasionally of covert behaviour, with thoughts and feelings being construed as internal behaviours (recall our discussion of mediational learning paradigms. They pay relatively little attention to direct alteration of the thinking and reasoning processes of the client. Perhaps it was in reaction to insight therapy that behaviour therapists initially discounted the importance of cognition, regarding any appeal to thinking as a return to structuralism, to which John Watson had vigorously objected in the early part of the 20th century.

Cognitive behaviour therapy (CBT) does incorporate theory and research on cognitive processes. Although we present it here as part of the cognitive paradigm, CBT has in fact become a blend of the cognitive and learning paradigms. Cognitive behaviour therapists pay attention to private events—thoughts, perceptions, judgments, self-statements, and even tacit (unconscious) assumptions—and have studied and manipulated these processes in their attempts to understand and modify overt and covert disturbed behaviour. Cognitive restructuring is a general term for changing a pattern of thought that is presumed to be causing a disturbed emotion or behaviour. This restructuring is implemented in several ways by cognitive behaviour therapists.

Beck's Cognitive Therapy The psychiatrist Aaron Beck is one of the leading cognitive behaviour therapists. He developed a cognitive therapy for depression based on the idea that depressed mood is caused by distortions in the way people perceive life experiences (Beck, 1976; Salkovskis, 1996). For example, a depressed person may focus exclusively on negative happenings and ignore positive ones, or interpret positive experiences in a negative manner. This is illustrated by revelations made in her autobiography by Canadian prima ballerina Karen Kain (see Kain, 1994). Kain admitted having experienced severe depression and had this to say about occasions when her performance did not meet her own exacting standards:

> Sometimes my lacklustre performance would be evident, and the applause would be muted, merely polite. But at other times—and these were even worse for a perfectionist like me—people would give me a warm reception, perhaps even stand and applaud, when I knew I'd been dreadful, and I would interpret their enthusiasm as proof positive that I'd never been any good. I had always danced badly, and somehow nobody had ever noticed. (Kain, 1994, p. 158)

Beck's therapy (examined in detail in Chapter 10) tries to persuade patients to change their opinions of themselves and the way in which they interpret life events. When a depressed person expresses feelings that nothing ever goes right, for example, the therapist offers counter-examples, pointing out how the client has overlooked favourable happenings. The general goal of Beck's therapy is to provide patients with experiences, both inside and outside the consulting room, that will alter their negative schemas.

Aaron Beck developed a cognitive theory of depression and a cognitive therapy for the cognitive biases of depressed people.

Ellis's Rational-Emotive Behaviour Therapy Albert Ellis is another leading cognitive behaviour therapist. His principal thesis is that sustained emotional reactions are caused by internal sentences that people repeat to themselves, and these self-statements reflect sometimes unspoken assumptions—irrational beliefs—about what is necessary to lead a meaningful life. In Ellis's rational-emotive therapy (RET), recently renamed rational-emotive behaviour therapy (REBT) (Ellis, 1993a, 1995), the aim is to eliminate self-defeating beliefs through a rational examination of them. Anxious persons, for example, may create their own problems by making unrealistic demands on themselves or others, such as "I must win the love of everyone." Or a depressed person may say several times a day, "What a worthless jerk I am." Ellis proposes that people interpret what is happening around them, that sometimes these interpretations can cause emotional turmoil, and that a therapist's attention should be focused on these beliefs rather than on historical causes or, indeed, on overt behaviour (Ellis, 1962, 1984).

Ellis used to list a number of irrational beliefs that people can harbour. One very common notion was that they must be thoroughly competent in everything they do. Ellis suggested that many people actually believe this untenable assumption and evaluate every event within this context. Thus, if a person makes an error, it becomes a catastrophe because it violates the deeply held conviction that he or she must be perfect (Ellis, 2002). It sometimes comes as a shock to clients to realize that they actually believe such strictures and have thus run their lives in a way that makes it is virtually impossible to live comfortably or productively.

More recently, Ellis (1991; Kendall et al., 1995) has shifted from a cataloguing of specific beliefs to the more general concept of "demandingness"—the musts or shoulds that people impose on themselves and others. Thus, instead of wanting something to be a certain way, feeling disappointed when it is not, and then engaging in behaviour that might bring about the desired outcome, the person demands that it be so. This unrealistic, unproductive demand is hypothesized to create severe emotional distress and behavioural dysfunction.

Clinical Implementation of REBT After becoming familiar with the client's problems, the therapist presents the basic theory of rational-emotive behaviour therapy so that the client can understand and accept it. The following transcript is from a session with a young man who had inordinate fears about speaking in front of groups. The therapist guides the client to view his inferiority complex in terms of the unreasonable things he may be telling himself. The therapist's thoughts during the interview are indicated in italics within square brackets.

Client: My primary difficulty is that I become very uptight when I have to speak in front of a group of people. I guess it's just my own inferiority complex.

Therapist: [*I don't want to get sidetracked at this point by talking about that conceptualization of his problem. I'll just try to finesse it and make a smooth transition to something else.*] I don't know if I would call it an inferiority complex but I do believe that people can, in a sense, bring on their own upset and anxiety in certain kinds of situations. When you're in a particular situation, your anxiety is often not the result of the situation itself, but rather the way in which you interpret the situation-what you tell yourself about the situation. For example, look at this pen. Does this pen make you nervous?

Client: No.

Therapist: Why not?

Client: It's just an object. It's just a pen.

Therapist: It can't hurt you?

Client: No...

Therapist: It's really not the object that creates emotional upset in people, but rather what you think about the object. [*Hopefully, this Socratic-like dialogue will eventually bring him to the conclusion that self-statements can mediate emotional arousal.*] Now this holds true for...situations where emotional upset is caused by what a person tells himself about the situation. Take, for example, two people who are about to attend the same social gathering. Both of them may know exactly the same number of people at the party, but one person can be optimistic and relaxed about the situation, whereas the other one can be worried about how he will appear, and consequently be very anxious. [*I'll try to get him to verbalize the basic assumption that attitude or perception is most important here.*] So, when these two people walk into the place where the party is given, are their emotional reactions at all associated with the physical arrangements at the party?

Client: No, obviously not.

Therapist: What determines their reactions, then?

Client: They obviously have different attitudes toward the party.

Therapist: Exactly, and their attitudes—the ways in which they approach the situation—greatly influence their emotional reactions. (Goldfried & Davison, 1994, pp. 163-165)

Having persuaded the client that his or her emotional problems will benefit from rational examination, the therapist proceeds to teach the person to substitute for irrational self-statements an internal dialogue meant to ease the emotional turmoil. Therapists who implement Ellis's ideas differ greatly on how they persuade clients to change their self-talk. Some therapists, like Ellis himself, argue with clients, cajoling and teasing them, sometimes in very blunt language. Others, believing that social influence should be more subtle and that individuals should participate more in changing themselves, encourage clients to discuss their own irrational thinking and then gently lead them to discover more rational ways of regarding the world (Goldfried & Davison, 1994).

Once a client verbalizes a different belief or self-statement during a therapy session, it must be made part of everyday thinking. Ellis and his followers provide patients with homework assignments designed to help them experiment with the new self-talk and to experience the positive consequences of viewing life in less catastrophic ways. Ellis emphasizes the importance of getting the patient to behave differently, both to test out new beliefs and to learn to cope with life's disappointments.

Meichenbaum's Cognitive-Behaviour Modification Donald Meichenbaum is also a leading cognitive behaviour therapist. In contrast to Beck and Ellis, who came from psychoanalytic backgrounds, Meichenbaum was trained first in the principles of behaviour modification. Nonetheless, his approach, originally referred to as cognitive-behaviour modification, also addresses issues that are typically focused on by psychodynamically oriented clinicians (see Canadian Contributions 2.2). In recent years, Meichenbaum has shifted in a "constructivist" direction (see Neimeyer & Raskin, 2001), emphasizing the narrative organization of experience (e.g., Meichenbaum, 1995; Meichenbaum & Fitzpatrick, 1995; Meichenbaum & Fong, 1993; also see Chapters 6 and 17). The term *constructivist* is used "to encompass the broad panoply of perspectives that emphasize those processes by which meaning is constructed by human beings in personal, interpersonal, and social contexts" (Neimeyer & Raskin, 2001, p. 423). Meichenbaum's approach is more integrative than that of Beck and Ellis. He addresses issues related to psychotherapy practice that will be explored in Chapter 17.

Behaviour Therapy and CBT in Groups Many of the behavioural and cognitive behaviour therapies we have described have been used with groups as well as with individuals. For example, the deep muscle relaxation of systematic desensitization can be efficiently taught to a group of people, and with a group of people with the same fear, the same hierarchy can be presented to everyone simultaneously. Group desensitization has been used effectively to treat the same kinds of fears that have been treated with individual desensitization (e.g., Meichenbaum, Gilmore, & Fedoravicius, 1971). Social and assertion skills have also been taught to groups of people. For example, depressed people have learned ways of interacting with others that are likely to bring them more reinforcement from others (e.g., Teri & Lewinsohn, 1986). The cognitive behaviour therapies of both Beck and Ellis have also been used in groups to treat anxiety disorders (Albano et al., 1995; Kobak, Rock, & Greist, 1995; Neron, Lacroix, & Chaput, 1995).

Canadian Contributions/2.2

Donald Meichenbaum

Donald Meichenbaum developed an integrative, collaborative, constructivist brand of CBT that includes strategies such as self-instructional training and stress inoculation, a focus on "barriers" to treatment, and the use of personal narratives.

Donald Meichenbaum, a Canadian clinical psychologist, is a pioneer in bridging the gap between the clinical concerns of psychodynamic psychotherapists and the behaviour technology of therapists such as B.F. Skinner, Joseph Wolpe, and T. Ayllon. Don Meichenbaum has developed a set of psychotherapeutic procedures that he now calls cognitive-behavioural therapy. Two illustrative cognitive-behavioural procedures include self-instructional training and stress-inoculation training.

In self-instructional training (Meichenbaum, 1977), the therapist helps the client prepare to make specific coping statements when confronted with difficult situations. In stress-inoculation training (Meichenbaum, 1975, 1977, 1985, 1992), Meichenbaum developed a multi-component coping-skills approach that incorporates self-instructional training and has proven to be a very effective therapeutic strategy. The approach emphasizes systematic acquisition of coping skills through learning to cope with small but manageable amounts of stress. This strategy is assumed to facilitate the maintenance of treatment gains and generalization to other stressful situations. The rationale is credible: people who learn to cope with relatively mild levels of stress can be "inoculated" against uncontrollable levels.

These cognitive behaviour procedures were employed initially with impulsive individuals who experienced self-control problems, such as hyperactive children (Meichenbaum & Goodman, 1971); children, adolescents, and adults who had problems with anger control (e.g., Meichenbaum & Novaco, 1977); children undergoing therapy (e.g., Burstein & Meichenbaum, 1979); schizophrenics who had attentional control problems (Meichenbaum, 1969); and people with pain management problems (e.g., Turk & Meichenbaum, 1987). In all of these cases, the therapy involved educating patients (and family members) about their disabilities and teaching them how to "think before they act." Clients were taught, by means of direct instruction, modelling rehearsal, and feedback, how to "notice, catch, interrupt, plan, monitor, and self-reinforce" their behaviour. In a problem-solving fashion, patients were taught a behavioural routine consisting of "goal, plan, do, check."

But Meichenbaum's cognitive behaviour approach did not stop there. Therapists and clients worked collaboratively to consider what factors might get in the way of patients using such coping skills. Sometimes, the barriers reflected the patient's beliefs (e.g., lack of self-confidence, perfectionistic standards) or lack of motivation (e.g., a "paralysis of will"). Sometimes the barriers were interpersonal in nature (e.g., lack of reinforcement, family members undermining improvement). The cognitive behaviour therapist and the clients worked on ways to anticipate and address these potential barriers. The psychodynamic features (e.g., Meichenbaum & Gilmore, 1980) found their way into cognitive behaviour treatment because sometimes the "barriers" to improvement come from early childhood/adolescent experiences. It is not merely the harsh developmental history experienced by many patients (e.g., about 50 percent of psychiatric patients have historical victimization), but also what patients tell themselves and others and the "stories" they construct about what they experienced that influence their current adjustment and future outlook (a constructivist-narrative approach). Cognitive behaviour therapists who adopt Meichenbaum's approach help clients understand the narratives they create and learn ways to alter how they appraise events and their abilities to handle stressful events. The cognitive behaviour intervention of stress-inoculation training has not only been used to treat individuals who have been traumatized (e.g., rape victims; Meichenbaum, 1994) and who experience ongoing stress (e.g., chronic physical pain; Turk, Meichenbaum, & Genest, 1983), but it has also been employed on a preventative basis with individuals who hold high-stress jobs (e.g., policemen, military personnel; Meichenbaum, 1992). Meichenbaum's (1994) comprehensive constructivist-narrative approach to the treatment of people with posttraumatic stress disorder is described in detail in Chapter 6.

Along with other cognitive therapists such as Albert Ellis and Aaron Beck, Don Meichenbaum has contributed significantly to the development of an integrative and empirically validated treatment approach. He is regarded as one of the 10 most influential psychotherapists of the 20th century. Dr. Meichenbaum is presently distinguished professor emeritus at the University of Waterloo and research director of the Melissa Institute for Violence Prevention and Treatment of Victims of Violence, in Miami, Florida.

Evaluating the Cognitive Paradigm

Some criticisms of the cognitive paradigm should be noted. The concepts on which it is based (e.g., schema) are abstract and not always well defined. Furthermore, cognitive explanations of psychopathology do not always explain much. That a depressed person has a negative schema tells us that the person thinks gloomy thoughts. However, such a pattern of thinking is actually part of the diagnosis of depression. What is distinctive in the cognitive paradigm is that the thoughts are given causal status; they are regarded as causing the other features of the disorder, such as sadness. Left unanswered is the question of where the negative schema came from in the first place. Cognitive explanations of psychopathology tend to focus more on current determinants of a disorder and less on its historical antecedents.

Is the cognitive point of view basically different and separate from the learning paradigm? Much of what we have just considered suggests that it is. The growing field of cognitive behaviour therapy gives us pause, however, for its workers study the complex interplay of beliefs, expectations, perceptions, and attitudes on the one hand and overt behaviour on the other. For example, as a leading advocate of changing behaviour through cognitive means, Bandura (1977) uses his concept of self-efficacy (see Canadian Contributions 2.1) to argue that different therapies produce improvement by increasing people's belief that they can achieve desired goals. At the same time, though, he argues that changing behaviour through behavioural techniques is the most powerful way to enhance self-efficacy. Therapists such as Ellis, in contrast, emphasize direct alteration of cognitions (through argument, persuasion, Socratic dialogue, and the like) to bring about improvements in emotion and behaviour. Complicating matters further, Ellis places importance on homework assignments that require clients to behave in ways they have been unable to previously because of negative thoughts. Ellis renamed his therapy "rational-emotive behaviour therapy" to highlight the importance of overt behaviour. Cognitive behaviour therapists work at both the cognitive and behavioural levels, and most of those who use cognitive concepts and try to change beliefs with verbal means also use behavioural procedures to alter behaviour directly.

This issue is reflected in the terminology used to refer to people such as Beck and Ellis. Are they cognitive therapists or cognitive behaviour therapists? For the most part we will use the latter term because it denotes both that the therapist regards cognitions as major determinants of emotion and behaviour and that he or she maintains the focus on overt behaviour that has always characterized behaviour therapy. Nonetheless, Beck, even though he assigns many behavioural tasks as part of his therapy, is usually referred to as the founder of cognitive therapy (CT); Ellis's rational-emotive therapy (RET) was once considered separate from behaviour therapy.

CONSEQUENCES OF ADOPTING A PARADIGM

The student who adopts a particular paradigm necessarily makes a prior decision concerning what kinds of data will be collected and how they will be interpreted. Thus, he or she may very well ignore possibilities and overlook other information in advancing what seems to be the most probable explanation. A behaviourist is prone to attribute the high prevalence of schizophrenia in lower-class groups to the paucity of social rewards that these people received, based on the assumption that normal development requires a certain amount of reinforcement patterning. A biologically oriented theorist will be quick to remind the behaviourist of the many deprived people who do not become schizophrenic. The behaviourist will undoubtedly counter with the argument that those who do not become schizophrenic had different reinforcement histories. The biologically oriented theorist will reply that such post hoc statements can always be made.

A biological theorist may suggest that biochemical factors that predispose a person both to schizophrenia and to deficiencies in the intellectual skills necessary for steady employment account for the correlation between social class and schizophrenia. The behaviourist will remind the biological theorist that these alleged factors have yet to be found, to which the biological theorist might answer, "Yes, but I'm placing my bets that they are there, and if I adopt your behavioural paradigm, I may not look for them." To which the behaviourist may reply, "Yes, but your assumption regarding biochemical factors makes it less likely that you will look for and uncover the subtle reinforcement factors that in all probability account for both the presence and the absence of schizophrenia."

Clearly, abnormal behaviour is much too diverse to be explained or treated adequately by any one of the current paradigms. It is probably advantageous that psychologists do not agree on which paradigm is the best. We know far too little to make hard-and-fast decisions on the exclusive superiority of any one paradigm. The best approach is often to assume multiple causation. A particular disorder may very well develop through an interaction of biological defects and environmental factors, a view we turn to next.

DIATHESIS-STRESS AND BIOPSYCHOSOCIAL: INTEGRATIVE PARADIGMS

A paradigm more general than the ones discussed so far, called diathesis-stress, links biological, psychological, and environmental factors. It is not limited to one particular school of thought, such as learning, cognitive, or psychodynamic, but focuses on the interaction between a predisposition toward disease—the diathesis—and environmental, or life, disturbances—the stress. Diathesis refers most precisely to a constitutional predisposition toward illness, but the term may be extended to any characteristic or set of characteristics that increases a person's chance of developing a disorder.

In the realm of biology, a number of disorders appear to have a genetically transmitted diathesis; that is, having a close relative with the disorder increases a person's risk for the disorder since there is a sharing of genetic endowment to some degree. Although the precise nature of these genetic diatheses is currently unknown (e.g., we don't know exactly what is inherited that makes one person more likely than another to develop schizophrenia), it is clear that a genetic predisposition is an important component of many psychopathologies. Other biological diatheses include oxygen deprivation at birth, poor nutrition, a maternal viral infection, or maternal smoking during pregnancy. Each of these conditions may lead to changes in the brain that predispose toward psychopathology.

In the psychological realm, a diathesis for depression may be the cognitive set already mentioned, the chronic feeling of hopelessness sometimes found in depressed people. Or, taking a psychodynamic view, it may be an extreme sense of dependency on others, perhaps because of frustrations during one of the psychosexual stages. Another psychological diatheses is the ability to be easily hypnotized, which may be a diathesis for dissociative identity disorder (formerly called multiple personality disorder).

Life stress, such as being overwhelmed at work or living in a war zone, is an important component of the diathesis-stress paradigm.

These psychological diatheses can arise for a variety of reasons. Some, such as hypnotizability, are personality characteristics that are in part genetically determined. Others, such as a sense of hopelessness, may result from childhood experiences with harshly critical parents. Abuse during childhood produces psychological changes that seem to predispose people to develop a number of different disorders. Socio-cultural influences also play an important role; for instance, cultural standards of beauty may lead to an intense fear of being fat and thus predispose some people toward eating disorders. The diathesis-stress paradigm is integrative because it draws on all these diverse sources of information about the causes of diatheses. In later chapters, we will see that concepts from the major paradigms we have already discussed apply differentially to different disorders. For example, a genetically determined biological diathesis plays a major role in schizophrenia. Cognitive diatheses, in contrast, are more influential in the anxiety disorders and depression. Psychoanalytic concepts figure prominently in theories of hysteria. A diathesis-stress paradigm allows us to draw on concepts from many sources and to make more or less use of them depending on the disorder being considered.

Possessing the diathesis for a disorder increases a person's risk of developing it but does not guarantee that the disorder will develop. It is the stress part of diathesis-stress that accounts for how a diathesis may be translated into an actual disorder. In this context, stress generally refers to some noxious or unpleasant environmental stimulus that triggers psychopathology. Psychological stressors include both major traumatic events (e.g., losing one's job, divorce, death of a spouse) and more mundane happenings (e.g., being stuck in traffic). The diathesis-stress model goes beyond the major paradigms we have already discussed by including these environmental events.

The key point of the diathesis-stress model is that both diathesis and stress are necessary in the development of disorders (see Figure 2.10). Some people, for example, inherit a biological predisposition that places them at high risk for schizophrenia (see Chapter 11); given a certain amount of stress, they stand a good chance of developing schizophrenia. Other people, at low genetic risk, are not likely to develop schizophrenia, regardless of how difficult their lives are.

Another feature of the diathesis-stress paradigm is that psychopathology is unlikely to result from any single factor. A genetically transmitted diathesis may be necessary for some disorders, but it is embedded in a network of other factors that also play a part: for example, genetically transmitted diatheses for other personality characteristics; childhood experiences that shape personality; the development of behavioural competencies and coping strategies; stressors encountered in adulthood; and cultural influences.

Some clinical scientists describe an integrative paradigm that is quite similar to and overlaps with the diathesis-stress perspective—the biopsychosocial paradigm. Biological, psychological, and social factors are conceptualized as different levels of analysis or subsystems within the paradigm. Like the diathesis-stress paradigm, the biopsychosocial paradigm is not limited to a particular school of thought. Figure 2.11 employs a Venn diagram to illustrate the biopsychosocial paradigm. The figure incorporates an array of the possible causal factors, including some of those described above in connection with the discussion of the diathesis-stress paradigm. The key point about the biopsychosocial paradigm is that explanations for the causes of disorders typically involve complex interactions among many biological, psychological,

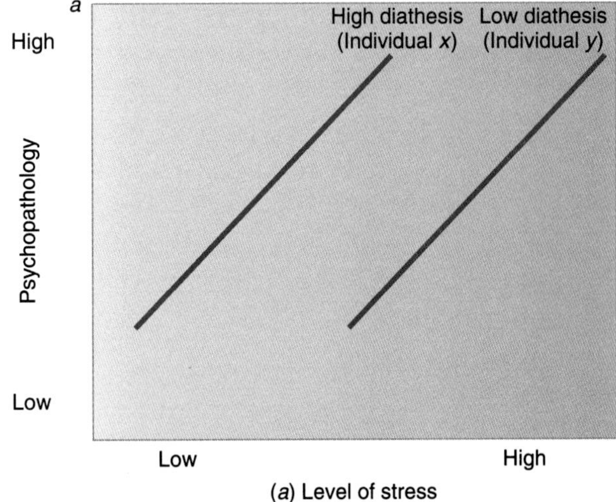

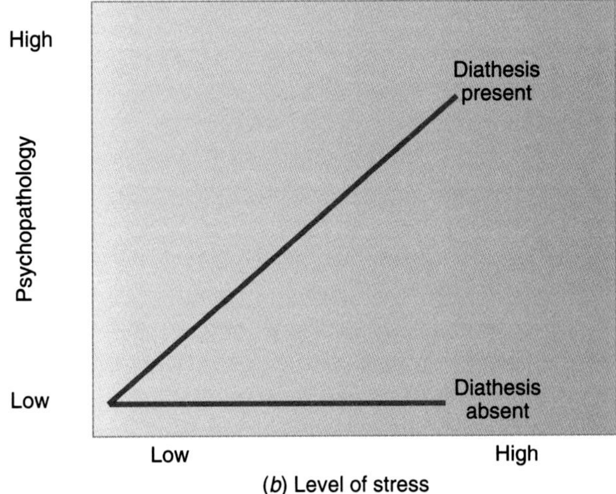

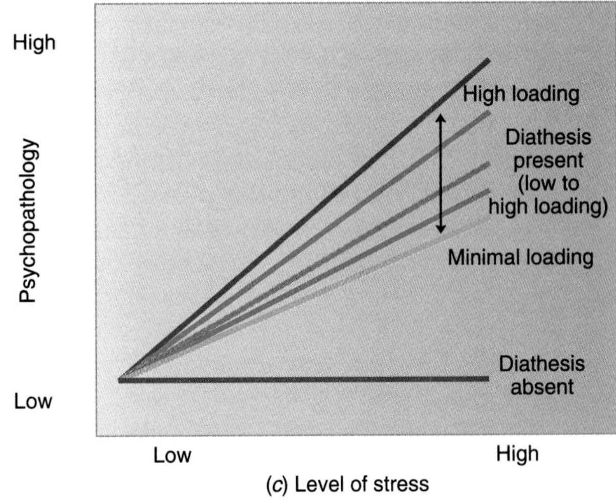

Figure 2.10 Three depictions of diathesis-stress models. (a) An individual with a large dose of the diathesis requires only a moderate amount of stress to develop psychopathology, whereas an individual with a small dose of the diathesis requires a large amount of stress to precipitate a breakdown. (b) The diathesis is dichotomous; stress level has no effect on those without the diathesis. (c) The diathesis is continuous; increasing stress increases psychopathology for all people with at least a minimal amount of the diathesis. After Monroe and Simons (1991).

and socio-environmental and socio-cultural factors. The actual variables and the degree of influence of the variables from the different domains typically differ from disorder to disorder. Thus, similar to the diathesis-stress paradigm, the biopsychosocial paradigm is integrative because it accepts the interplay of many factors and draws on diverse sources of information about the causes of psychological disorders.

Many scholarly articles and research papers are based on the diathesis-stress and biopsychosocial paradigms, a reflection of the now widely accepted view that psychological disorders develop from complex interactions involving multiple factors. Although both of these integrative paradigms tend to focus on the factors that interact to put people at greater risk of—or make them more vulnerable to—developing disorders, it should also be recognized that certain factors, if present, can help protect individuals from developing disorders. Protection from risk factors, or the ability to bounce back in the face of adversity, is referred to as resilience (Smith & Prior, 1995). Protective factors can occur within the individual (e.g., perseverance and courage in a child who suffers poverty; the ability to think and act independently in an adolescent whose parent is diagnosed with a psychiatric disorder) but can also reside in the environment (e.g., a close relationship with one parent; support from a caring teacher). (See Phares, 2003, for a more complete discussion of protective factors and resiliency.) Contemporary biopsychosocial models of psychopathology in

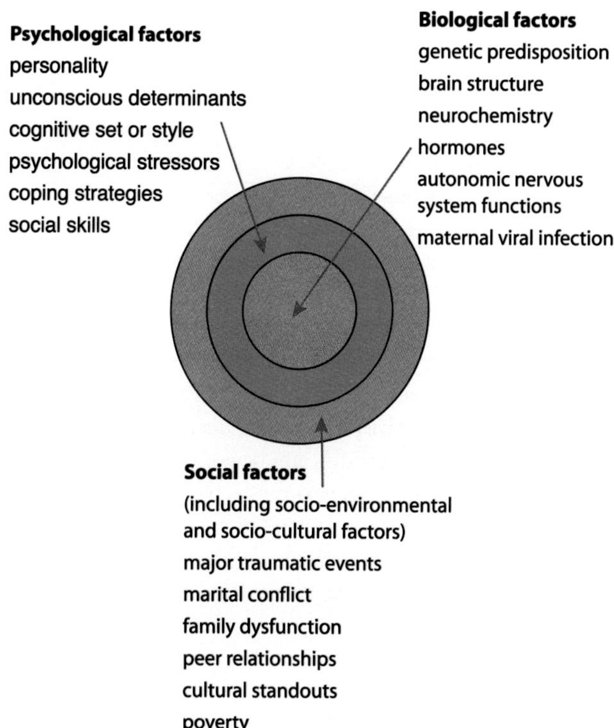

Figure 2.11 Diagram illustrating the biopsychosocial paradigm. Although disturbances in each area can contribute to the development of psychological disorders, the causes cannot be neatly divided, there is usually interaction among the three domains of influence.

children are described in Chapter 15. Throughout this book, you will discover elaborate explanations of disorders in which numerous variables, both risk and protective, work together to bring about maladaptive or adaptive outcomes.

DIFFERENT PERSPECTIVES ON A CLINICAL PROBLEM

To provide a concrete example of how it is possible to conceptualize a clinical case using different paradigms, we now return to the case of the police officer J. Brett Barkley with which this book began. The information provided there is open to a number of interpretations, depending on the paradigm adopted.

If you hold a biological point of view, you are attentive to the similarity between the man's alternately manic and depressed states and the cyclical mood swings of his father. You are probably aware of research (see Chapter 10) that suggests a genetic factor in mood disorders. You do not discount environmental contributions to Brett's problems, but you hypothesize that some inherited, probably biochemical, defect predisposes him to break down under stress. After all, not everyone who experiences a difficult childhood and adolescence develops the kinds of problems Brett has. For treatment, you may prescribe lithium carbonate, a drug that is generally helpful in reducing the magnitude of mood swings in manic-depression.

A psychoanalytic point of view casts Brett in yet another light. Believing that events in early childhood are of great importance in later patterns of adjustment, you hypothesize that Brett is still grieving for his mother and has blamed his father for her early death. Anger at the father has been repressed, but Brett has not been able to regard him as a competent, worthwhile adult or to identify with him. For treatment, you may choose dream analysis and free association to help Brett deal openly and consciously with his hitherto buried anger toward his father.

If you have a behavioural or cognitive behaviour perspective, you may focus on Brett's self-consciousness at college, which seems related to the fact that, compared with his fellow students, he grew up with few advantages. Economic insecurity and hardship may have made him unduly sensitive to criticism and rejection. Moreover, he regards his wife as warm and charming, pointing to his own perceived lack of social skills. Alcohol has been his escape from such tensions, but heavy drinking, coupled with persistent doubt about his own worth as a human being, has interfered with sexual functioning, worsening an already deteriorating marital relationship and further undermining his confidence. As a behaviour therapist, you may employ systematic desensitization. You teach Brett to relax deeply as he imagines a hierarchy of situations in which he is being evaluated by others. Or you may decide on rational-emotive behaviour therapy to convince Brett that he need not obtain universal approval for every undertaking. Or, given Brett's deficiency in social skills, you may choose behaviour rehearsal to teach him how to function effectively in social situations. You might follow more than one of these strategies.

Eclecticism in Psychotherapy: Practice Makes Imperfect

A word is needed about paradigms and the activities of therapists. The treatment approaches, as described so far, may appear to be separate, non-overlapping schools of therapy. You may have the impression that a behaviour therapist would never listen to a client's report of a dream, nor would a psychoanalyst be caught dead prescribing assertion training to a patient. Such suppositions could not be further from the truth. Many therapists subscribe to eclecticism, employing ideas and therapeutic techniques from a variety of schools (Hunsley & Lefebvre, 1990; Warner, 1991).

Therapists often behave in ways not entirely consistent with the theories they hold. For years, practising behaviour therapists have been listening empathically to clients, trying to make out their perspectives on events, on the assumption that this understanding would help them plan a better program for changing troublesome behaviour. Behavioural theories do not prescribe such a procedure, but on the basis of clinical experience, and perhaps through their own humanity, behaviour therapists have realized that empathic listening helps them establish rapport, determine what is really bothering the client, and plan a sensible therapy program. Freud himself is said to have been more directive and done far more to change immediate behaviour than would be concluded from his writings alone.

Today, psychoanalysts pay more attention to overt behaviour and the relief of symptoms than early theory prescribed. Some contemporary writers (e.g., Paul Wachtel, 1977, 1997) have even proposed that analysts employ behaviour therapy techniques, openly acknowledging that behaviour therapy has something to offer in the alleviation of behaviour pathology.

Treatment is a complex and ultimately highly individual process, and these are weighty issues. In Chapter 17, we will return to these and other issues and give them the attention they deserve. The reader should be aware of this complexity at the beginning, however, to better appreciate the intricacies and realities of psychotherapy.

Cultural Considerations

Despite our increasing understanding of biological and psychological factors in the nature and treatment of mental illness, and consistent with our discussion of the bio-psychosocial paradigm, social circumstances are ignored only at great risk. We must now visit the important issue of cultural diversity, especially as it pertains to Canada. This issue will be revisited throughout this book. Cultural diversity is important to highly heterogeneous countries such as Canada and to other countries as well, since most of our discussion of psychopathology is presented within the context and constraints of western European society.

Return once again to the case of J. Brett Barkley. We should consider his cultural, ethnic, or racial background. We noted earlier that the information provided in his case is open to different interpretations depending on the paradigm adopted. If his cultural background is known, will it make any difference to an understanding of his problems, including the approach to his diagnosis, assessment, and treatment? For example, what if Brett is French Canadian, the therapist is English Canadian, and neither is fluent in the other's language? Would Brett have more rapport with a French-Canadian clinician? Would he view a French-Canadian therapist as a more credible source of help?

What if Brett is of Asian descent? Brett realized that he needed help with his emotional problems after he abused his wife but if he is Asian, would he feel uncomfortable about seeking professional help because of the "loss of face" involved? What if he is an Aboriginal Canadian who has never fully accepted the values of the majority culture in Canada? Would he be guarded and less talkative with a white therapist and more open and spontaneous with an Aboriginal clinician?

Judgments about what is acceptable or normal vary considerably from culture to culture. Will it be more difficult for the therapist to understand what Brett is thinking and feeling if he comes from a cultural background very different from the therapist's? Will the therapist see more or perhaps less pathology in Brett's behaviour if he comes from another culture? These are legitimate questions. Unfortunately, we do not have clear answers to all of them.

Studies of the influences of culture on psychopathology—its diagnosis, assessment, and treatment—have proliferated in recent years. A caveat—our discussion of cultural and racial factors in psychopathology runs the risk of stereotyping because we are going to review generalizations that experts make about groups of people from different cultures. People from minority groups are, however, individuals who can differ as much from each other as their cultural or racial group differs from another cultural or racial group (cf. Lopez, 1994; Weizmann, Weiner, Wiesenthal, & Ziegler, 1991). It is critical to keep this point in mind as cultural differences are discussed in this and subsequent chapters. Nonetheless, a consideration of group characteristics is important and is part of a developing specialty called *minority mental health* (see Sue & Sue, 1999). The major paradigms have on occasion been revised to assist clinicians in their work with people from different cultural backgrounds. For example, cultural differences in internal dialogue and beliefs about adaptive coping have been incorporated into cognitive behaviour paradigms (e.g., Ivey, Ivey, & Simek-Morgan, 1997). Theories of multicultural counselling and therapy (e.g., Ivey et al., 1997; Sue & Sue, 1999) attempt to incorporate these revisions into an integrated perspective.

We will address cultural, ethnic, and racial factors related to people suffering from psychological disorders in the remainder of this section. While our focus is on Canadian culture, relatively little controlled research has been conducted in Canada. Therefore, we sometimes must extrapolate from relevant research conducted in the United States. Unfortunately, a majority of investigations with American minorities fail to provide information relevant to the assessment and treatment of people in Canada (Bowman, 2000).

Canada is a pluralistic society that has a policy of multiculturalism (Esses & Gardner, 1996). If clinicians in Canada are to do more than pay lip service to cultural considerations, it is important that they understand the cultural fabric of the country. Canadian Perspective 2.1 summarizes multiculturalism in Canada and compares and contrasts cultural diversity in Canada with that in the United States.

Canadian Perspectives/2.1

Canada: Collective Portrait of a Multicultural Country

"French-speaking Canadians and foreign-born immigrants represent the largest and most culturally significant minority groups in Canada. Visible groups consisting of African-Americans and Hispanics represent the largest and most significant minorities in the U. S. Further, Canada's largest minority represents a far larger portion (24%) of the population than does the Black minority group (13%) in the U.S."
—Bowman (2000, p. 237)

According to Queen's University researcher John Berry (1999), acculturation (where a dominant group values both diversity and equity) rather than assimilation (where a dominant group strives for cultural uniformity for everyone) better represents current Canadian goals of tolerance, diversity, and equity. Thus, a Canadian "cultural mosaic" model of preserving minority cultures contrasts with the American "melting pot" policy of assimilation. As Wintre, Sugar, Yaffe, and Costin (2000) have suggested, acculturation can be a difficult task, as it requires maintaining ethnic heritage while learning a new predominant culture.

What is the nature of cultural diversity in Canada? Recently, Marilyn Bowman (2000) from Simon Fraser University reviewed the differences between Canada and the U.S. in terms of well-being, social policy, and the nature of diversity within each country. She used several grouping variables for diversity (described below). As noted in the above quotation, the most dominant minorities in Canada are defined by first language and foreign birth. Much of our discussion focuses on differences between Canada and the U.S., in part because the published research in psychology is dominated by American influences, including powerful associations such as the American Psychological Association and the American Psychiatric Association. Although there are many similarities, differences between the two countries abound.

Language as a Grouping Variable for Diversity

Linguistic minorities represent a far more important issue in Canada than in the United States. Canada is a bilingual country with both English and French as official languages and thus, the largest minority group (22 percent of the population) has French as its "mother tongue." There is a significant francophone community outside of Quebec. According to Bowman (2000), there are more people who speak French at home in Canada than people who speak a non-English language at home in the U.S. (14 percent). Blacks form the largest minority group in the U.S. at 13 percent. In contrast to the socio-economic disadvantage of Blacks in the U.S., French Canadians typically earn more than people of British ethnicity (Lian & Mathews, 1999). Also, Canada has a greater proportion of first generation immigrants (many of whom enter the country unable to speak English) than the U.S. Thus, 40 percent of Canadians do not speak English as a first language (16 percent speaking neither English nor French), and they constitute a culturally powerful group in Canadian life. Fewer Canadians speak English at home (67 percent) than Americans (86 percent).

According to Bowman (2000), the impact of first language is particularly striking in Canadian cities. For example, in Richmond, B.C. (adjoining Vancouver), almost half of the elementary and high school students speak neither English nor French as their first language. Their first language is primarily Chinese. In Toronto, Ontario, almost 40 percent of residents speak neither English nor French. In fact, telephone translation is offered in 148 languages for people who contact the city (Purvis, 1999). In a study of over 1,000 first-year, unmarried students at York University, the participants reported 69 primary languages or combinations of languages spoken at home (Wintre et al., 2000). The most frequently spoken languages were English, Cantonese, Italian, and Greek. Data gathered by Statistics Canada in the 1996 census (see Ghafour, 2001) indicate that about 170 languages and dialects are spoken by immigrants and refugees in the

Greater Toronto Area. The most common first languages are Chinese, Italian, Portuguese, and Polish.

Foreign Birth as a Grouping Variable for Diversity

The participants in the Wintre et al. (2000) study revealed 94 countries of origin and identification with 203 cultural or ethnic groups. This reflects the fact that, among Western nations, Canada is the least culturally homogeneous (25 percent homogeneity relative to 50 percent in the U.S.). According to Bowman (2000), 57 percent of Canadian immigrants come from Asia (compared to only 17 percent in the U.S.). The next largest group comes from Europe, especially the United Kingdom.

Canada has entered a period of declining births and rising immigration that will further transform the Canadian mosaic. Further, the pattern of immigration has changed in the past decade. In 1990, 14 percent of immigrants came from Hong Kong and 39 percent came from other Asian countries. By 2000, only 0.5 percent came from Hong Kong and people from other Asian countries accounted for 61 percent of all immigrants (Frank, 2001). They ranged across East Asia (mainland China, Singapore, Vietnam, and Japan), Southeast Asia (the Philippines), South Asia (Pakistan, India, and Sri Lanka), and West Asia (Turkey and Lebanon). Immigrants from Europe had declined from 24 percent to 19 percent. In 2000, the next largest groups came from Africa (8 percent) and Central and South America (7.5 percent).

Visible Racial Differences as a Grouping Variable for Diversity

Minorities can be grouped on the basis of visible differences associated with geographic ancestry (Bowman, 2000). A race-based system is typically used in the U.S. to group minorities: Blacks, Hispanics, Asians, and Natives. In the U.S., Blacks comprise the largest visible minority group and most visible minorities speak English and are not foreign-born. Only 2 percent of the population in Canada is of African origin, and these individuals are far more culturally heterogeneous than Blacks in the U.S. Although the earliest Black immigrants were slaves who escaped from the U.S. during the Civil War and settled in Nova Scotia, most have come in recent years and have diverse origins (e.g., American Blacks who fled the Vietnam draft, as well as Caribbean and Somali immigrants). According to Bowman (2000, p. 234), "Each group represents a distinct historical, cultural, linguistic, religious, and racial mixture, and they are not a culturally homogeneous "Black" group."

During World War II, 22,000 Japanese Canadians were interned in camps such as this one.

During and following World War II, Japanese Canadians were resettled in other parts of Canada. Despite the fact that they were Canadian citizens they were required to carry identity cards.

In contrast to the U.S., where a majority of the Asian population have come from a narrow range of countries and have belonged to American society for more than a generation, the majority of Canada's Asian population came in recent years from a wide array of cultures and languages (Bowman, 2000; Frank, 2001). Although differences abound, a subset of people in both countries share an unfortunate past. Canadians and Americans of Japanese heritage living along the Pacific coast were interned or imprisoned in camps similar to concentration camps for several years during World War II, without any evidence that they posed a security threat. A majority of the 22,000 Japanese Canadians were born in Canada and were Canadian citizens. They lost virtually everything they owned. Most were eventually resettled in the interior of Canada and forced to carry identity cards for several years after the end of the war. Thousands were repatriated to war-ravaged Japan. In 1988 the Government of Canada apologized to Japanese Canadians on behalf of the people of Canada. No doubt some of the survivors still show the emotional scars of their treatment. More subtle but nonetheless hurtful discrimination is found in everyday occurrences in more recent times, not only toward the Japanese but toward other visible minorities as well.

Canada and the U.S. also differed with respect to relations between First Nations/Aboriginal peoples and European migrants (see Bowman, 2000). In early French Canada, the fur traders worked with and married Aboriginals and developed mutually advantageous policies and treaties in advance of migration that led to peaceful coexistence. There was little open conflict in Canada, but in the U.S., rapid and extensive agricultural settlement led to massive theft of treaty lands and decades of Plains Indian wars, resulting in decimation of the Aboriginal people. Thus, in contrast to the situation in the U.S., Aboriginal people in Canada survived at a relatively high rate, their population rising from 220,000 when the Europeans arrived to approximately 800,000 today (Bowman, 2000). Nonetheless, the history of Canada's Aboriginal people since the beginning of colonization is a history of suppression and oppression (see Canadian Perspectives 2.2).

Thinking Critically

1. Does the "cultural mosaic" model practised in Canada place more stress on new immigrants, as suggested by Maxine Wintre et al. (2000)? What practical suggestions do you have that could reduce or minimize the stress?
2. Imagine that you were a Japanese Canadian living with your family in British Columbia at the time of the December 7, 1941, attack on Pearl Harbor. As Toyo Takata wrote in Nikkei Legacy (1983), a nightmare that was to last many years began very quickly and unexpectedly:

   > Mary Nagata, a UBC student, was preparing for an exam when two Mounties appeared at the door seeking her businessman father. As they escorted him out, one officer scooped up her study notes, which were never returned. Near midnight, Zeiji Teramoto, a tomato grower, had just finished checking his hot house when the RCMP arrived. He was led away leaving behind his wife and seven frightened children, 16 and under. (p. 110)

   What do you think it was like for people like Mary Nagata or Zeiji Teramoto over the next several years of internment? What were the probable psychological and physical consequences of being put in an internment camp? As you read about disorders such as posttraumatic stress disorder (Chapter 6), psychophysiological disorders (Chapter 8), and mood disorders (Chapter 10), speculate about symptoms that some of the Japanese Canadians probably experienced. What factors, if any, would have protected them from the development of symptoms or disorders? What are the implications for our treatment of visible minorities today?

SOCIAL POLICY IMPLICATIONS OF CULTURAL DIVERSITY IN CANADA

The cultural features of minorities in Canada outlined in Canadian Perspectives 2.1 have implications for social policy:

1 Assimilation has been actively resisted by the main minority, French-speaking Quebecers. At the same time, there is a long history of attempts to preserve the unique culture of French Canadians. The Quebec Act of 1774 and subsequent policies guaranteed maintenance of language, religion, civil law, and the property ownership system. The Official Languages Act established French and English as official national languages. The 1982 Charter of Rights and Freedoms provided language rights in school instruction. The 1988 Multiculturalism Act established funding by the federal government in support of cultural diversity (Bowman, 2000). Nonetheless, in recent decades, there has been a strong movement in the province of Quebec toward actively seeking separation from Canada. Canada's most important minority group is a thriving culture, and the majority of Canadians want Quebec to remain part of Confederation.

2 In Canada, "mother tongue and foreign birth minorities are numerically and culturally far more important than are racial groups" (Bowman, 2000, p. 234). Because the main Canadian minorities have better social conditions than those in the U.S., there has been less impetus to develop social policies promoting selective income improvements for minorities. Nonetheless, smaller minority groups do experience some disadvantage, especially during the early years after migration. For example, Wintre et al. (2000) reported that immigrant groups of university students typically perceived themselves to belong to lower socio-economic classes and visible minorities. They reported experiencing less autonomy, less self-esteem, and more stress than Canadian-born students who had Canadian-born parents.

3 Recently migrated Asians—Canada's largest visible minority group-are an advantaged group on key indicators (such as education and income); this stands in sharp contrast to the U.S., where a great amount of social policy has been directed to minorities (especially Blacks) whose visibility is associated with social and economic disadvantage. Visible minorities in Canada are typically non-English-speaking immigrants, while in the U.S., the largest visible minority—Blacks—are English-speaking and born in the country. Thus, according to Bowman (2000, p. 234) it is inappropriate to use "racial visibility as if it were a culturally homogeneous and psychologically meaningful minority index within Canada."

4 Assimilation has been resisted by Canada's Aboriginal people, and there have been a number of high-profile conflicts between the different levels of government in Canada and Native groups. Currently, the Aboriginals and the federal government are in conflict over the federal government's plans to modernize the 1876 Indian Act (Lawton, 2001).

Mental Health Implications of Cultural Diversity in Canada

Our analysis of cultural diversity in Canada has implications for clinical practice and programs in Canada. Mental health practitioners, including psychologists, need to be aware of Canada's cultural diversity and how it is different from that in the United States. Cultural diversity has implications for our understanding of different psychological problems; for help-seeking and the use of mental health resources and facilities; for diagnosis and assessment; and for prevention, intervention, and treatment.

Clinicians must respect the dignity and worth of each individual, regardless of cultural background, as required by the codes of ethics of organizations such as the CPA (Canadian Psychological Association, 1991). Should members of minority groups be recruited into the mental health professions? Greater availability of clinicians from different cultures would no doubt better meet the needs of clients with values different from those of the majority culture (see Merali, 1999). Although group-targeted recruitment cannot guarantee cultural richness and raises the problem of stereotypes (Bowman, 2000), it is nonetheless important to recruit members of minority groups in Canada to mental health professional training programs. However, since questions about race open the possibility of discrimination, it is illegal in Canada to ask applicants questions about their ethnicity (Bowman, 2000).

Psychiatric Problems in Minority Groups The issue of whether psychiatric problems are more or less frequent in minority groups in Canada, relative to other groups, is complex because the answer depends on which minority group is being investigated. Do French Canadians differ from Anglo Canadians in the extent of their mental health problems? Probably not, at least not in any major way. Elisa Romano and her colleagues at the University of Montreal and McGill University (Romano, Tremblay, Vitaro, Zoccolillo, & Pagani, 2001) assessed a community sample of French-speaking 14-to17-year-old children in Quebec. Although it is often difficult to compare findings across different studies, Romano et al. noted that the prevalence of psychiatric disorders fell within the range reported in research with English-speaking children. Noh and his colleagues (Noh, Speechley, Kaspar, & Wu, 1992) studied 860 Korean immigrants in Toronto and reported that the frequency of depression is as high as it is in Caucasian counterparts. However, depression in Chinese people may be less prevalent. See Chapter 10 for a perspective on this point.

Although Aboriginal people constitute only 4 percent of the Canadian population, studies report high levels of mental health problems in many Canadian Aboriginal communities. We will examine the problem of suicide among young Native people, especially the Innu of Labrador, in Chapter 10 (Canadian Perspectives 10.3). The issue of abuse is discussed in Chapter 5 (Canadian Perspectives 5.1). Canadian Perspectives 2.2 provides an overview of these problems and discusses some of the historical and current social factors that can contribute to psychological distress and disorder in Aboriginal people, at both the individual and community levels.

Some cultural and religious groups receive attention not for elevated rates of mental disorder, but for atypically low rates of mental disorder. The Hutterites in Manitoba, who live in isolated, religious communities that are relatively free from outside influences, have remarkably low levels of mental illness. This German-speaking, Anabaptist sect emigrated in the 1870s from central Europe to Manitoba. Research conducted in 1953 (Eaton & Weil, 1953) found that they had the lowest lifetime prevalence of schizophrenia (1.1 per 1,000) of any group studied thus far in North America. A re-analysis of the original data (Torrey, 1995) and a recent study (Nimgaonkar et al., 2000) confirmed this finding. Genetic and lifestyle factors probably play a role in contributing to these low rates.

Research on the mental health of immigrants to Canada has found additional evidence for what is known as "the healthy immigrant effect." Consistent with research on physical health, a recent Statistics Canada report indicated that immigrants had comparatively lower rates of depression and alcohol dependence than Canadian-born members of the population (Ali, 2002). Lower rates of depression and alcohol dependence were unrelated to language proficiency in English or French, employment status, or sense of belonging. Secondary analyses found that Asian immigrants had the lowest rates of depression, while African immigrants had the lowest rates of alcohol dependence (Ali, 2002). The amount of time since arrival was also important because the healthy immigrant effect was stronger among recent arrivals than among those who had been living in Canada for some time.

Vicki Esses at the University of Western Ontario and her colleagues expressed the concern that Canadians are developing more negative attitudes toward immigration as a result of the terrorist attacks on September 11, 2001 (Esses, Dovidio, & Hodson, 2002). Overall, immigrants to Canada seem to be quite resilient and they can contribute to our society in a variety of meaningful ways.

Canadian Perspectives/2.2

Origins of Mental Health Problems Among Canada's Aboriginal People

Laurence Kirmayer of McGill University and his colleagues (Kirmayer, Brass, & Tait, 2000) recently reviewed research on the mental health of the First Nations, Inuit, and Metis of Canada. Depression, drug abuse (especially alcoholism and abuse of solvents), suicide, low self-esteem, symptoms of posttraumatic stress, and violence are widespread problems in many communities, especially among children and youth. Drug abuse frequently leads to child abuse, including child sexual abuse, an issue that also needs to be considered when there is family conflict. Kirmayer et al. (2000) attribute these mental health problems to cultural discontinuity and oppression, noting that Aboriginal Canadians have experienced institutional discrimination for over 300 years. In many cases, they have been forbidden to speak their own language, prohibited from engaging in religious and cultural practices, driven from the land they had inhabited for hundreds of years, and forced onto reservations in undesirable locations without regard for the special sanctity that land has for them. In one disastrous "experiment," Inuit people were relocated to the Far North to protect Canadian sovereignty (Tester & Kulchyski, 1994). Poverty and economic marginalization are endemic in many Aboriginal communities. Disproportionately high rates of obesity, diabetes, and other physical diseases are also a problem.

The governments of Canada and the provinces systematically sought the cultural assimilation of Aboriginal children through forced attendance at residential schools, followed by out-of-community adoption by non-Aboriginal families (Kirmayer et al., 2000). The residential schools were a 100-year failed experiment (e.g., Grant, 1996; Miller, 1996). Between 1879 and 1973, over 100,000 Aboriginal children were taken from their families and sent to church-run and government-administered boarding schools mandated to educate the children. Aboriginal parents were considered to be incapable of educating their children and passing on "proper" European values. Only recently has the extent of the physical, emotional, and sexual abuse that occurred in many of the schools been documented and acknowledged (e.g., Haig-Brown, 1988; Knockwood, 1992; Royal Commission on Aboriginal Peoples, 1996). Kirmayer et al. (2000) noted:

> Beyond the impact on individuals of abrupt separation from their families, multiple losses, deprivation, and brutality, the residential school system denied Aboriginal communities the basic human right to transmit their traditions and maintain their cultural identity. (p. 608)

About 6,000 Aboriginal people are involved in lawsuits against the federal government and the Anglican, United, and Roman Catholic churches for the abuses they suffered (Cox, 2000).

When the provinces took over responsibility for health, welfare, and educational services in the 1960s, child and welfare services focused on "child neglect," and social workers chose adoption and long-term foster care for many Aboriginal children. By the end of the 1960s, between 30 and 40 percent of children who were legal wards of the provinces were Aboriginal children (Kirmayer et al., 2000). In 1959 the rate was only 1 percent!

Fort Resolution, N.W.T: Bishop Breynat and Aboriginal pupils of Roman Catholic Mission. (National Archives of Canada.)

Kirmayer et al. (2000, p. 609) believe that it was short-sighted policies such as these (and many others) that produced the "collective trauma, loss, and grief" that, in conjunction with poverty, and the sense of deprivation created by "the values of consumer capitalism," led to the high rates of physical health problems and psychiatric disorders found in many Aboriginal communities. Conflicts about identification can be severe. Young Aboriginal people in particular can be torn between traditional values and those of the more privileged majority culture, and this in part, may underlie the high rates of psychological and social problems among Native Canadian young people. For most of them, there is little hope of wage-earning jobs and the pursuit of higher education is fraught with obstacles. Is it any wonder that so many Aboriginal youth have no clear sense of identity or life direction?

Aboriginal communities do differ, of course, in their political structure, religious activities, and social and psychological problems. Some communities have experienced cultural revitalization and political empowerment. The Cree of James Bay, for example, are politically active. In 1975 they won significant rights and major concessions (including monetary compensation, land-claims settlement, provisions for environmental and traditional activity protection, and some control over health, social, and education services) from the Government of Quebec in return for allowing hydroelectric development on traditional lands. In 1984 local self-government of Cree communities was legislated with the Cree-Naskapi (of Quebec) Act.

Within communities, potential protective factors (as well as risk factors) may be associated with levels of psychological distress in individuals. In one study of the Cree of James Bay, Kirmayer and his colleagues (Kirmayer, Boothroyd, Tanner, & Adelson, 2000) found that having a good relationship with other people in the community and "spending more time in the bush" predicted less distress. The Cree are noted for the degree to which extended families go to the bush to hunt and trap. Why should living in the bush be related to reduced distress?

> A large part of bush life involves contact with nature, spiritual relations with animals, consumption of valued foods and participation in other traditional activities. Increased time in the bush may confer mental health benefits by increasing family solidarity and social support, reinforcing cultural identity, improving physical health with nutritious bush foods and exercise, or providing respite from the pressures of settlement life. (Kirmayer, Boothroyd, et al., 2000)

Kirmayer, Boothroyd, et al. also hypothesized that time in the bush would benefit people with a history of abuse problems because a different ethic limits substance use in the bush and family violence is discouraged by social pressure. Consistent with findings for the majority culture, among the Cree of James Bay, depression is the most common psychological problem for women, whereas alcohol abuse is common among men. Noteworthy is the fact that their suicide rate is not any higher than the rate among non-Aboriginal Canadians.

Just as there are community success stories, we can cite many examples at the individual level where Aboriginal people have risen above the circumstances we have outlined. Paul Okalik is one success story. His story is eloquently told in a recent article from *Maclean's* magazine.

> At 17, Okalik went through an all-too-common rite of passage for troubled Inuit teenagers: he was thrown in jail. Okalik was drinking heavily, got kicked out of school, and then was caught trying to break into a post office to steal liquor. The three-month sentence he was given might have marked the start of a dissolute life. (Geddes, 2001, p.16)

In 1999, at the age of 34, Paul Okalik became premier of Canada's newest territory in the central and eastern Arctic—Nunavut.

Paul Okalik, who "wrestled personal demons to the ground" (Geddes, 2001, p. 17), became the first premier of the Territory of Nunavut.

Thinking Critically

1. Increased time in the bush appears to confer mental health benefits on the James Bay Cree. Since Kirmayer, Boothroyd, et al. (2000) collected all of their data at one point in time, is it possible that the direction of causality could be reversed? That is, people who are less distressed find it physically, economically, and socially easier to take part in bush life? See Chapter 5 for a discussion of the problem of causality in correlational investigations.
2. The survey used by Kirmayer, Boothroyd, et al. (2000) did not assess traditional pursuits other than time in the bush. Do you think that pursuits such as healing practices or dream interpretation could promote mental health among Aboriginal people?
3. How can you account for Paul Okalik's success at such a young age? Did he experience fewer risk factors than his peers, or did certain protective factors make it possible for him to take the harder path to success? Speculate about possible risk and protective factors.
4. Would you agree that solutions to mental health problems among Canada's Aboriginal people require societal and economic strategies, in addition to psychological interventions?

Help-Seeking Among Minority Groups Despite high rates of psychological problems and the accessibility of Canada's universal health care system, some minority groups consistently underutilize mainstream mental health services. The Greater Vancouver Mental Health Service Society (Peters, 1988) conducted a survey that determined that utilization by South Asian and Chinese Canadians was significantly lower than that of English Canadians. Roberts and Crockford (1997) reported that far fewer Asian Canadians were admitted to an adolescent in-patient unit in Calgary than would be expected on the basis of demographics. Indeed, numerous other studies conducted in Canada and the U.S. report consistently that Asians (relative to Caucasians and other ethnic groups) underutilize mental health facilities and services, regardless of the type of service. In general, Asian groups tend to show a greater tendency than whites to be ashamed of emotional suffering, to be relatively unassertive, and to experience greater reluctance to seek out professional help. Asians in Canada tend to rely on members of their families and various informal sources of support when they experience psychological difficulties (e.g., Naidoo, 1992).

Recently, Han Z. Li and Annette Browne (2000) conducted in-depth personal interviews with Asian Canadians (Chinese, Indian, and Filipino) in a northern community in B.C. What did the Asian Canadians perceive as insurmountable barriers to accessing and using mental health services? The two most serious difficulties were: (1) poor English language ability, especially among the Chinese and Indian respondents; and (2) a culturally determined interpretation of psychological disorders that decreased the likelihood of their seeking help (e.g., family problems remain inside the house).

Consistent with past research (e.g., Lai & Yue, 1990), participants tended to describe psychological problems as somatic illnesses, presumably an acceptable interpretation, since physical illnesses, in comparison to mental disorders, are considered to be treatable, curable, and no cause for shame. Li and Browne (2000, p. 153) cite the following quote by an Indian participant to illustrate the sense of shame attached to psychological problems: "If my neighbour knows that my husband has a mental health problem, he will not let his daughter marry my son."

Additional barriers included a lack of knowledge about how to access mental health services, especially among the Chinese and Indian respondents, and racial discrimination, especially among Indian and Filipino participants. The perceived barriers were reported less frequently when participants were accessing general health services. Length of stay in Canada was unrelated to the number of perceived barriers. Are the barriers perceived to be the same by all immigrant groups? Li and Browne (2000) indicated that Filipino participants reported fewer difficulties in accessing mental health services. Perhaps there is less stigmatization or shame attached to seeking help for psychological problems among Filipinos (Leong, 1994).

Li and Browne (2000) recommended that mental health agencies attempt to increase public awareness about how to access services, particularly among ethnic groups that experience language and cultural barriers. They also addressed issues of discrimination at both the individual and system levels. Since the Asian participants perceived that health care providers were unfamiliar with their cultures, Li and Browne (2000) recommended increased cultural awareness and sensitivity training for health care providers and an expanded range of culturally based mental health services for Asian Canadians. There is clearly a need for more bilingual and bicultural mental health professionals in different sectors of the Canadian mental health system, including psychiatric units of general hospitals, community mental health centres, and provincial psychiatric hospitals. Since Asian Canadians tend to look to their families for assistance, it is important for mental health workers to respect and make use of their clients' informal support networks (Cook, 1994; Roberts & Crockford, 1997).

Diagnosis and Assessment of Psychiatric Disorders Cultural diversity has implications for the diagnosis (see Chapter 3) and assessment (see Chapter 4) of psychological disorders. The latest version of a widely used manual of mental disorders (American Psychiatric Association, 2000) attempts to enhance clinicians' sensitivity to cultural and ethnic variations in psychopathology in several ways. The strategy is summarized in Focus on Discovery 3.2. As but one example, the manual asserts the importance of differentiating separation anxiety disorder, a problem seen in children (see Chapter 15), from the high value placed on strong interdependence among family members by some cultures. In terms of clinical assessment, it is problematic that clinicians often have to interact with clients who have difficulty conversing in one of the official languages of Canada. Imagine a distressed Portuguese-speaking mother having to take her 10-year-old daughter along to act as the interpreter when she talks to her therapist about her profound depression and suicidal thoughts! Further, few of the major standardized clinical tests have norms for Canada or norms for its major minority groups, including French Canadians.

Psychological Intervention As Bowman (2000, p. 239) has observed, "There are no texts about psychological treatment that attend to Canadian diversity with any depth of empirical content." She is critical of the quality and fragmented nature of information about minority-specific treatments. Indeed, few studies of empirically validated treatments with minorities are specific even to U.S. minority groups (Doyle, 1998). Bowman (2000, p. 240) is especially critical of specialized approaches proposed for small Canadian minorities, such as Aboriginals, since they are "typically based on impressionistic anecdotes published in obscure journals." Although it is important to consider that it is often the minority groups themselves who propose the minority-specific treatments, Bowman (2000, p. 240) believes it "unlikely that any major literature will develop for group-specific valid treatments for Canadian minorities" because minorities in Canada are so differentiated and their nature is continually changing.

Nonetheless, professional organizations share our belief that clinicians should be sensitive to cultural issues. In its Codes of Ethics, the Canadian Psychological Association (2000) acknowledges the need for psychologists to be sensitive to the needs and experiences of people from various cultures. Psychologists are given the responsibility to make themselves aware of and be sensitive to possible cultural differences in rights and responsibilities. If possible, in the delivery of services, assistance should be provided by "persons relevant to the culture or belief systems of those served." Moreover, CPA asserts that

> psychologists acknowledge that all persons have a right to their innate worth as human beings appreciated and that this worth is not dependent upon their culture, nationality, ethnicity, colour, race,

> religion, sex, gender, marital status, sexual orientation, physical or mental abilities, age, socio-economic status, or any other preference or personal characteristic, condition, or status. (Canadian Psychological Association, 2000; see <http://www.cpa.ca>)

With due regard for individual differences, such as the degree to which the person is assimilated into the majority culture, some generalizations can be made that pertain to interventions. We close this section by providing several examples.

It is generally assumed that patients do better with therapists who are similar to them in cultural and ethnic background. Therapists of similar background, perhaps even of the same gender, will better know the life circumstance of those in need and, most important, will be more acceptable to them. In psychoanalytic terms, similarity between patient and therapist may strengthen the therapeutic alliance. Although extensive research on modelling provides some justification for these assumptions (Rosenthal & Bandura, 1978), however, it has not been demonstrated that better outcomes are achieved when patient and therapist are similar in race or ethnicity (Beutler, Machado, & Neufeldt, 1994). The jury is out on this question. Although there is some evidence from American studies that people who choose to retain their distinct cultural identities not only prefer ethnically similar therapists but also do better in therapy (e.g., Sue, 1998), Merali (1999, p. 30) concluded that "similarity in values or cognitive match may be a better criterion for equating counsellors and clients than matching based on cultural background." Bowman (2000) agrees that an ability to identify a culture's key values (e.g., individualism/collectivism, tradition/change, empirical/spiritual explanations) is important in a country as culturally diverse as Canada in order to respond appropriately. For example, a value placed on co-operativeness rather than competitiveness could be misinterpreted by a culturally unaware therapist as lack of motivation.

Under some circumstances, the "linguistic divide" between client and therapist may be so great that it is very difficult to employ biological interventions and virtually impossible to practise traditional forms of psychotherapy. One of us knew a Japanese lady who came to Canada as a young woman. Although she remained in Canada for the remainder of her life, raised 12 children, and lived to be over 100 years old, she never learned to speak English! In some cultures, the use of an interpreter can create a risk—the interpreter may minimize the patient's problems to save face (Marcos, 1979).

Let us return to the distressed Portuguese mother who does not speak English. Toronto has a large Portuguese community and many of its members do not speak English very well, despite having lived in Canada for decades. Since the community has not integrated well in terms of language, it has been difficult for many Portuguese Canadians to take advantage of mainstream mental health services (Murray, 2000). However, Portuguese Mental Health and Addiction Services—a program attached to Toronto Western Hospital University Health Network—delivers language- and culture-specific services to Portuguese patients. The program sees about 1,000 people each year (Murray, 2000). Specialized programs are a possible solution to language barriers when the cultural group is large and professionals from that group are available.

We can extrapolate from a review by Sue and Sue (1999) and apply some of their wisdom to the treatment of Asian Canadians. They advise therapists to be sensitive to the personal losses that many Asian refugees have suffered, especially in light of the great importance that family connections have for them. To put it another way, therapists should appreciate the role of post-traumatic stress in Asian Canadians who have come to Canada as refugees. Therapists should also be aware of Asian Canadians' tendency to "somaticize"—to experience and to talk about stress in physical terms, such as headaches and fatigue, rather than in psychological terms, which Asian Canadians associate with being crazy or inferior. Their values are also different from the Western values of the majority culture in Canada. For example—and allowing for considerable individual variation—Asians respect structure and formality in interpersonal relationships, whereas a Western therapist is likely to favour informality and a less authoritarian attitude. Respect for authority may take the form of agreeing readily to what the therapist does and proposes—and perhaps, rather than discussing differences openly, just not showing up for the next session. The acceptability of psychotherapy as a way to handle stress is likely to be much lower among Asian Canadians, who probably tend to see emotional duress as something to be handled on one's own and through willpower. Asian Canadians may also consider some areas off-limits for discussion (e.g., the nature of the marital relationship, especially sex).

Asian Canadians born in Canada are often caught between two cultures. Some may seek to resolve this by identifying vigorously with majority values and denigrating anything Asian, a kind of racial self-hate. Others, torn by conflicting loyalties, may experience poorly expressed rage at a discriminatory Western culture but, at the same time, question aspects of their Asian background. Finally, as Peter Waxer of York University has reported, the therapist may have to be more directive and active than he or she otherwise might be, given the preference of many Asians for a directive, structured approach over a reflective one (Waxer, 1990).

Cognitive behaviour therapy may be more acceptable than insight-oriented psychotherapy to people from cultures that value tradition because it aims more at symptom relief, giving advice and guidance, and problem-solving around issues of immediate importance. (These characteristics would seem to apply generally to lower-income people, regardless of race or ethnicity.) The didactic style of cognitive behaviour therapy may also serve to demystify the process and render it more educational than psychotherapeutic in nature, thus reducing the possible stigmatizing effects of "having one's head shrunk" (Organista & Munoz, 1996).

Very little controlled research has been conducted on Aboriginal Canadians or Native Americans in therapy (Bowman, 2000; Kirmayer et al., 2000; Sue, Zane, & Young, 1994). Kirmayer et al. (2000) lament the fact that mental health services in urban areas have rarely been adapted to the needs of Aboriginal clients, resulting in low rates of use. They also point out that some of the features of Aboriginal communities make it difficult to deliver conventional treatment and prevention programs and that government policies lead to insufficient support for treatment programs. We need to be especially sensitive to cultural differences and needs involving Aboriginal children. Because Native Canadian children are often looked after in the households of various relatives, the pattern of a child's or young adult's moving among different households is not necessarily a sign of trouble. A youngster's avoidance of eye contact is a traditional sign of respect but may be misconstrued by someone unfamiliar with the culture as quite the opposite and regarded as a problem to be remedied (Everett, Proctor, & Cartmell, 1989). The importance of family may make it advisable to conduct treatment in the home with family members present and an integral part of the intervention. According to Kirmayer et al., many forms of traditional healing and traditional practices, such as the sweat lodge, are undergoing a renaissance. Kirmayer et al. (2000, p. 613) see some hope for the future: "A new generation of practitioners is emerging—people able to combine local knowledge about health and healing with the most useful aspects of psychiatry and psychology." We will discuss an example of this approach in Canadian Perspectives 12.2.

Studies suggest that racial differences are not insurmountable barriers to understanding between counsellor and client (Beutler et al., 1994). Therapists with considerable empathy are perceived as more helpful by clients, regardless of the racial mix. However, therapists need to know that many minority groups in Canada, like many African Americans, have encountered prejudice and racism, and some must wrestle with their anger and rage at a sometimes insensitive majority culture (Vontress & Epp, 1997). On the other hand, as Greene (1985) cautioned, therapists' sensitivity to social oppression should not translate into a paternalism that removes personal responsibility and empowerment from minority clients.

SUMMARY

- Scientific inquiry is a special way in which human beings acquire knowledge about their world. People may see only what they are prepared to see, and certain phenomena may go undetected because scientists can discover only the things about which they already have some general idea. One is better able to keep track of subjective influences by making explicit one's paradigm, or scientific perspective.
- Several major paradigms, or points of view, are current in the study of psychopathology and therapy. The biological paradigm assumes that psychopathology is caused by an organic defect. Two biological factors relevant to psychopathology are genetics and neurochemistry. Biological therapies attempt to rectify the specific biological defects underlying disorders or to alleviate symptoms of disorders, often using drugs to do so.
- Another paradigm derives from the work of Sigmund Freud. The psychoanalytic, or psychodynamic, point of view directs our attention to repressions and other unconscious processes traceable to early-childhood conflicts that have set in motion certain psychodynamics. Whereas present-day ego analysts, who are part of this tradition, place greater emphasis on conscious ego functions, the psychoanalytic paradigm has generally searched the unconscious and early life of the patient for the causes of abnormality. Therapeutic interventions based on psychoanalytic theory usually attempt to lift repressions so that the patient can examine the infantile and unfounded nature of his or her fears.
- Humanistic and existential therapies are insight oriented, like psychoanalysis, and regard freedom to choose and personal responsibility as key human characteristics. Rogers's client-centred therapy entails complete acceptance of and empathy for the client, restating the client's thoughts and feelings and sometimes offering new perspectives on the client's problem. The existential therapies emphasize personal growth and the need to confront the anxieties that attend the choices we have to make in life. Perls's Gestalt therapy tries to help patients better understand and accept their needs, desires, and fears. It focuses on the here and now and employs a number of techniques to help people get in better in touch with their feelings.
- Behavioural, or learning, paradigms suggest that aberrant behaviour has developed through classical conditioning, operant conditioning, or modelling. Investigators who believe that abnormal behaviour may have been learned examine all situations affecting behaviour and define concepts carefully. Behaviour therapists try to apply learning principles to bring about change in overt behaviour, thought, and emotion. Less attention is paid to the historical causes of abnormal behaviour than to what maintains it, such as the reward and punishment contingencies that encourage problematic response patterns.
- More recently, cognitive theorists have argued that certain schemas and irrational interpretations are major factors in abnormality. In both practice and theory, the cognitive paradigm has usually blended with the behavioural in an approach to intervention that is referred to as cognitive-behavioural.

- Because each of these paradigms seems to have something to offer to our understanding of mental disorders, there has recently been a movement to develop more integrative paradigms. The diathesis-stress paradigm, which integrates several points of view, assumes that people are predisposed to react adversely to environmental stressors. The diathesis may be biological, as appears to be the case in schizophrenia, or psychological, such as the chronic sense of hopelessness that seems to contribute to depression. Diatheses may be caused by early-childhood experiences, genetically determined personality traits, or socio-cultural influences. Similarly, the biopsychosocial paradigm presumes that disorders are a function of multifactorial interactions involving biological, psychological, and social variables.
- The most important implication of paradigms is that they determine where and how investigators look for answers. Paradigms necessarily limit perceptions of the world, for investigators will interpret data differently according to their points of view. In our opinion, it is fortunate that workers are not all operating within the same paradigm, for at this point too little is known about psychopathology and its treatment to settle on any one of them. Indeed, paralleling the current interest in integrative paradigms, most clinicians are eclectic in their approach to intervention, employing techniques that are outside their paradigm but that seem useful in dealing with the complexities of human psychological problems.
- Studies of the influences of culture on psychopathology have proliferated in recent years. The cultural and racial backgrounds of patients present a variety of challenges. Particular issues in Canada surround the assessment and treatment of French Canadians, Asian Canadians, foreign-born Canadians whose first language is not English, and Aboriginal Canadians, including the kinds of problems these groups may have and the kinds of sensitivities clinicians should possess to deal respectfully and effectively with patients from minority groups.
- Revisions are sometimes made to the major paradigms to assist clinicians in their work with people from different cultural backgrounds. However, it is critical to keep in mind that there are typically more differences within cultural groups than there are between them. Remembering this important point can help avoid the dangers of stereotyping members of a culture.

KEY TERMS

acculturation (p. 67)
action therapies (p. 43)
adoptees method (p. 35)
anal stage (p. 41)
assertion training (p. 57)
assimilation (p.67)
autonomic nervous system (ANS) (p. 39)
aversive conditioning (p. 56)
avoidance conditioning (p. 55)
behaviour genetics (p. 34)
behaviour modification (p. 55)
behaviour rehearsal (p. 57)
behaviour therapy (p. 55)
behaviourism (p. 52)
biological paradigm (p. 33)
biopsychosocial paradigm (p. 64)
brain stem (p. 38)
brief therapy (p. 45)
cerebellum (p. 38)
cerebral cortex (p. 37)
cerebral hemispheres (p. 37)
classical conditioning (p. 52)
client-centred therapy (p. 47)
cognition (p. 58)
cognitive behaviour therapy (CBT) (p. 59)
cognitive paradigm (p. 58)
cognitive restructuring (p. 59)
concordance (p. 35)
conditioned response (p.52)
conditioned stimulus (p. 52)
constructivist-narrative approach (p. 62)
corpus callosum (p. 37)
counterconditioning (p. 55)
countertransference (p. 44)
cultural diversity (p. 66)
defence mechanism (p. 42)
denial (p. 42)
diathesis-stress paradigm (p. 63)
diencephalons (p. 38)
discriminative stimulus (p. 53)
disease model (p. 33)
displacement (p. 42)
dizygotic (DZ) twins (p.35)
dream analysis (p. 44)
eclecticism (p. 66)
ego (p. 41)
ego analysis (p. 44)
Electra complex (p. 42)
extinction (p. 52)
family method (p. 34)
fixation (p. 42)
free association (p. 44)
frontal lobe (p. 37)
genes (p. 34)
genital stage (p. 41)
genotype (p. 34)
Gestalt therapy (p. 49)
gyri (p. 37)
humanistic and existential the rapies (p. 47)
hypothalamus (p. 38)
id (p. 41)
index cases (probands) (p. 34)
insight therapies (p. 43)
instrumental learning (p. 53)
Interpersonal Therapy (IPT) (p. 46)
interpretation (p. 44)
introspection (p. 51)
irrational beliefs (p. 59)
latency period (p. 41)
latent content (p. 44)
law of effect (p. 53)
learning (or behavioural) paradigm (p. 51)
libido (p. 41)
limbic system (p. 38)
linkage analysis (p. 35)
mediational theory of learning (p. 54)
mediator (p. 54)
medical model (p. 33)
medulla oblongata (p. 38)

meninges (p. 37)
midbrain (p. 38)
modelling (p. 53)
monozygotic (MZ) twins (p. 35)
moral anxiety (p. 42)
multicultural counselling and therapy (p. 67)
negative reinforcement (p. 53)
nerve impulse (p. 36)
neuron (p. 36)
neurotic anxiety (p. 42)
neurotransmitters (p. 36)
nuclei (p. 38)
objective (realistic) anxiety (p. 42)
occipital lobe (p. 37)
Oedipus complex (p. 42)
operant conditioning (p. 53)
oral stage (p. 41)
paradigm (p. 33)
parasympathetic nervous system (p. 39)
parietal lobe (p. 37)
phallic stage (p. 41)
phenotype (p. 34)
pleasure principle (p. 41)
pons (p. 38)
positive reinforcement (p. 53)
primary process thinking (p. 41)
projection (p. 42)
psychoanalytic (psychodynamic) paradigm (p.40)
psychodynamics (p. 41)
psychosexual stages (p. 41)
psychotherapy (p. 43)
rational-emotive behaviour therapy (REBT) (p. 59)
rationalization (p. 42)
reaction formation (p. 42)
reality principle (p. 41)
reductionism (p. 39)
regression (p. 42)
repression (p. 42)
resilience (p. 65)
resistance (p.44)
reticular formation (p. 38)
reuptake (p. 36)
risk (p. 65)
role-playing (p. 57)
schema (p. 58)
secondary process thinking (p. 41)
self-actualization (p. 47)
self-efficacy (p. 54)
self-instructional training (p. 61)
shaping (p. 53)
somatic nervous system (p. 39)
stress-inoculation training (p. 61)
sublimation (p. 42)
successive approximation (p. 53)
sulci (p. 37)
superego (p. 41)
sympathetic nervous system (p. 39)
synapse (p. 36)
systematic desensitization (p. 56)
temporal lobe (p. 37)
thalamus (p. 38)
time-out (p. 56)
token economy (p. 56)
transference (p. 44)
twin method (p. 35)
unconditional positive regard (p. 48)
unconditioned response (p. 52)
unconditioned stimulus (p. 52)
unconscious (p. 41)
ventricles (p. 38)
white matter (p. 37)

Reflections: Past, Present, and Future

- Recall the quote by von Liebig at the outset of this chapter. A "single cause" approach has been abandoned by most clinicians and psychopathologists, who now believe that psychological disorders arise from multiple causes. Assume that you are asked to name 10 major causes or "risk factors" for mental disorder. Based on your understanding of the different paradigms, which factors would you nominate?
- Our integrative paradigms focus on the interaction between a predisposition toward disease—the diathesis—and environmental, or life, disturbances—the stress, and the interaction among biological, psychological, and social factors. How would you incorporate your 10 causes into a diathesis-stress perspective or the biopsychosocial paradigm? Using a Venn diagram, illustrate your application of the biopsychosocial paradigm to J. Brett Barkley.
- Research has demonstrated a significant relationship between social factors, such as poverty, and risk for disorders, such as depression and substance abuse, especially among some of Canada's Aboriginal people, children, and the elderly. What can we do to reduce the correlation between poverty and mental disorder in Canada?
- Why and how do some people succumb to biopsychosocial risk factors while others react in adaptive ways, sometimes in the face of overwhelming adversity? We need to better understand the complexities of protective factors (resiliency) and the mechanisms underlying the consequences of such factors. Do various resiliency factors interact to produce protection from diatheses or multiple risk factors? What are the mechanisms or underlying processes that provide protection? Are there critical times in a person's life (e.g., childhood) when resiliency factors can play a vital role in the development of psychological outcomes?
- Do you agree with Bowman's assessment about the likelihood of developing minority-specific treatments in Canada? How would you develop and evaluate a specialized treatment program for depression or substance abuse among the Innu of Labrador (see Chapters 10 and 12)? Do you think it will ever be possible to develop valid treatments that are specific to other minority groups in Canada, such as Asian Canadians? What factors would need to be incorporated into the treatments described in this chapter?

3 chapter

Classification and Diagnosis

"It is more important to cure people than to make diagnoses."
— August Bier (1861-1949)

"In diagnosis think of the easy first."
— Martin H. Fischer (1879–1962), Fischerisms (Howard Fabing and Ray Marr)

"Progress will occur best through further critical review and through the exploration of alternative perspectives rather than through a premature embracement of the current manual."
— Widiger and Clark on the DSM (2000, pp. 958–959)

Marian Scott, *Tenants*, 1939–1940
oil on board, 63.6 x 42 cm, ART GALLERY OF ONTARIO, TORONTO
Gift from the J.S. McLean Collection, by Canada Packers Inc., 1990

Diagnosis is a critical aspect of the field of abnormal psychology. It is essential for professionals to be able to communicate accurately with one another about the types of cases they are treating or studying. Furthermore, a disorder must be classified correctly before its causes or best treatments can be found. For example, if one research group has found a successful treatment for depression but has defined the treatment in an unconventional manner, the finding is not likely to be replicated by another group of investigators. Only in recent years, however, has diagnosis been accorded the attention it deserves.

To beginning students of abnormal psychology, diagnosis can seem tedious because it sometimes relies on fine distinctions. For example, anxiety in social situations—being extremely tense around others—is a symptom of both schizotypal and avoidant personality disorders. In a person with schizotypal personality disorder, however, the anxiety does not decrease as the individual becomes more familiar with people, whereas in a person with avoidant personality disorder, exposure does tend to reduce social anxiety. This fine distinction could certainly be viewed as hairsplitting, but, as we will discuss later in the chapter, the decisive factor is whether the distinction is useful in differentiating the two diagnoses.

In this chapter we focus on the official diagnostic system widely employed by mental health professionals, the **Diagnostic and Statistical Manual of Mental Disorders**, now in its fourth edition, commonly referred to as **DSM-IV** (1994) or **DSM-IV-TR** (2000). The DSM is published by the American Psychiatric Association and has an interesting history.

A Brief History of Classification

By the end of the 19th century, medicine had progressed far beyond its practice during the Middle Ages, when bloodletting was at least part of the treatment of virtually all physical problems. Gradually, people recognized that different illnesses required different treatments. Diagnostic procedures were improved, diseases classified, and applicable remedies administered. Impressed by the successes that new diagnostic procedures had achieved in the field of medicine, investigators of abnormal behaviour also sought to develop classification schemes. Advances in other sciences, such as botany and chemistry, had followed the development of classification systems, reinforcing hope that similar efforts in the field of abnormal behaviour might bring progress. Unfortunately, progress in classifying mental disorders was not to be easily gained.

Early Efforts at Classification

During the 19th century and into the 20th as well, there was great inconsistency in the classification of abnormal behaviour. By the end of the 19th century, the diversity of classifications was recognized as a serious problem that impeded communication among people in the field, and several attempts were made to produce a system of classification that would be widely adopted. In the United Kingdom in 1882, for example, the Statistical Committee of the Royal Medico-Psychological Association produced a classification scheme; even though it was revised several times, however, it was never adopted by the association's members. In Paris in 1889 the Congress of Mental Science adopted a single classification system, but it was never widely used. In the United States the Association of Medical Superintendents of American Institutions for the Insane, a forerunner of the American Psychiatric Association, adopted a somewhat revised version of the British system in 1886. Then, in 1913, this group accepted a new classification scheme that incorporated some of Emil Kraepelin's ideas. Again, consistency was lacking. The New York State Commission on Lunacy, for example, insisted on retaining its own system (Kendell, 1975).

Development of the WHO and DSM Systems

More recent efforts at achieving uniformity of classification have not been totally successful either. In 1939 the World Health Organization (WHO) added mental disorders to the *International List of Causes of Death*. In 1948 the list was expanded to become the International Statistical Classification of Diseases, *Injuries, and Causes of Death (ICD)*, a comprehensive listing of all diseases, including a classification of abnormal behaviour. Although this nomenclature was unanimously adopted at a WHO conference, the mental disorders section was not widely accepted. Even though American psychiatrists had played a prominent role in the WHO effort, the American Psychiatric Association published its own *Diagnostic and Statistical Manual* (DSM) in 1952.

In 1969 the WHO published a new classification system that was more widely accepted. A second version of the American Psychiatric Association's DSM, DSM-II (1968), was similar to the WHO system, and in the United Kingdom a glossary of definitions was produced to accompany it (General Register Office, 1968). But true consensus still eluded the field. The WHO classifications were simply a listing of diagnostic categories; the actual behaviour or symptoms that were the bases for the diagnoses were not specified. DSM-II and the British *Glossary of Mental Disorders* provided some of this crucial information but did not specify the same symptoms for a given disorder. Thus, actual diagnostic practices still varied widely. In 1980 the American Psychiatric Association published an extensively revised diagnostic manual, DSM-III. A somewhat revised version, DSM-III-R, appeared in 1987.

In 1988 the American Psychiatric Association appointed a task force, chaired by psychiatrist Allen Frances, to begin work on DSM-IV. Working groups that included many psychologists were established to review sections of DSM-III-R, prepare literature reviews, analyze previously collected data, and collect new data if needed. An important change in the process for this edition of the DSM was the adoption of a conservative approach to making changes in the diagnostic criteria—the reasons for changes in diagnoses would be explicitly stated and clearly supported by data. In previous versions of the DSM, the reasons for diagnostic changes had not always been explicit. More than two-dozen Canadian psychologists and psychiatrists sat on the DSM-IV committees or participated in consultations with them. DSM-IV is used throughout the United States and Canada and is becoming widely accepted around much of the world.

DSM-IV was published in 1994 and the American Psychiatric Association subsequently completed a "text revision" of DSM-IV (DSM-IV-TR; APA, 2000). The revised version contains very few substantive changes to the different diagnostic categories and criteria, although some sections were rewritten to enhance clarity and incorporate recent research findings related to issues such as the prevalence, course, and etiology of disorders. Canadian psychologist Paula Caplan (1991, 1995) has been outspoken in her criticism of current and past versions of the DSM. She has been especially critical of the fact that many people with divergent viewpoints are not given the opportunity to participate in the decision-making process. Caplan will no doubt have stimulating and provocative comments about the next version of the DSM.

In this chapter we present the major DSM-IV-TR categories in brief summary. We then evaluate classification in general and the DSM in particular. In the next chapter we consider the assessment procedures that provide the data on which diagnostic decisions are based.

The Diagnostic System of the American Psychiatric Association (DSM-IV and DSM-IV-TR)

Definition of Mental Disorder

How does the DSM define the subject matter of this text? DSM-IV, recognizing that the term "mental disorder" is problematic and that "no definition adequately specifies precise boundaries for the concept," provided the following definition:

> Each of the mental disorders is conceptualized as a clinically significant behavioral or psychological syndrome or pattern that occurs in an individual and that is associated with present distress (e.g., a painful symptom) or disability (i.e., impairment in one or more important areas of functioning) or with a significantly increased risk of suffering death, pain, disability, or an important loss of freedom.

A number of conditions are excluded from consideration:

> In addition, this syndrome or pattern must not be merely an expectable and culturally sanctioned response to a particular event, for example the death of a loved one. Whatever its original cause, it must currently be considered a manifestation of a behavioral, psychological, or biological dysfunction in the individual. Neither deviant behavior (e.g., political, religious, or sexual) nor conflicts that are primarily between the individual and society are mental disorders unless the deviance or conflict is a symptom of a dysfunction in the individual.

Five Dimensions of Classification

Several major innovations distinguish the third edition and subsequent versions of the DSM. Perhaps the most sweeping change is the use of multiaxial classification, whereby each individual is rated on five separate dimensions, or axes (see Table 3.1 on pages 82 and 83). In this section we briefly discuss these five axes and then describe the major diagnostic categories. The five axes are:

- *Axis I.* All diagnostic categories except personality disorders and mental retardation.
- *Axis II.* Personality disorders and mental retardation.
- *Axis III.* General medical conditions.
- *Axis IV.* Psychosocial and environmental problems.
- *Axis V.* Current level of functioning.

The multiaxial system, by requiring judgments on each of the five axes, forces the diagnostician to consider a broad range of information.

Axis I includes all diagnostic categories except personality disorders and mental retardation, which make up Axis II. Thus, Axes I and II comprise the classification of abnormal behaviour. A detailed presentation of Axes I and II appears inside the front cover of the book. Axes I and II are separated to ensure that the presence of long-term disturbances is not overlooked. Most people consult a mental health professional for an Axis I condition, such as depression or an anxiety disorder, but prior to the onset of their Axis I condition, they may have had an Axis II condition, such as dependent personality disorder. The separation of Axes I and II is meant to encourage clinicians to be attentive to this possibility. The presence of an Axis II disorder along with an Axis I disorder generally means that the person's problems will be more difficult to treat.

Although the remaining three axes are not needed to make the actual diagnosis, their inclusion in the DSM indicates that factors other than a person's symptoms should be considered in an assessment so that the person's overall life situation can be better understood. On Axis III the clinician indicates any general medical conditions believed to be relevant to the mental disorder in question. For example, the existence of a heart condition in a person who has also been diagnosed with depression would have important implications for treatment; some antidepressant drugs could worsen the heart condition. Axis IV codes psychosocial and environmental problems that the person has been experiencing and that may be contributing to the disorder. These include occupational problems, economic problems, interpersonal difficulties with family members, and a variety of problems in other life areas that may influence psychological functioning. Finally, on Axis V, the clinician indicates the person's current level of adaptive functioning. Life areas considered are social relationships, occupational functioning, and use of leisure time. Ratings of current functioning are supposed to give information about the need for treatment.

DIAGNOSTIC CATEGORIES

In this section we provide a brief description of the major diagnostic categories of Axes I and II. Before presenting the diagnoses, we should note that for many of them the DSM indicates that the disorder may be due to a medical condition or substance abuse. For example, depression resulting from an endocrine gland dysfunction would be included in the depression section of the DSM but listed as caused by a medical problem. Clinicians must therefore be sensitive not only to the symptoms of their patients, but also to the possible medical causes of their patients' conditions. It should also be noted that beginning with DSM-III, there has been a dramatic expansion of the number of diagnostic categories. Eating disorders, some anxiety disorders (for example, posttraumatic stress disorder), several personality disorders (for example, schizotypal personality disorder), and many of the disorders of childhood were all added in DSM-III or subsequent editions. Focus on Discovery 3.1 describes some diagnoses and axes that are not regarded as well enough established to be included in DSM-IV-TR but are in need of further study.

Disorders Usually First Diagnosed in Infancy, Childhood, or Adolescence Within this broad-ranging category are the intellectual, emotional, and physical disorders that usually begin in infancy, childhood, or adolescence.

- The child with *separation anxiety disorder* has excessive anxiety about being away from home or parents.
- Children with *conduct disorder* repeatedly violate social norms and rules.
- Individuals with *attention-deficit/hyperactivity disorder* have difficulty sustaining attention and are unable to control their activity when the situation calls for it.
- Individuals with *mental retardation* (listed on Axis II) show subnormal intellectual functioning and deficits in adaptive functioning.
- The *pervasive developmental disorders* include autistic disorder, a severe condition in which the individual has problems in acquiring communication skills and deficits in relating to other people.
- *Learning disorders* refer to delays in the acquisition of speech, reading, arithmetic, and writing skills.

These disorders are discussed in Chapter 15.

Substance-Related Disorders *A substance-related disorder* is diagnosed when the ingestion of some substance—alcohol, opiates, cocaine, amphetamines, and so on—has changed behaviour enough to impair social or occupational functioning. The individual may become unable to control or discontinue ingestion of the substance and may develop withdrawal symptoms if he or she stops using it. These substances may also cause or contribute to the development of other Axis I disorders, such as mood or anxiety disorders. These disorders are examined in Chapter 12.

Schizophrenia For individuals with schizophrenia, contact with reality is faulty. Their language and communication are disordered, and they may shift from one subject to another in ways that make them difficult to understand. They commonly experience delusions, such as believing that thoughts that are not their own have been placed in their heads. In addition, they are sometimes plagued by hallucinations, commonly hearing voices that come from outside themselves. Their emotions are blunted, flattened, or inappropriate, and their social relationships and ability to work show marked deterioration. This serious mental disorder is discussed in Chapter 11.

Mood Disorders As the name implies, these diagnoses are applied to people whose moods are extremely high or low.

- In *major depressive disorder* the person is deeply sad and discouraged and is also likely to lose weight and energy and to have suicidal thoughts and feelings of self-reproach.
- The person with *mania* may be described as exceedingly euphoric, irritable, more active than usual, distractible, and possessed of unrealistically high self-esteem.
- *Bipolar disorder* is diagnosed if the person experiences episodes of mania or of both mania and depression.

The mood disorders are surveyed in Chapter 10.

Anxiety Disorders Anxiety disorders have some form of irrational or overblown fear as the central disturbance.

- Individuals with a *phobia* fear an object or situation so intensely that they must avoid it, even though they know that their fear is unwarranted and unreasonable and disrupts their lives.

- In *panic disorder* the person is subject to sudden but brief attacks of intense apprehension, so upsetting that he or she is likely to tremble and shake, feel dizzy, and have trouble breathing. Panic disorder may be accompanied by *agoraphobia* when the person is also fearful of leaving familiar surroundings.
- In people diagnosed with *generalized anxiety disorder*, fear and apprehension are pervasive, persistent, and uncontrollable. They worry constantly, feel generally on edge, and are easily tired.
- A person with *obsessive-compulsive disorder* is subject to persistent obsessions or compulsions. An obsession is a recurrent thought, idea, or image that uncontrollably dominates a person's consciousness. A compulsion is an urge to perform a stereotyped act, with the usually impossible purpose of warding off an impending feared situation. Attempts to resist a compulsion create so much tension that the individual usually yields to it.
- Experiencing anxiety and emotional numbness in the aftermath of a very traumatic event is called *posttraumatic stress disorder*. Individuals have painful, intrusive recollections by day and bad dreams at night. They find it difficult to concentrate and feel detached from others and from ongoing affairs.
- *Acute stress disorder* is similar to posttraumatic stress disorder, but the symptoms do not last as long.

The anxiety disorders are reviewed in Chapter 6.

Somatoform Disorders The physical symptoms of somatoform disorders have no known physiological cause but seem to serve a psychological purpose.

- People with *somatization disorder* have a long history of multiple physical complaints for which they have taken medicine or consulted doctors.

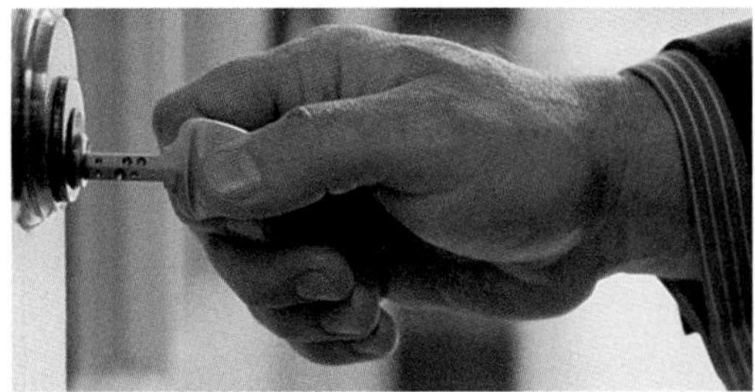

Constant checking, for example, to see if doors are locked, is a common compulsion in obsessive-compulsive disorder.

- People with *conversion disorder* report the loss of motor or sensory function, such as a paralysis, an anaesthesia (loss of sensation), or blindness.
- Individuals with *pain disorder* suffer from severe and prolonged pain.
- *Hypochondriasis* is the misinterpretation of minor physical sensations as serious illness.
- People with body *dysmorphic disorder* are preoccupied with an imagined defect in their appearance.

These disorders are covered in Chapter 7.

Dissociative Disorders Psychological dissociation is a sudden alteration in consciousness that affects memory and identity.

- People with *dissociative amnesia* may forget their entire past or lose their memory for a particular time period.
- With *dissociative fugue* the individual suddenly and unexpectedly travels to a new locale, starts a new life, and cannot remember his or her previous identity.

Table 3.1

DSM-IV Multiaxial Classification System

Axis I	Axis II	Axis III
Disorders usually first diagnosed in infancy, childhood, or adolescence	Mental retardation	General medical conditions
Delirium, demetia, amnestic and other cognitive disorders	Personality disorders	
Substance-related disorders		
Schizophrenia and other psychotic disorders		
Mood disorders		
Anxiety disorders		
Somatoform disorders		
Factitious disorders		
Dissociative disorders		
Sexual and gender identity disorders		
Eating disorders		
Sleep disorders		
Impulse control disorders not elsewhere classified		
Adjustment disorders		

Axis IV: Psychosocial and Environmental Problems

Check:

____ Problems with primary support group. Specify:
____ Problems related to the social environment. Specify:
____ Educational problem. Specify:
____ Occupational problem. Specify:
____ Housing problem. Specify:
____ Economic problem. Specify:
____ Problems with access to health care services. Specify:
____ Problems related to interaction with the legal system/crime. Specify:
____ Other psychosocial and environmental problems. Specify:

Axis V: Global Assessment of Functioning Scale (GAF Scale)

Consider psychological, social, and occupational functioning on a hypothetical continuum of mental health/illness. Do not include impairment in functioning due to physical (or environmental) limitations.

Code	
100–91	Superior functioning in a wide range of activities, life's problems never seem to get out of hand, is sought out by others because of his or her many positive qualities. No symptoms.
90–81	Absent or minimal symptoms (e.g., mild anxiety before an exam), good functioning in all areas, interested and involved in a wide range of activities, socially effective, generally satisfied with life, no more than everyday problems or concerns (e.g., an occasional argument with family members).
80–71	If symptoms are present, they are transient and expectable reactions to psychosocial stressors (e.g., difficulty concentrating after family argument); no more than slight impairment in social, occupational, or school functioning (e.g., temporarily falling behind in school work).
70–61	Some mild symptoms (e.g., depressed mood and mild insomnia) OR some difficulty in social, occupational, or school functioning (e.g., occasional truancy, or theft within the household), but generally functioning pretty well, has some meaningful interpersonal relationships.
60–51	Moderate symptoms (e.g., flat affect and circumstantial speech, occasional panic attacks) OR moderate difficulty in social, occupational, or school functioning (e.g., no friends, unable to keep a job).
50–41	Serious symptoms (e.g., suicidal ideation, severe obsessional rituals, frequent shoplifting) OR any serious impairment in social, occupational, or school functioning (e.g., no friends, unable to keep a job).
40–31	Some impairment in reality testing or communication (e.g., speech is at times illogical, obscure, or irrelevant) OR major impairment in several areas, such as work or school, family relations, judgment, thinking, or mood (e.g., depressed man avoids friends, neglects family, and is unable to work; child frequently beats up younger children, is defiant at home, and is failing at school).
30–21	Behaviour is considerably influenced by delusions or hallucinations OR serious impairment in communication or judgment (e.g., sometimes incoherent, acts grossly inappropriately, suicidal preoccupation) OR inability to function in almost all areas (e.g., stays in bed all day; no job, home, or friends).
20–11	Some danger of hurting self or others (e.g., suicide attempts without clear expectation of death, frequently violent, manic excitement) OR occasionally fails to maintain minimal personal hygiene (e.g., smears feces) OR gross impairment in communication (e.g., largely incoherent or mute).
10–1	Persistent danger of severely hurting self or others (e.g., recurrent violence) OR persistent inability to maintain minimal personal hygiene OR serious suicidal act with clear expectation of death.
0	Inadequate information.

Note: Reprinted with permission from DSM-IV, 1994, American Psychiatric Association.

- The person with *dissociative identity disorder* (formerly called multiple personality disorder) possesses two or more distinct personalities, each complex and dominant one at a time.
- *Depersonalization disorder* is a severe and disruptive feeling of self-estrangement or unreality.

These rare disorders are examined in Chapter 7.

Sexual and Gender Identity Disorders The sexual disorders section of DSM-IV-TR lists three principal subcategories:

- In the *paraphilias*, the sources of sexual gratification—as in exhibitionism, voyeurism, sadism, and masochism—are unconventional.
- People with *sexual dysfunctions* are unable to complete the usual sexual response cycle. Inability to maintain an

erection, premature ejaculation, and inhibition of orgasm are examples of their problems.

- People with *gender identity disorder* feel extreme discomfort with their anatomical sex and identify themselves as members of the opposite sex.

These disorders are studied in Chapter 14.

Sleep Disorders Two major subcategories of sleep disorders are distinguished in DSM-IV-TR:

- In the *dyssomnias*, sleep is disturbed in amount (e.g., the person is not able to maintain sleep or sleeps too much), quality (the person does not feel rested after sleep), or timing (e.g., the person experiences inability to sleep during conventional sleep times).
- In the *parasomnias*, an unusual event occurs during sleep (e.g., nightmares, sleepwalking).

These disorders are discussed in Chapter 16.

Eating Disorders Eating disorders fall into two major categories:

- In *anorexia nervosa*, the person avoids eating and becomes emaciated, usually because of an intense fear of becoming fat.
- In *bulimia nervosa*, frequent episodes of binge eating are coupled with compensatory activities such as self-induced vomiting and heavy use of laxatives.

These disorders are discussed in Chapter 9.

Factitious Disorder A diagnosis of *factitious disorder* is applied to people who intentionally produce or complain of physical or psychological symptoms, apparently because of a psychological need to assume the role of a sick person. This disorder is discussed in Chapter 7.

Adjustment Disorders An *adjustment disorder* involves the development of emotional or behavioural symptoms following the occurrence of a major life stressor. However, the symptoms that ensue do not meet diagnostic criteria for any other Axis I diagnosis.

Impulse-Control Disorder *Impulse-control disorders* include a number of conditions in which the person's behaviour is inappropriate and seemingly out of control.

- In *intermittent explosive disorder*, the person has episodes of violent behaviour that result in destruction of property or injury to another person.
- In *kleptomania*, the person steals repeatedly, but not for the monetary value or use of the object.
- In *pyromania*, the person purposefully sets fires and derives pleasure from doing so.
- In *pathological gambling*, the person is preoccupied with gambling, is unable to stop, and gambles as a way to escape from problems. See Canadian Perspectives 3.1 for a discussion of pathological gambling in Canada, factors related to a recent increase in problem and pathological gambling, and an example of a clinic for youth who are involved excessively in gambling activities.

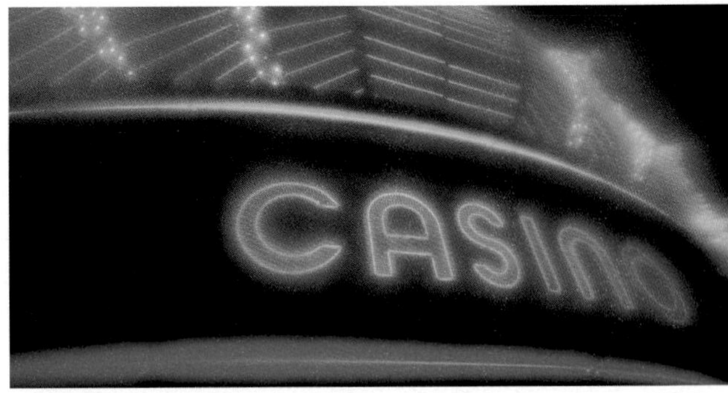

Pathological gambling is an example of an impulse-control disorder in which the person's behaviour is out of control.

- *Trichotillomania* is diagnosed when the person cannot resist the urge to pluck out his or her hair, often resulting in significant hair loss. This disorder is discussed further in Chapter 5.

Personality Disorders Personality disorders are defined as enduring, inflexible, and maladaptive patterns of behaviour and inner experience. They are listed on Axis II of the DSM.

- In *schizoid personality disorder*, the person is aloof, has few friends, and is indifferent to praise and criticism.
- The individual with a *narcissistic personality disorder* has an overblown sense of self-importance, fantasizes about great successes, requires constant attention, and is likely to exploit others.
- *Antisocial personality disorder* surfaces as conduct disorder before the person reaches age 15 and is manifested in truancy, running away from home, delinquency, and general belligerence. In adulthood the person is indifferent about holding a job, being a responsible partner or parent, planning for the future or even for tomorrow, and staying on the right side of the law. People with antisocial personality disorder—also called psychopathy—do not feel guilt or shame for transgressing social mores.

Chapter 13 covers the personality disorders.

Other Conditions That May Be a Focus of Clinical Attention This all-encompassing category comprises conditions that are not regarded as mental disorders per se but still may be a focus of attention or treatment. This category seems to exist so that anyone entering the mental health system can be categorized, even in the absence of a formally designated mental disorder.

If an individual's medical illness appears to be caused in part or exacerbated by a psychological condition, the diagnosis is ***psychological factors affecting physical condition***. Referred to previously as a psychophysiological or psychosomatic disorder, this condition is reviewed in detail

Canadian Perspectives/3.1

Pathological Gambling and the McGill Youth Gambling Research and Treatment Clinic

Several Canadian provinces have adopted liberal attitudes toward legalized gambling, primarily as a means of increasing revenue. There are now more than 50 permanent casinos in seven provinces and more are being built. By 1997 gambling revenue from provincial and territorial government-run casinos, lotteries, and video lottery terminals (VLTs) approached $7 billion (Marshall, 1998).

Does the frequency of persistent and maladaptive gambling increase as a function of government-owned legal gambling? In Chapter 5, we will discuss epidemiology as a research method. Briefly, epidemiology is the study of the frequency and distribution of a disorder in a population. In epidemiological research, data are gathered about the rates of a disorder and its possible correlates in a large sample or population. One focus of epidemiology is to determine the proportion of a population that has a disorder at a given time. This determination is known as prevalence. We now turn to several studies on the prevalence of "pathological" and "problem" gambling in Canada. The essential feature of pathological gambling is "persistent and recurrent maladaptive gambling behaviour... that disrupts personal, family or vocational pursuits" (American Psychiatric Association, 1994, p. 615). Epidemiological researchers typically use an instrument called the South Oaks Gambling Screen (Lesieur & Blume, 1987) or a multidimensional DSM-IV–based device known as the Canadian Problem Gambling Index (Ferris, Wynne, & Single, 1999) as a means of categorizing gambling problem severity.

Although there have been no Canadian national prevalence studies (Korn, 2000), in a 1996 review of older studies in Alberta, New Brunswick, Nova Scotia, Ontario, Quebec, and Saskatchewan, Ladouceur reported estimates of probable pathological gambling that ranged from 0.8 percent to 1.7 percent. Prevalence rates in the United States and Europe are comparable (see Sylvain, Ladouceur, & Boisvert, 1997).

Not surprisingly, problem gambling is more evident among substance abuses. Recent Canadian studies using the South Oaks Gambling Screen found that 10 percent of substance abusers in treatment at Niagara Falls had probable problem gambling (Toneatto, Ferguson, & Brennan, 2003), while 17.7 percent of those enrolled in a methadone maintenance program in Windsor met criteria for probable pathological gambling (Ledgerwood & Downey, 2002). Similarly, Doiron and Nicki (2001) assessed problem gamblers (relative to gamblers in general) in Prince Edward Island and found that they are more likely to have a drug or alcohol problem than the general population and to gamble while high or intoxicated. Fortunately, a recent Canadian study indicates that gambling treatment outcomes are unrelated to having a history of drug or medication use (Toneatto, Skinner, & Dragonetti, 2002).

Who is most likely to have a gambling problem? Problem gamblers are more likely to be male, single, under the age of 30, and to have begun gambling by age 18. Situational factors also play a role. Several Canadian studies provide information about the impact of the opening of a casino on gambling activities. The first major casino in Canada was opened in Winnipeg, Manitoba, in 1993. Cox, Kwong, Michaud, and Enns (2000) interviewed adults in Winnipeg and reported a "lifetime prevalence" (the proportion of the sample that had ever experienced the disorder up to the time of the interview) rate of 2.6 percent for "probable pathological gambling" and a further 3.0 percent who met criteria for problem gambling. They suggested that the latter group might experience other significant problems as a consequence of their gambling. Jacques, Ladouceur, and Ferland (2000) assessed respondents from the Hull area and the Quebec City area both before and a year after the opening of the Casino de Hull in 1996. The "experimental" group exposed to the casino reported an increase in the negative consequences of gambling among neighbours and relatives (e.g., increase in gambling on casino games; money lost gambling). In a similar vein, Room, Turner, and Ialomiteanu (1999) assessed the community impact of the opening of a casino in Niagara Falls, Ontario, also using a pre/post design. The opening led to increased gambling by local residents and an apparent increase in gambling problems.

Korn (2000) cited several studies that describe the negative impact of gambling in vulnerable or marginalized groups and special populations, including youth, women, older adults, Aboriginal people, other ethnocultural groups, and people with substance-use and mental disorders. Recently, Lepage, Ladouceur, and Jacques (2000) identified another such group—people who rely on community assistance for their survival. Lepage et al. found that 17.2 percent of the participants from this group met the criteria for pathological gambling (about eight times the prevalence for the general population). Korn (2000, p. 63) also refers to the high cost of gambling to families "in terms of dysfunctional relationships, violence and abuse, financial pressure, and disruption of growth and development of children."

We should be especially concerned about gambling in children and adolescents. A meta-analysis of available studies, including 35 Canadian studies, conducted by Shaffer, Hall, and Vander Bilt (1997) reported that the lifetime prevalence of combined problem and pathological gambling was 13.3 percent (relative to a rate of 5.5 percent in adults). Further, there appear to be rising prevalence rates of adolescent involvement in both legal and illegal gambling. In a recent study, Poulin (2000) examined the prevalence of problem gambling among students in grades 7, 9, 10, and 12 in the four Atlantic provinces and reported that 8.2 percent and 6.4 percent of the students met a "broad definition" of at-risk and problem gambling, respectively. Although prevalence did not vary according to age, lying about one's age or using fake identification was identified as an independent risk factor for problem gambling. Derevensky and Gupta from McGill University estimate that 10 to 14 percent of youth are at-risk for developing a serious problem and that 4 to 8 percent currently have a serious gambling problem (e.g., Derevensky & Gupta, 2000; Gupta & Derevensky, 1998). Pathological gambling can also be a serious problem among university and college students, with 2.8 percent estimated to be problem gamblers (Ladouceur, Dube, & Bujold, 1994).

Can pathological gamblers be helped? Although controlled studies of treatments developed specifically for pathological gamblers are relatively rare, Robert Ladouceur and his colleagues from the Université Laval have demonstrated the efficacy of cognitive-behavioural treatments in both adults and adolescents (e.g., Ladouceur et al., 2001; Ladouceur, Sylvain, Letarte, Giroux, & Jacques, 1998). A factor of obvious importance is whether pathological gamblers complete treatment. Leblond, Ladouceur, and Blaszczynski (2003) compared those who had completed treatment with those who had not and found no group differences on such variables as depression, anxiety, problem-solving skills, and alcohol use. However, non-completers did have significantly higher scores on a personality scale assessing impulsivity.

The need for assistance for people with gambling problems is underscored by the recent results of a community prevalence study that linked pathological gambling with attempted suicide (Newman & Thompson, 2003). This study found that after taking comorbid depression into account, there was still a strong, positive association between pathological gambling and attempted suicide.

In 1993 provincial governments began to fund services for pathological and problem gamblers. Numerous clinics and treatment programs have been opened across Canada, some of which focus on vulnerable, high-risk groups. The McGill Youth Gambling Research and Treatment Clinic (Clinique pour le traitement et la recherché des problèmes de jeux chez les jeunes) is one such service. The clinic employs an eclectic approach in the treatment of adolescents who become excessively involved in gambling and related activities "for the primary purpose of escaping life's difficulties." Consistent with a multifaceted, comprehensive assessment and intervention strategy, treatment is individually tailored to address the needs of each young person who presents with a gambling problem. The clinic's website provides a list of warning signs of adolescent problem gambling. A "Self-Quiz for Problem Gambling" is also available.

The treatment team, led by psychologists Jeffrey L. Derevensky and Rina Gupta, assumes that adolescents with gambling problems (1) suffer from an underlying clinical depression and seek out gambling in order to cope with their depression and (2) find gambling exciting and stimulating and seek it out in order to "feel good, 'alive,' and important." The youth are assumed to be more receptive to treatment when they are experiencing significant family, social, academic, and legal difficulties. The treatment that is employed targets underlying problem issues rather than gambling per se; these issues include depression, loss, poor coping skills, and ineffective social skills. Treatment continues until relevant underlying issues are resolved (typically three to nine months). Treatment emphasizes family involvement in order to facilitate a sense of social support. There is also an emphasis on helping the youth stand up to the influence of the peer group. Prior to ending treatment, therapists focus on alleviating academic problems and/or resolving employment issues.

Treatment at the McGill Youth Gambling Clinic is provided free of charge and is implemented by several psychologists and supervised doctoral-level graduate students. As would be expected, complete confidentiality is ensured (but see Chapter 18 for a discussion of possible exceptions). This treatment program is sponsored by Loto-Québec.

Research informs treatment at the McGill clinic (e.g., Gupta & Derevensky, 2000). Examples of current and recent research projects include the following:

1 evaluation of a province-wide gambling prevention program
2 changing cognitions and psychosocial factors involved in youth gambling
3 the relation between alcohol abuse and gambling addiction
4 coping skills and social support among adolescent problem gamblers

A recent study by the clinic's investigative team found that fewer than one-fifth of youth who met criteria for pathological gambling classified themselves as having a serious problem (Hardoon, Derevensky, & Gupta, 2003). This is unfortunate, as the vast majority may thus never seek help for their problem.

Because many problem gamblers do not seek out available treatments, it is vitally important for the future to develop innovative approaches to prevention. Dickson, Derevensky, and Gupta (2002) have outlined one such approach—a general risk-taking model that acknowledges common risk factors across various addictions. Korn (2000) outlined recommendations for ways to strengthen Canadian health and social policy related to gambling, including the following:

1 *Balance the public interest*: Policy-makers need "to ensure that there is a responsible balance between encouraging gambling as entertainment and protecting the public from gambling-related harm" (p. 63).
2 *Adopt harm reduction*: Policy-makers need "to adopt harm-reduction strategies directed toward minimizing the adverse health, social and economic consequences of gambling behaviour for individuals, families and communities" (p. 63).

In addition, Korn (2000) recommended that policy-makers monitor gambling advertising, assess the impact on quality of life, and foster a research agenda.

Source for McGill Youth Gambling Research and Treatment Clinic: <http://www.education.mcgill.ca/gambling/>.

Thinking Critically

1. Do you think governments in Canada should be in the business of promoting gambling for profit? What is the responsibility of government to address the economic, social, and psychological consequences of legalized, for-government-profit gambling?
2. In his harm-reduction recommendation, Korn (2000, p. 63) included strategies such as "healthy-gambling guidelines," "early identification" of gambling problems, and inclusion of "moderation and abstinence goals." How would you design a prevention and treatment program for a vulnerable, high-risk population such as young males who have concurrent substance-abuse or mental disorder problems? Would you add any critical elements to Korn's harm-reduction strategies?
3. What changes, if any, would you propose for the eclectic treatment program at the McGill Youth Gambling Clinic? Would Meichenbaum's self-instructional training be useful in facilitating appropriate changes to the thinking patterns of young gamblers? Would you make changes based on your evaluation of the cognitive-behavioural program developed by Ladouceur and his colleagues?
4. Gambling by means of the Internet is emerging as an issue. Do you think that parents should be concerned about the possibility of their children becoming involved in online "cybercasinos"? Should governments take steps to safeguard young people from such involvement?

in Chapter 8. Among the other diagnoses in this category are the following:

- academic problem (e.g., underachievement)
- antisocial behaviour (e.g., in professional thieves)
- malingering (faking physical or psychological symptoms to achieve a goal, such as avoiding work)
- relational problem (e.g., poor relationship with sibling or spouse)
- occupational problem (e.g., dissatisfaction with work)
- physical or sexual abuse
- bereavement
- noncompliance with treatment (e.g., refusing medication)
- religious or spiritual problem (e.g., questioning one's faith)
- phase-of-life problem (difficulties created by a life transition, such as beginning school)

In this context, it is interesting to recall our discussion of the difficulties of defining mental disorder. Should these life difficulties really be included in a listing of mental disorders? Are mental health professionals qualified, for example, to "treat" religious doubt? Many of these conditions will not be covered in this book, although malingering is discussed in Chapter 7, therapy for marital problems in Chapters 10 and 17, and physical and sexual abuse in Chapters 5, 7, and 14.

Delirium, Dementia, Amnestic, and Other Cognitive Disorders This category covers disorders in which cognition is seriously disturbed.

- *Delirium* is a clouding of consciousness, wandering attention, and an incoherent stream of thought. It may be caused by several medical conditions, such as malnutrition, as well as by substance abuse.
- *Dementia*, a deterioration of mental capacities, especially memory, is associated with Alzheimer's disease, stroke, and several other medical conditions as well as with substance abuse.
- *Amnestic syndrome* is an impairment in memory when there is no delirium or dementia.

Delirium and dementia are discussed in detail in Chapter 16 because they are often associated with aging. Amnestic syndrome is considered in Chapter 12 because it is often linked to alcohol abuse.

Now that we have briefly described the DSM's diagnostic categories and axes, we return to the case of J. Brett Barkley with which the book began. Table 3.2 shows how Brett's diagnosis would look. On Axis I, he is diagnosed with alcohol dependence, a condition that has also created a problem with sexual arousal. His current problems with his marriage are noted, as is his prior history of bipolar disorder. In addition, Brett is diagnosed on Axis II as having avoidant personality disorder. His feelings of inferiority, his self-consciousness when around others, and his avoidance of activities because of fear of criticism are the basis of this diagnosis. He has no general medical condition relevant to his problems, so he has no diagnosis on Axis III. His problems with his marriage are noted on Axis IV, and his current level of functioning is rated at 55 on the GAF (indicating a moderate level of impairment). Though alcohol may be Brett's most immediate problem, the multiaxial diagnosis gives clinicians a fairly full picture of the set of inter-related problems that will need to be addressed in treatment.

In Canadian Perspectives 3.2 we take an in-depth look at a comprehensive epidemiological study conducted in the province of Ontario. At appropriate points in this book, we will summarize the results of numerous other epidemiological studies conducted in Canadian settings. These studies often have a specific focus, such as the epidemiology of the DSM anxiety disorders (see Chapter 6).

Table 3.2

DSM-IV Multiaxial Diagnosis of J. Brett Barkley

Axis I	Alcohol dependence
	Alcohol-induced sexual problem, with impaired arousal
	Bipolar I disorder, most recent episode
	Manic, in full remission
	Partner relational problem
Axis II	Avoidant personality disorder
Axis III	None
Axis IV	Problem with primary support group
Axis V	GAF = 55

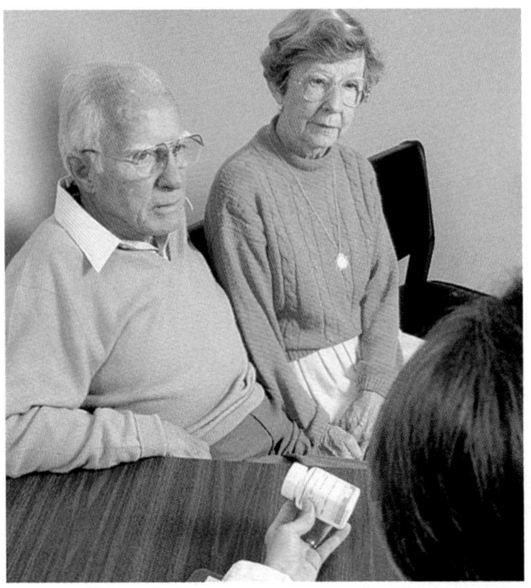

The frequency of Alzheimer's disease, which severely impairs cognitive functioning, increases with advanced age.

Canadian Perspectives/3.2

How Prevalent Are Psychological Disorders in Canada?

A pioneering study conducted in the 1950s (Leighton, 1959) provides a partial answer to our question. The *Stirling County Study* examined the impact of cultural and social factors on the mental health of about 20,000 people in a rural area of Nova Scotia. It used a procedure called *total case finding*—an attempt to discover every person in the community with some form of mental disorder. The researchers found many more cases than they expected. Although the procedures employed were flawed by today's standards and the researchers had to base their conclusions on information from many different sources (e.g., hospital records, informants, questionnaire assessments, etc.), it was concluded that about 20 percent of the population suffer from some type of psychological disorder that merits attention.

With this background, we will now introduce you to a relatively comprehensive and carefully designed epidemiological study conducted in Ontario as part of the Ontario Health Survey (*Mental Health Supplement*). The study was conducted in 1990 and 1991, and the preliminary results were first published in 1994 (Ontario Ministry of Health, 1994; also see Lin, Goering, Offord, Campbell, & Boyle, 1996; Offord, Boyle, Campbell, et al., 1996). Surprisingly, this was probably the first province-wide study in which respondents were chosen to be representative of the entire population. Information was collected using semi-structured interviews from 9,953 Ontarians, 15 years and older and living in private homes, who agreed to participate (76 percent of the 13,200 selected for participation). Most of the interview questionnaire was comprised of the Composite International Diagnostic Interview (CIDI), developed by the World Health Organization (1990) to measure mental disorders in a general population according to the definitions and criteria contained in DSM-III-R.

Figure 3.1 shows the one-year prevalence rates for the major categories of mental disorders assessed and included in the initial analyses. Rates are presented separately for males and females. The findings are shocking and consistent with the old Stirling County Study results. Clearly, mental disorders are common among the general population of people living in Ontario. Almost one in five (19 percent) of Ontarians aged 15 to 64 years have one or more of the mental disorders that were assessed. Although the overall rates of mental disorders are similar for men and women, specific disorders do vary by gender. Among women the most common conditions are anxiety and affective (mood) disorders, whereas among men the most prevalent conditions are anxiety disorders and substance-use disorders. Anxiety and mood disorders are significantly more prevalent in women than in men, while substance-use disorders and antisocial behaviour are more prevalent in men than in women. Note that antisocial behaviour was assessed as lifetime prevalence (the proportion of a sample that had experienced a disorder up to the time of the interview).

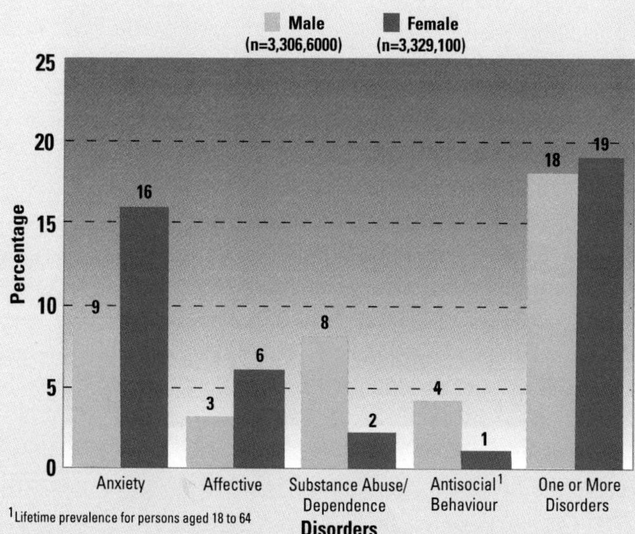

Source: Ontario Health Survey 1990, *Mental Health Supplement.*

Figure 3.1 One-year prevalence of mental disorders for people aged 15 to 64 by type of disorder.

Several other findings about the prevalence of psychological disorders in Ontario are of interest and importance:

1 Major depression (within the mood disorders category) is more common in women (5 percent) than in men (3 percent).
2 Alcohol abuse or dependence (within the substance-use disorders) is almost four times higher among men (7 percent) than among women (2 percent).
3 The one-year prevalence rate is especially high in individuals 15 to 24 years old (25 percent for both men and women). In this age range, women have the highest rates of both anxiety (20 percent) and mood (7 percent) disorders, while men have the highest rates of substance-use disorders (12 percent). The rate of substance abuse is also high in the 25 to 44 age range (10 percent).
4 There is a high rate of antisocial behaviour in men 18 to 24 years (12 percent lifetime prevalence rate).
5 Regional and urban-rural variations in prevalence are not marked.

Although the strengths of the Ontario study include a rigorous methodology, sophisticated sampling techniques, and a large sample of respondents, the study has a number of limitations. For example, results from people over 64 years were excluded because the prevalence rates of mental disorders were too low for meaningful analyses. Further, the sample did not include anyone living in an institution, homeless people, and Aboriginal people. Schizophrenia and related psychoses were not included in the report because few people were identified with these conditions. Surprisingly, despite the considerable current interest in eating disorders, anorexia nervosa was excluded "because of a mistake in the questionnaire" (Ontario Ministry of Health, 1994, p. 5). Nonetheless, comparable findings to those reported in Ontario's *Mental Health Supplement* have been reported in other Canadian studies. Bland and his colleagues (Bland, Orn, & Newman, 1988), for example, found similar results in a smaller-scale study in the city of Edmonton, Alberta.

Statistics Canada recently released (September 3, 2003) related findings based on the data collected between May 2002 and December 2002 as part of the Canadian Community Health Survey (CCHS). The survey collected information on the prevalence of five mental disorders (within the 12 months prior to the interview): major depression, mania, panic disorder, social phobia and agoraphobia, as well as alcohol and illicit drug dependence. The target population was household residents aged 15 and older throughout Canada (excluding the three territories, Native reserves, the armed forces, and people living in institutions and in some remote areas). The findings for this national epidemiological study are similar to and consistent with the results of the Ontario study. One out of every 10 Canadians (about 2.6 million people) reported symptoms associated with one of the five mental disorders or with drug dependence. Almost as many Canadians suffer from a mood disorder (4.9 percent) or anxiety disorder (4.7 percent) as from chronic diseases such as heart disease, diabetes, or a thyroid condition. Further, 1.7 percent of respondents were identified as "at risk" of developing an eating disorder whereas 3.7 percent admitted to having suicidal thoughts in the past 12 months. Consistent with other studies, the rates were highest among young people aged 15 to 24.

How prevalent are mental disorders when we examine prevalence over a person's lifetime? Unfortunately, except with respect to antisocial behaviour, lifetime prevalence was not assessed in the Ontario study or the CCHS. Earlier in this chapter, we reviewed Canadian studies on lifetime prevalence of pathological gambling. We will examine the available findings on the lifetime prevalence of other *specific* disorders in the Canadian setting when we look at different disorders in greater detail in subsequent chapters. However, recent and significant large-scale national studies conducted in the United States provide useful information about lifetime prevalence, especially for specific disorders. In the National Comorbidity Survey, structured interviews were used to collect information on the prevalence of several diagnoses (Kessler et al., 1994). Some data from this study are displayed in Table 3.3, which presents lifetime prevalence rates. From the table, we can see that major depression and alcoholism have much higher lifetime prevalences than do manic episodes or panic disorder. Bland, Orn, and Newman (1988) found a lifetime prevalence rate of approximately 33 percent in the Edmonton study. The largest epidemiologic investigation ever conducted in the United States—the Epidemiologic Catchment Area Study (Robins & Regier, 1991)—reported an overall lifetime prevalence rate of 32 percent. The National Comorbidity Survey (Kessler et al., 1994) included Axis II disorders and reported the one-year prevalence of any disorder to be 29.5 percent and the comparable lifetime prevalence to be a whopping 48 percent. In other words, almost half the population will have a diagnosable mental disorder at some time. If these estimates are accurate and the focus is on lifetime prevalence, it can be concluded that abnormality is almost the norm.

Table 3.3

Lifetime Prevalence Rates of Selected Diagnoses (%)

	Male	Female	Total
Major depressive episode	12.7	21.3	17.1
Manic episode	1.6	1.7	1.6
Dysthymia	4.8	8.0	6.4
Panic disorder	2.0	5.0	3.5
Agoraphobia without panic	3.5	7.0	5.3
Social phobia	11.1	15.5	13.3
Simple phobia	6.7	15.7	11.3
Generalized anxiety disorder	3.6	6.6	5.1
Alcohol dependence	20.1	8.2	14.1
Antisocial personality disorder	5.8	1.2	3.5

Source: From data collected in the National Comorbidity Survey (Kessler et al., 1994).

Additional findings from these studies of prevalence are even more alarming. The Ontario Health Survey's *Mental Health Supplement* (Offord, Boyle, Campbell, et al., 1996; Ontario Ministry of Health, 1994) reported that 5 percent of males and 4 percent of females could be diagnosed with two or more disorders. This comorbidity, or co-occurrence of different disorders, can be a major problem because it makes treatment planning more difficult, affects treatment compliance, and complicates the coordination of the delivery of services (Nathan & Langenbucher, 1999). Kessler et al. (1994) reported that the rate of comorbidity was very high in the National Comorbidity Survey—79 percent of people with one disorder also had another DSM disorder. Why is comorbidity so high? Perhaps factors involved in the development of one disorder, such as stress, also affect the development of other disorders.

The Ontario study found that 75 percent of those with a psychological disorder had never sought help for their problems. In the 15 to 24 years age range, 86 percent of the participants with a disorder were "untreated." Only 32 percent of those who suffered from any of the surveyed problems in the CCHS study (Statistics Canada, September 3, 2003) had seen or talked to a health care professional in the preceding year. These reports are especially disconcerting in the context of recent findings in Canada and the United States (e.g., Katz et al., 1998) that indicate that only a minority of people with psychological disorders receive adequate treatment, even though there is clear evidence that modern treatments are effective in treating many mental disorders. Hunsley et al. (1999), using data from the 1994–1995 Statistics Canada Population Health Survey, concluded that the high levels of psychological problems in the Canadian population are coupled with underutilization of effective psychological services. In a recent Alberta study, Bland, Newman, and Orn (1997a) reported that comorbidity plays a role in help-seeking; the help-seeking rate for those with one disorder was only 20.3 percent whereas the rate for those with more than one diagnosis was 42.8 percent. Different diagnoses, moreover, had different rates of help-seeking. While only 16 percent of people with alcohol abuse or dependence sought treatment, almost 50 percent (46.7 percent) of those with a major depressive episode sought assistance. Surprisingly, over one-third of help-seekers did not have a current disorder, indicating that many people with subclinical problems are distressed enough to seek treatment.

In a cross-national comparison, the WHO International Consortium in Psychiatric Epidemiology (2000) reported that mental disorders are often chronic; however, this chronicity is higher for anxiety disorders than for mood or substance use disorders. The Canadian data were based on interviews with over 3,000 adult residents of Edmonton (Bland, Newman, & Orn, 1997b). Although antisocial personality, drug abuse or dependence, and alcohol abuse or dependence appear to show increasing one-year remission rates with increasing age, the authors found that OCD and panic disorder had low rates of remission in all age groups, which indicated that these disorders "produce significant long-term morbidity" (p. 722). The overall remission rate for depression was less than 50 percent and was especially low between the ages of 55 and 64. Bland et al. (1997b) hypothesized that the stable low rate reflects both the difficulties of treatment and the low rates of treatment.

Thinking Critically

1. How do you think the prevalence of specific mental disorders in Canada and the United States compares to the prevalence of similar disorders in other places around the world (such as in Brazil, Mexico, Germany, the Netherlands, and Turkey)? If there are differences, what factors could account for them? What factors might lead to similar prevalence rates? For insight into this issue, read the WHO International Consortium (2000) paper.
2. The findings in the *Mental Health Supplement* of the Ontario Health Survey (Offord, Boyle, Campbell, et al., 1996; Ontario Ministry of Health, 1994) and from the *Canadian Community Health Survey* (Statistics Canada, September 3, 2003) indicates that there are significant differences in the prevalence rates of specific psychological disorders between Canadian males and females. What biological, psychological, and social factors could account for these differences? In the *Mental Health Supplement* study, people aged 15 to 24 were oversampled. Why do you suppose the designers of the project elected to do this?
3. Do you believe that the prevalence of mental disorders increased or decreased over the past quarter century? The WHO Consortium (2000) analyzed age-of-onset reports and concluded that lifetime prevalence rates have, in fact, recently increased in certain groups. However, the increase was less for the anxiety disorders than for both mood and substance-use disorders. What do you think will happen to prevalence rates in Canada and around the world over the new century? Do you think that the prevalence of specific disorders is likely to increase in the coming years? Why? What are the implications of changing prevalence rates and patterns?

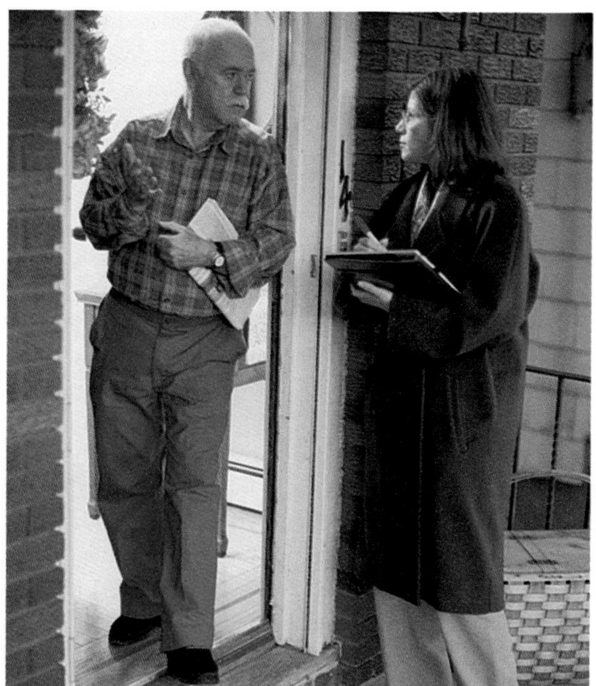

In some epidemiological research, interviewers go to homes in a community, conducting interviews to determine the rates of different disorders.

Issues in the Classification of Abnormal Behaviour

Our review of the major diagnostic categories of abnormal behaviour was brief because the diagnoses will be examined in more detail throughout this text. On the basis of this overview, however, we will examine here the usefulness of the current diagnostic system. Among those who are critical of the DSM, one group asserts that classification per se is irrelevant to the field of abnormal behaviour, and a second group finds specific deficiencies in the manner in which diagnoses are made in the DSM.

General Criticisms of Classification

Some critics of classification argue that to classify someone as depressed or anxious results in a loss of information about that person, thereby reducing some of the uniqueness of the individual being studied. In evaluating this claim, recall our earlier discussions of paradigms and their effect on how we glean information about our world. It appears to be in the nature of humankind to categorize whenever we perceive and think about anything. Those who argue against classification per se are overlooking the inevitability of classification and categorization in human thought.

Consider the simple example of casting dice. Any of the numbers one through six may come up on a given toss of a single die. Let us suppose, however, that we classify each outcome as odd or even. Whenever a one, three, or five comes up on a roll, we call out "odd," and whenever a two, four, or six appears, we say "even." A person listening to our calls will not know whether the call "odd" refers to a one, three, or five or whether "even" refers to a two, four, or six. In classification, some information must inevitably be lost.

What matters is whether the information lost is relevant, and relevance depends on the purposes of the classification system. Any classification is designed to group together objects sharing a common property and to ignore differences in the objects that are not relevant to the purposes at hand. If our intention is merely to count odd and even rolls, it is irrelevant whether a die comes up one, three, or five, or two, four, or six. In judging abnormal behaviour, however, we cannot so easily decide what is wheat and what is chaff, for the relevant and irrelevant dimensions of abnormal behaviour are uncertain. Thus, when we do classify, we may be grouping people together on rather trivial bases while ignoring their extremely important differences.

In Chapter 1, we discussed issues related to attitudes toward people with psychological disorders. We must revisit the topic in the present context to reinforce the fact that classification can have negative effects on a person. Consider how your life might be changed after being diagnosed as having schizophrenia. You might become guarded and suspicious lest someone recognize your disorder. Or you might be chronically on edge, fearing the onset of another episode. The fact that you are a "former mental patient" could have a stigmatizing effect. Friends and loved ones might treat you differently, and you might have difficulty obtaining employment.

There is little doubt that diagnosis can have such negative consequences. The existing research clearly shows that the general public holds a relatively negative view of mental patients, especially those diagnosed with one of the psychotic disorders, and that patients and their families believe that such stigmatizing effects are common (e.g., Martin et al., 2000; Phelan et al., 2000; Rabkin, 1974; Wahl & Harman, 1989). We must recognize and be on guard against the possible social stigma of a diagnosis.

The Value of Classification and Diagnoses

The various types of abnormal behaviour differ from one another in many ways, and thus classifying them is essential, for these differences may constitute keys to the causes and treatments of various deviant behaviours. For example, mental retardation is sometimes caused by phenylketonuria. A deficiency in the metabolism of the protein phenylalanine results in the release of incomplete metabolites that injure the brain. A diet drastically reduced in phenylalanine prevents some of this injury. As Mendels (1970) noted, however,

> had we taken 100, or even 1,000, people with mental deficiency and placed them all on the phenylalanine-free diet, the response would have been insignificant and the diet would have been discarded as a treatment. It was first necessary to recognize a subtype of mental deficiency [retardation], phenylketonuria, and then subject the value of a phenylalanine-free diet to investigation in this specific population, for whom it has been shown to have value in preventing the development of mental deficiency. (p. 35)

Forming categories furthers knowledge, for once a category is formed, additional information may be ascertained about it. Even though the category is only an asserted, and not a proved, entity, it may still be heuristically useful in that it facilitates the acquisition of new information. Only after a diagnostic category has been formed can we study people who fit its definition in the hope of uncovering factors responsible for the development of their problems and of devising treatments that may help them. For example, only a few decades ago, bipolar disorder (episodes of both mania and depression) was not typically distinguished from depression. If this distinction had not subsequently been made, it is unlikely that lithium would have been recognized as an effective treatment, as it is today.

Specific Criticisms of Classification

In addition to the general criticisms of classification described above, more specific criticisms are commonly made of psychiatric classification. The principal ones concern whether discrete diagnostic categories are justifiable and whether the diagnostic categories are reliable and valid. These criticisms were frequently levelled at DSM-I and DSM-II. At the close of this section, we will see how subsequent editions of the DSM have come to grips with them.

Discrete Entity versus Continuum The DSM represents a categorical classification, a yes–no approach to classification. Does the patient have schizophrenia or not? It may be argued that this type of classification, because it postulates discrete (separate) diagnostic entities, does not allow continuity between normal and abnormal behaviour to be taken into consideration. Those who advance the continuity argument hold that abnormal and normal behaviours differ only in intensity or degree, not in kind; therefore, discrete diagnostic categories foster a false impression of discontinuity.

In contrast, in dimensional classification, the entities or objects being classified must be ranked on a quantitative dimension (e.g., a 1-to-10 scale of anxiety, where 1 represents minimal and 10 extreme). Classification would be accomplished by assessing patients on the relevant dimensions and perhaps plotting the location of the patient in a system of coordinates defined by his or her score on each dimension. (See Figure 3.2 for an illustration of the difference between dimensional and categorical classification.) A dimensional system can subsume a categorical system by specifying a cutting point, or threshold, on one of the quantitative dimensions. This capability is a potential advantage of the dimensional approach.

A dimensional approach also allows for the possibility that certain individuals may experience a number of troubling symptoms of a disorder but not meet the number of symptoms required for an actual diagnosis. Contemporary research on disorders such as depression shows that there is substantial evidence for continuity and that people who experience symptoms of depression but do not meet the criteria for a diagnosis nevertheless experience significant levels of distress and impairment and appear to warrant treatment (see Flett, Vredenburg, & Krames, 1997; Lewinsohn, Solomon, Seeley, & Zeiss, 2000; Ruscio & Ruscio, 2000).

Clearly, a dimensional system can be applied to most of the symptoms that constitute the diagnoses of the DSM. Anxiety, depression, and the many personality traits that are included in the personality disorders are found in different people to varying degrees and thus do not seem to fit well with the DSM categorical model.

The choice between a categorical and a dimensional system of classification, however, is not as simple as it might seem initially. Consider hypertension (high blood pressure), a topic discussed at length in Chapter 8. Blood-pressure measurements form a continuum, which clearly fits a dimensional approach; yet researchers have found it useful to categorize certain people as having high blood pressure in order to research the causes and possible treatments for the condition. A similar situation could exist for the DSM categories. Even though anxiety clearly exists in differing degrees in different people and thus is a dimensional variable, it could prove useful to create a diagnostic category for those people whose anxiety is extreme. There is a certain inevitable arbitrariness to such a categorization (where exactly should the cutoff be?), but it could be fruitful nonetheless.

It is also possible that a variable that on the surface appears dimensional actually represents an underlying categorical, or off–on, process. This is a complex argument, but some of its flavour can be appreciated by considering a hypothetical single-gene cause for hypertension. Blood pressure might result from a complex interplay between the gene (off or on) and a variety of environmental influences—diet, weight, smoking, stress, and so on. Observed blood pressure is a dimensional variable, but hypertension might result principally from the operation of the single off–on gene, which is a categorical variable. Given that we can observe only the sur-

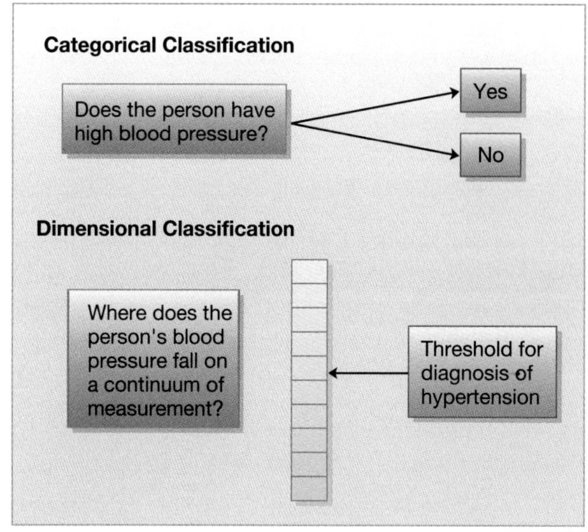

Figure 3.2 Categorical versus dimensional classification.

focus on discovery/3.1

Issues and Possible Categories in Need of Further Study

One of DSM-IV-TR's appendixes is entitled "Criteria Sets and Axes Provided for Further Study." It contains several proposals for new categories that the DSM-IV task force considers promising but not sufficiently established by data to merit inclusion in DSM-IV. By listing and describing these categories of disorders, the DSM task force hopes to encourage professionals to consider whether a future DSM should include any of these syndromes or axes as official ways of classifying mental disorders.

Possible New Syndromes

Here is a sampling of the more than two-dozen categories mentioned as meriting further study.

Caffeine Withdrawal As with withdrawal from other addicting substances, caffeine withdrawal (not drinking accustomed levels of beverages containing caffeine) results in significant distress or impairment in occupational or social functioning. Symptoms include headache, fatigue, anxiety, depression, nausea, and impaired thinking. Inclusion of caffeine withdrawal as a new category would certainly swell the ranks of the mentally disordered.

Premenstrual Dysphoric Disorder Written about a good deal in the press and assailed by feminists and sexists alike, this proposed syndrome occurs a week or so before menstruation for most months in a given year and is marked by depression, anxiety, anger, mood swings, and decreased interest in activities usually engaged in with pleasure. The symptoms are severe enough to interfere with social or occupational functioning. This category is to be distinguished from premenstrual syndrome, which is experienced by many more women and is not nearly as debilitating. Ongoing work by Steiner (1997) and others at St. Joseph's Hospital in Hamilton, Ontario, has shown that it is possible to confirm the diagnosis of premenstrual dysphoric disorder by establishing the presence of the symptoms described in DSM-IV and by conducting prospective daily charting of symptoms for at least two menstrual cycles.

Feminists may be pleased or displeased with this possible new category. On the plus side, inclusion might alert people to the hormonal bases of monthly mood changes linked to the menstrual cycle and thereby foster more tolerance and less blame. On the minus side, listing such mood changes in a manual of mental disorders could convey the message that women who experience these psychological changes are mentally disordered.

Mixed Anxiety-Depressive Disorder For a time during the development of DSM-IV, it seemed that this disorder would be formally listed, for clinicians have for many years sometimes found it difficult to decide whether to diagnose a person as having primarily a depressive disorder or primarily an anxiety disorder. In mixed anxiety-depressive disorder, a person would have been depressed for at least a month and have had at the same time at least four of the following symptoms: concentration or memory problems, sleep disturbances, fatigue or low energy, irritability, worry, crying easily, hypervigilance, anticipating the worst, pessimism about the future, and feelings of low self-esteem. The person must not be diagnosable as having a major depressive disorder, dysthymic disorder, panic disorder, or generalized anxiety disorder. We will return to this proposed category in Chapter 6.

Passive-Aggressive Personality Disorder (Negativistic Personality Disorder) This personality disorder was present in DSM-III and DSM-III-R but was moved to the appendix in DSM-IV. Not attributable to depression, symptoms include resenting, resisting, and opposing demands and expectations by means of passive activities, such as lateness, procrastination, forgetfulness, and intentional inefficiency. The inference is that the person is angry or resentful and is expressing these feelings by not doing certain things rather than by being assertive or aggressive. Such people often feel mistreated, cheated, or underappreciated.

Depressive Personality Disorder In lay terms, this personality disorder would be applied to people whose general lifestyle is characterized by gloominess, lack of cheer, and a tendency to worry a lot. This trait-like, long-term disorder may be a precursor to a full-blown major depressive disorder. The DSM admits that it is very difficult to distinguish between depressive personality disorder and the main depressive disorders. Research conducted in Canada by Bagby and Ryder (Bagby & Ryder, 1999; Ryder & Bagby, 1999) has shown that it is possible on a statistical basis to distinguish depressive personality disorder and dysthymia, which is a milder but long-lasting form of depression. However, they also found that 95 percent of the people who meet diagnostic criteria for depressive personality disorder also meet the diagnostic criteria for dysthymia, and they suggested that the high overlap limits the clinical utility of the depressive personality disorder diagnosis. Another disorder listed in the DSM-IV-TR appendix is minor depressive disorder, which may be distinguishable only by virtue of its not being as long-lasting as depressive personality disorder.

Proposed Axes in Need of Further Study

Professionals are being encouraged to consider whether a future axis should include defence mechanisms defined as "automatic psychological processes that protect the individual against anxiety and from the awareness of internal or external dangers or stressors" (DSM-IV-TR, 2000, p. 807). Defence mechanisms are divided into groups called defence levels and are measured by a proposed Defensive Functioning Scale. Although some of the defence mechanisms are similar to what many cognitive-behavioural theorists and practitioners describe as coping styles or strategies (see below), many of the mechanisms are derived from psychoanalytic theory.

There are seven defence levels, each with a set of defence mechanisms. The levels range from "high adaptive level" to "level of defensive dysregulation." The following examples are among the proposed levels and mechanisms.

High Adaptive Level This most adaptive, healthy defence level contains coping efforts that are realistic ways of handling stress and are conducive to achieving a good balance among conflicting motives. The following are some examples:

- *anticipation*—experiencing emotional reactions before a stressful event occurs and considering realistic, alternative courses of action; for example, carefully planning for an upcoming meeting with an employer who is unhappy with your performance
- *sublimation*—dealing with a stress by channelling negative feelings into socially acceptable behaviours; for example, working out at a gym

Disavowal Level This middle level is characterized by defences that keep troubling stressors or ideas out of conscious awareness.

- *denial*—refusing to acknowledge a degree of discomfort or threat that is obvious to an observer; for example, maintaining that your marriage is fine despite the obvious and repeated conflicts noticed by your friends
- *projection*—falsely attributing to another person one's own unacceptable feelings or thoughts; for example, believing that your professor is angry with you, rather than the reverse

Level of Defensive Dysregulation This lowest level is marked by a failure to deal with stress, leading to a break with reality.

- *psychotic denial*—denial that is so extreme as to be marked by a gross impairment in reality testing; for example, maintaining that the results of three biopsies showing a cancerous growth are wrong

The reliability of the defence mechanisms axis has recently been studied. Two clinicians rated a series of patients, using the axis, with disappointing results (Perry et al., 1998). Perhaps the axis would be more reliable if a better device were developed for the assessment of defence mechanisms, as happened when structured interviews began to be used to make DSM diagnoses. Recently, Vaillant (2000) outlined a prospective longitudinal strategy to provide more reliable definition and measurement of defences. Coping (changing cognitive and behavioural strategies to manage psychological stress, often through conscious awareness) can also mediate or moderate the link between stressful life circumstances and negative adaptational outcomes (e.g., Lazarus, 2000; Somerfield & McCrae, 2000; Tennen, Affleck, Armeli, & Carney, 2000). We will examine the scope, yield, and clinical applications of the coping research literature at different points in this book, but especially in Chapter 8.

face variable, how can we tell whether there might be an underlying categorical process? Although well beyond the scope of this book, complex mathematical procedures have been developed to test such questions (e.g., Meehl, 1986), and they have been used to test whether a dimensional or categorical approach is most applicable to several diagnoses (Tykra et al., 1995). We will return to this issue in our discussion of personality disorders in Chapter 13.

RELIABILITY: THE CORNERSTONE OF A DIAGNOSTIC SYSTEM

The extent to which a classification system, or a test or measurement of any kind, produces the same scientific observation each time it is applied is the measure of its reliability. An example of an unreliable measure would be a flexible, elastic-like ruler whose length changed every time it was used. This flawed ruler would yield different values for the height of the same object every time the object was measured. In contrast, a reliable measure, such as a standard wooden ruler, produces consistent results.

Interrater reliability refers to the extent to which two judges agree about an event. For example, suppose you wanted to know whether a child suspected of having attention deficit/hyperactivity disorder did indeed have difficulty paying attention and staying seated in the classroom. You could decide to observe the child during a day at school. To determine whether the observational data were reliable, you would want to have at least two people watch the child and make independent judgments about the level of attention and activity. The extent to which the raters agreed would be an index of interrater reliability (see Figure 3.3 for an illustration).

Reliability is a primary criterion for judging any classification system. For a classification system to be useful, those applying it must be able to agree on what is and what is not an instance of a particular category. A person diagnosed as having an anxiety disorder by one clinician should be given the same diagnosis by another clinician as well. After all, if someone is not diagnosed correctly, he or she may not receive the best treatment available. Prior to DSM-III, diagnostic reliability was not acceptable, mainly because the criteria for making a diagnosis were not presented clearly and methods of assessing a patient's symptoms were not standardized (Ward et al., 1962).

The two components of reliability—agreeing on who is a member of a class and who is not—are termed *sensitivity* and *specificity*. Sensitivity refers to agreement regarding the presence of a specific diagnosis; specificity refers to agreement concerning the absence of a diagnosis. As we will soon see, reliability for most current diagnostic categories is good.

HOW VALID ARE DIAGNOSTIC CATEGORIES?

Validity is a complex topic. We will describe the several types of validity in Chapter 4 but here we will focus on the type of validity that is most important for diagnosis—construct validity. The diagnoses of the DSM are referred to as constructs because they are inferred, not proven, entities. A diagnosis of schizophrenia, for instance, does not have the same status as a diagnosis of diabetes. In the case of diabetes, we know the symptoms, the biological malfunction that produces them, and some of the causes. For schizophrenia, we have a proposed set of symptoms but only very tentative information regarding mechanisms that may produce the symptoms.

Construct validity is determined by evaluating the extent to which accurate statements and predictions can be made about a category once it has been formed. In other words, to what extent does the construct enter into a network of lawful relationships? Some of these relationships may be about possible causes of the disorder, for example, a genetic predisposition or a biochemical imbalance. Others could be about characteristics of the disorder that are not symptoms but that occur frequently in association with it, for example, poor social skills in people with schizophrenia. Other relationships could refer to predictions about the course of the disorder or the probable response to particular treatments. The greater the number and strength of relationships into which a diagnosis enters, the greater the construct validity (see Figure 3.4).

We have organized this book around the major DSM diagnostic categories because we believe that they possess construct validity. Certain categories have greater validity than others, however, and we will discuss these differences in the chapters on each of the major diagnostic categories.

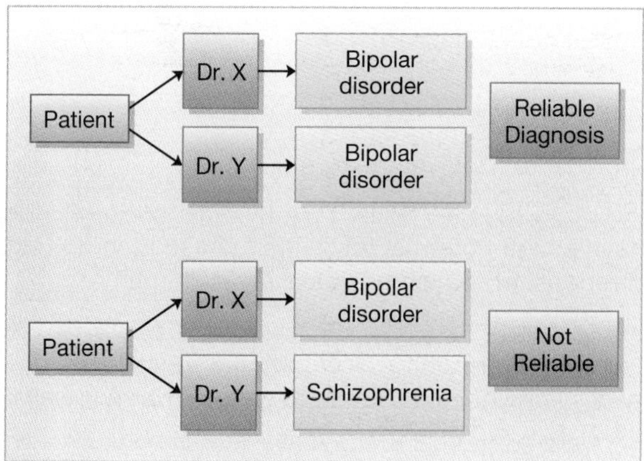

Figure 3.3 Interrater reliability.

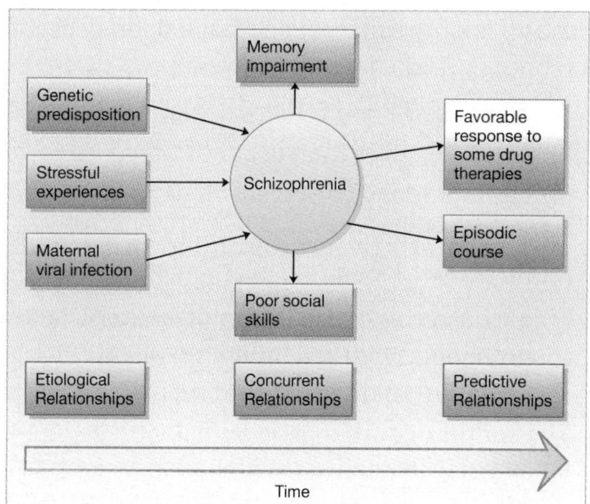

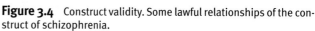

Figure 3.4 Construct validity. Some lawful relationships of the construct of schizophrenia.

THE DSM AND CRITICISMS OF DIAGNOSIS

As we have mentioned, the diagnoses in DSM-II were not very reliable. Beginning with DSM-III and DSM-III-R, an effort was made to create more reliable and valid diagnostic categories. Major improvements include the following:

1. The characteristics and symptoms of each diagnostic category in Axes I and II are now described much more extensively than they were in DSM-II. For each disorder, there is a description of essential features, then of associated features, such as laboratory findings (e.g., enlarged ventricles in schizophrenia), and results from physical exams (e.g., electrolyte imbalances in people who have eating disorders). Next are statements drawn from the research literature about age of onset, course, prevalence and sex ratio, familial pattern, and differential diagnosis (i.e., how to distinguish one diagnosis from another that is symptomatically similar to it).
2. Much more attention is now paid to how the symptoms of a given disorder may differ depending on the culture in which it appears. For example, the core symptoms of both schizophrenia (e.g., delusions and hallucinations) and depression (e.g., depressed mood and loss of interest or pleasure in activities) are similar cross-culturally (Draguns, 1989), but guilt is a frequent symptom of depression in Western society but an infrequent symptom in Japan and Iran. (Focus on Discovery 3.2 describes further efforts by the DSM to be more sensitive to the effects of culture and explores cultural factors from an assessment perspective).
3. Specific *diagnostic criteria*—the symptoms and other facts that must be present to justify the diagnosis—are spelled out more precisely, and the clinical symptoms that constitute a diagnosis are defined in a glossary. Table 3.4 compares the descriptions of a manic episode given in DSM-II with the diagnostic criteria given in DSM-IV-TR. The bases for making diagnoses are decidedly more detailed and concrete in DSM-IV-TR.

The improved explicitness of the DSM criteria has reduced the descriptive inadequacies that were the major source of diagnostic unreliability and thus has led to improved reliability. Another factor in improved reliability is the use of standardized, reliably scored interviews for collecting the information needed for a diagnosis. (We will describe such interviews in the next chapter.) Results of an extensive evaluation of the reliability of DSM-III-R are shown

Table 3.4

Description of Manic Disorder in DSM-II versus DSM-IV-TR

DSM-II (1968, p. 36)

Manic-depressive illness, manic type. This disorder consists exclusively of manic episodes. These episodes are characterized by excessive elation, irritability, talkativeness, flight of ideas, and accelerated speech and motor activity. Brief periods of depression sometimes occur, but they are never true depressive episodes.

DSM-IV-TR (2000, p. 362)

Diagnostic Criteria for a Manic Episode

A. A distinct period of abnormally and persistently elevated, expansive, or irritable mood, lasting at least 1 week (or any duration if hospitalization is necessary).

B. During the period of mood disturbance, three (or more) of the following symptoms have persisted (four if the mood is only irritable) and have been present to a significant degree:

(1) inflated self-esteem or grandiosity

(2) decreased need for sleep (e.g., feels rested after only three hours of sleep)

(3 more talkative than usual or pressure to keep talking

(4) flight of ideas or subjective experience that thoughts are racing

(5) distractibility (i.e., attention too easily drawn to unimportant or irrelevant external stimuli)

(6) increase in goal-directed activity (either socially, at work or school, or sexually) or psychomotor agitation

(7) excessive involvement in pleasurable activities that have a high potential for painful consequences (e.g., engaging in unrestrained buying sprees, sexual indiscretions, or foolish business investments)

C. The symptoms do not meet criteria for a Mixed Episode.

D. The mood disturbance is sufficiently severe to cause marked impairment in occupational functioning or in usual social activities or relationships with others, or to necessitate hospitalization to prevent harm to self or others, or there are psychotic features.

E. The symptoms are not due to the direct physiological effects of a substance (e.g., a drug of abuse, a medication, or other treatment) or a general medical condition (e.g., hyperthyroidism).

Note: DSM-IV-TR material reprinted with permission from the DSM-IV-TR, 2000, American Psychiatric Association.

in Table 3.4. The reliabilities vary but are quite acceptable for most of the major categories. The relatively low figures for anxiety disorders are higher in other studies that used an assessment interview specifically tailored for them (DiNardo et al., 1993). Although the data are not all in yet, the reliabilities of DSM-IV diagnoses look comparable to those shown in the table (e.g., Zanarini et al., 2000).

Thus far we have described the DSM in positive terms. The attainment of adequate diagnostic reliability is a considerable achievement, but a number of problems remain.

1 The discrete entity versus continuum issue, discussed earlier, has not been satisfactorily resolved.

2 It is unclear whether the rules for making diagnostic decisions are ideal. Examining Table 3.4, we see that for patients to be diagnosed as suffering from mania they must

The core symptoms of depression appear to be similar cross-culturally. However, guilt is less frequent in Japan than in Western cultures.

focus on discovery/3.2

Ethnic and Cultural Considerations in DSM-IV-TR

Previous editions of the DSM were criticized for their lack of attention to cultural and ethnic variations in psychopathology. DSM-IV-TR attempts to enhance its cultural sensitivity in three ways: (1) by including in the main body of the manual a discussion of cultural and ethnic factors for each disorder; (2) by providing in the appendix a general framework for evaluating the role of culture and ethnicity; and (3) by describing culture-bound syndromes in an appendix.

Among the cultural issues of which clinicians need to be aware are language differences between the therapist and the patient and the way in which the patient's culture talks about emotional distress. Many cultures, for example, describe grief or anxiety in physical terms—"I am sick in my heart" or "My heart is heavy"—rather than in psychological terms. Individuals also vary in the degree to which they identify with their cultural or ethnic group. Some value assimilation into the majority culture, whereas others wish to maintain close ties to their ethnic background. In general, clinicians are advised to be constantly mindful of how culture and ethnicity influence diagnosis and treatment, a topic discussed in the next chapter.

The DSM also describes "locality-specific patterns of aberrant behaviour and troubling experience that may or may not be linked to a particular DSM-IV diagnostic category" (DSM-IV-TR, 2000, p. 898). The following are some examples that may occur in clinical practices in North America.

- *amok*—a dissociative episode in which there is a period of brooding followed by a violent and sometimes homicidal outburst. The episode tends to be triggered by an insult and is found primarily among men. Persecutory delusions are often present as well. The term is Malaysian and is defined by the dictionary as a murderous frenzy. You have probably encountered the phrase "run amok."
- *brain fag*—originally used in West Africa, this term refers to a condition reported by high school and university students in response to academic pressures. Symptoms include fatigue, tightness in the head and neck, and blurring of vision. This syndrome resembles certain anxiety, depressive, and somatoform disorders.
- *dhat*—a term used in India to refer to severe anxiety and hypochondriasis linked to the discharge of semen.
- *ghost sickness*—extreme preoccupation with death and those who have died; found among certain Native American tribes.
- *koro*—reported also in south and east Asia, an episode of intense anxiety about the possibility that the penis or nipples will recede into the body, possibly leading to death.

Recently, Kirmayer and associates from Montreal provided an extensive discussion of the criteria included in the DSM-IV-TR "Outline for Cultural Formulation," which has been newly introduced to the DSM (see Kirmayer, Rousseau, Jarvis, & Guzder, 2003). The outline considers five key issues: (1) the ethnocultural identity of the individual (i.e., the individual's cultural reference groups and their positions in society); (2) cultural differences in explanations of the illness; (3) the psychosocial environment and levels of functioning; (4) the relationship between the individual and the clinician (including how the clinician's ethnocultural background influences the individual); and (5) the overall assessment with implications for diagnosis and care. Kirmayer, Rousseau, and Santhanam (2003) suggested that one viable approach is to work in multidisciplinary teams that are culturally diverse and reflective of the patient population. This may involve working closely with interpreters and "culture brokers" who would assist with the clarification of the cultural context.

We conclude this segment with some clinical vignettes taken from Kirmayer, Rousseau, Jarvis, and Guzder (2003) that illustrate the need for a complex and sensitive approach to diagnosis and clinical assessment that recognizes differences in cultural backgrounds.

Case Vignette #1

A woman from South Asia appears to have a severe depression with vegetative symptoms and persistent suicidal ideation. She does not respond to trials of several antidepressant medications. On reassessment with a clinician who speaks her language, she reveals that her husband has an unpaid debt of honor to her daughter's husband's family, and she is suffering from the ongoing feud, which has barred her from seeing her daughter and grandchildren. When this is addressed in a series of family therapy sessions, her "depression" lifts dramatically (Kirmayer et al., 2003, p. 24).

Case Vignette #2

A 35-year-old professional from Peru visited the emergency room because of high fever caused by pneumonia. While waiting to be seen, he suddenly became agitated and fled the hospital, breaking through the parking lot barrier. After the arrest the judge ordered a psychiatric assessment. The patient explained that on seeing the medical instruments in the ER he was reminded of his torture in Peru and felt convinced that he was back there and that his life was in danger. The combined effects of fever and reminders of the trauma had triggered a dissociative episode (Kirmayer et al., 2003, p. 24).

Case Vignette #3

A 16-year-old girl from Haiti presents with disorganized schizophrenia, which began around age 14 years. Her family has not been compliant with treatment and this has led to several hospitalizations of the patient in a dehydrated state. During the third hospitalization, the clinical team decide to explore the family's interpretation of the illness. A grand-aunt insists on sending the girl to Haiti for a traditional diagnosis. The traditional healer indicates that the problem is due to an ancestor's spirit in the mother's family and that for this reason it will be a prolonged illness. This explanation helps to restore cohesion in the extended family by rallying people around the patient, and her family receives much support. The traditional interpretation and treatment has broken the family's sense of shame and isolation and promoted an alliance with the medical team and the acceptance of antipsychotic medication (Kirmayer et al., 2003, p. 25)

have three symptoms from a list of seven, or four if their mood is irritable. But why require three symptoms rather than two or five (see Finn, 1982)? Just as there is a degree of arbitrariness about the point at which a person is diagnosed as having high blood pressure, so there is an element of arbitrariness to the DSM's diagnostic rules.

3 The reliability of Axes I and II may not always be as high in everyday practice as it is in formal research studies, for diagnosticians may not adhere as precisely to the criteria as do those whose work is being scrutinized.

4 Although the improved reliability of the DSM may lead to more validity, there is no guarantee that it will. The diagnoses made according to the DSM criteria may not reveal anything useful about the patients.

5 Subjective factors still play a role in evaluations made according to DSM-IV-TR. Consider again the criteria for manic syndrome in Table 3.4. What exactly does it mean to say that the elevated mood must be abnormally and persistently elevated? Or, what level of involvement in pleasurable activities with high potential for painful consequences is excessive? As another example, on Axis V the clinician must judge the patient's level of current functioning. The clinician determines the patient's level of adaptive functioning and how his or her behaviour compares with that of an average person. Such a judgment sets the stage for the insertion of cultural biases as well as the clinician's own personal ideas of what the average person should be doing at a given stage of life and in particular circumstances (C.B. Taylor, 1983). A male clinician might have a considerably different take on a single, 50-year-old female patient than would a female therapist; for example, the female therapist might view such a patient's childlessness more negatively than would the male therapist.

6 Not all of the DSM classification changes seem positive. Should a problem such as difficulty in learning arithmetic or reading be considered a psychiatric disorder? By expanding its coverage, the DSM seems to have made too many childhood problems into psychiatric disorders, without good justification for doing so.

In sum, although the DSM continues to improve, it is far from perfect. Throughout this book, as we present the literature on various disorders, we will have further opportunities to describe both the strengths and the weaknesses of DSM-IV-TR and to consider how it may deal with some of the problems that still exist. What is most heartening about the DSM is that

Table 3.5

Reliability of Selected DSM Diagnoses

Diagnosis	Kappa
Bipolar disorder	.84
Major depression	.64
Schizophrenia	.65
Alcohol abuse	.75
Anorexia nervosa	.75
Bulimia nervosa	.86
Panic disorder	.58
Social phobia	.47

Source: Williams et al., 1992.

Note: The numbers here are a statistic called "kappa", which measures the proportion of agreement over and above what would be expected by chance. Generally, kappas over .70 are considered good.

its attempts to be explicit about the rules for diagnosis make it easier to detect problems in the diagnostic system. We can expect more changes and refinements over the next several years. In a recent review, Widiger and Clark (2000) lamented the absence of adequate research to guide the construction of the DSM and discussed issues that deserve special attention in the development of DSM-V. These issues include the following: (1) the process by which the DSM is developed; (2) differentiation from normal functioning; (3) differentiation among diagnostic categories; (4) the longitudinal course of disorders; and (5) the role of laboratory instruments. Widiger and Clark favour a move toward a more dimensional model in which psychological functioning would be assessed using standardized psychological instruments.

SUMMARY

- Diagnosis is a critical aspect of the field of abnormal psychology. Having an agreed-upon system of classification makes it possible for clinicians to communicate effectively with one another and facilitates the search for causes and treatments for the various disorders.
- The recent editions of the *Diagnostic and Statistical Manual of Mental Disorders*, published by the American Psychiatric Association, reflect the continuing efforts by mental health professionals to categorize the various psychopathologies.
- A novel feature of the DSM is its multiaxial organization; every time a diagnosis is made, the clinician must describe the patient's condition according to each of five axes, or dimensions. Axes I and II make up the mental disorders per se; Axis III lists any physical disorders believed to bear on the mental disorder in question; Axis IV is used to indicate the psychosocial and environmental problems that the person has been experiencing; and Axis V rates the person's current level of adaptive functioning. A multiaxial diagnosis is believed to provide a more multidimensional and useful description of the patient's mental disorder.
- Several general and specific issues must be considered in evaluating the classification of abnormality. An important one is whether the categorical approach of the DSM, as opposed to a dimensional classification system, is best for the field.
- Because recent versions of the DSM are far more concrete and descriptive than was DSM-II, diagnoses based on these versions are more reliable; that is, independent diagnosticians are now likely to agree on the diagnosis they make of a particular case.
- Construct validity—how well the diagnosis relates to other aspects of the disorder, such as prognosis and response to treatment—however, remains more of an open question. In chapters dealing with specific disorders, we will see that validity varies with the diagnostic category being considered.

KEY TERMS

categorical classification (p. 92)
comorbidity (p. 90)
construct validity (p. 95)
Diagnostic and Statistical Manual of Mental Disorders (DSM) (p. 79)
dimensional classification (p. 92)
DSM-IV (p. 79)
DSM-IV-TR (p. 79)
epidemiology (p. 85)
help-seeking (p. 90)
interrater reliability (p. 95)
lifetime prevalence (p. 88)
mental disorder (p. 80)
multiaxial classification (p. 80)
pathological gambling (p. 85)
prevalence (p. 85)
reliability (p. 95)

Reflections: Past, Present, and Future

- How does the current DSM definition of mental disorder (and the exclusion criteria) compare and contrast with our discussion of definitional considerations in Chapter 1? How does the DSM definition compare with your own implicit or explicit definition?
- What is your own position on issues of classification and diagnosis of psychological disorders? Is the DSM-IV-TR really a major improvement over past versions? Will it lead to more effective and efficient treatment?
- How would you refine and improve upon the DSM-IV-TR? Would you propose additional axes for further study?
- In reaction to critics of the participation process in the development of the DSM, including P. Caplan (e.g., 1995), Sadler (in press) proposed that final decisions should be based on a democratic voting process. Would you agree? Could a scientifically valid decision be "politically incorrect" and thereby voted against?
- Although DSM-IV-TR is more culturally sensitive than previous versions, Draguns (1996) suggested that an axis that specifies the influence of cultural factors on a person's clinical condition should be included in future revisions to the DSM. Do you agree? What role can cultural diversity play in the assessment and treatment process?
- In the next chapter, we will examine clinical assessment procedures. Sometimes assessment is used to facilitate decisions about diagnosis or differential diagnosis. What other assessment questions would you propose? Are answers to these questions necessary for the development of comprehensive, multifaceted treatment or intervention plans?

chapter 4

Clinical Assessment Procedures

"The one thing psychologists can count on is that their subjects will talk, if only to themselves; and not infrequently whether relevant or irrelevant, the things people say to themselves determine the rest of the things they do."
— I. E. Farber, *The Things People Say to Themselves*

"Every man has reminiscences which he would not tell to everyone, but only to his friends. He has other matters in his mind which he would not reveal even to his friends, but only to himself, and that in secret. But there are other things which a man is afraid to tell even to himself, and every decent man has a number of such things stored away in his mind."
— Fyodor Dostoevsky, *Notes from Underground*

Renée Van Halm, *Upon Awakening She Becomes Aware*, 1983
acrylic on canvas mounted on wood; plaster, 249 x 318 cm
ART GALLERY OF ONTARIO, TORONTO

This book began with an account of a police officer, J. Brett Barkley, who had bipolar disorder as well as drinking and marital problems, and the preceding chapter included a diagnosis of his condition. Yet a DSM diagnosis is only a starting point. Many other questions remain to be answered. Why does J. Brett Barkley behave as he does? Do his mood swings and violent outbursts constitute a true disorder? Why does he doubt his wife's love for him? What can be done to resolve his marital conflicts? Is his difficulty maintaining an erection caused by physical or psychological factors or both? Has he performed up to his intellectual potential in school and in his career? What type of treatment would be helpful to him? What obstacles might interfere with treatment? Can his marriage be saved? Should it be saved? These are the types of questions that mental health professionals address before therapy begins and as it unfolds, and a clinical assessment helps them find answers.

All clinical assessment procedures are more or less formal ways of finding out what is wrong with a person, what may have caused a problem or problems, and what steps may be taken to improve the individual's condition. Some of these procedures are also used to evaluate the effects of therapeutic interventions.

In this chapter, we describe and discuss the most widely used psychological and biological assessment techniques—and some that are still in the early development phase. We also discuss a sometimes neglected aspect of assessment, the role of cultural diversity and clinician bias. The numerous linguistic minorities in Canada make this an especially important issue. We begin our discussion with two concepts that play a key role in assessment: reliability and validity.

RELIABILITY AND VALIDITY IN ASSESSMENT

The concepts of reliability and validity are extremely complex. There are several kinds of each, and an entire subfield of psychology—psychometrics—exists primarily for their study. We provide here a general overview that supplements our brief discussion in Chapter 3.

Reliability is an essential property of all assessment procedures. One means of determining reliability is to find if different judges agree, as happens when the court decides a case.

RELIABILITY

In the most general sense, reliability refers to consistency of measurement. There are several types of reliability, some of which we discuss here.

- **Interrater reliability**, discussed in the preceding chapter, refers to the degree to which two independent observers or judges agree. To take an example from baseball, the third-base umpire may or may not agree with the home-plate umpire as to whether a line drive down the left-field line is fair or foul.
- **Test-retest reliability** measures the extent to which people being observed twice or taking the same test twice, perhaps several weeks or months apart, score in generally the same way. This kind of reliability makes sense only when the theory assumes that people will not change appreciably between testings on the variable being measured; a prime example of a situation in which this type of reliability makes sense is in evaluating intelligence tests.
- Sometimes psychologists use two forms of a test rather than giving the same test twice, perhaps when there is concern that people will remember their answers from the first test and aim merely to be consistent. This approach enables the tester to determine **alternate-form reliability**, the extent to which scores on the two forms of the test are consistent.
- Finally, **internal consistency reliability** assesses whether the items on a test are related to one another. For example, with an anxiety questionnaire containing twenty items we would expect the items to be interrelated, or to correlate

with one another, if they truly tap anxiety. A person who reports a dry mouth in a threatening situation would be expected to report increases in muscle tension as well.

In each of these types of reliability, a correlation, a measure of how closely two variables are related, is calculated between raters or sets of items. The higher the correlation, the better the reliability.

VALIDITY

Validity is generally related to whether a measure fulfills its intended purpose. For example, if a questionnaire is intended to measure a person's hostility, does it in fact do so? Before we describe several types of validity, it is important to note that validity is related to reliability—unreliable measures will not have good validity. Because an unreliable measure does not yield consistent results (recall our example about trying to measure with a ruler whose length is constantly changing), an unreliable measure will not relate very strongly to other measures. For example, an unreliable measure of coping is not likely to relate well to how a person adjusts to a stressful life experience.

Content validity refers to whether a measure adequately samples the domain of interest. For example, later in this chapter we will describe an interview that is often used to make an Axis I diagnosis. It has excellent content validity because it contains questions about all the symptoms that are involved in Axis I diagnoses. As another example, refer to a measure of life stress that will be considered in more detail in Chapter 8. It consists of a list of 43 life experiences. Respondents indicate which of these experiences—for example, losing one's job—they have had in some time period, for example, the past year. Content validity is less certain here. After looking over the experiences in Table 8.2, you will likely think of stressors that are not on the list (e.g., the serious illness of someone close to you).

Criterion validity is evaluated by determining whether a measure is associated in an expected way with some other measure (the criterion). Sometimes these relationships may be concurrent (both variables are measured at the same point in time, and the resulting validity is sometimes referred to as *concurrent validity*). For example, we will describe later a measure of the distorted thoughts believed to play an important role in depression. Criterion validity for this test could be established by showing that the test is actually related to depression—that is, depressed people score higher on the test than do nondepressed people. Alternatively, criterion validity can be assessed by evaluating the ability of the measure to predict some other variable that is measured in the future; this kind of criterion validity is often referred to as *predictive validity*. For example, IQ tests were originally developed to predict future school performance. Similarly, a measure of distorted thinking could be used to predict the development of episodes of depression in the future.

Construct validity, discussed in Chapter 3, is relevant when we want to interpret a test as a measure of some characteristic or construct that is not simply defined (Cronbach & Meehl, 1955). A construct is an inferred attribute, such as anxiousness or distorted cognition, that a test is trying to measure. Consider an anxiety-proneness questionnaire as an example. The construct validity question is whether the variation we observe between people on a self-report test of anxiety proneness is really due to individual differences in anxiety proneness. Just because we call our test a measure of anxiety proneness and the items seem to be about the tendency to become anxious ("I find that I become anxious in many situations."), it is not certain that the test is a valid measure of anxiety proneness. People's responses to a questionnaire are determined by more variables than simply the construct being measured. For example, people vary in their willingness to admit to undesirable characteristics such as anxiety proneness; thus, scores on the questionnaire will be partly determined by this characteristic as well as by anxiety proneness itself.

Construct validity is evaluated by looking at a wide variety of data from multiple sources. For example, people diagnosed as having an anxiety disorder and people without such a diagnosis could be compared on their scores on the self-report measure of anxiety proneness. The self-report measure would achieve some construct validity if the people with anxiety disorders scored higher than a control group. Similarly, the self-report measure could be related to other measures thought to suggest anxiety, such as observations of fidgeting, trembling, or excessive sweating. When the self-report measure is associated with the observational one, its construct validity is increased. Studies may also examine change on the self-report measure. For example, if the measure has construct validity, we would expect scores of patients with anxiety disorders to become lower after a course of a therapy that is effective in reducing anxiety.

More broadly, the question of construct validity is related to a particular theory of anxiety proneness. For example, we might hypothesize that a proneness to anxiety is caused by certain childhood experiences. We could then obtain further evidence for the construct validity of our questionnaire by showing that it relates to these childhood experiences. At the same time, we would have also gathered support for our theory of anxiety proneness. Thus, construct validation is an important part of the process of theory testing.

PSYCHOLOGICAL ASSESSMENT

Psychological assessment techniques are designed to determine cognitive, emotional, personality, and behavioural factors in psychopathological functioning. We will see that beyond the basic interview, which is used in various guises almost universally, many of the assessment techniques stem from the paradigms presented in Chapter 2. We discuss here clinical interviews, psychological tests, many of which are psychodynamic in nature, and behavioural and cognitive assessment techniques.

CLINICAL INTERVIEWS

Most of us have probably been interviewed at one time or another, although the conversation may have been so informal that we did not regard it as an interview. To the layperson, the word "interview" connotes a formal, highly structured conversation, but we find it useful to construe the term as any interpersonal encounter, conversational in style, in which one person, the interviewer, uses language as the principal means of finding out about another, the interviewee. Thus, a pollster who asks a college student which candidate he or she will vote for in an upcoming presidential election is interviewing with the restricted goal of learning which candidate the student prefers. A clinical psychologist who asks a patient about the circumstances of his or her most recent hospitalization is similarly conducting an interview.

Characteristics of Clinical Interviews One way in which a clinical interview is perhaps different from a casual conversation and from a poll is the attention the interviewer pays to how the respondent answers—or does not answer—questions. For example, if a client is recounting marital conflicts, the clinician will generally be attentive to any emotion accompanying the comments. If the person does not seem upset about a difficult situation, the answers will probably be understood differently than they would be if the person were crying or agitated while relating the story.

The paradigm within which an interviewer operates influences the type of information sought, how it is obtained, and how it is interpreted. A psychoanalytically trained clinician can be expected to inquire about the person's childhood history. He or she is also likely to remain skeptical of verbal reports because the analytic paradigm holds that the most significant aspects of a disturbed or normal person's developmental history are repressed into the unconscious. Of course, how the data are interpreted is influenced by the paradigm. The behaviourally oriented clinician is likely to focus on current environmental conditions that can be related to changes in the person's behaviour—for example, the circumstances under which the person becomes anxious. Thus, the clinical interview does not follow one prescribed course but varies with the paradigm adopted by the interviewer. Like scientists, clinical interviewers in some measure find only the information for which they are looking.

Great skill is necessary to carry out good clinical interviews, for they are usually conducted with people who are under considerable stress. Clinicians, regardless of their theoretical orientation, recognize the importance of establishing rapport with the client. The interviewer must obtain the trust of the person; it is naive to assume that a client will easily reveal information to another, even to an authority figure with the title "Doctor." Even a client who sincerely, perhaps desperately, wants to recount intensely personal problems to a professional may not be able to do so without assistance. Psychodynamic clinicians assume that people entering therapy usually are not even aware of what is truly bothering them. Behavioural clinicians, although they concentrate more on what can be observed, also appreciate the difficulties people have in sorting out the factors responsible for their distress.

Most clinicians empathize with their clients in an effort to draw them out, to encourage them to elaborate on their concerns, and to examine different facets of a problem. Humanistic therapists employ specific empathy techniques to accomplish these goals. A simple summary statement of what the client has been saying can help sustain the momentum of talk about painful and possibly embarrassing events and feelings, and an accepting attitude toward personal disclosures dispels the fear that revealing "secrets of the heart" (London, 1964) to another human being will have disastrous consequences.

The interview can be a source of considerable information to the clinician. Its importance in abnormal psychology and psychiatry is unquestionable. Whether the information gleaned can always be depended on is not so clear, however. Clinicians often tend to overlook situational factors of the interview that may exert strong influences on what the patient says or does. Consider for a moment how a teenager is likely to respond to the question, "How often have you used illegal drugs?" when it is asked by a young, informally dressed psychologist as opposed to 60-year-old psychologist in a business suit.

Interviews vary in the degree to which they are structured. In practice, most clinicians operate from only the vaguest outlines. Exactly *how* information is collected is left largely up to the particular interviewer and depends, too, on the responsiveness and responses of the interviewee. Through years of clinical experience and both teaching and learning from students and colleagues, each clinician develops ways of asking questions with which he or she is comfortable and that seem to draw out the information that will be of maximum benefit to the client. Thus, to the extent that an interview is unstructured, the interviewer must rely on intuition and general experience. As a consequence, reliability for initial clinical interviews is probably low; that is, two interviewers may well reach different conclusions about the same patient. And because the overwhelming majority of clinical interviews are conducted within confidential relationships, it has not been possible to establish either their reliability or their validity through systematic research.

We need to look at the broader picture here to avoid a judgment that may be too harsh. Both reliability and validity may indeed be low for a single clinical interview that is conducted in an unstructured fashion. But clinicians usually do more than one interview with a given patient, and hence a self-corrective process is probably at work. The clinician may regard as valid what a patient said in the first interview, but then at the sixth recognize it to have been incorrect or only partially correct.

Structured Interviews At times, mental health professionals need to collect standardized information, particularly for making diagnostic judgments based on the DSM. Investigators have developed structured interviews, such as the Structured Clinical Interview Diagnosis (SCID) for Axis I of DSM-IV (Spitzer, Gibbon, & Williams, 1996), which assists researchers and clinicians in making diagnostic decisions. A structured interview is one in which the questions are set out in a prescribed fashion for the interviewer.

The SCID is a branching interview; that is, the client's response to one question determines the next question that is asked. It also contains detailed instructions to the interviewer concerning when and how to probe in detail and when to go on to questions bearing on another diagnosis. Most symptoms are rated on a three-point scale of severity, with instructions in the interview schedule for directly translating the symptom ratings into diagnoses. The initial questions pertaining to obsessive-compulsive disorder (discussed in Chapter 6) are presented in Figure 4.1. The interviewer begins by asking about obsessions. If the responses elicit a rating of 1 (absent), the interviewer turns to questions about compulsions. If the patient's responses again elicit a rating of 1, the interviewer is instructed to proceed to questions for posttraumatic stress disorder. On the other hand, if positive responses (two or three) are elicited about obsessive-compulsive disorder, the interviewer continues with further questions about that problem. The use of structured interviews such as the SCID is a major factor in the improvement of diagnostic reliability that we described in Chapter 3.

Structured interviews have also been developed for diagnosing personality disorders and more specific disorders, such as the anxiety disorders (DiNardo et al., 1993). With adequate training of clinicians, interrater reliability for structured interviews is generally good (Blanchard & Brown, 1998).

PSYCHOLOGICAL TESTS

Psychological tests are standardized procedures designed to measure a person's performance on a particular task or to assess his or her personality. If the results of a diagnostic interview are inconclusive, psychological tests can provide information that can be used in a supplementary way to arrive at a diagnosis. For example, a patient with schizophrenia may be very guarded during an interview and choose not to reveal information regarding delusional beliefs. Psychological tests may alert the clinician to the possible presence of schizophrenia. These tests also yield important information in their own right, such as personality characteristics or situational determinants of a person's problems.

Psychological tests further structure the process of assessment. The same test is administered to many people at different times, and the responses are analyzed to indicate how certain kinds of people tend to respond. Statistical norms for the test can thereby be established as soon as sufficient data have been collected. This process is called standardization. The responses of a particular person can then be compared with the statistical norms. We will examine the three basic types of psychological tests: self-report personality inventories, projective personality tests, and tests of intelligence.

Personality Inventories In a personality inventory, the person is asked to complete a self-report questionnaire indicating whether statements assessing habitual tendencies apply to him or her. The best-known and most frequently used and researched psychological test in the United States (see Butcher, Nezami, & Exner, 1999) is the Minnesota Multiphasic Personality Inventory (MMPI). The MMPI was developed in the early 1940s by Hathaway and McKinley (1943) and revised in 1989 (Butcher et al., 1989). Intended to serve as an inexpensive means of detecting psychopathology, the MMPI is called *multiphasic* because it was designed to detect a number of psychological problems. The MMPI has been widely used to screen large groups of people for whom clinical interviews are not feasible.

In developing the test, the investigators relied on factual information. First, many clinicians provided statements that they considered indicative of various mental problems. Second, these items were rated as self-descriptive or not by patients already diagnosed as having particular disorders and by a large group of individuals considered normal. Items that "discriminated" among the patients were retained; that is, items were selected if patients in one clinical group responded to them more often in a certain way than did those in other groups.

With additional refinements, sets of these items were established as scales for determining whether a respondent should be diagnosed in a particular way. If an individual answered a large number of the items in a scale in the same way as had a certain diagnostic group, his or her behaviour was expected to resemble that of the particular diagnostic group. The 10 scales are described in Table 4.1.

The revised MMPI-2 (Butcher et al., 1989) has several noteworthy changes designed to improve its validity and acceptability. The original sample of 60 years ago lacked representation of racial minorities, including African Americans and Native Americans; its standardization sample was restricted to white men and women—essentially to Minnesotans.

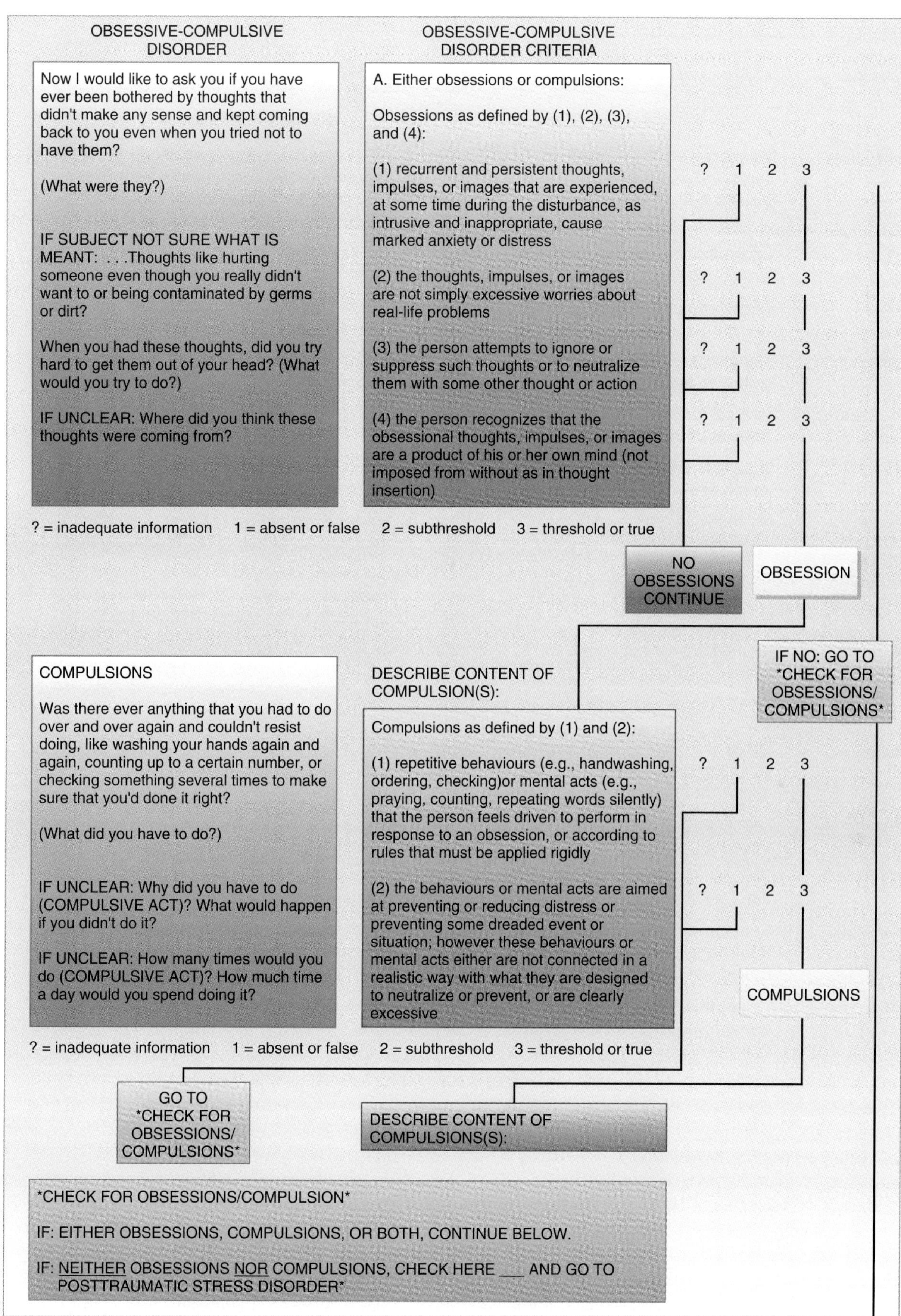
OBSESSIVE-COMPULSIVE DISORDER

Now I would like to ask you if you have ever been bothered by thoughts that didn't make any sense and kept coming back to you even when you tried not to have them?

(What were they?)

IF SUBJECT NOT SURE WHAT IS MEANT: . . .Thoughts like hurting someone even though you really didn't want to or being contaminated by germs or dirt?

When you had these thoughts, did you try hard to get them out of your head? (What would you try to do?)

IF UNCLEAR: Where did you think these thoughts were coming from?

OBSESSIVE-COMPULSIVE DISORDER CRITERIA

A. Either obsessions or compulsions:

Obsessions as defined by (1), (2), (3), and (4):

(1) recurrent and persistent thoughts, impulses, or images that are experienced, at some time during the disturbance, as intrusive and inappropriate, cause marked anxiety or distress — ? 1 2 3

(2) the thoughts, impulses, or images are not simply excessive worries about real-life problems — ? 1 2 3

(3) the person attempts to ignore or suppress such thoughts or to neutralize them with some other thought or action — ? 1 2 3

(4) the person recognizes that the obsessional thoughts, impulses, or images are a product of his or her own mind (not imposed from without as in thought insertion) — ? 1 2 3

? = inadequate information 1 = absent or false 2 = subthreshold 3 = threshold or true

NO OBSESSIONS CONTINUE

OBSESSION

IF NO: GO TO *CHECK FOR OBSESSIONS/ COMPULSIONS*

COMPULSIONS

Was there ever anything that you had to do over and over again and couldn't resist doing, like washing your hands again and again, counting up to a certain number, or checking something several times to make sure that you'd done it right?

(What did you have to do?)

IF UNCLEAR: Why did you have to do (COMPULSIVE ACT)? What would happen if you didn't do it?

IF UNCLEAR: How many times would you do (COMPULSIVE ACT)? How much time a day would you spend doing it?

DESCRIBE CONTENT OF COMPULSION(S):

Compulsions as defined by (1) and (2):

(1) repetitive behaviours (e.g., handwashing, ordering, checking)or mental acts (e.g., praying, counting, repeating words silently) that the person feels driven to perform in response to an obsession, or according to rules that must be applied rigidly — ? 1 2 3

(2) the behaviours or mental acts are aimed at preventing or reducing distress or preventing some dreaded event or situation; however these behaviours or mental acts either are not connected in a realistic way with what they are designed to neutralize or prevent, or are clearly excessive — ? 1 2 3

COMPULSIONS

? = inadequate information 1 = absent or false 2 = subthreshold 3 = threshold or true

GO TO *CHECK FOR OBSESSIONS/ COMPULSIONS*

DESCRIBE CONTENT OF COMPULSIONS(S):

CHECK FOR OBSESSIONS/COMPULSION

IF: EITHER OBSESSIONS, COMPULSIONS, OR BOTH, CONTINUE BELOW.

IF: NEITHER OBSESSIONS NOR COMPULSIONS, CHECK HERE ___ AND GO TO POSTTRAUMATIC STRESS DISORDER*

Figure 4.1 Sample item from the SCID. Reprinted by permission of New York State Psychiatric Institute Biometrics Research Division. Copyright © 1996 by the Board of Trustees of the Leland Stanford Junior University. Reprinted by permission of Stanford University Press.

Table 4.1

Typical Clinical Interpretations of Items Similar to Those on the MMPI-2

Scale	Sample Item	Interpretation
? (cannot say)	This is merely the number of items left unanswered or marked both true and false.	A high score indicates evasiveness, reading difficulties, or other problems that could invalidate the results of the test. A very high score could also suggest severe depression or obsessional tendencies.
L (Lie)	I approve of every person I meet. (True)	Person is trying to look good, to present self as someone with an ideal personality.
F (Infrequency)	Everything tastes sweet. (True)	Person is trying to look abnormal, perhaps to ensure getting special attention from the clinician.
K (Correction)	Things couldn't be going any better for me. (True)	Person is guarded, defensive in taking test, wishes to avoid appearing incompetent or poorly adjusted.
1. Hs (Hypochondriasis)	I am seldom aware of tingling feelings in my body. (False)	Person is overly sensitive to and concerned about bodily sensations as signs of possible physical illness.
2. D (Depression)	Life usually feels worthwhile to me. (False)	Person is discouraged, pessimistic, sad, self-deprecating, feeling inadequate.
3. Hy (Hysteria)	My muscles often twitch for no apparent reason. (True)	Person has somatic complaints unlikely to be due to physical problems; also tends to be demanding and histrionic.
4. Pd (Psychopathy)	I don't care about what people think of me. (True)	Person expresses little concern for social mores, is irresponsible, has only superficial relationships.
5. Mf (Masculinity –Femininity)	I like taking care of plants and flowers. (True, female)	Person shows non-traditional gender characteristics, e.g., men with high scores tend to be artistic and sensitive; women with high scores tend to be rebellious and assertive.
6. Pa (Paranoia)	If they were not afraid of being caught, most people would lie and cheat. (True)	Person tends to misinterpret the motives of others, is suspicious and jealous, vengeful and brooding.
7. Pt (Psychasthenia)	I am not as competent as most other people I know. (True)	Person is overanxious, full of self-doubts, moralistic, and generally obsessive-compulsive.
8. Sc (Schizophrenia)	I sometimes smell things others don't sense. (True)	Person has bizarre sensory experiences and beliefs, is socially seclusive.
9. Ma (Hypomania)	Sometimes I have a strong impulse to do something that others will find appalling. (True)	Person has overly ambitious aspirations and can be hyperactive, impatient, and irritable
10. Si (Social Introversion)	Rather than spend time alone, I prefer to be around other people. (False)	Person is very modest and shy, preferring solitary . activities.

Note: The first four scales assess the validity of the test; the numbered scales are the clinical or content scales.
Source: Hathaway and McKinley (1943); revised by Butcher et al. (1989).

The new version was standardized using a sample that was much larger and more representative of 1980 U.S. census figures. Several items containing allusions to sexual adjustment, bowel and bladder functions, and excessive religiosity were removed because they were judged in some testing contexts to be needlessly intrusive and objectionable. Sexist wording was eliminated, along with outmoded idioms. Several new scales deal with substance abuse, Type A behaviour, and marital problems.

Aside from these differences, MMPI-2 is quite similar to the original, having the same format, yielding the same scale scores and profiles (Ben-Porath & Butcher, 1989; Graham, 1988), and providing continuity with the vast literature already existing on the original MMPI (Graham, 1990). Items similar to those on the various scales are presented in Table 4.1. The extensive research literature shows that the MMPI is reliable and has adequate criterion validity when it is related to ratings made by spouses or clinicians (Graham, 1988).

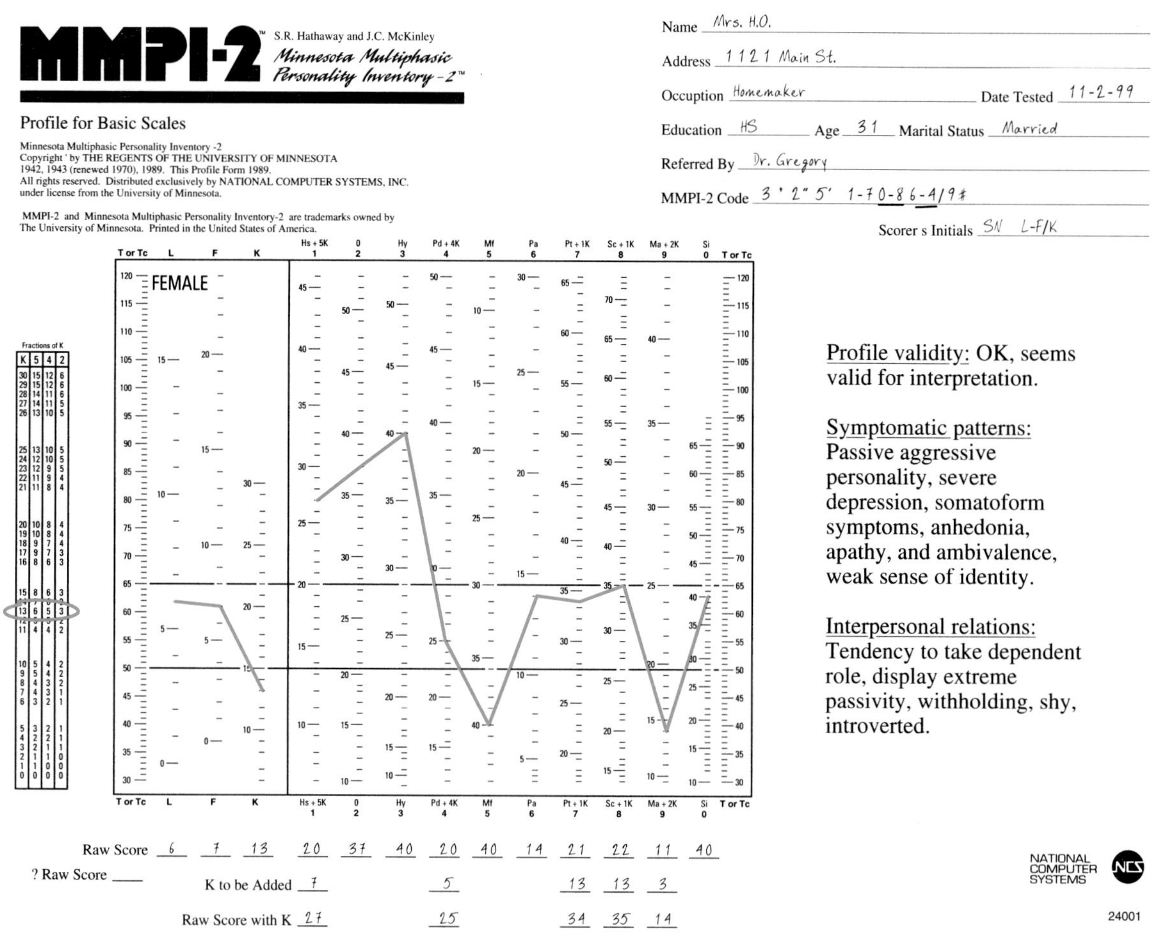

Figure 4.2 Hypothetical MMPI-2 profile.

Like many other personality inventories, the MMPI can now be administered by computer, and there are several commercial MMPI services that score the test and provide narratives about the respondent. Of course, the validity and usefulness of the printouts are only as good as the program, which in turn is only as good as the competency and experience of the psychologist who wrote it. Figure 4.2 shows a hypothetical profile. Such profiles can be used in conjunction with a therapist's evaluation to help diagnose a client, assess personality functioning and coping style, and identify likely obstacles to treatment.

We may well wonder whether answers that would designate a person as normal might not be easy to fake. A superficial knowledge of contemporary abnormal psychology, for example, would alert even a seriously disturbed person that in order to be regarded as normal, he or she must not admit to worrying a great deal about germs on doorknobs. There is evidence that these tests *can* be "psyched out." In most testing circumstances, however, people do not want to falsify their responses, for they *want* to be helped.

Moreover, as shown in Table 4.1, the test designers have included as part of the MMPI several so-called validity scales designed to detect deliberately faked responses. In one of these, the lie scale, a series of statements sets a trap for the person who is trying to look too good. An item on the lie scale might be, "I read the newspaper editorials every night." The assumption is that few people would be able to endorse such a statement honestly. Individuals who endorse a large number of the statements in the lie scale might well be attempting to present themselves in a particularly good light. Their scores on other scales are generally viewed with more than the usual skepticism. Being aware of these validity scales, however, does allow people to effectively fake a normal profile (Baer & Sekirnjak, 1997).

Projective Personality Tests A projective test is a psychological assessment device in which a set of standard stimuli—inkblots or drawings—ambiguous enough to allow variation in responses is presented to the individual. The assumption is that because the stimulus materials are unstructured, the patient's responses will be determined primarily by unconscious processes and will reveal his or her true attitudes, motivations, and modes of behaviour. This notion is referred to as the projective hypothesis. If a patient reports seeing eyes in an ambiguous inkblot, for example, the projective hypothesis might be that the patient tends toward paranoia.

The Rorschach Inkblot Test is perhaps the best-known projective technique. In the Rorschach test, a person is shown 10 inkblots, one at a time, and asked to tell what figures or objects he or she sees in each of them. Half the

During a ride in the country with his two children, Hermann Rorschach (1884–1922), a Swiss psychiatrist, noticed that what they saw in the clouds reflected their personalities. From this observation came the famous inkblot test.

inkblots are in black, white, and shades of grey, two also have red splotches, and three are in pastel colours.

The Thematic Apperception Test (TAT) is another well-known projective test. In this test, a person is shown a series of black-and-white pictures one by one and asked to tell a story related to each. For example, a patient seeing a picture of a prepubescent girl looking at fashionably attired mannequins in a store window may tell a story that contains angry references to the girl's parents. The clinician may, through the projective hypothesis, infer that the patient harbours resentment toward his or her parents.

As you might guess, projective techniques are derived from the psychoanalytic paradigm. The use of projective tests assumes that the respondent would be either unable or unwilling to express his or her true feelings if asked directly. Psychoanalytically oriented clinicians often favour such tests, a tendency consistent with the psychoanalytic assumption that people protect themselves from unpleasant thoughts and feelings by repressing them into the unconscious. Thus, the real purposes of a test are best left unclear so as to bypass the defence mechanism of repression and get to the basic causes of distress.

Our discussion of projective tests has focused on how they were conceptualized and used originally—as a stimulus to fantasy that was assumed to bypass ego defences. The content of the person's responses was viewed as *symbolic* of internal dynamics; for example, a man might be judged to have homosexual interests on the basis of his seeing buttocks in the Rorschach inkblots (Chapman & Chapman, 1969).

Other uses of the Rorschach test, however, concentrate more on the *form* of the person's responses (Exner, 1978). The test is considered more as a perceptual-cognitive task, and the person's responses are viewed as a sample of how he or she perceptually and cognitively organizes real-life situations (Exner, 1986). Erdberg and Exner (1984), for example, concluded from the research literature that respondents who see a great deal of human movement in the Rorschach inkblots (e.g., "The man is running to catch a plane") tend to use inner resources when coping with their needs, whereas those whose Rorschach responses involve colour ("The red spot is a kidney") are more likely to seek interaction with the environment. Rorschach suggested this approach in his original manual, *Psychodiagnostics: A Diagnostic Test Based on Perception* (1921), but he died only eight months after publishing his 10 inkblots and his immediate followers devised other methods of interpreting the test.

Though many, perhaps most, clinical practitioners still rely on the projective hypothesis in analyzing Rorschach responses, academic researchers have been paying a good deal of attention to Exner's work. Regarding its reliability and validity, this work has enthusiastic supporters as well as harsh critics (e.g., Garb, Florio, & Grove, 1998; Hunsley & Bailey, 1999, 2001; Wood, Nezworski, & Stejskal, 1997). Attempting to make a blanket statement about the validity of the Exner system for scoring the Rorschach is perhaps not the right approach, for the system may have more validity in some cases than in others. It appears, for instance, to have considerable validity in identifying people with schizophrenia or at risk of developing schizophrenia (Viglione, 1999). The utility of the Rorschach in this case can most likely be attributed to the fact that a person's responses on the test are highly related to the communication disturbances that are an important symptom of schizophrenia. However, as argued by Hunsley and Bailey (2001), even in this case it is possible that the information provided by the Rorschach could have been obtained more simply and directly through, for example, an interview.

The Roberts Apperception Test for Children (Roberts, 1982) illustrates how the use of projective tests has evolved to provide more standardized, objectively scored assessment tools. In this test, much as in the Thematic Apperception Test, pictures of children and families are presented to the child, who tells a story about each one. Whereas many scoring approaches to the TAT are impressionistic and nonstandardized, the Roberts test provides objective criteria for scoring, along with normative data to determine whether the child's pattern of responses is abnormal. Unique to this test are the scales that provide information about a child's coping skills. For example, the response "The boy asked his mother for help with his homework, and she helped him get started on his story" would be scored for both "Reliance on Others" and "Support from Others."

Intelligence Tests Alfred Binet, a French psychologist, originally constructed mental tests to help the Parisian school board predict which children were in need of special schooling. Intelligence testing has since developed into one of the largest psychological industries. An **intelligence test**, often referred as an IQ test, is a standardized means of assessing a person's current mental ability. Individually administered tests, such as the Wechsler Adult Intelligence Scale (WAIS), the Wechsler Intelligence Scale for Children (WISC), and the Stanford-Binet are all based on the assumption that a detailed sample of an individual's current intellectual functioning can predict how well he or she will perform in school. Intelligence tests are also used:

- in conjunction with achievement tests, to diagnose learning disabilities and to identify areas of strengths and weaknesses for academic planning;
- to help determine whether a person is mentally retarded;
- to identify intellectually gifted children so that appropriate instruction can be provided them in school; and
- as part of neuropsychological evaluations—for example, the periodic testing of a person believed to be suffering from a degenerative dementia so that deterioration of mental ability can be followed over time.

The French psychologist Alfred Binet developed the first IQ test to predict how well children would do in school.

IQ tests tap several functions asserted to constitute intelligence, including language skills, abstract thinking, nonverbal reasoning, visual-spatial skills, attention and concentration, and speed of processing. Scores on most IQ tests are standardized so that 100 is the mean and 15 or 16 is the standard deviation (a measure of how scores are dispersed above and below the average). Approximately 65 percent of the population receives scores between 85 and 115. Those with a score below 70 are two standard deviations below the mean of the population and are considered to have "significant subaverage general intellectual functioning." Those with scores above 130 (two standard deviations above the mean) are considered "intellectually gifted." Approximately 2.5 percent of the population falls at each of these extremes. In Chapter 15, we discuss people whose IQ falls at the low end of the distribution.

IQ tests are highly reliable (e.g., Carnivez & Walkins, 1998) and have good criterion validity. For example, they distinguish between individuals who are intellectually gifted and individuals with mental retardation and between people with different occupations or levels of educational attainment (Reynolds et al., 1997). They also predict later educational attainment and occupational success (Barody, 1985; Terman & Oldham, 1959).

Regarding construct validity, it is important to keep in mind that IQ tests measure only what psychologists consider intelligence. The tasks and items on IQ tests were, after all, invented by psychologists. In addition, factors other than what we think of as pure intelligence play an important role in how people will do in school, such as family and personal circumstances, motivation to do well, and difficulty of the curriculum. Though the correlations between IQ scores and school performance are statistically significant, IQ tests explain only a small part of the differences in people's school performance; much more is unexplained by IQ test scores than is explained.

Interest has recently focused on "emotional intelligence," reflected in such abilities as delaying gratification and being sensitive to the needs of others (Goleman, 1995). This aspect of human functioning may be as important to future success as the strictly intellectual achievements measured by traditional IQ tests. Research conducted in Canada and elsewhere indicates that emotional intelligence may also be an important protective factor in terms of levels of adjustment. High levels of emotional intelligence are associated negatively with alexithymia (see Parker, Taylor, & Bagby, 2001; Saklofske, Austin, & Minski, 2003), a condition of reduced emotional awareness that is a risk factor for a variety of adjustment problems. Moreover, high levels of emotional intelligence are associated with greater levels of subjective well-being and reduced proneness to depression (Saklofske et al., 2003).

BEHAVIOURAL AND COGNITIVE ASSESSMENT

Traditional assessment concentrates on measuring underlying personality structures and traits, such as obsessiveness, paranoia, coldness, aggressiveness, and so on. Behavioural and cognitively oriented clinicians, on the other hand, often use a system that involves the assessment of four sets of variables, sometimes referred to by the acronym SORC (Kanfer & Phillips, 1970).

- *S* stands for stimuli, the environmental situations that precede the problem. For instance, the clinician will try to ascertain which situations tend to elicit anxiety.

- *O* stands for organismic, referring to both physiological and psychological factors assumed to be operating "under the skin." Perhaps the client's fatigue is caused in part by excessive use of alcohol or by a cognitive tendency toward self-deprecation manifested in such statements as "I never do anything right, so what's the point in trying?"
- *R* refers to overt responses. These probably receive the most attention from behavioural clinicians, who must determine what behaviour is problematic, as well as the behaviour's frequency, intensity, and form. For example, a client might say that he or she is forgetful and procrastinates. Does the person mean that he or she does not return phone calls, arrives late for appointments, or both?
- Finally, *C* refers to consequent variables, events that appear to be reinforcing or punishing the behaviour in question. When the client avoids a feared situation, does his or her spouse offer sympathy and excuses, thereby unwittingly keeping the person from facing up to his or her fears?

A behaviourally oriented clinician attempts to specify SORC factors for a particular client. As might be expected, *O* variables are underplayed by Skinnerians, who focus more on observable stimuli and responses, and *C* variables receive less attention from cognitively oriented behaviour therapists than do *O* variables because these therapists' paradigm does not emphasize reinforcement.

Several alternative approaches to individual **cognitive-behavioural case formulation** have also been described by cognitive and cognitive-behaviour therapists (e.g., Meichenbaum, 1994; Persons & Tompkins, 1997). These approaches place considerably more emphasis on cognitive events such as people's distorted thinking patterns, negative self-instructions, irrational automatic thoughts and beliefs, and schemas. The strategy used by Jacqueline Persons and her colleagues is summarized in Focus on Discovery 4.1.

focus on discovery/4.1

Cognitive-Behavioural Case Formulation

Persons and her colleagues (e.g., Persons, 1992, 1993; Persons & Davidson, 2001; Persons & Tompkins, 1997) have described an approach that formulates an individualized cognitive-behavioural "theory" about a particular case with a view to helping a therapist develop an effective and efficient plan for treatment. The formulation is, of course, based on a general cognitive-behavioural theory (e.g., Beck's cognitive theory of psychological disorders). A key purpose of the formulation is to explain how a client's problems relate to one another in order to help the therapist select treatment "targets," since it is usually appropriate to first focus on problems that seem to play a causal role in other problems (e.g., depression causes marital problems, which contribute to behaviour problems in a child).

Different formulations imply different intervention strategies. Persons and Davidson (2001) described the case of a person complaining of severe fatigue. Two formulations appeared possible—abuse of sleep medication or negative thinking in reaction to a stressor. Either one of them could explain the fatigue, and each would lead to different treatments. As Persons and Davidson (2001, p. 89) noted, "All formulations are considered hypotheses, and the therapist is constantly revising and sharpening the formulations as the therapy proceeds."

Persons and Davidson (2001) use the case of "Judy," a 35-year-old single woman who lived alone and worked as a teacher, to illustrate the five components of their approach: problem list, diagnosis, working hypothesis, strengths and assets, and treatment plan.

Problem List A problem list includes difficulties the client is having in various domains—psychological, interpersonal, occupational, medical, financial, housing, legal, and leisure. A comprehensive list helps ensure that significant problems are not missed and facilitates the search for themes and speculation about causal relations. Psychological problems, in particular, are described in terms of cognitive, behavioural, and mood components (consistent with Beck's cognitive theory). Judy's problem list included the following: depressed, dissatisfied, passive; disorganized, unfocused, and unproductive; job dissatisfaction; social isolation; no relationship; and unassertive.

Diagnosis Although a psychiatric diagnosis is not a required part of cognitive-behavioural case formulations, Persons and Davidson include it because a diagnosis can lead to initial hypotheses about how to formulate the case and provide information about possible interventions. Judy received an Axis I diagnosis of DSM-IV dysthymic disorder (i.e., persistent and chronic depression that is milder in intensity than the depression in major depressive disorders). Although there was no Axis II or III diagnosis or information, Judy was described as socially isolated and as having occupational problems on Axis IV. Her GAF score on Axis V was 60, indicating some mild symptoms or difficulties in social or occupational functioning.

Working Hypothesis The working hypothesis is the "heart" of Persons and Davidson's formulation. The mini-theory of the case develops through adaptation of a general theory and describes relations among the problems. For example, according to Beck's theory, stressful events activate schemas (core beliefs) to produce problems and symptoms. Therefore, the working hypothesis would describe the hypotheses about the negative schemas (e.g., beliefs about self, others, world, and future) that appear to cause the problems, external precipitants (e.g., a poor work evaluation) or activating situations (e.g., attending meetings with the boss) that activate internal structures (schemas), and origins, or historical incidents or circumstances, that contributed to the development of the schemas or functional relationships among the problems. In a summary of the working hypothesis, the clinician "tells a story" that describes the relations among the components of the working hypothesis and integrates them with the problems on the list. Persons and Davidson (2001, p. 97) summarized Judy's working hypothesis as follows:

> When she was faced with taking actions to further her goals, her schemata that she was incapable and damaged were activated. She had learned from her mother's passive behaviours and from her father's abusive ones that she was damaged and incapable of taking action. When these schemata were activated, she became passive and inactive, with the result that she did not achieve her goals and felt dissatisfied and discouraged. This pattern occurred repeatedly in both work and social situations, and led to the difficulties she experienced in both those settings.

Figure 4.2 illustrates this "working hypothesis" for Judy in the form of a flow chart.

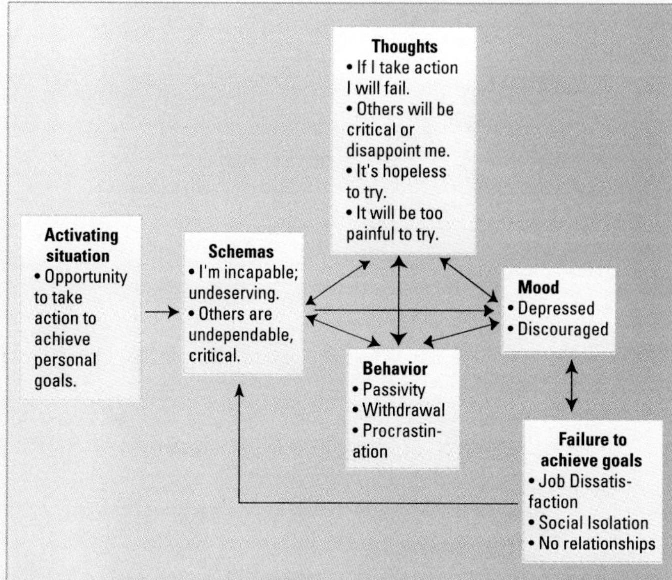

Figure 4.2 The working hypothesis for the client "Judy." From Persons and Davidson, "Cognitive-Behavioural Case Formulation," *Handbook of cognitive-behavioural therapies*, Guilford Press, 2001.

Strengths and Assets Information about strengths and assets (e.g., social skills, sense of humour, financial resources, social support, stable lifestyle, etc.) can help the therapist to develop the working hypothesis, can enhance the treatment plan, and can assist in the determination of realistic treatment goals. Judy had several strengths and assets, including a stable lifestyle, intelligence, excellent social skills, and a strong support network.

Treatment Plan According to Persons and Davidson, the treatment plan is based directly on the cognitive-behavioural case formulation and has six components: goals, modality, frequency, initial interventions, adjunct therapies, and obstacles. The "goals" and "obstacles" components are especially crucial. Judy's treatment plan had six goals, including the reduction of dysphoria and procrastination, an improvement in her ability to prioritize and organize, finding a more satisfying job, spending more time with friends, beginning to date in order to find a partner, and being more assertive. Obstacles to treatment included her procrastination, unassertiveness, and belief that she cannot be successful.

The clinical uses of the case formulation are multiple. In Judy's case, Persons and Davidson noted that it helped clarify treatment goals, helped the therapist to maintain a "clear focus" and address multiple problems, facilitated the client's taking an active and collaborative role, and assisted the therapist to cope with negative emotional reactions to working with the client. Of course, if the treatment plan based on the case formulation does not work, it is probably necessary to revise the formulation and the treatment plan.

Do you believe that individual cognitive-behavioural therapy is appropriate in Judy's case, and if so, how often should she meet with her therapist? What initial interventions would you propose? Under what circumstances would you employ adjunct treatments, such as pharmacotherapy?

The information necessary for a behavioural or cognitive assessment is gathered by several methods, including direct observation of behaviour in real life as well as in contrived settings, interviews and self-report measures, and various other methods of cognitive assessment (Bellack & Hersen, 1998; Blankstein &

Direct Observation of Behaviour It is not surprising that behaviour therapists have paid considerable attention to careful observation of overt behaviour in a variety of settings, but it should not be assumed that they simply go out and *observe*. Like other scientists, they try to fit events into a framework consistent with their points of view. The following excerpt from a case report by Gerald Patterson and his colleagues (1969), describing an interaction between a boy named Kevin and his mother, father, and sister Freida, serves as the first part of an example.

> Kevin goes up to father's chair and stands alongside it. Father puts his arms around Kevin's shoulders. Kevin says to mother as Freida looks at Kevin, "Can I go out and play after supper?" Mother does not reply. Kevin raises his voice and repeats the question. Mother says, "You don't have to yell; I can hear you." Father says, "How many times have I told you not to yell at your mother?" Kevin scratches a bruise on his arm while mother tells Freida to get started on the dishes, which Freida does. Kevin continues

to rub and scratch his arm while mother and daughter are working at the kitchen sink. (p. 21)

Behavioural assessment often involves direct observation of behaviour, as in this case, where the observer is behind a one-way mirror.

This informal description could probably be provided by any observer. But in formal behavioural observation, the observer divides the uninterrupted sequence of behaviour into various parts and applies terms that make sense within a learning framework.

> Kevin begins the exchange by asking a routine question in a normal tone of voice. This ordinary behaviour, however, is not reinforced by the mother's attention; for she does not reply. Because she does not reply, the normal behaviour of Kevin ceases and he yells his question. The mother expresses disapproval—punishing her son—by telling him that he does not have to yell. And this punishment is supported by the father's reminding Kevin that he should not yell at his mother.

This behavioural rendition acknowledges the consequences of ignoring a child's question. At some point, the behaviour therapist will undoubtedly advise the parents to attend to Kevin's requests when expressed in an ordinary tone of voice, lest he begin yelling. This example indicates an important aspect of behavioural assessment, its link to *intervention* (O'Brien & Hayes, 1995). The behavioural clinician's way of conceptualizing a situation typically implies a way to try to change it.

It is difficult to observe most behaviour as it actually takes place, and little control can be exercised over where and when it may occur. For this reason, many therapists contrive artificial situations in their consulting rooms or in a laboratory so that they can observe how a client or a family acts under certain conditions. For example, Barkley (1981) had a mother and her hyperactive child spend time together in a laboratory living room, complete with sofas and television set. The mother was given a list of tasks for the child to complete, such as picking up toys or doing arithmetic problems. Observers behind a one-way mirror watched the proceedings and reliably coded the child's reactions to the mother's efforts to control as well as the mother's reactions to the child's compliant or noncompliant responses. These behavioural assessment procedures yielded data that could be used to measure the effects of treatment.

Most of the research of the kind just described was conducted within an operant framework, employing no inferential concepts. But observational techniques can also be applied within a framework that makes use of mediators. Gordon Paul (1966) was interested in assessing the anxiety of public speakers. He decided to count the frequency of behaviours indicative of this emotional state. One of his principal measures was the Timed Behavioural Checklist for Performance Anxiety. Participants were asked to deliver a speech before a group. Some members of the group had been trained to reliably rate the participant's behaviour every 30 seconds and to record the presence or absence of 20 specific behaviours. By summing the scores, Paul arrived at a behavioural index of anxiety. This study provides one example of how observations of overt behaviour have been used to infer the presence of an internal state.

Self-Observation In Paul's study, people other than the public speaker made the observations. For many years, behaviour therapists and researchers have also asked individuals to observe their own behaviour and to keep track of various categories of response. This approach is called self-monitoring. Self-monitoring has been used to collect a wide variety of data of interest to both clinicians and researchers, including moods, stressful experiences, coping behaviours, and thoughts (Hurlburt, 1979; Stone et al., 1998).

Self-observation has also been referred to as ecological momentary assessment, or EMA (Stone & Shiffman, 1994). EMA involves the collection of data in real time as opposed to the more usual methods of having people reflect back over some time period and report on recently experienced thoughts, moods, or stressors. The methods for implementing EMA range from having people complete diaries at specified times during the day (perhaps signalled by a wristwatch that beeps at those times) to supplying them with palm-top computers that not only signal when reports are to be made but also allow them to enter their responses directly into the computer (Stone & Shiffman, 1994).

The main reason for using EMA is that the retrospective recall of moods, thoughts, or experiences may be inaccurate. Consider, for example, how difficult it would be for you to recall accurately the exact thoughts you had when you encountered a stressor. Memory researchers have shown not only that simple forgetting leads to inaccurate retrospective recall, but also that recalled information can be biased. For example, a report of a person's mood for a whole day is overly influenced by moods the person has experienced most recently (Strongman & Russell, 1986).

Given these problems in retrospective recall, some theories in the field of abnormal psychology almost demand the use of EMA. For example, current theories of both anxiety disorders and depression propose that emotional reactions to a stressor are determined by thoughts that the stressor elicits. It is unlikely, however, that these thoughts can be recalled accurately in retrospect. Consider also a prominent theory in the health psychology field that proposes that a person's response to a stressor depends on his or her appraising or evaluating it, attempting to cope with it, and then reappraising it (Lazarus & Folkman, 1984). It isn't at all likely that this process could be captured by retrospective recall.

Self-monitoring generally leads to increases in desirable behaviours and decreases in undesirable ones. A personal digital assistant can help people record their moods and thoughts at a given time as part of EMA.

EMA may also be useful in clinical settings, revealing information that traditional assessment procedures might miss. For example, Hurlburt (1997) describes a case of a man with severe attacks of anxiety. In clinical interviews, the patient reported that his life was going very well, that he loved his wife and children, and that his work was both financially and personally rewarding. No cause of the anxiety attacks could be discerned. The man was asked to record his thoughts as he went about his daily routine. Surprisingly, about a third of his thoughts were concerned with annoyance with his children (e.g., "He left the record player on again").

> Once the high frequency of annoyance thoughts was pointed out to him, he...accepted that he was in fact often annoyed with his children. However, he believed that anger at his children was sinful and felt unfit as a father for having such thoughts and feelings...[He] entered into brief therapy that focused on the normality of being annoyed by one's children and on the important distinction between being annoyed and acting out aggressively. Almost immediately, his anxiety attacks disappeared. (p. 944)

Although some research indicates that self-monitoring or EMA can provide accurate measurement of such behaviour, considerable research indicates that behaviour may be altered by the very fact that it is being self-monitored—that is, the self-consciousness required for self-monitoring affects the behaviour (Haynes & Horn, 1982). The phenomenon of behaviour changing because it is being observed is called **reactivity**. In general, desirable behaviour, such as engaging in social conversation, often increases in frequency when self-monitored (Nelson, Lipinski, & Black, 1976), whereas behaviour the person wishes to reduce, such as cigarette smoking, diminishes (McFall & Hammen, 1971). Such findings suggest that therapeutic interventions can take advantage of the reactivity that is a natural by-product of self-monitoring. Smoking, anxiety, depression, and health problems have all undergone beneficial changes in self-monitoring studies (Febbraro & Clum, 1998).

Interviews and Self-Report Inventories For all their interest in direct observation of behaviour, behavioural clinicians still rely very heavily on the interview to assess the needs of their clients (Sarwer & Sayers, 1998). Within a trusting relationship, the behaviour therapist's job is to determine, by skilful questioning and careful observation of the client's emotional reactions during the interview, the SORC factors that help the therapist conceptualize the client's problem.

Behaviour therapists also make use of self-report inventories. As we will see later, some of these questionnaires are similar to the personality tests we have already described. But others have a greater situational focus than traditional questionnaires. McFall and Lillesand (1971), for example, employed a Conflict Resolution Inventory containing 35 items that focused on the ability of the respondent to refuse unreasonable requests. Each item described a specific situation in which a person was asked for something unreasonable. For example, "You are in the thick of studying for exams when a person you know slightly comes into your room and says, 'I'm tired of studying. Mind if I come in and take a break for a while?'" Students were asked to indicate the likelihood that they would refuse such a request and how comfortable they would be in doing so. Concurrent validity for this self-report inventory was established by showing that it correlated with a variety of direct observational data on social skills (Frisch & Higgins, 1986). This and similar inventories, described in the next section, can be used by clinicians and have helped cognitive-behavioural researchers measure the outcome of clinical interventions as well.

Specialized Approaches to Cognitive Assessment

Perhaps the most widely employed cognitive assessment methods are self-report questionnaires that tap a wide range of cognitions, such as fear of negative evaluation, a tendency to think irrationally, and a tendency to make negative inferences about life experiences. "When someone criticizes you in class, what thoughts go through your mind?" is a question a client might be asked in an interview or on a paper-and-pencil inventory. When patients are asked about their thoughts in interviews and self-report inventories, they have to reflect backward in time and provide a retrospective and rather general report of their thoughts in certain situations. We have already seen how such retrospective reporting can provide inaccurate information.

As with all kinds of assessment, a key feature of contemporary approaches in cognitive assessment is that the development of methods is determined by theory as well as by the purposes of the assessment (Blankstein & Segal, 2001). For example, much research on depression is concerned with cognition—the things people consciously and sometimes unconsciously tell themselves as well as the underlying assumptions or attitudes that can be inferred from their behaviour and verbal reports. One cognitive theory (Beck, 1967), which we will examine in greater detail in Chapter 10, holds that depression is caused primarily by negative ideas people have about themselves, their world, and their future. People may believe, for instance, that they are not worth much and that things are never going to get better.

These pessimistic attitudes, or schemas, bias the way in which depressed people interpret events. So great is this bias that a misstep that might be taken in stride by a nondepressed person, such as forgetting to mail a birthday card, is construed by a depressed individual as compelling evidence of his or her ineptitude and worthlessness. Researchers employing cognitive assessment set themselves the task of trying to identify these different kinds of cognitions. They obtain their ideas both from clinical reports of practitioners who have firsthand experience with depressed patients and from controlled research that adheres to the methodological principles discussed in the next chapter.

One assessment device used in this context is the Dysfunctional Attitude Scale (DAS). The DAS contains items such as "People will probably think less of me if I make a mistake" (Weissman & Beck, 1978). Supporting the theory of construct validity, researchers have shown that they can differentiate between depressed and nondepressed people on the basis of their scores on this scale and that scores decrease (i.e., improve) after interventions that relieve depression. Furthermore, the DAS relates to other aspects of cognition in ways consistent with Beck's theory. For example, it correlates with an instrument called the Cognitive Bias Questionnaire (Krantz & Hammen, 1979), which measures the ways in which depressed patients distort information. An accumulating body of data is helping to establish both the validity and the reliability of these instruments (Glass & Arnkoff, 1997).

Cognitive assessment focuses on the person's perception of a situation, since the same event can be perceived differently by different people or at different times. For example, moving could be regarded as very stressful or seen in a positive light.

As mentioned, people's responses to inventories and to questions asked by interviewers about their thoughts in past situations may well differ from what they would report had they been able to do so in the immediate circumstance. Researchers have been working on ways to enable people to tap into their immediate, ongoing thought processes when confronted with particular circumstances (cf. Parks & Hollon, 1988). Can we show, for example, that a socially anxious person does in fact, as Ellis would predict, view criticism from others as catastrophic, whereas someone who is not socially insecure does not?

The Articulated Thoughts in Simulated Situations (ATSS) method of Davison and his associates (Davison, Robins, & Johnson, 1983) is one way to assess immediate thoughts in specific situations. In this procedure, a person pretends that he or she is a participant in a situation, such as listening to a teaching assistant criticize a term paper. Presented on audiotape, the scene pauses every 10 or 15 seconds. During the ensuing 30 seconds of silence, the participant talks aloud about whatever is going through his or her mind in reaction to the words just heard. One taped scene in which the participant overhears two pretend acquaintances criticizing him or her includes the following segments:

- First acquaintance: He certainly did make a fool of himself over what he said about religion. I just find that kind of opinion very closed-minded and unaware. You have to be blind to the facts of the universe to believe that. [Thirty-second pause for subject's response.]
- Second acquaintance: What really bugs me is the way he expresses himself. He never seems to stop and think, but just blurts out the first thing that comes into his head. [Thirty-second pause.]

Participants readily become involved in the pretend situations, regarding them as credible and realistic. Furthermore, the responses of participants can be reliably coded (Davison et al., 1983). Research using this approach indicates that socially anxious therapy patients articulate thoughts of greater irrationality (e.g., "Oh God, I wish I were dead. I'm so embarrassed.") than do nonanxious members of control groups (Bates, Campbell, & Burgess, 1990). In a study that directly compared ATSS data with overt behaviour (Davison, Haaga, et al., 1991), thoughts of positive self-efficacy were found to be inversely related to behaviourally indexed speech anxiety; that is, the more anxiously subjects behaved on a timed behavioural checklist measure of public-speaking anxiety, the less capable they felt they were while articulating thoughts in a stressful, simulated speech-giving situation. These and related findings (cf. Davison, Vogel, & Coffman, 1997) indicate that this method ferrets out people's thinking about both inherently bothersome and "objectively" innocuous situations.

Other cognitive assessment methods have also proved useful (cf. Blankstein & Segal, 2001). In **thought-listing**, for example, the person writes down his or her thoughts prior to or following an event of interest, such as entering a room to talk to a stranger, as a way to determine the cognitive components of social anxiety (Caccioppo, von Hippel, & Ernst, 1997). Open-ended techniques, such as the ATSS and thought-listing, may be preferable when investigators know relatively little about the participant and want to get general ideas about the cognitive terrain. For example, thought-listing studies conducted at the University of Toronto demonstrate that among test-anxious students there is a preponderance of negative thoughts about the "self" and a relative absence of positive thoughts about the self (e.g., Blankstein & Flett, 1990; Blankstein, Flett, Boase, & Toner, 1990). This focus on negative, self-referential thinking deflects attention from the task at hand and eats away at the motivation to succeed. The procedures and instructions for administering the thought-listing procedure and for coding the data must be considered carefully and the rated thoughts evaluated by independent trained raters or judges in order to make valid inferences about the meaning of the listed thoughts and to determine the reliability of assessment (e.g., Blankstein & Flett, 1990).

Videotape reconstruction (e.g., Meichenbaum & Butler, 1980) is an interesting strategy for assessing people's thoughts and feelings. The procedure involves videotaping an individual while he or she is engaged in some task or an actual or role-played problematic situation. The person then watches the videotape while attempting to *reconstruct* his or her thoughts and feelings at the time as accurately as possible. It is, of course, difficult to determine with certainty the degree to which people are actually reconstructing or are simply constructing the flow of thoughts and feelings as they observe themselves on videotape.

More focused techniques, such as questionnaires, may be better—and are certainly more easily scored—when investigators have more prior knowledge about the cognitions of interest. Blankstein and Segal (2001) recently reviewed structured endorsement and unstructured production approaches to thought assessment and summarized the advantages and limitations of the different methods. So far, the various cognitive assessment techniques often correlate poorly with one another (Blankstein & Segal, 2001; Clark, 1988, 1997), which presents an important challenge to researchers and clinicians alike. This challenge can be especially difficult when it comes to cognitive assessment of children (e.g., Lodge, Tripp, & Harte, 2000). Furthermore, some cognitive constructs, including automatic thoughts, schemas, and dysfunctional beliefs, have proved difficult to measure accurately (Blankstein & Segal, 2001). One implication, of course, is that we can have more confidence in the results of our assessments if several different strategies are employed.

Nonetheless, according to Blankstein and Segal (2001), the trend toward diversification is a healthy development within cognitive assessment that provides "a more enriched and vital armamentarium of assessment tools for the study of the relationship among cognition, emotion, and behavior" (p. 73). At the same time, it is important to achieve integration within cognitive assessment and integration with other approaches, including neurobiological perspectives.

Family Assessment

Much of the focus in abnormal psychology is on the problems of individuals. However, it is important to recognize that many forms of dysfunction have their developmental origins in problematic family interactions. Even if abnormal behaviour is not due, at least in part, to family characteristics, family factors can play a significant role in the persistence of abnormal behaviour. Thus, it is important to assess current or previous types and levels of **family functioning** before implementing the various forms of family therapy outlined in different sections of this book.

The possible role of the family in the development of abnormal behaviour is central to classical psychoanalytic theories, which trace abnormal behaviour back to conflicts between the child and parent that occur in the first four or five years of the child's life, and to more contemporary object-relations theories (e.g., Kernberg, 1985) that focus on an infant's attachment to the mother figure. However, familial processes play an important role in several other theories as well. Social learning theory, for example, with its emphasis on the role of imitation of powerful parent figures (e.g., Bandura & Walters, 1963), and interpersonal theories (e.g., Sullivan, 1953) that regard people as products of their social interactions assume that recurring social interactions with family members have great impact on the individual.

Contemporary views of the role of the family in psychopathology are based on a family systems perspective (e.g., Minuchin et al., 1975). A family systems approach holds that behaviours produced in the family environment reflect the various components that are present in the family setting, including the characteristics of each family member and the various transactions or interactions between family members. Accordingly, the therapist must focus on the entire family system rather than on a particular individual, and abnormal functioning in an individual is a reflection of a broader problem involving family dysfunction.

One key principle here is that the family is dynamic and changing rather than static, so it is important to measure ongoing changes in the family and not focus exclusively on the past. Another important principle of the systems approach involves the concept of *equifinality* (see Bertalanffy, 1968). Eqifinality is the notion that the same goal or endpoint can result from many different starting points and different processes. For example, two people can have the same symptoms of depression, but they can reach this point through very different background factors and different interpersonal processes.

Although the family systems concept is the predominant theory when familial factors are being considered, there is a tendency for clinicians and researchers to rely heavily on self-report measures of the family environment and family functioning, and these measures provide little insight into the family as an interacting system of various components. One such measure is the Family Environment Scale (FES) developed by Moos and colleagues (Moos & Moos, 1986). The FES is a 90-item, true-false measure consisting of 10 subscales that are divided into three main themes: (1) the family relationship, which is measured by subscales assessing the family environment in terms of cohesion, expression, and control; (2) personal growth, as measured by subscales tapping the family environment in terms of independence, active-recreational orientation, achievement orientation, moral-religious emphasis, and intellectual-cultural orientation; and (3) system maintenance, as assessed by organization and control in the family environment. The FES has many research applications, including a recent Canadian study in which it was used to examine the link between the perceived childhood family environment and levels of alcohol misuse and personality disorder as an adult (Jang, Vernon, & Livesley, 2000). An interesting feature of the FES is that it was designed not only to be used to measure the actual family environment (either now or in the past), but also to be used to assess perceptions of the ideal family environment and the family environment that the respondent feels ought to exist. Although the FES is generally regarded as a valid and reliable instrument, some researchers have questioned the validity of certain subscales when it is administered to specific clinical populations (see Sandford, Bingham, & Zucker, 1999).

The Family Adaptation and Cohesion Evaluation Scale—Third Edition (FACES-III; Olson, Portner, & Lavee, 1985) is a family assessment scale that stems from the circumplex model of family functioning outlined by Olson et al. (Olson, Sprenkle, & Russell, 1979). The two dimensions of the circumplex model are a family's degree of cohesion (i.e., closeness) and a family's degree of adaptability (i.e., ability to adjust by appropriate changes to roles and rules in the family). Both of these dimensions have four levels, with moderate levels reflecting appropriate family adjustment and the extremes reflecting maladjustment. The four levels of cohesion are (1) enmeshed (i.e., overly cohesive), (2) connected, (3) separated, and (4) disengaged (i.e., lack of involvement). A parent who is smothering and overcontrolling would contribute to a family situation of enmeshment, while a parent who is neglectful would contribute to a situation of disengagement.

The four levels of adaptability are (1) rigid (i.e., little or no flexibility), (2) structured, (3) flexible, and (4) chaotic (too much adaptability). The two dimensions assessed by the FACES measure have been used to distinguish functional versus dysfunctional families (see Rodick, Henggeler, & Hanson, 1986).

Two of the more widely used measures of family functioning have been developed in Canada. See Canadian Perspectives 4.1 for an overview of the McMaster Family Assessment Device and the Family Assessment Measure-III.

Other commonly used measures focus directly on the role of parental factors in family adjustment. One such measure is the Parental Bonding Inventory (PBI; Parker, Tupling, & Brown, 1979). The PBI can be completed for both the mother and the father. It consists of two subscales that assess the level of care or parental warmth, and the level of controlling parental behaviours. Research with the PBI has identified a condition known as *affectionless control* (i.e., an overcontrolling parent who lacks warmth and caring). The PBI has been used to identify a link between affectionless control and suicidal tendencies in several studies, including research conducted with Canadian adolescents (Adams et al., 1994; Tousignant, Bastien, & Hamel, 1993).

The Egna Minnen Betraffande Uppfostran ("Memories of My Childhood") or EMBU is another widely used measure developed to assess memories of parental rearing styles (Perris, Jacobsson, Lindstrom, Von Knorring, & Perris, 1980). This self-report questionnaire assesses several components of perceived parenting behaviour, including emotional warmth, rejection, and overprotection. Extensive research has confirmed a link between maladaptive parenting styles as assessed by the EMBU and psychological disorders (e.g., Gerlsma, Emmelkamp, & Arrindell, 1990; Perris, Arrindell, & Eisemann, 1994). A nagging concern with measures such as the PBI and the EMBU is the possibility that negative ratings of parents are, at least in part, a reflection of a mood bias; that is, dysphoric individuals will perceive their parents in a more negative way than nondepressed individuals.

The concern points to the primary limitation of these measures—they call for subjective responses. It is important to reiterate that these scales measure subjective appraisals of parental characteristics and may not assess actual parental characteristics. Gerlsma and his colleagues (Gerlsma, Snijders, van Duijn, & Emmelkamp, 1997) examined patterns of agreement and variability within families with regard to recalled parental behaviour and concluded that "perceptions of parental rearing styles are primarily tales by individuals, and to a much smaller extent tales about families, parents, or relationships" (p. 271). Self-report measures such as these also do not provide the opportunity to assess the dynamic interplay of factors in the family setting that contribute to dysfunction.

Behavioural assessment in the family context is a more objective approach that can provide richer sources of data that are less subject to cognitive biases. However, it must be acknowledged that these behavioural assessments have other limitations. The most important limitation involves the previously mentioned problem of reactivity—that is, the extent to which family members alter their usual ways of interacting when they know that they are being observed and evaluated. Reactivity is regarded as a significant problem, but this is not always the case. For example, a behavioural study of interactions in families with depressed and alcoholic members found little evidence of reactivity (Jacob, Tennenbaum, Seilhammer, Bargiel, & Sharon, 1994). Jacob et al. suggested that reactivity did not occur in their study because interaction patterns are well established and participants have little motivation to alter their behaviours, since they will have no long-term involvement with the researchers.

A segment of the CBC television show *The Fifth Estate* that aired in April 1994 (titled "The Trouble with Evan") illustrated that reactivity may not be a concern in the evaluation of some families. This show caused a national uproar because it depicted the emotional abuse of an 11-year-old boy named Evan who had engaged in antisocial behaviours, including stealing, lying, and putting paint in his teacher's coffee cup. The emotional abuse depicted in the show resulted in Evan and his 7-year-old sister being removed by the Children's Aid Society and placed in a foster home. One of the most remarkable aspects of this television program is that the abuse occurred despite the fact that family patterns were being videotaped for broadcast to a national television audience, and over the 10-week period, the parents themselves were quite cooperative, often loading new tapes into the recording

Table 4.2

Major Psychological Assessment Methods

Interviews	Clinical interviews	Conversational technique in which the clinician attempts tolearn about the patient's problems. Content of the interview varies depending on the paradigm of the interviewer.
	Structured interviews	Questions to be asked are spelled out in detail in a booklet; most often used for gathering information to make a diagnosis.
Psychological tests	Personality tests	Self-report questionnaires, used to assess either a broad range of characteristics, as in the MMPI, or a single characteristic, such as dysfunctional attitudes. Behaviourally oriented questionnaires tend to have a situational focus.
	Projective personality tests	Ambiguous stimuli, such as inkblots (Rorschach test), are presented and responses are thought to be determined by unconscious processes.
	Tests of family functioning	Self-report questionnaires used to assess perceptions of family environment and functioning or parental characteristics.
	Tests of cognition	Endorsement (self-report) and production (e.g., thought and listing) assessments of cognitive products, processes, structures.
	Intelligence tests	Assessments of current mental functioning. Used to predict school performance and diagnose mental retardation.
Direct observation		Used by behavioural clinicians to identify SORC factors. Also used to assess cognition, as in the Articulated Thoughts in Simulated Situations technique.
Self-observation		Individuals monitor and keep records of their own behaviour; also referred to as ecological momentary assessment.

equipment. Thus, reactivity may not happen in all instances, especially when automatic family interaction patterns are involved.

Another problem with behavioural assessment in a family context is that, ultimately, researchers must code their behavioural data into meaningful units of analysis, and different researchers may use different coding schemes, thereby making it difficult to compare findings across studies. These problems notwithstanding, some important findings have emerged from the use of behavioural measures to study the role of the family in psychopathology. For example, Gottman and associates (Gottman et al., 1995; Waltz, Babcock, Jacobsen, & Gottman, 2000), using both behavioural and physiological measures to assess interactions between spouse abusers and their wives, found two types of abusers: (1) a distressed group characterized by high levels of arousal and likely to restrict their violence to the family context (i.e., domestically violent batterers); and (2) a psychopathic group with exceptionally low levels of arousal who have general antisocial tendencies that operate inside and outside the family context (i.e., generally violent batterers). Psychopathy is described in detail in Chapter 13.

The psychological assessments we have described are summarized in Table 4.2.

Canadian Perspectives/4.1

Family Assessment in Canada:

THE MCMASTER FAMILY ASSESSMENT DEVICE AND THE FAMILY ASSESSMENT MEASURE–III

One of the earliest models of family functioning was developed in Canada by Nathan Epstein and Jack Santa-Barbera. It is called the McMaster model of family functioning because it was developed while Nathan Epstein was affiliated with McMaster University and Hamilton Psychiatric Hospital. The McMaster Family Assessment Device (Epstein, Baldwin, & Bishop, 1983) is a 60-item self-report measure that assesses family functioning in terms of problem-solving, communication, roles, affective responsiveness, affective involvement, and behaviour control. Problem-solving involves a six-stage process that includes (1) identifying the problem; (2) communicating the problem; (3) developing action alternatives; (4) selecting an alternative and carrying out the action associated with the alternative; (5) monitoring the action to see whether the choice is viable; and (6) evaluating the success of the solution. Communication assesses the extent to which messages are seen as clear versus masked and direct versus indirect. The roles subscale assesses the degree to which familial tasks are allocated and completed in an accountable manner; chaotic, maladaptive family situations arise when roles are not being fulfilled in a conscientiousness manner. Affective responsiveness assesses whether emotional expressions are appropriate; that is, family maladjustment is evident when there is too much restriction of emotion or the emotions expressed are more intense than the situation calls for (e.g., responding with rage to minor events). Affective involvement is similar to the concept of cohesion in Olson's circumplex model; that is, family members show adaptive responses to the extent that they are involved and do not engage in intrusiveness (enmeshed) or neglect. Finally, there are four types of behavioural control that vary in their adaptiveness. Families may be rigid, flexible, laissez-faire, or chaotic.

An important thing to remember about the McMaster Family Assessment Device is that it is used by an individual to assess the overall functioning of the family unit. It is useful as a general measure of perceived family adjustment, as shown in a study by Hewitt, Flett, and Mikail (1995). This investigation found that chronic pain patients from the Rehabilitation Centre in Ottawa reported lower overall levels of family adjustment if their spouse was overly demanding and wanted them to be perfect.

The process model of family functioning described by Steinhauer, Santa-Barbera, and Skinner (1984) is an improvement on the McMaster model because it includes a more explicit focus on the dynamic interactions of family functioning. This model includes the link between interpersonal aspects of family functioning and the intrapsychic needs of individual family members. The process model is currently assessed by the Family Assessment Measure-III (FAM-III), which is a modification of the original inventory developed by Skinner, Steinhauer, and Santa-Barbera (1983). The FAM-III has seven main subscales that assess task accomplishment, role performance, communication, affective expression, involvement, control, and values/norms. It has two important advantages, relative to the McMaster Family Assessment Device. First, the FAM-III can be administered to tap three difference levels of functioning, including the functioning of the entire family, certain dyadic relationships, and the individual's sense of his or her own level of functioning in the family context. Second, the FAM-III includes social desirability and defensiveness subscales that can be used to determine the validity of self-reports.

Although concerns have been raised about the length of time it would take to administer the FAM-III if it were used to assess the family, relationships, and the self, ongoing research in Canada and elsewhere has demonstrated the usefulness of this inventory. For example, research on eating-disorder patients from Toronto has confirmed the role of familial factors in the development of and recovery from eating disorders (Geist, Davis, & Heinmaa, 1998; Woodside, Lackstrom, Shekter-Wolfson, & Heinmaa, 1996). The role of familial factors in eating disorders will be explored in more detail in Chapter 9.

Thinking Critically

1. Do you believe that most psychological disorders are caused in part by dysfunction in the family or are at least exacerbated by such dysfunction?
2. Which dimensions or factors of the McMaster Family Assessment Device and the FAM-III would you hypothesize to be most strongly associated with psychological problems or disorders within an individual family member?
3. Is it actual family dysfunction or the individual's *perception or appraisal* of dysfunction in the family system that is most predictive of individual psychological dysfunction?
4. Do you think that it is generally appropriate and necessary to focus on the family system as a central component of case formulation and treatment planning?

BIOLOGICAL ASSESSMENT

Recall from Chapters 2 and 3 that some people interested in psychopathology have assumed, quite reasonably, that some malfunctions of the psyche are likely to be due to or at least reflected in malfunctions of the soma. We turn now to contemporary work in biological assessment.

BRAIN IMAGING: "SEEING" THE BRAIN

Because many behavioural problems can be brought on by brain abnormalities, neurological tests, such as checking the reflexes, examining the retina for any indication of blood-vessel damage, and evaluating motor coordination and perception, have been used for many years to diagnose brain dysfunction. More recently, devices have become available that allow clinicians and researchers a much more direct look at both the structure and functioning of the brain.

Computerized axial tomography, the **CT scan**, helps to assess structural brain abnormalities (and is able to image other parts of the body for medical purposes). A moving beam of X-rays passes into a horizontal cross-section of the patient's brain, scanning it through 360 degrees; the moving X-ray detector on the other side measures the amount of radioactivity that penetrates, thus detecting subtle differences in tissue density. A computer uses the information to construct a two-dimensional, detailed image of the cross-section, giving it optimal contrasts. Then the patient's head is moved, and the machine scans another cross-section of the brain. The resulting images can show the enlargement of ventricles, which signals degeneration of tissue and the locations of tumours and blood clots. Indeed, CT scans were used in a recent study in London, Ontario, to confirm that patients with a first episode of schizophrenia had a mild degree of enlargement of ventricles and cortical sulci (Malla et al., 2002).

Newer computer-based devices for seeing the living brain include **magnetic resonance imaging**, also known as **MRI**, which is superior to the CT scan because it produces pictures of higher quality and does not rely on even the small amount of radiation required by a CT scan. In MRI, the person is placed inside a large, circular magnet, which causes the hydrogen atoms in the body to move. When the magnetic force is turned off, the atoms return to their original positions and thereby produce an electromagnetic signal. These signals are then read by the computer and translated into pictures of brain tissue. The implications of this technique are enormous. For example, it has allowed physicians to locate and remove delicate brain tumours that would have been considered inoperable without such sophisticated methods of viewing brain structures.

More recently, a modification, called **fMRI (functional magnetic resonance imaging)**, has been developed that allows researchers to take MRI pictures so quickly that metabolic changes can be measured, providing a picture of the brain at work rather than of its structure alone. Using this technique, a recent study found that there was less activation in the frontal lobes of patients with schizophrenia than in the frontal lobes of normal people as they performed a cognitive task (Yurgelon-Todd et al., 1996).

A recent case study from Montreal illustrates the types of information that can emerge from fMRI assessments (Bentaleb, Beauregard, Liddle, & Stip, 2002). This research focused on a woman with schizophrenia who experienced auditory hallucinations that went away when she listened to loud external speech. She had learned to stop her hallucinations by turning up the volume of her radio or television. Comparisons using fMRI were made between her brain activity during the hallucinations and while listening to external speech, and these results were compared with the results for a matched control participant. The researchers found that auditory verbal hallucinations were linked with increased metabolic activity in the left primary auditory cortex and the right middle temporal gyrus. Overall, this case study clarified the mechanisms involved in aurditory hallucinations by showing that they stem jointly from aberrant activation of the auditory cortex and the misinterpreted inner speech of the patient with schizophrenia. Previous theorists did not consider the possibility that both factors might simultaneously play a role in auditory hallucinations.

Another recent study conducted in British Columbia used fMRI procedures to compare eight criminal psychopaths and eight criminals without psychopathy (Kiehl et al., 2001). The main focus in this investigation was on affective processing while completing a memory task. The researchers were able to obtain evidence consistent with the view that "criminal psychopathy is associated with abnormalities in the function of structures in the limbic system and frontal cortex while engaged in processing of affective stimuli" (p. 682).

Since the fMRI can be used to determine where in the brain activity occurs during cognitive tasks, it may prove useful in determining the mechanisms related to changes that occur during cognitive-behavioural therapy (Ingram & Siegal, 2000). Schwartz (1998) reported fMRI data indicating that obsessive-compulsive disorder appears to be characterized by abnormal activation in the orbital-frontal complex and that cognitive-behavioural treatment produced changes in left orbital-frontal activation, but only in treatment responders. Thus treatment may influence directly the parts of the brain affected by the disorder.

Positron emission tomography, the PET scan, a more expensive and invasive procedure, allows measurement of brain function. A substance used by the brain is labelled with a short-lived radioactive isotope and injected into the bloodstream. The radioactive molecules of the substance emit a particle called a positron, which quickly collides with an electron. A pair of high-energy light particles shoot out from the skull in opposite directions and are detected by the scanner. The computer analyzes millions of such recordings and converts them into a picture of the functioning brain. The images are in colour; fuzzy spots of lighter and warmer colours are areas in which metabolic rates for the substance are higher

Visual images of the working brain can indicate sites of epileptic seizures, brain cancers, strokes, and trauma from head injuries, as well as the distribution of psychoactive drugs in the brain. The PET scanner is also being used to study possible abnormal biological processes that underlie disorders, such as the failure of the frontal cortex of patients with schizophrenia to become activated while they attempt to perform a cognitive task. PET images are often overlaid on averaged MRI images to allow for the articulation of both function and structure.

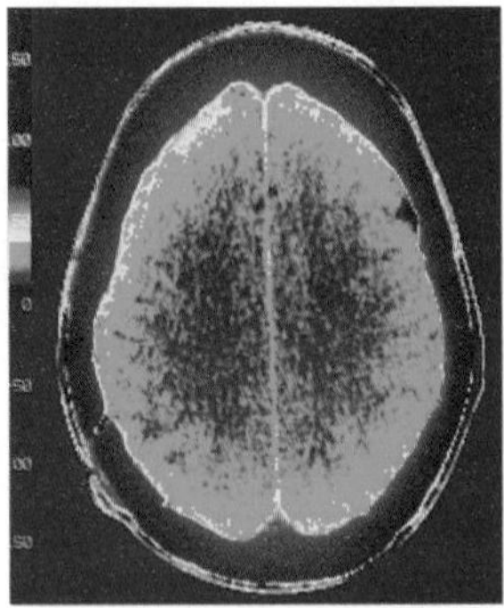
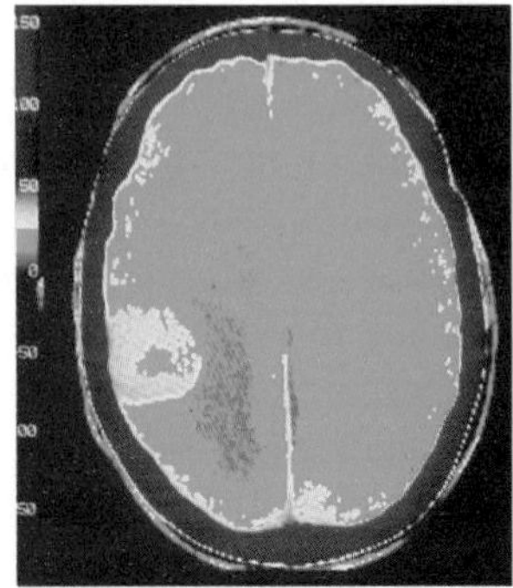

These two CT scans show a horizontal slice through the brain. The one on the left is normal; the one on the right has a tumour on the left side.

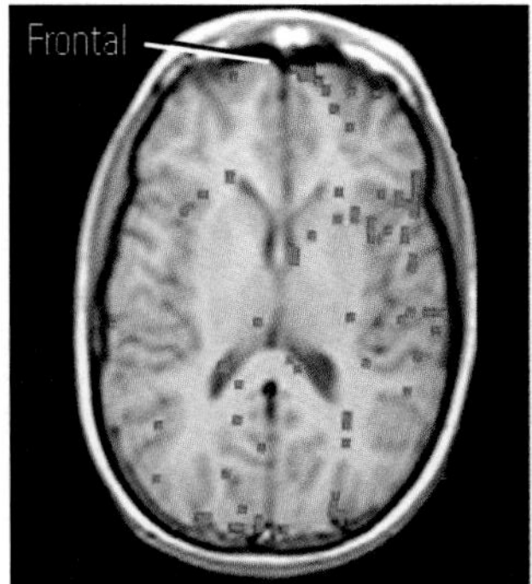

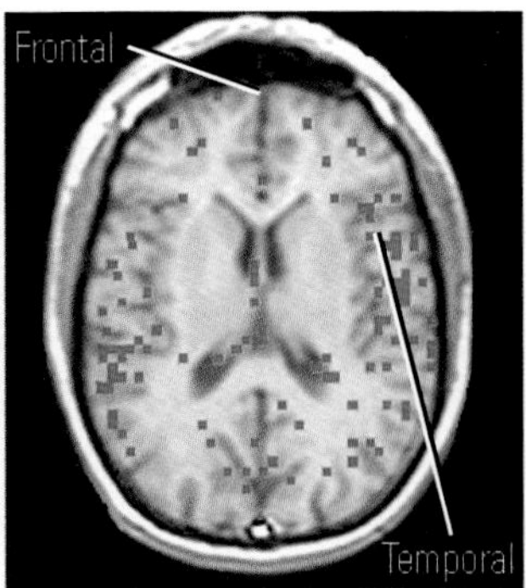

Functional magnetic resonance images (fMRI) of a patient diagnosed with schizophrenia (right) and a healthy individual (left). The red squares represent activation of the brain during a verbal task compared to baseline. The patient shows less frontal and more temporal activation. (Yurgelun-Todd et al., 1996)

Neurochemical Assessment

It might seem that assessing the amount of a particular neurotransmitter or the quantity of its receptors in the brain would be straightforward. But it is not. Only recently has PET scanning allowed an assessment of receptors in a living brain. Most of the research on neurochemical theories of psychopathology—of increasing importance in recent years—has relied on indirect assessments.

In postmortem studies, the brains of deceased patients are removed and the amount of specific neurotransmitters in particular brain areas can then be directly measured. Different brain areas can be infused with substances that bind to receptors, and the amount of binding can then be quantified; more binding indicates more receptors. In Chapter 11, we will discuss how this method has been used to study the dopamine theory of schizophrenia.

Another common method of neurochemical assessment involves analyzing the *metabolites* of neurotransmitters that have been broken down by enzymes. A metabolite, typically an acid, is produced when a neurotransmitter is deactivated. For example, the major metabolite of dopamine is homovanillic acid; of serotonin, 5 hydroxyindoleacetic acid. The metabolites can be detected in urine, blood, and cerebrospinal fluid (the fluid in the spinal column and in the brain's ventricles). A high level of a particular metabolite indicates a high level of a transmitter, and a low level indicates a low level of the transmitter. We will see in Chapter 10 that people with depression have low levels of the main metabolite of serotonin—a fact that has played an important role in the serotonin theory of depression.

Imaging and neurochemical techniques provide startling pictures of and insights into internal organs and permit the gathering of information about living tissue, including the brain. Results, however, are not strong enough for these methods to be used in diagnosing psychopathology. Clinicians and researchers in many disciplines are currently using these techniques both to discover previously undetectable tumours and other brain problems and to conduct inquiries into the neural and chemical bases of thought, emotion, and behaviour.

NEUROPSYCHOLOGICAL ASSESSMENT

"With such a wide array of eminent researchers and institutions, human neuropsychology in Canada should continue to thrive well into the foreseeable future, and Canadian investigators can be expected to remain respected leaders in this scientific endeavour."

—Hayman-Abello, Hayman-Abello and Rourke, 2003, (p. 120), on human neuropsychology in Canada during the 1990s.

The past decade has witnessed many advances in neuropsychological assessment. What exactly is neuropsychological assessment? It is important at this point to note a distinction between neurologists and neuropsychologists, even though both specialists are concerned with the study of the central nervous system. A neurologist is a physician who specializes in medical diseases that affect the nervous system, such as muscular dystrophy, cerebral palsy, or Alzheimer's disease. A neuropsychologist is a psychologist who studies how dysfunctions of the brain affect the way we think, feel, and behave. As the term implies, a neuropsychologist is trained as a psychologist—and as such is interested in thought, emotion, and behaviour—but one with a focus on how abnormalities of the brain affect behaviour in deleterious ways. Both kinds of specialists contribute much to each other as they work in different ways, often collaboratively, to learn how the nervous system functions and how to ameliorate problems caused by disease or injury to the brain.

The goals of neuropsychological testing were summarized recently by Seidman and Bruder (2003) as follows:

1. to measure as reliably, validly, and completely as possible, the behavioural correlates of brain functions
2. to identify the characteristic profile associated with a neurobehavioural syndrome (differential diagnosis)
3. to establish possible localization, lateralization, and etiology of a brain lesion
4. to determine whether neuropsychological deficits are present (i.e., cognitive, perceptual, or motor) regardless of diagnosis
5. to describe neuropsychological strengths, weaknesses, and strategy of problem-solving
6. to assess the patient's feelings about his or her syndrome
7. to provide treatment recommendations (i.e., to patient, family, school)

Adapted with permission from Seidman and Bruder (2003).

One might reasonably assume that neurologists and physicians, with the help of such procedures and technological devices as PET, CT, and MRI scans, can observe the brain and its functions more or less directly and thus assess all brain abnormalities. Many brain abnormalities and injuries, however, involve alterations in structure so subtle or slight in extent that they have thus far eluded direct physical examination.

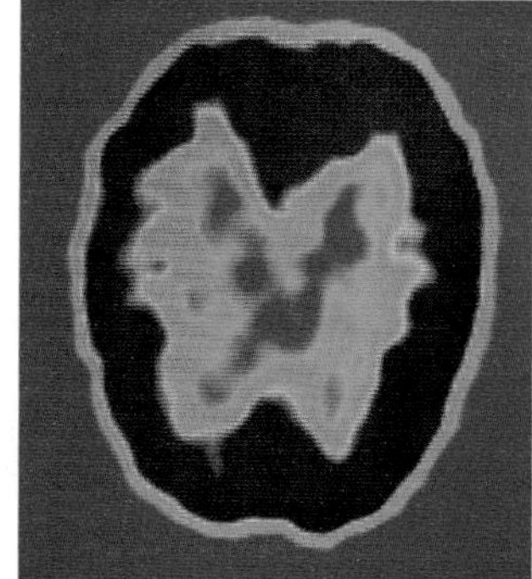
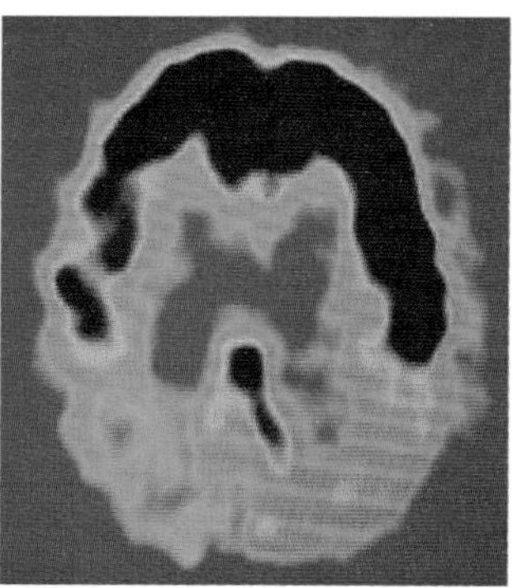

The PET scan on the left shows a normal brain; the one on the right shows the brain of a patient with Alzheimer's disease.

Neuropsychologists have developed tests to assess behavioural disturbances caused by brain dysfunctions. The literature on these tests is extensive, and as with most areas of psychology, so, too, is disagreement about them. The weight of the evidence does indicate that psychological tests have some validity in the assessment of brain damage, however, and they are often used in conjunction with the brain-scanning techniques just described. They are accordingly called neuropsychological tests. All are based on the idea that different psychological functions (e.g., motor speed, memory, language) are localized in different areas of the brain. Thus, finding a deficit on a particular test can provide clues about where in the brain some damage may exist.

One neuropsychological test is Reitan's modification of a battery or group of tests previously developed by Halstead. The concept of using a battery of tests, each tapping a different function, is critical, for only by studying a person's pattern of performance can an investigator adequately judge whether the person is brain damaged and where the damage is located. The following are four of the tests included in the Halstead-Reitan battery.

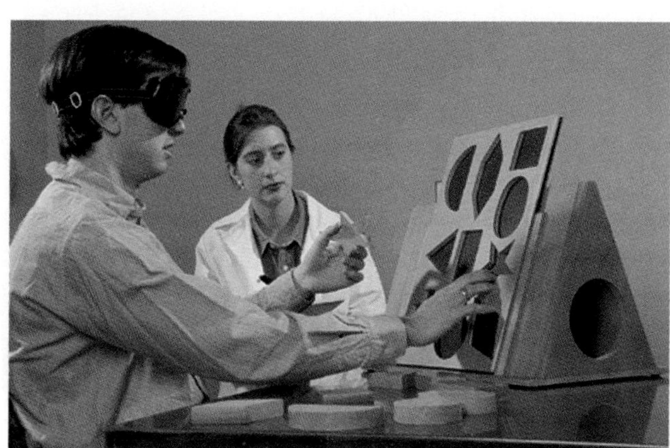

Neuropsychological tests assess various performance deficits in the hope of detecting a specific area of brain malfunction. Shown here is the Tactile Performance Test.

1 *Tactile Performance Test—Time.* While blindfolded, the patient tries to fit variously shaped blocks into spaces of a form board, first using the preferred hand, then the other, and finally both.

2 *Tactile Performance Test—Memory.* After completing the timed test, the participant is asked to draw the form board from memory, showing the blocks in their proper location. Both this and the timed test are sensitive to damage in the right parietal lobe.

3 *Category Test.* The patient, seeing an image on a screen that suggests one of the numbers from one to four, presses a button to show which number he or she thinks it is. A bell indicates that the choice is correct, a buzzer that it is incorrect. The patient must keep track of these images and signals in order to figure out the rules for making the correct choices. This test measures problem-solving, in particular the ability to abstract a principle from a nonverbal array of events. Impaired performance on this test is the best overall indicator of brain damage.

4 *Speech Sounds Perception Test.* Participants listen to a series of nonsense words, each comprising two consonants with a long "e" sound in the middle. They then select the "word" they heard from a set of alternatives. This test measures left-hemisphere function, especially temporal and parietal areas.

Extensive research has demonstrated that the battery is valid for detecting brain damage resulting from a variety of conditions, such as tumours, stroke, and head injury. Furthermore, this battery of tests can play an important role in making difficult diagnostic decisions, helping the clinician discriminate, for example, between dementia due to depression and dementia due to a degenerative brain disease (Reed & Reed, 1997).

The Luria-Nebraska battery (Golden, Hammeke, & Purisch, 1978), based on the work of the Russian psychologist Aleksandr Luria (1902–1977), is also in widespread use (Moses & Purisch, 1997). A battery of 269 items makes up 11 sections to determine basic and complex motor skills; rhythm and pitch abilities; tactile and kinesthetic skills; verbal and spatial skills; receptive speech ability; expressive speech ability; writing, reading, and arithmetic skills; memory; and intellectual processes. The pattern of scores on these sections, as well as on the 32 items found to be the most discriminating and indicative of overall impairment, helps reveal damage to the frontal, temporal, sensorimotor, or parietal-occipital area of the right or left hemisphere.

The Luria-Nebraska battery can be administered in two and a half hours, and research demonstrates that this test can be scored in a highly reliable manner (e.g., Kashden & Franzen, 1996). It also has an alternate form. Criterion validity has been established by findings such as a correct classification rate of over 86 percent when used with a sample of neurological patients and control groups (Moses et al., 1992). The Luria-Nebraska is also believed to pick up effects of brain damage that are not (yet) detectable by neurological examination; such deficits are in the cognitive domain rather than in the motor or sensory domains on which neurological assessments focus (e.g., assessing reflexes) (Moses, 1983). A particular advantage of the Luria-Nebraska tests is that one can control for educational level so that a less-educated person will not receive a lower score solely because of limited educational experience (Brickman et al., 1984). Finally, a version (Golden, 1981) for children ages 8 to 12 has been found useful in diagnosing brain damage and in evaluating the educational strengths and weaknesses of children (Sweet et al., 1986).

Canadian research in human neuropsychology has a long legacy of eminent contributions starting with the publication of Donald Hebb's Organization of Behaviour (1949), which described a theory of biological psychology that emphasized the role of behaviour. Canadian research in the various subspecialties of neuropsychology is in the vanguard of the field (cf. Costa, 1996; Fuerst & Rourke, 1995; Hayman-Abello, Hayman-Abello, & Rourke, 2003; Rourke, 2000). Indeed, Fuerst and Rourke (1995, p. 12) noted that, "In proportion to respective populations, Canada harbours more eminent researchers in the field than any other country, including the United States." Much of this current Canadian research is in the area of neuropsychological assessment. W. Gary Snow, for example, investigated the reliability and validity of numerous clinical neurospsychological tests, including the Halstead-Reitan Battery while at the Sunnybrook and the Women's College Health Science Centre in Toronto (e.g., Snow, 1987). Donald T. Stuss, currently director of the Rotman Research Institute of the Baycrest Centre of Geriatric Care, conducts neurobehavioural research with a focus on memory and frontal-lobe functions and on forms of dementia, including patterns of neuropsychological functioning in people with Alzheimer's disease. In one interesting series of studies, he and his colleagues assessed the long-term residual effects of prefrontal leucotomies on neuropsychological functions (e.g., Stuss & Benson, 1983). Claude Braun from the Université du Québec à Montréal has investigated the sensitivity of neuropsychological tests to impairments from diffuse brain damage and the possible role of cortical damage or dysfunction in psychiatric disorders, including anorexia nervosa, mood disorders, and antisocial personality disorder (see Hayman-Abello et al., 2003). One of the most prominent researchers in Canada is Byron Rourke from the University of Windsor. The contributions of Rourke and his colleagues include extensive work on the development of nonverbal methods for the neuropsychological assessment of children and adults with learning disabilities, research on subtypes of psychosocial functioning in children with learning disabilities, and work on subgroups of people with Alzheimer's disease (see Hayman-Abello et al., 2003).

In the late 1980s, the Canadian Department of National Health and Welfare allocated significant funding for a comprehensive, longitudinal study of the effects of dementia on Canadian society. This major research project involved the participation of over 10,000 Canadians at centres across Canada (Canadian Study of Health and Aging Working Group, 1994a; Costa, 1996) and is referred to as the Canadian Study of Health and Aging (CSHA). The study is described in some detail in Chapter 16, Canadian Perspectives 16.1. The full neuropsychological test battery administered to many of the participants was developed by a team of Canadian neuropsychologists who were charged with the task of producing a comprehensive neuropsychological battery that could be administered in approximately one hour. Details of the test battery and neuropsychological investigation are described by Holly Tuokko, from the University of Victoria, and her colleagues (Tuokko, Kristjansson, & Miller, 1995) and by Steenhuis and Ostbye (1995). According to Costa (1996), the CSHA is the largest epidemiological study of dementia to include a formal neuropsychological assessment.

One of the most widely used texts in neuropsychology was developed by neuropsychologists at the University of Victoria (Spreen & Strauss, 1998). At the University of Toronto, Konstantine Zakzanis and his colleagues (Zakzanis, Leach, & Kaplan, 1999) put together a compendium of neuropsychological profiles in which test sensitivities were compiled for several dementia (see Chapter 16) and neuropsychiatric disorders. The profiles were designed to help clinicians and researchers select neuropsychological tests on the basis of sensitivities of the tests to specific syndromes (as opposed to choosing tests on the basis of clinical lore, availability, past history of use, and so forth). The work by Spreen and Strauss (1998), Zakzanis et al. (1999), and other Canadian neuroscientists promises to place the selection and use of neuropsychological tests on firmer scientific ground.

PSYCHOPHYSIOLOGICAL ASSESSMENT

The discipline of **psychophysiology** is concerned with the bodily changes that accompany psychological events or that are associated with a person's psychological characteristics (Grings & Dawson, 1978). Experimenters have used measures such as heart rate, tension in the muscles, blood flow in various parts of the body, and brain waves to study the physiological changes that occur when people are afraid, depressed, asleep, imagining, solving problems, and so on. Like the brain-imaging methods we have already discussed, the assessments we describe here are not sensitive enough to be used for diagnosis. They can, however, provide important information. For example, in using exposure to treat a patient with an anxiety disorder, it would be useful to know the extent to which the patient shows physiological arousal when exposed to the stimuli that create anxiety. Patients who show higher levels of physiological arousal may be experiencing higher levels of fear, which predict more benefit from the therapy (Foa et al., 1995).

The activities of the autonomic nervous system (see Focus on Discovery 2.2) are frequently assessed by electrical and chemical measurements in attempts to understand the nature of emotion. One important measure is heart rate. Each heartbeat generates spreading changes in electrical potential, which can be recorded by an electrocardiograph, or on a suitably tuned polygraph, and graphically depicted in an **electrocardiogram**. Electrodes are usually placed on the chest and lead to an instrument for measuring electric currents. The deflections of this instrument may be seen as waves on a computer screen, or a pen recorder may register the waves on a continuously moving roll of graph paper. Both types of recordings are called electrocardiograms.

A second measure of autonomic nervous system activity is **electrodermal responding**, or skin conductance. Anxiety, fear, anger, and other emotions increase activity in the sympathetic nervous system, which then boosts sweat-gland activity. Increased sweat-gland activity increases the electrical conductance of the skin. Conductance is typically measured by determining the current that flows through the skin when a known small voltage derived from an external source is passed between two electrodes on the hand. This current shows a pronounced increase after activation of the sweat

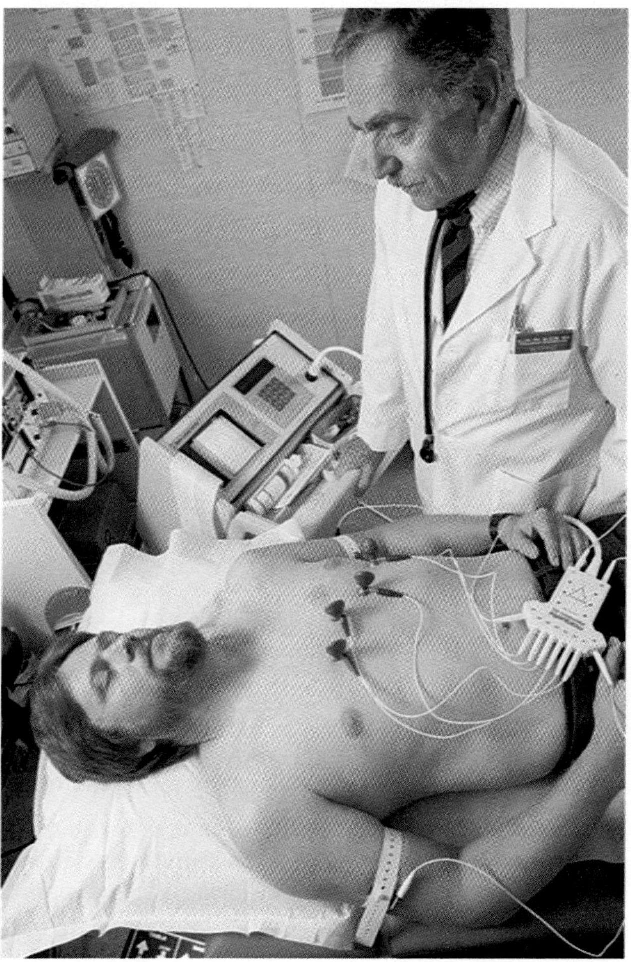

In psychophysiological assessment, physical changes in the body are measured. The electrocardiograph is one such assessment.

glands. Since the sweat glands are activated by the sympathetic nervous system, increased sweat-gland activity indicates sympathetic autonomic excitation and is often taken as a measure of emotional arousal. These measures are used widely in research in psychopathology.

Advances in technology allow researchers to track changes in physiological processes such as blood pressure in vivo, as people go about their normal business. Participants wear a portable device that automatically records blood pressure many times during the day. By combining these measures with self-reports recorded by the participants in specially designed diaries, researchers have been able to study how people's changing moods affect blood pressure—data of great interest to psychologically oriented researchers in hypertension (Kamarck et al., 1998; see Chapter 8).

Brain activity can be measured by an electroencephalogram, or EEG. Electrodes placed on the scalp record electrical activity in the underlying brain area. Abnormal patterns of electrical activity can indicate epilepsy or help in locating brain lesions or tumours.

As with the brain-imaging techniques reviewed earlier, a more complete picture of a human being is obtained when physiological functioning is assessed while the person is engaging in some form of behaviour or cognitive activity. If experimenters are interested in the psychophysiological responses of patients with obsessive-compulsive disorder, for example, they would likely study the patients while presenting stimuli, such as dirt, that would elicit the problematic behaviours.

The biological assessment methods we have described are summarized in Table 4.3.

A Cautionary Note

Inasmuch as psychophysiology employs highly sophisticated electronic machinery and many psychologists aspire to be as scientific as possible, psychologists sometimes believe uncritically in these apparently objective assessment devices without appreciating their real limitations and complications. Many of the measurements do not differentiate clearly among emotional states. Skin conductance, for example, increases not only with anxiety but also with other emotions—among them, happiness.

There is also no one-to-one relationship between a score on a given neuropsychological test or a finding on a PET or CAT scan on the one hand and psychological dysfunction on the other. This is especially so with chronic brain damage known or suspected to have been present for some years before the assessment is conducted. The reasons for these sometimes loose relationships have to do with such factors as how the person has, over time, reacted to and coped with the losses brought about by the brain damage. And, in turn, the success of efforts to cope has to do with the social environment in which the individual has lived. How understanding have parents and associates been, for example, or how well has the school system met the special educational needs of the individual? Therefore, in addition to taking into account the imperfect nature of the biological assessment instruments themselves and our incomplete understanding of how the brain actually functions, researchers must consider these experiential factors that operate over time to contribute to the clinical picture.

A final caution is reflected in the simple yet often unappreciated fact that in attempting to understand the neurocognitive consequences of any brain-injuring event, we must understand the abilities that the patient has brought to that event (Boll, 1985). This straightforward truth brings to mind the story of the man who, recovering from an accident that has broken all the fingers in both hands, earnestly asks the surgeon whether he will be able to play the piano when his wounds heal. "Yes, I'm sure you will," says the doctor reassuringly. "That's wonderful," exclaims the man, "I've always wanted to be able to play the piano."

Canadian Perspectives 4.2 summarizes an ongoing program of research undertaken by Connolly and his colleagues that shows how the complexities involved in clinical assessment may require an equally complex approach, one that combines various aspects of abnormal, cognitive, and physiological psychology.

Table 4.3

Biological Assessment Methods

Brain imaging	CT and MRI scans reveal the structure of the brain. PET and fMRI are used to study brain function.
Neurochemical assessment	Includes postmortem analysis of neurotransmitters and receptors, assays of metabolites of neurotransmitters, and PET scans of receptors.
Neuropsychological assessment	Behavioural tests such as the Halstead-Reitan and Luria-Nebraska assess abilities such as motor speed, memory, and spatial ability. Deficits on particular tests help localize an area of brain dysfunction.
Psychophysiological assessment	Includes measures of electrical activity in the autonomic nervous system, such as skin conductance, or in the central nervous system, such as the EEG and ERPs.

Canadian Perspectives/4.2

Cognitive Event-Related Potentials in Neuropsychological Assessment

A vexing problem in clinical assessment is how to assess levels of intellectual functioning and related processes in patients who have experienced a trauma (e.g., a stroke) that has had an impact on their cognitive abilities and capacities. Many standard assessment devices, in order to be useful, require that the patient have at least some communication ability and/or the ability to respond behaviourally. What can a clinician do when a person appears to lack the necessary communication abilities, but the clinician still must make some determination of neuropsychological functioning?

One innovative solution is outlined in a recent series of neuropsychological studies conducted by John Connolly and Ryan D'Arcy at Dalhousie University in Halifax, Nova Scotia (see Connolly, 2000; Connolly & D'Arcy, 2000; D'Arcy & Connolly, 1999; Marchand, D'Arcy, & Connolly, 2002). Their research is based on the use of cognitive event-related brain potentials. Cognitive **event-related potentials (ERPs)** are specific brain wave potentials that can be evoked by standardized neuropsychological tests modified for computer presentation. Research has demonstrated that ERPs are sensitive to aspects of language, attention, and memory. Different ERP components reflect different cognitive processes. Connolly and his colleagues (2000) summarized their work this way, "Our working hypothesis is that regardless of the ability to execute the behavioural activity, the engaging of specific cognitive functions should lead to different ERP patterns" (p. 100).

Connolly, D'Arcy, and associates argued that the use of cognitive ERPs in assessment offers a number of advantages in addition to addressing the problem inherent in evaluating patients who lack communication ability. Cognitive ERPs provide important information about the cognitive strategies used by an individual, for example, and the results can be clearly interpreted without ambiguity. Most importantly, these researchers have shown that it is possible to assess cognitive ERPs by creating and modifying computerized versions of standardized tests such as the Token Test (see D'Arcy & Connolly, 1999), the WISC-III and WAIS-R NI vocabulary subtests (Connolly, Major, Allen, & D'Arcy, 1999), the Wechsler Intelligence Scale for Children III, and the Peabody Picture Vocabulary Test—Revised (Marchand et al., 2002).

Gaetz (2002) noted that cognitive ERPS are particularly useful when brain damage is diffuse rather than focal, since other techniques, such as computed tomography (CT) and magnetic resonance imaging (MRI), focus on identifying deficits in localized, precise areas and are less able to detect more widespread damage. Gaetz (2002) suggested that cognitive ERPS are high in clinical utility because "they are practical, easily administered, cost effective and brief procedures" that can often be completed within 30 minutes.

Connolly et al. (2000) reported a number of case studies where cognitive ERPs were used. One case study of a young man with aphasia serves as a vivid illustration of the usefulness and significance of cognitive ERPs in clinical assessment (see Connolly, Mate-Kole, & Joyce, 1999). Connolly described the outcome of this case in the following manner:

> Confined to a wheelchair, aphasic, and with no apparent ability to engage in goal-directed behavior, the young man was judged to have lost all intellectual function and to be a poor candidate for rehabilitation. Just prior to being discharged, he was assessed using cognitive ERPs in a congruous/incongruous sentence paradigm and found to respond normally to speech stimuli. He was admitted into a rehabilitation program on the basis of these results. About four months later he was discharged having responded well to rehabilitation efforts of the hospital staff. Such a result demonstrates unequivocally what can be achieved with cognitive ERPS just as it validates the basic cognitive ERP research upon which the paradigm was based. (p. 101)

The potential of cognitive ERPs is clearly evident from this case study and related research investigations, even though this specific research is still in its early phases. In addition to the clinical applicability of this work, it also facilitates—through analysis of ERP component patterns assessed within the context of a particular test—understanding about how people perform particular neuropsychological tasks (D'Arcy, Connolly, & Crocker, 1999). Although the focus of Connolly and D'Arcy's work has been on the assessment of mental functions following neurological insult, it has been suggested by Ingram and Siegle (2001, p. 121) that physiological measurement, such as the ERP, can "be incorporated during therapy sessions to gauge aspects of cognition during techniques such as role plays and thought challenges."

Thinking Critically

1. In recent years there has been concern that the Canadian government is attempting to downplay its role as a major source of basic research funding by increasing demands for universities to collaborate with business and industry and by questioning the relevance or contribution of some areas of psychological research to the needs of taxpayers (e.g., health issues). Do you consider research such as that conducted by Connolly, D'Arcy, and their colleagues to be "relevant"?
2. Do you think that cognitive ERP research has the potential for significant "impact capability" in areas relevant to abnormal psychology during the next quarter century?
3. How likely is it that approaches that combine findings from the different assessment areas and approaches described in this chapter will lay a foundation for, and contribute to the development of, effective rehabilitative and therapeutic interventions?

Cultural Diversity and Clinical Assessment

The accuracy and validity of a clinical assessment may depend upon a clinician's skill and ability to take into account the cultural context in which a client's psychological difficulties occur. At the same time, as stated in Chapter 2, it is important for the clinician to avoid stereotyping members of a culture.

We should also note that the reliability and validity of various forms of psychological assessment have been questioned on the grounds that their content and scoring procedures reflect the culture of white European North Americans and so do not accurately assess people from other cultures. In this section we discuss problems of cultural bias in assessment and what can be done about them.

Cultural Bias in Assessment

The issue of **cultural bias** in assessment is not simple, nor is it clear that such biases make the assessment instruments useless. Some studies of bias in testing conducted in the United States have demonstrated that mainstream procedures, such as the Wechsler Intelligence Scale for Children—Revised, have equivalent predictive validity for minority and nonminority children (Sattler, 1992); IQ tests predict academic achievement equally well for both groups. Similarly, MMPI profiles relate equally well to clinician ratings among African Americans and Caucasians (McNulty et al., 1997).Nonetheless, some research studies suggest that there may be significant problems in using standardized intelligence testing with Native American and Canadian First Nations, Inuit, and Innu clients, especially children. Canadian Perspectives 4.3 addresses this issue.

Assessment must take the person's cultural background into account. Believing in possession by spirits is common in some cultures and thus should not always be taken to mean that the believer is psychotic.

Canadian Perspectives/4.3

IQ Testing and Aboriginal Canadians

"Apparently, many well-meaning but misinformed members of our profession are using intelligence testing in a completely inappropriate and even harmful manner. The clients involved may not have the power or may not believe they have the power to do anything about it. With such a power imbalance, it is all the more important that counsellors be absolutely scrupulous about the ethics of testing."
—Wes G. Darrow of the Canadian International Development Agency, commenting on the use of intelligence testing with Native Canadians (1986, p. 98.)

Is bias in assessment present when the norms of the majority population are applied to culturally different minority group children and adults? More specifically, are there problems in the assessment of intelligence using standardized IQ tests with culturally different Canadian Aboriginal people?

This possibility was addressed in a study by Wilgosh, Mulcahy, and Watters (1986) for a sample of Canadian Inuit children whose WISC-R scores, using the original norms, would fall below a scaled score of 70 (see the section on mental retardation in Chapter 15). Past studies with Native Canadian children had typically reported below average verbal scores and average or above average performance scores for the WISC (e.g., St. John, Krichev, & Bauman, 1976) and the WISC-R (e.g., Seyfort, Spreen, & Lahmer, 1980). Seyfort et al. (1980) identified an apparent lack of internal consistency for many of the WISC-R subtests for their Native sample. They suggested that the children had difficulty understanding numerous items and/or that many WISC-R items tapped different abilities and skills in the Native sample relative to the majority population. The participants in the Wilgosh et al. (1986) "Inuit Norming Study" were a randomly selected representative sample of girls and boys between the ages of 7 years 0 months and 14 years 11 months from the Kitikmeot and Keewatin Districts of Canada's Northwest Territories. The full WISC-R was administered by skilled psychometrists with special training related to the assessment of northern Native children. The children were assessed individually, and an effort was made to optimize the conditions of testing. Five items in the information subtest, one in the similarities subtest, and one in the comprehension subtest were modified to reflect Canadian content (e.g., Vernon, 1977). In addition, one similarities item and two arithmetic items were reworded to facilitate understanding.

What did Wilgosh et al. (1986) find? Over three-quarters of the children (77 percent) attained a verbal IQ scaled score less than 70, but only 5.7 percent of them had a performance scaled score less than 70. The respective percentage for full scale IQ was about 32. What do these results imply? Approximately 75 percent of Inuit children in the norming group would be classified as "retarded" *on the basis of their verbal IQ scores alone*. If the group had reflected the theoretical normal curve and the Wechsler normative group, the percentage would actually have approximated only 2.2 percent (Wilgosh et al., 1996). The authors concluded that, "using the Wechsler Verbal and Full Scale norms for the WISC-R would result in misclassification of great numbers of Inuit children" (p. 273). Further, a major factor resulting in the misclassification was presumed to be verbal comprehension of the English language, the second language for all of the Inuit children. The information and vocabulary subtests accounted for the majority of unanswered or incorrectly answered items.

Wilgosh et al. (1986) noted that "in actual educational programming for the Inuit children ... sole reliance is certainly not placed on the WISC-R scores" (p. 275). Nonetheless, Darou (1992) argued that many Aboriginal children are, in fact, streamed into special education programs on the basis of their IQ test results. Further, according to Darou, some Native administrative bodies perceive intelligence testing to be "just another tool of white domination" (p. 97). He believes that IQ tests are biased both *against* and *for* Native people in unusual and complicated ways, as illustrated in this anecdote about Zachary a hunter from a remote area near James Bay who was administered the Kohs Blocks subtest:

> The test involves showing the subject a square drawing on a small card. The subject recreates the design with four or nine red and white cubes. The subject is assigned certain points depending upon how quickly he or she completes the task. This test has the highest validity of all the WISC sub-tests. When Zachary did it, he appeared to be in no hurry, he placed the blocks by an 'S' pattern instead of by rows as most people do (the 'S' saving two arm movements), and at the end he would frame the blocks with his fingers for a few seconds, and sometimes adjust the blocks a little. He did the test so fast that he went off-scale on all seven examples. The test goes off scale at an I. Q. equivalent of 180.
>
> In discussions afterwards, Zachary explained that he believed the test was biased in his favour. He pointed out that, when he was young, his family ate or starved depending on his ability to recognize patterns. (p. 98)

Despite anecdotes such as these, the weight of the available evidence indicates that Aboriginal people often perform poorly on standardized tests of intelligence, especially on measures developed to assess verbal intelligence, in comparison to the original normative group.

Thinking Critically

1. Do you think that "renorming" a test such as the WISC-R to a higher or locally determined standard of performance would be a solution to the problem of bias in testing? Under what circumstances would a comparison with national norms be considered relevant and appropriate? As Wilgosh et al. (1986, p. 275) noted:

   > Whereas renorming of tests developed for use with the majority culture is useful in assessing the academic and intellectual performance of minority children, such tests do not assess social adaptability to the minority culture and adaptability to movement within the larger cultural context, and may mask differences in educational opportunity that render these children "retarded" in the broader cultural context.

2. Is it possible that the low scaled scores for verbal intelligence of the Inuit children, relative to the normative data, reflect, not a test bias, but differences in educational opportunities that have resulted in "real" differences in educational achievement?

3. Do you think that the findings reported by Wilgosh et al. (1986) are unique to the Inuit or do you think that they could apply to any minority group in Canada that has English as a second language, especially if that group lives in an isolated cultural and educational context?

4. What do you think should be the "culturally meaningful educational priorities" (Wilgosh et al., 1986, p. 275) for Aboriginal children in Canada? Should increased emphasis on comprehension of the English language be a high priority in the local cultural context? Or, as appeared to be the case with Zachary, should the focus be on adaptability within their own culture?

Cultural biases work in different ways—they may cause clinicians to over- or underestimate psychological problems in members of other cultures (Lopez, 1996). As noted in Canadian Perspectives 4.3, Aboriginal children may be overrepresented in special-education classes, which may be a result of subtle or not so subtle biases in the tests used to determine such placement. Yet consider the example of an Asian Canadian man who is very emotionally withdrawn. Should the clinician consider that lower levels of emotional expressiveness in men are viewed more positively in Asian cultures than in Euro–North American culture? A clinician who too quickly attributes the behaviour to a cultural difference rather than to a psychological disorder risks overlooking an emotional disorder that he or she would be likely to diagnose if the patient were a white male. Again, the effect of cultural bias in clinical assessment works both ways.

How do such biases come about? As noted in Chapter 2, cultural differences in Canada are many, and they may affect assessment in various ways. Language differences, differing religious and spiritual beliefs, illness beliefs, attitudes about family and relationships, cultural views of competition, the alienation or timidity of members of visible minority cultures when being assessed by clinicians of the Euro–North American culture—all these factors and more can play a role. For example, Native North Americans, taught by their culture to cooperate with others, are less likely to warm to the task of taking an aptitude test, which is by nature highly individualistic and competitive (O'Conner, 1989). Non–English-speaking people being assessed by English-speaking clinicians may be poorly served by translators (Sabin, 1975). Clinicians who encounter clients claiming to be surrounded by or possessed by spirits might view this belief as a sign of schizophrenia. Yet in Inuit culture such a belief often occurs in distressed people, perhaps as a culture-bound defence mechanism and/or attempt at problem-solving (e.g., Seltzer, 1983). Therefore, believing in spirit intrusion should probably not be taken as a sign of schizophrenia in an Inuit person. As noted in Chapter 2, language is a much more important diversity issue in Canada than in the United States.

Cultural differences can lead to different results on an IQ or aptitude test. For example, Aboriginal Canadian children may lack interest in the individualistic, competitive nature of IQ tests because of the co-operative, group-oriented values instilled by their culture

Although it is important to be aware of that cultural differences have the potential to bias clinical assessment, it is not clear that attempting to include cultural differences in one's assessment work necessarily contributes to a helpful diagnosis (e.g., Lopez & Hernandez, 1986). Assume that a clinician attaches less psychopathological significance to the hallucinations of an Asian Canadian woman because the clinician believes that hallucinations are more prevalent among Asian Canadians. This clinician would be minimizing the seriousness of the woman's problems by attributing them to a *perceived* subcultural norm. As a result, the clinician might not consider a diagnosis of schizophrenia, a decision that may not be in the woman's best interests.

Cultural biases can affect not only *who* is diagnosed, but also *how* the person is diagnosed. American studies have reported that clinicians were more likely to diagnose a patient as having schizophrenia if the case summary referred to the person as African American than if it described the person as white (Blake, 1973), that African American patients were overdiagnosed as having schizophrenia and underdiagnosed as having a mood disorder (Simon et al., 1973), and that, based on identical symptoms, lower-class African American patients were more likely to be diagnosed as alcoholic than were white, middle-class patients (this latter, given the symptoms exhibited, was a disservice to the white patients) (Luepnitz, Randolph, & Gutsch, 1982).

Cultural differences cannot be avoided. And the cultural biases that can creep into clinical assessment do not necessarily yield to efforts to compensate for them. There is no simple answer. DSM-IV-TR's inclusion of cultural factors in the discussion of every category of disorder may well sensitize clinicians to the issue, a necessary first step (Lopez & Guarnaccia, 2000). When practitioners were surveyed a number of years ago, they overwhelmingly reported taking culture into account in their clinical work (Lopez, 1994), so it appears that the problem, if not the solution, is clearly in focus.

Strategies for Avoiding Cultural Bias in Assessment

Clinicians can—and do—use various methods to minimize the negative effects of cultural biases when assessing patients. Sattler (1982) makes some helpful suggestions that can guide clinicians in the selection and interpretation of tests and other assessment data. First, clinicians should make efforts to learn about the culture of the person being assessed. This knowledge might come from reading, consultation with colleagues, and direct discussion with the client. Second, it is essential for clinicians to determine the client's preferred language and to consider testing in more than one language. The latter point is especially critical in Canada, given the importance of language as a grouping variable for diversity (Bowman, 2000). Recall that telephone translation is offered in 148 languages in the city of Toronto (Purvis, 1999)!

Language and Bias The issue of testing in another language is both complex and difficult—especially if the clinician wants to adapt to the client's language standardized tests that were developed in a different language (typically English in North America). This can be problematic even when the clinician is fluent in the client's language. We have already pointed out that language can be a problem in the assessment of intelligence in Aboriginal children. Since language is important in every culture, if language is involved in any psychological test, then an accurate translation is required. Butcher et al. (1999) summarized generally accepted, sophisticated, and rigorous test translation and adaptation methods, including the following:

- careful translation of items by multiple, bilingual translators
- use of informants to verify both the linguistic and social appropriateness of items
- integration of different translations of items into an experimental version

- "back-translation" of items with re-translation of problem items followed by further back-translation until the desired form of items is achieved
- pretesting of the experimental version on a bilingual sample

It is then vital for the test adapter to demonstrate that the test's validity (content, factorial, and predictive) is maintained in the target culture through rigorous research methodologies. The reader can readily see that appropriate test translation and validation is a difficult, time-consuming, and expensive process.

Although some widely used standardized tests have been translated into numerous languages and carefully validated in those languages, other tests (such as the many specialized inventories and measures developed for cognitive and behavioural assessment) are still in the adaptation process or are currently available in English only. Even if the test is available in the client's language, its use could be problematic if it was validated on a different cultural group. For example, Bowman (2000) noted that psychologists in Quebec typically use French versions of the Wechsler individual intelligence tests that do not have any Canadian norms. Although Douglas Jackson from the University of Western Ontario has developed a group test with both English-Canadian and French-Canadian norms—the Multidimensional Aptitude Battery (Jackson, 1984/1998)—there does not appear to be a good standardized test with norms for all the other minority groups in Canada.

The MMPI-2 has been extensively adapted for international use and translated into numerous languages, including French. Clinicians in Canada, therefore, have a validated French-language version of the MMPI-2 and access to norms based on the U.S. standardization sample or the nationally derived norms for France (which are very close to the American norms). Since Canada is a bilingual country with a significant francophone community outside of Quebec, it is essential for clinicians to have access to tests written and validated in both French and English. Unfortunately, psychologists working with francophones generally use the major American tests translated into French. Typically, contemporary Canadian standardization has not been completed. Although Jackson has also developed Canadian tests for the assessment of psychopathology (Jackson, 1988/1997) and the dimensions of personality disorders (Jackson & Livesley, 1999), according to Bowman (2000, p. 239), "These tests are less frequently used in Canadian clinical work or reported in research than are related American instruments."

In Chapter 6, we will examine the anxiety disorders. At this point, consider that there is a multitude of cognitive-behavioural measures that have been developed in the English language to assess these disorders and constructs hypothesized to be associated with them (e.g., dysfunctional attitudes). All of these measures should be translated into French (especially Canadian French) and validated for clinical and research use with the millions of people in Canada whose first language is French. Some progress has been made. For example, for the assessment of panic disorder, researchers from the University of Quebec at Montreal recently produced validated francophone versions of the Mobility Inventory for Agoraphobia (Stephenson, Marchand, & Lavallee, 1997), the Agoraphobic Cognitions Questionnaire, and the Body Sensations Questionnaire (Stephenson, Marchand, & Lavallee, 1998, 1999). Real Labelle and his colleagues (Labelle, Lachance, & Morval, 1996), also from the University of Quebec, validated a French-Canadian version of the Reasons for Living Inventory, which is often used in clinical and research work on depression and suicide risk (see Chapter 10). A French version of the widely used Beck Depression Inventory was previously developed by Bourque and Beaudette in 1982. However, these are but a few examples of the literally hundreds of cognitive-behavioural assessment instruments available in the English language, most of which are not validated for use with French Canadians.

There are, of course, other good examples of tests that have been translated and validated for use with French Canadians. As one example, recall our introduction to the Canadian Study of Health and Aging project. The sampling technique made it possible to test a representative sample of all Canadians, and participants could choose to respond in either English or French. The developers of the test battery, particularly the francophone neuropsychologists, were cognizant of the difference between literal test translation and the development of culturally equivalent tests and had to develop reliable and valid French versions of all of the tests that were part of the battery (Tuokko et al., 1995).

Can we assume that a test in English developed for one culture or country (e.g., the United States) is appropriate for another English-speaking culture or country (e.g., Canada). Perhaps not! A case in point is the information subtest of the revised version of the Wechsler Adult Intelligence Scale (WAIS-R). Many of the questions are problematic for Canadian clients because of the culturally specific American content (e.g., Boer & Pugh, 1988; Pugh & Boer, 1989). As many as 10 of the 29 items lack face validity for non-Americans and could be judged as unfair and inappropriate by Canadian respondents. Further, some of the culturally specific questions could be disproportionately difficult for Canadians. For example, a question about "Senators" could be significantly more difficult for Canadian respondents than for Americans because Americans should be expected to be more familiar with this component of the political system in the United States. A common but makeshift solution on the part of many Canadian psychologists has been to substitute what they perceive to be more culturally appropriate questions. Pugh and Boer (1989) addressed these issues and determined that empirical assessments of level of difficulty for Canadians differed significantly from the American normative sample for most of the items that lack face validity. They also determined that 9 of 10 Canadian face-valid substitutes reflected more accurately the difficulty level of the original standardization data. Thus, use of the original information subtest could inappropriately *lower* the individual IQs of Canadian clients. Nonetheless, Don Saklofske from the University of Saskatchewan and his colleagues (e.g., Saklofske & Hildebrand, 1999) have been involved in efforts to "renorm" the Wechsler tests of intelligence downward, since Canadian raw score means actually appear to be *higher* than the equivalent scores in the United States. Although certain items may lack validity and norms need to be adjusted, Saklofske and associates have also shown that the actual factor structure (or major dimensions or components) of the third edition of the WAIS was comparable to the factor model of the American standardization sample when the WAIS was administered to a representative Canadian sample of adults (Saklofske, Hildebrand, & Gorsuch, 2000). Overall, however, the cultural relevance of content and population-specific norms remain key issues.

Canadian Psychological Tests? Is there really a need for specifically Canadian psychological tests? Although the issue is controversial, according to Bowman (2000), the evidence that cognitive abilities, personality, or emotional condition is structured differently in different cultures is sparse. With the exception of intelligence tests, Bowman asserts that the need for Canadian tests is still an open empirical question. Assessment procedures can, of course, be modified to ensure that the person truly understands the requirements of the task. Consistent with Sattler's (1982) first suggestion, it is important for clinicians in Canada to be aware of the cultural diversity of our country and the implications of such diversity for understanding the clients seen in their clinical practice. For example, suppose that a First Nations Canadian child performed poorly on a test measuring psychomotor speed. The examiner's hunch is that the child did not understand the importance of working quickly and was overconcerned with accuracy instead. The test could be administered again after a more thorough explanation of the importance of working quickly without worrying about mistakes. If the child's performance improves, the examiner has gained an important understanding of him or her and has avoided diagnosing psychomotor-speed deficits when the child's test-taking strategy was more at issue.

When the examiner and client have different ethnic backgrounds, the examiner may need to make an extra effort to establish a rapport that will result in the person's best performance. For example, when testing a shy, Filipino elementary school student, one of the authors was unable to obtain a verbal response to test questions. However, the boy's mother was able to provide the clinician with an audio tape of the boy talking in an animated and articulate manner to his father, leading to a judgment that the test results did not represent a valid assessment of the child's language skills. When testing was repeated in the child's own home with his mother present, advanced verbal abilities were observed.

As Lopez (1994) pointed out, however, "the distance between cultural responsiveness and cultural stereotyping can be short" (p. 123). To minimize such problems, clinicians are encouraged to be particularly tentative in drawing conclusions about minority patients. Rather, they are advised to make *hypotheses* about the influence of culture on a particular client, entertain alternative hypotheses, and then test those hypotheses.

In a case from our files, a young man was suspected of having schizophrenia. One prominent symptom he reported was hearing voices. However, he claimed that he heard voices only while meditating and that within his (Buddhist) culture this experience was not uncommon. To test this hypothesis, the examiner (with the permission of the client) contacted the family's religious leader. The Buddhist priest indicated that the symptom reported by this young man was very unusual, and it turned out that the religious community to which he belonged was quite concerned about his increasingly bizarre behaviour. Thus, the hypothesis that his symptom should be attributed to cultural factors was refuted, and an error of failing to detect psychopathology was avoided.

Whenever practical, it is preferable that the mental health professional responsible for a patient's assessment (and treatment) come from a similar cultural and ethnic background, speak the same language, and be sensitive to and understand the values, life experiences, and issues facing the client.

SUMMARY

- Clinicians rely on several modes of assessment in trying to find out how best to describe a patient or client, search for the reasons a person is troubled, and design effective preventive or remedial treatments.
- Regardless of how unstructured an assessment method may appear, it inevitably reflects the paradigm of the investigator. Our earlier discussion of scientific paradigms in Chapter 2 is important to bear in mind when considering how information is gathered in the clinical context.
- However clinicians and researchers go about gathering assessment information, they must be concerned with both reliability and validity, the former referring to whether measurement is consistent and replicable, the latter to whether our assessments are tapping into what we want to be measuring. The many assessment procedures described in this chapter vary greatly in their reliability and validity.

- The two main approaches to assessment are psychological and biological. Psychological assessments include clinical interviews, structured or relatively unstructured conversations in which the clinician probes the patient for information about his or her problems; psychological tests, which range from the presentation of ambiguous stimuli, as in the Rorschach Inkblot Test and the Thematic Apperception Test, to empirically derived self-report questionnaires, such as the Minnesota Multiphasic Personality Inventory; and intelligence tests, which evaluate a person's intellectual ability and predict how well he or she will do in future academic situations.
- In behavioural and cognitive assessment, information is often gathered on four sets of factors (SORC): situational determinants, organismic variables, responses, and the consequences of behaviour. An alternative approach formulates an individualized cognitive-behavioural theory about a case with a view to helping the therapist develop a plan for treatment. Whereas traditional assessment seeks to understand people in terms of general traits or personality structure, behavioural and cognitive assessment is concerned more with how people act, feel, and think in particular situations. Specificity is the hallmark of cognitive and behavioural assessment, the assumption being that assessing psychological variables such as anxiety or distorted cognitions as they occur in specific situations will yield more useful information about people. Critics believe that such data may at times be too narrow to yield conclusions that are meaningful.
- Behavioural and cognitive assessment approaches include direct observation of behaviour either in natural surroundings or in contrived settings; interviews and self-report measures that are situational in their focus; and specialized, think-aloud cognitive assessment procedures that attempt to uncover beliefs, attitudes, and thinking patterns thought to be important in theories of psychopathology and therapy. Family assessment focuses on current or previous types and levels of family functioning.
- Biological assessments include sophisticated, computer-controlled imaging techniques, such as CT scans, that allow us to actually see various structures of the living brain; neurochemical assays that allow inferences about levels of neurotransmitters; neuropsychological tests, such as the Halstead-Reitan, that base inferences of brain defects on variations in responses to psychological tests; and psychophysiological measurements, such as heart rate, skin conductance, and event-related potentials.
- Cultural factors play a role in clinical assessment. Minority clients may react differently from majority clients to assessment techniques developed on the basis of research with majority populations. Clinicians can have biases when evaluating minority patients, which can lead to minimizing or overdiagnosing a patient's psychopathology. The numerous linguistic minorities represent an important diversity issue in Canada, one that has important implications for clinical assessment. Cultural differences and clinician bias are significant for scientific, practical, and ethical reasons.

KEY TERMS

alternate-form reliability (p. 101)
behavioural observation (p. 112)
clinical interview (p. 103)
cognitive-behavioural case formulation cognitive(p. 110)
construct validity (p. 102)
content validity (p. 102)
criterion validity (p. 102)
CT scan (p. 119)
cultural bias (p. 126)
ecological momentary assessment (EMA) (p. 112)
electrocardiogram (p. 123)
electrodermal responding (p. 123)
electroencephalogram (EEG) (p. 124)
event-related potential (ERP) (p. 125)
family functioning (p. 115)
functional magnetic resonance imaging (fMRI) (p. 119)
intelligence test (p. 109)
internal consistency reliability (p. 101)
magnetic resonance imaging (MRI) (p. 119)
Minnesota Multiphasic Personality Inventory (MMPI) (p. 104)
neurologist (p. 121)
neuropsychological tests (p. 121)
neuropsychologist (p. 121)
personality inventory (p. 104)
PET scan (p. 120)
projective hypothesis (p. 107)
projective test (p. 107)
psychological tests (p. 104)
psychophysiology (p. 123)
reactivity (of behaviour) (p. 113)
Rorschach Inkblot Test (p. 107)
self-monitoring (p. 112)
standardization (p. 104)
structured interview (p. 104)
test-retest reliability (p. 101)
Thematic Apperception Test (TAT) (p. 108)
thought-listing (p. 115)
videotape reconstruction (p. 115)

Reflections: Past, Present, and Future

- In Chapter 2, we examined prominent contemporary paradigms of abnormal psychology, summarized the consequences of adopting a particular paradigm, and introduced integrative paradigms. Assume that you are a practising clinical psychologist. Will your approach to clinical assessment and the assessment procedures that you choose be influenced by the conceptual framework that you prefer? Will your choice of assessment strategies be influenced by the nature of the specific psychological disorders presented by your clients? Return to this question once you have studied all of the disorders described in this book.
- In our discussion of the cognitive-behavioural approach to assessment, we described two different systems to guide the assessment: the traditional behavioural SORC and the more recent case formulation approaches that place a greater emphasis on cognitive factors. Which of these approaches seems most relevant to you, and why? Do you think that there is any value to an integration of the two approaches? What form would such integration take?
- Persons and Davidson (2001) described the case of "Judy" to illustrate a cognitive-behavioural case formulation approach. Among other problems, Judy was depressed. Based on the case formulation applied to Judy and your understanding of various cognitive-behavioral treatment strategies, and in particular the treatment of depression as described in Chapter 10, summarize the specific interventions you would employ in Judy's case. Develop a comprehensive treatment plan.

chapter 5

Research Methods in the Study of Abnormal Behaviour

"The great tragedy of science—the slaying of a beautiful hypothesis by an ugly fact."
—T.H. Huxley, *Biogenesis and Abiognesis*

"... it is clinical research which has dramatically altered the course of illness and of clinical care by taking us from ice wraps to lithium, from insulin shock to olanzepine, and from psychoanalytic regression to cognitive-behavioural therapy. This research has been meaningful at basic, clinical, and health-systems levels."
—Paul E. Garfinkel, president and CEO, and David S. Goldbloom, physician-in-chief, of the Centre for Addiction and Mental Health, Toronto (2000, p. 163)

Jean-Paul Riopelle, *Coups sur Coups,* 1953
oil on canvas, 73.0 x 100.3 cm; ART GALLERY OF ONTARIO, TORONTO
Gift from J.S. McLean, Canadian Fund, 1954

Given the different ways of conceptualizing and treating abnormal behaviour and the problems in its classification and assessment, it follows that there is also less than total agreement about how abnormal behaviour ought to be studied and what are the facts of the field. Yet it is precisely because facts about mental disorders are hard to come by that it is important to pursue them using the scientific research methods that are applied in contemporary psychopathology. This chapter discusses these methods and should provide a sense of the strengths and limitations of each. We hope, too, that the reader will gain respect for the information these methods have made available and the discoveries they have made possible.

Science and Scientific Methods

In current practice, science is the pursuit of systematized knowledge through observation. Thus, the term, which comes from the Latin *scire*, "to know," refers both to a method (the systematic acquisition and evaluation of information) and to a goal (the development of general theories that explain the information). It is always important for scientific observations and explanations to be testable (open to systematic probes) and reliable. In this section, we look briefly at the criteria of testability and reliability and in more depth at the key role theory plays. In the next section, we will examine the major research methods used in studying abnormal psychology.

Testability and Replicability

A scientific approach requires first that propositions and ideas be stated in a clear and precise way. Only then can scientific claims be exposed to systematic probes and tests, any one of which could negate the scientist's expectations about what will be found. Statements, theories, and assertions, regardless of how plausible they may seem, must be testable in the public arena and subject to disproof. The attitude of the scientist must be a doubting one. It is not enough to assert, for example, that traumatic experiences during childhood may cause psychological maladjustment in adulthood. This is no more than a possibility or proposition. According to a scientific point of view, such a hypothesis must be amenable to systematic testing that could show it to be false.

Closely related to testability is the requirement that each observation that contributes to a scientific body of knowledge be replicable or reliable. We have discussed the importance of reliability as it relates to diagnosis and assessment. It is equally important in the research process. Whatever is observed must be replicable; that is, it must occur under prescribed circumstances not once, but repeatedly. An event must be reproducible under the circumstances stated, anywhere, anytime. If the event cannot be reproduced, scientists become wary of the legitimacy of the original observation.

The Role of Theory

A theory is a set of propositions meant to explain a class of phenomena. A primary goal of science is to advance theories to account for data, often by proposing cause-effect relationships. The results of empirical research allow the adequacy of theories to be evaluated. Theories themselves can also play an important role in guiding research by suggesting that certain additional data be collected. More specifically, a theory permits the generation of hypotheses, expectations about what should occur if a theory is true, to be tested in research. For example, suppose you want to test a classical-conditioning theory of phobias. As a researcher, you begin by developing a specific hypothesis based on the theory. For example, if the classical-conditioning theory is valid, people with phobias should be more likely than those in the general population to have had traumatic experiences with the situations they fear, such as flying. By collecting data on the frequency of traumatic experiences with phobic stimuli among people with phobias and comparing this information with corresponding data from people without phobias, you could determine whether your hypothesis was confirmed, supporting the theory, or disconfirmed, invalidating the theory.

The generation of a theory is perhaps the most challenging part of the scientific enterprise—and one of the least understood. It is sometimes asserted, for example, that a scientist formulates a theory simply by considering data that have been previously collected and then deciding, in a rather straightforward fashion, that a given way of thinking about the data is the most economical and useful.

Although some theory-building follows this course, not all does. Aspects too seldom mentioned are the *creativity* of the act and the *excitement* of finding a novel way to conceptualize things. A theory sometimes seems to leap from the scientist's head in a wonderful moment of insight. New ideas suddenly occur, and connections previously overlooked are suddenly grasped. What formerly seemed obscure or meaningless makes a new kind of sense within the framework of the new theory.

Theories are *constructions* put together by scientists. In formulating a theory, scientists must often make use of theoretical concepts, unobservable states or processes that are inferred from observable data. Repression is a theoretical concept, as is the mediating fear response discussed in Chapter 2. Theoretical concepts are inferred from observable data. For example, behaviourists infer a mediating fear response based on a person's avoidance of a situation. Similarly, an analyst might infer the presence of a repressed conflict from a patient's continual avoidance of discussing his or her relationship with authority figures.

Several advantages can be gained by using theoretical terms. Theoretical concepts, for example, often bridge spatiotemporal relations. An example from early physics shows how a theoretical term may account for a spatial relationship. It had been observed that when a magnet was placed close to iron filings, some of the filings moved toward the magnet. How does one piece of metal influence another over the spatial distance? The inferred concept of magnetic fields proved useful in accounting for this phenomenon. Similarly, in abnormal psychology, we may want to bridge temporal gaps with theoretical concepts. If a child has had a particularly frightening experience and his or her behaviour changes for a lengthy period of time, we need to explain how the earlier event exerted an influence over subsequent behaviour. The unobservable and inferred concept of *acquired fear* has been very helpful in this regard.

Theoretical concepts can also summarize already observed relationships. We may observe that whether people are taking an examination, are expecting a momentary electric shock, or are arguing with a companion, they all have sweaty palms, trembling hands, and a fast heartbeat. If we ask them how they feel, they all report that they are tense. The relationships can be depicted as shown in Figure 5.1a. We could also say that all the situations have made these individuals anxious and that anxiety has in turn caused the reported tension, the sweaty palms, the faster heartbeat, and the trembling hands. Figure 5.1b shows anxiety as a theoretical concept explaining what has been observed. The first figure, which shows the relationships between the situations and the behaviour, is much more complex than the second, in which the theoretical concept of anxiety becomes a mediator of the relationships.

With these advantages in mind, we must consider the criteria to be applied in judging the legitimacy of a theoretical concept. One earlier school of thought, called *operationism,* proposed that each concept take as its meaning a single observable and measurable operation. In this way, each theoretical concept would be *nothing more* than one particular measurable event. For example, anxiety might be identified as nothing more than scoring above 50 on a particular anxiety questionnaire.

It soon became clear that this approach deprived theoretical concepts of their greatest advantage. If each theoretical concept is operationalized in only one way, its generality is lost. If the theoretical concept of learning, for instance, is identified as a single operation or effect that can be measured, such as how often a rat presses a bar, other behaviour, such as a child's performing arithmetic problems or a college student's studying this book, cannot also be called learning, and attempts to relate the different phenomena to one another might be discouraged.

The early operationist point of view quickly gave way to the more flexible position that a theoretical concept can be defined by sets of operations or effects. The concept can thus be linked to several different measurements, each of which taps a different facet of the concept. For example, in Figure 5.1b a subjective report of tension, physiological changes, and hand trembling form a set of operations defining anxiety. Theoretical concepts are better defined by sets of operations than by a single operation.

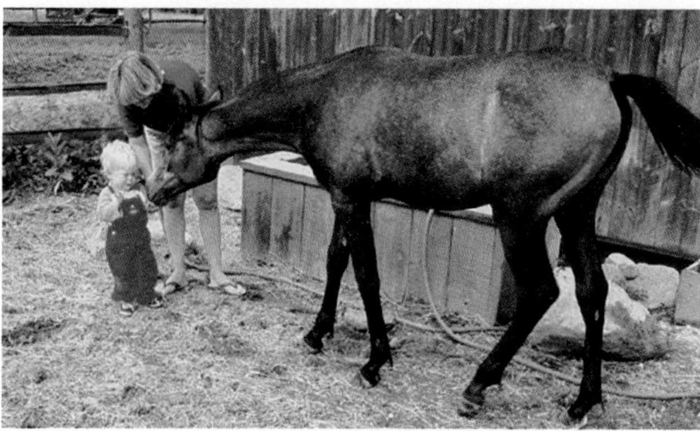

A theoretical concept, such as acquired fear, is useful in accounting for the fact that some earlier experience can have an effect on current behaviour.

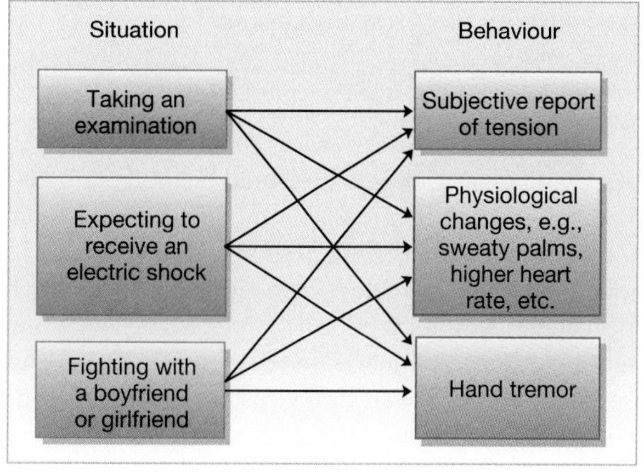

(a)

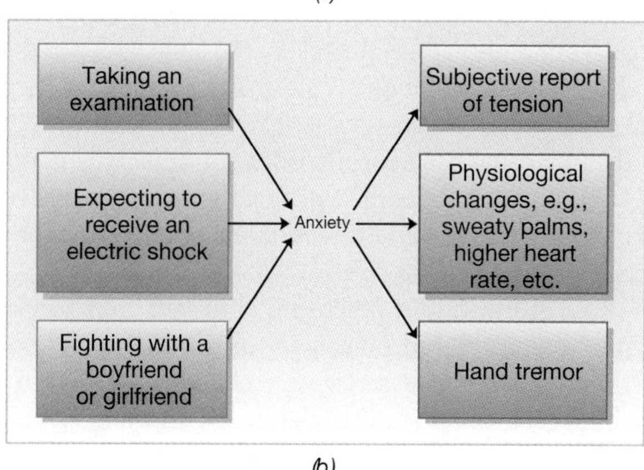

(b)

Figure 5.1 An illustration of the advantages of using anxiety as a theoretical concept. The arrows in (b) are fewer and more readily understood. After Miller (1959).

The Research Methods of Abnormal Psychology

All empirical research entails the collection of observable data. Sometimes research remains at a purely descriptive level, but often researchers observe several events and try to determine how they are associated or related. In the field of abnormal psychology, there is a large descriptive literature concerning the typical symptoms of people who have been diagnosed as having particular disorders. These symptoms can then be related to other characteristics, such as gender or social class; for example, eating disorders are more common in women than in men. But science demands more than descriptions of relationships. We often want to understand the causes of the relationships we have observed. For example, we want to know why eating disorders are found more often in women than in men. (Discussed more fully in Chapter 9, the answer may lie in social pressures for women to be thin.)

In this section, we describe the most commonly used research methods in the study of abnormal behaviour: the case study, epidemiological research, the correlational method, and various types of experiments. The methods vary in the degree to which they permit the collection of adequate descriptive data and the extent to which they allow researchers to infer causal relationships.

The Case Study

The most familiar and time-honoured method of observing others is to study them one at a time and record detailed information about them. As we did in Chapter 1 with J. Brett Barkley, clinicians prepare a **case study** by collecting historical and biographical information on a single individual, often including experiences in therapy. A comprehensive case study would cover family history and background, medical history, educational background, jobs held, marital history, and details concerning development, adjustment, personality, life course, and current situation. Important to bear in mind, though, is the role of the clinician's paradigm in determining the kinds of information actually collected and reported in a case study. To take but one example, case studies of psychoanalytically oriented clinicians contain more information about the client's early childhood and conflicts with parents than do reports made by behaviourally oriented practitioners.

Case studies from practising clinicians may lack the degree of control and objectivity of research using other methods, but these descriptive accounts have played an important role in the study of abnormal behaviour. Specifically, the case study has been used:

1. to provide a detailed description of a rare or unusual phenomenon and of important, often novel, methods or procedures of interviewing, diagnosis, and treatment;
2. to disconfirm allegedly universal aspects of a particular theoretical proposition; and
3. to generate hypotheses that can be tested through controlled research (Davison & Lazarus, 1994).

Providing Detailed Description Because it deals with a single individual, the case study can include much more detail than is typically included with other research methods. In a famous case history of multiple personality reported in 1954, psychiatrists Thigpen and Cleckley described a patient, Eve White, who assumed at various times three very distinct personalities. Their description of the case required an entire book, *The Three Faces of Eve*. The following brief summary emphasizes the moments in which new personalities emerged and what the separate selves knew of one another.

Eve White had been seen in psychotherapy for several months because she was experiencing severe headaches accompanied by blackouts. Her therapist (Dr. Thigpen) described her as a retiring and gently conventional figure. One day during the course of an interview, however, she changed abruptly and in a surprising way.

> As if seized by sudden pain, she put both hands to her head. After a tense moment of silence, both hands dropped. There was a quick, reckless smile, and, in a bright voice that sparkled, she said, "Hi there, Doc!" The demure and constrained posture of Eve White had melted into buoyant repose...This new and apparently carefree girl spoke casually of Eve White and her problems, always using she or her in every reference, always respecting the strict bounds of a separate identity...When asked her name, she immediately replied, "Oh, I'm Eve Black." (p. 137)

After this rather startling revelation, Eve was observed over a period of 14 months in a series of interviews that ran to almost 100 hours. A very important part of Eve White's therapy was to help her learn about Eve Black, her other, infectiously exuberant self, who added seductive and expensive clothing to her wardrobe and lived unremembered episodes of her life. During this period, a third personality, Jane, emerged while Eve White was recollecting an early incident in which she had been painfully scalded by water from a wash pot.

Jane, who from then on knew all that happened to the two Eves, although they did not share knowledge of her existence, was "far more mature, more vivid, more boldly capable, and more interesting than Eve White." Jane developed a deep and revering affection for the first Eve, who was considered somewhat a ninny by Eve Black. Jane knew nothing of Eve White's earlier life except what she learned through Eve's memories.

Some 11 months later, in a calamitous session with all three personalities present at different times, Eve Black emerged and reminisced for a moment about the many good times she had had in the past but then remarked that she did not seem to have real fun anymore. She began to sob, the only time Dr. Thigpen had seen her in tears. She told him that she wanted him to have her red dress to remember her by. All expression left her face and her eyes closed. Eve White opened them. When Jane was summoned a few minutes later, she soon realized that there was no longer any Eve Black or White and she began to experience a terrifying lost event. "No, no!...Oh no, Mother...I can't...Don't make me do it," she cried. Jane, who earlier had known nothing of Eve's childhood, was five years old and at her grandmother's funeral. Her mother was holding her high off the floor and above the coffin and saying that she must touch her grandmother's face. As she felt her hand leave the clammy cheek, the young woman screamed so piercingly that Dr. Cleckley, Dr. Thigpen's associate, came running from his office across the hall.

The two physicians were not certain who confronted them. In the searing intensity of the remembered moment, a new personality had been welded. Their transformed patient did not at first feel herself as apart and as sharply distinct a person as had the two Eves and Jane, although she knew a great deal about all of them. When her initial bewilderment lessened, she tended to identify herself with Jane. But the identification was not sure or complete, and she mourned the absence of the two Eves as though they were lost sisters. This new person decided to call herself Mrs. Evelyn White.

Chris Sizemore was the subject of the famous "three faces of Eve" case. She subsequently claimed to have had 21 separate personalities.

The case of Eve White, Eve Black, Jane, and eventually Evelyn constitutes a valuable classic in the literature because it is one of only a few detailed accounts of a rare phenomenon, multiple personality, now known as *dissociative identity disorder*. This controversial disorder is discussed in Chapter 7. In addition to illustrating the disorder itself, the original report of Thigpen and Cleckley provides valuable details about the interview procedures they followed and how the treatment progressed in this specific case.

However, the validity of the information gathered in a case study is sometimes questionable. Indeed, the real Eve, a woman named Chris Sizemore, wrote a book that challenged Thigpen and Cleckley's account of her case (Sizemore & Pittillo, 1977). She claimed that, following her period of therapy with them, her personality continued to fragment. In all, 21 separate and distinct strangers inhabited her body at one time or another. And, contrary to Thigpen and Cleckley's report, Sizemore maintains that nine of the personalities existed before Eve Black ever appeared. One set of personalities—they usually came in threes—would weaken and fade, to be replaced by others. Eventually, her personality changes were so constant and numerous that she might become her three persons in rapid switches resembling the flipping of television channels. The debilitating round-robin of transformations and the fierce battle for dominance among her selves filled her entire life. After resolving what she hoped was her last trio, by realizing finally that her alternate personalities were true aspects of herself rather than strangers from without, Chris Sizemore decided to reveal her story as a means of coping with past ordeals.

A more recent example of the use of case studies illustrates the value of combining a series of cases of an unusual phenomenon using a sophisticated and reliable data analytic strategy. In Chapter 3, we mentioned trichotillomania, one of the DSM-IV-TR impulse control disorders. The irresistible urge to pull out one's hair is an understudied, poorly understood, but chronic condition that affects predominantly adolescent girls and women. In an attempt to identify the concerns of compulsive hair pullers, Casati, Toner, and Yu (2000) from the Women's Mental Health Research Section of the Centre for Addiction and Mental Health in Toronto conducted focus interviews with seven women who met the diagnostic criteria for trichotillomania. The transcripts were analyzed using a procedure called the *constant comparative method* which consists of the identification of relevant units of information (unitizing), placing the units into categories that emerge from the data (categorizing), and providing organizational themes for the information (identifying themes). Casati et al. (2000) identified 10 major themes in the subjective experiences of the woman with compulsive hair pulling. Six themes related to the negative emotions the women experienced (embarrassment/shame, isolation, fear and guilt, anger/frustration, humiliation/pain, and body image). The following case illustrates the humiliation associated with trichotillomania:

> Ms. A.: "...I remember once sitting in class and I overheard someone behind me whispering to their friend that I had a bald spot. I remember being humiliated and thinking that next time I would sit at the back of the class. And that's exactly what I did for the rest of the year. I sat in desks that were located at the back of the classroom."

Three of the themes related to the issue of control (lack of control, self-disclosure, and lack of information from the medical community), and the last theme related to triggers or precipitants of the compulsive hair pulling. The latter varied considerably from woman to woman. Why is this study informative? In the past, treatments have focused primarily on symptom reduction, with limited effectiveness. The cases investigated by Casati et al. (2000) identified themes in the subjective experiences of compulsive hair pullers and demonstated the impact of their concerns on emotional, social, and psychological well-being. The authors concluded that practitioners should address these issues when assessing and treating women with trichotillomania.

The Case Study as Evidence Case histories are especially useful when they negate an assumed universal relationship or law. Consider, for example, the proposition that episodes of depression are always preceded by an increase in life stress. Finding even a single case in which this is not true would negate the theory or at least force it to be changed to assert that only some episodes of depression are triggered by stress.

The case study fares less well as evidence in support of a particular theory or proposition. Case studies do not provide the means for ruling out alternative hypotheses. To illustrate this problem, let us consider a clinician who has developed a new treatment for depression, tries it out on a client, and observes that the depression lifts after 10 weeks of the therapy. Although it would be tempting to conclude that the therapy worked, such a conclusion cannot legitimately be drawn because any of several other factors could also have produced the change. A stressful situation in the patient's life may have resolved itself, or perhaps episodes of depression are naturally time limited. Thus, several plausible rival hypotheses could account for the clinical improvement. The data yielded by the case study do not allow us to determine the true cause of the change.

Generating Hypotheses Although the case study may not play much of a role in confirming hypotheses, it does play a unique and important role in generating them. Through exposure to the life histories of a great number of patients, clinicians gain experience in understanding and interpreting them. Eventually, they may notice similarities of circumstances and outcomes and formulate important hypotheses that could not have been uncovered in a more controlled investigation. For example, in his clinical work with disturbed children, Kanner (1943) noticed that some children showed a similar constellation of symptoms, including failure to develop language and extreme isolation from other people. He therefore proposed a new diagnosis—infantile autism—which was subsequently confirmed by larger-scale research and eventually found its way into the DSM (see Chapter 15).

Some case studies are so unique that it is impossible to generalize to other individuals, including other people with the same disorder. A fascinating Canadian example is a case study of preferential bestiality (zoophilia) reported by Earls and Lalumiere (2002). A 54-year-old white male was serving a five-year prison sentence for cruelty to animals—a cruelty that had been exhibited in sexual activity with horses. He reported that his sexual attraction to animals developed while he grew up on a farm. The most distinguishing aspect of this case is reflected in the following excerpt:

> He also reported that his involvement with horses was not limited to sexual acts, but also included a strong emotional component. In his most recent offense, he inserted his arm to its full length into the vagina of a mare and punctured its vaginal wall. The horse subsequently died. The subject reported that the mare had shown interest in a stallion, and he had killed the mare as a result of jealousy (p. 86).

Case studies such as these are primarily informative in terms of the specific and unique manifestations of a disorder. Other sexual disorders are discussed in Chapter 14.

To sum up, the case study is an excellent way of examining the behaviour of a single individual in great detail and of generating hypotheses that can later be evaluated by controlled research. It is useful in clinical settings, where the focus is on just one person. Some investigators in the fields of clinical and personality psychology argue that the essence of psychological studies is the unique characteristics of an individual (e.g., Allport, 1961). The case history is an ideal method of study in such an individualistic context. But when general, universal laws are sought to explain phenomena, the case study is of limited use. Information collected on a single person may not reveal principles characteristic of people in general. Furthermore, the case study is unable to provide satisfactory evidence concerning cause-effect relationships.

Epidemiological Research

As described in Chapter 3, epidemiology is the study of the frequency and distribution of a disorder in a population. In epidemiological research, data are gathered about the rates of a disorder and its possible correlates in a large sample or population. This information can then be used to give a general picture of a disorder, how many people it affects, whether it is more common in men than in women, and whether its occurrence also varies according to social and cultural factors.

Epidemiological research focuses on determining three features of a disorder:

1 prevalence—the proportion of a population that has the disorder at a given point or period of time
2 incidence—the number of new cases of the disorder that occur in some period, usually a year
3 risk factors—conditions or variables that, if present, increase the likelihood of developing the disorder

Knowing the prevalence and incidence rates of various mental disorders and the risk factors associated with these disorders is important for planning health care facilities and services and for allocating provincial and federal grants for the study of disorders. Canadian Perspective 5.1 presents additional information on how epidemiological research can be used to clarify the relation between risk factors and mental disorder.

Canadian Perspectives/5.1

Early Risk Factors and Psychological Disorders in a Canadian Setting: THE ROLE OF ABUSE

The 1990 Ontario *Mental Health Supplement* study (Offord et al., 1996; Ontario Ministry of Health, 1994) examined the relation between selected early risk factors and mental disorders. Risk factors included the experience of severe physical or sexual abuse as a child, a history of parental mental disorder, and failure to graduate from high school. The relation between selected socio-demographic features (unemployment, public assistance, and low income) and mental disorders was also assessed. People with a disorder ("disordered group") were compared to those without a disorder ("healthy group"). Figure 5.2 provides information on two groups with mental disorders: those with only one disorder and those with two or more disorders. Clearly, those with two or more disorders are especially disadvantaged, relative to both the healthy group and the single-disorder group, on all of the theorized risk and socio-demographic factors.

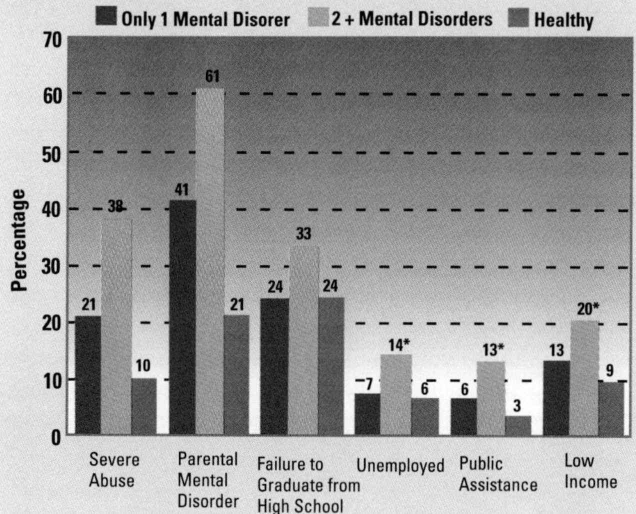

Figure 5.2 Early risk factors and associated socio-demographic features for people age 15 to 64 with one and two or more mental disorders. Ontario Health Survey, 1990, *Mental Health Supplement.*

Parental mental disorder and severe abuse are clearly the strongest risk factors from among the early risk and socio-demographic variables examined. For example, 61 percent of participants with two or more disorders and 41 percent of those with one disorder, reported that their parents had a mental disorder, whereas only 21 percent of the healthy group reported evidence of mental disorder in a parent. These results are consistent with the findings related to "parental psychopathologies" and "familial aggregation" from the U.S. National Comorbidity Study (Kendler, Davis, & Kessler, 1997; Kessler, Davis, & Kendler, 1997). Although a long history of research findings supports an association between mental disorder in parents and psychological problems in their offspring, evidence for the link between abuse, especially child sexual abuse (CSA), and mental disorders is relatively more recent. We will assess the link between child abuse and different disorders, including posttraumatic stress disorder, dissociative identity disorder, and eating disorders, in more detail in subsequent chapters. Issues related to intervention and prevention of CSA are also discussed in Chapter 14, Focus on Discovery 14.2.

Here we will further explore the issue of abuse in our Canadian setting. The Ontario epidemiological study found that 38 percent of people with two or more disorders reported experiencing severe sexual or physical abuse as a child and that the comparable figures for the one-disorder and healthy groups were 21 percent and 10 percent, respectively. Sexual abuse ranged from repeated indecent exposure to being sexually attacked, while physical abuse included being pushed, grabbed, shoved, and physically attacked. The authors (Ontario Ministry of Health, 1994) acknowledged that it is unclear how mistreatment in childhood leads to adult mental disorder but argued that research into the issue deserves government priority and that "there is an urgent need for effective programs both to prevent child abuse and to minimize its harmful after-effects" (p. 15). Similar results were reported by Kessler et al. (1997a) who found that interpersonal traumas (being molested, raped, mugged, or kidnapped; being physically attacked; suffering parental aggression) were the most consistent predictors of DSM-III-R disorders after parental psychopathologies.

Some cases of abuse are so appalling and disturbing as to defy credibility. Can these cases, even though rare, really happen in contemporary Canadian society? A high-profile case in the village of Blackstock, Ontario, was described by police officers as the worst case of child abuse they had ever seen (Huffman, 2001). The parents of two teenaged boys, 14 and 15 years old, were charged with forcible confinement, assault, assault with a weapon, aggravated assault, and failing to provide the necessities of life. The mother was also charged with administering a noxious substance. Police alleged that the boys were locked in separate covered cribs for long periods over the preceding 10 years. They were apparently forced to wear diapers, physically punished, and denied sufficient food. Can you imagine the possible long-term psychological consequences of abuse such as this?

What role should governments and individuals play in protecting children from abuse? Canada has had child protection legislation since 1893 (Walters, 1995). Since 1980, the provinces and territories have enacted "duty to report" legislation in order to provide further protection to those children whose safety and needs are at risk. Thus, it is now mandatory to report children who need "protection" using a "best interests of the child" test. In the case of the two teens described above, a local child welfare agency reported the suspicion of abuse to the police. One major incentive behind Canada's duty-to-report legislation is to reduce the long-term negative consequences of abuse and neglect (Walters, 1995). Organizers of Capital Health's Child and Adolescent Protection Centre, an Edmonton program for investigating alleged child abuse, reported that they saw 50 percent more children than expected during the first year of operation (CMAJ, 2000). More than half the 450 cases involved allegations of CSA and 236 cases involved children less than five years old!

Recall that Ontario's *Mental Health Supplement* study did *not* include Aboriginal people living on reserves. Although no formal studies have examined the prevalence of CSA among Canada's Aboriginal peoples, clinical and anecdotal data suggest that the prevalence may be as high as 80 percent (the Nechi Institute, The Four Worlds Development Project, 1988). Female children appear to be abused more than male children, but both male and female Native children are apparently abused at a much higher rate than non-Native children (McEvoy & Daniluk, 1995). McEvoy and Daniluk (1995) from the University of British Columbia summarized the many factors possibly associated with the high rate of sexual abuse among Native peoples in Canada, including the devastating impact of European contact (e.g., introduction of alcohol and diseases; assimilation and dislocation onto reserves; the isolationist residential school system, with attendant sexual exploitation; the breakdown of the extended family; lack of appropriate parental role models; identification with poverty values as opposed to traditional values; the lack of children's rights; non-Native attitudes of inferiority; domestic violence; and overcrowded, impoverished, and inadequate housing).

Distrust of outsiders, especially police and social workers, also makes it more difficult to deal with the problem of CSA among Canadian Aboriginal people. Previous government policy was to apprehend Native children suspected of being abused, many of whom would then lose contact with their families. Daily (1988) claimed that the rate was so high in the 1960s that some reserves lost most of a generation of children to the Native child welfare authorities. In 1995 McEvoy and Daniluk could not locate formal studies of the impact and treatment of CSA among Canadian Aboriginal populations. However, their phenomenological examination of the experiences of adult Aboriginal women sexually abused as children identified six "themes" common to the women's experiences: feelings of shame and guilt regarding the abuse; pervasive and debilitating feelings of vulnerability to harm (a perception that the world is not a safe place); fragmentation of personal identity and personal disempowerment; a sense of invalidation as women and cultural shame internalized as self-hatred; a need to understand and make sense of their abusive childhoods; and a need to experience "reintegration" and "healing." As children, the women had coped with the pain and horror of their lives by retreating into fantasy and dissociation (see Chapter 7); by adolescence, a majority had resorted to self-destructive behaviour, including alcohol and drug abuse, self-mutilation, suicide attempts, and sexual promiscuity (McEvoy & Daniluk, 1995). McEvoy and Daniluk (1995) outlined specific recommendations for working with Aboriginal survivors of sexual abuse (see Chapter 14).

Whatever the link between abuse and short-term effects or long-term psychological problems, most people deplore the sexual and physical abuse of children and adults. But what about the use of "spanking" as punishment for naughty children? Spanking is currently a hotly debated issue (whether or not it should ever occur, under what circumstances, at what age, etc.) among both mental health professionals and the Canadian general public. MacMillan and her colleagues (MacMillan, et al., 1999) from the Canadian Centre for Studies of Children at Risk at McMaster University examined the link between retrospective reports of slapping and spanking and lifetime prevalence of four categories of psychiatric disorder. Epidemiological data came from the *Mental Health Supplement* to the Ontario Health Survey. This study is perhaps the largest survey to date to examine the role of slapping and spanking in a sample from a general population. MacMillan, et al. (1999) concluded that there is a strong association between frequency of slapping and spanking and a lifetime prevalence of anxiety disorder, abuse of alcohol, and externalizing (or undercontrolled) disorders, such as conduct disorder. The association with major depression was not significant. The study is interesting in that the authors included respondents who reported being spanked or slapped "often" or "sometimes," but only from among those *without* a history of physical or sexual abuse during childhood. (Spanking was not included as a criterion for physical abuse.) Why were people who reported a history of physical or sexual abuse excluded from the analyses? They were excluded in order to remove the confounding effects of abusive experiences with physical punishment (spanking).

While the findings appeared to support a link between spanking in childhood and the prevalence of mental disorders, certain shortcomings and limitations must be acknowledged. Similar limitations are found in many, if not most, epidemiological studies. As noted by MacMillan et al. (1999), the measure of spanking experience was taken retrospectively and there was no opportunity for objective, independent corroboration. Furthermore, people's inability or limited ability to recall experiences that occur before the age of five (Brewin, Andrews, & Gotlib, 1993) may have led to an *underestimation* of the prevalence of spanking, although it is also possible, given the self-report methodology, that some respondents were unwilling to disclose painful and embarrassing memories. It is also possible that some recollections of spanking and slapping (and of physical and sexual abuse) were recovered memories (see Focus on Discovery 7.4; also discussed in Chapter 18). Finally, the cross-sectional nature of the research precludes making definitive statements about cause-effect relationships.

In summary, the results of the major epidemiological study conducted in the province of Ontario suggest that severe physical and sexual abuse and even spanking and slapping are risk factors for the onset and/or persistence of adult psychiatric disorders. However, analyses of data from the National Comorbidity Survey indicate that caution is needed in interpreting the findings of single-adversity, single-disorder studies. Kessler et al. (1997) reported a strong *clustering* among reported childhood adversities and lifetime comorbidity of DSM-IIIR disorders. Thus, it is possible that *specific* adversities that occur in childhood do not result in specific disorders found in adulthood.

Given that child maltreatment is a clear risk factor, there is an urgent need for additional empirical research. A New Emerging Team led by Christine Wekerle at the University of Western Ontario will be studying this topic over the next several years in a wide range of adjustment problems, including anxiety, depression, addiction, and personality disorders.

Thinking Critically

1. Not everyone who experiences severe physical or sexual abuse in childhood develops a mental disorder. What other factors play a role in determining how abuse affects a child? Do you think that severe abuse in childhood is a necessary or sufficient condition for adult psychological disorders? Why or why not? What other variables might coexist with or interact with abuse to increase or decrease the likelihood that a child will develop a psychological disorder as an adult?
2. Based on your understanding of the cultural and contextual factors surrounding child sexual abuse in Canada's Aboriginal population, how would you attempt to reduce the prevalence of abuse? Design a multifaceted intervention program for treating Native children and adults who have been sexually abused. What role should Native healing and spiritual activities play in your program?
3. MacMillan et al. (1999) reported a link between spanking and slapping and psychiatric disorders among people in Ontario. However, we should not conclude that spanking causes psychological problems. What other possible explanations for this association can you think of? Design a longitudinal, prospective study to test out your hypotheses.
4. Debate continues in Canada about whether or not slapping and spanking should be part of the spectrum of experiences that we classify as physical abuse (e.g., Cohen, 1995; Orwen, 2001). Section 43 of the Criminal Code of Canada permits spanking to be used on children provided that the force does not exceed what is "reasonable" under the circumstances. What force is reasonable? Currently, children's aid societies will remove children from a home only when the force used is severe or causes physical injuries. What is your own position on this emotional issue? Under what, if any, circumstances would you consider it appropriate to "spank" your own child?

It is clear that knowledge about risk factors can give clues to the causes of the disorder being studied. For example, recall that the Ontario study revealed that depression is about twice as common in women as in men. Thus, gender is a risk factor for depression. In Chapter 10, we will see that knowledge of this risk factor has led to a theory of depression that suggests that it is due to a particular style of coping with stress that is more common in women than in men. Similarly, it is known that the prevalence of schizophrenia is highest among members of the lowest social class; in other words, low social class is a risk factor for schizophrenia. If the cause of this relationship were known—it might be stress, poor nutrition, lack of high–quality medical care—it would provide clues to the causes of this disorder. The results of epidemiological research may thus provide hypotheses that can be more thoroughly investigated using other research methods.

THE CORRELATIONAL METHOD

A great deal of research in psychopathology relies on the correlational method. This method establishes whether there is a relationship between or among two or more variables, and it is often employed in epidemiological research as well as in studies that use smaller samples.

In correlational research, the variables being studied are measured as they exist in nature. This feature distinguishes the method from experimental research, in which variables are actually manipulated and controlled by the researcher. To understand this difference, consider that the possible role of stress in a disorder such as hypertension can be addressed with either a correlational or an experimental design. In a correlational study, we would measure stress levels by having people fill out a questionnaire or by interviewing them about their recent stressful experiences. Stress would then be correlated with blood pressure measurements collected from these same people. In an experimental study, in contrast, the experimenter would create or manipulate stress in the laboratory; for example, while their blood pressure was being monitored, some participants might be asked to give a speech to an audience about the aspect of their personal appearance they find least appealing (see Figure 5.3).

Numerous examples of correlation can be drawn from everyday life. Education correlates with income; the greater the educational level attained, the greater the earning power. Height tends to be positively correlated with weight; taller people are usually heavier. And a recent national study of Canadian preschoolers showed that behavioural problems were higher among children from less affluent neighbourhoods (Kohen, Brooks-Gunn, Leventhal, & Hertzman, 2002).

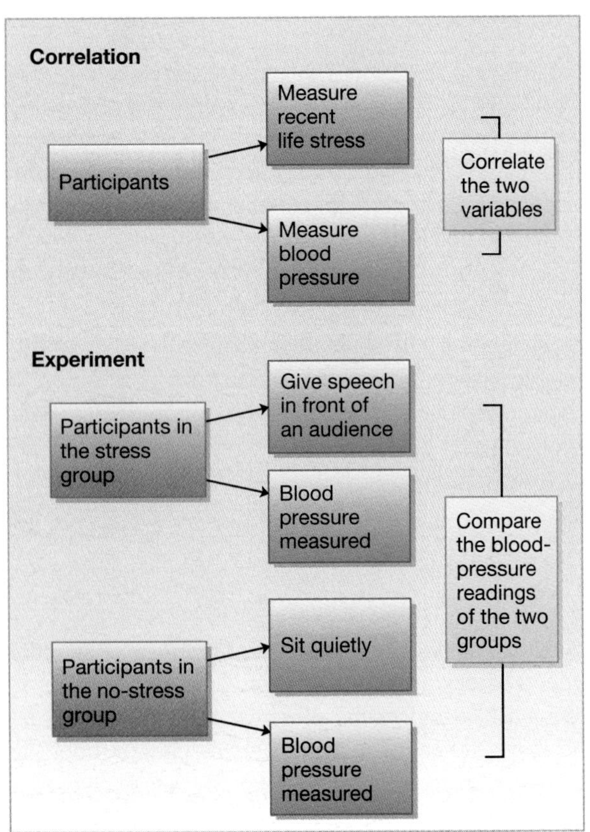

Figure 5.3 Correlational versus experimental studies.

Correlational studies, then, address questions of the form "Are variable *X* and variable *Y* associated in some way so that they vary together (co-relate)?" In other words, questions are asked concerning relationships; for example, "Is schizophrenia related to social class?" or "Are scores obtained on college examinations related to anxiety?"

Measuring Correlation The first step in determining a correlation is to obtain pairs of observations of the variables in question, such as height and weight, for each member of a group of participants. Once such pairs of measurements are obtained, the strength of the relationship between the two sets of observations can be computed to determine the correlation coefficient, denoted by the symbol *r*. This statistic may take any value between −1.00 and +1.00, and it measures both the magnitude and the direction of a relationship. The higher the absolute value of *r*, the larger or stronger the relationship between the two variables. An *r* of either +1.00 or −1.00 indicates the highest possible, or perfect, relationship, whereas an *r* of .00 indicates that the variables are unrelated. If the sign of *r* is positive, the two variables are said to be *positively related*; in other words, as the values for variable *X* increase, those for variable *Y* also tend to increase. For example, assume that the correlation between height and weight is +.88. This correlation would indicate a very strong positive relationship: as height increases, so does weight. Conversely, when the sign of *r* is negative, variables are said to be *negatively related*: as scores on one variable increase, those for the other tend to decrease. For example, the number of hours spent watching television is negatively correlated with grade point average.

Plotting a relationship graphically often helps make it clearer. Figure 5.4 presents what are called scatter diagrams of positive and negative correlations as well as unrelated variables. In the diagrams, each point corresponds to two values determined for a given person, the value of variable *X* and that of variable *Y*. In perfect relationships, all the points fall on a straight line; if we know the value of only one of the variables for an individual, we can state with certainty the value of the other variable. Similarly, when the correlation is relatively large, there is only a small degree of scatter about the line of perfect correlation. The values tend to scatter increasingly and become dispersed as the correlations become lower. When the correlation reaches .00, knowledge of a person's score on one variable tells us nothing about his or her score on the other.

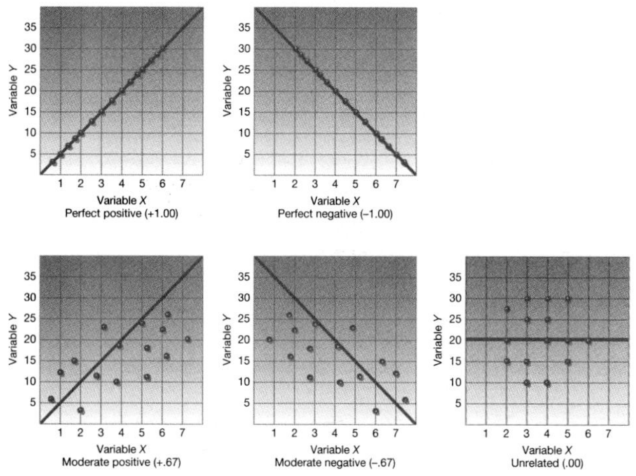

Figure 5.4 Scatter diagrams showing various degrees of correlational relationship.

Statistical Significance Thus far we have established that the magnitude of a correlation coefficient tells us the strength of a relationship between two variables. But scientists demand a more rigorous evaluation of the importance of correlations and use the concept of statistical significance for this purpose. Essentially, **statistical significance** refers to the likelihood that the results of an investigation are due to chance. A statistically significant correlation is one that is not likely to have occurred by chance.

Traditionally, in psychological research, a correlation is considered statistically significant if the likelihood or probability that it is a chance finding is 5 or less in 100. This level of significance is called the .05 level, commonly written as $p \leq .05$ (the p stands for probability). In general, as the size of the correlation coefficient increases, the result is more and more likely to be statistically significant. For example, a correlation of .80 is more likely than a correlation of .40 to be significant. Whether a correlation attains statistical significance also depends on the number of observations made. The greater the number of observations, the smaller r (the correlation) needs to be in order to reach statistical significance. For example, a correlation of $r = .30$ is statistically significant when the number of observations is large—say, 300—but it would not be significant if only 20 observations were made. Thus, if the alcohol consumption of 10 depressed and 10 nondepressed men was studied and the correlation between depression and drinking was found to be .32, the correlation would not be statistically significant. However, the same correlation would be significant if two groups of 150 men were studied.

Applications to Psychopathology The correlational method is widely used in the field of abnormal psychology. Whenever we compare people given one diagnosis with those given another or with normal people, the study is correlational. For example, two diagnostic groups may be compared to see how much stress members of each experienced before the onset of their disorders, or people with and people without an anxiety disorder may be compared on their physiological reactivity to a stressor administered in the laboratory.

When the correlational method is used in research on psychopathology, one of the variables is typically diagnosis—for example, whether the participant is diagnosed as having an anxiety disorder or not. To calculate a correlation between this variable and another one, diagnosis is quantified so that having an anxiety disorder is designated by a score of 1 and not having a disorder by a score of 2. (It does not matter what numbers are actually used.) The diagnosis variable can then be correlated with another variable, such as the amount of stress that has been recently experienced. An illustration of the data from such a study is presented in Table 5.1.

Table 5.1

Data for a Correlational Study

Participant Number	Diagnosis	Stress Score
1	1	65
2	1	72
3	2	40
4	1	86
5	2	72
6	2	21
7	1	65
8	2	40
9	1	37
10	2	28

Note: Diagnosis—having an anxiety disorder or not (with having an anxiety disorder designated as 1 and not having an anxiety disorder as 2)—is correlated with an assessment of recent life stress on a 0-100 scale. Higher scores indicate greater recent stress. As in previous examples, to make the point clearly, we present a smaller sample of cases than would be used in an actual research study. Notice that diagnosis is associated with recent life stress. Patients with an anxiety disorder tend to have higher stress scores than people without an anxiety disorder.

Often such investigations are not recognized as correlational, perhaps because participants come to a laboratory for testing. But the logic of such studies is correlational; the correlation between two variables—having an anxiety disorder or not and scores on the measure of recent life stress—is what is being examined. Variables such as having an anxiety disorder or not are called **classificatory variables**. The anxiety disorders were already present and were simply measured by the researcher. Other examples of classificatory variables are age, sex, social class, and body build. These variables are naturally occurring patterns and are not manipulated by the researcher, an important requirement for the experimental method discussed later. Thus, most research on the causes of psychopathology is correlational.

Problems of Causality The correlational method, although often employed in abnormal psychology, has a critical drawback: it does not allow determination of cause-effect relationships. A sizable correlation between two variables tells us only that they are related or tend to co-vary with each other, but we do not really know which is cause and which is effect or if either variable is actually the cause of the other.

The Directionality Problem When two variables are correlated, how can we tell which is the cause and which is the effect? For example, a correlation has been found between the diagnosis of schizophrenia and social class: lower-class people are more frequently diagnosed as having schizophrenia than are middle- and upper-class people. One possible explanation is that the stresses of living in the lowest social class cause an increase in the prevalence of schizophrenia. But a second and perhaps equally plausible hypothesis has been advanced. It may be that the disorganized behaviour patterns of individuals with schizophrenia cause them to perform poorly in their educational and occupational endeavours and thus to become impoverished. The directionality problem, as it is sometimes called, is present in many correlational research designs—hence the often-cited dictum "Correlation does not imply causation."

Although correlation does not imply causation, determining whether two variables correlate may serve to disconfirm certain causal hypotheses; that is, causation does imply correlation. For example, if an investigator asserts that cigarette smoking causes lung cancer, he or she is implying that lung cancer and smoking will be correlated. Studies of these two variables must show this positive correlation or the theory will be disconfirmed.

One way of overcoming the directionality problem is based on the idea that causes must precede effects. According to this idea, studies investigating the hypothesized causes of psychopathology would use a longitudinal design in which the hypothesized causes are studied before a disorder has developed. In this way, the hypothesized causes could be measured before the effect. The most desirable way of collecting information about the development of schizophrenia, for example, would be to select a large sample of babies and follow them, measuring certain hypothesized causes, for the 20 to 45 years that are the period of risk for the onset of schizophrenia. But such a method would be prohibitively expensive, for only about one individual in a hundred eventually develops schizophrenia. The yield of data from such a simple longitudinal study would be small indeed.

The high-risk method overcomes this problem. With this approach, only individuals with greater than average risk of developing schizophrenia in adulthood would be selected for study. Most current research using this methodology studies individuals who have a parent diagnosed with schizophrenia (having a parent with schizophrenia increases a person's risk for developing schizophrenia). The high-risk method is also used to study several other disorders, and we will examine these findings in subsequent chapters.

The Third-Variable Problem Another difficulty in interpreting correlational findings is called the third-variable problem; that is, the correlation may have been produced by a third, unforeseen factor. In the following example, an obvious third variable is identified.

> One regularly finds a high positive correlation between the number of churches in a city and the number of crimes committed in that city. That is, the more churches a city has, the more crimes are committed in it. Does this mean that religion fosters crime, or does it mean that crime fosters religion? It means neither. The relationship is due to a particular third variable—population. The higher the population of a particular community, the greater...the number of churches and...the frequency of criminal activity. (Neale & Liebert, 1980, p. 109)

Another example is the aforementioned study of Canadian preschoolers (see Kohen et al., 2002). Low neighbourhood income may be associated with child behaviour problems because of a third variable—children may be imitating frustrated parents who more frequently engage in behavioural dyscontrol.

Psychopathology research offers numerous examples of third variables. Biochemical differences between patients with schizophrenia and normal people have frequently been reported. These differences could reflect different diets or the fact that the patients are taking medication for their condition; the differences do not reveal anything telling about the nature of schizophrenia. Are there any solutions to the third-variable problem? In general, the answer is yes, although the solutions are only partially satisfactory and do not permit unambiguous causal inferences to be made from correlational data.

We have already noted that facts about the causes of abnormal behaviour are hard to come by. The issues we have just discussed are major reasons for this state of affairs. The psychopathologist is forced to make heavy use of the correlational method because diagnosis, a classificatory variable, is best suited to this strategy. But the relationships discovered between diagnosis and other variables are then clouded by the third-variable and directionality problems. Searching for the causes of the various psychopathologies will continue to be a challenging enterprise.

The Experiment

The factors causing the associations and relationships revealed by correlational research cannot be determined with absolute certainty. The experiment is generally considered the most powerful tool for determining causal relationships between events. It involves the random assignment of participants to the different conditions being investigated, the manipulation of an independent variable, and the measurement of a dependent variable. In the field of psychopathology, the experiment is most often used to evaluate the effects of therapies.

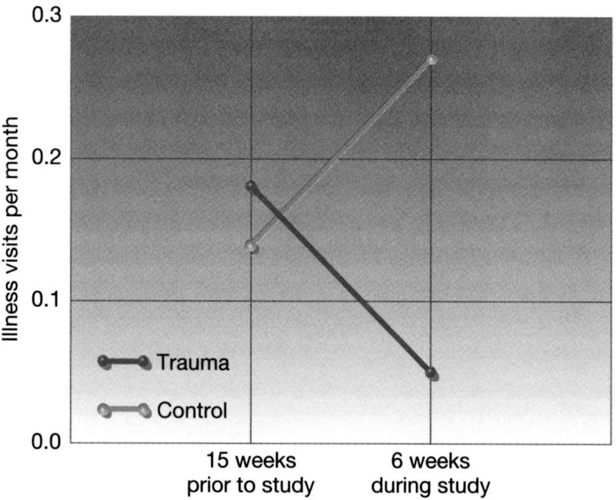

Figure 5.5 Visits to a health centre on account of illness for the periods before and during the experiment. After Pennebaker et al. (1987).

As an introduction to the basic components of experimental research, let us consider here the major aspects of the design and results of a study of how expressing emotions about past traumatic events is related to health (Pennebaker, Kiecolt-Glaser, & Glaser, 1988). In this experiment, 50 undergraduates participated in a six-week study, one part of which required them to come to a laboratory for four consecutive days. On each of the four days, half the students wrote a short essay about a past traumatic event. They were instructed as follows:

> During each of the four writing days, I want you to write about the most traumatic and upsetting experiences of your entire life. You can write on different topics each day or on the same topic for all four days. The important thing is that you write about your deepest thoughts and feelings. Ideally, whatever you write about should deal with an event or experience that you have not talked with others about in detail.

The remaining students also came to the laboratory each day, but they wrote essays describing such things as their daily activities, a recent social event, the shoes they were wearing, and their plans for the rest of the day.

Information about how often the participating undergraduates used the university health centre was obtained for the 15-week period before the study began and for the six weeks after it had begun. These data are shown in Figure 5.5. Members of the two groups had visited the health centre about equally prior to the experiment. After writing the essays, however, the number of visits declined for students who wrote about traumas and increased for the remaining students. (This increase may have been due to seasonal variation in rates of visits to the health centre for the second measure of number of visits was taken in February, just before midterm exams.) From these data the investigators concluded that expressing emotions has a beneficial effect on health.

Basic Features of Experimental Design The foregoing example illustrates many of the basic features of an experiment.

1. The researcher typically begins with an experimental hypothesis—that is, what he or she assumes will happen when a particular variable is manipulated. Pennebaker and his colleagues hypothesized that expressing emotion about a past event would improve health.
2. The investigator chooses an independent variable that can be manipulated—that is, some factor that will be under the control of the experimenter. In the case of the Pennebaker study, some students wrote about past traumatic events and others about mundane happenings.
3. Participants are assigned to the two conditions by random assignment so that each participant has an equal chance of being in each condition.
4. The researcher arranges for the measurement of a dependent variable, something that is expected to depend on or vary with manipulations of the independent variable. The dependent variable in this study was the number of visits to the health centre.
5. When differences between groups are found to be a function of variations in the independent variable, the researcher is said to have produced an experimental effect.

For instance, Dozois and Backs-Dermott (2000) conducted an experiment with University of Calgary students that tested the associations among personality traits, interpersonal feedback, self-descriptions, and cognitive processes. Students who were high or low in a personality trait known as sociotropy (i.e., an excessive need to maintain contact with and please other people; see Chapter 10) were asked to listen to an audiotape that emphasized the experience of either an interpersonal rejection (i.e., the breakup of a relationship) or an achievement failure (i.e., not being accepted into graduate school). Thus, the manipulated independent variable was the *type* of negative event that was described (referred to as either the rejection priming condition or the failure priming condition). The dependent measures included the number of negative and positive adjectives endorsed as self-descriptive when participants, following exposure to the audiotape, completed a self-description rating task. Dozois and Backs-Dermott (2000) found that students high in sociotropy who were exposed to the rejection priming situation did check off more negative adjectives and fewer positive adjectives as self-descriptive. Students with high versus low levels of sociotropy did not differ significantly in terms of the number of negative and positive adjectives rated as self-descriptive if they were in the failure priming situation. Additional dependent measures also indicated that sociotropic students showed a greater attentional bias to negative self-referential material after exposure to the rejection priming situation but not after the exposure to the failure priming situation.

To evaluate the importance of an experimental effect, as with correlations, researchers determine their statistical significance. To illustrate, consider a hypothetical study of the effectiveness of cognitive therapy in reducing depression among 20 depressed patients. (In the realm of actual research, 20 patients would be regarded as a very small sample; we present a small number of cases so that the example is easier to follow.) In brief, the independent variable is cognitive therapy versus no treatment; 10 patients are randomly assigned to receive cognitive therapy and 10 are randomly assigned to a no treatment control group. The dependent variable is scores on a standardized measure of the severity of depression, assessed after 12 weeks of treatment or no treatment; and higher scores reflect more severe depression.

Data for each of the patients in each group are presented in Table 5.2. Note that the average scores of the two groups differ considerably (8.3 for the cognitive-therapy group and 21.7 for the no-treatment group). This difference between groups, also called *between-group variance*, is the experimental effect; it has been caused by the independent variable. Note also from the table that the scores of individual participants within each group vary considerably; this is called *within-group variance*. Within the cognitive-therapy group, for example, most participants have low scores, but participant number 7 has a high score (18). Cognitive therapy did not seem to be of much help to this individual, but we don't know why. Similarly, most people in the no-treatment group have high scores, but participant number 17 has a low score (6). The cause of this within-group variability is unknown.

Statistical significance is tested by dividing the between-group variance (the difference between the average scores of the two groups—in this example 21.7−8.3=13.4) by a measure of the within-group variance. When the average difference between the two groups is large relative to the within-group variance, the result is more likely to be statistically significant. From the results of this hypothetical experiment, we would conclude that cognitive therapy is more effective in decreasing depression than no treatment at all.

Internal Validity An important feature of any experimental design is the inclusion of at least one control group that does not receive the experimental treatment (the independent variable). A control group is necessary for comparative purposes if the effects in an experiment are to be attributed to the manipulation of the independent variable. In the Pennebaker study, the control group wrote about mundane happenings. In the cognitive-therapy example, the control group received no treatment. The data from a control group provide a standard against which the effects of an independent variable (in this case, expressing emotion or cognitive therapy) can be compared.

Table 5.2

Results of a Hypothetical Study Comparing Cognitive Therapy with No Treatment for Depression

	Cognitive Therapy		No Treatment
Participant 1	8	Participant 11	22
Participant 2	6	Participant 12	14
Participant 3	12	Participant 13	26
Participant 4	4	Participant 14	28
Participant 5	3	Participant 15	19
Participant 6	6	Participant 16	27
Participant 7	18	Participant 17	6
Participant 8	14	Participant 18	32
Participant 9	7	Participant 19	21
Participant 10	5	Participant 20	23
Group Average	8.3		21.7

Note: Scores for each participant after treatment are shown.

To illustrate this point with another example, consider a study of the effectiveness of a particular therapy in modifying some form of abnormal behaviour. An experiment conducted in Quebec examined the efficacy of cognitive-behavioural therapy in the treatment of generalized anxiety disorder, a condition that involves a tendency to experience pathological, uncontrollable worry (see Chapter 6). Laberge, Dugas, and Ladouceur (2000) found that the treatment was successful in reducing dysfunctional beliefs about worry. If there had been no control group in this study, then it would not have been an experiment. However, the study did include a group of people with generalized anxiety disorder who were assigned randomly to a waiting list and had not yet received the therapeutic treatment. These individuals represented an effective comparison group because they were presumably similar in every respect to those who experienced the experimental treatment.

If there had been no control group against which to compare the improvement, valid conclusions could not have been drawn from such an investigation. The reduction in dysfunctional beliefs from the beginning of the treatment to the end could have been brought about by several factors in addition to or instead of the treatment employed, including the passage of time or the general influence of agreeing to participate in an experiment.

Variables such as the passage of time are often called **confounds**. Their effects are intermixed with those of the independent variable, and like the third variables in correlational studies, they make the results difficult or impossible to interpret. These confounds, as well as others described in this chapter, are widespread in research on the effects of psychotherapy, as is documented throughout this book. Studies in which the effect obtained cannot be attributed with confidence to the independent variable are called *internally invalid* studies. In contrast, research has **internal validity** when the effect can be confidently attributed to the manipulation of the independent variable.

In the study by Laberge et al. (2000), internal validity was improved by the inclusion of a control group. The changes in anxiety experienced by these control participants constituted a standard against which the effects of the independent variable could be assessed. If a change in anxiety is brought about by particular environmental events, quite beyond any therapeutic intervention, the experimental group receiving the treatment and the control group receiving no treatment are likely to be affected equally. On the other hand, if after six months the anxiety level of the treated group has lessened more than that of the untreated control group, we can be relatively confident that this difference is attributable to the treatment.

The inclusion of a control group does not always ensure internal validity, however. Consider yet another study of therapy, the treatment of two hospital wards of psychiatric patients. An investigator may decide to select one ward to receive an experimental treatment and another ward to be a control group. When the researcher later compares the frequencies of deviant behaviour in these two groups, he or she will want to attribute any differences between them to the fact that patients in one ward received treatment and those in the other did not. But the researcher cannot legitimately draw this inference, for there is a competing hypothesis that cannot be disproved. Even before treatment, the patients who happened to receive therapy might have had a lower level of deviant behaviour than the patients who became the control group. The principle of experimental design that was disregarded in this defective study is that of *random assignment*. This principle would be at work in a two-group experiment, if a coin were to be tossed for each participant. If the coin turns up heads, the participant is assigned to one group; if tails, he or she is assigned to the other. This procedure minimizes the likelihood that differences between the groups after treatment will reflect pretreatment differences in the samples rather than true experimental effects.

Furthermore, using both a control group and random assignment handles the type of confounds we described in our earlier example of treatment for high anxiety. When groups are formed by random assignment, confounds such as the resolution of a stressful life situation are equally likely to occur in both the treated group and the control group. There is no reason to believe that life stress would be resolved more often in one group than the other. Random assignment was employed in the experiments described earlier.

The Placebo Effect Experimental research on the effects of therapy—psychological or biological—should include a consideration of the **placebo effect**. This term refers to an improvement in a physical or psychological condition that is attributable to a patient's expectations of help rather than to any specific active ingredient in a treatment. J.D. Frank (1978) related placebo effects to faith healing in prescientific or nonscientific societies. For centuries, suffering human beings have made pilgrimages to sanctified places and ingested sometimes foul-smelling concoctions in the belief that these efforts would improve their condition. Sometimes they did.

Many people dismiss placebo reactions as not real or as "second best" to the benefits of actual treatments. After all, if a person has a tension headache, what possible benefit can he or she hope to get from a pill that is totally devoid of chemical action or direct physiological effect? The fact is, however, that the effects of placebos are sometimes significant and even long lasting (e.g., Turner et al., 1994). Furthermore, placebo effects may be the cause of a common finding in treatment research: treatments tend to be more effective when they are first introduced than a number of years later. An explanation could be that the initial enthusiasm for a treatment may increase its placebo value. The placebo effect is commonly found and universally accepted in drug research. It has been estimated, for example, that among depressed patients who respond favourably to antidepressant medication, half are actually showing a placebo response (Stewart et al., 1998).

It is not a simple matter, however, to extend the findings of research on chemical placebos directly to research on psychological placebos. In psychotherapy, the mere expectation of being helped can be an active ingredient. Why? If the theory adopted by the therapist holds that positive expectancy of improvement is an active ingredient, then improvement arising from the expectancy would by definition not be considered a placebo effect. Lambert, Shapiro, and Bergin (1986) argued that "placebo factors" should be replaced with the concept of "common factors" in the study of the effects of psychotherapy. They defined common factors as

> those dimensions of the treatment setting...that are not specific to a particular technique. Those factors that are common to most therapies (such as expectation for improvement, persuasion, warmth and attention, understanding, encouragement, etc.) should not be viewed as theoretically inert nor as trivial; they are central to psychological treatments and play an active role in patient improvement. (p. 163)

The effects of pilgrimages to shrines, such as Lourdes, may be placebo effects.

Because of the importance of the placebo effect, researchers studying the effects of psychotherapy often use what are called placebo control groups. Patients in such groups typically have regular contact with a therapist and receive support and encouragement, but they do not receive what is regarded as the active ingredient in the kind of therapy under study (e.g., gradual exposure to a feared situation in a behavioural treatment of a phobia).

When the placebo control group design is used, patients are randomly assigned to either the treatment or the placebo group; to reduce the possibility of bias, neither the researchers nor the patients are allowed to know to which group any specific individual is assigned. Because neither the researchers nor the patients are aware of who has been placed in the treatment and placebo control groups, the design is referred to as a double-blind procedure.

Research on psychotherapy reveals that patients in placebo control groups generally improve more than patients in no-treatment groups—though often not as much as patients in treatment groups (Lambert et al., 1986). Most psychotherapies, because they offer support and encouragement, may share a common factor that contributes to improvement. The issue of common factors is important in the movement toward psychotherapy integration, a topic examined in Chapter 17.

The place of placebo control groups in psychotherapy research is an often-debated and complex topic. A study that compares a particular therapy to no treatment at all and finds that therapy brings about more improvement does suggest that being treated is better than not being treated. This is not a trivial finding. But a given therapy usually tries to create improvement in a particular way—by removing the person's defences, by facilitating the individual's way to self-actualization, by enhancing responsible choices, by extinguishing fears, and so forth. To determine whether these processes are at work and are effective, a study needs a control group of patients who are instilled with expectancies of help, who believe that something worthwhile and beneficial is being done for them.

But using a placebo control group involves several problems. First, it raises ethical issues, for effective treatment is being withheld from some patients. Second, a double-blind placebo control group study is difficult to implement. Medications used in treating psychopathology typically produce side effects that are not produced by placebos. Therefore, both researchers and patients may come to know who is getting the active treatment and who is getting the placebo. Finally, informed consent is an issue. Potential participants in research must be informed about the details of the study in which they are being asked to participate. In a placebo control group study, participants must be told that they have some chance of being assigned to the placebo group. What does this knowledge do to the possibility of experiencing a placebo effect?

Problems such as these have led some researchers to suggest that placebo control groups should be abandoned (e.g., Rothman & Michels, 1994). Instead of comparing a group receiving a new treatment with a placebo control group, researchers could compare the group with one receiving the currently accepted standard treatment in the field. This approach is now frequently used in psychotherapy research, as will be seen throughout this book.

External Validity The extent to which the results of any particular piece of research can be generalized beyond the immediate experiment is the measure of external validity. If investigators have demonstrated that a particular treatment helps a group of patients, they will undoubtedly want to conclude that this treatment will be effective in ministering to other patients, at other times and in other places. For example, Pennebaker and his colleagues would hope that their findings would generalize to other instances of emotional expression (e.g., confiding to a close friend), to other situations, and to people other than those who actually participated in the experiment.

Determining the external validity of the results of a psychological experiment is extremely difficult. Merely knowing that one is a participant in a psychological experiment can alter behaviour, and thus the results produced in the laboratory may not automatically be produced in the natural environment. Furthermore, in the many instances where results are obtained from investigations with laboratory animals, such as rats, generalizations to human beings are risky indeed, since there are enormous differences between *Homo sapiens* and *Rattus norvegicus*. Researchers must be alert to the extent to which they claim generalization for findings, for there is no entirely adequate way of dealing with the questions of external validity. The best that can be done is to perform similar studies in new settings with new participants so that the limitations, or the generality, of a finding can be determined. This issue will be revisited in Chapter 17.

Analogue Experiments The experimental method is judged to be the most telling way to determine cause-effect relationships. The efficacy of treatments for psychopathology is usually evaluated by the experimental method, which has proved a powerful tool for determining whether a therapy reduces suffering. As mentioned earlier, however, this method has been little used by those seeking the causes of abnormal behaviour. Why?

Suppose that a researcher has hypothesized that a child's emotionally charged, overdependent relationship with his or her mother causes generalized anxiety disorder. An experimental test of this hypothesis would require assigning infants randomly to either of two groups of mothers. The mothers in one group would undergo an extensive training program to ensure that they would be able to create a highly emotional atmosphere and foster overdependence in children. The mothers in the second group would be trained not to create such a relationship with the children under their care. The researcher would wait until the participants in each group reached adulthood and then determine how many of them had developed generalized anxiety disorder.

Obviously, such an experimental design contains insurmountable practical problems. But practical issues are hardly the principal ones that must concern us. Consider the ethics of such an experiment. Would the potential scientific gain of proving that an overdependent relationship with a person's mother brings on generalized anxiety disorder outweigh the suffering that would be imposed on some of the participants? In almost any person's view, it would not. (Ethical issues are considered in detail in Chapter 18.)

In an effort to take advantage of the benefits of the experimental method, researchers seeking the causes of abnormal behaviour have sometimes used a format known as an analogue experiment. Investigators attempt to bring a related phenomenon—that is, an analogue—into the laboratory for more intensive study. Because a true experiment is now being conducted, results can be obtained that may be interpreted in cause-effect terms. However, the problem of external validity may be accentuated because the actual phenomenon in which the researchers are interested is not being studied.

In one type of analogue study, behaviour is rendered temporarily abnormal through experimental manipulations. For example, lactate infusion can elicit a panic attack, hypnotic suggestion can produce blindness similar to that seen in conversion disorder, and threats to self-esteem can increase anxiety and depression. If pathology can be experimentally induced by any one of these manipulations, the same process existing in the natural environment might well be a cause of the disorder.

The key to interpreting such studies lies in the validity of the independent variable as a reflection of some experience one might actually have in real life and of the dependent variable as an analogue of a clinical problem. Is a stressor encountered in the laboratory fundamentally similar to one

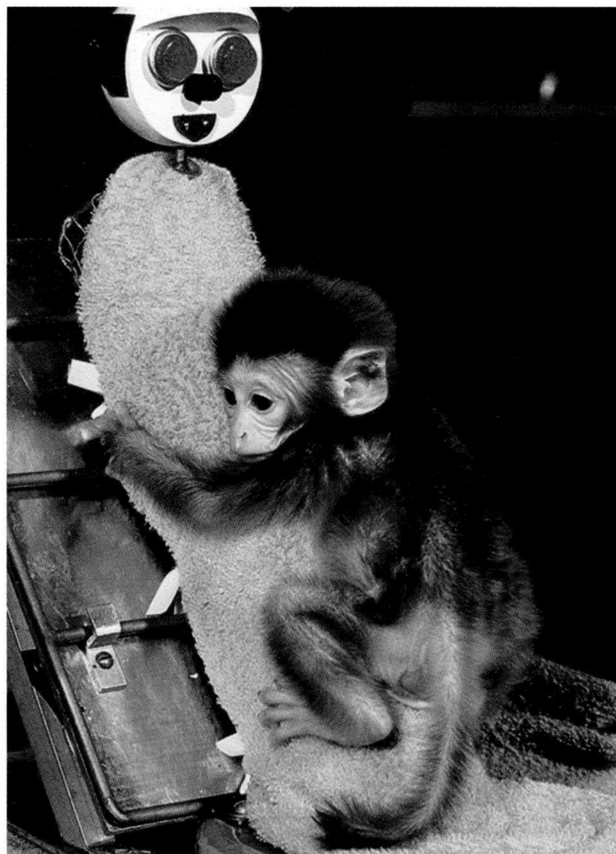

Harlow's famous analogue research examined the effects of early separation from the mother on infant monkeys. Even a cloth surrogate mother helps prevent the subsequent emotional distress and depression that would result from isolation.

that occurs in the natural environment? Are transient increases in anxiety or depression reasonable analogues of their clinical counterparts? Results of such experiments must be interpreted with great caution and generalized with care, although they can provide valuable information about the origins of psychopathology.

In another type of analogue study, participants are selected because they are considered similar to patients who have certain diagnoses. A large amount of research, for example, has been conducted with college students selected for study because they scored high on a questionnaire measure of anxiety or depression. The question is whether these somewhat anxious or depressed students, who do not have a clinical disorder, are adequate analogues for those with an anxiety disorder or major depression. Some research bearing on this issue is discussed in Chapter 10.

Whether an experiment is regarded as an analogue depends not on the experiment itself, but on the use to which it is put. We can very readily study avoidance behaviour in a white rat. The data collected from such studies are not analogue data if we limit our discussion to the behaviour of rats. They become analogue data only when we draw implications from them and apply them to other domains, such as anxiety in human beings.

Some of the animal experiments we have already examined are analogue in nature. For example, in Chapter 2, we described research on avoidance learning in rats that was very influential in the formulation of theories of anxiety in humans. It is important to keep in mind that we are arguing by analogy when we attempt to relate fear reactions of white rats to anxiety in people. At the same time, however, we do not agree with those who regard such analogue research as totally and intrinsically worthless for the study of human behaviour. Although human beings and other mammals differ on many important dimensions, it does not follow that principles of behaviour derived from animal research are necessarily irrelevant to human behaviour.

Single-Subject Experimental Research

We have been discussing experimental research as it is conducted on groups of participants, but experiments do not always have to be conducted on groups. In **single-subject experimental designs**, participants are studied one at a time and experience a manipulated variable.

The strategy of relying on a single person appears to violate many of the principles of research design that we have discussed. As with the case study, there is no control group to act as a check on a single subject. Moreover, generalization is difficult because the findings may relate to a unique aspect of the one individual whose behaviour has been explored. Hence, the study of a single individual would appear unlikely to yield any findings that could possess the slightest degree of internal or external validity. Nevertheless, the experimental study of a single subject can be an effective research technique for certain purposes (Hersen & Barlow, 1976).

A method developed by Tate and Baroff (1966) for reducing the self-injurious behaviour of a 9-year-old boy, Sam, serves as an example. The child engaged in a wide range of self-injurious behaviour, such as banging his head against the floors and walls, slapping his face with his hands, and kicking himself. Despite his self-injurious behaviour, Sam was not entirely antisocial. In fact, he obviously enjoyed contact with other people and would cling to them, wrap his arms around them, and sit on their laps. This affectionate behaviour gave the investigators the idea for an experimental treatment.

The study ran for 20 days. For a period of time on each of the first five days, the frequency of Sam's self-injurious actions was observed and recorded. Then, on each of the next five days, the two adult experimenters accompanied Sam on a short walk around the campus, during which they talked to him and held his hands continuously. The adults responded to each of Sam's self-injurious actions by immediately jerking their hands away from him and not touching him again until three seconds after such activity had ceased. The frequency of the self-injurious acts was again recorded. During the next part of the experiment, the experimenters reverted to the procedures of the first five days; there were no walks, and Sam's self-afflicting behaviour was again merely observed. Then, for the last five days, the experimenters reinstated their experimental procedure. The dramatic reduction in undesirable behaviour induced by the treatment is shown in Figure 5.6.

The design of such experiments, usually referred to as a **reversal design** or **ABAB** design, requires that some aspect of the participant's behaviour be carefully measured in a specific sequence:

1. during an initial time period, the baseline (A)
2. during a period when a treatment is introduced (B)
3. during a reinstatement of the conditions that prevailed in the baseline period (A)
4. finally, during a reintroduction of the experimental manipulation (B)

If behaviour in the experimental period is different from that in the baseline period, reverses when the experimentally manipulated conditions are reversed, and re-reverses when the treatment is again introduced, there is little doubt that the manipulation, rather than chance or uncontrolled factors, has produced the change.

The reversal technique cannot always be employed, however, for the initial state of a participant may not be recoverable, as when treatment aims to produce enduring change, the goal of all therapeutic interventions. Moreover, in studies of therapeutic procedures, reinstating the original condition of the patient would generally be considered an unethical practice. Most therapists would be extremely unwilling to act in any way that might bring back the very behaviour for which a client has sought help merely to prove that a particular treatment was indeed the effective agent in changing the behaviour. Fortunately, other single-subject experimental designs avoid these problems.

As indicated earlier, even though an experiment with a single participant can demonstrate an effect, generalization is usually not possible. The fact that a treatment works for a single subject does not necessarily imply that it will be universally effective. If the search for more widely applicable treatment is the major focus of an investigation, the single-subject design has a serious drawback. However, such a design may help investigators to decide whether large-scale research with groups is warranted. This strategy was used successfully by Robert Ladouceur and his colleagues at the Université Laval in the development of their cognitive-behavioural treatment of pathological gamblers (see Chapter 3). Bujold, Ladouceur, Sylvain, and Boisvert (1994) employed a single-subject experimental design to test a treatment program that had four components: cognitive correction of erroneous perceptions about gambling, problem-solving training, social skills training, and relapse prevention. Following the combined treatment, participants no longer met the criteria for pathological gambling and the positive outcome was maintained at a 9-month follow-up. This success led to evaluation of the efficacy of the treatment package in a controlled group study (see the next section on mixed designs). Sylvain et al. (1997) reported significant changes in the treatment group, relative to a wait-list control group, on various outcome measures. The therapeutic gains were maintained at 6- and 12-month follow-ups.

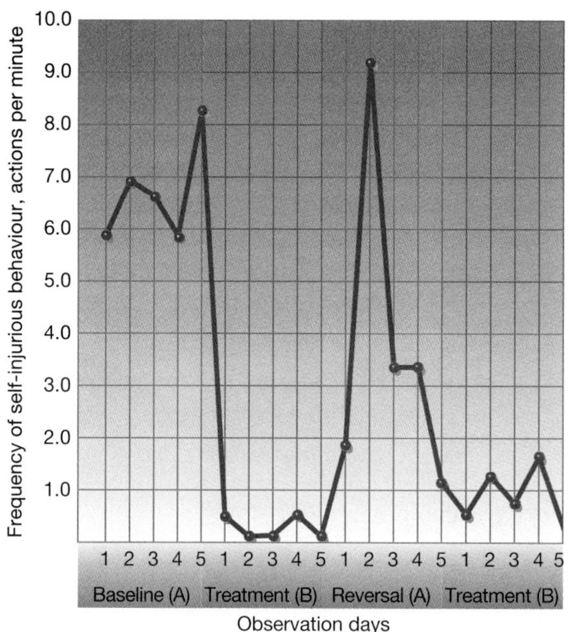

Figure 5.6 Effects of a treatment for self-injurious behaviour in an experiment with an ABAB single-subject design. Note the rapid shifts in frequency of problem behaviour as treatment is introduced (B), withdrawn (A), and finally reinstated (B). Adapted from Tate and Baroff (1966).

However, wouldn't it be useful to know more precisely what the active components of the program are? Ladouceur and his associates believed that the key factor in the development and maintenance of pathological gambling is the erroneous perceptions that gamblers have. According to their theory (Ladouceur & Walker, 1998), the core cognitive error relates to the gambler's misconception about randomness. Gamblers develop a set of false beliefs, thinking that they can control events governed by chance. They develop superstitious behaviours that they believe can increase the likelihood of winning (e.g., wearing a lucky tie while gambling). But, in fact, the "house" ultimately wins in all legalized forms of gambling! Ladouceur et al. (1998), therefore, evaluated the efficacy of an exclusively cognitive intervention to correct the pathological gambler's dysfunctional schema. Five pathological gamblers were treated in a single-subject multiple-baseline design. The treatment was successful for four of the participants, suggesting that a cognitive intervention that focuses on the gambler's misconception about the notion of randomness holds promise as a treatment for pathological gambling. Of course, the fact that the treatment was unsuccessful with one participant is an indication that other factors must also be considered.

Mixed Designs

Experimental and correlational research techniques can be combined in what is called a **mixed design**. Participants from two or more discrete and typically non-overlapping populations are assigned to each experimental condition. The two different types of populations—for example, patients with either schizophrenia or a phobia—constitute a classificatory variable; that is, the variables schizophrenia and phobia were neither manipulated nor created by the investigator, and they can only be correlated with the manipulated conditions, which are true experimental variables.

As an example of how a mixed design is applied, consider an investigation of the effectiveness of three types of therapy (the experimental variable) on patients divided into two groups on the basis of the severity of their illnesses (the classificatory or correlational variable). The question is whether the effectiveness of the treatments varies with the severity of illness. The hypothetical outcome of such a study is presented in Figure 5.7. Figure 5.7a illustrates the unfortunate conclusions that would be drawn were the patients not divided into those with severe and those with less severe illnesses. When all patients are grouped together, treatment 3 produces the greatest amount of improvement. Therefore, if no information about differential characteristics of the patients is available, treatment 3 would be preferred. When the severity of the patients' difficulties is considered, however, treatment 3 is no longer the therapy of choice for any of the patients. Rather, as seen in Figure 5.7b, treatment 1 would be selected for those with less severe illness and treatment 2 for patients with more severe illness. Thus, a mixed design can identify which treatment applies best to which group of patients.

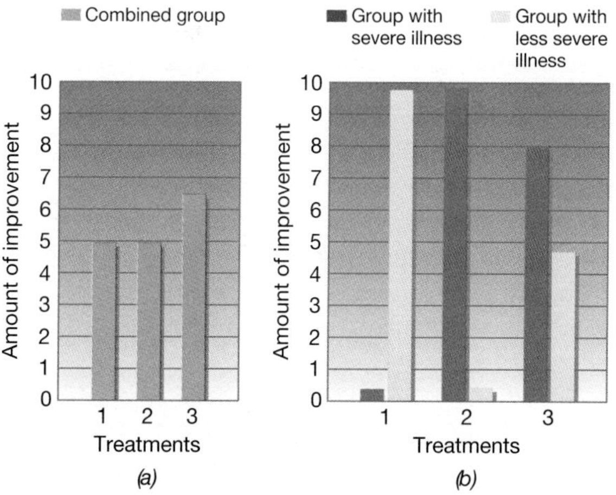

Figure 5.7 Effects of three treatments on patients whose symptoms vary in degree of severity. (a) When the severity of the illness is not known and the patients are grouped together, treatment number 3 appears to be the best. (b) The same data as in (a) are reanalysed, dividing patients by severity. Now treatment 3 is no longer best for any patients.

In interpreting the results of mixed designs, we must always be aware of the fact that one of the variables (severity of illness in our example) is not manipulated but is instead a classificatory or correlational variable. Therefore, the problems we have previously noted in interpreting correlations, especially the possible operation of third variables, arise in interpreting the results of mixed designs as well.

Figure 5.7 Effects of three treatments on patients whose symptoms vary in degree of severity. (a) When the severity of the illness is not known and the patients are grouped together, treatment number 3 appears to be the best. (b) The same data as in (a) are reanalyzed, dividing patients by severity. Now treatment 3 is no longer best for any patients.

Our survey of the major research methods of abnormal psychology is now complete. A summary appears in Table 5.3. Obviously, there is no perfect method that will easily reveal the secrets of psychopathology and therapy. Our task in subsequent chapters will be to attempt to synthesize the information yielded by investigations conducted with varying methodologies and to apply these results to advance knowledge. Focus on Discovery 5.1 discusses how scientists synthesize information using a method called *meta-analysis*.

Table 5.3

Research Methods in Abnormal Psychology

Method	Description	Evaluation
Case study	Collection of detailed historical and biographical information on a single individual	Excellent source of hypotheses but cannot determine causal relationships because cannot rule out alternative hypotheses
Epidemiology	Study of the frequency and distribution of a disorder in a population; determines incidence, prevalence, and risk factors	Knowledge of risk factors provides clues regarding causes of disorders
Correlation	Study of the relationship between two or more variables; variables are measured as they exist in nature	Cannot determine causality because of the directionality and third-variable problems; used extensively in research on the causes of psychopathology because diagnosis is a correlational or classifactory variable
Experiment with groups of participants	Includes a manipulated independent variable, a dependent variable, at least one control group, and random assignment	Most powerful method for determining causal relationships; used mainly in studies of the effectiveness of therapies
Experiment with single subjects	Includes a manipulated variable and contrasts behaviour during the time the manipulation is occurring with behaviour during a period when the manipulation is not occurring (as in the ABAB design)	Can demonstrate causal relationships, although generalization can be a problem
Mixed design	Includes both an experimental (manipulated) variable and a classificatory (correlational) variable	Can demonstrate that an experimental (e.g., a type of therapy) has variable different effects depending on the variable (e.g., severity of illness)

focus on discovery/5.1

Meta-analysis and the Effects of Psychotherapy

We have described the basic research methods of abnormal psychology and the strengths and weaknesses of individual studies. But scientific knowledge is based on integrating a body of evidence, not on merely considering individual studies one at a time. It is thus important to consider how a researcher goes about drawing conclusions from a series of investigations. A simple way of drawing conclusions is to read individual studies, mull them over, and decide what they mean overall. The disadvantage with this approach is that the researcher's biases and subjective impressions can play a significant role in determining what conclusion is drawn. It is fairly common for two scientists to read the same studies and reach very different conclusions.

Meta-analysis was developed as a partial solution to this problem. Devised by Smith, Glass, and Miller (1980), meta-analysis has played an important role in recent years in the evaluation of the effects of psychotherapy. The first step in a meta-analysis is a thorough literature search, usually by computer, so that all relevant studies are identified. Because these studies have typically reported their findings in different formats and used different statistical tests, meta-analysis then puts all the results into a common format, using a statistic called the *effect size*. The effect size offers a way of standardizing the differences in improvement between a therapy group and a control group (or between groups receiving two different types of therapy) so that the results of many different studies can be averaged.

The basis of comparison need not be type of therapy. One can compare on dimensions such as types of patients studied and settings in which therapy was administered (recall that this type of study is using a mixed design). The independent variables, in other words, can be any factors considered influential in the outcome of an intervention.

In their original and oft-cited report, Smith et al. (1980) meta-analyzed 475 psychotherapy outcome studies involving more than 25,000 patients and 1,700 effect sizes. They came to two conclusions that have attracted considerable attention and created some controversy. First, they concluded that a wide range of therapies produce more improvement than does no treatment. Specifically, treated patients were found to be better off than almost 80 percent of untreated patients. Subsequent meta-analyses by other authors have confirmed these early findings (Lambert & Bergin, 1994). Second, Smith et al. contended that effect sizes across diverse modes of intervention do not differ from one another; that is, different therapies are equally effective.

In a subsequent meta-analysis, Lambert et al. (1986) went beyond the findings of Smith et al. (1980) and reached the following further conclusions:

1. Many psychotherapeutic interventions are more effective than a number of placebo control groups. By the same token, what Lambert et al. call "common factors"—namely, warmth, trust, and encouragement—may themselves effect significant and even lasting improvement in a broad range of anxiety and mood disorders.
2. The positive effects of psychotherapy tend to be maintained for many months following termination. Lambert et al. (1986) based this conclusion on a meta-analysis of 67 outcome studies by Nicholson and Berman (1983), mostly behavioural in nature, with patients who had not been diagnosed as having a psychosis, a brain disorder, an antisocial personality, or substance dependence. This finding is obviously important to the client and to the individual therapist (who hopes that patients will continue to do well once they stop coming for regular sessions). It is important as well to psychotherapy researchers, who often have to undertake expensive and arduous follow-up measures to convince their colleagues that the effects of a given treatment are enduring.
3. There is considerable variability among participants in a given treatment condition, and thus, although treatment group X may on average show significant improvement, the group is likely also to include patients who get worse.
4. Meta-analytic studies comparing insight therapy with cognitive and behavioural interventions show a slight but consistent advantage over the latter, although some proponents of insight therapy contend that behavioural and cognitive therapies focus on milder disorders.

Meta-analysis has been criticized by a number of psychotherapy researchers. The central problem concerns the quality control of studies that are included in a meta-analysis. Therapy studies differ in their internal and external validity as judged by particular researchers. By giving equal weight to all studies, the meta-analyses of Smith et al. created a situation in which a poorly controlled outcome study (such as one that did not make clear what the therapists actually did in each session) received as much attention as a well-controlled one (such as a study in which therapists used a manual that specified what they were to do with each research participant). When Smith et al. attempted to address this problem by comparing effect sizes of good versus poor studies and found no differences, they were further criticized for the criteria they employed in separating the good from the not so good (Rachman & Wilson, 1980). O'Leary and Wilson (1987) considered other critiques as well and concluded that the ultimate problem is that someone has to make a judgment of good versus poor quality in psychotherapy research and that others can find fault with that judgment.

This seems an insoluble problem, one that has existed for years in reviews of therapy-outcome research. At times a scholar has no choice but to make his or her own judgment about the validity of a piece of research and to decide whether or not to ignore it. Perhaps Mintz (1983) was correct in saying that the move toward meta-analysis in this field has at least sensitized us to the subjectivity inherent in passing judgment on research and has also encouraged greater explicitness in the criteria used to accept or reject the findings of a given outcome study. Moreover, meta-analysis has uncovered deficiencies in some published research—for example, inadequate reporting of means and standard deviations or the collection of outcome data by persons who were aware of the treatment condition to which subjects were assigned (Shapiro & Shapiro, 1983). A long-term beneficial effect of meta-analysis may be an improvement in research practices and a tightening of publication standards (Kazdin, 1986).

SUMMARY

- Science represents an agreed-upon problem-solving enterprise, with specific procedures for gathering and interpreting data to build a systematic body of knowledge. Scientific statements must have the following characteristics: they must be testable in the public arena; they must be exposed to tests that could disconfirm them; they must derive from reliable observations; and although they may contain references to unobservable processes, the concepts inferred must be linked to observable and measurable events or outcomes.
- It is important to consider the various methods that scientists employ to collect data and arrive at conclusions. Clinical case studies serve unique and important functions in psychopathology, such as allowing rare phenomena to be studied intensively in all their complexity. Case studies also encourage the formulation of hypotheses that can be tested later through controlled research. However, the data they yield may not be valid, and they are of limited value in providing evidence to favour a theory.
- Epidemiological research gathers information about the prevalence and incidence of disorders and about risk factors that increase the probability of a disorder. Prevalence refers to the proportion of a population that has a disorder at a given point or period of time, whereas incidence refers to the number of new cases of the disorder that occur in some period. We examined abuse as a risk factor and determined that child maltreatment is a risk factor for numerous adult psychiatric disorders.
- Correlational methods are the most important means of conducting research on the causes of abnormal behaviour, for diagnoses are classificatory and not experimentally manipulated variables. In correlational studies, statistical procedures allow us to determine the extent to which two or more variables correlate, or co-vary. However, conclusions drawn from nearly all correlational studies cannot legitimately be interpreted in cause-effect terms. The directionality and third-variable problems are the source of this difficulty.
- The experimental method entails the manipulation of independent variables and the careful measurement of their effects on dependent variables. An experiment begins with a hypothesis to be tested. Participants are generally assigned to one of at least two groups: an experimental group, which experiences the manipulation of the independent variable; and a control group, which does not. If differences between the experimental and control groups are observed on the dependent variable, researchers can conclude that the independent variable did have an effect. Since it is important to ensure that experimental and control participants do not differ from one another before the introduction of the independent variable, they are assigned randomly to groups. If all these conditions are met, the experiment has internal validity.
- Placebo control groups are often used in psychotherapy research. Patients in such groups receive support and encouragement, but not what is hypothesized to be the active ingredient in the therapy administered to the group with which the placebo group is being compared.
- The external validity of research findings—whether they can be generalized to situations and people not studied within the experiment—can be assessed only by performing similar experiments in the actual domain of interest with new participants.
- Single-subject experimental designs (the reversal or ABAB design) that expose one person to different treatments over a period of time can provide internally valid results, although the generality of conclusions is typically limited.
- Mixed designs are combinations of experimental and correlational methods. For example, two different kinds of patients (the classificatory variable) may be exposed to various treatments (the experimental variable).
- A science is only as good as its methodology. Students of abnormal psychology must appreciate the strengths and limitations of the research methods of the field if they are to adequately evaluate the research and theories that form the subject matter of this book.

KEY TERMS

analogue experiment (p. 149)
case study (p. 136)
classificatory variables (p. 143)
confounds (p. 147)
control group (p. 146)
correlation coefficient (p. 142)
correlational method (p. 142)
dependent variable (p. 145)
directionality problem (p. 144)
double-blind procedure (p. 148)
epidemiology (p. 138)
experiment (p. 145)
experimental effect (p. 145)
experimental hypothesis (p. 145)
external validity (p. 148)
high-risk method (p. 144)
hypotheses (p. 134)
incidence (p. 139)
independent variable (p. 145)
internal validity (p. 147)
meta-analysis (p. 153)
mixed design (p. 151)
parental mental disorder (p. 139)
placebo control group (p. 148)
placebo effect (p. 147)
prevalence (p. 139)
random assignment (p. 145)
reversal (ABAB) design (p. 150)
risk factors (p. 139)
science (p. 134)
severe abuse (p. 139)
single-subject experimental design (p. 150)
statistical significance (p. 143)
theory (p. 134)
third-variable problem (p. 144)

Reflections: Past, Present, and Future

- In Chapter 1, we discussed the issue of reform of our health care system and management of costs of health services, including services for the care and treatment of the mentally ill. Ontario recently initiated a massive restructuring of the system in an attempt to reduce costs. Although it is vitally important that we maximize the efficient use of our psychological health care dollars, academics and policy-makers in Canada are starting to consider the costs of *failing* to prevent or treat psychological disorders (e.g., Hunsley et al., 1999; Nelson, Prilleltensky, Laurendeau, & Powell, 1996). What are the long-term costs of failing to invest in services for people with mental disorders? Can we develop effective prevention programs?
- What role should the different research methods and strategies described in this chapter play in your vision for the development of a long-term, comprehensive prevention and treatment strategy for Canada?
- In the next chapter, we will examine the anxiety disorders. Assume that the Government of Canada hired you to head a team that will conduct a long-term longitudinal study of risk factors for the development of anxiety disorders. You will track a large sample of infants, starting with the mother's pregnancy right through until they reach the age of 30. Assume that you are able to hire any experts that you desire as members of your team. What would be the composition of your team? What biopsychosocial "risk" (and protective) factors would you assess and why? How would your assessment change over time?

6 chapter

Anxiety Disorders

"Courage is resistance to fear, mastery of fear—not absence of fear."
— Mark Twain, letter to Annie Webster, September 1, 1876

"Fear and worry always lead to defeat."
"Go straight to the heart of danger, for there you will find safety."
— Ancient Chinese proverbs

"The trauma that causes posttraumatic stress disorder is a life-changing moment. It alters a person's belief in the components of the world, in safety and predictability, in the faith that bad things don't happen to good people. It alters the way people view the world and themselves in it. They are faced with reconstructing the beliefs they once held."
— David Lingley, Maple Ridge, B.C., psychologist who specializes in treating PTSD in emergency service workers (cited in Growe, 2000, p. F 7)

Frederick Varley, 1881–1969, *Dhârâna*, c.1932
oil on canvas, 86.4 x 101.6 cm, ART GALLERY OF ONTARIO, TORONTO
Gift from the Albert H. Robson Memorial Subscription Fund 1942, ©2001 Estate of Kathleen G. McKay

"I ALWAYS WAKE UP just before they kill me." This phrase summarizes the extreme anxiety and distress that some people experience. These particular words were uttered by Sergeant Bob Bilodeau to describe his dreams. Bilodeau, a 26-year veteran of the Royal Canadian Mounted Police, spent three months as a United Nations police officer inside the Muslim enclave of Srebrenica in the former Yugoslavia in 1993 (see Cowan, 1999). Bilodeau acknowledged that he has low self-esteem and problems concentrating. He experiences flashbacks and has many symptoms of an anxiety disorder known as posttraumatic stress disorder. Bilodeau turned to alcohol as a way to cope with his anxiety symptoms. He observed, "It's called self-medication. ... It works, but it will kill you in the end" (p. 29).

Bilodeau described a flashback that he experienced in October 1999. In talking about his experiences in Yugoslavia, he said, "It used to be very dangerous out there to drive at night because of robberies and car jackings. ...One time I was late, and as I came around a corner, there were two guys stopped in the middle of the road—I just did a U-turn and got out of there. A month ago, about dusk, I was going with my brother out to the lake lot we rent when we came across this vehicle with the doors open and two guys—my brain was just shouting 'danger, danger.'" Although Bilodeau has returned to the relative safety of Canada, he continues to experience nightmares involving the men on the road, but always, as he reported, "I always wake up before they kill me."

There is perhaps no single topic in abnormal psychology that touches as many of us as **anxiety**, that unpleasant feeling of fear and apprehension. This emotional state can occur in many psychopathologies and is a principal aspect of the disorders considered in this chapter. Anxiety also plays an important role in the study of the psychology of normal people, for very few of us go through even a week of our lives without experiencing some measure of anxiety or fear.

Anxiety disorders are diagnosed when subjectively experienced feelings of anxiety are clearly present. DSM-IV proposes six categories: phobias, panic disorder, generalized anxiety disorder, obsessive-compulsive disorder, posttraumatic stress disorder, and acute stress disorder. Table 6.1 provides a brief summary of the disorders we will be discussing. Often someone with one anxiety disorder meets the diagnostic criteria for another disorder as well. This comorbidity among anxiety disorders arises for two reasons:

1. Symptoms of the various anxiety disorders are not entirely disorder specific. For example, somatic signs of anxiety (e.g., perspiration, fast heart rate) are among the diagnostic criteria for panic disorder, phobias, and posttraumatic stress disorder.
2. The etiological factors that give rise to various anxiety disorders may be applicable to more than one disorder. Believing that you can't control stressors, for example, is common to both phobias and generalized anxiety disorder. Moreover, physical or sexual abuse during childhood may increase a person's risk for developing several disorders. Comorbidity could reflect the operation of common mechanisms.

Table 6.1

Summary of Major Anxiety Disorders

Disorder	Description
Phobia	Fear and avoidance of objects or situations that do not present any real danger.
Panic disorder	Recurrent panic attacks involving a sudden onset of physiological symptoms, such as dizziness, rapid heart rate, and trembling, accompanied by terror and feelings of impending doom; sometimes accompanied with agoraphobia, a fear of being in public places.
Generalized anxiety disorder	Persistent, uncontrollable worry, often about minor things.
Obsessive-compulsive disorder	The experience of uncontrollable thoughts, impulses, or images (obsessions) and repetitive behaviours or mental acts (compulsions).
Posttraumatic stress disorder	Aftermath of a traumatic experience in which the person experiences increased arousal, avoidance of stimuli associated with the event, and anxiety in recalling the event.
Acute stress disorder	Symptoms are the same as those of posttraumatic stress disorder, but last for four weeks or less.

As yet, theories of anxiety disorders tend to focus exclusively on a single disorder. The development of theories that take comorbidity into account is a challenge for the future.

According to the *Mental Health Supplement* to the Ontario Health Survey (Ontario Ministry of Health, 1994), 16 percent of women and 9 percent of men suffered from anxiety disorders in the preceding year. The highest one-year prevalence rates (i.e., almost one in five) were found in young women 15 to 24 years of age. Anxiety disorders were more common in women than in men across all age groups, although for both men and women the rates of anxiety disorders decreased with age.

We turn now to an examination of the defining characteristics, theories of etiology, and therapies for each of the anxiety disorders.

PHOBIAS

Psychopathologists define a **phobia** as a disrupting, fear-mediated avoidance that is out of proportion to the danger actually posed and is recognized by the sufferer as groundless. Extreme fear of heights, closed spaces, snakes, or spiders—provided that there is no objective danger—accompanied by sufficient distress to disrupt one's life is likely to be diagnosed as a phobia.

Fear and avoidance of heights is classified as a specific phobia. Other specific phobias include fears of animals, injections, and enclosed spaces.

Many specific fears do not cause enough hardship to compel an individual to seek treatment. For example, an urban dweller with an intense fear of snakes will probably have little direct contact with the feared object and may therefore not believe that anything is seriously wrong. The term phobia usually implies that the person suffers intense distress and social or occupational impairment because of the anxiety. A study of the fears and phobias of women in Calgary (Costello, 1982) found that about 5 percent were "incapacitated" by their phobias.

Over the years, complex terms have been formulated to name these unwarranted avoidance patterns. In each instance, the suffix *phobia* is preceded by a Greek word for the feared object or situation. The suffix is derived from the name of the Greek god Phobos, who frightened his enemies. Some of the more familiar terms are *claustrophobia*, fear of closed spaces; *agoraphobia*, fear of public places; and *acrophobia*, fear of heights. More exotic fears have also been given Greek-derived names, such as, *ergasiophobia*, fear of writing; pnigophobia, fear of choking; *taphephobia*, fear of being buried alive; and, believe it or not, *Anglophobia*, fear of England (McNally, 1997). These authoritative terms convey the impression that we understand how a particular problem originated and how it can be treated. Nothing could be further from the truth. As with so much in the field of abnormal psychology, there are more theories and jargon pertaining to phobias than there are firm findings.

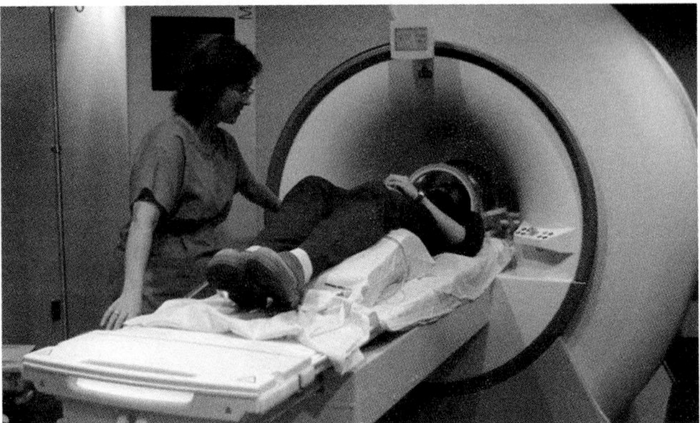

Claustrophobia, a fear of closed spaces, is a significant problem for people who must undergo MRI tests, since MRIs involve spending a prolonged amount of time in an enclosed chamber. Mock MRI studies have been conducted with university students to assess levels of claustrophobia (see McGlynn, Karg, & Lawyer, 2003).

Psychologists tend to focus on different aspects of phobias according to the paradigm they have adopted. Psychoanalysts focus on the content of the phobia and see the phobic object as a symbol of an important unconscious fear. In a celebrated case reported by Freud, a boy he called Little Hans was afraid of horses. Freud paid particular attention to Hans's reference to the "black things around horses' mouths and the things in front of their eyes." The horse was regarded as representing the father, who had a mustache and wore eyeglasses. Freud theorized that fear of the father had become transformed into fear of horses, which Hans then avoided. Thus, psychoanalysts believe that the content of phobias has important symbolic value. Behaviourists, on the other hand, tend to ignore the content of the phobia and focus instead on its *function*. For them, fear of snakes and fear of heights are equivalent in the means by which they are acquired, in how they might be reduced, and so on.
Let us look now at two types of phobias: specific phobias and social phobias.

SPECIFIC PHOBIAS

Specific phobias are unwarranted fears caused by the presence or anticipation of a specific object or situation. DSM-IV subdivides these phobias according to the source of the fear: blood, injuries and injections, situations (e.g., planes, elevators, enclosed spaces), animals, and the natural environment (e.g., heights, water).

Recent empirical research involving a nationally representative sample suggests that fears can be grouped into one of five factors: (1) agoraphobia; (2) fears of heights or water; (3) threat fears (e.g., blood/needles, storms/thunder); (4)

fears of being observed; and (5) speaking fears (Cox, McWilliams, Clara, & Stein, 2003). These fears were then classified under the two higher-order categories, specific fears and social fears.

Lifetime prevalence of specific phobias that involve specific objects was estimated at 7 percent for men and 16 percent for women in one U.S. study (Kessler et al., 1994). In a survey of 3,258 adults in Edmonton, Alberta, Bland, Orne, and Newman (1988) used structured interviews based on DSM-III criteria and determined a lifetime prevalence rate of 4.6 percent for men and 9.8 percent for women (average of 7.2 percent).

The specific fear focused on in a phobia can vary cross-culturally. In China, for example, a person with Pa-leng (a fear of the cold) worries that loss of body heat may be life-threatening. This fear appears to be related to the Chinese philosophy of yin and yang: yin refers to the cold, windy, energy-sapping, and passive aspects of life, while yang refers to hot, powerful and active aspects of life.

Another example is a Japanese syndrome called *taijin-kyofu-sho*, fear of other people. This is not a social phobia; rather, it is an extreme fear of embarrassing others—for example, by blushing in their presence, glancing at their genital areas, or making odd faces. It is believed that this phobia arises from elements of traditional Japanese culture, which encourages extreme concern for the feelings of others yet discourages direct communication of feelings (McNally, 1997).

What is feared in a phobia varies cross-culturally. In China, Pa-leng is a fear that loss of body heat will be life-threatening.

SOCIAL PHOBIAS

Social phobias are persistent, irrational fears linked generally to the presence of other people. They can be extremely debilitating. Individuals with a social phobia try to avoid particular situations in which they might be evaluated, fearing that they will reveal signs of anxiousness or behave in an embarrassing way. Speaking or performing in public, eating in public, using public lavatories, and other activities carried out in the presence of others can elicit extreme anxiety.

Social phobias can be either generalized or specific, depending on the range of situations that are feared and avoided. While generalized social phobias involve many different interpersonal situations, specific social phobias involve intense fear of one particular situation (e.g., public speaking). People with the generalized type have an earlier age of onset, more comorbidity with other disorders, such as depression and alcohol abuse, and more severe impairment (Mannuzza et al., 1995; Wittchen, Stein, & Kessler, 1999).

Social phobias are fairly common, with a lifetime prevalence in the National Comorbidity Survey of 11 percent in men and 15 percent in women (Kessler et al., 1994; Magee et al., 1996). The prevalence was actually much lower in Bland's Edmonton study (Bland et al., 1988). However, a telephone survey of 499 community residents from Winnipeg conducted by Stein, Walker, and Forde (1996) illustrates that different findings can occur as a result of the stringency of criteria used. In their study, the prevalence of a social phobia was about 7 percent when stringent criteria (DSM-III-R) were applied but about 33 percent when more liberal criteria were used. Social phobias have a high comorbidity rate with other disorders and often occur in conjunction with generalized anxiety disorder, specific phobias, panic disorder, avoidant personality disorder, and mood disorders (Jansen et al., 1994; Kessler et al., 1999; Lecrubier & Weiller, 1997). Onset generally takes place during adolescence, when social awareness and interaction with others become much more important in a person's life.

Findings from Canadian samples underscore the level of impairment associated with social phobia. In the Stein et al. (1996) study in Winnipeg, about 10 percent of the participants indicated that public-speaking anxiety had caused them significant distress or impairment. Similarly, analyses of data from Ontario's Mental Health Supplement (see Stein & Kean, 2000) found that diagnosed social phobia was associated with marked dissatisfaction and low functioning in terms of quality of life. Importantly, this study used a representative community sample, thereby supporting the generalizability of findings obtained with clinical samples (see Mendlowicz & Stein, 2000) that may have been biased by the inclusion of more severe cases of social phobia. Another unique aspect of the Ontario study is that a positive link was found between social phobia and dropping out of school (Stein & Kean, 2000).

Social phobias typically begin in adolescence and interfere with developing friendships with peers.

Etiology of Phobias

As is true for virtually all the disorders discussed in this book, proposals about the causes of phobias have been made by adherents of the psychoanalytic, behavioural, cognitive, and biological paradigms. We now look at the ideas of each of these paradigms.

Psychoanalytic Theories Freud was the first to attempt to account systematically for the development of phobic behaviour. According to Freud, phobias are a defence against the anxiety produced by repressed id impulses. This anxiety is displaced from the feared id impulse and moved to an object or situation that has some symbolic connection to it. These objects or situations—for example, elevators or closed spaces—then become the phobic stimuli. By avoiding them the person is able to avoid dealing with repressed conflicts. As discussed in Chapter 2, the phobia is the ego's way of warding off a confrontation with the real problem, a repressed childhood conflict. Freud thought that Little Hans had not successfully resolved the Oedipal conflict; as a result, his intense fear of his father was displaced onto horses and he became phobic about leaving his home. Arieti (1979) proposed that the repression stems from a particular interpersonal problem of childhood rather than from an id impulse. As with most psychoanalytic theorizing, most of the supporting evidence is restricted to conclusions drawn from clinical case reports.

Behavioural Theories Behavioural theories focus on learning as the way in which phobias are acquired. Several types of learning may be involved.

Avoidance Conditioning The main behavioural account of phobias is that such reactions are learned avoidance responses. Historically, the model of how a phobia is acquired is considered to be Watson and Rayner's (1920) demonstration of the apparent conditioning of a fear or phobia in Little Albert. The avoidance-conditioning formulation, which is based on the two-factor theory originally proposed by Mowrer (1947), holds that phobias develop from two related sets of learning.

1. Via classical conditioning, a person can learn to fear a neutral stimulus (the CS) if it is paired with an intrinsically painful or frightening event (the UCS).
2. The person can learn to reduce this conditioned fear by escaping from or avoiding the CS. This second kind of learning is assumed to be operant conditioning; the response is maintained by its reinforcing consequence of reducing fear.

An important issue exists in the application of the avoidance-conditioning model to phobias. The fact that Little Albert's fear was acquired through conditioning cannot be taken as evidence that all fears and phobias are acquired by this means. Rather, the evidence demonstrates only the *possibility* that some fears may be acquired in this particular way. Furthermore, attempts to replicate Watson and Rayner's experiment have for the most part not been successful (e.g., English, 1929). Very little experimental evidence supports the contention that human beings can be classically conditioned to develop a durable fear of neutral stimuli even when such stimuli are paired repeatedly with primary aversive stimuli, such as electric shock (e.g., Davison, 1968b).

Ethical considerations have restrained most researchers from employing highly aversive stimuli with human beings, but considerable evidence indicates that fear is extinguished rather quickly when the CS is presented a few times without the reinforcement of moderate levels of shock (Bridger & Mandel, 1965). The problem may be that a strong unconditioned physiological fear response is not being elicited in the laboratory and that such a response is critical to establishing conditioned fear (Forsyth & Eifert, 1998).

Outside the laboratory, the evidence for the avoidance-conditioning theory is also mixed. Some clinical phobias fit the avoidance-conditioning model rather well. A phobia of a specific object or situation has sometimes been reported after a particularly painful experience with that object. Some people become intensely afraid of heights after a bad fall; others develop a phobia of driving after experiencing a panic attack in their car (Munjack, 1984); and people with social phobias often report traumatic social experiences (Sternberger et al., 1995). Other clinical reports suggest that phobias may develop without a prior frightening experience. Many individuals with severe fears of snakes, germs, and airplanes tell clinicians that they have had no particularly unpleasant experiences with these objects or situations (Ost, 1987a). Can this problem with the avoidance-conditioning model be solved? One attempt to do so involves modelling.

Modelling In addition to learning to fear something as a result of an unpleasant experience with it, a person can also learn fears through imitating the reactions of others. Thus, some phobias may be acquired by modelling, not through an unpleasant experience with the object or situation that is feared. The learning of fear by observing others is generally referred to as vicarious learning.

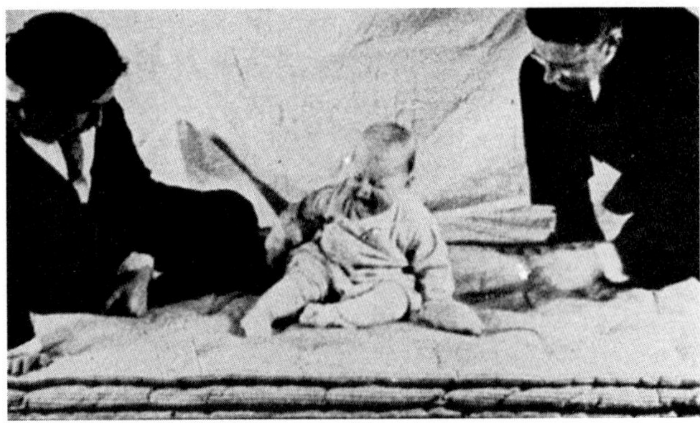

Little Albert, shown here with Watson and Rayner, was classically conditioned to develop a fear of a white rat.

In one study, Bandura and Rosenthal (1966) arranged for participants to watch another person, the model (a confederate of the experimenter), in an aversive-conditioning situation. The model was hooked up to an impressive-looking array of electrical apparatuses. On hearing a buzzer, the model withdrew his hand rapidly from the arm of the chair and feigned pain. The physiological responses of the participants witnessing this behaviour were recorded. After the participants had watched the model "suffer" a number of times, they showed an increased frequency of emotional responses when the buzzer sounded. Thus, they reacted emotionally to a harmless stimulus even though they had had no direct contact with a noxious event.

Vicarious learning may also be accomplished through verbal instructions. Thus, phobic reactions can be learned through another's description of what could happen. For example, a child may come to fear an activity after a parent has repeatedly warned him or her not to engage in it lest dire consequences ensue. Indeed, the *anxious-rearing model* is based on the premise that anxiety disorders in children are due to constant parental warnings that increase anxiety in the child.

Prepared Learning Another issue that the original avoidance-learning model fails to address is that people tend to fear only certain objects and events, such as spiders, snakes, and heights, but not others, such as lambs (Marks, 1969). The fact that certain neutral stimuli, called *prepared stimuli*, are more likely than others to become classically conditioned stimuli may account for this tendency. For example, rats readily learn to associate taste with nausea but not with shock when the two are paired (Garcia, McGowan, & Green, 1972). Some fears may well reflect classical conditioning, but only to stimuli to which an organism is physiologically prepared to be sensitive (Seligman, 1971). Conditioning experiments that show quick extinction of fear may have used CSs that the organism was not prepared to associate with UCSs.

Prepared learning is also relevant to learning fear by modelling. Cook and Mineka (1989) studied four groups of rhesus monkeys, each of which saw a different videotape showing a monkey seeming react with fear to different stimuli: a toy snake, a toy crocodile, flowers, or a toy rabbit. Only the monkeys exposed to the tapes showing the toy snake or toy crocodile acquired fear of the object shown, again demonstrating that not every stimulus is capable of becoming a source of acquired fear.

A Diathesis Is Needed A final question to consider is why some people who have traumatic experiences do not develop enduring fears. For example, 50 percent of people with a severe fear of dogs reported a prior traumatic experience, yet 50 percent of people who were not afraid of dogs reported a similar experience (DiNardo et al., 1988). Why did only some people develop this fear? A cognitive diathesis (predisposition)—a tendency to believe that similar traumatic experiences will occur in the future—may be important in developing a phobia. Another possible psychological diathesis is a history of not being able to control the environment (Mineka & Zinbarg, 1996).

In sum, the data suggest that while some phobias are learned through avoidance conditioning, avoidance conditioning should not be regarded as a totally validated theory; many people with phobias do not report either direct exposure to a traumatic event or exposure to fearful models (Merckelbach et al., 1989).

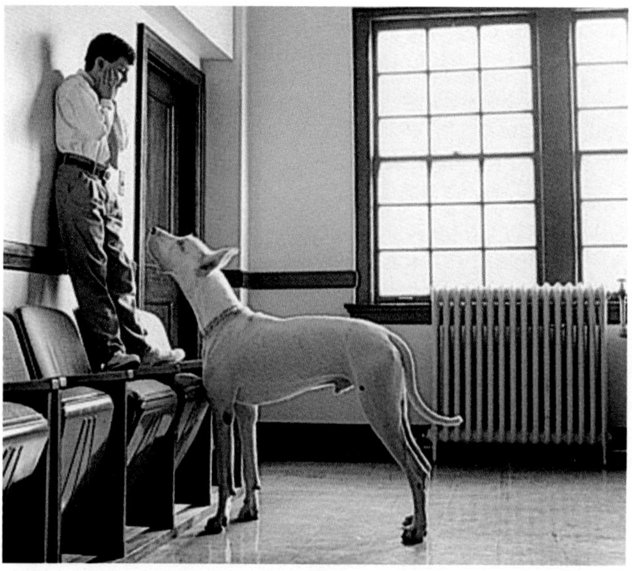

DiNardo's study showed that after a traumatic experience with a dog, those who developed a persistent fear of dogs were anxious about having similar future experiences.

Social Skills Deficits in Social Phobias A behavioural model of social phobia considers inappropriate behaviour or a lack of social skills as the cause of social anxiety. According to this view, the individual has not learned how to behave so that he or she feels comfortable with others, or the person repeatedly commits faux pas, is awkward and socially inept, and is often criticized by social companions. Support for this model comes from findings that socially anxious people are indeed rated as being low in social skills (Twentyman & McFall, 1975) and that the timing and placement of their responses in a social interaction, such as saying thank you at the right time and place, are impaired (Fischetti, Curran, & Wessberg, 1977).

Of course, social skills deficits may have arisen over time because the person was fearful for other reasons, such as classical conditioning, of interacting with others and therefore had little experience doing so. The lack of interpersonal skills in an adult who has a social phobia may therefore reveal little of etiological significance, though the information may be very important in planning effective therapeutic interventions.

Cognitive Theories Cognitive views of anxiety in general and of phobias in particular focus on how people's thought processes can serve as a diathesis and on how thoughts can maintain a phobia. Anxiety is related to being more likely to attend to negative stimuli, to interpret ambiguous information as threatening, and to believe that negative events are more likely than positive ones to occur in the future (Mathews & MacLeod, 1994). For instance, contemporary research suggests that spider phobia involves automatic thought processes and implicit cognitive associations involving themes of disgust and threat that occur without conscious introspection or awareness (Teachman & Woody, 2003).

Studies of socially anxious people have contributed to ideas about the cognitive factors related to social phobias. Socially anxious people are more concerned about evaluation than are people who are not socially anxious (Goldfried, Padawer, & Robins, 1984), are more aware of the image they present to others (Bates, 1990), and are preoccupied with hiding imperfections and not making mistakes in front of other people (Hewitt et al., 2003). Unfortunately, they tend to view themselves negatively even when they have actually performed well in a social interaction (Wallace & Alden, 1997).

Cognitive-behavioural models of social phobia outlined by Clark and Wells (1995) and Rapee and Heimberg (1997) link social phobia with certain cognitive characteristics: (1) an attentional bias to focus on negative social information (e.g., perceived criticism and hostile reactions from others); (2) perfectionistic standards for accepted social performances; and (3) a high degree of public self-consciousness. Research by Sheila Woody at the University of British Columbia has confirmed that excessive self-consciousness and self-focus tend to increase social anxiety (see Woody & Rodriguez, 2000).

Related research has shown that social phobia is linked with high self-criticism (Cox, Walker, Enns, & Karpinski, 2002). This self-criticism may underscore a general sensitivity to perceived criticism. Davison and Zighelboim (1987) used the Articulated Thoughts in Simulated Situations method to compare the thoughts of two groups of participants as they role-played participation in both a neutral situation and one in which they were being sharply criticized. One group comprised volunteers from an introductory psychology course; the other consisted of undergraduates referred from the student counselling centre and identified by their therapists as shy, withdrawn, and socially anxious. The thoughts articulated by the socially anxious students in both stressful and neutral situations were more negative than were those of the control subjects. Their reported thoughts as they imagined themselves being criticized included "I've been rejected by these people" and "I think I am boring when I talk to people."

Stanley Rachman from the University of British Columbia and his colleagues (Rachman, Gruter-Andrew, & Shafran, 2000) reported that socially anxious students not only anticipate negative social experiences, they also engage in extensive post-event processing of the negative social experiences, sometimes experiencing intrusive thoughts and images associated typically with obsessive-compulsive disorder.

Cognitive theories of phobias are also relevant to other features of these disorders—the persistence of the fears and the fact that the fears actually seem irrational to the person experiencing them. As noted earlier, these phenomena may occur because fear is elicited through early cognitive processes that are not available to conscious awareness. After this initial processing, the stimulus is avoided, so it is not processed fully enough to allow the fear to be extinguished (Amir, Foa, & Coles, 1998). In one study that partially tested this notion, people with high levels of fear of either snakes or spiders were presented with pictures of varying content, some expected to elicit fear (snakes and spiders) and some not (flowers and mushrooms). Each picture was followed 30 milliseconds later by another so that the content of the pictures could not be consciously recognized. Nevertheless, people high in fear of snakes showed increased skin conductance to the snake slides, and those high in fear of spiders showed increased skin conductance to the spider slides, indicating that phobic fears may be elicited by stimuli that are not available to consciousness and may therefore appear irrational (Öhman & Soares, 1994).

Predisposing Biological Factors Why do some people acquire unrealistic fears when others do not, given similar opportunities for learning? Perhaps those who are adversely affected by stress have a biological malfunction (a diathesis) that somehow predisposes them to develop a phobia following a particular stressful event. Research in two areas seems promising: the autonomic nervous system and genetic factors.

Autonomic Nervous System One way people differ in their reaction to certain environmental situations is the ease with which their autonomic nervous systems become aroused. Lacey (1967) identified a dimension of autonomic activity that he called stability-lability. Labile, or jumpy, individuals are those whose autonomic systems are readily aroused by a wide range of stimuli. Because of the extent to which the autonomic nervous system is involved in fear and hence in phobic behaviour, a dimension such as **autonomic lability** assumes considerable importance. Since there is reason to believe that autonomic lability is to some degree genetically determined (Gabbay, 1992), heredity may very well have a significant role in the development of phobias.

Genetic Factors Several studies have examined whether a genetic factor is involved in phobias. Blood-and-injection phobia is strongly familial. Sixty-four percent of patients with this phobia have at least one first-degree relative with the same disorder, whereas the disorder's prevalence in the general population is only 3 to 4 percent (Ost, 1992). Similarly, for both social (especially the generalized type) and specific phobias, prevalence is higher than average in first-degree relatives of patients (Fyer et al., 1995; Stein et al.,

1998). Twin studies have also provided evidence that phobias have a heritable component (Kendler, Karkowski, & Prescott, 1999), and another shows that genetic factors have a similar structure and role for men and women (Kendler, Prescott, Myers, & Neele, 2003).

Related to these findings is the work of Jerome Kagan on the trait of inhibition or shyness (Kagan & Snidman, 1997). Some infants as young as four months become agitated and cry when they are shown toys or other stimuli. This behaviour pattern, which may be inherited, may set the stage for the later development of phobias. In one study, inhibited children were shown to be more than five times more likely than uninhibited children to develop a phobia later (Biederman et al., 1990).

The data we have described do not unequivocally implicate genetic factors. Although close relatives share genes, they also have considerable opportunity to observe and influence one another. The fact that a son and his father are both afraid of heights may indicate a genetic component, the son's direct imitation of the father's behaviour, or both. Although there is some reason to believe that genetic factors may be involved in the etiology of phobias, there has as yet been no clear-cut demonstration of the extent to which they may be important.

THERAPIES FOR PHOBIAS

Most people suffer with their phobias and do not seek treatment (Magee et al., 1996). In fact, many people who could be diagnosed by a clinician as having a phobia do not feel they have a problem that merits attention. A decision to seek treatment often arises when a life change requires exposure to stimuli or situations that had for years been avoided or minimized.

AN INDUSTRIAL ENGINEER sought treatment for his fear of flying when a promotion required him to travel frequently. This professional recognition was a result of his having worked with distinction for several years in his firm at a job that kept him at his desk. Family trips were always by car or train, and those close to him worked around his debilitating fear of getting on an airplane. Imagine his mixed feelings at being informed that his excellence was to be rewarded by the promotion! His ambition and self-respect—and encouragement from family and friends—goaded him into seeking assistance.

Throughout the book, after reviewing theories about the causes of the various disorders, we will describe the principal therapies for them. The treatment sections of Chapters 1 and 2 were meant to furnish the reader with a context for understanding these discussions of therapy. We will now look at a number of therapeutic approaches used to treat phobias.

Psychoanalytic Approaches In general, all psychoanalytic treatments of phobias attempt to uncover the repressed conflicts believed to underlie the extreme fear and avoidance characteristic of these disorders. Because the phobia itself is regarded as symptomatic of underlying conflicts, it is usually not dealt with directly. Indeed, direct attempts to reduce phobic avoidance are contraindicated because the phobia is assumed to protect the person from repressed conflicts that are too painful to confront.

The analyst uses, in various combinations, the techniques developed within the psychoanalytic tradition to help lift the repression. During free association, the analyst listens carefully to what the patient mentions in connection with any references to the phobia. The analyst also attempts to discover clues to the repressed origins of the phobia in the manifest content of dreams. Exactly what the analyst believes the repressed conflict springs from depends on the particular psychoanalytic theory held. An orthodox analyst will look for conflicts related to sex or aggression, whereas an analyst holding to Arieti's interpersonal theory will encourage patients to examine their generalized fear of other people.

Contemporary ego analysts focus less on gaining historical insights and more on encouraging the patient to confront the phobia. However, they do view the phobia as an outgrowth of an earlier problem. Alexander and French, in their classic book *Psychoanalytic Therapy* (1946), wrote of the "corrective emotional experience" in therapy, by which they meant the patient's confrontation with what is so desperately feared. They observed that "Freud himself came to the conclusion that in the treatment of some cases, phobias for example, a time arrives when the analyst must encourage the patient to engage in those activities he avoided in the past" (p. 39). Wachtel (1977) recommended even more boldly that analysts employ the fear-reduction techniques of behaviour therapists. Many analytically oriented clinicians recognize the importance of exposure to what is feared, although they usually regard any subsequent improvement as merely symptomatic and not as a resolution of the underlying conflict that was assumed to have produced the phobia (Wolitzky & Eagle, 1990).

Behavioural Approaches Systematic desensitization was the first major behavioural treatment to be used widely in treating phobias (Wolpe, 1958). The individual with a phobia imagines a series of increasingly frightening scenes while in a state of deep relaxation. Clinical and experimental evidence indicates that this technique is effective in eliminating, or at least reducing, phobias (McGlynn, 1994). Many behaviour therapists, however, have come to recognize the critical importance of exposure to real-life phobic situations, sometimes during the period in which a patient is being desensitized in imagination and sometimes instead of the imagery-based procedure (Craske, Rapee, & Barlow, 1992). Historically, clinical researchers have regarded such **in vivo exposure** as superior to techniques using imagination, not a surprising finding given that imaginary stimuli are by definition not the real thing! However, some contemporary research comparing in vivo exposure with virtual reality (VR) exposure treatments has found VR exposure to be just as effective as in vivo exposure (Emmelkamp et al., 2002). Virtual reality involves exposure to stimuli that come in the form of computer-generated graphics. VR exposure can be tailored to involve graded exposures to threatening stimuli, similar to the increasingly frightening scenes used in systematic desensitization.

Blood-and-injection phobias have only recently, in DSM-IV, been distinguished from other kinds of severe fears and avoidances because of the distinctive reactions that people with these phobias have to the usual behavioural approach of relaxation paired with exposure (Page, 1994). Relaxation tends to make matters worse for people with blood-and-injection phobias. Why? Consider the typical reaction. After the initial fright, accompanied by dramatic increases in heart rate and blood pressure, a person with a blood-and-injection phobia often experiences a sudden drop in blood pressure and heart rate and faints (McGrady & Bernal, 1986). By trying to relax, patients with these phobias may well contribute to the tendency to faint, increasing their already high levels of fear and avoidance as well as their embarrassment (Ost, 1992). Patients with blood-and-injection phobias are now encouraged to tense rather than relax their muscles when confronting the fearsome situation (e.g., Hellstrom, Fellenius, & Ost, 1996).

Learning social skills can help people with social phobias who may not know what to do or say in social situations. Some behaviour therapists encourage patients to role-play interpersonal encounters in the consulting room or in small therapy groups (e.g., Marks, 1995). Several studies attest to the effectiveness of such an approach (e.g., Turner, Beidel, & Cooley-Quille, 1995). As noted by Herbert (1995), such practices may also expose the anxious person to anxiety-provoking cues, such as being observed by others, so that extinction of fear through real-life exposure takes place (Hope, Heimberg, & Bruch, 1995).

Modelling is another technique that uses exposure to feared situations. In modelling therapy, fearful clients are exposed to filmed or live demonstrations of other people interacting fearlessly with the phobic object (e.g., handling snakes). Flooding is a therapeutic technique in which the client is exposed to the source of the phobia at full intensity. The extreme discomfort that is inevitable has until recently discouraged therapists from using this technique, except perhaps as a last resort when graduated exposure has not worked. We will see more extensive use of flooding when we examine therapy for obsessive-compulsive disorder and posttraumatic stress disorder.

Behaviour therapists who favour operant techniques ignore the fear assumed to underlie phobias and attend instead to the overt avoidance of phobic objects and to the approach behaviour that must replace it. They treat approach to the feared situation as any other operant and shape it via the principle of successive approximations. Real-life exposures to the phobic object are gradually achieved, and the client is rewarded for even minimal successes in moving closer to it. Exposure is an inevitable aspect of any operant shaping of approach behaviours.

Many behaviour therapists attend both to fear and to avoidance, using techniques such as desensitization to reduce fear and operant shaping to encourage approach

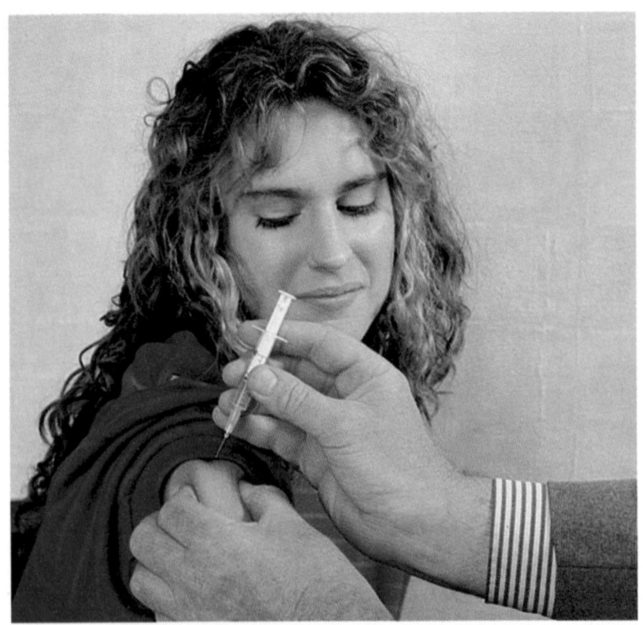

Blood-and-injection phobias are different from other specific phobias. Patients with this type of phobia are encouraged not to relax, but to tense their muscles when they encounter the feared situation.

In the most frequent treatment for phobias, patients are exposed to what they fear most, here, an enclosed space.

(Lazarus, Davison, & Polefka, 1965). In the initial stages of treatment, when fear and avoidance are both very great, the therapist concentrates on reducing the fear through relaxation training and graded exposures to the phobic situation. As therapy progresses, fear becomes less of an issue and avoidance more. A person with a phobia has often settled into an existence in which other people cater to his or her incapacities, in a way reinforcing the person's phobia (psychoanalysts call this phenomenon *secondary gain*). As the person's anxieties diminish, he or she is able to approach what used to be terrifying. This overt behaviour can then be positively reinforced—and avoidance discouraged—by relatives and friends as well as by the therapist.

Cognitive Approaches Cognitive treatments for specific phobias have been viewed with skepticism because of a central defining characteristic of phobias: the phobic fear is recognized by the individual as excessive or unreasonable. If the person already acknowledges that the fear is of something harmless, of what use can it be to alter the person's thoughts about it? Indeed, there is no evidence that the elimination of irrational beliefs alone, without exposure to the fearsome situations, reduces phobic avoidance (e.g., Turner et al., 1992).

With social phobias, on the other hand, such cognitive methods—sometimes combined with social skills training—are more promising. People with social phobias benefit from treatment strategies derived from Aaron Beck and Albert Ellis. They may be persuaded by the therapist to more accurately appraise people's reactions to them (e.g., the teacher's frown may reflect a bad mood rather than disapproval) but also to rely less on the approval of others for a sense of self-worth. Cognitive approaches have been used more often since the recognition that many people with social phobias have adequate social skills but do not use them because of self-defeating thoughts.

Even so, statistically significant differences between a treatment group undergoing, say, cognitive behaviour therapy and a control group does not mean that all or even most of the treated patients end up with no social anxiety at all. On the contrary—and this generalization applies to *all* the therapies judged effective—many patients do not respond at all to treatment and many achieve only a partial reduction of their anxiety (DeRubeis & Crits-Christoph, 1998).

All the behavioural and cognitive therapies for phobias have a recurrent theme, namely, the need for the patient to begin exposing himself or herself to what has been deemed too terrifying to face. Even Freud (1919) acknowledged that we must face our fears!

Biological Approaches Drugs that reduce anxiety are referred to as sedatives, tranquilizers, or anxiolytics (the suffix *lytic* comes from the Greek word meaning to loosen or dissolve). Barbiturates were the first major category of drugs used to treat anxiety disorders, but because they are highly addicting and present great risk of a lethal overdose, they were supplanted in the 1950s by two other classes of drugs, propanediols (e.g., Miltown) and benzodiazepines (e.g., Valium and Xanax). Valium and Xanax are still used today, although they have been largely supplanted by newer benzodiazepines, such as Ativan and Clonapam. As we will see, these drugs are of demonstrated benefit with some anxiety disorders. However, they are not used extensively with the specific phobias. Furthermore, although the risk of lethal overdose is not as great as with barbiturates, benzodiazepines are addicting and can produce a severe withdrawal syndrome (Schweizer et al., 1990).

In recent years, drugs originally developed to treat depression (antidepressants) have become popular in treating many anxiety disorders, phobias included. One class of these drugs, the monoamine oxidase (MAO) inhibitors, fared better in treating social phobias than did a benzodiazepine (Gelernter et al., 1991) and, in another study, was as effective as cognitive behaviour therapy at a 12-week follow-up (Heimberg et al., 1998). But MAO inhibitors, such as phenelzine (Nardil), can lead to weight gain, insomnia, sexual dysfunction, and hypertension. The more recently available selective serotonin reuptake inhibitors (SSRIs), such as fluoxetine (Prozac), were also originally developed to treat depression. They, too, have shown some promise in reducing social phobia in double-blind Canadian studies (Stein et al., 1999), and a recent meta-analysis of past studies has confirmed their effectiveness (Federoff & Taylor, 2001). However, the key problem in treating phobias and other anxiety disorders with drugs is that the patient may find it difficult to discontinue their use, relapse being a common result (Herbert, 1995).

PANIC DISORDER

In panic disorder, a person suffers a sudden and often inexplicable attack of a host of jarring symptoms—laboured breathing, heart palpitations, nausea, chest pain, feelings of choking and smothering; dizziness, sweating, and trembling; and intense apprehension, terror, and feelings of impending doom. Depersonalization, a feeling of being outside one's body, and derealization, a feeling of the world's not being real, as well as fears of losing control, of going crazy, or even of dying, may beset and overwhelm the patient.

Panic attacks may occur frequently, perhaps once weekly or more often; they usually last for minutes, rarely for hours; and they are sometimes linked to specific situations, such as driving a car. They are referred to as cued panic attacks when they are associated strongly with situational triggers. When their relationship with stimuli is present but not as strong, they are referred to as situationally predisposed attacks. Panic attacks can also occur in seemingly benign states, such as relaxation or sleep, and in unexpected situations; in these cases, they are referred to as uncued attacks.

In October 2001, Shayne Corson of the Toronto Maple Leafs revealed publicly that he had experienced crippling panic attacks throughout the preceding season. Corson decided he could no longer play when his symptoms reappeared during the 2003 playoffs.

Recurrent uncued attacks and worry about having attacks in the future are required for the diagnosis of panic disorder. The exclusive presence of cued attacks most likely reflects the presence of a phobia. Panic attacks are quite common among university and college students (see Canadian Perspectives 6.1).

The lifetime prevalence of panic disorder based on the National Comorbidity Survey is about 2 percent for men and more than 5 percent for women (Kessler et al., 1994). It typically begins in adolescence, and its onset is associated with stressful life experiences (Pollard, Pollard, & Corn, 1989). A comparative study of several countries found that the one-year rates were quite comparable across countries, with obtained rates of 0.9 percent of men and 1.9 percent of women from an Edmonton sample (Weissman et al., 1997). However, the prevalence of panic disorder does vary cross-culturally. For example, in Africa it was diagnosed in about 1 percent of men and 6 percent of women (Hollifield et al., 1990). However, in Taiwan the prevalence of panic disorder is quite low, perhaps because of a stigma about reporting a mental problem (Weissman et al., 1997).

Disorders that bear some relationship to panic disorder occur in other cultures. Among the Inuit of the Northwest Territories and west Greenland, *kayak-angst* occurs among seal hunters who are alone at sea. Attacks involve intense fear, disorientation, and concerns about drowning. *Ataque de nervios* was originally identified in Puerto Rico and involves physical symptoms and fears of going crazy in the aftermath of severe stress.

Disorders similar to panic attacks occur cross-culturally. Among the Inuit, kayak-angst is defined as intense fear in lone hunters.

In DSM-IV panic disorder is diagnosed as with or without agoraphobia. **Agoraphobia** (from the Greek *agora*, meaning "marketplace") is a cluster of fears centring on public places and being unable to escape or find help should one become incapacitated. Fears of shopping, crowds, and travelling are often present. Many patients with agoraphobia are unable to leave the house or do so only with great distress. Patients who have panic disorder typically avoid the situations in which a panic attack could be dangerous or embarrassing. If the avoidance becomes widespread, panic with agoraphobia is the result. Panic disorder with agoraphobia and agoraphobia without a history of panic disorder are both much more common among women than among men.

A crowd is likely to be very distressing to a person with agoraphobia, who typically is often afraid of having a panic attack in a public place.

More than 80 percent of patients diagnosed as having one of the other anxiety disorders also experience panic attacks, although not with the frequency that justifies a diagnosis of panic disorder (Barlow et al., 1985). Coexistence of panic disorder and major depression is also common (Johnson & Lydiard, 1998), as is comorbidity between panic disorder and generalized anxiety disorder (Kendler et al., 2002; Sanderson et al., 1990), phobias (Horwath et al., 1995), alcoholism, and personality disorders (Johnson, Weissman, & Klerman, 1990). As with many of the disorders discussed in this book, comorbidity in panic is associated with greater severity and poorer outcomes (Newman et al., 1998).

The following case in Canada described by Ananda Duquette (2001) illustrates what it is like to live with panic disorder with agoraphobia and provides some insight into possible causes.

Margot Paul answers the door slowly, with her head held down. "Come in quickly," she says, "before you let the cats out." Margot has four cats and they are often her only company. She lives alone and rarely goes outside, afraid she'll get hit by a car, fall and break her bones, or suffer a stroke. Margot suffers from agoraphobia, an anxiety condition that causes her extreme panic, or even terror, when she's subjected to any situation outside of her "safety zone." Like many agoraphobics, Margot's safety zone is her home. Margot, now in her eighties, traces her anxiety back to the age of 11 when a man in her First Nations community on Lennox Island, P.E.I., assaulted her. "He chased me and knocked me down," she says. "He tried to tear my clothes off, but I fought him off. I was terrified. He told me he'd kill me if I opened my mouth, so I didn't tell anybody." Margot remembers that after the incident she started making excuses for not leaving the house. "When I thought about that man, I was taken over with fear and trembling," she says. "I hid for a long, long time. I really believed he would kill me." At the age of 15, Margot ran away, but she couldn't run away from the fear. "When I saw people fighting, like a man and his girlfriend, panic would come on me," she says. Working for a travelling fair, Margot saw the man who assaulted her one more time. She says seeing him produced terror in her—"Sheer terror." But she says the assault wasn't the only thing that contributed to her condition. "Kids used to tell me how ugly I was," she says. "I was so afraid of being seen, I would always wear a hat to hide my face." Margot says she was also insecure because she grew up speaking only Mi'kmaq and her English was poor. She moved to Halifax when she was 18 years old and worked in restaurants, in bars, and for bootleggers. She says she would often suffer from anxiety and go into hiding, but then the symptoms would lift and she would be able to work again. Margot married and had five children. One of her sons comes over once or twice a week to take her grocery shopping or to the doctor. She calls him her "safe person," meaning he is one of the few people she trusts. Except for these trips, Margot hasn't been outside for over a year. ... One of her daughters, who also suffers from agoraphobia, lives upstairs from her. Margot's doctor tells her that her thought patterns fuel her fears. "What I think really does have an effect on how I feel," she says. "The mind is the computer of the body and what you feed it, it will produce. By changing the way I think, I've found a big difference." But Margot is still reluctant to join a self-help group. "I don't think I could even join a group," she says. "I feel like I don't fit in."... "It seems like all my life I've been hiding," she says. "My life is a sad, sad story."

Margot died of a heart attack on April 27, 2001. Documents indicated that she was older than realized—92 years old at the time of her death.

Canadian Perspectives/6.1

Panic Attacks and Panic Disorder in Canadian University Students

Extensive research has been conducted on panic attacks and panic disorder in Canadian students. Ron Norton and his colleagues at the University of Winnipeg found that panic is a common occurrence among students. Norton, Harrison, Hauch, and Rhodes (1985) administered a self-report measure known as the Panic Attack Questionnaire (PAQ) and found that 34 percent of undergraduates reported experiencing at least one panic attack in the previous year. While comparable rates have been found in other research (Norton, Dorward, & Cox, 1986), another Canadian study found that more than half of the students surveyed reported histories of panic (Wilson, Sandler, Asmundson, Larsen, & Ediger, 1991). Some researchers have suggested that these high rates of reported panic reflect methodological factors. For instance, the PAQ is an instrument that tends to yield a high false positive rate (Brown & Cash, 1989). Indeed, substantially lower rates of panic attacks are reported if the PAQ items are accompanied by a vignette that includes a detailed description of a person experiencing a severe panic attack (Wilson et al., 1991).

To what extent do the subclinical panic attack symptoms reported by students actually resemble the symptoms reported by patients with diagnosable panic disorders? Research on levels of "nonclinical panic" suggests that students who experience frequent panic attacks in a three-week period demonstrate phobic avoidance and psychological distress, while students who are less frequent panickers do not show these symptoms (Cox, Endler, & Norton, 1994). Wilson et al. (1992) examined the panic attacks described by two large samples of students from Winnipeg and a sample of panic disorder patients. They concluded that an alarmingly high 7.0 percent of the students in sample one and 8.1 percent of the students in sample two had symptoms consistent with clinical definitions of panic. However, because a key diagnostic feature (i.e., the frequency of attacks) was not assessed in a format that permits a diagnosis, it is not certain that all of these students met diagnostic criteria.

This problem was addressed in a study by McCabe and Blankstein (2000). The researchers screened a sample of 650 students twice for panic attacks with a self-report measure and then interviewed them using the panic disorder section of the Structured Clinical Interview for DSM-IV Axis I Disorders (SCID-IV; First, Spitzer, Gibbon, & Williams, 1996). Overall, 21 students (3 percent) were diagnosed with panic disorder and another 79 students (12 percent) experienced unexpected panic attacks and had significant levels of impairment and distress.

How comparable are clinical and subclinical forms of panic?

Cox, Endler, and Swinson (1991) examined the symptom structure and temporal characteristics of panic in outpatients suffering from panic disorder with agoraphobia and in university students who had experienced one or more panic attacks over a three-week period. They found that the main symptoms experienced by the two groups were quite similar. Both reported the experience of palpitations, tachycardia, difficulty concentrating, dizziness, and feelings of helplessness; the latter the most severe symptom reported. Cox et al. (1991) concluded that there is a continuity between nonclinical and clinical panic and that most group differences are quantitative rather than qualitative. However, one key qualitative difference did emerge: although students with panic attacks suffered from lifestyle impairment, lifestyle restriction was much more severe among the patients with panic disorder.

Thinking Critically

1. Would you count yourself among the many students who have experienced a subclinical panic attack in the past year? If so, did something trigger the attack, or did it seem to "come out of the blue"?
2. Do you agree that there is continuity between clinical and subclinical panic attacks? What about the fact that people with a diagnosed disorder appear to experience greater effects on their daily lives?

Etiology of Panic Disorder

Both biological and psychological theories have been proposed to explain panic disorder.

Biological Theories In a minority of cases, physical sensations caused by an illness lead some people to develop panic disorder. Mitral valve prolapse syndrome causes heart palpitations, and inner ear disease causes dizziness; both can be terrifying, leading to the development of panic disorder (Asmundson, Larsen, & Stein, 1998; Hamada et al., 1998).

Panic disorder runs in families (Goldstein et al., 1997) and has greater concordance in identical-twin pairs than in fraternal twins (Torgersen, 1983). Thus, a genetic diathesis may be involved, and specific chromosomes are being investigated.

Noradrenergic Activity Another biological theory suggests that panic is caused by overactivity in the noradrenergic system (neurons that use norepinephrine as a neurotransmitter). One version of this theory focuses on a nucleus in the pons called the locus ceruleus. Stimulation of the locus ceruleus causes monkeys to have what appears to be a panic attack, suggesting that naturally occurring attacks involve noradrenergic overactivation (Redmond, 1977). Subsequent research with humans has found that yohimbine, a drug that stimulates activity in the locus ceruleus, can elicit panic attacks in patients with panic disorder (Charney et al., 1987). However, more recent research is not consistent with this position. Importantly, drugs that block firing in the locus ceruleus have not been found to be very effective in treating panic attacks (McNally, 1994).

Another idea about noradrenergic overactivity is that it results from a problem in gamma-aminobutyric acid (GABA) neurons that generally inhibit noradrenergic activity. Consistent with this line of thinking, a recent PET study found fewer GABA-receptor binding sites in patients with panic disorder than in members of the control group (Malizia et al, 1998). Thus, while no definitive conclusions can as yet be drawn, noradrenergic overactivation remains an area of active research.

Cholecystokinin Canadian psychiatrist Jacques Bradwejn and his colleagues in Toronto, Ottawa, and Montreal initiated another stimulating line of research in the attempt to understand the neurobiology of panic disorder (e.g., Bradwejn, Koszycki, & Meterissian, 1990). They discovered that cholecystokinin (CCK), a peptide that occurs in the cerebral cortex, amygdala, hippocampus, and brain stem, induces anxiety-like symptoms in rats and that the effect can be blocked with benzodiazepines, suggesting that changes in CCK produce changes in the development or expression of panic (e.g., Bradwejn & Montigny, 1984; Harro, Vasar, & Bradwejn, 1993). Bradwejn hypothesizes that panic disorder is, at least in part, due to hypersensitivity to CCK. The mechanism of this sensitivity is not clear: CCK sensitivity may affect the action of other neurotransmitters or neurons in the noradrenergic system, or people may be reacting psychologically to the strong physical sensations caused by CCK (see below).

Creating Panic Attacks Experimentally Another line of biological inquiry has focused on experimental manipulations that can induce panic attacks in humans. One approach proposes that panic attacks are linked to hyperventilation, or overbreathing (Ley, 1987). Hyperventilation may activate the autonomic nervous system and trigger somatic aspects of a panic episode. Lactate (a product of muscular exertion) can also produce panic, and its level may become elevated in patients with panic disorder because of chronic hyperventilation. Oversensitive CO_2 receptors have also been proposed as a mechanism that could stimulate hyperventilation and then a panic attack, given evidence that breathing air containing higher than usual amounts of carbon dioxide (CO_2) can generate a panic attack in laboratory settings (Gorman et al., 1988; Klein, 1993). However, more recent research, which monitored patients with panic disorder in their natural environments, found that hyperventilation occurred in only one of 24 attacks (Garssen, Buikhuisen, & Van Dyck, 1996). Thus, this line of biological inquiry has not been supported.

Bradwejn and his colleagues (Bradwejn, Koszycki, & Shriqui, 1991) conducted a panic induction study that provides some further support for the possible role of CCK in panic disorder. Intravenous injections of either CCK4 (a tetrapeptide fragment form) or a placebo (saline solution) were administered to people with and without panic disorder. This injection led to a panic attack in everyone included in the panic disorder group and in almost half the normal control group participants. In contrast, the saline injection produced panic symptoms in fewer than 10 percent of the panic disorder group and in none of the control participants.

The data indicating that various biological challenges (e.g., carbon dioxide, hyperventilation) can induce panic also show that they do so only in those who have already been diagnosed with the disorder or those who are high in fear of their own bodily sensations. This could be taken to mean that these stimuli activate some kind of biological abnormality or diathesis in patients with the disorder. However, the physiological responses of people with panic disorder to these biological challenges are very similar to those of people without the disorder. Only the self-reported levels of fear induced by the challenge differentiate the two groups (Margraf, Ehlers, & Roth, 1986). Therefore, the results may indicate that it is the psychological reaction to the challenge that is central, a possibility that underlies a well-validated treatment for this disorder, as we will see. Further support for this hypothesis comes from a study that found that the effects of carbon dioxide on panic were markedly reduced when experienced in the presence of a person with whom the participant felt safe (Carter et al., 1995).

Psychological Theories The principal psychological theory of the agoraphobia that often accompanies panic disorder is the fear-of-fear hypothesis (e.g., Goldstein & Chambless, 1978), which suggests that agoraphobia is not a fear of public places per se, but a fear of having a panic attack in public.

As for panic attacks themselves, the foundation for their development may be an autonomic nervous system that is predisposed to be overly active (Barlow, 1988) coupled with a psychological tendency to become very upset by these sensations. When high physiological arousal occurs, some people construe these unusual autonomic reactions (such as rapid heart rate) as a sign of great danger or even as a sign that they are dying. After repeated occurrences, the person comes to fear having these internal sensations and, by worrying excessively, makes them worse and panic attacks more likely. Thus, the psychology of the person takes over from where the biology began. The person becomes more vigilant about even subtle signs of an impending panic attack, and this, too, makes an attack more probable. The result is a vicious circle—fearing another panic attack leads to increased autonomic activity; symptoms of this activity are interpreted in catastrophic ways; and these interpretations in turn raise the anxiety level, which eventually blossoms into a full-blown panic attack (Craske & Barlow, 1993).

Telch and Harrington (2000) studied students with no history of panic attacks who were divided into two groups (high and low scorers) based on their test scores on the Anxiety Sensitivity Index (ASI; Peterson & Reiss, 1987; 1992). The 16-item ASI measures the extent to which people respond fearfully to bodily sensations that could reflect a fear response. High scorers believe that these sensations have harmful somatic, psychological, or social consequences. Sample ASI items are shown in Table 6.2. All participants experienced two trials. In one trial they breathed room air, and in the other they breathed air with a higher than usual concentration of carbon dioxide. Half the participants in each group were told that the carbon dioxide would be relaxing, and half were told that it would produce symptoms of high arousal. The frequency of panic attacks in each group is shown in Table 6.3. Note that panic attacks did not occur in participants when they breathed room air, confirming previous findings. Also, the data show that the frequency of panic attacks was higher in participants who were high in fear of their own bodily sensations. Finally, and most important, the frequency of panic attacks was strikingly high in participants who feared their bodily sensations, breathed air

Table 6.2

Sample Items from the Anxiety Sensitivity Index and the Anxiety Sensitivity Profile

ASI Items	ASP Items by Factors
Unusual body sensations scare me.	You feel like you are suffocating (fear of respiratory symptoms).
When I notice that my heart is beating rapidly, I worry that I might have a heart attack.	Your heart is pounding (fear of cardiac symptoms).
It scares me when I feel faint.	Your thoughts seem jumbled (fear of cognitive dyscontrol).
It scares me when I feel "shaky" (trembling).	You have diarrhea (fear of gastrointestinal symptoms).

Sources: Peterson and Reiss, 1987; Taylor and Cox, 1998.
Note: People respond to each item on a 0 (very little) to 4 (very much) scale.

Table 6.3

Frequency of Panic Attacks as a Function of Breathing Room Air versus Breathing Air with Carbon Dioxide, Fear of Bodily Sensations, and Expectations

	High Fear of Bodily Sensations		*Low Fear of Bodily Sensations*	
Inhale	**Expect Relaxation**	**Expect Arousal**	**Expect Relaxation**	**Expect Arousal**
Room air	0	0	0	0
Carbon dioxide	52	17	5	5

containing a high concentration of carbon dioxide, and did not expect it to be arousing. This result is exactly what the theory predicts: unexplained physiological arousal in someone who is highly fearful of such sensations leads to panic attacks.

Thus, a heightened tendency to be afraid of fear sensations appears to play an important role. Additional Canadian contributions to research on anxiety sensitivity and the "fear of fear" are described in Canadian Perspectives 6.2.

Canadian Perspectives/6.2

Research on the Psychometric Properties and Applications of the Anxiety Sensitivity Index

Several Canadian research groups have examined the psychometric properties and research applications of the ASI as a way of finding out more about "the fear of fear," or the tendency to catastrophize the meaning of bodily symptoms. One question that has been asked is whether anxiety sensitivity is a unitary construct. While some research indicates that the ASI consists of only one factor, other research has identified as many as four factors within the scale; thus, the ASI may suffer from factorial instability (see Taylor, 1995, 1999). Some Canadian authors (e.g., Cox, Borger, & Enns, 1998; Taylor & Cox, 1998a) have suggested that psychometric problems associated with the ASI may stem from the fact that this 16-item scale is too brief to measure the factors that tap the anxiety sensitivity construct. Subsequent research by Taylor and Cox (1998b) examined the factor structure of an expanded 60-item version called the Anxiety Sensitivity Profile (ASP). When administered to a university sample, the ASP has four identifiable factors: fear of cardiac symptoms, fear of respiratory symptoms, fear of cognitive dyscontrol, and fear of gastrointestinal symptoms. Sample items from the ASP are also shown in Table 6.2.

Another version adapted by Taylor and Cox (1998a), known as Anxiety Sensitivity Index-Revised (ASI-R), consists of four factors, including the fear of publicly observable anxiety reactions (e.g., fear of blushing, fear of trembling). This ASI factor is particularly relevant in forms of social anxiety and in situations where the individual feels significant pressure to meet high social expectations (Flett, Greene, & Hewitt, 2004). Recent research on the ASI-R in a sample of 2,786 people from six countries, including Canada, France, and Spain, confirmed that the structure and nature of the anxiety sensitivity construct is generally similar across countries (Zvolensky et al., 2003).

Cox and his associates have conducted research with the ASI that shows that anxiety sensitivity is associated with personality traits such as neuroticism; however, anxiety sensitivity predicts unique variance in levels of panic, even given the link between panic and general personality traits such as neuroticism (Cox et al., 1999; Zvolensky et al., 2003).

Other research applications of the ASI include work on the cognitive aspects of anxiety sensitivity. For instance, Canadian researchers have used cognitive tasks to establish that high scorers on the ASI have a cognitive bias that involves an orientation toward the selective processing of threat cues. However, the pattern varies for women and men (Stewart, Conrod, Gignac, & Pihl, 1998); that is, high-anxiety-sensitive men tend to selectively process word cues reflecting social and psychological threats (e.g., embarrassment), while high-anxiety-sensitive women tended to selectively process cues involving physical threat (e.g., hospitalization).

McCabe (1999) compared high- and low-AS participants in terms of their memory for neutral words, positive words, anxiety words, and threatening words. She found that those with high ASI scores were more likely to recall words that connoted a sense of threat (e.g., harassment, assault) and concluded that a cognitive processing vulnerability exists in high-ASI scorers even before an actual panic attack occurs.

How do differences in anxiety sensitivity develop? Twin research shows that ASI scores are heritable, so this measure may be the source of the genetic diathesis for panic disorder (Stein, Jang, & Livesley, 1999). Retrospective research also suggests that people with high anxiety sensitivity may have learned to catastrophize their bodily sensations via parental modelling and parental reinforcement (Stewart et al., 2001; Watt & Stewart, 2000; Watt et al., 1998), and thus, developmental experiences should not be discounted when considering the etiology of panic disorder.

Is anxiety sensitivity associated uniquely with panic disorder? Cox and his colleagues (Cox, Enns, Walker, Kjernisted, & Pidlubny, 2001) found that the ASI cognitive dyscontrol subscale is a non-specific vulnerability factor that applies to both panic disorder and depression. Cognitive dyscontrol is also associated with cognitive rumination about depressive symptoms, leading Cox, Enns, and Taylor (2001) to suggest that this ASI factor may be associated with a "depression sensitivity." Other research has shown that anxiety sensitivity plays a role in substance abuse (Conrod, Pihl, Stewart, & Dongier, 2000).

Finally, other research has examined anxiety sensitivity and somatic factors. Gordon Asmundson at the Wascana Rehabilitation Centre in Regina has proposed that fear of pain plays a role in perpetuating chronic pain (see Chapter 8). His research suggests that fear of pain and physically unexplained chronic back pain are both influenced by anxiety sensitivity (Asmundson, 1995; Asmundson & Taylor, 1996). Thus, somatic concerns often reflect underlying issues involving anxiety and anxiety sensitivity.

Thinking Critically

1. Do you think that anxiety sensitivity is a construct that should be considered a risk factor in our attempts to understand the causes of disorders other than the anxiety disorders? What additional disorders would you nominate?
2. On August 24, 2001, an Air Transat Airbus on a transatlantic flight was forced to glide without fuel as the pilots attempted an emergency landing on a small airfield in the Azores. Although the pilot radioed that he would probably have to ditch in the ocean and the panic stricken passengers said their goodbyes to loved ones, the pilot made a miraculous landing and no one was killed. Air Transat was hit with the largest fine in Canadian aviation history because of faulty engine repairs and a class action lawsuit was launched on behalf of the passengers (Hall & Verma, 2001). What do you think will be the long-term psychological effects on the people who were on that plane? Will people high in anxiety sensitivity develop the most severe long-term symptoms? Assuming that anxiety sensitivity will predict long-term outcome, which component of the ASI should be linked most to negative effects?

The concept of control is also relevant to panic. Patients with the disorder have an extreme fear of losing control, which would happen if they had an attack in public. Sanderson, Rapee, and Barlow (1989) demonstrated the importance of control. Patients with panic disorder breathed carbon dioxide and were told that when a light turned on, they could turn a dial to reduce the concentration of carbon dioxide. For half the participants the light was on continuously, but it never came on for the other half. Turning the dial actually had no effect on CO_2 levels, so the study evaluated how the effects of perceived control affected the participants' reactions. Eighty percent of the group with no control had a panic attack, compared with only 20 percent of those who thought they could control CO_2 levels. Note that in addition to clearly demonstrating the importance of perceived control in panic disorder, the data again show that it is not the biological challenge per se that elicits panic; rather, it is the person's psychological reaction that is crucial.

THERAPIES FOR PANIC DISORDER AND AGORAPHOBIA

Therapies for panic disorder include both biological and psychological approaches. Some are quite similar to the treatments discussed for phobias.

Biological Treatments Several drugs have shown some success as biological treatments for panic disorder. They include antidepressants (both selective serotonin reuptake inhibitors, such as Prozac, and tricyclic antidepressants, such as Tofranil) and anxiolytics (such as alprazolam or Xanax) (Roy-Byrne & Cowley, 1998). Evidence for the effectiveness of alprazolam is particularly compelling, since it came from a large, multinational study (Ballenger et al., 1988).

Drug treatment must be continued indefinitely, for symptoms almost always return if it is stopped (Fyer, Sandberg, & Klein, 1991). However, as many as half of the patients on tricyclics drop out of treatment because of side effects such as jitteriness, weight gain, and elevated heart rate and blood pressure (Taylor et al., 1990). Furthermore, the benzodiazepines are addicting and produce both cognitive and motor side effects (i.e., memory lapses and difficulty driving). In their efforts to reduce anxiety, many patients use anxiolytics or alcohol on their own; the use and abuse of drugs is common in anxiety-ridden people.

Psychological Treatments Exposure-based treatments are often useful in reducing panic disorder with agoraphobia, and these gains are largely maintained for many years after therapy has ended (Fava et al., 1995). Married patients whose problem is primarily or solely agoraphobia have benefited from family-oriented therapies that involve the nonphobic spouse, who is encouraged to stop catering to his or her partner's avoidance of leaving the home. Barlow's clinical research program has found that the success of in vivo exposure treatment, in which the person with agoraphobia is encouraged to venture little by little from "safe" domains, is enhanced when the spouse is involved (Cerny et al., 1987). Contrary to the belief that one spouse somehow needs the other to be dependent on him or her (Milton &

Hafner, 1979), marital satisfaction tends to improve as the fearful spouse becomes bolder (e.g., Craske et al., 1992). Thus, although it is understandable that a spouse might become overly solicitous, perhaps from reasonable concern for his or her partner's well-being, perhaps from an inner need to have a spouse who is weak and dependent, the outcome data suggest that relationships improve when the spouse with agoraphobia becomes less fearful.

Because treating agoraphobia with exposure does not always reduce panic attacks (Michelson, Mavissakalian, & Marchione, 1985), psychological treatment of panic disorder also takes into account the idea mentioned earlier that some patients may become unduly alarmed by noticing and overreacting to innocuous bodily sensations. One well-validated therapy developed by Barlow and his associates (Barlow, 1988; Barlow & Craske, 1994) has three principal components:

1. relaxation training
2. a combination of Ellis- and Beck-type cognitive-behavioural interventions, including cognitive restructuring
3. exposure to the internal cues that trigger panic

Regarding the second component, Sanderson and Rego (2000) emphasize the need for patients to self-monitor the cognitions that occur *during the actual panic episode*. For the third—and most novel—component, the client practises behaviours in the consulting room that can elicit feelings associated with panic. For example, a person whose panic attacks begin with hyperventilation is asked to breathe fast for three minutes. When sensations such as dizziness, increased heart rate, and other signs of panic begin to be felt, the client (1) experiences them under safe conditions and (2) applies previously learned cognitive and relaxation coping tactics.

With practice and with encouragement or persuasion from the therapist, the client learns to reinterpret internal sensations, no longer seeing them as signals of loss of control and panic but rather as cues that are intrinsically harmless and can be controlled with certain skills. The intentional creation of these sensations by the client, coupled with success in coping with them, reduces their unpredictability and changes their meaning for the client (Craske, Maidenberg, & Bystritsky, 1995).

Two-year follow-ups have shown that therapeutic gains from this cognitive and exposure therapy have been maintained to a significant degree and are superior to gains resulting from the use of alprazolam (Xanax) (Craske, Brown, & Barlow, 1991), though many patients are not panic-free (Brown & Barlow, 1995). A multi-site study indicates that Barlow's panic-control therapy is superior to imipramine in reducing panic attacks. Furthermore, adding the drug to this psychological therapy does not bestow an advantage. These findings show up both immediately after the end of treatment and at a 15-month follow-up (Barlow, 1999). A similar cognitive-behavioural treatment independently developed by Clark (1989; Salkovskis & Clark, 1991) has also shown beneficial effects on panic disorder (Clark, Watson, & Mineka, 1994).

Comparative reviews of pharmacotherapy versus psychotherapy in the treatment of panic disorder (Barlow, Eisler, & Vitali, 1998; Gorman, 1994; Jacobson & Hollon, 1996) conclude that cognitive-behavioural treatments show better results in long-term follow-ups than tricyclics such as imipramine (Tofranil), monoamine oxidase inhibitors, and benzodiazepines, such as alprazolam. Relapse is typically the rule when drugs for panic and agoraphobia are discontinued.

GENERALIZED ANXIETY DISORDER

THE PATIENT, a 24-year-old mechanic, had been referred for psychotherapy by his physician, whom he had consulted because of dizziness and difficulties in falling asleep. He was quite visibly distressed during the entire initial interview, gulping before he spoke, sweating, and continually fidgeting in his chair. His repeated requests for water for a seemingly unquenchable thirst were another indication of his extreme nervousness. Although he first talked of his physical concerns, a more general picture of pervasive anxiety soon emerged. He reported that he nearly always felt tense. He seemed to worry about anything and everything. He was apprehensive of disasters that could befall him as he worked and interacted with other people. He reported a long history of difficulties in interpersonal relationships, which had led to his being fired from several jobs. As he put it, "I really like people and try to get along with them, but it seems like I fly off the handle too easily. Little things they do upset me too much. I just can't cope unless everything is going exactly right."

The individual with generalized anxiety disorder (GAD) is persistently anxious, often about minor items. Chronic, uncontrollable worry about all manner of things is the hallmark of GAD; the most frequent worries of patients with GAD concern their health and the hassles of daily life, such as being late for appointments or having too much work to do. The uncontrollable nature of the worries associated with GAD has been confirmed by both self-reports and laboratory data (Becker et al., 1998; Craske et al., 1989). Other features of GAD include difficulty concentrating, tiring easily, restlessness, irritability, and a high level of muscle tension.

Although people with GAD do not typically seek psychological treatment, the lifetime prevalence of the disorder is fairly high; it occurs in about 5 percent of the general population (Wittchen et al., 1994; National Comorbidity Survey). GAD typically begins in the person's mid-teens, though many people who have generalized anxiety disorder report having had the problem all their lives (Barlow et al., 1986). Stressful life events appear to play some role in its onset

(Blazer, Hughes, & George, 1987). It is twice as common in women as in men, and it has a high level of comorbidity with other anxiety disorders and with mood disorders (Brown, Barlow, & Liebowitz, 1994). It is difficult to treat GAD successfully. In one five-year follow-up study, only 18 percent of patients had achieved a full remission of symptoms (Woodman et al., 1999).

ETIOLOGY OF GENERALIZED ANXIETY DISORDER

Psychoanalytic View Psychoanalytic theory regards the source of generalized anxiety as an unconscious conflict between the ego and id impulses. The impulses, usually sexual or aggressive in nature, are struggling for expression, but the ego cannot allow their expression because it unconsciously fears that punishment will follow. Since the source of the anxiety is unconscious, the person experiences apprehension and distress without knowing why. The true source of anxiety—namely, desires associated with previously punished id impulses seeking expression—is ever-present. The patient with a phobia may be regarded as more fortunate, since, according to psychoanalytic theory, his or her anxiety is displaced onto a specific object or situation, which can then be avoided. The person with GAD has not developed this type of defence and is constantly anxious.

Cognitive-Behavioural Views In attempting to account for generalized anxiety, learning theorists (e.g., Wolpe, 1958) look to the environment. For example, a person anxious most of his or her waking hours might well be fearful of social contacts. If that individual spends a good deal of time with other people, it may be more useful to regard the anxiety as tied to these circumstances rather than to any internal factors. This behavioural model of generalized anxiety is identical to one of the learning views of phobias. The anxiety is regarded as having been classically conditioned to external stimuli, but with a broader range of conditioned stimuli.

The focus of other cognitive and behavioural views of generalized anxiety disorder mesh so closely that we will discuss them in tandem. Anxiety results when people are confronted with painful stimuli over which they have no control. Cognitive theory emphasizes the perception of not being in control as a central characteristic of all forms of anxiety (Mandler, 1966). Thus, a cognitive-behavioural model of generalized anxiety focuses on control and helplessness. Studies of humans have shown that stressful events over which people can exert some control are less anxiety provoking than are events over which they can exercise no control. Research also suggests that, in certain circumstances, it is sufficient for the control only to be perceived by the subject; control need not actually exist (e.g., Geer, Davison, & Gatchel, 1970). Linking these findings to GAD, Barlow (1988) has shown that these patients perceive threatening events as out of their control.

Related to this idea of control is the fact that predictable events produce less anxiety than do unpredictable events (see Mineka, 1992). For example, animals prefer a signalled, predictable shock to one that is not signalled (Seligman & Binik, 1977). The absence of the signal can serve as a sign of safety, indicating that there is no shock and no need to worry. Unsignalled and therefore unpredictable aversive stimuli may lead to chronic vigilance and fear—in humans, what we would call worry (Borkovec & Inz, 1990).

A perceived lack of control contributes to a sense of uncertainty. Extensive research has shown the role of an intolerance of uncertainty in the experience of chronic worry and GAD (Dugas, Freeston, & Ladouceur, 1997; Dugas, Gagnon, Ladouceur, & Freeston, 1998; Ladouceur, Gosselin, & Dugas, 2000). Researchers at Laval University and Concordia University have shown that manipulations designed to increase uncertainty intolerance lead to heightened levels of worry (Ladouceur et al., 2000) and that cognitive-behavioural interventions with individuals with GAD are effective to the extent that they focus on removing uncertainty intolerance (Dugas & Ladouceur, 2000; Dugas et al., 2003). Clinical improvement is associated with significant reductions in levels of uncertainty intolerance.

Several other cognitive processes tend to characterize patients with GAD. These patients often misperceive benign events, such as crossing the street, as involving threats, and their cognitions focus on anticipated future disasters (Beck et al., 1987; Kendall & Ingram, 1989). The attention of patients with GAD is easily drawn to stimuli that suggest possible physical harm or social misfortune, such as criticism, embarrassment, or rejection (MacLeod, Mathews, & Tata, 1986). People with GAD, for example, may be quick to notice when the person they are speaking with looks around the room from time to time, and they thus begin to worry about being rejected. Furthermore, patients with GAD are more inclined to interpret ambiguous stimuli as threatening and to believe that ominous events are more likely to happen to them (Butler & Mathews, 1983). The heightened sensitivity of GAD patients to threatening stimuli occurs even when the stimuli cannot be consciously perceived (Bradley et al., 1995).

Another cognitive view has been offered by Borkovec and his colleagues (e.g., Borkovec & Newman, 1998; Borkovec, Roemer, & Kinyon, 1995). Their focus is on the main symptom of uncontrollable worry. From a punishment perspective, why would anyone worry a lot? Since worry is thought to be a negative state, its repetition, one would think, should be avoided. Borkovec has shown that worry is actually negatively reinforcing; it distracts patients from negative emotions.

The key to understanding this position is to realize that worry does not produce much emotional arousal. It does not produce the physiological changes that usually accompany emotion, and it actually blocks the processing of emotional stimuli. Therefore, by worrying, people with GAD are avoiding certain unpleasant images and so their anxiety about these images does not extinguish. What are the anxiety-evoking images that patients with GAD are avoiding?

One possibility comes from data showing that people with GAD report more past trauma involving death, injury, or illness. Yet these are not the topics they worry about. Worry may distract patients with GAD from the distressing images of these past traumas.

Biological Perspectives Some studies indicate that GAD may have a genetic component. However, although greater prevalence of GAD in the relatives of GAD patients has been reported (Noyes et al., 1992), the results of twin studies are inconsistent (see Kendler et al., 1992). At this time, the data are equivocal, but the fact that neuroticism, a personality trait linked to all the anxiety disorders, is heritable indicates that genetic factors should not be ruled out as possible influences.

The most prevalent neurobiological model for GAD is based on knowledge of the operation of the benzodiazepines, a group of drugs that are often effective in treating anxiety. Researchers have discovered a receptor in the brain for benzodiazepines that is linked to the inhibitory neurotransmitter GABA. In normal fear reactions, neurons throughout the brain fire and create the experience of anxiety. This neural firing also stimulates the GABA system, which inhibits this activity and thus reduces anxiety. GAD may result from some defect in the GABA system, so that anxiety is not brought under control. The benzodiazepines may reduce anxiety by enhancing the release of GABA. Similarly, drugs that block or inhibit the GABA system lead to increases in anxiety (Insell, 1986). This approach seems destined to enhance our understanding of anxiety.

Therapies for Generalized Anxiety Disorder

Because they view generalized anxiety disorder as stemming from repressed conflicts, most psychoanalysts work to help patients confront the true sources of their conflicts. Treatment is much the same as that for phobias.

Behavioural clinicians approach generalized anxiety in various ways. If patients can construe the anxiety as a set of responses to identifiable situations, the free-floating anxiety can be reformulated into one or more phobias or cued anxieties, making it easier to treat. For example, a behaviour therapist may determine that the generally anxious client seems more specifically afraid of criticizing and of being criticized by others. The anxiety appears free-floating only because the client spends so many hours with other human beings. Systematic desensitization becomes a possible treatment.

Because it can be difficult to find specific causes of the anxiety suffered by such patients, behavioural clinicians tend to prescribe more generalized treatment, such as intensive relaxation training, in the hope that if patients learn to relax when beginning to feel tense, their anxiety will be kept from spiralling out of control (Barlow et al., 1984; Borkovec & Mathews, 1988; Ost, 1987b). Patients are taught to relax away low-level tensions, to respond to incipient anxiety with relaxation rather than with alarm (Suinn & Richardson, 1971). This strategy is quite effective in alleviating GAD (see Borkovec & Whisman, 1996; DeRubeis & Crits-Christoph, 1998).

If a feeling of helplessness seems to underlie the pervasive anxiety, the cognitively oriented behaviour therapist will help the client acquire skills that engender a sense of competence. The skills, including assertiveness, may be taught by verbal instructions, modelling, or operant shaping—and very likely some judicious combination of the three (Goldfried & Davison, 1994).

Because chronic worrying is central to GAD, it is not surprising that cognitive techniques have been employed in its treatment. A main ingredient in cognitive-behavioural approaches to worry is exaggerated exposure to the source of one's overly anxious concern. For example, a person worried about why his or her spouse is late coming home from a trip would be encouraged to imagine the worst possible outcome—that the plane has crashed. The patient is asked to imagine this extreme, unlikely outcome for half an hour or more and then to consider as many alternative explanations as possible for the tardiness, such as difficulties getting a cab or being caught in heavy traffic. Two processes are assumed to operate here to reduce worry:

1. Because the patient remains in a fearsome situation, anxiety is believed to extinguish
2. By considering the unlikelihood of the worst fears imagined, the patient alters his or her cognitive reactions to his or her spouse's not showing up when expected.

In other words, the patient learns to think about less catastrophic reasons for a particular event.

Outcome data from controlled clinical trials so far are inconsistent in demonstrating that the various cognitive-behavioural approaches are superior either to placebo treatments or to alternative therapies such as Rogerian therapy (Barlow et al., 1998). Of particular note, with the striking exception of a study by Borkovec and Costello (1993), is that few patients in the various therapies evaluated show what is called high end-state functioning—that is, levels of anxiety or worry that are so minimal as to resemble those of people not diagnosed as having GAD. At a one-year follow-up, more than 40 percent of patients in the cognitive-behaviour therapy group were not rated as high end-state in their functioning. In other words, many GAD patients, although they show improvement, continue to struggle with many symptoms of anxiety (e.g., Stanley et al., 1996). When compared with benzodiazepine treatment, however, cognitive-behaviour therapy appears to be superior; indeed, when it was combined with the drug treatment, the results were poorer than when it was used alone (Power et al., 1990).

Anxiolytics, such as those mentioned that treat phobias and panic disorder, are probably the most widespread treatment for GAD. Drugs, especially the benzodiazepines, such as Valium and Xanax, as well as buspirone (BuSpar), are often used because of the disorder's pervasiveness. Once the drugs take effect, they continue to work for several hours in whatever situations are encountered. A number of double-blind studies confirm that these drugs benefit GAD patients more than do placebos (Apter & Allen, 1999). Other studies show that certain antidepressants, such as Tofranil, are effective (Roy-Byrne & Cowley, 1998).

Unfortunately, many drugs have undesirable side effects, ranging from drowsiness, memory loss, and depression to physical addiction and damage to body organs. In addition, when patients stop taking these drugs, the gains achieved in treatment are usually lost (Barlow, 1988), perhaps because they (rightfully) attribute the improvement to an external agent, the medication, rather than to internal changes and their own coping efforts (Davison & Valins, 1969), thus re-establishing a sense of uncontrollability.

OBSESSIVE-COMPULSIVE DISORDER

BERNICE was 46 years old when she entered treatment. This was the fourth time she had been in outpatient therapy, and she had previously been hospitalized twice. Her obsessive-compulsive disorder had begun 12 years earlier, shortly after the death of her father. Since then, it had waxed and waned and currently was as severe as it had ever been.

Bernice was obsessed with a fear of contamination, a fear she vaguely linked to her father's death from pneumonia. Although she reported that she was afraid of nearly everything, because germs could be anywhere, she was particularly upset by touching wood, "scratchy objects," mail, canned goods, and "silver flecks." By silver flecks, Bernice meant silver embossing on a greeting card, eyeglass frames, shiny appliances, and silverware. She was unable to state why these particular objects were sources of possible contamination.

Bernice tried to reduce her discomfort by engaging in compulsive rituals that took up almost all her waking hours. She spent three to four hours in the morning in the bathroom, washing and rewashing herself. Between baths, she scraped away the outside layer of her bar of soap so that it would be totally free of germs. Mealtimes also lasted for hours because Bernice performed time-confusing rituals, eating three bites of food at a time, chewing each mouthful 300 times. These steps were meant magically to decontaminate her food. Even Bernice's husband was sometimes involved in these mealtime ceremonies, shaking a teakettle and frozen vegetables over her head to remove the germs. Bernice's rituals and fear of contamination had reduced her life to doing almost nothing else. She would not leave the house, do housework, or even talk on the telephone.

Obsessive-compulsive disorder (OCD) is an anxiety disorder in which the mind is flooded with persistent and uncontrollable thoughts and the individual is compelled to repeat certain acts again and again, suffering significant distress and interference with everyday functioning. Obsessive-compulsive disorder has a lifetime prevalence of 1 to 2 percent, and it affects women more than men (Karno & Golding, 1991; Stein et al., 1997). A comparative study of OCD in seven countries, including Canada, found that annual prevalence rates were remarkably consistent across countries (Weissman et al., 1994). OCD usually begins in early adulthood, often following some stressful event, such as pregnancy, childbirth, family conflict, or difficulties at work (Kringlen, 1970). Early onset is more common among men and is associated with checking compulsions; later onset is more frequent among women and is linked with cleaning compulsions (Noshirvani et al., 1991). Significant depression is often found in obsessive-compulsive patients (Rachman & Hodgson, 1980); epidemiological research conducted in Edmonton suggests that 30 percent of people with OCD also have major depression (Weissman et al., 1994). Obsessive-compulsive disorder shows comorbidity with other anxiety disorders as well, particularly with panic and phobias (Austin et al., 1990), and with various personality disorders (Baer et al., 1990; Mavissikalian, Hammen, & Jones, 1990). OCD may be associated with greater impairment than other anxiety disorders. A survey of seven anxiety clinics in Quebec found that OCD was the anxiety disorder associated with the highest-intensity use of mental health services (McCusker, Boulenger, Boyer, Bellavance, & Miller, 1997).

Obsessions are intrusive and recurring thoughts, impulses, and images that come unbidden to the mind and appear irrational and uncontrollable to the individual experiencing them. Whereas many of us may have similar fleeting experiences, the obsessive individual, as we saw in the case of Bernice, has them with such force and frequency that they interfere with normal functioning. Clinically, the most frequent obsessions concern fears of contamination, fears of expressing some sexual or aggressive impulse, and hypochondriacal fears of bodily dysfunction (Jenike, Baer, & Minichiello, 1986). Obsessions may also take the form of extreme doubting, procrastination, and indecision. Most people with OCD keep the content and frequency of their obsessions secret for many years (Newth & Rachman, 2001). In general, OCD is an especially debilitating disorder and the severity of obsessions has been identified as a factor that contributes to poorer quality of life among OCD patients (Masellis, Rector, & Richter, 2003).

A **compulsion** is a repetitive behaviour or mental act that the person feels driven to perform to reduce the distress caused by obsessive thoughts or to prevent some calamity from occurring. The activity is not realistically connected with its apparent purpose and is clearly excessive. Bernice did not need to chew each morsel of food 300 times, for

This famous scene from *Macbeth* illustrates compulsive handwashing. As noted by Shakespeare, "It is an accustomed action with her to seem thus washing her hands. I have known her continue in this a quarter of an hour" (Shakespeare, *Macbeth*, V, I).

example. Often an individual who continually repeats some action fears dire consequences if the act is not performed. The sheer frequency of repetition may be staggering. Some examples of commonly reported compulsions include:

- checking, going back many times to verify that already performed acts were actually carried out—for example:
  - "A 36-year-old single man had checking compulsions that focused on excrement, and he engaged in prolonged and meticulous inspection of any speck of brown, particularly on his clothes and shoes."
  - "A 40-year-old nursery school teacher checked that all rugs and carpets were absolutely flat, lest someone trip over them and spent long periods looking for needles and pins on the floor and in furniture."
  - "A 19-year-old clerk carried out 4 hours of checking after other members of the family retired at night. He checked all the electrical appliances, doors, taps and so on and was not able to get to bed before 3 or 4 o'clock in the morning" (Rachman, 2003a, pp. 142-143).
- pursuing cleanliness and orderliness, sometimes through elaborate ceremonies that take hours and even most of the day
- avoiding particular objects, such as staying away from anything brown
- performing repetitive, magical, protective practices, such as counting, saying certain numbers, or touching a talisman or a particular part of the body
- performing a particular act, such as eating extremely slowly.

With respect to the last point, when the slowness is the central problem and is not secondary to other OCD symptoms, such as checking, then it is a related condition known as *primary obsessional* slowness. How slow is slow? Rachman (2003b) described the case of a 38-year-old man who would take three hours each morning to get ready for work, including 45 minutes for teeth-brushing. A bath would take between three to five hours.

According to Rachman (2002), three "multipliers" that increase the intensity and frequency of compulsive checking are a sense of personal responsibility, the probability of harm if checking does not take place, and the predicted seriousness of harm.

We often hear people described as compulsive gamblers, compulsive eaters, and compulsive drinkers. Even though individuals may report an irresistible urge to gamble, eat, and drink, such behaviour is not clinically regarded as a compulsion because it is often engaged in with pleasure. A true compulsion is viewed by most OCD sufferers as somehow foreign to their personality (ego-dystonic). Stern and Cobb (1978) found that 78 percent of a sample of compulsive individuals viewed their rituals as "rather silly or absurd" but were still unable to stop them.

Canadian comedian Howie Mandel suffers from OCD. He refuses to shake hands with people because of contamination fears. Moreover, Howie has reported that he has a second house behind his home where only he can go to indulge his compulsion to clean.

Obsessive-compulsive disorder often has a negative effect on the individual's relations with other people, especially family members. People saddled with the irresistible need to wash their hands every 10 minutes, or to touch every doorknob they pass, or to count every tile in a bathroom floor, are likely to cause concern and even resentment in spouses, children, friends, or co-workers. Overt conflict may indicate the need for family therapy as a supplement to individual therapies

ETIOLOGY OF OBSESSIVE-COMPULSIVE DISORDER

Psychoanalytic Theory In psychoanalytic theory, obsessions and compulsions are viewed as similar, resulting from instinctual forces, sexual or aggressive, that are not under control because of overly harsh toilet training. The person is thus fixated at the anal stage. The symptoms observed represent the outcome of the struggle between the id and the defence mechanisms; sometimes the aggressive instincts of the id predominate, sometimes the defence mechanisms. For example, when obsessive thoughts of killing intrude, the forces of the id are dominant. More often, however, the observed symptoms reflect the partially successful operation of one of the defence mechanisms. For example, an individual fixated at the anal stage may, by reaction formation, resist the urge to soil and become compulsively neat, clean, and orderly.

Alfred Adler (1931) viewed obsessive-compulsive disorder as a result of feelings of incompetence. He believed that when children are kept from developing a sense of competence by doting or excessively dominating parents, they develop an inferiority complex and may unconsciously adopt compulsive rituals in order to carve out a domain in which they exert control and can feel proficient. Adler proposed that the compulsive act allows a person mastery of something, even if only the positioning of writing implements on a desk.

Behavioural and Cognitive Theories Behavioural accounts of compulsions consider them learned behaviours reinforced by fear reduction (Meyer & Chesser, 1970). Compulsive handwashing, for example, is viewed as an operant escape-response that reduces an obsessional preoccupation with and fear of contamination by dirt or germs. Similarly, compulsive checking may reduce anxiety about whatever disaster the patient anticipates if the checking ritual is not completed. Anxiety as measured by self-reports (Hodgson & Rachman, 1972) and psychophysiological responses (Carr, 1971) can indeed be reduced by such compulsive behaviour. The very high frequency of compulsive acts occurs in order to give the person reassurance because the stimuli that elicit anxiety are hard to discriminate. For example, it is hard to know when germs are present and when they have been eliminated by some cleaning ritual (Mineka & Zinbarg, 1996).

It has also been proposed that compulsive checking results from a memory deficit. An inability to remember some action accurately (such as turning off the stove) or to distinguish between an actual behaviour and an imagined behaviour ("Maybe I just thought I turned off the stove") could cause someone to check repeatedly. Although compulsive checkers believe that they have poor memory, actual tests of memory for specific actions have been inconsistent (Constans et al., 1995; Tallis, Pratt, & Jamani, 1999).

After reviewing cognitive biases in OCD, Canadian researchers concluded that there is only weak evidence for the existence of cognitive biases (Summerfeldt & Endler, 1998): that is, although individuals with other anxiety disorders may selectively process threat cues, evidence of selective processing of threat cues in OCD is far from convincing (see McNally, Kaspi, Riemann, & Zeitlin, 1990). Summerfeldt and Endler (1998) concluded that cognitive biases may only exist among the subset of OCD patients with contamination concerns.

So, how can we account for obsessive thoughts? The obsessions of patients usually make them anxious (Rabavilas & Boulougouris, 1974), much as do the somewhat similar intrusive thoughts of normal people after exposure to stressful stimuli, such as a scary movie (Horowitz, 1975). Most people occasionally experience unwanted ideas that are similar in content to obsessions (Rachman & deSilva, 1978). These unpleasant thoughts increase during times of stress (Parkinson & Rachman, 1981). Normal individuals can tolerate or dismiss these cognitions, but for individuals with OCD, the thoughts may be particularly vivid and elicit great concern, perhaps because childhood experiences taught them that some thoughts are dangerous or unacceptable. Persons with OCD also have trouble ignoring stimuli, and this can add to their difficulties (Clayton, Richards, & Edwards, 1999).

Rachman has advanced a cognitive theory of obsessions in OCD (see Rachman, 1998; Rachman & Shafran, 1998). He (1998) posited that unwanted intrusive thoughts are the roots of obsessions and that obsessions often involve catastrophic misinterpretations of the importance and significance of negative intrusive thoughts. Rachman and Shafran (1998) identified a range of cognitive factors involved in OCD in addition to the obsessions themselves, including an inflated sense of personal responsibility for outcomes and a cognitive bias involving thought-action-fusion. Thought-action-fusion involves two beliefs: (1) the mere act of thinking about unpleasant events increases the perceived likelihood that they will actually happen; and (2) at a moral level, thinking something unpleasant (e.g., imagining the self hurting others) is the same as actually having carried it out. Thus, thought-action-fusion involves a blurring of the distinction between thinking about something and reacting as if the behaviour has actually been expressed (Shafran et al., 1996).

Table 6.4 lists faulty cognitive appraisals, as summarized by David Clark (2001) at the University of New Brunswick. Themes represented here include a sense of being responsible for events that may or may not occur, the over-importance of thought control, an inability to tolerate uncertainty, and thought-action-fusion. Many of these thoughts are represented on a new measure known as the Meta-Cognitive Beliefs Questionnaire (Clark, Purdon, & Wang, 2003). Beliefs about thought control and the negative consequences of uncontrolled thoughts are highly predictive of obsessions (Clark et al., 2003). Other recent Canadian research suggests that there are meta-cognitive differences in OCD—specifically, that OCD patients have such highly developed cognitive self-consciousness that they reflect excessively on their cognitive processes (Janeck, Calamari, Riemann, & Heffelfinger, 2003). In other words, OCD patients engage in too much thinking about thinking itself!

What is distressing about intrusive thoughts? A recent study conducted at the University of Waterloo suggested that thoughts are especially upsetting if they are inconsistent with valued aspects of the self (Rowa & Purdon, 2003). Thus, people who pride themselves on their altruism would be highly distressed by repetitive, intrusive thoughts reflecting an urge to hurt other people.

People with obsessive-compulsive disorder may try actively to suppress intrusive thoughts, with unfortunate consequences. Wegner et al. (1987, 1991) studied what happens when people are asked to suppress a thought. Two groups of students were asked either to think or not think about a white bear. One group thought about the white bear and then was told not to; the other group did the reverse. Thoughts were measured by having participants voice their thoughts and also by having them ring a bell every time they thought about a white bear. Two findings are of particular note. First, attempts to not think about a white bear were not fully successful. Second, the students who began by inhibiting thoughts of a white bear had more subsequent thoughts about it once the inhibition condition was over. Trying to inhibit a thought may therefore have the paradoxical effect of inducing preoccupation with it. Furthermore, attempts to suppress unpleasant thoughts are typically associated with intense emotional states, resulting in a strong link between the suppressed thought and the emotion. After many attempts at suppression, a strong emotion may lead to the return of the thought, accompanied by an increase in negative mood (Wenzlaff, Wegner, & Klein, 1991). The result would be an increase in anxiety. Wegner has created a measure known as the White Bear Suppression Inventory to assess individual differences in people's preoccupation with trying to inhibit obsessive thoughts.

Canadian researchers (e.g., Purdon, 1999; Purdon & Clark, 2000) have reviewed research on the link between attempted thought suppression and obsessional phenomena and have concluded that an association does indeed exist. Research also indicates that attempted thought suppression is involved in either the etiology or persistence of other adjustment problems including depression, GAD, and post-traumatic stress disorder (see Purdon, 1999; Purdon & Clark, 1994).

Biological Factors Encephalitis, head injuries, and brain tumours have all been associated with the development of obsessive-compulsive disorder (Jenike, 1986). Interest has focused on two areas of the brain that could be affected by such trauma, the frontal lobes and the basal ganglia, a set of subcortical nuclei including the caudate, putamen, globus pallidus, and amygdala (see Figure 6.1). PET scan studies have shown increased activation in the frontal lobes of OCD patients, perhaps a reflection of the patients' overconcern with their own thoughts. The focus on the basal ganglia, a system linked to the control of motor behaviour, is due to its relevance to compulsions as well as to the relationship between OCD and Tourette's syndrome. Tourette's syndrome is marked by both motor and vocal tics and has been linked to basal ganglia dysfunction. Patients with Tourette's often have OCD as well (Sheppard et al., 1999).

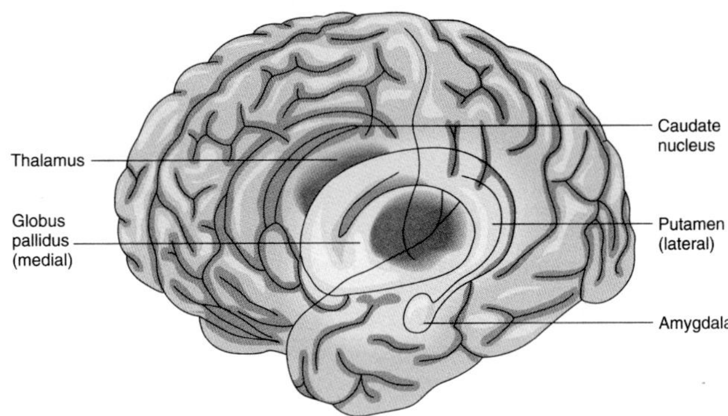

Figure 6.1 The basal ganglia.

Rauch et al. (1994) provided evidence in support of the importance to OCD of both brain regions mentioned above. They presented patients with stimuli selected for them, such as a glove contaminated with garbage or an unlocked door, and found that blood flow in the brain increased in the frontal area and to some of the basal ganglia. OCD patients also have smaller putamen than people in the control group (Rosenberg et al., 1997).

Research on neurochemical factors has focused on serotonin. As we describe later, antidepressants that inhibit the reuptake of serotonin have proved to be useful therapies for OCD (e.g., Pigott et al., 1990). The usual interpretation of this finding would be that because the drugs facilitate synaptic transmission in serotonin neurons, OCD is related to low serotonin or a reduced number of receptors. However, tests of these ideas have not yielded the expected results; in fact, research with drugs that stimulate the serotonin receptor shows that they can exacerbate rather than reduce OCD symptoms (Bastani, Nash, & Meltzer, 1990; Hollander et al., 1992). One possible explanation is that OCD is caused by a neurotransmitter system that is coupled to serotonin; when affected by antidepressants, the serotonin system causes changes in this other system, which is the real location of the therapeutic effect (Barr et al., 1994). Both dopamine and acetylcholine have been proposed as transmitters that are

Table 6.4

Faulty Appraisals Implicated in the Etiology and Persistence of Obsessions by Cognitive Behavioural Therapists

Faulty Appraisal	Explanation	Example
Overestimation of threat and negative consequences	The obsession is viewed as highly threatening and possibly resulting in very undesirable negative outcomes.	I have touched this doorknob. It is contaminated with germs that may now invade my body and cause cancer.
Inflated responsibility	The obsession is considered an indication that one has the power to bring about, or prevent, the occurrence of harm or other negative outcomes to self or others.	I notice a piece of glass on the road and think that it could cause a tire to blow and result in a fatal accident. Knowing this, I am responsible to ensure the glass is removed.
Overimportance of thoughts	The obsession is considered highly significant because of its prominence within the stream of consciousness.	The very fact that I am thinking unwanted intrusive thoughts of harming others means that these thoughts must be highly significant.
Overimportance of thought control	The obsession must be successfully dismissed from consciousness, and failure to do so represents a serious threat of possible negative consequences.	It is important that I suppress any intrusive thought of unwontedly touching a child because failure to control the thought means that I might lose control and actually commit such a horrible offence.
Thought-action fusion	The presence of the obsession increases the likelihood that the unwanted event will occur, and even thinking such a repugnant thought is morally equivalent to engaging in the forbidden act.	If I think about my father dying in a plane crash, this increases the probability that the event will actually happen; having unwanted intrusive thoughts of inappropriately touching a child is as morally reprehensible as actually doing it.
Catastrophic misinterpretation of significance	The obsession is interpreted as a sign or indication of something meaningful about the individual.	If I have unwanted intrusive thoughts of harming other people, this may mean that I am a latent psychopath.
Perfectionism	The best way to deal with the obsession is to achieve a perfect, complete, or just right" state.	If I keep saying this phrase over and over until I can repeat it perfectly, " then I will feel better and can get on with my daily activities.
Intolerance of uncertainty	It is intolerable to have any doubt or uncertainty associated with the obsession.	I cannot be certain that I understand this sentence, so I will reread it several times until I know that I understand what I have read.
Ego-dystonicity	The obsession is considered inconsistent, alien, and even threatening to one's self-definition.	A young man avoids public washrooms because of the obsessional doubt of whether he just molested a child in the washroom. Such a thought is completely contrary to his high moral standards and conscientiousness.

Note: Adapted with permission from Clark (2001), *Journal of Contemporary Psychotherapy*.

coupled to serotonin and play the more important role in OCD (Rauch & Jenike, 1993).

There is some evidence for a genetic side to OCD. High rates of anxiety disorders occur among the first-degree relatives of OCD patients (McKeon & Murray, 1987). The prevalence of OCD is also higher in first-degree relatives of OCD cases (10.3 percent) than in control relatives (1.9 percent) (Pauls et al., 1995). Thus, biological factors may predispose some people to OCD.

Therapies For Obsessive-Compulsive Disorder

OCD is one of the most difficult psychological problems to treat. For example, a 40-year follow-up study showed that only 20 percent of patients had recovered completely (Skoog & Skoog, 1999). The major therapeutic schools have had different impacts on this disorder.

Psychoanalytic Therapy Psychoanalytic treatment for obsessions and compulsions resembles that for phobias and generalized anxiety—namely, lifting repression and allowing the patient to confront what he or she truly fears. Because the intrusive thoughts and compulsive behaviour protect the ego from the repressed conflict, however, they are difficult targets for therapeutic intervention, and psychoanalytic procedures have thus not been effective in treating this disorder.

Such shortcomings have prompted some analytic clinicians to take a more active, behavioural approach to these disorders, using analytic understanding more as a way to increase compliance with behavioural procedures (Jenike, 1990). One psychoanalytic view hypothesizes that the indecision one sees in most obsessive-compulsive patients derives from a need for guaranteed correctness before any action can be taken (Salzman, 1985). Patients therefore must learn to tolerate the uncertainty and anxiety that all people feel as they confront the reality that nothing is certain or absolutely controllable in life. The ultimate focus of the treatment remains gaining insight into the unconscious determinants of the symptoms.

Exposure and Response Prevention (ERP) The most widely used and generally accepted behavioural approach to compulsive rituals, pioneered in England by Victor Meyer (1966), combines exposure with response prevention (ERP) (Rachman & Hodgson, 1980). In this method (sometimes called flooding), the person exposes himself or herself to situations that elicit the compulsive act—such as touching a dirty dish—and then refrains from performing the accustomed ritual—handwashing. The assumption is that the ritual is negatively reinforcing because it reduces the anxiety that is aroused by some environmental stimulus or event, such as dust on a chair. Preventing the person from performing the ritual will expose him or her to the anxiety-provoking stimulus, thereby allowing the anxiety to be extinguished. Controlled research (e.g., Duggan, Marks, & Richards, 1993; Stanley & Turner, 1995) suggests that this treatment is at least partially effective for more than half of patients with OCD, including children and adolescents (Franklin & Foa, 1998; March, 1995). In Meyer's original sample of 15 patients, only two had relapsed at a five-year follow-up (Meyer & Levy, 1973).

Sometimes control over obsessive-compulsive rituals is possible only in a hospital. Meyer (1966) created a controlled environment at Middlesex Hospital in London, England, to treat OCD. Staff members were trained to restrict the patients' opportunities for engaging in ritualistic acts. Adaptation of the treatment to the home required the involvement of family members. Preparing them for this work was no mean task, requiring skills and care beyond the necessary proficiency in whatever specific behavioural technique was being employed.

In the short term, the ERP treatment is arduous and unpleasant for clients. It typically involves exposures lasting upwards of 90 minutes for 15 to 20 sessions within a three-week period, with instructions to practise between sessions as well. Up to 25 percent of patients refuse treatment (Foa et al., 1985). In fact, refusal to enter treatment and dropping out are generally recognized problems for many interventions for OCD (Jenike & Rauch, 1994). Patients with OCD tend to procrastinate, fear changes, and be overly concerned about others controlling them—traits that can create special problems for manipulative approaches such as behaviour therapy.

Cognitive Behaviour Therapy A cognitive-behavioural approach is used rather than just a cognitive approach because an inherent part of any cognitive therapy is exposure and response prevention; to evaluate whether not performing a compulsive ritual will have catastrophic consequences, the patient must stop performing that ritual.

Salkovskis and Warwick (1985) provided one of the earliest demonstrations of the usefulness of a cognitive-behavioural approach when they showed that cognitive restructuring was able to assist an OCD patient who relapsed following ERP. This patient had developed the belief that her hand creams would cause cancer. Salkovskis (1996, 1998) has gone on to outline how cognitive procedures can eliminate the dysfunctional beliefs that contribute to the OCD patients' faulty appraisals. His recent model focuses on the notion of perceived responsibility, which is defined as "the belief that one has power which is pivotal to bring about or prevent subjectively crucial outcomes" (p. 40). Cognitive and behavioural techniques focus on the modification of dysfunctional beliefs involving this sense of personal responsibility. This can involve having the patient actually test whether something bad happens as a result of their being prevented from performing the ritual (see Van Oppen et al., 1995).

Several investigators based in Canada have extended the cognitive-behavioural interventions used to treat OCD. Freeston and Ladouceur and associates have outlined a five-step treatment program, with the fifth step being relapse prevention (see Freeston et al., 1997; Ladouceur et al., 1995). Another extension has been proposed by O'Connor and Robillard (1995, 2000) from Montreal. They focus on the OCD client's conviction that imaginary events may actually come true. Their modification, known as the "inference-based approach," is geared toward identifying and ameliorating the obsessional inference, which has become imbedded within a fictional account constructed by the patient. Over time, this imaginary account may be treated as if it were real. O'Connor and Robillard advocate a mixed approach that combines cognitive-behavioural therapy with their inference-based approach.

Biological Treatment Drugs that increase serotonin levels, such as the SSRIs and some tricyclics, are the biological treatments most often given to patients with obsessive-compulsive disorder. Both classes of drugs have yielded some beneficial results, though it is noteworthy that a review of pharmacological treatment by two psychiatrists underscores the importance of ERP as a first-line approach (Rauch & Jenike, 1998). Some studies found tricyclic antidepressants less effective than ERP (Balkom et al., 1994), and one study of antidepressants showed improvement in compulsive rituals only in those OCD patients who were also depressed (Marks et al., 1980). In another study, the benefits of a tricyclic antidepressant on OCD were found to be short-lived; withdrawal from this drug led to a 90 percent relapse rate, much higher than that found with response prevention (Pato et al., 1988). All in all, the picture is uncertain with regard to the effectiveness of tricyclic antidepressants.

Research has shown that serotonin reuptake inhibitors, such as fluoxetine (Prozac), produce more improvement in patients with OCD than do placebos or tricyclics (Kronig et al., 1999). However, treatment gains are modest, and symptoms return if the drugs are discontinued (e.g., Franklin & Foa, 1998). It is also not clear whether the drugs work specifically on OCD or on its associated depression (Barr et al., 1994; Tollefson et al., 1994). All antidepressant drugs have side effects that discourage some people from staying on them, such as nausea, insomnia, agitation, interference with sexual functioning, and even some negative effects on the heart and circulatory system (Rauch & Jenike, 1998).

Technological improvements in measuring various aspects of brain activity have encouraged researchers to look for brain changes from therapeutic interventions. One notable study compared fluoxetine with in vivo exposure plus response prevention and found that improvement in OCD produced by both treatments was associated with the same changes in brain function—namely, reduced metabolic activity in the right caudate nucleus, overactivity of which has been linked to OCD (Baxter et al., 1992). Only those patients who improved clinically showed this change in brain activity as measured by PET scans. Such findings suggest that markedly different therapies may work for similar reasons—they are just different ways of affecting the same factors in the brain. We should note that in the Baxter et al. study, the drug patients were still on medication during the posttreatment PET scan, whereas the behavioural-therapy patients were not and could not be, in any meaningful sense, in treatment—that is, still undergoing active response prevention for the rituals.

The desperation of mental health workers, surpassed only by that of the patients, explains the occasional use of psychosurgery in treating OCD. The procedure in current use, cingulatomy, involves destroying two to three centimetres of white matter in the cingulum, an area near the corpus callosum. Although some clinical improvement has been reported (Baer et al., 1995; Irle et al., 1998), this intervention is viewed as a treatment of very last resort, given its permanence, the risks of psychosurgery, and the poor understanding of how it works.

Regardless of treatment modality, OCD patients are seldom cured. Although a variety of interventions can result in significant improvement, OCD tendencies usually persist to some degree, albeit under greater control and less obtrusively (White & Cole, 1990).

Canadian Clinic Focus/6.1

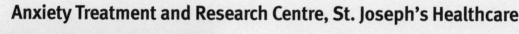

Anxiety Treatment and Research Centre, St. Joseph's Healthcare

Dr. Martin Antony, director of the Anxiety Treatment and Research Centre (ATRC) at St. Joseph's Healthcare in Hamilton, Ontario.

Various clinics in Canada are known for providing treatment and conducting research on anxiety disorders. One such clinic is the Anxiety Treatment and Research Centre (ATRC) at St. Joseph's Healthcare in Hamilton, Ontario, a specialty clinic focusing on the assessment and treatment of individuals with anxiety disorders. The centre is known internationally for its clinical services, scientific research, and training opportunities. The director of the centre is Martin M. Antony, a psychologist. Randi E. McCabe (also a psychologist) is the associate director, and Richard P. Swinson, a psychiatrist, is the medical director. The centre is affiliated with the Department of Psychiatry and Behavioural Neurosciences at McMaster University. More information about the ATRC can be found on their website, www.anxietytreatment.ca.

Clinical Services

REFERRAL PROCESS

Each year, the ATRC receives more than 400 referrals from across Southern Ontario. The mean age of the individuals referred is the mid-30s, although the range is from 18 to 75 years of age. About 60 percent of individuals referred to the centre are female. The most commonly presenting anxiety disorders include panic disorder (25 percent of referrals), social phobia (23 percent), and OCD (22 percent). The remaining patients suffer from a range of problems, including mood disorders, other anxiety disorders, and related conditions. All patients are referred by a physician. Referrals are typically made for the purpose of obtaining clarification regarding an individual's diagnosis, obtaining treatment recommendations (e.g., medications to be prescribed by the referring physician), or obtaining treatment at the ATRC (e.g., cognitive behaviour therapy).

ASSESSMENT

All individuals who are seen at the ATRC receive a comprehensive assessment. Initially, a battery of questionnaires is completed, including medical history and general measures of anxiety, depression, and functional impairment. In addition, a detailed life history questionnaire is completed to provide data on family history, schooling, and other background information. Most individuals are administered the Structured Clinical Interview for DSM-IV (SCID-IV; First et al., 1996), a semi-structured diagnostic interview that provides DSM-IV diagnoses for anxiety disorders, mood disorders, substance-use disorders, psychotic disorders, somatoform disorders, and eating disorders. This interview usually takes two to three hours. In addition, the assessment may include a one-hour clinical interview with a psychiatrist to confirm the diagnostic information obtained during the SCID-IV and to allow for medication recommendations, if appropriate. Patients often return for additional assessments following the initial interviews and questionnaires. For example, specialized questionnaires are completed by individuals with panic disorder, social phobia, and OCD to assess the features of these problems. In addition, individuals with OCD receive the clinician-administered Yale-Brown Obsessive Compulsive Scale (Y-BOCS; Goodman et al., 1989), a well-known measure that assesses the severity and content of an individual's OCD symptoms.

TREATMENT

The ATRC has specialized treatment programs for individuals suffering from OCD, panic disorder, and social phobia. These include group treatments (typically lasting about 12 to 15 sessions) and individual treatments. In some cases, brief treatments are also available for individuals suffering from GAD, health anxiety, and specific phobias. Treatment programs include cognitive-behavioural therapy, medications, or combinations of these approaches. Individuals who receive treatment in one of the ATRC's standard programs are later invited to attend a monthly booster group designed to reinforce the skills learned during initial treatment.

Cognitive-behavioural treatments typically involve cognitive therapy, exposure-based treatments, skills training (e.g., social skills training for social phobia), and response prevention (for individuals with OCD). These treatments are based on empirically supported protocols. Self-help materials are recommended, and suggestions for where to obtain additional information (e.g., Internet resources) are provided. In many cases, treatments are offered in the context of research studies. Measures are administered before and after treatment to assess treatment effectiveness. Also, patients rate their satisfaction with the centre's services.

Research

Research at the ATRC has focused on a number of broad areas. ATRC staff have studied brief interventions for anxiety disorders, including treatment of panic disorder in the emergency room, telephone treatments for panic disorder, and computer-administered treatments for OCD. Currently, the ATRC is developing a new treatment for individuals suffering from both panic disorder and depression. This treatment includes cognitive and behavioural strategies that have been shown to be useful for each condition. The centre is also studying a new home-based treatment for OCD.

ATRC staff has also been active in research on cognitive, biological, and personality variables associated with anxiety disorders. This work includes studies on memory processes in OCD, brain function in panic disorder, the effects of thought suppression in OCD, genetic transmission of OCD, impulsivity and anxiety disorders, symptom subtypes in OCD, social phobia and social comparison processes, the relationship between OCD and mood disorders, and the relationship between perfectionism and the anxiety disorders. A number of influential books have been published by ATRC staff, including books for clinicians who work with anxiety disorders (e.g., Antony & Barlow, 2002; Antony, Orsillo, & Roemer, 2001; Antony & Swinson, 2000a; Craske, Antony, & Barlow, 1997; Swinson, Antony, Rachman, & Richter, 1998) and self-help workbooks for individuals coping with social anxiety (Antony & Swinson, 2000b), specific phobias (Antony, Craske, & Barlow, 1995), perfectionism (Antony & Swinson, 1998), and depression (Bieling & Antony, 2003).

Training Programs

The ATRC is involved in training individuals from a broad range of health care disciplines. The centre regularly trains medical students, psychiatry residents, psychology interns, psychology practicum students, and social work students to provide clinical services for individuals with anxiety disorders. In addition, students frequently receive research training at the ATRC. Finally, individuals seeking additional training following completion of their degrees (e.g., post-doctoral fellows) often obtain placements at the ATRC. At any one time, between 15 and 20 students are receiving various types of training experience at the centre.

Case Example: CC

CC is a prototypical case from the ARTC. CC was referred for treatment of panic disorder and OCD. Her first panic attack occurred when she tried marijuana for the first time. CC experienced intense dizziness, feelings of unreality, and a number of other sensations during the initial attack. When she was assessed at the ATRC, she was experiencing panic attacks almost daily, many of which were uncued and some of which were cued by situations that she associated with the uncomfortable feared sensations. For example, CC avoided driving for fear that she might become very dizzy and crash her car. She also avoided all psychoactive substances, including alcohol and caffeine.

In the months following the onset of her panic disorder, CC also developed symptoms of OCD. In particular, she developed a fear of being contaminated by drugs or other substances that she came in contact with, especially while eating. She was fearful that impurities in her food might trigger a panic attack, which in turn might lead her to lose control or "go crazy." She avoided eating any foods that she had not prepared herself, and she avoided purchasing foods that were not wrapped. She also washed her hands many times per day to avoid contaminating her food or other objects in her home.

Because CC's symptoms of panic disorder and OCD were related (both were associated with a fear of developing feared symptoms), cognitive-behavioural treatment focused simultaneously on both problems. Cognitive restructuring was used to help CC to interpret her uncomfortable panic symptoms in a less anxiety-provoking way. CC was also encouraged to practise exposure to the symptoms she feared (e.g., spinning to cause dizziness), the activities she avoided (e.g., driving), and the foods she avoided. In addition, she was encouraged to touch objects in her home, without washing her hands. Treatment lasted 15 sessions. CC was still experiencing occasional panic attacks at the end, but much less frequently than before starting treatment. Her attacks were now occurring about once per month, and she was much less frightened of them. In addition, her heightened fear of contamination, her excessive washing, and her avoidance of particular foods were almost eliminated. However, she still feared drinking alcohol or caffeinated drinks.

Comment

The ARTC is a model specialized clinic that employs state-of-the-art treatment strategies for people suffering from the various anxiety disorders. However, it is important to note that such facilities are not available to the majority of Canadians. Swinson, Cox, Kerr, Kuch, and Fergus (1992) surveyed hospitals in Canada and reported that only about 15 percent of them had specialized anxiety treatment facilities. Most of these clinics are located in major metropolitan areas and are often associated with university-affiliated teaching hospitals. The improved training of students and professionals in the treatment of anxiety disorders, in clinical settings such as the ARTC, should lead to the increased availability of these treatments. However, governments and stakeholder organizations need to foster comprehensive, effective, and efficient treatment approaches for anxiety disorders in clinical settings throughout Canada. It is especially important to facilitate the accessibility of treatment for people who live in rural and remote areas.

We believe that people living in Canada deserve what Haaga (2000, p. 547) referred to as "an empirically supported treatment delivered competently by a well-trained practitioner." The task is difficult because both governments and third-party insurance providers are pressing for brief, cost-effective treatments in a managed health care system. Canadian investigators have demonstrated that brief, adapted cognitive-behavioural approaches can be useful. For example, Swinson and associates illustrated the effectiveness of telephone-administered treatment (Swinson, Fergus, Cox, & Wiskwire, 1995) and of giving people reassurance and exposure instructions in a general hospital emergency room (Swinson, Soulios, Cox, & Kuch, 1992), and Cote, Gauthier, Labarge, Plamondon, and Fournier (1994) reported that minimal therapist contact combined with use of a self-help book can be as effective as in-person cognitive-behavioural in treating panic disorder. Newman (2000) reviewed evidence indicating that many people with anxiety disorders can benefit from various low-cost interventions. Given the economic burden associated with untreated anxiety disorders (Greenberg et al., 1999), even more intensive, multi-faceted interventions may be cost-effective. When do we employ lower-cost interventions? When do we use more intensive but more costly interventions? We will address this question when we evaluate "Stepped Care" models in Chapter 17. These models seek to maximize the efficient allocation of limited health care resources (see Haaga, 2000; Davison, 2000).

POSTTRAUMATIC STRESS DISORDER

Posttraumatic stress disorder (PTSD), introduced as a diagnosis in DSM-III, entails an extreme response to a severe stressor, including increased anxiety, avoidance of stimuli associated with the trauma, and a numbing of emotional responses, as illustrated by the case of Sergeant Bilodeau at the start of this chapter. Although there had been prior awareness that the stresses of combat could produce powerful and adverse effects on soldiers, it was the aftermath of the Vietnam War that spurred the acceptance of the new diagnosis.

PTSD is defined by a cluster of symptoms. However, unlike the definitions of other psychological disorders, the definition of PTSD includes part of its presumed etiology—namely, a traumatic event or events that the person has directly experienced or witnessed involving actual or threatened death, serious injury, or a threat to the physical integrity of self or others. The event must have created intense fear, horror, or helplessness.

In addition to combat stress, prolonged abuse can trigger symptoms of PTSD. Indeed, a survey of inpatient adolescents from the Foothills Hospital in Calgary found that PTSD was diagnosed in 12 of the 13 adolescents with a history of physical or sexual abuse (Koltek, Wilkes, & Atkinson, 1998). McEvoy and Daniluk (1995) reported that Canadian Aboriginal women who experienced multiple forms of trauma, including sexual victimization, typically develop symptoms of PTSD.

In previous editions of the DSM, the traumatic event was defined as "outside the range of human experience." This definition was too restrictive, as it would have ruled out the diagnosis of PTSD following such events as automobile accidents or the death of a loved one. The current broadened definition may also be too restrictive, because it focuses on the event's objective characteristics rather than on its subjective meaning (King et al., 1995).

Unlike most other diagnoses, PTSD includes part of its cause, a traumatic event, in its definition. On September 11, 2001, terrorists hijacked two passenger jets and deliberately crashed them into the twin towers of the World Trade Center in New York City. Thousands of people perished in the explosions and collapse of the 110-storey buildings. Firefighters, police officers, and other rescue workers, such as these men at "ground zero," could be vulnerable to PTSD.

There is a difference between posttraumatic stress disorder and acute stress disorder, a new diagnosis in DSM-IV. Nearly everyone who encounters a trauma experiences stress, sometimes to a considerable degree. This is normal. If the stressor causes significant impairment in social or occupational functioning that lasts for less than one month, an acute stress disorder is diagnosed. The proportion of people who develop an acute stress disorder varies with the type of trauma they have experienced. Following rape, the figure is extremely high—over 90 percent (Rothbaum et al., 1992). Less severe traumas, such as exposure to a mass shooting or being in a motor vehicle accident, yield much lower figures, such as 13 percent for motor vehicle accident victims, for example (Bryant & Harvey, 1998; Classen et al., 1998). Although some people get over their acute stress disorder, a significant number develop PTSD (Brewin et al., 1999).

The inclusion in the DSM of severe stress as a significant causal factor of PTSD was meant to reflect a formal recognition that the cause of PTSD is primarily the event, not some aspect of the person. Instead of implicitly suggesting that the person would be all right were he or she made of sterner stuff, definition formally acknowledges the importance of the traumatizing circumstances (Haley, 1978). Yet the inclusion of this diagnostic criterion is controversial. Most people who encounter traumatic life events do not develop PTSD. In one study, for example, only 25 percent of people who experienced a traumatic event leading to physical injury subsequently developed PTSD (Shalev et al., 1996); thus, the event itself cannot be the sole cause of PTSD. Current research has moved in the direction of searching for factors that distinguish between people who do and people who do not develop PTSD after experiencing severe stress.

The symptoms for PTSD are grouped into three major categories. The diagnosis requires that symptoms in each category last longer than one month.

1. **Re-experiencing the traumatic event**. The individual frequently recalls the event and experiences nightmares about it. Intense emotional upset is produced by stimuli that symbolize the event (e.g., thunder, reminding a veteran of the battlefield) or on anniversaries of some specific experience. Kuch and Cox (1992) examined PTSD symptoms in a sample of 124 Holocaust survivors living in the Toronto area. This sample included subsamples of 78 concentration camp survivors and 20 tattooed concentration camp survivors. Nightmares were experienced by 87.2 percent of the concentration camp survivors and by 18 of the 20 tattooed concentration camp survivors.

   The importance of re-experiencing cannot be underestimated, for it is the likely source of the other categories of symptoms. Some theories of PTSD make re-experiencing the central feature by attributing the disorder to an inability to successfully integrate the traumatic event into an existing schema (the person's general beliefs about the world) (e.g., Foa, Zinbarg, & Rothbaum, 1992; Horowitz, 1986).
2. **Avoidance of stimuli associated with the event or numbing of responsiveness**. The person tries to avoid thinking about the trauma or encountering stimuli that will bring it to mind; there may be amnesia for the event. Numbing refers to decreased interest in others, a sense of estrangement, and an inability to feel positive emotions. These symptoms seem almost contradictory to those in item 1. In PTSD there is fluctuation: the person goes back and forth between re-experiencing and numbing.
3. **Symptoms of increased arousal**. These symptoms include difficulties falling or staying asleep, difficulty concentrating, hypervigilance, and an exaggerated startle response. Laboratory studies have confirmed these clinical symptoms by documenting the heightened physiological reactivity of PTSD patients to combat imagery (e.g., Orr et al., 1995) and their high-magnitude startle responses (Morgan et al., 1996, 1997).

Other problems often associated with PTSD are anxiety, depression, anger, guilt, substance abuse, marital problems, poor physical health, and occupational impairment (Bremner et al., 1996; Keane et al., 1992; Ouimette, Moos, & Finney, 2003; Zatzick et al., 1997). Suicidal thoughts and plans are common, as are incidents of explosive violence and stress-related psychophysiological problems, such as headaches and gastrointestinal disorders (Hobfoll et al., 1991).

PTSD has a prevalence rate of from 1 to 3 percent in the general U.S. population (Helzer, Robins, & McEvoy, 1987), representing over two million people. Research conducted in Canada suggests that even greater numbers have a subsyndromal form of PTSD, in which the person has symptoms of PTSD not severe or numerous enough to warrant the diagnosis but serious enough to cause considerable distress and impairment (Stein et al., 1997). The rate of PTSD was found to be very high (22 percent) among a southwestern Native American tribe (Robin et al., 1997). Given exposure to a traumatic event, the overall prevalence of PTSD rises to 9 percent (Breslau et al., 1998). Prevalences vary depending on the severity of the trauma experienced; it is about 3 percent among civilians who have been exposed to a physical attack, 20 percent among people wounded in Vietnam, and about 50 percent among rape victims and people who were POWs in either World War II or the Korean War (Engdahl et al., 1997; Rothbaum et al., 1992). Mitchell, Griffin, Stewart, and Loba (2004) found that 46% of community volunteers had probable PTSD after helping with the cleanup and recovery of bodies following the 1998 Swissair disaster off Canada's east coast. Overall, 69% of volunteers reported intrusive thoughts about the disaster. Factors that were deemed to increase PTSD symptoms included community silence, limited help-seeking (due to the stigma of seeking help), and insufficient proactive provision of therapeutic resources. Similar high rates of PTSD have been experienced by Canadian military personnel (see Canadian Perspectives 6.3). The most frequent trauma that precipitates PTSD is the loss of a loved one, accounting for about a third of all cases. When exposed to trauma, women are twice as likely as men to develop PTSD (Breslau et al., 1998). There is a high rate of comorbidity between PTSD and substance-use disorders; research suggests that PTSD symptoms typically precede, rather than follow, substance abuse (see Stewart, Pihl, Conrod, & Dongier, 1998).

Canadian Perspectives/6.3

PTSD in Canadian Veterans and Peacekeepers

Lt-Gen. Romeo Dallaire, former commander of United Nations forces in Rwanda who retired because of PTSD.

Most research on PTSD in military personnel has focused on American veterans of the Vietnam War, despite indications that Canadian Vietnam veterans who participated in the Vietnam War experienced comparable and even greater levels of distress than their American counterparts (Stretch, 1990, 1991). In fact, many people are unaware of the fact that an estimated 10,000 to 40,000 Canadians volunteered in the United States military to assist with the Vietnam War effort.

Published accounts of mental disorders in Canadian soldiers can be traced back to World War I. Farrar (1917) concluded that 10 percent of the World War I soldiers invalided to Canada were "nervous and mental cases" (p. 389). The majority of cases (58 percent) were said to suffer from "neurotic reactions," and of these, a subgroup suffered from "shell shock." The second group (14 percent) were said to suffer from "mental diseases and defects" (p. 389) that included cases of "dementia praecox," "primary mental defect," and "psychopathic inferiority."

Overall, there is a relative paucity of contemporary research on PTSD in Canadian military personnel, but the research that has been conducted has startling implications. For instance, Stretch (1990, 1991) examined the impact of participating in the Vietnam War in 164 Canadian veterans. These veterans had an average of 54 months of duty with 15 months in Vietnam. An alarming 107 of the 164 veterans (i.e., a prevalence rate of 65.4 percent) reported experiencing PTSD symptoms either during or after their Vietnam experience. PTSD was associated with poorer health, nervous system problems, depression, anxiety, anger, and shame. The sense of shame was, in part, a response to the perceived reaction of Canadian society. Comparisons of PTSD sufferers and veterans without PTSD showed that PTSD sufferers reported more negative reactions from people upon their return, more negative reactions to their involvement in the Vietnam War, and homecomings that were significantly worse. Stretch (1990) concluded that relative to American veterans, Canadian Vietnam veterans are particularly vulnerable to long-lasting forms of PTSD because they tend to be more isolated and receive less recognition and support for their war efforts.

A study conducted by Beal (1995) is arguably one of the most remarkable studies of the consequences of PTSD. This investigation is the longest follow-up study of PTSD published thus far. It was a 50-year follow-up that focused on 276 Canadian World War II veterans of the Dieppe Raid. The Dieppe Raid is regarded as one of the most bloody events of World War II with a casualty rate of 68 percent. One hundred and ninety-eight of the veterans in the study had become prisoners of war and 78 had not. Participants related their war experiences and completed a questionnaire that assessed PTSD symptoms evident in 1992. They also provided retrospective accounts of symptoms evident in 1946.

Beal (1995) found alarming levels of PTSD in both POWs and non-POWs. Overall, 43.4 percent of the POWs and 29.9 percent of the non-POWs were diagnosed with PTSD based on their 1992 self-reports. Comparisons of POWs with and without PTSD showed that those with PTSD reported more maltreatment in the form of beatings, personal intimidation, interrogation, group death threats, solitary confinement, and witnessing acts of torture. POWs with PTSD also had higher levels of depression, anxiety, and suicidal thoughts. The key point to remember in terms of their personal suffering is that these extreme levels of distress have persisted for 50 years. Most men reported experiencing little anxiety or depression prior to the Dieppe Raid. Beal (1995) noted further that despite the level of disability experienced by these veterans, with 37 percent of veterans having PTSD in 1992, relatively few qualified for government assistance, according to criteria used in 1992 by the Canadian government. Only 5.4 percent of the veterans were receiving psychological disability pensions from the Department of Veterans Affairs.

It is only recently that the Canadian government has opted to recognize PTSD symptoms as a form of disorder that merits a psychological disability pension (Thorne, 2000). This change was a response, in part, to the growing number of public accounts of severe forms of PTSD experienced by Canadian peacekeepers. The most well-known example involves retired Lt-Gen. Romeo Dallaire. Lt-Gen. Dallaire served as the United Nations commander in Rawanda in 1994 when over 800,000 Tutsis and Hutu moderates were killed by the ruling Hutu extremists. Dallaire and his men witnessed these atrocities (including children killing other children) as well as the slaughter of 10 Belgian soldiers by a machete-wielding mob. Dallaire's compelling account of his personal struggles and the genocide he witnessed has been summarized in his recent book (Dallaire, 2003).

Lieutenant-General Dallaire's personal difficulties became known to the public when he was discovered unconscious and apparently inebriated in a park in Hull, Quebec, on June 26, 2000. He revealed his difficulties in a letter that was sent to CBC Radio and read on-air on July 3, 2000. Dallaire has acknowledged his problems with PTSD and his suicide attempts (Growe, 2000). In his letter to CBC Radio, Dallaire said:

> The anger, the rage, the hurt and the cold loneliness that separates you from your family, friends and society's normal daily routine are so powerful that the option of destroying yourself is both real and attractive. That is what happened last Monday night. ... It appears, it grows, it invades and it overpowers you. In my current state of therapy, which continues to show very positive results, control mechanisms have not yet matured to always be on top of this battle.

This reference to "very positive results" was contradicted somewhat in a subsequent newspaper interview. Here, Dallaire stated, "You cannot put these things behind you. . . . And the more people say that, the more you get mad because you know these things will not disappear. Time does not help" (Growe, 2000, p. F1).

A recent Canadian investigation of deployed peacekeepers and non-deployed military personnel confirmed that PTSD symptoms have a direct negative impact on health status. Moreover, this link, the study showed, was evident for both deployed peacekeepers and non-deployed personnel (Asmundson, Stein, & McCreary, 2002). Thus, PTSD was associated with poor health, regardless of deployment status. PTSD in this sample was also closely linked with depression.

Thinking Critically

1. Lt-Gen. Dallaire, like so many Canadian peacekeepers, has had difficulty coping with the atrocities he witnessed. What steps would you take to help our peacekeepers better prepare for the psychological consequences of their missions? What preventive strategies would you recommend that the military employ during the missions? For example, would it be appropriate to have military psychologists available during the mission? What steps should be taken when the troops return home, in terms of both assessment and intervention? Should family therapy be one component of a multi-faceted intervention?

2. Lamerson and Kelloway (1996) from the University of Guelph developed a conceptual model of the stressors inherent in contemporary peacekeeping deployments and their consequences. They proposed that these deployments could be characterized as comprising exposure to traumatic stressors (e.g., witnessing the death or injury of others) in a context of chronic stressors (e.g., being separated from loved ones). Lamerson and Kelloway (1996, p. 199) further suggested that "the simultaneous experience of combat and contextual stressors may have multiplicative rather than additive effects." Do you agree with this hypothesis? What are the implications of this model for the management of "peacekeeping stress"?

ETIOLOGY OF POSTTRAUMATIC STRESS DISORDER

Research and theory on the causes of PTSD focus on risk factors for the disorder as well as on psychological and biological factors.

Risk Factors When examining risk factors, it is important to consider not only risk factors for PTSD, but also risk factors for the likelihood of being exposed to trauma. Research indicates that males, relative to females, have higher levels of trauma exposure, yet females have higher levels of PTSD (Breslau, 2002). Other factors associated with increased likelihood of being exposed to traumatic events include the personality traits of neuroticism and extraversion, early conduct problems, a family history of psychiatric disorders, and the presence of pre-existing psychiatric disorders (Breslau, 2002).

There are several risk factors for PTSD. Given exposure to a traumatic event, predictors of PTSD, in addition to gender, include perceived threat to life, early separation from parents, family history of a disorder, previous exposure to traumas, and a pre-existing disorder (an anxiety disorder or depression) (Breslau et al., 1997, 1999; Ehlers, Malou, & Bryant, 1998; Stein, 1997). Having high intelligence seems to be a protective factor, perhaps because it is associated with having better coping skills (Macklin et al., 1998). The prevalence of PTSD also increases with the severity of the traumatic event; for example, the greater the exposure to combat, the greater the risk. With a high degree of combat exposure, the rates of PTSD are the same in veterans who have family members with other disorders and those who do not. Among those with a family history of a disorder, even low combat exposure produces a high rate of PTSD (Foy et al., 1987). The initial reaction to the trauma is also predictive. More severe anxiety and depression increase the probability of later developing PTSD, as does a higher heart rate in the aftermath of the trauma (Shalev et al., 1996, 1998).

Dissociative symptoms (including depersonalization, derealization, amnesia, and out-of-body experiences) at the time of the trauma also increase the probability of developing PTSD, as does trying to push memories of the trauma out of one's mind (Ehlers, Mayou, & Bryant, 1998). Dissociation may play a role in maintaining the disorder, as it keeps the patient from confronting traumatic memories. A compelling study of dissociation assessed rape survivors within two weeks of the assault. While the women talked about either the rape or neutral topics, psychophysiological measures and self-reports of stress were taken. The women were divided into two groups based on their scores on a measure of dissociation during the rape (e.g., "Did you have moments of losing track of what was going on?"). Women with high dissociation scores were much more likely to have PTSD symptoms than were low scorers. High scorers also had a dissociation between their subjective stress ratings and their physiological responses. Although they reported high levels of stress when they were talking about being raped, they showed less physiological arousal than did the women with low dissociation scores.

Another risk factor was discovered in a study of Israeli veterans of the 1982 war with Lebanon. Development of PTSD was associated with a tendency to take personal responsibility for failures and to cope with stress by focusing on emotions ("I wish I could change how I feel") rather than on the problems themselves (Mikulincer & Solomon, 1988; Solomon, Mikulincer, & Flum, 1988). Similarly, a strong sense of commitment and purpose differentiated Gulf War veterans who did not develop PTSD from those who did (Sutker et al., 1995). A high level of social support may lessen the risk for the disorder (King et al., 1999; Taft et al., 1999). Access to social support also lessened the risk for PTSD in children who had experienced the trauma associated with Hurricane Andrew (Vernberg et al., 1996).

Attachment style has been identified as a PTSD risk factor by York University researcher Robert Muller and his associates in their study of high-risk adults with a history of childhood physical or sexual abuse (see Muller, Sicoli, & Lemieux, 2000). Attachment styles (e.g., how an infant reacts when left alone with a stranger when the mother leaves) are discussed in more detail in Chapter 15. Consistent with other studies that suggest an abused population is likely to be insecurely attached (e.g., Alexander et al., 1998), Muller et al. (2000) reported that 76 percent of the participants endorsed one of three insecure attachment styles (dismissing, fearful, or preoccupied). They found that PTSD is likely among people with an insecure attachment style that involves a negative view of the self; a negative view of others was not linked with PTSD symptoms despite this group's having a history of being abused by other people. Future longitudinal research is necessary to provide a clear ordering of cause and effect.

Of course, people in certain stressful occupations are at risk, as illustrated in a recent study of PTSD symptoms in Canadian and American firefighters (Corneil, Beaton, Murphy, Johnson, & Pike, 1999), as well as in Canadian studies of paramedics (Regehr et al., 2002) and emergency room personnel (Laposa & Alden, 2003). However, PTSD may also be experienced by more general workers who undergo traumatic events while at work. This was illustrated in a recent study of 44 workers from Alberta (Macdonald, Colotla, Flamer, & Karlinsky, 2003) who filed for worker compensation benefits after experiencing such traumatic events as armed robberies or physical assaults in non-robbery situations. Macdonald et al. (2003) found that fewer than half of these workers were able to return to their job.

Psychological Theories Learning theorists assume that PTSD arises from a classical conditioning of fear (e.g., Fairbank & Brown, 1987). A woman who has been raped, for example, may come to fear walking in a certain neighbourhood (the CS) because of having been assaulted there (the UCS). Based on this classically conditioned fear, avoidances are built up, and they are negatively reinforced by the reduction of fear that comes from not being in the presence of the CS. In a sense, PTSD is an example of the two-factor theory of avoidance learning proposed years ago by Mowrer (1947). There is a developing body of evidence in support of this view (Foy et al., 1990) and of related cognitive-behavioural theories that emphasize the loss of control and predictability felt by people with PTSD (Chemtob et al., 1988; Foa & Kozak, 1986).

Further support for the role of psychological factors is provided by research on the link between PTSD and anxiety sensitivity in a sample of people who had experienced serious motor vehicle accidents (Federoff, Taylor, Asmundson, & Koch, 2000). This study found that elevated levels of anxiety sensitivity and pain severity were significant predictors of PTSD symptoms, while specific beliefs about the nature of motor vehicle accidents were unrelated to PTSD symptoms.

A psychodynamic theory proposed by Horowitz (1986, 1990) posits that memories of the traumatic event occur constantly in the person's mind and are so painful that they are either consciously suppressed (by distraction, for example) or repressed. People are believed to engage in a kind of internal struggle to make some sense of a trauma by integrating it into their existing beliefs about themselves and the world.

Biological Theories Research on twins shows a possible diathesis for PTSD (True et al., 1993). A recent study conducted with 406 volunteer twin pairs from the Vancouver area demonstrated that exposure to certain kinds of trauma (i.e., violent crimes) was influenced by genetic and environmental factors, but only environmental factors contributed to other types of trauma (e.g., natural disasters); in addition, PTSD symptoms following exposure to non-combat trauma were moderately heritable (Stein, Jang, Taylor, Vernon, & Livesley, 2002). This study is unique in two ways: it is one of the few genetic studies conducted on a non-military, community sample, and it is the first study of its kind to include women. Stein et al. concluded that a personality characterized by trait neuroticism might be the genetic vulnerability factor that serves as a diathesis for PTSD.

Trauma may activate the noradrenergic system, raising levels of norepinephrine and thereby making the person startle and express emotion more readily than is normal (Krystal et al., 1989). Consistent with this view is the finding that levels of norepinephrine were higher in PTSD patients than in those diagnosed as having schizophrenia or mood disorders (Kosten et al., 1987). In addition, stimulating the noradrenergic system induced a panic attack in 70 percent and flashbacks in 40 percent of PTSD patients; none of the control participants had such experiences (Southwick et al., 1993). Finally, there is evidence for increased sensitivity of noradrenergic receptors in patients with PTSD (Bremner et al., 1998).

Therapies for Posttraumatic Stress Disorder

Most experts on trauma agree that it is best to intervene in some fashion as soon as possible after a traumatic event, well before PTSD has a chance to develop (Bell, 1995). Intervening when people are in the acute phase of a posttrauma period and are at risk of developing acute stress disorder is referred to as *crisis intervention*. As reviewed by Foa and Meadows (1997), intervention includes such procedures as recreating the event by having participants discuss with each other as many details as they can remember, encouraging them to describe their thoughts at the time of the event, and normalizing their anxiety reactions by reminding them that they have just been through an event that causes extreme distress for most people (Mitchell & Bray, 1990). A promising approach for people who have been sexually assaulted (a topic covered at greater length in Chapter 14) is a cognitive-behavioural strategy that involves, in combination, exposing patients to trauma-related cues in imagination, teaching them relaxation, and helping them think differently about what happened (e.g., to not blame themselves) (Foa et al., 1995).

As with the other anxiety disorders examined so far, the key to treating PTSD is exposure to thoughts and images of the frightening event (Keane, 1998). This common thread is found in a variety of treatment approaches for this disorder. Before any kind of exposure is attempted, however, therapists are advised to be sensitive to the typical aftermath of a traumatic experience, regardless of the specific cause (Keane et al., 1994). Common reactions include lack of trust, a frightening belief that the world is very dangerous and threatening (Janoff-Bulman, 1992), and maladaptive strategies for coping with the extreme stress, such as substance abuse (Keane & Wolfe, 1990). It can also be helpful to educate patients about the nature of PTSD and the kinds of symptoms most people experience (sleeplessness, being easily startled, depression, alienation from friends and loved ones, etc.). Such knowledge can provide a context for what the patients might be experiencing and reassure them that they are not losing their mind (Keane et al., 1994).

During World War II, "combat-exhausted" soldiers were often treated by narcosynthesis (Grinker & Spiegel, 1944), a procedure that might be considered a drug-assisted catharsis à la Breuer. A soldier was sedated with an intravenous injection of sodium pentothal, enough to cause extreme drowsiness. The therapist then stated in a matter-of-fact voice that the soldier was on the battlefield, in the front lines, and if necessary and possible, the therapist mentioned circumstances of the particular battle. The patient usually began to recall, often with intense emotion, frightening events that had perhaps been forgotten. The actual trauma was relived and even acted out by the patient. As the patient gradually

Twenty-six miners lost their lives in an explosion at the Westray Mine in Stellarton, Nova Scotia, in May 1992. The disaster triggered acute stress and PTSD disorders in many of the people involved with those who died. Westray provides a good example of the importance of community response to disasters and the importance of social support in reducing the risk of developing the disorder.

returned to the waking state, the therapist continued to encourage discussion of the terrifying events in the hope that the patient would realize that they were in the past and no longer a threat. In this fashion, a synthesis of the past horror with the patient's present life was sought (Cameron & Magaret, 1951).

Controlled research on the treatment of PTSD has accelerated in recent years as more attention has been focused on the aftermath of such traumas as natural disasters, rape, child abuse, combat and terrorist attacks. Recent work in cognitive behaviour therapy provides some findings based on studies that employed careful assessment, details of treatment, and appropriate control groups.

The basic principle of exposure-based behaviour therapy is that fears are best reduced or eliminated by having the person confront in some fashion whatever he or she most ardently wishes to avoid. A growing body of evidence indicates that structured exposure to trauma-related events, sometimes in imagination, as in systematic desensitization, contributes something beyond the benefits of medication, social support, or a safe therapeutic environment (Foa & Meadows, 1997; Keane, 1995).

In making the diagnosis of PTSD, we almost always know what triggered the problem, so the decision is a tactical one—that is, how to expose the frightened patient to what is fearsome. Many techniques have been employed. In one well-designed study involving Vietnam veterans suffering PTSD, for example, Terence Keane and his associates compared a no-treatment control group with a group that was subjected to imaginal flooding, in which patients visualized fearsome, trauma-related scenes for extended periods of time. The researchers found significantly greater reductions in depression, anxiety, re-experiencing of the trauma, startle reactions, and irritability in the veterans in the imaginal procedure (Keane et al., 1989). Conducting such exposure therapy is difficult for both patient and therapist, however, as it requires detailed review of the traumatizing events. As pointed out by Keane et al. (1992), patients may become temporarily worse in the initial stages of therapy, and therapists themselves may become upset when they hear about the horrifying events that their patients experienced.

How does exposure work? We have already discussed the possibility that it leads to the extinction of the fear response. But it may also change the meaning that stimuli have for people. This cognitive view has been elaborated by Edna Foa and her colleagues in a number of studies and theoretical papers. They emphasize the corrective aspects of exposure to what is feared:

> Exposure promotes symptom reduction by allowing patients to realize that, contrary to their mistaken ideas: (a) being in objectively safe situations that remind one of the trauma is not dangerous; (b) remembering the trauma is not equivalent to experiencing it again; (c) anxiety does not remain indefinitely in the presence of feared situations or memories, but rather it decreases even without avoidance or escape; and (d) experiencing anxiety/PTSD symptoms does not lead to loss of control. (Foa & Meadows, 1997, p. 462)

However exposure works, there is no doubt about its effectiveness in reducing the effects of trauma, including that arising from sexual assault.

In 1989, Shapiro (1989) began to promulgate an approach to treating trauma called Eye Movement Desensitization and Reprocessing (EMDR). This method is purported to be extremely rapid—often requiring only one or two sessions—and more effective than the standard exposure procedures just reviewed. In this procedure, the patient imagines a situation related to his or her problem, such as the sight of a horrible automobile accident. Keeping the image in mind, the patient follows with his or her eyes the therapist's fingers as the therapist moves them back and forth about a foot in front of the patient. This process continues for a minute or so or until the patient reports that the horror of the image has been reduced. Then the therapist has the patient verbalize whatever negative thoughts are going through his or her mind, again while following the moving target with his or her eyes. Finally, the therapist encourages the patient to think a more positive thought, such as "I can deal with this," and this thought, too, is held in mind as the patient follows the therapist's moving fingers.

A great deal of controversy surrounds this technique (or techniques, since the specifics of the therapy have been changing since it was initially proposed), and opinions are polarized in ways not often found in science. On the one hand are EMDR proponents who argue that combining eye movements with thoughts about the feared event promotes rapid deconditioning or reprocessing of the aversive stimulus (e.g., Shapiro, 1995, 1999). On the other hand are numerous studies that show that eye movements do not add anything to what may be happening as a result of exposure itself (e.g., Cahill, Carrigan, & Frueh, 1999), as well as a recent study showing that exposure therapy appears to be more effective than EMDR (Taylor et al., 2003). Moreover, claims of EMDR's effectiveness rest on experiments that have major methodological shortcomings (cf. Lohr, Tolin, & Lilienfeld, 1998; Rosen, 1999). In addition, the theorizing surrounding EMDR has been criticized as inconsistent with what is known about both the psychology and the neuroscientific foundations of learning and brain function (e.g., Keane, 1998; Lohr et al., 1998). However the many questions surrounding EMDR are resolved, no one disputes the important role played by exposure to memories or images of traumatic events, and the well-established role of exposure to aversive stimuli is probably the key ingredient in whatever efficacy EMDR has.

Another cognitive-behavioural approach conceptualizes PTSD more generally as an extreme stress reaction and therefore as amenable to the kind of multi-faceted approach to stress management described in Chapter 8, which entails relaxation, rational-emotive therapy, and training in problem-solving. Among the problems addressed within this broader framework is the anger felt by many patients with PTSD, especially those who have seen combat. Assertion training and couples therapy are often warranted to help patients deal with their anger more appropriately (Keane et al., 1992).

Donald Meichenbaum (see Canadian Contribution 2.1) developed a comprehensive CBT therapist's manual to be used in the treatment of adults with PTSD (Meichenbaum, 1994). Consistent with his recent clinical interests, it incorporates a constructive-narrative approach to PTSD. Narrative construction relies on the belief that people construct and reconstruct "accounts" or "stories" about important events in their lives. They develop these stories about significant life events in order to infuse them with some coherence and meaning. Thus, according to Meichenbaum (1994, p. 103), "People make meaning of their lives by organizing key events into stories which they incorporate into a larger life narrative." These client stories are considered to be open to change, and treatment for people with PTSD targets, in part, the meanings attached to traumatic events. The therapist works collaboratively with the client in the constructive-narrative process, intervening to highlight strengths and resilience and foster "survivorship," coping processes, and competence for future adaptive behaviour and thought: "You mean, in spite of this horrific event, you got through it?"; "How did you manage to do it?"; and, "Where did this courage come from?" Meichenbaum's goal is to have the client arrive at solutions about how to change. Through their actions, clients write a new "script," a new, more adaptive narrative. They "re-story" their lives.

In an interview with Michael Hoyt, Meichenbaum described the case of a woman who was home alone with her 10-year-old daughter (Meichenbaum, 2003). The woman woke up fearing that a robber had broken into the home. In a panicked state, she grabbed a pistol that her husband had given her, ran to protect her daughter, but accidentally discharged the gun and killed the little girl. What can you say or do in therapy? Meichenbaum responded, in part, with the following:

> I listened sympathetically to the tale of the horrendous events. And eventually asked the mother, "What did you see in your daughter that made your relationship with her so special? Please share with me the nature of the loss." In fact, I asked the bereaved mother to bring to therapy a picture album of her daughter and to review with me the special qualities of her daughter. The picture album permitted the client to tell the story of her relationship with her daughter in some developmental (time-line) context, and thus not delimit her memories to only the time of the shooting, which she played over and over again, with the accompanying narrative of, "if only"; "Why didn't I tell my husband I didn't want to own a gun?"; "Why my daughter?"... Moreover, the review of the picture album provided the opportunity to query further what she saw in her daughter, and, in turn, what did her daughter see in her.
>
> Following this exchange, I asked the client, "If your daughter, whom you described as being 'wise beyond her years' were here now, what advice, if any, might she have to help you get through this difficult period?" Fortunately, with some guidance I was able to help the client generate some suggestions that her daughter might have offered. I then noted, "I can now understand why you described your daughter as 'wise beyond her years.' "She does sound special." Moreover, if the client followed through on her notion to commit suicide in order to "stop the emotional pain," what would happen to the memory of her daughter? Did she feel that she owed her daughter more? Like many victims of traumatic events, this client found a mission in order to cope with her distress. She undertook the task of educating parents about the dangers of keeping guns in their homes. She became an expert on the incidence of accidental homicides and developed a foundation named after her daughter

designed to decrease the likelihood that this could happen to other children. She felt that if she could save one other child, then her daughter would not have died in vain.

(http://www.behavior.net/column/meichenbaum/index.html; January 28, 2001)

Although Meichenbaum advocates a constructive-narrative perspective, it is important to note that he also incorporates the full clinical array of cognitive-behavioural strategies. As is the case with all multi-component therapies, there is a need for empirical investigations to demonstrate the utility of the different treatment components in Meichenbaum's complex program for the treatment of PTSD.

Horowitz's (1988, 1990) psychodynamic approach has much in common with the cognitive-behavioural approach, for he encourages patients to discuss the trauma and otherwise expose themselves to the events that led to the PTSD. But Horowitz emphasizes the manner in which the trauma interacts with a patient's pretrauma personality, and the treatment he proposes also has much in common with other psychoanalytic approaches, including discussions of defences and analysis of transference reactions by the patient. This complex therapy awaits empirical verification. The few controlled studies conducted thus far lend a small degree of empirical support to its effectiveness (Foa & Meadows, 1997).

Finally, a range of psychoactive drugs have been used with PTSD patients, including antidepressants and tranquilizers (a summary of drugs used in treating all the anxiety disorders can be found in Table 6.5). Sometimes medication is used to deal with conditions comorbid with PTSD, such as depression; improvement in the depression can contribute to improvement in PTSD regardless of how the PTSD itself is treated (by a psychological intervention of the kinds just described, for example [Marshall et al., 1994]). Some modest successes have been reported for antidepressants, especially the serotonin reuptake inhibitors (e.g., Yehuda, Marshall, & Giller, 1998).

Whatever the specific mode of intervention, experts in PTSD agree that social support is critical. Sometimes finding ways to lend support to others can help the giver as well as the receiver (Hobfoll et al., 1991). Belonging to a religious group, having family, friends, or fellow traumatized individuals listen nonjudgmentally to one's fears and recollections of the trauma, and having other ways of feeling that one belongs and that others wish to help ease the pain may spell the difference between posttraumatic stress and posttraumatic stress disorder.

Table 6.5

Summary of Drugs Used to Treat Anxiety Disorders

Drug Category	Generic Name	Trade Name	Uses
Benzodiazepines	Diazepam, alprazolam, lorazepam, clonazepam	Valium, Xanax, Ativan, Clonapam	GAD, PTSD, panic disorder
Monoamine oxidase inhibitors	Phenelzine	Nardil	Social phobia
Selective serotonin reuptake inhibitors	Fluoxetine, sertraline, fluvoxamine	Prozac, Zoloft, Luvox	Social phobia, panic disorder OCD, PTSD
Tricyclic antidepressants	Imipramine, clomipramine	Tofranil, Anafranil	Panic disorder, GAD, OCD, PTSD
Azapirones	Buspirone	BuSpar	GAD, panic disorder, OCD

SUMMARY

- People with anxiety disorders feel an overwhelming apprehension that seems unwarranted. DSM-IV lists six principal diagnoses: phobic disorders, panic disorder, generalized anxiety disorder, obsessive-compulsive disorder, posttraumatic stress disorder, and acute stress disorder.
- Phobias are intense, unreasonable fears that disrupt the life of an otherwise normal person. They are relatively common. Social phobia is fear of social situations in which the person may be scrutinized by other people. Specific phobias are fears of animals, situations, the natural environment, and blood and injections. The psychoanalytic view of phobias is that they are a defence against repressed conflicts. Behavioural theorists have several ideas of how phobias are acquired—through classical conditioning, the pairing of an innocuous object or situation with an innately painful event; through

operant conditioning, whereby a person is rewarded for avoidance; through modelling, imitating the fear and avoidance of others; and through cognition, by making a catastrophe of a social mishap that could be construed in a less negative fashion. But not all people who have such experiences develop a phobia. It may be that a genetically transmitted physiological diathesis—lability of the autonomic nervous system—predisposes certain people to acquire phobias.

- A patient with panic disorder has sudden, inexplicable, and periodic attacks of intense anxiety. Panic attacks sometimes lead to fear and avoidance of being outside one's home, a condition known as agoraphobia. A number of laboratory manipulations (e.g., having the patient hyperventilate or breathe air with a high concentration of carbon dioxide) can induce panic attacks in those with the disorder. Panic disorder patients ruminate about serious illnesses, both physical and mental; they fear their own physical sensations and then amplify them until they are overwhelmed.
- In generalized anxiety disorder, sometimes called free-floating anxiety, the individual's life is beset with virtualy constant tension, apprehension, and worry. Psychoanalytic theory regards the source as an unconscious conflict between the ego and id impulses. Some behavioural theorists assume that with adequate assessment, this pervasive anxiety can be pinned down to a finite set of anxiety-provoking circumstances, thereby likening it to a phobia and making it more treatable. A sense of helplessness can also cause people to be anxious in a wide range of situations. Biological approaches focus on the therapeutic effects of the benzodiazepines and how they might enhance the activity of the neurotransmitter GABA.
- People with obsessive-compulsive disorder have intrusive, unwanted thoughts and feel pressured to engage in stereotyped rituals lest they be overcome by frightening levels of anxiety. This disorder can become disabling, interfering not only with the life of the person who experiences the difficulties but also with the lives of those close to that person. Psychoanalytic theory posits strong id impulses that are under faulty and inadequate ego control. In behavioural accounts, compulsions are considered learned avoidance responses. Obsessions may be related to stress and an attempt to inhibit these unwanted thoughts.
- Posttraumatic stress disorder is diagnosed in some people who have experienced a traumatic event that would evoke extreme distress in most individuals. It is marked by symptoms such as re-experiencing the trauma, increased arousal, and emotional numbing.
- There are many therapies for anxiety disorders. Psychoanalytic treatment tries to lift repression so that childhood conflicts can be resolved; direct alleviation of problems is discouraged. In contrast, behaviour therapists employ a range of procedures, such as systematic desensitization and modelling, to encourage exposure to what is feared. Preventing people with compulsions from performing their rituals is a useful, although initially arduous, technique.
- Perhaps the most widely employed treatments are anxiolytic and other drugs dispensed by medical practitioners. Drugs are subject to abuse, however, and their long-term use may have untoward and still inadequately understood side effects. Weaning a person from reliance on a chemical that reduces anxiety is problematic because many people become physically dependent on such drugs. Also, gains from using the drugs are usually lost when use is discontinued.

KEY TERMS

acute stress disorder (p. 184)
agoraphobia (p. 166)
anxiety (p. 157)
anxiety disorders (p. 157)
anxiety sensitivity (p. 170)
anxiolytics (p. 165)
autonomic lability (p. 162)
compulsion (p. 175)
depersonalization (p. 165)
derealization (p. 165)
flooding (p. 164)
generalized anxiety disorder (GAD) (p. 172)
in vivo exposure (p. 163)
obsessions (p. 175)
obsessive-compulsive disorder (OCD) (p. 175)
panic disorder (p. 165)
phobia (p. 158)
posttraumatic stress disorder (PTSD) (p. 183)
social phobias (p. 158)
specific phobias (p. 158)
vicarious learning (p. 160)
virtual reality exposure (p. 164)

Reflections: Past, Present, and Future

- In the previous chapter, you were asked to design a longitudinal study of risk factors for the development of anxiety disorders. Now that you have learned more about factors supported by empirical research, how would you redesign your long-term study? What risk factors would you retain? What new risk factors would you add to the design?
- Recall the quotations at the outset of this chapter. Assume that you are charged with the responsibility of designing a program to instill "courage" in elementary school children and to help them avoid "defeat." What would your program look like? How would you implement it? How would you evaluate the possible long-term effects?
- How does the treatment of PTSD induced by military conflict in the modern era compare with the treatment of shell shock in World War I veterans? What specific components used today should be most effective relative to earlier treatment approaches?
- Based on your evaluation of research on the causes, consequences, and management of PTSD, design a comprehensive program to be used to help people who developed, or will develop, PTSD (and other psychological problems) as a consequence of the terrorist attacks on the United States on September 11, 2001. (See Chapters 15 and 17 for a further discussion of the psychological consequences of, and appropriate reactions to, these horrific acts of terrorism.)
- Anxiety and stress are relevant to our understanding of many of the other disorders discussed in this book (e.g., somatoform and dissociative disorders, psychophysiological disorders, and schizophrenia). As you read about the different disorders, think about how you would adapt the treatment strategies outlined in this chapter for use with other disorders.

7 chapter

Somatoform and Dissociative Disorders

"If anything is sacred the human body is sacred."
—Walt Whitman, *I Sing the Body Electric*

"Every time I put another piece of this together, I can see more of what I have lost and have another wave of grief."
—A Winnipeg-area patient with a dissociative disorder, expressing the complex emotions associated with the recovery process (from Wakeman, 2002, p. 121)

"It is quite evident in talking to the patient that multiple personality is a disorder of the brain, not the result of witchcraft on the one hand, nor a vulgar put-up-job in search of publicity on the other. The research won't flourish if everyone is skeptical of it. It will flourish if it is recognized as an important clinical problem and equally important, a new avenue to the study of the mind."
—Donald O. Hebb, eminent Canadian psychologist (as cited by Klein, Doane, & Curtis, 1994, p. 3)

Mimmo Paladino, *Viandante, 1983*
oil, wood, plaster with papier mache on canvas mounted on wood, 320.0 cm (diameter),
ART GALLERY OF ONTARIO, TORONTO
Gift from the Volunteer Committee Fund, 1984

A 25-YEAR-OLD single female was referred by a psychiatrist who suspected the presence of MPD. Originally, he had thought drug and alcohol abuse were the reasons for her drastic personality changes and amnesic episodes. When seen, she was fearful for her own life, for there were homicidal threats written in lipstick on her walls. These were written at a time when she was in her apartment alone with the doors locked. She had a history of childhood sexual abuse and admitted to many episodes of amnesia, finding herself in locations to which she had no memory of travelling. Her boyfriend told her that at times she behaved and cried like a child and at other times she was violent and aggressive. Once she attacked him and fractured his jaw. With the use of hypnotic trance or guided imagery (Fraser, 1991), she readily dissociated into different personality patterns. Besides the present personality, which was very passive and introverted, she had within her a 6-year old male, a 5-year-old female, two 20-year-old sisters, a nonhuman state called "The Animal," and an 80-year-old grandmother.

These various personalities had "shared" her body for many years. Her knowledge of them was strictly through the reports of others, which generally corresponded to her periods of memory gaps. She admitted that she had heard inner voices of varying ages for a few years, but for the most part had tried to ignore them (Fraser, 1994, pp. 146–147).

Somatoform and dissociative disorders, our focus for this chapter, are related to anxiety disorders in that, in early versions of the DSM, all these disorders were subsumed under the heading of neuroses because anxiety was considered the predominant underlying factor in each case. Starting with DSM-III, classification came to be based on observable behaviour, not on presumed etiology. In the anxiety disorders, signs of anxiety are obvious, but anxiety is not necessarily observable in the somatoform and dissociative disorders. In **somatoform disorders**, the individual complains of bodily symptoms that suggest a physical defect or dysfunction—sometimes rather dramatic in nature—but for which no physiological basis can be found. In **dissociative disorders**, the individual experiences disruptions of consciousness, memory, and identity, as illustrated in the opening case study. The onset of both classes of disorders is typically related to some stressful experience, and the two classes sometimes co-occur. We will examine the somatoform and dissociative disorders in this chapter, focusing in more depth on those disorders about which more is known. As before, we will look at symptoms, etiology, and therapies throughout the discussion.

SOMATOFORM DISORDERS

As noted in Chapter 1, *soma* means "body." In somatoform disorders, psychological problems take a physical form. The physical symptoms of somatoform disorders have no known physiological explanation and are not under voluntary control. They are thought to be linked to psychological factors, presumably anxiety, and are assumed to be psychologically caused. In this section, we look at two somatoform disorders: conversion disorder and somatization disorder. But first we consider briefly three DSM-IV categories of somatoform disorders about which less information is available: pain disorder, body dysmorphic disorder, and hypochondriasis. (A summary of the somatoform disorders appears in Table 7.1.)

Table 7.1

Summary of Somatoform Disorders

Disorder	Description
Pain disorder	Psychological factors play a significant role in the onset and maintenance of pain.
Body dysmorphic disorder	Preoccupation with imagined or exaggerated defects in physical appearance.
Hypochondriasis	Preoccupation with fears of having a serious illness.
Conversion disorder	Sensory or motor symptoms without any physiological cause.
Somatization disorder	Recurrent, multiple physical complaints that have no biological basis.

In **pain disorder**, the person experiences pain that causes significant distress and impairment; psychological factors are viewed as playing an important role in the onset, maintenance, and severity of the pain. The patient may be unable to work and may become dependent on painkillers or tranquilizers. The pain may have a temporal relation to some conflict or stress, or it may allow the individual to avoid some unpleasant activity and to secure attention and sympathy not otherwise available. Accurate diagnosis is difficult because the subjective experience of pain is always a psychologically influenced phenomenon; that is, pain is not a simple sensory experience, as are vision and hearing. Therefore, deciding when a pain becomes a somatoform pain is difficult. Some differentiation may be achieved, however, in the way in which pain is described by patients with somatoform disorder as compared with descriptions by patients whose pain is clearly linked to a physical problem. Patients with physically based pain localize it more specifically, give more detailed sensory descriptions of their pain, and link their pain more clearly to situations that increase or decrease it (Adler et al., 1997). (Therapies for managing pain are discussed in Chapter 8.)

With body dysmorphic disorder, a person is preoccupied with an imagined or exaggerated defect in appearance, frequently in the face—for example, facial wrinkles, excess facial hair, or the shape or size of the nose. Women tend also to focus on the skin, hips, breasts, and legs, whereas men are more inclined to believe they are too short, that their penises are too small, or that they have too much body hair (Perugi et al., 1997). Some patients with the disorder may spend hours each day checking on their defect, looking at themselves in mirrors. Others take steps to avoid being reminded of the defect by eliminating mirrors from their homes or camouflaging the defect, for example by wearing very loose clothing (Albertini & Phillips, 1999). These concerns are distressing and sometimes lead to frequent consultations with plastic surgeons. Unfortunately, plastic surgery does little to allay patients' concerns (Phillips et al., 1993). Body dysmorphic disorder occurs mostly among women, typically begins in late adolescence, and is frequently comorbid with depression and social phobia (Veale et al., 1996).

As with pain disorder, subjective factors and matters of taste play a role. When, for example, does one's vanity become a body dysmorphic disorder? A survey (Fitts et al., 1989) found that 70 percent of students indicated at least some dissatisfaction with their appearance, with a higher figure for women than for men. Determining when these perceived defects become psychological disorders is difficult indeed. How much distress does the condition have to produce? Social and cultural factors surely play a role in how a person determines whether he or she is attractive, as they do with the eating disorders discussed in Chapter 9.

Actress Uma Thurman, star of *Kill Bill Volumes 1 & 2*, admitted in 2001 that she suffers from body dysmorphic disorder.

Despite there having been systematic studies of body dysmorphic disorder, it is unclear whether its status as a specific diagnosis is warranted. For example, people who are excessively preoccupied with their appearance and frequently check their looks might be diagnosed with OCD (McKay, Neziroglu, & Yarayura-Tobias, 1997). Others may hold a belief about a defect so unrelated to reality as to suggest a delusional disorder (Hollander, Cohen, & Simeon, 1993). Preoccupation with imagined defects in physical appearance may therefore not be a disorder itself, but a *symptom* that can occur in several disorders.

Hypochondriasis is a somatoform disorder in which individuals are preoccupied with persistent fears of having a serious disease, despite medical reassurance to the contrary. The disorder typically begins in early adulthood and tends to have a chronic course. In one study, over 60 percent of diagnosed cases still had the disorder when followed up five years later (Barsky et al., 1998). Patients with this little-used diagnosis are frequent consumers of medical services and are likely to have mood or anxiety disorders (Noyes, 1993). The theory is that they overreact to ordinary physical sensations and minor abnormalities, such as irregular heartbeat, sweating, occasional coughing, a sore spot, stomach ache, seeing these as evidence for their beliefs. Consistent with this idea, when asked to give a possible reason for a physical sensation, such as feeling that one's heart is pounding, people with high scores on a measure of hypochondriasis are more likely than others to attribute the feeling to an illness (MacLeod, Haynes, & Sensky, 1998). Similarly, patients with hypochondriasis make catastrophic interpretations of symptoms, such as believing that a red blotch on the skin is skin cancer (Rief, Hiller, & Margraf, 1998).

Asmundson, Taylor, Wright, and Cox (2001) cited a newspaper account of the compelling case study of James V. to support their observation that people who actually experience abnormally intense sensations may be particularly vulnerable to hypochondriasis.

> For reasons no one understood, Mr. V felt as if a million bugs crawled over him. To quiet his torment, he scratched himself so tenaciously that he ripped open his skin, even though he fell within the range of what is considered average intelligence and he was aware of the damage he was inflicting. ... Heavily scarred from his assaults ... [he] had a high tolerance for pain and would break his bones and tear off his fingernails as well as scratch himself. (Globe and Mail [Toronto], Saturday, October 30, 1999, A21, as cited by Asmundson et al., 2001, pp. 368-369).

Sadly, it was noted that Mr. V died at the young age of 25 from infections of the blood and spine.

In a review of prevalence studies, Asmundson, Taylor, Sevgur, and Cox (2001) concluded that hypochondriasis is evident in about 5 percent of the general population and is about as common as other psychiatric disorders. They noted that prevalence rates are higher in studies that selectively restrict their sample to individuals presenting at medical clinics.

Hypochondriasis is not well differentiated from somatization disorder, which is also characterized by a long history of complaints of medical illnesses (Noyes et al., 1994). Also, hypochondriasis often co-occurs with anxiety and mood disorders (Noyes et al., 1997).

Contemporary researchers focus on health anxiety rather than hypochondriasis per se. Health anxiety has been defined as "health-related fears and beliefs, based on interpretations, or perhaps more often, *misinterpretations*, of bodily signs and symptoms as being indicative of serious illness" (Asmundson, Taylor, Sevgur, & Cox, 2001, p. 4). Health anxiety is not limited to hypochondriasis but can also be linked with anxiety and mood disorders. According to Asmundson et al. (2001), health anxiety would be present in both hypochondriasis and an illness phobia. Whereas hypochondriasis is a fear of *having an illness*, an illness phobia is a fear of *contracting an illness*.

The Illness Attitudes Scale (IAS) by Kellner (1986) is one self-report measure that is used commonly by researchers to assess health anxiety. The IAS is intended to be a nine-factor scale, but according to Stewart and Watt (2001), recent factor analyses suggest that the IAS consists reliably of four factors: (1) worry about illness and pain (i.e., illness fears); (2) disease conviction (i.e., illness beliefs); (3) health habits (i.e., safety-seeking behaviours); and (4) symptom interference with lifestyle (i.e., disruptive effects). The IAS was used in a study by Cox, Borger, Asmundson, and Taylor (2000) to confirm a link between health anxiety and trait neuroticism. Indeed, a general neurotic syndrome is regarded as a contributing factor in the etiology of health anxiety along with more specific factors such as cognitive mechanisms (Asmundson, Taylor, Wright, & Cox, 2001).

Cognitive factors are featured in the model of health anxiety outlined by Salkovskis and Warwick (2001) presented in Figure 7.1. This model has four contributing factors: (1) a critical precipitating incident; (2) a previous experience of illness and related medical factors; (3) the presence of inflexible or negative cognitive assumptions (i.e., believing strongly that unexplained bodily changes are always a sign of serious illness); and (4) the severity of anxiety. This latter, the severity of anxiety, is a function of two factors that will increase anxiety and two that will decrease it. Health anxiety will increase multiplicatively as a function of related increases in (1) the perceived likelihood or probability of illness and (2) the perceived cost, awfulness, and burden of illness. Health anxiety will decrease as a function of (1) the perceived ability to cope and (2) the perceived presence of rescue factors (i.e., the availability and perceived effectiveness of medical help).

We turn now to a discussion of the symptoms of conversion disorder and somatization disorder and then to theories of etiology and therapies.

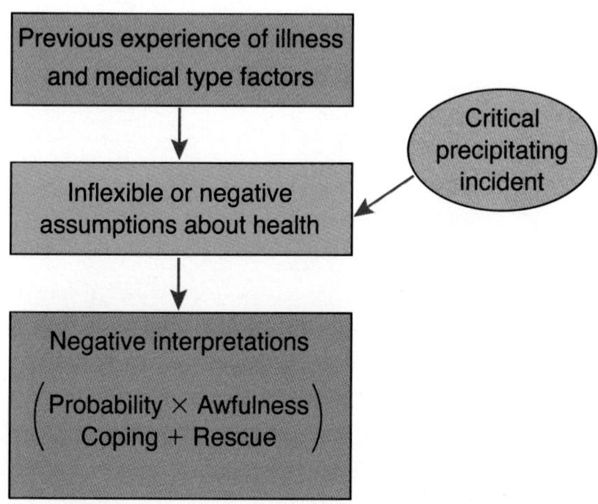

Source: "Making Sense of Hypochondriasis: A Cognitive Model of Health Activity," Paul M. Salkovskis and Hilary M.C. Warwick, *Health Anxiety*, eds. G.J.G Asmundson, S. Taylor & B.J. Cox, 2001. @ John Wiley & Sons Limited. Reproduced with permission.

Figure 7.1 Cognitive model of the development of health anxiety.

CONVERSION DISORDER

In **conversion disorder**, physiologically normal people experience sensory or motor symptoms, such as a sudden loss of vision or paralysis, suggesting an illness related to neurological damage of some sort, although the body organs and nervous system are found to be fine. Sufferers may experience paralysis of arms or legs; seizures and coordination disturbances; a sensation of prickling, tingling, or creeping on the skin; insensitivity to pain; or the loss or impairment of sensations, called **anesthesias**. Vision may be seriously impaired; the person may become partially or completely blind or have tunnel vision. *Aphonia*, loss of the voice and all but whispered speech, and *anosmia*, loss or impairment of the sense of smell, are other conversion disorders.

The psychological nature of conversion symptoms is demonstrated by the fact that they appear suddenly in stressful situations, allowing the individual to avoid some activity or responsibility or to receive badly wanted attention. The term *conversion* derived originally from Freud, who thought that the energy of a repressed instinct was diverted into sensory-motor channels and blocked functioning. Thus, anxiety and psychological conflict were believed to be *converted* into physical symptoms.

George Fraser (1994), while at the Royal Ottawa Hospital, reported two cases of conversion disorder that involved an apparent loss of eyesight:

> Both were young male military recruits who had been "strongly encouraged" to join the military by relatives. One of the cases was referred to psychiatry with a 2-week history of "blindness." He had been fully investigated neurologically and ophthalomologically. No pathology was found. All eye reflexes were normal, yet despite efforts to catch him in an unguarded moment, suggesting malingering, he persisted with his blindness. He had even sustained bruising by bumping into objects. History revealed his loss of vision occurred suddenly while doing combat manoeuvres on the bayonet range. Interestingly, he stated, "I just couldn't see myself killing people." He feared telling his parents that he was terrified to be in military life. After confirming the diagnosis and the cause, I told him that he would be released from military services, but it was only with hypnosis (one session, as was the case with the other soldier) that he immediately regained his vision. Also he was able to visually describe accurately all the locations he had been to during the 2 weeks of conversion blindness. (Fraser, 1994, p. 138)

The two military men described by Fraser suffered from a form of conversion disorder involving "hysterical" blindness. The cases illustrate the role that stress plays in the development of conversion disorders. **Hysteria**, the term originally used to describe what are now known as conversion disorders, has a long history, dating back to the earliest writings on abnormal behaviour. Hippocrates considered it an affliction limited solely to women and due to the wandering of the uterus through the body. (The Greek word *hystera* means "womb.") Presumably, the wandering uterus symbolized the longing for the production of a child.

Conversion symptoms usually develop in adolescence or early adulthood, typically after undergoing life stress. An episode may end abruptly, but sooner or later the disorder is likely to return, either in its original form or with a symptom of a different nature and site. Prevalence of conversion disorder is less than 1 percent, and more women than men are given the diagnosis (Singh & Lee, 1997). During both world wars, however, a large number of males developed conversion-like difficulties in combat (Ziegler, Imboden, & Meyer, 1960). Conversion disorder is also frequently comorbid with other Axis I diagnoses, such as, depression and substance abuse, and with personality disorders, notably borderline and histrionic personality disorders (Binzer, Anderson, & Kullgren, 1996; Rechlin, Loew, & Jorashky, 1997).

In making diagnoses, it is important to distinguish a conversion paralysis or sensory dysfunction from similar problems that have a true neurological basis (see Figure 7.2). Sometimes this task is easy, as when the paralysis does not make anatomical sense. A classic example is *glove anesthesia*, a rare syndrome in which the individual experiences little or no sensation in the part of the hand that would be covered by a glove (see Figure 7.2). For years this was the textbook illustration of anatomical nonsense because

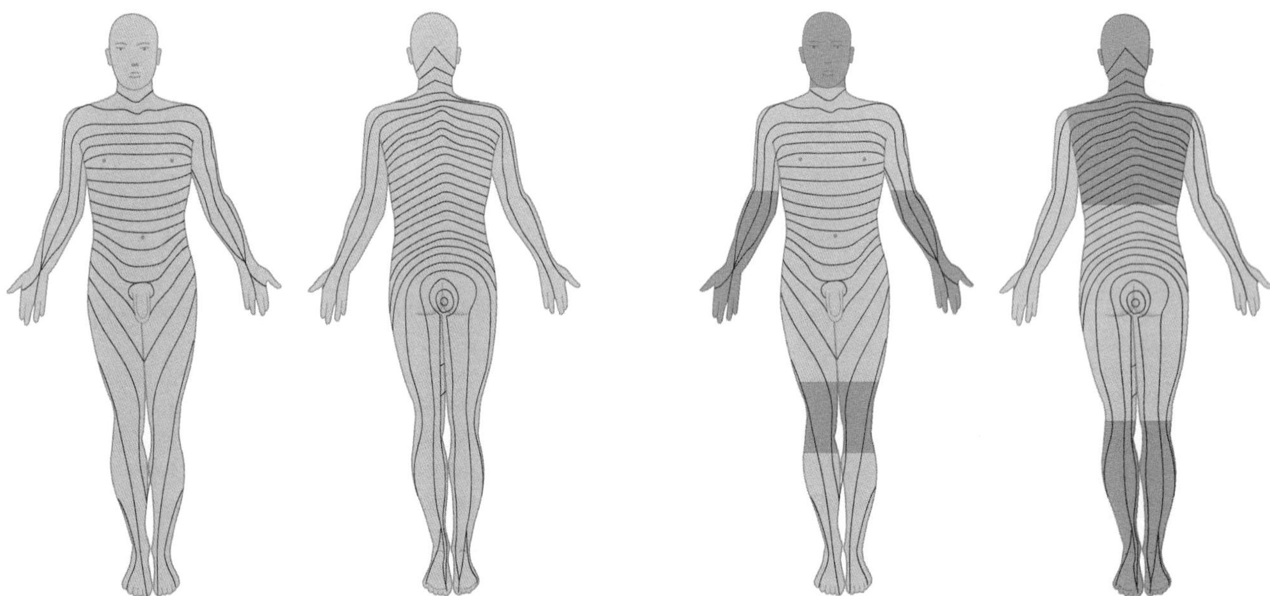

Figure 7.2 Hysterical anesthesias can be distinguished from neurological dysfunctions. The patterns of neural innervation are shown on the left. Typical areas of anesthesias in hysterical patients are superimposed on the right. The hysterical anesthesias do not make anatomical sense. Adapted from an original painting by Frank H. Netter, M.D. From *The CIBA Collection of Medical Illustrations*, copyright (c) by CIBA Pharmaceutical Company, Division of CIBA-GEIGY Corporation.

the nerves here run continuously from the hand up the arm. Yet, even in this case, it now appears that misdiagnosis can occur. A more recently recognized disease, *carpal tunnel syndrome*, can produce symptoms similar to those of glove anesthesia. Nerves in the wrist run through a tunnel formed by the wrist bones and membranes. The tunnel can become swollen and may pinch the nerves, leading to tingling, numbness, and pain in the hand.

Since the majority of paralyses, analgesias, and sensory failures do have biological causes, true neurological problems may sometimes be misdiagnosed as conversion disorders. Studies conducted during the 1960s indicated that on follow-up many patients diagnosed with conversion disorder may have been misdiagnosed. One of these studies found that nine years after diagnosis an alarming number—60 percent—of these individuals had either died or developed symptoms of physical disease! A high proportion had diseases of the central nervous system (Slater & Glithero, 1965). Fortunately, with technological advances in detecting brain disease (such as the MRI), the percentage of apparent conversion disorder patients who subsequently develop a neurological problem now seems to be much lower (Mace & Trimble, 1996). (See Focus on Discovery 7.1 for other diagnostic issues with this disorder.)

focus on discovery/7.1

Malingering and Factitious Disorder

In the case of conversion disorder described above, Fraser (1994) alluded to the fact that one diagnostic problem with conversion disorder is the difficulty of distinguishing it from **malingering**, listed in DSM-IV as a condition that may be a focus of clinical attention. In malingering, an individual fakes an incapacity in order to avoid a responsibility, such as work or military duty, or to achieve some goal, such as being awarded a large insurance settlement. Malingering is diagnosed when the conversion-like symptoms are determined to be under voluntary control, which is not thought to be the case in true conversion disorders.

In trying to discriminate conversion reactions from malingering, clinicians may attempt to determine whether the symptoms have been consciously or unconsciously adopted. This means of resolving the issue is dubious, for it is difficult, if not impossible, to know with any degree of certainty whether behaviour is consciously or unconsciously motivated. One aspect of behaviour that can sometimes help distinguish the two disorders is known as **la belle indifférence**, characterized by a relative lack of concern or a blasé attitude toward the symptoms that is out of keeping with their severity and supposedly long-term consequences. Patients with conversion disorder sometimes demonstrate this behaviour; they also appear willing and eager to talk endlessly and dramatically about their symptoms, but often without the concern one might expect. In contrast, malingerers are likely to be more guarded and cautious, perhaps because they consider interviews a challenge or threat to the success of the lie. But this distinction is not foolproof, for only about one-third of people with conversion disorders show la belle indifférence (Stephens & Kamp, 1962). Furthermore, a stoic attitude is sometimes found among patients with verified medical diseases.

Also related to the disorders we have been discussing is another DSM category, **factitious disorder**. In this disorder, patients intentionally produce physical symptoms (or sometimes psychological ones). They may make up symptoms—for example, reporting acute pain—or inflict injuries on themselves. In contrast to malingering, with factitious disorder the symptoms are less obviously linked to a recognizable goal; the motivation for adopting the physical or psychological symptoms is much less clear. The individual, for some unknown reason, wants to assume the role of patient.

Kathleen Bush is taken into custody, charged with child abuse and fraud for deliberately causing her child's illnesses.

Factitious disorder may also involve a parent creating physical illnesses in a child; in this case, it is called *factitious disorder by proxy* or *Munchausen syndrome by proxy*. In one extreme case, a 7-year-old girl was hospitalized over 150 times and experienced 40 surgeries at a cost of over $2 million. Her mother caused her illnesses by using drugs and even contaminating her feeding tube with faecal material (Time, 1996). The motivation in a case such as this appears to be the need to be regarded as an excellent parent and tireless in seeing to the child's needs. Munchausen syndrome by proxy has received a great deal of public attention in recent years, in part due to public claims by rap singer Eminem. He has stated that he was made ill during his childhood by his mother, who he alleges suffers from Munchausen syndrome by proxy.

While Munchausen syndrome by proxy involves making someone else ill, if someone is making themselves ill, the disorder is simply referred to as Munchausen syndrome. Two recent Canadian cases involved nurses who presented with urinary tract infections, flank pain, and gross hematuria (i.e., blood in the urine). Evidence in both cases suggested that these women had infused blood into their own bladders (Chew, Pace, & Honey, 2002).

Somatization Disorder

In 1859 the French physician Pierre Briquet described a syndrome that first bore his name, Briquet's syndrome, and now, in DSM-IV, is referred to as somatization disorder. The disorder is characterized by recurrent, multiple somatic complaints, with no apparent physical cause, for which medical attention is sought. To meet diagnostic criteria, the person must have

1. four pain symptoms in different locations (e.g., head, back, joint);
2. two gastrointestinal symptoms (e.g., diarrhea, nausea);
3. one sexual symptom other than pain (e.g., indifference to sex, erectile dysfunction); and
4. one pseudoneurological symptom (e.g., those of conversion disorder).

These symptoms, which are more pervasive than the complaints in hypochondriasis, usually cause impairment, particularly regarding work. DSM-IV notes that the specific symptoms of the disorder may vary across cultures. Burning hands or the experience of ants crawling under the skin are more frequent in Asia and Africa, for example, than in North America. The disorder may be more frequent in cultures that de-emphasize the overt display of emotion (Ford, 1995).

Somatization disorder and conversion disorder share many symptoms, and both diagnoses may be applicable to the same patient (e.g., Ford & Folks, 1985). Visits to physicians, sometimes to several simultaneously, are frequent, as is the use of medication. Hospitalization and even surgery are common (Guze, 1967). Menstrual difficulties and sexual indifference are frequent (Swartz et al., 1986). Patients present their complaints in a histrionic, exaggerated fashion or as part of a long, complicated medical history. Many believe that they have been ailing all their lives. Comorbidity is high with anxiety and mood disorders, substance abuse, and several personality disorders (Golding, Smith, & Kashner, 1991; Kirmayer, Robbins, & Paris, 1994).

The lifetime prevalence of somatization disorder is estimated at less than 0.5 percent of the population; it is more frequent among women (Escobar et al., 1987) and among patients in medical treatment. Prevalence is higher in some South American countries and in Puerto Rico (Tomasson, Kent, & Coryell, 1991).

Interpreting cultural differences is not straightforward (Kirmayer & Young, 1998). From a western European perspective, for example, a physical presentation of a psychological problem is sometimes considered somewhat primitive or unsophisticated. But this dualistic distinction between physical and psychological reflects a medical tradition that is not universally accepted (e.g., in Chinese medicine). It is more reasonable to view a person's culture as providing a concept of what distress is and how it should be communicated.

Somatization disorder typically begins in early adulthood (Cloninger et al., 1986). It may not be as stable as the DSM implies, though, for in one recent study, only one-third of patients with somatization disorder still met diagnostic criteria when reassessed 12 months later (Simon & Gureje, 1999). Anxiety and depression are often reported, as are behavioural and interpersonal problems, such as truancy, poor work records, and marital difficulties. Somatization disorder also seems to run in families; it is found in about 20 percent of the first-degree relatives of index cases, that is, individuals diagnosed with somatization disorder (Guze, 1993).

Etiology of Somatoform Disorders

Much of the theorizing in the area of somatoform disorders has been directed solely toward understanding hysteria as originally conceptualized by Freud. Consequently, it has focused on explanations of conversion disorder. Later in this section, we examine psychoanalytic views of conversion disorder and then look at what behavioural, cognitive, and biological theorists have to offer. First, we briefly discuss ideas about the etiology of somatization disorder.

Etiology of Somatization Disorder It has been proposed that patients with somatization disorder are more sensitive to physical sensations, overattend to them, or interpret them catastrophically (Kirmayer et al., 1994; Rief et al., 1998). A behavioural view of somatization disorder holds that the various aches, discomforts, and dysfunctions are the manifestation of unrealistic anxiety about bodily systems. In keeping with the possible role of anxiety, patients with somatization disorder have high levels of cortisol, an indication that they are under stress (Rief et al., 1998). Perhaps the extreme tension of an individual localizes in stomach muscles, resulting in feelings of nausea or in vomiting. Once normal functioning is disrupted, the maladaptive pattern may strengthen because of the attention it receives or the excuses it provides. In a related vein, the reporting of physical symptoms has been seen as a strategy to explain poor performance in evaluative situations. Attributing poor performance to illness is psychologically less threatening than attributing it to some personal failing (Smith, Snyder, & Perkins, 1983).

Psychoanalytic Theory of Conversion Disorder Conversion disorder occupies a central place in psychoanalytic theory, for it offered Freud a clear opportunity to explore the concept of the unconscious. Consider for a moment how you might try to make sense of a patient's report that she awakened one morning with a paralyzed left arm. Your first reaction might be to give her neurological tests to assess possible biological causes of the paralysis. Let us assume that these tests are negative; no evidence of neurological disorder is present. You are now faced with choosing whether to believe or doubt the patient's communication. She could be lying; she may know that her arm is not paralyzed but has decided to fake paralysis to achieve some end. This would be an example of malingering. But what if you believe the patient? Now you are almost forced to consider that unconscious processes are operating. On a conscious level, the patient is telling the truth; she believes that her arm is paralyzed. Only on a level that is not conscious does she know that her arm is actually normal.

In *Studies in Hysteria* (1895/1982), Breuer and Freud proposed that a conversion disorder is caused when a person experiences an event that creates great emotional arousal but the affect is not expressed and the memory of the event is cut off from conscious experience. The specific conversion symptoms were said to be related causally to the traumatic event that preceded them.

Anna O., for example, while watching at the bedside of her seriously ill father, had dropped off into a waking dream with her right arm over the back of her chair. She saw a black snake emerge from the wall and come toward her sick father to bite him. She tried to ward it off, but her right arm had gone to sleep. When she looked at her hand, her fingers turned into little snakes with death's heads. The next day, a bent branch recalled her hallucination of the snake, and at once her right arm became rigidly extended. After that, her arm responded in the same way whenever some object revived her hallucination. Later, when Anna O. fell into her "absences" and took to her own bed, the contracture of her right arm became chronic and extended to paralysis and anesthesia of her right side.

In his later writings, Freud hypothesized that conversion disorder in women is rooted in an unresolved Electra complex. The young female child becomes sexually attached to her father, and if her parents' responses to these feelings are harsh and disapproving, early impulses are repressed. The result is both a preoccupation with sex and at the same time an avoidance of it. At a later period of the person's life, sexual excitement or some event reawakens these repressed impulses, creating anxiety. The anxiety is then transformed or converted into physical symptoms.

A more contemporary psychodynamic interpretation of one form of conversion disorder, hysterical blindness, is based on experimental studies of hysterically blind people whose behaviour on visual tests showed that they were influenced by the stimuli even though they explicitly denied seeing them (Sackeim, Nordlie, & Gur, 1979). Two studies involved teenaged women. The first case, described by Theodor and Mandelcorn (1973), concerned a 16-year-old who had experienced sudden loss of peripheral vision and reported that her visual field had become tubular and constricted. Although a variety of neurological tests had proved negative, the authors wanted to be certain that they were not dealing with a neurological problem, so they arranged a special visual test. A bright, oval target was presented either in the centre or in the periphery of the patient's visual field. On each trial, there was a time interval bounded by the sounding of a buzzer. A target was either illuminated or not during the intervals, and the young woman's task was to report whether a target was present.

When the target was presented in the centre of the visual field, the patient always correctly identified it because she had not reported any loss of central vision. For the peripheral showings of the target, however, she was correct only 30 percent of the time. A person would be expected to be correct 50 percent of the time by chance alone if truly blind in the periphery. Therefore, she had performed significantly worse than would a person who was indeed blind! The clinicians reasoned that she had some awareness of the illuminated stimulus and she wanted, consciously or unconsciously, to preserve her blindness by performing poorly on the test.

The second case, reviewed by Sackeim et al. (1979) and reported by Grosz and Zimmerman (1970), was seemingly contradictory in that a hysterically blind adolescent girl showed almost perfect visual performance. Celia's initial symptom was a sudden loss of sight in both eyes, followed by severe blurring of vision. Celia claimed to be unable to read small or large print. She had set high standards for herself and did very well at school. Her busy parents, continually rushing off to their own many activities, professed concern about their four children's education but often left Celia responsible for the three younger children. When Celia's vision became so severely blurred, her parents became obligated to read her studies to her. Testing revealed that Celia could readily identify objects of various sizes and shapes and count fingers at a distance of 15 feet. When three triangles were projected on three display windows of a console, two of the triangles inverted, one of them upright, in

599 trials of 600 she pressed the switch under the upright triangle, the correct response.

Sackeim et al. proposed a two-stage defensive reaction to account for these conflicting findings:

1 Perceptual representations of visual stimuli are blocked from awareness, and on this basis people report themselves blind.
2 Information is nonetheless extracted from the perceptual representations.

If patients feel that they must deny being privy to this information, they perform more poorly than they would by chance on perceptual tasks. If patients do not need to deny having such information, they perform the task well but still maintain that they are blind. Whether or not hysterically blind people unconsciously need to deny receiving perceptual information is viewed as dependent on personality factors and motivation.

Are the people who claim that they are blind and yet on another level respond to visual stimuli being truthful? Sackeim and his colleagues reported that some patients with lesions in the visual cortex, rather than damage to the eye, said that they were blind yet performed well on visual tasks. Such patients have vision (sometimes called blindsight), but they do not *know* that they can see. Therefore, it is possible for people to claim truthfully that they cannot see but give evidence that they can. Moreover, a dissociation between awareness and behaviour has been reported in many perceptual and cognitive studies (see Bornstein, Leone, & Galley, 1987; Kunst-Wilson & Zajonc, 1980).

Contemporary investigators, many of whom would identify themselves as cognitive psychologists, have begun to corroborate Freud's view that some human behaviour is determined by unconscious processes. But the modern cognitive perspective understands the unconscious processes in a different way. Freud postulated the existence of *the* unconscious, a repository of instinctual energy and repressed conflicts and impulses. Contemporary researchers reject the notions of an energy reservoir and repression, holding more simply that we are not aware of everything going on around us or of some of our cognitive processes. At the same time, these stimuli and processes of which we are unaware can have a powerful influence on our behaviour. This recent research suggests that understanding the causes of human behaviour remains a difficult task. It is not sufficient merely to ask someone, "Why did you do that?"

Behavioural Theory of Conversion Disorder A behavioural account of conversion disorder was proposed by Ullmann and Krasner (1975). They view conversion disorder as similar to malingering in that the person adopts the symptom to secure some end. In their opinion, the person with a conversion disorder attempts to behave according to his or her conception of how a person with a disease affecting the motor or sensory abilities would act. This theory raises two questions: (1) Are people capable of such behaviour? and (2) Under what conditions would such behaviour be most likely to occur?

Considerable evidence indicates that the answer to the first question is yes: people can adopt patterns of behaviour that match many of the classic conversion symptoms. For example, paralyses, analgesias, and blindness, as we have seen, can be induced in people under hypnosis.

As a partial answer to the second question, Ullmann and Krasner specify two conditions that increase the likelihood that motor and sensory disabilities will be imitated. First, the individual must have had some experience with the role to be adopted; he or she may have had similar physical problems or may have observed them in others. Second, the enactment of a role must be *rewarded*; an individual will assume a disability only if it can be expected either to reduce stress or to reap other positive consequences.

Although this behavioural interpretation might seem to make sense, the literature does not support it completely. Grosz and Zimmerman's patient Celia, for example, did not act in accordance with Ullmann and Krasner's theory. The very intelligent Celia performed perfectly in the visual discrimination task while still claiming severely blurred vision. Such a pattern of behaviour seems a rather clumsy enactment of a role. If you wanted to convince someone that you could not see, would you always correctly identify the upright triangle?

Celia's actions seem more consistent with Sackeim's theory. On the level of conscious awareness, Celia probably saw only blurred images, as she claimed. But during the test the triangles were distinguished on an unconscious level, and she could pick out the upright one wherever it appeared. It is interesting to note that Celia's visual problems gained her crucial attention and help from her parents, which is in the nature of conversion disorder as well as of malingering. Three years after the onset of her visual difficulties, Celia dramatically recovered clear sight while on a trip with her parents. Earlier in the summer, Celia had graduated from high school with grades well above average. The need to receive reinforcement for poor vision had perhaps passed, and her eyesight returned.

Social and Cultural Factors in Conversion Disorder A possible role for social and cultural factors is suggested by the apparent decrease in the incidence of conversion disorder over the last century. Contemporary clinicians rarely see anyone with such problems. Several hypotheses have been proposed to explain this apparent decrease. Therapists with a psychoanalytic bent point out that in the second half of the nineteenth century, when the incidence of conversion reactions was apparently high in France and Austria, repressive sexual attitudes may have contributed to the increased prevalence of the disorder. The decrease in its incidence, then, may be attributed to a general relaxing of sexual mores and to the greater sophistication of contemporary culture, which is more tolerant of anxiety than it is of dysfunctions that do not make physiological sense.

Some psychoanalysts believe that the high frequency of conversion disorder in 18-century Europe was due to the repressive sexual attitudes of the time.

Support for the role of social and cultural factors also comes from studies showing that conversion disorder is more common among people with lower socioeconomic status and from rural areas (Binzer et al., 1996; Folks, Ford & Regan, 1984), who may be less knowledgeable about medical and psychological concepts. Further evidence derives from studies showing that the diagnosis of hysteria has declined in industrialized societies such as England (Hare, 1969) but has remained common in undeveloped countries such as Libya (Pu et al., 1986). These data, although consistent, are difficult to interpret. They could mean that increasing sophistication about medical diseases leads to decreased prevalence of conversion disorder. Alternatively, diagnostic practices may vary from country to country, producing different rates. A large-scale study conducted by diagnosticians trained to follow the same procedures is needed.

Biological Factors in Conversion Disorder Although genetic factors have been proposed as being important in the development of conversion disorder, research does not support this proposal. Slater (1961) investigated concordance rates in 12 identical and 12 fraternal pairs of twins. Probands of each pair had been diagnosed as having the disorder, but none of the co-twins in either of the two groups manifested a conversion reaction. Torgerson (1986) reported the results of a twin study of somatoform disorders that included 10 cases of conversion disorder, 12 of somatization disorder, and 7 of pain disorder. No co-twin had the same diagnosis as his or her proband! Even the overall concordance for somatoform disorders was no higher in the identical twins than in the fraternal twins. Genetic factors, then, from the studies done so far, seem to be of no importance.

There may be some relationship between brain structure and conversion disorder. Conversion symptoms are more likely to occur on the left side than on the right side of the body (Binzer et al., 1996; Ford & Folks, 1985). In most instances, these left-side body functions are controlled by the right hemisphere of the brain. Thus, the majority of conversion symptoms may be related to the functioning of the right hemisphere. Consistent with this idea, research has shown that in patients with left-sided conversion symptoms, stimulation of the right hemisphere yields smaller muscle responses than does stimulation of the left hemisphere (Foong et al., 1997). Research has shown that the right hemisphere can generate emotions, and it is suspected of generating more emotions, particularly unpleasant ones, than are generated by the left hemisphere. Conversion symptoms could be linked neurophysiologically to emotional arousal.

A recent report has documented an interesting biological difference between a patient with conversion disorder, who had complete loss of sensation below the elbow of his right arm, and another person, who was instructed to fake the same symptom during testing (Lorenz, Kunze, & Bromm, 1998). Various stimuli were administered to the left and right thumbs of both participants, and the electrical response of the brain to the stimuli was recorded. As expected, the brain responses indicating that a stimulus had been encountered were normal in both participants when either the right or the left thumb was stimulated. However, when the right thumb was stimulated, the brain of the person who was faking the symptom, but not of the patient, also showed another response, one that reflects more of a cognitive and less of a sensory response to stimuli. The authors interpreted this response as resulting from the malingerer's actively trying to withhold a response to the stimuli, and they thus believe that their data show that in conversion disorder there is an inability to use sensory information to direct behaviour.

Taken together these findings indicate that biological factors in conversion disorder are well worth pursuing further.

THERAPIES FOR SOMATOFORM DISORDERS

Because somatoform disorders are rarer than other disorders seen by mental health professionals, little controlled research exists on the efficacy of different treatments. Case reports and clinical speculation are the main sources of information on how to help people with these disorders.

People with somatoform disorders make many more visits to physicians than to psychologists, for they define their problems in physical terms. These patients interpret a referral from their physician to a psychologist or psychiatrist as an indication that the doctor thinks the illness is "all in their head"; therefore, they resent referrals to "shrinks." They try the patience of their physicians, who often prescribe one drug or medical treatment after another in the hope of remedying the somatic complaint.

The "talking cure" into which psychoanalysis developed was based on the assumption that a massive repression had forced psychic energy to be transformed into puzzling anesthesias or paralyses. The catharsis as the patient faced up to the infantile origins of the repression was assumed to help, and even today free association and other efforts to lift repression are used commonly to treat somatoform disorders. Psychoanalysis and psychoanalytically oriented psychotherapy have not been demonstrated to be useful with conversion disorder, however, except perhaps to reduce the patient's concern about the disabling problems (Simon, 1998).

When working with people with somatoform disorders, clinicians must be mindful that such patients often suffer from anxiety and depression. Cognitive and behavioural clinicians believe that the high levels of anxiety associated with somatization disorders are linked to specific situations. Alice, the woman described earlier, revealed that she was extremely anxious about her shaky marriage and about situations in which other people might judge her. Techniques such as exposure or any of the cognitive therapies could address her fears, the reduction of which would help lessen somatic complaints, but it is likely that more treatment would be needed, for a person who has been "sick" for a period of time has grown accustomed to weakness and dependency and to avoiding everyday challenges.

Chances are that the people who live with Alice have adjusted to her infirmity and are even unwittingly reinforcing her avoidance of normal adult responsibilities. Family therapy might help Alice and the members of her family change the web of relationships to support her movement toward greater autonomy. Assertion training and social skills training—for example, coaching Alice in how to approach and talk to people, maintain eye contact, give compliments, accept criticism, and make requests—could help her acquire, or reacquire, means of relating to others and meeting challenges that do not begin with the premise "I am a poor, weak, sick person."

In general, cognitive-behavioural approaches have proved effective in reducing hypochondriacal concerns. Treatment may entail such strategies as pointing out the patient's selective attention to bodily symptoms and discouraging the patient from seeking medical reassurance that he or she is not ill (e.g., Salkovskis & Warwick, 1986; Visser & Bouman, 1992).

In a widely accepted approach to somatization disorders, the physician does not dispute the validity of the physical complaints but minimizes the use of diagnostic tests and medications, maintaining contact with the patient regardless of whether the patient is complaining of illness or not (Monson & Smith, 1983). A study of this approach found that patients showed significant improvement in their physical medical condition and made less frequent use of health care services (Rost, Kashner, & Smith, 1994). Also of possible use is redirecting the patient's attention to sources of anxiety and depression that may underlie unexplained somatic symptoms or overattention to minor and benign pains. Techniques such as relaxation training and various forms of cognitive therapy have proved useful (e.g., Payne & Blanchard, 1995; Simon, 1998).

It is usually fruitless to make a sharp distinction between psychogenic pain and pain caused by actual medical factors, such as injury to muscle tissue. It is typically assumed that pain always has both components. Effective treatments tend to have the following ingredients:

- validating that the pain is real and not just in the patient's head
- relaxation training
- rewarding the person for behaving in ways inconsistent with the pain (toughing it out)

Evidence from a number of double-blind experiments shows that low doses of some antidepressant drugs, most especially imipramine (Tofranil), are superior to a placebo in reducing chronic pain and distress (Phillip & Fickinger, 1993). Interestingly, these antidepressants reduce pain even when—in the low dosages given—they don't alleviate the associated depression (Simon, 1998). The treatment of pain is described in greater detail in Chapter 8.

In general, it seems advisable to shift the focus away from what the patient cannot do because of illness and instead teach the patient how to deal with stress, encourage greater activity, and enhance a sense of control, despite the physical limitations or discomfort the patient is experiencing.

In treating somatoform disorders, behaviour therapists have applied a wide range of techniques intended to make it worthwhile for the patient to give up the symptoms. A case reported by Liebson (1967) provides an example. A man had relinquished his job because of pain and weakness in the legs and attacks of giddiness. Liebson helped the patient return to full-time work by persuading his family to refrain from reinforcing him for his idleness and by arranging for the man to receive a pay increase if he was able to get work. A reinforcement approach attempts to provide the patient with greater incentives for improvement than for remaining incapacitated.

Another important component of any such operant tactic, as noted by Walen, Hauserman, and Lavin (1977), is for the therapist to ensure that the patient does not lose face when relinquishing the disorder. The therapist should appreciate that the patient may feel humiliated at becoming better via treatment that does not deal with the medical problem.

Table 7.2

Summary of the Dissociative Disorders

Disorder	Description
Dissociative amnesia	Memory loss following a stressful experience.
Dissociative fugue	Memory loss accompanied by leaving home and establishing a new identity.
Depersonalization disorder	Experience of the self is altered.
Dissociative identity disorder	At least two distinct ego states—alters—that act independently of each other.

There is little controlled research on the treatment of conversion disorder. Case studies suggest that it is usually *not* a good idea to try to convince the patient that his or her conversion symptoms are related to psychological factors. Clinical lore advises a gentle, supportive approach along with rewards for the patient for any degree of improvement (Simon, 1998).

DISSOCIATIVE DISORDERS

In this section, we examine four dissociative disorders: dissociative amnesia, dissociative fugue, dissociative identity disorder (formerly known as multiple personality disorder), and depersonalization disorder, all of which are characterized by changes in a person's sense of identity, memory, or consciousness. (The dissociative disorders are summarized in Table 7.2). Individuals with these disorders may be unable to recall important personal events or may temporarily forget their identity or even assume a new identity. They may even wander far from their usual surroundings. We all have everyday dissociative experiences of one kind or another (see Canadian Perspectives 7.1)

Canadian Perspectives/7.1

Everyday Dissociative Experiences in Winnipeg

Colin Ross, a Canadian psychiatrist now based in Texas, did most of his extensive research on multiple personality disorder (what is now referred to in DSM-IV-TR as DID or dissociative identity disorder) in Canada. While he was in Winnipeg, he and his associates investigated whether typical Canadians living in the community have everyday occurrences of dissociation.

Have you ever sat at your desk studying, lapsed into daydreaming about the upcoming weekend, and become unaware of what was happening around you? Have you ever been so engrossed in imagining a "story" or engaged in a personal narrative with yourself that it actually seemed real? Have you ever had an impression that you were viewing yourself from outside your body? Have you ever found yourself wondering how you ended up in a certain place or situation? These are all dissociative experiences.

How did Colin Ross determine the frequency of dissociative experiences in a community sample? Ross, Joshi, and Currie (1990) tapped a representative sample of 1,055 adults in Winnipeg, having them complete a reliable and validated self-report measure of dissociative experiences—the Dissociative Experiences Scale (DES). The distribution of the respondents total scores (which can range between 0 and 100) is shown in Figure 7.3. The figure indicates that (1) a majority of people in the general population report having had at least a few dissociative experiences,

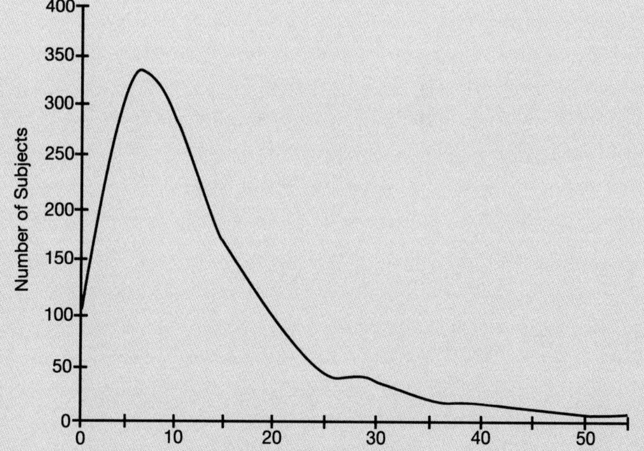

Figure 7.3 Distribution of Dissociative Experience Scale Scores in the General Population (N = 1,055).

although only a small number have had many; and (2) most people report never having experienced the most "pathological" items, although some have. Fewer than 75 people among the more than 1,000 participants reported having had no dissociative experiences at all. Ross re-analyzed the data and concluded that 3.3 percent of the sample had had pathological dissociative experiences, "and therefore presumptively had a dissociative disorder" (Ross, 1997, p. 105). Ross considers 3 percent to be a "conservative estimate," which, when extrapolated to all of North America, suggests that about 10 million North Americans have a dissociative disorder. However, note that the majority of DES items are not inherently pathological.

The results of the Winnipeg study indicate that the most common dissociative experiences include being able to ignore pain, missing part of a conversation, noticing that things that are typically difficult to do are done easily, and uncertainty about whether you actually did something or only thought about it. Less common experiences include being so involved in fantasy that it seems real, driving your car and realizing you don't remember part of the trip, not remembering important events in your life, and being in a familiar place but finding it unfamiliar. Relatively few people endorsed very unusual, even bizarre experiences, such as not recognizing your own reflection in a mirror, finding yourself dressed in clothes you don't remember putting on, finding yourself in a place but unaware of how you got there, or feeling as though your body is not your own.

Ross (1997) reported that there were no differences in overall DES scores due to ethnic background, gender, family composition, religion, or income. Similar findings have been reported in studies with students from around the world (e.g., Ray & Faith, 1995).

One further point about DID should be made. Before we conclude that over 3 percent of the general community population has DID, we should replicate the study using trained interviewers who employ a structured interview, such as the SCID (Spitzer et al., 1996), to confirm actual diagnoses. Certain DES items, when taken in isolation, seem dubious examples of dissociation (e.g., absorption in a television program or movie; staring into space), and this highlights discrepancies between self-report measures and what can be learned using the clinical interview.

What factors can cause everyday dissociation? Stress and fatigue are key factors. It is likely that these factors contributed to the high rates of dissociation that Laposa and Alden (2003) found in their study of PTSD in hospital emergency room workers. Almost half of their participants had "clinically meaningful dissociation" according to their responses on a self-report measure. Moreover, more than half reported periods of blanking out, going on "automatic pilot," and feeling unreal, like being in a movie or dream.

Another trigger for dissociation would be exposure to situations that actually require someone to portray himself or herself in a false manner. A recent simulation study conducted by researchers at the University of Ottawa focused on undercover agents who assumed false identities on the job (Girodo, Deck, & Morrison, 2002). This study of 48 federal police officers found that an alarming percentage of them (66 percent) had re-enacted their fabricated identity outside the operational context (i.e., they could not stop pretending to be someone else). Re-enactments were more likely among those who had gone to greater initial lengths to change their physical appearance. However, personal characteristics are also a factor. Self-reported identity re-enactments were higher among those police officers with prior dissociative tendencies, as assessed by the DES.

Other general triggers for dissociation would include binge drinking or the use of various psychoactive drugs. The hypnotic induction can also elicit dissociative symptoms, especially in suggestible people. Various cognitive disorders can lead to memory lapses, and older people often complain about forgetting things as their short-term memory deteriorates (see Chapter 16).

Finally, we remind you that dissociative experiences in the general population and among students are typically transient and are rarely a sign of serious psychological problems. However, if you are distressed by the type or frequency of any dissociative experiences you might have, or if they interfere with your daily functioning, then we encourage you to seek a professional opinion.

Thinking Critically

1. Which of the dissociative experiences described above have you experienced? Remember that dissociative experiences, even if recurrent, should not be considered problematic if they do not cause distress or impairment.
2. There can be numerous triggers for dissociative experiences other than traumatic life events. How do you explain the dissociative experiences that you had in the past? What do you think triggered these experiences? Could boredom also cause dissociative symptoms?

Few high-quality data concerning the prevalence of the various dissociative disorders are available. Perhaps the best study to date was conducted by Colin Ross (1991). This study found prevalences of 7.0 percent, 2.4 percent, and 0.2 percent for amnesia, depersonalization, and fugue, respectively. We will describe this study more fully when considering dissociative identity disorder.

Our examination of the four major dissociative disorders will first cover symptoms and then theories of etiology and therapies.

In Alfred Hitchcock's movie *Spellbound*, Gregory Peck played a man with amnesia. Dissociative amnesia is typically triggered by a stressful event.

DISSOCIATIVE AMNESIA

The person with dissociative amnesia is unable to recall important personal information, usually after some stressful episode. The information is not permanently lost, but it cannot be retrieved during the episode of amnesia. The holes in memory are too extensive to be explained by ordinary forgetfulness.

Fraser (1994) used case studies he had encountered in Canada to illustrate the symptoms of the various dissociative disorders. We refer to these compelling case examples throughout this chapter, and they include the case of dissociative disorder that began the chapter. Fraser described dissociative amnesia by outlining the case of a 17-year-old female student

> ...who was referred because of two episodes of amnesia. The first had happened while she was returning home from school by bus. She was just about to get off the bus, and then the very next moment she found herself in her home. She had no idea how she got home but did not dare to tell anyone. Several nights later, as she disembarked at the same bus stop, she suddenly found herself lying in a field alone, stripped to the waist. She had no idea of the time interval lost but felt it was the same evening. She went home and reported the incident. She was investigated neurologically, and all was normal, and she was referred to psychiatry. Under hypnosis she recalled that on the first incident, there were four boys who were at the bus stop. As they started to make sexual advances, she bolted away and ran home. It was assumed that she did this in a dissociated state. On the second incident, the same group of boys was waiting at the bus stop. This time they grabbed her and hauled her into a nearby field. They pulled off her brassiere and appeared to be intending to do more when somehow they were frightened off. (Fraser, 1994, pp. 144-145)

Most often the memory loss involves all events during a limited period of time following some traumatic experience, such as the one described above or such as witnessing the death of a loved one. More rarely the amnesia is for only selected events during a circumscribed period of distress, is continuous from a traumatic event to the present, or is total, covering the person's entire life (Coons & Milstein, 1992). The person's behaviour during the period of amnesia is otherwise unremarkable, except that the memory loss may bring some disorientation and purposeless wandering. With total amnesia, the patient does not recognize relatives and friends, but retains the ability to talk, read, and reason and also retains talents and previously acquired knowledge of the world and of how to function in it. The amnesic episode may last several hours or as long as several years. It usually disappears as suddenly as it came on, with complete recovery and only a small chance of recurrence.

There have been suggestions that "Mr. Nobody" should have regained his memory functioning by now since the alleged mugging that caused his memory loss occurred in 1999. He has become Canada's most famous possible case of faked amnesia. Questions have risen that he may be faking his amnesia for immigration purposes.

Memory loss is common in many brain disorders, as well as in substance abuse, but amnesia and memory loss caused by brain disorders or substance abuse can be fairly easily distinguished. In degenerative brain diseases, memory fails more slowly over time, is not linked to life stress, and is accompanied by other cognitive deficits, such as the inability to learn new information. Memory loss following a brain injury caused by some trauma (e.g., an automobile accident) or substance abuse can be easily linked to the trauma or the substance being abused.

There can be significant cultural differences in the expression of dissociative amnesia. This point is illustrated in the following case of an Inuit adolescent who apparently suffered from dissociative amnesia in the context of spirit possession.

> D.N. is a 19-year-old Inuit male student who is the eldest in his family. He described his father as teaching him the traditional skills; his mother he viewed as a scolding rejecting figure. He complained of several years of depression and suicidal ideation related to a confused sexual identity. While alone, hunting on the tundra, he felt a presence touch his shoulder and saying "Don't look back." He did nevertheless and saw a faceless apparition wearing a caribou parka. ...The latter named Nanonalok (Big Bear) said "Don't be afraid, I'm your grandfather." Initially friendly the spirit informed D.N. that he would leave him alone if he married "E," a young woman in whom D.N. had an ambivalent interest. He refused to obey and so began nightly battles associated with amnesia, from which he emerged with torn clothes, bruises and a gunshot wound "caused" by the spirit. (Seltzer, 1983, p. 53-54)

According to Seltzer (1983), this young man received treatment for dissociative disorder, since further assessment yielded no evidence of depression or thought disorder. D.N. received some of this treatment away from home because he insisted that the spirits would lose their energy if he were away from his arctic environment.

One concern involving dissociative amnesia was raised in a study involving a mixed sample of psychiatric patients in Kingston, Ontario (Horen, Leichner, & Lawson, 1995) using self-report scales and structured interviews, the investigation determined that dissociative amnesia was present in 8 percent of the sample, but the problem had gone undiagnosed by previous clinicians.

Dissociative Fugue

Memory loss is more extensive in dissociative fugue than in dissociative amnesia. The person not only becomes totally amnesic but suddenly leaves home and work and assumes a new identity. Sometimes the person takes a new name, a new home, a new job, and even a new set of personality characteristics. The person may even succeed in establishing a fairly complex social life. More often, however, the new life does not crystallize to this extent, and the fugue is of briefer duration. It consists for the most part of limited, but apparently purposeful, travel, during which social contacts are minimal or absent.

Fugues typically occur after a person has experienced some severe stress, such as marital quarrels, personal rejection, financial or occupational difficulties, war service, or a natural disaster. Recovery, although it takes varying amounts of time, is usually complete, and the individual does not recollect what took place during the flight from his or her usual haunts.

Fraser (1994) described a case in which a young man had engaged in three violent acts, including breaking a person's jaw in a fight, yet had total amnesia for these events. Further analysis focused on the time that this young man spent in prison. Fraser found that

> hypnosis helped him recall being gang-raped by a group of prison inmates who had singled him out because he was mild-mannered and of different racial origin. He had been sexually abused by these men on numerous occasions. Apparently, attempts to tell the prison guards only resulted in laughter by the guards, who told him the prison "was not the Holiday Inn and didn't cater to room change requests." When some of the more sadistic events were being recalled in hypnosis, a state that called itself "Empty" stated that it had taken over and accepted the severe episodes of anal intercourse. (p. 143)

According to Fraser, the young man committed the three assaults because "Empty" had overreacted and responded with rage to minimal touching.

Depersonalization Disorder

In depersonalization disorder, the person's perception or experience of the self is disconcertingly and disruptively altered. It, too, is included in DSM-IV as a dissociative disorder, although its inclusion is controversial, since depersonalization disorder, unlike other dissociative disorders, involves no disturbance of memory. In a depersonalization episode, which is typically triggered by stress, individuals rather suddenly lose their sense of self. They have unusual sensory experiences; for example, their limbs may seem drastically changed in size or their voices may sound strange to them. They may have the impression that they are outside their bodies, viewing themselves from a distance. Sometimes they feel mechanical, as though they and others are robots, or they move as though in a world that has lost its reality. Similar episodes sometimes occur in several other disorders: schizophrenia (see Chapter 11), panic attacks and posttraumatic stress disorder (Chapter 6), and borderline personality disorder (Chapter 13) (Maldonado, Butler, & Spiegel, 1998).

Depersonalization disorder usually begins in adolescence and has a chronic course; that is, it lasts a long time. Comorbid personality disorders are frequent, as are anxiety disorders and depression (Simeon et al., 1997). The following case illustrates the symptoms as well as the fact that sufferers often report childhood trauma.

> Mrs. A was a 43-year-old woman who was living with her mother and son and worked at a clerical job. She had felt depersonalized as far back as she could remember. "It's as if the real me is taken out and put on a shelf or stored somewhere inside of me. Whatever makes me me is not there. It is like

an opaque curtain ... like going through the motions and having to exert discipline to keep the unit together." She had suffered several episodes of depersonalization annually and found them extremely distressing. She had experienced panic attacks for 1 year when she was 35 and had been diagnosed with self-defeating personality disorder. Her childhood trauma history included nightly genital fondling and frequent enemas by her mother from earliest memory to age 10. (Simeon et al., 1997, p. 1109)

Some people experience symptoms of depersonalization but not the significant distress that is needed for a diagnosis of depersonalization disorder. However, these individuals have depersonalization experiences that seem similar in many respects to those reported by people with the disorder. Charbonneau and O'Connor (1999) analyzed the depersonalization experiences of 20 people from the Montreal area who responded to media advertisements. People were included in this study if it was confirmed via a clinical interview that they had experienced two or more depersonalization experiences in the past year. The authors found that the onset of depersonalization was associated with traumatic life events in general or specific events involving sexual abuse. The most common reaction was a sense of derealization, with statements such as "I am frequently looking on as if not part of things" and "I feel as if I am floating away from reality" endorsed by 90 percent or more of the participants. Desomatization was also reported, with 80 percent or more of the participants agreeing with statements such as "My body is not in harmony with my being" and "My body does not feel like it belongs." The most common thought or sensation accompanying the depersonalization experience involved worries about feeling isolated and detached from other people (reported by 60 percent), followed by a feeling of being vulnerable and embarrassed about the situation (reported by 45 percent). Additional analyses indicated that there was no single diagnosis associated consistently with depersonalization. The depersonalization group had higher levels of depression and trait anxiety relative to a community control group.

focus on discovery/7.2

Classification of Conversion Disorder and Dissociative Disorders

Now that both conversion disorder and the dissociative disorders have been described, we return to the manner in which they have been separately classified in DSM-IV—conversion as a somatoform disorder because it involves physical symptoms, and the dissociative disorders as a distinct category because they involve disruptions in consciousness. John Kihlstrom, a leading researcher in the field, has argued that this separation is a mistake. He believes that both disorders are disruptions in the normal controlling functions of consciousness. In the dissociative disorders, there is a dissociation between explicit and implicit memory. *Explicit memory* refers to a person's conscious recall of some experience, and it is what is disrupted in dissociative disorders. *Implicit memory* is reflected in the behavioural changes elicited by an event that cannot be consciously recalled. Kihlstrom (1994) cites numerous examples of patients with dissociative disorders whose implicit memory remains intact. One woman, for example, became amnesic after being the victim of a practical joke. Although she had no conscious memory of the event, she nonetheless became terrified when passing the location of the incident. The dissociation of explicit and implicit memory is the core of the dissociative disorders.

Kihlstrom argues that the same basic disruption of consciousness is found in conversion disorder, in this case affecting perception. As in the dissociative disorders, stimuli that are not consciously seen, heard, or felt nevertheless affect behaviour. (Our earlier descriptions of several cases of hysterical blindness clearly make this point.) So, we might consider conversion disorder as a disruption in explicit perception with unimpaired implicit perception. Empirical support for Kihlstrom's idea comes from research showing that dissociative symptoms are common in patients with conversion disorder (Spitzer et al., 1999).

DISSOCIATIVE IDENTITY DISORDER

Consider what it would be like to have dissociative identity disorder. This was what afflicted Chris Sizemore, the woman with the famous three faces of Eve. People tell you about things you have done that seem out of character, events of which you have no memory. You have been waking up each morning with the remains of a cup of tea by your bedside—and you do not like tea. How can you explain these happenings? If you think about seeking treatment, do you not worry whether the psychiatrist or psychologist will believe you?

We all have days when we are not quite ourselves. This is assumed to be normal and is not what is meant by multiple personality. According to DSM-IV, a proper diagnosis of **dissociative identity disorder (DID)** requires that a person have at least two separate ego states, or *alters*—different modes of being and feeling and acting that exist independently of each other and that come forth and are in control at different times. There is usually one primary personality, and treatment is typically sought by the primary alter. There are typically two to four alters at the time a diagnosis is made, but over the course of treatment several more often emerge. Gaps in memory occur in all cases and are produced because at least one alter has no contact with the others; that is, alter A has no memory for what alter B is like or even any knowledge of having this alternate state of being. The existence of different alters must also be chronic (long-lasting) and severe (causing considerable disruption in one's life); it cannot be a temporary change resulting from the ingestion of a drug, for example.

The film *Sybil* depicted a famous case of dissociative identity disorder. The title role was played by Sally Field.

Each alter may be quite complex, with its own behaviour patterns, memories, and relationships; each determines the nature and acts of the individual when it is in command. Usually, the personalities are quite different, even opposites of one another. They may have different handedness, wear glasses with different prescriptions, and have allergies to different substances. The original and subordinate alters are all aware of lost periods of time, and the voices of the others may sometimes echo into an alter's consciousness, even though the alter may not know to whom these voices belong.

Dissociative identity disorder usually begins in childhood, but it is rarely diagnosed until adulthood. It is more extensive than other dissociative disorders, and recovery may be less complete. It is much more common in women than in men. The presence of other diagnoses—in particular, depression, borderline personality disorder, and somatization disorder—is frequent (Boonn & Draijer, 1993). DID is often accompanied by headaches, substance abuse, phobias, hallucinations, suicide attempts, sexual dysfunction, and self-abusive behaviour, as well as by other dissociative symptoms such as amnesia and depersonalization (Scroppo et al., 1998). A study by Ross et al. (1990) of 102 multiple personality disorder patients, including a subset from Winnipeg and Ottawa, used a structured interview to determine that about 90 percent had a history of suicidal tendencies, depression, recurring headaches, and sexual abuse.

According to Liotti (1992), a related possibility is that individuals suffering from dissociative symptoms have a disorganized attachment style because they were exposed as young children to the frightening and chaotic behaviour of their caregiver. Indeed, a study of clinically treated adolescents from three Canadian cities confirmed that attachment-related trauma was linked significantly with self-reported symptoms of dissociation in this sample (West, Adam, Spreng, & Rose, 2001).

Cases of dissociative identity disorder are sometimes mislabelled in the popular press as schizophrenia. This diagnostic category, discussed in greater detail in Chapter 11, derives part of its name from the Greek root schizo, which means "splitting away from," hence the confusion. A split in the personality, wherein two or more fairly separate and coherent systems of being exist alternately in the same person, is very different from any recognized symptoms of schizophrenia.

Controversies in the Diagnosis of DID Although DID is recognized formally as a diagnosis by its inclusion in DSM-IV, its inclusion in the DSM is controversial. A survey of American psychiatrists found that two-thirds of the participants had reservations about the inclusion of DID in DSM-IV (Pope et al., 1999). A follow-up study of 550 Canadian psychiatrists found that more than two-thirds had reservations about including DID in DSM-IV (Lalonde, Hudson, Gigante, & Pope, 2001). Compared to the American sample, the Canadian respondents were significantly more skeptical about the scientific validity and diagnostic legitimacy of DID. There were no significant differences between the views of English-speaking and French-speaking respondents, a finding inconsistent with the hypothesis that French-speaking Canadian psychiatrists would be less accepting of DID diagnoses because there is little support for the diagnosis in the French-language research literature. However, consistent with the findings of the earlier study, psychoanalytically oriented psychiatrists were significantly more accepting of the validity of DID than were biologically oriented psychiatrists.

DID was first mentioned in the 19th century. In a review of the literature, Sutcliffe and Jones (1962) identified a total of 77 cases, most of which were reported in the period between 1890 and 1920. After that, reports of DID declined until the 1970s, when they increased markedly. More formal data on the prevalence of DID were collected on samples of adults in Winnipeg (Ross, 1991) and in Turkey (Akyuez et al., 1999). Prevalence was 1.3 percent in Winnipeg and 0.4 percent in Turkey. Although these prevalence figures may not seem high, they are—previously, prevalence was thought to be about one in one million.

What has caused the re-emergence of the DID diagnosis in the past 30 years? One possible explanation for the increase is that in DSM-III, which was published in 1980, the diagnostic criteria for DID were spelled out clearly for the first time (Putnam, 1996). But it is also possible that more people began to adopt the role of a patient with DID or that clinicians had always seen a similar number of cases but chose to report them only when interest in DID grew. We can also speculate that the earlier decline in the number of diagnoses of DID resulted from the increasing popularity of the concept of schizophrenia; that is, cases of DID may have been mistakenly diagnosed as cases of schizophrenia (Rosenbaum, 1980). However, the symptoms of the two disorders are actually not very similar. Although the voices of the alters may be experienced as auditory hallucinations, patients with DID do not show the thought disorder and behavioural disorganization of schizophrenia. Another diagnostic issue is that DSM-III-R did not require that the alters be amnesic for one another, raising the possibility that the diagnosis could have been applied to people with high levels of variability in their behaviour, as occurs with some personality disorders (Kihlstrom & Tataryn, 1991). Although DSM-IV and DSM-IV-TR restored the amnesia component to the diagnosis, we do not yet know what effect this will have on prevalence.

Another factor of possible relevance to the increase in DID diagnoses was the 1973 publication of *Sybil*, which presented a dramatic case with 16 personalities (Schreiber, 1973). This case attracted a great deal of attention and spawned much interest in the disorder. Some critics have hypothesized that this heightened interest led some therapists to suggest strongly to clients that they had DID, sometimes using hypnosis to probe for alters. It is notable that in the post-Sybil era, the number of alters in each case has risen dramatically, from two or three in the past to more than 12 (Goff & Simms, 1993).

Ironically, the Sybil case has been subject to some controversy. It has been claimed that Sybil's alters were created during therapy by a therapist who gave substance to the patient's different emotional states by giving them names (Rieger, 1998).

ETIOLOGY OF DISSOCIATIVE DISORDERS

The term *dissociative disorders* refers to the mechanism, dissociation, that is thought to cause the disorders. Historically, the concept comes from the writings of Pierre Janet, the French neurologist. The basic idea is that consciousness is usually a unified experience, including cognition, emotion, and motivation. But under stress, memories of a trauma may be stored in such a way that they are not accessible to awareness when the person has returned to a more normal state (Kihlstrom, Tataryn, & Holt, 1993). Possible outcomes are amnesia or fugue.

The behavioural view of dissociative disorders is somewhat similar to these early speculations. Behavioural theorists consider dissociation as an avoidance response that protects the person from stressful events and memories of these events. Because the person does not consciously confront these painful memories, the fear elicited has no opportunity to be extinguished.

A problem with any theory, be it psychoanalytic or behavioural, that holds that traumatic memories are forgotten or dissociated because of their painfulness is that research on both animals and humans shows that high levels of stress usually *enhance* rather than impair memory (Shobe & Kihlstrom, 1997). This is certainly what one finds in posttraumatic stress disorder, in which the person is overwhelmed by recurrent, intrusive images of past traumatic events. A response to this criticism, however, is that dissociative disorders are quite rare relative to the frequency with which people experience trauma. In other words, as Shobe and Kilhstrom (1997) have argued, while the *usual* response to trauma is enhanced memory, we are not talking about usual ways of responding when it comes to dissociative disorders.

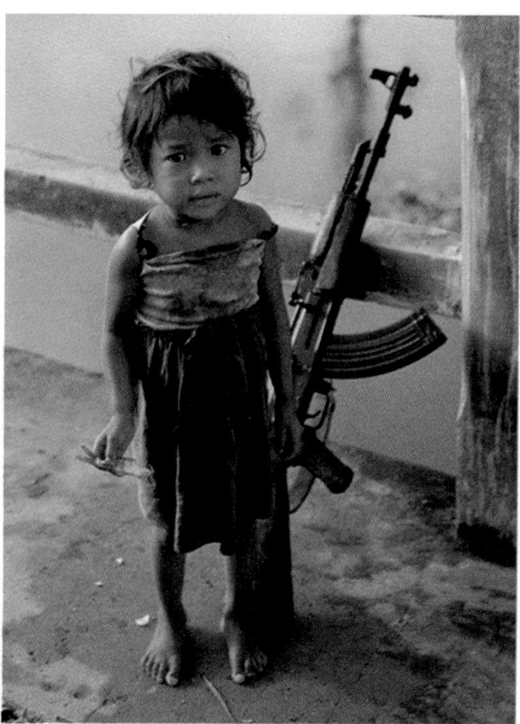

Severe trauma in childhood is regarded as a major cause of dissociative disorders.

Etiology of DID There are two major theories of DID. One assumes that DID begins in childhood as a result of severe physical or sexual abuse. The abuse causes dissociation and the formation of alters as a way of escaping the trauma (Gleaves, 1996). Since not everyone who experiences child abuse develops DID, it is further proposed that a diathesis is present among those who do develop DID. One idea is that being high in hypnotizability facilitates the development of alters through self-hypnosis (Bliss, 1983). Another proposed diathesis is that people who develop DID are very prone to engage in fantasy (Lynn et al., 1988).

The other DID theory considers the disorder to be an enactment of learned social roles. The alters appear in adulthood, typically due to suggestions by a therapist (Lilienfeld et al., 1999; Spanos, 1994). DID is not viewed as a conscious deception (or malingering) in this theory; the issue is not whether DID is real but how it developed and is maintained. See Canadian Contributions 7.1 for a more complete description of the views and contributions of Nicholas Spanos in this area.

Canadian Contributions/7.1

Nicholas P. Spanos and a Sociocognitive Perspective on DID

Nicholas Spanos believed that DID is essentially a socially constructed form of role-playing.

"Despite its current popularity, the notion that MPD is a naturally occurring disorder that results from severe child abuse is fraught with difficulties."

—Nick Spanos, *Multiple Identities and False Memories: A Sociocognitive Perspective* (1996, p. 2)

Nicholas Spanos was a prolific researcher who was a professor of psychology and director of the Laboratory for Experimental Hypnosis at Carleton University in Ottawa from 1975 to 1994. Spanos was also a pilot of small airplanes, and unfortunately, he died tragically in a plane crash while taking off from Martha's Vineyard in the Cape Cod area of Massachusetts in 1994. However, Spanos left a research legacy that continues to generate controversy and interest to this day. Spanos had over 250 publications, including some papers that were published posthumously (see Spanos, Burgess, Burgess, Samuels, & Blois, 1999). Also published posthumously was a major book submitted before his death (Spanos, 1996). In this book, he challenged the validity of DID as a distinct psychiatric disorder. Spanos developed a cognitive-behavioural model of hypnosis that has become the most influential in the field (Chaves & Jones, 1996). Although he made important contributions in several other areas, including demonic possession and the Salem witchcraft trials, in the area of dissociative disorders he is known primarily for three things.

First, Spanos (1994) has been a leading advocate of the idea that DID basically involves role-playing. He has pointed out that a small number of clinicians contribute most of the diagnoses of DID. A survey conducted in Switzerland, for example, found that 66 percent of the diagnoses of DID were made by fewer than 10 percent of the psychiatrists who responded (Modestin, 1992). Perhaps these clinicians have very liberal criteria for making the diagnosis. Alternatively, though, cases of DID may be referred to clinicians who have acquired a reputation for specializing in this condition (Gleaves, 1996). Therefore, the data are inconclusive.

Second, Spanos used role-playing studies with students to provide a unique perspective on the trial of an infamous serial murderer in California who came to be known as the Hillside Strangler (Spanos, Weekes, & Bertrand, 1985). The accused murderer, Ken Bianchi, unsuccessfully pled not guilty by reason of insanity, claiming that the murders had been committed by his alter, Steve. Bianchi was supposedly under hypnosis during a pretrial meeting with a mental health professional to determine his legal responsibility for his crimes. The interviewer (I) asked for a second personality to come forward.

I: I've talked a bit to Ken but I think that perhaps there might be another part of Ken that I haven't talked to. And I would like to communicate with that other part. And I would like that other part to come to talk with me. ... And when you're here, lift the left hand off the chair to signal to me that you are here. Would you please come, Part, so I can talk to you? ... Part, would you come and lift Ken's hand to indicate to me that you are here? ... Would you talk to me, Part, by saying "I'm here"? (Schwartz, 1981, pp. 142-143)

Bianchi (B) answered yes to the last question, and then he and the interviewer had thefollowing conversation.

I: Part, are you the same as Ken or are you different in any way...

B: I'm not him.

I: You're not him. Who are you? Do you have a name?

B: I'm not Ken.

I: You're not him? Okay. Who are you? Tell me about yourself. Do you have a name I can call you by?

B: Steve. You can call me Steve. (pp. 139–140)

In the Spanos et al. (1985) study, undergraduate students were told that they would play the role of an accused murderer and that, despite much evidence of guilt, a plea of not guilty had been entered. They were also told that they were to participate in a simulated psychiatric interview that might involve hypnosis. Then the students were taken to another room and introduced to the psychiatrist, actually an experimental assistant. After a number of standard questions, the interviews diverged depending on which of three experimental conditions the students were assigned to. In the most important of these, the Bianchi condition, students were given a rudimentary hypnotic induction and were instructed to let a second personality come forward, just as in the actual Bianchi case.

After the experimental manipulations, the possible existence of a second personality was probed directly by the "psychiatrist." In addition, students were asked questions about the facts of the murders. Finally, in a second session, those who had acknowledged the presence of another personality were asked to take two personality tests twice—once each for their two personalities. Eighty-one percent of the students in the Bianchi condition adopted a new name, and many of these admitted guilt for the murders. Even the personality test scores of the two personalities differed considerably.

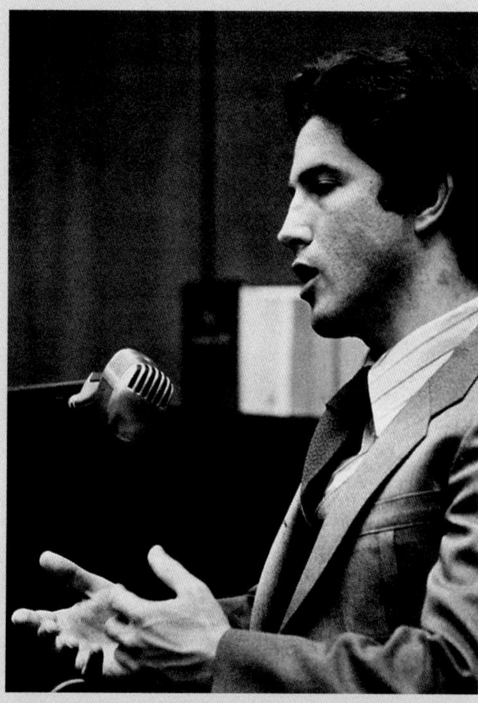

Ken Bianchi, the Hillside Strangler, attempted an insanity defence for his serial killings, but the court decided that he had merely tried to fake a multiple personality.

Clearly, when the situation demands, people can adopt a second personality. Spanos et al. suggested that some people who present as multiple personalities may have a rich fantasy life and considerable practice imagining that they are other people, especially when, like Bianchi, they find themselves in a situation in which there are inducements and cues to behave as though a previous bad act had been committed by another personality. We should remember, however, that this demonstration illustrates only that such role-playing is possible; it in no way determines that cases of multiple personality have such origins. Furthermore, the impact of such role-playing studies depends on how compelling the role-playing is as an analogue of DID. Critics have pointed out that DID is a complex disorder involving many symptoms, including auditory hallucinations, time loss, and depersonalization. None of these symptoms has been produced in role-playing studies (Gleaves, 1996).

In the actual trial of Bianchi, his insanity plea did not hold up, in part because of evidence from Martin Orne, a well-known expert on hypnosis. Orne subsequently interviewed Bianchi and demonstrated that his role enactment differed in important ways from how true multiple personalities and deeply hypnotized people act (Orne, Dinges, & Orne, 1984).

Finally, the third thing that Spanos is known for is his research, with Cross, Dickson, and DuBreuil (1993) on people who reported seeing actual UFOs (i.e., unidentified flying objects). These 49 people were recruited via a newspaper advertisement placed in an Ottawa newspaper, and then their psychological characteristics were compared with samples of students and community members who did not report seeing a UFO. Spanos et al. (1993) found that there was no evidence indicating that the UFO group had higher levels of psychopathology, higher levels of fantasy-proneness, and lower levels of intelligence relative to the other two groups. The factor that best distinguished the groups was the tendency for members of the UFO group to believe wholeheartedly in UFOs and alien life forms. Spanos et al. (1993) concluded that "with respect to UFO experiences, these ideas suggest that beliefs in alien visitation and flying saucers serve as templates against which people shape ambiguous external information, diffuse physical sensations, and vivid imaginings into alien encounters that are experienced as real events" (p. 631). According to Spanos, the alleged UFO incidents are byproducts of cognitive constructions that largely operate when people are asleep. They are complex false memories.

In his book, Spanos (1996) turned to an examination of the links among DID, false memories, and hypnosis, making a significant contribution to the scientific debate about the role that repressed memories of early childhood abuse play in the development of DID. Spanos was a skeptical scientist, as indicated in the following summary:

> Therapists who believe the false memories of MPD patients cite several reasons for their belief, all of which are problematic. Reliance on the strength of patients' emotional responses and the detail and apparent coherence of the memories are misleading because these attributes are also seen in demonstrably false recollections and can readily be created experimentally through suggestion. (Spanos, 1996, p. 114)

It is important to note that Spanos was not denying the reality of childhood abuse, including sexual abuse, and that people can have memories of that abuse.

According to Wagstaff (1995), with the premature death of Nicholas Spanos, psychology has "not just lost one of the greatest names in hypnosis research, we have lost one of the great psychologists of modern times" (p. 41).

A critical piece of evidence regarding the two theories is whether or not DID actually develops in childhood as a result of abuse. When patients with DID enter therapy, they are usually unaware of their alters, but as therapy progresses, alters emerge and patients report that their alters did begin in childhood. Typically, however, there has been no corroborating evidence for this, and we have previously cautioned about the uncritical acceptance of self-reports. The situation is similar regarding physical or sexual abuse: very high rates have been reported (e.g., Ross et al., 1990), but they have not been corroborated (see Focus on Discovery 7.3.).

One study, however, has come close to providing clearer data regarding both childhood onset and abuse in cases of DID, although it has been criticized by proponents of the role-enactment theory (Lilienfeld et al., 1999). The study, which was conducted over a period of two decades, examined 150 convicted murderers in detail (Lewis et al., 1997). Fourteen cases of DID were found. That the study was conducted on convicted murderers is important because in this situation adopting the role of a person with DID involves an obvious payoff. But the evidence indicated that 12 of the 14 cases had long-standing DID symptoms that preceded their incarceration: eight had experienced trances during childhood, nine had had auditory hallucinations, and 10 had had imaginary companions (a frequent report among DID patients). Each of these symptoms was corroborated by at least three outside sources (e.g., interviews with family members, teachers, parole officers). Furthermore, several participants showed distinctly different handwriting styles well before committing their crimes (see Figure 7.4).

Also important in this study was the documentation of physical or sexual abuse during childhood for 11 cases. Again, this was confirmed by outside sources and physical evidence such as scars. Indeed, the authors noted that "the term 'abuse' does not do justice to the quality of maltreatment these individuals endured. A more accurate term would be 'torture'!" One boy was set on fire, another was circumcised by his father at age 3, and another was forced to sit on a hot stove. These data, then, lend support to the proposition that DID does begin in childhood and that it is related to extreme stress.

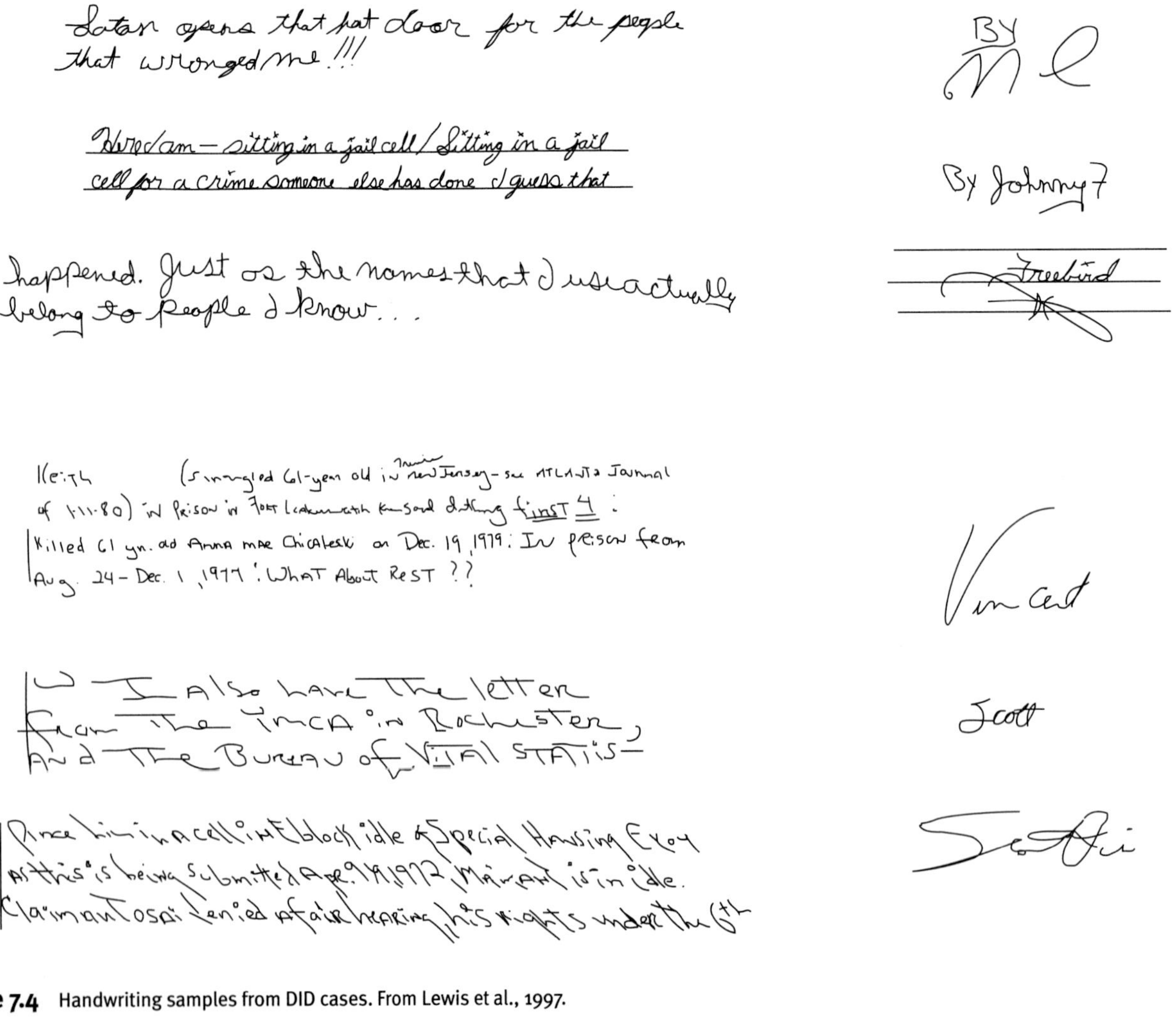

Figure 7.4 Handwriting samples from DID cases. From Lewis et al., 1997.

THERAPIES FOR DISSOCIATIVE DISORDERS

Dissociative disorders suggest, perhaps better than any other disorders, the possible relevance of psychoanalytic theorizing. In three disorders—amnesia, fugue, and dissociative identity disorder—people behave in ways that very assuredly indicate that they cannot access forgotten earlier parts of their lives. And since these people may at the same time be unaware of having forgotten something, the hypothesis that they have repressed or dissociated massive portions of their lives is compelling (MacGregor, 1996).

Consequently, psychoanalytic treatment is perhaps more widespread as a choice of treatment for dissociative disorders than for any other psychological problems. The goal of lifting repressions is the order of the day, pursued via the use of basic psychoanalytic techniques.

Because dissociative disorders are widely believed to arise from traumatic events that the person is trying to block from consciousness, there are links between therapies for these disorders and therapies for posttraumatic stress disorder. Indeed, PTSD is the most commonly diagnosed comorbid disorder with DID (Loewenstein, 1991). It is therefore no surprise that some mental health specialists propose strategies for these problems that are reminiscent of treatments for PTSD, such as encouraging the patients to think back to the traumatic events that are believed to have triggered the problem and to view them in a context of safety and support and with the expectation that they can come to terms with the horrible things that happened to them.

As discussed in Chapter 1, psychoanalysis had its beginnings in hypnosis, with Mesmer's work in the late 18th century and Charcot's work in the 19th century. Through the years, practitioners have continued to use hypnosis with patients diagnosed with dissociative disorders as a means of helping them gain access to hidden portions of their personality—to a lost identity or to a set of events precipitating or flowing from a trauma.

Treatment of DID As mentioned earlier, DID patients are unusually hypnotizable, and it is believed that they cope with stress by using their hypnotisability (unconsciously) to enter a dissociative, trancelike state (Butler et al., 1996). For these reasons, hypnosis is used commonly in the treatment of DID (Putnam, 1993). The general idea is that the recovery of repressed painful memories will be facilitated by recreating the state entered into during the original abuse, a hypothesis consistent with classic research conducted in Canada on state-dependent learning (Bower, 1981; Eich, 1995). Typically, the person is hypnotized (sometimes with the aid of drugs such as sodium Amytal) and encouraged to go back in his or her mind to events in childhood—a technique called age regression. The hope is that accessing these traumatic memories will allow the adult to realize that the dangers from childhood are not now present and that his or her current life need not be governed by these ghosts from the past (Grinker & Spiegel, 1944; Loewenstein, 1991). A long-term study of DID patients from Canada and the United States who received this treatment revealed that the patients showed significant improvements on a number of indicators, including dissociative symptoms and symptoms of borderline personality disorder (Ellason & Ross, 1997). This study represents initial evidence that DID patients may respond well to treatment, with the caveat that the results must be interpreted with some caution owing to the lack of control groups for comparison purposes.

It is ironic that family-based interventions are not as often discussed in the DID treatment literature as individual therapy, for DID is widely believed to result from problematic family relationships, specifically physical and/or sexual abuse in the patient's childhood (Simon, 1998). There have been some proposals to remedy this omission (e.g., Chiappa, 1994).

As DID is often comorbid with anxiety and depression, it is not surprising that case studies suggest that improvement in a DID patient's anxiety and depression is sometimes effected through psychoactive drugs such as tranquilizers and antidepressants, though without effect on the dissociative identity disorder itself (Simon, 1998).

focus on discovery/7.3

Repressed Memories of Childhood Sexual Abuse

We have seen that a history of abuse in childhood is thought to be an important cause of DID. In later chapters, we will learn that sexual abuse is considered to play a role in several other disorders. Until recently, childhood sexual abuse (CSA) was thought to be a relatively rare occurrence. Now it is estimated that between 15 and 30 percent of women experienced CSA (Finkelhor, 1993). Although the data on the frequency of CSA have been derived from the retrospective reports of patients and thus could be distorted, most researchers assume that the reports are fairly accurate.

Here we focus on the special instance of *recovered memories* of sexual abuse. In these cases the patient had no memory of abuse until it was recovered, typically during psychotherapy. Few issues are more hotly debated in psychology and in the courts than whether these recovered memories are valid. Memory and some hypnosis researchers caution against a blanket acceptance of memories of sexual or physical abuse recovered during therapy (Loftus, 1997; Spanos, 1996). It is important to raise such questions; good science requires it, and the issue is key for court cases where recovered memories may play a major role in convicting a parent or other person of sexual abuse (Pope, 1995). However, from a feminist perspective, Connie Kristiansen at Carleton University and her associates have outlined their concerns about ideologies prevailing over scientific research and the possibility that women who have indeed been abused will remain silent because the validity of recovered memories in general has been called into question; Kristiansen et al., 1999).

Recovered memories of CSA have assumed great importance in a series of court cases (Earleywine & Gann, 1995). In a typical scenario, a woman accuses one or both of her parents of having abused her during childhood and brings charges against them. Courts in several U.S. states allow plaintiffs to sue for damages within three years of the time they remember the abuse (Wakefield & Underwager, 1994). These cases depend on memories of CSA that were recovered in adulthood, often during psychotherapy, and that were apparently repressed for many years.

Williams (1995) conducted one of the most scientifically accurate studies of memories of sexual abuse by interviewing women whose abuse years earlier had been verified. Fully 38 percent of these women were unable to recall the abuse when they were asked about it almost two decades later. Williams (1995) concluded that forgetting CSA is a relatively common occurrence. More recently, however, Goodman et al. (2003) interviewed 175 adults with documented CSA histories and found that only 19 percent did not report the abuse. Rates of non-disclosure were substantially higher (30 percent) among African Americans relative to other racial groups, and the authors attributed this to a greater unwillingness for African Americans to disclose. Goodman et al. (2003) concluded that forgetting CSA may not be as common an experience as first thought.

These data notwithstanding, is it justifiable to assume that recovered memories are *invariably* accurate reports of repressed memories? This is a question of enormous legal and scientific importance. Studies have been conducted on women who have reported a history of sexual abuse. The women were asked whether there ever was a time when they could not remember the abuse. Based on these data, the frequency of "repression" ranges from 18 to 59 percent (Loftus, 1993). But a simple failure to remember does not mean that repression has occurred. Women could actively try to keep these thoughts out of mind because they are distressing. Or the abuse could have happened before the time of their earliest memories (generally around age 3 or 4). Nor has it been scientifically demonstrated that children repress or even forget traumatic events. As already mentioned, one of the hallmarks of posttraumatic stress disorder is the frequent reliving of the trauma in memory. Rather than repressing negative events, children recall them quite vividly (see Earleywine & Gann, 1995; Goodman et al., 2003).

Some allegedly recovered memories have no basis in fact, but if that is the case, where do they come from? Elizabeth Loftus (1993) suggests several possibilities:

1 **Popular writings.** *The Courage to Heal* (Bass & Davis, 1994) is a guide for victims of childhood sexual abuse and is widely known in the recovered-memory movement. It repeatedly suggests to readers that they were probably abused and offers as symptoms of abuse low self-esteem, feeling different from others, substance abuse, sexual dysfunction, and depression. In fact, symptoms such as these can result from many causal factors, not only from CSA.

2 **Therapists' suggestions**. By their own accounts, some therapists directly suggest to their clients, sometimes with the assistance of hypnotic age regression (itself a procedure with no established scientific validity), that childhood sexual abuse is likely. Note that one of the defining characteristics of hypnosis is heightened suggestibility. If a therapist believes in a given case that sexual abuse has been repressed, it is possible that memories recovered during hypnosis were planted there by the therapist (Kihlstrom, 1997; Loftus, 1997).

3 **Research on memory.** Cognitive psychologists have shown that it is possible for people to construct recollections of events that did not happen. Neisser and Harsch (1991) studied people's memories of where they were when they heard about the *Challenger* disaster on January 28, 1986. Participants were interviewed the day after the explosion and again two years later. Despite reporting vivid memories, none of the participants were entirely accurate in their later accounts and many were way off the mark.

There is little doubt that CSA exists and that it may be much more frequent than any of us would like to believe (Finkelhor, 1993). But we must be wary of uncritical acceptance of reports of abuse. Social scientists, lawyers, and the courts share a heavy responsibility in deciding whether a given recovered memory is a reflection of an actual (and criminal) event. Erring in either direction creates an injustice.

We will let Prout and Dobson (1998) from the University of Calgary have the final word on this issue. They have suggested quite reasonably that the best approach right now is a "middle ground perspective," one that recognizes that while child abuse claims can be quite legitimate, there is also the possibility that certain clinicians have facilitated false reports, and each case should be evaluated individually without preconceptions.

There seems to be widespread agreement on several principles in the treatment of dissociative identity disorder, whatever the clinician's orientation (Ross, 1989). The Executive Council of the International Society for the Study of Dissociation formulated a series of agreed-upon treatment guidelines at a meeting conducted in Vancouver in May 1994. The complete outline of the guidelines is available on the society's website (http://www.issd.org). The following are some of the guiding principles:

1 The goal is integration of the several personalities.

2 The optimal treatment modality is usually individual outpatient psychotherapy.

3 Regarding hypnotherapy, hypnotic techniques can be useful in crisis management to help patients stop spontaneous flashbacks.

4 In terms of recovered memories, therapists should take a respectful neutral stance, avoid suggestive and leading

interview techniques, but still afford the patient the freedom to evaluate the accuracy of their own memories.

5 When certain personalities are experienced as demons, exorcisms should be avoided; exorcism rituals have not been found to be effective.

The goal of any approach to DID should be to convince the person that forgetting or splitting into different personalities is no longer necessary to deal with traumas, either those in the past that triggered the original dissociation or those in the present or yet to be confronted in the future. In addition, assuming that DID and the other dissociative disorders are in some measure an escape response to high levels of stress, treatment can be enhanced by teaching the patient to cope better with present-day challenges.

Because of the rarity of DID and because it has often been misdiagnosed, there are no controlled outcome studies. Nearly all the well-reported outcome data come from the clinical observations of one highly experienced therapist, Richard Kluft (e.g., 1984a). Over a 10-year period, Kluft had contact with 171 cases. Of these, 83, or 68 percent, achieved integration of their alters that was stable for at least three months (33 remained stable for almost two and a half years). The greater the number of personalities, the longer the treatment lasted (Putnam et al., 1986); in general, therapy took almost two years and upwards of 500 hours per patient. In a more recent follow-up, Kluft reported that 103, or 84 percent of the original 123 patients, had achieved stable integration of their multiple personalities and another 10 percent were at least functioning better (Kluft, 1994). Sometimes complete integration of personalities cannot be achieved, and the most realistic outcome is some manner of "conflict-free collaboration" among the person's various personalities (Kluft, 1988, p. 578). Positive findings have been reported more recently by Ellason and Ross (1997). Canadian Perspectives 7.2 describes the provocative possibility that multiple personalities were once created for military purposes.

Canadian Perspectives/7.2

Interview with Colin Ross: The Creation of Multiple Personalities as Couriers for Military Purposes?

"Strange as it may seem, all of us appear to have another person living within our bodies besides ourselves. This other person, this unconscious mind, is quite as capable of handling our bodies as we are, and does so in the most startling manner."

—G.H. Estabrooks, in his book, *Spiritism* (1947, p. 30).

There are many things about the dissociative disorders that are highly controversial and thought-provoking. We conclude this chapter with an intriguing account of the use of thought control and the possible creation of multiple personalities for military purposes. In a radio interview conducted at Ryerson University in Toronto, Colin Ross related the following:

> ...But it is absolutely known for a fact that Dr. West and Dr. Orne had extensive funding from all branches of military intelligence from the CIA and had top secret clearance ... Martin Orne is tied in to a man named G. H. Estabrooks who was one of probably the top ten leading experts on hypnosis in the 20th century....G. H. Estabrooks was actually a Canadian by birth, he was a Rhodes Scholar, moved into Upper State New York, and basically spent his professional career in New York.* ... And he published starting in 1943 and going all the way up to 1971 ... very, very detailed accounts of creating Multiple Personalities during WWII for various branches of the U.S.A. military. Basically, he called these people Multiple Personalities. He talked about the Multiple Personality literature, and he referred to them as super-spies. The idea is that you create somebody artificially, using hypnosis and other mind control techniques who had no multiple personality before, but now has this second identity. And the second identity is hidden behind a memory barrier, an amnesia barrier, and there is a verbal access code that is used to call out the second identity. So, say this person is a Marine, they will be given some kind of courier assignment to take some documents to, for example, Tokyo, but G. H. Estabrooks then calls out the second personality and sticks in some classified information into this second personality. There is a switch-back to the main identity, and the person is just going on this routine trip to take documents or technical material over to Tokyo. When he gets to the far end, he uses the example of a Col. Brown who then uses the code signal, and the example he uses in the description is, "The moon is clear." As soon as Col. Brown says "The moon is clear," the second personality pops out, gives the classified message. Col. Brown inserts a classified response, then the person pops back to their regular identity, goes back to the States and thinks they have just gone on a routine assignment. But Estabrooks again says "The moon is clear," the identity pops out, and Estabrooks gets the classified message. He describes using these people

in classified courier missions for actual operations, extensively many times during WWII. (Ross, April 6, 1997) **

In his 1997 book, *Dissociative Identity Disorder: Diagnosis, Clinical Features, and Treatment of Multiple Personality*, Ross reviews the material that was the basis for his interview comments and states that Estabrooks is the only scientist,

> to describe systematically creating DID for military intelligence agencies, and the use of these individuals in covert operations. He describes this under a subheading "The Super Spy" in a chapter entitled "Psychological Warfare" in the 1957 edition of *Hypnotism*, and also in his *Science Digest article* (1971). (Ross, 1997, p. 42)

* George H. Estabrooks was born in Saint John, New Brunswick, on December 16, 1895. He completed his B.A. at Acadia University in Wolfville, Nova Scotia.

**Ross (1997) accepted Estabrooks's description of his artificial creation of DID as evidence that iatrogenic shaping of DID can actually occur. In fairness, he also argued that creating artificial secondary personalities in adults would require a great deal of time, persuasion, and control.

Thinking Critically

1. What are your thoughts on Ross's story about the creation of DID for military purposes? It sounds disturbingly like scenarios depicted in a Hollywood movie called *The Manchurian Candidate*. Is it really possible to create a second identity or does it defy credibility? Are you a "skeptic" or a "believer?"
2. Assume for the moment that you are a believer. Also assume that you are a psychologist with the Canadian Armed Forces and that you are charged with the responsibility of creating "multiples" for use by our military. Suspending for the moment the obvious ethical concerns that you should have (see Chapter 18), how would you go about creating a second identity that would be "hidden behind a memory barrier"? Obviously, you should not be allowed to administer traumatic experiences or stressors to trigger dissociation; however, we do know enough about various factors that make people vulnerable to the development of dissociative disorders that you could preselect people in such a way that you would increase the probability of some "success." Describe your ideal candidates for the project and then outline your training procedure. Don't forget the "code signal" to trigger the "switch-back."

SUMMARY

- In somatoform disorders, there are physical symptoms for which no biological basis can be found. The sensory and motor dysfunctions of conversion disorder, one of the two principal types of somatoform disorders, suggest neurological impairments, but ones that do not always make anatomical sense; the symptoms do, however, seem to serve some psychological purpose. In somatization disorder, multiple physical complaints, not adequately explained by physical disorder or injury, lead to frequent visits to physicians, hospitalization, and even unnecessary surgery.
- Anxiety plays a role in somatoform disorders, but it is not expressed overtly; instead, it is transformed into physical symptoms. Theory concerning the etiology of these disorders is speculative and focuses primarily on conversion disorder. Psychoanalytic theory proposes that in conversion disorder repressed impulses are converted into physical symptoms. Behavioural theories focus on the conscious and deliberate adoption of the symptoms as a means of obtaining a desired goal. In therapies for somatoform disorders, analysts try to help the client face up to the repressed impulses and behavioural treatments attempt to reduce anxiety and reinforce behaviour that will allow the patient to relinquish the symptoms.
- Dissociative disorders are disruptions of consciousness, memory, and identity. An inability to recall important personal information, usually after some traumatic experience, is diagnosed as dissociative amnesia. In dissociative fugue, the person moves away, assumes a new identity, and is amnesic for his or her previous life. In depersonalization disorder, the person's perception of the self is altered; he or she may experience being outside the body or changes in the size of body parts. The person with dissociative identity disorder has two or more distinct and fully developed personalities, each with unique memories, behaviour patterns, and relationships.
- Psychoanalytic theory regards dissociative disorders as instances of massive repression of some undesirable event or aspect of the self. In dissociative identity disorder, the role of abuse in childhood and a high level of hypnotizability are emerging as important. Behavioural theories consider dissociative reactions escape responses motivated by high levels of anxiety. Both analytic and behavioural clinicians focus their treatment efforts on understanding the anxiety associated with the forgotten memories, since it is viewed as etiologically significant.

KEY TERMS

anesthesias (p. 197)
body dysmorphic disorder (p. 196)
conversion disorder (p. 197)
depersonalization disorder (p. 208)
dissociative amnesia (p. 207)
dissociative disorders (p. 195)
dissociative fugue (p. 208)
dissociative identity disorder (DID) (p. 209)
factitious disorder (p. 199)
hypochondriasis (p. 196)
hysteria (p. 198)
la belle indifférence (p. 199)
malingering (p. 199)
pain disorder (p. 195)
somatization disorder (p. 200)
somatoform disorders (p. 195)

Reflections: Past, Present, and Future

- In Chapter 2, we pointed out that in some cultures, such as the Chinese, people tend to describe psychological problems as somatic or physical illnesses, perhaps in part because they can feel less shame if they have a somatic or physical illness rather than a psychological disorder. Do you think that their belief system increases the likelihood that diagnosable somatic disorders will be more prevalent in people from these cultures? The somatoform disorders are typically more prevalent in women than in men. Do you think that the prevalence of somatoform disorders in Chinese males will be as high as or higher than the prevalence of these disorders in Chinese women?
- Conversion disorder is often comorbid with other disorders, including depression, substance abuse, and borderline and histrionic personality disorders. Assume that you are a psychologist who is conducting CBT with a Chinese client who has a conversion disorder as well as an Axis I and Axis II disorder. How would this information influence your case conceptualization (see Chapter 4) and the development of your treatment plan?
- Recall the quotation by Donald Hebb at the outset of this chapter. Hebb first made this comment in an editorial for an issue of the *Canadian MPD Newsletter* back in 1982. Based on your own understanding of the past 20 years of research, do you consider DID to be a "disorder of the brain"?
- What are your thoughts on Nick Spanos's sociocognitive perspective on DID? Do you think that he is right in the following claim?

  > Expectations transmitted to patients, and the selective reinforcement of increasingly dramatic displays in MPD patients, frequently translate into an increase in the number of alters and ... an increase in the extent of abuse "remembered" by those alters. (Spanos, 1996, p. 233)

  Do you believe that at least some cases of DID are therapist produced? To what extent can iatrogenic influences account for DID?
- Do you think that DID should be allowed as an excusing condition for a criminal act? In the United States, Billy Milligan, a 23-year-old drifter, was acquitted of rape as a result of being diagnosed with MPD. Psychologists believed that Billy had 10 personalities (eight male and two female). His 19-year-old lesbian personality, Adelena, was held responsible for committing the rapes. We will return to this issue in Chapter 18. In the meantime, reflect on whether or not DID should be allowed as an "insanity" defence in Canada.

8 chapter

Psychophysiological Disorders and Health Psychology

"Worry affects circulation, the heart and the glands, the whole nervous system, and profoundly affects the heart. I have never known who died from overwork, but many who died from doubt."

—Charles H. Mayo

"Every stress leaves an indelible scar, and the organism pays for its survival after a stressful situation by becoming a little older."

—Hans Selye

"An hour of pain is as long as a day of pleasure."

—Proverb

Marian Dale Scott, *Atom, Bone and Embryo*, 1943
oil on canvas, 91.4 x 101.6 cm
ART GALLERY OF ONTARIO, TORONTO

MARK HOWARD was 38. After earning an M.B.A., he had joined the marketing division of a large conglomerate and had worked his way up the corporate ladder. His talent and long hours of work had recently culminated in a promotion to head of his division. The promotion left him with mixed feelings. On the one hand, it was what he had been working so hard to achieve, but on the other, he had never been comfortable giving orders to others and he especially dreaded the staff meetings he would have to run.

Soon after the promotion, during a routine checkup, Mark's physician discovered that Mark's blood pressure had moved into the borderline hypertension range, around 150 over 100. Before implementing any treatment, the physician asked Mark to wear an ambulatory monitor for a few days so that his blood pressure could be assessed as he went about his usual routine. The device was programmed to take blood pressure readings 20 times a day.

On the first day of monitoring, Mark had a staff meeting scheduled for ten o'clock. While he was laying out the marketing plans for a new product, the cuff inflated to take his blood pressure. A couple of minutes later, he checked the reading and became visibly pale. It was 195 over 140—not a borderline reading, but seriously high blood pressure. The next day he resigned his managerial role and returned to a less prestigious but, he hoped, less stressful position.

Psychophysiological disorders, such as asthma, hypertension, headache, and gastritis, are characterized by genuine physical symptoms that are caused by or can be worsened by emotional factors. The term *psychophysiological disorders* is preferred today to a term that was formerly used and is perhaps better known, psychosomatic disorders. Nevertheless, the term *psychosomatic* connotes quite well the principal feature of these disorders, that the psyche, or mind, is having an untoward effect on the soma, or body.

In contrast to many of the disorders described in Chapter 7 (e.g., hypochondriasis, somatization disorder, and conversion disorder), psychophysiological disorders are real diseases involving damage to the body (see Table 8.1). That such disorders are viewed as being related to emotional factors does not make the afflictions imaginary. People can just as readily die from psychologically produced high blood pressure or asthma as from similar diseases produced by infection or physical injury.

Psychophysiological disorders as such do not appear in DSM-IV, as they did in some earlier versions of the DSM. DSM-IV requires a diagnostic judgment to indicate the presence of psychological factors affecting medical condition, and this diagnosis is coded in the broad section that comprises "other conditions that may be a focus of clinical attention." The implication of this placement is that psychophysiological disorders are not a form of mental disorder. Nonetheless, we consider them here in some detail because of their historical link to the field of psychopathology.

The new approach to diagnosis is also broader in scope. Formerly, psychophysiological disorders were generally thought to include only some diseases (the classic psychosomatic diseases, such as ulcers, headaches, asthma, and hypertension). The new diagnosis is applicable to any disease, as it is now thought that any disease can be influenced by psychological factors, such as stress. Furthermore, the diagnosis of psychological factors affecting medical condition includes cases in which the psychological or behavioural factor influences the course or treatment of a disorder, not just cases in which it influences the onset, again broadening the definition. For example, a person with hypertension may continue to drink alcohol even though he or she knows that alcohol increases blood pressure, or a patient may fail to take prescribed medication regularly. The psychological or behavioural factors include Axis I and II diagnoses; personality traits; coping styles, such as holding anger in rather than expressing it; and lifestyle factors, such as failing to exercise regularly.

What is the evidence for the view that any illness may be in part stress related? For years, it has been known that various physical diseases can be produced in laboratory animals by exposure to severe stressors. Usually the diseases produced in such studies were the classic psychophysiological disorders, such as ulcers. More recently, studies have indicated that a broader range of diseases may be related to stress. Sklar and Anisman (1979) conducted research in Ottawa that involved inducing tumours in mice and then measuring the impact of stress—uncontrollable electric shocks—on growth of the tumours. The tumours grew more rapidly in animals exposed to electric shock, and these animals died earlier. Similarly, a 20-year follow-up of stress reactions in war veterans revealed unusually high rates of a broad range of diseases involving the circulatory, respiratory, digestive, musculoskeletal, endocrine, and nervous systems (Boscarino, 1997).

Table 8.1
Comparing Psychophysiological and Conversion Disorders

Type of Disorder	Organic Bodily Damage	Bodily Function Affected
Conversion	No	Voluntary
Psycho-physiological	Yes	Involuntary

The many demonstrations of the pervasive role of psychological factors in health form the basis for the fields of behavioural medicine and health psychology. Since the 1970s, these fields have dealt with the role of psychological factors in all facets of health and illness. Beyond examining the etiological role that stress can play in illness, researchers in these fields study psychological treatments (e.g., biofeedback for headache) and the health care system itself (e.g., how better to deliver services to underserved populations) (Appel et al., 1997; Schwartz & Weiss, 1977; Stone, 1982).

Prevention is also a major focus of health psychology. As the 20th century progressed and infectious diseases were brought under better control, people were dying more often from such illnesses as cardiovascular disease (CVD). It is estimated that 45 percent of all causes of death are cardiovascular in nature (Linden, 2003) and CVD remains the leading cause of death in Canada (Manuel et al., 2003). The causes of CVD involve behaviour—people's lifestyles—such as smoking, eating too much, and excessive alcohol use. Thus, it is believed that many CVD cases can be prevented by changing unhealthy lifestyles. Health psychologists are at the forefront of these preventative efforts, some of which we describe later in this chapter.

Health psychology and behavioural medicine are not restricted to a set of techniques or to particular principles of changing behaviour. Clinicians in the field employ a wide variety of procedures—from contingency management, to stress reduction, to cognitive-behavioural approaches—all of which share the goal of altering bad living habits, distressed psychological states, and aberrant physiological processes in order to improve a person's health.

STRESS AND HEALTH

We begin by reviewing general findings on the relationship between stress and health, as well as theories about how stress can produce illness.

DEFINING THE CONCEPT OF STRESS

In earlier chapters, the term stress was used to refer to some environmental condition that triggers psychopathology. Here we shall examine the term more closely and consider the difficulties in its definition.

The term stress was created by Hans Selye. Selye was and remains a world renowned researcher who eventually became a Canadian citizen and conducted much of his research in Montreal. Selye is also known for identifying the general adaptation syndrome (GAS), which is described more fully in Canadian Contributions 8.1.

Canadian Contributions/8.1

Hans Selye:
THE FATHER OF STRESS?

Dr. Hans Selye is regarded as the father of the *stress* concept and the inventor of the common term *stress*. Selye was born in Europe but immigrated to the United States when he was awarded a Rockefeller fellowship. In 1932 he immigrated to Canada when he was hired as an associate professor of histology at McGill University in Montreal. Selye was to remain in Canada the rest of his life. He became a Canadian citizen and was recognized as a Companion of the Order of Canada in 1968 for his pioneering research on the nature of stress. He authored 30 books and hundreds of research articles on the nature of stress in animals and people.

Most doctors focus on precise illnesses caused by specific factors, but Selye was an endocrinologist who was interested in the "general syndrome of being sick." He noticed early in his career that organisms exposed to a diverse array of stimuli (e.g., trauma, cold, heat, nervous irritation) often exhibit a similar, non-specific response. Accordingly, he viewed stress as a non-specific response of the body to any demand for change.

In 1936 Hans Selye introduced the general adaptation syndrome (GAS), a description of the biological response to sustained and unrelenting physical stress (i.e., a biological stress syndrome). There are three phases of the model, as shown in Figure 8.1.

1 During the first phase, the alarm reaction, the autonomic nervous system is activated by the stress. If the stress is too powerful, gastrointestinal ulcers form, the adrenal glands become enlarged, and the thymus undergoes atrophy (wasting away).

2 During the second phase, resistance, the organism adapts to the stress through available coping mechanisms. The length of resistance depends on the body's innate adaptability and the intensity of the stressor (Selye, 1974).

3 If the stressor persists or the organism is unable to respond effectively, the third phase, a stage of exhaustion, follows, and the organism dies or suffers irreversible damage (Selye, 1950).

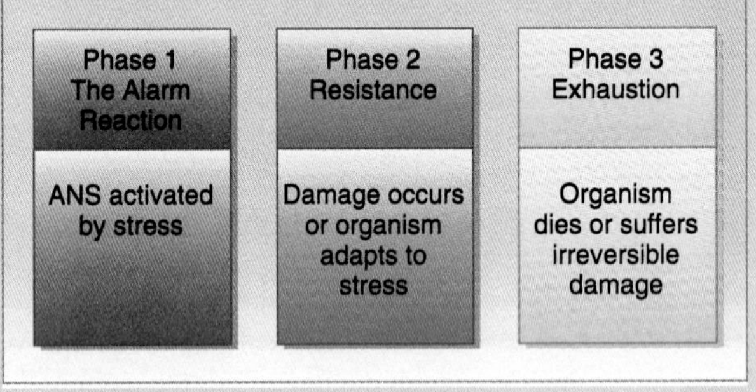

Figure 8.1 Selye's general adaptation syndrome.

Canada Post stamp commemorating the important contributions to our understanding of stress that were initiated by Hans Selye.

Selye is especially well-known for promoting the view that stress plays a role, for better or worse, in all diseases (see Selye, 1974). The role of stress in various illnesses is discussed in subsequent sections of this chapter.

Selye made an important distinction between negative and positive forms of stress, and this was reflected in his use of the terms distress and eustress. Distress was the term he used to describe damaging or unpleasant stress. Eustress was the term that he used to refer to positive, pleasant stress. He believed that pleasant and unpleasant emotional arousal result in increased levels of physiological stress, but only negative emotional arousal results in distress.

In time, Selye came to believe that the term stress was misleading and that he should have used the term *strain* instead, since "stress" had other meanings in the field of physics. But, according to Rosch (1998), Selye is regarded as the creator of the word as it is used commonly because many other languages lack a suitable word or phrase that can convey what is meant by the word stress.

Ironically, it appears that Selye's own medical history served as an illustration of the role that psychological factors play in stress and illness. According to Rosch (1998), at one point, Selye "developed a rare and usually fatal malignancy, and attributed his rather remarkable recovery to his strong desire to continue his research. He was convinced that stress could cause cancer, and that a strong faith could reverse this" (p. 5). Indeed, the role of psychological factors in cancer is detailed in a subsequent section of this chapter.

Selye's concept of stress eventually found its way into the psychological literature, but with substantial changes in its definition. Some researchers followed Selye's lead and considered stress a *response* to environmental conditions, defined on the basis of such diverse criteria as emotional upset, deterioration of performance, or physiological changes such as increased skin conductance or increases in the levels of certain hormones. The problem with these response-based definitions of stress is that the criteria are not clear-cut. Physiological changes in the body can occur in response to a number of stimuli that we would not consider stressful (e.g., anticipating a pleasurable event).

Other researchers looked on stress as a *stimulus*, often referred to as a stressor, and identified it with a long list of environmental conditions—electric shock, boredom, uncontrollable stimuli, catastrophic life events, daily hassles, and sleep deprivation. Stimuli that are considered stressors can be major (the death of a loved one), minor (being stuck in traffic), acute (failing an exam), or chronic (a persistently unpleasant work environment). According to one Canadian researcher, chronic stress can take many forms, including persistent threats, demands, and conflicts, as well as a sense of being under-rewarded and being deprived of essential resources, as might be the case with individuals from disadvantaged groups (see Wheaton, 1997).

Stressors can also be distinguished in terms of whether they are psychogenic or neurogenic (see Anisman & Merali, 1999). *Psychogenic stressors* stem from psychological factors (e.g., anticipation of an adverse event), while *neurogenic stressors* stem from a physical stimulus (e.g., bodily injury or recovery from surgery). Anisman and Merali (1999) noted that various stressors can differ in a number of ways, including whether they are controllable (i.e., stress can be lessened or eliminated by engaging in a certain response) or uncontrollable, predictable or unpredictable, short in duration or chronic, and intermittent or recurring. Anisman and Merali (1999) also described how different stressors have different physiological implications: for example, chronic, intermittent, and unpredictable stressors are less likely to result in neurochemical adaptation while intense and prolonged demands on neurochemical systems may create a condition known as allostatic load, which can lead to a variety of pathological outcomes.

Like response-based definitions, stimulus-based definitions also present problems. Stipulating exactly what constitutes a stressor is difficult. More than negativity is clearly involved; marriage, for instance, generally a positive event, is regarded as a stressor because it requires adaptation. Furthermore, people vary widely in how they respond to life's challenges. A given event does not elicit the same amount of stress in everyone. A family that has lost its home in a flood but has enough money to rebuild and a strong network of friends will experience less hardship than a family that has neither adequate money to rebuild nor a social network to provide support.

Some people believe that it is not possible to define

objectively what events or situations qualify as psychological stressors (e.g., Lazarus, 1966). They emphasize the cognitive aspects of stress; that is, the way we perceive or appraise the environment determines whether a stressor is present. When a person determines that the demands of a situation exceed his or her resources, the person experiences stress. A final exam may be merely challenging to one student, yet highly stressful to another who does not feel equipped to take it (whether his or her fears are realistic or not). Similarly, as shown in a recent study conducted with women from the Ottawa area, the stress experienced during breast cancer screening is closely tied to how the stressful situation is perceived and appraised (Sweet, Savoie, & Lemyre, 1999).

Also relevant to individual differences in responding to stressful situations is the concept of coping, how people try to deal with a problem or handle the emotions it produces. Even among those who appraise a situation as stressful, the effects of the stress may vary depending on how the individual copes with the event. Lazarus and his colleagues have identified two broad dimensions of coping (Lazarus & Folkman, 1984).

- *Problem-focused coping* involves taking direct action to solve the problem or seeking information that will be relevant to the solution. An example is developing a study schedule to pace assignments over a semester and thereby reduce end-of-semester pressure.
- *Emotion-focused coping* refers to efforts to reduce the negative emotional reactions to stress, for example, by distracting oneself from the problem, relaxing, or seeking comfort from others.

Coping can focus on solving the problem itself or on regulating the negative emotions it has created. Seeking comfort or social support from others is an example of emotion-focused coping.

Lazarus (1966) developed a transactional model of stress based on the premise that stress is not solely due to the situation or to an individual's cognitive appraisals and coping responses; rather, stress results from a transaction or interaction between situational factors and factors inside the person. A recent model of stress and coping developed by Neufeld (1999) at the University of Western Ontario also acknowledges the dynamic and ongoing interplay of these factors. A key element of this model is the recognition that stressors and related situations change over time.

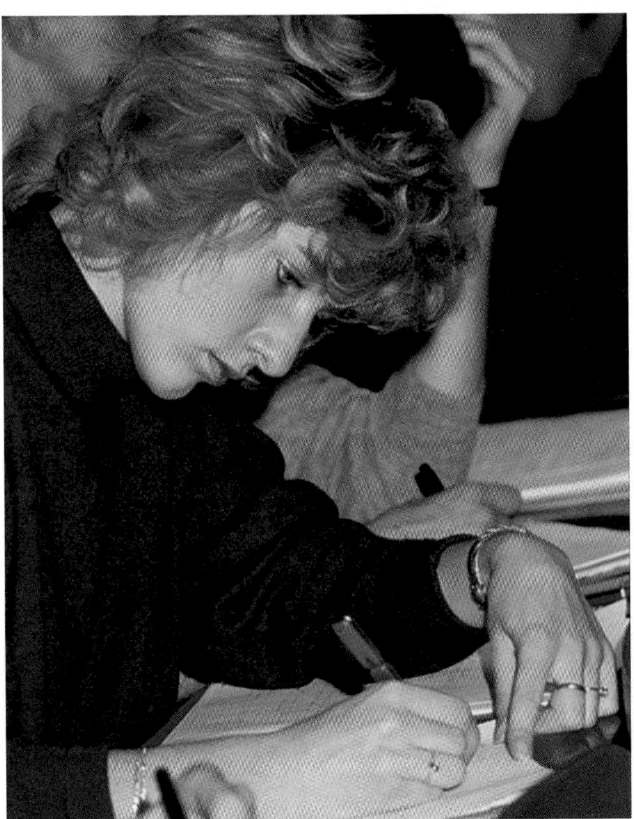

According to Richard Lazarus, the way a life event is appraised is an important determinant of whether it causes stress. An exam, for example, may be viewed as a challenge or as an extremely stressful event.

The effectiveness of attempts to cope varies with the situation. Various investigators (e.g., Endler, Speer, Johnson, & Flett, 2000; Felton & Revenson, 1984; Forsythe & Compas, 1987) have tested a "goodness of fit hypothesis" that suggests that the adaptivity of a particular coping response depends on the match between the coping response and what is called for ideally by the problem situation. Distraction may be an effective way of dealing with the emotional upset produced by impending surgery, but it would be a poor way to handle the upset produced by the discovery of a lump on the breast (Lazarus & Folkman, 1984). Similarly, continuing efforts to seek a solution to an unsolvable problem lead to increases in frustration rather than to any psychological benefit (Terry & Hynes, 1998).

A key factor is whether a problem or situation is controllable or uncontrollable. Problem-focused coping is most adaptive when there is something that an individual can do to improve the situation; emotion-focused coping is less adaptive in these situations. However, when a situation is uncontrollable, problem-focused coping is not adaptive; here it may be better to vent and express one's emotions to release tension (Stanton, Kirk, Cameron, & Danoff-Burg, 2000).

Canadian researchers Paul Wong, Ed Peacock, and Gary Reker have expanded on the notion of goodness of fit in their resource-congruence model of stress and coping (see Peacock & Wong, 1996; Peacock, Wong, & Reker, 1993; Wong, 1993). This model identifies five types of stressors as well as the congruent or matching coping strategies (see Wong, 1993). The five types of stressors are stressors controllable by the self, stressors controllable by others, emotional problems, attitudinal problems, and philosophical problems. We will illustrate the close link between stressors and coping strategies by analyzing how this model would predict the responses of someone writing an exam or test. Regardless of the exact stressor involved, the emphasis here is on determining which coping strategy is suited ideally to the particular stressor or problem that needs to be resolved.

According to Wong's model, stressors that are controllable by the self are best addressed with problem-focused coping and self-reliance. This may include a preventive, anticipatory schema that operates when stressors are expected but have not yet occurred and something can be done about them (i.e., anticipatory stress). For instance, students faced with a difficult test can use the problem-focused strategy of increasing their study time. Similarly, their anticipatory schema may help them figure out which questions are most likely to be on the test.

In contrast, stressors that are controllable by others require social support or dependence on others. Students writing a test constructed by an unrealistic professor (an unlikely occurrence!) could seek comfort from their classmates.

Emotional problems require palliative coping in the form of emotional expression and self-soothing. A student who is upset about his or her test performance might decide to comfort himself or herself by purchasing a new compact disc and relaxing by getting into the music.

Attitudinal problems (e.g., stressors that originate from a pessimistic outlook or perfectionistic beliefs) require attempts at cognitive restructuring. A pessimistic student who is convinced that the test will lead to certain failure can keep a daily log of his or her negative thoughts in order to see how these thoughts are causing and maintaining distress that may interfere with subsequent performance.

Philosophical problems, such as being distressed about an apparent lack of meaning in life, can be addressed by existential coping (e.g, relying on spiritual and religious strategies). A student who questions the value or meaning of a classroom test could be suffering more generally from concerns about the apparent lack of purpose of daily events. This student may turn to prayer or meditation as a way of gaining new insights.

Finally, it should be noted that, in terms of cognitive appraisals and strategies, people often respond with denial and avoidance when confronted with stressors of varying levels of severity, including shocking events. In general, however, the evidence indicates that escape/avoidance coping (such as wishing that the situation would go away or be over with) is the least effective method of coping with many life problems (Stanton & Snider, 1993; Suls & Fletcher, 1985), especially over the long term.

EFFORTS TO MEASURE STRESS

Given the difficulty of defining stress with precision, it is not surprising that measuring stress is difficult as well. Research on the effects of stress on human health has sought to measure the amount of life stress a person has experienced and then to correlate this measurement with illness. Various scales have been developed to measure life stress. Here we examine two: the Social Readjustment Rating Scale and the Assessment of Daily Experience.

The Social Readjustment Rating Scale In the 1960s two researchers, Holmes and Rahe (1967), gave a list of life events to a large group of people and asked them to rate each item according to its intensity and the amount of time they thought they would need to adjust to it. Marriage was arbitrarily assigned a stress value of 500; all other items were then evaluated using this reference point. For example, an event twice as stressful as marriage would be assigned a value of 1,000, and an event one-fifth as stressful as marriage would be assigned a value of 100. The average ratings assigned to the 12 most stressful events by the respondents in Holmes and Rahe's study are shown in Table 8.2.

Table 8.2

Social Readjustment Rating Scale

Rank	Life Event	Mean Value
1	Death of spouse	100
2	Divorce	73
3	Marital separation	65
4	Jail term	63
5	Death of close family member	63
6	Personal injury or illness	53
7	Marriage	50[a]
8	Fired from work	47
9	Marital reconciliation	45
10	Retirement	45
11	Change in health of family member	44
12	Pregnancy	40

Source: From Holmes and Rahe, 1967.

[a]Marriage was arbitrarily assigned a stress value of 500; no event was found to be any more than twice as stressful. Here the values are reduced proportionally and range up to 100.

Experiencing major life events such as marriage or starting school statistically increases risk for illness. Research on the effects of these major stressors assesses them with the Social Readjustment Rating Scale.

The Social Readjustment Rating Scale (SRRS) emerged from this study. A respondent checks off the life events experienced during the time period in question. Ratings are then totalled for all the events actually experienced to produce a Life Change Unit (LCU) score, a weighted sum of events.

Recently, Miller and Rahe (1997) rescaled the events on the SRSS and added some additional events in recognition of the possibility that the impact of life changes in the 1990s might be different from the impact experienced in the 1960s and 1970s. Once again, the event of marriage was used as the reference point, with this event being assigned a score of 50. The top five LCU ratings were given to death of a child (123), death of a spouse (119), death of a brother or sister (102), death of a parent (100), and divorce (96). Overall, Miller and Rahe (1997) found that the life-change intensity scores rose 45 percent. Changing to a different line of work, for example, went from an LCU of 36 to an LCU of 51.

The original LCU score has been related to several different illnesses, including heart attacks (Rahe & Lind, 1971), fractures (Tollefson, 1972), onset of leukemia (Wold, 1968), and colds and fevers (Holmes & Holmes, 1970). The results demonstrated a correlation between psychological stress and physical illness, but they do not mean that stress causes or contributes to illness. For example, illness itself could cause a high life-change score, as when chronic absenteeism caused by the illness brings dismissal from a job. Given the fact that it often takes many years for stress to contribute to illness, research on stress and health should, ideally, be longitudinal. Longitudinal research offers several advantages; for instance, the biases of retrospective self-reports are minimized and changes in stress can be shown to precede changes in health.

Assessment of Daily Experience Consideration of problems with the SRRS led Stone and Neale (1982) to develop a new assessment instrument, the Assessment of Daily Experience (ADE). Rather than relying on retrospective reports, the ADE allows individuals to record and rate their daily experiences in prospective or longitudinal investigations (see Chapter 15). A day was used as the unit of analysis because a thorough characterization of this period should be possible without major retrospective-recall bias. Although the events reported on a day will generally be less severe than those reported over a longer time period, there is now direct evidence that these minor events are related to illness (Jandorf et al., 1986). Part of the ADE is shown in Figure 8.2.

With an assessment of daily experiences in hand, Stone, Reed, and Neale (1987) began a study of the relationship between life experience and health. They examined the relationship between undesirable and desirable events and the onset of episodes of respiratory illness. Respiratory illness

WORK RELATED ACTIVITIES

Concerning Boss, Supervisor, Upper Management, etc.

- ➤ Praised for a job well done □ ○ ○ △ 01
- ➤ Criticism for job performance, lateness, etc. □ ○ ○ △ 02

Concerning Co-workers, Employees, Supervisees, and/or Clients

- ➤ Positive emotional interactions and/or happenings with co-workers, employees, supervisees, and/or clients (work related events which were fulfilling, etc.) □ ○ ○ △ 03
- ➤ Negative emotional interactions and/or happenings with co-workers, employees, supervisees, and/or clients (work related events which were frustrating, irritating, etc.) □ ○ ○ △ 04
- ➤ Firing or disciplining (by Target) □ ○ ○ △ 05
- ➤ Socializing with staff, co-workers, employees, supervisees, and/or clients □ ○ ○ △ 06

General Happenings Concerning Target at Work

- ➤ Promotion, raise □ ○ ○ △ 07
- ➤ Fired, quit, resigned □ ○ ○ △ 08
- ➤ Some change in job (different from the above, i.e., new assignment, new boss, etc.) □ ○ ○ △ 09
- ➤ Under a lot of pressure at work (impending deadlines, heavy workload, etc.) □ ○ ○ △ 10

Figure 8.2 Sample page from Assessment of Daily Experience scale (Stone & Neale, 1982). Respondents indicate whether an event occurred by circling the arrows to the left of the list of events. If an event has occurred, the respondents then rate it on the dimensions of desirability, change, meaningfulness, and control, using the enclosed spaces to the right.

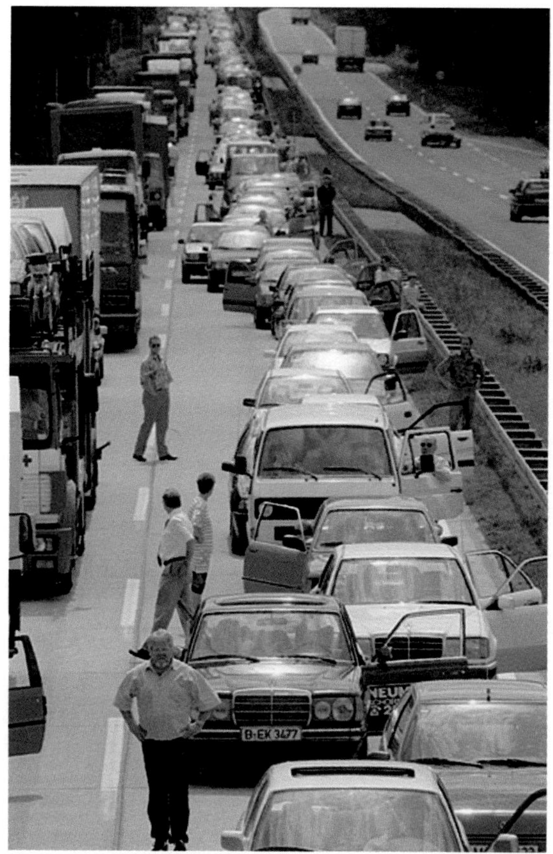

Daily hassles such as being stuck in traffic can be emotionally upsetting and also increase risk for illness.

was selected as the criterion variable because it occurs with sufficient frequency to allow it to be analyzed as a distinct outcome.

After reviewing the participants' data, the researchers identified 30 individuals who had experienced episodes of infectious illness during the assessment period. Next, they examined the daily frequency of undesirable and desirable events that occurred from one to 10 days before the start of an episode. For each person, a set of control days, without an episode, was also selected. The results showed that for desirable events there were significant decreases three and four days prior to the onset of respiratory infection; for undesirable events, there were significant increases at four and five days before the onset of the illness.

These results, which have been replicated (Evans & Edgerton, 1990), were the first to show a relationship between life events and health with both variables measured in a daily, prospective design. Most sources of confounding in prior life-events studies were avoided in this study, and we can now come much closer to asserting that life events play a causal role in increasing vulnerability to episodes of infectious illness.

Other research has studied daily events by having people complete self-report measures of their **daily hassles**. These studies often show that not only does a link exist between self-reported daily hassles and poor psychological and physical adjustment, but measures of daily hassles are often better than measures of major life events at predicting adjustment problems (DeLongis, Coyne, Dakof, Folkman, & Lazarus, 1982; Kanner, Coyne, Schaefer, & Lazarus, 1981).

In recent years, researchers have responded to two problems that plagued earlier research on daily hassles. First, the original Hassles Scale (Kanner et al., 1981) has been described as "contaminated" because it included items that could be construed as a symptom of distress (e.g., feeling tired) rather than a hassle per se. These symptoms were removed in a subsequent version of the Hassles Scale created by Anita DeLongis, who is now at the University of British Columbia (see DeLongis, Folkman, & Lazarus, 1988).

Second, the original Hassles Scale was developed for use with a middle-aged community sample, and as such, it contained daily hassles that may not be relevant to other populations. Researchers have addressed this problem by developing daily hassles tailored to the experiences of specific groups of people. Canadian researchers have developed hassles measures for university and college students (Blankstein, Flett, & Koledin, 1991; Kohn, Lafreniere, & Gurevich, 1990) and for adolescents (Kohn & Milrose, 1993). Hassles scales have also been devised for older men (Ewedemi & Linn, 1987) and elderly men and women (Holahan & Holahan, 1987).

In addition, a measure geared to people with specific illnesses was recently developed in Canada. Fillion, Kohn, and their associates have developed a hassles measure to assess the stressors faced by cancer patients, including stressors involving future concerns (e.g., thinking about how family members will manage if the patient dies), functional disability (e.g, difficulty walking and moving about), and body-image concerns (Fillion et al., 2001). Initial research with cancer patients from Quebec and Ontario indicates that this new measure is associated with higher levels of anger, fatigue, and depression. These population-specific measures are more precise and offer more meaningful ways of assessing hassles for respondents. It is important to remember, however, that the findings from this research apply to the specific group being studied and should not be overgeneralized to other groups.

ASSESSING COPING

We have already mentioned the importance of coping. Coping is most often measured by questionnaires that list a series of coping strategies and ask respondents to indicate to what extent they used each strategy to handle a recent stressor. An example of one such measure, the COPE, is presented in Table 8.3.

Table 8.3

Scales and Sample Items from the COPE

Active Coping
I've been concentrating my efforts on doing something about the situation I'm in.

Suppression of Competing Activities
I've been putting aside other activities in order to concentrate on this.

Planning
I've been trying to come up with a strategy about what to do.

Restraint
I've been making sure not to make matters worse by acting too soon.

Use of Social Support
I've been getting sympathy and understanding from someone.

Positive Reframing
I've been looking for something good in what is happening.

Religion
I've been putting my trust in God.

Acceptance
I've been accepting the reality of the fact that it happened.

Denial
I've been refusing to believe that it has happened.

Behavioural Disengagement
I've been giving up the attempt to cope.

Use of Humour
I've been making jokes about it.

Self-Distraction
I've been going to movies, watching TV, or reading, to think about it less.

Source: From Carver et al., 1993.

Canadian Contributions/8.2

Norman Endler and the Interaction Model of Anxiety, Stress, and Coping

Dr. Norman S. Endler was a Distinguished Research Professor from York University in Toronto. He was an international expert on anxiety, stress, and coping.

Dr. Norman Endler from York University was one of Canada's most influential psychologists prior to his death in 2003. For instance, in 1997 the Canadian Psychological Association gave him the Donald O. Hebb Award for Distinguished Contributions to Psychology as a Science, and the Royal Society of Canada gave him the Innis-Gerin medal "for distinguished and sustained contributions to the social sciences."

What contributions did he make? Endler was known initially for his interaction model of anxiety and his general work on interactionism with David Magnusson (see Endler & Magnusson, 1976; Endler, 1983). The essence of this model is that personality traits interact dynamically with situational factors to produce behaviours. The model's initial focus was on how different facets of trait anxiety (i.e., the person's usual level of anxiety) combine with congruent situational factors to produce immediate levels of anxiety (i.e., state anxiety). Endler hypothesized that people will experience state anxiety when they experience a situation that matches the aspect of trait anxiety that is central to their personal identity; that is, people high in physical danger anxiety, say, will be anxious in dangerous situations, while people concerned about social evaluation will be anxious in situations involving the possibility of public failures. Extensive research in specific contexts supports the interactionism model. For instance, people high in social evaluation anxiety become highly anxious when asked to give a speech (Muller, Endler, & Parker, 1990) or when taking a driving test to get a licence to drive (King & Endler, 1990). Similarly, studies of physical danger anxiety have shown that Canadian military recruits who are higher in physical danger trait anxiety experienced higher state anxiety when participating in their initial parachute jump training (Endler, Crooks, & Parker, 1992), and people high in physical danger anxiety were extremely anxious when under

SCUD missile attack in the Gulf War (Lobel, Gilat, & Endler, 1993). A more recent study conducted in Alberta shows that high physical danger anxiety predicts elevated physiological symptoms of anxiety following physical exercise that induces extreme exhaustion (Blanchard et al., 2002).

Other research examined anxiety in ambiguous situations. One study conducted during the most recent Quebec referendum on Quebec separation showed that students who usually tend to become anxious in ambiguous, uncertain, and novel situations actually did experience state anxiety when tested just before the referendum results were final (Flett, Endler, & Fairlie, 1999). Their high state anxiety was a joint reflection of their usual tendency to be anxious in ambiguous situations and the great situational uncertainty that existed about how the vote would turn out.

Endler extended his work in recent years by investigating specific trait components of social anxiety (see Endler, Flett, Macrodimitris, Corace, & Kocovski, 2002). This work focuses on people who are high in separation anxiety and self-disclosure anxiety (i.e., anxiety when asked to reveal secrets and other aspects of the self to others). New research here indicates that students high in trait separation anxiety are especially prone to feeling homesick in their first year of university.

In the past decade, Endler significantly extended the interaction model to include stress and coping components (for a summary, see Endler, 2002). This revised model is similar in some key respects to models described earlier (see Lazarus, 1966), but it places emphasize on coping as an aspect of personality; that is, when people deal with situational stressors, a key determinant of their emotional response is their typical coping style. Norman Endler teamed up with James Parker, currently at Trent University, to create a coping measure based on the premise that there are stable individual differences in coping styles. They created the Coping Inventory for Stressful Situations (CISS; Endler & Parker, 1990, 1994, 1999) to measure three stable, dispositional aspects of coping: (1) emotion-oriented coping; (2) task-oriented coping; and (3) avoidance-oriented coping. A key aspect of this work is the premise that coping styles are actually components of personality structure and, as such, are relatively stable and long-lasting. These stable coping styles interact with situational stressors and cognitive appraisals of these stressful situations to determine the nature (positive or negative) and intensity of the emotional response.

This model has implications for health outcomes, so Endler and Parker created a new coping measure with content geared specifically to how people cope with health problems. This problem-specific measure was developed because a person often copes with general problems differently than he or she would with a health problem (see Endler, Parker, & Summerfeldt, 1993). The scale that emerged from this work is called Coping with Health Injuries and Problems (CHIP; Endler & Parker, 2000). It has four scales that assess emotional preoccupation, distraction, instrumental coping (i.e., task-oriented strategies), and palliative coping (i.e., attempts to feel better via self-soothing and self-help by doing things such as staying in bed or resting when tired). Note that the CHIP scale measures coping responses rather than coping styles; that is, respondents are asked to complete the items with reference to specific illnesses rather than in response to illness in general. Thus far, the scale has been used to assess the ability of Canadians to cope with health problems such as cancer (Endler, Courbasson, & Fillion, 1998), Type II diabetes (Macrodimitris & Endler, 2001), and chronic pain (Hadjistavropoulos, Asmundson, & Norton, 1999), as well as to compare individuals with acute versus chronic illness (Endler, Kocovski, & Macrodimitris, 2001). The initial data indicate that the CHIP has adequate reliability and validity. For instance, Endler et al. (2001) predicted and confirmed that chronic illnesses tend to be associated primarily with the CHIP measure of emotional preoccupation.

Beyond Endler's important scientific contributions, his own personal story has proved uplifting to other people who have struggled with emotional distress. Endler was able to maintain a high level of productivity despite experiencing his own health problems. In fact, he took the brave step of chronicling his bout of bipolar depression in a well-known book *Holiday of Darkness* (Endler, 1982). Endler's experiences with depression are discussed in more detail in Chapter 10.

As with the effects of stressors, the best way to examine coping is to use a battery of measures and to conduct a longitudinal study; this approach would demonstrate that particular ways of coping with stress precede the outcomes in which the researcher is interested. Breast cancer has been investigated in this way. The diagnosis of breast cancer, which strikes about one woman in nine, is a major stressor on many levels. It is a life-threatening illness; surgical interventions are often disfiguring and thus have serious implications for psychological well-being; and both radiation therapy and chemotherapy have very unpleasant side effects.

Carver et al. (1993) selected women who had just been diagnosed with breast cancer and assessed how they were coping at several times during the following year. Women who accepted their diagnosis and retained a sense of humour had lower levels of distress (see Canadian Perspectives 8.1 for more information on the positive coping benefits of

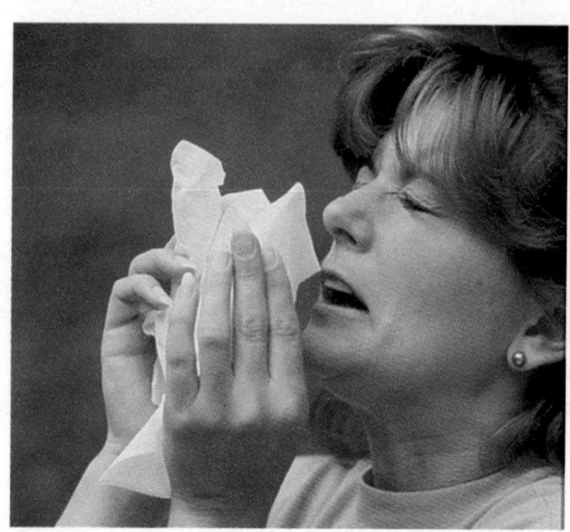

Stone and his colleagues have found that changes in the frequency of daily life events precede the onset of episodes of respiratory infection. The mechanism may be a stress-induced lowering of secretory IgA.

humour). Carver et al. also found that avoidant coping methods, such as denial and behavioural disengagement (see Table 8.3), were related to higher levels of distress. This negative effect of denial on adjustment to breast cancer has recently been replicated (Heim, Valach, & Schaffner, 1997). Another longitudinal study of several types of cancer found that avoidant coping ("I try not to think about it") predicted greater progression of the disease at a one-year follow-up (Epping-Jordan, Compas, & Howell, 1994). These data show that it is not merely the presence of stress that produces physical and emotional effects; how the person reacts to the stressor is crucial as well. In the case of cancer, reducing stress by ignoring the problem is not a good idea.

Canadian psychologist Norman Endler made important contributions to the research literature on coping, stress, and anxiety (see Canadian Contributions 8.2).

Canadian Perspectives/8.1

Humour and Coping with Stress

Canadian researchers have been very influential in illustrating the beneficial effects of relying on a sense of humour when confronted with a stressful situation. Extensive research has been conducted by Rod Martin and Nicholas Kuiper from the University of Western Ontario and by Herbert Lefcourt from the University of Waterloo. Much of this work is based on sense of humour measures created by Martin and Lefcourt (1983, 1984). The Coping Humour Scale (Martin & Lefcourt, 1983) is a seven-item scale that assesses the extent to which an individual uses humour as a way of coping with a demanding and stressful situation. It is regarded as a form of problem-focused coping and includes such items as "I usually look for something comical to say when I am in tense situations." In contrast, the Situational Humour Response Questionnaire (Martin & Lefcourt, 1984) asks respondents how likely they are to laugh in a variety of situations. It is believed to tap into an emotion-focused coping strategy that is designed to use humour expressively in order to avert a potentially stressful situation (e.g., you rush over to greet a friend only to discover you have the wrong person).

These measures treat humour as a unidimensional construct. More recent research treats humour as a multi-faced construct with positive and negative aspects (see Kirsh & Kuiper, 2003). The Humour Styles Questionnaire by Martin et al. (2003) has four subscales. It measures humour used to enhance social relationships (i.e., affiliative humour), humour used at the expense of others (i.e., aggressive humour), humour for self-enhancement (i.e., to cheer oneself up), and self-defeating humour that involves using humour (aimed at putting the self down).

Martin (2001) outlined four models that describe how humour and laughter can have a positive impact on health. First, a physiological model focuses on the possibility that physiological changes associated with laughter contribute to improved health. Second, an emotion model is based on the notion that humour leads to positive emotions, which in turn, contribute positively to health status. Third, a stress-moderation model has to do with the idea that humour and associated cognitive-appraisal processes (which involve a positive outlook on the world) act as buffers that mitigate stress, thereby improving health. Finally, a social support model suggests that the benefits of humour are mediated by the increased social support that comes from being a fun-loving and outgoing individual.

Many have linked humour with reduced stress and increased psychological well-being (Kuiper, Martin, Olinger, Kazarian, & Jette, 1998; Martin & Kuiper, 1999). Kuiper, Martin, and Olinger (1993) examined the links among sense of humour, stress, dysfunctional attitudes, and cognitive appraisals of performance on a classroom examination in a sample of university students. They found that a sense of humour was associated negatively with stress and dysfunctional attitudes involving unrealistic standards.

Higher levels of humour have been associated with immune system activity (see Lefcourt & Thomas, 1998). The physiological implications were shown in research by Lefcourt, Davidson, Prkachin, and Mills (1997). They found that women with high levels of coping humour had lower systolic blood pressure than women with low levels of coping humour; however, men with high levels of coping humour actually had higher blood pressure than men with lower levels of coping humour. Lefcourt et al. (1997) suggested that male humour often takes a hostile form that involves humour at the expense of someone else, while female humour is often more self-directed and promotes social cohesion. Presumably, men would derive more health benefits if their humour was more pro-social in its focus.

Although it seems logical that humour should be associated with better health, a critical review by Martin (2001) of existing research studies led him to conclude that existing studies have metholodological shortcomings and "provide little evidence for unique positive effects of humor and laughter on health-related variables" (p. 514). He was critical of the failure of some authors to include control groups in their experimental studies. Martin also noted the lack of research testing the possible mediating role of such factors as positive emotions and social support. Another concern was the relative lack of research examining the specific physiological mechanisms that can account for the positive effects of humour.

Clearly, future research still needs to establish exactly how and when humour contributes to reduced stress. One reason that humour is associated with stress reduction could be that it biases a person to attend to stimuli in a protective way. For example, Moran and Massan (1999) found that people exposed to sad cartoons felt less sad if they used coping humour. They suggested that people with asense of humour tend to focus on mood-enhancing stimuli in their environment.

Thinking Critically

1. How would you test the hypothesis of Lefcourt et al. (1997) as a way of explaining the finding that women with high levels of coping humour (relative to women with low levels of coping humour) had lower systolic blood pressure, whereas men with high levels of coping humour (relative to men with lower levels of coping humour) actually had higher levels of blood pressure? Assuming that the results of your study confirm the hypothesis, design a study to determine whether men benefit physiologically from more pro-social forms of humour.
2. We have seen, in the case of cancer, that reducing stress by ignoring the problem is not a good idea. Would it be a good idea to deliberately shape a greater sense of humour and encourage people with cancer to use this humour as a coping strategy? How would you go about inculcating a greater sense of humour and then testing the effectiveness of your strategy?

MODERATORS OF THE STRESS-ILLNESS LINK

Although we can demonstrate that life events are related to the onset of illness, important questions remain. We have already noted that the same life experience apparently can have different effects on different people. This situation raises the possibility that other variables moderate or change the general stress-illness relationship. We have described one significant moderator, coping, and we have seen that the use of avoidant coping increases the likelihood of both emotional and physical effects of stress. Social support is another important factor that can lessen the effects of stress.

There are various types and conceptualizations of social support. **Structural social support** refers to a person's basic network of social relationships, (e.g., marital status and number of friends). **Functional social support** is concerned more with the quality of a person's relationships, (e.g., whether the person believes he or she has friends to call on in a time of need) (Cohen & Wills, 1985).

Social support can also be discussed in terms of the kinds of assistance provided. **Emotional support** provides the recipient with a sense of being cared for by warm and sensitive others, while **instrumental support** provides the recipient with more tangible forms of assistance (e.g., someone helps by making dinner or by paying the bills). A recent study by Muller, Goh, Lemieux, and Fish (2000) serves as a reminder that different kinds of support vary in their relevance as a function of the stressful situation being experienced. This Canadian study found that adult survivors of abuse were more likely to receive emotional support than instrumental support and that friends were most likely to provide this emotional support.

Structural support is a well-established predictor of mortality. People with few friends or relatives tend to have a higher mortality rate than those with a higher level of structural support (Kaplan et al., 1994). Higher levels of functional support have been found to be related to lower rates of atherosclerosis (clogging of the arteries) (Seeman & Syme, 1989) and to the ability of women to adjust to chronic rheumatoid arthritis (Goodenow, Reisine, & Grady, 1990).

The benefits of social support are not limited to health outcomes. The actual or perceived presence of social support is a consistent predictor of mental health outcomes; this was demonstrated in a recent study in Quebec that found that psychiatric patients, in comparison to welfare recipients and people from the general population, reported less satisfaction with social support on all measures assessed in the study (Caron, Tempier, Mercier, & Leouffre, 1998). Moreover, social support is often operative in the link between personality traits and psychological distress (Dunkley, Blankstein, Halsall, Williams, & Winkworth, 2000): that is, personality vulnerability factors predict low social support, which in turn predicts distress. The role of social support in psychological adjustment will be examined further in Chapter 10 (mood disorders) and in Chapter 16 (regarding aging and psychological disorders).

How does social support exert its beneficial effects? One possibility is that people who have higher levels of social support perform positive health behaviours more frequently—eating a healthy diet, not smoking, and moderating alcohol intake. This possibility is consistent with the results of a University of Alberta study that found that adults who reported higher levels of social support also indicated a greater intention to exercise (Courneya, Plotnikoff, Hotz, & Birkett, 2000). Alternatively, social support (or lack of it) could have a direct effect on biological processes. Low levels of social support, for example, are related to an increase in negative emotions (Kessler & McLeod, 1985; see also our earlier discussion of PTSD in Chapter 6, which may affect some hormone levels and the immune system (Kiecolt-Glaser et al., 1984).

In recent years, social support has been studied in the laboratory, where cause and effect can be more readily established than in the naturalistic studies already described. In one such study, college-aged women were assigned to high- or low-stress conditions, which they experienced alone or with a close friend. In one part of the study, stress was created by having the experimenter behave coldly and impersonally, telling participants to improve their performance as they worked on a challenging task. In each case where the woman has the social-support of a close friend, the friend "silently cheered her on" and sat close to her, placing a hand

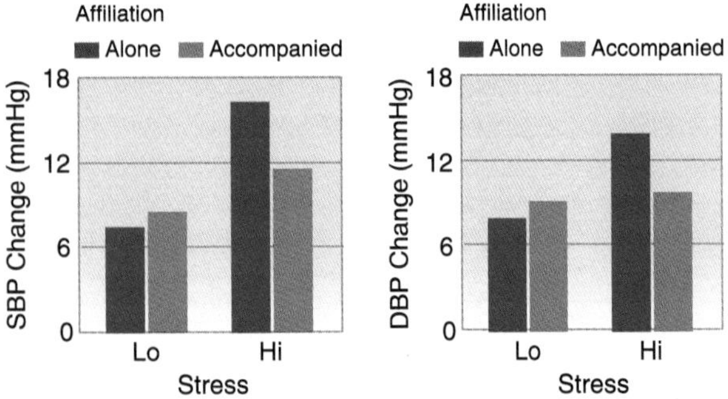

Figure 8.3 Results of a laboratory study of the effects of social support on blood pressure. Stress led to increased blood pressure, but the increase was less pronounced among people who experienced the stressor with a friend. From Kamarck et al. (1995).

on her wrist. The dependent variable was blood pressure, measured while participants performed the task. As expected, high stress led to higher blood-pressure levels. But, as Figure 8.3 shows, the high-stress condition produced its effects on blood pressure primarily in those women who experienced the stress alone (Kamarck, Annunziato, & Amateau, 1995). Social support was thus shown to have a causal effect on a physiological process. Further laboratory research has shown that such results are produced only when the support comes from a friend and not when it comes from a stranger (Christenfeld et al., 1997). Perhaps only a friend can lead someone to appraise a stressful situation as less threatening.

A possible biological mechanism for the stress-reducing effects of social support is suggested by some research with animals. A hormone called oxytocin may be released during social interaction. Oxytocin decreases activity of the sympathetic nervous system and may thereby lessen the physiological effects of a stressor (Carter, DeVries, & Getz, 1995; Uvnas-Mobert, 1997).

Not all research has found that social support has positive effects. With very severe stressors, the person may be so overwhelmed that support does no good. This point was well made in a study of social support and breast cancer, in which social support did not lead to reduced distress or less physical impairment (Bolger et al., 1996).

THEORIES OF THE STRESS-ILLNESS LINK

In considering the etiology of psychophysiological disorders, we are confronted with three questions:

1. Why does stress produce illness in only some people who are exposed to it?
2. Why does stress sometimes cause an illness and not a psychological disorder?
3. When stress produces a psychophysiological disorder, what determines which one of the many disorders will be produced?

Although answers to these questions have been sought by biologically and psychologically oriented researchers, theories in this domain are invariably diathesis-stress in nature. They differ primarily in whether the diathesis is described in psychological or biological terms.

Before we review some theories that describe how stress causes or exacerbates physical illness, it is important to note that much of the research in the field has attempted to link stress to *self-reports* of illness. The problem with this approach is that self-reports may not be an accurate reflection of physical illness, as we have already noted. Watson and Pennebaker (1989) concluded that an apparent association between negative emotional states and health was actually only a relationship between negative emotions and illness *reporting*. Similarly, Stone and Costa (1990) noted that neuroticism predicted reports of higher numbers of somatic complaints of all kinds (recall our discussion of hypochondriasis and somatization disorder) but did not predict "hard endpoints," such as death or verified coronary artery disease. Because of such problems, our discussion focuses mainly on research that goes beyond illness self-reports.

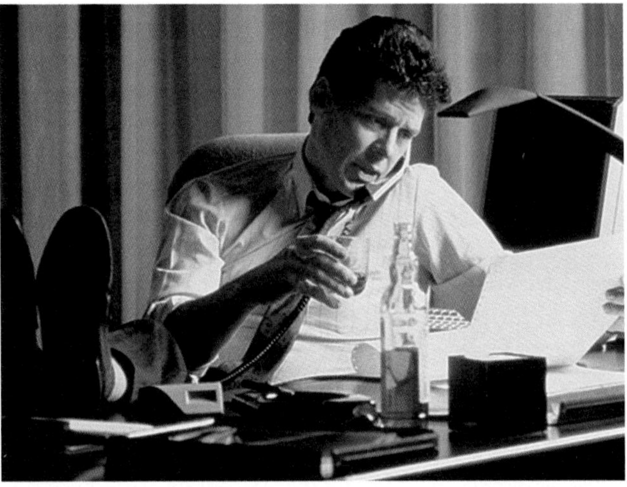

Stress may indirectly increase risk for illness by causing lifestyle changes such as increased consumption of alcohol.

In addition, the effects of stress may be indirect—that is, stress may lead to health changes that are not directly due to biological or psychological variables but are due to changes in health behaviour. High stress may result in increased smoking, disrupted sleep, increased alcohol consumption, and altered diet (the opposite of what we saw with social support). These behavioural changes may then increase risk for illness. Low socioeconomic status, for example, often thought of as a stressor, has been shown to be related to greater mortality from several diseases, but this relationship could be accounted for by increased rates of negative health behaviours, such as smoking and alcohol use (Lynch et al., 1996). The stress-illness association is real, but it may sometimes be mediated indirectly through changes in health behaviours rather than directly through some biological effect of the stress.

BIOLOGICAL THEORIES

Biological approaches attribute particular psychophysiological disorders to specific organ weaknesses, to overactivity of particular organ systems in responding to stress, to the effects of exposure to stress hormones, or to changes in the immune system that are caused by stress.

Somatic-Weakness Theory Genetic factors, prior illnesses, diet, and the like may disrupt a particular organ system, which may then become weak and vulnerable to stress. According to the somatic-weakness theory, the connection between stress and a particular psychophysiological disorder is a weakness in a specific body organ. For instance, a congenitally weak respiratory system might predispose the individual to asthma.

Specific-Reaction Theory People have been found to have their own individual patterns of autonomic response to stress. The heart rate of one individual may increase, whereas another person may react with an increased respiration rate but no change in heart rate (Lacey, 1967). According to the specific-reaction theory, individuals respond to stress in their own idiosyncratic ways, and the body system that is the most responsive becomes a likely candidate for the locus of a subsequent psychophysiological disorder. For example, someone reacting to stress with elevated blood pressure may be more susceptible to essential hypertension. Later in this chapter, when we consider specific psychophysiological disorders, evidence in support of both the somatic-weakness theory and the specific-reaction theory will be presented.

Prolonged Exposure to Stress Hormones A more recent theory attempts to deal with the fact that the biological changes that stress produces are adaptive in the short run—for example, the mobilization of energy resources in preparation for physical activity (McEwen, 1998). The major biological responses to stress involve activation of the sympathetic nervous system and the hypothalamic-pituitary-adrenal axis (HPA). Under conditions of stress, catecholamines such as epinephrine are released from nerves and from the adrenal medulla and lead to secretion of corticotropin from the pituitary. Corticotropin then leads to the release of cortisol from the cortex of the adrenal gland (see Figure 8.4).

The key to McEwen's theory is that the body pays a price if it must constantly adapt to stress. Through exposure to high levels of stress hormones, it may become susceptible to disease because of altered immune system functioning. Furthermore, high levels of cortisol can have direct effects on the brain; for example, high levels can kill cells in the hippocampus, which itself regulates the secretion of cortisol. Over time, the person may become even more susceptible to the effects of stress.

Some people may have consistently high levels of stress hormones because they experience frequent stress. Other people may have less difficulty in adapting to repeated exposure to stressful situations. Most people react to the stress of

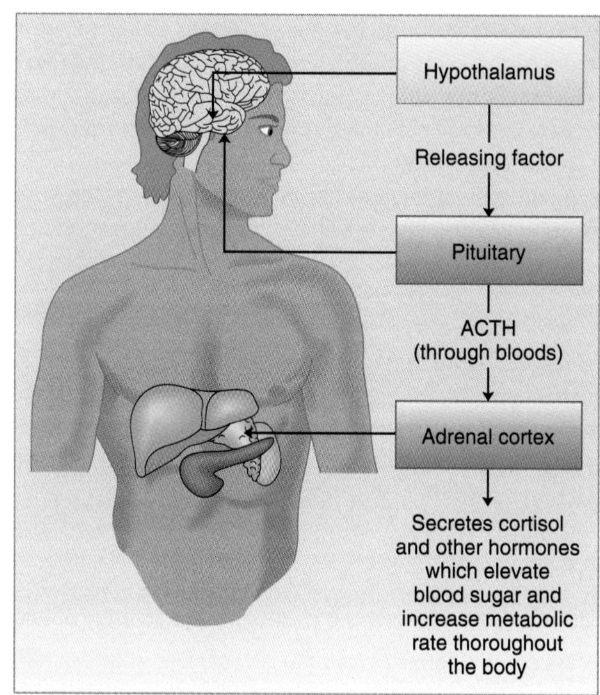

Figure 8.4 The HPA axis

public speaking, for example, with an increase in cortisol secretion but after repeated exposure, most adapt and the amount of cortisol secreted declines. However, about 10 percent of people show no adaptation and even increase their secretion of cortisol (Kirschbaum et al., 1995). According to McEwen's theory, these are the individuals at risk for disease.

Stress and the Immune System On a general level, stressors have multiple effects on various systems of the body—the autonomic nervous system, hormone levels, and brain activity. One major area of current interest is the immune system, an important consideration in infectious diseases, cancer, and allergies as well as in autoimmune diseases, such as rheumatoid arthritis, in which the immune system attacks the body. A wide range of stressors have been found to produce changes in the immune system—medical-school examinations, depression and bereavement, marital discord and divorce, job loss, caring for a relative with Alzheimer's disease, and the Three Mile Island nuclear disaster, among others (Cohen & Herbert, 1996). Whether such immune system changes lead to more negative clinical outcomes, such as early death from cancer or the onset of arthritis, is yet to be determined; that is, it is not yet certain that immune system changes that follow stress are great enough to actually increase risk for disease.

The area of research that comes closest to documenting a role for stress and immune system changes in actual illness is the study of infectious diseases. To illustrate, we will discuss one aspect of the immune system—secretory immunity—in some detail.

The secretory component of the immune system exists in the tears, saliva, and gastrointestinal, vaginal, nasal, and bronchial secretions that bathe the mucosal surfaces of the body. A substance found in these secretions, called secretory immunoglobulin A, or sIgA, contains antibodies that serve as the body's first line of defence against invading viruses and bacteria. They prevent the virus or bacterium from binding to mucosal tissues.

A study by Stone and his colleagues (Stone, Cox et al., 1987) showed that changes in the number of sIgA antibodies were linked to changes in mood. Throughout an eight-week study period, a group of dental students came to the laboratory three times a week to have their saliva collected and a brief psychological assessment conducted. On days when the students experienced relatively high levels of negative mood, fewer antibodies were present than on days when the students had low levels of negative mood. Similarly, antibody level was higher on days with higher levels of positive mood.

Prior research (e.g., Stone & Neale, 1984) had shown that daily events affect mood. It is therefore quite possible that daily events affect fluctuations in mood, which in turn affect the synthesis of the secretory sIgA antibodies. The process could operate as follows. An increase in undesirable life events coupled with a decrease in desirable life events produces increased negative mood, which in turn depresses antibody levels in secretory sIgA. If during this period a person is exposed to a virus, he or she will be at increased risk for infection (see Figure 8.5).

Several other studies have confirmed the relationship between stress and respiratory infection. In each of them, volunteers took nasal drops containing a mild cold virus and completed a battery of questionnaires concerning recent stress. The advantage of this method was that exposure to the virus was an experimental variable under the investigators' control. Researchers found that stress was clearly linked to developing a cold (Cohen, Tyrell, & Smith, 1991; Stone et al., 1992). The stressors most often implicated were interpersonal problems and work difficulties (Cohen et al., 1998). In a similar study, social support was found to moderate the relationship between viral exposure and colds (Cohen et al., 1997). People with more diverse social networks were less likely to develop a cold following exposure to a virus. These findings illustrate the complex interplay between psychological and biological variables in the etiology of psychophysiological disorders.

Psychological Theories

Psychological theories try to account for the development of various disorders by considering such factors as unconscious emotional states, personality traits, cognitive appraisals, and specific styles of coping with stress.

Psychoanalytic Theories Psychoanalytic theories propose that specific conflicts and their associated negative emotional states give rise to psychophysiological disorders. Franz Alexander is the psychoanalytic theorist who has the greatest impact here, relative to other psychoanalytic theorists. He maintained that each of the various psychophysiological disorders is the product of unconscious emotional states specific to that disorder. For example, undischarged hostile impulses are believed to create the chronic emotional state responsible for essential hypertension.

> The damming up of hostile impulses will continue and will consequently increase in intensity. This will induce the development of stronger defensive measures in order to keep pent-up aggressions in check. Because of the marked degree of their inhibitions, these patients are less effective in their occupational activities and for that reason tend to fail in competition with others ... [E]nvy is stimulated and hostile feelings toward more successful, less inhibited competitors are further intensified. (Alexander, 1950, p. 150)

Alexander formulated this theory of unexpressed-anger, or anger-in theory, on the basis of his observations of patients undergoing psychoanalysis. His hypothesis continues to be pursued in present-day studies of the psychological factors in essential hypertension, as discussed shortly.

Cognitive and Behavioural Factors Physical threats obviously create stress, but humans perceive more than merely physical threats (Simeons, 1961). We experience regrets about the past and worries about the future. All these perceptions can stimulate sympathetic-system activity and the secretion of stress hormones. But negative emotions, such as resentment, regret, and worry, cannot be fought or escaped as readily as can external threats, nor do they easily pass. They may keep the body's biological systems aroused and the body in a continual state of emergency, sometimes for far longer than it can bear, as suggested by McEwen's theory. In addition, the high level of cognition made possible in humans through evolution creates the potential for distressed thoughts, which can bring about bodily changes that persist longer than they were meant to. Our higher mental capacities, it is theorized, subject our bodies to physical storms that they were not built to withstand.

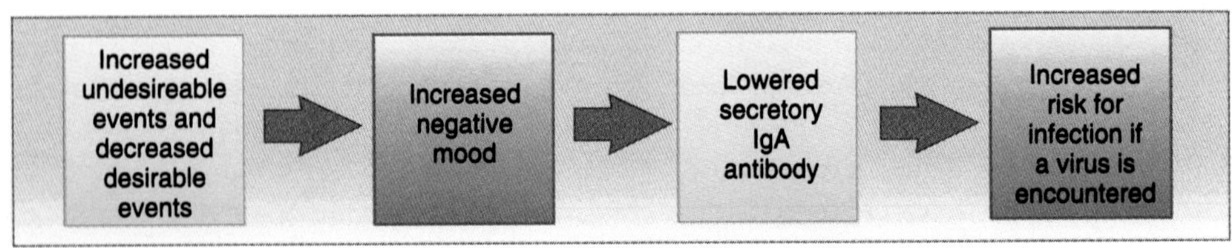

Figure 8.5 Mechanism through which stress could increase risk for viral infection

We saw in our general discussion of stress that the appraisal of a potential stressor is central to how it affects the person. People who continually appraise life experiences as exceeding their resources may be chronically stressed and at risk for the development of a psychophysiological disorder. How people cope with stress may also be relevant. We will shortly describe some findings that show that hypertension is related to how people cope with anger. Personality traits are implicated in several disorders, most notably cardiovascular disease (CVD). People who chronically experience high levels of negative emotions, for example, are at high risk for the development of heart problems. Finally, gender is an important variable in health; there are clear differences in the frequency with which men and women experience certain health problems (see Focus on Discovery 8.1).

focus on discovery/8.1

Gender and Health

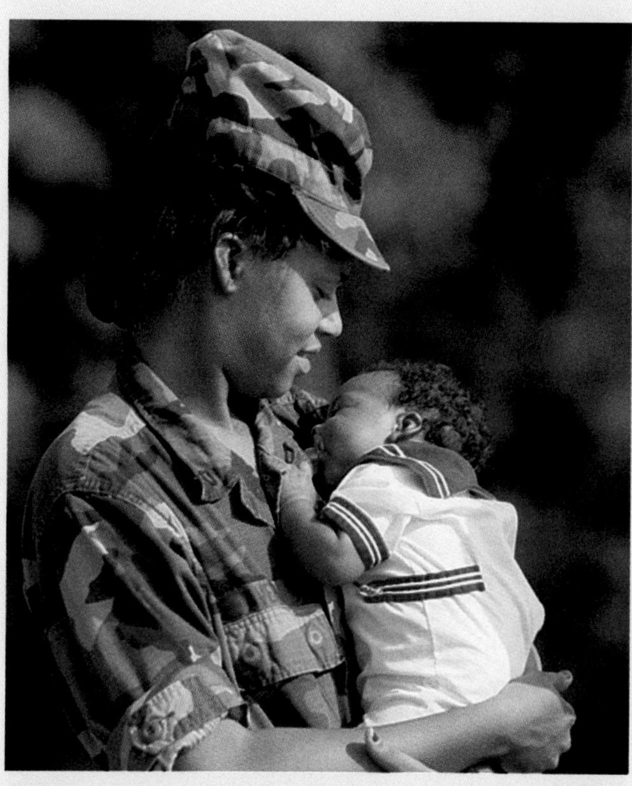

Women typically have higher rates of illness than do men. One source of stress for many women is the need to cope with the dual roles of homemaker and wage earner.

At every age from birth to 85 and older, more men die than women. Individual causes of death vary greatly between the sexes. Men are more than twice as likely to die in automobile accidents and of homicides, cirrhosis, heart disease, lung disease, lung cancer, and suicide. In spite of their reduced mortality, women have higher rates of morbidity—general poor health or the incidence of several specific diseases. For example, women have higher rates of diabetes, anemia, gastrointestinal problems, and rheumatoid arthritis; they report more visits to physicians and use more prescription drugs. In recent years, though, women's mortality advantage has been decreasing; for example, the death rate from CVD has declined among men in the last 30 years but stayed about the same in women (Rodin & Ickovics, 1990).

What are some of the possible reasons for the differences in mortality and morbidity rates between men and women, and why is mortality increasing? From a biological vantage point, it might be that women have some mechanism that protects them from life-threatening diseases. The female hormone, estrogen, may offer protection from cardiovascular disease, for example. Several lines of evidence support this idea. Postmenopausal women and those women who have had their ovaries removed—in both cases having lowered estrogen—have higher rates of cardiovascular disease than do premenopausal women. Hormone-replacement therapy lowers the rate of mortality from CVD, perhaps by maintaining elevated levels of high-density lipoprotein (HDL), the so-called good cholesterol (Matthews et al., 1989).

From a psychological viewpoint, women are less likely than men to be Type A personalities and are also less hostile than men (Waldron, 1976; Weidner & Collins, 1993). Eisler and Blalock (1991) hypothesize that the Type A pattern, discussed more fully later, is part and parcel of a rigid commitment to the traditional masculine gender role and its emphasis on achievement, mastery, competitiveness, not asking for help or emotional support, an excessive need for control, and the tendency to become angry and to express anger when frustrated. They link these attributes to the tendency for men to be more prone to coronary problems and other stress-related health risks, such as hypertension (Harrison, Chin, & Ficarrotto, 1989).

Denton and Walters (1999) believe that social structural factors are more important for women than men. Their analysis of data from the 1994 Canadian National Health Population Survey (N = 15,144) supported their position, finding evidence of striking gender differences. Specifically, factors such as caring for a family, the presence of social support, and being in the highest income category were more important predictors of outcomes for women than men. In contrast, smoking and alcohol consumption were more critical determinants of health status for men. As we shall see, both biological and psychological variables play important roles in CVD, and they could well be relevant to the lower levels of mortality of women.

Why is the gap between mortality rates in men and women decreasing? In the early 20th century, most deaths were due to epidemics and infection, but now most deaths result from diseases that are affected by lifestyle. One possibility, then, is that lifestyle differences between men and women account for the sex difference in mortality and that these lifestyle differences have become less evident. Men smoke more than women and consume more alcohol. These differences are likely contributors to men's higher mortality from CVD and lung cancer. In recent years, however, women have begun to smoke and drink more, changes paralleled by higher instances of lung cancer rates and the failure of the mortality rate for CVD to decrease among women (Rodin & Ickovics, 1990).

Another lifestyle change placing women at greater risk is that more women with families have been entering the workforce, thus taking on the stress of assuming the dual role of wage earner and homemaker. Frankenhaeuser et al. (1989) studied norepinephrine levels of men and women employed at an automobile-manufacturing plant in Gothenburg, Sweden. Levels were similar in both sexes during the day, but those of men declined after work, while those of women rose. Working women who have children at home do not have lower blood pressure at home than at work (Marco et al., 2000), and they excrete high levels of cortisol (Luecken et al., 1997).

There are several possible explanations for the difference in the morbidity rates of men and women. First, because women live longer than men, they may be more likely to experience several diseases associated with aging. Second, women may be more attentive to their health than are and thus may be more likely to visit physicians and be diagnosed. Finally, women may cope with stress in a way that increases their risk for some illnesses, for example, by focusing their attention on their responses to a negative event (Weidner & Collins, 1993).

The gathering of scientific data on how best to minimize women's risk for a number of disorders has likely been compromised by the tendency to exclude female subjects from studies. Women have been understudied in health research (Rodin & Ickovics, 1990). Future studies need to include equal samples of men and women and also to focus on the special health concerns of women. The Women's Health Initiative represents a promising step in this direction. Starting in 1993, this 12-year study looks at an ethnically diverse sample of more than 200,000 women. One part of the project involves evaluating preventive interventions such as a low-fat diet and hormone-replacement therapy for osteoporosis, coronary heart disease, and cancer. Other parts of the investigation include examining why women with low socioeconomic status are at high risk for various diseases and studying psychosocial factors such as life stress and personality that increase risk for these diseases (Matthews et al., 1997).

We turn now to a detailed review of two disorders that have attracted much attention from researchers—cardiovascular disorders and acquired immunodeficiency syndrome (AIDS). We then discuss issues of socioeconomic status and ethnicity that are related to health.

CARDIOVASCULAR DISORDERS

Cardiovascular disorders are diseases involving the heart and blood-circulation system. In this section, we focus on two forms of CVD that appear to be adversely affected by stress—hypertension and coronary heart disease. Of the cardiovascular diseases, coronary heart disease causes the greatest number of deaths. It is generally agreed that many of the deaths resulting from cardiovascular diseases could be prevented by dealing with one or more of the known risk factors.

It is estimated that the average annual cost of CVD to the Canadian medical system is $17 billion (Statistics Canada, 1997), even though rates of cardiovascular disease and associated outcomes (e.g., strokes) have declined substantially in Canada over the past two decades (see MacLean, 1999; Manuel et al., 2003). Some alarming results have emerged from recent analyses of the Canadian Heart Health Surveys conducted between 1986 and 1992. Langille et al. (1999) described the findings from probability samples of over 5,000 women and men between the ages of 55 and 74 drawn from all 10 provinces. Participants were visited by a trained nurse who collected demographic and lifestyle data, including an assessment of each participant's knowledge of cardiovascular disease risk factors. Blood pressure was measured at a clinic within two weeks of the initial visit. Blood samples were also provided. The results showed that 52 per cent of the participants were hypertensive, 26 percent suffered from isolated systolic hypertension, and 30 percent had levels of blood cholesterol requiring intervention. The presence of hypertension was untreated in 52 percent of the afflicted. Langille et al. (1999) found that almost 50 percent of the participants had three or more major risk factors, and they noted that this is particularly troubling because risk factors tend to act synergistically rather than in an additive fashion, resulting in a substantial magnification of risk.

A related study by Kirkland et al. (1999) used data from the same sample but focused on the participants' knowledge and awareness of risk factors for cardiovascular disease. Participants were asked, "Can you tell me what are the major causes of heart disease or heart problems?" (Kirkland et al., 1999, p. S10). The most frequently mentioned causes were stress (44 percent), worry (44 percent), and smoking (41 percent). High blood cholesterol was mentioned by only 23 percent of the respondents, and hypertension was mentioned by only 16 percent. The authors concluded that awareness of the major causes of cardiovascular disease is quite low among Canadians aged 55 to 74. They also noted that of those people in the study identified as having a risk factor, approximately two-thirds of the women and the men involved were unaware of their high cholesterol status, while 33 percent of the women and 43 percent of the men were unaware of their hypertensive status.

ESSENTIAL HYPERTENSION

Why is it important to be aware of hypertension? Hypertension, commonly called high blood pressure, disposes people to atherosclerosis (clogging of the arteries), heart attacks, and strokes; it can also cause death through kidney failure. Yet no more than 10 percent of all cases of hypertension in the United States are attributable to an identifiable physical cause. Hypertension without an evident biological cause is called essential (or sometimes primary) hypertension. Unless people have their blood pressure checked, they may go for years without knowing that they are hypertensive. Thus, this disease is known as the silent killer.

Blood pressure is measured by two numbers: one represents *systolic pressure*, and the other represents *diastolic pressure*. The systolic measure is the amount of arterial pressure when the ventricles contract and the heart is pumping; the diastolic measure is the degree of arterial pressure when the ventricles relax and the heart is resting. A normal blood pressure in a young adult is 120 (systolic) over 80 (diastolic) (Figure 8.6). A recent study by Wolf-Maier et al. (2003), using 140 over 90 as indicative of hypertension, found that 28 percent of Canadian and American adults had hypertension, while an astronomical 44 percent of Europeans had the condition.

Essential hypertension is viewed as a heterogeneous condition brought on by many possible disturbances in the various systems of the body that are responsible for regulating blood pressure. Genes play a substantial role in controlling blood pressure; other risk factors for hypertension include obesity, excessive intake of alcohol, and salt consumption. Blood pressure may be elevated by increased cardiac output (the amount of blood leaving the left ventricle of the heart), by increased resistance to the passage of blood through the arteries (vasoconstriction), or by both. The physiological mechanisms that regulate blood pressure interact in an extremely complex manner. Activation of the sympathetic nervous system is a key factor, but hormones, salt metabolism, and central nervous system mechanisms are all involved. Many of these physiological mechanisms can be affected by psychological stress. Current thinking is that, over the long term, frequent elevations in blood pressure eventually lead the arterial walls to thicken, resulting in sustained hypertension (National Heart, Lung, and Blood Institute [NHLBI], 1998).

Table 8.4 lists the 10 major risk factors for high blood pressure, as identified by the Canadian Expert Working Group (CEWG) on high blood pressure prevention and control. The conclusions of the CEWG are outlined in Canadian Perspectives 8.2. It can be seen in Table 8.4 that the risk factors are varied and include physical factors (e.g., excess weight) and the importance of exercise, but they also include lifestyle factors (e.g., degree of heavy alcohol use), socioeconomic status, and psychological factors involving stress and coping. The CEWG report summarized the results from the 1996 National Population Health Survey of Canadians aged 12 and older, which found that 5 percent of respondents engaged in heavy alcohol use, 48 percent had a body mass index of 25 or greater, and 57 percent were characterized by a lack of physical activity. These findings underscore the need for a national strategy and program to combat this problem.

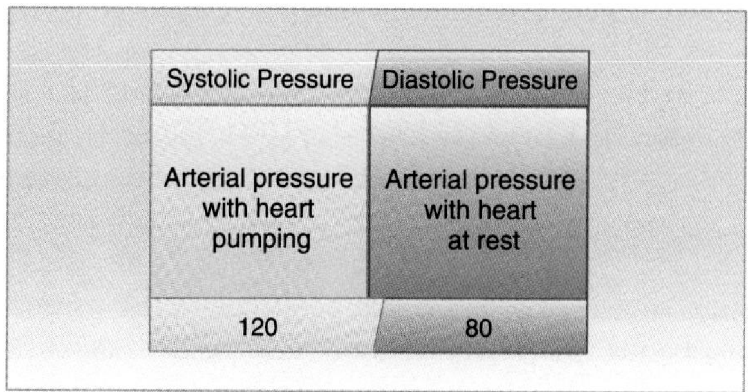

Systolic Pressure
Diastolic Pressure
Arterial pressure with heart pumping
Arterial pressure with heart at rest
120
80

Figure 8.6 Normal young-adult blood pressure

Table 8.4

Risk Factors for High Blood Pressure

Excess weight (body mass index greater than 25)
Central obesity (i.e., waist to hip ratio greater than 1)
Lack of regular physical activity
Heavy alcohol use (per week, 14 or more drinks for men, 9 or more drinks for women)
Lack of diet with high fibre, fruit, vegetables, and low saturated fat
Inadequate dietary intake of calcium and potassium
Excessive salt intake
Stress and coping response
Low socioeconomic status (reflecting its association with other risk factors and daily living challenges)
Low birth weight

Source: Adapted from Table 2, p. 25, Report of the Expert Working Group, Health Canada and the Canadian Coalition for High Blood Pressure Prevention and Control (2000).

Canadian Perspectives/8.2

Prevention and Control of Hypertension in Canada

An expert working group was put together in 1996 to devise a national strategy to combat hypertension in Canada. This committee was formed by Health Canada and the Canadian Coalition for High Blood Pressure Prevention and Control. It can be argued that their report, which was published in January 2000 and is updated annually, while aimed at policymakers, should nevertheless be required reading for all Canadians. The overarching goals of this committee are to reduce the prevalence of uncontrolled high blood pressure in Canada and reduce the proportion of Canadians who are entirely unaware of the fact that they have high blood pressure.

Their report identifies a number of short-term and long-term program objectives. Short-term objectives include increasing the general public's knowledge and improving their attitudes and skills involving healthy behaviours and the importance of regular blood pressure measurements; short-term objectives also include very specific outcomes, such as decreasing the amount of salt added to prepared food and food served in restaurants. The four stated long-term program outcomes are to achieve (1) an increase in a healthy lifestyle for all Canadians (i.e., healthy weight, regular physical activity, low risk alcohol use, and stress management) in order to prevent the onset of high blood pressure; (2) an increase in Canadians having regular blood pressure measurements; (3) an increase in high blood pressure investigation, diagnosis, and treatment; and (4) an increase in individuals with high blood pressure adopting healthy behaviours and appropriate use of prescribed medicine.

This important report also includes an analysis of why previous prevention programs have met with only limited success. One key factor that has undermined previous attempts at prevention is the fact that only 1 to 2 percent of the health care budget is dedicated to the promotion of healthy behaviours and this limits the overall impact of such programs. The report also suggests the need for an expanded approach to lifestyle counselling, one that does not rely so heavily on physicians but affords a greater role to psychologists, nurses, and nutritionists, among others. It recommended as well that physical environments be provided that are more conducive to people engaging in physical activity, that national attention be more focused on the need to minimize "the profound impact of poverty and low education" (p. 33), and that the failure of communities, regions, provinces, and territories to monitor progress in reducing risk factors be addressed. In this last regard, the report states that Saskatchewan is the only province or territory with plans in place to conduct an ongoing survey and monitoring of risk factors.

Although this working group has provided an important document, there is a need to further examine these issues in certain populations. Members of the working group suggest the importance of addressing hypertension in terms of the specific needs of children, pregnant women, and Aboriginal people (see Chockalingam et al., 2000). More generally, Campbell et al. (2002) suggest the need for greater participation by patients and involvement by multidisciplinary health care teams.

Thinking Critically

1. The Canadian Expert Working Group recommends an increase in a healthy lifestyle for all Canadians. Do you think that prevention programs could be implemented effectively in the workplace and supported and funded by business and industry? Why? How?

2. How would you address the issue of hypertension among Canada's Aboriginal people? Design a prevention program tailored specifically to our Aboriginal people. What key risk factors would you address in your program?

3. Design a model of hypertension that takes into account the various risk factors for hypertension that have been discussed in this chapter. Use lines and arrows to indicate the interrelationships among the factors. Develop a comprehensive, self-report assessment of lifestyle that could be used as an initial component of a lifestyle skills hypertension prevention program.

Psychological Stress and Blood-Pressure Elevation Various stressful conditions have been examined to determine their role in the etiology of essential hypertension. Stressful interviews, natural disasters such as earthquakes, and job stress have all been found to produce short-term elevations in blood pressure (e.g., Niedhammer et al., 1998).

It is also relatively easy to produce increased blood pressure in the laboratory. The induction of various emotional states, such as anger, fear, and sadness, all increase blood pressure (Caccioppo et al., 1993). Similarly, challenging tasks, such as mental arithmetic, mirror drawing, putting a hand in ice water (the cold pressor test), and giving a speech in front of an audience all lead to increased blood pressure (e.g., Manuck, Kaplan, & Clarkson, 1993; Tuomisto, 1997). A classic series of studies by Obrist and his colleagues (e.g., 1978) used a reaction-time task in which participants were told they would receive an electric shock if they did not respond quickly enough. Good performance led to a monetary bonus. The reaction-time task yielded significant increases in both heart rate and systolic blood pressure.

For ethical reasons, no experimental work has been done with human beings to determine whether short-term increases in blood pressure will develop into prolonged hypertension and structural changes. In research done on animals, sustained hypertension has proved elusive. In many studies using electric shock as a stressor, blood pressure increased during the period when the animal was stressed but returned to normal when the stressor was removed. Studies that have used more natural stressors, such as having to compete with other animals for food (Peters, 1977), have proved somewhat more successful in producing long-term blood-pressure elevations. But the overall picture indicates that some predisposing factor or factors, such as the activation of the sympathetic nervous system by anger, are required if stress is to bring on essential hypertension.

Although the results from these laboratory studies are interesting, ultimately we must understand why blood-pressure increases in people's natural environments. Therefore, researchers have also undertaken studies of ambulatory blood pressure, wherein participants wear a blood-pressure cuff that takes readings as they go about their daily lives. Many of these studies have asked participants about their emotional state at the time a blood-pressure reading is taken. The general finding has been that both positive and negative emotional states are associated with higher blood pressure (e.g., Jacob et al., 1999; Kamarck et al., 1998). There is also some indication that, of various negative emotions, anger is most strongly linked to elevated blood pressure (e.g., Schwartz, Warren, & Pickering, 1994).

Other ambulatory monitoring studies have examined environmental conditions associated with blood pressure. A series of studies examined the effects of stress on blood pressure among paramedics (Shapiro, Jamner, & Goldstein, 1993). In one of these analyses, ambulance calls were divided into high- and low-stress types. As expected, the high-stress calls were associated with higher blood pressure. Even more interesting were the results when the paramedics were divided into groups using personality-test measures of anger and defensiveness. The groups did not differ in blood pressure during the low-stress calls, but on the high-stress calls, paramedics high in anger and defensiveness had higher blood pressure.

In the ambulatory monitoring studies just described, the overall amount of blood-pressure increase associated with emotional states or environmental conditions was rather small. But it was also consistently found that a subset of participants had large increases. In the Kamarck study, for example, participants in the top 10 percent of the magnitude of association between negative mood and blood pressure showed, a 20-point increase in systolic blood pressure. These data suggest that only people who have some predisposition, or diathesis, will experience large blood-pressure increases that over time may lead to sustained hypertension. We turn next to these possible diatheses.

Predisposing Factors Some people and animals are genetically predisposed to hypertension. Research with animals has identified several powerful diatheses—rearing in social isolation (Henry, Ely, & Stephens, 1972), a high level of emotionality (Farris, Yeakel, & Medoff, 1945), and sensitivity to salt (Friedman & Dahl, 1975). In the salt study, the

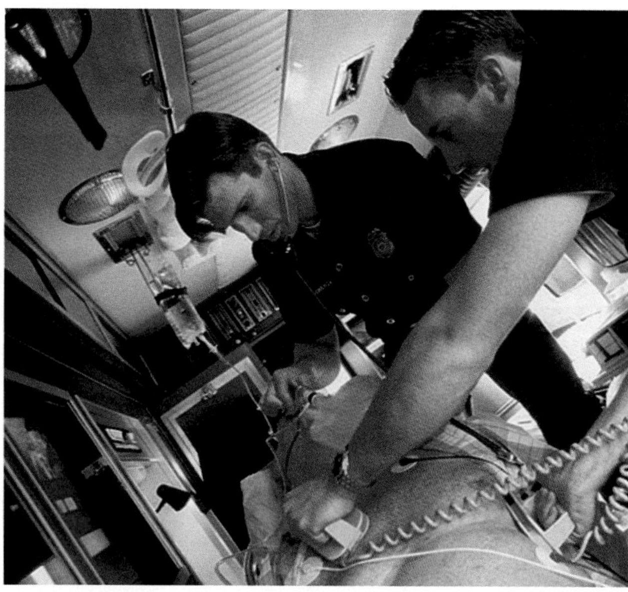

High-stress ambulance calls, such as those requiring the revival of the victim, led to greater blood-pressure increases than low-stress calls in the Shapiro, Jamner, and Goldstein study.

researchers worked with rats that had been bred to be either sensitive or insensitive to the impact of their diet. The sensitive rats developed hypertension and died on a high-salt diet. These salt-sensitive rats were also likely to show sustained blood-pressure elevations when placed in an experimentally created conflict situation.

As mentioned earlier, being easily angered could be a psychological diathesis. What is less clear about the anger variable is which aspect is most important: becoming angry easily, becoming angry and not expressing it, or having a cynical or suspicious attitude toward others. Recent research has not totally resolved this issue, but the data suggest that being easily angered is the most important variable (e.g., Raikkonen et al., 1999). Complicating the picture further, anger may function differently in men and women. Expressing anger has been related to increased blood-pressure reactivity in men, whereas suppressing anger has been linked to higher blood-pressure reactivity in women (Shapiro, Goldstein, & Jamner, 1995). Sex differences have also been found in the association between the tendency to anger easily and ambulatory blood pressure. Among men, but not among women, high trait anger is related to higher blood pressure (Guyll & Contrada, 1998). We return to this issue in our discussion of myocardial infarction.

In the past decade, there has been a great deal of interest in cardiovascular reactivity as a biological predisposition to hypertension (and coronary heart disease as well). Cardiovascular reactivity refers to the extent to which blood pressure and heart rate increase in response to stress. The general research strategy is to assess cardiovascular reactivity to a laboratory stressor (or, even better, a battery of stressors) among people who are not currently hypertensive and then to follow up the participants some years later to determine whether the reactivity measure (usually the amount of change from a baseline condition after exposure to the stressor) predicts blood pressure. Two important points must be demonstrated to ensure the success of this approach:

1 Reactivity must be reliable if it is going to have predictive power; that is, someone who is high in reactivity must be consistently high. Indications are that reactivity is reliable if it is measured in response to a battery of laboratory stressors (e.g., Kamarck et al., 1992).
2 The laboratory measure of reactivity must actually relate to what the person's cardiovascular system does during day-to-day activities. Because of what is called white-coat hypertension, a person's blood pressure may be high at the clinic or laboratory but normal elsewhere. Though the literature on this issue is somewhat conflicting (see Gerin et al., 1994; Swain & Suls, 1996), studies that have compared laboratory reactivity with reactivity to stressors in the natural environment have shown some relationship in at least some people (Matthews et al., 1992).

What are the results of the studies that have tried to predict blood pressure from reactivity? Again, there is some variability, but those from one well-conducted study are positive (Light et al., 1992). Cardiovascular measures were taken while participants performed a reaction-time task in which they were threatened with shock if their responses were slow. A follow-up 10 to 15 years later included both office-based measures of cardiovascular functioning and a day of ambulatory monitoring. Each of the cardiovascular-reactivity measures taken years earlier (heart rate and systolic and diastolic blood pressure) predicted later blood pressure; heart-rate reactivity was the strongest predictor. Importantly, these reactivity measures predicted subsequent blood pressure levels higher than those predicted by standard clinical predictors, such as family history of hypertension.

Further support for the importance of reactivity comes from high-risk research comparing individuals with and without a history for hypertension (e.g., Adler & Ditto, 1998; Lovallo & Al'Absi, 1998). People with a family history of hypertension show greater blood-pressure reactivity to various stressors. Coupled with research showing the heritability of hypertension, these findings suggest that blood-pressure reactivity is a good candidate for a genetically transmitted diathesis. Furthermore, reactivity is related to other known risk factors for hypertension, such as race and low social class (Gump, Matthews, & Raikkonen, 1999; Jackson et al., 1999), as well as obesity, excessive use of alcohol, and family history of hypertension (see Wielgosz & Nolan, 2000).

In spite of these findings, evidence that reactivity actually predicts hypertension in humans is limited. In one study in which reactivity predicted the development of hypertension, participants were the offspring of hypertensive parents, raising the issue of whether the relationship would hold in the general population (Falkner et al., 1981). A more recent study entailed a four-year follow-up of 508 Finnish men whose blood-pressure reactivity had been assessed as they anticipated a bicycle exercise test (Everson et al., 1996). Men whose systolic blood pressure increased by 30 points or more were almost four times more likely to have developed hypertension four years later. The obvious limitation of this study is that reactivity was assessed in an unusual situation. Thus, we can't be sure that the results would generalize to the more usual tests that have been used to assess reactivity.

Coronary Heart Disease

Coronary heart disease (CHD) takes two principal forms, angina pectoris and myocardial infarction, or heart attack.

Characteristics of the Disease The symptoms of angina pectoris are periodic chest pains, usually located behind the sternum and frequently radiating into the back and sometimes the left shoulder and arm. The major cause of these severe attacks of pain is an insufficient supply of oxygen to the heart (called ischemia), which in turn is due to coronary atherosclerosis, a narrowing or plugging of the coronary arteries by deposits of cholesterol, a fatty material, or to constriction of the blood vessels. In many patients with coronary artery disease, episodes of ischemia do not result in the report of pain. These are called episodes of silent ischemia. Both angina and episodes of silent ischemia are precipitated by physical or emotional exertion and are commonly relieved by rest or medication. Serious physical damage to heart muscle rarely results from an angina or ischemia attack, for blood flow is reduced but not cut off. If, however, the narrowing of one or more coronary arteries progresses to the point of producing a total blockage, a myocardial infarction, or heart attack, is likely to occur.

Myocardial infarction is a much more serious disorder. Like angina pectoris, it is caused by an insufficient supply of oxygen to the heart. But unlike angina, a heart attack usually results in permanent damage to the heart.

Several factors increase risk for CHD and the risk generally increases with the number and severity of these factors:

- age
- sex (males are at greater risk)
- cigarette smoking
- elevated blood pressure
- elevated serum cholesterol
- an increase in the size of the left ventricle of the heart
- obesity
- long-standing pattern of physical inactivity
- excessive use of alcohol
- diabetes

Stress and Myocardial Infarction In the short term, physical exertion can trigger a myocardial infarction, as can episodes of anger (Mittleman et al., 1997). Acute stress is another factor; the frequency of myocardial infarction, for example, increased among residents of Tel Aviv on the day of an Iraqi missile attack (NHLBI, 1998). More chronic stressors, such as marital conflict and financial worries, are also relevant. One of the most studied stressors is job strain (Karasek, 1979), an employment situation in which the person experiences a high level of demand—too much work and too little time in which to do it—coupled with little authority to make decisions and lack of opportunity to make full use of his or her skills on the job.

Many studies have found that a high level of job strain is associated with increased risk for myocardial infarction (Schall, Landsbergis, & Baker, 1994). In a recent study, over 10,000 British civil servants were assessed for the degree of control they could exercise on their jobs. They were then followed for about five years to determine the incidence of CHD. Replicating earlier studies, more CHD was found at follow-up among workers in lower-status jobs (e.g., clerical work). This result, in turn, was related to these workers' reports of having little control on the job (Marmot et al., 1997). In a large-scale study being conducted in Finland, highly demanding jobs have also been related to the progression of atherosclerosis (Lynch et al., 1997a) and to CVD mortality and morbidity (Lynch et al., 1997b).

Diatheses for Coronary Heart Disease The traditional risk factors, reviewed above, still leave at least half the instances of coronary heart disease unexplained (Jenkins, 1976). Indeed, people used to pay less attention to contributing causes, such as obesity, poor exercise habits, consumption of fatty foods, and smoking, than they do now, yet in earlier decades the incidence of CHD and related CVDs was much lower. Furthermore, in the Midwest United States, where people's diets are highest in saturated fats and smoking rates are especially high, the incidence of coronary heart disease is low compared with that in more industrialized parts of the United States. Anyone who has visited Paris is aware of the heavy smoking and the fat-rich diets of the French population, yet CHD is relatively low there. Why?

Psychological Diatheses The search for predispositions for coronary heart disease has begun to focus on psychological factors. Contemporary evidence linking CHD to psychological variables stems from investigations pioneered by two cardiologists, Meyer Friedman and Ray Rosenman (Friedman, 1969; Rosenman et al., 1975). In 1958 they identified a coronary-prone behaviour pattern called Type A behaviour pattern. As assessed by a structured interview, the Type A individual has an intense and competitive drive for achievement and advancement, an exaggerated sense of the urgency of passing time and of the need to hurry, and considerable aggressiveness and hostility toward others.

Type A behaviour is also assessed by self-report measures. The Survey of Work Styles developed by Jackson and Gray (1990) at the University of Western Ontario is an inventory that assesses six aspects of Type A behaviour: competitiveness, job dissatisfaction, impatience, anger, time urgency, and work involvement.

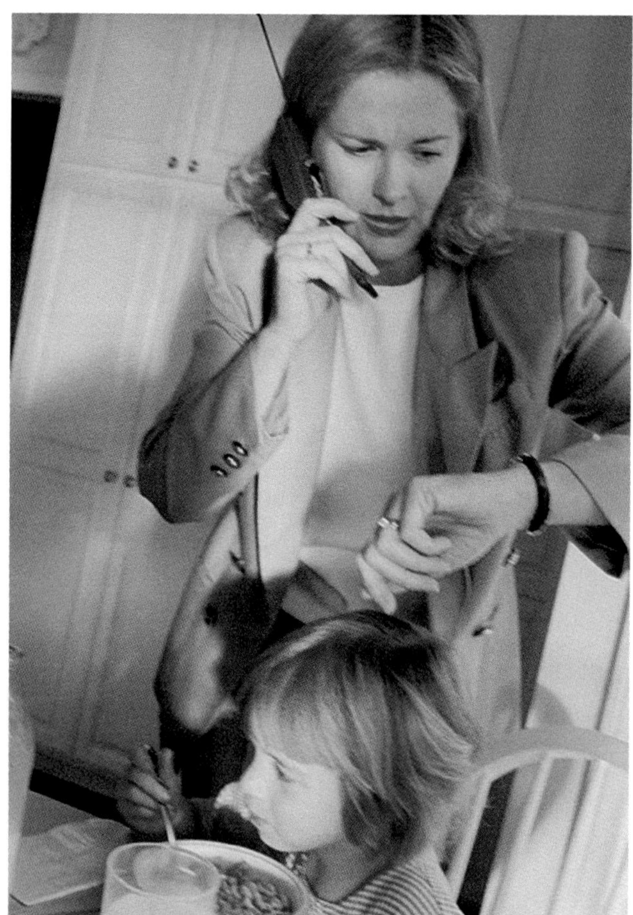

One characteristic of the Type A personality is feeling under time pressure and consequently trying to do several things at once.

Initial evidence supporting the idea that the Type A pattern predicts coronary heart disease came from the classic Western Collaborative Group Study (WCGS) (Rosenman et al., 1975). In this double-blind, prospective investigation, 3,154 men aged 39 to 59 were followed over a period of eight and a half years. Individuals who had been identified as Type A by interview were more than twice as likely to develop CHD as were Type B men, characterized by a less driven and less hostile way of life. Traditional risk factors, such as high levels of cholesterol, were also found to be related to CHD, but even when these factors were controlled for, Type A individuals were still twice as likely to develop CHD.

More recent research, however, has not supported the predictive utility of Type A behaviour. In several studies, Type A failed to predict either mortality or myocardial infarction (Eaker et al., 1992; Orth-Gomer & Unden, 1990; Shekelle et al., 1983), and other research has not found a relationship between Type A and coronary artery disease (Williams, 1987).

There are several reasons for these conflicting results. One is that later investigators used different methods of assessing Type A (e.g., questionnaires) that did not adequately measure it. Second, it became apparent that not all aspects of the Type A concept were truly related to CHD. In an analysis of the interview data from the WCGS done by Matthews and her colleagues (1977), for example, only seven of the whole set of items discriminated between Type A individuals who developed CHD and those who did not.

In further analyses of the WCGS data, anger and hostility have emerged as the major predictors of CHD (Hecker et al., 1988). A more recent longitudinal study has also found that difficulty controlling one's anger is related to higher rates of CHD (Kawachi et al., 1996). And higher levels of anger are related to several other variables that play a role in CHD, such as greater blood-pressure reactivity to stress, higher levels of cholesterol, cigarette smoking and alcohol use, and greater activation of platelets, which play a major role in the formation of blockages in the coronary arteries (Markovitz et al., 1996; Weidner et al., 1987; Weidner et al., 1989).

Other findings (e.g., Williams et al., 1986) suggest that cynicism (an approach to life that involves hostility) is a major factor within the Type A complex. The amount of coronary-artery blockage and coronary death was especially high in Type A participants who had earlier endorsed the Minnesota Multiphasic Personality Inventory (MMPI) items reflecting a cynical or hostile attitude (e.g., "Most people will use somewhat unfair means to gain profit or advantage, rather than lose it"). An earlier follow-up study of medical students who had been healthy when they took the MMPI 25 years earlier found a higher rate of CHD and death in those whose answers had indicated cynicism toward others (Barefoot, Dahlstrom, & Williams, 1983). More recently, in the large Finnish study mentioned earlier, cynicism was found to predict atherosclerosis, myocardial infarctions, and death from CHD (Everson et al., 1997; Kamarck et al., 1997).

What is not yet clear is the best way to conceptualize these results. Significant problems are the vague terminology that has been employed (anger, hostility, cynicism) and the lack of agreement among the measures that have been used to assess these concepts. One study followed a large sample of men for two years, using ultrasound to assess the progression of atherosclerosis (Julkunen et al., 1994). Three components of anger and hostility were assessed:

- *cognitive*—negative beliefs about others
- *affective*—impatience and irritability
- *experience*—whether anger is expressed or not

These measures did not correlate well, indicating that even though the terms sound similar, they cannot be readily substituted for one another. The affective component did not predict the progression of atherosclerosis, but the other two did. This study is not the last word on the issue, but it does illustrate the complexity of trying to determine whether anger is related to coronary heart disease. Another important issue is identifying the origin of anger and hostility. Research is just beginning on this topic, but indications are that it may lie in a high level of family conflict (Matthews et al., 1996).

Evidence that hostility may operate differently in men and women must also be taken into consideration. A study conducted by Wolfgang Linden and his associates at the University of British Columbia examined the correlates of ambulatory systolic pressure in a sample of students who wore an ambulatory monitor for a working day (Linden, Chambers, Maurice, & Lenz, 1993). High hostility and self-deception were associated with elevated blood pressure for men but these associations were not present for women.

Although interest in anger and hostility remains high, research has begun to examine the relationship between other negative emotions—particularly anxiety and depression—and CHD. Anxiety has been shown to be related to CHD in humans (Kawachi et al., 1994), and animal research demonstrates that inducing anxiety in animals with atherosclerosis can precipitate a heart attack (Carpeggio & Skinner, 1991). With regard to depression, it has been found that depressed patients have high rates of death from CVD. Similarly, cardiac patients who also have a depressive disorder are over five times more likely than others to die within six months (Glassman & Shapiro, 1998). Plausible biological mechanisms for these relationships have been proposed. Anxiety, for example, is associated with activation of the sympathetic nervous system, which can lead to both hypertension and atherosclerosis. Research has also shown that depression is linked to a greater tendency for platelets to aggregate and thus produce obstructions in the arteries. Furthermore, depression is often associated with increases in steroidal hormones, which increase blood pressure and damage cells in arteries (Musselman, Evans, & Nemeroff, 1998). When depression is combined with physical fatigue, it creates a condition known as **vital exhaustion**. Linden (2003) reviewed studies indicating that vital exhaustion is a predictor of CVD occurrence.

Tying together this interest in CHD and negative emotions—anger, anxiety, and depression—is the newly proposed Type D personality, with "D" standing for distressed type (Denollet & Brutsaert, 1997). Type D is defined as high scores on negative affectivity (a tendency to experience high levels of anxiety, anger, and depression) plus inhibiting the expression of these emotions. A recent review by Pederson and Denollet (2003) concluded unequivocally that Type D cardiac patients are at increased risk for cardiovascular morbidity and mortality, independent of other cardiac risk factors. Type D patients also had an impaired quality of life, benefited less from treatment, and had increased psychological distress. Distress can be a key predictor. Recent research in Canada has shown that a mildly depressed mood during the initial week of hospitalization predicts cardiac mortality following an acute myocardial infarction (Frasure-Smith et al., 1999). This research clearly needs replication and extension to samples of people who have not experienced a previous myocardial infarction. Whether Type D will replace Type A as a psychological risk factor remains to be seen.

Biological Diatheses As with research on hypertension, research on biological predispositions for myocardial infarction has focused on reactivity. Excessive changes in heart rate and the consequent alterations in the force with which blood is pumped through the arteries may injure them, increasing risk for a myocardial infarction. Heart-rate reactivity has been related to CHD in several research contexts. A series of experimental studies investigated monkeys that were on a special diet designed to promote atherosclerosis. On the basis of a stress test, the animals were divided into high versus low heart-rate reactors. Subsequently, the high heart-rate reactors developed twice as much atherosclerosis as did the low reactors (Kaplan, Manuck et al., 1993). In another investigation by the same group, stress was created experimentally by changing the monkeys' living groups every three months. Changing living groups stresses the animals because they are continually forced to re-establish a dominance hierarchy. In an earlier study, this manipulation had been found to promote atherosclerosis in dominant monkeys. This time, some animals were given drugs to reduce the sympathetic activation that the stress was expected to produce; these animals treated with the drugs did not show an increase in atherosclerosis.

In studies of humans, heart-rate reactivity and ischemia (lack of oxygen) elicited by laboratory stressors have predicted the development of CHD and the occurrence of cardiac events (Jiang et al., 1996; Keys et al., 1971). Thus, cardiovascular reactivity is a plausible candidate for a biological diathesis, and as we have already seen, it is associated with the psychological diathesis of anger and hostility.

SOCIOECONOMIC STATUS, ETHNICITY, AND HEALTH

Low socioeconomic status (SES) is associated with higher rates of mortality from all causes. One, but by no means the only, reason for this relationship is that people in lower social classes are more likely than people in higher classes to engage in behaviours that increase risk for disease, such as smoking, eating a high-fat diet, and drinking excessive amounts of alcohol (Lantz et al., 1998). The link between low SES and poorer health is also evident in Canada, where it has been referred to by Kosteniuk and Dickinson (2003) as the **social gradient of health** (i.e., inequalities in SES reflect inequalities in health status). These researchers analyzed data from the 1994–1995 Canadian National Population Health Survey and found that lower stressor levels were associated with higher household income, being retired, and growing older. Lower stressor levels were also linked with greater levels of control, self-esteem, and social support, and higher income was correlated with greater levels of control and social support.

Because people of ethnic minorities in North America are found in high numbers among the lower social classes, race is also a factor in research. Risk factors for cardiovascular disease (such as smoking) are higher among women from ethnic minorities than among white women. This finding holds even when members of the two groups have comparable socioeconomic statuses (Winkleby et al., 1998). The increased prevalence of some of these risk factors shows up in studies of children as young as 6 to 9 years of age. African American and Mexican American girls in this age range have higher body mass indexes and higher fat intake than do non-Hispanic white girls (Winkleby et al., 1999). Thus, both social class and ethnicity are important factors in health.

Ethnicity is also a variable of importance in how people cope with cancer. Research in the United States has demonstrated that the race of a person with cancer is associated with detection of illness, adherence to treatment regimens, survival, and quality of life. These relationships were recently examined in a review by Meyerowitz et al. (1998). Among the many findings based on data from the U.S. National Cancer Institute are the following:

- African Americans have the highest rates of cancer overall, as a result of very high rates of lung and prostate cancer among men.
- Although African American women have lower breast cancer rates than do white women, their mortality rates five years after diagnosis are the same, due to lower survival rates.
- Latinos have low rates of cancer in general, but high rates of cervical cancer. Asian Americans have low rates for all cancers except stomach cancer.

These and other findings are illustrative of ethnic differences in the incidence and outcomes of cancer. What might account for these differences? The answers appear to lie less with racial and biological factors than with social and psychological factors such as access to and willingness to seek out medical care. As one might expect, in the United States, the ability to afford skilled health care is not uniformly found across ethnic and socioeconomic lines. Canada's universal medicare system reduces this problem.

THERAPIES FOR PSYCHOPHYSIOLOGICAL DISORDERS

Since psychophysiological disorders are true physical dysfunctions, sound psychotherapeutic practice calls for close consultation with a physician. Whether high blood pressure is biologically caused or, as in essential hypertension, linked to psychological stress, a number of medications can reduce the constriction of the arteries. Mental health and medical professionals recognize, however, that most drug interventions treat only the symptoms; they do not address the fact that the person is reacting emotionally to psychological stress. Although the evidence suggests that the predisposition for breakdown of a particular organ is inherited, or at least somatically based, the importance of a person's psychological response nevertheless indicates that psychotherapeutic interventions are necessary.

Therapists of all persuasions agree that reducing anxiety, depression, or anger is the best way to alleviate suffering from psychophysiological disorders. The particular disorder—essential hypertension or coronary heart disease—is considered to be adversely affected, if not actually caused, by these emotions.

Psychoanalytically oriented therapists employ techniques such as free association and dream analysis, as they do with other patients experiencing anxiety, to help people confront the infantile origins of their fears. Ego analysts, such as Franz Alexander, believe that emotional states underlie the several disorders. Thus, they encourage patients with essential hypertension, whom they view as labouring under a burden of undischarged anger, to assert themselves and thereby release their anger.

Behavioural and cognitive therapists employ their usual range of procedures for reducing anxiety and anger—systematic desensitization, in vivo exposure, rational-emotive therapy, and assertion training—depending on the source of tension. Relaxation training, for example, has been used successfully to help asthmatic children exhale more fully (Lehrer et al., 1994). Behaviour rehearsal and shaping may help people learn to react in difficult situations with less emotional upset.

We turn now to an examination of several areas in which clinicians in the fields of behavioural medicine and health psychology have brought psychological perspectives and interventions to bear on the problem of helping people deal with medical illnesses.

Treating Hypertension and Reducing CHD Risk

Because some antihypertensive drugs have undesirable side effects, such as drowsiness, light-headedness, and for men, erectile difficulties, many investigations have been undertaken on non-pharmacological treatments for borderline essential hypertension. Efforts have been directed at weight reduction, restriction of salt intake, giving up cigarettes, aerobic exercise, and reduction in alcohol consumption. Losing weight, reducing salt intake, and exercising regularly can also help reduce harmful levels of cholesterol. Drugs, too, can lower cholesterol levels; for example, provastatin (trade name Mevacor) lowers low-density lipid cholesterol (LDL, the so-called bad cholesterol) and appears to be successful in forestalling the progression of atherosclerosis. Such drugs, plus improvements in eating habits observed in Canada and the United States since the 1960s, are associated with decreased mortality from cardiovascular diseases (Holme, 1990; Johnson et al., 1993; Weidner & Griffin, 1995).

A recent study with older adults highlights the importance of losing weight and reducing salt intake. The controlled 1998 Trial of Nonpharmacologic Interventions in the Elderly (TONE) (Whelton et al., 1998), indicated for the first time that significant benefits can be achieved by obese people between the ages of 60 and 80 who are taking blood-pressure medication. Specifically, half the overweight people in the study who reduced their salt intake by 25 percent and lost as little as eight pounds over the course of three months were able to come off their antihypertensive medications and maintain normal blood pressure. The ability to maintain normal blood pressure was achieved by 31 percent of the patients who reduced their salt intake, 36 percent of those who lost weight, and more than half of those who reduced both their salt intake and their weight. Furthermore, these results—the dietary and weight changes as well as the maintenance of normal blood pressure without medication—lasted for more than three years.

Regular exercise is another avenue for reducing blood pressure, one that is available to everyone at little or no cost. Recent research has shown that increasing exercise through so-called lifestyle activities—for example, walking up stairs rather than using an elevator or walking short distances rather than driving—yields as much benefit as a structured program of aerobic exercise (Dunn et al., 1999).

Other recent research (Dengel, Galecki, et al., 1998; Dengel, Hagberg, et al., 1998) indicates that people with essential hypertension, as well as those whose blood pressure is within the normal range, should adopt regular exercise habits, such as walking briskly most every day for about half an hour or engaging in other aerobic exercise that raises the heart and respiration rates. Most people can engage in such activity without even checking with their physician if the activity is not so strenuous that it prevents them from carrying on a conversation at the same time. In fact, the research suggests that people with high blood pressure and no other health complications should try exercise for about a year before turning to drugs to lower their blood pressure. For those already taking antihypertensive drugs, a regular and not necessarily strenuous exercise regimen can sometimes reduce or even eliminate dependence on medication. Decreases of 10 points in both systolic and diastolic blood pressure—a significant figure—can be achieved by most people after just a few weeks. Exercising regularly can also reduce mortality from cardiovascular disease (Wannamethee, Shaper, & Walker, 1998). All these beneficial results may be mediated by the favourable effects that exercise has on stress, weight, and blood cholesterol. And if the sense of well-being that accompanies regular exercise and weight loss leads to the adoption of other health-enhancing habits, such as stopping smoking and avoiding drinking to excess, the positive effects on blood pressure will be all the stronger and more enduring.

Another psychological approach has been to teach hypertensive individuals to lower sympathetic nervous system arousal, primarily via training in muscle relaxation, occasionally supplemented by biofeedback (Benson, Beary, & Carl, 1974; Blanchard, 1994). Results have been mixed (Kaufmann et al., 1988), and it is unclear how enduring the effects of relaxation treatment are (Patel et al., 1985). The success of this approach probably depends ultimately on whether the person maintains the acquired skill to relax, and that in turn depends on whether the person remains motivated to practise that skill.

DeQuattro and Davison (Lee et al., 1987) found that intensive relaxation, conducted in weekly sessions over two months and with practice sessions at home with audiotaped instructions, significantly reduced blood pressure immediately following treatment in borderline hypertensive people, more so than did a control group that received state-of-the-art medical advice and instructions concerning diet, weight loss, and other known risk factors. (The relaxation group also received the same medical information given to the control subjects.) Furthermore, these effects were stronger among hypertensive people previously found to have high sympathetic arousal than among those with lower arousal levels. This result supports the hypothesis of Esler et al. (1977) that there is a subset of hypertensive individuals with relatively high resting levels of sympathetic arousal who may be especially well suited for sympathetic-dampening therapies, such as relaxation.

Evidence suggesting the importance of cognitive change as well as the role of anger was reported by Davison, Williams, et al. (1991). Borderline hypertensive patients who achieved significant reductions in anger as expressed in their articulated thoughts had decreased blood pressure; that is, as their articulated thoughts became less angry, their blood pressure became lower. This finding is consistent with research linking anger with hypertension.

The recognition that cognition is probably a factor in hypertension has led to increased interest in cognitive-behavioural approaches to lowering blood pressure. A study from Nigeria reports that adding rational-emotive therapy to blood-pressure–lowering medication led to significantly greater reductions in systolic blood pressure than did drugs alone (Oluwatelure, 1997).

However, many studies have failed to find significant and enduring effects from relaxation training and other stress-management procedures (Johnston et al., 1993). One reason for negative findings may be that participants are inadequately trained in relaxation as well as inadequately motivated to apply it in their everyday lives. Another reason may relate to the Davison et al. findings just described: relaxation may work best or even only with people whose sympathetic nervous system arousal levels are particularly high, and these elevated levels may indicate high stress. Consistent with this hypothesis is one study's finding that relaxation has a strong effect in hypertensive elderly African American men (Schneider et al., 1995). The participants came from poor neighbourhoods where life was difficult. Perhaps these high-stress living conditions create hypertension that is more related to stress than is the hypertension studied in most research, which typically involves participants who are white and better off financially. In any case, continued research in this vein appears useful and promising (Johnston, 1997).

BIOFEEDBACK

A visit to the commercial exhibit area of any psychological or psychiatric convention will reveal a plentiful display of complex biofeedback apparatuses, touted as an efficient, even miraculous, means of helping people control one or another bodily-mental state. By using sensitive instrumentation, biofeedback gives a person prompt and exact information, otherwise unavailable, on muscle activity, brain waves, skin temperature, heart rate, blood pressure, and other bodily functions. It is assumed that a person can achieve greater voluntary control over these phenomena—most of which were once considered under involuntary control only—if he or she knows immediately, through an auditory or visual signal, whether a somatic activity is increasing or decreasing. Because anxiety has been viewed generally as a state involving the autonomic (involuntary) nervous system, and because psychophysiological disorders often afflict organs innervated by this system, researchers and clinicians have been intrigued by biofeedback. For a time, biofeedback was virtually synonymous with behavioural medicine.

In a series of classic studies at Harvard Medical School, Shapiro, Tursky, and Schwartz (1970; Schwartz, 1973) demonstrated that human volunteers could consciously achieve significant short-term changes in blood pressure and heart rate. They found that some people could even be trained to increase their heart rate while decreasing their blood pressure. Achievement of this fine-grained control lent impetus to biofeedback work with human beings and awakened hope that certain clinical disorders might be alleviated in this new way.

Research on using biofeedback to treat patients with essential hypertension has been somewhat encouraging, but results have not been certain enough to establish biofeedback as a standard treatment for the disease (Blanchard, 1994). Moreover, a recent meta-analysis of 22 randomized, controlled studies found that biofeedback was effective primarily if combined with relaxation training (Nakao, Yano, Nomura, & Kuboki, 2003). This is in keeping with earlier suggestions that relaxation training given in conjunction with biofeedback does more than the biofeedback to reduce blood pressure (Reed, Katkin, & Goldband, 1986).

Tension headaches, believed to be caused by excessive and persistent tension in the frontalis muscles of the forehead and in the muscles of the neck, have also been handled within this framework. The standard treatment entails feedback of tension in the frontalis muscles. Although such biofeedback has indeed been shown to be effective (e.g., Birbaumer, 1977), some studies suggest that cognitive factors may play a role. In a classic study, Holroyd et al. (1984) found that *believing* that one was reducing frontalis tension via biofeedback was associated with reductions in tension headaches, whether or not such reductions were actually being achieved. Enhanced feelings of self-efficacy and internal control appear to have inherent stress-reducing properties, a theme encountered in the discussion of control and anxiety in Chapter 6. Biofeedback may strengthen the sense of control, thus reducing general anxiety levels and ultimately reducing tension headaches (Bandura, 1997).

Other research (e.g., Blanchard et al., 1982) suggests that relaxation per se is the critical variable, much like the non-drug treatment of essential hypertension. Similar conclusions have been drawn about biofeedback in the treatment of migraine headache (Compas et al., 1998).

There is, then, very little evidence that biofeedback has any specific effects other than distraction, relaxation, and instilling a beneficial sense of control. In addition, clinicians must remain mindful of the complexities of human problems. A person with high blood pressure, for example, might have to alter a tense, driven lifestyle before he or she can significantly reduce blood pressure through biofeedback. It is unwise, and a sign of naive clinical practice, to assume that one technique focused on a specific malfunction or problem will invariably cure the patient.

Regardless of the specific processes involved, extensive evidence attests to the usefulness of biofeedback and other interventions in treating recurring headaches. A comparative review and analysis of past research by Janel Gauthier and his associates in Quebec led them to conclude that biofeedback, relaxation, and coping-skills training result in long-lasting improvements that are at least comparable to those obtained through medication (see Gauthier, Ivers, & Carrier, 1996).

Changing Type A Behaviour

Reducing anger and hostility as well as a grim and overly determined approach to life is the basis for treating people showing Type A behaviour. Over the past three decades, a great deal of research has been done to determine whether the behaviour patterns associated with Type A can be changed. These studies have generally involved men who have suffered a myocardial infarction, and the focus has been on reducing the likelihood of a second one. We will discuss the techniques used in one of the most comprehensive of these studies, the Recurrent Coronary Prevention Project (Friedman et al., 1982).

In this study, participants practised talking more slowly and listening to others more closely. They attempted to reduce the demands placed on them so that they could relax more and, in general, take a less time-pressured and less hostile approach to everyday challenges. In addition to the behavioural changes, participants were encouraged to ease up on the demanding beliefs identified as common among Type As—that events are direct personal threats and that the intensity of Type A behaviour is essential to success.

This study found that Type A behaviour can be changed. After three years of treatment, men who had received Type A counselling had nearly half the risk of a second heart attack. Their risk was 7.2 percent annually, compared with 13.2 percent for Type A men who received only cardiological counselling (Friedman et al., 1984; Friedman & Ulmer, 1984; Powell et al., 1984; Thoresen et al., 1985). Reductions in hostility shown in the study may have been particularly important, reflecting the increasing importance of hostility and anger in Type A research and in psychophysiological disorders generally (Haaga, 1987b).

Cardiac Rehabilitation Efforts

Frasure-Smith and her colleagues at the Montreal Heart Institute Research Centre have been evaluating the results of a long-term intervention program known as the Ischemic Heart Disease Life Stress Monitoring Program (IHDLSM) (Frasure-Smith & Prince, 1985, 1989). The IHDLSM is a cardiac rehabilitation program in which participants are assigned to a control condition or a stress-monitoring condition. The stress-monitoring condition involves the receipt of psychosocial support and advice from nurses who assess the patients' stress levels each month and intervene when stress is elevated. The initial results showed that this non-specific psychosocial intervention led to significant reductions in mortality and in reoccurrences of heart attacks (Frasure-Smith & Prince, 1985, 1989). Unfortunately, recent replication studies found less successful outcomes (Frasure-Smith et al., 1997, 2002). There was no treatment impact among men overall, and women in the treatment group actually had a worse prognosis. Secondary analyses showed that coping styles were important (Frasure-Smith et al., 2002). People characterized as repressors (i.e., those who have high arousal yet use defensive strategies to avoid acknowledging the arousal) had worse outcomes. Still, some findings from the IHDLSM project did show that some people can benefit from a focus on the alleviation of stress. Specifically, highly anxious men seemed to benefit from the program (Frasure-Smith et al., 2002). This finding with anxious men is more in line with the general pattern of findings across several studies. These studies tend to attest to the positive effects of psychosocial treatments for cardiac rehabilitation patients (see Linden, 2003).

The finding that women did worse in the Frasure-Smith et al. (2002) study is troubling in light of more general trends that have emerged from research on cardiac rehabilitation. A recent review conducted by researchers from Toronto associated with the University Health Network confirmed that there are widespread gender differences in cardiac rehabilitation outcomes (see Grace et al., 2002). They found that coronary recovery following an ischemic coronary event is poorer in women, relative to men, and women patients experience greater depression and anxiety but lower levels of social support and self-efficacy.

Jane Irvine from York University and her colleagues maintain that cognitive factors are extremely important in treating and rehabilitating cardiac patients (Irvine & Ritvo, 1998). They argue that since it is apparent that certain health-risk behaviours have been linked conclusively with heart disease, it follows that individual differences in health-risk appraisal play a vital role in determining adherence to treatment regimens. They have developed a cognitively-based model known as the Risk Adaptation Model, two key elements of which are risk expectancy (i.e., appraisals of the likelihood and magnitude of harm if no risk-reduction measures are taken) and risk-reduction expectancy (i.e., judgments of the efficacy of responses and a personal sense of an ability to reduce risks). Risk-reduction efficacy includes individual differences in optimism versus pessimism with respect to health outcomes. The third cognitive element of this model is attention regulation. Irvine and Ritvo (1998) recognize that people differ in their ability to focus their attention on specific activities and that people suffering from anxiety and intrusive memories triggered by traumatic stressors may not have the attentional processes required for changing health behaviours. Clearly, cognitive expectations are linked inextricably with health behaviours. The importance of cognitive and attitudinal factors is evident in other illnesses, too, such as cancer (see Focus on Discovery 8.2).

Reducing Type A behaviour is sometimes viewed as an instance of stress management, with the focus being on enhancing physical as well as mental health (Steptoe, 1997). We turn next to a consideration of the field of stress management.

focus on discovery/8.2

Coping with Cancer

A growing body of evidence indicates that interventions that alleviate anxiety and depression and foster a fighting spirit can help people cope with cancer (Telch & Telch, 1986). A non-passive attitude may even enhance the capacity to survive cancer (Greer, Morris, & Pettigale, 1979).

An optimistic, upbeat attitude is important in combating illness, including illnesses as serious as cancer (Carver et al., 1993) and HIV-positive status (Taylor et al., 1992). A recent study reported by Allison and colleagues from McGill University found that dispositional optimism was associated with higher levels of survival in patients from France with head or neck cancer (Allison, Guichard, Fung, & Gilain, 2003). Related research examines individual differences in hope and hopelessness (see Stanton, Danoff-Burg, & Huggins, 2002). One recent investigation of cancer patients from Princess Margaret Hospital in Toronto found that hopelessness predicted desire for a hastened death (Jones, Huggins, Rydall, & Rodin, 2003). The role of hopelessness will be explored further in Chapter 10 in the context of our discussion of suicide.

The mechanism by which an optimistic attitude helps people with life-threatening illnesses may be its link to adaptive coping. Optimistic people—for instance, people with high levels of self-efficacy (Bandura, 1997)—may be more likely to engage in risk-reducing health behaviours such as avoiding risky sex or engaging in prescribed regular exercise following coronary-bypass surgery (Scheier & Carver, 1987).

PSYCHOLOGICAL INTERVENTIONS TO HELP PEOPLE COPE

The quality of life and even the survival time of patients with terminal cancer can be improved by psychosocial interventions, as shown by research by Alastair Cunningham and his colleagues at the Ontario Cancer Institute (Cunningham, Edmonds, Phillips, et al., 2000; Cunningham, Phillips, Lockwood, et al., 2000; Edmonds, Lockwood, & Cunningham, 1999). Patients with metastatic breast cancer participate in weekly supportive group therapy, where they offer understanding and comfort to each other, openly discuss death and dying, express their feelings, and encourage each other to live life as fully as possible in the face of death. Edmonds et al. (1999) tracked the results of an eight-month intervention and found no significant improvements in self-reports of mood and quality of life, but profound clinical improvements were noted by the patients' therapists. In related research, Cunningham and associates sought to identify factors that predicted length of survival in 22 people with medically incurable metastatic cancer (Cunningham, Phillips, Lockwood, et al., 2000). One key factor was the amount of "psychological work" engaged in by the patients; that is, those who were rated as more involved psychologically in their recovery tended to live longer. Another important factor was the extent to which the patient held the expectancy that psychological efforts would have a positive effect. In contrast, standard psychometric measures of quality of life did not relate to survival.

Another recent Canadian study also examined the impact of group psychosocial support in a sample of women with metastatic breast cancer (Goodwin et al., 2001). Comparisons of women who did receive the intervention with those who did not showed no group differences in mortality rates; however, women in the supportive group condition, relative to women in the control group, reported less psychological distress and less pain.

Problem-solving therapy (PST) has shown its value in helping cancer patients cope with the myriad life challenges facing them, from daily hassles to dealing with isolation and depression (Nezu et al., 1997). An important component of PST (and of other approaches that can help cancer patients) is the enhanced sense of control that the patient learns to exercise. It would seem that such control is particularly important for people with a life-threatening illness who are experiencing the side effects of treatment.

A concern for men is prostate cancer. High-profile Canadians who have had prostate cancer include the late prime minister Pierre Trudeau and former health minister Allan Rock. The prostate is a small gland surrounding the urethra, the tube that carries urine from the bladder through the penis and outside the body. It is usually surgically excised if cancer is discovered in it. However, since this type of cancer grows slowly, some older men elect not to have the surgery because it is likely that they will die from other causes before the prostate cancer is advanced enough to kill them and, more important, because removal of the prostate often has two very negative side effects: marked diminution or loss of erectile capacity and loss of full urinary control. Recent research examining quality-of-life issues in men who have had prostatectomy surgery has found that quality of life is rated as quite high by post-surgery patients, especially when they are instructed in the use of erectile aids, such as rigid implants (Perez et al., 1997). With the recent availability of Viagra, a medication that can restore erectile function, the prospects are even better for good psychological adjustment following this kind of surgery. Indeed, a recent Canadian study of men receiving treatment found that sexual problems and other urinary and bowel problems were still common but had less of an impact on the quality of life than was reported in earlier studies (see Krahn et al., 2003).

Still, as shown by a qualititative study conducted in Toronto, men and their families may face many challenges post-surgery (see Gray et al., 2000). A primary focus is managing the impact of the illness. Gray et al. found that patients often struggle to stay in control of their emotions; they can be high in "fearful neediness" at some points but are high in "fierce self-reliance" at other times.

INTERVENTIONS TO ENCOURAGE PREVENTION

Psychological interventions in a community psychology model also focus on preventing cancer by encouraging healthy behaviours and discouraging unhealthy ones. When it comes to cancer, *primary prevention* is designed to decrease the occurrence of cancer, while *secondary prevention* focuses on identifying cancer in its early stages (see Kilbourn & Durning, 2003).

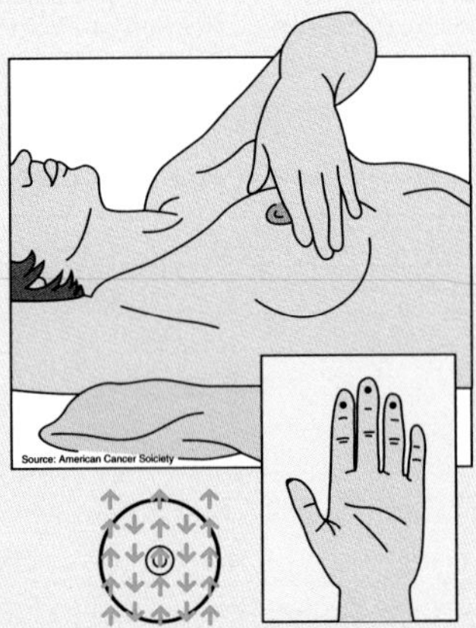

Encouraging women to perform breast self-examination (BSE) can lead to earlier detection of cancer and better treatment outcomes. Shown here is an advertisement from the American Cancer Society demonstrating how to perform BSE.

Table 8.5 provides an overview of recommended screening procedures that increase secondary prevention. Sadly, research indicates that the extent to which screening procedures are employed is often inadequate. A recent study by Isaacs et al. (2002) examined breast cancer and ovarian cancer screening behaviours in a sample of healthy women who were deemed to be high-risk candidates based on a family history of breast cancer or ovarian cancer. The authors concluded that the screening was "suboptimal," even for women over 50 years old who should be getting annual mammograms.

Table 8.5

Recommended Screening Procedures for Early Detection of Cancer

Cancer Site	Sex	Screening Test
Breast	F	Breast self-exam Clinical breast exam Mammogram
Cervix	F	Pap test
Endometrium/ Ovaries	F	Cervical pelvic exam
Colorectal	F/M	Faecal occult blood test Flexible sigmoidoscopy Screening colonoscopy
Skin	F/M	Clinical self-exam Skin self-exam
Prostate	M	Prostate specific antigen (PSA) blood test Digital rectal exam

Source: Adapted with permission from Kilbourn and Durning (2003, p. 107).

The most controversial procedure listed in Table 8.5 is the prostate specific antigen (PSA) blood test for men. The PSA is a protein molecule produced by the prostate glands. Healthy men have low levels of this antigen, but it can be substantially elevated in men with prostate cancer and a biopsy may be indicated. The test is controversial, in part because of uncertainty about the appropriate cut-off point value to use as an indicator of the possibility of prostate cancer. Test results are reported in nanograms per millilitre (ng/mL). A cut-off of 4 ng/mL has been used, but some clinicians have used a lower cut-off, and it is generally recognized that the cut-off point should be adjusted according to factors such as age and race.

Provinces throughout Canada have created brochures that instruct men to consider the risks and benefits of PSA testing. Clearly, the risk of prostate cancer increases with age, and both PSA tests and digital rectal exams (DREs) should be considered once a man hits the age of 45. At the same time, it is important to understand the limits of PSA testing and to carefully consider the negative side effects of interventions described earlier. Prostate cancer, if present, may be restricted to the prostate and may not spread to other areas of the body. Most men with prostate cancer die from causes other than prostate cancer, and there are concerns that some men are undergoing invasive, uncomfortable procedures that are unnecessary because the prostate cancer is restricted to the prostate and will not cause other difficulties. Still, for other men, the PSA test and DRE may ultimately save their lives, as prostate cancer is second only to lung cancer in terms of male deaths from cancer.

STRESS MANAGEMENT

Stress management involves a set of techniques that helps people who are seldom labelled as patients cope with the challenges that are a part of life. It is similar to the stress-inoculation training discussed in Chapter 2 in the sense that stress-inoculation training has been used on both a preventive and a treatment basis (Meichenbaum, 1992, 1994).

The increasing recognition of the role of stress in a variety of medical illnesses, including diseases affected by immune system dysfunction, has added impetus to stress management as a strategy for reducing stress-related malfunctioning of the immune system (Zakowski, Hall, & Baum, 1992). A Canadian consensus group concluded that individualized stress management is an effective intervention (Spence, Barnett, Linden, Ramsden, & Taenzer, 1999). Stress management has been used successfully for several health problems, large and small, including tension headaches, cancer, hypertension, and, as discussed later, chronic pain.

Stress management encompasses a variety of techniques, and more than one is typically used in any given instance (Lehrer & Woolfolk, 1993; Steptoe, 1997):

- *Arousal reduction*. In arousal reduction, the person is trained in muscle relaxation, sometimes assisted by biofeedback. Although the evidence is unclear as to the need to use the complex instrumentation required for proper biofeedback, there is confirmation that learning to relax deeply and to apply these relaxation skills to real-life stressors can help lower stress levels. It has also been shown that immune function can be improved by relaxation training (Kiecolt-Glaser et al., 1985), although enduring benefits are doubtful unless relaxation is practised regularly over a long period of time (Goldfried & Davison, 1994; Zakowski et al., 1992). Because stress itself can be seen as a reaction to situations perceived by the person as unpredictable, uncontrollable, or both, relaxation training may confer its benefits by virtue of enhancing the individual's sense of self-efficacy, the belief that one is not merely a pawn at the mercy of uncontrollable forces that are not always benign (Bandura, 1997).
- *Cognitive restructuring*. Included under cognitive restructuring are approaches such as those of Albert Ellis (1962) and Aaron Beck (1976). The focus is on altering people's belief systems and improving the clarity of their logical interpretations of experience, the assumption being that people's intellectual capacities can affect how they feel and behave. Providing information to reduce uncertainty and enhance people's sense of control, a theme from Chapter 6, has also been helpful in reducing stress. Promising findings have been reported for various stress-related problems, including genital herpes lesions (McLarnon & Kaloupek, 1988) and recovery from surgery (Johnston & Voegele, 1993).
- *Behavioural skills training*. Because it is natural to feel overwhelmed if one lacks the skills to execute a challenging task, stress management often includes instruction and practice in skills required as well as in general skills such as time management and effective prioritizing. Included also under this rubric is training in assertion skills—expressing likes and dislikes without encroaching on the rights of others.
- *Environmental-change approaches*. Whereas the other individual strategies aim at helping people deal with a particular environment, environmental-change approaches help those who believe that the environment is the problem and that change is best directed at altering it. One kind of environmental approach draws on research on the positive role of social support on health (discussed earlier in this chapter). If social support helps keep people healthy or helps them cope with illnesses, then it is reasonable to assume that enhancing such support can contribute to better functioning.

Another kind of environmental change can take place in the workplace. Altering management practices or providing greater privacy and fewer interruptions can reduce the stress-producing characteristics of the world in which people work and live for a significant portion of their waking hours (Murphy et al., 1995).

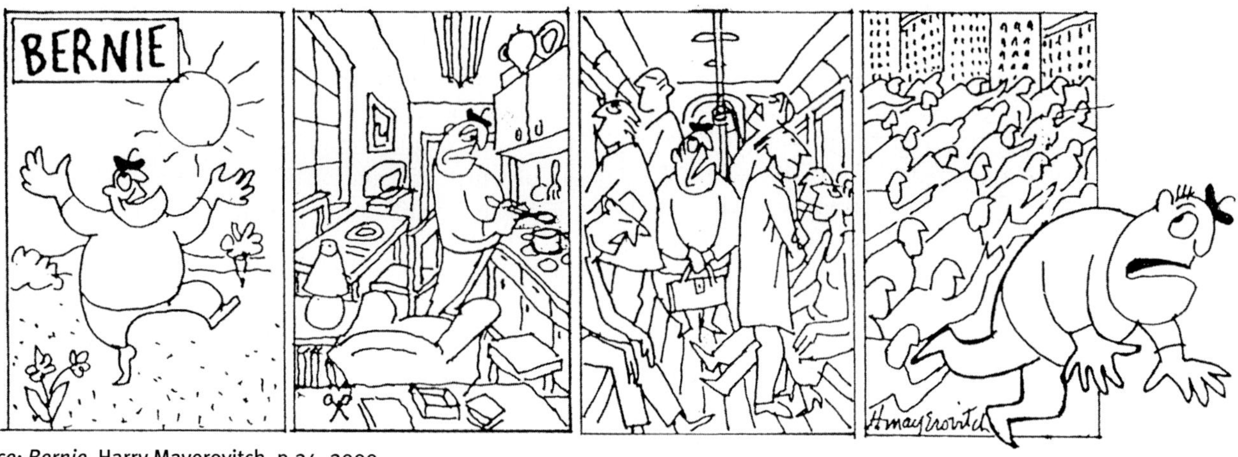

Source: Bernie, Harry Mayerovitch, p.24, 2000.

The Management of Pain

Like anxiety, pain can be adaptive. People with a congenital inability to feel pain are at an extreme disadvantage; indeed, they are at serious risk for injury. Our concern here is with pain that is maladaptive, pain that is out of proportion to the situation and unduly restricts a person's capacity for meaningful and productive living (Davison & Darke, 1991; Morley, 1997).

Recognition of the role of psychological factors in pain can be traced back to the gate-control theory of pain advanced by Melzack and Wall (1965, 1982) from McGill University. This influential theory holds that nerve impulses connoting pain reach the spinal column and the spinal column controls the pain sensations sent to the brain. How is it a gate-control model? The gate is an area of the spinal column known as the dorsal horns; the gate opens if sufficiently intense pain stimuli are experienced. However, the brain also plays a role in that it sends signals back down the spinal column that can affect the gate. The brain, therefore, can facilitate or inhibit the experience of pain, as is seen when people undergoing trauma do not acknowledge the pain to the degree that they should. Melzack (1998, 1999) proposed that the brain possesses a neural network, known as the body-self neuromatrix, that integrates multiple signals to produce a pattern leading to pain.

Indeed, we know enough about pain to appreciate that there is no one-to-one relationship between a stimulus that is capable of triggering the experience of pain, referred to as nociceptive stimulus, and the actual sensation of pain. Soldiers in combat can be wounded by a bullet and yet be so involved in their efforts to survive and inflict harm on the enemy that they do not feel any pain until later. This well-known fact tells us something important about pain, even as it hints at ways of controlling it: if one is distracted from a nociceptive stimulus, one may not experience pain, or at least not as much of it as when one attends to the stimulation (Turk, 1996).

The importance of distraction in controlling pain, both acute and chronic, is consistent with research findings in experimental cognitive psychology. Each person has only a limited supply of attentional resources, such that attention to one channel of input blocks the processing of input in other channels (Eccleston, 1995). This human limitation can thus be seen as beneficial when it comes to the experience of pain. In addition to distraction, other factors that reduce pain are lowered anxiety, feelings of optimism and control (Geer et al., 1970), and a sense that what one is engaged in has meaning and purpose (Gatchel, Baum, & Krantz, 1989).

Here are two examples of the use of distraction and refocused attention for controlling pain:

> [A] patient may be taught to construct a vivid mental image which includes features from a number of sensory dimensions, e.g., cutting a lemon and squeezing a drop of the juice onto the tongue. The elaborated sensory features of the image compete with the painful stimulus and reduces its impact. Alternatively the patient may be encouraged to alter the focus of their attention to the pain without switching attention directly away from the pain. In this instance, the subject may be asked to focus on the sensory qualities of the pain and transform it to a less threatening quality. For example, a young man with a severe "shooting" pain was able to reinterpret the sensory quality into an image that included him shooting at goal in a soccer match. As a result of this transformation, the impact of the pain was greatly reduced although its shooting quality remained. (Morley, 1997, p. 236)

Psychologists have contributed to our understanding of both acute and chronic pain. Acute pain is linked to nociception. Chronic pain can evolve from acute pain and refers to pain that is experienced after the time for healing has passed, when there is little reason to assume that nociception is still present. Whatever the specific psychological techniques employed to help alleviate a person's pain, the person is always informed the nature of the pain itself and the reasons he or she is experiencing it, including the fact that being in a negative mood can make the pain worse (Morley, 1997).

Acute Pain The importance of a sense of personal control in dealing with acute pain is readily seen in situations in which patients are allowed to administer their own painkillers (with a pre-set upper limit). This is known as PCA, patient-controlled analgesia. Patients who control the administration of the medication experience greater relief from pain and even use less analgesic medication than do patients who have to ask a nurse for pain medication, the more common hospital situation (White, 1986).

It is significant that PCA reduces pain even though it requires focusing on the pain, a finding that goes against the well-documented benefits of distraction. Apparently, the positive effects of control outweigh the negative consequences of focusing on the pain. Considerable research attests to the beneficial effects of a sense of control—less pain is experienced, mood is better (and thereby pain is less), and people engage in more normal daily activities, all of which enhance a stronger sense of well-being and bring about still further reductions in pain (Bandura, 1997). Of course, relying on a nurse to administer pain medication also requires the patient to attend to the pain—perhaps even more than when the patient administers the drug. With nurse-administered analgesia, the patient learns to wait until the pain is substantial before requesting medication; after making the request, the patient must usually wait until the nurse has time to fulfill it. This system obviously does not enhance distraction from the pain!

Chronic Pain Chronic pain is the lot of millions of North Americans, accounting for billions of dollars of lost work time and incalculable personal and familial suffering (Turk, 1996). A recent Canadian study found that the prevalence rate of chronic pain was 15 percent (Van Den Kerkhof et al., 2003). This prevalence may be overestimated, however, because the researchers relied solely on a self-report measure of chronic pain in existing datasets. Nevertheless, it is clear that this is a widespread problem.

Traditional medical treatments seldom help with this kind of pain. To understand chronic pain, it is useful to distinguish between pain per se—that is, the perception of nociceptive stimulation (as in acute pain)—and suffering and pain behaviours. Suffering refers to the emotional response to nociception and can be present even in the absence of pain, as when a loved one dies. Pain behaviours refer to observable behaviours associated with pain or suffering; examples include moaning, clenching teeth, irritability, and avoidance of activity (Turk, Wack, & Kerns, 1985). The treatment of chronic pain focuses on suffering and pain behaviours rather than on whether the person is actually experiencing pain. Patients usually have to be guided to the adoption of realistic goals—a pain-free existence may not be possible. The emphasis is on toughing it out, working through the pain rather than allowing oneself to be incapacitated by it. If handled properly, the result is often increased activity and function, which can sometimes even reduce the actual experience of pain. The most appropriate goals for each chronic pain patient can be established with the use of goal attainment scales to evaluate progress on an individual basis (see Zaza, Stolee, & Prkachin, 1999).

A well-researched example of chronic pain is lower back pain caused by severe muscle spasms. Initially, the person is unable to engage in activity any more vigorous than getting in and out of bed. In the acute phase, this is sensible behaviour. As the spasms ease, and if no other damage has occurred, such as to the disks between the vertebrae, the patient is advised to begin moving more normally, stretching, and eventually attempting exercises to strengthen the muscles that went into spasm. Of course, care must be taken not to push patients beyond what their bodies can actually handle.

Research on coping with chronic pain has identified a number of adaptive and maladaptive strategies. One maladaptive strategy is to engage in catastrophization. People who catastrophize engage in a repetitive cognitive process that involves negative self-statements and negative views of the future (i.e., the worst possible outcome will be experienced). According to Katz, Ritvo, Irvine, and Jackson (1996), catastrophizing in response to pain has been associated with a variety of negative outcomes, including depression, increased pain intensity, and psychosocial dysfunction. More generally, an emotion-oriented approach to coping with a health problem is linked with increased chronic pain (Endler, Corace, Summerfeldt, Johnson, & Rothbart, 2003). Passive coping strategies such as withdrawing or becoming resigned to one's fate also tend to be quite maladaptive. This was illustrated in a recent study of coping with neck and back pain conducted in Saskatoon (Mercado, Carroll, Cassidy, & Cote, 2000). Passive forms of coping were associated in this study with elevated levels of pain intensity.

In their classic work on pain, Fordyce and his colleagues (Fordyce, 1994; Fordyce et al., 1986) have shown the superiority of a behavioural over a traditional medical program for management of back pain. In the traditional program, patients exercised and otherwise moved about only until they felt pain; in the behavioural management program, patients were encouraged to exercise at a predetermined intensity for a predetermined period of time, even if they experienced pain. Patients with low back pain have also been given relaxation training and encouraged to relabel their pain as numbness or tickling (Rybstein-Blinchik, 1979), a cognitive-restructuring procedure. The implicit message seems to be that traditional medical practice has underestimated the capabilities of chronic pain patients (Keefe & Gil, 1986). A frequent finding of these studies was that increased activity improves muscle tone, which can reduce nociception over time and even reduce the likelihood of future reoccurrences of muscle spasms.

In a review of studies on the treatment of chronic pain, Blanchard (1994) concluded that strictly behavioural (operant conditioning) and cognitive-behavioural approaches are both important for effective treatment. There is also some evidence that biofeedback of muscle tension can be effective in alleviating chronic back pain by helping sufferers relax muscles in the lower back and thereby reduce nociception from sensory pain nerves around the spinal column (Flor & Birbaumer, 1993). Of course, pain may be experienced less if the relaxation associated with this kind of biofeedback calms the person down and improves his or her mood. Anxiety in general and health anxiety in particular may undermine treatment efforts. Indeed, contemporary research conducted in Canada found that patients with high health anxiety, relative to patients with low health anxiety, tended to experience greater anxiety, somatic sensations, and catastrophic cognitions during therapy, and only those with low health anxiety benefited from reducing pain behaviour (Hadjistavropoulos et al., 2002).

Canadian Clinic Focus 8.1 presents examples of pain treatment clinics and services in Canada.

Canadian Clinic Focus/8.1

Treatment of Chronic Pain Problems in Canada: Behavioural Medicine?

What can be done to alleviate the misery of the millions of Canadians who live with chronic pain, often on an unremitting daily basis despite the best efforts of the general practitioners they have consulted? How can they be helped to experience reduced pain, to minimize the impact of this pain on their levels of activity, productivity, and quality of life?

Psychologists certainly play an important role. Outcome studies have confirmed the effectiveness of psychological treatments, especially those that involve cognitive-behavioural interventions. Moreover, the importance of psychologists in the assessment and treatment of chronic pain has been recognized by numerous agencies and government bodies in Canada and the United States (see Turk & Monarch, 2003).

As is the case with many of the problems and disorders discussed in this book, there are numerous high-quality programs and clinics for the treatment of chronic pain in centres across Canada, especially in major metropolitan areas where hospitals are typically associated with comprehensive, medical universities. The McGill-Montreal General Hospital Pain Centre, for example, offers an integrated, multidisciplinary pain management program that treats all types of nonmalignant pain. The program integrates medical and psychological approaches and offers cognitive-behavioural group therapy, relaxation training, lifestyle counselling, and physiotherapy in addition to conventional pharmacological therapy (e.g., nerve blocks). The clinical teaching program offers formal courses for different professional groups and students at McGill University, including weekly Pain Rounds and an annual Pain Day. In addition, research teams evaluate pharmacological and non-pharmacological pain therapies, as well as alternative therapies, and conduct epidemiological studies. There are many similar clinics in the populated areas of Canada, and in many cases, the treatments are supported, in whole or in part, by provincial medicare plans.

But what do people do who continue to suffer from chronic pain but live in remote areas of the country or in areas not served by quality programs or clinics that have a specific focus on chronic pain? In such instances, individuals may choose to move temporarily, possibly at great personal expense, close to a major treatment facility in order to be able to participate in the appropriate programs. Alternatively, they may seek residential treatment at a private facility (at even greater expense), or they may be fortunate enough to be accepted for treatment by a skilled medical or mental health professional who specializes in pain management. The North American Chronic Pain Association of Canada (NACPAC) provides a "Directory of Canadian Pain Clinics and Pain Specialists." NACPAC approves clinics that meet or exceed a specific standard of care. The Chronic Pain Association of Canada, the Canadian Pain Society, and other national and regional organizations (e.g., the Fibromyalgia Association of British Columbia) also provide information and support to people interested in chronic pain. Many individuals, of course, also engage in self-help, either independently or with the encouragement of health professionals, and/or join a lay or volunteer organization that offers organized support groups as well as credible information.

The Yukon is one part of Canada that does not have a comprehensive, specialty chronic pain clinic, and until relatively recently, it lacked a specialist who offered more than traditional medical unimodal pain management. However, in 1992 a general practitioner who has had a full-time general practice in Whitehorse since 1977 decided to study and practise chronic pain management. Dr. Dave Skinner, who now focuses 75 percent of his work on helping people with chronic pain, believes that non-medical methods should be incorporated with traditional medical approaches to pain treatment and management. Following a comprehensive biopsychosocial assessment of each patient, he designs an individualized pain management plan that incorporates a combination of physical treatment, medication, and psychological interventions. Other treatments can include cognitive-behavioural techniques, yoga, physiotherapy, acupuncture, and trigger-point injections. Dr. Skinner believes that to help people regain a sense of control over their lives, physicians or therapists must help them change the way they think about and react to persistent pain. Office visits are coordinated with other therapies over a period of weeks or months. Books, audiocassettes, and instructional videos are loaned to patients in order to assist with the development of "informed, self-directed care." The effects of pain treatment or management are assessed in comprehensive follow-up assessments. The Yukon Health Care Insurance Plan covers the cost of the assessments and most of the treatments.

In some instances, people seek assistance from, or are referred to, the numerous private pain clinics that offer residential treatment programs. Although the cost of their programs are typically not covered by provincial medical plans, costs may be covered or subsidized by automobile insurance, workers' compensation boards, long-term disability plans, private health insurance, or other third-party coverage. Such programs can often be tailored to the needs of the individual or a particular group. They can, of course, be very expensive and beyond the reach of many of the people who are unable to rely on third-party payments. Some of these clinics may employ innovative, unconventional approaches that are not always accepted by mainstream medical authorities. The Victoria Pain Clinic in Victoria, British Columbia accepts clients who have been suffering pain for many years and have received various conservative conventional treatments without significant improvement. As one reporter (Rogers, 1994) noted, "They come here because nobody knows where else to send them." Except in emergency situations, the medical staff members do not prescribe medications. Although the Victoria clinic offers a number of programs and services, its primary program is the "Ten Day Residential Program," designed for clients who suffer from chronic pain, chronic stress, or stress-related disorders. Clients live at the clinic for 10 intensive days, during which they receive varied treatments, including individual counseling, group therapy, self-help classes, biofeedback, stretch and relax exercises, deep-tissue massage, and acupuncture. The program is tailored to the specific needs of individual clients. The multidisciplinary professional staff is located on site and available 24 hours per day. It is claimed that the results of the program compare favourably with most other chronic pain programs. It is not clear if cognitive-behavioural therapy is an integral part of the treatment package, although the use of relaxation and biofeedback, for example, is consistent with a broad health psychology and behavioural medicine approach.

Victoria Pain Clinic, centre buildings, http://www.vicpain.com.

Comment

It is clear that there are many clinics, programs, services, and dedicated professionals available to assist people in Canada who suffer from chronic pain. Although many resources emphasize conventional medical practices, others adopt a perspective consistent with the approach adopted in this book—that is, an integrated, biopsychosocial approach that necessitates a multi-faceted, individually tailored treatment plan that relies on the expertise of a multidisciplinary team for its implemenation. Psychologists who practise a behavioural medicine and health psychology approach, especially one based on empirically supported behavioural and cognitive-behavioural strategies (e.g., Turk, Meichenbaum, & Genest, 1983), are important contributors to this multidisciplinary approach.

However, it is not always clear that a majority of the available programs emphasize or incorporate all of the strategies that could be useful (e.g., stress management, cognitive restructuring, biofeedback, assertion and social skills training, coping-skills and problem-solving therapy). Further, the fact that many clinics and services are private or semi-private means that many needy people may not have easy access to the help they need. Public clinics are often overwhelmed with patients, necessitating long waiting lists and even turning people away. For example, the North Side General Hospital Pain Unit in North Sydney, Nova Scotia, is the only clinic that provides even conventional medical treatment in all of Cape Breton, which has a population of about 115,000 people. This small clinic sees as many as 50 patients a day, offering services such as intravenous trigger-point injections and nerve blocks. There is typically a 12- to 14-month waiting period. Also, in a majority of cases, the effectiveness and efficacy of the various clinic-based programs need to be evaluated.

Sources: NACPAC website: http://www.nacpa.ca; Chronic Pain Association of Canada website: http://www.chronicpaincanada.org; Victoria Pain Clinic website: http://vicpain.com; e-mail and telephone contacts (all information effective January-February 2001).

Our review of several therapeutic approaches to dealing with psychophysiological disorders, many of which can be subsumed under the rubric of behavioural medicine, illustrates the complex relationships between the soma and the psyche, the body and the mind. We come full circle to how we began this chapter, namely, to an appreciation of the inseparability of bodily and mental processes. Stress is a part of everyone's life. As much as it can pose problems, so, too, can it promote well-being as we learn ways to cope with it or manage it.

SUMMARY

- Psychophysiological disorders are physical diseases produced in part by psychological factors, primarily stress. Such disorders usually affect organs innervated by the autonomic nervous system, such as those of the respiratory, cardiovascular, gastrointestinal, and endocrine systems. Research has pursued a number of different paths to discover how psychological stress produces a particular psychophysiological disorder. Some researchers have looked at the specifics of the stressor or the psychological characteristics of the person, such as the links between anger/hostility and hypertension and between Type A personality and myocardial infarction. Others have emphasized that psychophysiological disorders occur only when stress interacts with a biological diathesis. Cardiovascular disorders occur in individuals who have a tendency to respond to stress with increases in blood pressure or heart rate. Although we have spoken of psychological stress affecting the body, it must be remembered that the *mind* and the *body* are best viewed as two different approaches to the same organism.

- Psychophysiological disorders no longer appear as a diagnostic category in the DSM. Instead, the diagnostician can make a diagnosis of psychological factors affecting a medical condition and then note the condition on Axis III. This change reflects the growing realization that life stress is relevant to all diseases and is not limited to those that were previously considered psychophysiological disorders.
- When events are appraised as stressful, coping efforts are engaged. If coping fails to lessen the amount of stress experienced, the risk of becoming ill increases. Important issues in current work on life stress and health include looking at moderators of the relationship (e.g., social support lessens the effects of stress) and specifying the physiological mechanisms (e.g., the immune system) through which stress can exert its effects.
- Psychophysiological disorders represent true physical dysfunctions. As a result, treatment usually includes medication. The general aim of psychotherapies for these disorders is to reduce anxiety or anger. Researchers in the field of behavioural medicine try to find psychological interventions that can improve the patient's physiological state by changing unhealthy behaviours and reducing stress. They have developed ways of helping people relax, smoke less, eat fewer fatty foods, and engage in behaviours that can prevent or alleviate illnesses, such as breast self-examination and adhering to medical treatment recommendations.
- The emergent field of stress management helps people without diagnosable problems avail themselves of techniques that allow them to cope with the inevitable stress of everyday life and thereby ameliorate the toll that stress can take on the body.

KEY TERMS

allostatic load (p. 223)
anger-in theory (p. 234)
angina pectoris (p. 240)
behavioural medicine (p. 221)
biofeedback (p. 245)
cardiovascular disorders (p. 236)
catastrophization (p. 251)
chronic pain (p. 250)
coping (p. 224)
coronary heart disease (CHD) (p. 240)
daily hassles (p. 227)
emotional support (p. 231)
essential hypertension (p. 237)
eustress (p. 223)
functional social support (p. 231)
general adaptation syndrome (GAS) (p. 222)
goodness of fit hypothesis (p. 224)
health psychology (p. 221)
instrumental support (p. 231)
interactionism (p. 228)
myocardial infarction (p. 240)
palliative coping (p. 225)
psychological factors affecting medical condition (p. 221)
psychophysiological disorders (p. 221)
psychosomatic disorders (p. 221)
social gradient of health (p. 243)
somatic-weakness theory (p. 233)
specific-reaction theory (p. 233)
stress (p. 222)
stress management (p. 249)
stressor (p. 223)
structural social support (p. 231)
Type A behaviour pattern (p. 241)
vital exhaustion (p. 242)

Reflections: Past, Present, and Future

- Jemmott and Magliore (1988) demonstrated that among college students who were experiencing the stress of final examinations, those students with more social support had superior immune function, as assessed by secretory immunoglobulin A. What are the implications of their finding? If you were working as a student mentor in a university academic skills centre, what advice would you give your charges?
- Research has shown that many people who develop psychological disorders also have various physical illnesses. Does this correlation allow us to conclude that mental disorders contribute to the development of physical illnesses? Design a study that would allow you to conclude that there is a causal effect of psychological disorders on physical illness.
- Diathesis-stress, biopsychosocial, and cognitive-behavioural paradigms all emphasize that psychological and social factors play a vital role in influencing people's health, including the experience of chronic pain. Does this mean that people are responsible for their own health? How might these perspectives affect public health policy in Canada?
- Research (e.g., Maccoby & Altman, 1988; Schooler, Flora, & Farquhar, 1993) has demonstrated that community-based programs have the potential to reduce significantly the incidence and seriousness of many medical illnesses beyond what is achievable by strictly medical practices. It is increasingly accepted that people's physical health is often very much in their own hands and that changing lifestyle practices is sometimes the best means of reducing the risk of illness (Bandura, 1986). How could you use the mass media to reduce cardiovascular disease? What would you inform people that they could do to reduce their risk of premature disease? Can people learn from properly designed and delivered mass media and other large-scale educational programs how to reduce their overall risk for cardiovascular and other diseases?

chapter 9

Eating Disorders

"What's come to perfection, perishes."
—R. Browning, *Old Pictures in Florence*, Stanza 17

"In fact, from any normal perspective, I was not fat. At five foot seven, even at my heaviest I had never weighed more than 130 pounds, which most physicians would think healthy and normal for that height.
But in the ballet world, having a few too many curves is obesity, and I was continually convinced that my excessive weight, which I saw as a real deformity, would doom me."
—Karen Kain, *Movement Never Lies* (1994, p. 23), commenting on her response to unrealistic pressures to be thin

"I still try to maintain as perfect an image as possible and I still seek to please my mother. My past has created the 'present day me' who needs to be successful in life, who needs to be perfect, who lacks self-confidence and fears failure, and who constantly strives to achieve the highest standards possible."
—An admission by a Canadian eating-disorder client, in recovery, who is known to the authors

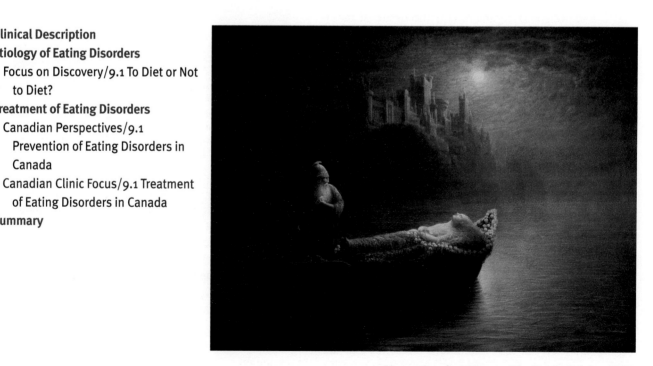

Homer Ransford Watson, *The Death of Elaine, 1877*
oil on canvas, 78.1 x 106.7 cm, ART GALLERY OF ONTARIO, TORONTO
Gift of Mrs. Mary King, Toledo, Ohio, 1937

LYNNE, 24, was admitted to the psychiatric ward of a general hospital for treatment of anorexia nervosa. Although she didn't really think anything was wrong with her, her husband and parents had consulted with a psychiatrist, and the four of them had confronted her with a choice of admitting herself or being committed involuntarily. At the time, Lynne had only 78 pounds on her five-foot-five-inch frame. She hadn't menstruated for three years and had a variety of medical problems—hypotension, irregularities in her heartbeat, and abnormally low levels of potassium and calcium.

Lynne had experienced several episodes of dramatic weight loss, beginning at age 18 when she was going through dissolution of her first marriage. But none of the prior episodes had been this severe, and she had not sought treatment before. She had an intense fear of becoming fat, and although she had never really been overweight, she felt that her buttocks and abdomen were too large. (This belief persisted even when she was at 78 pounds.) She severely restricted food intake and used laxatives heavily during the periods of weight loss. She had occasionally had episodes of binge eating, typically followed by self-induced vomiting so that she would not gain any weight.

Many cultures are preoccupied with eating. In North America today, gourmet restaurants abound and numerous magazines and television shows are devoted to food preparation. At the same time, many people are overweight. Dieting to lose weight is common, and the desire of many people, especially women, to be slimmer has created a multimillion-dollar-a-year business. Given this intense interest in food and eating, it is not surprising that this aspect of human behaviour is subject to disorder.

Although clinical descriptions of eating disorders can be traced back many years, these disorders only appeared in the DSM for the first time in 1980, as one subcategory of disorders beginning in childhood or adolescence. With the publication of DSM-IV, the eating disorders anorexia nervosa and bulimia nervosa formed a distinct category, reflecting the increased attention they have received from clinicians and researchers over the past three decades.

CLINICAL DESCRIPTION

We begin by describing anorexia nervosa and bulimia nervosa. The diagnoses of these two disorders share several clinical features, the most important being *an intense fear of being overweight*. There are some indications that these may not be distinct diagnoses but may be two variants of a single disorder. Co-twins of patients diagnosed with anorexia nervosa, for example, are themselves more likely than average to have bulimia nervosa (Walters & Kendler, 1994).

ANOREXIA NERVOSA

Lynne, the woman just described, had anorexia nervosa. *Anorexia* refers to loss of appetite, and *nervosa* indicates that this is for emotional reasons. The term is something of a misnomer because most patients with anorexia nervosa actually do not lose their appetite or interest in food. On the contrary, while starving themselves, most patients with the disorder become preoccupied with food; they may read cookbooks constantly and prepare gourmet meals for their families.

Anorexia nervosa can be a life-threatening condition. It is especially prevalent among young women who are under intense pressure to keep their weight low. Gymnast Christy Henrich died from the condition in 1994.

Lynne met all four features required for the diagnosis:

- The person must refuse to maintain a normal body weight; this is usually taken to mean that the person weighs less than 85 percent of what is considered normal for that person's age and height. Weight loss is typically achieved through dieting, although purging (self-induced vomiting, heavy use of laxatives or diuretics) and excessive exercise can also be part of the picture.
- The person has an intense fear of gaining weight, and the fear is not reduced by weight loss. They can never be thin enough.
- Patients with anorexia nervosa have a distorted sense of their body shape. They maintain that even when emaciated, they are overweight or that certain parts of their

bodies, particularly the abdomen, buttocks, and thighs, are too fat. To check on their body size, they typically weigh themselves frequently, measure the size of different parts of the body, and gaze critically at their reflections in mirrors. Their self-esteem is closely linked to maintaining thinness.

- In females, the extreme emaciation causes amenorrhea, the loss of the menstrual period. Of the four diagnostic criteria, amenorrhea seems least important; comparisons conducted in Canada show few differences between women who meet all four criteria and women who meet the other three but not amenorrhea. Moreover, amenorrhea occurs in a significant minority of women before any significant weight loss and the symptom can persist after weight gain (Garfinkel, 2002).

The distorted body image that accompanies anorexia nervosa has been assessed in several ways, most frequently by questionnaires such as the Eating Disorders Inventory (EDI; Garner, Olmsted, & Polivy, 1983). The EDI was developed in Canada and is one of the most widely used measures to assess self-reported aspects of eating disorders. The subscales and items on this questionnaire are presented in Table 9.1.

Table 9.1

Subscales and Illustrative Items from the Eating Disorders Inventory

Subscale	Illustrative items
Drive for thinness	I think about dieting. I feel extremely guilty after overeating. I am preoccupied with the desire to be thinner.
Bulimia	I stuff myself with food. I have gone on eating binges where I have felt that I could not stop. I have the thought of trying to vomit in order to lose weight.
Body dissatisfaction	I think that my thighs are too large. I think that my buttocks are too large. I think that my hips are too big.
Ineffectiveness	I feel inadequate. I have a low opinion of myself. I feel empty inside (emotionally).
Perfectionism	Only outstanding performance is good enough in my family. As a child, I tried hard to avoid disappointing my parents and teachers. I hate being less than best at things
Interpersonal distrust	I have trouble expressing my emotions to others. I need to keep people at a certain distance (I feel uncomfortable if someone tries to get too close).
Interoceptive awareness	I get confused about what emotion I am feeling. I don't know what's going on inside me. I get confused as to whether or not I am hungry.
Maturity fears	I wish that I could return to the security of childhood. I feel that people are happiest when they are children. The demands of adulthood are too great.

Source: From Garner, Olmsted, and Polivy, 1983.
Note: Respondents use a six-point scale ranging from always to never.

In another type of assessment, patients are shown line drawings of women with varying body weights and asked to pick the one closest to their own and the one that represents their ideal shape (see Figure 9.1). Patients with anorexia nervosa overestimate their own body size and choose a thin figure as their ideal.

DSM-IV distinguishes two types of anorexia nervosa. In the *restricting type*, weight loss is achieved by severely limiting food intake; in the *binge eating–purging type*, as illustrated in Lynne's case, the person also regularly engages in binge eating and purging. Numerous differences between these two subtypes support the validity of this distinction. The binging-purging subtype appears to be more psychopathological; patients exhibit more personality disorders, impulsive behaviour, stealing, alcohol and drug abuse, social withdrawal, and suicide attempts than do patients with the restricting type of anorexia (e.g., Pryor, Wiederman, & McGilley, 1996). Moreover, relative to the restricting type, binging-purging patients tend to weigh more in childhood, come from heavier families with greater familial obesity, and tend to use more extreme weight-control methods (Garfinkel, 2002).

However, Canadian research suggests that the differences between the two subtypes are becoming less distinct. Kruger, McVey, and Kennedy (1998) conducted a retrospective study comparing anorexic patients of the restricting subtype with those of the binge-purging subtype over three consecutive five-year periods (between 1978 and 1994). The participants were female outpatients at the University of Toronto Program for Eating Disorders. What did they find? An increasing proportion of patients were diagnosed with anorexia nervosa, the binge-purging subtype, during each time period. Over time, participants in both groups appeared to weigh more and were less likely to report amenorrhea. Further, patients from both groups reported higher frequencies of purging behaviour, impulsive behaviours, and associated affective symptoms in the later time periods.

Anorexia nervosa typically begins in the early to middle teenage years, often after an episode of dieting and exposure to life stress. It is about 10 times more frequent in women than in men, with a lifetime prevalence of a little less than 1 percent (Hsu, 1990; Walters & Kendler, 1994). When anorexia nervosa does occur in men, symptomatology and other characteristics, such as family conflict, are generally similar to those reported by women with the disorder (Olivardia et al., 1995). A recent comparison of the characteristics of 21 male adolescents and 136 female adolescents in the Eating Disorder Program of the Hospital for Sick Children in Toronto found that males had lower levels of drive for thinness and body dissatisfaction, but there were many more similarities than differences between the males and females (Geist, Heinmaa, Katzman, & Stephens, 1999). As we discuss more fully later, the gender difference in the prevalence of anorexia most likely reflects the greater importance women give to cultural standards of beauty, which have promoted a thin shape as the ideal over the past several decades.

Patients with anorexia nervosa are diagnosed frequently with depression, obsessive-compulsive disorder, phobias, panic disorder, alcoholism, oppositional defiant disorder, and various personality disorders (Geist, Davis, & Heinmaa, 1998; Kennedy & Garfinkel, 1992; Walters & Kendler, 1994). As is often the case, comorbidity declines when community rather than clinical samples are studied because clinical samples usually include people with more serious, multi-faceted problems (Welch & Fairburn, 1996). Women with anorexia nervosa are also likely to have sexual disturbances. In one study of women with an average age of 24 with the disorder, 20 percent had not had intercourse and more than 50 percent were either inorgasmic or had low sexual desire (Raboch & Faltus, 1991).

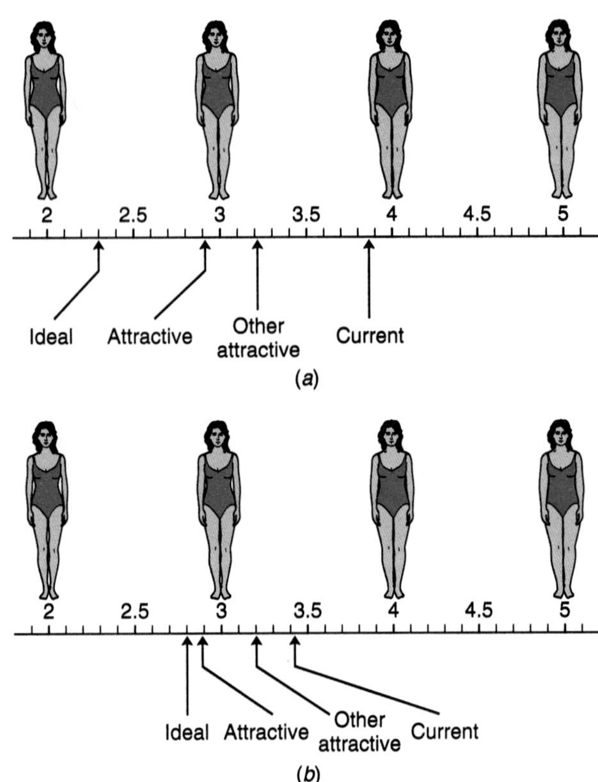

Figure 9.1 In this assessment of body image, respondents indicate their current shape, their ideal shape, and the shape they think is most attractive to the opposite sex. The figure actually rated as most attractive by members of the opposite sex is shown in both panels. Ratings of women who scored high on a measure of distorted attitudes toward eating are shown in (a); ratings of women who scored low are shown in (b). The high scorers overestimated their current size and chose a thin form as their ideal. From Zellner, Harner, and Adler (1988).

Physical Changes in Anorexia Nervosa Self-starvation and use of laxatives produce numerous undesirable biological consequences in patients with anorexia nervosa. Blood pressure often falls, heart rate slows, kidney and gastrointestinal problems develop, bone mass declines, the skin dries out, nails become brittle, hormone levels change, and mild anemia may occur. Some patients lose hair from the scalp, and they may develop laguna, a fine, soft hair, on their bodies. As in Lynne's case, levels of electrolytes, such as potassium and sodium, are altered. These ionized salts, present in various bodily fluids, are essential for the process of neural transmission, and lowered levels can lead to tiredness, weakness, cardiac arrhythmias, and even sudden death. Brain size declines in patients with anorexia, and EEG abnormalities and neurological impairments are frequent (Garner, 1997; Lambe, Katzman, Mikulis, Kennedy, & Zipursky, 1997). Research in Canada by Lambe and associates

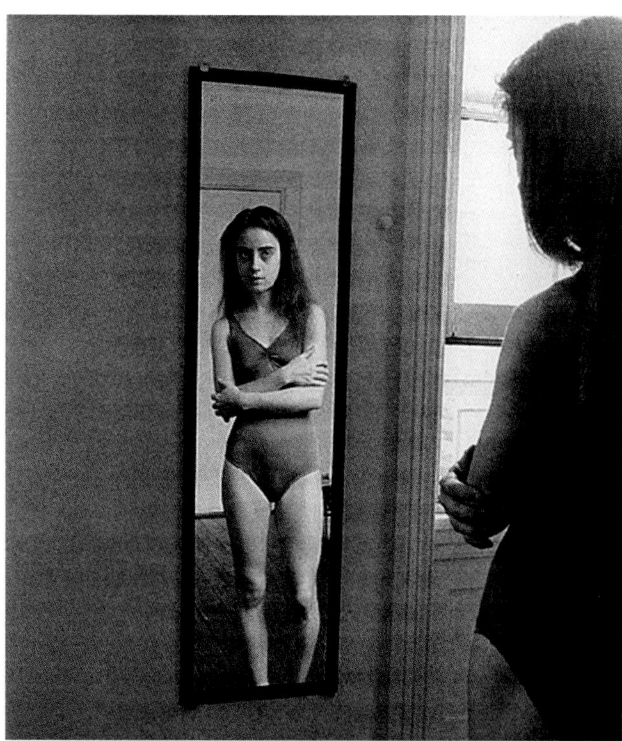

Despite being thin, women with anorexia believe that parts of their bodies are too fat, and they spend a lot of time critically examining themselves in front of mirrors.

has established that deficits in white-matter volumes in the brain are restored upon recovery from anorexia nervosa, but deficits in grey-matter volumes appear irreversible, at least in the short term.

Prognosis About 70 percent of patients with anorexia eventually recover. However, recovery often takes six or seven years, and relapses are common before a stable pattern of eating and maintenance of weight is achieved (Strober, Freeman, & Morrel, 1997). As we discuss later, changing these patients' distorted views of themselves is very difficult, particularly in cultures that value thinness.

Anorexia nervosa is a life-threatening illness; death rates are 10 times higher among patients with the disorder than among the general population and twice as high as among patients with other psychological disorders. Death most often results from physical complications of the illness—for example, congestive heart failure—and from suicide (Crisp et al., 1992; Sullivan, 1995).

BULIMA NERVOSA

JILL was the second child born to her parents. Both she and her brother became intensely involved in athletics at an early age, Jill in gymnastics and Tom in Little League baseball. At age 4, Jill was enrolled in gymnastics school, where she excelled. By the time Jill was 9, her mother had decided that her daughter had outstripped the coaching abilities of the local instructors and she began driving Jill to a nationally recognized coach several hundred miles distant, several times a week. Over the next few years, Jill continued to excel, her trophy case swelled, and aspirations for a place on the Olympic team grew. As she reached puberty, her thin frame began to fill out, raising concerns about the effects of her weight gain on her performance as a gymnast. She began to restrict her intake of food, but found that after several days of semi-starvation she would lose control and go on an eating binge. This pattern of dieting and binging lasted for several months, during which Jill's fear of becoming fat seemed to increase. At age 13, she hit on the solution of self-induced vomiting. She quickly fell into a pattern of alternating episodes of binging and vomiting three or four times per week. Although she maintained this pattern in secret for a while, eventually her parents caught on and initiated treatment for her.

Jill's behaviour illustrates the features of **bulimia nervosa**. *Bulimia* is from a Greek word meaning "ox hunger." This disorder involves episodes of rapid consumption of a large amount of food, followed by compensatory behaviours, such as vomiting, fasting, or excessive exercise, to prevent weight gain. The DSM defines a binge as eating an excessive amount of food within less than two hours. Bulimia nervosa is not diagnosed if the binging and purging occur only in the context of anorexia nervosa and its extreme weight loss; the diagnosis in such a case is anorexia nervosa, binge eating-purging type.

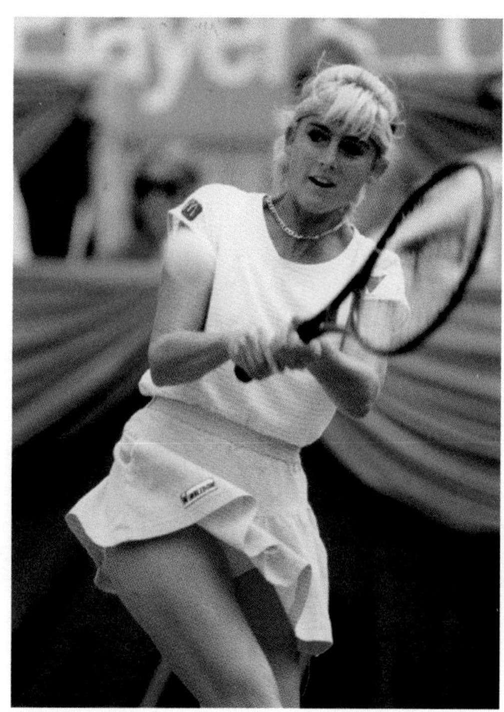

Carling Bassett-Seguso, an inductee into Canada's Sports Hall of Fame and Canada's top-ranked woman tennis player between 1982 and 1986, became bulimic shortly after experiencing the pressure of turning professional.

Binges typically occur in secret, may be triggered by stress and the negative emotions it arouses, and continue until the person is uncomfortably full (Grilo, Shiffman, & Carter-Campbell, 1994). Stressors that involve negative social interactions may be particularly potent elicitors of binges. Steiger and his associates in Quebec (Steiger, Gauvin, Jabalpurwala, Seguin, & Stotland, 1999) found in a study of daily experiences that bulimics have high levels of interpersonal sensitivity, as reflected in large increases in self-criticism following negative social interactions. Further, binge episodes tend to be preceded by poorer than average social experiences, self-concepts, and moods. Steiger et al. (1999) also reported that the binge episodes are followed by deterioration in self-concept, mood state, and social perception.

The person who is engaged in a binge often feels that he or she cannot control the amount of food that is being consumed. Foods that can be rapidly consumed, especially sweets such as ice cream or cake, are usually part of a binge. Although research suggests that patients with bulimia nervosa sometimes ingest an enormous quantity of food during a binge, often more than what a normal person eats in an entire day, binges are not always as large as the DSM implies, and there is wide variation in the caloric content consumed by individuals with bulimia nervosa during binges (e.g., Rossiter & Agras, 1990). Patients are usually ashamed of their binges and try to conceal them. They report that they lose control during a binge, even to the point of experiencing something akin to a dissociative state, perhaps losing awareness of what they are doing or feeling that it is not really they who are binging.

After the binge is over, disgust, feelings of discomfort, and fear of weight gain lead to the second step of bulimia nervosa, purging to undo the caloric effects of the binge. Patients most often stick fingers down their throats to cause gagging, but after a time many can induce vomiting at will without gagging themselves. Laxative and diuretic abuse (which do little to reduce body weight) as well as fasting and excessive exercises are also used to prevent weight gain.

Although many people binge occasionally and some people also experiment with purging, the DSM diagnosis of bulimia nervosa requires that the episodes of binging and purging occur at least twice a week for three months. Is twice a week a well-established cut-off point? Probably not. Epidemiological research conducted in Canada has found few differences between patients who binge twice a week and those who do so less frequently, suggesting that we are dealing with a continuum of severity rather than a sharp distinction (Garfinkel et al., 1995; Garfinkel, 2002).

Like patients with anorexia nervosa, patients with bulimia nervosa are afraid of gaining weight, and their self-esteem depends heavily on maintaining normal weight. Garfinkel (2002) observed that "a morbid fear of fat" is an essential diagnostic criterion for bulimia nervosa because (1) it covers what clinicians and researchers view as the "core psychopathology" of bulimia nervosa; (2) it makes the diagnosis more restrictive; and (3) it makes the syndrome more closely resemble the related disorder of anorexia nervosa.

People without eating disorders typically under-report their weight and say they are taller than they actually are; patients with bulimia nervosa are more accurate in their reports (Doll & Fairburn, 1998)

As with anorexia, two subtypes of bulimia nervosa are distinguished: a purging type and a non-purging type in which the compensatory behaviours are fasting or excessive exercise. Evidence for the validity of this distinction is mixed. In some studies, people diagnosed with non-purging bulimia were heavier, binged less frequently, and showed less psychopathology than did people with purging-type bulimia (e.g., Mitchell, 1992). But in other research, few differences emerged between the two types (e.g., Tobias, Griffing, & Griffing, 1997).

Bulimia nervosa typically begins in late adolescence or early adulthood. About 90 percent of cases are women, and prevalence among women is thought to be about 1 to 2 percent of the population (Gotesdam & Agras, 1995). Canadian studies of rates of eating disorders in community samples find that lifetime rates for females are approximately 1.1 percent of the population for bulimia nervosa and 0.5 percent of the population for anorexia nervosa (Garfinkel et al., 1995, 1996). Research conducted in Canadian public schools also suggests that bulimia is more common than anorexia among adolescents (Leichner, Arnett, Rallo, Srilcamesuaran, & Vulcano, 1986). An even greater number of females may not meet existing diagnostic criteria for eating disorders but show signs of vulnerability to subsequent problems. One study of Canadian high school students found that 7.5 percent of the females surveyed were characterized by disordered-eating attitudes (Chandarana, Helmes, & Benson, 1988). More recent surveys suggest that problems may be increasing. One study found that by the time that age 18 is reached, 80 percent of young women in British Columbia with normal height and weight indicate that they would like to weigh less (McCreary Centre Society, 1999). Another new study of over 1,800 females from Ottawa, Hamilton, and Toronto between the ages of 12 and 18 found that 27 percent had disordered-eating attitudes and behaviours, and approximately one in seven participants practised binge eating disorder with associated loss of control (Jones, Bennett, Olmsted, Lawson, & Rodin, 2001).

Comparisons across time suggest that the frequency of bulimia nervosa may be increasing. In a review paper, Dorian and Garfinkel (1999) concluded that there is evidence of a cohort effect, with rates being higher among individuals born after 1960, who also tend to have younger ages of onset. Cohort effects are described in more detail in Chapter 16.

Temporal studies of the course of the disorder indicate that many patients with bulimia nervosa are somewhat overweight before the onset of the disorder and that the binge eating often starts during an episode of dieting. Long-term follow-ups of patients with bulimia nervosa reveal that about 70 percent recover, although about 10 percent remain fully symptomatic (Keel et al., 1999).

Bulimia nervosa is associated with numerous other diagnoses, notably depression, personality disorders (especially borderline personality disorder, discussed in Chapter 13), anxiety disorders, substance abuse, and conduct disorder (discussed in Chapter 15) (Carroll, Touyz, & Beumont, 1996; Kennedy & Garfinkel, 1992; von Ransom, Iacono, & McGue, 2002). Suicide rates are much higher among people with bulimia nervosa than in the general population (Favaro & Santonastaso, 1998). A twin study has found that bulimia and depression are genetically related (Walters et al., 1992). Somewhat curiously, bulimia nervosa has been associated with stealing. Patients with bulimia who steal tend also to be illicit drug users and to be promiscuous (Rowston & Lacey, 1992). This combination of behaviours may reflect impulsivity or lack of self-control, characteristics that may be relevant to the behaviour of binge eating.

Like anorexia, bulimia is associated with several physical side effects. Frequent purging can cause potassium depletion. Heavy use of laxatives induces diarrhea, which can also lead to changes in electrolytes and cause irregularities in the heartbeat. Recurrent vomiting may lead to tearing of tissue in the stomach and throat and to loss of dental enamel as stomach acids eat away at the teeth, making them ragged. The salivary glands may become swollen. Bulimia nervosa, like anorexia, is a serious disorder with many unfortunate physical consequences (Garner, 1997). However, mortality appears to be much less common in bulimia nervosa than in anorexia nervosa (Keel & Mitchell, 1997).

Binge Eating Disorder

DSM-IV includes binge eating disorder as a diagnosis in need of further study rather than as a formal diagnosis. This disorder includes recurrent binges (two times per week for at least six months), lack of control during the binging episode, and distress about binging, as well as other characteristics, such as rapid eating and eating alone. It is distinguished from anorexia nervosa by the absence of weight loss and from bulimia nervosa by the absence of compensatory behaviours (purging, fasting, or excessive exercise).

Binge eating disorder appears to be more prevalent than either anorexia nervosa or bulimia nervosa. In a community sample, it was found in 6 percent of successful dieters (those who had kept their weight off for more than one year) and in 19 percent of unsuccessful dieters (Ferguson & Spitzer, 1995). One advantage of including this disorder as a diagnosis is that it would apply to many patients who are now given the vague diagnosis of "eating disorder not otherwise specified," since they do not meet criteria for anorexia or bulimia (Spitzer et al., 1993).

While it did not meet the threshold for inclusion in DSM-IV (see Fairburn, Welsh, & Hay, 1993), binge eating disorder has several features that support its validity. It occurs more often in women than in men and is associated with obesity and a history of dieting (Kinzl et al., 1999). It is linked to impaired work and social functioning, depression, low self-esteem, substance abuse, and dissatisfaction with body shape (Spitzer et al., 1993; Striegel-Moore et al., 1998). Risk factors for developing binge eating disorder include childhood obesity, critical comments regarding being overweight, low self-concept, depression, and childhood physical or sexual abuse (Fairburn et al., 1998).

An epidemiological study by Bulik, Sullivan, and Kendler (2000) provided strong evidence for the validity of binge eating disorder as a distinct category. This research was conducted on female community members from the state of Virginia. Six distinct clusters were identified on the basis of interview and self-report data, including three atypical groups and three other groups representing individuals with anorexia nervosa, bulimia nervosa, and binge eating disorder. Bulik et al. (2000) reported that only about half of the women with an apparent binge eating disorder reported feeling "out of control," and they suggested the need for further inquiry into binge eating and the cognitive feeling of being out of control.

Nevertheless, some researchers do not view binge eating disorder as a discrete diagnostic category, seeing it instead as a less severe version of bulimia nervosa. The reason is that some studies have found few differences between patients with binge eating disorder and the non-purging form of bulimia nervosa (Hay & Fairburn, 1998; Santonastaso, Ferrara, & Favaro, 1999).

ETIOLOGY OF EATING DISORDERS

As with other psychopathologies, a single factor is unlikely to cause an eating disorder. Several areas of current research—genetics, the role of the brain, sociocultural pressures to be thin, the role of the family, and the role of environmental stress—suggest that eating disorders result when several influences converge in a person's life.

Biological Factors

Genetics Both anorexia nervosa and bulimia nervosa run in families. First-degree relatives of young women with anorexia nervosa are about four times more likely than average to have the disorder themselves (Strober et al., 1990). Similar results are found for bulimia nervosa (Kassett et al., 1987). Furthermore, relatives of patients with eating disorders are more likely than average to have symptoms of eating disorders that do not meet the complete criteria for a diagnosis (Lilenfeld et al., 1998). Twin studies of eating disorders also suggest a genetic influence. Most studies of both anorexia and bulimia report higher identical than fraternal concordance rates (Fichter & Naegel, 1990; Holland et al., 1988). Research has also shown that key features of the eating disorders, such as dissatisfaction with one's body and a strong desire to be thin, appear to be heritable (Rutherford et al., 1993). These data are consistent with the possibility that a genetic diathesis is operating, but more sophisticated studies involving people who have been adopted are needed.

Eating Disorders and the Brain The hypothalamus is a key brain centre in regulating hunger and eating. Research on animals with lesions to the lateral hypothalamus (see Chapter 2) indicates that they lose weight and have no appetite (Hoebel & Teitelbaum, 1966); thus, it is not surprising that the hypothalamus has been proposed to play a role in anorexia. The paraventricular nucleus has also been implicated (Connan & Stanley, 2003). The level of some hormones regulated by the hypothalamus, such as cortisol, are indeed abnormal in patients with anorexia; rather than causing the disorder, however, these hormonal abnormalities occur as a result of self-starvation, and levels return to normal following weight gain (Doerr et al., 1980). Furthermore, the weight loss of animals with hypothalamic lesions does not parallel what we know about anorexia; these animals appear to have no hunger and become indifferent to food, whereas patients with anorexia continue to starve themselves despite being hungry and having an interest in food. Nor does the hypothalamic model account for body-image disturbance or fear of becoming fat. A dysfunctional hypothalamus thus does not seem highly likely as a factor in anorexia nervosa.

Endogenous opioids are substances produced by the body that reduce pain sensations, enhance mood, and suppress appetite, at least among those with low body weight. Opioids are released during starvation and have been viewed as playing a role in both anorexia and bulimia. Starvation among patients with anorexia may increase the levels of endogenous opioids, resulting in a positively reinforcing euphoric state (Marrazzi & Luby, 1986). Furthermore, the excessive exercise seen among some patients with eating disorders would increase opioids and thus be reinforcing (Davis, 1996; Epling & Pierce, 1992). Hardy and Waller (1988) hypothesized that bulimia is mediated by low levels of endogenous opioids, which are thought to promote craving; a euphoric state is then produced by the ingestion of food, thus reinforcing binging.

Some data support the theory that endogenous opioids do play a role in eating disorders, at least in bulimia (see Connan & Stanley, 2003). Waller et al. (1986) found low levels of the endogenous opioid beta-endorphin in patients with bulimia; they also observed that the more severe cases of bulimia had the lowest levels of beta-endorphin.

Finally, some research has focused on several neurotransmitters related to eating and satiety. Animal research has shown that serotonin promotes satiety (feeling full); therefore, it could be that the binges of patients with bulimia result from a serotonin deficit, which would cause them not to feel satiated as they eat. Researchers have examined levels of these (as well as other) neurotransmitters or their metabolites in patients with anorexia and bulimia. Several studies have reported low levels of serotonin metabolites in patients with bulimia (e.g., Steiger, Israel, Gauvin, Kin, & Young, 2003). Patients with bulimia also show smaller responses to serotonin agonists (chemicals that combine with receptors to initiate a reaction) (Levitan et al., 1997), again suggesting an underactive serotonin system. Furthermore, when patients who had recovered from bulimia nervosa had their serotonin levels reduced, they showed an increase in cognitions related to eating disorders, such as feeling fat (Smith, Fairburn, & Cowan, 1999). These data all suggest that a serotonin deficit may well be related to bulimia nervosa.

Though we can expect further biochemical research in the future, it is important to keep in mind that this work focuses principally on brain mechanisms relevant to hunger, eating, and satiety and does little to account for other key features of both disorders, particularly the intense fear of becoming fat. The social and cultural environments appear to play a role in the faulty perceptions and eating habits of those with eating disorders, and it is to these influences we now turn.

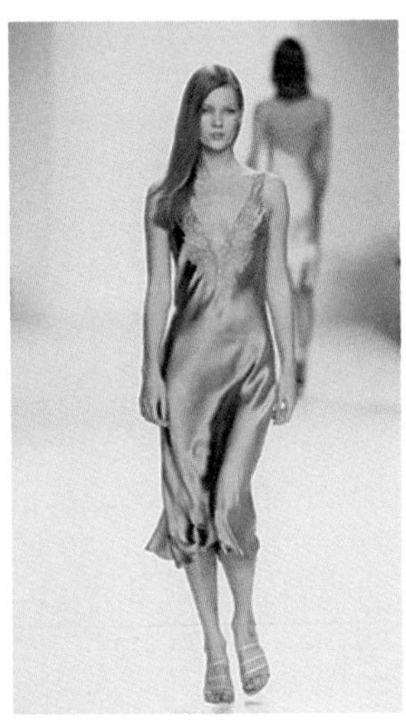

Cultural standards regarding the ideal feminine shape have changed over time. Even in the 1950s and 1960s, the feminine ideal was considerably heavier than what it has been since then.

Sociocultural Variables

Throughout history, the standards societies have set for the ideal body—especially the ideal female body—have varied greatly. Think of the famous nudes painted by Rubens in the 17th century; according to modern standards, these women are chubby. In recent times in our culture, there has been a steady progression toward increasing thinness as the ideal. *Playboy* magazine centrefolds became thinner between 1959 and 1978 (Garner, Garfinkel, Schwartz, & Thompson, 1980). Although one study found that the trend toward portrayals of increasing thinness was levelling off (Wiseman, Gray, Mosimann, & Ahrens, 1992), a recent analysis of *Playboy* centrefolds from 1960 to 1997 suggested that current *Playboy* centrefolds are becoming even thinner (Owen & Laurel-Seller, 2000). Moreover, this study showed that models shown on the Internet have unhealthy levels of thinness. Interestingly, a related study conducted at York University in Toronto not only examined the body sizes of *Playboy* centrefolds and Miss America winners, it also examined the attributes of *Playgirl* models over several decades, comparing them to the body sizes of young men in general (Spitzer, Henderson, & Zivian, 1999). The findings for female body sizes showed increasing thinness, in keeping with unrealistic cultural pressures; in contrast, analyses of the data for males indicated that over time the body sizes of *Playgirl* models had increased due to increases in muscularity, and that the body sizes of typical males had also increased, but because of increases in body fat. The researchers concluded that men featured in *Playgirl* and young men from the general population are becoming increasingly different in terms of the projected, desired image, and that these pressures may be contributing to the increases in body dissatisfaction among males that have been reported in more recent studies.

When it comes to the promotion of unrealistic images, it is still the case that females feel more pressure than males. Even toys reflect the unrealistic pressures on females; to achieve the same figure as another ideal, the Barbie doll, the average American woman would have to increase her bust by 12 inches, reduce her waist by 10, and grow to over seven feet in height (Moser, 1989)!

Patricia Pliner from the University of Toronto and Shelly Chaiken from New York University have advanced the theory that women respond to these sociocultural pressures by eating lightly in an attempt to project images of femininity (see Chaiken & Pliner, 1987; Mori, Pliner, & Chaiken, 1987; Pliner & Chaiken, 1990). Research in laboratory and naturalistic settings has confirmed that women who are portrayed as eating heavily are indeed seen as more masculine and less feminine than women who are portrayed as eating light meals. Pliner and Chaiken have coined the term the "Scarlett O'Hara effect" to refer to this phenomenon of eating lightly to project femininity. This is a reference to Mammy's admonition to Scarlett in *Gone with the Wind* that Scarlett should eat a meal prior to going to the barbecue so that she would appear dainty by eating very little when actually at the barbecue.

While cultural standards were moving in the direction of thinness and pressures were increasing, more and more people were becoming overweight. The prevalence of obesity has doubled since 1900; currently 20 to 30 percent of North Americans are overweight, perhaps because of an abundance of food and a sedentary lifestyle, setting the stage for greater conflict between the cultural ideal and reality. Pinel, Assanand, and Lehman (2000) attribute the increasing prevalence of obesity to an evolutionary tendency for humans to eat to excess in order to store energy in their personal warehouses (i.e., their bodies) for a time when food may be less plentiful. If so, this tendency to overconsume is clearly at odds with unrealistic pressures to maintain ideal bodyweights.

We know that the cultural ideal of extreme thinness has been internalized by the large percentage of young women who, although of normal weight, perceive themselves as fat. One study of 10th-grade girls found that one-third felt they were overweight even though they were not (Killen et al., 1986). Strong gender differences have been detected. A Canadian study of almost 30,000 people found that weight dissatisfaction was associated negatively with age among women, (i.e., younger women were more dissatisfied with their weight) but this association was not evident among men (Green et al., 1997). This study also found that women were more likely than men to wish they weighed less and were actually doing something to try to lose weight; this tendency was found regardless of whether their actual weight was in the acceptable range, as prescribed by body mass index tables. Another study conducted in Toronto with women and men of various ages found that women place greater importance on appearance than men do, and that this difference exists across the lifespan and can even be detected among the elderly (Pliner, Chaiken, & Flett, 1990).

As society has become more health and fat conscious, dieting to lose weight has become more common. The number of dieters increased from 7 percent of men and 14 percent of women in 1950 to 29 percent of men and 44 percent of women in 1999 (Serdula et al., 1999). A new study in southern Ontario found that in over 2000 girls aged 10-14, 29.3 percent were dieting and 1 in 10 girls had maladaptive eating attitudes suggesting the presence of an eating disorder (McVey, Tweed, & Blackmore, 2004). An earlier survey by Jones et al. (2001) found that 23 percent of Canadian adolescent females were on diets. The diet industry (books, pills, videos, special foods) is valued at more than $30 billion per year. Also, liposuction (vacuuming out fat deposits just under the skin) is a very common (and sometimes risky) procedure in plastic surgery (Brownell & Rodin, 1994).

There are some indications that this preoccupation with being thin has moderated somewhat. The Garner et al. (1980) study mentioned earlier found that the number of articles on dieting increased steadily during the period when centrefolds were becoming thinner. In a more recent study, Nemeroff et al. (1994) analyzed the content of three women's magazines, *Good Housekeeping, Cosmopolitan*, and *Ms*., for the years 1980 to 1991 and found that the number of articles on weight loss had decreased in *Cosmopolitan* and *Ms* over this period. Nemeroff et al. also analyzed the content of several men's magazines and found that the frequency of articles on weight loss, although lower in men's than in women's magazines, had increased during the time period studied. It would probably be incorrect to assume from these data, however, that we are about to witness an explosion of eating disorders in men, since the articles focus attention on the masculine ideal of normal body weight or on increased muscle mass (Mishkind et al., 1986). Other studies have found that the intensity of dieting and eating-disordered behaviours has lessened in recent years (Heatherton et al., 1995). Nevertheless, dissatisfaction with one's body is on the rise (Garner, 1997), so we should not expect a dramatic drop in the incidence of eating disorders.

Russian ballerina Anastasia Volochkova filed a lawsuit against the Bolshoi Theatre after being fired for allegedly being too heavy a dancer. She later won her job back.

The sociocultural ideal of thinness shared by most Western industrialized nations is the likely vehicle through which people learn to fear being or even feeling fat. In addition to creating an undesired physical shape, fat has negative connotations, such as being unsuccessful and having little self-control. Obese people are viewed by others as less smart and are stereotyped as lonely, shy, and greedy for the affection of others (DeJong & Kleck, 1986). Unfortunately, it appears that the media continues to promote these stereotypes. A content analysis of 18 prime-time television situation comedies conducted by researchers in Calgary found that females with below-average weights were overrepresented in these shows and that the heavier the female character, the more likely she was to have negative comments directed toward her (Fouts & Burggraf, 2000). Moreover, these negative comments were especially likely to be reinforced by audience laughter.

While society's negative attitude about fat became stronger, the prevalence of eating disorders increased. In an epidemiological study conducted in Switzerland, the incidence of anorexia nervosa was found to have quadrupled from the 1950s to the 1970s (Willi & Grossman, 1983). Similar increases have been found in other countries (Eagles et al., 1995; Hoek et al., 1995).

Regarding anorexia in athletes, Epling and Pierce from the University of Alberta have suggested that some people become anorexic because of a pursuit of fitness rather than a pursuit of thinness. They have outlined a theory of a phenomenon that they describe as activity anorexia (Epling & Pierce, 1992; Pierce & Epling, 1996). This concept refers to the loss of appetite when engaged in physical activity. These theorists used the concept of activity anorexia to explain why a comparative study conducted in Toronto by Garner and Garfinkel found that dancers, relative to models, had higher rates of anorexia and more disturbed eating attitudes (Garner & Garfinkel, 1980). Models and dancers share a pressure to maintain ideal appearance, but dancers also engage in much more strenuous physical activity. Epling and Pierce suggest that two interrelated motivational factors account for activity anorexia: food deprivation increases the reinforcement effectiveness of physical activity, and physical activity decreases the reinforcement effectiveness of food.

These processes are consistent with a recent theory of anorexia proposed by researchers from the University of British Columbia. Pinel et al. (2000) hypothesized that anorexics often display great interest in food and are sometimes obsessed with food, but lack positive incentives for actually eating the food. Pinel et al. observed that most starving people placed great positive incentive value when presented with food, but this is not the case with anorexics, for reasons that remain to be determined.

Gender Influences

The primary reason for the greater prevalence of eating disorders among women than among men is that women appear to have been more heavily influenced than men by the cultural ideal of thinness. Women are typically valued more for their appearance, whereas men gain esteem more for their accomplishments. Dieting to lose weight, the result of the prevalent tendency to be overweight, is especially common among white, upper-socioeconomic-status women—the same group with the highest rate of eating disorders. Women apparently are more concerned than men about being thin, are more likely to diet, and are thus more vulnerable to eating disorders. The risk for eating disorders among groups of women who might be expected to be particularly concerned with their weight, such as, models, dancers, and gymnasts, appears to be especially high (Garner et al., 1980). Furthermore, because the onset of eating disorders is typically preceded by dieting and other concerns about weight (e.g., perceived fatness, fear of weight gain), the role of social standards seems certain (see Focus on Discovery 9.1) (Killen et al., 1994). Of course, everyone who diets will not develop an eating disorder. Other factors are described in subsequent sections.

CROSS-CULTURAL STUDIES

Eating disorders appear to be far more common in industrialized societies, such as the United States, Canada, Japan, Australia, and Europe, than in non-industrialized nations. Moreover, according to a review conducted recently by University of Windsor researchers (Geller & Thomas, 1999), young women who immigrate to industrialized Western cultures may be especially prone to develop eating disorders owing to the experience of rapid cultural changes and pressures.

The wide variation in the prevalence of eating disorders across cultures suggests the importance of culture in establishing realistic versus potentially disordered views of one's body. In one study of 369 adolescent girls in Pakistan, none met diagnostic criteria for anorexia nervosa and only one met the criteria for bulimia (Mumford, Whitehouse, & Choudry, 1992). As yet, however, there have been no cross-cultural epidemiological studies employing similar assessments and diagnostic criteria, so it is difficult to compare prevalence rates across cultures accurately.

In one study supporting the notion of cross-cultural differences, Ugandan and British college students rated the attractiveness of drawings of nudes ranging from very emaciated to very obese (Furnham & Baguma, 1994). Ugandan students rated the obese females as more attractive than did the British students. Other studies have found that when women from cultures with low prevalence rates of eating disorders move into cultures with higher prevalence rates, their prevalence rates go up (Yates, 1989).

In spite of these findings, the cross-cultural variation in prevalence of eating disorders remains a supposition and a sometimes controversial one. Lee (1994), for example, has described a disorder similar to anorexia nervosa that exists in several non-industrialized Asian countries (India, Malaysia, the Philippines). This disorder involves severe emaciation, food refusal, and amenorrhea, but not a fear of becoming fat. Is this a cultural variant of anorexia or a different disorder, such as depression? This question is but one of the challenges that face cross-cultural researchers.

Finally, conclusions are complicated further by the possibility that the role of culture varies as a function of whether the focus is on anorexia nervosa or bulimia nervosa. Recently, a quantitative meta-analysis resulted in the conclusion that bulimia nervosa is a culture-bound syndrome, while anorexia nervosa is not (Keel & Klump, 2003). Thus, anorexia nervosa may be much more common across cultures, and the genetic heritability of anorexia, relative to bulimia nervosa, may show less variability across cultures.

Standards of beauty vary cross-culturally as shown by Gauguin's painting of Tahitian women.

RACIAL DIFFERENCES

In the United States, it was reported at one time that the incidence of anorexia was eight times greater in white women than in women of colour (Dolan, 1991). Although this difference may reflect the fact that women of colour have less access to health services or utilize them less often, it could also be a real difference. White teenage girls diet more frequently than do African American teenage girls and are more likely to be dissatisfied with their bodies (Story et al., 1995). Both these factors are related to an increased risk for developing an eating disorder. It does not appear, however, that race is the critical variable here; rather, social class is more important (Caldwell, Brownell, & Wilfley, 1997; French et al., 1997). The emphasis on thinness and dieting has now begun to spread beyond white upper- and middle-class women to women of the lower social classes, and the prevalence of eating disorders has increased among these latter groups (e.g., Root, 1990).

PSYCHODYNAMIC VIEWS

There are many psychodynamic theories of eating disorders. Most propose that the core cause lies in disturbed parent-child relationships and agree that certain core personality traits, such as low self-esteem and perfectionism, are found among individuals with eating disorders. Psychodynamic theories also propose that the symptoms of an eating disorder fulfill some need, such as the need to increase one's sense of personal effectiveness (the person succeeds in maintaining a strict diet) or to avoid growing up sexually (by being very thin, the person does not achieve the usual female shape) (Goodsitt, 1997). According to Canadian researchers Howard Steiger and Mimi Israel (1999), early psychodynamic mod-

focus on discovery/9.1

To Diet or Not to Diet?

As dieting has become more common and the diet industry has become a multibillion-dollar-a-year business, the incidence of both eating disorders and obesity has increased. Millions of North Americans are overweight. Is there a relationship among these facts? Studies of restrained eaters and patients with eating disorders show that dieting can lead to binging, and one recent study by Urbszat, Herman, and Polivy (2002) found that even the mere anticipation of going on a diet can trigger binges in restrained eaters (i.e., people who attempt to restrict their intake of food in general). Moreover, very "successful" dieters can become anorexic. Is dieting more dangerous than desirable?

Heredity plays a significant role in obesity. Between 20 percent and 50 percent of variability in obesity phenotypes is attributable to genetic factors (see Winchester & Collier, 2003). Adoption studies have found that children's weight is more strongly related to the weight of their biological parents than to the weight of their adoptive parents (Price et al., 1987). Similarly, 40 percent of the children of an obese parent will be obese, compared with 7 percent of the children of normal-weight parents. Heredity could produce its effects by regulating metabolic rate or through the hypothalamus and its impact on insulin level or the production of enzymes that make it easier to store fat and gain weight. Dieting may be of little use to people whose obesity is principally genetically caused. Their metabolic rate may simply slow down to help maintain body weight; when the diet is over, the lowered metabolic rate leads to weight gain.

But psychosocial factors are also clearly involved in gaining weight. Stress and its associated negative moods can induce eating in some people (Arnow, Kenardy, & Agras, 1992; Heatherton & Baumeister, 1991). And we are all subject to the continuing impact of advertisements, especially those promoting alluring high-fat, high-calorie products such as snack foods, desserts, and meals at fast-food restaurants.

The motivation to achieve thinness is generally tied to several possible goals:

- Being thin increases personal attractiveness, which in turn can produce both psychological (e.g., increased self-esteem) and social (e.g., advancement in the workplace) benefits.
- Being thin signifies self-discipline; obesity reflects a lack of self-control and failure.
- Thinness is associated with several health benefits; obesity is associated with health problems such as diabetes, hypertension, cardiovascular disease, and cancer.

Despite this drive to be thin, a backlash against dieting has been emerging (Brownell & Rodin, 1994). Feminist philosophy has challenged the view that women should be defined by their physical characteristics. On an empirical level, we have seen at least one potential danger in dieting—it is often a precursor to eating disorders. Moreover, in a review paper, McFarlane, Polivy, and McCabe (1999) from the University of Toronto concluded that dieting has a negative impact on psychological well-being, as made evident by established links between dieting and negative mood, low self-esteem, and cognitive preoccupations with food stimuli.

Polivy and Herman (Polivy, 2001; Polivy & Herman, 1999, 2002) underscored the negative aspects of dieting in their work on a phenomenon they refer to as the "false hope syndrome." They argued that attempts at self-change capitalize on false hopes that are reinforced by the initial positive outcomes that result from dieting (e.g., praise from other people). However, this sense of reward and related feelings of optimism and control lead to a tendency to pursue unrealistic weight-loss goals that ultimately result in extreme disappointment.

It is widely known that although many diets achieve weight loss in the short term (for example, one year), the weight is typically regained later (Polivy & Herman, 2002), suggesting that diets do not work in the long term. Weight fluctuation itself could be a health risk (e.g., for cardiovascular disease). Furthermore, the evidence concerning whether weight loss actually yields health benefits is conflicting. For example, the typical weight loss of 15 pounds may not be sufficient to produce any beneficial effects on health.

In trying to reconcile the competing positions on dieting, Brownell and Rodin (1994) acknowledged that all the data are not in. Nonetheless, they countered some of the points raised by anti-dieters. They noted that the samples in studies showing the long-term ineffectiveness of dieting typically contained large percentages of binge eaters and suggested that because binge eating is related to a poor prognosis for treating obesity, the data may underestimate the positive effects of dieting. Furthermore, some studies have found evidence of more favourable long-term outcomes. In one, participants with an average weight loss of 55 pounds maintained 75 percent of the weight loss at a one-year follow-up and 52 percent at two years (Nunn, Newton, & Faucher, 1992). Finally, they noted that returning to pre-diet weight sometime after dieting is not necessarily a bad outcome. Considering a return to baseline as a failure does not take into consideration what the person's weight would have been if no diet had ever been attempted.

Brownell and Rodin concluded that the decision to diet might be more profitably based on individualized risk-to-benefit ratios. Generally, these would be expected to favour dieting in very overweight people, but other characteristics could also be considered. The benefits of dieting could assume much more importance in someone with a family history of hypertension and cardiovascular disease, for example. Conversely, for someone with a family history of eating disorders, embarking on a diet would have to be viewed as a risky step.

els interpreted symptoms of anorexia from a *conflict* perspective (i.e., a defence against conflict drives, often of a sexual nature), while contemporary psychodynamic models interpret symptoms of anorexia from a *deficit* perspective, with a particular emphasis on anorexia as a way to compensate for defects in the self.

Several psychodynamic theories focus on family relationships. One view, proposed by influential theorist Hilde

Bruch (1980), is that anorexia nervosa is an attempt by children who have been raised to feel ineffectual to gain competence and respect and to ward off feelings of helplessness, ineffectiveness, and powerlessness. This sense of ineffectiveness is created by a parenting style in which the parents' wishes are imposed on the child without consideration of the child's needs or wishes. For example, parents may arbitrarily decide when the child is hungry or tired, failing to perceive the child's actual state. Children reared in this way do not learn to identify their own internal states and do not become self-reliant. When faced with the demands of adolescence, the child seizes on the societal emphasis on thinness and turns dieting into a means of acquiring control and identity. Steiger and Israel (1999) have a similar view of the origins of anorexia, and they maintain that "obstinate, avoidant, or controlling reactions on the part of these clients often constitute adaptations, justified by past experiences of parental overcontrol" (p. 745).

Another psychodynamic theory, described by Goodsitt (1997), proposes that bulimia nervosa in females stems from a failure to develop an adequate sense of self because of a conflict-ridden mother-daughter relationship. Food becomes a symbol of this failed relationship. The daughter's binging and purging represent the conflict between the need for the mother and the desire to reject her.

Family Systems Theory

Salvador Minuchin and his colleagues have proposed another influential position, known as *family systems theory*, a theory relevant to both anorexia and bulimia. This position holds that the symptoms of an eating disorder are best understood by considering both the patient and how the symptoms are embedded in a dysfunctional family structure. In this view, the child is seen as physiologically vulnerable (although the precise nature of this vulnerability is unspecified), and the child's family has several characteristics that promote the development of an eating disorder. Also, the child's eating disorder plays an important role in helping the family avoid other conflicts. Thus, the child's symptoms are a substitute for other conflicts within the family.

According to Minuchin et al. (1975), the families of children with eating disorders exhibit the following characteristics:

- **Enmeshment**. Families have an extreme form of overinvolvement and intimacy in which parents may speak for their children because they believe they know exactly how they feel.
- **Overprotectiveness**. Family members have an extreme level of concern for one another's welfare.
- **Rigidity**. Families have a tendency to try to maintain the status quo and avoid dealing effectively with events that require change (e.g., the demand that adolescence creates for increased autonomy).
- **Lack of conflict resolution**. Families either avoid conflict or are in a state of chronic conflict.

Evidence for these psychodynamic and family systems positions comes from two sources: studies of personality characteristics of patients with eating disorders and studies of the characteristics of their families. It is difficult to reach definitive conclusions in either area, however, because the disorder may have resulted in changes in personality or in the patient's family.

Characteristics of Families

Studies of the characteristics of families of patients with eating disorders are relevant to both family systems theory and psychodynamic theory. Results have been variable. Some of the variation stems, in part, from the different methods used to collect the data and from the sources of the information. For example, self-reports of patients consistently reveal high levels of conflict in the family (e.g., Hodges, Cochrane, & Brewerton, 1998). However, reports of parents do not necessarily indicate high levels of family problems. In one study in which the reports of parents of patients with eating disorders did differ from those of parents in the control group, parents of patients reported high levels of isolation and lower levels of mutual involvement and support (Humphrey, 1986). Disturbed family relationships do seem to characterize the families of some patients with eating disorders; however, the characteristics that have been observed, such as low levels of support, only loosely fit the family systems theory. And again, these family characteristics could be a result of the eating disorder and not a cause of it.

A study more directly linked to Minuchin's theory assessed both eating-disorder patients and their parents on tests designed to measure rigidity, closeness, emotional overinvolvement, critical comments, and hostility (Dare et al., 1994). Contrary to Minuchin's theory, the families showed considerable variation in enmeshment and were quite low in conflict (low levels of criticism and hostility). Though this latter finding could reflect the conflict-avoiding pattern Minuchin has described, the parents' lack of overinvolvement is clearly inconsistent with his clinical descriptions. Also inconsistent with Minuchin's theory is a family study conducted in Toronto in which assessments were conducted before and after treatment of the patient (Woodside et al., 1995). Ratings of family functioning improved after treatment, contradicting the idea that improvement in the patient should bring other family conflicts to light and supporting the idea that eating disorders may cause family problems rather than the other way around.

To better understand the role of family functioning, we must begin to study these families directly, by observational measures, rather than by reports alone. Although a child's *perception* of his or her family's characteristics is important, we also need to know how much of reported family disturbance is perceived and how much is real. In one of the few observational studies conducted thus far, parents of children with eating disorders did not appear to be very different from control parents. The two groups did not differ in the frequency of positive and negative messages given to their children, and the parents of children with eating disorders were more self-disclosing than were the control parents. The parents of eating-disorder children did lack some communication skills, however, such as the ability to request clarification of vague statements (van den Broucke, Vandereycken, & Vertommen, 1995). Observational studies such as this, coupled with data on perceived family characteristics, would help determine whether actual or perceived family characteristics are related to eating disorders.

Family functioning may also be important in terms of the extent to which there is a focus on the importance of appearance. One Canadian study of 918 high school students found that family preoccupation with appearance had a direct impact on body dissatisfaction and symptoms of eating disorders (Leung, Schwartzman, & Steiger, 1996). A follow-up study conducted in Toronto found that a family focus on appearance predicted body dissatisfaction among young women had a neurotic personality style and tended to be anxious individuals (Davis, Shuster, Blackmore, & Fax, 2004). Thus, family factors may interact with the vulnerable individual's personality characteristics. Parents may also be important in terms of the transmission of abnormal eating attitudes, either through reinforcement and punishment or through modelling and imitation (Pike & Rodin, 1991). One study examined the mothers, fathers, and sisters of eating-disorder patients and found a link between the abnormal eating concerns of daughters and mothers (Steiger, Stotland, Trottier, & Ghadirian, 1998). Once again, however, a key issue is whether any effects on the patients are due to actual parental characteristics or to perceived parental characteristics. Baker, Whisman, and Brownell (2000) studied eating attitudes in university students and their parents and found that the students' attitudes and behaviours were tied more closely to perceived parental characteristics (i.e., criticism from parents) than to actual parental characteristics.

Child Abuse and Eating disorders

Some studies have indicated that self-reports of childhood sexual abuse are higher than normal among patients with eating disorders, especially those with bulimia nervosa (Deep et al., 1999; Steiger & Zanko, 1990). A study conducted in Toronto found that 25 percent of women with eating disorders reported the experience of previous sexual abuse; it also correlated a past history of sexual abuse with greater psychological disturbance (DeGroot, Kennedy, Rodin, & McVey, 1992). Similarly, a recent study conducted in Verdun, Quebec, confirmed that bulimic women, relative to normal eaters, had higher levels of childhood abuse and that the presence and the severity of abuse predicted more extreme psychopathology (Leonard, Steiger, & Kao, 2003).

Patients with eating disorders consistently report that their family life was high in conflict.

Since, as discussed in Chapter 7, some data indicate that reports of abuse may be created in therapy, it is notable that high rates of sexual abuse have been found among people with eating disorders who have not been in treatment as well as those who have (Welch & Fairburn, 1994). However, high rates of childhood sexual abuse are found among people in many diagnostic categories, so if it plays some role, it is not highly specific to eating disorders (Fairburn et al., 1999).

Research has also found higher rates of childhood physical abuse among patients with eating disorders. These data suggest that future studies should focus on a broad range of abusive experiences. Furthermore, it has been suggested that the presence or absence of abuse may be too general a variable. Abuse at a very early age, involving force by a family member, may bear a stronger relationship to eating disorders than abuse of any other type (Everill & Waller, 1995).

Personality and Eating Disorders

Researchers study personality factors in the hope of identifying vulnerability factors that may be involved in the etiology of eating disorders. In assessing the role of personality, it is important to keep in mind that the eating disorder itself can affect personality. A study of semi-starvation in male conscientious objectors conducted in the late 1940s supports the idea that the personality of patients with eating disorders, particularly those with anorexia, is affected by their weight loss (Keys et al., 1950). For a period of six weeks, the men were given two meals a day, totalling 1,500 calories, to simulate the meals in a concentration camp. On average, they lost 25 percent of their body weight. All the men soon became preoccupied with food. They also reported increased fatigue, poor concentration, lack of sexual interest, irritability, moodiness, and insomnia. Four became depressed, and one developed bipolar disorder. This research shows vividly how severe restriction of food intake can have powerful effects on personality and behaviour; we need to consider these effects when evaluating the personality of patients with anorexia and bulimia.

In part as a response to the findings just mentioned, some researchers have collected retrospective reports of personality before the onset of an eating disorder. This research described patients with anorexia as having been perfectionistic, shy, and compliant before the onset of the disorder. It described patients with bulimia as having the additional characteristics of histrionic features, affective instability, and an outgoing social disposition (Vitousek & Manke, 1994). It is important to remember, however, that retrospective reports in which a patient and his or her families recall what the person was like before diagnosis can be inaccurate and biased by awareness of the patient's current problem.

Numerous studies have also measured the current personality of patients with eating disorders, relying on results from established personality questionnaires such as the MMPI. Both patients with anorexia and patients with bulimia are high in neuroticism and anxiety and low in self-esteem (Bulik et al., 2000). They also score high on a measure of traditionalism, indicating strong endorsement of family and social standards. Some differences emerged between the two groups on the MMPI: patients with anorexia nervosa reported depression, social isolation, and anxiety, whereas patients with bulimia nervosa exhibited more diffuse and serious psychopathology, scoring higher than the anorexic patients on several of the MMPI scales (Vitousek & Manke, 1994).

Researchers have also examined the personality trait of narcissism in patients with eating disorders. Narcissists are characterized by an excessive focus on the self and a heightened sense of self-importance and grandiosity. These individuals are believed to be overcompensating for a fragile sense of self-esteem, however, and they are highly sensitive and reactive to criticism. Pathological narcissism at extreme levels can take the form of a narcissistic personality disorder (see Chapter 13). Recent studies by Steiger and his associates have shown that patients with anorexia nervosa and bulimia nervosa are characterized by high levels of narcissism and that this narcissism appears to be a persistent personality feature even when the eating disorder is in remission (Lehoux, Steiger, & Jabalpurlawa, 2000; Steiger, Jabalpurwala, Champagne, & Stotland, 1997).

As suggested earlier, perfectionism is believed to be highly relevant to an understanding of eating disorders. The initial research in this area was conducted with the perfectionism subscale of the Eating Disorder Inventory (EDI; see Table 9.1), and it confirmed that perfectionism is elevated in individuals with eating disorders (Garner et al., 1983). The EDI perfectionism subscale provides a single, global measure of perfectionism. Subsequent researchers, however, have found that the perfectionism construct is multidimensional, and consistent with this finding, contemporary research in this area has sought to determine which aspects of the perfectionism construct are involved in eating disorders.

Frost and his colleagues at Smith College in Massachusetts created a multidimensional perfectionism scale that assesses six dimensions: concern over mistakes, high personal standards, doubts about actions, organization, high parental expectations, and high parental criticism (Frost, Marten, Lahart, & Rosenblate, 1990). Meanwhile, in Canada, Hewitt and Flett (1989, 1991) created a multidimensional perfectionism scale that assesses self-oriented perfectionism (setting high standards for oneself), other-oriented perfectionism (setting high standards for others), and socially prescribed perfectionism (the perception that high standards are imposed on the self by others). One possible manifestation of socially prescribed perfectionism of relevance here is a sense that there is social pressure to attain unrealistic standards of physical perfection.

Research with the Frost et al. measure has shown that almost all of the perfectionism dimensions are elevated in eating disorders (Bastiani, Rao, Weltzin, and Kaye, 1995) and that these dimensions of perfectionism remain elevated in women who have recovered from a bout of anorexia nervosa (Srinivasagam et al., 1995). Such findings indicate that the link between perfectionism and eating disorders can still be detected even in the absence of current psychopathology.

Eating-disorder research with the Hewitt and Flett (1991) Multidimensional Perfectionism Scale suggests that self-oriented and socially prescribed perfectionism are both elevated in eating disorders. Bastiani et al. (1995) reported that weight-restored and underweight anorexics had elevated scores on self-oriented perfectionism. In addition, the underweight anorexics had higher scores on socially prescribed perfectionism, relative to the control group.

Davis (1997) examined levels of perfectionism and correlates of perfectionism in a sample of 123 eating-disorder patients receiving treatment at Toronto Hospital. This study revealed that the eating-disorder patients had substantially higher levels of self-oriented perfectionism and socially prescribed perfectionism, relative to established norms for these measures. Similarly, another recent study conducted with eating-disorder patients from the Toronto Hospital showed that they had elevated levels of self-oriented and socially prescribed perfectionism (McCabe, McFarlane, Blankstein, & Olmsted, 2000). Other research conducted in Toronto found that these two perfectionisms were elevated once again in eating-disorder patients, and that anorexics who engage in excessive exercise are distinguished by remarkably high levels of self-oriented perfectionism (Davis, Kaptein, Kaplan, Olmsted, & Woodside, 1998).

In the McCabe et al. (2000) study, participants completed a relatively new multidimensional measure of perfectionism—the Almost Perfect Scale-Revised (Slaney, Mobley, Trippi, Ashby, & Johnson, 1996). A unique aspect of this study is that it showed that the eating-disorder groups also differed from control groups on a measure of discrepancy (discrepancy reflects the perception that one consistently fails to meet one's own self-imposed standards). This finding is in keeping with extensive research by Cash and his associates that shows that self-ratings of the discrepancy between actual body image and the body-image ideals is a factor that predicts distress and low self-esteem (e.g., Szymanski & Cash, 1995).

Perfectionism is relevant to both anorexia and bulimia. One line of investigation has provided supported for a three-factor interactive model of bulimic symptom development (Bardone, Vohs, Abramson, Heatherton, & Joiner, 2000; Vohs et al., 2001). According to this interactive model, bulimic symptoms are elevated among females who are characterized not only by perfectionism, but also by body dissatisfaction and low self-esteem. This model is relevant to work by Cash and his associates because presumably those females who have body dissatisfaction and low self-esteem have a substantial discrepancy between their perceptions of their body and body-image ideals.

Contemporary research is testing the possibility that some individuals respond to social pressures to be perfect by engaging in a form of behaviour known as perfectionistic self-presentation; that is, these individuals try to create an image of perfection and are highly focused on minimizing the mistakes they make in front of other people (see Hewitt, Flett, & Ediger, 1995; Hewitt et al., 2003). Perfectionistic self-presentation is reflected by the quote at the start of this chapter from the student with an eating disorder (i.e., "I still try to maintain as perfect an image as possible and I still seek to please my mother").

A focus on perfectionistic self-presentation is in keeping with indications that women with eating disorders are high in public self-consciousness and overly concerned with presentation of self to others, in part because they often feel like imposters and frauds who have not been detected yet by other people and are mistakenly seen by them as competent (Strigel-Moore, Silberstein, & Rodin, 1993). People who feel like imposters and fear detection of their self-perceived inadequacies can respond defensively by trying to create an impression of being perfect; this strategy can include attempts to portray their physical appearance in the best possible way. Although still in its early stages, research on perfectionistic self-presentation has already established that women with anorexia nervosa are characterized by elevated levels of perfectionistic self-presentation (Cockell et al., 2002) and patients with this personality style are characterized by self-silencing and the inhibited expression of negative emotions (Geller, Cockell, Hewitt, Goldner, & Flett, 2000; Goldner, Srikameswaran, & Cockell, 2002). This tendency to minimize conflict by not expressing personal concerns is common among people suffering from eating disorders.

Overall, the studies outlined above suggest that various perfectionism dimensions are indeed elevated in the various eating disorders. However, one significant limitation of this work is that the causal role of these dimensions of perfectionism has yet to be established by longitudinal, prospective research on the role of these dimensions in the onset of eating disorders. Prospective studies would examine personality characteristics before an eating disorder is present. These studies are just beginning, and the data are not in yet, but research in progress has yielded some interesting information (e.g., Leon et al., 1995). More than 2,000 students in a suburban Minneapolis school district completed a variety of tests for three consecutive years. Among the measures were assessments of personality characteristics as well as an index of the risk for developing an eating disorder based on the Eating Disorders Inventory. Strong predictors of risk for eating disorders were a measure of *interoceptive awareness* (the extent to which people can distinguish different biological states of their bodies) (see Table 9.1 for items that assess interoceptive awareness) and a propensity to experience negative emotions.

Data from some studies of the personalities of those with eating disorders are somewhat consistent with psychodynamic theory. Patients with eating disorders have consistently been found to have low self-esteem (e.g., Garner et al., 1983) and elevated levels of orality and dependency (Narduzzi & Jackson, 2000), characteristics that reflect oral fixations. Furthermore, in line with Bruch's theory, patients with anorexia nervosa tend to be compliant, inhibited, and perfectionistic. Leon et al.'s finding that a lack of interoceptive awareness predicts risk for eating disorders confirms Bruch's idea that these people are poor at identifying their own internal states.

Cognitive-Behavioural Views

Anorexia Nervosa Cognitive-behavioural theories of anorexia nervosa emphasize fear of fatness and body-image disturbance as the motivating factors that make self-starvation and weight loss powerful reinforcers. Behaviours that achieve or maintain thinness are negatively reinforced by the reduction of anxiety about becoming fat. Furthermore, dieting and weight loss may be positively reinforced by the sense of mastery or self-control they create (Fairburn, Shafran, & Cooper, 1999; Garner, Vitousek, & Pike, 1997). Some theories also include personality and sociocultural variables to explain how fear of fatness and body-image disturbances develop. For example, perfectionism and a sense of personal inadequacy may lead a person to become especially concerned with his or her appearance, making dieting a potent reinforcer.

Similarly, the media's portrayal of thinness as an ideal, being overweight, and a tendency to compare oneself with especially attractive others all contribute to dissatisfaction with one's body (Stormer & Thompson, 1996). As shown in one Canadian study, even brief exposure to pictures of fashion models can instill negative moods in young women, and women who are dissatisfied with their bodies seem especially vulnerable when exposed to these images (Pinhas, Toner, Ali, Garfinkel, & Stuckless, 1999).

Somewhat ironically, recent research by Jennifer Mills from York University and her associates showed that, initially, chronic dieters actually feel thinner after looking at idealized images of the thin body and this motivates them to diet (Mills, Polivy, Herman, & Tiggemann, 2002). This effect, labelled the "thinspiration effect," can begin a process of dieting that can ultimately lead to distress among dieters unable to attain unrealistic body-image standards.

Another important factor in producing a strong drive for thinness and disturbed body image is criticism from peers and parents about being overweight (Paxton et al., 1991). In one study supporting this conclusion (Paxton et al., 1991), adolescent girls aged 10 to 15 were evaluated twice, with a three-year interval between assessments. Obesity at the first assessment was related to being teased by peers and at the second assessment to dissatisfaction with their bodies. Dissatisfaction was in turn related to symptoms of eating disorder.

It is known that binging frequently results when diets are broken (Polivy & Herman, 1985). Thus, a lapse that occurs in the strict dieting of a person with anorexia nervosa is likely to escalate into a binge. The purging following an episode of binge eating can again be seen as motivated by the fear of weight gain that the binge elicited. Patients with anorexia who do not have episodes of binging and purging may have a more intense preoccupation with and fear of weight gain (Schlundt & Johnson, 1990) or may be more able to exercise self-control.

To match the proportions of a Barbie doll, a woman with a normal shape (left) would have to transform her height, waist, and bust to appear like the figure on the right.

Bulimia Nervosa Patients with bulimia nervosa are thought to be overconcerned with weight gain and body appearance; indeed, they judge their self-worth mainly by their weight and shape. They also have low self-esteem, and because weight and shape are somewhat more controllable than other features of the self, they tend to focus on weight and shape, hoping their efforts in this area will make them feel better generally. They try to follow a rigid pattern of eating that has strict rules regarding how much to eat, what kinds of food to eat, and when to eat. These rules are inevitably broken, and the lapse escalates into a binge. After the binge, feelings of disgust and fear of becoming fat build up, leading to compensatory actions such as vomiting (Fairburn, 1997). Although purging temporarily reduces the anxiety from having eaten too much, this cycle lowers the person's self-esteem, which triggers still more binging and purging, a vicious circle that maintains desired body weight but has serious medical consequences (see Figure 9.2 for a summary of this theory).

Patients with bulimia nervosa typically binge when they encounter stress and experience negative moods. This was confirmed in a study conducted with bulimic patients receiving treatment at Toronto Hospital (see Davis, Freeman, & Garner, 1988) who were asked to keep hourly records of their behaviours and moods. Bulimic patients reported more negative moods in the hour just prior to their binges. The binge may therefore function as a means of regulating negative moods (also see Stice et al., 1999). Evidence also supports the idea that anxiety is relieved by purging. Patients with bulimia report increased levels of anxiety when they eat a meal and are not allowed to purge (Leitenberg et al., 1984), and these self-reports have been validated by physiological measures, such as skin conductance (e.g., Williamson et al., 1988). Similarly, anxiety levels decline after purging (Jarrell, Johnson, & Williamson, 1986), again

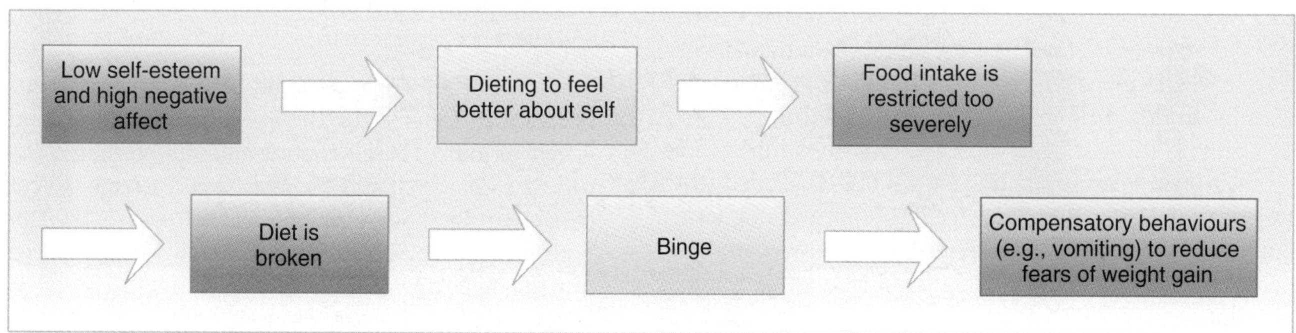

Figure 9.2 Schematic of the cognitive-behavioural theory of bulimia nervosa.

supporting the idea that purging is reinforced by anxiety reduction.

TREATMENT OF EATING DISORDERS

It is often difficult to get a person with an eating disorder into treatment because the person typically denies that he or she has a problem. For this reason, the majority of people with eating disorders—up to 90 percent of them—are not in treatment (Fairburn et al., 1996).

Hospitalization is frequently required to treat people with anorexia so that the patient's ingestion of food can be gradually increased and carefully monitored. Weight loss can be so severe that intravenous feeding is necessary to save the patient's life. The medical complications of anorexia, such as electrolyte imbalances, also require treatment. For both anorexia and bulimia, both biological and psychological interventions have been employed.

Biological Treatments

Because bulimia nervosa is often comorbid with depression, it has been treated with various antidepressants. Interest has focused on fluoxetine (Prozac) (e.g., Fluoxetine Bulimia Nervosa Collaborative Study Group, 1992). In one multi-centre study, 387 women with bulimia were treated as outpatients for eight weeks. Fluoxetine was shown to be superior to a placebo in reducing binge eating and vomiting; it also decreased depression and lessened distorted attitudes toward food and eating. Findings from most studies, including double-blind studies with placebo control groups, confirm the efficacy of a variety of antidepressants in reducing purging and sometimes even bringing about complete remission (Goldstein et al., 1999; Wilson & Fairburn, 1998).

On the negative side, many more patients drop out of drug therapy in studies on bulimia than drop out of the kind of cognitive-behavioural interventions described later (Fairburn, Agras, & Wilson, 1992). In the multi-centre fluoxetine study cited, almost one-third of the patients dropped out before the end of the eight-week treatment, primarily because of the side effects of the drug; this figure compares with drop-out rates of under 5 percent with cognitive-behavioural therapy (Agras et al., 1992). Moreover, most patients relapse when various kinds of antidepressant medication are withdrawn (Mitchell & de Zwaan, 1993; Wilson & Pike, 1993), as is the case with most psychoactive drugs. In a recent review, Ferguson and Pigott (2000) concluded that two strategies in combination seem to improve long-term outcome in bulimia nervosa: treatment with cognitive-behaviour therapy and changing to an alternative antidepressant.

Drugs have also been used in attempts to treat anorexia nervosa. Unfortunately, they have not been very successful. In a recent review paper, researchers from the Centre for Addiction and Mental Health in Toronto concluded that attempts to treat anorexics with drugs have "proven to be simplistic and, to date, no drug or class of drugs has emerged as an effective agent to treat patients with this disorder" (Kruger & Kennedy, 2000, p. 498). No drug has led to significant weight gain, changed core features of anorexia, or even added significant benefit to a standard inpatient treatment program (Attia et al., 1998; Johnson, Tsoh, & Varnado, 1996).

Psychological Treatment of Anorexia Nervosa

There is little in the way of controlled research on psychological interventions for anorexia nervosa, but we will present what appear to be the most promising approaches to this life-threatening disorder.

Therapy for anorexia is generally believed to be a two-tiered process. The immediate goal is to help the patient gain weight in order to avoid medical complications and the possibility of death. The patient is often so weak and physiological functioning so disturbed that hospital treatment is medically imperative (in addition to being needed to ensure that the patient ingests some food). Operant-conditioning behaviour therapy programs have been somewhat successful in achieving weight gain in the short term (Hsu, 1991). In these programs, the hospitalized patient is isolated as much as possible and then rewarded with mealtime company, access to a television set, radio, or stereo, walks with a student nurse, mail, and visitors for eating and gaining weight. However, the second goal of treatment—long-term maintenance of weight gain—has not yet been reliably achieved by medical, behavioural, or traditional psychodynamic interventions (Wilson, 1995), though fluoxetine (Prozac) may contribute to a maintenance of inpatient weight gain as long as the person remains on the drug (Kaye et al., 1997).

Recently, Fairburn and his colleagues (Fairburn, Shafran, & Cooper, 1999) proposed a cognitive-behavioural theory of the maintenance of anorexia nervosa. They argued that the central feature of the disorder is an extreme need to control eating. A tendency to judge self-worth in terms of shape and weight is assumed to be superimposed on the need for self-control. According to Fairburn et al. (1999) the theory has two major treatment implications:

- The issue of self-control should be the principal focus of treatment, including "the use of eating, shape, and weight as indices of self-control, and self-worth, the disturbed eating itself and the associated extreme weight behaviour, the body checking and, of course, the low body weight" (p. 10). They suggest that other targets for change in traditional cognitive-behavioural approaches (e.g., Garner, Vitousek, & Pike, 1997), such as low self-esteem, difficulty recognizing and expressing emotions, interpersonal and family difficulties, do not need to be addressed unless they interfere with treatment progress.

- Treatment should also focus on the client's need for self-control in general. Thus, the "focus of control can be gradually shifted away from eating by helping patients derive satisfaction and a sense of achievement from other activities, and by demonstrating that control over eating does not provide what they are seeking" (p. 10).

Some evidence has indicated that an individual ego-analytic psychotherapy focused on encouraging greater autonomy can be somewhat effective (Robin, Siegel, & Moye, 1995). However, family therapy is the principal mode of treatment for anorexia. Like most other treatments, it has not yet been sufficiently studied for its long-term effects. One report, however, suggests that as many as 86 percent of 50 anorexic daughters treated with their families were still functioning well when assessed at times ranging from three months to four years after treatment (Rosman, Minuchin, & Liebman, 1976). A better-controlled follow-up study of psychodynamically oriented family therapy has recently confirmed these earlier findings. Patients with early-onset anorexia and a short history of it maintained their gains from family therapy for five years following treatment termination (Eisler et al., 1997).

Let us take a closer look at the well-known family therapy of Salvador Minuchin and his colleagues, which is based on the family systems theorizing described earlier. In Minuchin's view, the family member with an eating disorder deflects attention away from underlying conflicts in family relationships. To treat the disorder, Minuchin attempts to redefine it as interpersonal rather than individual and to bring the family conflict to the fore. In this way, he theorizes, the symptomatic family member is freed from having to maintain his or her problem, for it no longer deflects attention from the dysfunctional family.

How is this accomplished? The therapist sees the family at a family lunch session, since the conflicts related to anorexia are believed to be most evident then. These lunch sessions have three major goals:

- to change the patient role of the patient with anorexia
- to redefine the eating problem as an interpersonal problem
- to prevent the parents from using their child's anorexia as a means of avoiding conflict

One strategy is to instruct each parent to try individually to force the child to eat. The other parent may leave the room. The individual efforts are expected to fail. But through this failure and frustration, the mother and father may now work *together* to persuade the child to eat. Thus, rather than being a focus of conflict, the child's eating will produce co-operation and increase parental effectiveness in dealing with the child (Rosman, Minuchin, & Liebman, 1975).

Family therapy is the main treatment for anorexia nervosa.

Psychological Treatment of Bulimia Nervosa

The cognitive behaviour therapy (CBT) approach of Fairburn (1985; Fairburn, Marcus, & Wilson, 1993) is the best validated and current standard for the treatment of bulimia. In Fairburn's therapy, the patient is encouraged to question society's standards for physical attractiveness. Patients must also uncover and then change beliefs that encourage them to starve themselves to avoid becoming overweight. They must be helped to see that normal body weight can be maintained without severe dieting and that unrealistic restriction of food intake can often trigger a binge. They are taught that all is not lost with just one bite of high-calorie food and that snacking need not trigger a binge that would be followed by induced vomiting or taking laxatives. Altering this all-or-nothing thinking can help patients begin to eat more moderately. They are also taught assertion skills to help them cope with unreasonable demands placed on them by others, and they learn as well more satisfying ways of relating to people.

The overall goal of treatment in bulimia nervosa is to develop normal eating patterns. Patients need to learn to eat three meals a day and even to eat some snacks between meals without sliding back into binging and purging. Regular meals control hunger and thereby, it is hoped, the urge to eat enormous amounts of food, the effect of which—being overweight—is counteracted by purging. To help patients develop less extreme beliefs about themselves, the cognitive behaviour therapist gently but firmly challenges such irrational beliefs as "No one will love or respect me if I am a few pounds heavier than I am now." A generalized assumption underlying such cognitions for female patients might be that a woman has value to a man only if she is a few pounds underweight—a belief that is put forth in the media and advertisements.

This CBT approach has the patient bring small amounts of forbidden food to eat in the session. Relaxation is employed to control the urge to induce vomiting. Unrealistic demands and other cognitive distortions—such as the belief that eating a small amount of high-calorie food means that the patient is an utter failure and doomed never to improve—are continually challenged. The therapist and patient work together to determine the events, thoughts, and feelings that trigger an urge to binge and then to learn more adaptive ways to cope with these situations. For example, if the therapist and the patient, usually a young woman, discover that binging often takes place after the patient has been criticized by her boyfriend, therapy could entail any or all of the following:

- encouraging the patient to assert herself if the criticism is unwarranted
- teaching her, à la Ellis, that it is not a catastrophe to make a mistake and it is not necessary to be perfect, even if the boyfriend's criticism is valid
- desensitizing her to social evaluation and encouraging her to question society's standards for ideal weight and the pressures on women to be thin—not an easy task by any means

The outcomes of CBTs are promising, at least in the short term. A recent meta-analysis showed that CBT yielded better results than antidepressant drug treatments (Whittal, Agras, & Gould, 1999). Findings from a number of other studies indicated that CBT often results in less frequent binging and purging, with reductions ranging from 70 to more than 90 percent; extreme dietary restraint is also reduced significantly, and there is improvement in attitudes toward body shape and weight (Compas et al., 1998; Garner et al., 1993; Wilson et al., 1991). These data have led some authors to conclude that no other treatment has greater efficacy than CBT (see Ricca, Mannucci, Zucchi, Rotella, & Favarelli, 2000). However, if we focus on the patients themselves rather than on numbers of binges and purges *across* patients, we find that at least half of those treated with CBT improve very little (Wilson, 1995) and almost half relapse after four months (Halmi et al., 2002). Predictors of relapse include less initial motivation for change and higher initial levels of food and eating preoccupation (Halmi et al., 2002).

Waller and associates have argued that if CBT is extended and takes the form of a schema-focused cognitive behaviour therapy (SFCBT), it will prove to be more effective in treating bulimia (see Waller & Kennerley, 2003). The goal of this approach is to identify and modify deeply ingrained and painful core belief systems that reflect the individual's cognitive schemas (i.e., mental filters). Waller argues that a negative core belief system involving negative aspects of the self (e.g., I am unlovable) must be replaced by positive core beliefs in order for improvements to occur. Research on SFCBT is still in its early stages.

Other investigators are conducting what are called component analyses of the CBT therapy package just described. One important aspect that has been examined is the response prevention and exposure component (recall this aspect of the behavioural treatment of obsessive-compulsive disorder). This component involves discouraging the patient from purging after eating foods that usually elicit an urge to vomit. Indications are that this is an important component; CBT minus this element does not appear to be as efficacious as the total treatment package (Fairburn et al., 1995; Wilson et al., 1991).

Are outcomes better when CBT is combined with antidepressant pharmacotherapy? Adding drug treatment to CBT does not enhance the effectiveness of CBT, and CBT alone is more effective than any available drug treatment (Compas et al., 1998). Adding antidepressant drugs, however, may be useful in alleviating the depression that often occurs with bulimia (Wilson & Fairburn, 1998). Walsh et al. (1997) found that a treatment combining CBT and medication was superior to medication alone. In fact, medication alone was no better than a placebo.

Patients who are successful in overcoming their urge to binge and purge also improve in associated problems such as depression and low self-esteem. This result is not surprising. If a person is able to achieve normal eating patterns after viewing bulimia as an uncontrollable problem, the person can be expected to become less depressed and to feel generally better about himself or herself. One last finding from the empirical CBT literature is that self-help groups that follow a manual based on Fairburn's treatment model and are minimally supervised by a mental health professional can achieve significant benefits (Cooper, Coker, & Fleming, 1994).

Is CBT superior to other psychological interventions for the treatment of bulimia? Based on research so far, the answer is mostly yes (Wilson & Fairburn, 1998). A study that compared the effects of CBT with those of a psychodynamically oriented supportive therapy (Walsh, Wilson et al., 1997) determined that CBT was better at reducing the symptoms of bulimia nervosa.

In several other studies, Weissman and Klerman's Interpersonal Therapy (IPT) fared well in comparisons with CBT, though it may not produce results as quickly (see Wilfley, Stein, & Welch, 2003). The two modes of intervention are equivalent at one-year follow-up in effecting change across all four of the specific aspects of bulimia: binge eating, purging, dietary restraint, and maladaptive attitudes about body shape and weight (Wilson, 1995). (Similar results were achieved by these two treatment approaches in the large outcome study on depression conducted by the National Institute of Mental Health.) It is noteworthy that IPT is effective at all, considering that it does not focus, as CBT does, on maladaptive eating patterns, but focuses instead on improving interpersonal functioning. Such success suggests that, at least for some patients, disordered-eating patterns might be caused by poor interpersonal relationships and associated negative feelings about the self and the world.

Although the outcomes from these two leading psychological treatments, especially the cognitive-behavioural one, appear to be superior to those from other modes of intervention, including drugs, a good deal more remains to be learned about how best to treat bulimia nervosa. Part of the reason at least half of the patients in the controlled studies do not recover may be that significant numbers of the patients in these studies have psychological disorders in addition to eating disorders, such as borderline personality disorder, depression, anxiety, and marital distress (Wilson, 1995). Such patients show less improvement from CBT and from other therapies as well. Gleaves and Eberenz (1994), for example, examined cognitive-behavioural therapy outcomes among 464 women with bulimia in a residential treatment setting and found that those with a history of multiple therapists or hospitalizations, suicide attempts, and sexual abuse derived significantly less benefit from therapy than did those without such backgrounds. The poor therapeutic outcomes could have resulted because such patients simply have more pervasive and more serious psychopathology. Alternatively, the poor prognosis could result from the patients' failure to engage in the therapy, perhaps because of lack of trust in authority figures owing to earlier sexual abuse (therapists are authority figures, and if the patient was abused by a parent, the ensuing distrust and anger may very well be generalized to a therapist).

Given the difficulties associated with the treatment of individuals with eating disorders, serious consideration has to be given to prevention of the disorders before onset. Efforts to prevent eating disorders in Canada and elsewhere are summarized in Canadian Perspectives 9.1.

People seldom seek therapy for only a single problem, and something as serious as an eating disorder is probably bound up with other psychological problems, such as depression. When we consider that depression itself undoubtedly has multiple causes, the lesson to be learned is that controlled outcome studies are limited in what they can tell us about how best to deal with a particular patient in a real-life therapy setting. The complexities that practising clinicians face and try to deal with in individual cases cannot be addressed in comparative outcome studies in which therapists must strive to follow a treatment manual. In a Canadian study, Steiger and Stotland (1996) demonstrated that Axis-II comorbidity is linked to unfavourable outcomes after therapy in bulimic patients. Specifically, bulimics with comorbid borderline personality disorder (see Chapter 13 for a description) relative to non-borderlines showed more initial psychiatric symptoms and retained clinical disturbances at the completion of treatment and at three- and 12-month post-treatment follow-ups. The differences were less dramatic on specific eating symptoms.

Canadian Perspectives/9.1

Prevention of Eating Disorders in Canada

Austin (2000) provided a comprehensive review of past studies designed to prevent the occurrence of eating disorders. According to Austin, 20 published studies have been conducted thus far, including 10 studies in the United States and three in Canada (Moriarty, Shore, & Maxim, 1990; Porter, Morrell, & Moriarty, 1986; Piran, 1999). Overall, the results have been quite disappointing; only four of the 20 studies have shown any sign of positive behavioural changes, and a number of studies have actually reported that attempts at prevention have made the situation even worse!

The Canadian studies that have reported thus far have provided encouraging results, though the studies differ substantially in the approach taken and the scope of the respective projects. The Porter et al. (1986) study consisted of only one session, but improvements in attitudes about weight-related concerns were detected. Improvements have also been noted in terms of knowledge (Moriarty et al., 1990) and actual behaviours (Piran, 1999). One factor that distinguishes the Canadian studies from most other studies is that they have all incorporated participatory techniques, allowing the target audience to take an active role in the process rather than simply be lectured to by a teacher and/or eating-disorder expert.

The Piran (1999) study is regarded as one of the most unique and successful preventive interventions to have taken place. This study is part of an ongoing intervention program at an internationally acclaimed ballet school in Toronto. What makes it relatively unique? According to Piran, it is the first study conducted in a high-risk setting and, in contrast to most other studies, it involves attempts to intervene at the systemic level by changing the school culture. In addition, it involves a long-term focus on the evaluation of outcomes.

Piran (1999) reported results from three time phases involving various cohorts of students- 1987 (i.e., when the study began), 1991, and 1996. Extremely positive results have been obtained thus far. For instance, among students in grades 10 to 12, the proportion of students with abnormal eating attitudes has gone from almost 50 percent in 1987 to approximately 15 percent in 1991 and 1996. There have also been significant, striking reductions in the proportion of students who binged, vomited, or used laxatives.

So, how have these positive outcomes been achieved? First and foremost, as noted above, the prevention program involves a participatory focus as well as attempts to change the school culture. The goal is "to reduce body weight and shape preoccupation through creating a school environment where students feel comfortable with the processes of puberty and growth and believe in their right to feel both safe and positive in their diverse bodies" (Piran 1999, p. 79). Specific interventions include replacing a focus on body shape with a focus on stamina and body conditioning, not permitting teachers to make negative comments about body shape to their students, and having a staff member available to discuss body-shape concerns. The students also meet in groups of their peers up to six times a year to analyze body-shape experiences, including discussions of ways to minimize teasing and mutual evaluations of body shape.

Other research on the prevention of eating disorders is ongoing in Canadian settings. McVey and Davis (2000) have put together a program designed to reduce the impact of media portrayals of unrealistic body images and to promote a non-dieting approach to eating and exercise. This multi-faceted program also includes a focus on stress-management skills and social problem-solving strategies, along with strategies to promote a positive self-image. An additional aspect is parent education on the nature and prevention of eating problems. Initial results have found no specific effects of the program because both the prevention and control groups in this study showed increases in body-image satisfaction and decreases in eating problems over time (McVey & Davis, 2002).

The newest approach to prevention involves forming school-based peer support groups (McVey, Lieberman, Voorberg, Wardrope, & Blackmore, 2003; McVey et al., 2003). Thus far, McVey and colleagues have found mixed evidence for the impact of peer support groups, with one study leading to improvements in grades 7 and 8 girls and another study finding no improvement. Regardless, this multi-faceted approach to prevention recognizes that a multitude of factors can contribute to the development of eating disorders and that a complex prevention program is required to combat this problem.

Information on eating disorders can be obtained from the National Eating Disorder Information Centre (http://www.nedic.ca) located in Toronto.

Thinking Critically

1. What explanations do you have for why some prevention programs appear to have backfired and led to increases in maladaptive eating tendencies? What factors do you think contributed to this negative outcome? How would you avoid or decrease the likelihood of such outcomes?

2. Prevention efforts often take place under the auspices of school boards. Do you think that all school boards should be required to include a focus on the prevention of disorders such as eating disorders and depressive disorders? If you were to set up such a program for eating disorders, what would you emphasize?

3. Governments have taken steps to make sure that there are warning labels on products such as cigarettes because they can be harmful to your health. Do you think there is merit in including warnings about television shows that promote unhealthy body images and/or restricting ads that promote unhealthy body images? Or would this simply draw even more attention to these body images?

Canadian Clinic Focus/9.1

Treatment of Eating Disorders in Canada

Eating-disorders clinics and treatment centres can be found across Canada in major metropolitan areas and sometimes in smaller communities, from St. John's, Newfoundland, in the east (e.g., St. Clare's Mercy Hospital) across the prairies (e.g., Bridge Point Centre for Eating Disorders in Milden, Saskatchewan) to Vancouver Island (e.g., the Cedric Centre in Victoria). While the majority of these treatment facilities are available as part of Canada's universal medicare system, a smaller number are, at least in part, private facilities (e.g., Pickhaven Centre in Calgary, Alberta; Homewood Health Centre in Guelph, Ontario). Some of these facilities have eating-disorders programs, such as the programs at the Toronto Hospital and the Hospital for Sick Children, that are world-renowned for their treatment, research, and training activities. The mandate of such programs is, typically, to provide comprehensive, integrated, and cost-effective treatments within the constraints of the available resources. Further, the focus is often on specialized interventions that are not otherwise readily available in the individual's community. Programs are usually staffed by multidisciplinary teams that include professionals from psychology, psychiatry, social work, occupational therapy, nutrition, and nursing.

St. Paul's Hospital and the British Columbia Children's Hospital in Vancouver both offer hospital-based treatment programs. The two hospitals are affiliated and offer programs tailored to adults (17 years and older) and younger patients. These are the government-designated tertiary provincial resource programs for adults and children with anorexia nervosa, bulimia, and related disorders and their families. We will focus here on the program for children.

B.C. Children's Hospital Eating Disorders Program

MANDATE

The mandate is to "provide leadership and excellence in the areas of clinical services, education and teaching, family-focused child and adolescent health promotion, and research and outreach activities in the area of eating disorders." In the hospital's mission statement, it is stated that there is support for the integration of tertiary care and locally based treatment resources in the community throughout the province of British Columbia. The goal is to provide the "highest possible standard of care."

REFERRALS

Referrals are received from various regions of British Columbia. Following comprehensive evaluations, referring agencies are provided with a report of assessment findings and recommendations.

The results of the assessment and treatment options are discussed with the children and their families.

SERVICES

The cornerstone of the program is multidisciplinary collaboration and includes the following:

- **Intake service**. Patients receive medical, nursing, nutritional, psychiatric/psychological, and family assessments, as well as an eating-disorders diagnostic interview, to determine the most appropriate services.
- **Day treatment**. "Capella" is designed for children and adolescents with a moderate to severe disorder that necessitates intensive treatment. Operating five days per week with space for 10 patients, treatment is primarily group-based and emphasizes patient management rather than inpatient hospital care. Goals include normalization of eating behaviour, weight restoration (when applicable), and psychosocial treatment with a strong family-focused component.
- **Outpatient services**. Includes ongoing medical and dietary assessment as well as psychotherapy (individual and family). Individuals are helped to gain control over eating difficulties and to address self-image and family dynamics problems. Aftercare and relapse prevention are provided for people who have undergone more intensive treatment.
- **Inpatient unit**. This is located on the Adolescent Care Unit, and its goals are medical stabilization and nutritional rehabilitation, support and counselling, and preparation for further treatment within the program or within the community. Patients are helped to regain normal metabolic functioning and to develop healthy eating patterns. When medically able, patients may begin to attend Day Treatment.
- **Residence**. Hudson House is a residential setting that gives accessibility to Capella (the day treatment program) to patients and families throughout British Columbia. Staff provide continuous support and care: meal support, recreational activities, assistance with lifestyle normalization, and recovery promotion.
- **Parent support group**. A support group is open to parents of individuals in any component of the program.
- **Outreach provincial services**. Outreach services include community education, training of staff in local eating-disorders programs, telephone consultation with health care professionals, assistance with the development of local assessment and treatment services, specialized training for trainees from all disciplines, support of research projects and ongoing evaluation of treatment services, and liaison with other organizations (e.g., Provincial Eating Disorders Steering Committee, St. Paul's Hospital Eating Disorders Program).

ANAB Quebec and Sheena's Place

There is usually a long waiting list for admission to programs such as those at the B. C. Children's Hospital, since only a limited number of individuals can participate at a given time. Waiting periods as long as seven or eights months can occur. However, various non-profit, community-based organizations provide support programs. These programs are an excellent "waiting room" for people waiting for admission to the comprehensive hospital-based treatment programs, and they are beneficial to individuals who may not be quite ready to make a commitment to go into treatment. They also provide information and support to families and significant others. Anorexia Nervosa and Bulimia Quebec (ANAB) and Sheena's Place are representative examples of such non-profit organizations. Although these organizations may employ professional personnel, volunteerism is their lifeblood.

ANAB QUEBEC

ANAB Quebec offers professionally run support groups, provides advice and current information to family and friends through its Coping Course, and gives prevention and awareness talks on topics such as body image and nutrition. Part of its mission is to match people "whose lives are touched by an eating disorder" with appropriate resources. In 2002, representatives spoke to over 5,000 students, parents, educators, and community organizers. Follow-up, in-depth discussion groups are also available to schools and include training, handouts, in-group exercises, homework assignments, and topic sheets. The school supplies an interested teacher, parent, administrator, or peer helper.

The support groups (as many as 12 at a time, in both French and English, at essentially free cost) are a cornerstone of ANAB Quebec. Each group is comprised of five to eight participants who meet weekly for a period of six to 10 months. The priority is to provide a "safe place" for members to express their fears and feelings. Topics introduced through in-group exercises and homework assignments include body image, effects of eating disorders, perfectionism, anger, irrational thoughts, and family dynamics. Participants explore the reasons for the development of their eating disorder and are provided with concrete strategies to stop starving, binging, and purging. Each group consults with specific student dieticians from McGill's School of Dietetics and Human Nutrition. Group leaders participate in a comprehensive training program, are provided with a comprehensive guide, and participate in continuing education.

One important feature of ANAB Quebec is its willingness to provide information and training to groups wanting to offer similar services. ANAB Quebec recently published a 350-page development manual (*Through Thick and Thin: A Complete Guide to Running a Support Group for Eating Disorders*) and a companion guide for support group participants.

SHEENA'S PLACE

Sheena's Place, a registered charity, offers "hope and support services ... in a warm, comfortable and safe environment." The services are provided at no cost to people with eating disorders and their families. A poignant story surrounds its formation. Sheena Carpenter died in 1993 as a consequence of her anorexia. Friends and colleagues of her mother were motivated to create a centre in a non-institutional environment in downtown Toronto for people like Sheena. The objective is to work with the existing system, acting "as a conduit between those affected or living with eating disorders and the various systems." Like ANAB Quebec, Sheena's Place has a comprehensive support-group program and a focus on outreach and education. Its 2001 spring program included over 60 groups (e.g., "Mothers and daughters"), ongoing programs (e.g., "Family members, friends and partners support group"), and workshops (e.g., "Fat phobia").

Comment

Clearly, there is widespread interest in the prevention and treatment of eating disorders in Canada as reflected in the number and variety of lay and professional organizations and programs dedicated to these disorders throughout the country. Although the primary focus of most programs has been on the traditional eating disorders, anorexia nervosa and bulimia nervosa, obesity and binge eating disorder are also receiving attention owing to the recognition of the health consequences of obesity, coupled with the increasing prevalence of obesity and the inclusion of binge eating disorder in the DSM-IV as a diagnosis in need of further study. For example, obesity is treated in a group setting in the Eating Disorders and Obesity Treatment Program at Montreal General Hospital. The two-year program is based primarily on cognitive-behavioural therapy. A 10-week CBT group program also focuses on compulsive eating. We expect to see the development of many more such programs in the future given that about 50 percent of Canadians are obese or overweight and that the cost of treating the resulting diseases (e.g., diabetes, heart disease, respiratory problems, gallstones, osteoarthritis, cancer) is estimated to be as high as $15 billion per year (Nichols, 1999). According to Dr. David Lau, the head of Obesity Canada (Talaga, 2001), adult-onset diabetes, which typically has its onset in white North Americans in their 50s, is appearing now in First Nations teenagers. The cause is assumed to be obesity, physical inactivity, and poverty.

Although research and evaluation is a very important aspect of the mission of most eating disorders treatment programs, there are too few published evaluations of the efficacy or effectiveness of programs. Nonetheless, such reports do exist. For example, research conducted as part of the Eating Disorders Programs at the Toronto Hospital has demonstrated that seven additional sessions of group psychotherapy did not provide additional benefit to bulimia nervosa outpatients over and above that achieved through five sessions of group psychoeducation (Davis, Olmsted, Rockert, Marques, & Dolhanty, 1997). Similarly, research at the Hospital for Sick Children compared the effects of four months of two family-oriented treatments, family therapy and family psychoeducation, on female adolescents who required hospitalization for anorexia nervosa (Geist, Heinmaa, Stephens, Davis, & Katzman, 2000). Although weight restoration was achieved following the four months of treatment in both groups, there were no significant changes in self-reported psychological functioning by either the patients or their parents. However, participants in both groups admitted to more family psychopathology, as assessed by the Family Assessment Measure (see Chapter 4), at the end of treatment. Further, there were no significant group differences on any of the self-report measures of eating-disorder pathology, leading Geist et al. (2000, p. 178) to conclude that family group psychoeducation "appears to be a cost-effective, clinically useful method of involving the parents as treatment allies to support weight gain during the first months of treatment for severely ill anorexic patients." Although controlled outcome and long-term follow-up studies are difficult to conduct in real-life settings, careful records of results should be kept for purposes of accountability and program improvement .

What constitutes success in these programs? In the case of anorexia, weight gain and avoidance of medical complications that can lead to death are obvious immediate goals. Long-term maintenance of normal eating patterns and weight gain is also desirable.

Centres in Canada are starting to employ graduated approaches to the treatment of eating disorders consistent with the current interest in empirically guided stepped-care models (e.g., Wilson, Vitousek, & Loeb, 2000). The basis for such models is research on predictors of response to treatment and of the most effective but least costly interventions. In such a flexible intervention system, people with eating disorders who are identified as relatively likely to benefit from a minimal approach, such as outpatient brief psychoeducational groups, would be assigned to such approaches. People judged to require and benefit from more intensive and expensive interventions, such as family, cognitive-behavioural, or behavioural interventions, typically conducted in day treatment or inpatient settings, would be assigned to the more intensive, expensive interventions.

The treatment of eating disorders can raise certain ethical and legal issues. For example, should people with anorexia nervosa be force-fed? The Montreux Clinic, a controversial private clinic for eating disorders situated in Victoria, B.C., was forced to close down in 2000. We will discuss some of the issues related to this closing in Chapter 18 in the context of our discussions about legal and ethical issues.

Clinic Sources: ANAB Quebec website: http://www.anebque.ca; British Columbia Children's Hospital website: http://www.cw.bc.ca.org.ca; Sheena's Place website: http://www.sheenasplace.org.ca; St. Paul's Hospital Eating Disorders Program website: http://www.eating disorders-sph.org.ca; e-mail and telephone contacts (all information effective January-February, 2001).

Canadian singer Anne Murray has been a source of inspiration to children and families fighting eating disorders because she shared with the public the story of her daughter, Dawn Langstroth, who has struggled with anorexia nervosa. Anne Murray is honorary director of Sheena's Place.

SUMMARY

- The two main eating disorders are anorexia nervosa and bulimia nervosa. The symptoms of anorexia nervosa include refusal to maintain normal body weight, an intense fear of being fat, a distorted sense of body shape, and, in women, amenorrhea. Anorexia typically begins in the mid-teens, is 10 times more frequent in women than in men, and is comorbid with several other disorders, notably depression. Its course is not favourable, and it can be life threatening. The symptoms of bulimia nervosa include episodes of binge eating followed by purging, fear of being fat, and a distorted body image. Like anorexia, bulimia begins in adolescence, is much more frequent in women than in men, and is comorbid with other diagnoses, such as depression. Prognosis is somewhat more favourable than for anorexia.
- Biological research in the eating disorders has examined both genetics and brain mechanisms. Evidence is consistent with a possible genetic diathesis, but adoption studies have not yet been done. Endogenous opioids and serotonin, both of which play a role in mediating hunger and satiety, have been examined in eating disorders. Low levels of both these brain chemicals have been found in such patients (see Steiger et al., 2001).
- On a psychological level, several factors play important roles. As cultural standards changed to favour a thinner shape as the ideal for women, the frequency of eating disorders increased. The prevalence of eating disorders is higher in industrialized countries, where the cultural pressure to be thin is strongest. The prevalence of eating disorders is very high among people who are especially concerned with their weight, such as models, dancers, and athletes.
- Psychodynamic theories of eating disorders emphasize parent-child relationships and personality characteristics. Bruch's theory, for example, proposes that the parents of children who later develop eating disorders impose their wishes on their children without considering the children's needs. Children reared in this way do not learn to identify their own internal states and become highly dependent on standards imposed by others. Research on characteristics of families with an eating-disordered child have yielded different data depending on how the data were collected. Reports of patients show high levels of conflict, but actual observations of the families do not find them especially deviant. Studies of personality have found that patients with eating disorders are high in neuroticism and perfectionism and low in self-esteem.
- Cognitive-behavioural theories of eating disorders propose that fear of being fat and body-image distortion make weight loss a powerful reinforcer. Among patients with bulimia nervosa, negative mood and stress precipitate binges that create anxiety, which is then relieved by purging.
- The main biological treatment of eating disorders is the use of antidepressants. Although drugs are somewhat effective, drop-out rates from drug-treatment programs are high and relapse is common when patients stop taking the medication. Treatment of anorexia often requires hospitalization to reduce the medical complications of the disorder. Providing reinforcers for weight gain, such as visits from friends, has been somewhat successful, but no treatment has yet been shown to produce long-term maintenance of weight gain.
- Cognitive-behavioural treatment for bulimia focuses on questioning society's standards for physical attractiveness, challenging beliefs that encourage severe food restriction, and developing normal eating patterns. Outcomes are promising, at least in the short term.

KEY TERMS

activity anorexia (p. 264)
amenorrhea (p. 257)
anorexia nervosa (p. 256)
binge eating disorder (p. 261)
bulimia nervosa (p. 259)
false hope syndrome (p. 266)
lateral hypothalamus (p. 262)
Scarlett O'Hara effect (p. 263)

Reflections: Past, Present, and Future

- What are the theoretical and practical implications of the changes in the clinical profile of anorexia nervosa in Canadian women as described by Kruger et al. (1998)?
- Bulimia nervosa and depression are often associated with each other. Do you think that bulimia nervosa plays a causal role in the development of depression, or that depression contributes to the development of bulimia, or is each of the disorders caused by common third variables? What biological, personality, family, or sociocultural factors might lead to the development of both bulimia nervosa and depression?
- If you had a friend, loved one, or significant other with an eating disorder how would you want that person to be treated? Assume that members of the individual's family

would be included in the treatment program. Would you recommend cognitive or cognitive-behavioural therapy, behaviour therapy (no cognitive elements), interpersonal therapy, family therapy, or antidepressant medication such as Prozac? Defend the reasons for your choice.

- Assume that you were able to design and implement the "perfect" multi-faceted intervention program for a specific eating disorder. What would it look like? What elements would you include? Would the program differ from one person to another even though they might receive the same DSM-IV diagnosis (review our discussions about assessment strategies in Chapter 4)? How would you deal with comorbid conditions or associated problems, including mood disorders (see the next chapter), anxiety disorders (refer back to Chapter 6), substance-related disorders (Chapter 12), personality disorders (Chapter 13), and even sexual problems (Chapter 14)?
- Binge eating disorder was included in DSM-IV as a diagnosis "in need of further study." Although it did not reach the threshold for inclusion in 1994, based on your evaluation of the available research, do you think it should be included as a separate diagnostic category in DSM-V?

chapter 10

Mood Disorders

"What other dungeon is so dark as one's own heart! What jailer so inexorable as oneself!"
—Nathaniel Hawthorne, *The House of the Seven Gables*

"I want to ask you gentlemen, if I cannot give consent to my own death, then whose body is this? Who owns my life?"
—Sue Rodriguez, victim of ALS (amyotrophic lateral sclerosis, Lou Gehrig's disease, a terminal illness), appearing in a videotaped presentation to a Government of Canada House of Commons' subcommittee in November 1992, in which she urged amendments to the section of the Criminal Code that makes it a crime for any person to assist another's suicide

"I certainly did try my very best to kill myself and from what they have told me I nearly succeeded. They gave me up for hopeless three or four times."
—A. Roy Brown, Canadian ace fighter pilot in World War I who downed the Red Baron and went into a severe depression, from the letter he addressed to his father, August 1, 1918

Marian Dale Scott, *Passengers*, c. 1940
oil on canvas, 63.6 x 38.5 cm, ART GALLERY OF ONTARIO, TORONTO
Gift from the J.S. McLean Collection by Canada Packers Inc., 1990

JOHN BENTLEY MAYS has suffered from chronic depression for many years and has received psychotherapy for over 30 years. Mays had a brief period as a professor at York University before working for many years as an art critic for the *Globe and Mail* newspaper. More recently, he worked for the *National Post*. Mays described his experiences with severe depression in his book *In the Jaws of the Black Dogs: A Memoir of Depression* (Mays, 1996). The "black dog" is the well-known metaphor for depression that was used by Sir Winston Churchill in describing his years of suffering and being hounded by "the black dog of depression."

In various segments of his book, Mays (1996) provides poignant accounts of what it feels like to experience severe depression:

> I complained of a decline in vital energy; a weakened ability to enjoy the fulfilment of needs or of aesthetic desire. Even the most reasonable goals had become difficult or impossible to set, and, when established, impossible to fulfil ...I complained of sleep troubles, eating troubles. I found myself avoiding all but the most urgently necessary contact with other people. The ill feeling that, for some depressives, does not get much worse than a generalized unhappiness would in my case often degenerate into overwhelming self-loathing, climaxing in sudden, surprising relief, or thoughts of suicide (Mays, 1996, p. 64).

Mays achieved some relief when prescribed the drug Prozac, but his severe depression returned. In the final chapter of his book, Mays concludes that "[d]epression has always been for me, and remains, a self-punishing language, a prolonged sensation of filthiness and worthlessness, of embarrassment at being alive; a sickening deadness I enviously compare to the liveliness other people seem to enjoy" (p. 216).

In this chapter we discuss the mood disorders. We begin by describing the DSM categories of depression, bipolar disorder, and chronic mood disorders. We then present research on biological and psychological factors relevant to these disorders and discuss their treatment. In the final section we examine suicide.

GENERAL CHARACTERISTICS OF MOOD DISORDERS

Mood disorders involve disabling disturbances in emotion, from the sadness of depression to the elation and irritability of mania.

DEPRESSION—SIGNS AND SYMPTOMS

As illustrated by the case of John Bentley Mays, depression is an emotional state marked by great sadness and feelings of worthlessness and guilt. Additional symptoms include withdrawal from others and loss of sleep, appetite, sexual desire, and interest and pleasure in usual activities. Just as most of us experience occasional anxiety, so, too, do we experience sadness during the course of our lives, although perhaps not to a degree or with a frequency that warrants the diagnosis of depression. Depression is often associated with other psychological problems, such as panic attacks, substance abuse, sexual dysfunction, and personality disorders.

Paying attention is exhausting for people who are depressed. They cannot take in what they read and what other people say to them. Conversation is also a chore; depressed individuals may speak slowly, after long pauses, using few words and a low, monotonous voice. Many prefer to sit alone and remain silent. Others are agitated and cannot sit still. They pace, wring their hands, continually sigh and moan, or complain. When depressed individuals are confronted with a problem, no ideas for its solution occur to them. Every moment has a great heaviness, and their heads fill and reverberate with self-recriminations. Depressed people may neglect personal hygiene and appearance and make numerous complaints of somatic symptoms with no apparent physical basis (Simon et al., 1999). Utterly dejected and completely without hope and initiative, they may be apprehensive, anxious, and despondent much of the time.

The symptoms and signs of depression vary somewhat across the lifespan. Depression in children often results in somatic complaints, such as headaches or stomach aches. In older adults, depression is often characterized by distractibility and complaints of memory loss (see Chapter 16). Symptoms of depression exhibit some cross-cultural variation, probably resulting from differences in cultural standards of acceptable behaviour. A recent review of depression in Chinese people led to the conclusion that depression is substantially less prevalent in China than in North America, and this is due in part to cultural mores that make it less appropriate for Chinese people to display emotional symptoms (Parker, Gladstone, & Chee, 2001). It is commonly believed that people from non-Western cultures (such as the Chinese) emphasize somatic symptoms of depression, while people from Western cultures emphasize emotional symptoms of depression. This tendency does exist but it is a matter of degree. Studies by Montreal researcher Lawrence Kirmayer suggested that people from various cultures, including Canadians, tend to emphasize somatic symptoms of depression rather than the emotional symptoms, especially when they are being evaluated in a medical setting (for a summary, see Kirmayer, 2001). Overall, only 15 percent of depressed primary care patients in Canada are what Kirmayer refers to as "psychologizers" (i.e., people who emphasize the psychological aspects of depression). More "psychologizers" are likely to be found in Canada than in a nation such as China, but most people in most cultures tend to emphasize physical symptoms.

Fortunately, most depression, although recurrent, tends to dissipate with time. But an average untreated episode may stretch on for three to five months or even longer and may seem to be of even greater duration to patients and their families. Also, about one-third of depressed people suffer from chronic depression. And as we discuss later, suicide is a risk. In cases where depression becomes chronic, the patient does not completely snap back to an earlier level of functioning between bouts.

Mania—Signs and Symptoms

Mania is an emotional state or mood of intense but unfounded elation accompanied by irritability, hyperactivity, talkativeness, flight of ideas, distractibility, and impractical, grandiose plans. Some people who experience episodic periods of depression may at times suddenly become manic. Although there are clinical reports of individuals who experience mania but not depression, this condition is quite rare.

The person in the throes of a manic episode, which may last from several days to several months, is readily recognized by his or her loud and incessant stream of remarks, sometimes full of puns, jokes, rhyming, and interjections about objects and happenings that have attracted the speaker's attention. This speech is difficult to interrupt and reveals the manic patient's so-called flight of ideas. Although small bits of talk are coherent, the individual shifts rapidly from topic to topic. The patient's need for activity may cause the person to be annoyingly sociable and intrusive, constantly and sometimes purposelessly busy, and, unfortunately, oblivious to the obvious pitfalls of his or her endeavours. Any attempt to curb this momentum can bring quick anger and even rage. Mania usually comes on suddenly over a period of a day or two.

The following description of a case of mania is from our files. The irritability that is often part of this state was not evident in this patient.

Mr. W., a 32-year-old postal worker, had been married for eight years. In retrospect, there appeared to be no warning of what was to happen. One morning, Mr. W. told his wife that he was bursting with energy and ideas, that his job as a mail carrier was unfulfilling, and that he was just wasting his talent. That night he slept little, spending most of the time at a desk, writing furiously. The next morning, he left for work at the usual time but returned home at 11:00 a.m., his car filled to overflowing with aquariums and other equipment for tropical fish. He had quit his job, then withdrawn all the money from the family's savings account and spent it on tropical fish equipment. Mr. W. reported that the previous night he had worked out a way to modify existing equipment so that fish "won't die anymore. We'll be millionaires." After unloading the paraphernalia, Mr. W. set off to canvass the neighbourhood for possible buyers, going door-to-door and talking to anyone who would listen.

The following bit of conversation from the period after Mr. W. entered treatment indicates his incorrigible optimism and provocativeness.

Therapist: Well, you seem pretty happy today.

Client: Happy! Happy! You certainly are a master of understatement, you rogue! [*Shouting, literally jumping out of his seat.*] Why I'm ecstatic. I'm leaving for the West Coast today, on my daughter's bicycle. Only 3,100 miles. That's nothing, you know. I could probably walk, but I want to get there by next week. And along the way I plan to contact a lot of people about investing in my fish equipment. I'll get to know more people that way—you know, Doc, "know" in the biblical sense [*leering at the therapist seductively*]. Oh, God, how good it feels. It's almost like a nonstop orgasm.

Formal Diagnostic Listings of Mood Disorders

Two major mood disorders are listed in DSM-IV-TR, major depression, also referred to as unipolar depression, and bipolar disorder.

Diagnosis of Depression The formal DSM-IV-TR diagnosis of a major depression, also referred to as unipolar depression, requires the presence of five of the following symptoms for at least two weeks. Either depressed mood or loss of interest and pleasure must be one of the five symptoms:

- sad, depressed mood, most of the day, nearly every day
- loss of interest and pleasure in usual activities
- difficulties in sleeping (insomnia); not falling asleep initially, not returning to sleep after awakening in the middle of the night, and early morning awakenings; or, in some patients, a desire to sleep a great deal of the time
- shift in activity level, becoming either lethargic (psychomotor retardation) or agitated
- poor appetite and weight loss, or increased appetite and weight gain
- loss of energy, great fatigue
- negative self-concept; self-reproach and self-blame; feelings of worthlessness and guilt
- complaints or evidence of difficulty in concentrating, such as slowed thinking and indecisiveness
- recurrent thoughts of death or suicide

Canadian actress Margot Kidder has experienced episodes of both mania and depression and therefore would be regarded as having had bipolar disorder.

There is no question that these are the major symptoms of depression. What is controversial, though, is whether a patient with five symptoms and a two-week duration is distinctly different from one who has only three symptoms for 10 days. In an evaluation of this issue with a sample of twins, the number of symptoms and the duration of depression were used to predict the likelihood of future episodes and the probability that a co-twin would also be diagnosed as depressed. Even with fewer than five symptoms and a duration of less than two weeks, co-twins were also likely to be diagnosed with depression and patients were likely to have recurrences (Kendler & Gardner, 1998). Other research suggests that depression exists on a continuum of severity (Flett, Vredenburg, & Krames, 1997). The DSM diagnostic criteria identify patients at a relatively severe end of the continuum.

Major depression is one of the most prevalent of the disorders described in this book. Lifetime prevalence rates have ranged from 5.2 percent to 17.1 percent in two large-scale American studies (Kessler et al., 1994; Weissman et al., 1996). This large discrepancy reflects differences between the studies in diagnostic criteria used, in the amount of training of the interviewers, and in the use of interviews for collecting symptom information.

The one-year prevalence of depression in Canada tends to vary between 4 and 6 percent (see Patten et al., 2003), but some studies have found much higher prevalence rates. Patten (2000) found a prevalence of 11 percent in a community study conducted via telephone in Calgary. A follow-up study found a prevalence of 10.6 percent in rural areas and 17.1 percent in urban areas, leading the authors to suggest that people seeking treatment had migrated to urban areas (Patten et al., 2003). Previously, a prevalence of 10.3 percent was found in a Toronto community study (DeMarco, 2000). In contrast, the *Mental Health Supplement* of the Ontario Health Survey found a prevalence rate of 4.1 percent (Offord et al., 1996). Patten (2000) noted that the variability in results should be attributed, in part, to differences in the measures and methods used to make diagnoses. Recent results from the Canadian Community Health Survey found that 4.5 percent of Canadians reported experiencing symptoms of major depression (Statistics Canada, 2003). This prevalence information was derived from a sample of 37,000 people who were surveyed in 2002. The survey found that rates of depression in Canadians are comparable to the rates of chronic medical conditions such as heart disease, diabetes, and thyroid problems.

As seen in our earlier discussion of people from China, prevalence of depression can also vary across cultures. In a major cross-cultural study that used the same diagnostic criteria and structured interview in each country, including Canada, prevalence varied from a low of 1.5 percent in Taiwan to a high of 19 percent in Beirut, Lebanon (Weissman et al., 1996). The estimated prevalence in Edmonton was 4.6 percent, well within the 4 to 6 percent range cited above. The reasons for these large differences are not understood, though the political upheavals in Beirut may help account for the high prevalence there.

Regardless of these differences in overall prevalence, depression is at least two times more common in women than in men, in Canada and elsewhere (see Focus on Discovery 10.1). A consistent finding across many studies is that current and lifetime prevalence rates of depression are higher among younger than older persons (see Murphy et al., 2000). Moreover, depression occurs more frequently among members of the lower socioeconomic classes.

focus on discovery/10.1

Depression in Females Versus Males: Why Is There a Gender Difference?

"She sat by the window, looking inward rather than looking out. Her thoughts were consumed with her sadness. She viewed her life as a broken one, and yet she could not place her finger on the exact moment it fell apart. 'How did I get to feel this way?' she repeatedly asked herself. By asking, she hoped to transcend her depressed state; through understanding, she hoped to repair it. Instead her questions led her deeper and deeper inside herself—further away from the path that would lead to her recovery."

—Reported by Treynor, Gonzalez, and Nolen-Hoeksema, *Rumination Reconsidered* (2003)

Depression occurs about twice as often in women as in men. Research involving patients in treatment as well as surveys of community residents consistently yield a female-male ratio of almost 2 to 1 (e.g., Patten, 2001). For example, Offord et al. (1996) examined Ontario data and reported a one-year prevalence rate for people aged 15 to 64 of 3 percent for males and 6 percent for females. The highest rate was in young women aged 15 to 24 (7 percent). The gender difference does not appear in pre-adolescent children, but it emerges consistently by mid-adolescence (Hankin et al., 1998). Analyses of data from the 1994-1996 Canadian National Health Population Survey show that the gender gap emerges at age 14 and seems to be maintained across the lifespan (Cairney & Wade, 2002; Wade, Cairney, & Pevalin, 2002). Clues to the etiology of depression may come from understanding the cause and timing of this gender difference.

Nolen-Hoeksema and Girgus (1994) concluded that girls are more likely than boys to have certain risk factors for depression even before adolescence, but it is only when these risk factors interact with the challenges of adolescence that the gender differences in depression emerge. Nolen-Hoeksema and her associates have focused on gender differences in ruminative coping versus distraction when feelings of depression are experienced. Females are more likely than males to engage in ruminative coping. They focus their attention on their depressive symptoms (e.g., saying things to themselves such as "What does it mean that I feel this way?"). In contrast, males are more likely to rely on distraction, on doing something that diverts their attention (e.g., engaging in physical activity, watching television). An 18-month longitudinal study confirmed that the ruminative-coping style predicts the onset of episodes of depression and is associated with more severe depressive symptoms (Just & Alloy, 1997). A study by Nolen-Hoeksema, Larson, and Gray (1999) showed that rumination was more common in women and was key to the gender difference in depressive symptoms. More recently, Nolen-Hoeksema and her colleagues (Treynor, Gonzalez, & Nolen-Hoeksema, 2003) suggested important refinements of the theory, including the need to differentiate between a reflective pondering component of rumination and a component referred to as brooding (or moody pondering). They concluded that the relationship between gender and depression could be due to the brooding component of rumination (e.g., "What am I doing to deserve this?").

Another possible explanation for the gender difference is that females and males differ in the stressors they experience. A stress-process model has been used to account for the tendency of single mothers to have higher levels of depression than married mothers. In their analysis of the 1994 National Population Health Survey, Cairney, Thorpe, Rietschlin, and Avison (1999) reported that married mothers had a depression prevalence rate of 6.8 percent, while single mothers with a child under 5 years old had a rate of 17.3 percent.

A related explanation is that females are more likely than males to be exposed to various forms of victimization, including childhood sexual abuse. A Canadian study provided clear evidence that a history of abuse is a risk factor for depression (Levitan et al., 1998). Another study conducted at Women's College Hospital in Toronto found that 52 percent of women receiving inpatient treatment for depression had been sexually victimized in childhood and adulthood (Sahay, Piran, & Maddocks, 2000). This study showed that greater levels of sexual violation were associated with lower levels of self-esteem and an external locus of control (powerlessness).

Canadian singers Alanis Morissette and Sarah McLachlan have both acknowledged bouts of depression.

But are females more likely than males to be targets of abuse and can this help explain the gender difference? Valerie Whiffen and Sharon Clark (1997) from the University of Ottawa compared levels of depression and victimization histories in 91 men and 76 women seeking outpatient psychotherapy. Women had substantially higher levels of depression and were much more likely to have a history of childhood sexual abuse. Moreover, the women also reported higher levels of victimization as an adult. Of course, this is not to say that victimized men will not experience depression, but depression is apparently more common among women and perhaps it is exacerbated by related differences in rumination.

Finally, explanations provided by feminist scholars may help account for the gender difference in depression. Janet Stoppard from the University of New Brunswick has criticized mainstream theories of the development of depression, including cognitive theories, for not focusing attention on why gender differences exist (see 1999, 2000). She argues that depression must be interpreted within the broad sociocultural context and the societal conditions that influence the everyday lives of women, including stressors more germane to women and feelings of disempowerment. Stoppard's views are consistent with the position that single mothers may experience depression because of the psychosocial stressors and societal circumstances they experience.

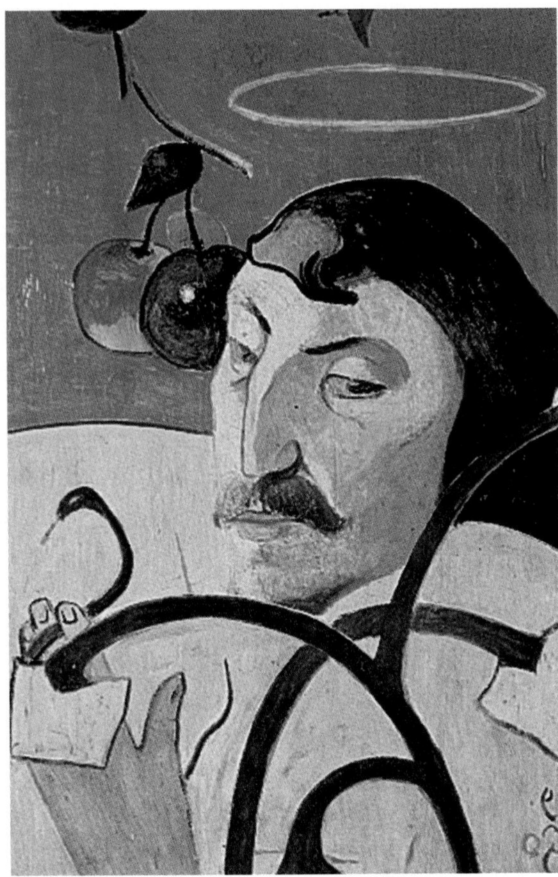

Self-portrait by Paul Gauguin. He is but one of the many artists and writers who apparently suffered from a mood disorder.

Depression tends to be a recurrent disorder. About 80 percent of those with depression experience another episode, and the average number of episodes, which typically last for three to five months, is about four (Judd, 1997). In about 12 percent of cases, depression becomes a chronic disorder that lasts more than two years. Even among those who improve sufficiently to be no longer diagnosable, subclinical depression can remain for years (Judd et al., 1998).

Diagnosis of Bipolar Disorder DSM-IV-TR defines bipolar I disorder as involving episodes of mania or mixed episodes that include symptoms of both mania and depression. Most individuals with bipolar I disorder also experience episodes of depression. A formal diagnosis of a manic episode requires the presence of elevated or irritable mood plus three additional symptoms (four if the mood is irritable). Notably, some clinicians do not regard euphoria as a core symptom of mania and report that irritable mood and even depressive features are more common (e.g., Goodwin & Jamison, 1990). The symptoms, listed here, must be sufficiently severe to impair social and occupational functioning:

- increase in activity level at work, socially, or sexually
- unusual talkativeness; rapid speech
- flight of ideas or subjective impression that thoughts are racing
- less than the usual amount of sleep needed
- inflated self-esteem; belief that one has special talents, powers, and abilities
- distractibility; attention easily diverted
- excessive involvement in pleasurable activities that are likely to have undesirable consequences, such as reckless spending

Bipolar disorder occurs less often than major depression, with a lifetime prevalence rate of about 1 percent of the population (Myers et al., 1984). The average age of onset is in the twenties, and it occurs equally often in men and women. Among women, episodes of depression are more common and episodes of mania less common than among men (Leibenluft, 1996). Like major depression, bipolar disorder tends to recur; over 50 percent of cases have four or more episodes (Goodwin & Jamison, 1990). The severity of the disorder is indicated by the fact that at 12 months after release from hospital, 76 percent of patients are rated as impaired and 52 percent are sufficiently symptomatic that the original diagnosis is still applicable (Keck et al., 1998).

Heterogeneity within the Categories

A problem in the classification of mood disorders is their great heterogeneity—that is, people with the same diagnosis can vary greatly from one another. Some bipolar patients, for example, experience the full range of symptoms of both mania and depression almost every day, termed a *mixed episode*. Other patients have symptoms of only mania or only depression during a clinical episode. So-called bipolar II disorder patients have episodes of major depression accompanied by hypomania (*hypo* comes from the Greek for "under"), a

Mood disorders are common among artists and writers. Van Gogh, Tchaikovsky (shown here), and Whitman were all affected.

change in behaviour and mood that is less extreme than full-blown mania.

Some depressed patients may be diagnosed as having psychotic features if they are subject to delusions and hallucinations. The presence of delusions appears to be a useful distinction among people with unipolar depression (Johnson, Horvath, & Weissman, 1991); depressed patients with delusions do not generally respond well to the usual drug therapies for depression, but they do respond favourably to these drugs when they are combined with the drugs commonly used to treat other psychotic disorders, such as schizophrenia. Furthermore, depression with psychotic features is more severe than depression without delusions and involves more social impairment and less time between episodes (Coryell et al., 1996).

According to DSM-IV-TR, some patients with depression may have melancholic features. In the DSM, the term *melancholic* refers to a specific pattern of depressive symptoms. Patients with melancholic features find no pleasure in any activity and are unable to feel better even temporarily when something good happens. Their depressed mood is worse in the morning. They awaken about two hours too early, lose appetite and weight, and are either lethargic or extremely agitated. These individuals had no personality disturbance prior to their first episode of depression and respond well to biological therapies.

Studies of the validity of the distinction between depressions with or without melancholic features have yielded mixed results. However, one study found that patients with melancholic features had more comorbidity (e.g., with anxiety disorders), more frequent episodes, and more impairment, suggesting it may be a more severe type of depression (Kendler, 1997).

Both manic and depressive episodes may be characterized as having catatonic features, such as motor immobility or excessive, purposeless activity. Both manic and depressive episodes may also occur within four weeks of childbirth; in this case, they are noted to have a postpartum onset. Postpartum depression research in Canada is summarized in Canadian Perspectives 10.1.

Canadian Perspectives/10.1

Postpartum Depression in Canadian Women

Many people find it difficult to understand the phenomenon of postpartum depression (PD). How is it possible that some mothers experience profound depression even though they may be delighted by their "new arrival"? Even more difficult to understand are extreme cases such as that of Suzanne Killinger-Johnson, a physician and psychotherapist who apparently suffered from postpartum depression. In August 2000 she took her own and her infant son's life by committing suicide at a Toronto subway station.

Canadian researchers have conducted several studies in an attempt to uncover the nature of PD. In a broad investigation, researchers at the University of Western Ontario (Gotlib, Whiffen, Mount, Milne, & Cordy, 1989) assessed 360 women during their pregnancies and after having given birth. Depression was assessed on the basis of self-report measures and clinical interviews. They found that 10 percent of the women were depressed during pregnancy and 6.8 percent had postpartum depression. Of those women who had PD, half had been depressed during the pregnancy and the postpartum depression was a continuation, while the other half experienced depression only after giving birth.

These same researchers also investigated factors associated with the onset of PD and recovery from PD (Gotlib, Whiffen, Wallace, & Mount, 1991). Onset was predicted by levels of depression in the pregnancy period as well as by a reported lack of warmth and care from one's own parents while growing up (Gotlib, Whiffen, Wallace, & Mount, 1991). These findings are in keeping with past indications of a high correlation between depression during the pregnancy and postpartum periods. Indeed, it is believed that the best predictor of PD is whether the mother-to-be was depressed prior to giving birth.

Several studies of postpartum depression have been conducted in Quebec. One study evaluated 213 pregnant women during the second trimester of pregnancy and six months postpartum (Bernazzi, Saucier, David, & Borgeat, 1997). They found that postpartum depression was predicted by several variables, among them depression during pregnancy, negative life events, and lower socioeconomic status. Lower socioeconomic status was also associated with postpartum depression in a telephone survey of child-bearing women (Zelkowitz & Milet, 1995). The link between stress and postpartum depression has also been confirmed by Seguin, Potvin, St.-Denis, and Loiselle (1999). They reported that chronic postnatal stressors and low perceived social support were associated with postpartum depression, even after taking depressive symptoms during pregnancy and lower socioeconomic factors into account. Regarding social support, a recent study in British Columbia found that telephone-based peer support decreased levels of postpartum depression and new mothers were highly satisfied with this form of support (Dennis, 2003).

One stressor of significance in postpartum depression is having an infant with a difficult, irritable temperament (Whiffen & Gotlib, 1989). Given the link between stressors and postpartum depression, how a woman copes with motherhood becomes quite important. A Canadian study showed that an emotion-oriented coping style is linked with postpartum depression (Da Costa, et al., 2000). Research conducted elsewhere also suggests that an emotion-oriented form of wishful thinking and a lack of problem-focused coping contribute to postpartum depression (Terry, Mayocchi, & Hynes, 1996).

The stress of natural disasters may also play a role. New research shows that pregnant mothers with high levels of stress during the 1998 Quebec Ice Storm delivered children with lower cognitive ability when assessed at the age of 2 with the Bayley Mental Developmental Index (LaPlante et al., in press). Evaluation of the "Ice Storm" babies showed that higher prenatal stress in the mother-to-be predicted poorer cognitive ability; in fact, children exposed to high stress, relative to those with low stress, had IQs that were 20 points lower on average. Higher stress also predicted more behavioural problems and anxiety in children at 4 years of age. Physical differences were also found; the children of mothers with high stress had abnormalities in their fingerprint profiles, suggesting that stress impacted on prenatal development during the crucial 14 to 22 week segment of gestation.

Are the depressions experienced by new mothers different from the depressions experienced by other women? Whiffen and Gotlib (1993) compared the symptom expressions, psychiatric histories, and social adjustments of women with postpartum depression and women with non-postpartum depression. Overall, very few differences were found. Whiffen (1992), now at the University of Ottawa, reviewed existing findings and concluded that postpartum depression is not qualitatively different from other depressions. Moreover, postpartum depressive episodes tend to be relatively mild and are quickly resolved for most women. Whiffen suggested that PDs are best conceptualized as adjustment disorders that are experienced as a result of the stressors associated with giving birth. The diagnosis "adjustment disorder" is used to indicate bouts of depression or anxiety that stem from stressful life events. According to diagnostic criteria, if someone is depressed due to a life event, then they would receive a diagnosis of adjustment disorder and not major depressive disorder.

Finally, what about fathers? Montreal researchers Zelkowitz and Milet (1996, 1997) compared the characteristics of fathers who have a spouse with PD with the characteristics of those without a depressed spouse. They found that fathers married to women with PD report greater levels of dissatisfaction with marital and family changes and greater stress, especially in terms of work and economic pressures. Follow-up research indicates that psychiatric disturbance is just as persistent over time for mothers and fathers, with approximately three-fifths of mothers and fathers having a disorder at six months postpartum (Zelkowitz & Milet, 2001). These findings underscore the need to adopt a family focus that includes fathers when seeking to help sufferers of postpartum depression.

Thinking Critically

1. The evidence suggests that postpartum depression is linked most strongly to the stress in women's lives. But what about the role of hormonal changes? There have been debates and controversy over the issue of whether the so-called ovarian hormones, estrogen and progesterone, play a role in the development of women's depression (e.g., Nolen-Hoeksema, 1995). Is it possible that certain women have a general vulnerability that can be triggered by either the physiological changes or the stressful events of the postpartum period?
2. Prospective parents typically attend prenatal classes prior to the child's birth. Given that both mothers and fathers may experience various stresses and strains prior to and following the birth, is it possible to develop prevention programs in connection with the prenatal classes that would decrease the probability of the development of postpartum depression in mothers? What strategies would you incorporate into such programs? Despite the best possible prevention efforts, some women will still develop depression. Design an intervention to minimize the severity and impact of these depressions. Were fathers included in this intervention?

Finally, DSM-IV-TR states that both bipolar and unipolar disorders can be subdiagnosed as seasonal if there is a regular relationship between an episode and a particular time of the year. Most research has focused on depression in the winter (i.e., winter depression or seasonal affective disorder), and the most prevalent explanation is that it is linked to a decrease in the number of daylight hours. **Seasonal affective disorder (SAD)** was first described in a study of 29 patients by Rosenthal et al. (1984). Rosenthal noted that the patients' symptoms varied in response to changes in climate and latitude in a manner that suggested that reduced exposure to sunlight was causing their depressions. Most of these patients had been diagnosed with bipolar depression.

In Canada, a study of community members interviewed via telephone found that the seasonal subtype of major depression was detected in 11 percent of the people diagnosed with depression in the overall sample (Levitt, Boyle, Joffe, & Baumal, 2000). The prevalence of SAD was 2.9 percent. A more recent study of 111 randomly selected people from an Inuit community in the Canadian Arctic found that one in five people were depressed (Haggarty et al., 2002). Collectively, 18 percent of the population had either SAD or subsyndromal SAD (i.e., milder SAD that does not quite meet DSM criteria), and the authors noted that this is the highest rate of SAD found thus far in research involving DSM-based assessments.

Icelanders go without light for many months in the winter, yet, as a group, they have surprising low levels of SAD. A study of Icelanders who emigrated to the Interlake District in Manitoba found a prevalence rate of only 1.2 percent (Magnusson & Axellson, 1993). The authors of the study speculated that Icelanders might have lower rates because they have adapted genetically to reduced sunlight exposure and are somehow protected from experiencing SAD.

Reduced light does cause decreases in the activity of serotonin neurons of the hypothalamus, and these neurons regulate some behaviours, such as sleep, that are part of the syndrome of SAD (Schwartz et al., 1997). Therapy for these winter depressions involves exposing the patients to bright, white light (Blehar & Rosenthal, 1989; Wirz-Justice et al., 1993). According to the Canadian Consensus Guidelines, exposure to bright, white light (known as **phototherapy**) is a highly effective treatment for SAD (Lam & Levitt, 1999). Lam and his co-workers at the University of British

Columbia have shown that phototherapy does indeed alleviate SAD and associated symptoms of depression, including suicidal tendencies (Lam, 1994; Lam et al., 2000). Recent research indicates that people with SAD and those with subsyndromal SAD have comparable recovery rates, and longer light exposure is associated with better outcomes (Levitt, Lam, & Levitan, 2002).

CHRONIC MOOD DISORDERS

DSM-IV lists two long-lasting, or chronic, disorders in which mood disturbances are predominant. Although the symptoms of these disorders must have been evident for at least two years, they are not severe enough to warrant a diagnosis of a major depressive or manic episode.

In cyclothymic disorder, the person has frequent periods of depressed mood and hypomania. These periods may be mixed with, may alternate with, or may be separated by periods of normal mood lasting as long as two months. People with cyclothymic disorder have paired sets of symptoms in their periods of depression and hypomania. During depression, they feel inadequate; during hypomania, their self-esteem is inflated. They withdraw from people, then seek them out in an uninhibited fashion. They sleep too much and then too little. Depressed cyclothymic patients have trouble concentrating, and their verbal productivity decreases; during hypomania, their thinking becomes sharp and creative and their productivity increases. Patients with cyclothymia may also experience full-blown episodes of mania and depression.

Seasonal depression is one of the subtypes of major depressive disorder. This woman is demonstrating light therapy, an effective treatment for patients whose seasonal depression occurs during the winter.

The person with dysthymic disorder is chronically depressed. Besides feeling blue and losing pleasure in usual activities and pastimes, the person experiences several other signs of depression, such as insomnia or sleeping too much; feelings of inadequacy, ineffectiveness, and lack of energy; pessimism; an inability to concentrate and to think clearly; and a desire to avoid the company of others. Data collected by Klein and his associates (1988) on dysthymia as a form of depression indicate that it causes severe impairment. Many patients with dysthymic disorder have episodes of major depression as well, a condition known as double depression.

PSYCHOLOGICAL THEORIES OF MOOD DISORDERS

Depression has been studied from several perspectives. Here, we discuss psychoanalytic views, which emphasize the unconscious conflicts associated with grief and loss; cognitive theories, which focus on the depressed person's self-defeating thought processes; and interpersonal factors, which emphasize how depressed people interact with others. These theories, for the most part, describe different diatheses in a general diathesis-stress theory that require stressful life events in order to trigger bouts of depression (Brown & Harris, 1978; Kendler, Karkowski, & Prescott, 1999). The theories we discuss address the question, What are the psychological characteristics of people who respond to stress with an episode of mood disorder?

PSYCHOANALYTIC THEORY OF DEPRESSION

In his celebrated paper "Mourning and Melancholia," Freud (1917/1950) theorized that the potential for depression is created early in childhood. During the oral period, a child's needs may be insufficiently or oversufficiently gratified, causing the person to become fixated in this stage and dependent on the instinctual gratifications particular to it. With this arrest in psychosexual maturation, this fixation at the oral stage, the person may develop a tendency to be excessively dependent on other people for the maintenance of self-esteem.

From this happenstance of childhood, how can the adult come to suffer from depression? The complex reasoning is based on an analysis of bereavement. Freud hypothesized that after the loss of a loved one, whether by death or, most commonly for a child, separation or withdrawal of affection, the mourner first introjects, or incorporates, the lost person; he or she identifies with the lost one, perhaps in a fruitless attempt to undo the loss. Because, Freud asserted, we unconsciously harbour negative feelings toward those we love, the mourner then becomes the object of his or her own hate and anger (anger turned inward); in addition, the mourner resents being deserted and feels guilt for real or imagined sins against the lost person.

The period of introjection is followed by a period of mourning work, when the mourner recalls memories of the lost one and thereby separates himself or herself from the person who has died or disappointed him or her and loosens the bonds imposed by introjection. But the grief work can go astray and develop into an ongoing process of self-abuse, self-blame, and depression in overly dependent individuals. These individuals do not loosen their emotional bonds with the lost person; rather, they continue to castigate themselves for the faults and shortcomings perceived in the loved one who has been introjected. The mourner's anger toward the lost one continues to be directed inward.

Some research has been generated by psychoanalytic points of view, but it has been limited and does not give strong support to the theory. Dreams and projective tests should theoretically be means of expressing unconscious needs; however, Beck and Ward (1961) analyzed the dreams of depressed people and found themes of loss and failure, not of anger turned inward. Also, if depression comes from anger turned inward, we would expect depressed people to express little hostility toward others; yet depressed individuals often express intense anger and hostility toward people close to them (Weissman, Klerman, & Paykel, 1971). On the positive side, some depressed people are high in dependency and prone to depression following a rejection (see Canadian Perspectives 10.2).

Cognitive Theories of Depression

Earlier discussions of the role of cognition in anxiety (Chapter 6) and of Ellis's concept of irrational beliefs (Chapter 2 and elsewhere) indicate that cognitive processes play a decisive role in emotional behaviour. In some theories of depression, as in some theories of anxiety, thoughts and beliefs are regarded as major factors in causing or influencing the emotional state.

Because cognitive theories of depression are those pursued most actively in controlled studies, we now discuss two of them in some detail—Beck's schema theory and the helplessness/hopelessness theory.

Beck's Theory of Depression Aaron Beck (1967, 1987) is responsible for the most important contemporary theory that regards thought processes as causative factors in depression. His central thesis is that depressed individuals feel as they do because their thinking is biased toward negative interpretations. Figure 10.1 illustrates the interactions among the three levels of cognitive activity that Beck believes underlie depression. According to Beck, in childhood and adolescence, depressed individuals acquired a negative schema—a tendency to see the world negatively—through loss of a parent, an unrelenting succession of tragedies, the social rejection of peers, the criticisms of teachers, or the depressive attitude of a parent. All of us have schemata of many kinds; by these perceptual sets, we order our lives. The negative schemata acquired by depressed persons are activated whenever they encounter new situations that resemble in some way, perhaps only remotely, the conditions in which the schemata were learned. Moreover, the negative schemata of depressed people fuel and are fuelled by certain cognitive biases that lead these people to misperceive reality. Thus, an ineptness schema can make depressed individuals expect to fail most of the time, a self-blame schema burdens them with responsibility for all misfortunes, and a negative self-evaluation schema constantly reminds them of their worthlessness.

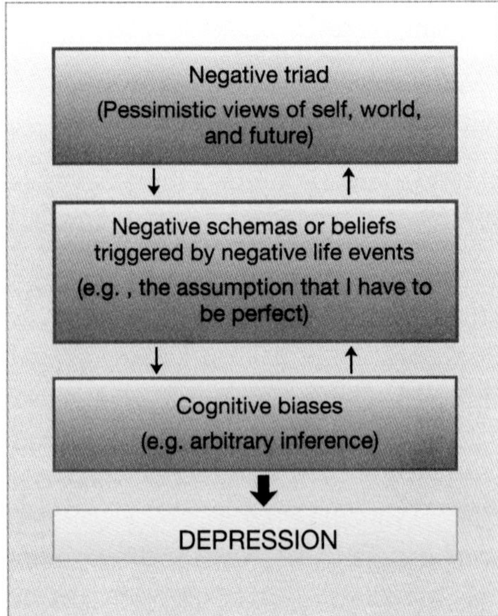

Figure 10.1 The interrelationships among different kinds of cognitions in Beck's theory.

Negative schemata, together with cognitive biases or distortions, maintain what Beck called the negative triad: negative views of the self, the world, and the future. The world part of Beck's depressive triad refers to the person's judgment that he or she cannot cope with the demands of the environment. Rather than having to do with a concern for global events that do not implicate the self directly (e.g., "The world has been going south since the American League adopted the designated hitter rule"), it is highly personal ("I cannot possibly cope with all these demands and responsibilities") (Haaga, Dyck, & Ernst, 1991, p. 218).

Being rejected by peers may lead to the development of the negative schema that Beck's theory suggests plays a key role in depression.

The following list describes some of the principal cognitive biases of depressed individuals according to Beck.

- Arbitrary inference—a conclusion drawn in the absence of sufficient evidence or of any evidence at all. For example, a man concludes that he is worthless because it is raining the day he is hosting an outdoor party.
- Selective abstraction—a conclusion drawn on the basis of only one of many elements in a situation. A worker feels worthless when a product fails to function, even though she is only one of many people who contributed to its production.
- Overgeneralization—an overall sweeping conclusion drawn on the basis of a single, perhaps trivial, event. A student regards her poor performance in a single class on one particular day as final proof of her worthlessness and stupidity.
- Magnification and minimization—exaggerations in evaluating performance. A man, believing that he has completely ruined his car (magnification) when he notices a slight scratch on the rear fender, regards himself as good for nothing; a woman believes herself worthless (minimization) in spite of a succession of praiseworthy achievements.

In Beck's theory, our emotional reactions are a function of how we construe our world. The interpretations of depressed individuals do not mesh well with the way most people view the world, and they become victims of their own illogical self-judgments.

A review by Rector, Segal, and Gemar (1998) noted that much of the depression research conducted in Canada has tested predictions involving Beck's schema notion. Clearly, Beck's theory has served as the impetus for more general research on the link between cognition and depression. The research investigations conducted thus far can be differentiated in terms of whether they have focused on cognitive products (i.e., the stimuli that are recalled), cognitive processes or operations involving the deployment of attention, or cognitive structures in terms of the organization of cognitive schemas. Recently, the emphasis has shifted away from initial research on cognitive products and toward cognitive processes and organization.

Initial Canadian research on cognition and depression was dominated by investigations conducted by Nicholas Kuiper and his associates at the University of Western Ontario (Derry & Kuiper, 1981; Kuiper & MacDonald, 1983; MacDonald & Kuiper, 1984). They used a self-referent encoding task that involved presenting participants with positive and negative word adjectives (e.g., smart, stupid) and asking them to indicate whether the adjectives applied to them by indicating "yes" or "no." Three important dependent measures can be derived from this procedure. First, researchers can compare depressed and non-depressed participants in terms of how many positive versus negative adjectives were seen as self-descriptive. They can also assess response times (i.e., how fast the words are reacted to) of depressed and non-depressed individuals. Finally, researchers can assess incidental recall by waiting a certain time after the rating period and then asking participants to recall as many of the words as possible; this is a measure of cognitive production and retention.

Two key findings emerged from this research. First, depressed individuals, relative to non-depressed individuals, endorse more negative words and fewer positive words as self-descriptive. Second, they exhibit a cognitive bias: they have greater recall of adjectives with depressive content, especially if the adjectives were rated as self-descriptive. Overall, this research tests the notion that the presence or absence of depression reflects differences in the *cognitive availability* of negative versus positive thoughts about the self.

The next wave of research on cognition and depression tested the possibility that the main differences of importance involved *cognitive accessibility* rather than cognitive availability per se. In other words, depressed and non-depressed people do not differ in terms of whether their schemas involve positive or negative content; rather, they differ in terms of cognitive processing. Depressed people pay greater attention to negative stimuli and can more readily access negative as opposed to positive information.

Differences in cognitive processing are assessed via the Stroop task. Participants are provided with a series of words in different colours and are asked to identify the colour of each word and ignore the actual word itself (i.e., if the word "sad" is presented in red ink, the correct answer is red). The Stroop task assesses the latency or length of time it takes to respond.

Gotlib and McCann (1984) examined response patterns when students were asked to colour-name words that varied in their content. Some words were neutral, while other words were depression-oriented (e.g., "bleak") or manic-oriented (i.e., overly euphoric). Non-depressed students did not differ in their response latencies across the word types, but depressed students took longer to colour-name the depression-oriented words, suggesting that these themes were more cognitively accessible for them.

In subsequent research on cognitive accessibility, Marlene Moretti at Simon Fraser University and her associates examined whether depressed and non-depressed individuals differ in terms of accessibility to them of positive versus negative expressions directed toward the self or to other people (Moretti et al., 1996). They found that depressed individuals have reduced accessibility to positive information that is specific to themselves, not to other people.

Recent investigations by Scott McCabe from the University of Waterloo and his associates have shed light on cognitive processes in depression by focusing on differences in attentional processes. This experimental research has used a deployment-of-attention task to show that dysphoric and clinically depressed individuals do not seem to selectively attend to negative or positive material but that non-depressed individuals have a protective bias that involves diverting their attention away from negative stimuli and focusing instead on positive stimuli (McCabe & Gotlib, 1995; McCabe & Tonan, 2000). In related research, people who had a history of depression but were in a neutral mood tended to divert their attention when presented with negative stimuli, once again suggesting the presence of a protective bias (McCabe, Gotlib, & Martin, 2000). However, people with a history of depression who were induced into a negative mood state were less able to keep themselves from noticing and paying attention to negative stimuli.

Recent Canadian studies in this area were conducted by Dozois and Dobson (Dozois, 2002; Dozois & Dobson, 2001; Dozois & Dobson, 2003). The Dozois and Dobson (2001) study is remarkable because it used multiple tasks to determine whether people with and without clinical depression differed, not only in cognitive accessibility, but also in cognitive organization. (Unfortunately, there have been only a few empirical attempts thus far to measure depression and cognitive structures [see Segal & Gemar, 1997].) Dozois and Dobson had their participants complete a variety of cognitive tasks, including the self-referent encoding task, the modified Stroop task, and two tasks designed to assess cognitive structure. Four groups of participants took part (i.e., 24 depressed people, 26 depressed and anxious people, 25 never-depressed, anxious people, and 25 non-psychiatric controls). Patients with anxiety disorders were included to determine whether the findings were specific to depression. Several interesting findings emerged from this study. First, on the self-referent encoding task, depressed individuals endorsed a relatively equal number of positive and negative words as self-relevant. Dozois and Dobson suggested that this shows that the self-schema of clinically depressed people is not devoid of positive content and that there is not a lack of cognitive availability. The main group differences that emerged involved cognitive processing and cognitive organization. The investigators summarized the cognitive structure findings by concluding that "depressed individuals have an interconnected negative self-representational system and lack a well-organized positive template of self" (p. 2), a pattern that was not evident among the anxious group and the control group. Follow-up research by Dozois (2002) on a sample of dysphoric students found additional evidence for a deterioration of positive interconnectedness as levels of depression increased. Once again, there was evidence of greater organization of negative content among severely dysphoric students. A further follow-up study by Dozois and Dobson (2003) showed that self-schematas involving greater organization of negative content and less interconnectedness of positive content were associated with more recurrent depression.

Evaluation Much has been learned about cognition and depression, but we must come back to two key issues when evaluating Beck's theory. The first is whether depressed patients actually think in the negative ways enumerated by Beck. Beck initially confirmed this point in clinical observations (Beck, 1967). Further support comes from a number of sources: self-report questionnaires, laboratory studies of processes such as memory, and the Articulated Thoughts in Simulated Situations method described in Chapter 4 (Dobson & Shaw, 1986; Segal et al., 1995; White et al., 1992). The recent studies outlined above confirm the presence of related differences in terms of cognitive accessibility and organization.

The second issue represents perhaps the greatest challenge for cognitive theories of depression—whether it could be that the negative beliefs of depressed people do not follow the depression, but in fact cause the depressed mood. While many studies in experimental psychology have shown that a person's mood can be influenced by how he or she construes events, it has also been shown that manipulating affect can change thinking (e.g., Isen et al., 1978). Beck and others have found that depression and certain kinds of thinking are correlated, but a specific causal relationship cannot be determined from such data—depression could cause negative thoughts, or negative thoughts could cause depression. The relationship in all likelihood works both ways: depression can make thinking more negative, and negative thinking can probably cause and can certainly worsen depression. In recent years Beck himself has come to this more bidirectional position.

Longitudinal studies have assessed this issue. One study followed a sample of people for 45 days, collecting measures of mood and cognitions each day (Stader & Hokanson, 1998). Episodes of mild depression were identified, and the investigators evaluated whether these episodes were preceded by an increase in negative cognitions. Although an increase in interpersonal stress and dependency did precede the episodes of depression, negative cognitions did not. Thus, at present, the data do not unequivocally support the idea that negative thinking causes depression.

Beck has extended his theory in recent years by suggesting a need to focus on personality styles known as sociotropy and autonomy. The role of these factors and other personality traits is discussed in Canadian Perspectives 10.2. Despite uncertainties, Beck's theory has the advantage of being testable. It has engendered considerable research on the treatment of depression. Beck's work has encouraged therapists to focus on the thinking of depressed patients in order to change their feelings.

Canadian Perspectives/10.2

Canadian Research on Personality Orientations in Depression

The past 20 years have seen extensive research on the role of personality factors in depression, with much of this research conducted in Canada. There is great interest in personality research because personality factors may be associated with susceptibility to the onset and long-term persistence of depression. Personality factors may also predict specific depressive symptom profiles. Finally, if it can be established that certain personality factors are reliable predictors of depression, then prevention programs can be developed to reduce the possibility that vulnerable people will become afflicted with depression.

Beck (1983) proposed that depression is associated with two personality styles, sociotropy and autonomy. Sociotropic individuals are dependent on others. They are especially concerned with pleasing others, avoiding disapproval, and avoiding separation. Autonomy is an achievement-related construct that focuses on self-critical goal striving, a desire for solitude, and freedom from control. The Sociotropy-Autonomy Scale (SAS; Beck et al., 1983) was developed to assess these constructs. Research with this measure has tended to show that sociotropy is linked with depression but autonomy is not correlated consistently with it (Sato & McCann, 2000); this latter finding may be due, in part, to problems associated with the low reliability of the autonomy subscale (see Flett, Hewitt, Endler, & Bagby, 1995, for a review).

The problems inherent in the SAS necessitated the development of alternative measures of autonomy and sociotropy, including a multidimensional scale developed by David Clark at the University of New Brunswick and Aaron Beck (Clark & Beck, 1991). Their revised Sociotropy-Autonomy Scale assesses sociotropy and two aspects of autonomy known as solitude and independence (Clark, Steer, Beck, & Ross, 1995).

Sidney Blatt from Yale University is another major personality theorist. Blatt (1974, 1995) suggested that the introjective and anaclitic personality styles are associated with vulnerability to depression. The *introjective orientation* involves excessive levels of self-criticism. The *anaclitic orientation* involves excessive levels of dependency on others. Blatt developed the Depressive Experiences Questionnaire (DEQ) to assess self-criticism and dependency. Canadian researchers such as David Zuroff from McGill University have collaborated with Blatt in this research and tested his predictions (see Blatt & Zuroff, 1992). Darcy Santor from Dalhousie University, along with Zuroff and his colleagues (Santor, Zuroff, Mongrain, & Fielding, 1998), developed a revised version of Blatt's measure known as the McGill DEQ (see Table 10.1).

Table 10.1

Sample Items on the McGill Revision of the DEQ

Self-Criticism

If I fail to live up to expectations, I feel unworthy.

I tend to be very critical of myself.

I often feel guilty.

Dependency

I become frightened when I feel alone.

I would feel like I'd be losing an important part of myself if I lost a very close friend.

After a fight with a friend, I must make amends as soon as possible.

Extensive research has shown a strong association between self-criticism and depression and a weaker but still significant link between dependency and depression (Mongrain & Zuroff, 1994; Zuroff & Mongrain, 1987). One reason why dependency has shown a reduced association with depression is that it has been discovered that the DEQ actually measures a needy, maladaptive form of dependency as well as a healthy, adaptive form of dependency that reflects positive affiliations with other people (Blatt, Zohar, Quinlan, Zuroff, & Mongrain, 1995). Recent research conducted at the University of Toronto (Dunkley, Blankstein, Zuroff, Lecce, & Hui, 2003) determined that "neediness" reflects self-consciousness and unassertiveness, whereas "connectedness" (the term for the relatively more adaptive dimension) reflects warmth, agreeableness, and the valuing of relationships. In other words, dependency is not always a bad thing and the adaptive component of dependency may actually protect someone from being depressed.

The concept of self-criticism is linked closely with perfectionism (Blatt, 1995). Several Canadian studies have examined the link between perfectionism dimensions and depression (for an earlier description of the perfectionism dimensions, see Chapter 9). Hewitt and Flett (1991a) found that depressed patients had elevated levels of self-oriented and socially prescribed perfectionism (i.e., expectations imposed on the self by others). Enns and Cox (1999) assessed depression, self-criticism, and levels of perfectionism in psychiatric patients. They found that socially prescribed perfectionism, excessive concern over mistakes, and self-criticism were the strongest correlates of depression. Perfectionism has also been linked with chronic symptoms of unipolar and bipolar depression (Hewitt, Flett, Ediger, Norton, & Flynn, 1998).

We will conclude our discussion of this topic by focusing on four substantive research approaches. First, one line of investigation tests the congruency hypothesis. This hypothesis reflects the diathesis-stress approach outlined in Chapter 2. Before outlining the hypothesis, we should reiterate that extensive research highlights the role of stressful life events in depression. Kate Harkness from Queen's University and her associates, for example, have found that negative life events are linked with depression (see Harkness, Monroe, Simons, & Thase, 1999; Wildes, Harkness, & Simons, 2002). Consistent with Hammen's (1991) notion of stress generation (i.e., people prone to depression might actually engage in behaviours or choices that generate or cause stress to occur), this research shows that depressed individuals have indeed experienced more stressful events that may be attributable to their own actions and choices (Harkness & Luther, 2001; Harkness et al., 1999).

In terms of personality and stress, the essence of the congruency hypothesis is that if a non-depressed person with a personality style (i.e., a diathesis) that makes him or her vulnerable to depression also experiences a negative life event that is congruent with or matches their vulnerability in some way, then this person will become depressed. For instance, depression could be experienced by a student who wants to be perfect but fails a test.

The congruency hypothesis highlights the distinction between interpersonal and achievement-based vulnerabilities. Thus, a person characterized by interpersonal needs that indicate sociotropy and dependency will become depressed if she or he experiences interpersonal rejection or the loss of a significant other, but a person characterized by an achievement vulnerability that indicates a need to be perfect and to work autonomously will become depressed if she or he experiences a failure at school or work.

The congruency hypothesis has received only mixed support. Some personality studies have found some evidence of congruency (e.g., Hewitt, Flett, & Ediger, 1996; Segal, Shaw, Vella, & Katz, 1992); others have found a non-specific effect (i.e., stress in general combines with personality factors to produce depression); and still others have found no evidence for the congruency hypothesis (see Clark & Oates, 1995).

The lack of consistent support for the congruency hypothesis across studies could signify that this hypothesis does not apply. However, methodological factors must also be considered. Most studies conducted thus far have relied on self-report measures of stress that can be criticized for being imprecise. The events listed on these measures may not fully represent the stressors that participants have experienced. A recommended alternative is to increase measurement precision by assessing stressful events via structured interviews. In addition, more research should address the possibility that personality combines with other variables besides stress to produce depression. One such factor is social support. Dunkley, Blankstein, and colleagues (Dunkley, Blankstein, Halsall, Williams, & Winkworth, 2000; Dunkley, Zuroff, & Blankstein, 2003) found that low perceived social support combines with perfectionism to predict depressive symptoms and daily negative mood.

The second research focus involves personality factors, interpersonal processes, and depression. Personality factors such as sociotropy, dependency, and self-criticism may be linked with depression through their association with maladaptive interpersonal processes. Bieling and Alden (1998) tested the extent to which sociotropy and autonomy were associated with interpersonal ratings in a dyadic interaction involving a participant and a confederate. Depressed students high in autonomy were rated as low in likeability when compared to depressed students high in sociotropy and non-depressed students.

Mongrain, Vettese, Shuster, and Kendal (1998) from York University staged a conflict-resolution task as a way of examining the interpersonal processes between women with varying levels of self-criticism and depression and their romantic partners. Analyses showed that women with high self-criticism were rated by observers as relatively low in lovingness but high in hostility. A follow-up analysis by Vettese and Mongrain (2000) had participants evaluate their own and their partner's performance in the conflict-resolution task. The main finding was that self-critics were more negative than other participants in their appraisal of themselves and their partners; in turn, the partners of the self-critics responded with more negative feedback than other partners. This suggests that self-criticism may be associated with the negative interpersonal cycles that characterize troubled relationships. This is supported further by evidence indicating that self-critical women and men had partners who were especially likely to have numerous complaints about them (Whiffen & Aube, 1999).

The third area of research attempts to link personality and interpersonal processes with cognitive factors. Dozois and Backs-Dermott (2000) tested the associations among personality traits, interpersonal feedback, self-descriptions, and cognitive processes in a study of information processing in students with high sociotropy. They found that people with high sociotropy who are exposed to an audiotaped situation emphasizing interpersonal rejection tend to endorse more negative and fewer positive adjectives as self-descriptive in cognitive-processing tasks. In another recent study at McGill University, researchers found, as expected, that students high in sociotropy tend to recall an interpersonal event when asked to remember what made them most upset during the past year (Abela, McIntyre-Smith, & Dechef, 2003). Perhaps surprisingly, however, rather than remember an achievement-based event, students high in autonomy also tend to recall an interpersonal event.

In the fourth area of research, the role of personality factors in treatment outcomes is explored. A study led by Neil Rector at the Centre for Addiction and Mental Health (Rector, Bagby, Segal, Joffe, & Levitt, 2000) investigated the ability of self-criticism and dependency to predict treatment response among depressed patients who received either pharmacotherapy or cognitive therapy. The overall results suggested that the personality factors had little impact on the outcomes associated with pharmacotherapy, but that the personality trait of self-criticism predicted a poor response to cognitive treatment. Further, the extent to which self-critical patients became less self-critical over the course of treatment was the best predictor of treatment response to cognitive therapy. These findings combine with the results of the NIMH treatment study to suggest that whether a person will respond to certain kinds of treatment will be determined, in part, by personality vulnerabilities.

It should be noted that there is considerable overlap among some personality constructs. Autonomy, self-criticism, and socially prescribed perfectionism developed out of different theoretical frameworks, but they are conceptually and empirically related (see Blankstein & Dunkley, 2002; Dunkley & Blankstein, 2000). These personality factors likely coexist in actual people. For instance, Karen Kain has acknowledged being perfectionistic, self-critical, and, at times, without a sense of autonomy (Kain, 1994).

Thinking Critically

1. What other variables, in addition to stress and social support, might interact with specific personality vulnerability factors to moderate the relationship between personality and depression?
2. Assuming that there is a link between certain personality factors and depression, how would you attempt to prevent the onset of depression in vulnerable people?
3. Design a modified treatment program that incorporates the treatment implications of the findings presented here as components of more traditional cognitive-behavioural and interpersonal treatment for depression.

Helplessness/Hopelessness Theories In this section, we discuss the evolution of an influential cognitive theory of depression—actually, three theories—the original helplessness theory; its subsequent, more cognitive, attributional version; and its transformation into the hopelessness theory (see Figure 10.2 for a summary).

Learned Helplessness The basic premise of the **learned helplessness theory** is that an individual's passivity and sense of being unable to act and to control his or her own life is acquired through unpleasant experiences and traumas that the individual tried unsuccessfully to control.

This theory began as a mediational learning theory formulated to explain the behaviour of dogs who received inescapable electric shocks. Soon after receiving the first shocks, the dogs seemed to give up and passively accept the painful stimulation. Later, when the shocks could be avoided, these dogs did not acquire the avoidance response as efficiently and effectively as did control animals that had not experienced the inescapable shocks. Rather, most of them lay down in a corner and whined. Seligman (1974) proposed that animals acquire a sense of helplessness when confronted with uncontrollable aversive stimulation. Later, this sense of helplessness impairs their performance in stressful situations that can be controlled. They appear to lose the ability and motivation to learn to respond in an effective way to painful stimulation.

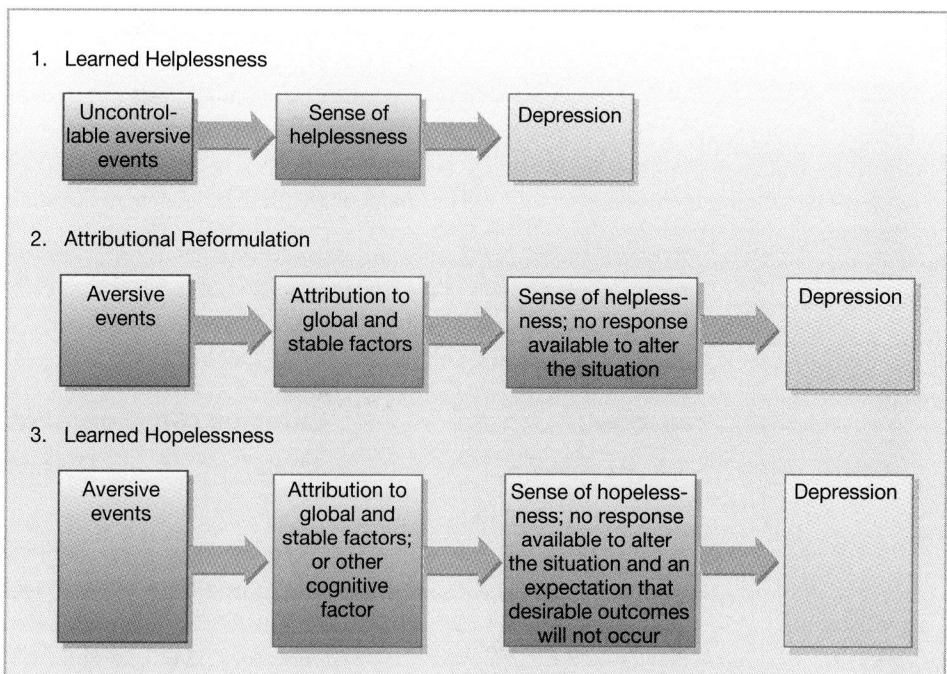

Figure 10.2 The three helplessness theories of depression.

Seligman concluded that learned helplessness in animals could provide a model for at least certain forms of human depression. Like many depressed people, the animals appeared passive in the face of stress, failing to initiate actions that might allow them to cope. They had difficulty eating or retaining what they ate, and they lost weight. Further, one of the neurotransmitter chemicals implicated in depression, norepinephrine, was depleted in Seligman's animals.

Attribution and Learned Helplessness After the original research with animals, investigators conducted similar studies with humans. By 1978, several inadequacies of the theory and unexplained aspects of depression had become apparent, and a revised learned helplessness model was proposed by Abramson, Seligman, and Teasdale (1978). Some studies with humans, for example, had indicated that helplessness inductions sometimes led to subsequent improvement of performance (e.g., Wortman & Brehm, 1975). Also, many depressed people hold themselves responsible for their failures. If they see themselves as helpless, how can they blame themselves? This characteristic of feeling helpless yet blaming oneself is referred to as the **depressive paradox**.

The essence of the revised theory is the concept of **attribution**—the explanation a person has for his or her behaviour (Weiner et al., 1971). When a person has experienced failure, he or she will try to attribute the failure to some cause. Table 10.2 applies the Abramson, Seligman, and Teasdale formulation to various ways in which a college student might attribute a low score on the mathematics portion of the Graduate Record Examination (GRE). The formulation is based on answers to three questions:

1. Are the reasons for failure believed to be internal (personal) or external (environmentally caused)?
2. Is the problem believed to be stable or unstable?
3. How global or specific is the inability to succeed perceived to be?

The attributional revision of the helplessness theory postulates that the way in which a person cognitively explains failure will determine its subsequent effects:

- Global attributions ("I never do anything right") increase the generality of the effects of failure.
- Attributions to stable factors ("I never test well") make them long term.
- Attributions to internal characteristics ("I am stupid") are more likely to diminish self-esteem, particularly if the personal fault is also global and persistent.

The theory suggests that people become depressed when they attribute negative life events to stable and global causes. Whether self-esteem also collapses depends on whether they blame the bad outcome on their own inadequacies. The individual prone to depression is thought to show a depressive attributional style, a tendency to attribute bad outcomes to personal, global, and stable faults of character. When people with this style (a diathesis) have unhappy, adverse experiences (stressors), they become depressed (Peterson & Seligman, 1984).

Where does the depressive attributional style come from? In Chapter 2, we noted that the failure to answer such a central question is a problem with most cognitive theories of psychopathology. In general terms, the answer is thought to lie in childhood experiences (a common theme in many psychological theories), but few data have been collected to support this view. A promising start is the finding that depressive attributional style is related to sexual abuse in childhood, parental overprotectiveness, and harsh discipline (Rose et al., 1994).

Hopelessness Theory The latest version of the theory (Abramson, Metalsky, & Alloy, 1989) has moved even further away from the original formulation. Some forms of depression (hopelessness depressions) are now regarded as caused by a state of hopelessness, an expectation that desirable outcomes will not occur or that undesirable ones will occur and that the person has no responses available to change this situation. (The latter part of the definition of hopelessness, of course, refers to helplessness, the central concept of earlier versions of the theory.) As in the attributional reformulation, negative life events (stressors) are seen as interacting with diatheses to yield a state of hopelessness.

Table 10.2

Attributional Schema of Depression: Why I Failed My GRE Math Exam

	Internal (Personal)		External (Environmental)	
Degree	**Stable**	**Unstable**	**Stable**	**Unstable**
Global	I am stupid.	I am exhausted.	These tests are all unfair.	It's an unlucky day, Friday the 13th.
Specific	I lack mathematical ability.	I am fed up with math.	The math tests are unfair.	My math test was numbered "13."

One diathesis is the attributional pattern already described—attributing negative events to stable and global factors. However, the hopelessness theory now considers the possibility of two other diatheses—low self-esteem and a tendency to infer that negative life events will have severe negative consequences.

Metalsky and his colleagues (1993) conducted the first test of the hopelessness theory in a prospective study that examined how students differing in attributional style responded to success versus failure on a class test. Two new features were the direct measurement of hopelessness and one of the newly proposed diatheses, low self-esteem. As in the earlier study, attributing poor grades to global and stable factors led to more persistent depressed mood. This pattern supported the hopelessness theory, for it was found only among students whose self-esteem was low and was mediated by an increase in feelings of hopelessness. A similar study conducted with children in the sixth and seventh grades yielded almost identical results (Robinson, Garber, & Hillsman, 1995). Lewinsohn and his colleagues (1994) also found that depressive attributional style and low self-esteem predicted the onset of depression in adolescents.

An advantage of the hopelessness theory is that it can deal directly with the comorbidity of depression and anxiety disorders. Alloy and her colleagues proposed that an expectation of helplessness creates anxiety. When the expectation of helplessness becomes certain, a syndrome with elements of anxiety and depression emerges. Finally, if the perceived probability of the future occurrence of negative events becomes certain (a phenomenon known as **depressive predictive certainty**), hopelessness depression develops.

Issues in the Helplessness/Hopelessness Theories Although these theories are promising, there are some problems worth noting:

1. Which type of depression is being modelled? In his original paper, Seligman attempted to document the similarity between learned helplessness and what used to be called reactive depression, depression thought to be brought on by stressful life events. Similarly, Abramson et al. (1989) now talk about a hopelessness depression, referring both to the presumed cause of the depression and to a set of symptoms that do not exactly match the DSM criteria. Only future research will tell whether these proposals are more than circular statements (hopelessness depression is caused by hopelessness).
2. Are the findings specific to depression? Because of the high correlation between anxiety and depression, it becomes important for theories to document that they are truly about depression and not about negative affect in general. Depressive attributional style does not appear to be specific to depression but is related to anxiety and general distress as well (Clark, Watson, & Mineka, 1994; Ralph & Mineka, 1998).
3. Are attributions relevant? Do people actively attempt to explain their own behaviour to themselves and do the attributions they make have subsequent effects on their behaviour? Some research indicates that making attributions is not a process in which everyone engages (Hanusa & Schulz, 1977). Furthermore, Nisbett and Wilson (1977) showed that people are frequently unaware of the causes of their behaviour.
4. One key assumption of the helplessness/hopelessness theories is that the depressive attributional style is a persistent part of the makeup of depressed people; that is, the depressive attributional style must already be in place when the person encounters some stressor. However, research shows that the depressive attributional style disappears following an episode of depression (Hamilton & Abramson, 1983).

Despite all their problems, the helplessness/hopelessness theories have clearly stimulated much research and theorizing about depression and seem destined to do so for many years to come.

INTERPERSONAL THEORY OF DEPRESSION

In this section, we discuss behavioural aspects of depression that generally involve relationships between the depressed person and others. Some data we present may be relevant to the etiology of depression and some to its course.

In Chapter 8, we discussed the role of social support in health. This concept has also been applied depression. Depressed individuals tend to have sparse social networks and to regard them as providing little support. Reduced social support may lessen an individual's ability to handle negative life events and increase vulnerability to depression (Billings, Cronkite, & Moos, 1983).

Depressed people also elicit negative reactions from others (Coyne, 1976). This feature of depression has been studied in a variety of ways, ranging from conducting telephone conversations with depressed patients, to listening to audiotapes of depressed patients, to participating in face-to-face interactions. Data show that the behaviour of depressed people elicits rejection. For example, the roommates of depressed students rated social contacts with them as low in enjoyment and reported high levels of aggression toward them; mildly depressed students were likely to be rejected by their roommates (Joiner, Alfano, & Metalsky, 1992).

Bieling and Alden (2001) investigated the interpersonal theory of depression by examining the social behaviours of depressed patients. They discovered that one reason why depressed people may elicit negative reactions from others is that depressed people tend to reject their partners and display relatively few positive social behaviours. This tendency was especially evident among people high in autonomy, as described by Beck. It seems that depressed individuals with an autonomous orientation are oriented toward themselves rather than toward other people. When they are oriented toward others, they can act in a negative, rejecting manner.

Given the interpersonal problems of depressed people, it is not surprising that depression and marital discord frequently co-occur and that the interactions of depressed people and their spouses involve mutual hostility (Kowalik & Gotlib, 1987). Critical comments of spouses of depressed people are a significant predictor of recurrence of depression (Hooley & Teasdale, 1989). Couples in which one partner has a mood disorder report less marital satisfaction than do couples in which neither has a mood disorder (Beach, Sandeen, & O'Leary, 1990).

What other factors help explain why depressed people elicit these negative reactions? Several studies have demonstrated that depressed people are low in social skills across a variety of measures—interpersonal problem-solving (Gotlib & Asarnow, 1979), speech patterns (speaking very slowly, with silences and hesitations, and more negative self-disclosures), and maintenance of eye contact (Gotlib & Robinson, 1982).

Related to the general concept of a social skills deficit is the more specific idea that constant seeking of reassurance is the critical variable in depression (Joiner & Schmidt, 1998). Perhaps as a result of being reared in a cold and rejecting environment (Carnelly, Pietomonaco, & Jaffe, 1994), depressed people seek reassurance that others truly care, but even when reassured, they are only temporarily satisfied. Their negative self-concept causes them to doubt the truth of the feedback they have received, and their constant efforts to be reassured come to irritate others. Later, they actually seek out negative feedback, which, in a sense, validates their negative self-concept. Rejection ultimately occurs because of the depressed person's inconsistent behaviour. Data collected by Joiner and Metalsky on mildly depressed students have shown that this inconsistent pattern in seeking reassurance predicts increases in depressed mood.

Do any interpersonal characteristics of depressed people precede the onset of depression, suggesting a causal relationship? Some research using the high-risk method suggests the answer is yes. For example, the behaviour of elementary school-age children of depressed parents was rated negatively by both peers and teachers (Weintraub, Liebert, & Neale, 1975; Weintraub, Prinz, & Neale, 1978); low social competence predicted the onset of depression among children (Cole et al., 1990); and poor interpersonal problem-solving skills predicted increases in depression among adolescents (Davila et al., 1995). Thus, social skills deficits may be a cause and consequence of depression. Interpersonal behaviour clearly plays a major role in depression.

Psychological Theories of Bipolar Disorder

Bipolar disorder has been neglected by psychological theorists and researchers, although, as with unipolar depression, life stress seems important in precipitating episodes (Johnson & Miller, 1997; Malkoff-Schwartz et al., 1998). Cognitive factors may also play a role. Scott et al. (2001) showed that patients with bipolar depression have elevated levels of the dysfunctional attitudes described by Beck, as well as problems in autobiographical memory and the ability to generate solutions in a problem-solving task.

The manic phase of the disorder is seen as a defence against a debilitating psychological state. The specific negative state that is being avoided varies from theory to theory. One of our own cases illustrates why many theorists have concluded that the manic state serves a protective function.

A 42-YEAR-OLD MAN was experiencing his third manic episode. During each episode, he had exhibited the classic pattern of manic symptoms, and much of his manic behaviour centred on a grandiose delusion that he was the world's greatest businessman. "Did you know that I've already bought 20 companies today?" he asked at the beginning of a therapy session. "Not even Getty or Rockefeller has anything on me." From sessions between episodes it was apparent that success in business was indeed a central concern to the patient, but he was far from successful. His parents had lent him money to start several companies, but each had gone bankrupt. He was obsessed with matching the business successes of his wealthy father, but as the years passed, his opportunities to do so were slipping away. It seemed, therefore, that his manic grandiosity was protecting him from a confrontation with his lack of business success—a realization that would likely have plunged him into a deep depression.

Clinical experience with manic patients and studies of their personalities when they are in remission indicate that they appear relatively well-adjusted between episodes. But if mania is a defence, it must be a defence against something, suggesting that the apparently good adjustment of manic people between episodes may not be an accurate reflection of their true state. Using a specially developed test designed to bypass defensive responding, Winters and Neale (1985) showed that manic individuals, even when between episodes, have very low self-esteem. A recent study came to a similar conclusion (Lyon, Startup, & Bentall, 1999).

BIOLOGICAL THEORIES OF MOOD DISORDERS

Since biological processes are known to have considerable effects on moods, it is not surprising that investigators have sought biological causes for depression and mania. Furthermore, disturbed biological processes must be part of the causal chain if a predisposition for a mood disorder can be genetically transmitted, and evidence that a predisposition for a mood disorder is heritable would provide some support for the view that the disorder has a biological basis. In the treatment of mood disorders, the effectiveness of drug therapies that increase the levels of certain neurotransmitters suggests that biological factors are important.

In this section, we will look at some of the research in the areas of genetics, neurochemistry, and the neuroendocrine system. There is also a growing literature on structural abnormalities of the brains of patients with mood disorders. Because these abnormalities are similar to those found in schizophrenia, we will discuss them in the next chapter.

THE GENETIC DATA

Research on genetic factors in bipolar disorder and unipolar depression has used the family, twin, and adoption methods discussed in Chapter 2. About 10 to 25 percent of the first-degree relatives of bipolar patients have experienced an episode of mood disorder (Gershon, 1990). The risk is higher among the relatives of those patients with early onset of the disorder. These figures are higher than those for the general population. Curiously, among the first-degree relatives of bipolar probands, there are more cases of unipolar depression than of bipolar disorder. James and Chapman (1975) found that the risk estimates for the first-degree relatives of bipolar patients were 6.4 percent for bipolar disorder and 13.2 percent for unipolar depression. Overall, the concordance rate for bipolar disorder is about 72 percent in identical twins and about 14 percent in fraternal twins (Allen, 1976). These data plus the results of adoption studies (e.g., Wender et al., 1986) support the notion that bipolar disorder has a heritable component.

The information available on unipolar depression indicates that genetic factors, although influential, are not as decisive as they are in bipolar disorder. Kendler et al. (1993) found that relatives of depressed individuals had only slightly higher than normal risk. Furthermore, if the relatives of unipolar probands are at somewhat increased risk for unipolar depression, this risk is less than the risk among relatives of bipolar probands (Andreasen et al., 1987).

Linkage analysis, described in Chapter 2, has also been applied to mood disorders. In a widely reported linkage study of the Old Order Amish, Egeland and her colleagues (1987) found evidence favouring the hypothesis that bipolar disorder results from a dominant gene on the 11th chromosome. However, attempts to replicate the Egeland study as well as other apparently successful linkage studies have had mixed success (e.g., Berrettini et al., 1990; Smyth et al., 1996). Research on linkage continues and has broadened to focus on other genes on other chromosomes, especially chromosomes 18 and 21.

NEUROCHEMISTRY AND MOOD DISORDERS

Over the past several decades, researchers have sought to understand the role played by neurotransmitters in mood disorders. The two most-studied neurotransmitters have been: norepinephrine and serotonin. The theory involving norepinephrine is most relevant to bipolar disorder and posits that a low level of norepinephrine leads to depression and a high level to mania. The serotonin theory suggests that a low level of serotonin produces depression.

The actions of drugs that were used to treat depression provided the clues on which both theories are based. In the 1950s, two groups of drugs, tricyclics and monoamine oxidase inhibitors, were found effective in relieving depression. **Tricyclic drugs** (e.g., imipramine, trade name Tofranil) are a group of antidepressant medications so named because their molecular structure is characterized by three fused rings. They prevent some of the reuptake of both norepinephrine and serotonin by the presynaptic neuron after it has fired, leaving more of the neurotransmitter in the synapse so that transmission of the next nerve impulse is made easier (see Figure 10.3). **Monoamine oxidase (MAO) inhibitors** (e.g., tranylcypromine, trade name Parnate) are antidepressant drugs that keep the enzyme monoamine oxidase from deactivating neurotransmitters, thus increasing the levels of both serotonin and norepinephrine in the synapse. This action produces the same facilitating effect described for tricylics, compensating for the abnormally low levels of these neurotransmitters in depressed people. These drug actions suggest that depression and mania are related to serotonin and norepinephrine. Newer antidepressant drugs, called *selective serotonin reuptake inhibitors* (e.g., fluoxetine, Prozac), act more selectively than the older ones, specifically inhibiting the reuptake of serotonin. Because these drugs are effective in treating unipolar depression, a stronger link has been shown between low levels of serotonin and depression.

Two main approaches have been used to further evaluate the theories. The first measures metabolites of these neurotransmitters, the byproducts of the breakdown of serotonin and norepinephrine found in urine, blood serum, and the cerebrospinal fluid. The problem with such measurements is that they are not direct reflections of levels of either serotonin or norepinephrine in the brain; metabolites measured in this way could reflect neurotransmitters anywhere in the body. Indeed, the majority of neurons that use serotonin are found in the intestines and norepinephrine is also an important neurotransmitter in the peripheral nervous system.

A second strategy is to investigate the behavioural effects of drugs other than the antidepressants that are known either to increase or to decrease the brain levels of serotonin and norepinephrine. A drug raising the level of serotonin should alleviate depression; one reducing it should deepen depression or induce it in normal subjects. Similarly, a drug that increases norepinephrine might induce a manic episode. This strategy also has its problems, however. Most drugs have multiple effects, making it difficult to choose one that accomplishes a specific purpose without complicating side effects.

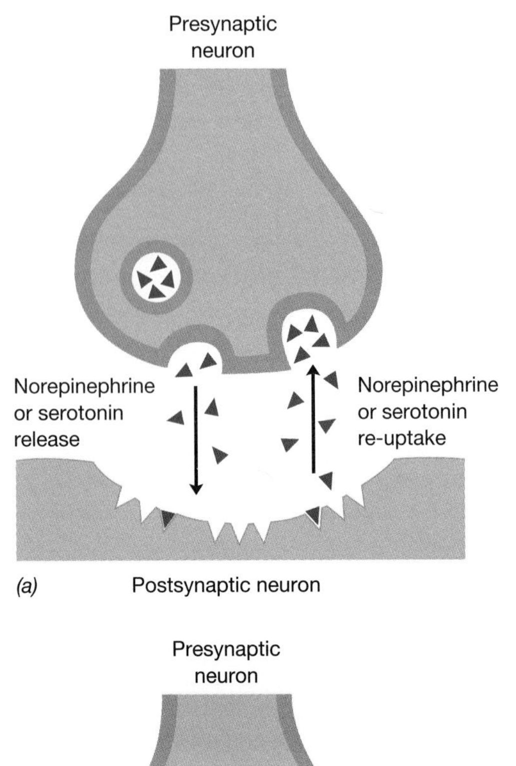

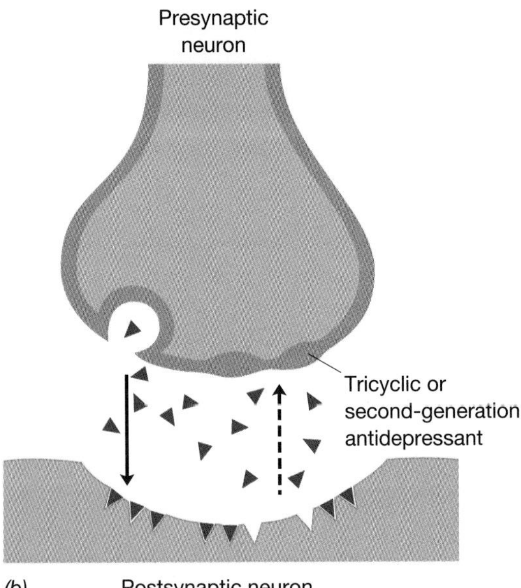

Figure 10.3 (a) When a neuron releases norepinephrine or serotonin from its endings, a pump-like reuptake mechanism immediately begins to recapture some of the neurotransmitter molecules before they are received by the postsynaptic (receptor) neuron. (b) Tricyclic drugs block this reuptake process, enabling more norepinephrine or serotonin to reach, and thus fire, the postsynaptic (receptor) neuron. Serotonin reuptake inhibitors act more selectively on serotonin. Adapted from Snyder (1986, p. 106).

These problems notwithstanding, what can be said of the validity of theories that implicate low levels of norepinephrine or serotonin in depression and high levels of norepinephrine in mania? First, a series of studies conducted by Bunney and Murphy and their colleagues at the National Institute of Mental Health monitored closely the urinary levels of norepinephrine in a group of bipolar patients as they cycled through stages of depression, mania, and normalcy. Urinary levels of norepinephrine decreased as patients became depressed (Bunney et al., 1970) and increased during mania, confirming the hypothesis that low levels of norepinephrine are associated with depression and high levels with mania (Bunney, Goodwin, & Murphy, 1972). A problem in interpreting these data, however, is that such changes could result from increases in activity level because increased motor activity in mania can increase norepinephrine activity. Nonetheless, there is evidence that increasing norepinephrine levels can precipitate a manic episode in bipolar patients (Altshuler et al., 1995).

The principal metabolite of norepinephrine is 3-methoxy-4-hydroxyphenyl glycol (MHPG); low levels of norepinephrine should be reflected in low levels of MHPG. As expected, depressed bipolar patients have generally been shown to have low levels of urinary MHPG (Muscettola et al., 1984); further, MHPG levels are higher during a manic than during a depressed episode and higher in manic patients than in normal people (Goodwin & Jamison, 1990). As with studies that directly measured norepinephrine, however, the MHPG results could reflect differences in activity levels.

Studies of serotonin have examined its major metabolite, 5-hydroxyindoleacetic acid (5-HIAA). A fairly consistent body of data indicates that 5-HIAA levels are low in the cerebrospinal fluid of depressed patients (see McNeal & Cimbolic, 1986). Studies also show that ingestion of L-tryptophan, from which serotonin is subsequently produced, is somewhat effective as a treatment for depression, especially when used in combination with other drugs (Coppen et al., 1972; Mendels et al., 1975). Furthermore, a drug that suppresses serotonin synthesis reduces the therapeutic effect of drugs that usually lessen depression (Shopsin, Friedman, & Gershon, 1976). Delgado et al. (1990) used a special diet to reduce the level of serotonin in depressed patients in remission by lowering the level of its precursor, tryptophan. They found that 67 percent of patients experienced a return of their symptoms. A gradual remission followed when patients resumed their normal diet. Similar results have been found in Canadian research conducted with patients with seasonal depression (Lam et al., 1996). A recent study used this same tryptophan-depletion strategy in normal participants who had either a positive or a negative family history of depression. Again, as predicted by the low-serotonin theory, those with a positive family history experienced an increase in depressed mood (Benkelfat et al., 1994).

We have indicated that effective antidepressants increase levels of norepinephrine and serotonin and that knowledge of this action formed a keystone of the norepinephrine and serotonin theories of depression. It now appears that the explanation of why these drugs work is not as straightforward as it seemed at first. The therapeutic effects of tricyclics and MAO inhibitors do not depend solely on an increase in levels of neurotransmitters. The earlier findings were correct—tricyclics and MAO inhibitors do indeed increase levels of norepinephrine and serotonin when they are first taken—but after several days the neurotransmitters return to their earlier levels. This information is crucial because it does not fit with data on how much time must pass before antidepressants become effective. Both tricyclics and MAO inhibitors take from seven to 14 days to relieve depression but by that time, the neurotransmitter level has already returned to its previous state. It would seem, then, that a simple increase in norepinephrine or serotonin is not a sufficient explanation for why the drugs alleviate depression.

What is the impact of these new findings? Researchers are focusing on the postsynaptic effects of antidepressants and are developing theories of depression that implicate postsynaptic mechanisms. One line of research is examining whether antidepressants alter the chemical messengers that a postsynaptic receptor sends into the postsynaptic neuron (Duman, Heninger, & Nestler, 1997). No definitive answers are as yet available.

Research on bipolar disorder is also moving away from the older norepinephrine theory. One major reason for this shift is that lithium, the most widely used and effective treatment for bipolar disorder, is useful in treating both the manic and the depressive episodes of the disorder, suggesting that it acts by affecting some neurochemical that can either increase or decrease neural activity. Current research is focusing on G-proteins (guanine nucleotide-binding proteins), which are found in postsynaptic cell membranes and play an important role in modulating activity in the postsynaptic cell. High levels of G-proteins have been found in patients with mania and low levels in patients with depression (Avisson et al., 1997, 1999), suggesting that the therapeutic effects of lithium may be due to its ability to regulate G-proteins (Manji et al., 1995).

THE NEUROENDOCRINE SYSTEM

The hypothalamic-pituitary-adrenocortical axis may also play a role in depression (see Figure 8.6). The limbic area of the brain is closely linked to emotion and also affects the hypothalamus. The hypothalamus in turn controls various endocrine glands and thus the levels of hormones they secrete. Hormones secreted by the hypothalamus also affect the pituitary gland and the hormones it produces. Because of its relevance to the so-called vegetative symptoms of depression, such as disturbances in appetite and sleep, the hypothalamic-pituitary-adrenocortical axis is thought to be overactive in depression.

Various findings support this proposition. Levels of cortisol (an adrenocortical hormone) are high in depressed patients, perhaps because of oversecretion of thyrotropin-releasing hormone by the hypothalamus (Garbutt et al., 1994). The excess secretion of cortisol in depressed persons also causes enlargement of their adrenal glands (Rubun et al., 1995). These high levels of cortisol have even led to the development of a biological test for depression—the dexamethasone suppression test (DST). Dexamethasone suppresses cortisol secretion, but when given dexamethasone during an overnight test, some depressed patients, especially those with delusional depression, do not experience cortisol suppression (Nelson & Davis, 1997). It is believed that the failure of dexamethasone to suppress cortisol reflects overactivity in the hypothalamic-pituitary-adrenocortical axis of patients. The failure to show suppression ceases when the depressive episode ends, suggesting such failure is a non-specific response to stress.

The hypothalamic-pituitary-thyroid axis is also of possible relevance to bipolar disorder. Disorders of thyroid function are often seen in bipolar patients (Lipowski et al., 1994), and thyroid hormones can induce mania in these patients (Goodwin & Jamison, 1990).

Finally, a recent review of contemporary research on the neuropsychology of depression led the authors to conclude that there is solid evidence implicating both the right and left hemispheres in the experience of depression (Shenal, Harrison, & Demaree, 2003). However, the depression itself may vary: right hemisphere dysfunction involves symptoms of indifference or flat affect, while left hemisphere dysfunction involves more overt symptoms of agitation and sadness.

Table 10.3

Summary of Biological Hypotheses about Unipolar Depression and Bipolar Disorder

Unipolar depression	Genetic diathesis; low serotonin or serotonin-receptor dysfunction; high levels of cortisol.
Bipolar disorder	Genetic diathesis; low serotonin or low norepinephrine in depressed phase; high norepinephrine in manic phase; may also be linked to G-proteins.

All these data lend some support to theories that mood disorders have biological causes (see Table 10.3 for a summary of major biological positions). Does this mean that psychological theories are irrelevant or useless? Not in the least. To assert that behavioural disorders have a basis in biological processes is to state the obvious. No psychogenic theorist would deny that behaviour is mediated by some bodily changes. The biological and psychological theories may well be describing the same phenomena, but in different terms (such as learned helplessness versus low serotonin). They should be thought of as complementary, not incompatible.

THERAPIES FOR MOOD DISORDERS

Most episodes of depression lift after a few months, although the time may seem immeasurably longer to the depressed individual and to those close to him or her. That most depressions are self-limiting is fortunate. However, depression is too widespread and too incapacitating, both to the depressed person and to those around him or her, simply to wait for the disorder to go away untreated. Bouts of depression tend to recur, and suicide is a risk for people who are depressed. Thus, it is important to treat major depression as well as bipolar disorder. Current therapies are both psychological and biological; singly or in combination, they are somewhat effective.

Psychological Therapies

Psychodynamic Therapies Because depression is considered to be derived from a repressed sense of loss and from anger unconsciously turned inward, psychoanalytic treatment tries to help the patient achieve insight into the repressed conflict and often encourages outward release of the hostility directed inward. The aim of psychoanalytic therapy is to uncover latent motivations for the patient's depression. People may, for example, blame themselves for a lack of parental affection but repress this belief because of the pain it causes. The therapist must first guide the patients to confront the fact that they feel this way and then help them realize that any guilt is unfounded. The recovery of memories of stressful circumstances of the patients' childhood should also bring relief.

Research on the effectiveness of dynamic psychotherapy in alleviating depression is sparse (Craighead, Evans, & Robins, 1992; Klerman, 1988a) and characterized by mixed results, in part owing to the high degree of variability among approaches that come under the rubric of psychodynamic or psychoanalytic psychotherapy. A report from the American Psychiatric Association (1993) concluded that there are no controlled data attesting to the efficacy of long-term psychodynamic psychotherapy or psychoanalysis in treating depression. Although a more contemporary meta-analytic review by Leichsenring (2001) concluded that short-term psychodynamic treatment and cognitive behaviour therapy are equally effective in alleviating depression, it was acknowledged that this conclusion must remain tentative because of the relatively small number of studies conducted.

This more favourable conclusion reflects findings from a well-known large-scale study (Elkin et al., 1989) that suggests that a form of psychodynamic therapy that concentrates on present-day interactions between the depressed person and the social environment—Klerman and Weissman's interpersonal therapy (IPT) (Klerman et al., 1984)—is effective for alleviating unipolar depression as well as for maintaining treatment gains (Frank et al., 1990). The core of the therapy is to help depressed patients examine the ways in which their current interpersonal behaviour might interfere with obtaining pleasure from relationships. For example, the patients might be taught how to improve communication with others to meet their own needs better and to have more satisfying social interactions and support. This psychodynamic therapy is not as much intrapsychic as it is interpersonal. It emphasizes better understanding of the interpersonal problems assumed to give rise to depression and aims at improving relationships with others. As such, the focus is on better communication, reality testing, developing effective social skills, and meeting present social-role requirements. The focus is on the patients' *current* life, not on an exploration of past, often-repressed causes of present-day problems. Actual techniques include somewhat non-directive discussion of interpersonal problems, exploration of and encouragement to express unacknowledged negative feelings, improvement of both verbal and non-verbal communications, problem-solving, and suggesting new and more satisfying modes of behaviour.

A recent study by Harkness et al. (2002) attested to the effectiveness of IPT. In this particular study, IPT helped buffer the impact and possible etiological role of stressful interpersonal events in the recurrence of depression.

Cognitive and Behaviour Therapies In keeping with their contention that depression is caused by errors in thinking, Beck and his associates devised a cognitive therapy aimed at altering maladaptive thought patterns. The therapist tries to persuade depressed persons to change their opinions of events and of the self. When a client expresses worthlessness because "Nothing goes right; everything I try to do ends in a disaster," the therapist offers examples contrary to this overgeneralization, such as citing abilities that the client is either overlooking or discounting. The therapist also instructs patients to monitor private monologues and to identify all patterns of thought that contribute to depression. The therapist then teaches patients to think through negative prevailing beliefs to understand how these beliefs prevent them from making more realistic and positive assumptions.

Although developed independently of Ellis's rational-emotive method described in Chapter 2, Beck's analyses are similar to it in some ways. For example, Beck suggests that depressed people are likely to consider themselves totally inept and incompetent if they make a mistake (see Brown & Beck, 2002). This schema can be considered an extension of one of Ellis's irrational beliefs (i.e., the individual must be competent in all things in order to be worthwhile).

Beck also includes behavioural components in his treatment. When patients are severely depressed, Beck encourages them to do things, such as get out of bed in the morning or go for a walk. He gives his patients activity assignments to provide them with successful experiences and allow them to think well of themselves. But the overall emphasis is on cognitive restructuring, on persuading the person to think differently. If a change in behaviour will help achieve that goal, fine. However, behavioural change by itself is not expected to alleviate depression.

Over the past two decades, considerable research has been conducted on Beck's therapy, beginning with a widely cited study by Rush et al. (1977), which indicated that cognitive therapy was more successful than the tricyclic imipramine (Tofranil) in alleviating unipolar depression. The unusually low improvement rate found for the drug in this clinical trial suggests that these patients might have been poorly suited for pharmacotherapy and that this was therefore not a fair comparison. Nonetheless, the efficacy of Beck's therapy in this study and in a 12-month follow-up (Kovacs et al., 1981) encouraged many other researchers to conduct additional evaluations, which have confirmed its efficacy (see Dobson, 1989). In addition, research shows that Beck's therapy has a prophylactic effect in preventing subsequent bouts of depression (Evans et al., 1993; Hollon, DeRubeis, & Seligman, 1993). However, a recent meta-analysis by Hamilton and Dobson (2002) from the University of Calgary, while confirming the efficacy of cognitive therapy, identified a number of factors that contribute to less favourable outcomes. They found that cognitive therapy is less effective when used to treat patients with high levels of dysfunctional attitudes and high pre-treatment severity scores on measures of depression; it is also less effective for those with more chronic forms of depression, an increased number of previous episodes, and earlier onsets of depression.

Mindfulness-Based Cognitive Therapy In recent years, a treatment known as mindfulness-based cognitive therapy (MBCT) has been developed specifically to prevent relapse among clinically depressed people. MBCT is an extension of Kabat-Zinn's stress-reduction program that teaches people how to combat stress through mindful mediation. In contrast, the MBCT approach developed by Zindel Segal from Toronto, John Teasdale from England, and Mark Williams from Wales combines relaxation and related techniques designed to increase awareness of changes in the body and the mind with standard cognitive intervention techniques (see Segal, Williams, & Teasdale, 2002). The key component is developing meta-cognitive awareness (i.e., a sense of how *cognitive sets* are related to emotional feelings and vice versa). Initial research indicates that MBCT has a great deal of promise. Rates of relapse are substantially reduced among patients who have had at least three previous episodes of depression (Teasdale et al., 2000), and reduced relapse following either MBCT or cognitive therapy is associated with the increased presence of meta-cognitive sets (Teasdale et al., 2002).

Zindel Segal from Toronto's Centre for Addiction and Mental Health, Clarke Division is one of the developers of Mindfulness-Based Cognitive Therapy.

Williams, Teasdale, Segal, and Soulsby (2000) also showed that MBCT reduces the overgenerality of autobiographic memory effect. When asked to recall specific past events in their lives, depressed people, relative to non-depressed people, tend to provide broad, categorical memories lacking in specificity (e.g., my father was cruel) rather than specific, detailed events. This overgenerality effect is believed to reflect the negative schema described by Beck. Depressed people who receive MBCT show reduced overgenerality; they have learned new encoding and retrieval skills that involve processing their past and current experiences in non-judgmental ways.

Teasdale, Segal, and Williams (2003) observed that mindfulness-based interventions are multi-faceted. Potentially helpful aspects of training include exposure to negative moods and arousal states, cognitive change, self-management, relaxation, and acceptance of unwanted experiences. Because MBCT involves general principles that could apply broadly, MBCT interventions are seen as relevant for other disorders, such as substance abuse (Breslin, Zack, & McMain, 2002). However, the developers of MBCT caution that it is important that therapists using this approach adhere closely to the principles of MBCT, and to assist them, they have developed the MBCT Adherence Scale (Segal, Teasdale, Williams, & Gemar, 2002). This scale involves an evaluation of such issues as the extent to which the therapist used systematic awareness exercises, conveyed the link between thinking and feeling, and facilitated relating to one's experiences from a standpoint of acceptance, not rejection or avoidance.

We turn now to an examination of a widely cited study that compares Beck's therapy with the interpersonal therapy described above and with an antidepressant drug.

The NIMH Treatment of Depression Collaborative Research Program In 1977 the National Institute of Mental Health (NIMH) undertook a large three-site study of Beck's cognitive therapy (CT), comparing it with interpersonal psychotherapy (IPT) and pharmacotherapy (Elkin et al., 1985). Called the Treatment of Depression Collaborative Research Program (TDCRP), this was the first multi-site coordinated study initiated by the NIMH in the field of psychotherapy. We will describe it in some detail because it is a widely cited and controversial study, that illustrates a number of issues in therapy research.

The pharmacological therapy imipramine (Tofranil), a well-tested tricyclic drug widely regarded at the time as a standard therapy for depression, was used as a reference treatment against which to evaluate the two psychotherapies, the second and third treatments. Dosages were adjusted according to predetermined guidelines that were flexible enough to allow the psychiatrist to apply some clinical judgment in the context of clinical management (support and advice), that is, in a warm, supportive atmosphere (Fawcett et al., 1987). Elkin et al. (1985) regarded this almost as a drug-plus-supportive-therapy condition, supportive referring to the nature of the doctor-patient relationship.

A fourth and final "treatment" involved a placebo–clinical management group against which to judge the efficacy of imipramine. This treatment was also conceived of as a partial control for the two psychotherapies because of the presence of strong support and encouragement. In a double-blind design similar to that used in the imipramine condition, patients in this group received a placebo that they believed might be an effective antidepressant medication; they were also given direct advice when considered necessary. As placebo conditions go, this was a very strong one; it included much more psychological support and even intervention than do most placebo control groups in both the psychotherapy and the pharmacotherapy literatures. Clinical management was common to both this and the imipramine group.

All treatments lasted 16 weeks, with slight differences in numbers of sessions, depending on the treatment manuals. A wide range and large number of assessments were made at pre- and post-treatment of the 60 participants in each of the four conditions, as well as three times during treatment and again at six-, 12-, and 18-month follow-ups. Measures included some that might provide answers to questions about processes of change. For example, do interpersonal-therapy patients learn to relate better to others during therapy, and if so, is this improvement correlated with clinical outcome? Do cognitive-therapy patients manifest less cognitive distortion during the later sessions than at the beginning of treatment, and if so, is this shift associated with better clinical outcome? Other assessment instruments tapped the perspectives of the patient, the therapist, an independent clinical evaluator blind to treatment condition, and, whenever possible, a significant other from the patient's life (e.g., a spouse). Three domains of change were assessed: depressive symptomatology, overall symptomatology and life functioning, and functioning related to particular treatment approaches (e.g., the Dysfunctional Attitudes Scale of Weissman and Beck [1978], to assess cognitive change).

Analyses of the data suggest variations among research sites, between those who completed treatment and the total sample (including dropouts), and among assessments with different perspectives (e.g., patient versus clinical-evaluator judgments). Some of the complex findings are summarized here (Elkin et al., 1986, 1989, 1996; Imber et al., 1990; Shea et al., 1990, 1992).

- At termination, there were no significant differences in reduction of depression or improvement in overall functioning between cognitive therapy (CT) and interpersonal therapy (IPT) or between either of them and imipramine plus clinical management. In general, the three active treatments achieved significant *and equivalent* degrees of success and were for the most part superior to the placebo group. The placebo-plus-clinical-management patients did show significant improvement, however.
- Imipramine was faster than the other treatments in reducing depressive symptoms during treatment. By the end of 16 weeks of therapy, however, the two psychotherapies had caught up with the drug.
- On some measures, the less severely depressed placebo patients were doing as well at termination as were the less depressed people in the three active treatment conditions.
- Severely depressed patients in the placebo condition did not fare as well as those in the three active treatments.
- There was some evidence that IPT was more effective than CT with the more severely depressed patients, most notably in terms of recovery rates.
- There was some evidence that particular treatments effected change in expected domains. For example, IPT patients showed more improvements in social functioning than imipramine or CT patients, and CT reduced certain types of dysfunctional attitudes more than the other treatments did.
- For IPT and pharmacotherapy, but not for CT, patients diagnosed with personality disorders (see Chapter 13) were more likely to have residual depressive symptoms after therapy than those without these Axis II diagnoses.

At the 18-month follow-up, the active treatment conditions did *not* differ significantly, and of those patients across the four conditions who had markedly improved immediately after treatment, only between 20 and 30 percent remained completely without depression.

Subsequent analyses have sought to identify various factors that may account for the different outcomes experienced by patients. The competency of the therapist is one variable examined by Brian Shaw and associates from the Hospital for Sick Children in Toronto (Shaw et al., 1999). They looked at the outcomes of cognitive therapy and reported that patients had lower levels of depression if their therapists were rated as especially competent, especially in terms of their ability to structure and organize the treatment approach.

Other analyses have shown the importance of taking personality differences between participants into account. Research with the Dysfunctional Attitudes Scale showed that patients who endorsed perfectionistic attitudes tended to experience less positive outcomes overall than other patients in the study, and this held across all treatment modalities (Blatt, Quinlan, Pilkonis, & Shea, 1995; Blatt & Zuroff, 2002). One reason why perfectionists had less successful outcomes is that they were characterized by a poorer working alliance and a less positive relationship with their therapist throughout the course of treatment (see Shahar, Blatt, Zuroff, & Pilkonis, 2003; Zuroff et al., 2000). Blatt et al. (1995) suggested that these individuals may be more difficult to treat because they suffer from emotional and interpersonal isolation.

Much remains to be learned about how to effect even short-term improvement in depressed patients. Even less is known about how to maintain any benefits that are evident right after treatment ends. Certainly, there is little in the many findings from this milestone study of comparative outcome that can gladden the hearts of proponents of any of the interventions. Indeed, a recent comparative analysis of existing studies by a research team based in Montreal found that rates of remission were virtually identical (46.4 percent versus 46.3 percent, respectively) for patients receiving medication and patients receiving psychotherapy (Cascalenda, Perry, & Looper, 2002). However, either form of treatment was superior to no treatment.

Social Skills Training Since a key feature of depression is a lack of satisfying experiences with other people, behavioural treatments have focused on helping patients improve social interactions. Although there are cognitive components in these approaches—for example, encouraging the depressed patient not to evaluate his or her performance too harshly—evidence supports the effectiveness of a focus on enhancing overt social behaviours by such techniques as assertion and social skills training (Hersen et al., 1984; Lewinsohn, 1974; Lewinsohn & Gotlib, 1995). One large-scale collaborative study by Neil Jacobson at the University of Washington and Keith Dobson at the University of Calgary and their colleagues compared this social skills approach with cognitive therapy and found them to be equally effective, both in terms of alleviating depression and preventing relapses (Gortner, Gollan, Dobson, & Jacobson, 1998; Jacobson et al., 1996). In general, reductions in interpersonal conflicts found in a distressed marriage or other intimate relationships alleviate depression (O'Leary & Beach, 1990).

Psychological Treatment of Bipolar Disorder Psychological therapies alone also show promise in dealing with many of the interpersonal, cognitive, and emotional problems of bipolar patients. If a patient in a manic phase commits an indiscretion such as having an extramarital affair or spending everything in the family bank account, the consequences of this behaviour last much longer than improvements in mood brought about by lithium. Stress is likely to be higher as a result, and stress can trigger a subsequent mood swing. A cognitive-behavioural intervention targeted at the thoughts and interpersonal behaviours that go awry during wide mood swings appears to be effective (Basco & Rush, 1996).

One problem in getting bipolar patients to take their medication regularly is that they often lack insight into the self-destructive nature of their behaviour. A small but significant number of empirical studies show that careful education about bipolar disorder and its treatment can improve adherence to medication such as lithium, which is helpful in reducing the mood swings of this disorder and thereby brings more stability into the patient's life (Craighead et al., 1998; Peet & Harvey, 1991). Obviously, an effective drug is beneficial only to the extent that it is taken as prescribed. It is also important to recognize, that, in addition to improving adherence to a drug regimen, education about the illness is likely to increase social support from family and friends (Craighead et al., 1998).

As with patients with schizophrenia, bipolar patients relapse more quickly if they return from hospital to family settings characterized by high levels of hostility and over-involvement (called "expressed emotion") than if they returned to a less-charged emotional climate in the home (Miklowitz et al., 1996). This points to the need for interventions aimed at the family and not merely at the patient. Research indicates the effectiveness of educating the family about the disorder, the desirability of working to reduce stress at home, and the need to continue medication to help maintain improvements of the discharged bipolar patient (Glick et al., 1991).

Researchers are investigating a problem-solving approach called interpersonal and social rhythm therapy (see Craighead et al., 1998). This approach is designed to help the patient deal better with life events that trigger stress and manic episodes. The patient is taught to appreciate how manic episodes interfere with relationships and learns how to deal with daily challenges without allowing moods to sink into depressive despair or escalate to levels that create embarrassment or lead to self-destructive behaviour. Reality-based thinking and behaviour are taught and encouraged, including the acceptance that the disorder is chronic, may be lifelong, and requires that the patient take proper medication and pay attention to altering behaviour and thought patterns (Frank et al., 1994).

Final Comment Determining the best therapy for each individual can be a challenge. For instance, a woman who is disheartened because of the way she is treated by men might be better advised by a feminist therapist, who will encourage her to resist continued subjugation by an overbearing spouse or boss, than by an equally well-intentioned cognitive therapist, who might try to teach her that the treatment she receives from husband or supervisor is not all that bad. A central question in this context is whether the therapist should help the client alter his or her life situation. Indeed, the very fact that a person is depressed may indicate that he or she is ready for a change in social and personal relations with others.

BIOLOGICAL THERAPIES

There are a variety of biological therapies for depression and mania. The two most common are electroconvulsive shock and various drugs.

Electroconvulsive Therapy Perhaps the most dramatic, and controversial, treatment for severe depression is electroconvulsive therapy (ECT). ECT was introduced in the early 20th century by two Italian physicians, Cerletti and Bini. More rudimentary treatment methods were used prior to the advent of ECT; for instance, in the 16th century, electric catfish were used to induce shock in patients in an attempt to expel devils (see Endler & Persad, 1988).

Previously, Cerletti was interested in epilepsy and sought a means to induce seizures. The solution became apparent to him during a visit to a slaughterhouse, where he saw seizures and unconsciousness induced in animals by electric shocks administered to the head. Shortly thereafter, he found that by applying electric shocks to the sides of the human head, he could produce full epileptic seizures. Then, in Rome in 1938, he used the technique on a patient with schizophrenia (see Endler, 1988, for a full account of the first use of ECT).

In the decades that followed, ECT was administered to patients with both schizophrenia and severe depression, usually in hospital settings. Its use is restricted today to profoundly depressed individuals. Canadian research indicates that ECT is more likely to be administered to people with longer hospital stays and a greater number of previous admissions (Malla, 1988). Both factors are associated with more severe and persistent forms of depression.

Currently, there are indications that ECT is being used with increasing frequency in Canada and elsewhere. Why? One reason is that when it works, it is faster than antidepressants and psychotherapy. The increased use of ECT was brought to the attention of the Canadian public thanks to an independent review conducted in British Columbia. A psychiatrist had expressed concern that the use of ECT had increased dramatically at the Riverview Hospital in Coquitlam, B.C. (i.e., the province's largest mental health facility). Indeed, it was determined that ECT use had more than doubled between 1996 and 1999 as a way of treating depression in people aged 65 or older. The review panel concluded that the use of ECT at the hospital was appropriate.

ECT entails the deliberate induction of a seizure and momentary unconsciousness by passing a current between 70 and 130 volts through the patient's brain. Electrodes were formerly placed on each side of the forehead, allowing the current to pass through both hemispheres, a method known as **bilateral ECT**. Today, **unilateral ECT**, in which the current passes through the non-dominant (right) cerebral hemisphere only (e.g., Abrams, Swartz, & Vedak, 1991), is more commonly used. In the past, the patient was usually awake when the current triggered the seizure and the electric shock often created frightening contortions of the body, sometimes even causing bone fractures. Now the patient is given a short-acting anaesthetic, then an injection of a strong muscle relaxant before the current is applied. The convulsive spasms of the body muscles are barely perceptible to onlookers, and the patient awakens a few minutes later remembering nothing about the treatment. The mechanism through which ECT works is unknown. It reduces metabolic activity and blood circulation to the brain and may thus inhibit aberrant brain activity.

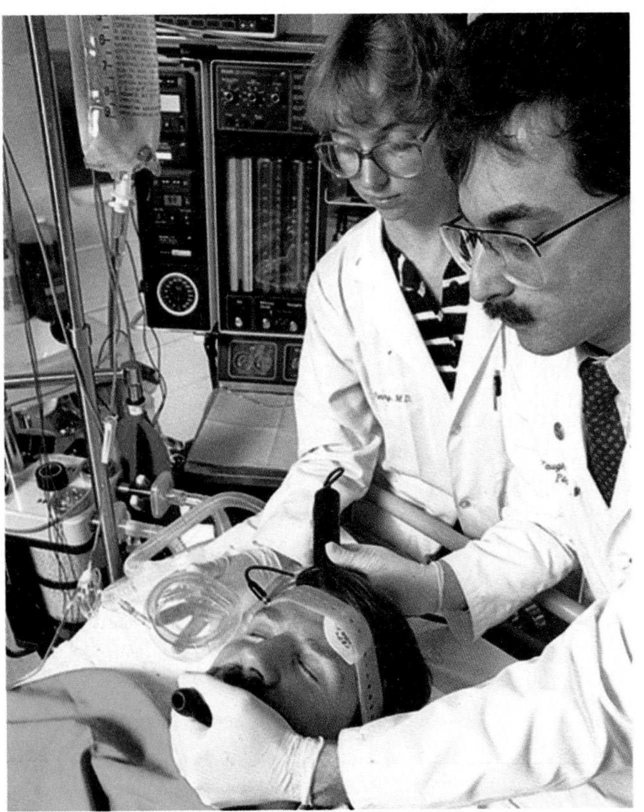

ECT was first used on a patient with schizophrenia in 1938.

Inducing a seizure is still a drastic procedure. Why should anyone agree to undergo such radical therapy? How could a parent or a spouse consent to such treatment for a patient judged legally incapable of giving consent? The answer is simple. Although we don't know why, ECT may be the optimal treatment for extremely severe depression (Klerman, 1988a). Most professionals acknowledge the risks involved—confusion and memory loss that can be prolonged. However, unilateral ECT to the non-dominant hemisphere erases fewer memories than does bilateral ECT, and no detectable changes in brain structure result (Devanand et al., 1994). Clinicians typically resort to ECT only when the depression is unremitting and after less-drastic treatments have been tried and found wanting. In considering any treatment that has negative side effects, the person making the decision must be aware of the consequences of not providing any treatment at all. Given that suicide is a real possibility among depressed people, the use of ECT, at least after other treatments have failed, is regarded by many as defensible and responsible.

One issue that has emerged is the high relapse rate of people treated with ECT. A new study by Sackeim et al. (2001) used a sophisticated methodological approach (i.e., a randomized, double-blind, placebo-controlled trial) and found that without active follow-up treatment, virtually all patients in remission relapsed within six months of no longer receiving ECT. However, the relapse rate was only 39 percent for those patients who received follow-up nortriptyline-lithium treatment.

Over the years, many activist groups have expressed their concerns about the use of ECT, and these protests continue. The groups maintain that the procedure is inhumane, involves considerable risk, and is not effective. In addition, there are published accounts by former patients who believe that ECT led to permanent damage. Wendy Funk of Cranbook, B.C., for example, wrote a book detailing her negative experiences and claimed that ECT wiped out her lifetime of memories (see Funk, 1998). Clearly, as with most treatments, there is variability in the outcomes experienced, for other people feel that ECT saved their lives. Several public inquiries conducted throughout Canada led to conclusions

Ernest Hemingway, famous author and former reporter for the *Toronto Daily Star*, shot himself in 1961. He attributed the fatal step he would take, in part, to receiving more than 20 sessions of ECT. He questioned: "What is the sense of ruining my head and erasing my memory, which is my capital, and putting me out of business? It was a brilliant cure, but we lost the patient" (see Bohuslawsky, *Ottawa Sun*, August 5, 2001).

that support the use of ECT (Endler & Persad, 1988). The Clark Committee Report from Ontario (Clark, 1985) concluded that ECT is effective but that appropriate safeguards must remain in place to protect the well-being of patients, including the continuing right to informed consent. Full, informed consent is crucial, given that some patients have indeed had negative experiences with ECT.

Norman Endler (see Canadian Contributions 7.1) was one of Canada's leading proponents of ECT. Why? Because Endler was twice treated successfully with ECT when he suffered from bipolar depression. He chronicled his experiences in his memoir *Holiday of Darkness* (Endler, 1982). Endler also examined ECT from a scientific perspective in a book entitled *Electroconvulsive Therapy: The Myths and the Realities* (see Endler & Persad, 1988).

Drug Therapy Drugs are the most commonly used treatments—biological or otherwise—for mood disorders. The use of antidepressants is increasing exponentially. A recent analysis by Hemels, Koren, and Einarson (2002) of antidepressant use in Canada from 1981 to 2000 found that the number of prescriptions increased from 3.2 million to over 14 million in 20 years. However, antidepressants do not work for everyone and side effects are sometimes serious (see Table 10.4). Moreover, it is difficult to identify personal characteristics that might predict treatment response. Response to drug treatment is not predicted by age, sex, age at onset, symptom duration, or number of reoccurrences of the disorder. However, there is some evidence of a better response among people with higher levels of social support (see Bagby, Ryder, & Cristi, 2002).

Specific Drug Therapies for Depression In our earlier discussion of biological research on depression, we mentioned three major categories of antidepressant drugs:

1. tricyclics, such as imipramine (Tofranil) and amitriptyline (Elavil)
2. selective serotonin reuptake inhibitors (SSRIs), such as fluoxetine (Prozac) and sertraline (Zoloft)
3. monoamine oxidase (MAO) inhibitors, such as tranylcypromine (Parnate)

Since the MAO inhibitors have by far the most serious side effects, the other two classes of drugs are more widely used. These medications have been established as effective in a number of double-blind studies, with improvement rates of 50 to 70 percent among patients who complete treatment (Depression Guideline Panel, 1993; Nemeroff & Schatzberg, 1998). Although early indications were that the SSRIs were clinically more effective than either tricyclics or MAO inhibitors, it now seems that the clinical effectiveness of all three types of drugs is similar. However, the SSRIs do have the advantage of producing fewer side effects (Enserink, 1999).

Although the various antidepressants hasten a patient's recovery from an episode of depression, relapse is still common after the drugs are withdrawn. Continuing to take imipramine after remission is of value in preventing recurrence, provided that maintenance doses are as high as the effective treatment doses (instead of lower, as is usually the

Table 10.4

Drugs for Treating Mood Disorders

Category	Generic Name	Trade Name	Side Effects
Tricyclic antidepressants	Imipramine Amitriptyline	Tofranil Elavil	Heart attack, stroke, hypotension, blurred vision, anxiety, tiredness, dry mouth, constipation, gastric disorders, erectile failure, weight gain
MAO inhibitors	Tranylcypromine	Parnate	Possibly fatal hypertension, dry mouth, dizziness, nausea, headaches
Selective serotonin reuptake inhibitors	Fluoxetine	Prozac	Nervousness, fatigue, gastrointestinal complaints, dizziness, headaches, insomnia
Lithium	Lithium	Lithium	Tremors, gastric distress, lack of coordination, dizziness, cardiac arrhythmia, blurred vision, fatigue, death

case) and that the drug therapy was given in conjunction with a psychological treatment (Frank et al., 1990).

Antidepressant medication can be and often is used in combination with some kind of psychotherapy. If, for example, a person's depression is (partly) caused by lack of personal satisfaction because of social skills problems, it is probably essential for the drug treatment to be supplemented by attention to those behavioural deficits (Klerman, 1988a). A recent review led to the conclusion that combination therapy involving medication and cognitive therapy works better than either in isolation, but this conclusion is qualified by the relatively small number of participants in existing studies (Segal, Vincent, & Levitt, 2002). Thus, a definitive answer is not yet available.

Even if a chemical agent manages to alleviate a bout of depression only temporarily, that benefit in itself should not be underestimated, given the potential for suicide in depression and given the extreme anguish and suffering borne by the individual and, usually, his or her family. The judicious use of a drug may make unnecessary an avenue of intervention and control that many regard as very much a last resort—namely, being placed in a mental hospital.

Although some studies suggest that antidepressants should always be used for severe depression, others indicate that cognitive or interpersonal therapy is just as effective (DeRubeis et al., 1999; Jarrett et al., 1999), with the added benefit that, at the end of treatment, there are no drug-produced side effects or relapse as there is when medication is withdrawn (Hollon et al., 1992; Persons et al., 1996).

Drug Therapy for Bipolar Disorder People with the mood swings of bipolar disorder are often helped by carefully monitored dosages of the element lithium, taken in a salt form, lithium carbonate. Up to 80 percent of bipolar patients experience at least some benefit from taking this drug (Prien & Potter, 1993). Lithium is effective for bipolar patients when they are depressed as well as when they are manic, and it is much more effective for bipolar patients than for unipolar patients-another bit of evidence that these two mood disorders are basically different from each other. Because the effects of lithium occur gradually, therapy typically begins with both lithium and an antipsychotic, such as Haldol, which has an immediate calming effect. Several hypotheses concerning how lithium works are being pursued (recall our earlier discussion of the effects of lithium on G-proteins). Conclusive evidence is not yet available, but it is interesting to note that a research team led by Paul Grof in Ottawa has established that responsiveness or non-responsiveness to lithium treatment seems to be an inherited family trait (see Duffy et al., 2002; Grof et al., 2002). Offspring of lithium–non-responsive patients also experience chronic mood disorders and poor premorbid functioning compared with the offspring of lithium-responsive patients.

Because of possibly serious, even fatal, side effects, lithium has to be prescribed and used very carefully. Although it has great value in the elimination of a manic episode and forestalling future episodes if it is taken regularly, discontinuation of lithium actually increases the risk of recurrence (Suppes et al., 1991). Thus, it is recommended that lithium be used continually. Unfortunately, many patients discontinue treatment after release from the hospital (Maj et al., 1998).

Robert Munsch, well-known author of children's books, lives in Guelph, Ontario. Munsch experienced depression for many years and attributes his recovery to taking Prozac. Here his receiving the Order of Canada from Governor-General Adrienne Clarkson.

Two drugs originally used to control seizures offer promise of helping patients with bipolar disorder. Carbamazapine (Tegretol) and divalproex sodium (Depakote) are both effective treatments and are tolerated by some patients who are unable to withstand lithium's side effects (Small et al., 1991). However, neither has been established as preventing future episodes if taken regularly.

Although lithium is the treatment of choice for bipolar disorder (Keck & McElroy, 1998), the psychological aspects of the disorder must be considered, if only, as discussed earlier, to encourage the person to continue taking the medication (Goodwin & Jamison, 1990). A friend of one of the authors put it this way (paraphrased): "Lithium cuts out the highs as well as the lows. I don't miss the lows, but I have to admit that there were some aspects of the highs that I do miss. It took me a while to accept that I had to give up those highs. Wanting to keep my job and my marriage helped!" A drug alone does not address this kind of concern.

SUICIDE

Suicide was not condemned in Western thought until the fourth century, when Saint Augustine proclaimed it a crime because it violated the Sixth Commandment, Thou shalt not kill. Saint Thomas Aquinas elaborated on this view in the 13th century, declaring suicide a mortal sin because it usurped God's power over life and death. Thus, although neither the Old Testament nor the New Testament explicitly forbids suicide, the Western world came to regard it as a crime and a sin (Shneidman, 1973).

The irony is that the Christian injunctions against suicide, deriving from a profound respect for life, contributed to persecution of those who attempted to or actually did take their own lives. As late as 1823, anyone in London who committed suicide was buried with a stake pounded through the heart, and not until 1961 did suicide cease to be a criminal offence in the United Kingdom. Suicide ceased being a criminal offence in Canada in 1972.

Suicide is discussed in this chapter because many depressed persons and persons with bipolar disorder have suicidal thoughts and sometimes make attempts to take their own lives. It is believed that more than half of those who try to kill themselves are depressed and despondent at the time of the act (Henriksson et al., 1993), and it is estimated that 15 percent of people who have been diagnosed with major depression ultimately commit suicide (Maris et al., 1992). A significant number of people who are not depressed, however, make suicidal attempts, some with success—most notably people diagnosed with borderline personality disorder (Links, Gould, & Ratnayake, 2003). The suicide rate for male alcoholics is greater than that for the general population of men, and it becomes extremely high in alcoholic men who are also depressed (Linehan, 1997). Up to 13 percent of individuals with schizophrenia commit suicide (Roy, 1982), and a recent Canadian study of completed suicides found that the number of completed suicides among people with schizophrenia (84) was comparable to the number of completed suicides among people with depression (92) (see Martin, 2000). Given that people with various diagnoses commit suicide, our focus here is on issues and factors in suicide that transcend specific diagnoses.

FACTS ABOUT SUICIDE

Self-intentioned death is a complex and multi-faceted act (Berman & Jobes, 1991; Fremouw, Perczel, & Ellis, 1990; Moscicki, 1995; National Center for Health Statistics, 1988, 1994; Wright, 1992). No single theory can hope to explain it. Some facts about suicide are listed here (see Focus on Discovery 10.2 for myths about suicide):

Suicide involving violent death, such as jumping off a building, is more common among men than among women.

- According to estimates from the World Health Organization, over one million people died from suicide in 2000 and suicide rates have increased 60 percent worldwide in the past 45 years.
- According to statistics, every 17 minutes someone in the United States kills himself or herself. This figure, translating into almost 30,000 suicides a year, is probably a gross underestimate. The overall suicide rate in the United States is about 11.3 per 100,000. It rises in old age; between the ages of 75 and 84 the rate reaches 24 per 100,000.
- Suicide rates in Canada have decreased for females but not for males. In 1999 a total of 4,074 people in Canada committed suicide (Sakinofsky, 2003).
- Suicide rates in Canada and the United States were comparable until the 1970s when the Canadian rate significantly surpassed the American rate (Sakinofsky, 1998). In recent years, there have been reductions in the number of suicides in Canada by firearms and drug poisonings, but there has been an increased number of suicides by methods such as hanging and gassing. The highest rates of suicide are found in the Northwest Territories, Alberta, and Quebec, and the lowest rates are found typically in Newfoundland (Sakinofsky, 1998).
- The World Health Organization estimates globally that suicide attempts outnumber completed suicides by a 20 to 1 ratio.
- About half of those who commit suicide have made at least one previous attempt, but most attempters never make another attempt. Most do not really intend to die, especially children and adolescents. Some differences between attempters and completers are shown in Table 10.5.
- In Canada, men are four times more likely than women to kill themselves.
- Three times as many women as men attempt to kill themselves but do not die.
- Being divorced or widowed increases suicide risk by four or five times and may be a risk factor that becomes more influential with age.
- Suicide is found at all social and economic levels but is especially common among psychiatrists, physicians, lawyers, and psychologists, even more so if they are women. Also at higher risk are law enforcement officers, musicians, and dentists.
- No other kind of death leaves friends and relatives with such long-lasting feelings of distress, shame, guilt, puzzlement, and general disturbance. These survivors are themselves victims, having an especially high mortality rate in the year after the loved one's suicide.
- Guns are by far the most common means of committing suicide in the United States, accounting for about 60 percent of all suicides. The availability of firearms in U.S.

homes increases suicide risk independent of other known risk factors. Men usually choose to shoot or hang themselves; women are more likely to use sleeping pills, which may account for their lower rate of completed suicide. The implementation of gun control legislation restricting access to firearms in Canada in 1977 was associated with long-term reductions in the rates of suicide for both men and women with no corresponding increase in suicide by other methods (Carrington, 1999; Leenaars & Lester, 1996).

- It is estimated that each year upwards of 10,000 American college students attempt to kill themselves and as many as 20 percent consider suicide at least once during college.
- The rates of suicide for adolescents and children in the United States are increasing dramatically. As many as 3,000 young people between the ages of 15 and 19 are believed to kill themselves each year, and attempts are made by children as young as 6 years old. But the rates are far below those of adults. As with adults, *thinking* about suicide occurs much more often than making an actual attempt; one estimate is that suicidal imaginings occur at least once among 40 percent of children and adolescents.
- Gay and lesbian adolescents are at higher risk for suicide than heterosexual adolescents.
- Physical illness, for example, AIDS and multiple sclerosis, is a contributing factor in as many as half of all suicides.
- Suicide rates rise during depression years, remain stable during years of prosperity, and decrease during war years.

focus on discovery/10.2

Some Myths about Suicide

There are many prevalent misconceptions about suicide (Fremouw et al, 1990; Pokorny, 1968; Shneidman, 1973). It is as important to be familiar with them as it is to know the facts.

1. **People who discuss suicide will not commit the act.** At least three-quarters of those who take their own lives have communicated their intention beforehand, perhaps as a cry for help. A recent study of suicides in the Montreal subway system (the Montreal Metro) found that 81 percent of people committing suicide had expressed a prior suicide intent (Mishara, 1999).
2. **Suicide is committed without warning.** The falseness of this belief is shown by the preceding statement. The person usually gives many warnings, such as saying that the world would be better off without him or her or making unexpected and inexplicable gifts to others.
3. **Only people of a certain class commit suicide.** Suicide is neither the curse of the poor nor the disease of the rich. People in all socioeconomic classes commit suicide.
4. **Membership in a religious group is a good predictor that a person will not consider suicide.** It is mistakenly thought that the strong Catholic prohibition against suicide makes the risk that Catholics will take their lives much lower. This belief is not supported by the evidence.
5. **The motives for suicide are easily established.** The truth is that we do not fully understand why people commit suicide. For example, that a severe reverse in finances precedes a suicide does not mean that it adequately explains the suicide.
6. **All who commit suicide are depressed.** This fallacy may account for the fact that signs of impending suicide are often overlooked. Many people who take their lives are not depressed; some even appear calm and at peace with themselves.
7. **A person with a terminal physical illness is unlikely to commit suicide.** A person's awareness of impending death does not preclude suicide. Perhaps the wish to end their own suffering or that of their loved ones impels many to choose the time of their death.
8. **Improvement in emotional state means lessened risk of suicide.** People, especially those who are depressed, often commit suicide after their spirits and energy begin to rise.
9. **Suicide is a lonely event.** Although the debate whether to commit suicide is waged within the individual's head, deep immersion in a frustrating, hurtful relationship with another person—a spouse, a child, a lover, a colleague—may be a principal cause.
10. **Suicidal people clearly want to die.** Most people who contemplate suicide appear to be ambivalent about their own deaths. Some suffer from depression or alcoholism, the alleviation of which would reduce the suicidal desire. For many people, the suicidal crisis passes, and they are grateful for having been prevented from self-destruction.
11. **Thinking about suicide is rare.** Lifetime prevalence estimates from various studies suggest that among nonclinical populations, suicidal ideation runs from 40 percent to as high as 80 percent; that is, these percentages of people have thought about committing suicide at least once in their lives.
12. **Asking a person, especially a depressed person, about suicide will push him or her over the edge and cause a suicidal act that would not otherwise have occurred.** One of the first things clinicians learn in their training is to inquire about suicide when treating a deeply troubled patient. Asking about it can give the person permission to talk about what he or she might harbour as a terrible, shameful secret, one that could otherwise lead to further isolation and depression.

Table 10.5

Comparison of Suicide Attempters and Completers

Characteristics	Attempters	Completers
Gender	Majority female	Majority male
Age	Predominantly young	Risk increases with age
Method	Low lethality (pills, cutting)	More violent (gun, jumping)
Common diagnoses	Dysthymic disorder Borderline personality disorder Schizophrenia	Major mood disorder Alcoholism
Dominant affect	Depression with anger	Depression with hopelessness
Motivation	Change in situation Cry for help	Death
Hospital course	Quick recovery from dysphoria	
Attitude toward attempt	Relief to have survived Promises not to repeat	

Source: Adapted from Fremouw et al., 1990, p. 24. Reprinted by permission of Simon and Schuster International.

PERSPECTIVE ON SUICIDE

When imagining a suicide, we usually think of a person deliberately performing a dramatic act explicitly chosen to end life almost immediately—the woman sitting in a car in a garage with the motor running, the man with the gun next to his temple, the child with the bottle of a parent's sleeping pills. But suicidologists also regard people as suicidal when they act in self-destructive ways that can cause serious injury or death after a prolonged period of time, such as a diabetic patient who neglects taking insulin or adhering to a dietary regimen or an individual with alcoholism who continues to drink and does not seek help despite awareness of the damage being done to his or her body. Sometimes termed *subintentioned death*, these apparent suicides complicate still further the task of understanding and gathering statistics (Shneidman, 1973).

Ideas about the nature and causes of suicide can be found in many places (Shneidman, 1987). Letters and diaries can provide insights into the phenomenology of people who commit suicide. Novelists, such as Herman Melville and Leo Tolstoy, have provided insights on suicide, as have writers who have killed themselves, such as Virginia Woolf and Sylvia Plath.

Studies of suicide notes from ordinary people have found that those who follow through with suicide often leave specific, detailed instructions; as well, their notes show evidence of more anguish and hostility than do simulated suicide notes written by individuals who were not thinking about suicide but who were matched demographically and asked to write a suicide note as if they were planning to kill themselves (Ogilvie et al., 1983; Shneidman & Farberow, 1970). Lacking in real suicide notes is the type of general and philosophical content that characterizes those written by simulators; "Be sure to pay the electric bill" would more likely appear in a real suicide note than "Be good to others" (Baumeister, 1990).

Many motives for suicide have been suggested (Mintz, 1968): aggression turned inward; retaliation by inducing guilt in others; efforts to force love from others; efforts to make amends for perceived past wrongs; the desire to rejoin a dead loved one; and the desire or need to escape from stress, deformity, pain, or emotional vacuum. Many contemporary mental health professionals regard suicide in general as an individual's attempt at problem-solving, conducted under considerable stress and marked by consideration of a

Writers who killed themselves, such as Sylvia Plath, have provided insights about the causes of suicide.

very narrow range of alternatives of which self-annihilation appears the most viable (Linehan & Shearin, 1988).

A theory about suicide based on work in social and personality psychology holds that some suicides arise from a strong desire to escape from aversive self-awareness, that is, from the painful awareness of shortcomings and failures that the person attributes to himself or herself (Baumeister, 1990). This awareness is assumed to produce severe emotional suffering, perhaps depression. Unrealistically high expectations—and therefore the probability of failing to meet these expectations (cf. Beck and Ellis)—play a central role in this perspective on suicide. Of particular importance is a discrepancy between high expectations for intimacy and a reality that falls short, such as when someone's expectations for intimacy are dashed because a loved one cannot possibly deliver what the person needs (Stephens, 1985). Because perfectionists have impossibly high standards, they are more likely to experience such discrepancies and are at increased risk for suicide, especially if it is perceived that perfection is socially prescribed and is expected or perhaps even demanded by others (Hewitt, Flett, Sherry, & Caelian, in press).

Media reports of suicide may spark an increase in suicides. This disturbing possibility was discussed by Bandura (1986), who reviewed research by Phillips (1974, 1977, 1985) that showed several relationships:

1. Suicides rose by 12 percent in the month following Marilyn Monroe's death.
2. Publicized accounts of self-inflicted deaths of people who are not famous also are followed by significant increases in suicide, suggesting that it is the publicity rather than the fame of the person who committed suicide that is important.
3. Publicized accounts of murder-suicides are followed by increases in automobile and plane crashes in which the driver and others are killed.
4. Media reports of natural deaths of famous people are not followed by increases in suicide, suggesting that it is not grief per se that is the influential factor.

We turn now to several other perspectives on suicide, each of which attempts to shed light on this disturbing aspect of humankind.

Freud's Psychoanalytic Theory Freud proposed that suicide is murder, an extension of his anger-in theory of depression. When a person loses someone whom he or she has ambivalently loved and hated, and introjects that person, aggression is directed inward. If these feelings are strong enough, the person will commit suicide.

Durkheim's Sociological Theory Emile Durkheim (1897, 1951), a renowned sociologist, analyzed the records of suicide for various countries and during different historical periods and concluded that self-annihilation could be understood in sociological terms. He distinguished three different kinds of suicide. Egoistic suicide is committed by people who have few ties to family, society, or community. These people feel alienated from others, cut off from the social supports that are important to keep them functioning adaptively as social beings.

The suicide of Nirvana's lead singer, Kurt Cobain, triggered an increase in suicide among teenagers.

Altruistic suicide is viewed as a response to societal demands. Some people who commit suicide feel very much a part of a group and sacrifice themselves for what they take to be the good of society. The self-immolations of Buddhist monks and nuns to protest the fighting during the Vietnam War fits into this category. Some altruistic suicides, such as the hara-kiri of the Japanese, are required as the only honourable recourse in certain circumstances.

Finally, anomic suicide may be triggered by a sudden change in a person's relationship to society. A successful executive who suffers severe financial reverses may experience anomie, a sense of disorientation, because what he or she believed to be a normal way of living is no longer possible.

Anomie can pervade a society in disequilibrium, making suicide more likely. An example of anomic suicide occurred among a rural Brazilian tribe, the Guarani Indians. Their suicide rate in 1995 was 160 per 100,000, markedly higher than it was a year earlier and dramatically higher than Canadian and U.S. rates. The reason for this high suicide rate may be found in a sudden change in their living conditions. The Guarani have recently lost most of their ancestral lands to industrialization. Communities that used to live by hunting and fishing are now crowded onto reservations too small to support that way of life. Nearby cities tempt the Guarani with consumer goods that they desire and yet can ill afford on their low wages. Because hunting, farming, and family life have religious significance, their demise has significantly affected religious life. Life has lost its meaning for many of the Guarani (Long, 1995).

As with all sociological theorizing, Durkheim's hypotheses have difficulty accounting for the differences among individuals in a given society in their reactions to the same demands and conditions. Not all those who unexpectedly lose their money commit suicide, for example. It appears that Durkheim was aware of this problem, for he suggested that individual temperament would interact with any of the social pressures that he found causative.

The high suicide rate of the Guarani Indians of Brazil, who were forced onto crowded reservations, illustrates Durkheim's concept of anomic suicide. Maurice da Silva Goncalves is one of the local Guarani leaders who accused Norwegian millionaire Erling Lorentzen of stealing their land.

Shneidman's Approach to Suicide While acknowledging that perhaps 90 percent of suicides could be given a DSM diagnosis, Shneidman (1987), a pioneer in the study of suicide and its prevention, reminds us that the overwhelming majority of people with schizophrenia and mood disorders do not commit suicide. He suggests that the perturbation of mind that he posits as a key feature in a person who commits suicide is not a mental illness.

Shneidman's psychological approach to suicide is summarized in Table 10.6, which lists the 10 most frequent characteristics of suicide, not all of them found in each and every case. Shneidman regards suicide as a conscious effort to seek a solution to a problem that is causing intense psychological suffering, or what he refers to as "psychache." To the sufferer, this solution ends consciousness and unendurable pain—what Melville in *Moby Dick* termed an "insufferable anguish." Hope and a sense of constructive action are gone.

Shneidman's concept of psychological pain was referred to in the journal of Richard Edmunds, who killed himself by hanging in Calgary at age 27. Edmunds wrote, "I was born and bred to be frustrated. I cannot stand the pain any longer. I negate the past, and I have negated all of the future" (Edmunds, 1998, p. 371). This excerpt is from a moving account of the impact of a family member's suicide on survivors, as related by Anne Edmunds, the mother of the deceased.

Still—and this is of central importance in prevention—most people who contemplate or actually commit suicide are ambivalent. "The prototypical suicidal state is one in which an individual cuts his or her throat, cries for help at the same time, and is genuine in both of these acts. . . . Individuals would be happy not to do it, if they didn't have to" (Shneidman, 1987, p. 170). There is a narrowing of the perceived range of options. When not in a highly perturbed suicidal state, the person is capable of seeing more choices for dealing with stress. People planning suicide usually communicate their intention, sometimes as a cry for help, sometimes as a withdrawal from others. Typical behaviours include giving away treasured possessions and putting financial affairs in order.

Table 10.6

The Ten Commonalities of Suicide

I. The common purpose of suicide is to seek a solution.

II. The common goal of suicide is the cessation of consciousness.

III. The common stimulus in suicide is intolerable psychological pain.

IV. The common stressor in suicide is frustrated psychological needs.

V. The common emotion in suicide is hopelessness-helplessness.

VI. The common cognitive state in suicide is ambivalence.

VII. The common perceptual state in suicide is constriction.

VIII. The common action in suicide is egression.

IX. The common interpersonal act in suicide is communication of intention.

X The common consistency in suicide is with lifelong coping patterns.

Source: From Shneidman, 1985, p. 167.

Neurochemistry and Suicide Just as research has shown that low levels of serotonin appear to be related to depression, research has also established a connection among serotonin, suicide, and impulsivity. Low levels of serotonin's major metabolite, 5-HIAA, have been found in people in several diagnostic categories—depression, schizophrenia, and various personality disorders—who committed suicide (see Brown & Goodwin, 1986; van Praag, Plutchik, & Apter, 1990). Post-mortem studies of the brains of people who committed suicide have revealed increased binding by serotonin receptors (presumably a response to a decreased level of serotonin itself) (Turecki et al., 1999). The link between 5-HIAA levels and suicide is especially compelling in the case of violent and impulsive suicide (e.g., Roy, 1994). Finally, 5-HIAA levels are negatively correlated with questionnaire measures of aggression and impulsivity (Brown & Goodwin, 1986).

Prediction of Suicide from Psycological Tests

It would be of considerable theoretical and practical value to be able to predict suicide on the basis of psychological tests, and several efforts have been made to do so. Significant correlations have been found between suicide intent and hopelessness. Especially noteworthy are Aaron Beck's findings, based on prospective data, that hopelessness is a strong predictor of suicide (Beck et al., 1985, 1990), even stronger than depression (Beck, Kovacs, & Weissman, 1975). The expectation that at some point in the future things will be no better than they are right now—which, to be sure, an aspect of depression but can be found among non-depressed people as well—seems to be more instrumental than depression per se in propelling a person to take his or her life. Hopelessness is a predominant theme in Canadian Perspectives 10.3, which addresses the exceptionally high levels of suicide among certain Aboriginal groups.

Another self-report instrument is Marsha Linehan's Reasons for Living (RFL) Inventory (Ivanoff et al., 1994; Linehan, 1985; Linehan et al., 1983). Clusters of items tap six themes of importance to the individual: (1) survival and coping beliefs, (2) responsibility to family, (3) concerns about children, (4) fear of social disapproval, (5) fear of suicide, and (6) moral objections (i.e., it is morally wrong). This approach is different from, and possibly more useful than, scales that focus only on negativism and pessimism, because knowing what there is in a person's life that *prevents* him or her from committing suicide has both assessment and intervention value. This instrument can discriminate between suicidal and non-suicidal individuals and can help the clinician with intervention by identifying the reasons the person has for not wanting to die. The RFL also appears to be generalizable. It was found to have good psychometric qualities and was associated negatively with suicide ideation when the scale was adapted for use with French Canadian populations (see Labelle, Lachance, and Morval, 1996).

Another avenue of research has focused on the cognitive characteristics of people who attempt suicide. It has been suggested that suicidal individuals are more rigid in their approach to problems (e.g., Neuringer, 1964) and less flexible in their thinking (Levenson, 1972). Constricted thinking could account for the apparent inability to seek solutions to life's problems other than that offered by taking one's own life (Linehan et al., 1987). Research confirms the hypothesis that people who attempt suicide are more rigid than others, lending support to the clinical observations of Shneidman and others that people who attempt suicide seem incapable of thinking of alternative solutions to problems.

Overall, it has proved difficult to predict suicide based on the kind of trait approach that characterizes these research efforts. As we saw in Chapter 4, behaviour is influenced a great deal by the environment, and the environment includes stressful events that themselves can be difficult to predict. We can seldom know, for example, whether a given individual is going to lose employment, experience serious marital problems, suffer the loss of a loved one, or be involved in a serious accident. In addition, it is hard to predict with accuracy an infrequent event such as suicide, even

Canadian Perspectives/10.3

Suicide Among Canadian Aboriginal People

"Innu youth talk openly about their pain and sense of hopelessness. They acknowledge that they drink, take drugs and sniff gasoline to forget the boredom, the beatings, the abuse."

—DeMont, "The Tragedy of Andrew Rich", *Maclean's*, November 22, 1999, p. 40.

"This is a wounded community. A nightmare place where no one seems to have any hope."

—Lynne Gregory, addictions counsellor in Sheshatshiu (DeMont, 1999, p. 39)

"The prospect of a future without change is too much for some to bear."

—DeMont (1999, p.40)

In recent years, world attention has been focused on Canada because of the alarming situation that has emerged in Davis Inlet and Sheshatshiu, Newfoundland and Labrador, where excessively high rates of suicide and widespread dysfunctional behaviours, such as solvent abuse, sexual abuse, and domestic violence, have been documented.

One tragic story among many is that of Andrew Rich, the son of Jean-Pierre Ashini. Andrew went with his father to the airport in Goose Bay to see him off to London, England. Ashini was going to address a news conference about the "suicide epidemic" among Canada's Innu people.

> But he worried about his son, a shy 15-year-old who went by the nickname of 'Mr. T.' Andrew spoke little English and had always seemed most comfortable camping and hunting in Nitassinan, the name the Innu gave to their homeland in the Labrador wilderness. But in Sheshatshiu, 32 km north of Goose Bay, he had, like so many Innu youths, fallen into despair. He drank, did drugs and inhaled gasoline fumes when nothing else was available to dull the pain of his life. Sometimes, he talked about suicide. Preparing to board the plane, Ashini, a tee-totalling [sic] shrimp fisherman, urged his son to stay clean and behave himself while he was away. Once on the plane, he recalls, "I mouthed the words 'don't drink' through the glass of the window. I saw him nod yes, and I felt good when I left."
>
> But 45 minutes after arriving in London, Ashini received news from home that shattered his world. Sometime in the early morning of Nov. 6, Andrew had swallowed a vial of pills. He then walked into his bedroom and shot himself in the head while his 13-year-old girlfriend sat a few rooms away—the third youth in the past year to commit suicide in the community of 1,500. (DeMont, 1999, p. 36)

According to a report released in 2000 by the human rights group Survival for Tribal People, the Innu people of Labrador and Quebec are 13 times more likely to kill themselves than other people in Canada and the Innu of Davis Inlet, 200 kilometres north of Sheshatshiu, have the highest suicide rate in the world (178 per 100,000 people). Moreover, the suicide rate among children and adolescents is extremely high, with estimates ranging from three to seven times the national average for children.

What factors contribute to such high suicide rates? The organization's report points to a multitude of factors that have contributed to the suicide rate, including loss of cultural identity, industrial development and depletion of natural resources on Innu land, and even physical and sexual abuse experienced when the Innu visited Roman Catholic missionaries at trading posts (see Samson, Wilson, & Mazower, 2000).

Although the Innu situation has recently garnered most of the public attention, other Native groups also experience high levels of suicide. Shortly after the recent Innu situation came to light, British sociologist Colin Samson, co-author of the Innu study, reported that the Ojibwa reserve in Pikangijum (300 kilometres northeast of Winnipeg) had the even higher rate of 213 per 100,000 people between 1992 and 2000; these data included the suicides of eight females (including five 13-year-olds) who killed themselves in 2000 (Canadian Press, 2000; Harries, 2001). Michael Kral of the University of Windsor conducted a comparative analysis of this suicide rate and concluded that "[a]t this point, it's off the scale" and the situation is "horrendous" (Canadian Press, 2000).

Some Native communities have experienced "cluster suicide," which involves multiple suicides by groups of individuals in the same community. Ward and Fox (1977) reported "a true suicide epidemic" among a rural community of just 37 families on a reservation on Manitoulin Island, Ontario. A 17-year-old boy, upset by the expected separation of his parents, consumed a large volume of alcohol and shot himself. In less than a year, eight other youths were dead, an astronomical suicide rate of 267 per 100,000. Wilkie, Macdonald, and Hildahl (1998) described a small First Nations community in Manitoba of less than 1,500 people that had six suicides and many more attempted suicides in a three-month span in 1995. Alcohol and previous sexual assault were factors in four suicides. Wilkie et al. also noted that those who had attempted suicide in this community reported that they had experienced dreams of beckoning in which voices urged them to kill themselves.

These alarming situations have led Canadian researchers to focus their attention on this issue. A study of 99 Inuit between the ages of 14 and 25 found that 34 percent had attempted suicide and 20 percent had made two or more suicide attempts (Kirmayer, Malus, & Boothroyd, 1996). Risk factors associated with *suicide attempts* included being male, having a friend who had attempted or committed suicide, a history of physical abuse, solvent abuse, and having a parent with an alcohol or drug problem. Two protective factors were degree of church attendance and doing well at school. A follow-up study of 203 Inuit youth found some gender differences (Kirmayer, Boothroyd, & Hodgins, 1998). The strongest predictors of attempted suicide among females were the presence of a psychiatric problem, recent alcohol abuse, and cocaine or crack use. The strongest predictors among males were solvent use and number of recent life events.

As is generally the case, males are much more likely to commit suicide. One recent study of Inuit people from Nunavik found that the ratio of male suicides to female suicides was 5 to 1 (Boothroyd et al., 2001). The two principal means of suicide were by hanging and by gunshot.

Alcohol may be a disinhibiting factor. A comparative study of suicides in Manitoba from 1988 to 1994 found that Aboriginal people who committed suicide had higher blood alcohol levels than non-Aboriginals who committed suicide (Malchy, Enns, Young, & Cox, 1997). Furthermore, Aboriginal people were less likely than non-Aboriginal people to have sought help.

Chandler and Lalonde (1998) noted that there are substantial differences in suicide rates among the various indigenous and First Nations groups, with some communities having rates that are 800 times the national average. They suggested that a key contributing factor is the degree to which cultural identity is maintained and preserved over time. Their analysis of 196 bands in British Columbia showed that a key factor that mitigates against suicide is the extent to which the community makes a collective effort to maintain and strengthen its own cultural continuity. Cooper, Corrado, Karlberg, and Adams (1992) also reported risk factors among bands in British Columbia with high suicide rates, including overcrowding, numerous low-income and single-parent families, large households with numerous children, and very few elders in the community. They also reported that the rates of suicide for registered Natives who lived outside of the reserves were comparable to suicide rates for the general population.

Finally, a study by Enns et al. (1997) illustrated the need to consider the possibility that the factors associated with suicide attempts in Caucasians may not be the same factors associated with suicide attempts in Aboriginals. They found that hopelessness was the only predictor of suicide intent in Caucasian adolescents, while depression was the only predictor of suicide intent in Aboriginal adolescents.

The problem of suicide among Aboriginal people resulted in the formation of the Suicide Prevention Advisory Group (SPAG) in 2001. The SPAG was appointed jointly by then national chief Matthew Coon Come of the Assembly of First Nations and then minister of health Allan Rock. The initial SPAG report entitled *Acting on What We Know: Preventing Youth Suicide in First Nations*, was published in January 2003 (Advisory Group on Suicide Prevention, 2003). The recommendations address four primary themes: (1) increasing knowledge about what works in suicide prevention; (2) developing more effective and integrated health care services; (3) supporting community-driven approaches; and (4) creating strategies for building youth identity, resilience, and culture. More generally, the SPAG acknowledged that no single approach will be effective by itself and that multi-level changes to family and community systems are needed.

Thinking Critically

1. As indicated by the SPAG report, it should be clear that solutions to the problem of suicide among our Aboriginal peoples will require, not only psychological interventions, but also societal and economic interventions. Does the fact that the suicide rate is relatively low in some First Nations and Innu communities suggest to you that community-based solutions are, in fact, possible?
2. Do you think that young Innu like Andrew Rich feel pressure to belong to traditional Innu culture and at the same time pressure to achieve in mainstream Canadian culture? Is it possible that they perceive a lack of support in both directions?

with a highly reliable test (Fremouw et al., 1990; Roy, 1995).

Preventing Suicide

The need to prevent suicide is garnering increased attention, not only in Canada, but around the world. In 1999 the World Health Organization began a worldwide initiative—known as SUPRE-MISS—to prevent suicidal behaviours (World Health Organization, 2000). "SUPRE" refers to suicide prevention, and "MISS" refers to the multi-site intervention study on suicidal behaviours. The study focuses on the evaluation of treatment strategies for people attempting suicide, as well as on community surveys of suicidal thoughts and behaviours. But just what can be done to prevent suicides from occurring?

Treating the Underlying Mental Disorder One way to look at the prevention of suicide is to bear in mind that most people who attempt to kill themselves are suffering from a treatable mental disorder such as depression, schizophrenia, substance abuse, or borderline personality disorder. A Canadian study of young men who committed suicide showed that almost everyone who had beenn examined had a diagnosable Axis I disorder such as depression and 57.3 percent had a diagnosable personality disorder (Lesage et al., 1994). Thus, when someone following Beck's cognitive approach successfully lessens a patient's depression, that patient's prior suicidal risk is reduced; the same is true for the dialectical behaviour therapy of Marsha Linehan (1993b), whose therapy with borderline patients is described in Chapter 13.

The view that efforts to prevent suicide should focus on the underlying psychological disorder is held by many experts (e.g., Moscicki, 1995). However, no controlled studies have demonstrated that psychological or pharmacological treatments that reduce depression have a beneficial impact on suicide (Linehan, 1997). The absence of such a positive effect on suicide therefore casts doubt on the strategy of treating a disorder presumed to underlie suicidality.

Treating Suicidality Directly Another tradition in suicide prevention downplays mental disorder and concentrates instead on the particular characteristics of suicidal people that transcend mental disorders. One of the best-known approaches of this nature is that of Edwin Shneidman. We have already reviewed some of his thinking on suicide. His general strategy of suicide prevention (1985, 1987) is threefold:

1 Reduce the intense psychological pain and suffering.
2 Lift the blinders, that is, expand the constricted view by helping the individual see options other than the extremes of continued suffering or nothingness.
3 Encourage the person to pull back even a little from the self-destructive act.

Shneidman cited the example of a wealthy college student who was single, pregnant, and suicidal and had a clearly formed plan. The only solution she could think of besides suicide was never to have become pregnant, even to be virginal again.

> I took out a sheet of paper and began to widen her blinders. I said something like, "Now, let's see: You could have an abortion here locally." She responded, "I couldn't do that." I continued, "You could go away and have an abortion." "I couldn't do that." "You could bring the baby to term and keep the baby." "I couldn't do that." "You could have the baby and adopt it out." Further options were similarly dismissed. When I said, "You can always commit suicide, but there is obviously no need to do that today," there was no response. "Now," I said, "let's look at this list and rank them in order of your preference, keeping in mind that none of them is optimal." (Shneidman, 1987, p. 171)

Shneidman reported that just drawing up the list had a calming effect. The student's lethality—her drive to kill herself very soon—receded, and she was able to rank the list even though she found something wrong with each item. But an important goal had been achieved; she had been pulled back from the brink and was in a frame of mind to consider courses of action other than dying or being a virgin again. "We were then simply 'haggling' about life, a perfectly viable solution" (p. 171).

Dr. Isaac Sakinofsky (centre), head of the Clarke Institute's High Risk Consultation Clinic, received the Doug Lear Memorial Suicide Award from the Council on Suicide Prevention. Shown presenting the award are Dr. Fred Lowy, head of the University of Toronto's Centre for Bioethics, and Dr. Frances Newman, president of the Council on Suicide Prevention.

Suicide Prevention Centres Many **suicide prevention centres** are modelled after the Los Angeles Suicide Prevention Center, founded in 1958 by Farberow and Shneidman. There are at present more than 200 such centres in the United States and many abroad as well (Lester, 1995). According to the Canadian Association for Suicide Prevention (1994) there are over 200 suicide prevention and crisis centres in Canada.

Staffed largely by nonprofessionals under the supervision of psychologists or psychiatrists, these centres attempt to provide 24-hour consultation to people in suicidal crises. Usually the initial contact is made by telephone, and the centre's phone number is well publicized in the community. Workers rely heavily on demographic factors to assess risk (Shneidman, Farberow, & Litman, 1970). They have before them a checklist to guide their questioning of each caller. For example, a caller would be regarded as a lethal risk if he were male, middle-aged, divorced, and living alone and had a history of previous suicide attempts. Usually the more detailed and concrete the suicide plan, the higher the risk. The worker tries to assess the likelihood that the caller will make a serious suicide attempt and, most important, tries to establish personal contact and dissuade the caller from suicide. Staffers are taught to adopt a phenomenological stance, to view the suicidal person's situation as he or she sees it and not to convey in any way that the patient is a fool or is crazy to have settled on suicide as a solution to his or her woes. This empathy for suicidal people is sometimes referred to as *tuning in*.

Many students who take abnormal psychology are eager to "make a difference" in the lives of others, and one common route to achieving this goal is to volunteer as a member of a suicide or crisis telephone line. Indeed, according to Leenaars (2000), throughout the world, suicide prevention depends on "volunteerism." The telephone service is available in many locations throughout Canada and is becoming increasingly available in more remote regions. Levy and Fletcher (1998) described the origins and development of the first crisis line in the North, Kamatsiaqtut, the Baffin Crisis Line, "a community response to the cries of hopelessness and helplessness that have been vibrating through the North" (p. 355). The first two phone lines were established in 1990, after start-up funds were provided by CBC employees who put together a curl-a-thon. The crisis line received over 400 calls the first year, a large number considering that these lines served only the 3,700 people in Iqaluit. Currently, there are 45 active volunteers and about three calls are received per night. Callers report a number of problems, but the most common centre on losses involving relationships, family members, and friends.

Levy and Fletcher (1998) noted that the decision to provide a crisis line in the North is inconsistent with Inuit culture beliefs because the crisis line focuses on the individual, while Inuit society emphasizes the importance of community. Still, the crisis line is made available by the volunteer efforts of the community, and Levy and Fletcher (1998) concluded that it plays a vital role in providing distressed individuals with a chance to express their concerns and not simply keep things to themselves.

According to Leenaars (2000) review of suicide prevention in Canada, the first telephone centre in Canada was started in Sudbury, Ontario, in 1965; however, the real push in Canada came from the Suicide Prevention and Distress

Centre in Toronto. The 48 trained volunteers started answering the telephones on November 1, 1967, and the first three calls came from people contemplating suicide. It is estimated that the centres in the Greater Toronto Area now receive approximately 800,000 calls each year (Leenaars, 2000). Suicide Action in Montreal is the largest French-language telephone crisis service in Canada.

Such community facilities are potentially valuable because people who attempt suicide give warnings—cries for help—before taking their lives. Ambivalence about living or dying is the hallmark of the suicidal state (Shneidman, 1976). Usually, pleas are directed first to relatives and friends, but many people contemplating suicide are isolated from these sources of emotional support. A hotline service may save the lives of such individuals.

Victims of suicide include survivors, especially those among the unfortunate 25 percent who were speaking to or in the presence of the person when the act was committed (Andress & Corey, 1978). Sometimes these survivors are therapists or hospital emergency room personnel. All are subject to strong feelings of guilt and self-recrimination, second-guessing what they might have done to prevent the suicide. Even dispassionate analysis does not invariably allay the guilt and anger. Grieving after a suicide death tends to last much longer than a death that is not self-inflicted. For these many reasons, peer support groups exist to help survivors cope with the aftermath of a suicide. They provide social support, opportunities to ventilate feelings, constructive information, and referrals to professionals if that seems advisable (Fremouw et al., 1990).

Government Suicide Prevention Programs in Canada

Dyck and White (1998) provided a comprehensive overview of suicide prevention programs in Canada. They noted that the provinces differ substantially in this regard. Alberta has the longest-standing suicide prevention program in the nation. This contrasts substantially with three provinces (i.e., Ontario, Quebec, and Saskatchewan) that do not have well-articulated suicide prevention programs.

Alberta is also distinguished by the fact that it is one of the few provinces to document its evaluation efforts (see Dyck & White, 1998). Provincial assessments led to an updated approach in Alberta in 1993 (White et al., 1993). The three goals of this approach, as stated by Dyck and White (1998), were: (1) prevent fatal and non-fatal suicidal behaviours; (2) reduce the impact of suicidal behaviours on individuals; and (3) improve access and availability to appropriate services for people who are at-risk and/or vulnerable. Six province-wide strategies were identified: (1) community coordination of a full range of prevention strategies (this entails mental health promotion, prevention, early intervention, crisis intervention, treatment, bereavement counselling for survivors, and post-vention); (2) suicide

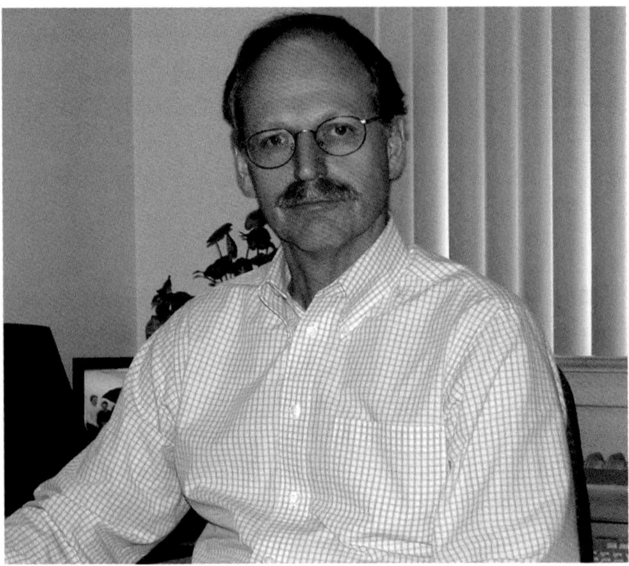

Paul Links holds the only endowed research chair in suicide studies in North America. He conducts research on the prevention and etiology of suicide and holds the Arthur Sommer Rotenberg Chair in Suicide Studies at St. Michael's Hospital in Toronto. The chair is named after Dr. Arthur Sommer Rotenberg, a family physician from Toronto, who committed suicide.

awareness education; (3) training in suicide intervention and suicide bereavement; (4) research; (5) evaluation of suicide prevention activities as well as the overall program; and (6) advocacy for improving public health policy. The Suicide Information and Education Centre (SIEC), initiated in 1981, has grown into the world's largest information centre for English-language literature on suicide (Leenaars, 2000).

Provinces such as Quebec and Ontario lack a coordinated suicide prevention approach at the governmental level. In 1992 the Quebec provincial government set a goal of reducing suicide by 15 percent by 2002, but no resources were provided to achieve this goal (Dyck & White, 1998). Nevertheless, Quebec and Ontario have a community-based approach that includes crisis lines, suicide intervention training, and public education. Quebec was identified by Dyck and White (1998) as a province that utilizes a community-based approach similar to the U.S. suicide prevention centres described earlier.

It is exceedingly difficult to do controlled research on suicide, and outcome studies have yielded inconsistent results. A U.S. meta-analysis of five studies on the effectiveness of suicide prevention centres failed to demonstrate that rates decline after the implementation of services (Dew et al., 1987). A similarly negative finding was reported from Canada (Leenaars & Lester, 1995). However, another study found that suicide rates declined in the years following the establishment of suicide prevention centres in several cities (Lester, 1991). These inconclusive findings are consistent with the paucity of data on suicide prevention by other means, though the most promising approach appears to be a cognitive-behavioural one that emphasizes social problem-solving (e.g., Linehan et al., 1991). The despair and hopelessness of suicidal people may make them see suicide as the only solution, the only exit from an unbearable existence. The therapist encourages consideration of other ways to change the distressed state by construing problems as soluble and then generating life-affirming strategies for dealing with them.

We are left with conflicting and inconclusive evidence. Human lives are precious, however, and since many people who contact suicide prevention centres and crisis lines weather a suicidal crisis successfully, these efforts will continue.

CLINICAL AND ETHICAL ISSUES IN DEALING WITH SUICIDE

Professional organizations charge their members to protect people from harming themselves even if doing so requires breaking the confidentiality of the therapist-patient relationship. The suicide of a therapist's patient is frequently grounds for a malpractice lawsuit, and therapists tend to lose such suits if it can be proved that the therapist failed to make adequate assessments and to take reasonable precautions according to generally accepted standards of care for suicide prevention (e.g., Roy, 1995).

It is not easy to agree about what constitutes reasonable care, particularly when the patient is not hospitalized and therefore not under surveillance and potential restraint. Clinicians must work out their own ethic regarding a person's right to end his or her life. What steps are the professional willing to take to prevent a suicide? Confinement in a hospital? Or, as is more common today, sedation administered against the patient's wishes and strong enough that the person is virtually incapable of taking any action at all? And for how long should extraordinary measures be taken? Clinicians realize that most suicidal crises pass; the suicidal person is likely to be grateful afterward for having been prevented from committing suicide.

Physician-Assisted Suicide Physician-assisted suicide is currently a highly charged issue. It came to the fore in the early 1990s when a Michigan physician, Jack Kevorkian, helped a 54-year-old Oregonian woman in the early stages of Alzheimer's disease, a degenerative and fatal brain disease, to commit suicide. Not yet seriously disabled, she was helped by Kevorkian to press a button on a machine designed by him to inject a drug that induced unconsciousness and a lethal dose of potassium chloride that stopped her heart (Egan, 1990). Death was painless. For almost 10 years, Kevorkian played an active role in assisting upwards of 100 terminally ill people take their lives.

One such person was Austin Bastable from Windsor, Ontario. Bastable suffered from multiple sclerosis and went public (primarily through his website) with his desire to die. Bastable travelled with his wife across the border to Detroit on May 6, 1996. He died later that same night in the presence of four physicians, including Kevorkian, who was standing trial at that time for the death of two people. Kevorkian was acquitted in 1996; he was brought to trial several times but was not convicted of murder or professional misconduct until the spring of 1999, when he was found guilty of murder and sentenced to 10 to 25 years in prison. As for Bastable, he became an activist prior to his death and lobbied the Canadian government to legalize assisted suicide. His story drew nationwide attention when it was broadcast on CBC's *Man Alive* on February 8, 1996. Right-to-life advocates attempted to intervene by pleading with Austin, via a "Save Austin Bastable" website, not to commit suicide.

Jack Kevorkian has provoked a searching and emotional discussion about the conditions under which a physician may take the life of a dying patient—an issue made all the more heated by knowledge that health professionals every day pull the plug on brain-dead patients who are being kept physically alive by sophisticated medical apparatus. Passionate arguments pro and con continue. Right-to-life advocates in the U.S. claim that, especially in this era of managed health care, patients will be pressured, albeit subtly, to ask to have their suffering lives terminated in order to spare their families the high costs of medical care. Opponents fear that physicians, too, will lean in this direction, perhaps pressured by insurance companies that want to save money on expensive terminal medical care, and will influence the patient and his or her family to end the person's life. Among powerful groups opposing assisted suicide are the American Medical Association and the Catholic Church. Kevorkian's supporters and others, such as the American Civil Liberties Union, believe that terminally ill people should have the right to

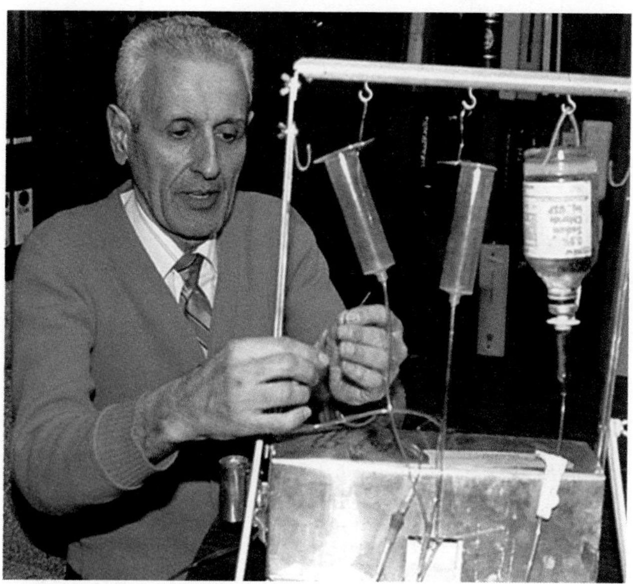

Jack Kevorkian, a Michigan physician, assisted many patients in taking their own lives. The controversy stimulated by his actions focused attention on the moral issues surrounding suicide

end their suffering. Many of these supporters have for years objected to the intrusion of the state on what they regard as a person's inalienable right to make such life or death decisions.

Interestingly, a 1999 study sought to determine physicians' attitudes towards assisted suicide (Heath, Wood, Bally, Cornelisse, & Hogg, 1999). Anonymous questionnaires were sent to almost 3,000 family physicians in Canada. It was found that 60 percent of physicians with an opinion on this issue were in favour of the legalization of assisted suicide. One factor that predicted a more positive view was whether the physician provided care to HIV patients. Another factor was the physician's location, with more favourable attitudes coming from physicians practising in British Columbia, Ontario, and Quebec.

Comment on Treating the Suicidal Person

Cases such as that of Jack Kevorkian are unusual. For the most part, mental health workers try to prevent suicide, and in that context they should not hesitate to inquire directly whether a client has thought of suicide. Above all, the clinician treating a suicidal person must be prepared to devote more energy and time than usual. Late-night phone calls and visits to the patient's home may be frequent. The therapist should realize that he or she is likely to become a singularly important figure in the suicidal person's life and should be prepared both for the extreme dependency of the patient and for the hostility and resentment that sometimes greet efforts to help.

SUMMARY

- DSM-IV-TR lists two principal kinds of mood disorders. In major, or unipolar, depression, a person experiences profound sadness as well as related problems such as sleep and appetite disturbances and loss of energy and self-esteem. In bipolar I disorder, a person has episodes of mania alone, distinct episodes of mania and of depression, or mixed episodes, in which both manic and depressive symptoms occur together. With mania, mood is elevated or irritable, and the person becomes extremely active, talkative, and distractible. DSM-IV also lists two chronic mood disorders, cyclothymia and dysthymia; both must last for two years. In cyclothymia, the person has frequent periods of depressed mood and hypomania; in dysthymia, the person is chronically depressed.
- Psychological theories of depression have been couched in psychoanalytic, cognitive, and interpersonal terms. Psychoanalytic formulations stress fixation in the oral stage (leading to a high level of dependency) and unconscious identification with a lost loved one whose desertion of the individual has resulted in anger turned inward. Beck's cognitive theory ascribes causal significance to negative schematas and cognitive biases and distortions. According to helplessness/hopelessness theory, early experiences in inescapable, hurtful situations instill a sense of hopelessness that can evolve into depression. Individuals are likely to attribute failures to their own general and persistent inadequacies and faults. Interpersonal theory focuses on the problems depressed people have in relating to others and on the negative responses they elicit from others. These same theories are applied to the depressive phase of bipolar disorder. The manic phase is considered a defence against a debilitating psychological state, such as low self-esteem.
- There may be an inherited predisposition for mood disorders, particularly for bipolar disorder. Linkage analyses may provide information about the chromosome on which the gene is located. Early neurochemical theories related depression to low levels of serotonin and bipolar disorder to norepinephrine (high in mania and low in depression). Recent research has focused on the postsynaptic receptors rather than on the amount of various transmitters. Overactivity of the hypothalamic-pituitary-adrenal axis is also found among depressive patients, indicating that the endocrine system may influence mood disorders.
- Several psychological and somatic therapies are effective for mood disorders, especially for depression. Psychoanalytic treatment tries to give the patient insight into childhood loss and inadequacy and later self-blame. The aim of Beck's cognitive therapy is to uncover negative and illogical patterns of thinking and to teach more realistic ways of viewing events, the self, and adversity. Interpersonal therapy, which focuses on the depressed patient's social interactions, also is an effective therapy.
- Biological treatments are often used in conjunction with psychological treatment and can be effective. ECT and several antidepressant drugs (tricyclics, selective serotonin reuptake inhibitors, and MAO inhibitors) have proved their worth in lifting depression, with the caveat that recent evidence indicates that ECT patients relapse at high rates if they do not receive follow-up antidepressant treatment. Other findings indicate that patients may avoid the excesses of manic and depressive periods through careful administration of lithium carbonate.
- Our exploration of suicide reveals that self-annihilatory

tendencies are not restricted to those who are depressed. Many methods can be applied to help prevent suicide, although no single theory is likely to account for the wide variety of motives and situations behind it. Most perspectives on suicide regard it as usually an act of desperation to end an existence that the person feels is unendurable.

- Physician-assisted suicide has become controversial in recent years as legislatures and the courts wrestle with the issue of the proper role of doctors in releasing terminally ill patients from the extreme pain and disability that can accompany the last months or days of life.
- Most large communities have suicide prevention centres, and most therapists at one time or another have to deal with patients in suicidal crisis. Suicidal persons need to have their fears and concerns understood but not judged; clinicians must gradually and patiently point out to them that there are alternatives to self-destruction to be explored.

KEY TERMS

altruistic suicide (p. 312)
anomic suicide (p. 312)
attribution (p. 296)
autonomy (p. 293)
bilateral ECT (p. 306)
bipolar I disorder (p. 286)
bipolar II disorder (p. 286)
brooding (p. 285)
congruency hypothesis (p. 294)
cyclothymic disorder (p. 289)
depression (p. 282)
depressive paradox (p. 296)
depressive predictive certainty (p. 297)
double depression (p. 289)
dysthymic disorder (p. 289)
egoistic suicide (p. 312)
electroconvulsive therapy (ECT) (p. 305)
hypomania (p. 286)
learned helplessness theory (p. 295)
lithium carbonate (p. 308)
major depression (p. 283)
mania (p. 283)
monoamine oxidase (MAO) inhibitors (p. 299)
mood disorders (p. 282)
negative triad (p. 290)
phototherapy (p. 288)
postpartum depression (p. 287)
psychologizer (p. 282)
ruminative coping (p. 285)
seasonal affective disorder (SAD) (p. 288)
sociotropy (p. 293)
Stroop task (p. 291)
suicide prevention centres (p. 317)
tricyclic drugs (p. 299)
unilateral ECT (p. 306)

Reflections: Past, Present, and Future

- Research suggests that there is a genetic predisposition for major depression and bipolar disorder that probably affects brain neurochemistry in some way. Is it possible that traumatic life events and other negative life experiences lead to neurochemical changes that create the same effect as a genetic predisposition? Post and Weiss (1995) proposed a *kindling-sensitization model* that argues that neurotransmitter systems become increasingly sensitive to stressors (biological or environmental) with repeated episodes of depression or mania. The consequence is that the brain becomes more easily affected by stressors and eventually minor events or mild stressors cause dysregulation and trigger episodes. Did you know that monkeys raised without their mothers and with only peers for support had low serotonin levels as early as 14 days of age and continuing into adulthood (APA Monitor, April, 1997)?
- Currently, most of the abnormalities in neurotransmitters that have been identified in people with the various mood disorders are "state dependent," meaning that the differences are evident when the mood disorder occurs but tend to dissipate when mood changes. What are the implications of this fact for our understanding of the mood disorders?
- In Chapter 15, we will discuss the issue of depression in children. Do you think depression occurs in younger children or does it develop during adolescence? Does depression in young people differ from depression in adults? Is it possible to find a way to prevent first depressions in vulnerable children?
- In Chapter 5, we discussed the issue of sexual abuse among Canada's Aboriginal peoples. In this chapter, we discussed the extremely high rates of suicide among Aboriginals. In Chapter 12, you will learn that Aboriginal people have a very high rate of substance abuse. Based on your understanding of the history of the treatment of Aboriginal peoples, their current life circumstances, the identified risk factors for different psychological disorders, and factors related to suicide and substance abuse, design a comprehensive, diathesis-stress model to explain the psychological problems seen in Aboriginal people, especially children.
- If you had the power and resources to try to change the destiny of Innu children, what would you do? Outline a comprehensive, multi-faceted intervention plan. What role would the Innu themselves play in the design and implementation of the plan?

11 chapter

Schizophrenia

"Schizophrenic behaviour is a special strategy that a person invents in order to live in an unlivable situation."
—R.D. Laing

"If you talk to God, you are praying. If God talks to you, you have schizophrenia."
—Thomas Szasz, "Schizophrenia," in *The Second Sin*

"Many people don't realize that most people with schizophrenia are not violent—and actually, we are more likely to harm ourselves, than others. If it wasn't for my medication, and the assistance I've had with support and housing, I don't think I could do what I am now doing. The stigma I've had to face could have been devastating, but I've learned to deal with it and I'm now helping others through advocacy work and peer-counselling."
—Linda Chamberlain, now 51, who was diagnosed with schizophrenia at the age of 20 and who was in and out of hospital until, eventually, she became homeless (Schizophrenia Society of Canada, 2002, p. 5).

"The humanity, decency, and respect for human rights of any society can be measured by the way it treats its most afflicted and unfortunate patients, the schizophrenics. A humane society treats these patients in hospitals, or asylums, or good shelters with decent food, proper care, respect, dignity, and privacy—and it does so until they are well enough to look after themselves in the community. A less humane society houses them in prisons, rundown hostels, decrepit hotels, nursing homes, and on the streets—in doorways, cardboard boxes, parks, and city sidewalk grates."
—Abram Hoffer, former director of psychiatric research for the Province of Saskatchewan, currently in private practice in Victoria, B.C., and president of the Canadian Schizophrenia Foundation (2000, p. 144)

Harry Mayerovitch, *The Defeatists*

As an Air Canada ticket agent in Calgary during the early 1980s, Michele Misurelli was convinced that Communist agents were plotting against her. "I believed that some of the people I worked with were Communist spies who travelled from airport to airport trying to blow things up," recalls Misurelli, 31, whose own illness has now been largely controlled by antipsychotic drugs. She adds, "You take in information from all five senses properly but you interpret it wrong. If someone followed me down a hallway, I thought they were going to kill me." Overwhelmed by paranoia, Misurelli finally resigned from Air Canada in June 1988 to evade the colleagues she believed were trying to kill her. "I thought," she says, "that I was thinking normally."

The turning point came two months later. "I thought Communists sprayed gas under my apartment door at night and performed brain surgery on me while I was sleeping," says Misurelli, who at the time was obsessed with politics and wanted to run for public office. "I thought they stuck a pick in my ear and pulled my brain out bit by bit. I woke up screaming in my apartment. I phoned my mother and told her that the Communists were going to kill me." Misurelli finally agreed to go to the local hospital, where doctors diagnosed her as schizophrenic and put her on antipsychotic drugs.

Over the next year, as she struggled with schizophrenia, Misurelli tried several times to hold a job. She lasted only a couple of days as a receptionist in Calgary because she repeatedly disconnected callers. "Again, I thought the phones were bugged," she remembers. "I became paranoid and had another confrontation." Several months later, Misurelli landed a ticket agent's job with American Airlines and was sent to Montreal for on-the-job training. But the stress triggered a new bout of psychotic paranoia. "I was afraid in my hotel room," she says. "I thought the walls were closing in on me. I needed to be surrounded by friends and family, so I said that I had the flu and went back to Calgary. My boss fired me for leaving the training."

Although stress can still cause her to experience hallucinations, Misurelli works as a volunteer for the Schizophrenia Society of Alberta, visiting schools and talking to senior students about her illness. In 1993, Misurelli, who is unmarried, gave birth to a daughter, Jennifer, after a brief relationship, and she now lives in Calgary with her parents. "With schizophrenia," says Misurelli, "everything was taken away from me. All my hopes and opportunities were gone. Now, my job is to look after my daughter. I have a purpose" (from "Schizophrenia: Hidden Torment," by Mark Nichols, *Maclean's*, January 30, 1995).

Although the diagnosis of schizophrenia has existed now for over a century and the disorder has spawned more research than any other psychological problem, we are far from understanding this serious mental disorder.

Schizophrenia is a psychotic disorder characterized by major disturbances in thought, emotion, and behaviour—disordered thinking in which ideas are not logically related, faulty perception and attention, flat or inappropriate affect, and bizarre disturbances in motor activity. Patients with schizophrenia withdraw from people and reality, often into a fantasy life of delusions and hallucinations.

Schizophrenia is one of the most severe psychopathologies we will describe in this book; its lifetime prevalence is about 1 percent and it affects men and women equally. Although it sometimes begins in childhood, it usually appears in late adolescence or early adulthood, somewhat earlier for men than for women. People with schizophrenia typically have a number of acute episodes of their symptoms. Between episodes, they often have less severe but still very debilitating symptoms. Comorbid substance abuse is a major problem for patients with schizophrenia, occurring in about 50 percent of them (Kosten & Ziedonis, 1997).

A recent meta-analysis of prevalence and incidence rates conducted by Canadian researchers (see Goldner, Hsu, Waraich, & Somers, 2002) concluded that there may be real variation in schizophrenia across geographical regions around the world, with Asian populations having lower prevalence rates.

In this chapter, we first describe the clinical features of schizophrenia; we then consider the history of the concept and how it has changed over the years; and, finally, we examine research on the etiology of schizophrenia and therapies for the disorder.

CLINICAL SYMPTOMS OF SCHIZOPHRENIA

"When I'm psychotic I feel like I'm a disembodied soul. I'm in contact with fairy kings, delusionary people. Sometimes I'm not even aware there are normal people around me, I'm so caught up in the fantasy. Sometimes I've thought I was Peter Rabbit and I would only eat rabbit food. Sometimes, like when I thought I was Brother Michael, Michael the Archangel, I thought I had the power to heal people. One time I felt like I had electricity flowing through my body and that it was controlling me and if I didn't keep control of it that it would kill people. It's very frightening. It's not imaginary. It's real at the time."

—Sandy, a 37-year-old woman with schizophrenia. From the National Film Board of Canada film *Full of Sound and Fury*.

The symptoms of patients with schizophrenia involve disturbances in several major areas—thought, perception, and attention; motor behaviour; affect or emotion; and life functioning. The range of problems of people diagnosed as schizophrenic is extensive, although only some of these problems may be present at any given time. The DSM determines for the diagnostician how many problems must be present and in what degree to justify the diagnosis. The duration of the disorder is also important in diagnosis.

Unlike most of the diagnostic categories we have considered, no essential symptom must be present for a diagnosis of schizophrenia. Thus, patients with schizophrenia can differ from each other more than do patients with other disorders. Walter Heinrichs (1993) of York University has suggested that the key to understanding schizophrenia is to recognize the heterogeneity of schizophrenia, at the empirical and conceptual levels. He noted that

> the presentation, course, and outcome of schizophrenia are variable and diverse. Some patients develop delusions but no hallucinations. Others become isolated socially and show "positive" psychotic symptoms only later. Some patients have histories of poor social and academic adjustment that predate their illness. Other patients seem to have thrived until stricken with their first psychotic episode....Current evidence indicates that it is hard to find specific traits or characteristics that are shared by all persons with a diagnosis of schizophrenia. (p. 222)

The heterogeneity of schizophrenia suggests that it may be appropriate to subdivide patients into types that manifest particular constellations of problems. We will examine several recognized types later in this chapter, but here we present the main symptoms of schizophrenia in two categories, positive and negative, and also describe some symptoms that do not fit neatly into these two categories.

Positive Symptoms

Positive symptoms comprise excesses or distortions, such as disorganized speech, hallucinations, and delusions. They are what define, for the most part, an acute episode of schizophrenia. Positive symptoms involve the presence of a behaviour (i.e., too much) that is not apparent in most people, while the negative symptoms described below involve deficits of functions and behaviours (i.e., too little) that should be evident in most people. We will now discuss positive symptoms involving excesses.

Disorganized Speech Also known as formal thought disorder, disorganized speech refers to problems in organizing ideas and in speaking so that a listener can understand.

Interviewer: Have you been nervous or tense lately?
Patient: No, I got a head of lettuce.
Interviewer: You got a head of lettuce? I don't understand.
Patient: Well, it's just a head of lettuce.
Interviewer: Tell me about lettuce. What do you mean?
Patient: Well, ... lettuce is a transformation of a dead cougar that suffered a relapse on the lion's toe. And he swallowed the lion and something happened. The ... see, the ... Gloria and Tommy, they're two heads and they're not whales. But they escaped with herds of vomit, and things like that.
Interviewer: Who are Tommy and Gloria?
Patient: Uh, ... there's Joe DiMaggio, Tommy Henrich, Bill Dickey, Phil Rizzuto, John Esclavera, Del Crandell, Ted Williams, Mickey Mantle, Roy Mantle, Ray Mantle, Bob Chance ...
Interviewer: Who are they? Who are those people?
Patient: Dead people ... they want to be fucked ... by this outlaw.
Interviewer: What does all that mean?
Patient: Well, you see, I have to leave the hospital. I'm supposed to have an operation on my legs, you know. And it comes to be pretty sickly that I don't want to keep my legs. That's why I wish I could have an operation.
Interviewer: You want to have your legs taken off?
Patient: It's possible, you know.
Interviewer: Why would you want to do that?
Patient: I didn't have any legs to begin with. So I would imagine that if I was a fast runner, I'd be scared to be a wife, because I had a splinter inside of my head of lettuce. (Neale & Oltmanns, 1980, pp. 103–104)

This excerpt illustrates the incoherence sometimes found in the conversation of individuals with schizophrenia. Although the patient may make repeated references to central ideas or a theme, the images and fragments of thought are not connected; it is difficult to understand exactly what the patient is trying to tell the interviewer.

Speech may also be disordered by what are called loose associations, or derailment. In these cases, the patient may be more successful in communicating with a listener but has difficulty sticking to one topic. He or she seems to drift off on a train of associations evoked by an idea from the past. Patients have themselves provided descriptions of this state.

> My thoughts get all jumbled up. I start thinking or talking about something but I never get there. Instead, I wander off in the wrong direction and get caught up with all sorts of different things that may be connected with things I want to say but in a way I can't explain. People listening to me get more lost than I do.... My trouble is that I've got too many thoughts. You might think about something, let's say that ashtray and just think, oh yes, that's for putting my cigarette in, but I would think of it and then I would think of a dozen different things connected with it at the same time. (McGhie & Chapman, 1961, p. 108)

Disturbances in speech were at one time regarded as the principal clinical symptom of schizophrenia, and they remain one of the criteria for the diagnosis. But evidence indicates that the speech of many patients with schizophrenia is not disorganized and that the presence of disorganized speech does not discriminate well between schizophrenia and other psychoses, such as some mood disorders (Andreasen, 1979). For example, patients in a manic episode exhibit loose associations as much as do patients with schizophrenia.

Delusions Consider the anguish you would feel if you were firmly convinced that many people did not like you—indeed, that they disliked you so much that they were plotting against you. Imagine that your persecutors have sophisticated listening devices that allow them to tune in on your most private conversations and gather evidence in a plot to discredit you. Those around you, including your loved ones, are unable to reassure you that these people are not spying on you. Even your closest friends are gradually joining your tormentors and becoming members of the persecuting community. You are naturally quite anxious or angry about your situation, and you begin your own counteractions against the imagined persecutors. You carefully check any new room you enter for listening devices. When you meet people for the first time, you question them at great length to determine whether they are part of the plot against you.

Such **delusions**, beliefs held contrary to reality, are common positive symptoms of schizophrenia. Persecutory delusions like these were found in 65 percent of a large, cross-national sample (Sartorius, Shapiro, & Jablonsky, 1974). Delusions may take several other forms as well. Some of the most important delusions were described by the German psychiatrist Kurt Schneider (1959). The following descriptions of these delusions are drawn from Mellor (1970).

- The patient may be the unwilling recipient of bodily sensations or thoughts imposed by an external agency.

  A twenty-nine-year-old teacher described "X-rays entering the back of my neck, where the skin tingles and feels warm, they pass down the back in a hot tingling strip about six inches wide to the waist. There they disappear into the pelvis which feels numb and cold and solid like a block of ice. They stop me from getting an erection." (p. 16)

- Patients may believe that their thoughts are broadcast or transmitted, so that others know what they are thinking.

  A twenty-one-year-old student [observed], "As I think, my thoughts leave my head on a type of mental ticker-tape. Everyone around has only to pass the tape through their mind and they know my thoughts." (p. 17)

- Patients may think their thoughts are being stolen from them, suddenly and unexpectedly, by an external force.

  A twenty-two-year-old woman [described such an experience]: "I am thinking about my mother, and suddenly my thoughts are sucked out of my mind by a phrenological vacuum extractor, and there is nothing in my mind, it is empty." (pp. 16-17)

- Some patients believe that their feelings are controlled by an external force.

  A twenty-three-year-old female patient reported, "I cry, tears roll down my cheeks and I look unhappy, but inside I have a cold anger because they are using me in this way, and it is not me who is unhappy, but they are projecting unhappiness onto my brain. They project upon me laughter, for no reason, and you have no idea how terrible it is to laugh and look happy and know it is not you, but their emotions." (p. 17)

- Some patients believe that their behaviour is controlled by an external force.

  A twenty-nine-year-old shorthand typist described her [simplest] actions as follows: "When I reach my hand for the comb it is my hand and arm which move, and my fingers pick up the pen, but I don't control them.... I sit there watching them move, and they are quite independent, what they do is nothing to do with me.... I am just a puppet who is manipulated by cosmic strings. When the strings are pulled my body moves and I cannot prevent it." (p. 17)

- Some patients believe that impulses to behave in certain ways are imposed on them by some external force.

  A twenty-nine-year-old engineer [who had] emptied the contents of a urine bottle over the ward dinner trolley [tried to explain the incident]. "The sudden impulse came over me that I must do it. It was not my feeling, it came into me from the X-ray department, that was why I was sent there for implants yesterday. It was nothing to do with me, they wanted it done. So I picked up the bottle and poured it in. It seemed all I could do." (p. 18)

Kurt Schneider, a German psychiatrist, proposed that particular forms of hallucinations and delusions, which he calls first-rank symptoms, are central to defining schizophrenia.

Although delusions are found among more than half of the people with schizophrenia, as with speech disorganization, they are also found among patients with other diagnoses—notably, mania and delusional depression. The delusions of patients with schizophrenia, however, are often more bizarre than are those of patients in other diagnostic categories; that is, the delusions of patients with schizophrenia are highly implausible, as shown by the delusions just described (Junginger, Barker, & Coe, 1992).

Hallucinations and Other Disorders of Perception Patients with schizophrenia often report that the world seems somehow different or even unreal to them. A patient may mention changes in how his or her body feels, or the patient's body may become so depersonalized that it feels like a machine. As described in the case beginning this chapter, some people report having difficulty in attending to what is happening around them.

> I can't concentrate on television because I can't watch the screen and listen to what is being said at the same time. I can't seem to take in two things like this at the same time especially when one of them means watching and the other means listening. On the other hand I seem to be always taking in too much at the one time, and then I can't handle it and can't make sense of it. (McGhie & Chapman, 1961, p. 106)

The most dramatic distortions of perception are hallucinations, sensory experiences in the absence of any stimulation from the environment. They are more often auditory than visual; 74 percent of one sample reported having auditory hallucinations (Sartorius et al., 1974). Like delusions, hallucinations can be very frightening experiences.

Some hallucinations are thought to be particularly important diagnostically because they occur more often in patients with schizophrenia than in other psychotic patients. These types of hallucinations include the following (taken from Mellor, 1970):

- Some patients with schizophrenia report hearing their own thoughts spoken by another voice.

  > [The] thirty-two-year-old housewife complained of a man's voice speaking in an intense whisper from a point about two feet above her head. The voice would repeat almost all the patient's goal-directed thinking—even the most banal thoughts. The patient would think, "I must put the kettle on," and after a pause of not more than one second the voice would say, "I must put the kettle on." It would often say the opposite, "Don't put the kettle on." (p. 16)

- Some patients claim that they hear voices arguing.

  > A twenty-four-year-old male patient reported hearing voices coming from the nurse's office. One voice, deep in pitch and roughly spoken, repeatedly said, "G. T. is a bloody paradox," and another higher in pitch said, "He is that, he should be locked up." A female voice occasionally interrupted, saying, "He is not, he is a lovely man." (p. 16)

- Some patients hear voices commenting on their behaviour.

  > A forty-one-year-old housewife heard a voice coming from a house across the road. The voice went on incessantly in a flat monotone describing everything she was doing with an admixture of critical comments. "She is peeling potatoes, got hold of the peeler, she does not want that potato, she is putting it back, because she thinks it has a knobble like a penis, she has a dirty mind, she is peeling potatoes, now she is washing them." (p. 16)

Negative Symptoms

As noted earlier, the negative symptoms of schizophrenia consist of behavioural deficits, such as avolition, alogia, anhedonia, flat affect, and asociality, all of which are described below. These symptoms tend to endure beyond an acute episode and have profound effects on the lives of patients with schizophrenia. They are also important prognostically, as the presence of many negative symptoms is a strong predictor of a poor quality of life (e.g., occupational impairment, few friends) two years following hospitalization (Ho et al., 1998).

When assessing negative symptoms, it is important to distinguish among those that are truly symptoms of schizophrenia and those that are due to some other factor (Carpenter, Heinrichs, & Wagman, 1988). For example, flat affect (a lack of emotional expressiveness) can be a side effect of antipsychotic medication. Observing patients over extended time periods is probably the only way to address this issue. Also, as Heinrichs (1993) has noted, negative symptoms such as flat affect and anhedonia are difficult to distinguish from aspects of depression, so specificity becomes an issue.

Avolition Apathy or avolition refers to a lack of energy and a seeming absence of interest in or an inability to persist in what are usually routine activities. Patients may become inattentive to grooming and personal hygiene, with uncombed hair, dirty nails, unbrushed teeth, and dishevelled clothes. They have difficulty persisting at work, school, or household chores and may spend much of their time sitting around doing nothing.

Alogia A negative thought disorder, alogia can take several forms. In poverty of speech, the sheer amount of speech is greatly reduced. In poverty of content of speech, the amount of discourse is adequate, but it conveys little information and tends to be vague and repetitive. The following excerpt illustrates poverty of content of speech.

Interviewer: O.K. Why is it, do you think, that people believe in God?

Patient: Well, first of all because, He is the person that is their personal savior. He walks with me and talks with me. And uh, the understanding that I have, a lot of peoples, they don't really know their personal self. Because they ain't, they all, just don't know their personal self. They don't know that He uh, seems to like me, a lot of them don't understand that He walks and talks with them. And uh, show 'em their way to go. I understand also that, every man and every lady, is not just pointed in the same direction. Some are pointed different. They go in their different ways. The way that Jesus Christ wanted 'em to go. Myself. I am pointed in the ways of uh, knowing right from wrong, and doing it, I can't do any more, or not less than that. (American Psychiatric Association, 1987, pp. 403-404)

Anhedonia An inability to experience pleasure is called **anhedonia**. It is manifested as a lack of interest in recreational activities, failure to develop close relationships with other people, and lack of interest in sex. Patients are aware of this symptom and report that pleasurable activities are not enjoyable for them.

Flat Affect In patients with **flat affect**, virtually no stimulus can elicit an emotional response. The patient may stare vacantly, the muscles of the face flaccid, the eyes lifeless. When spoken to, the patient answers in a flat and toneless voice. Flat affect was found in 66 percent of a large sample of patients with schizophrenia (Sartorius et al., 1974).

The concept of flat affect refers only to the outward expression of emotion and not to the patient's inner experience, which may not be impoverished at all. In a study by Kring and Neale (1996), patients with schizophrenia and normal participants watched excerpts from films while their facial reactions and skin conductance were recorded. After each film clip, participants self-reported on the moods the films had elicited. While the patients were much less facially expressive than were the non-patients they reported about the same amount of emotion and were even more physiologically aroused.

Asociality Some patients with schizophrenia have severely impaired social relationships, a characteristic referred to as **asociality**. They have few friends, poor social skills, and little interest in being with other people. A study of patients from the Hamilton (Ontario) Program for Schizophrenia showed that people diagnosed with schizophrenia have lower sociability and greater shyness (Goldberg & Schmidt, 2001). Schizophrenics also reported more childhood "social troubles." Indeed, as will be seen later, these manifestations of schizophrenia are often the first to appear, beginning in childhood before the onset of more psychotic symptoms.

Some of these interpersonal deficits could reflect related deficits in the ability to recognize emotional cues displayed by others. Kerr and Neale (1993) showed that people with schizophrenia, compared to nonpsychiatric members of control groups, did less well on facial affect recognition and facial recognition tasks. A recent prospective study conducted in Alberta compared patients with schizophrenia and patients with bipolar disorder and confirmed that patients with schizophrenia did less well on the facial affect recognition and facial recognition tasks (Addington & Addington, 1998). Moreover, these deficits persisted and were evident when the patients were reassessed three months later, even though there were substantial improvements in the number of both positive and negative symptoms since initial hospitalization.

OTHER SYMPTOMS

Some authors (e.g., Heinrichs, 1993) have taken issue with the usefulness of the positive versus negative symptom distinction. One problem is that the positive and negative symptoms do not necessarily reflect exclusive subtypes because they are dimensions that often coexist within the same patient (Heinrichs, 1993). Moreover, several other symptoms of schizophrenia do not fit neatly into the positive-negative scheme we have presented. Two important symptoms in this category are catatonia and inappropriate affect. Many patients also exhibit various forms of bizarre behaviour. They may talk to themselves in public, hoard food, or collect garbage.

An 1896 photo showing a group of patients with catatonic immobility. These men held these unusual positions for long periods of time.

Catatonia *Catatonia* is defined by several motor abnormalities. Some patients gesture repeatedly, using peculiar and sometimes complex sequences of finger, hand, and arm movements that often seem to be purposeful, odd as they may be. Others manifest an unusual increase in their overall level of activity, which might include much excitement, wild flailing of the limbs, and great expenditure of energy similar to that seen in mania. At the other end of the spectrum is catatonic immobility: patients adopt unusual postures and maintain them for very long periods of time. A patient may stand on one leg, with the other tucked up toward the buttocks, and remain in this position virtually all day. Catatonic patients may also have waxy flexibility, whereby another person can move the patient's limbs into strange positions that the patient will then maintain for extended periods.

Inappropriate Affect Some people with schizophrenia have inappropriate affect. The emotional responses of these individuals are out of context; for example, the patient may laugh on hearing that his or her mother just died or become enraged when asked a simple question about how a new garment fits. These patients are likely to shift rapidly from one emotional state to another for no discernible reason. This symptom is quite rare, but its appearance is of considerable diagnostic importance because it is relatively specific to schizophrenia.

Taken together, these symptoms of schizophrenia have a profound effect on patients' lives as well as the lives of their families and friends. Their delusions and hallucinations may cause considerable distress, which is compounded by the fact that their hopes and dreams have been shattered. Their cognitive impairments and avolition make stable employment difficult, with impoverishment and often homelessness the result. Their strange behaviour and social-skills deficits lead to loss of friends and a solitary existence. A review by Peter Liddle (2000), formerly of the University of British Columbia, indicates that the strongest predictor of this social disability is chronic cognitive impairment. Substance abuse rates are high (Fowler et al., 1998), perhaps reflecting an attempt to achieve some relief from negative emotions (Blanchard et al., 1999). Little wonder, then, that the suicide rate among patients with schizophrenia is high.

Emil Kraepelin (1856–1926), a German psychiatrist, articulated descriptions of dementia praecox that have proved remarkably durable in the light of contemporary research.

Eugen Bleuler (1857–1939), a Swiss psychiatrist, contributed to our conceptions of schizophrenia and coined the term.

HISTORY OF THE CONCEPT OF SCHIZOPHRENIA

We turn now to a review of the history of the concept of schizophrenia and how ideas about this disorder have changed over time.

EARLY DESCRIPTIONS

The concept of schizophrenia was formulated by two European psychiatrists, Emil Kraepelin and Eugen Bleuler. Kraepelin first presented his notion of dementia praecox, the early term for schizophrenia, in 1898. He differentiated two major groups of endogenous, or internally caused, psychoses: manic-depressive illness and dementia praecox. Dementia praecox included several diagnostic concepts—dementia paranoides, catatonia, and hebephrenia—that had been regarded as distinct entities by clinicians in the previous few decades. Although these disorders were symptomatically diverse, Kraepelin believed that they shared a common core. His term *dementia praecox* reflected what he believed was the common core—an early onset (praecox) and a deteriorating course marked by a progressive intellectual deterioration (dementia). The "dementia" in dementia praecox is not the same as the dementias we discuss in the chapter on aging (Chapter 16). The latter are defined principally by severe memory impairments, whereas Kraepelin's term refers to a general "mental enfeeblement."

The formulation of the next major figure, Eugen Bleuler, represented both a specific attempt to define the core of the disorder and a move away from Kraepelin's emphasis on age of onset and course in the definition. Bleuler broke with Kraepelin on two major points: he believed that the disorder did not necessarily have an early onset, and he believed that it did not inevitably progress toward dementia. Thus, the label *dementia praecox* was no longer appropriate, and in 1908 Bleuler proposed his own term, *schizophrenia*, from the Greek words *schizein*, meaning "to split," and *phren*, meaning "mind," to capture what he viewed as the essential nature of the condition.

With age of onset and deteriorating course no longer considered defining features of the disorder, Bleuler faced a conceptual problem. Since the symptoms of schizophrenia could vary widely among patients, he needed some justification for putting them into a single diagnostic category. Bleuler therefore tried to specify a common denominator, or essential property, that would link the various disturbances. The metaphorical concept that he adopted for this purpose was the "breaking of associative threads."

For Bleuler, associative threads joined not only words but thoughts. Thus, goal-directed, efficient thinking and communication were possible only when these hypothetical structures were intact. The notion that associative threads were disrupted in patients with schizophrenia could then account for other problems. Bleuler viewed attentional difficulties—for example, as might result from a loss of purposeful direction in thought—as the cause of passive responses to objects and people in the immediate surroundings. Also, he viewed blocking, an apparently total loss of a train of thought, as a complete disruption of the person's associative threads.

Although Kraepelin recognized that a small percentage of patients who originally manifested symptoms of dementia praecox did not deteriorate, he preferred to limit this diagnostic category to patients who had a poor prognosis. Bleuler's work, in contrast, led to a broader concept of schizophrenia. He diagnosed patients with a good prognosis as schizophrenic, and he also included in his concept of schizophrenia many patients who would have received different diagnoses from other clinicians.

THE HISTORICAL PREVALENCE OF SCHIZOPHRENIA

As noted earlier, it is estimated that schizophrenia has a current prevalence of about 1 percent in the population. Data from several countries throughout the world suggest that rates of schizophrenia have fallen sharply since the 1960s. Recently, a case registry analysis of data from Kingston, Ontario, confirmed that there was a substantial decrease in inpatient prevalence rates of schizophrenia between 1986 and 1996, with no corresponding increase in outpatient prevalence rates (Woogh, 2001). It is unlikely that this decrease reflects changes in methods of service delivery, since the prevalence rates for major affective disorders over the same time period in the same location increased nonsignificantly for inpatients and significantly for outpatients. However, because Woogh (2001) conducted the first Canadian study on this topic in Kingston, it is not clear whether this trend can be generalized to other regions of the country. Also, these decreases in prevalence rates over time do not obscure the fact that millions of people around the world suffer from schizophrenia.

Over the years, the number of people diagnosed with schizophrenia has varied considerably depending on how schizophrenia has been conceptualized and defined, and this has hampered attempts to determine accurately the extent of changes in prevalence over time. Bleuler had a great influence on the concept of schizophrenia as it developed in the United States. Over the first part of the 20th century, the breadth of the diagnosis was extended considerably. At the New York State Psychiatric Institute, for example, about 20 percent of the patients were diagnosed as schizophrenic in the 1930s. The numbers increased through the 1940s and in 1952 peaked at a remarkable 80 percent. In contrast, the concept of schizophrenia prevalent in Europe remained narrower. The percentage of patients diagnosed as schizophrenic at the Maudsley Hospital in London, for example, stayed relatively constant, at 20 percent, for a 40-year period (Kuriansky, Deming, & Gurland, 1974).

The reasons for the increase in the frequency of diagnoses of schizophrenia in the United States are easily discerned. Several prominent figures in U.S. psychiatry expanded Bleuler's already broad concept of schizophrenia even more. In 1933, for example, Kasanin described nine patients who had been diagnosed with dementia praecox. For all of them, the onset of the disorder had been sudden and recovery relatively rapid. Noting that theirs could be said to be a combination of both schizophrenic and affective symptoms, Kasanin suggested the term schizoaffective psychosis to describe the disturbances of these patients. This diagnosis subsequently became part of the U.S. concept of schizophrenia and was listed in DSM-I (1952) and DSM-II (1968).

The concept of schizophrenia was further broadened by three additional diagnostic practices:

1 U.S. clinicians tended to diagnose schizophrenia whenever delusions or hallucinations were present. Because these symptoms, particularly delusions, occur also in mood disorders, many patients with a DSM-II diagnosis of schizophrenia may actually have had a mood disorder (Cooper et al., 1972).

2 Patients whom we would now diagnose as having a personality disorder (notably schizotypal, schizoid, borderline, and paranoid personality disorders, discussed in Chapter 13) were diagnosed as schizophrenic according to DSM-II criteria.

3 Patients with an acute onset of schizophrenic symptoms and a rapid recovery were diagnosed as having schizophrenia.

The DSM-IV-TR Diagnosis

Beginning in DSM-III (American Psychiatric Association, 1980) and continuing in DSM-IV-TR (American Psychiatric Association, 2000), the U.S. concept of schizophrenia shifted considerably from the former broad definition to a new definition that narrows the range of patients diagnosed as schizophrenic in five ways:

1. The diagnostic criteria are presented in explicit and considerable detail.
2. Patients with symptoms of a mood disorder are specifically excluded. Schizophrenia, schizoaffective type, is now listed as schizoaffective disorder in a separate section as one of the psychotic disorders. Schizoaffective disorder comprises a mixture of symptoms of schizophrenia and mood disorders.
3. DSM-IV-TR requires at least six months of disturbance for the diagnosis. The six-month period must include at least one month of the active phase, which is defined by the presence of at least two of the following: delusions, hallucinations, disorganized speech, grossly disorganized or catatonic behaviour, and negative symptoms (only one of these symptoms is required if the delusions are bizarre or if the hallucinations consist of voices commenting or arguing). The remaining time required within the minimum six months can be either a prodromal (before the active phase) or a residual (after the active phase) period. Problems during the prodromal and residual phases include social withdrawal, impaired role functioning, blunted or inappropriate affect, lack of initiative, vague and circumstatial speech, impairment in hygiene and grooming, odd beliefs or magical thinking, and unusual perceptual experiences. These criteria eliminate patients who have a brief psychotic episode, often stress related, and then recover quickly. DSM-II's acute schizophrenic episode is now diagnosed as either *schizophreniform disorder* or *brief psychotic disorder*, both also listed in a new section in DSM-IV-TR. The symptoms of schizophreniform disorder are the same as those of schizophrenia but last only from one to six months. Brief psychotic disorder lasts from one day to one month and is often brought on by extreme stress, such as bereavement.
4. Some of what DSM-II regarded as mild forms of schizophrenia are now diagnosed as personality disorders (e.g., schizotypal personality disorder).
5. DSM-IV-TR differentiates between paranoid schizophrenia, to be discussed shortly, and **delusional disorder**. A person with delusional disorder is troubled by persistent persecutory delusions or by delusional jealousy, the unfounded conviction that a spouse or lover is unfaithful. There are also delusions of being followed, somatic delusions (believing that some internal organ is malfunctioning), and delusions of erotomania (believing that one is loved by some other person, usually a complete stranger with a higher social status). A highly publicized case of apparent erotomania occurred when Tricia Miller, a 31-year-old factory worker, was arrested in July 1995 at the Skydome Hotel in Toronto. Miller was obsessed with Roberto Alomar, a former star of the Toronto Blue Jays, and was frustrated that she was unable to reach him despite her persistent attempts. Miller had a loaded gun and reported to police that she had been planning to kill Alomar and then commit suicide, despite having no prior relationship or face-to-face contact with the athlete.

   Unlike the person with paranoid schizophrenia, the person with delusional disorder does not have disorganized speech or hallucinations, and his or her delusions are less bizarre. Delusional disorder is quite rare and typically begins later in life than does schizophrenia. In most family studies, it appears to be related to schizophrenia, perhaps genetically (Kendler & Diehl, 1993).

Are the DSM-IV-TR diagnostic criteria applicable across cultures? Data bearing on this question were collected in a World Health Organization study of both industrialized and developing countries (Jablonsky et al., 1994). The symptomatic criteria held up well cross-culturally. However, patients in developing countries have a more acute onset and a more favourable course than those in industrialized societies. The cause of this intriguing finding is unknown (Susser & Wanderling, 1994).

Categories of Schizophrenia in DSM-IV-TR

Earlier, we mentioned that the heterogeneity of schizophrenic symptoms suggested the presence of subtypes of the disorder. Three types of schizophrenic disorders included in DSM-IV-TR—disorganized (hebephrenic), catatonic, and paranoid—were initially proposed by Kraepelin many years ago. The present descriptions of Kraepelin's original types demonstrate the great diversity of behaviour that relates to the diagnosis of schizophrenia.

Disorganized Schizophrenia Kraepelin's hebephrenic form of schizophrenia is called **disorganized schizophrenia** in DSM-IV-TR. Speech is disorganized and difficult for a listener to follow. Patients may speak incoherently, stringing together similar-sounding words and even inventing new words, often accompanied by silliness or laughter. They may have flat affect or experience constant shifts of emotion, breaking into inexplicable fits of laughter and crying. Their behaviour is generally disorganized and not goal directed; for example, a patient may tie a ribbon around a big toe or move incessantly, pointing at objects for no apparent reason. Patients sometimes deteriorate to the point of incontinence, voiding anywhere and at any time, and completely neglect their appearance, never bathing, brushing teeth, or combing hair.

Catatonic Schizophrenia The most obvious symptoms of catatonic schizophrenia are the catatonic symptoms described earlier. Patients typically alternate between catatonic immobility and wild excitement, but one of these symptoms may predominate. These patients resist instructions and suggestions and often echo (repeat back) the speech of others. The onset of catatonic reactions may be more sudden than the onset of other forms of schizophrenia, although the person is likely to have previously shown some apathy and withdrawal from reality.

Catatonic schizophrenia is seldom seen today, perhaps because drug therapy works effectively on these bizarre motor processes. Boyle (1991) has argued that, during the early part of the century, the apparent high prevalence of catatonia reflected misdiagnosis and that apparent catatonic schizophrenia was actually lethargica (sleeping sickness). This was portrayed in the film *Awakenings*, which was based on the writings of Oliver Sacks.

Paranoid Schizophrenia The diagnosis paranoid schizophrenia is assigned to a substantial number of recently admitted patients to mental hospitals. The key to this diagnosis is the presence of prominent delusions. Delusions of persecution are most common, but patients may experience grandiose delusions, in which they have an exaggerated sense of their own importance, power, knowledge, or identity. Some patients are plagued by delusional jealousy, the unsubstantiated belief that their sexual partner is unfaithful. The other delusions described earlier, such as the sense of being persecuted or spied on, may also be evident. Vivid auditory hallucinations may accompany the delusions. Patients with paranoid schizophrenia often develop ideas of reference; they incorporate unimportant events within a delusional framework and read personal significance into the trivial activities of others. For instance, they think that overheard segments of conversations are about them, that the frequent appearance of a person on a street where they customarily walk means that they are being watched, and that what they see on television or read in magazines somehow refers to them. Individuals with paranoid schizophrenia are agitated, argumentative, angry, and sometimes violent. They remain emotionally responsive, although they may be somewhat stilted, formal, and intense with others. They are also more alert and verbal than are patients with other types of schizophrenia. Their language, although filled with references to delusions, is not disorganized.

Evaluation of the Subtypes Although these subtypes form the basis of current diagnostic systems and certain distinctions seem valid, such as the presence versus the absence of paranoid characteristics (Nicholson & Neufeld, 1993), the overall usefulness of subtypes is often questioned. Because diagnosing types of schizophrenia is extremely difficult, diagnostic reliability is dramatically reduced. Furthermore, these subtypes have little predictive validity; that is, the diagnosis of one over another form of schizophrenia provides little information that is helpful either in treating or in predicting the course of the problems. There is also considerable overlap among the types. For example, patients with all forms of schizophrenia may have delusions. Kraepelin's system of subtyping has not proved to be a useful way of dealing with the variability in schizophrenic behaviour.

Supplemental types included in DSM-IV-TR are also flawed. The diagnosis of undifferentiated schizophrenia applies to patients who meet the diagnostic criteria for schizophrenia but not for any of the three subtypes. The diagnosis of residual schizophrenia is used when the patient no longer meets the full criteria for schizophrenia but still shows some signs of the illness.

In spite of the problems with current subtyping systems, there is continuing interest in differentiating different forms of schizophrenia. A radically different and promising approach focuses on schizophrenia subtypes that differ qualitatively in terms of neurocognitive features that involve brain abnormalities. Regarding the heterogeneity issue, Heinrichs and Awad (1993) conducted a cluster analysis that identified subtypes of schizophrenics based on their performances on a battery of neuropsychological tests that included the Wisconsin Card Sorting Test (a test of executive functioning), the Weschler Adult Intelligence Scale (WAIS), and measures of motor function and verbal memory. The cluster analysis identified five subtypes, including one group with normative, intact cognition. The other four groups included an "executive subtype," which was distinguished by impairment on the Wisconsin Card Sorting Test, an "executive-motor subtype," which had deficits in terms of card sorting and motor functioning; a "motor subtype," which had deficits only in motor functioning; and a "dementia subtype," which had pervasive and generalized cognitive impairment. This study also showed that these subtypes differed on other variables, such as length of illness and extent of hospitalization. A subsequent study of a subset of the patients in this same study showed that most of the neurocognitive and functional differences persisted over time, even though there were no apparent symptom differences among the subtypes (Heinrichs, Ruttan, Zakzanis, & Case, 1997). It appears from this research that a continuing focus on neuropsychological differences in future research may provide some important insights into the heterogeneity of schizophrenia.

The system that distinguishes between positive and negative symptoms, described earlier (Crow, 1980; Strauss, Carpenter, & Bartko, 1974), is continuing to receive much attention. Andreasen and Olsen (1982) evaluated 52 patients with schizophrenia and found that 16 could be regarded as having predominantly negative symptoms, 18 predominantly positive symptoms, and 18 mixed symptoms. Although these data suggest that it is possible to talk about types of schizophrenia, subsequent research has indicated that most patients with schizophrenia show mixed symptoms (e.g., Andreasen, Flaum et al., 1990) and that very few patients fit into the pure positive or pure negative types.

Subsequent analyses have revealed three dimensions, not two (Lenzenweger, Dworkin, & Wethington, 1991). These studies have shown that positive symptoms should be divided into two categories—a positive symptom component consisting of delusions and hallucinations and a disorganized component that includes bizarre behaviour and disorganized speech (see Table 11.1).

A distinction between positive and negative symptoms (as opposed to between types of patients) continues to be used increasingly in research on the etiology of schizophrenia. We will present evidence relevant to the validity of this distinction in the discussion of the possible roles of genetics, dopamine, and brain pathology in the etiology of schizophrenia.

Table 11.1

Summary of the Major Symptom Dimensions in Schizophrenia

Positive Symptoms	Negative Symptoms	Disorganization
Delusions, hallucinations	Avolition (apathy), alogia (poverty of speech and poverty of content of speech), anhedonia, flat affect, asociality	Bizarre behaviour, disorganized speech

ETIOLOGY OF SCHIZOPHRENIA

We have described how patients with schizophrenia differ from normal people in thought, speech, perception, and imagination. What can explain the disconnection of their thoughts, their inappropriate emotions or lack of emotion, their misguided delusions and bewildering hallucinations? Because broad theoretical perspectives, such as psychoanalysis, have not contributed substantially to research in schizophrenia, we look here at other major areas of etiological research.

THE GENETIC DATA

What would you do if you wanted to find an individual who had a very good chance of being diagnosed one day as schizophrenic and you could not consider any behaviour patterns or other symptoms? Indeed, imagine that you could not even meet the person. This problem, suggested by Paul Meehl (1962), has a solution that offers you a close-to-even chance of picking a person who is potentially schizophrenic: find an individual who has an identical twin with schizophrenia.

A convincing body of literature indicates that a predisposition to schizophrenia is transmitted genetically. The family, twin, and adoption methods employed in this research, as in other behaviour-genetics research projects, have led researchers to conclude that a predisposition to schizophrenia is inherited. Furthermore, according to a contemporary review by Anne Bassett of the Centre for Addiction and Mental Health and her associates (Bassett, Chow, Waterworth, & Brzustowicz, 2001), researchers are now beginning to focus on a small, specific number of chromosomal locations that confer genetic susceptibility to schizophrenia.

Though many genetic studies of schizophrenia were conducted before the publication of DSM-III, genetic investigators collected extensive descriptive data on their subjects, allowing them to be rediagnosed with newer diagnostic criteria. Reanalyses using DSM-III criteria have substantiated the conclusions reached earlier (e.g., Kendler & Gruenberg, 1984).

Family Studies Table 11.2 presents a summary of the risk for schizophrenia in various relatives of index cases with schizophrenia. (In evaluating the figures, keep in mind that the risk for schizophrenia in the general population is a little less than 1 percent.) Quite clearly, relatives of patients with schizophrenia are at increased risk, and the risk increases as the genetic relationship between proband and relative becomes closer.

More recent data confirm what is shown in Table 11.2 (Kendler, Larkowski-Shannon, & Walsh, 1996). The relatives of patients with schizophrenia are also at increased risk for other disorders (e.g., schizotypal personality disorder)

Table 11.2

Summary of Major European Family and Twin Studies of the Genetics of Schizophrenia

Relation to Proband	Percentage with Schizophrenia
Spouse	1.00
Grandchildren	2.84
Nieces/nephews	2.65
Children	9.35
Siblings	7.30
DZ twins	12.08
MZ twins	44.30

Source: After Gottesman, McGuffin, and Farmer, 1987.

that are thought to be less severe forms of schizophrenia (Kendler, Neale, & Walsh, 1995). The data gathered by the family method thus support the notion that a predisposition to schizophrenia can be transmitted genetically. Of course, relatives of a schizophrenic index case may share not only genes but also common experiences. The behaviour of a parent with schizophrenia, for example, could be very disturbing to a developing child. Therefore, the influence of the environment cannot be discounted as a rival explanation for the higher morbidity risks.

Twin Studies Concordance rates for MZ and DZ twins are also given in Table 11.2. Concordance for identical twins (44.3 percent), although greater than that for fraternal twins (12.08 percent), is less than 100 percent. Similar results have been obtained in more recent studies (e.g., Cannon et al., 1998; Cardno et al., 1999). The less than 100 percent concordance in MZ twins is important: if genetic transmission alone accounted for schizophrenia and one twin had schizophrenia, then the other twin would also have schizophrenia because MZ twins are genetically identical. Consistent with a genetic interpretation of these data, concordance among MZ twins does increase when the proband is more severely ill (Gottesman & Shields, 1972).

There is, of course, a critical problem in interpreting the results of twin studies. A common "deviant" environment rather than common genetic factors could account for the concordance rates. By common environment we mean not only similar child-rearing practices, but also a more similar intrauterine environment, for MZ twins are more likely than DZ twins to share a single blood supply.

A clever analysis supporting a genetic interpretation of the high concordance rates found for identical twins was performed by Fischer (1971). She reasoned that if these rates indeed reflected a genetic effect, the children of even the discordant, or nonschizophrenic, identical co-twins of patients with schizophrenia should be at high risk for the disorder. These nonschizophrenic twins would presumably have the genotype for schizophrenia, even though it was not expressed behaviourally, and thus might pass along an increased risk for the disorder to their children. In agreement with this line of reasoning, the rate of schizophrenia and schizophrenic-like psychoses in the children of nonschizophrenic co-twins of patients with schizophrenia was 9.4 percent. The rate among the children of the patients with schizophrenia themselves was only slightly and nonsignificantly higher, 12.3 percent. Both rates are substantially higher than the 1 percent prevalence found in an unselected population.

Dworkin and his colleagues reevaluated the major twin studies according to the positive-negative symptom distinction discussed earlier (Dworkin & Lenzenweger, 1984; Dworkin, Lenzenweger, & Moldin, 1987). Ratings of positive and negative symptoms were compiled from published case histories of the twins and compared for probands of concordant and discordant pairs. No differences emerged for positive symptoms, but probands from concordant pairs were higher in negative symptoms than were probands from discordant pairs. These data suggest that negative symptoms have a stronger genetic component than do positive ones.

Adoption Studies The study of children whose mothers had schizophrenia but who were reared from early infancy by nonschizophrenic adoptive parents has provided more-conclusive information on the role of genes in schizophrenia by eliminating the possible effects of a deviant environment. Heston (1966) was able to follow up 47 people born between 1915 and 1945 to women with schizophrenia in a state mental hospital. The infants were separated from their mothers at birth and raised by foster or adoptive parents. Fifty control participants were selected from the same foundling homes that had placed the children of the women with schizophrenia.

The follow-up assessment, conducted in 1964, included an interview, the MMPI, an IQ test, and social class ratings. A dossier on each participant was rated independently by two psychiatrists, and a third evaluation was made by Heston. Clinical ratings were made on a 0 to 100 scale of overall disability. Overall, the control participants were rated as less disabled than the children of mothers with schizophrenia. Thirty-one of the 47 children of mothers with schizophrenia (66 percent) but only nine of the 50 controls (18 percent) were given a DSM diagnosis. None of the controls was diagnosed as schizophrenic, but 16.6 percent of the offspring of women with schizophrenia were so diagnosed. Children of women with schizophrenia were also more likely to be diagnosed as mentally defective, psychopathic, and neurotic (Table 11.3). They had been involved more frequently in criminal activity, had spent more time in penal institutions, and had more often been discharged from the armed services for psychiatric reasons. Heston's study provides strong support for the importance of genetic factors in the development of schizophrenia. Children reared without contact with their so-called pathogenic mothers were still more likely to become schizophrenic than were the control participants.

A similar study was conducted in Denmark under Kety's direction (Kety et al., 1976, 1994). This study began with a culling of the records of children who had been adopted at a young age. All adoptees who had later been admitted to a psychiatric facility and diagnosed as schizophrenic were selected as the index cases. From the remaining cases, the investigators chose a matched control group of people who had no psychiatric history. Both the adoptive and the biological parents and the siblings and half-siblings of the two groups were then identified, and a search was made to determine who among them had a psychiatric history. As might be expected if genetic factors figure in schizophrenia, the biological relatives of the index cases were diagnosed as schizophrenic more often than occurs in the general population; the adoptive relatives were not.

Table 11.3

Characteristics of Participants Separated from Their Mothers in Early Infancy

Assessment	Offspring of Schizophrenic Mothers	Control Offspring
Number of participants	47	50
Mean age at follow-up	35.8	36.3
Overall ratings of disability (low score indicates more pathology)	65.2	80.1
Number diagnosed schizophrenic	5	0
Number diagnosed mentally defective	4	0
Number diagnosed psychopathic	9	2
Number diagnosed neurotic	13	7

Source: From Heston, 1966.

Evaluation of the Genetic Data The data indicate that genetic factors play an important role in the development of schizophrenia. Early twin and family studies were criticized because they did not separate the effects of genes and environment. However, more recent studies of children of parents with schizophrenia who were reared in foster and adoptive homes, plus the follow-up of relatives of adopted children who developed schizophrenia, have virtually removed the potential confounding influence of the environment.

Despite this evidence, we cannot conclude that schizophrenia is a disorder completely determined by genetic transmission, for we must keep in mind the distinction between phenotype and genotype. Like other mental disorders, schizophrenia is defined by behaviour; it is a phenotype and thus reflects the influence of both genes and environment. The role of both factors is suggested by outcomes experienced by the Genain quadruplets (see Focus on Discovery 11.1). The diathesis-stress model introduced in Chapter 2 seems appropriate for guiding theory about and research into the etiology of schizophrenia. Genetic factors can only predispose individuals to schizophrenia. Some kind of stress is required to render this predisposition an observable pathology.

The genetic research into schizophrenia has some further limitations as well. First, it has not been possible to specify exactly how a predisposition to schizophrenia is transmitted. It does not appear that the predisposition is transmitted by a single gene; several multi- or polygenic models remain viable. Contemporary gene analyses point to the role of several specific genes, including the serotonin type 2A receptor (5—HT2a) gene, the dopamine D3 receptor gene, and chromosomal regions on chromosomes 6, 8, 13, and 22, including microdeletion on chromosome 22ql1 (see Walker, Kestler, Bollini, & Hochman, 2004).

A second limitation is that the nature of the inherited diathesis remains unknown. What exactly is inherited that puts some people at risk for schizophrenia? One way of addressing this question is to study relatives of patients with schizophrenia. Although not necessarily disordered, individuals genetically at risk for schizophrenia may reveal signs of the genetic predisposition. A major area of research is the study of how well the eyes track a moving target, such as a pendulum. Patients with schizophrenia do poorly on this task, as do about 50 percent of their first-degree relatives (Holzman, 1985). The importance of eye tracking is supported by data showing that it is influenced by genetic factors (Iacono et al., 1992) and may even be linked to chromosome 6 (Arolt et al., 1996). Deficient eye tracking may reflect a problem in several areas of the brain, including the frontal and temporal lobes as well as the cerebellum (Chen et al., 1999). We will soon see that these brain areas are thought to be very important in schizophrenia.

Despite the problems and loose ends in the genetic data, these data represent an impressive body of evidence. The strong positive correlation between genetic relatedness and the prevalence of schizophrenia remains one of the strongest links in the chain of information about the causes of schizophrenia. Accordingly, Canadian authors have made a strong recommendation that genetic counselling should be made available to everyone with schizophrenia and their families (see Hodgkinson, Murphy, O'Neill, Brzustowicz, & Bassett, 2001). *Genetic counselling* is a process of communication that involves conveying information about risk to patients and their relatives in order to help them make decisions, deal with current issues, and anticipate other issues associated with schizophrenia.

focus on discovery/11.1

The Genain Quadruplets—Heredity or Environment in Schizophrenia?

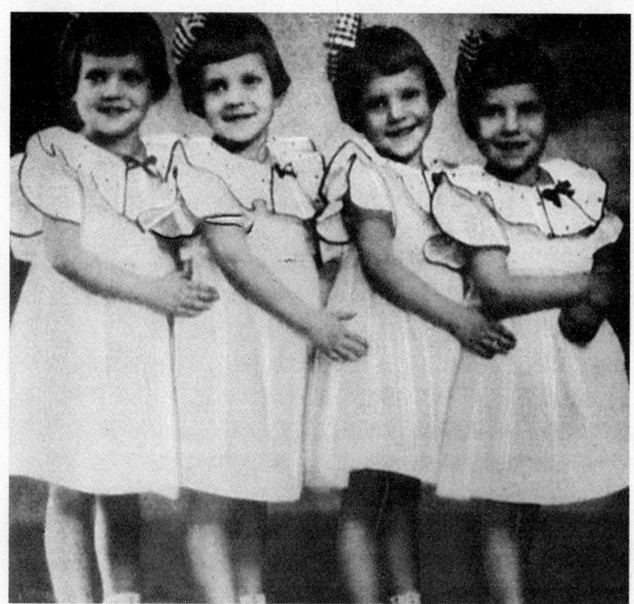

Childhood photograph of the Genain quadruplets. All of the girls developed schizophrenia later in life.

The schizophrenia manifested by the Genain quadruplets represents a fascinating illustration of the mutual influence played by genetic factors and life experiences. All of the Genain sisters had developed schizophrenia by the time they had reached the age of 24. Genain is a pseudonym used to protect the identity of the four sisters who live in a U.S. Midwestern state. The story of Hester, Nora, Iris, and Myra is fascinating for many reasons. First, it was estimated in 1963 that the odds of identical quadruplets all developing schizophrenia were one in 1.5 billion births! Second, the Genain sisters have been studied throughout much of their life, initially, by David Rosenthal and his associates at the U.S. National Institute of Mental Health (NIMH) and more recently by Allan Mirsky and his co-investigators. The latter recently published a 39-year follow-up investigation of the sisters (see Mirsky et al., 2000; Mirsky & Quinn, 1988). The sisters have experienced very different life outcomes even though they share the same genetic background. One sister (Hester) experienced severe impairment, never completed high school, and was incapable of independent functioning. Two other sisters (Iris and Nora) showed better functioning but never had substantial careers and never got married. In contrast, Myra was able to work, marry and raise a family despite becoming schizophrenic.

The differences between the sisters demonstrate that the course of the illness can be variable and, clearly, that all people diagnosed with schizophrenia are not alike. The sisters' different outcomes illustrate the need to consider genetic factors and factors jointly, consistent with the diathesis-stress approach. Scholars such as Mirsky point to the differential treatment of the girls by their father, who was especially cruel to Hester and Iris and kinder to Myra and Nora.

Of course, it is impossible to pinpoint exactly the factors that contributed to the outcomes experienced by the Genain quadruplets. Still, the lives of the four sisters were quite different despite their common history of schizophrenia.

BIOCHEMICAL FACTORS

The demonstrated role of genetic factors in schizophrenia suggests that biochemicals should be investigated, for it is through body chemistry and biological processes that heredity may have an effect. Present research is examining several different neurotransmitters, including norepinephrine and serotonin. No biochemical theory has unequivocal support, but because of the great effort being spent in the search for biochemical causes of schizophrenia, we shall review one of the best-researched factors, dopamine.

Dopamine Activity The theory that schizophrenia is related to excess activity of the neurotransmitter dopamine is based principally on the knowledge that drugs effective in treating schizophrenia reduce dopamine activity. Antipsychotic drugs, in addition to being useful in treating some symptoms of schizophrenia, produce side effects resembling the symptoms of Parkinson's disease. Parkinsonism is known

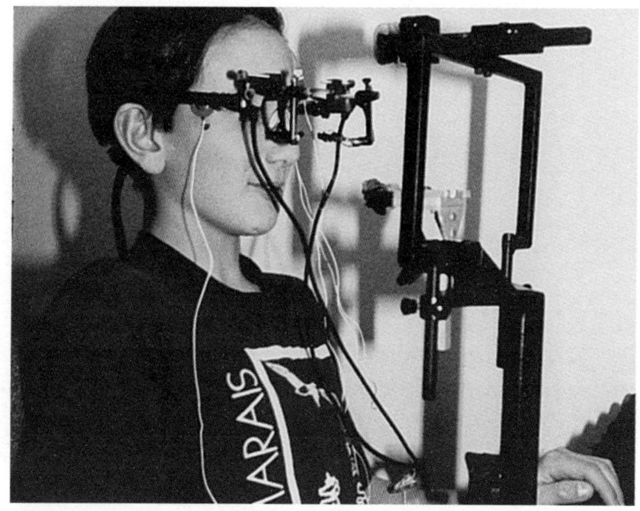

This apparatus is used to assess a person's ability to track a moving target. This ability is impaired in both patients with schizophrenia and their relatives, suggesting that eye tracking is a genetic marker for the disorder.

to be caused in part by low levels of dopamine in a particular nerve tract of the brain. It has been confirmed that because of their structural similarities to the dopamine molecule (Figure 11.1), molecules of antipsychotic drugs fit into and thereby block postsynaptic dopamine receptors. The dopamine receptors that are blocked by antipsychotics are called D2 receptors. (Like other neurotransmitters, there are several subclasses of dopamine receptors that differ in the specifics of how they signal the postsynaptic neuron.) From this knowledge about the action of the drugs that help patients with schizophrenia, it is but a short inductive leap to view schizophrenia as resulting from excess activity in dopamine nerve tracts.

Further indirect support for the **dopamine theory** of schizophrenia comes from the literature on amphetamine psychosis. Amphetamines can produce a state that closely resembles paranoid schizophrenia, and they can exacerbate the symptoms of schizophrenia (Angrist, Lee, & Gershon, 1974). The amphetamines cause the release of catecholamines, including norepinephrine and dopamine, into the synaptic cleft and prevent their inactivation. We can be relatively confident that the psychosis-inducing effects of amphetamines are a result of increasing dopamine rather than of increasing norepinephrine, because antipsychotics are antidotes to amphetamine psychosis.

Based on the data just reviewed, researchers at first assumed that schizophrenia was caused by an excess of dopamine. But as other studies progressed, this assumption did not gain support. For example, the major metabolite of dopamine, homovanillic acid (HVA), was not found in greater amounts in patients with schizophrenia (Bowers, 1974).

Such data, plus improved technologies for studying neurochemical variables in humans, has led researchers to propose excess or oversensitive dopamine receptors, rather than a high level of dopamine, as factors in schizophrenia. Research on the antipsychotics' mode of action suggests that the dopamine receptors are a more likely locus of disorder than the level of dopamine itself. Some postmortem studies of brains of schizophrenic patients, as well as PET scans of schizophrenic patients, have revealed that dopamine receptors are greater in number or are hypersensitive in some people with schizophrenia (Goldsmith, Shapiro, & Joyce, 1997; Hietala et al., 1994). Having too many dopamine receptors would be functionally akin to having too much dopamine. The reason is that when dopamine (or any neurotransmitter) is released into the synapse, only some of it actually interacts with postsynaptic receptors. Having more receptors gives a greater opportunity for the dopamine that is released to stimulate a receptor.

Excess dopamine receptors may not be responsible for all the symptoms of schizophrenia; in fact, they appear to be related mainly to positive symptoms. Some studies have shown, for example, that amphetamines do not worsen the symptoms of all patients (e.g., Kornetsky, 1976); one study has reported that symptoms actually lessen after an amphetamine has been administered (van Kammen et al., 1977). Furthermore, antipsychotics have been shown to ameliorate only some of the symptoms of schizophrenia. It turns out that these divergent results are related to the positive-negative symptom distinction noted earlier. Amphetamines worsen positive symptoms and lessen negative ones. Antipsychotics lessen positive symptoms, but their effect on negative symptoms is less clear; some studies show no benefit (e.g., Haracz, 1982), while others show a reduction in negative symptoms (e.g., van Kammen, Hammer, & Malas, 1987).

Subsequent developments in the dopamine theory (e.g., Davis et al., 1991) have expanded its scope. The key change involves the recognition of differences among the neural pathways that use dopamine as a transmitter. The excess dopamine activity that is thought to be most relevant to schizophrenia is localized in the mesolimbic pathway (see Figure 11.2), and the therapeutic effects of antipsychotics on positive symptoms occur by blocking dopamine receptors there, thereby lowering activity in this neural system.

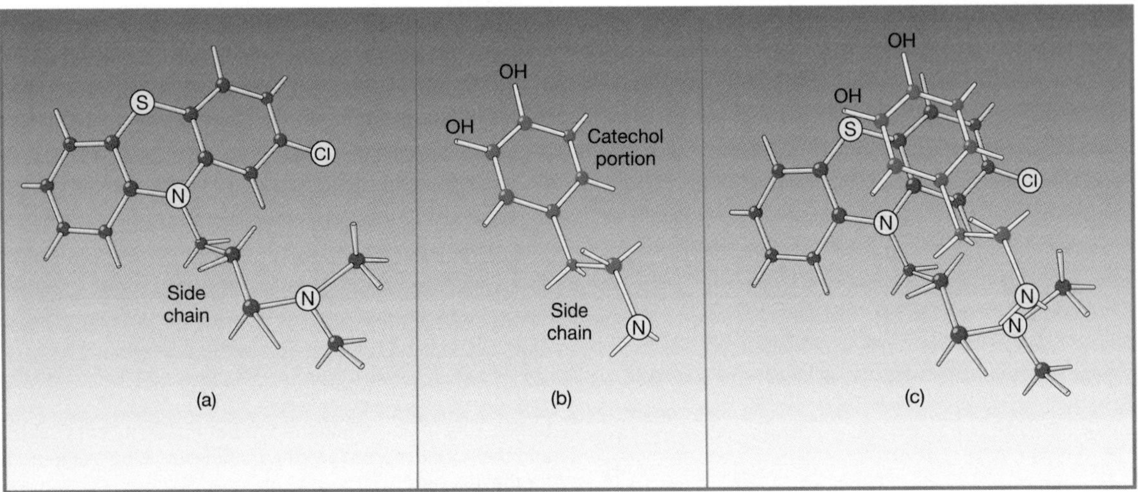

Figure 11.1 Conformation of (*a*) chlorpromazine, an antipsychotic, and (*b*) dopamine, and (*c*) their superimposition, determined by X-ray crystallographic analysis. Chlorpromazine blocks impulse transmission by dopamine by fitting into its receptor sites. Adapted from Horn and Snyder (1971).

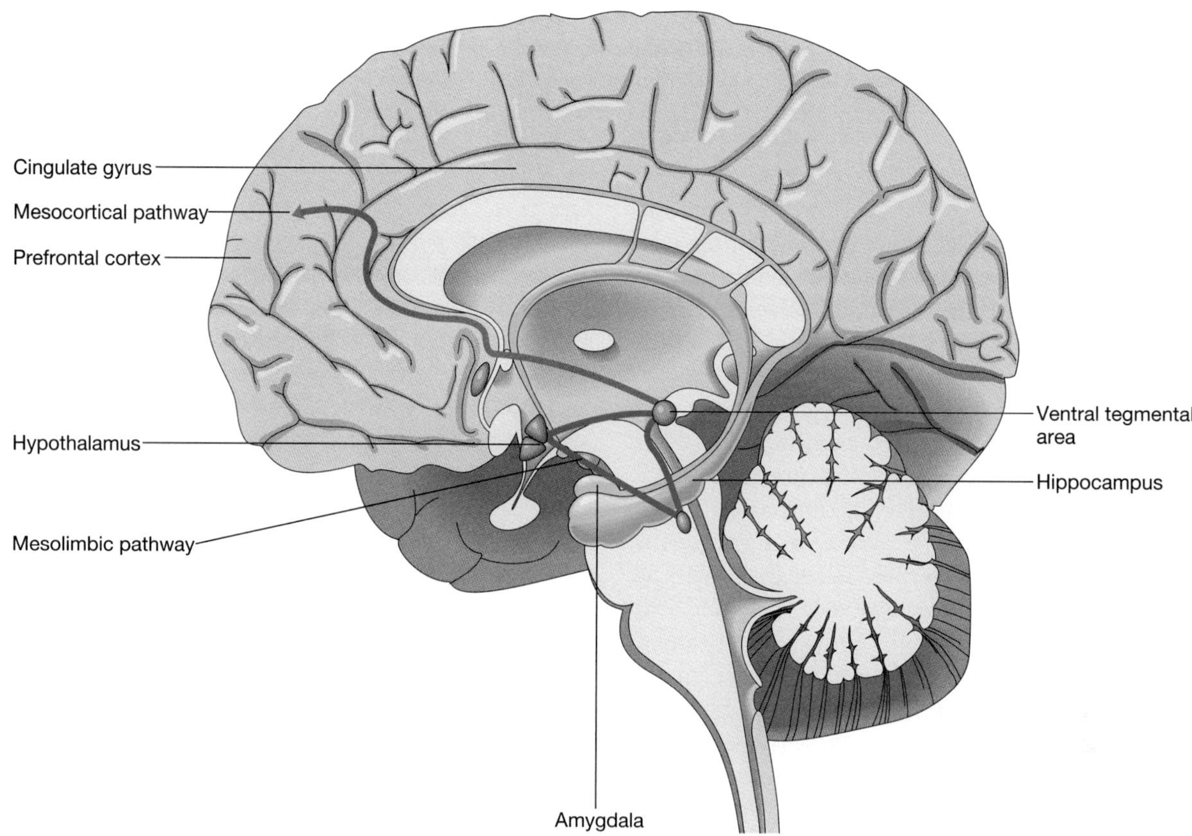

Figure 11.2 The brain and schizophrenia. The mesocortical pathway begins in the ventral tegmental area and projects to the prefrontal cortex. The mesolimbic pathway also begins in the ventral tegmental area, but projects to the hypothalamus, amygdala, hippocampus, and nucleus accumbens.

The mesocortical dopamine pathway begins in the same brain region as the mesolimbic, but it projects to the prefrontal cortex. The prefrontal cortex also projects to limbic areas that are innervated by dopamine. These dopamine neurons in the prefrontal cortex may be underactive and thus fail to exert inhibitory control over the dopamine neurons in the limbic area, with the result that there is overactivity in the mesolimbic dopamine system. Because the prefrontal cortex is thought to be especially relevant to the negative symptoms of schizophrenia, the underactivity of the dopamine neurons in this part of the brain may also be the cause of the negative symptoms of schizophrenia (see Figure 11.3). This proposal has the advantage of allowing the simultaneous presence of positive and negative symptoms in the same patient with schizophrenia. Furthermore, because antipsychotics do not have major effects on the dopamine neurons in the prefrontal cortex, we would expect them to be relatively ineffective as treatments for negative symptoms, and they are. When we examine research on structural abnormalities in the brains of patients with schizophrenia, we will see some close connections between these two domains.

Evaluation of the Biochemical Data Despite the positive evidence we have reviewed, the dopamine theory does not appear to be a complete theory of schizophrenia. For example, it takes several weeks for antipsychotics to gradually lessen positive symptoms of schizophrenia, although they begin blocking dopamine receptors rapidly (Davis, 1978). This disjunction between the behavioural and pharmacological effects of antipsychotics is difficult to understand within the context of the theory. One possibility is that although antipsychotics do indeed block D_2 receptors, their ultimate therapeutic effect may result from the effect this blockade has on other brain areas and other neurotransmitter systems (Cohen et al., 1997).

It is also puzzling that to be therapeutically effective, antipsychotics must reduce dopamine levels or receptor

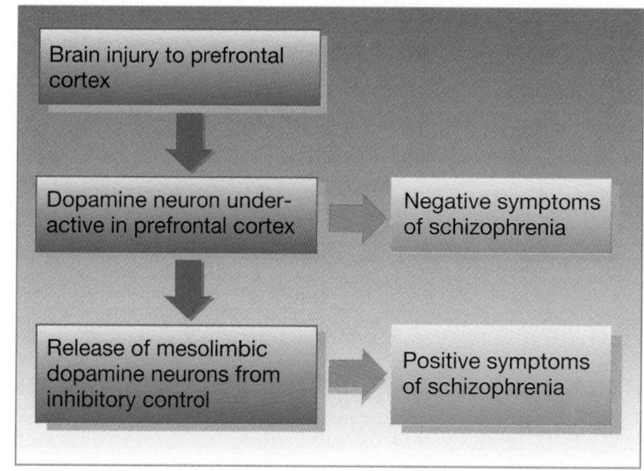

Figure 11.3 Dopamine theory of schizophrenia.

activity to *below normal*, producing Parkinsonian side effects. According to the theory, reducing dopamine levels or receptor activity to normal should be sufficient for a therapeutic effect.

Furthermore, newer drugs used in treating schizophrenia implicate other neurotransmitters, such as serotonin, in the disorder. Dopamine neurons generally modulate the activity of other neural systems; for example, in the prefrontal cortex, they regulate GABA neurons. Similarly, serotonin neurons regulate dopamine neurons in the mesolimbic pathway. Thus, dopamine may be only one piece in a much more complicated jigsaw puzzle.

Glutamate, a transmitter that is widespread in the human brain, may also play a role (Carlsson et al., 1999). Low levels of glutamate have been found in cerebrospinal fluid of patients with schizophrenia (Faustman et al., 1999), and postmortem studies have revealed low levels of the enzyme needed to produce glutamate (Tsai et al., 1995). The street drug PCP can induce a psychotic state, including both positive and negative symptoms, in normal people, and it produces this effect by interfering with one of glutamate's receptors (O'Donnell & Grace, 1998). Furthermore, a decrease in glutamate inputs from either the prefrontal cortex or the hippocampus (both of these brain areas are implicated in schizophrenia) to the corpus striatum (a temporal-lobe structure) can result in increased dopamine activity (O'Donnell & Grace, 1998).

Although dopamine remains the most actively researched biochemical factor in schizophrenia, it is not likely to provide a complete explanation of the biochemistry of the illness. Schizophrenia is a disorder with widespread symptoms covering perception, cognition, motor activity, and social behaviour. It is unlikely that a single neurotransmitter, such as dopamine, could account for all of them. Biochemically oriented schizophrenia researchers are starting to cast a broader biochemical net, moving away from an almost exclusive emphasis on dopamine. Glutamate and serotonin may well be at the forefront of these inquiries, perhaps in conjunction with dopamine activity.

The Brain and Schizophrenia

The search for a brain abnormality that causes schizophrenia began as early as the syndrome was identified, but the research did not prove promising, as the different studies did not yield the same findings. Interest gradually waned over the years. In the last 25 years, however, spurred by a number of technological advances, the field has reawakened and yielded some promising evidence. Some patients with schizophrenia have been found to have observable brain pathology.

Postmortem analyses of the brains of patients with schizophrenia are one source of evidence. Such studies consistently reveal abnormalities in some areas of the brain, although the specific problems reported vary from study to study and many of the findings are contradictory. The most consistent finding is of enlarged ventricles, which implies a loss of subcortical brain cells. Moderately consistent findings indicate structural problems in subcortical temporal-limbic areas, such as the hippocampus and the basal ganglia, and in the prefrontal and temporal cortex (Dwork, 1997; Heckers, 1997).

Even more impressive are the images obtained in CT scan and MRI studies. Researchers were quick to apply these new tools to brains of living patients with schizophrenia. Thus far, these images of living brain tissue have most consistently revealed that some patients, especially males (Nopoulos, Flaum, & Andreasen, 1997), have enlarged ventricles. Research also shows a reduction in cortical grey matter in both the temporal and frontal regions (Goldstein et al., 1999) and reduced volume in basal ganglia (e.g., the caudate nucleus) and limbic structures (Keshavan et al., 1998; Velakoulis et al., 1999), suggesting deterioration or atrophy of brain tissue.

Further evidence concerning large ventricles comes from an MRI study of 15 pairs of MZ twins who were discordant for schizophrenia (Suddath et al., 1990). For 12 of the 15 pairs, the twin with schizophrenia could be identified by simple visual inspection of the scan. Because the twins were genetically identical, these data suggest that the origin of these brain abnormalities may not be genetic.

Large ventricles in patients with schizophrenia are correlated with impaired performance on neuropsychological tests, poor adjustment prior to the onset of the disorder, and poor response to drug treatment (Andreasen et al., 1982; Weinberger et al., 1980). A recent Canadian study found that large ventricles can be detected both in people with a first episode of schizophrenia and in patients with chronic schizophrenia. It is likely that the large ventricles have a neurodevelopmental origin and are not progressive. Thus, enlarged ventricles do not simply reflect chronic, untreated schizophrenia (see Malla, Mitall, et al., 2002). The extent to which the ventricles are enlarged, however, is modest, and many patients do not differ from normal people in this respect. Furthermore, enlarged ventricles are not specific to schizophrenia, as they are also evident in the CT scans of patients with other psychoses, such as bipolar disorder (Rieder et al., 1983; Zipursky et al., 1997) (see Focus on Discovery 11.2).

A variety of data suggest that the prefrontal cortex is of particular importance in schizophrenia.

- The prefrontal cortex is known to play a role in behaviours such as speech, decision-making, and willed action, all of which are disrupted in schizophrenia. Comparisons of patients diagnosed with schizophrenia and other patients, in terms of their performance on cognitive tasks that are believed to tap this area (e.g., the Wisconsin Card Sorting Task), show that people with schizophrenia give poorer responses and make more errors (Everitt, Lavoie, focus on discovery/11.2

Mood Disorders and Schizophrenia

As we have mentioned, enlarged ventricles are not specific to schizophrenia; other psychotic patients, notably those with mood disorders, show ventricular enlargement almost as great as that seen in schizophrenia (Elkis et al., 1995). One recent study conducted in Toronto found that a group of patients with bipolar disorder had larger ventricles than the group diagnosed with schizophrenia (Zipursky et al., 1997). Similarly, increased density of dopamine receptors has been reported among psychotic patients with bipolar disorder (Pearlson et al., 1995). Maternal exposure to an influenza virus during the second trimester of pregnancy also increases the risk for mood disorders (Machon, Mednick, & Huttunen, 1997). The phenothiazines, used most often to treat schizophrenia, are also effective with mania and psychotic depression. Finally, the twin literature reports a set of identical triplets, two with bipolar disorder and one with schizophrenia.

These data suggest that the diagnostic categories of schizophrenia and psychotic mood disorders may not be totally separate entities. They share some common symptoms (notably delusions) and some possible etiological factors (increased dopamine activity), and they respond similarly to biological treatments. An important implication is that researchers would do well to focus some of their efforts on psychotic symptoms across diagnostic groups, rather than only on the diagnosis of schizophrenia.

Gagnon, & Gosselin, 2001). Moreover, tests of verbal fluency in patients and control participants show differences in fluency performance that are believed to reflect deficits involving the frontal lobe (Zakzanis, Troyer, Rich, & Heinrichs, 2000).

- Donald Young from the Centre for Addiction and Mental Health in Toronto and his colleagues have been examining the relation between insight, or, more specifically, a lack of awareness of their disorder, and neuropsychological performance in chronic schizophrenics. In one study, Young et al. (1998) determined that lack of illness awareness was related to poorer neuropsychological performance (Wisconsin Card Sorting Task) more often in patients with schizophrenia than in bipolar participants, supporting the hypothesis that lack of awareness is related to defective frontal-lobe functioning. A recent meta-analysis conducted by researchers at the University of Calgary found a small negative association between insight and global positive and negative symptoms of schizophrenia (Mintz, Dobson, & Romney, 2003).
- MRI studies have shown reductions in grey matter in the prefrontal cortex (Buchanan et al., 1998).
- In a type of functional imaging in which glucose metabolism is studied in various brain regions while patients perform psychological tests, patients with schizophrenia have shown low metabolic rates in the prefrontal cortex (Buchsbaum et al., 1984). Glucose metabolism in the prefrontal cortex has also been studied while patients are performing neuropsychological tests of prefrontal function. Because the tests place demands on the prefrontal cortex, glucose metabolism normally goes up as energy is used. Patients with schizophrenia do poorly on the tests and also fail to show activation in the prefrontal region (Fletcher et al., 1998; Weinberger, Berman, & Illowsky, 1988). Failure to show frontal activation has also been detected by the more recently developed fMRI (Curtis et al., 1998).
- The frontal hypoactivation is less pronounced in the nonschizophrenic twin of discordant MZ pairs, again suggesting that this brain dysfunction may not have a genetic origin (Torrey et al., 1994). Failure to show frontal activation is related to the severity of negative symptoms (O'Donnell & Grace, 1998) and thus parallels the work on dopamine underactivity in the frontal cortex already discussed.

A possible interpretation of these brain abnormalities is that they are the consequence of damage during gestation or birth. Many studies have shown high rates of delivery

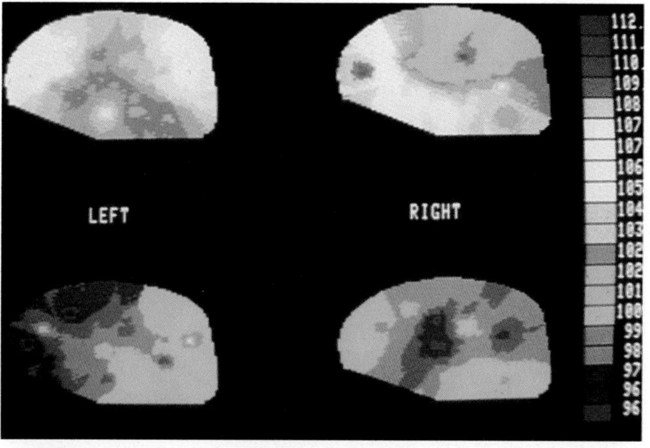

Differences in regional cerebral blood flow for each hemisphere between people diagnosed with schizophrenia (*bottom*) and normal individuals (*top*). The values shown were scored as the percentage change in cerebral blood flow from a control task to the Wisconsin Card Sort, which was expected to activate the prefrontal cortex. The normal participants showed greater prefrontal cortical activation as indexed by the "hotter" colour of this brain region. *Source*: Weinberger, Berman, and Illowsky, 1988.

complications in patients with schizophrenia; such complications could have led to a reduced supply of oxygen to the brain, resulting in damage (e.g., Verdoux et al., 1997). These obstetrical complications do not raise the risk of schizophrenia in everyone who experiences them; rather, the risk for schizophrenia is increased in those who experience complications *and* have a genetic predisposition (Cannon & Mednick, 1993).

Although the data are not entirely consistent (Westergaard et al, 1999), another possibility is that a virus invades the brain and damages it during fetal development (Mednick, Huttonen, & Machon, 1994; Mednick et al., 1988). During a five-week period in 1957, Helsinki experienced an epidemic of influenza virus. Researchers examined rates of schizophrenia among adults who had likely been exposed during their mothers' pregnancies. People who had been exposed to the virus during the second trimester of pregnancy had much higher rates than those who had been exposed in either of the other trimesters or in nonexposed control adults. This finding is intriguing because we know that cortical development is in a critical stage of growth during the second trimester. During this period, neurons are being produced in the rudimentary brain called the neural tube. These neurons then have to move to their appropriate location, passing through layers of cells as they do so. Perhaps this process of cell migration is disrupted in people who later develop schizophrenia.

Consistent with this speculation, postmortem analyses of neurons in the brains of individuals with schizophrenia have shown reduced numbers of cells in the outer layers of the cortex in both the prefrontal and the temporal areas (Akbarian et al., 1995). Similarly, a widespread thinning of the cortex of patients with schizophrenia has been reported, apparently resulting from loss of dendrites and axons (Selemon, Rajkowska, & Goldman-Rakic, 1995), and neurons in the frontal cortex have been shown to be smaller than normal in patients with schizophrenia (Rajkowska, Selemen, & Goldman-Rakic, 1998).

If, as the findings we have just reviewed suggest, the brains of people with schizophrenia are damaged early in their development, why does the disorder begin many years later, in adolescence or early adulthood? Weinberger (1987) proposed that the brain injury interacts with normal brain development and that the prefrontal cortex is a brain structure that matures late, typically in adolescence. Thus, an injury to this area may remain silent until the period of development when the prefrontal cortex begins to play a larger role in behaviour. Notably, dopamine activity also peaks in adolescence, which may further set the stage for the onset of schizophrenic symptoms.

Further work on the relationship of the brain and schizophrenia is proceeding at a rapid rate. Recognizing that the symptoms of schizophrenia implicate many areas of the brain, the research has moved away from trying to find some highly specific "lesion" and has started to examine neural systems and the way different areas of the brain interact with one another. This work is beginning to call attention to the possible role of a wider range of brain structures (e.g., the thalamus, cerebellum) in schizophrenia (Andreasen, Paradiso, & O'Leary, 1998; Levitt et al., 1999). Indeed, quantitative and conceptual reviews such as those conducted in Canada by Zakzanis and Heinrichs and their associates (see Heinrichs & Zakzanis, 1998; Zakzanis & Heinrichs, 1999; Zakzanis, Poulis, Hansen, & Jolic, 2000) have led these authors to conclude that the specific role of deficits in the temporal lobes has been overstated and that more diffuse dysfunction exists. Moreover, the extent of a more broad-based cognitive impairment needs to be examined with respect to the heterogeneity of schizophrenia. It may be the case that specific deficits exist in only a subset of those afflicted with schizophrenia.

Psychological Stress and Schizophrenia

We have discussed several possible biological diatheses for schizophrenia, but more than biology is responsible. Psychological stress plays a key role by interacting with a biological vulnerability to produce this illness. Data show that, as with other disorders, increases in life stress increase the likelihood of a relapse (Hirsch et al., 1996; Ventura et al., 1989). Moreover, as shown in a recent Canadian study, patients who take part in a stress-management program are less likely to be readmitted to the hospital in the year following treatment, especially if they had attended treatment sessions regularly (Norman et al., 2002). We turn now to the role of life stress in the actual development of schizophrenia. Two stressors that have played an important part in schizophrenia research are social class and the family.

Social Class and Schizophrenia For many years, we have known that the highest rates of schizophrenia are found in central city areas inhabited by people in the lowest socioeconomic class (e.g., Harvey et al., 1996; Hollingshead & Redlich, 1958; Srole et al., 1962). The relation between

The prevalence of schizophrenia is highest among people in the lowest socioeconomic class. Seaton House in Toronto provides a safeplace for those who are homeless & suffering from severe mental illness, including schizophrenia.

social class and schizophrenia does not show a continuous progression of higher rates of schizophrenia as the social class becomes lower. Rather, there is a decidedly sharp difference between the number of people with schizophrenia in the lowest social class and the number in other social classes. In the classic 10-year Hollingshead and Redlich study of social class and mental illness in New Haven, Connecticut, the rate of schizophrenia was found to be twice as high in the lowest social class as in the next lowest class. This finding has been confirmed cross-culturally by similar community studies carried out in countries such as Denmark, Norway, and the United Kingdom (Kohn, 1968).

The correlations between social class and schizophrenia are consistent, but they are difficult to interpret in causal terms. Some people believe that stressors associated with being in a low social class may cause or contribute to the development of schizophrenia—the sociogenic hypothesis. The degrading treatment a person receives from others, the low level of education, and the lack of rewards and opportunity taken together may make membership in the lowest social class such a stressful experience that an individual—at least one who is predisposed—develops schizophrenia. Alternatively, the stressors encountered by those in the lowest social class could be biological; for example, we know that children of mothers whose nutrition during pregnancy was poor are at increased risk for schizophrenia (Susser et al., 1996).

Another explanation of the correlation between schizophrenia and low social class is the social-selection theory, which reverses the direction of causality between social class and schizophrenia. During the course of their developing psychosis, people with schizophrenia may drift into the poverty-ridden areas of the city. The growing cognitive and motivational problems besetting these individuals may so impair their earning capabilities that they cannot afford to live elsewhere. Or, they may choose to move to areas where little social pressure will be brought to bear on them and they can escape intense social relationships.

One way of resolving the conflict between these opposing theories is to study the social mobility of schizophrenic people. Consistent with the social-selection theory, three studies (Lystad, 1957; Schwartz, 1946; Turner & Wagonfeld, 1967) found that people with schizophrenia are downwardly mobile in occupational status. But an equal number of studies have shown that people with schizophrenia are not downwardly mobile (Clausen & Kohn, 1959; Dunham, 1965; Hollingshead & Redlich, 1958). Clearly, this approach has not resolved the issue.

Kohn (1968) suggested another way of examining this question: Are the fathers of patients with schizophrenia also from the lowest social class? If they are, this could be considered evidence in favour of the sociogenic hypothesis that lower-class status is conducive to schizophrenia, for class would be shown to *precede* schizophrenia. If the fathers are from a higher social class, the social-selection hypothesis would be the better explanation. Turner and Wagonfeld (1967) found evidence for the social-selection hypothesis: of 26 patients in the lowest social class, only four had fathers in the lowest class.

A subsequent study in Israel employed a new methodology, simultaneously investigating both social class and ethnic background (Dohrenwend et al., 1992). The rates of schizophrenia were examined in Israeli Jews of European ethnic background and in more recent immigrants to Israel from North Africa and the Middle East. Those in the latter group experience considerable racial prejudice and discrimination. The sociogenic hypothesis would predict that because all social classes of this disadvantaged ethnic group experience high levels of stress, all should have consistently higher than normal rates of schizophrenia. However, this pattern did not emerge, supporting the social-selection theory.

In sum, the data are more supportive of the social-selection theory than of the sociogenic theory. But we should not conclude that the social environment plays no role in schizophrenia. For example, the prevalence of schizophrenia among Africans from the Caribbean who remain in their native country is much lower than among those who have emigrated to London (Bhugra et al., 1996). This difference could well be caused by the stress associated with trying to assimilate into a new culture.

The Family and Schizophrenia Early theorists regarded family relationships, especially those between a mother and her son, as crucial in the development of schizophrenia. At one time, the view was so prevalent that the term schizophrenogenic mother was coined to describe the supposedly cold and dominant, conflict-inducing parent who was said to produce schizophrenia in her offspring (Fromm-Reichmann, 1948). These mothers were characterized as rejecting, overprotective, self-sacrificing, impervious to the feelings of others, rigid and moralistic about sex, and fearful of intimacy.

Controlled studies evaluating the schizophrenogenic mother theory have not yielded supporting data. Studies of families of individuals with schizophrenia have, however, revealed that they differ in some ways from normal families, exhibiting, for example, vague patterns of communication and high levels of conflict. It is plausible, though, that the conflict and unclear communication are family members' responses to having a young family member with schizophrenia.

Some findings do suggest that the faulty communications of parents may play a role in the etiology of schizophrenia. One type of communication deviance is illustrated in the following example. Note how the father not only ignores his daughter's concern, but ridicules her choice of words.

Daughter (complainingly): Nobody will listen to me. Everybody is trying to still me.

Mother: Nobody wants to kill you.

Father: If you're going to associate with intellectual people, you're going to have to remember that still is a noun and not a verb. (Wynne & Singer, 1963, p. 195)

In an important study of communication deviance, adolescents with behavioural problems were studied along with their families. A five-year follow-up revealed that a number of the young people had developed schizophrenia or schizophrenia-related disorders. The investigators were then able to relate the disorders discovered at follow-up to any deviance in the communications of parents that had been evident five years earlier (Goldstein & Rodnick, 1975). Communication deviance in the families was indeed found to predict the later onset of schizophrenia in their offspring, supporting its significance (Norton, 1982). However, it does not appear that communication deviance is a specific etiological factor for schizophrenia, since parents of manic patients are equally high on this variable (Miklowitz, 1985).

Further evidence favouring some role for the family comes from a substantial adoption study by Tienari and his colleagues (1994) that is continuing in Finland. A large sample of adopted offspring of mothers with schizophrenia is being studied along with a control group of adopted children. Extensive data were collected on various aspects of family life in the adoptive families, and these family data were related to the adjustment of the children. The families were categorized into levels of maladjustment based on material from clinical interviews as well as psychological tests. Long-term follow-up investigation has confirmed that more serious psychopathology is evident among the adoptees if they were reared in a disturbed family environment; children having a biological parent with schizophrenia showed a greater increase in psychopathology than did the control participants who were reared in a disturbed family environment (Tienari et al., 2004). Although it is tempting to conclude that both a genetic predisposition and a noxious family environment are necessary to increase risk for psychopathology, a problem in interpretation remains. The disturbed family environment could be a response to a disturbed child. Thus, we can only tentatively say that an etiological role for the family has been established.

A series of studies initiated in London indicate that the family can have an important impact on the adjustment of patients after they leave the hospital. Brown and his colleagues (1966) conducted a nine-month follow-up study of a sample of patients with schizophrenia who returned to live with their families after being discharged from the hospital. Interviews were conducted with parents or spouses before discharge and rated for the number of critical comments made about the patient and for expressions of hostility toward or emotional overinvolvement with him or her. The following statement is an example of a critical comment made by a father about his daughter's behaviour. The father is expressing the idea that his daughter is deliberately symptomatic to avoid housework: "My view is that Maria acts this way so my wife doesn't give her any responsibilities around the house" (Weissman et al., 1998). Unfortunately, a recent study conducted at Laval University showed that the tendency to perceive symptoms of schizophrenia as intentional is far too evident among caregivers of people with schizophrenia (see Provencher & Fincham, 2000).

A variable identified by Brown and associates in families of schizophrenics is known as **expressed emotion (EE)**. On the basis of this expressed emotion variable, families were divided into two groups: those revealing a great deal of expressed emotion, called high-EE families, and those revealing little, called low-EE families. At the end of the follow-up period, 10 percent of the patients returning to low-EE homes had relapsed. In marked contrast, in the same period, 58 percent of the patients returning to high-EE homes had gone back to the hospital!

How is expressed emotion assessed? The standard procedure is to obtain ratings of expressed emotion via the Camberwell Family Interview (CFI), which was developed by Vaughn and Leff (1976). However, the CFI is lengthy to administer, trained evaluators are required, and one or more family members must be available to be interviewed. Alternatives are self-report measures of expressed emotion. One such measure, the Level of Expressed Emotion (LEE) Scale, was developed by Canadian researchers (see Cole & Kazarian, 1988). Research suggests that the LEE Scale provides information that supplements the CFI (Kazarian, Malla, Cole, & Baker, 1990), and long-term follow-ups over a five-year period showed that elevated scores on the LEE Scale are associated with relapse and rehospitalization (Cole & Kazarian, 1993). However, in recent years, authors have expressed concern about the validity of the original four-factor structure of the LEE Scale (Gerlsma & Hale, 1997; Gerlsma, van der Lubbe, & van Nieuwenhuizen, 1992; Startup, 1999). The three factors identified in a Dutch study by Gerlsma et al. (1992) were lack of emotional support from family members, intrusiveness, and general irritability in the family environment.

Regardless of the method of assessment, a meta-analysis of research findings conducted by Butzlaff and Hooley (1998) indicates that the environment into which patients are discharged has great bearing on how soon they are rehospitalized. It has also been found that negative symptoms of schizophrenia are the ones most likely to elicit critical comments (King, 2000) and that relatives who make the most critical comments tend to view the patients as being able to control their symptoms (Lopez et al., 1999; Weissman et al., 1998). Family research conducted in Quebec has established further that high EE mothers are highly sensitive to excitement and depression in the patient and report a high level of burden associated with their child's illness (King et al., 2003). These mothers also have a personality characterized by high levels of conscientiousness and low levels of neuroticism.

What is not yet clear is exactly how to interpret the effects of EE. Is EE causal, or do these critical comments reflect a reaction to the patients' behaviour? For example, if the condition of a patient with schizophrenia begins to deteriorate, does family concern and involvement increase? Indeed, bizarre or dangerous behaviour by the patient might seem to warrant the setting of limits and other familial efforts that could increase the level of expressed emotion.

Research indicates that both interpretations of the operation of EE—the causal and the reactive—may be correct (Rosenfarb et al., 1994). Recently discharged schizophrenic patients and their high-or low-EE families were observed as they engaged in a discussion of a family problem. Two key findings emerged:

1. The expression of unusual thoughts by the patients ("If that kid bites you, you'll get rabies") elicited higher levels of critical comments by family members who had previously been characterized as high in EE.
2. In high-EE families critical comments by family members led to increased expression of unusual thoughts.

Thus, this study found a bidirectional relationship: critical comments by members of high-EE families elicited the higher expression of higher levels of unusual thoughts by patients; and unusual thoughts expressed by patients led to increased critical comments in high-EE families. Another recent study conducted in Montreal with 28 people with schizophrenia and their mothers is more consistent with the position that critical comments and emotional overinvolvement may be responses to schizophrenia (i.e., effects) rather than causes (see King, 2000).

How does stress, such as a high level of EE, increase the symptoms of schizophrenia and precipitate relapses? In attempting to answer this question, some researchers have related the effects of stress on the hypothalamic-pituitary-adrenal (HPA) axis to the dopamine theory (Walker & DiForio, 1997). Stress is known to activate the HPA axis, causing cortisol to be secreted. In turn, cortisol is known to increase dopamine activity and may thereby increase the symptoms of schizophrenia. Furthermore, heightened dopamine activity itself can increase HPA activation, which may make a person overly sensitive to stress. Thus, the theory suggests a bidirectional relationship between HPA activation and dopamine activity. Another possibility is that stress may increase substance abuse. Patients report, for example, that alcohol reduces their anxiety, apathy, sleep difficulties, and anhedonia (Noorsdy et al., 1991). However, the irony is that drugs of abuse stimulate dopamine systems in the brain and may thereby increase the positive symptoms of the disorder.

HIGH-RISK STUDIES OF SCHIZOPHRENIA

What are people who develop schizophrenia like before their symptoms begin, typically in adolescence or early adulthood? An early method of answering this question was to construct developmental histories by examining the childhood records of those who had later become schizophrenic. Such research revealed that individuals who became schizophrenic were different from their contemporaries even before any serious problems were noted in their behaviour.

In the 1960s, Albee and Lane and their colleagues repeatedly found that children who later developed schizophrenia had lower IQs than did members of various control groups, usually comprising siblings and neighbourhood peers (Albee, Lane, & Reuter, 1964; Lane & Albee, 1965). Investigations of the social behaviour of preschizophrenic patients yielded some interesting findings as well. For example, teachers described preschizophrenic boys as disagreeable in childhood and preschizophrenic girls as passive (Watt, 1974; Watt et al., 1970). Both men and women were described as delinquent and withdrawn in childhood (Berry, 1967).

Researchers have also examined home movies of normal family life taken before the onset of a child's schizophrenia (Walker, Davis, & Savoie, 1994; Walker et al., 1993). Compared with their siblings who did not later become schizophrenic, preschizophrenic children showed poorer motor skills and more expressions of negative affect.

As intriguing as these findings are, the major limitation of such developmental research is that the data were not originally collected with the intention of describing preschizophrenic patients or of predicting the development of schizophrenia from childhood behaviour. More specific information is required if developmental histories are to provide clear evidence regarding etiology.

The high-risk method, described in Chapter 5, can yield this information. The first such study of schizophrenia was begun in the 1960s by Sarnoff Mednick and Fini Schulsinger (Mednick & Schulsinger, 1968). They chose Denmark because the Danish registries of all people make it possible to keep track of them for long periods of time. Mednick and Schulsinger selected as their high-risk subjects 207 young people whose mothers had chronic schizophrenia. The researchers decided that the mother should be the parent with the disorder because paternity is not always easy to determine. Then, 104 low-risk subjects, individuals whose mothers did not have schizophrenia, were matched to the high-risk subjects on variables such as sex, age, father's occupation, rural or urban residence, years of education, and institutional upbringing versus rearing by the family.

In 1972 the now-grown men and women were followed up with a number of measures, including a diagnostic battery. Fifteen of the high-risk subjects were diagnosed as schizophrenic; none of the control men and women was so diagnosed. Looking back to the information collected on the subjects when they were children, the investigators found that several circumstances predicted the later onset of schizophrenia. These data, albeit from a small study, suggest that the etiology of schizophrenia may differ for positive- and negative-symptom patients. In the most recent analysis of the data, the patients with schizophrenia were divided into two groups, those with predominantly positive and those with predominantly negative symptoms (Cannon, Mednick, & Parnas, 1990). Variables predicting schizophrenia were different for the two groups. Negative-symptom schizophrenia was preceded by a history of pregnancy and birth complications and by a failure to show electrodermal responses to simple stimuli. Positive-symptom schizophrenia was preceded by a history of family instability, such as

Sarnoff Mednick, a psychologist at the University of Southern California, pioneered the use of the high-risk method for studying schizophrenia. He has also contributed to the hypothesis that a maternal viral infection is implicated in this disorder.

separation from parents and placement in foster homes or institutions for periods of time.

In the wake of Mednick and Schulsinger's pioneering study, several other high-risk investigations were undertaken, some of which have also yielded information concerning the possible causes of adult psychopathology. The New York High-Risk Study found that a composite measure of attentional dysfunction predicted behavioural disturbance at follow-up (Cornblatt & Erlenmeyer-Kimling, 1985). Furthermore, low IQ was a characteristic of the first high-risk children to be hospitalized (Erlenmeyer-Kimling & Cornblatt, 1987). In an Israeli study, poor neurobehavioural functioning (poor concentration, poor verbal ability, lack of motor control and coordination) predicted schizophrenia-like outcomes, as did earlier interpersonal problems (Marcus et al., 1987). As participants in other high-risk studies mature, we will gain further glimpses into the development of this debilitating disorder.

THERAPIES FOR SCHIZOPHRENIA

The puzzling, often frightening array of symptoms displayed by people with schizophrenia makes treatment difficult. The history of psychopathology, reviewed in Chapter 1, is in many respects a history of humankind's efforts, often brutal and unenlightened, to deal with schizophrenia, arguably the most serious of the disorders described in this book. Although some of the profoundly disturbed people confined centuries ago in foul asylums may have suffered from problems as prosaic as syphilis, there seems little doubt that many, if examined now, would carry a diagnosis of schizophrenia. Today we know a good deal about the nature and etiology of schizophrenia, but although we can treat its symptoms somewhat effectively, a cure remains elusive.

With the notable exception of an intensive behaviour-therapy project described in Focus on Discovery 11.3, research indicates, for the most part, that traditional hospital care does little to effect meaningful, enduring changes in the majority of mentally disordered patients (see description of mental hospitals in Chapter 1). The overwhelming body of evidence shows rehospitalization rates of 40 to 50 percent after one year and upwards of 75 percent after two years (Paul & Menditto, 1992). Studies designed specifically to follow patients with schizophrenia after discharge from the hospital show generally poor outcomes as well (Robinson et al., 1999).

focus on discovery/11.3

A Classic Behaviour Therapy Project with Hospitalized Schizophrenic Patients

Although the trend over the past 30-plus years has been to have people with schizophrenia spend as little time as possible in a mental hospital, even with advances in psychoactive medication, there are still hundreds of thousands of people living in institutional settings, some for many years. As described in Chapter 2, behaviour therapists introduced an innovation known as the *token economy* into hospital settings in the 1960s. The most comprehensive and impressive of these efforts was reported by Gordon Paul and Robert Lentz (1977). Because this project was a milestone in the treatment of schizophrenia and an exemplar of comparative-therapy research, we describe it here in some detail.

The long-term, regressed, and chronic schizophrenic patients in the program were the most severely debilitated institutionalized adults ever studied systematically. Some patients screamed for long periods, some were mute; many were incontinent, a few assaultive. Most of them no longer used silverware, and some buried their faces in their food. The patients were matched for age, sex, socioeconomic background, symptoms, and length of hospitalization and then assigned to one of three wards—social learning (behavioural—basically a token economy), milieu therapy, and routine hospital management. Each ward had 28 residents. The two treatment wards shared ambitious objectives: to teach self-care, housekeeping, communication, and vocational skills; to reduce symptomatic behaviour; and to release patients to the community.

SOCIAL-LEARNING WARD

Located in a new mental health centre, the social-learning ward operated on a token economy that embraced all aspects of the residents' lives. The patients' appearance had to pass muster in 11 specific ways each morning for them to earn a token. Well-made beds, good behaviour at mealtime, classroom participation, and socializing during free periods were other means of earning tokens. Residents learned through modelling, shaping, prompting, and instructions. They were also taught to communicate better with one another, and they participated in problem-solving groups. Tokens were a necessity, for they purchased meals as well as small luxuries. In addition to living by the rules of the token economy, individuals received behavioural treatments tailored to their needs—for example, assertion training to deal with a specific interpersonal conflict they might be having with a staff member. Residents were kept busy 85 percent of their waking hours learning to behave better.

MILIEU-THERAPY WARD

This ward operated according to the principles of Jones's (1953) therapeutic community, an approach reminiscent of Pinel's moral treatment of the late 18th century. These residents, too, were kept busy 85 percent of their waking hours. Both individually and as a group, they were expected to act responsibly and to participate in decisions about how the ward was to function. In general, they were treated more as normal individuals than as incompetent mental patients. Staff members impressed on the residents their positive expectations and praised them for doing well. When patients behaved symptomatically, staff members stayed with them, making clear their expectation that the patients would soon behave more appropriately.

ROUTINE HOSPITAL MANAGEMENT

These patients continued their accustomed hospital existence in an older state institution, receiving custodial care and heavy antipsychotic medication. Except for the 5 percent of their waking hours occupied by occasional activity and recreational, occupational, and individual and group therapies, these people were on their own.

Before the program began, the staffs of the two treatment wards were carefully trained to adhere to detailed instructions in therapy manuals. Regular observations then confirmed that they were implementing the principles of a social-learning or a milieu-therapy program. Over the four and a half years of hospitalization and the one and a half years of follow-up, the patients were carefully evaluated at regular six-month intervals on the basis of structured interviews and meticulous, direct, behavioural observations.

The results? Both social learning and milieu therapy reduced positive and negative symptoms, with the social-learning ward achieving better results than the milieu ward on a number of measures. The residents had also acquired self-care, housekeeping, social, and vocational skills. The behaviour of members of these two groups within the institution was superior to that of the residents of the hospital ward, and by the end of treatment, more of them had been discharged. Over 10 percent of the social-learning patients and 7 percent of the milieu patients left the centre for independent living, while none of the hospital-treatment patients achieved this goal.

An interesting finding emerged concerning medication use. About 90 percent of the patients in all three groups were receiving antipsychotic drugs at the outset of the study. Over time, use among the routine-hospital-management group increased to 100 percent, while in the other two groups the percentage of patients on drugs dropped dramatically, to 18 percent in the milieu group and 11 percent in the social-learning ward. This is a remarkable finding for the medical staff had assumed that without their medication, these chronic patients would be too difficult for the staff to manage. In addition, many patients from all three groups were discharged to community placements, such as boarding homes and halfway houses, where there was supervision but also considerably less restraint than they had experienced for an average of 17 years. Members of the social-learning group did significantly better at remaining in these community residences than did patients in the other two groups.

Considering how poorly these patients were functioning before this treatment project, these results are extraordinary. That the social-learning program was superior to the milieu program is also significant, for milieu treatment is used in many mental hospitals. As implemented by Paul's team of clinicians, the milieu treatment provided patients with more attention than was given to those on the social-learning ward. This greater amount of attention would appear to control well for the positive expectancy effect of the social-learning therapy.

These results, though, should not be accepted as confirming the usefulness of token economies per se, for the social-learning therapy contained elements that went beyond operant conditioning of overt motor behaviour. Staff provided information to residents about appropriate behaviour and attempted verbally to clarify misconceptions. Paul (personal communication, 1981) relegated the token economy to a secondary, although not trivial, role. He saw it as a useful device for getting the attention of severely regressed patients in the initial stages of treatment. The token economy created the opportunity for his patients to acquire new information, or, in Paul's informal phrase, to "get good things into their heads."

Paul and Lentz never claimed that any one of the social-learning patients was cured. Although they were able to live outside the hospital, most continued to manifest many signs of mental disorder and few of them had gainful employment or participated in the social activities that most people take for granted. The outcome, however, is not to be underestimated: chronic mental patients, those typically shut away on back wards and forgotten by society, can be resocialized and taught self-care. They can learn to behave normally enough to be discharged from mental institutions. This is a major achievement in mental health care. Reports published since the Paul and Lentz study support the effectiveness of social-learning programs (see Mueser & Liberman, 1995; Paul & Menditto, 1992; Paul, Stuve, & Cross, 1997).

A major problem with any kind of treatment for schizophrenia is that many patients with schizophrenia lack insight into their impaired condition and refuse any treatment at all (Amador et al., 1994). As they don't believe they have an illness, they don't see the need for professional intervention, particularly when it includes hospitalization or drugs. This is especially true of those with paranoid schizophrenia, who may regard any therapy as a threatening intrusion from hostile outside forces. Family members therefore face a major challenge in getting their relatives into treatment, which is one reason they sometimes turn to involuntary hospitalization via civil commitment as a last resort or lobby for community treatment orders.

Biological Treatments

Shock and Psychosurgery The general warehousing of patients in mental hospitals earlier in the 20th century, coupled with the shortage of professional staff, created a climate that allowed, perhaps even subtly encouraged, experimentation with radical biological interventions. In the early 1930s, the practice of inducing a coma with large dosages of insulin was introduced by Sakel (1938), who claimed that up to three-quarters of the schizophrenics he treated showed significant improvement. Later findings by others were less encouraging, and insulin-coma therapy—which presented serious risks to health, including irreversible coma and death—was gradually abandoned. As discussed in Chapter 10, electroconvulsive therapy (ECT) was also used after its development in 1938 by Cerletti and Bini; it, too, proved to be only minimally effective.

In 1935, Moñiz, a Portuguese psychiatrist, introduced the **prefrontal lobotomy**, a surgical procedure that destroys the tracts connecting the frontal lobes to lower centres of the brain. His initial reports claimed high rates of success (Moñiz, 1936), and for 20 years thereafter, thousands of mental patients—not only those diagnosed with schizophrenia—underwent variations of psychosurgery. A related procedure known as a *leukotomy* is a more circumscribed and specific procedure than a lobotomy. The lobotomy procedure was used especially for those whose behaviour was violent. Many patients did indeed quiet down after undergoing a lobotomy and could even be discharged from hospitals. During the 1950s, however, this intervention fell into disrepute for several reasons. After surgery, many patients became dull and listless and suffered serious losses in their cognitive capacities (e.g., becoming unable to carry on a coherent conversation with another person). This is not surprising given the destruction of parts of their brains believed responsible for thought. Controlled studies comparing chronic schizophrenics with and without surgery, including a recent one of patients in Quebec who received leukotomies, showed relatively few cognitive deficits associated with brain lesions (Black et al., 2000). Overall, the principal reason for the abandonment of lobotomies was the introduction of drugs that seemed to reduce the behavioural and emotional excesses of many patients.

Scene from *One Flew Over the Cuckoo's Nest*. The character on whose shoulders Jack Nicholson is sitting was lobotomized in the film.

Drug Therapies Without question, the most important development in the treatment of schizophrenia was the advent in the 1950s of several medications collectively referred to as **antipsychotic drugs**. These drugs are also referred to as *neuroleptics* because they produce side effects similar to the symptoms of a neurological disease. One of the more frequently prescribed antipsychotic drugs, *phenothiazine*, was first produced by a German chemist in the late 19th century. Not until the discovery of the antihistamines, which have a phenothiazine nucleus, in the 1940s did phenothiazines receive much attention.

Reaching beyond their use to treat the common cold and asthma, the French surgeon Laborit pioneered the use of antihistamines to reduce surgical shock. He noticed that they made his patients somewhat sleepy and less fearful about the impending operation. Laborit's work encouraged pharmaceutical companies to reexamine antihistamines in light of their tranquilizing effects. Shortly thereafter, a French chemist, Charpentier, prepared a new phenothiazine derivative, which he called chlorpromazine. This drug proved very effective in calming patients with schizophrenia. As already mentioned, phenothiazines derive their therapeutic properties from their ability to block dopamine receptors in the brain, thus reducing the influence of dopamine on thought, emotion, and behaviour.

Chlorpromazine (trade name Thorazine) was first used therapeutically in the United States in 1954 and rapidly became the preferred treatment for schizophrenia. Thorazine was actually introduced to North America by Canadian psychiatrist Heinz Lehmann, as described in Canadian Contributions 11.1. By 1970 more than 85 percent of all patients in state and provincial mental hospitals in the United States and Canada were receiving chlorpromazine or another phenothiazine. Other antipsychotics that have been used for years in the treatment of schizophrenia include the *butyrophenones* (e.g., haloperidol, Haldol) and the *thioxanthenes* (e.g., thiothixene, Navane). Both types seem generally as effective as the phenothiazines and work in similar ways. These classes of drugs reduce the positive symptoms of schizophrenia but have much less effect on the negative symptoms.

Canadian Contributions/11.1

Heinz E. Lehmann and the "Discovery" of Neuroleptics in North America

Recall for a moment the contributions of Phillipe Pinel (described in Chapter 1) who in 1793 removed the chains of mentally ill people at La Bicêtre asylum in Paris and ushered in many humanitarian reforms. Pinel lived on the asylum grounds and took his meals with the patients in order to be available to them and to practise his compassionate treatment of them throughout the day. Perhaps his intent was to serve as an appropriate role model for his charges. Can you imagine the director of a mental hospital living on the institution's grounds in the modern era? One such person was Heinz Lehmann. Lehmann, who passed away in 1999, must be considered one of the most important historical and contemporary figures in Canadian psychiatry.

In 1937 a young physician escaped from the Nazis in Germany and made his way to Canada, where he soon obtained a position at the Verdun Protestant Hospital in Montreal, a psychiatric hospital now known as the Douglas Hospital. According to Dongier (1999), at Verdon, Lehmann was initially placed in charge of about 750 patients, who accounted for almost half the beds at the hospital during that era. By 1947 he was clinical director. Subsequently, he became the director of research and education (1962), a full professor at McGill University (1965), and chair of the Department of Psychiatry (1971-1974). For 60 years, Lehmann remained on staff at the Douglas, where he lived with his family in a small house on the hospital grounds. Until his retirement in 1968, he kept a personal tradition of meeting and shaking hands with all of his patients on Christmas Day.

In the early years, Lehmann was unable to purchase phenobarbital, the main sedative used at the time, in capsule form. However, the resourceful physician overcame the obstacle: "At night, once my visits to patients were over, I was busy making capsules using bottles of powder. Incidentally, this started the rumour that I was an addict because nobody in his right mind would work in the pharmacy at 2 am" (Dongier, 1999, p. 362). In the 1950s, Lehmann and some of his patients were featured in a series of short films produced by the National Film Board of Canada. He interviewed patients and summarized the symptoms of the disorders that led to commitment to a mental hospital during the era when available drugs and psychosocial interventions were not especially effective. The disorders included the schizophrenias, manic depression, depression, and organic psychoses. These films are informative and educational even today, especially because the patients demonstrated some of the more florid symptoms of psychotic disorders that are now frequently controlled by modern neuroleptic drugs. Today it would be considered unethical to deprive people suffering from schizophrenia and other serious mental disorders of an intervention that could reduce their suffering.

The favourite film of one of the authors, *Folie à Deux* (literally, *Madness in Two*), illustrates a disorder of the same name, now referred to in the DSM-IV-TR as *shared psychotic disorder*—the development of a delusional system within a close relationship

Heinz E. Lehmann (1911-1999) published the first North American paper on the treatment of schizophrenia using chlorpromazine. Following upon his success at the Verdun Protestant Hospital (now the Douglas) in Montreal, the use of neuroleptics spread to the rest of the continent.

with a delusional person. In the film, Zena developed delusions that she was being persecuted by doctors, the police, lawyers, and judges following what she perceived to be unsuccessful cosmetic surgery on her nose. Her mother subsequently developed the same delusions. Zena attributed her problems to a conspiracy on the part of the entire criminal justice system, whereas her mother, who was less sophisticated medically and psychologically, blamed "witches" hidden among the patients and staff. You might ask, if Zena's mother's delusions are caused by her close association with Zena's delusions, why not separate the two of them? Presumably, when no longer influenced by her daughter, the mother would give up her own delusions. This would seem to be a logical strategy. In fact, Dr. Lehmann did exactly this, and as predicted, the mother's delusions disappeared. Unfortunately, she became so clinically depressed and suicidal that, for humane reasons, Lehmann decided to put mother and daughter back together on the same ward. Parenthetically, the case of Zena and her mother illustrates an important difference between the treatment of the mentally ill during that era and the treatment today. Despite ongoing concerns about current practices, it is very improbable that today's doctors would lock Zena and her mother away for much of the remainder of their lives, as often occurred back in the 1950s. We will discuss current mental health laws in Canada, especially as they relate to civil commitment, in Chapter 18.

In 1953 Heinz Lehmann noticed in a French journal an article about the effects of chlorpromazine as a tranquilizer and antipsychotic medication and decided that it would be worth trying the new drug with his own patients. He managed to obtain a supply from the drug manufacturer's representative and administered it with considerable success to over 200 patients who had a diagnosis of schizophrenia. He published his findings in the scientific journal *Archives of Neurology and Psychiatry*. This journal article was the very first paper to be published North American on the use of a neuroleptic to control symptoms of psychosis. At about the same time, Dr. Ruth Kajander tested chlorpromazine on 25 patients with schizophrenia at London Psychiatric Hospital in Ontario and presented her results at a meeting of the Ontario Neuropsychiatric Association in late 1953 (Griffin, December 1993). Just as Philippe Pinel unchained the chained in the asylums of Paris, Heinz Lehmann attempted to liberate his schizophrenic patients from the torments of their delusional thoughts. The use of chlorpromazine soon spread throughout North America. Subsequently, Lehmann read in a Swiss journal the first published paper on the use of the tricyclic antidepressant imipramine for the treatment of major depression. According to Dongier (1999), Lehmann deserves the credit for introducing this treatment advance to North America.

Although he received numerous international honours for his clinical psychopharmacology research, it should be noted that Heinz Lehmann's research and clinical interests were not wedded to biological interventions. Some of his over 300 publications in journals and books focused on psychotherapy, psychosocial approaches to treatment of the mentally ill, aftercare services in the community, community psychiatry, and assessment tools to measure the severity of psychiatric disorders (Dongier, 1999). In fact, Lehmann was opposed to the reductionist trends in biological psychology. He also resisted the process of psychiatric hospital deinstitutionalization when it was not accompanied by appropriate supports in the community.

In the concluding section of his eulogy to Lehmann in the Canadian Medical Association's Journal of Psychiatry and Neuroscience, Dongier (1999, p. 362) stated, "Without any doubt, no contemporary Canadian psychiatrist had the international prestige or commanded such high unanimous respect as Heinz Lehmann." His body rested at Douglas Hall, in the heart of the hospital to which he had devoted his life.

Primary Source: Adapted from Dongier (1999)

Although the antipsychotics reduce positive symptoms of schizophrenia, allowing the release of many patients from hospital, they are not a cure. Furthermore, about 30 percent of patients with schizophrenia do not respond favourably, although some of these patients may respond to some of the newer antipsychotic drugs (e.g., clozapine), which will be discussed later. Because of the side effects of the whole range of antipsychotic drugs, one American study found that about half the patients who take them quit after one year and up to three-quarters quit after two years (Harvard Mental Health Letter, 1995). A Canadian survey of 100 patients found that 56 percent reported that, without seeking their doctor's approval, they had stopped taking their medication; the most common reason given for noncompliance was drug side effects (Schizophrenia Society of Canada, 2002). Because of these high noncompliance rates, patients are frequently treated with long-lasting antipsychotics (e.g., fluphenazine decanoate, Prolixin), which are injected every two to six weeks.

Other drugs are used adjunctively, that is, along with antipsychotics, to treat depression or anxiety or to stabilize mood. These adjunctive medications include lithium, antidepressants, anticonvulsants, and tranquilizers. Antidepressants are also used with schizophrenic patients who become depressed after a psychotic episode (Hogarty et al., 1994; Siris et al., 1994).

Patients who respond positively to antipsychotics are kept on so-called *maintenance doses* of the drug, just enough to continue the therapeutic effect. They take their medication and return to the hospital or clinic on occasion for adjustment of the dose level. Released patients who are maintained on medication may make only marginal adjustment to the community, however. For example, they may be unable to live unsupervised or to hold down the kind of job for which they would otherwise be qualified. Their social relationships are likely to be sparse. And again, although antipsychotics keep positive symptoms from returning, they have little effect on negative symptoms such as flat affect. Reinstitutionalization is frequent. Antipsychotics have significantly reduced long-term institutionalization, but they have also initiated the revolving-door pattern of admission, discharge, and readmission seen in some patients.

Commonly reported side effects of antipsychotics include dizziness, blurred vision, restlessness, and sexual dysfunction. In addition, a group of particularly disturbing side effects, termed *extrapyramidal side effects*, stem from dysfunctions of the nerve tracts that descend from the brain to spinal motor neurons. Extrapyramidal side effects resemble the symptoms of Parkinson's disease. People taking antipsychotics usually develop tremors of the fingers, a shuffling gait, and drooling. Other side effects include *dystonia*, a state of muscular rigidity, and *dyskinesia*, an abnormal motion of voluntary and involuntary muscles, producing chewing movements as well as other movements of the lips, fingers, and legs. Together, these side effects cause arching of the back and a twisted posture of the neck and body. *Akasthesia* is an inability to remain still; people pace constantly and fidget. These perturbing symptoms can be treated by drugs used with patients who have Parkinson's disease.

In a muscular disturbance of older patients with schizophrenia, called *tardive dyskinesia*, the mouth muscles involuntarily make sucking, lip-smacking, and chin-wagging motions. In more severe cases, the whole body can be subject to involuntary motor movements. This syndrome affects about 10 to 20 percent of patients treated with antipsychotics for a long period of time and is not responsive to any known treatment (Sweet et al., 1995). Finally, a side effect called *neuroleptic malignant syndrome* occurs in about 1 percent of cases. In this condition, which can sometimes be fatal, severe muscular rigidity develops, accompanied by fever. The heart races, blood pressure increases, and the patient may lapse into a coma.

Because of these serious side effects, some clinicians believe it is unwise to take high doses of antipsychotics for extended periods of time. Current clinical practice calls for treating patients with the smallest possible doses of drugs. This situation puts the clinician in a quandary: if medication is reduced, the chance of relapse increases; but if medication is continued, serious and untreatable side effects may develop. One possible solution is to keep medication levels low but monitor patients closely so that when symptoms worsen, medication can be increased. Unfortunately, this strategy has not yet been shown to be effective (Marder et al., 1994; Schooler et al., 1997).

In the decades following the introduction of these antipsychotic drugs, there appeared to be little interest in developing new drugs to treat schizophrenia. This situation has changed markedly in recent years, following the introduction of clozapine (Clozaril), which can produce therapeutic gains in schizophrenics who do not respond well to traditional antipsychotics (Buchanan et al., 1998; Kane et al., 1988) and has produced greater therapeutic gains than traditional antipsychotics (Rosenheck et al., 1999; Wahlbeck et al., 1999). A survey of patients' attitudes conducted at Hamilton Psychiatric Hospital concluded that most patients had a favourable view of clozapine, reporting improvements in levels of satisfaction, quality of life, thinking, mood, and alertness (Waserman & Criollo, 2000).

A recent international study that included data obtained in Montreal found that clozapine, relative to olanzapine, resulted in fewer suicide attempts among patients with schizophrenia (Meltzer et al., 2003). Clozapine also produces fewer motor side effects than do traditional antipsychotics. Furthermore, maintaining discharged patients on clozapine reduces relapse rates (Conley et al., 1999). Although the precise biochemical mechanism of the therapeutic effects of clozapine is not yet known, we do know that it has a major impact on serotonin receptors.

Clozapine does have serious side effects, however. It can impair the functioning of the immune system in a small percentage of patients (about 1 percent) by lowering numbers of white blood cells, making patients vulnerable to infection and even death; for this reason, patients taking clozapine have to be carefully monitored. It also can produce seizures and other side effects, such as dizziness, fatigue, drooling, and weight gain (Meltzer, Cola, & Way, 1993; Waserman & Criollo, 2000).

The success of clozapine stimulated drug companies to begin a more earnest search for other drugs that might be more effective than traditional antipsychotics. Two results of this search are olanzapine (Zyprexa) and risperidone (Risperdal). Both have the advantage of producing fewer motor side effects than traditional antipsychotics, and they appear to be as effective as traditional antipsychotics in reducing symptoms (Bondolf et al., 1998; Conley et al., 1998; Wirshing et al., 1999), perhaps even better (Sanger et al., 1999). Iskedjian, Hux, and Remington (1998) stated that Canadian investigators have played a leading role in the development and ongoing research on risperidone. For instance, the Canadian Risperidone Study compared the effects of risperidone and haloperidol in an eight-week, double-blind, randomized study (Chouinard et al., 1993). This study found that 6 mg of risperidone was the most effective dosage level and that risperidone was significantly more effective than haloperidol at reducing negative and positive symptoms. Another recent study conducted in Canada showed that risperidone is quite effective and may lead to reduced use of health services because it was associated with a lower length of first hospitalization and less use of inpatient beds (Malla, Norman, Scholten, Zirul, & Kotteda, 2001). See Table 11.4 for a summary of other major drugs used in treating schizophrenia, in addition to resperidone.

Table 11.4

Summary of Major Drugs Used in Treating Schizophrenia

Drug Category	Generic Name	Trade Name
Phenothiazine	Chlorpromazine	Thorazine
	Fluphenazine decanoate	Prolixin
Butyrophenone	Haloperidol	Haldol
Thioxanthene	Thiothixene	Navane
Tricyclic dibenzodiazepine	Clozapine	Clozaril
Thienbenzodiazepine	Olanzapine	Zyprexa
Benzisoxazole	Risperidone	Risperdal

A psychological approach to the study of risperidone would involve examining fundamental aspects of cognition, such as attention and memory, that are known to be deficient in many patients with schizophrenia (e.g., Green, 1993) and are associated with poor social adaptation (Green, 1996). Evidence is emerging that risperidone improves verbal working memory (e.g., remembering a phone number long enough to be able to dial it) more than other antipsychotic drugs, apparently by reducing the activity of serotonin-sensitive receptors in the frontal cortex (Green et al., 1997). Research has also shown that improvements in verbal working memory are correlated with improvements in learning social skills in psychosocial rehabilitation programs (Green, 1996). Risperidone may thus make possible more thoroughgoing changes in schizophrenia and its behavioural consequences than do drugs that do not have these cognitive effects.

Antipsychotics block dopamine D_2 receptors. In a recent double-blind PET (positron emission tomography) study with patients with first-episode schizophrenia, Shitij Kapur and his colleagues from the Centre for Addiction and Mental Health (Kapur et al., 2000) confirmed that D_2 occupancy is an important mediator of clinical response and side effects in antipsychotic treatment. Their findings are consistent with a "target and trigger" hypothesis of the action of antipsychotics. The idea is that "the D_2 specificity of antipsychotics permits them to target discrete neurons and that their antagonistic properties trigger within those neurons intracellular changes that ultimately beget antipsychotic response" (Kapur et al., 2000). Although this study was limited to haloperidol, the authors concluded that the results help explain observed differences between typical and atypical antipsychotics.

Antipsychotic drugs are an indispensable part of treatment for schizophrenia and will undoubtedly continue to be an important component. They are surely preferable to the straitjackets formerly used to restrain patients. Furthermore, the recent success of clozapine, olanzapine, and risperidone has stimulated a continued effort to find new and more effective drug therapies for schizophrenia. Many other drugs are currently being evaluated, and we may be on the verge of a new era in the treatment this illness. Nevertheless our growing knowledge of biological diatheses for schizophrenia and the continuing improvement in antipsychotic medications should not lead to a neglect of the psychosocial factors in both the causes of and the efforts to control schizophrenia. The case has recently been put clearly by two psychiatrists in their review of empirically supported psychological treatments for schizophrenia. We would do well to keep their sentiments in mind as we turn to such interventions:

> For veteran practitioners who have long considered only biological treatments as effective in protecting schizophrenic individuals from stress-induced relapse and disability ... evidence [on reducing expressed emotion in families, reviewed later] that supports the protective value of psychosocial treatments ... may serve as an antidote to the insidious biological reductionism that often characterizes the field of schizophrenia research and treatment.... It is essential to view treatments of schizophrenia in their biopsychosocial matrix—leaving out any of the three components ... will diminish the impact and efficacy of treatment. (Kopelowicz & Liberman, 1998, p. 192)

Similarly, in his review of dopamine dysregulation and related biological factors, Kapur (2003) from the University of Toronto concluded eloquently that "[d]opamine dysregulation may provide the driving force, but the subject's cognitive, psychodynamic, and cultural context gives form to the experience. Psychosis is seen as a dynamic interaction between a bottom-up neurochemical drive and a top-down psychological process, not an inescapably determined outcome of a biology" (p. 17). This view is very much in keeping with the tenets of the biopsychosocial model.

Psychological Treatments

It is increasingly understood by mental health professionals, as well as by patients and families, that the cognitive impairments inherent in schizophrenia are likely to limit the degree to which patients with this illness (or group of illnesses) can profit from psychological interventions (Bowen et al., 1994). Add to this the accumulating evidence that whatever the biological diathesis for schizophrenia, this vulnerability is likely to persist throughout the person's life (Neuchterlein et al., 1994), and you have a situation that might discourage clinicians from even trying to implement psychosocial treatments. But as we have just seen, as promising as many of the newer antipsychotic drugs are, a neglect of the psychological and social aspect of schizophrenia compromises efforts to deal with people and their families who are struggling with that illness. We turn now to a consideration of various psychological treatments of schizophrenia as we come to appreciate both their limitations and their strengths.

Psychodynamic Therapies Freud did little, either in his clinical practice or through his writings, to adapt psychoanalysis to the treatment of patients with schizophrenia. He believed that these patients were incapable of establishing the close interpersonal relationship with the physician essential for analysis. It was Harry Stack Sullivan, an American psychiatrist, who pioneered the use of psychotherapy with schizophrenic hospital patients. Sullivan established a ward at the Sheppard and Enoch Pratt Hospital in Towson, Maryland, in 1923 and developed a psychoanalytic treatment that was reported to be markedly successful.

Sullivan held that schizophrenia reflects a return to early childhood forms of communication. The fragile ego of the individual with schizophrenia, unable to handle the extreme stress of interpersonal challenges, regresses. Therapy therefore requires the patient to learn adult forms of communication and to achieve insight into the role the past has played in current problems. Sullivan advised the very gradual, nonthreatening development of a trusting relationship. For example, he recommended that the therapist sit somewhat to the side of the patient in order not to force eye contact, which he considered too frightening in the early stages of treatment. After many sessions and with the establishment of greater trust and support, the analyst begins to encourage the patient to examine his or her interpersonal relationships.

A similar ego-analytic approach was proposed by Frieda Fromm-Reichmann (1889-1957), a German psychiatrist who emigrated to the United States and worked for a period of time with Sullivan at Chestnut Lodge, a private mental hospital in Rockville, Maryland. Fromm-Reichmann was sensitive to the symbolic and unconscious meaning of behaviour, attributing the aloofness of patients with schizophrenia to a wish to avoid the rebuffs suffered in childhood and thereafter judged inevitable. She treated them with great patience and optimism, making it clear that they need not take her into their world or give up their sickness until they were completely ready to do so. Along with Sullivan, Fromm-Reichmann (1952) helped establish a variant of psychoanalysis as a major treatment for schizophrenia.

The overall evaluation of analytically oriented psychotherapy with such patients justifies little enthusiasm, however (Katz & Gunderson, 1990). In fact, the problems that patients with schizophrenia have just thinking clearly about things may well make such therapy harmful, at least during the more acute, florid phases of a psychotic episode (Mueser & Berenbaum, 1990). Results from a long-term follow-up of patients bearing a diagnosis of schizophrenia and discharged between 1963 and 1976 after treatment at the New York State Psychiatric Institute confirm the lack of success (Stone, 1986). Such treatment may in itself be too intrusive and too intense for some patients with schizophrenia to handle. Earlier, great claims of success were made for the analyses done by Sullivan and Fromm-Reichmann, but a close consideration of the patients they saw indicates that many were only mildly disturbed and might not even have been diagnosed as schizophrenic by the strict DSM-IV-TR criteria for the disorder.

More recent psychosocial interventions take a more active, present-focused, and reality-oriented turn as therapists try to help patients and their families deal more directly with the everyday problems they face in coping with this disruptive and debilitating illness. Inherent to this work is the assumption that a good deal of the stress experienced by people with schizophrenia is due to their difficulties in negotiating everyday social challenges, including the pressures that arise in their families when they return home after hospitalization. We turn now to these newer and more effective approaches.

Social Skills Training Social skills training is designed to teach people with schizophrenia behaviours that can help them succeed in a wide variety of interpersonal situations—discussing their medications with their psychiatrist, ordering meals in a restaurant, filling out job applications, saying no to offers to buy drugs on the street, reading bus schedules—all things that most of us take for granted and give little thought to in our daily lives. For people with schizophrenia, these life skills are not to be taken for granted; such individuals need to work hard to acquire or reacquire them.

In an early demonstration of social skills training, Bellack, Hersen, and Turner (1976) contrived social situations for three chronic schizophrenic patients and then observed whether they behaved appropriately. For instance, a patient was told to pretend that he had just returned home from a weekend trip to find that his lawn had been mowed. As he gets out of the car, his next-door neighbour approaches him and says that he has cut the patient's grass because he was already cutting his own. The patient must then respond to the situation. As expected, patients were initially not very good at making a socially appropriate response, which in this instance might have been some sort of thank-you. Training followed. The therapist encouraged the patients to respond, commenting helpfully on their efforts. If necessary, the therapist also modelled appropriate behaviour so that the patients could observe and then try to imitate it.

This combination of role-playing, modelling, and positive reinforcement effected significant improvement in all three patients. There was even generalization to social situations that had not been worked on during the training. This study and others conducted with larger groups of patients (e.g., Lieberman et al., 1998; Marder et al., 1996) indicate that severely disturbed patients can be taught new social behaviour that may help them function better for over two years following treatment. Unfortunately, generalization to life outside the hospital is far from a reliable finding (Hayes, Halford, & Varghese, 1995). Despite the equivocal results, social skills training nowadays is usually a component of treatments for schizophrenia that go beyond the use of medications alone, including family therapies for lowering expressed emotion. We turn to that work now.

Family Therapy and Reducing Expressed Emotion

Many patients with schizophrenia who are discharged from mental hospitals go home to their families. Earlier we discussed research showing that high levels of expressed emotion (including being hostile, hypercritical, and overprotective within the family) have been linked to relapse and rehospitalization. Accordingly, a number of family interventions have been developed. While they differ in length, setting, and specific techniques, these family therapies have several features in common beyond the overall purpose of calming things down for the patient by calming things down for the family.

- *They educate patients and families about schizophrenia, specifically about the biological vulnerability that predisposes some people to the illness, cognitive problems inherent to schizophrenia, the symptoms of the illness, and signs of impending relapse.* High-EE families are typically not well informed about schizophrenia, and acquisition of some basic knowledge is intended to help reduce the tendency of family members to be overly critical of the relative with schizophrenia. Knowing, for example, that biology has a lot to do with having schizophrenia and that the illness impairs the patient's ability to think clearly and rationally might help the family be more accepting and understanding of the patient's inappropriate or ineffectual actions. Therapists encourage family members to lower their expectations of their schizophrenic kin and thereby become less critical. Therapists make clear to family and patient alike that schizophrenia is primarily a biochemical illness and that proper medication and the kind of therapy they are receiving can reduce stress on the patient and prevent deterioration.

- *They provide information about and advice on the monitoring of the effects of antipsychotic medication.* Therapists impress on both the family and the patient the importance of the patient's taking his or her antipsychotic medication, becoming better informed about the side effects of the medication, and taking initiative and responsibility for seeking medical consultation rather than just discontinuing the drugs.
- *They encourage family members to blame neither themselves nor the patient for the illness and for the difficulties all are having in coping with it.*
- *They help improve communication and problem-solving skills within the family.* Therapists focus on teaching the family ways to express both positive and negative feelings in a constructive, empathic, nondemanding manner rather than in a finger-pointing, critical, or overprotective way. They focus as well on defusing tense personal conflicts by teaching family members ways to work together to solve everyday problems.
- *They encourage patients as well as their families to expand their social contacts, especially their support networks.*
- *They instill a degree of hope that things can improve, including the hope that the patient may not have to return to the hospital.*

Programs employ various techniques to implement these several strategies. Examples include identifying stressors that could cause relapse, training in communication and problem solving, and having high-EE family members watch videotapes of interactions of low-EE families (Penn & Mueser, 1996). Compared with standard treatments (usually just medication only), family therapy plus medication has typically lowered relapse over periods of one to two years. This positive finding is particularly evident in studies in which the treatment lasted for at least nine months (Hogarty et al., 1986, 1991; Kopelowicz & Liberman, 1998; Penn & Mueser, 1996).

Cognitive-Behavioural Therapy We turn next to several new cognitive-behavioural approaches in the treatment of schizophrenia. Whereas it used to be assumed that it was futile to try to alter the cognitive distortions, including delusions, of patients with schizophrenia, a developing clinical and experimental literature is demonstrating that the maladaptive beliefs of some patients can in fact be changed with cognitive-behavioural interventions. In fact, in recent reviews, Aaron Beck from the Beck Institute of Cognitive Therapy and Neil Rector from the Centre for Addiction and Mental Health, Clarke Division, concluded that schizophrenics with psychosis can benefit from cognitive techniques designed to address their delusions and hallucinations (Beck & Rector, 2000; Rector & Beck, 2001, 2002). Furthermore, they suggested that cognitive-behavioural therapy (CBT) can facilitate motivation and engagement in social and vocational activities. This is in keeping with observations that patients who have been psychotic for some time incorporate their psychotic beliefs into their broader cognitive schemas (see Kapur, 2003). Initial comparative research conducted by Rector and associates indicates that CBT plus enriched treatment as usual is as effective as treatment as usual alone and that CBT seems to be particularly effective at reducing negative symptoms of schizophrenia (Rector, Seeman, & Segal, 2003).

Ross Norman and Laurel Townsend (1999) from the University of Western Ontario and the London Health Sciences Centre have attributed the growing interest in cognitive-behavioural approaches to the following factors: (1) the success of cognitive-behavioural techniques in treating other disorders such as anxiety and depression; (2) evidence that schizophrenics sometimes develop their own cognitive coping strategies as a way of combating their symptoms; (3) research suggesting that social-environmental factors may contribute to the course of schizophrenia; (4) the need to find treatments for the significant proportion of schizophrenics who do not respond to drug treatment; and (5) an increased acceptance that a psychiatric, pharmacologically based approach and a psychological approach may be complementary rather than incompatable. Norman and Townsend, too, conclude that cognitive-behavioural therapy may be clinically useful, but at the same time, they acknowledge that research in this area is still in the preliminary stages and that controlled studies with more sophisticated methods are needed to more accurately evaluate the benefits of cognitive-behavioural treatments for schizophrenia.

Norman and Townsend (1999) provided a succinct summary of several cognitive-behavioural treatment interventions designed for schizophrenia. Two key goals are to help the patient reframe the psychosis (i.e., help him or her develop a cognitive understanding of the psychosis) and self-identify triggers for the psychosis (i.e., learn which external conditions and internal mood states elicit the psychosis). Other interventions involve teaching patients how to reduce physiological arousal, enhancing their coping skills in general, and modifying aberrant beliefs directly.

Personal Therapy As encouraging as the family EE-lowering studies were, most patients were still returning to the hospital and the clinical outcomes of those who managed to remain in the community left a lot to be desired (Hogarty et al., 1997a). What more could be done for discharged patients with schizophrenia to increase their chances of being able to remain longer outside the hospital, whether or not they could do so within their family of origin? This question led to the formulation of a new approach by one of the groups that had published positive, though limited, findings on lowering EE (Hogarty et al., 1995, 1997a, 1997b).

What Hogarty et al. call *personal therapy* is a broad-spectrum cognitive-behavioural approach to the multiplicity of problems of patients with schizophrenia who have been discharged from the hospital. This individualistic therapy is conducted both one-on-one and in small groups (workshops). A key element in this approach, based on the finding in EE research that a reduction in emotional reactions by family members leads to less relapse following hospital discharge, is teaching the patient how to recognize inappropriate affect. If ignored, inappropriate affect can build up and lead to cognitive distortions and inappropriate social behaviour. Patients are also taught to notice small signs of relapse, such as social withdrawal or inappropriate threats against others, and they learn skills to reduce these problems. Such behaviours, if left unchecked, will likely interfere with the patients' efforts to live by conventional social rules, including being able to keep a job and make and maintain social contacts. The therapy also includes some rational-emotive behaviour therapy to help patients avoid turning life's inevitable frustrations and challenges into catastrophes and thus to help them lower their stress levels.

In addition, many patients are taught muscle-relaxation techniques as an aid to detecting the gradual buildup of anxiety or anger; they also learn how to apply the relaxation skills in order to control these emotions better. The operating assumption is that emotional dysregulation is part of the biological diathesis in schizophrenia and a factor that patients must learn to live and cope with rather than eliminate (or cure) altogether. But there is also a strong focus on teaching specific social skills as well as on encouraging patients to continue to take their antipsychotic medication in a maintenance mode, that is, in a dose that is typically lower than what is necessary in the earliest, acute, and most florid phase of the illness.

Hogarty's individual therapy includes non-behavioural elements, especially warm and empathic acceptance of the patient's emotional and cognitive turmoil along with realistic but optimistic expectations that life can be better. In general, patients are taught that they are emotionally vulnerable to stress, that their thinking is not always as clear as it should be, that they have to continue with their medication, and that they can learn a variety of skills to make the most of the hand that nature has dealt them. This is not a short-term treatment; it can extend over three years of weekly to biweekly therapy contacts.

Note that the focus of much of personal therapy is on the patient, not on the family. Whereas the focus in the family studies was on reducing the high EE of the patient's family—an environmental change from the point of view of the patient—the goal of personal therapy is to teach the patient internal coping skills, new ways of thinking about and controlling his or her own affective reactions to whatever challenges are presented by his or her environment. Specific instruction in social skills is also an integral part of this treatment.

Finally, this therapy is important because of what Hogarty et al. call "criticism management and conflict resolution." This phrase refers to learning how to deal with negative feedback from others and how to resolve the interpersonal conflicts that are an inevitable part of dealing with others. Indications are that this form of intervention can help many people with schizophrenia stay out of the hospital and function better, with the most favourable outcomes achieved by those who can live with their family of origin (Hogarty et al., 1997a, 1997b).

Reattribution Therapy We have just reviewed some recent work of Hogarty et al. (1995, 1997a, 1997b) that includes attempts to apply rational-emotive behaviour therapy to help patients with schizophrenia catastrophize less when things don't go their way. There is also evidence that some patients can be encouraged to test out their delusional beliefs in much the same way as normal people do. Through collaborative discussions (and in the context of other modes of interventions, including antipsychotic drugs), some patients have been helped to attach a nonpsychotic meaning to paranoid symptoms and thereby reduce their intensity and aversive nature, similar to what is done in Beck's cognitive therapy of depression and Barlow's approach to panic disorder (Haddock et al., 1998). This rather intellectual approach is probably suitable for only a minority of patients with schizophrenia.

Attending to Basic Cognitive Functions According to a recent review (see Walker et al., 2004), it is well established that people diagnosed with schizophrenia, as a group, have deficits in virtually all facets of cognitive functioning and show performance deficits on a range of simple and complex tasks. Moreover, these deficits are apparent in first-episode, non-medicated patients, so deficits are not a byproduct of receiving treatment. Consequently, researchers have been attending to fundamental aspects of cognition that are disordered in schizophrenia in an attempt to improve these functions and thereby produce a favourable effect on behaviour. This more molecular approach concentrates on trying to normalize such fundamental cognitive functions as attention and memory, which are known to be deficient in many patients with schizophrenia (e.g., Green, 1993) and are associated with poor social adaptation (Green, 1996).

Efforts are underway at the Clinical Research Center for Schizophrenia and Psychiatric Rehabilitation at UCLA, under the leadership of research psychiatrist Robert Paul Liberman, to use psychological means to enhance basic cognitive functions such as verbal learning ability. Another goal is to construct intervention strategies that make maximum use of those cognitive functions that remain relatively intact in schizophrenia, such as the ability to understand and remember what is presented in a picture. For example, photographs relevant to learning a necessary social skill are being employed in addition to the usual verbal means of teaching such skills (Kopelowicz & Liberman, 1998).

The assumption—yet to be borne out—is that improvement in these cognitive functions will lead to increased clinical improvement (Liberman & Green, 1992). Recall from our discussion of drug therapy that positive clinical outcomes from risperidone are associated with improvements in certain kinds of memory (Green et al., 1997), lending support to the more general notion that paying attention to fundamental cognitive processes—the kind that nonclinical cognitive psychologists study—holds promise for improving the social and emotional lives of people with schizophrenia.

Recent Canadian research conducted by Young and Zakzanis and their colleagues has demonstrated the utility of *scaffolding* in the remediation of cognitive deficits. Scaffolded instruction is a concept derived from Vygotsky's (1986) cognitive development research. Vygotsky proposed that everyone has a zone of current development and that the complexity of tasks must be tailored to account for individuals' current skill level and level of potential development. The scaffolding model of instruction requires instructors to select tasks that reflect the patients' current capabilities so that eventually they are able to solve problems for themselves. The ultimate goal is to develop general problem-solving skills and processes that patients can generalize to new situations. Young et al. (2002) found that the delivery of scaffolded instruction to patients with schizophrenia, relative to direct instruction, significantly increased the number of categories created during the Wisconsin Card Sorting Task and that cognitive improvements were still evident one month later. The scaffolded group also had relatively higher levels of positive affect and self-esteem. Thus, scaffolding may lead to improvements in self-regulation and self-conceptualizations.

Case Management

After deinstitutionalization began in the 1960s in Canada and the United States, many patients with schizophrenia no longer resided in mental hospitals and often had to fend for themselves in securing needed services. Without a centralized hospital as the site where most services were delivered, the mental health system became more complex. In 1997, fearing that many patients were not accessing services, the NIMH established a program that gave grants to states to be directed toward helping patients cope with the mental health system. Out of this program, a new mental health specialty, the case manager, was created. Canada has adopted the strategy (Health Canada, 1991), but the practice varies widely across provinces and territories and in different places in the same province or territory.

Initially, case managers were basically brokers of services. Being familiar with the system, they were able to get patients into contact with providers of whatever services the patients required. As the years passed, different models of case management developed. The major innovation was the recognition that case managers often needed to provide direct clinical services and that services might best be delivered by a team rather than brokered out. The Assertive Community Treatment model (Stein & Test, 1980) and the Intensive Case Management model (Surles et al., 1992) both entail a multidisciplinary team that provides community services ranging from medication, treatment for substance abuse, help in dealing with the kind of stressors patients face regularly (such as managing money), psychotherapy, vocational training, and assistance in obtaining housing and employment.

The Greater Vancouver Mental Health Service Agency is considered to be one of the best of its kind in North America (Nichols, 1995). The agency serves about 5,000 people with serious mental disorders each year, many of them suffering from schizophrenia. It provides housing, special programs for older patients, and community response teams that can act very quickly in crisis situations involving their clients. The latter approach is proving to be effective in Ontario. Community-based teams of doctors, nurses, and social workers called PACT (Program for Assertive Community Treatment) have been set up to ease the pressure caused by the closing of provincial psychiatric hospitals and to reduce the number of people with schizophrenia and other serious psychiatric disorders who end up in hospital emergency wards (Sumi, 1998). The mental health teams are available 24 hours a day and even make "house calls" to mentally ill people in their homes and workplaces.

Indications are that this more intensive treatment is more effective than less intensive methods in reducing time spent in the hospital, improving housing stability, and ameliorating symptoms (Mueser, 1998). However, more intensive case management has not shown positive effects on other domains, such as time spent in jail or social functioning. The actual procedures that come under the rubric of case management vary a great deal from study to study. The services provided by a case management team will have positive effects only to the extent that those services are appropriate and effective.

General Trends in Treatment

Only a generation ago, many, if not most, mental health professionals and laypeople believed that the primary culprit in the etiology of schizophrenia was the child's psychological environment—most especially, the family. As we have seen throughout this chapter, the thinking now is that biological factors predispose a person to develop schizophrenia and that stressors, principally of a psychological nature, trigger the illness in a predisposed individual and interfere with that person's adaptation to community living. The most promising contemporary approaches to treatment make good use of this increased understanding and emphasize the importance of both pharmacological and psychosocial interventions.

- Families and patients are given realistic and scientifically sound information about schizophrenia. They learn that it is a disability that can be controlled but is probably lifelong. They also learn that, as with many other chronic disabilities, medication is necessary to help maintain control and allow them to perform daily activities. What is *not* necessary, and is even counterproductive, is the guilt of family members, especially parents, who may have been led to believe that something in the patient's upbringing initiated the problem. Considerable effort is devoted in many treatment programs to dispelling this sense of culpability while encouraging a focus on the biological diathesis and the associated need for medication.

- Medication is only part of the whole treatment picture. Family-oriented treatment aims to lessen the stress experienced by the patient after discharge from the hospital by reducing hostility, overinvolvement, intrusiveness, and criticality in the family (EE). Evidence is also emerging on the importance of cognitive-behavioural interventions that teach patients with schizophrenia how to notice and control their own stress reactions before they snowball and lead to emotional dysregulation and disruptive behaviours.
- It is increasingly recognized that early intervention is important in influencing the course of schizophrenia over time; that is, losing no time getting patients onto the right medications and providing support and information to the family and appropriate psychotherapy to the patient can reduce the severity of relapses in the future (Drury et al., 1996). Ongoing research in Canada and elsewhere on a variable identified as *duration of untreated psychosis* (DUP) has found that DUP predicts remission and positive symptom outcome after one year of treatment (see Malla, Norman, et al., 2002), underscoring the importance of early intervention. It is also important to teach patients social skills and more reality-based thinking so that they can control their emotions and function more normally outside the hospital and probably reduce the EE encountered both inside and outside the home. Families affected by schizophrenia are encouraged to join support groups and formal organizations, such as the Alliance for the Mentally Ill or the Schizophrenia Society of Canada or its provincial or local counterparts, to combat and reduce the isolation and stigma associated with having a family member who has schizophrenia (Greenberg et al., 1988; Health Canada, 1991). Examples of Canadian early intervention programs for schizophrenia are summarized in Canadian Clinic Focus 11.1.
- Though the kind of integrated treatment we have been describing is promising, the sad fact is that it is not widely available or accessible to most patients and their families. The reasons for this are unclear (Baucom et al., 1998; Dixon et al., 1997) (see the "Comment" concluding Canadian Clinic Focus 11.1 for a discussion of a recent U.S. study on this issue). One factor, however, is likely the increasing popularity and use of psychoactive medications, a trend that, although helpful to many, too narrowly defines schizophrenia as a medical disease that is relatively uninfluenced by social context. Commenting on the

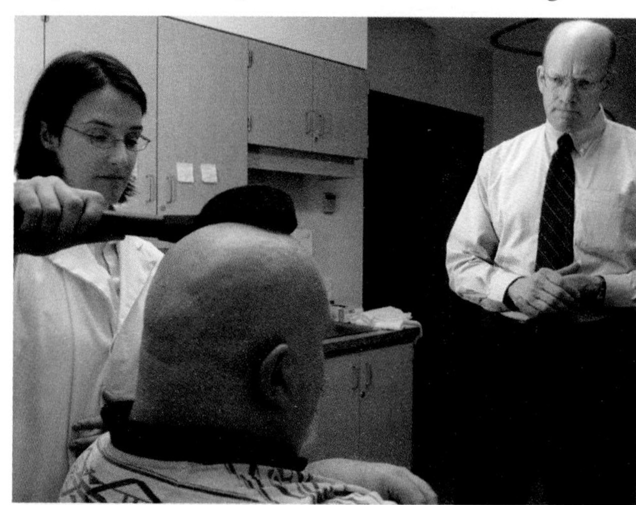

Dr. Doug Urness (right), Clinical Director of Telemental Health Service at the Alberta Hospital, Ponoka, speaks with a refractory depression patient, as Nurse Kellie Erickson treats the condition with transcranial magnetic stimulation (TMS). Modern scientists are returning to the use of magnets to treat mental illness from depression to schizophrenia.

Canadian Clinic Focus/11.1

Early Detection and Prevention of Schizophrenia: The PRIME Clinic

"It's quite horrendous. First of all, you've got somebody that you love, a child that you've raised. And then suddenly, the child becomes a crazy person."

—June Beeby, former executive director of the Ontario Friends of Schizophrenics (now the Schizophrenia Society of Ontario) speaking about her 19-year-old son, Mathew, whose schizophrenia drove him to commit suicide (Nichols, 1995)

"Medication may diminish the symptoms, but not completely. Part of what we do is to teach people how to deal with voices, or paranoia, so that they can say to themselves, The reason I hear a voice coming out of that radiator is because I have schizophrenia."

-Calgary General Hospital psychiatrist Dr. Ruth Dickson (Nichols, 1995)

In recent years, early psychosis intervention projects have been developed in major centres across Canada. These programs include the Early Psychosis Program at the Nova Scotia Hospital in Halifax, the First Episode Psychosis Clinic at the Clarke Division of the Centre for Addiction and Mental Health (CAMH) in Toronto, the Therapeutic Partnership Program of the Psychotic Disorders Clinic at Chedoke-McMaster Hospitals in Hamilton, the Early Psychosis Program at Victoria Hospital in London, and the Early Psychosis Treatment and Prevention Program at Calgary's Foothills Hospital.

Most programs are outpatient services for young people and most treatment is done in the participant's home. The hope is that early intervention will help people function at the highest level possible, despite their disorder. A research component is an important feature of many of the early detection programs.

The PRIME Clinic: Prevention through Risk Identification Management and Education

The CAMH First Episode Psychosis Clinic was established in 1992 to help individuals with schizophrenia and their families deal with the complexities of managing an initial episode of schizophrenia. In 1999 Dr. Irvin Epstein became the director of the new PRIME Clinic at CAMH, unique in Canada, established to facilitate early identification and treatment of people aged 12 to 45 who are possibly in the earliest stages of a first episode of psychosis (prodromal phase) and are at risk of "transitioning" to the active phase of psychosis. The phase preceding acute psychosis is often confusing and traumatic for people. In addition to presenting with mild pre-psychotic symptoms, people at risk may also be experiencing a decline in their usual day-to-day functioning or way of relating to others. They may also have a family history of psychotic disorders such as schizophrenia. The PRIME Clinic is fully affiliated with the Department of Psychiatry at the University of Toronto.

CLINICAL SERVICES

Goal The goal is to intervene during the prodromal phase to prevent (1) the onset of active phase symptoms and (2) the decline in cognitive, social, and occupational functioning typically associated with schizophrenia. Thus, the expectation is that through careful monitoring of identified high-risk individuals, it will be possible to prevent, delay, or attenuate the active phase symptoms and to improve the long-term course and outcome of the disorder. Thus, treatment should begin as soon as possible to ensure the best possible chance of recovery.

Identification A strong educational component is offered for hospital staff, psychiatrists, and general practitioners in order to raise awareness about schizophrenia both in the general medical community and in the general public. Early signs of risk can include confusion, exaggerated self-opinion, suspiciousness, altered perceptions, odd thinking and speaking processes, lack of close friends, difficulty with social activities, flat emotions, and difficulty performing functions at school or at work.

Referral Process Referrals are typically made by family physicians, child or general psychiatrists, and pediatricians. All referred individuals are given an initial consultation. If participation in clinic programs is not deemed appropriate, people are provided with further referrals.

Intervention The program attempts to intervene on three levels to better treat and support both the individual and his or her family or other caregivers. The three levels entail coping and stress management strategies, medication, and education.

Follow-up Follow-up is offered to individuals assessed in the prodromal phase.

RESEARCH

The PRIME Clinic and a clinic affiliated with the University of Calgary are both participating in a multi-centre North American clinical trial that is examining the benefits of using low-dose atypical neuroleptics (see McGlashan et al., 2003). This research has unique methodological aspects; for example, it is the first double-blind and placebo-controlled clinical trial of olanzapine in patients at risk of being prodromally symptomatic for psychosis, and it is testing for prevention versus delay in psychosis onset. Some participants are also given the opportunity to participate in ongoing research studies conducted through both clinics. The long-term effectiveness of the PRIME Clinic is currently being evaluated.

COMMENT

In this chapter, we have been describing the best available therapeutic approaches to schizophrenia. They are both biological and psychosocial in nature, and many published reports attest to the positive impact they make on many patients with schizophrenia. However, there is often a gap between what is available in an ideal world and what the experiences of people actually are, especially when they do not live near large metropolitan centres where most of the research is conducted and where most of the state-of-the-art psychosocial treatments are obtainable.

Although comprehensive Canadian data are not available, this issue was highlighted in an article by A.F. Lehman et al. (1998) in the *Schizophrenia Bulletin*, a quarterly periodical published by the Division of Clinical and Treatment Research of the National Institute of Mental Health. (NIMH is the principal source of U.S. federal funds for supporting research into mental disorders, their prevention, and their treatment.) Lehmann et al. collected data by interviewing over 700 patients and reviewing their medical records. As expected, almost 90 percent had been prescribed antipsychotic drugs, but of these patients only 62 percent received a dose in the recommended range; about 15 percent got too little, and the remainder too much. Further, although over 90 percent of patients were prescribed maintenance doses of drugs, only 29 percent of these received a dose in the recommended range; of the 71 percent who did not receive a recommended dose, about half were getting too much and half too little. African Americans were much more likely to be prescribed maintenance doses that were too high. We do not know whether or not minority groups in Canada receive excessively high maintenance doses of neuroleptics, but it is a real possibility that should be investigated.

Psychosocial treatments were also examined in the Lehman et al. (1998) study, but these were more difficult to evaluate because records or patient reports did not indicate whether the treatment was one of those considered effective (such as family-EE intervention or social skills training). Just in terms of whether any psychosocial treatments at all were prescribed for these patients, the data show that some sort of individual or group therapy was provided for over 90 percent of inpatients. For patients who had regular contact with their families, family treatment of some sort was prescribed for only about 40 percent. For unemployed patients, vocational rehabilitation (teaching job skills) was prescribed for only about 30 percent.

Conclusion? Many patients with schizophrenia are not getting anything near optimal therapy. Critics in Canada are also concerned that provincial governments burdened by deficits may cut funding to various services in the community that are even more essential at a time when psychiatric beds in provincial psychiatric hospitals and general hospitals are being closed. These services include subsidized housing, crisis response centres, and rehabilitation programs (Nichols, 1995). It must also be noted that such community services vary greatly in both availability and quality in different parts of Canada. In most places, including many of our major cities, the services are also very fragmented, with numerous government-funded and private organizations offering a range of community services for people suffering from schizophrenia.

Sources for Early Psychosis Programs: Dr. Irvin Epstein, director of the PRIME Clinic at CAMH; Nichols (1995).

reliance on the use of drugs in the treatment of schizophrenia, Dr. Abram Hoffer (2000, p. 146), president of the Canadian Schizophrenia Foundation, stated that "tranquilizers convert a natural psychosis (schizophrenia) into an iatrogenic psychosis (tranquilizer psychosis) ... characterized by a decrease in symptoms and by an increase in apathy. .... The only treatment for tranquilizer psychosis is to discontinue the drug."

Ongoing Issues in the Care of Patients with Schizophrenia

As patients with schizophrenia grow older, they are less likely to be living with their families. The transition to living arrangements outside the parents' home is fraught with risk. Aftercare is one of society's thorniest social problems; we describe it in more detail in Focus on Discovery 11.4. Do people with schizophrenia end up on the streets by falling through cracks in the mental health system? Though a relatively small proportion of homeless people in the United States are mentally ill, many people with schizophrenia are among those without residences. In Canada, the situation is much different—the mentally ill comprise a large proportion of the homeless. For example, a United Way (1997) report on homelessness in Metropolitan Toronto concluded that about 86 percent of the homeless have experienced a mental health or addiction problem at some point in their lives. Many of these individuals have been diagnosed with schizophrenia. The 1999 Mayor's Homelessness Action Task Force concluded that "between 30 per cent and 35 per cent of homeless people are living with mental illness"; among its 105 recommendations was one that called for 5,000 supportive housing units for those who were currently suffering from mental disorders and addictions. However, the problem of the homeless mentally ill is not found only in Canada's largest cities, such as Toronto, Vancouver, and Montreal. A recent study of homeless shelter users in Calgary (Stuart & Arboleda-Florez, 2000) employed a semi-structured interview and determined that three-quarters of the sample of 250 homeless people presented some psychiatric symptoms, and a third had a significant mental health problem. The lifetime prevalence of alcohol abuse was 33.6 percent. The downward spiral in functioning among homeless people with schizophrenia is difficult to reverse. Welfare and other social service benefits are available to those with schizophrenia, but many do not receive all they are entitled to because of inadequately staffed bureaucracies. And many patients with schizophrenia have lost contact with their post-hospital treatment programs. Despite the existence for mental health care services, however inadequate, the homeless mentally ill often do not know where to access them (Stuart & Arboleda-Florez, 2000). The Calgary Urban Project Society (CUPS) treats about 1,000 homeless street people each month, 30 to 40 percent of whom are mentally ill (Bakogeorge, 2000). Lorraine Melchior, director of the storefront health clinic and aid agency, describes the case of a schizophrenic homeless man who trusted CUPS and allowed the agency's physician to treat him and persuade him to accept hospital admission: "So here you had a physician ... in an alley, doing an assessment. We need to try to change the system ... [and] we need to go to where the people are" (Bakogeorge, 2000). This issue is discussed further in Chapter 18.

Obtaining employment poses a major challenge for people with schizophrenia because of bias against those who have been in mental hospitals. Although laws in most provinces and territories prohibit employers from asking applicants if they have a history of serious mental illness, former mental hospital patients still have a difficult time obtaining regular employment. Also a factor is how much leeway employers are willing to give former mental patients, whose thinking, emotions, and behaviour are usually unconventional to some degree.

There are some positive signs, however. Twenty or 30 years after first developing symptoms of schizophrenia, about half of patients with schizophrenia are able to look after themselves and participate meaningfully in society at large. Some continue to take medications, but many do not and yet still function well enough to stay out of the hospital (*Harvard Mental Health Letter*, 1995). Welfare, community, and other social service agencies in Canada try to provide rent subsidies or affordable housing to former mental patients to help them live in their own apartments or group homes, where they are occasionally checked on by mental health workers. Nonetheless, there is a chronic shortage of subsidized housing for psychiatric patients in most places in Canada. The jury at the inquest into the highly publicized case of Edmond Yu (Coyle, 1999), who was diagnosed with paranoid schizophrenia and was shot at age 35 by a police officer while brandishing a small hammer aboard a Toronto bus, recommended provision of safe houses for psychiatric patients and more affordable housing. The jury's list of 24 recommendations also included the provision of jobs with flexible or part-time hours that would offer the dignity of work. On January 22, 2004, the Edmond Yu Safe House Project was officially launched at the Gerstein Crisis Centre in Toronto. The house will provide transition for 16 people who will be able to stay for up to 18 months while working their way into permanent housing. The organizers hoped that the city and federal governments would share the $2-million start-up costs and that the Province of Ontario would provide the annual budget ($790,000).

Preventing substance abuse among patients with schizophrenia is largely an unmet challenge. The lifetime prevalence rate for substance abuse among people with schizophrenia is an astounding 50 percent (Kosten & Ziedonis, 1997); the rate is even higher among the homeless mentally ill population. Programs for treating substance abuse usually exclude people who are seriously mentally ill, and programs for treating people who are seriously mentally ill usually exclude substance abusers; in both instances, the reason is that the comorbid condition is considered disruptive to the treatment (Mueser, Bellack, & Blanchard, 1992). Additional problems arise because patients with schizophrenia who are substance abusers often do not continue to take their antipsychotic medication and, as a result, lose ground in their efforts to lead a more normal life. This situation is gradually changing in Canada as a consequence of attempts to integrate mental health facilities and programs. For example, in 1997, in Toronto, the provincial Health Services Restructuring Commission ordered the merging of four facilities associated with the treatment of mental disorders and substance abuse: the Clarke Institute of Psychiatry, the Queen Street Mental Health Centre, the Addiction Research Foundation, and the Donwood Institute. According to psychiatrist Paul Garfinkel, the chief executive officer of the larger umbrella institution, the Centre for Addiction and Mental Health is expected to be a stronger and more effective force to address issues related to funding, advocacy, service fragmentation, and patient capacity (Hall, 1998).

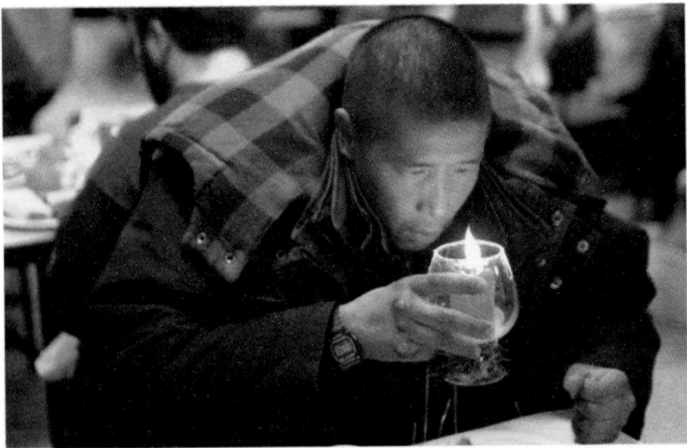

Edmond Wai-Kong Yu, a one-time University of Toronto medical student who deteriorated into schizophrenia and homelessness.

Further progress in the destigmatization of schizophrenia must occur. Stip, Caron, and Lane (2001) examined people's perceptions of schizophrenia in Quebec. The findings were both heartening and disheartening. Fifty-four percent of the 1,001 people interviewed indicated that people with schizophrenia should be considered violent and dangerous, and 31 percent felt that an employee with schizophrenia would be fired from his or her job. With respect to the issue of integration into the community of people with schizophrenia, 49 percent agreed with rehabilitation in the community but 40 percent disagreed. On a positive note that bodes well for the future, the youngest respondents were more likely to agree with rehabilitation in the community (57 percent) than older respondents (29 percent).

As part of a pilot project for the World Psychiatric Association's Global Campaign to Fight Stigma and Discrimination Because of Schizophrenia, Stuart and Arboleda-Florez (2001) surveyed attitudes toward people with schizophrenia in two adjacent rural and urban health regions in Alberta. Half the respondents knew someone who had been treated for schizophrenia or another mental illness. Social distance increased with the level of intimacy required, ranging from a low of 20 percent who claimed that they would be unable to remain friends with someone with schizophrenia to a high of 75 percent who would be unwilling to marry someone with schizophrenia. Consistent with Stip et al. (2000), respondents over 60 years of age were the least knowledgeable or enlightened about schizophrenia and the ones who practiced the most social distancing. Stuart and Arboleda-Florez (2001, p. 245) did, however, conclude that "[m]ost respondents were relatively well informed and progressive in their reported understanding of schizophrenia." Thus, the majority believed that people with schizophrenia could be treated with some success outside of a psychiatric facility, needed to take antipsychotic medications to control their symptoms, could function adequately in regular employment, and were not a public nuisance or threat to safety. The authors further concluded that it is people's knowledge of schizophrenia rather than exposure to the mentally ill that is the "central modifiable correlate of schizophrenia" (p. 245).

Finally, much of the stigma around schizophrenia has been attributed to negative media accounts of people with the illness. A recent media intervention attempt in Calgary sought to promote more positive attitudes among Calgary newspaper journalists by providing the media with accurate information and liaisons to mental health experts. Unfortunately, the intervention yielded mixed findings. In general, the number of positive stories about mental illness increased following the intervention, but the number of negative stories about patients with schizophrenia also increased (Stuart, 2003). Stuart suggested that local positive stories might be undermined by a phenomenon dubbed "The CNN effect"—that is, sensationalized television stories may overshadow local anti-stigma initiatives.

focus on discovery/11.4

Halfway Houses, Group Homes, and Aftercare

"I have something to offer society. It may not be as much as the next guy, but I feel my contribution is valuable and I want to offer it. There are times when I can't, when I'm sick and I have to stay in the hospital. But when I'm well, I have something I want to give, to share. I want to be part of the world."

—Sandy, from a National Film Board of Canada film about three people in Toronto who suffer from schizophrenia (*Full of Sound and Fury*)

Some people with mental problems function too well to remain in a mental hospital and yet do not function independently enough to live on their own or even with their own families. For such individuals, there are halfway houses or group homes; Fairweather's "community lodge" is a classic example (Fairweather et al., 1969). These are protected living units, typically located in large, formerly private residences. Here, patients discharged from a mental hospital live, take their meals, and gradually return to ordinary community life by holding a part-time job or going to school. As part of what is called vocational rehabilitation, these former hospital patients learn marketable skills that can help them secure employment and thereby increase their chances of remaining in the community. Living arrangements may be relatively unstructured, and some houses set up money-making enterprises that help train and support the residents

Depending on how well funded the halfway house or group home is, the staff may include psychiatrists or clinical psychologists. The most important staff members are often paraprofessionals—sometimes undergraduate psychology majors or graduate students in clinical psychology or social work—who live in the house and act both as administrators and as friends to the residents. Group meetings, at which residents talk out their frustrations and learn to relate to others in honest and constructive ways, are often part of the routine. More than 100 programs modelled after Fairweather's pioneering efforts have been founded across the United States and Canada. These programs have helped thousands of patients, most of them with schizophrenia, make enough of a social adaptation to be able to remain out of the hospital. The integration of therapy with gainful employment is increasingly recognized as important in keeping people with schizophrenia (and also mental retardation; see Chapter 15) out of institutional settings (Kopelowicz & Liberman, 1998).

The need in Canada and the United States for effective halfway houses and group homes for ex-mental patients cannot be underestimated, especially in light of deinstitutionalization trends that have seen tens of thousands of patients discharged from mental hospitals who 30 years ago would have remained in the protected hospital setting. Although civil-rights issues are very important in shielding mental patients from ill-advised and even harmful detention—a topic discussed in depth in Chapter 18—discharge has all too often led to shabbily dressed former patients having to fend for themselves on the streets or being rehospitalized in the revolving-door syndrome. Discharge is a desirable goal, but ex-patients usually need follow-up community-based services, and these are scarce. However, the study by Stuart and Arboleda-Florez (2001) on community attitudes found that most people would not oppose a group home for people with schizophrenia in their own neighbourhood.

A model of what aftercare can be is part of the Paul and Lentz (1977) comparative treatment study discussed in Focus on Discovery 11.4. When patients were discharged from any of the three wards of the program—social learning, milieu therapy, or routine hospital management—they usually went to live in nearby boarding homes. These homes, often converted motels, were staffed by workers who had been trained by the Paul-Lentz project to treat the ex-patients according to social-learning principles. The workers, some of whom had Bachelor of Arts degrees, attended to the specific problems of the ex-patients, using rewards, including tokens, to encourage more independence and normal functioning. They positively reinforced the appropriate behaviour of the residents and paid little attention to bizarre behaviour.

Because assessment was careful and ongoing, the staff knew at all times how a particular patient was doing. Paul's mental-health-centre-project—and this is of paramount importance—acted as consultant to these community boarding homes, helping their staffs work with the ex-patients in as effective a manner as possible. Some boarding homes for ex-mental patients are supported financially by the state in the U.S. or by the provinces and territories in Canada as part of the mental health system, but only rarely have the procedures followed in these homes been carefully planned and monitored by professional mental health staff.

In spite of many practical problems, such as staff layoffs, the results for the ex-patients were as positive as those of the social-learning inpatient program. The ex-patients derived significant benefits from the aftercare; more than 90 percent of the patients discharged from the social-learning ward were able to remain continuously in the community residences during the year-and-a-half follow-up period, and some remained for as long as four years more. The revolving-door syndrome in this instance was halted. Finally, in a finding rather critical in these days of diminishing public funds, the full social-learning program—the mental health centre treatment combined with the aftercare—was much less expensive than the institutional care.

Some communities in Canada have non-profit organizations that have been modelled on the highly regarded Fountain House Project that started in New York City (Health Canada, 1991). The "club-house program" is designed specifically for people with psychiatric disorders, including schizophrenia, and "the club" is the focus of services that are provided, including reasonably priced meals, social and recreational activities, and sheltered employment. Organizations like this attempt to develop positive working relations with local employers and arrange employment where appropriate. The clubs sometimes provide housing.

Most aftercare programs are paying increasing attention to preparing patients for the work world, teaching them how to obtain and retain employment for which they can qualify. Governments have begun to recognize the importance of employment to people with mental disabilities such as schizophrenia, since having a job can increase their chances of living independently or at least outside a mental hospital. There is a recognition, too, of the harmful effects of not working and not being able to live in a reasonably independent manner. The trend seems to be to do whatever is necessary to help people work and live in as autonomous a manner as their physical and mental condition will allow (Kopelowicz & Liberman, 1998).

SUMMARY

- The symptoms of schizophrenia are typically divided into positive and negative types. Positive symptoms refer to behavioural excesses, such as delusions, hallucinations, and disorganized speech. Negative symptoms refer to behavioural deficits, such as flat affect, avolition, alogia, and anhedonia. Individuals with schizophrenia also show deterioration in functioning in occupational and social roles.
- The diagnosis requires that symptoms be present for at least one month and that a prodromal or residual phase, in which some symptoms are present but at a lower level of severity, lasts for at least five months.
- Schizophrenia is typically divided into subtypes, such as paranoid, catatonic, and disorganized. These subtypes are based on the prominence of particular symptoms (e.g., delusions in the paranoid subtype) and reflect the considerable variations in behaviour found among people diagnosed with schizophrenia.
- The concept of schizophrenia arose from the pioneering efforts of Kraepelin and Bleuler. Kraepelin's work fostered a descriptive approach and a narrow definition, whereas Bleuler's theoretical emphasis led to a broad diagnostic category. Bleuler had a great influence on the American concept of schizophrenia, making it extremely broad. By the middle of the 20th century, the differences between the diagnosis of schizophrenia in the United States and the diagnosis of schizophrenia in Europe were vast.
- Subsequent to the publication of DSM-III in 1980, the American concept of schizophrenia has become narrower and more like the European view.
- Research has tried to determine the etiological role of specific biological variables, such as genetic and biochemical factors and brain pathology, as well as of stressors, such as low social class and family conflict. The data on genetic transmission are impressive. Adoption studies, which generally escape the criticisms levelled at family or twin studies, show a strong relationship between having a schizophrenic parent and the likelihood of developing the disorder. Perhaps the genetic predisposition has biochemical correlates, although research in this area permits only tentative conclusions.
- At this point, it appears that an increased sensitivity of dopamine receptors in the limbic area of the brain is related to the positive symptoms of schizophrenia. The negative symptoms may be due to dopamine underactivity in the prefrontal cortex. Research into biochemical factors in schizophrenia is beginning to examine the possible role played by other neurotransmitters, such as serotonin.
- The brains of patients with schizophrenia, especially those with negative symptoms, have enlarged lateral ventricles and prefrontal atrophies, as well as reduced metabolism and structural abnormalities in the frontal and limbic areas. Some of these structural abnormalities could result from maternal viral infection during the second trimester of pregnancy or from damage sustained during a difficult birth.
- The diagnosis of schizophrenia is most frequently applied to members of the lowest social class. Available information indicates that this is so mainly because the disorder keeps people from achieving higher social status.
- Vague communications and conflicts are evident in the family life of patients with schizophrenia and probably contribute to their disorder. A high level of expressed emotion (EE)—criticism, hostility, and emotional overinvolvement—in families has been shown to be an important determinant of relapse. Increases in general life stress have also been shown to be important precipitants of relapse. These stressors may increase cortisol levels, which, in turn, stimulate dopamine activity.
- Much of the available information is consistent with a diathesis-stress or biopsychosocial view of schizophrenia. Investigators have turned to the high-risk method, studying children who are particularly vulnerable to schizophrenia by virtue of having a schizophrenic parent. Mednick and Schulsinger found that circumstances predicting maladjustment in adulthood differ depending on whether positive or negative symptoms are most prominent.
- There are both biological and psychological therapies for schizophrenia. Insulin and electroconvulsive treatments and even surgery were in vogue in the early 20th century, but they are no longer much used, primarily because

of the availability of antipsychotic drugs, in particular, the phenothiazines. In numerous studies, these medications have been found to have a major beneficial impact on the disordered lives of people with schizophrenia. Newer medications such as clozapine and risperidone are at least as effective as the phenothiazines and produce fewer motor side effects. Drugs have also been a factor in the deinstitutionalization of hospital patients.

- Drugs alone are not a completely effective treatment, as patients with schizophrenia need to be taught or retaught ways of dealing with the challenges of everyday life. Furthermore, most antipsychotic drugs have serious side effects, especially after long-term use, and many patients with schizophrenia do not benefit from them.
- Psychoanalytic theory assumes that schizophrenia represents a retreat from the pain of childhood rejection and mistreatment. The relationship gradually and patiently established by the analyst offers the patient a safe haven in which to explore repressed traumas. Good evidence for the efficacy of analytic treatments does not exist, although case studies of dramatic cures have been presented in both the professional and the popular literature.
- Family therapy, aimed at reducing high levels of expressed emotion, has been shown to be valuable in preventing relapse.
- More recently, behavioural treatments, such as social skills training, have helped patients discharged from mental hospitals meet the inevitable stresses of family and community living or, when discharge is not possible, lead more ordered and constructive lives within an institution.
- Recent efforts to change the thinking of people with schizophrenia are showing much promise.
- The most effective treatments for schizophrenia are likely to involve both biological and psychological components.

KEY TERMS

alogia (p. 326)
anhedonia (p. 327)
antipsychotic drugs (p. 346)
asociality (p. 327)
avolition (p. 326)
catatonic immobility (p. 328)
catatonic schizophrenia (p. 331)
delusional disorder (p. 330)
delusional jealousy (p. 331)
delusions (p. 325)
dementia praecox (p. 328)
disorganized schizophrenia (p. 330)
disorganized speech (thought disorder) (p. 324)
dopamine theory (p. 336)
expressed emotion (EE) (p. 342)
flat affect (p. 327)
grandiose delusions (p. 331)
group homes (p. 359)
halfway houses (p. 359)
hallucinations (p. 326)
ideas of reference (p. 331)
inappropriate affect (p. 328)
incoherence (p.324)
loose associations (derailment) (p. 324)
negative symptoms (p. 326)
paranoid schizophrenia (p. 331)
positive symptoms (p. 324)
prefrontal lobotomy (p. 346)
residual schizophrenia (p. 331)
schizophrenia (p. 323)
schizophrenogenic mother (p. 341)
social-selection theory (p. 341)
sociogenic hypothesis (p. 341)
undifferentiated schizophrenia (p. 331)
waxy flexibility (p. 328)

Reflections: Past, Present, and Future

- In his famous quotation at the beginning of this chapter, R.D. Laing suggested that people who receive a diagnosis of schizophrenia are using a strategy invented to help them cope with an untenable life situation. Now that you have read this chapter, you are in a better position to evaluate the credibility and validity of Laing's thesis. What is your own position on this issue? How would you challenge his thinking based on your understanding and evaluation of current theories and empirical research? What is your reaction to the quote by Thomas Szasz?
- Most people diagnosed with schizophrenia lead a tortured, tormented existence; however, even when they respond favourably to antipsychotic medication, they often experience severe side effects and stop taking their medication. Some advocates have argued that for this reason people with schizophrenia should have the right to choose to continue to be psychotic. Do you agree or disagree with these advocates? Under what circumstance, if any, should we be allowed to impose treatment on psychiatric patients?
- Assume that that you are engaged to be married. Although your future partner appears to be extremely well adjusted, he or she has a fraternal twin who has been diagnosed with schizophrenia. The two of you are concerned about the genetic implications for your children. Will they be at elevated risk for schizophrenia? What other factors could put your children at risk of developing schizophrenia? What future scientific findings would help you to decide whether or not to have children?

- Assume that you are a psychologist who has been given *carte blanche* to develop a comprehensive and effective psychosocial treatment for schizophrenia (to be used in conjunction with traditional medical management). What would you focus on? Assume that the very best programs include the following components: individual case managers to work as advocates to help clients obtain necessary services; social supports that can "wrap around" clients to keep them in the community (e.g., safe houses and peer support groups); individualized proactive plans to facilitate crisis avoidance and management; and specific vocational rehabilitation plans that identify needed skills for occupational goals. Design and implement your program. Be specific. Assume that the financial cost or the availability of human resources becomes a factor. Which component(s) would you delete from your program?

chapter 12

Substance-Related Disorders

"I don't know what is marijuana. Perhaps I will try it when it will no longer be criminal. I will have my money for my fine and a joint in the other hand."
—Former prime minister Jean Chretien, as quoted in a 2003 story in the *Winnipeg Free Press*

"I also have experienced with my own family, in the most painful way possible, the consequence of excessive drinking."
—British Columbia Premier Gordon Campbell, during his 2003 apology for his drunk driving incident, alluding to his father, a doctor and medical school professor who suffered from alcoholism and committed suicide when Campbell was 13 years old

Harriet Clench, 1982, *A Country Tavern near Cobourg, Canada West,* 1849
oil on canvas, 29.5 x 37.2 cm, ART GALLERY OF ONTARIO, TORONTO
Purchase with assistance from Wintario, 1980

"The blackouts became regular. Each time I drank there would be hours, even days I could not remember. I would start to work and manage to get three pages done. Then, thinking three pages was a wonderful amount, I would go to the bookshelf where I kept my bottle of rum and have one drink, then two. ... Yet now, when I really wanted to stop, when I prayed to be able to drink normally, I could not. Nor could I control anything I did or said once I started drinking. It was a terrible feeling, not to know what was to happen to me once I went outside. Three-day drunks became three-week drunks, and then three-month drunks."

—Richards, 2001, pp. 115-116

The above excerpt is from the personal account of the award-winning author from New Brunswick, David Adams Richards. His story is but one of 10 compelling essays by Canadian authors in an edited book entitled *Addicted: Notes from the Belly of the Beast* (see Crozier & Lane, 2001). Fortunately, Richards was able to quit drinking over 20 years ago when a friend took him to an Alcoholics Anonymous meeting. His story illustrates that some people with extreme forms of addiction can overcome it.

From prehistoric times, humankind has used various substances in the hope of reducing physical pain or altering states of consciousness. Almost all peoples have discovered some intoxicant that affects the central nervous system, relieving physical and mental anguish or producing euphoria. Despite the often-devastating consequences of taking such substances into the body, their initial effects are usually pleasing, a factor that is perhaps at the root of substance abuse.

North America is a drug culture. North Americans use drugs to wake up (coffee or tea), to stay alert throughout the day (cigarettes, soft drinks), to relax (alcohol), and to reduce pain (aspirin). The widespread availability and frequent use of various drugs sets the stage for the potential abuse of drugs, the topic of this chapter.

The pathological use of substances falls into two categories: substance abuse and substance dependence. **Substance dependence** is characterized by DSM-IV-TR as the presence of at least three of the following:

- The person develops **tolerance**, indicated by either (a) larger doses of the substance being needed to produce the desired effect or (b) the effects of the drug becoming markedly less if the usual amount is taken.
- **Withdrawal** symptoms, negative physical and psychological effects, develop when the person stops taking the substance or reduces the amount. The person may also use the substance to relieve or avoid withdrawal symptoms.
- The person uses more of the substance or uses it for a longer time than intended.
- The person recognizes excessive use of the substance; he or she may have tried to reduce usage but has been unable to do so.
- Much of the person's time is spent in efforts to obtain the substance or recover from its effects.
- Substance use continues despite psychological or physical problems caused or exacerbated by the drug (e.g., smoking despite knowledge that it increases the risk for cancer and cardiovascular disease).
- The person gives up or cuts back participation in many activities (work, recreation, socializing) because of the use of the substance.

Substance dependence is diagnosed as being accompanied by physiological dependence (also called addiction) if either tolerance or withdrawal is present. In general, physical dependence on a drug is associated with more severe problems (Schuckit et al., 1999).

For the less serious diagnosis of **substance abuse**, the person must experience one of the following as a result of recurrent use of the drug:

- failure to fulfill major obligations (e.g., absences from work or neglect of children)
- exposure to physical dangers (e.g., operating machinery or driving while intoxicated)
- legal problems (e.g., arrests for disorderly conduct or traffic violations)
- persistent social or interpersonal problems (e.g., arguments with a spouse)

The DSM-IV-TR section on substance-related disorders includes several other diagnoses. Substance intoxication is diagnosed when the ingestion of a substance affects the central nervous system and produces maladaptive cognitive and behavioural effects. If a person addicted to a drug is denied it and then experiences withdrawal, that person receives a diagnosis of both substance dependence and substance withdrawal. An example of substance withdrawal is alcohol withdrawal delirium, commonly known as the DTs (delirium tremens). Furthermore, drugs can cause dementia and the symptoms of other Axis I disorders.

We turn now to an overview of the major substance-related disorders, considering problem drinking, nicotine and cigarette smoking, marijuana, sedatives and stimulants, and the hallucinogens. We will then look at etiological factors suspected in substance abuse and dependence and conclude with an examination of available therapies.

ALCOHOL ABUSE AND DEPENDENCE

The term *alcoholic* is familiar to most people, yet it does not have a precise meaning. To some, it implies a person slumped against a building, to others an abusive husband or co-worker, and to still others a man or woman sneaking drinks during the day. All these images are to some extent accurate, yet none provides a full or useful definition. DSM-IV-TR distinguishes between alcohol dependence and alcohol abuse. This distinction is not always made in the research literature. The term *abuse* is often used to refer to both aspects of the excessive and harmful use of alcohol.

Canadian hockey player Theoren Fleury had to leave the New York Rangers of the National Hockey League in 2001 to take part in a rehabilitation program for alcohol abuse. Fleury's struggles continued. He was suspended for six months in 2003 and prohibited from playing for his new team, the Chicago Blackhawks, because of continuing addiction problems and related behavioural difficulties.

Alcohol dependence may include tolerance or withdrawal reactions. People who are physically dependent on alcohol generally have more severe symptoms of the disorder (Schuckit et al., 1998). Those who begin drinking early in life develop their first withdrawal symptoms in their thirties or forties. The effects of the abrupt withdrawal of alcohol in a chronic, heavy user may be dramatic because the body has become accustomed to the drug. Subjectively, the patient is often anxious, depressed, weak, restless, and unable to sleep. Tremors of the muscles, especially of the small musculatures of the fingers, face, eyelids, lips, and tongue, may be marked, and pulse, blood pressure, and temperature are elevated.

In relatively rare cases, a person who has been drinking heavily for a number of years may also experience **delirium tremens (DTs)** when the level of alcohol in the blood drops suddenly. The person becomes delirious as well as tremulous and has hallucinations that are primarily visual but may be tactile as well. Unpleasant and very active creatures—snakes, cockroaches, spiders, and the like—may appear to be crawling up the wall or over the person's body or they may fill the room. Feverish, disoriented, and terrified, the person may claw frantically at his or her skin to get rid of the vermin or may cower in the corner to escape an advancing army of fantastic animals. The delirium and physiological paroxysms caused by withdrawal of alcohol indicate that the drug is addictive.

Increased tolerance is evident following heavy, prolonged drinking. Some alcohol abusers can drink a quart of bourbon a day without showing signs of drunkenness (Mello & Mendelson, 1970). Moreover, levels of alcohol in the blood of such people are unexpectedly low after what is usually viewed as excessive drinking, suggesting that the body adapts to the drug and becomes able to process it more efficiently.

Although changes in the liver enzymes that metabolize alcohol can account to a small extent for tolerance, most researchers now believe that the central nervous system is implicated. Some research suggests that tolerance results from changes in the number or sensitivity of GABA or glutamate receptors (Tsai et al., 1998). Withdrawal may be the result of increased activation in some neural pathways to compensate for alcohol's inhibitory effects in the brain. When drinking stops, the inhibitory effects of alcohol are lost, resulting in a state of overexcitation.

Although tolerance is mostly due to physiological factors, research by Vogel-Sprott and associates at the University of Waterloo has shown that psychological factors may also play a role. This research has shown that response expectations and the consequences of behaviour can have a direct influence on tolerance and the effects of alcohol (see Vogel-Sprott, Kartechner, & McConnell, 1989; Zinatelli & Vogel-Sprott, 1993). Similarly, the development of addictions often reflects the interplay of biological and psychological factors.

The drinking pattern of people who are alcohol dependent indicates that their drinking is out of control. They need to drink daily and are unable to stop or cut down despite repeated efforts to abstain completely or to restrict drinking to certain periods of the day. They may go on occasional binges, remaining intoxicated for two, three, or more days. Sometimes they consume a litre of alcohol at a time. They may suffer blackouts and have no memory of events that took place during a bout of intoxication; their craving may be so overpowering that they are forced to ingest alcohol in a non-beverage form, such as hair tonic. Such drinking, of course, causes social and occupational difficulties, quarrels with family or friends, violent behaviour, frequent absences from work, loss of job, and arrests for intoxication or traffic accidents.

The person who abuses alcohol, in contrast to the person physically dependent on it, experiences negative social and occupational effects from the drug but does not show tolerance, withdrawal, or the compulsive drinking patterns seen in the person who is alcohol dependent.

Alcohol abuse or dependence is often part of **polydrug abuse**, using or abusing more than one drug at a time. It is estimated, for example, that 80 to 85 percent of alcohol abusers are smokers. Unfortunately, while at present just over half of Canadian addiction programs offer smoking cessation

Polysubstance abuse involves the use of multiple drugs. Alcohol and nicotine are a common combination, although most people who smoke and drink in social situations do not become substance abusers.

services for those with other addictions, available help is often informal and most programs place little emphasis on smoking cessation (Currie, Nesbitt, Wood, & Lawson, 2003). Alcohol serves as a cue for smoking; smoking is twice as frequent in situations where a person is also drinking (Shiffman et al., 1994). This very high level of comorbidity may occur because alcohol and nicotine are cross-tolerant; that is, nicotine can induce tolerance for the rewarding effects of alcohol and vice versa. Thus, consumption of both drugs may be increased to maintain their rewarding effects.

Polydrug abuse can create serious health problems because the effects of some drugs when taken together are synergistic—the effects of each combine to produce an especially strong reaction. For example, mixing alcohol and barbiturates is a common means of suicide, intentional and accidental (Lesage et al., 1994). Alcohol is also believed to contribute to deaths from heroin, for it can reduce the amount of the narcotic needed to make a dose lethal.

Prevalence of Alcohol Abuse and Comorbidity with Other Disorders

Lifetime prevalence rates for alcohol dependence defined by DSM criteria were greater than 20 percent for men and just over 8 percent for women in a large U.S. epidemiological study (Kessler et al., 1994). The prevalence of alcohol dependence declines with advancing age, both because of early death among long-term abusers and because of achievement of stable abstinence from alcohol among others (Vaillant, 1996). Rates of problem drinking among young women are approaching those of men. Alcohol abuse is common among some Native American peoples and is associated with 40 percent of deaths and with virtually all crimes committed by Native Americans (Yetman, 1994). According to Health Canada (2003), alcohol abuse and abuse of other substances is an extremely serious problem in many Aboriginal communities in Canada.

The prototypical heavy drinker in Canada is a young adult male who is not married and who is relatively well off financially (Single et al., 1995). Problem drinking is comorbid with several personality disorders; in fact, Canadian researchers have sought to identify genetic factors that are common to personality disorders and alcohol misuse (Jang, Vernon, & Livesley, 2000). Problem drinking is also comorbid with mood and anxiety disorders, as shown in a study of six countries, including Canada (Merikangas et al., 1998), and with other drug use and schizophrenia. It is a factor in 25 percent of suicides (Kessler et al., 1997; Morgenstern et al., 1997).

Canadian Perspectives/12.1

Binge Drinking at Universities, Colleges, and Schools

Alcohol use is frequent among university and college students. A 1993 survey in the United States revealed that 50 percent of men and 40 percent of women engaged in binge drinking, defined as having five drinks in a row for men and four for women (Wechsler et al., 1994). The 1993 survey was repeated in 1997 and 1999, and similar findings emerged. The 1999 survey evaluated over 14,000 students from 119 sites and found that 44 percent had engaged in binge drinking, a rate similar to those obtained in previous surveys (Wechsler, Lee, Kuo, & Lee, 2000). Also, 23 percent of students were frequent binge drinkers. The survey results have received a great deal of attention and not just because of the alarming levels of binge drinking. Other findings point to the harmful consequences of excessive drinking on campuses. Students who binge drink are substantially more likely to damage property, get into legal trouble, miss classes, and experience injuries (Wechsler et al., 1994). Binge drinkers are more willing to engage in unsafe sexual practices, and non-drinking students in close proximity to binge drinkers are more likely to be the target of unwanted sexual advances and physical assaults.

What about binge drinking on Canadian campuses? The results of the first comprehensive survey of Canadian campuses was reported by Gliksman, Demers, Adlaf, Newton-Taylor, and Schmidt (2000). This study, conducted 1998, used representative sampling techniques to survey 7,800 undergraduate students at 16 universities across Canada. This broad survey assessed alcohol problems and other forms of drug use. Students were questioned on a number of other topics, including mental health, sexual activity, and assault experiences. We will refer to several findings in various segments of this chapter.

The data confirmed that binge drinking is a very significant problem on Canadian campuses. Overall, 62.7 percent of students reported drinking five or more drinks on a single occasion since the start of the school year and 34.8 percent reported drinking eight or more drinks. Men were more likely than women to have five or more drinks on a single occasion (70.6 percent versus 56.1 percent) and eight or more drinks on a single occasion (46.5 percent versus 25.2 percent).

Most drinking tended to occur off-campus. Beer was the most popular drink in terms of total consumption (55.4 percent), followed by spirits (32.1 percent) and wine (12.5 percent). There were no regional differences in terms of the consumption of beer or spirits, but students in Quebec reported a slightly higher level of wine drinking.

Problems associated with excessive drinking included hangovers (37.6 percent), regret for actions (12.6 percent), memory loss (11.2 percent), missing classes due to a hangover (10.5 percent), unplanned sexual relations (6.5 percent), drinking and driving (4.9 percent), and unsafe sex (2.7 percent). In terms of student views of the most serious problems on campus, student alcohol use placed fourth (mentioned by 37 percent of respondents). The other problems were (1) vandalism and theft of property; (2) safety concerns; and (3) sexual assaults on campus.

How do students compare at Canadian and American universities? The Canadian and American research teams combined their data and found that a greater proportion of Canadian students drink but heavy alcohol use is higher among American students (Kuo et al., 2002). Data from both countries showed that students living at home were less likely to be heavy drinkers, but the protective effect of living at home was much stronger for students at American universities.

It was found in both countries that students who report having had their first experience of drunkenness prior to age 16 are substantially more likely to be heavy drinkers in college (Kuo et al., 2002). In many respects, the data from university samples seems to reflect a pre-existing problem among high school and junior high school students. The annual Ontario Student Drug Use Survey of over 6,000 students revealed in 2003 that 39.1 percent of grade 7 students and 48.9 percent of grade 8 students admitted drinking alcohol and 82.5 percent of grade 12 students admitted drinking alcohol (Adlaf & Paglia, 2003). Overall, 26 percent of students reported binge drinking at least once during the month prior to the survey, and 10 percent of drinkers reported binge drinking four or more times. A similar survey of high school students in Manitoba found that 81 percent of students admitted drinking in the past year, with 33 percent of male students and 20 percent of female students drinking at least once a week (Patton, Brown, Broszeit, & Dhaliwal, 2001). One shocking trend is the lack of parental awareness of their child's substance use. A study conducted in Alberta found that only 34 percent of parents were aware of their child's alcohol use, and only 11 percent were aware of their child's use of illicit drugs (Williams, McDermitt, Bertrand, & Davis, 2003). Single parents, parents from blended families, and parents of higher-achieving students were more likely to be "clued in" about the illicit drug use.

Follow-up analyses of the data obtained from Canadian university students have shown that the likelihood of having at least one session that involves eight or more drinks is predicted by male gender, living in residence, and having a high recreational orientation and a low academic orientation (Gliksman, Adlaf, Demers, & Newton-Taylor, 2003). Other analyses of alcohol intake and the reasons for drinking have provided clear evidence that the amount of drinking varies substantially across various situational contexts (Demers et al., 2002; Kairouz, Gliksman, Demers, & Adlaf, 2002). Situational factors associated with increased drinking include drinking at a party, in a bar/disco, off-campus, during the weekend, and, more generally, in peer-oriented drinking environments, which illustrates the relevance of social reasons for drinking. At the high school, a key situational factor is the school setting and whether a peer drinking culture exists (Kairouz & Adlaf, 2003).

What can be done about the binge-drinking problem? A survey of U.S. college administrators indicated that many preventive steps are being taken (Wechsler, Kelley, Weitzman, San Giovanni, & Seibring, 2000). (A comparable survey has not been conducted in Canada.) Prevention efforts include providing general education about the effects of alcohol, use of policy controls to limit access to alcohol (including "dry" residences and "dry" campuses), and restrictions on media advertising involving alcohol. Most U.S. campuses now have an alcohol specialist on staff and many colleges have task forces.

Alan Marlatt has conducted extensive research on high-risk college drinkers (see Canadian Contributions 12.1). He and his associates have tested the usefulness of brief interventions that focus on controlling and reducing the drinking behaviour of high-risk students rather than on striving for complete abstinence. They have shown that even brief interventions can reduce the harmful consequences of heavy drinking and that these improvements persist over a two-year period (see Marlatt, Baer, & Larimer, 1995; Marlatt et al., 1998). However, despite these improvements, the high-risk group still experiences more alcohol-related problems than the low-risk participants.

Thinking Critically

1. Is binge drinking a problem on your university or college campus? How would you rank it relative to other possible concerns (such as vandalism, safety, and sexual assaults)?
2. If binge drinking is a problem, what can be done about it? Who should be responsible for doing something about it if it is a problem? Should it be the administration, faculty, the students themselves, or a coordinated effort on the part of all stakeholders?
3. Do you think that an intervention that focuses on moderating the drinking behaviour of high-risk students, such as the program tested by Alan Marlatt, would work on your campus? How would you go about setting up a program?

Course of the Disorder

At one time, the life histories of alcohol abusers were thought to have a common, downhill progression. On the basis of an extensive survey of 2,000 members of Alcoholics Anonymous, Jellinek (1952) described the male alcohol abuser as passing through four stages, beginning with social drinking and progressing to a stage at which he lives only to drink.

Although Jellinek's description has been widely cited, the available evidence does not always corroborate it. The histories of alcohol-dependent people do indeed show a progression from alcohol abuse to alcohol dependence (Langenbucher & Chung, 1995); however, data reveal considerable fluctuations in drinking patterns, from heavy drinking for some periods of time to abstinence or lighter drinking at others (Vaillant, 1996). Furthermore, patterns of maladaptive use of alcohol are more variable than Jellinek implied. Heavy use of alcohol may be restricted to weekends, or long periods of abstinence may be interspersed with binges of continual drinking for several weeks (Robins et al., 1988). There is no single pattern of alcohol abuse.

Evidence also indicates that Jellinek's account does not apply to women. Difficulties with alcohol usually begin at a later age in women than in men and often after an inordinately stressful experience, such as a serious family crisis. For women, the time interval between the onset of heavy drinking and alcohol abuse is briefer than it is for men (Mezzich et al., 1994). Women with drinking problems tend to be steady drinkers who drink alone and are more unlikely than men to binge (Hill, 1980; Wolin, 1980).

Jason Priestley, Canadian actor and co-star of *Beverley Hills 90210*, pleaded no contest to a misdemeanour charge for driving under the influence, following a 1999 car crash that resulted in his friend suffering a broken arm. He was ordered to take a three-month alcohol counselling program. In 2002 the acknowledged risk-taker had a near-fatal car crash while practising for a car race.

Costs of Alcohol Abuse and Dependence

Comparative analyses, including data gathered by the World Health Organization, indicate that alcohol abuse is the fourth leading cause of worldwide disability. Moreover, alcohol abuse accounts for more years lost to death or disability than the use of either tobacco or illegal drugs (see Aronson, 2003).

Although most people who have a drinking problem do not seek professional help, people who abuse alcohol constitute a large proportion of new admissions to mental and general hospitals. Problem drinkers use health services four times more than do non-abusers, and their medical expenses are twice as high as those of non-drinkers (*Harvard Mental Health Letter*, 1987). As mentioned in Chapter 10, the suicide rate for alcohol abusers is much higher than that for the general population. Although alcohol-related traffic fatalities have declined substantially in Canada (including an overall decrease of 31 percent in the 1980s), 1997 national statistics indicate that it was still the case in 1997 that 31 percent of fatally injured drivers had blood alcohol concentrations over the legal limit (Mayhew, Beirness, & Simpson, 2000). According to statistics from the Traffic Injury Research Foundation in Ottawa, as summarized by the Canadian division of Mothers Against Drunk Driving (MADD; 2001), drunk drivers kill an average of 4.5 people and injure 125 people in Canada every day. Alcohol increases both the likelihood and severity of traffic accidents. The prototypical drinking driver in Canada is a male between the ages of 25 and 34 who drinks large amounts of alcohol on a regular basis or is a social drinker who occasionally drinks heavily (MADD, 2001).

It seems that a substantial proportion of impaired drivers have a general tendency to engage in antisocial acts. Stewart, Boase, and Lamble (2000) examined a random sample of 100 Canadian drivers with alcohol-related driving offences and found that 45 percent had a history of charges or convictions for such things as robbery, assault, and narcotic offences.

A recent analysis of 1995 statistics indicated that over 82,000 Canadians were admitted to hospital because of alcohol misuse (Single, Rehm, Robson, & van Truong, 2000). This includes people who were killed or injured because other people misused alcohol. The financial and human capital cost of alcohol-related injuries in Canada was $3.9 billion in 1992, and this was for only one year (Robson, Single, Xie, & Rehm, 1998). The likelihood of experiencing alcohol-related harm may be especially high in smaller communities. A survey of residents from Yukon found that over three-quarters reported alcohol-related harm in the previous year because of someone else's drinking, and the problem was greater in smaller communities (Kellner, Webster, & Chanteloup, 1996).

Alcohol may contribute to other injuries as well; it may be a factor in airplane crashes, industrial accidents, and mishaps in the home. Alcohol also presents law-enforcement problems. Rape, assault, and family violence are alcohol-related crime, as is homicide—it is believed that over half of all murders are committed under its influence (Murdoch, Pihl, & Ross, 1990). A recent review by Canadian researchers concluded that alcohol is the drug with the most evidence of there being a direct link between intoxication and violence (Hoaken & Stewart, 2003). The link between alcohol and violence was underscored by a study of hospital emergency rooms in Canada (Macdonald, Wells, Giesbrecht, & Cherpitel, 1999). It was found that people with violent injuries (i.e., intentional injuries inflicted by another or oneself) were much more likely to be feeling the effects of alcohol at the time of the injury than people with accidental injuries, with drunkenness involved in 42 percent of the violent injuries. Another telephone survey of over 1,000 Canadian adults confirmed that alcohol intoxication is associated with physical aggression (Wells, Graham, & West, 2000). This study found that either the perpetrator or victim was drinking in over two-thirds of reported cases of physical aggression.

These data illustrate the pervasive negative impact that excessive drinking can have on drinkers and the people around them. The human costs, in terms of broken lives, are incalculable.

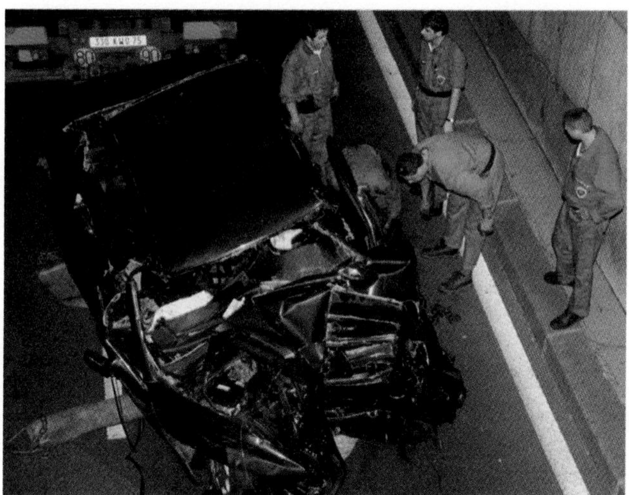

Princess Diana was killed in an automobile accident in Paris. Her driver was intoxicated.

SHORT-TERM EFFECTS OF ALCOHOL

How does alcohol produce its short-term effects? Alcohol is metabolized by enzymes after being swallowed and reaching the stomach. Most of it goes into the small intestines where it is absorbed into the blood. It is then broken down, mostly in the liver, which can metabolize about one ounce of 100-proof (50 percent alcohol) whisky per hour. Quantities in excess of this amount stay in the bloodstream. Absorption of alcohol can be rapid, but removal is always slow. The effects of alcohol vary with the level of concentration of the drug in the bloodstream, which in turn depends on the amount ingested in a particular period of time, the presence or absence of food in the stomach to retain the alcohol and reduce its absorption rate, the size of a person's body, and the efficiency of the liver. The effects of two ounces of alcohol would vary greatly for a 180-pound man who has just eaten and a 110-pound woman with an empty stomach.

Because drinking alcoholic beverages is accepted in most societies, alcohol is rarely regarded as a drug. But it is indeed a drug, and it has a biphasic effect. This means that the initial effect of alcohol is stimulating—the drinker experiences an expansive feeling of sociability and well-being as the blood-alcohol level rises—but after the blood-alcohol level peaks and begins to decline, alcohol acts as a depressant that may lead to negative emotions. Large amounts of alcohol interfere with complex thought processes. Motor coordination, balance, speech, and vision are also impaired. At this stage of intoxication, some people become depressed and withdrawn. Alcohol can also blunt pain. Large doses may induce sedation, sleep, and even death.

Alcohol produces its effects through its interactions with several neural systems in the brain. It stimulates GABA receptors, which may be responsible for reducing tension. (GABA is a major inhibitory neurotransmitter; the benzodiazepines, such as Valium, have an effect on the GABA receptor similar to that of alcohol.) Alcohol also increases levels of serotonin and dopamine, and this may be the source of its ability to produce pleasurable effects. Finally, alcohol inhibits glutamate receptors, which may cause the cognitive effects of alcohol intoxication, such as slurred speech and memory loss (U.S. Department of Health and Human Services, 1994).

There are many beliefs about the effects of alcohol—it is thought to reduce anxiety, increase sociability, relax inhibitions, and so on. But it appears that some of the short-term effects of ingesting small amounts of alcohol are as strongly related to the drinker's expectations about the effects of the drug as they are to its chemical action on the body. For example, alcohol is commonly thought to stimulate aggression and increase sexual responsiveness, but research has shown that these reactions may not be caused by alcohol itself but by the drinker's beliefs about alcohol's effects. In experiments demonstrating these points, participants are told that they are consuming a quantity of alcohol when they are actually given an alcohol-free beverage with its taste disguised. They subsequently become more aggressive (Lang et al., 1975) and report increased sexual arousal (Wilson & Lawson, 1976). People who actually drink alcohol also report increased sexual arousal, even though alcohol actually lowers physiological arousal (Farkas & Rosen, 1976). Once again, cognitions have a demonstrably powerful effect on behaviour. We shall see later that beliefs about the effects of drugs are linked with their abuse.

Long-Term Effects of Prolonged Alcohol Abuse

Chronic drinking creates severe biological damage in addition to psychological deterioration. Almost every tissue and organ of the body is affected adversely by prolonged consumption of alcohol. Malnutrition may be severe. Because alcohol provides calories—a pint of 80-proof spirits supplies about half a day's caloric requirements—heavy drinkers often reduce their intake of food. But the calories provided by alcohol are empty; they do not supply the nutrients essential for health. Alcohol also contributes directly to malnutrition by impairing the digestion of food and absorption of vitamins. In older chronic alcohol abusers, a deficiency of B-complex vitamins can cause amnestic syndrome, a severe loss of memory for both recent and long-past events. Memory gaps are often filled in with reports of imaginary, improbable events.

Prolonged alcohol use with reduction in the intake of proteins contributes to the development of cirrhosis of the liver, a disease in which some liver cells become engorged with fat and protein, impeding their function; some cells die, triggering an inflammatory process. When scar tissue develops, blood flow is obstructed. Cirrhosis ranks ninth among causes of death in the United States (U.S. Department of Health and Human Services [USDHHS], 1990b). Paralleling a decrease in drinking in the late 1980s, this figure represents a decline in deaths from cirrhosis, which peaked at over 14 per 100,000 in the 1970s.

Other common physiological changes include damage to the endocrine glands and pancreas, heart failure, hypertension, stroke, and capillary hemorrhages, which are responsible for the swelling and redness in the face, especially the nose, of chronic alcohol abusers. Prolonged use of alcohol appears to destroy brain cells; a five-year longitudinal study found significant loss of grey matter from the temporal lobes (Pfefferman et al., 1998). Even shorter-term abuse may produce some cognitive impairment; alcohol-abusing college students show impairment on neuropsychological tests (Sher et al., 1997). Alcohol also reduces the effectiveness of the immune system and increases susceptibility to infection and cancer. For example, women's risk of breast cancer increases steadily with the amount they drink; there is a linear-dose response such that each daily drink increases risk by about 7 percent (see Aronson, 2003).

Heavy alcohol consumption during pregnancy is the leading cause of mental retardation. The growth of the fetus is slowed, and cranial, facial, and limb anomalies are produced, a condition known as fetal alcohol syndrome. Even moderate drinking by mothers-to-be can produce less severe but undesirable effects on the fetus, so total abstention is recommended. Currently, it is estimated that 90 percent of Canadian women realize that drinking alcohol is not good for the unborn baby, and many recognize that drinking alcohol confers risk for the unborn (Koren, Nulman, Chudley, & Loocke, 2003). Given that at least half of Canadian and American women drink socially and half of all pregnancies are unplanned, each year about 100,000 Canadian infants are exposed to some alcohol during gestation (Koren et al., 2003). About one-quarter of pregnant women in Canada drink alcohol prior to realizing that they have conceived (Koren et al., 2003). Still, substantial exposure to alcohol is typically the case in extreme fetal alcohol syndrome.

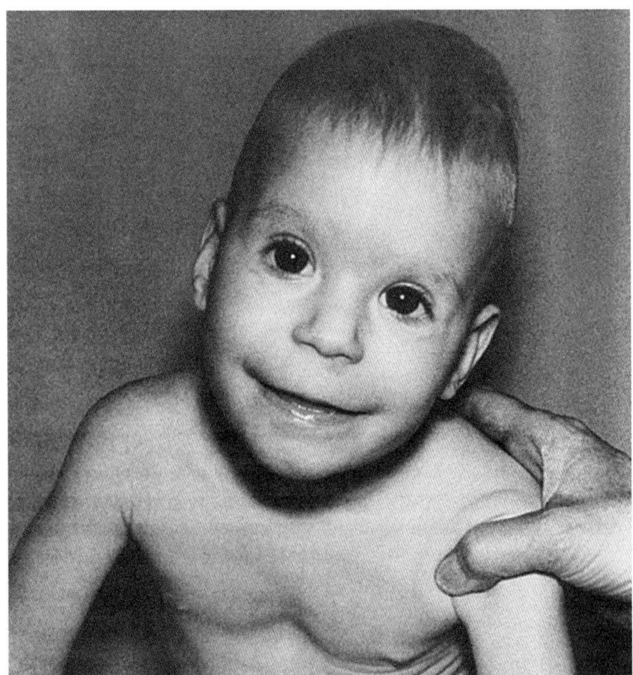

Heavy drinking during pregnancy causes fetal alcohol syndrome. These children have facial abnormalities as well as mental retardation.

Although it is appropriate and accurate to concentrate on the deleterious effects of alcohol, tantalizing evidence suggests positive health benefits for some people. Light drinking (fewer than three drinks a day), especially of wine, has been related to decreased risk for coronary heart disease and stroke (Sacco et al., 1999; Stampfer et al., 1988). Not all researchers, however, accept this finding at face value. Some people who abstain may have done so for health reasons—hypertension, for example. Comparing these abstainers to light drinkers could result in misleading conclusions. If alcohol does have a beneficial effect, it could be either physiological or psychological (a less-driven lifestyle and decreased levels of hostility).

Research on this topic was stimulated by the so-called French paradox—despite diets rich in saturated fats, the French have relatively low cholesterol levels. Some hypothesize that consumption of low to moderate amounts of red wine may lower cholesterol levels. Of course, the French lifestyle has other characteristics that may result in lower risk for heart disease; the French eat more fresh foods and get more daily exercise than North Americans. Promoting alcohol in North America may set the stage for a dangerous flirtation with alcohol abuse.

The psychological, biological, and social consequences of prolonged consumption of alcohol are extremely serious.

Because the alcohol abuser's own functioning is so severely disrupted, the people with whom he or she interacts are also deeply affected and hurt.

INHALANT USE DISORDERS

We will mention briefly another class of disorders that may be a stepping-stone for developing other disorders involving alcohol and drug abuse—inhalant use disorders. Although inhalant use is not confined to children and adolescents, an alarming number of young people begin their substance abuse by inhaling such substances as glue, white-out correction fluid, spray paint, cosmetics, gasoline, household aerosol sprays, and the nitrous oxide found in spray cans of whipped cream. According to the Canadian Paediatric Society (1998), the peak age of inhalant use is 14 to 15 years of age, with initial onsets in children as young as 6 years old. Inhalants are dangerous because they are inexpensive and readily available. Inhalant use disorders can involve behaviours such as sniffing (i.e., nasal inhalation of a substance), huffing (i.e., breathing fumes from a small rag stuffed in the mouth), and bagging (i.e., breathing fumes from a plastic bag held up to the mouth). Gasoline sniffing is a widespread problem among certain groups in northern Canada and is especially prevalent among Native children and adolescents (Barnes, 1989). For instance, a study conducted with Native and rural high school students in Quebec found that solvent use was considerably higher among Native students. This finding reflected a general tendency for the Native students to make greater use of illicit drugs, while the francophone students consumed more alcoholic beverages (Lalinec-Michaud, Martine-Subak, Ghadirian, & Kovess, 1991). In Chapter 10 we discussed the high rate of drug abuse, especially gasoline sniffing, in the context of our discussion of the alarming rates of suicide among Native youth. Harries (2001) asked children in Pikangikum what the gas does for them.

> "It makes you dizzy, it makes you high," Sylvester says. "You get hungry."
>
> Is there anything else they could be doing?
>
> "No," Erroll says. "It's boring," Sylvester says.
>
> What would make a difference?
>
> "We wanted a community centre so we could go there, play pool," Erroll says.
>
> "We could paint," Sylvester suggests.
>
> "We want some ..." Erroll's voice trails away. He brings the bag up to his face.
>
> "Chips and pop," Sylvester is sniffing from a bag too.
>
> Erroll finds his voice. "We want clothing, we want food, I wish that people had—I don't know." His hands are shaking and he sniffs again to compose himself.
>
> "To play games at the school—soccer, hockey, baseball ..." (p. A16)

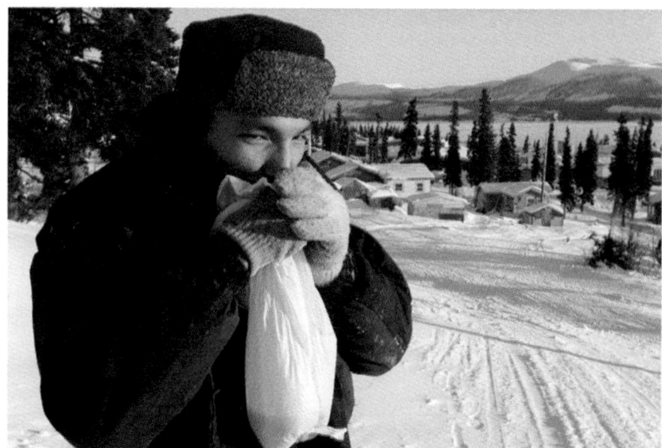

Young people from Davis Inlet, Sheshatshui, and Pikangikum have engaged in inhalant abuse. Unfortunately, the $150 million move from Davis Inlet to the new town of Natuashish in February, 2002 has not solved the problems of the Mushuau Innu from Davis Inlet (Toughill, 2003). The children are still sniffing gasoline.

Most inhalants act as depressants and, as such, can be seen as similar to alcohol and sedatives. The inhaled substance can result in feelings of euphoria and psychic numbing, but inhalants can cause damage to the central nervous system and can involve a number of side effects, including hallucinations, memory problems, and dizziness. Nausea and subsequent headaches are experienced eventually in almost all cases.

Inhalant use is linked with other adjustment problems. Howard and Jenson (1999) compared delinquents who did or did not use inhalants and found that those with inhalant use had higher levels of suicide, criminal behaviour, and family problems.

NICOTINE AND CIGARETTE SMOKING

The history of tobacco smoking bears much similarity to that of other addictive drugs (Brecher, 1972). It was not long after Columbus's first commerce with Native North Americans that sailors and merchants began to imitate the Natives' habit of smoking rolled leaves of tobacco and experienced, as they did, the increasing craving for it. When not smoked, tobacco was—and is—chewed or ground into small pieces and inhaled as snuff.

Nicotine is the addicting agent of tobacco. It stimulates receptors, called nicotinic receptors, in the brain. Then the neural pathways that become activated stimulate the dopamine neurons in the mesolimbic area that seem to be involved in producing the reinforcing effects of most drugs (Stein et al., 1998). Some idea of the addictive qualities of tobacco can be appreciated by considering how much people have sacrificed to maintain their supplies. In 16th-century England, for example, tobacco was exchanged for silver ounce for ounce. Poor people squandered their meagre resources for their several daily pipefuls. Even the public tortures and executions engineered as punishment by Sultan Murad IV of Turkey during the 17th century could not dissuade those of his subjects who were addicted to the weed.

Prevalence and Health Consequences of Smoking

The threat to health posed by smoking has been documented convincingly since 1964. It is estimated that smoking causes more than 45,000 deaths annually in Canada (Makomaski-Illing & Kaiserman, 1999) and more than 430,000 American tobacco users die prematurely each year (Schultz, 1991). Cigarette smoking is responsible in some way for one of every six deaths in the United States, killing more than 1,100 people each day. It is the single most preventable cause of premature death. The health risks of smoking are significantly less for cigar and pipe smokers because they seldom inhale the smoke into their lungs, but cancers of the mouth are increased.

Among the medical problems associated with, and almost certainly caused or exacerbated by, long-term cigarette smoking are lung cancer, emphysema, cancer of the larynx and of the esophagus, and a number of cardiovascular diseases. The most probable harmful components in the smoke from burning tobacco are nicotine, carbon monoxide, and tar; the latter consists primarily of certain hydrocarbons, including known carcinogens (Jaffe, 1985). Health risks from smoking decline greatly over a period of five to 10 years after quitting, to levels only slightly above those of non-smokers, but the destruction of lung tissue is not reversible (Jaffe, 1985).

Reports from Health Canada (2003), Statistics Canada (2004), the United States Surgeon General (USDHHS, 1989, 1990a) and the Centers for Disease Control (Cimons, 1992), as well as other publications (Cherner, 1990; Jansen, Glynn, & Howard, 1996; Tye, 1991; Youth Risk Behaviour Survey, 1997), draw several conclusions from more than 25 years of focused government efforts to discourage cigarette smoking:

- Approximately 21 percent of Canadians aged 15 or older are current smokers, totalling 5.4 million Canadians. Annual comparisons indicate that fewer Canadians are smoking and smokers are smoking fewer cigarettes on a daily basis (Health Canada, 2003). A greater proportion of men than women are current smokers (22 percent versus 20 percent), and men smoke a greater number of cigarettes on a daily basis.
- More than half (57 percent) of Aboriginal people in Canada smoke, and this rises to 71 percent in the Northwest Territories (see Stephens, 1991).
- Rates of smoking have been increasing among teenagers since 1991, as illustrated in a recently published study conducted in Atlantic Canada (Poulin et al., 1999), and have now reached or surpassed the levels found in 1979.
- About 17 percent of Canadian university students smoke cigarettes daily, and an additional 10 percent report the occasional use of cigarettes (Gliksman et al., 2003). Students are more likely to smoke if they live off-campus but

I WILL QUIT SMOKING. I WILL QUIT SMOKING AND I WILL QUIT TALKING TO MYSELF

WICKS

Impotent
WARNING: SMOKING CAUSES IMPOTENCE

California's Tobacco Education Media Campaign parodies tobacco ads to illustrate potential health effects of smoking and to attack pro-tobacco influences.

not with their parents. Rates are above average among students in the Atlantic provinces and below average in the western provinces. Overall, Canadian students smoke less than their U.S. counterparts (Cairney & Lawrance, 2002).

- Prevalence remains high among Native North Americans, blue-collar workers, and less educated individuals. Prevalence is lowest among college graduates and people over 75.
- Rates of smoking among Canadian youth in grades 5 to 9 have declined by more than half between 1994 and 2002. The top reasons stated for smoking were peer pressure, cusiosity, and because popular kids do it.

As with alcohol, the socioeconomic cost of smoking is staggering. American surveys indicated that smokers compile over 80 million lost days of work and 145 million days of disability each year, considerably more than do their non-smoking peers. This loss of productivity coupled with the health care costs associated with smoking runs to more than $65 billion annually in the United States.

Emerging data that cigarette smoking contributes to erectile problems in men—not surprising, given that nicotine constricts blood vessels—gave rise in 1998 to several televised public service announcements aimed at creating some second thoughts about how sexy smoking is. One ad shows a well-dressed young man looking with interest at an attractive woman at a fancy cocktail party. He lights up a cigarette, and when she looks over in his direction, the cigarette goes limp. She shakes her head and walks away (Morain, 1998).

Consequences of Second-Hand Smoke

As we have known for many years, the health hazards of smoking are not restricted to those who smoke. The smoke coming from the burning end of a cigarette, so-called second-hand smoke, or environmental tobacco smoke (ETS), contains higher concentrations of ammonia, carbon monoxide, nicotine, and tar than does the smoke actually inhaled by the smoker. Environmental tobacco smoke is blamed for more than 50,000 deaths a year in the United States. In 1993 the U.S. Environmental Protection Agency classified ETS as a hazard as dangerous as asbestos and radon. Health Canada has launched "The Blue Ribbon Campaign" to "clear the air" of second-hand smoke. The campaign website lists the following facts:

- Two-thirds of smoke from a cigarette is not inhaled by the smoker but enters the air around the smoker.
- Second-hand smoke has at least twice the nicotine and tar as the smoke inhaled by the smoker.
- Regular exposure to second-hand smoke increases the chances of contracting lung disease by 25 percent and heart disease by 10 percent.
- Second-hand smoke aggravates symptoms in people with allergies and asthma, and can cause eye, nose, and throat irritations, headaches, dizziness, nausea, coughing and wheezing in otherwise healthy people.
- Infants and children exposed to second-hand smoke are more likely to suffer chronic respiratory illness, impaired lung function, middle ear infections, and food allergies, and can even succumb to sudden infant death syndrome.
- In Canada, 2.4 million homes with children under 12 years of age report regular exposure to second-hand smoke.

At present, over 300 communities across Canada have passed ordinances regulating cigarette smoking in public places and work settings. Smoking is banned in many supermarkets, buses, restaurants, hospitals, government buildings, and on all airline flights. Many non-smokers express enthusiastic approval of such measures, but some smokers object strongly to what they view as undue infringement on their rights and the general stigmatization of smokers.

MARIJUANA

Marijuana consists of the dried and crushed leaves and flowering tops of the hemp plant, *Cannabis sativa*. It is most often smoked, but it may be chewed, prepared as a tea, or eaten in baked goods. Hashish, much stronger than marijuana, is produced by removing and drying the resin exudate of the tops of high-quality cannabis plants.

Originally, the hemp plant was extensively cultivated in the United States, not for smoking, but for its fibres, which were used in the manufacture of cloth and rope. By the 19th century, the medicinal properties of cannabis resin had been noted, and it was marketed by several drug companies as a treatment for rheumatism, gout, depression, cholera, and neuralgia. It was also smoked for pleasure, though little seen in the United States until 1920. At that time, the passage of the Eighteenth Amendment prohibiting the sale of alcohol prompted some people to begin smoking marijuana brought across the border from Mexico. Unfavourable reports in the press attributing crimes to marijuana use led to the enactment of a federal law against the sale of the drug in 1937. Today marijuana use is illegal in most countries, including Canada, many of them bound by a United Nations treaty prohibiting its sale (Goodwin & Guze, 1984). However, in 2003 the Canadian federal government moved toward decriminalizing simple possession of small amounts (up to 15 grams) of marijuana (Lawton, 2003).

Effects of Marijuana

Like most other drugs, marijuana has its risks. Generally, the more we learn about a drug, the less benign it turns out to be, and marijuana is no exception (see Focus on Discovery 12.1).

Psychological Effects The intoxicating effects of marijuana, like most drugs, depend in part on its potency and

In January 2004 police raided a massive computer-controlled, hydroponic marijuana growing operation in Barrie, Ontario. The former Molson Brewery plant contained over 30,000 plants growing in converted beer vats. It was called the largest pot "bust" in North America, with the total value of the marijuana produced yearly estimated at $100 million.

size of dose. Smokers of marijuana find it makes them feel relaxed and sociable. Large doses have been reported to bring rapid shifts in emotion, to dull attention, to fragment thoughts, and to impair memory. Time seems to move more slowly. Extremely heavy doses sometimes induce hallucinations and other effects similar to those of LSD, including extreme panic. Dosage can be difficult to regulate because it may take up to half an hour after smoking marijuana for its effects to appear; many users thus get much higher than intended. People with psychological problems are generally believed to be at highest risk for negative reactions to marijuana or any psychoactive drug, perhaps because lack of control is frightens them.

The major active chemical in marijuana is delta-9-tetrahydrocannabinol (THC). The amount of THC in marijuana is variable, but in general marijuana is more potent now than it was two decades ago (Zimmer & Morgan, 1995). In the late 1980s, cannabis receptors were discovered in the brain; shortly thereafter, it was found that the body produces its own cannabis-like substance, anandamide, named for the Sanskrit word for bliss (Sussman et al., 1996). Unfortunate-

focus on discovery/12.1

The Stepping-Stone Theory—From Marijuana to Hard Drugs

A concern prevalent for some time is expressed in the so-called stepping-stone theory of marijuana use. According to this view, marijuana is dangerous not only in itself, but also because it is a first step that can lead young people to become addicted to other drugs, such as heroin. If so, this magnifies the significance of recent indications in Canada that regular use of marijuana among adolescents has increased dramatically since the early 1990s (Adlaf, Ivis, & Smart, 1997), hitting a 25-year peak in 2003, according to a Health Canada survey (see Tibbetts and Rogers, 2003). Canada is a high-use country, according to a comparative study of adolescents in 36 countries (Smart & Ogborne, 2000). The Canadian Campus Survey found that 47 percent of students reported using marijuana at some point in their lives and 28.7 percent had used marijuana in the previous year (Gliksman et al., 2000). Marijuana use in Canada is associated with smoking, heavy drinking, and cocaine use (Ogborne, Smart, & Adlaf, 2000).

New statistics derived from the 2002 Canadian Community Health Survey indicate that among people aged 15 or older, marijuana use has doubled between 1989 and 2002 (Statistics Canada, 2004). An estimated 3 million Canadians smoked marijuana in 2002. Cannabis use was significantly higher among males, and age group comparisons indicated that usage peaked in the 18 to 19 year old age group.

But is marijuana a stepping-stone to more serious substance abuse? The question is not difficult to answer. About 40 percent of regular marijuana users do not go on to use such drugs as heroin and cocaine (Stephens, Roffman, & Simpson, 1993). So if by stepping-stone we mean that there is an inevitability of escalating to a more serious drug, then marijuana is not a stepping-stone. Still, we do know that many, but far from all, who use heroin and cocaine began their drug experimentation with marijuana. Moreover, users of marijuana are more likely than non-users to experiment later with heroin and cocaine (Kandel, 1984; Miller & Volk, 1996), and the single best predictor of cocaine use in adulthood is heavy use of marijuana during adolescence (Kozel & Adams, 1986). These data are in accordance with the results of a recent survey conducted in Montreal of rave participants (Gross, Barrett, Shestowsky, & Pihl, 2002). This study found a linear trend of experimentation with substances; that is rave participants reported a history of using first alcohol, then cannabis, LSD, psilocybin, amphetamines, cocaine, and ecstasy.

Nevertheless, perhaps a network theory is more appropriate than a stepping-stone theory. *Network* implies a complex set of relationships in which cause and effect are virtually impossible to isolate but some degree of association among many variables is acknowledged. Some regular users of heroin and cocaine, for example, turn to marijuana as a safer substitute, or lesser evil (Sussman et al., 1996). Marijuana is part of the picture, but only one of many factors contributing to involvement in harmful substance use.

Early recreational use of hashish occurred in a fashionable apartment in New York City. An 1876 issue of the *Illustrated Police News* carried this picture with the title "Secret Dissipation of New York Belles: Interior of a Hasheesh Hell on Fifth Avenue."

ly, problems associated with heavy marijuana use are not confined to cognitive difficulties. A recent Ontario study of people seeking treatment for cannabis-related problems compared daily marijuana users with non-daily users. This study confirmed that more of the daily users than the non-daily users reported cannabis-related cognitive problems (60 percent versus 42 percent). Daily users were also more likely to report psychological problems, health problems, financial problems, and vocational problems (Strike, Urbanoski, & Rush, 2003). Daily users were found to be more likely to use multiple substances and suffer from an anxiety disorder. Additional results showed that almost four-fifths of those seeking treatment were single males.

Several studies have found that being high on marijuana impairs the complex psychomotor skills necessary for driving. Highway fatality and driver-arrest figures indicate that marijuana plays a role in a significant proportion of accidents and arrests (Brookoff et al., 1994). Marijuana has similarly been found to impair manipulation of flight simulators. Some performance decrements measurable after smoking one or two marijuana cigarettes containing 2 percent THC can persist for eight hours after a person believes he or she is no longer high, creating the very real danger that people will attempt to drive or fly when they are not functioning adequately.

Does chronic use of marijuana affect intellectual functioning even when the person is not using the drug? Studies of memory and problem-solving conducted in Egypt and India in the late 1970s indicated some deterioration in users compared with non-users (Soueif, 1976; Wig & Varma, 1977). A subsequent study found memory impairment but not a general intellectual inefficiency (Millsaps, Azrin, & Mittenberg, 1994). It is impossible to know from this study whether these problems existed before heavy drug use. However, a more recent longitudinal study conducted by researchers at Carleton University in Ottawa found that current marijuana use resulted in an average decrease of 4.1 IQ points, but only among heavy users who smoked at least five joints per week (Fried, Watkinson, James, & Gray, 2002). Lighter use did not result in diminished IQ scores.

Survey findings suggest that heavy use of marijuana during teenage years may well contribute to psychological problems in adulthood. Kandel et al. (1986) interviewed 1,004 adults in their mid-twenties who had been part of an earlier New York public high school survey of drug use. Those who reported using marijuana in high school tended to have higher rates of separation or divorce, more delinquency, increased tendencies to consult mental health professionals, and, among women, less-stable employment patterns. The authors caution, however, that the specific effects of a single drug such as marijuana are very difficult to disentangle from the effects of other drugs that marijuana smokers sometimes use, in particular, alcohol and cocaine.

Somatic Effects The short-term effects of marijuana include bloodshot and itchy eyes, dry mouth and throat, increased appetite, reduced pressure within the eye, and somewhat raised blood pressure. There is no evidence that smoking marijuana has untoward effects on a normal heart but the drug apparently poses a danger to people with already abnormal heart functioning, for it elevates heart rate, sometimes dramatically.

Long-term use of marijuana seriously impairs lung structure and function (Grinspoon & Bakalar, 1995). Even though marijuana users smoke far fewer cigarettes than do tobacco smokers, most inhale marijuana smoke more deeply and retain it in their lungs for much longer periods of time. Since marijuana has some of the same carcinogens found in tobacco cigarettes, its harmful effects are much greater than would be expected were only the absolute number of cigarettes or pipefuls considered. For example, one marijuana cigarette is the equivalent of five tobacco cigarettes in carbon monoxide intake, four in tar intake, and 10 in terms of damage to cells lining the airways (Sussman et al., 1996).

Is marijuana addictive? Contrary to widespread earlier belief, it may be. The development of tolerance began to be suspected when American service personnel returned from Vietnam accustomed to concentrations of THC that would be toxic to domestic users. Controlled observations have confirmed that habitual use of marijuana does produce tolerance (Compton, Dewey, & Martin, 1990; Nowlan & Cohen, 1977). In Canada, a recent analysis of data from over 2,700 lifetime marijuana users in the Ontario Health Survey identified a threshold of use (100 to 199 uses of marijuana) that was associated with substantially greater risk for developing marijuana disorders (DeWit, Hance, Offord, & Ogborne, 2000). Interestingly, this threshold was lower for females, with using marijuana between 50 and 99 times being associated with the development of marijuana disorders. This study also found that the timing of marijuana use matters. Ontarians who were late starters and began using after the age of 17 were less likely to have a subsequent marijuana disorder than those who initiated use before the age of 14. It is less clear whether long-term users experience physical withdrawal when accustomed amounts of marijuana are not available (Johnson, 1991). If people do develop a physical dependency on marijuana, it is less serious than dependency on nicotine, cocaine, and alcohol.

The question of physical addiction to marijuana is complicated by reverse tolerance. Experienced smokers need only a few hits or puffs to become high from a marijuana cigarette, whereas less experienced users puff many times to reach a similar state of intoxication. Reverse tolerance is the direct opposite of the tolerance that occurs with an addicting drug, such as heroin. The substance THC, after being rapidly metabolized, is stored in the body's fatty tissue and then released very slowly, perhaps for a month, which may explain reverse tolerance for it.

Therapeutic Effects In a seeming irony, therapeutic uses of marijuana came to light just as the negative effects of regular and heavy usage of the drug were being uncovered. In the 1970s, several double-blind studies (e.g., Salan, Zinberg, & Frei, 1975) showed that THC and related drugs can reduce the nausea and loss of appetite that accompany chemotherapy for some cancer patients. Later findings confirmed this result (Grinspoon & Bakalar, 1995). Marijuana often appears to reduce nausea when other anti-nausea agents fail. Marijuana is also a treatment for the discomfort of AIDS (Sussman et al., 1996), as well as glaucoma, epilepsy, and multiple sclerosis. These observations have been confirmed in laboratory research using animal models. THC has been demonstrated to relieve pain by blocking pain signals from injuries or inflammation (as in arthritis) and thereby preventing them from reaching the brain. The analgesic effects have been shown with both injections of THC and by direct application to an affected area (Attias et al., 1997; Meng et al., 1997; Richardson, Kilo, & Hargreaves, 1997).

On August 3, 2001, then federal minister of health Alan Rock toured the plant where marijuana is being grown for medical purposes. The hydroponic lab (dubbed the Rock Garden by workers), located in an old shaft at Trout Lake Mine in Flin Flon, Manitoba, is Canada's first legal growing operation.

The potential benefits of smoking marijuana were also confirmed in a 1998 report to the U.S. National Institutes of Health (NIH) by a panel of experts. The panel suggested that medical researchers and clinicians should take the benefits more seriously (Ad Hoc Advisory Group of Experts, 1998). The NIH agreed to fund research on the subject, including research on whether the benefits from taking THC in pill form are comparable to what patients report from smoking marijuana. However, the panel warned that undesirable effects from smoking marijuana, such as suppression of immune function, had to be considered, especially with people whose immune system is already compromised, as with AIDS.

In 1999 a committee of the U.S. Institute of Medicine recommended that patients with "debilitating symptoms" or terminal illnesses be allowed to smoke marijuana under close medical supervision for up to six months; the rationale for smoking was based on findings that THC swallowed by mouth does not provide the same level of relief. But the committee also emphasized the dangers of smoking per se and urged the development of alternative delivery systems, such as inhalers.

In light of this evidence and following a request from two men with AIDS, Health Canada set up a process in June 1999 whereby people wishing to use marijuana for medical reasons could apply to be exempt from the federal ban. Although exemptions were granted and are evaluated on a case-by-case basis, the Government of Canada could not find a supplier who could grow the marijuana without the purchaser and seller being charged with a crime. The problem was rectified in December 2000 when a Saskatoon company known as Prairie Plant Systems was awarded a contract to provide a legal supply of marijuana. Also, in April 2001, the Government of Canada announced that people with other medical conditions (e.g., arthritis) might be eligible for medical marijuana, with the caveat that the people had to first demonstrate that other means (e.g., painkillers) did not alleviate their suffering. Research on the use of medical marijuana is limited at present, but a recent survey found that about 2 percent of Canadians reported using marijuana for medical reasons (Ogborne et al., 2000), with the vast majority using it for pain or persistent nausea.

SEDATIVES AND STIMULANTS

Addiction to drugs, including sedatives, was disapproved of but tolerated in the United States until 1914, when the Harrison Narcotics Act made the unauthorized use of various drugs illegal and those addicted to them criminals. The drugs we discuss here, some of which may be obtained legally with a prescription, can be divided into two general categories, sedatives and stimulants.

SEDATIVES

The major sedatives, often called *downers*, slow the activities of the body and reduce its responsiveness. This group of drugs includes the opiates—opium and its derivatives, morphine, heroin, and codeine—and the synthetic barbiturates and tranquilizers, such as secobarbital (Seconal) and diazepam (Valium).

Opiates The opiates are a group of addictive sedatives that relieve pain and induce sleep when taken in moderate doses. Foremost among them is opium, originally the principal drug of illegal international traffic and known to the people of the Sumerian civilization as long ago as 7000 B.C. They gave the poppy that supplied this drug its name (i.e., the plant of joy).

In 1806 the alkaloid morphine, named after Morpheus, the Greek god of dreams, was separated from raw opium. This bitter-tasting powder proved to be a powerful sedative and pain reliever. Before its addictive properties were noted, it was used in patent medicines. In the middle of the 19th century, when the hypodermic needle was introduced, morphine began to be injected directly into the veins to relieve pain. Many soldiers wounded in battle during the Civil War were treated with morphine and returned home addicted to the drug.

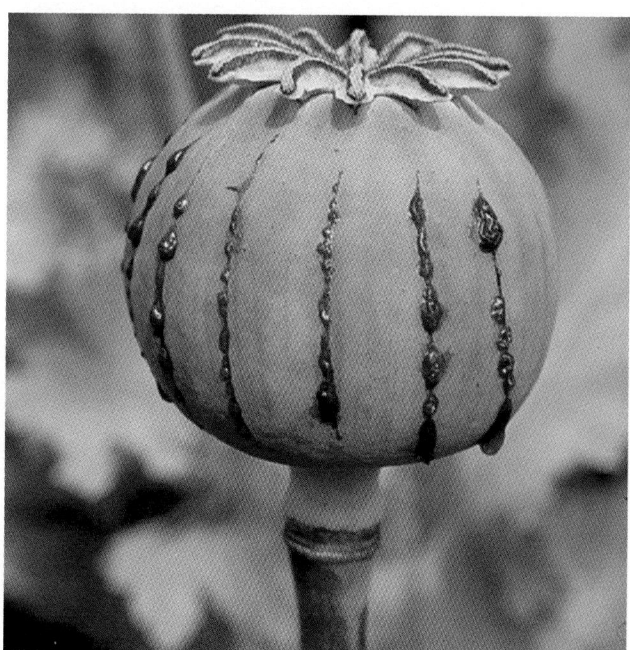

An opium poppy. Opium is harvested by slitting the seed capsule, which allows the raw opium to seep out.

Heroin was synthesized from opium in 1874 and was soon being added to a variety of medicines that could be purchased without prescription. This ad shows a teething remedy containing heroin. It probably worked.

Concerned about administering a drug that could disturb the later lives of patients, scientists began studying morphine. In 1874 they found that morphine could be converted into another powerful pain-relieving drug, which they named heroin. Used initially as a cure for morphine addiction, heroin was substituted for morphine in cough syrups and other patent medicines. So many maladies were treated with heroin that it came to be known as G.O.M., or "God's own medicine" (Brecher, 1972). However, heroin proved to be even more addictive and more potent than morphine, acting more quickly and with greater intensity. In 1909 American president Theodore Roosevelt called for an international investigation of opium and the other opiates.

Psychological and Physical Effects Opium and its derivatives, morphine and heroin, produce euphoria, drowsiness, reverie, and a lack of coordination. Heroin has an additional initial effect—the rush, a feeling of warm, suffusing ecstasy immediately following an intravenous injection. The user sheds worries and fears and has great self-confidence for four to six hours, but then experiences letdown, bordering on stupor.

Opiates produce their effects by stimulating neural receptors of the body's own opioid system. Heroin, for example, is converted into morphine in the brain and then binds to opioid receptors. The body produces opioids, called endorphins and enkephalins, and opium and its derivatives fit into their receptors and stimulate them.

Opiates are clearly addicting, for users show both increased tolerance of the drugs and withdrawal symptoms when they are unable to obtain another dose. Reactions to not having a dose of heroin may begin within eight hours of the last injection, at least after high tolerance has built up. The individual typically has muscle pain, sneezes, sweats, becomes tearful, and yawns a great deal over the next few hours. The symptoms resemble those of influenza. The withdrawal symptoms become more severe within 36 hours. There may be uncontrollable muscle twitching, cramps, chills alternating with excessive flushing and sweating, and

Canadian boxing great George Chuvalo has dedicated his time to warning students about the dangers of using drugs such as heroin. Three of his four sons became addicted to heroin. Unfortunately, his sons George Lee Chuvalo and Steven Chuvalo died of heroin overdoses, and Jesse Chuvalo committed suicide by shooting himself. Chuvalo's wife, Lynn, could not cope with these losses and also committed suicide.

a rise in heart rate and blood pressure. The addicted person is unable to sleep, vomits, and has diarrhea. These symptoms typically persist for about 72 hours and then diminish gradually over a five- to 10-day period.

It is believed that there are more than a million heroin addicts in the United States (Goldstein, 1994). Dependence is many times higher among physicians and nurses than in any other group with a comparable educational background. This problem is a joint reflection of the availability of opiates in medical settings and high job stress (Jaffe, 1985).

Heroin used to be confined to poor neighbourhoods and the inner city. In Canada, less than 1 percent of Canadians report using heroin in their lifetime, but heroin and cocaine abuse are quite prevalent among street youth; one study found that 5 percent of street youth in Montreal report using heroin everyday (see Poulin et al., 1998). A comparison of six Canadian cities (Vancouver, Calgary, Winnipeg, Toronto, Montreal, and Halifax) identified Vancouver as first in terms of per capita number of heroin- and cocaine-related hospital separations and deaths (Poulin et al., 1998). In recent years, heroin has started to become the cool drug for middle- and upper-middle-class college students and young professionals, and it is beginning to vie with cocaine for popularity among these groups. The Canadian Campus Survey (Gliksman et al., 2000) found that 2.3 percent of university students had used such illicit drugs as heroin, cocaine, and anabolic steroids.

American surveys indicate that the number of new users of heroin has been increasing steadily since 1992 (NIDA, 1997). In 1988, 1,250 people were seen in emergency rooms after injecting or snorting heroin; in 1994 this figure increased more than 2,000 percent, to 27,300. Drug rehabilitation centres have seen commensurate increases in traffic (Corwin, 1996).

Some of these increases in drug casualties are due to the nature of the heroin now available. The substantial increase in the mortality rate due to heroin or cocaine use recorded in British Columbia between 1990 and 1993 was attributed to the increased purity of the drugs (Office of the Chief Coroner of British Columbia, 1994). Fifteen years ago, the heroin sold in southern California, for example, was in a powder form that was less than 5 percent pure. Today heroin ranges from 25 to 50 percent pure and is sold in a gummy form that is difficult to dilute, or "step down," making it more likely that users will overdose (Corwin, 1996).

Opiates present a serious set of problems for the abuser. In a 24-year follow-up of 500 heroin addicts, about 28 percent had died by age 40; half of these deaths were from homicide, suicide, or accident, and one-third were from overdoses (Hser, Anglin, & Powers, 1993). Equally serious are the social consequences of using an illegal drug. The drug and obtaining it become the centre of the abuser's existence, governing all activities and social relationships. The high cost of these drugs—addicts must often spend upwards of $200 per day for their opiates—means they either have great wealth or must acquire money through illegal activities, such as prostitution or selling drugs. The correlation between opiate addiction and criminal activities is high, undoubtedly contributing to the notion that drug addiction per se causes crime. An additional problem now associated with intravenous drug use is exposure, through sharing needles, to the human immunodeficiency virus (HIV) and AIDS (see Chapter 8).

Synthetic Sedatives **Barbiturates**, another major type of sedative, were synthesized as aids for sleeping and relaxation. The first barbiturate was produced in 1903, and since then hundreds of derivatives of barbituric acid have been made. These drugs were initially considered highly desirable and were frequently prescribed. A campaign was mounted against them in the 1940s because they were discovered to be addicting, and physicians began to prescribe barbiturates less often. Today, the benzodiazepines, such as Valium, are more commonly used and abused. Methaqualone, a sedative sold under the trade names Quaalude and Sopor, is similar in effect to barbiturates and has become a popular street drug.

Sedatives relax the muscles, reduce anxiety, and in small doses produce a mildly euphoric state. Like alcohol, they are thought to produce these psychological effects by stimulating the GABA system. With excessive doses, however, speech becomes slurred and gait unsteady. Judgment, concentration, and ability to work may be severely impaired. The user loses emotional control and may become irritable and combative before falling into a deep sleep. Very large doses can be fatal because the diaphragm muscles relax to such an extent that the individual suffocates. As indicated in Chapter 10, sedatives are frequently chosen as a means of suicide.

However, many users accidentally kill themselves by drinking alcohol, which potentiates, or magnifies, the depressant effects of sedatives. The brain can become damaged and personality deteriorates with prolonged excessive use.

Increased tolerance follows prolonged use of sedatives, and the withdrawal reactions after abrupt termination are particularly severe and long-lasting and can cause sudden death. The delirium and convulsions resemble the symptoms that follow abrupt withdrawal of alcohol.

Three types of abusers can be distinguished:

1 The first group fits the stereotype of the illicit drug abuser: adolescents and young adults, usually male and often antisocial, who use synthetic sedatives to alter their moods and consciousness, sometimes mixing them with other drugs.
2 The second group consists of middle-aged, middle-class individuals who begin their use of sedatives under a physician's orders, to alleviate sleeplessness and anxiety, and then come to use larger and larger doses until they are addicted. These people rely less on street purchases because they are generally able to obtain refills of their drug prescriptions whenever they wish, sometimes changing physicians so as not to raise suspicion.
3 The third group comprises health professionals—physicians and nurses—who have easy access to these drugs and often use them to self-medicate for anxiety-related problems.

STIMULANTS

Stimulants, or uppers, such as cocaine, act on the brain and the sympathetic nervous system to increase alertness and motor activity. Cocaine is a natural stimulant extracted from the coca leaf The amphetamines, such as Benzedrine, are synthetic stimulants. Focus on Discovery 12.2 discusses a less risky and more prevalent stimulant, caffeine.

Amphetamines Seeking a treatment for asthma, the Chinese American pharmacologist Chen studied ancient Chinese descriptions of drugs. He found that a desert shrub, *mahuang*, was described as an effective remedy. After systematic effort, Chen isolated an alkaloid from this plant belonging to the genus *Ephedra*, and the result, ephedrine, proved highly successful in treating asthma. But relying on the shrub for the drug was not efficient, and so efforts to develop a synthetic substitute began. Amphetamines resulted from these efforts (Snyder, 1974).

The first amphetamine, Benzedrine, was synthesized in 1927. Almost as soon as it became commercially available in the early 1930s as an inhalant to relieve stuffy noses, the public discovered its stimulating effects. Physicians thereafter prescribed it and the other amphetamines that were soon synthesized to control mild depression and appetite. Soldiers on both sides in World War II were supplied with the drugs to ward off fatigue, and today amphetamines are sometimes used to treat hyperactive children.

Amphetamines, such as Benzedrine, Dexedrine, and Methedrine, produce their effects by causing the release of norepinephrine and dopamine and blocking the reuptake of these neurotransmitters. They are taken orally or intravenously and can be addicting. Wakefulness is heightened, intestinal functions are inhibited, and appetite is reduced—hence their use in dieting. The heart rate quickens, and blood vessels in the skin and mucous membranes constrict. The individual becomes alert, euphoric, and outgoing and is possessed with seemingly boundless energy and self-confidence. Larger doses can make people nervous and confused, subjecting them to palpitations, headaches, dizziness, and sleeplessness. Sometimes heavy users become so suspicious and hostile that they can be dangerous to others. Large doses taken over time can induce a state similar to paranoid schizophrenia, including its delusions.

Tolerance to amphetamines develops rapidly, so that more and more of the drug is required to produce the stimulating effect. As tolerance increases, the user may stop taking pills and inject Methedrine, the strongest of the amphetamines, directly into the veins. The so-called speed freaks give themselves repeated injections of the drug and maintain intense and euphoric activity for a few days, without eating or sleeping (a run), after which they are exhausted and depressed and sleep, or crash, for several days. Then the cycle starts again. After several repetitions of this pattern, physical and social functioning deteriorates considerably. Behaviour is erratic and hostile, and speed freaks may become a danger to themselves and to others.

Amphetamine use in the workplace has been increasing. Under time pressure to produce—the saying of the 1990s was "do more with less"—many white-collar workers turned to speed to stay awake, be more productive, and in general feel more energized, even euphoric. In some instances, supervisors encouraged use, even supplying the drug to an already-motivated employee. Although this may work in the short run, extreme irritability sets in over time and people may take more and more of the addicting substance to combat these angry feelings. Sometimes they use alcohol in the evening to wind down. The emotional and physical costs are steep as personal relationships and job performance begin to deteriorate.

In 1994 and 1995, 35 percent of admissions to California drug-treatment centres were for amphetamine abuse; in comparison, 27 percent were for heroin, and 24 percent were for cocaine. Emergency admissions to California hospitals for amphetamine abuse have also skyrocketed in recent years (Marsh, 1996). The problem is apparently more serious in California because of the high concentration there of clandestine laboratories that manufacture this easily made and inexpensive drug. Chemicals for manufacturing amphetamines are readily available, but highly volatile and dangerous to breathe. Inherent in the manufacturing process

focus on discovery/12.2

Our Tastiest Addiction—Caffeine

What may be the world's most popular drug is seldom viewed as a drug at all, and yet it has strong effects, produces tolerance in people, and even subjects habitual users to withdrawal (Hughes et al., 1991). Users and non-users alike joke about it. We are, of course, referring to caffeine, a substance found in coffee, tea, cocoa, cola, some cold remedies, and some diet pills.

Two cups of coffee, containing between 150 and 300 milligrams of caffeine, affect people within half an hour. Metabolism, body temperature, and blood pressure all increase; urine production goes up, as most of us will attest; there may be hand tremors, appetite can diminish, and, most familiar of all, sleepiness is warded off. Panic disorder can be exacerbated by caffeine because of the heightened arousal of the sympathetic nervous system occasioned by the drug. Extremely large doses can cause headache, diarrhea, nervousness, severe agitation, even convulsions and death. Death, however, is virtually impossible unless someone grossly overuses caffeine tablets, since the drug is excreted by the kidneys without any appreciable accumulation.

Although it has long been recognized that drinkers of very large amounts of regular coffee daily can experience withdrawal symptoms when consumption ceases, people who drink no more than two cups of regular coffee a day can suffer from clinically significant headaches, fatigue, and anxiety if caffeine is withdrawn from their daily diet (Silverman et al., 1992). These symptoms, moreover, can markedly interfere with social and occupational functioning.

As is the case with other drugs, people ingest caffeine to obtain positive outcomes and avoid negative outcomes. Research by Kathryn Graham (1988) examined the reasons that Canadian undergraduates gave for heavy consumption of coffee and tea. Students reported drinking for reasons of sociability and affiliation with others, but also to obtain relief from aversive states. Of course, the need for a stimulant was also important. Analyses showed that relief and stimulation as reasons for caffeine use were the best predictors of overall consumption and caffeine dependence.

The caffeine found in coffee, tea, and soft drinks is probably the world's favourite drug.

are frequent explosions and fires, and the release of the hazardous chemicals causes damage ranging from eye irritation and nausea to coma and death.

Cocaine The natives of the Andean uplands, to which the coca shrubs are native, chew the leaves. Europeans, introduced to coca by Spanish conquistadors, chose instead to brew the leaves in beverages. The alkaloid **cocaine** was extracted from the leaves of the coca plant in the mid-1800s and has been used since then as a local anesthetic. In 1884, while still a young neurologist, Sigmund Freud began using cocaine to combat his depression. Convinced of its wondrous effects, he prescribed it to a friend who had a painful disease. Freud published one of the first papers on the drug, "Song of Praise," which was an enthusiastic endorsement of the exhilarating effects he had experienced. Freud subsequently lost his enthusiasm for cocaine after nursing a physician friend, to whom he had recommended the drug, through a night-long psychotic state brought on by it. Perhaps the most famous fictional cocaine addict was Sherlock Holmes.

Cocaine has other effects in addition to reducing pain. It acts rapidly on the brain, blocking the reuptake of dopamine in mesolimbic areas that are thought to yield pleasurable states; the result is that dopamine is left in the synapse and thereby facilitates neural transmission and resultant positive feelings. Self-reports of the pleasure induced by cocaine are strongly related to the extent that cocaine has blocked dopamine reuptake (Volkow et al., 1997). Cocaine increases sexual desire and produces feelings of self-confidence, well-being, and indefatigability. An overdose may bring on chills, nausea, and insomnia, as well as a paranoid breakdown and terrifying hallucinations of insects crawling beneath the skin. Chronic use often leads to changes in personality, which include heightened irritability, impaired social skills, paranoid thinking, and disturbances in eating and sleeping (Scientific Perspectives on Cocaine Abuse, 1987). Ceasing cocaine use appears to cause a severe withdrawal syndrome. Cocaine can take hold of people with as much tenacity as do the established addictive drugs. As with alcohol, developing fetuses are markedly and negatively affected

Cocaine freebase is produced by heating cocaine with ether. Comedian and actor Richard Pryor was burned severely and nearly died when the ether he used caught fire.

in the womb by the mother's use of cocaine during pregnancy, and many babies are born addicted to the drug.

Cocaine, a vasoconstrictor, causes the blood vessels to narrow. As users take larger doses of the purer forms of cocaine now available, they are more frequently rushed to emergency rooms and may die of an overdose, often from a myocardial infarction (Kozel, Crider, & Adams, 1982). Cocaine also increases a person's risk for stroke and causes cognitive impairments, including problems with memory and attention. Because of its strong vasoconstricting properties, cocaine poses special dangers in pregnancy, for the blood supply to the fetus may be compromised.

Cocaine can be sniffed (snorted), smoked in pipes or cigarettes, swallowed, or injected into the veins; some heroin addicts mix the two drugs. In the 1970s, cocaine users began to separate, or free, a component of cocaine by heating it with ether. The cocaine base—or freebase—produces very powerful effects because it is absorbed so rapidly. It is smoked in a water pipe or sprinkled on a tobacco or marijuana cigarette. It is rapidly absorbed into the lungs and carried to the brain in a few seconds, where it induces an intense two-minute high, followed by restlessness and discomfort. Some freebase smokers go on marathon binges lasting up to four days (Goodwin & Guze, 1984). The freebasing process is hazardous, however, because ether is flammable.

In the mid-1980s a new form of freebase, called crack, appeared on the streets. The presence of crack brought about an increase in freebasing and in casualties. Because it was available in small, relatively inexpensive doses ($10 for about 100 milligrams versus the $100 per gram that users formerly had to pay to obtain cocaine), younger and less-affluent buyers began to experiment with the drug and to become addicted (Kozel & Adams, 1986).

Cocaine use in general soared in the 1970s and 1980s, increasing by more than 260 percent between 1974 and 1985. The use of cocaine dramatically decreased in the late 1980s and early 1990s. However, among 12th graders, use increased from 1996 to 1997 (NIDA, 1998). The frequency of use of crack has not shown any decline. Figures for crack use in 1991 (based on reported use during the past month) were about 0.3 percent for young people (ages 18 to 34) (NIDA, 1991), but in 1996 had increased to 0.8 percent (NIDA, 1996). Many public health and police officials regard crack as the most dangerous illicit drug in society today.

LSD AND OTHER HALLUCINOGENS

In 1943 a Swiss chemist, Albert Hofmann, described an illness he had seemingly contracted:

> Last Friday .... I had to interrupt my laboratory work ... I was seized with a feeling of great restlessness and mild dizziness. At home, I lay down and sank into a not unpleasant delirium, which was characterized by extremely exciting fantasies. In a semiconscious state with my eyes closed ... fantastic visions of extraordinary realness and with an intense kaleidoscopic play of colors assaulted me. (Cited in Cashman, 1966, p. 31)

Earlier in the day Hofmann had manufactured a few milligrams of d-lysergic acid diethylamide, a drug that he had synthesized in 1938. Reasoning that he might have unknowingly ingested some and that this had caused his unusual experience, he deliberately took a dose and confirmed his hypothesis.

After Hofmann's experiences with **LSD** in 1943, the drug was referred to as psychotomimetic because it was thought to produce effects similar to the symptoms of a psychosis. Then the term *psychedelic*, from the Greek words for "soul" and "to make manifest," was applied to emphasize the subjectively experienced expansions of consciousness reported by users of LSD and often referred to by them as a trip. The term in current use for LSD is **hallucinogen**, which describes one of the main effects of such drugs—hallucinations.

Four other important hallucinogens are mescaline, psilocybin, and the synthetic compounds MDA and MDMA. In 1896 **mescaline**, an alkaloid and the active ingredient of peyote, was isolated from small, disk-like growths on the top of the peyote cactus. The drug has been used for centuries in the religious rites of Native peoples living in the Southwest and northern Mexico. **Psilocybin** is a crystalline powder that Hofmann isolated from the mushroom *Psilocybe mexicana* in 1958. The early Aztec and Mexican cultures called the sacred mushrooms "God's flesh," and the Natives of Mexico still use them in their worship. Each of

In the 1960s, psychologist Timothy Leary was one of the leading proponents of the use of hallucinogens to expand consciousness.

these substances is structurally similar to several neurotransmitters, but their effects are thought to be due to the stimulation of serotonin receptors.

During the 1950s, researchers gave LSD, mescaline, and psilocybin to people in research settings so that they could study what were thought to be psychotic experiences. In 1960 Timothy Leary and Richard Alpert of Harvard University began an investigation of the effects of psilocybin on institutionalized prisoners. Their early results were encouraging: released prisoners who had taken psilocybin proved less likely to be rearrested. The investigators started taking trips themselves and soon had gathered around them other people interested in experimenting with psychedelic drugs. Their activities had attracted the attention of law-enforcement agencies by 1962. As the police investigation continued, the situation became a scandal, culminating in Leary's and Alpert's departures from Harvard. The affair gave tremendous impetus to the use of the hallucinogens, particularly since the manufacture of LSD and the extraction of mescaline and psilocybin were relatively easy and inexpensive. There is no evidence of withdrawal symptoms during abstinence, but tolerance seems to develop rapidly (McKim, 1991).

The use of LSD and other hallucinogens peaked in the 1960s, and by the 1980s only 1 or 2 percent of people were regular users. Even those who used hallucinogens did not indulge more than once or twice every two weeks (NIDA, 1982, 1983a). LSD use increased in the 1990s (NIDA, 1998), and its use is rising sharply in certain groups. For instance, a study of adolescents from Atlantic Canada found that 11.5 percent used LSD in 1996, up from 8 percent in 1991-1992 (Poulin et al., 1999) and a Montreal study showed that almost one-third of the adolescents surveyed had used illegal drugs more than five times (Zoccolillo, Vitaro, & Tremblay, 1999). The majority of the Montreal students reported going to school and playing sports while high on drugs.

A new hallucinogen joined the ranks of illegal drugs in 1985. Ecstasy, which refers to two closely similar synthetic compounds, MDA (methylenedioxyamphetamine) and MDMA (methylenedioxymethamphetamine), is chemically similar to mescaline and the amphetamines and is the psychoactive agent in nutmeg. Ecstasy is a designer-drug produced via chemical synthesis. It comes in many different sizes and shapes, depending on how it is manufactured. MDA was first synthesized in 1910, but it was not until the 1960s that its psychedelic properties came to the attention of the drug-using, consciousness-expanding generation of the times. Today it is popular on some college campuses, and the use of ecstasy is associated with "raves," gigantic parties attended by young people in warehouse-like settings (see Gross et al., 2002). The Canadian Campus Survey found that 4.4 percent of university students reported using ecstasy sometime in the previous year (Gliksman et al., 2000). Ecstasy use among Ontario students in grades 7 to 13 increased steadily in the 1990s, with 4.8 percent of students reporting use in 1999 (Adlaf et al., 2000).

Users report that the drug enhances intimacy and insight, improves interpersonal relationships, elevates mood, and promotes aesthetic awareness. It can also cause muscle tension, rapid eye movements, increased heart rate and blood pressure, nausea, faintness, chills or sweating, and anxiety, depression, and confusion. Lasting side effects that include paranoia, confusion, and memory complaints are beginning to be reported in the literature, and research with animals has shown that recreational doses of ecstasy cause permanent nerve damage (Centre for Addiction and Mental Health, 2001). The U.S. Drug Enforcement Administration considers the use of ecstasy and other so-called designer drugs unsafe and a serious health threat. Several deaths have come from accidental overdoses, with hyperthermia being the leading cause of death (see Gross et al., 2002).

A drug not easy to classify is PCP, phencyclidine, often called angel dust. Developed as a tranquilizer for horses and other large animals, it generally causes serious negative reactions, including severe paranoia and violence. Coma and death are also possible. Though often as terrifying to the user as to observers, its use increased in the 1990s.

Effects of Hallucinogens

The following excerpt describes the general effects of LSD, but it also applies to other hallucinogens.

> Synesthesias, the overflow from one sensory modality to another, may occur. Colors are heard and sounds may be seen. Subjective time is also seriously altered, so that clock time seems to pass extremely slowly. The loss of boundaries [between one's

> sense of self and one's environment] and the fear of fragmentation create a need for a structuring or supporting environment; and in the sense that they create a need for experienced companions and an explanatory system, these drugs are "cultogenic." During the "trip," thoughts and memories can vividly emerge under self-guidance or unexpectedly, to the user's distress. Mood may be labile, shifting from depression to gaiety, from elation to fear. Tension and anxiety may mount and reach panic proportions. After about 4 to 5 hours, if a major panic episode does not occur, there may be a sense of detachment and the conviction that one is magically in control. ... The user may be greatly impressed with the drug experience and feel a greater sensitivity for art, music, human feelings, and the harmony of the universe. (Jaffe, 1985, p. 564)

The effects of hallucinogens depend on a number of psychological variables in addition to the dose itself. A person's set—that is, attitudes, expectations, and motivations with regard to taking drugs—is widely held to be an important determinant of his or her reactions to hallucinogens. The setting in which the drug is experienced is also important.

Among the most prominent dangers of taking LSD is the possibility of experiencing a bad trip. A bad trip can sometimes develop into a full-blown panic attack and is far more likely to occur if some aspect of taking the drug creates anxiety. Often the specific fear is of going crazy. These panics are usually short-lived and subside as the drug is metabolized. A minority of people, however, go into a psychotic state that can require hospitalization and extended treatment.

Flashbacks, a recurrence of psychedelic experiences after the physiological effects of the drug have worn off, also sometimes occur, most frequently in times of stress, illness, or fatigue (Kaplan & Sadock, 1991). Flashbacks are not believed to be caused by drug-produced physical changes in the nervous system, in part because only 15 to 30 percent of users of hallucinogenic drugs are estimated ever to have flashbacks (e.g., Stanton & Bardoni, 1972). Moreover, there is no independent evidence of measurable neurological changes in these drug users. Flashbacks seem to have a force of their own, haunting and upsetting people weeks and months after they have taken the drug.

ETIOLOGY OF SUBSTANCE ABUSE AND DEPENDENCE

In considering the causes of substance abuse and dependence disorders, we must recognize that becoming substance-dependent is generally a developmental process. The person must first have a positive attitude toward the substance, then begin to experiment with using it, then begin using it regularly, then use it heavily, and finally abuse or become physically dependent on it (see Figure 12.1). The general idea is that the person becomes ensnared by the biological processes of tolerance and withdrawal after engaging in prolonged, heavy use.

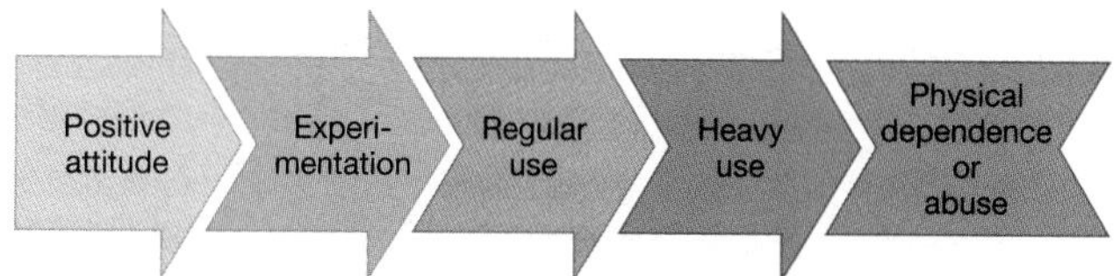

Figure 12.1 The process of becoming a drug abuser.

Although researchers are just beginning to consider the stages of this process separately (Stice, Barrera, & Chassin, 1998), variables that cause substance dependence appear to depend on the stage being considered. For example, developing a positive attitude toward smoking and beginning to experiment with tobacco are strongly related to the smoking of other family members (Robinson et al., 1997). In contrast, becoming a regular smoker is more strongly related to smoking by peers and being able to acquire cigarettes readily (Holowaty, Feldman, Harvey, & Shortt, 2000; Robinson et al., 1997; Wang et al., 1997).

This developmental model does not account for all cases of substance abuse or dependence. There are documented cases in which heavy use of tobacco or heroin did not end in addiction. Moreover, progression through the stages is not inevitable. Some people have periods of heavy use of a substance and then return to moderate use. Nevertheless, guided by this model, most research has examined variables related to initial use and its subsequent escalation. In the following sections, we discuss sociocultural, psychological, and biological variables related to substance abuse. Note that these factors can relate to various substances differently (e.g., a genetic diathesis may contribute to alcoholism but not to hallucinogen abuse).

SOCIAL VARIABLES

Sociocultural variables can play a widely varying role in drug abuse. Various aspects of the social world (e.g., peers, parents, media portrayals) can affect people's interest in and access to drugs. At the broadest level, we can look at great cross-national variations in alcohol consumption. The data in Figure 12.2, from a large-scale longitudinal study, illustrate the commonalities in the alcohol consumption of various regions. First, over the study period (1950–1980), alcohol consumption rose greatly in each area studied. Second, variations in consumption across locations decreased with the passage of time, although great differences still exist. Other research has found striking cross-national differences in the prevalence of substance use despite widespread

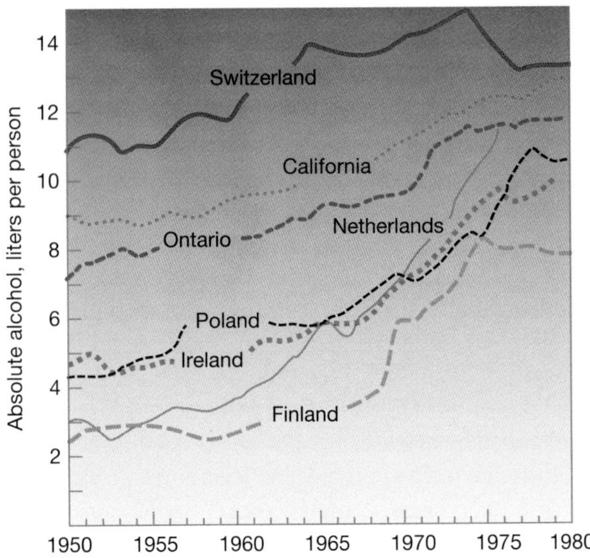

Figure 12.2 Annual consumption of alcoholic beverages among people aged 15 years and over in countries from 1950 to 1980, including data from Ontario. After Mäkelä et al., 1981.

similarities in the average onset of first use (see Vega et al., 2002). For example, the highest alcohol consumption rates have typically been found in wine-drinking countries, such as France, Spain, and Italy, where drinking alcohol regularly is widely accepted (deLint, 1978). Cultural attitudes and patterns of drinking thus influence the likelihood of drinking heavily and therefore of abusing alcohol.

Ready availability of the substance is also a factor. For example, in the wine-drinking cultures just mentioned, wine is present in many social settings, even in university cafeterias. Rates of alcohol abuse are also high among bartenders and liquor store owners, people for whom alcohol is readily available (Fillmore & Caetano, 1980). As for smoking, rates of smoking increase if cigarettes are perceived as being easy to get and affordable (Robinson et al., 1997).

Family variables are also important sociocultural influences. If both parents smoke, a child is four times more likely to do so than if no other family member smokes. Similarly, exposure to alcohol use by parents increases children's likelihood of drinking (Hawkins et al., 1997), and a recent study of adolescents in Canada and the eastern United States who were receiving treatment for amphetamine use showed that they tended to come from homes where one or more parent used illicit drugs and drank regularly (Hawke, Jainchill, & De Leon, 2000). Psychiatric, marital, or legal problems in the family are related to drug abuse, and a lack of emotional support from parents is linked with increased use of cigarettes, cannabis, and alcohol (Cadoret et al., 1995a; Wills, DuHamel, & Vaccaro, 1995). Finally, a lack of parental monitoring leads to increased association with drug-abusing peers and subsequent use of drugs (Chassin et al., 1996).

Results from the Ontario Health Survey suggest that any analysis of family factors should be extended to include the role of siblings. This study of substance abuse found that the dominant family influence in terms of behaviour was from older siblings to younger siblings, especially if the siblings were less than two years apart in age (Boyle et al., 2001). Moreover, this effect was stronger than the link between substance use in parents and their children. These data suggest the need for an extended family focus that includes the possible role of siblings.

The social milieu in which a person operates can also affect substance abuse. Having friends who smoke predicts smoking (Killen et al., 1997). Tobacco use among high school students is highest in certain subgroups—those with poor grades, behaviour problems, and a taste for heavy metal music (Sussman et al., 1990). In longitudinal studies, peer-group identification in the 7th grade predicted smoking in the 8th (Sussman et al., 1994), and in a three-year study, it predicted increased drug use in general (Chassin et al., 1996). Peer influences are also important in promoting alcohol and marijuana use (Karouz & Aflaf, 2003; Stice et al., 1998; Wills & Cleary, 1999). Although peer influence is important in the decisions adolescents make about using substances, those who have a high sense of self-efficacy (Bandura, 1997) are influenced less by their peers. Adolescents with this quality agree with statements like "I can imagine refusing to use tobacco with students my age and still have them like me" (Stacy et al., 1992, p. 166).

The role of the media must also be considered. We are bombarded with TV commercials in which beer is associated with athletic-looking males, bikini-clad women, and good times. In Canada, the recent "I am Canadian campaign" even implicitly suggested a link between beer and patriotic interests. Supporting the role of advertising in promoting alcohol use is an analysis of consumption in 17 countries between 1970 and 1983. Those countries that banned ads for spirits had 16 percent less consumption than those that did not (Saffer, 1991).

A particularly pernicious example of the role of the media was the Joe Camel campaign for Camel cigarettes. With the number of smokers declining, the tobacco industry's profitability depends on recruiting new smokers to replace those who are quitting. Elementary and high school students are obvious targets. Camel launched its campaign in 1988 with the Joe Camel character modelled after James Bond or the character played by Don Johnson in the television program *Miami Vice*, a popular show of the time. Prior to the campaign, from 1976 to 1988, Camels were the preferred brand of less than 0.5 percent of 7th through 12th graders. By 1991, Camel's share of this illegal market had increased to 33 percent (DiFranza et al., 1991)!

Additional evidence also indicates that advertising does influence smoking. In a longitudinal study of nonsmoking adolescents, those who had a favourite cigarette ad were twice as likely subsequently to begin smoking or to be willing to do so (Pierce et al., 1998).

The days of Joe Camel and other cartoon characters that appeal to young people are over. On March 13, 1996, the Liggett Group, manufacturers of cigarettes, agreed to stop using such advertising tools and to take other steps to discourage smoking among minors. These actions were part of a settlement in a class action lawsuit against the U.S. cigarette industry that charged companies with manipulating nicotine levels to keep smokers addicted.

PSYCHOLOGICAL VARIABLES

Next, we examine three classes of psychological variables. The first class essentially comprises the effects of alcohol on mood, the situations in which a tension-reducing effect occurs, and the role of cognition in this process. The second concerns beliefs about the prevalence of the drug's use and health risks associated with that drug. The third includes the personality traits that may make it more likely for some people to use drugs heavily.

Mood Alteration, Situations, and Role of Cognition

Why do people drink? One team of Canadian investigators proposed that it is possible to approach this issue from a cost versus benefit perspective; for example, drinking occurs if the perceived benefits outweigh the costs (Cunningham et al., 1997). Cox and Klinger (1988) proposed another motivational model of alcohol use that suggested that drinking motives vary along two dimensions: the valence of reinforcement (positive versus negative) and locus (external reasons versus internal, personal reasons): that is, people can drink to obtain pleasurable outcomes or avoid negative outcomes, and they can drink in response to external, social stimulation or in response to internal, personal cues. Four combinations involving these two dimensions are possible.

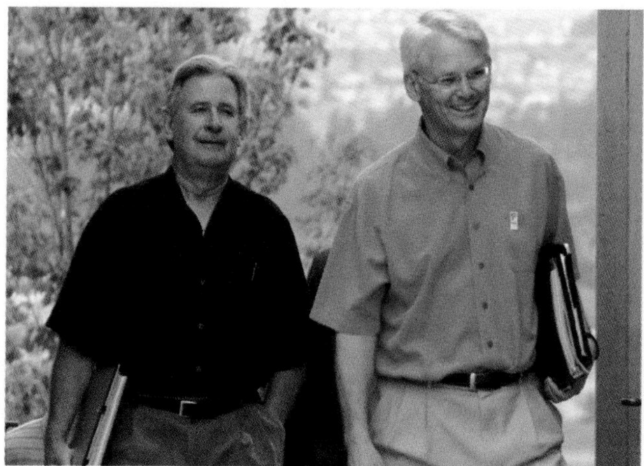

Canadian premiers Ralph Klein of Alberta and Gordon Campbell of British Columbia have both been identified as having drinking problems. Klein acknowledged his problem in December 2001 following a bizarre incident in which an inebriated Klein stopped outside a shelter and berated homeless people, while Campbell was arrested for drunk driving in Hawaii in January 2003.

Drinking for positive, internal reasons reflects drinking to enhance positive mood. Drinking for negative, internal reasons reflects drinking to reduce or avoid experiencing negative emotions. Drinking for positive, external reasons reflects drinking to obtain social rewards, and drinking for negative, external reasons would involve drinking to escape punishment or to avoid being embarrassed by other people.

Cooper (1994) created a multifactorial scale to assess these four drinking motives. Positive, internal reasons are measured by the enhancement scale (e.g., drinking because it gives you a pleasant feeling). Negative, internal reasons are reflected by the coping scale (e.g., drinking because it cheers you up when you are in a bad mood). Positive, external reasons are assessed via the social scale (e.g., drinking because it makes social gatherings more fun). Finally, negative, external reasons are assessed via the conformity scale (e.g., drinking because you do not want to feel left out). Sherry Stewart and her associates at Dalhousie University in Halifax used Cooper's measure to show that personality factors such as neuroticism and extraversion are more closely associated with the internal motives rather than the external motives and that the coping subscale is the drinking-motive subscale that is the strongest predictor of a measure of alcohol-related problems (Stewart & Devine, 2000; Stewart, Loughlin, & Rhyno, 2001). Other Canadian research shows that people who drink to cope do so even though they clearly recognize the risk of experiencing personal harm (Wild & Cunningham, 2001). Coping-based needs predict problem-drinking behaviour (Bonin, McCreary, & Sadava, 2000). Also, research by Stan Sadava at Brock University has shown that problem drinkers attach great importance to drinking in order to cope (Sadava & Pak, 1993).

In terms of internal motives, a principal psychological reason for using drugs is to enhance positive moods and diminish negative ones. Most early research in this area focused on the tension-reducing properties of alcohol. Early animal experiments (Conger, 1951) showed that alcohol impairs avoidance learning, which is usually regarded as mediated by anxiety. Studies with humans (e.g., Sher & Levenson, 1982) confirmed that alcohol reduces tension in people who are not yet alcohol abusers, but conflicting data have emerged (e.g., Thyer & Curtis, 1984).

Subsequent research on reasons for these inconsistent results has focused on the situation in which alcohol is consumed—specifically, situations in which distraction is present. Findings indicate that alcohol may produce its tension-reducing effect by altering cognition and perception (Curtin et al., 1997; Steele & Josephs, 1990). Alcohol impairs cognitive processing and narrows attention to the most immediately available cues, resulting in what Steele and Josephs term "alcohol myopia"—the intoxicated person has less cognitive capacity to distribute between ongoing activity and worry. If a distracting activity is available, attention will be diverted to it rather than to worrisome thoughts, with a resultant decrease in anxiety. However, alcohol may increase tension when no distractors are present as an intoxicated person may focus all his or her limited processing capacity on unpleasant thoughts or personal shortcomings. This person may brood and become more depressed while drinking.

Another situational variable that influences the tension-reducing effects of alcohol is the temporal relationship between alcohol consumption and stress—that is, whether alcohol consumption precedes or follows stress. The notion most people have is that an increase in tension (e.g., a bad day at the office) leads to increased consumption to reduce the effects of the earlier stressor. Empirical support for this idea comes from studies showing that increases in life stress precede relapses in reformed alcoholics (e.g., Brown et al., 1990). However, experimental research on the tension-reducing properties of alcohol has typically reversed the order of the two variables, having subjects drink and then encounter a stressor. One study compared alcohol's effects in both orders (stress-alcohol vs. alcohol-stress) and found tension reduction only in the alcohol-stress sequence (Sayette & Wilson, 1991). Thus, alcohol may not be a potent tension reducer in many life situations when it is consumed after stress.

If it is true that alcohol does not reduce stress when consumed after the fact, why do so many people believe that it helps them unwind? Perhaps people use alcohol after stress not because it reduces distress directly but because they expect it to reduce tension. Indeed, people who expect alcohol to reduce stress are likely to be frequent users (Sher et al., 1991; Tran, Haaga, & Chambless, 1997).

Extensive research has been conducted on the role of positive versus negative expectations in drinking behaviour. Positive alcohol expectations have been linked consistently with higher levels of consumption and alcohol-related problems, while negative expectations tend to inhibit consumption. The belief that alcohol helps one cope with stress is one of several positive beliefs. Other positive beliefs are that drinking enhances sexual pleasure and that it makes a person more friendly and assertive in social situations (see MacLatchy-Gaudet & Stewart, 2001). Negative alcohol expectations include beliefs such as drinking contributes to physical problems (i.e., hangovers), is linked with cognitive deficits, increases negative moods, and increases one's willingness to engage in unsafe and risky behaviours.

It seems that positive expectations are stronger predictors of drinking behaviour than negative ones (Goldman, Del Boca, & Darkes, 1999). A strong self-protective bias also seems to exist. A recent Canadian study found that there is a discrepancy in people's beliefs about the effects of alcohol on themselves versus others, with most people believing that alcohol has a stronger effect on other people than on themselves (Paglia & Room, 1999).

Some evidence indicates that males and females differ in the link between alcohol expectations and drinking behaviour. For instance, a Canadian study found that the expectation of risk and aggression predicted drinking behaviour for men, but the expectation of negative self-evaluation predicted drinking behaviour in women (McKee, Hinson, Wall, & Spriel, 1998). This study also found that coping measures and expectation measures were independent predictors of drinking behaviour for men and women, suggesting that alcohol expectations and coping orientations represent distinct variables of importance.

Several factors may be involved in the development of alcohol expectations, including direct personal experiences and more indirect, vicarious influences that involve the imitation and internalization of parental beliefs and beliefs displayed in the media (see Goldman et al., 1999). For instance, having an alcoholic parent and experiencing high levels of abuse while growing up are factors that contribute to negative alcohol expectations (Wall, Wekerle, & Bissonette, 2000). Alcohol expectations are also influenced by situational factors. A recent Canadian study assessed the alcohol expectations of students who were surveyed either in a laboratory or in an on-campus bar (Wall, McKee, & Hinson, 2000). Students tested in the on-campus bar reported higher expectations of pleasurable disinhibition and stimulation from drinking. Furthermore, positive expectations about alcohol and drinking appear to influence each other. The expectation that drinking will reduce anxiety increases drinking, which in turn makes the positive expectations even stronger (Smith et al., 1995). Similarly, positive expectations about a drug's effects predict increased drug use in general (Stacy, Newcomb, & Bentler, 1991).

Canadian researchers have attempted to identify factors within the person that would make the tension-reducing effects of alcohol especially reinforcing. People for whom alcohol produces a very strong reduction in tension tend to have elevated scores on the Anxiety Sensitivity Index (see Chapter 6) (Conrod, Pihl, & Vassileva, 1998; Stewart, Peterson, & Pihl, 1995). These findings fit with additional data indicating that alcohol abuse is comorbid with posttraumatic stress disorder (Bonin, Norton, Asmundson, Dicurzio, & Pidlubney, 2000). In short, alcohol may be particularly reinforcing for people who tend to have anxiety problems.

Tension reduction is only one aspect of the possible effects of drugs on mood. Some people may use drugs to reduce negative affect, whereas others use drugs when they are bored or underaroused to increase positive affect (Cooper et al., 1995). In both cases, drug use reflects a failure of other means of coping with emotional states.

Beliefs about Prevalence and Risks Two other psychological variables related to drug use are the extent to which a person believes a drug is harmful and the perceived prevalence of use by others (Jackson, 1997). Marijuana use peaked in 1978, when almost 11 percent of high school seniors reported daily use. At that time, only 12 percent of seniors believed there was risk associated with occasional use and only 35 percent believed there was risk with regular use. Compare this with 1985, when daily use had plummeted to 5 percent: 25 percent of high school seniors believed marijuana was harmful if used occasionally, and 70 percent believed it was harmful if used on a regular basis (Kozel & Adams, 1986). This twofold increase indicates that as beliefs change, so does behaviour. The dramatic increase in marijuana use in the 1990s was mainly among those adolescents who considered marijuana harmless (USDHHS, 1994). Similarly, many smokers do not believe that they are at increased risk for cancer or cardiovascular disease (Ayanian & Cleary, 1999).

Personality and Drug Use Neither sociocultural factors nor mood-alteration theories can completely account for individual differences in drug use. Not all members of a particular culture or subculture are heavy users, nor do all who experience stress increase drug usage. Personality variables attempt to explain why certain people are drawn to substance abuse.

Personality variables are stable individual differences that can be detected early in childhood and are believed to be relatively stable across the lifespan. Developmental factors that contribute to personality traits include related individual differences in genetic background and experiential factors, including exposure to parental models. The possible existence of an addiction-prone personality has been studied extensively, including research by the Winnipeg Health and Drinking Survey (Barnes, Murray, Patton, Bentler, & Anderson, 2000). Theoretical and empirical attempts to link personality factors with various forms of substance abuse have focused on two main classes of variables. First, theorists have focused on a class of personality variables involved in behavioural disinhibition. Zuckerman (1994) has studied a personality style known as sensation seeking. High-sensation seekers are thrill seekers who enjoy heightened levels of arousal. One way to increase arousal is to ingest certain drugs.

Cloninger and Eysenck are other theorists who have attempted to link alcohol and drug use with personality factors believed to be associated with behavioural disinhibition. Cloninger (1987a, 1987b) suggested that brain systems associated with behavioural activation and behavioural inhibition are associated with three genetically inherited dimensions of personality—novelty seeking, harm avoidance, and reward dependence. Novelty seeking is the dimension most relevant to alcohol dependence (Cloninger, 1987a).

Hans Eysenck conducted research throughout his lifetime on his three-factor model of personality (see Eysenck, 1967, 1981). He believed that the three key dimensions of personality were extraversion-introversion (i.e., outgoing versus reserved), neuroticism versus emotional stability, and psychoticism (i.e., aggressive, antisocial, tough-minded). Eysenck took issue with the five-factor model outlined in Chapter 13 and suggested instead that three core personality dimensions were sufficient to account for most outcomes. According to his model, substance use and abuse are likely among individuals characterized by high levels of neuroticism and psychoticism (Eysenck & Eysenck, 1977). Eysenck's suggested link between psychoticism and drug use is in keeping with several studies that link antisocial tendencies with drug use. An association has also been found between drug use in general and antisocial personality disorder (Ball et al., 1994). Drug abuse may be part of the thrill-seeking behaviour of the psychopath, to be discussed in Chapter 13. Furthermore, alcohol use is comorbid with several personality disorders, most notably antisocial personality disorder for men and borderline personality disorder for women (Morgenstern et al., 1997). Similarly, research conducted with adolescents from Montreal found that rebelliousness and a high level of aggression are also related to substance abuse (Masse & Trembley, 1997).

Cognitive processes and negative affect in the form of trait neuroticism may be inextricably linked in some drinkers. Studies of cognitive processing at the Centre for Addiction and Mental Health in Toronto found that negative affective cues in the environment seem to activate alcohol-related concepts (e.g. target words such as beer) in problem drinkers with high levels of psychological distress (Zack, Toneatto, & MacLeod, 1999; Zack et al., 2003). Thus, it seems that an orientation toward negative affect moods has cognitive implications for certain alcohol abusers.

One problem that plagues most research in this area is that the studies are cross-sectional rather than longitudinal while these studies show that personality and substance abuse are related, it cannot be assumed that personality factors create a vulnerability to substance abuse. However, two prospective studies do suggest that personality factors are risk factors. In one study demonstrating these points, kindergarten children were rated by their teachers on several personality traits and were followed up several years later. Anxiety (e.g., worries about things, afraid of new things or situations) and novelty seeking (e.g., restless, fidgety) predicted the onset of getting drunk, using drugs, and smoking. Depression was related to the initiation of smoking (Killen et al., 1997).

In another study, Sher, Bartholow, and Wood (2000) had 489 university students participate in a diagnostic interview and complete measures reflecting the models outlined by Cloninger and Eysenck. These students also had the diagnostic interview a second time six years later. This research design enabled Sher et al. to examine the role of personality factors in predicting the development of substance-use disorders in students who did not already have a history of substance abuse or other disorders. The study revealed that students characterized by novelty seeking or psychoticism were more likely to develop substance-use disorders. Traits related to negative emotionality (i.e., neuroticism) were correlated with substance-use disorders, but prospective analyses could not determine whether negative emotionality was a cause or a result of substance abuse.

When personality factors are identified as contributors to substance abuse, they tend to be regarded as distal factors that are less important than more proximal predictors, such as drinking motives. However, it is generally accepted that individual differences in temperament and personality organization create a potential for substance abuse that becomes realized if the vulnerable individual experiences situational factors or other life experiences that lead to the development of related differences in such factors as drinking motives and alcohol expectations.

Biological Variables

Most of the research on biological factors in substance abuse has addressed the possibility that there is a genetic predisposition for problem drinking. We will focus primarily on these data in our consideration of the biological variables that contribute to substance use.

Evidence for a genetic predisposition for alcohol abuse is found in studies of animals that have been bred to prefer alcohol to other beverages (Li et al., 1981). Data also indicate that problem drinking in human beings runs in families, suggesting a genetic component. Relatives and children of problem drinkers have higher than expected rates of alcohol abuse or dependence (e.g., Chassin et al., 1999). Furthermore, family studies show that the relatives of substance abusers are at increased risk for abusing many substances, not just the one that was the basis for selecting the proband (Bierut et al., 1998; Merilcangas et al., 1998). Twin studies have revealed greater concordance in identical twins than in fraternal twins for alcohol abuse (e.g., McGue, Pickens, & Svikis, 1992), caffeine use (Kendler & Prescott, 1999), smoking (True et al., 1993), heavy use or abuse of cannabis (Kendler & Prescott, 1998), and drug abuse (Tsuang et al., 1998).

Adoption studies add further support for the importance of a genetic diathesis in both alcohol and drug abuse (Cadoret et al., 1995a; Goodwin et al., 1973). Large-scale adoptee research conducted in Sweden has raised the possibility that there are subtypes of alcohol abuse with different genetic bases (Cloninger, Bohman, & Sigvardson, 1981). The investigators identified two groups of adopted children who were problem drinkers. Type I problem drinking occurred in both men and women and was not too severe. It was associated with mild, adult-onset problem drinking in the biological parents and exposure to alcohol abuse in the adoptive home. Thus, both genes and the environment seemed to play a role. In contrast, Type II alcohol abuse or dependence was found only in men, had an early age of onset, was associated with antisocial behaviour in the adoptees, and was linked to alcohol abuse in biological parents. Although other research has not replicated all these results, an early age of onset of alcohol abuse in men seems to be the crucial factor in this type of alcohol abuse (Fils-Aime et al., 1996). Linking these findings to the effects of alcohol on mood would suggest that Type I drinkers may consume alcohol to reduce tension, whereas Type II drinkers may drink to increase pleasure.

The ability to tolerate alcohol may be what is inherited as a diathesis for alcohol abuse or dependence (Goodwin, 1979). To become a problem drinker, a person first has to be able to drink a lot; in other words, the person must be able to tolerate large quantities of alcohol. Some ethnic groups, such as Asians, may have a low rate of alcohol abuse because of physiological intolerance, which is caused by an inherited deficiency in an enzyme that metabolizes alcohol. About three-quarters of Asians experience unpleasant effects from small quantities of alcohol. Noxious effects of the drug may thus protect a person from alcohol abuse.

This hypothesis focuses on short-term effects, possibly on how alcohol is metabolized or on how the central nervous system responds to alcohol. Animal research indicates that genetic components are at work in both these processes (Schuckit, 1983). Corroborating this notion are findings from research using the high-risk method. These studies have compared young, nonalcoholic adults with a first-degree alcohol-abusing relative to similar individuals without a positive family history of the disorder. Two variables predicted the development of alcohol abuse in men in a 10-year follow-up (Schuckit, 1994; Schuckit & Smith, 1996): (1) self-report of a low level of intoxication after a dose of alcohol and (2) less body sway (a measure of steadiness while standing) after drinking. Both findings indicate that alcohol abuse is more likely to occur in those in whom alcohol has little effect. Notably, these variables predict alcohol abuse among men with and without an alcohol-abusing father.

The smaller response to alcohol of the men who later became alcohol abusers may at first seem puzzling, but it fits with the notion that you have to drink a lot to become a problem drinker. A small response to alcohol may set the stage for heavier than normal drinking. The size of the response to alcohol is also related to our earlier discussion of alcohol's biphasic effects. In the research just discussed, the largest differences between sons of problem drinkers and control-group participants occurred when their blood levels of alcohol were declining. Therefore, sons of alcohol abusers may experience fewer of the negative, depressing effects of alcohol. Other research indicates that sons of alcohol abusers experience greater effects of alcohol (e.g., more tension reduction), as their blood-alcohol levels are on the rise. Thus, they receive more reinforcement and less punishment from the drug (Newlin & Thomson, 1990).

Although biological factors are clearly important, Siegel from McMaster University in Hamilton has developed a **conditioning theory of tolerance** that underscores the need to jointly consider biological processes and environmental stimuli that may be involved in the acquisition and maintenance of addictive behaviours (Siegel, 1975, 1999; Siegel, Baptista, Kim, McDonald, & Weise-Kelly, 2000). Siegel's initial research on the "associative basis of tolerance" was conducted with rats, but similar findings have been obtained with humans. The conditioning theory of tolerance is based on the notion that tolerance is a learned response, and the environmental cues that are present when addictive behaviours are developed can influence behaviours because these cues have come to be associated with the addictive substances via Pavlovian conditioning. For instance, if a person developed an addiction by drinking excessively in his or her recreation room at home, the room itself can become a conditioned stimulus. Drug-associated environmental cues can also elicit withdrawal symptoms.

One consistent research finding is that the presentation of environmental cues previously associated with the drug can attenuate or reduce an already established tolerance. Siegel has also postulated "Feedforward mechanisms," which are defined as anticipatory regulatory responses made in anticipation of a drug (Siegel, 1991; Siegel, Krank, & Hinson, 1987). Feedforward mechanisms reflect the fact that we learn to anticipate drug effects before they actually occur.

What are the implications of the conditioning theory of tolerance for addicted individuals? One clear implication is that factors pertaining to the environmental cues that were present when conditioning first occurred may be quite alluring and will thus have an impact when they reoccur (Siegel, 1999); that is, these environmental factors may contribute to relapses among drug addicts who have been successfully treated. Siegel's work reminds us that physiological processes must be evaluated within the context of situational factors.

Finally, exciting research has recently emerged on the mechanism behind the role of genetics in smoking. Like most drugs, nicotine derives its reinforcing properties by stimulating dopamine release and inhibiting its reuptake. Research has examined a link between a gene that regulates the reuptake of dopamine and smoking. One form of this gene has been related to being less likely to begin smoking (Lerman et al., 1999) and more likely to have quit (Sabo et al., 1999). A possible explanation for these results is that people who have this particular form of this gene experience less reinforcement from nicotine, making it less likely that they will start smoking and enabling them to quit more easily if they do.

Having reviewed the nature and possible causes of the several kinds of substance-related disorders, we turn now to their treatment and prevention.

THERAPY FOR ALCOHOL ABUSE AND DEPENDENCE

The havoc created by problem drinking, both for the drinker and for his or her family, friends, employer, and community, makes this problem a serious public health issue. Consequently, a great deal of research and clinical effort has gone into the design and evaluation of treatments.

Treatment of alcohol abuse is difficult, not only because of the addictive nature of the drug, but also because of related psychological problems involving depression, anxiety, and severe disruptions in social and occupational functioning. As indicated in Chapter 10, the risk of suicide is also very high. Although some of these problems may have preceded and even contributed to the abuse of alcohol, by the time an abuser is treated, it is seldom possible to know what is cause and what is effect. But what is certain is that the person's life is usually a shambles, and any treatment that has any hope of success has to address more than merely the excessive drinking.

Interventions for problem drinking are both biological and psychological. Whatever the intervention, the first step is for the person to admit the problem and decide to do something about it.

ADMITTING THE PROBLEM

To admit to having a serious drinking problem may sound straightforward to someone who has never had a drinking problem or has never known someone who did. However, substance abusers of all kinds are adept at denying that they have a problem and may react angrily to any suggestion that they do. Moreover, because patterns of problem drinking are highly variable—someone physically dependent on alcohol, for example, does not always drink uncontrollably—the need for intervention is not always recognized by friends or even by health professionals.

There have been very few Canadian investigations of the willingness of problem drinkers to seek help. One study does not paint a very rosy picture. Ogborne and DeWit (1999) found that, overall, only 2 percent of lifetime drinkers reported seeking help; this rose to 9 percent if the focus was restricted to those who felt that their alcohol use had resulted in some harm. Ogborne and DeWit concluded that the help-seeking rate in Canada is much lower than that among lifetime drinkers in the United States (5 percent). Canadians report that they would much rather receive assistance by obtaining a self-help book or getting computerized feedback than by contacting a counsellor or therapist, and this is the case even among people who have experienced drinking-related harm in at least two life domains (Koski-Jannes & Cunningham, 2001).

A contemporary analysis of Canadian survey data has found higher help-seeking rates, with one in three people with alcohol abuse or dependence seeking treatment (Cunningham & Breslin, 2004). Still we must ask: Why did two out of three people not seek help?

Enabling the drinker to take the first step to betterment—what has been called the contemplation stage (Prochaska, DiClimente, & Norcross, 1992)—can be achieved through questions that get at the issue somewhat indirectly.

Do you sometimes feel uncomfortable when alcohol is not available?

Do you drink more heavily than usual when you are under pressure?

Are you in more of a hurry to get to the first drink than you used to be?

Do you sometimes feel guilty about your drinking?

Are you annoyed when people talk about your drinking?

When drinking socially, do you try to sneak in some extra drinks?

Are you constantly making rules for yourself about what and when to drink?

(*Harvard Mental Health Letter*, 1996c, pp. 1-2)

Once the alcohol abuser recognizes that a problem exists, many treatment approaches are available.

Traditional Hospital Treatment

Public and private hospitals worldwide have for many years provided retreats for alcohol abusers, sanctums where people can dry out and avail themselves of a variety of individual and group therapies. The withdrawal from alcohol, detoxification, can be difficult, both physically and psychologically, and usually takes about one month. Tranquilizers are sometimes given to ease the anxiety and general discomfort of withdrawal. Because many alcohol abusers misuse tranquilizers, some clinics try a gradual tapering off without tranquilizers rather than a sudden cut-off of alcohol. This non-drug-assisted withdrawal works for most problem drinkers (Wartenburg et al., 1990). To help get through withdrawal, alcohol abusers also need carbohydrate solutions, B vitamins, and, sometimes, anticonvulsants.

When is inpatient treatment needed? One analysis indicated that an inpatient approach is probably best for people with few sources of social support who are living in environments that encourage the alcohol abuse, especially individuals with serious psychological problems in addition to their substance abuse (Finney & Moos, 1998).

Biological Treatments

Some problem drinkers who are in treatment, inpatient or outpatient, take disulfiram, or Antabuse, a drug that discourages drinking by causing violent vomiting if alcohol is ingested. It blocks the metabolism of alcohol so that noxious byproducts are created. Adherence to an Antabuse regimen can be a problem. The drinker must already be committed to change. If an alcohol abuser is able or willing to take the drug every morning as prescribed, the chances are good that drinking will lessen because of the negative consequences of imbibing (Sisson & Azrin, 1989). However, in a large, multicentre study with placebo controls, Antabuse showed no specific benefit and dropout rates were as high as 80 percent (Fuller, 1988; Fuller et al., 1986). Antabuse can also cause serious side effects, such as inflammation of nerve tissue (Moss, 1990).

Biological treatments are best viewed as adjunctive; that is, they may offer some benefit when combined with a psychological intervention. Drugs such as naltrexone and naloxone are more effective than a placebo in reducing drinking and add to overall treatment effectiveness when combined with cognitive-behavioural therapy (Volpicelli et al., 1995, 1997; Ward et al., 1998). Like many other drug treatments we have discussed, the benefits of naltrexone continue only for as long as the person continues to take it and long-lasting compliance with the treatment is difficult to achieve (O'Malley et al., 1996). The serotonin agonist buspirone is also of some therapeutic value (Kranzler et al., 1994). Clonidine, which reduces noradrenergic activity in the brain, also has some value in reducing withdrawal effects from several drugs, including alcohol, opiates, and nicotine (Baumgartner & Rowen, 1987).

The use of drugs to treat alcohol-abusing patients carries some risk because liver function is often impaired in the patient and, therefore, the metabolism of the prescribed drug in the liver can be adversely affected, leading to undesirable side effects (Klerman et al., 1994).

Alcoholics Anonymous

Alcoholics Anonymous (AA) is the largest and most widely known self-help group in the world. It was founded in 1935 in the United States by two recovered alcoholics. It currently has about 70,000 chapters in more than 100 other countries throughout the world. Consistent with the experiences of David Adams Richards, even though relatively few Canadians seek help, of those that do, the majority (60 percent) seek help from Canadian chapters of AA (Ogborne & DeWit, 1999). An AA chapter runs regular and frequent meetings at which newcomers rise to announce that they are

Alcoholics Anonymous is the largest self-help group in the world. At their regular meetings, newcomers rise to announce their addiction and receive advice and support from others.

alcoholics, and older, sober members give testimonials, relating the stories of their problem drinking and indicating how their lives are better now. The group provides emotional support, understanding, and close counselling for the problem drinker as well as a social life to relieve isolation. Members are urged to call on one another around-the-clock when they need companionship and encouragement not to relapse into drink. About 70 percent of Americans who have ever been treated for alcohol abuse have attended at least one AA meeting. Programs modelled after AA are available for other substance abusers—for example, Cocaine Anonymous and Marijuana Anonymous. There are even similar 12-step programs called Overeaters Anonymous and Gamblers Anonymous.

The belief is instilled in each AA member that alcohol abuse is a disease that can never be cured, so continuing vigilance is necessary to resist taking even a single drink lest uncontrollable drinking begin all over again. The basic tenet of AA was articulated vividly in the classic film *Lost Weekend*, for which Ray Milland won an Oscar for best actor. In one scene, his brother confronts him about his denial of the seriousness of his drinking problem: "Don't you ever learn that with you it's like stepping off a roof and expecting to fall just one floor?" The spiritual aspect of AA is apparent in the 12 steps of AA shown in Table 12.1, and there is evidence that belief in this philosophy is important for achieving abstinence (Gilbert, 1991).

Two related self-help groups have developed from AA. The relatives of problem drinkers meet in Al-Anon Family Groups for mutual support in dealing with their family members and in realizing that they cannot make them change their ways. Similarly, Alateen is for the children of alcohol abusers, who also require support and understanding to help them overcome the sense that they are in some way responsible for their parents' problems and responsible also for changing them. Other self-help groups do not have the religious overtones of AA, relying instead on social support, reassurance, encouragement, and suggestions for leading a life without alcohol. People often see mental health professionals while attending self-help meetings.

The claims made by AA about the effectiveness of its treatment have been empirically tested. Although AA does seem to confer significant benefits (Ouimette, Finney, & Moos, 1997), it has high dropout rates, and the dropouts are not always factored into the results. In addition, there is only limited long-term follow-up of AA clients. Results from the best-controlled study to date are mixed (Walsh & Hingson, 1991). It does appear that many people who choose AA and stay with it for more than three months—a select group, to be sure—remain abstinent for at least a few years (Emrick et al., 1993). The needs of such people seem to be met by the fellowship, support, and religious overtones of AA. For them, it becomes a way of life; members often attend meetings regularly for many years, as often as four times a week. As with other forms of intervention, it remains to be determined for whom this particular mode is best suited.

Canadian Perspectives 12.2 describes an Aboriginal treatment centre—Poundmaker's Lodge—that combines the goals of AA with Native values that emphasize cultural awareness.

Table 12.1

Twelve Suggested Steps of Alcoholics Anonymous

1. We admitted we were powerless over alcohol—that our lives had become unmanageable.
2. Came to believe that a power greater than ourselves could restore us to sanity.
3. Made a decision to turn our will and our lives over to the care of God as we understood Him.
4. Made a searching and fearless moral inventory of ourselves.
5. Admitted to God, to ourselves, and to another human being the exact nature of our wrongs.
6. Were entirely ready to have God remove all these defects of character.
7. Humbly asked Him to remove our shortcomings.
8. Made a list of all persons we had harmed, and became willing to make amends to them all.
9. Made direct amends to such people wherever possible, except when to do so would injure them or others.
10. Continued to take personal inventory and, when we were wrong, promptly admitted it.
11. Sought through prayer and meditation to improve our conscious contact with God as we understood Him, praying only for knowledge of His will for us and the power to carry that out.
12. Having had a spiritual awakening as the result of these steps, we tried to carry this message to alcoholics and to practice these principles in all our affairs.

Source: The Twelve Steps and Twelve Traditions. Copyright © 1952 by Alcoholics Anonymous World Services, Inc. Reprinted with permission of Alcoholics Anonymous World Services, Inc

Canadian Perspectives/12.2

Poundmaker's Lodge

"To join Poundmaker/Nechi requires a commitment to our mission against alcohol and drug use—in body as well as in spirit. Since total abstinence is the only solution for the Native client, staff cannot just 'talk the talk'; they must also 'walk the walk.'"
—From the Mission Statement of Poundmaker's Lodge.

Many drug abuse programs in Canada are designed for and often run by Aboriginal people. Poundmaker's Lodge (named after a 19th-century Native leader), located outside of Edmonton, Alberta, is an excellent example of a Native alcohol, drug, and gambling treatment centre. The non-profit centre, founded in 1973 and managed by the Aboriginal people themselves, has the oldest Aboriginal-oriented inpatient (54-bed, 28-day) alcoholism program in Canada. In addition, it operates an outpatient centre, an adolescent treatment program, and a prison program. Poundmaker's Lodge is also an agent for positive initiatives in the Native community (e.g., education, self-esteem building, increasing cultural awareness, and so forth).

At Poundmaker's Lodge, the facilities are designed to closely resemble nature, thereby providing inspiration to the clients.

Philosophy and Structure

Consistent with many traditional treatment approaches, the centre's overall philosophy is simple: addiction is viewed as a disease and complete abstinence is the goal. Also, in keeping with Native values, it is crucial to treat the entire person—spiritual, mental, emotional, and physical. The assumption is that the Aboriginal client will respond best to an approach that embraces both Aboriginal cultural awareness and the philosophy of Alcoholics Anonymous or Narcotics Anonymous (NA): "At Poundmaker's Lodge, the setting, the facility, the staff, and the treatment model harmonize to create an environment for recovery."

Treatment staff includes elders, two treatment directors, counsellors, psychologists, and medical care. An executive director manages the 50-member treatment and support staff, as well as trainees and consulting professionals. Many of the staff have a unique common bond—personal experience with the addictions they are treating. The programs were founded on the principle that substance abusers are treated most effectively by "sober" people who have been trained to address problems of abuse.

The core structure of all programs is composed of four components: education, skills development, counselling, and Native culture. In addition to group therapy sessions, other treatment activities are considered essential for a comprehensive, effective experience (e.g., "community-building activities that allow people to share fun as well as sadness"). The cultural component includes sweat lodge and pipe ceremonies, sweetgrass ceremonies, and sessions by an in-residence elder. The burning of sweetgrass, for example, is intended to cleanse the body and mind (a process called "smudging"). An annual powwow attracts over 5,000 "sober" people for a three-day event. The following description of the Adolescent Treatment Centre provides an example of the way the core structure is implemented.

ADOLESCENT TREATMENT CENTRE

Poundmaker's Adolescent Treatment Centre provides an intensive 90-day treatment program for Aboriginal children between 12 and 17 years old. It has been given "Open Custody" status, which allows Alberta Justice to refer young offenders. However, it is a treatment centre, not a correctional institution. The program's goals include stopping the children's drug consumption; detoxifying them from their addictive subculture; integrating them back into families and communities; dealing with physical and mental health; and developing strategies for relapse prevention.

The centre provides a comprehensive, structured program that includes several components: addictions treatment; school education; family program; Native culture/spiritual values; follow-up and aftercare; medical care; recreational activities; and behavioural management.

Although all of these components are probably very important, we believe that the family program is especially vital. Families are invited to attend a one-week program to show support for their child and to learn the consequences of substance abuse. Perhaps most important, they are taught how to resolve conflicts, practise effective communication and problem-solving skills, and work together as a family unit to overcome problems.

OUTCOMES

Poundmaker's Lodge claims that its programs have helped thousands of Aboriginal people overcome their alcohol and drug problems and rebuild their lives. Although there is no doubt that the centre has helped many Aboriginal people, it is very difficult to determine accurately the long-term effects of its programs, much less determine the "active" components of its programs. In some cases, it is clear that success has been short-lived. For example, many of the children from Davis Inlet have been taken thousands of kilometres away from their community and families to Poundmaker's Lodge for treatment of their inhalant and alcohol abuse. Unfortunately, it is difficult to implement the family program when the entire family cannot be physically present. Despite some success, when the children are returned home to the same circumstances that contributed to their problems in the first place, many go back to a life of substance abuse, suicidal despair, behavioural problems, and so forth. As a result of recent media attention, children have been taken to traditional treatment centres in St. John's, despite resistance from families and Native leaders. The Innu of Labrador would prefer to have Aboriginal treatment facilities, such as Poundmaker's Lodge, in their own communities.

Primary Source: Adapted from "Poundmaker's Lodge." (January 21, 2001). [On-line]. Available: http://poundmaker.org

Thinking Critically

1. Do you think that the programs at Poundmaker's Lodge would be more successful if they incorporated, in some cases, a philosophically different approach that allowed for the possibility of controlled drinking or moderation in drinking? Would the guided self-change approach described in Canadian Clinic Focus 12.1 or Marlatt's harm reduction therapy (Canadian Contributions 12.1) increase the probability of success?
2. After you have read about the various approaches to treating drug abuse presented in this chapter, design a treatment program that you believe would lead to more successful treatment of substance abuse, especially the use of inhalants and alcohol in Aboriginal children.
3. Is it realistic to assume that the Poundmaker's Lodge program can have lasting success when (1) it is not always feasible to work with all of the family members and (2) the children are typically returned to the same social, psychological, cultural, and economic environment that contributed to the development of the children's problems in the first place?

COUPLES AND FAMILY THERAPY

Alcohol severely disrupts the lives of problem drinkers. For this reason, many live fairly solitary lives. Moreover when problem drinkers do remain married or in some other close relationship, they often physically abuse members of their families (O'Farrell & Murphy, 1995; Wekerle & Wall, 2001).

This intertwining of alcohol abuse and family conflict (the cause-effect relationship goes both ways [O'Farrell, 1993]) has led to the use of various kinds of couples and family therapy to help the drinker abstain or control his or her excessive drinking. Behaviourally oriented marital or couples therapy has been found to achieve some reductions in problem drinking as well as some improvement in couples' distress generally (e.g., McCrady & Epstein, 1995). A focus of this therapy is involving the spouse in helping the drinker take his or her Antabuse on a regular basis.

The need to consider drinking problems from a couples perspective is illustrated by studies on drinking behaviour conducted in Quebec (Demers, Bisson, & Palluy, 1999) and in Ontario (Graham & Braun, 1999). These studies have replicated previous findings suggesting that there is a substantial concordance between husbands and wives in terms of their frequency of drinking and overall amount consumed, especially among older couples (Graham & Braun, 1999); that is, husbands who drink excessively often have wives who also drink to excess. Possible reasons for this concordance include shared life experiences, the impact of the husband's drinking on the wife, and the tendency for people with similar drinking patterns to get married (Leonard & Eiden, 1999). When such situations exist, a joint focus on the drinking of both partners is essential.

The importance of a partner's support in the problem drinker's effort to deal with life's stresses is not to be underestimated. But also not to be underestimated is the difficulty of maintaining moderate drinking or abstinence beyond the one- and two-year follow-ups regardless of the mode of marital intervention and its short-term positive effects (Alexander et al., 1994; Baucom et al., 1998).

COGNITIVE AND BEHAVIOURAL TREATMENT

Behavioural and cognitive-behavioural researchers have been studying the treatment of alcohol abuse for many years. Indeed, one of the earliest articles on behaviour therapy concerned aversive conditioning as a treatment for alcoholism (Kantorovich, 1930). In general, cognitive and behavioural therapies represent the most effective psychological treatments for alcohol abuse (Finney & Moos, 1998).

Aversion Therapy In aversion therapy, problem drinkers are shocked or made nauseous while looking at, reaching for, or beginning to drink alcohol. In one procedure, called covert sensitization (Cautela, 1966), problem drinkers are instructed to imagine being made violently and disgustingly sick by their drinking.

Despite some evidence that aversion therapy may slightly enhance the effectiveness of inpatient treatment (Smith, Frawley, & Polissar, 1991), some well-known behaviour therapists discourage its use because it lacks empirical support and causes great discomfort (e.g., Wilson, 1991). Aversion therapy, if used at all, seems best implemented in the context of broad programs that attend to the patient's particular life circumstances—for example, marital conflict, social fears, and other factors associated with problem drinking (Tucker, Vuchinich, & Downey, 1992).

Contingency-Management Therapy Contingency-management therapy (a term often used interchangeably with operant conditioning) for alcohol abuse involves teaching patients and those close to them to reinforce behaviours inconsistent with drinking—for example, taking Antabuse and avoiding situations associated with past drinking. This therapy also includes teaching job-hunting and social skills as well as assertiveness training for refusing drinks. Socially isolated individuals are encouraged and helped to establish contacts with other people who are not associated with drinking. As noted earlier, this approach includes couples therapy. Often referred to as the community-reinforcement approach, contingency-management therapy has generated very promising results (Azrin et al., 1982; Baucom et al., 1998; Sisson & Azrin, 1989).

A strategy that is sometimes termed behavioural self-control training (Tucker et al., 1992) builds on the work just described. This approach emphasizes patient control and includes one or more of the following:

- **stimulus control**, whereby one narrows the situations in which one allows oneself to drink (e.g., with others on a special occasion)
- **modification of the topography of drinking** (e.g., having only mixed drinks and taking small sips rather than gulps)
- **reinforcing abstinence** (e.g., allowing oneself a nonalcoholic treat if one resists the urge to drink)

An issue not formally addressed by advocates of behavioural self-control training is how to get the person to abide by restrictions and conditions that, if implemented, will reduce or eliminate drinking. In other words, the challenge with such therapies seems not so much to discover the means necessary to control drinking as to get the alcohol abuser to employ these tools without constant external supervision and control. There is evidence for the general effectiveness of this approach (Hester & Miller, 1989), some of it in the context of controlled-drinking programs, to which we turn now.

Moderation in Drinking Until recently, it was generally agreed that alcohol abusers had to abstain completely if they were to be cured, for they were believed to have no control over imbibing once they had taken that first drink. Although this continues to be the belief of AA, this assumption has been called into question by research mentioned earlier indicating that drinkers' beliefs about themselves and alcohol may be as important as the physiological addiction to the drug itself. Considering the difficulty in society of avoiding alcohol altogether, it may even be preferable to teach the problem drinker to imbibe with moderation. A drinker's self-esteem will certainly benefit from being able to control a problem and from feeling in charge.

Controlled drinking in alcohol treatment was introduced by the Sobells while they were located at the Addiction Research Foundation in Toronto (see Sobell & Sobell, 1993). This approach is currently much more widely accepted in Canada and Europe than in the United States. Controlled drinking refers to a moderate pattern of alcohol consumption that avoids the extremes of total abstinence and inebriation. The results of the Sobells' initial treatment program suggested that at least some alcohol abusers can learn to control their drinking and improve other aspects of their lives as well (Sobell & Sobell, 1976). Problem drinkers attempting to control their drinking were given shocks when they chose straight liquor rather than mixed drinks, gulped their drinks down too fast, or took large swallows rather than sips. They also received problem-solving and assertiveness training, watched videotapes of themselves inebriated, and identified the situations that precipitated their drinking so that they could settle on a less self-destructive course of action. Their improvement was greater than that of alcohol abusers who tried for total abstinence and were given shocks for any drinking at all.

Patients in contemporary controlled-drinking treatment programs are taught to respond adaptively to situations in which they might otherwise drink excessively. They learn various social skills to help them resist pressures to drink; they receive assertiveness, relaxation, and stress-management training, sometimes including biofeedback and meditation; and they are encouraged to exercise and maintain a healthy diet.

Patients are also taught—or more precisely, are encouraged to believe—that a lapse will not inevitably precipitate a total relapse and should be regarded as a learning experience rather than as a sign that the battle is lost, a marked contrast from the AA perspective (Marlatt & Gordon, 1985). This noncatastrophizing approach to relapse after therapy—falling off the wagon—is important because the overwhelming majority of problem drinkers who become abstinent do experience a relapse over a four-year period (Polich, Armor, & Braiker, 1980). In this therapy, alcohol abusers examine sources of stress in their work, family, and relationships so that they can become active and responsible in anticipating and resisting situations that might tempt excessive drinking (Marlatt, 1983; Sobell, Toneatto, &

Sobell, 1990). The controlled-drinking approach has now been supplemented by the *guided self-change approach*, which was developed in Toronto. This approach is the subject of Canadian Clinic Focus 12.1.

Harm reduction therapy is another alternative to an approach that focuses on complete abstinence. The principles of harm reduction therapy are outlined in Canadian Contributions 12.1.

Canadian Clinic Focus/12.1

The Addiction Research Foundation and Guided Self-Change

Linda and Mark Sobell's current approach to breaking addiction was developed while they were based in Toronto at the Addiction Research Foundation (ARF). ARF is now part of the Centre for Addiction and Mental Health (CAMH) in Toronto. The Sobells' approach to teaching moderation to problem drinkers is primarily cognitive. Their basic assumption is that people have more potential control over their immoderate drinking than they typically believe and that heightened awareness of the costs of drinking to excess as well as of the benefits of abstaining or cutting down can be of material help. Termed guided self-change, this outpatient approach emphasizes personal responsibility and control.

A major impetus of the guided self-change focus is the recognition that many drinkers are able to stop drinking without seeking clinical treatment. For instance, a CAMH study of people who had recovered from alcohol abuse or alcohol dependence found that 50 percent of the respondents had done so without accessing formal sources of help or treatment (Cunningham, Lin, Ross, & Walsh, 2000). An earlier Canadian survey found that over three-quarters of problem drinkers who had broken their habit for at least a year had not sought treatment (Sobell, Cunningham, & Sobell, 1996). A reasonable assumption is that some form of guided self-change took place with these individuals. Surprisingly, according to a survey conducted with five different groups, including general members of the community visiting the Ontario Science Centre, most people do not know about the role played by guided self-change (Cunningham, Sobell, & Sobell, 1998). It is important that they be made aware of this factor.

So what is involved in guided self-change? The Guided Self-Change Program (GSCP; Addiction Research Foundation, 1994) is an early intervention program designed for people with mild to moderate drinking problems. As stated in the GSCP manual, the goals of the program are to (1) help clients help themselves; (2) allow clients to make informed choices; (3) teach a general problem-solving approach; (4) strengthen client motivation and commitment to change; and (5) encourage self-reliance, empowerment, and personal competence.

The features of the GSCP include a clinical assessment with personalized feedback, four sessions with a therapist, a focus on goal setting and self-monitoring, as well as reading and homework exercises. The client is also assisted in identifying high-risk situations, and the therapist is available for additional support if needed after the final treatment session.

Problem drinkers typically overestimate how heavily other people drink. Providing accurate information on the drinking patterns of others—social comparison—is part of this treatment approach. Patients are encouraged to view themselves, not as victims of an addictive disease, but as basically healthy people who have been making unwise, often self-destructive choices about how to deal with life's inevitable stresses.

The therapist is empathic and supportive while he or she makes the problem drinker aware of the negative aspects of excessive drinking that the person may have been overlooking. For example, most problem drinkers don't calculate the expense of drinking to excess (the cost of drinking at home can easily run to more than $2,000 a year; the cost of drinking in a bar or restaurant is double or triple that amount) or the amount of weight gain attributable to alcohol. They also seldom try to identify seemingly minor behavioural changes that can help them drink less, such as finding a new route home that does not take them by a bar they have been frequenting. Sometimes, getting problem drinkers to delay 20 minutes before taking a second or third drink can help them reflect on the costs versus the benefits of drinking to excess. Evidence supports the effectiveness of this approach in helping problem drinkers moderate their intake and otherwise improve their lives (Sobell & Sobell, 1993).

Comment

Available research indicates that the Guided Self-Change Program is relatively effective, especially in view of the difficulties in effecting significant and lasting reductions in excessive drinking in problem drinkers. The most recent published study (Sobell, Sobell, & Leo, 2000) found results in keeping with previous reports (e.g., Sobell & Sobell, 1998)—about a 50 percent reduction in problem drinking. Perhaps most importantly, the greatest improvement in drinking behaviour was found among the heavier drinkers rather than among those engaged in lower-risk, moderate drinking. Despite these initial positive results, a number of issues and questions still need to be addressed, including (1) determining the "active" ingredients in the Guided Self-Change Program; (2) improving the effectiveness of the program; (3) conducting more full-scale evaluations in which guided self-change is compared to and/or combined with other treatment programs and appropriate control conditions; (4) assessing long-term outcome; and (5) determining the effectiveness of the strategy with different cultural groups.

Canadian Contributions/12.1

G. Alan Marlatt and Harm Reduction Therapy

G. Alan Marlatt has outlined harm reduction therapy as an alternative to treatments stemming from the medical model.

G. Alan Marlatt, a Canadian psychologist, is currently the director of the Addictive Behaviors Research Center at the University of Washington in Seattle. He has had a substantial impact on the assessment and treatment of addictions, and his work has been widely recognized. For instance, in 1990 he was given the Jellinek Memorial Award for outstanding contributions to knowledge in the field of alcohol studies. He has also been given the Senior Scientist Award from the U.S. National Institute of Alcohol Abuse and Alcoholism. In 1996 Marlatt was appointed as a member of the U.S. National Advisory Council on Drug Abuse.

Marlatt's research on employing brief interventions to help control and reduce binge drinking among students was discussed earlier. His harm reduction therapy (HRT) is having an increasing impact as a general approach that can be used to treat a variety of high-risk behaviours, including addictions. The basic tenets of HRT are discussed below.

- First, contrary to moral/criminal models or disease models of drug use, addiction is not a crime deserving of punishment. Rather, it is an adjustment problem that needs intervention.
- Second, HRT recognizes that abstinence is an ideal outcome, but it is not the only outcome, especially for those beginning treatment. It is quite acceptable to strive for outcomes that involve the reduction of harm rather than striving in an all-or-none fashion to eliminate harm altogether. HRT recognizes that striving for more extreme goals may be self-defeating.
- Third, HRT is a bottom-up approach that is more in line with the needs of the addict and is focused on reducing their level of suffering. It contrasts with the top-down approach favoured by those who make drug policy.
- Fourth, because HRT does not require complete abstinence, more people should be able to gain access to what Marlatt refers to as "low-threshold" services. Marlatt (1999) has suggested that the difference is reflected in the phrase "We'll meet you where you are" (p. 55)—not "where you should be."
- Finally, Marlatt (1999) argues that HRT is based on the principle of "compassionate pragmatism" rather than on "moralistic idealism." Specifically, harm reduction is non-judgmental and acknowledges the realistic struggles of people as they attempt to manage their everyday affairs.

Harm reduction involves a number of goals: to stabilize the maladaptive behaviour and prevent further harm; to help the patient develop an awareness of high-risk behaviours; and to give the patient coping training in how to deal with high-risk situations. Another important goal is to facilitate health-promoting and risk-reducing strategies.

Marlatt's Alcohol Skills Training Program (ASTP) for students incorporates the harm reduction model. The ASTP is based on the view that drinking is normal behaviour for students and that interventions may be needed; thus, a focus on moderation rather than abstinence is more realistic. Students participate in eight sessions over several weeks. The initial sessions focus on helping student become more aware of alcohol's impact and learning practical things such as how to calculate their own blood-alcohol levels. Subsequent sessions challenge overly positive beliefs about the benefits of drinking. Students also learn specific skills and role-play so that they will know how to deal with stressful situations without turning to alcohol.

HRT can be controversial, as some of the things that are done to reduce initial harm may involve initiatives that are not accepted by everyone. These could include such things as encouraging controlled drinking or the moderate (as opposed to extensive) use of amphetamines or setting up needle-exchange programs to limit additional health risks. Marlatt has acknowledged that his approach has been criticized for "enabling" drug use (see Marlatt, Blume, & Parks, 2001). Another criticism is that HRT does not have the goal of abstinence. Marlatt et al. (2001), however, have noted that abstinence is a goal at the endpoint of the continuum once the addicted individual starts to improve.

According to Marlatt and Witkiewitz (2002), empirical research shows that harm reduction is at least as effective as abstinence-oriented approaches in reducing alcohol consumption and alcohol-related consequences. Moreover, Marlatt, a firm believer in the importance of education, maintains that the basic tenets of harm reduction therapy can be taught in educational programs. High school and university students respond well to this approach. If they are heavy drinkers, for example, they can adopt the goal of drinking less and in a more responsible manner rather than strive for absolute abstinence. According to

Marlatt et al. (2001), one advantage that HRT has over other treatment approaches is that with HRT a positive alliance between the client and therapist is more easily forged, since the realistic goals of HRT are more in keeping with the needs of the client.

In Canada, the harm reduction debate reached a peak during the 2003 mayoral election in Vancouver, when successful candidate Larry Campbell proposed the use of a harm reduction model as a way of combating rampant drug use in downtown Vancouver. The overall strategy, known as the Four Pillars Drug Strategy, includes the creation of supervised drug-injection sites. According to the City of Vancouver, these sites would be a "vital part of a harm reduction plan to reduce overdose and overdose deaths and the spread of HIV/AIDS and hepatitis C, and to provide access to primary health care to drug users in Vancouver." The strategy's four pillars are harm reduction, prevention, treatment, and law enforcement. Hopefully, this innovative approach will prove to be successful.

CLINICAL CONSIDERATIONS IN TREATING ALCOHOL ABUSE

Many attempts to treat problem drinking are impeded by the therapist's often unstated assumption that all people who drink to excess do so for the same reasons. From what we have examined thus far in this chapter, we know that this assumption is unlikely to be correct.

A comprehensive clinical assessment considers what place drinking occupies in the person's life (Tucker et al., 1992). A woman in a desperately unhappy marriage, with time on her hands now that her children are in school, may seek the numbing effects of alcohol to help pass the time and avoid facing life's dilemmas. Making the taste of alcohol unpleasant for this patient by pairing it with shock or a drug that induces vomiting seems neither sensible nor adequate. The therapist should concentrate on the marital and family problems and try to reduce the psychological pain that permeates the patient's existence. She will also need help in tolerating the withdrawal symptoms that come with reduced consumption. Without alcohol as a reliable anesthetic, she will need to mobilize other resources to confront her hitherto-avoided problems. Social skills training and rewarding activities outside the home may help her do so.

We have seen that problem drinking is sometimes associated with other mental disorders, in particular anxiety disorders, mood disorders, and psychopathy. Therapists of all orientations have to recognize that depression is often comorbid with alcohol abuse and that suicide is also a risk. The clinician must therefore conduct a broad-spectrum assessment of the patient's problem.

Alcohol researchers recognize that different kinds of drinkers may require different treatment approaches (Mattson et al., 1994). The challenge is to determine which factors in the drinkers should be aligned with which factors in treatment. Client-treatment matching, or what the psychotherapy literature describes as aptitude-treatment interaction (ATI), has been cited by the Institute of Medicine (1990a) as a critical issue in the development of better interventions for problem drinking. A large-scale effort to address the question was Project Match, a multi-site clinical trial designed to test the hypothesis that certain kinds of treatments are good matches for certain kinds of problem drinkers. This project is described in Focus on Discovery 12.3.

focus on discovery/12.3

Matching Patient to Treatment—Project Match

For many years, both practitioners and researchers have understood the importance of employing treatments that are suitable for particular patients. This notion goes beyond the question of the general kind of therapy best suited for a particular kind of problem; rather, it involves an approach called *aptitude-treatment interaction* (ATI), which focuses on characteristics of patients with the same disorder that might make them more suitable candidates for one generally effective treatment than for another.

The question of matching patient to treatment was tested in Project Match, a large, eight-year, multi-site study on alcohol abuse (Project Match Research Group, 1997). This study is controversial in professional circles because it failed to find what it was looking for, namely, a way to match particular kinds of alcoholic patients with specific interventions.

Ten matching variables, among them severity of alcohol dependency, severity of cognitive impairment, motivation to change, severity of psychological disturbance (referred to as "psychiatric severity"), support from one's social milieu for drinking, and sociopathic tendencies, were chosen, having been found in previous research to be associated with outcomes of intervention. There were three treatments:

- The 12-step facilitation treatment (TSF) was designed to convert patients to the AA view of alcoholism as an incurable but manageable disease and to encourage their involvement in AA.
- The motivational-enhancement therapy (MET), based on William Miller's approach (Miller et al., 1992), attempted to

mobilize patients' own resources to reduce drinking. Part of this intervention involved highlighting the ways in which current maladaptive behaviour was interfering with their valued goals.

- A cognitive-behavioural coping-skills therapy (CBT) presented to patients the idea that drinking is functionally related to problems in their lives; this treatment taught patients skills to help them cope with situations that trigger drinking or for preventing relapse.

Some of the predicted interactions were that drinkers under heavy pressure to stop would do best with the 12-step facilitation therapy; those with psychological problems would do best with the cognitive therapy; and those with low motivation to change would do best with the motivational-enhancement therapy.

All treatments were carefully administered in individual sessions by trained therapists over a 12-week period. The principal dependent (outcome) measures were percentage of days abstinent and drinks per drinking day during a one-year posttreatment assessment period. Figure 12.3 portrays the main results of this study. Significant within-group improvement was observed—all treatments were very helpful on average, consistent with a subsequent study by Ouimette et al. (1997). However, interactions between treatments and matching variables (the main purpose of the study) were not found except for the interaction involving psychiatric severity. Patients in better psychological shape had more abstinent days after the 12-step facilitation program than did patients in the cognitive-behavioural condition, although patients in worse psychological condition did not fare differently across the three treatments.

According to Marlatt (1999), one shortcoming of the Project Match study as a treatment efficacy study is that it did not include a no-treatment, assessment-only control group. The extensive assessment sessions undergone by the participants may have had a positive influence on their behaviour, independent of treatment. Another criticism of Project Match raised by Canadian researchers (Conrod et al., 2000) is that the therapies chosen were not precise enough and were not tailored to the specific therapy needs of the individual clients. Conrod et al. (2000) conducted their own study and showed that personality-specific motivational and coping-skills training was substantially more effective than a motivational control intervention in reducing the frequency and severity of alcohol and drug use. They concluded that matching strategies that link client personality characteristics and treatments have substantial promise.

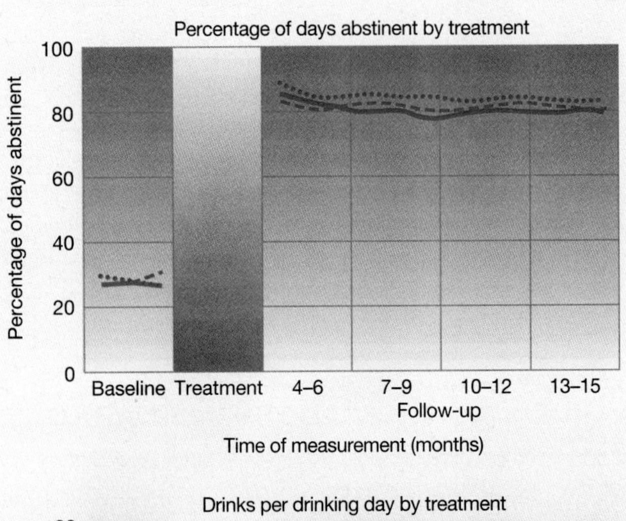

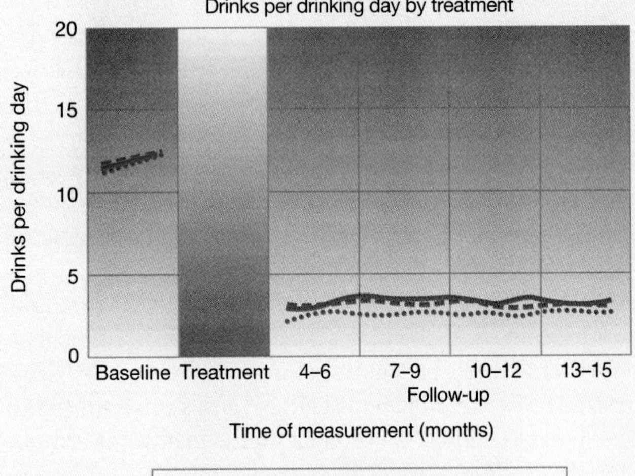

Figure 12.3 Monthly percentage of days abstinent and drinks per drinking day (DDD) for baseline (averaged over three months prior to treatment) and for each month of the posttreatment period (months 1–15).

It is doubtful that a single event, even a dramatic one, can bring about the kind of profound changes necessary to wean a person from an addiction. It is more probable that successful abstinence, whether resulting from treatment or not, relies on a confluence of many life events and forces that can support the recovering alcoholic's efforts to lead a life without substance abuse. Whatever combination of factors helps problem drinkers become abstinent or controlled drinkers, a key element is social support for their efforts from family, friends, work, or self-help groups such as AA (McCrady, 1985).

THERAPY FOR THE USE OF ILLICIT DRUGS

Some factors involved in treatment for alcohol abuse are relevant also to treatment for addiction to illegal drugs. We focus here on issues that pertain to those who abuse illicit drugs.

People turn to drugs for many reasons, and even though in most instances drug use becomes controlled primarily by a physical addiction, the entire pattern of an addict's existence is bound to be affected by the drug and must therefore be addressed in any treatment. As seen in our earlier discussion of conditioning theory of tolerance, one of the chief difficulties of maintaining abstinence is the negative influence of many stimuli on the recovering addict. The presence of needles, neighbourhoods, and people with whom a person used to take drugs can elicit a craving for the substance (Wikler, 1980).

Central to the treatment of people who use addicting drugs, such as heroin and cocaine, is detoxification—withdrawal from the drug itself. Heroin-withdrawal reactions range from relatively mild bouts of anxiety, nausea, and restlessness for several days to more severe and frightening bouts of delirium and panic anxiety, depending primarily on the purity of the heroin that the individual has been using. Someone high on amphetamines can be brought down by appropriate dosages of one of the phenothiazines, a class of drugs used to treat schizophrenia, although it is important to remember that the person may also have been using other drugs in conjunction with amphetamines. Withdrawal reactions from barbiturates are especially severe, even life-threatening, beginning about 24 hours after the last dose and peaking two or three days later. They usually abate by the end of the first week but may last for a month if large doses were taken. Withdrawal from barbiturates is best undertaken gradually, not cold turkey (a term that derives from the goosebumps that occur during withdrawal, making the person's skin resemble that of a plucked turkey), and should take place under close medical supervision.

Detoxification is the first way in which therapists try to help an addict or drug abuser, and it may be the easiest part of the rehabilitation process. Enabling the drug user to function without drugs after detoxification is an arduous task that promises more disappointment and sadness than success for both helper and client. A variety of approaches are available, both biological and psychological.

BIOLOGICAL TREATMENTS

Two widely used drug-therapy programs for heroin addiction involve the administration of **heroin substitutes**, drugs chemically similar to heroin that can replace the body's craving for it, or **heroin antagonists**, drugs that prevent the user from experiencing the heroin high. The first category includes **methadone**, levomethadyl acetate, and bupreophine, synthetic narcotics designed to take the place of heroin. Since these drugs are themselves addicting, successful treatment essentially converts the heroin addict into someone who is addicted to a different substance. This conversion occurs because these synthetic narcotics are **cross-dependent** with heroin; that is, by acting on the same central nervous system receptors, they become a substitute for the original dependency. Of course, methadone used as described here is legal, whereas heroin is not.

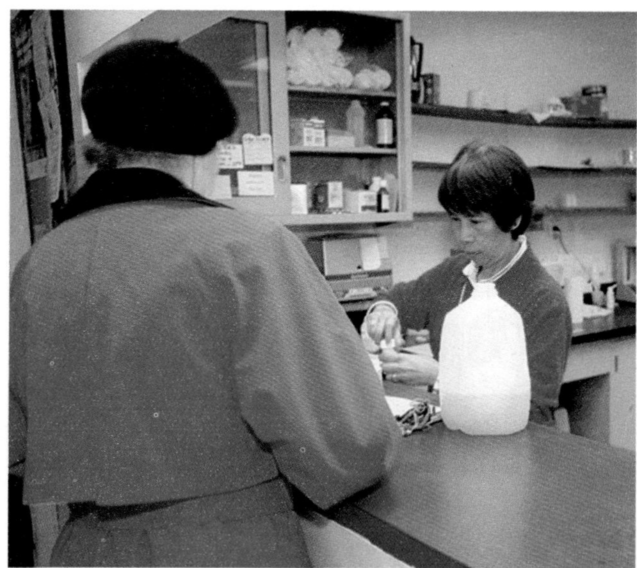

Methadone is a synthetic narcotic substitute. Former heroin addicts come to clinics each day and swallow their dose.

Abrupt discontinuation of methadone results in its own pattern of withdrawal reactions. Because these reactions are less severe than those of heroin, methadone can wean the addict altogether from drug dependence (Strain et al., 1999).

For treatment with heroin substitutes, the addict must go to a clinic and swallow the drug in the presence of a staff member, once a day for methadone and three times a week for levomethadyl acetate and bupreophine. Some users under treatment are able to hold jobs, commit no crimes, and refrain from using other illicit drugs (Cooper et al., 1983; Eissenberg et al., 1997), but many users are unable to do so (Condelli et al., 1991). The effectiveness of methadone treatment is improved if combined with regular psychological counselling (Ball & Ross, 1991).

Preexisting behavioural patterns and life circumstances play a role in how the individual will react to methadone treatment. Since methadone does not provide a euphoric high, many addicts will return to heroin if it becomes available to them. Many people drop out of methadone programs in part because of side effects, such as insomnia, constipation, excessive sweating, and diminished sexual functioning. Yet in this era of AIDS and the transmission of the human immunodeficiency virus through shared needles, this treatment has a big advantage because methadone can be swallowed.

In treatment with the opiate antagonists cyclazocine and naloxone, addicts are first gradually weaned from heroin. They then receive increasing dosages of one of these drugs and are thereby prevented from experiencing any high should they later take heroin. These drugs have great affinity for the receptors to which opiates usually bind; their molecules occupy the receptors without stimulating them, leaving heroin molecules with no place to go. As with methadone, however, addicts must make frequent and regular visits to a clinic, and this takes motivation and responsibility on their part. In addition, addicts do not lose the craving for heroin for some time. Thus, patient compliance with therapy involving opiate antagonists is very poor, and the overall outcomes are only fair (Ginzburg, 1986; Goldstein, 1994).

The search is now on for drugs that will ease the symptoms of withdrawal and perhaps attack the physical basis of cocaine addiction. Although some favourable results with antidepressants were reported earlier, findings from two more recent and better-controlled studies were decidedly less positive. In the first of two similarly conducted double-blind experiments, use of the tricyclic desipramine (Norpramine) by cocaine abusers, as compared with a placebo, did not lead to decreased use of cocaine at the end of eight weeks of treatment (Kosten et al., 1992). The second study found that cocaine use was significantly greater than that of placebo patients at three- and six-month follow-ups after a 12-week treatment period (Arndt et al., 1992). Similarly, while imipramine (Tofranil) helped alleviate depression in cocaine abusers who were depressed, it did not help the patients achieve abstinence from cocaine (Nunes et al., 1998). On the other hand, desipramine fared better in another study, which will be discussed shortly (Carroll, Rounsaville, & Gordon, 1994).

Clonidine, an antihypertensive medication, may ease withdrawal from a variety of addicting drugs, including cocaine (Baumgartner & Rowen, 1987). Bromocriptine also shows some promise in reducing craving, perhaps by reversing the depletion of dopamine that is believed to underlie cocaine's addicting properties (Moss, 1990).

Psychological Treatments

Drug abuse is sometimes treated in the consulting rooms of psychiatrists, psychologists, and other mental health workers. Several kinds of psychotherapy are applied to drug-use disorders, as they are to other human maladjustments, often in combination with biological treatments aimed at reducing the physical dependence.

In the first direct comparison in a controlled study, the tricyclic antidepressant desipramine and a cognitive-behavioural treatment were found to be somewhat effective in reducing cocaine use as well as in improving abusers' family, social, and general psychological functioning. In a 12-week study by Carroll and associates (Carroll, Rounsaville, & Gordon, 1994; Carroll et al., 1995), desipramine was more effective than a placebo for patients with a low degree of dependence on cocaine, whereas the cognitive treatment was better in reducing cocaine use in patients with a high degree of dependence. This finding illustrates the significance of the psychological aspects of substance abuse.

In Carroll's study, patients receiving cognitive treatment learned how to avoid high-risk situations (e.g., being around people who use cocaine), recognize the lure of the drug for them, and develop alternatives to using cocaine (e.g., recreational activities with nonusers). Cocaine abusers in this

Group therapy in residential settings is frequently used to treat heroin addiction.

study also learned strategies for coping with the craving and for resisting the tendency to regard a slip as a catastrophe ("relapse prevention training," per Marlatt & Gordon, 1985). The more depressed the patient, the more favourable the outcome from both the antidepressant drug and the cognitive therapy. Overall, the results for the psychosocial treatment were superior to those for the antidepressant drug in reducing cocaine use, and this pattern was maintained at a one-year follow-up (Carroll, Rounsaville, & Nich, 1994).

A more operant-type of program has shown some promise as well. Modelled after the token economy employed in hospital settings, this program rewards patients with vouchers for not using cocaine or heroine (verified by urine samples). The tokens are exchangeable for things that patients would like to have more of (Higgins et al., 1993, 1999; Silverman et al., 1996). Some evidence also exists for the effectiveness of programs that follow a psychodynamic approach combined with methadone (Woody et al., 1990).

Self-help residential homes or communes are the most widespread psychological approach to dealing with heroin addiction and other drug abuse. Modelled after Synanon, a therapeutic community of former drug addicts founded in 1958 by Charles Dederich in Santa Monica, California, these residences are designed to restructure radically the addict's outlook on life so that illicit drugs no longer have a place. Daytop Village, Phoenix House, Odyssey House, and other drug-rehabilitation homes share the following features:

- separation of addicts from previous social contacts, on the assumption that these relationships have been instrumental in fostering the addictive lifestyle
- a comprehensive environment in which drugs are not available and continuing support is offered to ease the transition from regular drug use to a drug-free existence
- the presence of charismatic role models, former addicts who appear to be meeting life's challenges without drugs
- direct, often brutal confrontation in group therapy, in which addicts are goaded into accepting responsibility

for their problems and for their drug habits and are urged to take charge of their lives

- a setting in which addicts are respected as human beings rather than stigmatized as failures or criminals

There are several obstacles to evaluating the efficacy of residential drug-treatment programs. Since entrance is voluntary, only a small minority of dependent users enter such settings. Furthermore, because the dropout rate is high, those who remain cannot be regarded as representative of the population of people addicted to illicit drugs; their motivation to go straight is probably much stronger than that of the average addict. Any improvement that participants in these programs make may reflect their uncommonly strong desire to rid themselves of the habit rather than the specific qualities of the treatment program. Such self-regulating residential communities do, however, appear to help a large number of those who remain in them for a year or so (Institute of Medicine, 1990b; Jaffe, 1985).

As successful as these efforts are, the fact remains that most people who participate in these various individual and group programs do not achieve abstinence by the end of formal contact with the treatment, and of those who do, the majority fail to remain abstinent. The abuse of illicit drugs remains a serious societal and health problem that resists intensive therapeutic efforts.

TREATMENT OF CIGARETTE SMOKING

As we mentioned earlier, numerous laws today prohibit smoking in restaurants, trains, airplanes, and public buildings. These laws are part of a social context that provides more incentive and support to stop smoking than existed in the past. Of the more than 40 million smokers in the United States who have quit since 1964, it is believed that 90 percent did so without professional help (National Cancer Institute, 1977; USDHHS, 1982, 1989). Each year more than 30 percent of cigarette smokers try to quit with minimal outside assistance, but fewer than 10 percent succeed even in the short run (Fiore et al., 1990). Research is ongoing on smokers' use of self-help methods outside the framework of formal smoking-cessation programs (DiClemente, 1993; Orleans et al., 1991).

Laws that have banned smoking in many places have probably increased the frequency of quitting.

Some smokers attend smoking clinics or consult with professionals for specialized smoking-reduction programs. It is estimated that about half of those who go through smoking-cessation programs succeed in abstaining by the time the program is over; only about 20 percent of those who have succeeded in the short term actually remain nonsmoking after a year. The greatest success overall is found among smokers who are better educated, are older, or have acute health problems (USDHHS, 1998).

BIOLOGICAL TREATMENTS

Reducing a smoker's craving for nicotine by providing it in a different way is one biological approach to treatment. Attention to nicotine dependence is clearly important because the more cigarettes a person smokes daily, the less successful attempts to quit will be. Gum containing nicotine may help smokers endure the nicotine withdrawal that accompanies any effort to stop smoking. The nicotine in gum is absorbed much more slowly and steadily than that in tobacco. The long-term goal is for the former smoker to be able to cut back on the use of the gum as well, eventually eliminating reliance on nicotine altogether.

There is some controversy around this treatment, however, as ex-smokers can become dependent on the gum. Moreover, in doses that deliver an amount of nicotine equivalent to smoking one cigarette an hour, the gum causes cardiovascular changes (e.g., increased blood pressure) that can be dangerous to people with cardiovascular diseases. Nevertheless, some experts believe that even prolonged, continued use of the gum is healthier than obtaining nicotine by smoking, since at least the poisons in the smoke are avoided. The best results are obtained when the gum is combined with a behaviourally oriented treatment (Hughes, 1995; Killen et al., 1990), although one well-controlled study showed no additional benefit from the gum over a behavioural intervention that emphasized educational information (e.g., health risks) and environmental changes (e.g., the removal of ashtrays from home and work settings) (Hill et al., 1995).

Hughes (1995) pointed out that although nicotine replacement alleviates withdrawal symptoms—which justifies its use in gum and in the nicotine patches to be described next (Hughes et al., 1990)—the severity of withdrawal is related only minimally to success in stopping smoking (Hughes & Hatsukami, 1992). Thus, the logic of employing nicotine replacement to help people stop smoking appears a bit shaky.

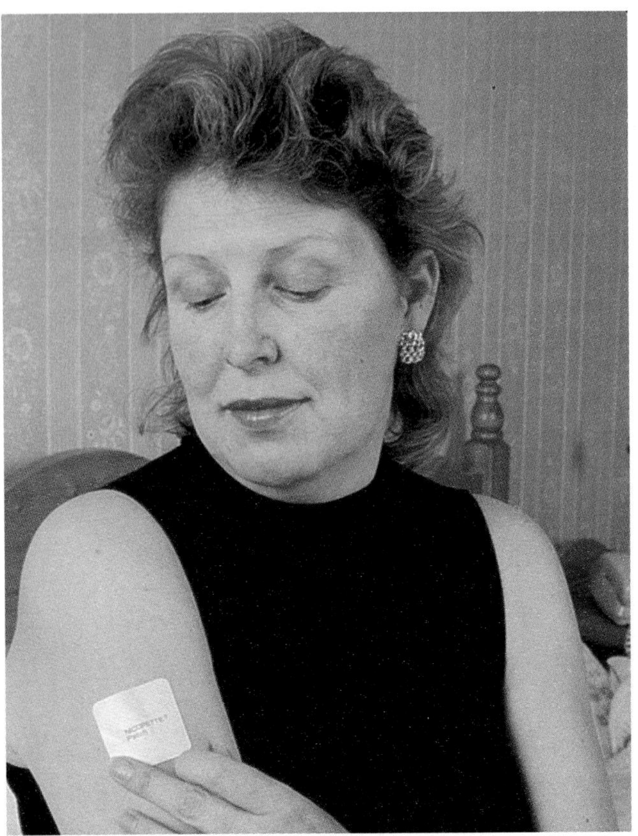

Nicotine patches are now available over the counter to help relieve withdrawal symptoms.

Nicotine patches first became available in December 1991 with a doctor's prescription and in 1996 over the counter. A polyethylene patch taped to the arm serves as a transdermal (through the skin) nicotine delivery system that slowly and steadily releases the drug into the bloodstream and thence to the brain. An advantage of the patch over nicotine gum is that the person needs only to apply the patch each day and not remove it, making compliance easier. A program of treatment usually lasts 10 to 12 weeks, with smaller and smaller patches used as treatment progresses. A drawback is that a person who continues smoking while wearing the patch risks increasing the amount of nicotine in the body to dangerous levels.

Evidence suggests that the nicotine patch is superior to the use of a placebo patch in terms of abstinence as well as subjective craving (see Hughes, 1995). However, as with nicotine gum, the patch is not a panacea. Abstinence rates are less than 40 percent immediately following the termination of treatment, and at nine-month follow-ups, differences between the drug and a placebo disappear. The manufacturers state that the patch is to be used only as part of a psychological smoking-cessation program and then for not more than three months at a time.

The newest nicotine replacement therapy involves an inhaler. The user inhales the nicotine through a plastic tube shaped like a cigarette holder; unlike gum or patches, this method of nicotine delivery has some resemblance to smoking, as the person handles the device and inhales. In a comparison of these inhalers with placebo inhalers that did not actually contain nicotine, one-year abstinence rates were 28 percent for the treatment group and 18 percent for the placebo group (Hjalmarson et al., 1997).

Given that attempting to quit smoking can precipitate an episode of depression in someone who has previously been depressed, interest has also focused on the possible role of antidepressants in aiding smoking cessation. Thus far, the evidence shows that antidepressants that have strong effects on dopamine do have some benefit, regardless of whether the person has a history of depression (Hall et al., 1998; Hurt, Sachs, & Glover, 1997). Patients are typically given an amount of the antidepressant that is less than would be used to treat depression. They take the drug for some period of time before trying to stop smoking and then continue taking the antidepressant for some amount of time (e.g., seven weeks) as they try to give up smoking. Hurt et al. (1997) combined brief counselling with either buproprion (an antidepressant sold under the names of Wellbutrin and Zyban) or a placebo and found one-year abstinence rates of 23 percent in the treated group and 12 percent in the placebo group. Combining buproprion and nicotine patches has yielded an impressive 12-month abstinence rate of 35 percent (Jorenby et al., 1999).

Psychological Treatments

Although short-term results of psychological treatments are often very encouraging (some programs [e.g., Etringer, Gregory, & Lando, 1984] have reported as many as 95 percent of smokers abstinent by the end of treatment), longer-term results are far less positive. Most smokers return to smoking within a year (DiClemente, 1993) and do so quickly if they have been heavy smokers (USDHHS, 1998). This evidence does not belie the fact that a substantial minority of smokers can be helped; clearly, however, the task is not easy.

Many techniques have been tried. The idea behind some of them is to make smoking unpleasant, even nauseating. In the 1970s, there was considerable interest in rapid smoking treatment, in which a smoker sits in a poorly ventilated room and puffs much faster than normal, perhaps as often as every six seconds (e.g., Lando, 1977). Newer variations include rapid puffing (rapid smoking without inhaling), focused smoking (smoking for a long period of time but at a normal rate), and smoke holding (retaining smoke in the mouth for several minutes but without inhaling). Although such treatments reduce smoking and foster abstinence more than no-treatment control conditions, they usually do not differ from each other or from other credible interventions, showing high rates of relapse at follow-ups (Schwartz, 1987; Sobell et al., 1990).

Cognitively oriented investigators have tried to encourage more control in people who smoke with treatments that have them develop and utilize various coping skills, such as relaxation and positive self-talk, when confronted with tempting situations (e.g., following a good meal). Results are not very promising (Hill, Rigdon, & Johnson, 1993).

According to Compas et al. (1998), scheduled smoking shows real promise. The strategy is to reduce nicotine intake gradually over a period of a few weeks by getting the smoker to agree to increase the time intervals between cigarettes. For example, during the first week of treatment, a pack-a-day smoker would be put on a schedule allowing only 10 cigarettes per day; during the second week, only five cigarettes are allowed; and during the third week, the person would taper off to zero. These cigarettes have to be smoked on a schedule provided by the treatment team, not when the smoker feels an intense craving. In this way, smoking cigarettes is controlled by the passage of time rather than by urges, mood states, or situations. Breaking this link—assuming the smoker is able to comply with the agreed-upon schedule—has led to 44 percent abstinence after one year, a very impressive outcome (Cinciripini et al., 1994).

Another approach, in the spirit of tailoring treatment to factors believed to underlie the smoking, is applying cognitive therapy to depressed mood in certain smokers. Available results are encouraging (Hall, Munoz, & Reus, 1994; Hall et al., 1996).

Probably the most widespread intervention is advice or direction from a physician to stop smoking. Each year millions of smokers are given this counsel because of hypertension, heart disease, lung disease, diabetes, or on general grounds of preserving or improving health. Indeed, by age 65, most smokers have managed to quit (USDHHS, 1998). There is some evidence that a physician's advice can get some people to stop smoking, at least for a while, especially when the patients also chew nicotine gum (Law & Tang, 1995; Russell et al., 1983). But much more needs to be learned about the nature of the advice, the manner in which it is given, its timing, and other factors that must surely play a role in determining whether an addicted individual is prepared and able to alter his or her behaviour primarily on a physician's say-so (USDHHS, 1998).

As with other addictions, psychological factors may make it difficult for smokers to quit. As these factors can vary significantly among addicts, one treatment package cannot be expected to help all smokers. People have trouble quitting for many different reasons, and diverse methods need to be developed to help them. Yet in their zeal to make an impact on the smoking problem, clinicians have until recently put smokers in standardized programs.

RELAPSE PREVENTION

Mark Twain quipped that stopping smoking was easy—he'd done it hundreds of times! Most smokers relapse within a year of stopping, regardless of the means used to stop. As might be expected, people who smoked the most—and are presumably more addicted to nicotine—relapse more often and more quickly than moderate or light smokers. It is very difficult for ex-smokers to maintain their abstinence. Data (and common sense) tell us that ex-smokers who do not live with a smoker do better at follow-up than do those who do live with a smoker (McIntyre-Kingsolver, Lichtenstein, & Mermelstein, 1986). So-called booster or maintenance sessions help, but in a very real sense they represent a continuation of treatment; when they stop, relapse is the rule (Brandon, Zelman, & Baker, 1987). However, there is considerably more social support for not smoking than there was just 10 years ago. Perhaps as time goes on, societal sanctions against smoking will help those who have succeeded in quitting remain abstinent.

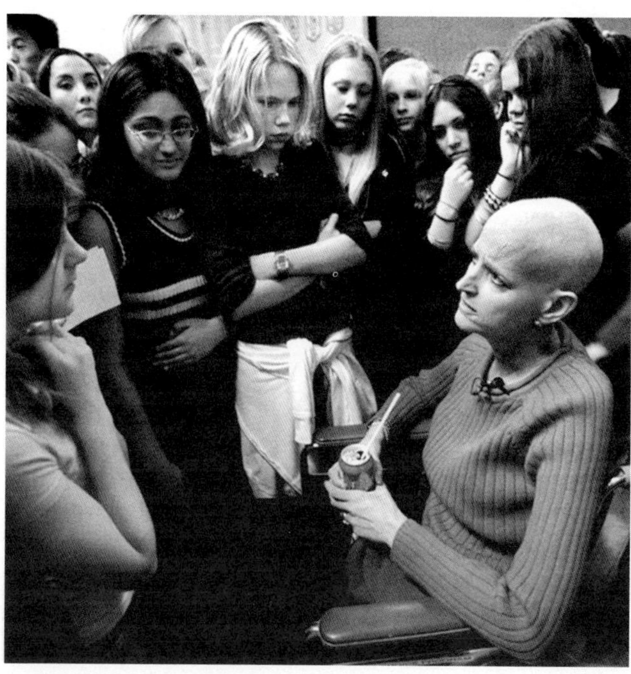

Life-long smoker Barbara Tarbox spoke to young people across Canada about the dangers of smoking before she died of lung cancer at age 42.

One approach to the relapse problem is to focus on the cognitions of ex-smokers (Baer & Lichtenstein, 1988). Using the articulated thoughts paradigm (Davison et al., 1983), Haaga (1989) found that recent ex-smokers who tended to think of smoking without prompting relapsed more readily three months later. However, if they learned some effective ways of countering these smoking-related thoughts, such as distracting themselves with other concerns, their abstinence was better months later. Using a questionnaire measure, Haaga found that ex-smokers' self-efficacy in their most difficult challenge situation (e.g., having coffee and dessert following a pleasant dinner) was a good predictor of abstinence a year later (Haaga, 1990). These and related studies indicate that we can more reliably predict the maintenance or relapse in smoking cessation if we access the cognitions of ex-smokers. Such information may help therapists design programs that will improve the ability of a person to remain a nonsmoker (Compas et al., 1998).

PREVENTION OF SUBSTANCE ABUSE

From all that is known about the etiology of substance abuse, discouraging people from beginning to abuse drugs makes the most sense. It is difficult—and for many, impossible—to loosen oneself from substances that create both psychological and physical dependency. We turn our attention next to prevention efforts involving alcohol abuse, drug abuse, and smoking.

Many prevention efforts have been aimed at adolescents because substance abuse in adulthood often follows experimentation in the teens and earlier. Programs, usually conducted in schools, have been directed at enhancing the young adolescent's self-esteem, teaching social skills, and encouraging the young person to say no to peer pressure. The results are mixed (Hansen, 1993; Jansen et al., 1996). Self-esteem enhancement, sometimes called affective education, has not demonstrated its effectiveness. In contrast, social skills training and resistance training (learning to say no) have shown some positive results, particularly with girls. A highly publicized program, Project DARE (Drug Abuse Resistance Education), which combines affective education and resistance training and is delivered by police officers in 5th- and 6th-grade classrooms, has shown disappointing results (Clayton, Catterello, & Walden, 1991; Ringwalt, Ennett, & Holt, 1991). Other preventive efforts, yet to be adequately evaluated, include the following:

- parental involvement in school programs for their children
- warning labels on containers of alcoholic beverages
- informing consumers that drinking alcohol during pregnancy can cause birth defects in the fetus and that alcohol impairs driving a car and operating machinery
- cautionary announcements in the media about stiff legal penalties for driving under the influence and exhortations to arrange for designated drivers before imbibing at social occasions
- testing for alcohol and drugs in the workplace

Developing ways of discouraging young people from experimenting with tobacco has become a top priority among health researchers and politicians. Canada is among the world leaders in taking an aggressive stand against tobacco advertising as well as in providing the public with warnings about the use of tobacco. On June 28, 2000, Canada's health minister, Alan Rock, announced new regulations for tobacco advertisements that mandated that all cigarette packages sold in Canada will carry health warnings that cover 50 percent of the front and back of the package. According to Senior (2000), these warnings are the most stringent and graphic in the world. They also seem to be effective. According to Senior (2000), research conducted by Health Canada in 1999 showed that the larger and more emotional the message on the package, the more impact it had on potential users. The use of warning labels, the recent decision to raise taxes to make it more difficult for young people to smoke, and preventive lectures on the topic given to Canadian schoolchildren by people such as Dr. Jeffrey Wigand (see the movie, *The Insider*) are all part of a multifaceted Health Canada strategy designed to decrease the number of young smokers and limit the long-term costs to the health system.

Another approach has been to increase the cost of cigarettes through taxes. However, Canadian research indicates that pricing has a differential impact on men versus women (Dedobbeleer et al., 2004). Higher prices appear to decrease the prevalence of smoking among men but have no effect among women, who, it was suggested, tend to smoke in response to life stressors.

Regarding the potential financial savings, not to mention the savings in terms of well-being and quality of life, an analysis of health costs suggested that a national prevention program in Canada could be implemented for as little as $67 per student (Stephens, Kaiserman, McCall, & Sutherland, 2000). The net savings over time due to improved public health as a result of decreased smoking was estimated at $619 million per year. Thus, substantial savings would result. However, as noted by Stephens et al. (2000), preventive efforts currently underway are not extensive enough to realize these enormous benefits.

The measures that hold promise for persuading young people to resist smoking may also be useful in dissuading them from trying illicit drugs and alcohol. Many smokers do fear disastrous consequences later in life and try to cut down on cigarettes, yet others, both young and old, seem able to discount the possibility that they are at higher risk for coronary heart disease or lung cancer. This is the "It won't happen to me" syndrome.

Recent years have seen scores of school-based programs aimed at preventing young people from starting to use tobacco. By and large, such programs have succeeded in delaying the onset of smoking (Sussman et al., 1995). They share some common components (Hansen, 1992; Hansen et al., 1988; Sussman, 1996):

1. **Peer-pressure resistance training**. Students learn about the nature of peer pressure and ways to say no. For example, specially prepared films portray teenagers resisting appeals from friends to try smoking, not an easy matter for young people for whom peer approval and acceptance are so important.
2. **Correction of normative expectations**. Many young people believe that cigarette smoking is more prevalent (and by implication, more okay) than it actually is. Changing beliefs about the prevalence of smoking is an effective strategy, perhaps because of the sensitivity young people have to what others their age do and believe.

3 **Inoculation against mass-media messages**. Some prevention programs try to counter any positive images of smokers that are put forth in the media.

4 **Information about parental and other adult influences**. Since it is known that parental smoking is strongly correlated with and most probably contributes to smoking by their children, some programs note that this aspect of parental behaviour should not be imitated.

5 **Peer leadership**. Most smoking and other drug-prevention programs involve peers of recognized status to enhance the impact of the anti-use messages being conveyed.

6 **Affective education, self-image enhancement**. Several programs focus on the idea that intrapsychic factors, such as poor self-image and inability to cope with stress, underlie the onset of smoking in young people. However, there are indications that such programs may actually increase drug use, perhaps because their focus on drugs as a poor way to resolve self-esteem issues unintentionally suggests drug use as a way to deal with life stress.

7 **Other components**. Additional features include providing information about the harmful effects of smoking or of drug use (in addition to that provided in warnings on cigarette packages) and encouraging students to make a public commitment not to smoke (e.g., making a commitment on videotape).

SUMMARY

- Using substances to alter mood and consciousness is a human characteristic and so, too, is the tendency to abuse them. DSM-IV-TR distinguishes between substance dependence and substance abuse.
- Dependence refers to a compulsive pattern of substance use and consequent serious psychological and physical impairments. It can involve physiological dependence, or addiction, when tolerance and withdrawal are present.
- In substance abuse, drug use leads to failure to meet obligations and to interpersonal and legal problems.
- Alcohol has a variety of short-term and long-term effects on human beings. Many of these effects are tragic in nature, ranging from poor judgment and motor coordination and their dire consequences for the alcohol-abusing person and society, to addiction, which makes an ordinary, productive life impossible and is extremely difficult to overcome. As with other addicting drugs, people come to rely on alcohol not so much because it makes them feel good as because it provides an escape from feeling bad.
- Less prevalent but more notorious, perhaps because of their illegality, are the opiates, which include heroin; the barbiturates, which are sedatives; and the amphetamines and cocaine, which are stimulants. All these substances are addicting, and cocaine, including crack, is especially so. Heroin has been the focus of concern in recent years because usage is up and stronger varieties have become available. Barbiturates have for some time been implicated in both intentional and accidental suicides; they are particularly lethal when taken with alcohol.
- Nicotine, especially when taken into the body via the inhaled smoke from a cigarette, has worked its addictive power on humankind for centuries, and despite sombrely phrased warnings from public health officials, it continues in widespread use. Smoking by school-age youngsters and teenagers is a notable concern because nearly all adult smokers began their use in their teens. Each year, the government and private individuals spend millions of dollars to dissuade people from beginning the habit or to help those already addicted to stop smoking.
- Marijuana is smoked by a large number of young North Americans. Its use declined in the 1980s but increased in the 1990s. Arguments for deregulation of marijuana have stressed its supposed safety in comparison with the known harm caused by the habitual use of alcohol, which is a legal and integral part of North American culture. But currently available evidence indicates that when used regularly, marijuana is not benign; it can damage the lungs and cardiovascular system and lead to cognitive impairments. There is also evidence that constituents of marijuana may adversely affect fetal development, heart function in people who already have coronary problems, and pulmonary function. Further, marijuana appears to be addicting.
- The hallucinogens—LSD, mescaline, and psilocybin—are taken to alter or expand consciousness. Their use reflects humankind's desire not only to escape from unpleasant realities, but also to explore inner space.
- Several factors are related to the etiology of substance abuse and dependence. Social attitudes and culture play a role in encouraging the abuse of drugs, alcohol, and cigarettes. Sociocultural variables, such as attitudes toward the substance, peer pressure, and how the substance is portrayed by the media, are all related to how frequently a substance is used. Many substances are used to alter mood (e.g., to reduce tension or increase positive affect), and people with certain personality traits, such as

those high in negative affect or psychopathy, are especially likely to use drugs. Cognitive variables, such as the expectation that the drug will yield positive effects, are also important. Finally, biological factors, most notably a genetic predisposition or diathesis, play a role in the use of some substances, particularly alcohol.

- Therapies of all kinds have been used to help people refrain from the use of both legal (e.g., alcohol and nicotine) and illegal (e.g., heroin and cocaine) drugs. As all the drugs discussed in this chapter are addictive, biological treatments have attempted to release users from their physiological dependency. Some benefits have been observed for treatments using such drugs as clonidine, naltrexone, and methadone. Recently, nicotine replacement via gum or patches has met with some success in reducing cigarette smoking. None of these somatic approaches appears to lead to enduring change unless accompanied by psychological treatments with such goals as helping patients resist pressures to indulge, cope with normal life stress, control emotions without relying on chemicals, and make use of social supports such as AA.
- Health professionals recognize that substance abuse is a multi-faceted problem requiring a broad range of interventions and that different people use and abuse drugs for different reasons, making it necessary to assess carefully those factors of particular importance for a given individual. Since it is far easier never to begin using drugs than to stop using them, considerable effort has been expended in recent years on attempts to prevent substance abuse by implementing educational and social programs to equip young people with the skills they need to develop their lives without a reliance on drugs.

KEY TERMS

amphetamines (p. 379)
Antabuse (p. 390)
barbiturates (p. 378)
clonidine (p. 400)
cocaine (p. 380)
conditioning theory of tolerance (p. 388)
controlled drinking (p. 394)
covert sensitization (p. 394)
cross-dependent (p. 399)
delirium tremens (DTs) (p. 365)
detoxification (p. 390)
Ecstasy (p. 382)
feedforward mechanisms (p. 389)
fetal alcohol syndrome (p. 370)
flashback (p. 383)
guided self-change (p. 395)
hallucinogen (p. 381)
harm reduction therapy (p. 395)
hashish (p. 373)
heroin (p. 377)
heroin antagonists (p. 399)
heroin substitutes (p. 399)
LSD (p. 381)
marijuana (p. 373)
mescaline (p. 381)
methadone (p. 399)
morphine (p. 377)
nicotine (p. 371)
opiates (p. 377)
opium (p. 377)
polydrug abuse (p. 365)
psilocybin (p. 381)
second-hand smoke (p. 373)
sedatives (p. 377)
stimulants (p. 379)
substance abuse (p. 364)
substance dependence (p. 364)
tolerance (p. 364)
withdrawal (p. 364)

Reflections: Past, Present, and Future

- The Government of Canada has eliminated sponsorship of entertainment and sporting events by tobacco companies. Should they consider similar prohibitions for beer companies in Canada? Although beer commercials on television cannot portray people actually drinking beer, these commercials emphasize positive lifestyles in association with beer. Should there be a move away from these beer commercials on television?
- Should pot be legalized in Canada? Is prohibition more harmful than marijuana itself? Or, are there numerous reasons not to legalize? Where do you stand on this controversial issue? What is your position on the medical use of marijuana?
- Do you think the goal of substance abuse treatment should be total abstinence, or do you favour a harm reduction approach? What is your view on harm reduction efforts that involve supplying addicts with needles? Is this a wise decision? Do you think that it will ever be possible to reduce the prevalence of inhalant abuse or other substance abuse by means of psychological interventions among Canada's Aboriginal peoples?

chapter 13

Personality Disorders

"Every man has three characters: that which he exhibits, that which he has, and that which he thinks he has."
—Alphonse Karr

"People, I know I've done some terrible things ... and I've caused a lot of sadness and sorrow to a lot of people and I'm really sorry for that and I know I deserve to be punished. But I didn't kill these girls."
—Paul Bernardo, *The Toronto Star*, August 15, 1995

Harry Mayerovitch, Musée du Quebec, *Self Portrait.*

MARY WAS 26 years old at the time of her first admission to a psychiatric hospital. She had been in outpatient treatment with a psychologist for several months when her persistent thoughts of suicide and preoccupation with inflicting pain on herself (by cutting or burning) led her therapist to conclude that she could no longer be managed as an outpatient.

Mary's first experience with some form of psychological therapy occurred when she was an adolescent. Her grades declined sharply in the 11th grade, and her parents suspected she was using drugs. She began to miss curfews and even failed to come home at all on a few occasions. She was frequently truant. Family therapy was undertaken, and it seemed to go well at first. Mary was enthusiastic about her therapist and asked for additional, private sessions with him.

Her parents' fears were confirmed during the family sessions, as Mary revealed an extensive history of drug use, including "everything I can get my hands on." She had been promiscuous and had prostituted herself several times to get drug money. Her relationships with her peers were changeable, to say the least. The pattern was a constant parade of new friends, at first thought to be the greatest ever but who soon disappointed Mary in some way and were cast aside, often in a very unpleasant way. Except for the one person with whom she was currently enamoured, Mary had no friends. She reported that she stayed away from others for fear that they would harm her in some way.

After several weeks of therapy, Mary's parents noticed that her relationship with the therapist had cooled appreciably. The sessions were marked by Mary's angry and abusive outbursts toward the therapist. After several more weeks had passed, Mary refused to attend any more sessions. In a subsequent conversation with the therapist, Mary's father learned that Mary had behaved seductively toward the therapist during their private sessions and that her changed attitude toward him coincided with the rejection of her advances, despite the therapist's attempt to mix firmness with warmth and empathy.

Mary managed to graduate from high school and enrolled in a local community college, but the old patterns returned. Poor grades, cutting classes, continuing drug use, and lack of interest in her studies finally led her to quit in the middle of the first semester of her second year. After leaving school, Mary held a series of clerical jobs. Most of them didn't last long, as her relationships with co-workers paralleled her relationships with her peers in high school. When Mary started a new job, she would find someone she really liked, but something would come between them and the relationship would end angrily. Mary was frequently suspicious of her co-workers and reported that she often heard them talking about her, plotting how to prevent her from getting ahead on the job. She was quick to find hidden meanings in their behaviour; for example, she interpreted being the last person asked to sign a birthday card to mean that she was the least liked person in the office. She indicated that she "received vibrations" from others and that, even in the absence of any direct evidence, she could tell when they really didn't like her.

Mary's behaviour includes many characteristic symptoms of several personality disorders, in particular, borderline personality disorder. Her frequent mood swings, with periods of depression and extreme irritability, led her to seek therapy several times. But after initial enthusiasm, her relationship with her therapist always deteriorated, resulting in premature termination of therapy. The therapist she was seeing just before her hospitalization was her sixth.

Personality disorders (PDs) are a heterogeneous group of disorders that are coded on Axis II of the DSM. They are regarded as long-standing, pervasive, and inflexible patterns of behaviour and inner experience that deviate from the expectations of a person's culture and that impair social and occupational functioning. Some, but not all, can cause emotional distress.

As we examine the personality disorders, some may seem to fit people we know, not to mention ourselves! Although the symptoms of the personality disorders come close to describing characteristics that we all possess from time to time and in varying degrees, an actual personality disorder is defined by the extremes of several traits and by the inflexible way these traits are expressed. People with personality disorders are often rigid in their behaviour and cannot change it in response to changes in the situations they experience.

The personality each of us develops over the years reflects a persistent means of dealing with life's challenges, a certain style of relating to other people. One person is overly dependent; another is challenging and aggressive; another is shy and avoids social contact; and still another is concerned more with appearance and bolstering his or her vulnerable ego than with relating to others. These individuals would not be diagnosed as having personality disorders unless the patterns of behaviour were long-standing, pervasive, and dysfunctional. For example, on entering a crowded room and hearing a loud burst of laughter, you might feel that you are the target of some joke and that people are talking about you. Such concerns become symptoms of paranoid personality disorder only if they occur frequently and intensely and prevent the development of close personal relationships.

One final prefatory comment. In addition to being viewed as clinical syndromes in their own right, personality disorders are often comorbid with an Axis I disorder. Personality disorders can serve as a context for Axis I problems, shaping them in different ways (Millon, 1996). A person diagnosed with an anxiety disorder on Axis I and obsessive-compulsive personality disorder on Axis II will express anxiety in ways such as perfectionism and indecision.

In this chapter, we look first at how we classify personality disorders and at the challenges associated with classification and assessment. Then we turn to the personality disorders themselves, the theory and research on their etiology, and therapies for dealing with them. The extent of our coverage of the specific personality disorders varies depending on how much is known about them; for example, there are very few empirical data about histrionic personality disorder but a vast literature on antisocial personality disorder.

CLASSIFYING PERSONALITY DISORDERS: CLUSTERS, CATEGORIES, AND PROBLEMS

The idea that personality can be disordered goes back at least to the time of Hippocrates and his humoral theory, which we discussed in Chapter 1. Personality disorders were listed in the early DSMs, but the diagnoses were very unreliable. One clinician might diagnose a flamboyant patient as narcissistic, whereas another might consider him or her psychopathic. As with other diagnoses, the publication of DSM-III began a trend toward improved reliability (Coolidge & Segal, 1998). Beginning with DSM-III, personality disorders were also placed on a separate axis, Axis II, to ensure that diagnosticians would pay attention to their possible presence. Although a diagnostic interview sometimes points directly to the presence of a personality disorder, more often a person arrives at a clinic with an Axis I disorder (such as panic disorder) that, quite naturally, is the primary focus of attention. With personality disorders on Axis II, the clinician must consider whether a personality disorder is also present.

The reliability of personality disorder diagnoses, then, have been improved because of two developments:

1. the publication of specific diagnostic criteria
2. the development of structured interviews specially designed for assessing personality disorders

Data now indicate that good reliability can be achieved, even across cultures (Loranger et al., 1987; Widiger et al., 1988). Interrater reliability (the extent to which raters agree) from a recent study of the DSM-IV diagnostic criteria is presented in Table 13.1 (Maffei et al., 1997); the figures compare favourably with reliability figures for Axis I disorders (Chapter 3). Thus, by using structured interviews, reliable diagnoses of personality disorders can be achieved. Interviews with people who know the patient well are sometimes part of the diagnostic workup and improve the accuracy of diagnosis (Bernstein et al., 1997).

Because personality disorders are presumed to be more stable over time than some episodic Axis I disorders (e.g., depression), test-retest reliability—a comparison of whether patients receive the same diagnosis when they are assessed twice with some time interval separating the two assessments—is also an important factor in their evaluation. A summary of test-retest reliability is also given in Table 13.1 (Zimmerman, 1994). Note the wide variability of the figures. Antisocial personality disorder has a high test-retest reliability, indicating that it is a stable diagnosis—a patient given the diagnosis is very likely to receive the same diagnosis when evaluated later. The figures for schizotypal and dependent personality disorders are very low, indicating that the symptoms of people with these latter two diagnoses are not stable over time. Thus it appears that many of the personality disorders are not as enduring as the DSM asserts.

Another major problem with personality disorders is that it is often difficult to diagnose a single, specific personality disorder because many disordered people exhibit a wide range of traits that make several diagnoses applicable (Marshall & Serin, 1997). In the case opening this chapter, Mary met the diagnostic criteria not only for borderline personality disorder but also for paranoid personality disorder, and she came close to meeting the criteria for schizotypal disorder as well. One study found that 55 percent of patients with borderline personality disorder also met the diagnostic criteria for schizotypal personality disorder; 47 percent, the criteria for antisocial personality disorder, and 57 percent, the criteria for histrionic personality disorder (Widiger, Frances, & Trull, 1987). Such data are particularly discouraging when we try to interpret the results of research that

Table 13.1

Interrater and Test-Retest Reliability for the Personality Disorders

Diagnosis	Interrater Reliability	Test-Retest Reliability
Paranoid	.93	.57
Schizoid	.90	—
Schizotypal	.91	.11
Borderline	.91	.56
Histrionic	.92	.40
Narcissistic	.98	.32
Antisocial	.94	.84
Dependent	.86	.15
Avoidant	.97	.41
Obsessive-compulsive	.83	.52

Source: Figures for interrater reliability are from the Maffei et al. 1997 study and reflect the amount of agreement above chance. Test-retest figures are rates of agreement from Zimmerman's 1994 summary of longer (generally more than a year) studies.

compares patients who have a specific personality disorder with some control group. If, for example, we find that people with borderline disorder differ from normal people, is what we have learned specific to borderline personality disorder or is it related to personality disorders in general or perhaps even applicable to an Axis I diagnosis?

Although some decrease in comorbidity occurred with the publication of DSM-IV (Blais, Hilsenroth, & Castlebury, 1997), the data still suggest that the categorical diagnostic system of DSM-IV-TR may not be ideal for classifying personality disorders. The personality traits that constitute the data for classification form a continuum; that is, most of the relevant characteristics are present in varying degrees in most people. Although Canadian researchers have provided some evidence to suggest that the psychopathy underscoring antisocial personality may represent a discrete category (Harris, Rice, & Quinsey, 1994; Skilling, Harris, Rice, & Quinsey, 2002), a dimensional approach seems to apply to most other personality characteristics. Research by John Livesley from the University of British Columbia and his associates shows that when people with a personality disorder take a general personality inventory, what is revealed is a personality with a structure that is similar to that of normal people but is simply more extreme (Clark et al., 1996; Livesley, Jang, & Vernon, 1998; Livesley & Schroeder, 1993). Similar research by O'Connor and Dyce at Lakehead University in Thunder Bay, Ontario, has shown that dimensional differences exist when characterizing normal versus abnormal personality; personality disorders reflect extreme and rigid response tendencies that differ in degree, not in kind, from the responses of people without disorders (O'Connor, 2002; O'Connor & Dyce, 2001). Thus, the personality disorders can be construed as the extremes of characteristics we all possess. A dimensional approach to classification of personality disorders, then, may be more appropriate.

How is it first determined whether a personality disorder exists? Livesley, Schroeder, Jackson, and Jang (1994) regard personality disorder as a failure or inability to come up with adaptive solutions to life tasks. Livesley (1998) identified three types of life tasks as important and proposed that failure with any one of these tasks is enough to warrant a personality disorder diagnosis. The three tasks are (1) to form stable, integrated, and coherent representations of self and others; (2) to develop the capacity for intimacy and positive affiliations with other people; and (3) to function adaptively in society by engaging in prosocial and cooperative behaviours. Once one of these conditions exists, disorder is evident and the focus can shift to dimensional ratings.

A dimensional system was considered for inclusion in both DSM-III-R and DSM-IV, but consensus could not be reached on which dimensions to include. A promising effort to develop a dimensional classification system is described later (Focus on Discovery 13.1).

Despite problems with the diagnosis of personality disorders, we should not dismiss the utility of trying to make such diagnoses. These disorders are prevalent, and they cause severe impairment in people's lives. As research continues, the diagnostic categories will most likely be refined, perhaps with a dimensional system, and many of these problems may be solved.

ASSESSING PERSONALITY DISORDERS

Some key points need to be made about the assessment of personality disorders. A significant challenge with assessing personality dysfunction is that many disorders are *ego-syntonic*—that is, the person with a personality disorder is unaware that a problem exists and may not be experiencing significant personal distress. However, the people who interact with these individuals may have a great deal of discomfort and upset. This suggests that the assessment and diagnosis of personality disorders are enhanced when the significant others in an individual's life become informants. Furthermore, because of the lack of personal awareness in many cases, disorders may need to be diagnosed via clinical interviews led by trained personnel.

Although clinical interviews are preferable, researchers often rely on the use of self-report measures when assessing personality disorder symptoms. The MMPI-2 that was described in Chapter 4 is a personality inventory that can also be used for this purpose. Scoring schemes using MMPI items have been created to assess the symptoms of specific personality disorders (e.g., Morey, Waugh, & Blashfeld, 1985). Harkness, McNulty, and Ben-Porath (1995) described a set of MMPI-2 scales that they developed to assess five dimensional personality constructs to reflect psychopathology. This framework, known as the "PSY-5," consists of dimensions assessing negative emotionality/neuroticism, lack of positive emotionality, aggressiveness, lack of constraint, and psychoticism. Research has confirmed that the PSY-5 dimensions can be identified via confirmatory factor analyses (Bagby et al., 2002), and other research has shown that these dimensions are associated in the expected manner with personality disorder symptom counts (Trull, Useda, Costa, & McCrae, 1995). As Trull et al. (1995) noted, a measure such as the PSY-5 constraint scale should be associated with antisocial personality disorder symptoms given that the constraint scale has items that assess lying, stealing, and getting into legal trouble.

Perhaps the most widely used measure of personality disorder symptoms is the Millon Clinical Multiaxial Inventory, which is now in its third edition (MCMI-III; Millon, 1994). The MCMI-III is a 175-item true-false inventory that was revised to parallel DSM-IV. The MCMI-III provides subscale measures of 11 clinical personality scales (i.e., schizoid, avoidant, depressive, dependent, histrionic, narcissistic, antisocial, aggressive [sadistic], compulsive, passive-aggressive, and self-defeating) and three severe personality pathology scales (i.e., schizotypal, borderline, and paranoid). The

MCMI-III also provides symptom ratings for clinical syndromes located on Axis I of the DSM-IV, such as somatoform disorder and posttraumatic stress disorder. Importantly, the MCMI-III includes a validity index and three response-style indices (known as modifying indices) that correct for such tendencies as denial and random responding. The inclusion of these scales reflects Millon's recognition of the need to assess response biases and other self-report tendencies that can undermine the data obtained via self-report scales.

Although the MCMI-III provides extensive information, significant concerns remain about the use of this measure. For instance, it appears that the MCMI-III is only moderately effective in terms of its ability to detect faking (see Daubert & Metzler, 2000). Also, certain MCMI-III items are questionable because they are used to assess personality characteristics involving both Axis II and Axis I disorders, even though Axis II disorders are chronic and long-lasting, while Axis I disorders are often episodic. Widiger, Verheul, and van den Brink (1999) noted that an item such as "I have given serious thought recently to doing away with myself" is scored as an indicator of Axis II borderline personality and Axis I major depression. They observed that such items may reflect current mood disorders rather than a long-standing personality trait or style.

Two other issues involving self-report measures of personality disorder (PD) need to be considered. First, empirical tests comparing the various self-report measures show that they differ in their content and are not equivalent. A study done at the University of Alberta examined the prevalence of personality disorders in university students by administering three self-report personality disorder scales, including the MCMI-II, the MMPI personality disorder scale, and the Coolidge Axis Two scale (CATI) (Sinha & Watson, 2001). For men, narcissistic PD was the most prevalent disorder according to the MCMI-II and CATI results, but the MMPI measure indicated that paranoid PD was the most prevalent. For women, the most prevalent disorder according to MCMI-II results was avoidant PD, but it was narcissistic PD according to CATI responses and paranoid PD according to the MMPI responses.

Second, a general concern involving self-report measures, including PD measures, is that the cut-off points used to determine the presence of a personality disorder often overestimate the number of people who meet diagnostic criteria for particular disorders. For instance, the Sinha and Watson (2001) study described above found that 26.28 percent (i.e., more than one in four) of women surveyed had an avoidant PD, yet a community study conducted in Oslo, Norway, using a structured clinical interview, established that the prevalence of any PD was just 13.4 percent (Torgerson, Kringlen, & Cramer, 2001). A common pattern in comparative research is that only a proportion of those who appear to have a diagnosable disorder on the basis of the self-report measure actually are diagnosed with the disorder following more detailed examination using clinical criteria.

Ideally, if the goal is to obtain accurate diagnoses, a measure such as the MCMI-III is best used in conjunction with a clinical interview such as the Personality Disorder Examination (Loranger, 1988; Loranger et al., 1987). This extensive structured interview provides dimensional and categorical assessments. An international version was developed for a study done by the World Health Organization (Loranger et al., 1994). The advent of this interview led to the finding that the personality disorders described by diagnostic systems appear to exist across various cultures.

PERSONALITY DISORDER CLUSTERS

When a categorical approach is used and DSM-IV-TR criteria are involved, personality disorders are grouped into three clusters:

1. Individuals in cluster A (paranoid, schizoid, and schizotypal) seem odd or eccentric. These disorders reflect oddness and avoidance of social contact.
2. Those in cluster B (antisocial, borderline, histrionic, and narcissistic) seem dramatic, emotional, or erratic. Behaviours are extrapunitive and hostile.
3. Those in cluster C (avoidant, dependent, and obsessive-compulsive) appear fearful.

Although the empirical evidence on the validity of these clusters is mixed, they form a useful organizational framework for this chapter. It is worth noting that patients with both borderline and schizotypal personality disorders would probably have been diagnosed as schizophrenic using DSM-II criteria. Designating the behaviour of these people as the criteria for these two personality disorders is one way in which DSM-III-R and DSM-IV narrowed the schizophrenia diagnosis (see Chapter 11).

ODD/ECCENTRIC CLUSTER

The odd/eccentric cluster comprises three diagnoses—paranoid, schizoid, and schizotypal PDs. The symptoms of these disorders bear some similarity to the symptoms of schizophrenia, especially to the less severe symptoms of its prodromal and residual phases.

PARANOID PERSONALITY DISORDER

The individual with **paranoid personality** disorder (PPD) is suspicious of others. People with this diagnosis expect to be mistreated or exploited by others and thus are secretive and always on the lookout for possible signs of trickery and abuse. Such individuals are reluctant to confide in others and tend to blame them even when they themselves are at fault. They can be extremely jealous and may unjustifiably question the fidelity of a spouse or lover.

Patients with PPD are preoccupied with unjustified doubts about the trustworthiness or loyalty of others. They may read hidden negative or threatening messages into events (e.g., the individual may believe that a neighbour's dog deliberately barks in the early morning to disturb him or her). This diagnosis is different from schizophrenia, paranoid type, because symptoms such as hallucinations are not present and there is less impairment in social and occupational functioning. It differs from delusional disorder because full-blown delusions are not present.

PPD occurs most frequently in men and co-occurs most frequently with schizotypal, borderline, and avoidant personality disorders (Bernstein, 1993; Morey, 1988). Its prevalence is about 1 percent (Weissman, 1993).

Schizoid Personality Disorder

Patients with schizoid personality disorder do not appear to desire or enjoy social relationships and usually have no close friends. They appear dull, bland, and aloof and have no warm, tender feelings for others. They rarely report strong emotions, have no interest in sex, and experience few pleasurable activities. Indifferent to praise and criticism, individuals with this disorder are loners with solitary interests. The prevalence of schizoid personality disorder is less than 1 percent. It is slightly less common among women than men (Weissman, 1993).

Comorbidity is highest for schizotypal, avoidant, and paranoid personality disorders, most likely because of the similar diagnostic criteria in the four categories. The diagnostic criteria for schizoid personality disorder are also similar to some of the symptoms of the prodromal and residual phases of schizophrenia.

Schizotypal Personality Disorder

The concept of the schizotypal personality grew out of Danish studies of the adopted children of schizophrenic parents (Kety et al., 1968). Although some of these children developed full-blown schizophrenia as adults, an even larger number developed what seemed to be an attenuated form of schizophrenia. The diagnostic criteria for schizotypal personality disorder were devised by Spitzer, Endicott, and Gibbon (1979) to describe these individuals. These criteria were incorporated in DSM-III and were narrowed somewhat in DSM-III-R and DSM-IV.

Patients with schizotypal personality disorder usually have the interpersonal difficulties of the schizoid personality and excessive social anxiety that does not diminish as they get to know others. Several additional, more eccentric symptoms, identical to those that define the prodromal and residual phases of schizophrenia, occur in schizotypal personality disorder.

Patients with schizotypal personality disorder may have odd beliefs or magical thinking, (e.g., superstitiousness, beliefs that they are clairvoyant and telepathic) and recurrent illusions (they may sense the presence of a force or a person not actually there). In their speech, they may use words in an unusual and unclear fashion—for example, "I'm not a very talkable person." Their behaviour and appearance may also be eccentric; they may talk to themselves, for example. Also common are ideas of reference (the belief that events have a particular and unusual meaning for the person), suspiciousness, and paranoid ideation. Affect appears to be constricted and flat. Widiger et al. (1987) found that paranoid ideation, ideas of reference, and illusions were the symptoms most relevant for making a diagnosis. The prevalence of this disorder is about 3 percent. It is slightly more frequent among men than women (Zimmerman & Coryell, 1989).

A significant problem in the diagnosis of schizotypal personality disorder is its comorbidity with other personality disorders. Morey (1988) found that 33 percent of people diagnosed with schizotypal personality also met the diagnostic criteria for borderline personality disorder; 59 percent, the criteria for avoidant personality disorder; 59 percent, the criteria for paranoid personality disorder; and 44 percent, the criteria for schizoid personality disorder. Clearly, these comorbidity figures are unsatisfactory if we want to consider schizotypal personality disorder a discrete diagnostic entity.

Etiology of the Odd/Eccentric Cluster

What causes the odd, sometimes paranoid thinking, bizarre behaviour, and interpersonal difficulties that appear in this cluster of personality disorders? The search for causes has been guided by the idea that these disorders are genetically linked to schizophrenia, perhaps as less severe variants of this Axis I disorder. The evidence for this idea varies depending on which of the odd/eccentric disorders is considered.

- Family studies have shown that the relatives of patients with schizophrenia are at increased risk for this disorder (Nigg & Goldsmith, 1994). However, Squires-Wheeler et al. (1993) found increased rates in the first-degree relatives of patients with depression, suggesting that schizotypal personality disorder is related to disorders other than schizophrenia.
- Family studies of paranoid personality disorder for the most part find higher than average rates in the relatives of patients with schizophrenia or delusional disorder (Bernstein, Useda, & Siever, 1993).
- No clear pattern has emerged from behaviour-genetic research on schizoid personality disorder, though a family study found higher prevalence of schizoid personality disorder among the relatives of people with schizotypal personality disorder (Battaglia et al., 1995).

Thus, family studies provide at least some evidence that personality disorders of the odd/eccentric cluster are related to schizophrenia. Patients with schizotypal personality disorder have deficits in cognitive and neuropsychological functioning (Cadenhead et al., 1999; Chen et al., 1998; Keefe et al., 1997) that are similar to those seen in schizophrenia. Also in keeping with schizophrenia research, patients with schizotypal personality disorder have enlarged ventricles and less temporal-lobe grey matter (Dickey et al., 1999; Siever et al., 1995).

DRAMATIC/ERRATIC CLUSTER

The diagnoses in the dramatic/erratic cluster—borderline, histrionic, narcissistic, and antisocial personality disorders—include patients with a wide variety of symptoms, ranging from variable behaviour to inflated self-esteem, exaggerated emotional displays, and antisocial behaviour.

BORDERLINE PERSONALITY DISORDER

Borderline personality disorder (BPD) was adopted as an official DSM diagnosis in 1980. The core features of this disorder are impulsivity and instability in relationships, mood, and self-image (Blais, Hilsenroth, & Castlebury, 1997; Links, Heslegrave, & van Reekum, 1999). For example, attitudes and feelings toward other people may vary considerably and inexplicably over short periods of time. Emotions are erratic and can shift abruptly, particularly from passionate idealization to contemptuous anger. Patients with BPD are argumentative, irritable, sarcastic, quick to take offence, and very hard to live with. Their unpredictable and impulsive behaviour may include gambling, spending, indiscriminate sexual activity, and eating sprees, and is thus potentially self-damaging. This impulsivity is not specific to borderline personalities; researchers in Montreal have argued that impulsivity is one trait that underscores all four disorders in the dramatic and erratic cluster (Looper & Paris, 2000).

These individuals have not developed a clear and coherent sense of self and remain uncertain about their values, loyalties, and career choices. They cannot bear to be alone, have fears of abandonment, and demand attention. Subject to chronic feelings of depression and emptiness, they often attempt suicide and engage in self-mutilating behaviour, such as slicing into their legs with a razor blade. Research in Canada and elsewhere indicates that one in 10 patients with BPD commit suicide (Paris, 2002). According to Montreal psychiatrist Joel Paris, in contrast to typical patterns with other patients, most BPD patients who kill themselves are female rather than male and most suicides occur after multiple attempts rather than on the first attempt.

Clinicians and researchers have used the term *borderline personality* for some time but have given it many meanings. Originally, the term implied that the patient was on the borderline between neurosis and schizophrenia. The DSM concept of borderline personality no longer has this connotation. The current conceptualization derives from two main sources. First, Gunderson, Kolb, and Austin (1981) proposed a set of specific diagnostic criteria similar to those that ultimately appeared in DSM-III. The second source of the diagnostic criteria was a study of the relatives of patients with schizophrenia done by Spitzer et al. (1979). As discussed earlier, some of these relatives had schizotypal personality disorder, but Spitzer et al. also identified another syndrome in the relatives, the characteristics of which came to identify borderline personality disorder.

BPD typically begins in early adulthood, has a prevalence of 1 to 2 percent, and is more common in women than in men (Swartz et al., 1990). Borderline patients are likely to have an Axis I mood disorder (Zanarini et al., 1998), and their parents are more likely than average to have mood disorders and other forms of psychopathology (Shachnow et al., 1997; Trull, 2001). Comorbidity is found with substance abuse, PTSD, eating disorders, and personality disorders from the odd/eccentric cluster (Skodol, Oldham, & Gallaher, 1999; Zanarini et al., 1998).

For many years, it has been assumed that the prognosis of BPD is not favourable. In a seven-year follow-up in Canada, for instance, about 50 percent of a sample still had the disorder (Links, Heslegrave, & van Reekum, 1998). However, the results of a 27-year investigation conducted in Montreal qualify this conclusion. Gradual improvement over time occurred for most patients such that only 7.8 percent met criteria for BPD 27 years later (Paris & Zweig-Frank, 2001; Zweig-Frank & Paris, 2002). Still, the mortality rate of the sample as a whole was substantially elevated, relative to Canadian norms, as many BPD patients had premature deaths.

Borderline features are combined with antisocial tendencies in some individuals. The role of borderline personality characteristics in spouse abuse is outlined in Canadian Perspectives 13.1.

Susanna Kaysen, the actual person portrayed by Winona Ryder in the movie *Girl Interrupted*, was diagnosed with BPD. Her autobiography is an insightful account of what it means to have BPD.

Canadian Perspectives/13.1

Borderline Personality and Spouse Abuse

Don Dutton from the University of British Columbia is an expert on the origins of spouse battering and of the abusive personality. He has been called on as a witness in trials involving spouse abusers and worked for the prosecution in the original O.J. Simpson trial.

The presence of a personality dominated by borderline characteristics is an important aspect of his theory of batterers (Dutton, 1994b, 1995, 1999). His analysis of etiological factors has focused on three central characteristics of the abusive personality—borderline personality characteristics, anger, and the chronic experience of traumatic symptoms. In addition, Dutton (1995, 1999) has suggested that batterers are characterized by an anxious and angry attachment style instead of the secure attachment style that is linked with interpersonal and personal adjustment.

Dutton and his colleagues (e.g., Dutton & Starzomski, 1993) have confirmed the importance of these characteristics. Dutton suggests that the BPD characteristics of abusive men are responsible for many of the interpersonal problems in abusive relationships. Dutton (1995, p. 146) noted that:

> Borderlines blame their partners when things go wrong in intimate relationships. And things are always going wrong, because they set impossibly high standards and double-binds for others. As their tension mounts, their need for perfect control in an imperfect world generates inevitable failure. People are fallible. One man would inspect the house after his wife did the chores, running his finger under the refrigerator, looking for dust. Eventually, he found some. Then a two-hour harangue would ensue in which he screamed at her about her lousy housekeeping. This personality profile creates an environment in which relationship conflict and abuse are inevitable.

Several studies attest to the link between spouse abuse and borderline personality characteristics. Tweed and Dutton (1998) reported the results of a cluster analysis conducted on the MCMI-II responses of batterers and identified two groups of batterers. The first group was described as generally violent and antisocial in many respects. Elevated distress and dysphoria and higher scores on measures of borderline personality organization characterized the second group. Dutton and Starzomski (1994) found that male spouse abusers with elevated scores on measures of borderline personality organization had scores comparable to those obtained by patients diagnosed with BPD.

BPD characteristics also appear to undermine attempts at treatment. Dutton et al. (1997) found that men with certain personality disorders (i.e., borderline, antisocial, and avoidant) have higher levels of posttreatment recidivism in terms subsequent spouse abuse.

In summary, it has been suggested by some that anyone has the potential to be aggressive and abusive in certain situations. However, Dutton's work shows that men who characteristically engage in abuse are not simply responding to situational factors; instead, they have a personality style with many borderline features.

Thinking Critically

1. Tweed and Dutton (1998) identified two seemingly distinct types of batterers, those who were generally violent and those with borderline, dysphoric features. Do you think this is a valid distinction? If so, what different developmental histories might characterize these types?
2. Therapists often report that the treatment process with borderline personality disorder patients is challenging because of their interpersonal styles, including the tendency to experience and express their feelings of anger and rage. Which treatment or treatments would you employ if you were the therapist given the task of treating someone with this disorder? What additional steps would you take for the borderline individual who also has a history of spouse abuse? Consider these issues when you read the section on therapies for BPD.

Etiology of Borderline Personality Disorder There are several views concerning the causes of BPD. Here, we discuss object-relations theory, biological research, and Linehan's diathesis-stress theory.

Object-Relations Theory Object-relations theory, an important variant of psychoanalytic theory, is concerned with the way children incorporate (or introject) the values and images of important people, such as their parents. In other words, the focus is on the manner in which children identify with people to whom they have strong emotional attachments. These introjected people (object representations) become part of the person's ego, but they can come into conflict with the wishes, goals, and ideals of the developing adult. For example, a college-age woman who has adopted her mother's notion of the proper role of a woman in society may find herself drawn to more modern ideals of feminism.

Object-relations theorists hypothesize that people react to their world through the perspectives of people from their past, primarily their parents or primary caregivers. As noted, sometimes these perspectives conflict with the person's own wishes. Two leading object-relations theorists are Otto Kernberg and Heinz Kohut (Kohut's views on narcissism will be discussed later).

Kernberg (1985) proposed that adverse childhood experiences—for example, having parents who provide love and attention inconsistently, perhaps praising achievements but being unable to offer emotional support and warmth—cause children to develop insecure egos.

Although people with borderline personality disorder have weak egos and need constant reassuring, they retain the capacity to test reality. As a result, these patients are in touch with reality but frequently engage in a defence mechanism called *splitting*—dichotomizing objects into all good or all bad and failing to integrate positive and negative aspects of another person or the self into a whole. This tendency causes extreme difficulty in regulating emotions because the borderline patient sees the world, including himself or herself, in black-and-white terms. Somehow this defence protects the patient's weak ego from intolerable anxiety.

A number of studies have yielded data relevant to Kernberg's theory. As expected, BPD patients report a low level of care by their mothers (Patrick et al., 1994). They view their families as emotionally inexpressive, low in cohesion, and high in conflict. Research conducted in Toronto by Links and van Reekum (1993) indicates that they also frequently report childhood sexual and physical abuse. A history of abuse has been verified in some studies (Johnson et al., 1999). Also, as demonstrated by researchers in Montreal, many BPD patients have experienced separation from parents during childhood (Paris, Zweig, & Guzder, 1994).

Biological Factors BPD runs in families, suggesting that it has a genetic component (Baron et al., 1985). BPD patients are also high in neuroticism, a heritable trait (Nigg & Goldsmith, 1994).

Some data suggest poor functioning of the frontal lobes, which may play a role in impulsive behaviour. BPD patients perform poorly on neurological tests of frontal-lobe functioning and show low glucose metabolism in the frontal lobes (Goyer et al., 1994; Van Reekum et al., 1993).

Consistent with the idea that low levels of the neurotransmitter serotonin are associated with impulsivity, when borderline patients were administered a drug to increase serotonin levels, their level of anger decreased (Hollander et al., 1993). Thus, biological research on BPD patients has yielded some promising leads concerning their impulsive behaviour.

Linehan's Diathesis-Stress Theory Linehan proposes that borderline personality disorder develops when people with a biological diathesis (possibly genetic) for having difficulty controlling their emotions are raised in a family environment that is invalidating; that is, a diathesis for what Linehan calls *emotional dysregulation* can interact with experiences that invalidate the developing child, leading to the development of borderline personality.

An invalidating environment is one in which the person's wants and feelings are discounted and disrespected, and efforts to communicate one's feelings are disregarded or even punished. An extreme form of invalidation is child abuse, sexual and nonsexual: Daddy says he loves me and yet he is hurting me and threatening even more if I tell. A recent humorous example of our own illustrates invalidation between a husband and a wife.

Wife: Honey, could you help me with something for a minute?
Husband: Sure, but I have to go to the bathroom first.
Wife: No, you don't.

The two main hypothesized factors—dysregulation and invalidation—interact with each other in a dynamic fashion (see Figure 13.1). For example, the emotionally dysregulated child makes enormous demands on his or her family. The exasperated parents ignore or even punish the child's outbursts. This response can lead to the child suppressing emotions, only to have them build up to an explosion, which then gets parental attention. Parents can end up reinforcing the very behaviours they find aversive. Other patterns are possible, but they share a constant back-and-forth, a vicious circle, between the diathesis for dysregulation and the stress of invalidation.

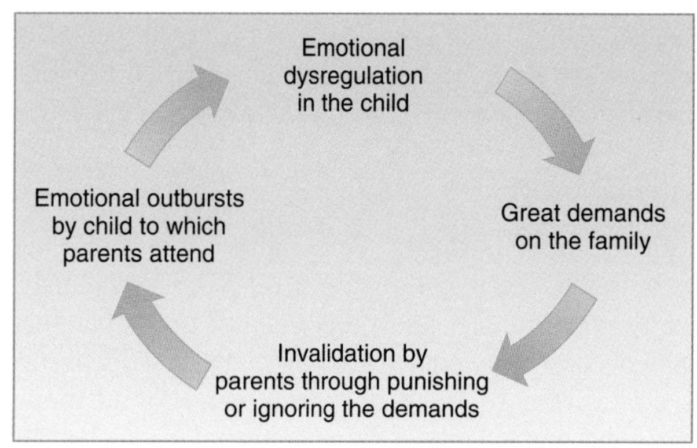

Figure 13.1 Linehan's diathesis–stress theory of borderline personality disorder.

A key piece of evidence supporting Linehan's theory concerns childhood physical and sexual abuse. As noted above, abuse is more frequent among people with BPD than among people diagnosed with most other disorders (Herman et al., 1989; Wagner, Linehan, & Wasson, 1989). One exception to this general pattern is dissociative identity disorder, which is also linked with very high rates of childhood abuse. Given the high rates of dissociative symptoms in borderline personality, the two disorders may be related and dissociation in both disorders may reflect the extreme stress of child abuse. Indeed, a study by Ross et al. (1998) found that the link between child abuse and borderline symptoms was mediated by dissociative tendencies.

As Linehan herself has cautioned, most aspects of her theory of etiology remain to be investigated. For example, self-reports by BPD patients that they suffered invalidating experiences as children are subject to the same kinds of questions as any retrospective self-report from a patient in therapy. Considering how sensitive such patients are to invalidating experiences as adults, it is conceivable that their recollections of invalidating childhood experiences are coloured by their current psychological turmoil.

Histrionic Personality Disorder

The diagnosis of histrionic personality, formerly called hysterical personality, is applied to people who are overly dramatic and attention-seeking. They often use features of their physical appearance, such as unusual clothes, makeup, or hair colour, to draw attention to themselves. These individuals, although displaying emotion extravagantly, are thought to be emotionally shallow. They are self-centred, overly concerned with their attractiveness, and uncomfortable when not the centre of attention. They can be inappropriately sexually provocative and seductive and are easily influenced by others. Their speech is often impressionistic and lacking in detail. For example, they may state a strong opinion yet be unable to give any supporting information.

This diagnosis has a prevalence of 2 to 3 percent and is more common among women than among men (Corbitt & Widiger, 1995). The prevalence of histrionic personality disorder (HPD) is higher among separated and divorced people, and it is associated with high rates of depression and poor physical health (Nestadt et al., 1990). Comorbidity with BPD is high.

Etiology of Histrionic Personality Disorder Little research has been conducted on HPD. Psychoanalytic theory predominates and proposes that emotionality and seductiveness were encouraged by parental seductiveness, especially father to daughter. Patients with HPD are thought to have been raised in a family environment in which parents talked about sex as something dirty but behaved as though it was exciting and desirable. This upbringing may explain the preoccupation with sex, coupled with a fear of actually behaving sexually. The exaggerated displays of emotion on the part of histrionic persons are seen as symptoms of such underlying conflicts, and their need to be the centre of attention is seen as a defence mechanism, a way to protect themselves from their true feelings of low self-esteem (Apt & Hurlbert, 1994; Stone, 1993).

Narcissistic Personality Disorder

People with a narcissistic personality disorder (NPD) have a grandiose view of their own uniqueness and abilities. They are preoccupied with fantasies of great success. To say that they are self-centred is an understatement. They require almost constant attention and excessive admiration and believe that only high-status people can understand them.

Narcissistic personality disorder draws its name from Narcissus of Greek mythology. He fell in love with his own reflection, was consumed by his own desire, and was then transformed into a flower.

Their interpersonal relationships are disturbed by their lack of empathy, feelings of envy, arrogance, and their tendency to take advantage of others. Relationships are also problematic because of their feelings of entitlement—they expect others to do special, not-to-be-reciprocated favours for them. Most of these characteristics, with the exception of lack of empathy and extreme reactions to criticism, have been validated in empirical studies as aspects of NPD (Ronningstan & Gunderson, 1990). The prevalence of NPD is less than 1 percent. It most often co-occurs with BPD (Morey, 1988).

Etiology of Narcissistic Personality Disorder The diagnosis of NPD is rooted in modern psychoanalytic writings. Many psychoanalytically oriented clinicians have regarded it as a product of our times and our system of values. On the surface, the person with NPD has a remarkable sense of self-importance, complete self-absorption, and fantasies of limitless success, but it is theorized that these characteristics mask a very fragile self-esteem.

Constantly seeking attention and adulation, narcissistic personalities are very sensitive to criticism and deeply fearful of failure. Sometimes they seek out others whom they can idealize because they are disappointed in themselves, but others are not allowed to become genuinely close. Their relationships are few and shallow. People with NPD become angry with others and reject them when they fall short of their unrealistic expectations. Their inner lives are impoverished because, despite their self-aggrandizement, they actually think very little of themselves.

At the centre of contemporary interest in narcissism is Heinz Kohut, whose two books, *The Analysis of the Self* (1971) and *The Restoration of the Self* (1977), have established a variant of psychoanalysis known as *self-psychology*. According to Kohut, the self emerges early in life as a bipolar structure with an immature grandiosity at one pole and a dependent overidealization of other people at the other. A failure to develop healthy self-esteem occurs when parents do not respond with approval to their children's displays of competency; that is, the child is not valued for his or her own self-worth but rather as a means to foster the parents' self-esteem.

Kohut suggests that when parents respond to a child with respect, warmth, and empathy, the child is endowed with healthy self-esteem. But when parents further their own needs rather than directly approve of their children, the result may be a narcissistic personality.

> A little girl comes home from school, eager to tell her mother about some great successes. But this mother, instead of listening with pride, deflects the conversation from the child to herself [and] begins to talk about her own successes which overshadow those of her little daughter. (Kohut & Wolf, 1978, p. 418)

Children neglected in this way do not develop an internalized, healthy self-esteem and have trouble accepting their own shortcomings. They develop into narcissistic personalities, striving to bolster their sense of self through unending quests for love and approval from others.

Heinz Kohut has played a major role in conceptualizing narcissistic personality disorder.

ANTISOCIAL PERSONALITY DISORDER AND PSYCHOPATHY

In current usage, the terms *antisocial personality disorder* and psychopathy (sometimes referred to as sociopathy) are often used interchangeably, although there are important differences between the two. Antisocial behaviour is an important component of both terms.

Characteristics of Antisocial Personality Disorder The DSM-IV-TR concept of antisocial personality disorder (APD) involves two major components:

1. A conduct disorder (described in Chapter 15) is present before the age of 15. Truancy, running away from home, frequent lying, theft, arson, and deliberate destruction of property are major symptoms of conduct disorder. Upwards of 60 percent of children with conduct disorder later develop APD (Myers, Stewart, & Brown, 1998).
2. This pattern of antisocial behaviour continues in adulthood.

Thus, the DSM diagnosis involves not only certain patterns of antisocial behaviour but patterns that began in childhood. Adults with antisocial personality disorder show irresponsible and antisocial behaviour by working only inconsistently, breaking laws, being irritable and physically aggressive, defaulting on debts, and being reckless. They are impulsive and fail to plan ahead and, although completely aware of lies and misdeeds, may neither show regard for truth nor experience remorse for their misdeeds.

It is estimated that about 3 percent of adult men and 1 percent of women in the United States are antisocial personalities (Robins et al., 1984). Similarly, a community study conducted in Edmonton found that about 3 percent of people met DSM criteria for APD (Swanson, Bland, & Newman, 1994). Rates are much higher among younger than among older adults and among people of low socioeconomic status. APD is comorbid with a number of other diagnoses, most notably substance abuse. Swanson et al. (1994) found that over 90 percent of the Canadians in their sample with APD had at least one other lifetime psychiatric diagnosis in addition to APD.

Characteristics of Psychopathy The concept of psychopathy is linked closely to the writings of Hervey Cleckley and his classic book *The Mask of Sanity* (1976). On the basis of his clinical experience, Cleckley formulated a set of criteria for recognizing the disorder. Unlike the DSM criteria for antisocial personality disorder, Cleckley's criteria for psychopathy refer less to antisocial behaviour per se than to the psychopathic individual's thoughts and feelings. One of the key characteristics of psychopathy is poverty of emotions, both positive and negative. Psychopathic people have no sense of shame, and even their seemingly positive feelings for others are merely an act. The psychopath is superficially charming and manipulates others for personal gain. Their lack of anxiety may make it impossible for psychopaths to learn from their mistakes, and their lack of positive emotions leads them to behave irresponsibly and often cruelly toward others. Another key point in Cleckley's description is that the antisocial behaviour of the psychopath is performed impulsively, as much for thrills as for something like financial gain.

Most researchers diagnose psychopathy using a checklist developed by Robert Hare and his associates (Hare et al., 1990). An extensive description of this measure and related research is provided in Canadian Contributions 13.1.

Canadian Contributions/13.1

Robert Hare and the Conceptualization and Assessment of Psychopathy

Robert Hare retired recently from the University of British Columbia after conducting decades of influential research on the nature and assessment of psychopathy. Hare's work has received widespread recognition, including an award from the Canadian Psychological Association for distinguished contributions in applied psychology and citations from the director of the Federal Bureau of Investigation (FBI) for exceptional service in the public interest. Hare's most well-known measure is the Psychopathy Checklist-Revised (PCL-R; Hare, 1991). The PCL-R consists of 20 items that are rated on a three-point scale. The 20 items on the checklist assess two major clusters of psychopathic behaviours. Factor 1, referred to as emotional detachment, describes a selfish, remorseless individual with inflated self-esteem who exploits others. This factor focuses on affective and interpersonal characteristics associated with psychopathy. It assesses attributes such as egocentricity, manipulativeness, callousness, and lack of guilt. Factor 2 characterizes an unstable and antisocial lifestyle marked by impulsivity and irresponsibility. Unfortunately, the Hare checklist does not include items to assess an absence of anxiety, a key feature of psychopathy according to Cleckley (Schmidt & Newman, 1999).

Although these two factors are highly correlated with each other and extreme psychopaths tend to receive substantially elevated scores on both, extensive research evidence indicates that the factors differ in their associations with other personality, behavioural, and demographic factors. Harpur and Hare (1994) examined whether scores on the PCL-R factors vary as a function of age in a sample of 889 male prisoners. They found that scores on Factor 1 remained stable across the age span, but scores on Factor 2 decreased with age, suggesting that psychopaths may became less impulsive and lower in sensation-seeking with age.

Research conducted with the Hare PCL-R shows that psychopathy occurs more among men than among women (Salekin, Rogers, & Sewell, 1997). Among Axis I diagnoses, psychopathy is frequently comorbid with abuse of alcohol and other drugs (Smith & Newman, 1990).

The PCL-R has been used extensively with forensic populations. A recent study in British Columbia used the PCL-R to identify criminal psychopaths; subsequent functional magnetic resonance imaging tests showed that, compared to criminal non-psychopaths and control participants, criminal psychopaths had less affect-related activity in the amygdala/hippocampal formation, suggesting that the hypoemotionality of psychopaths reflects limbic system deficiencies (Kiehl et al., 2001).

Stephen Porter at Dalhousie University and his colleagues use the PCL-R to study offenders who have committed homicides. They have shown that criminal homicides committed by psychopathic murderers are cold-blooded acts that are almost always premeditated and motivated by an external goal (e.g., material gain or revenge), while homicides committed by non-psychopaths are more likely to be impulsive crimes of passion (Woodworth & Porter, 2002). Other research found that most sexual murderers have moderate to high scores on the PCL-R and that psychopaths are especially likely to exhibit sadistic behaviour in their homicides (Porter, Woodworth, Earl, Drugge, & Boer, 2003).

In research conducted around the world, the PCL-R has proven to be one of the best predictors of recidivism (see Hare, Clark, Grann, & Thornton, 2000). A review of research conducted with the PCL-R led Hemphill, Hare, and Wong (1998) to conclude that psychopaths are three times more likely than non-psychopaths to recidivate in general and four times more likely to recidivate by committing acts of violence. Both factors of the PCL-R predicted violent recidivism, while only Factor 2 predicted general recidivism.

Overall, the PCL-R is regarded as the measure of choice when one is seeking to identify violent recidivists. For instance, a Canadian study conducted by Serin (1996) found that the PCL-R was the best predictor of violent recidivism when pitted against other factors. Thus, the PCL-R is regarded as a key component of risk appraisal in forensic assessment (see Serin & Brown, 2000).

Additional research suggests that the PCL-R is a predictor of treatment outcome. Ogloff, Wong, and Greenwood (1990) evaluated 80 male federal inmates in a therapeutic community program in British Columbia and found that the psychopaths in their sample showed less clinical improvement and had lower levels of motivation.

The PCL-R can also be used successfully with adolescents. A study of juvenile psychopaths aged 14 to 18 from Quebec used the PCL-R to distinguish psychopaths and non-psychopaths and confirmed that high PCL-R scores are associated with a lack of behavioural inhibition (Roussy & Toupin, 2000). A separate version of the Hare checklist, developed for use with children and relying on ratings by mothers to make diagnoses (Lynam, 1997), has revealed that psychopathic children are similar to psychopathic adults—they are impulsive and severely delinquent.

Controversies with Diagnoses of APD and Psychopathy We have seen that these two diagnoses—APD and psychopathy—are related, but they are by no means identical. One study found that only about 20 percent of people with APD scored high on the Hare PCL-R (Rutherford, Cacciola, & Alterman, 1999). Harpur and Hare (1994) observed that almost all psychopaths are diagnosed with APD but many people diagnosed with APD do not meet the criteria for psychopathy on the PCL-R. The question of which diagnosis is preferable has raised several issues.

Hare, Hart, and Harpur (1991) criticized the DSM diagnosis of APD because it requires accurate reports of events

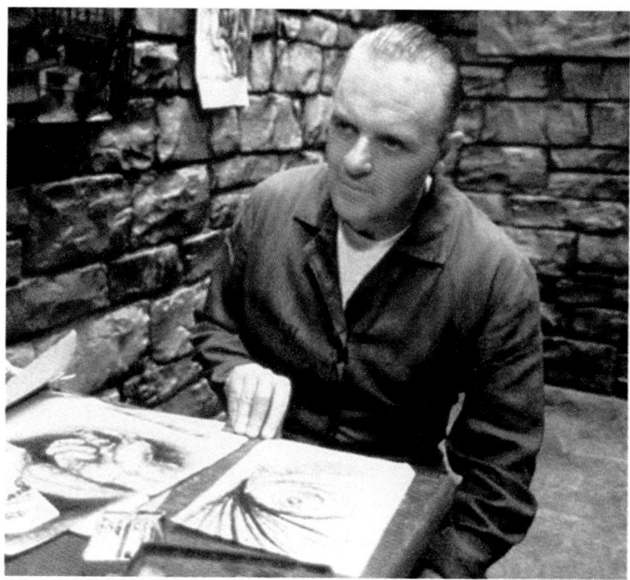

The character played by Anthony Hopkins in *The Silence of the Lambs* and *Hannibal* displayed many of the characteristics of the psychopath, especially total lack of regard for the rights of others.

from many years earlier by people who are habitual liars (recall the onset-in-childhood criterion), and many researchers believe that a DSM diagnostic concept should not be synonymous with criminality. Nevertheless, 75 to 80 percent of convicted felons meet the criteria for APD, while only 15 to 25 percent of convicted felons meet the criteria for psychopathy (Hart & Hare, 1989). Moreover, lack of remorse, a hallmark of psychopathy, is but one of seven criteria for the DSM's antisocial personality diagnosis, and only three of these criteria need to be present to make the diagnosis. Therefore, the person diagnosed with APD by the DSM may not have the lack of remorse that is central to psychopathy.

The differences between APD and psychopathy were described by Hare (1996) in a discussion of people who kill law enforcement officers. Hare stated that a 1992 FBI report described these killers as having an antisocial personality when, in fact, psychopathy was evident. Hare (1996) noted, "These killers were not simply persistently antisocial individuals who met DSM-IV criteria for APD; they were psychopaths—remorseless predators who use charm, intimidation, and, if necessary, impulsive and cold-blooded violence to attain their ends" (p. 39). Unfortunately, in recent years, Canada has had its share of these individuals, including infamous characters such as Clifford Olson, Paul Bernardo, and Karla Homolka, who have killed children and/or young women.

As we review the research in this area, it is important to keep in mind that it has been conducted on individuals diagnosed in different ways—some as antisocial personalities and some as psychopaths—which makes integrating these findings somewhat difficult.

The Case of Dan Before considering current research on psychopathy, we will examine an excerpt from a case history compiled by psychologist Elton McNeil (1967), a personal friend of the subject. This case illustrates the classic characteristics of the psychopath, but it is unusual in that the person described was neither a criminal nor in psychiatric treatment at the time the data were collected. This is an important point, for the majority of psychopaths who are the subjects of research studies have broken the law and been caught for doing so. Only rarely do we have the opportunity to examine in detail the behaviour of an individual who fits the diagnostic definition and yet has managed not to break the law.

Dan was a wealthy actor and disc jockey who lived in an expensive house in an exclusive suburb and generally played his role as a "character" to the hilt. One evening, when he and McNeil were out for dinner, Dan made a great fuss over the condition of the shrimp de Johnge he had ordered. McNeil thought that Dan had deliberately contrived the whole scene for the effect it might produce, and he said to his companion:

> "I have a sneaking suspicion this whole scene came about just because you weren't really hungry." Dan laughed loudly in agreement and said, "What the hell, they'll be on their toes next time." "Was that the only reason for this display?"
>
> "No," he replied, "I wanted to show you how gutless the rest of the world is. If you shove a little they all jump. Next time I come in, they'll be all over me to make sure everything is exactly as I want it. That's the only way they can tell the difference between class and plain ordinary. When I travel I go first class."
>
> "Yes, but how do you feel about you as a person—as a fellow human being?"
>
> "Who cares?" he laughed. "If they were on top they would do the same to me. The more you walk on them, the more they like it. It's like royalty in the old days. It makes them nervous if everyone is equal to everyone else. Watch. When we leave I'll put my arm around that waitress, ask her if she still loves me, pat her on the fanny, and she'll be ready to roll over any time I wiggle my little finger." (McNeil, 1967, p. 85)

Another incident occurred when a friend of Dan's committed suicide. Other friends were concerned and called McNeil to see whether he could provide any information about why the man had taken his life. Dan did not. Later, when McNeil mentioned the suicide, all Dan could say was, "That's the way the ball bounces." In his public behaviour, however, Dan's attitude seemed quite different. He was the one who collected money and presented it to the widow. In keeping with his character, Dan noted that the widow had a sexy body that really interested him.

These two incidents convey the flavour of Dan's behaviour. McNeil had witnessed a long succession of similar events, which led him to conclude:

> [The incidents] painted a grisly picture of life-long abuse of people for Dan's amusement and profit. He was adept at office politics and told me casually of an unbelievable set of deceptive ways to deal with the opposition. Character assassination, rumor mongering, modest blackmail, seduction, and barefaced lying were the least of his talents. He was a jackal in the entertainment jungle, a jackal who feasted on the bodies of those he had slaughtered professionally. (p. 91)

In his conversations with Dan, McNeil was also able to inquire into Dan's life history. One early and potentially important event was related by Dan.

> I can remember the first time in my life when I began to suspect I was a little different from most people. When I was in high school my best friend got leukemia and died and I went to his funeral. Everybody else was crying and feeling sorry for themselves and as they were praying to get him into heaven I suddenly realized that I wasn't feeling anything at all. He was a nice guy but what the hell. That night I thought about it some more and found that I wouldn't miss my mother and father if they died and that I wasn't too nuts about my brothers and sisters for that matter. I figured there wasn't anybody I really cared for but, then, I didn't need any of them anyway so I rolled over and went to sleep. (p. 87)

(Copyright (c) 1967. Adapted by permission of Prentice-Hall.)

An extreme callousness toward others clearly marks Dan's behaviour. A person may be otherwise quite rational and show no loss of contact with reality and yet behave in a habitually and exceedingly unethical manner. The final excerpt illustrated Dan's complete lack of feeling for others, a characteristic that is very relevant in explaining the behaviour of the psychopath.

Research and Theory on the Etiology of Antisocial Personality Disorder and Psychopathy We now turn to research and theory on the etiology of APD and psychopathy. We examine genetics as well as the psychological factors that operate in the family and in emotions. A final section on response modulation and impulsivity ties together several of the individual research domains. Note again, however, that most research has been conducted on psychopathic individuals who have already been convicted as criminals. Thus, the available literature may not allow generalization to the behaviour of psychopaths who elude arrest.

The Role of the Family Since much psychopathic behaviour violates social norms, many investigators have focused on the primary agent of socialization, the family, in their search for the explanation for such behaviour. McCord and McCord (1964) concluded, on the basis of a literature review, that lack of affection and severe parental rejection were the primary causes of psychopathic behaviour. Several other studies have related psychopathic behaviour to parents' physical abuse, inconsistencies in disciplining their children, and failure to teach them responsibility toward others (Bennett, 1960; Johnson et al., 1999). Furthermore, the fathers of psychopaths are likely to be antisocial in their behaviour.

Self-reported data on early rearing must be interpreted cautiously, as they were gathered by means of retrospective reports—individual recollections of past events. Information obtained in this way cannot be accepted uncritically. When people are asked to recollect early events in the life of someone now known to be psychopathic, their knowledge of the person's adult status may well affect what they remember or report about these early events. They may be more likely to recall deviant incidents and overlook more normal events. It is also risky to trust the retrospective reports of psychopaths because lying is a key feature of this disorder.

The problems of retrospective data can be avoided by conducting a follow-up study in adulthood of individuals who as children were seen at child-guidance clinics. In one such study, detailed records had been kept on the children, including the type of problem that had brought them to the clinic and related family information (Robins, 1966). Ninety percent of an initial sample of 584 cases were located 30 years after their referral to the clinic. Also interviewed in adulthood were 100 control participants who had lived in the geographic area served by the clinic but who had not been referred to it. By interviewing the now-adult people in the two samples, the investigators were able to diagnose and describe any maladjustments of these individuals. They then related the adult problems to the characteristics that these people had had as children to find out which characteristics predicted psychopathic behaviour in adulthood. Robins's summary brings to mind conduct disorder, mentioned earlier in relation to APD and discussed in Chapter 15.

> If one wishes to choose the most likely candidate for a later diagnosis of [psychopathy] from among children appearing in a child guidance clinic, the best choice appears to be a boy referred for theft or aggression who has shown a diversity of antisocial behaviour in many episodes, at least one of which could be grounds for Juvenile Court appearance, and whose antisocial behaviour involves him with strangers and organizations as well as with teachers

> and parents.... More than half of the boys appearing at the clinic [with these characteristics were later] diagnosed sociopathic personality. Such boys had a history of truancy, theft, staying out late, and refusing to obey parents. They lied gratuitously, and showed little guilt over their behaviour. They were generally irresponsible about being where they were supposed to be or taking care of money. (p. 157)

In addition to these characteristics, several aspects of family life were found to be consequential. Both inconsistent discipline and no discipline at all predicted psychopathic behaviour in adulthood, as did antisocial behaviour of the father.

Two important limitations to this research should be noted: (1) the harsh or inconsistent disciplinary practices of parents could be reactions to trying to raise a child who is displaying antisocial behaviour; and (2) many individuals who come from disturbed social backgrounds do not become psychopaths or develop any other behaviour disorders. This second point is important. Adults may have no problems whatsoever in spite of an inconsistent and otherwise problematic upbringing. Thus, although family experience is probably a significant factor in the development of psychopathic behaviour, it is not the sole factor. A diathesis also is required.

Genetic Correlates of APD Research suggests that both criminality and antisocial personality disorder have heritable components. Adoption and twin studies, including those of twins reared apart, indicate that genetic factors play a significant role in the likelihood that a person will commit a criminal act (Gottesman & Goldsmith, 1994; Grove et al., 1990; Mednick, Gabrielli, & Hutchings, 1984). For APD, twin studies show higher concordance for MZ than DZ pairs (Lyons et al., 1995). Moreover, adoption studies reveal higher than normal prevalence of antisocial behaviour in adopted children of biological parents with APD and substance abuse (Cadoret et al., 1995b; Ge et al., 1996).

Both twin and adoption studies also show that the environment plays a substantial role in antisocial personality disorder. In the Cadoret adoption study referred to above, an adverse environment in the adoptive home (such as marital problems and substance abuse) was related to the development of antisocial personality disorder whether or not the adoptive parents had antisocial personality disorder. Furthermore, high levels of conflict and negativity and low levels of parental warmth predicted antisocial behaviour in a twin study by Reiss et al. (1995).

Adoption research has also shown that some characteristics of adoptive families that are related to antisocial behaviour in their children appear to be reactions to a "difficult" child (Ge et al., 1996); that is, the child's genetically influenced antisocial behaviour leads to environmental changes involving harsh discipline, which, in turn, exacerbate the child's antisocial tendencies.

As noted earlier, Canadian researchers such as Kerry Jang and John Livesley at the University of British Columbia and Philip Vernon at the University of Western Ontario have been instrumental in extending research on the role of genetic factors in personality disorders such as APD (see Jang, Vernon, & Livesley, 2001; Livesley et al., 1998). They have used twin studies to show that a large genetic component accounts for much of the variability in individual differences in the personality dimension known as "dissocial behaviour" (i.e., antisocial behaviour). Twin studies have provided extensive evidence for the importance of genetic factors, but little progress has been made in identifying the specific genes involved in the etiology of specific personality disorders (see Jang et al., 2001).

Finally, most genetic research has focused on antisocial personality disorder and has not focused specifically on psychopathy. However, a recent study of male twins in Minnesota used the Minnesota Temperament Inventory, a 19-item measure of psychopathy, to test the relative roles of genetic versus environmental influences in the dimensions of psychopathy (Taylor et al., 2003). This study found that variance in dimensions of psychopathy was attributable to

Psychopathic serial killer Clifford Olson murdered 11 children in British Columbia. In 1982 he was sentenced to life in prison without eligibility for parole for 25 years. In 1997 he asked to have his parole eligibility reconsidered under the "faint hope" clause. The jury at his hearing rejected his application. How does he compare himself with the cannibalistic killer of *Silence of the Lambs*? "Hannibal Lecter is fiction—I'm real" (Worhington, 1997, p. 15). Robert Pickton, a pig farmer from Port Coquitlam, B.C., may have surpassed Olson's acts. He is to stand trial in 2004 accused of at least 22 counts of first-degree murder. Many of the victims were prostitutes who had disappeared from the Vancouver area.

genetic factors and that scale scores were not predicted by shared environmental factors. Similar findings were reported by Blonigen et al. (2003). However, it should be noted that both studies relied on males from the general community, so the heritability of psychopathy in clinical samples remains to be established.

Emotion and Psychopathy In defining the psychopathic syndrome, Cleckley pointed out the inability of such persons to profit from experience or even from punishment; they seem to be unable to avoid the negative consequences of social misbehaviour. Many are chronic lawbreakers despite their experiences with jail sentences. They seem immune to the anxiety or pangs of conscience that help keep most of us from breaking the law or lying to or injuring others, and they have difficulty curbing their impulses. In learning-theory terms, psychopaths have not been well socialized because they were unresponsive to punishments for their antisocial behaviour. Thus, they do not experience conditioned fear responses when they encounter situations in which the conditioned fear response should inhibit antisocial behaviour.

In a classic study based on Cleckley's clinical observations, Lykken (1957) tested the idea that psychopaths may have few inhibitions about committing antisocial acts because they experience so little anxiety. He performed several tests to determine whether psychopaths do indeed have low anxiety. One of the most important tests involved avoidance learning, which is assumed to be mediated by anxiety. Lykken studied the ability of psychopaths and control-group participants to avoid shock. He found that the psychopaths were poorer than the controls at avoiding the shocks, which supported the idea that psychopaths are low in anxiety.

Studies of the activity of the autonomic nervous system also indicate that psychopaths respond less anxiously to fear-eliciting stimuli. Psychopaths have lower than normal levels of skin conductance in resting situations, and their skin conductance is less reactive when they are confronted with intense or aversive stimuli or when they anticipate an aversive stimulus (Harpur & Hare, 1990). However, a different picture emerges when heart rate is examined. The heart rate of psychopaths is normal under resting conditions and remains normal when neutral stimuli are presented, but in situations in which they anticipate a stressful stimulus, their hearts beat faster than those of normal people anticipating stress.

These physiological reactions indicate that psychopaths cannot be regarded as simply underaroused, since their heart rates are higher than normal in anticipation of a stressor. Basing his theorizing in part on Lacey's work (1967), Hare (1978) focused on the *pattern* of psychophysiological responses of psychopaths. Faster heartbeats are viewed as an indication that a person is tuning out or reducing sensory input. Thus, the increased heart rate of psychopaths who are anticipating an aversive stimulus indicates that they are tuning out the stimulus. Their skin conductance is then less reactive to an aversive stimulus because they are effective in ignoring it.

This interpretation of the physiological reactions of psychopaths is plausible and consistent with Lykken's study on avoidance learning. It has also been directly confirmed in subsequent research conducted at Simon Fraser University (Ogloff & Wong, 1990). Further research by Hare and his associates has confirmed that, in both their behaviour and their biological response (Jutai & Hare, 1983), psychopaths are particularly adept at ignoring certain stimuli and focusing their attention on what interests them (Forth & Hare, 1989).

The research we have described thus far has been based on the idea that punishment does not arouse strong emotions in psychopaths and thus does not inhibit antisocial behaviour. But some researchers do not believe that punishment is the critical agent of socialization. They think that empathy, being in tune with the emotional reactions of others, is more important. For example, empathizing with the distress that callous treatment might cause in someone else could inhibit such behaviour. Some features of psychopathy may arise from a lack of empathy.

This idea has been tested by monitoring the skin conductance of psychopathic and nonpsychopathic men as they viewed slides of varying content. Three types of slides were used: threatening (e.g., gun, shark), neutral (e.g., book), and distress (e.g., a crying person). No differences were found between the two groups in their responses to the first two types of slides, but the psychopaths were less responsive to the distress slides (Blair et al., 1997). Thus, the psychopaths indeed appeared to show less empathy for the distress of others (see Figure 13.2).

Response Modulation, Impulsivity, and Psychopathy Similarities between aspects of psychopathy and the behaviour of animals who have had parts of their brains destroyed have led some researchers to propose that heightened impulsivity is a key element of psychopathy (Gorenstein & Newman, 1980). Lesioned animals show deficits in avoidance learning as well as impulsive responding to immediate rewards. The

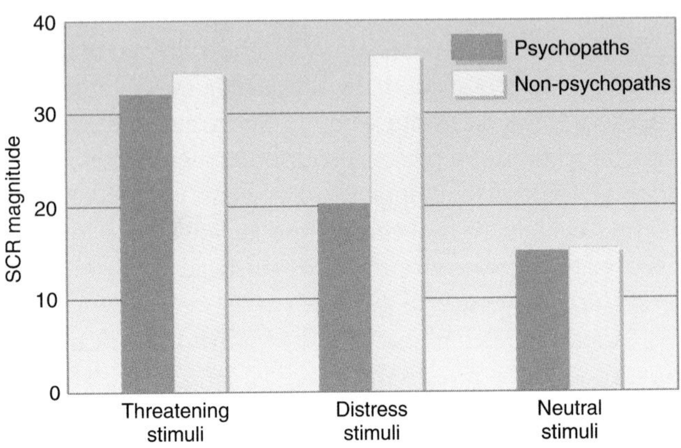

Figure 13.2 Skin-conductance response (SCR) of psychopathic and nonpsychopathic men to three types of stimuli. The psychopathic men showed less responsiveness to the distress stimuli, indicating a deficit in empathy.

idea that a key feature of psychopathy is impulsivity is also supported by studies of the brain waves of psychopaths, which reveal slow waves and spikes in the temporal area. These are often linked to impulsivity (Syndulko, 1978).

Impulsivity shows up when psychopaths attempt tasks designed to test their ability to modify their responses to success or failure (Patterson & Newman, 1993). In one study, participants viewed playing cards on a computer-generated video display (Newman, Patterson, & Kosson, 1987). Psychopaths continued playing the game much longer than non-psychopaths and appeared to ignore numerous cues indicating that they were unlikely to be rewarded and should quit. The insensitivity to contextual information appears to be a general feature of psychopathy; it occurs even in situations that do not involve threat of punishment (Newman, Schmitt, & Voss, 1997). Because social interactions are heavily dependent on context, this characteristic might well relate to psychopaths' insensitivity to other people.

Thus, psychopaths do not react as most of us do. In particular, they have little anxiety, so anxiety can have little deterrent effect on their antisocial behaviour. Their callous treatment of others may also be inked to their lack of empathy. Because psychopaths are deficient in using contextual information and in planning ahead, they behave impulsively. These are possible reasons for the psychopath's misconduct without regret.

ANXIOUS/FEARFUL CLUSTER

This cluster comprises three personality disorders:

- Avoidant personality disorder applies to people who are fearful in social situations.
- Dependent personality disorder refers to those who lack self-reliance and are overly dependent on others.
- Obsessive-compulsive personality disorder applies to those who have a perfectionistic approach to life.

AVOIDANT PERSONALITY DISORDER

The diagnosis of avoidant personality disorder applies to people who are keenly sensitive to the possibility of criticism, rejection, or disapproval and are reluctant to enter into relationships unless they are sure they will be liked. They may avoid employment that entails a lot of interpersonal contact. They are restrained in social situations owing to an extreme fear of saying something foolish or of being embarrassed by blushing or other signs of anxiety. They believe they are incompetent and inferior to others and are reluctant to take risks or try new activities.

The prevalence of avoidant personality disorder is about 1 percent (Weissman, 1993), and it is highly comorbid with dependent personality disorder (Trull, Widiger, & Frances, 1987) as well as BPD (Morey, 1988). According to one recent review, the only symptom that reliably differentiates avoidant personality disorder from dependent personality is that the avoidant person has great difficulty approaching and initiating social relationships (Alden, Laposa, Taylor, & Ryder, 2002). Avoidant personality is also comorbid with depression and generalized social phobia (Alpert et al., 1997). The comorbidity with generalized social phobia is likely due to the similarity between the diagnostic criteria for these disorders; avoidant personality disorder may be a more severe variant of generalized social phobia (Hofmann et al., 1995).

Both avoidant personality disorder and social phobia are related to a syndrome that occurs in Japan called *taijin kyoufu* (taijin means "interpersonal" and *kyoufu* means "fear"). Like patients with avoidant personality disorder and social phobia, those with *taijin kyoufu* are overly sensitive and avoid interpersonal contact. But what they fear is somewhat different from the usual fears of those with the DSM diagnoses. Patients with *taijin kyoufu* tend to be ashamed about how they appear to others, fearing, for example, that they are ugly or have body odor (Ono et al., 1996).

DEPENDENT PERSONALITY DISORDER

The core feature of dependent personality disorder (DPD) is a lack of both self-confidence and a sense of autonomy. Patients with DPD view themselves as weak and other people as powerful. They also have an intense need to be taken care of, which makes them feel uncomfortable when alone; they may be preoccupied with fears of being left alone to take care of themselves. They subordinate their own needs to ensure

Children normally go through a phase in which separation from a parent is distressing. People with dependent personality disorder may be experiencing a similar phenomenon in their adult relationships.

that they do not break up protective relationships. When a close relationship ends, they urgently seek another relationship to replace the old one.

The DSM criteria also include some features that are not well supported by the research literature. These diagnostic criteria portray people with DPD as being very passive (e.g., having difficulty initiating projects or doing things on their own, not being able to disagree with others, allowing others to make decisions for them). Research indicates, however, that dependent people do what is necessary to maintain a close relationship. This could involve being very deferential and passive, but may also entail taking active steps to preserve a relationship (Bornstein, 1997).

The prevalence of DPD is a little over 1.5 percent; higher figures are found in India and Japan, perhaps because these societies encourage dependent behaviour. It occurs more frequently among women than among men, possibly because of different childhood socialization experiences (Corbitt & Widiger, 1995; Weissman, 1993). DPD co-occurs frequently with borderline, schizoid, histrionic, schizotypal, and avoidant personality disorders as well as with the Axis I diagnoses of bipolar disorder, depression, anxiety disorders, and bulimia.

Obsessive-Compulsive Personality Disorder

The **obsessive-compulsive personality** is a perfectionist, preoccupied with details, rules, schedules, and the like. These people often pay so much attention to detail that they never finish projects. They are work rather than pleasure oriented and have inordinate difficulty making decisions (lest they err) and allocating time (lest they focus on the wrong thing). Their interpersonal relationships are often poor because they are stubborn and demand that everything be done their way. "Control freak" is a popular term for these individuals. They are generally serious, rigid, formal, and inflexible, especially regarding moral issues. They are unable to discard worn-out and useless objects, even those with no sentimental value. A dysfunctional attention to work and productivity is found more often in men than in women.

Obsessive-compulsive personality disorder (OCPD) is quite different from obsessive-compulsive disorder; it does not include the obsessions and compulsions that define the latter. Although the use of the "obsessive-compulsive" in both disorders suggests that the two disorders are related, the relationship does not appear to be very strong. Although obsessive-compulsive personality disorder is found more frequently among patients with OCD than among patients with panic disorder or depression (Diaferia et al., 1997), it is found in only a minority of OCD cases (Baer & Jenike, 1992). Obsessive-compulsive personality disorder is most highly comorbid with avoidant personality disorder and has a prevalence of about 1 percent (Lassano, del Buoeno, & Latapano, 1993).

See Focus on Discovery 13.1 for a comparison of a dimensional approach and the DSM-IV-TR discrete entity approach to diagnosing personality disorders.

focus on discovery/13.1

A Dimensional Approach to Personality Disorders

According to the most promising dimensional approach to personality disorders, these disorders represent extremes of personality traits found in everyone. Although literally hundreds of traits could be considered, much contemporary research in personality focuses on a model of personality called the five-factor model (McCrae & Costa, 1990). The five factors, or major dimensions, of personality are neuroticism, extraversion/introversion, openness to experience, agreeableness/antagonism, and conscientiousness. Table 13.2 presents questionnaire items that assess each of these dimensions. You can acquire a sense of what each dimension means by reading the table.

We will illustrate the five-factor model by examining its link with certain forms of personality dysfunction. For instance, how does psychopathy, as measured by Hare's PCL-R, relate to the five-factor model? Harpur, Hart, and Hare (1994) found that psychopaths are high in neuroticism and low in agreeableness and conscientiousness, with extreme antagonism and disagreeableness being the most definitive personality traits.

Other forms of personality dysfunction have been examined with the five-factor model. Widiger and Costa (1994) summarized the results of several studies that linked these personality traits to schizoid, borderline, and avoidant personality disorders. Patients with schizoid personality disorder and those with avoidant personality disorder are high in introversion. Thus, the five-factor model would predict that these two disorders would be hard to differentiate, and this has indeed been found to be true. However, there is some differentiation between the two disorders on the neuroticism dimension; patients with avoidant personality disorder are higher than those with schizoid personality disorder. In fact, according to Alden et al. (2002), avoidant personality disorder is the only personality disorder characterized by high neuroticism and introversion. Rather than forcing each patient into a discrete category and encountering problems in distinguishing between avoidant personality disorder and schizoid personality disorder, the dimensional approach would simply describe patients on their levels of neuroticism and introversion.

Borderline personality disorder is most strongly related to neuroticism and antagonism. Because high scores on neuroticism are found in many personality disorders and in Axis I disorders, it is not surprising that borderline personality is comorbid with these other conditions. Borderline patients also score high on antagonism, which distinguishes them from patients with avoidant personality disorder. High scores on antagonism are also found in patients with paranoid and antisocial disorders, so comorbidity with these disorders would be expected. Again, the dimensional approach does not force patients into discrete categories, but simply describes their scores on the five factors.

A dimensional model thus appears to have several distinct advantages. First, it handles the comorbidity problem, because comorbidity is a difficulty only in a categorical classification system like the DSM. Further, because the dimensional system forges a link between normal and abnormal personality, the findings on personality development in general become relevant to the personality disorders. For example, since genetic researchers have found that most of the traits of the five-factor model are heritable (Bouchard et al., 1990), genetic factors become plausible as variables related to the causes of personality disorders. Similarly, because there are sex differences in scores on the five factors, the model becomes relevant to sex differences in the prevalence of the personality disorders. Women, for example, score higher than men on neuroticism, agreeableness, and extraversion (Costa & McRae, 1988). Thus, women would be expected to be more likely than men to experience histrionic personality disorder (high scores on extraversion and neuroticism), dependent personality disorder (high scores on agreeableness and neuroticism), and BPD (high scores on neuroticism). Conversely, antisocial personality disorder (low scores on agreeableness) should be more frequent in men. Data confirm these expectations.

The utility of the five-factor model has also been supported by more formal statistical techniques that compare actual data on the interrelationships among the personality disorders to predictions about these relationships made by both the DSM system and the five-factor model. Researchers from Lakehead University showed that the data were more supportive of the predictions of the five-factor model than of the predictions from DSM-IV (O'Connor & Dyce, 1998).

Obviously, the five-factor model is not the only system for describing personality; other models with other dimensions are being considered. The PSY-5 described earlier is one example, and another is Livesley and Jackson's (2002) self-report scale known as the Dimensional Assessment of Personality Pathology—Basic Questionnaire (DAPP-BQ). The DAPP-BQ has 22 scales that assess 18 personality trait dimensions (e.g., anxiousness, affective lability, callousness, insecure attachment, narcissism, etc.) and various response styles. Statistical tests show that DAPP-BQ trait scales reflect the higher-order factors of emotional dysregulation (i.e., affective lability and impulsivity), dissocial behaviour (i.e., callousness, conduct problems, and narcissism), inhibitedness (i.e., avoidance of intimacy and restricted expression of emotions), and compulsivity (Livesley, Jang, & Vernon, 1998). The twin study at the University of British Columbia found that the DAPP-BQ personality traits have a large genetic component (Jang & Livesley, 1999). Other research linking the DAPP-BQ with the five-factor model and Eysenck's dimensions of psychoticism, extraversion, and neuroticism shows that neuroticism is linked with emotional dysregulation, dissocial behaviour is linked with high psychoticism, inhibitedness is linked with low extraversion, and compulsivity is linked with high conscientiousness (Larstone, Jang, Livesley, Vernon, & Wolf, 2002).

Given that the dimensional approach to personality disorders is valid and offers distinct advantages, it is possible that subsequent diagnostic systems will make a greater effort to incorporate a dimensional framework into the personality disorder section. Indeed, Livesley and Jang (2000) have proposed a two-phase approach in which clinicians first determine whether a personality disorder exists in general terms and then establish the specific nature of the disorder via dimensional ratings on a series of personality trait dimensions.

Table 13.2

The Five-Factor Model: Sample Items from the Revised NEO Personality Inventory

Factor	Sample items
Neuroticism	I am not a worrier. (-) I often feel tense or jittery. (+)
Extroversion/introversion	I'm known as a warm and friendly person. (+) Many people think of me as somewhat cold and distant. (-)
Openness to experience	I have a very active imagination. (+) I don't like to waste my time daydreaming. (-)
Agreeableness/antagonism	I believe that most people will take advantage of you if you let them. (-) I think most people I deal with are honest and trustworthy. (+)
Conscientiousness	I keep myself informed and usually make intelligent decisions. (+) I often come into situations without being prepared. (-)

Source: Costa and McCrae, 1992.

Note: Agreeing with an item marked with a + increases one's score on that factor; agreeing with an item marked - decreases it.

ETIOLOGY OF THE ANXIOUS/FEARFUL CLUSTER

Few data exist on the causes of the personality disorders in this cluster. Speculation about their causes has focused on parent-child relationships. It has been argued, for example, that dependent personality disorder results from an overprotective and authoritarian parenting style that prevents the development of feelings of self-efficacy (Bornstein, 1997).

Dependent personality disorder could also be a reflection of what are referred to as attachment problems (Livesley, Schroeder, & Jackson, 1990). Attachment has been studied by developmental psychologists and is regarded as important for personality development (see Chapter 15). The basic idea is that the young infant becomes attached to an adult and uses the adult as a secure base from which to explore and pursue other goals. Separation from the adult leads to anger and distress. As development proceeds, the child becomes less dependent on the attachment figure for security. The abnormal attachment behaviours seen in dependent personalities may reflect a failure in the usual developmental process arising from a disruption in the early parent-child relationship owing to death, neglect, rejection, or overprotectiveness. Persons with dependent personality disorder engage in a number of tactics (originally established to maintain their relationship with their parents) to keep their relationships with other people at any cost—for example, always agreeing with them (Stone, 1993).

Much like the fears and phobias discussed in Chapter 6, avoidant personality disorder may reflect the influence of an environment in which the child is taught to fear people and situations that most of us regard as harmless. For example, the abnormal fears of one of the child's parents may be transmitted through modelling.

Freud viewed obsessive-compulsive personality traits as being due to fixation at the anal stage of psychosexual development. More contemporary psychodynamic theories emphasize a fear of loss of control that is handled by overcompensation. For example, the man who is a compulsive workaholic may fear that his life will fall apart if he relaxes and has fun.

THERAPIES FOR PERSONALITY DISORDERS

There is not much research-based information on treating personality disorders (Crits-Christoph, 1998). There is, however, a lively and burgeoning clinical case literature on therapies for many disorders. The ideas outlined here are thus based mostly on the clinical experiences of a small number of mental health professionals and not on studies that contain suitable controls. These therapeutic guidelines are almost all that is available on treating personality disorders.

It is important to bear in mind that a therapist working with patients with personality disorders is typically also concerned with Axis I disorders, since most patients with PDs enter treatment because of an Axis I disorder rather than a personality disorder. For example, a person with antisocial personality disorder is likely to have substance abuse problems; a person with avoidant personality disorder may seek treatment for a social phobia; and a patient with obsessive-compulsive personality disorder may be seen for depression. In this connection, it should be mentioned that patients with Axis I disorders as well as personality disorders tend not to show as much improvement in various forms of psychotherapy as do patients with Axis I diagnoses alone (Crits-Christoph, 1998). The reason seems pretty clear: people with diagnoses on both axes are more seriously disturbed than are those with only Axis I diagnoses and therefore may require therapy that is both more intensive (because of the long-standing nature of personality disorders) and more extensive (i.e., focused on a broad range of psychological problems).

Psychoactive drugs are often used to treat the various personality disorders. The choice of drug is determined by the Axis I problem that the personality disorder resembles. Patients with avoidant personality disorder, for instance, can be prescribed a tranquilizer, such as the benzodiazepine Xanax, in the hope of reducing their social anxieties and phobias. When depression is present in an Axis II disorder, antidepressant medication, such as fluoxetine (Prozac), can be helpful. Fluoxetine has also reduced the impulsivity and aggressiveness of a group of patients with a variety of personality disorders (Coccaro & Kavousi, 1997).

Psychodynamic therapists aim to alter the patient's present-day views of the childhood problems assumed to underlie a personality disorder. For example, they may help a compulsive personality to realize that the childhood quest to win the love of his or her parents by being perfect need not be carried into adulthood, that he or she need not be perfect to win the approval of others, that it is possible to take risks and make mistakes without being abandoned.

Behavioural and cognitive therapists, in keeping with their focus on situations rather than traits, had little to say about specific treatments for the personality disorders until the publication of a book edited by Beck and Freeman (1990) on the cognitive therapy of personality disorders. Little empirical research on treatment has been done, although a notable exception is some research in Canada that is described in more detail below (see Howes & Vallis, 1996; Vallis, Howes, & Standage, 2000). Behavioural and cognitive therapists tend to analyze the individual problems that taken together reflect a personality disorder. For example, a person diagnosed as having a paranoid or an avoidant personality is extremely sensitive to criticism. This sensitivity may be treated by systematic desensitization or rational-emotive behaviour therapy (Renneberg et al., 1990). The paranoid personality's argumentativeness and hostility when faced with a contrary opinion pushes others away and provokes counterattacks from them. The behaviour therapist may help the paranoid individual learn more adaptive ways of disagreeing with other people. Social skills training in a support group might be suggested to encourage avoidant personalities to be more assertive with other people. One controlled study done in Vancouver confirmed that this is a promising strategy (Alden, 1989). Such an approach, perhaps combined with rational-emotive behaviour therapy, may help these patients cope when efforts to reach out do not succeed, as is bound to happen at times (Millon, 1996).

In looking at cognitive therapy for personality disorders, Beck, Freeman, and associates (1990) apply the same kind of analysis that has been found promising in the treatment of depression (see Chapter 10). Each disorder is analyzed in terms of logical errors and dysfunctional schemata. For example, treating obsessive-compulsive personality with cognitive therapy entails first persuading the patient to accept the essence of the cognitive model, that feelings and behaviours are primarily a function of thoughts. Errors in logic are then explored, such as the patient concluding that he or she cannot do anything right because of failing in one particular endeavour (an example of overgeneralization). The therapist also looks for dysfunctional assumptions or schemata that might underlie the person's thoughts and feelings—for example, the belief that it is critical for every decision to be correct (adherents of Ellis's methods would also take this step). Beck's approach to personality disorders represents a combination of a variety of behavioural and cognitive-behavioural techniques, all designed to address the particular, long-standing, and pervasive difficulties experienced by patients.

Vallis and his associates at Dalhousie University in Halifax examined whether short-term cognitive therapy is suitable for treating symptoms of personality disorder (Vallis et al., 2000). They found that patients with higher levels of personality dysfunction were less suitable for cognitive therapy, in terms of both self-ratings and clinician ratings of the therapeutic alliance. However, the authors suggested that there are still grounds for "cautious optimism" when it comes to treating personality disorders with cognitive therapy because they found indications that severe personality disorder would pose significant challenges for any form of short-term psychotherapy and that the problems may not be specific to cognitive therapy per se.

THERAPY FOR THE BORDERLINE PERSONALITY

Whatever the intervention modality, one thing is certain: few patients pose a greater challenge to treatment than do those with BPD. The problems that borderline personalities have with other people are replicated in the consulting room.

With the borderline patient, trust is inordinately difficult to create and sustain, thus handicapping the therapeutic relationship. The patient alternately idealizes and vilifies the therapist, demanding special attention and consideration one moment—such as therapy sessions at odd hours—and refusing to keep appointments the next, imploring for understanding and support but insisting that certain topics are off-limits.

Suicide is always a serious risk, but it is often difficult for the therapist to judge whether a frantic phone call at 2:00 a.m. is a call for help or a manipulative gesture designed to see how special the patient is to the therapist and to what lengths the therapist will go to meet the patient's needs at the moment. As happened in the case presented at the beginning of this chapter, hospitalization is often necessary when the behaviour of the patient becomes unmanageable on an outpatient basis or when the threat of suicide cannot be managed without the greater supervision possible only in the controlled setting of a psychiatric hospital.

Seeing such patients is so stressful that it is common practice for therapists to have regular consultations with another therapist, sometimes for support and advice, sometimes for professional help in dealing with their own emotions as they try to cope with the extraordinary challenges of helping borderline patients. (In psychoanalytic terms, these feelings of the therapist are called *countertransference*.) In her own cognitive-behavioural approach to therapy with borderlines (discussed later), Linehan makes this kind of ongoing consultation an integral part of the treatment.

A number of drugs have been tried in the pharmacotherapy of BPD, most notably antidepressants and antipsychotic medications. There is little to recommend antidepressants, but antipsychotics show some modest effects on borderline patients' anxiety, suicidality, and psychotic symptoms (Bendetti et al., 1998; Gitlin, 1993). Because such patients often abuse drugs and are suicide risks, extreme caution must be used in any drug-therapy regimen (Waldenger & Frank, 1989).

Otto Kernberg, one of the leading object-relations theorists, has been very influential in the study of borderline personality disorder.

Object-Relations Psychotherapy As noted earlier, object-relations theory focuses on how children identify with people to whom they have strong emotional attachments. Earlier in the chapter, we described the views of two object-relations theorists: Heinz Kohut, on narcissism, and Otto Kernberg, on the borderline personality.

As noted earlier, Kernberg (1985) operates from the basic assumption that borderline personalities have weak egos and therefore inordinate difficulty tolerating the probing that occurs in psychoanalytic treatment. Kernberg's modified analytic treatment has the overall goal of strengthening the patient's weak ego so that he or she does not fall prey to splitting, or dichotomizing. Splitting is the result of an inability to form complex ideas (object representations) that do not fit a simple good-bad dichotomy. For example, the patient may see the therapist as a godlike genius only to be crushed and furious when the therapist later mentions that the patient is behind in therapy payments; in an instant, the therapist becomes evil and incompetent. The therapist employs interpretive techniques, pointing out how the patient is allowing his or her emotions and behaviour to be regulated by such defences as splitting.

Kernberg's approach is more directive than that of most analysts. In addition to interpreting defensive behaviour, he gives patients concrete suggestions for behaving more adaptively and will hospitalize patients whose behaviour becomes dangerous to themselves or others. Kernberg's opinion that such patients are unsuitable for classical psychoanalysis because of their weak egos is consistent with a long-term study conducted at the world-famous analytically oriented Menninger Clinic (Stone, 1987).

Dialectical Behaviour Therapy Marsha Linehan (1987) introduced an approach that combines client-centred empathy and acceptance with cognitive-behavioural problem-solving and social skills training. What she calls dialectical behaviour therapy (DBT) has three overall goals for borderline individuals:

1 that they learn to modulate and control their extreme emotionality and behaviours
2 that they learn to tolerate feeling distressed
3 that they learn to trust their own thoughts and emotions

Why does Linehan use the word dialectical in describing her therapy? The concept of dialectics comes from the German philosopher Hegel (1770–1831). For our purposes, it is enough to know that *dialectics* refers to a worldview that holds that reality is an outcome of a constant tension between opposites. Any event—called the thesis—tends to generate a force in opposition to it—its *antithesis*. The tension between the opposites is resolved by the creation of a new event—the *synthesis*. For example, John loves Mary (thesis). But he finds in her some qualities that annoy him, creating in him some doubt as to whether he truly loves her (antithesis). John then comes to realize that he can love Mary in spite of her faults, perhaps even because of them (synthesis). This synthesis can then split into another pair of dialectical opposites, with a new synthesis eventually emerging that can reconcile them into yet another synthesis. And so on and on.

Linehan uses the term *dialectic* to describe the seemingly paradoxical stance that the therapist must take with borderline patients—accepting the patients as they are and yet helping them change. Linehan also uses the term to refer to the borderline patients' realization that they need not split the world into black and white, but can achieve a synthesis of apparent opposites. For example, instead of a friend being either all bad (thesis) or all good (antithesis), the friend can be a person with both kinds of qualities (synthesis)

DBT centres on the therapist's full acceptance of borderline personalities with all their contradictions and acting out, empathically validating their (distorted) beliefs with a matter-of-fact attitude toward their suicidal and other dysfunctional behaviour. Shelley McMain and Lorne Korman from the Centre of Addiction and Mental Health in Toronto and Linda Dimeff from the University of Washington recently described the role of DBT in treating emotion dysregulation (McMain, Korman, & Dimeff, 2001). They illustrated the concept of therapist acceptance by relating the case study of Jane, a BPD client with substance abuse disorder. Jane had a history of sexual abuse and experienced intense emotions of sadness, fear, and anger, along with intense self-criticism and shame. The following account stems from Jane's failure to keep self-monitoring diary cards and her emotional reactions to the treatment sessions:

Marsha Linehan created dialectical behaviour therapy, which combines cognitive behaviour therapy with Zen and Rogerian notions of acceptance.

CLIENT: Sometimes it's so upsetting. Because sometimes I could come in a good mood and then leave depressed. I end up leaving here so upset.

THERAPIST: No, I agree, that doesn't sound too comfortable.

CLIENT: It's like my mother in the past, reminding me of all my faults all the time.

THERAPIST: Yeah, it's so painful to bring up this stuff. Why would anyone want that?

CLIENT: Yeah, exactly!

THERAPIST: Now here's the dilemma. We could not talk about your problems, and if this would take away your pain and misery, I'd be all for it. On the other hand, if we help you figure out how to tolerate your bad feelings, then you won't have to rely on your pain medicine or resort to thinking of killing yourself when these feelings come up. (from McMain et al., 2001, p. 192-193).

This exchange illustrates the therapist's acceptance and acknowledgement of Jane's emotional experiences. At the same time, the therapist suggests that learning to develop some emotional self-control can be substituted for the extreme emotional reactions that Jane has relied on in the past.

The cognitive-behavioural aspect of the treatment, conducted both individually and in groups, involves helping patients learn to solve problems, to acquire more effective and socially acceptable ways of handling their daily living problems and controlling their emotions. Work is also done on improving their interpersonal skills and controlling their anger and anxieties. After many months of intensive treatment, limits are set on their behaviour, consistent with what Kernberg advocates. Basically, DBT is cognitive behaviour therapy within the paradoxical context of validating and accepting the person for who he or she is. In Linehan's words:

> Stylistically, DBT blends a matter-of-fact, somewhat irreverent, and at times outrageous attitude about current and previous parasuicidal and other dysfunctional behaviours with therapist warmth [and] flexibility.... [A] focus ... on active problem-solving [is] balanced by a corresponding emphasis on validating the patient's current emotional, cognitive, and behavioural responses just as they are. (1993b, p. 19)

Linehan and her associates published the results of the first randomized, controlled study of a psychological intervention for BPD (Linehan et al., 1991). Patients were assigned randomly either to DBT or to treatment as usual, meaning any therapy available in the community (Seattle, Washington). Patients were assessed after one year of treatment and again six and 12 months later (Linehan, Heard, & Armstrong, 1993). The findings immediately after treatment revealed the highly significant superiority of DBT on measures of intentional self-injurious behaviour, including suicide attempts; dropping out of treatment; and inpatient hospital days. At the follow-ups superiority was maintained; additionally, DBT patients had better work histories, reported less anger, and were judged as better adjusted overall than the comparison therapy patients. A subsequent study showed that DBT was reasonably effective in reducing drug use in BPD patients with substance dependence (Linehan et al., 1999). As a result of Linehan's (1993a, 1993b) work, there is widespread interest in this approach to BPD, and many outcome studies are in progress around the world to evaluate its effectiveness.

THERAPY FOR PSYCHOPATHY

As for the treatment of psychopathy, there is unusual—and unfortunate—agreement among therapists of varying theoretical persuasions: psychopathy is virtually impossible to treat (Cleckley, 1976; McCord & McCord, 1964; Palmer, 1984). This issue is revisited in the description of work by Rice and her colleagues (see Chapter 18).

It may be that people with the classic symptoms listed by Cleckley are by their very natures incapable of benefiting from any form of psychotherapy. In fact, it is unlikely that psychopaths would even want to be in therapy. The primary reason for their unsuitability for psychotherapy is that they are unable and unmotivated to form any sort of trusting, honest relationship with a therapist. People who lie almost without knowing it, who care little for the feelings of others and understand their own even less, who appear not to realize that what they are doing is morally wrong, who lack any motivation to obey society's laws and mores, and who, living only for the present, have no concern for the future are, all in all, extremely poor candidates for therapy.

Many valiant attempts have been made to establish tenable connections with psychopaths, but both the published literature and informal communications among mental health professionals support the conclusion that true psychopathy cannot be reached through psychological efforts. Similar negative conclusions may be drawn about somatic methods—electroconvulsive shock; drugs such as Dilantin, stimulants, and sedatives; and psychosurgery. There is, however, some evidence that large doses of antianxiety agents can reduce hostility in psychopaths (Kellner, 1982), and there is some tentative evidence that psychopaths who had attention-deficit disorder as children might benefit from the stimulant drug Ritalin, which has had some positive effects with hyperactive youngsters (Stringer & Josef, 1983; see Chapter 15). A failed attempt to treat the psychopath using a controlled social environment in combination with drugs is described in Canadian Clinic Focus 13.1

The cognitive therapy of Beck and his associates (1990) conceptualizes psychopaths in terms of particular kinds of thoughts and assumptions:

> [They have] self-serving beliefs that emphasize immediate, personal satisfactions and minimize future consequences. The underlying belief that they are always right makes it unlikely that they will question their actions.... Instead of evaluating the potential helpfulness of [guidance and counseling from others, such] patients tend to dismiss input from others as irrelevant to their purposes.... Antisocial

> patients' lack of concern for future outcomes might be placed on the opposite end of a continuum from obsessive-compulsive patients' excessive striving toward perfectionistic future goals. (p. 154)

Specific beliefs are said to include justification (merely wanting something justifies any actions to attain it), personal infallibility (believing that one always makes good choices), the impotence of others (what others think doesn't matter), and low-impact consequences (negative outcomes may happen, but they will not matter).

The general goal of cognitive therapy is to challenge such beliefs and to try to bring the patient's ideas and behaviours in line with those of a lawful society in which people respect the rights and sensibilities of others and are responsive to social controls. In this view, efforts should be made to demonstrate to the patient that his or her goals can be achieved more readily by altering behaviour so that it is less impulsive and more empathic and, in general, better conforms to societal standards. Considering the feelings of others might be more advantageous to the psychopathic patient than continuing to ignore others' feelings. It remains to be seen whether this cognitive-behavioural conceptualization will generate interventions any more successful than others that have been tried in vain.

Many psychopaths spend time in prison for committing crimes, and the discouraging results of imprisonment as a means of rehabilitation may be traced at least in part to the inability to modify psychopathic behaviour. As criminologists have often stated, our prison system seems to operate more as a school for crime than as a place where criminals, and psychopaths, are rehabilitated.

An interesting argument in favour of incarceration is that psychopaths often settle down in middle age and thereafter (Craft, 1969). Whether through biological changes, insight into their self-defeating natures, or simply becoming worn out and unable to continue in their finagling and often violent ways, many psychopaths grow less disruptive as they approach age 40. Prison protects society from the antisocial behaviour of active psychopaths, with release more plausible when the prisoner enters a stage of life in which the excesses of the disorder are less in evidence.

Canadian Clinic Focus/13.1

Treatment of Psychopaths: The Oak Ridge "Experiment"

"Patients drugged in experiments at psychiatric facility suit claims: Programs abused criminally insane, documents allege"

—Headline to report by Tracey Tyler, *The Toronto Star*, January 23, 2001, p. A18

Were "criminally insane" patients, including many psychopaths, drugged and tortured in the name of treatment while the Government of Ontario sat idly by and did nothing? This is the basis of allegations in a $150-million class-action lawsuit filed against both the Government of Ontario and the psychiatrist who initiated the program at the Oak Ridge division of the Penetanguishene Mental Health Centre. The major allegation of the lead plaintiff, Vance Egglestone, is that he was one of hundreds of patients who were "no more than human guinea pigs" when allegedly subjected to mental and physical abuse and various mind-altering experiments, including the administration of LSD, between 1965 and 1982 as part of treatment programs designed to "reconstruct" their personalities.

Oak Ridge Division of the Penetanguishene Mental Health Centre

Oak Ridge is the only maximum-security psychiatric hospital in Ontario, and it is reserved exclusively for men. Most men confined to Oak Ridge in the era described in the lawsuit were held "at the Pleasure of the Lieutenant Governor" (warrant) for an indeterminate period of time. Further, there was no obligation to treat individuals or specification of criteria for discharge. Men who had been acquitted of murder on grounds of "insanity" were usually destined to remain confined until they died (Wiesman, 1995). In addition to men referred by the courts, Oak Ridge drew its population from men transferred from prison (especially following riots at the federal penitentiary at Kingston in 1971) or reformatories, and from referrals from other mental hospitals. Oak Ridge developed a reputation as a place that could control behaviour that could not be controlled in other facilities. Escape from Oak Ridge was virtually impossible. No wonder it became known as "the Alcatraz of Canada" (Boyd, 1963)! It was the final stage in government attempts to control "dangerous" behaviour. Male attendants controlled the lives of the patients using numerous rules and rituals. Thus, prior to 1965, there was essentially no psychological treatment of any form for the men committed to Oak Ridge.

The Social Therapy Unit (STU)

In 1965 the new medical director, Dr. Barry Boyd, hired a young psychiatrist named Dr. Elliot Barker. Barker set about developing an experiment in social engineering that became known as the Social Therapy Unit program. He started in 1965 with 38 patients on the now infamous "G Ward" and by 1968 had expanded the program to include half the population of Oak Ridge (about 150 patients) (Weisman, 1995).

The novel program generated much public attention worldwide, most of it favourable. Over the decade between 1966 and 1976, reporters and film crews from Canada and abroad shared with the public a reassuring view of the treatment of the "criminally insane." Weisman (1995, p. 266) interpreted the portrayals of the filmmakers and journalists in the following way:

> [H]ere were young, handsome, and intelligent men discussing their violent actions with insight and understanding, and apparently interacting with their peers in a manner that was both honest and compassionate.... That somehow men who had committed the most heinous acts of multiple murder, rape, and arson, and that, more improbably, those branded as psychopaths, could be brought to the point of confronting their defenses on a daily basis and choosing caring over cruelty and hope over despair was the psychiatric equivalent to walking on water.

What was this miraculous approach to treating the psychopath? What exactly happened on the STU? The therapeutic community was peer-run with very minimal professional staff contact. Patients were involved in compulsory, structured, intensive group therapy for about 80 hours each week. They participated in daily sessions with other patients, sat on committees that structured and observed every aspect of life in the institution, spent minimal time in organized recreational, academic, or vocational programs, and had no opportunity for diversion, such as through reading, watching television, and even ordinary social interaction. Men who performed well and showed the appropriate talent could be appointed to leadership roles, leading groups and sitting on security and administrative committees (Rice & Harris, 1993; Weisman, 1995). Indeed, one patient, Michael Mason, not only played a vital role in the development of the program but also co-authored with Dr. Barker several major theoretical publications that described the STU (e.g., Barker & Mason, 1968; Barker, Mason, & Wilson, 1969). Mason was a warrant patient who had been tried on murder charges.

The patient committee system had real and extensive powers. A medication committee determined which drugs a patient could or should take, and decisions were invariably enforced. Patients could be escorted forcibly to meetings, placed in cuffs, and watched over by an assigned patient. The objective of the therapeutic community was "a major reconstruction of personality."

Should this strategy be the focus of lawsuits a generation later? Perhaps not, but for the fact that the STU involved much more than drastic changes in hospital routine. The radical vision was that the major reconstruction "required a break with normality and a re-experiencing of one's pathology, and that the resources of the community would be mobilized both to accelerate these changes and to make sure that they resulted in greater health" (Weisman, 1995, p. 275). Some of the strategies designed to make the patients surrender their defences, risk loss of control, and let their pathology show included the following:

1 The STU deliberately employed various medications that were cathartic, hypnotic, disorienting, or hallucinogenic. The drugs were often used in combination in attempts to eliminate defensive behaviour (Defence-Disruptive Therapy) and raise the level of tension in the individual and in the community. The drugs included sodium amytal, methedrine, scopolamine, and LSD.

2 The STU tested the limits of interpersonal communication by developing social situations that were unusual and extreme. These included the "small group encounter," the "forced dyadic encounter," "compressed encounter therapy," and, the ultimate tool for bringing down defences, the "total encounter capsule." This latter was

> a windowless, safe, and self-contained room equipped with tubes for feeding and an open toilet, together with a one-way mirror overhead for constant monitoring, in which patients could be together unclothed and undistracted by external stimuli, free to express themselves with no inhibitions and secure in the realization that should they overstep the generous limits that had been allowed, they would be restrained. (Weisman, 1995, p. 275)

Weisman (1995, p. 285) noted further that "[i]n the culture of the Social Therapy Unit, the capsule was to be the site of extraordinary events—of breakthroughs and recovery."

Consent was rarely solicited at Oak Ridge. Coercion on the part of the attendants and other patients was apparently the norm. The class-action suit alleges that even when consent was sought, it was of little legal value because it was obtained "under duress, coercion or intimidation" (Tyler, 2001, A18). It is certainly true that, according to today's ethical standards, many aspects of the STU program would violate the rights of patients (see Chapter 18) and would also be questioned on clinical grounds. Nonetheless, many professionals of the era viewed the program favourably on both ethical and clinical grounds. Indeed, the chair of a parliamentary subcommittee that evaluated the program concluded that the techniques used "are the most fruitful anywhere in the universe at the present time, based on the knowledge we have gathered" (Government of Canada, 1977, p. 45).

The Violent Self Reconstructed?

How successful was the Oak Ridge experiment? Unfortunately, it was a failure. Although the non-psychopaths fared somewhat better after their release than offenders with similar characteristics who went to prison, retrospective evaluations determined that the psychopaths who received treatment in the program had even higher rates of recidivism involving violence than their counterparts in prison (Rice & Harris, 1993). The experiment is yet another failure in the long history of valiant attempts to encourage the psychopath to think, feel, and act in non-violent, prosocial ways. This failure is echoed in the assertions of the lawsuit filed against the Government of Ontario and Dr. Barker: "There was no scientifically proven value to these experiments" and they were carried out "for years and even decades without the crown questioning the value" or the adverse effects on the participants (Tyler, 2001).

Comment

The bold experiment at Oak Ridge, however misguided, was an attempt to change the especially violent behavioural, cognitive, and affective reactions of a group of men who included many of the most antisocial psychopaths who at that point had not responded favourably to any conventional type of biological and psychological treatment or management strategies. Many of the techniques were unorthodox, to say the least. It is also clear that some of the specific strategies used on the STU mirrored some of the mind-altering experiments employed by Dr. Ewen Cameron at McGill's Allan Memorial Institute (see Chapter 2). Would society ever allow a similar program of "coercive resocialization" to be employed today? Very unlikely! As stated by Weisman (1995, p. 289), the STU "is still remembered by some as a successful venture in utopian experimentation; for others, it embodies the ultimate of modern tyrannies—the state-authorized subjection of the individual without any countervailing restraint." We will address pertinent ethical and legal issues in detail in Chapter 18. There are now strict legal controls on psychiatric authority, including the patient's right under most circumstances to refuse treatment.

What became of Dr. Barker's intensive and radical program of treatment on the STU? What factors led to the demise of the program? According to Rice and Harris (1993, p. 198), "the program began a slow death in 1978 when local administration and bureaucrats at the Ministry of Health head office in Toronto gave in to demands of the attendants (who were in conflict with professional staff over control of the program), and permanently banished the unit's entire clinical team from the building." Further, the more stringent, legislated criteria for treatment consent (revised in 1978, in 1987, and subsequently) and pressure from advocacy groups, as well as negative evaluations about the success of the program, would have eventually coalesced to terminate the program on the STU (Rice & Harris, 1993). Subsequent programs tended to try to blend considerations about security with traditional clinical interventions, including behaviour modification and pharmacotherapy. According to Rice and Harris (1993), these new programs failed to reduce recidivism of criminal behaviours when patients were released.

What will the future hold with respect to the possible treatment of the psychopath? Although the current Zeitgeist is a pessimistic view and the problem of the "violent psychopath" has been shifted from psychology and psychiatry to criminal justice (Weisman, 1995), Wong and Hare (in press) have developed promising program guidelines for the institutional treatment of violent psychopathic offenders. Their cognitive-behavioural approach concentrates especially on relapse prevention, a major shortcoming of past attempts to change the psychopath. Perhaps future research will finally confirm a useful and effective treatment for the violent psychopath. Will Wong and Hare's approach stand the test of time and long-term follow-up, or will we look back on it as yet another failure?

What became of Dr. Barker? Elliot Barker is president of the Canadian Society for the Prevention of Cruelty to Children.

The Oak Ridge Division serves all of Ontario.

Primary Sources: Rice and Harris (1993); Tyler (2001); Weissman (1995); Wong and Hare (in press)

SUMMARY

- Coded on Axis II in DSM-IV-TR, personality disorders are defined as enduring patterns of behaviour and inner experience that disrupt social and occupational functioning. They are usually codiagnosed with such Axis I disorders as depression and anxiety disorders. Although these diagnoses have become reliable in recent years, they overlap considerably and it is usual for a person to meet diagnostic criteria for more than one personality disorder. This high comorbidity, coupled with the fact that personality disorders are seen as the extremes of continuously distributed personality traits, has led to proposals to develop a dimensional rather than a categorical means of classifying these disorders.
- Personality disorders are grouped into three clusters in DSM-IV-TR. Specific diagnoses in the first cluster—odd/eccentric—include paranoid, schizoid, and schizotypal. These disorders are usually considered to be less severe variants of schizophrenia, and their symptoms are similar to those of the prodromal or residual phases of schizophrenia. Behaviour-genetic research gives some support to this assumption, especially for schizotypal personality disorder.

- The dramatic/erratic cluster includes borderline, histrionic, narcissistic, and antisocial personality disorders. The major symptom of borderline personality disorder is unstable, highly changeable emotions and behaviour; of histrionic personality disorder, exaggerated emotional displays; of narcissistic personality disorder, highly inflated self-esteem; and of antisocial personality disorder, seriously antisocial behaviour. Theories of the etiology of the first three of this cluster of diagnoses focus on early parent-child relationships. For example, object-relations theorists, such as Kernberg and Kohut, have proposed detailed explanations for borderline and narcissistic personality disorders, focusing on the child developing an insecure ego because of inconsistent love and attention from the parents. Linehan's cognitive-behavioural theory of borderline personality disorder proposes an interaction between a deficit in emotional regulation and an invalidating family environment. Psychopathy is related to the antisocial personality disorder but it is not an official DSM diagnosis.
- More is known about antisocial personality disorder and psychopathy than about other disorders in the dramatic/erratic cluster. Though they overlap a great deal, the two diagnoses are not exactly equivalent. The diagnosis of antisocial personality focuses on antisocial behaviour, whereas that of psychopathy, influenced by the writings of Cleckley, emphasizes emotional deficits, such as a lack of fear, regret, or shame. Psychopaths are thought to be unable to learn from experience, to have no sense of responsibility, and to be unable to establish genuine emotional relationships with other people.
- Research on their families indicates that psychopaths tend to have fathers who themselves were antisocial and that discipline during their childhoods was either absent or inconsistent. Genetic studies, particularly those using the adoption method, suggest that a predisposition to antisocial personality disorder is inherited.
- The core problem of the psychopath may be that impending punishment creates no inhibitions about committing antisocial acts. A good deal of overlapping evidence supports this view: (1) psychopaths are slow to learn to avoid shock; (2) according to their electrodermal responses, psychopaths show little anxiety, but as indicated by their faster heart rates, they seem more able than normal people to tune out aversive stimuli; and (3) psychopaths have difficulty altering their responses, even when their behaviour is not producing desirable consequences. A lack of empathy may also be a factor in the psychopath's callous treatment of others.
- The anxious/fearful cluster includes avoidant, dependent, and obsessive-compulsive personality disorders. The major symptom of avoidant personality disorder is fear of rejection or criticism; of dependent personality disorder, low self-confidence; and of obsessive-compulsive personality disorder, a perfectionistic, detail-oriented style. Theories of etiology focus on early experience. Avoidant personality disorder may result from the transmission of fear from parent to child via modelling. Dependent personality may be caused by disruptions of the parent-child relationship (e.g., through separation or loss) that lead to the fear of losing other relationships in adulthood.
- Little has been discovered about effective therapy for the various personality disorders for several reasons. The high level of comorbidity among the diagnoses makes it difficult to evaluate reports of therapy. Some promising evidence is emerging, however, for the utility of dialectical behaviour therapy for borderline personality disorder. This approach combines client-centred acceptance with a cognitive-behavioural focus on making specific changes in thought, emotion, and behaviour.
- Psychotherapy for psychopathy is rarely successful. In addition to the pervasiveness and apparent intractability of an uncaring and manipulative lifestyle, the psychopath is by nature a poor candidate for therapy. People who habitually lie and lack insight into their own or others' feelings—and have no inclination to examine emotions—will not readily establish a trusting and open working relationship with a therapist.

KEY TERMS

antisocial personality (p. 417)
avoidant personality (p. 423)
borderline personality (p. 413)
dependent personality (p. 423)
dialectical behaviour therapy (DBT) (p. 428)
histrionic personality (p. 416)
narcissistic personality (p. 416)
obsessive-compulsive personality (p. 424)
paranoid personality (p. 411)
personality disorders (p. 408)
psychopathy (p. 417)
schizoid personality (p.412)
schizotypal personality (p. 412)

Reflections: Past, Present, and Future

- Assume that you are a counselling psychologist at a university counselling centre who has a female undergraduate student as a client. She has been referred to you with a diagnosis on Axis I of the DSM-IV-TR of panic disorder with agoraphobia (see Chapter 6). You already have a treatment plan in mind based on your experience in working with anxious students. However, during your assessment, you realize that the woman also meets the criteria for a dependent personality disorder. How would your case conceptualization (see Chapter 4) and intervention change as a result of this new Axis II information?
- The beginning of this chapter included the now famous quote from Paul Bernardo that was made at the time of his trial. Do you think that Bernardo was telling the truth or is he, as Crown Attorney Ray Houlahan stated at the time, a "master of deception"? Was he showing genuine remorse or was his sorrow yet another "con"?
- Psychopaths do not seem to respond to attempts to change their antisocial behaviour through rehabilitation and treatment efforts. In fact, the clever ones probably do learn from their experiences—but only to become more successful predators and even less likely to be caught in the future. How should we then cope with them? Should Canada consider reinstating the death penalty (abolished in 1976) for serial killers and multiple murderers such as Clifford Olson and Paul Bernardo? Should such people be incarcerated for the rest of their lives as punishment for their crimes and/or because they are likely to reoffend? Or, should they be considered criminally insane and committed for treatment? We will discuss the issue of criminal insanity, or what is now called "not criminally responsible on account of a mental disorder," and the prediction of violence in Chapter 18.
- Battered women often perceive that they are trapped in their abusive relationships. Do you think it possible that Karla Homolka was actually a battered wife whose involvement in the murders of Leslie Mahaffey and Kristen French was motivated out of fear of her husband? Or should she be considered as culpable as Bernardo?
- In the next chapter, we will discuss the various sexual disorders. Some psychopaths are also diagnosed with a DSM-IV-TR paraphilia. Paul Bernardo, for example, has reportedly been diagnosed with sexual sadism (Black, 2000). A current approach to treating sex offenders is to attempt to teach them to feel more empathy for their victims. Thus, the purpose of empathy training is to encourage the offender to envision the feelings and thoughts of his victims, thereby making him aware of the pain, suffering, and harm that he has caused. Although this strategy may be effective with some sexual offenders (see Chapter 14), do you think that it can work with sexual sadists who are also psychopaths (especially very intelligent psychopaths like Bernardo)? Is it possible that psychopaths can turn the empathy training to their own advantage by learning how to prey in an even more effective way on vulnerable children and women?

chapter 14

Sexual and Gender Identity Disorders

"[O]nce it starts happening, it is brutal. You are always trying to run and hide from him and he is always tracking you down. It is something that you just can't tell anybody. ... Graham knew I needed a father figure coming from home because it was brutal at home and he preys on that. He knows. He knows exactly what he is doing. He put me in a position right off the top that screwed my whole life for me."
—Sheldon Kennedy, former NHL hockey player, describing the effects of being sexually abused at the age of 14 by his hockey coach in junior hockey, Graham James (Adams, 1997, A1)

"A crown psychiatrist would later categorize him as a sexual sadist, who enjoyed and relived every single second that he was raping both girls. ... In his world there was only one commandment: Take what you want, no matter who got hurt."
—Pron, Duncanson, and Rankin (1995) on Paul Bernardo

Alfred Pellan, 1906–1988, *Femme d'une Pomme*, 1943
oil on canvas, 161 x 129.7 cm, ART GALLERY OF ONTARIO, TORONTO
Gift of Mr. and Mrs. Charles S. Band, 1956

WILLIAM V. is a 28-year-old computer programmer who lives alone. He grew up in a rural area within a conservative family with strong religious values. He has two younger brothers and an older sister. William began to masturbate at age 15; his first masturbatory experience took place while he watched his sister urinate in an outdoor toilet. Despite considerable feelings of guilt, he continued to masturbate two or three times a week while having voyeuristic fantasies....

On a summer evening at about 11:30 p.m. William was arrested for climbing a ladder and peeping into the bedroom of a suburban home. Just before this incident he had been drinking heavily at a cocktail lounge featuring a topless dancer... Feeling lonely and depressed [after leaving the bar], he had begun to drive slowly through a nearby suburban neighborhood, where he noticed a lighted upstairs window. With little premeditation, he had parked his car, erected a ladder he found lying near the house, and climbed up to peep. The householders, who were alerted by the sounds, called the police, and William was arrested. Although this was his first arrest, William had committed similar acts on two previous occasions....

[In therapy] William described a lonely and insecure life. ... Six months before the arrest, he had been rejected in a long-term relationship. ... As an unassertive and timid individual, he had responded by withdrawing from social relationships, and increasing his use of alcohol. His voyeuristic fantasies, which were present to begin with, became progressively more urgent as William's self-esteem deteriorated. His arrest had come as a great personal shock, although he recognized that his behaviour was both irrational and self-destructive. (Rosen & Rosen, 1981, pp. 452–453. Reprinted by permission of McGraw-Hill Book Company)

Table 14.1

Sexual and Gender Identity Disorders

A. Gender identity disorder
B. Paraphilias
   1. Fetishism
   2. Transvestic fetishism
   3. Pedophilia
   4. Exhibitionism
   5. Voyeurism
   6. Frotteurism
   7. Sexual masochism
   8. Sexual sadism
   9. Paraphilias not otherwise specified (e.g., zoophilia, necrophilia)
C. Sexual dysfunctions
   1. Sexual desire disorders
      a. Hypoactive sexual desire disorder
      b. Sexual aversion disorder
   2. Sexual arousal disorders
      a. Female sexual arousal disorder
      b. Male erectile disorder
   3. Orgasmic disorders
      a. Female orgasmic disorder (inhibited female orgasm)
      b. Male orgasmic disorder (inhibited male orgasm)
      c. Premature ejaculation
   4. Sexual pain disorders
      a. Dyspareunia
      b. Vaginismus

Source: From DSM-IV-TR; APA, 2000.

Sexuality is one of the most personal—and generally private—areas of an individual's life. Each of us is a sexual being with preferences and fantasies that may surprise or even shock us from time to time. These are part of normal sexual functioning. But when our fantasies or desires begin to affect us or others in unwanted or harmful ways, as with William's peeping, they begin to qualify as abnormal. This chapter considers the full range of human sexual thoughts, feelings, and actions that are generally regarded as abnormal and dysfunctional and are listed in DSM-IV-TR as sexual and gender identity disorders (Table 14.1).

Our study of these disorders is divided into three major sections. First we examine theory and research in gender identity disorder, a diagnosis used to describe people who believe they are of the opposite sex. Next we consider the paraphilias, in which people are attracted to unusual sexual activities or objects. We include a discussion of rape, which, although not a diagnostic listing in DSM-IV-TR, merits examination in an abnormal psychology textbook. The third major section of the chapter addresses sexual dysfunctions, disruptions in normal sexual functioning found in many people who are in otherwise reasonably sound psychological health.

GENDER IDENTITY DISORDER

"Are you a boy or a girl?" "Are you a man or a woman?" For virtually all people—even those with serious mental disorders such as schizophrenia—the answer to such questions is immediate and obvious. And others would also agree unequivocally with the answer. Our sense of ourselves as male or female, our gender identity, is so deeply ingrained from earliest childhood that whatever stress is suffered at one time or another, the vast majority of people are certain beyond a doubt of their gender. In contrast, sexual identity or sexual orientation is the preference we have for the sex of a partner. For example, a man may be attracted to men—a matter of sexual orientation—without believing he is a woman—a matter of gender identity.

CHARACTERISTICS OF GENDER IDENTITY DISORDER

People with gender identity disorder (GID), sometimes referred to as transsexualism, feel deep within themselves, usually from early childhood, that they are of the opposite sex. They have an aversion to same-sex clothing and activities. The evidence of their anatomy—normal genitals and the usual secondary sex characteristics, such as beard growth for men and developed breasts for women—does not persuade them that they are what others see them to be. A man can look at himself in a mirror, see the body of a biological man, and yet personally experience that body as belonging to a woman. He may try to pass as a member of the opposite sex and may even want to have his body surgically altered to bring it in line with his gender identity.

Much of what is known about GID is due to research conducted at the Child and Adolescent Gender Identity Clinic at the Clarke Division of the Centre for Addiction and Mental Health in Toronto. This clinic first opened in 1978, and experts affiliated with it include Kenneth Zucker, Susan Bradley, and Ray Blanchard. The impact of these researchers on the field is reflected by the fact that they were part of the advising team that provided feedback on the DSM-IV diagnostic criteria for GID (see Bradley et al., 1991).

When GID begins in childhood, it is associated with cross-gender behaviours, such as dressing in opposite-sex clothes, preferring opposite-sex playmates, and engaging in play that would usually be considered more typical of the opposite sex (e.g., a boy playing with Barbie dolls). GID is associated with a developmental lag in achieving a sense of gender constancy or stability (i.e., acceptance that one is a boy or girl for life) (see Zucker et al., 1999). GID in a child is usually recognized by parents when the child is between 2 and 4 years old (Green & Blanchard, 1995). A review of 275 referrals showed that gender identity disorder is about 6.6 times more frequent in boys than in girls (Zucker, Bradley, & Sanikhani, 1997). Zucker et al. (1997) conducted an empirical analysis of possible explanations and concluded that social factors partly account for the difference in referral rates; that is, cross-gender behaviour is less tolerated when exhibited by boys and a higher threshold has to be met in order for a girl to be referred.

Zucker (2000) conducted a chart review that identified several factors associated with the decision to seek a clinical assessment. These factors included (1) a belief that the behaviour was no longer a phase that the child would grow out of; (2) a threshold violation (i.e., a boy wanting to cross-dress at nursery school, not just at home); (3) belief that the child was experiencing intense distress about being a boy or a girl; and (4) concerns about potential or actual rejection by peers. This last issue is a growing concern in light of the findings of a recent study of children with GID that was done in Toronto and the Netherlands (see Cohen-Kettenis et al., 2003). This study found that poor peer relations was the strongest predictor of behaviour problems in both samples. This study is unique in that it is the first cross-national investigation of this disorder. Overall, comparisons showed more similarities than differences across the two samples, and the predictors of behaviour problems were comparable.

A person with gender identity disorder, or transsexualism, experiences great discomfort with his or her gender and may have sex-reassignment surgery to become like someone of the opposite sex. The person shown here was voted Miss Transsexual in Italy.

Most children with GID do not grow up to be disordered in adulthood, even without professional intervention (Zucker et al., 1984). However, many demonstrate a homosexual orientation (Green, 1985).

Excluded from GID are people with schizophrenia who on very rare occasions claim to be of the other sex, as well as hermaphrodites, so-called intersexed individuals, who have both male and female reproductive organs. GID is also differentiated from transvestic fetishism, which is one of the paraphilias discussed later in this chapter. Although they often dress in clothing typical of the opposite sex, transvestites do not identify themselves as of the opposite sex.

A male with GID experiences his sexual interest in men as a conventional heterosexual preference, since he considers himself a woman. Predictably, those with GID often arouse the disapproval of others and experience discrimination in employment when they choose to cross-dress. Cross-dressing is less of a problem for women with GID because contemporary fashions allow women to wear clothing similar to that worn by men. People with GID often experience anxiety and depression, not surprising given their psychological predicament and the negative attitudes most people have toward them. GID in childhood is linked with separation anxiety disorder (Bradley & Zucker, 1997). The prevalence rates for GID are slight, one in 30,000 for men and one in 100,000 to 150,000 in women (American Psychiatric Association, 1994).

Causes of Gender Identity Disorder

The categorization of boys and girls as having their own masculine and feminine ways is so heavily laden with value judgments and stereotyping that considering cross-gender behavioural patterns in children to be abnormal may seem unjustified. Recently, in fact, a team of Canadian scholars from Concordia University and the University of Lethbridge conducted a conceptual analysis of the existing data on GID with a view to determining whether gender identity disorder in children should be considered a mental disorder according to DSM-IV criteria for mental disorder (Bartlett, Vasey, & Bukowski, 2000). Bartlett et al. (2000, p. 753) concluded that children who

> experience a sense of inappropriateness in the culturally prescribed gender role of their sex but who do not experience discomfort with their biological sex should not be considered to have GID. Because of flaws in the DSM-IV-TR definition of mental disorder, and limitations of the current research base, there is insufficient evidence to make any conclusive statement regarding children who experience discomfort with their biological sex.

These authors went on to suggest that GID in children should be removed from the DSM. Moreover, they expressed their concern that viewing GID as a mental disorder may contribute to a labelling process that stigmatizes those children with GID who go on to develop homosexuality.

Clearly, more information is needed on the causes of GID in order to resolve this debate. Research investigations examining the etiology of GID have yielded some data indicating that these patterns can come from a physical disturbance. (Also see Focus on Discovery 14.1 for a discussion of nature vs. nurture in gender identity.) Specifically, evidence indicates that gender identity is influenced by hormones. A study demonstrating this point was conducted on the members of an extended family in the Dominican Republic (Imperato-McGinley et al., 1974). Participants were unable to produce a hormone that shapes the penis and scrotum in males during fetal development. They were born with very small penises and scrotums that looked like labial folds. Two-thirds of them were raised as girls. However, when they reached puberty and testosterone levels increased, their sex organs changed. The penis enlarged, and the testicles descended into the scrotum. Seventeen of 18 participants then developed a male gender identity.

focus on discovery/14.1

Joan/John: Nature versus Nurture in Gender Identity

In 1965 Linda Thiessen gave birth to twin boys. Seven months later, she noticed that the boys' foreskins were closing, making urination difficult. Her pediatrician recommended circumcision to correct the problem. However, because of either an equipment problem or an error by the surgeon, the penis of John, one of the twins, was destroyed. Although the Thiessens consulted with several physicians, none held out much hope of surgically reconstructing John's penis.

In December 1966, the Thiessens happened to see a television program on which John Money, a well-known sex researcher at Johns Hopkins, described the successful use of sex-change surgery for transsexuals. The Thiessens contacted Money, who proposed that turning John into Joan was the best option. The plan involved castration, construction of female genitals, and later treatment with sex hormones.

Several years later, Money shared the details of the case, describing it as a total success, consistent with his theory that gender identity is determined by the environment. Over subsequent years, he wrote several follow-ups, again claiming success. The facts reveal otherwise. Two researchers who managed to find Joan several years later conducted interviews with her and her parents and discovered a picture very different from the one Money had painted, one that suggests that there is a strong biological influence on gender identity.

Despite having been instructed to encourage feminine behaviour in Joan, her parents reported that Joan behaved in a very boyish way. At age 2 she ripped off her first dress, and during her preschool years, her play activities were clearly masculine. The same pattern continued into her elementary school years. When she reached age 11, it was time to begin her treatment with female hormones to promote the development of breasts and other feminine characteristics. Vaginal surgery was also recommended to construct a more feminine vagina. Although she reluctantly began taking estrogen, Joan steadfastly held out against the surgery.

By age 14, Joan decided to stop living as a girl. She adopted male attire, began to urinate standing up, and enrolled in a technical high school. Given Joan's refusal to have the surgery and a life filled with considerable distress, Joan's physicians finally recommended that she be told the whole story. She immediately changed her name back to John and decided to do everything possible to reverse the earlier treatments. She took male hormones, had her breasts removed, and had an artificial penis constructed. At age 21, John had another operation to improve his artificial penis, and at age 25, he was married.

Clearly, this case demonstrates a strong biological underpinning for gender identity; despite not having a penis, being encouraged to behave in a feminine way, and developing breasts as a result of taking estrogen, John never developed a female gender identity (Colapinto, 1997).

It has since been revealed in Colapinto's (2000) book entitled *As Nature Made Him: The Boy Who Was Raised as a Girl* that this case involved a family in Winnipeg and is actually the tragic story of Brenda/David Reimer. Reimer asked Colapinto to reveal her/his actual identity and provide more details of the case. These revelations have caused various societies to rethink their position. For instance, the American Association of Pediatrics now recommends that various factors should be taken into account when deciding whether a child should be raised as male or female.

This ultimate outcome of the John/Joan case contrasts with the reports of a similar case in Canada reported by Bradley, Oliver, Chernick, and Zucker (1998). A two-month-old boy suffered a burn of his penile shaft during an electrocautery circumcision and eventually his penis sloughed off. The decision was made to reassign the child as a female and raise her as a girl. According to Bradley et al. (1998), long-term follow-up of this person has taken place, including an interview when she was 26 years old. In this case study, the reassigned girl continues to have a female gender identity, which Bradley et al. (1998) attribute to her being raised as a girl. However, they also noted that this young Canadian woman has a bisexual sexual identity and has had sexual experiences with both women and men. Also, she has many masculine interests and is employed in a blue-collar job that is usually dominated by men. Bradley et al. raised the possibility that this behavioural masculinity is a remnant of the masculine sexual biology and prenatal androgenization of the central nervous system. Nevertheless, the fact remains that unlike the outcome for John/Joan, this Canadian case study shows that the reassigned female gender identity is still evident, despite the presence of masculine tendencies.

Other research shows that human and other primate offspring of mothers who have taken sex hormones during pregnancy frequently behave like members of the opposite sex and have anatomical abnormalities. For example, girls whose mothers took synthetic progestins, which are precursors to male sex hormones, to prevent uterine bleeding during pregnancy were found to be tomboyish during their preschool years (Ehrhardt & Money, 1967). Young boys whose mothers ingested female hormones when pregnant were found to be less athletic as young children and to engage less in rough-and-tumble play than their male peers (Yalom, Green, & Fisk, 1973). Although such children were not necessarily abnormal in their gender identity, the mothers' ingestion of prenatal sex hormones did apparently give them higher than usual levels of cross-gender interests and behaviour.

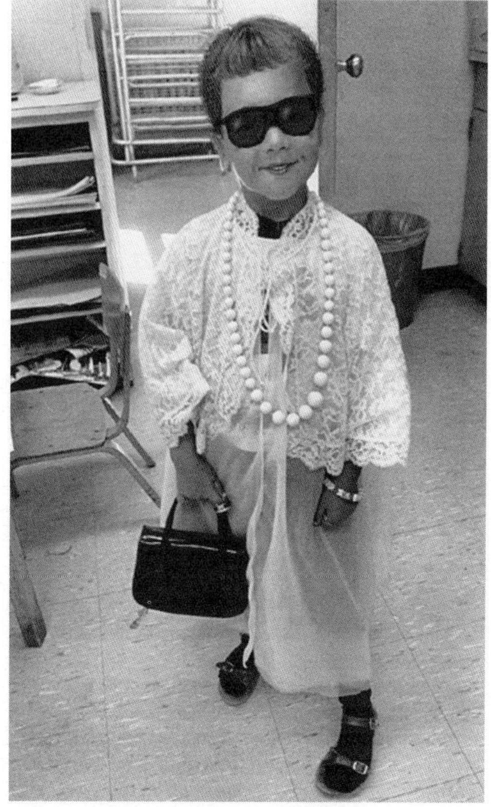

Although dressing up is normal in childhood, most transsexuals trace their gender identity disturbance to childhood and report dressing in gender-inappropriate clothes.

Levels of sex hormones have also been studied in adults with gender identity disorder. In a review of several such investigations, Gladue (1985) found few, if any, differences in hormone levels among men with GID, male heterosexuals, and male homosexuals. A more recent study found equivocal results: some women with GID had elevated levels of male hormones, but others did not (Bosinski et al., 1997). Even when differences are found, they are difficult to interpret because many people with GID use sex hormones in an effort to alter their bodies in the direction of the sex to which they believe they belong.

The available data, then, do not clearly support an explanation of adult transsexualism solely in terms of hormones. Even less conclusive is the research on possible chromosomal abnormalities, and efforts to find differences in brain structure between transsexuals and control group subjects have likewise been negative (Emory et al., 1991).

What about the possible role of the environment? Many, perhaps most, young children engage in cross-gender behaviour now and then. In some homes, such behaviour may receive too much attention and reinforcement from parents and other relatives. Interviews with the parents of children who show signs of GID often reveal that they did not discourage, and in many instances clearly encouraged, cross-dressing behaviour in their atypical children. This holds true especially for feminine boys. Female relatives found it cute when the boys dressed in the mother's old dresses and high-heeled shoes. Family albums typically contain photographs of the young boys attired in women's clothing. Such reactions of the family to an atypical child probably contribute in a major way to the conflict between his or her anatomical sex and the acquired gender identity (Green, 1987; Zuckerman & Green, 1993). The child's attractiveness is a factor that may contribute to this pattern of parental behaviour. Boys with GID have been rated as more attractive than control children, and girls with GID as less attractive (Fridell et al., 1996; Zucker et al., 1993). Also, male patients with GID report having had a distant relationship with their fathers; females often report a history of physical or sexual abuse (Bradley & Zucker, 1997).

A novel hypothesis is that stereotypically feminine behaviour in boys is encouraged by mothers who, prior to the child's birth, wanted very much to have a girl. This hypothesis was not confirmed in a recent study: mothers whose sons did not have a childhood feminine identity reported that they had had the same level of interest in having a girl as mothers whose sons did manifest a feminine identification (Zucker et al., 1994).

Investigators working in this field are very much aware of the culture-related aspects of masculinity and femininity and of the difference between enjoying activities more typical of the opposite sex and actually believing that one is of the opposite sex. The vast majority of little boys engage in varying amounts of traditional feminine play and little girls in varying amounts of traditional masculine play with no identity conflicts whatsoever (Green, 1976). This is not to say that feminine boys are not subject to considerable stress. Our society has a low tolerance for boys who engage in activities more typical of girls, whereas girls can play games and dress in a manner more typical of boys and still conform to acceptable standards of behaviour for girls (Williams, Goodman, & Green, 1985). In any event, GID is far less prevalent than would be indicated by the numbers of boys who play with dolls and girls who engage in contact sports.

Therapies for Gender Identity Disorder

We turn now to the interventions available to help people with GID. These are of two main types. One attempts to alter the body to suit the person's psychology; the other is designed to alter the psychology to match the person's body.

Body Alterations A person with GID who enters a program that entails alteration of the body is generally required to undergo six to 12 months of psychotherapy. The therapy typically focuses not only on the anxiety and depression that the person has likely been experiencing but also on options available to the person for altering his or her body. Some people with GID may choose to have only cosmetic surgery; a male-to-female transsexual may have electrolysis to remove facial hair and surgery to reduce the size of the chin and Adam's apple. Many transsexuals also take hormones to

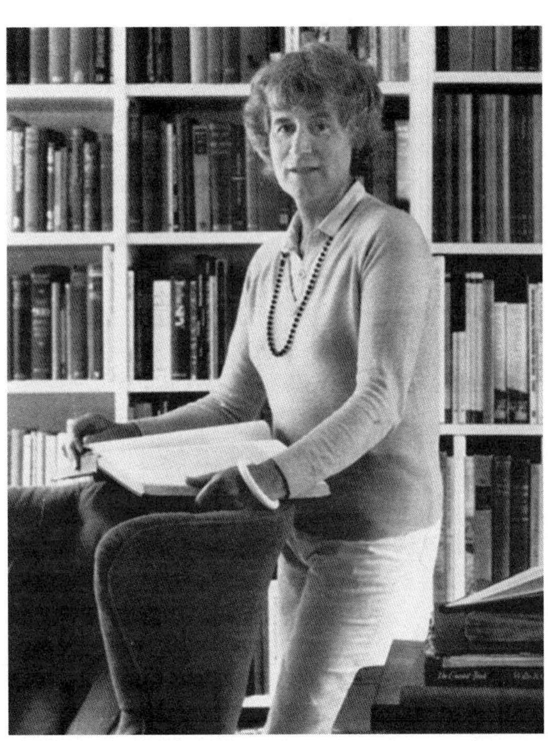

After sex-reassignment surgery, author and historian James Morris (in a 1960 picture) became Jan Morris (in a 1974 photograph)

bring their bodies physically closer to their beliefs about their gender. For example, female hormones will promote breast growth and soften the skin of male-to-female transsexuals (Schaefer, Wheeler, & Futterweit, 1997). Many people with GID go no further than using such methods, but some take the next step of having sex-reassignment surgery.

Sex-reassignment surgery is an operation in which the existing genitalia are altered to make them more like those of the opposite sex. The first sex-reassignment operation took place in Europe in 1930, but the surgery that attracted worldwide attention was performed on an ex-soldier, Christine (originally George) Jorgensen, in Copenhagen, Denmark, in 1952.

Sex-reassignment surgery is an option much more frequently exercised by men than by women. How beneficial is sex-reassignment surgery? There has been much controversy over this question. One of the most controversial outcome studies (Meyer & Reter, 1979) found no advantage to the individual "in terms of social rehabilitation" (p. 1015). The findings of this study led to the termination of the Johns Hopkins University School of Medicine sex-reassignment program, the largest such program in the United States. Other researchers criticized the Meyer-Reter findings. A review of 20 years of research showed an overall improvement in social adaptation rates because of the surgery, with female-to-male transsexuals having greater success than male-to-female transsexuals (Abramovitz, 1986).

A subsequent review by Green and Fleming (1990) of reasonably controlled outcome studies published between 1979 and 1989, with at least a one-year follow-up, drew even more favourable conclusions. Of 130 female-to-male surgeries, about 97 percent could be judged satisfactory; of 220 male-to-female surgeries, 87 percent were satisfactory. Preoperative factors that seemed to predict favourable postsurgery adjustment were (1) reasonable emotional stability, (2) successful adaptation in the new role for at least one year before the surgery, (3) adequate understanding of the actual limitations and consequences of the surgery, and (4) psychotherapy in the context of an established gender identity program. The authors cautioned, however, that satisfactory ratings meant only that the patients reported that they did not regret having had the surgery. Such patient reports may be an overly generous criterion for favourable outcome, especially since they follow the investment of considerable time, money, and energy in an outcome that is, for the most part, irreversible. A more recent report from the University of Pennsylvania indicated that sexual responsiveness and sexual satisfaction increase dramatically in both male-to-female and female-to-male transsexuals, with an overall high level of satisfaction with the results of the surgery (Lief & Hubschman, 1993).

Sex-reassignment programs continue in many medical-psychological settings. It is estimated that, each year in the United States, more than 1,000 transsexuals are surgically altered to the opposite sex. The long-term effectiveness, or even wisdom, of sex-reassignment surgery is still difficult to evaluate. Given that people who go to great lengths to have this surgery claim that their future happiness depends on the change, should this surgery be evaluated in terms of how happy such people are afterward? If so, it can probably be said that most GID patients who have crossed over anatomically are generally better off, although some are not. But if a surgically altered transsexual becomes dismally unhappy, is the surgery to be indicted as antitherapeutic? Consider this: people who undergo these procedures often cut their ties to former friends and family members and to many aspects of their previous lives. A person who has sex-reassignment surgery confronts challenges few others have occasion to face, and this adjustment may well have to be made without the social support of family and friends.

People who focus on the discrepancy between their gender identity and their biological makeup tend to blame present dissatisfactions on the horrible trick nature has played on them. But these people usually find that sex reassignment falls short of solving life's problems. It may handle this one set of them, but it usually leaves untouched other difficulties to which all human beings are subject, such as conflicts at work, with intimates, and even within oneself.

Alterations of Gender Identity Is sex reassignment the only option? Surgery and associated hormone administration used to be considered the only viable treatment for gender identity disorder because psychological attempts to shift gender identity had consistently failed. Gender identity was assumed to be too deep-seated to alter. Some apparently successful procedures for altering gender identity through behaviour therapy have been reported, however.

In one case, the patient was a 17-year-old male who wanted to change his gender identity rather than—the choice of most transsexuals—change his anatomy to fit his feminine gender identity (Barlow, Reynolds, & Agras, 1973). The treatment involved shaping various specific behaviours, such as mannerisms and interpersonal behaviour—how to talk to young women, for instance—but it also included attention to cognitive components, such as fantasies. One technique paired slides of women with slides of men, the idea being that the sexual arousal from the latter might be transferred, or classically conditioned to, the former. This positive approach to changing the arousal properties of images and fantasies was complemented by aversion therapy to reduce the attractiveness of men. After half a year of intensive treatment, the young man was thinking of himself as a man, not as a woman, and was finding women sexually attractive. At a five-year follow-up, these changes were still present (Barlow, Abel, & Blanchard, 1979).

Two additional cases treated in the same way were reported by Barlow et al. Two men in their mid-twenties were on route to sex-reassignment surgery but had second thoughts. The behavioural retraining succeeded in altering their gender identity but not their attraction to men; that is, their sexual orientation remained homosexual.

This work demonstrates that cross-gender identity may be amenable to change. But as the researchers point out, their clients might have been different from others with GID because they consented to participate in a therapy program aimed at changing gender identity. Most transsexuals refuse such treatment. For them, physically altering their bodies is the only legitimate goal. But if the surgical option did not exist, would more professional energy be expended on developing psychological procedures for altering gender identity? And if those procedures involved teaching men to be more traditionally masculine and women more traditionally feminine, would that be desirable or ethically defensible? These are but two of the ethical conundrums associated with treating disorders of gender identity.

Canadian Perspectives/14.1

Transsexuals and the Complex Case of Kimberly Nixon

Kimberly Nixon is a former airline pilot who had a sex-change operation in 1990. Overall, Nixon has lived as a woman for approximately 20 years. Nixon has a young son and, while a woman, was sexually abused by a man.

The case of Kimberly Nixon first became known to the public in 1995. She applied to be a volunteer rape counsellor for the Vancouver Rape Relief Society (VRRS), a women-only rape counselling organization (with an associated shelter for women) that was founded in 1973 and does not accept men as volunteers or members. Nixon was asked to leave when she acknowledged her previous past as a man. One day later, Nixon filed a human rights complaint with the British Columbia Human Rights Commission. First, however, she contemplated suicide. She stated that after being asked to leave, "I could barely see because of the tears in my eyes. ... All I could think of was the Lion's Gate Bridge—jumping off the bridge" (Wente, 2000, p. 1).

VRRS representatives contended that it would be traumatic for female rape victims to receive counsel from a woman who appeared to be a man in drag. At issue was the legal question of "What is a woman?" Regardless of these arguments, on June 7, 2000, the B.C. Supreme Court rejected the attempt by the VRRS to prevent the human rights commission from hearing Nixon's discrimination complaint, and the case went forward to a human rights tribunal.

The complexities inherent in this case were illustrated by comments made by Judy Rebick, one of Canada's foremost feminists and a former president of the National Action Committee on the Status of Women. Rebick testified on behalf of the VRRS before the tribunal in December 2000, arguing that women's groups have the right to decide who their members are. However, outside the hearing room, she observed, "What makes this tense is there's no question that transgendered people suffer from discrimination, they suffer a great deal. So, of course, [in] your heart as a feminist you want to be on their side in every fight but you can't because there is a conflict of rights" (Bailey, 2000, p. 1).

Kimberly Nixon, a transsexual, filed a human rights complaint against the Rape Relief Society of Vancouver. The Human Rights Tribunal ruled in her favour, but this decision was overturned by the British Columbia Supreme Court.

The tribunal's decision included the determination that the VRRS acted in good faith and meant no harm, but was nevertheless in breach of the Human Rights Code. The VRRS was ordered to pay $7,500 to Nixon.

In 2002 the VRRS requested a judicial review of the decision by the B.C Supreme Court because it was concerned that men would now be able to gain access to the shelter as a result of the decision. In December 2003, the Court overturned the tribunal's decision on the grounds that the VRRS is protected by section 41 of the Human Rights Code, which protects charitable groups and their right to freedom of association. The monetary award was also overturned.

Thinking Critically

1. Do you agree with the final decision reached by the B.C. Supreme Court? Do you think discrimination has taken place here? Should an organization such as the VRRS have the right to exclude transsexuals even though other organizations have accepted them?
2. Whose rights matter the most in this situation? The rights of Kimberly Nixon? The rights of victims seeking assistance from the VRRS? Or the rights of the VRRS? Explain your selection.

THE PARAPHILIAS

In DSM-IV-TR, the **paraphilias** are a group of disorders involving sexual attraction to unusual objects or sexual activities that are unusual in nature. In other words, there is a deviation (*para*) in what the person is attracted to (*philia*). The fantasies, urges, or behaviours must last at least six months and cause significant distress or impairment. A person can have the behaviours, fantasies, and urges that a person with a paraphilia has (such as exhibiting the genitals to an unsuspecting stranger or fantasizing about doing so) but not be diagnosed with a paraphilia if the fantasies or behaviours are not recurrent or if he or she is not markedly distressed by them. Indeed, surveys have shown that many people occasionally fantasize about some of the activities we will be describing. A Canadian survey found that 50 percent of men report voyeuristic fantasies of peeping at unsuspecting naked women (Hanson & Harris, 1997).

The DSM diagnostic criterion of distress or impairment has created some problems because many people with the behavioural features of a paraphilia are neither distressed nor impaired (Hudson & Ward, 1997). For example, according to the DSM criteria, someone who has repeatedly had sex with young children but is not distressed or impaired cannot be diagnosed as having pedophilia. Therefore, many researchers in this field hold a more behavioural definition of paraphilias and ignore the distress and disability parts of the DSM definition.

People often exhibit more than one paraphilia, and such patterns can be aspects of other mental disorders, such as schizophrenia, depression, or one of the personality disorders. Accurate prevalence statistics are not available for most of the paraphilias. Many people with paraphilias may choose not to reveal their deviance when responding to a community survey. Similarly, statistics on arrests are likely to be underestimated because many crimes go unreported and some paraphilias (e.g., voyeurism) involve an unsuspecting victim. The data do indicate, though, that most people with paraphilias, whatever their sexual orientation, are male; even with masochism and pedophilia, which do occur in noticeable numbers of women, men vastly outnumber women. As some persons with paraphilias seek nonconsenting partners, these disorders often have legal consequences.

FETISHISM

Fetishism involves a reliance on an inanimate object for sexual arousal. The person with fetishism, almost always a male, has recurrent and intense sexual urges toward nonliving objects, called fetishes (e.g., women's shoes), and the presence of the fetish is strongly preferred or even necessary for sexual arousal to occur.

Feet and shoes, sheer stockings, rubber products such as raincoats, gloves, toilet articles, fur garments, and especially underpants are common sources of arousal for fetishists. Some can carry on their fetishism by themselves in secret by fondling, kissing, smelling, sucking, placing in their rectum, or merely gazing at the adored object as they masturbate. Others need their partner to don the fetish as a stimulant for intercourse. Fetishists sometimes become interested in acquiring a collection of the desired objects, and they may commit burglary week after week to add to their hoard.

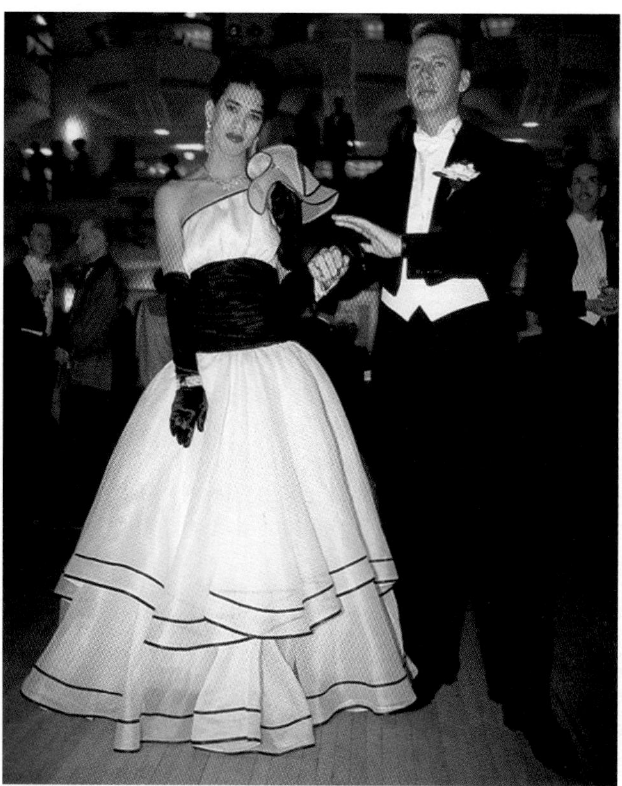

Transvestic fetishism, or transvestism, is diagnosed when the person sexually arouses himself by dressing in opposite-sex clothing. This transvestite is attending a fundraiser for AIDS at the Waldorf Astoria in New York.

The attraction felt by the fetishist toward the object has a compulsive quality; it is experienced as involuntary and irresistible. It is the degree of the erotic focalization—the exclusive and very special status the object occupies as a sexual stimulant—that distinguishes fetishisms from the ordinary attraction that, for example, high heels and sheer stockings may hold for heterosexual men in Western cultures. The boot fetishist must see or touch a boot to become aroused, and when the fetish is present, the arousal is overwhelmingly strong.

The disorder usually begins by adolescence, although the fetish may have acquired special significance even earlier, during childhood. Fetishists often have other paraphilias, such as pedophilia, sadism, and masochism (Mason, 1997).

TRANSVESTIC FETISHISM

When a man is sexually aroused by dressing in women's clothing, although he still regards himself as a man, the term **transvestic fetishism**, or transvestism, applies. The extent of transvestism varies from wearing women's underwear under conventional clothing to full cross-dressing. Some transvestites may enjoy appearing socially as women; some female impersonators become performers in nightclubs, catering to the delight that many sexually conventional people take in observing skilled cross-dressing. However, these impersonators are not considered transvestic unless the cross-dressing is associated with sexual arousal. Transvestism should not be confused with the cross-dressing associated with GID or with the cross-dressing preferences of some homosexuals.

The term *autogynephilia* was coined by Ray Blanchard (1989) at the Clarke Institute in Toronto to refer to a man's tendency to become sexually aroused at the thought or image of himself as a woman. Blanchard (1992) noted that autogynephilia is typically, but not always, found in association with transvestism.

Transvestic fetishism usually begins with partial cross-dressing in childhood or adolescence. Transvestites are heterosexual, always males, and by and large cross-dress episodically rather than on a regular basis. They tend to be otherwise masculine in appearance, demeanour, and sexual preference. Many are married. Cross-dressing usually takes place in private and in secret and is known to few members of the family. This is one of the paraphilias for which the DSM distress and disability criteria do not seem to apply at all.

The urge to cross-dress may become more frequent over time and sometimes is accompanied by gender dysphoria—discomfort with one's anatomical sex—but not to the extent found in GID. Transvestism is comorbid with other paraphilias, notably masochism (Zucker & Blanchard, 1997).

Pedophilia and Incest

"If I can help just one person ... then all of this will have been worth it."

—Martin Kruze on *Jane Hawtin Live*, February 26, 1997, concerning his revelations about being sexually abused as a child by employees at Maple Leaf Gardens

According to the DSM, individuals who practise **pedophilia** (*pedos*, Greek for "child") are adults who derive sexual gratification through physical and often sexual contact with prepubescent children unrelated to them. DSM-IV-TR requires that the offender be at least 16 years old and at least five years older than the child. Research does not appear to support the DSM's statement that all pedophiles prefer prepubescent children; an analysis by Marshall (1997) at Queen's University revealed that some of them victimize postpubescent children who are younger than the legal age to consent to having sex with an adult.

Pedophilia occurs much more frequently in men than in women, though case studies of female pedophiles have been reported, including a Canadian case involving a young woman who had sexual relations with two 4-year-old daughters of acquaintances (see Chow & Choy, 2002). Pedophilia

On June 17, 2004 Michael Briere was sentenced to 25 years in prison for the brutal sexual attack and strangulation of 10-year-old Holly Jones. Briere's "dark secret," was an overwhelming desire to have sex with a young child. His fantasy was fuelled by child pornography readily downloaded from the Internet. Canada's child pornography laws became an issue in the June 2004 federal election.

is often comorbid with mood and anxiety disorders, substance abuse, and other paraphilias (Raymond et al., 1999). The pedophile can be heterosexual or homosexual. In recent years, the Internet has played an increasing role in pedophilia; pedophiles use the Internet to acquire child pornography and to contact potential victims (Durkin, 1997). As a result, convicted pedophiles who are granted parole often have their access to the Internet restricted as a condition of their release. This was the case for Robert Noyes, who was released in December 2000. Noyes, a teacher and a school principal in British Columbia, was arrested in 1985 and charged in connection with approximately 600 separate assaults on children, including at least 65 children (mostly boys) between the ages of 6 and 15. Noyes was one of the first pedophiles to be designated as a dangerous offender, so he could have been in prison for an indefinite term.

Pedophilia in Canada has received great public attention because of the number of highly publicized cases reported in the media. These cases include the Maple Leaf Gardens scandal. It was revealed in 1997 that about 90 children had been sexually abused by some Maple Leaf Gardens employees, including George Hannah, Gordon Stuckless, and John Paul Roby. The tragedy of Martin Kruze, one of the boys victimized who "blew the whistle" on a shameful period in Canadian sport history, is told by Cathy Vine and Paul Challen's (2002) moving account, *Gardens of Shame*. Kruze worked as a spokesperson for sexual abuse survivors. Sadly, he jumped off a bridge to his death at age 35 just three days after Stuckless was sentenced to two years less a day in a reformatory. In December 2003, a woman alleged that she had been sexually abused by former owner Harold Ballard

Convicted pedophile Karl Toft. The group Mad Mothers against Pedophiles planned rallies to protest his release.

when she was 10 years old. Previously, we also learned of the abuse experienced by Sheldon Kennedy, former player in the National Hockey League. In 1997 Kennedy's coach in junior hockey, Graham James, pleaded guilty to charges of sexual assault.

Another disturbing case occurred in New Brunswick at the Kingsclear Youth Training Facility near Fredericton. Karl Toft, who worked at the facility, is a convicted pedophile who was found guilty in 1992 of buggery, bestiality, and over 30 counts of sexual assault involving children. Toft has since admitted to abusing over 150 children over two decades. He was denied parole as recently as August 2000. The parole board's decision at that time was based on several factors, including Toft's apparent lack of empathy for his victims, his lack of "internal control mechanism," and his unwillingness to submit to medication as a form of treatment. Then, in August 2001, the decision was made to grant Toft parole and send him to a halfway house in Edmonton. The Edmonton Police Service issued a public warning that outlined his convictions, noted his participation in a sex offender program, and included a physical description with a photo. In response to vigorously expressed public concern, the Correctional Service of Canada reversed the decision and sent him to a regional psychiatric centre in Saskatoon, a secure treatment facility (Auld, 2000).

Violence is seldom a part of the molestation, although it can be, as occasionally comes to people's attention through lurid media accounts. But even if most pedophiles do not physically injure their victims, some intentionally frighten the child by, for example, killing a pet and threatening further harm if the youngster tells his or her parents. Sometimes the pedophile is content to stroke the child's hair, but he may also manipulate the child's genitalia, encourage the child to manipulate his, and, less often, attempt intromission. Molestations may be repeated for weeks, months, or years if they are not discovered by other adults or if the child does not protest.

A minority of pedophiles, who might also be classified as sexual sadists or antisocial (psychopathic) personalities, inflict serious bodily harm on the object of their passion. These individuals, whether psychopathic or not, are perhaps best viewed as child rapists and are different from pedophiles in that they wish to hurt the child physically at least as much as they wish to obtain sexual gratification (Groth, Hobson, & Guy, 1982). Indeed, research by Firestone et al. (1998, 2000) at the University of Ottawa shows that although it is often difficult to distinguish homicidal child molesters from nonhomicidal child molesters, it is still the case that homicidal child molesters show a greater physiological response to and preference for descriptions of assaults on children. Although psychopathy is more elevated in these men than in incest offenders, rapists tend to have even higher levels of psychopathy when assessed by Hare's PCL-R (Firestone et al., 2000).

Incest refers to sexual relations between close relatives for whom marriage is forbidden. It is most common between brother and sister. The next most common form is between father and daughter. Although father-daughter incest is considered more pathological, recent data from Quebec question this conclusion because brother-sister incest was associated with just as much distress among victims as incest involving fathers or stepfathers; moreover, brother-sister incest was associated with a much higher frequency of sexual penetration (Cyr, Wright, McDuff, & Perron, 2002).

The taboo against incest seems virtually universal in human societies (Ford & Beach, 1951), a notable exception being the marriages of Egyptian pharaohs to their sisters or other females of their immediate families. In Egypt it was believed that the royal blood should not be contaminated by that of outsiders. The incest taboo makes sense according to present-day scientific knowledge. The offspring from a father-daughter or a brother-sister union have a greater probability of inheriting a pair of recessive genes, one from each parent. For the most part, recessive genes have negative biological effects, such as serious birth defects. The incest taboo, then, has adaptive evolutionary significance.

There is evidence that the structure of families in which incest occurs is unusually patriarchal and traditional, especially with respect to the subservient position of women (Alexander & Lupfer, 1987). Parents in these families also tend to neglect and remain emotionally distant from their children (Madonna, Van Scoyk, & Jones, 1991). Furthermore, it is believed that incest is more prevalent when the mother is absent or disabled (Finkelhor, 1979), as mothers usually protect their daughters from intrafamilial sexual abuse.

Incest is listed in DSM-IV-TR as a subtype of pedophilia. Several major distinctions are drawn between incest and pedophilia. First, incest is by definition between members of the same family. Second, incest victims tend to be older than the victims of a pedophile's desires. It is more often the case that a father becomes interested in his daughter when she begins to mature physically, whereas the pedophile is usually interested in the youngster precisely because he or she is sexually immature. The term *gynephile* refers to an adult who is incestuous with a child in the absence of a mature, adult sex partner.

An archival study of cases in Saskatchewan examined the nature of incest versus extrafamilial forms of child sexual abuse and found that incest had an earlier onset and longer duration (Fischer & McDonald, 1998). Also, victims of incest had comparatively greater levels of physical injury and emotional distress.

A study by Studer et al. (2000) at the Alberta Hospital–Edmonton Site yielded evidence suggesting that risk assessments of incest offenders have substantially underestimated the threat actually posed by incest offenders. First, it has generally been believed that incest offenders have a low likelihood of being a repeat incest offender (between 4 and 10 percent). Studer et al. (2000), however, found that 22 percent had prior incestuous offences and were, in fact, repeat offenders. Also, almost two-thirds of the incest offenders reported having nonincestuous victims as well, which suggests they are also pedophiles. Studer et al. concluded that for these men, the main issue is one of opportunity; they have a general sexual attraction to children that may indeed go beyond members of their own family. The researchers cited earlier work indicating the need to distinguish the family-only incest offender from incest offenders who have an intense craving for young children in general.

Further empirical work by Rice and Harris (2002) indicates that daughter-only molesters have lower levels of psychopathy than incestuous fathers who also engage in extrafamilial offences. Although these daughter-only child molesters have less deviant sexual preferences and lower recidivism rates than molesters who commit offences inside and outside the family, their sexual preferences are still deviant overall and the recidivism risk is not low in absolute terms.

Data from penile plethysmography studies (see Figure 14.1 for an explanation of these measures) conducted in Canada confirm that men who molest children unrelated to them are sexually aroused by photographs of nude children. Men who molest children within their families show more arousal to adult heterosexual cues (Marshall, Barbaree, & Christophe, 1986).

One of the first rudimentary versions of the penile plethysmograph was developed by Kurt Freund, who developed his first device in Czechoslovakia. Freund then worked for several decades at the Clarke Institute of Psychiatry in Toronto (see Freund, 1967; Freund & Blanchard, 1989; Freund & Watson, 1991). Plethysmograph measures have been described as "phallometric tests," and they have been used to identify males—both adults (Laws, Hanson, Osborn, & Greenbaum, 2000) and adolescents (Seto, Lalumière, & Blanchard, 2000)—with pedophilic interests. Once established, phallometric testing results show little variance, indicating that it is very difficult to change sexual preferences (Lalumière & Quinsey, 1998).

Although phallometric testing is used routinely with sex offenders, concerns have been raised about the reliability and validity of these measures (see Marshall & Fernandez, 2000). In particular, Marshall and Fernandez expressed concern about the demonstrated ability of some people to fake their responses when being measured.

It is generally believed that a history of exposure to pornography is a cause of sexual offending. However, in a review paper, a team of Canadian researchers concluded that pornography only plays a role among men who are already

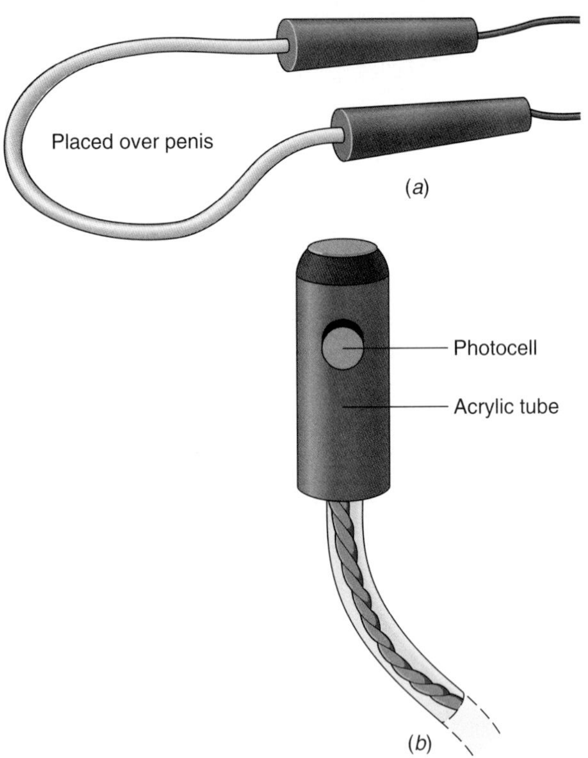

Figure 14.1 Behavioural researchers use two genital devices for measuring sexual arousal. Both are sensitive indicators of vasocongestion of the genitalia (i.e., the flooding of the veins with blood, a key physiological process in sexual arousal); both provide specific measurements of sexual excitement (e.g., Adams et al., 1992; Barlow et al., 1970; Heiman et al., 1991). (a) For men, the penile plethysmograph measures changes in the circumference of the penis by means of a strain gauge, consisting of a very thin rubber tube filled with mercury. As the penis is engorged with blood, the tube stretches, changing its electrical resistance, which can then be measured by a suitably configured polygraph. (b) For women, sexual arousal can be measured by a vaginal plethysmograph, such as the device invented by Sintchak and Geer (1975). Shaped like a menstrual tampon, this apparatus can be inserted into the vagina to provide direct measurement of the increased blood flow characteristic of female sexual arousal.

predisposed to sexually offend (Seto, Maric, & Barbaree, 2001)-that is, men who are not predisposed show little effect.

It is sometimes alleged that child pornography is a critical ingredient in motivating child molestation in predisposed people, but a clinical study of male pedophiles indicates that such materials may not even be necessary. These men were arousable by media materials widely available, such as television ads and clothing catalogues picturing young children in underwear. In other words, rather than using explicitly pornographic materials, these men appeared to construct in their minds their own sexually stimulating material from sources generally viewed as innocuous (Howitt, 1995).

As in most paraphilias, a strong subjective attraction impels pedophilic behaviour. According to Gebhard and his colleagues (1965), pedophiles generally know the children they molest; they are neighbours or friends of the family.

Alcohol use and stress increase the likelihood that a pedophile will molest a child. Research by Looman at the Regional Treatment Centre in Kingston suggests that child molesters have sexual fantasies about children when their mood is negative, perhaps as a way to cope with their unease; however, it also appears that having a pedophilic fantasy enhances the negative affect. Perhaps this downward spiral can eventually lead to the person's acting on the impulse to molest a child (Looman, 1995). Indeed, recent research using inmates from Canadian federal penitentiaries confirmed that sexual offenders, relative to nonsexual violent offenders, are more likely to report using consensual and nonconsensual sex as a coping strategy (Cortoni & Marshall, 2001). Data also suggest that pedophiles are low in social maturity, self-esteem, impulse control, and social skills (Kalichman, 1991; Marshall, Cripps, Anderson, & Cortoni, 1999; Overholser & Beck, 1986). Most older heterosexual pedophiles are or have been married.

One-half of all child molestations, including those that take place within the family, are committed by adolescent males (Becker, Kaplan, et al., 1986; Morenz & Becker, 1995). About 50 percent of adult offenders began their illegal behaviour in their early teens. These juveniles have typically experienced a chaotic and negative family life. Their homes often lack structure and positive support (Blaske et al., 1989). Research conducted in Canada by Worling (1995, 1999) as part of the Sexual Abuse: Family Education and Treatment (SAFE-T) Program has shown that many of these teenagers were themselves sexually abused as children (Worling, 1995). Worling (2001) reported that 39 percent of his sample had experienced childhood sexual victimization and 45 percent reported receiving abusive physical discipline from parents. Another recent study conducted in Alberta found that 79 percent of adolescent child molesters had experienced sexual abuse, often in combination with physical abuse (Alywin, Studer, Reddon, & Clelland, 2003). A history of sexual abuse increased the likelihood that the molester would choose boys as victims.

Worling (2001) has also shown that there is substantial heterogeneity in terms of the personality characteristics of adolescent male sexual offenders. Cluster analyses of scores on the California Psychological Inventory have identified four types of offenders: antisocial/impulsive, unusual/isolated, overcontrolled/reserved, and confident/aggressive. Worling suggested that the overcontrolled/reserved adolescents have a more positive orientation toward others and are overly shy. Similarly, the confident/aggressive adolescents have a relatively positive orientation toward others, but they can be narcissistic and hostile at times. These two groups contrast with the antisocial/impulsive and unusual/isolated groups, which have more pathological characteristics. Worling (2001) reported that the antisocial/impulsive group was the largest group, comprising more than half of his sample. This group was most likely to have criminal charges for their sexual assaults and be the recipients of abusive physical discipline from their parents. The four groups were equally likely to have a history of childhood sexual victimization.

Overall, adolescents who engage in child molestation are more socially isolated and have poorer social skills than peers who are in trouble with the law for nonsexual crimes (Awad & Saunders, 1989). Social isolation is most characteristic of the unusual/isolated group identified by Worling (2001), who suggested that these adolescents are most likely to benefit from training in basic social skills, such as learning how to listen, how to start a conversation, and how to introduce oneself to someone else. Academic problems are also common (Becker & Hunter, 1997). In general, these young males (females are much less often found among the ranks of sex offenders) are what one would call juvenile delinquents, in frequent trouble with the police for a wide variety of lawbreaking. Not surprisingly, conduct disorder and substance abuse are frequent diagnoses made of these youths. Somewhat more surprisingly, depression and anxiety disorders are also common features (Becker et al., 1991; Galli et al., 1999).

Because overt physical force is seldom used in incest or pedophilia, the child molester often denies that he is actually forcing himself on his victim. Sometimes the molester rationalizes that he is doing something good for the child, despite the betrayal of trust that is inherent in child sexual abuse and despite the serious negative psychological consequences that can befall the abused child some years later.

New developments involving the assessment of child molesters continue to emerge, and researchers based in Canada have played a substantial role. For instance, Seto and Lalumière (2001) developed a brief measure known as the Screening Scale for Pedophilic Interests (SSPI) and have shown that this screening instrument is quite successful in distinguishing pedophilic child molesters and nonchild molesters who have abused older victims. This instrument was developed on the basis of earlier work that compared adult child molesters and molesters of adolescents (see Freund & Blanchard, 1989; Freund & Watson, 1991; Seto, Lalumière, & Kuban, 1999).

One of the scale items refers to whether an "unrelated" victim (i.e., outside the victim's family, or extrafamilial) was involved. Greater pedophilic interest is present when an unrelated victim was involved. Item analyses by Seto and Lalumière (2001) found that having a male victim was twice as predictive as the other items in identifying child molesters. A recent study of pedophiles by Blanchard et al. (1999) found that lower levels of intellectual functioning are associated with greater interest in boys and in younger children in general.

VOYEURISM

Now and then, a man may by chance happen to see a nude woman without her knowing he is watching her. If his sex life is primarily conventional, his act is voyeuristic, but he would not generally be considered a voyeur. Similarly, voyeuristic fantasies are quite common in men but do not by themselves warrant a diagnosis (Hanson & Harris, 1997). Voyeurism involves a marked preference for obtaining sexual gratification by watching others in a state of undress or

focus on discovery/14.2

Child Sexual Abuse: Effects on the Child and Modes of Intervention

According to a recent analysis of data collected in 1997, a survey of 179 police forces in six provinces found that 62 percent of all victims of a sexual offence were young people under the age of 18, with 30 percent being young children under the age of 12 (Statistics Canada, 1999). The prototypical act is a sexual offence committed against a female by someone familiar to her. More than four of five victims are females, but the proportion of males being victimized rises to 31 percent for children under the age of 12. Half of the sexual offences were committed by a friend or acquaintance, and another 28 percent were committed by family members.

Pedophilia and incest are forms of child sexual abuse (CSA) and should be distinguished from nonsexual child abuse. Both sexual and nonsexual abuse can have negative consequences, and sometimes the two forms of abuse co-occur. Nonsexual child abuse may include neglecting the child's physical and mental welfare—punishing the child unfairly; belittling the child; intentionally withholding suitable shelter, food, and medical care; or striking or otherwise inflicting physical pain and injury. Many parents who engage in nonsexual abuse of their children never abuse them sexually. Both types of abuse are reportable offences. In Canada, anyone aware of abuse taking place is required by law to report it to the police or child protective agencies.

Comedian Drew Carey admitted in his autobiography that he was sexually abused as a child, has suffered from depression, and had attempted suicide on two occasions

EFFECTS ON THE CHILD

The short-term effects of CSA are variable. Almost half of the children who are exposed to CSA do not appear to experience adverse effects (Kuehnle, 1998). Among those who are negatively affected, problems include anxiety, depression, low self-esteem, and conduct disorder.

Several factors likely contribute to how CSA affects a child. One is the nature of the abuse itself. Consider, for example, the probable differences in consequences between a case involving the repeated rape of a 7-year-old girl by her father and that of a 12-year-old boy who has a sexual relationship with an older woman. Sometimes the aftermath of CSA is posttraumatic stress disorder (PTSD). Indeed, DSM-IV-TR lists sexual assault as one of the stressors that can be traumatic. A high level of self-blame and lack of a supportive family environment increase the chances that the CSA will produce negative reactions (Kuehnle, 1998).

Regarding long-term effects, we have seen in previous chapters that a history of CSA is found among patients in many diagnostic categories—notably, dissociative identity disorder, eating disorders, and borderline personality disorder. It has also been proposed that CSA is related to the development of depression (Culter & Nolen-Hoeksema, 1991), and we will see later in this chapter that it is related to sexual dysfunctions. Some sexually abused children may even become suicidal in subsequent years.

Victims of child sexual abuse such as comedian Drew Carey and former NHL hockey player Sheldon Kennedy have both acknowledged that they have had suicidal tendencies. Among clinically disordered adults, CSA probably served as but one of many factors that combined to produce a clinical disorder. We suggest this possibility because studies of the relationship between CSA alone and adjustment in the general population do not find a strong association between the two variables (Rind, Tromovitch, & Bauserman, 1998).

The strength of the association between CSA and adjustment may vary according to the way that adjustment is assessed. A recent review of the research on female survivors of childhood sexual abuse conducted by Canadian researchers led to the conclusion that, in terms of interpersonal outcomes, CSA is indeed associated with interpersonal distress such as marital distress and with problems in sexual functioning (see Rumstein-McKean & Hunsley, 2001). However, the researchers also noted that conclusions about the long-term effects of CSA in general are limited by numerous problems associated with past research, including concerns about low generalizability owing to the researcher's tendency to rely on select clinical samples rather than on randomly selected community samples and the need for improved assessment measures with better psychometric features (i.e., reliability and validity).

PREVENTION

An important goal of any prevention program is to reduce the incidence, prevalence, and severity of a particular problem. For CSA, prevention efforts have focused on elementary schools. The ESPACE program is offered in schools throughout Quebec. A recent evaluation of this program found that the grades 1 and 3 students who took part were better able to identify appropriate behavioural responses when presented with vignettes of situations that could involve abuse (Hebert, Lavoie, Piche, & Poitras, 2001). Parents reported that this program also had indirect, unintended effects, such as raising the level of self-confidence and assertiveness among children, even to the point that approximately 29 percent of the children became so assertive that they started to disobey appropriate requests from their parents!

Summaries of prevention efforts provided by Canadian researchers (Hebert et al., 2001; Wolfe, 1990) indicate that their content varies from program to program, but common elements include teaching children to recognize inappropriate adult behaviour, resist inducements, leave the situation quickly, and report the incident to an appropriate adult. Children are taught to say no in a firm, assertive way when an adult talks to or touches them in a manner that makes them feel uncomfortable. Instructors may use comic books, films, and descriptions of risky situations to try to teach children about the nature of sexual abuse and how they can protect themselves.

Evaluations of school programs on sexual abuse support the notion that, like the ESPACE program, they increase awareness of sexual abuse among children. However, less is known about whether the children are able to translate what they have learned into overt behaviour and whether such changes reduce the problem (Wolfe, 1990). These programs seem to legitimize discussion of the problem at home (Wurtele & Miller-Perrin, 1987) and might therefore achieve one important goal—namely, to increase the reporting of the crime by encouraging and empowering children to tell their parents or guardians that an adult has made a sexual overture to them.

DEALING WITH THE PROBLEM

When they suspect something is awry, parents must raise the issue with their children, but many adults are uncomfortable doing so. Physicians also need to be sensitized to signs of abuse.

For a child, reporting sexual abuse can be extremely difficult. We tend to forget how helpless and dependent a youngster feels, and it is difficult to imagine how frightening it would be to tell one's parents that one had been fondled by a brother or grandfather.

The vast majority of cases of sexual abuse do not leave any physical evidence, such as torn vaginal tissue. Furthermore, there is no behavioural pattern, such as anxiety, depression, or increased sexual activity, that unequivocally indicates that abuse has occurred (Kuehnle, 1998). Therefore, the primary data regarding CSA must come from the child's self-report. The problem is that leading questions may be needed to facilitate disclosure and these leading questions may lead to some false reports. In questioning a child about possible sexual abuse, the adult needs great skill to ensure that the report is accurate, to avoid biasing the youngster one way or the other, and to minimize the inevitable stress. Some jurisdictions use innovative procedures that can reduce the stress on the child while protecting the rights of the accused adult (e.g., videotaped testimony, closed-courtroom trials, closed-circuit televised testimony, and special assistants and coaching sessions to explain courtroom etiquette and what to expect) (Wolfe, 1990). In Canada, the legal system has implemented several reforms to safeguard the rights of child witnesses, especially those who reveal sexual abuse (Welder, 2000).

Having the child play with anatomically correct dolls can be useful in getting at the truth, but it should be but one part of an assessment since many nonabused children portray such dolls having sexual intercourse (Jampole & Weber, 1987). All things considered, it is little wonder that many, perhaps most, occurrences of child molestation within families go unreported and become a developing adult's terrible secret that can lower self-esteem, distort what could otherwise be positive relationships, and even contribute to serious mental disorders.

Parents go through their own crisis when they become aware that someone has been molesting their child. If incest is involved, it is a true family crisis. If it is the father, then there is often conflict about what to do, for he is frequently the dominant figure in the family and is feared as well as loved. Shame and guilt abound within the home. The family may be struggling with other serious problems as well, such as alcoholism in one or both parents. Decisions have to be made about how to protect the youngster from further sexual abuse or vindictive threats or actions from a frightened, angry perpetrator. The incest victim's mother is in a particularly difficult situation, sometimes torn between her partner and her child, sometimes facing financial uncertainty should the father leave the home or be arrested. It is impossible to know what percentage of incest cases are not reported to the police, but it is safe to say that it is sizable, perhaps the great majority (Finkelhor, 1983). Pedophilic offences, when the perpetrator is not a member of the family, are more frequently reported to police and prosecuted in court.

After the immediate crisis is past, many children may need continued professional attention (Wolfe, 1990). Like adult survivors of rape—and in a very real sense molested children are often rape victims—PTSD can be a consequence. However, symptom expression should differ somewhat for children (as opposed to adults). It has been observed that symptoms such as psychogenic amnesia and numbing are difficult to assess among children, in part because it is hard to determine whether children are simply refusing to talk about what happened (Wolfe & Gentile, 1992). Also, children are less likely to experience full-blown flashbacks but may relive the events through play activities or in dreams.

Wolfe (1999) from the University of Western Ontario proposed a model of PTSD in sexually abused children that distinguishes between Type I and Type II symptoms. This model is adapted from earlier work by Terr (1995), who suggested the need to distinguish between PTSD arising from a single traumatic event (Type I) and PTSD arising from long-standing and chronic experiences (Type II), as would be the case in children experiencing repeated sexual abuse. According to Wolfe (1999), among those with CSA, Type II traumas will have four consequences: (1) a helpless attributional style; (2) dissociative states; (3) ineffective coping when faced with daily situations and traumatic stress; and (4) an extreme and negative response to anger-inducing situations. A team of researchers from Laval University and the University of Quebec at Montreal conducted a study in which they compared the characteristics of three groups of children between the ages of 7 to 12, including a sexually abused group, a medical control group, and a community group (Tremblay, Hebert, & Piche, 2000). The authors found that the sexually abused group had higher levels of symptoms than the other two groups, in terms of both Type I and Type II symptoms.

Many interventions are similar to those used for PTSD in adults. The emphasis is on exposure to memories of the trauma through discussion in a safe and supportive therapeutic atmosphere (Johnson, 1987). It is also important that the child learn that healthy human sexuality is not about power and fear, that it can be a bolstering part of one's personality as one continues to mature (McCarthy, 1986). Inhibitions about bodily contact can be addressed in group therapy settings via structured, nonsexual hand-holding and back rubs (Wolfe, 1990). As with rape, it is important to externalize the blame for what happened, changing the individual's attribution of responsibility from an "I was bad" self-concept to "He/she was bad." Intervention varies with the person's age; a 14-year-old does not need dolls to recount what was done, and a 3-year-old is not an appropriate candidate for group therapy. As yet, there has been no controlled research on these various and complex interventions, but clinical reports are encouraging.

What about treatment of adult survivors of CSA? How can we help them to cope and resolve the long-term effects of CSA, including a sense of shame and guilt, the feeling of being unlovable or unworthy, and the need to make sense of their abuse (e.g., Cole & Putnam, 1992)? Although there is minimal actual research that is specific to adults who were abused as children, the strategies developed to treat PTSD (described above and in Chapter 6) and for counselling sexual assault and rape victims (see Canadian Clinic Focus 14.1) are often used. In his comprehensive treatment manual, Meichenbaum (1994) outlines in detail appropriate assessment, conceptualization, and treatment strategies, including the use of the constructivist-narrative approach (see Chapter 17). He emphasizes the importance of soliciting the client's permission before assessing abuse components, abuse-related events, and long-term impact. After the client tells her or his story of "emotional pain," the therapist must make clear that continued support is offered.

Let us return to the Aboriginal women who were "survivors" of CSA, described in Chapter 5. McEvoy and Daniluk (1995) proposed several treatment principles specific to therapy for Aboriginal women who have experienced sexual abuse.

1 Therapists must typically work on multiple levels and address the complex issues related to culture, class, and so forth, and the consequences of multiple forms of abuse (e.g., verbal and physical abuse, alcoholism, poverty) in addition to repeated sexual victimization. It is difficult to tease apart the specific consequences of sexual abuse.
2 Therapists must help clients reconcile the importance of the extended family with the reality of experiencing abuse from a family member.
3 Therapists must deal with a lack of trust of mainstream institutions, since the women have typically sought help from the white community (e.g., social workers, police) and received little concrete support or help.
4 Therapists must help Aboriginal women work through issues related to cultural shame and the other themes common to their experiences (see Chapter 5), to explore the meaning of being an Aboriginal woman in order "to understand the abuse and the ways in which they attempted to cope with the painful realities of their lives" (McEvoy & Daniluk, 1995, p. 231).
5 Therapists should be familiar with the nature, goals, and consequences of Aboriginal healing and spiritual activities and ceremonies (e.g., sweat lodges, talking circles, powwows) and with the available literature on treating Aboriginal women.
6 Consistent with Meichenbaum's narrative approach, the women should tell their stories and share them with other Aboriginal women to help them understand and connect their experiences.
7 Mainstream therapists should avoid stereotyping and be familiar with the different values and beliefs of Aboriginal people.

A caveat is in order. We are not aware of any comprehensive, controlled outcome study that has evaluated a therapy program that has incorporated suggestions such as these, but we agree with McEvoy and Daniluk (1995) that effective and enduring intervention is probably extremely difficult.

In closing, we should point out that both incest and pedophilia occur much more often in the majority North American culture than was formerly assumed. A study of 796 college students found that an astounding 19 percent of the women and 8.6 percent of the men reported that they had been sexually abused as children. Of the abused women, 28 percent had had incestuous relations; of the men, 23 percent had (Finkelhor, 1979). Other survey data confirm these findings (Siegel et al., 1987). Analyses of Ontario's *Mental Health Supplement* data found that 13 percent of women and 4 percent of men drawn from the general population reported having been sexually abused during childhood or adolescence (MacMillan et al., 1997).

having sexual relations. For some men, voyeurism is the only sexual activity in which they engage; for others, it is preferred but not absolutely essential for sexual arousal (Kaplan & Kreuger, 1997). As in the case of William at the beginning of this chapter, the looking, often called peeping, is what helps the individual become sexually aroused. The voyeur's orgasm is achieved by masturbation, either while watching or later, remembering what he saw. Sometimes the voyeur fantasizes about having sexual contact with the observed person, but it remains a fantasy. In voyeurism, there is seldom contact between the observer and the observed.

A true voyeur, almost always a man, does not find it particularly exciting to watch a woman who is undressing for his special benefit. The element of risk seems important, for the voyeur is excited by the anticipation of how the woman would react if she knew he was watching. Some voyeurs derive special pleasure from secretly observing couples having sexual relations. As with all categories of behaviour that are against the law, frequencies of occurrence are difficult to assess, since the majority of all illegal activities go unnoticed by the police. Indeed, voyeurs are most often charged with loitering rather than with peeping itself (Kaplan & Kreuger, 1997).

Voyeurism typically begins in adolescence. It is thought that voyeurs are fearful of more direct sexual encounters with others, perhaps because they lack social skills. Their peeping serves as a substitute gratification and possibly gives them a sense of power over those watched. Voyeurs often have other paraphilias, but they do not seem to be otherwise disturbed.

In Denmark, following the lifting of all restrictions against the sale of pornographic materials to adults, a significant reduction in peeping, at least as reported to the police, was observed (Kutchinsky, 1970). It may be that the increased availability of completely frank pictorial and written material, typically used in masturbation, partially satisfied the needs that had made voyeurs of some men in the absence of other outlets. Perhaps the ready availability of pornography on the Internet will have a similar, but more global, effect.

EXHIBITIONISM

Exhibitionism is a recurrent, marked preference for obtaining sexual gratification by exposing one's genitals to an unwilling stranger, sometimes a child. It typically begins in adolescence (Murphy, 1997). As with voyeurism, there is seldom an attempt to have actual contact with the stranger. However, some exhibitionists do get arrested for other crimes involving contact with a victim (Sugarman et al., 1994). Sexual arousal comes from fantasizing that one is exposing himself or from actually doing so, and the exhibitionist masturbates either while fantasizing or even during the actual exposure. In most cases, there is a desire to shock or embarrass the observer.

Voyeurism and exhibitionism together account for a majority of all sexual offences that come to the attention of the police. The frequency of exhibitionism is much greater among men, who are often arrested for what is legally termed *indecent exposure*. Other paraphilias are very common in exhibitionists, notably voyeurism and frotteurism (Freund, 1990).

The urge to expose seems overwhelming and virtually uncontrollable to the exhibitionist, or flasher, and is apparently triggered by anxiety and restlessness as well as by sexual arousal. One exhibitionist persisted in his practices even after suffering a spinal cord injury that left him without sensation or movement from the waist down (DeFazio et al., 1987). Because of the compulsive nature of the urge, the exposures may be repeated rather frequently and even in the same place and at the same time of day. Apparently, exhibitionists are so strongly driven that at the time of the act, they are usually oblivious to the social and legal consequences of what they are doing (Stevenson & Jones, 1972). In the desperation and tension of the moment, they may experience headaches and palpitations and have a sense of unreality. Afterward, they flee in trembling and remorse (Bond & Hutchinson, 1960). Generally, exhibitionists are immature in their approaches to the opposite sex and have difficulty in interpersonal relationships. Over half of all exhibitionists are married, but their sexual relationships with their spouses are not satisfactory (Mohr, Turner, & Jerry, 1964).

The penile plethysmograph was used in a study of male exhibitionists in an effort to determine whether they were sexually aroused by stimuli that do not arouse nonexhibitionists (Fedora, Reddon, & Yeudall, 1986). Compared with normal people and with sex offenders who had committed violent assaults, the exhibitionists showed significantly greater arousal in response to slides of fully clothed women in nonsexual situations, such as riding on an escalator or sitting in a park, but they showed similar levels of sexual interest in response to erotic and sexually explicit slides. These results are consistent with the hypothesis that exhibitionists misread cues in the courtship phase of sexual contact, in the sense that they construe certain situations as sexual that are judged nonerotic by nonexhibitionists.

Frotteurism

Frotteurism involves the sexually oriented touching of an unsuspecting person. The frotteur may rub his penis against a woman's thighs or buttocks or fondle her breasts or genitals. These attacks typically occur in places that provide an easy means of escape, such as a crowded bus or sidewalk. Frotteurism has not been studied very extensively. It appears to begin in adolescence (DSM-IV-TR, 2000) and typically occurs along with other paraphilias (Krueger & Kaplan, 1997).

The sexual sadist obtains sexual gratification from inflicting pain or humiliation on another person, often a sexual masochist, who is aroused by being dominated or humiliated.

Sexual Sadism and Sexual Masochism

A marked preference for obtaining or increasing sexual gratification by inflicting pain or psychological suffering (such as humiliation) on another is the key characteristic of sexual sadism. A marked preference for obtaining or increasing sexual gratification through subjecting oneself to pain or humiliation is the key characteristic of sexual masochism.

Both these disorders are found in heterosexual and homosexual relationships, though it is estimated that upwards of 85 percent of people with these disorders are exclusively or predominantly heterosexual (Moser & Levitt, 1987). Some sadists and masochists are women; surveys have found that 20 to 30 percent of the members of sadomasochistic clubs are female (Moser & Levitt, 1987). Alcoholism is common among sadists (Allnut et al., 1996). The disorders seem to begin in early adulthood, and most sadists and masochists are relatively comfortable with their unconventional sexual practices (Spengler, 1977). The majority of sadists and masochists lead otherwise conventional lives, and there is some evidence that they are above average in income and educational status (Moser & Levitt, 1987; Spengler, 1977).

The majority of sadists establish relationships with masochists to derive mutual sexual gratification. From 5 to 10 percent of the population have engaged in some form of sadomasochistic activity, such as blindfolding one's partner, but few do so regularly, and even fewer prefer such activities during sex (Baumeister & Butler, 1997). The sadist may derive full orgasmic pleasure by inflicting pain on his or her partner, and the masochist may be completely gratified by being subjected to pain. For other partners, sadistic and masochistic practices, such as spanking, are a prelude to or an aspect of sexual intercourse.

Although a great many people are switchable—that is, able to take both dominant and submissive roles—masochists outnumber sadists. For this reason, bondage-and-discipline services may constitute a considerable portion of the business of a house of prostitution. The manifestations of sexual masochism are varied. Examples include restraint (physical bondage), blindfolding (sensory bondage), spanking, whipping, electric shocks, cutting, humiliation (e.g., being urinated or defecated on, being forced wear a collar and bark like a dog, or being put on display naked), and taking the role of slave and submitting to orders and commands. The term *infantilism* refers to a desire to be treated like a helpless infant and clothed in diapers. One particularly dangerous form of masochism, called hypoxyphilia, involves sexual arousal by oxygen deprivation, which can be achieved using a noose, a plastic bag, chest compression, or a chemical that produces a temporary decrease in brain oxygenation by peripheral vasodilation (American Psychiatric Association, 1994).

The shared activities of a sadist and a masochist are heavily scripted (Gagnon & Simon, 1977). The loss of control that masochists seem to desire is partly illusory, since they have typically established clear rules about what activities they want to engage in. Pain, humiliation/domination, or both take place as part of a story that the two participants agree to act out together. Themes of submission/domination seem as important as the infliction of physical pain.

Occasionally, sadists murder and mutilate; some are sex offenders who are imprisoned for torturing victims, mostly strangers, and deriving sexual satisfaction from doing so (Dietz, Hazelwood, & Warren, 1990). Sadists who commit acts of aggression against people have a different pattern of offences than that of nonsadistic sex offenders. Sadistic offenders are more likely to impersonate police officers, commit serial murders, tie up their victims, and conceal corpses (Gratzer & Bradford, 1995).

PARAPHILIAS NOT OTHERWISE SPECIFIED

In addition to the paraphilias described above, the DSM-IV-TR also lists several disorders in the category of "paraphilias not otherwise specified." This includes such disorders as necrophilia (sex with dead people), zoophilia (bestiality), telephone scatalogia (repeated urge to make obscene phone calls), and coprophilia (the use of feces for sexual excitement).

The high level of dysfunction that can be involved in paraphilias not otherwise specified is underscored by the report of a 54-year-old man incarcerated in a Canadian federal penitentiary (Earls & Lalumière, 2002). This man had been convicted four times for cruelty to animals. He was diagnosed with bestiality and an antisocial personality disorder. He had developed a sexual attraction to horses and killed a horse by puncturing its vaginal wall with his arm when he became jealous of the horse's interest in a stallion. Phallometric testing confirmed that he was sexually aroused by horses and not at all sexually aroused by people.

ETIOLOGY OF THE PARAPHILIAS

Of the many theories and hypotheses about the etiology of the paraphilias, the principal ones come from psychodynamic and behavioural perspectives; others are from the biological perspective.

Psychodynamic Perspectives The paraphilias are viewed by psychodynamic theorists as defensive in nature, protecting the ego from having to deal with repressed fears and memories and representing fixations at pregenital stages of psychosexual development. The person with a paraphilia is seen as someone who is fearful of conventional heterosexual relationships, even of heterosocial relationships that do not involve sex. His (less often, her) social and sexual development is immature, stunted, and inadequate for both social and heterosexual intercourse with the adult world (Lanyon, 1986). For example, the fetishist and the pedophile are viewed as men whose castration anxiety makes heterosexual sex with other adults too threatening. Castration anxiety leads the exhibitionist to reassure himself of his masculinity by showing his manhood (his genitals) to others; it results in the sadist dominating others.

Behavioural and Cognitive Perspectives Some theorists operating within a behavioural paradigm hold the view that the paraphilias arise from classical conditioning that by chance has linked sexual arousal with classes of stimuli deemed by the culture to be inappropriate causes of sexual arousal (Kinsey, Pomeroy, & Martin, 1948; Kinsey et al., 1953). For example, a young man may masturbate to pictures or images of women dressed in black leather boots. According to this theory, repetitions of these experiences endow boots with properties of sexual arousal. Similar proposals have been made for transvestism, pedophilia, voyeurism, and exhibitionism. Although there is some minor support from clinical case studies (e.g., McGuire, Carlisle, & Young, 1965) and controlled experimentation (e.g., Rachman, 1966), this orgasm-conditioning hypothesis has very little empirical support (O'Donohue & Plaud, 1994). However, as described later, some innovative therapeutic strategies have been developed based on this etiological speculation.

Most current behavioural and cognitive theories of the paraphilias are multidimensional and propose that a paraphilia results when a number of factors impinge on an individual. The childhood histories of individuals with paraphilias reveal that often they were subjected to physical and sexual abuse and grew up in a family in which the parent-child relationship was disturbed (Mason, 1997; Murphy, 1997). These early experiences may well contribute to the low level of social skills, low self-esteem, loneliness, and lack of intimate relationships often seen among those with paraphilias (Kaplan & Kreuger, 1997; Marshall et al., 1997). Paraphilias such as exhibiting or peeping may thus be activities that substitute for more conventional relationships and sexual activity. Distorted parent-child relationships may also create in an individual hostility or a general negative attitude and lack of empathy toward women, which may increase the chances of his victimizing a woman. Alcohol and negative affect are often triggers of incidents of pedophilia, voyeurism, and exhibitionism. Marshall (1996) reported that 50 percent of the sex offenders in his sample were intoxicated at the time of their offence, and a recent study by Abracen, Looman, and Anderson (2000) of men incarcerated in Canadian federal penitentiaries found that a group of sexual offenders (including a subset of 34 child molesters) were much more likely than a group of nonsexual violent offenders to abuse alcohol. These data are consistent with what we know about the disinhibiting effects of alcohol (see Chapter 12). Deviant sexual activity, like alcohol use, may be a means of escaping from negative affect (Baumeister & Butler, 1997).

Cognitive distortions also play a role in the paraphilias. A voyeur, for example, may believe that a woman who left her blinds up while undressing really wanted someone to look at her (Kaplan & Kreuger, 1997). Hypotheses that focus on cognitions sometimes sound psychoanalytic in nature. For instance, some clinicians of a cognitive-behavioural perspective and some of a psychodynamic persuasion regard transvestism as a beleaguered male's refuge from responsibilities he sees himself saddled with solely by virtue of being a man. Women's clothing, then, is believed to have a particular meaning for the male transvestite beyond any sexual arousal he experiences by donning it. Perhaps less rigid gender roles will alter the meaning that women's clothes have for such men.

From an operant conditioning perspective, many paraphilias are considered an outcome of inadequate social skills or reinforcement of unconventionality by parents or relatives. Case histories of transvestites, for example, often refer to childhood incidents in which the little boy was praised and fussed over for looking cute in his mother's dresses.

Biological Perspectives As the overwhelming majority of people with paraphilias are male, there has been speculation that androgen, the principal male hormone, plays a role. Because the human fetus begins as a female, with maleness emerging from later hormonal influences, perhaps something can go wrong during fetal development. Findings of hormonal differences between normal people and people with paraphilias are inconclusive, however. As to differences in the brain, a dysfunction in the temporal lobe may be relevant to a minority of cases of sadism and exhibitionism (Mason, 1997; Murphy, 1997). If biology turns out to be important, it most likely will be but one factor in a complex network of causes that includes experience as a major, if not the major, player (Meyer, 1995).

Therapies for the Paraphilias

Because most paraphilias are illegal, many people diagnosed with them are imprisoned and their treatment is ordered by the court. Outcomes for incarcerated adult sex offenders are highly variable; published success rates range from more than 90 percent to as low as 30 percent (Marshall et al., 1991). Juvenile sex offenders have also been the focus of some research, as most offenders begin in adolescence. The results, as with the findings on adults, are variable (Becker & Hunter, 1997). Published data are hard to interpret for several reasons. Experimental designs are not the rule here, as ethical considerations have led most researchers to conclude that control groups should not be used. Some programs select the most problematic prisoners for treatment, whereas others treat those with the most promising prognoses (e.g., first offenders). Some programs do not have follow-up sessions after release, whereas others do. Recidivism increases as the years go by, especially after two years have passed since termination of treatment (Marshall & Barbaree, 1990).

As we have seen with substance abusers, sex offenders often lack the motivation to try to change their illegal behaviour. Undermining their motivation for treatment are such factors as denial of the problem (see Marshall, Thornton, Marshall, Fernandez, & Mann, 2001), minimization of the seriousness of their problem, a belief that their victims will not be credible witnesses, and the confidence that they can control their behaviour without professional assistance. Some blame the victim—even a child—for being overly seductive. Such people are frequently judged to be inappropriate for treatment programs (Dougher, 1988), for when they do become involved, they frequently drop out (Knopp, 1984). There are several methods to enhance their motivation to commit to treatment (Miller & Rollnick, 1991):

1. The therapist can empathize with the offender's reluctance to admit that he is an offender, thereby reducing the defensiveness and hostility.
2. The therapist can point out to the offender the treatments that might help him control his behaviour better and emphasize the negative consequences of refusing treatment (e.g., transfer to a less attractive incarceration setting if the person is already in custody) and of offending again (e.g., stiffer legal penalties).
3. Having elaborated on the possible benefits of treatment, the therapist can implement a paradoxical intervention by expressing doubt that the person is motivated to enter into or continue in treatment, thereby challenging him to prove wrong the therapist whom he has been resisting.
4. The therapist can explain that there will be a psychophysiological assessment of the patient's sexual arousal, the implication being that the patient's sexual proclivities can be revealed without his admitting to them (Garland & Dougher, 1991).

There is also the issue of what happens to motivation levels after the offender is released back into the community. A recent study conducted with sex offenders from Ontario showed that motivation to change sexually deviant behaviour increased substantially throughout the course of treatment but decreased significantly, relative to posttreatment levels, after conditional release to the community (Barrett, Wilson, & Long, 2003). Barrett et al. (2003) concluded that motivation is dynamic rather than static and that many clinicians in community settings will find it difficult to re-engage the offender in the treatment process. With the foregoing as background, we now describe treatments for the paraphilias.

Psychoanalytic Therapy A prevalent psychoanalytic view of the paraphilias is that they arise from a character disorder, an older term for personality disorder, and are therefore exceedingly difficult to treat with any reasonable expectation of success. This perspective is probably also held by the courts and by the lay public (Lanyon, 1986). Psychoanalytic views have made few contributions to effective therapy for these disorders.

Behavioural Techniques Behaviour therapists have been less interested in presumed deep-seated personality defects among people with paraphilias and more focused on the particular pattern of unconventional sexuality. Consequently, they have tried to develop therapeutic procedures for changing only the sexual aspect of the individual's makeup. Some successes have been achieved, especially when a variety of techniques are used in a broad-spectrum, multi-faceted treatment (Becker, 1990; Maletzky, 1991; Marshall et al., 1991).

In the earliest years of behaviour therapy, paraphilias were narrowly viewed as attractions to inappropriate objects and activities. Looking to experimental psychology for ways to reduce these attractions, researchers fixed on aversion therapy. Thus, a boot fetishist would be given shock (on the hands or feet) or an emetic (a drug that produces nausea) when looking at a boot, a transvestite when cross-dressing, a pedophile when gazing at a photograph of a nude child, and so on. Although aversion therapy may not completely eliminate the attraction, in some cases, it provides the patient with a greater measure of control over the overt behaviour (McConaghy, 1990, 1994). Another method is called *satiation*; with this method, the man masturbates for a long time, typically after ejaculating, while fantasizing out loud about his deviant activity. There is reason to believe that both aversion therapy and satiation, especially when combined with other psychological interventions, such as social skills training, can have beneficial effects (Brownell, Hayes, & Barlow, 1977; Laws & Marshall, 1991; Marshall & Barbaree, 1990).

Orgasmic reorientation has been employed to help the patient learn to become more aroused by conventional sexual stimuli. In this procedure, patients (again, most of whom are men) are confronted with a conventionally arousing stimulus (e.g., a photograph of a woman) while they are responding sexually for other, undesirable reasons. In the first clinical demonstration of this technique, Davison (1968a) instructed a young man troubled by sadistic fantasies to masturbate at home in the following manner:

> When assured of privacy in his dormitory room ... he was first to obtain an erection by whatever means possible—undoubtedly with a sadistic fantasy, as he indicated. He was then to begin to masturbate while looking at a picture of a sexy, nude woman (the target sexual stimulus). ... If he began losing his erection, he was to switch back to his sadistic fantasy until he could begin masturbating effectively again. Concentrating again on the ... picture, he was to continue masturbating, using the fantasy only to regain the erection. As orgasm was approaching, he was at all costs to focus on the ... picture. (p. 84)

The client was able to follow these instructions and, over a period of weeks, began to find conventional pictures, ideas, and images sexually arousing. However, the therapist had to complement the orgasmic procedure with some imaginal aversion therapy (e.g., imagining receiving a painful electric shock contingent on inappropriate thoughts) for the sadistic fantasies. The follow-up after a year and a half found the client capable of conventional arousal, although he apparently reverted at will to his sadistic fantasies every now and again. This dubious outcome has been reported for other instances of orgasmic reorientation. Behaviour therapists continue to explore its possibilities, despite no clear evidence of its effectiveness (Laws & Marshall, 1991).

In addition to the arousal-based procedures just described, several other techniques are in widespread use. Social skills training is often used because of the well-established fact that many individuals with paraphilias have social skills deficits. Another technique, *alternative behavioural completion*, entails imagining a typical deviant activity but changing its ending.

> As you drive home one night you notice an attractive woman driver on your right in a van. She can see right into your car. You slow down and drive parallel with her as you begin to get aroused. You want to rub your penis and take it out to show her. However, the urge this time is weaker and you drive past her quickly without exposing. You feel good about yourself for being able to exert control. (Maletzky, 1997, p. 57)

Cognitive Treatment Cognitive procedures are often used to counter the distorted thinking of individuals with paraphilias. For example, an exhibitionist might claim that the girls he exposes himself to are too young to be harmed by it. The therapist would counter this distortion by pointing out that the younger the victim the worse the harm will be (Maletzky, 1997). Training in empathy toward others is another cognitive technique. Teaching the patient to consider how his behaviour would affect someone else may lessen the sex offender's tendency to engage in such activities. Relapse prevention, modelled after the work on substance abuse described in Chapter 12, is also an important component of many treatment programs.

Cognitive and behavioural approaches have become more sophisticated and broader in scope since the 1960s, when the paraphilias were addressed almost exclusively in terms of sexual attraction to inappropriate environmental stimuli. In many instances, therapy is modelled on the approach of Masters and Johnson (1970) under the assumption that some paraphilias develop or are maintained as a result of unsatisfactory sexual relationships with consenting adults (Marshall & Barbaree, 1990). Overall, both institution-based and outpatient programs that follow a cognitive-behavioural model with sex offenders reduce recidivism to a greater degree than would be expected were no treatment at all attempted. These outcomes are much better for child molesters than for rapists. Although sex offenders generally evoke disgust and fear more than genuine interest, society tends to overlook the fact that even minimally effective efforts to treat such people not only are cost-effective but may protect others when the person is released from prison (Prentky & Burgess, 1990).

Biological Treatment A variety of biological interventions have been tried on sex offenders. Castration, or removal of the testes, was used a great deal in western Europe a generation ago, with some apparent efficacy in terms of reducing the incidence of paraphilic behaviour (e.g., Langeluddeke, 1963). However, those operated on were a heterogeneous group that included homosexuals involved in noncoercive sex with other adults (Marshall et al., 1991). It is unclear how many were offenders whose crimes harmed innocent others—that is, it is unclear how many were child molesters and rapists. The lack of clarity of outcome, coupled with major ethical concerns, has led to infrequent use of castration today, although there are trends to use chemical means.

Biological efforts to control illegal and socially disapproved paraphilic behaviour among sex offenders have more recently involved the use of drugs. Treatment has employed medroxyprogesterone acetate (MPA, trade name Depo-Provera), which lowers testosterone levels in men. By reducing the frequency of erections and ejaculations, use of this drug presumably inhibits sexual arousal (to both conventional and unconventional stimuli) and consequent disapproved behaviour. Cyproterone acetate, which lowers androgen levels, has been used to produce similar effects (Hall, 1995).

Results so far are mixed. Berlin and Meinecke (1981) found that after periods of MPA administration ranging from 5 to 20 years, 17 of 26 offenders did not engage in paraphilic behaviours; however, when the drug was discontinued, most reverted to such behaviour. If these sexual appetite suppressants have to be taken indefinitely, many ethical issues are raised, particularly as these drugs may have serious side effects (i.e., infertility, diabetes) with long-term use (Gunn, 1993). The high dropout rate among participants is another problem.

We have mentioned rape several times in our discussion of the paraphilias, especially in connection with pedophilia and incest. Forced sexual contact, however, occurs far more often between adults than between an adult and a child. We now examine the important topic of rape.

RAPE

In legal terms, rape falls into two categories—forced and statutory. Forced rape is sexual intercourse with an unwilling partner. Statutory rape refers to sexual intercourse with a minor, someone under the age of consent. The age of consent is decided by statutes and is typically 18, although in recent years people have suggested lowering the age. It is assumed that a person younger than the age of consent should not be held responsible for her sexual activity. A charge of statutory rape can be made even if it is proved that the person entered into the situation knowingly and willingly. Thus, statutory rape need not involve force, only consummated intercourse with a minor that is reported to the police. We focus in this section on forced rape.

THE CRIME

The specifics of rape cases vary widely. Some rapes are planned, and some are thought to be more impulsive, spur-of-the moment crimes. Up to 70 percent of rapes are associated with intoxication (Marshall & Barbaree, 1990). Some rapes seem motivated by a desire to control the other person Others are more clearly sexually motivated, although many rapists experience erectile failure or fail to reach organism (Groth & Burgess, 1977; Hudson & Ward, 1997). In what is sometimes termed *sadistic rape*, the rapist severely injures the victim's body, for example, by inserting foreign objects into her vagina or pulling and burning her breasts; some rapists also murder their victims. Little wonder, then, that rape is considered as much an act of violence, aggression, and domination as an act of sex. In many jurisdictions, the definition of rape includes oral and anal entry as well as vaginal penetration. Although men can be victims of sexual assault—especially by other men in prison—our discussion focuses on women because rape is primarily an act committed by men against women.

Rape that occurs on dates is called acquaintance rape, or date rape. Rapes of this kind outnumber rapes by strangers by as much as three to one (Kilpatrick & Best, 1990). In general, the vast majority of rapes in Canada are committed by people who are known to the victim (Stermac, Du Mont, & Dunn, 1998; Stermac, Du Mont, & Kalemba, 1995), with one Canadian study finding that 81 percent of sexual assaults were perpetrated by men who were familiar to their victim (Canadian Panel on Violence against Women, 1993). Unfortunately, many students are sexually assaulted. One study of 259 Canadian undergraduate women found that about one-third of those who dated had experienced physical, verbal, or psychological sexual coercion during the previous year (DeKeseredy, Schwartz, & Tait, 1993). In a subsequent survey of over 3,600 female students at six Ontario universities, 15 percent reported being sexually assaulted (including 2 percent who reported date rape) and 24 percent reported being physically assaulted (Newton-Taylor, DeWit, & Gliksman, 1998). First-year students were more likely to be assaulted than were students in their second, third, or fourth years. Problems arise among adolescents as well. For instance, in a study conducted in British Columbia of students in grades 8 through 12, 26 percent reported being forced into some kind of sexual activity (Rhynard, Krebs, & Glover, 1997). A comparable study in Alberta found that 23 percent of an adolescent sample had been assaulted at least once and that those who had experienced a higher number of sexual assaults were more likely than other students to suffer from clinically significant levels of emotional distress (Bagley, Bolitho, & Bertrand, 1997).

A recent development with regard to date rape is the use of the tranquilizer Rohypnol. This drug is odourless and tasteless and can be easily slipped into a drink; if ingested, it causes the person to pass out and have little if any memory of what happens. Men have used Rohypnol to enable them to rape women when on a date.

As many as 25 percent of American women will be raped during their lifetime (Kilpatrick & Best, 1990), most often by someone they know (Hudson & Ward, 1997), and it is likely that more than 80 percent of sexual assaults are not reported. If we consider coerced sexual activity that stops short of rape, findings show that as many as 75 percent of female college students have been subjected to some type of unwanted sexual activity (Koss, 1985).

THE VICTIM, THE ATTACK, AND THE AFTERMATH

A prevalent belief is that all women who are raped are young and attractive. This is a myth. Although many victims do fit this description, many others do not. Age and physical appearance are no barriers to some rapists; they may choose children as young as 1 year old or women in their eighties.

Rape victims are usually traumatized by the attack, both physically and mentally (Resick, 1993; Rothbaum et al., 1992). In the minutes or seconds preceding rape, the woman begins to recognize her dangerous situation but can scarcely believe what is about to happen to her. During the assault she is first and foremost in great fear for her life. The physical violation of her body and the ripping away of her freedom of choice are enraging, but the victim also feels her vulnerability in not being able to fight off her typically stronger attacker. Moreover, the attacker usually has the element of surprise and sometimes a weapon to intimidate and coerce. Resistance is seriously compromised by terror.

For weeks or months following the rape, many victims feel extremely tense and deeply humiliated. They feel guilt that they were unable to fight harder and may have angry thoughts of revenge. Many have nightmares about the rape. Depression and loss of self-esteem are common. Some victims of rape develop phobias about being outdoors or indoors or in the dark, depending on where the rape took place. They may also fear being alone or in crowds or having anyone behind them. Unfortunately, some of these reactions are exacerbated by insensitivity on the part of police and even friends and loved ones, some of whom may question the victim's complicity in what happened (more on this later). Sometimes an unwanted pregnancy results from a rape, and justifiable concern about sexually transmitted diseases, including AIDS, adds to the trauma of the attack. For good reason, DSM-IV-TR mentions rape as one of the traumas that can give rise to posttraumatic stress disorder.

Many women who have been raped subsequently develop a negative attitude toward sex and experience difficulty in their relationships with their husbands or lovers (Becker, Skinner, et al., 1986). So certain are Calhoun and Atkeson (1991), two experienced clinical researchers on rape, that sexual problems are a frequent long-term consequence of untreated rape trauma that they urge clinicians to consider the possibility that rape or sexual assault has occurred in women who come to therapy for many of the sexual dysfunctions discussed later in this chapter. For some women, even though frequency of sex and of orgasms may not be diminished, satisfaction with sex can be reduced for years (Feldman-Summers, Gordon, & Mengler, 1979).

Without intervention, symptoms of anxiety and depression—and in some cases, full-blown PTSD—an persist in some women for many years following an assault (Calhoun & Atkeson, 1991; Resick, 1993). Suicidal risk is also high for many rape survivors (Kilpatrick, Edmunds, & Seymour, 1992; Kilpatrick et al., 1985), as is substance abuse (Burnam et al., 1988), which might have begun as an attempt to self-medicate to reduce anxiety.

The nature and duration of what some call *rape trauma syndrome* (Burgess & Holmstrom, 1974) depend a great deal on the person's life both prior to and following the attack. Factors that can mitigate the negative aftermath of rape include a supportive spouse and friends as well as the kind of crisis intervention described later (Atkeson et al., 1982; Ruch & Leon, 1983). Research is inconclusive, however, as to whether the negative emotional consequences of rape correlate with the violence of the assault, the setting, or the familiarity of the rapist (Resick, 1993). These complexities led Calhoun and Atkeson (1991) to conclude that the aftermath is more a function of how the person appraises the events than of the circumstances themselves.

THE RAPIST

As documented some years ago in a classic book on the politics of rape, the fact that men with their generally superior strength can usually overpower women buttresses the view that rape has served in the past and still serves to control and intimidate women (Brownmiller, 1975).

Who Is the Rapist? Is the rapist primarily the psychopath who seeks the thrill of dominating and humiliating a woman through intimidation and often brutal assault? Is he an ordinarily unassertive man with a fragile ego who, feeling inadequate after disappointment and rejection in work or love, takes out his frustrations on an unwilling stranger? Is he an otherwise respectable, even honoured, man in authority who takes advantage of his position of power over a woman? Is he a teenager, provoked by a seductive and apparently available young woman who, it turns out, was not as interested as he in sexual intimacy? Is he a man whose inhibitions against expressing anger have been dissolved by alcohol? The best answer is that the rapist is all these men, often operating under a combination of several of these circumstances.

Research on rapists in Canada suggests that heterogeneity does exist and that one can make meaningful distinctions between types of rapists, such as psychopathic and nonpsychopathic rapists (see Brown & Forth, 1997). How-

Paul Bernardo and Karla Homolka were involved in the death of Homolka's sister and in the murder of two teenaged girls in Ontario. Paul Bernardo was also the "Scarborough Rapist," who allegedly raped, brutalized, and terrorized over two dozen women in Toronto.

ever, what many rapists probably have in common is unusually high hostility toward women, arising from beliefs of having been betrayed, deceived, or demeaned by them or from exposure to parental violence and physical or sexual abuse during childhood (Duke & Durham, 1990; Malamuth et al., 1993). Reports from rapists indicate that the urge to rape is heightened by feelings of loneliness, anger, humiliation, inadequacy, and rejection (McKibben, Proulx, & Lusignan, 1994). Some rapists also seem to have problems distinguishing friendliness from seductiveness and in accurately reading cues from a woman indicating that she wants intimacies to cease (Malamuth & Brown, 1994). They often lack social skills, have low self-esteem, and have demonstrably low levels of empathy for their victims (Hudson & Ward, 1997; Marshall & Moulden, 2001). Follow-up research conducted in Kingston, Ontario, indicates that rapists may repress empathy toward their own victim rather than suffer from a general deficit in empathy (Fernandez & Marshall, 2003).

From a sociological perspective, the more a society accepts interpersonal violence as a way to handle conflict and solve problems, the higher the frequency of rape (Sanday, 1981). It seems worth noting that in a controlled experiment, male college students who stated that they regarded rape as unacceptable were aroused by video portrayals of rape if the woman was depicted as having an orgasm during the assault (Malamuth & Check, 1983). This research suggests that rape may be encouraged by pornography that depicts women enjoying coerced sexual relations.

Therapy for Rapists and Rape Victims

Unlike most of the disorders discussed in this book, rape has the dubious distinction of presenting two different challenges to the mental health professional: treating the man who has committed the act and treating the woman who has been the victim.

Therapy for Rapists Therapy programs for incarcerated rapists are typically multidimensional in nature and are evaluated by following men after release from prison to determine recidivism rates. Among the components of these programs are cognitive techniques aimed at rapists' distorted beliefs (such as that women want to be raped) and inappropriate attitudes toward women, attempts to increase empathy with their victims, anger management, techniques to improve self-esteem, and efforts to reduce substance abuse. These methods are often implemented in confrontational group-therapy sessions that attempt to goad the rapist into taking responsibility for his aggressive behaviour and include an explicit focus on relapse prevention (Marshall, 1999). As with the paraphilias, this psychologically based therapy is sometimes supplemented with the use of biological treatments to reduce the rapist's sex drive. Although these programs typically have not had adequate control groups, meta-analyses (quantitative reviews of past studies) have led to the conclusion that cognitive therapy and the biological interventions may lower recidivism somewhat, especially among men who complete the treatment programs (Hall, 1995; Hanson & Bussière, 1998). The meta-analysis technique is described in more detail in Canadian Perspectives 14.2.

Therapy for Rape Victims Efforts to counsel rape victims have expanded considerably in recent years. Rape crisis centres and telephone hotlines have been established throughout

Rape counsellors support a victim's decision to prosecute the rapist. The Ottawa Rape Crisis Centre provides assistance with a 24-hour crisis line as well as acting as a liason with police, hospitals, lawyers, and other social service resources.

Canadian Perspectives/14.2

Canadian Research on Sex Offender Recidivism

A number of studies and quantitative reviews of sex offender recidivism have been conducted in Canada. A review that spanned a period of four decades was conducted by Greenberg (1998) at the Royal Ottawa Hospital. He concluded that incest offenders, relative to extrafamilial offenders, are less likely to re-offend, while rapists and exhibitionists have higher levels of recidivism.

One of the most widely cited papers in recent years was a meta-analysis conducted by Karl Hanson and Monique Bussière (1998) from the Department of the Solicitor General of Canada that examined the factors associated with sexual recidivism in 61 follow-up studies. They found that demographic variables (e.g., being young and single) and criminal lifestyle variables (e.g., total number of prior offences) were reliable but modest predictors of sexual recidivism. Examination of psychological adjustment variables found that measures of psychological maladjustment had little predictive utility. Only antisocial personality disorder predicted sexual recidivism. This general association has been replicated in recent research showing that psychopathy is one personality variable that predicts recidivism. A recent Canadian study found that men with elevated levels of psychopathy and deviant sexual arousal tended to recidivate sooner and at much higher rates than men low in these factors (Serin, Mailloux, & Malcolm, 2001).

Overall, Hanson and Bussière found that sexual criminal history variables (e.g., prior sexual offences, victimization of strangers) had small to moderate correlations with sexual recidivism. Measures of sexual deviancy proved to be the strongest predictors, with sexual interest in children as measured by phallometric testing being the most robust predictor. Examination of the clinical presentation variables showed that low remorse did not predict recidivism, but recidivism was predicted by the failure to complete treatment.

Subsequent research in Canada on the treatment of sexual offenders and levels of recidivism has yielded inconsistent findings. Nicholaichuk, Gordon, Gu, and Wong (2000) studied the efficacy of cognitive-behavioural treatment at the Regional Psychiatric Centre in Saskatoon. They compared 296 treated and 283 untreated offenders over a six-year period and found that 14.5 percent of treated offenders and 33.2 of untreated offenders were convicted for new sexual offences. In contrast, Quinsey, Khanna, and Malcolm (1998) examined inmates in the Regional Treatment Centre (RTC) program in Ontario between 1976 and 1989 and revealed a less positive picture. Their pattern of results indicated that treatment resulted in a decrease in violent recidivism in general, but levels of sexual recidivism actually increased as a result of treatment! Analyses of a composite variable that combined the levels of violent and sexual recidivism showed that treatment had no effect whatsoever. The picture is complicated further by a study by Seto and Barbaree (1999) that found that men rated as having more appropriate treatment behaviour while receiving group treatment (i.e., higher attendance, less disruptive interactions) actually were the most likely to reoffend. The authors concluded that offenders, paricularly those high in psychopathy, may learn social skills in group treatment that enable them to gain access to and manipulate potential victims.

A contemporary meta-analysis by Hanson et al. (2002)—known as the ATSA study because it was commissioned by the Association for the Treatment of Sexual Abusers—has clarified and resolved this issue. This quantitative summary of 43 studies provided clear evidence of treatment effectiveness. In contrast to the untreated group, the treated group had lower recidivism levels for sexual crimes (12.8 percent versus 16.8 percent) and crimes in general (27.9 percent versus 39.2 percent). The benefits of treatment were even stronger when analyses compared the efficacy of current treatments (i.e., cognitive-behavioural therapy together with relapse prevention) with that of earlier interventions. Additional results showed that treatment effects were comparable for juvenile and adult offenders.

Recently, Marshall and McGuire (2003) expressed concern that some may still question the magnitude of the treatment effects (i.e., there is not a great difference between 12.8 and 16.8 percent), and noted that the treatment-effect sizes are comparable to those that emerge from psychological treatments of other disorders. In addition, they argued convincingly in favour of a harm reduction approach and suggested that the effects of treatment would be even more evident if the outcome variable was the number of victims involved, since sexual reoffenders often have multiple victims.

Thinking Critically

1. On the basis of the available data, do you believe that treatment for sex offenders is essential? If you feel that it is essential, would you change your view if you knew the person was a psychopath?
2. When people learn that a former sex offender is now living in their community following release, they have often responded by harassing the offender until he leaves the area. Do you think communities have the right to do this? How would you respond upon learning that one of your new neighbours is a former sex offender who has responded well to treatment? How do you weigh the former offender's right to privacy against the possible risk of harm to the public?

Canadian Clinic Focus/14.1

Rape Crisis Centres in Canada

Staffed both by professionals and by female volunteers who may themselves have been rape victims, rape crisis centres offer support and advice within a crisis-intervention framework. They focus on normalizing the victim's emotional reactions—"Everyone goes through this emotional turmoil after an assault"—encouraging her to talk about her feelings and helping her meet immediate needs, such as arranging for child care or improving the security arrangements in her home. In short, the goal is to help the victim solve problems and cope with the immediate aftermath of the traumatic event (Calhoun & Atkeson, 1991; Sorenson & Brown, 1990). Discouraging self-blame is also important (Frazier, 1990), especially when the rapist was someone the woman knew (Stewart et al., 1987).

The Victoria Women's Sexual Assault Centre in Victoria, British Columbia, has a 24-hour crisis line that provides support and information for people dealing directly or indirectly with sexual assault or childhood sexual abuse (see http://www.islandnet.com/~vwsac/). Immediate crisis counselling is also available. This assault centre is similar to many others in that rape counsellors urge the woman not to withdraw or become inactive, and women from the crisis centre often accompany the rape victim to the hospital and to the police station, where they help her with the legal procedures and with recounting the events of the attack. They may later arrange for examinations for pregnancy and venereal diseases and for professional therapy if necessary. The possibility of HIV infection also has to be addressed. Empathic companions from the crisis centre help the victim begin to express her feelings about the ordeal, and they urge her to continue venting with her own relatives and friends. If the attacker or attackers have been apprehended, women from the centre support the victim in her decision to go through with prosecuting the rapist, and they assist with the formulation of victim impact statements. Counselling is made available in individual sessions as well as in 12-week counselling groups facilitated by professional counsellors.

The Lloydminster Sexual Assault and Information Centre in Lloydminster, Saskatchewan, also provides a 24-hour crisis line, and volunteers assist in accompanying the victim to the hospital and to the police station (see http://lloydminster.org/sexualassault/). Another important aspect of this centre is that it includes a number of preventive programs for children, including such programs as "Safe & Happy," "It's O.K. to Say No," and "My Body Belongs to Me!" Their purpose is to enhance awareness and provide the skills needed to ensure personal safety. Support is also made available for "secondary survivors" (i.e., parents, siblings, partners, etc.).

Finally, the Fredericton Sexual Assault Centre in New Brunswick had its origins in the summer of 1975, and a 24-hour crisis line was added the next year. It is a feminist organization that also provides crisis-intervention counselling and assistance to the hospital and police station. The center is prototypical in that it also offers both individual counselling and group counselling (see http://www.discribe.ca/fsacc). It has a dating-violence program that includes a focus on prevention and classroom presentations for students in grades 8 through 12. Importantly, this program includes a peer-training component in recognition of the significant benefits that accrue when teens speak with each other about dating violence. Other features include community workshops designed to increase awareness of warning signs.

Comment

There can be no doubt that these centres provide a range of valuable services. A major problem in Canada is that approximately 94 percent of sexual assaults are never reported. Women who have been raped by a nonstranger and who have no readily observable physical injuries are especially unlikely to report the sexual assault (see McGregor, Wiebe, Marion, & Livingstone, 2000). Therefore, the support provided by these centres is very important. However, there are at least two ways that obvious improvements can be made.

First, the centres are typically underfunded, and hence no one is in a position to conduct the type of program evaluation research that would determine their effectiveness. In the absence of research, we can only assume that the services provided are highly valued in the aftermath of personal crisis.

Second, concerns have been raised about the relative paucity of services for sexually abused males. A report compiled for Health Canada concluded that male-centred assessment is almost non-existent and treatment programs for males are rare (Mathews, 1996). In fact, according to the report, "Canada lags far behind other western democracies in the study of male victims and their male and female abusers.... Social policy development, public education, treatment programs and research funding, and the evolution of a more inclusive discourse on interpersonal violence that reflects the male experience are long overdue" (Mathews, 1996, p. 2).

North America. Some are associated with hospitals and clinics; others operate on their own. See Canadian Clinic Focus 14.1 on page 460 for a discussion of some rape crisis centres in Canada.

Mental health professionals who attend rape victims typically focus on the woman's ongoing relationships, which may be disrupted or negatively affected by the rape. Friends and family, especially spouses and lovers, will need help handling their own emotional turmoil so that they can provide the kind of nonjudgmental support that rape victims need.

Much of the therapy for rape has a great deal in common with the treatment for PTSD (Keane et al., 1989). The victim is asked to relive the fearsome events of the attack by discussing them with the therapist, perhaps also imagining them in vivid detail. Such repeated exposure to the trauma is designed to extinguish the fear (or, in psychoanalytic terms, work it through) (Calhoun & Atkeson, 1991; Calhoun & Resick, 1993; Rothbaum & Foa, 1992). As is the case with other kinds of anxieties, it is no easy task to succeed in getting the person to reflect on her fears, since denial and avoidance are the typical coping methods used by rape victims—for the most part unsuccessfully. Depression can be addressed by helping the woman reevaluate her role in the rape, as many victims tend to see themselves as at least partially responsible. A little-researched topic is the anger and rage many victims have toward their assailants; women are often afraid of expressing or are socialized not to express such feelings (Calhoun & Atkeson, 1991).

A cognitive-behavioural intervention that is beginning to be empirically validated is the cognitive processing therapy of Patricia Resick (1992; Resick & Schnicke, 1992). This therapy combines exposure to memories of the trauma (as is done in other anxiety reduction interventions) with the kind of cognitive restructuring found in the work of Ellis and Beck. For example, the rape victim is encouraged to dispute any tendency to attribute the blame to herself and to consider fully those aspects of the attack that were beyond her control.

Social attitudes and support systems encourage the victim to report rape and pursue the prosecution of the alleged rapist, but the legal situation is still problematic. Interviews with half a million women indicated three reasons for reluctance to report rape:

1. They consider the rape a private matter.
2. The fear reprisals from the rapist or his family or friends.
3. They believe that the police would be inefficient or insensitive (Wright, 1991).

It is estimated that only a very small percentage of rapists are ultimately convicted of their crimes. Furthermore, there is no denying that going to trial is very stressful. Any familiarity of the victim with her assailant argues strongly against conviction, and the victim's role in her own assault is almost always examined by defence attorneys. Finally, even though many rapists rape hundreds of times, they are only occasionally imprisoned for an offence. Society must be attentive and active to ensure that the victim's rights are defended by the legal system.

SEXUAL DYSFUNCTIONS

Having discussed the unconventional patterns of the sexual behaviour of a small minority of the population, we turn now to sexual problems that interfere with conventional sexual enjoyment during the course of many people's lives. Our concern here is with **sexual dysfunctions**, the range of problems considered to represent inhibitions in the normal sexual response cycle.

What is defined as normal and desirable in human sexual behaviour varies with time and place. The contemporary view that inhibitions of sexual expression underlie abnormality can be contrasted with views held during the 19th and early 20th centuries in the Western world, when excess was regarded as the culprit. We must keep these varying temporal and cultural norms in mind as we study human sexual dysfunctions.

Psychological problems have consequences not only for the people who experience them but also for those with whom they are involved. This aspect of human emotional problems is especially important in our consideration of sexual dysfunctions, which usually occur in the context of intimate personal relationships. A marriage is bound to suffer if one of the partners fears sex. And most of us, for better or for worse, base part of our self-concept on our sexuality. Do we please the people we love, do we gratify ourselves, or, more simply, are we able to enjoy the fulfillment and relaxation that can come from a pleasurable sexual experience? Sexual dysfunctions can be so severe that human tenderness itself is lost, let alone the more intense satisfaction of sexual activity.

We look first at the human sexual response cycle as it normally functions. With that as context, we examine the several sexual dysfunctions. Then we discuss etiologies and therapies for these problems.

SEXUAL DYSFUNCTIONS AND THE HUMAN SEXUAL RESPONSE CYCLE

As indicated in Table 14.2, DSM-IV-TR divides sexual dysfunctions into four principal categories: sexual desire disorders, sexual arousal disorders, orgasmic disorders, and sexual pain disorders. The difficulty should be persistent and recurrent, a clinical judgment acknowledged in the DSM to entail a degree of subjectivity. The disturbance should cause marked distress or interpersonal problems. This requirement was new in DSM-IV and allows the person's own reactions to, say, having no interest in sex play a role in whether he or she should be diagnosed. A diagnosis of sexual dysfunction is not made if the disorder is believed to be due entirely to a medical illness (such as advanced diabetes, which can cause erectile problems in men) or if it is due to another Axis I disorder (such as major depression).

Most contemporary conceptualizations of the sexual response cycle are a distillation of proposals by Masters and Johnson (1966) and Kaplan (1974). More than 30 years ago, the work of Masters and Johnson signalled a revolution in the nature and intensity of research in and clinical attention to human sexuality. These researchers extended the earlier interview-based breakthroughs of the Kinsey group (Kinsey et al., 1948, 1953) by making direct observations and physiological measurements of people masturbating and having sexual intercourse. Four phases in the human sexual response cycle are typically identified; they are considered quite similar in men and women.

1 **Appetitive**. Introduced by Kaplan (1974), this stage refers to sexual interest or desire, often associated with sexually arousing fantasies.

2 **Excitement**. In this phase, originally Masters and Johnson's first stage, a subjective experience of sexual pleasure is associated with physiological changes brought about by increased blood flow to the genitalia and, in women, also to the breasts. This tumescence, the flow of blood into tissues, shows up in men as erection of the penis and in women as enlargement of the breasts and changes in the vagina, such as increased lubrication.

3 **Orgasm**. In this phase, sexual pleasure peaks in ways that have fascinated poets and the rest of us ordinary people for thousands of years. In men, ejaculation feels inevitable and indeed almost always occurs. In women, the walls of the outer third of the vagina contract. In both sexes, there is general muscle tension and involuntary pelvic thrusting.

4 **Resolution**. This last of Masters and Johnson's stages refers to the relaxation and well-being that usually follow an orgasm. In men, there is an associated refractory period, during which further erection and arousal are not possible. Women may be able to respond again with sexual excitement almost immediately, a capability that permits multiple orgasms.

This four-stage view is one of many conceivable ways to organize and discuss the relevant body of information (Gagnon, 1977; Kuhn, 1962). We are about to see how the DSM uses this scheme to describe sexual dysfunctions.

The pioneering work of the sex therapists William H. Masters and Virginia Johnson helped launch a candid and scientific appraisal of human sexuality.

Descriptions and Etiology of Sexual Dysfunctions

The prevalence of occasional disturbances in sexual functioning is quite high. Table 14.2 presents data from a survey of over 3,000 men and women who were asked whether they had experienced various symptoms of sexual dysfunction in the past 12 months (Laumann, Paik, & Rosen, 1999). The overall prevalence of symptoms of sexual dysfunction was 43 percent for women and 31 percent for men. Because these symptoms are so common, people should not assume that they need treatment if they sometimes experience one or more of the problems described in this section. In the diagnostic criteria for each sexual dysfunction, the phrase "persistent or recurrent" is used to underscore the fact that a problem must be serious indeed for the diagnosis to be made. In addition, there is a fair amount of comorbidity among the sexual dysfunctions. For example, almost half of both men and women diagnosed with hypoactive sexual disorder (low sexual desire) also have at least one other dysfunction (Segraves & Segraves, 1991). As we review the various disorders, their interconnectedness will become evident.

Sexual Desire Disorders DSM-IV-TR distinguishes two kinds of sexual desire disorders. **Hypoactive sexual desire disorder** refers to deficient or absent sexual fantasies and urges; in **sexual aversion disorder**, a more extreme form of the disorder, the person actively avoids nearly all genital contact with another person. Twenty to 30 percent of the general adult population, more often women than men, may have hypoactive sexual desire disorder (Laumann et al., 1994), although accurate estimates are difficult to obtain because of the inevitable problem of getting people to report

Table 14.2

Self-Reported Rates of Experiencing Various Sexual Problems in the Past 12 Months

Problem	Men	Women
Lacked interest in sex	13–17%	27–32%
Unable to achieve orgasm	7–9%	22–28%
Climax too early	28–32%	N/A
Sex not pleasurable	6–8%	17–24%
Trouble maintaining/ achieving erection	11–18%	N/A
Trouble lubricating	N/A	18–27%
Pain during sex	N/A	8–15%

Source: After Loumann et al., 1999.

Note: The ranges reflect the fact that rates vary according to age.

accurately on something as personal as a sexual dysfunction. Among people seeking treatment for sexual dysfunctions, more than half complain of low desire, and among these people, it is often comorbid with an orgasmic disorder. Hypoactive sexual desire disorder increased in clinical samples for both men and women from the 1970s to the 1990s (Beck, 1995).

Of all the DSM-IV-TR diagnoses, the sexual desire disorders, often colloquially referred to as low sex drive, seem the most problematic. How frequently should a person want sex? And with what intensity or urgency? The reason a person goes to a clinician in the first place and ends up with this diagnosis is probably that someone else is dissatisfied with that person's interest in sex. The hypoactive desire category appeared for the first time in DSM-III in 1980, under the title of "inhibited sexual desire," and may owe its existence to the high expectations some people have about being sexual. It is striking that entire books—for example, Leiblum and Rosen (1988)—have been written about a disorder that 25 years ago was hardly mentioned in professional sexology circles. Data attest to the significance of subjective factors in the extent to which a person believes he or she has a low sex drive; for example, hypoactive sexual desire disorder was reported more often by American men than by British (Hawton et al., 1986) or German men (Arentewicz & Schmidt, 1983).

We know little about the causes of either hypoactive sexual desire or sexual aversion disorder. Because women with the disorder show normal sexual responses to sexual stimuli in laboratory studies, it does not appear that they are incapable of becoming fully aroused (Kaplan, 1997). Among the causes of low sex drive in people seen clinically are religious orthodoxy, trying to have sex with a partner of the nonpreferred sex, fear of loss of control, fear of pregnancy, depression, side effects from such medications as antihypertensives and tranquilizers, and lack of attraction resulting from such factors as poor personal hygiene in the partner (LoPiccolo & Friedman, 1988).

Relationship factors may also be part of the picture, as women with sexual desire disorder report that their communication with their husband is poor and that they are unhappy with the way conflicts are resolved (Stuart et al., 1987). Other possible causes include a past history of sexual trauma, such as rape or childhood sexual abuse (Stuart & Greer, 1984), and fears of contracting sexually transmitted diseases, such as AIDS (Katz et al., 1989). Two empirical studies indicate that anger is a major factor in reducing sexual desire in both men and women, though it has a smaller role for women (Beck & Bozman, 1995; Bozman & Beck, 1991). Sexual desire is lower when people complain of high levels of everyday stress (Morokoff & Gilliland, 1993). There are also data pointing to the importance of testosterone levels in men—the lower the levels, the lower the sexual desire (Bancroft, 1988).

Sexual Arousal Disorders Some people have little or no trouble experiencing sexual desire but do have difficulty attaining or maintaining sexual arousal, the next stage of the sexual response cycle described by Masters and Johnson. The two subcategories of arousal disorders are **female sexual arousal disorder** and **male erectile disorder**. The former used to be called frigidity, and the latter, impotence.

Replacement of the words *impotence* and *frigidity* by the phrase sexual arousal disorder can be considered an advance. Impotence implies that the man is not potent, in control, or truly masculine, and negatively supports the macho conception of masculinity that many people today challenge. Frigidity implies that the woman is emotionally cold, distant, unsympathetic, and unfeeling. Both terms are derogatory and encourage a search for causes within the person rather than focus attention on the relationship, a domain that many contemporary investigators explore for answers and solutions.

The diagnosis of arousal disorder is made for a woman when there is consistently inadequate vaginal lubrication for comfortable completion of intercourse and for a man when there is persistent failure to attain or maintain an erection through completion of the sexual activity. The prevalence rate for female arousal disorder is about 20 percent (Laumann et al., 1994). For male erectile disorder, prevalence is estimated at between 3 and 9 percent (e.g., Ard, 1977; Frank, Anderson, & Rubenstein, 1978) and increases greatly in older adults (Feldman et al., 1994; Kinsey et al., 1948). Arousal problems account for about half the complaints of men and women who seek help with sexual dysfunctions (Frank, Anderson, & Kupfer, 1976; Renshaw, 1988).

As many as two-thirds of erectile problems have some biological basis, usually in combination with psychological factors (LoPiccolo, 2002). In general, any disease, drug, or hormonal imbalance that can affect the nerve pathways or blood supply to the penis can contribute to erectile problems. Examples are certain drugs, such as Thorazine, Prozac, and some antihypertensive medications, and illnesses, such as diabetes, kidney problems, and chronic alcoholism. As indicated, though, somatic factors usually interact with psychological factors to produce and maintain erectile difficulties. For example, anxiety and depression are common among men with erectile disorder (Araujo et al., 1998; Schiavi, 1997). Research using a measure of sexual self-efficacy developed by researchers in Quebec (Libman, Rothenberg, Fichten, & Amsel, 1985) shows that men with erectile dysfunction often have low levels of sexual self-efficacy and that depression is linked closely with this sense of inefficacy (see Fichten, Libman, Takefman, & Brender, 1988; Holden, 1999; Libman et al., 1985). Once the disorder has begun, fears of sexual failure arise and could certainly inhibit subsequent sexual responding (Rowland, Cooper, & Slob, 1996).

Orgasmic Disorders Three kinds of orgasmic disorders are described in DSM-IV-TR, one found in women and two in men.

Female Orgasmic Disorder Formerly called inhibited female orgasm, **female orgasmic disorder** refers to absence of orgasm after a period of normal sexual excitement. The published prevalence rates for female orgasmic disorder vary widely. One review of this literature found prevalences ranging from 5 to 20 percent (Spector & Carey, 1990). A more recent study, which involved interviewing a large sample of women, found a prevalence of 24 percent (Laumann et al., 1994). Whatever the true prevalence rate, this is the problem that most often brings women into therapy (Kaplan, 1974; Spector & Carey, 1990). Failure to achieve orgasm is not only a problem for women, it is also an important aspect of sex for their partners, who may come to believe that they are unskilled or insensitive lovers. This last point probably accounts for the fact that up to 60 percent of women report faking an orgasm on occasion (McConaghy, 1993).

There is an important distinction between problems a woman may have in becoming sexually aroused and those she may have in reaching an orgasm. Although as many as 10 percent of adult women have never experienced an orgasm (Anderson, 1983), far fewer are believed to remain unaroused during sexual activity. Indeed, laboratory research has shown that women with orgasmic disorder are as responsive to erotic stimuli as are control women (Meston & Gorzalka, 1996).

Numerous reasons have been put forward to explain the problem. Perhaps many women, unlike men, have to learn to become orgasmic; that is, the capacity to have an orgasm may not be innate in females as it is in males. In men, ejaculation, which almost always is accompanied by orgasm, is necessary for reproduction. Survey findings indicate that women who masturbated little or not at all before they began to have intercourse were much more likely to be nonorgasmic than those who had masturbated to orgasm before becoming sexually active with a partner (Hite, 1976; Hoon & Hoon, 1978; Kinsey et al., 1953). These are, of course, correlational data; some third factor may be responsible both for infrequent masturbation and for diminished ability to have orgasms. Lack of sexual knowledge also appears to play a role according to clinical data. Many nonorgasmic women, as well as those who experience little excitement during sexual stimulation, are unaware of their own genital anatomy and therefore have trouble knowing what their needs are and communicating them to a partner. Chronic use of alcohol may be a somatic factor in orgasmic dysfunction in women (Wilsnak, 1984).

Another factor is that women have different thresholds for orgasm. Although some have orgasms quickly and without much clitoral stimulation, others seem to need intense and prolonged stimulation during foreplay or intercourse. A man may conclude that he and his penis are inadequate if the female asks for or herself provides manual stimulation of her clitoris during intercourse, and his reaction can contribute to the problem.

Another possibility arose from research examining the sexual responses of inorgasmic women to erotic films (Meston & Gorzalka, 1996). One feature of this study was determining whether activation of the sympathetic nervous system (achieved by riding a stationary bicycle) would increase genital responding to erotic films. It did in normal women but not in those with orgasmic dysfunction. Meston and Gorzalka speculate that women with orgasmic dysfunction may have a lower threshold for optimal sympathetic activation. Among normal women, low to moderate levels of sympathetic activation (as was induced by bicycle riding in their study) augment vaginal responses to erotic stimuli, but higher levels of sympathetic arousal inhibit sexual responding. Women with an orgasmic disorder may not be able to tolerate even moderate levels of sympathetic arousal and respond to it in a way that interferes with sexual response.

Yet another factor may be fear of losing control. The French have an expression for orgasm, la petite mort, "the little death." Some women fear that they will scream uncontrollably, make fools of themselves, or faint. A related source of inhibition is a belief, perhaps poorly articulated, that to let go and allow the body to take over from the conscious, controlling mind is somehow unseemly.

Male Orgasmic Disorder and Premature Ejaculation Male orgasmic disorder and premature ejaculation are the two orgasmic disorders of men in DSM-IV-TR. Male orgasmic disorder, or difficulty in ejaculating, is relatively rare, occurring in 3 to 8 percent of patients in treatment (Spector & Carey, 1990). Causes that have been put forth include fear of impregnating a female partner, withholding love, expressing hostility, and, as with female orgasmic problems, fear of letting go. In some instances, the problem may be traced to a physical source, such as spinal cord injury or certain tranquilizers (Rosen, 1991).

Premature ejaculation is probably the most prevalent sexual dysfunction among males. It is a problem for as many as 40 percent of men at some time in their lives (Laumann et al., 1994; St. Lawrence & Madakasira, 1992). Sometimes premature ejaculation occurs even before the penis enters the vagina, but it more usually occurs within a few seconds of intromission. Premature ejaculation is generally associated with considerable anxiety.

There is some laboratory-based evidence that men who have premature ejaculation problems are more sexually responsive to tactile stimulation (a vibrator) than men who don't have this problem (Rowland et al., 1996). Perhaps, then, their penises are very sensitive, causing them to ejaculate more quickly. Men with premature ejaculation also have longer periods of abstinence from climactic sex than do men who are not premature ejaculators (Spiess, Geer, & O'Donohue, 1984). Learning has also been proposed as a factor. For example, a man may acquire the tendency to ejaculate quickly as a result of having hurried sex because of not being in a private place and fearing detection (Metz et al., 1997). Relationship problems and a sexually dysfunctional partner can also play a role (Metz et al., 1997).

Sexual Pain Disorders Two pain disorders associated with sex are listed in the DSM, dyspareunia and vaginismus.

Dyspareunia is diagnosed when there is persistent or recurrent pain during sexual intercourse. Some women report that the pain starts at entry, whereas others report pain only after penetration (Meana et al., 1997). Not surprisingly, women with dyspareunia show normal levels of sexual arousal to films of oral sex, but their arousal declines when they watch a depiction of intercourse (Wouda et al., 1998). In women, the diagnosis of dyspareunia should not be made when the pain is believed to be due to lack of vaginal lubrication (when presumably female sexual arousal disorder would be diagnosed); nor should it be made when the pain is judged to be a function of the second pain disorder, vaginismus.

Vaginismus is marked by involuntary spasms of the outer third of the vagina to a degree that makes intercourse impossible. Despite not being able to have intercourse, women with vaginismus have normal sexual arousal and have orgasms from manual or oral stimulation that does not involve penetration.

Prevalence rates for dyspareunia in women range from 8 percent (Schover, 1981) to 15 percent (Laumann et al., 1994). It is generally accepted that the disorder is far less often found in men, perhaps in as few as 1 percent (Bancroft, 1989). Estimates for vaginismus range from 12 to 17 percent of women seeking sex therapy (Rosen & Leiblum, 1995), and it is a very common complaint seen by gynecologists (Leiblum, 1997).

Genital pain associated with intercourse is usually caused by a medical problem, such as an infection of the vagina, bladder, or uterus or of the glans of the penis (McCormick, 1999; Meana et al., 1997). Depressive symptoms, anxiety, and marital problems are also associated with dyspareunia (Meana et al., 1998). One theory regarding the source of vaginismus supposes that the woman wishes, perhaps unconsciously, to deny herself, her partner, or both the pleasures of sexual intimacy. As plausible as this idea may seem, no evidence supports it. However, fear of pregnancy, anxiety, relationship problems, and negative attitudes toward sex in general may play a role in vaginismus (e.g., Reissing, Binik, & Khalife, 1999; Tugrul & Kabacki, 1997). Negative attitudes often are traceable to molestation in childhood or to rape (LoPiccolo & Stock, 1987). Masters and Johnson found that for a number of couples the man's inability to maintain an erection preceded the development of vaginismus in his partner. For some women, then, the sexual problems of their partners may be so anxiety provoking as to result in the development of this disorder.

General Theories of Sexual Dysfunctions

Having reviewed descriptions of the sexual dysfunctions and some of the causes believed to underlie each, we turn now to a consideration of general theoretical perspectives.

At one time, sexual dysfunctions were generally viewed as a result of moral degeneracy. As recently reviewed by

In the early 20th century, corn flakes were promoted as part of a bland diet to reduce sexual desire.

LoPiccolo (in press), excessive masturbation in childhood was widely believed to lead to sexual problems in adulthood. Von Krafft-Ebing (1902) and Havelock Ellis (1910) postulated that early masturbation damaged the sexual organs and exhausted a finite reservoir of sexual energy, resulting in lessened abilities to function sexually in adulthood. Even in adulthood, excessive sexual activity was thought to underlie such problems as erectile failure. The general Victorian view was that dangerous sexual appetite had to be restrained. To discourage handling of the genitals by children, metal mittens were promoted, and to distract adults from too much sex, outdoor exercise and a bland diet were recommended. In fact, Kellogg's Corn Flakes and graham crackers were developed as foods that would lessen sexual interest. They didn't.

Psychoanalytic views have assumed that sexual dysfunctions are symptoms of underlying repressed conflicts. The analyst considers the symbolic meaning of the symptom both to understand its etiology and to guide treatment. Since sexual dysfunctions bring discomfort and psychological pain to the individual and to his or her partner, and since unimpaired sexuality is inherently pleasurable, the theme of repressed anger and aggression competing with the gratification of sexual needs pervades psychoanalytic writings. Thus, a man who ejaculates so quickly that he frustrates his female partner may be expressing repressed hostility toward women, who remind him unconsciously of his mother. A woman with vaginismus may be expressing her hostility toward men, perhaps as a result of childhood sexual abuse or more directly because of her husband's overbearing manner.

Many contemporary psychoanalysts supplement their therapy with cognitive-behavioural techniques (LoPiccolo, 1977). The spirit of rapprochement has also affected cognitive-behavioural approaches to the treatment of sexual dysfunctions, as these therapists are coming to appreciate the role of psychodynamic themes in what used to be straightforward behavioural treatments.

The most comprehensive account of the etiology of human sexual dysfunctions was offered by Masters and Johnson in their widely acclaimed book *Human Sexual Inadequacy* (1970), based on case studies from their practice. We will first examine their suggestions and then consider subsequent modifications and extensions of their ideas.

The Theoretical Model of Masters and Johnson Masters and Johnson (1970) used a two-tier model of current and historical causes to conceptualize the etiology of human sexual inadequacy (Figure 14.2).

Current Causes The current or proximal causes can be distilled down to two: fears about performance and the adoption of a spectator role. Fear of performance refers to being overly concerned with how one is performing during sex. The spectator role refers to being an observer rather than a true participant in a sexual experience. Both involve a pattern of behaviour in which the individual's focus on and concern for sexual performance impedes his or her natural sexual responses.

We have no conclusive evidence, however, that these factors are the causal agents in sexual dysfunctions. This is because of the directionality problem, discussed first in Chapter 5 and again in many places throughout this book. Researchers have consistently shown that performance fears do exist in people with sexual dysfunctions, but the data do not show that the fear preceded and caused the dysfunction. Someone with an erectile dysfunction, for example, may well become fearful that he will not attain an erection in a sexual encounter, and that anxiety may ensure that he is unable to become erect. But the anxiety may be functioning here as a factor that is maintaining the disorder, not one that caused it in the first place.

Historical Causes In the Masters and Johnson model, the current, or proximal, reasons for sexual dysfunctions were hypothesized to have one or more historical antecedents.

- **Religious orthodoxy**. Some conservative religious upbringing styles look askance at sexuality for the sake of pleasure, particularly outside marriage. Masters and Johnson found that many of their sexually dysfunctional patients had negative views of sexuality as a consequence. One female patient, for example, had been taught as she was growing up not to look at herself naked in the mirror and that intercourse was reserved for marriage and then only to be endured for purposes of having children.
- **Psychosexual trauma**. Some dysfunctions can be traced to rape or other degrading encounters. One young male patient of Masters and Johnson's was told by a prostitute that he would never be able to "get the job done" with other women if he didn't "get it done here and now with a pro."
- **Homosexual inclination**. Sexual enjoyment is understandably less if a person with homosexual inclinations tries to engage in heterosexual sex.
- **Inadequate counselling**. This phrase is a euphemism for comments made by professionals that are incorrect and destructive, such as a health care worker telling a healthy 65-year-old man to forget about sex or a cleric saying that erectile dysfunction is God's punishment for sins.
- **Excessive intake of alcohol**. As Shakespeare wrote in Macbeth, "It provokes the desire but it takes away the performance" (act II, scene 3). If an inebriated man cannot achieve or maintain an erection, he may begin to fear

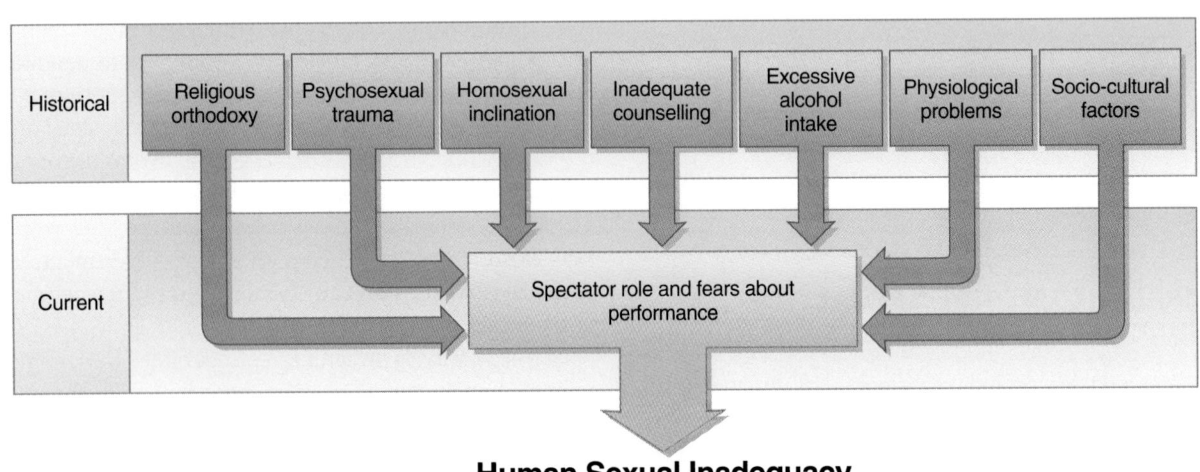

Figure 14.2 Historical and current causes of human sexual inadequacies, according to Masters and Johnson.

that his erectile problem will recur rather than attribute the problem to alcohol.

- **Biological causes**. Masters and Johnson alerted us back in 1970 to somatic factors contributing to sexual dysfunction. Now even more is known about such factors; we have reviewed this information in our discussions of the individual dysfunctions.
- **Sociocultural factors**. Expectations and concerns differ between women and men and as a function of social class. For example, men have the blessing, even demand, of society to develop sexual expressiveness and to take the initiative. Despite the changes that have resulted from the feminist movement of the past 30 years, it remains questionable whether this holds true for women.

Other Contemporary Views Masters and Johnson considered sexual dysfunctions as problems in and of themselves that could be treated directly, rather than as symptoms of other intrapsychic or nonsexual interpersonal difficulties. The couples whose treatment formed the basis of their book *Human Sexual Inadequacy* (1970) had marriages that, in spite of sexual problems, were marked by caring and closeness. But as the Masters and Johnson therapy techniques became widespread and as the social milieu changed so as to allow more people to feel comfortable seeking help, sex therapists began to see people whose relationships were seriously impaired. In such situations, by the time a therapist is consulted, it is impossible to know whether the hostility between the two people caused the sexual problem or vice versa.

The working assumption of most contemporary sex therapists is that sexually dysfunctional couples have both sexual and interpersonal problems (Rosen & Leiblum, 1995). It is unrealistic to expect a satisfying sexual encounter when, for example, the man is angry with the woman for spending more and more time outside the home or the woman resents the man's insensitive dealings with their children. Such negative thoughts and emotions can intrude into the sexual situation and thereby inhibit whatever arousal and pleasure might otherwise be found.

A couple's sexual difficulties may serve a purpose not immediately obvious to the therapist or even to the couple themselves. Joseph LoPiccolo (2002), a leading cognitive-behavioural sex therapist, offers some psychodynamic reasons for the hidden meaning a sexual problem might have in a person's life or within a relationship.

> For some patients, sexual dysfunction is a way of resolving negative feelings about their sexuality.... Sexual dysfunction may ward off depression about some highly distressing life situation, by simply giving the patient another problem upon which to focus. A man with erectile failure who is very unhappy in his marriage but who finds divorce too threatening an idea to process, exemplifies this issue.... Other patients may find that during intercourse [with an adult partner], deviant fantasies such as sex with a child occur. In such cases, sexual dysfunction fosters repression of unacceptable sexual impulses, allows maintenance of one's self image as a decent, moral person.... Sexual dysfunction may almost be a psychic necessity to maintain self esteem.

Such hidden benefits—known in the psychoanalytic paradigm as secondary gain—may underlie the occasional sabotaging therapists encounter when a therapy seems to be proceeding well. For example, a man who is angry with his wife may derive satisfaction from knowing that his erectile problems interfere with her sexual gratification. As the kind of direct sex therapy described later in this chapter begins to show the intended effect, the man finds reasons not to attend therapy sessions or "forgets" appointments. The secondary gain of the sexual problem represents a familiar psychoanalytic theme that has recently begun to be recognized in the largely cognitive-behavioural field of sex therapy (LoPiccolo, in press).

Many other causes of sexual dysfunction have been identified. As mentioned earlier, people who have sexual problems are often found to lack knowledge and skill (LoPiccolo & Hogan, 1979). Sometimes their partners may have deficiencies—the husbands of nonorgasmic women are often reported to be awkward lovers (Kaplan, 1974; LoPiccolo, 1977). Simply caring for the partner may not be enough to establish a mutually satisfying sexual relationship. In fact, Kaplan (1974) suggested that inhibiting anxiety can arise when one partner wants too much to please the other; the feeling of being in the spotlight may result in a kind of performance anxiety. Another proposed cause of sexual dysfunction is response anxiety—anxiety about not being aroused (Apfelbaum, 1989).

Poor communication between partners also contributes to sexual dysfunction. For any number of reasons—embarrassment, distrust, dislike, resentment, depression, to name but a few—one lover may not inform the other of his or her preferences, likes, and dislikes and then may misinterpret the failure of the partner to anticipate or mind read as a sign of not really caring.

In considering these hypothesized etiological factors, it is important to keep two things in mind. First, many people have unsatisfying episodes in their sex lives, perhaps after a bruising argument with their partner or when preoccupied with problems at work. Usually these periods pass, and the sexual relationship returns to normal. Second, many people who currently have in their lives or had in the past one or more of the pathogenic factors discussed do not develop persistent sexual dysfunctions. Although to date there is little real understanding of this phenomenon, there is speculation that other variables, such as an unusually supportive network of friends or a particularly understanding sexual partner, must be operating in these people's present lives to mitigate the putative negative effects of the pathogenic factors.

Therapies for Sexual Dysfunctions

The treatment of sexual dysfunctions was pioneered by Masters and Johnson (1970), who virtually created the sex-therapy movement. With some variations, their approach is still followed by many practitioners conducting therapy for sexual dysfunctions (LoPiccolo, 2002). The overall aim of Masters and Johnson was to reduce or eliminate fears of performance and to take the participants out of the maladaptive spectator role. They hoped that these steps would enable the couple to enjoy sex freely and spontaneously.

In this approach, assessment interviews took place over the first few days. These interviews placed considerable focus on the so-called sexual value system, the ideas of each partner about what was acceptable and needed in a sexual relationship. Sometimes the sexual value system of one or both partners had to be changed before sexual functioning could improve. For example, if one partner persisted in regarding sexuality as ugly and unacceptable, even the most powerful therapy would not be likely to help the partner enjoy sex.

On the third day, the therapists began to offer interpretations about why problems had arisen and why they were continuing. In all cases, the emphasis was on the problems in the relationship, not on individual difficulties of either partner. A basic premise of the Masters and Johnson therapy was that "there is no such thing as an uninvolved partner in any marriage in which there is some form of sexual inadequacy" (1970, p. 2). Whatever the problem, the couple was encouraged to see it as their mutual responsibility. At this time, the clients were introduced to the idea of the spectator role. They were told, for example, that a male with erectile problems—and often his partner as well—usually worries about how well or poorly he is doing rather than participating freely and that this pattern of observing the state of the erection, although totally understandable in context, blocks his natural responses and greatly interferes with sexual enjoyment.

At the end of the third day an all-important assignment was given to the couple, namely, to engage in sensate focus. The couple was instructed to choose a time when both partners felt "a natural sense of warmth, unit compatibility ... or even a shared sense of gamesmanship" (Masters & Johnson, 1970, p. 71). They were to undress and give each other pleasure by touching each other's bodies. The co-therapists appointed one marital partner to do the first pleasuring, or giving; the partner who was "getting" was simply to be allowed to enjoy being touched. The one being touched was not required to feel a sexual response and was responsible for immediately telling the partner if something became distracting or uncomfortable. Then the roles were to be switched. Attempts at intercourse were still forbidden. To Masters and Johnson, this approach was a way of breaking up the frantic groping common among these couples. The sensate-focus assignment usually promoted contact where none had existed for years, constituting a first step toward gradually reestablishing sexual intimacy. Once this sense of intimacy was established, couples received explicit instructions involving specific techniques.

Over the past 30 years, therapists and researchers have devised new procedures for the clinicians who seek to improve the sexual lives of dysfunctional patients. We will describe several strategies and procedures that extend Masters and Johnson's work. A therapist may choose only one technique for a given case, but the complex and multifaceted nature of sexual dysfunctions usually demands several. These approaches are suitable for homosexual as well as heterosexual sex.

Anxiety Reduction Well before the publication of the Masters and Johnson therapy program, behaviour therapists appreciated that their dysfunctional clients needed gradual and systematic exposure to anxiety-provoking aspects of the sexual situation. Wolpe's systematic desensitization and in vivo desensitization (desensitization by real-life encounters) have been employed with high degrees of success (Anderson, 1983; Hogan, 1978), especially when combined with skills training. For example, a woman with vaginismus might first be trained in relaxation and then practise inserting her fingers or dilators into her vagina, starting with small insertions and working up to larger ones (Leiblum, 1997). In vivo desensitization would appear to be the principal technique of the Masters and Johnson program, although additional components probably contribute to its overall effectiveness.

Directed Masturbation We have previously mentioned that women with orgasmic disorder frequently lack knowledge of their own sexual anatomy. Directed masturbation, devised by LoPiccolo and Lobitz (1972), is a multi-step program that supplements the Masters and Johnson program. The first step is for the woman to carefully examine her nude body, including her genitals, and identify various areas with the aid of diagrams. Next, she is instructed to touch her genitals and locate areas that produce pleasure. With this accomplished, she then increases the intensity of masturbation using erotic fantasies. If orgasm has not been achieved by this time, she is instructed to buy a vibrator and use it in her masturbation. Finally, her partner enters the picture, first watching his mate masturbate, then doing for her what she has been doing for herself, and finally having intercourse in a position that allows him to stimulate the woman's genitals manually or with a vibrator. Directed masturbation appears to add significantly to the effectiveness of treatment of orgasmic disorder (O'Donohue, Dopke, & Swingen, 1997).

Procedures to Change Attitudes and Thoughts In what are called sensory-awareness procedures, clients are encouraged to tune in to the pleasant sensations that accompany even incipient sexual arousal. The sensate-focus exercises described by Masters and Johnson, for example, are a way of opening the individual to truly sensual and sexual feelings. Rational-emotive behaviour therapy tries to substitute less self-demanding thoughts for "musturbation," the "I must" thoughts that often cause problems for people with sexual dysfunctions. A therapist might try to reduce the pressure a man with erectile dysfunction feels by challenging his belief that intercourse is the only true form of sexual activity. Kaplan (1997) recommends several procedures to try to increase the attractiveness of sex. She has clients engage in erotic fantasies and gives them courtship and dating assignments, such as getting away for a weekend.

Skills and Communication Training To improve sexual skills and communication, therapists assign written materials, show clients videotapes and films demonstrating explicit sexual techniques, and discuss techniques (McMullen & Rosen, 1979). Of particular importance for a range of sexual dysfunctions is encouraging partners to communicate their likes and dislikes to each other (Hawton, Catalan, & Fagg, 1992; Rosen, Leiblum, & Spector, 1994). Taken together, skills and communication training also expose patients to anxiety-provoking material—such as seeing one's partner naked—which allows for a desensitizing effect. Telling one's partner one's preferences in sex is often made more difficult by tensions that go beyond the sexual relationship, which leads us to the next strategy.

Couples Therapy Sexual dysfunctions are often embedded in a distressed marital or other close relationship, and troubled couples usually need special training in nonsexual communication skills. As noted earlier, recent writings on sex therapy emphasize the need for a systems perspective—that is, for the therapist to appreciate that a sexual problem is embedded in a complex network of relationship factors (Wylie, 1997). Sometimes a therapy that focuses on nonsexual issues, such as difficulties with in-laws or with child rearing, is necessary and appropriate, either in addition to or instead of a Masters and Johnson type of sex therapy.

Psychodynamic Techniques and Perspectives A man may not at first admit that he cannot have an erection, in which case the therapist must listen for clues in what he says. A woman may be reluctant to initiate sexual encounters because, although she may not verbalize it to the therapist, she considers such assertiveness unseemly and inappropriate to her traditional female role. In such instances, the general psychodynamic view that clients are often unable to express clearly to their therapists what truly bothers them can help in proper assessment and planning for behavioural treatment (Kaplan, 1974). No doubt, elements of psychodynamic therapy are to be found in the actual practices of sex therapists, even if they are usually not made explicit by these workers when they discuss their techniques in journals or with colleagues. Our earlier discussion of eclecticism in therapy may serve as a reminder of the complexity of the therapeutic enterprise.

Medical and Physical Procedures As more discoveries are made about biological factors in sexual dysfunctions, it becomes increasingly important for therapists to consider whether underlying somatic problems are contributing to the dysfunction (LoPiccolo, 1992b; Rosen & Leiblum, 1995). Consideration of possible somatic factors is especially important for the disorders of dyspareunia and complete erectile dysfunction.

Dyspareunia can be ameliorated in postmenopausal women by estrogen treatments, which can reduce the thinning of vaginal tissue and improve vaginal lubrication (Masters, Johnson, & Kolodny, 1988; Walling, Anderson, & Johnson, 1990). When depression, along with severely diminished sex drive, is part of the clinical picture, antidepressant drugs can be helpful. Tranquilizers are also used as an adjunct to anxiety-reduction techniques. However, a complicating factor is that some of these psychoactive drugs themselves interfere with sexual responsiveness.

Surgical procedures are also available. A semi-rigid silicone rod can be implanted in a chronically flaccid penis, or a device can be implanted in the penis that can be stiffened with fluid from a reservoir and a small pump that is implanted in the scrotum. However, long-term follow-ups of men who have had such operations indicate that poor sexual functioning continues in many cases (Tiefer, Pedersen, & Melman, 1988). If the psychological components of the problem are not addressed, men with rod implants may continue to have sexual problems, but with a penis that is never flaccid. (With a rod, sexual interest and arousal are not necessary for intercourse, and this situation is usually not favourable for long-term psychological adjustment.) Vascular surgery involves correction of problems with blood inflow via arteries or outflow via veins in the penis. Results are mixed at best (Melman & Rossman, 1989), but the possibility exists for restoration of normal functioning because, unlike the case with implants, erection will occur only with desire and arousal (Wincze & Carey, 1991).

A nonsurgical intervention entails the use of a cylinder attached to a vacuum pump. The penis is placed in the cylinder, and when air is pumped out, blood is drawn into the penis, producing an erection. When the penis is erect, the cylinder is removed and an elastic band is put around its base to trap the blood and maintain the erection. This device is one of the treatments that has been recommended as effective by the American Urological Association (Skolnick, 1998).

Several drugs have been used in the treatment of sexual dysfunctions. One group of drugs (including alprostadil and paparevine hydrochloride) has to be injected; it dilates the arteries and thus produces an erection, even in the absence of sexual stimulation. Antidepressants have had mixed results with erectile dysfunction, as have testosterone injections; however, antidepressants have produced some good results with premature ejaculation (Haensel et al., 1998; Strassberg et al., 1999).

Viagra (sildenafil) is a relative newcomer to drug treatment of erectile dysfunction. It was approved by the U.S. Food and Drug Administration in March 1998 and in its first three months was prescribed over 3 million times. It is even being sold illegally over the Internet. Viagra relaxes smooth muscles and thereby allows blood to flow into the penis during sexual stimulation, creating an erection. It is taken one hour before sex, and its effects last about four hours, thus allowing an erection to be maintained for a substantial time period. Thus far, research indicates that seven of 10 men who take Viagra report improvement, whether the cause of their erectile dysfunction is biological (e.g., diabetes) or psychological (Lamberg, 1998). Generally, Viagra produces modest side effects, such as headaches. However, it may be dangerous for men with cardiovascular disease.

In all instances of medical intervention, consideration of psychosocial factors remains important, for sexual dysfunctions are almost always embedded in a complex set of interpersonal and intrapsychic conflicts. The current trend toward viewing sexual dysfunctions as medical or biological problems may divert the attention of therapists and patients from the inherently interpersonal nature of these problems, giving rise to a quick-fix mentality that is probably ill-advised (Rosen & Leiblum, 1995).

Montreal Canadiens hockey legend Guy Lafleur became the spokesperson for the first Canadian campaign for the impotence wonder drug Viagra.

SUMMARY

- Gender identity disorder (GID) involves the deep and persistent conviction of the individual that his or her anatomic sexual makeup and psychological sense of self as man, woman, boy, or girl are discrepant. Thus, a man with GID is physically male but considers himself a woman and desires to live as a woman. Child-rearing practices may have encouraged the young child to believe that he or she was of the opposite sex. Hormonal causes (e.g., too much male hormone in a woman) have also been considered, but the data are equivocal.
- For a time, the only kind of help available to people with GID was sex-reassignment surgery to bring certain bodily features into line with their gender identity. Now, however, there is preliminary evidence that behaviour therapy can help bring gender identity into line with anatomy in some cases.
- In the paraphilias, unusual imagery and acts are persistent and necessary for sexual excitement or gratification. The principal paraphilias are fetishism, reliance on inanimate objects for sexual arousal; transvestic fetishism, sometimes called transvestism, the practice of dressing in the clothing of the opposite sex, usually for the purpose of sexual arousal but without the gender identity confusion of a person with GID; pedophilia and incest, marked preferences for sexual contact with minors and, in the case of incest, for members of one's own family; voyeurism, a marked preference for watching others in a state of undress or in sexual situations; exhibitionism, obtaining sexual gratification by exposing oneself to unwilling strangers; frotteurism, obtaining sexual contact by rubbing against or fondling women in public places; sexual sadism, a reliance on inflicting pain and humiliation on another person to obtain or increase sexual gratification; and sexual masochism, obtaining or enhancing sexual gratification through being subjected to pain, usually from a sadist.
- Many hypotheses have been put forward to account for the several paraphilias. Psychoanalytic theories generally hold that they are defensive in nature, protecting the person from repressed conflicts and representing fixations at immature stages of psychosexual development. According to this perspective, the person with a paraphilia is basically fearful of conventional heterosexual relationships. Fetishists and pedophiles, for example, are hypothesized to suffer from castration anxiety that makes it too threatening to engage in conventional sex with adults.
- Behavioural and cognitive theorists focus more directly on the sexual behaviour itself. One view is that a fetishistic attraction to objects, such as boots, arises from accidental classical conditioning of sexual arousal. Another behavioural hypothesis posits social skills deficiencies that make it difficult for the person to interact normally with other adults. Cognitive distortions appear to be involved, as voyeurs may claim that the women they viewed wanted to be seen.
- Efforts have also been made to detect hormonal anomalies in people with paraphilias, but the findings are inconclusive at this time.

- Rape, although it is not separately diagnosed in DSM-IV-TR, is a pattern of behaviour that results in considerable social and psychological trauma for the victim. The inclusion of rape in a discussion of human sexuality is a matter of some controversy, as many theorists regard rape as an act of aggression and violence rather than of sex.
- The most promising treatments for the paraphilias are multi-dimensional, entailing several behavioural and cognitive components. One procedure is reducing the arousal to the stimulus that is involved in the paraphilia. Another, orgasmic reorientation, tries to increase arousal to conventional sexual stimuli. Cognitive methods focus on the cognitive distortions of the person with a paraphilia; social skills training and empathy training are also used frequently.
- Few emotional problems are of greater interest to people than the sexual dysfunctions. These disruptions in the normal sexual response cycle are often caused by inhibitions, and they rob many people of sexual enjoyment. DSM-IV-TR categorizes these disturbances in four groups: sexual desire disorders, sexual arousal disorders, orgasmic disorders, and sexual pain disorders. The disorders can vary in severity, chronicity, and pervasiveness, occurring generally or only with certain partners and in particular situations. In no instance should a person believe that he or she has a sexual dysfunction unless the difficulty is persistent and recurrent; most people normally experience sexual problems on an intermittent basis throughout their lives.
- Although biological factors must be considered, especially for dyspareunia and erectile failure, the etiology of the disorders usually lies in a combination of unfavourable attitudes, difficult early experiences, fears of performance, assumption of a spectator role, relationship problems, and lack of specific knowledge and skills.
- Sex-role stereotypes may play a part in some dysfunctions. For example, a man who has trouble maintaining his erection is often called impotent, with the implication that he is not much of a man, and a woman who does not have orgasms with regularity is often termed frigid, with the implication that she is generally cold and unresponsive. The problems of women in particular appear to be linked to cultural prejudices against their sexuality, ironic in light of laboratory data indicating that women are capable of more frequent orgasms than men.
- Information on the causes of sexual dysfunctions derives almost entirely from uncontrolled case studies and must therefore be viewed with caution. The absence of solid data on etiology, however, has not deterred therapists from devising effective interventions, many of them cognitive and behavioural in nature, often blended with psychodynamic perspectives and techniques.
- Direct sex therapy, aimed at reversing old habits and teaching new skills, was propelled into public consciousness by the work of Masters and Johnson. Their method hinges on gradual, non-threatening exposure to increasingly intimate sexual encounters and the sanctioning of sexuality by credible and sensitive therapists. Other means applied by sex therapists include educating patients in sexual anatomy and physiology; reducing anxiety; teaching communication skills; and working to change patients' attitudes and thoughts about sex and their own sexuality.
- Couples therapy is appropriate when the sexual problem is embedded, as it often is, in a snarled relationship. Biological treatments such as Viagra may also be used, especially when the sexual dysfunction is primarily physical rather than psychological in nature, as in erectile dysfunction.
- Controlled data are just beginning to appear, but there is good reason to be optimistic about the ultimate ability of the mental health professions to help many people achieve at least some relief from sexual problems.

KEY TERMS

acquaintance (date) rape (p. 456)
child sexual abuse (p. 448)
dyspareunia (p. 465)
exhibitionism (p. 451)
fear of performance (p. 466)
female orgasmic disorder (p. 463)
female sexual arousal disorder (p. 463)
fetishism (p. 443)
forced rape (p. 456)
frotteurism (p. 452)
gender identity (p. 436)
hypoactive sexual desire disorder (p. 462)
incest (p. 445)
male erectile disorder (p. 463)
male orgasmic disorder (p. 464)
orgasmic reorientation (p. 455)
paraphilias (p. 443)
pedophilia (p. 444)
premature ejaculation (p. 464)
secondary gain (p. 467)
sensate focus (p. 468)
sensory-awareness procedures (p. 468)
sex-reassignment surgery (p. 441)
sexual and gender identity disorders (p. 436)
sexual aversion disorder (p. 462)
sexual dysfunctions (p. 461)
sexual masochism (p. 452)
sexual sadism (p. 452)
sexual value system (p. 468)
spectator role (p. 466)
statutory rape (p. 456)
transsexualism (p. 437)
transvestic fetishism (p. 443)
vaginismus (p. 465)
voyeurism (p. 448)

Reflections: Past, Present, and Future

- Do you think that gender identity disorder should be regarded as a mental disorder? Why, or why not?
- Paul Bernardo has been diagnosed as having an antisocial personality disorder. He has also been identified as a psychopath and described as a narcissist. Apparently, he is also quite bright. Do you think that he also meets the criteria for sexual sadism? Although there is no simple explanation, do you think that the combination of psychopathy and sexual sadism can be a "deadly combination" (Black, 2000) that contributes to the likelihood that people can turn out to be multiple murderers like Paul Bernardo or serial killers like Clifford Olson?
- Tragically for the victims, it appears to be the case that high intelligence also contributes to "successful" multiple murder and serial killing. Paul Bernardo, Clifford Olson, Jeffrey Dahmer, and Ted Bundy are (or were) endowed with above average, even superior, intelligence. Why would intelligence be a critical consideration in our understanding of some multiple and serial killers? What role would narcissism play in the case of Paul Bernardo (and possibly in other cases, too)?
- During the development of DSM-III, experts considered including "rape" in the list of sexual disorders. The specific disorder to be included was to be called something like "paraphilic coercive disorder." Why do you think the decision was made not to include the proposed disorder in the 1980 and subsequent revisions of the manual? Should rape, or some specific subtype of rape, be included in the next revision of the DSM? Why, or why not?
- Suppose that you specialize in sex therapy. A couple has initiated therapy with you because they are concerned that the male partner is unable to maintain an erection. What would you need to focus on during your initial meeting? Would it be important for you to make a referral to a physician? How will your conceptualization of the case influence the treatment plan that you develop?

chapter 15

Disorders of Childhood

"Parents, I think, are probably in the best position of all to notice a behavioural change. And behavioural change is one of the fundamental signs of mental illness. If you see that your child is moving in one direction suddenly, is a different person, there's a reason for it. It doesn't just happen."
—Michael Wilson, former federal finance minister and advocate for the mentally ill, commenting on conditions leading up to his son's suicide (Nunes & Simmie, 2002, pp. 33–34)

"A common frustration expressed by parents is that services for children and adolescents are splintered and uncoordinated. Four different ministries—health, education, corrections, community and social services—are involved, to varying degrees."
—Scott Simmie on mental health services for children in Ontario, from "Mental illness also hits the very young," *The Toronto Star*, October 5, 1998

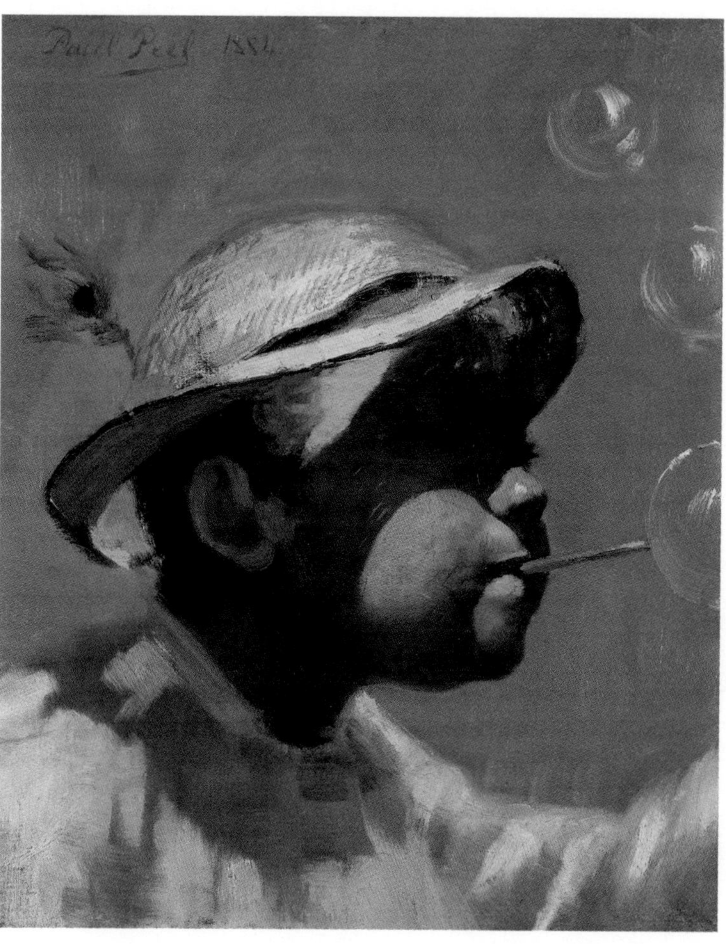

Paul Peel, Canadian 1860–1892, *The Bubble Boy*, 1884
oil on canvas, 43.2 x 35.9 cm,
ART GALLERY OF ONTARIO, TORONTO
Bequest of Mrs. Majorie F. Barlow, Toronto, 1968,
in memory of her grandfather, James McGee

"ERIC. ERIC? ERIC!!" His teacher's voice and the laughter of his classmates roused the boy from his reverie. Glancing at the book of the girl sitting next to him, he noticed that the class was pages ahead of him. He was supposed to be answering a question about the Confederation of Canada, but he had been lost in thought about what seats he and his father would have for the baseball game they'd be attending that evening. A tall, lanky 12-year-old, Eric had just begun 7th grade. His history teacher had already warned him about being late for class and not paying attention, but Eric just couldn't seem to get from one class to the next without stopping for drinks of water or investigating an altercation between classmates. In class, he was rarely prepared to answer when the teacher called on him, and he usually forgot to write down the homework assignment. He already had a reputation among his peers as a "space cadet."

Eric's relief at the sound of the bell was quickly replaced by anxiety as he reached the playground for his physical education class. Despite his speed and physical strength, Eric was always picked last for baseball teams. His team was up to bat first, and Eric sat down to wait his turn. Absorbed in studying a pile of pebbles at his feet, he failed to notice his team's third out and missed the change of innings. The other team had already come in from the outfield before Eric noticed that his team was out in the field—too late to avoid the irate yells of his P.E. teacher to take his place at third base. Resolved to watch for his chance to field the ball, Eric nonetheless found himself without his glove on when a sharply hit ball rocketed his way; he had taken it off to toss it in the air in the middle of the pitch.

At home, Eric's father told him he had to finish his homework before they could go to the Blue Jays game. He had only one page of math problems and was determined to finish them quickly. Thirty minutes later, his father emerged from the shower to find Eric building an elaborate Lego structure on the floor of his room; the math homework was half done. In exasperation, Eric's father left for the game without him.

By bedtime, frustrated and discouraged, Eric was unable to sleep. He often lay awake for what seemed like hours, reviewing the disappointments of the day and berating himself for his failures. On this night, he ruminated about his lack of friends, his teachers' disappointment in him, and his parents' exhortations to pay attention and "get with the program." Feeling that it was hopeless to do better despite his daily resolve, Eric found himself thinking—as he often did—of suicide. Tonight he reviewed his fantasy of wandering out into the street in front of a passing car. Although Eric had never acted on his suicidal thoughts, he frequently replayed in his mind his parents' sorrow and remorse, his classmates' irritation with him, and the concern of his teachers.

Eric's difficulty in focusing his attention is characteristic of attention-deficit/hyperactivity disorder—just one of the disorders clinicians encounter when they work with children. The clinical problems loosely characterized as disorders of childhood cover a wide range of difficulties, from an attentional problem such as that suffered by Eric to depression, fear, the sometimes serious intellectual deficits found in mental retardation, the gross and sometimes callous disregard for the rights of others found in conduct disorder, and the social isolation of autistic disorder. Children typically have access to fewer social, financial, and psychological resources than do adults in dealing with such problems. The extreme dependency of troubled children on their parents and guardians adds to the sense of responsibility these people feel and to their guilt, justified or not. Whether such children receive professional attention at all usually depends on the adults in their lives—parents, teachers, school counsellors.

Most theories consider childhood experience and development critically important to adult mental health. Most theories also regard children as better able to change than adults and thus as particularly suitable for treatment. Although earlier research devoted little attention to childhood disorders, recent years have brought a dramatic increase in professional interest in the nature, etiology, prevention, and treatment of child psychopathology. This interest stems from a growing realization of the widespread mental health problems facing our children and youth. It is now estimated that 14 percent of children (1.1 million children in Canada) have clinically important disorders, with anxiety disorders being most prevalent (Waddell et al., 2002).

In this chapter, we discuss emotional and behavioural disorders that are most likely to arise in childhood and adolescence. We begin by considering disorders of attention and of socially acceptable behaviour and then turn to disorders in which the acquisition of cognitive, language, motor, or social skills is disturbed, including learning disabilities and the most severe of developmental disorders, mental retardation and pervasive developmental disorders (especially autism), which are usually chronic and often persist into adulthood. We conclude by examining mood and anxiety disorders in these age groups.

CLASSIFICATION OF CHILDHOOD DISORDERS

To classify abnormal behaviour in children, diagnosticians must first consider what is normal for a particular age. The diagnosis for a child who lies on the floor kicking and screaming when he or she doesn't get his or her way must take into account whether the child is 2 years old or 7. The field of developmental psychopathology involves disorders of childhood within the context of normal lifespan development, enabling us to identify behaviours that are appropriate at one stage but considered disturbed at another.

Table 15.1

Disorders of Childhood and Adolescence in DSM-IV-TR

I. DISORDERS USUALLY FIRST DIAGNOSED IN INFANCY, CHILDHOOD, OR ADOLESCENCE

Mental retardation: Intellectual functioning that is significantly below average, is accompanied by concurrent deficits in adaptive functioning, and is noticeable before age 18.

Learning disorders: Academic achievement in reading, mathematics, or written expression substantially below that expected for age, schooling, and level of intelligence.

Motor skills disorder: Problems in motor coordination.

Communication disorders: Problems in expressing and/or understanding speech.

Pervasive developmental disorders: Severe and pervasive impairment in several areas of development, including interaction and communication with others and the exhibition of stereotyped behaviour.

Attention-deficit/hyperactivity disorder: A persistent pattern of inattention and/or hyperactivity-impulsivity that is more frequent or severe than is typically observed in individuals at a comparable level of development. Symptoms must be present before age 7 and interfere with functioning in at least two settings.

Conduct disorder: A repetitive and persistent pattern of seriously antisocial behaviour, usually criminal in nature and marked by extreme callousness.

Oppositional defiant disorder: A recurrent pattern of defiant, disobedient, and hostile behaviour toward authority figures.

Feeding and eating disorders of infancy or early childhood: Persistent feeding and eating disorders, such as eating nonnutritive substances (pica), repeated regurgitation and rechewing of food (rumination disorder), or persistent failure to eat adequately, as reflected in significant weight loss or failure to gain weight (feeding disorder of infancy or early childhood).

Tic disorders (e.g., Tourette syndrome): Characterized by sudden, rapid, recurrent, nonrhythmic, stereotyped motor movements or vocalizations.

Elimination disorders: Repeated defecation in inappropriate places after age 4 (encopresis) or voiding of urine in bed or clothes after age 5 (enuresis).

Separation anxiety disorder: Excessive anxiety concerning separation from the home or from those to whom the person is attached, to the extent that it causes distress or impairs functioning.

Selective mutism: Persistent failure to speak in specific social situations (e.g., at school), despite speaking in other situations (e.g., with parents).

Reactive attachment disorder of infancy or early childhood: Markedly disturbed and developmentally inappropriate social-relatedness in most contexts that begins before age 5 and is associated with grossly pathological care by parents or other caregivers.

II. DIAGNOSES THAT MAY BE APPLIED TO ADULTS, ADOLESCENTS, OR CHILDREN

Substance-related disorders: See Chapter 12.

Schizophrenia: See Chapter 11.

Mood disorders: See Chapter 10 and this chapter.

Anxiety disorders, such as specific phobia, social phobia, obsessive-compulsive disorder, posttraumatic stress disorder, generalized anxiety disorder: See Chapter 6 and this chapter; for aftermath of child sexual abuse, see Chapter 14.

Somatoform disorders: See Chapter 7.

Dissociative disorders: See Chapter 7.

Gender identity disorders: See Chapter 14.

Eating disorders, such as anorexia nervosa and bulimia nervosa: See Chapter 9.

Parasomnias: Abnormal behavioural or physiological events occurring in association with sleep. For example, **nightmare disorder**, **sleep terror disorder**, and **sleepwalking disorder**.

Source: Adapted from DSM-IV-TR.

Table 15.1 outlines the principal childhood disorders included in DSM-IV-TR. Some disorders included in the DSM, such as separation anxiety disorder, are unique to children, whereas others, such as depression, are subsumed under the criteria used for adults. Still others, such as attention-deficit/hyperactivity disorder, have been conceptualized primarily as childhood disorders but may continue into adulthood. Eric, the distressed boy described at the beginning of this chapter, might be given the following multiaxial DSM-IV-TR diagnosis:

Axis I: Attention-deficit/hyperactivity disorder, predominantly inattentive type; dysthymic disorder, early onset

Axis II: No diagnosis on Axis II

Axis III: No general medical conditions

Axis IV: Educational problems: discord with teacher and classmates

Axis V: Global assessment of functioning = 50 (suicidal ideation; no friends; behind in schoolwork)

Childhood disorders may be conceptualized by a dimensional model rather than a categorical model such as that represented by the DSM. As discussed earlier, a dimensional model portrays dysfunctional behaviour as existing on a continuum. One dimension often employed by child psychopathologists is the degree to which behaviour is controlled. At one end of the continuum of control, undercontrolled behaviour is characterized by excess, such as extreme aggressiveness. At the other end of the continuum, children are overcontrolled and show emotional inhibitions, such as school phobia (Achenbach & Edelbrock, 1978). A distinction sometimes drawn between these two extremes is whether the child creates a problem primarily for others (undercontrolled) or primarily for the self (overcontrolled). Children and adolescents may exhibit symptoms from both extremes, as Eric did.

Undercontrol problems are consistently found more often among boys and overcontrol more often among girls across cultures (Weisz et al., 1987). Problems of undercontrol and overcontrol can lead to significant distress in children and their families, often at great cost to society. Additional information on the adjustment problems of children and adolescents is therefore vital. Accordingly, in 1994, Canada undertook an important national research study—the National Longitudinal Survey of Children and Youth (NLSCY)—to gather data. This ongoing study is the subject of Canadian Perspectives 15.1. Canadian Perspectives 15.2 looks at McMaster University's Offord Centre for Child Studies, recognized around the world for its research on the psychological disorders of children, including research on the epidemiology of these disorders.

Tourette syndrome involves involuntary tics, both motor and vocal (phonic) and can be found in children and adults. Canadian actress Neve Campbell's younger brother has Tourette's, and they both participate actively as members of the spokes family for the Tourette Syndrome Foundation of Canada (see http://www.tourette.ca).

There is considerable controversy about categorical versus dimensional systems (Kazdin & Kagan, 1994). We have organized our discussion of childhood psychopathology partially in dimensional terms, considering problems as lying on a continuum ranging from undercontrol to overcontrol; but we also follow the DSM in its categorical approach, considering discrete diagnostic categories into which a person fits or does not fit.

Canadian Perspectives/15.1

The National Longitudinal Survey of Children and Youth

The National Longitudinal Survey of Children and Youth (NLSCY) involves approximately 23,000 children in Canada, ranging from birth to 11 years old at the outset of the study. Participants will be studied prospectively throughout their childhood into adulthood by an extensive network of Canadian researchers at many sites. Because the study is in its initial phases, at present it can only provide interesting information about the associations among variables assessed cross-sectionally, with much information to come from the prospective data.

With this in mind, it is already the case that the NLSCY project has yielded some illuminating findings, many of which are described in the initial report "Growing Up In Canada." The following are some of the findings to date:

1 Low birth weight is associated with numerous childhood health problems and is more likely if a mother smokes during pregnancy. As discussed in Chapter 12, having a mother who smokes during pregnancy is also a risk factor for birth defects.

2 Children with difficult temperaments, relative to those with easy temperaments, have parents characterized by greater hostility, and, to some degree, a child's temperament reflects the particular family environments in which he or she is reared.

3 Children between the ages of 4 and 11 with emotional and/or behavioural problems tend to have multiple problems. For instance, of those with an identified adjustment problem, 47.9 percent had a conduct disorder, and over half of these children had at least one other problem.

4 Children from single-mother families are more likely to be poor financially, and economic disadvantage increases the likelihood of physical aggression on the part of the child.

The website for Human Resources Development Canada (HRDC), Applied Research Branch contains numerous research reports from the first stage of this project (see http://www.hrdc-drhc.gc.ca/arb/publications/research). We will mention a few specific studies derived from the NLSCY to illustrate the rich findings that are emerging. For instance, Pepler and Sedighdeilami (1998) determined that the problems of aggressive girls were quite similar to those experienced by aggressive boys. Comparisons of aggressive and non-aggressive girls indicated that aggressive girls suffered in terms of interpersonal relationships, low self-esteem, difficult behaviour, and academic problems. Other NLSCY findings showed that boys and girls in the most extreme cluster of children with antisocial behaviour came from a situation of "material disadvantage" (Wade, Pevalin, & Brannigan, 1999).

Another study by Hodinott, Lethbridge, and Phipps (2002) illustrated the negative impact of "bundles" of household characteristics. "Disadvantaged" children (i.e., having a young mother who did not complete high school and had a low income) obtained substantially lower mathematics scores than children from households with an older mother with a university degree at the 75th percentile of income. Longitudinal analyses showed that differences in children's levels of achievement tended to be quite similar over time.

O'Connor and Jenkins (2000) focused on the 5 percent of families who experienced a divorce or separation. Individual, family, and sociocultural variables all predicted the likelihood of separation. Although marital separation increased emotional problems in children, a positive parenting style mitigated the negative impact of the separation.

Finally, Beiser, Hou, Hyman, and Tousignant (1998) compared children who immigrated to Canada with children born in Canada. They found that immigrant children actually had better adjustment overall than children born in Canada! New immigrant children had lower prevalence rates of hyperactivity (3.8 percent vs. 10.8 percent), emotional disorders (5.3 percent vs. 9.1 percent), and conduct disorders (6.7 percent vs. 13.2 percent). Beiser et al. (1998) concluded that poor immigrant families may provide a supportive environment that fosters a greater sense of resilience relative to the poor families of children born in Canada. However, the researchers expressed concern that one-third of immigrant families were financially impoverished, as this could lead to subsequent problems.

Thinking Critically

1. To what do you attribute the findings reported by Beiser et al.? Can you think of some plausible uncontrolled or unmeasured factors that may have contributed to these differences between the immigrant families and families of Canadian-born children?
2. Assume that you are the NLCSY project director and that the initial findings point to some interventions that could improve the well-being of children in the study. From an ethical perspective, should you implement the intervention, even though it will mean that the study will be compromised? What would you do in this situation?

DISORDERS OF UNDERCONTROLLED BEHAVIOUR

The child who is undercontrolled does not behave in a given setting in a way that is expected or is appropriate to his or her age. Eric, for example, should be able to follow his teacher's lessons as well as his team's progress at bat. The undercontrolled child is therefore frequently an annoyance to adults and peers and usually gets the attention of parents and teachers more often than children who are overcontrolled. Two general categories of undercontrolled behaviour are typically differentiated: attention-deficit/hyperactivity disorder and conduct disorder.

Problems of undercontrol are defined by the type, form, and frequency of the behaviour. The high frequency of some problem behaviour, such as fidgeting in class, in the general population of children brings into question whether isolated incidents should be considered abnormal. Other behaviour, such as assaulting a teacher, is considered abnormal by most people.

ATTENTION-DEFICIT/HYPERACTIVITY DISORDER

The term *hyperactive* is familiar to most people, especially parents and teachers. The child who is constantly in motion, tapping fingers, jiggling legs, poking others for no apparent reason, talking out of turn, and fidgeting is often called hyperactive. This is the child who, in colloquial terms, drives parents and teachers nuts. These children also have difficulty concentrating on the task at hand for an appropriate period of time. The current diagnostic term is **attention-deficit/hyperactivity disorder (ADHD)**.

Canadian Perspectives/15.2

The Offord Centre for Child Studies

"... the burden of suffering from child psychiatric disorders is extremely high, and one-to-one interventions can never make a large dent in reducing this burden."
—Daniel Offord, 1995, p. 287

The Offord Centre for Child Studies (OCCS), formerly known as the Canadian Centre for Studies of Children at Risk, is a world-renowned organization comprised of a team of clinical researchers based in Hamilton, Ontario, many of whom also hold appointments at McMaster University. The director and founder of the centre was David (Dan) Offord. Other researchers include Kathryn Bennett, Michael Boyle, Charles Cunningham, Ellen Lipman, Harriett MacMillan, Mark Sanford, and Peter Szatmari. Their individual descriptions are located on the centre's website (see http://www.fhs.mcmaster.ca/cscr).

The stated mission of the OCCS is "to improve the life quality of children in Canada by reducing the suffering and disadvantage associated with children's emotional and behavioural problems" (see website). The interrelated goals of the centre are listed as follows:

1 to increase scientific knowledge about the range of influences on children's emotional and behavioural development
2 to determine, through rigorous evaluations, which programs are most effective in terms of improving mental health and functioning
3 to generate information useful to decision-makers in formulating and implementing the best policies for improving children's mental health
4 to develop, in an environment that fosters collaboration and mentoring, a national education and resource centre that trains professionals and educates the public about children's mental health

The OCCS has played a leading role in epidemiological research on mental health problems in children and adolescents. Known primarily for the Ontario Child Health Study, a cross sectional investigation of 1,869 families and 3,294 children, the centre is also involved in the National Longitudinal Study of Children and Youth as well as numerous projects on several topics, including (1) the prevention and modification of antisocial behaviour, especially in children at risk; (2) identifying the clinical and familial characteristics of depressed children; (3) establishing the factors associated with the incidence and prevention of substance abuse in youth; (4) determining the amount of child abuse and predictors of child abuse in Ontario; and (5) assessing the health and well-being and associated correlates in First Nations youth. Collectively, these research initiatives have already yielded many important findings. For instance, recent analyses of the role of family influences on substance use by adolescents found that the most robust family influence is from an older sibling to a younger sibling and not from parents to their children (Boyle et al., 2001).

Dr. Dan Offord died peacefully at home in Ottawa on April 10, 2004 after a battle with cancer. He was one of Canada's preeminent child psychiatrists, a renowned clinician, researcher, teacher, and recipient of the Order of Canada. He taught practitioners about the major problems facing children—including poverty, abuse, and depression. However, to the thousands of children he helped, he was simply Dr. Dan (Kravitz, 2004, B3).

Thinking Critically

1. It is disturbing that in Ontario and elsewhere stories continue to emerge of massive waiting lists of children and adolescents with an identified or suspected disorder that requires intervention. According to Offord, one-to-one interventions cannot cope adequately with the problem. Do you think that a major focus for the future must be on the prevention of childhood disorders? Do you think that, to some degree, a lack of government funding is a critical issue because widespread preventive programs are simply not possible with the current resources available? We will revisit this issue in Chapter 17.
2. Do you believe that, in addition to an increased commitment of resources toward prevention, there is a great need for more trained clinicians who specialize in the treatment of disorders in children and adolescents?

Virginia Douglas has played an instrumental role in refining our understanding of ADHD (see Canadian Contributions 15.1). Her views and research became well known in the 1970s. Until that time, hyperactive children were identified as having "minimal brain damage" or "minimal brain dysfunction" because of apparent similarities between their hyperactive behaviours and the behaviours expressed by certain children with brain damage. Because brain damage could not be detected, more emphasis was placed on the hyperactivity, and the disorder came to be known as "hyperactive child syndrome" and "hyperkinetic reaction of childhood." The importance of attentional difficulties is now recognized, in large measure, because of the pioneering work of Douglas.

Studies of symptoms, including a recent investigation conducted in Canada with Native and non-Native children

Canadian Contributions/15.1

Virginia Douglas and the Development of the ADHD Concept

Virginia Douglas has gained international recognition for her contributions to the understanding of ADHD. A professor emeritus of the McGill University Department of Psychology, past chair of the Department of Psychology at McGill, and Senior Psychologist at the Montreal Children's Hospital, Douglas has published almost 100 journal articles and book chapters. She also served as the president of the Canadian Psychological Association and was the first recipient of the Canadian Psychological Association Award for Distinguished Contributions to Psychology as a Profession. She was also awarded the Outstanding Achievement Award from the Association for Children and Adults with Attention Deficit Disorders.

Douglas is credited with being the first researcher to note the attentional problems in ADHD. She outlined these deficits and her theoretical observations as part of her presidential address to the Canadian Psychological Association in 1970. Her views were later published in a 1972 paper titled "Stop, look, and listen—The problem of sustained attention and impulse control in hyperactive and normal children." This paper, published in the *Canadian Journal of Behavioural Sciences*, has become a citation classic because of its impact.

Douglas has gone on to conduct a lifetime of experimental research on the attentional deficits and problems with inhibition that comprise ADHD. A central aspect of her work is the development of a self-regulation theory with the premise that poor self-regulation is the primary deficit in ADHD. Experimental research studies are designed to elicit these hypothesized deficits in self-regulation. Douglas documented how ADHD children are underaroused by boring tasks and overaroused by stimulating tasks (see Douglas, 1983). One recent study comparing recall performance and rehearsal strategies in boys with and without ADHD found that ADHD boys recall fewer words and spend less time rehearsing (O'Neill & Douglas, 1996). Another study showed that low doses of the drug methylphenidate slowed performance in an adaptive way in ADHD children engaged in a complex cognitive processing task, suggesting that the drug was effective because it improved self-regulatory ability (Berman, Douglas, & Barr, 1999).

In 1994 the American Psychiatric Association further refined the diagnosis of ADHD to include three possible diagnoses (see below). There can be little doubt that the research by Douglas paved the way for this refinement.

Virginia Douglas from McGill University began the study of attentional problems in ADHD children.

(Beiser, Dion, & Gotowiec, 2000), suggest that attention-deficit and hyperactivity-impulsivity are two separate but correlated dimensions that coexist in children with ADHD. Beiser et al. concluded that symptoms of ADHD are similar across cultural groups.

Children with ADHD seem to have particular difficulty controlling their activity in situations that call for sitting still, such as in the classroom or at mealtimes. They appear unable to stop moving or talking when required to be quiet. They are disorganized, erratic, tactless, obstinate, and bossy. Their activities and movements seem haphazard. They smash their toys and exhaust their family and teachers. It is difficult, however, to distinguish them from normal children during free play, when fewer restrictions are placed on a child's behaviour.

Many hyperactive children find it difficult to get along with peers and establish friendships (Whalen & Henker, 1985), probably because their behaviour is often aggressive and annoying to others. Although these children are usually friendly and talkative, they tend to miss subtle social cues, such as noticing when playmates are tiring of their constant jiggling. They also frequently misinterpret the wishes and intentions of their peers and make inadvertent social mistakes, such as reacting aggressively because they assume that a neutral action by a peer was meant to be aggressive. (Such cognitive misattributions are also found in some children with conduct disorder.) Children with ADHD can know what the socially correct action is in hypothetical situations but be unable to translate this knowledge into appropriate behaviour in real-life social interactions (Whalen & Henker, 1999).

A recent study compared the attributions and perceptions of boys with ADHD and control participants in a social interaction situation (Hoza, Waschbusch, Pelham, Molina, & Milich, 2000). Participants engaged in a get-acquainted task that involved receiving success or failure feedback. Objective raters viewed the performance of the boys with ADHD as poorer in quality, relative to that of controls, but the boys saw themselves in much more positive terms and had more positive performance self-evaluations than the control group. Thus, boys with ADHD may have an illusory bias concerning the quality of their social behaviours.

An observational study of children playing tabletop football demonstrated that children with ADHD, particularly those who are also aggressive, have different social goals than comparison children. The aggressive ADHD children approached the game with sensation-seeking goals, such as making trouble, seeking domination, and showing off, whereas comparison children were more likely to have a goal of playing fair (Melnick & Hinshaw, 1996).

About 15 to 30 percent of children with ADHD have a learning disability in math, reading, or spelling (e.g., Casey, Rourke, & DelDotto, 1996), and about half of ADHD children are placed in special education programs because of their difficulty in adjusting to a typical classroom environment (Barkley, DuPaul, & McMurray, 1990).

The ADHD diagnosis does not properly apply to youngsters who are rambunctious, active, or slightly distractible, for in the early school years children are often so (Whalen, 1983). To use the label simply because a child is more lively and more difficult to control than a parent or teacher would like represents a misuse of the term. The diagnosis of ADHD is reserved for truly extreme and persistent cases.

Because the symptoms of ADHD are varied, DSM-IV-TR has three subcategories:

1 children whose problems are primarily those of poor attention
2 children whose difficulties result primarily from hyperactive-impulsive behaviour
3 children who have both sets of problems

The third subcategory comprises the majority of ADHD children. Children with both attentional problems and hyperactivity are more likely to develop conduct problems and oppositional behaviour, to be placed in special classes for behaviour-disordered children, and to have peer difficulties (Barkley, DuPaul, & McMurray, 1990; Faraone et al., 1998). Children with attentional problems but with normal activity levels appear to have more difficulty focusing their attention or processing information at a reasonable speed (Barkley, Grodzinsky, & DuPaul, 1992), believed to stem from some problem in the right frontal lobe (Posner, 1992). Studies suggest that it may be best to think of two separate disorders (Barkley, 1998), but most of the theory and research does not make this distinction.

It is difficult to differentiate between ADHD and conduct disorder in making a diagnosis. An overlap of 30 to 90 percent between the two categories (Hinshaw, 1987) has led to assertions that the two types of undercontrolled behaviour are actually the same disorder (Quay, 1979). There are differences, however. Hyperactivity is associated more with off-task behaviour in school, cognitive and achievement deficits, and a better long-term prognosis. Conduct disorder is associated more with acting out in school and elsewhere, being much more aggressive, and having antisocial parents. The home life of children with conduct disorder is marked by family hostility and low socioeconomic status, and these children are much more at risk for delinquency and substance abuse in adolescence (Faraone et al., 1997; Hinshaw, 1987; Jensen, Martin, & Cantwell, 1997).

When these two disorders occur in the same youngster, the worst features of each are manifested. A study at the University of Sherbrooke in Quebec concluded that "children with CD and ADHD are especially at risk for persistent antisocial behaviour" (Toupin et al., 2000, p. 422). Such children exhibit the most serious antisocial behaviour and have the poorest prognosis (Biederman, Newcorn, & Sprich, 1991; Cadoret & Stewart, 1991; Moffitt, 1990). It has been suggested that children with ADHD and conduct disorder form a distinct category highly likely to progress to the adult psychopathic patterns of antisocial personality disorder (Lynam, 1996). It may be that ADHD comes first, with the child's aggravating behaviour eliciting hostile reactions from peers and adults; then the situation escalates with more extreme attacks and counterattacks, finally resulting in the aggressive behaviours characteristic of conduct disorder. Unfortunately, much of the research on hyperactive children confounds ADHD with conduct problems and aggressiveness, making the findings about hyperactivity less clear.

The prevalence of ADHD has been difficult to establish because of varied definitions of the disorder over time and differences in the populations sampled. Estimates vary from 2 to 7 percent in the United States (e.g., August et al., 1996), New Zealand (e.g., Fergusson, Horwood, & Lynskey, 1993), and Germany (Esser, Schmidt, & Woerner, 1990), with somewhat higher rates found in India (Bhatia et al., 1991) and China (Leung et al., 1996). The consensus is that about 3 to 5 percent of children worldwide currently have ADHD (DSM-IV-TR, 2000).

It is generally believed that the disorder is more common in boys than in girls, but research findings depend on whether the sample is taken from clinic referrals or from the general population. Boys are more likely to be referred to clinics because of a higher likelihood of aggressive and antisocial behaviour. Earlier research found few differences between girls and boys with ADHD, with the exception that the boys with ADHD are more likely to have comorbid conduct disorder and oppositional defiant disorder (e.g., Biederman, 1997; Faraone, 1997; Millberger, 1997). However, a comparative study in Toronto showed that ADHD girls, relative to ADHD boys and control participants, have significantly greater impairment on a wide range of measures, despite an absence of differences between the ADHD girls and boys in terms of Axis I disorders (Rucklidge & Tannock, 2001). For instance, ADHD girls had greater levels of psychological distress, a more external locus of control (beliefs that reinforcements are determined by other people, luck, or fate), and lower vocabulary scores. This study is unique because it is the first comprehensive effort to evaluate psychiatric, psychosocial, and cognitive functioning in ADHD girls and boys and control participants in a controlled design.

Although many preschoolers are considered inattentive and overactive by their parents and teachers, the majority of these youngsters are going through a normal developmental stage that will not become a persistent pattern of ADHD

(Campbell, 1990). On the other hand, most children who do develop ADHD exhibit excessive activity and temperamental behaviour quite early in life. Their insatiable curiosity and vigorous play make childproofing a necessity to avoid such tragedies as accidental poisoning and falling out of windows. Although the preschool years are stressful for parents whose children have ADHD, the problems become salient when the children enter school and are suddenly expected to sit in their seats for longer periods of time, complete assignments independently, and negotiate with peers on the playground.

It was once thought that hyperactivity simply went away by adolescence. This belief has been challenged by numerous longitudinal studies (e.g., Biederman et al., 1996; Claude & Firestone, 1995; Weiss & Hechtman, 1993). Although these studies do show reduced severity of symptoms in adolescence (Hart et al., 1995), 65 to 80 percent of children with ADHD still meet criteria for the disorder in adolescence and adulthood. Table 15.2 provides a catalogue of behaviours that are found more often among adolescents with ADHD than among normal adolescents. In addition to having these fidgety, distractible, impulsive behaviours, adolescents with ADHD are far more likely to drop out of high school and develop antisocial behaviour than their peers. In adulthood, while most are employed and financially independent, these individuals generally reach a lower socioeconomic level and change jobs more frequently than would normally be expected (Mannuzza et al., 1993; Weiss & Hechtman, 1993). A recent study in Montreal found that family and marital functioning was impaired in families with an ADHD adult (Minde et al., 2003). Although most adults with a history of ADHD continue to exhibit some symptoms of the disorder, many learn to adapt to these symptoms, perhaps by finding a niche for themselves in the working world. Still, there are some noteworthy exceptions. A study of adult women with ADHD in Toronto found that they had impairments in social functioning, reduced self-esteem, elevated stress, and a self-blaming attributional style (Rucklidge & Kaplan, 1997).

Biological Theories of ADHD The search for causes of ADHD is complicated by the heterogeneity of children given this diagnosis; any factor found to be associated with the syndrome is perhaps linked with only some of the diagnosed cases.

Genetic Factors Research suggests that a genetic predisposition toward ADHD may play a role. When parents have ADHD, half of their children are likely to have the disorder

Table 15.2

Prevalence of Symptoms in ADHD and Normal Adolescents

Symptom	ADHD %	Normal %
Fidgets	73.2	10.6
Difficulty remaining seated	60.2	3.0
Easily distracted	82.1	15.2
Difficulty waiting turn	48.0	4.5
Blurts out answers	65.0	10.6
Difficulty following instructions	83.7	12.1
Difficulty sustaining attention	79.7	16.7
Shifts from one uncompleted task to another	77.2	16.7
Difficulty playing quietly	39.8	7.6
Talks excessively	43.9	6.1
Interrupts others	65.9	10.6
Doesn't seem to listen	80.5	15.2
Loses things needed for tasks	62.6	12.1
Engages in physically dangerous activities	37.4	3.0

Source: Adapted from Barkley, DuPaul, and Murray (1990).

(Biederman et al., 1995). Adoption studies (e.g., van den Oord, Boomsma, & Verhulst, 1994) and numerous large-scale twin studies (e.g., Levy et al., 1997) indicate a genetic component to ADHD. Family environment does not make a significant contribution (Consensus Statement on ADHD, 2002).

Exactly what is inherited is as yet unknown, but recent studies point to differences in brain function and structure. Studies have documented that the frontal lobes of children with ADHD are underresponsive to stimulation (e.g., Rubia et al., 1999) and that cerebral blood flow is reduced (Sieg et al., 1995). Moreover, parts of the brains (frontal lobes, caudate nucleus, globus pallidus) of ADHD children are smaller than normal (Castellanos et al., 1996; Filipek et al., 1997; Hynd et al., 1993). The evidence from neurological studies indicates that the brains of children with ADHD have developed differently but are not damaged. Evidence from other research shows poorer performance of ADHD children on neuropsychological tests of frontal-lobe functioning (such as inhibiting behavioural responses), providing further support for the theory that a basic deficit in this part of the brain may be related to the disorder (e.g., Barkley, 1997).

Environmental Toxins Popular theories of ADHD over the years have involved the role of environmental toxins in the development of hyperactivity. A biochemical theory of hyperactivity put forth by Feingold (1973) enjoyed much attention. He proposed that food additives upset the central nervous systems of hyperactive children, and he prescribed a diet free of such additives. It is unlikely, however, that more than a small percentage of cases of hyperactivity are caused by sensitivity to food additives. Well-controlled studies of the Feingold diet have found that very few ADHD children respond positively to it (Goyette & Conners, 1977). Similarly, the popular view that refined sugar can cause ADHD (Smith, 1975) has not been supported by careful research (Wolraich, Wilson, & White, 1995).

Nicotine—specifically, maternal smoking—is an environmental toxin that may play a role in the development of ADHD. Milberger et al. (1996) reported that 22 percent of mothers of children with ADHD reported smoking a pack of cigarettes per day during pregnancy, compared to 8 percent of mothers whose children were normal. Animal studies indicate that chronic exposure to nicotine increases dopamine release in the brain and causes hyperactivity (e.g., Fung & Lau, 1989). Milberger and associates hypothesize that maternal smoking can affect the dopaminergic system of the developing fetus, leading to behavioural disinhibition and ADHD.

Psychological Theories of ADHD The child psychoanalyst Bruno Bettelheim (1973) proposed a diathesis-stress theory of ADHD, suggesting that hyperactivity develops when a predisposition to the disorder is coupled with an authoritarian upbringing. If a child with a disposition toward overactivity and moodiness is stressed by a parent who easily becomes impatient and resentful, the child may have difficulty complying with the parent's demands for obedience. As the parent becomes more and more negative and disapproving, the parent-child relationship becomes a battleground. With a disruptive and disobedient pattern established, the child cannot handle the demands of school, and his or her behaviour is often in conflict with the rules of the classroom.

Learning may have a role in hyperactivity as well. Hyperactivity could be reinforced by the attention it elicits, thereby increasing in frequency or intensity. Or, as Ross and Ross (1982) have suggested, hyperactivity may be modelled on the behaviour of parents and siblings. However, such theories have not been supported by research. Neurological and genetic factors have far greater research support than psychological factors in the etiology of ADHD.

In any event, the parent-child relationship is bidirectional. Just as parents of hyperactive children give their offspring more commands and have negative interactions with them, so hyperactive children have been found to be less compliant and more negative in interactions with parents (Barkley, Karlsson, & Pollard, 1985). As we will describe shortly, stimulant medication has been shown to reduce hyperactivity and increase compliance in ADHD children. When such medication is used, the parents' commands and negative behaviour decrease (see Barkley, 1990), suggesting that it is the child's behaviour that negatively affects the parents rather than the reverse.

Treatment of ADHD In 2002 a consensus statement on ADHD by international experts indicated that fewer than half of those with ADHD receive treatment. The need for treatment is underscored by the fact that those with ADHD, relative to normal people, are more likely to drop out of school, have no or few friends, engage in antisocial activities, use tobacco or illicit drugs, contract a sexually transmitted disease, and drive at excessive speeds and have multiple car accidents (International Consensus Statement on ADHD, 2002).

ADHD is typically treated with drugs and behavioural methods based on operant conditioning. Recently, an international team of experts led by Stan Kutcher from Dalhousie University concluded that the optimal treatment for ADHD and disruptive behaviour disorders—including conduct disorders—is to "combine pharmacotherapy, which addresses core biological symptoms, with psychosocial intervention, which focuses on the youngsters' and families' attitudes and life strategies" (Kutcher et al., 2004, p. 19). This international consensus statement was motivated, in part, by concerns that children may not be receiving appropriate treatment even though effective therapies are available. Specific treatment approaches for ADHD are outlined below.

Stimulant Drugs Stimulant drugs, in particular methylphenidate (MPH), or Ritalin, have been prescribed for ADHD since the early 1960s (Sprague & Gadow, 1976). The stimulating effects of these drugs somehow reduce disruptive behaviour in ADHD children and improve their ability to concentrate. One survey found that 6 percent of elementary schoolchildren and 25 percent of those in special-education classrooms were receiving stimulant medication (Safer & Krager, 1988). The prescription of these medications has sometimes continued into adolescence and adulthood in light of the accumulating evidence that the symptoms of ADHD do not usually disappear with the passage of time.

One perception that has emerged is that ADHD is overdiagnosed and overtreated. These concerns have been fuelled by dramatic increases in the 1990s in the use of Ritalin to treat ADHD. Canadian surveys indicate that there was almost no change in the use of Ritalin between 1983 and 1990 but that use between 1990 and 1996 has increased by 3 to 4.5 times the previous levels of use (Canadian Council on Social Development, 1997; Miller et al., 1998). A Manitoba study confirmed that there are regional variations in the rates of diagnosing ADHD, with urban areas having higher rates than rural areas (Brownell & Yogendran, 2001). In rural areas, however, rates of ADHD diagnosis and medication increase as a function of income level, leading the authors to suggest that ADHD is underdiagnosed in regions that may lack access to adequate resources.

Numerous double-blind studies comparing stimulants with placebos have shown short-term improvements in concentration, goal-directed activity, classroom behaviour, and social interactions with parents, teachers, and peers, and reductions in aggressiveness and impulsivity in about 75 percent of ADHD children taking stimulants (Spencer et al., 1996; Swanson et al., 1995). An experiment by Brodeur and Pond (2001) investigated selective attention in control children and children with ADHD from Nova Scotia. The performance of children with ADHD was more disrupted by the presence of distracters in a selective attention task, but comparisons of performance when the ADHD participants were on or off MPH treatment showed that MPH was associated with enhanced performance.

A comparison of Ritalin with an operant intervention indicates better outcomes with the drug than with the behaviour-therapy program. A treatment combining the two was not superior to the drug alone but did show an advantage of not requiring as high a dosage of Ritalin to reduce ADHD symptoms. The combined treatment also improved positive functioning, such as social skills, more than the drug alone (MTA Cooperative Group, 1999).

Research indicates that stimulant drugs may not improve academic achievement over the long haul (Weiss & Hechtman, 1993; Whalen and Henker, 1991). Further, stimulant medication has side effects. In addition to transient loss of appetite and sleep problems, a risky side effect of the widespread prescription of stimulants has emerged. *Newsweek* magazine reported that children are beginning to use Ritalin and other stimulants obtained from their siblings or friends as recreational drugs (Leland, 1995). Its use is also spreading among high school and college students not suffering from ADHD but finding that snorting it like cocaine helps them focus better on their schoolwork and ward off fatigue (Tennant, 1999).

Finally, two additional points should be noted. First, a key issue is the extent to which ADHD children adhere to drug treatment in the long-term. It is often readily apparent when an ADHD child is no longer taking his or her medication. A recent study in Toronto examined the predictors of long-term adherence to medication treatment (Thiruchelvam, Charach, & Schachar, 2001). Overall, only about half of the participants were adhering by taking their medication three years after the start of the study. Greater adherence was associated with younger age at the start of treatment and absence of oppositional defiant disorder (discussed below).

Second, the MTA Cooperative Group Study (1999) deserves additional discussion because it is the first study of its kind in treatment research on the disorders of childhood and adolescence. MTA refers to the Multimodal Treatment Study of Children with ADHD. According to Schachar (1999), the MTA study is noteworthy because it involved six collaborating academic sites, including one site in Canada, and multi-site studies have seldom been conducted on childhood disorders. More importantly, the MTA Cooperative Group Study is state-of-the-art in that it is the largest and most methodologically rigorous study conducted thus far (Schachar, 1999). This lends credence to its main finding that a carefully managed medication approach is superior to behavioural treatment and routine community care in treating ADHD symptoms, but that more general areas of functioning (i.e., social skills and academic performance) were enhanced by a combined form of medication and behavioural treatment (see Jensen, 1999). Secondary analyses of the data from this study have confirmed the benefits of the combined treatment, which have come to be referred to as "the multimodality superiority effect" (Swanson et al., 2001). Other results indicate that the multimodality superiority effect is reduced among families who have a child with extreme ADHD symptoms and at least one depressed parent (Owens et al., 2003).

Psychological Treatment Other than medication, the most promising treatments for ADHD children involve parent training and changes in classroom management based on operant-conditioning principles. These programs have demonstrated at least short-term success in improving both social and academic behaviour. The children are monitored at home and in school and are reinforced for behaving appropriately—for example, for remaining in their seats and working on assignments. Point systems and star charts are typical components of these programs. Youngsters earn points and younger children earn stars for behaving in certain ways; the children can then spend their earnings for rewards. The focus of these operant programs is on improving academic work, completing household tasks, or learning specific social skills, not on reducing signs of hyperactivity, such as running around or jiggling. Evidence is accumulating in support of the efficacy of parent-training programs, although it is unclear whether they improve children's behaviour beyond the effects of treatment with medication (Abikoff & Hechtman, 1996; Anastopoulos et al., 1993; Pisterman et al., 1992). Research by Kerns from the University of Victoria and associates also suggests that direct intervention designed to enhance attentional processes can be quite effective (Kerns, Eso, & Thomson, 1999).

School interventions for children with ADHD include training teachers to understand the unique needs of these children and to apply operant techniques in the classroom (Welsh et al., 1997), peer tutoring in academic skills (DuPaul & Henningson, 1993), and having teachers provide daily reports to parents about in-school behaviour, with follow-up rewards and consequences at home (Kelley, 1990). Research has shown that certain classroom structures have a favourable impact on children with ADHD. In the ideal classroom environment, for example, teachers vary the presentation format and the materials used for tasks, keep assignments brief, providing immediate feedback on accuracy, have an enthusiastic and task-focused style, provide breaks for physical exercise, use computer-assisted drill programs, and schedule academic work during the morning hours. Such environmental changes are designed to accommodate the limitations imposed by this disorder rather than to change the disorder itself (Pfiffner & Barkley, 1998).

Although these advances are encouraging, it is important to recognize that there is substantial heterogeneity among individuals with ADHD. In fact, Waschbusch, Kipp, and Pelham (1998) have made a strong case for a more individualized approach to treatment. They describe a series of case studies to demonstrate the considerable heterogeneity of treatment responses among ADHD children, often varying according to the domain of functioning being assessed, the treatment setting, and the intensity or strength of the treatment.

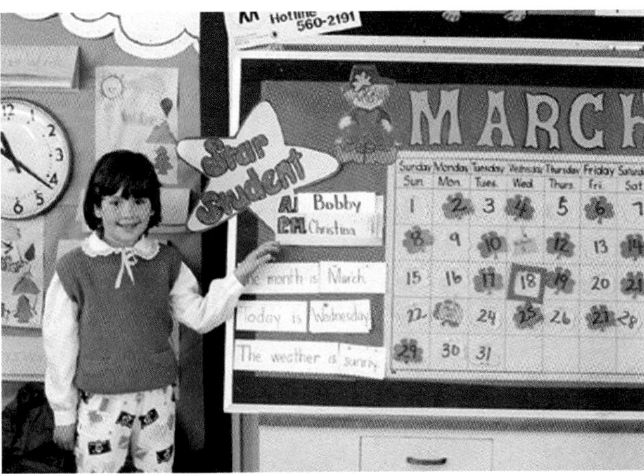

Point systems and star charts, which are common in classrooms, are particularly useful in the treatment of attention-deficit/hyperactivity disorder.

Conduct Disorder

The term **conduct disorder** encompasses a wide variety of undercontrolled behaviour. DSM-IV-TR focuses on behaviours that violate the basic rights of others and major societal norms. Nearly all such behaviour is illegal. The types of behaviour considered symptomatic of conduct disorder include being aggressive and cruel toward people or animals, damaging property, lying, and stealing. Conduct disorder denotes a frequency and severity of acts that go beyond the mischief and pranks common among children and adolescents. Often the behaviour is marked by callousness, viciousness, and lack of remorse, making conduct disorder one of the criteria for antisocial personality disorder.

A related but lesser-known category in the DSM is **oppositional defiant disorder (ODD)**. There is a debate as to whether ODD is distinct from conduct disorder, a precursor to it, or merely an earlier manifestation of it (Loeber et al., 1993). ODD is diagnosed if a child does not meet the criteria for conduct disorder—most especially, extreme physical aggressiveness—but exhibits such behaviours as losing his or her temper, arguing with adults, repeatedly refusing to comply with requests from adults, deliberately doing things to annoy others, and being angry, spiteful, touchy, or vindictive. The DSM also mentions that such children, most of them boys, seldom see their conflicts with others as their fault; they justify their oppositional behaviour by claiming that unreasonable demands are being placed on them.

According to the international consensus statement, comorbidity is the norm rather than the exception for children with ODD, conduct disorder, and ADHD (Kutcher et al., 2004). Problems commonly comorbid with ODD are ADHD, learning disorders, and communication disorders, but ODD differs from ADHD in that the defiant behaviour is not thought to arise from attentional deficits or sheer impulsiveness. This difference is evident in the ODD children's tendency to be more deliberate in their obstreperousness than ADHD children. (An operant theorist would see ODD behaviour as more instrumental in nature than the ADHD behaviour.) Interestingly, the DSM observes that mothers with a depressive disorder are more likely to have children with ODD; less clear, the manual goes on to say, is whether the depression contributes to or is caused by the child's behaviour (DSM-IV-TR, 2000). Because of ODD's questionable status, we focus here on the more serious diagnosis of conduct disorder.

Perhaps more than any other childhood disorder, conduct disorder is defined by the impact of the child's behaviour on people and surroundings. Schools, parents, peers, and the criminal justice system usually determine which undercontrolled behaviour constitutes unacceptable conduct. Preadolescents and adolescents are often identified as conduct problems by legal authorities, in which case they might be considered juvenile delinquents—a legal, not a psychological, term.

Many children with conduct disorder display other problems as well. We have noted the high degree of comorbidity between conduct disorder and ADHD. This link is underscored by the results of a Quebec study (Toupin et al., 2000) which showed that even after controlling for ADHD symptoms, children with conduct disorder revealed significant cognitive deficits on attentional tests of executive functioning (e.g., the number of perseveration [repeated] errors made on the Wisconsin Card Sorting Test, a measure of cognitive set).

Substance abuse also commonly co-occurs with conduct problems. Investigators from the Pittsburgh Youth Study, a longitudinal study of conduct problems in boys, found a strong association between substance use and delinquent acts (vanKammen, Loeber, & Stouthamer-Loeber, 1991). For example, among 7th graders who reported having tried marijuana, over 30 percent had attacked someone with a weapon and 43 percent admitted breaking and entering; fewer than 5 percent of children who reported no substance use had committed these acts.

Anxiety and depression are common among children with conduct disorder, with comorbidity estimates varying from 15 to 45 percent (Loeber & Keenan, 1994). There is some evidence that conduct-disordered boys with a comorbid anxiety disorder are less antisocial than those with conduct disorder alone (Walker et al., 1991).

Population-based studies indicate that conduct disorder is fairly common. The Ontario Child Health Study found that 8 percent of boys and about 3 percent of girls aged 4 to 16 met the DSM criteria for conduct disorder (Offord et al., 1987). Rates may climb as high as 16 percent in boys when surveyed during adolescence (Cohen et al., 1993). Burglary and violent crimes such as forcible rape and aggravated assault are largely crimes of male adolescents. As shown in Figure 15.1, both the incidence and the prevalence of serious lawbreaking peak sharply at around age 17 and drop precipitously in young adulthood (Moffitt, 1993). Although not all these criminal acts are marked by the viciousness and callousness that can be part of conduct disorder, these data illustrate the problem of antisocial behaviour in children and adolescents.

The prognosis for children diagnosed as having conduct disorder is mixed. Robins (1978) summarized longitudinal studies that examined antisocial behaviour in cohorts from the 1920s to the 1970s, with follow-ups over as long as 30 years. She concluded that the vast majority of highly antisocial adults were highly antisocial as children, but noted that more than half the children with conduct disorder did not become antisocial adults. These findings have been replicated in more recent studies (e.g., Zoccolillo et al., 1992). Thus, conduct problems in childhood do not inevitably lead to antisocial behaviour in adulthood, but they certainly are a predisposing factor. Furthermore, a longitudinal study indicated that while about half of the boys with conduct disorder did not meet full criteria for the diagnosis at a later assessment (one to four years later), almost all of them still had some conduct problems (Lahey et al., 1995).

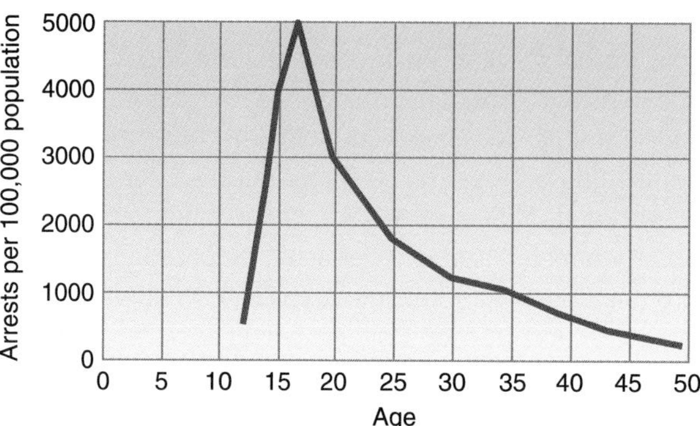

Figure 15.1 Arrest rates across ages for the crimes of homicide, forcible rape, robbery, aggravated assault, and auto theft. From "Criminal Career Research: Its Value for Criminology," by A. Blumstein, J. Cohen, and D.P. Farrington, 1988. *Criminology*, 26, p. 11. Copyright (c) 1988 by the American Society of Criminology. Adapted by permission.

Moffitt (1993) has theorized that two different courses of conduct problems should be distinguished. Some individuals show a "life-course-persistent" pattern of antisocial behaviour, beginning their conduct problems by age 3 and continuing with serious transgressions into adulthood. Others are "adolescence-limited." These people had normal childhoods, engaged in high levels of antisocial behaviour during adolescence, and returned to nonproblematic lifestyles in adulthood. Moffitt proposes that the temporary form of antisocial behaviour is the result of a maturity gap—that is, the gap between the adolescent's physical maturation and his or her opportunity to assume adult responsibilities and obtain the rewards usually accorded such behaviour.

Canadian research by Tremblay et al. (see Canadian Contributions 15.2) has found that there is much more heterogeneity than previously believed in the developmental trajectories associated with conduct disorder and violent behaviour. The term developmental trajectory refers to changing or stable behavioural patterns and characteristics that emerge when individuals are studied in longitudinal research designs. Research conducted in Montreal, studying boys from kindergarten through to the age of 17 years old, identified as many as six different developmental trajectories in antisocial behaviour (see LaCourse et al., 2002). The study revealed that only 11.4 percent of participants were on a rising trajectory of physical aggression. This is inconsistent with the **age crime curve hypothesis**, which maintains that there is a substantial increase in physical violence during adolescence. In fact, LaCourse et al. (2002) found that most boys were either on a low-level antisocial behaviour trajectory or a declining trajectory that was especially apparent when they were between the ages of 11 and 17.

It is important to be able to identify which youths are most likely to persist in their antisocial behaviour. The Developmental Trends Study has shed some light on this issue. Lahey et al. (1995) found that boys with conduct disorder were much more likely to persist in their antisocial behaviour if they had a parent with antisocial personality disorder or if they had low verbal intelligence. Boys with higher verbal IQs and no antisocial parent apparently had a more transient form of the disorder. Other factors, including socioeconomic status and ethnicity, did not predict which boys would continue to show conduct disorder over time.

Although almost all research on conduct disorder has focused on males, a study conducted by Zoccolillo at McGill University followed 55 hospitalized adolescent girls with the disorder (Zoccolillo & Rogers, 1991). As with boys, the majority of these girls had a history of substance use, and most also met diagnostic criteria for depression or an anxiety disorder. The outcome for these girls paralleled the poor prognosis found in boys; 88 percent had a high frequency of such problems as premature death (6 percent), dropping out of school (41 percent), encounters with the legal system (50 percent), running away (48 percent), pregnancy before age 17 (32 percent), and suicide attempts (22 percent). Evidence suggests that girls with conduct disorder have higher risk than boys with the disorder for developing comorbid disorders (e.g., depression, substance abuse, and hyperactivity), and this may indicate greater severity of psychopathology (Loeber & Keenan, 1994).

Etiology of Conduct Disorder Numerous proposals have been put forward for the causes of conduct disorder, including biological, psychological, and sociological factors.

Biological Factors The evidence for genetic influences in conduct disorder is mixed, although heritability may well play a part. A study of over 3,000 Vietnam-era veteran twin pairs indicated only modest genetic influence on childhood antisocial behaviour; family-environment influences were more significant (Lyons et al., 1995). However, a study of 2,600 twin pairs in Australia found a substantial genetic influence and almost no family-environment influence for childhood symptoms of conduct disorder (Slutske et al., 1997). The authors of the latter study point out that differences in the samples may have accounted for the different findings. For example, the veterans in the sample from the earlier study of Lyons et al. were better educated and apparently had lower rates of conduct disorder than the general population. Furthermore, the problem of contradictory findings might be resolved if the types of conduct problems are distinguished. Evidence from twin studies indicates that aggressive behaviour (e.g., cruelty to animals, fighting) is clearly heritable, whereas other delinquent behaviour (e.g., stealing, running away, truancy) may not be (Edelbrock et al., 1995).

Neuropsychological deficits have been implicated in the childhood profiles of children with conduct disorder (Moffitt, 1993; Moffitt, Lynam, & Sylva, 1994). These deficits include poor verbal skills, difficulty with executive functioning (the ability to anticipate, plan, use self-control, and problem-solve), and problems with memory. A Canadian study showed that even when executive function deficits cannot be detected, conduct disorder is associated with language deficits, as revealed by a neuropsychological battery (Dery et al., 1999). Unfortunately, more direct investigations of conduct disorder with structural magnetic resonance imaging (MRI) have not been performed (see Kutcher et al., 2004).

Psychological Factors An important part of normal child development is the growth of moral awareness, acquiring a sense of what is right and wrong and the ability, even desire, to abide by rules and norms. Most people refrain from hurting others not only because it is illegal but because it would make them feel guilty to do otherwise. Children with conduct disorder, like psychopathic individuals (see Chapter 13), often seem to be deficient in this moral awareness, lacking remorse for their wrongdoing and viewing antisocial acts as exciting and rewarding—indeed, as central to their very self-concept (Ryall, 1974).

Research into the backgrounds of conduct-disordered youngsters has shown a pattern of family life lacking in factors that contribute to a strong moral sense. Parents who are affectionate with their children and each other, who clearly express moral principles and demand that their children uphold them, who use punishment justly and consistently, and who use reasoning and explanations with the child do not usually raise conduct-disordered children (e.g., Herbert, 1982). Conversely, lax parental discipline and parental adjustment difficulties appear to contribute to conduct-disordered behaviour (Verlaan & Schwartzman, 2002).

Learning theories that look to both modelling and operant conditioning provide useful explanations for the development and maintenance of conduct problems. As mentioned in Chapter 2, Bandura and Walters (1963) were among the first researchers to appreciate the significance of the fact that children can learn aggressiveness from parents who behave aggressively. Children may also imitate aggressive acts they see elsewhere, such as on television (Huesmann & Miller, 1994). Since aggression is an effective, albeit unpleasant, means of achieving a goal, it is likely to be reinforced. Thus, once imitated, aggressive acts will probably be maintained.

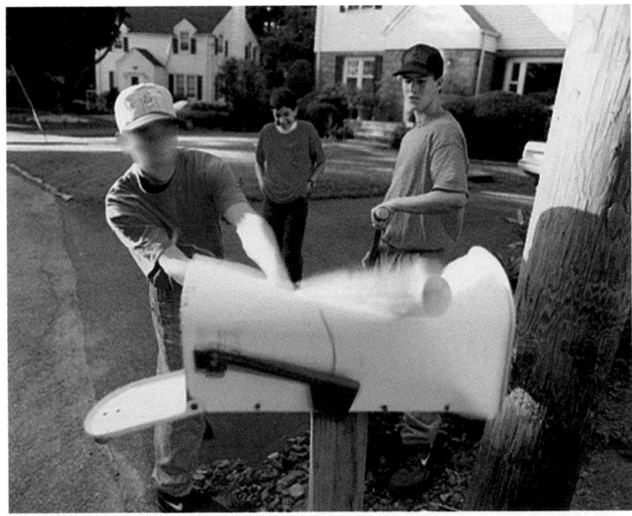

Conduct disorder is diagnosed among those who act aggressively, steal, lie, and vandalize property.

This social mimicry may at least partially explain the dramatic surge in delinquent behaviour in adolescents who had not previously shown conduct problems. Moffitt (1993) proposed that these adolescents imitate the behaviour of persistently antisocial peers because they see them as enjoying high-status possessions and sexual opportunities.

A cognitive perspective on aggressive behaviour (and, by extension, conduct disorder) comes from the work of Kenneth Dodge and his associates. Dodge and Frame (1982) found that the cognitive processes of aggressive children had a particular bias; these youngsters interpreted ambiguous acts, such as being bumped in line, as evidence of hostile intent. Perceptions like this may lead such children to retaliate aggressively for actions that may not have been intended to be provocative. Subsequently, their peers, remembering these aggressive behaviours, may tend to treat them more aggressively, further angering the already aggressive children and continuing a cycle of rejection and aggression (see Figure 15.2). Crick and Dodge (1994) have constructed a social-information processing theory of child behaviour that focuses on how children process information about their world and how these cognitions affect their behaviour.

Recently, Dodge's cognitive theory was incorporated into a comprehensive biopsychosocial model of the development of conduct disorder (Dodge & Pettit, 2003). According to this model, biological predisposition and sociocultural context operate both as distal factors (i.e., more remote influences) and as proximal factors (see Figure 15.2). Sociocultural context factors include the influence of neighbourhood and classroom environments. In addition to the acknowledged roles played by life experiences that the child has with parents and peers (see Figure 15.2), the child's mental processes (i.e., cognitive factors) play a central role in this model because it is the cognitive and emotional mental factors that are the final determinants of how distal factors eventually get translated into antisocial behaviour. Thus, malevolent cognitions still play an important role, but biological and sociocultural factors are also recognized.

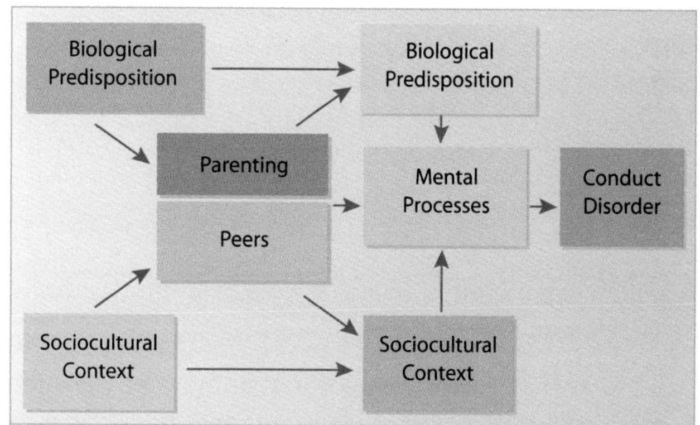

Figure 15.2 A biopsychosocial model of the development of conduct disorder

Treatment of Conduct Disorder The management of conduct disorder poses a formidable challenge. Sociologists, politicians, and community psychologists, working on the assumption that poor economic conditions create most of the problem, argue for a fairer distribution of income and for job programs and other large-scale efforts to alleviate the material deprivation of people in the lower socioeconomic classes. Here, however, we emphasize psychological methods aimed at particular individuals and their families rather than such sociological considerations. Nevertheless, as we will see, working to influence the multiple systems involved in the life of a youngster (family, peers, school, neighbourhood) may be critical to the success of treatment efforts.

Some young people with conduct disorder are the psychopaths of tomorrow. And like psychopaths, young people who commit violent and antisocial acts with little remorse or emotional involvement are extraordinarily difficult to reach. Incarceration, release, and recidivism are the rule. An enduring societal problem is how to deal with people whose social consciences appear grossly underdeveloped. A critical issue in the area of conduct-disordered young people is whether the treatment is designed for a child or an adolescent. According to a review by Canadian researchers, interventions for younger children are more effective than interventions for adolescents (Moretti et al., 1997).

Simply jailing juvenile delinquents will not reduce crime. A longitudinal study demonstrated that punitive discipline (e.g., juvenile incarceration) leads to lower job stability and more adult crime. Thus, harsh discipline, whether imposed by government or by parents, appears to contribute in a major way to further delinquency and criminal activity in adulthood (Laub & Sampson, 1995).

Canadian Perspectives/15.3

The Youth Criminal Justice Act

The Government of Canada tried for many years to pass legislation designed to overhaul the old Young Offenders Act. The new Youth Criminal Justice Act (YCJA; Bill C-7) finally passed the last major parliamentary hurdle on February 4, 2002, and came into effect on April 1, 2003 after delays caused by disputes with the provinces over some significant details of the proposed act (Bailey, 2002; MacCharles, 2001).

As noted by MacCharles (2001), "The bill provides tougher sentences for violent youth crime, but more community based alternatives and diversion programs for non-violent offenders."

Although the overarching principle remains the "protection of society," the preamble emphasizes both "meaningful consequences" for and rehabilitation of young offenders. The new act introduced by then justice minister Anne McLellan

1 lowers the age from 16 to 14 for possible adult sentences for serious crimes;

2 allows publication of names when a youth receives an adult sentence, or in certain other serious cases;

3 creates the new category of "repeat offender" for more than two convictions of a violent crime;

4 requires a kind of mandatory probation after all custodial sentences;

5 gives victims a greater role in the court process—judges can allow publication of the names of young victims and witnesses with their consent and the consent of their parents;

6 promotes alternatives to court for non-violent crimes (e.g., police warnings and community service)—judges are directed to refer offenders to the child welfare system when appropriate;

7 creates a special sentence for mentally or emotionally disturbed violent offenders that requires that they receive treatment while in custody; and

8 leaves children under the age of 12 outside the criminal justice system, to be handled under child welfare laws.

The government wanted to introduce more consistency into the system. For example, youth judges are directed to impose sentences that are "proportional" to similar sentences within a particular region of the country. It goes without saying that judges cannot levy sentences that would be greater than what an adult would receive for a similar crime.

Why did the federal government have so much difficulty getting members of Parliament, provincial governments, and other stakeholders to accept the proposed legislation? The federal Canadian Alliance and Progressive Conservative parties viewed the legislation as unwieldy, expensive, and too lenient on the worst delinquents. On the other hand, the Bloc Québécois perceived it to be excessively harsh. Unfortunately, the provinces, too, could not agree to the new bill initially. Nevertheless, the justice department received qualified support from the Canadian School Boards Association, the Canadian Association of Chiefs of Police, the Canadian Bar Association, and the John Howard Society of Canada (McCharles, 2001).

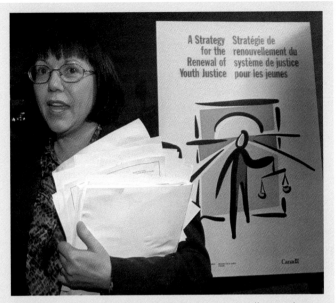

As justice minister, Deputy Prime Minister Anne McLellan was instrumental in shepherding the Youth Criminal Justice Act through Parliament.

In February 2004, a court in Brampton, Ontario, heard the case of the first Canadian teen charged with murder under the YCJA. He killed a 14-year-old boy from his school by strangling him with a belt. Testimony indicated that the youth charged had an unhappy home life, had been thinking about suicide and felt that being in jail was better than living at home (Canadian Press, 2004). Ironically, the murder took place the first day that the YCJA came into effect, April 1, 2003. The 15-year-old teen pleaded guilty to first-degree murder. The presiding judge had to decide whether the youth would be sentenced as a youth or as an adult. Sentencing as a youth carries a maximum 10-year term with no parole for six years; however, an adult conviction carries a life sentence with no parole for at least seven years. On April 22, 2004, Justin Morton was sentenced as an adult (Mitchell, 2004).

Thinking Critically

1. Do you think that the new Youth Criminal Justice Act will solve problems in Canada's youth justice system, or do you think that it will create further problems?
2. Do you think that the new act should have been tougher (Ontario's initial position) or more lenient (Quebec's position)?
3. Do you think that "repeat offenders" should receive even more intensive rehabilitation and treatment efforts, or should society adopt a punishment philosophy with youth who repeat serious, violent offences?
4. Ontario has done less than the other Canadian provinces to implement the community-justice provisions of the YCJA (see Lockett, 2003). Do you think that Ontario should put more emphasis on the notion of restorative or Aboriginal justice in order to reduce recidivism rates? This approach typically involves dealing with all parties involved—the offender, the victim, the families, police, and the community—in an attempt to "shame" and rehabilitate the offender while at the same time bringing closure for the victim.

Nonetheless, the current *Zeitgeist* in Canada is to consider dealing with children who engage in criminal activity in a more stringent manner. The federal government enacted the new Youth Criminal Justice Act, described in Canadian Perspectives 15.3, to provide a better balance between punishment and rehabilitation.

Family Interventions Some of the most promising approaches to treating conduct disorder involve intervening with the parents or families of the antisocial child. Gerald Patterson and his colleagues have worked for over three decades on a behavioural program of parental management training in which parents are taught to modify their responses to their children so that prosocial rather than antisocial behaviour is consistently rewarded. Parents are taught to use techniques such as positive reinforcement when the child exhibits positive behaviours and time-out and loss of privileges for aggressive or antisocial behaviours. Parents' and teachers' reports of children's behaviour and direct observation of behaviour at home and at school both support the program's effectiveness (Patterson, 1982). Parental management training has also been shown to improve the behaviour of siblings and reduce depression in mothers involved in the program (Kazdin, 1985). A study of chronic adolescent offenders by Patterson's group (Bank et al., 1991) found that both parent training and court-provided family treatment reduced rates of criminal offence. The parent-training approach, which included teaching parents to monitor their adolescents more closely and use age-appropriate rewards and consequences, led to more rapid improvement.

Multisystemic Treatment A new treatment for serious juvenile offenders has demonstrated reductions in arrests four years following treatment (Borduin et al., 1995). Henggeler's multisystemic treatment (MST) involves delivering intensive and comprehensive therapy services in the community, targeting the adolescent, the family, the school, and in some cases the peer group. See Canadian Perspectives 15.4 for a further description of MST, a recent application of MST in Ontario, and examples of other approaches in various provinces.

Few prevention programs for antisocial behaviour and conduct disorder have proven to be effective. An influential Canadian study conducted by Richard Tremblay and his colleagues is described in Canadian Contributions 15.2 on page 491.

Canadian Perspectives/15.4

Multisystemic Treatment in Ontario and Alternative Canadian Approaches to the Rehabilitation of Young Offenders

Multisystemic Therapy: Model and Strategies

Consistent with the focus on family assessment in Chapter 4, MST interventions reflect the view that conduct problems are influenced by multiple contexts within the family and between the family and other social systems. MST is derived from Bronfenbrenner's (1979) social-ecological model of development and its notion that behaviours, both adaptive and maladaptive, originate and are maintained by transactions that involve multiple systems within an individual's family, the immediate social environment, including the community, as well as broader, global systems that reflect cultural influences.

The strategies used by MST therapists are varied, incorporating behavioural, cognitive, family-systems, and case-management techniques. A major implication of MST is that youths receive treatment in their homes and stay in their communities rather than be incarcerated. This approach may result in reduced financial costs, and it recognizes that real changes must also occur in the troubled youth's environment. The therapy's uniqueness and perhaps its effectiveness (see Henggeler et al., 1998) lie in its emphasizing individual and family strengths, identifying the context for the conduct problems, using present-focused and action-oriented interventions, and using interventions that require daily or weekly efforts by family members. Treatment is provided in "ecologically valid" settings, such as the home, school, or local recreational centre, to maximize generalization of therapeutic changes.

Efficacy and Mechanism of Change

Henggeler et al. (1998) compared the results for a MST group with those for a control group that received an equivalent number of sessions (about 25) of traditional individual therapy in an office setting. They found that adolescents in the MST group showed reduced behaviour problems and far fewer arrests over the following four years; 70 percent of adolescents receiving traditional therapy were arrested in the four years following treatment, while only 22 percent of those completing MST were arrested. In addition, family assessments indicated that parents who were involved in MSTs showed reductions in psychiatric symptoms and that MST families showed improved supportiveness and decreased conflict and hostility in videotaped interactions. In contrast, the quality of interactions in the families of the adolescents receiving traditional individual therapy deteriorated following treatment. Even the adolescents in the MST group who dropped out of treatment after about four sessions demonstrated significantly reduced arrest rates compared to adolescents who completed the full course of traditional individual therapy.

Huey, Henggeler, Brondino, and Pickrel (2000) examined the specific MST mechanisms of change that led to the improvements. They found that the therapist's adherence to the MST protocol facilitated a sequence in which improved family functioning decreased the adolescents' affiliation with delinquent peers, which in turn decreased their delinquent behaviour.

Multisystemic Therapy in Ontario

A team of researchers led by Allan Leschied and Alison Cunningham implemented MST in Ontario in a project started in 1997 (see Cunningham, 2002; Leschied & Cunningham, 2000; Leschied, Cunningham, & Hawkins, 2000). This project, known as "The Clinical Trials of Multisystemic Therapy in Ontario," involved coordination with agencies located in London, Mississauga, Ottawa, and Simcoe County. MST was seen as a cost-efficient community alternative to custodial residential placement for high-risk Ontario youth. Participants were eligible for the study if they had a history of criminal offences and a high level of risk for reoffending. Leschied et al. (2000) maintain that the study has high ecological validity because the youths in the study are those who have been identified as providing the greatest challenge for local agencies.

Unfortunately, although data are still being collected (follow-up will end in 2004) and some early findings appear to favour the MST participants, the most recent results indicate that the MST group and the treatment-as-usual group do not differ significantly on any outcome measure. Although there is no significant treatment effect, there is a trend suggesting a lower number of subsequent convictions among MST recipients (Cunningham, 2002). Overall, 79 percent of the 409 youth in the study have been convicted at least once during the three years since the study's inception. Cunningham (2002) concluded that "at this point. It is not possible to recommend the adoption of MST in Canada."

Alternative Approaches in Canada

MST may, or may not, ultimately prove to be a successful alternative to custody for young offenders in Ontario. What are the current alternatives when closed custody is ordered in Canadian youth courts? The irony in research on MST in Ontario should be noted, given the more general response to conduct disorder adopted by that province. A review paper by Moretti et al. (1997) provided a clear description of the various approaches adopted in four provinces (i.e., British Columbia, Ontario, Quebec, and New Brunswick). Ontario was identified as being the least progressive because of its unique decision to rely on so-called boot camps (strict discipline facilities) as a form of incarceration for young offenders, many of whom meet diagnostic criteria for conduct disorder. Moretti et al. maintain that boot camps in the United States have been largely ineffective and involve considerable financial cost. In fact, in fairness to the government, Ontario's secure custody program, finally implemented in July 1997 amid controversy and media focus, is quite different from the American boot camp model, though still considered a strict discipline facility (Wormith, Wright, Sauve, & Fleury, 1998). "Project Turnaround," run by the private sector in a jail converted for the purpose, accepted as many as 50 repeat young male offenders, between 16 and 19 years of age, for a period of up to six months. Children serving time for murder, arson, or sexual assault were not eligible for the program. A philosophy of the program is that troubled youth need more order in their lives. The military milieu provided a structure where attention was focused on positive activities and progress was rewarded by "promotion." The busy 16-hour days involved the young people in high school classes, anger-management courses, substance abuse counselling, sexual assault and abuse counselling, problem-solving and life skills activities, a values and moral reasoning program, a behaviour-management program, a positive peer culture program, and physical fitness. Each youth (cadet) was assigned a case manager (counsellor) and a primary worker (sergeant) who monitored progress and provided individualized services. A second phase of the program (aftercare) attempted to ease the youth back into the community. The new provincial government in Ontario indicated that they planned to close the first boot camp (Canadian Press, November 26, 2003) for practical reasons (because of toxic mould in the camp itself and the associated financial cost) rather than on ideological grounds. The Government of Saskatchewan had previously announced its plan to initiate its own boot camps (Canadian Press, October 10, 2003).

The boot camp approach contrasts with the approach adopted in British Columbia at the Maples Adolescent Centre where the Response Program is offered (see Moretti et al., 1997). This program includes a focus on lifestyle, home life, and school issues; personal and family dynamics are examined from an attachment-style perspective within each of these domains. The guiding premise of the Maples program is that an insecure attachment style is at the root of the conduct disorder. Interventions include family therapy and parent training, as well as individually focused treatment. The goal is to involve the community and return the child with conduct disorder to his or her community. Moretti et al. conclude, on the basis of evaluation research, that the program is effective in reducing problem behaviour and psychological distress.

The boot camp approach also contrasts sharply with the therapeutic youth jail opened in New Brunswick in 1998. The New Brunswick Youth Centre is a prison that has cottage-like cell blocks and mixes compassion with discipline (Canadian Press, 1998). It claims to be the first correctional facility in Canada to base its full rehabilitation program on therapeutic community principles, although the program was adapted from a program developed in Quebec (the "Portage Program") that was used for about 30 years in that province. The New Brunswick program is described by government sources as "a structured milieu that facilitates personal growth, self-awareness and self-respect" (Canadian Press, 1998). It relies heavily on peer pressure to change young offenders' attitudes.

It is premature to determine the impact of these different programs on recidivism and other desired outcomes (e.g., increased family cohesion, reduced aggression with peers). Only future research can determine which of these alternative models for the rehabilitation of young offenders, if any, is effective over the longer term.

Moretti et al. (1997) were highly critical of governments everywhere for not adopting a preventive approach that addresses possible problems involving conduct disorder and implements change before a problem emerges.

Thinking Critically

1. Many of the currently available services and programs for serious and persistent conduct-disordered youth are of limited effectiveness. However, the MST strategy appears to offer more hope of success than typical single and short-term treatments. Assuming that rigorous outcome research ultimately supports its effectiveness, are you in favour of seeing MST extended throughout Canada? Would a program such as MST be most effective with children identified as "at risk" at a very young age? Does the best hope for the future lie in the development of early intervention and prevention programs?

2. For older conduct-disordered youngsters, do you favour the types of treatment approach used in British Columbia and New Brunswick or the "get tough" boot camp approach previously applied in Ontario? Which approach will have the best long-term results? Why?

3. Why do you think that relatively few government prevention programs exist for conduct-disordered children, even though such programs probably play a critical role in reducing dysfunction and distress?

Cognitive Approaches Although research by Patterson's and Henggeler's groups suggests that intervention with parents and families is a critical component of success, such treatment is expensive and time-consuming (though clearly less so than incarceration). Indeed, some families may not be able or willing to become involved in it. Moretti et al. (1997) observed that the parents of youths with conduct disorder have often disengaged by the time their children come into contact with the mental health system, and thus, if parental involvement is not forthcoming, these youths will be excluded from treatment research that has a parental component.

In light of these issues, it is noteworthy that other research indicates that individual cognitive therapy with conduct-disordered children can improve their behaviour even without the involvement of the family. For example, programs that teach children cognitive skills to control their anger show real promise in helping them reduce their aggressive behaviour. In anger-control training, aggressive children are taught self-control in anger-provoking situations. To withstand verbal attacks without responding aggressively, they learn to use distracting techniques such as humming a tune, saying calming things to themselves, or turning away. The children then apply these self-control methods while a peer provokes and insults them (e.g., Lochman & Wells, 1996).

Another strategy involves focusing on the deficient moral development of conduct-disordered children. The teaching of moral-reasoning skills to groups of behaviour-disordered adolescents in school has achieved far-reaching success (Arbuthnot & Gordon, 1986). Adolescents who were identified by their teachers as having behaviour problems (e.g., stealing, aggressiveness, and vandalism) participated for four to five months in weekly groups at school that encouraged higher levels of moral reasoning. Group sessions included discussion of vignettes such as the following:

> Sharon and her best friend, Jill, are shopping in a boutique. Jill finds a blouse she wants but cannot afford. She takes it into a fitting room and puts it on underneath her jacket. She shows it to Sharon and, despite Sharon's protests, leaves the store. Sharon is stopped by a security guard. The manager searches Sharon's bag, but finding nothing, concludes that Jill shoplifted the blouse. The manager asks Sharon for Jill's name, threatening to call both Sharon's parents and the police if she doesn't tell. Sharon's dilemma is whether or not to tell on her best friend.

The group members were encouraged to debate the merits of alternative perspectives and the rights and responsibilities of characters in the dilemmas as well as of other people and society. Compared with a control group of nominated students who received no intervention, adolescents participating in the groups showed improvement in moral-reasoning skills and school grades, as well as reductions in tardiness, referrals to the principal for behaviour problems, and contacts with police or juvenile courts. Follow-ups in the next school year showed increased differences between the groups, with the adolescents who had received the intervention showing continued advances in moral reasoning and further reductions in behaviour problems.

This improvement is impressive, but other research cautions that behavioural changes produced by altering cognitive patterns may yield only short-term gains—improvements that may be lost when the youngsters return to their familiar, "bad" neighbourhoods. Environmental contingencies—the communities in which people live—need to be considered when dealing with the complexities of aggression (Guerra & Slaby, 1990).

Canadian Contributions/15.2

Richard Tremblay and the GRIP Research Unit

"Aggression does not suddenly erupt in our teens or when conflicts arise in a couple. All humans make spontaneous use of physical aggression very early in life—and it is then that we learn to control our violent reactions. Unfortunately, those who don't learn alternatives to physical aggression tend to use it later against their parents and partners."

—Richard Tremblay

Richard E. Tremblay, director of the Group de recherché sur l'inadaptation psychosocial chez l'enfant (GRIP; Research Unit on Children's Psychosocial Maladjustment)

Richard Tremblay was identified by *Time* magazine (Blumstein, 2003) as one of the most innovative researchers in Canada. He is a professor of pediatrics, psychiatry, and psychology at the University of Montreal, and holds a Canada research chair in child development. Tremblay is a fellow of the Royal Society of Canada and was honoured in 2003 with the Innis-Gerin Medal from the Royal Society of Canada. This award is for distinguished and sustained contribution to the literature of the social sciences. In 2002 Tremblay won the Jacques-Rousseau Interdisciplinary Research Award.

Tremblay is perhaps best known for his involvement in the Montreal Longitudinal-Experimental Study. The purpose of this study was to help prevent antisocial behaviour in boys who were disruptive in kindergarten (see Tremblay et al., 1992). The study tested the hypothesis that poor parental management and deficits in social skills contribute to the development of antisocial behaviour. The results after two years of treatment (when the children were 7 and 8) and after three years of follow-up were encouraging. The treated disruptive boys were less physically aggressive, were more often in an age-appropriate regular classroom, had less-serious school-adjustment problems, and engaged in fewer delinquent behaviours.

The LaCourse et al. (2002) longitudinal study of developmental trajectories, described earlier in this chapter, also included a preventative component. Recall that this study tracked boys from kindergarten until they were 17 years old. A subset of participants in this study received an intervention that consisted of social skills training for the at-risk boys as well as parent training. A comparison of boys who received the intervention versus those in the non-intervention control group showed that boys who received the intervention were significantly more likely, over time, to follow the lowest level trajectory and were substantially less likely to follow the high level trajectory of aggressive and violent behaviour. This is an impressive outcome because, as LaCourse et al. noted, this is the first intervention program with a long-term follow-up component that has been able to demonstrate a significant impact on the developmental course of physical aggression. This study represents solid evidence that well-designed and well-timed interventions can make a difference!

The longitudinal study also focused on the causes and correlates of developmental trajectories of aggression. Recently, Tremblay and Vitaro, also from the University of Montreal, were part of an international multi-site team of investigators that examined the developmental course of physical aggression in childhood (see Broidy et al., 2003). This study found that a small but identifiable number of boys and girls chronically exhibit aggression throughout childhood and that, for boys, this chronic physical aggression predicted later violent delinquency as well as nonviolent offending; chronic physical aggression did not consistently predict girls' aggression in adolescence.

Additional research themes address the biological and physical correlates of physical aggression. For example, one study showed that obstetrical complications (e.g., umbilical cord prolapse) predicted the risk of violence at 6 and 17 years of age in 849 boys from Montreal (Arsenault, Tremblay, Boulerice, & Saucier, 2002). Research has also investigated the comorbidity of chronic physical aggression with other disorders, such as ADHD, conduct disorder, and depression. One study confirmed that there are substantial gender differences in the profiles that confer risk for conduct disorders (Cote, Tremblay, Nagin, Zoccolillo, & Vitaro, 2002).

Tremblay is also the director of the Group de recherché sur l'inadaptation psychosocial chez l'enfant (GRIP; Research Unit on Children's Psychosocial Maladjustment). This highly productive research unit consists of scholars from three sites (Laval University, McGill University, and the University of Montreal) and a host of associate investigators, including some who are affiliated with other universities, such as Tracy Vaillancourt of McMaster University and Philip Zelazo of the University of Toronto. According to its website (www.grip.umontreal.ca), GRIP's mandate is to investigate risk and protective factors that influence child development from birth through adolescence. This multidisciplinary research program has three objectives: (1) to describe the prevalence and development of maladjustment in children and examine the influence of environmental variables such as the family, the school, and peers; (2) to identify risk factors that interfere with children's development as well as factors that increase resilience in children; and (3) to investigate the impact of preventive interventions with children from high-risk populations.

The research findings identified by Tremblay and his colleagues have important societal implications, and certain findings have already led to positive changes in "the real world." In this regard, after showing empirically that aggressive boys who become violent teenagers tend to have poor, uneducated mothers who gave birth as teenagers (Nagin & Tremblay, 2001), Tremblay has been able to convince the provincial government to develop a prenatal care and parenting-skills program for at-risk mothers.

LEARNING DISABILITIES

SEVERAL YEARS AGO, a young man in one of our undergraduate courses showed an unusual pattern of strengths and difficulties. His oral comments in class were exemplary, but his handwriting and spelling were sometimes indecipherable. After the instructor had noted these problems on the student's mid-term examination, the undergraduate came to see him and explained that he was dyslexic and that it took him longer to complete the weekly reading assignments and to write papers and exams. The instructor decided to accord him additional time for preparing written work. The student was obviously of superior intelligence and highly motivated to excel. Excel he did, earning an A in the seminar and on graduation being admitted to a leading law school.

Learning disabilities signify inadequate development in a specific area of academic, language, speech, or motor skills that is not due to mental retardation, autism, a demonstrable physical disorder, or deficient educational opportunities. Children with these disorders are usually of average or above-average intelligence but have difficulty learning some specific skill (e.g., arithmetic or reading), and thus their progress in school is impeded.

The term *learning disabilities* is not used by DSM-IV-TR but is used by most health professionals to group together three disorders that do appear in the DSM: learning disorders, communication disorders, and motor skills disorder. Any of these disorders may apply to a child who fails to develop to the degree expected of his or her intellectual level in a specific academic, or language, or motor skill area. Learning disabilities are usually identified and treated within the school system rather than through mental health clinics. Although they are widely believed to be far more common in males than in females, evidence from population-based studies (which avoid the problem of referral biases) indicates that, like ADHD, the disorders are only slightly more common in males (e.g., Shaywitz et al., 1990). Even though individuals with learning disabilities usually find ways to cope with their problems, their academic and social development is nonetheless affected, sometimes quite seriously.

LEARNING DISORDERS

DSM-IV-TR divides learning disorders into three categories: reading disorder, disorder of written expression, and mathematics disorder. None of these diagnoses is appropriate if the disability can be accounted for by a sensory deficit, such as a visual or auditory problem.

- Children with reading disorder, better known as dyslexia, have significant difficulty with word recognition, reading comprehension, and typically written spelling as well. When reading out loud, they omit, add, or distort the pronunciation of words to an extent unusual for their age. In adulthood, problems with reading, comprehension, and written spelling persist (Bruck, 1987). This disorder, present in 2 to 8 percent of school-age children, does not preclude great achievements. For example, it is widely known that inventor Alexander Graham Bell, who stayed at his summer home in Baddeck, Nova Scotia, suffered from dyslexia.
- Disorder of written expression describes an impairment in the ability to compose the written word (including spelling errors, errors in grammar, or very poor handwriting) that is serious enough to interfere significantly with academic achievement or daily activities that require writing skills. Few systematic data have yet been collected on the prevalence of this disorder, which the college student in our case had in addition to his dyslexia.

Alexander Graham Bell suffered from dyslexia.

- Children with mathematics disorder may have difficulty rapidly and accurately recalling arithmetic facts, counting objects correctly and quickly, or aligning numbers in columns.

Communication Disorders

Several categories of communication disorders have been distinguished:

- In expressive language disorder, the child has difficulty expressing himself or herself in speech. The youngster may seem eager to communicate but have inordinate difficulty finding the right words; for example, he or she may be unable to come up with the word "car" when pointing to a car passing by on the street. By age 4, this child speaks only in short phrases. Old words are forgotten when new ones are learned, and the use of grammatical structures is considerably below age level.
- Unlike children who have trouble finding words, youngsters with phonological disorder comprehend and are able to use a substantial vocabulary, but their speech sounds like Elmer Fudd; "blue" comes out "bu", and "rabbit" sounds like wabbit, for example. They have not learned articulation of the later-acquired speech sounds, such as *r*, *sh*, *th*, *f*, *z*, *l*, and *ch*. With speech therapy, complete recovery occurs in most cases and milder cases may recover spontaneously by age 8.
- A third communication disorder is stuttering, a disturbance in verbal fluency characterized by one or more of the following speech patterns: frequent repetitions or prolongations of sounds, long pauses between words, substituting easy words for those that are difficult to articulate (e.g., words beginning with certain consonants), and repeating whole words (e.g., saying "go-go-go-go" instead of just a single "go"). Sometimes bodily twitching and eye blinking accompany the verbal dysfluencies. Stuttering can interfere with academic, social, and occupational functioning and can prevent otherwise capable people from fulfilling their potential. About three times as many males as females have the problem, which usually shows up at around age 5 and almost always before the age of 10. The DSM estimates that up to 80 percent of stutterers recover, most of them without professional intervention, before the age of 16.

A speech therapist works with a child with phonological disorder by having him practise the sounds he finds difficult.

A Canadian study highlights the serious dysfunction and impairment that tends to accompany language difficulties. Cohen et al. (2000) compared functioning in ADHD children with no language impairment with functioning in ADHD children with language impairment and in psychiatric control groups comprised of children with or without impairment. Children with language impairment were the most disadvantaged, regardless of their diagnosis. In fact, in terms of predicting executive functioning, language impairment was a stronger predictor than having an ADHD diagnosis.

Beitchman et al. (2001) from the Centre of Addiction and Mental Health in Toronto undertook a 14-year prospective study of the outcomes experienced by language-impaired children. This study shows clearly that there is a link between language problems in early childhood and psychiatric disorders years later. Thus, early remediation of language problems is an important goal.

The most recent data from this project indicate that by age 19, language-impaired boys (relative to those without language impairment), have greater symptoms of delinquency based on parental reports, though differences are not evident in terms of self-reports of delinquency. Moreover, these language-impaired boys have higher rates of arrests and convictions (Brownlie et al., 2004).

Motor Skills Disorder

In motor skills disorder, also referred to as *developmental coordination disorder*, children show marked impairment in the development of motor coordination that is not explainable by mental retardation or a known physical disorder such as cerebral palsy. The young child may have difficulty tying shoelaces and buttoning shirts and, when older, building models, playing ball, and printing or handwriting. The diagnosis is made only if the impairment interferes significantly with academic achievement or with the activities of daily living.

Etiology of Learning Disabilities

Most research on learning disabilities concerns dyslexia, perhaps because it is the most prevalent of this group of disorders. Although studies on mathematics disorder are beginning to emerge, the literature has advanced more slowly in this area.

Etiology of Dyslexia Family and twin studies show there is a heritable component to dyslexia (Pennington, 1995), possibly controlled by chromosome 6 (e.g., Grigorenko et al., 1997). A study of the branches of five Canadian families of Celtic ancestry who submitted to DNA testing showed that hereditary factors appear to cause specific language impairment, a known precursor of dyslexia. Moreover, chromosome 13 (13q21) is directly implicated as a dyslexia phenotype (Bartlett et al., 2002). According to a review by Gilger and Kaplan at the University of Calgary, other evidence continues to suggest that brain abnormalities, possibly heritable, may be responsible for dyslexia and other learning disorders (Gilger & Kaplan, 2001). Autopsies of the brains of right-handed individuals with childhood dyslexia have revealed microscopic abnormalities in the location, number, and organization of neurons on the right side of the brain in what is called the *posterior language* area of the cortex (Galaburda, 1993).

PET scans made of dyslexic and normal children as they performed a variety of cognitive tasks reveal differences in how another part of the cortex functions. During a test that required children to detect rhymes, the left temporoparietal cortex was activated in the normal children but not in the dyslexic children. This finding is significant because the temporoparietal cortex is important in an aspect of language processing called *phonological awareness*, believed to be critical to the development of reading skills (Rumsey et al., 1994).

Past psychological theories have focused on perceptual deficits as the basis for dyslexia. One popular hypothesis suggested that children with reading problems perceive letters in reverse order or mirror image, mistaking, for example, a *d* for a *b*. However, more recent findings have not supported simple perceptual deficits as characterizing dyslexia (Wolff & Melngailis, 1996); most children make letter reversals when first learning to read, but even dyslexic individuals very rarely make letter reversals after age 9 or 10. No link has been found between letter confusions at age 5 or 6 and subsequent reading ability (Calfee, Fisk, & Piontkowski, 1985), nor does a person need to be able to see to have reading problems—blind people may have difficulty learning to read Braille (McGuiness, 1981).

Other research points to one or more problems in language processing that might underlie dyslexia, including perception of speech and analysis of the sounds of spoken language and their relation to printed words (Mann & Brady, 1988). A series of longitudinal studies suggests that some early language problems can predict later dyslexia. Children are more likely to develop dyslexia if they have difficulty recognizing rhyme and alliteration at age 4 (Bradley & Bryant, 1985), have problems rapidly naming familiar objects at age 5 (Scarborough, 1990; Wolf, Bally, & Morris, 1986), or are behind in learning syntactic rules at age 2 and a half (Scarborough, 1990). These language-processing difficulties and the visual-processing deficits noted earlier may arise from the same neurological problem, namely, a deficit in the brain structures that are used to process stimuli rapidly (Eden & Zeffiro, 1996).

TREATMENT OF LEARNING DISABILITIES

The anxiety of parents whose otherwise normal child lags behind in reading or cannot speak effectively and normally for his or her age cannot be underestimated. Professional attempts to remedy learning disabilities have been subject to somatic, educational, and psychological fads—from using stimulants and tranquillizers to training the child in motor activities (such as crawling) believed to have been inadequately mastered at a younger age—in the hope of reorganizing neuronal connections in the brain.

Most treatment for learning disabilities occurs within special-education programs in the public schools. Educational approaches include identifying and working with the child's cognitive strengths while circumventing his or her deficits; targeting study skills and organizational strategies; and teaching verbal self-instruction strategies (Culbertson, 1998). Although special-education interventions are extremely common, their effectiveness in improving the academic performance of children with learning disabilities has not been carefully evaluated (Council for Exceptional Children, 1993).

Several strategies are currently being used to treat learning disabilities, both in school programs and in private tutoring. Traditional linguistic approaches, used primarily in cases of reading and writing difficulties, focus on instruction in listening, speaking, reading, and writing skills in a logical, sequential, and multisensory manner, such as having the child read out loud under close supervision (Lyon & Moats, 1988). In young children, readiness skills, such as letter discrimination, phonetic analysis, and learning letter-sound correspondences, may need to be taught before explicit instruction in reading is attempted. Individuals with dyslexia often can succeed in university or college with the aid of instructional supports, such as tape-recorded lectures, tutors, editorial assistance, and untimed tests (Bruck, 1987). Most universities and colleges have special services to help such students. Public schools are now required to provide transitional vocational and career planning for older adolescents with learning disabilities.

There has been an exciting development in the treatment of communication disorders (Merzenich et al., 1996; Tallal et al., 1996). Given indications that children with such disorders have difficulty discriminating certain sounds, researchers developed special computer games and audiotapes that slow speech sounds. After intensive training with these modified speech stimuli for one month, children with severe language disorders were able to improve their language skills by approximately two years, to the point where they were functioning as normal children do. Similar training using unmodified speech stimuli resulted in very little progress. Although the number of participants in these initial studies was small, the remarkable gains suggest a promising new approach that will surely be investigated further. The researchers speculate that this training method may even help prevent dyslexia, since many reading-disordered children had difficulties understanding language as young children.

Most children with learning disabilities experience frustration and failure, which erodes their motivation and confidence. Whatever their design, treatment programs should provide opportunities for children to experience feelings of mastery and self-efficacy. Rewarding small steps can help increase the child's motivation, focus his or her attention on the learning task, and reduce behavioural problems caused by frustration. In addition to targeting academic skills, those treating children with learning disabilities should include strategies to address the secondary social and emotional adjustment problems the children experience. For example, educating children and parents about the disability, addressing their emotional reactions to the disability, and teaching them strategies to adapt are all helpful approaches to improving overall adjustment (Culbertson, 1998).

MENTAL RETARDATION

Mental retardation, an Axis II disorder, is defined in DSM-IV-TR as (1) significantly subaverage intellectual functioning along with (2) deficits in adaptive behaviour and (3) occurring prior to age 18. We first examine traditional criteria and then discuss some newer perspectives from the American Association of Mental Retardation (AAMR), the principal professional organization devoted to research, education, and application in the field of mental retardation. Although founded in the United States, this organization has many international chapters, including local chapters in Alberta, Manitoba, Quebec, Nova Scotia, and Prince Edward Island. Mentally retarded children and adults are often referred to as "developmentally delayed" or "intellectually handicapped" by the public and the media in Canada.

TRADITIONAL CRITERIA FOR MENTAL RETARDATION

Intelligence-Test Scores The first component of the DSM definition requires a judgement of intelligence. As discussed in Chapter 4, approximately two-thirds of the population achieve IQ (intelligent quotient) test scores between 85 and 115. Those with a score below 70 to 75, two standard deviations below the mean of the population, meet the criterion of "significant subaverage general intellectual functioning." Approximately 3 percent of the population fall within this category.

The determination of IQ should be based on tests administered by a competent, well-trained professional. Interpretation of scores must take into account cultural, linguistic, and sensory or motor limitations that may affect performance. For example, when testing a child with cerebral palsy who has limited use of his or her hands, the examiner might select IQ tests that require verbal responses or simple gestural responses, rather than the traditional intellectual tests, which include a nonverbal or performance component requiring fairly complex and rapid motor movements. Similarly, a child who speaks Farsi at home and English at school cannot be tested in a valid way using only English-language measures (American Association of Mental Retardation [AAMR], 1992).

Adaptive Functioning Adaptive functioning refers to mastering childhood skills such as toileting and dressing; understanding the concepts of time and money; being able to use tools, to shop, and to travel by public transportation; and becoming socially responsive. An adolescent, for example, is expected to be able to apply academic skills, reasoning, and judgement to daily living and to participate in group activities. An adult is expected to be self-supporting and to assume social responsibilities.

Tests constructed to assess adaptive behaviour include the Adaptive Behaviour Scale, or ABS (Nihira et al., 1975), and the Vineland Adaptive Behaviour Scales (Sparrow, Ballo, & Cicchetti, 1984; see Table 15.3). Although impairments in adaptive functioning have long been included in the definition of mental retardation, only recently have tests been adequately standardized with firmly established norms. A problem with many assessments of adaptive behaviour is

Table 15.3

Sample Items from the Vineland Adaptive Behaviour Scales

Age, Years	Adaptive Ability
2	Says at least fifty recognizable words.
	Removes front-opening coat, sweater, or shirt without assistance.
5	Tells popular story, fairy tale, lengthy joke, or plot of television program.
	Ties shoelaces into a bow without assistance.
8	Keeps secrets or confidences for more than one day.
	Orders own meal in a restaurant.
11	Uses the telephone for all kinds of calls without assistance.
	Watches television or listens to radio for information about a particular area of interest.
16	Looks after own health.
	Responds to hints or indirect cues in conversation.

Source: From Sparrow, Ballo, and Cicchetti, 1984.

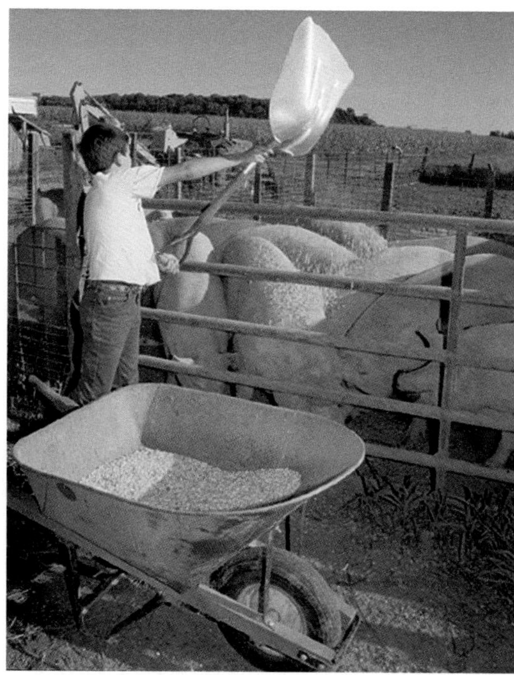

When assessing normal adaptive behaviour, the environment must be considered. A person living in a rural community may not need the same skills that someone living in Vancouver or St. John's needs, and vice-versa.

that they fail to consider the environment to which the person must adapt. Youngsters who are competent working at farm chores, walking to school, and shopping at the local store may, when transported to a city, be considered deficient in adaptive behaviour if they are not able to ride the subway to school or buy groceries at a store where a foreign language is spoken. By the same token, city children may find themselves at a loss with some of the activities expected of youngsters living on a farm. An effective and valid assessment of adaptive behaviour should therefore consider how well the child interacts with the surroundings in which he or she must function.

Age of Onset A final definitional criterion is that mental retardation be manifest before age 18, to rule out classifying as mental retardation any deficits in intelligence and adaptive behaviour from traumatic accidents or illnesses occurring later in life. Children with severe impairments are often diagnosed during infancy. Most children considered mentally retarded, however, are not identified as such until they enter school. These children have no obvious physiological, neurological, or physical manifestations, and their problems become apparent only when they are unable to keep up with their peers in school.

CLASSIFICATION OF MENTAL RETARDATION

Four levels of mental retardation are recognized by DSM-IV-TR, each corresponding to a specific subaverage range on the far left of the normal distribution curve of measured intelligence (recall Figure 1.1). Again, the IQ ranges are not the sole basis of diagnosis; deficiencies in adaptive behaviour are also a criterion of mental retardation. Some persons falling within the mildly retarded range based on IQ may have no deficits in adaptive behaviour and thus would not be considered mentally retarded. In fact, the IQ criterion is usually applied only after deficits in adaptive behaviour have been identified. The following is a brief summary of characteristics of people at each level of mental retardation (DSM-IV-TR; Robinson & Robinson, 1976).

- *Mild mental retardation* (50-55 to 70 IQ). About 85 percent of all those with IQs less than 70 are classified as having **mild mental retardation**. They are not always distinguishable from normal youngsters before they enter school. By their late teens, they can usually learn academic skills at about a 6th-grade level. As adults, they are likely to be able to maintain themselves in unskilled jobs or in sheltered workshops, although they may need help with social and financial problems. They may marry and have children.
- *Moderate mental retardation* (35-40 to 50-55 IQ). About 10 percent of those with IQs less than 70 are classified as having **moderate mental retardation**. Brain damage and other pathologies are frequent. People with moderate mental retardation may have physical defects and neurological dysfunctions that hinder fine motor skills, such as grasping and colouring within lines, and gross motor skills, such as running and climbing. They may learn to travel alone in a familiar locality. Many live in institutions, but most live dependently within the family or in supervised group homes.
- *Severe mental retardation* (20-25 to 35-40 IQ). Of those people with IQs less than 70, about 3 to 4 percent come under the category of **severe mental retardation**. These people often have congenital physical abnormalities and limited sensorimotor control. Most are institutionalized and require constant supervision. Adults with severe retardation may be friendly but usually can communicate only briefly on a very concrete level. They engage in little independent activity and are often lethargic, for their severe brain damage leaves them relatively passive. They may be able to perform very simple work under close supervision.
- *Profound mental retardation* (below 20 to 25 IQ). One to 2 percent of people with mental retardation are classified as having **profound mental retardation**, requiring total supervision and often nursing care all their lives. Most have severe physical deformities as well as neurological damage and cannot get around on their own. The mortality rate during childhood for people with profound mental retardation is very high.

A recent Canadian study of adolescents established that the overall prevalence of mental retardation is 7.18 per 1,000, with the prevalence of severe mental retardation being 3.64 per 1,000 (Bradley, Thompson, & Bryson, 2002). The prevalence estimate was similar to previous Canadian estimates and the estimated prevalence worldwide. Mental retardation was defined in this study as an IQ of 75 or less, which is higher than the IQ cut-off of 70 described above.

The Approach of the American Association of Mental Retardation

We turn now to a very different approach to mental retardation, one being followed by increasing numbers of professionals. In the ninth edition of its classification system, the American Association of Mental Retardation (AAMR, 1992) shifted its focus from identifying severity of disability to determining what remedial supports are necessary to facilitate higher functioning. Professionals are now encouraged to identify an individual's strengths and weaknesses on psychological, physical, and environmental dimensions with a view toward determining the kinds and intensities of environmental supports needed to enhance a person's functioning in different domains.

This approach encourages a more individualized assessment of a person's skills and needs. For example, a survey of over 200 people with severe retardation (IQs between 20 and 40) found that individuals varied greatly in their communication skills, with some communicating only through nonverbal signals that could seldom be interpreted by caregivers and others able to combine symbols (through spoken words, manual signs, or communication boards) to make their needs known (McLean, Brady, & McLean, 1996). This approach also focuses more on what people can do than on what they cannot do, and directs professional attention to how best to make positive changes in the person's life.

As an example of the AAMR approach to classification, consider Roger, a 24-year-old man with an IQ of 45 who has attended a special program for mentally retarded children since he was six. According to the DSM, he would be considered moderately mentally retarded, and on that basis, he would not be expected to be able to live independently, get around on his own, or progress beyond grade 2. The AAMR classification system, however, would emphasize what is needed to maximize Roger's functioning. A clinician might discover that Roger can use the bus system if he takes a route familiar to him, and thus he might be able to go to a movie by himself from time to time. And although he cannot prepare complicated meals, he might be able to learn to prepare frozen entrées in a microwave oven. The assumption is that by concentrating and building on what he can do, Roger will make more progress.

In the schools, an individualized placement is based on the person's strengths and weaknesses and on the amount of instruction needed. A student who needs considerable one-on-one instruction because of deficient intellectual functioning may be placed in the same classroom as a child who needs intensive instruction because of emotional problems or physical disabilities. Students are identified by the classroom environment they are judged to need. This approach can lessen the stigmatizing effects of being considered retarded, rather than encouraging a focus on what to label a child, it may direct attention to what can be done to improve the student's learning.

Etiology of Mental Retardation

In only 25 percent of the population with mental retardation can the primary cause be identified at this time. When specific causes can be identified, they are typically biological.

No Identifiable Etiology People with mild or moderate mental retardation do not, as far as is known at this time, have an identifiable brain defect. And whereas individuals whose mental retardation is associated with identifiable biological impairments are found in much the same percentages throughout all socioeconomic, ethnic, and racial groups, those with mild or moderate mental retardation are overrepresented in the lower socioeconomic classes, suggesting that certain social conditions of deprivation are major factors in retarding their intellectual and behavioural development.

Baumeister, Kupstas, and Klindworth (1991) have suggested several variables that might act in concert to produce milder forms of mental retardation. These include predisposing variables (diatheses), such as undetermined genetic factors, and resource variables, such as educational and health care resources. Consider two young people with the same biological brain impairment, so subtle as to be undetectable by the neurological methods currently available. One youngster comes from a high socioeconomic level, the other from a low level. The first individual's slight deficit could be compensated for by the enriched social and educational environment made possible by the family's financial resources. In contrast, the second individual's deficit might be exaggerated by impoverished circumstances. To show signs of retardation, a socially advantaged person would have to have more extensive damage—damage that is less responsive or even impervious to the benefits of an enriched upbringing.

Known Biological Etiology As noted, about 25 percent of people have mental retardation for which there is a known

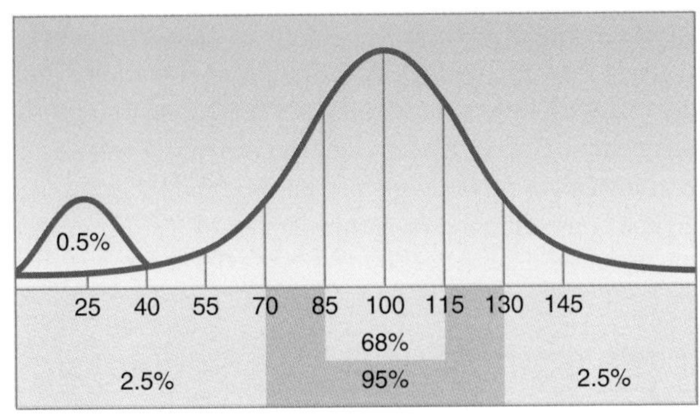

Figure 15.3 Normal curve showing the theoretical distribution of IQ scores. The bump on the left represents the actual frequency of severe and profound retardation with biological causes.

biological cause. These individuals create what is referred to as a bump at the far left end of the normal curve, as shown in Figure 15.3. The bump indicates that the prevalence of mental retardation at this point in the curve is greater than would be statistically expected, other things being equal. Causes of impairment include genetic factors, infectious diseases, accidents, and environmental hazards.

Genetic or Chromosomal Anomalies Chromosomal abnormalities occur in just under 5 percent of all recognized pregnancies. The majority of these pregnancies end in spontaneous abortions or miscarriages. In all, about one-half of 1 percent of the babies who are born have a chromosomal abnormality (Smith, Bierman, & Robinson, 1978). A significant proportion of these infants die soon after birth. Of the babies who survive, the majority have **Down syndrome**, or trisomy 21.

People with Down syndrome have moderate to severe retardation as well as several distinctive physical signs, such as short and stocky stature; oval, upward-slanting eyes; a prolongation of the fold of the upper eyelid over the inner corner of the eye; sparse, fine, straight hair; a wide and flat nasal bridge; square-shaped ears; a large, furrowed tongue, which protrudes because the mouth is small and its roof low; and short, broad hands with stubby fingers.

About 40 percent of children with Down syndrome have heart problems; a small minority may have blockages of the upper intestinal tract; and about one in six dies during the first year. Mortality after age 40 is high. At autopsy, brain tissue generally shows deterioration similar to that in Alzheimer's disease. Despite having mental retardation, some of these children learn to read, write, and do arithmetic.

Down syndrome is named after the British physician Langdon Down, who first described its clinical signs in 1866. In 1959 the French geneticist Jerome Lejeune and his colleagues identified its genetic basis. Human beings normally possess 46 chromosomes, inheriting 23 from each parent. Individuals with Down syndrome almost always have 47 chromosomes instead of 46. During maturation of the egg, the two chromosomes of pair 21, the smallest ones, fail to separate. If the egg unites with a sperm, there will be three of chromosome 21-thus the technical term *trisomy 21*. Down syndrome is found in about one in 800 to 1,200 live births.

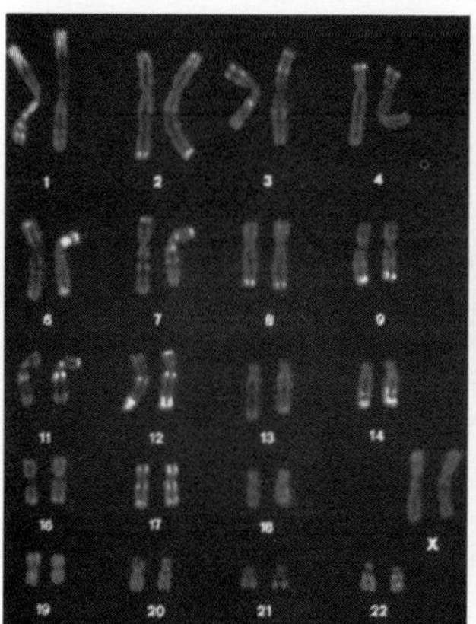
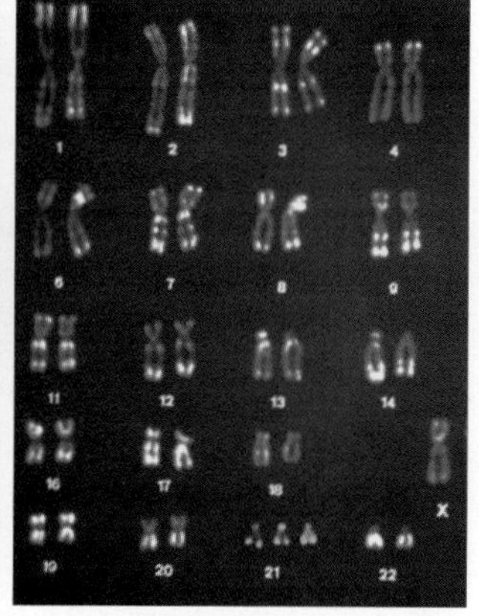

The normal complement of chromosomes is 23 pairs (left). In Down syndrome, there is a trisomy of chromosome 21 (right).

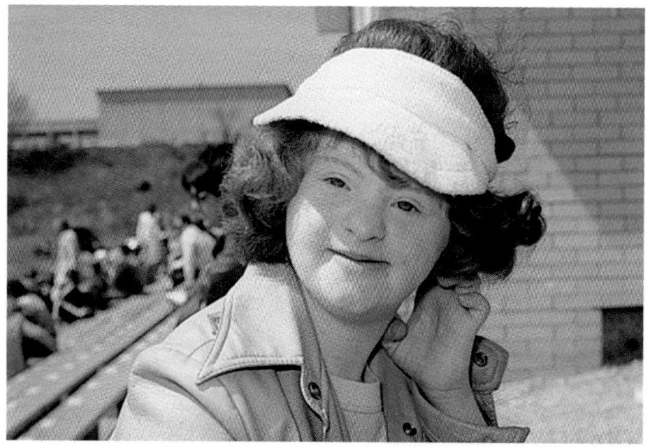

Child with Down syndrome.

Another chromosomal disease that can cause mental retardation is **fragile X syndrome**, in which the X chromosome breaks in two. Fragile X is the second leading cause, after Down syndrome, of mental retardation with a chromosomal basis (Dykens et al., 1988). Physical symptoms associated with fragile X include such facial features as large, underdeveloped ears, a long, thin face, and a broad nasal root. In males, the testicles may be enlarged. Recent studies using DNA testing have provided evidence for a spectrum of dysfunctions in individuals with different forms of fragile X (Hagerman, 1995). Many such individuals exhibit mental retardation and behaviour problems. Others have normal IQ but show such problems as learning disabilities, difficulties with frontal-lobe and right-hemisphere tasks, and mood lability. Some cases of autistic disorder may be caused by a form of fragile X. Some individuals with fragile X have very few problems but suffer social difficulties, such as shyness or poor eye contact (Dykens et al., 1988).

Recessive-Gene Diseases Several hundred recessive-gene diseases have been identified, and many of them cause mental retardation. Genetic counselling can help future parents determine whether their backgrounds suggest that they are at risk for carrying certain of these recessive genes. Here we discuss one recessive-gene disease, phenylketonuria.

In **phenylketonuria (PKU)**, the infant, born normal, soon suffers from a deficiency of a liver enzyme, phenylalanine hydroxylase. This enzyme is needed to convert phenylalanine, an amino acid found in protein, to tyrosine, an amino acid essential for the development of such hormones as epinephrine. Because of this enzyme deficiency, phenylalanine and its derivative phenylpyruvic acid are not broken down and instead build up in the body's fluids. This build-up eventually causes irreversible brain damage because the unmetabolized amino acid interferes with the process of myelination, the sheathing of neuron axons, which is essential for the rapid transmittal of impulses and thus of information. The neurons of the frontal lobes, the site of many important mental functions (e.g., rational decision-making), are particularly affected, and thus mental retardation is profound.

Although PKU is rare, with an incidence of about one in 14,000 live births, it is estimated that one person in 70 is a carrier of the recessive gene. A blood test is available for prospective parents who have reason to suspect that they might be carriers. After the newborn with PKU has consumed milk for several days, an excess amount of unconverted phenylalanine can be detected in the blood. If the test is positive, parents should provide the infant with a diet low in phenylalanine as early as possible.

Studies have indicated that children with PKU whose dietary restrictions stop at age 5 to 7 begin to show subtle declines in functioning, particularly in IQ, reading, and spelling (e.g., Legido et al., 1993). A study in Toronto showed that children with PKU and good dietary control had substantially higher comprehension scores than children with PKU and poor dietary control (Dennis et al., 1999). Even among children with PKU who maintain the diet, deficits in perceptual skills and arithmetic may emerge over time. It is especially important that pregnant women who carry the recessive gene follow the dietary regimen so that the fetus will not be exposed to toxic levels of phenylalanine (Baumeister & Baumeister, 1995).

Infectious Diseases While in utero, the fetus is at increased risk of mental retardation resulting from maternal infectious diseases such as rubella (German measles). The consequences of these diseases are most serious during the first trimester of pregnancy, when the fetus has no detectable immunological response. Cytomegalovirus, toxoplasmosis, rubella, herpes simplex, and syphilis are all maternal infections that may cause both physical deformities and mental retardation in the fetus. The mother may experience slight or no symptoms from the infection, but the effects on the developing fetus can be devastating. Pregnant women who go to prenatal clinics are given a blood test for syphilis. Women can also have their blood tested to determine whether they are immune to rubella; nearly 85 percent of North American women are. Women who are not immune should be vaccinated six months before becoming pregnant. If a fetus contracts rubella from the mother, the child is likely to be born with brain lesions that cause mental retardation.

HIV infection has become a significant cause of mental retardation. When not treated for HIV infection during pregnancy and delivery, an HIV-positive woman is more likely to pass on the virus to the developing fetus, and about half of these infected infants develop mental retardation. Some develop normally at first, but decline in their cognitive and motor functioning as their HIV condition worsens; some remain HIV-infected for many years without any impairment in intelligence.

Infectious diseases can also affect a child's developing brain after birth. Encephalitis and meningococcal meningitis may cause irreversible brain damage and even death if contracted in infancy or early childhood. These infections in adulthood are usually far less serious, probably because the brain is largely developed by about age 6. There are several forms of childhood meningitis, a disease in which the protective membranes of the brain are acutely inflamed and fever is very high. Some children who survive without severe retardation may become mildly to moderately retarded. Other disabling after-effects are deafness, paralysis, and epilepsy.

Although lead-based paint is now illegal, it can still be found in older homes. Eating these paint chips can cause lead poisoning and mental retardation.

Accidents In Canada and the United States accidents are the leading cause of severe disability and death in children over one year of age. Falls, near drowning, and automobile accidents are among the most common mishaps in early childhood, causing varying degrees of head injuries and mental retardation. The institution of laws mandating that children riding in automobiles wear seat belts and that they wear protective helmets when bicycling may play a major role in reducing the incidence of mental retardation in children.

Environmental Hazards Several environmental pollutants can cause poisoning and mental retardation. One such pollutant is mercury, which may be ingested by eating affected fish. Another is lead, which is found in lead-based paints, smog, and the exhaust from automobiles that burn leaded gasoline. Lead poisoning can cause kidney and brain damage as well as anemia, mental retardation, seizures, and death.

Prevention and Treatment of Mental Retardation

In the early part of the 20th century, many large institutions were built in Canada and the United States to house retarded individuals apart from the rest of the population. Many were no more than warehouses for anyone unfortunate enough to do poorly on newly constructed intelligence tests

Canadian Perspectives/15.5

Eugenics and the Sexual Sterilization of Canadians with Mental Retardation

"Nobody has the right to play God. Nobody."
—Leilani Muir (June 1, 1995), who was sexually sterilized as an adolescent without her knowledge or consent, under the Sexual Sterilization Act in Alberta.

In Chapter 1, we referred to C.M. Hincks and his support of the sexual sterilization of mentally ill Canadians. Throughout the 20th century, Canadians with mental retardation were often the targets of the eugenics movement. According to the proponents, elimination of the possibility that mentally retarded people would reproduce was one way of "perfecting" the gene pool.

Two provinces, Alberta and British Columbia, were particularly active in terms of the number of sexual sterilizations performed (Park & Radford, 1998; Woodhill, 1992). The Sexual Sterilization Act was approved initially in Alberta in 1928 and modified in 1937 so that any form of consent was no longer required. Overall, 2,822 people were sexually sterilized in Alberta before the act was finally repealed in 1972 (Woodhill, 1992); this included 2,102 people identified as "mental defectives" and 370 psychotics (Park & Radford, 1998). British Columbia was the only other province that put a sterilization law into place, in 1933 (McLaren, 1986). Sterilizations were also performed in other parts of Canada, even without similar laws. For instance, there are reports of mentally retarded children being sterilized at the request of their parents, and one of the authors of this text received clinical training at a site where sterilizations took place in Ontario.

Dickin and Ryan (1983) provided a cogent summary of the arguments made both for and against the sexual sterilization of mentally retarded Canadians. They outlined three main arguments put forth by those in favour of nonconsensual sterilization:

1 Sterilization of the mentally retarded serves the well-being of the handicapped individual. Mentally retarded individuals have a right to protection from participating in a role (i.e., parenting) that they are not prepared for, and they should not have to be concerned about possible pregnancies.
2 It serves the well-being of potential children (in terms of whether they will receive proper care and whether they will be at risk for mental retardation, assuming that genetic factors play a role).
3 It serves the well-being of society (in terms of decreasing the proportional incidence of mental retardation in the population—the central concern of the eugenics movement).

In response, four arguments have been raised by those vehemently opposed to sterilization:

1 Evidence for the genetic inheritance of mental retardation is not strong, and genetic theory and research does not support the unmitigated sterilization of mentally retarded people.
2 Serious human-rights violations are involved, including the right to equal treatment under the law.
3 Negative psychological consequences involving the loss of self-esteem may ensue from being sterilized and being degraded and treated as less human than other people.
4 The practice of sterilization is open to bias and discrimination such that those people who are considered "unfit" actually are fit and may not receive fair and impartial treatment.

The fourth point raised above applies to the case of Leilani Muir. Much of the focus in Canada has been on sterilizations in Alberta, partly because of the life story of Leilani Muir but also because Alberta was the province most involved in sterilizations. Ms. Muir's story is depicted in the National Film Board of Canada documentary *The Sterilization of Leilani Muir* (National Film Board of Canada, 1996).

It was often the case that people became candidates for sexual sterilization not because they were mentally deficient, but rather because they were not wanted by their families or were immigrants with language problems and thus misunderstood in terms of their actual capabilities. Leilani grew up on a farm in Alberta. She had an abusive mother who beat her, starved her, and locked her away. In 1955, at the age of 11, Leilani was essentially abandoned by her mother, who left her at the Provincial Training School for Mental Defectives in Red Deer, Alberta. Leilani's mother lied about Leilani's true mental abilities and Leilani was confined improperly for 10 years. The only IQ test she received while at the training school was administered in 1957, and she scored a 65, thereby obtaining the label "moron."

Leilani was sterilized surgically in 1957 at the age of 14. She was told that she was going to have her appendix out. According to Wahlsten (1997), the order for Muir's sterilization was signed by John MacEachran, founder of the Department of Philosophy and Psychology at the University of Alberta and chair of the Eugenics Board from 1929 to 1965. The Eugenics Board was a four-person committee that listened briefly to the children and adolescents deemed suitable for sexual sterilization and then made their decision.

Muir left the training school at the age of 21, but having been institutionalized for so long, she had difficulty functioning in the outside world. Later, she dated and married the first man she met. When she was in her mid-twenties, a medical examination determined that she had been sterilized earlier and that her "insides looked like they had been through a slaughterhouse" (National Film Board of Canada, 1996).

Leilani and her first husband eventually divorced. She remarried, and she and her second husband considered the possibility of adoption, but that fell through. He turned to alcohol and Leilani experienced depression and considered suicide.

Meanwhile, her IQ was retested several times and was always found to be in the normal range (i.e., it varied from 90 to 101).

Muir pursued legal action against the Alberta government and was awarded approximately $740,000 in 1996 and an additional $230,000 in legal costs. She became a symbol for all people who were affected by the Sexual Sterilization Act. In 1996, based on a ruling by Alberta's public trustee, hundreds of other people began comparable legal action that would lead to settlements of over $140 million. One of these people was Ken Nelson. Because of a speech impediment caused by mild cerebral palsy, he was deemed to be mentally defective while at the Michener Centre in Red Deer between 1955 and 1973 (Cooper, 1999). On those grounds, he was sterilized.

In 2003, 18 plaintiffs (17 women and 1 man) lost a lawsuit for sexual assault against the British Columbia provincial government. These people were sterilized between 1940 and 1968 at the Essondale Provincial Mental Hospital, now Riverview Hospital (Canadian Press, 2003). The plaintiffs are appealing the ruling. The lawsuit alleges that sterilizations were done for convenience and for reasons of "institutional management" in the absence of evidence that the children of the patients would inherit mental disorder and mental deficiencies.

Thinking Critically

1. The rights of mentally retarded individuals are now protected under the Charter of Rights and Freedoms. Some public opinion polls found that a significant number of people felt that Muir's family was to blame and that the government should not be held accountable. Do you think it is justified that these settlements were awarded? Is the government responsible?
2. Why do you think that Leilani's first IQ test showed that she had an IQ of 65 while at least one subsequent test showed that she had an IQ of 101? What factors could account for the discrepancy?

(Blatt, 1966). The majority of residents were recently arrived immigrants, members of ethnic or racial minorities, children with physical disabilities, and indigents.

This forced segregation did not stop couples within institutions from bearing children. The first mandatory sterilization law for women with mental retardation in the U.S. was passed in Indiana in 1907. By 1930, 28 states had these laws. Although its constitutionality was questioned, forced sterilization—especially for undereducated minority and immigrant groups—continued to be practised in many institutions through the 1950s. In the 1960s, safeguards were passed to protect the rights of individuals with mental retardation to marry and bear children. Canada's track record in this area was equally deplorable. The situation in Alberta and the tragic case of Leilani Muir are featured in Canadian Perspectives 15.5.

Current workers in the field promote the right of mentally retarded adults to freedom of sexual expression as well as to marry and have children.

Children with mental retardation are still warehoused in many parts of the world. In Russia, for example, the old Soviet ideal of "perfect children" still encourages parents to give up their disabled children to the care—actually neglect—of state-run institutions (Bennett, 1997). The cruelty and neglect experienced by children in Russian orphanages was documented in a report by the organization Human Rights Watch in December 1998 (see www.hrw.org).

Prevention of mental retardation depends on understanding its causes. The field of medical genetics is not yet equipped to prevent the more severe genetic causes of mental retardation, but startling advances in genetics may change this situation in the not-too-distant future. When the causes of mental retardation are unknown, prevention is not possible, but treatment to improve the person's ability to live on his or her own is an option. When an impoverished environment is the source of mild retardation, enrichment programs can prevent further deficits and sometimes even overcome existing ones.

Environmental Interventions and Enrichment Programs Children whose mild to moderate mental retardation is believed to have been caused by the lack of a stimulating environment can participate in such programs as Head Start. Head Start, a federally funded program in the United States, strives to prepare children, socially and culturally, to succeed in the regular school setting by giving them experiences that they may be missing at home. The impetus for the program came during the 1960s, when national attention was directed to problems of hunger and civil rights.

The core of the Head Start program is community-based preschool education that focuses on the early development of cognitive and social skills. Head Start contracts with professionals in the community to provide children with health and dental services, including vaccinations, hearing and vision testing, medical treatment, and nutrition information (North, 1979). Mental health services are another important component of these programs. Psychologists identify children with psychological problems and consult with teachers and staff to help make the preschool environment sensitive to psychological issues; for example, they share knowledge of child development, consult on an individual case, and help staff address parents' concerns (Cohen, Solnit, & Wohlford, 1979). Social workers can serve as advocates for the child's family, linking families with needed social services and encouraging parents to get involved with their children's education (Lazar, 1979).

A comparison of Head Start children with other disadvantaged youngsters who attended either a different preschool or no preschool showed that Head Start children improved significantly more than both control groups on social-cognitive ability and motor impulsivity; the relative improvement was strongest for African American children, particularly those with below average initial ability. Although the Head Start program succeeded in enhancing the functioning of the neediest children, these children were still behind their peers in terms of absolute cognitive levels after one year in the program (Lee, Brooks-Gunn, & Schnur, 1988). Other reports confirm the value of Head Start in helping poor youngsters improve their intellectual functioning (e.g., Hubbs-Tait et al., 2002).

A similar Canadian federal government initiative ("Aboriginal Head Start") was described in Chapter 1.

Residential Treatment Since the 1960s, there have been serious and systematic attempts to educate children with mental retardation as fully as possible. Most people with mental retardation can acquire the competence needed to function effectively in the community. The trend has been to provide these individuals with educational and community services rather than with largely custodial care in big mental hospitals.

Individuals with mental retardation have a right to expect appropriate treatment in the least-restrictive setting. Ideally, adults with moderate retardation live in small- to medium-sized homelike residences that are integrated into the community. Medical care is provided, and trained, live-in supervisors and aides attend to the residents' special needs around the clock. Residents are encouraged to participate in the household routines to the best of their abilities. Many adults with mild retardation have jobs and are able to live independently in their own apartments. Others live semi-independently in apartments housing three to four retarded adults, with the aid of a counsellor generally provided in the evening. Severely retarded children may live at home or in foster-care homes provided with educational and psychological services. Only people with severe and profound retardation and with physical disabilities tend to remain in institutions (Cunningham & Mueller, 1991).

Behavioural Interventions Based on Operant Conditioning Whereas programs such as Head Start can help prevent mild mental retardation, other early-intervention programs using cognitive and behavioural techniques have been developed to improve the level of functioning of individuals with more serious retardation. Several pilot projects have intervened with children with Down syndrome during infancy and early childhood in an attempt to improve their functioning. These programs typically include systematic home- and treatment-centre-based instruction in language skills, fine and gross motor skills, self-care, and social development. Specific behavioural objectives are defined, and in an operant fashion, children are taught skills in small, sequential steps (e.g., Reid, Wilson, & Faw, 1991).

Children with severe mental retardation usually need intensive instruction to be able to feed, toilet, and groom themselves. To teach a severely retarded child a particular routine, the therapist usually begins by analyzing the targeted behaviour, such as eating, and dividing it into smaller components: pick up spoon, scoop food from plate onto spoon, bring spoon to mouth, remove food with lips, chew and swallow food. Operant-conditioning principles are then applied to teach the child these components of eating. For example, the child may be reinforced for successive attempts to pick up the spoon until he or she is able to do so.

This operant approach, sometimes called **applied behaviour analysis** or ABA, is also used to reduce inappropriate and self-injurious behaviour. Children with severe and profound mental impairment who live in institutions are especially prone to performing stereotyped behaviours in isolation—repetitive, rhythmic, self-stimulatory motions, such as rocking back and forth, swaying, rolling the head—and to acting aggressively toward the self or other children and staff. These maladaptive movements and injurious actions can be reduced by reinforcing substitute responses.

Studies of these programs indicate consistent improvements in fine motor skills, acceptance by others, and self-help skills. However, the programs appear to have little effect on gross motor skills and linguistic abilities, and show no long-term improvements in IQ or school performance. It is not yet clear whether the programs provide greater benefits than can be provided in the home by parents with no special training (Gibson & Harris, 1988).

The significance of learning self-care and of reducing stereotyped and injurious actions in people with severe or profound retardation must be recognized. Toilet-trained children, for example, are more comfortable, are liked better by the staff and by other children, and can leave the ward for other rooms and leave the building to play on the grounds. Mastering toilet training and learning to feed and dress themselves may even mean that children with mental retardation can live at home. Most people with mental retardation face discrimination from others, based in part on violations of social norms. Being able to act more normally increases their chances of interacting meaningfully with others. Moreover, the self-esteem that comes from learning to take better care of themselves is extremely bolstering.

Cognitive Interventions Many children with mental retardation fail to use strategies in solving problems, and when they do have strategies, they often apply them ineffectively. **Self-instructional training** teaches these children to guide their problem-solving efforts through speech. Meichenbaum and Goodman (1971) outlined a five-step procedure:

Computer-assisted instruction is well suited for application in the field of mental retardation.

1 The teacher performs the task, speaking instructions aloud to himself or herself while the child watches and listens.
2 The child listens and performs the task while the teacher says instructions to the child.
3 The child repeats the task while giving himself or herself instructions aloud.
4 The child repeats the task again while whispering the instructions.
5 Finally, the child is ready to perform the task while uttering instructions silently to himself or herself.

Children with more severe retardation use signs rather than speech to guide themselves through the tasks.

Self-instructional training has been employed to teach retarded children self-control as well as how to pay attention and how to master academic tasks. Children with severe retardation can effectively master self-help skills through this technique. Hughes, Hugo, and Blatt (1996), for example, taught high school students with IQs below 40 to make their own buttered toast and clean up after themselves. A teacher would demonstrate and verbalize the steps to solving a problem, such as a toaster being upside down or unplugged. The children learned to talk themselves through the steps using simple verbal or signed instructions. When the toaster was presented upside down, the child would be taught to first state the problem ("Won't go in"), state the response ("Turn it"), self-evaluate ("Fixed it"), and self-reinforce ("Good"). Children were rewarded with praise and high fives when they verbalized and solved the problem correctly. Several studies have demonstrated that even individuals with severe mental retardation can learn self-instructional approaches to problem-solving and then generalize the strategy to new tasks (Hughes & Agran, 1993).

Of course, the benefits of self-instruction are not limited to children. Researchers in Kingston, Ontario, demonstrated that self-instructional manuals are effective in teaching child care skills to mothers with mild mental retardation (Feldman, Ducharme, & Case, 1999).

Computer-Assisted Instruction Computer-assisted instruction is increasingly found in educational settings of all kinds. It is especially well suited to the education of individuals with mental retardation. The visual and auditory components of computers maintain the attention of distractible students; the level of the material can be geared to the individual, ensuring successful experiences; and the computer can meet the need for numerous repetitions of material. Computer-assisted instruction programs have been shown to be superior to traditional methods for teaching people with mental retardation spelling, money handling, arithmetic, text reading, word recognition, handwriting, and visual discrimination (Conners, Caruso, & Detterman, 1986).

AUTISTIC DISORDER

A psychology student walks into a special-education classroom for children. She is taking a course on child disabilities, and one requirement is to volunteer some time in this class. As several children rise to greet her, she becomes aware of their minor or major physical characteristics. One child has slanted eyes and a flat nose, typical of Down syndrome. Another makes spastic movements, a sign of cerebral palsy. A third child calls to her from a wheelchair with grunting noises and communicates with a combination of hand gestures and pictures.

Then this psychology student notices a fourth child in the room, standing in front of the fish tank. She approaches him and notices his graceful, deft movements, the dreamy, remote look in his eyes. She wonders if he is a visitor to the class or a sibling of one of the students. She starts talking to him about the fish. Instead of acknowledging her comment or even her presence, he begins rocking back and forth while continuing to smile, as if enjoying a private joke. When the teacher enters the room, she tells the psychology student that he is autistic.

CHARACTERISTICS OF AUTISTIC DISORDER

From the time it was first distinguished, autistic disorder has had a somewhat mystical aura. The syndrome was identified in 1943 by a Harvard psychiatrist, Leo Kanner, who noticed in his clinical work that 11 disturbed children behaved in ways that were uncommon in children with mental retardation or schizophrenia. He named the syndrome early infantile autism because he noted that "there is from the start an extreme autistic aloneness that, whenever possible, disregards, ignores, shuts out anything that comes to the child from the outside" (Kanner, 1943).

Kanner considered autistic aloneness the most fundamental symptom. He also found that these 11 children had been unable from the beginning of life to relate to people in the ordinary way. They were severely limited in language and had a strong obsessive desire for everything about them to remain exactly the same. Despite its early description by Kanner and others (e.g., Rimland, 1964), the disorder was not accepted into official diagnostic nomenclature until the publication of DSM-III in 1980.

Official acceptance of the diagnosis was delayed by general confusion in the classification of serious disorders that begin in childhood. DSM-II used the diagnosis of childhood schizophrenia for these conditions, implying that autism was simply an early-onset form of adult schizophrenia, but the available evidence indicates that childhood-onset schizophrenia and autism are separate disorders (Frith, 1989; Rutter & Schopler, 1987). Although the social withdrawal and inappropriate affect seen in autistic children may appear similar to the negative symptoms of schizophrenia, autistic children do not exhibit hallucinations and delusions and do not grow up to become schizophrenic adults (Wing & Attwood, 1987). Further, people with autism do not have a higher prevalence of schizophrenia in their families, as do children and adults with schizophrenia. Other features associated with autism but not with schizophrenia include a higher male-female ratio (more boys than girls have autism), onset in infancy or very early childhood, and co-occurrence of mental retardation and epileptic seizures.

In part to clarify the differentiation of autism from schizophrenia, DSM-III introduced (and DSM-III-R and DSM-IV and DSM-IV-TR have retained) the term **pervasive developmental disorders**. This term emphasized that autism involves a serious abnormality in the developmental process itself and thus differs from the mental disorders that originate in adulthood. In DSM-IV-TR, autistic disorder is but one of several pervasive developmental disorders; the others are Rett's disorder, child disintegrative disorder, and Asperger's syndrome.

- Rett's disorder is very rare and found only in girls. Development is entirely normal until the first or second year of life, when the child's head growth decelerates. She loses the ability to use her hands for purposeful movements, instead engaging in stereotyped movements such as hand-wringing or handwashing; walks in an uncoordinated manner; learns only poorly to speak and understand others; and is profoundly retarded. The child relates poorly to others, though this may improve later in life.
- Childhood disintegrative disorder occurs in children who have had normal development in the first two years of life but then suffer significant loss of social, play, language, and motor skills. Abnormalities in social interaction and communication and the presence of stereotyped behaviour are very similar to those in autism.
- Asperger's syndrome is often regarded as a mild form of autism. Social relationships are poor and stereotyped behaviour is intense and rigid, but language and intelligence are intact. Extensive research on Asperger's syndrome has been conducted by Peter Szatmari and his research team, who are part of the Centre for Studies of Children at Risk described in Canadian Perspectives 15.1. They have conducted comparative research on Asperger's syndrome and autism to address the controversy over whether Asperger's disorder should be a separate diagnostic entity or viewed as a less severe form of autism. There are some subtle but important differences between the two disorders. One key difference is that children with Asperger's syndrome have better communication skills than children with autism (Szatmari, 1995). One study compared 21 children with either Asperger's syndrome or autism and found that those with Asperger's had higher levels of language competence but that the two groups did not differ in nonverbal communication and nonverbal cognition (Szatmari et al., 1995). A longitudinal study of autism versus Asperger's in children found that the children with Asperger's had better social skills and fewer autistic symptoms two years after being in the study than the autistic children (Szatmari et al., 2000). Overall, on the basis of her review of empirical evidence, Mary Konstantereas (2001) from the University of Guelph concluded that Asperger's syndrome is distinct from high-functioning autism. However, causative factors distinguishing autism and Asperger's syndrome have not been identified (Szatmari, 2003).

Because these newly included categories have received less empirical attention, our focus here is on autism.

Autistic disorder begins in early childhood and can be evident in the first months of life. Current estimates indicate that, in the general population, autism occurs in 16 infants in 10,000, or 0.16 percent of births (Szatmari, 2003). To put this in perspective, recall that the prevalence of schizophrenia is estimated at a little less than 1 percent, more than six times greater. However, the prevalence rises to 63 per 10,000 when all autistic spectrum disorders are included (Szatmari, 2003). Studies show that about 4.3 times more boys than girls have autism (Fombonne, 2003). Comorbidity is high, with depression, anxiety, and ADHD being common (Tidmarsh & Volkmar, 2003). Autism is found in all socio-economic classes and in all ethnic and racial groups.

Autism and Mental Retardation Approximately 80 percent of autistic children score below 70 on standardized IQ tests, and it is sometimes difficult to differentiate autism and mental retardation. There are important differences, however. Although children with mental retardation usually score poorly on all parts of an intelligence test, the scores of children with autism may have a differentiated pattern. Generally, children with autism do worse on tasks requiring abstract thought, symbolism, or sequential logic, all of which may be associated with their language deficits (Carpentieri & Morgan, 1994). They usually obtain better scores on items requiring visual-spatial skills, such as matching designs in block-design tests and putting together disassembled objects (Rutter, 1983). In addition, they may have isolated skills that reflect great talent, such as the ability to multiply two four-digit numbers rapidly in their heads. They may also have exceptional long-term memory, being able to recall the exact words of a song heard years earlier. Sensorimotor develop-

Table 15.4

Parental Report of Social Relatedness in Autistic Children Before Age 6

	Percentage of Responses				
Relatedness Measure	**Never**	**Rarely**	**Often**	**Very Often**	**Almost Always**
1. Ignored people	0	4	22	29	45
2. Emotionally distant	0	8	23	19	50
3. Avoided eye contact	2	4	20	16	58
4. No affection or interest when held	11	11	35	26	17
5. Going limp when held	30	33	17	17	2
6. Stiff/rigid when held	33	24	7	18	18
7. Ignored affection	6	30	34	11	19
8. Withdrew from affection	12	33	29	10	15
9. Cuddling when held	26	24	29	10	15
10. Accept/return affection	30	34	26	4	6
11. Looked through people	4	10	22	22	41
12. Seemed not to need mother	12	20	32	8	28
13. Responsive smile to mother	14	30	30	14	12
14. Unaware of mother's absence	17	25	25	14	19

Source: Adapted from F.R. Volkmar, D.J. Cohen, and R. Paul, 1986. "An Evaluation of DSM-III Criteria for Infantile Autism," *Journal of the American Academy of Child Psychiatry*, 25, p. 193. Copyright (c) 1986 by the American Academy of Child Psychiatry. Adapted by permission..

ment is the area of greatest relative strength among children with autism. These children, who may show severe or profound deficits in cognitive abilities, can be quite graceful and adept at swinging, climbing, or balancing, whereas children with mental retardation are much more delayed in areas of gross-motor development (e.g., learning to walk).

Extreme Autistic Aloneness In a sense, autistic children do not withdraw from society—they never joined it to begin with. Table 15.4 shows how they have been described by their parents.

Normally infants show signs of attachment, usually to their mothers, as early as three months of age. In children with autism, this early attachment is less pronounced. Parents of autistic children must work harder to make contact and share affection with their babies. Autistic children rarely try to engage their parents in play, and they do not point to, show, or share objects of play with others.

Children with autism rarely approach others and may look through or past people or turn their backs on them. One study found that autistic children rarely offered a spontaneous greeting or farewell, either verbally or through smiling, making eye contact, or gesturing, when meeting or departing from an adult (Hobson & Lee, 1998). However, when play is initiated by someone else, autistic children may be compliant and engage in the selected activity for a period of time. Physical play, such as tickling and wrestling, may be enjoyable to children with autism. Observations of their spontaneous play in an unstructured setting reveal that children with autism spend much less of their time engaged in symbolic play, such as making a doll drive to the store or pretending that a block is a car, than do either mentally retarded or normal children of comparable mental age (Sigman et al., 1987). Autistic children are more likely to twirl a favourite block continually for hours on end.

Few children with autism initiate play with other children, and they are usually unresponsive to any who may approach them. Children with autism do make eye contact, but their gaze has a different quality. Normal children gaze to gain someone's attention or to direct the other person's attention to an object; autistic children generally do not (Mirenda, Donnellan, & Yoder, 1983)-they just stare.

Some autistic children appear not to recognize or distinguish one person from another. They become preoccupied with and form strong attachments to inanimate objects (e.g., keys, rocks, a wire-mesh basket, light switches, a large blanket) and to mechanical objects (e.g., refrigerators, vacuum cleaners). If the object is something they can carry, they may walk around with it in their hands, which keeps them from learning to do more useful things.

It may be that the autistic child's social isolation is the source of his or her retarded development in other areas, such as language (Kanner, 1943). On the other hand, the core deficit may be an inability to process certain kinds of sensory input, leaving the child incapable of understanding and responding to the world around him or her (Ornitz, 1989).

Some researchers have proposed that a deficiency in the autistic child's "theory of mind" represents the core deficit and leads to the kinds of social dysfunctions we have described here (Sigman, 1994). *Theory of mind* refers to our understanding that other people have desires, beliefs, intentions, and emotions that may be different from our own. Children with autism seem unable to understand others' perspectives and emotional reactions; they lack empathy. When a parent shows distress or pain, the child with autism withdraws rather than show concern; this withdrawal may indicate the child's inability to understand and empathize with another's feelings. Although high-functioning autistic children can learn to understand emotional experiences, they "answer questions about . . . emotional experiences like normal children answer difficult arithmetic questions" (Sigman, 1994, p. 15), with concentrated cognitive effort.

Communication Deficits Even before they acquire language, autistic children show deficits in communication. Babbling, a term describing the utterances of infants before they actually begin to use words, is less frequent in infants with autism and conveys less information than it does in other infants (Ricks, 1972). By 2 years of age, most normally developing children use words to represent objects in their surroundings and construct one- and two-word sentences to express more complex thoughts, such as "Mommy go" or "Me juice." About 50 percent of all autistic children never learn to speak at all (Paul, 1987; Rutter, 1966). The speech of those who do learn includes various peculiarities.

One such feature is **echolalia**, in which the child echoes, usually with remarkable fidelity, what he or she has heard another person say. The teacher may ask an autistic child, "Do you want a cookie?" The child's response may be "Do you want a cookie?" This is immediate echolalia. In delayed echolalia, the child may be in a room with the television on and appear to be completely uninterested. Several hours later or even the next day, the child may echo a word or phrase from the television program. Mute autistic children who later acquire some functional speech through training usually first pass through a stage of echolalia.

In the past, most educators and researchers believed that echolalia served no functional purpose. Echolalia may, however, be an attempt to communicate (Prizant, 1983). The child who was offered a cookie may decide later that he or she does want one. The child will approach the teacher and ask, "Do you want a cookie?" Although the child may not know what each individual word means, he or she has learned that the phrase is connected with getting a cookie.

Another abnormality common in the speech of autistic children is **pronoun reversal**. Children refer to themselves as "he," "she," or "you" or by their own proper names. Pronoun reversal is closely linked to echolalia. Since autistic children often use echolalic speech, they refer to themselves as they have heard others speak of them. For example:

Parent: What are you doing, Johnny?

Child: He's here.

Parent: Are you having a good time?

Child: He knows it.

If speech continues to develop more normally, this pronoun reversal might disappear. In most instances, however, it is highly resistant to change (Tramontana & Stimbert, 1970). Some children have required very extensive training even after they have stopped parroting the phrases of other people.

Neologisms, made-up words or words used in unusual ways, are another characteristic of the speech of autistic children. A 2-year-old autistic child might refer to milk as "moyee" and continue to do so well beyond the time when a normal child has learned to say "milk."

Children with autism are very literal in their use of words. If a father provided positive reinforcement by putting the child on his shoulders when he or she learned to say the word "yes," then the child might say yes to mean that he or she wants to be lifted onto the father's shoulders. Or the child may say, "Do not drop the cat" to mean "no," because his or her mother had used these emphatic words when the child was about to drop the family feline.

These communication deficiencies may be the source of the social retardation in children with autism rather than the other way around. Such a causal relationship is made plausible by the often spontaneous appearance of affectionate and dependent behaviour in these children after they have been trained to speak (e.g., Churchill, 1969). Even after they learn to speak, however, people with autism often lack verbal spontaneity, are sparse in their verbal expression, and do not always use language appropriately (Paul, 1987).

Obsessive-Compulsive and Ritualistic Acts Children with autism become extremely upset over changes in their daily routines and surroundings. An offer of milk in a different drinking cup or a rearrangement of furniture may make them cry or precipitate a temper tantrum. One child had to be greeted with the set phrase "Good morning, Lily, I am very, very glad to see you." If any word, even one "very," was omitted, or another added, the child would begin to scream (Diamond, Baldwin, & Diamond, 1963).

An obsessional quality pervades the behaviour of autis-

Autistic children frequently engage in stereotyped behaviour, such as ritualistic hand movements.

tic children in other ways. In their play, they may continually line up toys or construct intricate patterns with household objects. As they grow older, they may become preoccupied with train schedules and number sequences.

Children with autism are also given to stereotypical behaviour, peculiar ritualistic hand movements, and other rhythmic movements, such as endless body rocking, hand flapping, and walking on tiptoe. They spin and twirl string, crayons, sticks, and plates, twiddle their fingers in front of their eyes, and stare at fans and spinning things. These are often described as self-stimulatory activities. They may become preoccupied with manipulating a mechanical object and be very upset when interrupted.

Prognosis for Autistic Disorder What happens to such severely disturbed children when they reach adulthood? Kanner (1973) reported on the adult status of nine of the 11 children whom he had described in his original paper on autism. Two developed epileptic seizures; one of these died, and the other was in a state mental hospital. Four others had spent most of their lives in institutions. Of the remaining three, one was still mute but was working on a farm and as an orderly in a nursing home. The other two showed considerable improvement. Although both still lived with their parents and had little social life, they were gainfully employed and had developed some recreational interests.

Early follow-up studies corroborated this generally gloomy picture of adults with autism (e.g., Treffert, McAndrew, & Dreifuerst, 1973). From his review of all published studies, Lotter (1978) concluded that only 5 to 17 percent of autistic children had made a relatively good adjustment in adulthood, leading independent lives but with some residual problems, such as social awkwardness. Most of the others led limited lives, and about half were institutionalized.

Similar outcomes have been found in more recent population-based, follow-up studies (e.g., von Knorring & Hagglof, 1993). Generally, children with higher IQs who learned to speak before age 6 have the best outcome, and a few of these function nearly normally in adulthood. Follow-up studies focusing on non-mentally retarded, high-functioning autistic individuals have indicated that most do not require residential care and some even attend college and support themselves through employment (Yirmiya & Sigman, 1991).

Prior to the passage in the United States of the Developmentally Disabled Assistance and Bill of Rights Act in 1975 and similar laws in Canada at about the same time (see Bowlby & Regan, 1998, for a discussion of federal [e.g., the 1981 Canadian Charter of Rights and Freedoms] and provincial human rights legislation; and Bowlby, Peters, & Mackinnon, 2001, for a discussion of special-education laws for "exceptional" children), children with autism (and other children with special needs) were often excluded from educational programs in the public schools. Thus, most of the autistic children followed into adulthood had not had the benefit of intensive educational interventions or behavioural programs. In contrast, newer studies involving early, intensive interventions paint a considerably more promising picture. After reviewing several new studies on early detection and early interventions, often in school settings, and a group of Canadian authors (Bryson, Rogers, & Fombonne, 2003) indicated that they share the conclusion reached by several international groups: [It seems that] outcomes for children with autism can be significantly enhanced by offering many hours weekly of targeted and individualized teaching that is carefully planned, delivered, and monitored.... It seems clear that we must leave behind several truisms about autism, including the assumptions that 50% of affected children will not speak, and 75% will have mental retardation. These older findings need to be considered as reflecting untreated children with autism, rather than as the expected course and outcome for children with autism today" (p. 511).

Etiology of Autistic Disorder

The earliest theorizing about the etiology of autism was that it was psychogenic, that is, that psychological factors were responsible for its development. This narrow perspective has been replaced in recent years by speculation about and evidence supporting the importance of biological factors, some of them genetic, in the etiology of this puzzling syndrome.

Psychological Bases Some of the same reasons that led Kanner to believe that autistic children were of average intelligence—their normal appearance and apparently normal physiological functioning—led early theorists to discount the importance of biological factors. People may have assumed tacitly that for a biological cause to underlie something as devastating as autism, it would have other obvious signs, such as the physical stigmata of Down syndrome.

Thus, the early focus was on psychological factors, primarily family influences very early in life.

Psychoanalytic Theories One of the best known of the psychological theories was formulated by Bruno Bettelheim (1967), who worked extensively with autistic children. His basic supposition was that autism closely resembles the apathy and hopelessness found among inmates of German concentration camps during World War II and that therefore something very negative must take place in early childhood. Bettelheim hypothesized that the young infant with rejecting parents is able to perceive their negative feelings. The infant finds that his or her own actions have little impact on the parents' unresponsiveness. The child thus comes to believe "that [his or her] own efforts have no power to influence the world, because of the earlier conviction that the world is insensitive to [his or her] reactions" (Bettelheim, 1967, p. 46). The autistic child never really enters the world but builds the "empty fortress" of autism against pain and disappointment.

A more recent psychoanalytic theory proposes that autism is an infantile version of PTSD (Tustin, 1994). When the breast-feeding mother and vulnerable child are overly close, weaning feels like a catastrophic and traumatic separation. As a result, the infant develops a "deadening insulation," which is the autistic behaviour.

Another psychoanalytic theory, called the intersubjective theory, asserts that autism results when a biologically vulnerable child has an anxious or preoccupied mother who is unable to read the cues of her unusually difficult baby (Roser & Buchholz, 1996).

Behavioural Theory Some behavioural theorists have postulated that certain childhood learning experiences cause autism. In an extremely influential article, Ferster (1961) suggested that the inattention of the parents, especially of the mother, prevents establishment of the associations that make human beings social reinforcers. Because the parents have not become reinforcers, they cannot control the child's behaviour, and the result is autistic disorder.

Evaluation of Psychological Theories of Autistic Disorder Both Bettelheim and Ferster, as well as others, have stated that parents play the crucial role in the etiology of autism. Many investigators have therefore studied the characteristics of these parents. For a psychogenic theory of a childhood disorder to have any plausibility at all, something very unusual and damaging about the parents' treatment of their children would have to be demonstrated.

Kanner described the parents of autistic children as cold, insensitive, meticulous, introverted, distant, and highly intellectual (Kanner & Eisenberg, 1955). Systematic investigations, however, have failed to confirm these clinical impressions (e.g., Cantwell, Baker, & Rutter, 1978); moreover, such parents raise other normal and healthy siblings.

Even if we ignore these findings, the direction of a possible correlation between parental characteristics and autism is not easily determined. As noted in earlier discussions of ADHD and many other disorders, any deviant parental behaviour could be a reaction to the child's abnormality rather than the other way around. Overall, there is no evidence that the family life of autistic children is characterized by the kind of extreme emotional maltreatment, deprivation, or neglect that could conceivably produce behaviour resembling the dramatically pathological symptoms of autism (Ornitz, 1973; Wing, 1976).

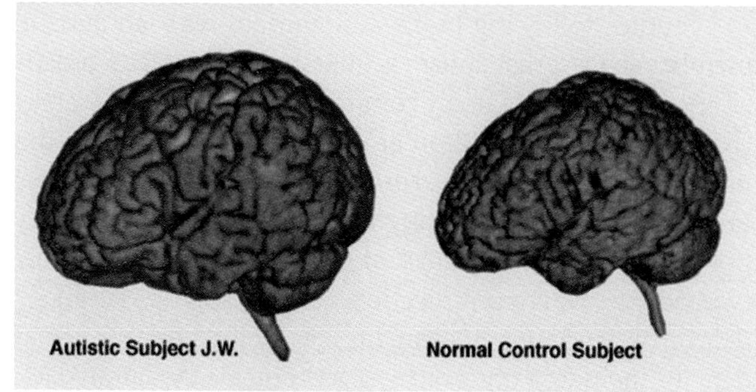

A case of extreme macroencephaly. The 3-D MRI image of 3.4-year-old autistic subject J.W. (left) is compared to that of a normal male child whose brain volume was scaled to equal normal average size (right). J.W.'s brain volume (1816 ml) was much larger than the normal average (1162 ml) for his age.

The early popularity of psychogenic hypotheses may have had an unintended negative consequence (Rimland, 1964). Consider, for a moment, what your feelings might be if a psychiatrist or psychologist were to tell you that your unconscious hostility has caused your child to be mute at the age of 6. Over the years, a tremendous emotional burden has been placed on parents who have been told that, on the basis of psychogenic theories, they are at fault.

Biological Bases The very early onset of autism, along with an accumulation of neurological and genetic evidence, strongly implicates a biological basis for this disorder.

Genetic Factors Genetic studies of autism are difficult to conduct because the disorder is so rare. The family method presents special problems because autistic persons almost never marry. Nonetheless, emerging evidence strongly suggests a genetic basis for autistic disorder. The risk of autism in the siblings of people with the disorder is about 75 times greater than it is if the index case does not have autistic disorder (McBride, Anderson, & Shapiro, 1996). Even stronger evidence for genetic transmission of autism comes from twin studies, which have found 60 to 91 percent concordance for autism between identical twins, compared with concordance rates of 0 to 20 percent in fraternal twins (e.g., Bailey et al., 1995; LeCouteur et al., 1996). According to Nicholson and Szatmari (2003), autism is the most heritable psychiatric disorder, with heritability estimates (i.e., the extent to which clinical variance is due to genetic factors) that are even higher than those for schizophrenia and bipolar disorder.

Studies following twins and families with an autistic member suggest that autism is linked genetically to a broader spectrum of deficits in communicative and social areas (Bailey et al., 1995; Bolton et al., 1994). For example, the nonautistic identical twin of an autistic adult is almost always unable to live independently or maintain a confiding relationship. In addition, most of these nonautistic identical twins evidence communication deficits, such as language delays or reading impairments, as well as severe social deficits, including no social contacts outside the family, lack of responsiveness to social cues or conventions, and little or no spontaneous affection with caregivers. In contrast, the nonidentical twin of an autistic child is almost always normal in social and language development and marries and lives independently in adulthood (LeCouteur et al., 1996). Taken together, the evidence from family and twin studies strongly supports a genetic basis for autistic disorder.

Neurological Factors Early EEG studies of autistic children indicated that many had abnormal brain-wave patterns (e.g., Hutt et al., 1964). Other types of neurological examinations also revealed signs of damage in many autistic children (e.g., Gillberg & Svendsen, 1983). Studies using magnetic resonance imaging (MRI) showed that autistic people have larger brains than normal people (Hardan et al., 2001; Sparks et al., 2002); as noted by Nicolson and Szatmari (2003), this is unique to autism, as other neurodevelopmental disorders and mental retardation are associated with reduced brain volume. Further evidence supporting the possibility of brain dysfunction derives from 16 MRI and autopsy studies from nine independent research groups, all finding abnormalities in the cerebellum of autistic children (Haas et al., 1996). Studies of neurological patients indicate that those with parietal damage have a greatly narrowed attentional focus and those with damage to the cerebellum are unable to shift their attention quickly. Therefore, it is possible that the specific areas of brain dysfunction found in people with autism may partly explain their observed lack of response to information outside their attentional focus (Haas et al., 1996).

Jenna Flanagan, a child with autism, experiences the Snoezelen Room at Magnetic Hill School in Moncton N.B. The room has soft, soothing lights that shift colours continually, and various tactile oriented surfaces.

In adolescence, 30 percent of those who had severe autistic symptoms as children begin having epileptic seizures, another sign that a brain defect is involved in the disorder. The prevalence of autism in children whose mothers had rubella during the prenatal period is approximately 10 times higher than in the general population of children, and we know that rubella in the mother during pregnancy can harm the developing fetus's brain. A syndrome similar to autism sometimes follows in the aftermath of meningitis (a bacterial disease which causes inflammation of the membrane enveloping the brain), encephalitis (inflammation of the brain), fragile-X, and tuberous sclerosis (a hardening of brain tissue), all of which may affect central nervous system functioning. These findings, together with the degree of mental retardation commonly found in autism, seem to link autism and brain damage (Courchesne et al., 1988).

Treatment of Autistic Disorder

Because their isolation is so moving and their symptoms so pronounced, a great deal of attention has been given to trying to improve the condition of children with autism. As with theories of etiology, the earliest efforts were psychological in nature, and some of them have shown considerable promise. More recently, various psychopharmacotherapies have been studied as well, with few positive results. Treatments for autistic children usually try to reduce their un-usual behaviour and improve their communication and social skills. Sometimes an eagerly sought-after goal for a family is simply to be able to take their autistic child to a restaurant or market without attracting negative attention.

Special Problems in Treating Children with Autism Children with autism have several characteristics that make teaching them difficult. First, they do not adjust well to changes in routine, yet change is the essence of treatment. Second, their isolation and self-stimulatory movements may interfere with effective teaching. Although the similar behaviour of children with other disabilities may intrude on the teacher's efforts, it does not do so with the same frequency and severity.

Third, it is particularly difficult to find ways to motivate children with autism. To be effective with these children, reinforcers must be explicit, concrete, and highly salient. A widely used way to increase the range of reinforcers that autistic children respond to is to pair social reinforcement, such as praise, with primary reinforcers, such as a highly desired food (Davison, 1964).

A further problem that often interferes with the learning of children with autism is their overselectivity of attention. When the child's attention becomes focused on one particular aspect of a task or situation, other properties, including relevant ones, may not be noticed (Lovaas et al., 1971). This overselectivity makes it especially difficult for the children to generalize or apply their learning to other areas. For example, the child who has learned several words by watching the instructor's lip movements may not comprehend the same words spoken by another person with less-pronounced lip movements.

In spite of these problems, educational programs for students with autism have achieved some positive results, and we turn to these now.

Behavioural Treatment of Children with Autism Using modelling and operant conditioning, behaviour therapists have taught autistic children to talk (Hewett, 1965), modified their echolalic speech (Carr, Schreibman, & Lovaas, 1975), encouraged them to play with other children (Romanczyk et al., 1975), and helped them become more generally responsive to adults (Davison, 1964).

Ivar Lovaas, a leading clinical researcher at the University of California at Los Angeles, conducted an intensive operant program with very young (under 4 years old) autistic children (Lovaas, 1987). Therapy encompassed all aspects of the children's lives for more than 40 hours a week over more than two years. Parents were trained extensively so that treatment could continue during almost all the children's waking hours. Nineteen children receiving this intensive treatment were compared with 40 control youngsters who received a similar treatment for less than 10 hours per week. All children were rewarded for being less aggressive, more compliant, and more socially appropriate—for example, talking and playing with other children. The goal of the program was to mainstream the children, the assumption being that autistic children, as they improve, benefit more from being with normal peers than from remaining by themselves or with other seriously disturbed children.

The results of this landmark study were dramatic and encouraging for the intensive-therapy group. Their measured IQs averaged 83 in grade 1 (after about two years in the intensive therapy) compared with about 55 for the control children; 12 of the 19 reached the normal range, compared with only two (of forty) in the control group. Furthermore, nine of the 19 in the intensive-therapy group were promoted to grade 2 in a regular public school, whereas only one of the much larger control group achieved this level of normal functioning. A follow-up of these children four years later indicated that the intensive-treatment group maintained their gains in IQ, adaptive behaviour, and grade promotions in school (McEachin, Smith, & Lovaas, 1993). Although critics have pointed out weaknesses in the study's methodology and outcome measures (Schopler, Short, & Mesibov, 1989), this ambitious program confirms the benefits of the heavy involvement of both professionals and parents in dealing with the extreme challenge of autistic disorder.

Ivar Lovaas is noted for his operant-conditioning treatment of autistic children.

There is reason to believe that the education provided by parents is more beneficial to the child than clinic- or hospital-based treatment. Parents are present in many different situations and thus can help children generalize the gains they make. Koegel and his colleagues (1982) demonstrated that 25 to 30 hours of parent training was as effective as 200 hours of direct clinic treatment in improving the behaviour of autistic children. Subsequently, Koegel's research group compared different strategies for behavioural parent training, with interesting discoveries. While parents had traditionally been taught to focus on changing individually targeted problem behaviours in a sequential manner, Koegel, Bimbela, and Schreibman (1996) found that they could be more effective when taught to focus on increasing their autistic children's general motivation and responsiveness. For example, allowing the child to choose the teaching materials, providing natural reinforcers (e.g., play and social praise) instead of edible reinforcers, and reinforcing attempts to respond as well as correct responses all led to improved family interactions and the parents' more positive communication with their autistic children.

It must be clearly understood, however, that some autistic and other severely disturbed children can be adequately cared for only in a hospital or in a group home staffed by mental health professionals. Moreover, the circumstances of some families preclude the home care of a seriously disturbed child. That effective treatments can be implemented by parents does not mean that this is the appropriate course for all families.

Psychodynamic Treatment of Children with Autism Because he viewed attachment difficulties and emotional deprivation as the sources of autism, Bruno Bettelheim (1967, 1974) argued that a warm, loving atmosphere must be created to encourage the child to enter the world. Patience and what Rogerians would call unconditional positive regard were believed to be necessary conditions for the child with autism to begin to trust others and to take chances in establishing relationships. At his Orthogenic School at the University of

Chicago, Bettelheim and his colleagues reported many instances of success, but the uncontrolled nature of their observations makes it difficult to evaluate their claims. Furthermore, the accuracy of Bettelheim's reports on the procedures used and the successes achieved with the students at his school have been called into question, casting serious doubt on the validity of his claims (Gardner, 1997; Pollak, 1997).

Drug Treatment of Children with Autism The most commonly used medication for treating problem behaviours in autistic children is haloperidol (brand name Haldol), an antipsychotic medication frequently used in the treatment of schizophrenia. Some controlled studies have shown that this drug reduces social withdrawal, stereotyped motor behaviour, and maladaptive behaviour, such as self-mutilation and aggression (Anderson et al., 1989; McBride et al., 1996; Perry et al., 1989), and a more recent Canadian study showed that it was superior to clomipramine (Remington et al., 2001). Many autistic children do not respond positively to this drug, however, and it has not shown any positive effects on other aspects of autistic disorder, such as abnormal interpersonal relationships and language impairment (Holm & Varley, 1989). Haloperidol also has potentially serious side effects. One study showed that over 30 percent of autistic children developed drug-related dyskinesias, or jerky muscle disturbances, although most were reversible after the drug was withdrawn (Campbell et al., 1997). Recent efforts to substitute olanzapine, an atypical neuroleptic, showed it

Canadian Perspectives/15.6

The Canadian Autism Intervention Research Network (CAIRN): Early Detection and Intervention?

The prognosis for autism remains poor in general, despite the fact that some psychological interventions have shown promise. Can autism and other pervasive developmental disorders be detected at an early age and the diagnosis be followed by intervention leading to more favourable outcomes? As we have seen, autism is usually detected at an early age (typically before the age of 2 and a half). But can we detect signs of the disorder even earlier and then develop interventions that will prevent or minimize the development of some or all of the major symptoms? One recent initiative in Canada under the direction of Peter Szatmari with the Centre for Studies of Children at Risk (CSCR) is named "CAIRN: The Canadian Autism Intervention Research Network." CAIRN is a national network of researchers who share a focused interest in early intervention. It involves researchers from numerous disciplines, including psychiatry, psychology, pediatrics, education, speech and language pathology, and early childhood education.

The objective of CAIRN was spelled out during a network workshop held in Toronto, November 11–12, 2000: "to bring together various stakeholders in developing a research agenda and then to provide high quality evidence in early intervention to insure long-term outcomes for children with autism spectrum disorders (see http://www.fhs.mcmaster.ca/cscr)."

It is generally agreed, of course, that early intervention with the pervasive developmental disorders (as with all disorders) is extremely important and can have a favourable impact on long-term outcomes. However, the members of CAIRN identified two serious problems with the current status of the clinical treatment literature: (1) systematic reviews have pointed to significant limitations to the available evidence on the effectiveness of various early intervention programs for autism, and (2) research experts, front-line clinicians, and the parents of children with pervasive developmental disorders often disagree about what form early interventions should take and what strategies appear to work. Regarding the latter point, there is clearly great variation in the type and availability of programs across the country. It was concluded that there is an urgent need in Canada for new research to inform important treatment decisions involving young children who show symptoms of autism spectrum disorders.

Members of CAIRN have taken on the shared responsibility of advocating for increased research on early intervention and additional training for those physicians and clinicians in a position to detect these disorders in young children.

Although an effective early intervention has yet to be developed, CAIRN is currently pursuing two major issues. First, families with two or more children with autism are being asked to participate in an investigation of the role of genetic factors in autism. Second, CAIRN has undertaken a long-term follow-up investigation of the outcomes experienced by children with various pervasive developmental disorders; the study includes a comparison between children with autism and those with Asperger's syndrome. Initial research indicates that language skills predict outcome in high-functioning children with either autism or Asperger's syndrome, though this link is stronger in the autistic group (Szatmari et al., 2003). Other research projects are collaborative efforts involving investigators at other sites. They include a study of the infant siblings of children with pervasive developmental disorders and a brain-imaging study that examines the neurotransmitter functioning of children with autism. The CAIRN area of the CSCR website contains a description of the preliminary research findings from these projects prior to project completion. For instance, the infant siblings study has found that certain siblings do display atypical patterns of development, and CAIRN researchers have developed a new observational tool to detect these atypical behaviours. This measure will assist in terms of early detection. Also, a general investigation of children with autism revealed that two-thirds of them have an anxiety or mood disorder. This finding has implications for the development of a comprehensive intervention with children who have already developed a pervasive developmental disorder.

Thinking Critically

1. Early detection and intervention is critical. As a result of the efforts of researchers and clinicians such as those at the CSCR and the stakeholder members of CAIRN, there is hope that more effective and efficient early interventions for the pervasive developmental disorders will be developed in the future. Do you believe that these programs will be available to the parents of autistic children who desperately need them?

2. By and large, governments pay lip service to the importance of early interventions, but often the level of funding is simply not sufficient to meet the needs of the burgeoning Canadian population (see Chapter 18). For example, in Ontario, many autistic children remain on long waiting lists for the special funding for intensive early-intervention ABA therapy for children aged 2 to 5. Funding currently stops when the child reaches age 6. Many parents spend as much as $50,000 a year to provide treatment for their autistic children. In 2002 the province spent $39 million to treat 500 children, but 900 others were on waiting lists (Orwen, 2003). In 2003 the Ministry of Community, Family and Children's Services promised support of almost $100 million by 2006/07 for children with autism and their families; the funding was also to cover new (unspecified) services for older children with autism. A lawsuit was initiated by 29 families seeking to force Ontario to provide intensive treatment for autistic children beyond age 6 and continuing as the child progresses through the school system. On January 20, 2004, the Ontario Human Rights Commission joined the battle to force the province to fund treatment for older children with autism. An estimated 2,000 children had passed age 6 and would not benefit from intensive behavioural intervention treatment unless the government changed its policy (Boyle, 2004). Do you think governments have an obligation to provide the best possible treatment for all autistic children? Should they provide programs and services for older children or should these children be the responsibility of the parents or caregivers?

to be a safer alternative in terms of fewer side effects, but it was less effective in terms of symptom improvement (Kemner et al., 2002).

Evidence that autistic children may have elevated blood levels of serotonin (Anderson & Hoshino, 1987) encouraged research on medications (e.g., fenfluramine) that reduce the action of serotonin. Although fenfluramine may have modest positive effects in some autistic children—improving social adjustment, attention span, activity level, and stereotyped behaviour—no consistent effect has been shown on cognitive measures such as IQ or language functioning. Reviews concur that the effects of fenfluramine are at best subtle, and the drug certainly does not represent a cure for autism (Campbell, Anderson, & Small, 1990; Leventhal et al., 1993).

Researchers have also studied an opioid receptor antagonist, naltrexone, and found that this drug reduces hyperactivity in autistic children (Campbell et al., 1993; Willemsen-Swinkels, Buitelaar, & van Engeland, 1996). One controlled study suggested mild improvements in initiation of communication as well (Kolmen et al., 1995), but others found no changes in social behaviour (Willemsen-Swinkels et al., 1995, 1996). The drug does not appear to affect the core symptoms of autism, and some evidence suggests that, at some doses, it may increase self-injurious behaviour (Anderson et al., 1997).

Canadian Perspectives 15.6 describes a new initiative in Canada to develop an early detection and intervention program for children with autism or other pervasive developmental disorders.

DISORDERS OF OVERCONTROLLED BEHAVIOUR

This chapter began by highlighting the distinction between undercontrolled and overcontrolled behaviour. We conclude the chapter by examining overcontrolled behaviour in the form of anxiety disorders and depressive disorders in children and adolescents. The symptoms of these disorders as experienced by adults have already been discussed at length, with anxiety disorders described in Chapter 6 and depressive disorders described in Chapter 10. Accordingly, our analysis will focus on aspects of anxiety and depression that are relatively unique to children and adolescents. We begin with an examination of childhood fears and anxiety disorders.

CHILDHOOD FEARS AND ANXIETY DISORDERS

Most children experience fears and worries as part of the normal course of development. A classic report by Jersild and Holmes (1935) indicated that children between the ages of 2 and 6 average about five fears, and similar findings have been reported by later investigators (e.g., Lapouse & Monk, 1959). Common fears, most of which are outgrown, include fear of the dark and of imaginary creatures (in children under 5) and fear of being separated from parents (in children under 10).

The general prevalence of fearfulness was documented in a comparative survey of children from five countries, including Canada (see Phipps, 1999). It was found that over one-third of Canadian children between the ages of 4 and 11 years old were rated by their parents as too fearful or anxious, and that Canadian children were three times more anxious and fearful than children from Norway. It is important to take note of an important methodological factor involving these data: this study was based solely on parental reports and did not involve child self-reports. Discrepancies often exist between parental, teacher, and child reports, significantly affecting prevalence rates and the correlates of disorders and dysfunction (see Breton et al., 1999; Offord, Boyle, & Racine, 1989). Parental bias may have contributed to another finding from this research: when asked to assess their children's happiness, almost all of the parents surveyed (98.8 percent) indicated that their children were happy or somewhat happy (Phipps, 1999). This finding emerged despite the high levels of fearfulness acknowledged by these same parents and the substantial rates of depression and other disorders identified in epidemiological studies conducted in Canada.

In general, as with adults, fears and phobias are reported more often for girls than for boys (King et al., 1989), though this sex difference may be due at least in part to social pressures against boys' admitting that they are afraid of things. For fears and worries to be classified as disorders, children's functioning must be impaired; unlike adults, however, children might not regard their fear as excessive or unreasonable, as they sometimes lack the insight to make such judgements. Using this definition, about 10 to 15 percent of children and adolescents have an anxiety disorder, making these the most common disorders of childhood (Cohen et al., 1993). Although most unrealistic childhood fears dissipate over time, most anxious adults can trace their problems back to childhood. The seriousness of some childhood anxiety problems should therefore not be underestimated.

Separation Anxiety

Separation anxiety involves an unrealistic concern about separation from major attachment figures, with the levels of anxiety being above the level typically associated with the child's developmental level. The DSM-IV-TR description of separation anxiety disorder emphasizes that the eight symptoms associated with separation anxiety disorder must be experienced for at least eight weeks. These symptoms include unrealistic and persistent worries about harm to major attachment figures along with fears of abandonment, refusal to attend school owing to a need to stay close to an attachment figure, an avoidance of being alone, the experience of nightmares involving separation themes, and the experience of physical complaints in anticipation of being separated from attachment figures. Separation anxiety disorder is considered to be specific to childhood and adolescence, and DSM-IV-TR diagnostic criteria stipulate that the symptoms apply to individuals under the age of 18.

Developmental analyses indicate that the experience of separation anxiety is a natural reaction among very young children, with some scholars suggesting that levels of separation anxiety reach their peak when toddlers are 18 months of age (Wachtel & Strauss, 1995). Investigations with older children and adults indicate that a significant proportion of children and adolescents continue to manifest symptoms of separation anxiety. Although there is an overall tendency for levels of separation anxiety to decrease with age, with lower levels being reported by adolescents (Spence, 1997, 1998), recent research (e.g., Manicavasagar, Silove, & Curtis, 1997) indicates that some adults may meet diagnostic criteria for separation anxiety disorder.

Much of our understanding of separation anxiety comes from the seminal work of attachment theorists such as Ainsworth and Bowlby. An "anxious attachment style" among infants predicts subsequent anxiety disorders. Canadian Contributions 15.3 focuses on Ainsworth's work.

School Phobia

Separation anxiety and school phobia are related, with some children expressing their separation anxiety by refusing to go to school. However, separation anxiety and school phobia are considered as distinct problems because some children have no difficulty leaving attachment figures for extended periods but are afraid to go to school. School phobia, sometimes called school refusal, has serious academic and social consequences for the youngster and can be extremely disabling. Two types of school phobia have been identified. In the more common type, which is associated with separation anxiety, children worry constantly that some harm will befall their parents or themselves when they are away from their parents; when at home, they shadow one or both of their parents and often try to join them in bed.

Since many children have their first experience of lengthy and frequent separations from their parents when they begin school, separation anxiety is often a principal cause of school phobia. One study found that 75 percent of children who have school refusal caused by separation anxiety have mothers who also avoided school in childhood (Last & Strauss, 1990). It has been hypothesized that the child's refusal or extreme reluctance to go to school stems from some difficulty in the mother-child relationship. Perhaps the mother communicates her own separation anxieties and unwittingly reinforces the child's dependent and avoidant behaviour.

The second major type of school refusal is associated with a true phobia of school—either a fear specifically related to school or a more general social phobia. Children with this type of phobia generally begin refusing to go to school later in life and have more severe and pervasive avoidance of school. Their fear is more likely to be related to specific aspects of the school environment, such as worries about academic failure or discomfort with peers.

Experts agree that if untreated (or if it doesn't dissipate without professional intervention), school phobia in childhood can have long-term negative consequences as the person grows into adolescence and adulthood. The child with a school phobia can grow up to be a seriously dependent and fearful person.

Social Phobia

Most classrooms include at least one or two children who are extremely quiet and shy. Often these children will play only with family members or familiar peers, avoiding strangers both young and old. Their shyness may prevent them from acquiring skills and participating in a variety of activities enjoyed by most of their age-mates, for they avoid playgrounds and games played by neighbourhood children. Although some shy youngsters may simply be slow to warm up, withdrawn children never do, even after prolonged exposure to new people. Extremely shy children may refuse to speak at all in unfamiliar social circumstances; this condition is called selective mutism. In crowded rooms, they cling and whisper to their parents, hide behind the furniture, cower in corners, and may even have tantrums. At home, they ask their parents endless questions about situations that worry them. Withdrawn children usually have warm and satisfying relationships with family membersand family friends, and they show a desire for affection and acceptance.

Because the point at which shyness or withdrawal becomes a problem varies, few reliable statistics have been compiled on the frequency of this disorder. One estimate is that 1 percent of children and adolescents can be diagnosed with social phobia (Kashani & Orvaschel, 1990). It is more of a problem with adolescents, who are of an age when concern about the opinions of others can be acute.

Some children exhibit intense anxiety in specific social situations, showing social phobia similar to that of adults. When such children were asked to keep daily diaries of anxiety-producing events, they reported experiencing anxiety

Canadian Contributions/15.3

Mary Ainsworth, Attachment Styles, and Distress

Although she was actually born in the United States, Mary Ainsworth (née Salter) is widely regarded as one of the top psychologists produced in Canada. Ainsworth spent most of her childhood in Toronto and completed her undergraduate and graduate work at the University of Toronto. She obtained her Ph.D. in 1939. Eventually, she became a professor at the University of Toronto. She was a research fellow at the Institute of Child Study at the University of Toronto from 1946 to 1950. In 1950 she married World War II veteran Leonard Ainsworth and moved to England, where she began her lifelong research collaboration with attachment-style theorist John Bowlby (see Ainsworth & Bowlby, 1953).

Ainsworth is known primarily for her work on infant attachment styles. She developed a paradigm known as the Strange Situation, in which an infant was left in a room for a brief period of time with a stranger, the mother having left the room. Observational data indicated that three distinct types of infants reflect the differences between secure attachment and anxious attachment (Ainsworth, Blehar, Waters, & Wall, 1978). A securely attached infant shows little distress and interacts quite willingly with the stranger, secure in the knowledge that his or her mother will return. This pattern of behaviour contrasts with the pattern expressed by two types of insecurely attached infants. An anxiously attached infant becomes very distressed when his or her mother leaves the room. These infants have been described as "clingy" and are at risk of being overly dependent and prone to feelings of separation anxiety. When mothers of anxiously attached infants return to the room, their babies tend to express their upset by making a fuss as a form of protest, as if they are saying, "Don't do that to me again." In contrast, an infant with an avoidant attachment style displays little emotion when the mother leaves the room and shows little reaction upon her return, almost if an attachment bond has never been formed in the first place. Avoidantly attached infants can become withdrawn and socially isolated.

Psychologist Mary Ainsworth, a pioneer in the field of infant-caregiver attachment styles.

Research by Ainsworth and her associates established that insecure forms of attachment are likely to develop when a child is exposed to harsh or inconsistent parenting (see Ainsworth, 1984). Secure attachment emerges when the parent responds to the infant's needs in a warm and predictable manner, so that the infant comes to believe that the parent will be available as a source of comfort on a regular basis.

A fourth attachment style has been identified in recent years. The **disorganized attachment style** is evident in infants who seem totally confused by their surroundings. This style results from being exposed to chaotic and abusive environments.

Research on attachment styles has established that there are longstanding individual differences between secure and insecure attachments and that it is possible to distinguish older children, adolescents, and adults in terms of whether they have a secure or insecure style (see Bowlby, 1969). Research has sought to establish the early experiences and related factors that contribute to insecure attachment. A recent meta-analytic study conducted by researchers in Canada and involving an analysis of several studies concluded that maternal mental health variables are associated with degree of attachment security (Atkinson et al., 2000). Significant correlates of attachment security included the amount of social support available to the mother, marital satisfaction, maternal stress, and maternal depression.

Numerous studies have linked forms of insecure attachment with personal and interpersonal adjustment problems in children and adolescents. One longitudinal study assessed children exposed to the Strange Situation at 1 year of age and then used interviews 18 years later to determine which children had developed an anxiety disorder (Warren, Huston, Egeland, & Sroufe, 1997). This study found that an anxious attachment style among infants did predict subsequent anxiety disorders, while an avoidant attachment style predicted other types of psychiatric disorders. Another study conducted by researchers from Simon Fraser University found that fearful, insecure attachment in adolescents was associated with the severity of suicide risk in a clinical sample (Lessard & Moretti, 1998). Attachment style is also associated with maladaptive interpersonal styles. A study conducted by Canadian researchers yielded evidence that male adolescents with an avoidant attachment style are more likely than males with a secure attachment style to express and receive coercive behaviours in dating relationships (Wekerle & Wolfe, 1998).

Ainsworth is unique for more than her important research contributions on attachment style and achievements while at the University of Toronto. This remarkable woman was also in the Canadian military from 1942 to 1945 during World War II, and it is here that she achieved the rank of major. After the war was over, she served as a psychology advisor for the Department of Veterans' Affairs.

Mary Ainsworth died in 1999 after being given a number of awards, including the American Psychological Association Gold Medal Award in 1998 for "Lifetime Achievement in the Science of Psychology." There is little doubt that Ainsworth's work on attachment styles will be highly valued for many future generations.

three times more frequently than children in a normal control group, with concerns about such activities as reading aloud before a group, writing on the board, and performing in front of others. They reported crying, avoidance, and somatic complaints such as shakiness and nausea when faced with these events (Beidel, 1991).

Theories of the etiology of social phobia in children are not well worked out. It has been suggested that anxiety interferes with social interaction, causing the child to avoid social situations and thus not to get much practice at social skills. Another suggestion is that withdrawn children may simply not have the social know-how that facilitates interaction with their age-mates. The finding that isolated children make fewer attempts to make friends and are less imaginative in their play may indicate a deficiency in social skills. Finally, isolated children may have become so because they have spent most of their time with adults; these children interact more freely with adults than with other children (Scarlett, 1980). Having a parent with social phobia may also play a role. A study by Mancini and her associates in Hamilton found that among 47 children who had a parent with social phobia, 49 percent had at least one anxiety disorder diagnosis (Mancini et al., 1996). Overall, 23 percent of the children had social phobia, and 19 percent had separation anxiety disorder. The specific processes and mechanisms in social phobia can involve social learning (i.e., imitation of the parent), exposure to an overly anxious parenting style, and increased risk due to genetic factors.

Treatment of Childhood Fears and Phobias

How are childhood fears overcome? Many simply dissipate with time and maturation. For the most part, treatment of such fears is similar to that employed with adults, with suitable modifications to accommodate the different abilities and circumstances of childhood.

Perhaps the most popular method for helping children overcome fears, employed by millions of parents, is to expose them gradually to the feared object, often while simultaneously performing some action to inhibit their anxiety. If a little girl fears strangers, a parent takes her by the hand and walks her slowly toward the new person.

Contemporary therapists generally agree that exposure is the most effective way of eliminating baseless fear and avoidance. Modelling has also proved effective, both in laboratory studies (e.g., Bandura, Grusec, & Menlove, 1967) and in countless clinical treatments (Barrios & O'Dell, 1989). Another child—for example, one the fearful child is likely to imitate—could be asked to demonstrate fearless behaviour. In one innovative study, youngsters were helped by films showing other isolated children gradually engage in and come to enjoy play with their peers (O'Connor, 1969). Another group of researchers paired undergraduate volunteers with socially isolated children on the playground during recess (Allen et al., 1976). The goal was to include the target children in group games and give *in vivo* feedback to the child about which behaviours promoted or inhibited positive interactions with other children. By the end of the six-month program, the volunteers were standing on the sidelines observing the children playing with their peers.

Offering rewards for moving closer to a feared object or situation can also be help a fearful child. Both modelling and operant treatments involve exposure to what is feared. When the fear and avoidance of a child with school phobia are very great and of long duration, the child may require desensitization through direct, graduated exposure plus operant shaping.

In one case (Lazarus, Davison, & Polefka, 1965), the therapist began by walking to school with 9-year-old Paul. Then, on the successive days, the boy was exposed more and more to school, with lessening contact with the therapist. First, Paul entered the schoolyard and returned home; next, he entered an empty classroom after school; then he attended the opening morning exercises and left. Later he sat at a desk and spent time in school, first with the therapist beside him, then with the therapist out of sight but still nearby. In the last steps, when anxiety seemed to have lessened, the therapist provided reinforcement for Paul in the form of comic books and tokens that would eventually earn him a baseball glove.

Like adults, children may find some new situations threatening because they lack the knowledge and skills to deal with them. Thus, a child's fear of the water may very well be based on a reasonable judgement that danger lurks there because he or she cannot swim. Some shy children lack specific social skills needed for peer interaction. Skills such as asking questions (Ladd, 1981), giving compliments, and starting conversations with age-mates (Michelson et al., 1983) may be taught in small groups or in pairs, with interactions videotaped so the child and coach can observe and modify the new behaviours.

Manassis and Monga (2001) from the Hospital for Sick Children in Toronto have pointed out that there is a need for treatment that focuses on the family more generally, in addition to the anxious child. They noted that parents can play a role both in the etiology and treatment of anxiety disorders in children. Parents may contribute to the etiology of anxiety disorders by being anxious themselves and providing a model who can be imitated. Further, anxiety in the child can be a response, at least in part, to being the target of parental frustration. Manassis and Monga suggest that parents who learn to reduce their frustration and respond calmly when faced with stress will be less likely to express frustration to their children and will themselves become a model of self-control.

Contemporary research on anxiety disorders in children has evaluated the effectiveness of cognitive behaviour therapy (CBT). Comprehensive programs developed by Kendall and his associates, among others, include between 16 and 20 sessions (see Kendall, 1996; Kendall et al., 1997). The first part of treatment involves training the child to recognize physiological signs of anxiety, challenge and change cognitions and internal dialogue, and learn new problem-solving and coping plans. The last half of treatment involves having the child implement these new skills when exposed to anxiety-provoking situations. The final session requires the child to make a videotaped commercial describing the steps of CBT and how they are used to combat anxiety (for a detailed description, see Kazdin, 2003).

CBT is regarded as an evidence-based psychotherapy that is highly effective in treating childhood anxiety (Kazdin, 2003; Liashko & Manassis, 2003). Numerous studies attest to its usefulness (e.g., Barrett et al., 2001), including research conducted by investigators at the Hospital for Sick Children in Toronto (see Mendlowitz et al., 1999). However, as alluded to above, this research team has also established that high levels of parental frustration can undermine treatment gains (see Crawford & Manassis, 2001; Liashko & Manassis, 2003).

A recent follow-up investigation of 43 adolescents who had received CBT seven years earlier through the Hospital for Sick Children attested to the long-term effectiveness of

focus on discovery/15.1

After the Terrorist Attacks: PTSD in Children

"... lost is the sleep of the innocent since the Sept. 11 terrorist attacks in the U.S. stole the peaceful slumber of the young ..."

— Frank Calleja in "Traumatized young make a stand," *The Toronto Star*, September 24, 2001

"I think there is going to be another war. I am very scared about this because lots of people are going to die."

— Jonathon, quoted by Calleja (2001)

Calleja (2001) tells the story of a 9-year-old Toronto boy who has had negative reactions in the aftermath of the suicide passenger jet attacks on the United States. Jonathon's symptoms include inability to sleep, waking up in the night afraid, worry about more terrorist attacks, and worry about war. Although Jonathon's symptoms seem more consistent with generalized anxiety than with PTSD, it is premature to give him any diagnosis at this point and it is likely that none is warranted. Further, we should hope and expect that he will be able to cope adaptively and that his symptoms will be short-lived.

PTSD IN CHILDREN

But what about the children who were affected directly by the attacks, either because they escaped from the disaster area or because a loved one perished in the conflagration? What about those affected indirectly through watching countless television replays of the disaster, listening to family talk about it, and hearing different things about it at school and on the playground? We should anticipate that a relatively large number of children and adolescents will develop at least some symptoms of the anxiety disorders, especially PTSD. Is PTSD expressed in children in the same way that it is in an adult? Although there is considerable overlap with the adult expression of symptoms, in children there may be disorganized or agitated behaviour (American Psychiatric Association, 1994) instead of or in addition to the typical intense fear, helplessness, or horror experienced by adults. According to the DSM-IV-TR, distressing dreams of the event seen in the younger children may, within weeks, evolve into more generalized nightmares (e.g., of monsters, of having to rescue others, or of threats to self or others) or frightening dreams that do not have recognizable content.

In very young children, themes or aspects of the trauma can be expressed in their repetitive play. DSM-IV-TR also notes that trauma-specific reenactments are sometimes seen in young children (e.g., a child repeatedly reenacts the collapse of the World Trade Center with toy buildings). Some children may develop a belief that life will be too short for them to become an adult (sense of foreshortened future). They may develop "omen formation,"a belief in the ability to predict future negative events. Some of them will express the impact of the trauma through physical symptoms (e.g., headaches or stomach aches). Most children will experience distress at reminders of the trauma, as well as the repetitive, intrusive thoughts typically reported by adults. Some children will develop specific fears to stimuli or situations related to the trauma (e.g., fear of high-rise buildings, fear of flying). Many children will be terrified about the possibility of war. Many will develop separation difficulties and become "clingy" or dependent. Some will resist going to school or insist on sleeping with an adult.

It is very important that parents, teachers, and other observers recognize that there could be a delay of months or even longer before the appearance of serious symptoms. It should also be noted that many children will exhibit symptoms but not meet the formal diagnostic criteria for the diagnosis of PTSD. Nonetheless, they may experience considerable distress and impairment in important areas of functioning. For example, children's performance at school may suffer; adolescents may experience disruptions in their pursuit of higher education and careers; and some children will exhibit other psychological problems (e.g., depressed mood, anhedonia, irritability and anger, and behavioural problems such as aggressive outbursts) or meet criteria for other psychiatric disorders (e.g., a conversion or dissociative disorder). Like some adults, some children will express guilt because they survived or because they feel somehow responsible for the death of a loved one. Although symptoms of PTSD can be expected to decline over time, one study reported that as many as three-quarters of young children (grades 3 through 5) who experienced Hurricane Andrew in Florida continued to report re-experiencing symptoms 10 months later (LaGreca, Silverman, Vernberg, & Prinstein, 1996).

A MODEL OF PTSD IN CHILDREN

What factors can put some children at risk for the development of PTSD? PTSD can develop in children even when there are no predisposing conditions, especially when the stressor is as extreme as the September 11 terrorist attacks. Nonetheless, several factors appear to affect the pattern, intensity, and persistence of symptoms. LaGreca, Silverstein, and Wasserstein (1998) developed a model to predict children's reactions to a natural disaster (Hurricane Andrew), one we believe is relevant to our understanding of children's reactions to traumas of human design such as September 11. The conceptual model requires us to consider four factors: (1) exposure to a traumatic event, (2) preexisting characteristics of the child (e.g., anxiety sensitivity, separation anxiety disorder), (3) the child's attempts to process and cope with the trauma, and (4) the availability of social support. As noted previously, in the case of the World Trade Center and Pentagon attacks, a child's exposure can include being a survivor of the actual attack, losing an attachment figure, or simply being a vicarious witness to seemingly endless images and descriptions of explosions, fire, death, and incalculable human suffering. We have discussed these different components at different points in this book.

HELPING TRAUMATIZED CHILDREN

How can we help the tens of thousands of children traumatized by the terrorist attacks and their consequences? Help has, of course, been provided in the form of immediate trauma counselling followed, where necessary, with long-term psychological interventions (see Chapter 17). Canadian psychologists and other professionals have responded to the appeals for help with the crisis intervention efforts. But what can ordinary people do—the parents and other caregivers, schoolteachers, people in the community, and, of course, other children? Although they can never take the place of professional intervention when needed and never be an answer when a child has lost a mother, father, or other loved one, the following strategies should be helpful to many children and possibly short-circuit the development of more serious problems in some cases. We discuss these strategies as if the tragic events had just occurred.

1 We must talk to the children and acknowledge that the terrorist attacks are incomprehensible, even to adults. We must try to answer children's questions in an open, honest, straightforward, and simple manner and admit it to them when we don't have the answers.

2 We must talk to them repeatedly over days and weeks, if necessary, unless the child is showing signs of increasing upset, which would be a sign that it is time to consult a professional. We must listen to their concerns and share our own concerns with them. Some people might believe that very young children should be told as little as possible. However, it is also possible that if we attempt to hide information from young children, they will manufacture their own realities based on misinformation, since trying to understand the traumatic event is a natural response (see Tremblay et al., 2000; Wolfe, 1999). They may imagine future threats and consequences far beyond the realm of realistic probability.

3 We must focus on all the things that haven't changed in the world—their homes, their families, their neighbourhood—and assure them that the world is still a safe place. Even though we can't deny that many people were killed and injured, it is a rare event and the children are safe. Reassurance that their immediate world is unchanged is vitally important. They need to have a sense of stability.

4 We should try to minimize the children's exposure to the horrific images. The repeated images and vivid descriptions can serve as repeated triggers for anxiety and other reactions. We must help very young children understand that the events, as tragic as they were, occurred only once in a single day. Perhaps some children are too young to understand that the same footage is being replayed on television over and over again and actually that the attacks have not occurred a multitude of times.

5 Let the children play. We mentioned that reenactment of the disaster during play often occurs in younger children. Initially, this play may be a part of the "re-experiencing" of the trauma. However, play can also be a critical part of the recovery process and thus can be encouraged by caretakers and others. For example, following Hurricane Hugo in South Carolina, the play of many children progressed from blowing homes down to pretending that they were roofers rebuilding their homes (Saylor, Powell, & Swenson, 1992).

6 Get the children involved in helping other children (and adults) through a difficult time. At one Toronto junior high school, the children made over 6,000 friendship bracelets with messages of hope and support to be delivered to schoolchildren in New York City.

7 An editorial in the *Toronto Star* on September 24, 2001, complained that the Ontario education ministry failed to provide advice to school boards despite the traumatic effects of the attacks, especially for immigrant or refugee children recently arrived from countries of social unrest and civil conflict (American Psychiatric Association, 1994). When appropriate, school boards should send tragic-events response teams to the schools to counsel and provide support for the children and their teachers.

8 School boards need to ensure that tensions over the terrorist attacks do not "spill over" into the classrooms in the form of teasing, bullying, blaming, and inappropriate comments directed toward different ethnic groups.

We do not have any detailed information about the prevalence and severity of PTSD and related symptoms and problems among children in North America that could be considered a direct consequence of the terrorist attacks. It is clear, however, that many were adversely affected. Schuster et al. (2001) interviewed almost 600 randomly selected adults across the United States in the week after the attacks and reported that 44 percent of the adults and 35 percent of their children had significant stress reactions. A year later, 58 percent of children polled reported that they thought about the attacks at least a few times a month, 51 percent felt that future bombings or other attacks are somewhat likely, and 46 percent felt less safe travelling (*Time* Poll, 2002). Further, people in both the United States and Canada claimed that they changed their approach or attitudes toward family life as a consequence of the attacks (Gardwyn, 2002; *Maclean's* Year-End Poll, 2001/2002). For example, 78 percent of American parents considered family more of a priority, and 35 percent indicated that they were designating more family time to their children. Among Canadians, 9 percent of women and 66 percent of men reported that they were more appreciative of family life.

We end on a positive note by pointing out that the majority of children are resilient. Their strength and resourcefulness, coupled with their family's love and support, no doubt helped them rebound from the trauma of September 11, 2001. How did Jonathon cope? He set about helping the victims. He and his siblings set up a lemonade stand draped in a large American flag and sold lemonade and red, white, and blue cookies. They raised over $300 for the American Red Cross disaster fund.

Thinking Critically

1. What other strategies would you employ to help prevent the development of serious psychological problems in children who were possibly traumatized by the terrorist attacks on the United States on September 11, 2001?
2. We have focused on the anxiety reactions of children directly or indirectly involved with the traumatic events. However, we predict that some predisposed children will experience other psychological difficulties, including depression and aggressive acting out. Do you agree with this hypothesis? What suggestions do you have for helping these children?

treatment for the majority of participants with a previous anxiety disorder. Manassis, Avery, Butalia, and Mendlowitz (2004) found that almost all of the adolescents still experienced some anxiety-related impairment, but 70 percent required no further treatment for anxiety disorder or other mental health problems. However, these data were based on telephone surveys and did not involve actual diagnostic interviews. Manassis et al. (2004) also emphasized that about one-third of their sample still required treatment and this was somewhat unexpected given the higher levels of long-term effectiveness demonstrated in a previous study by Barrett et al. (2001).

Children also experience the other anxiety disorders described in the DSM-IV-TR. Focus on Discovery 15.1 examines the potential impact on children of the September 11, 2001 terrorist attacks on the United States. A discussion of some of the approaches that may have been employed to help people who were directly or indirectly affected by the horrific events of that day can be found in Chapter 17 in the context of our presentation on community psychology.

DEPRESSION IN CHILDHOOD AND ADOLESCENCE

We conclude our discussion of the disorders in childhood and adolescence by turning our attention to depressive disorders. Considering our typical image of children as happy-go-lucky, it is distressing to observe that major depression and dysthymia occur in children and adolescents as well as in adults. DSM-IV-TR diagnoses mood disorders in children using the adult criteria, while allowing for age-specific features such as irritability and aggressive behaviour instead of or in addition to depressed mood.

Symptoms and Prevalence of Childhood and Adolescent Depression

There are similarities and differences in the symptomatology of children and adults with major depression (Mitchell et al., 1988). Children and adolescents ages 7 to 17 resemble adults in depressed mood, inability to experience pleasure, fatigue, concentration problems, and suicidal ideation. Symptoms that differ are higher rates of suicide attempts and guilt among children and adolescents, and more frequent waking up early in the morning, loss of appetite, weight loss, and early morning depression among adults.

It is also possible for adolescents to develop an early-onset form of bipolar disorder. A study by Robertson, Kutcher, and associates at Dalhousie University (Robertson, Kutcher, Bird, & Grasswick, 2001) compared levels of family adjustment in adolescents with bipolar depression, unipolar depression, and control participants, and found relatively few group differences, unlike other studies that have found a link between depression in adolescents and poor family functioning. The authors suggested the need for additional research with observer ratings of family functioning rather than self-report measures of family assessment alone. This shortcoming notwithstanding, the study is relatively unique in terms of its focus on bipolar depression in adolescents, as most studies either focus on unipolar depression or simply measure depressive symptoms in samples obtained in school settings rather than clinical settings.

As in adults, depression in children is recurrent. Longitudinal studies have demonstrated that both children and adolescents with major depression are likely to continue to exhibit significant depressive symptoms when assessed even four to eight years later (Garber et al., 1988; Hammen et al., 1990).

Estimates of the prevalence of childhood depression vary depending on the age of the child, the country being studied, the type of samples (community based or clinic referred), the diagnostic criteria, and the methods used to make the assessment (e.g., clinical interviews, questionnaires, reports from parents or teachers [Kazdin, 1989; Nottelmann & Jensen, 1995]). Sometimes depression—often called **masked depression**—is inferred from behaviours that would not, in adults, be viewed as reflecting an underlying depression, for example, acting aggressively or misbehaving at school or at home.

In general, depression occurs in less than 1 percent of preschoolers (Kashani & Carlson, 1987; Kashani, Hoalcomb, & Orvaschel, 1986) and in 2 to 3 percent of school-age children (Cohen et al., 1993; Costello et al., 1988). In adolescents, rates of depression are comparable to those of adults, with particularly high rates for girls. A four-year longitudinal study in Canada used interview data from the National Population Health Survey to show that the annual prevalence of depression is about 9 percent in females and between 3 to 5 percent in males (Galambos, Leadbeater, & Barker, 2004). The lifetime prevalence was 21.4 percent for females and 10.7 percent for males.

One problem complicating the diagnosis of depression in children is frequent comorbidity with other disorders (Hammen & Compas, 1994). Up to 70 percent of depressed children also have an anxiety disorder or significant anxiety symptoms (Anderson et al., 1987; Kovacs, 1990; Manassis & Menna, 1999). Depression is also common in children with conduct disorder and attention-deficit disorder (Fleming & Offord, 1990; Kashani et al., 1987; Rohde et al., 1991). Youngsters with both depression and another disorder have been found to experience more severe depression and to take longer to recover (Keller et al., 1988).

Etiology of Depression in Childhood and Adolescence

What causes a young person to become depressed? As with adults, evidence suggests that genetic factors play a role (Puig-Antich et al., 1989; Tsuang & Faraone, 1990). Indeed, the genetic data on adults reviewed earlier in Chapter 10 naturally apply to children and adolescents, since genetic influences are present from birth, though they may not be expressed right away.

Studies of depression in children have also focused on family and other relationships as sources of stress that might interact with a biological diathesis. Research conducted in Canada (Bergeron et al., 2000) suggests that having a parent with a depressive disorder is associated moderately with internalizing and externalizing mental disorders among children. Having a mother who is depressed increases the chances of a child being depressed; less is known about the influence of fathers (Kaslow, Deering, & Racusin, 1994) or the reasons for these linkages.

An impressive longitudinal study by Mark Ellenbogen from Concordia University and Sheilagh Hodgins from the University of Montreal examined parents with bipolar disorder, major depression, or no disorder. This study showed that the personality trait of neuroticism (i.e., low trait levels of emotional stability) in the parent contributed to numerous deficits in the parent, and ultimately, to the development of maladaptive coping styles (e.g., high emotion-oriented and low task-oriented coping), as assessed by Endler and Parker's Coping Inventory for Stressful Situations. These parents also had deficits in terms of the predictability, organization, and consistency of their parenting behaviours. These data suggest that a personality style involving neuroticism in the parent may be implicated directly in the intergenerational transmission of depression from parents to their children.

It is possible that depression in a youngster is caused by any serious emotional problem in a parent because of the disruption in home life that parental illnesses can create (Weintraub, Winters, & Neale, 1986). And childhood problems other than depression—conduct disorder, for example—are associated with depressed parents (Orvaschel, Walsh-Allis, & Ye, 1988). We know that depression in either or both spouses is often associated with marital conflict; we should expect, therefore, that depression would have negative effects on the children in a household, and it does (Hammen, 1997).

Depressed children and their parents have been shown to interact with each other in negative ways, showing less warmth and more hostility toward each other, for example, than is the case with nondepressed children and their parents (Chiariello & Orvaschel, 1995; Puig-Antich et al., 1985). Children and adolescents experiencing major depression also have poor social skills and impaired relationships with siblings and friends (Lewinsohn et al., 1994; Puig-Antich et al., 1993). These behavioural patterns are likely to be both a cause and a consequence of depression. Depressed youngsters have fewer and less-satisfying contacts with their peers (Brendgen, Vitaro, Turgeon, & Poulin, 2002), who often reject them because they are not pleasant to be around (Kennedy, Spence, & Hensley, 1989). These negative interactions in turn aggravate the negative self-image and sense of worth that the depressed youngster already has (cf. Coyne, 1976). Frequent criticism from parents may be especially harmful to the child's sense of competency and self-worth (Cole & Turner, 1993; Stark et al., 1996).

New longitudinal research, by investigators from Dalhousie University using time-lagged models, shows that depression in mothers from the Halifax area predicted subsequent oppositional/defiant behaviour in the child, but maternal distress was also predicted by the child's prior behavioural problems. Maternal depression and anxiety predicted the child's impulsive and overactive behaviour, while maternal confusion predicted the child's oppositional/defiant behaviour. However, it was also the case that maternal anger, fatigue, and confusion were a reflection of the child's inattentiveness and impulsive, overactive behaviour. Thus, mothers and children had a mutual influence on each other, rather than just a unidirectional influence of the mother on the child (see Elgar, Waschbusch, McGrath, Stewart, Curtis, 2004b). The researchers concluded that negative maternal moods and disruptive child behaviour are "intrinsically intertwined" (p. 245).

This same team of investigators analyzed separate data from the National Longitudinal Survey of Children and Youth (see Canadian Perspectives 15.1). They found further compelling evidence indicating that exposure to a depressed mother contributes to children's maladjustment (see Elgar, Curtis, McGrath, Waschbusch, & Stewart, 2003). That is, depression in the mother predicted child problems involving aggression and hyperactivity. However, emotional problems in the child were associated with subsequent depression in the mother. Thus, once again, bi-directional influences were apparent.

These researchers conducted a thorough review of the literature and incorporated their findings and related research into a new biopsychosocial model of vulnerability to depression (see Elgar, McGrath, Waschbusch, Stewart, & Curtis, 2004a). According to this model, depression in children stems from a complex interplay of biological vulnerability factors, parental factors (e.g., maternal depression), psychosocial factors (e.g., attachment style differences, modeling, child discipline techniques, and general family functioning), and "social capital" resources, including the availability of social support and other social resources.

A growing number of studies have investigated the role of stress in depression among children and adolescents. Stress may operate by itself to produce depression or it may operate in conjunction with vulnerability factors involving personality factors and maladaptive cognitive styles to produce depression in children and adolescents. Dumont and Provost (1999) at the University of Quebec at Trois-Rivières have also examined protective factors associated with resiliency, and their research has shown that higher self-esteem and problem-focused coping are two factors that seem to lessen the impact of stress on depression. Other Canadian research indicates that social support (Galambos et al., 2004) and the absence of the habit of dwelling on things when depressed (Abela, Brozina, & Haigh, 2002) may protect children and adolescents from depression.

Personality research on depression in children and adolescents tends to parallel research conducted with adults.

Investigators at McGill University have shown that self-criticism and dependency are associated with depressive symptoms in adolescents (Fichman, Koestner, & Zuroff, 1996, 1997). Similarly, socially prescribed perfectionism (i.e., the belief that others expect us to be perfect) is associated with depressive symptoms and suicide ideation in Canadian youths (Hewitt et al., 2002; Hewitt, Newton, Flett, & Callander, 1997).

Consistent with both Beck's theory (1967) and the learned helplessness theory of depression (Abramson et al., 1988), cognitive distortions and negative attributional styles are associated with depression in children and adolescents in ways similar to what has been found with adults (e.g., Gotlib et al., 1993; Kaslow et al., 1992). For example, cognitive research with depressed children indicates that their outlooks (schemata) are more negative than those of nondepressed children and resemble those of depressed adults (Prieto, Cole, & Tageson, 1992). An investigation by Abela (2001) from McGill University found that a negative attributional style interacted with the experience of stressful events to predict increases in depression among children in grade 7 but not among children in grade 3. Perhaps negative attributional styles have more impact on older children, who are more aware of the long-term implications of negative attributions involving personal weaknesses. Other findings reported by Abela provide general support for hopelessness models of depression (Abela, 2002; Abela & Sarin, 2002). Such findings suggest a useful connection between childhood depression and research and theory on cognitive factors in depressed adults. Accumulating evidence indicates that experiences in the home, primarily the manner in which parents deal with their children, cause the cognitions and thoughts that can lead to depression (Stark et al., 1996).

The gender difference in depression that is seen in adults also exists in adolescents. This issue was highlighted in Focus on Discovery 10.1.

Treatment of Childhood and Adolescent Depression

Far less research has been done on therapy with depressed children and adolescents than on therapy with adults (Hammen, 1997; Kaslow & Racusin, 1990). One reason suggested for this relative neglect is that depressed young people don't attract as much adult attention as those who act out, such as the youngsters with conduct disorder described previously (Kaslow & Thompson, 1998).

Drug therapies do not seem to be very effective. A recent review by researchers at the Royal Ottawa Hospital indicated that there is only limited evidence of robust, effective therapeutic interventions, and one interpretive problem is that placebos have yielded a high rate of improvement (Milin, Walker, & Chow, 2003). The authors point to recent findings suggesting that selective serotonin reuptake inhibitors (SSRIs) can be effective, but they caution that much more investigation is needed. Indeed, on February 3, 2004, Health Canada issued a rare public warning, advising individuals under 18 to consult with their physicians before taking SSRIs and SNRIs because of safety concerns involving an increased rate of "suicide-related events," suicides, and suicide attempts in adolescents who took certain of these newer classes of drugs. The drugs identified were Prozac, Paxil, Celexa, Luvox, Remeron, Zoloft, and Effexor. In Canada, the drugs are not approved for use with children and adolescents; however, they are often prescribed in a practice called "off label use." Britain and the United States took similar actions (Picard, 2004). The U.S. Food and Drug Administration appointed an advisory panel that held public hearings on the issue, and it was expected that Canada's health department would take further action based on the panel's recommendations.

The link between antidepressants and increased risk of suicide and violent behaviour was suggested by British psychiatrist David Healy (2003), who, in his testimony at the U.S. hearings, was also critical of the volume of prescriptions written for children and teenagers. In 2000 Healy was awarded a senior position at the Centre for Addiction and Mental Health (a University of Toronto teaching hospital), but the appointment was revoked following a speech he delivered on SSRIs and suicide. Although the centre denied the decision had anything to do with alleged pressure from Eli Lilly, the maker of Prozac and a significant donor to the centre, the ensuing major debate about academic freedom thrust the issue of antidepressants and suicide into public consciousness (Picard, 2003).

Most psychosocial interventions are modelled after clinical research with adults. Interpersonal therapy (IPT), for instance, has been modified for use with depressed adolescents, focusing on issues of concern to adolescents, such as peer pressure, separation from parents, and authority issues (Moreau et al., 1992; Mufson et al., 1994). Recent findings indicate that IPT is quite effective in treating depression in adolescents and has led to significant improvements in interpersonal functioning (Mufson, Weissman, Moreau, & Garfinkel, 1999; Rosello & Bernal, 1999).

A cognitive-behavioural group intervention involving instruction in coping with depression was found to be effective with depressed adolescents, particularly when parents were involved in treatment (Clarke et al., 1992; Lewinsohn et al., 1990). Quantitative reviews suggest that CBT is effective in reducing depression among children and adolescents (Lewinsohn & Clarke, 1999; Reinecke, Ryan, & Dubois, 1998). However, even in studies that yield improvements following CBT (Kolko et al., 2002), it is difficult to identify the specific cognitive mechanisms or processes responsible for improvement.

Fifth and 6th graders showed improvement in depression after a small-group role-playing intervention that concentrated on instructions in social skills and social problem-solving in stressful situations (Butler et al., 1980).

Social skills training can help depressed young people by providing them with the behavioural and verbal means to gain access to pleasant, reinforcing environments, such as making friends and getting along with peers (Frame et al., 1982; Stark, Reynolds, & Kaslow, 1987). Relating to others in better ways can also break into the cycle of depression, negative behaviour, and rejection from others that Coyne (1976) has discussed and that has been noted in other research with young people (e.g., Blechman et al., 1986). However, findings from Stark et al. (1996) indicate that some depressed children know how to relate appropriately to others but are apparently inhibited from doing so by negative thoughts and physiological arousal, suggesting that cognitive interventions and, for some, such procedures as relaxation training could also be useful. Overall, treatments that include social skills training, problem-solving, and cognitive techniques similar to those employed successfully with adults are effective (Kaslow & Thompson, 1998).

Treatment of depressed children and adolescents may be best accomplished with a broad-spectrum approach that involves not only the child or adolescent but also the family and the school (Hammen, 1997; Stark et al., 1996, 1998). Therapy might well have to focus on a depressed parent in addition to the depressed child. Depressed parents probably communicate to their children their own pessimistic views of themselves and the world, and children are influenced strongly by the ideas of their parents. The proposal to include the family and school environments is based on the hypothesis that, for young people more than for adults, environmental stressors can be more important than cognitive biases, expectations, and attributions (Cole & Turner, 1993). This approach also highlights the importance of teaching the young person ways to cope with interpersonal stress via more effective overt behaviour—for example, interacting more effectively with others and being appropriately assertive with overbearing peers—so that the person has alternatives other than the polar extremes of anger or withdrawal. The involvement of the family is now recognized as important when dealing with younger people who are depressed (Kaslow & Thompson, 1998).

A case report by Braswell and Kendall (1988) illustrates a cognitive-behavioural therapy with a depressed 15-year-old girl.

WHEN INITIALLY SEEN, Sharon was extremely dysphoric, experienced recurrent suicidal ideation, and displayed a number of vegetative signs of depression. ... [After being] placed on antidepressant medication ... she was introduced to a cognitive-behavioural approach to depression. ... She was able to understand how her mood was affected by her thoughts and behaviour and was able to engage in behavioural planning to increase the occurrence of pleasure and mastery-oriented events. Sharon manifested extremely high standards for evaluating her performance in a number of areas, and it became clear that her parents also ascribed to these standards, so that family therapy sessions were held to encourage Sharon and her parents to reevaluate their standards.

Sharon had difficulty with the notion of changing her standards and noted that when she was not depressed she actually valued her perfectionism. At that point she resisted the therapy because she perceived it as trying to change something she valued in herself. With this in mind, we began to explore and identify those situations or domains in which her perfectionism worked for her and when and how it might work against her. She became increasingly comfortable with this perspective and decided she wanted to continue to set high standards regarding her performance in mathematical coursework (which was a clear area of strength), but she did not need to be so demanding of herself regarding art or physical education. (p. 194)

Can depression in children and adolescents be prevented? Asarnow, Jaycox, and Tompson (2001) conducted a review of empirical research on the prevention of depression in youths and concluded that the relatively few studies that have been done thus far have yielded encouraging results overall. Asarnow et al. (2001) proposed a model to guide the treatment of depression in youths, their working assumption being that the same cognitive-behavioural factors that are suggested as the focus of treatment will also yield benefits if they are the focus of preventive efforts aimed at children and adolescents.

SUMMARY

- Attention-deficit/hyperactivity disorder and conduct disorder are marked by undercontrolled behaviour. ADHD is a persistent pattern of inattention and/or impulsivity that is judged to be more frequent and more severe than what is typically observed in youngsters of a given age. There is growing evidence for genetic and neurological factors in its etiology, but parents can be helpful in improving the behaviour of children with ADHD. Stimulant drugs, such as Ritalin, and reinforcement for staying on task have some effectiveness in reducing the intensity of ADHD.
- Conduct disorder is often a precursor to antisocial personality disorder in adulthood, although many children carrying the diagnosis do not progress to that extreme. It is characterized by high and widespread levels of aggression, lying, theft, vandalism, cruelty to other people and to animals, and other acts that violate laws and social norms. Among the apparent etiological factors are a

genetic predisposition, inadequate learning of moral awareness, modelling and direct reinforcement of anti-social behaviour, and living in impoverished and crime-ridden areas. The most promising approach to treating young people with conduct disorder involves intensive intervention in multiple systems, including the family, school, and peer systems.

- Learning disorders are diagnosed when a child fails to develop to the degree expected by his or her intellectual level in a specific academic, language, or motor skill area. These disorders are usually identified and treated within the school system rather than through mental health clinics. There is mounting evidence that the most widely studied of the learning disorders, dyslexia, has genetic and other biological components. The most widespread interventions for dyslexia, however, are educational.
- The diagnostic criteria for mental retardation are sub-average intellectual functioning and deficits in adaptive behaviour, with onset before the age of 18. Contempor-ary analyses focus more on the strengths of individuals with mental retardation than on their assignment to a particular level of severity. This shift in emphasis is associated with increased efforts to design psychological and educational interventions that make the most of individuals' abilities.
- The more severe forms of mental retardation have a biological basis, such as the chromosomal trisomy that causes Down syndrome. Certain infectious diseases in the pregnant mother (e.g., HIV, rubella, and syphilis), and illnesses that affect the child directly, (e.g., encephalitis) can stunt cognitive and social development, as can malnutrition, severe falls, and automobile accidents that injure the brain. Environmental factors are considered the principal causes of mild retardation. Thus far, no brain damage has been detected in people with mild retardation, who often are from lower-class homes and live in an environment of social and educational deprivation.
- Researchers try to prevent mild retardation by giving children at risk through impoverished circumstances special preschool training and social opportunities. The best-known and largest of these programs is Head Start, which has been shown to be helpful in equipping children to benefit from school. Many children with mental retardation who would formerly have been institutionalized are now being educated in the public schools under the provisions of various laws. In addition, using applied behavioural analysis, self-instructional training, and modelling, behaviour therapists have been able to treat successfully many of the behavioural problems of individuals with mental retardation and to improve their intellectual functioning.
- Autistic disorder, one of the pervasive developmental disorders, begins before the age of 2 and a half. The major symptoms are extreme autistic aloneness, a failure to relate to other people; communication problems consisting of either a failure to learn any language or speech irregularities, such as echolalia and pronoun reversal; and preservation of sameness, an obsessive desire to keep daily routines and surroundings exactly the same. The disorder was originally believed to be the result of parents' coldness and aloofness and their rejection of their children, but recent research gives no credence to such notions. Although no specific biological basis of autism has been found, a biological cause is suspected for a number of reasons: its onset is very early; family and twin studies give compelling evidence of a genetic predisposition; abnormalities have been found in the brains of autistic children; a syndrome similar to autism can develop following meningitis and encephalitis; and many autistic children have the low intelligence associated with brain dysfunctions.
- The most promising psychological treatments for autism involve procedures that rely on modelling and operant conditioning. Although the prognosis for autistic children remains poor in general (except for some startling cases), recent work suggests that intensive behavioural treatment involving the parents as their children's therapists may allow some of these children to participate meaningfully in normal social intercourse. Recent drug treatments, notably those that lower serotonin, show little promise in treating the core deficits of the disorder.
- While ADHD and conduct disorder are undercontrolled behaviours, other children and adolescents experience difficulties that involve overcontrolled behaviours. Anxiety disorders and related fears in children reflect over-controlled tendencies. These disorders include separation anxiety disorder, school phobia, and social phobia. Theorists seeking to account for the etiology of these disorders are increasingly focusing on the role of attachment style, first described by theorists such as Ainsworth and Bowlby. Family factors are also seen as important in the etiology and treatment of anxiety disorders in children and adolescents. By and large, treatments for children are similar to those used with adults, including the role of exposure to the feared object or situation.
- Various types of depression are regarded as forms of over-controlled behaviour. The core symptoms of depression in children and adults are similar, though it is recognized that there are age-specific features, not only distinguishing between children and adults with depression, but also between children and adolescents with depression. Extensive research has shown the negative impact of exposure to a depressed parent, as this factor is linked with depression in children. Gender differences in depression emerge in adolescence, and investigators have suggested several hypotheses to explain the causes of these gender differences. As is the case with research on adults, research has examined the role of stress in childhood and adolescent depression, either by itself or in combination with personality factors such as self-criticism, dependency, and attributional style.

KEY TERMS

anxious attachment (p. 515)
applied behaviour analysis (p. 503)
attention-deficit/hyperactivity disorder (ADHD) (p. 477)
autistic disorder (p. 504)
avoidant attachment style (p. 515)
conduct disorder (p. 484)
disorder of written expression (p. 493)
disorganized attachment style (p. 516)
Down syndrome (trisomy 21) (p. 499)
echolalia (p. 507)
expressive language disorder (p. 494)
fragile X syndrome (p. 499)
learning disabilities (p. 493)
learning disorders (p. 493)
masked depression (p. 520)
mathematics disorder (p. 494)
mild mental retardation (p. 497)
moderate mental retardation (p. 497)
motor skills disorder (p. 494)
oppositional defiant disorder (ODD) (p. 484)
pervasive developmental disorders (p. 505)
phenylketonuria (PKU) (p. 499)
phonological disorder (p. 494)
profound mental retardation (p. 497)
pronoun reversal (p. 507)
reading disorder (dyslexia) (p. 493)
school phobia (p. 514)
secure attachment (p. 515)
selective mutism (p. 515)
self-instructional training (p. 503)
separation anxiety (p. 514)
severe mental retardation (p. 497)
social phobia (p. 515)
stuttering (p. 494)

Reflections: Past, Present, and Future

- Effective early intervention programs for children at risk for developing conduct disorder probably require the cooperation of multiple social service and mental health agencies that employ "individualized care" or "wrap-around" services involving interdisciplinary teams that develop individualized and comprehensive plans. Such programs would employ multiple-component, flexible treatments that would involve the child, the family, and the school (see Frick, 2001). Do you think that in some cases multiple interventions will be required throughout the youngster's life, including into adulthood (see Waddell, Lipman, & Offord, 1999; Wicks-Nelson & Israel, 2000). Would any intervention work with those children who are "Bad to the Bone" (Barovick, 1999), that is, who are predisposed to become the worst psychopaths as adults? The approach we are recommending would be extremely expensive. Would it be worth the cost in the long run if it could "save" an Eric Harris or a Dylan Klebold (the teenagers responsible for the massacre at Columbine High School in April 1999)?
- With respect to learning disabilities, it is often stated that most professionals use a "definition of exclusion." What does that mean? What are the implications?
- Paralleling attempts to educate children with mental retardation as fully as possible has been a movement for deinstitutionalization and the provision of alternative living arrangements in an attempt to integrate people with mental retardation into their communities. What are the most compelling arguments for deinstitutionalization? We all should treat retarded children and adults with decency and dignity and, if possible, facilitate their participation in our communities. What could you do that would help them develop a sense of purpose, pride, and self-esteem? In your judgement, who should be responsible for caring for the severely and profoundly retarded?
- You learned in the section on autistic disorder that many children with autism (perhaps two-thirds of them) also have an anxiety or mood disorder. What are the implications of this fact for the treatment of autistic children? In light of your understanding of possible treatments for autism, anxiety, and depression, design a comprehensive treatment program for autistic children with comorbid anxiety and depression. The treatment and legal rights of children must be recognized and protected. Under what circumstances, if any, should it be permissible for clinicians to use punishment (e.g., a squirt of water in the face) in an attempt to eliminate self-injury in autistic children? Who should decide? (See Chapter 18 for a discussion of ethical dilemmas.)
- An anxious attachment style among infants seems to be a risk factor for the subsequent development of anxiety disorders. Do you think that a prevention program will be developed in the future that will target such high-risk infants at a very early age? What form would such an intervention take? What other risk factors should be targeted?
- Separation/loss is a major theme in many theories of depression, although cognitive and behaviour theories hypothesize other factors in the development of depression. What are the implications of this theme for the many children who lost a parent in the September 11 terrorist attacks on the United States? What role should this information play in the development of possible interventions for these children? Do you think that we will ever be able to prevent depression in vulnerable children before it begins?

16 chapter

Aging and Psychological Disorders

"Oh God, don't let me die stupid."
— Robertson Davies, expressing his concerns about cognitive declines associated with aging, from *The Toronto Star*, October 20, 1989

"Please, my near & dear ones, forgive me & understand. I hope this potion works. My spirit is already in another country & my body has become a damn nuisance. I have been so fortunate."
— from the suicide note of Canadian author Margaret Laurence, who was diagnosed with terminal cancer and took her own life via a drug overdose at age 60 (see King, 1997, p. 388)

David Brown Milne, Canadian 1882–1953, *The Blue Rocker*, 1914
oil on canvas, 50.8 x 50.8 cm, ART GALLERY OF ONTARIO, TORONTO
Anonymous gift in memory of J.S. McLean, Esquire, 1958

The story of Brendan Shanahan, Canadian NHL hockey player, and his father, Donal Shanahan, illustrates with poignancy the symptoms and difficulties associated with disorders related to aging.

BRENDAN'S FATHER never played hockey himself but being a hockey dad, he was just as fascinated as his son with this truly Canadian sport. "My father was always there for me, driving me to practices and games religiously. ..."

Brendan was barely 14 when he started noticing a change in his father's behaviour; the year was 1983. Early on, his father showed signs of confusion that gradually became worse. A full year went by before Donal Shanahan was diagnosed with Alzheimer's Disease at age 52. During this time, Brendan recalls feeling frustrated and impatient. "I didn't know what was happening and couldn't understand. I never heard of Alzheimer's until my dad was diagnosed with it—even then, the whole thing was foreign to me."

The symptoms appeared gradually as the disease took its course. Often, simple tasks became big challenges. Brendan remembers his father being puzzled by a pen. "He had forgotten how to use a pen and would hold it the wrong way. Driving was also a problem and he was no longer confident driving me to the games. Sometimes he would get lost getting to or from the game—other times he didn't know where to insert the car keys. On my 16th birthday, we drove to the licensing bureau to get my driving permit. It was the last time my father drove a car; he was 54." (See http://www.alzheimer.ca.)

Shanahan's father passed away when Brendan was 21. Brendan Shanahan has been an active fundraiser for research on Alzheimer's disease.

If you are fortunate, you will grow old one day. As you do, physiological changes are inevitable, and there may be many emotional and mental changes as well. Are aged people at higher risk for mental disorders than young people? Are earlier emotional problems, such as anxiety and depression, likely to become worse in old age? Do these emotional problems develop in people who did not have them when younger?

Most segments of North American society tend to have certain assumptions about old age. We fear that we will become doddering and befuddled. We worry that our sex lives will become unsatisfying. This chapter examines such issues and considers whether some therapies are better suited than others to deal with the psychological problems of older adults. We shall consider also whether, as life expectancy extends well into the seventies and beyond, society is devoting enough intellectual and monetary resources to studying aging and helping older adults.

In contrast to the esteem in which they are held in most Asian countries, older adults are generally not treated very well in North America, and numerous myths abound. The process of growing old, although inevitable for us all, is resented, even abhorred, by many. Perhaps this lack of regard for older adults stems from our own deep-seated fear of and misconceptions about growing old. The old person with serious infirmities is an unwelcome reminder that any one of us may one day walk with a less steady gait, see less clearly, taste food less keenly, and fall victim to some of the diseases and maladies that are the lot of many old people.

The general public endorses many mistaken beliefs about the elderly. For instance, considerable mythology has surrounded sexuality and aging, the principal assumption being that at the age of 65 sex becomes improper, unsatisfying, and even impossible. Evidence indicates otherwise. Barring serious physical disability, older people, well into their eighties and beyond, are capable of deriving enjoyment from sexual intercourse and other kinds of lovemaking.

The social problems of aging may be especially severe for women. Even with the consciousness-raising of the past four decades, our society does not readily accept in women the wrinkles and sagging that become more and more prominent with advancing years. Although grey hair at the temples and even a bald head are often considered distinguished in a man, signs of aging in women are not valued in society. The cosmetics and plastic-surgery industries make billions of dollars each year exploiting the fear inculcated in women about looking their age.

The physical realities of aging are complicated by **ageism**, which can be defined as discrimination against any person, young or old, based on chronological age. Ageism can be seen when a professor in her or his sixties is considered too old to continue teaching at a university or when a person over 75 is ignored in a social gathering on the assumption that he or she has nothing to contribute to the conversation. Like any prejudice, ageism ignores the diversity among people in favour of employing stereotypes (Gatz & Pearson, 1988).

Mental health professionals have until recently paid little attention to the psychological problems of older adults. This situation is gradually changing, as illustrated by the formation in 2002 of the Canadian Coalition for Seniors Mental Health (see http://www.ccsmh.ca). Another important initiative with mental health implications is the Canadian Longitudinal Study on Aging (CLSA), launched in 2004. The CLSA will provide basic information about healthy aging, health care utilization, and risk factors for diseases and disabilities. Its goals include preventive interventions and cost-efficient treatments. Hebert (2003) has indicated that this nationwide research initiative is vital in light of what he refers to as "The Big Boom," which is the impact that Canada's baby boomers will have on the country's health system when they become senior citizens en masse in less than a decade.

In the past, mental health professionals operated under the popular misconceptions that intellectual deterioration is prevalent and inevitable, that depression among old people is widespread and untreatable, that sex is a lost cause. Although those who provide mental health services are probably not extremely ageist (Gatz & Pearson, 1988), their attitudes and practices merit special attention because of the influence they have on policies that affect the lives of older adults. Since the 1980s, many schools and universities that prepare people for the health professions have added research and training in gerontology to their curricula, yet there is still a dearth of professionals committed primarily to serving the needs of older adults (Gatz & Smyer, 1992; Knight, 1996). The need for greater experience and more understanding in general is underscored by a survey conducted in Kingston, Ontario, that showed that family physicians feel less prepared to identify older patients with psychological problems than younger patients with psychological problems (Mackenzie, Gekoski, & Knov, 1999). They also reported that they were much less likely to treat or to refer older patients for treatment, and they rated psychotherapy as less effective with older people. These findings are disturbing because while elderly people seldom seek help for psychological problems, when they do, they are most likely to turn to their physicians.

In any discussion of the differences between the old and the not yet old, the old are usually defined as those over the age of 65. The decision to use this age was set largely by social policies, not because age 65 is some critical point at which the physiological and psychological processes of aging suddenly begin. To have some rough demarcation points, gerontologists usually divide people over age 65 into three groups: the young-old, those aged 65 to 74; the old-old, those aged 75 to 84; and the oldest-old, those over age 85. The health of these groups differs in important ways. According to a report by the National Advisory Council on Aging (Harper, 1999), in 1998 about 3.7 million Canadians (12.3 percent of the population) were 65 or older. This number is expected to jump about 10 million by 2041. The old-old segment of the Canadian population (those between 75 and 84) is growing at a rate of 3.5 percent per year, relative to the general growth rate of 1 percent (Gnaedinger, 1989). Thus, it is important to examine what we know about the psychological and neuropsychological issues facing older adults and to expose some of our misconceptions about aging.

In this chapter, we review some general concepts and topics critical to the study of aging. We look next at brain disorders of old age. Then, we examine psychological disorders—most of which were discussed earlier—focusing especially on how these disorders are manifested in old age. Finally, we discuss general issues of treatment and care for older adults.

ISSUES, CONCEPTS, AND METHODS IN THE STUDY OF OLDER ADULTS

Theory and research bearing on older adults require an understanding of several specialized issues, ranging from diversity among old people to problems unique to old age.

DIVERSITY IN OLDER ADULTS

The word *diversity* is well suited to the older population. Not only are older people different from one another, but they are more different from one another than are individuals in any other age group. People tend to become less alike as they grow older. That all old people are alike is a prejudice held by many people. The many differences among people who are 65 and older will become increasingly evident as you read this chapter.

Advancing age need not lead to a curtailment of activities. Hazel McCallion, the mayor of Mississauga, Ontario, celebrated her 80th birthday in 2001. She is one of Canada's most active citizens.

AGE, COHORT, AND TIME-OF-MEASUREMENT EFFECTS

Chronological age is not as simple a variable in psychological research as it might seem. Because other factors associated with age may be at work, we must be cautious when we attribute differences in age groups solely to aging. In the field of aging, as in studies of earlier development, a distinction is made among three kinds of effects (see Table 16.1):

- Age effects are the consequences of being a given chronological age.

Table 16.1

Age, Cohort, and Time-of-Measurement Effects

Age Effects	Cohort Effects	Time-of-Measurement Effects
The consequences of being a chronological age (e.g., Jewish boys are bar mitzvahed at age 13).	The consequences of having been born in a given year and having grown up during a particular time period (e.g., people who invested money in the stock market in the late 1990s viewed investments in equities as a reasonably safe and very lucrative place to put their money—unlike people who lost a lot of money in the bear markets of the 1930s or late 1960s).	The consequences of the effects that a particular factor can have at a particular time (e.g., people responding in the 1990s to surveys about their sexual behaviour were more likely to be frank than people responding to the same questions in the 1950s since public discussions of sex were much more the norm in the 1990s).

- **Cohort effects** are the consequences of having been born in a given year and having grown up during a particular time period with its own unique pressures, problems, challenges, and opportunities. For instance, the 1991 Canadian Study of Health and Aging is a national cohort study that investigated the prevalence and characteristics of dementia and Alzheimer's disease in a sample of over 9,000 people who were aged 65 or older when assessed in 1991 (see Canadian Perspectives 16.1 for more information).
- **Time-of-measurement effects** are confounds that arise because events at an exact point in time can have a specific effect on a variable being studied over time (Schaie & Hertzog, 1982).

The two major research designs used to assess developmental change, the cross-sectional and the longitudinal, clarify these terms. In **cross-sectional studies**, the investigator compares different age groups at the same moment in time on the variable of interest. Suppose that in 1995 we took a poll and found that many interviewees over age 80 spoke with a European accent, whereas those in their forties and fifties did not. Could we conclude that as people grow older, they develop European accents? Hardly! Cross-sectional studies do not examine the same people over time; consequently, they allow us to make statements only about age effects in a particular study or experiment, not about age changes over time.

In **longitudinal studies**, the researcher selects one cohort—say, the graduating class of 2002—and periodically retests it using the same measure over a number of years. This design allows us to trace individual patterns of consistency or change over time—cohort effects—and to analyze how behaviour in early life relates to behaviour in old age.

However, because each cohort is unique, conclusions drawn from longitudinal studies are restricted to the cohort chosen. If members of a cohort studied from 1956 to 1996 are found to decline in sexual activity as they enter their sixties, we cannot conclude that the sexuality of those in a cohort studied from 1996 to 2036 will decline when they reach the same age.

An additional problem with longitudinal studies is that participants often drop out as the studies proceed, creating a bias commonly called **selective mortality**. The least-able people are the most likely to drop out, leaving a nonrepresentative group of people who are usually healthier than the general population. Thus, findings based on longitudinal studies may be overly optimistic about the rate of decline of a variable such as sexual activity over the lifespan.

Cohort effects refer to the fact that people of the same chronological age may differ considerably depending on when they were born.

DIAGNOSING AND ASSESSING PSYCHOPATHOLOGY IN LATER LIFE

The DSM-IV-TR criteria for older adults are basically the same as those for younger adults. The nature and manifestations of mental disorders are usually assumed to be the same in adulthood and old age, even though little research supports this assumption (Gatz, Kasl-Godley, & Karel, 1996; LaRue, Dessonville, & Jarvik, 1985). We often do not know what certain symptoms in older adults mean because we have few specifics about psychopathology in old age (Zarit, Eiler, & Hassinger, 1985). For example, somatic symptoms are generally more prevalent in late life, but they are also evident in depression in older adults. Are the somatic symptoms of a depressed older adult necessarily a part of depression, or might they reflect physical changes?

Accurate assessment of elderly people for the purposes of establishing diagnoses and conducting research requires assessment measures tailored to elderly people. A measure of cognitive functioning is often included as standard practice in research to determine whether the elderly respondent has experienced declines in cognitive ability. Researchers often assess cognitive functioning with the Mini-Mental State Examination (MMSE; Folstein, Folstein, & McHugh, 1975) in its original or modified form (i.e., the Modified Mini-Mental State Exam). The MMSE is a brief measure of an individual's cognitive state, assessing "orientation, memory, and attention ... ability to name, follow verbal and written commands, write a sentence spontaneously, and copy a complex polygon" (Folstein et al., 1975, p. 190).

Because some elderly people will have diminished attention spans, one goal is to develop short but reliable measures suitable for screening purposes. One relatively simple measure used to detect dementia and Alzheimer's disease is the clock drawing subtest of the Clock Test. The Clock Test was developed by Holly Tuokko of the University of Victoria and her associates (Tuokko et al., 1992, 1995). Respondents are presented with a previously drawn circle (7 cm in diameter) and are asked to imagine that the circle is the face of a clock and to put the numbers on the clock and then draw the hand placement for the time of 11:10. Up to 25 different types of errors can occur, including omissions, perseverations (i.e., repetitions), rotations, misplacements, distortions, substitutions, and additions. This simple test has been found to be reliable and valid, though results vary depending on the scoring system used (see Tuokko et al., 2000).

Another assessment goal is to create measures whose item content is tailored directly to the concerns and symptoms reported by elderly people, not to those of younger respondents. One well-known measure crafted for the elderly is the Geriatric Depression Scale (GDS; Yesavage et al., 1983), a true-false self-report measure. The GDS has acceptable psychometric characteristics and is regarded as the standard measure for assessing depression in the elderly. Another self-report measure created for the elderly is the Geriatric Hopelessness Scale (GHS; Fry 1984). The GHS was constructed on the basis of a factor analysis of pessimistic themes that emerged during semi-structured interviews with 60 elderly Canadians. Although the GHS is linked consistently with depression in the elderly, concerns have been raised about the reliability of the GHS and its factor structure (Hayslip, Lopez, & Nation, 1991). This underscores the need to carefully evaluate the properties of measures created for the elderly.

Range of Problems

We know that mental health may be tied to the problems in a person's life. As a group, no other people have more of these problems than the aged. They have them all—physical decline and disabilities, sensory and neurological deficits, loss of loved ones, the cumulative effects of a lifetime of many unfortunate experiences, and social stresses such as ageism. One concern expressed by the World Health Organization (WHO; 2002) is that elderly people with a mental disorder may suffer from "double jeopardy"—that is, they suffer the stigmas associated with being older and being mentally ill. Unfortunately, almost no research has explored stigma associated with mental illness among older adults (WHO, 2002).

It is important to remember that in addition to a lifetime of exposure to losses and to other stressors, older adults have many positive life experiences, coping mechanisms, and wisdom on which to draw. Moreover, older adults who belong to groups that provide meaningful, strong roles for them seem to have an easier time adjusting to growing old (Keith, 1982).

OLD AGE AND BRAIN DISORDERS

Although the majority of older people do not have brain disorders, these problems account for more admissions and hospital inpatient days than any other geriatric condition (Christie, 1982). We will examine two principal types of brain disorders, dementia and delirium.

Dementia

Dementia—what laypeople call senility—is a general descriptive term for gradual deterioration of intellectual abilities to the point that social and occupational functions are impaired. Difficulty remembering things, especially recent events, is the most prominent symptom, and reported memory problems in people who objectively have normal cognition predict subsequent dementia (St. John & Montgomery, 2002). People with dementia may leave tasks unfinished because they forget to return to them after an interruption. The person who had started to fill a teakettle at the sink leaves the water running; a parent is unable to remember the name of a daughter or son. Hygiene may be poor and appearance slovenly because the person forgets to bathe or how to dress. Patients with dementia also get lost, even in familiar settings.

Judgement may become faulty, and the person may have difficulty comprehending situations and making plans or decisions. People with dementia relinquish their standards and lose control of their impulses; they may use coarse language, tell inappropriate jokes, or shoplift. The ability to deal with abstract ideas deteriorates, and disturbances in emotions are common, including symptoms of depression, flatness of affect, and sporadic emotional outbursts. Patients with dementia are likely to show language disturbances as well, such as vague patterns of speech. Although the motor system is intact, they may have difficulty carrying out motor activities, such as those involved in brushing the teeth or dressing themselves. They may also have trouble recognizing familiar surroundings or naming common objects. Episodes of delirium, a state of great mental confusion (discussed in detail later), may also occur.

The course of dementia may be progressive, static, or remitting, depending on the cause. Many people with progressive dementia eventually become withdrawn and apathetic. In the terminal phase of the illness, the personality loses its sparkle and integrity. Relatives and friends say that the person is just not himself or herself anymore. Social involvement with others keeps narrowing. Finally, the person is oblivious to his or her surroundings.

The prevalence of dementia increases with advancing age. One U.S. study found a prevalence of 1 percent in people aged 65 to 75, 4 percent in those aged 75 to 84, and 10 percent in those over age 84 (George et al., 1991). The annual incidence—that is, the number of new cases developing in a year—in the United States is more than 5 percent for those over age 85 (Gao et al., 1998).

An increasing number of Canadians are projected to suffer from various forms of dementia, including Alzheimer's disease. According to the Canadian Study of Health and Aging Working Group (1994a), about 161,000 Canadians had Alzheimer's disease in 1991; this will increase to 314,000 in 2011 and 509,000 in 2031. These estimates reflect increases in longevity and in the proportion of elderly people in the population. The Alzheimer Society of Canada estimates that more than 750,000 Canadians will develop Alzheimer's and other dementias in the next 30 years.

Causes of Dementia Dementias are typically classified into three types. Alzheimer's disease is the most common. Then, there are the frontal-temporal and frontal-subcortical dementias, which are defined by the areas of the brain that are most affected.

Alzheimer's Disease **Alzheimer's disease** was described in the case that began this chapter. It accounts for about 50 percent of dementia in older people. About one in 13 Canadians over the age of 65 has Alzheimer's disease or a related dementia. In Alzheimer's disease, initially described by the German neurologist Alois Alzheimer in 1906, the brain tissue deteriorates irreversibly, and death usually occurs 10 or 12 years after the onset of symptoms. The median survival time is 3.1 years for Canadians with Alzheimer's disease and 3.3 years for Canadians with vascular dementia (Wolfson et al., 2001). Gender is a factor. Women with Alzheimer's disease live longer than men with Alzheimer's disease, but more women than men die as a result of this disease (Alloul et al., 1998). In fact, Alzheimer's disease is the 10th leading cause of death for women and the 15th leading cause of death for men in Canada (Stokes & Lindsay, 1996). The person may at first have difficulties only in concentration and in memory for newly learned material, and may appear absentminded and irritable, shortcomings that can be overlooked for several years but that eventually interfere with daily living. Indeed, well before the onset of any clinical symptoms, subtle deficits in learning and memory are revealed by neuropsychological tests in people who will later develop the disease (Linn et al., 1995). As the disease develops, the person often blames others for personal failings and may have delusions of being persecuted. Memory continues to deteriorate, and the person becomes increasingly disoriented and agitated. A study at the University of Victoria found that patients are wholly unaware of the extent of their memory decline (Correa, Graves, & Costa, 1996).

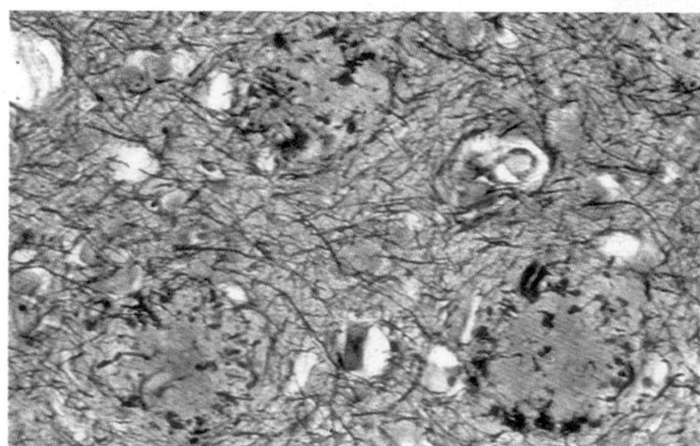

In the photograph above of brain tissue from a patient with Alzheimer's disease, the waxy amyloid shows up as areas of dark pink. Below are computer-generated images of a brain of a patient with Alzheimer's disease (left) and a normal brain. Note that the patient's brain has shrunk considerably owing to the loss of nerve cells.

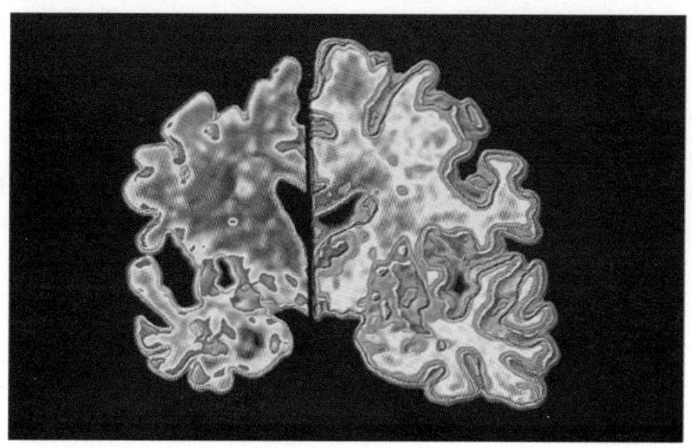

Canadian Perspectives/16.1

The Canadian Study of Health and Aging

The Canadian Study of Health and Aging (CSHA) began in February 1991 and the first phase of data collection ended in May 1992. This nationwide project is coordinated by the University of Ottawa and Health Canada, Division of Aging and Seniors, and involves researchers from at least 18 universities throughout Canada and 9,008 seniors aged 65 or older drawn from 36 communities, as well as 1,255 institutionalized elderly people. Participants were selected by random sampling with stratification by area. They underwent interviews and medical examinations as part of being in this study. The 45-minute interview focused on gathering demographic data and information on daily living and health status. Participants were also administered the modified version of the Mini-Mental State Examination (MMSE). The medical examination focused on confirming whether dementia was evident. It included neuropsychological testing and a structured interview with an examination. The test battery assessed memory, abstract thinking, judgement, language, recognition of familiar objects, attention, and psychomotor speed (CSHA Working Group, 1994a).

The CSHA website outlines the four main goals of this massive project:

1 to use a common research protocol to estimate prevalence of dementia in Canadians aged 65 and older

2 to identify risk factors associated with Alzheimer's disease

3 to examine patterns of caring for Canadians with dementia

4 to develop a uniform database for subsequent longitudinal investigations

The fourth objective refers to the fact that this study will be continued in phases, with the results of phase two just beginning to emerge (e.g., Hogan & Ebly, 2000).

Many studies from the initial phase of this project have already been published, and much has been learned about forms of dementia in Canadians. Several findings are described in other parts of this chapter. Other noteworthy results include the following:

1 The prevalence of Alzheimer's disease and other forms of dementia is 8 percent in Canada. Furthermore, another 16.8 percent of Canadians who are 65 or over have some cognitive impairment but no dementia, with many of these people having circumscribed memory loss (see Graham et al., 1997). This study found that cognitive impairment in the absence of dementia (i.e., subclinical dementia) still involves a need for institutional care, and follow-up research showed that subclinical dementia predicted negative outcomes such as death and dementia over a five-year period (Tuokko et al., 2003). MMSE scores that are low but still in the normal range have been shown to predict death and institutionalization (St. John et al., 2002).

2 Confirmed risk factors for Alzheimer's disease in this study were a family history of Alzheimer's disease, head trauma, and lower education (CSHA Working Group, 1994b).

3 Approximately one-half of Canadians with dementia are institutionalized, and the other half are community residents. Most primary caregivers are female and married. Wives are most likely to be the informal caregiver (i.e., family member or friend) for seniors in the community, while adult daughters are most likely to be the informal caregiver for institutionalized seniors (CSHA Working Group, 1994a).

4 A re-evaluation in 1996 of the original participants revealed that there are over 60,000 new cases of dementia per year in Canada (CSHA Working Group, 2000).

5 A follow-up study of which Canadians subsequently developed dementia showed that having a greater chronological age, lower MMSE scores, and identification of memory difficulties by caregivers are risk factors for dementia (Hogan & Ebly, 2000).

Thinking Critically

1. The cause or causes of Alzheimer's disease have received increased attention from clinical scientists in the last few years. Why is this disorder considered one of the most pressing problems in Canadian society? What are the implications of the findings thus far from the Canadian Study of Health and Aging?
2. Would you be prepared to make "eldercare" one of your responsibilities in the future should a loved one develop dementia? Would you put your own life on hold in order to care for a loved one? Or, do you think that this is the government's responsibility?

The main physiological change in the brain, evident at autopsy, is an atrophy (wasting away) of the cerebral cortex, first the entorhinal cortex and the hippocampus and later the frontal, temporal, and parietal lobes. As neurons and synapses are lost, the fissures widen and the ridges become narrower and flatter. The ventricles also become enlarged. **Plaques**—small, round areas comprising the remnants of the lost neurons and b-amyloid, a waxy protein deposit—are scattered throughout the cortex. Tangled, abnormal protein filaments—**neurofibrillary tangles**—accumulate within the cell bodies of neurons. These plaques and tangles are present throughout the cerebral cortex and the hippocampus.

A recent quantitative review of neuroimaging studies involving 3,411 patients led Toronto researchers to conclude that, in terms of structural imaging, volume loss within the hippocampus (and episodic memory impairment) best discriminated people in the early stages of Alzheimer's disease from control participants. However, volume loss within the medial temporal lobes (and associated naming deficits) was the most sensitive measure when identifying patients with Alzheimer's disease for four or more years (Zakzanis, Graham, & Campbell, 2003).

The cerebellum, spinal cord, and motor and sensory areas of the cortex are less affected, which is why Alzheimer's patients do not appear to have anything physically wrong with them until late in the disease process. For some time, patients are able to walk around normally, and their overlearned habits, such as making small talk, remain intact, so that in short encounters strangers may not notice anything amiss.

About 25 percent of patients with Alzheimer's disease also have brain deterioration similar to the deterioration in Parkinson's disease. Neurons are lost in the nigrostriatal pathway.

There is a lively controversy over the relative importance of the amyloid deposits and the neurofibrillary tangles in Alzheimer's disease (Wischik, 1994). Both substances can disrupt brain function. The cell dies when amyloid builds up in it. Neurofibrillary tangles are associated with changes in tau proteins, which are crucial for maintaining the transport of essential components of neural function (such as synaptic vesicles) from the axon to the synaptic terminal. Evidence favouring the importance of amyloid comes primarily from genetic studies. However, an increase in amyloid is found in normal aging and is not unique to Alzheimer's disease. The tangles, in contrast, are more specific to Alzheimer's and thus may be more important in its etiology. Furthermore, when amyloid and tangles are correlated with cognitive deficits, tangles show a stronger association (Berg et al., 1998).

Although neural pathways using other transmitters (e.g., serotonin, norepinephrine) deteriorate in Alzheimer's (Wester et al., 1988), those using acetylcholine (ACh) are of particular importance. Evidence suggests that anticholinergic drugs (those that reduce ACh) can produce memory impairments in normal people similar to those found in Alzheimer's patients. There are fewer acetylcholine terminals in the brains of patients with Alzheimer's disease (Strong et al., 1991), and levels of the major metabolite of acetylcholine are also low and are associated with greater mental deterioration (Wester et al., 1988).

There is very strong evidence for a genetic basis for Alzheimer's. The risk for Alzheimer's is increased in first-degree relatives of afflicted individuals (Silverman et al., 1994), and concordance for MZ twins is greater than for DZ twins (Bergen, Engedal, & Kringlen, 1997). The role of genetic factors is the main focus of the MIRAGE (Multi-Institutional Research in Alzheimer Genetic Epidemiology) Project that examined predictors at 13 centres in Canada, Germany, and the United States. This project found that by the time they reach the age of 80, children of parents who both developed Alzheimer's disease will themselves have a cumulative risk of 54 percent, which is 1.5 times the level of risk for children with one parent who developed the disease and five times the level of risk for children whose parents did not (Lautenschlager et al., 1996). Among early-onset (before age 60) cases, which account for less than 5 percent of cases, the inheritance pattern suggests the operation of a single dominant gene.

Because people with Down syndrome often develop Alzheimer's disease if they survive until middle age, interest focused initially on chromosome 21, which is aberrant in Down syndrome. A gene controlling the protein responsible for the formation of b-amyloid was found on the long arm of chromosome 21, and studies have demonstrated that this gene causes the development of about 5 percent of cases of early-onset Alzheimer's. Dominant genes causing the disease have also been found on chromosomes 1 and 14; the gene on chromosome 14 accounts for 75 percent of early-onset cases (Levy-Lahad & Bird, 1996). Note that we used the verb *cause* in the previous two sentences. Unlike the genetic diatheses we have described in earlier chapters, the presence of these Alzheimer's disease genes does not appear to require activation by a stressor to result in the disease. No person with the gene on chromosome 21 has survived beyond the age of 67 without developing Alzheimer's disease.

The majority of late-onset cases of Alzheimer's disease exhibit a particular form of a gene (called the apolipoprotein E 4 allele) on chromosome 19, which functions more like the genetic diatheses we have considered so often before. Having one E 4 allele increases the risk for Alzheimer's disease to almost 50 percent, and having two alleles brings the risk to above 90 percent (Farlow, 1997). Having a different form of this gene (the E 2 allele) lowers the risk of developing Alzheimer's disease.

How, exactly, does the gene increase the risk for Alzheimer's disease? While the answer is not certain, the gene appears to be related to the development of both plaques and tangles, and it seems to increase the likelihood that the brain will incur damage from free radicals (unstable molecules derived from oxygen that attack proteins and DNA).

Finally, the environment is likely to play a role in most cases of Alzheimer's, as demonstrated by reports of long-lived MZ twins who are discordant for the disorder. The reasoning is the same as for judging the importance of genetic and environmental factors in any disorder—if two people with the same genetic material (i.e., MZ twins) do not both develop a particular disorder, then environmental factors must play a role.

A July 2004 international conference on Alzheimer's disease included reports of two new longitudinal studies on this topic (see www.alz.org). A study of World War II veterans by Brenda Plassman from Duke University showed that, if one identical twin had the disease, there was a 40 percent chance that his or her twin would contract the disease (see www.alz.org). Another study of the Swedish Twin Registry by Margaret Gatz from the University of Southern California showed there was a 59 percent chance that the identical twin would also develop Alzheimer's disease. Gatz highlighted the role of environmental factors and reported that lower education is a risk factor because lower education is related to a host of environmental factors.

A history of head injury is a risk factor for developing Alzheimer's disease (Rasmussen et al., 1995). This finding was confirmed by results from the MIRAGE Project (see Guo et al., 2000), described earlier. Analyses of longitudinal data from the Mirage Project also show that depression increases the risk for Alzheimer's disease (Green et al., 2003).

Some environmental factors appear to offer protection against developing Alzheimer's. Nonsteroidal anti-inflammatory drugs such as aspirin appear to reduce the risk of Alzheimer's (Stewart et al., 1997), as does nicotine (Whitehouse, 1997). Of course, both these protective factors also have undesirable effects—liver damage from anti-inflammatories and cardiovascular damage from smoking.

General research on cognitive decline in the elderly supports the phrase "Use it or lose it!" As part of the Victoria Longitudinal Study, Hultsch, Hertzog, Small, and Dixon (1999) tested 250 middle-aged and older adults over a six-year period and showed a link between undergoing changes in intellectually related activities and changes in cognitive functioning. Their results suggest that remaining active at

focus on discovery/16.1

The Nun Study: Unlocking the Secrets of Alzheimer's?

"It's the day after Easter, and the first crocus shoots have ventured tentatively above the ground at the convent on good Counsel Hill. This is Minnesota, however; the temperature is 23 F and the wind chill makes it feel far colder. Yet even though she's wearing only a skirt and sweater, Sister Ada, 91, wants to go outside. She wants to feed the pigs.

But the pigs she and the other nuns once cared for have been gone for 30 years. Sister Ada simply can't keep that straight. In recent years, her brain, like a time machine gone awry, has been wrenching her back and forth between the present and the past, depositing her without warning into the days when she taught primary schoolchildren in Minnesota or to the years when she was a college student in St. Paul. Or to the times when she and the sisters had to feed the pigs several times a day."

— Michael D. Lemonick and Alice Park, *Time: Canadian Edition*, May 14, 2001

The Nun Study is arguably one of the most remarkable research investigations in recent years. David Snowdon from the University of Kentucky has been studying 678 Catholic nuns from the American School Sisters of Notre Dame since 1986. The sisters have consented to allow Snowdon and colleagues to research their personal and medical histories, and they have undergone cognitive testing on an annual basis. They have also agreed to donate their brains for analysis via autopsies after they die.

This study is providing insight from a long-term perspective on the factors associated with the development of Alzheimer's disease and other forms of dementia. For instance, the nuns had written autobiographies in the weeks preceding their religious vows. These autobiographies were analyzed for their grammatical complexity and idea density, concepts related to general knowledge, vocabulary skills, and other cognitive abilities. Excerpts from two sisters illustrate the differences in linguistic ability that were found:

> *Low linguistic ability:* I was born in Eau Claire, Wis. on May, 24, 1913 and was baptized in St. James church.
>
> *High linguistic ability:* The happiest day of my life so far was my First Communion Day which was in June nineteen hundred and twenty when I was but eight years of age, and four years later I was confirmed by Bishop D. D. (Snowden et al., 1996, p. 530)

Low linguistic ability was found in 90 percent of those who developed Alzheimer's disease and in only 13 percent of those who didn't (Snowden et al., 1996).

Danner, Snowden, and Friesen (2001) also investigated the expression of positive and negative emotions in the previous writings of 180 nuns. Nuns who expressed more positive emotions lived longer, and nuns who eventually succumbed to Alzheimer's disease gradually expressed fewer positive emotions prior to the disease's onset. A related analysis of language samples taken over 60 years used a grammatical complexity measure to confirm earlier findings suggesting that reduced language ability was a precursor for dementia (Kemper et al., 2001).

One drawback of the Nun Study is that even though it is longitudinal, it does not enable the researchers to make definitive cause and effect statements about the factors of importance in aging and Alzheimer's disease. Nevertheless, this study is remarkable, not only because of the extreme cooperation that the nuns have given in the name of science, but also because the nuns are all experiencing a common environment and have similar experiences, which reduces the likelihood that other factors have biased the results.

the cognitive level may buffer or protect an individual in terms of the degree of cognitive decline experienced. Having a high level of cognitive ability may also offer protection. This possibility was demonstrated in a well-known study of nuns that is receiving increasing media attention (see Focus on Discovery 16.1).

A related protective factor is being bilingual. Innovative research by Ellen Bialystok from York University and Fergus Craik from the Rotman Research Institute and their colleagues indicates that being bilingual protects against the negative effects of aging on cognitive control (Bialystok, Craik, Klein, & Viswanathan, 2004). Tests of older adults showed that bilingual participants responded much more quickly, relative to unilingual participants, in experimental conditions that placed heavy demands on working memory.

Frontal-Temporal Dementias This type of dementia accounts for 10 to 15 percent of cases. It typically begins in a person's late fifties. In addition to the usual cognitive impairments of a dementia, frontal-temporal dementias are marked by extreme behavioural and personality changes. Sometimes patients are very apathetic and unresponsive to their environment; at other times, they show an opposite pattern of euphoria, overactivity, and impulsivity (Levy et al., 1996). Unlike Alzheimer's disease, frontal-temporal dementias are not closely linked to loss of cholinergic neurons. Serotonin neurons are most affected, and there is widespread loss of neurons in the frontal and temporal lobes. *Pick's disease* is one cause of frontal-temporal dementia. Like Alzheimer's disease, Pick's disease is a degenerative disorder in which neurons are lost. It is also characterized by the presence of Pick bodies, spherical inclusions within neurons. Frontal-temporal dementias have a strong genetic component (Usman, 1997).

Frontal-Subcortical Dementias Because these dementias affect subcortical brain areas, which are involved in the control of motor movements, both cognition and motor activity are affected. Types of frontal-subcortical dementias include the following:

- *Huntington's chorea* is caused by a single dominant gene located on chromosome 4 and is diagnosed principally by neurologists on the basis of genetic testing. Its major behavioural feature is the presence of writhing (choreiform) movements. Perhaps the best-known person with this disease is the late folk-song writer and singer Woody Guthrie.
- *Parkinson's disease* is marked by muscle tremors, muscular rigidity, and akinesia (an inability to initiate movement), and can lead to dementia. Canadian Michael J. Fox has Parkinson's disease.
- *Vascular dementia* is the second most common type, next to Alzheimer's disease. It is diagnosed when a patient with dementia has neurological signs, such as weakness in an arm or abnormal reflexes, or when brain scans show evidence of cerebrovascular disease. Most commonly, the patient had a series of strokes in which a clot formed, impairing circulation and causing cell death. Genetic factors appear to be of no importance (Bergen et al., 1997), and risk for vascular dementia increases with the same risk factors generally associated with cardiovascular disease—for example, a high level of "bad" cholesterol (Moroney et al., 1999).

Canadian actor Michael J. Fox has Parkinson's disease.

Other Causes of Dementia A number of infectious diseases can produce irreversible dementia. *Encephalitis*, a generic term for any inflammation of brain tissue, is caused by viruses that enter the brain either from other parts of the body (such as the sinuses or ears) or from the bites of mosquitoes or ticks. *Meningitis*, an inflammation of the membranes covering the outer brain, is usually caused by a bacterial infection. The organism that produces the venereal disease syphilis (*Treponema pallidum*) can invade the brain and cause dementia.

Finally, head traumas, brain tumours, nutritional deficiencies (especially of B-complex vitamins), kidney or liver failure, and endocrine-gland problems such as hyperthyroidism can result in dementia. Exposure to toxins, such as lead or mercury, as well as chronic use of drugs, including alcohol, are additional causes.

Treatment of Dementia If the dementia has a reversible cause, appropriate medical treatment (such as correcting a hormonal imbalance) can be beneficial. Despite numerous investigations, no clinically significant treatment has been found that can halt or reverse Alzheimer's disease, although some drugs, as described here, show promise in effecting modest improvement in certain cognitive functions for a short period of time.

Biological Treatments of Alzheimer's Disease Because Alzheimer's disease involves the death of brain cells that secrete acetylcholine, various studies have attempted to increase the levels of this neurotransmitter. Research using choline (a precursor of the enzyme that catalyzes the reaction that produces acetylcholine) and physostigmine (a drug that prevents the breakdown of acetylcholine) has been disappointing. Tetrahydroaminoacridine (tacrine, brand name Cognex), which inhibits the enzyme that breaks down acetylcholine, produces mild improvement or slows the progression of cognitive decline (Qizilbash et al., 1998). Tacrine cannot be used in high doses, however, because it has severe side effects; for example, it is toxic to the liver. Donepezil (Aricept) is similar to tacrine in its method of action and results but produces fewer side effects (Rogers et al., 1998). Hydergine is another drug approved for use in Alzheimer's disease; its effects appear to be very modest at best (Schneider & Olin, 1994).

Long-term strategies focus on slowing the progression of the disease. Operating on the hypothesis that the buildup of b-amyloid is the crucial factor in Alzheimer's, researchers are focusing on ways of blocking the creation of amyloid from its precursor protein (Whyte, Bayreuther, & Masters, 1994). Findings also indicate that antioxidants, such as vitamin E, may be useful in slowing the progression of the disease (Sano et al., 1997). Management of other symptoms of Alzheimer's includes many of the drugs previously discussed, (e.g., phenothiazines for paranoia, antidepressants for depression, benzodiazepines for anxiety, and sedatives for sleep difficulties).

Psychosocial Treatments for Patients and Their Families
Although effective medical treatment for Alzheimer's is not yet available, patients and their families can be helped to deal with the effects of the disease. The general psychological approach is supportive. The overall goal is to minimize the disruption caused by the patient's behavioural changes. Health workers achieved this by allowing the person and the family the opportunity to discuss the illness and its consequences, providing accurate information about it, helping family members care for the patient in the home, and encouraging a realistic attitude in dealing with the disease's specific challenges (Knight, 1996; Zarit, 1980).

Counselling the person with Alzheimer's is difficult. Because of cognitive losses, psychotherapy provides little long-term benefit for those with severe deterioration. However, some patients seem to enjoy and be reassured by occasional conversations with professionals and with others not directly involved in their lives—in both individual and group settings. Interventions employed with normally functioning older adults, like Butler's life review (described below), can also be useful for early- to mid-stage Alzheimer's patients, whose cognitive abilities have not markedly deteriorated (Kasl-Godley & Gatz, 2002). In contrast to approaches taken with other psychological problems, it may be desirable not to make an effort to get patients to admit to their problems, for denial may be the best coping mechanism available (Zarit, 1980).

For every institutionalized individual with a severely disabling dementia, there are at least two individuals with dementia living in the community, usually supported by a spouse, daughter, or other family member. As the care of the older adult with dementia generally falls on family members, psychosocial treatment concerns not only the individual, but the family as well. Caring for a person with Alzheimer's has been shown to be extremely stressful (Anthony-Bergstone, Zarit, & Gatz, 1988). Analyses reported by the Canadian Study of Health and Aging Working Group (1994b) indicate that depression is twice as evident among caregivers as among non-caregivers. This CSHA study is important because it is one of the few caregiver studies that began with a nationally representative sample of individuals suffering from dementia and their caregivers.

Follow-up analyses of the CSHA data by Chappell and Penning (1996) indicate that depression and feelings of being burdened are highly correlated among caregivers. Caregivers were especially likely to feel burdened in response to apathy and an apparent lack of interest on the part of the patient, despite the best efforts of the caregiver. Subsequent research has confirmed that objective and subjective indicators of burden predict psychological distress and reduced well-being in caregivers (Chappell & Reid, 2002; Provencher et al., 2003).

The CSHA Working Group (1994a) found that caregivers are also more likely than non-caregivers to experience chronic health problems. Other studies have found more physical illness (McDowell et al., 2002; Zunzunegui et al., 2002) and decreased immune functioning (Kiecolt-Glaser et al., 1991) among caregivers. In many instances, the disorders seem to be attributable to the stresses of caregiving; prior to these challenges, the families of caregivers usually did not experience such health difficulties (Gatz, Bengtson, & Blum, 1990).

Some resources are available to assist caregivers. In Canada, the Alzheimer Society of Canada has an online caregivers' forum that enables caregivers to share their experiences via the Internet and seek support and comfort from others (see http://www.alzheimer.ca). Expressing one's concerns online is a compelling way to achieve a better understanding within society of the challenges faced by caregivers.

Caregivers of patients with dementia can also benefit from participating in psychoeducation groups. Hebert et al. (2003) found that participants in weekly sessions on stress appraisal and coping reported significant improvements in their reactions to the behavioural problems of care receivers.

Dispositional factors involving personality traits of the caregivers themselves also seem important. A recent study conducted in Guelph, Ontario showed that levels of functioning were much higher in family caregivers of relatives with dementia if the caregivers were relatively high in optimism (Gottlieb & Rooney, 2004). Specific outcome expectancies in terms of more positive self-efficacy beliefs about specific aspects of the caregiving process were also beneficial.

Because the family members are affected so powerfully, it is often recommended that they be given respites from their task. The patient may be hospitalized for a week, or a health care worker may take over and give the family a much-needed break. Unfortunately, a review of respite programs in Canada by Gottlieb and Johnson (2000) concluded that the phrase "too little too late" can be applied; that is, when respites are utilized, which is infrequently, the use occurs quite late and the pattern of use is not intense or protracted in time. Typically, up to one-half of caregivers do not avail themselves of available programs, and when they do participate, it is between two and four and a half years after assuming the caregiver role.

Perhaps the most wrenching decision facing caregivers is whether to institutionalize the person with dementia. A qualitative study of caregivers in Northern Canada suggested that feelings of guilt among caregivers are intense when a person must be institutionalized, but their most predominant emotion is worry (Loos & Boyd, 1997). One wife who had assumed the caregiver role stated, "Putting him in the [institution], even though the care is good, is like putting him in jail. It haunts you" (Loos & Bowd, 1997, p. 510). For many people, custodial care (e.g., in-home assistance with bathing and grooming) can delay the need for placement in a nursing home. However, the patient's nursing needs may become so onerous and mental state so deteriorated that placement in a nursing home is the only realistic option for both the person and the family. The conflicts people face when making this decision are considerable. Extensive research in Canada and elsewhere has evaluated the predictors associated with the decision to institutionalize someone with dementia. Alloul et al.'s (1998) review concluded that the three best predictors of institutionalization are the elderly person's level of aggressivity, incontinence, and the presence of psychiatric disturbances.

Not everyone has a caregiver. Over 3,000 people in Canada with dementia continue to live in the community despite the fact that they don't have any formal or informal caregiver (CSHA Working Group, 1994a). A study of Canadians "home alone" with dementia showed that these people (predominantly women) were perceived as having much greater risk for accidents and injuries than people with dementia living with their spouses, but in fact, they did not die at comparatively higher rates (Tuokko, MacCourt, & Heath, 1999).

DELIRIUM

The term delirium is derived from the Latin words *de*, meaning "from" or "out of," and *lira*, meaning "furrow" or "track." The term implies being off track or deviating from the usual state (Wells & Duncan, 1980). Delirium is typically described as "a clouded state of consciousness." The patient, sometimes rather suddenly, has great trouble concentrating and focusing attention and cannot maintain a coherent and directed stream of thought. In the early stages, the person with delirium is frequently restless, particularly at night. The sleep-waking cycle becomes disturbed, so that the person is drowsy during the day and awake, restless, and agitated during the night. The individual is generally worse during sleepless nights and in the dark. Vivid dreams and nightmares are common.

Delirious patients may be impossible to engage in conversation because of their wandering attention and fragmented thinking. In severe delirium, speech is rambling and incoherent. Bewildered and confused, some delirious individuals lose their sense of time and place. They are often so inattentive that they cannot be questioned about orientation. Memory impairment, especially for recent events, is common. In the course of a 24-hour period, however, delirious people have lucid intervals and become alert and coherent. These daily fluctuations help distinguish delirium from other syndromes, especially Alzheimer's disease.

Perceptual disturbances are frequent. Individuals mistake the unfamiliar for the familiar, stating, for example, that they are at home instead of in a hospital. Although illusions and hallucinations are common, particularly visual and mixed visual-auditory ones, they are not always present. Paranoid delusions have been noted in 40 to 70 percent of delirious older adults. These delusions tend to be poorly worked out, fleeting, and changeable.

Swings in activity and mood accompany disordered thoughts and perceptions. Delirious people can be erratic, ripping their clothes one moment and sitting lethargically the next. They are in great emotional turmoil and may shift rapidly from one emotion to another—depression, fright, anger, euphoria, and irritability. Fever, flushed face, dilated pupils, tremors, rapid heartbeat, elevated blood pressure, and incontinence are common. If the delirium proceeds, the person will completely lose touch with reality and may become stuporous (Lipowski, 1983).

Although delirium is one of the most frequent biological mental disorders in older adults, it has been neglected in research and, like dementia, is often misdiagnosed (Knight, 1996). Progress in diagnosis has been impeded by terminological chaos. The literature reveals 30 or more synonyms signifying delirium (Liston, 1982); acute confusional state and acute brain syndrome are the two most common. It is often the case that delirium is simply not detected (Zarit & Zarit, 1998), and this problem seems to apply to emergency department in Canadian hospitals, where the prevalence of delirium in elderly patients could be as high as 9.6 percent (Elie et al., 2000).

The following is a typical example. An older woman found in a filthy apartment with no food was believed by a poorly informed physician to have dementia and was given routine custodial care in a nursing home. A professional knowledgeable about delirium learned that she had become depressed over the loss of a loved one and had neglected her diet. Once this was recognized, appropriate attention was given to her nutritional deficiencies, and her condition improved such that she was discharged to her own home after one month (Zarit, 1980).

Unfortunately, neglect of delirium is fairly typical. Cameron et al. (1987) assessed 133 consecutive admissions to an acute medical ward. They found 15 cases of delirium, only one of which had been detected by the admitting physician. Older adults are frequently misdiagnosed as having an irreversible dementia and therefore considered beyond hope. Long-term institutional care is all too often viewed as the only option.

People of any age are subject to delirium, but it is more common in children and older adults, especially hospitalized older adults, with perhaps up to one-quarter of older adult inpatients experiencing delirium at some point during their hospitalization. The rates of delirium are even higher in certain subgroups of inpatients, such as postoperative older adults who have undergone heart surgery or orthopedic surgery for hip fracture (Zarit & Zarit, 1998). Older inpatients who develop delirium stay longer in the hospital and have a greater chance of dying (Pompei et al., 1994). One Canadian study compared 38 elderly patients with delirium (including 22 with dementia as well) and 148 patients with no delirium or dementia (Rockwood et al., 1999). Delirium was a significant risk factor for the development of dementia and dying early, with those with delirium living less than half as long as the patients without delirium. Independent research in Montreal has confirmed that delirium is a risk factor for mortality as well as for functional status and cognitive difficulties in the 12 months following hospital admission (McCusker et al., 2001, 2002).

Rates of delirium in nursing homes also appear to be high. One study found that between 6 and 12 percent of nursing-home residents may develop delirium in the course of one year (Katz, Parmalee, & Brubaker, 1991).

Clearly, delirium is a serious health problem for older adults. The mortality rate for delirium is extremely high. Approximately 40 percent of patients die, either from exhaustion or from the conditions that caused the delirium, such as a drug overdose or malnutrition (Rabins & Folstein, 1982). When fatality rates for dementia and delirium are compared over a one-year period, rates are higher for delirium (37.5 percent versus 16 percent).

Causes of Delirium The causes of delirium in older adults can be grouped into several general classes: drug intoxications and drug-withdrawal reactions, metabolic and nutritional imbalances (as in uncontrolled diabetes and thyroid dysfunction), infections or fevers, neurological disorders, and the stress of a change in the person's surroundings (Knight, 1996). As mentioned earlier, delirium may also occur following major surgery, most commonly hip surgery (Zarit & Zarit, 1998); during withdrawal from psychoactive substances; and following head trauma or seizures. Common physical illnesses that cause delirium in older adults include congestive heart failure, pneumonia, urinary tract infection, cancer, kidney or liver failure, malnutrition, and cerebrovascular accidents or strokes. Probably the most frequent cause of delirium in this age group is intoxication with prescription drugs (Besdine, 1980; Lipowski, 1983). However, delirium usually has more than one cause. A contemporary review of the existing literature conducted by Canadian researchers (see Elie et al., 1998) concluded that the top five correlates of delirium among elderly hospitalized patients are dementia, being on medication, medical illness, age, and male gender.

Although delirium usually develops swiftly (within a matter of hours or days), the exact mode of onset depends on the underlying cause. Delirium resulting from a toxic reaction or concussion has an abrupt onset; when infection or metabolic disturbance underlies delirium, the onset of symptoms is more gradual.

Why are older adults especially vulnerable to delirium? Many explanations have been offered: the physical declines of aging, the increased general susceptibility to chronic diseases, the many medications prescribed for older patients, the greater sensitivity to drugs, and vulnerability to stress. One other factor, brain damage, increases the risk of delir-

Table 16.2

Comparative Features of Dementia and Delirium

Dementia	Delirium
Gradual deterioration of intellectual abilities, especially memory for recent events	Trouble concentrating and staying with a train of thought
Difficulties in everyday problem-solving	Restlessness at night, nightmares
Loss of control of impulses, can result in antisocial behaviour (e.g., shoplifting or making sexual advances	Rambling speech; appearance of intoxication or psychosis
Periods of depression	Frequent lucid intervals
Problems naming common objects	Hallucinations; sometimes loss of contact with reality
Faulty orientation to time (e.g., day of week), place (e.g., location), and person (e.g., who the self is or others are)	Large swings in mood and activity
Usually progressive and irreversible	Usually reversible but potentially fatal if cause (e.g., malnutrition) not treated
Increased prevalence with age	Prevalence high in the very young as well as the old

ium. Older individuals with dementing disorders appear to be the most susceptible to delirium. A retrospective review of 100 hospital admissions of people with delirium revealed that 44 percent had delirium superimposed on another brain condition (Purdie, Honigman, & Rosen, 1981).

Treatment of Delirium Complete recovery from delirium is possible if the syndrome is identified correctly and the underlying cause promptly treated. It generally takes one to four weeks for the condition to clear; it takes longer in older patients than in younger patients. If the underlying cause is not treated, however, permanent brain damage and death can ensue.

Primary prevention strategies appear to reduce the high rates of delirium as well as the duration of delirium episodes in hospitalized older adults (Inouye et al., 1999). The intervention addresses such risk factors for delirium as sleep deprivation, immobility, dehydration, visual and hearing impairment, and cognitive impairment.

One often-neglected aspect of the management of delirium is educating the family of a person with dementia to distinguish the manifestations of dementia and delirium. Table 16.2 compares the features of dementia and delirium, and serves as a useful summary of the nature of delirium.

OLD AGE AND PSYCHOLOGICAL DISORDERS

Although a psychological disorder at any age may have at least a partial physical explanation, this explanation can be misleading, since much psychopathology found in older adults has not been linked directly to the physiological processes of aging. Indeed, the maladaptive personality traits and inadequate coping skills that the person brings into old age play a role in psychological disturbances, as do health, genetic predisposition, and life stressors.

We look first at the prevalence of mental disorders in late life and then survey a number of them, paying specific attention to their characteristics in older adults.

Overall Prevalence of Mental Disorders in Late Life

Is age itself a contributing factor to emotional and mental malfunction? Do more old people than young people have mental disorders?

It is not entirely clear whether mental disorders become more prevalent with age, partly because of the methodological and conceptual difficulties we have already discussed. An extensive cross-sectional study conducted by the U.S. National Institute of Mental Health (NIMH) yielded valuable data on mental disorders in all age groups, including the old (Myers et al., 1984; Regier et al., 1988).

Current prevalence data indicate that persons over age 65 have the lowest overall rates of mental disorder of all age groups when the various disorders are grouped together. The primary problem detected was cognitive impairment, not as a separate DSM category but as an important characteristic of more than one disorder (e.g., depression, dementia, delirium). Rates for mild cognitive impairment were about 14 percent for older men and women; for severe cognitive impairment, rates were 5.5 percent for older men and 4.7 percent for older women.

The majority of persons 65 years of age and older are free from serious psychopathology, but 10 to 20 percent do have psychological problems severe enough to warrant professional attention (Gatz et al., 1996; Gurland, 1991).

Depression

According to the U.S. NIMH and other data, mood disorders are less prevalent in older adults than in younger adults—under 3 percent compared with as high as 20 percent among younger people (Eaton et al., 1989; Myers et al., 1984; Regier et al., 1988)—but they are estimated to account for nearly half the admissions of older adults to acute psychiatric care (Wattis, 1990). However, a study conducted in Quebec found that rates of major depression and dysthymia were not significantly less prevalent in elderly participants than in younger participants (Kovess, Murphy, & Tousignant, 1987). Estimates of the prevalence of depression in elderly people may actually be underestimates if researchers rely exclusively on DSM criteria. Researchers in Edmonton using DSM-III-R criteria for major depression estimated that the six-month prevalence of depression was 1.2 percent (Bland, Newman, & Orn, 1988). However, subsequent community surveys of depression that used a measure known as the Geriatric Mental State (GMS), a semi-structured questionnaire accompanied by an automated computer diagnostic program, found much higher rates of depression among elderly Albertans, with prevalence estimates of over 11 percent (Newman, Bland, & Orn, 1998; Newman, Sheldon, & Bland, 1998). These prevalence rates are more in keeping with reported rates of depression in elderly people from Europe. The GMS yields higher rates because it assesses a wider range of symptoms, including crying, hopelessness, irritability, and loneliness, and notes whether the person is someone who cried or appeared sad during the interview.

Most depressed older adults are not experiencing depression for the first time; rather, their depression is a continuation of a condition present earlier in life (Cole & Dendukuri, 2003). The depression of those older adults who do have true late-onset depression can often be traced to a specific biological cause (Fiske et al., 1998).

Unipolar depression is much more common than bipolar depression among older patients (Regier et al., 1988). The emergence of bipolar disorder after the age of 65 is rare

(Jamison, 1979; Regier et al., 1988; Shulman, 1993). Our discussion therefore addresses unipolar depression in older adults.

Women have more periods of depression than men for most of their lives. An epidemiological study in Edmonton showed that elderly women have substantially higher rates of depression regardless of whether they are between 65 and 74 years old or 85 years old and older (Newman, Bland, & Orn, 1998).

As many as 40 percent of older people who have chronic health problems or are confined in hospitals are depressed (Rapp, Parisi, & Walsh, 1988). People with a dementing disorder, such as Alzheimer's, may also be depressed. In addition to the 30 percent of patients with dementia of the Alzheimer's type who are estimated to have a superimposed major depressive disorder, many more have some symptoms of depression that interfere with their lives (Burns, 1991).

Characteristics of Depression in Older versus Younger Adults Worry, feelings of uselessness, sadness, pessimism, fatigue, inability to sleep, and difficulties getting things done are common symptoms of depression in both older (Blazer, 1982) and younger adults. The cognitive correlates of depression (i.e., negative automatic thoughts, dysfunctional attitudes) are also apparent among elderly Canadians (Vezina & Borque, 1984). A recent study conducted with older adults in Ottawa showed that dysfunctional attitudes reflecting sociotropic-dependency themes interacted with high-impact social events to predict depression relapse (Voyer & Cappeliez, 2002), and this finding is generally in keeping with personality research on depression in younger samples. But there are also some age-related differences (Blazer, 1982; Small et al., 1986). Feelings of guilt are less common and somatic complaints more common in depressed older adults. Furthermore, older depressed patients show greater motor retardation, more weight loss, more of a general physical decline, less hostility, and less suicidal ideation than younger depressed patients (Musetti et al., 1989). Despite the difference in suicidal ideation, however, actual suicide attempts and completed suicides increase as men enter old age; such increases are not found in older women. Finally, memory complaints—not necessarily actual memory problems—are more common in older than in younger depressed individuals (O'Connor et al., 1990).

The use of standard DSM-IV-TR criteria may lead to the underdiagnosis of depression in older adults. Older adults are less likely to demonstrate impaired social and occupational functioning as a result of their depression because they are less likely than younger people to be working (Fiske et al., 1998). Some researchers (Fogel & Fretwell, 1985; Newmann et al., 1996) have described a subtype of depression more commonly seen in older adults, called depletion syndrome. This syndrome is characterized chiefly by loss of pleasure, vitality, and appetite as well as hopelessness and somatic symptoms; in contrast to other forms of depression, self-blame, guilt, and dysphoric mood are either absent or less prominent.

Causes of Depression in Older Adults Many aged patients in poor physical health are depressed. A survey of 900 older adults in the community found that 44 percent with depressive symptoms were medically ill (Blazer & Williams, 1980). In a study of hospitalized medical patients who were old, about 15 percent were found to be clinically depressed (Reifler, 1994). Older men who have their first onset of depression in late life are likely to have undergone surgery before their episode of depression, to have unusually high rates of chronic illness, and to have had more medical conditions than other people (Roth & Kay, 1956). Many physicians who care for older medical patients are insensitive to the likelihood of depression coexisting with physical illnesses. More often than not they do not diagnose, and therefore do not treat, the psychological condition (Rapp, Parisi, Wallace, & Walsh, 1988). This oversight can lead to the worsening not only of the depression but also of the medical problem itself (Wolfe et al., 1996).

Physical illness and depression are linked for reasons other than the disheartening aspects of an illness. A genetic diathesis for depression, for example, may play a role. This idea is supported by a study showing a higher prevalence of depression among the relatives of Alzheimer's disease patients who became depressed after the onset of the disease (Strauss & Ogrocki, 1996). Medications prescribed to treat a chronic condition can aggravate a depression that already exists, cause a depression to start, or produce symptoms that resemble the disorder but are not in fact a true depression (Klerman, 1983). The drugs most likely to have these effects are antihypertensive medications (Spar & LaRue, 1990). On the other side of the coin, longitudinal and retrospective studies have pointed out that individuals who are depressed may be predisposed to develop physical illness (Vaillant, 1979; Wigdor & Morris, 1977), and because of their discouraged and lethargic state of mind, they may not seek appropriate medical treatment for symptoms they are experiencing.

As we grow older, we almost inevitably experience a number of life events that could cause depression. Bereavement after the loss of a loved one has been hypothesized to be the most important risk factor for depression in the elderly (see Vinkers et al., 2004). Bereavement also contributes to poorer prognosis in elderly people already suffering from depression (Denihan et al., 2000). The predictiveness of bereavement was also confirmed in a recent meta-analysis conducted by researchers from McGill University (Cole & Dendukuri, 2003). Significant risk factors for depression across 20 prospective studies were bereavement, sleep disturbance, disability, prior depression, and female gender.

Contemporary longitudinal research on bereavement suggests that while bereavement contributes in general to depression, the extent of its effect depends on the nature of the loss and the timing of assessment. For instance, in a well-designed prospective study, Carnelley, Wortman, and Kessler (1999) found that widowed women reported more depression than control participants up to two years following the loss. However, widowed women whose husbands were ill when the study started did not experience more depression when their husbands died. Carnelley et al. (1999) suggest that there is a timing effect in being forewarned; that is, women with ill husbands anticipate the loss and may become depressed prior to their spouse's death.

A longitudinal study by Turvey et al. (1999) assessed reactions to the death of the spouse in elderly people aged 70 years and older. They found that newly bereaved individuals had rates of diagnosable depression that were nine times higher and levels of self-reported depression that were nearly four times higher than married and non-bereaved individuals. Elevated levels of depression were evident up to two years after the loss. However, lower rates of depression among the long-time widowed group attest to the fact that most people adjust eventually, though some elderly people continue to suffer from unresolved grief.

Clearly, there is a link between bereavement and depression. Although opinions vary, several authors have suggested that diagnostic systems should be revised to include a separate category for the pathological grief experienced by people who suffer a prolonged reaction to bereavement (see Bonanno & Kaltman, 2001; Stroebe et al., 2001). This call for a separate category is based on evidence that grief-stricken individuals have grief-related symptoms that are distinguishable from existing definitions of depression (see Stroebe et al., 2001). A key issue is how to distinguish between normal and abnormal grief reactions.

Given the different reactions to bereavement, researchers have identified factors associated with resilient reactions to the death of one's spouse. Prem Fry at Trinity Western University in British Columbia has found that existential factors are quite important. For instance, a study of widows and widowers between the ages of 65 to 87 years found that people who were optimistic and found meaning in their lives had better psychological adjustment than people lacking these attributes (Fry, 2001). An involvement in organized religion was also associated with better adjustment.

As with younger adults, psychological stress plays a role in depression in older adults, but a stressor that might trigger or exacerbate a depressive episode in a younger person may not do so in an older adult (George, 1994). For example, social isolation is not as strongly linked to depression in old age as it is in middle age (Musetti et al., 1989). Still, many factors that contribute to the link between stress and depression in younger people also play a role among the elderly. After reviewing existing data on coping resources, Cappeliez (1993) concluded that depressed elderly people are less inclined than nondepressed elders to use active coping strategies with either a behavioural focus (i.e., active problem-solving) or a cognitive focus (i.e., positive reappraisal of stressful events).

Numerous findings point to the importance of social support as a stress buffer for elderly people faced with life challenges (e.g., Cappeliez, 1993; Fry, 1993). Ostbye, Steenhuis, Walton, and Cairney (2000) examined the correlates of dysphoria in elderly Canadians living in the community who did not have dementia. Correlates of dysphoria included lower perceived social support, chronic pain, poor health, and functional dependency. Lefrancois et al. (2000) examined psychological distress in elderly people from Quebec between the ages of 81 and 86 and found that social-support satisfaction was associated with less psychological distress. However, in this study, social support did not moderate the link between stress and distress.

Although retirement has been assumed to have negative consequences, research does not generally support this assumption (George, 1980). Any ill effects of retirement may have more to do with the poor health and low incomes of some retirees and less with retirement per se (Pahkala, 1990). Retirement often ushers in a satisfying period of life (Wolfe et al., 1996).

Each older person brings to late life a developmental history that makes his or her reactions to common problems unique. Each person's coping skills and personality determine how effectively that individual will respond to new life events (Butler & Lewis, 1982). Overall, adaptation rather than depression is the more common reaction to stress in late life.

Treatment of Depression A substantial proportion of older people who suffer from depression have persistent forms of depression. Meta-analytic reviews conducted by researchers in Montreal indicate that depression in elderly people is associated with a poor prognosis and is undertreated (Cole & Bellavance, 1997; Cole, Bellavance, & Mansour, 1999). One meta-analysis of studies that examined the course of depression found that only 33 percent of the participants recovered, while another 33 percent were still depressed and 21 percent had died (Cole et al., 1999). A one-year follow-up study conducted in Montreal of a sample of elderly people with depression found that fewer than half of the depressed elderly in the study were improved; this study showed that major depression superimposed on dysthymic disorder (i.e., double depression) was especially persistent (see Fenton, Cole, Engelsmann, & Mansouri, 1998). An epidemiological study in Alberta comparing rates of remission among older people found that depression, obsessive-compulsive disorder, and panic disorder all had low rates of remission (Bland, Newman, & Orn, 1997). The low remission rate of depression was attributed to lack of treatment intervention.

Although clinical lore holds that depressions in older patients are more resistant to treatment than the depressions in younger people, we have known for some time that these claims are not substantiated (Small & Jarvik, 1982). Rather, there is considerable evidence that depressed older adults can be helped by both psychological and pharmacological interventions, but there must be access to treatment. A review by Canadian researchers showed that a small but consistent number of studies attest to the usefulness of psychotherapy in treating geriatric depression (O'Rourke & Hadjistavropoulos, 1997).

Gallagher and Thompson (1982, 1983) compared cognitive, behavioural, and brief psychodynamic psychotherapies for older individuals with depression. These three methods were found equally effective, and in subsequent studies (Gallagher-Thompson & Thompson, 1995a, 1995b; Thompson, Gallagher, & Breckenridge, 1987), about three-quarters of the patients were judged either completely cured or markedly improved. These rates compare very favourably with the outcomes of psychotherapy in younger people with depression. Supplementary analyses by Louise Gaston at McGill University and her associates show that the quality of the alliance between the elderly patient and his or her therapist is a key factor in determining whether there is a positive treatment response (Gaston et al., 1998). Another notable finding is that untreated control patients did not improve, as younger untreated depressed patients often do, suggesting that older adults are less likely than younger patients to recover without treatment.

A study with depressed elderly patients from Ottawa showed that they responded quite well to cognitive therapy, with decreases in depressive symptoms comparable to those obtained in other research investigations (Cappeliez, 2000). However, as is often the case with younger participants, depressed elders had a less positive response to treatment if they had more severe levels of depression to begin with. It was also found that depressed elders with negative self-views had less positive responses to the cognitive interventions.

Another treatment study compared cognitive therapy and bibliotherapy (the reading of a self-help book) as treatments for the depressed elderly (Floyd et al., 2004). Both these therapies were superior to delayed treatment in a control group.

Interpersonal psychotherapy (IPT; also discussed in Chapter 10) has also been used successfully to treat depression in older adults. IPT is a short-term psychotherapy that addresses themes such as role loss, role transition, and interpersonal disputes, problem areas prominent in the lives of many older adults. Although it is not yet considered a well-established treatment for depression in older adults (Gatz et al., 1998), it has shown great promise (Hinrichsen, 1997).

A form of treatment known as *reminiscence therapy* can be effective for treating depression in the elderly. Reminiscence therapy is also known as *life review therapy*. It is a cognitive process that requires individuals to reflect on previous negative events and address any remaining conflicts; it also requires that they strive to find life's meaning while examining the present situation and the past. One focus here is to re-examine the role of the self in events in an attempt to achieve a sense of self-acceptance and reduced self-blame. For instance, a self-critical perfectionist could dredge up previous mistakes from the past and re-examine his or her role, working toward the ultimate goal of achieving a less self-critical interpretation.

A recent meta-analysis of 20 studies showed that reminiscence and life review had both statistical and clinical significance in terms of reducing depression in elderly people (Bohlmeijer, Smit, & Cuijpers, 2003). The treatment effect was comparable to those obtained with pharmacotherapy and other psychological treatments.

According to Watt and Cappeliez (2000), the type of reminiscence involved determines the effectiveness of reminiscence therapy. Clearly, reflecting on the past is maladaptive if it involves obsessively ruminating about past shortcomings or, as Watt and Cappeliez suggest, if it serves as a way of escaping from and not coping with current problems. However, reminiscence therapy can be effective if it takes the form of integrative or instrumental reminiscence (see Watt & Cappeliez, 2000). Integrative reminiscence is a nonjudgemental way of looking back that emphasizes cognitive re-attribution and the consideration of realistic causes of life events that go beyond the self. It focuses on establishing a sense of purpose and meaning in life. To provide an example of integrative reminiscence, Watt and Cappeliez (2000) described a woman, who, through integrative reminiscence, learned to attribute her failure to obtain a teaching degree in the 1930s to the economic depression of the era rather than to personal failings. *Instrumental reminiscence* is remembering past coping responses, such as the plans that were used to address challenging situations, goal-directed activities, and recalling when goals were met. For instance, remembering what you did to fix a flooded basement would reflect instrumental reminiscence.

Research on the use of drugs to treat depression is not as extensive for older adults as it is for younger adults, but emerging evidence suggests that certain antidepressants can

Reminiscence (or life review) therapy for depression requires individuals to reflect on their past and present situation to help achieve a sense of self-acceptance and reduce self-blame.

be useful, particularly selective serotonin reuptake inhibitors such as fluoxetine (Prozac) (Hale, 1993). A longitudinal study conducted over a four-year period in Toronto found that antidepressant medication was highly effective and 70 percent of the depressed elderly receiving treatment did not experience a recurrence of their depressions (Flint & Rifat, 2000). However, the use of certain antidepressant drugs with older adults is complicated by side effects, such as postural hypotension (a fall in blood pressure when standing up), which causes some patients to become dizzy when they stand up and then to fall. These drugs also pose a risk to the cardiovascular system, with the danger of a heart attack. Moreover, older people generally are at high risk for toxic reactions to medications. For these reasons, nonpharmacological approaches to depression in older adults are particularly important (Bressler, 1987; Scoggin & McElerath, 1994).

Perhaps the side effects of medication account for the results of a study by Philippe Landreville and his associates at Laval University (Landreville, Landry, Baillargeon, Gurette, & Matteau, 2001). They recruited 200 people aged 65 and over from family medicine clinics to rate the acceptability of antidepressant medication, cognitive therapy, and cognitive bibliotherapy for geriatric depression. Cognitive interventions were preferred over antidepressant medication.

Electroconvulsive therapy is back in favour among many geriatric psychiatrists (Hay, 1991), particularly for patients who had an earlier favourable response to it (Janicak et al., 1993). ECT does, however, carry significant risks, and it should be considered only when other treatments have not been effective or are contraindicated or when a rapid response (such as in the case of an acutely suicidal patient) is needed (Zarit & Zarit, 1998).

We now turn to a discussion of anxiety disorders in the elderly. Although depression and anxiety are discussed separately, they are often correlated and comorbid in older people, as they are in younger people. Research conducted in Canada and elsewhere has shown that a mixed subtype of depression and anxiety in certain elderly individuals is associated with poor treatment response and higher relapse rates (Flint & Rifat, 1996, 1997; Lynch, Compton, Mendelson, Robins, & Krishnan, 2000).

ANXIETY DISORDERS

Anxiety disorders are more prevalent than depression among older adults (Gatz et al., 1996; Regier et al., 1988; Scoggin, 1998; Wetherell, 2002). Anxiety disorders in old age can be a continuation or reemergence of problems experienced earlier in life, or they can develop for the first time in the senior years. Like depression, DSM-defined anxiety disorders appear to be less prevalent among older than among younger adults (Flint, 1994; Kessler et al., 1994). As nearly all the available data are cross-sectional, however, it is wise to be cautious about this conclusion.

A further complicating factor in determining prevalence is that, as with younger people, symptoms of anxiety among older adults are more predominant than those of diagnosable anxiety disorders, indicating that unwarranted anxiety among seniors is fairly common (Gurian & Miner, 1991). The quality of a person's life, however, can be compromised by symptoms that, although not severe, frequent, or enduring enough to warrant a formal DSM diagnosis, could still justify professional concern and intervention (Fisher & Noll, 1996).

In general, symptoms of anxiety disorders do not differ as people enter old age, although as in the case of depression, diagnostic criteria for anxiety may be insufficient or ill suited for diagnosis of the disorder in older adults, thus rendering current prevalence rates underestimates (Fuentes & Cox, 1997; Wetherell, 1998). For example, there appear to be age-related differences in the symptom expression of generalized anxiety disorder. Stanley and Novy (2000) identified a number of differences. First, elderly people report more worries about health and fewer about work-related issues than younger people do; worry about health matters was confirmed as the predominant focus in a study of older adults from Quebec (Doucet, Ladouceur, Freeston, & Dugas, 1998), followed by worries about relationships with family members and friends. Second, differences exist in the structure of affect, with elderly people placing less emphasis on feelings of guilt and self-blame. Third, elderly people tend to emphasize the somatic aspects of anxiety rather than the cognitive aspects. Finally, symptoms of anxiety in the elderly may be more closely intertwined with symptoms reflecting sleep difficulties and declines in cognitive capabilities (see Skarborn & Nicki, 1996).

It should be noted that findings obtained with younger samples may not be generalizable to older people. For instance, in their study of levels of anxiety and correlates of anxiety in a mixed Canadian sample of middle-aged adults and elderly participants, Fuentes and Cox (2000) found no gender differences among the younger participants but did find them among the elderly, with women reporting significantly more anxiety.

After reviewing the literature, Alistair Flint (1994, 1999) from the University of Toronto concluded that the most prevalent anxiety disorders among the elderly are generalized anxiety disorder (GAD) and agoraphobia. Flint (1999) also noted that because there have been few empirical investigations into the treatment of anxiety disorders in elderly people, treatment guidelines often have to be extrapolated from studies with younger participants.

Clearly, more information is needed on GAD in elderly people. One contemporary study compared a sample of elderly people with GAD with an age-matched control group (Diefenbach, Stanley, & Beck, 2001). The two groups did not differ in the pattern of worry content, with family/interpersonal worries being most predominant in both groups. Further comparisons with a younger group of participants confirmed the anticipated tendency for elderly people to have more health worries and fewer worries about work.

As alluded to above, causes of anxiety disorders reflect some of the circumstances of getting older (Fisher & Noll, 1996). Anxiety problems are often associated with medical illness (Fuentes & Cox, 1997; Heidrich, 1993), being reactions to worries about being sick and becoming infirm. Sometimes an older person's anxieties are reactions to medication or part of the delirium that frequently accompanies medical illness in older patients (Lipowski, 1990).

Many other medical diseases can create anxiety symptoms that are not properly considered part of an anxiety disorder but still warrant professional attention. Metabolic conditions, such as hypoglycemia and anemia; endocrine disorders, such as hyperthyroidism; cardiovascular conditions, such as angina and congestive heart failure; and excessive caffeine consumption all may cause such symptoms as a faster heart rate, which is also a symptom of anxiety (Fisher & Noll, 1996) or can be construed by the person as a symptom of anxiety. Age-related deterioration in the vestibular system (inner-ear control of one's sense of balance) can account for panic symptoms such as severe dizziness (Raj, Corvea, & Dagon, 1993).

Scoggin (1998) remarks that PTSD and acute stress disorder, two anxiety disorders that may be especially relevant to the lives of older adults, have received scant attention from researchers. We noted in Chapter 6 that Beal's (1995) study revealed long-term PTSD in Canadian veterans of the Dieppe Raid. PTSD has also been observed in older patients following such trauma as major health crises (Scoggin, 1998). The only prevalence study conducted thus far found PTSD in 0.9 percent of the elderly and subthreshold PTSD in 13.1 percent. The strongest predictors of both forms of PTSD were neuroticism and adverse events in early childhood (van Zelst et al., 2003).

Anxiety problems in older adults respond to the same kinds of psychological treatments found useful with younger adults. For instance, accumulating evidence attests to the value of cognitive behaviour therapy (CBT) in the treatment of generalized anxiety disorder in elderly adults (Stanley et al., 2003; Wetherell, Gatz, & Craske, 2003). CBT consisting of three main components (relaxation training, cognitive therapy, and exposure-based procedures), according to Stanley et al. (2003), is useful for older adults because it is time-limited, symptom-focused, and collaborative in nature.

Because the physician usually hears the psychological complaints of older adults, psychoactive medications are in widespread use. However, potentially dangerous interactions with other drugs, along with the elderly's increased sensitivity to any drug, make antianxiety medication a risky intervention (Fisher & Noll, 1996).

Delusional (Paranoid) Disorders

A 66-YEAR-OLD married woman reluctantly agreed to a clinical evaluation. She [had] a six-week history of bizarre delusions and hallucinations of her husband spraying the house with a fluid that smelled like "burned food." She complained that he sprayed the substance everywhere around the house, including draperies and furniture, although she had never seen him do it. She could smell the substance almost constantly, and it affected her head, chest, and rectum. She also complained that someone in the neighborhood had been throwing bricks and rocks at her house. In addition, she suspected her husband of having affairs with other women, whose footprints she claimed to have seen near home....

Interviews revealed a sullen woman who was extremely hostile toward her husband. She focused on the delusion that he was spraying an unusual substance in an attempt to upset her; other issues in the relationship seemed secondary. She looked very sad at times and would occasionally wipe away a tear; but her predominant affect was extreme hostility and consternation about her husband's alleged behaviour. (Varner & Gaitz, 1982, p. 108)

In addition to the distress experienced by the patient, paranoia may have a disturbing and immediate impact on others, often bringing angry reactions and contributing to a decision to institutionalize the older adult (Berger & Zarit, 1978). Paranoid symptomatology is found in many older psychiatric patients (Heston, 1987; Pfeiffer, 1977).

Tuokko, Frerichs, Halpern, and Eisner (1999) examined delusional symptoms in elderly people evaluated by a community outreach team. This study showed that 15 percent of the elderly people assessed had delusional beliefs and three-quarters of these delusional individuals had two or more delusions. The most predominant paranoid delusion was a sense of being plotted against, and this applied both to elderly people with delusions but not dementia and to those characterized jointly by delusions and dementia. These groups were similar in most respects, with about half of the members of both groups also experiencing hallucinations. However, the delusions of the group without dementia were psychosomatic and reflected a grandiose sense of self-worth.

Causes of Delusional Disorder Paranoia in older patients may be the continuation of a disorder that began earlier in life or it may accompany brain diseases, such as delirium and dementia. Paranoia may even serve a function for patients with dementia, filling in the gaps caused by memory loss. Instead of admitting, "I can't remember where I left my keys," they think, "Someone must have come in and taken my keys" (Zarit, 1980).

Paranoid ideation has also been linked to sensory losses, in particular to loss of hearing. Some believe that older people with severe paranoid disorders tend to have longstanding hearing loss in both ears (Eastwood et al., 1985; Pearlson & Rabins, 1988). An older person who is deaf may believe that other people are whispering because they are talking about the person and do not want him or her to hear what is being said. The person's paranoid reactions may be an attempt to fill in the blanks caused by sensory loss (Pfeiffer, 1977). By explaining bewildering events, delusions are in a sense adaptive and understandable. There is, however, conflicting evidence about this presumed link between hearing problems and delusional disorders. Whereas some researchers report that hearing loss precedes the onset of paranoid symptoms, others report that such sensory losses are not common among people with delusional disorder (Jeste et al., 1988).

Since people who become paranoid also have poor social adjustment, the onset of their symptoms may follow a period of increasing isolation (Gurland, 1991). This isolation itself limits people's opportunities to check their suspicions about the world, making it easier for delusions to take hold. They build a pseudocommunity—a private world of their own—rather than social relations based on communication and mutual trust (Cameron, 1959).

Older people are especially vulnerable to all kinds of abuse from others (see Canadian Perspectives 16.3). Others may talk about them behind their backs, or even to their faces, as though they were not present. People take advantage of older adults in many ways. An older person's complaint of persecution should not be blithely dismissed. An older client of one of the authors complained bitterly about being followed by a detective hired by her evil husband. Inquiry revealed that the husband was worried that she was having an affair and had indeed hired someone to follow her!

Treatment of Delusional Disorder The treatment of paranoia is much the same for older and younger adults. Although controlled data are lacking, clinicians suggest that a patient and supportive approach is best, with the therapist providing empathic understanding of the person's concerns. Directly challenging the paranoid delusion or attempting to reason the person out of his or her beliefs is seldom effective. By the time the patient sees a health professional, many others—family, friends, the police—have probably tried this approach. Nonjudgemental recognition of the distress caused by the paranoia is more likely to promote a therapeutic relationship with the patient. When the patient trusts and feels safe with the therapist, the delusions can gradually be questioned.

If an auditory or visual problem is present, a hearing aid or corrective lenses may alleviate some of the paranoid symptoms. If the individual is socially isolated, efforts can be made to increase his or her activities and contacts. Regular supportive therapy may help the patient reestablish relations with family members and friends. Positive reinforcement can be provided for appropriate behaviour; for example, the therapist may pay special attention to comments by the patient that are not paranoid in nature. Even if these straightforward measures do not relieve paranoia, they may be beneficial in other areas of the person's life.

Studies of therapy outcomes indicate that delusions in older patients can be treated with some success with phenothiazines (Schneider, 1996), although paranoid individuals are generally suspicious of the motives of those who give them drugs. In their study conducted in British Columbia, Tuokko et al. (1999) found that medications were prescribed to more than half of the elderly people being treated for delusions and that the only thing distinguishing the group of people with delusions from those with delusions and dementia was noncompliance with taking medication, with this being a problem for the majority in the delusional group. Toxicity from medications must also be considered, given the particular sensitivity of older people to drugs. Institutionalization, best viewed as a last resort, may do little good. In practice, this decision depends more on the level of tolerance in the person's social environment than on the severity and disruptiveness of the paranoid beliefs.

SCHIZOPHRENIA

As discussed in Chapter 11, the symptoms of schizophrenia include delusions, cognitive impairment, hallucinations, and negative symptoms such as flat affect. The prevalence of schizophrenia in older adults overall is lower than it is in the total population. This difference is attributable to two factors. First, individuals with this disorder die at a higher rate than members of the general population and thus more tend to die before they reach old age (Karon & VandenBos, 1998). Second, many people with schizophrenia show a marked reduction, sometimes a complete remission, of symptoms when they reach old age (Zarit & Zarit, 1998).

Does schizophrenia ever appear for the first time in old age? Debate on this question has raged for years. Even Kraepelin had doubts that it was always appropriate to use the adjective *praecox*—meaning early onset—to describe schizophrenia. It is estimated that 90 percent of cases of schizophrenia have onset before the person reaches age 60. Late-onset schizophrenia, then, is indeed rare, though it does occur (Karon & VandenBos, 1998).

When schizophrenia does appear for the first time in older adults, it is often called paraphrenia (Howard, 1993). Although paraphrenia is now excluded from the DSM, some researchers believe that it can be distinguished from schizophrenia and delusional disorder and is a viable diagnostic entity (Ravindran, Yatham, & Munro, 1999). Symptoms differ from those seen in early-onset schizophrenia, paraphrenia typically involving more hallucinations and paranoid delusions (Howard, Almeida, & Levy, 1993). Patients tend to be unmarried, live in isolation, have few surviving relatives, experience hearing loss, have a family history of schizophrenia, and belong to the lower socioeconomic classes (Harris & Jeste, 1988; Post, 1987).

With older adults, biological factors that have little or nothing to do with mental disturbance per se must be considered with special care in the diagnosis of a mental illness such as paraphrenia. For example, several reversible medical and surgical problems can produce signs and symptoms that mimic schizophrenia (Marengo & Westermeyer, 1996), including hyperthyroidism, hypothyroidism, Addison's disease, Cushing's disease, Parkinson's disease, Alzheimer's disease, and vitamin deficiencies (Jeste, Manley, & Harris, 1991).

Antipsychotic medications, such as the phenothiazines discussed earlier, are effective in the treatment of schizophrenia in older adults (Jeste et al., 1993), though side effects and interactions with other drugs taken by the patient can pose a challenge to the prescribing physician. A supportive therapeutic relationship is also helpful and bolstering (Marengo & Westermeyer, 1996).

Substance-Related Disorders

Substance abuse is less prevalent in today's cohorts of older adults than among younger adults, but it is a problem nonetheless. One reason for the lower prevalence may be increased mortality among those who have abused drugs in the past (Gilhooly & McDonach, 2003). However, many researchers (e.g., Gomberg & Zucker, 1998; Zarit & Zarit, 1998) predict that as successive cohorts enter old age, the prevalence of substance abuse and dependence in older adults will begin to rise.

Alcohol Abuse and Dependence Historically, it has been assumed that alcohol abuse is less prevalent in older than in younger cohorts, yet the problem is not trivial. Prevalence rates for DSM-defined alcohol abuse or dependence have been pegged at 3.1 percent for older men and 0.46 percent for older women (Helzer, Burnam, & McEvoy, 1991; Myers et al., 1984), averaging out to less than 2 percent. This rate is much lower than the rates that have been determined for the general adult population. However, a Canadian study painted a very different picture (see Thomas & Rockwood, 2001). A subset of over 2,000 participants in the Canadian Study of Health and Aging underwent clinical examinations by physicians rather than more standardized forms of assessment. While this is a significant limitation of the study, it nevertheless found that 8.9 percent of the participants had definite alcohol abuse, another 3.7 percent had "questionable alcohol abuse," and men had higher rates of alcohol abuse than women. All participants were aged 65 or older when this cohort study began in 1991. Additional analyses showed that participants diagnosed with definite or questionable alcohol abuse had significantly greater risk of short-term mortality over the next 18 months. The authors concluded that alcohol abuse among older people might be more common than first realized. These findings emerged even though many alcohol abusers do not survive to old age. The peak years for death from cirrhosis are between 55 and 64 years of age. Mortality from cardiovascular problems is also higher in heavy drinkers than in those who have not drunk to excess (Shaper, 1990).

It might be assumed that problem drinking in older adults is always a continuation of a pattern established earlier in life, but this is not the case. Many problem drinkers begin having alcohol-related problems after the age of 60—so-called late-onset alcoholism. Estimates vary widely, but a review of the literature concluded that between one-third and one-half of those who have drinking problems in old age began their problem drinking after the age of 60 (Liberto, Oslin, & Ruskin, 1996).

As noted, tolerance for alcohol diminishes with age, in part because the ratio of body water to body mass decreases with age, resulting in higher blood-alcohol concentration per unit of alcohol imbibed (Morse, 1988). In addition, older people metabolize alcohol more slowly. Thus, the drug may cause greater changes in brain chemistry and more readily bring on toxic effects, such as delirium, in older people. Several neuropsychological studies have shown that cognitive deficits associated with alcohol abuse, such as memory problems, are likely to be more pronounced in the aged alcoholic than in younger individuals with comparable drinking histories (Brandt et al., 1983). Although some intellectual functioning is recovered with abstinence, residual effects may remain long after the older person has stopped drinking.

Clinicians are less likely to look for alcohol abuse in older people than in younger patients and may instead attribute

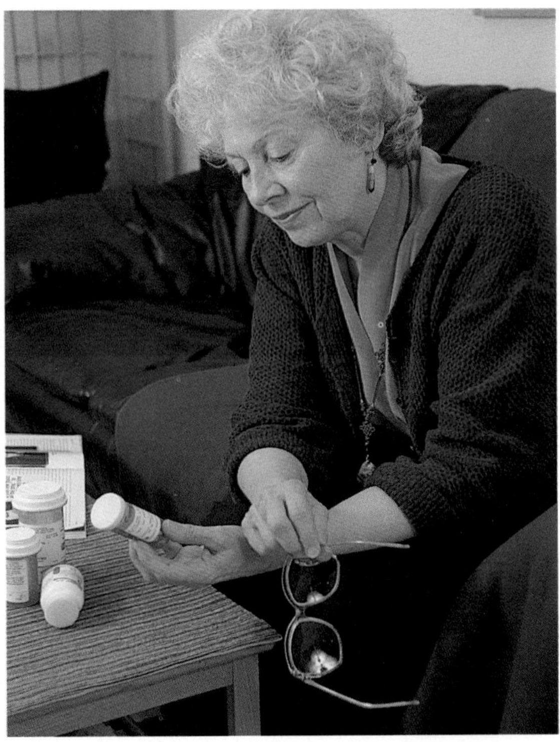

Medication misuse, whether deliberate or inadvertent, is a serious problem among older patients and can cause delirium.

symptoms such as poor motor coordination and impaired memory to a medical problem or to late-life depression. Indeed, alcohol problems often are comorbid with major depression and brain damage (Liberto et al., 1996).

Abuse of Illegal Drugs Although comprehensive figures have been difficult to obtain, it seems certain that the current older population abuses illegal drugs less frequently than do other age groups. In the previously cited NIMH survey (Regier et al., 1988), no one aged 65 and older, and only 0.1 percent of those between 45 and 64 years of age, had a drug abuse or dependency disorder, much lower rates than for younger groups. However, many experts believe that the abuse of illegal drugs is higher than indicated by these formal estimates. As successive cohorts enter old age, it is expected that rates of illegal drug use and abuse will rise.

Some studies of older narcotics abusers indicate that they began their habit early in life and reduced their drug intake as they grew older (Ball & Chambers, 1970), and it has been assumed that all addicts either stop using or die before reaching old age. However, it now appears that a growing proportion of heroin addicts are aged 60 or older. One study (Pascarelli, 1985) found that people aged 60 and older constituted only 0.005 percent of methadone-program consumers in 1974 but accounted for 2 percent of methadone-program consumers in 1985—a 400 percent increase in a time span of only 11 years. Current data on cocaine and cannabis use in older adults are scarce; however, rates will likely rise as adults who came of age in the 1960s and 1970s—a period of widespread use of illegal drugs, especially marijuana—reach their later years.

Medication Misuse The misuse of prescription and over-the-counter medicines is a much greater problem than drug or alcohol abuse in the aged population (LaRue et al., 1985). Elderly people have a higher overall rate of legal drug intake than any other group; although they constitute only 13 percent of the population, they consume about one-third of all prescribed medications (Weber, 1996). Older patients use more anti-anxiety medications than any other age group. Rates of benzodiazepine use among community-dwelling older adults have been estimated at 14 to 37 percent, while rates among nursing-home residents are thought to be even higher (Wetherell, 1998). Some of this use reflects serious drug abuse.

Abuse of prescription or legal drugs is often inadvertent but can be deliberate. Some people obtain medications from a number of sources—for example, by going to more than one physician, filling their prescriptions at different pharmacies, and paying cash instead of using credit cards to reduce the chances that their multiple prescriptions will be discovered (Weber, 1996). One study of 141 well-functioning, middle-class older adults living in their own homes found that almost half reported having misused prescription or over-the-counter drugs at least once over a period of six months (Folkman, Bernstein, & Lazarus, 1987).

Older adults may abuse tranquillizers, antidepressants, or sleep aids prescribed years earlier to deal with postoperative pain or the grief and anxiety of losing a loved one. These drugs often create physical as well as psychological dependency. However, because older adults tend not to go to work regularly and may sometimes not even be seen in public for days or weeks at a time, they can hide their abuse for years. The slurred speech and memory problems caused by drugs may be attributed by others to old age and dementia (LaRue et al., 1985), another example of how popular stereotypes can interfere with proper diagnosis and treatment. Said one addiction specialist, "They're not like a 25-year-old mixing it up [using drugs and alcohol] to get high.... They're trying to make a lonely, miserable life less miserable" (Weber, 1996, p. A36). A former Valium addict and now a leader of Pills Anonymous in California stated the problem this way: "Closet junkies, that's what we call them here. They're at home. They're alone. They're afraid. They're just hiding. Their drug pusher is their doctor" (Weber, 1996, p. A36).

Since the current cohort of older adults is not as acculturated as younger people to seeking help for psychological problems, including drug problems, many make unsupervised efforts to abstain, sometimes going cold turkey. Doing so can be very dangerous, even life-threatening, because withdrawal reactions place great demands on the cardiovascular system.

Some older addicts end up in places where one doesn't expect to find an older adult.

> Her skin itched as if an invisible case of hives were creeping across her flesh. She would shiver, then sweat. She felt suffocated by despair.
>
> She was 65, a doctor's wife, a proud grandma with a purseful of photographs. But there she was, curled in a ball like any other junkie at the ... drug treatment center, sobbing as her body withdrew from a diet of painkillers and tranquilizers.
>
> She couldn't believe it had come to this.
>
> People her age, the woman said, "don't associate themselves with the lowlifes [who] sneak into doorways to shoot up. No, they sneak into the bathroom for a pill." (Weber, 1996, p. A1)

HYPOCHONDRIASIS

Older adults may experience a multitude of physical problems, among them sore feet and backs, poor digestion, constipation, laboured breathing, and cold extremities. All are to be taken seriously by health professionals. However, some older adults believe they are ill and complain unendingly about aches and pains for which there are no plausible physical causes.

It is widely believed that hypochondriasis is especially common in the older population, but its prevalence may not be any greater among older adults than among others (see Snyder & Stanley, 2001). Taken as a group, older adults tend to underreport somatic symptoms rather than overreport them and often fail to seek help for serious illnesses (Besdine, 1980), perhaps because of a belief—probably true—that aches and pains are an inevitable part of aging and may not reflect a specific medical problem.

Some data suggest that while prevalence is not greater among older people, hypochondriasis and health anxiety among the elderly may result in greater functional disability (Snyder & Stanley, 2001). Two key risk factors associated with hypochondriasis and health anxiety in the elderly are social isolation and an elevated prevalence of other psychological disorders that may have somatic concerns as a secondary feature (Snyder & Stanley, 2001).

No controlled studies of the treatment of hypochondriasis in older adults have been done. Clinicians generally agree that reassuring the person that he or she is healthy is useless, for these people are not swayed by negative laboratory tests or authoritative pronouncements from official sources. Some tentative evidence suggests that ignoring the somatic complaints and focusing instead on more positive aspects of existence can be helpful (Goldstein & Birnbom, 1976). Diverting activities may allow these people to function in the face of their perceived medical ills.

Sleep Disorders

Insomnia is a frequent complaint among older adults. One survey found insomnia in 25 percent of respondents aged 65 to 79, as compared with 14 percent in the 18 to 34 age group; another 20 percent had less serious but still problematic insomnia (Mellinger, Balter, & Uhlenhuth, 1985). Overall, insomnia in the elderly (especially in late life) is more frequent and severe and is associated with more complications (Lichstein & Morin, 2000).

The most common sleep problems experienced by older adults are waking often at night, frequent early-morning awakenings, difficulty falling asleep, and daytime fatigue (Miles & Dement, 1980). These complaints parallel the physiological changes that occur normally as people enter old age (Bootzin, Engle-Friedman, & Hazelwood, 1983). Older adults sleep somewhat less or the same amount of time as younger adults do, but their sleep is also more often spontaneously interrupted; in addition, they take longer to fall back to sleep after awakening (Webb & Campbell, 1980). Thus, older people generally sleep less in relation to the total time they spend in bed at nighttime; they tend to make up for this loss with daytime naps.

Older adults also spend less absolute time in a phase known as rapid eye movement (REM) sleep, and stage 4 sleep—the deepest stage—is virtually absent. Instead, older adults spend more time in light sleep (i.e., stage 1). Older men generally experience more disturbances of their sleep than older women do, a difference found to a lesser extent in young adults (Dement, Laughton, & Carskadon, 1981). The sleep problems of older adults must be treated seriously, as the symptoms of chronic insomnia have been found to be associated with higher rates of morbidity and mortality (Neckelmann, 1996).

Causes of Sleep Disorders In addition to the changes associated with aging, various illnesses, medications, caffeine, stress, anxiety, depression, lack of activity, and poor sleep habits may make insomniacs of older adults. Depressed mood has been shown to be related to sleep disturbances in older adults, especially early-morning awakening (Rodin, McAvay, & Timko, 1988). Since the prevalence of insomnia greatly exceeds the prevalence of depression in old age, however, not all geriatric sleep problems should be attributed to an underlying depression (Morgan, 1992).

Pain, particularly arthritis, is a principal disrupter of sleep for older adults (Prinz & Raskin, 1978). Sleep problems are also strongly associated with Alzheimer's disease, and progressive disruptions of the normal sleep phases occur as dementia advances (Hoch et al., 1992).

Whatever the cause of insomnia at any age, it is worsened by self-defeating actions such as ruminating over it and counting the number of hours slept and those spent waiting to fall asleep. Sleeping problems can also be worsened by medications that are taken to deal with them.

Sleep apnea is a respiratory disorder in which breathing ceases repeatedly for a period of a few seconds to as long as two minutes as the person sleeps. It seriously disrupts normal sleep and can lead to fatigue, muscle aches, and elevation in blood pressure over a period of time. The disruption in normal breathing is usually due to markedly reduced airflow caused by relaxation-produced obstruction from excess tissue at the back of the throat. These interruptions in breathing can occur upwards of 200 times an hour! Both snoring and sleep apnea increase as people get older (Bliwise et al., 1984). Reliable diagnosis of sleep apnea requires the person to spend a night in a sleep lab, where various parameters of sleep (e.g., eye movements, respiration, muscle tension) are monitored.

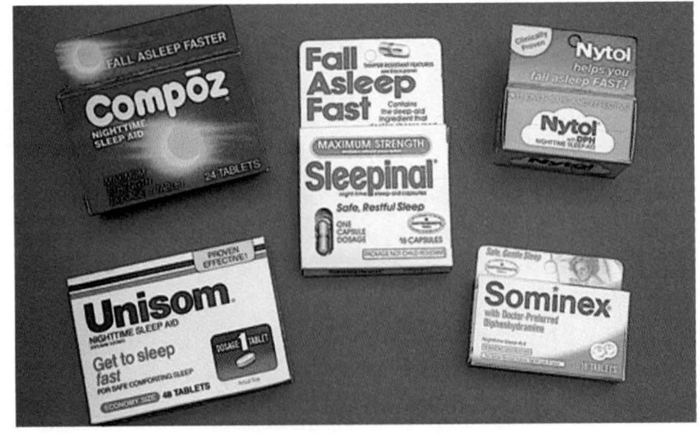

Over-the-counter sleep aids can have serious side effects.

Treatment of Sleep Disorders Over-the-counter medications and prescription drugs are taken by many older people with insomnia. Older adults are major consumers of sleep aids; more than 60 percent of users of prescription sleep drugs are over the age of 50 (Mellinger et al., 1985). According to Morin, Bastien, Brink, and Brown (2003), pharmacotherapy is the most common form of treatment for sleep disorders for people of all ages, but this is especially true for the elderly, who receive one-third of the sedatives/hypnotics that are used. Yet sleep drugs rapidly lose their effectiveness and, with continuous use, may make sleep light and fragmented. REM rebound sleep, an increase in REM sleep after prolonged reliance on drugs, is fitful (Bootzin et al., 1996). Medications can even bring about what is called a drug-dependent insomnia. These so-called aids can also give people drug hangovers and increase respiratory difficulties, which in older adults is a great hazard.

There is considerable evidence that tranquillizers are not the appropriate treatment for patients of any age with chronic insomnia, and particularly not for older patients with insomnia. Side effects of tranquillizers such as the benzodiazepines (e.g., Valium) include problems in learning new

Canadian Contributions/16.1

Charles Morin and the Treatment of Insomnia in Older Adults

Charles Morin is a professor in the Department of Psychology at Laval University in Quebec City. He is also the director of the Sleep Disorders Research Centre in the same city and president of the Canadian Sleep Society (http://www.css.to). In 1995 Morin received the American Psychological Association's Distinguished Award for Early Career Contributions in the field of health psychology.

For the past 15 years, Morin and his colleagues have been engaged in a comprehensive program of research on all aspects of sleep disorders. Much of what we know about the nature and psychological treatment of insomnia in elderly adults is due to the impressive efforts of Morin and his colleagues.

In one of their first studies, Morin and Gramling (1989) compared the sleep characteristics and associated factors for older adults with insomnia and without insomnia. The main sleep variable that distinguished those with from those without insomnia was the amount of time awake after sleep onset. This was in keeping with the general situation of older poor sleepers having trouble staying asleep, while younger poor sleepers have trouble getting to sleep in the first place. Morin and Gramling (1989) also established that poor sleepers had substantially elevated levels of depression and anxiety. The extent of physical illness and medication usage did not distinguish the two groups.

More recent research has focused on pharmacological and psychological treatments for chronic insomnia in older adults. Morin and associates provided incontrovertible evidence that older adults can benefit greatly from cognitive-behavioural intervention for their sleep difficulties. In fact, these interventions may, in the long run, be superior to drug therapies (Morin et al., 1999). In a controlled, randomized study of older adults, one-fourth were assigned to a drug-treatment-only group (they were administered the sleep aid Restoril, one of the benzodiazepines), one-fourth to a behavioural-treatment-only group (90-minute sessions once a week for eight weeks), one-fourth to a combination drug-and-behavioural-treatment group, and the remainder to a placebo control group. The behavioural treatment consisted of many components (e.g., education about sleep hygiene, correction of faulty expectations about sleep, the teaching and practising of good sleep habits, and relaxation training).

At the end of the study, the members of all three treatment groups were sleeping much better, and the amount of improvement across groups was essentially the same. However, at the two-year follow-up, the group that had received the behavioural treatment had largely maintained its gains, whereas the group that had received the sleep medication had not. Most surprising, the group that had received a combination of medication and behavioural treatment did not maintain as much improvement as the group that had received the behavioural treatment alone. The authors suggest that the former group might have attributed improvement to the medication and consequently may not have invested as much time and energy in the behavioural treatment.

Follow-up analyses of the data from this study examined predictors of treatment response (see Gagne & Morin, 2001). Treatment response was assessed with subjective self-reports of sleep quality and objective physiological recordings of sleep quality (i.e., polysomnography) based on three nights of laboratory assessment. Poorer treatment outcome was associated with more advanced age and longer duration and greater severity of insomnia. However, the overall finding was that there were no reliable predictors of treatment outcome that held across all treatment modalities and methods of assessment. The authors concluded that elderly people with insomnia do benefit from cognitive-behavioural interventions but that we need to identify those elderly people suffering from insomnia who are most likely to benefit from these interventions.

A recent investigation examined the side effects of the drug temazepam, a short-term benzodiazepine, when administered to older adults with chronic insomnia. Morin et al. (2003) found that the overall level of adverse effects following use of temazepam was low and that concurrent psychological treatment further reduced the number of adverse effects. Other research shows that a supervised medication-tapering program and cognitive behaviour therapy are both effective in reducing long-term use of benodiazepine medications (Morin et al., 2004).

Morin and Savard (2002) also showed that cognitive behaviour therapy resulted in reductions in dysfunctional attitudes about sleep and that these reductions were linked directly with improvements in sleep efficiency (i.e., the ratio of total sleep time to total time spent in bed) as assessed by daily sleep diaries and polysomnography (e.g., electroencephalaographic monitoring). Dysfunctional attitudes were assessed with Morin's (1994) Dysfunctional Beliefs and Attitudes about Sleep (DBAS) Scale. The DBAS assesses five themes: (1) misconceptions about causes of insomnia (e.g., "I believe that insomnia is essentially the result of aging and there isn't much that can be done about this problem"); (2) diminished perception of control and predictability of sleep (e.g., "When I sleep poorly on one night, I know it will disturb my sleep schedule for the whole week"); (3) unrealistic sleep expectations (e.g., "I must get eight hours of sleep to feel refreshed and function well during the day"); (4) misattribution or amplification of the consequences of insomnia (e.g., "I am concerned that chronic insomnia may have serious consequences on my physical health"); and (5) faulty beliefs about sleep-promoting practices (e.g., "When I have trouble sleeping, I should stay in bed and try harder").

A more recent study by Bastien, Morin, Ouellet, Blais, and Bouchard (2004) compared three methods of delivering cognitive behaviour therapy: individual therapy, group therapy, and telephone consultations. All three methods led to significant improvements in sleep that were still evident six months after treatment, and there were no significant differences in terms of their effectiveness.

What's next for Morin? One of his goals is to evaluate a new self-help treatment based on psychoeducational theory. This treatment could go a long way toward reducing the consequences of insomnia, both for older and younger people.

information and serious difficulties in thinking clearly the day after taking the medication (Ghoneim & Mewaldt, 1990; Schatzberg, 1991). Nonetheless, tranquillizers are prescribed for most nursing-home residents, and in many instances, they are administered daily, even without evidence of a sleep disturbance (Bootzin et al., 1996; Cohen et al., 1983).

Melatonin, a hormone secreted by the pineal gland, plays an important role in regulating sleep and is known to decrease with aging. Thus, it is not surprising that it has been used to treat sleep disorders in older adults and has had some success (Garfinkel et al., 1995).

Jokes have been told for years about taking a little nip of alcohol to help get to sleep. As a central nervous system depressant, alcohol does induce relaxation and drowsiness in most people, but like nearly all other drugs, alcohol has negative effects on what is called the architecture of sleep—that is, the different stages of sleep, such as rapid eye movement (REM) sleep, which is associated with dreaming. Alcohol markedly reduces REM sleep, resulting in such problems as fatigue and difficulty thinking clearly the next day.

People with sleep disturbances, including older adults, sometimes mix alcohol with sedatives or tranquillizers. These combinations—which can lead to unintended death—can be particularly dangerous for older adults because of their greater sensitivity to biochemicals. Finally, alcohol exacerbates sleep apnea.

In general, explaining the nature of sleep and the changes that take place as a normal part of the aging process can reduce the worry that older persons have about their sleep patterns, a concern that itself can interfere with sleep. The therapist can also reassure patients that going without sleep from time to time is not a calamity; it will not cause irreversible brain damage or mental illness, as some people fear.

Worrying less about sleeping usually helps one sleep. Some individuals are given relaxation training to help them fall asleep and tips to help them develop good sleep habits: rising at the same time every day; avoiding activities at bedtime that are inconsistent with falling asleep; lying down only when sleepy; and if unable to go to sleep, getting up and going into another room. Regular exercise can also help (Stevenson & Topp, 1990). All these tactics can loosen the grip of insomnia on adults of all ages (Bootzin et al., 1996; Morin & Azrin, 1988).

For years, practitioners have believed that medication was the most effective treatment for sleep problems in older adults. Recent research into non-pharmacological treatment of sleep disorders in this population, however, has yielded extremely promising results. Charles Morin from Laval University is one of the leading scholars in this area. His work is described in Canadian Contributions 16.1.

SUICIDE

Several factors put people in general at especially high risk for suicide: serious physical illness, feelings of hopelessness, social isolation, loss of loved ones, dire financial circumstances, and depression (see Chapter 10). Because these problems are widespread among older adults, it should not be surprising that suicide rates for people over age 65 are high, perhaps three times greater than the rate for younger individuals (McIntosh, 1995).

An examination of cross-sectional data indicates that the association between suicide rates and age is not as straightforward as it initially appears. The U.S. suicide rate for men rises from youth and increases in a linear fashion with age, whereas the rate for women peaks in middle age—in their fifties—and then slightly yet steadily declines across the rest of the lifespan (McIntosh et al., 1994). Older white men in the U.S. are more likely to commit suicide than are members of any other group; the peak ages for committing suicide in this group are from 80 to 84 (Conwell, 1994). As for Canada, according to 1997 statistics (World Health Organization, 1997), rates of suicide in men remain fairly constant and quite high across the various age ranges, including old age, while rates for women decline somewhat. Men have higher suicide rates than women throughout the lifespan, but the difference is most notable in people aged 75 and older.

A study of suicide in Alberta showed that elderly men were more likely than elderly women to use lethal methods (e.g., guns) as a means of committing suicide (Quan & Arboleda-Florez, 1999). A study of suicide rates in 21 health units in British Columbia (Agbayewa, Marion, & Wiggins, 1998) found that the elderly had a higher suicide rate in every region and that the male suicide rate was higher than the female in every region.

Older persons are less likely than younger persons to communicate their intentions to commit suicide, and they make fewer attempts (Conwell, 2001). When older people attempt suicide, they use more lethal methods and more often kill themselves (McIntosh et al., 1994), so the ratio of attempted to completed suicides for elderly people tends to be much lower than for younger people. According to Pearson and Brown (2000), the ratio of attempted suicides to completed suicides is about 4 to 1 for elderly people but ranges between 8 to 1 and 20 to 1 for the overall population. Several factors contribute to this difference. Conwell (2001) mentions such factors as elderly people having fewer physical resources, so they are less likely to survive self-inflicted damage. Also, elderly people are often more socially isolated and less likely to be rescued prior to death. Finally, the suicide acts themselves are more planned and determined in older people. Unfortunately, the statistics are probably underestimates. Older adults have many opportunities to give up on living, such as by neglecting their diet or medications, thus killing themselves in a more passive fashion. As more and more people survive longer, the number of suicides in people over age 65 is almost certain to increase (see Conwell, 2001).

Numerous factors play a role in suicide among the elderly. Conwell (2001) alluded to the role of psychosocial factors. Individual differences in loneliness and feelings of isolation predicted suicide ideation in the elderly in Canadian studies (Mireault & deMan, 1996; Stravynski & Boyer, 2001). Heisel, Flett, and Besser (2002) showed that poor cognitive functioning, depression, general hopelessness, and interpersonal hopelessness were predictors of suicide ideation in a sample of seniors from the Toronto area, and they presented a model in which depression and hopelessness mediated the link between poor cognitive functioning and suicide ideation. Suicide ideation was assessed with the Geriatric Suicide Ideation Scale, the first measure of suicide ideation created specifically for the elderly.

Brown, Bongar, & Cleary (2004) asked a sample of 681 practising psychologists with expertise on aging to rate the importance of 36 potential suicide risk factors. Factors deemed of critical importance for suicides by elderly people included a history of suicide attempts, severe hopelessness, the seriousness of previous suicide attempts, depression, isolation, losses and separations, and a family history of suicide.

Butler and Lewis (1982) argued that the suicide of older adults might more often represent a rational or philosophical decision than it does for younger people.

Two of the most common methods of suicide amongst the elderly are firearms and self poisoning.

Consider, for example, the older person facing the intractable pain of a terminal illness who knows that each passing day brings more physical agony to him- or herself and more emotional suffering to his or her family. Physical illness is often cited as a reason for suicide among the elderly, but empirical research on this topic is not extensive. However, a recent Alberta study found that suicide was higher than the norm among elderly men suffering from illnesses such as cancer and prostatic disorders, but that other illnesses (e.g., diabetes, heart disease) were not predictive (Quan et al., 2002). The link between suicide and specific terminal illnesses and the issue of physician-assisted suicide are likely to focus increased attention on suicide among the elderly.

A recent study conducted in Toronto found that treatment for multiple illnesses (i.e., multiple health problems) was strongly related to a higher risk of suicide (Juurlink et al., 2004). Overall, 1,354 elderly people were deemed to have committed suicide in Ontario between 1992 and 2000. The most common methods of suicide were firearms (28 percent), hanging (24 percent), and self-poisoning (21 percent).

Intervention to prevent the suicide of an older person is similar to that discussed in Chapter 10. In general, the therapist tries to persuade the person to regard his or her problems in less desperate terms. Mental health professionals, who are usually younger and healthier than their older patients, may unwittingly try less hard to prevent an older person's suicide attempt, but older people—like people of any age—are usually grateful to have another chance at life once a crisis has passed.

Unfortunately, only a small number of suicidal elderly people actually seek help from a mental health professional. About 70 percent of those who commit suicide visit their physician sometime during the month prior to committing suicide, but their profound depression and despair often goes undetected (see Pearson & Brown, 2000). The Toronto study cited above found that almost half of those who committed suicide visited their physician in the week prior to their suicide (see Juurlink et al., 2004). As a result, it has been suggested that, in primary care settings, doctors should conduct routine screenings for depression and suicidal tendencies when assessing their elderly patients.

Clearly, the elderly are neglected when it comes to suicide prevention. A survey of American and Canadian crisis prevention centres found that only one-quarter of Canadian centres have specialty programs for elderly people (versus 46 percent having programs for adolescents) and only 14.3 percent have outreach programs for suicidal elderly people (Adamek & Kaplan, 1996). In addition, more than two-thirds of the volunteers and almost half of the program managers did not realize that older adults represent the age group with the highest suicide rate. Perhaps this lack of outreach and awareness accounts, at least in part, for the reluctance of elderly people to seek help from crisis prevention centres.

Finally, in his review of suicide prevention in Canada, Leenaars (2000) lamented the fact that even though Canada's elderly have been identified as at high risk for suicide, successive national task forces (1987, 1994) cite primarily American studies on the elderly. This has occurred despite the availability of numerous Canadian studies (e.g., Abayewa, 1993; Bagley & Ramsay, 1993; Leenaars et al., 1991).

TREATMENT AND CARE OF OLDER ADULTS

Older adults sometimes go to mental health centres or seek private psychotherapy through referrals. Yet older people are less likely than younger adults to be referred (Knight, 1996), which could be a reflection of the attitudes uncovered in the Kingston study, described earlier in this chapter. One problem is that general practitioners usually fail to detect depression in older patients (Bowers et al., 1990). This situation may be due in part to inadequate geriatric training for medical professionals.

Clinicians tend to expect less success in treating older patients than in treating young patients (Knight, 1996; Settin, 1982). In one study, therapists in Canada and the United States were provided with descriptions of people of various ages with personality disorders requiring treatment (Zivian et al, 1992). The results showed that therapists overwhelmingly preferred to provide treatment to middle-aged and younger adults than to the elderly. Psychotherapists were less likely to respond this way if they themselves were older, had taken three or more professional courses focusing on older adults, or had practices in which at least one in 10 of their clients was 65 or older.

The views of psychotherapists are paralleled by equally negative views of the elderly endorsed by people in the general population. The same team of researchers assessed public opinions of psychotherapy for the elderly in a large sample of visitors to the Ontario Science Centre (see Zivian et al., 1994). The respondents were presented with the same scenarios used in the previous study and were asked to evaluate the value of psychotherapy if provided to the target people in the scenarios. Zivian et al. found that older people were seen as less likely to benefit from psychotherapy; they also found that this negative view was especially pronounced among the older people in the sample.

These findings have emerged even though research does not show that psychotherapy is less successful for older patients (Gallagher-Thompson & Thompson, 1995a, 1995b; Knight, 1996; Knight, Kelly, & Gatz, 1992; Scoggin & McElreath, 1994). If older patients are viewed as having limited possibilities for improvement, they may not be treated.

There is an irony in questioning whether psychotherapy is appropriate for older adults. As people grow older, they tend to become increasingly reflective and philosophical about life (Neugarten, 1977). Running counter to pessimism about the capacity for older people to change, both of these traits augur well for the suitability of older adults for psychotherapeutic interventions, and indeed, this suitability is borne out by the data.

Admissions of older adults to mental hospitals and to psychiatric units of general hospitals have decreased substantially in recent years owing to changes in mental health policy in most provinces and territories. Most older people needing mental health treatment now live in nursing homes or receive community-based care. The importance of home care is shown in Canadian Perspectives 16.2.

NURSING HOMES

The prevalent myth regarding nursing homes is that families dump their older relatives into these institutions at the first sign of frailty. However, families usually explore all their alternatives and exhaust their own resources before they institutionalize an older relative. The decision to institutionalize comes as a last resort, not as a first choice. While institutionalization can sometimes have a negative impact on family relations, one U.S. study found that moving the parent to a nursing home tended to strengthen family ties and brought a renewed closeness between the parent and the child who was the primary caregiver. The care provided by the nursing home alleviated the strain caused by the parent's multiple physical or mental problems. Relations grew worse in only about 10 percent of families (Smith & Bengston, 1979).

Nursing homes are now the major locus for institutional care for older adults with severe chronic illnesses and mental disorders (Gatz & Smyer, 1992; Horgas, Wahl, & Baltes, 1996). Given projected future needs, it does not appear that enough people are being trained to provide mental health services within nursing homes. This is a matter of concern in both the United States and Canada. In the United States, a minority of the approximately 15,000 nursing homes offer counselling as a routine service, and the great majority of patients have diagnosed mental disorders (including dementia) (National Center for Health Statistics, 1989; Rovner et al., 1986). The situation is similar in Canada. Worse still, nursing-home operators prefer to exclude older adults with mental disorders, a step likely to place further strains on caregivers and families.

Even a good nursing home—and not all of them are run well—may have unintended negative consequences on some residents. This caution is based on a classic study by Blenker (1967). Older adults who went to a medical health centre were assigned randomly to one of three treatments: intensive, intermediate, and minimal. Intensive treatment involved the services of a nurse and a social worker; intermediate treatment involved somewhat less professional attention; and minimal treatment consisted of information and referral to community-based services. One might expect intensive treatment to have been the most effective, but after half a year, the death rate of members of the intensive-care group was four times that of people in the minimal-care group. The intermediate-care group was better off than the intensive-care group, the death rate of its members being "only" twice that of the minimal-care group.

What happened? It turned out that the major factor was whether or not a patient was placed in an institution, such as a nursing home. People were much more likely to be institutionalized if a nurse and social worker were intensively involved in planning their care, and the excessive death rates were found in institutionalized patients. Since people had been assigned randomly to the three treatments, the death rates were not due to related differences existing before treatment began.

What is it about some nursing homes that could contribute to such decline? First, relocation to a new setting is in itself stressful and plays a role in increased mortality (Schultz & Brenner, 1977). Once the person is in the nursing home, the extent and nature of care discourage rehabilitation and even maintenance of whatever self-care skills and autonomous activities the resident may be capable of. For example, a resident able to feed himself or herself will be assisted or even fed like a child at mealtimes to shorten the time devoted to serving meals.

During the late 1980s and 1990s, a series of investigations into lax practices in nursing homes in both the United States and Canada led to a number of governmental reforms. Despite resulting improvements in most nursing homes, there remain serious problems with some of them. These deficiencies undermine the belief that residents reliably receive satisfactory care. The situation has been much worse in the United States than in Canada. In the United States, for example, nursing assistants are often inadequately trained, overworked, and underpaid, and it is the nursing assistants, not the professional nursing staff or physicians, who have by far the most contact with nursing-home residents. Many nursing assistants do not speak the same language as the residents; they are often high school dropouts and homeless; and some work two jobs for as many as 18 hours a day. Turnover in these positions is high. Despite the best intentions, nursing assistants are presented with an overwhelming set of challenges, owing in part to cutbacks in government funding to nursing homes and the resulting unreasonably heavy workload. In a study in California, some residents were reported to have been harmed, sometimes fatally, through errors of omission and of commission by nursing assistants (Pyle, 1999). The possibility of abuse of nursing-home residents is discussed in Canadian Perspectives 16.3.

Nursing homes play a major role in the institutional care of the aged. They have often been criticized for the poor care they provide as well as for the lack of stimulation in the environment.

Canadian Perspectives/16.2

Home Care in Canada

In a policy statement, the Canadian Association of Gerontology (CAG; 1999) decried the fact that Canada does not have a universally accessible, comprehensive home care policy or program. Each province has a different approach to home care delivery (see Romanow & Marchildon, 2003; Woodward et al., 2004). Should home care be a vital part of a comprehensive health care system? According to the CAG, numerous groups have advised different levels of government to establish comprehensive community-focused health and support services as an essential component of the Canadian health care system. These include the National Forum on Health, the National Advisory Council on Aging, the Canadian Home Care Association, and the Victorian Order of Nurses of Canada. As noted in Chapter 1, their efforts paid off. Roy Romanow, who led the Commission on the Future of Health

Care in Canada, concluded that home care should definitely be expanded to include mental health services (Romanow & Marchildon, 2003).

A key group in this effort is the Canadian Association of Retired Persons (CARP), a national, nonpartisan organization for Canadians aged 50 or older (for its website, see http://www.50plus.com). CARP conducted a national survey of 300 organizations involved in home care. The results were summarized in the report entitled *Home Care by Default, Not by Design* (Parent & Anderson, 2001). CARP's "report card" concluded that home care in Canada is a "system-by-default," and the organization reiterated previous calls for a national strategy, national standards, and a common national definition of home care.

Are home care services both appropriate and cost-effective? Unfortunately, research on cost-effectiveness, much of which is U.S. based, has been inconclusive. Despite the fact that recipients typically report higher quality of life, home services are not always cost-effective.

A recent report prepared for the Canadian Mental Health Association (Parent, Anderson, Neuwelt, & Elliott, 2002) examined the link between senior's mental health and home care. This report summarized the results of a national study that surveyed home care organizations, governments, seniors' organizations, physicians, seniors, and family caregivers. The first segment focused on a number of factors deemed to contribute to mental health in the elderly, including physical health, spirituality, the ability to cope with losses, a sense of independence and personal control over one's life, and a sense of dignity and purpose in life. Home care factors were seen as broad situational factors that contributed to mental health, such as the quality of the home environment, the accessibility of services, the role played by the formal care provider, and the flexibility of service provision. The formal care provider was seen as playing a key role. Respondents indicated that it is vitally important to have a highly competent provider who is both compatible with the care recipient and who provides continuity of care (i.e., a single formal care provider). One focus group participant noted that her husband, who suffered a stroke, had 35 different workers in just one month.

Is home care adequately funded in Canada? The CAG concluded that it is chronically underfunded. For example, in 1997–1998, public home care expenditures accounted for only 4 percent of total public health care spending (Health Canada, 1998). This is an increase from 1.2 percent in 1980-81. Despite the fact that home care budgets are increasing in Canada, the CAG argues that these increases cannot keep up with increased demands for services. The increased demand is due, in part, to changing demographics—that is, to an increase in the proportion of frail elderly who need home care and related services if they are to remain in their homes (Woodward et al., 2004).

CARP's 2001 national report identified funding as the top home care issue (Parent & Anderson, 2001). The top five issues identified, in order, were (1) funding; (2) human resources; (3) needs of the population not being fully met; (4) coordination with other parts of the health care system; and (5) leadership and strategic direction.

Given that over 70 percent of personal care to the elderly is provided by informal networks of family and friends (Kane & Kane, 1985), the consequences of health care restructuring in Canada (e.g., closing of hospitals, restrictions on building long-term care beds) mean an increased burden on caregivers unless there are major increases in the funding of home care. According to CARP's 2001 national report card, most provinces in Canada are not considering official policies for family caregivers. Newfoundland and Labrador is the only province with such a policy in place. Many of Canada's largest provinces, including British Columbia, Ontario, and Quebec, also lack respite policies as support for family caregivers (Parent & Anderson, 2001).

In its position paper, the CAG (1999) recommends that the Canadian federal, provincial, and territorial governments institute a universal and comprehensive home care program as part of Medicare. The program would include

1 adequate funding for training, the delivery of services, and evaluation of services;
2 national standards for training, service delivery, and evaluation; and
3 appropriate services available to informal caregivers.

Although visions of health care reform over the last decade (e.g., Mhatre & Deber, 1992) identified home care as a "cornerstone" of the ideal health care system in Canada, not just for the elderly but for Canadians of all ages, the promise has been largely unfulfilled. Indeed, some individuals and organizations have argued that recent developments are regressive. The situation in Ontario is representative of what has happened and continues to occur across Canada. In response to the government's announced budget freeze for home care (Potter, 2001), at a time of massive restructuring of the hospital system, the 43 Community Care Access Centres (CCAC) confirmed that service cuts and waiting lists would be initiated immediately.

Ontario has a long history of home care, with the first services established in 1958. In 2001, \$1.6 billion was budgeted for home care (a 78 percent increase from the levels in 1995). Although six other provinces in Canada require means-testing or cost-sharing for some home care services, in Ontario no direct fees are charged to clients. The amount Ontario spends on home care services (approximately \$128 per person) is, in fact, the highest in Canada (Potter, 2001). Almost 450,000 Ontarians were estimated to receive home care in 2000–2001.

Why is there a problem? For one thing, the system used to focus on the frail elderly and disabled, including people with mental health problems, but now, according to some experts in the field (see Potter, 2001), the system is directed primarily toward acute care patients. As one CEO of a not-for-profit service provider put it, "the chronic who are not in immediate danger get marginalized out of the equation because they aren't in immediate danger.... It amounts to basic abandonment of frail elderly in favour of the sicker" (Potter, 2001, p. A4). The situation is exacerbated because registered nurses, registered practical nurses, and personal support workers are leaving the home care sector for better-paying positions in hospitals and institutions. A report commissioned by the health ministry concluded that there is a "critical shortage" of human resources and recommended increased funding (see Boyle, 2001). The report also noted that over 30,000 people were on waiting lists to get into long-term care facilities in August 2000. Finally, it was noted that Ontarians receive different levels of service in different parts of the province. In her response to the report, MPP Frances Lankin stated, "We need to stabilize this system very quickly to end the government-sanctioned elder abuse that is now taking place" (Boyle, 2001, pp. A1, A26).

A recent qualitative study by Aronson (2002) concluded that some elderly people in Ontario respond to home care by proactively taking charge, but a substantial proportion of the elderly saw home care as something beyond their control. In essence, they felt that home care "pushed them over the edge." They found home care to be insufficient and depersonalizing in that it involved a succession of care providers who never really got to know them personally and who often did not have enough time for them.

Thinking Critically

1. Do you think that home care should be available as part of Medicare in Canada? Should every citizen have access on a universal basis?
2. What criteria should be used to determine access? Would all elderly people with dementia be eligible? Would adults with mental retardation living in supportive housing receive home care? What about people with chronic schizophrenia living on their own?
3. Should means-testing and cost-sharing be a part of the home care system everywhere in Canada? Should all services be privatized?

Depression is a particular problem among the residents of nursing homes. The type of intervention employed is usually a drug, and the psychoactive drug prescribed is more likely to be a tranquillizer than an antidepressant—a less agitated, relatively inactive patient is easier to handle. Psychological interventions are virtually unheard of, for staff members either are untrained in their implementation or operate under the belief that such therapy is inappropriate for an old person (Zarit, 1980). This situation is unfortunate, as interventions such as behaviour therapy have been found to be quite effective in reducing unwanted behaviours and improving overall functioning in nursing-home residents with dementia (Mansdorf et al., 1999).

In sum, all the problems of institutionalization are exhibited in bold and exaggerated relief in some nursing homes. Independence is inadvertently, but with sad consequences, discouraged, and both physical and mental deterioration occur, in part because they are expected.

ALTERNATIVE LIVING SETTINGS

Recently, the United States and Canada have seen a dramatic rise in assisted-living or retirement homes, a viable alternative to placement in nursing homes for many older adults who require assistance of one sort or another. The American Association of Retired Persons (AARP) reports that assisted living is the fastest-growing category of housing for older adults in the United States. (AARP, 1999). In contrast to nursing homes, assisted-living facilities resemble hotels, with separate rooms and suites for the residents as well as dining rooms and on-site amenities such as beauty and barber shops. The philosophy of assisted living stresses autonomy, independence, dignity, and privacy (AARP, 1999). Many such residences are quite luxurious, with attentive staff, nursing and medical assistance readily available, daily activities, such as bingo and movies, and other services all designed to provide assisted care for older adults too infirm to live on their own but not so infirm as to require a nursing home. However, as with nursing homes, there is a great deal of variability in quality of care.

COMMUNITY-BASED CARE

At any given time, 95 percent of older persons reside in the community. Many of these individuals are frail and have an urgent need for help with daily living arrangements. Some communities and for-profit agencies are organized to provide various services, such as

- telephone reassurance;
- daily phone calls to old persons living alone to check that they are all right;
- home services (e.g., Meals on Wheels, which brings a hot meal each day to the person's door);
- visits from volunteers who cook meals and do household chores;
- shopping help from young people or other seniors and light repair work by volunteers;
- community and/or seniors' centres, which may also serve hot lunches and provide help with government forms;
- sheltered housing (i.e., apartments in which several old people may live together semi-independently);
- home visits by health professionals and social workers, who can assess the actual needs of old people and treat them; and
- regular social visits from community neighbours.

Canadian Perspectives/16.3

Elder Abuse in Canada: A "Hidden Horror"?

DESPITE EVERYTHING, Janet* still remembers the good things about her son, Brian. The 69-year-old retired Alberta day-care worker says Brian, an only child, was devoted to her husband, a former oil company technician who suffers from Parkinson's disease. "My son always took great care of his dad," she says, but then added: "It was always me he picked on." "Picked on" hardly describes the pain and suffering Brian inflicted if Janet refused his demands for money or said anything he didn't like. "He would pin me up against the wall and grab my face or my neck, and squeeze until I'd repeat whatever he wanted me to," she says, her voice trembling.

The worst attacks occurred when her son, in his 30s, moved back to his parents' home after he lost his job last year. Janet says she knew she ought to have called the police, but after each incident, she succumbed to Brian's appeasements, believing his contrition was real. But instead, the abuse grew worse, both in ferocity and frequency. The last straw for Janet came last January when, for the first time, she says, Brian attacked his partially paralyzed father, knocking him from his walker, pinning him to the ground and repeatedly spitting and screaming into the 70-year-old man's face. Janet fled to a neighbour's house and called authorities. "I lived in terror for years," she says, her voice breaking, 'and I became increasingly fearful for my life.' "(Oh, 1999, p. 48)

*All names of victims and their family members have been changed.

Elder abuse was recently in the news because of revelations in newspapers and on the CTV show *W-5* about the abuse experienced by 87-year-old Norma Stenson at two separate retirement and long-term care facilities in Brantford, Ontario (see Canadian Press, 2004). A videotape that aired on *W-5* showed footage of two workers mistreating Stenson. This frail, elderly woman was smacked and tossed about, had a pillow put over her face, was pulled roughly from bed at 4 a.m., injuring her arm and knee, and had money stolen from her. Stenson requires the use of a wheelchair, and she can barely speak as a result of experiencing several strokes prior to the incidents.

Definitions and Types of Abuse

"Elder abuse" refers to the abuse of people over the age of 65 years by caregivers, family members, or other people who may be in a position of trust (Trevitt & Gallagher, 1996). It includes any act that harms or threatens to harm the physical health and/or psychological well-being of an older person. Elder abuse victims in Canada experience more serious physical health problems and have shorter life expectancies than people who are not abused (Oh, 1999).

Experts have identified a number of different subtypes of abuse, including the following:

1 *Financial abuse*. This involves the misappropriation of the elder's legally owned assets (e.g., a mother cannot account for large sums of money because her son misuses his power of attorney for personal gain). This is the most prevalent type of abuse. A study in Winnipeg found that women over 80 years old were especially likely to be targets (Bond et al., 1999). This study also found that unpaid personal care home bills that should have been paid were the best indicators of financial abuse. Spencer's (1996) analysis in British Columbia revealed that social and physical isolation is a deliberate aspect that facilitates financial abuse.

2 *Neglect*. Active neglect is the failure to provide the necessities of life (e.g, an elderly man has an unkempt appearance and appears to be weak and dehydrated). Neglect is sometimes unintentional (passive neglect) due to a failure of the caregiver to understand the elderly person's needs (e.g., caregiver not knowing the nutritional requirements of the person under care).

3 *Psychological or emotional abuse*. Psychological abuse can occur many ways: screaming or yelling or any behaviour that insults, threatens, humiliates, intimidates, denies privileges, or removes the power of the elder to make decisions (e.g., an elderly woman shows low self-esteem, is depressed and fearful, especially when the caregiver is present).

4 *Physical abuse*. Physical abuse entails the infliction of pain, discomfort, or injury (e.g., the elderly person shows physical signs of possible abuse such as bruises, welts, swelling, grip marks, or fractures).

5 *Sexual abuse*. Here, the abuse is of a sexual nature (e.g., an elderly person is sexually assaulted by a neighbour).

Of course, it is possible for the elderly person to experience several types of abuse, and all forms of abuse can have adverse psychological consequences. For example, Janet and her husband experienced psychological, physical, and financial abuse from their son. It is probable that they would soon have experienced neglect as well.

Prevalence of Elder Abuse in Canada

Officially, the prevalence of elder abuse in Canada, as determined by a national telephone survey, is 4 percent (Podneiks & Pillemer, 1990). However, elder abuse is rarely reported and the figure of 4 percent likely underestimates the magnitude of the problem. A chart review of patients affiliated with a geriatric psychiatry service in Montreal found suspected or confirmed elder abuse in 16 percent of cases, with the most common forms being financial abuse (13 percent) and neglect (6 percent) (Vida, Monk, & Des Rosiers, 2002). A history of family disruption owing to death, divorce, or separation was higher among the abused. Kosberg (1988) estimated that five out of every six cases of abuse can go unreported. Why? Out of shame, guilt, or fear, victims rarely report mistreatment. Often the abuse is difficult to detect by others, who may be reluctant to "see it" or are unaware of the signs and symptoms of abuse. Further, police and prosecutors can be reluctant to pursue what may be viewed as a family dispute. Elizabeth Podneiks, who chairs the Ontario Network for the Prevention of Elder Abuse, estimates that between 7 and 10 percent of the 3.7 million seniors in Canada experience some form of abuse, primarily by their children and grandchildren. Thus, although a majority of elderly people cared for by their families receive good care, tragic cases such as that of Janet are not uncommon or unusual in Canada.

Although abuse may be difficult to detect, a Canadian study identified some reliable signs of impending or actual abuse of the elderly (Mendonca, Velamoor, & Sauve, 1996). Indications of poor physical care are often clues that physical abuse is likely occurring. Other indicators include obvious signs of psychological distress, irritability, and defensiveness in the abuser. Alcohol abuse by the abuser has also been identified as a contributing factor in approximately 15 percent of Canadian cases (Bradshaw & Spencer, 1999).

Robert Gordon from Simon Fraser University and Deborah Brill have reviewed the hypotheses offered as explanations for elder abuse (see Gordon & Brill, 2001). These explanations include the stressed-caregiver hypothesis (i.e., abuse is a byproduct of overworked, burdened caregivers), the learned-violence hypothesis (i.e., a family member, once the target of violence or neglect, learned these behaviours and can now exact revenge on an elderly parent), and the psychopathology hypothesis (i.e., abuse is a reflection of a pre-existing disorder in the abuser, such as substance dependence). Gordon and Brill (2001) posited an "integrated theory" of abuse and neglect of the elderly that includes aspects of the caregiver (caregiver stress, caregiver pathology, learned violence), aspects of the elderly victim (e.g., victim pathology and excessive dependency behaviour), and ongoing environmental stressors.

Mandatory Reporting of Elder Abuse?

Legislation for the reporting of elder abuse by both individuals and social service agencies varies across Canada. In Ontario, there is currently no mandatory reporting of elder abuse in the community. However, mandatory reporting is required in cases of abuse, neglect, or improper treatment of residents in homes for the aged and nursing homes, a provision in response, in part, to research studies and media accounts in Ontario of preventable deaths of nursing home residents (see Gordon & Verdun-Jones, 1992).

Legislation tends to be most stringent in the Maritimes. The Adult Protection Act in Nova Scotia provides a means whereby anyone 16 years of age or older who lacks the ability to adequately care for themselves can be protected from abuse and neglect. People must report suspected abuse, even if the information is privileged or confidential. Prince Edward Island and British Columbia also have mandatory reporting in place. Social workers and other health care professionals in the Atlantic provinces are given a great deal of latitude, based on legislation modelled after laws pertaining to the abuse of children, to intervene directly to protect elderly people. Legislation is in place in all of the provinces and territories mandating the police to deal with physical and financial abuse of the elderly, although the laws are not always applied (Oh, 1999).

Prevention, Detection, and Treatment of Elder Abuse in Canada

What can our society and the various professionals who come in contact with the elderly do to detect abuse and protect seniors? Most experts agree that elder abuse is part of a larger social context that requires responsibility on the part of government, the community, and the individual caregiver (Trevitt & Gallagher, 1996).

PREVENTION AND DETECTION

Role of Governments Various levels of government throughout Canada are taking some initiative to try to put a stop to elder abuse. In 1999, the Ontario government formed the "Round Table for Ontario's Elder Abuse Strategy." The goal is to enhance the ability of communities in Ontario to combat elder abuse through staff training, services coordination, and public awareness. In 2002, the Ontario government provided $4.3 million in funding for the strategy.

Role of Professional Personnel Although psychiatrists and psychologists can play important roles in the detection and prevention of elder abuse, front-line workers such as general practitioners, nurses, and social workers play more critical roles, since they are more likely to encounter situations of actual abuse and situations where an elderly person is at risk for abuse. Unfortunately, a survey of transition houses in the Yukon and in British Columbia found that only 4 percent of the facilities had special services available for older women (Hightower et al., 1999).

Role of Physicians General practitioners can play a vital role in the prevention, identification, and treatment of elder abuse. Nonetheless, many physicians believe that they do not have the skills and resources to deal with elder abuse, even if they are able to identify it. The Canadian Medical Association (CMAJ, 1997) polled general practitioners in Ontario to determine what strategies for dealing with elder abuse they would be likely to use. More than 80 percent of respondents indicated that they would be "fairly" or "very likely" to use the following: a single agency overseeing all cases of elder abuse, a directory of services for seniors, a list of resource people to provide advice them, and professional guidelines or protocols for both the detection and the management of elder abuse.

Role of Nurses, Social Workers, and Personal Support Workers Nurses in community practice and health care facilities often have a unique opportunity to play a significant role in the prevention and treatment of elder abuse. However, a study of registered nurses involved in care of the elderly in various health care settings in Victoria, B.C. (Trevitt & Gallagher, 1996), concluded that the nurses were not knowledgeable about different types of elder abuse. Further, the nurses perceived themselves as unskilled and felt uncomfortable when dealing with actual cases of abuse. The nurses also identified relevant problems within the community, such as few trained personnel, a lack of co-operation between agencies, a lack of legal guidelines, and a reluctance to become involved.

Role of Community Organizations Community organizations, either alone or in partnership with various levels of government, are making efforts to educate the general public and professionals about elder abuse. For example, the non-profit Ontario Network for Prevention of Elder Abuse supports several initiatives. In an attempt to prevent future elder abuse, the network has developed a new program to influence positively children's attitudes toward seniors. The program involves the use of interactive storytelling and "skit" kits for children as young as 4 years old. The "Grandpa is a Grump" story for younger children explains why an elderly person's face can look grumpy and how to see beyond the physical appearance. With assistance from Health and Welfare Canada, the network has produced a video that can be used by groups and individuals concerned about elder abuse. The video explores various situations of abuse, one example being an older man attempting to forget the shame of having been beaten by his son.

CARING FOR VICTIMS

A number of community organizations in Canada help seniors who are victims of abuse. In Nova Scotia, the Senior Support Network (King's County) offers support through non-judgemental peer counselling to seniors who have experienced abuse. One goal is to help elderly people identify alternatives to their current situation and to empower them to make adaptive decisions. The network also gives support to elderly people who need help accessing services in the community, and it makes appropriate referrals when necessary.

Sometimes support and counselling is not sufficient for the needs of abused elderly people. In 1999 the Kerby Centre, a long-established nonprofit resource facility for seniors, opened a 32-bed shelter for the elderly abused in Calgary. The centre had previously developed a handbook (*Golden Years—Hidden Fears: Elder Abuse*) to help professionals and volunteers identify and address elder abuse. In Edmonton, Catholic Social Services joined forces with the police and other agencies to respond to crisis calls. Their purpose is to educate both the victims and the abusers and to explore viable options for the families involved (Oh, 1999).

Psychiatrists, psychologists, and social workers often see abused elderly people in clinic situations or in their private practices. Perhaps these professionals could be especially effective as members of an interdisciplinary team trained to care for victims of elderly abuse and their abusers. Psychologists could also be effective in assisting with the planning, implementation, and evaluation of programs and in facilitating the development of appropriate counselling skills in the volunteer and paraprofessional staff members of community organizations.

ELDER ABUSE IN NURSING, RETIREMENT HOMES, AND HOSPITALS

Thus far, we have focused on the abuse of the elderly in their own homes. However, we began this discussion with a case of horrific abuse in a nursing home and long-term care facility. What about the abuse of the elderly in retirement homes and nursing homes? In recent years, there have been numerous highly publicized cases of elder abuse in these institutions throughout Canada. Nursing homes and homes for the aged are subject to quite stringent regulations. In contrast, retirement homes are unregulated. Furthermore, no provincial operating standards outlining the quality of care that people should receive have been established for the over 600 retirement homes in Ontario. Following an investigation by a local newspaper, the City of Toronto set up a special retirement home hotline. Seniors called and complained about poor-quality food, dirty sheets, and unclean rooms. They also complained about patients forced to lie in wet diapers (Priest, 1999). Is the use of restraints, both physical and chemical, in hospitals a form of abuse? Legislators in Ontario were opposed to a practice that was carried out each day in Ontario hospitals. On June 27, 2001, the Legislative Assembly of Ontario passed legislation to end restraints on elderly hospital patients (Boyle, 2001). The Ontario Hospital Association opposed the legislation.

In the fall of 2003, the *Toronto Star* published a series of investigative reports on nursing-home neglect and abuse in Ontario. The investigation into the province's 544 nursing homes analyzed the health ministry's own data to reveal widespread

Dr. Elizabeth Podnieks received the Order of Canada for research on elder abuse.

neglect and inadequate care for the 65,000 residents in the system; for example, the residents were left for long periods in dirty diapers, went hungry, and suffered from toxic bed sores (leading to death in at least one case). Many homes were able to "cheat" on annual inspections thanks to advance warnings. The new health minister, George Smitherman, promised a "revolution" in long-term care (Welsh, 2004). He began by introducing surprise annual inspections and surprise dietary and environmental inspections, and he created a toll-free phone number (1-866-434-0144) for families to register complaints. The president of Concerned Friends of Ontario, the chief advocacy group for nursing-home residents, expressed disappointment that the announcement did not include family councils.

Thinking Critically

1. Elder abuse is a complicated issue. Although we cannot ever condone the behaviour, do you think that some instances of abuse might occur because of the unrelenting demands of caregiving? Would this be a further indication of the need for respite care for both the elderly and their caregivers?
2. Should reporting of suspected abuse be mandatory? Some professionals have suggested that mandatory reporting takes away the right of a competent person suspected of being abused to make choices regarding what they want to do. Further, if the reporting of suspected abuse is mandatory, it will be necessary to have increased services in place to deal with the probable increased demand for assistance.
3. In some states in the United States (e.g., California), public databases rate nursing homes on the basis of indicators of quality care (e.g., hours left in bed, use of restraints, inspection results). Do you think such ratings should be a mandatory component of the system in Canada so that families can determine if the homes they are considering for a loved one provide good care?
4. The Canadian government is in the process of enacting whistle-blower protection legislation for government agencies. Do you think we should legislate whistle-blower protection so that staff in long-term care facilities can report instances of neglect and abuse without fear of reprisal?

Primary Sources: Brockville (Ontario) Police; Muskoka-Parry Sound (Ontario) Health Unit; National Clearing House on Family Violence; Nova Scotia Senior Citizen's Secretariat; Ontario Network for Prevention of Elder Abuse; Ontario Senior's Secretariat (Ministry of Citizenship, Culture and Recreation with Responsibility for Seniors and Women); Senior Support Network (King's County, Nova Scotia); the *Toronto Star*.

A range of available services allows a true match with the needs of the older person so that he or she will not have too much or too little help. The availability of home care has become a major issue in Canada (see Canadian Perspectives 16.2). Home care is defined as "the provision of an array of health and social services designed to support living at home" (Woodward et al., 2004, p. 177). In addition to improving the quality of life for the elderly person, home care helps to prevent burnout in informal caregivers and plays an important role in preventing abuse of the elderly, (see Canadian Perspectives 16.3). Although our focus here is on home care for the elderly, it should be noted that home care is intended to help diverse groups in our society, including the disabled mentally ill. Research indicates that such community-based home care projects enhance the quality of life of older people and reduce their dependency on institutional care (e.g., Knight, 1983; Nocks et al., 1986).

Mere availability of services is not enough. Services must be coordinated, but they are not coordinated in most localities. All too often, an older person and his or her family are shuffled from one agency to another, getting lost in bureaucracies. Even professionals who have experience with the system often have difficulty working through it to get need-

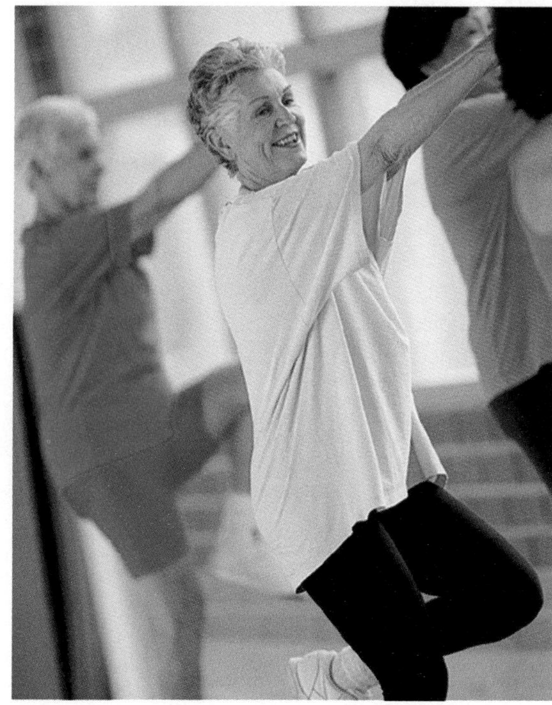

Among community-based services are daycare centres, where older people participate in various activities, such as exercise classes.

ed services for their clients. Frustrating rules can interfere with the very goals for which programs were instituted.

When it comes to health care for older adults, one of the main difficulties is that the chronic health problems of old people are not appealing to physicians because they seldom diminish. Many, if not most, of the maladies of old people—hearing loss; visual impairments; loss of mobility; aches and pains, especially in the feet (Pearson & Gatz, 1982); and a steadily declining cardiovascular system—are unlikely to get better and must somehow be adjusted to. Older persons rely heavily on their relationships with health care providers, but these providers may become impatient with them because, as Zarit (1980) suggested, the illnesses of older people are often incurable and therefore violate a "law" by which most medical professionals live. Moreover, older people do not always take medication as instructed (Leach & Roy, 1986).

In addition, older people's relations with family caregivers are likely to suffer. Ailing older patients are sometimes torn both by feelings of guilt for needing so much from others and feelings of anger toward these younger people for whom, at one time, they sacrificed so much. The sons and daughters also have feelings of guilt and anger (Zarit, 1980), and this sometimes leads to abuse, as seen in Canadian Perspectives 16.3.

ISSUES SPECIFIC TO THERAPY WITH OLDER ADULTS

It is important that we consider a few general issues concerning the conduct of therapy for older people. They can be divided into issues of content and issues of process (Zarit, 1980).

CONTENT OF THERAPY

The incidence of brain disorders increases with age, but other mental health problems of older adults are not that different from those experienced earlier in life. Although clinicians should appreciate how physical incapacities and medications may intensify psychological problems, they should also noted the importance of consistency and continuity from earlier decades of the older person's life.

For older people, medical illnesses can create irreversible difficulties in walking, seeing, and hearing. Finances may be a problem. Therapists treating psychological distress in older adults must bear in mind that much of it is an understandable response to real-life challenges rather than a sign of psychopathology. Professional intervention, however, may still be helpful.

Therapy with older adults must take into account the social contexts in which they live, something that cannot be accomplished merely by reading the professional literature. The therapist who, for example, urges a lonely widower to seek companionship in a neighbourhood recreation centre for senior citizens may be misguided if the centre is not suited to the particular patient (Knight, 1996); this could make the patient feel even lonelier. All social organizations, even those as loosely structured as a senior centre, develop their own local mores and practices, or what social scientists have come to call *social ecology*. Some may be tolerant of physical frailty, others not. Some may be frequented primarily by people who used to be well-paid professionals; others may have mostly former psychiatric hospital patients as regulars. Mental health care workers need to know and understand the social environments in which their older patients live. We take this need for granted when dealing with younger patients but, Knight points out, often neglect to consider it with older adults.

The social needs of older patients often differ from those of younger people. The widespread concern that old people are socially isolated and need to be encouraged to interact more with others appears to be ill-founded. There is no link between level of social activity and psychological well-being among old people (Carstensen, 1996). As we age, our interests shift away from seeking new social interactions to cultivating those few social relationships that really matter to us, such as those with family and with close friends and associates.

What some therapists see as psychologically harmful social withdrawal may be social selectivity. When we have less time ahead of us, we tend to place a higher value on emotional intimacy than on learning more about the world. This preference applies not just to older people, but also to younger people who see themselves as having limited time, such as when they are preparing to move far away from those they feel closest to (Frederickson & Carstensen, 1990) or if they have AIDS.

Women may suffer doubly as psychotherapy patients, as not only ageist but also sexist attitudes can negatively influence the direction of psychotherapy (Steuer, 1982). For example, stress in an older couple can increase when the husband retires. A common therapeutic goal is not so much to help the husband make accommodations as to help the woman accommodate to the husband's loss of status and learn to spend more time with him each day.

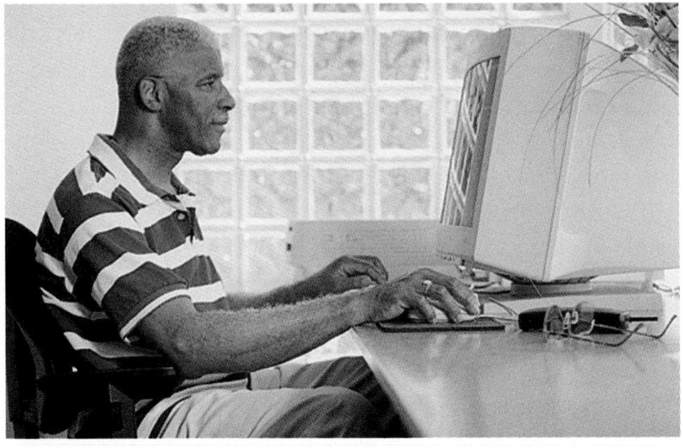

Being able to use a computer and access the Internet is one way older adults can increase their social contacts.

The expectations and values that present-day cohorts of older adults place on marriage can be quite different from those of people in their fifties and younger. Most readers of this book probably expect a marriage to provide happiness and personal fulfillment and believe that divorce is a logical step if expectations are not met. But people who are now in their seventies and older may have different expectations (Knight, 1996). These people married when stability and commitment were the essence of a marital union and often took precedence over personal fulfillment.

Death and dying figure prominently in therapy with older patients. They may need help dealing with the fear of facing death or an illness that requires life support. It may be helpful to counsel some older clients to examine their lives from a philosophical or a religious perspective. These perspectives may help them transcend the limitations that aging imposes on human existence. When the person is dying, discussions of the meaning of the individual's life can facilitate self-disclosure and enhance his or her sense of well-being and personal growth (see the discussion of life review that follows). The person's loved ones may also benefit from such discussions.

Process of Therapy

We have already indicated that traditional individual, group, family, and marital therapies are effective with older adults (Gatz et al., 1985). Some clinicians adapt these therapies to here-and-now practical problems. They hold that therapy with older patients needs to be more active and directive, and thus they provide information and take the initiative in seeking out agencies for necessary services.

Some characteristics of aging may mean that therapy will proceed differently (Knight, 1996; Light, 1990). Certain kinds of thinking simply take longer for many older people. Older people also tend to experience some diminution in the number of things that can be held in mind at any one time. Therapists may find that it helps to move with greater deliberation when seeing an older adult. Explanations may have to be more elaborate and conversation more extended.

In a historical overview of psychotherapy with older adults, Knight, Kelly, and Gatz (1992) discussed life review, proposed by Butler (1963) as a psychotherapeutic approach uniquely suitable for older adults. This approach reflects the influence of Erik Erikson's (1950, 1968) lifespan developmental theory, which postulates stages of conflict and growth extending well into the senior years. Life review facilitates what appears to be a natural tendency of older adults to reflect on their lives and to try to make sense of what has happened to them. In Eriksonian terms, it helps the person address the conflict between ego integrity and despair. *Ego integrity* refers to a process of finding meaning in the way one has led one's life, and *despair* reflects the discouragement that can come from unreached goals and unmet desires. Life-review methods include having the patient bring in old photographs, travel to a childhood home, and write an autobiography. People can feel worse or better from this kind of therapy; it takes considerable skill on the part of the therapist to guide the patient to a positive view of life and its coming end.

Canadian Clinic Focus/16.1

Efficacy of a Multidimensional Preventive Program for the Elderly at Risk of Functional Decline

In our discussion of home care, we described the Canadian Association on Gerontology's recommendation that governments set aside funding to evaluate home care programs. Research by Dr. Réjean Hebert and colleagues illustrates how important it is to conduct controlled clinical evaluations. Hebert is the founding scientific director of the Canadian Institutes of Health Research—Institute of Aging. He is known internationally for developing the Functional Autonomy Measurement System, which is a disability rating scale.

In a previous study, Hebert and his colleagues determined that the annual incidence of functional decline in individuals over 75 years of age who are living at home is almost 12 percent (Hebert, Brayne, & Spiegelhalter, 1997). The prevalence of disabilities is approximately 80 percent in people in Quebec over age 85 (Saucier, 1986). Can early detection of elderly individuals at risk of losing their autonomy and the application of an assessment and surveillance program prevent or delay functional decline?

Hebert and his team (Hebert, Robichaud, Roy, Bravo, & Voyer, 2001) used a selective two-stage strategy: screening for individuals at risk and then an intervention where appropriate, an approach expected to be more effective and efficient than an intervention that targeted all older people in an area. The outcome measure for testing the efficacy of the intervention was the autonomy and well-being of the elderly participants. The participants were a representative sample of elderly people (over age 75) who were living at home and who were identified by Hebert's scale as being at risk of functional decline.

Multidimensional Preventive Program

Participants were assigned randomly to a study group or a control condition. Participants in the study group were assessed at home by a nurse. The nurse used standardized instruments to evaluate 12 different dimensions of functioning, such as depressive mood, cognitive functions, social support, medication, and so forth. The results of the assessment were sent to the participant's family physician along with suggestions for the diagnosis or treatment. For example, if the participant was depressed as assessed by the Geriatric Depression Scale, geriatric psychiatric assessment and treatment were recommended. If cognitive dysfunction was evident, then referral for assessment at the memory clinic was advised. The nurse then monitored the proposed interventions and followed the participant's progress via monthly telephone contact. The outcome measures were administered at the baseline interview and after one year.

How did the study group fare relative to the control group? The primary outcomes of interest were functional decline as assessed in five areas (activities of daily living, mobility, communication, mental functions, and instrumental activities of daily living), admission to a nursing home or long-term care hospital, and death. Surprisingly, the groups did not differ in terms of functional decline. Further, there were no differences on the secondary measures examined: functional autonomy, general well-being, perceived social support, and the use of health care services. The authors concluded that "the efficacy of structured screening programs for preventing functional decline in the older population remains to be demonstrated" (Hebert et al., 2001, p. 152). Further, they proposed that increased effort be placed on attempts to improve the efficacy of specific interventions, such as prevention of cognitive decline prior to the use of multidimensional screening programs.

Comment

Although the results of this study were disappointing, the findings are very important because they illustrate the critical importance of carefully designed and implemented outcome studies. The Hebert et al. (2001) study was based on the best available information about intervention, carefully controlled and rigorously implemented. The authors examined several alternative explanations before concluding that the program was ineffective. Interestingly, although compliance was acceptable, it was the participants themselves rather than the physicians who typically failed to comply with the recommendations. This study can be placed in the context of a review for Health Canada by Roberts et al. (2000). The review examined the literature on the effectiveness of services or models of care for people with dementia who were living in their own homes, in specialized care, and in assisted-living centres or congregate homes. Although the authors found some evidence for the effectiveness of respite care, day programs, counselling, congregate living, and special care units in institutions, they were unable to find any rigorous effectiveness studies for hospice care, case management, or psychogeriatric outreach mental health programs. The ubiquitous "more research" was recommended, an important conclusion given the current emphasis on "evidence based" approaches. (See Chapter 17 for a further discussion.) In their assessment of Canada's health care system, Ritchie and Edwards (1998, p. 386) concluded, "Evidence-based decision making is regarded as a key element in making the future health-care system appropriate to meeting health needs and in controlling costs."

The very process of being in therapy can foster dependency. Older adults, whether institutionalized or living at home with caregivers, often receive much more social reinforcement (attention, praise) for dependent behaviours, such as asking for help or being concerned about the opinion of their therapist, than for instances of independent functioning (Baltes, 1988). The growing specialization of behavioural gerontology (Nemeroff & Karoly, 1991) emphasizes helping older people to enhance their self-esteem by focusing on specific, deceptively minor behaviours, such as controlling their toileting better (Whitehead, Burgio, & Engel, 1985), increasing self-care and mobility (Burgio et al., 1986), and improving their telephone conversational skills, thus enhancing social contacts (Praderas & MacDonald, 1986). One development, though hardly a formal therapy, involves teaching older adults computer skills so that they can access the Internet and expand their social contacts (Cody et al., 1999).

All therapists must be able to interpret the facial expressions of their patients and thereby understand the meaning of the patients' words or reactions and appreciate their phenomenological experience of the world. Research on emotional changes over the lifespan suggests real potential for error when the therapist is younger than the patient (Knight, 1996). Because of their more varied and extensive life exper-iences, older people's emotions can be more complex and subtle than those of younger adults (Schulz, 1982). Younger people tend to commit more errors when trying to identify the emotions reflected in the faces of elders (see Malatesta & Izard, 1984).

Finally, clinicians may encounter aspects of the concept of countertransference when they use psychotherapy with older patients. Therapists can be troubled by the patients' problems, for these difficulties can touch on sensitive areas in their own lives, such as unresolved conflicts with their own parents, worries about their own aging process, and a fear of death and dying. As Knight, Kelly, and Gatz (1992) speculated, "the perception that therapy is different with older adults is now thought to be due more to the emotional impact on the therapists of working with the elderly than to actual differences in technique, process, or likelihood of success.... [Working with older adults] will challenge therapists intellectually and emotionally to reach a maturity beyond their years" (pp. 540, 546).

We will conclude with a statement on the overall amount and quality of care available to seniors in Canada. In their position paper on the delivery of mental health services to elderly people, the CAG (2000) stated: "The current range of community services are inadequate and insufficient to meet the needs of older mental health clients, but no money to expand or improve community services seems immediately forthcoming." In particular, there is a lack of focus on prevention and too much of the current funding and available treatment is medically driven, even though, as the CAG notes, many issues facing the elderly are non-medical in nature. Given the increasing proportion of the population that will be elderly in the years to come, this is a problem deserving of more attention at the national level. It is also important to conduct rigorous scientific evaluations of preventive and treatment programs (see Canadian Clinic Focus 16.1).

SUMMARY

- Until recently, the psychological problems of older people were neglected by mental health professionals. As the proportion of people who live beyond age 65 continues to grow, it will become ever more important to learn about the disorders suffered by some older people and the most effective means of preventing or ameliorating them. Although physical deterioration is an obvious aspect of growing old, most of the emotional distress to which old people are prone is psychologically produced.
- Serious brain disorders affect a small minority of older people, fewer than 10 percent. Two principal disorders have been distinguished, dementia and delirium. In dementia, the person's intellectual functioning declines; memory, abstract thinking, and judgement deteriorate. If the dementia is progressive, as most are, the individual seems another person altogether and is, in the end, oblivious to his or her surroundings. A variety of diseases can cause this deterioration. The most important is Alzheimer's disease, a progressive, irreversible illness in which cortical cells waste away. Genes figure prominently in the etiology of Alzheimer's, particularly the early-onset forms. Head injury and depression are also risk factors.
- In delirium, there is sudden clouding of consciousness and other problems in thinking, feeling, and behaving—fragmented and undirected thought, incoherent speech, inability to sustain attention, hallucinations, illusions, disorientation, lethargy or hyperactivity, and mood swings. The condition is reversible, provided that the underlying cause is self-limiting or adequately treated. Brain cells malfunction but are not necessarily destroyed. Causes include overmedication, infection of brain tissue, high fevers, malnutrition, dehydration, endocrine disorders, head trauma, cerebrovascular problems, and surgery.
- The treatments of these two disorders are quite different from each other. If delirium is suspected, there should be a search for the cause—for example, nutritional deficiencies or a toxic reaction to medication—so that it can be rectified. Progressive dementia usually cannot be treated, but the person and the family affected by the disease can be counselled on how to make the remaining time manageable and even rewarding. If adequate support is given to caregivers, many patients with dementia can be looked after at home. There usually comes a time, however, when the burden of care impels most families to place the person in a nursing home or hospital.
- Older people may experience the entire spectrum of psychological disorders, in many instances brought with them from their earlier years. Yet it appears that, overall, the prevalence of depression and anxiety is lower among older adults than among those younger than 65. The newer cognitive behaviour therapies as well as various psychodynamic therapies are being applied to depression in older patients, and results are encouraging.
- Although not as widespread as depression, paranoia is a problem for older people and for those who have a relationship with them. Paranoia is sometimes brought on by brain damage in dementia, but it can also be caused by psychological factors. Delusional thinking may be a reaction to hearing difficulties. Isolation can be a factor as well; when a person has little social intercourse, it is difficult to verify impressions and suspicions, setting the stage for the development of delusions.
- Other psychological disorders experienced in old age include rare cases of schizophrenia (sometimes called paraphrenia); hypochondriasis; substance abuse, in particular the misuse of medication; sexual dysfunctions; and sleep disorders. All are treatable.
- More of the suicide attempts of old people result in death than do those of younger people. Mental health professionals may assume that people who are old and debilitated have nothing to live for. This attitude may reflect their own fear of growing old.
- Nursing homes and other extended-care facilities sometimes do little to encourage residents to maintain or enhance whatever skills and capacities they have. Both physical and mental deterioration are possible. Serious neglect can be found in some nursing homes, despite efforts to correct the deficiencies.
- Today, care is provided in the community whenever possible. Comprehensive services, such as Meals on Wheels, regular home visits by health professionals, and support for caregivers, seem to be beneficial when they are available and coordinated so that people do not have to confront a bureaucratic maze. All intervention should be minimal so that older adults remain as independent as their circumstances permit.
- Many older people can benefit from psychotherapy, but several issues specific to treating older adults need to be kept in mind. The emotional distress of older adults is often realistic in content. Many have experienced irreplaceable losses and face real medical and financial problems. It is unwise always to attribute their complaints to

a psychopathological condition. Death is a more immediate issue as well.

- As for the process of therapy, clinicians should sometimes be active and directive, providing information and seeking out the agencies that provide the services needed by their clients. Therapy should also foster a sense of control and hope and should help the older patient elucidate a sense of meaning as he or she approaches the end of life.

KEY TERMS

age effects (p. 528)
ageism (p. 527)
Alzheimer's disease (p. 531)
cohort effects (p. 529)
cross-sectional studies (p. 529)
delirium (p. 537)
dementia (p. 530)
longitudinal studies (p. 529)
neurofibrillary tangles (p. 532)
paraphrenia (p. 545)
plaques (p. 532)
selective mortality (p. 529)
sleep apnea (p. 548)
time-of-measurement effects (p. 529)

Reflections: Past, Present, and Future

- Are Canada's economic, social, and medical resources sufficient to provide for the coming dramatic increase in the population of elderly people? Are we facing a caregiving crisis in the future? What can the people of Canada and different levels of government in Canada do to prepare for the aging of the Canadian population?
- If you were consulted by the federal, provincial, and territorial governments about how best they might cope with the increase in disorders of the elderly owing to the aging of the Canadian population, what would you advise them to do? Why?
- A leading American neurologist and ethicist, Dr. Ron Crawford, has suggested that people with Alzheimer's disease should have the right to choose to die rather than being required to live with the possibility that they will become a burden on their families (Vienneau, 1999). However, Dr. Margaret Somerville, director of McGill University's Centre for Medicine, Ethics and Law is appalled by Crawford's ideas:

  Despite its overlay of empathy, it is a "gene machine" approach to human life. It focuses on cognitive, neural processes as identifying us as human ... and when these are absent we should be disposed of. (Vienneau, 1999, p. L8). Crawford believes that his own position is ahead of its time and "pushes the moral envelope," but he believes that it is "the reality of what we are going to have to face" in the future (Vienneau, 1999, p. L8). What is your own position on this controversial issue? Refer back to Chapter 10 if you need more background information.
- In 1999, the year dedicated to the elderly by the United Nations, Pope John Paul, who suffers from Parkinson's disease, decried the fact that some cultures cherish the elderly, whereas other cultures seem to dismiss them as disposable items (Reuters, 1999). What is the situation in your own culture? Are the elderly "cherished" or "disposable"?

chapter 17

Outcomes and Issues in Psychological Intervention

"People, when they are looking for psychotherapy, often don't know what they are getting. They get a psychiatrist or GP who does therapy and get anything from holotropic breathing to long-term psychoanalytic psychotherapy. So consumers need to educate themselves about what they're looking for and knowing how to identify it."
— Zindel V. Segal, cited in Simmie and Nunes, 2001, p. 158

"Don't ever do anything to someone that you can't reverse."
— D. Ewen Cameron, quoted by Don Gillmor in *I Swear by Apollo: Dr. Ewen Cameron and the CIA-Brainwashing Experiments* (1987).

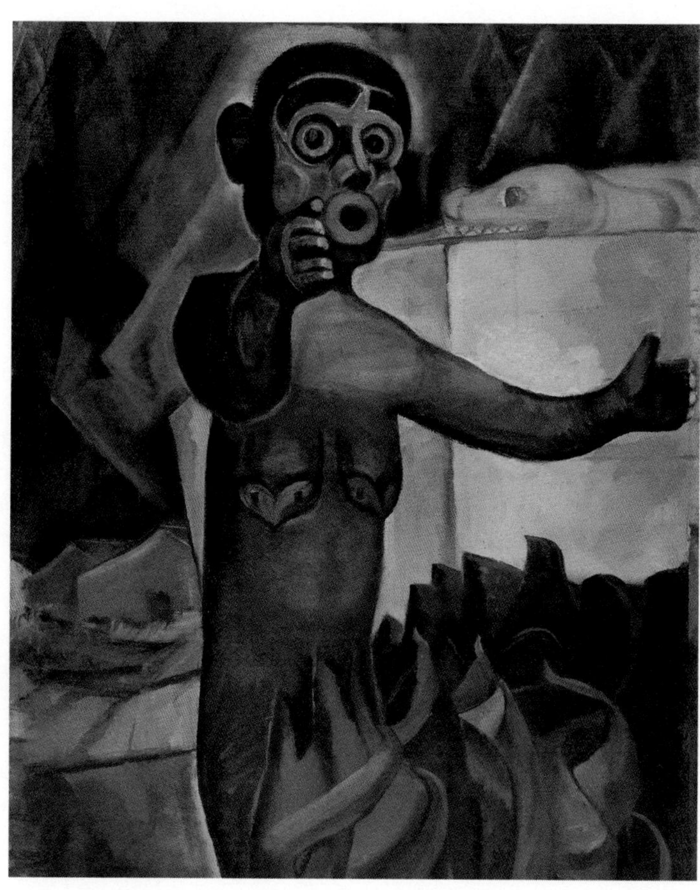

Emily Carr 1871-1945, *Guyasdoms D'Sonoqua*, 1928-1930
oil on canvas, 100.3 x 65.4 cm, ART GALLERY OF ONTARIO, TORONTO
Gift from the Albert H. Robson Memorial Subscription Fund, 1942

THERAPY FOCUSED on a client with multiple presenting concerns, including major depression, anxiety disorder and interpersonal problems overcoming her core maladaptive fear by accessing her sadness at loss and anger at violation, and mobilizing her current abilities to protect herself.... Having spent the first three sessions establishing an empathic bond the therapy first focused on her primary fear of her abusive parents and her fear of her dependence/weakness and vulnerability. Her frequent experiences of shame and embarrassment in therapy were often mixed with her fear. Her parents had disciplined her with harsh criticism and ridicule, as well as physical abuse, and she stated that her greatest pain was that "they never believed in me." She was called stupid, crazy, a whore and a slut and grew up utterly paralyzed in interpersonal relationships. Interventions were aimed at [her] becoming aware of and accessing her fear and shame in the session by talking about her childhood. This led to [her] experiencing and reprocessing these emotions and to a strengthening of her sense of self.

One of her earliest memories was of her father forcing her and her siblings to watch him drown a litter of kittens. This was to "teach her a lesson about life" and the client believed he enjoyed it. The client accessed a core self-organization, which included her "suppressed scream of horror" from this experience. While [she] imaginally reliv[ed] this scene in therapy the therapist *guided her attention* to the expression of disgust in her mouth while she was feeling afraid. This mobilized this subdominant adaptive emotion as a resource to begin building a stronger sense of self. Rather than feeling afraid she accessed her alternate emotions of disgust and anger, which she actively expressed toward her father in an empty chair. She mobilized her *adaptive needs* to not be violated by her father and to be protected by her mother and *expressed* these to her parent in the empty chair dialogues. Expression and exploration of her vulnerability (fear and sadness) took place, not to the imagined father, but in the affirming and safe dialogue with the therapist. . . . These imaginary confrontations with the father evoked her fear and her painful memories of childhood beatings, of being told she was bad, and of being aware of nothing but her desperate need to escape. . . . Her anger undid her fear and the therapist supported the client's new found sense of power, heightening her awareness of her strengths. This motivated further assertion and self-validation. The client acknowledged that she was worthy and had *deserved more* than she got from her parents. She began to create a new identity narrative, one in which she was worthy and had unfairly suffered abuse at the hands of cruel parents. She also began to feel that it would be possible to need love and she was now open to learn love." (Greenberg, 2004, p.p. 13-14).

The case study outlined above illustrates how people requiring treatment often have very complex concerns and idiosyncratic experiences that require an equally complex and multi-faceted intervention in a supportive therapeutic environment. The client described above received emotion-focused therapy, a form of treatment described later in this chapter.

In Chapter 2, we outlined the major approaches to therapeutic intervention, and in Chapters 6 through 16 we reviewed how these approaches have treated various psychopathologies. We turn now to a critical appraisal of a number of psychological interventions. We discuss the research on their effectiveness and offer as well some general comments that, we hope, will enrich the reader's understanding of the complexities of psychotherapy.

GENERAL ISSUES IN EVALUATING PSYCHOTHERAPY RESEARCH

We begin with a few general issues that will inform our understanding and appreciation of research in psychotherapy.

THERAPY AS RESEARCHED AND THERAPY AS PRACTISED

Therapist manuals are detailed guides on how to conduct a particular therapy, stipulating specific procedures to be followed at different stages of treatment. The use of such manuals has become the norm in psychotherapy research (e.g., Addis, 1997; Nathan & Gorman, 1998). Indeed, it is impossible nowadays to obtain funding to study the outcome of psychotherapy without first explicitly defining the independent variables via a manual that the therapists in the study must follow as closely as possible.

The use of therapist manuals began with the earliest controlled studies on Wolpe's technique of systematic desensitization (Davison, 1968b; Lang & Lazovik, 1963; Paul, 1966). In contrast, in earlier psychotherapy research of the 1940s and 1950s, the activity of the therapist was, for the most part, described only in terms of his or her theoretical orientation (psychodynamic, client centred, etc.). But what therapists actually do in the consulting room is often difficult to know on the basis of what they say they do and their allegiance to a particular orientation (London, 1964). Specifying via manuals what therapists are to do in a controlled study and then monitoring what they actually do in their sessions with patients has thus been hailed as a significant advance in the scientific study of therapeutic interventions (see Hunsley & Rumstein-McKean, 1999). It allows someone reading a psychotherapy study to know what actually happened to patients in a given experimental condition.

Hunsley and Rumstein-McKean (1999) endorsed the use of treatment manuals as an adjunct to research involving randomized clinical trials. At the same time, they acknowledged that several concerns involving some current treatment manuals need to be addressed. The most common criticism, they suggested, is that manuals are too unwieldy for actual clinical practice, with some situations requiring a more specific approach and others requiring a more general approach. They also expressed concern that "many manuals inadvertently promote rule-governed behaviour that may not be appropriate in all instances" (p. 1511), and noted that more attention needs to be given to contextual factors, including timing issues, such as advice on when a particular technique is appropriate. This latter issue reflects the more general concern that treatment manuals lose sight of the individuality of people because they are based on abstract representations of the typical patient and therapists may thus have to rely on their own clinical judgement to deal with the unique issues facing certain patients (see Nathan, Stuart, & Dolan, 2000). Finally, Hunsley and Rumstein-McKean pointed to an urgent need for research that examines the extent to which treatment manuals, accompanied by little or no supervision, do indeed result in treatments that are accurate and effective. These concerns notwithstanding, they suggested that, for treatments supported by randomized clinical trials, "working knowledge of the treatment manual would be essential to practitioners" (p. 1510).

A moment's reflection suggests another problem. Although the use of manuals buys us greater internal validity—results obtained can be attributed with some confidence to the action of the independent variable—what about external validity? Do the results obtained from manual-based studies generalize to the actual practice of psychotherapy outside the constraints of a controlled study? There is perhaps no more important and more hotly debated topic in psychotherapy than this (Beutler, 1999; Goldfried & Davison, 1994).

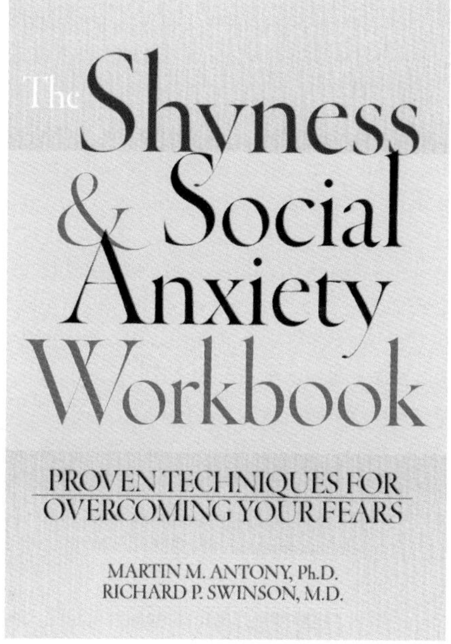

Workbooks such as this are designed for patients and are commonly used in conjunction with a manual that guides the therapist in treating the patient.

Finally, another overarching problem is that treatment manuals are based on mental disorders. This is problematic because manuals are disorder-based rather than theory-based (Nathan et al., 2000).

Here's a way to look at the issue. Because many therapists describe themselves as eclectic, controlled studies of specific techniques (e.g., desensitization) or approaches (e.g., client-centred therapy) are limited in what they can tell us about the nature and outcomes of therapy as actually practised (Lambert & Bergin, 1994); that is, we know that most therapists seldom behave strictly in line with a particular theoretical orientation—whether psychoanalytic, client centred, or behavioural. Therefore, the kinds of controlled studies emphasized in this chapter and earlier in the book are limited in what they can tell us about the effectiveness of the psychotherapy available to patients who are not participants in research studies. This situation is ironic, for it is these controlled studies that provide the evidence used by proponents of particular techniques or general theoretical approaches to support their positions!

A common characteristic of today's controlled studies is the exclusion of people on various grounds. For example, people may be excluded from a study if they have problems in addition to the one being studied (the comorbidity issue). Moreover, studies rely on people who are willing to be seen in a highly structured treatment protocol. In short, the patients who volunteer and are accepted as participants in controlled studies are different from many—and perhaps the vast majority of—patients in psychotherapy. This point was underscored by the results of a provocative study that compared psychotherapy research participants in randomized controlled trials (RCTs) with general community outpatients (Stirman, DeRubeis, Crits-Cristoph, & Brody, 2003). This study found that 58 percent of the community sample had primary diagnoses that had never been studied in RCTs, indicating that some diagnoses are common but not represented in psychotherapy research. Common diagnoses overlooked in research studies included adjustment disorder, dysthymia, and mood and anxiety disorders not otherwise specified. Findings such as these suggest that it is quite risky to generalize from controlled studies to the actual practice of psychotherapy and the people receiving this psychotherapy.

Another related attribute of controlled studies is the widespread use of a DSM diagnosis and thereby the definition of patients as homogeneous. For example, the large-scale NIMH study of depression that we examined in Chapter 10 followed the DSM criteria in defining people as having major depression and then randomly assigned them to different experimental conditions. But as we have seen many times, people are depressed, anxious, or dependent on alcohol or cigarettes for many different reasons. What is not possible in such studies is an *idiographic analysis* of a person—that is, an analysis of the unique features of a single case—to determine which factors are most important in making that one person feel, think, and behave in a certain way (Beutler, 1997; Goldfried & Davison, 1994). Note that psychotherapy researchers do not really believe that the people who are diagnosed as, for example, depressed and then assigned randomly to different treatment conditions are depressed for the same reasons (e.g., biased thinking). Rather, for the sake of creating an experiment with as much internal validity as possible, they pretend that this is the case. For this reason, large numbers of participants are needed in psychotherapy research; the differences that are present among people are assumed to "randomize out" with large groups.

Therapy as actually practised takes a more idiographic approach; that is, it is tailored to the particular needs and characteristics of a particular patient. When they are working in clinical settings, therapists make continual adjustments that are not constrained by the demands of a scientific study. In contrast, the very essence of treatment manuals is to minimize the tailoring of intervention to individual patients. It remains a challenge to researchers and clinicians alike to reconcile the seemingly incompatible needs of these two approaches (Davison, 1998; Fishman, 1999). The Society for Clinical Psychology (Division 12 of the American Psychological Association) has responded to this challenge by striking the Task Force on the Identification of Principles of Therapeutic Change (see Beutler, 2002). Their mandate is to incorporate empirically supported findings into practice but with treatment approaches that are flexible and can be modified to suit the particular needs and concerns of the individual client

In this regard, psychotherapy researchers make an important distinction between efficacy and effectiveness. The **efficacy** of an intervention is what we determine from a controlled outcome study, typically conducted in an academic research setting. The **effectiveness** of an intervention refers to what is offered to and received by people in the everyday world. According to Dobson and Hamilton (2002), efficacy researchers emphasize maximizing the internal validity of research, often conducted in controlled laboratory settings, while effectiveness researchers hope to optimize the external validity or generalizability of the intervention. Whereas the elimination of observable, well-defined problems, such as a person with agoraphobia being unable to venture far from his or her home, is the usual focus of efficacy studies, effectiveness is usually judged subjectively by patients themselves on the basis of more global criteria, such as the level of satisfaction people have with their therapy, how much they believe they have been helped, and how much the quality of their life has improved (cf. Consumer Reports, 1995; Seligman, 1995, 1996).

Troubled people may talk about their problems with friends or seek professional therapy. Therapy is typically sought by those for whom the advice and support of family or friends have not provided relief.

The efficacy-effectiveness distinction is another topic of lively debate in the field. The Consumers Report Study (1995) is cited widely as a clear example of research that examines the effectiveness of treatment rather than its efficacy. A survey was mailed to 180,000 readers and 22,000 answered; about 7,000 gave responses to the mental health questions, and 4,100 of these people said that they received assistance from some combination of mental health professionals, doctors, and support groups. The main conclusions were summarized by Seligman (1995):

1. The treatment usually worked; in fact, of the 786 people who said they felt poor at the outset, 92 percent reporting feeling very good, good, or so-so after treatment.
2. Long-term treatment was associated with more improvement than short-term treatment.
3. There was no benefit to psychotherapy plus medication versus psychotherapy alone in terms of perceived effectiveness.
4. Family doctors were just as effective as mental health professionals in the short term, but mental health professionals were much more effective in the long term.
5. Alcoholics Anonymous fared especially well and was rated as doing substantially better than mental health professionals.
6. Active participants had better outcomes than more passive recipients.
7. Comparisons among the various psychotherapies showed that no particular type of treatment was superior in terms of effectiveness.

Controlled follow-up studies are needed to confirm the Consumer Report findings. One of the most glaring shortcomings of this report is the absence of a control group (for a discussion, see Nathan et al., 2000). This factor and other limitations led Nathan et al. (2000) to conclude that although this study reached an encouraging conclusion about the effectiveness of treatment, it should be regarded as a consumer survey rather than a research study per se, and as such, it tells us little about efficacy.

Although this study is not without its flaws, it did reach some conclusions that replicated other research findings, including confirmation of the Dodo bird effect. The **Dodo bird effect** refers to the tendency for various therapies to achieve similar results. The term was coined by Rosenzweig

focus on discovery/17.1

Consensus Beliefs Involving Psychotherapy Research

A recent study by Boisvert and Faust (2003) involved surveying the beliefs of an international group of experts who conduct psychotherapy research. Each researcher was asked to indicate his or her degree of agreement with 20 statements about psychotherapy, based on existing research. The experts demonstrated strong agreement that research supported the following claims:

1 Therapy is helpful to the majority of clients.
2 Most people achieve some change relatively quickly in therapy.
3 In general, therapies achieve similar outcomes (i.e., the Dodo bird effect).
4 People change more because of "common factors" than because of "specific factors" associated with therapies.
5 The client-therapist relationship is the best predictor of treatment change.
6 Most therapists learn more about effective therapy techniques from their experience than from research.
7 About 10 percent of clients get worse as a result of therapy.

Boisvert and Faust (2003) observed that, given the researchers' acceptance of the view that a small proportion of clients actually get worse as a result of treatment, perhaps informed-consent procedures should be modified so that potential clients are made aware of the potential risk, as well as the potential benefits, of treatment. Do you agree?

(1936), who adapted it from *Alice in Wonderland*. In this famous book, a Dodo bird judges the outcome of a race and concludes that everyone has won. Indeed, a recent "meta-meta-analysis" of 17 meta-analyses concluded that differences between therapies are small and not statistically significant (Luborsky et al., 2002).

The Dodo bird effect is but one of several beliefs and principles shared by most psychotherapy researchers. Other consensus beliefs are outlined in Focus on Discovery 17.1.

Practising clinicians and other mental health service providers must make daily decisions about how to treat their clients. In some settings, they now use a stepped care approach in making treatment decisions (see Haaga, 2000). The approach offers guidelines for both efficient and effective delivery of psychological services and does this at both the individual and the community service level (Sobell & Sobell, 2000). Focus on Discovery 17.2 presents a brief summary and evaluation of the stepped care approach.

The Challenge of Managed Care

No doubt you have heard of managed care. In the United States, health care is most likely provided to people via an insurance company that attempts to control costs (and maximize profits) by requiring prior approval of the nature and extent of treatment and by reducing the amount of payment provided to hospitals, clinics, and medical and psychological personnel.

Run for the most part by businesspeople rather than by health care providers, managed-care organizations (MCOs) have indeed brought down the costs of care in the United States over the past few decades. They have also demanded increased accountability from providers. MCOs look to scientific evidence to justify what health professionals do with their patients. Surgical, dental, and medical procedures are justified by scientific evidence. Drugs approved by the Food and Drug Administration for use in the United States are

focus on discovery/17.2

Stepped Care Models and the Treatment Process: Can We Do More with Less?

The concept of stepped care involves the notion that clinicians should match the level of the required treatment to the seriousness of the adjustment problem being addressed, but that they should begin with less involved and less costly interventions, with more complex interventions following if the initial interventions are not successful. Lower cost is seen by many as the guiding principle in stepped care (see Haaga, 2000), but it has been suggested by Sobell and Sobell (2000) that the preferred treatment option is the one that is least restrictive for the individual. In this context, "restrictive" refers to such considerations as physical effects of treatment as well as issues involving lifestyle restrictions and economic considerations. Sobell and Sobell (2000) also suggest that treatment must be individualized to reflect the client's beliefs and resources and that the tailoring of treatment to the individual must be consistent with the current research literature.

Figure 17.1 is a diagram of the stepped care approach as conceptualized by Sobell and Sobell (2000). The left-hand portion of the figure clearly shows how the intensity of treatment increases in response to negative treatment outcomes when more basic interventions are used. Davison (2000) has been critical of this figure, stating that the illustration needs to be adapted to reflect the fact that the treatment process is inherently complex. He holds that, according to a stepped care approach, it is indeed the case that feedback-based adjustments are made, but sometimes these adjustments are made very quickly, perhaps even on a moment-by-moment basis. Thus, it needs to be appreciated that the treatment process is ongoing and dynamic and that small procedural steps may be implemented with very little notice.

The usefulness of a stepped care approach will vary depending on the problem in question. Wilson, Vitousek, and Loeb (2000) observed that a low-intensity solution is not well suited to such situations as someone with anorexia nervosa being close to starving to death. In such a potentially life-threatening situation, unless other complications need to be considered, high-intensity treatments designed to provide immediate relief should begin immediately.

Another qualifying condition was identified by Otto, Pollack, and Maki (2000) in the course of their evaluation of the usefulness of stepped care to treat panic disorder. They observed that a substantial proportion of panic disorder patients receive medical treatment before psychological treatment is considered and approximately half of their patients prefer this kind of treatment and likely would not participate in a stepped-care program.

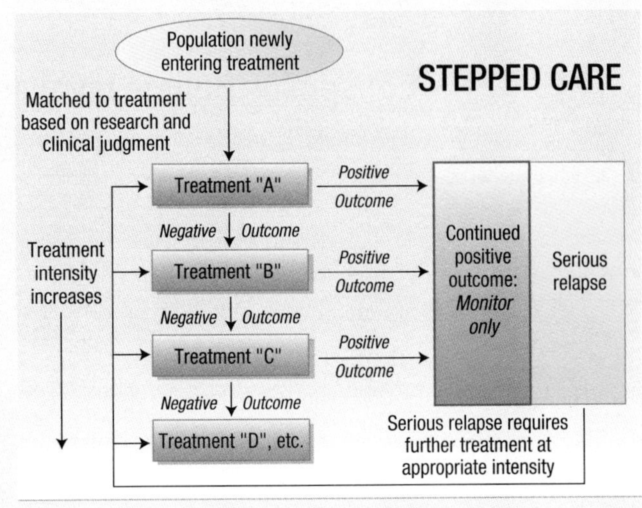

Figure 17.1 A stepped care approach to the delivery of health care services. From M.B. Sobell and L.C. Sobell, "Stepped Care As a Heuristic Approach to the Treatment of Alcohol Problems," *Journal of Consulting and clinical Psychology*, Vol. 68. No. 4, American Psychological Association.

judged from controlled research to be safe and effective for particular conditions. More recently, these standards have been applied to assessments and treatments of mental disorders. The scrutiny that physicians and dentists have been accustomed to for many years is now being brought to bear on mental health professionals.

The situation is considerably different in Canada owing to our universal health care system, where there is an expectation that every citizen will have equal opportunity to receive the best care available (e.g., Romanow & Marchildon, 2003). Nonetheless, in recent years, there has been considerable pressure on governments at the federal, provincial and territorial, and local levels to increase the efficiency of our system, to reduce costs, and to be accountable for the use of tax dollars. Although the Canadian Medicare system does not currently allow user fees, Prime Minister Jean Chrétien indicated a willingness to examine this possibility as part of future health care reforms (Lawton, 2001). Of course, as in the United States, some services, such as private psychotherapy sessions provided by psychologists, can require personal payment or reimbursement by insurance providers. Although American-style managed care has not been loudly advocated by private sector third-party insurers in Canada (Ritchie & Edwards, 1998), insurance providers are beginning to demand the increased accountability that is part of U.S. managed care in conjunction with employee assistance programs (Dobson & Khatri, 2000). As pointed out in Chapter 1, governments in Canada are currently focused on best practice models of service delivery.

In Chapter 1, we introduced the issue of evidence-based treatment or empirically supported therapies (ESTs) (e.g., Hunsley & Johnston, 2000). These treatments have been demonstrated to be effective in research studies with appropriate scientific controls with a specific population, such as patients diagnosed with major depression (Chambless & Ollendick, 2001). Cognitive therapy (CT) has been linked to this issue because it has been evaluated through various empirical outcome studies. It is attractive to managed-care companies because it is not only effective, but typically time-limited. Even though managed-care companies tend to prefer the more widely used medications, such as antidepressants, and CT is more expensive than medications in the short term, DeRubeis, Tang, and Beck (2001) believe that cost-benefit analyses could reveal that CT pays for itself soon after treatment is terminated. Why? CT has the potential to reduce the likelihood of relapse or recurrence (DeRubeis et al., 2001). Neimeyer and Raskin (2001) also believe that constructivist and narrative approaches are well positioned to compete in the managed-care climate, given their emphasis on therapist accountability and short-term interventions.

There are numerous problems with the evidence-based approach. Clearly, practitioners should use effective treatments. But how do we judge effectiveness? How do we reach a consensus on the treatments that qualify to make the "list"? Dobson and Khatri (2000) summarized future needs as follows:

> The future of EST needs to include multisite, longitudinal research trials in clinical settings to improve outcome generalizability. Also, other issues such as process of change, client factors (e.g., ethnicity, age, gender), chronic mental illness (e.g., schizophrenia), and the study of nondominant clinical paradigms need to be explored through EST research if

the outcomes of this research are to be the basis for treating diverse populations in clinical settings ....Overall, there is a need for outcome studies that use randomized designs, appropriate comparison conditions, and follow up at least 6 months post treatment. In addition, results of controlled studies must be interpreted in the context of normative functioning. Lastly, it is important to keep in mind that all of these scientific developments occur against a backdrop of social and technological change that affects the science and profession of psychology." (pp. 914–915)

How should therapists proceed in the meantime? We concur with the recommendation of the Canadian Psychological Association Task Force (Hunsley et al., 1999) as presented by Hunsley and Johnston (2001, p. 271):

> [T]here should be clear statements about the availability of clearly preferable, first-line treatments based on scientific data and about the limitations inherent in the classification of treatments as empirically supported (e.g., the difference between a treatment having support and having been empirically evaluated).

As described by Hunsley and Johnston (2000), rather than redeveloping lists of empirically supported therapies (as was done in the U.S.), the Canadian Psychological Association Task Force focused on promoting evidence-based practice in Canada, promoting collaboration among stakeholders, and providing information about the limitations of current empirical knowledge.

Given that some approaches currently have more empirical support than others, how is evidence-based treatment practised in the real world? Rowa, Antony, Brar, Summerfeldt, and Swinson (1999) sought to determine the extent to which empirically supported psychological and pharmacological treatments were used in Canada for people with panic disorder, social phobia, or obsessive-compulsive disorder. They found that the types of pharmacological treatment received by patients were consistent with findings from the empirical literature. In contrast, empirically validated cognitive and behavioural treatments had been tried by less than one-half of the participants. This result is consistent with other recent studies that report a preference on the part of psychiatrists and many psychologists for traditional but non-validated treatments, such as psychodynamic approaches. Rowa et al. (1999) also reported that the most frequently used psychological intervention for the anxiety disorders was "supportive" therapy. Why is there a discrepancy between treatments identified as effective and treatments actually received by clients in clinical practice? Rowa et al. observed that

> these numbers are a cause for concern. It is possible that these results can be explained in part by the fact that psychiatric services in Canada are government funded and thus are more accessible for patients, and that training for psychiatrists has traditionally focused on psychodynamic approaches. (Rowa et al., 1999, p. 97)

They recommended improved efforts to educate people about empirically supported treatments, improvement in the training of mental health professionals in all fields in methods of cognitive behaviour therapy, and finding ways to make cognitive-behavioural treatments more available and affordable.

Many of the concerns outlined above about randomized controlled trials method and ESTs are summarized in Western, Novotny, and Thompson-Brenner's (2004) insightful, critical review of empirically supported therapies. They concluded that ESTs are well-suited to some disorders (e.g. anxiety disorders) but are poorly suited to treating other disorders. They issued a call for **empirically informed therapies** that are more focused on intervention strategies and change processes that are guided by the clinician's insights rather than rigidly invoking a manualized approach that may not take into account important factors such as the personality characteristics of the client, the presence of co-morbid disorders, and so on. As noted by Goldfried and Eubanks-Carter (2004), when it comes to more complex cases, there is a widening gap between clinical practice and the EST-driven outcome research that has high internal validity but questionable external validity.

With these general observations and the consensus beliefs of psychotherapy experts as background, we turn now to an evaluation of several therapeutic approaches, both the data on their effectiveness and some issues pertaining to them.

REVIEW OF PSYCHOANALYTIC THERAPIES

Before we evaluate several psychoanalytic psychotherapies, it will be good to review and summarize their core features. Information on the whole range of psychotherapy was presented in greater detail in Chapter 2.

Basic Concepts and Techniques in Classical Psychoanalysis and Its Variations

At the heart of classical psychoanalysis is the therapeutic attempt to remove repressions that have prevented the ego from helping the individual grow into a healthy adult. Psychopathology is assumed to develop when people remain unaware of their true motivations and fears. They can be restored to healthy functioning only by becoming conscious of what has been repressed. When people can understand what is motivating their actions, they have a greater number of choices. Where id is, let there ego be, to paraphrase a maxim of psychoanalysis. The ego—the primarily conscious, deliberating, choosing portion of the personality—can better guide the individual in rational, realistic directions if repressions are minimal.

As described in Chapter 2, psychoanalysts employ a variety of techniques to achieve the goal of insight into repressed conflicts. Among these are free association (in which the patient, reclining on a couch, is encouraged to give free rein to thoughts and feelings and to verbalize whatever comes to mind); the analysis of dreams (in which the therapist guides the patient in remembering and later analyzing his or her dreams, the assumption being that during sleep the ego defences are lowered, allowing repressed material to come forth, usually in disguised form); and interpretation (whereby the therapist helps the person finally face the emotionally loaded conflict that was previously repressed; at the right time the analyst begins to point out the patient's defences and the underlying meaning of his or her dreams, feelings, thoughts, and actions).

The concept of transference is of particular importance to psychoanalysts. Freud noted that his patients sometimes acted toward him in an emotion-charged and unrealistic way. For example, a patient much older than Freud would behave in a childish manner during a therapy session. Although these reactions were often positive and loving, they could also be negative and hostile. Since these feelings seemed out of character with the ongoing therapy relationship, Freud assumed that they were relics of attitudes transferred to him from those held in the past toward important people in the patient's childhood, most often parents. In other words, Freud felt that patients responded to him as though he were one of the important people in their past. Freud used this transference of attitudes, which he came to consider an inevitable aspect of psychoanalysis, as a means of explaining to patients the childhood origin of many of their concerns and fears. This revelation and explanation, he believed, tended also to help lift repressions and allow the patient to confront buried impulses. In psychoanalysis, transference is regarded as essential to a complete cure. It is precisely when analysts notice transference developing that they take hope that the important repressed conflict from childhood is getting closer to the surface.

Those who have modified classical psychoanalysis to make it more efficient—generally referred to as *psychodynamic therapists*—are more oriented toward the present than was Freud. However, they still emphasize unconscious motivation and the need for patients to understand the hidden reasons for their current feelings and behaviour.

Therapists identified as *ego analysts* focus more than classical psychoanalysts do on people's ability to influence what happens around them. The basic assumption is that the individual is as much ego as id. In addition, ego analysts attend more to the patient's current life than Freud did.

Ego analysts emphasize ego functions that are primarily conscious, that are capable of controlling id instincts as well as the environment, and that operate on energy of their own, separately from the id. And whereas Freud viewed society essentially as an obstacle to the unrestrained gratification of id impulses, ego analysts assert that an individual's social interactions provide their own special kind of gratification.

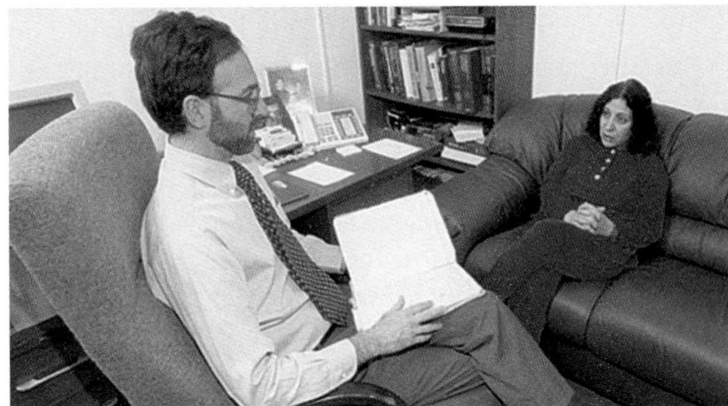

Sadly, many needs go unfulfilled because the majority of people who need help do not seek help.

Brief therapy, or brief psychodynamic therapy, is similar to ego analysis but focuses more on practical, real-life problems—still within the general framework of psychoanalysis. The different forms of brief therapy share several common elements (Koss & Shiang, 1994):

- Assessment tends to be rapid and early.
- It is made clear right away that therapy will be limited and that improvement is expected within a small number of sessions, from six to 25.
- Goals are concrete and focused on the amelioration of the patient's worst symptoms, on helping the patient understand what is going on in his or her life, and on enabling the patient to cope better in the future.
- Interpretations are directed more toward present life circumstances and patient behaviour than on the historical significance of feelings.
- Development of transference is not encouraged, but some positive transference to the therapist is fostered to encourage the patient to follow the therapist's suggestions and advice.
- There is a general understanding that psychotherapy does not cure, but that it can help troubled individuals learn to deal better with life's inevitable stressors.

A variant of psychodynamic therapy, often referred to as *interpersonal therapy* (IPT), emphasizes the interactions between a patient and the social environment. Harry Stack Sullivan was a pioneer in the development of this approach. He held that a patient's basic difficulty lies in misperceptions of reality stemming from disorganization in the interpersonal relations of childhood, primarily those between child and parents. Sullivan departed from Freud in his conception of the analyst as a "participant observer" in the therapy process. He argued that the therapist, like the scientist, is inevitably a part of the process being studied. An analyst does not see patients without also affecting them. IPT includes strategies from both psychodynamic and cognitive-behavioural therapies (Klerman et al., 1984). Its focus is on here-and-now problems rather than on childhood or developmental issues. A therapist practising IPT is much more active and directive, as he or she concentrates on the patient's present-day interactions with others and how the patient could have more satisfying interpersonal relationships.

EVALUATION OF CLASSICAL PSYCHOANALYSIS

Some General Issues The paradigm one holds bears on any evaluation of the effectiveness of psychoanalysis. What are the criteria for improvement? A principal criterion is the lifting of repressions, making the unconscious conscious. But how is that to be demonstrated? Attempts to assess outcome have sometimes relied on projective tests, such as the Rorschach, which in turn rely on the concept of the unconscious (Cook, Blatt, & Ford, 1995). For those who reject the very concept of an unconscious, data from projective tests will not be very convincing.

The central concept of insight has also been questioned. Rather than accept insight as the recognition by the client of some important, externally valid, historical connection or relationship, several writers (e.g., Bandura, 1969; London, 1964) have proposed that the development of insight is better understood as a *social conversion process* whereby the patient comes to accept the belief system of his or her therapist. Marmor (1962) suggested that insight means different things, depending on the school of therapy; a patient treated by a proponent of any one of the various schools develops insights along the lines of its particular theoretical predilections. Freudians tend to elicit insights regarding oedipal dilemmas, Sullivanians insights regarding interpersonal relationships, and so forth.

If an insight is part of a social conversion process, do we need to be concerned with its truth? Therapists who encourage clients to look at things differently—as do all insight-oriented therapists as well as cognitive behaviour therapists—believe that an insight may help the client change. Furthermore, because of the immense complexity of human lives, it is sometimes impossible to know with any degree of certainty whether an event really happened, and if it did, whether it caused the current problem.

This issue has other ramifications. In our discussion of ethics in therapy in Chapter 18, we examine the proposal that psychotherapy is inherently, ultimately, a moral enterprise; that is, therapists, sometimes unwittingly, convey to clients messages about how to live their lives. Therapists assume the role of secular priests (London, 1964, 1986). In this framework, the usefulness of a given insight depends on whether it helps the client lead a life more consonant with a particular set of shoulds and oughts. Whether a given insight is true or not is irrelevant; indeed, it may be impossible to determine whether it is true at all.

It is difficult to distinguish between classical psychoanalysis and psychodynamic psychotherapy in practice (Henry et al., 1994). It is generally held that most classical psychoanalysts act in a fairly passive way, in contrast to those who practise psychodynamic psychotherapy. However, Freud seems to have been a good deal less remote and more directive than the classical analysts who have followed him. In a report of a large psychoanalytic psychotherapy project from the famous Menninger Foundation, a psychoanalytic clinical and research centre in Kansas, Wallerstein (1989) downplayed clear distinctions between psychoanalysis and forms of treatment based on Freud's thinking but containing greater amounts of direct support and direction from the therapist: "Real treatments in *actual practice* [italics added] are intermingled blends of expressive-interpretive and supportive-stabilizing elements; all treatments (including even pure psychoanalyses) carry many more supportive components than they are usually credited with" (p. 205).

With all these cautions in mind, let us consider the efforts researchers have made to evaluate the efficacy of classical psychoanalytic, ego-analytic, and interpersonal therapies.

Outcomes of Research As Bachrach et al. (1991) have pointed out, there are only four outcome studies of long-term psychoanalytic treatment. Each study has methodological problems, the most limiting of which is the lack of a no-treatment control group. Although some people argue that the inclusion of a control group may be unethical (Wolitzky, 1995), it is difficult to make a substantive case for the efficacy of any therapy given such an omission.

Perhaps the most ambitious attempt to evaluate the effectiveness of psychoanalysis was the Menninger Foundation Psychotherapy Research Project, which began in the mid-1960s. In this study, 42 patients—mostly whites with anxiety, depression, or both (what used to be referred to as "garden-variety neuroses")—were seen in either psychoanalysis (22) or short-term psychodynamic psychotherapy (20). In both groups, about 60 percent of the patients improved. There were no significant differences between the two groups either immediately after treatment or at follow-ups of two to three years (Wallerstein, 1986, 1989).

Research on classical psychoanalysis suggests the following conclusions (Henry et al., 1994; Luborsky & Spence, 1978):

- Patients with severe psychopathology (e.g., schizophrenia) do not do as well as those with anxiety disorders, understandable in view of Freud's admitted emphasis on neurosis rather than on psychosis and the heavy reliance of psychoanalysis on rationality and verbal abilities.
- The more education a patient has, the better he or she does in analysis, probably because of the heavy emphasis on verbal interaction.
- A key ingredient is the therapist's identifying and interpreting transference reactions—for example, indicating to a male patient that his behaviour toward the therapist seems to reflect unresolved conflicts with his mother. It appears, though, that a high frequency of such interpretations is often not helpful either to the patient-therapist

relationship or to the treatment outcome. This problem is also evident in briefer, time-limited interventions. A study at the University of British Columbia showed convincingly that the frequency of transference interpretations was related inversely to both the quality of the therapeutic alliance between the patient and therapist and the favourability of treatment outcome (Ogrodniczuk, Piper, Joyce, & McCallum, 1999). The term **therapeutic**, or **working, alliance** (see Horvath & Greenberg, 1994) refers here to rapport and trust and to a sense that the therapist and the patient are working together to achieve mutually agreed-upon goals. Another psychotherapy study done in Quebec found that even when a good therapeutic alliance is in place, transference interpretations that occur early in psychotherapy are followed by increased defensiveness (Banon, Evan-Grenier, & Bond, 2001).

- There is conflicting evidence as to whether the outcome of psychoanalysis is any better than what would be achieved through the mere passage of time or by engaging other health professionals, such as a family doctor (Bergin, 1971). This is not to say that psychoanalysis does no good, only that clear evidence is lacking.

Evaluation of Brief Psychodynamic and Interpersonal Therapies

We look first at outcome research—whether a therapy works—and then at research aimed at elucidating the processes by which favourable outcomes might be achieved.

Outcome Research The picture emerging from outcome studies on brief psychodynamic therapy is inconsistent but generally positive. Koss and Butcher (1986) reached the conclusion that brief therapy is no less effective than time-unlimited psychoanalysis, perhaps because both patient and therapist work harder and focus on goals that are more specific and manageable than a major restructuring of the personality. Two other reviews indicate either no superiority (Crits-Christoph, 1992) or modest superiority (Svartberg & Stiles, 1991) of brief therapy compared with nonpsychotherapeutic interventions such as self-help groups. In their review, Goldfried, Greenberg, and Marmar (1990) concluded that brief psychodynamic therapy is effective in treating stress and bereavement (Marmar & Horowitz, 1988), late-life depression (Thompson, Gallagher, & Breckenridge, 1987), and mood and personality disorders (Marziali, 1984). Other literature reviews have found that brief psychodynamic therapy is useful with job-related distress and a variety of anxiety disorders (Koss & Shiang, 1994), including PTSD (Horowitz, 1988). The NIMH Treatment of Depression Collaborative Research Program, described in detail in Chapter 10, provides additional evidence that interpersonal psychotherapy is effective in treating depression, confirming some earlier research by Weissman, Klerman, and associates (DiMascio et al., 1979). Moreover, a meta-analysis of six studies found that brief psychodynamic therapy was as effective as cognitive-behavioural therapies for depression (Leichsenring, 2001).

Another study assessed the maintenance of treatment gains from interpersonal psychotherapy three years following termination of therapy for depression (Frank et al., 1990). This study was a randomized controlled trial complete with all the methodological rigour needed to establish efficacy. The conclusions point to the potential of IPT to bring about long-term improvement (Frank & Kupfer, 1994). Thus, IPT may be successful in relapse prevention, always a concern in the arena of psychotherapy effectiveness.

One especially interesting outcome study pitted IPT against cognitive and behavioural therapies in the treatment of bulimia nervosa. IPT was seen to be as effective as the other therapies in the treatment of this disorder immediately after treatment (Fairburn et al., 1991) and had surpassed the other therapies in some assessment areas at a one-year follow-up (Fairburn et al., 1993), with the caveat that only one-third of the patients had maintained their treatment gains. IPT showed these positive effects even with no discussion at all of eating behaviours or body image. Frank and Spanier (1995) suggested that this study may indicate the centrality of interpersonal conflict in the development of a variety of psychological conditions.

Process Research What are the active ingredients in IPT? Frank and Spanier (1995) observed that IPT may exert its therapeutic effect by enhancing social support, decreasing adversity, and/or improving the patient's ability to cope with hardship. However, process studies are needed to illuminate fully the mechanism of effect. In this connection, Frank and Spanier related a conversation with the late Daniel Freedman, a leading academic psychiatrist, on the subject of IPT's active ingredient(s). Freedman suggested the possibility that IPT may work through what it does not do rather than through what it does. Specifically, the focus on current and future issues may preclude the patient's preoccupation with the past, thereby preventing the individual's rumination on past events that cannot be changed. Indeed, research with a measure developed in Canada shows that people who are excessively preoccupied with and unable to accept the past are prone to experience psychological distress (Santor & Zuroff, 1994).

Process research in brief therapy has improved since 1980, with more careful delineation of therapeutic procedures, the use of manuals, and more operational measurement of concepts such as the working alliance between therapist and patient (Hartley & Strupp, 1983; Howard & Orlinsky, 1989). A study by Kolden (1991) found that the better this bond, the more favourable the outcome after an average of 25 sessions. Reviews of other studies conducted over two decades confirm that the stronger the therapeutic relationship, or alliance, the better the outcome (see Horvath, 2001). Horvath (2001) also suggests that the most clinically useful indicator may be the client's report of the early alliance.

The need for a good working alliance is a nonspecific factor that is relevant to various treatment approaches. For instance, Piper et al. (1999) compared 22 dropouts and 22 "completers" who were given time-limited, individual psychotherapy in British Columbia. Demographic and diagnostic factors did not differentiate people in the two groups. However, dropout status was predicted by a weaker working alliance and greater focus on transference. Recent work by Hunsley, Aubry, Vestervelt, and Vito (1999) also suggests that dissatisfaction with therapy and the therapist predicts treatment termination and that there may be substantial discrepancies between the therapist's and client's understanding of why therapy was terminated. Other research conducted in Edmonton shows that a positive therapeutic alliance enhances the tendency for clients with positive therapy expectations to actually do better as a result of treatment (Joyce, Ogrodniczuk, Piper, & McCallum, 2003).

Rector, Zuroff, and Segal (1999) demonstrated how the therapeutic bond and change in depressive cognitions are closely intertwined. After following depressed patients who received 20 weeks of cognitive therapy, they reached three main findings. First, higher levels of dysfunctional attitudes at the start of treatment were associated with poorer ratings of the therapeutic bond. Second, one aspect of the working alliance—the extent to which patients agreed with the goals and tasks of therapy—predicted subsequent improvement in terms of changes in dysfunctional attitudes. Finally, the quality of the therapeutic bond (or working alliance) combined with the amount of cognitive change to produce what Rector et al. referred to as a multiplier effect (i.e., the positive impact of reducing dysfunctional beliefs was substantially greater when a positive therapeutic bond was in place). The authors concluded that there is a clear need for a joint focus on technical aspects of cognitive therapy (i.e., specific techniques) and more general factors involving the therapeutic relationship.

There are different views on how a good working alliance works (Henry et al., 1994). It might have a direct therapeutic effect (Henry & Strupp, 1994), or it might have an indirect effect by making the therapist's interpretations more effective. Research on therapist factors indicates that the therapist's skills and personal characteristics are both key factors, while the therapist's level of training is relatively inconsequential (see Horvath, 2001). Nevertheless, Horvath (2001) allows for the realistic possibility that therapists need more extensive training if they are to be able to form a good alliance with a client suffering from extreme psychopathology.

Another issue to consider is the fact that the working alliance is multi-faceted, and one or more of its aspects may be involved in a given case. Horvath and Greenberg (1989) developed the Working Alliance Inventory to assess three components of the alliance—the bond between the client and therapist, agreement on the goals of treatment, and agreement on the tasks of therapy. Louise Gaston from McGill University is one of a team of contributors who has conducted extensive research on another multidimensional assessment device, known as the California Psychotherapy Alliance Scales. The four subscales of this measure assess the patient's commitment (i.e., seeing the therapy as important, being willing to make sacrifices and see it through to the conclusion), the patient-therapist working alliance, degree of therapist understanding and involvement, and a working strategy consensus scale that assesses the perceived agreement between the patient and therapist on the goals and tasks involved in therapy. Gaston (1991) found that all four subscales are associated significantly with client satisfaction ratings and all but the therapist understanding and involvement subscale are associated with lower levels of psychological distress and interpersonal problems involving a lack of intimacy.

Research in this area should not rule out the possibility that a strong working alliance is the result, rather than the cause, of therapeutic change; that is, patients might feel better about their relationship with their therapist if they have improved. However the alliance works, it seems to be an important factor for any therapeutic approach, not only for psychodynamic approaches.

As suggested earlier, recent studies of interpretations of the transference relationship suggest that higher frequencies of interpretations may be related to poorer outcome (Henry et al., 1994). Frequent interpretations may get in the way of the therapeutic alliance, perhaps by making the patient feel criticized and defensive if he or she is not in agreement with the therapist's views. Although findings such as these arise from correlational studies that have certain methodological problems, they do tend to confirm the wisdom of briefer forms of dynamic and cognitive-behavioural therapies, which discourage the development and interpretation of transference.

REVIEW OF CLIENT-CENTRED THERAPY

Basic Concepts and Techniques of Client-Centred Therapy

Usually regarded as a humanistic psychotherapy, Rogers's *client-centred therapy* rests on the basic premise that people can be understood only in terms of their own phenomenology—the immediate experience that they have of themselves and their world—and that they become disordered when they fail to attend to their own inner nature and instead guide their behaviour according to what others wish. Client-centred therapy places great emphasis on people's freedom to choose and on the responsibility that comes from having that freedom. We are what we make of ourselves, according to Rogerian and other humanistic and existential therapists.

The therapist's principal role is to create conditions in

therapy that are totally accepting and nonjudgemental, and the therapist should accomplish this by being empathic rather than directive. The result is that clients gradually come to better understand their own wishes, needs, fears, and aspirations and gain the courage to pursue their own goals rather than the goals that others have set.

Evaluation of Client-Centred Therapy

Many efforts have been made to evaluate client-centred therapy, largely because of Rogers's insistence that the outcome and process of therapy be carefully scrutinized and empirically validated. Indeed, Rogers is rightfully credited with originating the field of psychotherapy research. He and his students deserve the distinction of being the first to remove the mystique and excessive privacy of the consulting room. For example, they pioneered the tape-recording of therapy sessions for subsequent analysis by researchers.

Most research on Rogerian therapy has focused principally on relating outcome to the personal qualities of therapists. Results have been inconsistent, casting doubt on the widely held assumption that positive outcome is strongly related to the therapist's empathy and genuineness (Beutler, Crago, & Arizmendi, 1986; Greenberg, Elliott, & Lietaer, 1994; Lambert, Shapiro, & Bergin, 1986). And yet it probably makes sense to continue emphasizing these qualities in the training of clinicians, as such qualities are likely to help create an atmosphere of trust and safety within which the client can reveal the deep inner workings of the self (Bohart & Greenberg, 1997). It is not justifiable, however, from a research perspective, to assert that these qualities by themselves are sufficient to help clients change.

A strong relationship between therapist and patient is widely regarded as essential for implementing therapy procedures.

A meta-analysis of studies on client-centred therapy from 1978 to 1992 conducted by Les Greenberg at York University and his colleagues concluded clients were better off after the intervention than about 80 percent of comparable people who had not received any professional therapy (see Greenberg et al., 1994). Although not bad, this outcome is no better than that achieved by comparison therapies, such as brief psychodynamic treatment, with people who are not severely disturbed. Of the studies in the meta-analysis, only eight that had a control group.

In keeping with Rogers's phenomenological approach, the outcome of this type of therapy has been assessed primarily by client self-reports. The basic data have been the individual's own phenomenological evaluation of and reaction to the self and events in his or her world. The overt behaviour believed to follow from these perceptions—that is, how patients actually behave following therapy—has not been the focus of study by client-centred therapy researchers.

According to a recent historical review of developments involving the client-therapist relationship by Adam Horvath (2000) from Simon Fraser University, one finding that was not anticipated by Rogers is entirely in keeping with his emphasis on subjective, phenomenological experiences—that is, the patient's perception of the therapist's behaviour is more important in terms of predicting therapy outcome than the therapist's actual behaviour in the therapeutic relationship. Thus, the patient's cognitive appraisals are quite important.

Rogers's emphasis on subjective experience raises epistemological problems, for the therapist must be able to make accurate inferences about what the client is feeling or thinking. Validity is a real issue. Rogers relied on what the client said, yet he also asserted that clients can be unaware of their true feelings; it is this lack of awareness that brings most of them into therapy in the first place.

The exclusive use of self-descriptive measures of outcome in the earliest research on client-centred therapy has been supplemented with more direct assessment of how well the patient functions in daily life, such as how adequately he or she performs social roles. An associated trend is the use of multiple methods to assess therapeutic change, as investigators have come to appreciate the complex nature of behaviour and the need to assess it along many dimensions (Beutler, 1983; Lambert et al., 1986). Patient self-reports, for example, can be supplemented by physiological meas-ures as well as by reports from significant others (e.g., spouses).

Rogers may be criticized for assuming that self-actualization is the principal human motivation. He inferred this motive from his observation that people seek out situations offering fulfillment, but then he proposed the self-actualization tendency as an explanation for the search for these situations—an example of circular reasoning (i.e., a tautology).

Finally, Rogers assumed both that the psychologically healthy person makes choices to satisfy self-actualizing tendencies and that people are by their very natures good. But some social philosophers have taken a less optimistic view of human nature. Thomas Hobbes, for example, stated that life is "nasty, brutish, and short." How do we explain people who engage in abhorrent behaviour that injures or kills others? Are these people basically good?

It may be that the problem of extreme unreasonableness was not adequately addressed by Rogers because he and his colleagues concentrated on people who were only mildly disturbed. As a way to help unhappy but not severely disturbed people understand themselves better (and perhaps even to behave differently), client-centred therapy may be appropriate and effective.

Gestalt therapists use the empty-chair technique to help clients confront their feelings more directly.

REVIEW OF GESTALT THERAPY

Generally regarded as an existential therapy, Gestalt therapy has not benefited from the kind of controlled research that is characteristic of the client-centred tradition we have just examined and the cognitive-behavioural approach we will examine later. Instead, the focus here has often been on case studies. One reason for this difference is that existential therapists tend to see the experimental methodologies of contemporary science as dehumanizing and thus to be avoided. They believe that applying scientific principles denies people their uniqueness and humanity.

BASIC CONCEPTS AND TECHNIQUES OF GESTALT THERAPY

Fritz Perls and his Gestalt therapy followers hold, like Rogers, that there is an innate goodness in people and that therapy should serve the goal of enabling people to become aware of their basic needs and desires and to trust their instincts. But whereas the Rogerians shy away from specific techniques, Gestalt therapy is full of what may be the most imaginative and creative techniques on the entire psychotherapy scene—from having people talk to empty chairs to having them assume that they are part of every image in every dream they have. True to their roots in existentialism, Gestalt therapists emphasize that people create their own existence every day, in fact every minute, of their lives. People can change, and the Gestalt therapist, in sometimes very confrontational ways, does not tolerate stagnation.

If a patient is crying, the Gestalt therapist might ask the patient to regard the tears as being in an empty chair opposite him or her and to speak *to* the tears. This tactic often seems to help people confront their feelings (see Clarke & Greenberg, 1988). Indeed, according to Gestalt therapists, to ask a person to instead talk *about* his or her tears is to encourage the person to establish an even greater distance from his or her feelings—a condition that Gestalt therapists assert would interfere with psychological well-being.

The empty-chair technique is often used to resolve unfinished business—that is, issues from the past that are still a source of distress for the individual, including feelings toward significant others from the past (Paivio & Bahr, 1998). A modification of this technique is the two-chair technique, which has been used extensively by Les Greenberg at York University as part of time-limited Gestalt therapy (Greenberg, 1992). This technique involves a dialogue between the client and therapist and can be used to resolve intrapsychic conflict between opposing or conflicting aspects of the self. When clients discover something about their internal conflict, they have an "emerging experience" that leads to a new understanding or insight and helps them move beyond an impasse (Greenberg, 1984). Recent data indicate that clients improve if they use this technique to express their unmet needs; the key aspect is whether they experience a shift in their view of the significant other (Greenberg & Malcolm, 2002). However, in a study with students from the University of Western Ontario that examined client performance using the two-chair method, Sicoli and Hallberg (1998) speculated that certain emerging experiences may be too threatening for certain individuals and could result in premature exits from treatment.

EVALUATION OF GESTALT THERAPY

A few studies have attempted to examine aspects of Gestalt therapy, in particular, the empty-chair technique. In an analogue study with college undergraduates, Conoley and colleagues (1983) found that self-rated anger was reduced after a 20-minute empty-chair exercise. Greenberg and Rice (1981) reported that the technique increases awareness and emotional expression, and Clarke and Greenberg (1986) found it superior to problem-solving in helping people make decisions. Other research has examined the effectiveness of a process-experiential form of therapy versus cognitive therapy in the treatment of depression (Greenberg & Watson, 1998; Watson et al., 2003). *Process-experiential therapy* combines Gestalt techniques with client-centred techniques. These studies indicate that both process-experiential and cognitive therapy are effective in the treatment of depression and that their effects are comparable in size. Watson et al. (2003) also found some evidence indicating that process-experiential therapy is more effective in treating interpersonal problems. Although these findings are encouraging, there is relatively little controlled research on this and other humanistic and existential approaches (except client-centred therapy).

All therapies are subject to abuse. Gestalt is no exception, and it may indeed present special problems. It is not difficult, even for trainees with a minimum of experience, to induce clients to express their feelings. Some Gestalt techniques may be so powerful in opening people up that clients can be harmed unintentionally. The forcefulness of Perls's personality and his confrontational style have led some therapists to try to mimic him, though they lack the thoughtfulness, skill, and caring he appeared to possess in unusual abundance. The responsible Gestalt therapist is a professional who keeps the client's interests at the forefront and who understands that the expression of strong emotion for its own sake is seldom enough to ease an individual's suffering. Because of the nature of Gestalt therapy and the fact that a cult has grown up around the memory of Fritz Perls, practising Gestalt therapists should strive for an extra measure of caution.

REVIEW OF BEHAVIOURAL AND COGNITIVE THERAPIES

Behavioural and cognitive therapies attempt to use the investigative methods of experimental psychology to study, develop, and evaluate specific therapeutic interventions. Many principles are drawn from animal research on classical and operant conditioning, but the more recent cognitive trends understandably rely on research and theory with humans. Because the techniques vary greatly, we provide summary details of the several behavioural and cognitive therapies in the separate sections devoted to evaluating each one.

Evaluation of Counterconditioning and Exposure Methods

Clinicians have treated many different anxiety-related problems by systematic desensitization, an approach developed by Joseph Wolpe in the 1950s. The technique appears deceptively simple. It involves having a deeply relaxed person imagine a hierarchy of situations that he or she finds unduly fear provoking in real life. However, as with any therapy for people in emotional distress, its proper application is a complicated affair. The clinician must first determine, by means of a comprehensive behavioural assessment, that the situations eliciting the patient's anxious reactions do not warrant such reactions. If a person is anxious because he or she lacks the skills to deal with a given set of circumstances, then desensitization is inappropriate. Desensitization is appropriate, however, if a person seems to be inhibited by anxiety from behaving in customary and known ways. Sometimes the technique can be used when the patient does not appear obviously anxious, as when depression is caused by an unfulfilling lifestyle that, in turn, arose from social anxiety (cf. our later discussion of underlying causes in behaviour therapy).

As with all the techniques we describe, systematic desensitization is very rarely used exclusively. A person fearful of social interactions might well be given training in conversational and other social skills in addition to undergoing desensitization. The applicability of desensitization depends largely on the therapist's ingenuity in discovering the source of the anxiety underlying a patient's problems (Goldfried & Davison, 1994).

Researchers became interested in desensitization when clinical reports indicated that the technique was effective. It has been well documented that exposing fearful people to what they are frightened of or uneasy about—whether in imagination as in Wolpe's technique or in real life—usually leads to marked reductions in their unrealistic fears. Whether it is necessary to associate exposure with a relaxed state is far less certain; there are indications that relaxation may operate almost like a "safety blanket" that encourages the anxious person to expose himself or herself to fearsome events they have usually avoided (Wilson & Davison, 1971).

The demonstrated importance of exposure has benefited patients with a wide variety of anxiety disorders, including simple phobias, PTSD, OCD, panic disorder, and agoraphobia (DeRubeis & Crits-Christoph, 1998). Although most of the research has been done with adults, fearful children have also benefited from exposure-based procedures (Kazdin & Weisz, 1998).

Evaluation of Operant Methods

Operant methods have proved successful with a wide range of behavioural problems. Recall the token economy work described earlier and Paul's classic study with seriously impaired patients in a mental hospital. Systematically rewarding desirable behaviour and extinguishing undesirable behaviour have been particularly successful in the treatment of many childhood problems, as reviewed in some detail in Chapter 15.

Perhaps one reason operant-conditioning behaviour therapy has been so effective with children is that much of their behaviour is subject to the control of others. Children tend more than adults to be under continual supervision. At school their behaviour is scrutinized by teachers, and at home their parents often oversee their play and other social activities. The behaviour therapist works with the parents and teachers in an effort to change the ways in which they reward and punish children. It is assumed that altering the reinforcement practices of the adults in a child's life will ultimately change the child's behaviour.

The range of childhood problems dealt with through operant conditioning is broad, including bedwetting, thumb-sucking, nail-biting, aggression, tantrums, hyperactivity, disruptive classroom behaviour, poor school performance, language deficiency, extreme social withdrawal, and asthmatic attacks (Kazdin & Weisz, 1998). Self-mutilation has also been treated effectively with punishment procedures, sometimes involving the response-contingent application of painful electric shock to the hands or feet. Such extreme measures are used only when less drastic interventions are ineffective and problem behaviours are life-threatening (Sandler, 1991).

Before applying operant techniques, the therapist must determine that the problem behaviour is, in fact, operant behaviour—that can be controlled by a contingent reinforcer. A child who is crying because of physical pain, for example, should be attended to. Encouraging results have been achieved by applying operant techniques to therapy with children with mental retardation and autism. Therapists who apply operant-conditioning techniques have challenged assumptions about the limited trainability of such children, much to their benefit.

Evaluation of Cognitive Behaviour Therapy

The core assumption of all cognitive therapies is that the way people construe their world is a major—if not *the* major—determinant of their feelings and behaviour. Our examination of cognitive behaviour therapy (CBT) focuses first on Albert Ellis's rational-emotive behaviour therapy (REBT), then on Beck's cognitive therapy, and then on a comparison of the two. Finally we offer some general reflections on CBT as a whole.

Ellis's Rational-Emotive Behaviour Therapy The basic premise of REBT is that emotional suffering is due primarily to the often unverbalized assumptions and demands that people carry around with them as they negotiate their way in life. Demanding perfection from oneself and from others is, Ellis hypothesizes, a principle cause of emotional distress. Expecting that one has to be approved of by everyone and for everything one does is another belief that Ellis regards as irrational and that other writers (e.g., Goldfried & Davison, 1994) have called unproductive or self-defeating. The rational-emotive behavioural therapist challenges these assumptions and persuades the patient that living a life without imposing on oneself unattainable demands and goals will be less stressful and more satisfying.

Several conclusions can be offered on the outcome research on REBT (Baucom et al., 1998; Engels, Garnefski, & Diekstra, 1993; Haaga & Davison, 1989; Kendall et al., 1995):

- REBT reduces self-reports of general anxiety, speech anxiety, and test anxiety.
- REBT improves both self-reports and behaviour for social anxiety, though it may be less effective than systematic desensitization.
- REBT is inferior to exposure-based treatments for agoraphobia.
- Preliminary evidence suggests that REBT may be useful in treating excessive anger, depression, and antisocial behaviour.
- REBT is useful only as part of more comprehensive behavioural programs for sexual dysfunction.
- As described in Chapter 8, REBT shows promise in reducing the Type A behaviour pattern.
- REBT may be useful as a preventive measure for untroubled people; that is, it helps emotionally healthy people cope better with everyday stress.
- There is tentative evidence (e.g., Smith, 1983) that REBT achieves its effects through a reduction in the irrationality of thought. The importance of the support REBT gives patients to confront what they fear and to take risks with new, more adaptive behaviour should not be underestimated.

As with most other clinical procedures, the relevance of REBT to a given problem depends in part on how the clinician conceptualizes the patient's predicament. Thus, a therapist who is trying to help an overweight person lose pounds might conceptualize eating as a way of reducing anxiety; in turn, the anxiety might be viewed as due to social distress that is caused by extreme fear of rejection arising from an irrational need to please everyone and never make a mistake.

Beck's Cognitive Therapy Like Ellis, Beck hypothesizes that people in emotional distress operate with assumptions—he calls them schemas—that are impossible to live with, such as believing that one has to be a perfect parent or student. But in contrast to Ellis, Beck focuses a great deal on the lack of objective evidence that depressed and anxious people have for maintaining their maladaptive schemas. Beck engages the patient in a process very much like a scientific investigation, asking such questions as what evidence the patient has for believing that he or she is totally inept and worthless. A principal focus is on cognitive biases, errors in information processing—such as selective abstraction and overgeneralization—that filter experience in a way that contributes to negative beliefs about oneself and the world.

The effectiveness of Beck's cognitive therapy (CT) has been under intensive study for over 20 years. Several studies attest to the favourable impact it has on depression (see Clark, Beck, & Alford, 1999; Hamilton & Dobson, 2002), and an earlier meta-analysis by Keith Dobson from the University of Calgary of outcome studies of diverse therapies for depression concluded that Beck's therapy achieves greater short-term improvement than wait-list controls, drug therapies, non-cognitive behavioural treatments, and a heterogen-eous group of other psychotherapies (Dobson, 1989). CT may also be better than drug treatment at preventing future episodes, a consideration of major importance in light of the oft-observed tendency for depressive episodes to recur (Freeman & Reinecke, 1995; Hollon, DeRubeis, & Evans, 1996). Perhaps CT patients acquire some useful CT skills that they are able to use following termination of therapy. As seen in Chapter 16, because older patients can be extremely sensitive to medications and can also have medical problems that contraindicate prescribing psychoactive drugs, non-pharmacological interventions are especially appropriate for them.

The great interest in CT led to the widely publicized comparative outcome study sponsored by the National Institute of Mental Health (Elkin et al., 1985), a study that did not find CT superior to a drug therapy or to interpersonal psychotherapy (IPT) but nonetheless supported the utility of Beck's approach to the treatment of depression. (Recall our in-depth discussion of this study in Chapter 10.) Further, a task force of the clinical division of the American Psychological Association has concluded that Beck's cognitive therapy is an effective treatment for panic disorder, generalized anxiety disorder, social phobia, chronic pain, irritable bowel syndrome, and bulimia nervosa, and that it often fares better than medications alone (Chambless et al., 1996).

Emerging data indicate that when cognitive therapy works, it does so because—as originally hypothesized by Beck—it helps patients change their cognitions. Predictable changes in cognitions do occur in cognitive therapy (Hollon & Beck, 1994; Hollon et al., 1996), but such changes are found as well in successful treatment of depression by drugs (e.g., Rush et al., 1982). Cognitive change may therefore be the consequence of change produced by other means (Jacobson et al., 1996). Or, at least with depression (the disorder in which cognitive therapy has been most researched), cognitive change may be the mediator of therapeutic improvement brought about by any therapy, including Beck's cognitive therapy, interpersonal therapy, and pharmacotherapy.

In a recent study conducted in Toronto at the Rotman Research Institute (Goldapple et al., 2004), the brain changes underlying response to CBT were examined using positron emission tomography in unmedicated, unipolar depressed outpatients. The patients were scanned before and after a 15 to 20 session course of CBT. Treatment resulted in significant clinical improvement in the patients who completed the program, and the treatment response was associated with modulated functioning of specific sites in limbic and cortical regions, consistent with findings for other antidepressant treatments, including drugs. The authors suggested that the unique directional changes in the frontal cortex, cingulate, and hippocampus that occur more with CBT than with an independent group of paroxetine responders possibly reflects modality-specific effects due to CBT. We anticipate that more controlled, comparative outcome imaging investigations will be conducted in the future, since the results have implications for our understanding of the mechanisms underlying treatment strategies.

Research on cognitive behaviour therapy for depression has sought to identify the specific treatment components that are most effective. Initially, this research indicates that it is the behavioural interventions rather than the cognitive interventions that are most beneficial, both in the short term (Jacobson et al., 1996) and in the longer term (Gortner, Gollan, Dobson, & Jacobson, 1997). Dobson and Khatri (2000) noted that there have been few attempts to conduct "component analyses" when CBT is applied to other types of disorders, even though, according to these authors, exposure to anxiety-provoking stimuli seems to be a key element in treatments of various anxiety disorders, including PTSD (see Howes & Vallis, 1996). An important goal for future research is to undertake these more fine-grained analyses of components.

Beck and his colleagues believe that research into the mechanisms of CT might be even more important to the future of CT than research into its efficacy:

> In order to serve our patients better, and to assure that the progress of cognitive therapy keeps pace with that of alternative treatments, clinical researchers need to improve and refine cognitive therapy and the training of cognitive therapists, so that more patients can benefit from it. To do so, we need first to understand better how cognitive therapy achieves its effects. (DeRubeis, Tang, & Beck , 2001, p. 386)

According to Bieling and Kuyken (2003), even though cognitive therapy seems to be effective, until research on the validity of cognitive case formulation is conducted "researchers cannot conclude that cognitive therapy is effective *because its statements about etiology and the mechanisms of change are correct*" (p. 53). The ultimate goal is to move from a descriptive approach toward a more explanatory approach by identifying and testing specific, hypothesized cognitive mechanisms that contribute to the presentation of problems and by identifying and testing the distal and proximal factors believed to be involved when a person begins to develop dysfunctional beliefs and cognitive styles.

Because cognitive therapy involves patients in logical analysis and empirical study of their life situation—a challenging intellectual task—it has been assumed that more intelligent individuals are better suited to this approach (Whisman, 1993). This does not seem to be the case, however (Haaga, Dyck, & Ernst, 1991). Perhaps intelligence is too general a concept, entailing as it does a variety of human cognitive processes, such as memory, reasoning, verbal facility, and quantitative skills. A more focused search for cognitive variables might prove more fruitful (Haaga, Rabois, & Brody, 1999).

Some Comparisons between the Therapies of Beck and Ellis The theories and techniques of Ellis and Beck are used widely by therapists. With the inevitable changes that inventive clinicians make as they apply the work of others, and with the evolution in the thinking of the theorists themselves, the differences between the therapies can be difficult to discern. However, they do contrast in interesting, important ways (Haaga & Davison, 1991, 1992).

To a parent who became depressed on learning that his or her child had failed a test at school, Ellis would say immediately, in essence, "So what if you are an inadequate parent? It is irrational to demand perfection from yourself and then to become depressed when you fall short." Ellis (2002) advocates challenging the irrationality of perfectionism. Beck, in contrast, would first examine the evidence for the conclusion. His is a more empirical approach. "What evidence is there for thinking that you are an inadequate parent?" If proof is lacking, this discovery in itself will be therapeutic. Ellis regards his own type of solution as more thoroughgoing. Even if the person is wanting as a parent, the world will not end, for a person does not have to be competent in everything he or she does. Beck, too, will eventually question with the patient whether one has to be competent in everything to feel good about oneself, but perhaps not until accumulated evidence suggests that the person is in fact an inadequate parent.

The therapist adopting Beck's approach certainly has preconceptions about negative schemas (which seem to us very similar to Ellis's irrational beliefs) and especially about the forms that maladaptive, illogical, or biased thinking takes, such as overgeneralization. But working with a depressed individual is a collaborative, inductive procedure by which patient and therapist attempt to discover, by examining the patient's biased thinking, the particular dysfunctional assumptions underlying the person's negative thoughts. Rational-emotive behaviour therapists, in contrast, operate much more deductively; they are confident that a distressed person subscribes to one or more irrational beliefs from a predetermined list or that they make unrealistic demands of themselves or others and then seek out evidence to support their hypotheses.

Beck's therapy and standard rational-emotive practices differ in style on this inductive-deductive basis. Beck suggests that the therapist should avoid being overly didactic, while Ellis often uses mini-lectures and didactic speeches. Beck proposes calling negative thoughts "unproductive ideas" to promote rapport. He does not favour adjectives such as "irrational" or "nutty", which might be heard—with supportive humour—from Ellis. Finally, Beck recommends that the therapist begin by acknowledging the patient's frame of reference and asking for an elaboration of it. Having had a chance to present his or her case and feel understood, the person may be more willing to go through the collaborative process of questioning his or her beliefs. In contrast, Ellis supposes that quite forceful interventions are necessary to disrupt a well-learned maladaptive pattern of thinking. He will directly confront the patient's irrational beliefs, sometimes within minutes in the first session.

Both approaches have one thing in common, and this factor makes Beck and Ellis soul mates in terms of the humanistic and existential therapists. They both convey the message that people can change their psychological predicaments by thinking differently. They emphasize that how a person construes himself or herself and the world is a major determinant of the kind of person he or she will be—and that people have *choice* in how they construe things. They assert that people can, sometimes with great effort, choose to think, feel, and behave differently. Unlike behaviour therapists, who are not cognitive, but like the humanists and existentialists, Beck and Ellis believe that new behaviour is important primarily for the evidence it can provide about how the person looks at himself or herself and the world. Thus, their focus remains on the cognitive dimension of humankind and on the abiding belief that people's minds can be set free and that their thinking is the key to positive psychological change.

Reflections on Cognitive Behaviour Therapy We turn now to some general issues surrounding cognitive behaviour therapy. Some are of historical significance, others focus more on the present, and still others concern the future.

CBT: A Return to Psychology's Cognitive Roots As we indicated in Chapter 2, behaviour therapy initially aligned itself with the study of classical and operant conditioning, under the assumption that principles and procedures derived from conditioning experiments could be applied to lessen psychological suffering. What developed into cognitive behaviour therapy (or cognitive therapy) may appear to be a radical and novel departure, given the earlier focus of behaviour therapists on conditioning and their de-emphasis or even total avoidance of cognition as a controlling variable in behaviour and emotion. But in a historical sense, CBT represents a return to the cognitive foci of the earliest period of experimental psychology (e.g., Bartlett's [1932] classic work on memory). Many experimental psychologists have continued through the years to do research into cognition—into the mental processes of perceiving, recognizing, conceiving, judging, and reasoning, of problem-solving, imagining, and other symbolizing activities. CBT has actually caught up with what has been going on for years in experimental psychology.

Restructuring versus Replacing Cognitions Two distinctions are often drawn in cognitive behaviour therapy on the basis of whether its strategy is to restructure cognitions or replace them (Arnkoff, 1986). A restructuring strategy is found in Beck's and Ellis's approaches to treatment, which assume that cognitive-change efforts should be directed toward changing particular thoughts the patient is having. In contrast, a replacement strategy has the therapist assume nothing about the patient's cognitions other than that they are interfering with his or her life; the goal is simply to teach the patient a way of thinking that is believed to be more adaptive than the cognitions with which the patient is operating, whatever they may be. An example is the problem-solving therapy of D'Zurilla and Goldfried (1971). In this approach, the therapist teaches the patient a set of problem-solving strategies believed to be generally applicable to a wide range of situations. No effort is expended in determining—as Ellis and Beck do—the aspects of the person current cognitions that are getting him or her into psychological trouble (Haaga et al., 2002).

Early Behaviour Therapy's Cognitive Features Ellis and Beck try to change cognitive processes directly to relieve psychological distress. From the beginning, however, behaviour therapists have relied heavily on the human being's capacity to symbolize, to process information, to represent the world in words and images. Wolpe's systematic desensitization is a clear example. This technique is inherently a cognitive procedure because the patient imagines what is fearful. The most exciting overt behavioural event during a regimen of desensitization is the person's occasional signalling of anxiety by raising an index finger. If anything important is happening, it is surely going on under the skin, and some of this activity is surely cognitive.

The Continuing Importance of Behaviour Change in CBT As behaviour therapy goes cognitive, however, it is important to bear in mind that many contemporary researchers continue to believe that behavioural *procedures* are more powerful than strictly verbal ones in affecting cognitive processes (Bandura, 1977). That is, they favour behavioural techniques while maintaining that it is important to alter a person's beliefs to effect an enduring change in behaviour and emotion. Bandura suggests that all theraputic procedures, to the extent that they are effective, work their improvement by giving the person a sense of mastery, of self-efficacy (Bandura, 1997). At the same time he finds that the most effective way to gain a sense of self-efficacy is by changing behaviour. Regardless of whether we believe self-efficacy is as important as Bandura does, a distinction can be made between processes that underlie improvement and *procedures* that set these processes in motion.

Cognitive behaviour therapists continue to be behavioural in their use of performance-based procedures and in their commitment to behavioural change (Dobson & Jackman-Cram, 1996; Jacobson et al., 1996), but they are cognitive in the sense that they believe that cognitive change (e.g., enhanced self-efficacy) is an important mechanism that accounts for the effectiveness of at least some behavioural procedures. Cognition and behaviour continually and reciprocally influence each other—new behaviour can alter thinking, and that new mode of thinking can in turn facilitate the new behaviour. In addition, the environment influences both thought and action and is influenced by them. This model, termed **triadic reciprocality** by Bandura (1986), highlights the close interrelatedness of thinking, behaving, and the environment.

The Importance of Emotion in CBT As Salovey and Singer (1991) have noted, Bandura's triadic reciprocality underemphasizes the concept of emotion. People have many cognitions that are affect laden–sometimes referred to as "hot cognitions"—and these tend to relate to the self (Cantor et al., 1986), to one's dreams and fantasies, fondest hopes, and most dire fears, what Singer (1984) called the private personality. "The therapist must be alert to emotions that color the maladaptive cognitions that are traditionally the focus of treatment. Even though feelings often also arise as a consequence of cognition, it may still be possible to alter maladaptive cognitions by first assessing and then intervening at the level of feelings" (Salovey & Singer, 1991, p. 366). Both clinical observations (Greenberg & Safran, 1984) and experimental findings (e.g., Snyder & White, 1982) point to the importance of emotion in personality and suggest that it should be included more systematically in cognitive-behavioural conceptions of disorder and treatment.

Dobson and Khatri (2000) argue that cognitive therapy does include an explicit focus on emotion as a consequence of cognitions. Specifically, they note that "[b]oth Ellis and Beck have developed sophisticated models of various emotions and their cognitive substrates.…Although they do hypothesize that emotions are largely consequential to various thought patterns, they do not, as some authors have argued (Coyne & Gotlib, 1983), see them as epiphenomenal" (p. 909).

The Phenomenological Essence of CBT All cognitive behaviour therapists heed the mental processes of their patients in another way: they pay attention to the world as it is perceived by the patient. It is not what impinges on us from the outside that controls our behaviour, the assumption that has guided behavioural psychology for decades; rather, it is our view of the world that determines our feelings and behaviour. Hamlet, in the famous Shakespearean play, put it this way: "There is nothing either good or bad, but thinking makes it so" (*Hamlet*, act II, scene 2). CBT is being brought closer to the humanistic and existential therapies. A central thesis of experiential therapists, such as Rogers and Perls, is that clients must be understood from their own frame of reference, from their phenomenological world, for it is this experience of the world that controls life and behaviour.

From a philosophical point of view, such assumptions on the part of those who would understand people and try to help them are profoundly important. Experimentally minded clinicians and researchers are intrigued by how much CBT has have in common with the experientialists, and their attention to the phenomenological world of their patients. To be sure, the techniques used by cognitive behaviour therapists are usually quite different from those of the followers of Rogers and Perls, but these surface differences should not blind us to the links between the two approaches. Further discussion of integration among diverse therapeutic modalities is found at the end of this chapter.

GENERALIZATION AND MAINTENANCE OF TREATMENT EFFECTS IN BEHAVIOURAL AND COGNITIVE THERAPIES

We turn now to a problem that is common to all treatments but perhaps especially to the behavioural and, to a lesser extent, the cognitive therapies—generalizing to real life and maintaining whatever gains have been achieved while the patient is in regular contact with the therapist. Brian Shaw, a well-known cognitive therapist and researcher from Toronto, observed that perhaps the most disappointing and challenging problem today is that the confidence placed in the effectiveness of treatment is not accompanied by concerns about sustaining treatment effects over time and the narrow range of patients included in clinical trials (see Shaw, 1999).

Insight therapists assume that therapeutic effects are enduring because of the restructuring of the personality. In contrast, behaviour therapists, who look a good deal to the environment for factors that affect people, wonder how therapeutic changes can be made to last once clients return to their everyday situations, often assumed to have been instrumental in creating their problems in the first place. This challenge has been addressed by behaviourists in several ways.

Intermittent and Naturalistic Reinforcement Because laboratory findings indicate that intermittent reinforcement—rewarding a response only a portion of the times it appears—makes new behaviour more enduring, many operant programs take care to move away from continuous schedules of reinforcement once desired behaviour is occurring with satisfactory regularity. For example, if a teacher has succeeded in helping a disruptive child spend more time sitting down by praising the child generously for each arithmetic problem finished while seated, the teacher will gradually reward the child for every other success and, ultimately, only infrequently.

Another strategy is to move from artificial reinforcers to those that occur naturally in the social environment. A token program might be maintained only long enough to encourage certain desired behaviour, after which the person is weaned to naturally occurring reinforcers, such as praise from peers.

Environmental Modification Another approach to bringing about generalization takes the therapist into the province of community psychology. Behaviour therapists manipulate surroundings, or attempt to do so, to support changes brought about in treatment. For example, Lovaas and his colleagues (1987; McEachin, Smith, & Lovaas, 1993) found that the gains painstakingly achieved in therapy for autistic children were sustained only when their parents continued to reinforce their good behaviour.

Eliminating Secondary Gain Most behaviour therapists assign their clients homework tasks to do between sessions. Patients may be asked to listen to audiotapes containing relaxation-training instructions, for example. They sometimes fail to follow through in a consistent fashion, however, complaining of not having enough quiet time at home to listen to the tapes or saying that they forgot about the assignment. Many patients are so resistant to doing on their own what they consciously and rationally agree is in their best interest that therapists sometimes invoke as an explanation the psychoanalytic concept of secondary gain, that the patients derive benefit from their problem. For complex and poorly understood reasons, people sometimes act as though they unconsciously wish to keep their symptoms. Therapists, whatever their persuasion, may have to examine a client's interpersonal relationships for clues that might explain why he or she seems to prefer to hold on to a problem that causes distress.

Relapse Prevention Marlatt (1985) proposed the *abstinence violation effect* as a focus of concern in relapse prevention. His research on alcoholism sensitized him to the generally negative effects of a slip, as when a former drinker, after a successful period of abstinence, imbibes to a stupor after taking a single drink. Marlatt suggested that the manner in which the person reacts cognitively to the slip determines whether he or she will overcome the setback or relapse and resume drinking to excess. The consequences of the slip are hypothesized to be worse if the person attributes it to internal, stable, and global factors believed to be uncontrollable—much as Abramson, Seligman, and Teasdale (1978) theorized

Source: Bernie, Harry Mayerovitch.

about helplessness and depression. An example would be a belief, fostered by Alcoholics Anonymous, that the lapse was caused by an uncontrollable disease process that overwhelms the person once a single drink is taken. In contrast, relapse is assumed to be less likely if the individual attributes the slip to causes that are external, unstable, specific, and controllable, such as an unexpectedly stressful life event. In essence, the person is encouraged to distinguish between a lapse and relapse. Cognitive behaviour therapists attempt to minimize the abstinence violation effect by encouraging attributions to external, unstable, and specific factors and by teaching strategies for coping with life stressors. In this way, it is hoped that gains achieved in therapy will persist once formal contact with the therapist has ended.

Attribution to Self The concept of attribution may also offer insight into how to maintain treatment gains once therapy is over. How people explain to themselves why they are behaving or have behaved in a particular way presumably helps determine their subsequent actions. A person who has terminated therapy might attribute improvement in behaviour to an external cause, the therapist, and could relapse once that attributed factor is no longer present.

Davison, Tsujimoto, and Glaros (1973) demonstrated in an experiment with people having sleep difficulties that real problems may be treated by helping patients attribute improvements to themselves. Individuals attempting to reduce smoking (Chambliss & Murray, 1979), lose weight (Jeffrey, 1974), and reduce panic attacks (Basoglu et al., 1994) have similarly benefited from attributing gains to their own efforts and changes in attitudes rather than to external forces. Frank (1976) also found that anxious and depressed patients who attributed their gains to a drug did not maintain their improvement as much as did those who attributed their changes to their own efforts.

What are the implications of attribution research? Since behaviour therapy, especially therapy relying on operant manipulation, attributes much improvement to environmental forces, it might be wise for behaviour therapists to help their clients feel more responsible. By encouraging an "I did it" attitude, perhaps by motivating them to practise new skills and expose themselves to challenging situations, therapists may help their clients depend less on therapy and the therapist and better maintain their treatment gains. However, care must be taken to make sure that this added sense of responsibility does not foster a self-blaming attributional style for negative events, which would only serve to undermine self-esteem. Also, an increased sense of responsibility could be maladaptive for people who already have an excessive sense of personal responsibility, as is the case with obsessive-compulsive disorder (see Chapter 6).

Finally, it is often assumed that patients who maintain their improvement after termination of treatment are continuing to apply specific skills acquired during treatment. A controlled comparative outcome study, discussed in Chapter 12, on the treatment of cocaine dependence (Carroll, Rounsaville, Gordon et al., 1994; Carroll, Rounsaville, Nick et al., 1994) found two important instances of generalization at a one-year follow-up: patients treated with the drug desipramine maintained their treatment-produced gains, and patients treated with cognitive behaviour therapy not only maintained their improvement but showed signs of even further improvement, or what the authors called "delayed emergence of effects" (Carroll, Rousaville, Nich, et al., 1994, p. 995). That the drug-produced effects were maintained at one-year follow-up is a welcome exception to the general finding of relapse following drug withdrawal. That the CBT gains were actually greater at one-year follow-up prompted the investigators to speculate that CBT had taught patients coping skills that they were able to implement long after formal therapy had ended, something lacking in the drug-therapy group.

Since one purpose of professional intervention is to make the professional helper superfluous, we can expect increasing formal attention to be focused on what it is that patients take away from treatment that can help them maintain and enhance their gains as well as deal with the new challenges that await them in their day-to-day lives.

Some Basic Issues in Cognitive and Behavioural Therapy

We complete our discussion of cognitive and behavioural therapy with a consideration of some general problems and issues. An understanding of what follows will help the reader appreciate both the strengths and limitations of this approach to psychotherapy.

Internal Behaviour and Cognition In Chapter 5, we discussed how the inference of intervening processes and other explanatory factors is useful in interpreting data and generating fruitful hypotheses. Behaviour therapists are sometimes thought to hold only the radical behaviouristic positions of Watson and Skinner, such as that it is not useful or legitimate to make inferences about internal processes of the organism. But behaviour therapy, as applied experimental psychology, is legitimately concerned with internal as well as external events, provided that the internal mediators such as thoughts and feelings, are securely anchored to observable stimuli or responses.

Unconscious Factors and Underlying Causes With the growing interest in cognitive factors, cognitive therapists have focused their assessments and interventions on unconscious internal mediators (Bowers & Meichenbaum, 1984; Mahoney, 1993). Ellis, for example, assumes that people are distressed by beliefs that he designates irrational—even though a patient seldom states the problem in such terms and may be unaware of these beliefs. Based on what the patient says and how it is said, and working from rational-emotive theory, Ellis may infer the operation of a belief such as "It is a dire necessity that I be perfect in everything I do." He then persuades the

Canadian Perspectives/17.1

Relaxing with the Radio in Quebec

We have often wondered about the extent to which radio and television can be used proactively to prevent mental disorders. This issue was examined directly in a remarkable study in Quebec in the 1980s. Borgeat and Chaloult (1985) investigated whether material presented via the radio could be used to lessen the levels of anxiety and sleep difficulty experienced by many people. They reached an agreement with radio station CIME-FM (99.5) to broadcast a show for half an hour per night, starting at 11:30 p.m. about a basic relaxation method. That show included subliminal messages below the level of conscious awareness that involved themes designed to relax listeners, such as "My arms and legs are heavy," "My face feels warm," and "I'm relaxing now."

This show proved to be quite popular and was on the air for at least six years. According to Borgeat and Chaloult (1985), the broadcast started out with an audience of approximately 3,500, but eventually reached audiences of 21,600 each night in 1983. It also spawned two best-selling records.

A survey of 100 respondents indicated that listeners had no unpleasant reactions to the show and its subliminal messages. Three-quarters of the respondents found that the show helped lower their levels of tension and stress (Borgeat & Chaloult, 1985). Nine out of 10 people indicated that the show helped their minds go blank and increased their sleepiness.

Of course, as a research study, this survey has many limitations. Respondents were self-selected volunteers rather than randomly selected participants, and there were no comparison groups of people exposed to other stimuli. Still, the results are encouraging, suggesting that mediums such as the radio and television can be used effectively as a form of primary prevention.

Thinking Critically

1. Realistically, do you think that radio and television can help people cope with adjustment problems?
2. Do you think that the use of the radio in this manner was appropriate? Do you have any ethical concerns involving the issue of informed consent when it comes to unsuspecting people who may have tuned into this radio show without knowing about the subliminal messages (see Chapter 18)?

patient to accept the notion that this belief underlies the problems. Therapy is directed at altering that belief. Although he tends to work more slowly and more inductively than Ellis, Beck infers similar beliefs, which he calls negative schemas or dysfunctional assumptions, including a dysfunctional belief in the need to be perfect (Brown & Beck, 2002).

This is an interesting turn of events for an approach that initially rejected the notion of unconscious motivation and thought! Yet it is consistent with decades of research by experimental cognitive psychologists, who infer sets, beliefs, attitudes, and other abstract cognitive concepts of which the person is often unaware (e.g., Bruner, Goodnow, & Austin, 1956). To be sure, appreciation of factors of which a person may be unaware does not make any of the cognitive therapies equivalent to psychoanalysis, but it does demonstrate the wisdom of some of Freud's clinical insights and is reflected in the kinds of rapprochements we explore later.

One of the clearest laboratory demonstrations of the role of exposure to stimuli below conscious awareness was provided by Canadian researcher Mark Baldwin and his associates (Baldwin, Carrell, & Lopez, 1990). In their first study, they used a tachistoscope to present graduate students with either the image of the scowling face of the chair of the psychology department or the image of a more pleasant face, but below the participants' conscious level of awareness. In their second study, devout Roman Catholic women were presented with a picture of the Pope making a disapproving face or a picture of an unfamiliar person assuming a more pleasant expression. Baldwin et al. found that being exposed to negative expressions from the chair of the department or the Pope had the effect of increasing the participants' levels of state anxiety and caused them to endorse more negative self-evaluations, even though the participants were unable to verbally express the material that had been presented to them.

A growing number of studies demonstrate the effects that unconscious or preconscious stimuli can have on mood, cognition, and behaviour. Canadian Perspectives 17.1 describes a remarkable experiment conducted in Canada that involved preconscious messages.

Cognitive behaviour therapists, like their analytic counterparts, have come to believe that, generally, there is more to the patient than immediately meets the eye (Goldfried & Davison, 1994). Guidano and Liotti (1983) spoke of the "protective belt" behind which one must search for core beliefs, which themselves are generally related to one's idea of oneself, such as a negative self-image. According to Mahoney (1982, 1990), core cognitions may be extremely difficult to change, even when uncovered, because they stem from one's earlier developmental history. And well before the popularity of cognitive behaviour therapy, George Kelly (1955) distinguished between "core constructs" and "peripheral constructs," the former relating to the person's basic sense of self or identity.

Although changing core beliefs is not a simple matter for either patient or therapist, it is believed by many contemporary researchers to be essential to cognitive therapy if the positive effects of therapy are to endure (see Chapter 2). The subtlety required in assessing variables that are not immediately apparent is similar to that of advanced accurate empathy, discussed earlier, as illustrated in the following case from Safran et al. (1986).

> A client who failed an exam ... accessed the automatic thought: "I can't handle university." At this point the therapist could have challenged this belief or encouraged the client to examine evidence relevant to this belief. Instead she decided to engage in a process of vertical exploration. In response to the therapist's probes a constellation of automatic thoughts emerged that revolved around the client's beliefs that he was not smart enough. The client at this point spontaneously recalled two memories of situations in which he had felt humiliated and worthless because he felt he had "been stupid" at the time. As he recounted these memories he became visibly more emotional. Further exploration revealed that these feelings of intellectual inferiority and associated feelings of worthlessness cut across a number of problem situations for the client. It also emerged that he believed that his value as a person was completely dependent upon his intellectual performance. In this situation had the therapist intervened when the first automatic thought emerged, she may not have accessed the entire chain of self-evaluative cognitions and higher level constructs that underlay the client's distress. (p. 515)

Broad-Spectrum Treatment In clinical practice, behaviour therapists usually employ several procedures at once or sequentially in an attempt to deal with all the important controlling variables; this approach is generally referred to as *broad-spectrum behaviour therapy* (Lazarus, 1971). For example, a patient fearful of leaving home might well undergo in vivo desensitization by walking out the door and gradually engaging in activities that take place farther from that safe haven. Over the years, however, the person may also have built up a dependent relationship with his or her spouse. As the person becomes bolder in venturing forth, this change in behaviour may disrupt the equilibrium of the relationship that the couple has worked out over the years. To attend only to the fear of leaving home would be incomplete (Lazarus, 1965) and might even lead to replacement of the agoraphobia with another difficulty that would serve to keep the person at home—a problem frequently called *symptom substitution*.

A variation of CBT proposed by Rutgers University psychologist Arnold Lazarus (1989, 1997) is called multimodal therapy. Lazarus's basic premise is that people are a composite of seven dimensions, described through the acronym BASIC IB: behaviour, affective processes, sensations, images, cognitions, interpersonal relationships, and biological functions. Effective therapy must attend to problems in all or in some subset of these areas, decide the order in which problems should be treated, and then apply to each problem area the techniques best suited to it. Most significantly, these techniques may well come from other theoretical orientations, such as the empty chair of Gestalt therapy.

In a related vein, cognitive and behavioural therapists do not invariably focus only on the patient's complaint as stated during the first interview (Goldfried & Davison, 1994). As an illustration, one of us was supervising a clinical graduate student who was desensitizing an undergraduate for test anxiety. The patient made good progress up the hierarchy of imagined situations but was not improving at all in the real world of test taking. The supervisor suggested that the therapist find out whether the patient was studying for the tests. It turned out that he was not; worry about the health of his mother was markedly interfering with his attempts to study. Thus, the goal of making the person nonchalant about taking tests was inappropriate, for he was approaching the tests themselves without adequate preparation. On the basis of additional assessment, the therapy shifted away from desensitization to a discussion of how the client could deal with his realistic fears about his mother's possible impending death. Further explication of this issue and a detailed model of the assessment, conceptualization, and treatment of "test anxiety" are presented in Flett and Blankstein (1994).

Relationship Factors A good relationship between patient and therapist is important for many reasons and regardless of the particular theoretical orientation. It is doubtful that people will reveal deeply personal information if they do not trust or respect their therapists. Furthermore, since therapy can seldom be imposed on an unwilling client, a therapist must obtain the co-operation of the person if the techniques are to have their desired effect.

The importance of the therapeutic relationship is central to Linehan's dialectical behaviour therapy. She argues that, with patients who have borderline personality disorder, it is essential to create an atmosphere of acceptance and empathy within which specific cognitive-behavioural techniques can be implemented. An atmosphere of empathy and warmth is also endorsed as facilitating the recovery process for sexual offenders (Serran, Fernandez, Marshall, & Mann, 2003). Although behaviour therapists seldom use the term *therapeutic alliance*, the strongly affective interpersonal bond between therapist and patient is increasingly recognized as a necessary condition for implementing cognitive and behavioural procedures (Goldfried & Davison, 1994).

It is worth noting that transference—minus the psychosexual overtones of psychoanalysis—is a subject of research by experimental cognitive psychologists, who find value in studying how people's present-day interactions are affected by their relationships with significant others (Andersen & Berk, 1998; Chen & Andersen, 1999). There is nothing mysterious about the fact that our perceptions of others in the here and now are coloured by our feelings toward others from our past or from other aspects of our current life. If behaviour therapists are to be true to their credo that their clinical interventions derive from basic (nonclinical) research, they should not be as reluctant as they used to be to examine the therapist-patient relationship.

REVIEW OF COUPLES AND FAMILY THERAPY

BASIC CONCEPTS AND TECHNIQUES IN COUPLES AND FAMILY THERAPY

We turn now to a discussion of couples and family therapy, with a particular emphasis on marital conflict. In a recent review paper, Johnson and Lebow (2000, p. 23) noted, "Distress in an intimate relationship is recognized as the single most frequent presenting problem in psychotherapy," and couples therapy is now the preferred mode of treatment for such problems.

Clearly, marital conflict can have a profound negative impact on the well-being of family members. This is underscored by a re-analysis of the data from the Ontario Health Survey's *Mental Health Supplement* by Whisman, Sheldon, and Goering (2000), who found that marital problems were associated with six disorders, including generalized anxiety disorder, panic disorder, major depression, and drinking problems. In contrast, an inability to get along with friends and relatives was unrelated to the various psychiatric disorders when other social relationships were controlled. Given the negative impact that marital troubles apparently have, how effective are the therapies that are designed to improve functioning?

When a problem involves a couple, therapy is most effective if the couple is seen together.

THE NORMALITY OF CONFLICT

There is almost universal agreement among couples therapists and researchers, regardless of theoretical orientation, that conflict is inevitable in a marriage or in any other long-term relationship. The aura of the honeymoon passes when the couple makes unromantic decisions about where to live, where to seek employment, how to budget money, what kinds of meals to prepare and how to share that responsibility, when to visit in-laws, if and when to have children, and whether to experiment with novel sexual techniques. Today, in addition, couples have the changed nature of gender roles to negotiate. For example, if both spouses work, will their place of residence be determined by the husband's employment or by the wife's? These sources of conflict must be handled by any two people living together, whether they are married or not, whether they are of the opposite sex or not. Authorities agree that how couples deal with such inherent conflicts will often determine the quality and duration of their cohabitation relationship (e.g., Schwartz & Schwartz, 1980).

A strategy some couples adopt, deliberately or unconsciously, is to avoid acknowledging disagreements and conflicts. Because they believe in the reality of the fairy-tale ending "And they lived happily ever after," any sign that their relationship is not going smoothly is threatening and must be ignored. Such patterns may keep peace in the short term but usually to run the risk of serious dysfunction in the long term (Gottman & Krokoff, 1989). Dissatisfaction and resentment develop and begin to take their toll as time goes by. Because the partners do not quarrel, they may appear to be a perfect couple to observers, but without opening the lines of communication, they may drift apart emotionally. Conversely, whereas disagreement and even the expression of anger are related to unhappiness in couples in the short term, they actually are predictive of more satisfaction over time (Gottman & Krokoff, 1989).

FROM INDIVIDUAL TO CONJOINT THERAPY

The terms *family therapy* and *couples therapy* do not denote a set procedure. They tell us that therapeutic focus is on at least two people in a relationship, but they leave undefined such issues as how the therapist views the nature and causes of the problem, what techniques are chosen to alleviate it, how often clients are seen, and whether children and even grandparents are included.

Couples and family therapy share some theoretical frameworks with individual therapy. Psychoanalytic marital therapists, for example, focus on how a person seeks or avoids a partner who resembles, to his or her unconscious, the opposite-sexed parent (Segraves, 1990). Frustrated and unsatisfied by his love-seeking attempts as a child, the adult man may unconsciously seek maternal nurturing from his wife and make excessive, even infantile, demands of her. Much of the discussion in this kind of couples therapy focuses on the conflicts he is having with his wife and, presumably, on the repressed striving for maternal love that underlies his immature ways of relating to her. These unconscious forces are plumbed, with the wife assisting and possibly revealing some of her own unresolved yearnings for her father. Transference is explored, but in analytic couples therapy, it is the transference between the two partners rather than between the client and the therapist that is usually the focus. The overall goal is to help each partner see the other as he or she actually is rather than as a symbolic parent (Fitzgerald, 1973). Sometimes, each partner is seen separately by different therapists (Martin & Bird, 1953), sometimes separately by the same therapist (Greene, 1960), and sometimes conjointly by the same therapist (Ackerman, 1966).

Ellis's rational-emotive behaviour therapy has also been applied to family conflict. Again, the perspective is primarily individualistic or intrapsychic. The therapist assumes that something going on within one or both of the partners is causing the distress in the relationship. Ellis (2002) cited the example of a man with both marital and work difficulties who demanded absolute perfection, not only from himself, but also from his wife and business associates. Therapy emphasized this irrational need for perfection.

With this as background to the shift from individual to conjoint therapies, we describe now some of the details of conjoint therapy. Some methods are common to all couples and family therapies, whereas others differ according to theoretical orientation.

The Approaches to Couples and Family Therapy

The Mental Research Institute Tradition Couples and family therapy seems to have begun in the 1950s at the Mental Research Institute (MRI) in California, where the focus was on faulty communication patterns, uneasy relationships, and inflexibility. Family members were shown how their behaviour affected their relations with others. They were then persuaded to make specific changes, such as making their needs and dislikes more clearly known to others. Few family therapists who identify themselves with the MRI approach are concerned with past history. Their focus is on how current problems are being maintained and how they might be changed. Whatever the problem, the family therapist takes a family systems approach, a general view of etiology and treatment that focuses on the complex interrelationships within families.

Cognitive-Behavioural Approaches Distressed couples do not react very positively toward each other, and this antagonism is usually evident in the very first session. It is not uncommon for one partner to feel coerced into attending conjoint therapy, even for an initial session. In a pioneering treatise on behavioural marital therapy, Jacobson and Margolin (1979) recommended that the therapist attend to this problem of antagonism as a first step in helping partners improve their marriage. One strategy is the "caring days" idea of Richard Stuart (1976), which applies an operant strategy to the couple's conflict. The husband, for example, is cajoled into agreeing to devote himself to doing nice things for his wife all day on a given day, without expecting anything in return. The agreement is that the wife will do the same for him the next day. If successful, this strategy accomplishes at least two important things: first, it breaks the cycle of distance, suspicion, and aversive control of each other; and second, it shows the giving partner that he or she is able to affect the spouse in a positive way. This enhanced sense of positive control is achieved simply by pleasing the partner. The improved atmosphere that develops as a consequence of their doing nice things for each other and having nice things done for them in return helps each of them become motivated to please the other on future occasions.

Behavioural couples therapists generally adopt Thibaut and Kelley's (1959) exchange theory of interaction. According to this view, people value others if they receive from them a high ratio of benefits to costs—that is, if they see themselves getting at least as much from the other person as they give. Furthermore, people are assumed to be more disposed to continue a given relationship if other alternatives are less attractive to them, promising fewer benefits and costing more. Therapists therefore try to encourage a mutual dispensing of rewards by partner A and partner B.

Behavioural marital or couples therapy shares with other approaches a focus on enhancing communication skills between the partners, but the emphasis is more on increasing the ability of each partner to please the other. The core assumption is that "the relative rates of pleasant and unpleasant interactions determine the subjective quality of the relationship" (Wood & Jacobson, 1985). Indeed, behavioural couples therapists consider this more than an assumption, for they can point to data supporting the view that distressed couples differ from nondistressed couples in that they have lower frequencies of positive exchanges and higher frequencies of unsatisfying exchanges. Also, as Camper et al. (1988) found, spouses in distressed marriages view negative behaviour on the part of their partners as global and stable—"There is nothing I can do to please him, and it's never going to change"—whereas they construe positive behaviour as less so—"Well, he was happy with me today, but it's not going to last." Distressed couples also tend to get upset by immediate and recent negative events, like the weather's being bad when an outdoor project was scheduled, whereas nondistressed couples are better able to overlook such minor annoyances (Margolin, 1981; Wood & Jacobson, 1985).

Canadian Perspectives/17.2

Emotion-Focused Couples Therapy

Susan Johnson, from the University of Ottawa, is a co-founder of emotion-focused couples therapy, which was developed with Les Greenberg.

Emotion-focused therapy (EFT) was developed originally by Les Greenberg of York University and Susan Johnson, now at the University of Ottawa (see Greenberg & Johnson, 1988; Johnson & Greenberg, 1985a, 1985b). The essence of EFT is that marital distress stems from maladaptive and distressed forms of emotion in the marital context and the destructive interactions that follow from this maladaptive emotion. This focus on negative emotions is consonant with the humanistic, experiential approach adopted originally by Greenberg and Johnson, as well as with general findings indicating that the emotional processing in therapy is associated with improvements in psychological functioning (Pos, Greenberg, Goldman, & Korman, 2003).

The most recent version of EFT has incorporated a contemporary focus on adult attachment styles in relationships (Johnson, 2002; Johnson & Whiffen, 2003), and this includes an emphasis on attachment bonds among couples influenced by traumatic experiences (Johnson, 2002). This therapy integrates components from attachment theory, which has been used to conceptualize adult romantic relationships (see also Bartholomew & Horowitz, 1991), and focuses on the "innate adaptive needs for protection, security, and connectedness with significant others" (Johnson & Greenberg, 1995, p. 124). From this vantage point, relationship distress occurs when the attachment needs have not been met and the relationship does not provide a secure base for one or both partners. The overall goal of treatment is for couples to maintain emotional engagement and be accessible and responsive to each other's needs.

Typically, EFT involves 12 to 15 sessions (Johnson, 2000). The process of change via EFT is broken down into three general phases that span nine steps altogether (see Johnson, 2000; Johnson, Hunsley, Greenberg, & Schindler, 1999). The goal of the first phase is to de-escalate the maladaptive cycle. The four steps that comprise this phase are (1) assessing the current conflicts experienced by the couple and fostering an alliance; (2) identifying the problematic interaction cycle that is maintaining problems in the relationship; (3) accessing underlying emotions; and (4) trying to reframe the problem in terms of associated emotions and attachment needs.

The goal of the second phase is to change interactional positions. This second phase consists of three steps: (1) helping the couple to identify needs and aspects of the self that have been denied and incorporate these into the relationship; (2) learning to accept the partner's new emotional experience and related responses; and (3) learning to express specific needs and developing a sense of positive emotional engagement.

According to Johnson et al. (1999), the goal of the third phase is consolidation and integration and this involves two main steps: (1) attempts are made to arrive at new solutions to old problems; and (2) new positions and new cycles of attachment behaviour must be consolidated.

Empirical evaluations suggest that EFT is an effective treatment. Johnson et al. (1999) reported the results of a meta-analysis of seven studies that assessed EFT and marital distress. It showed that the majority of couples reported clinical improvement on the outcome measure (i.e., the Dyadic Adjustment Scale), and that 70-73 percent had recovered from marital distress.

Dessaulles, Johnson, and Denton (2003) reported the results of a pilot study that tested emotion-focused therapy as a treatment for depression in couples with marital problems. Depression was diagnosed in the women in the study. Comparisons of those who received EFT with those who received pharmacotherapy showed that both treatments were equally effective in reducing depressive symptoms. Improvements were deemed to be both statistically and clinically significant. Another study in Ottawa showed that EFT treatment gains in marital functioning are maintained among couples with a chronically ill child (Cloutier, Manion, Walker, & Johnson, 2002).

Johnson and Talitman (1997) conducted a study that showed the importance of the working alliance with the ther-apist. Specifically, they found that a positive working alliance was more predictive of successful treatment than even the initial level of marital distress. This finding is surprising because it is generally the case that initial distress is among the top predictors of subsequent marital distress. The finding underscores the importance of developing a solid therapeutic alliance in EFT. Others factors linked with more positive EFT outcomes include the female partner's trust in the care provided by the partner, higher emotional involvement, and lower levels of coercive behaviour (see Johnson & Lebow, 2000). Another key element involves events know as "softenings," in which partners express their vulnerabilities (Johnson & LeBow, 2000).

Recent developments show that EFT can be modified and tailored to address specific issues and specific adjustment problems. Whiffen and Johnson (1998) described how EFT from an attachment-style perspective can be used to address some of the interpersonal conflicts that contribute to postpartum depression, while Johnson and Williams-Keeler (1998) outlined ways in which EFT can be combined with "constructivist" self-development theories (see Neimyer & Raskin, 2001) to treat distressed couples who have recently experienced a severe trauma. Also, therapists in Toronto have outlined how EFT can be modified to incorporate concepts addressed by feminist family therapy and emotional issues involving gender roles (Vatcher & Bogo, 2001).

Thinking Critically

1. Theorists have discussed the suitability of using couples treatment to address more severe disorders that are experienced by individuals but may not yet involve a marital component (e.g., a depressed spouse). Do you think EFT could be used to address severe disorders experienced by individuals?
2. It is usually suggested that men are low in emotional expression. Do you think that men, relative to women, will benefit more, less, or the same from EFT? Explain your answer.

Thus, behavioural couples therapy concentrates on increasing positive exchanges in the hope not only of increasing short-term satisfaction but also of laying a foundation for long-term trust and positive feelings, qualities that are characteristic of nondistressed relationships. Cognitive change is also seen as important, for couples often need training in problem-solving and encouragement to acknowledge positive changes. Distressed couples often perceive inaccurately the ratio of positive to negative exchanges, as they focus on the negative (Gottman et al., 1976).

Behavioural couples therapists have become increasingly interested in cognitive components of relationships and relationship distress, a reflection of the cognitive trend in behaviour therapy as a whole (Baucom, Epstein, & Rankin, 1995). The interest in cognition in couples therapy can also be traced to the influence of attribution theory in social psychology (the study of how people explain the reasons for their own and others' behaviour) and the overlap between marital distress and depression. As a result of adding this cognitive component and broadening its treatment strategies, behavioural marital therapy is now frequently referred to as cognitive-behavioural marital therapy (CBMT). CBMT focuses on each person's attributions, for example, paying close attention to whether one partner decides that the other is responsible or blameworthy for an event that was actually not under anyone's control.

Integrative Behavioural Couples Therapy *Integrative behavioural couples therapy* (IBCT) was developed by Andrew Christensen and Neil S. Jacobson (Christensen, Jacobson, & Babcock, 1995). IBCT uses reinforcement principles as well as the behavioural exchange and communication training strategies just described, but it also incorporates the Rogerian notion of acceptance and provides a series of procedures designed to foster acceptance in couples (Cordova & Jacobson, 1993).

The assumption of IBCT is that traditional behaviour therapy for couples focuses on superficial variables rather than on trying to uncover the major controlling variables. For example, traditional behaviour therapists might focus on discrete observable behaviour, such as lack of sex or frequent arguments, rather than on a partner's feeling that he or she is not loved or valued by the other partner. This latter consideration would be the focus in IBCT. This shift in therapeutic attention is not new to the approach introduced next.

Emotion-Focused Therapy The approach to conjoint treatment known as *emotion-focused therapy* (EFT) (Alexander, Holtzworth-Munroe, & Jameson, 1994; Johnson & Greenberg, 1987, 1988, 1995) contains psychodynamic elements, but its humanistic emphasis on feelings strikes us as more salient. See Canadian Perspectives 17.2 for a detailed description and evaluation of this therapy.

It should be noted that emotion-focused therapy consists of principles and processes that can also be used to treat individuals. According to Greenberg (2004), the three major empirically supported principles of EFT are (1) emotion awareness and the acceptance of emotion, (2) emotion regulation, and (3) emotion utilization or transformation in order to move on from or transform core feelings. Emotion-regulation skills include identifying and labelling emotions, allowing and tolerating emotions, increasing positive emotions, reducing vulnerability to negative emotions, self-soothing, breathing, and distraction. The case study described at the beginning of this chapter illustrates a number of these key principles.

General Features of All Couples Therapy In all forms of couples therapy, each partner is trained to listen empathically to the other and to state clearly to the partner what he or she understands is being said and what feelings underlie those remarks. One way to improve communication is to distinguish between the intent of a remark and its impact. Partner A, for example, may wish to be helpful by asking whether partner B would like him or her to get something from the store, but this question may have a negative impact if partner B would prefer partner A to stay home and help with a project. Intent and impact can differ.

The communications of distressed and happy couples may differ in impact more than in intent. Gottman and his colleagues (1976) found that both types of couples made the same number of positive statements to partners, but distressed spouses reported having heard fewer positive statements. Gottman proposed a technique for clarifying intent. One partner calls, "Stop action," and asks the other to indicate what he or she believes the first is trying to say. The feedback indicates immediately whether remarks are having the intended impact.

An interaction pattern known as the *demand-withdraw cycle* is recognized as particularly destructive for couples. First described by MRI people (Watzlawick, Beavin, & Jackson, 1967) and in a contemporary research study by others (Christensen & Pasch, 1993; Christensen & Shenk, 1991), the demand-withdraw pattern is characterized by one partner attempting to discuss a problem and the other avoiding or withdrawing from such efforts. This withdrawal generates more demands from the first spouse, who tries harder and harder to engage the other, only to be met with more avoidance. And so the cycle escalates. Christensen and Heavey (1990) suggest that there are sex differences in this pattern: women tend to assume the demanding role whereas men usually withdraw. This pattern is found in couples that have a conflict surrounding closeness; the person demanding change may be trying to generate closeness and the person avoiding the interaction may be struggling to seek or maintain autonomy (Christensen, 1987).

Couples and family therapy have for years made creative use of videotape equipment. A couple can be given a problem to solve during part of a therapy session, such as where to go on vacation, and can be videotaped while they attempt to solve it. The ways in which they push forward their own wishes—or fail to—and the ways in which they accommodate the other's wishes—or fail to—are but two aspects of their communication patterns that a therapist can come to understand from later viewing the tape, often with the couple watching also. Patterns of communication and miscommunication can be readily discerned using this tool.

A common practice among family therapists is to give couples specific homework assignments so that they can practice the new patterns of interaction they have learned during sessions and begin the important process of generalizing change from the consulting room to their everyday lives. Couples may be asked to practise paraphrasing each other's sentences for a specified time period, such as a half hour after dinner, as part of an active listening assignment. In essence, couples are taught Rogerian empathy skills. They may also be instructed to practise a new parenting skill with their children. Some therapists ask couples to tape-record their assignment so that the therapist can review their progress during the next therapy session.

General Issues and Special Considerations

The severity and nature of marital dysfunction treated by therapists vary considerably, as Margolin and Fernandez (1985) have pointed out. One couple may seek professional assistance when there is merely dissatisfaction in the relationship, but another may wait until the crisis is so great that one or both partners have already consulted a divorce lawyer. Thus, there are different stages of marital distress (Duck, 1984; Weiss & Cerreto, 1980), and different therapeutic approaches may be used, depending on the couple's starting point. For example, a couple married for five years and on the verge of divorce, with some threat of physical violence, needs a more directive, intensive approach than a couple drifting apart after 10 years.

An important issue is deciding who the patient is. The term *identified patient* is often used when more than one family member is being seen by a therapist, especially when parents consult a therapist because their child is having problems. Treatment proceeds best when family members agree on what problem will be addressed. For example, should the husband be less demanding and the wife more malleable—an issue that has been the subject of feminist writings for several decades? Difficulties also arise when only one partner wants to end the relationship. Finally, couples therapy varies depending on whether children are involved.

Family therapy is further complicated when sexual or nonsexual physical abuse is present. The therapist must consider what effect saving the relationship may have on the abused spouse and possibly on the abused children, for when there is spousal abuse there is a high likelihood of child abuse as well. Regardless of who the identified patient is, the therapist must be sensitive to the needs of all those whose lives are affected by the relationship (Kadis & McClendon, 1995).

Other ethical considerations in family therapy include how to deal with the disclosure of secrets by one spouse when the other spouse is not present. Some therapists handle this at the outset of treatment by telling the couple that nothing that is told to the therapist by one of the partners will be kept secret from the other. Other therapists feel that this policy may keep them from obtaining valuable information (Kadis & McClendon, 1995).

An interesting line of research has focused on individual problems in one of the partners and how such problems respond to conjoint therapy versus how they respond to an intervention targeting only the individual problems. Noting that depression in at least one of the partners is often a part of a distressed couple's relationship and that relapse into depression is more likely if the formerly depressed partner is in a troubled marriage (Hooley & Teasdale, 1989), researchers (Beach & O'Leary, 1986; Jacobson et al., 1989, 1991; O'Leary & Beach, 1990) have studied behavioural marital therapy (BMT) as a treatment for depression. The findings indicate that Beck's individualized cognitive therapy for the depressed partner is no more effective than BMT in alleviating depression and that cognitive therapy is not as effective as BMT in enhancing marital satisfaction. In other words, someone who is depressed and in a troubled relationship can be helped as much by a systems-oriented approach to the relationship as by an individualized intervention—with the advantage of also deriving benefit for relationship problems. This research highlights both the interpersonal nature of depression—a theme examined earlier in Chapter 10— and the role of depression in a distressed intimate relationship. Moreover, the finding that individualized cognitive therapy does not improve a marriage in the same way that improvement in a marriage lifts depression shows the limits of a nonsystems individualized therapy, such as cognitive therapy, as well as the strengths of a systems approach, such as BMT.

There is great variety within couples and family therapy—from psychoanalytic to Gestalt to behavioural. The techniques employed reflect the particular theoretical orientation of the therapist. A psychoanalytically oriented couples therapist will attend to possible unconscious factors in each person's behaviour toward the other, whereas a cognitive-behavioural marital therapist will focus instead on unrealistic demands the partners have of each other and on maladaptive behavioural patterns that are unwittingly reinforced in the relationship. What all couples and family therapies have in common is the view that conflicts and tensions are inevitable when people live together and that the best way to address these problems is to involve all members of the family unit in therapy. A principal focus is improving communication among members so that personal needs can be met without sacrificing the needs and wishes of others.

Evaluation of Couples and Family Therapy

A meta-analysis of 20 carefully selected outcome studies meeting stringent methodological standards concluded that, overall, couples therapy has beneficial effects for many relationship problems (Hazelrigg, Cooper, & Borduin, 1987). Subsequent reviews by Baucom et al. (1998), Gurman and Kniskern (1978), Gurman, Kniskern, and Pinsoff (1986), Jacobson and Addis (1993), and Lebow and Gurman (1995) have reached the following specific conclusions about outcome and process in couples and family therapy:

- Conjoint therapy for couples problems appears to be more successful than individual therapy with one partner. The state of about 10 percent of patients seen individually for couples problems worsens.
- Behavioural couples therapy (BCT), which focuses on here-and-now skills training in communication and on increasing positive exchanges between the partners, has been shown to relieve distress in the relationship and/or increase partner satisfaction (Hahlweg & Markman, 1988). BCT has stronger effects than both no treatment and placebo-controlled treatments, and these positive outcomes sometimes last for up to a year.
- Adding a cognitive component to BCT (e.g., encouraging empathy) has not been shown to add to the positive outcomes (Baucom, Sayers, & Sher, 1990).
- Positive findings from a small number of studies have been reported for an insight-oriented therapy (Snyder & Wills, 1989). This approach encourages partners to explore their feelings and needs and to share these innermost aspects of themselves with the other. One study found an extremely low divorce rate in couples treated with an insight-oriented couples therapy (Snyder & Wills, 1989; Snyder, Wills, & Grady-Fletcher, 1991). At a four-year follow-up, Snyder's insight couples therapy was found to be superior to BCT in terms of divorce rates and marital satisfaction (Snyder et al., 1991). Emotion-focused therapy is also an insight-oriented approach.
- Although statistically significant, the outcomes of couples therapy research are not all clinically significant (Jacobson et al., 1984). For example, across all studies, no more than half the treated couples were really happily married at the end of treatment (even if they had improved in a strictly statistical sense). Few studies included much in the way of follow-ups, and those that did—and these were mostly behaviourally oriented—found frequent relapse (Alexander, Holtzworth-Munroe, & Jameson, 1994; Jacobson et al., 1987) and divorce (Snyder et al., 1991). As Jacobson and Addis have cautioned, these findings should temper premature enthusiasm for the efficacy of conjoint therapies, regardless of their theoretical bases.
- Although focused on the fearfulness of one partner, Barlow's exposure treatment, which involves the encouragement and collaboration of the spouse, has proved effective in reducing agoraphobia (see Chapter 6) and has avoided the deterioration in the marital relationship that has sometimes been reported when the agoraphobic partner gets better (Brown & Barlow, 1995; Himadi et al., 1986).
- The results of couples therapy are generally better for younger couples and when no steps have been taken toward divorce.

- Predictors of poor outcome include what Jacobson and Addis (1993) call "emotional disengagement," manifested by poor communication of feelings and by low frequency of sexual activity. Another sign of a poor prognosis in couples therapy is a relationship marked by rigidly held traditional gender roles, when the wife is oriented to affiliation and relationships and the husband is oriented primarily to work and autonomy (Jacobson, Follette, & Pagel, 1986). Finally, depression in one of the partners does not bode well for couples therapy (even though, as noted, behavioural couples therapy can have a positive impact both on a person's depression and on the relationship).
- Brief training in communication skills can enhance future satisfaction with the relationship and even result in lower divorce rates when compared with no-intervention controls (Markman et al., 1988). Since couples therapy generally works better when people are younger and highly involved with each other, prevention efforts seem particularly sensible and promising.
- Despite the growing use of "couples" rather than "marital" therapy, practically no research has been done on same-sex or unmarried heterosexual couples. Also, as noted by Johnson and Lebow (2000), there is increasing recognition of the need for research that incorporates a focus on cultural diversity; much of the field has focused on white, middle-class couples.

REVIEW OF COMMUNITY PSYCHOLOGY

Basic Concepts and Techniques of Community Psychology

Reaching out to large populations in an attempt to prevent the onset or spread of a physical illness or a mental disorder characterizes **community psychology**. The means of doing so may involve mass-media campaigns, instructional programs in schools, or other techniques designed to prevent disorder in groups of people. As with individual psychotherapy, the theoretical rationales and the techniques used vary greatly. There is a long history of activity in community psychology and psychiatry in Canada (Benjafield & Boudreau, 2000). In fact, in 1951 Canadian psychologist William Line was the first to use the term *community psychology* (see Babarik, 1979). A paper by Babarik (1979) provides an excellent overview of the history of community psychology in Canada. Line was one of the major contributors, and he served as the President of the World Federation for Mental Health. According to Babarik, Line was the most influential person in terms of extending the focus on mental health to primary prevention.

Prevention of mental disorders has always been a primary mission of the Canadian Mental Health Association (CMHA). Key historical figures were C.M. Hincks (see Chapter 1) and G. Brock Chisholm. Chisholm was a World War I sniper who eventually became the Canadian deputy minister of health and subsequently assumed the role of director general of the World Health Organization (WHO) (see Babarik, 1979). As a result of these men's efforts, the definition of health embraced by the CMHA formed the basis for the WHO definition of health, which includes physical, mental, social, and economic well-being (Babarik, 1979). The National Institute of Mental Health (NIMH) committee's widely promoted terminology of prevention (see Prilleltensky & Nelson, 2000) describes the various types of preventive interventions.

> *Universal* preventive interventions are targeted to the general public or a whole population group that has not been identified on the basis of individual risk. An example of a universal preventive intervention for physical health is childhood immunization. *Selective* preventive interventions are targeted to individuals or subgroups of the population whose risk of developing problems is significantly higher than average. A Head Start or other early childhood programmes for all children living in an economically depressed neighbourhood is an example of a selective prevention intervention. *Indicated* preventive interventions are targeted to high risk individuals who are identified as already having minimal, but detectable signs or symptoms, or biological markers, indicating predisposition for the mental disorder, but who do not meet diagnostic criteria. An intervention to prevent depression in children with one or both clinically depressed parents is an example of an indicated preventive intervention. (NIMH Committee on Prevention Research, 1995, pp. 6–7)

Many of the prevention programs in Canada focus on children (see Prilleltensky & Nelson, 2000). Further, while numerous programs focus on prevention—that is, interventions that reduce the incidence of disorder—governments in Canada, led by the federal government, are increasingly focusing on **mental health promotion**; that is, they are focusing on enhanced functioning, well-being, and optimal functioning. (For a discussion of the distinctions between prevention and promotion and Canadian guidelines and proposals, see Epp [1988], *Mental Health for Canadians: Striking a Balance*.) Prilleltensky and Nelson (2000) also proposed a new focus for psychological and social interventions, presenting a framework that would have interventions foster the well-being of children and families.

We have previously described many community psychology programs. These programs often focus on attempting both to reduce risk factors and to facilitate the development of protective factors. Examples of these programs include

- Canadian eating-disorder prevention programs;

- Canadian programs for the early detection and prevention of schizophrenia;
- school-based programs for the prevention of cigarette smoking;
- the establishment of suicide prevention centres with telephone hot lines that desperate people can use to survive a suicidal crisis;
- efforts through Head Start programs to prevent educational deficits and associated social and economic disadvantages, including Canada's Aboriginal Head Start initiative;
- a parent and child training program with francophones in Montreal to prevent early onset of delinquent behaviour; and
- a program in which material was presented via the radio to lessen the levels of anxiety and sleep difficulties experienced by many people.

Some other innovative, comprehensive, and possibly effective large-scale programs have emerged in Canada in recent years, including the Better Beginnings, Better Futures Project launched by Ontario under the direction of Ray DeV. Peters at Queen's University (Peters, 1994; Peters et al., 2000; Peters, Petrunka, & Arnold, 2003). This study, started in 1990, is a 25-year longitudinal investigation to evaluate the effectiveness of prevention as a policy for children. It involves a combined focus on the child, his or her family, childcare and school programs, and the involvement of the community. The most recent findings are based on results in three disadvantaged communities in Ontario, and the results are quite encouraging (Peters et al., 2003). Longitudinal analyses of changes over the first five years indicate significant improvements in children's and parents' social-emotional functioning and physical health. Parenting behaviours have also improved, and positive changes have occurred in the neighbourhood and school setting. Peters et al. (2003) concluded that the project has provided "unique evidence for the extent to which a universal, comprehensive, community-based prevention strategy can promote the longer term development of young children, their families, and their neighbourhoods" (p. 215). In short, the Better Beginnings, Better Futures Project is an excellent example of a primary or "universal" prevention program.

As noted above, "selective" and "indicated" preventive interventions use a high-risk approach that targets people who are exposed to specific, known risk factors. An example of these interventions would be approaches employed to help people who were directly or indirectly affected by the terrorist attacks on the Pentagon and the World Trade Center on September 11, 2001. Past research on the consequences of traumatic events taught us to expect (see Chapter 6) that a significant number of the survivors, as well as many of the firemen, police, rescue workers, and members of the families, significant others, and even friends and co-workers of the thousands of people killed or missing, would be at risk of developing traumatic stress disorders (acute stress disorder and PTSD) immediately after the event or as a delayed reaction. Other symptoms or disorders, including dissociative reactions, substance abuse, depression, health problems, and social conflicts, were also expected. Although some of these consequences have necessitated long-term treatment efforts, early intervention with people at high risk for the development of psychological problems eased the suffering and emotional pain associated with trying to cope with the consequences of the tragedies and likely short-circuited or reduced the probability of the development of PTSD and other serious psychological problems.

Canadian Perspectives/17.3

Back to the Future: Therapy and Technology

It seems apparent that future therapeutic techniques will increasingly incorporate advances in technology and the result will be a broadening in the range of services available to people in the community who are seeking treatment. This will be an important change in Canada, particularly in remote and rural areas.

One possibility was outlined by Klein and Richards (2001). Australians with panic disorder participated in a study in which one group of participants received an Internet-based, self-help treatment for three weeks, while the other group of participants experienced a self-monitoring condition. A self-paced treatment program was placed on the Internet and accessed via password by panic disorder patients. The program utilized principles of cognitive therapy; specifically, it examined the nature, causes, and effects of panic as well as useful and less useful ways of managing its symptoms. In addition, participants completed self-assessment quizzes and received immediate feedback. Daily assessments of anxiety and depression were obtained, as well as measures of frequency of panic and anticipatory fear of panic. The participants completed measures of depression, trait anxiety, and anxiety sensitivity before and after the study. Group comparisons at the conclusion of treatment showed that the treatment group had significant reductions in panic, anticipatory anxiety, and daily anxiety, but there were no group differences in depression or anxiety sensitivity. Overall, they concluded that the intervention was effective.

Researchers in Canada have demonstrated the potential usefulness of technology in the treatment of people who otherwise might not receive treatment. The Alberta Mental Health Board (AMHB) developed a "telemental health service" that has been in existence since 1996. The service uses videoconferences to make psychiatric consultations available to health practitioners in rural parts of the province. There are videoconference sites throughout Alberta, including such places as Drumheller, Slave Lake, Peace River, and Fort Chipewyan. Published studies and information on the AMHB website (http://www.amhb.ab.ca) indicate that the program is quite effective (see Doze, Simpson, Hailey, & Jacobs, 1999; Simpson, Doze, Urness, Hailey, & Jacobs, 2001a, 2001b). For instance, 96.2 percent of rural physicians indicate that they are satisfied or very satisfied with the telemental health service, and 80.8 percent indicate that they are satisfied with the mental health improvement of clients they have referred for service. Surveys indicate that approximately nine out of 10 people were satisfied with their sessions, felt that the doctor listened to them, felt supported and encouraged, and felt that the sessions could provide the same information that would have been presented in person. Importantly, nine out of 10 also felt that they would rather use telepsychiatry than have to spend time on a waiting list to obtain treatment. Still, assessment showed that about 50 percent of patients would have preferred a face-to-face session over telepsychiatry (Simpson et al., 2001). Nevertheless, the study found an average saving of more than $200 per client because travel costs to the treatment site were no longer required. On the basis of these findings, the AMHB identified future telemental goals, including additional services (e.g., forensic, brain injury) and an explicit focus on children's services.

Numerous other such innovations are emerging in Canada. For instance, the first emergency telehealth consultation for a mental health issue occurred in January 2002 in Saint John, New Brunswick, when the existing telehealth services were expanded (see Palmer, Montgomery, & Harland, 2003). Whereas patients in remote areas previously required airlifts and were escorted by the local sheriff, they are now assessed by a psychiatrist in Saint John who evaluates each person in the emergency department of his or her own local hospital.

In one specific case, telehealth technology was used to deliver family therapy to family members who remained in their rural Ontario home while an anorexic adolescent female member of the family was being treated in an urban hospital (Goldfried & Boachie, 2003). The family members were highly satisfied with telehealth and had no concerns about confidentiality issues.

Technological advances also expand the training opportunities for mental health professionals. A project in Atlantic Canada involving training via satellite showed that mental health professionals in rural areas reported many positive outcomes, including expanded knowledge, greater sensitivity to mental health issues, and greater cohesion among professionals (Cournish et al., 2003).

Finally, Bouchard and associates at the University of Quebec have conducted preliminary research on the efficacy of cognitive behaviour therapy via videoconference as a way of treating panic disorder with agoraphobia (Bouchard et al., 2000). In their preliminary investigation, they examined the effects of 12 sessions of cognitive behaviour therapy delivered via videoconference by trained therapists operating according to a standardized treatment manual. The "telepsychotherapy" resulted in substantial improvements in terms of the frequency of panic attacks, severity of panic disorder, trait anxiety, and self-efficacy. Importantly, the authors indicated that "a very good therapeutic alliance was built after only the first telepsychotherapy session" (p. 999). The authors conducted a large investigation that included a direct comparison of patients treated with cognitive therapy delivered via videoconference or face-to-face interactions (Bouchard et al., 2004). Both methods were equally effective, and 91 percent of those who were treated via videoconference were free of panic symptoms six months after treatment was over. Once again, an "excellent therapeutic alliance" could be identified as early as the first video conference therapy session.

Bouchard et al. (2000) make a number of provocative observations when discussing their results. They suggest that this form of treatment may be especially well suited to people with disorders such as panic disorder with agoraphobia because these people may be more comfortable receiving treatment in their home environment where they feel less threatened. However, the authors point out that the videoconference approach does involve some significant limitations that have a bearing on the therapist's ability to establish rapport and enhance the therapeutic alliance (e.g., the inability to shake hands, provide tissues to a crying patient, look directly into the person's eyes, etc). At an even more practical level, client and therapist must quickly learn to keep their movements within the camera's field of view.

As technology advances and the need for therapeutic services increases, it is likely that more and more people will avail themselves of these technologically based forms of treatment. Regulatory bodies are currently working on ethics and standards protocols for the therapeutic services often delivered through the Internet. Key issues to consider include ways to safeguard the client's confidentiality and right to anonymity, as well as to maximize the safety of these individuals.

Thinking Critically

1. Preliminary research results confirm the potential usefulness of innovative technological approaches in delivering mental health services, including therapy, especially in more rural areas of Canada. There is no doubt that "telemental health" services can be cost-effective, relatively efficient alternatives to traditional consultation and treatment

approaches. However, the study by Simpson et al. (2001) reported that about half the participants would have preferred face-to-face sessions despite the cost saving. What are the implications of this finding for the treatment of people in remote and rural places in Canada?

2. The studies by Klein and Richards (2001) and Bouchard et al. (2000) used principles of cognitive therapy and cognitive behaviour therapy to treat panic disorder. These studies used brief, Internet-based self-help treatment and longer-term videoconferencing using trained therapists, respectively. Although these approaches seem effective with a disorder such as panic disorder, will they be effective with psychological problems such as depression? Note that participants in Klein and Richards's self-help group did not experience significant reductions in depression. Is this because the treatment did not target their depression or because technology-based strategies are less likely to be effective with depression?

3 . What other disorders or psychological problems should be treated next with technology-based forms of therapy? Would the approach work well with, for example, the stress-related health problems described in Chapter 9.

Presumably, crisis intervention strategies such as Critical Incident Stress Debriefing (see Meichenbaum, 1994) were usefully employed to help the survivors and rescue personnel. According to Meichenbaum (1994), people who respond in such circumstances in a dissociative fashion or appear calm, composed, and unfazed should not be overlooked by debriefers or rescue workers, for they are at high risk for maladjustment. A focus on the provision of social support (e.g., the creation of temporary "communities" near the disaster sites for the victims' families, where they received necessary information and professional counselling for grief, anger, guilt, self-blame, and shock) was helpful to people at risk, and a family centre was established near "ground zero" soon after the tragedy. The media played a meaningful role by providing stress-reducing radio and television programs and programs on coping efforts. The mental health community helped to establish telephone hotlines, provided appropriate material for dissemination to the public by the media, and guided outreach programs. It was expected that the greatest need for psychological interventions would occur one or two months following the disaster, once immediate needs had been met and after support systems had worn down. Future research will determine exactly which strategies were employed in response to the September 11 terrorist attacks and how effective emergency intervention programs actually were. Although some studies find that crisis interventions are efficacious, others do not (e.g., Everly, Boyle, & Lating, 1999).

Canadian Perspectives 17.3 summarizes research that illustrates the potential usefulness of innovative technological approaches delivering mental health services to communities. These approaches may reduce the subsequent need for more intensive mental health services.

Evaluation of Community Psychology

It has been suggested that the results of community psychology have been disappointing (Bernstein & Nietzel, 1980; Phares & Trull, 1997), but some projects have shown their worth in recent years. One infrequently discussed reason for the limited effectiveness of prevention efforts is that some problems are not readily amenable to environmental or social manipulation because they have major genetic or biological components. As we saw in Chapter 11, for example, there is very strong evidence that schizophrenia has some kind of biological diathesis. Although an environmental preventive effort may conceivably reduce the amount of stress that a predisposed individual is subject to in normal daily living, it seems unlikely that any realistic social change could keep stress levels low enough to prevent episodes of schizophrenia from occurring or recurring in high-risk people. Family therapy for reducing expressed emotion is a prototype of what might be necessary on a societal scale to have a positive impact on the recurrence of episodes of schizophrenia. However, how practical is it to apply such an approach on a broad scale?

Another problem in terms of the implementation of prevention programs is the lack of government commitment to providing the resources that would facilitate their creation. Widespread prevention programs are simply not possible in Canada with the current resources available. For more than a decade, the federal government has been drastically reducing transfer payments to the provinces for health, welfare, social services, and education. Nelson, Prilleltensky, Laurendeau, and Powell (1996) reviewed the situation as of 1993 and noted that there have been many good prevention programs (e.g., preschool enrichment for children at risk and youth suicide prevention) that have been matched by government rhetoric in terms of stated policies, but there have not been corres-ponding reallocations and increases of financial resources. They concluded that the relevant provincial ministries allocated a very small proportion of their budgets (less than 1 percent) to such programs. Health funding, in particular, has not been redirected from direct treatment efforts toward preventing disorders in children and youth (e.g., McCain & Mustard, 1999; Nelson et al., 1996; Prilleltensky & Nelson, 2000). As a result, preventive efforts have been limited and community psychology efforts in Canada marginalized in many respects, in contrast to the strong beginning thanks to the efforts of people such as Line, Hincks, and Chisholm, among others (see Walsh-Bowers, 1998).

Overall, an evaluation of community-psychology efforts is particularly challenging because the interventions occur in the field, where it is difficult to set up experimental controls and thus harder to draw causal inferences (Linney, 1989). There are many alternative explanations for the effect of a preventive intervention. For example, a reduction in gang activity following a school-based intervention aimed at that goal may largely be the consequence of the opening of a community centre, such as the YMCA, or even the actions of a single, inspirational teacher. Another concern in the current practice of prevention science is the problem of attrition, or loss of participants (Mrazek & Haggerty, 1994). Those who drop out of an intervention must be monitored in some fashion, for these individuals could be at the highest risk.

Political and Ethical Factors in Community Psychology

The study of community psychology raises an interesting question. In the 1960s and 1970s, there was a shift throughout Western nations, including Canada and the United States, to community activism in the prevention of mental disorders. Why? The answer is complex.

For many years, it was obvious that few people could avail themselves of psychotherapeutic services, which were usually very expensive, in short supply, and geared to so-called YAVIS clients— individuals who are young, attractive, verbal, intelligent, and successful (Schofield, 1964). Eysenck (1952) had earlier questioned the effectiveness of most kinds of psychotherapy, finding treated patients' rates of improvement no better than the spontaneous remission rate. Although Eysenck's criticisms were compellingly rebutted by many scholars (see Bergin, 1971), the idea took hold among mental health professionals that psychotherapy aimed at changing the individual might not be the best way to alleviate the psychological problems of the majority of people. Focus began to shift from repressions, conflicts, and neurotic fears to large-scale social problems, such as poverty, overcrowding, poor education, segregation, the alienation felt in large cities, and the impersonal nature of many aspects of present-day living. The emphasis on prevention became especially significant in the United States, where a large gap developed between the need for mental health care and the availability of services (Weissberg, Caplan, & Sivo, 1989).

The shift from intrapsychic to social factors probably also reflected the *Zeitgeist*, or tenor of the times, especially in the United States. The 1960s and early 1970s were a period of tremendous social upheaval and activism. Institutions of all kinds were being challenged. Cities and college campuses in the United States erupted in riots, and a range of minority groups, from African Americans to gays, charged racism and political repression. This social upheaval, which at times seemed to border on revolution, spilled over into Canada and further encouraged looking at social institutions for causes of individual suffering.

Community psychology has as its goal the change of large systems and groups of people rather than the treatment of individual problems. And it is primarily in the seeking mode—psychologists take the initiative in serving people rather than waiting for individuals in need to come to them. On the face of it, this is a tall order. What do we know about the principles that operate to produce change in societal values and institutions? If the community psychologist hopes to take actions that meet the wishes and needs of the community, how does he or she determine them? Recall from Chapters 3 and 4 the difficulties the psychologist has in assessing the needs of an individual client with whom there is extensive direct contact. How much more difficult, then, to assess the needs of thousands of people!

Community psychologists become social activists to some degree, which raises the danger that these well-meaning professionals may impose values and goals on their clients. What is mental health? Who is to decide how people should live their lives? To what extent do the people being served by community psychologists have a say in how they are to be helped? These are but a few of the nettlesome questions that must continually be posed if community psychology is to act responsibly and effectively. The focus of this field is on large-scale factors. Many people are involved; many lives, then, will be affected by decisions and actions. Questions of values and of effectiveness are inherent in any effort to alter the human condition, but they are of special importance when the clients themselves do not seek the intervention.

Psychotherapy Integration

Having reviewed the theory and research on the major psychological interventions, we turn now to the question of whether useful connections can be made among them. We examine first whether contemporary psychoanalysis is compatible with behaviour therapy. We then turn to more general questions about eclecticism and integration in psychotherapy.

Psychoanalysis and Behaviour Therapy: A Rapprochement?

The question as to whether there is common ground between psychoanalysis and behaviour therapy has been discussed for many years. Few professionals are optimistic about a meaningful rapprochement, arguing that these two points of view are incompatible paradigms. But Paul Wachtel, in his work on just such an integration (1977,1997, 2002), offers a scheme that holds considerable promise.

As indicated earlier, ego analysts place much more emphasis on current ego functioning than did Freud. Sullivan, for example, suggested that patients would feel better about themselves and function more effectively if they focused on problems in their current interpersonal behaviour. But it appears that Sullivan was ambivalent about the wisdom of working directly on how people act and feel in the present if doing so meant that they would not recover memories of repressed infantile conflicts. Wachtel, on the other hand, suggests that therapists, including those working within a psychoanalytic paradigm, should help the client change current behaviour, not only so that he or she can feel better in the here and now, but, indeed, so that he or she can also resolve repressed conflicts from the past.

Wachtel bases his principal position on Horney (1939), Sullivan (1953), and Erikson (1950) and calls it "cyclical psychodynamics" (1982). He believes that people's current behaviour maintains repressed problems via feedback from present-day interactions with others. Wachtel holds to the psychoanalytic notion that people's problems are set in motion by repressed past events, but he departs from psychoanalysis and from most ego analysts as well when he suggests that people act in ways that maintain these problems.

Wachtel suggests that therapy should attempt to alter current behavioural patterns both for their own sake, which is the behaviour therapist's credo, and for the purpose of uncovering and changing the underlying psychodynamics, which is the focus of psychoanalytic approaches. By pointing out that a direct alteration of behaviour may help patients attain a more realistic understanding of their repressed past conflicts, Wachtel hopes to interest his analytic colleagues in the techniques employed by behaviour therapists. He also holds that behaviour therapists can learn much from their analytic colleagues, especially concerning the kinds of problems people tend to develop. For example, psychoanalytic theory tells us that children have strong and usually ambivalent feelings about their parents, some of which are so unpleasant that people repress them or at least have difficulty focusing on them and talking about them openly. Wachtel also wants behaviour therapists to be attuned to unconscious motivation, to the possibility that a person may be motivated or reinforced by a set of events of which he or she is unaware.

Contemporary psychoanalytic thought may help behaviour therapists become aware of the meaning that a particular intervention has for a patient. Consider the case of a young woman with whom a behaviour therapist decided to do assertion training. As the therapist began to describe role-playing procedures, she stiffened in her chair and then began to sob. To proceed with the training without dealing with her reaction to its description would have been insensitive and poor clinical practice. An awareness of psychoanalytic theory had sensitized the therapist to the possibility that assertion symbolized something to the woman. The therapist gently encouraged her to talk freely, to free-associate about the idea of assertion training. She recalled a series of incidents from childhood in which her parents had criticized the way she acted with her friends without providing support and constructive suggestions about other ways to behave. Without initially being aware of it herself, the patient was reminded of this pain from the past when the therapist suggested that she learn more assertive ways of dealing with others. The psychologist was able to explain to her the current enterprise, assertion training, and to distinguish it from the unhelpful and negative criticisms made in the past. He was able thereby to persuade the young woman to try role-playing. This incident also reflected the patient's unresolved problems with her parents and with authority figures in general.

In our view, the actual practices of experienced behavioural clinicians often reflects the kind of subtlety characteristic of psychodynamic clinicians such as Wachtel. What is unclear is the degree to which a sophisticated practice can be derived from the theories that constitute contemporary cognitive and behaviour therapy. The disjunction between theory and practice lies at the core of Wachtel's critical discussion of behaviour therapy and the ways in which psychoanalysis might enrich both behavioural theory and practice. We turn now to some general issues in eclecticism and psychotherapy integration.

Eclecticism and Theoretical Integration in Psychotherapy

Wachtel's efforts at rapprochement are part of a long tradition in the field of psychotherapy (e.g., Dollard & Miller, 1950). More than 35 years ago, Perry London (1964), in his critical analysis of insight and behavioural therapies, wrote:

> There is a quiet blending of techniques by artful therapists of either school, a blending that takes account of the fact that people are considerably simpler than the Insight schools give them credit for, but that they are also more complicated than the Action [behaviour] therapists would like to believe. (London, 1964, p. 39)

The use of an eclectic approach is quite common (Hunsley & Lefebvre, 1990; Warner, 1991) but not necessarily increasing in prevalence. For instance, a random sampling survey in the United States based on the *National Register of Health Service Providers in Psychology* for the years 1981, 1985, and 1989 found that approximately two-fifths of respondents listed their primary theoretical orientation as eclectic and that there was no significant increase over time in the proportion of eclectic therapists (Milan, Montogomery, & Rogers, 1994).

Three Types of Psychotherapy Integration Distinctions have been drawn among three modes of psychotherapy integration (Arkowitz, 1989): **technical eclecticism**, common factorism, and theoretical integration. In technical eclecticism, exemplified in Lazarus's multimodal approach and in Beutler's prescriptive psychotherapy (Beutler & Harwood, 1995), the therapist works within a particular theoretical framework, (e.g., cognitive behaviour therapy) but sometimes imports from other orientations techniques deemed effective, though without subscribing to the theories that spawned them. "Use whatever works" is the operating principle of the technical eclectic, but one should rationalize the use of a technique from one's own framework. Lazarus, for example, sometimes uses the Gestalt empty chair as a method of behavioural rehearsal rather than as a way to help the patient reclaim disowned parts of his or her personality, which is how the technique is conceived in Gestalt therapy.

Common factorism (e.g., Frank, 1961; Goldfried, 1991; Schofield, 1964) seeks strategies that all therapy schools might share. For example, informing a patient how he or she affects others is a strategy employed by many different kinds of therapists and believed by many (e.g., Brady et al., 1980) to be an important component of effective psychotherapy.

An approach that could be considered common factorism was outlined in a book on treatment planning by Sheila Woody and associates (see Woody, Detweiler-Bedeil, Teachman, & O'Hearn, 2003). Woody, located at the University of British Columbia, is a member of the APA Division 12 Task Force on empirically supported treatments (ESTs). Woody et al. (2003) outlined an eclectic treatment planning system that favours evidence-based approaches. They described a phase approach to treatment planning that includes steps toward identifying problems, establishing clear treatment goals and aims, and measuring treatment progress after implementing ESTs. It represents common factorism because, other than a general preference for ESTs, no single theoretical orientation is imposed and therapists are free to adopt techniques and conceptualizations from various approaches.

The third approach, theoretical integration, tries to synthesize not only techniques but also theories. Wachtel's efforts to justify and make sense of assertion training within a modified psychoanalytic framework is a prime example of an effort toward theoretical integration. The resulting theory is itself something different because of the blending of psychoanalytic and behavioural elements.

Arguments Against Premature Integration

In contemplating efforts at theoretical integration, we have wondered whether a grand, all-encompassing theory or approach is necessarily desirable or even possible. We believe not, and our own use of different paradigms in the study of both psychopathology and intervention aligns us more with the views of Garfield and Bergin:

> [H]uman personality may operate in accordance with a complex interaction of seemingly disparate processes that act together, though each differently and in its own sphere. Thus, it is conceivable that the same individual may suffer at one time from a repressed conflict, a conditioned response, an incongruent self-image, and irrational cognitions; and that each of these dysfunctions may operate in semi-independent systems of psychic action that are amenable to rather different interventions, each of which is compatible with the "system" to which it is being applied. Diagnosis and therapy might then become concerned with the locus of the disorder or with which portion or portions of the multisystem psyche is involved. (1986, p. 10)

Indeed, not all those interested in psychotherapy integration agree with the overall notion that the more blurring between conceptual frameworks, the better. In an article entitled "Disappearing Differences Do Not Always Reflect Healthy Integration," Haaga and Davison (1991) pointed out several ways in which Ellis's REBT and Beck's CT have begun to merge. Beck originally focused almost entirely on cognitive biases and how they might distort a person's analysis of a situation. Thus, a depressed person who complains that he or she has no friends is encouraged, like a scientist, to determine whether in fact this is true. In contrast, Ellis emphasized the belief or assumption under which a person operates, such as "I must be perfect in everything I do." Now, however, Beck devotes considerable time to talking about "dysfunctional schemas," which can look a great deal like Ellis's "irrational beliefs." And Ellis does not ignore social realities, for even at the beginning (Ellis, 1962) he advocated teaching someone without social skills how to better interact with others, with the goal of improving relationships (rather than merely encouraging the person to care little about turning people off).

Haaga and Davison caution that we may lose something by blurring such distinctions, especially if integration is not based on research (and they argue that it is not). If we preserve the uniqueness of these two therapies, we might then be more inclined to construct a more integrative therapy that uses the particular strengths of each. For example, perhaps for certain people under certain circumstances, it is best to focus on changing social realities, whereas other circumstances might call for changing people's interpretations of an unchanging and perhaps unchangeable social reality. Creating this kind of integration requires (1) holding on to at least some of the original distinctions between REBT and CT and, more important, (2) constructing or utilizing a superordinate theory that can subsume both REBT and CT and specify when a particular aspect of one is suitable and when a feature of the other is appropriate. Science sometimes moves forward more readily when rapprochement among divergent theories is *not* encouraged.

We conclude this chapter with a discussion of an effective integrative approach that combines cognitive and behavioural factors with other characteristics.

An Integrative Approach: Meichenbaum's Constructivist Cognitive-Behavioural Treatment Model

As noted in Chapter 2, Donald Meichenbaum (e.g., 1977, 1992, 1994, 1995) has developed several empirically supported treatments, with supporting manuals, using cognitive-behavioural approaches, including self-instructional training and stress inoculation. These approaches are effective in treating a wide range of psychological problems and disorders and were designed to overcome barriers to effective outcomes and to facilitate maintenance and generalization of treatment effects. We also noted in Chapter 2 (and illustrated in Chapter 6) Meichenbaum's adoption of a constuctivist-narrative approach.

Meichenbaum's current approach is both comprehensive and integrative. It is partly based on the cognitive-behavioural underpinnings derived from his earlier contributions, the literature on common factors in psychotherapy, the constructivist-narrative approach, barriers to treatment adherence and resistance, relapse prevention, and his interests in the psychotherapy integration movement.

The following tasks of psychotherapy form the core of his current constructivist cognitive-behavioural treatment approach. He also views these as the common elements in all successful therapy.

1. Develop a therapeutic alliance and help clients tell their stories.
2. Educate clients about the clinical problem.
3. Help clients reconceptualize their "problems" in a more hopeful fashion.
4. Ensure that clients have coping skills.
5. Encourage clients to perform "personal experiments."
6. Ensure that clients take credit for changes they have brought about.
7. Conduct relapse prevention.

The constructivist narrative perspective (which Meichenbaum adds to traditional CBT) is probably the most controversial component of his approach. It is based on a view of people as "meaning-making agents" who construct their own stories to explain their lives and experiences. For instance, the constructivist narrative perspective could involve your being asked to describe your most memorable experience after making the transition to college or university. What does this experience mean to you? How does it connect with your other experiences? How does it fit into your life narrative? What are your choices in this world? In contrast to traditional cognitive or cognitive-behavioural therapy, Meichenbaum's approach is less structured, more exploratory, and more discovery-oriented. As you learned in Chapter 6, where we described his innovative approach to treating people with PTSD, clients are assisted in telling their stories and in creating new stories through therapy.

Attempts to include a greater focus on the process of thinking and the generation of meaning, as advocated by Meichenbaum, may account, at least in part, for the recent growth of CBT. Dobson and Pusch (1993) observed that CBT has grown in terms of breadth (application to diverse psychological disorders and problems) and depth (greater focus on difficult core features of cognitive structure and function that have great personal salience). Although Meichenbaum's approach is applicable to a wide array of problems, as pointed out by Neimeyer and Raskin (2001), constructivism has made its most significant contributions to Dobson and Pusch's depth dimension.

There are several varieties of constructivism in psychotherapy (see Neimeyer & Raskin, 2001), but Meichenbaum borrowed most directly from only two of the five thematic emphases: (1) psychotherapy as personal science and (2) psychotherapy as narrative reauthoring. Dobson and Dozois (2001) wondered what the effect of Meichenbaum's adoption of the narrative-constructionist approach will have on continuing interest in stress inoculation and his other early contributions. Neimeyer and Raskin (2001) asked how constructivist developments will be received by more traditional CBT theorists and therapists.

SUMMARY

- Research on the effectiveness of various forms of psychotherapy has been conducted for many decades, with sometimes complicated and inconsistent results. The evaluation of the effects of psychotherapy has grown in significance as increased demands for accountability are being imposed. Several general issues provide a context for the study of psychotherapeutic interventions.
- There are differences between the way therapies have been examined in experimental settings and the way they are actually practised by clinicians. Recent research has employed treatment manuals that specify what experimenters are to do when applying given therapies to research participants. Although this practice enhances the internal validity of psychotherapy research, the contrast with therapy as practised—making adjustments depending on the needs of the individual patient—limits the limited external validity of such research.
- Classical psychoanalysis tries to uncover childhood repressions so that infantile fears of libidinal expression can be examined by the adult ego in the light of present-day realities. Brief psychodynamic therapy puts more emphasis on the need and ability of the patient to achieve greater control over both the environment and

instinctual gratification. It is a time-limited therapy in which expectations are set for fewer than two-dozen sessions. There is a focus on setting concrete goals and learning ways to cope with life's inevitable stressors, forsaking the goal of psychoanalysis to obtain a personality overhaul through analysis of the transference neurosis.

- Research on psychoanalytic and brief psychodynamic therapies suggests that they can be useful for a variety of anxiety and depressive disorders but not as useful for more serious psychopathology. Process research on such factors as interpretation raises questions about the positive effects of certain variables on the outcome of treatment. Interpreting hypothesized transference reactions, for example, can sometimes be detrimental for the patient.
- Rogers trusted the basic goodness of the drive to self-actualize, and he proposed the creation of nonjudgemental conditions in therapy. Through empathy and unconditional positive regard, client-centred therapists help their clients view themselves more accurately and trust their own instincts for self-actualization. Research on client-centred therapy has investigated whether such factors as empathy and genuineness on the part of the therapist are associated with good outcomes. Results are inconsistent. Moreover, the assumption that people are by nature good and that they have an innate drive to self-actualization does not apply to many disorders.
- The Gestalt therapy of Perls stresses living in the now, and the many techniques he and his followers have introduced are designed to help clients experience their current needs and feel comfortable about satisfying them as they emerge. Gestalt and other humanistic and existential therapies have engendered little research, perhaps because of the objection that research is an objectifying, dehumanizing process.
- The cognitive and behaviour therapies attempt to apply the methodologies and principles of experimental psych-ology to the alleviation of psychological distress. Because of their emphasis on research, the various behavioural and cognitive-behavioural therapies account for the lion's share of both process and outcome research in psych-otherapy. Evidence attests to the efficacy of counterconditioning, exposure, operant, and cognitive-behavioural interventions in alleviating a wide range of disorders. However, the fact that high end-state functioning is often not achieved even by patients whose improvement is significant highlights the fact that much remains to be learned.
- Cognitive therapies, such as Ellis's rational-emotive behaviour therapy and Beck's cognitive therapy, alter the thoughts that are believed to underlie emotional disorders. They reflect the increasing importance of cognition in experimentally based psychological interventions.
- Of particular importance for the cognitive and behavioural therapies, as well as for other approaches, is the generalization of treatment effects once the client is no longer seeing the therapist on a regular basis. Several procedures hold promise for maintaining whatever gains have been achieved during treatment. Of particular importance for techniques that are directive and therefore heavily reliant on influence from the therapist is how patients attribute or explain to themselves why they have improved. Encouraging an internal "I was a major factor in my own improvement" attribution is gaining popularity as a way to help people maintain their gains.
- Marital or couples therapy helps distressed couples resolve the conflicts inevitable in any ongoing relationship of two adults living together. Behavioural and some insight-oriented therapies show promise in easing the stress that many couples experience.
- Community psychology aims primarily at the prevention of disorder. It adopts a seeking rather than the traditional waiting mode in helping communities cope with large-scale stressors and other life challenges. Political and ethical issues are intrinsic aspects of any therapeutic effort that aims to help people who have not actually asked for assistance.
- Eclecticism and theoretical integration in psychotherapy represent a trend that reflects growing awareness on the part of many clinicians and researchers of the limitations of their respective theoretical approaches. Psychoanalysis and behaviour therapy might inform each other and take advantage of the strengths each can offer the other to help professionals better understand the human condition and design effective therapeutic interventions. There are risks, however, in integrating diverse theoretical perspectives, such as glossing over differences that might better be examined and evaluated.

KEY TERMS

common factorism (p. 599)
community psychology (p. 593)
Dodo bird effect (p. 568)
effectiveness (p. 568)
efficacy (p. 568)
mental health promotion (p. 593)
multimodal therapy (p. 586)
stepped care (p. 569)
technical eclecticism (p. 598)
theoretical integration (p. 599)
therapeutic (working) alliance (p. 574)
triadic reciprocality (p. 582)

Reflections: Past, Present, and Future

- Think back to our discussion of Dr. Ewen Cameron's treatment of his patients at the Allan Memorial Institute in the 1950's and recall the lesson of history presented in Chapter 1. Now read Cameron's quotation at the outset of this chapter: "Don't ever do anything to someone that you can't reverse." Through the wisdom of hindsight, we now know tht he did irreversible damage to so many of the people under his care. Do you think that the strategies used today, including psychological and biological interventions, cause irreversible damage to people? How can we continue to guard against this possibility? Do you think that we really have learned from out past mistakes?
- In Canadian Perspectives 17.3, we discussed recent approaches that employ technology to make mental health services available in the remote and rural areas of Canada. At different points in this book, we have focused on the plight of many of Canada's Aboriginal people, and in particular on rampant substance abuse, suicide, and child abuse. Do you think that some of the technology-based strategies described in this chapter could be adapted for use with Native people? How would you go about doing this? Would you develop approaches similar in mission and philosophy to, say, Poundmaker's Lodge (see Chapter 12) that would be run by the Aboriginal people themselves? Could this approach be helpful in to reducing the devastating consequences of alcohol abuse in adults and gasoline sniffing in children, or is it really more essential to focus on developing on-site programs? Would telemental health services be useful adjuncts to, or provide helpful support for, community programs?
- Reflect on the different approaches to psychotherapy that we have discussed in this book and evaluated in the current chapter. If you were asked to pick the approach that had the most personal meaning for you, the one that would best fit into your own life narrative, which treatment would you select and why?
- Review the framework of Meichenbaum's constructivist cognitive-behavioural treatment model. Using this framework, evaluate the major therapies to determine which therapies have these elements in common.
- The issue of psychotherapy integration is controversial. While some theorists and researchers embrace it, others eschew it. We recognize that there are some risks in integration but that there also seems to be a strong trend toward it. For example, Neimeyer and Raskin (2001, p. 421) concluded that "it seems to be a safe prediction that cognitive theorists will continue to build bridges to constructivist approaches." Where do you stand on issues of eclecticism and integration? Is integration feasible or desirable?
- In the next chapter, we will examine ethical issues that are important in both treatment and research. Ewen Cameron conducted research on the people who came to him for help. He didn't tell them that they were being used as research subjects or that they were receiving experimental treatments. What was unethical about what Cameron did? Why was it unethical? According to psychiatric historians (e.g., Collins, 1988; Weinstein, 1990), Cameron was driven by blind ambition in his misguided quest to discover a quick, effective "cure" for schizophrenia and other severe mental disorders. He hoped that his discoveries would bring him fame, power, and glory and also the ultimate prize—the Nobel Prize in Medicine and Physiology (just as Egas Moniz of Portugal won the prize in 1955, 20 years after discovering lobotomy for the treatment of schizophrenia). What if Cameron had discovered an effective treatment? Should we have then made, or even now make, allowances for the consequences of his zeal? Would his treatment of his patients be any less unethical?

chapter 18

Legal and Ethical Issues

"The myth is that if people exhibit bizarre behaviour, men in white coats will come and take you away. There aren't any people who can do that. If only there were."
— Fay Herrick, Calgarian whose son suffers from schizophrenia (Nichols, 1995)

"The idea that patients would heal faster within their communities is bizarre. These same patients originally came from the communities whose healing qualities clearly were not sufficient to prevent them from becoming sick in the first place. The notion that patients would heal faster in the bosom of their families is equally problematic. Many families are too sick, or too tired, or simply do not have the resources or the energy to cope with very sick patients."
—Abram Hoffer, former director of psychiatric research for the Province of Saskatchewan, currently in private practice in Victoria, B.C. and president of the Canadian Schizophrenia Foundation (2000, p. 145)

George Agnew Reid, 1860 – 1947, *The Other Side of the Question*, 1890
oil on canvas, 104.0 x 132.5 cm,
ART GALLERY OF ONTARIO, TORONTO
Purchase, 1985

Section 1—Guarantee of Rights and Freedoms. The Canadian Charter of Rights and Freedoms guarantees the rights and freedoms set out in it subject only to such reasonable limits prescribed by law as can be demonstrably justified in a free and democratic society.

Section 2—Fundamental Freedoms. Everyone has the following fundamental freedoms: 1. freedom of conscience and religion; 2. freedom of thought, belief, opinion and expression; including freedom of the press and other media of communication; 3. freedom of peaceful assembly; and 4. freedom of association.

Section 3—Democratic Rights. Every citizen of Canada has the right to vote in an election of members of the House of Commons or as a legislative assembly and to be qualified for membership therein.

Section 7—Legal Rights. Every one has the right to life, liberty and security of the person and the right not to be deprived thereof except in accordance with the principles of fundamental justice.

Section 8—Everyone has the right to be secure against unreasonable search or seizure.

Section 9—Everyone has the right not to be arbitrarily detained or imprisoned.

Section 12—Everyone has the right not be subjected to any cruel and unusual treatment or punishment.

Section 15—Equality before and under law and equal protection and benefit of law. Every individual is equal before and under the law and has the right to equal protection and benefits of the law without discrimination, and, in particular, without discrimination based on race, national, or ethnic origin, colour, religion, sex, age or mental or physical disability.

Section 16—Official Languages of Canada. English and French are the official languages of Canada and have equality of status and equal rights and privileges as to their use in all institutions of the Parliament and government of Canada.

We open our final chapter in this way, with sections of the Canadian Charter of Rights and Freedoms (1982), for two reasons. First, the legal and mental health systems collaborate continually, although often subtly, to deny a substantial proportion of the Canadian population their basic civil rights. With the best of intentions, judges, tribunals, governing boards of hospitals, bar associations, and professional mental health groups have worked over the years to protect society at large from the actions of people regarded as mentally ill or mentally disordered and considered dangerous to themselves or to others. However, in so doing, they have denied many thousands of people their basic civil rights.

Second, Section 15 (1) of the Charter of Rights and Freedoms (i.e., Equality before and under Law) is especially significant because it extends the right of equality to mentally ill people. According to Eaves, Lamb, and Tien (2000, p. 615) Canada "is one of the few countries in the world that explicitly extends the general rights found in our constitution to people who are mentally ill." It is up to each province to formulate and implement laws that are in keeping with the Charter of Rights and Freedoms. Although all provinces share the same Charter-driven principles in their legislation, differences exist in terms of how these principles are realized. Another possible source of differences between the provinces is the "notwithstanding clause," which permits provinces to opt out of the Charter if they perceive a conflict between their goals and values and the overall goals and values of the nation.

Although mentally ill people are extended rights under the equality provision, there are situations in which other principles come into effect. Specifically, the Charter of Rights and Freedoms also includes provisions that allow for some people to be removed from society if they act in a way that infringes on the rights of other people to a free and democratic society. In other words, at times, the needs of the society as a whole may outweigh the needs of any one individual. Mentally ill individuals who have broken the law, or who are alleged to have done so, may be subject to a loss of liberty where their mental disorder becomes relevant to the criminal prosecution either because of concerns regarding fitness to stand trial or criminal responsibility. In other words, they may be subject to **criminal commitment**, a procedure that may confine a person in a mental institution either for determination of competency to stand trial or after a verdict of not criminally responsible on account of mental disorder. Part XX.1 of the Criminal Code of Canada provides a 'mini-code' that sets out the procedures for dealing with mentally disordered individuals who find themselves before the criminal courts. **Civil commitment**, provided for in provincial statutes, is a procedure by which a mentally ill and dangerous person who may not have broken a law can be deprived of liberty and incarcerated in a mental hospital. Both committal procedures—one federal, the other provincial—may result in a loss of liberty as a result of mental disorder. In this chapter, we look at these legal procedures in depth. We then turn to an examination of some important ethical issues as they relate to therapy and research.

CRIMINAL COMMITMENT

Historically, most of Canadian law has derived from English common law, reflecting the British influence in Canada. The exception is Quebec, where Napoleonic law has been incorporated into civil statutes. In Canada, criminal law is a matter of federal statute and is therefore the same in every province. Matters of health law, however, are determined at a provincial level and will differ from province to province. Our criminal code was first enacted in 1892, when we adopted a "draft" British code that was never enacted in Britain. Britain, to this day, has no criminal code. Almost as early as the concept of *mens rea*, or "guilty mind," and the rule "No crime without an evil intent" had begun to be accepted in English common law, "insanity" had to be taken into consideration, for a disordered mind may be regarded as unable to formulate and carry out a criminal purpose (Morse, 1992). In other words, a disordered mind cannot be a guilty mind; only a guilty mind can engender culpable actions.

Initially, insanity was not a trial defence, but in England, the Crown sometimes granted pardons to people who had been convicted of homicide if they were judged completely and totally "mad" (A.A. Morris, 1968). By the reign of Edward I (1272–1307), the concept of insanity had begun to be argued in court and could lessen punishment. It became the rule of law during the course of the 14th century that a person proved to be wholly and continually mad could be defended against a criminal charge.

In today's courts, judges and lawyers call on psychiatrists and clinical psychologists for assistance in dealing with criminal acts thought to result from the accused person's disordered mental state rather than from free will. Are such emotionally disturbed perpetrators less criminally responsible than those who are not distraught but commit the same crimes? Should such individuals even be brought to trial for transgressions against society's laws? Although efforts to excuse or protect an accused person by invoking the insanity defence or by judging him or her unfit to stand trial are undoubtedly well intentioned, invoking these doctrines can often subject those accused to a greater denial of liberty than they would otherwise experience.

THE NOT CRIMINALLY RESPONSIBLE DEFENCE

IN HAMILTON, Lucia Piovesan had been diagnosed as having had paranoid schizophrenia for over 20 years, but she received minimal treatment because she did not take her antipsychotic drugs. Moreover, she resisted family requests to get additional treatment. Tony Antidormi and his wife, Lori Triano-Antidormi (a former graduate student in psychology at York University), tried unsuccessfully on several occasions to convince police that their neighbour (Piovesan) was dangerous. In March 1997, Piovesan stabbed to death the Antidormi's 2-year-old son, Zachery, after becoming convinced that he was the soul of her dead son and was asking for release (see Prete, 2000). Piovesan was found not criminally responsible because of her paranoid schizophrenia.

Dorothy Joudrie, a wealthy Calgary socialite, apparently endured years of abuse from her former husband, Earl Joudrie, and as a result, developed a problem with alcoholism. The situation escalated in January 1995 when Joudrie shot her former husband six times and was arrested for attempted murder. Her lawyer argued that, at the time of the crime, Joudrie was in a dissociative, trance-like state (a condition known as automatism) and had no recollection of her actions. In May 1996, a jury found her not criminally responsible owing to a mental disorder, and she was confined at the Alberta Hospital in Edmonton for five months. Joudrie's mental state improved greatly over time, and she received an absolute discharge on October 20, 1998 (Martin, 1998). Until her death in 2002, she acted as an advocate for the rights of mentally ill people.

On May 28, 1998, two teenagers from British Columbia were killed when struck by a car driven by Julia Campagna of Seattle, Washington. Campagna's car was speeding and smashed into the back of the teenagers' car at the Canadian Customs border crossing. The driver was charged with dangerous driving causing death, but on September 3, 1999, a B.C. court ruled that Campagna was not criminally responsible on account of mental disorder. The accident occurred while Campagna was in a psychotic state. She had symptoms of psychosis after taking the diet drug Xenadrine to lose weight for a marathon running race. Campagna thought that she was in an airplane rather than a car and that she was hearing the voice of Canadian NHL hockey player Joe Nieuwendyk on her radio. She was following the voice's instructions, believing she was on her way to a rendezvous with Nieuwendyk to conceive a child with him.

Because her symptoms were deemed to be due to the pills she was taking (a finding that was confirmed by a B.C. Children's Commission investigation [see McLintock, 2001]), Campagna was released and allowed to go free, having been found not criminally responsible. The court ruled that Campagna posed no risk to the public and could not be held. Don Egleston, a University of British Columbia law professor, observed, "Before, this woman would have been locked up in a mental hospital for the criminally insane, and she probably would have spent 15 or 20 years there....It's an unhappy situation from the victims' point of view—a woman got off, and two girls are dead. But the only justification for keeping a person in custody now, the court says, is if they need treatment" (Ith, 1999). Julie Campagna subsequently launched a civil lawsuit against the drug manufacturer and other parties, and the families of the deceased launched civil lawsuits against Campagna and the drug manufacturer (see the Canadian Press, 2000).

The three cases described above all involved high-profile situations in which defendants in Canadian courts were found **not criminally responsible** for their acts on account of mental disorder (NCRMD). The so-called insanity defence, NCRMD involves the legal argument that a defendant should not be held responsible for an otherwise illegal act if it is attributable to mental illness that interferes with rationality or that results in some other excusing circumstance, such as not knowing right from wrong. Mental disorder may operate to negate the requisite mental element (*mens rea*), or it may operate to render the act (*actus reus*) involuntary. Or, it may operate to provide a supervening defence even where the requisite mental element and act have been proven. For example, an accused may specifically intend to kill his neighbour, believing him to be an alien sent to destroy the world. Here, the court may find that, notwithstanding the requisite elements having been proved, the accused did not appreciate the nature and consequences of his act or know it to be wrong. A staggering amount of material has been written on this defence, and public outcries continue to emerge in prominent cases in which the defendant is found not criminally responsible.

Concerns abound even though a review conducted by Canadian researchers (see Lymburne & Roesch, 1999) confirmed past findings suggesting that (1) the insanity defence is very rare, (2) it is usually only successful when applied to severely disordered individuals, and (3) people who are found to be insane are still detained for long periods of time that may greatly exceed the otherwise appropriate sentence. It is important to note that being found not criminally responsible does not result in an acquittal.

Stone (1975), a professor of law and psychiatry at Harvard University, proposed an intriguing reason for this great interest in finding certain people not guilty by reason of insanity (NGRI or later NCRMD in Canada). Criminal law rests on the assumption that people have free will and that if they do wrong, they have chosen to do so, are blameworthy, and should be punished. Stone suggested that the insanity defence strengthens the concept of free will by pointing to the few people who constitute an exception because they do not have it—namely, those judged to be insane. These individuals are assumed to have less responsibility for their actions because of a mental disorder, an inability to distinguish between right and wrong, or both. They lack the degree of free will that would justify holding them legally accountable for criminal acts. By exclusion, everyone else has free will! "The insanity defence is in every sense the exception that proves the rule. It allows the courts to treat every other defendant as someone who chose 'between good and evil'" (Stone, 1975, p. 222).

Landmark Cases in Canada In modern Anglo-American criminal law, several court rulings and established principles bear on the problems of legal responsibility and mental illness. Table 18.1 summarizes these rulings and principles.

According to Schneider et al. (2000), Canada's modern history with respect to the legal treatment of mentally disordered people began with the case of *Rex v. Hadfield* (1800) (see Table 18.1). Hadfield fired a shot in the direction of King George III because he believed that the king's death would herald the end of the world and the second advent of Christ (Ogloff & Whittemore, 2001). Hadfield was found not guilty by reason of insanity. This case is noteworthy because the chief justice overseeing the case returned Hadfield to prison but remarked that neither the prison environment nor the community were proper alternatives. This case led the British Parliament to enact the Criminal Lunatics Act, (1800), which provided the leeway for people to be sent to a place deemed fit by the court (i.e., a mental institution) rather than be incarcerated or set free. This provision was incorporated into a draft of the British Criminal Code and the first Criminal Code of Canada in 1892 (see Schneider et al., 2000, for a more complete description).

The M'Naghten Rules The well-known criteria, the M'Naghten Rules, were formulated in the aftermath of a murder trial in England in 1843. The accused, Daniel M'Naghten, had set out to kill the British prime minister, Sir Robert Peel, but had mistaken Peel's secretary, Sir Edward Drummond, for Peel. M'Naghten claimed that he had been instructed to kill Lord Peel by the "voice of God." As a result of a post-trial reference to the House of Lords, the M'Naghten Rules were articulated as follows:

> to establish a defence of insanity, it must be clearly proved that, at the time of the committing of the act, the party accused was labouring under such a defect of reason, from disease of the mind, as not to know the nature and quality of the act he was doing; or if he did know it, that he did not know he was doing what was wrong.

The rules are unique in that they are never read as part of a court's ruling at the conclusion of the trial, and they were not part of any legislation. Nevertheless, the M'Naghten Rules have had an unprecedented impact, as they were adopted not only in Britain but throughout all of the Commonwealth and most American jurisdictions as the test to be met in an insanity defence. Prior to the House of Lords' articulation as to the law, a defence of insanity could be raised, although different tests were employed in a haphazard, inconsistent manner. A key point to emphasize here is that the M'Naghten Rules apply to insanity at the time of the criminal act or omission.

The issue of being able to tell right from wrong as a component of the insanity defence has been the subject of some debate. According to Ogloff and Whittemore (2001), the Canadian legal system defined "wrong" in terms of legally wrong, but this was expanded by the Supreme Court of Canada in *Regina v. Chaulk* to include morally wrong as well.

The case of *Regina v. Swain* (1991) led to the proclamation of Bill C-30, which received royal assent on December 13, 1991, and was proclaimed on February 4, 1992. Bill C-30 created the mini-code in Part XX.1 within the Criminal Code of Canada dealing exclusively with the mentally disordered accused. The case involved a man who had acted in a threatening manner toward members of his family and was subsequently arrested for the crime of assault causing bodily harm. When the police arrived, they discovered that Swain "had swung his children over his head, scored a cross on his wife's chest, spoken about spirits, and fought with the air. At his arrest, he was speaking excitedly in religious themes" (Stuart et al., 2001, p. 528). He later testified that he was trying to save his family from the devil.

Swain recovered after receiving drug treatment and had lived in the community for over a year without incident when the day of his trial finally came. The insanity defence was raised by the Crown over his objections. Swain was found to be NGRI, but according to the Criminal Code provisions, he had to be held in "strict custody," even though he had been out on bail and problem-free at the time of the verdict. The Supreme Court, in reviewing the legislative scheme, found that the failure of the provisions to set a maximum time within which the accused's status must be reviewed constituted a violation of his Charter rights. The court noted that for many other similar situations Parliament had set limits on the amount of time that could pass before an accused's status had to be reviewed. While the case turned on this narrow point, the court expressed "concern" with respect to other features of the legislative scheme. Accordingly, Parliament was given six months to bring the legislation into Charter compliance. This gave birth to Bill C-30.

Bill C-30 included a key change in terminology. The phrase "not guilty by reason of insanity" was altered to "not criminally responsible on account of mental disorder" (NCRMD). Another change concerned the party to be responsible for the individual found NCRMD. Previously, the mentally disordered individual had been kept at the "pleasure" of the lieutenant governor, but now legal authority was allocated to provincial review boards. Ogloff and Whittemore (2001) noted that, prior to changes made to the Criminal Code in 1992, people who were found not guilty by reason of insanity were detained for an indeterminate length of time. However, as a result of *Regina v. Swain* (1991) and the subsequent proclamation of Bill C-30, review boards now determine the individual's fate within 45 days of the verdict and thereafter not less than annually. Review boards must weigh many factors, including the individual's current mental status and the risk to society posed by the individual. They can discharge the individual with or without conditions, or alternatively, they can order detention in a hospital setting.

Included in Bill C-30, which constitutes Part XX.1 of the Criminal Code of Canada, is a list of issues for which assessments may be ordered. The issues include fitness to stand trial, criminal responsibility, infanticide, and, the least onerous, disposition. Specific time limits are set for the assessment of the various issues. It is presumed, for example, that a fitness assessment will be completed within five days, but the maximum period of assessment is set at 60 days for com-

Table 18.1

Landmark Cases and the Disposition of the Mentally Ill in Canada

Case	Date	Significance
Rex v. Hadfield	1800	Led to changes such that mentally ill could be institutionalized rather than returned to prison or community. Accused were held at "His or Her Majesty's Pleasure."
Rex v. M'Naghten	1843	Was followed by a reference to the House of Lords that set a standard test for "insanity" that was subsequently adopted as the standard, with modifications, for the Western world. Is seen to mark the beginning of the modern insanity defence.
Regina v. Swain	1991	Led to creation of Bill C-30 and establishes jurisdiction of provincial review boards that can balance the individual's and the community's concerns; changes verdict from "not guilty by reason of insanity" to "not criminally responsible on account of mental disorder."
Regina v. Chaulk	1990	Specifies that "wrong" means morally wrong as well as legally wrong.
Regina v. Oommen	1994	The accused must not only be able to know what is wrong but be able to apply that knowledge at the time of the act.
Winko v. British Columbia	1999	If it cannot be determined whether a mentally disordered person is a significant threat to public safety, he or she must be discharged absolutely.

pelling situations. It is also presumed that all assessments will take place out of custody unless the Crown shows why this should not occur. Notwithstanding this presumption, most assessments take place on an inpatient basis because the subject of the assessment is often too unwell to be released into the community. While being assessed, an accused is not to be treated against his or her will. However, if the accused is found to be unfit to stand trial, the Crown may bring an application for the court to order that the accused be treated for up to 60 days in order to render him or her fit. This order, if the evidentiary hurdles are met, will be effected with or without the accused's consent.

Initial research on the impact of Bill C-30 was conducted in British Columbia. A comparison of a cohort of people found NGRI versus a newer cohort of those found NCRMD found a substantial increase in the number of cases following the enactment of Bill C-30, including a shift toward an increased number of cases involving people charged with less serious offences (Livingston, Wilson, Tien, & Bond, 2003). The average length of hospitalization for the NCRMD cohort (9.8 months) was much lower than for the NGRI cohort (47.7 months). Livingston et al. (2003) concluded, "The Bill C-30 provisions have made the NCRMD defence an attractive option for defendants and legal counsel" (p. 408).

Insanity and Mental Illness In general, the insanity defence requires applying an abstract principle to specific life situations. As in all aspects of the law, terms can be interpreted in a number of ways—by defendants, defence lawyers, prosecutors, judges, and jurors—and testimony can be presented in diverse fashion, depending on the skill of the interrogators and the intelligence of the witnesses. Furthermore, because the defendant's mental condition only at the time the crime was committed is in question, retrospective, often speculative, judgement on the part of attorneys, judges, jurors, and psychiatrists is required. And disagreement between defence and prosecution psychiatrists and psychologists is the rule.

A final point should be emphasized. There is an important difference between insanity and mental illness or defect. A person can be diagnosed as mentally ill and yet be held responsible for a crime. *Insanity* is a legal concept, not a psychiatric or psychological concept. And, while the Criminal Code of Canada defines "mental disorder"—the legal term—to mean "disease of the mind," the presence of mental disorder is a necessary but not a sufficient condition to make the defence of insanity. This distinction was made vivid by the February 15, 1992, conviction of Jeffrey Dahmer in Milwaukee, Wisconsin. He admitted to butchering, cannibalizing, and having sex with the corpses of 15 boys and young men. Dahmer plead guilty but mentally ill, and his sanity was the sole focus of an unusual trial that had jurors listening to conflicting testimony from mental health experts about the defendant's state of mind during the serial killings to which he had confessed. They had to decide whether he had had a mental disease that prevented him from knowing right from wrong or from being able to control his action. Even though there was no disagreement that he was mentally ill, diagnosable as having some sort of paraphilia, Dahmer was deemed sane and therefore legally responsible. He was sentenced by the judge to 15 consecutive life terms.

Insanity is a legal concept and differs from the psychological concept of mental illness. Jeffrey Dahmer, a serial killer and paraphiliac, seemed clearly psychopathological but was not judged insane because he was regarded as knowing right from wrong and as able to control his behaviour.

FITNESS TO STAND TRIAL

The insanity defence concerns the accused person's mental state at the time of the crime. A question that first arises is whether the person is competent or fit to stand trial at all. The mental fitness of individuals to stand trial must be decided before it can be determined whether they are responsible for the crime of which they are accused. The requirement that an accused be fit to stand trial was a refinement of the older principle that an accused had to be present before the state could proceed with its prosecution. The requirement of mere physical presence was expanded to require the accused to be "mentally present" as well. It is possible for a person to be judged competent to stand trial yet subsequently be deemed not criminally responsible by reason of mental disorder. In fact, that is the case for all accused raising the NCRMD defence in that they must be fit prior to commencing their trial. Fitness has to do with the accused's present condition—not how he or she might have been functioning at the time of the alleged offence.

Decisions may be changed on appeal if the fitness of the defendant is in question and has not been adequately assessed. For instance, Schneider (2001) related a recent case in which an Ontario Court of Appeal overturned a conviction for attempted murder because of a judge's failure to assess the fitness of the defendant. In this case, although the

Canadian Perspectives/18.1

Louis Riel and the Issue of Fitness to Stand Trial

Louis Riel is one of the most controversial figures in the history of Canada. Riel, of French Canadian and Métis background, was executed for his role in the Métis uprising in 1885 known as the North-West Rebellion. This armed rebellion stemmed from political and land disputes in Western Canada between the Métis and the federal government, and it involved the deaths of several North-West Mounted Police. Riel was executed for high treason after a jury found him guilty but recommended mercy.

One vexing question that remains to this day was whether Riel should have been deemed not criminally responsible due to mental disorder. An equally important and related issue is whether he was fit to stand trial. Riel had spent time in mental institutions on two separate occasions prior the uprising. His lawyers based his defence on the insanity plea, after other options failed, despite his vehement protests that he did not support this strategy.

Was Riel insane at the time of the act or, at the very least, unfit to stand trial because of an inability to participate in his own defence? Riel displayed many symptoms of megalomania (see Perr, 1992). He believed that he had been specially selected by the spirits to bring forth the message of the Métis. Similar tendencies to put aside one's personal identity and take on another identity (referred to as "misidentification of the self") have come to be described as "The Riel Phenomenon" (see Perr & Federoff, 1992).

The actual documents filed on Riel's behalf by his lawyer (Francois-Xavier Lemieux) and two psychiatrists (Dr. Roy and Dr. Clarke) contain vivid accounts of Riel's apparent deterioration (The *Queen vs. Louis Riel*, 1886). Lemieux noted in his declaration:

> While he was speaking he suddenly stops showing me his hand. "Do you see, says he, blood flowing in the veins; the telegraph is operating actively, and I feel it, they are talking about me, and questioning authorities, in Ottawa, about me."
>
> It is of similar fantastic visions he speaks with me every day. I am convinced that he is not acting a part, he speaks with a conviction and a sincerity which leave no doubt in my mind about the state of his mind, he has retracted his errors but he believes himself today to be a prophet and invested with a divine mission to reform the world on the day he has spoken to the Court and when I reprove him for his foolish and extravagant ideas, he answers that he submits, but that he cannot stifle the voice that speaks in him and the spirit that commands him to communicate to the world the revelations he receives. One must have the ferocious hatred of a fanatic or the stupidity of an idiot, to say that Riel is not a fool, because he is intelligent in other matters, as if history was not filled with such anomalies, among certain men who, remarkable in certain subjects, have lost the balance which contains intelligence within the limits from which it cannot escape without losing its privilege of guiding us or making us responsible for our own acts.
>
> ...The experience I have gained of this man by continual contact with him has only confirmed me more and more in the opinion I had already formed of him, that he is crazy and insane. ... I have just been visiting him, and during an hour he spoke of extraordinary revelations made to him by the spirit the previous night, and that he has been ordered to communicate to me and to all the Catholic clergy: "The great cause of sin in the world is the revolt of the body against the spirit, it is because we do not chew our food enough, and by this want of mastication it communicates animal life only to the body while by masticating and chewing it well, it spiritualizes the body." (p. 204)

The opinion offered by Lemieux was echoed by the two psychiatrists who concluded that Riel was insane and unable to discern right from wrong. However, the medical petition failed and Riel was eventually executed.

Thinking Critically

1. Do you think that Riel was not criminally responsible by reason of mental disorder, or was this simply a desperate attempt on the part of his defence team to avoid his execution? On the basis of your understanding of current legislation, do you think the same sentence and result would have been reached today?
2. Do you think it was ethical of Riel's lawyers and psychiatrists to proceed with the insanity defence against their client's wishes? What would you have done if you had been in their situation? Note that Riel felt that to argue his insanity would, in effect, undermine the cause of his people and the strength of his views.

attorney representing the Crown suggested to the judge that fitness might be an issue, the judge simply asked the accused whether he felt fit to stand trial (Schneider, 2001). Obviously, fitness needs to be established by trained professionals. Canadian Perspectives 18.1 further examines the fitness to stand trial issue (as well as the use of the insanity defence) in the complex case of Louis Riel.

Rather than relying on subjective clinical judgements to determine an individual's fitness (or lack of fitness) to stand trial, another alternative is to adopt measures developed in Canada to assist with the decision. One measure developed in Canada is the Fitness Interview Test—Revised (FIT-R;

Roesch, Zapf, Webster, & Eaves, 1999). The three components of this interview-based measure assess (1) whether the person understands the nature and purpose of the legal proceedings; (2) whether the person understands the possible or likely consequences of the proceedings; and (3) whether the person is capable of communicating with his or her lawyer. The FIT-R appears to have an exceptional level of validity; for example, a study conducted by Zapf and Roesch (1997) found that the measure resulted in no false negative errors (i.e., it did not call someone fit who is really not fit to stand trial). More recent research found that defendants with primary psychotic disorders had greater legal impairment than defendants with other psychiatric disorders in terms of their understanding of various aspects of the legal process and their rights (Viljoen, Roesch, & Zapf, 2002). However, impairment was widespread among other groups as well. For instance, 27 percent of those with no diagnosed mental disorder were deemed to have impaired understanding. It seems that IQ level is a key factor. In general, those with higher IQs were less likely to have a problem in understanding. The authors cautioned that a case-by-case functional assessment of legal abilities is required, and special efforts are needed to enhance the legal abilities of all suspects.

What role do psychologists play in fitness and criminal responsibility evaluations? According to a recent article by Viljoen, Roesch, Ogloff, and Zapf (2003), psychologists are regarded as qualified to provide assessments under the Youth Criminal Justice Act and dangerous offender legislation, but only medical practitioners are qualified to provide court-ordered assessments of fitness and criminal responsibility. However, as noted by Viljoen et al. (2003), psychologists often assist physicians by conducting psychological evaluations when requested. These authors also predicted that, in time, psychologists will play a larger role in fitness and criminality responsibility evaluations in Canada.

Judgements about the fitness to stand trial are still exceedingly difficult at times, and the possible influence of a dissociative state is an issue that further complicates the decision-making process. As noted earlier, in the Dorothy Joudrie case, the determination of a dissociative state was key to the court decision that she was not criminally responsible for shooting her husband. Focus on Discovery 18.1 delves into this issue by summarizing the unusual challenge posed by dissociative identity disorder in criminal commitments.

focus on discovery/18.1

Dissociative Identity Disorder and the Insanity Defence

Imagine that as you are having a cup of coffee, you hear pounding at the front door. You hurry to answer and find two police officers staring grimly at you. One of them asks, "Are you John Smith?" "Yes," you reply. "Well, sir, you are under arrest for grand theft and for the murder of Jane Doe." The officer then reads you your rights against self-incrimination, handcuffs you, and takes you to the police station, where you are allowed to call your lawyer. This would be a scary situation for anybody. What is particularly frightening and puzzling is that you have absolutely no recollection of having committed the crime that a detective later describes to you. You are aghast that you cannot account for the time period when the murder was committed—in fact, your memory is startlingly blank for that entire time. And, as if this were not bizarre enough, the detective then shows you a videotape in which you are clearly firing a shotgun at a bank teller during a holdup. "Is that you in the videotape?" asks the detective. You confer with your lawyer, saying that it certainly looks like you, including the clothes, but your lawyer advises you not to admit anything one way or the other.

Let's move forward in time now to your trial some months later. Witnesses have come forward and identified you beyond a reasonable doubt. You know of no one who can testify that you were somewhere other than at the bank on the afternoon of the crimes. And it is clear that the jury is going to find you descriptively responsible for the crimes. But did you murder the teller in the bank? You are able to assert honestly to yourself and to the jury that you did not. And yet even you have been persuaded that the person in the videotape is you and that that person committed the robbery and the murder.

The film *Primal Fear* with Richard Gere and Edward Norton portrayed an insanity defence in a case of dissociative identity disorder.

Because of the strange nature of the case, your lawyer arranged prior to the trial to have you interviewed by a psychiatrist and a clinical psychologist, both of them well-known experts in forensics. Through extensive questioning, they have decided that you have dissociative identity disorder (DID, formerly called multiple personality disorder) and that the crimes were committed not by you, John Smith, but by your rather violent alter, Dick. Indeed, during one interview, Dick emerged and boasted about the crime, even chuckling because you, John, would be imprisoned for it.

This fictional account is not as far-fetched as you might think. Mental health lawyers have for some time been concerned with such scenarios as they have wrestled with various aspects of the insanity defence, and psychologists are searching for research paradigms that can assist in determining the nature (i.e., validity) of amnesia in legal cases involving DID (see Allen & Iacono, 2001).

Note that nearly all the people who successfully use an insanity defence are diagnosable as having schizophrenia (or more generally, as psychotic) and that DID is regarded as a dissociative disorder (and used to be classified as one of the neuroses). Can DID be an excusing condition for a criminal act? Should John Smith be held ascriptively responsible for a crime committed by his alter, Dick? The quandary is clearly evident in the title of an article that addresses the DID issue: "Who's on Trial?" (Appelbaum & Greer, 1994).

Consider the legal principle that people accused of crimes should be punished only if they are blameworthy. In recent reviews of the DID literature and forensic implications, Saks (1992, 1997) argues that DID should be regarded as a special case in mental health law, that a new legal principle should be established, "irresponsibility by virtue of multiple personality disorder." Her argument takes issue with legal practice that would hold a person with DID responsible for a crime as long as the personality acting at the time of the crime intended to commit it.

What is intriguing about Saks's argument is that she devotes a major portion of it to defining personhood. What is a person? Is a person the body we inhabit? Well, usually our sense of who we are as persons does not conflict with the bodies we have come to know as our own or, rather, as us. But in DID, there is a discrepancy. The body that committed the crimes at the bank was John Smith. But it was his alter, Dick, who committed the crimes. Saks argues that, peculiar as it may sound, the law should be interested in the body only as a container for the person. It is the person who may or may not be blameworthy, not the body. They are usually one and the same, but in the case of DID, they are not. In a sense, Dick committed the murder by using John's body.

Then, is John blameworthy? The person John did not commit the crime; he did not even know about it. Saks argues that it would be unjust for the judge to sentence John, or more specifically, the body in the courtroom who usually goes by that name, because John is descriptively innocent. To be sure, sending John to prison would punish Dick, for whenever he would emerge, he would find himself imprisoned. But what of John? Saks concludes that we cannot imprison John because he is not blameworthy. Rather, we must find him not guilty by reason of dissociative identity disorder and remand him for treatment of the disorder.

Dissociative identity disorder would not, however, be a justification for a verdict of not criminally responsible if the alter that did not commit the crime was aware of the other alter's criminal intent and did not do anything to prevent the criminal act. Under these circumstances, argues Saks, the first alter would be complicit in the crime and blameworthy. Saks draws a comparison to Robert Louis Stevenson's fictional character of Dr. Jekyll and Mr. Hyde. Jekyll made the potion that caused the emergence of Mr. Hyde, his alter, with the foreknowledge that Hyde would do evil. So even though Jekyll was not present when Hyde was in charge, he would nonetheless be blameworthy because of his prior knowledge of what Hyde would do—not to mention that he, Jekyll, had concocted the potion that created his alter, Hyde.

Saks is optimistic about the effectiveness of therapy for DID and believes that people like John/Dick can be integrated into one personality and then released to rejoin society. Saks goes so far as to argue that people with DID who are judged dangerous but who have not committed a crime should be subject to civil commitment, even though this would be tantamount to preventive detention. In this way, she suggests, future crimes might be avoided.*

*It should be recalled that a substantial number of mental health professionals dispute the existence of DID. For them, Saks's arguments would not be persuasive.

CIVIL COMMITMENT

Historically, governments have had a duty to protect their citizens from harm. We take for granted the right and duty of government to set limits on our freedom for the sake of protecting us. Few drivers, for example, question the legitimacy of imposing limits on them by providing traffic signals that often make them stop when they would rather go. Government has a long-established right as well as an obligation to protect us both from ourselves—the *parens patriae*, "power of the state"—and from others—the police power of the state. *Civil commitment* is one further exercise of these powers.

In virtually all jurisdictions, a person can be committed to a psychiatric hospital against his or her will if a judgement is made that he or she is (1) mentally ill and (2) a danger to self, (i.e., unable to provide for the basic physical needs of food, clothing, and shelter) or a danger to others (Perlin, 1994). (There is also a form of outpatient commitment, which we describe later.)

Specific commitment procedures generally fit into one of two categories: formal or informal. Formal or judicial commitment is by order of a court. It can be requested by any responsible citizen: usually the police, a relative, or a friend seeks the commitment. If the judge believes that there is a good reason to pursue the matter, he or she will order a mental health examination. The person has the right to object to these attempts to "certify" him or her, and a court hearing can be scheduled to allow the person to present evidence against commitment. In Canada, this procedure is covered by provincial legislation that permits an *ex parte* hearing before a justice of the peace. Generally, this legislation permits a justice of the peace to have an individual held against his or her will a period of time (e.g. up to 72 hours in Ontario) for the purposes of assessment only. If, after that period of assessment, the individual meets the certification criteria, she or he may be held for longer periods, and most provinces have a process for subsequent involuntary treatment. Alternatively, where the prospective patient is compliant, a person may be brought to a physician who may, where the individual is seen as a danger to him/herself or to others, issue the same process. For example, in Ontario the form signed by the physician (Form 1) is in effect for seven days and is authority for a peace officer to take the individual to a psychiatric facility for assessment for up to 72 hours.

If seven days elapse, and an order of a physician or justice of the peace has not been effected, it is no longer valid.

Informal, emergency commitment of mentally ill persons can be accomplished without initially involving the courts. For example, if a hospital administrative board believes that a voluntary patient requesting discharge is too disturbed and dangerous to be released, it can detain the patient with a temporary, informal commitment order.

Civil commitment affects far more people than criminal commitment. It is beyond the scope of this book to examine the intricacies of civil commitment laws. Our aim is to present an overview that will provide a basic understanding of the issues and current directions of change.

Table 18.2 provides an overview of the current Canadian criteria for involuntary admission for the provinces and territories (see Gray & O'Reilly, 2001). Inspection of this table reveals considerable differences among the provinces in the criteria used. One overarching difference is that some jurisdictions use a broad definition of mental disorder, while others use a specific definition. Douglas and Koch (2001) noted that provinces with a specific definition actually use a functional definition of mental illness (cf. Robertson, 1994) that is quite detailed. The definition of mental disorder in Saskatchewan, for example, is "a disorder of thought, perceptions, feelings or behaviour that seriously impairs a person's judgment, capacity to recognize reality, ability to associate with others or ability to meet the ordinary demands of life, in which respect treatment is available" (p. 355). In contrast, as seen in Table 18.2, Ontario, Quebec, Nova Scotia, and Newfoundland and Labrador do not utilize such precise and detailed definitions of the impact of mental illness. In Ontario, mental disorder is defined simply as "a disease or disability of the mind" (see Douglas & Koch, 2001, p. 355).

The provinces and territories also differ in terms of how they define harm to self or others. Ontario, Alberta, and the Northwest Territories and Nunavut focus on a definition that emphasizes the possibility of physical harm. Douglas and Koch (2001) state that Alberta is particularly stringent in its conceptualization of dangerousness. Other jurisdictions have an expanded definition of harm that includes the possibility of a wider range of harmful acts that may or may not involve direct physical damage involving the self or others. Gray and O'Reilly (2001) note that four provinces include the additional criterion that the person is deemed likely to suffer further deterioration, either mental or physical.

The column on the far right of Table 18.2 shows that, at present, Saskatchewan is distinct in that even if other criteria are satisfied, individuals are not committed in this province if they are capable of making a treatment decision. Gray and O'Reilly (2001) indicated that this caveat exists to

Table 18.2

Canadian Criteria for Involuntary Admission by Jurisdiction

Jurisdiction	Definition of Mental Disorder	Harm Criterion	Deterioration as Alternative to Harm	Need for Treatment	Not Capable of Treatment Decision
British Columbia	Specific	Broad	Yes †	Yes	No
Alberta	Specific	Physical	No	No	No
Saskatchewan	Specific	Broad	Yes	Yes	Yes
Manitoba	Specific	Broad	Yes	Yes	No
Ontario	Broad	Physical	Yes	Yes & No	No
Quebec	Broad	? *	No	No	No
Nova Scotia	Broad	?	No	Implied	No
New Brunswick	Specific	Broad	No	Implied	No
Prince Edward Island	Specific	Broad	No	Implied	No
Newfoundland and Labrador	Broad	Broad	No	Implied	No
Yukon	Specific	Broad	No	No	No
Northwest Territories & Nunavut	Specific	Physical	No	No	No

Note: * The "?" signifies that it is not clear from the legislation or court cases how to classify. † The "Yes and No" represents yes for deterioration and no for bodily harm. Adapted with permission from Gray & O'Reilly (2001).

rule out situations in which a person is committed but then refuses the treatment needed in order to recover and eventually be discharged.

So, who experiences civil commitment in Canada? Crisanti and Love (2001) examined the admissions at the Department of Psychiatry at Calgary General Hospital for the years 1987 to 1995. Involuntary commitment was more likely to apply to males (54 percent); those who were committed involuntarily had substantially longer hospital stays than voluntary people; and involuntarily committed people were also more likely to be diagnosed with schizophrenia and be known to the justice system.

COMMUNITY COMMITMENT: COMMUNITY TREATMENT ORDERS

One controversial issue that has arisen in Canada involves the concepts of *involuntary community commitment* and *community treatment orders* (CTOs). The latter can be characterized as a form of **community commitment** designed to ensure treatment compliance. At present, four provinces have implemented some form of community treatment orders (i.e., Saskatchewan, Manitoba, British Columbia, and Ontario). In July 1995, Saskatchewan was the first province to implement CTOs (see Goering et al., 2000; O'Reilly, Keegan, & Elias, 2000), and Ontario is the most recent province to do so. CTOs stipulate that the individual will only be released back into the community if he or she adheres to recommended treatments. It is controversial topic because this condition of release essentially forces people to be treated, regardless of their wishes.

The Province of Saskatchewan has outlined several criteria that must be met in order for a CTO to be invoked (see O'Reilly et al., 2000):

1 Obviously, the person must have a mental disorder that requires treatment and the treatment can be provided in the community.
2 The person has received inpatient involuntary treatment for 60 cumulative days or more, has been in an inpatient facility on three or more occasions in the last two years, or has previously been the subject of a CTO.
3 The person may harm themselves or others or suffer from physical deterioration without care or supervision.
4 Services must exist in the community and must be available.
5 The person is unable to understand or is incapable of making an informed decision about the need for care and treatment as a result of his or her mental disorder.
6 The person is capable of complying with the requirements of a CTO.

According to the Centre for Addiction and Mental Health (CAMH), 63 CTOs were given over a three-year period (from a population of 6,000 people with serious mental illness) and 95 percent of people in Saskatchewan with a CTO had a diagnosis of schizophrenia (CAMH Best Advice Paper, 2000). A survey of Saskatchewan psychiatrists found that 62 percent were satisfied or extremely satisfied with the effects of CTOs on their patients, while only 10 percent were dissatisfied or extremely dissatisfied. However, CTOs are issued for only three months in Saskatchewan (as opposed to six months in Ontario), and survey respondents felt that the three-month period was too short (see O'Reilly et al., 2000).

The law establishing CTOs in Ontario came into effect and was proclaimed on December 1, 2000. It is named "Brian's Law" in memory of a popular Ottawa sportscaster who was killed by a man with paranoid schizophrenia who did not adhere to his prescribed treatment. The CTO criteria in Ontario differ slightly from those in Saskatchewan. A CTO may be issued if the person has two admissions or 30 cumulative days as an inpatient over a three-year period (see Gray & O'Reilly, 2001). Thus, the provinces differ in terms of the specific CTO details.

Although concerns have been raised about the coercive aspects of CTOs, it is interesting that the Province of Ontario, in describing the legislation, still maintains that all protections involving the issue of informed consent still exist. Also, according to this legislation (see Brian's Law [Mental Health Legislative Reform], 2000), individuals subjected to a CTO retain a number of rights, including

1 a right of review by the Consent and Capacity Board with appeal to the courts each time a CTO is issued or reviewed;
2 a mandatory review by the Consent and Capacity Board every second time a CTO is reviewed;
3 a right to request a re-examination by the issuing physician to determine if the CTO is still needed in order for the person to live in the community; and
4 a right of review of findings of incapacity to consent to treatment.

In Ontario, the procedure should really be referred to as a "community treatment agreement" because the patient is free to withdraw his or her consent at any time. When that is done, the "Order" comes to an end. There is a relative lack of research on the impact of CTOs in Canada, but there has been extensive research conducted in those American states that have implemented CTOs. By and large, these investigations point to the benefits of CTOs. For example, a current investigation in North Carolina by Swanson et al. (2001) found that patients who received long-term outpatient commitment had lower probabilities of being arrested than a comparison group, and the key factor accounting for this outcome was a reduced risk of violent behaviour. Thus, for the most part, these people seem to have benefited from the extended opportunity to experience a form of outpatient commitment.

Preventive Detention and Problems in Risk Assessment

The perception is widespread that mentally ill people account for a significant proportion of the violence that besets contemporary society, but this is not the case (Bonta, Law, & Hanson, 1998; Monahan, 1992). Only about 3 percent of the violence in the United States is linked clearly to mental illness (Swanson et al., 1990). Moreover, about 90 percent of people diagnosed as psychotic (primarily schizophrenia) are not violent (Swanson et al., 1990). Mentally ill persons—even allowing for their relatively small numbers—do not account for a large proportion of violent offences, especially when compared with substance abusers and people who are in their teens and twenties, are male, and are poor (Mulvey, 1994). Indeed, one recent study suggests that former mental patients who are not substance abusers are no more likely to engage in violence than are non-mentally ill individuals who are not substance abusers. Thus, if substance abuse is not involved, mentally ill people are no more prone to violence than the average person. Also, when former patients do act aggressively, it is usually against family members or friends and the incidents tend to occur at home (Steadman et al., 1998). By and large, then, the general public is seldom affected by violence from former mental patients. Thus, certain case studies outlined in this chapter are atypical in the sense that they involve violent and aggressive acts committed by people with mental disorders.

Nevertheless, there is a strong connection in the public mind between violence and mental illness, and this belief is central to society's justification of civil commitment (Monahan & Shah, 1989; Steadman et al., 1998) as well as to the stigma attached to having been a patient in a psychiatric institution (Link et al., 1987; Steadman et al., 1998). In fact, there is some evidence that mental disorder may sometimes contribute to violence, enough to justify preventive detention. In the Steadman et al. (1998) study just mentioned, for example, substance abuse increased the chances of violent behaviour more among discharged mental patients than among non-patient controls. We now examine the issues and the evidence.

The Prediction of Dangerousness The likelihood of committing an act that is dangerous to the self or others is central to civil commitment. Historically, the focus of assessment has been on the prediction of dangerousness, but more-contemporary approaches focus on the assessment of risk rather than the prediction of dangerousness (see Lyon, Hart, & Webster, 2001). Lyon et al. (2001) attribute the shift in emphasis to several factors, including results indicating that professionals tended to overestimate the incidence of violence when the institutionalized were released. Moreover, a focus on the dangerousness inherent in the individual promotes a tendency to attribute outcomes entirely to the dispositional traits of the individual and fail to take into account circumstantial and situational factors.

Regardless of which term is used, is dangerousness easily predicted or is risk easily assessed? Early studies examining the accuracy of predictions that a person would commit a dangerous act found that mental health professionals were poor at making this judgement (e.g., Kozol, Boucher, & Garofalo, 1972; Monahan, 1973, 1976; Stone, 1975). Collectively, there is an extensive literature on the limited validity of clinical judgements, including several studies conducted in Canada (e.g., Harris, Rice, & Quinsey, 1993; Menzies & Webster, 1995). The meta-analytic, quantitative review by Hanson and Bussière (1998) found that the ability of clinicians to predict recidivism among sex offenders is only slightly better than chance. The low validity of these judgements is a serious problem because of the weight given to such information. In fact, a recent Canadian study found that the senior clinician's testimony was the strongest predictor of the decision reached by tribunals in deciding whether to continue to detain forensic patients in maximum security (Hilton & Simmons, 2001).

One alternative is to make decisions on the basis of actuarial prediction. Actuarial prediction involves the use of statistical formulas comprised of factors that are significant predictors of dangerousness. The factors are weighted statistically in terms of their importance, based on the outcomes of previous studies.

Several actuarial measures have been developed in Canada to assist decision-makers. The PCL-R (Hare, 1991), discussed in Chapter 13, is a consistent predictor of criminal recidivism (see Heilbrun, Ogloff, & Picarrello, 1999) and is often included in risk assessment batteries, either as a stand-alone measure or as part of a broader assessment battery.

Recently, Lyon et al. (2001) summarized the strengths and criticisms of the actuarial approach. First, actuarial assessments are more likely than clinical ratings to use quantitative ratings and less likely to be influenced by subjective biases. Second, actuarial measures involve greater consistency because the creators of the measures have already specified with precision the information involved, the strategies for data coding, and required analyses. Also, according to Lyon et al., actuarial decisions are easy for others to review. However, these same authors note that actuarial approaches may be too rigid and cannot be altered to take into account individual factors of potential importance. In addition, actuarial measures are derived from specific populations, so the generalizability of statistical formulae to other populations is always an issue.

Lyon et al. (2001) noted that another alternative that is growing in popularity is to rely on more structured forms of clinical judgements instead of unstructured clinical judgements or actuarial approaches. The HCR-20 is a more structured assessment device developed in Canada (see Webster, Douglas, Eaves, & Hart, 1997). The "HCR" refers to historical variables, clinical variables, and risk variables. Historical variables include such factors as previous violence, early maladjustment at home or at school, history of serious mental disorder, other personality disorders, and so on. Current clinical variables include such indicators as being unresponsive to treatment, a lack of insight, and acting in an impulsive manner. Finally, additional risk variables include consideration of such factors as lack of social support and experience of stressful events.

Quinsey, Harris, Rice, and Cormier (1998) have criticized the HCR-20 on the grounds that it includes certain factors (e.g., a past history of serious mental disorder) that have not been robust predictors of risk in previous studies. Moreover, they have observed that the HCR-20 is not an actuarial measure in the truest sense because the checklist items were not selected on the basis of empirical links with outcomes. The assessment package they advocate using is described in Canadian Contributions 18.1, which examines the contributions of Marnie Rice.

Regardless of the criticism expressed by Quinsey et al. (1998), a growing number of studies attest to the predictive usefulness of the HCR-20. For instance, research led by Douglas from Simon Fraser University indicated that the HCR-20 is better than the Psychopathology CheckList Revised (PCL-R) at post-dicting previous acts of violence and antisocial behaviour in a sample of incarcerated offenders (Douglas & Webster, 1999). Note that post-diction involves the identification of variables that are found, after the fact, to distinguish violent tendencies. Another study by Douglas, Ogloff, Nicholls, and Grant (1999) demonstrated that the HCR-20 had predictive validity in terms of predicting subsequent acts of violence in a sample of 193 civilly committed patients, and once again, the HCR-20 outperformed the PCL-R screening version.

A more recent investigation conducted in the United Kingdom showed that even though the PCL-R had moderate predictive ability, the HCR-20 outperformed it in terms of subsequent acts of verbal aggression, physical aggression, and violence to property (Gray et al., 2003). However, Gray et al. (2003) also noted that studies with the HCR-20 have been conducted with psychiatric patients and, thus far, no study has been conducted with non-mentally disordered prisoners.

A recent court decision in the case of *Winko versus British Columbia* (see Table 18.1) further increases the importance of making accurate risk assessments. This case established that where there is uncertainty about whether an offender poses a risk, the onus is on the province in question to resolve this uncertainty, and if it cannot be resolved, the former offender must be released (see Schneider et al., 2000). In other words, unless the provincial review board can find affirmatively that the accused poses a significant threat to the safety of the public, he or she must be discharged absolutely. Previously, the law was interpreted such that if there was uncertainty about risk, then the person in question would remain subject to the jurisdiction of the provincial review board.

Parenthetically, another aspect of this case involved the issue of "capping provisions" and setting a standard for the maximum amount of time that a person could be detained. The issue was whether Winko and three other offenders with similar appeals could be detained, perhaps indefinitely, if risk of dangerousness was still evident (see Schneider et al., 2000). The court ruled that these individuals could indeed still be held if there was a risk in terms of dangerousness, with the caveat mentioned above that the risk of dangerousness had to be demonstrated.

Canadian Contributions/18.1

Marnie Rice and Actuarial Risk Assessment

Marnie Rice was made a fellow of the Royal Society of Canada in 2003. She has been a vital member of an effective research team based at the Oak Ridge Mental Health Centre in Penetanguishene, Ontario. Other team members include Grant Harris, Vernon Quinsey, and Catherine Cormier. Rice is the former director of research at the centre and, upon her recent retirement, holds the title of director of research emerita. Her collaborative work has contributed greatly to our understanding of forensic patients and risk assessment, and in recognition of this, she was the 1995 recipient of the American Psychological Association Award for Contribution to Research in Public Policy. She was given the award for "pioneering the rigorous empirical evaluation of risk assessment and risk reduction in difficult forensic populations. . . . With her colleagues Grant Harris and Vernon Quinsey, she has established a remarkable program of cutting-edge research on the actuarial assessment of violence risk" (American Psychological Association, 1996, p. 342). She has also studied social skills deficits and clinical treatment, and she developed a program for preventing institutional violence.

Marnie Rice has furthered the actuarial approach to risk assessment.

Rice and her colleagues developed the Violence Risk Appraisal Guide (VRAG; Rice & Harris, 1995) for the purposes of actuarial assessments of risk. The construction and development of the VRAG is described at length in Quinsey et al. (1998). Rice and her associates hoped to create an assessment tool that could predict over time which institutionalized offenders would have a new criminal charge from a violent act upon being released. The 12 variables that comprise the VRAG are displayed in Table 18.3. This table indicates that the two best predictors within the VRAG are scores on the revised Psychopathy Checklist (Hare, 1991) and a variable of elementary school maladjustment. The negative correlation between violent recidivism and age at the time of the index offence indicates that risk is higher to the extent that the offender was relatively young. Similarly, the negative correlation with schizophrenia indicates that it is associated with less risk (also see Rice & Harris, 1995). This variable underscores one of the main findings emerging from the work of Rice and her associates—namely, that mental disorder per se is not a risk factor. In fact, Rice (1997, p. 420) concluded that "violent recidivism among mentally disordered individuals is related to the same variables as among nonmentally disordered individuals," so there is no basis for public perceptions that link mental disorder with the possibility of violence.

A recent comparative study found that the VRAG predicted general recidivism, as well as sexual and violent recidivism, thus supporting the actuarial approach (Barbaree, Seto, Langston, & Peacock, 2001). Prospective research involving a five-year follow-up of the original cohort of forensic patients found that the VRAG was a strong predictor of violent recidivism and a robust predictor of extreme violence (Harris, Rice, & Cormier, 2002). Comparative research of four actuarial measures found that the VRAG was comparable or superior to these measures in predicting violent recidivism and sexually motivated recidivism (Harris et al., 2003). Finally, in a very specific context, Rice and Harris (2003) found that the VRAG was a good predictor of violent and sexual recidivism by father-daughter child molesters, even though it was the case that these child molesters had lower scores on the VRAG and lower rates of recidivism than non-familial child molesters.

A general finding that has emerged from research conducted in Canada is that it is the psychopaths among us who are especially likely to reoffend in a violent manner (see Rice & Harris, 1995; Serin & Amos, 1995). Rice (1997) is quite pessimistic about the chances of treating and rehabilitating the psychopaths who have participated in her research investigations, in part because some findings indicate that treatment actually yields worse outcomes. For these people, treatment is a chance to improve their social skills and increase their charm in order to further mislead unsuspecting victims. As a result, Rice has decided to concentrate her efforts on developing measures such as the VRAG that may be used to identify these people, so members of the court and review boards will be aware of whom they are evaluating. Evidence continues to attest to the validity of the measure. For instance, Rice and Harris (1997) showed that the VRAG predicted violent recidivism among sex offenders. One extension of work in this area is a version of the VRAG designed specifically for sex offenders, the Sex Offenders Risk Appraisal Guide (SORAG; see Quinsey et al., 1998).

Table 18.3

Violence Risk Appraisal (VRAG) Variables and Pearson Correlations with Violent Recidivism

Variable	Correlation
Revised Psychopathy Checklist score	.34
Elementary School Maladjustment score	31
Meets DSM-III criteria for any personality disorder	.26
Age at the time of the index offence	-.26
Separation from either parent (except death) under age 16	.25
Failure on prior conditional release	.24
Non-violent offence history score (using the Cormier-Lang scale)	.20
Never married (or equivalent)	.18
Meets DSM-III criteria for schizophrenia	-.17
Most serious victim injury (from the index offence)	-.16
Alcohol abuse score	.13
Female victim in the index offence	-.11

Note: Adapted from Quinsey et al. (1988, p. 147), Exhibit 8.1. Reprinted with permission from the American Psychological Association.

Litwack (2001) concluded that the VRAG is the best actuarial tool for assessing dangerousness to date. Still, significant concerns remain. First, we are still a long way from being able to use actuarial measures to determine levels of dangerousness with absolute certainty. The correlation between the VRAG and the outcome measure of violent recidivism is approximately $r = .44$ (see Rice, 1997), which means that almost four-fifths of the variance in this important outcome measure still remains to be predicted. Indeed, in our discussions with numerous clinical practitioners who have used the VRAG in their own work, we learned that a significant number found the VRAG not very useful in helping them make meaningful predictions. Violence is a product of the individual's personal characteristics (including the consumption of drugs and/or alcohol) and the environment within which he or she is functioning. To make the point, you could take two clinically similar individuals with identical VRAG scores and place them in two very different environments—one will probably reoffend, whereas the other possibly will not. Much of the variance in violent recidivism is accounted for by environmental factors that are probably not captured by instruments such as the VRAG. Second, although Litwack (2001) concluded that the VRAG is the best assessment device available, he feels that it must receive more validation in order to be used to make the important decision of whether a person should be detained because of his or her dangerousness. Third, as a general criticism of the actuarial approach, Rogers (2000) noted that current measures are limited by their focus on negative predictors involving risk instead of protective factors that increase an offender's resilience when back in society.

Finally, as noted earlier, other risk assessment measures, such as the HCR-20, have been developed. Proponents of the HCR-20 believe that it is more suitable because it includes an assessment of dynamic, changing clinical risks factors. In addition, these researchers emphasize the importance of a multi-faceted approach that incorporates actuarial assessment within a model that also includes structured clinical judgements by trained professionals (Douglas, Ogloff, & Hart, 2003). Rice, Harris, and Quinsey (2002), however have suggested that while dynamic predictors help predict *when* an individual is likely to offend or reoffend, they are of limited usefulness in determining *who* is at greatest risk of offending.

Overall, in light of these concerns, the prediction of dangerousness remains a complicated and very difficult enterprise. Nevertheless, the work and contributions of Marnie Rice and her colleagues have illustrated the potential usefulness of actuarial measures.

Some researchers have gone so far as to argue that civil commitment for the purposes of preventive detention should be abolished. Reconsideration of earlier research suggests that greater accuracy can be achieved in predicting dangerousness in the longer term (Monahan, 1984; Monahan & Steadman, 1994; Steadman et al., 1998). Violence prediction becomes more accurate under the following conditions (note the role played by situational factors, sometimes in interaction with personality variables) (e.g., Campbell, Stefan, & Loder, 1994):

- If a person has been repeatedly violent in the recent past, it is reasonable to predict that he or she will be violent in the near future unless there have been major changes in the person's attitudes or environment. Thus, if a violent person is placed in a restrictive environment, such as a prison or high-security psychiatric hospital facility, he or she may well not be violent, given the markedly changed environment.
- If violence is in the person's distant past and constituted a single but very serious act, and if that person has been incarcerated for a period of time, then violence can be expected on release if there is reason to believe that the person's pre-detention personality and physical abilities have not changed and the person is going to return to the same environment in which he or she was previously violent.
- Even with no history of violence, violence can be predicted if the person is judged to be on the brink of a violent act—for example, if the person is pointing a loaded gun at an occupied building.

In addition, as stated earlier, the presence of substance abuse significantly raises the rate of violence (Steadman et al., 1998). This finding supports the inclusion of substance abuse among the factors to be considered when attempting to predict violence. (Substance abuse predicts violence also among non-mentally disordered individuals [Gendreau, Little, & Goggin, 1996].) Violence in discharged mental patients is usually attributable to that small percentage of individuals who do not take their medication (Monahan, 1992) or, possibly, who self-medicate. Outpatient commitment is one way to increase medication compliance.

For a detailed discussion of the responsibility of therapists to predict dangerousness, see Focus on Discovery 18.2.

focus on discovery/18.2

The Tarasoff Case—The Duty to Warn and to Protect

The client's right to privileged communication—the legal right of a client to require that what goes on in therapy remain confidential—is an important protection, but it is not absolute. Society has long stipulated certain conditions in which confidentiality in a relationship should not be maintained because of harm that can befall others. A famous California court ruling in 1974[1] described circumstances in which a therapist not only may but must breach the sanctity of a client's communication. The facts in this case are outlined below.

IN 1968, Prosenjit Poddar, a graduate student from India studying at the University of California at Berkeley, met Tatiana (Tanya) Tarasoff at a folk dancing class. They saw each other weekly during the fall, and she kissed him on New Year's Eve. Poddar interpreted this act as a sign of formal engagement (as it might have been in India, where he was a member of the Harijam or "untouchable caste"). [But] Tanya told him that she was involved with other men, and indicated that she did not wish to have an intimate relationship with him.

Poddar was depressed as a result of the rebuff, but he saw Tanya a few times during the spring (occasionally tape recording their conversations in an effort to understand why she did not love him). Tanya left for Brazil in the summer, and Poddar at the urging of a friend went to the student health facility where a psychiatrist referred him to a psychologist for psychotherapy. When Tanya returned in October 1969, Poddar discontinued therapy. Based in part on Poddar's stated intention to purchase a gun, the psychologist notified the campus police, both orally and in writing, that Poddar was dangerous and should be taken to a community mental health centre for psychiatric commitment.

The campus police interviewed Poddar, who seemed rational and promised to stay away from Tanya. They released him and notified the health service. No further efforts at commitment were made because the supervising psychiatrist apparently decided they were not needed and, as a matter of confidentiality, requested that the letter to the police and certain therapy records be destroyed.

On October 27, Poddar went to Tanya's home armed with a pellet gun and a kitchen knife. She refused to speak to him. He shot her with the pellet gun. She ran from the house, was pursued, caught, and repeatedly and fatally stabbed by him. Poddar was found guilty of voluntary manslaughter rather than first- or second-degree murder. The defence established with the aid of the expert testimony of three psychiatrists that Poddar's diminished mental capacity, paranoid schizophrenia, precluded the malice necessary for first- or second-degree murder. After his prison term, he returned to India, where, according to his own report, he is happily married (Schwitzgebel & Schwitzgebel, 1980, p. 205).

Under the privileged communication statute of California, the counselling centre psychologist properly breached the confidentiality of the professional relationship and took steps to have Poddar civilly committed, for he judged Poddar to be an imminent danger. Poddar had stated that he intended to purchase a gun, and he had convinced the therapist that he was desperate enough to harm Tarasoff. What the psychologist did not do, and what the court decided he should have done, was to warn the likely victim, Tanya Tarasoff, that her former friend had bought a gun and might use it against her. Such a warning would have been consistent with previous court decisions requiring physicians to warn the public when they are treating people with contagious diseases and requiring mental institutions to warn others when a dangerous patient has escaped (Knapp & Vandecreek, 1982). The Tarasoff ruling, now being applied in other states as well,[2] requires clinicians, in deciding when to violate confidentiality, to use the very imperfect skill of predicting dangerousness.

EXTENDING PROTECTION TO FORESEEABLE VICTIMS

A subsequent California court ruling[3] held, by a bare majority, that foreseeable victims include those in close relationship with the identifiable victim. In this instance, a mother was hurt by a shotgun fired by a dangerous patient, and her 7-year-old son was present when the shooting took place. The boy later sued the psychologists for damages brought on by emotional trauma. Since a young child is likely to be in the company of his or her mother, the court concluded in this case that the Tarasoff ruling extended to the boy.

CHILLING EFFECT OF TARASOFF?

In the years since the Tarasoff ruling, professionals have wondered whether it would have a negative effect, perhaps even a chilling effect, on psychotherapists. If clients are informed of this limitation to confidentiality, they may become reluctant to express feelings of extreme anger to therapists for fear that therapists will notify the people with whom they are angry. Clients might become less open with their therapists, perhaps derive less benefit from therapy, and even become more likely to inflict harm if they have not disclosed their fury as a first step toward controlling it. The welfare of the people whom the Tarasoff decision intended to protect might be endangered by the very ruling itself!

It is unclear whether these concerns are well-founded. A survey of psychologists and psychiatrists in California soon after Tarasoff became law indicated that the court decision was affecting their thinking and practices (Wise, 1978). On the plus side, one-third reported consulting more often with colleagues concerning cases in which violence was an issue. This practice should have a good outcome, since input from other professionals may improve the solitary clinician's decision-making, presumably to the benefit of the client. (Consultation can also demonstrate that the clinician took extra steps to adhere to Tarasoff, which can reduce legal liability [Monahan, 1993].) On the minus side, about 20 percent of the respondents indicated that they avoided asking their clients questions about violence, an ostrichlike stance that may keep the clinician from obtaining important information and yet reduces his or her legal liability should the client harm someone. A substantial number of therapists were keeping less detailed records, again in an effort to reduce legal liability.

As for Canada, the courts have not established that it is the duty of psychologists to warn or protect others (see Heilbrun, Ogloff, and Picarello, 1999), but codes of ethics by professional organizations such as the Canadian Psychological Association stipulate clearly that psychologists must breach confidentiality when there is reason to suspect that a third party is at risk (see Ogloff, 1999). Thus, although confidentially typically prevails in the therapeutic setting, certain circumstances can lead the therapist to inform others of the possible dangers.

In a Tarasoff situation, the clinician is seeing a client in a counselling capacity and comes to suspect that third persons may be at risk. What about the forensic context? The Supreme Court of Canada has visited this issue with results that are as "chilling" as the civil context of Tarasoff. In *Smith versus Jones* (1999), Jones (an alias), the accused, was charged with a number of sexual assaults on prostitutes in the Vancouver area. Counsel for the accused retained the services of a psychiatrist—Smith (also an alias)—to conduct a psychiatric assessment of his client. This is a routine procedure for defence counsel and is usually perceived to be risk-free, as the psychiatrist's assessment would be privileged in that he or she is acting in the capacity of counsel's agent or, alternatively, under the umbrella of the "solicitor-client brief." In *Smith versus Jones*, the psychiatrist, Smith, contacted counsel for the accused to inquire when the trial was to commence. Counsel advised Smith repeatedly that he would not be needed (in that his report was quite negative). Smith persisted, indicating that Jones was very dangerous and prospective victims should be warned. Counsel continued to rebuff Smith. Finally, Smith retained counsel and sought to intervene. The case went to the B.C. Trial Division, Court of Appeal, and finally to the Supreme Court of Canada, where it was held that, notwithstanding the privilege that would normally be expected in a situation of this sort, where a mental health professional is retained by counsel to perform an assessment and as a result of that assessment the accused is seen as a an imminent threat of serious bodily harm to an identifiable victim or class of victims, the clinician has an obligation to notify whoever, including the police, may be appropriate in the circumstances.

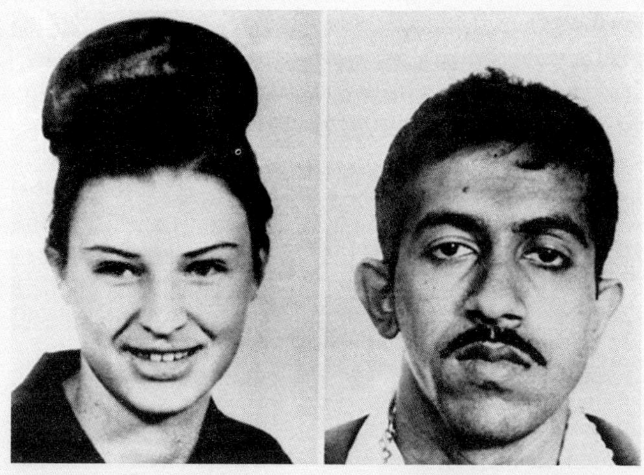

Prosenjit Poddar was convicted of manslaughter in the death of Tatiana Tarasoff. The court ruled that his therapist, who had become convinced Poddar might harm Tarasoff, should have warned her of the impending danger.

In this instance, Jones had outlined to Smith his detailed plans to kidnap and kill a small prostitute who could be physically overpowered. Jones planned to strangle the victim and dispose of her body in the bush near Hope, B.C. Jones had been diagnosed with multiple paraphilias, including sexual sadism, as well as drug abuse problems.

As a result of this decision, the defence bar is no longer able to rely upon the law of agency or the privilege that would attach to the gathering of information in anticipation of litigation—the solicitor-client brief. The frequency of referrals for assessments is anticipated to plummet, and ironically, it can be argued that the public safety concern driving the decision of the Supreme Court has actually been set back because now the prospectively dangerous accused will not be sent off for assessment by the defence bar unless the assessment is absolutely crucial. It is ironic because this is the clearest statement in Canada of a duty to warn and the decision is based on the principle that concerns about public safety outweigh the interest of doctor-patient confidentiality (Canadian Psychiatric Association, 2000). The Canadian Psychiatric Association (2004) has responded to the case of *Smith versus Jones* by concluding that the position about the duty to warn taken by the Supreme Court of Canada is to be accepted as a professional standard of practice.

[1] *Tarasoff v. Regents of the University of California*, 529 P.2d 553 (Cal. 1974), vacated, reheard in bank, and affirmed, 131 Cal. Rptr. 14, 551 P.2d 334 (1976). The 1976 California Supreme Court ruling was by a four-to-three majority.

[2] *White vs. United States*, 780 F2D 97 (D.C. Cir. 1986); *Soutear vs. United States*, 646 F.Supp. 524 (1986); *Dunkle vs. Food Services East Inc.*, 582 A.2d. 1342 (1990); *People vs. Clark*, 50 Cal. 3d 583, 789 P.2d 127 (1990).

[3] *Hedlund vs. Superior Court*, 34 Cal.3d 695 (1983).

Recent Trends Towards Greater Protection

We turn now to a discussion of several issues and trends that revolve around the greater protections being provided to mental patients in recent years: the right to treatment, the right to refuse treatment, and questions of free will in the law. We begin with a discussion of how to resolve complicated situations in which several themes may conflict in efforts to provide humane mental health treatment while respecting individual rights. We shall see that competing interests operate to create a complex and continually changing picture.

Choosing among Ethical Principles The ethical code prescribed by the American Psychological Association (APA) first appeared in 1953, and it was adopted and used for many years with minor changes by the Canadian Psychological Association and provincial associations (Sinclair, Poizner, Gilmour-Barrett, & Randall, 1987). One factor that provided the impetus for a separate code for Canadian psychologists was dissatisfaction with changes made to the APA code in 1979 (see Sinclair, 1993). Specifically, Canadian psychologists were concerned about a change that loosened restrictions on advertising by psychologists. As a result, work was undertaken on a Canadian code of ethics in the 1980s, leading in 1986 to the first Canadian Code of Ethics for Psychologists. The third edition of this code was recently published (Canadian Psychological Association, 2000).

A particularly useful aspect of the Canadian ethics code is that it assists psychologists who must make decisions in situations where various ethics may be in conflict (Sinclair et al., 1987). Psychologists were surveyed about how they would respond to hypothetical scenarios, and the four most relevant principles were identified and rank-ordered in terms of their importance. These are the four principles:

1. *Respect for the dignity of persons*. This principle is given the most weight, especially when there is the possibility that anyone will be exposed to physical danger.
2. *Responsible caring*. This provision includes the notion that responsible caring only occurs when it is provided by competent individuals who are able to respect the dignity of other people.
3. *Integrity in relationships*. This principle applies to all relationships, but it is noted in the code of ethics that there may be times when a need to be open and candid with an individual may conflict with the need to respect the dignity of others, and if so, the emphasis is on respecting the dignity of others.
4. *Responsibility to society*. The ranking of this ethical principle as the fourth consideration in no way suggests that this is not an important guideline. Rather, the Canadian Code of Ethics for Psychologists emphasizes that when there is a conflict between the needs of the individual and the needs of society, the need to preserve the dignity of the individual should prevail.

The notion of responsibility to society is important because it stipulates that psychologists have a general duty to promote the welfare of human beings and enhance our society. This principle was seen as particularly important by Dobson, Dobson, and Ritchie (1993). In their call for involvement, they observed that "sustained advocacy by professional psychology on a range of issues linking psychological knowledge, expertise and practice with the public good is both an ethical requirement, particularly from the perspective of social responsibility, as well as a matter of enlightened self-interest. Although there have been some examples of political advocacy, there are other areas in which psychology has been mute or passively acquiescent. The profession requires a system to derive clear and defensible social policy positions as well as the ability to act upon these positions" (p. 451). The importance of this approach is certainly evident to the many psychology students in Canada who embrace similar values and become actively involved as volunteers in their local communities.

Right to Treatment Another aspect of civil commitment that has received the attention of the courts is the so-called right to treatment, a principle first articulated by Birnbaum (1960). If a person is deprived of liberty because he or she is mentally ill and is a danger to self or others, is the state not required to provide treatment to alleviate these problems? Is it not unconstitutional (and even indecent) to incarcerate someone without then providing the required help? This key question has been the subject of several court cases since Birnbaum first articulated the issue.

In *O'Connor versus Donaldson* (1975), a celebrated case in the United States that eventually went to the Supreme Court, a civilly committed mental patient sued two state hospital doctors for his release and for monetary damages on the grounds that he had been incarcerated against his will for 14 years without being treated and without being dangerous to himself or to others. In January 1957, at the age of 49, Kenneth Donaldson had been committed to a Florida state hospital on petition of his father, who felt that his son was delusional. A county judge had found that Donaldson had paranoid schizophrenia and committed him for "care, maintenance, and treatment." The Florida statute then in effect allowed for such commitment on the usual grounds of mental illness and dangerousness, the latter defined as inability to manage property and to protect oneself from being taken advantage of by others.

In 1971 Donaldson sued Dr. O'Connor, the hospital superintendent, and Dr. Gumanis, a hospital psychiatrist, for release. Evidence presented at the trial indicated that the hospital staff could have released Donaldson at any time following a determination that he was not a dangerous person. Testimony made it clear that at no time during his hospitalization had Donaldson's conduct posed any real danger to others or to himself. Furthermore, just before his commitment in 1957, he had been earning a living and taking adequate care of himself (and immediately on discharge he secured a job in hotel administration). Nonetheless, O'Connor had repeatedly refused the patient's requests for release, feeling it was his duty to determine whether a committed patient could adapt successfully outside the institution. His judgement was that Donaldson could not. Several responsible people had attempted to obtain Donaldson's release by guaranteeing that they would look after him. O'Connor refused, saying that the patient could be released only to his parents, who by this time were quite old.

The evidence indicated that Donaldson received only custodial care during his hospitalization. No treatment that could conceivably alleviate or cure his assumed mental illness was undertaken. The milieu therapy that O'Connor claimed Donaldson was undergoing consisted of being kept in a large room with 60 other patients, many of whom were under criminal commitment. Donaldson had been denied privileges to stroll around the hospital grounds or even to discuss his case with Dr. O'Connor. O'Connor also regarded as delusional Donaldson's expressed desire to write a book about his hospital experiences (which Donaldson did after his release; the book sold well).

The original trial and a subsequent appeal concluded that Donaldson was not dangerous and had been denied his constitutional right to treatment. Throughout this litigation, Donaldson declared that he was neither dangerous nor mentally ill. But, said his claim, even if he were mentally ill, he should be released because he was not receiving treatment. The Supreme Court ruled on June 26, 1975, that "a State cannot constitutionally confine...a nondangerous individual who is capable of surviving safely in freedom by himself or with the help of willing and responsible family members or friends." In 1977 Donaldson settled for $20,000 from Dr. Gumanis and the estate of Dr. O'Connor, who died during the appeals process.

The Supreme Court decision on *O'Connor versus Donaldson* created a stir when it was issued and has since given mental health professionals pause in detaining patients. Although this decision is often cited as yet another affirmation of the right to treatment, the Supreme Court did not, in fact, rule on the constitutionality of this doctrine. The Donaldson decision did say that a committed patient's status must be periodically reviewed, for the grounds on which a patient was committed cannot be assumed to continue in effect forever. In other words, people can change while in a mental hospital and may no longer require confinement. This position seems straightforward enough, yet it may still be overlooked. Take for example, a 1986 court decision involving a woman with mental retardation who had spent her entire adult life in a state institution for the retarded after having been committed at age 15; during her 20 years of confinement, she was never given a hearing to reconsider the grounds for the original commitment (*Clark versus Cohen*, 1986).

Presumably, a situation such as that found in *Donaldson versus O'Connor* would not occur in Canada in that a precondition to civil commitment is a finding of danger to self or others, which is reviewed every 90 days or upon the patient's request.

Right to Refuse Treatment If a committed patient has the right to expect appropriate treatment, does he or she have the right to refuse treatment or a particular kind of treatment? The answer is yes, depending on the province in question.

The case of *Regina versus Rogers* (1991; see Table 18.1), in British Columbia reiterated that mentally disordered individuals have the right to refuse treatment, even if they were civilly committed against their personal wishes. Currently, the situation is more complicated when viewed from a national perspective. Douglas and Koch (2001) have provided an up-to-date summary of how the right to refuse treatment varies from province to province. Some provinces maintain the patient's right to refuse treatment (e.g., Nova Scotia, Quebec, Ontario, and Manitoba), while others (e.g., Prince Edward Island, Newfoundland and Labrador, New Brunswick, and British Columbia) have provisions that allow for treatment without the individual's consent. The situation is more complicated in Alberta, where mental health officials having the opportunity to apply to a review panel in order to override the patient's right to refuse treatment (Douglas & Koch, 2001). Typically, when the patient's right to refuse treatment is circumvented, a substitute decision-maker (i.e., family member) is asked to provide consent.

One alternative in provinces where a person can be given treatment without his or her consent is to have the person outline his or her wishes during a time when they were of sounder mind. According to Simmie and Nunes (2001), this concept is known as establishing a person's **prior capable wish** and this wish has been ruled valid in court cases in both Canada and the United States.

In Ontario, patients can only be treated against their will civilly where they are determined to be incapable of consent. In such cases, a scheme exists whereby substitute consent to treatment may be obtained. A potentially more interesting question arises around patients who do consent to treatment! Curiously, the issue of capacity to consent is rarely raised where the patient does consent to treatment. What percentage of those patients currently being treated "voluntarily" are actually incapable of consenting to their treatment?

Recently, in the case of *Starson versus Swayze* (2003), the Supreme Court of Canada confirmed the patient's right to refuse treatment. This case is the subject of Canadian Perspectives 18.2.

Canadian Perspectives/18.2

"A Beautiful Mind" in Canada? Scott Starson and the Right to Refuse Treatment

In some respects, Scott Starson is similar to John Nash, who was the subject of the book *A Beautiful Mind* by Nasar and the subsequent Academy Award winning movie starring Russell Crowe. Nash won a Nobel Prize in Economics for his contribution to game theory. He has a history of schizophrenia. Starson is a highly intelligent person with an abiding interest and expertise in physics as it pertains to the study of discrete antigravity and its implications for space travel.

Starson, who prefers to be referred to as Professor Starson, has authored some highly regarded articles in scientific journals despite not having any formal training in physics and not being an actual professor. Starson suffers from schizoaffective disorder, a condition that combines symptoms of schizophrenia and bi-polar depression. In 1998 he was found not criminally

Scott Starson is a physics savant.

responsible on account of mental disorder after uttering death threats. Specifically, he phoned his work colleagues and informed them that he was in a phone booth with a rifle and was going to shoot the sales manager of a car dealership where he had been turned down for a lease or loan (Wente, 2003). He also threatened to kill his psychiatrist (Bailey, 2002).

Starson is an involuntary psychiatric patient who has been detained in psychiatric hospitals in Penetanguishene and Ottawa and has experienced mental difficulties since 1985. There is no doubt that he suffers from mental illness. According to one interview account, he indicated that "Pope John Paul II works for me now." He also indicated that he had plans to wed comedian Joan Rivers, though he had never met her. He also believes that former prime minister Pierre Elliott Trudeau was killed by an alien (see Bailey, 2003).

Starson has gained notoriety for successfully winning a legal case in which his right to refuse treatment was upheld by the Supreme Court of Canada in a 6 to 3 decision. He argued that the drug medication was ineffective and would take away his mental faculties. In his statement to the Court of Appeal for Ontario, he observed:

> Well, like all psychiatrists that I've met before them, they all think the same way, that the only thing they can do is to give you these chemicals—and I've been through these chemicals that they propose before—and I know the effects and what they want to achieve is slow down my brain, basically, and to slow down my brain which means I can't do what I've been trying to do—or what I have been doing for 30 years and will be successful at doing. And that would just be like worse than death.

In its ruling, the Supreme Court of Canada supported the ruling of two previous courts that had overturned the initial ruling of the Ontario Consent and Capacity Board (CCB), which ruled that Starson had to consent to treatment.

The Supreme Court of Canada based its decision on the observation that the Ontario CCB based its initial ruling on what the board felt was in the best treatment interests of Starson rather than on a strict interpretation of his legal rights (see Brooks, O'Reilly, & Gray, 2003). It is still the case that patients have the right to refuse treatment if they are deemed to be capable of making this decision, but if it can be shown that they are incapacitated based on "a balance of probabilities," then treatment can be forced on them (Brooks et al., 2003).

Regardless of whether one agrees with the Supreme Court decision, it is hard not to feel sorry for Starson's mother, Jeanne Stevens. According to Bailey (2003), she wants her son to receive treatment and, in reaction to the court decision, she stated, "I'm devastated. I don't think what they did was a humane judgement. It's a disaster because they have destroyed his life and his dream."

Starson does acknowledge that he has mental problems, but he notes that he distrusts psychiatry, which he views as a religion. By the way, Starson's original surname is Schutzman. According to his mother, he changed it in 1993 because "he actually thought he was the son of the stars."

Thinking Critically

1. Do you agree or disagree with the Supreme Court decision? Do you think Starson should have the right to refuse treatment?
2. The Supreme Court decision was based on a strict interpretation of Starson's legal rights. What about the feelings and wishes of Starson's mother? Does she have any right to support forced treatment? Was the Court's decision inhumane?
3. Are there any circumstances when it is in society's best interests for a person to be treated against his or her will?

Opponents of the right to refuse treatment are concerned that mental hospitals will revert to being warehouses of poorly treated patients. Psychiatrists fear that lawyers and judges will not accept that some people are too mentally ill to be believed, too mentally disturbed to be able to make sound judgements about their treatment. In a book on what he calls America's mental health crisis, psychiatrist E. Fuller Torrey asserts that upwards of 90 percent of psychotic patients have no insight into their condition. Believing that they do not need any treatment, they subject themselves and loved ones to sometimes desperate and frightening situations by refusing medication or other modes of therapy, most of which involve hospitalization (Torrey, 1996).

Deinstitutionalization, Civil Liberties, and Mental Health

Since the 1960s, provinces throughout Canada have embarked on a policy of deinstitutionalization, discharging as many patients as possible from mental hospitals and discouraging admissions. The maxim is now "Treat them in the community," the assumption being that virtually anything is preferable to institutionalization.

Barnes and Toews (1983) assessed deinstitutionalization in Canada and concluded that deinstitutionalization had occurred at the same rate in Canada as in the United States. They cited a previous study (see Kedward, Eastwood, Allodi, & Duckworth, 1974) that indicated that there was a 43 percent reduction in the number of patients in public mental institutions between 1960 and 1972, as well as a Statistics Canada (1979) report showing a decrease by 50 percent of beds in institutions. Barnes and Toews also noted that patients fare no worse in the community than in an institution, with the vital provision that this depended substantially on the quality of care and provisions for care made available when people were released to the community. Research studies on care in the hospital versus care in the home in Montreal (Fenton, Tessier, & Streuning, 1979; Smith, Fenton, Benoit, & Barzell, 1976) and in Vancouver

(Goodacre et al., 1975) yielded few differences. Other research suggests that the quality of life can even be significantly better in the community (Lord & Pedlar, 1991), but Canadian investigators continue to emphasize that the quality and availability of aftercare is a vital consideration (e.g., Bigelow, McFarland, Gareau, & Young, 1991; Lesage & Morissette, 1993). Ideally, most discharged people will get into highly supervised settings, as was shown to be the case in a study conducted in Quebec by Lesage et al. (2000). This study found that long-stay patients released from Canada's largest psychiatric hospital (i.e., the Louis-H Lafontaine Hospital) were not abandoned.

Deinstitutionalization is a phenomenon that has taken place across Canada. Simmie and Nunes (2001, p. 162) observed:

> New Brunswick recently demolished its oldest psychiatric hospital, and former residents are now doing well in the community. Many of these people have spent years, even decades, on the inside. "I never thought that some of the people coming out would make it," says the director of a community mental health centre in Fredericton, "but in fact their needs have declined."

But what is this community that former mental hospital patients are supposed to find more helpful to them on discharge? Facilities outside hospitals are often not prepared to cope with the influx of these patients. Some promising programs were described in Chapter 11, but these are very much the exception, not the rule. The state of affairs in many large metropolitan areas is an unrelenting social crisis, for hundreds of thousands of chronically ill mental patients across North America have been released without sufficient job training and without community services to help them. It is doubtful, too, that deinstitutionalization has reduced the rate of chronic mental illness. As Gralnick (1987) argued, acutely ill persons are largely neglected because it is difficult to commit them unless they are found to be a danger to themselves and others, a state that can take years to develop; by that time their problems may have become chronic and more difficult to deal with. The irony is that deinstitutionalization may be contributing to the very problem it was designed to alleviate, chronic mental illness.

Indeed, *de*institutionalization may be a misnomer. *Trans*institutionalization may be more apt, for declines in the census of public mental hospitals have occasioned increases in the numbers of mentally ill people in prisons, nursing homes, and the mental health departments of nonpsychiatric hospitals (Cloud, 1999; Kiesler, 1991), and these settings are often not equipped to handle the particular needs of mental patients. The oft-mentioned revolving door is seen in the increase in readmission rates, from 25 percent before the deinstitutionalization movement to around 80 percent by the 1980s (Paul & Menditto, 1992).

Many patients discharged from mental hospitals are eligible for social benefits, but a large number are not receiving this assistance. Financial and occupational concerns are very salient. A qualitative study examined the deinstitutionalization experience and the issues that faced 139 people who were previously institutionalized in Eastern Canada (Herman & Smith, 1989). Six significant themes emerged: (1) stigmatization of people with a history of mental illness; (2) an absence of basic living skills; (3) poor housing; (4) poverty; (5) difficulties getting a job; and (6) accessing aftercare programs.

Homeless persons do not have fixed addresses and need help in establishing eligibility and residency for the purpose of receiving benefits. Nowadays, especially in larger cities, it is common to see people who have been discharged from psychiatric hospitals living in the streets, in train and bus terminals, in abandoned buildings, on subways, and in shelters operated by public agencies, churches, and charitable organizations. In Toronto alone, there are about 25,000 such people (Goering et al., 2000), and comparable situations exist in other major cities throughout Canada. The lives of these individuals are desperate.

> [In a train station at 11:00 p.m.] the attendant goes off duty and women rise from separate niches and head for the bathroom. There they disrobe, and wash their clothes and bodies. Depending on the length of [the] line at the hand dryers, they wait to dry their clothes, put them in their bags or wear them wet. One woman cleans and wraps her ulcerated legs with paper towels every night. The most assertive claim toilet cubicles, line them with newspapers for privacy and warmth and sleep curled around the basin. Once they are taken, the rest sleep along the walls, one on a box directly beneath the hand dryer which she pushes for warm air. One of the women regularly cleans up the floors, sinks and toilets so that no traces of their uncustomary use remain. (Baxter & Hopper, 1981, p. 77)

Discharged mental patients who are not homeless may live marginal lives in nursing homes, jails, and run-down hotels. Although a visible part of the population, their visibility may be diminishing, as many other people have been dispossessed from their homes and have lost their jobs. The state of homelessness exacerbates the emotional suffering of former mental patients. Mentally ill persons are an especially defenceless segment of the homeless population. And what is worse, they are ending up in the criminal courts in unprecedented numbers. Schneider (2000) reported that across Canada the number of mentally disordered accused coming before provincial review boards has been increasing at a minimum of 10 percent per year since the early 1990s while overall prosecution rates have been decreasing. It may be naive to expect that the community from which the mentally disordered individual came is the one best suited to provide support and treatment.

The links between homelessness and mental illness have been extensively documented. In Chapter 11, we discussed homelessness with respect to the case of Edmund Yu, a homeless young man who suffered from schizophrenia prior to his death. The homelessness issue was analyzed in the United States by a committee of the National Academy of Sciences (NAS; Committee on Health Care for Homeless People, 1988, as summarized in Leeper, 1988). The committee estimated that 25 to 40 percent of the homeless population are alcoholics and similar proportions have some form of serious mental illness, usually schizophrenia. A study of homelessness in Toronto found that approximately two-thirds of the 300 people assessed had lifetime diagnoses of mental illness (Tolomic-Zenko & Goering, 1998). Moreover, two-thirds of the participants had some form of substance abuse. Stuart and Arboleda-Florez (2000) assessed homeless shelter users in Calgary and found that approximately one-third had a significant mental health problem and that the lifetime prevalence of alcohol abuse was 33.6 percent. Greater psychiatric problems were associated with a wider range of hardships, health risks, victimization, negative life events (including economic problems), and a sense of dissatisfaction. Research in British Columbia also points to the association between homelessness and mental illness. Acorn (1993) surveyed users of an emergency shelter and found that depression, anxiety, and tension were quite common; approximately one-fifth of the respondents acknowledged a current mental disorder, with schizophrenia and bipolar depression being most evident. Another investigation of jail detainees confirmed links between homelessness and severe mental disorder as well as prior psychiatric history (Zapf, Roesch, & Hart, 1996). Such problems are probably aggravated by a nomadic and dangerous existence. Homeless people, especially women, are likely victims of violence and rape, even when living in shelters for the homeless (D'Ercole & Struening, 1990).

Children are also found among the homeless population. These youngsters are forced to live their formative years in chaotic and dangerous situations, with parents under severe stress. One NAS committee member noted that "many children have developmental delays. I've seen two-year-olds who can't walk, six-month-olds who don't cuddle in your arms, and four-year-olds acting like mothers to one-year-olds because their mother isn't giving them the care they need" (Leeper, 1988, p. 8). It comes as no surprise that these children are often subject to abuse and many drop out of school and suffer from anxiety, depression, and substance abuse.

Do such appalling conditions, still found today, justify reversing the policy of deinstitutionalization? In the view of the NAS committee, no, because in its opinion the problem lies with the failure of communities to provide suitable living and rehabilitation conditions, a theme sounded earlier in this book.

There are signs that the pendulum may begin to swing back in the direction of more involuntary hospitalization, even when the person does not pose a real danger to self or to others but is wandering homeless on the streets and living in squalor. Being "persistently and acutely disabled" is, in some jurisdictions, replacing "being a danger to oneself or to others" (Shogren, 1994). It remains to be seen how this trend will develop in the light of laws and court rulings that have been making it more and more difficult to keep people institutionalized against their will.

Some people fear that individuals with schizophrenia are increasingly being seen as misfits, drug abusers, and panhandlers rather than as ill people in need of professional care (Gralnick, 1986). They end up more often in jails, shelters, and church basements than in mental wards. A large-scale field study (Teplin, 1984) found that police officers were 20 percent more likely to arrest people if they were showing signs of mental disorder than if they were (merely) committing offences for which arrest was an option.

Canadian Perspectives 18.3 describes recommended solutions to the problems of deinstitutionalization in Canada.

Canadian Perspectives/18.3

Solutions to the Consequences of Deinstitutionalization in Canada

"Whether it's a friend, a colleague or someone living in a bus shelter, there are really only eight kinds of people affected by mental health problems: Someone's mother, daughter, sister or wife; someone's father, husband, brother or son. People. Like me."

—Scott Simmie, October 10, 1998, author of the "Atkinson Fellowship Investigation into Mental Health," published as the eight-part "Out of Mind" series in *The Toronto Star* (October 3-10, 1998). Simmie has suffered from bipolar disorder.

In the spring of 1998, two investigative reporters for The Toronto Star, Donovan Vincent and Theresa Boyle, wrote a seven-part series (entitled "Madness") that was based on their investigations of the human tragedy of mental illness. Later, in the fall of 1998, Scott Simmie, winner of the Atkinson Fellowship in Public Policy, wrote an eight-part *Toronto Star* series (entitled "Out of Mind") that was based on his year-long explorations of mental health reform. Both series of articles concluded with long lists of recommendations and steps that should be taken for the benefit of people with serious and chronic mental illness. In our opinion, these series covered the issues in a constructive, responsible, and fair way.

Scott Simmie, author of the "Out of Mind" series about the plight of the mentally ill. His investigations led to many proposed and implemented solutions to the consequences of deinstitutionalization.

In their assessment of the Simmie series, Goering et al. stated:

> The combination of personal account and careful investigative reporting created a powerful series that was educational, destigmatizing, and much appreciated by mental health consumers and providers. Unfortunately, such coverage of mental health by the Canadian Press is the exception, not the rule. (Goering et al., 2000)

In the final segment of his own series, Scott Simmie prefaced his proposed solutions in a poignant way, as follows:

> Today is World Mental Health Day. Its theme: human rights and mental health. As a country, we love to talk about human rights and point an admonishing finger abroad when we see things we don't like. It's time we looked closer to home. We are abusing the human rights of many of our citizens. People stricken with serious and chronic mental health problems. We marginalize them in every way. We abandon them as friends, avoid them on the street. And we provide them with income supports that keep them in second-hand clothes—at best. But our greatest shame is our failure to supply the most fundamental need of any human being. A home. That's where true mental health reform must begin.... Drugs are critical for schizophrenia—but the best medication means nothing if your home is a bus shelter. (Simmie, from "True reform is up to all of us," *The Toronto Star*, October 10, 1998)

Steps to Take

Boyle and Vincent (1998) and Simmie (1998) listed steps that must be taken in Ontario to help people with serious and chronic mental health problems. Most of their recommendations can be applied right across Canada. Throughout this section, we use the preferred term for current and former psychiatric patients, as determined by the patients and former patients themselves—*consumers/survivors*. The following is an integrated list of the steps, plus some additional recommendations:

- Reinvestment of funds (approximately $400 million) into community mental health services (such as crisis centres, crisis lines, and child and adolescent programs). In particular, there is a need for 80 assertive-community response teams. This reinvestment would not only be humane, there would be substantial cost savings coupled with a reduction of disability and mortality.
- Review and changes to the Mental Health Act consistent with change from the old and outdated "institutional model" to a "community-oriented system" model.
- A variety of supportive housing, ranging from independent apartments to group homes, coupled with monitoring of standards and maintenance, particularly for boarding homes and rooming houses. At least 14,000 units are needed.
- In addition to supportive housing, there is a need for an expanded home care program for people with serious mental disorders.
- Community mental health centres as standard access points to the mental health "system" where people can receive assistance on site and appropriate referrals. Consumer/survivor advocates would be a part of multidisciplinary teams.
- Incentives to adequately staff provincial psychiatric hospitals (professional as well as support staff), especially those slated for closure.
- Development, evaluation, and implementation of risk assessment tools for forensic patients to facilitate the best use of resources and bed space.
- Opening of additional forensic beds for mentally ill offenders, to eliminate the problem of the mentally ill being incarcerated in jails.
- Diversion of the mentally ill from the criminal justice system if possible, as well as the hiring of additional mental health workers in jails.
- Community treatment orders should be a last resort.
- The most effective (but sometimes most expensive) medications for schizophrenia should be available as "first-line" treatment.
- Increased emphasis on early detection and treatment of mental disorders in children. Emphasis on "defragmenting" children's services should have high priority.
- More non-medical safe houses for people in crisis, patterned after Toronto's Gerstein Centre.
- Government-established 24-hour information/crisis lines staffed by consumers/survivors who are trained to refer people to appropriate resources.
- Expansion of consumer/survivor alternative businesses to provide work and "restore dignity and hope" to former psychiatric patients (survivors). For example, the Ontario Council of Alternative Businesses helps consumer/survivors initiate and operate businesses, such as A-Way Express, a courier service.

Fresh Start, another example, is a cleaning and maintenance company staffed and run by psychiatric survivors.

- Expanded income supports and reduction of penalties for consumers/survivors who attempt to supplement their income. (In 1998, typical monthly benefits under the Ontario Disability Support Program were about $700 per month.)
- Extension or subsidizing of drug benefits under the Ontario Drug Benefits Program for consumers/survivors who want to fully rejoin the work force.
- Development of alternative payment schemes that will encourage psychiatrists to treat people with severe, persistent mental illnesses. Awareness by psychiatrists of, and referral to where appropriate, all the services and resources in their local community. General practitioners (usually the initial point of contact) should consult actively with psychiatrists.
- Support for anti-stigma campaigns by the Ministry of Health or Health Canada, in consultation with the Canadian Mental Health Association.
- Encouragement of co-operation among community service providers. (Such co-operation should not be legislated.)
- Support on the part of employers for employees with mental health problems.
- Encouraging the mentally ill to seek help from each other through various associations (such as the local chapter of the Mood Disorders Association).
- Increased training for the police in ways to deal with the mentally ill, including alternative "use of force" strategies to prevent the deaths of psychotic individuals.
- Appropriate contextual statements in all stories linking violence and mental illness, since the seriously mentally ill are responsible for only 4 percent of the violence in society.
- A decision on how a reformed mental health system should be managed. As noted by Boyle and Vincent, as of 1998, in Ontario, there were 10 provincial hospitals (e.g., Queen Street Mental Health Centre in Toronto), 65 general hospital psychiatric units, four specialty psychiatric hospitals, and more than 300 community mental health and addiction programs. They summarized the system as follows: "It's an uncoordinated patchwork of services with too few bridges between them and too many mentally ill falling through the cracks" (p. F4). Simmie recommended that the Government of Ontario create a "mental health commission" with a mandate to create a mental health "system," adequate transitional funding, and authority to fund and build supportive housing.
- The public must re-examine their views of mental illness, help to reduce stigma, and lobby politicians to instigate changes.

Sources: This section was adapted primarily from Boyle and Vincent (1998) and Simmie (1998).

Changes?

These two series of carefully researched, thoughtful, provocative, and timely articles on mental health garnered tremendous public support and sympathy for consumers/survivors. They compelled various levels of government to begin to make many of the proposed changes, at least as pilot projects, and forced an ongoing consideration and evaluation of other options. The following are some of the positive changes that are already affecting the treatment of serious and chronic mental illness in our society:

- The creation of the restructured and integrated Centre for Addiction and Mental Health
- Diversion of the mentally ill from jails through the establishment of special courts and judges with special training (Ontario Court of Justice mental health court)
- Expansion of the assertive-response team program
- Expanded training of the police, such as the creation of special teams that include social workers riding in the patrol cars
- Creation of additional forensic beds in Toronto
- Input on the part of stakeholders, including consumers/survivors, into the final legislation creating community treatment orders
- Creation of anti-stigma campaigns
- Additional government funding targeted to community supports
- Promises of funding for supportive housing

There is obviously a long way to go toward full implementation of the proposed steps, not only in Ontario but also throughout Canada. It is clear from Simmie's series that he considers supportive housing to be a critical step, and a number of initiatives have been taken in this area. However, progress has been slow. A year after the Ontario government had committed $100 million to fight homelessness, only about $30 million had been spent (Brennan, 2000). About half the money designated for the homeless mentally ill ($45 million) had been paid out to community organizations in Toronto, Hamilton, and Ottawa.

Of course, provinces can also learn from each other's strategies and efforts, and Ontario is not the only province facing significant challenges. The B.C. Early Intervention Study (see Macnaughton, 1998) was a survey conducted by the B.C. chapter of the CMHA to evaluate people's first experiences with the mental health system. This report documented, among other things, the length of time for people to get treatment. According to Macnaughton (1998), it took three years on average from first onset for people with schizophrenia and schizoaffective disorder to access treatment, and it took one year to access care from the time of acute onset. It took seven to eight years on average from first onset for people with mood disorders to access care, and it took six months to access care from the time of acute onset. A related problem that undermined treatment was that almost half of the survey's participants received an incorrect diagnosis during the early years of treatment. The most common misdiagnoses were interpreting bipolar depression and early psychosis as depression and failing to make dual diagnoses involving various mental illnesses in combination with substance abuse. Community-based crisis response systems may not address the misdiagnosis issue but could perhaps result in quicker care.

Concerns about access to psychological services have also been raised in Alberta. The Alberta Alliance on Mental Illness and Mental Health (a coalition that includes the Psychologists'

Association of Alberta) issued a call in March 2000 for the Alberta government to implement a comprehensive community care strategy. This group expressed concern about rates of suicide in Alberta and outlined a strategy with four components to address this problem (see http://www.psychologistsassociation.ab.ca):

- continuing efforts to promote public awareness of suicide as a preventable, public health problem
- eliminating barriers in public and private insurance programs and establishing incentives for treating people with co-existing mental illness and substance-abuse disorders
- increasing the use of schools and workplaces as access and referral points for services
- increasing research on risk and protective factors, as well as prevention programs, psychological treatment for suicidal individuals, and culture-specific interventions

In October 2003, this same group reiterated that all Albertans should have equal and timely access to mental health services (see Position Paper Regarding The Future of Mental Health Services in Alberta).

According to Goering et al. (2000), community-based crisis response systems (connected interventions that range from least to most intrusive) are most well developed in the province of Manitoba. In Manitoba, most regions count heavily on "mobile crisis teams" as well as on "free-standing crisis centres" in support of people with serious and chronic mental health problems.

Thinking Critically

1. Some recommendations in this section have already been implemented, but the majority have not. Review all of the proposed steps and choose the five recommendations that you consider to be most critical. Explain why you chose them. Outline a plan for implementing your recommendations.
2. What steps do you believe it will be most difficult to gain acceptance for—from politicians, practitioners, and possibly the consumers/survivors themselves?

ETHICAL DILEMMAS IN THERAPY AND RESEARCH

In this textbook, we have examined a variety of theories and a multitude of data that focus on what is and what is thought to be. Ethics and values, often embodied in laws, are a different order of discussion. They concern what ought to be, having sometimes little to do with what is. It is extremely important to recognize the difference.

Within a given scientific paradigm, we are able to examine what we believe is reality. As the study of philosophy and ethics reveals, however, the statements people have made for thousands of years about what should be are another matter. The Ten Commandments are such statements. They are prescriptions and proscriptions about human conduct.

The Nuremberg trials

The legal trends reviewed thus far in this chapter place limits on the activities of mental health professionals. These legal constraints are important, for laws are one of society's strongest means of encouraging all of us to behave in certain ways. Mental health professionals also have professional and ethical constraints. All professional groups promulgate shoulds and should nots, and by guidelines and mandates, they limit to some degree what therapists and researchers should do with their patients, clients, and research participants. Courts, too, have ruled on some of these questions. Most of the time what we believe is unethical is also illegal, but sometimes existing laws are in conflict with our moral sense of right and wrong. We examine now the ethics of making psychological inquiries and interventions into the lives of other human beings.

Ethical Restraints on Research

Basic to the nature of science is the saying "What can be done will usually be attempted." The most reprehensible ethical insensitivity was evidenced in the brutal experiments conducted by German physicians on concentration camp prisoners during World War II. One experiment, for example, investigated how long people lived when their heads were bashed repeatedly with a heavy stick. Even if important information might be obtained from this kind of experiment, such actions violate our sense of decency and morality. The Nuremberg Trials, conducted by the Allies following the war, brought these Nazis and other barbarisms to light and meted out severe punishment to some of the soldiers, physicians, and Nazi officials who had engaged in or contributed to such actions, even when they claimed that they had merely been following orders.

It would be reassuring to be able to say that such gross violations of human decency take place only during incredible and cruel epochs, such as the Third Reich, but unfortunately, this is not the case. Spurred on by a blind enthusiasm for their work, researchers have sometimes dealt with human subjects in reproachable ways.

Henry K. Beecher, a research professor at Harvard Medical School, surveyed medical research since 1945 and found that "many of the patients [used as subjects in experiments] never had the risk satisfactorily explained to them, and ...further hundreds have not known that they were the subjects of an experiment although grave consequences have been suffered as the direct result" (1966, p. 1354). One experiment compared penicillin with a placebo as a treatment to prevent rheumatic fever. Even though penicillin had already been acknowledged as the drug most successful in protecting people with a streptococcal respiratory infection from later contracting rheumatic fever, placebos were administered to 109 service personnel without their knowledge or permission. More subjects received penicillin than received the placebo, but three members of the control group contracted serious illnesses—two had rheumatic fever and one acute nephritis, a kidney disease. No one who received penicillin contracted such illnesses.

Half a century later, in January 1994, spurred on by Eileen Welsome, a journalist who won a Pulitzer Prize for her investigative reporting on the issue, the U.S. Energy Department began to publicize numerous experiments conducted in the 1950s through the 1970s that had exposed hundreds of people—usually without their informed consent or prior knowledge—to harmful doses of radiation. There was particular concern over the fact that the overwhelming majority were people of low socioeconomic status, members of racial minorities, people with mental retardation, nursing home patients, or prisoners. The scientists, for the most part supported in their research with federal funds, clearly understood that the risks were great, even though relatively little was known about the harmful effects of radiation at the time, for, as was pointed out, "they were doing it to poor and black people. You didn't see them doing it at the Mayo Clinic" (lawyer arguing for compensation for some of the subjects, quoted in Healy, 1994). Some of these experiments involved giving women in the third trimester of pregnancy a radioactive tonic to determine safe levels of exposure and irradiating the testicles of prisoners to find out the degree of radiation that service personnel could endure without negative effects on sperm production. It is particularly troubling that these studies took place many years after the Nuremberg Trials.

The training of scientists equips them splendidly to pose interesting questions, sometimes even important ones, and to design research that is as free as possible of confounding elements. They have no special qualifications, however, for deciding whether a particular line of inquiry that involves humankind should be followed. Society needs knowledge, and a scientist has a right in a democracy to seek that knowledge. However, the ordinary citizens employed as participants in experiments must be protected from harm, risk, humiliation, and invasion of privacy.

Several international codes of ethics pertain to the conduct of scientific research—the Nuremberg Code formulated in 1947 in the aftermath of the Nazi war-crime trials, the 1964 Declaration of Helsinki, and statements from the British Medical Research Council. As for Canada, it has been noted by Young (1998) that medical research (including psychiatric investigations) in Canada is governed by four documents: the Nuremberg Code, the Declaration of Helsinki, the Medical Research Council of Canada's document Guidelines on Research Involving Human Subjects (1987), and the Tri-Council Working Group on Ethics (1998) document Ethical Conduct for Research Involving Humans (final report). The three councils that comprise the Tri-Council Working Group are the Medical Research Council of Canada (MRC), the Natural Sciences and Engineering Research Council of Canada (NSERC), and the Social Sciences and Humanities Research Council of Canada (SSHRC).

In 1974 the U.S. Department of Health, Education, and Welfare began to issue guidelines and regulations governing scientific research that employs human and animal subjects. In addition, a blue-ribbon panel, the National Commission for the Protection of Human Subjects of Biomedical and Behavioral Research, issued a report in 1978 that arose from hearings and inquiries into restrictions that the U.S. government might impose on research performed with prisoners, children, and patients in psychiatric institutions. These various codes and principles are continually being reevaluated and revised as new challenges are posed to the research community (e.g., Brennan, 1999; Levine, 1999).

For the past 25 years, the proposals of behavioural researchers, many of whom conduct experiments related to psychopathology and therapy, have been reviewed for safety and general ethical propriety by institutional review boards in hospitals, universities, and research institutes. Such committees—and this is significant—comprise not only behavioural scientists but also citizens from the community, lawyers, students, and specialists in a variety of disciplines, such as professors of English, history, and comparative religion. They are able to block any research proposal or require questionable aspects to be modified if, in their collective judgement, the research would put participants at too great a risk. Such committees also now pass judgement on the scientific merits of proposals, the rationale being that it is not ethical to recruit participants for studies that will not yield valid data (Capron, 1999; Rosenthal, 1995).

Changes in the Declaration of Helsinki are being debated, spurred on by two recent developments in biomedical research. The first is an increase in research sponsored by for-profit organizations such as pharmaceutical companies. Faced with fierce competition and marketplace pressures to maximize profits, such companies may push for research that would not be approved by human subjects committees in nonprofit organizations such as universities. Recently, this issue came to a head when the International Committee of Medical Journal Editors (ICMJE), a group that includes the *Canadian Medical Association Journal* (*CMAJ*), issued an extensive set of rules and new policies that will govern the publication of results in major journals (see CMAJ, 2001). A *CMAJ* editorial on this issue stated:

> Henceforth, these 11 leading journals will require authors to attest that they "had full access to all of the data in [the] study and ... [would] take complete responsibility for the integrity of the data and the accuracy of the data analysis." In addition, editors will retain the right to review the study protocol as well as funding contracts for the study before accepting the paper for publication. CMAJ will not accept reports on research that was conducted under a contractual arrangement that did not meet these ethical standards. (CMAJ, 2001, p. 733)

This position was reached in response to concerns that results could have been altered or even suppressed if the findings did not yield the results anticipated by the funding body.

The internationalization of research is a second factor in the possible attenuation of protection of human subjects. Developing countries are particularly eager for partnerships in research and do not always have the same historical commitment to individual informed consent and safety that is prevalent in more industrialized and democratic countries. A danger seen by some is that utilitarian standards (e.g., will the research yield generally useful results?) are becoming more important than the focus of the past half-century on the rights and safety of individual research participants.

> The proposed revisions to the Declaration of Helsinki weaken the principle of the researcher's moral commitment to the research subject and provide diminished protection of the rights of research subjects. Utilitarian efficiency, aligned with marketplace values, is more prominent. (Brennan, 1999, p. 529)

In reaction to some ethical lapses in hospital-based research with mental patients, the National Bioethics Advisory Commission recommends special precautions to ensure that research subjects with mental illness fully understand the risks and benefits of any research they are asked to participate in and that particular care be taken to make certain that they can decline or withdraw from research without feeling coerced. Specifically, instead of simply allowing a guardian or family member to make the decision for the patient, the commission proposes that a health professional who has nothing to do with the particular study make a judgement on whether a given patient can give informed consent. The commission recommends also that if a guardian is allowed to give consent on behalf of a patient judged incompetent to do so, then the guardian's own ability to give consent must be evaluated (Capron, 1999).

INFORMED CONSENT

This recent concern about conducting research with mental patients underscores the all-important concept of informed consent. Just as committed mental patients are gaining some right to refuse treatment, so may anyone refuse to be a participant in an experiment. The investigator must provide enough information to enable people to judge whether they want to accept any risks inherent in being a participant. Prospective participants must be legally capable of giving consent, and there must be no deceit or coercion in obtaining it. For example, an experimental psychologist might wish to determine whether imagery helps college students associate one word with another. One group of students might be asked to associate pairs of words in their minds by generating a fanciful image connecting the two, such as a cat riding on a bicycle. Current standard operating procedure allows a prospective participant to decide that the experiment is likely to be boring and to decline to participate. Furthermore, those who begin to participate as research subjects are free to withdraw at any time without fear of penalty.

Paired-associates research such as that just described is relatively innocuous, but what if the experiment poses real risks, such as ingesting a drug, or what if a patient with schizophrenia whose condition has improved by taking a drug is withdrawn from it so that the investigator can assess the effects of "drug washout"? Or what if the prospective participant is a committed mental patient, or a child with mental retardation, unable to understand fully what is being asked? Such a person may not feel free or even be able to refuse participation. Although recent research mentioned earlier shows that even committed patients with schizophrenia may be competent to understand and participate in treatment decisions, the degree of coercion that is part and parcel of being in a hospital setting must not be overlooked.

A further complication is that it is not always easy to demonstrate that a researcher has obtained informed consent. Epstein and Lasagna (1969) found that only one-third of those volunteering for an experiment really understood what the experiment entailed. In a more elaborate study, Stuart (1978) discovered that most college students could not accurately describe a simple experiment, even though it had just been explained to them and they had agreed to participate. A signature on a consent form is no assurance that informed consent has been obtained, which poses a challenge to investigators and members of review panels who are committed to upholding codes of ethics governing participation of human subjects in research.

As suggested earlier (Capron, 1999), such problems are especially pronounced in clinical settings where patients may or may not understand the nature of antipsychotic medication. Irwin et al. (1985) found that although most patients said they understood the benefits and side effects of their drugs, only a quarter of them could actually demonstrate such understanding when queried specifically. The authors concluded that simply reading information to hospitalized patients—especially the more disturbed ones—is no guarantee that they fully comprehend; therefore, informed consent cannot be said to have been obtained. The recent report of the National Bioethics Advisory Commission pointed to many published experiments involving mental patients in which no effort was made to determine whether the research participants had the decision-making capacity to give informed consent (Capron, 1999).

Still, as with the right to refuse treatment, there is recognition that being judged mentally ill—more specifically, being diagnosed with schizophrenia and being hospitalized—does not necessarily mean being incapable of giving informed consent (Appelbaum & Gutheil, 1991; Grisso, 1986). An experiment by Grisso and Applebaum (1991) found that although patients with schizophrenia on average understood issues relating to treatment involving medication less well than nonpsychiatric patients did, there was a wide range of understanding among the patients; in fact, the understanding of some was as good as that of nonpsychiatric patients. These results suggest that it is important to examine each person individually for ability to give informed consent, rather than assume that a person is unable to do so by virtue of being hospitalized.

Confidentiality and Privileged Communication

When an individual consults a physician, psychiatrist, or clinical psychologist, he or she is assured by professional ethics codes that what goes on in the session will remain confidential. **Confidentiality** means that nothing will be revealed to a third party, except to other professionals and those intimately involved in the treatment, such as a nurse or medical secretary.

A **privileged communication** goes even further. It is communication between parties in a confidential relationship that is protected by law. The recipient of such a communication cannot legally be compelled to disclose it as a witness. The right of privileged communication is a major exception to the access courts have to evidence in judicial proceedings. Society believes that in the long term the interests of people are best served if communications to a spouse and to certain professionals remain off limits to the prying eyes and ears of the police, judges, and prosecutors. The privilege applies to such relationships as those between husband and wife, physician and patient, pastor and penitent, attorney and client, and psychologist and patient. The legal expression is that the patient or client "holds the privilege," which means that only he or she may release the other person to disclose confidential information in a legal proceeding.

There are important limits to a client's right of privileged communication, however. For example, according to the current California psychology licensing law (similar elements are present in other state laws), this right is eliminated for any of the following reasons:

- The client has accused the therapist of malpractice. In such a case, the therapist can divulge information about the therapy in order to defend himself or herself in any legal action initiated by the client.
- The client is less than 16 years old and the therapist has reason to believe that the child has been a victim of a crime such as child abuse. In fact, the psychologist is required to report to the police or to a child welfare agency within 36 hours any suspicion he or she has that the child client has been physically abused, including any suspicion of sexual molestation.
- The client initiated therapy in hopes of evading the law for having committed a crime or for planning to do so.
- The therapist judges that the client is a danger to self or to others and disclosure of information is necessary to ward off such danger (recall Focus on Discovery 18.3 on Tarasoff).

In Canada, as seen above in the Supreme Court of Canada's decision in *Smith versus Jones*, even formally privileged solicitor-client relationships may be pierced where an individual is seen by a consulting mental health practitioner to constitute an imminent risk of serious bodily harm to an identifiable person or class of persons.

Who is the Client or Patient?

Is it always clear to the clinician who the client is? In private therapy, when an adult pays a clinician a fee for help with a personal problem that has nothing to do with the legal system, the consulting individual is clearly the client. But an individual may be seen by a clinician for an evaluation of his or her competency to stand trial, or the clinician may be hired by an individual's family to assist in civil commitment proceedings. Perhaps the clinician is employed by a provincial mental hospital as a regular staff member and sees a particular patient about problems in controlling aggressive impulses.

It should be clear, although it seldom is clear, that in these instances the clinician is serving more than one client. In addition to the patient, he or she serves the family or the province, and it is incumbent on the mental health professional to inform the patient that this is so. Verdun-Jones (2000) from Simon Fraser University has written extensively on the conflict faced by clinicians who must be true to their clinical role and protect the client's rights while at the

Which environment best fosters learning: traditional classroom (above) or open classroom (below)?

same time ensuring that the rights of the general public are also protected. This dual allegiance does not necessarily indicate that the patient's own interests will be sacrificed, but it does mean that discussions will not inevitably remain secret and that the clinician may in the future act in a way that displeases the individual.

Choice of Goals

Ideally, the client sets the goals for therapy, but in practice, it is naive to assume that some goals are not imposed by the therapist and may even go against the wishes of the client. For example, a school system may want to institute a program that will teach children to "be still, be quiet, be docile" (Winett & Winkler, 1972, p. 499). Many behaviour therapists have assumed that young children should be compliant, not only because the teacher can then run a more orderly class, but because children are assumed to learn better when they are so. But do we really know that the most efficient and most enjoyable learning takes place when children are forced to remain quietly in their seats? Some advocates of open classrooms believe that curiosity and initiative, even in the youngest elementary school pupil, are at least as important as the acquisition of academic skills.

As is generally the case in psychology, evidence is less plentiful than strongly held and vehemently defended opinions. But it is clear that any professionals consulted by a school system have to be mindful of their own personal biases with respect to goals and should be prepared to work toward different ones if the parents and school personnel so wish. Any therapist has the option of not working for a client whose goals and proposed means of attaining them are abhorrent in his or her view.

This question of goals is particularly complex in family and couples therapy (Margolin, 1982). If several people are clients simultaneously—inevitable in family treatment—an intervention that benefits one or more individuals may well work to the disadvantage of one or more others. This can happen if one partner in couples therapy really wants to end the relationship, but the other sees the therapy as a way to save it. Because people often do not openly express their real concerns and wishes at the very beginning of therapy, the therapist can already be deeply enmeshed in their lives before learning that the two partners have conflicting goals. For this reason, among others, couples and family therapy is particularly challenging.

Choice of Techniques

The end does not justify the means. This canon is said to be intrinsic to a free society. For years, questions concerning behavioural techniques have been debated among professionals and have been the subject of court rulings. Perhaps because the various insight therapies de-emphasize direct efforts to change behaviour, they have seldom been scrutinized in the way behaviour therapy has. The very concreteness, specificity, and directiveness of behavioural techniques have called attention to them, as has their alignment with experimental psychology. Some find it offensive to believe that our understanding of human beings could possibly be advanced by employing rats and pigeons as analogues to humans.

Particular concern has been expressed about the ethics of inflicting pain for purposes of therapy. For some people, the term behaviour therapy conjures up an image of the violent protagonist in Kubrick's classic film *A Clockwork Orange*, eyes propped open with a torturous apparatus, being made nauseous by a drug while scenes of violence flash on a screen. Aversion-therapy programs never reach this level of coercion and drama, but certainly any such procedure entails making the patient uncomfortable, sometimes extremely so. Making patients vomit or cringe with pain from electric shock applied to the extremities are two aversion techniques worthy of their name. Can there be any circumstances that justify therapists' inflicting pain on clients?

Before quickly exclaiming, "No!" consider the following report.

THE PATIENT was a nine-month-old baby who had already been hospitalized three times for treatment of vomiting and chronic rumination (regurgitating food and rechewing it in the mouth). A number of diagnostic tests, including an EEG, plus surgery to remove a cyst on the right kidney, had revealed no biological basis for the problems, and several treatments, including a special diet, had been attempted without success. When referred to Lang and Melamed (1969), two behaviour therapists, the child was in critical condition and was being fed by tubes leading from the nose directly into the stomach. The attending physician had stated that the infant's life was in imminent danger if the vomiting could not be halted.

Treatment consisted of delivering a series of one-second-long electric shocks to the infant's calf each time he showed signs of beginning to vomit. Sessions followed feeding and lasted under an hour. After just two sessions, shock was rarely required, for the infant learned quickly to stop vomiting in order to avoid the shock. By the sixth session, he was able to fall asleep after eating. Nurses reported that the in-session inhibition of vomiting generalized as the infant progressively reduced his vomiting during the rest of the day and night. About two weeks later, the mother began to assume some care of the hospitalized child, and shortly thereafter the patient was discharged with virtually complete elimination of the life-threatening pattern of behaviour. Throughout the three weeks of treatment and observation, the child gained weight steadily. One month after discharge, the child weighed 21 pounds and was rated as fully recovered by the attending physician. Five months later, he weighed 26 pounds and was regarded as completely normal, both physically and psychologically (Lang & Melamed, 1969).

The use of aversion therapy has been subject to an understandably high degree of regulation. An additional reason for administrative and judicial concern is that aversion techniques smack more of research than of standard therapy. The more established a therapeutic procedure, whether medical or psychological, the less likely it is to attract the attention of the courts or other governmental agencies. Paul and Lentz (1977) had a few very assaultive patients. Their account of administrative problems demonstrates that patients might be subject to more extreme procedures because of restrictions placed on the use of new techniques.

> Some consideration was given to the contingent use of mild electric shock....However, early in the explorations of the necessary safeguards and review procedures to be followed before evaluating such methods, the department director telephoned to explain that aversion conditioning was a politically sensitive issue. Therefore, more than the usual proposal, preparation, documentation, and committee reviews would be required—to the extent that approval would probably take about eighteen months. Instead, it was suggested that convulsive shock...be employed since "ECT is an accepted medical treatment." With those alternatives, our choice was to abandon either use of shock. (p. 499)

But should we be concerned only with physical pain? The anguish we suffer when a loved one dies is psychologically painful. It is perhaps more painful than an electric shock of 1,500 microamperes. Who is to say? Since we allow that pain can be psychological, should we forbid a Gestalt therapist from making a patient cry by confronting the patient with feelings that have been avoided for years? Should we forbid a psychoanalyst from guiding a patient to an insight that will likely cause great anguish, all the more so for the conflict's having been repressed for years?

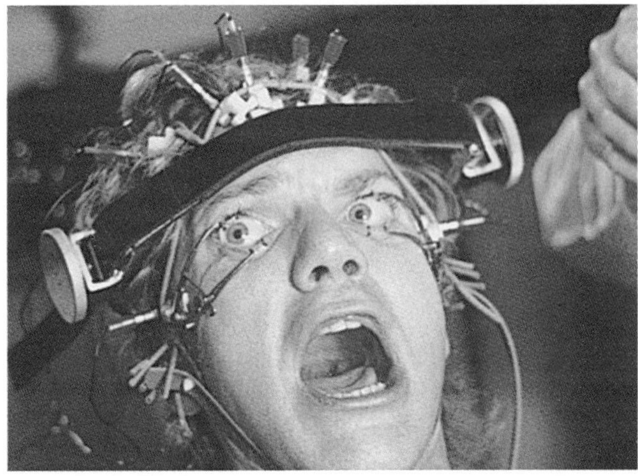

***A Clockwork Orange* depicted an extreme and fanciful example of aversion therapy.**

The Right to Competent Treatment

Most readers of this text would assume that an important ethical principle that can almost go without saying is that people have a right to receive treatment from competent and highly trained individuals. Indeed, this provision is clearly stated in the ethical guidelines and standards of practice endorsed by the Canadian Psychological Association (see Sinclair, 1993). It is important to remain vigilant and ensure that the quality of care meets or exceeds expectations. This point is illustrated in Canadian Clinic Focus 18.1.

Canadian Clinic Focus/18.1

Ethical Concerns and the Montreux Clinic

The Montreux Clinic, an eating-disorder clinic in British Columbia run by Peggy Claude-Pierre, initially caused quite a sensation because eating disorders are notoriously difficult to treat. However, the Montreux Clinic appeared to have a very high success rate in terms of curing the eating disorders of its clients. Claude-Pierre and her clinic received extensive coverage on a number of television shows, including ABC's *20/20*, *The Oprah Winfrey Show*, and, here in Canada, *The Pamela Wallin Show*. Claude-Pierre's approach received further attention when it was learned that Diana, Princess of Wales, had sought her advice for her bulimia problem.

Claude-Pierre's approach involved intensive treatment designed to restore the patient's sense of self-esteem in a safe and loving atmosphere. According to Claude-Pierre (1997), a vulnerability for eating disorders stems from "a confirmed negativity condition" that involves excessive self-criticism. A central goal of treatment was to reverse the negative mind through a variety of techniques and by treating the patient with unconditional love. Much of this treatment was based on insights that Claude-Pierre obtained as a result of her experiences as a mother of two daughters with eating disorders (see Claude-Pierre, 1997).

Unfortunately, problems eventually emerged at the Montreux Clinic. The clinic was investigated when a former employee made allegations to officials in the Victoria area that patients had been mistreated and that the staff were not trained adequately to address the problems of the eating-disorder patients. On December 1, 1999, the local medical officer, Dr. Richard Stanwick, ordered that the clinic be closed on January 31, 2000, because "the facility put the lives of its patients in danger with dishonesty and poor qualifications" (Sutherland, 1999, A23). Stanwick's report indicated that staff at the facility had physically restrained some patients and had forced others (including a 3-year-old boy who had been admitted even though the clinic's licence restricted it to patients 19 years or older) to eat. Also, few of the staff had university degrees and overall training was characterized as woefully inadequate. As director of the Montreux Clinic, Claude-Pierre did not have a graduate degree in psychology or a related discipline.

Initially, the Montreux Clinic appealed the order to close. However, the appeal was dropped and its operating licence was surrendered on August 25, 2000 (Meissner, 2000).

Comment

Unfortunately, it seems that the Montreux Clinic did indeed fail to meet a number of ethical standards prescribed by the Canadian Psychological Association. Which ones were violated? One was an ethical principle described by the Canadian Psychological Association (1991) as the "Competence and Self-Knowledge" principle. The essence of this principle is that help providers must limit their assistance to those activities for which they have established their competence in carrying out to the benefit of others. Moreover, there should be no attempt to delegate activities to people who lack the competence to carry them out. This standard would have been violated if indeed it was the case that the staff lacked adequate training. A related principle that apparently was not met is one that involves maximizing the benefit to the patient—that is, clinicians must provide the best possible service for those needing and seeking psychological services. This may include, but is not limited to, selecting interventions that are relevant to the needs and characteristics of the client and that have reasonable theoretical or empirically supported efficacy in light of those needs and characteristics. Another related concern with regard to the Montreux Clinic involved the general caring provisions set forth by the Canadian Psychological Association. If adequate treatment is not provided and coercive physical interventions are used, the best interests of the clients have not been served in terms of protecting and promoting their welfare.

THE ETHICAL AND LEGAL DIMENSIONS OF RECOVERED MEMORIES

In Chapter 7, we examined the scientific controversies raised by so-called recovered memories. The growing debate over the validity and reliability of reports of child abuse that surface when adults are in therapy has created considerable ethical and legal concern (Ceci & Hembrooke, 1998). One of the most important of the guidelines issued by the American Psychiatric Association (1993) stipulates that therapists should remain neutral when a patient reports abuse. Because a given symptom—for example, avoidance of sexual contact—may have many possible origins, it is not ethical, according to the APA, to attribute such symptoms to repressed memories of childhood sexual abuse without corroborating evidence.

A problem with this laudable stance is the notion that therapists can maintain neutrality. Furthermore, as mentioned in Chapter 14, some experts on sexual dysfunctions recommend that therapists inquire into possible sexual abuse whenever patients, especially women, report aversions to or disinterest in sex. The basic difficulty, then, is that many therapists are predisposed by their theorizing or by personal biases to believe that sexual abuse lies behind a wide range of psychological disorders. By the same token, therapists who do not believe that traumatic memories are often repressed may overlook childhood sexual abuse when it has taken place.

The statute of limitations has been extended in the United States, allowing those who believe they were abused as children to file suit 20 or more years after the abuse purportedly occurred. However, there has been a backlash against these kinds of lawsuits, as accused parents and others (e.g., clergy, youth leaders, and other professionals in positions of trust with children and adolescents) have begun to deny such charges vigorously, and some patients have recanted their allegations. This turn of events has resulted in lawsuits being filed against therapists both by the accused parties and by the patients (MacNamara, 1993).

Probably the best-known legal incident concerned Gary Romona, whose daughter sued him father for allegedly having molested her when she was a child. Romona, in turn, sued his daughter's therapist for having allegedly planted this erroneous idea into his daughter's mind. The father won a nearly half-million-dollar judgement (Kramer, 1995), at which point the daughter's suit against her father was dismissed. It is estimated that thousands of parents and other third parties either have already filed or plan to file lawsuits against therapists (Lazo, 1995). In addition to a concern with possible therapist bias, these lawsuits are also concerned with particular treatments that may increase susceptibility to suggestion, such as hypnosis and sodium amytal (truth serum).

It is not clear, however, whether such lawsuits will be allowed to go forward in the future. In a recent case in California, a parent falsely accused of molesting a child on the basis of repressed memories elicited during therapy was not allowed to sue the therapist. The court ruled that a therapist must be free to act solely in the interests of the client and can be sued only by the client for negligent diagnosis or treatment. A therapist, the court said, is entitled to examine the possibility of past sexual abuse and should not be inhibited by the possibility of a suit by the alleged abuser. "The therapist risks utter professional failure in his or her duty to the patient if possible childhood sexual abuse is ignored," the judge said (Associated Press, February 18, 1999).

With the scientific status of the validity of recovered memories very much in dispute, legal scholars as well as professional associations advise extreme caution in dealing with the issue. The danger of false positives—concluding that there was abuse when there was not—is as serious a matter as the danger of false negatives—concluding that there was no abuse when there was.

CONCLUDING COMMENT

An underlying theme of this book concerns the nature of knowledge. How do we decide that we understand a phenomenon? The rules of science that govern our definition of and search for knowledge require theories that can be tested, studies that can be replicated, and data that are public. But given the complexity of abnormal behaviour and the vast areas of ignorance, far more extensive than the domains that have already been mapped by science as it is currently practised, we have great respect for theoreticians and clinicians, those inventive souls who make suppositions, offer hypotheses, follow hunches—all based on rather flimsy data, but holding some promise that scientific knowledge will be forthcoming (Davison & Lazarus, 1995, 1997).

This final chapter demonstrates again something emphasized at the very beginning of this book—namely, that the behavioural scientists and mental health professionals who conduct research and give treatment are only human beings. They suffer from the same foibles that sometimes plague nonspecialists. They occasionally act with a certainty their evidence does not justify, and they sometimes fail to anticipate the moral and legal consequences of the ways in which they conduct research and apply the tentative findings of their young discipline. When society acts with great certainty on the basis of expert scientific opinion, particularly when that opinion denies to an individual the rights and respect accorded others, it may be well to let Szasz (1963) remind us that Sir Thomas Browne, a distinguished English physician, testified in an English court of law in 1664 that witches did indeed exist, "as everyone knew."

We hope that we have communicated in some measure our love for the subject matter and, more important, our commitment to the kind of questioning, doubting stance that wrests useful knowledge from nature and will yield more as new generations of scholars build on the achievements of their predecessors.

SUMMARY

- There are many legal and ethical issues related to treatment and research in psychopathology and intervention. Some civil liberties are rather routinely set aside when mental health professionals and the courts judge that mental illness has played a decisive role in determining an individual's behaviour.
- Criminal commitment sends a person to a hospital either before a trial for an alleged crime, because the person is deemed incompetent to stand trial, or after an acquittal by reason of not being criminally responsible on account of mental disorder.

- Several landmark cases in Canada and principles in Anglo-American law inform current thinking about the conditions under which a person who has committed a crime might be excused from legal responsibility for it. These decisions involve the notion that some people may not be able to distinguish between right and wrong (the M'Naghten Rules).
- There is an important difference between mental illness and insanity. The latter is a legal concept. A person can be diagnosed as mentally ill and yet be deemed sane enough both to stand trial and to be found guilty of a crime.
- A person who is considered mentally ill and dangerous to self and to others, though he or she has not broken a law, can be civilly committed to an institution or be allowed to live outside of a hospital but sometimes only under supervision and with restrictions placed on his or her activities.
- There are a number of ethical issues concerning therapy and research: ethical restraints on what kinds of research are allowable, the duty of scientists to obtain informed consent from prospective human subjects, the right of clients to confidentiality, the setting of therapy goals, the choice of techniques, and memories of sexual abuse in childhood recovered during psychotherapy when the person is an adult.

KEY TERMS

civil commitment (p. 604)
confidentiality (p. 630)
community commitment (p. 613)
criminal commitment (p. 604)
informed consent (p. 629)
insanity defence (p. 605)
M'Naghten Rules (p. 606)
not criminally responsible (p. 605)
prior capable wish (p. 621)
privileged communication (p. 630)

Reflections: Past, Present, and Future

- Revisit the quote by Abram Hoffer at the beginning of this chapter. One strict interpretation is that people with serious and chronic mental disorders can't be rehabilitated while living in the community ("whose healing qualities clearly were not sufficient to prevent them from becoming sick in the first place") or staying with their families ("too sick, or too tired, or simply do not have the resources or the energy to cope with very sick patients"). What does Hoffer really mean? What is the implication of his statements? How do they tie in to the implications of our discussions about the problems with deinstitutionalization?
- We reviewed recommended changes to the mental health "system" and the treatment of people with chronic mental health problems. What changes do you think will occur in the next 25 years? What reforms will be implemented? Will there be discoveries of new drugs that will act as "magic bullets" in the fight against disorders such as schizophrenia and bipolar disorder? Will there be breakthroughs in psychotherapy? What will it be like for the mentally ill in the next millennium? Will mental illness be all but eradicated, just as some illnesses such as leprosy or polio have been eliminated, at least in the Western world?
- Do you think that we will ever get rid of the stigma associated with mental illness? Do you think that the goal of integrating people with serious and chronic mental health problems will ever become "reality rather than rhetoric" (Goering, 2000, p. 356)? Do you think that scarce dollars in the mental health area will be allocated to other priorities in health care as a consequence of the "baby boomer" generation developing physical health problems that put pressure on the health care system in Canada?

Glossary

abnormal behaviour: Patterns of emotion, thought, and action deemed pathological for one or more of the following reasons: infrequent occurrence, violation of norms, personal distress, disability or dysfunction, and unexpectedness.

accountability: The Romanow report on the future of health care in Canada includes a recommendation that accountability, i.e. a requirement that the system and provinces be held responsible for the quality of the care provided, be a part of a new Health Care Act.

acculturation: The process that unfolds as different cultures come into contact with each other and diversity is experienced.

accurate empathic understanding: In client-centred therapy, an essential quality of the therapist, referring to the ability to see the world through the client's phenomenology as well as from perspectives of which the client may be only dimly aware.

acetylcholine: A neurotransmitter of the central, somatomotor, and parasympathetic nervous systems and of the ganglia and the neuron–sweat gland junctions of the sympathetic nervous system.

acquaintance (date) rape: Forcible sex when the people involved know each other, sometimes occurring on a date.

action therapies: Behavioural therapies are sometimes referred to as "action therapies" because they involve work on behaviour as opposed to work on dreams or transference as occurs in psychodynamic therapies. .

activity anorexia: The loss of appetite that results from being engaged in extreme physical activity. Activity anorexia could apply to ballet dancers or athletes, for example.

acute stress disorder: New in DSM-IV, a short-lived anxiety reaction to a traumatic event; if it lasts more than a month, it is diagnosed as posttraumatic stress disorder.

addiction: See *substance dependence.*

adoptees method: Research method which studies children who were adopted and reared completely apart from their abnormal parents, thereby eliminating the influence of being raised by disordered parents.

adrenal glands: Two small areas of tissue located just above the kidneys. The inner core of each gland, the medulla, secretes epinephrine and norepinephrine; the outer cortex secretes cortisol and other steroid hormones.

adrenaline: A hormone that is secreted by the adrenal glands; also called epinephrine.

adrenergic system: All the nerve cells for which epinephrine and norepinephrine are the transmitter substances, as contrasted with the cholinergic system, which consists of the nerve cells activated by acetylcholine.

advanced directive: Legal document in which an individual prescribes and proscribes certain courses of action that are to be taken to preserve his or her health or terminate life support. These instructions are prepared before the person becomes incapable of making such decisions.

advanced accurate empathy: A form of empathy in which the therapist infers concerns and feelings that lie behind what the client is saying; it represents an interpretation. Compare with primary empathy.

affect: A subjective feeling or emotional tone often accompanied by bodily expressions noticeable to others.

age effects: The consequences of being a given chronological age. Compare with *cohort effects.*

ageism: Discrimination against someone because of his or her age.

agoraphobia: A cluster of fears centring on being in open spaces and leaving the home. It is often linked to panic disorder.

AIDS (acquired immune deficiency syndrome): A fatal disease transmitted by transfer of the human immunodeficiency virus, usually during sexual relations or by using needles previously infected by an HIV-positive person; it compromises the immune system to such a degree that the person ultimately dies from cancer or from one of any number of infections.

alcoholism: A behavioural disorder in which consumption of alcoholic beverages is excessive and impairs health and social and occupational functioning; a physiological dependence on alcohol. See *substance dependence.*

alkaloid: An organic base found in seed plants, usually in mixture with a number of similar alkaloids. Alkaloids are the active chemicals that give many drugs their medicinal properties and other powerful physiological effects.

allostatic load: A maladaptive condition based in neurochemical reactions that reflect prolonged exposure to unpredictable stressors.

amenorrhea: The loss of a woman's menstrual period due to extreme weight loss and emaciation.

alogia: A negative symptom in schizophrenia, marked by poverty of speech and of speech content.

alternate form reliability: See *reliability.*

altruistic suicide: As defined by Durkheim, self-annihilation that the person feels will serve a social purpose, such as the self-immolations practised by Buddhist monks during the Vietnam War.

Alzheimer's disease: A dementia involving a progressive atrophy of cortical tissue and marked by memory impairment, involuntary movements of limbs, occasional convulsions, intellectual deterioration, and psychotic behaviour.

ambivalence: The simultaneous holding of strong positive and negative emotional attitudes toward the same situation or person.

amenorrhea: Loss of menstrual period that is sometimes caused by eating disorders.

American Law Institute guidelines: Rules proposing that insanity is a legitimate defence plea if during criminal conduct, an individual could not judge right from wrong or control his or her behaviour as required by law. Repetitive criminal acts are disavowed as a sole criterion. Compare *M'Naghten* rule and *irresistible impulse.*

amino acid: One of a large class of organic compounds important as the building blocks of proteins.

amnesia: Total or partial loss of memory that can be associated with a dissociative disorder, brain damage, or hypnosis.

amniocentesis: A prenatal diagnostic technique in which fluid drawn from the uterus is tested for birth defects, such as Down syndrome.

amphetamines: A group of stimulating drugs that produce heightened levels of energy and, in large doses, nervousness, sleeplessness, and paranoid delusions.

anaesthesia: An impairment or loss of sensation, usually of touch but sometimes of the other senses, that is often part of conversion disorder.

anal personality: An adult who, when anal retentive, is found by psychoanalytic theory to be stingy and sometimes obsessively clean; when anal expulsive, to be aggressive. Such traits are assumed to be caused by fixation through either excessive or inadequate gratification of id impulses during the anal stage of psychosexual development.

anal stage: In psychoanalytic theory, the second psychosexual stage, which occurs during the second year of life when the anus is considered the principal erogenous zone.

analgesia: An insensitivity to pain without loss of consciousness, sometimes found in conversion disorder.

analogue experiment: An experimental study of a phenomenon different from but related to the actual interests of the investigator.

analysand: A person being psychoanalyzed.

analysis of defences: The study by a psychoanalyst of the ways in which a patient avoids troubling topics by the use of defence mechanisms.

analyst: See *psychoanalyst.*

analytical psychology: A variation of Freud's psychoanalysis introduced by Carl Jung and focusing less on biological drives and more on factors such as self-fulfillment, collective unconscious, and religious symbolism.

anesthesias: In a conversion disorder a patient may experience a loss or impairment of sensation defined as an anesthesia.

anger-in theory: The view that psychophysiological disorders, such as essential hypertension, arise from a person's not expressing anger or resentment.

angina pectoris: See *coronary heart disease*.

anhedonia: A negative symptom in schizophrenia in which the individual is unable to feel pleasure.

animal phobia: The fear and avoidance of small animals.

anomic suicide: As defined by Durkheim, self-annihilation triggered by a person's inability to cope with sudden and unfavourable change in a social situation.

anorexia nervosa: A disorder in which a person refuses to eat or to retain any food or suffers a prolonged and severe diminution of appetite. The individual has an intense fear of becoming obese, feels fat even when emaciated, refuses to maintain a minimal body weight, and loses at least 25 percent of his or her original weight.

anoxia: A deficiency of oxygen reaching the tissues that is severe enough to damage the brain permanently.

Antabuse (trade name for disulfiram): A drug that makes the drinking of alcohol produce nausea and other unpleasant effects.

antidepressant: A drug that alleviates depression, usually by energizing the patient and thus elevating mood.

antipsychotic drug: Psychoactive drugs, such as Thorazine, that reduce psychotic symptoms but have long-term side effects resembling symptoms of neurological diseases.

antisocial personality: Also called a psychopath or a sociopath, a person with this disorder is superficially charming and a habitual liar, has no regard for others, shows no remorse after hurting others, has no shame for behaving in an outrageously objectionable manner, is unable to form relationships and take responsibility, and does not learn from punishment.

anxiety: An unpleasant feeling of fear and apprehension accompanied by increased physiological arousal. In learning theory, it is considered a drive that mediates between a threatening situation and avoidance behaviour. Anxiety can be assessed by self-report, by measuring physiological arousal, and by observing overt behaviour.

anxiety disorders: Disorders in which fear or tension is overriding and the primary disturbance: phobic disorders, panic disorder, generalized anxiety disorder, obsessive-compulsive disorder, acute stress disorder, and posttraumatic stress disorder. These disorders form a major category in DSM-IV and cover most of what used to be referred to as the neuroses.

anxiety neurosis: DSM-II term for what are now diagnosed as panic disorder and generalized anxiety disorder.

anxiety sensitivity: A cognitive preoccupation that involves a fear of fear itself and thus contributes to a heightened sense of panic.

anxiolytics: Tranquilizers; drugs that reduce anxiety.

anxious attachment style: An attachment orientation in which the infant expresses great distress when left alone by the caregiver, but perhaps still in the presence of a stranger.

aphasia: The loss or impairment of the ability to use language because of lesions in the brain: executive, difficulties in speaking or writing the words intended; receptive, difficulties in understanding written or spoken language.

apnea: Cessation of breathing for short periods of time, sometimes occurring during sleep.

applied behaviour analysis: The study of the antecedent conditions and reinforcement contingencies that control behaviour. See also *operant conditioning*.

aptitude test: A paper-and-pencil assessment of a person's intellectual functioning that is supposed to predict how the person will perform at a later time; well-known examples include the Scholastic Aptitude Test and the Graduate Record Examination.

aptitude-treatment interaction: The suitability of a particular therapeutic intervention to a particular patient characteristic.

arousal: A state of behavioural or physiological activation.

ascriptive responsibility: The social judgment assigned to someone who has committed an illegal act and who is expected by society to be punished for it. Contrast with descriptive responsibility.

asociality: A negative symptom of schizophrenia marked by an inability to form close relationships and to feel intimacy.

Asperger's disorder: Believed to be a mild form of autism in which social relationships are poor, and stereotyped behaviour is intense and rigid, but language and intelligence are intact.

assertion training: Behaviour therapy procedures that attempt to help a person more easily express thoughts, wishes, beliefs, and legitimate feelings of resentment or approval.

assimilation: The process of absorbing a minority group into a dominant group as they adapt and establish greater uniformity.

asthma: A psychophysiological disorder characterized by narrowing of the airways and increased secretion of mucus, often causing extremely labored and wheezy breathing.

asylums: Refuges established in western Europe in the fifteenth century to confine and provide for the mentally ill; the forerunners of the mental hospital.

attention-deficit/hyperactivity disorder (ADHD): A disorder in children marked by difficulties in focusing adaptively on the task at hand, by inappropriate fidgeting and antisocial behaviour, and by excessive non-goal-directed behaviour.

attribution: The explanation a person has for his or her behaviour.

autistic disorder: In this pervasive developmental disorder, the child's world is one of profound aloneness. Speech is often absent, and the child has an obsessive need for everything to remain the same.

automatic thoughts: In Beck's theory, the things people picture or tell themselves as they make their way in life.

autonomic lability: Tendency for the autonomic nervous system to be easily aroused.

autonomic nervous system (ANS): The division of the nervous system that regulates involuntary functions; innervates endocrine glands, smooth muscle, and heart muscle; and initiates the physiological changes that are part of the expression of emotion. See *sympathetic* and *parasympathetic nervous systems*.

autonomy: A personality style associated with vulnerability to depression. It involves a need to work toward achievement goals while being free from constraints imposed by others.

aversion therapy: A behaviour therapy procedure that pairs a noxious stimulus, such as a shock, with situations that are undesirably attractive to make the situations less appealing.

aversive conditioning: Process believed to underlie the effectiveness of aversion therapy.

aversive stimulus: A stimulus that elicits pain, fear, or avoidance.

avoidance conditioning: Learning to move away from a stimulus that has previously been paired with an aversive stimulus such as electric shock.

avoidance learning: An experimental procedure in which a neutral stimulus is paired with a noxious one so that the organism learns to avoid the previously neutral stimulus.

avoidant attachment style: An attachment orientation in which the infant is withdrawn and detached from the caregiver, almost as if no attachment bond was formed in the first place.

avoidant personality disorder: Individuals with this disorder have poor self-esteem and thus are extremely sensitive to potential rejection and remain aloof even though they very much desire affiliation and affection.

avolition: A negative symptom in schizophrenia in which the individual lacks interest and drive.

barbituates: A class of synthetic sedative drugs that are addictive and in large doses can cause death by almost completely relaxing the diaphragm.

baseline: The state of a phenomenon before the independent variable is manipulated, providing a standard against which the effects of the variable can be measured.

bedlam: A term that describes a scene or place involving a wild uproar or confusion. The term is derived from the scenes at Bethlehem Hospital in London, where unrestrained groups of mentally ill people interacted with each other.

behaviour genetics: The study of individual differences in behaviour that are attributable to differences in genetic makeup.

behaviour modification: A term sometimes used interchangeably with behaviour therapy.

behaviour rehearsal: A behaviour therapy technique in which a client practices new behaviour in the consulting room, often aided by demonstrations and role-play by the therapist.

behaviour therapy: A branch of psychotherapy narrowly conceived as the application of classical and operant conditioning to the alteration of clinical problems, but more broadly conceived as applied experimental psychology in a clinical context.

behavioural assessment: A sampling of ongoing cognitions, feelings, and overt behaviour in their situational context. Contrast with projective test and personality inventory.

behavioural medicine: An interdisciplinary field concerned with integrating knowledge from medicine and behavioural science to understand health and illness and to prevent as well as to treat psychophysiological disorders and other illnesses in which a person's psyche plays a role. See also *health psychology*.

behavioural observation: A form of behavioural assessment that entails careful observation of a person's overt behaviour in a particular situation.

behavioural pediatrics: A branch of behavioural medicine concerned with psychological aspects of childhood medical problems.

behaviourism: The school of psychology associated with John B. Watson, who proposed that observable behaviour, not consciousness, is the proper subject matter of psychology. Currently, many who consider themselves behaviourists do use mediational concepts, provided they are firmly anchored to observables.

bell and pad: A behaviour therapy technique for eliminating nocturnal enuresis; if the child wets, an electric circuit is closed and a bell sounds, waking the child.

best practices model: An approach to treatment that focuses on the most efficacious interventions as determined by empirical research.

bilateral ECT: Electroconvulsive therapy in which electrodes are placed on each side of the forehead and an electrical current is passed between them through both hemispheres of the brain.

binge eating disorder: Categorized in DSM-IV as a diagnosis in need of further study; includes recurrent episodes of unrestrained eating.

biofeedback: Procedures that provide an individual immediate information on minute changes in muscle activity, skin temperature, heart rate, blood pressure, and other somatic functions. It is assumed that voluntary control over these bodily processes can be achieved through this knowledge, thereby ameliorating to some extent certain psychophysiological disorders.

biological paradigm: A broad theoretical view that holds that mental disorders are caused by some aberrant somatic process or defect.

bipolar I disorder: A term applied to the disorder of people who experience episodes of both mania and depression or of mania alone.

bipolar II disorder: A type of bipolar disorder in which episodes of major depression are followed by a type of manic phase that is less severe than in Bipolar I disorder.

Biopsychosocial paradigm: A paradigm that suggests that all normal and abnormal behaviour is caused by an interaction of biological, psychological and social factors.

bisexuality: Sexual desire or activity directed toward both men and women.

blocking: A disturbance associated with thought disorders in which a train of speech is interrupted by silence before an idea is fully expressed.

body dysmorphic disorder: A somatoform disorder marked by preoccupation with an imagined or exaggerated defect in appearance, for example, facial wrinkles or excess facial or body hair.

borderline personality disorder: People with a borderline personality are impulsive and unpredictable, with an uncertain self-image, intense and unstable social relationships, and extreme mood swings.

brain stem: The part of the brain connecting the spinal cord with the cerebrum. It contains the pons and medulla oblongata and functions as a neural relay station.

brief reactive psychosis: A disorder in which a person has a sudden onset of psychotic symptoms—incoherence, loose associations, delusions, hallucinations—immediately after a severely disturbing event; the symptoms last more than a few hours but no more than two weeks. See *schizophreniform disorder*.

brief therapy: Time-limited psychotherapy, usually ego-analytic in orientation and lasting no more than twenty-five sessions.

Briquet's syndrome: See *somatization disorder*.

brooding: A moody contemplation of depressive symptoms, "What am I doing to deserve this?", that is more common in females than males.

bulimia nervosa: A disorder characterized by episodic uncontrollable eating binges followed by purging either by vomiting or by taking laxatives.

Canadian Mental Health Association: A national organization that provides information about mental illness and acts as an advocate for mentally ill people.

Cannabis sativa: See *marijuana*.

cardiovascular disorder: A medical problem involving the heart and the blood circulation system, such as hypertension or coronary heart disease.

case study: The collection of historical or biographical information on a single individual, often including experiences in therapy.

castration: The surgical removal of the testes.

castration anxiety: The fear of having the genitals removed or injured.

catastrophization: A cognitive tendency that involves magnifying or amplifying the impact of a problem, symptom, or stressful situation by interpreting it is a major catastrophe.

catatonic immobility: A fixity of posture, sometimes grotesque, maintained for long periods, with accompanying muscular rigidity, trancelike state of consciousness, and waxy flexibility.

catatonic schizophrenia: A subtype of schizophrenia whose primary symptoms alternate between stuporous immobility and excited agitation.

catecholamines: Monoamine compounds, each having a catechol portion. Catecholamines known to be neurotransmitters of the central nervous system are norepinephrine and dopamine; another, epinephrine, is principally a hormone.

categorical classification: An approach to assessment in which the basic decision is whether a person is or is not a member of a discrete grouping. Contrast with *dimensional classification*.

cathartic method: A therapeutic procedure introduced by Breuer and developed further by Freud in the late nineteenth century whereby a patient recalls and relives an earlier emotional catastrophe and re-experiences the tension and unhappiness, the goal being to relieve emotional suffering.

central nervous system: The part of the nervous system that in vertebrates consists of the brain and spinal cord, to which all sensory impulses are transmitted and from which motor impulses pass out; it also supervises and coordinates the activities of the entire nervous system.

cerebellum: An area of the hindbrain concerned with balance, posture, and motor coordination.

cerebral atherosclerosis: A chronic disease impairing intellectual and emotional life, caused by a reduction in the brain's blood supply through a buildup of fatty deposits in the arteries.

cerebral contusion: A bruising of neural tissue marked by swelling and hemorrhage and resulting in coma; it may permanently impair intellectual functioning.

cerebral cortex: The thin outer covering of each of the cerebral hemispheres; it is highly convoluted and composed of nerve cell bodies which constitute the gray matter of the brain.

cerebral hemisphere: Either of the two halves that make up the cerebrum.

cerebral hemorrhage: Bleeding onto brain tissue from a ruptured blood vessel.

cerebral thrombosis: The formation of a blood clot in a cerebral artery that blocks circulation in that area of brain tissue and causes paralysis, loss of sensory functions, and possibly death.

cerebrovascular disease: An illness that disrupts blood supply to the brain, such as a stroke.

cerebrum: The two-lobed structure extending from the brain stem and constituting the anterior (frontal) part of the brain. The largest and most recently developed portion of the brain, it coordinates sensory and motor activities and is the seat of higher cognitive processes.

character disorder: The old term for personality disorder.

child sexual abuse: Sexual abuse of children that involves direct physical contact, such as pedophilia or incest.

childhood disintegrative disorder: A lifelong developmental disorder characterized by significant loss of social, play, language, and motor skills after the second year of life. Abnormalities in social interaction and communication are similar to autism.

chlorpromazine: One of the phenothiazines, the generic term for one of the most widely prescribed anti-psychotic drugs, sold under the name Thorazine.

cholinergic system: All the nerve cells for which acetylcholine is the transmitter substance, in contrast to the *adrenergic system*.

choreiform: Pertaining to the involuntary, spasmodic, jerking movements of the limbs and head found in Huntington's chorea and other brain disorders.

chromosomes: The threadlike bodies within the nucleus of the cell, composed primarily of DNA and bearing the genetic information of the organism.

chronic: Of lengthy duration or recurring frequently, often with progressing seriousness.

chronic brain syndrome: See *senile dementia*.

chronic pain: Persistent and debilitating pain that continues to be present long after the anticipated time for healing has passed.

chronic schizophrenic: A psychotic patient who deteriorated over a long period of time and has been hospitalized for more than two years.

civil commitment: A procedure whereby a person can be legally certified as mentally ill and hospitalized, even against his or her will.

classical conditioning: A basic form of learning, sometimes referred to as Pavlovian conditioning, in which a neutral stimulus is repeatedly paired with another stimulus (called the unconditioned stimulus, UCS) that naturally elicits a certain desired response (called the unconditioned response, UCR). After repeated trials the neutral stimulus becomes a conditioned stimulus (CS) and evokes the same or a similar response, now called the conditioned response (CR).

classificatory variables: The characteristics that people bring with them to scientific investigations, such as sex, age, and mental status; studied by correlational research and mixed designs.

client-centred therapy: A humanistic-existential insight therapy, developed by Carl Rogers, which emphasizes the importance of the therapist's understanding the client's subjective experiences and assisting the client to gain more awareness of current motivations for behaviour; the goal is not only to reduce anxieties but also to foster actualization of the client's potential.

clinical interview: General term for conversation between a clinician and a patient that is aimed at determining diagnosis, history, causes for problems, and possible treatment options.

clinical psychologist: An individual who has earned a Ph.D. degree in psychology or a Psy.D. and whose training has included an internship in a mental hospital or clinic.

clinical psychology: The special area of psychology concerned with the study of psychopathology, its diagnosis, causes, prevention, and treatment.

clinician: A health professional authorized to provide services to people suffering from one or more pathologies.

clitoris: The small, heavily innervated structure located above the vaginal opening; the primary site of female responsiveness to sexual stimulation.

clonidine: An anti-hypertensive drug that shows some promise in helping people wean themselves from substance dependence.

cocaine: A pain-reducing, stimulating, and addictive alkaloid obtained from coca leaves, which increases mental powers, produces euphoria, heightens sexual desire, and in large doses causes paranoia and hallucinations.

cognition: The process of knowing; the thinking, judging, reasoning, and planning activities of the human mind; behaviour is now often explained as depending on these processes.

cognitive-behavioural case formulation: A process in which a cognitive-behavioural therapist attempts to ascertain how the various problems experienced by a client are related in order to pick out target behaviours that will become the focus of therapy.

cognitive behaviour therapy (CBT): Behaviour therapy which incorporates theory and research on cognitive processes such as thoughts, perceptions, judgments, self-statements, and tacit assumptions. A blend of both the cognitive and behavioural paradigms.

cognitive event related potential (ERP): Specific brain wave potentials that can be evoked by standardized neuropsychological tests modified for computer presentation.

cognitive paradigm: General view that people can best be understood by studying how they perceive and structure their experiences.

cognitive restructuring: Any behaviour therapy procedure that attempts to alter the manner in which a client thinks about life so that he or she changes overt behaviour and emotions.

cognitive therapy (CT): A cognitive restructuring therapy associated with the psychiatrist Aaron T. Beck, concerned with changing negative schemata and certain cognitive biases or distortions that influence a person to construe life in a depressing or otherwise maladaptive way.

cohort effects: The consequences of having been born in a given year and having grown up during a particular time period with its own unique pressures, problems, challenges, and opportunities. To be distinguished from *age effects*.

coitus: Sexual intercourse.

collective unconscious: Jung's concept that every human being has within, the wisdom, ideas, and strivings of those who have come before.

common factorism: A method that seeks therapeutic strategies that are common to all forms of psychotherapy.

communication disorders: Learning disabilities in a child who fails to develop to the degree expected by his or her intellectual level in a specific language skill area. Includes expressive language disorder, phonological disorder, and stuttering.

community mental health: The delivery of services to needy, under-served groups through centres that offer outpatient therapy, short-term inpatient care, day hospitalization, twenty-four-hour emergency services, and consultation and education to other community agencies, such as the police.

community psychology: An approach to therapy that emphasizes prevention and the seeking out of potential difficulties rather than waiting for troubled individuals to initiate

consultation. The location for professional activities tends to be in the person's natural surroundings rather than in the therapist's office. See *prevention*.

community treatment orders (CTOs): A legal tool that specifies the terms of treatment that must be adhered to in order for a mentally ill person to be released and live in the community.

comorbidity: The co-occurrence of two disorders, as when a person is both depressed and alcoholic.

competency to stand trial: A legal decision as to whether a person can participate meaningfully in his or her own defence.

compulsion: The irresistible impulse to repeat an irrational act over and over again.

concordance: As applied in behaviour genetics, the similarity in psychiatric diagnosis or in other traits within a pair of twins.

concurrent validity: See *validity*.

concussion: A jarring injury to the brain produced by a blow to the head that usually involves a momentary loss of consciousness followed by transient disorientation and memory loss.

conditioned response (CR): See *classical conditioning*.

conditioned stimulus (CS): See *classical conditioning*.

conditioning theory of tolerance: A theory that involves the notion that tolerance and extinction are learned responses and environmental cues become associated with addictive substances through Pavlovian conditioning.

conduct disorder: Patterns of extreme disobedience in youngsters, including theft, vandalism, lying, and early drug use; may be precursor of antisocial personality disorder.

confabulation: Filling in gaps in memory caused by brain dysfunction with made-up and often improbable stories that the person accepts as true.

confidentiality: A principle observed by lawyers, doctors, pastors, psychologists, and psychiatrists that dictates that the goings-on in a professional and private relationship are not divulged to anyone else. See *privileged communication*.

conflict: A state of being torn between competing forces.

confounds: Variables whose effects are so intermixed that they cannot be measured separately, making the design of an experiment internally invalid and its results impossible to interpret.

congenital: Existing at or before birth but not acquired through heredity.

congruency hypothesis: This hypothesis is derived from research on personality, stress, and depression. The congruency hypothesis involves the prediction that people are likely to be depressed if they have a personality vulnerability that is matched by congruent life events (i.e., perfectionists who experience a failure to achieve).

conjoint therapy: Couples or family therapy where partners are seen together and children are seen with their parents and possibly with an extended family.

construct: An entity inferred by a scientist to explain observed phenomena. See also *mediator*.

construct validity: The extent to which scores or ratings on an assessment instrument relate to other variables or behaviours according to some theory or hypothesis.

constructivist-narrative approach: An approach that focuses on the cognitive meaning that people attach to life events by assessing the stories they have constructed to account for their personal situation.

content validity: See *validity*.

contingency: A close relationship, especially of a causal nature, between two events, one of which regularly follows the other.

control group: Those in an experiment for whom the independent variable is not manipulated, thus forming a baseline against which the effects of the manipulation of the experimental group can be evaluated.

controlled drinking: A pattern of alcohol consumption that is moderate and avoids the extremes of total abstinence and of inebriation.

conversion disorder: A somatoform disorder in which sensory or muscular functions are impaired, usually suggesting neurological disease, even though the bodily organs themselves are sound; anaesthesias and paralyses of limbs are examples.

convulsive therapy: See *electroconvulsive therapy*.

coronary heart disease (CHD): Angina pectoris, chest pains caused by insufficient supply of blood and thus oxygen to the heart; and myocardial infarction, or heart attack, in which the blood and oxygen supply is reduced so much that heart muscles are damaged.

corpus callosum: The large band of nerve fibres connecting the two cerebral hemispheres.

correlation: The tendency for two variables, such as height and weight, to covary.

correlation coefficient: A statistic that measures the degree to which two variables are related.

correlational method: The research strategy used to establish whether two or more variables are related. Relationships may be positive—as values for one variable increase, those for the other do also—or negative—as values for one variable increase, those for the other decrease.

cortisol: A hormone secreted by the adrenal cortices.

co-twin: In behaviour genetics research using the twin method, the member of the pair who is tested later to determine whether he or she has the same diagnosis or trait discovered earlier in the birth partner.

counselling psychologist: A doctoral level mental health professional whose training is similar to that of a clinical psychologist, though usually with less emphasis on research and serious psychopathology.

counterconditioning: Relearning achieved by eliciting a new response in the presence of a particular stimulus.

countertransference: Feelings that the psychoanalyst unconsciously directs to the patient, stemming from his or her own emotional vulnerabilities and unresolved conflicts.

couples (marital) therapy: Any professional intervention that treats relationship problems of a couple.

covert sensitization: A form of aversion therapy in which the person is told to imagine undesirably attractive situations and activities while unpleasant feelings are being induced by imagery.

criminal commitment: A procedure whereby a person is confined in a mental institution either for determination of competency to stand trial or after acquittal by reason of insanity.

criterion validity: See *validity*.

critical period: A stage of early development in which an organism is susceptible to certain influences and during which important irreversible patterns of behaviour are acquired.

cross-dependent: Acting on the same receptors, as methadone does with heroin. See *heroin substitutes*.

cross-sectional studies: Studies in which different age groups are compared at the same time. Compare with *longitudinal studies*.

CT scan: Refers to computerized axial tomography, a method of diagnosis in which X- rays are taken from different angles and then analyzed by computer to produce a representation of the part of the body in cross section; often used on the brain.

cultural bias: The degree to which assessment devices, such as intelligence tests, have content that is not representative and meaningful for individuals from various cultural backgrounds.

cultural diversity: The differences that exist in an area or region due to the heterogeneity and varying backgrounds of the members of that region.

cultural-familial retardation: A mild backwardness in mental development with no indication of brain pathology but evidence of similar limitation in at least one of the parents or siblings.

cunnilingus: The oral stimulation of female genitalia.

Cushing's syndrome: An endocrine disorder usually affecting young women, produced by oversecretion of cortisone and marked by mood swings, irritability, agitation, and physical disfigurement.

cyclical psychodynamics: The reciprocal relations between current behaviour and repressed conflicts, such that they mutually reinforce each other.

cyclothymic disorder: Chronic swings between elation and depression not severe enough to warrant the diagnosis of bipolar disorder.

daily hassles: The relatively minor yet chronic and persistent life stressors that combine to have a strong, negative influence on personal well-being.

defence mechanisms: In psychoanalytic theory, reality-distorting strategies unconsciously adopted to protect the ego from anxiety.

deinstitutionalization: The increasing tendency for treatment to take place in the community, perhaps on an outpatient basis, rather than having patients reside in a public institution, such as a provincial mental hospital.

delay of reward gradient: The learning theory term for the finding that rewards and punishments lose their effectiveness the further they are removed in time from the response in question.

delayed echolalia: See *echolalia*.

delirium: A state of great mental confusion in which consciousness is clouded, attention cannot be sustained, and the stream of thought and speech is incoherent. The person is probably disoriented, emotionally erratic, restless or lethargic, and often has illusions, delusions, and hallucinations.

delirium tremens (DTs): One of the withdrawal symptoms that sometimes occurs when a period of heavy alcohol consumption is terminated; marked by fever, sweating, trembling, cognitive impairment, and hallucinations.

delusional (paranoid) disorder: A disorder in which the individual has persistent persecutory delusions or delusional jealousy and is very often contentious but has no thought disorder or hallucinations.

delusional jealousy: The unfounded conviction that one's mate is unfaithful; the individual may collect small bits of "evidence" to justify the delusion.

delusions: Beliefs contrary to reality, firmly held in spite of evidence to the contrary; common in paranoid disorders; **of control**, belief that one is being manipulated by some external force such as radar, television, or a creature from outer space; **of grandeur**, belief that one is an especially important or powerful person; **of persecution**, belief that one is being plotted against or oppressed by others.

dementia: Deterioration of mental faculties—memory, judgment, abstract thought, control of impulses, intellectual ability—that impairs social and occupational functioning and eventually changes the personality. See *Alzheimer's disease*.

dementia praecox: An older term for schizophrenia, chosen to describe what was believed to be an incurable and progressive deterioration of mental functioning beginning in adolescence.

demographic variable: A varying characteristic that is a vital or social statistic of an individual, sample group, or population, for example, age, sex, socioeconomic status, racial origin, education.

demonology: The doctrine that a person's abnormal behaviour is caused by an autonomous evil spirit.

denial: Defence mechanism in which a thought, feeling, or action is disavowed by the person.

dependent personality disorder: Lacking in self-confidence, such people passively allow others to run their lives and make no demands on them so as not to endanger these protective relationships.

dependent variable: In a psychological experiment, the behaviour that is measured and is expected to change with manipulation of the independent variable.

depersonalization: An alteration in perception of the self in which the individual loses a sense of reality and feels estranged from the self and perhaps separated from the body. It may be a temporary reaction to stress and fatigue or part of panic disorder, depersonalization disorder, or schizophrenia.

depersonalization disorder: A dissociative disorder in which the individual feels unreal and estranged from the self and surroundings enough to disrupt functioning. People with this disorder may feel that their extremities have changed in size or that they are watching themselves from a distance.

depression: A disorder marked by great sadness and apprehension, feelings of worthlessness and guilt, withdrawal from others, loss of sleep, appetite, sexual desire, loss of interest and pleasure in usual activities, and either lethargy or agitation. Called major depression in DSM-IV and unipolar depression by others. It can be an associated symptom of other disorders.

depressive paradox: A cognitive tendency for depressed individuals to accept personal responsibility for negative outcomes despite feeling a lack of personal control.

depressive predictive certainty: This concept, derived from the hopelessness theory of depression, states that people become prone to depression when they perceived that an anticipated state of helplessness is certain to occur.

derealization: Loss of the sense that the surroundings are real; present in several psychological disorders, such as panic disorder, depersonalization disorder, and schizophrenia.

descriptive responsibility: In legal proceedings, the judgment that the accused performed an illegal act. Contrast with *ascriptive responsibility*.

deterioration effect: In abnormal psychology, a harmful outcome from being in psychotherapy.

detoxification: The initial stage in weaning an addicted person from a drug; involves medical supervision of the sometimes painful withdrawal.

detumescence: The flow of blood out of the genital area.

diagnosis: The determination that the set of symptoms or problems of a patient indicates a particular disorder.

Diagnostic and Statistical Manual of Mental Disorders (DSM) DSM-IV_TR : A publication of the American Psychiatric Association that is an attempt to delineate specific and discrete syndromes or mental disorders. It has been through several revisions and the current one is the Fourth Editon (IV)

dialectical behaviour therapy: A therapeutic approach to borderline personality disorder that combines client-centred empathy and acceptance with behavioural problem solving, social-skills training, and limit setting.

diathesis: Predisposition toward a disease or abnormality.

diathesis–stress paradigm: As applied in psychopathology, a view that assumes that individuals predisposed toward a particular mental disorder will be particularly affected by stress and will then manifest abnormal behaviour.

dichotic listening: An experimental procedure in which a person hears two different taped messages simultaneously through earphones, one in each ear, usually with the instruction to attend to only one of the messages.

diencephalon: The lower area of the forebrain, containing the thalamus and hypothalamus.

dimensional classification: An approach to assessment according to which a person is placed on a continuum. Contrast with *categorical classification*.

directionality problem: A difficulty that arises in the correlational method of research when it is known that two variables are related but it is unclear which is causing the other.

discriminative stimulus: An event that informs an organism that if a particular response is made, reinforcement will follow.

disease: The medical concept that distinguishes an impairment of the normal state of the organism by its particular group of symptoms and its specific cause.

disease model: See *medical model*.

disorder of written expression: Difficulties writing without errors in spelling, grammar, or punctuation.

disorganized attachment style: An attachment orientation in which the infant demonstrates a confused attachment style that emerges after being raised in a chaotic and abusive environment.

disorganized schizophrenia: In this subtype of schizophrenia the person has diffuse and regressive symptoms; the individual is given to silliness, facial grimaces, and inconsequential rituals and has constantly changeable moods and poor hygiene. There are few significant remissions and eventually considerable deterioration. This form of schizophrenia was formerly called hebephrenia.

disorganized speech (thought disorder): Speech found in schizophrenics that is marked by problems in the organization of ideas and in speaking so that others can understand.

disorientation: A state of mental confusion with respect to time, place, identity of self, other persons, and objects.

displacement: A defence mechanism whereby an emotional response is unconsciously redirected from an object or concept perceived as dangerous to a substitute less threatening to the ego.

dissociation: A process whereby a group of mental processes is split off from the mainstream of consciousness, or behaviour loses its relationship with the rest of the personality.

dissociative amnesia: A dissociative disorder in which the person suddenly becomes unable to recall important personal information to an extent that cannot be explained by ordinary forgetfulness.

dissociative disorders: Disorders in which the normal integration of consciousness, memory, or identity is suddenly and temporarily altered; dissociative amnesia, dissociative fugue, dissociative identity disorder (multiple personality), and depersonalization disorder are examples.

dissociative fugue: Disorder in which the person experiences total amnesia, moves, and establishes a new identity.

dissociative identity disorder (DID): A rare dissociative disorder in which two or more fairly distinct and separate personalities are present within the same individual, each with his or her own memories, relationships, and behaviour patterns, with only one of them dominant at any given time. Formerly called multiple personality disorder.

divorce mediation: A form of couples (marital) therapy in which a distressed couple is helped to collaborate on issues such as child custody outside the adversarial framework of a formal legal process.

dizygotic (DZ) twins: Birth partners who have developed from separate fertilized eggs and who are only 50 percent alike genetically, no more so than siblings born from different pregnancies; sometimes called fraternal twins.

Dodo bird effect: The general finding that all forms of psychotherapies achieve similar outcomes.

dominant gene: One of a pair of genes that predominates over the other and determines that the trait it fosters will prevail in the phenotype.

dopamine: A catecholamine that is both a precursor of norepinephrine and itself a neurotransmitter of the central nervous system. Disturbances in certain of its tracts apparently figure in schizophrenia and Parkinson's disease.

dopamine activity theory (dopamine theory): The view that schizophrenia arises from an increase in the number of dopamine receptors.

double-bind theory: An interpersonal situation in which an individual is confronted over long periods of time by mutually inconsistent messages to which she or he must respond, formerly believed by some theorists to cause schizophrenia.

double-blind procedure: A method for reducing the biasing effects of the expectations of research participant and experimenter; neither is allowed to know whether the independent variable of the experiment is being applied to the participant.

double depression: A comorbid condition that applies to someone characterized by both dysthymia and major depression.

Down syndrome (trisomy 21): A form of mental retardation generally caused by an extra chromosome. The child's IQ is usually less than 50, and the child has distinctive physical characteristics, most notably slanted eyes.

dream analysis: A key psychoanalytic technique in which the unconscious meanings of dream material are uncovered.

drive: A construct explaining the motivation of behaviour, or an internal physiological tension impelling an organism to activity.

drug abuse: See *substance abuse*.

drug addiction: See *substance dependence*.

DSM-IV: The current Diagnostic and Statistical Manual of the American Psychiatric Association.

dualism: Philosophical doctrine, advanced most definitively by Descartes, that a human being is both mental and physical and that these two aspects are separate but interacting. Contrast with *monism*.

Durham decision: A 1954 U.S. court ruling that an accused person is not ascriptively responsible if his or her crime is judged attributable to mental disease or defect.

dysfunction: An impairment or disturbance in the functioning of an organ, organ system, behaviour, or cognition.

dyslexia: A disturbance in the ability to read; it is one of the learning disorders.

dyspareunia: Painful or difficult sexual intercourse; the pain or difficulty is usually caused by infection or a physical injury, such as torn ligaments in the pelvic region.

dysthymic disorder: State of depression that is long lasting but not severe enough for the diagnosis of major depression.

echolalia: The immediate repetition of the words of others, often found in autistic children. In **delayed echolalia** this inappropriate echoing takes place hours or weeks later.

eclecticism: In psychology, the view that more is to be gained by employing concepts and techniques from various theoretical systems than by restricting oneself to a single approach.

ecological momentary assessment (EMA): Form of self-observation involving collection of data in real time (e.g., diaries) regarding thoughts, moods, and stressors.

Ecstasy: A relatively new hallucinogen that is chemically similar to mescaline and the amphetamines.

effectiveness: Research into psychotherapy has made a distinction between the efficacy of an intervention and its effectiveness which is defined as what is offered to and received by clients in the real world.

ego: In psychoanalytic theory, the predominantly conscious part of the personality, responsible for decision making and for dealing with reality.

ego analysis: An important set of modifications of classical psychoanalysis, based on a conception of the human being as having a stronger, more autonomous ego with gratifications independent of id satisfactions. Sometimes called ego psychology.

ego analysts: Those who practice ego analysis.

ego-alien: Foreign to the self, such as a compulsion.

ego-dystonic homosexuality: According to DSM-III, a disorder of people who are persistently dissatisfied with their homosexuality and wish instead to be attracted to members of the opposite sex.

egoistic suicide: As defined by Durkheim, self-annihilation committed because the individual feels extreme alienation from others and from society.

Electra complex: See *Oedipus complex*.

electrocardiogram: A recording of the electrical activity of the heart, made with an electrocardiograph.

electroconvulsive therapy (ECT): A treatment that produces a convulsion by passing electric current through the brain. Though an unpleasant and occasionally dangerous procedure, it can be useful in alleviating profound depression.

electrodermal responding: A recording of the minute electrical activity of the sweat glands on the skin, allowing the inference of an emotional state.

electroencephalogram (EEG): A graphic recording of electrical activity of the brain, usually of the cerebral cortex, but sometimes of lower areas.

emotional support: A sense of being cared for and comforted by other people.

empathy: Awareness and understanding of another's feelings and thoughts. See *primary empathy* and *advanced accurate empathy*.

empty-chair technique: A Gestalt therapy procedure for helping the client become more aware of denied feelings; the client talks to important people or to feelings as though they were present and seated in a nearby vacant chair.

encephalitis: Inflammation of brain tissue caused by a number of agents, the most significant being several viruses carried by insects.

encephalitis lethargica: Known as sleeping sickness, a form of encephalitis that occurred early in this century and was characterized by lethargy and prolonged periods of sleeping.

encopresis: A disorder in which, through faulty control of the sphincters, the person repeatedly defecates in his or her clothing after an age at which continence is expected.

encounter group: See *sensitivity training group*.

endocrine gland: Any of a number of ductless glands that release hormones directly into the blood or lymph. The secretions of some endocrine glands increase during emotional arousal.

endogenous: Attributable to internal causes.

endorphins: Opiates produced within the body; they may have an important role in the processes by which the body builds up tolerance to drugs and is distressed by their withdrawal.

enuresis: A disorder in which, through faulty control of the bladder, the person wets repeatedly during the night (nocturnal enuresis) or during the day after an age at which continence is expected.

enzyme: A complex protein produced by the cells to act as a catalyst in regulating metabolic activities.

epidemiology: The study of the frequency and distribution of illness in a population.

epilepsy: An altered state of consciousness accompanied by sudden changes in the usual rhythmical electrical activity of the brain.

epinephrine: A hormone (a catecholamine) secreted by the medulla of the adrenal gland; its effects are similar, but not identical, to those of stimulating the sympathetic nerves. It causes an increase in blood pressure, inhibits peristaltic movements, and liberates glucose from the liver. Also called adrenaline.

erogenous: Capable of giving sexual pleasure when stimulated.

Eros (libido): Freud's term for the life-integrating instinct or force of the id, sometimes equated with sexual drive. Compare *Thanatos*.

essential hypertension: A psychophysiological disorder characterized by high blood pressure that cannot be traced to an organic cause. Over the years it causes degeneration of small arteries, enlargement of the heart, and kidney damage.

estrogen: A female sex hormone produced especially in the ovaries that stimulates the development and maintenance of the secondary sex characteristics, such as breast enlargement.

etiological validity: See *validity*.

etiology: All the factors that contribute to the development of an illness or disorder.

eugenics: The field concerned with improving the hereditary qualities of the human race through social control of mating and reproduction.

eustress: A term coined by Hans Selye to refer to pleasant stress arising from environmental conditions.

evidence-based treatment: Treatments and interventions that have been shown to be effective according to controlled experimental research.

***ex post facto* analysis**: In the correlational method of research, an attempt to reduce the third-variable problem by picking people who are matched on characteristics that may be confounds.

excitement phase: As applied by Masters and Johnson, the first stage of sexual arousal, which is initiated by any appropriate stimulus.

executive aphasia: See *aphasia*.

executive functioning: The cognitive capacity to plan how to do a task, how to devise strategies, and how to monitor one's performance.

exhibitionism: Marked preference for obtaining sexual gratification by exposing one's genitals to an unwilling observer.

existential analysis: See *existential therapy*.

existential therapy: An insight therapy that emphasizes choice and responsibility to define the meaning of one's life. In contrast with humanistic therapy, it tends to be less cheerful or sanguine in outlook, focusing more on the anxiety that is inherent to confronting one's ultimate aloneness in the world.

exogenous: Attributable to external causes.

exorcism: The casting out of evil spirits by ritualistic chanting or torture.

experiment: The most powerful research technique for determining causal relationships, requiring the manipulation of an independent variable, the measurement of a dependent variable, and the random assignment of participants to the several different conditions being investigated.

experimental effect: A statistically significant difference between two groups experiencing different manipulations of the independent variable.

experimental hypothesis: What the investigator assumes will happen in a scientific investigation if certain conditions are met or particular variables are manipulated.

expressed emotion (EE): In the literature on schizophrenia, the amount of hostility and criticism directed from other people to the patient, usually within a family.

expressive language disorder: Difficulties expressing oneself in speech.

external validity: See *validity*.

extinction: The elimination of a classically conditioned response by the omission of the unconditioned stimulus. In operant conditioning, the elimination of the conditioned response by the omission of reinforcement.

extradural hematoma: Hemorrhage and swelling between the skull and dura mater when a meningeal artery is ruptured by a fractured bone of the skull.

factitious disorders: Disorders in which the individual's physical or psychological symptoms appear under voluntary control and are adopted merely to assume the role of a sick person. The disorder can also involve a parent producing a disorder in a child and is then called factitious disorder by proxy or Munchausen syndrome.

false hope syndrome: A tendency for the initial positive results of attempts at weight loss to foster an overly positive tendency to pursue unrealistic weight loss goals, resulting eventually in profound disappointment.

falsifiability: The extent to which a scientific assertion is amenable to systematic probes, any one of which could negate the scientist's expectations.

familiar: In witchcraft, a supernatural spirit often embodied in an animal and at the service of a person.

family functioning: The adjustment of the family system as a whole in terms of the family environment and performance of assigned roles to family members.

family interaction method: A procedure for studying family behaviour by observing family members' interactions in a structured laboratory situation.

family method: A research strategy in behaviour genetics in which the frequency of a trait or of abnormal behaviour is determined in relatives who have varying percentages of shared genetic background.

family systems approach: A general approach to etiology and treatment that focuses on the complex interrelationships within families.

family therapy: A form of group therapy in which members of a family are helped to relate better to one another.

fear drive: In the Mowrer–Miller theory, an unpleasant internal state that impels avoidance. The necessity to reduce a fear drive can form the basis for new learning.

fear of performance: Being overly concerned with one's behaviour during sexual contact with another, postulated by Masters and Johnson as a major factor in sexual dysfunction.

fear response: In the Mowrer–Miller theory, a response to a threatening or noxious situation that is covert and unobservable but that is assumed to function as a stimulus to produce measurable physiological changes in the body and observable overt behaviour.

feedforward mechanisms: Anticipatory, regulatory responses made in anticipation of a drug that enables us to anticipate drug effects before they occur.

female orgasmic disorder: A recurrent and persistent delay or absence of orgasm in a woman during sexual activity adequate in focus, intensity, and duration; in many instances the woman may experience considerable sexual excitement.

female sexual arousal disorder: Formally called frigidity, the inability of a female to reach or maintain the lubrication–swelling stage of sexual excitement or to enjoy a subjective sense of pleasure or excitement during sexual activity.

fetal alcohol syndrome: Retarded growth of the developing fetus and infant; cranial, facial, and limb anomalies; and mental retardation caused by heavy consumption of alcohol by the mother during pregnancy.

fetishism: Reliance on an inanimate object for sexual arousal.

first-rank symptoms: In schizophrenia, specific delusions and hallucinations proposed by Schneider as particularly important for its more exact diagnosis.

fixation: In psychoanalytic theory, the arrest of psychosexual development at a particular stage through too much or too little gratification at that stage.

flashback: An unpredictable recurrence of psychedelic experiences from an earlier drug trip.

flat affect: A deviation in emotional response wherein virtually no emotion is expressed whatever the stimulus, emotional expressiveness is blunted, or a lack of expression and muscle tone is noted in the face.

flight of ideas: A symptom of mania that involves a rapid shift in conversation from one subject to another with only superficial associative connections.

flooding: A behaviour therapy procedure in which a fearful person is exposed to what is frightening, in reality or in the imagination, for extended periods of time and without opportunity for escape.

follow-up study: A research procedure whereby individuals observed in an earlier investigation are contacted at a later time for further study.

forced rape: The legal term for rape, forced sexual intercourse or other sexual activity with another person. **Statutory rape** is sexual intercourse between an adult male and someone who is under the age of consent, as fixed by local statute.

forced-choice item: A format of a personality inventory in which the response alternatives for each item are equated for social desirability.

forensic psychiatry or psychology: The branch of psychiatry or psychology that deals with the legal questions raised by disordered behaviour.

fragile X syndrome: Malformation (or even breakage) of the X chromosome associated with moderate mental retardation. Symptoms include large, underdeveloped ears, a long, thin face, a broad nasal root, and enlarged testicles in males; many individuals show attention deficits and hyperactivity.

free association: A key psychoanalytic procedure in which the patient is encouraged to give free rein to his or her thoughts and feelings, verbalizing whatever comes into the mind without monitoring its content. The assumption is that over time, repressed material will come forth for examination by the patient and psychoanalyst.

freebase: The most potent part of cocaine, obtained by heating the drug with ether.

free-floating anxiety: Continual anxiety not attributable to any specific situation or reasonable danger. See *generalized anxiety disorder*.

frotteurism: A form of sexual disorder or paraphilia in which an individual receives sexual pleasure from rubbing against people in public places.

frontal lobe: The forward or upper half of each cerebral hemisphere, in front of the central sulcus, active in reasoning and other higher mental processes.

fugue: See *dissociative fugue*.

functional magnetic resonance imaging (fMRI): Modification of magnetic resonance imaging (MRI) which allows researchers to take pictures of the brain so quickly that metabolic changes can be measured, resulting in a picture of the brain at work rather than its structure alone.

functional social support: The quality of a person's relationships, for example, a good versus a distressed marriage. Contrast with *structural social support*.

gay: A colloquial term for homosexual, now often adopted by homosexuals who have openly announced their sexual orientation.

gay liberation: The often militant movement seeking to achieve civil rights for homosexuals and recognition of the normality of homosexuality.

gender identity: The deeply ingrained sense a person has of being either a man or a woman.

gender identity disorder: Disorder in which there is a deeply felt incongruence between anatomic sex and the sensed gender; transsexualism and gender identity disorder of childhood are examples.

gene: An ultramicroscopic area of the chromosome; the gene is the smallest physical unit of the DNA molecule that carries a piece of hereditary information.

general adaptation syndrome (GAS): Hans Selye's model to describe the biological reaction of an organism to sustained and unrelenting stress; there are several stages, culminating in death in extreme circumstances.

general paresis: See *neurosyphilis*.

generalized anxiety disorder (GAD): In this anxiety disorder, anxiety is so chronic, persistent, and pervasive that it seems free-floating. The individual is jittery and strained, distractible, and worried that something bad is about to happen. A pounding heart, fast pulse and breathing, sweating, flushing, muscle aches, a lump in the throat, and an upset gastrointestinal tract are some of the bodily indications of this extreme anxiety.

genital stage: In psychoanalytic theory, the final psychosexual stage, reached in adulthood, in which heterosexual interests predominate.

genotype: An individual's unobservable, genetic constitution; the totality of genes possessed by an individual. Compare *phenotype*.

genuineness: In client-centred therapy, an essential quality of the therapist, referring to openness and authenticity.

germ theory (of disease): The general view in medicine that disease is caused by infection of the body by minute organisms and viruses.

gerontology: The interdisciplinary study of aging and of the special problems of the elderly.

Gestalt therapy: A humanistic therapy developed by Fritz Perls, which encourages clients to satisfy emerging needs so that their innate goodness can be expressed, to increase their awareness of unacknowledged feelings, and to reclaim parts of their personality that have been denied or disowned.

gestation period: The length of time, normally nine months in human beings, during which a fertilized egg develops into an infant ready to be born.

glans: The heavily innervated tip of the penis.

glove anaesthesia: A lack of sensation in the part of the arm that would be covered by a glove. One of the conversion disorders.

goodness of fit hypothesis: The notion that the effectiveness of a coping response depends on whether it is appropriate for a particular problem; that is, different situations call for different coping responses.

grandiose delusions: Found in paranoid schizophrenia, delusional disorder, and mania, an exaggerated sense of one's importance, power, knowledge, or identity.

Graves' disease: An endocrine disorder resulting from oversecretion of the hormone thyroxin, in which metabolic processes are speeded up, producing apprehension, restlessness, and irritability.

gray matter: The neural tissue made up largely of nerve cell bodies that constitutes the cortex covering the cerebral hemisphere, the nuclei in lower brain areas, columns of the spinal cord, and the ganglia of the autonomic nervous system.

grimace: A distorted facial expression, often a symptom of schizophrenia.

group homes: Care facilities in which groups of individuals live semi-cooperatively in one home or facility. Group homes are often recommended for schizophrenics for the social support they provide outside of an institutional setting.

group therapy: Method of treating psychological disorders whereby several persons are seen simultaneously by a single therapist.

guided self-change: An approach to treating addiction and other types of disorders that emphasizes personal responsibility and problem-solving techniques that foster a sense of self-reliance.

gyrus: A ridge or convolution of the cerebral cortex.

habituation: In physiology, a process whereby an organism's response to the same stimulus lessens with repeated presentations.

halfway house: A homelike residence for people who are considered too disturbed to remain in their accustomed surroundings but do not require the total care of a mental institution.

hallucinations: Perceptions in any sensory modality without relevant and adequate external stimuli.

hallucinogen: A drug or chemical whose effects include hallucinations. Hallucinogenic drugs such as LSD, psilocybin, and mescaline are often called psychedelic.

harm reduction therapy: A form of treating addiction and other types of disorders that focuses on reducing the harmful consequences to some degree rather than striving initially for absolute abstinence.

hashish: The dried resin of the Cannabis plant, stronger in its effects than the dried leaves and stems that constitute marijuana.

health psychology: A branch of psychology dealing with the role of psychological factors in health and illness. See also *behavioural medicine*.

hebephrenia: See *disorganized schizophrenia*.

help seeking: The act of obtaining assistance from informal sources (i.e., friends or family members) or formal sources (i.e., mental health professionals).

helplessness. A construct referring to the sense of having no control over important events; considered by many theorists to play a central role in anxiety and depression. See *learned helplessness theory*.

hermaphrodite: A person with parts of both male and female genitalia.

heroin: An extremely addictive narcotic drug derived from morphine.

heroin antagonists: Drugs, such as naloxone, that prevent a heroin user from experiencing any high.

heroin substitutes: Narcotics, such as methadone, that are cross-dependent with heroin and thus replace it and the body's craving for it.

heterosexual: A person who desires or engages in sexual relations with members of the opposite sex.

high-risk method: A research technique involving the intensive examination of people who have a high probability of later becoming abnormal.

histrionic personality disorder: This person is overly dramatic and given to emotional excess, impatient with minor annoyances, immature, dependent on others, and often sexually seductive without taking responsibility for flirtations; formerly called hysterical personality.

homophobia: Fear of, or aversion to homosexuality.

homosexuality: Sexual desire or activity directed toward a member of one's own sex.

homovanillic acid: A major metabolite of dopamine.

hormone: A chemical substance produced by an endocrine gland and released into the blood or lymph for the purpose of controlling the function of a distant organ or organ system. Metabolism, growth, and development of secondary sexual characteristics are among the functions so controlled.

humanistic and existential therapies: A generic term for insight psychotherapies that emphasize the individual's subjective experiences, free will, and ever-present ability to decide on a new life course.

humanistic therapy: An insight therapy that emphasizes freedom of choice, growth of human potential, the joys of being a human being, and the importance of the patient's phenomenology; sometimes called an experiential therapy. See also *existential therapy*.

Huntington's chorea: A fatal disease passed on by a single dominant gene. Symptoms include spasmodic jerking of the limbs, psychotic behaviour, and mental deterioration.

5-hydroxyindoleacetic acid (5-HIAA): The major metabolite of serotonin.

hyperactivity: See *attention-deficit/hyperactivity disorder*.

hyperkinesis: See *attention-deficit/hyperactivity disorder*.

hypertension: Abnormally high arterial blood pressure, with or without known organic causes. See *essential hypertension*.

hyperventilation: Very rapid and deep breathing associated with high levels of anxiety; causes the level of carbon dioxide in blood to be lowered with possible loss of consciousness.

hypnosis: A trancelike state or behaviour resembling sleep, induced by suggestion, characterized primarily by increased suggestibility.

hypoactive sexual desire disorder: The absence of or deficiency in sexual fantasies and urges.

hypochondriasis: A somatoform disorder in which the person, misinterpreting rather ordinary physical sensations, is preoccupied with fears of having a serious disease and is not dissuaded by medical opinion. Difficult to distinguish from somatization disorder.

hypomania: An above-normal elevation of mood, but not as extreme as mania.

hypothalamus: A collection of nuclei and fibres in the lower part of the diencephalon concerned with the regulation of many visceral processes, such as metabolism, temperature, and water balance.

hypothesis: In an experiment, the specific prediction about the outcome of the experiment. It is based on the assumption that the theory in question is accurate.

hysteria: A disorder known to the ancient Greeks in which a physical incapacity—a paralysis, an anaesthesia, or an analgesia—is not due to a physiological dysfunction, for example, glove anaesthesia; an older term for conversion disorder. In the late nineteenth century dissociative disorders were identified as such and considered hysterical states.

hysterical neurosis: The DSM-II category for dissociative and somatoform disorders.

id: In psychoanalytic theory, that part of the personality present at birth, composed of all the energy of the psyche, and expressed as biological urges that strive continually for gratification.

ideas of reference: Delusional thinking that reads personal significance into seemingly trivial remarks and activities of others and completely unrelated events.

identity crisis: A developmental period in adolescence marked by concerns about who one is and what one is going to do with his or her life.

idiographic: In psychology, relating to investigative procedures that consider the unique characteristics of a single person, studying them in depth, as in the case study. Contrast with *nomothetic*.

idiot savant: An individual with a rare form of mental retardation, extraordinarily talented in one or a few limited areas of intellectual achievement; sometimes called autistic savant.

illusion: A misperception of a real external stimulus, such as hearing the slapping of waves as footsteps.

imipramine: An antidepressant drug, one of the tricyclic group, trade name Tofranil.

in absentia: Literally, "in one's absence." Courts are concerned that a person be able to participate personally and meaningfully in his or her own trial and not be tried in absentia because of a distracting mental disorder.

in vivo: As applied in psychology, taking place in a real-life situation.

in vivo exposure: The process of having a phobic individual encounter or experience the subject of their phobia in a real-life situation.

inappropriate affect: Emotional responses that are out of context, such as laughter when hearing sad news.

incest: Sexual relations between close relatives, most often between daughter and father or between brother and sister.

incidence: In epidemiological studies of a particular disorder, the rate at which new cases occur in a given place at a given time. Compare with *prevalence*.

incoherence: In schizophrenia, an aspect of thought disorder wherein verbal expression is marked by disconnectedness, fragmented thoughts, and jumbled phrases.

independent variable: In a psychological experiment, the factor, experience, or treatment that is under the control of the experimenter and that is expected to have an effect on participants as assessed by changes in the dependent variable.

index case (proband): The person who in a genetic investigation bears the diagnosis or trait in which the investigator is interested.

individual psychology: A variation of Freud's psychoanalysis introduced by Alfred Adler and focusing less on biological drives and more on such factors as people's conscious beliefs and goals for self-betterment.

infectious disease: An illness caused when a microorganism, such as a bacterium or a virus, invades the body, multiplies, and attacks a specific organ or organ system; pneumonia is an example.

informed consent: The agreement of a person to serve as a research participant or to enter therapy after being told the possible outcomes, both benefits and risks.

inhibited male orgasm: A recurrent and persistent delay or absence of ejaculation after an adequate phase of sexual excitement.

insanity defence: The legal argument that a defendant should not be held ascriptively responsible for an illegal act if the conduct is attributable to mental illness.

insight therapy: A general term for any psychotherapy that assumes that people become disordered because they do not adequately understand what motivates them, especially when their needs and drives conflict.

instrumental learning: See *operant conditioning*.

instrumental support: The provision of tangible assistance (e.g., meal preparation) to people in need.

intelligence quotient (IQ): A standardized measure indicating how far an individual's raw score on an intelligence test is from the average raw score of his or her chronological age group.

intelligence test: A standardized means of assessing a person's current mental ability, for example, the Stanford–Binet test and the Wechsler Adult Intelligence Scale.

interactionism: The notion that behaviour is a joint function of personal characteristics and the properties of the situations that are experienced.

internal consistency reliability: See *reliability*.

internal validity: See *validity*.

interpersonal therapy: A psychodynamic psychotherapy that focuses on the patient's interactions with others and that directly teaches how better to relate to others.

interpretation: In psychoanalysis, a key procedure in which the psychoanalyst points out to the patient where resistance exists and what certain dreams and verbalizations reveal about impulses repressed in the unconscious; more generally, any statement by a therapist that construes the client's problem in a new way.

interrater reliability: See *reliability*.

introjection: In psychoanalytic theory, the unconscious incorporation of the values, attitudes, and qualities of another person into the individual's own ego structure.

introspection: A procedure whereby trained subjects are asked to report on their conscious experiences. This was the principal method of study in early twentieth-century psychology.

irrational beliefs: Self-defeating assumptions that are assumed by rational-emotive therapists to underlie psychological distress.

irresistible impulse: The term used in an 1834 Ohio court ruling on criminal responsibility that determined that an insanity defence can be established by proving that the accused had an uncontrollable urge to perform the act.

Korsakoff's psychosis: A chronic brain disorder marked by loss of recent memories and associated confabulation and by additional lesions in the thalamus.

la belle indifférence: The blasé attitude people with conversion disorder have toward their symptoms.

labelling theory: The general view that serious psychopathology, such as schizophrenia, is caused by society's reactions to unusual behaviour.

labile: Easily moved or changed, quickly shifting from one emotion to another, or easily aroused.

language disorder: Difficulties understanding spoken language (receptive) or expressing thoughts verbally (expressive).

lanugo: A fine soft hair that develops on the bodies of people with anorexia nervosa.

latency period: In psychoanalytic theory, the years between ages six and twelve, during which id impulses play a minor role in motivation.

latent content: In dreams, the presumed true meaning hidden behind the manifest content.

lateral hypothalamus: A section of the brain that, if lesioned, is associated with a dramatic loss of appetite.

law of effect: A principle of learning that holds that behaviour is acquired by virtue of its consequences.

learned helplessness theory: The theory that individuals acquire passivity and a sense of being unable to act and to control their lives; this happens through unpleasant experiences and traumas against which their efforts were ineffective; according to Seligman, this brings on depression.

learning disabilities: General term for learning disorders, communication disorders, and motor skills disorder.

learning disorders: A set of developmental disorders encompassing dyslexia, mathematics disorder, and disorder of written expression and characterized by failure to develop in a specific academic area to the degree expected by the child's intellectual level. Not diagnosed if the disorder is due to a sensory deficit.

learning (behavioural) paradigm: In abnormal psychology, a set of assumptions that abnormal behaviour is learned in the same way as other human behaviour.

least restrictive alternative: The legal principle according to which a committed mental patient must be treated in a setting that imposes as few restrictions as possible on his or her freedom.

lesion: Any localized abnormal structural change in organ or tissue caused by disease or injury.

libido. See *Eros*.

Life Change Unit (LCU) score: A score produced by totaling ratings of the stressfulness of recently experienced life events; high scores are found to be related to the contraction of a number of physical illnesses.

life-span developmental psychology: The study of changes in people as they grow from infancy to old age.

lifetime prevalence rate: The proportion of a sample that has ever had a disorder.

limbic system: The lower parts of the cerebrum, made up of primitive cortex; controls visceral and bodily changes associated with emotion and regulates drive-motivated behaviour.

linkage analysis: A technique in genetic research whereby occurrence of a disorder in a family is evaluated alongside a known genetic marker.

lithium carbonate: A drug useful in treating both mania and depression in bipolar disorder.

lobotomy: A brain operation in which the nerve pathways between the frontal lobes of the brain and lower brain structures are cut in hopes of effecting beneficial behavioural change.

logotherapy: An existential psychotherapy, developed by Viktor Frankl, aimed at helping the demoralized client restore meaning to life by placing his or her suffering in a larger spiritual and philosophical context. The individual assumes responsibility for his or her existence and for pursuing a meaningful life.

longitudinal studies: Investigation that collects information on the same individuals repeatedly over time, perhaps over many years, in an effort to determine how phenomena change. Compare with *cross-sectional studies*.

loose associations (derailment): In schizophrenia, an aspect of thought disorder wherein the patient has difficulty sticking to one topic and drifts off on a train of associations evoked by an idea from the past.

LSD: d-lysergic acid diethylamide, a drug synthesized in 1938 and discovered by accident to be a hallucinogen in 1943.

Luria–Nebraska test: A battery of neuropsychological tests that can detect impairment in different parts of the brain.

magical thinking: The conviction of the individual that his or her thoughts, words, and actions may in some manner cause or prevent outcomes in a way that defies the normal laws of cause and effect.

magnetic resonance imaging (MRI): A technique for measuring the structure (or, in the case of functional magnetic resonance imaging, the activity) of the living brain. The person is placed inside a large circular magnet that causes hydrogen atoms to move; the return of the atoms to their original positions when the current to the magnet is turned off is translated by a computer into pictures of brain tissue.

mainstreaming (immersion): A policy of placing children with disabilities in regular classrooms; although special classes are provided as needed, the children share as much as possible in the opportunities and ambience afforded youngsters without disabilities.

maintenance dose: An amount of a drug designed to enable a patient to continue to benefit from a therapeutically effective regimen of medication. It is often less than the dose required to initiate the positive change.

major (unipolar) depression: A disorder of individuals who have experienced episodes of depression but not of mania.

male erectile disorder: A recurrent and persistent inability to attain or maintain an erection until completion of sexual activity.

male orgasmic disorder: See *inhibited male orgasm*.

malingering: Faking a physical or psychological incapacity in order to avoid a responsibility or gain an end; the goal is readily recognized from the individual's circumstances. To be distinguished from conversion disorder, in which the incapacity is assumed to be beyond voluntary control.

malleus maleficarum ("the witches' hammer"): A manual written by two Dominican monks in the fifteenth century to provide rules for identifying and trying witches.

mammillary body: Either of two small rounded structures located in the hypothalamus and consisting of nuclei.

mania: An emotional state of intense but unfounded elation evidenced in talkativeness, flight of ideas, distractibility, grandiose plans, and spurts of purposeless activity.

manic-depressive illness, manic-depressive psychosis: Originally described by Kraepelin, a mood disorder characterized by alternating euphoria and profound sadness or by one of these moods. Called bipolar disorder in DSM-IV.

manifest content: The immediately apparent, conscious content of dreams. Compare with *latent content*.

marathon group: A group therapy session run continuously for a day or even longer, typically for sensitivity training, the assumption being that defences can be worn down by the physical and psychological fatigue generated through intensive and continuous group interaction.

marijuana: A drug derived from the dried and ground leaves and stems of the female hemp plant, Cannabis sativa.

marital therapy: See *couples therapy*.

masked depression: A depression that is expressed in atypical ways not usually associated with the symptoms of depression, such as misbehaving at school.

masochism: See *sexual masochism*.

mathematics disorder: Difficulties dealing with arithmetic symbols and operations; one of the learning disorders.

mediational theory of learning: In psychology, the general view that certain stimuli do not directly initiate an overt response but activate an intervening process, which in turn initiates the response. It explains thinking, drives, emotions, and beliefs in terms of stimulus and response.

mediator: In psychology, an inferred state intervening between the observable stimulus and response, activated by the stimulus and in turn initiating the response; in more general terms, a thought, drive, emotion, or belief. Also called a construct.

medical (disease) model: As applied in abnormal psychology, a set of assumptions that conceptualizes abnormal behaviour as similar to physical diseases.

medicare: The term for the system of health care in Canada.

medulla oblongata: An area in the brain stem through which nerve fibre tracts ascend to or descend from higher brain centres.

megalomania: A paranoid delusion of grandeur in which an individual believes that he or she is an important person or is carrying out great plans.

melancholia: A vernacular diagnosis of several millennia's standing for profound sadness and depression. In major depression with melancholia the individual is unable to feel better even momentarily when something good happens, regularly feels worse in the morning and awakens early, and suffers a deepening of other symptoms of depression.

meninges: The three layers of nonneural tissue that envelop the brain and spinal cord. They are the dura mater, the arachnoid, and the pia mater.

meningitis: An inflammation of the meninges through infection, usually by a bacterium, or through irritation. Meningococcal, the epidemic form of the disease, takes the lives of 10 percent of those who contract it and causes cerebral palsy, hearing loss, speech defects, and other forms of permanent brain damage in one of four people who recover.

mental age: The numerical index of an individual's cognitive development determined by standardized intelligence tests.

mental disorder: A behavioural or psychological syndrome associated with current distress and/or disability.

mental health promotion: Methods used to foster primary prevention of mental disorders through the teaching of skills or attitudes that have been shown to correlate with mental health.

mental health status: An individual's level of distress and cognitive impairment.

mental retardation: Subnormal intellectual functioning associated with impairment in adaptive behaviour and identified at an early age.

meprobamate: Generic term for Miltown, an anxiolytic, the first introduced and for a time one of the most widely used.

mescaline: A hallucinogen and alkaloid that is the active ingredient of peyote.

mesmerize: The first term for hypnotize, after Franz Anton Mesmer, an Austrian physician who in the late eighteenth century treated and cured hysterical or conversion disorders with what he considered the animal magnetism emanating from his body and permeating the universe.

meta-analysis: A quantitative method of analyzing and comparing various therapies by standardizing their results.

metabolism: The sum of the intracellular processes by which large molecules are broken down into smaller ones, releasing energy and wastes, and by which small molecules are built up into new living matter by consuming energy.

metacognition: The knowledge people have about the way they know their world, for example, recognizing the usefulness of a map in finding their way in a new city.

methadone: A synthetic addictive heroin substitute for treating heroin addicts that acts as a substitute for heroin by eliminating its effects and the craving for it.

methedrine: A very strong amphetamine, sometimes shot directly into the veins.

3-methoxy-4-hydroxyphenylethylene glycol (MHPG): A major metabolite of norepinephrine.

midbrain: The middle part of the brain that consists of a mass of nerve fibre tracts connecting the spinal cord and pons, medulla, and cerebellum to the cerebral cortex.

migraine headaches: Extremely debilitating headaches caused by sustained dilation of the extracranial arteries, the temporal artery in particular; the dilated arteries trigger pain-sensitive nerve fibres in the scalp.

mild mental retardation: A limitation in mental development measured on IQ tests at between 50–55 and 70; children with such a limitation are considered the educable mentally retarded and are usually placed in special classes.

milieu therapy: A treatment procedure that attempts to make the total environment and all personnel and patients of the hospital a therapeutic community, conducive to psychological improvement; the staff conveys to the patients the expectation that they can and will behave more normally and responsibly.

Miltown: The trade name for meprobamate, one of the principal anxiolytics.

Minnesota Multiphasic Personality Inventory (MMPI): A lengthy personality inventory by which individuals are diagnosed through their true–false replies to groups of statements indicating states such as anxiety, depression, masculinity–femininity, and paranoia.

mixed design: A research strategy in which both classificatory and experimental variables are used; assigning people from discrete populations to two experimental conditions is an example.

mixed receptive-expressive language disorder: Difficulties producing and understanding spoken language.

M'Naghten rule. An 1843 British court decision stating that an insanity defence can be established by proving that the defendant did not know what he or she was doing or did not realize that it was wrong.

modelling: Learning by observing and imitating the behaviour of others.

moderate mental retardation: A limitation in mental development measured on IQ tests between 35–40 and 50–55; children with this degree of retardation are often institutionalized, and their training is focused on self-care rather than on development of intellectual skills.

mongolism: See Down syndrome.

monism: Philosophical doctrine that ultimate reality is a unitary organic whole and that therefore mental and physical are one and the same. Contrast with dualism.

monoamine: An organic compound containing nitrogen in one amino group (NH). Some of the known neurotransmitters of the central nervous system, called collectively brain amines, are catecholamines and indoleamines, which are monoamines.

monoamine oxidase (MAO): An enzyme that deactivates catecholamines and indoleamines within the presynaptic neuron, indoleamines in the synapse.

monoamine oxidase inhibitors: A group of antidepressant drugs that prevent the enzyme monoamine oxidase from deactivating neurotransmitters of the central nervous system.

monozygotic (MZ) twins: Genetically identical siblings who have developed from a single fertilized egg; sometimes called identical twins.

mood disorders: Disorders in which there are disabling disturbances in emotion.

moral anxiety: In psychoanalytic theory, the ego's fear of punishment for failure to adhere to the superego's standards of proper conduct.

moral treatment: A therapeutic regimen, introduced by Philippe Pinel during the French Revolution, whereby mental patients were released from their restraints and were treated with compassion and dignity rather than with contempt and denigration.

morbidity risk: The probability that an individual will develop a particular disorder.

morphine: An addictive narcotic alkaloid extracted from opium, used primarily as an analgesic and as a sedative.

motor skills disorder: A learning disability characterized by marked impairment in the development of motor coordination that is not accounted for by a physical disorder such as cerebral palsy.

mourning work: In Freud's theory of depression, the recall by a depressed person of memories associated with a lost one, serving to separate the individual from the deceased.

multi-axial classification: Classification having several dimensions, each of which is employed in categorizing; DSM-IV is an example.

multicultural counselling and therapy: Treatments with interventions that have been modified to address issues, beliefs, and dialogues that characterize people from various cultures.

multifactorial: Referring to the operation of several variables influencing in complex fashion the development or maintenance of a phenomenon.

multimodal therapy: A cognitive-behavioural therapy introduced by Arnold Lazarus, which employs techniques from diverse approaches in an effort to help people make positive changes in their BASIC IB: behaviour, affects, sensations, images, cognitions, interpersonal relationships, and biological functioning.

multiple personality disorder (MPD): See *dissociative identity disorder (DID)*.

multiple-baseline design: An experimental design in which two behaviours of a single person are selected for study and a treatment is applied to one of them. The behaviour that is not treated serves as a baseline against which the effects of the treatment can be determined. This is a common design in operant conditioning research.

mutism: The inability or refusal to speak.

myocardial infarction: Heart attack. See *coronary heart disease*.

narcissistic personality disorder: Extremely selfish and self-centred, people with a narcissistic personality have a grandiose view of their uniqueness, achievements, and talents and an insatiable craving for admiration and approval from others. They are exploitative to achieve their own goals and expect much more from others than they themselves are willing to give.

narcosynthesis: A psychiatric procedure originating during World War II in which a drug was employed to help stressed soldiers recall the battle traumas underlying their disorders.

narcotics: Addictive sedative drugs, for example, morphine and heroin, that in moderate doses relieve pain and induce sleep.

negative reinforcement: The strengthening of a tendency to exhibit desired behaviour by rewarding responses in that situation with the removal of an aversive stimulus.

negative symptoms: Behavioural deficits in schizophrenia, such as flat affect and apathy.

negative triad: In Beck's theory of depression, a person's baleful views of the self, the world, and the future; the triad is in a reciprocal causal relationship with pessimistic assumptions (schemata) and cognitive biases such as selective abstraction.

neo-Freudian: A person who has contributed to the modification and extension of Freudian theory.

neologism: A word made up by the speaker that is usually meaningless to a listener.

nerve impulse: A change in the electric potential of a neuron; a wave of depolarization spreads along the neuron and causes the release of neurotransmitter.

neurofibrillary tangles: Abnormal protein filaments present in the cell bodies of brain cells in patients with Alzheimer's disease.

neurologist: A physician who studies the nervous system, especially its structure, functions, and abnormalities.

neuron: A single nerve cell.

neuropsychological tests: Psychological tests, such as the Luria–Nebraska, that can detect impairment in different parts of the brain.

neuropsychologist: A psychologist concerned with the relationships among cognition, affect, and behaviour on the one hand, and brain function on the other.

neuroses: Old term for a large group of non-psychotic disorders characterized by unrealistic anxiety and other associated problems, for example, phobic avoidances, obsessions, and compulsions. See *anxiety disorders*.

neurosyphilis (general paresis): Infection of the central nervous system by the spirochete Treponema pallidum, which destroys brain tissue; marked by eye disturbances, tremors, and disordered speech as well as severe intellectual deterioration and psychotic symptoms.

neurotic anxiety: In psychoanalytic theory, a fear of the consequences of expressing previously punished and repressed id impulses; more generally, unrealistic fear.

neurotransmitter: A chemical substance important in transferring a nerve impulse from one neuron to another; for example, serotonin and norepinephrine.

nicotine: The principal alkaloid of tobacco (an addicting agent).

Niemann-Pick disease: An inherited disorder of lipid (fat) metabolism that produces mental retardation and paralysis and brings early death.

nitrous oxide: A gas that, when inhaled, produces euphoria and sometimes giddiness.

nomenclature: A system or set of names or designations used in a particular discipline, such as the DSM-IV.

nomothetic: Relating to the universal and to the formulation of general laws that explain a range of phenomena. Contrast with idiographic.

norepinephrine: A catecholamine that is a neurotransmitter of the central nervous system. Disturbances in its tracts apparently figure in depression and mania. It is also a neurotransmitter secreted at the nerve endings of the sympathetic nervous system, a hormone liberated with epinephrine in the adrenal medulla and similar to it in action, and a strong vasoconstrictor.

normal curve: As applied in psychology, the bell-shaped distribution of a measurable trait depicting most people in the middle and few at the extremes.

nosology: A systematic classification of diseases.

not criminally responsible: Phrase used in the Canadian Criminal Code to refer to a situation in which an individual has taken actions that are defined as illegal but due to the effects of a mental disorder are not held legally responsible for their actions. Formally referred to as "not guilty by reason of insanity."

nucleus: In anatomy, a mass of nerve cell bodies (gray matter) within the brain or spinal cord by which descending nerve fibres connect with ascending nerve fibres.

nuclei: The plural of nucleus.

object choice: In the psychology of sex, the type of person or thing selected as a focus for sexual desire or activity.

objective (realistic) anxiety: In psychoanalytic theory, the ego's reaction to danger in the external world; realistic fear. Contrast with *neurotic anxiety*.

observer drift: The tendency of two raters of behaviour to begin to agree with each other, achieving unusually high levels of reliability; their way of coding behaviour differentiates their scores from those of another pair of raters. This is regarded as a threat to reliable and valid behavioural assessment.

obsession: An intrusive and recurring thought that seems irrational and uncontrollable to the person experiencing it.

obsessive-compulsive disorder (OCD): An anxiety disorder in which the mind is flooded with persistent and uncontrollable thoughts or the individual is compelled to repeat certain acts again and again, causing significant distress and interference with everyday functioning.

obsessive-compulsive personality disorder: People with an obsessive-compulsive personality have inordinate difficulty making decisions, are overly concerned with details and efficiency, and relate poorly to others because they demand that things be done their way. They are unduly conventional, serious, formal, and stingy with their emotions.

occipital lobe: The posterior area of each cerebral hemisphere, situated behind the parietal lobe and above the temporal lobes, responsible for reception and analysis of visual information and for some visual memory.

Oedipus complex: In Freudian theory, the desire and conflict of the four-year-old male child who wants to possess his mother sexually and to eliminate the father rival. The threat of punishment from the father causes repression of these id impulses. Girls have a similar sexual desire for the father, which is repressed in analogous fashion and is called the Electra complex.

operant behaviour: A response that is supposedly voluntary and operates on the environment, modifying it so that a reward or goal is attained.

operant conditioning: The acquisition or elimination of a response as a function of the environmental contingencies of reward and punishment.

operationism: A school of thought in science that holds that a given concept must be defined in terms of a single set of identifiable and repeatable operations that can be measured.

opiates: A group of addictive sedatives that in moderate doses relieve pain and induce sleep.

opium: One of the opiates, the dried, milky juice obtained from the immature fruit of the opium poppy. This addictive narcotic produces euphoria and drowsiness and reduces pain.

oppositional defiant disorder: An under-controlled disorder of children marked by high levels of disobedience to authority but lacking the extremes of conduct disorder.

oral stage: In psychoanalytic theory, the first psychosexual stage, which extends into the second year; during this stage the mouth is the principal erogenous zone.

organismic variable: A physiological or psychological factor assumed to be operating "under the skin"; these variables are a focus of behavioural assessment.

orgasm (climax): The involuntary, intensely pleasurable, climactic phase in sexual arousal that lasts a number of seconds and usually involves muscular contractions and ejaculation in the male and similar contractions in the genitalia of the female.

orgasmic reorientation: A behaviour therapy technique for altering classes of stimuli to which people are sexually attracted; individuals are confronted by a conventionally arousing stimulus while experiencing orgasm.

outcome research: Research on the efficacy of psychotherapy. Contrast with *process research*.

outpatient commitment: A form of civil commitment whereby the person is not institutionalized, rather is allowed to be free in the community but under legal-medical constraints that ensure, for example, that prescribed medication and other measures are taken to maximize the chances of the patient being able to live outside of a mental hospital. Consistent with the principle of least restrictive alternative.

overcontrolled (behaviour): In reference to childhood disorders, problems that create distress for the child, such as anxiety and social withdrawal.

pain disorder: A somatoform disorder in which the person complains of severe and prolonged pain that is not explainable by organic pathology; it tends to be stress-related or permits the patient to avoid an aversive activity or to gain attention and sympathy.

palliative coping: The tendency to respond to emotional problems through emotional expression and acts that are designed to soothe the self.

panic disorder: An anxiety disorder in which the individual has sudden and inexplicable attacks of jarring symptoms, such as difficulty breathing, heart palpitations, dizziness, trembling, terror, and feelings of impending doom. In DSM-IV, said to occur with or without agoraphobia.

paradigm: A set of basic assumptions that outlines the universe of scientific inquiry, specifying both the concepts regarded as legitimate and the methods to be used in collecting and interpreting data.

paradoxical intervention: A therapeutic strategy that asks patients to increase or observe the frequency or intensity of a symptom, for example, having anxious patients make themselves more anxious or note when and how severely they become anxious.

paranoia: The general term for delusions of persecution, of grandiosity, or both; found in several pathological conditions, delusional disorders, paranoid schizophrenia, and paranoid personality disorder. It can also be produced by large doses of certain drugs, such as cocaine or alcohol.

paranoid disorder: See *delusional disorder*.

paranoid personality disorder: The person with this personality expects to be mistreated by others, becomes suspicious, secretive, jealous, and argumentative. He or she will not accept blame and appears cold and unemotional.

paranoid schizophrenia: A type of schizophrenia in which the patient has numerous systematized delusions as well as hallucinations and ideas of reference. He or she may also be agitated, angry, argumentative, and sometimes violent.

paraphilias: Sexual attraction to unusual objects and sexual activities unusual in nature.

paraphrenia: A term sometimes used to refer to schizophrenia in an older adult.

paraprofessional: In clinical psychology, an individual lacking a doctoral degree but trained to perform certain functions usually reserved for clinicians, for example, a college student trained and supervised by a behavioural therapist to shape the behaviour of autistic children through contingent reinforcers.

parasympathetic nervous system: The division of the autonomic nervous system that is involved with maintenance; it controls many of the internal organs and is active primarily when the organism is not aroused.

parental mental disorder: The presence of a behavioural or psychological syndrome in one's mother or father.

paresthesia: Conversion disorder marked by a sensation of tingling or creeping on the skin.

parietal lobe: The middle division of each cerebral hemisphere, situated behind the central sulcus and above the lateral sulcus; the receiving centre for sensations of the skin and of bodily positions.

Parkinson's disease: A disease characterized by uncontrollable and severe muscle tremors, a stiff gait, a mask-like, expressionless face, and withdrawal.

pathological gambling: A tendency to engage in persistent and recurring gambling behaviour that is self-defeating and detrimental to the well-being and goal attainments of the self or family members.

pathology: The anatomical, physiological, and psychological deviations of a disease or disorder; the study of these abnormalities.

PCP: See *phencyclidine*.

Pearson product moment correlation coefficient (r): A statistic, ranging in value from -1.00 to +1.00; the most common means of denoting a correlational relationship. The sign indicates whether the relationship is positive or negative, and the magnitude indicates the strength of the relationship.

pedophilia: The sexual disorder of a pedophile (see pedophile).

pedophile: Person with a marked preference for obtaining sexual gratification through contact with youngsters defined legally as underage; pedophilia is a paraphilia.

penile plethysmograph: A device for detecting blood flow and thus for recording changes in size of the penis.

perseveration: The persistent repetition of words and ideas, often found in schizophrenia.

personality disorders: A heterogeneous group of disorders, listed separately on Axis II, regarded as longstanding, inflexible, and maladaptive personality traits that impair social and occupational functioning.

personality inventory: A self-report questionnaire by which an examinee indicates whether statements assessing habitual tendencies apply to him or her.

personality structure: See *trait*.

pervasive developmental disorders: Severe childhood problems marked by profound disturbances in social relations and oddities in behaviour. Autistic disorder is one.

PET scan: Computer-generated picture of the living brain, created by analysis of radioactive particles from isotopes injected into the bloodstream.

peyote: A hallucinogen obtained from the root of the peyote cactus; the active ingredient is mescaline, an alkaloid.

phallic stage: In psychoanalytic theory, the third psychosexual stage, extending from ages three to six, during which maximal gratification is obtained from genital stimulation.

phencyclidine (PCP): Also known as angel dust, PeaCE Pill, zombie, and by other street names, this very powerful and hazardous drug causes profound disorientation, agitated and often violent behaviour, and even seizures, coma, and death.

phenomenology: As applied in psychology, the philosophical view that the phenomena of subjective experience should be studied because behaviour is considered to be determined by how people perceive themselves and the world, rather than by objectively described reality.

phenothiazine: The name for a group of drugs that relieve psychotic symptoms; their molecular structure, like that of the tricyclic drugs, consists of three fused rings. An example is chlorpromazine (Thorazine).

phenotype: The totality of observable characteristics of a person. Compare with *genotype*.

phenylketonuria (PKU): A genetic disorder that, through a deficiency in a liver enzyme, phenylalanine hydroxylase, causes severe mental retardation unless phenylalanine can be largely restricted from the diet.

phobia: An anxiety disorder in which there is intense fear and avoidance of specific objects and situations, recognized as irrational by the individual.

phonological disorder: A learning disability in which some words sound like baby talk because the person is not able to make certain speech sounds.

phototherapy: A treatment designed for people with seasonal affective disorder. It involves exposure to intense white light.

physiology: The study of the functions and activities of living cells, tissues, and organs and of the physical and chemical phenomena involved.

placebo: Any inactive therapy or chemical agent, or any attribute or component of such a therapy or chemical, that affects a person's behaviour for reasons related to his or her expectation of change.

placebo control group: A group in an experiment which receives contact, support, and encouragement from a therapist, but not the active ingredient in the particular kind of therapy under study.

placebo effect: The action of a drug or psychological treatment that is not attributable to any specific operations of the agent. For example, a tranquilizer can reduce anxiety both because of its special biochemical action and because the recipient expects relief. See placebo.

plaques: Small, round areas composed of remnants of lost neurons and beta-amyloid, a waxy protein deposit; present in the brains of patients with Alzheimer's disease.

plateau phase: According to Masters and Johnson, the second stage in sexual arousal, during which excitement and tension have reached a stable high level before orgasm.

play therapy: The use of play as a means of uncovering what is troubling a child and of establishing rapport.

pleasure principle: In psychoanalytic theory, the demanding manner by which the id operates, seeking immediate gratification of its needs.

plethysmograph: An instrument for determining and registering variations in the amount of blood present or passing through an organ.

polydrug abuse: The misuse of more than one drug at a time, such as drinking heavily and taking cocaine.

pons: An area in the brain stem containing nerve-fibre tracts that connect the cerebellum with the spinal cord and with motor areas of the cerebrum.

positive reinforcement: The strengthening of a tendency to behave in a certain situation by presenting a desired reward following previous responses in that situation.

positive spikes: An EEG pattern recorded from the temporal lobe of the brain, with frequencies of 6 to 8 cycles per second and 14 to 16 cycles per second, often found in impulsive and aggressive people.

positive symptoms: In schizophrenia, behavioural excesses, such as hallucinations and bizarre behaviour. Compare with *negative symptoms*.

postpartum depression: The depression experienced by some mothers after giving birth.

posttraumatic stress disorder (PTSD): An anxiety disorder in which a particularly stressful event, such as military combat, rape, or a natural disaster, brings in its aftermath intrusive re-experiencings of the trauma, a numbing of responsiveness to the outside world, estrangement from others, a tendency to be easily startled, and nightmares, recurrent dreams, and otherwise disturbed sleep.

poverty of content: Reduced informational content in speech, one of the negative symptoms of schizophrenia.

poverty of speech: Reduced amount of talking, one of the negative symptoms of schizophrenia.

predictive validity: See *validity*.

predisposition: An inclination or diathesis to respond in a certain way, either inborn or acquired; in abnormal psychology, a factor that lowers the ability to withstand stress and inclines the individual toward pathology.

prefrontal lobotomy: A surgical procedure that destroys the tracts connecting the frontal lobes to lower centres of the brain; once believed to be an effective treatment for schizophrenia.

premature ejaculation: Inability of the male to inhibit his orgasm long enough for mutually satisfying sexual relations.

premorbid adjustment: In research on schizophrenia, the social and sexual adjustment of the individual before the onset or diagnosis of the symptoms. Patients with good premorbid adjustment are those found to have been relatively normal earlier; those with poor premorbid adjustment had inadequate interpersonal and sexual relations.

preparedness: In classical conditioning theory, a biological predisposition to associate particular stimuli readily with the unconditioned stimulus.

prevalence: In epidemiological studies of a disorder, the percentage of a population that has the disorder at a given time. Compare with *incidence*.

prevention: Primary prevention comprises efforts in community psychology to reduce the incidence of new cases of psychological disorder by such means as altering stressful living conditions and genetic counselling; secondary prevention includes efforts to detect disorders early, so that they will not develop into full-blown, perhaps chronic, disabilities; tertiary prevention attempts to reduce the long-term consequences of having a disorder, equivalent in most respects to therapy.

primary empathy: A form of empathy in which the therapist understands the content and feeling of what the client is saying and expressing from the client's phenomenological point of view. Compare with *advanced accurate empathy*.

primary prevention: See *prevention*.

primary process: In psychoanalytic theory, one of the id's means of reducing tension, by imagining what it desires.

prior capable wish: The process of getting a person to outline his or her treatment wishes at an earlier time when he or she is of sounder mind and is not incapacitated.

privileged communication: The communication between parties in a confidential relationship that is protected by statute. A spouse, doctor, lawyer, pastor, psychologist, or psychiatrist cannot be forced, except under unusual circumstances, to disclose such information.

proband: See *index case*.

process research: Research on the mechanisms by which a therapy may bring improvement. Compare with *outcome research*.

process-reactive dimension (of schizophrenia): A dimension used to distinguish people with schizophrenia; patients with process schizophrenia suffer long-term and gradual deterioration before the onset of their illness, whereas those with reactive schizophrenia have a better premorbid history and a more rapid onset of symptoms. See premorbid adjustment.

profound mental retardation: A limitation in mental development measured on IQ tests at less than 20–25; children with this degree of retardation require total supervision of all their activities.

progestins: Steroid progestational hormones that are the biological precursors of androgens, the male sex hormones.

prognosis: A prediction of the likely course and outcome of an illness. Compare with *diagnosis*.

projection: A defence mechanism whereby characteristics or desires unacceptable to the ego are attributed to someone else.

projective hypothesis: The notion that highly unstructured stimuli, as in the Rorschach, are necessary to bypass defences in order to reveal unconscious motives and conflicts.

projective test: A psychological assessment device employing a set of standard but vague stimuli on the assumption that unstructured material will allow unconscious motivations and fears to be uncovered. The Rorschach series of inkblots is an example.

pronoun reversal: A speech problem in which the child refers to himself or herself as "he," "she," or "you" and uses "I" or "me" in referring to others; often found in the speech of children with autistic disorder.

provincial psychiatric hospital: A location where chronic patients are treated. Such hospitals provide protection, but treatment is often custodial and may involve little psychosocial treatment.

pseudo-community: An illusory world built up by a paranoid person, dominated by false beliefs that are not properly verified and shared by others.

psilocybin: A psychedelic drug extracted from the mushroom Psilocybe mexicana.

psyche: The soul, spirit, or mind as distinguished from the body. In psychoanalytic theory, it is the totality of the id, ego, and superego, including both conscious and unconscious components.

psychedelic: A drug that expands consciousness. See also *hallucinogen*.

psychiatric nurse: a nurse who has obtained additional training in the mental health field.

psychiatrist: A physician (M.D.) who has taken specialized postdoctoral training, called a residency, in the diagnosis, treatment, and prevention of mental disorders.

psychoactive drugs: Chemical compounds having a psychological effect that alters mood or thought process. Valium is an example.

psychoanalysis: A term applied primarily to the therapy procedures pioneered by Freud, entailing free association, dream analysis, and working through the transference neurosis. More recently the term has come to encompass the numerous variations on basic Freudian therapy.

psychoanalyst (analyst): A therapist who has taken specialized postdoctoral training in

psychoanalysis after earning an M.D. or a Ph.D. degree.

psychoanalytic (psychodynamic) paradigm: General view based on psychoanalysis.

psychodynamics: In psychoanalytic theory, the mental and emotional forces and processes that develop in early childhood and their effects on behaviour and mental states.

psychogenesis: Development from psychological origins, as distinguished from somatic origins. Contrast with *somatogenesis*.

psychological autopsy: The analysis of an individual's suicide through the examination of his or her letters and through interviews with friends and relatives in the hope of discovering why the person committed suicide.

psychological deficit: The term used to indicate that performance of a pertinent psychological process is below that expected of a normal person.

psychological dependency: The term sometimes applied as the reason for substance abuse; a reliance on a drug but not a physiological addiction.

psychological factor influencing a medical condition: A diagnosis in DSM-IV that a physical illness is caused in part or exacerbated by psychological stress. See *psychophysiological disorders*.

psychological tests: Standardized procedures designed to measure a person's performance on a particular task or to assess his or her personality.

psychologizer: An individual who emphasizes the psychological aspects and symptoms of depression.

psychopath: See *antisocial personality*.

psychopathologists: Mental health professionals who conduct research into the nature and development of mental disorders. Their academic backgrounds can differ; some are trained as experimental psychologists, others as psychiatrists, and still others as biochemists.

psychopathology: The field concerned with the nature and development of mental disorders.

psychopathy: See *antisocial personality*.

psychophysiological disorders: Disorders with physical symptoms that may involve actual tissue damage, usually in one organ system, and that are produced in part by continued mobilization of the autonomic nervous system under stress. Hives and ulcers are examples. No longer listed in DSM-IV in a separate category, such disorders are now diagnosed on Axis I as psychological factor influencing a medical condition; on Axis III the specific physical condition is given.

psychophysiology: The discipline concerned with the bodily changes that accompany psychological events.

psychosexual stages: In psychoanalytic theory, critical developmental phases that the individual passes through, each stage characterized by the body area providing maximal erotic gratification. The adult personality is formed by the pattern and intensity of instinctual gratification at each stage.

psychosexual trauma: As applied by Masters and Johnson, an earlier frightening or degrading sexual experience that is related to a present sexual dysfunction.

psychosis: A severe mental disorder in which thinking and emotion are so impaired that the individual is seriously out of contact with reality.

psychosocial stages of development: In Erik Erikson's theory, phases through which people pass from infancy through old age, each characterized by a particular challenge or crisis.

psychosomatic (disorder): See *psychophysiological disorders*.

psychosurgery: Any surgical technique in which neural pathways in the brain are cut in order to change behaviour. See *lobotomy*.

psychotherapy: A primarily verbal means of helping troubled individuals change their thoughts, feelings, and behaviour to reduce distress and to achieve greater life satisfaction. See *insight therapy* and *behaviour therapy*.

psychotic (delusional) depression: A profound sadness and unjustified feelings of unworthiness, which also include delusions.

punishment: In psychological experiments, any noxious stimulus imposed on an organism to reduce the probability that it will behave in an undesired way.

random assignment: A method of assigning people to groups in an experiment that gives each person an equal chance of being in each group. The procedure helps to ensure that groups are comparable before the experimental manipulation begins.

rape: See *forced rape*.

rapid-smoking treatment: A behaviour therapy technique for reducing cigarette smoking in which the person is instructed to puff much more quickly than usual in an effort to make the whole experience aversive.

rapport: A close, trusting relationship, believed to be essential for effective psychotherapy.

rational-emotive behaviour therapy (REBT): New term for rational-emotive therapy.

rational-emotive therapy (RET): A cognitive-restructuring behaviour therapy introduced by Albert Ellis and based on the assumption that much disordered behaviour is rooted in absolutistic demands that people make on themselves. The therapy aims to alter the unrealistic goals individuals set for themselves, such as, "I must be universally loved."

rationalization: A defence mechanism in which a plausible reason is unconsciously invented by the ego to protect itself from confronting the real reason for an action, thought, or emotion.

Raynaud's disease: A psychophysiological disorder in which capillaries, especially of the fingers and toes, are subject to spasm. It is characterized by cold, moist hands, is commonly accompanied by pain, and may progress to gangrene.

reaction formation: A defence mechanism whereby an unconscious and unacceptable impulse or feeling that would cause anxiety is converted into its opposite so that it can become conscious and can be expressed.

reaction-time test: A procedure for determining the interval between the application of a stimulus and the beginning of the subject's response.

reactivity (of behaviour): The phenomenon whereby behaviour is changed by the very fact that it is being observed.

reading disorder: See *dyslexia*.

reality principle: In psychoanalytic theory, the manner in which the ego delays gratification and otherwise deals with the environment in a planned, rational fashion.

receptive aphasia: See *aphasia*.

receptor: Proteins embedded in the membrane covering a neural cell that interact with one or more neurotransmitters.

recessive gene: A gene that must be paired with one identical to it in order to determine a trait in the phenotype.

recovery time: The period it takes for a physiological process to return to baseline after the body has responded to a stimulus.

reductionism: Refers to the view that whatever is being studied can, and should, be reduced to its most basic elements or constituents. Biological reductionism proposes that mental and emotional responses can best be understood by understanding basic biological variables such as neurotransmitter levels and balanaces.

refractory phase: The brief period after stimulation of a nerve, muscle, or other irritable element during which it is unresponsive to a second stimulus; or the period after intercourse during which the male cannot have another orgasm.

regression: A defence mechanism in which anxiety is avoided by retreating to the behaviour patterns of an earlier psychosexual stage.

reinforcement: In operant conditioning, increasing the probability that a response will recur either by presenting a contingent positive event or by removing a negative one.

reliability: The extent to which a test, measurement, or classification system produces the same scientific observation each time it is applied. Some specific kinds of reliability include **test-retest**, the relationship between the scores that a person achieves when he or she takes the same test twice; **interrater**, the relationship between the judgments that at least two raters make independently about a phenomenon; **split half**, the relationship between two halves of an assessment instrument that have been determined to be equivalent; **alternate form**, the relationship between scores achieved by people when they complete two versions of a test that are judged to be equivalent; **internal consistency**, degree to which different items of an assessment are related to one another.

repression: A defence mechanism whereby impulses and thoughts unacceptable to the ego are pushed into the unconscious.

residual schizophrenia: Diagnosis given to patients who have had an episode of schizophrenia but who presently show no psychotic symptoms, though signs of the disorder do exist.

resilience: Protection from risk factors or the ability to recover from emotional difficulties or trauma is referred to as an individual's resilience.

resistance: During psychoanalysis, the defensive tendency of the unconscious part of the ego to ward off from consciousness particularly threatening repressed material.

resistance to extinction: The tendency of a conditioned response to persist in the absence of any reinforcement.

resolution phase: The last stage in the sexual arousal cycle, during which sexual tensions abate.

response cost: An operant conditioning punishment procedure in which the misbehaving person is fined already earned reinforcers.

response deviation: A tendency to answer questionnaire items in an uncommon way, regardless of their content.

response hierarchy: The ordering of a series of responses according to the likelihood of their being elicited by a particular stimulus.

response prevention: A behaviour therapy technique in which the person is discouraged from making an accustomed response; used primarily with compulsive rituals.

response set: The tendency of an individual to respond in a particular way to questions or statements on a test—for example, with a False—regardless of the content of each query or statement.

reticular formation: Network of nuclei and fibres in the central core of the brain stem that is important in arousing the cortex and maintaining alertness, in processing incoming sensory stimulation, and in adjusting spinal reflexes.

retrospective reports: Recollections by an individual of past events.

Rett's disorder: A very rare disorder found only in girls, with onset in the first or second year of life. Symptoms include decelerated head growth, lost ability to use hands purposefully, uncoordinated walking, poor speech production and comprehension, and poor interpersonal relations. Child may improve later in life, but usually will remain severely or profoundly mentally retarded.

reuptake: Process by which released neurotransmitters are pumped back into the pre-synaptic cell, making them available for enhancing transmission of nerve impulses.

reversal (ABAB) design: An experimental design in which behaviour is measured during a baseline period (A), during a period when a treatment is introduced (B), during the reinstatement of the conditions that prevailed in the baseline period (A), and finally during a reintroduction of the treatment (B). It is commonly used in operant research to isolate cause–effect relationships.

reward: Any satisfying event or stimulus that, by being contingent on a response, increases the probability that the person will make that response again.

Rh factor: A substance present in the red blood cells of most people. If the Rh factor is present in the blood of a fetus but not in that of the mother, her system produces antibodies that may enter the bloodstream of the fetus and indirectly damage the brain.

right to refuse treatment: A legal principle according to which a committed mental patient may decline to participate in treatment.

right to treatment: A legal principle according to which a committed mental patient must be provided some minimal amount and quality of professional intervention, enough to afford a realistic opportunity for meaningful improvement.

risk factor: A condition or variable that, if present, increases the likelihood of developing a disorder.

role-playing: A technique that teaches people to behave in a certain way by encouraging them to pretend that they are in a particular situation; it helps people acquire complex behaviours in an efficient way. See also *behaviour rehearsal*.

Rorschach Inkblot Test: A projective test in which the examinee is instructed to interpret a series of ten inkblots reproduced on cards.

Rosenthal effect: The tendency for results to conform to experimenters' expectations unless stringent safeguards are instituted to minimize human bias; named after Robert

Rosenthal, who performed many of the original experiments revealing the problem.

rubella (German measles): An infectious disease that, if contracted by the mother during the first three months of pregnancy, has a high risk of causing mental retardation and physical deformity in the child.

ruminative coping: A tendency to focus cognitively (perhaps to the point of obsession) on the causes of depression and associated feelings rather than engaging in forms of distraction.

sadism: See *sexual sadism*.

Scarlett O'Hara Effect: A tendency to eat lightly in an attempt to project an image of femininity.

schema: A mental structure for organizing information about the world.

schizoaffective disorder: Diagnosis applied when a patient has symptoms of both mood disorder and either schizophreniform disorder or schizophrenia.

schizoid personality disorder: The person with a schizoid personality is emotionally aloof, indifferent to the praise, criticism, and feelings of others, and usually a loner with few, if any, close friends and with solitary interests.

schizophrenia: A group of psychotic disorders characterized by major disturbances in thought, emotion, and behaviour; disordered thinking in which ideas are not logically related; faulty perception and attention; bizarre disturbances in motor activity; flat or inappropriate emotions; and reduced tolerance for stress in interpersonal relations. The patient withdraws from people and reality, often into a fantasy life of delusions and hallucinations. See *schizoaffective disorder*, *schizophreniform disorder*, and *brief reactive psychosis*.

schizophreniform disorder: Diagnosis given to people who have all the symptoms of schizophrenia, except that the disorder lasts more than two weeks but less than six months. See *brief reactive psychosis*.

schizophrenogenic mother: A cold, dominant, conflict-inducing mother formerly believed to cause schizophrenia in her child.

schizotypal personality disorder: The person with a schizotypal personality is eccentric, has oddities of thought and perception (magical thinking, illusions, depersonalization, derealization), speaks digressively and with overelaborations, and is usually socially isolated. Under stress he or she may appear psychotic.

school phobia: An acute, irrational dread of attending school, usually accompanied by somatic complaints. It is the most common phobia of childhood.

science: The pursuit of systematized knowledge through reliable observation.

seasonal affective disorder: The "winter depressions" that stem from reduced exposure to daylight.

secondary gain: Benefits that a person unconsciously obtains from a disability.

secondary prevention: See *prevention*.

secondary process: The reality-based decision-making and problem-solving activities of the ego. Compare with primary process.

secondhand smoke: Also referred to as sidestream smoke, the smoke from the burning end of a cigarette, which contains higher concentrations of ammonia, carbon monoxide, nicotine, and tar than does the smoke inhaled by the smoker.

secure attachment style: An attachment orientation in which the infant can tolerate separations from the caregiver and will interact comfortably with a stranger.

sedative: A drug that slows bodily activities, especially those of the central nervous

system; it is used to reduce pain and tension and to induce relaxation and sleep.

selective abstraction: A cognitive bias in Beck's theory of depression whereby a person picks out from a complex situation only certain features and ignores aspects that could lead to a different conclusion.

selective mortality: A possible confound in longitudinal studies, whereby the less healthy people in a sample are more likely to drop out over time.

selective mutism: A pattern of continuously refusing to speak in almost all social situations, including school, even though the child understands spoken language and is able to speak.

self-actualization: Fulfilling one's potential as an always growing human being; believed by client-centred therapists to be the master motive.
self-efficacy: In Bandura's theory, the person's belief that he or she can achieve certain goals.
self-instructional training: A cognitive-behavioural approach that tries to help people improve their overt behaviour by changing how they silently talk to themselves.
self-monitoring: In behavioural assessment, a procedure whereby the individual observes and reports certain aspects of his or her own behaviour, thoughts, or emotions.
self-psychology: Kohut's variant of psychoanalysis, in which the focus is on the development of the person's self-worth from acceptance and nurturance by key figures in childhood.
senile plaques: Small areas of tissue degeneration in the brain, made up of granular material and filaments.
sensate focus: A term applied to exercises prescribed at the beginning of the Masters and Johnson sex therapy program; partners are instructed to fondle each other to give pleasure but to refrain from intercourse, thus reducing anxiety about sexual performance.
sensitivity training group (T-group): A small group of people who spend a period of time together both for therapy and for educational purposes; participants are encouraged or forced to examine their interpersonal functioning and their often overlooked feelings about themselves and others.
sensory-awareness procedures: Techniques that help clients tune into their feelings and sensations, as in sensate-focus exercises, and to be open to new ways of experiencing and feeling.
separation anxiety disorder: A disorder in which the child feels intense fear and distress when away from someone on whom he or she is very dependent; said to be a significant cause of school phobia.
serotonin: An indoleamine that is a neurotransitter of the central nervous system. Disturbances in its tracts apparently figure in depression.
severe abuse: The traumatic experience of extreme mistreatment by someone else (e.g., childhood sexual abuse).
severe mental retardation: A limitation in mental development measured in IQ tests at between 20–25 and 35–40. Individuals often cannot care for themselves, communicate only briefly, and are listless and inactive.
sex-reassignment surgery: An operation removing existing genitalia of a transsexual and constructing a substitute for the genitals of the opposite sex.
sexual and gender identity disorders: In DSM-IV, disorders comprising the paraphilias, sexual dysfunctions, and gender identity disorders.
sexual aversion disorder: Avoidance of nearly all genital contact with other people.
sexual dysfunctions: Dysfunctions in which the appetitive or psychophysiological changes of the normal sexual response cycle are inhibited.
sexual masochism: A marked preference for obtaining or increasing sexual gratification through subjection to pain or humiliation.
sexual orientation disturbance: An earlier term for DSM-III's ego-dystonic homosexuality.
sexual response cycle: The general pattern of sexual physical processes and feelings, building to an orgasm by stimulation and made up of five phases: interest, excitement, plateau, orgasm, and resolution.
sexual sadism: A marked preference for obtaining or increasing sexual gratification by inflicting pain or humiliation on another person.
sexual script: Rules people have for guiding their actions in sexual situations.
sexual value system: As applied by Masters and Johnson, the activities that an individual holds to be acceptable and necessary in a sexual relationship.
shaping: In operant conditioning, reinforcing responses that are successively closer approximations to the desired behaviour.
shell shock: A term from World War I for what is now referred to as posttraumatic stress disorder; it was believed to be due to sudden atmospheric changes from nearby explosions.
significant difference: See *statistical significance*.
single-subject experimental design: A design for an experiment conducted with a single subject, for example, the reversal and multiple-baseline designs in operant conditioning research.
situational determinants: The environmental conditions that precede and follow a particular piece of behaviour, a primary focus of behavioural assessment.
skeletal (voluntary) muscle: Muscle that clothes the skeleton of the vertebrate, is attached to bone, and is under voluntary control.
Skinner box. A laboratory apparatus in which an animal is placed for an operant-conditioning experiment. It contains a lever or other device that the animal must manipulate to obtain a reward or avoid punishment.
sleep apnea: Respiratory disorder in which breathing ceases repeatedly for a period of ten seconds or more hundreds of times throughout the night.
sleeping sickness. See encephalitis *lethargica*.
smooth (involuntary) muscle. Thin sheets of muscle cells associated with viscera and walls of blood vessels, performing functions not usually under direct voluntary control.
social desirability: In completion of personality inventories, the tendency of the responder to give what he or she considers the socially acceptable answer, whether or not it is accurate.
social gradient of health: The link between low SES and poor health..
social phobia: A collection of fears linked to the presence of other people.
social problem solving: A form of cognitive behaviour therapy that has people construe their psychological difficulties as stemming from soluble problems in living and then teaches them how to generate useful solutions.
social selection theory: An attempt to explain the correlation between social class and schizophrenia by proposing that people with schizophrenia move downward in social status.
social worker: A mental health professional who holds a master of social work (M.S.W.) degree.
social-skills training: Behaviour therapy procedures for teaching socially unknowledgeable individuals how to meet others, talk to them and maintain eye contact, give and receive criticism, offer and accept compliments, make requests and express feelings, and otherwise improve their relations with other people. Modeling and behaviour rehearsal are two such procedures.
socioeconomic status: A relative position in the community as determined by occupation, income, and level of education.
sociogenic hypothesis: Generally, an idea that seeks causes in social conditions, for example, that being in a low social class can cause one to become schizophrenic.
sociopath: See *antisocial personality*.
sociotropy: A personality style associated with vulnerability to depression. It involves high levels of dependency and an excessive need to please others.
sodomy: Originally, penetration of the male organ into the anus of another male; later broadened in English law to include heterosexual anal intercourse and by some U.S. state statutes to cover unconventional sex in general.
soma: The totality of an organism's physical makeup.
somatic nervous system: That part of the nervous system that controls muscles under voluntary control.
somatic weakness: The vulnerability of a particular organ or organ system to psychological stress and thereby to a particular psychophysiological disorder.
somatization disorder (Briquet's syndrome): A somatoform disorder in which the person continually seeks medical help for recurrent and multiple physical symptoms that have no discoverable physical cause. The medical history is complicated and dramatically presented. Compare with hypochondriasis.
somatoform disorders: Disorders in which physical symptoms suggest a physical problem but have no known physiological cause; they are therefore believed to be linked to psychological conflicts and needs but not voluntarily assumed. Examples are somatization disorder (Briquet's syndrome), conversion disorder, pain disorder, hypochondriasis.
somatoform pain disorder: A somatoform disorder in which the person complains of severe and prolonged pain that is not explainable by organic pathology; it tends to be stress related or permits the patient to avoid an aversive activity or to gain attention and sympathy.
somatogenesis: Development from bodily origins, as distinguished from psychological origins. Compare with *psychogenesis*.
SORC: An acronym for the four sets of variables that are the focus of behavioural assessment: situational determinants, organismic variables, (overt) responses, and reinforcement contingencies.
specific phobia: An unwarranted fear and avoidance of a specific object or circumstance, for example, fear of nonpoisonous snakes or fear of heights.

specific-reaction theory: The hypothesis that an individual develops a given psycho-physiological disorder because of the innate tendency of the autonomic nervous system to respond in a particular way to stress, for example, by increasing heart rate or developing tension in the forehead.

spectator role: As applied by Masters and Johnson, a pattern of behaviour in which the individual's focus on and concern with sexual performance impedes his or her natural sexual responses.

split-half reliability: See *reliability*.

stability–lability: A dimension of classifying the responsiveness of the autonomic

nervous system. Labile individuals are those in whom a wide range of stimuli can elicit autonomic arousal; stable individuals are less easily aroused.

standardization: The process of constructing an assessment procedure that has norms and meets the various psychometric criteria for reliability and validity.

state-dependent learning: The phenomenon whereby an organism shows the effects of learning that took place in a special condition, such as while intoxicated, better than in another condition.

state-dependent memory: The phenomenon whereby people are more able to remember an event if they are in the same state as when it occurred. If they are in a greatly different state when they try to remember—happy now, and sad then, for example—memory is poorer.

statistical significance: A result that has a low probability of having occurred by chance alone and is by convention regarded as important.

statutory rape: See *forced rape*.

stepped care: A treatment strategy that begins with less complex and costly interventions followed by more complex attempts if initial attempts are not successful.

stepping-stone theory: The belief that the use of one kind of drug, such as marijuana, leads to the use of a more dangerous one, such as cocaine.

stereotyping: A fixed belief that typically involves a negative generalization about a group or class of people. Members of the general public often endorse a number of negative beliefs about mentally ill people, and thus engage in stereotyping.

stigmatization: A reduction in the status of a group of people - such as mentally ill people - due to perceived deficiencies.

stimulant: A drug that increases alertness and motor activity and at the same time reduces fatigue, allowing an individual to remain awake for an extended period of time. Examples are cocaine and amphetamines.

strategic processing: The use of cognitive strategies to solve problems; said to be defective in people with mental retardation.

stress: State of an organism subjected to a stressor; it can take the form of increased autonomic activity and in the long term can cause the breakdown of an organ or development of a mental disorder.

stress inoculation training: The act of teaching someone how to cope with small, manageable amounts of stress so they will be "protected" and will respond favourably when faced with more stressful circumstances.

stress management: A range of psychological procedures that help people control and reduce their stress or anxiety.

stressor: An event that occasions stress in an organism, for example, loss of a loved one.

stroke: A sudden loss of consciousness and control followed by paralysis; caused when a blood clot obstructs an artery or by hemorrhage into the brain when an artery ruptures.

Stroop task: A measure of cognitive processing that requires respondents to identify the colour of a word while ignoring the word's content or meaning. It takes longer to colour-name a word if the word reflects a theme that is cognitively accessible for a particular individual.

structural social support: A person's network of social relationships, for example, number of friends. Contrast with functional social support.

structured interview: An interview in which the questions are set out in a prescribed fashion for the interviewer. Assists professionals in making diagnostic decisions based upon standardized criteria.

stuttering: One of the communication disorders of childhood, marked by frequent and pronounced verbal dysfluencies, such as repetitions of certain sounds.

subdural hematoma: Hemorrhage and swelling of the arachnoid torn by a fractured bone of the skull.

sub-intentioned death: A form of suicide that is believed to have been caused in some measure by the person's unconscious intentions.

sublimation: Defence mechanism entailing the conversion of sexual or aggressive impulses into socially valued behaviours, especially creative activity.

substance abuse: The use of a drug to such an extent that the person is often intoxicated throughout the day and fails in important obligations and in attempts to abstain, but there is no physiological dependence. See *psychological dependency*.

substance dependence: The abuse of a drug sometimes accompanied by a physiological dependence on it, made evident by tolerance and withdrawal symptoms; also called addiction.

substance-related disorders: Disorders in which drugs such as alcohol and cocaine are abused to such an extent that behaviour becomes maladaptive; social and occupational functioning are impaired, and control or abstinence becomes impossible. Reliance on the drug may be either psychological, as in substance abuse, or physiological, as in substance dependence, or addiction.

successive approximations: Responses that closer and closer resemble the desired response in operant conditioning. See *shaping*.

suicide: The taking of one's own life intentionally.

suicide prevention centres: Based on the assumption that people are often ambivalent about taking their own lives, these centres are staffed primarily by paraprofessionals who are trained to be empathic and to encourage suicidal callers to consider nondestructive ways of dealing with what is bothering them.

sulci: The cerebral cortex or outer layer of the brain is composed or ridges and depressions between the ridges which are called fissures or sulci.

sulcus (fissure): A shallow furrow in the cerebral cortex separating adjacent convolutions or gyri.

superego: In psychoanalytic theory, the part of the personality that acts as the conscience and reflects society's moral standards as learned from parents and teachers.

symbolic loss: In psychoanalytic theory, the unconscious interpretation by the ego of an event such as the rebuff of a loved one as a permanent rejection.

sympathetic nervous system: The division of the autonomic nervous system that acts on bodily systems—for example, contracting the blood vessels, reducing activity of the intestines, and increasing the heartbeat—to prepare the organism for exertion, emotional stress, or extreme cold.

symptom: An observable physiological or psychological manifestation of a disease, often occurring in a patterned group to constitute a syndrome.

synapse: A small gap between two neurons where the nerve impulse passes from the axon of the first to the dendrites, cell body, or axon of the second.

syndrome: A group or pattern of symptoms that tends to occur together in a particular disease.

systematic desensitization: A major behaviour therapy procedure that has a fearful person, while deeply relaxed, imagine a series of progressively more fearsome situations. The two responses of relaxation and fear are incompatible and fear is dispelled. This technique is useful for treating psychological problems in which anxiety is the principal difficulty.

systematic rational restructuring: A variant of rational-emotive therapy in which the client imagines a series of increasingly anxiety-provoking situations while attempting to reduce distress by talking about them to the self in a more realistic, defusing fashion.

systems perspective: A general viewpoint that holds that a phenomenon, for example, a child's conduct problem, is best understood in the broad context in which it occurs, for example, the child's family and school environments.

tachycardia: A racing of the heart, often associated with high levels of anxiety.

tardive dyskinesia: A muscular disturbance of older patients who have taken phenothiazines for a very long time, marked by involuntary lip smacking and chin wagging.

Taylor Manifest Anxiety Scale: Fifty items drawn from the MMPI, used as a self-report questionnaire to assess anxiety.

technical eclecticism: A method of psychotherapy integration in which a particular style or school of psychotherapy is employed but one in which the therapist is free to borrow from other schools or methods deemed effective..

temporal lobe: A large area of each cerebral hemisphere situated below the lateral sulcus and in front of the occipital lobe; contains primary auditory projection and association areas and general association areas.

tertiary prevention: See *prevention*.
testes: Male reproductive glands or gonads; the site where sperm develop and are stored.
testosterone: Male sex hormone secreted by the testes that is responsible for the development of sex characteristics, such as enlargement of the testes and growth of facial hair.
test-retest reliability: See *reliability*.
tetrahydrocannabinol (THC): The major active chemical in marijuana and hashish.
T-group: See *sensitivity training group*.
thalamus: A major brain relay station consisting of two egg-shaped lobes located in the diencephalon; it receives impulses from all sensory areas except the olfactory and transmits them to the cerebrum.
Thanatos: In psychoanalytic theory, the death instinct; with Eros, the two basic instincts within the id.
Thematic Apperception Test (TAT): A projective test consisting of a set of black-and-white pictures reproduced on cards, each depicting a potentially emotion-laden situation. The examinee, presented with the cards one at a time, is instructed to make up a story about each situation.
theory: A formally stated and coherent set of propositions that purport to explain a range of phenomena, order them in a logical way, and suggest what additional information might be gleaned under certain conditions.
therapeutic community: A concept in mental health care that views the total environment as contributing to prevention or treatment.
therapeutic working alliance: A method of psychotherapy used in some schools in which the patient or client is enlisted as an active partner in the planning and implementation of the procedures.
thiamine: One of the complex of B vitamins.
third-variable problem: The difficulty in the correlational method of research whereby the relationship between two variables may be attributable to a third factor.
Thorazine: Trade name for chlorpromazine, one of the antipsychotic drugs and a member of the phenothiazine group.
thought disorder: A symptom of schizophrenia, evidenced by problems such as incoherence, loose associations, poverty of speech, and poverty of content of speech.
thought listing: A cognitive assessment technique that involves a person writing down his or her thoughts upon experiencing an event, such as taking a test or meeting a person.
thyroid gland: An endocrine structure whose two lobes are located on either side of the windpipe; it secretes thyroxin.
time-of-measurement effects: A possible confound in longitudinal studies whereby conditions at a particular point in time can have a specific effect on a variable that is being studied over time.
time-out: An operant conditioning punishment procedure in which, after bad behaviour, the person is temporarily removed from a setting where reinforcers can be obtained and placed in a less desirable setting, for example, in a boring room.
token economy: A behaviour therapy procedure, based on operant conditioning principles, in which institutionalized patients are given scrip rewards, such as poker chips, for socially constructive behaviour. The tokens can be exchanged for desirable items and activities such as cigarettes and extra time away from the ward.
tolerance: A physiological process in which greater and greater amounts of an addictive drug are required to produce the same effect. See *substance dependence*.
trait: A somatic characteristic or an enduring psychological predisposition to respond in a particular way, distinguishing one individual from another.
tranquilizer: A drug that reduces anxiety and agitation, such as Valium. See *anxiolytics*.
transference: The venting of the patient's emotions, either positive or negative, by treating the psychoanalyst as the symbolic representative of someone important in the past. An example is the patient's becoming angry with the psychoanalyst to release emotions actually felt toward his or her father.
transference neurosis: A crucial phase of psychoanalysis during which the patient reacts emotionally toward the psychoanalyst, treating the analyst as a parent and reliving childhood experiences in his or her presence. It enables both psychoanalyst and patient to examine hitherto repressed conflicts in the light of present-day reality.
transsexual: A person who believes he or she is opposite in sex to his or her biological endowment; sex-reassignment surgery is frequently desired.
transexualism: The state of being a transsexual (see transsexual).
transvestic fetishism: The practice of dressing in the clothing of the opposite sex, for the purpose of sexual arousal.
trauma: A severe physical injury or wound to the body caused by an external force, or a psychological shock having a lasting effect on mental life.
traumatic disease: An illness produced by external assault, such as poison, a blow, or stress; for example, a broken leg.
tremor: An involuntary quivering of voluntary muscle, usually limited to small musculature of particular areas.
trepanning: The act of making a surgical opening in a living skull. This act was sometimes performed because of the belief that it would allow evil spirits to leave the body.
triadic reciprocality: The influence of cognition and behaviour on each other through the relationships among thinking, behaviour, and the environment.
tricyclic drugs: A group of antidepressants with molecular structures characterized by three fused rings. Tricyclics are known to interfere with the reuptake of norepinephrine and serotonin by a neuron after it has fired.
trisomy: A condition wherein there are three rather than the usual pair of homologous chromosomes within the cell nucleus.
tumescence: The flow of blood into the genitals.
tumour (neoplasm): Abnormal growth that when located in the brain can either be malignant and directly destroy brain tissue or be benign and disrupt functioning by increasing intra-cranial pressure.
twin method: Research strategy in behaviour genetics in which concordance rates of monozygotic and dizygotic twins are compared.
two-factor theory: Mowrer's theory of avoidance learning according to which (1) fear is attached to a neutral stimulus by pairing it with a noxious unconditioned stimulus, and (2) a person learns to escape the fear elicited by the conditioned stimulus, thereby avoiding the unconditioned stimulus. See *fear-drive*.
Type A behaviour pattern: One of two contrasting psychological patterns revealed through studies seeking the cause of coronary heart disease. Type A people are competitive, rushed, hostile, and over-committed to their work, and are believed to be at heightened risk for heart disease. Those who meet the other pattern, Type B people, are more relaxed and relatively free of pressure.
unconditional positive regard: According to Rogers, a crucial attitude for the client-centred therapist to adopt toward the client, who needs to feel complete acceptance as a person in order to evaluate the extent to which current behaviour contributes to self-actualization.
unconditioned response (UCR): See *classical conditioning*.
unconditioned stimulus (UCS): See *classical conditioning*.
unconscious: A state of unawareness without sensation or thought. In psychoanalytic theory, it is the part of the personality, in particular the id impulses, or id energy, of which the ego is unaware.
under-controlled (behaviour): In reference to childhood disorders, problem behaviour of the child that creates trouble for others, such as disobedience and aggressiveness.
undifferentiated schizophrenia: Diagnosis given for patients whose symptoms do not fit any listed category or meet the criteria for more than one subtype.
unilateral ECT: Electroconvulsive therapy in which electrodes are placed on one side of the forehead so that current passes through only one brain hemisphere.
unipolar depression: A term applied to the disorder of individuals who have experienced episodes of depression but not of mania; referred to as major depression in DSM-IV.
vagina: The sheath-like female genital organ that leads from the uterus to the external opening.
vaginal barrel: The passageway of the vaginal canal leading from the external opening to the uterus.
vaginal orgasm: Sexual climax experienced through stimulation of the vagina.
vaginal plethysmograph: A device for recording the amount of blood in the walls of the vagina and thus for measuring arousal.
vaginismus: Painful, spasmodic contractions of the outer third of the vaginal barrel, which make insertion of the penis impossible or extremely difficult.

validity: Different types of validity include **internal**, the extent to which experimental results can be confidently attributed to the manipulation of the independent variable; **external**, the extent to which research results may be generalized to other populations and settings. Validity as applied to psychiatric diagnoses includes **concurrent**, the extent to which previously undiscovered features are found among patients with the same diagnosis; **predictive**, the extent to which predictions can be made about the future behaviour of patients with the same diagnosis; **etiological**, the extent to which a disorder in a number of patients is found to have the same cause or causes. Validity as applied to psychological and psychiatric measures includes **content validity**, the extent to which a measure adequately samples the domain of interest; **criterion**, the extent to which a measure is associated in an expected way with some other measure (the criterion). See also *construct validity*.

Valium: An anxiety-reducing drug, or anxiolytic; one of the benzodiazepines.

value self-confrontation: A procedure whereby a person's values and behaviour are changed by demonstrating that the values of people he or she wishes to emulate are different from the ones currently held by the person.

variable: A characteristic or aspect in which people, objects, events, or conditions vary.

vasoconstriction: A narrowing of the space within the walls (lumen) of a blood vessel; implicated in diseases such as hypertension.

ventricles: Deep within the brain are cavities called ventricles that are continuous with the central canal of the spinal cord and are filled with cerebrospinal fluid.

vicarious learning: Learning by observing the reactions of others to stimuli or by listening to what they say.

videotape reconstruction: A technique for assessing a person's thoughts and feelings. It involves having the person recall his or her reactions while watching a videotape of a previous time when they were engaged in a task.

Vineland Adaptive Behaviour Scale: An instrument for assessing how many age-appropriate, socially adaptive behaviours a child engages in.

virtual reality exposure: The use of a computer generated graphics and sound to construct an experience similar to one that a patient fears.

viscera: The internal organs of the body located in the great cavity of the trunk proper.

vitamins: Various organic substances that are, as far as is known, essential to the nutrition of many animals, acting usually in minute quantities to regulate various metabolic processes.

voyeurism: Marked preference for obtaining sexual gratification by watching others in a state of undress or having sexual relations.

vulnerability schema: The schema of people who are socially anxious and who generally think about danger, harm, and unpleasant events that may come to them.

waxy flexibility: An aspect of catatonic immobility in which the patient's limbs can be moved into a variety of positions and maintained that way for unusually long periods of time.

white matter: The neural tissue, particularly of the brain and spinal cord, consisting of tracts or bundles of myelinated (sheathed) nerve fibres.

withdrawal: Negative physiological and psychological reactions evidenced when a person suddenly stops taking an addictive drug; cramps, restlessness, and even death are examples. See *substance abuse*.

woolly mammoth: A metaphor for the way in which the repressed conflicts of psychoanalytic theory are encapsulated in the unconscious, making them inaccessible to examination and alteration; thus maintained, the conflicts cause disorders in adulthood.

working through: In psychoanalysis, the arduous, time-consuming process through which the patient confronts repressed conflicts again and again and faces up to the validity of the psychoanalyst's interpretations until problems are satisfactorily solved.

Zeitgeist: The German word for the trends of thought and feeling of culture and taste of a particular time period.

zygote: The fertilized egg cell formed when the male sperm and female ovum unite.

References

Recent Canadian references, (since and including 1997), are highlighted with the authors names appearing in bold.

Abela, J.R.Z. (2001). The hopelessness theory of depression: A test of the diathesis-stress and causal mediation components in third and seventh grade children. *Journal of Abnormal Child Psychology, 29*, 241-254.

Abela, J.R.Z. (2002). Depressive mood reactions to failure in the achievement domain: A test of the integration of the hopelessness and self-esteem theories of depression. *Cognitive Therapy and Research, 26*, 531-552.

Abela, J.R.Z., Brozina, K., & Haigh, E.P. (2002). An examination of the response styles theory of depression in third- and seventh-grade children: A short-term longitudinal study. *Journal of Abnormal Child Psychology, 30*, 515-527.

Abela, J.R.Z., McIntyre-Smith, A., & Dechef, M.L.E. (2003). Personality predispositions to depression: A test of the specific vulnerability and symptom specificity hypotheses. *Journal of Social and Clinical Psychology, 22*, 493-514.

Abela, J.R.Z., & Sarin, S. (2002). Cognitive vulnerability to hopelessness depression: A chain is only as strong as its weakest link. *Cognitive Therapy and Research, 26*, 811-829.

Abikoff, H.B. & Hechtman, L. (1996). Multimodal therapy and stimulants in the treatment of children with attention-deficit hyperactivity disorder. In E.D. Hibbs & P.S. Jensen (Eds.), *Psychosocial treatments for child and adolescent disorders: Empirically based strategies for clinical practice* (pp. 341-369). Washington, D.C.: American Psychological Association.

Abracen, J., Looman, J., & Anderson, D. (2000). Alcohol and drug abuse in sexual and nonsexual violent offenders. *Sexual Abuse: A Journal of Research and Treatment, 12*, 261-272.

Abrams, R., Swartz, C.M., & Vedak, C. (1991). Antidepressant effects of high-dose right unilateral electroconvulsive therapy. *Archives of General Psychiatry, 48,* 746-748.

Abramson, L.Y., Metalsky, G.I., & Alloy, L.B. (1989). Hopelessness depression: A theory-based subtype of depression. *Psychological Review, 96,* 358-372.

Abramson, L.Y., Seligman, M.E.P., & Teasdale, J.D. (1978). Learned helplessness in humans: Critique and reformulation. *Journal of Abnormal Psychology, 87,* 49-74.

Achenbach, T.M., & Edelbrock, C.S. (1978). The classification of child psychopathology: A review of empirical efforts. *Psychological Bulletin, 85,* 1275-1301.

Achenbach, T.M., Hensley, V.R., Phares, V., & Grayson, D. (1990). Problems and competencies reported by parents of Australian and American children. *Journal of Child Psychology and Psychiatry, 31,* 265-286.

Ackerman, N.W. (1966). *Treating the troubled family*. New York: Basic Books.

Acorn, S. (1993). Mental and physical health of homeless persons who use emergency shelters in Vancouver. *Hospital and Community Psychiatry, 44*, 854-857.

Adamek, M.E., & Kaplan, M.S. (1996). Managing elder suicide: A profile of American and Canadian crisis prevention centers. *Suicide and Life-Threatening Behavior, 26*, 122-131.

Adams, A. (1997, January 6). NHLer tells of horror of sex abuse. *The Toronto Star,* p. A1.

Adams, H.E., Wright, L.W., Jr., & Lohr, B.A. (1996). Is homophobia associated with homosexual arousal? *Journal of Abnormal Psychology, 105,* 440-445.

Adams, K.M. (1980). In search of Luria's battery: A false start. *Journal of Consulting and Clinical Psychology, 48,* 511-516.

Adams, K.S., Keller, A., West, M., Larose, S., et al. (1994). Parental representation of suicidal adolescents: A controlled study. *Australian and New Zealand Journal of Psychiatry, 28,* 418-425.

Adams, P., & Laghi, B. (2000, November). Medicare debate boils over. *The Globe and Mail*, A1, A7.

Addiction Research Foundation (1994). *Guided Self-Change: Clinical training manual.* Toronto: Author.

Addington, J. (2003). The prodromal stage of psychotic illness: Observation, detection, or intervention? *Journal of Psychiatry and Neuroscience, 28*, 93-97.

Addington, J., & Addington, D. (1998). Facial affect recognition and information processing in schizophrenia and bipolar disorder. *Schizophrenia Research, 32*, 171-181.

Addington, J., & Addington, D. (2000). Neurocognitive and social functioning in schizophrenia: A 2.5 year follow-up study. *Schizophrenia Research, 44*, 47-56.

Addis, M.E. (1997). Evaluating the treatment manual as a means of disseminating empirically validated psychotherapies. *Clinical Psychology: Science and Practice, 4,* 1-11.

Adelmann, P.K. (1994). Multiple roles and psychological well-being in a national sample of older adults. *Journal of Gerontology, 49,* S277-S285.

Adlaf, E.M., Gliksman, L., Demers, A., & Newton-Taylor, B. (2003). Cigarette use among Canadian undergraduates. *Canadian Journal of Public Health, 94*, 22-24.

Adlaf, E.M., Ivis, F.J., & Smart, R.G. (1997). *Ontario student drug use survey: 1977-1997.* Toronto: Addiction Research Foundation.

Adlaf, E.M., & Paglia, A. (2003). *Drug use among Ontario students: Detailed OSDUS findings (1997-2003).* Toronto: Centre For Addiction and Mental Health.

Adler, A. (1929). *Problems of neurosis*. New York: Harper & Row.

Adler, A. (1930). *Guiding the child on the principles of individual psychology*. New York: Greenberg.

Adler, P.S., & Ditto, B. (1998). Psychophysiological effects of interviews about emotional events on offspring of hypertensives and normotensives. *International Journal of Psychophysiology, 28,* 263-271.

Adler, R.H., Zamboni, P., Hofer, T., & Hemmeler, W. (1997). How not to miss a somatic needle in a haystack of chronic pain. *Journal of Psychosomatic Research, 42,* 499-505.

Advisory Group For Suicide Prevention. (2003). *Acting on what we know: Preventing youth suicide in First Nations*. Ottawa: Government of Canada, First Nations and Inuit Health Branch.

Agbayewa, M.O. (1993). Elderly suicide in British Columbia: An exploration of regional variation and related factors. *Canadian Journal of Public Health, 84*, 231-236.

Agbayewa, M.O., Marion, S.A., & Wiggins, S. (1998). Socioeconomic factors associated with suicide in elderly populations in British Columbia: An 11-year review. *Canadian Journal of Psychiatry, 43*, 829-836.

Agras, W.S., Rossiter, E.M., Arnow, B., Schneider, J.A., Telch, C.F., Raeburn, S.D., Bruce, B., Perl, M., & Koran, L.M. (1992). Pharmacologic and cognitive-behavioral treatment for bulimia nervosa: A controlled comparison. *American Journal of Psychiatry, 149,* 82-87.

Ainsworth, M.D. (1984). Attachment. In N. S. Endler & J. McV. Hunt (Eds.),*Personality and the behavioral disorders* (Vol. 1, 2nd ed., pp. 559-602). New York: Wiley.

Ainsworth, M.D., Blehar, M.C., Waters, E., & Wall, S. (1978). *Patterns of attachment: A psychological study of the strange situation*. Hillsdale, NJ: Erlbaum.

Ainsworth, M.D., & Bowlby, J. (1953). *Research strategy in the study of mother-child separation*. Paris: Coumer de la Centre International de l'Enfance.

Akbarian, S., Kim, J.J., Potkin, S.G., Hagman, J.O., Tafazzoli, A., et al. (1995). Gene expression for glutamic acid decarboxylase is reduced without loss of neurons in prefrontal cortex of schizophrenics. *Archives of General Psychiatry, 52,* 258-266.

Akillas, E., & Efran, J.S. (1995). Symptom prescription and reframing: Should they be combined? *Cognitive Therapy and Research, 19,* 263-279.

Akyuez, G., Dogan, O., Sar, V., Yargic, L.I., & Tutkun, H. (1999). Frequency of dissociative disorder in the general population in Turkey. *Comprehensive Psychiatry, 40,* 151-159.

Al-Absim, M., & Rokke, P.D. (1991). Can anxiety help us tolerate pain? *Pain, 46,* 43-51.

Albano, A.M., Marten, P.A., Holt, C.S., Heimberg, R.G., et al. (1995). Cognitive-behavioral group treatment for social phobia in adolescents: A preliminary study. *Journal of Nervous and Mental Disease, 183,* 649-656.

Albee, G.W., Lane, E.A., & Reuter, J.M. (1964). Childhood intelligence of future schizophrenics and neighborhood peers. *Journal of Psychology, 58,* 141-144.

Albertini, R.S., & Phillips, K.A. (1999). Thirty-three cases of body dysmorphic disorder in children and adolescents. *Journal of the American Academy of Child and Adolescent Psychiatry, 38,* 453-459.

Alcohol, Drug Abuse, and Mental Health Administration. (1996). Reports of the Secretary's Task Force on Youth Suicide. *Vols. 1-4,* Washington, DC. U.S. Government Printing Office.

Alden, L.E. (1989). Short-term structured treatment for avoidant personality disorder. *Journal of Consulting and Clinical Psychology, 57,* 756-764.

Alden, L.E., Laposa, J.M., Taylor, C.T., & Ryder, A.G. (2002). Avoidant personality disorder: Current status and future directions. *Journal of Personality Disorders, 16,* 1-29.

Alexander, F. (1950). *Psychosomatic medicine.* New York: Norton.

Alexander, F., & French, T.M. (1946). *Psychoanalytic therapy.* New York: Ronald Press.

Alexander, J.F., Holtzworth-Munroe, A., & Jameson, P. (1994). The process and outcome of marital and family therapy: Research review and evaluation. In A.E. Bergin & S.L. Garfield (Eds.), *Handbook of psychotherapy and behavior change.* Fourth edition (pp. 595-630). New York: Wiley.

Alexander, P.C., Anderson, C.L., Brand, B., Schaeffer, C.M., Grelling, B.Z., & Kretz, L. (1998). Adult attachment and long-term effects in survivors of incest. *Child Abuse and Neglect, 22,* 45-61.

Alexander, P.C., & Lupfer, S.L. (1987) Family characteristics and long-term consequences associated with sexual abuse. *Archives of Sexual Behavior, 16,* 235-245.

Allderidge, P. (1979). Hospitals, mad houses, and asylums: Cycles in the care of the insane. *British Journal of Psychiatry, 134,* 321-324.

Allen, G.J., Chinsky, J.M., Larsen, S.W., Lockman, J.E., & Selinger, H.V. (1976). *Community psychology and the schools: A behaviorally oriented multilevel preventive approach.* Hillsdale, NJ: Erlbaum.

Allen, J.J.B., & Iacono, W.G. (2001). Assessing the validity of amnesia in dissociative identity disorder: A dilemma for the DSM and the courts. *Psychology, Public Policy, and Law, 7,* 311-344.

Allen, M.G. (1976). Twin studies of affective illness. *Archives of General Psychiatry, 33,* 1476-1478.

Allison, P.J., Guichard, C., Fung, K., & Gilain, L. (2003). Dispositional optimism predicts survival status 1 year after diagnosis in head and neck cancer patients. *Journal of Clinical Oncology, 21,* 543-548.

Allison, R.B. (1984). Difficulties diagnosing the multiple personality syndrome in a death penalty case. *International Journal of Clinical and Experimental Hypnosis, 32,* 102-117.

Allnutt, S.H., Bradford, J.M., Greenberg, D.M., & Curry, S. (1996). Co-morbidity of alcoholism and the paraphilias. *Journal of Forensic Science, 41,* 234-239.

Alonso-Zaldivar, R. (1999, February 23). Alcohol-related road deaths analyzed. *Los Angeles Times,* A12.

Alloul, K., Sauriol, L., Kennedy, W., Laurier, C., Tessier, G., Novosel, S., & Contandriopoulos, A. (1998). Alzheimer's disease: A review of the disease, its epidemiology, and economic impact. *Archives of Gerontology and Geriatrics, 27,* 189-221.

Alloy, L.B., Kelly, K.A., Mineka, S., & Clements, C.M. (1990). Comorbidity in anxiety and depressive disorders: A helplessness/hopelessness perspective. In J.D. Maser & C.R. Cloninger (Eds.), *Comorbidity in anxiety and mood disorders.* Washington, DC: American Psychiatric Press.

Allport, G.W. (1937). *Personality: A psychological interpretation.* New York: Holt, Rinehart & Winston.

Allport, G.W. (1961). *Pattern and growth in personality.* New York: Holt, Rinehart & Winston.

Alpert, J.E., Uebelacker, L.A., McLean, N.E., Nierenberg, A.A., & et al. (1997). Social phobia, avoidant personality disorder and atypical depression: Co-occurrence and clinical implications. *Psychological Medicine, 27,* 627-633.

Altman, D.G., Flora, J.A., & Farquhar, J.W. (1986, August). *Institutionalizing community-based health promotion programs.* Paper presented at the annual meeting of the American Psychological Association, Washington, DC.

Altshuler, L.L., Post, R.M., Leverich, G.S., Mikalauskas, K., Rusoff, A., & Ackerman, L. (1995).

Antidepressant-induced mania and cycle acceleration: A controversy revisited. *American Journal of Psychiatry, 152,* 1130-1138.

Alzheimer's Association. (2004, July 21). *Biology is not always destiny in Alzheimer's, says new twins data* (see http://www.alz.org/internationalconference/Pressreleases/072104_genetics_studies.asp)

Amador, X.F., Flaum, M., Andreasen, N.C., Strauss, D.H., Yale, S.A., et al. (1994). Awareness of illness in schizophrenia and schizoaffective and mood disorder. *Archives of General Psychiatry, 51,* 826-836.

American Association of Mental Retardation. (1992). *Mental retardation: Definition, classification, and systems of support.* Washington, DC: Author.

American Law Institute. (1962). *Model penal code: Proposed official draft.* Philadelphia: Author.

American Psychiatric Association. (1993). Practice guidelines for major depressive disorder in adults. *American Journal of Psychiatry, 150,* All.

American Psychiatric Association (1994). *Diagnostic and statistical manual of mental disorders.* Fourth edition (DSM-IV). Washington, DC: Author.

American Psychiatric Association (2000). *Diagnostic and statistical manual of mental disorders.* Fourth edition, Text Revision (DSM-IV-TR). Washington, DC: Author.

American Psychiatric Association. *Diagnostic and statistical manual of mental disorders.* First edition, 1952; second edition, 1968; third edition, 1980; revised, 1987. Washington, DC: Author.

American Psychiatric Association Board of Trustees. (1993). *Statement on memories of sexual abuse.* Washington, DC: American Psychiatric Association.

Amir, N., Foa, E.B., & Coles, M.E. (1998). Automatic activation and strategic avoidance of threat-relevant information in social phobia. *Journal of Abnormal Psychology, 107,* 285-290.

Anastasi, A. (1990). *Psychological testing* (6th ed.). New York: Macmillan.

Anastopoulos, A.D., Shelton, T., DuPaul, G.J., & Guevremont, D.C. (1993). Parent training for attention deficit hyperactivity disorder: Its impact on parent functioning. *Journal of Abnormal Child Psychology, 20,* 503-520.

Andersen, B.L., Kiecolt-Glaser, J.K., & Glaser, R. (1994). A biobehavioral model of cancer stress and disease course. *American Psychologist, 49,* 389-404.

Andersen, S.M., & Berk, M.S. (1998). The social-cognitive model of transference: Experiencing past relationships in the present. *Current Directions in Psychological Science, 7,* 109-115.

Anderson, B.L. (1992). Psychological interventions for cancer patients to enhance quality of life. *Journal of Consulting and Clinical Psychology, 60,* 552-568.

Anderson, C.A. (1991). How people think about causes: Examination of the typical phenomenal organization of attributions for success and failure. *Social Cognition, 9,* 295-329.

Anderson, L.T., Campbell, M., Adams, P., Small, A.M., Perry, R., & Shell, J. (1989). The effects of haloperidol on discrimination learning and behavioral symptoms in autistic children. *Journal of Autism and Developmental Disorders, 19,* 227-239.

Anderson, R.E., Crespo, C.J., Bartlett, S.J., Cheskin, L.J., & Pratt, M. (1998). Relationship of physical activity and television watching with body weight and level of fatness among children: Results from the third National Health and Nutrition Examination survey. *Journal of the American Medical Association, 279,* 938-942.

Anderson, S., Hanson, R., Malecha, M., Oftelie, A., Erickson, C., & Clark, J.M. (1997). The effectiveness of naltrexone in treating task attending, aggression, self-injury, and stereotypic mannerisms of six young males with autism or pervasive developmental disorders. *Journal of Developmental and Physical Disabilities, 9,* 211-221.

Andreasen, N.C. (1979). Thought, language, and communication disorders: 2. Diagnostic significance. *Archives of General Psychiatry, 36,* 1325-1330.

Andreasen, N.C., Flaum, M., Swayze, V.W., Tyrrell, G., & Arndt, S. (1990). Positive and negative symptoms in schizophrenia: A critical reappraisal. *Archives of General Psychiatry, 47,* 615-621.

Andreasen, N.C., & Olsen, S.A. (1982). Negative versus positive schizophrenia. Definition and validation. *Archives of General Psychiatry, 39,* 789-794.

Andreasen, N.C., Olsen, S.A., Dennert, J.W., & Smith, M.R. (1982). Ventricular enlargement in schizophrenia: Relationship to positive and negative symptoms. American *Journal of Psychiatry, 139,* 297-302.

Andreasen, N.C., Paradiso, S., & O'Leary, D.S. (1998). "Cognitive Dysmetria" as an intergrative thory of schizophrenia: A dysfunction in cortical-subcortical-cerebrellar circuitry. *Schizophrenia Bulletin, 24,* 203-218.

Andreasen, N.C ., Rice, J., Endicott, J., Coryell, W., Grove, W.W., & Reich, T. (1987). Familial rates of affective disorder. *Archives of General Psychiatry, 44,* 461-472.

Andreasen, N.C., Swayze, V.W., Flaum, M., Yates, W.R., et al. (1990). Ventricular enlargement in schizophrenia evaluated with computed tomographic scanning: Effects of gender, age, and stage of illness. *Archives of General Psychiatry, 47,* 1008-1015.

Andress, V.R., & Corey, D.M. (1978). Survivor-victims: Who discovers or witnesses suicide? *Psychological Reports, 42,* 759-764.

Angrist, B., Lee, H.K., & Gershon, S. (1974). The antagonism of amphetamine-induced symptomatology by a neuroleptic. *American Journal of Psychiatry, 131,* 817-819.

Angus, L., & Hardtke, K. (1994). Narrative processes in psychotherapy. *Canadian Psychology, 35,* 190-203.

Angus, L., Levitt, H., & Hardtke, K. (1999). The Narrative Processes Coding System: Research applications and implications for psychotherapy practice. Journal of Clinical Psychology, *55,* 1255-1270.

Anisman, H., & Merali, Z. (1999). Understanding stress: Characteristics and caveats. *Alcohol Research and Health, 23,* 241-249.

Annis, H.M., Sklar, S.M., & Moser, A.M. (1998). Gender in relation to relapse crisis situations, coping, and outcome among treated alcoholics. *Addictive Behaviors, 23,* 127-131.

Anthony-Bergstone, C., Zarit, S.H., & Gatz, M. (1988). Symptoms of psychological distress among caregivers of dementia patients. *Psychology and Aging, 3,* 245-248.

Antoni, M.H., Baggett, L., Ironson, G., LaPerriere, A., August, S., Klimas, N., Schneiderman, N., & Fletcher, M.A. (1991). Cognitive-behavioral stress management intervention buffers distress responses and immunologic changes following notification of HIV-1 seropositivity. *Journal of Consulting and Clinical Psychology, 59,* 906-915.

Antoni, M.H., Schneiderman, N., Fletcher, M.A., Goldstein, D.A., Ironson, G., & Laperriere, A. (1990). Psychoneuroimmunology and HIV-1. *Journal of Consulting and Clinical Psychology, 58,* 38-49.

Antony, M.M., & Barlow, D.H. (Eds.) (2002). *Handbook of assessment and treatment planning for psychological disorders.* New York, NY: Guilford Publications.

Antony, M.M., Craske, M.G., & Barlow, D.H. (1995). *Mastery of your specific phobia (client workbook).* San Antonio, TX: The Psychological Corporation.

Antony, M.M., Orsillo, S.M., & Roemer, L. (Eds.) (2001). *Practitioner's guide to empirically-based measures of anxiety.* New York, NY: Kluwer Academic/Plenum.

Antony, M.M., & Swinson, R.P. (1998). *When perfect isn't good enough: Strategies for coping with perfectionism.* Oakland, CA: New Harbinger Publications.

Antony, M.M., & Swinson, R.P. (2000a). *Phobic disorders and panic in adults: A guide to assessment and treatment.* Washington, DC: American Psychological Association.

Antony, M.M., & Swinson, R.P. (2000b). *The shyness and social anxiety workbook: Proven, step-by-step techniques for overcoming your fear.* Oakland, CA: New Harbinger Publications.

Antony, M.M., Orsillo, S.M., & Roemer, L. (Eds.) (in press). *Practitioner's guide to empirically-based measures of anxiety.* New York, NY: Kluwer Academic/Plenum.

Apfelbaum, B. (1989). Retarded ejaculation: A much-misunderstood syndrome. In S.R. Leiblum & R.C. Rosen (Eds.), *Principles and practice of sex therapy: Update for the 1990s* (pp. 168-206). New York: Guilford.

Appel, L.J., Moore, T.J., Obarzanek,E., Vollmer, W.M., Svetkey, L.P., Sacks, F.M., Bray, G.A., Vogt, T.M., Cutler, J.A., Windhauser, M.M., Lin, P-H, Karanja, N., for the DASH Collaborative Research Group. (1997). A clinical trial of the effects of dietary patterns on blood pressure. *New England Journal of Medicine, 336,* 1117-1124.

Appelbaum, P.S. (1985). Tarasoff and the clinician: Problems in fulfilling the duty to protect. *American Journal of Psychiatry, 142,* 425-429.

Appelbaum, P.S., & Greer, A. (1994). Who's on trial? Multiple personalities and the insanity defense. *Hospital and Community Psychiatry, 45,* 965-966.

Appelbaum, P.S., & Grisso, T. (1995). The MacArthur Treatment Competence Study: 1. Mental illness and competence to consent to treatment. *Law and Human Behavior, 19,* 105-126.

Appelbaum, P.S., Grisso, T., Frank, E., O'Donnel, S., & Kupfer, D. (1999). Capacities of depressed patients to consent to research. *American Journal of Psychiatry, 156,* 1380-1384

Appelbaum, P.S., & Gutheil, T. (1980). The Boston State Hospital case: "Involuntary mind control," the Constitution, and the "right to rot." *American Journal of Psychiatry, 137,* 720-727.

Appelbaum, P.S., & Gutheil, T. (1991). *Clinical handbook of psychiatry and the law.* Baltimore: Williams & Wilkins.

Apt, C., & Hurlbert, D.H. (1994). The sexual attitudes, behavior, and relationships of women with histrionic personality disorder. *Journal of Sex and Marital Therapy, 20,* 125-133.

Apter, J.T., & Allen, L.A. (1999). Buspirone: Future directions. *Journal of Clinical Psychopharmacology, 19,* 86-93.

Araujo, A.B., Durante, R., Feldman, H.A., Goldstein, I., & McKinley, J.B. (1998). The relationship between depressive symptoms and male erectile dysfunction: Cross-sectional results from the Massachusetts Male Aging Study. *Psychosomatic Medicine, 60,* 458-465.

Arbuthnot, J., & Gordon, D.A. (1986). Behavioral and cognitive effects of a moral reasoning development intervention for high-risk behavior disordered adolescents. *Journal of Consulting and Clinical Psychology, 54,* 208-216.

Ard, B.N., Jr. (1977). Sex in lasting marriages: A longitudinal study. *Journal of Sex Research, 13,* 274-285.

Arentewicz, G., & Schmidt, G. (1983). *The treatment of sexual disorders: Concepts and techniques of couple therapy.* New York: Basic Books.

Arieti, S. (1979). New views on the psychodynamics of phobias. *American Journal of Psychotherapy, 33,* 82-95.

Arkowitz, H. (1989). The role of theory in psychotherapy integration. *Journal of Integrative and Eclectic Psychotherapy, 8,* 8-16.

Arkowitz, H. (1992). Integrative theories of therapy. In D. Freedheim (Ed.), *The history of psychotherapy: A century of change.* Washington, DC: American Psychological Association.

Arndt, I.O., Dorozynsky, L., Woody, G.E., McLellan, A.T., & O'Brien, C.P. (1992). Desipramine treatment of cocaine dependence in methadone-maintained patients. *Archives of General Psychiatry, 49,* 888-893.

Arnow, B., Kenardy, J., & Agras, W.S. (1992). Binge eating among the obese. *Journal of Behavioral Medicine, 15,* 155-170.

Arolt, V., Lencer, R., Nolte, A., Muller-Myhsok, B., Purmann, S., et al. (1996). Eye-tracking dysfunction is a putative phenotypic susceptibility marker for schizophrenia and maps to a locus on chromosome 6p in families with multiple occurrence of the disease. *American Journal of Medical Genetics, 67,* 564-579.

Aronson, E. (1972). *The social animal.* San Francisco: Freeman.

Aronson, E., & Carlsmith, J.R. (1968). Experimentation in social psychology. In G. Lindzey & E. Aronson (Eds.), *The handbook of social psychology: Vol 2. Research methods.* Menlo Park, CA: Addison-Wesley.

Aronson, J. (2002). Elderly people's accounts of home care rationing: Missing voices in long-term care policy debates. *Aging and Society, 22,* 399-418.

Aronson, K. (2003). Alcohol: A recently identified risk factor for breast cancer. *Canadian Medical Association Journal, 168,* 1147-1148.

Arseneault, L., Tremblay, R.E., Boulerice, B., & Saucier, J.F. (2002). Obstetrical complications and violent delinquency: Testing two developmental pathways. *Child Development*, *73*, 496-508.

Asarnow, J.R., Jaycox, L.H., & Tompson, M.C. (2001). Depression in youth: Psychosocial interventions. *Journal of Clinical Child Psychology*, *30*, 33-47.

Ascher, L.M., & Turner, R.M. (1979). Paradoxical intention and insomnia: An experimental investigation. *Behaviour Research and Therapy, 17,* 408-411.

Asmundson, G.J., Larsen, D.K., & Stein, M.B. (1998). Panic disorder and vestibular disturbance: An overview of empirical findings and clinical implications. *Journal of Psychosomaitc research, 44,* 107-120.

Asmundson, G.J., Stein, M.B., & McCreary, D.R. (2002). Posttraumatic stress disorder symptoms influence health status of deployed peacekeepers and nondeployed military personnel. *Journal of Nervous and Mental Disease*, *190*, 807-815.

Asmundson, G.J., Taylor, S., Sevgur, S., & Cox, B.J. (2001). Health anxiety: Classification and clinical features. In G.J.G. Asmundson, S. Taylor, & B.J. Cox (Eds.), *Health anxiety: Clinical and research perspectives on hypochondriasis and related conditions* (pp. 3-21). Toronto: Wiley.

Asmundson, G.J., Taylor, S., Wright, K.D., & Cox, B.J. (2001). Future directions and challenges in assessment, treatment, and investigation. In G.J.G. Asmundson, S. Taylor, & B.J. Cox (Eds.), *Health anxiety: Clinical and research perspectives on hypochondriasis and related conditions* (pp. 365-381). Toronto: Wiley.

Associated Press. (1998a). Bill aims to thwart assisted suicides. *Los Angeles Times*, A18

Associated Press. (1998b). Bosnian Serb admits to raping four women. *Los Angeles Times*, A6

Atkeson, B.M., Calhoun, K.S., Resick, P.A., & Ellis, E.M. (1982). Victims of rape: Repeated assessment of depressive symptoms. *Journal of Consulting and Clinical Psychology, 50,* 96-102.

Atkinson, D.R., Brown, M.T., Matthews, L.G., Landrum-Brown, J., & Kim, A.U. (1996). African American client skin tone and clinical judgments of African American and European American psychologists. *Professional Psychology: Research and Practice, 27,* 500-505.

Atkinson, D.R., & Lowe, S.M. (1995). The role of ethnicity, cultural knowledge, and conventional techniques in counseling and psychotherapy. In J.G. Ponterotto, J.M. Casas, L.A. Suzuki, & C.M. Alexander (Eds.), *Handbook of multicultural counseling*. (pp. 387-414). Thousand Oaks, CA: Sage.

Atkinson, L., Paglia, A., Coolbear, J., Niccols, A., Parker, K.C.H., & Guger, S. (2000). Attachment security: A meta-analysis of maternal mental health correlates. *Clinical Psychology Review*, *20*, 1019-1040.

Attia, E., Haiman, C., Walsh, B.T., & Flater, S.R. (1998). Does fluoxetine augment the inpatient treatment of anorexia nervosa? *American Journal of Psychiatry, 155,* 548-551.

August, G.J., Realmuto, G.M., MacDonald, A.W., Nugent, S.M., & Crosby, R. (1996). Prevalence of ADHD and comorbid disorders among elementary school children screened for disruptive behavior. *Journal of Abnormal Child Psychology, 24,* 555-569.

Auld, A. (2001, August 2). Convicted pedophile will be released from prison, but will go to psych centre. *The Canadian Press.*

Austin, J.P., Azia, H., Potter, L., Thelmo, W., Chen, P., Choi, K., Brandys, M., Macchia, R.J., & Rotman, M. (1990). Diminished survival of young Blacks with adenocarcinoma of the prostate. *American Journal of Clinical Oncology, 13,* 465-469.

Austin, S.B. (2000). Prevention research in eating disorders: Theory and new directions. *Psychological Medicine*, *30*, 1249-1262.

Author (1994). *AIDS and behavior: An integrated approach.* Washington,DC: National Academy Press.

Author (1995). *Job stress interventions.* Washington,DC: American Psychological Association.

Author (1996). Why Jenifer got sick: The mother of a poster child is accused of causing her daughter's illness. *Time, 147,* 70.

Author (1997). Workshop on the medical utility of marijuana: Report to the Director, National Institutes of Health, by the Ad Hoc Group of Experts.

Author (1998). *Expert witnesses in child abuse cases: What can and should be said in court.* Washington,DC: American Psychological Association.

Avison, W.R., & McAlpine, D.D. (1992). Gender differences in symptoms of depression among adolescents. *Journal of Health and Social Behavior*, *33*, 77-96.

Avissar, S., Nechamkin, Y., Barki-Harrington, L., Roitman, G., & Schreiber, G. (1997). Differential G protein measures in mononuclear leucocytes of patients with bipolar mood disorder are state dependent. *Journal of Affective Disorders, 43,* 85-93.

Avissar, S., Schreiber, G., Nechamkin, Y., Nehaus, I., Lam, G., et al. (1999). The effects of seasons and light therapy on G protein levels in mononuclear leukocytes in patients with seasonal; affective disorder, *Archives of General Psychiatry, 56,* 178-184.

Awad, G.A., & Saunders, E. (1989). Adolescent child molesters: Clinical observations. *Child Psychiatry and Human Development, 19,* 195-206.

Ayanian, J.Z., & Cleary, P.D. (1999). Perceived risks of heart disease and cancer among cigarete smokers. *JAMA, 281,* 1019-1021.

Aycan, Z., & Berry, J. W. (1996). Impact of employment-related experiences on immigrants' psychological well-being and adaptation to Canada. *Canadian Journal of behavioural Science, 28,* 240-251.

Ayllon, T., & Azrin, N.H. (1968). *The token economy: A motivational system for therapy and rehabilitation.* New York: Appleton-Century-Crofts.

Ayllon, T., & Michael, J. (1959). The psychiatric nurse as a behavioral engineer. *Journal of the Experimental Analysis of Behavior, 2,* 323-335.

Aylwin, A.S., Studer, L.H., Reddon, J.R., & Clelland, S.R. (2003). Abuse prevalence and victim gender among adult and adolescent child molesters. *International Journal of Law and Psychiatry*, *26*, 179-190.

Azrin, N.H., Sisson, R.W., Meyers, R., & Godley, M. (1982). Alcoholism treatment by disulfiram and community reinforcement therapy. *Journal of Behaviour Therapy and Experimental Psychiatry, 13,* 105-112.

Azrin, N.H., Sneed, T.J., & Foxx, R.M. (1973). Dry bed: A rapid method of eliminating bedwetting (enuresis) of the retarded. *Behaviour Research and Therapy, 11,* 427-434.

Babarik, P. (1979). The buried Canadian roots of community psychology. *Journal of Community Psychology*, *7*, 362-367.

Bach, G.R. (1966). The marathon group: Intensive practice of intimate interactions. *Psychological Reports, 181,* 995-1002.

Bachrach, H., Galatzer-Levy, R., Skolnikoff, A., & Waldron, S. (1991). On the efficacy of psychoanalysis. *Journal of the American Psychoanalytic Association, 39,* 871-916.

Badian, N.A. (1983). Dyscalculia and nonverbal disorders of learning. In H.R. Myklebust (Ed.), *Progress in learning disabilities* (Vol. 5). New York: Grune & Stratton.

Baer, J.S., & Lichtenstein, E. (1988). Cognitive assessment. In D.M. Donovan & G.A. Marlatt (Eds.), *Assessment of addictive behaviors* (pp. 189-213). New York: Guilford.

Baer, L., & Jenike, M.A. (1992). Personality disorders in obsessive-compulsive disorder. *Psychiatric Clinics of North America, 15,* 803-812.

Baer, L., Jenike, M.A., Ricciardi, J.N., Holland, A.D., Seymour, R.J., et al. (1990). Standardized assessment of personality disorders in obsessive compulsive disorder. *Archives of General Psychiatry, 47,* 826-831.

Baer, L., Rauch, S.L., Ballantine, H.T., Martuza, R., Cosgrove, R., et al. (1995). Cingulatomy for intractable obsessive-compulsive disorder. *Archives of General Psychiatry, 52,* 384-392.

Baer, R.A., & Sekirnjak, G. (1997). Detection of underreporting on the MMPI-II in a clinical population. Effects of information about validity scales. *Journal of Personality Assessment, 69,* 555-567.

Bagby, R.M., & Ryder, A.G. (1999). Diagnostic discriminability of dysthymia and depressive personality disorder. *Depression and Anxiety*, *10*, 41-49.

Bagby, R.M., Ryder, A.G., Ben-Dat, D., Bacchiochi, J., & Parker, J.D.A. (2002). Validation of the dimensional factor structure of the Personality Psychopathology Five in clinical and nonclinical samples. *Journal of Personality Disorders*, *16*, 304-316.

Bagby, R.M., Ryder, A.G., & Christi, C. (2002). Psychosocial and clinical predictors of response to pharmacotherapy for depression. *Journal of Psychiatry and Neuroscience, 27, 250-257.*

Bagley, C., Bolitho, F., & Bertrand, L. (1997). Sexual assault in school, mental health and suicidal behaviors in adolescent women in Canada. *Adolescence*, *32*, 361-366.

Bagley, C., & Ramsay, R. (1993). Suicidal ideas and behavior in contrasted generations: Evidence from a community mental health survey. *Journal of Community Psychology*, *21*, 26-34.

Bailey, A., LeCouteur, A., Gottesman, I., Bolton, P., Simonoff, E., Yuzda, E., & Rutter, M. (1995). Autism as a strongly genetic disorder: Evidence from a British twin study. *Psychological Medicine, 25,* 63-77.

Bailey, I. (2000, December 19). *Rebick defends rape centre's right to reject* *transsexual*. The National Post.

Bailey, S. (2002, April 18). Genius physicist's fight to decline anti-psychotic drug goes to top court. *Canadian Press*.

Bailey, S. (2003, June 6). Man can't be forced to take drugs; Top court stresses individual rights in decision. *Hamilton Spectator*, D03 (from the Canadian Press).

Baker, C.W., Whisman, A., & Brownell, K.D. (2000). Studying intergenerational transmission of eating attitudes and behaviors: Methodological and conceptual questions. *Health Psychology*, *19*, 376-381.

Baker, T., & Brandon, T.H. (1988). Behavioral treatment strategies. In *A report of the Surgeon General: The health consequences of smoking: Nicotine addiction*. Rockville, MD: U.S. Department of Health and Human Services.

Bakogeorge, P. (2000, January 8). Mentally ill left out in new Calgary. *The Toronto Star*, p.

Bakwin, H. (1973). The genetics of enuresis. In J. Kolvin, R.C. MacKeith, & S.R. Meadow (Eds.), *Enuresis and encopresis*. Philadelphia: Lippincott.

Baldwin, M.W., Carrell, S.E., & Lopez, D.F. (1990). Priming relationship schemas: My advisor and the Pope are watching me from the back of my mind. *Journal of Experimental Social Psychology*, *26*, 435-454.

Ball, J.C., & Chambers, C.D. (Eds.). (1970). *The epidemiology of opiate addiction in the United States*. Springfield, IL: Charles C. Thomas.

Ball, J.C., & Ross, A. (1991). *The effectiveness of methadone maintenance treatment*. New York: Springer-Verlag.

Ball-Rokeach, S.J., Rokeach, M., & Grube, J.W. (1984). *The great American values test*. New York: Free Press.

Ballenger, J.C., Burrows, G.O., DuPont, R.L., Lesser, M., Noyes, R.C., Pecknold, J.C., Rifkin, A., & Swinson, R.P. (1988). Alprazolam in panic disorder and agoraphobia, results from multicenter trial. *Archives of General Psychiatry, 45,* 413-421.

Baltes, M.M. (1988). The etiology and maintenance of dependency in the elderly: Three phases of operant research. *Behavior Therapy, 19,* 301-319.

Ban, T.A., Healy, D., & Shorter, E. (1998). *The rise of psychopharmacology and the story of CINP.* Budapest, Hungary: Animula Publishing House.

Bancroft, J. (1988). Sexual desire and the brain. *Sexual and Marital Therapy, 3,* 11-29.

Bancroft, J.H. (1989). *Human sexuality and its problems* (2nd ed.). Edinburgh: Churchill Livingston.

Bandura, A. (1969). *Principles of behavior modification*. New York: Holt, Rinehart & Winston.

Bandura, A. (1982). The psychology of chance encounters. *American Psychologist, 37,* 747-755.

Bandura, A. (1986). *Social foundations of thought and action: A social cognitive theory*. Englewood Cliffs, NJ: Prentice-Hall.

Bandura, A. (1997). *Self-efficacy: The exercise of control*. New York: Freeman.

Bandura, A., Blanchard, E.B., & Ritter, B. (1969). Relative efficacy of desensitization and modeling approaches for inducing behavioral, affective, and attitudinal changes. *Journal of Personality and Social Psychology, 13,* 173-199.

Bandura, A., Grusec, J.E., & Menlove, F.L. (1967). Vicarious extinction of avoidance behavior. *Journal of Personality and Social Psychology, 5,* 16-23.

Bandura, A., Jeffrey, R.W., & Bachicha, D.L. (1974). Analysis of memory codes and cumulative rehearsal in observational learning. *Journal of Research in Personality, 7,* 295-305.

Bandura, A., & Menlove, F.L. (1968). Factors determining vicarious extinction of avoidance behavior through symbolic modeling. *Journal of Personality and Social Psychology, 8,* 99-108.

Bandura, A., & Perloff, B. (1967). Relative efficacy of self-monitored and externally imposed reinforcement systems. *Journal of Personality and Social Psychology, 7,* 111-116.

Bandura, A., & Rosenthal, T.L. (1966). Vicarious classical conditioning as a function of arousal level. *Journal of Personality and Social Psychology, 3,* 54-62.

Bandura, A., & Walters, R.H. (1963). *Social learning and personality development*. New York: Holt, Rinehart & Winston.

Banis, H.T., Varni, J.W., Wallander, J.L., Korsch, B.M., Jay, S.M., Adler, R., Garcia-Temple, E., & Negrete, V. (1988). Psychological and social adjustment of obese children and their families. *Child: Care, Health, and Development, 14,* 157-173.

Bank, L., Marlowe, J.H., Reid, J.B., Patterson, G.R., & Weinrott, M.R. (1991). A comparative evaluation of parent-training interventions for families of chronic delinquents. *Journal of Abnormal Child Psychology, 19,* 15-33.

Banks, S.M., Salovey, P., Greener, S., Rothman, A.J., et al. (1995). The effects of message framing on mammography utilization. *Health Psychology, 14,* 178-184.

Banon, E., Marcella, E.-G., & Bond, M. (2001). Early transference interventions with male patients in psychotherapy. *Journal of Psychotherapy Practice and Research*, *10*, 79-92.

Barbaree, H.E., Marshall, W.L., Yates, E., & Lightfoot, L. (1983). Alcohol intoxication and deviant sexual arousal in male social drinkers. *Behaviour Research and Therapy, 21,* 365-373.

Barbaree, H.E., & Seto, M.C. (1997). Pedophilia: Assessment and treatment. In D.R. Laws & W. O'Donohue (Eds.), *Sexual deviance*. (pp. 175-193). NY: Guilford Press.

Barbaree, H.E., Seto, M.C., Langton, C.M., & Peacock, E.J. (2001). Evaluating the predictive accuracy of six risk assessment instruments for adult sex offenders. *Criminal Justice and Behavior*, *28*, 490-521.

Barbarin, O.A., & Soler, R.E. (1993). Behavioral, emotional, and academic adjustment in a national probability sample of African-American children: Effects of age, gender, and family structure. *Journal of Black Psychology, 19,* 423-446.

Barclay, D.R., & Houts, A.C. (1995). Childhood enuresis. In C. Schaefer (Ed.), *Clinical handbook of sleep disorders in children* (pp. 223-252). Northvale, NJ: Jason Aronson.

Bardone, A.M., Vohs, K.D., Abramson, L.Y., Heatherton, T.F., & Joiner, T.E., Jr. (2000). The confluence of perfectionism, body dissatisfaction, and low self-esteem predicts bulimic symptoms: Clinical implications. *Behavior Therapy*, *31*, 265-280.

Barefoot, J.C., Dahlstrom, G., & Williams, R.B. (1983). Hostility, CHD incidence, and total mortality: A 25-year follow-up study of 255 physicians. *Psychosomatic Medicine, 45,* 59-63.

Barker, E., & Mason, M. (1968). Buber behind bars. *Canadian Psychiatric Association Journal, 13,* 61-72.

Barker, E., Mason, & Wilson, J. (1969). Defence-disrupting therapy. *Canadian Psychiatric Association Journal, 14,* 355-359.

Barkley, R.A. (1981). *Hyperactive children: A handbook for diagnosis and treatment*. New York: Guilford.

Barkley, R.A. (1990). *Attention-deficit hyperactivity disorder: A handbook for diagnosis and treatment*. New York: Guilford.

Barkley, R.A. (1997). Behavioral inhibition, sustained attention, and executive function: Constructing a unifying theory of ADHD. *Psychological Bulletin, 121,* 65-94.

Barkley, R.A. (1998). *Attention-deficit hyperactivity disorder: A handbook for diagnosis and treatment*, 2nd Edition. New York, NY: Guilford Press.

Barkley, R.A. (2002). Consensus statement on ADHD. *European Child and Adolescent Psychiatry*, *11*, 96-98.

Barkley, R.A., DuPaul, G.J., & McMurray, M.B. (1990). A comprehensive evaluation of attention deficit disorder with and without hyperactivity defined by research criteria. *Journal of Consulting and Clinical Psychology, 58,* 775-789.

Barkley, R.A., Grodzinsky, G., & DuPaul, G.J. (1992). Frontal lobe functions in attention deficit disorder with and without hyperactivity: A review and research report. *Journal of Abnormal Child Psychology, 20,* 163-188.

Barkley, R.A., Karlsson, J., & Pollard, S. (1985). Effects of age on the mother-child interactions of hyperactive children. *Journal of Abnormal Child Psychology, 13,* 631-638.

Barkowski, J.G. & Varnhagen, C.K. (1984). Transfer of learning strategies: Contrast of self-instructional and traditional learning formats with EMR children. American *Journal of Mental Deficiency, 88,* 369-379.

Barlow, D.H. (1988). *Anxiety and its disorders: The nature and treatment of anxiety and panic*. New York: Guilford.

Barlow, D.H. (1999). *NIMH Collaborative Trial on the Treatment of Panic Disorder*. Paper presented at the annual convention of the Association for Advancement of Behavior Therapy, Toronto.

Barlow, D.H. (2002). *Anxiety and its disorders: The nature and treatment of anxiety and panic*. New York: Guilford.

Barlow, D.H., Abel, G.G., & Blanchard, E.B. (1979). Gender identity change in transsexuals. *Archives of General Psychiatry, 36,* 1001-1007.

Barlow, D.H., Becker, R., Leitenberg, H., & Agras, W.S. (1970). A mechanical strain gauge for recording penile circumference. *Journal of Applied Behavior Analysis, 3,* 73-76.

Barlow, D.H., Blanchard, E.B., Vermilyea, J.A., Vermilyea, B.B., & DiNardo, P.A. (1986). Generalized anxiety and generalized anxiety disorder: Description and reconceptualization. *American Journal of Psychiatry, 143,* 40-44.

Barlow, D.H., Cohen, A.B., Waddell, M.T., Vermilyea, B.B., Klosko, J.S., Blanchard, E.B., & DiNardo, P.A. (1984). Panic and generalized anxiety disorders: Nature and treatment. *Behavior Therapy, 15,* 431-449.

Barlow, D.H., Craske, M.G., Cerny, J.A., & Klosko, J.S. (1989). Behavioral treatment of panic disorder. *Behavior Therapy, 26,* 261-282.

Barlow, D.H., Esler, J.L., & Vitali, A.E. (1998). Psychosocial treatments for panic disorders, phobias, and generalized anxiety disorder. In P.E. Nathan & J.M. Gorman (Eds.), *A guide to treatments that work.* (pp. 288-318). New York: Oxford University Press.

Barlow, D.H., Vermilyea, J., Blanchard, E., Vermilyea, B., DiNardo, P., & Cerny, J. (1985). The phenomenon of panic. *Journal of Abnormal Psychology, 94,* 320-328.

Barlow, D.H., Reynolds, E.J., & Agras, W.S. (1973). Gender identity change in a transsexual. *Archives of General Psychiatry, 29,* 569-576.

Barnes, G.E. (1989). Gasoline sniffing in northern Canada. In S. Einstein (Ed.), *Drug and alcohol use: Issues and factors* (pp. 363-385). New York: Plenum Press.

Barnes, G.E., Murray, R.P., Patton, D., Bentler, P.M., & Anderson, R.E. (2000). *The addiction-prone personality.* New York: Kluwer Academic/Plenum Publishers.

Barnes, G.E., & Toews, J. (1983). Deinstitutionalization of chronic mental patients in the Canadian context. *Canadian Psychology, 24,* 22-36.

Baron, M., Risch, N., Levitt, M., & Gruen, R. (1985). Familial transmission of schizotypal and borderline personality disorders. *American Journal of Psychiatry, 142,* 927-934.

Barr, L.C., Goodman, W.K., McDougle, C.J., Delgado, P.L., Heninger, G.R., et al. (1994). Tryptophan depletion in patients with obsessive-compulsive disorder who respond to serotonin reuptake blockers. *Archives of General Psychiatry, 51,* 309-317.

Barrett, M., Wilson, R.J., & Long, C. (2003). Measuring motivation to change in sexual offenders from institutional intake to community treatment. *Sexual Abuse, 15,* 269-283.

Barrios, B.A., & O'Dell, S.I. (1989). *Fears and anxieties.* In E.J. Mash & R.A. Barkley

(Eds.)*Treatment of childhood disorders.* New York: Guilford.

Barsky, A.J., Brener, J., Coeytaux, R.R., & Cleary, P.D. (1995). Accurate awareness of heartbeat in hypochondriacal and non-hypochondriacal patients. *Journal of Psychosomatic Research, 39,* 489-497.

Barsky, A.J., Fama, J.M., Bailey, E.D., & Ahern, D.K. (1998). A prospective 4- to 5-year study of DSM-III-R hyponchondriasis. Archives of General Psychiatry, 55, 737-744.

Bartholomew, K., & Horowitz, L.M. (1991). Attachment styles among young adults: A test of a four-category model. *Journal of Personality and Social Psychology, 61,* 226-244.

Bartlett, C.W. et al. (2002). A major susceptibility locus for specific language impairment is located on 13q21. *American Journal of Human Genetics, 71,* 45-55.

Bartlett, F. (1932). *Remembering.* Cambridge: Cambridge University Press.

Bartlett, J. (1992). *Familiar quotations: A collection of passages, phrases and proverbs traced to their sources in ancient and modern literature.* Boston: Little, Brown and Company.

Bartlett, J.G. (1993). *The Johns Hopkins Hospital guide to medical care of patients with HIV infection.* Baltimore: Williams & Wilkins.

Bartlett, N.H., Vasey, P. L., & Bukowski, W.M. (2000). Is gender identity disorder in children a mental disorder? *Sex Roles, 43,* 753-785.

Bartlett, P. (2000). Structures of confinement in 19th-century asylums: A comparative study using England and Ontario. *International Journal of Law and Psychiatry, 23,* 1-13.

Bartzokis, G., Liberman, R.P., & Hierholzer, R. (1990). Behavior therapy in groups. In I.L. Kutash & A. Wolf (Eds.), *The group psychotherapist's handbook: Contemporary theory and technique.* New York: Columbia University Press.

Basco, M.R., & Rush, A.J. (1996). *Cognitive-behavioral therapy for bipolar disorder.* New York: Guilford.

Basoglu, M., Marks, I.M., Kilic, C., Brewin, C.R., & Swinson, R.P. (1994). Alpralzolam and exposure for panic disorder with agoraphobia: Attribution of improvement to medication predicts subsequent relapse. *British Journal of Psychiatry, 164,* 652-659.

Bass, E., & Davis, L. (1994). *The courage to heal: A guide for women survivors of child sexual abuse.* New York: Harper Collins.

Bassett, A.S., Chow, E.W.C., Waterworth, D.M., & Brzustowicz, L. (2001). Genetic insights into schizophrenia. *Canadian Journal of Psychiatry, 46,* 131-137.

Bastiani, A.M., Rao, R., Weltzin, T., & Kaye, W.H. (1995). Perfectionism in anorexia nervosa. *International Journal of Eating Disorders, 17, 147-152.*

Bastani, B., Nash, J.F., & Meltzer, H.Y. (1990). Prolactin and cortisol responses to MK-212, a serotonin agonist, in obsessive compulsive disorder. *Archives of General Psychiatry, 47,* 833-839.

Bastien, C.H., Morin, C.M., Ouellet, M-C., Blais, F.C., & Bouchard, S. (2004). Cognitive-behavioral therapy for insomnia: Comparison of individual therapy, group therapy, and telephone consultations. *Journal of Consulting and Clinical Psychology, 72,* 653-659.

Bates, G.W. (1990). *Social anxiety and self-presentation: Conversational behaviours and articulated thoughts of heterosexually anxious males.* Unpublished doctoral dissertation, University of Melbourne, Australia.

Bates, G.W., Campbell, T.M., & Burgess, P.M. (1990). Assessment of articulated thoughts in social anxiety: Modification of the ATSS procedure. *British Journal of Clinical Psychology, 29,* 91-98.

Battaglia, M., Bernardeschi, L., Franchini, L., Bellodi, L., & et al. (1995). A family study of schizotypal disorder. *Schizophrennia Bulletin, 21,* 33-45.

Baucom, D., Epstein, N., & Rankin, L. (1995). Integrative couple therapy. In N.S. Jacobson & A.S. Gurman (Eds.), *Clinical handbook of couple therapy* (pp. 65-90). New York: Guilford.

Baucom, D.H., Epstein, N., Sayers, S.L., & Sher, T.G. (1989). The role of cognitions in marital relationships: Definitional, methodological, and conceptual issues. *Journal of Consulting and Clinical Psychology, 57,* 31-38.

Baucom, D.H., & Hoffman, J.A. (1986). The effectiveness of marital therapy: Current status and application to the clinical setting. In N.S. Jacobson & A.S. Gurman (Eds.), *Clinical handbook of marital therapy* (pp. 597-620). New York: Guilford.

Baucom, D.H., Sayers, S.L., & Sher, T.G. (1990). Supplementing behavioral marital therapy with cognitive restructuring and emotional expressiveness training: An outcome investigation. *Journal of Consulting and Clinical Psychology, 58,* 636-645.

Baumeister, A. A., & Baumeister, A. A. (1995). Mental retardation. In M. Hersen, & R. T. Ammerman (Eds.), *Advanced abnormal child psychology* (pp. 283-303). Hillsdale, NJ: Lawrence Erlbaum Associates.

Baumeister, A.A., Kupstas, F.D., & Klindworth, L.M. (1991). The new morbidity: A national plan of action. *American Behavioral Scientist, 34,* 468-500.

Baumeister, R.F. (1990). Suicide as escape from self. *Psychological Review, 97,* 90-113.

Baumeister, R.F., & Butler, J.L. (1997). Sexual masochism: Deviance without pathology. In D.R. Laws & W. O'Donohue (Eds.), *Sexual deviance.* (pp. 225-239). NY: Guilford Press.

Baumgartner, G.R., & Rowen, R.C. (1987). Clonidine vs. chlordiazepoxide in the management of acute alcohol withdrawal. *Archives of Internal Medicine, 147,* 1223-1226.

Baxter, E., & Hopper, K. (1981). *Private lives/public places: Homeless adults on the streets of New York City.* New York: Community Service Society.

Baxter, L.R., Schwartz, J.M., Bergman, K.S., Szuba, M.P., Guze, B.H., Mazziotta, J.C., Alazraki, A., Selin, C.E., Ferng, H., Munford, P., & Phelps, M.E. (1992). Caudate glucose metabolic rate changes with both drug and behavior therapy for obsessive-compulsive disorder. *Archives of General Psychiatry, 49,* 681-689.

Beach, S.R.H., & O'Leary, K.D. (1986). The treatment of depression occurring in the context of marital discord. *Behavior Therapy, 17,* 43-49.

Beach, S.R.H., Sandeen, E.E., & O'Leary, K.D. (1990). *Depression in marriage.* New York: Guilford.

Beal, A.L. (1995). Post-traumatic stress disorder in prisoners of war and combat veterans of the Dieppe raid: A 50-year follow-up. *Canadian Journal of Psychiatry, 40,* 177-184.

Beck, A.T. (1967). *Depression: Clinical, experimental and theoretical aspects.*

New York: Harper & Row.

Beck, A.T. (1976). *Cognitive therapy and the emotional disorders*. New York: International Universities Press.

Beck, A.T. (1983). Cognitive therapy of depression: New perspectives. In P. J. Clayton & J. E. Barnett (Eds.), *Treatment of depression: Old controversies and new approaches* (pp. 265-290). New York: Raven Press.

Beck, A.T., Epstein, N., Harrison, R.P., & Emery, G. (1983). *Development of the Sociotropy-Autonomy Scale: A measure of personality factors in psychopathology*. Unpublished manuscript, University of Pennsylvania, Philadelphia.

Beck, A.T. (1986). Cognitive therapy: A sign of retrogression or progress. *The Behavior Therapist, 9,* 2-3.

Beck, A.T. (1987). Cognitive models of depression. *Journal of Cognitive Psychotherapy: An International Quarterly, 1,* 5-37.

Beck, A.T., Brown, G., Berchick, R.J., Stewart, B.L., & Steer, R.A. (1990). Relationship between hopelessness and ultimate suicide: A replication with psychiatric outpatients. *American Journal of Psychiatry, 147,* 190-195.

Beck, A.T., Brown, G., Steer, R.A., Eidelson, J.I., & Riskind, J.H. (1987). Differentiating anxiety and depression: A test of the cognitive-content-specificity hypothesis. *Journal of Abnormal Psychology, 96,* 179-183.

Beck, A.T., Freeman, A, and associates (1990). *Cognitive therapy of personality disorders*. New York: Guilford.

Beck, A.T., Kovacs, M., & Weissman, A. (1975). Hopelessness and suicidal behavior: An overview. *Journal of the American Medical Association, 234,* 1146-1149.

Beck, A.T., Kovacs, M., & Weissman, A. (1979). Assessment of suicidal ideation: The Scale for Suicide Ideation. *Journal of Consulting and Clinical Psychology, 47,* 343-352.

Beck, A.T., & Rector, N.A. (2000). Cognitive therapy of schizophrenia: A new therapy for the new millennium. *American Journal of Psychotherapy, 54,* 291-300.

Beck, A.T., Schuyler, D., & Herman, I. (1974). Development of suicidal intent scales. In A.T. Beck, H.L.P. Resnik, & D.J. Lettieri (Eds.), *The prediction of suicide*. Bowie, MD: Charles Press.

Beck, A.T., Steer, R.A., Kovacs, M., & Garrison, B. (1985). Hopelessness and eventual suicide: A 10-year prospective study of patients hospitalized with suicidal ideation. *American Journal of Psychiatry, 142,* 559-563.

Beck, J.G. (1995). Hypoactive sexual desire disorder: An overview. *Journal of Consulting and Clinical Psychology, 63,* 919-927.

Beck, J.G., & Bozman, A. (1995). Gender differences in sexual desire: The effects of anger and anxiety. *Archives of Sexual Behavior, 24,* 595-612.

Becker, E.S., Rinck, M., Roth, W.T., & Margraf, J. (1998). Don't worry and beware of white bears: Thought suppression in anxiety patients. *Journal of Anxiety Disorders, 12,* 39-55.

Becker, J.V. (1990). Treating adolescent sexual offenders. *Professional Psychology: Research and Practice, 21,* 362-365.

Becker, J.V., & Hunter, J.A. (1999). Understanding and treating child and adolescent sexual offenders. In T.H. Ollendick & R.J. Prinz (Eds.), *Advances in clinical child psychology.* (pp. 177-196). New York: Plenum Press.

Becker, J.V., Kaplan, M.S., Cunningham-Rathner, J., & Kavoussi, R.J. (1986). Characteristics of adolescent incest sexual perpetrators: Preliminary findings. *Journal of Family Violence, 1,* 85-97.

Becker, J.V., Kaplan, M.S., Tenke, C.E., & Tartaglini, A. (1991). The incidence of depressive symptomatology in juvenile sex offenders with a history of abuse. *Child Abuse and Neglect, 15,* 531-536.

Becker, J.V., Skinner, L.J., Abel, G.G., & Cichon, J. (1986). Level of postassault sexual functioning in rape and incest victims. *Archives of Sexual Behavior, 15,* 37-49.

Bedell, J.R., Archer, R.P., & Marlow, H.A. (1980). A description and evaluation of a problem-solving skills training program. In D. Upper & S.M. Ross (Eds.), *Behavioral group therapy: An annual review* (pp. 3-35). Champaign, IL: Research Press.

Bednar, R.L., & Kaul, T.J. (1994). Experiential group research: Can the canon fire? In A.E. Bergin & S.L. Garfield (Eds.), *Handbook of psychotherapy and behavior change* (4th edition.) New York: Wiley.

Beecher, H.K. (1966). Ethics and clinical research. *New England Journal of Medicine, 274,* 1354-1360.

Begelman, D.A. (1975). Ethical and legal issues of behavior modification. In M. Hersen, R. Eisler, & P.M. Miller (Eds.), *Progress in behavior modification*. New York: Academic Press.

Beidel, D.C. (1991). Social phobia and overanxious disorder in school-age children. *Journal of the American Academy of Child and Adolescent Psychiatry, 30,* 545-552.

Beiser, M., Dion, R., & Gotowiec, A. (2000). The structure of attention-deficit and hyperactivity symptoms among Native and non-Native elementary school children. *Journal of Abnormal Child Psychology*, *28*, 425-437.

Beiser, M., Hou, F., Hyman, I., and Tousignant, M. (1998). *Growing up Canadian—A study of new immigrant children* (No. W-98-24E). Ottawa: Human Resources Development Canada.

Beitchman, J.H., Wilson, B., Johnson, C.J., Atkinson, L., Young, A., Adlaf, E., Escobar, M., & Douglas, L. (2001). Fourteen-year follow-up of speech/language-impaired and control children: Psychiatric outcome. *Journal of the American Academy of Child and Adolescent Psychiatry*, *40*, 75-82.

Bell, J.E. (1961). *Family group therapy*. Washington, DC: U.S. Department of Health, Education, and Welfare.

Bellack, A.S., & Hersen, M. (1998). *Behavioral assessment: A practical handbook.* Fourth edition. Boston: Allyn and Bacon.

Bellack, A.S., Hersen, M., & Turner, S.M. (1976). Generalization effects of social skills training in chronic schizophrenics: An experimental analysis. *Behavior Research and Therapy, 14,* 391-398.

Bellack, A.S., Morrison, R.L., & Mueser, K.T. (1989). Social problem solving in schizophrenia. *Schizophrenia Bulletin, 15,* 101-116.

Bellack, A.S., & Mueser, K.T. (1993). Psychosocial treatments for schizophrenia. *Schizophrenia Bulletin, 19,* 317-336.

Ben-Porath, Y.S., & Butcher, J.N. (1989). The comparability of MMPI and MMPI-2 scales and profiles. *Psychological Assessment, 1,* 345-347.

Ben-Tovim, M.V., & Crisp, A.H. (1979). Personality and mental state within anorexia nervosa. *Journal of Psychosomatic Research, 23,* 321-325.

Bendetti, F., Sforzini, L., Colombo, C., Marrei, C., & Smeraldi, E. (1999). Low-dose clozapine in acute and continuation treatment of borderline personality disorder. *Journal of Clinical Psychiatry, 59,* 103-107.

Benes, F.M., McSparren, J., Bird, T.D., SanGiovanni, J.P., Vincent, S.L., et al. (1991). Deficits in small interneurons in prefrontal and cingulate cortices of schizophrenic and schizoaffective patients. *Archives of General Psychiatry, 48,* 986-1001.

Benjafield, J.G., & Boudreau, F. *(2000).* Introduction: Canadian community mental health: Our past, our future. *Canadian Journal of Community Mental Health, 19, 5-8.*

Benkelfat, C., Ellenbogen, M.A., Dean, P., Palmour, R.M., & Young, S.N. (1994b). Mood-lowering effect of tryptophan depletion: Enhanced susceptibility in young men at genetic risk for major affective disorders. *Archives of General Psychiatry, 51,* 687-700.

Bennett, C.C., Anderson, L.S., Cooper, S., Hassol, L., Klein, D.C., & Rosenblum, G. (Eds.). (1966). *Community psychology: A report of the Boston Conference on the education of psychologists for community mental health.* Boston: Boston University Press.

Bennett, I. (1960). *Delinquent and neurotic children*. London: Tavistock.

Bennett, V. (1997, February 22). *Russia's forgotten children*. Los Angeles Times, pp. A1, A10.

Benson, H., Beary, J.F., & Carl, M.P. (1974). The relaxation response. *Psychiatry, 37,* 37.

Bentaleb, L.A., Beauregard, M., Liddle, P., & Stip, E. (2002). Cerebral activity associated with auditory verbal hallucinations: A functional magnetic resonance imaging case study. *Journal of Psychiatry and Neuroscience*, *27*, 110-115.

Berg, L., McKeel, D.W., Miller, J.P., Storandt, M., Rubin, E.H., et al. (1998). Clinicopathologic studies in cognitively healthy aging and Alzheimer disease. *Archives of Neurology, 55,* 326-335.

Bergem, A.L., Engedal, K., & Kringlen, E. (1997). The role of heredity in late-onset Alzheimer's disease and vascular dementia: A twin study. *Archives of General Psychiatry, 54,* 264-270.

Berger, K.S., & Zarit, S.H. (1978). Late life paranoid states: Assessment and treatment. *American Journal of Orthopsychiatry, 48,* 528-537.

Bergeron, L., Valla, J.-P., Breton, J.-J., Gaudet, N., et al. (2000). Correlates of mental disorders in the Quebec general population of 6 to 14-year olds. *Journal of Abnormal Child Psychology, 28*, 47-62.

Bergin, A.E. (1971). The evaluation of therapeutic outcomes. In A.E. Bergin & S.L. Garfield (Eds.), *Handbook of psychotherapy and behavior change: An empirical analysis*. New York: Wiley.

Bergin, A.E., & Garfield, S.L. (Eds.). (1994). *Handbook of psychotherapy and behavior change*. Fourth edition. New York: Wiley.

Bergin, A.E., & Lambert, M.J. (1978). The evaluation of therapeutic outcomes. In S.L. Garfield & A.E. Bergin (Eds.), *Handbook of psychotherapy and behavior change: An empirical analysis* (2nd ed.). New York: Wiley.

Berlin, F.S., & Meinecke, C.F. (1981). Treatment of sex offenders with antiandrogenic medication: Conceptualization, review of treatment modalities, and preliminary findings. *American Journal of Psychiatry, 138,* 601-607.

Berman, A.L., & Jobes, D.A. (1996). *Adolescent suicide: Assessment and intervention*. Washington, DC: American Psychological Association.

Berman, E.M., & Lief, H.I. (1976). Sex and the aging process. In W.W. Oaks, G.A. Melchiode, & I. Ficher (Eds.), *Sex and the life cycle*. New York: Grune & Stratton.

Berman, J.S., & Norton, N.C. (1985). Does professional training make a therapist more effective? *Psychological Bulletin, 98,* 401-407.

Berman, T., Douglas, V.I., & Barr, R.G. (1999). Effects of methylphenidate on complex cognitive processing in attention-deficit hyperactivity disorder. *Journal of Abnormal Psychology, 108*, 90-105.

Bernazzani, O., Saucier, J.-F., David, H., & Borgeat, F. (1997). Psychosocial predictors of depressive symptomatology level in postpartum women. *Journal of Affective Disorders, 46*, 39-49.

Bernstein, D. (1993). Paranoid personality disorder: A review of the literature and recommendations for DSM-IV. *Journal of Personality Disorders, 7,* 53-62.

Bernstein, D.A., & Nietzel, M.T. (1980). *Introduction to clinical psychology*. New York: McGraw-Hill.

Bernstein, D.P., Kasapis, C., Bergman, A., Weld, E., Mitropoulou, V., & et al. (1997). Assessing Axis II disorders by informant interview. *Journal of Personality Disorders, 11,* 158-167.

Bernstein, D.P., Useda, D., & Siever, L.J. (1993). Paranoid personality disorder: Review of the literature and recommendations for DSM-IV. *Journal of Personality Disorders, 7,* 53-62.

Berrenberg, J.L., Dougherty, K.L., Erikson, M.S., Loew, J.L., Pacot, D.M., & Rousseau, C.N.S. (1993). *Saturation in AIDS education: Can we still make a difference?* Paper presented at the annual meeting of the Rocky Mountain and Western Psychological Associations, Phoenix, AZ,

Berrettini, W.H., Goldin, L.R., Gelernter, J., Geiman, P.Z., Gershon, E., et al. (1990). X-chromosome markers and manic-depressive illness: Rejection of linkage to Xq28 in nine bipolar pedigrees. *Archives of General Psychiatry, 47,* 366-373.

Berry, J.C. (1967). *Antecedents of schizophrenia, impulsive character and alcoholism in males*. Paper presented at the 75th Annual Convention of the American Psychological Association, Washington, DC.

Berry, J.W. (1999). Intercultural relations in plural societies. *Canadian Psychology, 40,* 12-21.

Bertalanffy, L. von. (1968). *General systems theory: Foundation, development, applications*. New York: Braziller.

Besdine, R.W. (1980). Geriatric medicine: An overview. In C. Eisodorfer (Ed.), *Annual review of gerontology and geriatrics*. New York: Springer.

Bettelheim, B. (1967). *The empty fortress*. New York: Free Press.

Bettelheim, B. (1973). Bringing up children. *Ladies Home Journal, 90,* 28.

Bettelheim, B. (1974). *A home for the heart*. New York: Knopf.

Beutler, L.E. (1979). Toward specific psychological therapies for specific conditions. *Journal of Consulting and Clinical Psychology, 47,* 882-897.

Beutler, L.E. (1983). *Eclectic psychotherapy: A systematic approach*. New York: Pergamon.

Beutler, L.E. (1991). Have all won and must all have prizes? Revisiting Luborsky et al.'s verdict. *Journal of Consulting and Clinical Psychology, 59,* 226-232.

Beutler, L.E. (1997). The psychotherapist as a neglected variable in psychotherapy: An illustration by reference to the role of therapist experience and training. *Clinical Psychology: Science and Practice, 4,* 44-52.

Beutler, L.E. (2002). It isn't the size, but the fit. *Clinical Psychology: Science and Practice, 9*, 434-438.

Beutler, L.E., Crago, M., & Arizmendi, T.G. (1986). Therapist variables in psychotherapy process and outcome. In S.L. Garfield & A.E. Bergin (Eds.), *Handbook of psychotherapy and behavior change* (3rd ed.). New York: Wiley.

Beutler, L.E., & Davison, E.H. (1995). What standards should we use? In S.C. Hayes, V.M. Follette, R.M. Dawes, & K.E. Grady (Eds.), *Scientific standards of psychological practice: Issues and recommendations* (pp. 11-24). Reno, NV: Context Press.

Beutler, L.E., & Harwood, T.M. (1995). Prescriptive psychotherapies. *Applied and Preventive Psychology, 4,* 89-100.

Beutler, L.E., Machado, P.P.P., & Neufeldt, S.A. (1994). Therapist variables. In A.E.

Bergin & S.L. Garfield (Eds.), *Handbook of psychotherapy and behavior change*. Fourth edition (pp. 229-269). New York: Wiley.

Beutler, L.E., Scogin, F., Kirkish, P., Schretlen, D., Corbishley, A., Hamblin, D., Meredith, K., Potter, R., Bamford, C.R., & Levenson, A.I. (1987). Group cognitive therapy and alprazolam in the treatment of depression in older adults. *Journal of Consulting and Clinical Psychology, 55,* 550-556.

Bhatia, M.S., Nigam, V.R., Bohra, N., & Malik, S.C. (1991). Attention deficit disorder with hyperactivity among pediatric outpatients. *Journal of Child Psychology and Psychiatry, 32,* 297-306.

Bialystok, E., Craik, F.I.M., Klein, R., & Viswanathan, M. (2004). Bilingualism, aging, and cognitive control: Evidence from the Simon task. *Psychology and Aging, 19*, 290-303.

Biederman, J. (1997, October). *Comorbidity in girls with ADHD*. Paper presented at the American Academy of Child and Adolescent Psychiatry, Toronto, Canada.

Biederman, J., Faraone, S., Mick, E., Spencer, T., Wilens, T., Kiely, K., Guite, J., Ablon, J.S., Reed, E., & Warbuton, R. (1995). High risk for attention deficit hyperactivity disorder among children of parents with childhood onset of the disorder: A pilot study. *American Journal of Psychiatry, 152,* 431-435.

Biederman, J., Faraone, S., Milberger, S., Curtis, S., Chen, L., Marrs, A., Ouellette, C., Moore, P., & Spencer, T. (1996). Predictors of persistence and remission of ADHD into adolescence: Results from a four-year prospective follow-up study. *Journal of the American Academy of Child and Adolescent Psychiatry, 35,* 343-351.

Biederman, J., Newcorn, J., & Sprich, S. (1991). Comorbidity of attention deficit hyperactivity disorder with conduct, depressive, and other disorders. *American Journal of Psychiatry, 148,* 564-577.

Biederman, J., Rosenbaum, J., Hirschfeld, D., Faraone, S., Bolduc, E., et al. (1990). Psychiatric correlates of behavioral inhibition in young children of parents with and without psychiatric disorders. *Archives of General Psychiatry, 47,* 21-26.

Bieling, P.J., & Alden, L.E. (1998). Cognitive-interpersonal patterns in dysphoria: The impact of sociotropy and autonomy. *Cognitive Therapy and Research, 22,* 161-178.

Bieling, P.J., & Alden, L.E. (2001). Sociotropy, autonomy, and the interpersonal model of depression: An integration. *Cognitive Therapy and Research, 25,* 167-184.

Bieling, P.J., & Antony, M.M. (2003). *Ending the depression cycle: A step-by-step guide for preventing relapse.* Oakland, CA: New Harbinger Publications.

Bieling, P.J., & Kuyken, W. (2003). Is cognitive case formulation science or science fiction? *Clinical Psychology: Science and Practice, 10*, 52-69.

Bieri, D., Reeve, R.A., & Champion, C.E. (1989). The Faces Pain Scale for the self-assessment of the severity of the pain experience by children: Development, initial validation, and preliminary investigation for ratio scale properties. *Pain, 41,* 139-150.

Bierut, L.J., Dinwiddie, S.H., Begleiter, H., Crowe, R.R., Hesselbrock, V., et al. (1998). Familial transmission of substance dependence: Alcohol, marijuana, cocaine, and habitual smoking: A report from the Collaborative Study on the Genetics of Alcoholism. *Archives of General Psychiatry, 55,* 982-994.

Bigelow, D.A., McFarland, B.H., Gareau, M J., & Young, D.J. (1991). Implementation and effectiveness of a bed reduction project. *Community Mental Health Journal, 27,* 125-133.

Billings, A. (1979). Conflict resolution in distressed and nondistressed married couples. *Journal of Consulting and Clinical Psychology, 47,* 368-376.

Billings, A.G., Cronkite, R.C., & Moos, R.H. (1983). Social-environmental factors in unipolar depression: Comparisons of depressed patients and non-depressed controls. *Journal of Abnormal Psychology, 92,* 119-133.

Binzer, M., Andersen, P.M., & Kullgren, G. (1997). Clinical characteristics of patients with motor disability due to conversion disorder: A prospective control group study. *Journal of Neurology, Neurosurgery, and Psychiatry, 63,* 83-88.

Bion, W. (1959). *Experiences in groups.* New York: Basic Books.

Birbaumer, H. (1977). Biofeedback training: A critical review of its clinical applications and some possible future directions. *European Journal of Behavioral Analysis and Modification, 4,* 235-251.

Birnbaum, M. (1960). The right to treatment. *American Bar Association Journal, 46,* 499-505.

Birren, J.E., & Schaie, K.W. (Eds). (1996). *Handbook of the psychology of aging.* Fourth edition. San Diego, CA: Academic Press.

Black, D. (1995, December 4). Deadly combination: New research on the brains of psychopaths and serial killers may help experts identify the makings of a monster. *The Toronto Star,* pp. C1, C3.

Black, D.N., Stip, E. Bedard, M-A., Kabay, M., Paquette, I., & Bigras, M-J. (2000). Leukotomy revisited: Late cognitive and behavioral effects in chronic institutionalized schizophrenics. *Schizophrenia Research, 43,* 57-64.

Blackburn, I.M., Eunson, K.M., & Bishop, S. (1986). A two-year naturalistic follow-up of depressed patients treated with cognitive therapy, pharmacotherapy, and a combination of both. *Journal of Affective Disorders, 10,* 67-75.

Blair, R.J.D., Jones, L., Clark, F., & Smith, M. (1997). The psychopathic individual: A lack of responsiveness to distress cues? *Psychophysiology, 34,* 192-198.

Blais, M.A., Hilsenroth, M.J., & Castlebury, F.D. (1997). Content validity of the newly revised Diagnostic and Statistical Manual of Mental Disorders-IV (DSM-IV) narcissitic personality disorder (NPD) and borderline personality disorder (BPD) criteria sets. *Comprehensive Psychiatry, 38,* 31-37.

Blake, W. (1973). The influence of race on diagnosis. *Smith College Studies in Social Work, 43,* 184-192.

Blanchard, C.M., Rodgers, W.M., Bell, G., Wilson, P.M., & Gesell, J. (2002). An empirical test of the interaction model of anxiety in an acute exercise setting. *Personality and Individual Differences, 32,* 329-336.

Blanchard, E.B. (1994). Behavioral medicine and health psychology. In A.E. Bergin & S.L. Garfield (Eds.), *Handbook of psychotherapy and behavior change.* Fourth edition (pp. 701-733). New York: Wiley.

Blanchard, E.B., Andrasik, F., Neff, D.F., Arena, J.G., Ashles, T.A., Jurish, S.E., Pallmeyer, T.P., Saunders, N.L., & Teders, S.J. (1982). Biofeedback and relaxation training with three kinds of headache: Treatment effects and their prediction. *Journal of Consulting and Clinical Psychology, 50,* 562-575.

Blanchard, J.J., & Brown, S.B. (1998). Structured diagnostic interviews. In C.R. Reynolds (Ed.), *Comprehensive clinical psychology, vol 3, assessment.* (pp. 97-130). New York: Elsevier.

Blanchard, J.J., Squires, D., Henry, T., Horan, W.P., Bogenschutz, M., et al. (1999). Examining an affect regulation model of substance abuse in schizophrenia: The role of traits and coping. *Journal of Nervous and Mental Disease, 187,* 72-79.

Blanchard, R. (1989). The classification and labeling of nonhomosexual gender dysphorias. *Archives of Sexual Behavior, 18,* 315-334.

Blanchard, R. (1992). Nonmonotonic relation of autogynephilia and heterosexual attraction. *Journal of Abnormal Psychology, 101,* 271-276.

Blanchard, R., Watson, M.S., Choy, A., Dickey, R., Klassen, P., Kuban, M., & Ferren, D.J. (1999). Pedophiles: Mental retardation, maternal age, and sexual orientation. *Archives of Sexual Behavior, 28,* 111-127.

Bland, R.C. (1988). Psychiatry and the burden of mental illness. *Canadian Journal of Psychiatry, 43,* 801-810.

Bland, R.C., Newman, S.C., & Dyck, R.J. (1994). The epidemiology of parasuicide in Edmonton. *Canadian Journal of Psychiatry, 39,* 391-396.

Bland, R.C., Newman, S.C., & Orn, H. (1988). Period prevalence of psychiatric disorders in Edmonton. *Acta Psychiatrica Scandinavica, 77* (Supplement), 33-42.

Bland, R.C., Newman, S.C., & Orn, H. (1997a). Age and remission of psychiatric disorders. *Canadian Journal of Psychiatry, 42,* 722-729.

Bland, R.C., Newman, S.C., & Orn, H. (1997b). Help-seeking for psychiatric disorders. *Canadian Journal of Psychiatry, 42,* 935-942.

Bland, R.C., Orn, H., & Newman, S.C. (1988). Lifetime prevalence of psychiatric disorders in Edmonton. *Acta Psychiatrica Scandinavica, 77* (Suppl. 338), 24-32.

Blankstein, K. R., & Dunkley, D. (2002). Evaluative concerns, self-critical, and personal standards perfectionism: A structural equation modeling strategy. In G. L. Flett and P. L. Hewitt (Eds.), *Perfectionism: Theory, research, and treatment.* (pp. 285-315). Washington: American Psychological Association Press.

Blankstein, K.R., Flett, G.L., Boase, P., & Toner, B.B. (1990). Thought listing and endorsement measures of self-referential thinking in test anxiety. *Anxiety Research, 2, 103-111.*

Blankstein, K.R., Flett, G.L., & Koledin, S. (1991). The Brief College Students Hassles Scale: Development, validation, and relation with pessimism. *Journal of College Student Development, 32,* 258-264.

Blankstein, K.R., & Flett, G.L. (1990). Cognitive components of test anxiety: A comparison of assessment and scoring methods. *Journal of Social Behavior and Personality, 5,* 187-202.

Blankstein, K.R., & Segal, S. V. (2001). Cognitive assessment: Issues and methods. In K.S. Dobson (Ed.), *Handbook of cognitive-behavioral therapies, 2nd ed.* (pp. 40-85). New York: Guilford Press.

Blaske, D.M., Borduin, C.M., Hengeler, S.W., & Mann, B.J. (1989). Individual, family, and peer characteristics of adolescent sex offenders and assaultive offenders. *Developmental Psychology, 25,* 846-855.

Blatt, B. (1966). The preparation of special educational personnel. *Review of Educational Research, 36,* 151-161.

Blatt, S.J. (1974). Levels of object representation in anaclitic and introjective depression. *Psychoanalytic Study of the Child, 29,* 107-157.

Blatt, S.J. (1995). The destructiveness of perfectionism: Implications for the treatment of depression. *American Psychologist, 50,* 1003-1020.

Blatt, S.J., Quinlan, D.M., Pilkonis, P.A., & Shea, M.T. (1995). Impact of perfectionism and

need for approval on the brief treatment of depression: The National Institute of Mental Health Treatment of Depression Collaborative Research Program revisited. *Journal of Consulting and Clinical Psychology, 63,* 125-132.

Blatt, S.J., & Zuroff, D.C. (1992). Interpersonal relatedness and self-definition: Two prototypes for depression. *Clinical Psychology Review, 12,* 527-562.

Blatt, S.J., & Zuroff, D.C. (2002). Perfectionism and the therapeutic context. In G. L. Flett, & P. L. Hewitt (Eds.), *Perfectionism: Theory, research, and treatment* (pp. 393-406). Washington, DC: American Psychological Association.

Blau, Z.S., Oser, G.T., & Stephens, R.C. (1979). Aging, social class, and ethnicity: A comparison of Anglo, Black, and Mexican-American Texans. *Pacific Sociological Review, 22,* 501-525.

Blazer, D.G. (1982). *Depression in late life.* St. Louis: Mosby.

Blazer, D.G., Bachar, J.R., & Manton, K.G. (1986). Suicide in late life: Review and commentary. *Journal of the American Geriatrics Society, 34,* 519-525.

Blazer, D.G., Hughes, D., & George, L.K. (1987). Stressful life events and the onset of a generalized anxiety syndrome. *American Journal of Psychiatry, 144,* 1178-1183.

Blazer, D.G., Kessler, R.C., & McGonagle, K.A. (1994). The prevalence and distribution of major depression in a national community sample: The National Comorbidity Survey. *American Journal of Psychiatry, 151,* 979-986.

Blazer, D.G., & Williams, C.D. (1980). Epidemiology of dysphoria and depression in the elderly population. *American Journal of Psychiatry, 137,* 439-444.

Blechman, E.A., McEnroe, M.J., Carella, E.T., & Audette, D.P. (1986). Childhood competence and depression. *Journal of Abnormal Psychology, 95,* 223-227.

Blenker, M. (1967). Environmental change and the aging individual. *Gerontologist, 7,* 101-105.

Blinebury, E. (2001, September 17). Raptor star fears a backlash: Images, reports called damaging to Muslims. *Toronto Star,* B2.

Bliss, E.L. (1980). Multiple personalities: A report of 14 cases with implications for schizophrenia and hysteria. *Archives of General Psychiatry, 37,*

1388-1397.

Bliss, E.L. (1983). Multiple personalities, related disorders, and hypnosis. *American Journal of Clinical Hypnosis, 26,* 114-123.

Bliwise, D., Carskadon, M., Carey, E., & Dement, W. (1984). Longitudinal development of sleep-related respiratory disturbance in adult humans. *Journal of Gerontology, 39,* 290-293.

Block, J. (1971). *Lives through time.* Berkeley, CA: Bancroft Books.

Blonigen, D.M., Carlson, S.R., Krueger, R.F., & Patrick, C.J. (2003). A twin study of self-reported psychopathic personality traits. *Personality and Individual Differences, 35,* 179-197.

Bloomfield, H.H. (1973). Assertive training in an outpatient group of chronic schizophrenics: A preliminary report. *Behavior Therapy, 4,* 277-281.

Blumstein, A. (2003, May 26). Canada's Best: The kid whiz, Richard Tremblay. *Time: Canadian Edition,* 54.

Blumstein, A., & Cohen, J. (1987). Characterizing criminal careers. *Science, 237,* 985-991.

Board of Inspectors of Asylums, Prisons, & c. (1865). *Report of the Board of Inspectors of ASYLUMS, PRISONS, &c., for the year 1864.* Quebec: Hunter, Rose, and Co.

Bockhoven, J. (1963). *Moral treatment in American psychiatry.* New York: Springer.

Boer, D.P., & Pugh, G.M. (1988). Canadianization of the WAIS-R Information subtest: Implications for psychiatric assessment. *Canadian Journal of Behavioural Assessment, 20,* 273-286.

Bohart, A.C., & Greenberg, L.S. (1997) (Eds.), *Empathy reconsidered: New directions in psychotherapy.* Washington, DC: American Psychological Association.

Bohlmeijer, E., Smit, F., & Cuijpers, P. (2003). Effects of reminiscence and life review on late-life depression: A meta-analysis. *International Journal of Geriatric Psychiatry, 18,* 1088-1094.

Bohuslawsky, M. (2001, August 5). *Medicine's shocking new trend.* Ottawa Citizen (http://www.ottawacitizen.com/city/990712/2596182.html, accessed on August 12, 2001).

Boisvert, C.M., & Faust, D. (2003). Leading researchers' consensus on psychotherapy research findings: Implications for the teaching and conduct of psychotherapy. *Professional Psychology: Research and Practice, 34,* 508-513.

Bolger, N., Foster, M., Vinokur, A.D., & Ng, R. (1996). Close relationships and adjustment to a life crisis: The case of breast cancer. *Journal of Personality and Social Psychology, 70,* 283-294.

Boll, T.J. (1985). Developing issues in clinical neuropsychology. *Journal of Clinical and Experimental Neuropsychology, 7,* 473-485.

Bolton, P., MacDonald, H., Pickles, A., Rios, P., Goode, S., Crowson, M., Bailey, A., & Rutter, M. (1994). A case-control family history study of autism. *Journal of Child Psychology and Psychiatry, 35,* 877-900.

Bonanno, G.A., & Kaltman, S. (2001). The varieties of grief experience. *Clinical Psychology Review, 21,* 705-734.

Bond, J.B., Cuddy, R., Dixon, G.L., Duncan, K.A., & Smith, D.L. (1999). The financial abuse of mentally incompetent older adults: A Canadian study. *Journal of Elder Abuse and Neglect, 11,* 23-38.

Bondolfi, G., Dufour, H., Patris, M., May, J.P., Baumann, P., & the Risperidone Study Group. (1998). Respiridone versus clozapine in treatment-resistant chronic schizophrenia: A randomized,double-blind study. *American Journal of Psychiatry, 155,* 499-504.

Bonin, M.P., McCreary, D.R., & Sadava, S.W. (2000). Problem drinking behavior in two community-based samples of adults: Influence of gender, coping, loneliness, and depression. *Psychology of Addictive Behaviors, 14,* 151-161.

Bonin, M.F., Norton, G.R., Asmundson, G.J.G., Dicurzio, S., & Pidlubney, S. (2000). Drinking away the hurt: The nature and prevalence of PTSD in substance abuse patients attending a community-based treatment program. *Journal of Behavior Therapy and Experimental Psychiatry, 31,* 55-66.

Bonta, J., Law, M., & Hanson, K. (1998). The prediction of criminal and violent recidivism among mentally disordered offenders. *Psychological Bulletin, 123,* 123-142.

Boon, S., & Draijer, N. (1993). *Multiple personality disorder in the Netherlands.* Amsterdam: Swets & Zeitlinger.

Boon, S., & Draijer, N. (1993). Multiple personality disorder in the Netherlands: A clinical investigation of 71 cases. *American Journal of Psychiatry, 150,* 489-494.

Boothroyd, L.J., Kirmayer, L.J., Spreng, S., Malus, M., & Hodgins, S. (2001). Completed suicides among the Inuit of norther Quebec, 1982-1996: A case control study. *Canadian Medical Association Journal, 165,* 749-755.

Bootzin, R.R., & Engle-Friedman, M. (1987). Sleep disturbances. In L.L. Carstensen & B.A. Edelstein (Eds.), *Handbook of clinical gerontology.* New York: Pergamon.

Bootzin, R.R., Engle-Friedman, M., & Hazelwood, L. (1983). Sleep disorders and the elderly. In P.M. Lewinsohn & L. Teri (Eds.), *Clinical geropsychology: New directions in assessment and treatment.* New York: Pergamon.

Borduin, C.M., Mann, B.J., Cone, L.T., Henggeler, S.W., Fucci, B.R., Blaske, D.M., & Williams, R.A. (1995). Multisystemic treatment of serious juvenile offenders: Long-term prevention of criminality and violence. *Journal of Consulting and Clinical Psychology, 63,* 569-578.

Borgeat, F., & Chaloult, L. (1985). A relaxation experiment using radio broadcasts. *Canada's Mental Health, 33,* 11-13.

Borkovec, T.D., & Costello, E. (1993). Efficacy of applied relaxation and cognitive behavioral therapy in the treatment of generalized anxiety disorder. *Journal of Consulting and Clinical Psychology, 61,* 611-619.

Borkovec, T.D., & Inz, J. (1990). The nature of worry in generalized anxiety disorder: A predominance of thought activity. *Behaviour Research and Therapy, 28,* 153-158.

Borkovec, T.D., & Mathews, A. (1988). Treatment of nonphobic anxiety disorders: A comparison of nondirective, cognitive and coping desensitization therapy. *Journal of Consulting and Clinical Psychology, 56,* 877-884.

Borkovec, T.D., & Newman, M.G. (1998). Worry and generalized anxiety disorder. In P. Salkovskis (Ed.), *Comprehensive clinical psychology.* Oxford: Elsevier.

Borkovec, T.D., Roemer, L., & Kinyon, J. (1995). Disclosure and worry: Opposite sides of the emotional processing coin. In J.W. Pennebaker (Ed.), *Emotion, disclosure, and health.* Washington, DC: American Psychological Association.

Borkovec, T.D., & Whisman, M.A. (1996). Psychosocial treatment for generalized anxiety disorder. In M. Mavissakalian & R.E. Prien (Eds.), *Long-term treatment of anxiety disorders* (pp. 171-199). Washington, DC: American Psychiatric Association.

Bornstein, P.E., Clayton, P.J., Halikas, J.A., & Robins, E. (1973). The depression of widowhood after thirteen months. *British Journal of Psychiatry, 122,* 561-566.

Bornstein, R.F. (1997). Dependent personality disorder in the DSM-IV and beyond. *Clinical Psychology: Science and Practice, 4,* 175-187.

Bornstein, R.F., Leone, D.R., & Galley, D.J. (1987). The generalizability of subliminal mere exposure effects: Influence of stimuli perceived without awareness on social behavior. *Journal of Personality and Social Psychology, 53,* 1070-1079.

Boscarino, J.A. (1997). Diseases among men 20 years after exposure to severe stress: Implications for clinical research and care. *Psychosomatic Medicine, 59,* 605-614

Bosinski, H.A., Peter, M., Bonatz, G., Arndt, R., Heidenreich, M., et al. (1997). A higher rate of hyperadrenergic disorders in female-to-male transsexuals. *Psychoneuroendocrinology, 22,* 361-380.

Botvin, G.J., & Tortu, S. (1988). Peer relationships, social competence, and substance abuse prevention: Implications for the family. *Journal of Chemical Dependency Treatment, 1,* 245-273.

Bouchard, S., et al. (2004). Delivering cognitive-behavior therapy for panic disorder with agoraphobia in videoconference. *Telemedicine Journal and e-health, 10,* 13-25.

Bouchard, S., Payeur, R., Rivard, V., Allard, M., Paquin, B., Renaud, P., & Goyer, L. (2000). Cognitive behavior therapy for panic disorder with agoraphobia in videoconference: Preliminary results. *CyberPsychology and Behavior, 3,* 999-1007.

Bouchard, T.J., Lykken, D.T., McGue, M., Segal, N.L., & Tellegen, A. (1990). Sources of human psychological differences: The Minnesota Study of Twins Reared Apart. *Science, 250,* 223-228.

Bourque, P., & Beaudette, D. (1982). Etude psychometrique du Questionnaire de Depression de Beck aupres d'un echantillon d'etudiantsuniversitaires francophones [Psychometric study of the Beck Depression Inventory in a sample of francophone university students]. *Canadian Journal of Behavioural Science, 14,* 211-218.

Bowen, L., Wallace, C.J., Glynn, S.M., Nuechterlein, K.H., Lutzger, J.R., & Kuehnel, T.G. (1994). Schizophrenics' cognitive functioning and performance in iinterpersonal interactions and skills training procedures. *Journal of Psychiatric Research, 28,* 289-301.

Bower, G.H. (1981). Mood and memory. American Psychologist, 36, 129-141.

Bowers, J., Jorm, A.F., Henderson, S., & Harris, P. (1990). General practitioners' detection of depression and dementia in elderly patients. *The Medical Journal of Australia, 153,* 192-196.

Bowers, K.S., & Meichenbaum, D. (Eds.). (1984). *The unconscious reconsidered.* New York: Praeger.

Bowers, M.B., Jr. (1974). Central dopamine turnover in schizophrenic syndromes. *Archives of General Psychiatry, 31,* 50-54.

Bowlby, J. (1969). *Attachment and loss: Vol. 1. Attachment.* New York: Basic Books.

Bowman, M. L. (2000). The diversity of diversity: Canadian-American differences and their implications for clinical training and APA accreditation. *Canadian Psychology, 41,* 244-256.

Boyd, B. (1993). Correctional service training. *Canadian Journal of Corrections, 5,* 343-346.

Boyle, M. (1991). *Schizophrenia: A scientific delusion?* New York: Routledge.

Boyle, M.H., Sanford, M., Szatmari, P., Merikangas, K., & Offord, D.R. (2001). Familial influences on substance use by adolescents and young adults. *Canadian Journal of Public Health, 92,* 206-208.

Boyle, T. (2001, June 12). Cash crisis threatens home care report says: Lack of staff, long waits sinking Ontario system. *The Toronto Star,* pp. A1, A26.

Boyle, T. (2001, June 28). Retraints on patients curbed as Ontario approves new law: Lankin's private members bill wins full support. *The Toronto Star,* p. A6.

Bozman, A., & Beck, J.G. (1991). Covariation of sexual desire and sexual arousal: The effects of anger and anxiety. *Archives of Sexual Behavior, 20,* 47-60.

Bradley, B.P., Mogg, K., Millar, N., & White, J. (1995). Selective processing of negative information: Effects of clinical anxiety, concurrent depression, and awareness. *Journal of Abnormal Psychology, 104,* 532-536.

Bradley, E.A., Thompson, A., & Bryson, S.E. (2002). Mental retardation in teenagers: Prevalence data from the Niagara region, Ontario. *Canadian Journal of Psychiatry, 47,* 652-659.

Bradley, L., & Bryant, P.E. (1985). *Rhyme and reason in reading and spelling.* Ann Arbor: University of Michigan Press.

Bradley, S.J., Blanchard, R., Coates, S., Green, R., Levine, S.B., Meyer-Bahlburg, H. F. L., Pauly, I. B., & Zucker, K. J. (1991). Interim report of the DSM-IV subcommittee on gender identity disorders. *Archives of Sexual Behavior, 20,* 333-343.

Bradley, S.J., Oliver, G.D., Chernick, A.B., & Zucker, K.J. (1998). Experiment of nurture: Albatio penis at 2 months, sex reassignment at 7 months, and a psychosexual follow-up in young adulthood. *Pediatrics, 102,* e1-e9.

Bradley, S.J., & Zucker, K.J. (1997). Gender identity disorder: A review of the past 10 years. *Journal of the American Academy of Child and Adolescent Psychiatry, 36,* 872-880.

Bradshaw, D., & Spencer, C. (1999). The role of alcohol in elder abuse cases. In J. Pritchard (Ed.), *Elder abuse work: Best practices in Britain and Canada* (pp. 332-353). London: Jessica Kingsley Publications.

Bradwejn, J., & Montigny, C. (1984). Benzodiazepines antagonize cholecystokinin-induced activation of rat hippocampal neurons. *Nature, 312,* 363-364.

Bradwejn, J., Koszycky, D., & Meterissian, G. (1990). Cholecystokinin-tetrapeptide induced panic attacks in patients with panic disorder. *Canadian Journal of Psychiatry, 35,* 83-85.

Bradwejn, J., Koszycky, D., & Shriqui, C. (1991). Enhansed sensitivity to Cholecystokinin tetrapeptide in panic disorder. *Archives of General Psychiatry, 48,* 603-610.

Brady, J.P., Davison, G.C., DeWald, P.A., Egan, G., Fadiman, J., Frank, J.D., Gill, M.M., Hoffman, I., Kempler, W., Lazarus, A.A., Raimy, V., Rotter, J.B., & Strupp, H.H. (1980). Some views on effective principles of psychotherapy. *Cognitive Therapy and Research, 4,* 269-306.

Brandon, Y.H., Zelman, D.C., & Baker, T.B. (1987). Effects of maintenance sessions on smoking relapse: Delaying the inevitable? *Journal of Consulting and Clinical Psychology, 55,* 780-782.

Brandt, J., Buffers, N., Ryan, C., & Bayog, R. (1983). Cognitive loss and recovery in chronic alcohol abusers. *Archives of General Psychiatry, 40,* 435-442.

Bransford, J.D., & Johnson, M.K. (1973). Considerations of some problems of comprehension. In W.G. Chase (Ed.), *Visual information processing.* New York: Academic Press.

Braswell, L., & Kendall, P.C. (1988). Cognitive-behavioral methods with children. In K.S. Dobson (Ed.), *Handbook of cognitive-behavioral therapies.* New York: Guilford.

Bray, N.W. & Turner, L.A. (1987). Production anomalies (not strategic deficiencies) in mentally deficient individuals. *Intelligence, 11,* 49-60.

Brecher, E.M., & the Editors of Consumer Reports. (1972). *Licit and illicit drugs.* Mount Vernon, NY: Consumers Union.

Brehm, J.W. (1966). *A theory of psychological reactance.* New York: Academic Press.

Brehm, S.S., & Brehm, J.W. (1981). *Psychological reactance: A theory of freedom and control.* New York: Academic Press.

Breier, A., Schreiber, J.L., Dyer, J., & Pickar, D. (1991). National Institute of Mental Health longitudinal study of chronic schizophrenia: Prognosis and predictors of outcome. *Archives of General Psychiatry, 48,* 239-246.

Bremner, J.D., Innis, R.B., Ng, C.K., Staib, L.H., Salomon, R.A., et al. (1997). Positron emission tomography measurement of cerebral metabolic correlates of yohimbine administration in combat-related posttraumatic stress disorder. *Archives of General Psychiatry, 54,* 246-256.

Bremner, J.D., Southwick, S.M., Darnell, A., & Charney, D.S. (1996). Chronic post-traumatic stress disorder in Vietnam combat veterans: Course of illness and substance abuse. *American Journal of Psychiatry, 153,* 369-375.

Brendgen, M., Vitaro, F., Turgeon, L., & Poulin, F. (2002). Assessing aggressive and depressed children's social relations with classmates and friends: A matter of perspective. *Journal of Abnormal Child Psychology, 30,* 609-624.

Breslau, N. (2002). Epidemilogic studies of trauma, posttraumatic stress disorder, and other psychiatric disorders. *Canadian Journal of Psychiatry, 47,* 923-929.

Breslau, N., Davis, G.C., Andreski, P., Peterson, E.L., & Schultz, L.R. (1997). Sex differences in posttraumatic stress disorder. *Archives of General Psychiatry, 54,* 1044-1048.

Breslau, N., Chilcoat, H.D., Kessler, R.C., & Davis, G.C. (1999). Previous exposure to trauma and PTSD effects of subsequent trauma: Results from the Detroit area survey of trauma. *American Journal of Psychiatry, 156,* 902-907.

Breslau, N., Holmes, J.P., Carlson, D.C., Pelton, G.H., et al. (1998). Trauma and posttraumatic stress disorder in the community: The 1996 Detroit area survey of trauma. *Archives of General Psychiatry, 55,* 626-632.

Breslin, F.C., Zack, M., & McMain, S. (2002). An information-processing analysis of mindfulness: Implications for relapse prevention in the treatment of substance abuse. *Clinical Psychology: Science and Practice, 9,* 275-299.

Breton, J.-J., Bergeron, L., Valla, J.-P., Berthiaume, C., Gaudet, N., Lambert, J., et al. (1999). Quebec Mental Health Survey; Prevalence of DSM-III-R mental health disorders. *Journal of Child Psychology and Psychiatry, 40,* 375-384.

Breuer, J., & Freud, S. (1982). *Studies in hysteria.* (J. Strachey, Trans. and Ed., with the collaboration of A. Freud). New York: Basic Books. (Original work published 1895.)

Brewin, C.R., Andrews, B., & Gotlib, I. H. (1993). Psychopathology and early experience: A reappraisal of retrospective reports. *Psychological Bulletin, 113,* 82-98.

Brewin, C.R., Andrews, B., Rose, S., & Kirk, M. (1999). Acute stress disorder and posttraumatic stress disorder in victims of violent crime. *American Journal of Psychiatry, 156,* 360-366.

Brickman, A.S., McManus, M., Grapentine, W.L., & Alessi, N. (1984). Neuropsychological assessment of seriously delinquent adolescents. Journal of the *American Academy of Child Psychiatry, 23,* 453-457.

Bridger, W.H., & Mandel, I.J. (1965). Abolition of the PRE by instructions in GSR conditioning. *Journal of Experimental Psychology, 69,* 476-482.

Brodeur, D. A., & Pond, M. (2001). The development of selective attention in children with attention deficit hyperactivity disorder. *Journal of Abnormal Child Psychology, 29*, 229-239.

Brody, N. (1985). The validity of tests of intelligence. In B.B. Wolman (Ed.), *Handbook of intelligence* (pp. 353-389). New York: Wiley.

Broidy, L. M. et al. (2003). Developmental trajectories of childhood disruptive behaviors and adolescent delinquency: A six-site, cross-national study. *Developmental Psychology, 39*, 222-245.

Bronfenbrenner, U. (1979). Contexts of child rearing: Problems and prospects. *American Psychologist, 34*, 844-850.

Brookoff, D., Cook, C.S., Williams, C., & Mann, C.S. (1994). Testing reckless drivers for cocaine and marijuana. *The New England Journal of Medicine, 331,* 518-522.

Brooks, S.A., O'Reilly, R.L., & Gray, J.E. (2003, August). Implications for psychiatrists of the Supreme Court of Canada Starson vs. Swayze decision. *Canadian Psychiatric Association Bulletin*, 28.

Brown, G.K., Beck, A.T., Steer, R.A., & Grisham, J.R. (2000). Risk factors for suicide in psychiatric outpatients: A 20-year prospective study. *Journal of Consulting and Clinical Psychology, 68*, 371-377.

Brown, G.L., & Goodwin, F.K. (1986). Cerebrospinal fluid correlates of suicide attempts and aggression. *Annals of the New York Academy of Science, 487,* 175-188.

Brown, G.P., & Beck, A.T. (2002). Dysfunctional attitudes, perfectionism, and models of vulnerability to depression. In G.L. Flett & P.L. Hewitt (Eds.), *Perfectionism: Theory, research, and treatment* (pp. 231-251). Washington, DC: American Psychological Association.

Brown, G.W., & Birley, J.L.T. (1968). Crises and life changes and the onset of schizophrenia. *Journal of Health and Social Behavior, 9,* 203-214.

Brown, G.W., Bone, M., Dalison, B., & Wing, J.K. (1966). *Schizophrenia and social care*. London: Oxford University Press.

Brown, G.W., & Harris, T.O. (1978). *Social origins of depression*. London: Tavistock.

Brown, L.M., Bongar, B., & Cleary, K.M. (2004). A profile of psychologists' views of critical risk factors for completed suicide in older adults. *Professional Psychology: Research and Practice, 35*, 90-96.

Brown, S.A., Vik, P.W., McQuaid, J.R., Patterson, T.L., Irwin, M.R., et al. (1990). Severity of psychosocial stress and outcome of alcoholism treatment. *Journal of Abnormal Psychology, 99,* 344-348.

Brown, S.L., & Forth, A.E. (1997). Psychopathy and sexual assault: Static risk factors, emotional precursors, and rapist subtypes. *Journal of Consulting and Clinical Psychology, 65*, 848-857.

Brown, T.A., & Barlow, D.H. (1995). Long-term outcome in cognitive-behavioral treatment of panic disorder: Clinical predictors and alternative strategies for assessment. *Journal of Consulting and Clinical Psychology, 63,* 754-765.

Brown, T.A., Barlow, D.H., & Liebowitz, M.R. (1994). The empirical basis of generalized anxiety disorder. *American Journal of Psychiatry, 151,* 1272-1280.

Brown, T.A., & Cash, T.F. (1989). The phenomenon of panic in nonclinical populations: Further evidence and methodological considerations. *Journal of Anxiety Disorders, 3*, 139-148.

Brownell, K.D., & Rodin, J. (1994). The dieting maelstrom: Is it possible or advisable to lose weight? *American Psychologist, 49,* 781-791.

Brownell, K.D., Stunkard, A.J., & Albaum, J.M. (1980). Evaluation and modification of exercise patterns in the natural environment. *American Journal of Psychiatry, 137,* 1540-1545.

Brownell, K.D., & Wadden, T.A. (1992). Etiology and treatment of obesity: Toward understanding a serious, prevalent, and refractory disorder. *Journal of Consulting and Clinical Psychology, 60,* 505-517.

Brownell, M.D., & Yogendran, M.S. (2001). Attention-deficit hyperactivity disorder in Manitoba children: Medical diagnosis and psychostimulant treatment rates. *Canadian Journal of Psychiatry, 46*, 264-271.

Brownmiller, S. (1975). *Against our will: Men, women and rape.* New York: Simon & Schuster.

Bruch, H. (1980). Preconditions for the development of anorexia nervosa. *American Journal of Psychoanalysis, 40,* 169-172.

Bruck, M. (1987). The adult outcomes of children with learning disabilities. *Annals of Dyslexia, 37, 252*-263.

Bruder, G.E., Stewart, J.W., Mercier, M.A., Agosti, V., Leite, P., Donovan, S., & Quitkin, F.M. (1997). Outcome of cognitive-behavioral therapy for depression: Relation to hemispheric dominance for verbal processing. *Journal of Abnormal Psychology, 106,* 138-144.

Bryant, R.A. (1995). Autobiographical memory across personalities in dissociative identity disorder. *Journal of Abnormal Psychology, 4,* 625-632.

Bryant, R.A., & Harvey, A.G. (1998). Relationship between acute stress disorder and posttraumatic stress disorder following mild traumatic brain injury. *American Journal of Psychiatry, 155,* 625-629.

Bryson, S.E., Rogers, S.J., & Fombonne, E. (2003). Autism spectrum disorders: Early detection, intervention, education, and psychopharmacological management. *Canadian Journal of Psychiatry, 48*, 506-516.

Buchanan, A., Reed, A., & Weseley, S., et al. (1993). Acting on delusions . II: The phenomenological correlates of acting on delusions. *British Journal of Psychiatry, 163,* 77-81.

Buchanan, R.W., Breier, A., Kirkpatrick, B., Ball, P., & Carpenter, W.T. (1998). Positive and negative symptom response to clozapine in schizophrenic patients with and without the deficit syndrome. *American Journal of Psychiatry, 155,* 751-760.

Buchanan, R.W., Vladar, K., Barta, P.E., & Pearlson, G.D. (1998). Structural evaluation of the prefrontal cortex in schizophrenia. *American Journal of Psychiatry, 155,* 1049-1055.

Buchsbaum, M.S., Kessler, R., King, A., Johnson, J., & Cappelletti, J. (1984). Simultaneous cerebral glucography with positron emission tomography and topographic electroencephalography. In G. Pfurtscheller, E.J. Jonkman, & F.H. Lopes da Silva (Eds.), *Brain ischemia: Quantitative EEG and imaging techniques*. Amsterdam: Elsevier.

Bujold, A., Ladouceur, R., Sylvain, C., & Boisvert, J.-M.. (1994). Treatment of pathological gamblers: An experimental study. *Journal of Behavioural Therapy and Experimental Psychiatry, 25,* 275-282.

Bulfinch's mythology. (1979). New York: Avenel Books.

Bulik, C.M., Sullivan, P.F., Fear, J.L., & Joyce, P.R. (1997). Eating disorders and antecedent anxiety disorders: A controlled study. *Acta Psychiatrica Scandanavica, 96,* 101-107.

Bulik, C. M., Sullivan, P. F., & Kendler, K. S. (2000). An empirical study of the classification of eating disorders. *American Journal of Psychiatry, 157,* 886-895.

Bunney, W.E., Goodwin, F.K., & Murphy, D.L. (1972). The "Switch Process" in manic-depressive illness. *Archives of General Psychiatry, 27,* 312-317.

Bunney, W.E., Murphy, D.L., Goodwin, F.K., & Borge, G.F. (1970). The switch process from depression to mania: Relationship to drugs which alter brain amines. *Lancet, 1,* 1022.

Burgess, A.W., & Holmstrom, L.L. (1974). *Rape: Victim of crisis. Bowie*, MD: Robert J. Brady Company.

Burgio, L.D., Burgio, K.L., Engel, B.T., & Tice, L.M. (1986). Increasing distance and independence of ambulation in elderly nursing home residents. *Journal of Applied Behavior Analysis, 19,* 357-366.

Burns, A. (1991). Affective symptoms in Alzheimer's disease. *International Journal of Geriatric Psychiatry, 6,* 371-376.

Buss, A.H. (1966). *Psychopathology*. New York: Wiley.

Butcher, J.N., Dahlstrom, W.G., Graham, J.R., Tellegen, A., & Kraemer, B. (1989). *Minnesota Multiphasic Personality Inventory-2: Manual for administration and scoring*. Minneapolis: University of Minnesota Press.

Butcher, J.N., Nezami, E. & Exner, J. (1998*)*. Psychological assessment of people in diverse cultures. In S. S. Kazarian and D. R. Evans (Eds.), *Cultural clinical psychology,* pp. 61-105.

Butler, G., & Mathews, A. (1983). Cognitive processes in anxiety. *Advances in Behaviour Research and Therapy, 5,* 51-62.

Butler, L., Miezitis, S., Friedman, R., & Cole, I.D. (1980). The effect of two school-based intervention programs on depressive symptoms. *American Educational Research Journal, 17,* 111-119.

Butler, L.D., Duran, R.E.F., Jasiukaitis, P., Koopman, C., & Spiegel, D. (1996). Hypnotizability and traumatic experience: A diathesis-stress model of dissociative symptomatology. *American Journal of Psychiatry, 153,* 42-63.

Butler, R.N. (1963). The life review: An interpretation of reminiscence in the aged. *Psychiatry, 119,* 721-728.

Butler, R.N., & Lewis, M.I. (1982). *Aging and mental health: Positive psychosocial approaches* (3rd ed.). St. Louis: Mosby.

Butterfield, E.C., & Belmont, J.M. (1977). Assessing and improving the cognitive functions of mentally retarded people. In I. Bialer & M. Sternlicht (Eds.), *The psychology of mental retardation: Issues and approaches*. New York: Psychological Dimensions.

Butzlaff, R.L., & Hooley, J.M. (1998). Expressed emotion and psychiatric relapse: A meta-analysis. *Archives of General Psychiatry, 55,* 547-553.

Caccioppo, J.T., Glass, C.R., & Merluzzi, T.V. (1979). Self-statements and self-evaluations: A cognitive-response analysis of heterosexual social anxiety. *Cognitive Therapy and Research, 3,* 249-262.

Cacioppo, J.T., Klein, D.J., Bernston, G.G., & Hatfield, E. (1998). The psychophysiology of emotion. In M. Lewis & E. Haviland (Eds.), *Handbook of emotions*. (pp. 119-142). New York: Guilford.

Cacioppo, J.T., von Hippel, W., & Ernst, J.M. (1997). Mapping cognitive structures and processes through verbal content: The thought-listing technique. *Journal of Consulting and Clinical Psychology, 65,* 928-940.

Caddy, G.R. (1983). Alcohol use and abuse. In B. Tabakoff, P.B. Sutker, & C.L. Randell (Eds.), *Medical and social aspects of alcohol use*. New York: Plenum.

Cadenhead, K.S., Perry, W., Shafer, K., & Braff, D.L. (1999). Cognitive functions in schizotypal personality disorder. *Schizophrenia Research, 37,* 123-132.

Cadoret, R.J., & Stewart, M.A. (1991). An adoption study of attention deficit/aggression and their relationship to adult antisocial personality. *Archives of General Psychiatry, 47,* 73-82.

Cadoret, R.J., Yates, W.R., Troughton, E., Woodworth, G., & Stewart, M.A. (1995a). Adoption study demonstrating two genetic pathways to drug abuse. *Archives of General Psychiatry, 52,* 42-52.

Cadoret, R.J., Yates, W.R., Troughton, E., Woodworth, G., & Stewart, M.A. (1995b). Genetic-environment interaction in the genesis of aggressivity and conduct disorders. *Archives of General Psychiatry, 52,* 916-924.

Cahill, S.P., Carrigan, M.H., & Frueh, B.C. (1999). Does EMDR work? And if so, why?: A critical review of controlled outcome and dismantling research. *Journal of Anxiety Disorders, 13,* 5-33.

Cairney, J., & Lawrence, K. (2002). Smoking on campus: An examination of smoking behaviours among post-secondary students in Canada. *Canadian Journal of Public Health, 93,* 313-316.

Cairney, J., Thorpe, C., Rietschlin, J., & Avison, W.R. (1999). 12-month prevalence of depression among single and married mothers in the 1994 National Population Health Survey. *Canadian Journal of Public Health, 90,* 320-324.

Cairney, J., & Wade, T.J. (2002). The influence of age on gender differences in depression: Further population-based evidence on the relationship between menopause and the sex difference in depression. *Social Psychiatry and Psychiatric Epidemiology, 37,* 401-408.

Caldwell, M.B., Brownell, K.D., & Wilfley, D. (1997). Relationship of weight, body dissatisfaction, and self-esteem in African American and white female dieters. *International Journal of Eating Disorders, 22,* 127-130.

Calfee, R. C., Fisk, L., & Piontkowski, D. (1975). "On-off" tests of cognitive skills in reading acquisition. In M. P. Douglass (Ed.), *Claremont Reading Conference 39th Yearbook 1975*. Claremont, CA: Claremont Graduate School.

Calhoun, J.B. (1970). Space and the strategy of life. Ekistics, 29, 425-437.

Calhoun, K. S., & Resick, P. A. (1993). Post-traumatic stress disorder. In D. H. Barlow (Ed.) *Clinical handbook of psychological disorders: A step-by-step treatment manual.* 2nd edition (pp. 48-98). New York: Guilford Press.

Calleja, F. (2001, September 24). Traumatized young make a stand: Troubled by attack, children raise cash for relief in U.S. *The Toronto Star*, B5.

Cameron, D.J., Thomas, R.I., Mulvhill, M., & Bronheim, H. (1987). Delirium: A test of the Diagnostic and Statistical Manual III criteria on medical inpatients. *Journal of the American Geriatrics Society, 35,* 1007-1010.

Cameron, N. (1959). The paranoid pseudocommunity revisited. *American Journal of Sociology, 65,* 52-58.

Cameron, N., & Magaret, A. (1951). *Behavior pathology*. Boston: Houghton Mifflin.

Campbell, J., Stefan, S., & Loder, A. (1994). Putting violence in context. *Hospital and Community Psychiatry, 45,* 633.

Campbell, M., Anderson, L.T., & Small, A.M. (1990). Pharmacotherapy in autism: A summary of research at Bellevue/New York University. *Brain Dysfunction, 3,* 299-307.

Campbell, M., Anderson, L.T., Small, A.M., Adams, P., Gonzales, N.M., & Ernst, M. (1993). Naltrexone in autistic children: Behavioral symptoms and attentional learning. *Journal of the American Academy of Child and Adolescent Psychiatry, 32,* 1283-1291.

Campbell, M., Armenteros, J.L., Malone, R.P., Adams, P.B., Eisenberg, Z.W., & Overall, J.E. (1997). Neuroleptic-related dyskinesias in autistic children: A prospective, longitudinal study. *Journal of the American Academy of Child and Adolescent Psychiatry, 36,* 835-843.

Campbell, N.R.C., Drouin, D., Feldman, R.D., for the Canadian Hypertension Recommendations Working Group. (2002). The 2001 Canadian hypertension recommendations: Take-home messages. *Canadian Medical Association Journal, 167,* 661-668.

Campbell, S.B. (1990). *Behavioral problems in preschoolers: Clinical and developmental issues*. New York: Guilford.

Camper, P.M., Jacobson, N.S., Holtzworth-Munroe, A., & Schmaling, K.B. (1988). Causal attributions for interactional behaviors in married couples. *Cognitive Therapy and Research, 12,* 195-209.

Campos, P.E., & Hathaway, B.E. (1993). Behavioral research on gay issues 20 years after Davison's ethical challenge. *the Behavior Therapist, 16,* 193-197.

Canadian Association on Gerontology (2000a). *Position paper: Issues in the delivery of mental health services to older adults (http://www.cagacg.ca/english/pubs/pol-mentalhealth.html; accessed December 15, 2000).*

Canadian Association on Gerontology (2000b). *Policy statement: Home care in Canada (http://www.cagacg.ca/english/pubs/pol-mentalhealth.html; accessed December 15, 2000).*

Canadian Centre for Studies of Children at Risk (2001). *Past research (http://www-fhs.mcmaster.ca.cscr/abindex1.html; accessed November 15, 2000).*

Canadian Council on Social Development. (1997). *The controversy over attention deficit hyperactivity disorder (ADHD) and ritalin.* In *The Progress of Canada's Children.* Ottawa: Renouf Publishing.

Canadian Medical Association. (1997). Detecting and managing elder abuse: Challenges in primary care. *Canadian Medical Association Journal, 157,* 1094-1095.

Canadian Medical Association. (2000). Alberta child abuse program swamped. *Canadian Medical Association Journal, 163,* 1492.

Canadian Mental Health Association. (2001, May 7). *Media Release: An astounding 91% of Canadians say maintaining mental health is very important, yet fewer Canadians willing to disclose receiving treatment. (http://www.pressi.com/pressi-html; accessed May 9, 2001).*

Canadian Medical Association Journal (2001). Editorial: Look no strings: Publishing industry-funded research. *Canadian Medical Association Journal, 165,* 733.

Canadian Panel on Violence Against Women (1993). *Changing the landscape. Ending violence and achieving equality* (Catalogue No. SW45-1/1993E). Canada: Ministry of Supply and Services, Ottawa.

Canadian Paediatric Society. (1998). Inhalant abuse: Position statement. *Paediatrics and Child Health, 3,* 123-126.

Canadian Press (2003, August 13th). *People sterilized under old law appeal lawsuit against B.C. government.*

Canadian Press (2004, February 8th). *Police investigate allegations of elder abuse at nursing home.*

Canadian Press (2004, February 17th). *First Canadian teen charged under revised youth law wanted jail, court hears.*

Canadian Psychological Association (1991). *Canadian Code of Ethics for Psychologists,* revised edition. Ottawa: Author.

Canadian Psychological Association (2000). *Canadian Code of Ethics for Psychologists,* 3rd edition. Ottawa: Author.

Canadian Psychological Association (2002, December). *Psychology specific analysis of the report of the Royal Commission on the Future of Health Care in Canada.* Ottawa: Author.

Canadian Study of Health and Aging Working Group. (1994a). Canadian Study of Health and Aging: Study methods and prevalence of dementia. *Canadian Medical Association Journal, 150,* 899-913.

Canadian Study of Health and Aging Working Group. (1994b). Patterns of caring for people with dementia. *Canadian Journal on Aging, 13,* 470-487.

Canadian Study of Health and Aging Working Group. (2000). The incidence of dementia in Canada. *Neurology, 55,* 66-73.

Canetto, S.S. (1992). Gender and suicide in the elderly. *Suicide and Life-*

Threatening Behavior, 22, 80-97.

Canivez, G.L., & Watkins, M.W. (1998). Long-term stability of the Wechsler Intelligence Scale for Children-Third edition. *Psychological Asessment, 10,* 285-291.

Cannon, D.S., Baker, T.B., Gino, A., & Nathan, P.E. (1986). Alcohol-aversion therapy: Relation between strength of aversion and abstinence. *Journal of Consulting and Clinical Psychology, 54,* 825-830.

Cannon, T.D., Kaprio, J., Lonnqvist, J., Huttunen, M., & Koskenvuo, M. (1998). The genetic epidemiology of schizophrenia in a Finnish twin cohort: A population-based modeling study. *Archives of General Psychiatry, 55,* 67-74.

Cannon, T.D., & Mednick, S.A. (1993). The schizophrenia high-risk project in Copenhagen: Three decades of progress. *Acta Psychiatrica Scandanavica,* 33-47.

Cannon, T.D., Mednick, S.A., & Parnas, J. (1990). Antecedents of predominantly negative and predominantly positive-symptom schizophrenia in a high-risk population. *Archives of General Psychiatry, 47,* 622-632.

Cantor, N., Markus, H., Niedenthal, P., & Nurius, P. (1986). On motivation and the self-concept. In R.M. Sorrentino & E.T. Higgins (Eds.), *Handbook of motivation and cognition: Foundations of social behavior* (pp. 96-121). New York: Guilford.

Cantos, A.L., Neidig, P.H., & O'Leary, K.D. (1994). Injuries of women and men in a treatment program for domestic violence. *Journal of Family Violence, 9,* 113-124.

Cantwell, D.P., Baker, L., & Rutter, M. (1978). Family factors. In M. Rutter & E. Schopler (Eds.), *Autism: A reappraisal of concepts and treatment.* New York: Plenum.

Caplan, G. (1964). *Principles of preventive psychiatry.* New York: Basic Books.

Caplan, M., Weissberg, R.P., Grober, J.S., Sivo, P.J., et al. (1992). Social competence promotion with inner-city and suburban young adolescents: Effects on social adjustment and alcohol use. *Journal of Consulting and Clinical Psychology, 66,* 56-63.

Caplan, P. (1991). How do they decide who is normal? The bizarre, but true, tale of the DSM process. *Canadian Psychology, 32,* 162-170.

Caplan, P. (1995). *They say you're crazy: How the world's most p[owerful psychiatrists decide who's normal.* Reading, MA: Addison-Weley.

Cappeliez, P. (1993). Depression in elderly persons: Prevalence, predictors, and psychological intervention. In P. Cappeliez & R. J. Flynn (Eds.), *Depression and the social environment: Research and intervention with neglected populations* (pp. 332-368). Montreal: McGill-Queen's University Press.

Cappeliez, P. (2000). Presentation of depression and response to group cognitive therapy with older patients. *Journal of Clinical Geropsychology, 6,* 165-174.

Capron, A.M. (1999). Ethical and human rights issues in research on mental disorders that may affect decision-making capacity. *The New England Journal of Medicine, 340,* 1430-1434.

Cardno, A.G., Marshall, E.J., Coid, B., Macdonald, A.M., Ribchester, T.R., et al. (1999). Heritability estimates for psychotic disorders: The Maudsley Twin Psychosis Series. *Archives of General Psychiatry, 56,* 162-170.

Carey, E. (1999, November 4). Strain of caring for ill grows, report finds: As relatives age, many are juggling jobs, caregiving. *The Toronto Star,* p. A16.

Carlsson, A., Hanson, L.O., Waters, N., & Carlsson, M.L. (1999). A glutamatergic defiency model of schizophrenia. *British Journal of Psychiatry, 174,* 2-6.

Carnelly, K.B., Pietomonaco, P.R., & Jaffe, K. (1994). Depression, working models of others and relationship functioning. *Journal of Personality and Social Psychology, 66,* 127-141.

Carnelley, K.B., Wortman, C.B., & Kessler, R.C. (1999). The impact of widowhood on depression: Findings from a prospective survey. *Psychological Medicine, 29,* 1111-1123.

Caron, J., Tempier, R., Mercier, C., & Leouffre, P. (1998). Components of social support and quality of life in severely mental ill, low income individuals and a general population group. *Community and Mental Health Journal, 34,* 459-475.

Carone, B.J., Harrow, M., & Westermeyer, J.F. (1991). Posthospital course and outcome in schizophrenia. *Archives of General Psychiatry, 48,* 247-253.

Carpeggiani, C., & Skinner, J.E. (1991). Coronary flow and mental stress: Experimental findings. *Circulation, 83,* 90-93.

Carpenter, W.T., Heinrichs, D.W., & Wagman, A.M.I. (1988). Deficit and non-deficit forms of schizophrenia: The concept. *American Journal of Psychiatry, 145,* 578-583.

Carpentieri, S.C. & Morgan, S.B. (1994). Brief report: A comparison of patterns of cognitive functioning of autistic and nonautistic retarded children on the Stanford-Binet, Fourth Edition. *Journal of Autism and Developmental Disorders, 24,* 215-223.

Carpentieri, S.C. & Morgan, S.B. (1996). Adaptive and intellectual functioning in autism. *Journal of Autism and Developmental Disorders, 26,* 611-620.

Carr, A.T. (1971). Compulsive neurosis: Two psychophysiological studies. *Bulletin of the British Psychological Society, 24,* 256-257.

Carr, E.G., Schreibman, L., & Lovaas, O.I. (1975). Control of echolalic speech in psychotic children. *Journal of Abnormal Child Psychology, 3,* 331-351.

Carrington, P.J. (1999). Gender, gun control, suicide and homicide in Canada. *Archives of Suicide Research, 5,* 71-75.

Carroll, B.J. (1982). The dexamethasone suppression test for melancholia. *British Journal of Psychiatry, 140,* 292-304.

Carroll, J.M., Touyz, S.M., & Beumont, P.J. (1996). Specific comorbidity between bulimia nervosa and personality disorders. *International Journal of Eating Disorders, 19,* 159-170.

Carroll, K.M. (1996). Relapse prevention as a psychosocial treatment: A review of controlled clinical trials. *Experimental and Clinical Psychopharmacology, 4,* 46-54.

Carroll, K.M., Rounsaville, B.J., Gordon, L.T., Nich, C., Jatlow, P., Bisighini, R.M., & Gawin, F.H. (1994). Psychotherapy and pharmacotherapy for ambulatory cocaine abusers. *Archives of General Psychiatry, 51,* 177-187.

Carroll, K.M., Rounsaville, B.J., Nich, C., Gordon, L.T., & Gawin, F. (1995). Integrating psychotherapy and pharmacotherapy for cocaine dependence: Results from a randomized clinical trial. In L.S. Onken, J.D. Blaine & J.J. Boren (Eds.), *Integrating behavioral therapies with medications in the treatment of drug dependence* (pp. 19-36). Rockville, MD: National Institute on Drug Abuse.

Carroll, K.M., Rounsaville, B.J., Nich, C., Gordon, L.T., Wirtz, P.W., & Gawin, F. (1994). One-year follow-up of psychotherapy and pharmacotherapy for cocaine dependence. *Archives of General Psychiatry, 51,* 989-997.

Carstensen, L.L. (1996). Evidence for a life-span theory of socioemotional selectivity. *Current Directions in Psychological Science, 4,* 151-156.

Carter, M.M., Hollon, S.D., Carson, R., & Shelton, R.C. (1995). Effects of a safe person on induced distress following a biological challenge in panic disorder with agoraphobia. *Journal of Abnormal Psychology, 104,* 156-163.

Carver, C.S., Pozo, C., Harris, S.D., Noriega, V., Scheier, M., Robinson, D., Ketcham, A., Moffat, F.L., & Clark, K. (1993). How coping mediates the effect of optimism on distress: A study of women with early stage breast cancer. *Journal of Personality and Social Psychology, 65,* 375-390.

Casacalenda, N., Perry, J.C., & Looper, K. (2002). Remission in major depressive disorder: A comparison of pharmacotherapy, psychotherapy, and control conditions. *American Journal of Psychiatry, 159,* 1354-1360.

Casati, J., Toner, B. B., & Yu, B. (2000). *Comprehensive Psychiatry, 41,* 344-351.

Casey, J.E., Rourke, B.P., & Del Dotto, J.E. (1996). Learning disabilities in children with attention deficit disorder with and without hyperactivity. *Child Neuropsychology, 2,* 83-98.

Cashman, J.A. (1966). *The LSD story.* Greenwich, CT: Fawcett.

Casriel, D. (1971). The dynamics of Synanon. In R.W. Siroka, E.K. Siroka, & G.A. Schloss (Eds.), *Sensitivity training and group encounter.* New York: Grosset & Dunlap.

Castellanos, F.X., Giedd, J.N., Marsh, W.L., Hamburger, S.D., Vaituzis, A.C., Dickstein, D.P., Sarfatti, S.E., Vauss, Y.C., Snell, J.W., Lange, N., Kaysen, D., Krain, A.L., Ritchie, G.F., Rajapaske, J.C., & Rapoport, J.L. (1996). Quantitative brain magnetic resonance imaging in attention-deficit/hyperactivity disorder. *Archives of General Psychiatry, 53,* 607-616.

Castle, D.J., & Murray, R.M. (1993). The epidemiology of late-onset schizophrenia. *Schizophrenia Bulletin, 19,* 691-700.

Cautela, J.R. (1966). Treatment of compulsive behavior by covert sensitization. *Psychological Record, 16,* 33-41.

CBC News (2003, February 7th). *B.C. faces forced sterilization lawsuit* (www.cbc.ca).

Centre For Addiction and Mental Health (2000). *Social stigma cited as top reason why people don't seek treatment for depression: Former Toronto Maple Leaf hockey star speaks out in time for World Mental health Day. (http://www.camh.net/events/thereishelp_campaign.html; accessed on*

November 10, 2000).

Centre For Addiction and Mental Health (2000). *CAMH Best Advice Paper: Community Treatment Orders: Overview and recommendations. (http://www.camh.net).*

Centre For Addiction and Mental Health (2001). *Information Bulletin: Ecstasy. (http://www.camh.net/bulletins/ecstasy.html; accessed on April 10, 2001).*

Cerny, J.A., Barlow, D.H., Craske, M.G., & Himadi, W.G. (1987). Couples treatment of agoraphobia: A two year follow-up. *Behavior Therapy, 18,* 401-415.

Chaiken, S., & Pliner, P. (1987). Women, but not men, are what they eat—The effects of meal size and gender on perceived femininity and masculinity. *Personality and Social Psychology Bulletin, 13,* 166-176.

Chaimowitz, G., & Glancy, G. (2004). *The duty to protect.* Canadian Psychiatric Association Position Paper (available January 18, 2004 on www.cpa-apc.org)

Chambers, K.C., & Bernstein, I.L. (1995). Conditioned flavor aversions. In R.L. Doty (Ed.), *Handbook of olfaction and gustation* (pp. 745-773). New York: Marcel Dekker.

Chambless, D. L., & Ollendick, T. H. (2001). Empirically supported psychological interventions: Controversies and evidence. *Annual Review of Psychology, 52,* 685-716.

Chambless, D.L., Sanderson, W.C., Shoham, V., Johnson, S.B., Pope, K.S., Crits-Christoph, P., Baker, M., Johnson, B., Woody, S.R., Sue, S., Beutler, L.E., Williams, D.A., & McCurry, S. (1996). An update on empirically validated therapies. *The Clinical Psychologist, 49,* 5-18.

Chambliss, C.A., & Murray, E.J. (1979). Efficacy attribution, locus of control, and weight loss. *Cognitive Therapy and Research, 3,* 349-353.

Chappell, N.L., & Reid, R.C. (2002). Burden and well-being among caregivers. *Gerontologist, 42,* 772-780.

Chandarana, P., Helmes, E., & Benson, N. (1988). Eating attitudes as related to demographic characteristics: A high school survey. *Canadian Journal of Psychiatry, 33,* 834-837.

Chandler, M.J., & Lalonde, C. (1998). Cultural continuity as a hedge against suicide in Canada's First Nations. *Transcultural Psychiatry, 35,* 191-220.

Chaney, E.F., O'Leary, M.R., & Marlatt, G.A. (1978). Skills training with alcoholics. *Journal of Consulting and Clinical Psychology, 46,* 1092-1104.

Chapman, L.J., & Chapman, J.P. (1969). Illusory correlation as an obstacle to the use of valid psychodiagnostic signs. *Journal of Abnormal Psychology, 74,* 271-287.

Chappell, N.L., & Penning, M. (1996). Behavioural problems and distress among caregivers of people with dementia. *Ageing and Society, 16,* 57-73.

Charbonneau, J., & O'Connor, K. (1999). Depersonalization in a non-clinical sample. *Behavioral and Cognitive Psychotherapy, 27,* 377-381.

Charney, D.A., Paraherakis, A.M., Negrete, J.C., & Gill, K.J. (1998). The impact of depression on the outcome of addictions treatment. *Journal of Substance Abuse Treatment, 15,* 123-130.

Charney, D.S., Woods, S.W., Goodman, W.K., & Heninger, G.R. (1987). Neurobiological mechanisms of panic anxiety: Biochemical and behavioral correlates of yohimbine-induced panic attacks. *American Journal of Psychiatry, 144,* 1030-1036.

Charter of Rights and Freedoms (1982). *The Charter of Rights and Freedoms: A Guide For Canadians.* Ottawa: Publications Canada.

Chassin, L., Curran, P.J., Hussong, A.M., & Colder, C. R. (1996). The relation of parent alcoholism to adolescent substance abuse: A longitudinal follow-up. *Journal of Abnormal Psychology, 105,* 70-80.

Chassin, L., Pitts, S.C., DeLucia, C., & Todd, M. (1999). A longitudinal study of children of alcholics: Predicting young adult substance use disoders, anxiety, and depression. *Journal of Abnormal Psychology, 108,* 106-119.

Chemtob, C., Roitblat, H.C., Hamada, R.S., Carlson, J.G., & Twentyman, C.T. (1988). A cognitive action theory of posttraumatic stress disorder. *Journal of Anxiety Disorders, 2,* 253-275.

Chen, E., Bush, J.P., & Zeltzer, L. (1997). Psychologic issues in pediatric pain management. *Current Review of Pain, 1,* 153-164.

Chen, S., & Andersen, S.M. (1999). Relationships from the past in the present: Significant-other representations and transference in interpersonal life. In M.P. Zanna (Ed.), *Advances in experimental social psychology.* San Diego: Academic Press.

Chen, W.J., Liu, S.K., Chang, C.-G., Lien, Y.-J., et al. (1998). Sustained attention deficit and schizotypal personality features in nonpsychotic relatives of schizophrenic patients. *American Journal of Psychoatry, 155,* 1214-1220.

Chen, Y., Levy, D.L., Nakayama, K., Matthysse, S., et al. (1999). Dependence of impaired eye tracking on velocity discrimination in schizophrenia. *Archives of General Psychiatry, 56,* 155-161.

Cherner, J. (1990). *A smoke-free America.* New York: Smokefree Educational Services.

Chew, B.H., Pace, K.T., & Honey, J. D'A. (2002). Munchausen syndrome presenting as gross hematuria in two women. *Urology, 59,* 601i-601iii.

Chiappa, F. (1994). Effective management of family and individual interventions in the treatment of dissociative disorders. *Dissociation, 7, 185*-190.

Chiariello, M.A., & Orvaschel, H. (1995). Patterns of parent-child communication: Relationship to depression. *Clinical Psychology Review, 15,* 395-407.

Chipperfield, J.G., & Havens, B. (2001). Gender differences in the relationship between marital status transitions and life satisfaction in later life. *Journal of Gerontology: Social Sciences, 56B,* P176-P186.

Chockalingam, A., Campbell, N., Ruddy, T., Taylor, G., & Stewart, P. (2000). Canadian National High Blood Pressure Prevention and Control Strategy. *Canadian Journal of Cardiology, 16,* 1087-1093.

Chouinard, G., Jones, B., Remington, G., Bloom, D., Addington, D., MacEwan, G. W. et al. (1993). A Canadian multicentre placebo-controlled study of fixed doses of risperidone and haloperidol in the treatment of chronic schizophrenia patients. *Journal of Clinical Psychopharmacology, 13,* 25-40.

Chow, E.W., & Choy, A.L. (2002). Clinical characteristics and treatment response to SSRI in a female pedophile. *Archives of Sexual Behavior, 31,* 211-215.

Chow, T.W., Miller, B.L., Hayashi, V.N., & Geschwind, D.H. (1999). Inheritance of frontotemporal dementia. *Archives of Neurology, 56,* 817-822.

Christenfeld, N., Gerin, W., Linden, W., Sanders, M., Mathur, J.D., et al. (1998). Social support efects on cardiovascular reactivity: Is a stranger as effective as a friend? *Psychosomatic Medicine, 59,* 388-398.

Christensen, A., & Heavey, C.L. (1990). Gender and social structure in the demand/withdraw pattern of marital interaction. *Journal of Personality and Social Psychology, 59,* 73-81.

Christensen, A., & Jacobson, N.S. (1993). Who or what can do psychotherapy? *Psychological Science, 5,* 8-14.

Christensen, A., Jacobson, N.S., & Babcock, J.C. (1995). Integrative behavioral couples therapy. In N.S. Jacobson & A.S. Gurman (Eds.), *Clinical handbook of couples therapy* (pp. 31-64). New York: Guilford.

Christensen, A., & Shenk, J.L. (1991). Communication, distress, and psychological distance in nondistressed, clinic, and divorcing couples. *Journal of Consulting and Clinical Psychology, 59,* 458-463.

Christie, A.B. (1982). Changing patterns in mental illness in the elderly. *British Journal of Psychiatry, 140,* 154-159.

Chua, S.T., & McKenna, P.T. (1995). Schizophrenia-a brain disease? *British Journal of Psychiatry, 166,* 563-582.

Churchill, D.W. (1969). Psychotic children and behavior modification. *American Journal of Psychiatry, 125,* 1585-1590.

Cimons, M. (1992, May 22). Record number of Americans stop smoking. *Los Angeles Times,* p. A4.

Cimons, M. (1995, December 16). Smoking, illegal drug use still rising among teens, national survey shows. *Los Angeles Times,* p. A25.

Cimons, M. (1996, March 19). Firm adjusted nicotine in cigarettes, affidavits say. *Los Angeles Times,* pp. A1, A13.

Cimons, M. (1998, April 3). Study finds sharp rise in teenage tobacco use. *Los Angeles Times,* A1, A26.

Cimons, M. (1999, May 21). Marijuana studies to be aided by likely policy reversal. *Los Angeles Times,* A15

Cinciripini, P.M., Lapitsky, L., Seay, S., Wallfisch, A., Kitchens, K., & Van Vunakis, H. (1995). The effect of smoking schedules on cessation outcome: Can we improve on common methods of gradual and abrupt nicotine withdrawal? *Journal of Consulting and Clinical Psychology, 63,* 388-399.

Cinciripini, P.M., Lapitsky, L.G., Wallfisch, A., Mace, R., Nezami, E., & Van Vunakis, H. (1994). An evaluation of a multicomponent treatment program involving scheduled smoking and relapse prevention procedures: Initial findings. *Addictive Behaviors, 19,* 13-22.

Cioffi, D. (1991). Beyond attentional strategies: A cognitive-perceptual model of somatic interpretation. *Psychological Bulletin, 109,* 25-41.

Clark, C.C. (1985). *Report of the Electro-Convulsive Therapy Review Committee*. Toronto: Ontario Ministry of Health.

Clark, D.A. (1997). Twenty years of cognitive assessment: Current status and future directions. *Journal of Consulting and Clinical Psychology, 65,* 996-1000.

Clark, D.A., & Beck, A.T. (1991). Personality factors in dysphoria: A psychometric refinement of Beck's Sociotropy-Autonomy Scale. *Journal of Psychopathology and Behavioral Assessment, 13*, 369-388.

Clark, D.A., & Oates, T. (1995). Daily hassles, major and minor life events, and their interaction with sociotropy and autonomy. *Behaviour Research and Therapy, 33*, 819-823.

Clark, D.A., Purdon, C., & Wang, A. (2003). The Meta-Cognitive Beliefs Questionnaire: Development of a measure of obsessional beliefs. *Behaviour Research and Therapy, 41*, 655-659.

Clark, D.A., Steer, R.A., Beck, A.T., & Ross, L. (1995). Psychometric characteristics of revised sociotropy and autonomy scales in college students. *Behaviour Research and Therapy, 33*, 325-334.

Clark, D.A. (1988). The validity of measures of cognition: A review of the literature. *Cognitive Therapy and Research, 12,* 1-20.

Clark, D.A. (2000). Cognitive behavior therapy for obsessions and compulsions: New applications and emerging trends. *Journal of Contemporary Psychotherapy, 30*, 129-147.

Clark, D.A., Beck, A.T., & Alford, B.A. (1999). *Scientific foundations of cognitive theory and therapy of depression*. New York: Wiley.

Clark, D.M. (1989). Anxiety states: Panic and generalized anxiety. In K. Hawton, P. Salkovskis, J. Kirk, & D.M. Clark (Eds.), *Cognitive behavior therapy for psychiatric problems: A practical guide*. Oxford,U.K. Oxford University Press.

Clark, D.M., Salkovskis, P.M., Hackmann, A., Middleton, H., Anastasiades, P., & Gelder, M. (1994). A comparison of cognitive therapy, applied relaxation, and imipramine in the treatment of panic disorder. *British Journal of Psychiatry, 164,* 759-769.

Clark, D.M., & Wells, A. (1995). A cognitive model of social phobia. In R.G. Heimberg, M.R. Liebowitz, D.A. Hope, & F.R. Schneier (Eds.), *Social phobia: Diagnosis, assessment, and treatment* (pp. 69-93). New York: Guilford.

Clark, L.A., Livesley, W.J., Schroeder, M.L., & Irish, S.L. (1996). Convergence of two systems for assessing personality disorder. *Psychological Assessment, 8*, 294-303.

Clark, L.A., Watson, D., & Mineka, S. (1994). Temperament, personality, and the mood and anxiety disorders. *Journal of Abnormal Psychology, 103,* 92-102.

Clark, R.F., & Goate, A.M. (1993). Molecular genetics of Alzheimer's disease. *Archives of Neurology, 50,* 1164-1172.

Clarke, G., Hops, H., Lewinsohn, P.M., Andrews, J., Seeley, J.R., & Williams, J. (1992). Cognitive-behavioral group treatment of adolescent depression: Prediction of outcome. *Behavior Therapy, 23,* 341-354.

Clarke, K.M., & Greenberg, L. (1986). Differential effects of the gestalt two chair intervention and problem solving in resolving decisional conflict. *Journal of Counseling Psychology, 33,* 48-53.

Clarke, K. M., & Greenberg, L. S. (1988). Clinical research on Gestalt methods. In F. N. Watts (Ed.), *New developments in clinical psychology (*Vol. 2, pp. 5-19). NY: Wiley.

Clarkin, J.F., Marziali, E., & Munroe-Blum, H. (Eds.). (1992). *Borderline personality disorder: Clinical and empirical perspectives*. New York: Guilford.

Clary, M. (1998, May 8). Teen-driven ad campaign puts heat on big tobacco. *Los Angeles Times,* A1, A25.

Classen, C., Koopman, C., Hales, R., & Spiegel, D. (1998). Acute stress disorder as a predictor of posttraumatic stress disorder. *American Journal of Psychiatry, 155,* 620-624.

Claude, D., & Firestone, P. (1995). The development of ADHD boys: A 12-year follow-up. *Canadian Journal of Behavioral Science, 27,* 226-249.

Claude-Pierre, P. (1997). The secret language of eating disorders. Toronto: Random House of Canada Limited.

Clausen, J.A., & Kohn, M.L. (1959). Relation of schizophrenia to the social structure of a small city. In B. Pasamanick (Ed.), *Epidemiology of mental disorder.* Washington, DC: American Association for the Advancement of Science.

Clayton, D., & Barcelo, A. (1999). The cost of suicide mortality in New Brunswick, 1996. *Chronic Diseases in Canada, 20*, 89-95.

Clayton, E.W. (1988). From Rogers to Rivers: The rights of the mentally ill to refuse medications. *American Journal of Law and Medicine, 13,* 7-52.

Clayton, I.C., Richards, J.C., & Edwards, C.J. (1999). Selective attention in obsessive-compulsive disorder. *Journal of Abnormal Psychology, 108,* 171-175.

Clayton, R.R., Catterello, A., & Walden, K.P. (1991). Sensation seeking as a potential mediating variable for school-based prevention intervention: A two-year follow-up of DARE. *Health Communication, 3,* 229-239.

Cleckley, H. (1976). *The mask of sanity* (5th ed.). St. Louis: Mosby.

Clomipramine Collaborative Study Group. (1991). Clomipramine in the treatment of patients with obsessive-compulsive disorder. *Archives of General Psychiatry, 48,* 730-738.

Cloninger, C.R. (1987a), Neurogenetic adaptive mechanisms in alcoholism. *Science, 236*, 410-416.

Cloninger, C.R. (1987b). A systematic method for clinical description and classification of personality variants. *Archives of General Psychiatry, 44*, 573-588.

Cloninger, R.C., Martin, R.L., Guze, S.B., & Clayton, P.L. (1986). A prospective follow-up and family study of somatization in men and women. *American Journal of Psychiatry, 143,* 713-714.

Cloud, J. (1999, June 7). Mental health reform: What it would really take. *Time Magazine,* 54-56.

Cloutier, P.R., Manion, I.G., Walker, J.G., & Johnson, S.M. (2002). Emotionally focused interventions for couples with chronically ill children: A 2-year follow-up. *Journal of Marital and Family Therapy, 28*, 391-398.

CMAJ (2001). Can we afford medicare? Romanow to find out. *Canadian Medical Association Journal, 164,* 1609.

Cocarro, E.F., & Kavousi, R.J. (1997). Fluoxetine and impulsive aggressive behavior in personality-disordered subjects. *Archives of General Psychiatry, 54,* 1081-1088.

Cody, M., Wendt, P., Dunn, D., Ott, J., Pierson, J., & Pratt, L. (1997). Friendship formation and community development on the Internet. International Communication Association Meeting, Montreal, May.

Cody, M.J., Dunn, D., Hoppin, S., & Wendt, P. (1999). Silver surfers: Training and evaluating Internet use among older adult learners. *Communication Education, 48,* 269-286.

Cohen, D., Eisdorfer, C., Prinz, P., Breen, A., Davis, M., & Gadsby, A. (1983). Sleep disturbances in the institutionalized aged. *Journal of the American Geriatrics Society, 31,* 79-82.

Cohen, D.J., Solnit, A.J., & Wohlford, P. (1979). Mental health services in Head Start. In E. Zigler & J. Valentine (Eds.), *Project Head Start*. New York: Free Press.

Cohen, N.J., Davine, M., Horodezky, N., Lipsett, L., & Isaacson, L. (1993). Unsuspected language impairment in psychiatrically disturbed children: Prevalence and language and behavioral characteristics. *Journal of the American Academy of Child and Adolescent Psychiatry, 32*, 595-603.

Cohen, N.J., Menna, R., Vallance, D.D., Barwick, M. A., Im, N., & Horodezky, N. (1998). Language, social cognitive processing, and behavioral characteristics of psychiatrically disturbed children with previously identified and suspected language impairments. *Journal of Child Psychology and Psychiatry, 39*, 853-864.

Cohen, N.J., Vallance, D.D., Barwick, M., Im, N., Menna, R., Horodezky, N.B., & Isaacson, L. (2000). The interface between ADHD and language impairment: An examination of language, achievement, and cognitive processing. *Journal of Child Psychology and Psychiatry, 41*, 353-362.

Cohen, P., Cohen, J., Kasen, S., Velez, C.N., Hartmark, C., Johnson, J., Rojas, M., Brook, J., & Streuning, E.L. (1993). An epidemiological study of disorders in late childhood and adolescence: 1. Age and gender-specific prevalence. *Journal of Child Psychology and Psychiatry, 34,* 851-867.

Cohen, R.M., Nordahl, T.E., Semple, W.E., Andreason, P., et al. (1997). The brain metabolic patterns of clozapine and fluphenazine-treated patients with schizophrenia during a continous performance task. *Archives of General Psychiatry, 54,* 481-486.

Cohen, S., Doyle, W.J., Skoner, D.P., Rabin, B.S., & Gwaltney, J.M. (1997). Social ties and susceptibility to the common cold. *JAMA, 277,* 1940-1945.

Cohen, S., Frank, E., Doyle, W.J., Rabin, B.S., et al. (1998). Types of stressors that increase susceptibility to the common cold in healthy adults. *Health Psychology, 17,* 214-223.

Cohen, S., & Herbert, T.B. (1996). Health psychology: Psychological factors and physical disease from the perspective of human psychoneuroimmunology. In J.T. Spence, J.M. Darley, & D.J. Foss (Eds.), *Annual review of psychology* (pp. 123-142). Stanford, CA: Stanford University Press.

Cohen, S., Tyrell, D.A.J., & Smith, A.P. (1991). Psychological stress and susceptibility to the common cold. New England Journal of Medicine, 325, 606-612.

Cohen, S., & Wills, T.A. (1985). Stress, social support, and the buffering process. *Psychological Bulletin, 98,* 310-357.

Cohen-Kettenis, P.T., Owen, A., Kaijser, V.G., Bradley, S.J., & Zucker, K.J. (2003). Demographic characteristics, social competence, and behavior problems in children with gender identity disorder: A cross-national, cross-clinic comparative analysis. *Journal of Abnormal Child Psychology*, *31*, 41-53.

Colapinto, J. (1997). *The true story of Joan/John*. Rolling Stone, 55-ff.

Colapinto, J. (2000). *As nature made him: The boy who was raised as a girl.* Toronto: Harper Collins.

Cole, D., & Turner, J., Jr. (1993). Models of cognitive mediation and moderation in child depression. *Journal of Abnormal Psychology, 102,* 271-281.

Cole, D.A., Martin, J.M., Powers, B., & Truglio, R. (1990). Modeling causal relations between academic and social competence and depression: A multitrait-multimethod longitudinal study of children. *Journal of Abnormal Psychology, 105,* 258-270.

Cole, J., Watt, N., West, S., Hawkins, J., Asarnow, J., Markman, H., Ramey, S., Shure, M., & Long, B. (1993). The science of prevention: A conceptual framework and some directions for a national research program. *American Psychologist, 48,* 1013-1022.

Cole, J.D. (1988). Where are those new anti-depressants they promised us? *Archives of General Psychiatry, 45,* 193-194.

Cole, J.D., & Kazarian, S.S. (1988). The Level of Expressed Emotion Scale: A new measure of expressed emotion. *Journal of Clinical Psychology*, *44*, 392-397.

Cole, J.D., & Kazarian, S.S. (1993). Predictive validity of the Level of Expressed Emotion (LEE) Scale: Readmission follow-up data for 1, 2, and 5-year periods. *Journal of Clinical Psychology*, *49*, 216-218.

Cole, K.C. (1996, November 22). Trying to solve the riddle of the rock. *Los Angeles Times*, pp. A1, A29.

Cole, M.G., & Bellavance, F. (1997). The prognosis of depression in old age. *American Journal of Geriatric Psychiatry*, *5*, 4-14.

Cole, M.G., Bellavance, F., & Mansour, A. (1999). Prognosis of depression in elderly community and primary care populations: A systematic review and meta-analysis. *American Journal of Psychiatry*, *156*, 1182-1189.

Cole, M.G., & Dendukuri, N. (2003). Risk factors for depression among elderly community subjects: A systematic review and meta-analysis. *American Journal of Psychiatry*, *160*, 1147-1156.

Coleman, H.L.K., Wampold, B.E., & Casali, S.L. (1995). Ethnic minorities: ratings of ethnically similar and European American counselors: A meta-analysis. *Journal of Counseling Psychology, 42,* 55-64.

Colletti, G., & Kopel, S.A. (1979). Maintaining behavior change: An investigation of three maintenance strategies and the relationship of self-attribution to the long-term reduction of cigarette smoking. *Journal of Consulting and Clinical Psychology, 47,* 614-617.

Collins, A. (1988). *In the sleep room: The story of the CIA brainwashing experiments in Canada.* Toronto: Lester and Orpen Dennys Limited.

Collins, L.F., Maxwell, A.E., & Cameron, C. (1962). A factor analysis of some child psychiatric clinic data. *Journal of Mental Science, 108,* 274-285.

Combs, G., Jr., & Ludwig, A.M. (1982). Dissociative disorders. In J.H. Greist, J.W. Jefferson, & R.L. Spitzer (Eds.), *Treatment of mental disorders*. New York: Oxford University Press.

Committee on Government Operations. (1985). *The federal response to the homeless crisis*. Washington, DC: U.S. Government Printing Office.

Committee on Health Care for Homeless People. (1988). *Homelessness, health, and human needs*. Washington, DC: National Academic Press.

Compas, B.E., Ey, S., & Grant, K.E. (1993). Taxonomy, assessment and diagnosis of depression during adolescence. *Psychological Bulletin, 144,* 323-344.

Compas, B.E., Haaga, D.A.F., Keefe, F.J., Leitenberg, H., & Williams, D.A. (1998). Sampling of empirically supported psychological treatments from health psychology: Smoking, chronic pain, cancer, and bulimia nervosa. *Journal of Consulting and Clinical Psychology, 66,* 89-112.

Compton, D.R., Dewey, W.L., & Martin, B.R. (1990). Cannabis dependence and tolerance production. *Advances in Alcohol and Substance Abuse, 9,* 129-147.

Condelli, W.S., Fairbank, J.A., Dennis, M.L., & Rachal, J.V. (1991). Cocaine use by clients in methadone programs: Significance, scope, and behavioral interventions. *Journal of Substance Abuse Treatment, 8,* 203-212.

Conger, J.J. (1951). The effects of alcohol on conflict behavior in the albino rat. *Quarterly Journal of Studies on Alcohol, 12,* 129.

Conley, R.R., Love, R.C., Kelly, D.L., & Bartko, J.J. (1999). Rehospitalization rates of patients recently discharged on a regimen of risperidone or clozapine. *American Journal of Psychiatry, 156,* 863-868.

Connan, F., & Stanley, S. (2003). Biology of appetite and weight regulation. In J. Treasure, U. Schmidt, & van Furth, E, *Handbook of eating disorders* (2nd edition, pp. 63-87). Chichester, West Sussex: Wiley.

Connelly, M. (1992, March 7). 3 found dead after inhaling laughing gas. *Los Angeles Times*, pp. A1, A23.

Conners, C.K. (1969). A teacher rating scale for use in drug studies with children. *American Journal of Psychiatry, 126,* 884-888.

Conners, F.A., Caruso, D.R., & Detterman, D.K. (1986). Computer-assisted instruction for the mentally retarded. In N.R. Ellis & N.W. Bray (Eds.), *International review of research in mental retardation* (Vol. 14). New York: Academic Press.

Connolly, J.F. (2000). Applying cognitive research in the twenty-first century: Event-related potentials in assessment. *Brain and Cognition*, *42*, 99-101.

Connolly, J.F., & D'Arcy, R.C.N. (2000). Innovations in neuropsychological assessment using event-related brain potentials. *International Journal of Psychophysiology*, *37*, 31-47.

Connolly, J.F., D'Arcy, R.C.N., Newman, R.L., & Kemps, R. (2000). The application of cognitive event-related brain potentials (ERPs) in language-impaired individuals: Review and case studies. *International Journal of Psychophysiology*, *38*, 55-70.

Connolly, J.F., Major, A.M., Allen, S.L., & D'Arcy, R.C.N. (1999). Performance on WISC-III and WAIS-R NI vocabulary subtests assessed with event-related brain potentials: An innovative method of assessment. *Journal of Clinical and Experimental Neuropsychology*, *21*, 444-464.

Connolly, J.F., Mate-Kole, C.C., & Joyce, B.M. (1999). An innovative assessment approach in a case of global aphasia. *Archives of Physical Medicine and Rehabilitation*, *80*, 1309-1315.

Conoley, C.W., Conoley, J.C., McConnell, J.A., & Kimzey, C.E. (1983). The effect of the ABCs of rational emotive therapy and the empty-chair technique of Gestalt therapy on anger reduction. *Psychotherapy: Theory, Research, and Practice, 20,* 112-117.

Conrod, P.J., Pihl, R.O., Stewart, S.H., & Dongier, M. (2000). Validation of a system of classifying female substance abusers on the basis of personality and motivational risk factors for substance abuse. *Psychology of Addictive Behaviors*, *14*, 243-256.

Conrod, P.J., Pihl, R.O., & Vassileva, J. (1998). Differential sensitivity to alcohol reinforcement in groups of men at risk for distinct alcoholic syndromes. *Alcoholism: Clinical and Experimental Research, 22,* 585-597.

Conrod, P.J., Stewart, S.H., Pihl, R.O., Cote, S., Fontaine, V., & Dongier, M. (2000). Efficacy of brief coping skills interventions that match different personality profiles of female substance abusers. *Psychology of Addictive Behaviors*, *14*, 231-242.

Constans, J.I., Foa, E.B., Franklin, M.E., & Mathews, A. (1995). Memory for actual and imagined events in obsessive-compulsive disorder. *Behaviour Research and Therapy, 33,* 665-671.

Consumer Reports. (1995, November). Mental health: Does therapy help? *Consumer Reports*, pp. 734-739.

Conwell, Y. (1994). Suicide in elderly patients. In L.S. Schneider, C.F. Reynolds, III, B.D. Lebowitz, & A.J. Friedhoff (Eds.), *Diagnosis and treatment of depression in late life* (pp. 397-418). Washington, DC: American Psychiatric Press.

Conwell, Y. (2001). Suicide in later life: A review and recommendations for prevention. *Suicide and Life-Threatening Behavior*, *31*, 32-47.

Cook, B., Blatt, S.J., & Ford, R.Q. (1995). The prediction of therapeutic response to long-term intensive treatment of seriously disturbed young adult inpatients. *Psychotherapy Research, 5,* 218-230.

Cook, M., & Mineka, S. (1989). Observational conditioning of fear to fear-relevant versus fear-irrelevant stimuli in rhesus monkeys. *Journal of Abnormal Psychology, 98,* 448-459.

Cook, P. (1994). Chronic illness beliefs and the role of social networks among Chinese, Indians, and Angloceltic Canadians. *Journal of Cross-Cultural Psychology, 25,* 452-464.

Coolidge, F.L., & Segal, D.L. (1998). Evolution of personality disorder diagnosis in the Diagnostic and Statistical Manual of Mental Disorders. *Clinical Psychology Review, 18,* 585-589.

Coons, P.M., & Milstein, V. (1992). Psychogenic amnesia: A clinical investigation of 25 cases. *Dissociation: Progress in the Dissociative Disorders, 5,* 73-79.

Coons, W.H. (1957). Interaction and insight in group psychotherapy. *Canadian Journal of Psychology, 11,* 1-8.

Coons, W. H. (1967). The dynamics of change in psychotherapy. *Canadian Psychiatric Association Journal, 12,* 239-245.

Coons, W. H., & Peacock, T. P. (1970). Interpersonal interaction and personality change in group psychotherapy. *Canadian Psychiatric Association Journal, 15,* 347-355.

Cooper, A.F., Kay, D.W.K., Curry, A.R., Garside, R.F., & Roth, M. (1974). Hearing loss in paranoid and affective psychoses of the elderly. *Lancet, 2,* 851-854.

Cooper, J.E., Kendell, R.E., Gurland, B.J., Sharpe, L., Copeland, J.R.M., & Simon, R. (1972). *Psychiatric diagnosis in New York and London*. London: Oxford University Press.

Cooper, M.L. (1994). Motivations for alcohol use among adolescents: Development and validation of a four-factor model. *Psychological Assessment, 6,* 117-128.

Cooper, M.L., Frone, M.R., Russell, M., & Mudar, P. (1995). Drinking to regulate positive and negative emotion: A motivational model of alcoholism. *Journal of Personality and Social Psychology, 69, 961*-974.

Cooper, P.J., Coker, S., & Fleming, C. (1994). Self-help for bulimia nervosa: A preliminary report. *International Journal of Eating Disorders, 16,* 401-404.

Coppen, A., Prange, A.J., Whybrow, P.C., & Noguera, R. (1972). Abnormalities in indoleamines in affective disorders. *Archives of General Psychiatry, 26,* 474-478.

Corbitt, E.M., & Widiger, T.A. (1995). Sex differences in the personality disorders: An exploration of the data. *Clinical Psychology: Science and Practice, 2,* 225-238.

Cordova, J.V., & Jacobson, N.S. (1993). Couple distress. In D.H. Barlow (Ed.), *Clinical handbook of psychological disorders*. 2nd ed. (pp. 461-512). New York: Guilford.

Cornblatt, B., & Erlenmeyer-Kimling, L.E. (1985). Global attentional deviance in children at risk for schizophrenia: Specificity and predictive validity. *Journal of Abnormal Psychology, 94,* 470-486.

Corneil, W., Beaton, R., Murphy, S., Johnson, C., & Pike, K. (1999). Exposure to traumatic events and prevalence of posttraumatic stress symptomatology in urban firefighters in two countries. *Journal of Occupational Health Psychology, 4,* 131-141.

Cornelius, J.R., Salloum, I.M., Mezzich, J., Cornelius, M.D., Fabrega, H., et al. (1995). Disproportionate suicidability in patients with comorbid major depression and alcoholism. *American Journal of Psychiatry, 152,* 358-364.

Correa, D.D., Graves, R.E., & Costa, L. (1996). Awareness of memory deficit in Alzheimer's disease patients and memory-impaired older adults. *Aging, Neuropsychology, and Cognition, 3,* 215-228.

Cortoni, F., & Marshall, W.L. (2001). Sex as a coping strategy and its relationship to juvenile sexual history and intimacy in sexual offenders. *Sexual Abuse: A Journal of Research and Treatment, 13,* 27-43.

Corwin, M. (1996). Heroin's new popularity claims unlikely victims. *Los Angeles Times,* A1.

Coryell, W., Winokur, G., Shea, T., Maser, J.W., Endicott, J., & Akiskal, H.S. (1994). The long-term stability of depressive subtypes. *American Journal of Psychiatry, 151,* 199-204.

Costa, L. (1996). Lifespan neuropsychology. *The Clinical Neuropsychologist, 10,* 365-374.

Costa, P.T., Jr., & McCrae, R.R. (1988). Personality in adulthood: A six-year longitudinal study of self-reports and spouse ratings on the NEO Personality Inventory. *Journal of Personality and Social Psychology, 54,* 853-863.

Costa, P.T., Jr., & McCrae, R.R. (1992). *NEO-PI-R*. Odessa, FL: Psychological Assessment Resources.

Costello, C.G. (1982). Fears and phobias in women: A community survey. *Journal of Abnormal Psychology, 91,* 280-286.

Costello, E.J., Costello, A.J., Edelbrock, C., Burns, B.J., Dulcan, M.K., Brent, D., & Janiszewski, S. (1988). Psychiatric disorders in pediatric primary care. *Archives of General Psychiatry, 45,* 1107-1116.

Cote, G., Gauthier, J., Laberge, B., Cormier, H.J., & Plamondon, J. (1994). Reduced therapist contact in the cognitive-behavioral treatment of panic disorder. *Behavior Therapy, 25,* 123-145.

Cote, S., Tremblay, R.E., Nagin, D.S., Zoccolillo, M., & Vitaro, F. (2002). Childhood behavioral profiles leading to adolescent conduct disorder: Risk trajectories for boys and girls. *Journal of the American Academy of Child and Adolescent Psychiatry, 41,* 1086-1094.

Council for Exceptional Children (1993). *Inclusion: What does it mean for children with learning disabilities? Reston,* VA: Division for Learning Disabilities.

Courchesne, E., Yeung-Courchesne, R., Press, G.A., Hesselink, J.R., & Jernigan, T.L. (1988). Hypoplasia of cerebellar vermal lobules VI and VII in autism. *New England Journal of Medicine, 318,* 1349-1354.

Courneya, K.S., Plotnikoff, R.C., Hotz, S.B., & Birkett, N.J. (2000). Social support and the theory of planned behavior in the exercise domain. *American Journal of Health Behavior, 24,* 300-308.

Cournish, P.A., et al. (2003). Rural interdisciplinary mental health team building via satellite: A demonstration project. *Telemedia Journal and e-Health, 9,* 63-71.

Covi, L., Lipman, R.S., Derogatis, L.R., Smith, J.E., & Pattison, J.H. (1974). Drugs and group psychotherapy in neurotic depression. *American Journal of Psychiatry, 131,* 191-197.

Cowan, P. (1999, November 7). Traumatic memories dog veteran; "I always wake up before they kill me." *Edmonton Sun,* 29.

Cox, B.J., Borger, S.C., Asmundson, G.J.G., & Taylor, S. (2000). Dimensions of hypochondriasis and the five-factor model of personality. *Personality and Individual Differences, 29,* 99-108.

Cox, B.J., Borger, S.C., & Enns, M.W. (1999). Anxiety sensitivity and emotional disorders: Psychometric studies and their theoretical implications. In S. Taylor, (Ed). *Anxiety sensitivity: Theory, research, and treatment of the fear of anxiety* (pp. 115-148). Mahwah, NJ: Erlbaum.

Cox, B.J., Borger, S.C., Taylor, S., Fuentes, K., & Ross, L.M. (1999). Anxiety sensitivity and the five-factor model of personality. *Behaviour Research and Therapy, 37,* 633-641.

Cox, B.J., Endler, N.S., & Norton, G.R. (1994). Levels of "nonclinical panic." *Journal of Behavioural Therapy and Experimental Psychiatry, 25,* 35-40.

Cox, B.J., Endler, N.S., & Swinson, R.P. (1991). Clinical and nonclinical panic attacks: An empirical test of a panic anxiety continuum. *Journal of Anxiety Disorders, 5,* 21-34.

Cox, B.J., Enns, M.W., & Taylor, S. (2001). The effect of rumination as a mediator of elevated anxiety sensitivity in major depression. *Cognitive Therapy and Research, 25,* 525-534.

Cox, B.J., Enns, M.W., Walker, J.R., Kjernisted, K., & Pidlubny, S.R. (2001). Psychological vulnerabilities in patients with major depression vs. panic disorder. *Behaviour Research and Therapy, 39,* 567-573.

Cox, B.J., Kwong, J., Michaud, V., & Enns, M.W. (2000). Problem and probable pathological gambling: Considerations from a community survey. *Canadian Journal of Psychiatry, 45,* 548-553.

Cox, B.J., McWilliams, L.A., Clara, I.P., & Stein, M.B. (2003). The structure of feared situations in a nationally representative sample. *Anxiety Disorders, 17,* 89-101.

Cox, B.J., Walker, J.R., Enns, M.W., & Karpinski, D.C. (2002). Self-criticism in generalized social phobia and response to cognitive-behavioral treatment. *Behavior Therapy, 33,* 479-491.

Cox, D.J., Freundlich, A., & Meyer, R.G. (1975). Differential effectiveness of electromyographic feedback, verbal relaxation instructions, and medication placebo with tension headaches. *Journal of Consulting and Clinical Psychology, 43,* 892-898.

Cox, M., & Klinger, E. (1988). A motivational model of alcohol use. *Journal of Abnormal Psychology, 97,* 168-180.

Cox, W. (2000, December 27). Aboriginals seek tribunal on residential school abuse. *The Toronto Star, p. A6.*

Coyne, J.C. (1976). Depression and the response of others. *Journal of Abnormal Psychology, 85,* 186-193.

Coyne, J.C. (1994). Self-reported distress: Analog or ersatz depression? *Psychological Bulletin, 116,* 29-45.

Coyne, J.C., & Gotlib, I.H. (1983). The role of cognition in depression: A critical appraisal. *Psychological Bulletin, 84,* 472-505.

Craft, M.J. (1969). The natural history of psychopathic disorder. *British Journal of Psychiatry, 115,* 39-44.

Craig, M.M., & Glick, S.J. (1963). Ten years' experience with the Glueck social prediction table. *Crime and Delinquency, 9,* 249-261.

Craighead, W.E., Evans, D.D., & Robins, C.J. (1992). Unipolar depression. In S.M. Turner, K.S. Calhoun, & H.E. Adams (Eds.), *Handbook of clinical behavior therapy.* 2nd ed. (pp. 99-116). New York: Wiley.

Craske, M.G., Antony, M.M., & Barlow, D.H. (1997). *Mastery of your specific phobia (therapist guide).* San Antonio, TX: Psychological Corporation.

Craske, M.G., Brown, A.T., & Barlow, D.H. (1991). Behavioral treatment of panic disorder: A two-year follow-up. *Behavior Therapy, 22,* 289-304.

Craske, M.G., Maidenberg, E., & Bystritsky, A. (1995). Brief cognitive-behavioral versus nondirective therapy for panic disorder. *Journal of Behavior Therapy & Experimental Psychiatry, 26,* 113-120.

Craske, M.G., Rapee, R.M., & Barlow, D.H. (1992). Cognitive-behavioral treatment of panic disorder, agoraphobia, and generalized anxiety disorder. In S.M. Turner, K.S. Calhoun, & H.E. Adams (Eds.), *Handbook of clinical behavior therapy.* 2nd ed. (pp. 39-65). New York: Wiley.

Craske, M.G., Rapee, R.M., Jackel, L., & Barlow, D.H. (1989). Quantitative dimensions of worry in DSM-III-R generalized anxiety disorder subjects and non-anxious controls. *Behaviour Research and Therapy, 27,* 397-402.

Crawford, A.M., & Manassis, K. (2001). Familial predictors of treatment outcome in childhood anxiety disorders. *Journal of the American Academy of Child and Adolescent Psychiatry, 40,* 1182-1189.

Crick, N.R., & Dodge, K.A. (1994). A review and reformulation of social information-processing mechanisms in children's social adjustment. *Psychological Bulletin, 115,* 74-101.

Crisanti, A.S., & Love, E.J. (2001). Characteristics of psychiatric inpatients detained under civil commitment legislation: A Canadian study. *International Journal of Law and Psychiatry, 24,* 399-410.

Crisp, A.H., Callender, J.S., Haleck, C., & Hsu, L.K.G. (1992). Long-term mortality in anorexia nervosa. *British Journal of Psychiatry, 161,* 104-107.

Crits-Christoph, P. (1992). The efficacy of brief dynamic psychotherapy. *American Journal of Psychiatry, 149,* 151-158.

Cronbach, L.J., & Meehl, P.E. (1955). Construct validity in psychological tests. *Psychological Bulletin, 52,* 281-302.

Crow, T.J. (1980). Molecular pathology of schizophrenia: More than one disease process? *British Medical Journal, 280,* 784-788.

Crowe, R.R., Noyes, R., Pauls, D.I., & Slyman, D.J. (1983). A family study of panic disorder. *Archives of General Psychiatry, 40,* 1065-1069.

Cruz, D.B. (1999). Controlling desires: Sexual orientation conversion and the limits of knowledge and law. *Southern California Law Review, 72,* 1297-1400.

Csikszentmihalyi, M., & Figurski, T.J. (1982). Self-awareness and aversive experience in everyday life. *Journal of Personality, 50,* 15-28.

Culbertson, J.L. (1998). Learning disabilities. In Ollendick, T.H. & Hersen, M. (Eds.), *Handbook of child psychopathology*, 3rd Ed. New York: Plenum Press.

Culter, S.E., & Nolen-Hoeksema, S. (1991). Accounting for sex differences in depression through female victimization: Childhood sexual abuse. *Sex Roles, 24,* 425-438.

Cummings, E.M., Davies, P.T., & Simpson, K.S. (1994). Marital conflict, gender, and children's appraisals and coping efficacy as mediators of child adjustment. *Journal of Family Psychology, 8,* 141-149.

Cunningham, A. (2002). *One step forward: Lessons learned from a randomized study of multisystemic therapy in Canada.* London: Centre For Children and Families in the Justice System.

Cunningham, A.J., Edmonds, C.V., Phillips, C., Soots, K.I., Hedley, D., & Lockwood, G.A. (2000). A prospective longitudinal study of the relationship of psychological work to duration of survival in patients with metastatic cancer. *Psychooncology, 9,* 323-329.

Cunningham, A.J., Phillips, C., Lockwood, G.A., Hedley, D.W., & Edmonds, C.V. (2000). Association of involvement in psychological self-regulation with longer survival in patients with metastatic cancer: An exploratory study. *Advances in Mind and Body Medicine, 16,* 276-287.

Cunningham, J.A. (1999). Resolving alcohol-related problems with and without treatment. *Journal of Studies on Alcohol, 60,* 463-?

Cunningham, J.A., & Breslin, F.C. (2004). Only one in three people with alcohol abuse ever seek treatment. *Addictive Behaviors, 29,* 221-223.

Cunningham, J.A., Lin, E., Ross, H.E., & Walsh, G.E. (2000). Factors associated with untreated remissions from alcohol abuse or dependence. *Addictive Behaviors, 25,* 317-321.

Cunningham, J.A., Sobell, L.C., Gavin, D.R., Sobell, M.B., & Breslin, F.C. (1997). Assessing motivation for change: Preliminary development and evaluation of a scale measuring the costs and benefits of changing alcohol or drug use. *Psychology of Addictive Behaviors, 11,* 107-114.

Cunningham, J.A., Sobell, L.C., & Sobell, M.B. (1998). Awareness of self-change as a pathway to recovery for alcohol abusers: Results from five different groups. *Addictive Behaviors, 23,* 399-404.

Cunningham, P.J., & Mueller, C.D. (1991). Individuals with mental retardation in residential facilities: Findings from the 1987 National Medical Expenditure Survey. *American Journal on Mental Retardation, 96,* 109-117.

Currie, S.R., Nesbitt, K., Wood, C., & Lawson, A. (2003). Survey of smoking cessation services in Canadian addiction programs. *Journal of Substance Abuse Treatment, 24,* 59-65.

Curtin, J.J., Lang, A.R., Patrick, C.J., & Strizke, W.G.K. (1998). Alcohol and fear-potiantiated startle: The role of competing cognitive demands in the stress-reducing effects of intoxication. *Journal of Abnormal Psychology, 107,* 547-557.

Curtis, V.A., Bullmore, E.T., Bramer, M.J., Wright, I.C., Williams, S.C.R., et al. (1998). Attenuated frontal activation during a verbal fluency task in patients with schizophrenia. *American Journal of Psychiatry, 155,* 1056-1063.

Cyr, M., Wright, J., McDuff, P., & Perron, A. (2002). Intrafamilial sexual abuse: Brother-sister incest does not differ from father-daughter and stepfather-stepdaughter incest. *Child Abuse and Neglect, 26,* 957-973.

D'Arcy, R.C.N., & Connolly, J.F. (1999). An event-related brain potential study of receptive speech comprehension using a modified Token Test. *Neuropsychologia, 37,* 1477-1489.

D'Ercole, A., & Struening, E. (1990). Victimization among homeless women: Implications for service delivery. *Journal of Community Psychology, 18,* 141-152.

D'Zurilla, T.J. (1986). *Problem-solving therapy: A social competence approach to clinical intervention.* New York: Springer.

D'Zurilla, T.J. (1990). Problem-solving training for effective stress management and prevention. *Journal of Cognitive Psychotherapy: An International Quarterly, 4,* 327-355.

D'Zurilla, T.J., & Goldfried, M.R. (1971). Problem-solving and behavior modification. *Journal of Abnormal Psychology, 78,* 107-126.

D'Zurilla, T.J., & Sheedy, C.F. (1991). Relation between social problem-solving ability and subsequent level of psychological stress in college students. *Journal of Personality and Social Psychology, 61,* 841-846.

D'Zurilla, T.J., & Sheedy, C.F. (1992). The relation between social problem-solving ability and subsequent level of academic competence in college students. *Cognitive Therapy and Research, 16,* 589-599.

Da Costa, D., Larouche, J., Dritsa, M., & Brender, W. (2000). Psychosocial correlates of prepartum and postpartum depressed mood. *Journal of Affective Disorders, 59,* 31-40.

DaCosta, M., & Halmi, K.A. (1992). Classifications of anorexia nervosa: Question of subtypes. *International Journal of Eating Disorders, 11,* 305-313.

Dahmen, W., Hartje, W., Bussing, A., & Sturm, W. (1982). Disorders of calculation in aphasic patients-Spatial and verbal components. *Neuropsychologia, 20,* 145-153.

Daily, B. (1988). The roots of the problem in native communities. In T. Martens (Ed.), *The spirit weeps* (pp. 107-122). Edmonton, Alta : Nechi Institute.

Dallaire, R. (2003). *Shake hands with the devil: The failure of humanity in*

Rwanda. Toronto : Random House of Canada.

*Dana, (1998).

Daneman, E.A. (1961). Imipramine in office management of depressive reactions (a double-blind study). *Diseases of the Nervous System, 22,* 213-217.

Daniolos, P.T., & Holmes, V.F. (1995). HIV public policy and psychiatry: An examination of ethical issues and professional guidelines. *Psychosomatics, 36,* 12-21.

Dare, C., LeGrange, D., Eisler, I., & Rutherford, J. (1994). Redefining the psychosomatic family: Family process of 26 eating disordered families. *International Journal of Eating Disorders, 16,* 211-226.

Darou, W.G. (1992). Native Canadians and intelligence testing. *Canadian Journal of Counselling, 26,* 96-99.

Daubert, S.D., & Metzler, A.E. (2000). The detection of fake-bad and fake-good responding on the Millon Clinical Multiaxial Inventory III. *Psychological Assessment, 12,* 418-424.

Davies, P.T., & Cummings, E.M. (1994). Marital conflict and child adjustment: An emotional security hypothesis. *Psychological Bulletin, 116,* 387-411.

Davila, J., Hammen, C.L., Burge, D., Paley, B., & Daley, S.E. (1995). Poor interpersonal problem solving as a mechanism of stress generation in depression among adolescent women. *Journal of Abnormal Psychology, 104,* 592-600.

Davis, C. (1996). The interdependence of obsessive-compulsiveness, physical activity, and starvation: A model for anorexia nervosa. In W.F. Epling & W.D. Pierce (Eds.), *Activity nervosa: Theory, research, and treatment.* (pp. 209-218). Mahwah,NJ: Erlbaum.

Davis, C. (1997). Normal and neurotic perfectionism in eating disorders: An interactive model. *International Journal of Eating Disorders, 22,* 421-426.

Davis, C. Kaptein, S., Kaplan, A.S., Olmsted, M.P., & Woodside, D.B. (1998). Obsessionality in anorexia nervosa: The moderating influence of exercise. *Psychosomatic Medicine, 60,* 192-197.

Davis, C., Shuster, B., Blackmore, E., & Fox, J. (2004). Looking good: Family focus on appearance and the risk for eating disorders. *International Journal of Eating Disorders, 35,* 136-144.

Davis, J.M. (1978). Dopamine theory of schizophrenia: A two-factor theory. In L.C. Wynne, R.L. Cromwell, & S. Matthysse (Eds.), *The nature of schizophrenia.* New York: Wiley.

Davis, K.L., Kahn, R.S., Ko, G., & Davidson, M. (1991). Dopamine and schizophrenia: A review and reconceptualization. *American Journal of Psychiatry, 148,* 1474-1486.

Davis, R., Freeman, R. J., & Garner, D. M. (1988). A naturalistic investigation of eating behavior in bulimia nervosa. *Journal of Consulting and Clinical Psychology, 56,* 273-279.

Davis, R., Olmsted, M., Rockert, W. Marques, & Dolhanty, J. (1997). Group psychoeducation for bulimia nervosa with and without additional psychotherapy process sessions. *International Journal of Eating Disorders, 22,* 25-34.

Davison, E.H. (1996). Women and aging. Unpublished manuscript, University of California at Santa Barbara.

Davison, E. H. (1999). The interrelationships among subjective well-being, gender role flexibility, perceived sexism, and perceived ageism in older women. Unpublished dissertation, University of California at Santa Barbara.

Davison, G.C. (1964). A social learning therapy programme with an autistic child. *Behaviour Research and Therapy, 2,* 146-159.

Davison, G.C. (1966). Differential relaxation and cognitive restructuring in therapy with a "paranoid schizophrenic" or "paranoid state." *Proceedings of the 74th Annual Convention of the American Psychological Association.* Washington, DC: American Psychological Association.

Davison, G.C. (1968a). Elimination of a sadistic fantasy by a client-controlled counterconditioning technique. *Journal of Abnormal Psychology, 73,* 84-90.

Davison, G.C. (1968b). Systematic desensitization as a counterconditioning process. *Journal of Abnormal Psychology, 73,* 91-99.

Davison, G.C. (1973). Counter countrol in behavior modification. In L.A. Hamerlynck, L.C. Handy, & E.J. Mash (Eds.), *Behavior change: Methodology, concepts and practice.* Champaign, IL: Research Press.

Davison, G.C. (1974). *Homosexuality: The ethical challenge.* Presidential address to the Eighth Annual Convention of the Association for Advancement of Behavior Therapy, Chicago.

Davison, G.C. (1976). Homosexuality: The ethical challenge. *Journal of Consulting and Clinical Psychology, 44,* 157-162.

Davison, G.C. (1978). Not can but ought: The treatment of homosexuality. *Journal of Consulting and Clinical Psychology, 46,* 170-172.

Davison, G.C. (1991). Constructionism and therapy for homosexuality. In J. Gonsiorek & J. Weinrich (Eds.), *Homosexuality: Research findings for public policy.* Newbury Park, CA: Sage.

Davison, G.C. (2000). Stepped care: Doing more with less? *Journal of Consulting and Clinical Psychology, 68,* 580-585.

Davison, G.C., & Darke, L. (1991). Managing pain. In R. Bjork & D. Druckman (Eds.), *In the mind's eye: Understanding the basis of human performance.* Washington, DC: National Academy Press.

Davison, G.C., Feldman, P.M., & Osborn, C.E. (1984). Articulated thoughts, irrational beliefs, and fear of negative evaluation. *Cognitive Therapy and Research, 8,* 349-362.

Davison, G.C., Haaga, D.A., Rosenbaum, J., Dolezal, S.L., & Weinstein, K.A. (1991). Assessment of self-efficacy in articulated thoughts: "States of Mind" analysis and association with speech anxious behavior. *Journal of Cognitive Psychotherapy: An International Quarterly, 5,* 83-92.

Davison, G.C., & Lazarus, A.A. (1995). The dialectics of science and practice. In S.C. Hayes, V.M. Follette, T. Risley, R.D. Dawes, & K. Grady (Eds.), *Scientific standards of psychological practice: Issues and recommendations* (pp. 95-120). Reno, NV: Context Press.

Davison, G.C., Navarre, S.G., & Vogel, R.S. (1995). The articulated thoughts in simulated situations paradigm: A think-aloud approach to cognitive assessment. *Current Directions in Psychological Science, 4,* 29-33.

Davison, G.C., & Neale, J.M. (1996). *Abnormal psychology.* Revised sixth edition. New York: Wiley.

Davison, G.C., Robins, C., & Johnson, M.K. (1983). Articulated thoughts during simulated situations: A paradigm for studying cognition in emotion and behavior. *Cognitive Therapy and Research, 7,* 17-40.

Davison, G.C., Tsujimoto, R.N., & Glaros, A.G. (1973). Attribution and the maintenance of behavior change in falling asleep. *Journal of Abnormal Psychology, 82,* 124-133.

Davison, G.C., Williams, M.E., Nezami, E., Bice, T.L., & DeQuattro, V. (1991). Relaxation, reduction in angry articulated thoughts, and improvements in borderline essential hypertension and heart rate. *Journal of Behavioral Medicine, 14,* 453-468.

Davison, G.C., & Wilson, G.T. (1973). Attitudes of behavior therapists toward homosexuality. *Behavior Therapy, 4,* 686-696.

Davison, G.C., & Zighelboim, V. (1987). Irrational beliefs in the articulated thoughts of college students with social anxiety. *Journal of Rational-Emotive Therapy, 5,* 238-254.

Dawes, R.M. (1994). *House of cards: Psychology and psychotherapy built on myth.* New York: Free Press.

Dawson, G., & Lewy, A. (1989). Reciprocal subcortical-cortical influences in autism. In G. Dawson (Ed.), *Autism: Nature, diagnosis, and treatment* (pp. 144-173). New York: Guilford.

Dedobbeleer, N., Beland, F., Contandriopoulos, A-P., & Adrian, M. (2004). Gender and the social context of smoking behaviour. *Social Science and Medicine, 58,* 1-12.

Deep, A.L., Lilenfeld, L.R., Plotnicov, K.H., Pollice, C., & Kaye, W.H. (1999). Sexual abuse in eating disorder subtypes and control women: The role of cormorbid substance dependence in bulimia nervosa. *International Journal of Eating Disorders, 25,* 1-10.

DeGroot, J. M., Kennedy, S., Rodin, G., & McVey, G. (1992). Correlates of sexual abuse in women with anorexia nervosa and bulimia nervosa. *Canadian Journal of Psychiatry, 37,* 516-518.

DeJong, W., & Kleck, R.E. (1986). The social psychological effects of overweight. In C.P. Herman, M.P. Zanna, & E.T. Higgins (Eds.), *Physical appearance, stigma, and social behavior.* Hillside, NJ: Erlbaum.

DeKeseredy, W. S., Schwartz, M. D., & Tait, K. (1993). Sexual assault and stranger aggression on a Canadian university campus. *Sex Roles, 28,* 263-277.

Delgado, P.L., Charney, D.S., Price, L.H., Aghajanian, G.K., Landis, H., et al. (1990). Serotonin function and the mechanism of antidepressant action: Reversal of antidepressant induced remission by rapid depletion of plasma tryptophan. *Archives of General Psychiatry, 47,* 411-418.

deLint, J. (1978). Alcohol consumption and alcohol problems from an epidemiological perspective. *British Journal of Alcohol and Alcoholism, 17,*

109-116.

DeLongis, A., Coyne, J.C., Dakof, G., Folkman, S., & Lazarus, R.S. (1982). Relationship of daily hassles, uplifts, and major life events to health status. *Health Psychology*, *1*, 119-136.

DeLongis, A., Folkman, S., & Lazarus, R.S. (1988). The impact of daily stress on health and mood: Psychological and social resources as mediators. *Journal of Personality and Social Pscyhology*, *54*, 486-495.

DeMarco, R.R. (2000). The epidemiology of major depression: Implications of occurrence, recurrence, and stress in a Canadian community sample. *Canadian Journal of Psychiatry*, *45*, 67-74.

Dement, W.C., Laughton, E., & Carskadon, M.A. (1981). "White paper" on sleep and aging. *Journal of the American Geriatrics Society, 30,* 25-50.

Demers, A., Bisson, J., & Palluy, J. (1999). Wives' convergence with their husbands' alcohol use: Social conditions as mediators. *Journal of Studies on Alcohol*, *60*, 368-377.

Demers, A., Kairouz, S., Adlaf, E.M., Gliksman, L., Newton-Taylor, B., & Marchand, A. (2002). Multilevel analysis of situational drinking among Canadian undergraduates. *Social Science and Medicine*, *55*, 415-424.

Denihan, A., Kirby, M., Bruce, I., Cunningham, C., Coakley, D., & Lawlor, B. A. (2000). Three-year prognosis of depression in the community-dwelling elderly. *British Journal of Psychiatry*, *176*, 453-457.

Dennis, C-L. (2003). The effect of peer support on postpartum depression: A pilot randomized controlled trial. *Canadian Journal of Psychiatry*, *48*, 115-124.

Dennis, M., Lockyer, L., Lazenby, A. L., Donnelly, R. E., Wilkinson, M., & Schoonheyt. (1999). Intelligence patterns among children with high-functioning autism, phenylketonuria, and childhood head injury. *Journal of Autism and Developmental Disorders, 29,* 5-16.

Denollet, J., & Brutsaert, D.L. (1998). Personality, disease severity, and the risk of long-term cardiac events in patients with a decreased ejection fraction after myocardial infarction. *Circulation, 97,* 167-173.

Denton, (2000). From humane care to prevention. *Canadian Journal of Community Mental Health, 19,* 127-134.

Denton, M., & Walters, V. (1999). Gender differences in structural and behavioral determinants of health: An analysis of the social production of health. *Social Science and Medicine*, *48*, 1221-1235.

Depression Guideline Panel. (1997). *Depression in primary care: Detection and diagnosis.* Rockville, MD: U.S. Department of Health and Human Services.

Derevensky, J. L., & Gupta, R. (2000). Prevalence estimates of adolescent gambling: A comparison of the SOGS-RA, DSM-IV-J, and the G. A. 20 questions. *Journal of Gambling Studies, 16, (2/3),* 227-251.

Derry, P.H., & Kuiper, N.A. (1981). Schematic processing and self-reference in clinical depression. *Journal of Abnormal Psychology*, *90*, 286-297.

Dershowitz, A. (1994a, May 15). "Abuse Excuse" du jour victimizes many. *Los Angeles Times*, B5.

Dershowitz, A. (1994b). *The abuse excuse and other cop-outs, sob stories, and evasions of responsibility.* Boston: Little Brown.

DeRubeis, R.J., & Crits-Christoph, P. (1998). Empirically supported individual and group psychological treatments for adult mental disorders. *Journal of Consulting and Clinical Psychology, 66,* 37-52.

DeRubeis, R.J., Gelfand, L.A., Tang, T.Z., & Simons, A.D. (1999). Medications versus cognitive behavior therapy for severely depressed outpatients: MegaAnalysis of four randomized comparisons. *American Journal of Psychiatry, 156,* 1007-1013.

DeRubeis, R.J., Hollon, S.D., Evans, M.D., & Bemis, K.M. (1982). Can psychotherapies for depression be discriminated? A systematic investigation of cognitive therapy and interpersonal therapy. *Journal of Consulting and Clinical Psychology, 50,* 744-760.

Dery, M., Toupin, J., Pauze, R., Mercier, H., & Fortin, L. (1999). Neuropsychological characteristics of adolescents with conduct disorder: Association with attention-deficit-hyperactivity and aggression. *Journal of Abnormal Child Psychology*, *27*, 225-236.

Dessaulles, A., Johnson, S.M., & Denton, W.H. (2003). Emotion-focused therapy for couples in the treatment of depression: A pilot study. *The American Journal of Family Therapy*, *31*, 345-353.

Detterman, D.K. (1979). Memory in the mentally retarded. In N.R. Ellis (Ed.), *Handbook of mental deficiency, psychological theory and research* (2nd ed.). Hillsdale, NJ: Erlbaum.

Deutsch, A. (1949). *The mentally ill in America.* New York: Columbia University Press.

Devanand, D.P., Dwork, A.J., Hutchinson, E.R., Bolwig, T.G., & Sackeim, H.A. (1994). Does ECT alter brain structure? *American Journal of Psychiatry, 151,* 957-970.

Devine, V., Adelson, R., Goldstein, J., Valins, S., & Davison, G.C. (1974). Controlled test of the analgesic and relaxant properties of nitrous oxide. *Journal of Dental Research, 53,* 486-490.

DeVries, H.A. (1975). Physiology of exercise and aging. In D.S. Woodruff & J.E. Birren (Eds.), *Aging: Scientific perspectives and social issues.* New York: Van Nostrand-Reinhold.

Dew, M.A., Bromet, E.J., Brent, D., & Greenhouse, J.B. (1987). A quantitative literature review of the effectiveness of suicide prevention centers. *Journal of Consulting and Clinical Psychology, 55,* 239-244.

Dewar, K.M., & Stravynski, A. (2001). The quest for biological correlates of social phobia: An interitem assessment. *Acta Psychiatrica Scandinavica*, *103*, 244-251.

Dewit, D.J., Hance, J., Offord, D.R., & Ogborne, A. (2000). The influence of early and frequent use of marijuana on the risk of desistance and of progression to marijuana-related harm. *Preventive Medicine*, *31*, 455-464.

DeWit, D.J., Ogborne, A., Offord, D.R., & Macdonald, K. (1999). Antecedents of the risk of recovery from DSM-III-R social phobia. *Psychological Medicine*, *29*, 569-582.

Dewys, W.D., Begg, C., & Lavin, P.T. (1980). Prognostic effect of weight loss prior to chemotherapy in cancer patients. *American Journal of Medicine, 69,* 491-497.

Diaferia, P., Bianchi, I., Bianchi, M.L., Cavedini, P., et al. (1997). Relationship beteewn obsessive-compulsive personality disorder and obsessive-compulsive disorder. *Comprehensive Psychiatry, 38,* 38-42.

Diamond, S., Baldwin, R., & Diamond, R. (1963). *Inhibition and choice.* New York: Harper & Row.

Dickey, C.C., McCarley, R.W., Volgmaier, M.M., Niznikiewicz, M.A., Seidman, L.J., et al. (1999). Schizotypal personality disorder and MRI abnormalities of temporal grey matter. *Biological Psychiatry, 45,* 1392-1402.

Dickin, K.L., & Ryan, B.A. (1983, March). Sterilization and the mentally retarded. *Canada's Mental Health*, *31*, 4-8.

Dickson, L.M., Derevensky, J.L., & Gupta, R. (2002). The prevention of gambling problems in youth: A conceptual framework. *Journal of Gambling Studies*, *18*, 97-159.

DiClemente, C.C. (1993). Changing addictive behaviors: A process perspective. *Current Directions in Psychological Science, 2,* 101-106.

Diefenbach, G.J., Stanley, M.A., & Beck, J.G. (2001). Worry content reported by older adults with and without generalized anxiety disorder. *Aging and Mental Health*, *5*, 269-274.

Dietz, P.E., Hazelwood, R.R., & Warren, J. (1990). The sexually sadistic criminal and his offenses. *Bulletin of the American Academy of Psychiatry and the Law, 18,* 163-178.

DiFranza, J.R., Richards, J.W., Paulman, P.M., Wolf-Gillespie, N., Fletcher, C., et al. (1991). RJR Nabisco's cartoon camel promotes Camel cigarettes to children. *Journal of the American Medical Association, 266,* 3149-3153.

DiMascio, A., Weissman, M.M., Prusoff, B.A., Neu, C., Zwilling, M., & Klerman, G.L. (1979). Differential symptom reduction by drugs and psychotherapy in acute depression. *Archives of General Psychiatry, 36,* 1450-1456.

DiNardo, P.A., Guzy, L.T., Jenkins, J.A., Bak, R.M., Tomasi, S.F., & Copland, M. (1988). Etiology and maintenance of dog fears. *Behaviour Research and Therapy, 26,* 241-244.

DiNardo, P.A., O'Brien, G.T., Barlow, D.H., Waddell, M.T., & Blanchard, E.B. (1993). Reliability of the DSM-III-R anxiety disorders categories using the Anxiety

Disorders Interview Schedule-Revised (ADIS-R). *Archives of General Psychiatry, 50,* 251-256.

Dion, K.L., Dion, K.K., & Pak, A. (1992). Personality-based hardiness as a buffer for discrimination-related stress in members of Toronto's Chinese community. *Canadian Journal of Behavioural Science, 24,* 517-536.

Dixon, L., Scott, J., Lyles, A., Fahey, A., Skinner, A., & Shore, A. (1997). Adherence to schizophrenia PORT family treatment recommendations. *Schizophrenia Research, 24,* 221

Dobson, K.S. (1986). The self-schema in depression. In L. M. Hartmann & K.

R. Blankstein (Eds.), *Perception of self in emotional disorders and psychotherapy* (pp. 187-217). New York: Plenum Press.

Dobson, K.S. (1989). A meta-analysis of the efficacy of cognitive therapy for depression. *Journal of Consulting and Clinical Psychology, 57,* 414-419.

Dobson, K.S., Dobson, D.J.G., & Ritchie, P.L.-J. (1993). Professional psychology in Canada: Present status and future promises. In K. G. Dobson & D. J. G. Dobson (Eds.), *Professional psychology in Canada* (pp. 433-454). Toronto: Hogrefe and Huber.

Dobson, K.S., & Dozois, D.J.A. (2001). Historical and philosophical bases of the cognitive-behavioral therapies. In K.S. Dobson (Ed.), *Handbook of cognitive-behavioral therapies, 2nd ed.* (pp. 3-39). New York: Guilford Press.

Dobson, K.S., & Hamilton, K.E. (2002). The stage model for psychotherapy manual development: A valuable tool for promoting evidence-based practice. *Clinical Psychology: Science and Practice*, *9*, 407-409.

Dobson, K.S., & Jackman-Cram, S. (1996). Common change processes in cognitive-behavioral therapies. In K.S. Dobson & K.D. Craig (Eds.), *Advances in cognitive-behavioral therapy*. (pp. 63-82). Thousand Oaks, CA: Sage Publications.

Dobson, K.S., & Khatri, N. (2000). Cognitive therapy: Looking forward, looking backward. *Journal of Clinical Psychology*, *56*, 907-923.

Dobson, K. S., & Pusch, D. (1993). Towards a definition of the conceptual and empirical boundaries of cognitive therapy. *Australian Psychologist, 28,* 137-144.

Dobson, K.S., & Shaw, B.F. (1986). Cognitive assessment with major depressive disorders. *Cognitive Therapy and Research, 10,* 13-29.

Dodge, K.A., & Coie, J.D. (1987). Social information-processing factors in reactive and proactive aggression in children's peer groups. *Journal of Personality and Social Psychology, 53,* 1146-1158.

Dodge, K.A., & Frame, C.L. (1982). Social cognitive biases and deficits in aggressive boys. *Child Development, 53,* 620-635.

Dodge, K.A., & Pettit, G.S. (2003). A biopsychosocial model of the development of chronic conduct problems in adolescence. *Developmental Psychology*, *39*, 349-371.

Doerr, P., Fichter, M., Pirke, K.M., & Lund, R. (1980). Relationship between weight gain and hypothalamic-pituitary-adrenal function in patients with anorexia nervosa. *Journal of Steroid Biochemistry, 13,* 529-537.

Dohrenwend, B.P., Levav, P.E., Schwartz, S., Naveh, G., Link, B.G., Skodol, A.E., & Stueve, A. (1992). Socioeconomic status and psychiatric disorders: The causation-selection issue. *Science, 255,* 946-952.

Doidge, N. (1999). Who is in psychoanalysis now? Empirical data and reflection on some common misperceptions. In H. Kaley, M. N. Eagle, & D. L. Wolitzky (Eds.), *Psychoanalytic therapy as health care: Effectiveness and economics in the 21st century* (pp. 177-198). Hillsdale, NJ: The Analytic Press.

Doidge, N., Simon, B., Brauer, L. et al. (2002). Psychoanalytic patients in the U.S., Canada, and Australia: I. DSM-III-R disorders, indications, previous treatment, medications, and length of treatment. *Journal of the American Psychoanalytic Association*, *50*, 575-614.

Doidge, N., Simon, B., Gillies, L. A., & Ruskin, R. (1994). Characteristics of psychoanalytic patients under a nationalized health plan: DSM-III-R diagnoses, previous treatment and childhood trauma. *American Journal of Psychiatry, 151,* 586-590.

Doidge, N., Simon, B., Lancee, W.J., et al. (2002). Psychoanalytic patients in the U.S., Canada, and Australia: II. A DSM-III-R validation study. *Journal of the American Psychoanalytic Association*, *50*, 615-627.

Doiron, J. P., & Nicki, R. M. (2001). Epidemiology of problem gambling in Prince Edward Island: A Canadian microcosm? *Canadian Journal of Psychiatry, 46,* 413-417.

Dolan, B. (1991). Cross-cultural aspects of anorexia and bulimia: A review. *International Journal of Eating Disorders, 10,* 67-78.

Dollard, J., & Miller, N.E. (1950). *Personality and psychotherapy*. New York: McGraw-Hill.

Dongier, M. (1999). In memoriam—Heinz E. Lehmann, 1911-1999. *Journal of Psychiatry and Neuroscience, 24,* 362.

Dorian, B. J., & Garfinkel, P. E. (1999). The contributions of epidemiologic studies to the etiology and treatment of the eating disorders. *Psychiatric Annals*, *29*, 187-192.

Doucet, C., Ladouceur, R., Freeston, M. H., & Dugas, M. J. (1998). Worry themes and the tendency to worry in older adults. *Canadian Journal on Aging*, *17*, 361-371.

Dougher, M.J. (1988). Clinical assessment of sex offenders. In B.K. Schwartz (Ed.), *A practitioner's guide to treating the incarcerated male sex offender* (pp. 77-84). Washington, DC: U.S. Department of Justice.

Douglas, K.S., & Koch, W.J. (2001). Civil commitment and civil competence: Psychological issues. In R. A. Schuller & J. R. Ogloff (Eds.), *Introduction to psychology and law: Canadian perspectives* (pp. 351-374). Toronto: University of Toronto Press.

Dennis, M., Lockyer, L., Lazenby, A.L., Donnelly, R.E., Wilkinson, M., & Schoonheyt, W. (1999). Intelligence patterns among children with high-functioning autism, phenylketonuria, and childhood head injury. *Journal of Autism and Developmental Disorders*, *29*, 5-17.

Doiron, J.P., & Nicki, R.M. (2001). Epidemiology of problem gambling in Prince Edward Island: A Canadian microcosm? *Canadian Journal of Psychiatry*, *46*, 413-417.

Douglas, K.S., Ogloff, J.R.P., & Hart, S.D. (2003). Evaluation of a model of violence risk assessment among forensic psychiatric patients. *Psychiatric Services*, *54*, 1372-1379.

Douglas, K.S., & Webster, C.D. (1999). The HCR-20 violence risk assessment scheme: Concurrent validity in a sample of incarcerated offenders. *Criminal Justice and Behavior, 26*, 3-19.

Douglas, V.I. (1972). Stop, look, and listen—The problem of sustained attention and impulse control in hyperactive and normal children. *Canadian Journal of Behavioural Science*, *4*, 259-282.

Douglas, V.I. (1999). Cognitive control processes in attention-deficit/hyperactivity disorder. In H. C. Quay & A. E. Hogan (Eds.), *Handbook of disruptive behavior disorders* (pp. 105-138). New York: Kluwer Academic/Plenum Publishers.

Dowd, J.J., & Bengston, V.L. (1978). Aging in minority populations: An examination of the double jeopardy hypothesis. *Journal of Gerontology, 33,* 427-436.

Dowson, J.H. (1992). Associations between self-induced vomiting and personality disorder in patients with a history of anorexia nervosa. *Acta Psychiatrica Scandinavica, 86,* 399-404.

Doyle, A.B. (1998). Are empirically validated treatments valid with culturally diverse populations? In K.S. Dobson & K.D. Craig (Eds.), *Best practice: Developing and promoting empirically validated interventions* (pp. 93-103). Newbury Park, CA: Sage.

Doze, S., Simpson, J., Hailey, D., & Jacobs, P. (1999). Evaluation of a telepsychiatry pilot project. *Journal of Telemedicine and Telecare*, *5*, 38-46.

Dozois, D.J.A. (2002). Cognitive organization of self-schematic content in nondysphoric, mildly dysphoric, and moderately-severely dysphoric individuals. *Cognitive Therapy and Research*, *26*, 417-429.

Dozois, D.J.A., & Backs-Dermott, B.J. (2000). Sociotropic personality and information processing following imaginal priming: A test of the congruency hypothesis. *Canadian Journal of Behavioural Science*, *32*, 117-126.

Dozois, D.J.A., & Dobson, K.S. (2001). Information processing and cognitive organization in unipolar depression: Specificity and comorbidity issues. *Journal of Abnormal Psychology*, *110*, 236-246.

Draguns, J.G. (1989). Normal and abnormal behavior in cross-cultural perspective: Specifying the nature of their relationships. In J.J. Berman (Ed.), *Nebraska symposium on motivation*. Lincoln: University of Nebraska Press.

Drummond, T. (1999, June 7). Never too old: Sexually active seniors are one of the fastest-growing HIV-infected populations in the U.S. *Time Magazine*, p. 84H.

Dubbert, P. (1995). Behavioral (life style) modification in the prevention and treatment of hypertension. *Clinical Psychology Review, 15,* 187-216.

Duck, S. (1984). *A perspective on the repair of personal relationships. In S. Duck (Ed.), Personal relationships: 5. Repairing personal relationships.* New York: Academic Press.

Duffy, A., Alda, M., Kutcher, S., Cavazzoni, P., Robertson, C., Grof, E., & Grof, P. (2002). A prospective study of the offspring of bipolar parents responsive and nonresponsive to lithium treatment. *Journal of Clinical Psychiatry*, *63*, 1171-1178.

Dugas, M.J., Freeston, M.H., & Ladouceur, R. (1997). Intolerance of uncertainty and problem orientation in worry. *Cognitive Therapy and Research*, *21*, 593-606.

Dugas, M J., Gagnon, F., Ladouceur, R., & Freeston, M.H. (1998). Generalized anxiety disorder: A preliminary test of a conceptual model. *Behaviour Research and Therapy*, *36*, 215-226.

Dugas, M.J., Ladouceur, R., Leger, E., Freeston, M.H., Langlois, F., Provencher, M.D., & Boisvert, J-M. (2003). Group cognitive-behavioral therapy for generalized anxiety disorder: Treatment outcome and long-term follow-up. *Journal of Consulting and Clinical Psychology*, *71*, 821-825.

Duggan, C.E., Marks, I., & Richards, D. (1993). Clinical audit of behavior therapy training of nurses. *Health Trends, 25,* 25-30.

Duggan, C.F., Lee, A.S., & Murray, R.M. (1991). Do different subtypes of hospitalized depressives have different long term outcomes? *Archives of General Psychiatry, 48,* 308-312.

Duman, R.S., Heninger, G.R., & Nestler, E.J. (1997). A molecular and cellular theory of depression. *Archives of General Psychiatry, 54,* 597-606.

Dumont, M. (2000). Experience du stress a l'adolescence. *International Journal of Psychology*, *35*, 194-206.

Dumont, M., & Provost, M.A. (1999). Resilience in adolescents: Protective role of social support, coping strategies, self-esteem, and social activities on experience of stress and depression. *Journal of Youth and Adolescence*, *28*, 343-361.

Dunham, H.W. (1965). *Community and schizophrenia: An epidemiological analysis*. Detroit: Wayne State University Press.

Dunkley, D.M., & Blankstein, K.R. (2000). Self-critical perfectionism, coping, hassles, and current distress: A structural equation modeling strategy. *Cognitive Therapy and Research, 24,* 713-730.

Dunkley, D.M., Blankstein, K.R., Halsall, J., Williams, M., & Winkworth, G. (2000). The relation between perfectionism and distress: Hassles, coping, and perceived social support as mediators and moderators. *Journal of Counseling Psychology*, *47*, 437-453.

Dunkley, D. M., Blankstein, K. R., Zuroff, D. C., Lecce, S., & Hui, D. (2004). Maladaptive and more adaptive components of relatedness located in the five-factor model of personality. [Manuscript submitted].

Dunkley, D.M., Zuroff, D.C., & Blankstein, K.R. (2003). Self-critical perfectionism and daily affect: Dispositional and situational influences on stress and coping. *Journal of Personality and Social Psychology*, *84*, 234-252.

Dunn, A.L., Marcus, B.H., Kampert, J.B., Garcia, M.E., et al. (1999). Comparison of lifestyle and structured interventions to increase physical activity and cardiorespiratory fitness. *JAMA, 281,* 327-324.

DuPaul, G.J. (1991). Parent and teacher ratings of ADHD symptoms: Psychometric properties in a community-based sample. *Journal of Clinical Child Psychology, 20,* 245-253.

DuPaul, G.J. & Henningson, P.N. (1993). Peer tutoring effects on the classroom performance of children with attention deficit hyperactivity disorder. *School Psychology Review, 22,* 134-143.

Duquette, A. (2001, February 2). *Living with agoraphobia*. (Atlantic Journalism Awards) www.aja.kings.ns.ca.

Dura, J.R., Stukenberg, K.W., & Kiecolt-Glaser, J.K. (1991). Anxiety and depressive disorders in adult children caring for demented parents. *Psychology and Aging, 6,* 467-473.

Durkheim, E. (1951). *Suicide*. (J.A. Spaulding & G. Simpson, Trans.). New York: Free Press. (Original work published 1897; 2nd ed., 1930)

Durkin, K.L. (1997). Misuse of the internet by pedophiles: Implications for law enforcement and and probation practice. *Federal Probation, 61,* 14-18.

Dutton, D.G. (1994a). Behavioral and affective correlates of borderline personality organization in wife assaulters. *International Journal of Law and Psychiatry*, *17*, 265-277.

Dutton, D.G. (1994b). The origin and structure of the abusive personality. *Journal of Personality Disorders*, *8*, 181-191.

Dutton, D.G. (1995). *The batterer: A psychological profile*. New York: Basic Books.

Dutton, D.G. (1999). Traumatic origins of intimate rage. *Aggression and Violent Behavior*, *4*, 431-447.

Dutton, D.G., Bodnarchuk, M., Kropp, R., Hart, S.D., & Ogloff, J.P. (1997). Client personality disorders affecting wife assault post-treatment recidivism. *Violence and Victims*, *12*, 37-50.

Dutton, D.G., & Starzomski, A.J. (1993). Borderline personality in perpetrators of physical and psychological abuse. *Violence and Victims*, *8*, 327-337.

Dutton, D.G., & Starzomski, A.J. (1994). Psychological differences between court-referred and self-referred wife assaulters. *Criminal Justice and Behavior*, *21*, 203-222.

Dwork, A.J. (1997). Postmortem studies of the hippocampal formation in schizophrenia. *Schizophrenia Bulletin, 23,* 385-402.

Dworkin, R.H., & Lenzenwenger, M.F. (1984). Symptoms and the genetics of schizophrenia: Implications for diagnosis. *American Journal of Psychiatry, 141,* 1541-1546.

Dworkin, R.H., Lenzenwenger, M.F., & Moldin, S.O. (1987). Genetics and the phenomenology of schizophrenia. In P.D. Harvey and E.F. Walker (Eds.), *Positive and negative symptoms of psychosis*. Hillsdale, NJ: Erlbaum.

Dyck, R.J., & White, J. (1998). Suicide prevention in Canada: Work in progress. In A. A. Leenaars, S. Wenckstern, I. Sakinofsky, R. J. Dyck, M. J. Kral, & R. C. Bland (Eds.), *Suicide in Canada* (pp. 256-274). Toronto: University of Toronto Press.

Dykens, E., Leckman, J., Paul, R., & Watson, M. (1988). Cognitive, behavioral, and adaptive functioning in fragile X and non-fragile A retarded men. *Journal of Autism and Developmental Disorders, 18,* 41-52.

Dysken, M.W. (1979). Clinical usefulness of sodium amobarbital interviewing. *Archives of General Psychiatry, 36,* 789-794.

Eagles, J.M., Johnston, M.I., Hunter, D., Lobban, M., & Millar, H.R. (1995). Increasing incidence of anorexia nervosa in the female population of northeast Scotland. *American Journal of Psychiatry, 152,* 1266-1271.

Eaker, E.D., Pinsky, J., & Castelli, W.P. (1992). Myocardial infarction and coronary death among women: Psychosocial predictors from a 20 year follow-up of women in the Framingham study. *American Journal of Epidemiology, 135,* 854-864.

Earleywine, M., & Gann, M.K. (1995). Challenging recovered memories in the courtroom. In J. Ziskin (Ed.), *Coping with psychiatric and psychological testimony* (pp. 1100-1134). Los Angeles: Law and Psychology Press.

Earls, C.M., & Lalumiere, M.L. (2002). A case study of preferential bestiality (zoophilia). *Sexual Abuse*, *14*, 83-88.

Eastwood, M.R., Corbin, S., Reed, M., Nobbs, H., & Kedward, M.B. (1985). Acquired hearing loss and psychiatric illness: An estimate of prevalence and co-morbidity in a geriatric setting. *British Journal of Psychiatry, 147,* 552.

Eaton, J.W., & Weil, R.J. (1953). The mental health of the Hutterites. *Scientific American*, *189*, 31-37.

Eaton, W.W., Kramer, M., Anthony, J.C., Dryman, A., Shapiro, S., et al. (1989). The incidence of specific DIS/DSM-III mental disorders: Data from the NIMH Epidemiologic Catchment Area Programs. *Acta Psychiatrica Scandinavica, 79,* 163-178.

Eaves, D., Lamb, D., & Tien, G. (2000). Forensic psychiatric services in British Columbia. *International Journal of Law and Psychiatry*, *23*, 615-631.

Ebly, E.M., Parhad, I.M., Hogan, D.B., & Fung, T.S. (1994). Prevalence and types of dementia in the very old: Results from the Canadian Study of Health and Aging. *Neurology*, *44*, 1593-1600.

Eccleston, C. (1995). Chronic pain and distraction: An experimental investigation into the role of sustained and shifting attention in the processing of chronic persistent pain. *Behaviour Research and Therapy, 33,* 391-406.

Eckhardt, C.I., Barbour, K.A., & Stuart, G.L. (1997). Anger and hostility in maritally violent men: Conceptual distinctions, measurement issues, and literature review. *Clinical Psychology Review, 17,* 333-358.

Edelbrock, C., Rende, R., Plomin, T., & Thompson, L.A. (1995). A twin study of competence and problem behavior in childhood and early adolescence. *Journal of Child Psychology and Psychiatry and Allied Disciplines, 36,* 775-789.

Eden, G. F., & Zeffiro, T. A. (1996). PET and fMRI in the detection of task-related brain activity: Implications for the study of brain development. In R.W. Thatcher & G.R. Lyon (Eds.), *Developmental neuroimaging: Mapping the development of brain and behavior*. (pp. 77-90). San Diego, CA: Academic Press.

Editorial (2001, June 12). Door-to-door troubles in health care. *The Toronto Star,* p. A28.

Edmonds, C.V., Lockwood, G.A., & Cunningham, A.J. (1999). Psychological response to long-term group therapy: A randomized trial with metastatic breast cancer patients. *Psychooncology*, *8*, 74-91.

Edmunds, A. (1998). My story: Thoughts of a survivor. In A. A. Leenaars, S. Wenckstern, I. Sakinofsky, R. J. Dyck, M. J. Kral, & R. C. Bland (Eds.), *Suicide in Canada* (pp. 369—374). Toronto: University of Toronto Press.

Egan, G. (1975). *The skilled helper*. Monterey, CA: Brooks/Cole.

Egan, T. (1990). As memory and music faded, Alzheimer patient met death. The *New York Times*, 89, pp. A1, A16.

Egeland, J.A., Gerhard, D.S., Pauls, D.L., Sussex, J.N., Kidd, K.K., Allen, C.R., Hosterer, A.M., & Housman, D.E. (1987). Bipolar affective disorders linked to DNA markers on chromosome 11. *Nature, 325,* 783-787.

Ehlers, A., Mayou, R.A., & Bryant, B. (1998). Psychological predictors of chronic posttraumatic stress disorder after motor vehicle accidents. *Journal of Abnormal Psychology, 107,* 508-519.

Ehrhardt, A., & Money, J. (1967). Progestin-induced hermaphroditism: IQ and psychosexual identity in a study of ten girls. *Journal of Sex Research, 3,* 83-100.

Eiberg, H., Berendt, I., & Mohr, J. (1995). Assignment of dominant inherited nocturnal enuresis to chromosome 13Q. *Nature Genetics, 10,* 354-356.

Eich, E. (1995). Searching for mood-dependent memory. *Psychological Science, 6,* 67-75.

Eich, E., Macaulay, D., Loewenstein, R.J., & Dihle, P.H. (1997). Memory, identity, and dissociative identity disorder. *Psychological Science, 8,* 417-422.

Eisler, R.M., & Blalock, J.A. (1991). Masculine gender role stress: Implications for the assessment of men. *Clinical Psychology Review, 11,* 45-60.

Eissenberg, T., Bigelow, G.E., Strain, E.C., & Walsh, S.L. (1997). Dose-related efficacy of levomethadyl acetate for treatment of opioid dependence. *JAMA, 277,* 1945-1951.

Elgar, F.J., Curtis, L.J., McGrath, P.J., Waschbusch, D.A., & Stewart, S.H. (2003). Antecedent-consequence conditions in maternal mood and child adjustment: A four-year cross-lagged study. *Journal of Clinical Child and Adolescent Psychology, 32,* 362-374.

Elgar, F.J., McGrath, P.J., Waschbusch, D.A., Stewart, S.H., & Curtis, L.J. (2004). Mutual influences on maternal depression and child adjustment problems. *Clinical Psychology Review, 24,* 441-459.

Elgar, F.J., Waschbusch, D.A., McGrath, P.J., Stewart, S.H., & Curtis, L.J. (2004). Temporal relations in daily-reported maternal mood and disruptive child behavior. *Journal of Abnormal Child Psychology, 32,* 237-247.

Elias, M., & Clabby, J.F. (1989). *Social decision making skills: A curriculum for the elementary grades.* Rockville, MD: Aspen Publishers.

Elie, M., Cole, M.G., Primeau, F.J., & Bellavance F. (1998). Delirium risk factors in elderly hospitalized patients. *Journal of General Internal Medicine, 13,* 204-212.

Elie, M., Rousseau, F., Cole, M., Primeau, F., McCusker, J., & Bellavance, F. (2000). Prevalence and detection of delirium in elderly emergency department patients. *Canadian Medical Association Journal, 163,* 977-981.

Elkin, I. (1994). Treatment of Depression Collaborative Research Program: Where we began and where we are. In A.E. Bergin & S.L. Garfield (Eds.), *Handbook of psychotherapy and behavior change.* Fourth edition (pp. 114-139). New York: Wiley & Sons.

Elkin, I., Gibbons, R.D., Shea, M.T., & Shaw, B.F. (1996). Science is not a trial (but it can sometimes be a tribulation). *Journal of Consulting and Clinical Psychology, 64,* 92-103.

Elkin, I., Gibbons, R.D., Shea, M.T., Sotsky, S.M., Watkins, J.T., Pilkonis, P.A., & Hedeker, D. (1995). Initial severity and differential treatment outcome in the NIMH Treatment of Depression Collaborative Research Program. *Journal of Consulting and Clinical Psychology, 63,* 841-847.

Elkin, I., Parloff, M.B., Hadley, S.W., & Autry, J.H. (1985). NIMH Treatment of Depression Collaborative Research Program. *Archives of General Psychiatry, 42,* 305-316.

Elkin, I., Shea, M.T., Watkins, J.T., Imber, S.D., Sotsky, S.M., Collins, J.F., Glass, D.R., Pilkonis, P.A., Leber, W.R., Docherty, J.P., Fiester, S.J., & Parloff, M.B. (1989). NIMH Treatment of Depression Collaborative Research Program: 1. General effectiveness of treatments. *Archives of General Psychiatry, 46,* 971-983.

Elkin, I., Shea, T., Imber, S., Pilkonis, P., Sotsky, S., Glass, D., Watkins, J., Leber, W., & Collins, J. (1986). *NIMH Treatment of Depression Collaborative Research Program: Initial outcome findings.* Paper presented to the American Association for the Advancement of Science.

Elkis, H., Friedman, L., Wise, A., & Meltzer, H.T. (1995). Meta-analysis of studies of ventricular enlargement and cortical sulcal prominence in mood disorders. *Archives of General Psychiatry, 52,* 735-746.

Ellason, J.W., & Ross, C.A. (1997). Two-year follow-up of inpatients with dissociative identity disorder. *American Journal of Psychiatry, 154,* 832-839.

Ellenberger, H.F. (1972). The story of "Anna O": A critical review with new data. *Journal of the History of the Behavioral Sciences, 8,* 267-279.

Ellenbogen, M.A., & Hodgins, S. (2004). The impact of high neuroticism in parents on children's psychosocial functioning in a population at high risk for major affective disorder: A family-environment pathway of intergenerational risk. *Development and Psychopathology, 16,* 113-136.

Ellis, A. (1962). *Reason and emotion in psychotherapy.* New York: Lyle Stuart.

Ellis, A. (1984). Rational-emotive therapy. In R.J. Corsini (Ed.), *Current psychotherapies* (3rd ed.). Itasca, IL: Peacock Press.

Ellis, A. (1991). The revised ABC's of rational-emotive therapy (RET). *Journal of Rational-Emotive and Cognitive Behavior Therapy, 9,* 139-172.

Ellis, A. (1993a). Changing rational-emotive therapy (RET) to rational emotive behavior therapy (REBT). *the Behavior Therapist, 16,* 257-258.

Ellis, A. (1993b). Fundamentals of rational-emotive therapy for the 1990s. In W. Dryden & L. Hill (Eds.), *Innovations in rational-emotive therapy.* Newbury Park, CA: Sage.

Ellis, A. (2002). The role of irrational beliefs in perfectionism. In G. L. Flett & P. L. Hewitt (Eds.), *Perfectionism: Theory, research, and treatment* (pp. 217-229). Washington, DC: American Psychological Association.

Ellis, H. (1906). *Studies in the psychology of sex.* New York: Random House.

Ellis, H. (1910). *Studies in the psychology of sex.* Philadelphia: FA Davis.

Ellis, J.A. & Spanos, N.P. (1994). Cognitive-behavioral interventions for children's distress during bone marrow aspirations and lumbar punctures: A critical review. *Journal of Pain and Symptom Management, 9,* 96-108.

Ellis, N.R., Deacon, J.R., & Wooldridge, P.W. (1985). Structural memory deficits of mentally retarded persons. *American Journal of Mental Deficiency, 89,* 393-402.

Ellis, R.J., Jan, K., Kawas, C., Koller, W.C., Lyons, K.E., et al. (1998). Diagnostic validity of the Questionnaire for Alzheimer Disease. *Archives of Neurology, 55,* 360-365.

Elmore, A.M., & Tursky, B. (1978). The biofeedback hypothesis: An idea in search of a theory and method. In A.A. Sugerman & R.E. Tarter (Eds.), *Expanding dimensions of consciousness.* New York: Springer.

Elmore, J.L., & Sugerman, A.A. (1975). Precipitation of psychosis during electroshock therapy. *Diseases of the Nervous System, 3,* 115-117.

EMDR Institute (1995). *International EMDR conference: Research and clinical application.* Pacific Grove, CA: Author.

EMDR Institute (1998). Promotional advertisement. *APA Monitor, 28,* 65

Emery, R.E., & O'Leary, K.D. (1979). *Children's perceptions of marital discord and behavior problems of boys and girls.* Paper presented at the annual meeting of the Association for Advancement of Behavior Therapy, San Francisco.

Emmelkamp, P.M.G., et al. (2002). Virtual reality treatment versus exposure in vivo: A comparative evaluation in acrophobia. *Behaviour Research and Therapy, 40,* 509-516.

Emmelkamp, P.M.G., Visser, S., & Hoekstra, R.J. (1988). Cognitive therapy versus exposure in vivo in the treatment of obsessive-compulsives. *Cognitive Therapy and Research, 12,* 103-114.

Emmons, R.A., & Diener, E. (1986). Situation selection as a moderator of response consistency and stability. *Journal of Personality and Social Psychology, 51,* 1013-1019.

Emory, L.E., Williams, D.H., Cole, C.M., Amparo, E.G., & Meyer, W.J. (1991). Anatomic variation of the corpus callosum in persons with gender dysphoria. *Archives of Sexual Behavior, 20,* 409-417.

Emrick, C.D., Tonigan, J.S., Montgomery, H., & Little, L. (1993). Alcoholics Anonymous: What is currently known? In B.S. McCrady & W.R. Miller (Eds.), *Research on Alcoholics Anonymous: Opportunities and alternatives* (pp. 41-76). New Brunswick, NJ: Rutgers Center of Alcohol Studies.

Endler, N.S. (1982). *Holiday of darkness.* New York: Wiley.

Endler, N.S. (1983). Interactionism: A personality model, but not yet a theory. In M. M. Page (Ed.), *Nebraska Symposium on Motivation 1982: Personality—Current theory and research* (pp. 241-266). San Francisco, CA: Jossey Bass.

Endler, N.S. (1988). The origins of Electroconvulsive Therapy (ECT). *Convulsive Therapy, 4,* 5-23.

Endler, N.S. (2002). Multidimensional interactionism: Stress, anxiety, and coping. In L. Backman & R.C. von Hofsen (Eds.), *Psychological science 2000: Social, personality, and health perspectives* (Volume 2, pp. 281-304).

Brighton, UK: Taylor & Francis, Psychology Press.

Endler, N.S., Corace, K.M., Summerfeldt, L.J., Johnson, J.M., & Rothbart, P. (2003). Coping with chronic pain. *Personality and Individual Differences, 34*, 323-346.

Endler, N.S., Courbasson, C.M.A., & Fillion, L. (1998). Coping with cancer: The evidence for the temporal stability of the French Canadian version of the Coping With Health, Injuries, and Problems (CHIP). *Personality and Individual Differences, 25*, 711-717.

Endler, N.S., Crooks, D.S., & Parker, J.D.A. (1992). The interaction model of anxiety: An empirical test in a parachute jumping situation. *Anxiety, Stress and Coping, 5,* 301-311.

Endler, N.S., & Flett, G.L. (2003). *Endler Multidimensional Anxiety Scales (EMAS) - Social Anxiety Scales (SAS): Manual.* Los Angeles, CA: Western Psychological Services.

Endler, N.S., Flett, G.L., Macrodimitris, S., Corace, K., & Kocovski, N. (2002). Separation, self-disclosure, and social evaluation anxiety as facets of trait social anxiety. *European Journal of Personality, 16*, 239-269.

Endler, N.S., Kocovski, N.L., & Macrodimitris, S.D. (2001). Coping, efficacy, and perceived control in acute vs chronic illnesses. *Personality and Individual Differences, 30*, 617-625.

Endler, N.S., & Magnusson, D. (1976). Toward an interactional psychology of personality. *Psychological Bulletin, 83*, 956-979.

Endler, N.S., & Parker, J.D.A. (1990). *The Coping Inventory for Stressful Situations (CISS): Manual.* Toronto: Multi-Health Systems, Inc.

Endler, N.S., & Parker, J.D.A. (1994). Assessment of multidimensional coping: Task, emotion, and avoidance strategies. *Psychological Assessment, 6*, 50-60.

Endler, N.S., & Parker, J.D.A. (1999). *The Coping Inventory for Stressful Situations (CISS): Manual (2nd ed.).* Toronto: Multi-Health Systems, Inc.

Endler, N.S., & Parker, J.D.A. (2000). *Coping With Health, Injuries and Problems (CHIP): Manual.* Toronto: Multi-Health Systems, Inc.

Endler, N.S., Parker, J.D.A., & Summerfeldt, L.J. (1993). Coping with health problems: Conceptual and methodological issues. *Canadian Journal of Behavioural Science, 25*, 384-399.

Endler, N.S., & Persad, E. (1988). *Electroconvulsive therapy: The myths and the realities.* Toronto: Hans Huber Publishers.

Endler, N.S., Speer, R.L., Johnson, J.M., & Flett, G.L. (2000). Controllability, coping, efficacy, and distress. *European Journal of Personality, 14*, 245-264.

Engdahl, B., Dikel, T.N., Eberly, R., & Blank, A. (1997). Posttraumatic stress disorder in a community group of former prisoners of war: A normative response to severe trauma. *American Journal of Psychiatry, 154,* 1576-1581.

Engels, G.I., Garnefski, N., & Diekstra, R.F.W. (1993). Efficacy of rational-emotive therapy: A quantitative analysis. *Journal of Consulting and Clinical Psychology, 61,* 1083-1090.

English, H.B. (1929). Three cases of the "conditioned fear response." *Journal of Abnormal and Social Psychology, 34,* 221-222.

Enns, M.W., & Cox, B.J. (1999). Perfectionism and depressive symptom severity in major depressive disorder. *Behaviour Therapy and Research, 37*, 783-794.

Enns, M.W., Inayatulla, M., Cox, B.J., & Cheyne, C. (1997). Prediction of suicide intent in aboriginal and non-aboriginal adolescent inpatients: A research note. *Suicide and Life-Threatening Behavior, 27*, 218-224.

Enright, J.B. (1970). An introduction to Gestalt techniques. In J. Fagan & I.L. Shepherd (Eds.), *Gestalt therapy now: Theory, techniques, applications.* Palo Alto, CA: Science & Behavior Books.

Enserink, M. (1999). Drug therapies for depression: From MAO inhibitors to substance. *Science, 284,* 239.

Epling, W.F., & Pierce, W.D. (1992). *Solving the anorexia puzzle.* Toronto, Can.: Hogrefe & Huber.

Epp, J. (Ed.). (1988). *Mental health for Canadians: Striking a balance.* Ottawa: Ministry of National Health and Welfare.

Epping-Jordan, J.E., Compas, B.E., & Howell, D.C. (1994). Predictors of cancer progression in young adult men and women: Avoidance, intrusive thoughts, and psychological symptoms. *Health Psychology, 13,* 539-547.

Epstein, L.C., & Lasagna, L. (1969). Obtaining informed consent. *Archives of Internal Medicine, 123,* 682-688.

Epstein, L.H., Beck, S., Figneroa, J., Farkas, G., Kazdin, A.E., Danema, D., & Becker, D. (1981). The effects of point economy and parent management on urine glucose and metabolic control in children with insulin dependent diabetes. *Journal of Applied Behavior Analysis, 14,* 365-375.

Epstein, L.H., Masek, B.J., & Marshall, W.R. (1978). A nutritionally based school program for control of eating in obese children. *Behavior Therapy, 9,* 766-788.

Epstein, L.H., Wing, R.R., Thompson, J.K., & Griffen, W. (1980). Attendance and fitness in aerobics exercise: The effects of contract and lottery procedures. *Behavior Modification, 4,* 465-479.

Epstein, N.B., Baldwin, L.M., & Bishop, D.S. (1983). The McMaster Family Assessment Device. *Journal of Marital and Family Therapy, 9*, 171-182.

Epstein, S. (1979). The stability of behavior: On predicting most of the people much of the time. *Journal of Personality and Social Psychology, 37,* 1097-1126.

Erdberg, P., & Exner, J.E., Jr. (1984). Rorschach assessment. In G. Goldstein & M. Hersen (Eds.), *Handbook of psychological assessment.* New York: Pergamon.

Erikson, E.H. (1950). *Childhood and society*. New York: Norton.

Erikson, E.H. (1959). *Identity and the life cycle*. Selected papers. New York: International Universities Press.

Erikson, E.H. (1968). *Identity: Youth and crisis.* New York: Norton.

Erlenmeyer-Kimling, L.E., & Cornblatt, B. (1987). The New York high-risk project: A follow-up report. *Schizophrenia Bulletin, 13,* 451-461.

Ernst, M., Liebenauer, L.L., King, A.C., Fitzgerald, G.A., Cohen, R.M., & Zametkin, A.J. (1994). Reduced brain metabolism in hyperactive girls. *Journal of the American Academy of Child and Adolescent Psychiatry, 33,* 858-868.

Escobar, J.I., Burnam, M.A., Karno, M., Forsythe, A., Golding, J.M., et al. (1987). Somatization in the community. *Archives of General Psychiatry, 44,* 713-720.

Esler, J., Julius, S., Sweifler, A., Randall, O., Harburg, E., Gardiner, H., & DeQuattro, V. (1977). Mild high-renin essential hypertension: A neurogenic human hypertension. *New England Journal of Medicine, 296,* 405-411.

Esser, G., Schmidt, M.H., & Woerner, W. (1990). Epidemiology and course of psychiatric disorders in school-age children: Results of a longitudinal study. *Journal of Child Psychology and Psychiatry, 31,* 243-263.

Esses, V.M., Dovidio, J.F., & Hodson, G. (2002). Public attitudes toward immigration in the United States and Canada in response to the September 11, 2001 "Attack on America." *Analyses of Social Issues and Public Policy*, 2, 69-85.

Esses, V.M., & Gardner, R.C. (1996). Multiculturalism in Canada: Context and current status. *Canadian Journal of Behavioural Science, 28,* 145-152.

Estes, C.L. (1995). Mental health services for the elderly: Key policy elements. In M. Gatz (Ed.), *Emerging issues in mental health and aging* (pp. 303-327). Washington, DC: American Psychological Association.

Estes, C. L, Gerard, L., & Clarke, A. (1985). Women and the economics of aging. In B. B. Hess & E. W. Markson (Eds.), *Growing old in America: New perspectives on old age* (3rd ed.) (pp. 546-562). New Brunswick: Transaction Books.

Etringer, B.D., Gregory, V.R., & Lando, H.A. (1984). Influence of group cohesion on the behavioral treatment of smoking. *Journal of Consulting and Clinical Psychology, 52,* 1080-1086.

Evans, M.D., Hollon, S.D., DeRubeis, R.J., Piasecki, J.M., Grove, W.M., et al. (1992). Differential relapse following cognitive therapy, pharmacotherapy, and combined cognitive-pharmacotherapy for depression. *Archives of General Psychiatry, 49,* 802-808.

Evans, P.D., & Edgerton, N. (1990). Life events as predictors of the common cold. *British Journal of Medical Psychology, 64,* 35-44.

Everett, F., Proctor, N., & Cartmell, B. (1989). Providing psychological services to American Indian children and families. In D.R. Atkinson, G. Morten, & D.W. Sue (Eds.), *Counseling American minorities* (3rd ed.). Dubuque, IA: W.C. Brown.

Everill, J.T., & Waller, G. (1995). Reported sexual abuse and eating psychopathology: A review of the evidence for a causal link. *International Journal of Eating Disorders, 18,* 1-11.

Everitt, J., Lavoie, K., Gagnon, J-F., & Gosselin, N. (2001). Performance of patients with schizophrenia on the Wisconsin Card Sorting Task (WCST). *Journal of Psychiatry and Neuroscience, 26*, 123-130.

Everson, S.A., Kaplan, G.A., Goldberg, D.A., & Salonen, J.T. (1996). Anticipatory blood pressure response to exercise predicts future high blood pressure in middle-aged men, *Hypertension, 27,* 1059-1064.

Everson, S.A., Kauhanen, J., Kaplan, G.A., Goldberg, D.E., Julkunen, J., et al. (1997). Hostility and increased risk of mortality and acute myocardial infarction: The mediating role of behavioral risk factors. *American Journal of Edidemiology, 146,* 142-152.

Ewedemi, F., & Linn, M.W. (1987). Health and hassles in older and younger men. *Journal of Clinical Psychology, 43,* 347-353.

Exner, J.E. (1978). *The Rorschach: A comprehensive system: Vol. 2. Current research and advanced interpretation.* New York: Wiley.

Exner, J.E., Jr. (1986). *The Rorschach: A comprehensive system: Vol. 1. Basic foundations* (2nd ed.). New York: Wiley.

Eysenck, H.J. (1952). The effects of psychotherapy: An evaluation. *Journal of Consulting Psychology, 16,* 319-324.

Eysenck, H.J. (1967). *The biological basis of personality.* Springfield, IL: Charles C. Thomas.

Eysenck, H.J. (1981). General features of the model. In H. J. Eysenck (Ed.), *A model for personality* (pp. 1-37). New York; Springer-Verlag.

Eysenck, H.J. (1975). Crime as destiny. *New Behaviour, 9,* 46-49.

Eysenck, S.B.G., & Eysenck, H.G. (1977). The place of impulsiveness in a dimensional system of personality description. *British Journal of Social and Clinical Psychology, 16,* 57-68.

Fairbank, J.A., & Brown, T.A. (1987). Current behavioral approaches to the treatment of posttraumatic stress disorder. *the Behavior Therapist, 3,* 57-64.

Fairbank, J.A., DeGood, D.E., & Jenkins, C.W. (1981). Behavioral treatment of a persistent post-traumatic startle response. *Journal of Behaviour Therapy and Experimental Psychiatry, 12,* 321-324.

Fairburn, C.G. (1985). Cognitive-behavioral treatment for bulimia. In D.M. Garner, & P.E. Garfinkel (Eds.), *Handbook of psychotherapy for anorexia nervosa and bulimia* (pp. 160-192). New York: Guilford.

Fairburn, C.G. (1997). Eating disorders. In D.M. Clark & C.G. Fairburn (Eds.), *Science and practice of cognitive behavior therapy.* (pp. 209-243). New York: Oxford.

Fairburn, C.G., Agras, W.S., & Wilson, G.T. (1992). The research on the treatment of bulimia nervosa: Practical and theoretical implications. In G.H. Anderson & S.H. Kennedy (Eds.), *The biology of feast and famine: Relevance to eating disorders.* New York: Academic Press.

Fairburn, C.G., Cooper, Z., Doll, H.A., & Welch, S.L. (1999). Risk factors for anorexia nervosa: Three integrated case-control comparisons. *Archives of General Psychiatry, 56,* 468-478.

Fairburn, C.G., Marcus, M.D., & Wilson, G.T. (1993). Cognitive behaviour therapy for binge eating and bulimia nervosa: A comprehensive treatment manual. In C.G.

Fairburn & G.T. Wilson (Eds.), *Binge eating: Nature, assessment, and treatment.* New York: Guilford.

Fairburn, C.G., Norman, P.A., Welch, S.L., O'Connor, M.E., Doll, H.A., & Peveler, R.C. (1995). A prospective study of outcome in bulimia nervosa and the long-term effects of three psychological treatments. *Archives of General Psychiatry, 52,* 304-312.

Fairburn, C.G., Shafran, R., & Cooper, Z. (1999). A cognitive behavioural theory of anorexia nervosa. *Behaviour Research and Therapy, 37,* 1-13.

Fairburn, C.G., Welch, S.L., & Hay, P.J. (1993). The classification of recurrent overeating: The "binge eating disorder" proposal. *International Journal of Eating Disorders, 13,* 155-159.

Fairburn, C.G., Welch, S.L., Norman, P.A., O'Conner, M.E., & Doll, H.E. (1996). Bias and bulimia nervosa: How typical are clinic cases? *American Journal of Psychiatry, 153,* 386-391.

Fairweather, G.W. (Ed.). (1964). *Social psychology in treating mental illness: An experimental approach.* New York: Wiley.

Fairweather, G.W., Sanders, D.H., Maynard, H., & Cressler, D.L. (1969). *Community life for the mentally ill: An alternative to institutional care.* Chicago: Aldine-Atherton.

Falkner, B., Kusher, H., Oresti, G., & Angelakus, E.T. (1981). Cardiovascular characteristics in adolescents who develop essential hypertension. *Hypertension, 3,* 496-505.

Fallon, B., Liebowitz, M.R., Salmon, E., Schieier, F.R., Jusino, C., Hollander, E., & Klein, D.F. (1998). Fluoxetine for hypochondriacal patients without major depression. *Journal of Clinical Psychopharmacology, 13,* 438-441.

Faraone, S.V. (1997, October). *Familial aggregation of ADHD in families of girls with ADHD.* Paper presented at the American Academy of Child and Adolescent Psychiatry, Toronto, Canada.

Faraone, S.V., Biederman, J., Chen, W.J., Milberger, S., Warburton, R., & Tsuang, M.T. (1995). Neuropsychological functioning among the nonpsychotic relatives of schizophrenic patients: A diagnostic efficiency anaylsis. *Journal of Abnormal Psychology, 104,* 286-304.

Faraone, S.V., Biederman, J., Jetton, J.G., & Tsuang, M.T. (1997). Attention deficit disorder and conduct disorder: Longitudinal evidence for a family subtype. *Psychological Medicine, 27,* 291-300.

Faraone, S.V., Biederman, J., Weber, W., & Russell, R.L. (1998). Psychiatric, neuropsychological, and psychosocial features of DSM-IV subtypes of attention-deficit/hyperactivity disorder: Results from a clinically referred sample. *Journal of the American Academy of Child and Adolescent Psychiatry, 37,* 185-193.

Farina, A. (1976). *Abnormal psychology.* Englewood Cliffs, NJ: Prentice-Hall.

Farkas, G., & Rosen, R.C. (1976). The effects of alcohol on elicited male sexual response. *Studies in Alcohol, 37,* 265-272.

Farlow, M. (1997). Alzheimer's disease: Clinical implications of the apolipoprotein E genotype. *Neurology, 48, Supplement 6,* s30-s34.

Farquhar, J.W. (1991). The Stanford cardiovascular disease prevention programs. *Annals of the New York Academy of Sciences, 623,* 327-331.

Farquhar, J.W., Fortmann, S.P., Flora, J.A., & Maccoby, N. (1990). Methods of communication to influence behaviour. In W. Holland, R. Detels, & G. Knox (Eds.), *Oxford textbook of public health* (2nd ed.). New York: Oxford University Press.

Farquhar, J.W., Fortmann, S.P., Flora, J.A., Taylor, B., Haskell, W.L., Williams, P.T., Maccoby, N., & Wood, P.D. (1990). Effects of communitywide education on cardiovascular disease risk factors: The Stanford Five-City Project. *Journal of the American Medical Association, 264,* 359-365.

Farrar, C.B. (1917). The problem of mental disease in the Canadian army. *Mental Hygiene, 1,* 389-391.

Farris, E.J., Yeakel, E.H., & Medoff, H. (1945). Development of hypertension in emotional gray Norway rats after air blasting. *American Journal of Physiology, 144,* 331-333.

Fassinger, R.E. (1991). The hidden minority: Issues and challenges in working with lesbian women and gay men. *The Counseling Psychologist, 19,* 157-176.

Fassinger, R.E. (1991). Counseling lesbian women and gay men. *The Counseling Psychologist, 19, 157*-176.

Fassinger, R.E., & Richie, B.S. (1997). Sex matters: Gender and sexual orientation in training for multicultural competency. In D.B. Pope-Davis & H.L.K. Coleman (Eds.), *Multicultural counseling competencies: Assessment, education and training, and supervision.* (pp. 83-110). Thousand Oaks,CA: Sage Publications.

Faustman, W.O., Bardgett, M., Faull, K.F., Pfefferman, A., & Cseransky, J.G. (1999). Cerebrospinal fluid glutamate inversely correlates with positive symptom severity in unmedicated male schizophrenic/ schizoaffective patients. *Biological Psychiatry, 45,* 68-75.

Fava, G.A., Zielezny, M., Savron, G., & Grandi, S. (1995). Long-term effects of behavioural treatment for panic disorder with agoraphobia. *British Journal of Psychiatry, 166,* 87-92.

Fava, M., Rosenbaum, J.F., Pava, J.A., McCarthy, M.K., et al. (1993). Anger attacks in unipolar depression. Part I. Clinical correlates and response to fluoxetine treatment. *American Journal of Psychiatry, 150,* 1158-1163.

Favaro, A., & Santonastaso, P. (1997). Suicidality in eating disorders: Clinical and psychological correlates. *Acta Psychiatrica Scandanavica, 95,* 508-514.

Fawcett, J., Epstein, P., Fiester, S.J., Elkin, I., & Autry, J.H. (1987). Clinical Management-Imipramine/placebo administration manual: NIMH Treatment of Depression Collaborative Research Program. *Psychopharmacology Bulletin, 23,* 309-324.

Febbraro, G.A.R., & Clum, G.A. (1998). Meta-analytic investigation of the effectiveness of self-regulatory components in the treatment of adult behavior problems. *Clinical Psychology Review, 18,* 143-161.

Federoff, I.C., & Taylor, S. (2001). Psychological and pharmacological treatments of social phobia: A meta-analysis. *Journal of Clinical Psychopharmacology, 21,* 311-324.

Federoff, I.C., Taylor, S., Asmundson, G.J.G., & Koch, W.J. (2000). Cognitive factors in traumatic stress reactions: Predicting PTSD symptoms from anxiety sensitivity and beliefs about harmful events. *Behavioural and Cog-*

nitive Psychotherapy, 28, 5-15.

Federoff, J.P., Fishell, A., & Federoff, B. (1999). A case series of women evaluated for paraphilic sexual disorders. *Canadian Journal of Human Sexuality, 8,* 127-140.

Fedora, O., Reddon, J.R., & Yeudall, L.T. (1986). Stimuli eliciting sexual arousal in genital exhibitionists: A possible clinical application. *Archives of Sexual Behavior, 15,* 417-427.

Fein, D., Pennington, B., Markowitz, P., Braverman, M., & Waterhouse, L. (1986). Toward a neuropsychological model of infantile autism: Are the social deficits primary? *Journal of the American Academy of Child Psychiatry, 25,* 198-212.

Feingold, B.F. (1973). *Introduction to clinical allergy.* Springfield, IL: Charles C. Thomas.

Feinsilver, D.B., & Gunderson, J.G. (1972). Psychotherapy for schizophrenics—Is it indicated? *Schizophrenia Bulletin, 1,* 11-23.

Feldman, H., Gauthier, S., Hecker, J., Vellas, B., Subbiah, P., & Whalen, E. (2001). A 24-week, randomized, double-blind study of donzepil in moderate to severe Alzheimer's disease. *Neurology, 57,* 613-620.

Feldman, H.A., Goldstein, I., Hatzichristou, G., Krane, R.J., & McKinlay, J.B. (1994). Impotence and its medical and psychosocial correlates: Results of the Massachusetts male aging study. *Journal of Urology, 151,* 54-61.

Feldman, M.A., Ducharme, J.M., & Case, L. (1999). Using self-instructional pictorial manuals to teach child-care skills to mothers with intellectual disabilities. *Behavior Modification, 23,* 480-497.

Felner, R.D., Farber, S.S., & Primavera, J. (1983). Transition and stressful events: A model for primary prevention. In R.A. Felner, L.A. Jason, J.N. Mortisugu, & S.S. Farber (Eds.), *Preventive psychology: Theory, research, and practice* (pp. 199-229). New York: Pergamon.

Felton, B.J., & Revenson, T.A. (1984). Coping with chronic illness: A study of illness controllability and the influence of coping strategies on psychological adjustment. *Journal of Consulting and Clinical Psychology, 12,* 343-353.

Fenigstein, A. (1979). Self-consciousness, self-attention, and social interaction. *Journal of Personality and Social Psychology, 37,* 75-86.

Fenigstein, A., Scheier, M.F., & Buss, A.H. (1975). Public and private self-consciousness: Assessment and theory. *Journal of Consulting and Clinical Psychology, 43,* 522-527.

Fentiman, L.C. (1985). Guilty but mentally ill: The real verdict is guilty. *Boston College Law Review, 26,* 601-653.

Fenton, F. R., Cole, M.G., Engelsmann, F., & Mansouri, I. (1997). Depression in older medical inpatients: One-year course and outcome. *International Journal of Geriatric Psychiatry, 12,* 389-394.

Fenton, F.R., Tessier, L., & Streuning, E.L. (1979). A comparative trial of home and hospital psychiatric care: One-year follow-up. *Archives of General Psychiatry, 36,* 1073-1079.

Ferenczi, S. (1952). *First contributions to psychoanalysis.* New York: Brunner/Mazel.

Ferguson, K.J., & Spitzer, R.L. (1995). Binge eating disorder in a community-based sample of successful and unsuccessful dieters. *International Journal of Eating Disorders, 18,* 167-172.

Fergusson, D.M., Horwood, L.J., & Lynskey, M.T. (1993). Prevalence and comorbidity of DSM-III-R diagnoses in a birth cohort of 15 year olds. *Journal of the American Academy of Child and Adolescent Psychiatry, 32,* 1127-1134.

Fernandez, Y.M., & Marshall, W.L. (2003). Victim empathy, social self-esteem, and psychopathy in rapists. *Sexual Abuse, 15,* 11-26.

Ferris, J., Wynne, H., & Single, E. (1999). *Measuring problem gambling in Canada: Final report—phase I.* Ottawa: Canadian Centre on Substance Abuse.

Ferster, C.B. (1961). Positive reinforcement and behavioral deficits of autistic children. *Child Development, 32,* 437-456.

Fichten, C.S., Libman, E., Takefman, J., & Brender, W. (1988). Self-monitoring and self-focus in erectile dysfunction. *Journal of Sex and Marital Therapy, 14,* 120-128.

Fichter, M.M., & Noegel, R. (1990). Concordance for bulimia nervosa in twins. *International Journal of Eating Disorders, 9,* 425-436.

Filipek, P.A., Semrud-Clikeman, M., Steingard, R.J., Renshaw, P.F., Kennedy, D.N., & Biederman, J. (1997). Volumetric MRI analysis comparing subjects having attention-deficit hyperactivity disorder with normal controls. *Neurology, 48,* 589-601.

Fillion, L., Kohn, P., Gagnon, P., van Wijk, M., & Cunningham, A. (2001). The Inventory of Recent Life Experiences for Cancer Patients (IRLE-C): A decontaminated measure of cancer-based hassles. *Psychology and Health, 16,* 443-459.

Fillmore, K.M. (1987). Prevalence, incidence and chronicity of drinking patterns and problems among men as a function of age: A longitudinal and cohort analysis. *British Journal of Addiction, 82,* 77-83.

Fillmore, K.M., & Caetano, R. (1980, May 22). *Epidemiology of occupational alcoholism.* Paper presented at the National Institute on Alcohol Abuse and Alcoholism's Workshop on Alcoholism in the Workplace, Reston, VA.

Fils-Aime, M.L., Eckardt, M.J., George, D.T., Brown, G.L., Mefford, I., & Linnoila, M. (1996). Early-onset alcoholics have lower cerebrospinal fluid 5-hydroxyindoleacetic acid levels than late-onset alcoholics. *Archives of General Psychiatry, 53,* 211-216.

Finkelhor, D. (1979). *Sexually victimized children.* New York: Free Press.

Finkelhor, D. (1983). Removing the child-Prosecuting the offender in cases of sexual abuse: Evidence from the national reporting system for child abuse and neglect. *Child Abuse and Neglect, 7,* 195-205.

Finkelhor, D. (1993). Epidemiological factors in the clinical identification of child sexual abuse. *Child Abuse and Neglect, 17,* 67-70.

Finkelhor, D., Hotaling, G., Lewis, I.A., & Smith, C. (1990). Sexual abuse in a national survey of adult men and women: Prevalence, characteristics, and risk factors. *Child Abuse and Neglect, 14,* 19-28.

Finn, S.E. (1982). Base rates, utilities, and DSM-III: Shortcomings of fixed-rule systems of psychodiagnosis. *Journal of Abnormal Psychology, 91,* 294-302.

Finney, J.W., & Moos, R.H. (1998). Psychosocial treatments for alcohol use disorders. In P.E. Nathan & J.M. Gorman (Eds.), *A guide to treatments that work.* (pp. 156-166). New York: Oxford University Press.

Fiore, M.C., Novotny, T.F., Pierce, J.P., Giovino, G.A., Hatziandreu, E.J., Newcomb, P.A., Surawicz, T.S., & Davis, R.M. (1990). Methods used to quit smoking in the United States: Do cessation programs help? *Journal of the American Medical Association, 263,* 2760-2765.

Fiore, M.C., Smith, S.S., Jorenby, D.E., & Baker, T.B. (1994). The effectiveness of the nicotine patch for smoking cessation: A meta-analysis. *Journal of the American Medical Association, 271,* 1940-1947.

Firestone, P., Bradford, J.M., Greenberg, D.M., & Larose, M.R. (1998). Homicidal sex offenders: Psychological, psychometric, and diagnostic features. *Journal of the American Academy of Psychiatry and the Law, 26,* 57-552.

Firestone, P., Bradford, J.M., Greenberg, D.M., & Nunes, K.L. (2000). Differentiation of homicidal child molesters, nonhomicidal child molesters, and nonoffenders by phallometry. *American Journal of Psychiatry, 157,* 1847-1850.

Firestone, P., Bradford, J.M., Greenberg, D.M., & Serran, G.A. (2000). The relationship of deviant sexual arousal and psychopathology in incest offenders, extrafamilial child molesters, and rapists. *Journal of the American Academy of Psychiatry and the Law, 28,* 303-308.

First, M.B., Spitzer, R.L., Gibbon, M., & Williams, J.B. (1995). The Structured Clinical Interview for DSM-IIIR Personality Disorders (SCID-II): Part I: Description. *Journal of Personality Disorders, 9,* 83-91.

First, M.B., Spitzer, R.L., Gibbon, M., & Williams, J.B.W. (1996). *Structured Clinical Interview for DSM-IV Axis I Disorders - Patient Edition (SCID-I/P, Version 2.0).* New York: Biometrics Research Department, New York State Psychiatric Institute.

Fischer, D.G., & McDonald, W.L. (1998). Characteristics of intrafamilial and extrafamilial child sexual abuse. *Child Abuse and Neglect, 22,* 915-929.

Fischer, M. (1971). Psychoses in the offspring of schizophrenic monozygotic twins and their normal co-twins. *British Journal of Psychiatry, 118,* 43-52.

Fischetti, M., Curran, J.P., & Wessberg, H.W. (1977). Sense of timing. *Behavior Modification, 1,* 179-194.

Fisher, J.E., Goy, E.R., Swingen, D.N., & Szymanski, J. (1994, November). *The functional context of behavioral disturbances in Alzheimer's disease patients.* Paper presented at the annual convention of the Association for Advancement of Behavior Therapy.

Fisher, J.E., & Noll, J.P. (1996). Anxiety disorders. In L.L. Carstensen, B.A. Edelstein, & L. Dornbrand (Eds.), *The practical handbook of clinical gerontology* (pp. 304-323). Thousand Oaks: Sage.

Fishman, D.B. (1999). *The case for pragmatic psychology*. New York: NYU Press.

Fishman, D.B., Rodgers, F., & Franks, C.M. (Eds.). (1988). *Paradigms in behavior therapy: Present and promise* (pp. 254-293). New York: Springer.

Fiske, A., Kasl-Godley, J. E., & Gatz, M. (1998). Mood disorders in late life. In A. S. Bellack & M. Hersen (Eds.), *Comprehensive clinical psychology: Vol. 7.* (pp. 193-229). New York: Elsevier.

Fitts, S.N., Gibson, P., Redding, C.A., & Deiter, P.J. (1989). Body dysmorphic disorder: Implications for its validity as a DSM-III-R clinical syndrome. *Psychological Reports, 64,* 655-658.

Fitzgerald, R.V. (1973). *Conjoint marital therapy*. New York: Jason Aronson.

Fleming, J.E., & Offord, D.R. (1990). Epidemiology of childhood depressive disorders: A critical review. *Journal of the American Academy of Child and Adolescent Psychiatry, 29,* 571-580.

Fletcher, P.C., McKenna, P.J., Frith, C.D., Friston, K.J., & Dolan, R.J. (1998). Brain activations in schizophrenia during a graded memory task studied with functional imaging. *Archives of General Psychiatry, 55,* 1001-1009.

Flett, G. L., & Blankstein, K.R. (1994). Worry as a component of test anxiety: A multidimensional analysis. In G.C.L. Davey & F. Tallis (Eds.), *Worrying: Perspectives on theory, assessment and treatment,* (pp. 135-181). London: Wiley.

Flett, G. L., Blankstein, K.R., & Martin, T.R. (1995). Procrastination, negative self-judgments, and stress in depression and anxiety: A review and preliminary model. In J. R. Ferrari, J. L. Johnson, & W. G. McCown, (Eds.), *Procrastination and task avoidance: Theory, research, and treatment* (pp. 137-167). NY: Plenum.

Flett, G.L., Endler, N.S., & Fairlie, P. (1999). The interaction model of anxiety and the threat of Quebec's separation from Canada. *Journal of Personality and Social Psychology, 76,* 143-150.

Flett, G.L., Greene, A., & Hewitt, P.L. (2004). Dimensions of perfectionism and anxiety sensitivity. *Journal of Rational-Emotive and Cognitive-Behavior Therapy, 22,* 39-57.

Flett, G.L., Hewitt, P.L., Endler, N.S., & Bagby, R.M. (1995). Conceptualization and assessment of personality factors in depression. *European Journal of Personality, 9,* 309-350.

Flett, G.L., Vredenburg, K., & Krames, L. (1997). The continuity of depression in clinical and nonclinical samples. *Psychological Bulletin, 121,* 395-416.

Flint, A.J. (1994). Epidemiology and comorbidity of anxiety disorders in the elderly. *American Journal of Psychiatry, 151,* 640-649.

Flint, A.J. (1999). Anxiety disorders in late life. *Canadian Family Physician, 45,* 2672-2679.

Flint, A.J., & Rifat, S.L. (1996). The effect of sequential antidepressant treatment on geriatric depression. *Journal of Affective Disorders, 36,* 95-105.

Flint, A.J., & Rifat, S.L. (1997). Two-year outcome of elderly patients with anxious depression. *Psychiatry Research, 66,* 23-31.

Flint, A.J., & Rifat, S.L. (2000). Maintenance treatment for recurrent depression in late life: A four-year outcome study. *American Journal of Geriatric Psychiatry, 8,* 112-116.

Flor, H., & Birbaumer, N. (1993). Comparison of the efficacy of electromyographic biofeedback, cognitive-behavioral therapy, and conservative medical interventions in the treatment of chronic musculoskeletal pain. *Journal of Consulting and Clinical Psychology, 61,* 653-658.

Floyd, M., Scogin, F., McKendree-Smith, N. L., Floyd, D.L., & Rokke, P.D. (2004). Cognitive therapy for depression: A comparison of individual psychotherapy and bibliotherapy for depressed older adults. *Behavior Modification, 28,* 297-318.

Fluoxetine Bulimia Nervosa Collaborative Study Group. (1992). Fluoxetine in the treatment of bulimia nervosa: A multicenter, placebo-controlled, double blind trial. *Archives of General Psychiatry, 49,* 139-147.

Foa, E.B. (1996). Psychological treatment for obsessive-compulsive disorder. In M.R. Mavissakalian & R.F. Prien (Eds.), *Long-term treatments of anxiety disorders*. (pp. 285-309). Washington, DC: American Psychiatric Press.

Foa, E.B., Feske, U., Murdock, T. B., Kozak, M.J., & McCarthy, P.R. (1991). Processing of threat-related information in rape victims. *Journal of Abnormal Psychology, 100,* 156-165.

Foa, E.B., & Kozak, M.J. (1986). Emotional processing of fear: Exposure to corrective information. *Psychological Bulletin, 99,* 20-35.

Foa, E.B., Kozak, M.J., Steketee, G.S., & McCarthy, P.R. (1992). Treatment of depressive and obsessive-compulsive symptoms in OCD by imipramine and behavior therapy. *British Journal of Clinical Psychology, 31,* 279-292.

Foa, E., Riggs, D.S., Marsie, E.D., & Yarczower, M. (1995). The impact of fear activation and anger on the efficacy of exposure treatment for posttraumatic stress disorder. *Behavior Therapy, 26,* 487-499.

Foa, E.B., Zinbarg, R., & Rothbaum, B.O. (1992). Uncontrollability and unpredictability in post-traumatic stress disorder: An animal model. *Psychological Bulletin, 112,* 218-238.

Fodor, I. (1978). Phobias in women: Therapeutic approaches. In *Helping women change: A guide for professional counseling*. New York: BMA Audio Cassette Program.

Folkman, S., Bernstein, L., & Lazarus, R.S. (1987). Stress processes and the misuse of drugs in older adults. *Psychology and Aging, 2,* 366-374.

Folks, D.G., Ford, C.V., & Regan, W.M. (1984). Conversion symptoms in a general hospital. *Psychosomatics, 25,* 285-295.

Follette, V.M. (1994). Acceptance and commitment in the treatment of incest survivors: A contextual approach. In S.C. Hayes, N.S. Jacobson, V.M. Follette, & M. Dougher (Eds.), *Acceptance and change: Content and context in psychotherapy*. Reno, NV: Context Press.

Folstein, M.F., Folstein, S.E., & McHugh, P.R. (1975). "Mini-mental state: A practical method for grading the cognitive state of patients for the clinician. *Journal of Psychiatric Research, 12,* 189-198.

Fombonne, E. (2003). Epidemiology of pervasive developmental disorders. *Trends in Evidence-Based Neuropsychiatry, 5,* 29-36.

Foong, J., Ridding, M., Cope, H., Mardsen, C.D., & Ron, M.A. (1997). Corticospinal function in conversion disorder. *Journal of Neuropsychiatry and Clinical Neurosciences, 9,* 302-303.

Foot, D. (with D. Stoffman). (1996). *Boom, bust & echo: How to profit from the coming demographic shift.* Toronto: Macfarlane, Walter, & Ross.

Ford, C.S., & Beach, F.A. (1951). *Patterns of sexual behavior*. New York: Harper.

Ford, C.V. (1995). Dimensions of somatization and hypochondriasis. Special Issue: Malingering and conversion reactions. *Neurological Clinics, 13,* 241-253.

Ford, C.V., & Folks, D.G. (1985). Conversion disorders: An overview. *Psychosomatics, 26,* 371-383.

Ford, D.H., & Urban, H.B. (1963). *Systems of psychotherapy: A comparative study*. New York: Wiley.

Fordyce, W.E. (1994). Pain and suffering: What is the unit? *Quality of Life Research: An International Journal of Quality of Life Aspects of Treatment, Care, and Rehabilitation, 3,* S51-S56.

Fordyce, W.E., Brockway, J.A., Bergman, J.A., & Spengler, D. (1986). Acute back pain: A control-group comparison of behavioral vs. traditional methods. *Journal of Behavioral Medicine, 9,* 127-140.

Forsythe, C.J., & Compas, B.E. (1987). Interaction of cognitive appraisals of stressful events and coping: Testing the goodness of fit hypothesis. *Cognitive Therapy and Research, 11,* 473-485.

Forsyth, J.P., & Eifert, G.H. (1998). Reponse intensity in content-specific fear conditioning comparing 20% versus 13% CO2-enriched air as unconditioned stimuli. *Journal of Abnormal Psychology, 107,* 291-304.

Forsythe, W.I., & Redmond, A. (1974). Enuresis and spontaneous cure rate: Study of 1129 enuretics. *Archives of Disease in Childhood, 49,* 259-263.

Forth, A.E., & Hare, R.D. (1989). The contingent negative variation in psychopaths. *Psychophysiology, 26,* 676-682.

Foucault, M. (1965). *Madness and civilization*. New York: Random House.

Foulkes, S.H. (1964). *Therapeutic group analysis*. New York: International Universities Press.

Fouts, G., & Burggraf, K. (2000). Television situation comedies: Female weight, male negative comments, and audience reactions. *Sex Roles, 42,* 925-932.

Fowler, I.L., Carr, V.J., Carter, N.T., & Lewin, T.J. (1998). Patterns of current and lifetime substance use in schizophrenia. *Schizophrenia Bulletin, 24,* 443-455.

Foy, D.W., Resnick, H.S., Carroll, E.M., & Osato, S.S. (1990). Behavior therapy. In A.S. Bellack & M. Hersen (Eds.), *Handbook of comparative treatments for adult disorders* (pp. 302-315). New York: Wiley.

Foy, D.W., Resnick, H.S., Sipprelle, R.C., & Carroll, E.M. (1987). Premilitary, military, and postmilitary factors in the development of combat-related posttraumatic stress disorder. *the Behavior Therapist, 10,* 3-9.

Frame, C., Matson, J.L., Sonis, W.A., Fialkov, M.J., & Kazdin, A.E. (1982).

Behavioral treatment of depression in a prepubertal child. *Journal of Behaviour Therapy and Experimental Psychiatry, 3,* 239-243.

Frances, A., Pincus, H.A., Widiger, T.A., Davis, W.W., & First, M.B. (1990). DSM-IV: Work in progress. *American Journal of Psychiatry, 147,* 1439-1448.

Frances, R., Franklin, J., & Flavin, D. (1986). Suicide and alcoholism. *Annals of the New York Academy of Science, 287,* 316-326.

Frank, E., Anderson, C., & Kupfer, D.J. (1976). Profiles of couples seeking sex therapy and marital therapy. *American Journal of Psychiatry, 133,* 559-562.

Frank, E., Anderson, C., & Rubenstein, D. (1978). Frequency of sexual dysfunctions in "normal" couples. *New England Journal of Medicine, 299,* 111-115.

Frank, E., & Kupfer, D.J. (1994). Maintenance therapy in depression: In reply. *Archives of General Psychiatry, 51,* 504-505.

Frank, E., Kupfer, D.J., Ehlers, C.L., & Monk, T.H. (1994). Interpersonal and social rhythm therapy for bipolar disorder: Integrating interpersonal and behavioral approaches. *the Behavior Therapist, 17,* 143.

Frank, E., Kupfer, D.J., Perel, J.M., Cornes, C., Jarrett, D.B., et al. (1990). Three-year outcomes for maintenance therapies in recurrent depression. *Archives of General Psychiatry, 47,* 1093-1099.

Frank, E., Kupfer, D.J., Wagner, E.F., McEachran, A.B., & Cornes, C. (1991). Efficacy of interpersonal psychotherapy as a maintenance treatment of recurrent depression: Contributing factors. *Archives of General Psychiatry, 48,* 1053-1059.

Frank, J.D. (1961). *Persuasion and healing.* Baltimore: Johns Hopkins University Press. Second edition, 1973; third edition, 1978.

Frank, J.D. (1976). Psychotherapy and the sense of mastery. In R.L. Spitzer & D.F. Klein (Eds.), *Evaluation of psychotherapies: Behavioral therapies, drug therapies and their interactions.* Baltimore: Johns Hopkins University Press.

Frank, J.D. (1982). Therapeutic components shared by all psychotherapies. In J.H. Harvey & M.M. Parks (Eds.), *The Master Lecture Series: Vol. 1. Psychotherapy research and behavior change* (pp. 73-122). Washington, DC: American Psychological Association.

Frank, S. (2001, May 7). Canada: The next generation. *Time, Canadian Edition,* pp. 18-26.

Frankenhaeuser, M.U., Lundberg, M., Fredriksson, B., Melin, M., Thomisto, A., et al. (1989). Stress on and off the job as related to sex and occupational status in whitecollar workers. *Journal of Organizational Behavior, 10,* 321-346.

Frankl, V. (1959). *From death camp to existentialism.* Boston: Beacon.

Frankl, V. (1963). *Man's search for meaning.* New York: Washington Square.

Frankl, V. (1967). *Psychotherapy and existentialism.* New York: Simon & Schuster.

Franklin, J.C., Schiele, B.C., Brozerk, J., & Keys, A. (1948). Observations on human behavior in experimental semistarvation and rehabilitation. *Journal of Clinical Psychology,* 4, 28-45.

Franklin, M.E., & Foa, E.B. (1998). Cognitive-behavioral treatments for obsessive-compulsive disorder. In P.E. Nathan & J.M. Gorman (Eds.), *A guide to treatments that work.* (pp. 339-357). New York: Oxford University Press.

Franks, C.M., Wilson, G.T., Kendall, P.C., & Foreyt, J.P. (1990). *Review of behavior therapy: Theory and practice.* New York: Guilford.

Fraser, G.A. (1994). Dissociative phenomena and disorders: Clinical presentations. In R. M. Klein & B. K. Doane (Eds.), *Psychological concepts and dissociative disorders* (pp.131-151). Hillsdale, NJ: Erlbaum.

Frasure-Smith, N., Lesperance, F., Gravel, G., Masson, A., Juneau, M., & Bourassa, M.G. (2002). Long-term survival differences among low-anxious, high-anxious and repressive copers enrolled in the Montreal Heart Attack Readjustment Trial. *Psychosomatic Medicine, 64,* 571-579.

Frasure-Smith, N., Lesperance, F., Juneau, M., Talajic, M., & Bourassa, M.G. (1999). Gender, depression, and one-year prognosis after myocardial infarction. *Psychosomatic Medicine, 61,* 26-37.

Frasure-Smith, N., Lesperance, F., Prince, R.H., Verrier, P., Garber, R.A., Juneau, M., Wolfson, C., & Bourassa, M.G. (1997). Randomized trial of home-based psychosocial nursing intervention for patients recovering from myocardial infarction. *Lancet, 350,* 473-479.

Frasure-Smith, N., & Prince, R. (1985). The Ischemic Heart Disease Life Stress Monitoring Program: Impact on mortality. *Psychosomatic Medicine, 47,* 431-445.

Frasure-Smith, N., & Prince, R. (1989). Long-term follow-up of the Ischemic Heart Disease Life Stress Monitoring Program. *Psychosomatic Medicine, 51,* 485-513.

Frayn, D. H. (1996). *The Clarke and its founders: The thirteeth anniversary: A retrospective look at the impossible dream (Clarke Monograph Series No. 6).* Toronto: Clarke Institute of Psychiatry.

Frazier, P.A. (1990). Victim attributions and post-rape trauma. *Journal of Personality and Social Psychology, 59,* 298-304.

Frederickson, B.L., & Carstensen, L.L. (1990). Choosing social partners: How old age and anticipated endings make people more selective. *Psychology and Aging, 5,* 335-347.

Freeman, A., & Reinecke, M.A. (1995). Cognitive therapy. In A.S. Gurman & S.B. Messer (Eds.), *Essential psychotherapies: Theory and practice.* New York: Guilford.

Freeman, V.G., Rathore, S.S., Weinfurt, K.P., Schulman, K.A., & Sulmasy, D.P. (1999). Lying for patients: Physician deception of third party payers. *Archives of Internal Medicine, 159,* 2263-2270.

Freeston, M.H., Ladouceur, R., Gagnon, F., Thibodeau, N., Rheaume, J., Letarte, H., & Bujold, A. (1997). Cognitive-behavioral treatment of obsessive thoughts: A controlled study. *Journal of Consulting and Clinical Psychology, 65,* 405-413.

Freud, A. (1946). *The ego and mechanisms of defense.* New York: International Universities Press.

Freud, A. (1966). *The ego and the mechanisms of defense.* New York: International Universities Press.

Freud, S. (1917). Mourning and melancholia. In *Collected papers* (Vol. 4). London: Hogarth and the Institute of Psychoanalysis, 1950.

Freud, S. (1937). Analysis terminable and interminable. *International Journal of Psychoanalysis, 18,* 373-391.

Freud, S. (1955). Lines of advance in psychoanalytic therapy. In *The complete psychological works of Sigmund Freud. J. Strachey* (Ed. and Trans.) London: Hogarth and the Institute of Psychoanalysis. (Original work published 1918)

Freud, S. (1956). Analysis of a phobia in a five-year-old boy. In *Collected works of Sigmund Freud* (Vol. 10). London: Hogarth. (Original work published 1909)

Freund, K. (1967). Diagnosing homo- or heterosexuality and erotic age-preference by means of a psychophysiological test. *Behaviour Research and Therapy, 5,* 209-228.

Freund, K. (1990). Courtship disorders. In W.L. Marshall, D.R. Laws, & H.E. Barbaree (Eds.), *Handbook of sexual assault: Issues, theories, and treatment.* (pp. 195-207). NY: Plenum Press.

Freund, K., & Blanchard, R. (1989). Phallometric diagnosis of pedophilia. *Journal of Consulting and Clinical Psychology, 57,* 100-105.

Freund, K., & Kuban, M. (1994). The basis of the abused abuser theory of pedophilia: A further elaboration on an earlier study. *Archives of Sexual Behavior, 23,* 553-563.

Freund, K., & Watson, R. (1991). Assessment of the sensitivity and specificity of a phallometric test: An update of phallometric diagnosis of pedophilia. *Psychological Assessment, 3,* 254-260.

Frick, P.J. (2001). Effective interventions for children and adolescents with conduct disorder. *Canadian Journal of Psychiatry, 46,* 597-608.

Fridell, S., R., Zucker, K.J., Bradley, S.J., & Maing, D.M. (1996). Physical attractiveness of girls with gender identity disorders. *Archives of Sexual Behavior, 25,* 17-31.

Fried, P., Watkinson, B., James, D., & Gray, R. (2002). Current and former marijuana use: Preliminary findings of a longitudinal study of effects of IQ in young adults. *Canadian Medical Association Journal, 166,* 887-891.

Friedman, J.M., & Hogan, D.R. (1985). Sexual dysfunction: Low sexual desire. In D.H. Barlow (Ed.), *Clinical handbook of psychological disorders.* New York: Guilford.

Friedman, M. (1969). *Pathogenesis of coronary artery disease.* New York: McGraw-Hill.

Friedman, M., Thoresen, C.E., Gill, J.J., Powell, L.H., Ulmer, D., Thompson, L., Price, V.A., Rabin, D.D., Breall, W.S., Dixon, T., Levy, R., & Bourg, E. (1984). Alteration of type A behavior and reduction in cardiac recurrences in postmyocardial infarction patients. *American Heart Journal, 108,* 237-248.

Friedman, M., Thoresen, C.E., Gill, J.J., Ulmer, D., Thompson, L., Powell, L., Price, A., Elek, S.R., Rabin, D.D., Breall, W.S., Piaget, G., Dixon, T., Bourg, E., Levy, R., & Tasto, D.I. (1982). Feasibility of altering type A behavior pattern after myocardial infarction. *Circulation, 66,* 83-92.

Friedman, M., & Ulmer, D. (1984). *Treating type A behavior and your heart.* New York: Fawcett Crest.

Friedman, R., & Dahl, L.K. (1975). The effects of chronic conflict on the blood pressure of rats with a genetic susceptibility to experimental hypertension. *Psychosomatic Medicine, 37,* 402-416.

Friend, R. A. (1991). Older lesbian and gay people: A theory of successful aging. *Journal of Homosexuality, 20,* 99-118.

Frisch, M.B., & Higgins, R.L. (1986). Instructional demand effects and the correspondence among role-play, self-report, and naturalistic measures of social skill. *Behavioral Assessment, 8,* 221-236.

Frise, S., Steingart, A., Sloan, M., Cotterchio, M., & Kreiger, N. (2002). Psychiatric disorders and the use of mental health services by Ontario women. *Canadian Journal of Psychiatry, 47,* 849-856.

Frith, U. (1989). *Autism: Explaining the enigma.* Cambridge, MA: Basil Blackwell.

Fromm-Reichmann, F. (1948). Notes on the development of treatment of schizophrenics by psychoanalytic psychotherapy. *Psychiatry, 11,* 263-273.

Fromm-Reichmann, F. (1952). Some aspects of psychoanalytic therapy with schizophrenics. In E. Brady & F.C. Redlich (Eds.), *Psychotherapy with schizophrenics.* New York: International Universities Press.

Fry, P.S. (1984). Development of a geriatric scale of hopelessness: Implications for counseling and intervention with the depressed elderly. *Journal of Counseling Psychology, 31,* 322-331.

Fry, P.S. (1993). Mediators of depression in community-based elders. In P. Cappeliez & R. J. Flynn (Eds.), *Depression and the social environment: Research and intervention with neglected populations* (pp. 369-394). Montreal: McGill-Queen's University Press.

Fry, P.S. (2001). The unique contribution of key existential factors to the prediction of psychological well-being of older adults following spousal loss. *The Gerontologist, 41,* 69-81.

Fuentes, K., & Cox, B.J. (1997). Prevalence of anxiety disorders in elderly adults: A critical analysis. *Journal of Behavior Therapy and Experimental Psychiatry, 28,* 269-279.

Fuentes, K., & Cox, B.J. (2000). Assessment of anxiety in older adults: A community-based survey and comparison with younger adults. *Behaviour Research and Therapy, 38,* 297-309.

Fuerst, K.B., & Rourke, B.P. (1995). Human neuropsychology in Canada: The 1980s. *Canadian Psychology, 36,* 12-45.

Fuller, R.K. (1988). Disulfiram treatment of alcoholism. In R.M. Rose & J.E. Barrett (Eds.), *Alcoholism: Treatment and outcome.* New York: Raven.

Fuller, R.K., Branchey, L., Brightwell, D.R., Derman, R.M., Emrick, C.D., Iber, F.L., James, K.E., & Lacoursiere, R.B. (1986). Disulfiram treatment of alcoholism: A Veterans Administration cooperative study. *Journal of the American Medical Association, 256,* 1449-1455.

Funk, W. (1998). *What difference does it make? The journey of a soul survivor.* Cranbrook, BC: Wild Flower Publishing.

Furnham, A., & Baguma, P. (1994). Cross-cultural differences in the evaluation of male and female body shapes. *International Journal of Eating Disorders, 15,* 81-89.

Fyer, A.J., Mannuzza, S., Chapman, T.F., Martin, L.Y., & Klein, D.F. (1995). Specificity in familial aggregation of phobic disorders. *Archives of General Psychiatry, 52,* 564-573.

Fyer, A.J., Sandberg, D., & Klein, D.F. (1991). The pharmacological treatment of panic disorder and agoraphobia. In J.R. Walker, G.R. Norton, & C.A. Ross (Eds.), *Panic disorder and agoraphobia: A comprehensive guide for the practitioner* (pp. 211-251). Belmont, CA: Brooks/Cole.

Gabbay, F.H. (1992). Behavior genetic strategies in the study of emotion. *Psychological Science, 3,* 50-55.

Gaetz, M. (2002). An emerging role for event-related potentials in the assessment of brain injury. *Clinical Neurophysiology, 113,* 1665-1666.

Gagne, A., & Morin, C.M. (2001). Predicting treatment response in older adults with insomnia. *Journal of Clinical Geropsychology, 7,* 131-143.

Gagnon, J.H. (1977). *Human sexualities.* Chicago: Scott, Foresman.

Gaines, J. (1974). The founder of Gestalt therapy: A sketch of Fritz Perls. *Psychology Today, 8,* 117-118.

Galaburda, A.M. (1993). Neuroanatomical basis of developmental dyslexia. *Neurologic Clinics, 11,* 161-173.

Galambos, N.L., Leadbeater, B.J., & Barker, E.T. (2004). Gender differences in and risk factors for depression in adolescence: A 4-year longitudinal study. *International Journal of Behavioral Development, 28,* 16-25.

Galanter, M., & Castaneda, R. (1985). Self-destructive behavior in the substance abuser. *Psychiatric Clinics of North America, 8,* 251-261.

Gallagher, D., Breckenridge, J.N., Thompson, L.W., Dessonville, C., & Amaral, P. (1982). Similarities and differences between normal grief and depression in older adults. *Essence, 5,* 127-140.

Gallagher, D., & Thompson, L.W. (1982). *Elders' maintenance of treatment benefits following individual psychotherapy for depression: Results of a pilot study and preliminary data from an ongoing replication study.* Paper presented at the annual meeting of the American Psychological Association, Washington, DC.

Gallagher, D., & Thompson, L.W. (1983). Cognitive therapy for depression in the elderly. A promising model for treatment and research. In L.D. Breslau & M.R. Haug (Eds.), *Depression and aging: Causes, care and consequences.* New York: Springer.

Gallagher-Thompson, D., & Thompson, L.W. (1995a). Efficacy of psychotherapeutic interventions with older adults. *The Clinical Psychologist, 48,* 24-30.

Gallagher-Thompson, D., & Thompson, L.W. (1995b). Psychotherapy with older adults in theory and practice. In B. Bongar & L.E. Beutler (Eds.), *Comprehensive textbook of psychotherapy: Theory and practice* (pp. 359-379). New York: Oxford University Press.

Galli, V., McElroy, S.L., Soutullo, C.A., Kizer, D., Raute, N., et al. (1999). The psychiatric diagnoses of twenty-two adolescents who have sexually molested children. *Comprensive Psychiatry, 40,* 85-88.

Gammell, D.J., & Stoppard, J.M. (1999). Women's experiences of treatment of depression: Medicalization or empowerment? *Canadian Psychology, 40,* 112-128.

Gann, M.K., & Davison, G.C. (1999). *Assessing psychological reactance: Defiant thoughts at the ATSS paradigm.* Unpublished manuscript. University of Southern California.

Gao, S., Hendrie, H.C., Hall, K.S., & Hui, S. (1998). Relationships between sex, age, and the incidence of dementia and Alzheimer's disease: A meta-analysis. *Archives of General Psychiatry, 55,* 809-816.

Garb, H.N., Florio, C.M., & Grove, W.M. (1998). The validity of the Rorschach and the Minnesota Multiphasic Personality Inventory: Results from meta-analyses. *Psychological Science, 5,* 402-404.

Garber, J., Kriss, M.R., Koch, M., & Lindholm, L. (1988). Recurrent depression in adolescents: A follow-up study. *Journal of the American Academy of Child and Adolescent Psychiatry, 27,* 49-54.

Garbutt, J.C., Mayo, J.P., Little, K.Y., Gillette, G.M., Mason, G.A., et al. (1994). Dose-response studies with protirelin. *Archives of General Psychiatry, 51,* 875-883.

Garcia, J., McGowan, B.K., & Green, K.F. (1972). Biological constraints on conditioning. In A.H. Black & W.F. Prokasy (Eds.), *Classical conditioning: 2. Current research and theory.* New York: Appleton-Century-Crofts.

Garcia-Andrade, C., Wall, T.L., & Ehlers, C.L. (1997). The firewater myth and response to alcohol in Mission Indians. *American Journal of Psychiatry, 154,* 983-988.

Gardner, H. (1997, January 19). Review of "The Creation of Dr. B." *Los Angeles Times,* Book Review, p. 3.

Garfield, S.L. (1978). Research on client variables in psychotherapy. In S.L. Garfield & A.E. Bergin (Eds.), *Handbook of psychotherapy and behavior change* (2nd ed.). New York: Wiley.

Garfield, S.L., & Bergin, A.E. (1986). Introduction and historical overview. In S.L. Garfield & A.E. Bergin (Eds.), *Handbook of psychotherapy and behavior change* (3rd ed.). New York: Wiley.

Garfinkel, D., Laudon, M., Nof, D., & Zisapel, N. (1995). Improvement of sleep quality in elderly people by controlled-release melatonin. *Lancet, 346,* 541-543.

Garfinkel, P.E. (2002). Classification and diagnosis of eating disorders. In C.G. Fairburn & K. D. Brownell (Eds.), *Eating disorders and obesity: A comprehensive handbook* (2nd edition, pp. 155-161). New York: Guilford.

Garfinkel, P.E., Goering, E.L., Goldbloom, S.D., Kennedy, S., Kaplan, A.S., & Woodside, D.B. (1996). Should amenorrhea be necessary for the diagnosis of anorexia nervosa? *British Journal of Psychiatry, 168,* 500-506.

Garfinkel, P.E., & Goldbloom, D.S. (2000). Significant developments in psychiatry: Implications for community mental health. *Canadian Journal of Community Mental Health, 19,* 161-165.

Garfinkel, P.E., Kennedy, S.H., & Kaplan, A.S. (1995). Views on classification and diagnosis of eating disorders. *Canadian Journal of Psychiatry, 40,* 445-456.

Garfinkel, P.E., Lin, B., Goering, P., Spegg, C., Goldbloom, D.S., Kennedy, S., Kaplan, A.S., & Woodside, D.B (1995). Bulimia nervosa in a Canadian community sample: Prevalence and comparison of subgroups. *American Journal of Psychiatry, 152,* 1052-1058.

Garland, R.J., & Dougher, M.J. (1991). Motivational interviewing in the treatment of sex offenders. In W.R. Miller & S. Rollnick (Eds.), *Motivating interviewing: Preparing people to change addictive behavior* (pp. 303-313). New York: Guilford.

Garner, D.M. (1997b). Psychoeducational principles. In D.M. Garner & P.E. Garfinkel (Eds.), *Handbook of treatment for eating disorders.* (pp. 145-177). New York: Guilford Press.

Garner, D.M., & Garfinkel, P.E. (1980). Sociocultural factors in the development of anorexia nervosa. *Psychological Medicine, 10,* 647-656.

Garner, D.M., Garfinkel, P.E., Schwartz, D., & Thompson, M. (1980). Cultural expectation of thinness in women. *Psychological Reports, 47,* 483-491.

Garner, D.M., Olmsted, M.P., & Polivy, J. (1981). The Eating Disorder Inventory: A measure of cognitive-behavioral dimensions of anorexia nervosa and bulimia. In P.L. Darby, P.E. Garfinkel, D.M. Garner, & D.V. Coscina (Eds.), *Anorexia nervosa: Recent developments in research.* New York: Liss.

Garner, D.M., Olmsted, M.P., & Polivy, J. (1983). Development and validation of a multi-dimensional eating disorder inventory for anorexia nervosa and bulimia. *International Journal of Eating Disorders, 2,* 15-34.

Garner, D.M., Rockert, W., Davis, R., Garner, M.V., Olmsted, M.P., & Eagle, M. (1993). Comparison between cognitive-behavioral and supportive-expressive therapy for bulimia nervosa. *American Journal of Psychiatry, 150,* 37-46.

Garner, D.M., Vitousek, K.M., & Pike, K.M. (1997). Cognitive-behavioral therapy for anorexia nervosa. In D.M. Garner & P.E. Garfinkel (Eds.), *Handbook of treatment for eating disorders.* (pp. 94-144). New York: Guilford Press.

Garnets, L., Herek, G.M., & Levy, B. (1990). Violence and victimization of lesbians and gay men: Mental health conseqences. *Journal of Interpersonal Violence, 5,* 366-383.

Garrison, C.Z., McKeown, R.E., Valois, R.F., & Vincent, M.L. (1993). Aggression, substance use, and suicidal behaviors in high school students. *American Journal of Public Health, 83,* 179-184.

Garssen, B., Buikhuisen, M., & Van Dyck, R. (1996). Hyperventilation and panic attacks. *American Journal of Psychiatry, 153,* 513-518.

Gaston, L. (1991). Reliability and criterion validity of the California Psychotherapy Alliance Scales-Patient version. *Psychological Assessment, 3,* 68-74.

Gaston, L., Thompson, L., Gallagher, D., Cournoyer, L.G., & Gagnon, R. (1998). Alliance, technique, and their interactions in predicting outcome of behavioral, cognitive, and brief dynamic therapy. *Psychotherapy Research, 8,* 190-209.

Gatchel, R.J., Baum, A., & Krantz, D.S. (1989). *An introduction to health psychology* (2nd ed.). New York: Random House.

Gatz, M., Fiske, A., Fox, L. S., Kaskie, B., Kasl-Godley, J. E., McCallum, T. J., & Wetherell, J. L. (1998). Empirically validated psychological treatments for older adults. *Journal of Mental Health and Aging, 4,* 9-46.

Gatz, M., Kasl-Godley, J.E., & Karel, M.J. (1996). Aging and mental disorders. In J.E. Birren & K.W. Schaie (Eds.), *Handbook of the psychology of aging.* San Diego: Academic Press.

Gatz, M., & Pearson, C.G. (1988). Ageism revised and the provision of psychological services. *American Psychologist, 43,* 184-188.

Gatz, M., Popkin, S.J., Pino, C.D., & VandenBos, G.R. (1985). Psychological interventions with older adults. In J.E. Birren & W.K. Schaie (Eds.), *Handbook of the psychology of aging.* (pp. 755-785). New York: Van Nostrand Reinhold.

Gatz, M., & Smyer, M.A. (1992). The mental health system and older adults in the 1990s. *American Psychologist, 47,* 741-751.

Gauthier, J.G. (2002). Facilitating mobility for psychologists through a competency-based approach for regulation and accreditation: The Canadian experiment. *European Psychologist, 7,* 203-212.

Gauthier, J.G., Ivers, H., & Carrier, S. (1996). Nonpharmacological approaches in the treatment of recurrent headache disorders and their comparison and combination with pharmacotherapy. *Clinical Psychology Review, 16,* 543-571.

Ge, X., Conger, R.D., Cadoret, R.J., Neiderhiser, J.M., Yates, W., et al. (1996). The developmental interface between nature and nurture: A mutual influence model of child antisocial behavior and parent behaviors. *Developmental Psychology, 32,* 574-589.

Geary, D.C., Brown, S.C., & Samaranayake, V.A. (1991). Cognitive addition: A short longitudinal study of strategy choice and speed-of-processing differences in normal and mathematically disabled children. *Developmental Psychology, 27,* 787-797.

Geary, D.C. (1993). Mathematical disabilities: Cognitive, neuropsychological, and genetic components. *Psychological Bulletin, 114,* 345-362.

Geary, D.C. & Brown, S.C. (1991). Cognitive addition: Strategy choice and speed-of-processing differences in gifted, normal, and mathematically disabled children. *Developmental Psychology, 27,* 398-406.

Gebhard, P.H., Gagnon, J.H., Pomeroy, W.B., & Christenson, C.V. (1965). *Sex offenders.* New York: Harper & Row.

Geddes, J. (2001, April 23). Northern Son. *Maclean's, April 23,* pp. 16-20.

Geer, J.H., Davison, G.C., & Gatchel, R.I. (1970). Reduction of stress in humans through nonveridical perceived control of aversive stimulation. *Journal of Personality and Social Psychology, 16,* 731-738.

Geist, R., Davis, R., & Heinmaa, M. (1998). Binge/purge symptoms and comorbidity in adolescents with eating disorders. *Canadian Journal of Psychiatry, 43,* 507-512.

Geist, R., Heinmaa, M., Katzman, D., & Stephens, D. (1999). A comparison of male and female adolescents referred to an eating disorders programme. *Canadian Journal of Psychiatry, 44,* 374-378.

Geist, R., Heinmaa, M., Stephens, D., Davis, R., & Katzman, D.K. (2000). Comparison of family therapy and family group psychoeducation in adolescents with anorexia nervosa. *Canadian Journal of Psychiatry, 45,* 173-178.

Gelernter, C.S., Uhde, T.W., Cimbolic, P., Arnkoff, D.B., Vittone, B.J., et al. (1991). Cognitive behavioral and pharmacological treatments of social phobia: A controlled study. *Archives of General Psychiatry, 48,* 938-945.

Geller, G., & Thomas, C.D. (1999). A review of eating disorders in immigrant women: Possible evidence of a cultural-change model. *Eating Disorders: The Journal of Treatment and Prevention, 7,* 279-297.

Geller, J., Cockell, S.J., Hewitt, P.L., Goldner, E.M., & Flett, G.L. (2000). Inhibited expression of negative emotions and interpersonal orientation in anorexia nervosa. *International Journal of Eating Disorders, 28,* 8-19.

Gendlin, E.T. (1962). *Experiencing and the creation of meaning: A philosophical and psychological approach to the subject.* New York: Free Press.

General Register Office. (1968). *A glossary of mental disorders.* London: Author.

George, L.K. (1980). *Role transitions in later life.* Monterey, CA: Brooks/Cole.

George, L.K. (1994). Social factors and depression in late life. In L.S. Schneider, C.F. Reynolds, III, B.D. Lebowitz, & A.J. Friedhoff (Eds.), *Diagnosis and treatment of depression in late life* (pp. 131-153). Washington, DC: American Psychiatric Press.

George, L.K., Landoman, R., Blazer, D.G., & Anthony, J.C. (1991). Cognitive impairment. In L.N. Robins & D.A. Regier (Eds.), *Psychiatric disorders in America.* New York: Free Press.

Gerber, L.M. (1983). Ethnicity still matters: Socio-demographic profiles of the ethnic elderly in Ontario. *Canadian Ethnic Studies, 15,* 60-80.

Gergen, K.J. (1982). *Toward transformation in social knowledge.* New York: Plenum.

Gerin, W., Rosofsky, M., Pieper, C., & Pickering, T.G. (1994). A test of generalizability of cardiovascular reactivity using a controlled ambulatory procedure. *Psychosomatic Medicine, 56,* 360-368.

Gerlsma, C., Emmelkamp, P. M. G., & Arrindell, W. A. (1990). Anxiety, depression, and perception of early parenting: A meta-analysis. *Clinical Psychology Review, 10,* 251-257.

Gerlsma, C., & Hale, W.W. (1997). Predictive power and construct validity of the Level of Expressed Emotion (LEE) Scale. *British Journal of Psychiatry, 170,* 520-525.

Gerlsma, C., Snijders, T. A. B., van Duijn, M. A. J., & Emmelkamp, P. M. G. (1997). Parenting and psychopathology: Differences in family members' perceptions of parental rearing styles. *Personality and Individual Differences, 23,* 271-282.

Gerlsma, C., van der Lubbe, P.M., & van Nieuwenhuizen, C. (1992). Factor analysis of the Level of Expressed Emotion Scale: A questionnaire intended to measure "perceived expressed emotion." *British Journal of Psychiatry, 160*, 385-389.

Gesten, E.L., & Jason, L.A. (1987). Social and community interventions. *Annual Review of Psychology, 38,* 427-460.

Ghafour, H. (2001, May 27). The English patients: Newcomers struggle with new language. *The Toronto Star,* p. A6.

Ghoneim, M.M., & Mewaldt, S.P. (1990). Benzodiazepines and human memory: A review. *Anesthesiology, 72,* 926-938.

Gibbons, D.C. (1975). *Delinquent behavior*. Englewood Cliffs, NJ: Prentice-Hall.

Gibson, D., & Harris, A. (1988). Aggregated early intervention effects for Down's syndrome persons: Patterning and longevity of benefits. *Journal of Mental Deficiency Research, 32,* 1-17.

Gielen, A.C., Faden, R.R., O'Campo, P., Kass, N., & Anderson, J. (1994). Women's protective sexual behaviors: A test of the health belief model. *AIDS Education and Prevention, 6,* 1-11.

Gilbert, F.S. (1991). Development of a "steps questionnaire." *Journal of Studies on Alcohol, 52,* 353-360.

Gilger, J.W., & Kaplan, B.J. (2001). Atypical brain development: A conceptual framework for understanding developmental learning disabilities. *Developmental Neuropsychology*, *20*, 465-481.

Gillberg, C., & Svendsen, P. (1983). Childhood psychosis and computed tomographic brain scan findings. *Journal of Autism and Developmental Disorders, 13,* 19-32.

Gillis, J.J. & DeFries, J.C. (1991). Confirmatory factor analysis of reading and mathematics performance measures in the Colorado Reading Project. *Behavior Genetics, 21,* 572-573.

Gillmor, D. (1987*). I swear by Apollo: Dr. Ewen Cameron and the CIA-brainwashing experiments*. Montréal : Eden Press.

Ginzburg, H.M. (1986). Naltrexone: Its clinical utility. In B. Stimmel (Ed.), *Advances in alcohol and substance abuse* (pp. 83-101). New York: Haworth.

Girodo, M., Deck, T., & Morrison, M. (2002). Dissociative-type identity disturbances in undercover agents: Socio-cognitive factors behind false-identity appearances and reenactments. *Social Behavior and Personality*, *30*, 631-644.

Gitlin, M.J. (1993). Pharmacotherapy of personality disorders: Conceptual framework and clinical strategies. *Journal of Clinical Psychopharmacology, 13,* 343-353.

Gittelman, R., Abikoff, H., Pollack, E., Klein, D., Katz, F., & Mattes, J. (1980). A controlled trial of behavior modification and methylphenidate in hyperactive children. In C. Whalen & B. Henker (Eds.), *Hyperactive children: The social ecology of identification and treatment* (pp. 221-246). New York: Academic Press.

Gladue, B.A. (1985). Neuroendocrine response to estrogen and sexual orientation. *Science, 230,* 961.

Glass, C.R., & Arnkoff, D.B. (1997). Questionnaire methods of cognitive self-statement assessment. *Journal of Consulting and Clinical Psychology, 65,* 911-927.

Glassman, A.H., & Shapiro, P.A. (1998). Depression and the course of cardiovascular disease. *American Journal of Psychiatry , 155,* 4-11.

Gleaves, D.H. (1996). The sociocognitive model of dissociative identity disorder: A reexamination of the evidence. *Psychological Bulletin, 120,* 42-59.

Gleaves, D.H., & Eberenz, K.P. (1994). Sexual abuse histories among treatment-resistant bulimia nervosa patients. *International Journal of Eating Disorders, 15,* 227-231.

Gleick, J. (1987). *Chaos: Making a new science*. New York: Penguin Books.

Glick, I.D., Clarkin, J.F., Haas, G.L., Spencer, J.H., & Chen, C.L. (1991). A randomized clinical trial of inpatient family intervention: VI. Mediating variables and outcome. *Family Process, 30,* 85-99.

Gliksman, L., Adlaf, E.M., Demers, A., & Newton-Taylor, B. (2003). Heavy drinking on Canadian campuses. *Canadian Journal of Public Health, 94,* 17-21.

Gliksman, L., Demers, A., Adlaf, E., Newton-Taylor, B., & Schmidt, K. (2000). *Canadian Campus Survey 1998.* Toronto: Centre For Addiction and Mental Health.

Gnaedinger, N. (1989). *Elder abuse: A discussion paper.* Prepared for Working Together, National Forum on Family Violence.

Goeree, R., O'Brien, B. J., Goering, P., Blackhouse, G., Agro, K., Rhodes, A., & Watson, J. (1999). The economic burden of schizophrenia in Canada. *Canadian Journal of Psychiatry, 44,* 464-472.

Goering, P., Wasylenki, & Durbin, J. (2000). Canada's mental health system. *International Journal of Law and Psychiatry, 23,* 345-359.

Goff, D.C., & Simms, C.A. (1993). Has multiple personality disorder remained consistent over time? A comparison of past and present cases. *Journal of Nervous and Mental Disease, 181,* 595-600.

Goldapple, K., Segal, Z., Garson, C., Lau, M., Bieling, P., Kennedy, S., & Mayberg, H. (2004). Modulation of cortical-limbic pathways in major depression: Treatment-specific effects of cognitive behavior therapy. *Archives of General Psychiatry, 61,* 34-41.

Goldberg, E.M., & Morrison, S.L. (1963). Schizophrenia and social class. *British Journal of Psychiatry, 109,* 785-802.

Goldberg, J.O., & Schmidt, L.A. (2001). Shyness, sociability, and social dysfunction in schizophrenia. *Schizophrenia Research*, *48*, 343-349.

Golden, C.J. (1981a). The Luria-Nebraska Children's Battery: Theory and formulation. In G.W. Hynd & J.E. Obrzut (Eds.), *Neuropsychological assessment and the school-age child: Issues and procedures*. New York: Grune & Stratton.

Golden, C.J. (1981b). A standardized version of Luria's neuropsychological tests: A quantitative and qualitative approach to neuropsychological evaluation. In S.B. Filskov & T.J. Boil (Eds.), *Handbook of clinical neuropsychology*. New York: Wiley.

Golden, C.J., Hammeke, T., & Purisch, A. (1978). Diagnostic validity of a standardized neuropsychological battery derived from Luria's neuropsychological tests. *Journal of Consulting and Clinical Psychology, 46,* 1258-1265.

Goldfield, G.S., & Boachie, A. (2003). Delivery of family therapy in the treatment of anorexia nervosa using telehealth. *Telemedicine Journal and e-Health*, *9*, 111-114.

Goldfried, M.R. (1991). Research issues in psychotherapy integration. *Journal of Psychotherapy Integration, 1,* 5-25.

Goldfried, M.R., & D'Zurillia, T.J. (1969). A behavioral-analytic model for assessing competence. In C.D. Speilberger (Ed.), *Current topics in clinical and community psychology* (Vol. 1). New York: Academic Press.

Goldfried, M.R., & Davison, G.C. (1994). *Clinical behavior therapy*. Expanded edition. New York: Wiley.

Goldfried, M.R., & Eubanks-Carter, C. (2004). On the need for a new psychotherapy research paradigm: Comment on Westen, Novotny, and Thompson-Brenner (2004). *Psychological Bulletin*, *130*, 669-673.

Goldfried, M.R., Greenberg, L.S., & Marmar, C. (1990). Individual psychotherapy: Process and outcome. *Annual Review of Psychology, 41,* 659-688.

Goldfried, M.R., Padawer, W., & Robins, C. (1984). Social anxiety and the semantic structure of heterosocial interactions. *Journal of Abnormal Psychology, 93,* 87-97.

Golding, J.M., Smith, G.R., & Kashner, T.M. (1991). Does somatization disorder occur in men? Clinical characteristics of women and men with unexplained somatic symptoms. *Archives of General Psychiatry, 48,* 231-235.

Goldman, A., & Greenberg, L. (1992). Comparison of integrated systemic and emotionally focussed approaches to couples therapy. *Journal of Consulting and Clinical Psychology, 60,* 962-969.

Goldman, L., & Haaga, D.A.F. (1995). Depression and the experience of anger in marital and other relationships. Journal of Nervous and Mental Disease, 183, 505-509.

Goldman, M.S., Del Boca, F.K., & Darkes, J. (1999). Alcohol expectancy theory: The application of cognitive neuroscience. In K. E. Leonard & H. T. Blane (Eds.), *Psychological theories of drinking and alcoholism* (2nd ed., pp. 203-246). New York: Guilford.

Goldmeier, J. (1988). Pets or people: Another research note. *The Gerontologist, 26,* 203-206.

Goldner, E.M., Hsu, L., Waraich, P., & Somers, J.M. (2002). Prevalence and incidence studies of schizophrenic disorders: A systematic review of the literature. *Canadian Journal of Psychiatry*, *47*, 833-843.

Goldner, E.M., Srikameswaran, S., & Cockell, S.J. (2002). Perfectionism and eating disorders. In G. L. Flett & P. L. Hewitt (Eds.), *Perfectionism: Theory, research, and treatment* (pp. 319-340). Washington, DC: American Psychological Association.

Goldstein, A. (1994). *Addiction: From biology to drug policy*. New York: W.H. Freeman.

Goldstein, A.J., & Chambless, D.L. (1978). A reanalysis of agoraphobic behavior. *Behavior Therapy, 9,* 47-59.

Goldstein, J.L. (1999). *Snoring can kill*. Pacific Palisades, CA: Caren Publishing Group.

Goldstein, J.M., Goodman, J.M., Seidman, L.J., Kennedy, D.N., Makris, N., et al. (1999). Cortical abnormalities in schizophrenia identified by structural magnetic resonance imaging. *Archives of General Psychiatry, 56,* 537-547.

Goldstein, M.J., & Rodnick, E. (1975). The family's contribution to the etiology of schizophrenia: Current status. *Schizophrenia Bulletin, 14,* 48-63.

Goldstein, R.B., Wickramaratne, P.J., Horwath, E., & Weissman, M.M. (1997). Familal aggregation and phenomenology of "early"-onset (at or before age 20 years) panic disorder. *Archives of General Psychiatry, 54,* 271-278.

Goldstein, S.E., & Birnbom, F. (1976). Hypochondriasis and the elderly. *Journal of the American Geriatrics Society, 24,* 150-154.

Goleman, D. (1995). *Emotional intelligence*. New York: Bantam.

Gomberg, E. S. L., & Zucker, R. A. (1998). Substance use and abuse in old age. In I.H. Nordhus, G.R. VandenBos, S. Berg, & P. Fromholt, (Eds.), *Clinical geropsychology* (pp. 189-204). Washington, D.C.: American Psychological Association.

Goodacre, R. H. (1975) et al.. Hospitalization and hospital bed replacement. *Canadian Psychiatric Association Journal*, *20*, 7-14

Goodenow, C., Reisine, S.T., & Grady, K.E. (1989). Quality of social support and associated social and psychological functions in women with rheumatoid arthritis. *Health Psychology, 9,* 266-284.

Goodman, G. S., et al. (2003). A prospective study of memory for child sexual abuse: New findings relevant to the repressed-memory controversy. *Psychological Sciences*, *14*, 113-118.

Goodman, L.A., Koss, M.P., Fitzgerald, L.F., Russo, N.F., et al. (1993). Male violence against women: Current research and future directions. *American Psychologist, 48,* 1054-1058.

Goodman, R., & Stevenson, J. (1989). A twin study of hyperactivity: 2. The aetiological role of genes, family relationships, and perinatal adversity. *Journal of Child Psychology and Psychiatry, 30,* 691-709.

Goodsitt, A. (1997). Eating disorders: A self-psychological perspective. In D.M. Garner & P.E. Garfinkel (Eds.), *Handbook of treatment for eating disorders*. (pp. 205-228). New York: Guilford Press.

Goodwin, D.W. (1979). Alcoholism and heredity: A review and hypothesis. *Archives of General Psychiatry, 36,* 57-61.

Goodwin, D.W., & Guze, S.B. (1984). *Psychiatric diagnosis* (3rd ed.). New York: Oxford University Press.

Goodwin, D.W., Schulsinger, F., Hermansen, L., Guze, S.B., & Winokur, G.A. (1973). Alcohol problems in adoptees raised apart from alcoholic biological parents. *Archives of General Psychiatry, 128,* 239-243.

Goodwin, F., & Jamison, K. (1990). *Manic-depressive illness*. New York: Oxford University Press.

Goodwin, P.J., et al. (2001). The effect of group psychosocial support on survival in metastatic breast cancer. *New England Journal of Medicine*, *345*, 1719-1726.

Gordon, R.M., & Brill, D. (2001). The abuse and neglect of the elderly. *International Journal of Law and Psychiatry*, *24*, 183-197.

Gordon, R.M., & Verdun-Jones, S.N. (1992). *Adult guardianship law in Canada*. Toronto: Carswell Thomson.

Gorenstein, E.E., & Newman, J.P. (1980). Disinhibitory psychopathology: A new perspective and a model for research. *Psychological Review, 87,* 301-315.

Gorman, J.M. (1994). New and experimental pharmacological treatments for panic disorder. In B.E. Wolfe & J.D. Maser (Eds.), *Treatment of panic disorder: A consensus development conference* (pp. 83-90). Washington, DC: American Psychiatric Press.

Gorman, J.M., Fyer, M.R., Goetz, R., Askanazi, J., Leibowitz, M.R., Fyer, A.J., Kinney, J., & Klein, D.F. (1988). Ventilatory physiology of patients with panic disorder. *Archives of General Psychiatry, 45,* 53-60.

Gortner, E., Gollan, J., Dobson, K.S., & Jacobson, N.S. (1997). Cognitive-behavioral treatment for depression: Relapse prevention. *Journal of Consulting and Clinical Psychology*, *66*, 377-384.

Gotesdam, K.G., & Agras, W.S. (1995). General population-based epidemiological survey of eating disorders in Norway. *International Journal of Eating Disorders, 18,* 119-126.

Gotlib, I.H., & Asarnow, R.F. (1979). Interpersonal and impersonal problem-solving skills in mildly and clinically depressed students. *Journal of Consulting and Clinical Psychology, 47,* 86-95.

Gotlib, I.H., Lewinsohn, P.M., Seeley, J.R., Rohde, P., & Rednew, J.E. (1993). Negative cognitions and attributional style in depressed adolescents: An examination of stability and specificity. *Journal of Abnormal Psychology, 102,* 607-615.

Gotlib, I.H., & McCann, C.D. (1984). Construct accessibility and depression: An examination of cognitive and affective factors. *Journal of Personality and Social Psychology*, *47*, 427-439.

Gotlib, I.H., & Robinson, L.A. (1982). Responses to depressed individuals: Discrepancies between self-report and observer-rated behavior. *Journal of Abnormal Psychology, 91,* 231-240.

Gotlib, I.H., Whiffen, V.E., Mount, J.H., Milne, K., & Cordy, N.I. (1989). Prevalence rates and demographic characteristics associated with depression in pregnancy and the postpartum. *Journal of Consulting and Clinical Psychology*, *57*, 269-274.

Gotlib, I.H., Whiffen, V.E., Wallace, P., & Mount, J. (1991). A prospective investigation of postpartum depression: Factors involved in onset and recovery. *Journal of Abnormal Psychology*, *100*, 122-132.

Gottesman, I., & Shields, J. (1972). *Schizophrenia and genetics: A twin study vantage point*. New York: Academic Press.

Gottesman, I.I., & Goldsmith, H.H. (1994). Developmental psychopathology of antisocial behavior: Inserting genes into its ontogenesis and epigenesis. In C.A. Nelson (Ed.), *Threats to optimal development*. Hillside, NJ: Erlbaum.

Gottesman, I.I., McGuffin, P., & Farmer, A.E. (1987). Clinical genetics as clues to the "real" genetics of schizophrenia. *Schizophrenia Bulletin, 13,* 23-47.

Gottlieb, B.H., & Johnson, J. (2000). Respite programs for caregivers of persons with dementia: A review with practice implications. *Aging and Mental Health*, *4*, 119-129.

Gottlieb, J. (1990). Mainstreaming and quality education. *American Journal on Mental Retardation, 95,* 16-25.

Gottman, J.M. (1979). *Marital interaction: Experimental investigations*. New York: Academic Press.

Gottman, J.M., & Krokoff, L.J. (1989). Marital interaction and satisfaction: A longitudinal view. *Journal of Consulting and Clinical Psychology, 57,* 47-52.

Gottman, J.M., Notarius, C., Gonso, J., & Markman, H. (1976). *A couple's guide to communication*. Champaign, IL.: Research Press.

Gould, M.S., Wallenstein, S., & Kleinman, M.H. (1990). Time-space clustering of teenage suicide. *American Journal of Epidemiology, 131,* 71-78.

Government of Canada (1977). Minutes of proceedings and evidence of the subcommittee on the penitentiary system in Canada. House of Commons Issue No. 36, Tuesday March 8. Available: Canadian Government Publishing Centre, Supply and Services Canada, Ottawa, Canada, K1A 0S9.

Goyer, P., Andreason, P.J., Semple, W.E., Clayton, A.H., et al. (1994). Positron-emission tomography and personality disorders. *Neuropsychopharmacology, 10,* 21-28.

Goyette, C.H., & Conners, C.K. (1977). *Food additives and hyperkinesis*. Paper presented at the 85th Annual Convention of the American Psychological Association.

Grace, S.L., Abbey, S.E., Shnek, Z.M., Irvine, J., Franche, R-L., & Stewart, D.E. (2002). Cardiac rehabilitation I: Review of psychosocial factors. *General Hospital Psychiatry*, *24*, 121-126.

Graham, J.E., Rockwood, K., Beattie, B. L., Eastwood, R., Gauthier, S., & Tuokko, H., & McDowell, I. (1997). Prevalence and severity of cognitive impairment with and without dementia in an elderly population. *The Lancet*, *349*, 1793-1796.

Graham, J.R. (1988). Establishing validity of the revised form of the MMPI. Symposium presentation at the 96th Annual Convention of the American Psychological Association, Atlanta.

Graham, J.R. (1990). *MMPI-2: Assessing personality and psychopathology*. New York: Oxford University Press.

Graham, K. (1988). Reasons for consumption and heavy caffeine use: Generalization of a model based on alcohol research. *Addictive Behaviors*, *13*,

209-214.

Graham, K., & Braun, K. (1999). Concordance of use of alcohol and other substances among older adult couples. *Addictive Behaviors, 24,* 839-856.

Gralnick, A. (1986). Future of the chronic schizophrenic patient: Prediction and recommendation. *American Journal of Psychotherapy, 40,* 419-429.

Gramling, S.E., Clawson, E.P., & McDonald, M.K. (1996). Perceptual and cognitive abnormality model of hypochondriasis: Amplification and physiological reactivity in women. *Psychosomatic Medicine, 58,* 423-431.

Grant, A. (1996). No end of grief: Indian residential schools in Canada. Winnipeg: Pemmican Publications.

Gratzer, T., & Bradford, J.M.W. (1995). Offender and offense characteristics of sexual sadists: A comparative study. *Journal of Forensic Sciences, 40,* 450-455.

Gray, E.B. (1983). *Final report: Collaborative research of community and minority group action to prevent child abuse and neglect: Vol. 3. Public awareness and education using the creative arts.* Chicago: National Committee for Prevention of Child Abuse.

Gray, J.E., & O'Reilly, R.L. (2001). Clinically significant differences among Canadian mental health acts. *Canadian Journal of Psychiatry, 46,* 325-321.

Gray, R.E., Fitch, M., Phillips, C., Labreque, M., & Fergus, K. (2000). Managing the impact of illness: The experiences of men with prostate cancer and their spouses. *Journal of Health Psychology, 5,* 531-548.

Gray, N.S. et al. (2003). Prediction of violence and self-harm in mentally disordered offenders: A prospective study of the efficacy of HCR-20, PCL-R, and psychiatric symptomatology. *Journal of Consulting and Clinical Psychology, 71,* 443-451.

Green, K.L., Cameron, R., Polivy, J., Cooper, K., Liu, L.Y., Leiter, L., et al. (1997). Weight dissatisfaction and weight loss attempts among Canadian adults. *Canadian Medical Association Journal, 157,* S17-S25 (Supplement).

Green, M.F. (1993). Cognitive remediation in schizophrenia. *American Journal of Psychiatry, 150,* 178-187.

Green, M.F. (1996). What are the functional consequences of neurocognitive deficits in schizophrenia? *American Journal of Psychiatry, 153,* 321-330.

Green, M.F., Marshall, B.D., Wirshing, W.C., Ames, D., Marder, S.R., McGurk, S., Kern, R.S., & Mintz, J. (1997). Does risperidone improve verbal working memory in treatment-resistant schizophrenia? *American Journal of Psychiatry, 154,* 799-804.

Green, R. (1969). Mythological, historical and cross-cultural aspects of transsexualism. In R. Green & J. Money (Eds.), *Transsexualism and sex reassignment.* Baltimore: Johns Hopkins University Press.

Green, R. (1976). One hundred ten feminine and masculine boys: Behavioral contrasts and demographic similarities. *Archives of Sexual Behavior, 5,* 425-446.

Green, R. (1985). Gender identity in childhood and later sexual orientation: Follow-up of 78 males. *American Journal of Psychiatry, 142,* 339-341.

Green, R. (1987). *The "sissy boy syndrome" and the development of homosexuality.* New Haven: Yale University Press.

Green, R. (1992). *Sexual science and the law.* Cambridge, MA: Harvard University Press.

Green, R., & Blanchard, R. (1995). Gender identity disorders. In H.I. Kaplan & B.J. Sadock (Eds.), *Comprehensive textbook of psychiatry.* (pp. 1347-1360). Baltimore, MD: Williams & Wilkins.

Green, R., & Fleming, D.T. (1990). Transsexual surgery follow-up: Status in the 1990s. In J. Bancroft, C. Davis, & D. Weinstein (Eds.), *Annual review of sex research* (pp. 163-174).

Green, R., & Money, J. (1969). *Transsexualism and sex reassignment.* Baltimore: Johns Hopkins University Press.

Green, R.C. et al. (2003). Depression as a risk factor for Alzheimer disease: The *MIRAGE* study. *Archives of Neurology, 60,* 753-759.

Greenberg, D.M. (1998). Sexual recidivism in sex offenders. *Canadian Journal of Psychiatry, 43,* 459-465.

Greenberg, J. (1996, August 21). Teen drug use has doubled in 4 years, U.S. says. *Los Angeles Times,* pp. A1, A17.

Greenberg, L.S. (1984). A task analysis of conflict resolution. In L. N. Rice & L. S. Greenberg (Eds.), *Patterns of change* (pp. 67-123). NY: Guilford.

Greenberg, L.S. (1992). Task analysis: Identifying components of intrapersonal conflict resolution. In S. G. Toukmanian & D. L. Rennie (Eds.), *Psychotherapy process research: Paradigmatic and narrative approaches.* Newbury Park, CA: Sage.

Greenberg, L.S. (2004). Emotion-focused therapy. *Clinical Psychology and Psychotherapy, 11,* 3-16.

Greenberg, L.S., & Bolger, E. (2001). An emotion-focused approach to the overregulation of emotion and emotional pain. *Journal of Clinical Psychology/In Session: Psychotherapy in Practice, 57,* 197-211.

Greenberg, L., Elliott, R., & Lietaer, G. (1994). Research on experiential therapies. In A.E. Bergin & S.L. Garfield (Eds.), *Handbook of psychotherapy and behavior change.* Fourth edition (pp. 509-539). New York: Wiley.

Greenberg, L.S., & Johnson, S.M. (1988). *Emotionally focussed couples therapy.* New York: Guilford.

Greenberg, L.S., & Malcolm, W. (2002). Resolving unfinished business: Relating process to outcome. *Journal of Consulting and Clinical Psychology, 70,* 406-416.

Greenberg, L.S., & Rice, L.N. (1981). The specific effects of a gestalt intervention. *Psychotherapy: Theory, Research, and Practice, 18,* 31-37.

Greenberg, L.S., & Safran, J. (1984). Integrating affect and cognition: A perspective on the process of therapeutic change. *Cognitive Therapy and Research, 8,* 559-578.

Greenberg, L.S., & Watson, J. (1998). Experiential therapy of depression: Differential effects of client-centered relationship conditions and process experiential interventions. *Psychotherapy Research, 8,* 210-224.

Greenberg, P.E., Sisitsky, T., Kessler, R. C., Finkelstein, S.N., Berndt, E.R., Davidson, J.R. T., Ballenger, J. C., & Fyer, A.J. (1999). The economic burden of anxiety disorders in the 1990s. *Journal of Clinical Psychiatry, 60,* 427-435.

Greenblatt, M., Solomon, M.H., Evans, A.S., & Brooks, G.W. (Eds.). (1965). *Drugs and social therapy in chronic schizophrenia.* Springfield, IL: Charles C. Thomas.

Greene, B.A. (1985). Considerations in the treatment of black patients by white therapists. *Psychotherapy, 22,* 115-122.

Greene, B.L. (1960). Marital disharmony: Concurrent analysis of husband and wife. *Diseases of the Nervous System, 21,* 1-6.

Greenland, C. (1996). Origins of the Toronto Psychiatric Hospital. In E. Shorter (Ed.), *TPH: History and memories of the Toronto Psychiatric Hospital, 1925-1966.* Toronto: Wall & Emerson.

Greer, S., Morris, T., & Pettigale, K.W. (1979). Psychological response to breast cancer: Effect on outcome. *Lancet, 2,* 785-787.

Griffin, J. (1989). *In search of sanity: A chronicle of the Canadian Mental Health Association, 1918-1988.* London, Ontario: Third Eye Publications.

Griffin, J. D. (1993, December). An historical oversight. *Newsletter of the Ontario Psychiatric Association,* 9-10.

Griffith, D., & Bartholomew, K. (1994). The metaphysics of measurement: The case of adult attachment. In K. Bartholomew & D. Perlman (Eds.), *Advances in personal relationships: Vol. 5: Attachment processes in adulthood* (pp. 17-52). London: Jessica Kingsley Publishers.

Grifin, M.G., Resick, P.A., & Mechanic, M.B. (1997). Objective assessment of peritraumatic dissociation: Psychophysiological indicators. *American Journal of Psychiatry, 154,* 1081-1088.

Grigorenko, E.L. (1997). Susceptibility for distinct components of developmental dyslexia on chromosomes 6 and 15. *American Journal of Human Genetics, 60,* 27-39.

Grigorenko, E.L., Wood, F.B., Meyer, M.S., Hart, L.A., Speed, W.C., Shuster, A., & Pauls, D.L. (in press). Susceptibility loci for distinct components of developmental dyslexia on chromosome 6 and 15. *American Journal of Human Genetics.*

Grilo, C.M., Shiffman, S., & Carter-Campbell, J.T. (1994). Binge eating antecedents in normal weight nonpurging females: Is there consistency? *International Journal of Eating Disorders, 16,* 239-249.

Grings, W.W., & Dawson, M.E. (1978). *Emotions and bodily responses: A psychophysiological approach.* New York: Academic Press.

Grinker, R.B., & Spiegel, J.P. (1945). *Men under stress.* Philadelphia: Blakiston.

Grinker, R.R., & Spiegel, J.P. (1944). *Management of neuropsychiatric casualties in the zone of combat: Manual of military neuropsychiatry.* Philadelphia: W.B. Saunders.

Grinker, R.R., & Spiegel, J.P. (1979). *War neuroses.* New York: Arno Press.

Grinspoon, L., & Bakalar, J.B. (1995). Marijuana as medicine: A plea for reconsideration. *Journal of the American Medical Association, 273,* 1875-1876.

Grisso, T. (1986). *Evaluating competencies: Forensic assessments and instruments.* New York: Plenum.

Grisso, T., & Appelbaum, P.S. (1991). Mentally ill and non-mentally ill patients' abilities to understand informed consent disclosures for medication: Preliminary data. *Law and Human Behavior, 15,* 377-388.

Grisso, T., & Appelbaum, P.S. (1992). Is it unethical to offer predictions of future violence? *Law and Human Behavior, 16,* 621-633.

Grisso, T., & Appelbaum, P.S. (1995). The MacArthur Treatment Competence Study: 3. Abilities of patients to consent to psychiatric and medical treatments. *Law and Human Behavior, 19,* 149-174.

Gross, M.D. (1984). Effects of sucrose on hyperkinetic children. *Pediatrics, 74,* 876-878.

Gross, S.R., Barrett, S.P., Shestowsky, J.S., & Pihl, R.O. (2002). Ecstasy and drug consumption patterns: A Canadian rave population study. *Canadian Journal of Psychiatry, 47,* 546-550.

Grosz, H.J., & Zimmerman, J. (1970). A second detailed case study of functional blindness: Further demonstration of the contribution of objective psychological laboratory data. *Behavior Therapy, 1,* 115-123.

Groth, N.A., & Burgess, A.W. (1977). Sexual dysfunction during rape. *New England Journal of Medicine, 297,* 764-766.

Groth, N.A., Hobson, W.F., & Guy, T.S. (1982). The child molester: Clinical observations. In J. Conte & D.A. Shore (Eds.), *Social work and child sexual abuse.* New York: Haworth.

Grove, W.R., Eckert, E.D., Heston, L., Bouchard, T., et al. (1990). Heritability of substance abuse and antisocial behavior in monozygotic twins reared apart. *Biological Psychiatry, 27,* 1293-1304.

Grych, J.H., & Fincham, F.D. (1990). Marital conflict and children's adjustment: A cognitive-contextual framework. *Psychological Bulletin, 108,* 267-290.

Guerra, N., & Slaby, R. (1990). Cognitive mediators of aggression in adolescent offenders: 2. Intervention. *Developmental Psychology, 26,* 269-277.

Guidano, V.F., & Liotti, G. (1983). *Cognitive processes and emotional disorders.* New York: Guilford.

Gump, B.S., Matthews, K.A., & Raikkonen, K. (1999). Modeling relationships among socioeconomic status, hostility, cardiovascular reactivity, and left ventricular mass in African American and White children. *Health Psychology, 18,* 140-150.

Gunderson, J.G., Kolb, J.E., & Austin, V. (1981). The diagnostic interview for borderline patients. *American Journal of Psychiatry, 138,* 896-903.

Gunn, J. (1993). Castration is not the answer. *British Medical Journal, 307,* 790-791.

Guo, Z., Cupples, L.A., Kurz, A., Auerbach, S.H., Volicer, L., Chui, H., et al. (2000). Head injury and the risk of Alzheimer's disease in the MIRAGE study. *Neurology, 28,* 1316-1323.

Gupta, R., & Derevensky, J. L. (1998). Adolescent gambling behavior: A prevalence study and examination of the correlates associated with problem gambling. *Journal of Gambling Studies, 14, (4),* 319-345.

Gupta, R., & Derevensky, J. L. (2000). Adolescents with gambling problems: From research to treatment. *Journal of Gambling Studies, 16, (2/3),* 315-342.

Gurian, B., & Miner, J.H. (1991). Clinical presentation of anxiety in the elderly. In C. Salzman & B.D. Lebowitz (Eds.), *Anxiety in the elderly.* New York: Springer.

Gurland, B. (1991). Epidemiology of psychiatric disorders. In J. Sadavoy, L.W. Lazarus, & L.F. Jarvik (Eds.), *Comprehensive review of geriatric psychiatry* (pp. 25-40). Washington, DC: American Psychiatric Press.

Gurman, A.S., & Kniskern, D.P. (1978). Research on marital and family therapy: Progress, perspective, and prospect. In S.L. Garfield & A.E. Bergin (Eds.), *Handbook of psychotherapy and behavior change: An empirical analysis* (2nd ed.). New York: Wiley.

Gurman, A.S., & Kniskern, D.P. (1981). Family therapy outcome research: Knowns and unknowns. In A.S. Gurman & D.P. Kniskern (Eds.), *Handbook of family therapy.* New York: Brunner/Mazel.

Gurman, A.S., Kniskern, D.P., & Pinsoff, W.M. (1986). Research on the process and outcome of marital and family therapy. In S.L. Garfield & A.E. Bergin (Eds.), *Handbook of psychotherapy and behavior change* (3rd ed.). New York: Wiley.

Gustafson, Y., Berggren, D., Bucht, B., Norberf, A., Hansson, L.I., & Winblad, B. (1988). Acute confusional states in elderly patients treated for femoral neck fracture. *Journal of the American Geriatrics Society, 36,* 525-530.

Guyll, M., & Contrada, R.J. (1998). Trait hostility and ambulatory cardiovascular activity: Responses to social interaction. *Health Psychology, 17,* 30-39.

Guze, S.B. (1967). The diagnosis of hysteria: What are we trying to do? *American Journal of Psychiatry, 124,* 491-498.

Guze, S.B. (1993). Genetics of Briquet's syndrome and somatization disorder: A review of family, adoption, and twin studies. *Annals of Clinical Psychiatry, 5,* 225-230.

Haaga, D.A. (1987a). *Smoking schemata revealed in articulated thoughts predict early relapse from smoking cessation.* Paper presented at the 21st Annual Convention of the Association for Advancement of Behavior Therapy, Boston.

Haaga, D.A. (1987b). Treatment of the type A behavior pattern. *Clinical Psychology Review, 7,* 557-574.

Haaga, D.A. (1988). *Cognitive aspects of the relapse prevention model in the prediction of smoking relapse.* Paper presented at the 22nd Annual Convention of the Association for Advancement of Behavior Therapy, New York.

Haaga, D.A.F. (2000). Introduction to the special section on stepped care models in psychotherapy. *Journal of Consulting and Clinical Psychology, 68,* 547-548.

Haaga, D.A., & Davison, G.C. (1989). Outcome studies of rational-emotive therapy. In M.E. Bernard & R. DiGiuseppe (Eds.), *Inside rational-emotive therapy.* New York: Academic Press.

Haaga, D.A.F. (1989). Articulated thoughts and endorsement procedures for cognitive assessment in the prediction of smoking relapse. *Psychological Assessment: A Journal of Consulting and Clinical Psychology, 1,* 112-117.

Haaga, D.A.F. (1990). Issues in relating self-efficacy to smoking relapse: Importance of an "Achilles' Heel" situation and of prior quitting experience. *Journal of Substance Abuse, 2,* 191-200.

Haaga, D.A.F. (2000). Introduction to the special section on stepped care models in psychotherapy. *Journal of Consulting and Clinical Psychology, 68,* 547-548.

Haaga, D.A.F., & Davison, G.C. (1991). Cognitive change methods. In F.H. Kanfer & A.P. Goldstein (Eds.), *Helping people change: A textbook of methods* (4th ed.). Elmsford, NY: Pergamon.

Haaga, D.A.F., & Davison, G.C. (1992). Disappearing differences do not always reflect healthy integration: An analysis of cognitive therapy and rational-emotive therapy. *Journal of Psychotherapy Integration, 1,* 287-303.

Haaga, D.A.F., DeRubeis, R.J., Stewart, B.L., & Beck, A.T. (1991). Relationship of intelligence with cognitive therapy outcome. *Behaviour Research and Therapy, 29,* 277-281.

Haaga, D.A.F., Dyck, M.J., & Ernst, D. (1991). Empirical status of cognitive theory of depression. *Psychological Bulletin, 110,* 215-236.

Haaga, D.A.F., Rabois, D., & Brody, C. (1999). Cognitive behavior therapy. In M. Hersen & A.S. Bellack (Eds.), *Handbook of comparative treatments for adult disorders.* New York: Wiley.

Haas, R.H., Townsend, J., Courchesne, E., Lincoln, A.J., Schreibman, L., & Yeung-Courchesne, R. (1996). Neurologic abnormalities in infantile autism. *Journal of Child Neurology, 11,* 84-92.

Haddock, G., Tarrier, N., Spaulding, W., Yusupoff, L. K., & McCarthy, E. (1998). Individual cognitive-behavior therapy in the treatment of hallucinations and delusions: A review. *Clinical Psychology Review, 18,* 821-838.

Hadjistavropoulos, H.D., Asmundson, G.J.G., LaChapelle, D.L., & Quine, A. (2002). The role of health anxiety among patients with chronic pain in determining response to therapy. *Pain Research and Management, 7,* 127-133.

Hadjistavropoulos, H.D., Asmundson, G.J.G., & Norton, G.R. (1999). Validation of the Coping with Health, Injuries, and Problems Scale in a chronic pain sample. *Clinical Journal of Pain, 15,* 41-49.

Haensel, S.M., Klem, T.M., Hop, C.J., & Slob, A.K. (1998). Fluoxetine and premature ejaculation: A double-blind, cross-over, placebo-controlled trial. *Journal of Clinical Psychopharmacology, 18,* 72-77.

Hagerman, R.J. (1995). Molecular and clinical correlations in Fragile X syndrome. *Mental Retardation and Developmental Disabilities Research Reviews, 1,* 276-280.

Haggarty, J.M., Cernovsky, Z., Husni, M., Minor, K., Kermeen, P., & Merskey, H. (2002). Seasonal affective disorder in an Arctic community. *Acta Psychiatrica Scandinavica, 105,* 378-384.

Haggbloom, S.J., et al. (2002). The 100 most eminent psychologists of the 20th century. *Review of General Psychology, 6,* 139-152.

Hahlweg, K., & Markman, H.J. (1988). The effectiveness of behavioral marital therapy: Empirical status of behavioral techniques in preventing and alleviating marital distress. *Journal of Consulting and Clinical Psychology, 56,* 440-447.

Haig-Brown, C. (1988). *Resistance and renewal: Surviving Indian residential school.* Vancouver, Canada: Tillacum Library.

Hale, A.S. (1993). New antidepressants: Use in high-risk patients. *Journal of Clinical Psychiatry, 54,* 61-70.

Haley, S.A. (1978). Treatment implications of post-combat stress response syndromes for mental health professionals. In C.R. Figley (Ed.), *Stress disorders among Vietnam veterans.* New York: Brunner/Mazel.

Hall, C.S., Lindzey, G., Loehlin, J.C., & Manosevitz, M. (1985). *Introduction to theories of personality.* New York: Wiley.

Hall, E. (1900). The unofficial gynaecological treatment of the insane in British Columbia. *Medical Sentinel* (see www.canadiana.org).

Hall, G.C.N. (1995). Sexual offender recidivism revisited: A meta-analysis of treatment studies. *Journal of Consulting and Clinical Psychology, 63,* 802-809.

Hall, J. (1998, February 1). Merger of Clarke, Addiction Centre seen as 'win, win': New organization will treat mental illness and drug abuse problems. *The Toronto Star,* A4.

Hall, S.M., Munoz, R.F., & Reus, V.I. (1994). Cognitive-behavioral intervention increases abstinence rates for depressive-history smokers. *Journal of Consulting and Clinical Psychology, 62,* 141-146.

Hall, S.M., Munoz, R.F., Reus, V.I., Sees, K.L., Duncan, C., Humfleet, G.L., & Hartz, D.T. (1996). Mood management and nicotine gum in smoking treatment: A therapeutic contract and placebo-controlled study. *Journal of Consulting and Clinical Psychology, 64,* 1003-1009.

Hall, S.M., Reuss, V.I., Munoz, R.F., Sees, K.L., Humfleet, G., et al. (1998). Nortriptyline and cognitive-behavioral therapy in the treatment of cigarette smoking. *Archives of General Psychiatry, 55,* 683-690.

Halmi, K.A., Agras, W.S., Mitchell, J., Wilson, G.T., Crow, S., Bryson, S.W., & Kraemer, H. (2002). Relapse predictors of patients with bulimia nervosa who achieved abstinence through cognitive behavioral therapy. *Archives of General Psychiatry, 59,* 1105-1109.

Halmi, K.A., Sunday, S.R., Strober, M., Kaplan, A., Woodside, B., et al. (2000). Perfectionism in anorexia nervosa: Variation by clinical subtype, obsessionality, and pathological eating behavior. *American Journal of Psychiatry, 157,* 1799-1805.

Hamada, T., Koshino, Y., Misawa, T., Isaki, K., & Geyjo, F. (1998). Mitral valve prolapse and autonomic function in panic disorder. *Acta Psychiatrica Scandanavica, 97,* 139-143.

Hamilton, E.W., & Abramson, L.Y. (1983). Cognitive patterns and major depressive disorder: A longitudinal study in a hospital setting. *Journal of Abnormal Psychology, 92,* 173-184.

Hamilton, K.E., & Dobson, K.S. (2002). Cognitive therapy of depression: Pretreatment patient predictors of outcome. *Clinical Psychology Review, 22,* 875-893.

Hammen, C. (1997). Depression. East Sussex, Great Britain: Psychology Press.

Hammen, C.L. (1980). Depression in college students: Beyond the Beck Depression Inventory. *Journal of Consulting and Clinical Psychology, 48,* 126-128.

Hammen, C., & Compas, B.E. (1994). Unmasking unmasked depression in children and adolescents: The problem of comorbidity. *Clinical Psychology Review, 14,* 585-603.

Hankin, B.J., Abramson, L.Y., Moffitt, T.E., Silva, P.A., McGee, R., et al. (1998). Development of depression from preadolescence to young adulthood: Emerging gender differences in a 10-year longitudinal study. *Journal of Abnormal Psychology, 107,* 128-140.

Hansen, W.B. (1992). School-based substance abuse prevention: A review of the state of the art in curriculum, 1980-1990. *Health Education Research: Theory and Practice, 7,* 403-430.

Hansen, W.B. (1993). School-based alcohol prevention programs. *Alcohol Health and Research World, 18,* 62-66.

Hansen, W.B., Johnson, C.A., Flay, B.R., Graham, J.W., & Sobel, J. (1988). Affective and social influence approaches to the prevention of multiple substance abuse among seventh grade students. *Preventive Medicine, 17,* 135-154.

Hanson, R.K., & Bussiere, M.T. (1998). Predicting relapse: A meta-analysis of sexual offender recidivism studies. *Journal of Consulting and Clinical Psychology, 66,* 348-362.

Hanson, R.K., Gordon, A., Harris, A.J.R., Marques, J.K., Murphy, W., Quinsey, V.L., & Seto, M. (2002). First report of the Collaborative Outcome Data project on the effectiveness of psychological treatment for sex offenders. *Sexual Abuse: A Journal of Research and Treatment, 14,* 169-194.

Hanson, R.K., & Harris, A.J.R. (1997). Voyeurism: Assessment and treatment. In D.R. Laws & W. O'Donohue (Eds.), *Sexual deviance.* (pp. 311-331). NY: Guilford Press.

Hanusa, B.H., & Schulz, R. (1977). Attributional mediators of learned helplessness. *Journal of Personality and Social Psychology, 35,* 602-611.

Haracz, J.L. (1982). The dopamine hypothesis: An overview of studies with schizophrenic patients. *Schizophrenia Bulletin, 8,* 438-469.

Hardan, A.Y., Minshew, N.J., Mallikarjuhn, M., & Keshevan, M.S. (2001). Brain volume in autism. *Journal of Child Neurology, 16,* 421-424.

Hardoon, K., Derevensky, J.L., & Gupta, R. (2003). Empirical measures versus perceived gambling severity among youth: Why adolescent problem gamblers fail to see treatment. *Addictive Behaviors, 28,* 933-946.

Hardy, B.W., & Waller, D.A. (1988). Bulimia as substance abuse. In W.G. Johnson (Ed.), *Advances in eating disorders.* New York: JAI.

Hardy, J. (1993). Genetic mistakes point the way to Alzheimer's disease. *Journal of NIH Research, 5,* 46-49.

Hare, E. (1969). *Triennial statistical report of the Royal Maudsley and Bethlem Hospitals.* London: Bethlem and Maudsley Hospitals.

Hare, R.D. (1978). Electrodermal and cardiovascular correlates of sociopathy. In R.D. Hare & D. Schalling (Eds.), *Psychopathic behavior: Approaches to research.* New York: Wiley.

Hare, R.D. (1991). *The Hare Psychopathy Checklist-Revised.* Toronto: Multi-Health Systems.

Hare, R.D. (1996). Psychopathy and antisocial personality disorder: A case of diagnostic confusion. *Psychiatric Times, 13,* 39-40.

Hare, R.D., Clark, D., Grann, M., & Thornton, D. (2000). Psychopathy and the predictive utility of the PCL-R: An international perspective. *Behavioral Sciences and the Law, 18,* 623-645.

Hare, R.D., Harpur, T.J., Hakstian, R.A., Forth, A.E., Hart, S.D., et al. (1990). The revised Psychopathy Checklist: Reliability and factor structure. *Psychological Assessment, 2,* 338-341.

Hare, R.D., Hart, S.D., & Harpur, T.J. (1991). Psychopathy and the DSM-IV criteria for antisocial personality disorder. *Journal of Abnormal Psychology, 100,* 391-398.

Harkness, A.R., McNulty, J.L., & Ben-Porath, Y.S. (1995). The Personality Psychopathology Five (PSY-5): Constructs and MMPI-2 scales. *Psychological Assessment, 7,* 104-114.

Harkness, K.L., Frank, E., et al. (2002). Does interpersonal psychotherapy protect women from depression in the face of stressful life events? *Journal of Consulting and Clinical Psychology, 70,* 908-915.

Harkness, K.L., & Luther, J. (2001). Clinical risk factors for the generation of life events in major depression. *Journal of Abnormal Psychology, 110,* 564-572.

Harkness, K.L., Monroe, S.M., Simons, A.D., & Thase, M. (1999). The generation of life events in recurrent and non-recurrent depression. *Psychological Medicine, 29,* 135-144.

Harpur, T.J., & Hare, R.D. (1990). Psychopathy and attention. In J. Enns (Ed.), *The development of attention: Research and theory.* Amsterdam: New Holland.

Harpur, T.J., & Hare, R.D. (1994). Assessment of psychopathy as a function of age. *Journal of Abnormal Psychology, 103,* 604-609.

Harpur, T.J., Hart, S.D., & Hare, R.D. (1994). Personality of the psychopath. In P. T. Costa, Jr., & T. A. Widiger (Eds.), *Personality disorders and the five-factor model of personality* (pp. 149-173). Washington, DC: American Psychological Association.

Harries, K. (2001, August 18). The plight of Pikangikum: Suicides haunt remote reserve. *The Toronto Star,* pp. A1, A16-A17.

Harris, G.T., Rice, M.E., Lalumiere, M.L., Boer, D., & Lang, C. (2003). A multisite comparison of actuarial risk instruments for sex offenders. *Psychological Assessment, 15,* 413-425.

Harris, G.T., Rice, M.E., & Cormier, C.A. (2002). Prospective replication of the Violence Risk Appraisal Guide in predicting violent recidivism among forensic patients. *Law and Human Behavior, 26*, 377-394.

Harris, G.T., Rice, M.E., & Quinsey, V.L. (1993). Violent recidivism of mentally disordered offenders: The development of a statistical prediction instrument. *Criminal Justice and Behavior, 20*, 315-335.

Harris, G.T., Rice, M.E., & Quinsey, V.L. (1994). Psychopathy as a taxon: Evidence that psychopaths are a discrete class. *Journal of Consulting and Clinical Psychology, 62*, 387-397.

Harris, M.J., & Jeste, D.V. (1988). Late-onset schizophrenia: A review. *Schizophrenia Bulletin, 14,* 39-55.

Harrison, J., Chin, J., & Ficarrotto, T. (1989). Warning: Masculinity may be dangerous to your health. In M.S. Kimmel & M.A. Messner (Eds.), *Men's lives* (pp. 296-309). New York: Macmillan.

Harro, J., Vassar, E., & Bradwejn, J. (1993). Cholecystokinin in animal and human research on anxiety. *Trends in Pharmacological Science, 14,* 244-249.

Hart, E.L., Lahey, B.B., Loeber, R., Applegate, B., & Frick, P.J. (1995). Developmental changes in attention-deficit hyperactivity disorder in boys: A four-year longitudinal study. *Journal of Abnormal Child Psychology, 23,* 729-750.

Hart, S.D., Dutton, D., & Newlove, T. (1993). The prevalence of personality disorder among wife assaulters. *Journal of Personality Disorders, 7*, 329-341.

Hart, S.D., & Hare, R.D. (1989). Discriminant validity of the Psychopathy Checklist in a forensic psychiatric population. *Psychological Assessment, 1,* 211-218.

Hartley, D.E., & Strupp, H.H. (1983). The therapeutic alliance: Its relationship to outcome in brief psychotherapy. In J. Masling (Ed.), *Empirical studies of psychoanalytical theories* (Vol. 1). Hillsdale, NJ: Analytical Press.

Hartmann, H. (1958). *Ego psychology and the problem of adaptation*. New York: International Universities Press.

Harvard Mental Health Letter. (1994a, July). *Borderline personality-Part III, 11,* 1-3.

Harvard Mental Health Letter. (1994b, July). *Borderline personality-Part I and II, Special Supplement, 11,* 1-3.

Harvard Mental Health Letter. (1995, July). *Schizophrenia update-Part II, 12,* 1-5.

Harvard Mental Health Letter. (1996a, August). *Treatment of alcoholism-Part I, 13,* 1-4.

Harvard Mental Health Letter. (1996b, February). *Personality disorders: The anxious cluster-Part I, 12,* 1-3.

Harvard Mental Health Letter. (1996c, March). *Personality disorders: The anxious cluster-Part II, 12,* 1-3.

Hastrup, J.L., Light, K.C., & Obrist, P.A. (1982). Parental hypertension and cardiovascular response to stress in healthy young adults. *Psychophysiology, 19,* 615-622.

Hathaway, S.R., & McKinley, J.C. (1943). *MMPI manual*. New York: Psychological Corporation.

Hawke, J.M., Jainchill, N., & De Leon, G. (2000). Adolescent amphetamine users in treatment: Client profiles and treatment outcomes. *Journal of Psychoactive Drugs, 32*, 95-105.

Hawkins, J.D., Graham, J.W., Maguin, E., Abbott, R., et al. (1998). Exploring the effects of age of alcohol use initiation and psychosocial risk factors on subsequent alcohol misuse. *Journal of Studies on Alcohol, 58,* 280-290.

Hawton, K., Catalan, J., & Fagg, J. (1992). Sex therapy for erectile dysfunction: Characteristics of couples, treatment outcome, and prognostic factors. *Archives of Sexual Behavior, 21,* 161-176.

Hawton, K., Catalan, J., Martin, P., & Fagg, J. (1986). Long-term outcome of sex therapy. *Behaviour Research and Therapy, 24,* 665-675.

Hay, D.P. (1991). Electroconvulsive therapy. In J. Sadavoy, L.W. Lazarus, & L.F. Jarvik (Eds.), *Comprehensive review of geriatric psychiatry* (pp. 469-485). Washington, DC: American Psychiatric Press.

Hay, P., & Fairburn, C.G. (1998). The validity of the DSM-IV scheme for classifying eating disorders. *International Journal of Eating Disorders, 23,* 7-15.

Hayashi, K., Toyama, B., & Quay, H.C. (1976). A cross-cultural study concerned with differential behavioral classification: 1. The Behavior Checklist. *Japanese Journal of Criminal Psychology, 2,* 21-28.

Hayes, R.L., Halford, W.K., & Varghese, F.T. (1995). Social skills training with chronic schizophrenic patients: Effects on negative symptoms and community functioning. *Behavior Therapy, 26,* 433-449.

Hayes, S.C. (1987). A contextual approach to therapeutic change. In N.S. Jacobson (Ed.), *Psychotherapists in clinical practice: Cognitive and behavioral perspectives*. New York: Guilford.

Hayman-Abello, B.A., Hayman-Abello, S.E., & Rourke, B.P. (2003). Human neuropsychology in Canada: The 1990s (A review of research by Canadian neuropsychologists over the past decade). *Canadian Psychology, 44*, 100-138.

Haynes, S.N., & Horn, W.F. (1982). Reactivity in behavioral observation: A review. *Behavioral Assessment, 4,* 369-385.

Hayslip, B., Lopez, F.G., & Nation, P. (1991). Hopelessness in community-residing aging persons: A viable construct? *Journal of Personality Assessment, 57*, 498-505.

Hazelrigg, M.D., Cooper, H.M., & Borduin, C.M. (1987). Evaluating the effectiveness of family therapies: An integrative review and analysis. *Psychological Bulletin, 101,* 428-442.

Health Canada (1991). *Schizophrenia: A handbook for families*. Ottawa: Ministry of Supply and Services Canada.

Health Canada (1996a). *Smoking among Francophones: Preliminary assessment of the needs of Francophones for smoking prevention and cessation programs in Canada*. Ottawa: Minister of Supply and Services Canada.

Health Canada (1996b). *Francophone women's tobacco use in Canada*. Ottawa: Minister of Supply and Services Canada.

Health Canada (1998). *The aboriginal headstart on reserve program. (http://www.hc-sc.gc.ca/msb/fnihp/ahs_e.htr; accessed December 7, 2000).*

Health Canada (2000). *Canadian tobacco use monitoring survey: I. Summary of results*. Ottawa: Health Canada.

Health Canada (2002, November 28). *Building on values: The future of health care in Canada.* Saskatoon, SK: Commission on the Future of Health Care in Canada [R. J. Romanow, Chair]. *(http://finalreport.healthcarecommission.ca)*

Health Canada (2003). *Canadian Tobacco Use Monitoring Survey (CTUMS): Summary of results for 2002 (February to December)*. Ottawa: Health Canada.

Health Canada and the Canadian Coalition For High Blood Pressure Prevention and Control (2000). *National High Blood Pressure Prevention and Control Strategy: Report of the Expert Working Group*. Ottawa, Canada: Health Canada.

Healy, M. (1994, January 8). Science of power and weakness. *Los Angeles Times*, pp. A1, A12.

Heath, K.V., Wood, E., Bally, G., Cornelisse, P.G., & Hogg, R.S. (1999). Experience in treating persons with HIV/AIDS and the legalization of assisted suicide: The views of Canadian physicians. *AIDS Care, 11*, 501-510.

Heatherton, T.F., & Baumeister, R.F. (1991). Binge eating as escape from self-awareness. *Psychological Bulletin, 110,* 86-108.

Heatherton, T.F., Herman, C.P., & Polivy, J. (1991). Effects of physical threat and ego threat on eating behavior. *Journal of Personality and Social Psychology, 60,* 138-143.

Heatherton, T.F., Nichols, P., Mahamedi, F., & Keel, P. (1995). Body weight, dieting, and eating disorder symptoms among college students, 1982 to 1992. *American Journal of Psychiatry, 152,* 1623-1630.

Hebert, M., Lavoie, F., Piche, C., & Poitras, M. (2001). Proximate effects of a child sexual abuse prevention program in elementary school children. *Child Abuse and Neglect, 25*, 505-522.

Hebert, R. (2003). The big boom: What CIHR's Canadian longitudinal study on aging means to the baby boomer generation and Canada's healthcare system. *Hospital Quarterly* (Spring), 19-20.

Hebert, R., et al. (2003). Efficacy of a psychoeducative group program for caregivers of demented persons living at home: A randomized control trial. *Journals of Gerontology: B. Psychological Sciences and Social Sciences, 58,* S58-S67.

Hebert, R., Robichaud, L., Roy, P-M., Bravo, G., & Voyer, L. (2001). Efficacy of a nurse-led multidimensional preventive programme for older people at risk of functional decline. A randomized controlled trial. *Age and Ageing, 30,* 147-153.

Hecker, M.H.L., Chesney, M., Black, G.W., & Frautsch, N. (1988). Coronary-prone behavior in the Western Collaborative Group Study. *Psychosomatic Medicine, 50,* 153-164.

Heckers, S. (1997). Neuropathology of schizophrenia: Cortex, basal ganglia, and neurotransmitter-specific projection systems. *Schizophrenia Bulletin, 23,* 403-421.

Heidrich, S.M. (1993). The relationship between physical health and psychological well-being in elderly women: A developmental perspective. *Research in Nursing and Health, 16,* 123-130.

Heilbrun, K., Ogloff, J.R., & Picarello, K. (1999). Dangerous offender statutes in the United States and Canada: Implications for risk assessment. *International Journal of Law and Psychiatry*, *22*, 393-415.

Heim, E., Valach, L., & Schaffner, L. (1997). Coping and psychosocial adaptation: Longitudinal effects over time and stages in breast cancer. *Psychosomatic Medicine, 59,* 408-418.

Heiman, J.R., & Verhulst, J. (1990). Sexual dysfunction and marriage. In F.D. Fincham, & T.N. Bradbury (Eds.), *The psychology of marriage: Basic issues and applications* (pp. 299-322). New York: Guilford.

Heiman, J.R., Rowland, D.L., Hatch, J.P., & Gladue, B.A. (1991). Psychophysiological and endocrine responses to sexual arousal in women. *Archives of Sexual Behavior, 20,* 171-186.

Heimberg, R.G., Liebowitz, M.R., Hope, D.A., Schneir, F.R., Holt, C.S., et al. (1998). Cognitive behavioral group therapy vs phenelzine therapy for social phobia: 12-week outcome. *Archives of General Psychiatry, 55,* 1133-1142.

Heinrichs, R.W. (1993). Schizophrenia and the brain: Conditions for a neuropsychology of madness. *American Psychologist*, *48*, 221-233.

Heinrichs, R.W., & Awad, A.G. (1993). Neurocognitive subtypes of chronic schizophrenia. *Schizophrenia Research*, *9*, 49-58.

Heinrichs, R.W., & Zakzanis, K.K. (1998). Neurocognitive deficit in schizophrenia: A quantitative review of the evidence. *Neuropsychology*, *12*, 426-445.

Heisel, M.J., Flett, G.L., & Besser, A. (2002). Cognitive functioning and geriatric suicide ideation: Testing a mediational model. *American Journal of Geriatric Psychiatry*, *10*, 428-436.

Heller, J. (1966). *Something happened.* New York: Knopf.

Heller, K.A., Holtzman, W.H., & Messick, S. (Eds.). (1982). *Placing children in special education: A strategy for equity*. Washington, DC: National Academy Press.

Hellstrom, K., Fellenius, J., & Ost, I. (1993). One versus five sessions of applied tension in the treatment of blood phobia. *Behaviour Research and Therapy, 34,* 101-112.

Helzer, J.E., Burnam, A., & McEvoy, L.T. (1991). Alcohol abuse and dependence. In L. Robins & D. Reiger (Eds.), *Psychiatric disorders in America: The Epidemiologic Catchment Area Study* (pp. 9-38). New York: Free Press.

Helzer, J.E., Robins, L.N., & McEvoy, L. (1987). Post-traumatic stress disorder in the general population. *New England Journal of Medicine, 317,* 1630-1634.

Hembree, W.C., Nahas, G.G., & Huang, H.F.S. (1979). Changes in human spermatozoa associated with high dose marihuana smoking. In G.G. Nahas & W.D.M. Paton (Eds.), *Marihuana: Biological effects*. Elmsford, NY: Pergamon.

Hemels, M.E.H., Koren, G., & Einarson, T.R. (2002). Increased use of antidepressants in Canada: 1981-2000.

Hemphill, J.R., Hare, R.D., & Wong, S. (1998). Psychopathy and recidivism: A review. *Legal and Criminological Psychology*, *3*, 139-170.

Henderson, H. (2000, May 19). Orphans of schizophrenia: When a parent has the mental disorder, children feel isolated. *The Toronto Star,* pp. D1-D2.

Henggeler, S.W., Schoenwald, S.D., Borduin, C.M., Rowland, M.D., & Cunningham, P.B. (1998). *Multisystemic treatment of antisocial behavior in children and adolescents*. New York: Guilford Press.

Henkel, H., & Lewis-Thomé, J. (1976). *Verhaltenstherapie bei männlichen Homosexuellen*. Diplomarbeit der Studierenden der Psychologie. University of Marburg, Germany.

Henker, B., & Whalen, C.K. (1999). The child with attention-deficit/hyperactivity disorder in school and peer settings. In H.C. Quay, & A. E. Hogan, *Handbook of disruptive behavior disorders* (pp. 157-178). New York: Kluwer Academic/Plenum.

Henriksson, M.M., Aro, H.M., Marttunen, M.J., Heikkinen, M.E., Isometsa, E.T., Kuoppasalmi, K.I., & Lonnqvist, J.K. (1993). Mental disorders and comorbidity in suicide. *American Journal of Psychiatry, 150,* 935-940.

Henry, J.P., Ely, D.L., & Stephens, P.M. (1972). Changes in catecholamine-controlling enzymes in response to psychosocial activation of defense and alarm reactions. In *Physiology, emotion, and psychosomatic illness*. Ciba Symposium 8. Amsterdam, Netherlands: Associated Scientific Publishers.

Henry, R.M. (1996). Psychodynamic group therapy with adolescents: Exploration of HIV-related risk taking. *International Journal of Group Psychotherapy, 46,* 229-253.

Henry, W.P., & Strupp, H.H. (1994). The therapeutic alliance as interpersonal process. In A. Horvath & L. Greenberg (Eds.), *The working alliance: Theory, research and practice* (pp. 51-84). New York: Guilford.

Henry, W.P., Strupp, H.H., Schacht, T.E., & Gaston, L. (1994). Psychodynamic approaches. In A.E. Bergin & S.L. Garfield (Eds.), *Handbook of psychotherapy and behavior change*. Fourth edition (pp. 467-508). New York: Wiley.

Herbert, J.D. (1995). An overview of the current status of social phobia. *Applied and Preventive Psychology, 4,* 39-51.

Herbert, M. (1982). Conduct disorders. In B.B. Lahey & A.E. Kazdin (Eds.), *Advances in clinical child psychology* (Vol. 5). New York: Plenum.

Herek, G.M. (1989). Hate crimes against lesbians and gay men: Issues for research and policy. *American Psychologist, 44,* 948-955.

Herek, G.M. (1994). Assessing heterosexuals' attitudes towards lesbians and gay

men: A review of the empirical research with the ATLG scale. In B. Greene & G.M.

Herek (Eds.), *Contemporary perspectives on lesbian and gay issues in psychology*. (pp. 206-228). Newbury Park, CA: Sage.

Herek, G.M., Gillis, R., Kogan, J.C., & Glunt, E.K. (1996). Hate crime victimization among lesbian, gay, and bisexual adults. Journal of Interpersonal Violence, 12, 195-215.

Herman, C.P., & Polivy, J. (1980). Restrained eating. In A. Stunkard (Ed.), *Obesity*. Philadelphia: Sanders.

Herman, C.P., Polivy, J., Lank, C., & Heatherton, T.F. (1987). Anxiety, hunger, and eating. *Journal of Abnormal Psychology, 96,* 264-269.

Herman, J.L., Perry, J.C., & van der Kolk, B.A. (1989). Childhood trauma in borderline personality disorder. *American Journal of Psychiatry, 146,* 490-495.

Herman, N.J., & Smith, C.M. (1989). Mental hospital depopulation in Canada: Patient perspectives. *Canadian Journal of Psychiatry*, *34*, 386-391.

Herrell, R., Goldberg, J., True, W.R., Ramakrishnan, V., Lyons, M., Eisen, S., & Tsuang, M.T. (1999). Sexual orientation and suicidality: A co-twin control study of adult men. *Archives of General Psychiatry, 56,* 867-874.

Hersen, M., & Barlow, D.H. (1976). *Single case experimental designs: Strategies for studying behavior change*. New York: Pergamon.

Hersen, M., Bellack, A.S., Himmelhoch, J.M., & Thase, M.E. (1984). Effects of social skill training, amitriptyline, and psychotherapy in unipolar depressed women. *Behavior Therapy, 15,* 21-40.

Herzog, A. R. (1989). Physical and mental health in older women: Selected research issues and data sources. In A. R. Herzog, K. C. Holden, & M. M. Seltzer (Eds.), *Health and economic status of older women: Research issues and data sources* (pp. 35-91). Amityville, NY: Baywood Publishing Co.

Hester, R.K., & Miller, W.R. (1989). Self-control training. In R.K. Hester & W.R. Miller (Eds.), *Handbook of alcoholism treatment approaches: Effective alternatives* (pp. 141-149). New York: Pergamon.

Heston, L.L. (1966). Psychiatric disorders in foster home reared children of schizophrenic mothers. *British Journal of Psychiatry, 112,* 819-825.

Heston, L.L. (1987). The paranoid syndrome after mid-life. In N.E. Miller & G.D. Cohen (Eds.), *Schizophrenia and aging* (pp. 249-257). New York: Guilford.

Hewett, F.M. (1965). Teaching speech to an autistic child through operant conditioning. *American Journal of Orthopsychiatry, 33,* 927-936.

Hewitt, P.L., Caelian, C.F., Flett, G.L., Sherry, S.B., Collins, L., & Flynn, C.A. (2002). Perfectionism in children: Associations with depression, anxiety, and anger. *Personality and Individual Differences*, *32*, 1049-1061.

Hewitt, P.L., & Flett, G.L. (1991). Perfectionism in the self and social contexts: Conceptualization, assessment, and association with psychopathology. *Journal of Personality and Social Psychology*, *60*, 456-470.

Hewitt, P.L., Flett, G.L., & Ediger, E. (1996). Perfectionism and depression:

Longitudinal assessment of a specific vulnerability hypothesis. *Journal of Abnormal Psychology, 105,* 276-280.

Hewitt, P.L., Flett, G.L., Ediger, E., Norton, G.R., & Flynn, C.A. (1998). Perfectionism in chronic and state symptoms of depression. *Canadian Journal of Behavioural Science, 30,* 234-242.

Hewitt, P. L., Flett, G. L., Sherry, S. B., & Caelian, C. F. (in press). Trait perfectionism dimensions and suicide behavior. In T. E. Ellis (Ed.), *Cognition and suicide: Theory, research, and practice*. Washington, DC: American Psychological Association.

Heyd, D., & Bloch, S. (1981). The ethics of suicide. In S. Bloch & P. Chodoff (Eds.), *Psychiatric ethics*. New York: Oxford University Press.

Hietala, J., Syvalahti, E., Vuorio, K., Nagren, K., Lehikoinen, P., et al. (1994). Striatal D2 dopamine receptor characteristics in drug-naive schizophrenic patients studied with positive emission tomography. *Archives of General Psychiatry, 51,* 116-123.

Higgins, S.T., Roll, J.M., Wong, C.J., Tidey, J.W., & Dantona, R. (1999). Clinic and laboratory studies on the use of incentives to decrease cocaine and other substance use. In S.T. Higgins & K. Silverman (Eds.), *Motivating behavior change among illicit drug-abusers: Research on contingency management interventions*. (pp. 35-56). Washington, DC: APA.

Hightower, J., Smith, M.J., Ward-Hall, C.A., & Hightower, H.C. (1999). Meeting the needs of abused older women? A British Columbia and Yukon transition house survey. *Journal of Elder Abuse and Neglect, 11,* 39-57.

Hill, C.E., O'Grady, K.E., & Elkin, I. (1992). Applying the Collaborative Study Psychotherapy Rating Scale to rate therapist adherence to cognitive-behavior therapy, interpersonal therapy, and clinical management. *Journal of Consulting and Clinical Psychology, 60,* 73-79.

Hill, J.H., Liebert, R.M., & Mott, D.E.W. (1968). Vicarious extinction of avoidance behavior through films: An initial test. *Psychological Reports, 12,* 192.

Hill, S.Y. (1980). *Introduction: The biological consequences. In Alcoholism and alcohol abuse among women: Research issues*. Rockville, MD: National Institute on Alcohol Abuse and Alcoholism.

Hilsenroth, M. J., Ackerman, S. J., Blagys, M. D., Baumann, B. D., Baity, M. R., Smith, S. R., Price, J. L., Smith, C. L., Heindselman, T. L., Mount, M. K., Holdwick, D. J. Jr. (2000). Reliability and v validity of DSM-IV Axis V. (2000). *American Journal of Psychiatry, 157,* 1858-1863.

Hilton, N.Z., & Simmons, J.L. (2001). The influence of actuarial risk assessment in clinical judgments and tribunal decisions about mentally disordered offenders in maximum security. *Law and Human Behavior, 25,* 393-408.

Hinrichsen, G. A. (1997). Interpersonal psychotherapy for depressed older adults. *Journal of Geriatric Psychiatry, 30,* 239-257.

Hinshaw, S.P. (1987). On the distinction between attentional deficits/hyperactivity and conduct problems/aggression in child psychopathology. *Psychological Bulletin, 101,* 443-463.

Hinshaw, S.P. (1991). Stimulant medication and the treatment of aggression in children with attentional deficits. *Journal of Clinical Child Psychology, 20,* 301-312.

Hinshaw, S.P., Henker, B., & Whalen, C.K. (1984a). Cognitive-behavioral and pharmacologic interventions for hyperactive boys: Comparative and combined effects. *Journal of Consulting and Clinical Psychology, 52,* 739-749.

Hirschi, T. (1969). *Causes of delinquency*. Berkeley, CA: University of California Press.

Hite, S. (1976). *The Hite Report: A nationwide study of female sexuality*. New York: Dell.

Ho, B-C., Nopoulos, P., Flaum, M., Arndt, S., & Andreasen, N.C. (1998). Two-year outcome in first-episode schizophrenia: Predictive value of symptoms for quality of life. *American Journal of Psychiatry, 155,* 1196-1201.

Hoaken, P.N.S., & Stewart, S.H. (2003). Drugs of abuse and the elicitation of human aggressive behavior. *Addictive Behaviors, 28,* 1533-1554.

Hobbs, S.A., Beck, S.J., & Wansley, R.A. (1984). Pediatric behavioral medicine: Directions in treatment and prevention. In M. Hersen, R.M. Eisler, & P.M. Miller (Eds.), *Progress in behavior modification* (Vol. 16). New York: Academic Press.

Hobfoll, S.E., Spielberger, C.D., Breznitz, S., Figley, C., Folkman, S., Lepper-Green, B., Meichenbaum, D., Milgram, N.A., Sandler, I., Sarason, I., & van der Kolk, B. (1991). War-related stress: Addressing the stress of war and other traumatic events. *American Psychologist, 46,* 848-855.

Hobson, R.P. & Lee, A. (1998). Hello and goodbye: A study of social engagement in autism. *Journal of Autism and Developmental Disorders, 28,* 117-127.

Hoddinott, J., Lethbridge, L., & Phipps, S. (2002). *Is history destiny? Resources, transitions and child education attainments in Canada*. Ottawa: Government of Canada

Hodges, E.L., Cochrane, C.E., & Brewerton, T.D. (1998). Family characteristics of binge-eating disorder patients. *International Journal of Eating Disorders, 23,* 145-151.

Hodges, L.F., Rothbaum, B.O., Kooper, R., Opdyke, D., Meyer, T., de Graff, J.J., & Williford, J.S. (1994). *Presence as the defining factor in a VR application: Virtual reality graded exposure in the treatment of acrophobia*. Tech Rep GIT-GVU-94-96, Georgia Institute of Technology.

Hodgson, R.J., & Rachman, S.J. (1972). The effects of contamination and washing on obsessional patients. *Behaviour Research and Therapy, 10,* 111-117.

Hoebel, B.G., & Teitelbaum, P. (1966). Weight regulation in normal and hypothalamic hyperphagic rats. *Journal of Comparative and Physiological Psychology, 61,* 189-193.

Hofmann, S.G., Newman, M.G., Ehlerr, A., & Roth, W. (1995). Psychophysiological differences between subgroups of social phobia. *Journal of Abnormal Psychology, 104,* 224-231.

Hogan, D. (1978). The effectiveness of sex therapy: A review of the literature. In J. LoPiccolo & L. LoPiccolo (Eds.), *Handbook of sex therapy*. New York: Plenum.

Hogan, D.B., & Ebly, E.M. (2000). Predicting who will develop dementia in a cohort of Canadian seniors. *Canadian Journal of Neurological Sciences, 27,* 18-24.

Hogarty, G.E. (1993). Prevention of relapse in chronic schizophrenic patients. *Journal of Clinical Psychiatry, 54,* 18-23.

Hogarty, G.E., Anderson, C.M., Reiss, D.J., Kornblith, S.J., Greenwald, D.P., et al. (1986). Family psychoeducation, social skills training, and maintenance chemotherapy in the aftercare treatment of schizophrenia: 1. One-year effects of a controlled study on relapse and expressed emotion. *Archives of General Psychiatry, 43,* 633-642.

Hogarty, G.E., Anderson, C.M., Reiss, D.J., Kornblith, S.J., Greenwald, D.P., Ulrich, R.F., Carter, M., & The Environmental-Personal Indicators in the Course of Schizophrenia (EPICS) Research Group. (1991). Family psychoeducation, social skills training, and maintenance chemotherapy in the aftercare treatment of schizophrenia. *Archives of General Psychiatry, 48,* 340-347.

Hogarty, G.E., Greenwald, D., Ulrich, R.F., Kornblith, S.J., DiBarry, A.L., Cooley, S., Carter, M., & Flesher, S. (1997a). Three-year trials of personal therapy among schizophrenic patients living with or independent of family, II: Effects on adjustment of patients. *Archives of General Psychiatry, 154,* 1514-1524.

Hogarty, G.E., Kornblith, S.J., Greenwald, D., DiBarry, A.L., Cooley, S., Ulrich, R.F., Carter, M., & Flesher, S. (1997b). Three-year trials of personal therapy among schizophrenic patients living with or independent of family, I: Description of study and effects on relapse rates. *Archives of General Psychiatry, 154,* 1504-1513.

Hogarty, G.E., Kornblith, S.J., Greenwald, D., DiBarry, A.L., Cooley, S., Flesher, S., Reiss, D., Carter, M., & Ulrich, R. (1995). Personal therapy: A disorder-relevant psychotherapy for schizophrenia. *Schizophrenia Bulletin, 21,* 379-393.

Hogarty, G.E., McEvoy, J.P., Ulrich, R.F., DiBarry, A.L., Bartone, P., et al. (1994). Pharmacotherapy of impaired affect in recovering schizophrenic patients. *Archives of General Psychiatry, 52,* 29-41.

Hoge, S., Lidz, C., Eisenberg, M., Gardner, W., Monahan, J., Mulvey, E., Roth, L., & Bennet, N. (1997). Perceptions of coercion in the admission of voluntary and involuntary psychiatric patients. *International Journal of Law and Psychiatry, 20,* 167-181.

Holahan, C.K., & Holahan, C.J. (1987). Life stress, hassles, and self-efficacy in aging: A replication and extension. *Journal of Applied Social Psychology, 17,* 574-592.

Holden, C. (1972). Nader on mental health centers: A movement that got bogged down. *Science, 177,* 413-415.

Holden, R.R. (1999). The Holden Psychological Screening Inventory and sexual efficacy in urological patients with erectile dysfunction. *Psychological Reports, 84,* 255-258.

Holland, A.J., Hall, A., Murray, R., Russell, G.F.M., & Crisp, A.H. (1984).

Anorexia nervosa: A study of 34 twin pairs and one set of triplets. *British Journal of Psychiatry, 145,* 414-419.

Hollander, E., Cohen, L.J., & Simeon, D. (1993). Body dysmorphic disorder. *Psychiatric Annals, 23,* 359-364.

Hollander, E., DeCaria, C.M., Nitescu, A., Gully, R., Suckow, R.F., et al. (1992). Serotonergic function in obsessive-compulsive disorder: Behavioral and neuroendocrine responses to oral m-chlorophenylpiperazine and fenfluramine in patients and healthy volunteers. *Archives of General Psychiatry, 49,* 21-27.

Hollander, E., Stein, D.J., Decaria, D.M., Cohen, L.J., Saond, J.B., et al. (1994). Serotonergic sensitivity in borderline personality disorder. *American Journal of Psychiatry, 151,* 277-280.

Hollifield, M., Katon, W., Spain, D., & Pule, L. (1990). Anxiety and depression in a village in Lesotho, Africa: A comparison with the United States. *British Journal of Psychiatry, 156,* 343-350.

Hollingshead, A.B., & Redlich, F.C. (1958). *Social class and mental illness: A community study.* New York: Wiley.

Hollon, S.D., & Beck, A.T. (1986). Cognitive and cognitive-behavioral therapies. In S.L. Garfield & A.E. Bergin (Eds.), *Handbook of psychotherapy and behavior change* (3rd ed.). New York: Wiley.

Hollon, S.D., & Beck, A.T. (1994). Cognitive and cognitive behavioral therapies. In A.E. Bergin & S.L. Garfield (Eds.), *Handbook of psychotherapy and behavior change.* Fourth edition (pp. 428-466). New York: Wiley.

Hollon, S.D., De Rubeis, R.J., & Evans, M.D. (1996). Cognitive therapy in the treatment and prevention of depression. In P.M. Salkovskis (Ed.), *Frontiers of cognitive therapy* (pp. 293-317). New York: Guilford.

Hollon, S.D., DeRubeis, R.J., & Seligman, M.E.P. (1992). Cognitive therapy and the prevention of depression. *Applied and Preventive Psychology, 1,* 89-95.

Hollon, S.D., DeRubeis, R.J., Evans, M.D., Wiemer, J.J., Garvey, J.G., Grove, W.M., & Tuason, V.B. (1992). Cognitive therapy and pharmacotherapy for depression: Singly and in combination. *Archives of General Psychiatry, 49,* 774-781.

Hollon, S.D., & Kendall, P.C. (1980). Cognitive self-statements in depression: Development of an automatic thoughts questionnaire. *Cognitive Therapy and Research, 4,* 383-395.

Holm, V.A., & Varley, C.K. (1989). Pharmacological treatment of autistic children. In G. Dawson (Ed.), *Autism: Nature, diagnosis, and treatment* (pp. 386-404). New York: Guilford.

Holme, I. (1990). An analysis of randomized trials on cholesterol reduction on total mortality and coronary heart disease risk. *Circulation, 82,* 1916-1924.

Holmes, T.H., & Rahe, R.H. (1967). The social readjustment rating scale. *Journal of Psychosomatic Research, 11,* 213-218.

Holmes, T.S., & Holmes, T.H. (1970). Short-term intrusions into the life style routine. *Journal of Psychosomatic Research, 14,* 121-132.

Holowaty, P., Feldman, L., Harvey, B., & Shortt, L. (2000). Cigarette smoking in multicultural, urban high school students. *Journal of Adolescent Health, 27,* 281-288.

Holroyd, K., Penzien, D., Hursey, K., Tobin, D., Rogen, L., Holm, J., Marcille, P., Hall, J., & Chila, A. (1984). Change mechanisms in EMG biofeedback training: Cognitive changes underlying improvements in tension headache. *Journal of Consulting and Clinical Psychology, 52,* 1039-1053.

Holtzworth-Munroe, A., Markman, H., O'Leary, K.D., Neidig, P., Leber, D., Heyman, R., Hulbert, D., & Smutzler, N. (1995). The need for marital violence prevention efforts: A behavioral cognitive secondary prevention program for engaged and newly married couples. *Applied and Preventive Psychology, 4,* 77-88.

Holzman, P.S. (1985). Eye movement dysfunctions and psychosis. *Review of Neurobiology, 27,* 179-205.

Hooley, J.M., & Teasdale, J.D. (1989). Predictors of relapse in unipolar depressives: Expressed emotion, marital distress, and perceived criticism. *Journal of Abnormal Psychology, 98,* 229-235.

Hoon, E.F., & Hoon, P.W. (1978). Styles of sexual expression in women: Clinical implications of multivariate analyses. *Archives of Sexual Behavior, 7,* 105-116.

Hope, D.A., Heimberg, R.G., & Bruch, M.A. (1995). Dismantling cognitive-behavioral group therapy for social phobia. *Behaviour Research and Therapy, 33,* 637-650.

Horen, S.A., Leichner, P.P., & Lawson, J.S. (1995). Prevalence of dissociative symptoms and disorders in an adult psychiatric inpatient population in Canada. *Canadian Journal of Psychiatry, 40,* 185-191.

Horn, A.S., & Snyder, S.H. (1971). Chlorpromazine and dopamine: Confirmational similarities that correlate with the anti-psychotic activity of phenothiazine drugs. *Proceedings of the National Academy of Sciences, 68,* 2325-2328.

Hornblower, M., & Svoboda, W. (1987, November 23). Down and out—but determined: Does a mentally disturbed woman have the right to be homeless? *Time,* p. 29.

Horney, K. (1939). *New ways in psychoanalysis.* New York: International Universities Press.

Horney, K. (1942). *Self-analysis.* New York: Norton.

Horowitz, M.J. (1975). Intrusive and repetitive thoughts after experimental stress. *Archives of General Psychiatry, 32,* 223-228.

Horowitz, M.J. (1986). *Stress response syndromes.* Northvale, NJ: Aronson.

Horowitz, M.J. (1988). *Introduction to psychodynamics: A new synthesis.* New York: Basic Books.

Horowitz, M.J. (1990). Psychotherapy. In A.S. Bellack & M. Hersen (Eds.), *Handbook of comparative treatments for adult disorders* (pp. 289-301). New York: Wiley.

Horvath, A.O. (2000). The therapeutic relationship: From transference to alliance. *Journal of Clinical Psychology/In Session: Psychotherapy in Practice, 56,* 163-173.

Horvath, A.O. (2001). The alliance. *Psychotherapy, 38,* 365-372.

Horvath, A.O., & Greenberg, L. (1989). Development and validation of the Working Alliance Inventory. *Journal of Counseling Psychology, 36,* 223-233.

Horvarth, A.O., & Greenberg, L. (Eds.). (1994). *The working alliance: Theory, research, and practice.* New York: Wiley.

Horwath, E., Wolk, S.I., Goldstein, R.B., Wickramaratne, P., Sobin, C., et al. (1995). Is the comorbidity between social phobia and panic disorder due to familial cotransmission or other factors? *Archives of General Psychiatry, 52,* 574-581.

Horwitz, L. (1974). Clinical prediction in psychotherapy. New York: Jason Aronson.

House, J.S., Landis, K.R., & Umberson, D. (1988). Social relationships and health. *Science, 241,* 540-544.

Houts, A.C. (1991). Nocturnal enuresis as a biobehavioral problem. *Behavior Therapy, 22,* 133-151.

Houts, A.C., Berman, J., & Abramson, H. (1994). Effectiveness of psychological and pharmacological treatments for nocturnal enuresis. *Journal of Consulting and Clinical Psychology, 62,* 737-745.

Howard, M.O., & Jenson, J.M. (1999). Inhalant abuse among antisocial youth. *Addictive Behaviors, 24,* 59-74.

Howard, R. (1993). Late paraphrenia. *International Review of Psychiatry, 5,* 455-460.

Howard, R., Almeida, O.P., & Levy, R. (1993). Schizophrenic symptoms in late paraphrenia. *Psychopathology, 26,* 95-101.

Howard, R., Castle, D., O'Brien, J., Almeida, O., & Levy, R. (1991). Permeable walls, floors, ceilings, and doors: Partition delusions in late paraphrenia. *International Journal of Geriatric Psychiatry, 7,* 719-724.

Howard, R., Castle, D., Wessely, S., & Murray, R. (1993). A comparative study of 470 cases of early-onset and late-onset schizophrenia. *British Journal of Psychiatry, 163,* 352-357.

Howes, J.L., & Vallis, T.M. (1996). Cognitive therapy with nontraditional populations: Application to post-traumatic stress disorder and personality disorders. In K.S. Dobson & K.D. Craig (Eds.), *Advances in cognitive-behavioral therapy* (pp. 237-272). Thousand Oaks, CA: Sage.

Howitt, D. (1995). Pornography and the paedophile: Is it criminogenic? *British Journal of Medical Psychology, 68,* 15-27.

Hoza, B., Waschbusch, D.A., Pelham, W.E., Molina, B.S.G., & Milich, R. (2000). Attention-deficit/hyperactivity disordered and control boys' responses to social success and failure. *Child Development, 71,* 432-446.

Hser, Y., Anglin, M.D., & Powers, K. (1993). A 24-year follow-up of California narcotics addicts. *Archives of General Psychiatry, 50,* 577-584.

Hsu, L.K.G. (1990). *Eating disorders.* New York: Guilford.

Hubbs-Tait, L., Culp, A.M., Culp, R.E., & Miller, C.E. (2002). Relation of maternal cognitive stimulation, emotional support, and intrusive behavior during Head Start to children's kindergarten cognitive abilities. *Child Development, 73*, 110-131.

Hudson, J.I., Pope, H.G., Yurgelun-Todd, D., Jonas, J.M., & Frankenburg, F.R. (1987). A controlled study of lifetime prevalence of affective and other psychiatric disorders in bulimic patients. *American Journal of Psychiatry, 144,* 1283-1287.

Hudson, S.M., & Ward, T. (1997). Rape: Psychopathology and theory. In D.R. Laws & W. O'Donohue (Eds.), *Sexual deviance*. (pp. 332-355). NY: Guilford Press.

Huesmann, L.R., & Miller, L.S. (1994). Long-term effects of repeated exposure to media violence in childhood. In L.R. Huesmann (Ed.), *Aggressive behavior: Current perspectives* (pp. 153-186). New York: Plenum.

Huey, S.J., Jr., Henggler, S.W., Brondino, M.J., & Pickrel, S.G. (2000). Mechanisms of change in multisystemic therapy: Reducing delinquent behavior through therapist adherence and improved family and peer functioning. *Journal of Consulting and Clinical Psychology*, *68*, 451-467.

Huffman, T. (2001, July 20). Abused boys' parent given bail: Second man charged in disciplining of children. *The Toronto Star*, B4.

Hughes, C. & Agran, M. (1993). Teaching persons with severe disabilities to use self-instruction in community settings: An analysis of applications. *The Journal of the Association for Persons with Severe Handicaps, 18,* 261-274.

Hughes, C., Hugo, K., & Blatt, J. (1996). Self-instructional intervention for teaching generalized problem-solving within a functional task sequence. *American Journal on Mental Retardation, 100,* 565-579.

Hughes, J.R., & Hatsukami, D.K. (1992). The nicotine withdrawal syndrome: A brief review and update. *International Journal of Smoking Cessation, 1,* 21-26.

Hughes, J.R., Higgins, S.T., Bickel, W.K., Hunt, W.K., & Fenwick, J.W. (1991). Caffeine self-adminstration, withdrawal, and adverse effects among coffee drinkers. *Archives of General Psychiatry, 48,* 611-617.

Hughes, J.R., Higgins, S.T., & Hatsukami, D.K. (1990). Effects of abstinence from tobacco: A critical review. In L.T. Kozlowski, H. Annis, H.D. Cappell, F. Glaser, M. Goodstadt, Y. Israel, H. Kalant, E.M. Sellers, & J. Vingilis (Eds.), *Research advances in alcohol and drug problems*. New York: Plenum.

Hultsch, D.F., Hertzog, C., Small, B.J., & Dixon, R.A. (1999). Use it or lose it: Engaged lifestyle as a buffer of cognitive decline in aging? *Psychology and Aging, 14,* 245-263.

Humphrey, L.L. (1986). Family relations in bulimic-anorexic and nondistressed families. *International Journal of Eating Disorders, 5,* 223-232.

Humphreys, K., & Rappaport, J. (1993). From the community mental health movement to the war on drugs: A study in the definition of social problems. *American Psychologist*, 892-901.

Hundert, J., Boyle, M.H., Cunningham, C.E., Duku, E., Heale, J., McDonald, J. et al. (1999). Helping children adjust—A tri-Ministry study: II. Program effects. *Journal of Child Psychology and Psychiatry*, *40*, 1061-1073.

Hunsley, J., Aubry, T.D., Vestervelt, C.M., & Vito, D. (1999). Comparing therapist and client perspectives on reasons for psychotherapy termination. *Psychotherapy*, *36*, 380-388.

Hunsley, J., & Bailey, J.M. (1999). The clinical utility of the Rorschach: Unfulfilled promises and an uncertain future. *Psychological Assessment, 11,* 266-277.

Hunsley, J., & Bailey, J.M. (2001). Whither the Rorschach? An analysis of the evidence. *Psychological Assessment*, *13*, 423-432.

Hunsley, J., Dobson, K. S., Johnston, C., & Mikail, S. F. (1999). Empirically supported treatments in psychology: Implications for Canadian professional psychology. *Canadian Psychology, 40,* 239-302.

Hunsley, J., & Johnston, C. (2000). The role of empirically supported treatments in evidence-based psychological practice: A Canadian perspective. *Clinical Psychology: Science and Practice*, *7*, 269-275.

Hunsley, J., Lee, C.M., & Aubry, T. (1999). Who uses psychological services in Canada? *Canadian Psychology, 40,* 232-240.

Hunsley, J., & Lefebvre, M. (1990). A survey of the practices and activities of Canadian clinical psychologists. *Canadian Psychology*, *31*, 350-358.

Hunsley, J., & Rumstein-McKean, O. (1999). Improving psychotherapeutic services via randomized clinical trials, treatment manuals, and component analysis designs. *Journal of Clinical Psychology*, 55, 1507-1517.

Hunter, J.E. (1986). Cognitive ability, cognitive aptitudes, job knowledge, and job performance. *Journal of Vocational Behavior, 29,* 340-362.

Hurd, H. (1916-1917). *The institutional care of the insane in the United States and Canada,* Volumes I and IV. Baltimore, MD: The John Hopkins Press. (Reprint Edition, 1973. New York: Arno Press.)

Hurlburt, R.T. (1979). Random sampling of cognitions and behavior. *Journal of Research on Personality, 13,* 103-111.

Hurlburt, R.T. (1997). Randomly sampling thinking in the natural environment. *Journal of Consulting and Clinical Psychology, 65,* 941-949.

Hurst, J. (1992, March). Blowing smoke. *Los Angeles Times*, pp. A3, A29.

Hurst, S.A., & Genest, M. (1995). Cognitive-behavioural therapy with a feminist orientation: A perspective for therapy with depressed women. *Canadian Psychology*, *36*, 236-257.

Hurt, R.D., Eberman, K.M., & Croghan, J.T. (1994). Nicotine dependence treatment during inpatient treatment for other addictions: A prospective intervention trial. *Alcohol: Clinical and Experimental Research, 18,* 867-872.

Hurt, R.D., Sachs, D.P.L., & Glover, E.D. (1997). A comparison of sustained release buprioprion versus placebo for treatment of nicotine dependence. *New England Journal of Medicine, 337,* 1195-1202.

Hussian, R.A., & Lawrence, P.S. (1980). Social reinforcement of activity and problem-solving training in the treatment of depressed institutionalized elderly patients. *Cognitive Therapy and Research, 5,* 57-69.

Hutt, C., Hutt, S.J., Lee, D., & Ountsted, C. (1964). Arousal and childhood autism. *Nature, 204,* 908-909.

Hynde, G.W., Hern, K.L., Novey, E.S., Eliopulos, D., Marshall, R., Gonzalez, J.J., & Voeller, K.K. (1993). Attention-deficit hyperactivity disorder and asymmetry of the caudate nucleus. *Journal of Child Neurology, 8,* 339-347.

Iacono, W.G., Morean, M., Beiser, M., Fleming, J.A., et al. (1992). Smooth pursuit eye-tracking in first episode psychotic patients and their relatives. *Journal of Abnormal Psychology, 101,* 104-116.

Imber, S.D., Elkin, I., Watkins, J.T., Collins, J.F., Shea, M.T., Leber, W.R., & Glass, D.R. (1990). Mode-specific effects among three treatments for depression. *Journal of Consulting and Clinical Psychology, 58,* 352-359.

Imperato-McGinley, J., Guerrero, L., Gautier, T., & Peterson, R.E. (1974). Steroid 5a-reductase deficiency in man: An inherited form of pseudohermaphroditism. *Science, 186,* 1213-1215.

Ingram, C. (1996, September 26). Bill signed to let police tell of sex offenders' whereabouts. *Los Angeles Times*, pp. A3, A19.

Ingram, R. E., & Siegle, G. J. (2000). Cognition and clinical science: From revolution to evolution. In K. S. Dobson (Ed.), *Handbook of cognitive-behavioral therapies, 2nd ed.* (pp. 111-138). New York: Guilford Press.

Inouye, S. K., Bogardus, S. T., Jr., Charpentier, P. A., Leo-Summers, L., Acampora, D., Holford, T. R., & Cooney, L. M., Jr. (1999). A multicomponent intervention to prevent delirium in hospitalized older patients. *New England Journal of Medicine, 340,* 669-676.

Insell, T.R. (1986). The neurobiology of anxiety. In B.F. Shaw, Z.V. Segal, T.M. Wallis, & F.E. Cashman (Eds.), *Anxiety disorders*. New York: Plenum.

Institute of Medicine. (1990a). Matching. In *Broadening the base of treatment for alcohol problems* (pp. 279-302). Washington, DC: National Academy Press.

Institute of Medicine. (1990b). *Treating drug problems*. Washington, DC: National Academy Press.

Insull, W. (Ed.). (1973). *Coronary risk handbook*. New York: American Heart Association.

Irle, E., Exner, C., Thielen, K., Weniger, G., & Ruther, E. (1998). Obsessive-compulsive disorder and ventromedial lesions: Clinical and neuropsychological findings. *American Journal of Psychiatry, 155,* 255-263.

Irwin, M., Lovitz, A., Marder, S.R., Mintz, J., Winslade, W.J., Van Putten, T., & Mills, M.J. (1985). Psychotic patients' understanding of informed consent. *American Journal of Psychiatry, 142,* 1351-1354.

Irvine, J., & Ritvo, P. (1998). Health risk behaviour change and adaptation in cardiac patients. *Clinical Psychology and Psychotherapy*, *5*, 86-101.

Isaacs, C., Peshkin, B.N., Schwartz, M., Demarco, T.A., Main, D., & Lerman, C. (2002). Breast and ovarian cancer screening practices in healthy women with a strong family history of breast or ovarian cancer. *Breast Cancer Research and Treatment*, *71*, 103-112.

Isaacs, S., Keogh, S., Menard, C., & Hockin, J. (1998). Suicide in the Northwest Territories: A descriptive review. *Chronic Diseases in Canada*, *19*, 152-156.

Isen, A.M., Shaiken, T.F., Clark, M., & Karp, L. (1978). Affect, accessibility of material in memory, and behavior: A cognitive loop? *Journal of Personality and Social Psychology, 36,* 1-12.

Iskedjian, M., Hux, M., & Remington, G. J. (1998). The Canadian experience with risperidone for the treatment of schizophrenia: An overview. *Journal of Psychiatry and Neuroscience*, *23*, 229-239.

Issidorides, M.R. (1979). Observations in chronic hashish users: Nuclear aberrations in blood and sperm and abnormal acrosomes in spermatozoa. In G.G. Nahas & W.D.M. Paton (Eds.), *Marihuana: Biological effects*. Elmsford, NY: Pergamon.

Ivanoff, A., Jang, S.J., Smyth, N.J., & Linehan, M.M. (1994). Fewer reasons for staying alive when you are thinking of killing yourself: The Brief Reasons for Living Inventory. *Journal of Psychopathology and Behavioral Assessment, 16,* 1-13.

Ivey, A. E., Ivey, M. B., & Simek-Morgan, L. (1997). Counseling and psychotherapy: A multicultural perspective. Needham Heights, MA: Allyn and Bacon.

Jablensky, A., Sartorius, N., Cooper, J.E., Anker, A., Korten, A., & Bertelson, A. (1994). Culture and schizophrenia. *British Journal of Psychiatry, 165,* 434-436.

Jackson, A.M. (1973). Psychotherapy: Factors associated with the race of the therapist. *Psychotherapy: Theory, Research, and Practice, 10,* 273-277.

Jackson, C. (1997). Testing a multi-stage model for the adoption of alcohol and tobacco behaviors by children. *Addictive Behaviors, 22,* 1-14.

Jackson, C., Winkleby, M.A., Flora, J.A., & Fortmann, S.P. (1991). Use of educational resources for cardiovascular risk reduction in the Stanford Five-City Project. *American Journal of Preventive Medicine, 7,* 82-88.

Jackson, R.L., & Murphy, K. (1998, June 6). U.S. won't block Oregon suicide law, Reno says. *Los Angeles Times*, A1, A14.

Jackson, R.L., & Weinstein, H. (1996, March 16). Liggett agrees to pay 5 states for tobacco illnesses. *Los Angeles Times*, pp. A1, A15.

Jackson, R.W., Treiber, F.A., Turner, J.R., Davis, H., & Strong, W.B. (1999). Effects of race,sex, and socioeconomic status upon cardiovascular stress responsivity and recovery in youth. *International Journal of Psychophysiology, 31,* 111-119.

Jacob, R.G., Thayer, J.F., Manuck, S.B., Muldoon, M.F., Tamres, L.K., et al. (1999). Ambulatory blood pressure responses and the circumplex model of mood: A 4-day study. *Psychosomatic Medicine, 61,* 319-333.

Jacobs, M., Jacobs, A., Gatz, M., & Schaible, T. (1973). Credibility and desirability of positive and negative structured feedback in groups. *Journal of Consulting and Clinical Psychology, 40,* 244-252.

Jacob, T., Tennenbaum, D., Seilhammer, R. A., Bargiel, K., & Sharon, T. (1994). Reactivity effects during naturalistic observation of distressed and nondistressed families. *Journal of Family Psychology, 8,* 354-363.

Jacobson, A., & Herald, C. (1990). The relevance of childhood sexual abuse to adult psychiatric inpatient care. *Hospital and Community Psychiatry, 41,* 154-158.

Jacobson, E. (1929). *Progressive relaxation*. Chicago: University of Chicago Press.

Jacobson, N. S. (1983). Beyond empiricism: The politics of marital therapy. *American Journal of Family Therapy, 11,* 11-24.

Jacobson, N.S. (1984). A component analysis of behavioral marital therapy: The relative effectiveness of behavior exchange and problem solving training. *Journal of Consulting and Clinical Psychology, 52,* 295-305.

Jacobson, N. S. (1989). The therapist-client relationship in cognitive behavior therapy: Implications for treating depression. *Journal of Cognitive Psychotherapy, 3,* 85-96.

Jacobson, N.S. (1992). Behavioral couple therapy: A new beginning. *Behavior Therapy, 23,* 493-506.

Jacobson, N.S., & Addis, M.E. (1993). Research on couples and couple therapy: What do we know? Where are we going? *Journal of Consulting and Clinical Psychology, 61,* 85-93.

Jacobson, N.S., & Christensen, A. (1996). *Integrative couple therapy: Promoting acceptance and change.* New York: Norton.

Jacobson, N.S., Christensen, A., Prince, S. E., Cordova, J., & Eldridge, K. (2000). Integrative behavioral couple therapy: An acceptance-based, promising new treatment for couple discord. *Journal of Consulting and Clinical Psychology*, *68*, 351-355.

Jacobson, N.S., Dobson, K.S., Truax, P.A., Addis, M.E., Koerner, K., Gollan, J.K., Gortner, E., & Prince, S.E. (1996). A component analysis of cognitive-behavioral treatment for depression. *Journal of Consulting and Clinical Psychology, 64,* 295-304.

Jacobson, N.S., Dobson, K., Fruzzetti, A.E., Schmaling, K.B., & Salusky, S. (1991). Marital therapy as a treatment for depression. *Journal of Consulting and Clinical Psychology, 59,* 547-557.

Jacobson, N.S., Follette, W.C., & Pagel, N. (1986). Predicting who will benefit from behavioral marital therapy. *Journal of Consulting and Clinical Psychology, 54,* 518-522.

Jacobson, N.S., Follette, W.C., Revenstorf, D., Baucom, D.H., Hahlweg, K., & Margolin, G. (1984). Variability of outcome and clinical significance of behavioral marital therapy: A reanalysis of outcome data. *Journal of Consulting and Clinical Psychology, 52,* 497-504.

Jacobson, N.S., Fruzzetti, A.E., Dobson, K., Whisman, M., & Hops, H. (1993). Couple therapy as a treatment for depression. 2: The effects of relationship quality and therapy on depressive relapse. *Journal of Consulting and Clinical Psychology, 61,* 516-519.

Jacobson, N.S., Gottman, J.M., Waltz, J., Rushe, R., Babcock, J., & Holtzworth-Munroe, A. (1994). Affect, verbal content, and psychophysiology in the arguments of couples with a violent husband. *Journal of Consulting and Clinical Psychology, 62,* 982-988.

Jacobson, N.S., & Hollon, S.D. (1996). Cognitive-behavior therapy versus pharmacotherapy: Now that the jury's returned its verdict, it's time to present the rest of the evidence. *Journal of Consulting and Clinical Psychology, 64,* 74-80.

Jacobson, N.S., Holzworth-Munroe, A., & Schmaling, K.B. (1989). Marital therapy and spouse involvement in the treatment of depression, agoraphobia, and alcoholism. *Journal of Consulting and Clinical Psychology, 57,* 5-10.

Jacobson, N.S., & Margolin, G. (1979). *Marital therapy: Strategies based on social learning*. New York: Brunner/Mazel.

Jacobson, N.S., Schmaling, K.B., & Holtzworth-Munroe, A. (1987). Component analysis of behavioral marital therapy: Two-year follow-up and prediction of relapse. *Journal of Marital and Family Therapy, 13,* 187-195.

Jacobson, N.S., Waldron, H., & Moore, D. (1980). Toward a behavioral profile of marital distress. *Journal of Consulting and Clinical Psychology, 48,* 696-703.

Jacques, C., Ladouceur, R., & Ferland, F. (2000). Impact of availability on gambling: A longitudinal study. *Canadian Journal of Psychiatry, 45,* 810-815.

Jaffe, J.H. (1985). Drug addiction and drug abuse. In *Goodman and Gilman's the pharmacological basis of therapeutic behavior*. New York: Macmillan.

James, N., & Chapman, J. (1975). A genetic study of bipolar affective disorder. *British Journal of Psychiatry, 126,* 449-456.

Jamison, K.R. (1979). Manic-depressive illness in the elderly. In O.J. Kaplan (Ed.), *Psychopathology of aging*. New York: Academic Press.

Jamison, K.R. (1992). *Touched with fire: Manic depressive illness and the artistic temperament*. New York: Free Press.

Jampole, L., & Weber, M.K. (1987). An assessment of the behavior of sexually abused and nonsexually abused children with anatomically correct dolls. *Child Abuse and Neglect, 11,* 187-192.

Jandorf, L., Deblinger, E., Neale, J.M., & Stone, A.A. (1986). Daily vs. major life events as predictors of symptom frequency. *Journal of General Psychology, 113,* 205-218.

Janeck A.S., Calamari, J.E., Riemann, B.C., & Heffelfinger, S.K. (2003). Too much thinking about thinking?: Metacognitive differences in obsessive-compulsive disorder. *Anxiety Disorders*, *17*, 181-195.

Jang, K.L., & Livesley, W.J. (1999). Why do measures of normal and disordered personality correlate? A study of genetic morbidity. *Journal of Personality Disorders*, *13*, 10-17.

Jang, K.L., Livesley, W.J., Vernon, P.A., & Jackson, D.N. (1996). Heritability of personality disorder traits: A twin study. *Acta Psychiatrica Scandinavica, 94,* 438-444.

Jang, K.L., Vernon, P.A., & Livesley, W.J. (2000). Personality disorder traits, family environment, and alcohol misuse: A multivariate behavioural genetic analysis. *Addiction*, *95*, 873-888.

Janicak, P.G., Davis, J.M., Preskorn, S.H., & Ayd, F.J. (1993). *Principles and practice of psychopharmacological therapy*. Baltimore: Williams & Wilkins.

Janoff-Bulman, R. (1992). *Shattered assumptions: Toward a new psychology of trauma*. New York: Free Press.

Jansen, M.A., Arntz, A., Merckelbach, H., & Mersch, P.P.A. (1994). Personality disorders and features in social phobia and panic disorder. *Journal of Abnormal Psychology, 103,* 391-395.

Jansen, M.A., Glynn, T., & Howard, J. (1996). Prevention of alcohol, tobacco and other drug abuse. *American Behavioral Scientist, 39,* 790-807.

Jarrell, M.P., Johnson, W.G., & Williamson, D.A. (1986). *Insulin and glucose response in the binge purge episode of bulimic women.* Paper presented at the annual convention of the Association for Advancement of Behavior Therapy, Chicago.

Jarrett, R.B., Schaffer, M., McIntire, D., Witt-Browder, A., Kraft, D., & Risser, R.C. (1999). Treatment of atypical depression with cognitive therapy or phenelzine: A double blind, placebo controlled trial. *Archives of General Psychiatry, 56,* 431-437.

Jarvelin, M.R., Moilanen, I., Vikevainen-Tervonen, L., & Huttunen, N.P. (1990). Life changes and protective capacities in enuretic and non-enuretic children. *Journal of Child Psychology and Psychiatry, 31,* 763-774.

Jary, M.L., & Stewart, M.A. (1985). Psychiatric disorder in the parents of adopted children with aggressive conduct disorder. *Neuropsychobiology, 13,* 7-11.

Jay, S.M., Elliott, C.H., Ozolins, M., & Olson, R.A. (1982). *Behavioral management of children's distress during painful medical procedures.* Paper presented at the annual meeting of the American Psychological Association, Washington, DC.

Jay, S.M., Elliott, C.J., Woody, P.D., & Siegel, S. (1991). An investigation of cognitive-behavioral therapy combined with oral Valium for children undergoing painful medical procedures. *Health Psychology, 10,* 317-322.

Jeffrey, D.B. (1974). A comparison of the effects of external control and self-control on the modification and maintenance of weight. *Journal of Abnormal Psychology, 83,* 404-410.

Jeffrey, R.W. (1991). Weight management and hypertension. *Annals of Behavioral Medicine, 13,* 18-22.

Jeffrey, R.W., Forster, J.L., & Schmid, T.L. (1989). Worksite health promotion: Feasibility testing of repeated weight control and smoking cessation classes. *American Journal of Health Promotion, 3,* 11-16.

Jellinek, E.M. (1952). Phases of alcohol addiction. *Quarterly Journal of Studies on Alcohol, 13,* 673-684.

Jenike, M.A. (1986). Theories of etiology. In M.A. Jenike, L. Baer, & W.E. Minichiello (Eds.), *Obsessive-compulsive disorders.* Littleton, MA: PSG Publishing.

Jenike, M.A. (1990). Psychotherapy. In A.S. Bellack & M. Hersen (Eds.), *Handbook of comparative treatments for adult disorders* (pp. 245-255). New York: Wiley.

Jenike, M.A., Baer, L., & Minichiello, W.E. (1986). *Obsessive-compulsive disorders: Theory and management.* Littleton, MA: PSG Publishing.

Jenike, M.A., & Rauch, S.L. (1994). Managing the patient with treatment-resistant obsessive-compulsive disorder: Current strategies. *Journal of Clinical Psychiatry, 55,* 11-17.

Jenkins, C.D. (1976). Recent evidence supporting psychologic and social risk factors for coronary disease. *New England Journal of Medicine, 294,* 1033-1038.

Jenkins, J.M., & Smith, M.A. (1991). Marital disharmony and children's behaviour problems: Aspects of a poor marriage that affect children adversely. *Journal of Child Psychology & Psychiatry & Allied Disciplines, 32,* 793-810.

Jensen, P.S., Martin, D., & Cantwell, D.P. (1997). Comorbidity in ADHD: Implications for research, practice, and DSM-V. *Journal of the American Academy of Child and Adolescent Psychiatry, 27,* 742-747.

Jeste, D.V., Harris, M.J., Pearlson, G.D., Rabins, P.V., Lesser, I., Miller, B., Coles, C., & Yassa, R. (1988). Late-onset schizophrenia: Studying clinical validity. *Psychiatric Annals of North America, 11,* 1-13.

Jeste, D.V., Lacro, J.P., Gilbert, P.L., Kline, J., & Kline, N. (1993). Treatment of late-life schizophrenia with neuroleptics. *Schizophrenia Bulletin, 19,* 817-830.

Jeste, D.V., Manley, M., & Harris, M.J. (1991). Psychoses. In J. Sadavoy, L.W. Lazarus, & L.F. Jarvik (Eds.), *Comprehensive review of geriatric psychiatry* (pp. 353-368). Washington, DC: American Psychiatric Press.

Jiang, V., Babyak, M., Krantz, D.S., Waugh, R.A., Coleman, E., et al. (1996). Mental stress-induced myocardial ischemia and cardiac events. *JAMA, 275,* 1651-1656.

Johnson, B.A. (1991). Cannabis. In I.B. Glass (Ed.), *International handbook of addiction behavior.* London: Tavistock/Routledge.

Johnson, C.L., Rifkind, B.M., & Sempos, C.T., et al. (1993). Declining serum total cholesterol levels among U.S. adults. *Journal of the American Medical Association, 269,* 3002-3008.

Johnson, D.R. (1987). The role of the creative arts therapist in the diagnosis and treatment of psychological trauma. *The Arts in Psychotherapy, 14,* 7-13.

Johnson, G.R, Krug, E.G., & Potter, L.B. (2000). Suicide among adolescents and young adults: A cross-national comparison of 34 countries. *Suicide and Life-Threatening Behavior, 30,* 74-82.

Johnson, J., Horvath, E., & Weissman, M.M. (1991). The validity of depression with psychotic features based on a community study. *Archives of General Psychiatry, 48,* 1075-1081.

Johnson, J., Weissman, M.M., & Klerman, G.L. (1990). Panic disorder, comorbidity, and suicide attempts. *Archives of General Psychiatry, 47,* 805-808.

Johnson, J.G., Cohen, P., Brown, J., Smailes, E.M., & Bernstein, D.P. (1999). Childhood maltreatment increases risk for personality disorders during early adulthood. *Archives of General Psychiatry, 56,* 600-606.

Johnson, K.W., Anderson, N.B., Bastida, E., Kramer, B.J., Williams, D., & Wong, M. (1995). Macrosocial and environmental influences on minority health. *Health Psychology, 14,* 601-612.

Johnson, L. (1995). *Psychotherapy in the age of accountability.* New York: Norton.

Johnson, M.R., & Lydiard, R.B. (1998). Comorbidity of major depression and panic disorder. *Journal of Clinical Psychlogy, 54,* 201-210.

Johnson, S.L., & Miller, I. (1997). Negative life events and time to recovery from episodes of bipolar disorder. *Journal of Abnormal Psychology, 196,* 449-457.

Johnson, S.M. (2000). Emotionally focused couples therapy. In F. M. Dattilio & L. J. Bevilacqua (Eds.), *Comparative treatments for relationship dysfunction: Springer series on comparative treatments for psychological disorders* (pp. 163-185). New York: Springer.

Johnson, S.M. (2002). *Emotionally focused couple therapy with trauma survivors: Strengthening attachment bonds.* New York: Guilford.

Johnson, S.M., & Greenberg, L.S. (1985a). Differential effects of experiential and problem-solving interventions in resolving marital conflict. *Journal of Consulting and Clinical Psychology, 53,* 175-184.

Johnson, S.M., & Greenberg, L.S. (1985b). Emotionally focused couples therapy: An outcome study. *Journal of Marital and Family Therapy, 11,* 313-317.

Johnson, S.M., & Greenberg, L.S. (1987). Emotionally focused marital therapy: An overview. *Psychotherapy, 24,* 552-560.

Johnson, S.M., & Greenberg, L.S. (1995). The emotionally focused approach to problems in adult attachment. In N.S. Jacobson & A.S. Gurman (Eds.), *Clinical handbook of couples therapy* (pp. 121-141). New York: Guilford.

Johnson, S.M., Hunsley, J., Greenberg, L., & Schlinder, D. (1999). Emotionally focused couples therapy: Status and challenges. *Clinical Psychology: Science and Practice, 6,* 67-79.

Johnson, S.M., & LeBow, J. (2000). The "coming of age" of couple therapy: A decade review. *Journal of Marital and Family Therapy, 26,* 23-38.

Johnson, S.M., Makinen, J.A., & Milliken, J. W. (2001). Attachment injuries in couple relationships: A new perspective on impasses in couples therapy. *Journal of Marital and Family Therapy, 27,* 145-155.

Johnson, S.M., & Talitman, E. (1997). Predictors of success in emotionally focused marital therapy. *Journal of Marital and Family Therapy, 23,* 135-152.

Johnson, S.M., & Whiffen, V. (2003). *Attachment processes in couples and families.* New York: Guilford.

Johnson, S.M., & Williams-Keeler, L. (1998). Creating healing relationships for couples dealing with trauma: The use of emotionally focused marital therapy. *Journal of Marital and Family Therapy, 24,* 25-40.

Johnson, W.G., Tsoh, J.Y., & Varnado, P.J. (1996). Eating disorders: Efficacy of pharmacological and psychological interventions. *Clinical Psychology Review, 16,* 457-478.

Johnston, D.W. (1997). Hypertension. In A. Baum, S. Newman, J. Weinman, R. West, & C. McManus (Eds.), *Cambridge handbook of psychology, health and medicine*. (pp. 500-501). Cambridge, UK: Cambridge University Press.

Johnston, D.W., Gold, A., Kentish, J., Leach, G., & Robinson, B. (1993). Effect of stress management on blood pressure in mild primary hypertension. *British Medical Journal, 306,* 963-966.

Johnston, H.F., & Fruehling, J.J. (1994). Pharmacotherapy for depression in children and adolescents. In W.M. Reynolds & H.F. Johnston (Eds.), *Handbook of depression in children and adolescents*. New York: Plenum Press.

Johnston, M., & Voegele, C. (1993). Benefits of psychological preparation for surgery: A meta-analysis. *Annals of Behavioral Medicine, 15,* 245-256.

Johnston, M.B., Whitman, T.L., & Johnson, M. (1980). Teaching addition and subtraction to mentally retarded children: A self-instructional program. *Applied Research in Mental Retardation, 1,* 141-160.

Joiner, T.E. (1999). The clustering and contagion of suicide. *Current Directions in Psychological Science, 8,* 89-92.

Joiner, T.E., Alfano, M.S., & Metalsky, G.I. (1992). When depression breeds contempt: Reassurance seeking, self-esteem, and rejection of depressed college students by their roommates. *Journal of Abnormal Psychology, 101,* 165-173.

Joiner, T.E., & Schmidt, N.B. (1998). Excessive reassurance-seeking predicts depressive but not anxious reactions to acute stress. *Journal of Abnormal Psychology, 107,* 533-537.

Jones, G.M. (1987). Elderly people and domestic crime: Reflections on ageism, sexism, victimology. *British Journal of Criminology, 27,* 191-201.

Jones, J.M., Bennett, S., Olmsted, M.P., Lawson, M.L., & Rodin, G. (2001). Disordered eating attitudes and behaviours in teenaged girls: A school-based study. *Canadian Medical Association Journal, 165,* 547-552.

Jones, J.M., Huggins, M.A., Rydall, A.C., & Rodin, G.M. (2003). Symptomatic distress, hopelessness, and the desire for hastened death in hospitalized cancer patients. *Journal of Psychosomatic Research, 55,* 411-418.

Jones, M. (1953). The therapeutic community. New York: Basic Books.

Jones, M.C. (1924). A laboratory study of fear: The case of Peter. *Pedagogical Seminary, 31,* 308-315.

Jones, R.T. (1980). *Human effects: An overview. In Marijuana research findings*. Washington, DC: U.S. Government Printing Office.

Jorenby, D.E., Leischow, S.J., Nides, M.A., Rennard, S.I., Johnston, J.A., et al. (1999). A controlled trial of sustained-release buproprion, a nicotine patch, or both for smoking cessation. *New England Journal of Medicine, 340,* 685-691.

Joyce, A.S., Ogrodniczuk, J.S., Piper, W.E., & McCallum, M. (2003). The alliance as mediator of expectancy effects in short-term individual therapy. *Journal of Consulting and Clinical Psychology, 71,* 672-679.

Judd, L.J., Akiskal, H.S., Maser, J.D., Zeller, P.J., Endicott, J., et al. (1998). A prospective 12-year study of subsyndromal and syndromal depressive symptoms in unipolar major depressive disorders. *Archives of Gerneral Psychiatry, 55,* 694-701.

Judd, L.L. (1997). The clinical course of unipolar depressive disorders. *Archives of General Psychiatry, 54,* 989-992.

Julkunen, J.T., Salonen, R., Kaplan, G.A., Chesney, M.A., & Salonen, J.T. (1994). Hostility and the progression of carotid atherosclerosis. *Psychosomatic Medicine, 56,* 519-525.

Jung, C.G. (1935). Fundamental psychological conceptions. In M. Barker & M. Game (Eds.), *A report of five lectures*. London: Institute of Medical Psychology.

Junginger, J., Barker, S., & Coe, D. (1992). Mood theme and bizarreness of delusions in schizophrenia and mood psychosis. *Journal of Abnormal Psychology, 101,* 287-292.

Just, N., & Alloy, L.B. (1997). The response styles theory of depression: Tests and an extension of the theory. *Journal of Abnormal Psychology, 106,* 221-229.

Jutai, J.W., & Hare, R.D. (1983). Psychopathy and selective attention during performance of a complex perceptual-motor task. *Psychophysiology, 20,* 140-151.

Juurlink, D.N., Herrmann, N., Szalai, J.P., Kopp, A., & Redelmeier, D.A. (2004). Medical illness and risk of suicide in the elderly. *Archives of Internal Medicine, 164,* 1179-1184.

Kagan, J., & Snidman, N. (1991a). Infant predictors of inhibited and uninhibited profiles. *Psychological Science, 2,* 40-44.

Kahana, R.J. (1987). Geriatric psychotherapy: Beyond crisis management. In J. Sadavoy & M. Leszcz (Eds.), *Treating the elderly with psychotherapy.* Madison, CT: International Universities Press.

Kahneman, D. (1973). *Attention and effort.* Englewood Cliffs, NJ: Prentice-Hall.

Kail (1992). General slowing of information-processing by persons with mental retardation. *American Journal on Mental Retardation, 97,* 333-341.

Kain, K. (1994). *Movement never lies: An autobiography.* Toronto: McClelland and Stewart.

Kairouz, S., & Adlaf, E.M. (2003). Schools, students and heavy drinking: A multilevel analysis. *Addiction Research and Theory, 11,* 427-439.

Kairouz, S., Gliksman, L., Demers, A., & Adlaf, E.M. (2002). For all these reasons, I do … drink: A multilevel analysis of contextual reasons for drinking among Canadian undergraduates. *Journal of Studies on Alcohol, 63,* 600-608.

Kalichman, S.C. (1991). Psychopathology and personality characteristics of criminal sexual offenders as a function of victim age. *Archives of Sexual Behavior, 20,* 187-198.

Kamarck, T.W., Annunziato, B., & Amateau, L.M. (1995). Affiliations moderate the effects of social threat on stress-related cardiovascular responses: Boundary conditions for a laboratory model of social support. *Psychosomatic Medicine, 57,* 183-194.

Kamarck, T.W., Everson, S.A., Kaplan, G.A., Manuck, S.B., Jennings, J.R., et al. (1997). Exaggerated blood pressure responses during mental stress are associated with enhanced carotid atherosclerosis in middle-aged Finnish men. *Circulation, 96,* 3842-3848.

Kamarck, T.W., Jennings, J.R., Debski, T.T., Glickman-Weiss, E., Johnson, P.S., et al. (1992). Reliable measures of behaviorally-evoked cardiovascular reactivity from a PC-based test battery: Results from student and community samples. *Psychophysiology, 29,* 17-28.

Kamarck, T.M., Shiffman, S.M., Smithline, L., Goodie, J.L., Paty, J.A., et al. (1998). Effects of task strain, social conflict, and emotional activation on ambulatory cardiovascular activity: Daily life consequences of recurring stress in a multiethnic adult sample. *Health Psychology, 17,* 17-29.

Kammen, D.P. van, Bunney, W.E., Docherty, J.P., Jimerson, J.C., Post, R.M., et al. (1977). Amphetamine induced catecholamine activation in schizophrenia and depression. *Advances in Biochemical Psychopharmacology, 16,* 655-659.

Kandel, D.B., Davies, M., Karus, D., & Yamaguchi, K. (1986). The consequences in young adulthood of adolescent drug involvement. *Archives of General Psychiatry, 43,* 746-754.

Kane, J., Honigfeld, G., Singer, J., Meltzer, H., and the Clozapine Collaborative Study Group. (1988). Clozapine for treatment resistant schizophrenics. *Archives of General Psychiatry, 45,* 789-796.

Kane, J.M., Woerner, M., Weinhold, P., Wegner, J., Kinon, B., & Bernstein, M. (1986). Incidence of tardive dyskinesia: Five-year data from a prospective study. *Psychopharmacology Bulletin, 20,* 387-389.

Kane, R.A., & Kane, R.L. (1985). Feasibility of universal long-term-care benefits: Ideas from Canada. *New England Journal of Medicine, 312,* 1357-1364.

Kane, R.L., Parsons, D.A., & Goldstein, G. (1983). Statistical relationships and discriminative accuracy of the Halstead-Reitan, Luria-Nebraska, and Wechsler IQ scores in the identification of brain damage. *Journal of Clinical and Experimental Neuropsychology, 7,* 211-223.

Kanfer, F.H., & Busenmeyer, J.R. (1982). The use of problem-solving and decision making in behavior therapy. *Clinical Psychology Review, 2,* 239-266.

Kanfer, F.H., & Phillips, J.S. (1970). *Learning foundations of behavior therapy*. New York: Wiley.

Kanner, A.D., Coyne, J.C., Schaefer, C., & Lazarus, R.S. (1981). Comparison of two modes of stress measurement: Daily hassles and uplifts versus major life events. *Journal of Behavioral Medicine, 4,* 1-39.

Kanner, L. (1943). Autistic disturbances of affective contact. *Nervous Child, 2,* 217-250.

Kanner, L. (1973). *Childhood psychosis: Initial studies and new insights*. Washington, D.C.: V. H. Winston and Sons.

Kanner, L., & Eisenberg, L. (1955). Notes on the follow-up studies of autistic children. In P. Hoch & J. Zubin (Eds.), *Psychopathology of childhood*. New York: Grune & Stratton.

Kantorovich, N.V. (1930). An attempt at associative-reflex therapy in alcoholism. *Psychological Abstracts, 4,* 493.

Kaplan, H.I., & Sadock, B.J. (1991). *Synopsis of psychiatry: Behavioral sci-*

ences, clinical psychiatry. Baltimore: Williams & Williams.

Kaplan, H.S. (1991). Sex therapy with older patients. In W.A. Myers (Ed.), *New techniques in the psychotherapy of older patients* (pp. 21-37). Washington, DC: American Psychiatric Press.

Kaplan, H.S. (1997). Sexual desire disorders (hypoactive sexual desire and sexual aversion). In G.O. Gabbard & S.D. Atkinson (Eds.), *Synopsis of treatments of psychiatric disorders*. Second edition. (pp. 771-780). Washington,DC: American Psychiatric Press.

Kaplan, J.R., Manuck, S.B., Williams, J.K., & Strawn, W. (1993). *Psychosocial influences on atherosclerosis: Evidence for effects and mechanisms in nonhuman primates. In J. Blascovich & E.S. Katkin (Eds.), Cardiovascular reactivity*. (pp. 3-26). Washington, DC: American Psychological Association.

Kaplan, M.S., & Kreuger, R.B. (1997). Voyeurism: Psychopathology and theory. In D.R. Laws & W. O'Donohue (Eds.), *Sexual deviance*. (pp. 297-310). NY: Guilford Press.

Kapur, S. (2003). Psychosis as a state of aberrant salience: A framework linking biology, phenomenology, and pharmacology in schizophrenia. *American Journal of Psychiatry*, *160*, 13-23.

Kapur, S., Zipursky, R., Jones, C., Remington, G., & Houle, S. (2000). Relationship between dopamine D_2 occupancy, clinical response, and side effects: A double-blind PET study of first-episode schizophrenia. *American Journal of Psychiatry*, *157*, 514-520.

Karagianis, J. (1994). Frequency of electroconvulsive therapy use at a provincial mental hospital: A retrospective study. *Canadian Journal of Psychiatry, 39*, 551-556.

Karasek, R.A. (1979). Job demands, job decision latitude, and mental strain: Implications for job redesign. *Administrative Science, 24,* 285-308.

Karasu, T.B., Stein, S.P., & Charles, E.S. (1979). Age factors in the patient-therapist relationship. *Journal of Nervous and Mental Disease, 167,* 100-104.

Karno, M., & Golding, J.M. (1991). Obsessive-compulsive disorder. In L.N. Robinson & D.A. Regier (Eds.), *Psychiatric disorders in America*. New York: Free Press.

Karon, B. P., & VandenBos, G. R. (1998). Schizophrenia and psychosis in elderly populations. In I.H. Nordhus, G.R. VandenBos, S. Berg, & P. Fromholt, (Eds.), *Clinical geropsychology* (pp. 219-227). Washington, D.C.: American Psychological Association.

Kasanin, J. (1933). The acute schizoaffective psychoses. *American Journal of Psychiatry, 13,* 97-123.

Kashani, J.H., & Carlson, G.A. (1987). Seriously depressed preschoolers. *American Journal of Psychiatry, 144,* 348-350.

Kashani, J.H., Holcomb, W.R., & Orvaschel, H. (1986). Depression and depressive symptoms in preschool children from the general population. *American Journal of Psychiatry, 143,* 1138-1143.

Kasl-Godley, J., & Gatz, M. (1999). *Psychosocial interventions for individuals with dementia: An integration of theory, therapy, and a clinical understanding of dementia*. Unpublished manuscript, University of Southern California.

Kasl-Godley, J. E., Gatz, M., & Fiske, A. (1998). Depression and depressive symptoms in old age. In I.H. Nordhus, G.R. VandenBos, S. Berg, & P. Fromholt (Eds.), *Clinical geropsychology* (pp. 211-217). Washington, D.C.: American Psychological Association.

Kaslow, N.J., Brown, R.T., & Mee, L. (1994). Cognitive and behavioral correlates of childhood depression: A developmental perspective. In W.M. Reynolds & H.F. Johnston (Eds.), *Handbook of depression in children and adolescents*. New York: Plenum Press.

Kaslow, N.J., & Racusin, G.R. (1990). Childhood depression: Current status and future directions. In A.S. Bellack, M. Hersen, & A.E. Kazdin (Eds.), *International handbook of behavior modification and therapy* (2nd ed.). New York: Plenum.

Kaslow, N.J., Stark, K.D., Printz, B., Livingston, R., & Tsai, Y. (1992). Cognitive Triad Inventory for Children: Development and relationship to depression and anxiety. *Journal of Clinical Child Psychology, 21,* 339-347.

Kaslow, N.J., & Thompson, M.P. (1998). Applying the criteria for empirically supported treatments to studies of psychosocial interventions for child and adolescent depression. *Journal of Clinical Child Psychology, 27,* 146-155.

Kasprowicz, A.L., Manuck, S.B., Malkoff, S., & Kranz, D.S. (1990). Individual differences in behaviorally evoked cardiovascular response: Temporal stability and hemodynamic patterning. *Psychophysiology, 27,* 605-619.

Kassett, J.A., Gershon, E.S., Maxwell, M.E., et al. (1989). Psychiatric disorders in the first-degree relatives of probands with bulimia nervosa. *American Journal of Psychiatry, 146,* 1468-1471.

Kaszniak, A.W., Nussbaum, P.D., Berren, M.R., & Santiago, J. (1988). Amnesia as a consequence of male rape: A case report. *Journal of Abnormal Psychology, 97,* 100-104.

Katz, E.R. (1980). *Illness impact and social reintegration. In J. Kellerman (Ed.), Psychological aspects of childhood cancer*. Springfield, IL: Charles C. Thomas.

Katz, E.R., Kellerman, J., & Siegel, S.E. (1980). Behavioral distress in children with leukemia undergoing bone marrow aspirations. *Journal of Consulting and Clinical Psychology, 48,* 356-365.

Katz, E.R., Varni, J.W., Rubenstein, C.L., Blew, A., & Hubert, N. (1992). Teacher, parent, and child evaluative ratings of a school reintegration program for children with newly diagnosed cancer. *Children's Health Care, 21,* 69-75.

Katz, H.M., & Gunderson, J.G. (1990). Individual psychodynamically oriented psychotherapy for schizophrenic patients. In M.I. Herz, S.J. Keith, & J.P. Docherty (Eds.), *Handbook of schizophrenia: Psychosocial treatment of schizophrenia*. (pp. 69-90). Amsterdam, The Netherlands: Elsevier Science Publishers.

Katz, J., Ritvo, P., Irvine, M.J., & Jackson, M. (1996). Coping with chronic pain. In M. Zeidner & N. S. Endler (Eds.), *Handbook of coping: Theory, research, and applications* (pp. 252-278). New York: Wiley.

Katz, R.C., Gipson, M.T., Kearl, A., & Kriskovich, M. (1989). Assessing sexual aversion in college students: The Sexual Aversion Scale. *Journal of Sex and Marital Therapy, 15,* 135-140.

Katz, S. J. et al. (1998). Medication management of depression in the United States and Ontario. *Journal of General internal Medicine, 13,* 77-85.

Katzelnick, D.J., Kobak, K.A., Greist, J.H., Jefferson, J.W., Mantle, J.M., & Serlin, R.C. (1995). Sertraline for social phobia: A double-blind, placebo-controlled crossover study. *American Journal of Psychiatry, 152,* 1368-1371.

Kaufmann, P.G., Jacob, R.G., Ewart, C.K., Chesney, M.A., Muenz, L.R., Doub, N., Mercer, W., & HIPP Investigators. (1988). Hypertension intervention pooling project. *Health Psychology, 7,* 209-224.

Kaw, E. (1993). Medicalization of racial features: Asian American women and cosmetic surgery. *Medical Anthropology Quarterly, 7,* 74.

Kawachi, I., Colditz, G.A., Ascherio, A., Rimm, E.B., Giovannucci, E., et al. (1994). Prospective study of phobic anxiety and risk of coronary heart disease in men. *Circulation, 89,* 1992-1997.

Kawachi, I., Sparrow, D., Spiro, A., Vokonas, P., & Weiss, S.T. (1996). A prospective study of anger and coronary heart disease: The normative aging study. *Circulation, 94,* 2090-2094.

Kawas, C., Resnick, S., Morrison, A., Brookmeyer, R., et al. (1997). A prospective study of estrogen replacement therapy (ERT) and the risk of developing Alzheimer's disease: The Baltimore longitudinal study of aging. *Neurology, 48,* 1517-1521.

Kaye, W.H., Greeno, C.G., Fernstrom, J., Fernstrom, M., Moss, H., et al. (1998). Alterations in serotonin activity and psychiatric symptoms after recovery from bulimia nervosa. *Archives of General Psychiatry, 55,* 927-935.

Kazarian, S. S., Malla, A., Cole, J. D., & Baker, B. (1990). Comparisons of two expressed emotion scales with the Camberwell Family Interview. *Journal of Clinical Psychology*, *46*, 306-309.

Kazdin, A.E. (1985). *Treatment of antisocial behavior in children and adolescents*. Homewood, IL: Dorsey Press.

Kazdin, A.E. (1994). Psychotherapy for children and adolescents. In A.E. Bergin & S.L. Garfield (Eds.), *Handbook of psychotherapy and behavior change*. Fourth edition (pp. 543-594). New York: Wiley.

Kazdin, A.E. (2003). Psychotherapy for children and adolescents. *Annual Review of Psychology*, *54*, 253-276.

Kazdin, A.E., & Kagan, J. (1994). Models of dysfunction in developmental psychopathology. *Clinical Psychology: Science and Practice, 1,* 35-52.

Kazdin, A.E., & Weisz, J.R. (1998). Identifying and developing empirically supported child and adolescent treatments. *Journal of Consulting and Clinical Psychology, 66,* 19-36.

Keane, T.M. (in press). The role of exposure therapy in the psychological treatment of PTSD. PTSD *Clinical Quarterly*.

Keane, T.M., Fairbank, J.A., Caddell, J.M., & Zimering, R.T. (1989). Implosive (flooding) therapy reduces symptoms of PTSD in Vietnam combat veterans. *Behavior Therapy, 20,* 245-260.

Keane, T.M., Fisher, L.M., Krinsley, K.E., & Niles, B.L. (1994). Posttraumatic stress disorder. In M. Hersen & R.T. Ammerman (Eds.), *Handbook of prescriptive treatments for adults* (pp. 237-260). New York: Plenum.

Keane, T.M., Foy, D.W., Nunn, B., & Rychtarik, R.G. (1984). Spouse contracting to increase Antabuse compliance in alcoholic veterans. *Journal of Clinical Psychology, 40,* 340-344.

Keane, T.M., Gerardi, R.J., Quinn, S.J., & Litz, B.T. (1992). Behavioral treatment of post-traumatic stress disorder. In S.M. Turner, K.S. Calhoun, & H.E. Adams (Eds.), *Handbook of clinical behavior therapy* (2nd ed., pp. 87-97). New York: Wiley.

Keane, T.M., & Wolfe, J. (1990). Co-morbidity in post-traumatic stress disorder: An analysis of community and clinical studies. *Journal of Applied Social Psychology, 20,* 1776-1788.

Kearns, R.A., & Taylor, S.M. (1989). Daily life experience of people with chronic mental disabilities in Hamilton, Ontario. *Canada's Mental Health, 37,* 1-4.

Keck, P.E., McElroy, S.L., Strakowski, S.M., West, S.A., Sax, K.W., et al. (1998). 12-month outcome of patients with bipolar disorder following hospitalization for a manic or mixed episode. *American Journal of Psychiatry, 155,* 646-652.

Keck, P.E., & McElroy, S.L. (1998). Pharmacological treatment of bipolar disorders. In P.E. Nathan & J.M. Gorman (Eds.), *A guide to treatments that work.* (pp. 249-269). New York: Oxford University Press.

Kedward, H.B., Eastwood, M.R., Allodi, F., & Duckworth, G.S. (1974). The evaluation of chronic psychiatric care. *Canadian Medical Association Journal, 110,* 519-523.

Keefe, F.J., & Gil, K.M. (1986). Behavioral concepts in the analysis of chronic pain syndromes. *Journal of Consulting and Clinical Psychology, 54,* 776-783.

Keefe, R.S., Silverman, J.M., Mohs, R.C., Siever, L.J., et al. (1997). Eye tracking, attention, and schizotypal symptoms in nonpsychotic relatives of patients with schizophrenia. *Archives of General Psychiatry, 54,* 169-176.

Keel, P.K., & Klump, K.L. (2003). Are eating disorders culture-bound syndromes? Implications for conceptualizing their etiology? *Psychological Bulletin, 129,* 747-769.

Keel, P.K., & Mitchell, J.E. (1997). Outcome in bulimia nervosa. *American Journal of Psychiatry, 154,* 313-321.

Keel, P.K., Mitchell, J.E., Miller, K.B., Davis, T.L., & Crowe, S.J. (1999). Long-term outcome of bulimia nervosa. *Archives of General Psychiatry, 56,* 63-69.

Keith, J. (1982). *Old people as people.* Boston: Little, Brown.

Keller, M.B., Beardslee, W., Lavori, P.W., Wunder, J., Dils, D.L., & Samuelson, H. (1988). Course of major depression in non-referred adolescents: A retrospective study. *Journal of Affective Disorders, 15,* 235-243.

Keller, M.B., Kocsis, J.H., Thase, M.E., Gelenberg, A.J., Rush, J., et al. (1998). Maintenance phase efficacy of Sertraline for chronic depression. *JAMA, 280,* 1665-1672.

Keller, M.B., Shapiro, R.W., Lavori, P.W., & Wolpe, N. (1982). Relapse in major depressive disorder: Analysis with the life table. *Archives of General Psychiatry, 39,* 911-915.

Kellerman, J., & Varni, J.W. (1982). Pediatric hematology/oncology. In D.C. Russo & J.W. Varni (Eds.), *Behavioral pediatrics: Research and practice.* New York: Plenum.

Kelley, M.L. (1990). *School-home notes: Promoting children's classroom success.* New York: Guilford Press.

Kellner, F., Webster, I., & Chanteloup, F. (1996). Describing and predicting alcohol use-related harm: An analysis of the Yukon Alcohol and Drug Survey. *Substance Use and Misuse, 31,* 1619-1638.

Kellner, R. (1982). Disorders of impulse control (not elsewhere classified). In J.H. Griest, J.W. Jefferson, & R.L. Spitzer (Eds.), *Treatment of mental disorders.* New York: Oxford University Press.

Kellner, R. (1986). *Somatization and hypochondriasis.* New York: Praeger-Greenwood.

Kelly, G.A. (1955). *The psychology of personal constructs.* New York: Norton.

Kelly, J.A. (1985). Group social skills training. *the Behavior Therapist, 8,* 93-95.

Kelly, K. (1992). *Visible Minorities: A diverse group* [Online] www.statcan.ca/english/ads/11-008-XPE/vismin.html Ottawa, ON: Statistics Canada.

Kemner, C., Willemsen-Swinkels, S.H., de Jonge, M., Tuynman-Qua, H., & van Engeland, H. (2002). Open-label study of olanzapine in children with pervasive developmental disorder. *Journal of Clinical Psychopharmacology, 22,* 455-460.

Kemper, S., Greiner, L.H. Marquis, J.G., Prenovost, K., & Mitzner, T.L. (2001). Language decline across the life span: Findings from the Nun Study. *Psychology and Aging, 16,* 227-239.

Kempster, N. (1996, August 25). Clinton orders tracking of sex offenders. *Los Angeles Times,* p. A20.

Kendall, P., Haaga, D.A.F., Ellis, A., Bernard, M., DiGiuseppe, R., & Kassinove, H. (1995). Rational-emotive therapy in the 1990s and beyond: Current status, recent revisions, and research questions. *Clinical Psychology Review, 15,* 169-185.

Kendall, P.C. (1990). Cognitive processes and procedures in behavior therapy. In C.M. Franks, G.T. Wilson, P.C. Kendall, & J.P. Foreyt (Eds.), *Review of behavior therapy: Theory and practice* (Vol. 12, pp. 103-137). New York: Guilford.

Kendall, P.C., & Braswell, L. (1985). *Cognitive-behavioral therapy for impulsive children.* New York: Guilford.

Kendall, P.C., Flannery-Schroeder, E., Panichelli-Mindel, S.M., Southam-Gerow, M., Henin, A., & Warman, M. (1997). Therapy for youths with anxiety disorders: A second randomized clinical trial. *Journal of Consulting and Clinical Psychology, 65,* 366-380.

Kendall, P.C., & Ingram, R.E. (1989). Cognitive-behavioral perspectives: Theory and research on depression and anxiety. In P.C. Kendall & D. Watson (Eds.), *Anxiety and depression: Distinctive and overlapping features* (pp. 27-54). New York: Academic Press.

Kendell, R.E. (1975). *The role of diagnosis in psychiatry.* London: Blackwell.

Kendler, K., Pedersen, N., Johnson, L., Neale, M.C., & Mathe, A. (1993). A Swedish pilot twin study of affective illness, including hospital and population-ascertained subsamples. *Archives of General Psychiatry, 50,* 699-706.

Kendler, K.S. (1993). Twin studies of psychiatric illness: Current status and future directions. *Archives of General Psychiatry, 50,* 905-914.

Kendler, K.S. (1997). The diagnostic validity of melancholic major depression in a population-based sample of female twins. *Archives of General Psychiatry, 54,* 299-304.

Kendler, K.S., Davis, C. G., & Kessler, R. C. (1997). The familial aggregation of common psychiatric and substance use disorders in the National Comorbidity Survey: A family history study. *British Journal of Psychiatry, 170,* 541-548.

Kendler, K.S., & Gardner, C.O. (1998). Boundaries of major depression: An evaluation of DSM-IV criteria. *American Journal of Psychiatry, 155,* 172-177.

Kendler, K.S., & Gruenberg, A.M. (1984). Independent analysis of Danish adoption study of schizophrenia. *Archives of General Psychiatry, 41,* 555-562.

Kendler, K.S., Karkowski, L.M., & Prescott, C.A. (1999). Causal relationship between stressful life events and the onset of major depression. *American Journal of Psychiatry, 156,* 837-841.

Kendler, K.S., Karkowski, L.M., & Prescott, C.A. (1999). Fears and phobias: Reliability and heritability. *Psychological Medicine, 29,* 539-553.

Kendler, K.S., Karkowski-Shuman, L., & Walsh, D. (1996). Age of onset in schizophrenia and risk of illness in relatives. *British Journal of Psychiatry, 169,* 213-218.

Kendler, K.S., Neale, M.C., Kessler, R.C., Heath, A.C., & Eaves, L.J. (1992). Generalized anxiety disorder: Same genes, (partly) different environments. *Archives of General Psychiatry, 49,* 716-722.

Kendler, K.S., Neale, M.C., Kessler, R.C., Heath, A.C., & Eaves, L.J. (1992). The genetic epidemiology of phobias in women: The interrelationship of agoraphobia, social phobia, and simple phobia. *Archives of General Psychiatry, 49,* 273-281.

Kendler, K.S., Neale, M.C., & Walsh, D. (1995). Evaluating the spectrum concept of schizophrenia in the Roscommon Family Study. *American Journal of Psychiatry, 152,* 749-754.

Kendler, K.S., & Prescott, C.A. (1998). Cannabis use, abuse, and dependence in a population-based sample of female twins. *American Journnal of Psychiatry, 155,* 1016-1022.

Kendler, K.S., & Prescott, C.A. (1999). Caffeine intake, tolerance, and withdrawal in women: A population-based twin study. *American Journal of Psychiatry, 156,* 223-228.

Kendler, K.S., Prescott, C.A., Myers, J., & Neale, M.C. (2003). The structure of genetic and environmental risk factors for common psychiatric and substance use disorders in men and women. *Archives of General Psychiatry, 60,* 929-937.

Kennedy, E., Spence, S.H., & Hensley, R. (1989). An examination of the relationship between childhood depression and social competence amongst primary school children. *Journal of Child Psychology and Psychiatry, 30,* 561-573.

Kennedy, M., & Jones, E. (1995). Violence from patients in the community: Will UK courts impose a duty of care on mental health professionals? *Criminal Behaviour and Mental Health, 5,* 209-217.

Kennedy, S. H. (1990). A multifaceted programme for preventing and treating eating disorders. *Hospital and Community Psychiatry, 41,* 1120-1123.

Kennedy, S.H., & Garfinkel, P.E. (1992). Advances in the diagnosis and treatment of anorexia nervosa and bulimia nervosa. *Canadian Journal of Psychiatry, 37,* 309-315.

Kent, H. (1999). The Yukon takes native health a step further at Whitehorse hospital (Native healing building). *Canadian Medical Association Journal, 161,* 1312.

Kent, J.S., & Clopton, J.R. (1992). Bulimic women's perceptions of their family relationships. *Journal of Clinical Psychology, 48,* 281-292.

Kernberg, O.F. (1985). *Borderline conditions and pathological narcissism.* Northvale, NJ: Jason Aronson.

Kerns, K.A., Eso, K., & Thomson, J. (1999). Investigation of a direct intervention for improving attention in young children with ADHD. *Developmental Neuropsychology, 16,* 273-295.

Kerr, S. L., & Neale, J. M. (1993). Emotional perception in schizophrenia: Specific deficit or further evidence of generalized poor performance? *Journal of Abnormal Psychology, 102,* 312-318.

Keshavan, M.S., Rosenberg, D., Sweeney, J.A., & Pettegrew, J.W. (1998). Decreased caudate volume in neuroleptic-naive psychotic patients. *American Journal of Psychiatry, 155,* 774-778.

Kessel, N., & Grossman, G. (1961). Suicide in alcoholics. *British Medical Journal, 2,* 1671-1672.

Kessler, R.C., Andrade, L.H., Bijl, R.V., Offord, D.R., Demler, O.V., & Stein, D.J. (2002). The effects of co-morbidity on the onset and persistence of generalized anxiety disorder in the ICPE surveys. *Psychological Medicine, 32,* 1213-1225.

Kessler, R.C., Crum, R.M., Warner, L.A., Nelson, C.B., et al. (1997). Lifetime co-occurrence of DSM-IIIR alcohol dependence with other psychiatric disorders in the National Comorbidity Study. *Archives of General Psychiatry, 54,* 313-321.

Kessler, R.C., Davis, C. G., & Kendler, K. S. (1997). Childhood adversity and adult psychiatric disorder in the US National Comorbidity Survey. *Psychological Medicine, 27,* 1101-1119.

Kessler, R.C., Frank, R.G., Edlund, M., Katz, S.J., Lin, E., & Leaf, P. (1997). Differences in the use of psychiatric outpatient services between the United States and Ontario. *New England Journal of Medicine, 336,* 551-557.

Kessler, R.C., McGonagle, K.A., Zhao, S., Nelson, C.B., Hughes, M., et al. (1994). Lifetime and 12-month prevalence rates of DSM-III-R psychiatric disorders in the United States: Results from the National Comorbidity Survey. *Archives of General Psychiatry, 51,* 8-19.

Kessler, R.C., & McLeod, J.D. (1985). Social support and mental health in community samples. In S. Cohen & L. Syme (Eds.), *Social support and health.* (pp. 219-240). Orlando,FL: Academic Press.

Kessler, R.C., Wittchen, H.-U., Stein, M., & Walters, E.E. (1999). Lifetime comorbidities between social phobia and mood disorders in the US National Comorbidity Survey. *Psychological Medicine, 29,* 555-567.

Kety, S.S., Rosenthal, D., Wender, P.H., & Schulsinger, F. (1968). The types and prevalence of mental illness in the biological and adoptive families of adopted schizophrenics. In D. Rosenthal & S.S. Kety (Eds.), *The transmission of schizophrenia* Elmsford, NY: Pergamon.

Kety, S.S., Rosenthal, D., Wender, P.H., & Schulsinger, F. (1975). Mental illness in the adoptive and biological families of adopted individuals who have become schizophrenic. In R.R. Fieve, D. Rosenthal, & H. Brill (Eds.), *Genetic research in psychiatry.* Baltimore: Johns Hopkins University Press.

Kety, S.S., Wender, P.H., Jacobsen, B., Ingraham, L.T., Jansson, L., et al. (1994). Mental illness in the biological and adoptive relatives of schizophrenic adoptees: Replication of the Copenhagen study in the rest of Denmark. *Archives of General Psychiatry, 51,* 442-468.

Keys, A., Brozek, J., Hsu, L.K.G., McConoha, C.E., & Bolton, B. (1950). *The biology of human starvation.* Minneapolis: Univ of Minnesota Press.

Keys, A., Taylor, H.L., et al. (1971). Mortality and coronary heart disease in men studied for 23 years. *Archives of Internal Medicine, 128,* 201-214.

Kidd, G.E. (1946). Trepanation among the early Indians of British Columbia. *Canadian Medical Association Journal, 55,* 513-516.

Kiecolt-Glaser, J., Dura, J.R., Speicher, C.E., & Trask, O. (1991). Spousal caregivers of dementia victims: Longitudinal changes in immunity and health. *Psychosomatic Medicine, 54,* 345-362.

Kiecolt-Glaser, J., Glaser, R., Strain, E., Stout, J.C., Tarr, K.L., Holliday, J.E., & Speicher, C.E. (1986). Modulation of cellular immunity in medical students. *Journal of Behavioral Medicine, 9,* 5-21.

Kiecolt-Glaser, J.K., Garner, W., Speicher, C.E., Penn, G.M., Holliday, J., & Glaser, R. (1984). Psychosocial modifiers of immunocompetence in medical students. *Psychosomatic Medicine, 46,* 7-14.

Kiecolt-Glaser, J.K., Glaser, R., Williger, D., Stout, J., Messick, G., Sheppard, S., Ricker, D., Romischer, S.C., Briner, W., Bonnell, G., & Donnerberg, R. (1985). Psychosocial enhancement of immunocompetence in a geriatric population. *Health Psychology, 4,* 25-41.

Kiehl, K.A., Smith, A.M., Hare, R.D., Mendrek, A., Forster, B.B., Brink, J., & Liddle, P.F. (2001). Limbic abnormalities in affective processing by criminal psychopaths as revealed by functional magnetic resonance imaging. *Biological Psychiatry, 50,* 677-684.

Kiesler, C.A. (1991). Changes in general hospital psychiatric care. *American Psychologist, 46,* 416-421.

Kihlstrom, J.F. (1994). Dissociative and conversion disorders. In D.J. Stein & J.E. Young (Eds.), *Cognitive science and clinical disorders.* San Diego, CA. Academic Press.

Kihlstrom, J.F. (1997). Exhumed memory. In S.J. Lynn, K.M. McConkey, & N.P. Spanos (Eds.), *Truth in memory.* New York: Guilford.

Kihlstrom, J.F., & Tataryn, D. J. (1991). Dissociative disorders. In P.B. Sutker & H.E. Adams (Eds.), *Comprehensive handbook of psychopathology* (2nd ed.). New York: Plenum.

Kilbourn, K.M., & Durning, P.E. (2003). Oncology and psycho-oncology. In S. Llewelyn & P. Kennedy (Eds.), *Handbook of clinical health psychology* (pp. 103-129). Chichester, West Sussex, England: Wiley.

Kihlstrom, J.F., Tataryn, D.J., & Hoyt, I.P. (1993). Dissociative disorders. In P.B. Sutker & H.E. Adams (Eds.), *Comprehensive handbook of psychopathology.* (pp. 203-234). NY: Plenum.

Killen, J.D., Fortmann, S.P., Newman, B., & Varady, A. (1990). Evaluation of a treatment approach combining nicotine gum with self-guided behavioral treatments for smoking relapse prevention. *Journal of Consulting and Clinical Psychology, 58,* 85-92.

Killen, J.D., Robinson, T.N., Haydel, K.F., Hayward, C., et al. (1997). Prospective study of risk factors for the initiation of cigarette smoking. *Journal of Consulting and Clinical Psychology, 65,* 1011-1016.

Killen, J.D., Taylor, C.B., Hayward, C., Wilson, D.M., Haydel, K.F., et al. (1994). Pursuit of thinness and onset of eating disorders in a community sample of adolescent girls. *International Journal of Eating Disorders, 16,* 227-238.

Killen, J.D., Taylor, C.B., Telch, M.J., Saylor, K.E., Maron, D.J., & Robinson, T.N. (1986). Self-induced vomiting and laxative and diuretic use among teenagers: Precursors of the binge-purge syndrome. *Journal of the American Medical Association, 255,* 1447-1449.

Kilpatrick, D.G., & Best, C.L. (1990, April). *Sexual assault victims: Data from a random national probability sample.* Paper presented at the annual convention of the Southeastern Psychological Association, Atlanta.

Kilpatrick, D.G., Best, C.L., Veronen, L.J., Amick, A.E., Villeponteaux, L.A., & Ruff, G.A. (1985). Mental health correlates of criminal victimization: A random community survey. *Journal of Consulting and Clinical Psychology, 53,* 866-873.

Kilpatrick, D.G., Edmunds, C.N., & Seymour, A.K. (1992). *Rape in America: A report to the nation.* Arlington,VA: National Victim Center.

King, D.W., King, L.A., Foy, D.W., Keane, T.M., & Fairbank, J.A. (1999).

Posttraumatic stress disorder in a national sample of female and male Vietnam veterans: Risk factors, war-zone stressors, and resilience-recovery variables. *Journal of Abnormal Psychology, 198,* 164-170.

King, D.W., King, L.A., Gudanowski, D.M., & Vreven, D.L. (1995). Alternative representations of war zone stressors: Relationship to posttraumatic stress disorder in male and female Vietnam veterans. *Journal of Abnormal Psychology, 104,* 184-196.

King, J. (1997). The life of Margaret Laurence. Toronto: Knopf.

King, P.R., & Endler, N.S. (1990). Interactional anxiety and the evaluation of driving skills: An empirical examination of a composite predictor for state anxiety. *Canadian Journal of Behavioural Science*, *22*, 13-19.

King, S. (2000). Is expressed emotion cause or effect in the mothers of schizophrenic young adults? *Schizophrenia Research*, *45*, 65-78.

King, S., Ricard, N., Rochon, V., Steiger, H., & Nelis, S. (2003). Determinants of expressed emotion in mothers of schizophrenia patients. *Psychiatry Research*, *117*, 211-222.

Kinsey, A.C., Pomeroy, W.B., Main, C.E., & Gebhard, P.H. (1953). *Sexual behavior in the human female*. Philadelphia: Saunders.

Kinsey, A.C., Pomeroy, W.B., & Martin, C.E. (1948). *Sexual behavior in the human male*. Philadelphia: Saunders.

Kinzl, J.F., Traweger, C., Trefalt, E., Mangweth, B., & Biebl, W. (1999). Binge eating disorder in females: A population based investigation. *International Journal of Eating Disorders, 25,* 287-292.

Kipke, M.D., Montgomery, S., & MacKenzie, R.G. (1993). Substance use among youth who attend community-based health clinics. *Journal of Adolescent Health, 14,* 289-294.

Kirkland, S.A., MacLean, D.R., Langille, D.B., Joffres, M.R., MacPherson, K.M., & Andreou, P. (1999). Knowledge and awareness of risk factors for cardiovascular disease among Canadians 55 to 74 years of age: Results from the Canadian Health Surveys, 1986-1992. *Canadian Medical Association Journal*, *161 (8, Supplement)*, S10-S16.

Kirmayer, L.J. (1994). Suicide among Canadian Aboriginal peoples. *Transcultural Psychiatric Research Review, 31,* 3-58.

Kirmayer, L.J. (2001). Cultural variations in the clinical presentation of depression and anxiety: Implications for diagnosis and treatment. *Journal of Clinical Psychiatry*, *62 (Supplement 13)*, 22-28.

Kirmayer, L.J., Boothroyd, L.J., & Hodgins, S. (1998). Attempted suicide among Inuit youth: Psychosocial correlates and implications for prevention. *Canadian Journal of Psychiatry*, *43*, 816-822.

Kirmayer, L.J., Boothroyd, L.J., Tanner, A., Adelson, N., & Robinson, E. (2000). Psychological distress among the Cree of James Bay. *Transcultural Psychiatry, 37,* 35-56.

Kirmayer, L.J., Brass, G.M., & Tait, C.L. (2000). The mental health of Aboriginal peoples: Transformations of identity and community. *Canadian Journal of Psychiatry, 45,* 607-616.

Kirmayer, L.J., Malus, M., & Boothroyd, L.J. (1996). Suicide attempts among Inuit youth: A community survey of prevalence and risk factors. *Acta Psychiatrica Scandinavica*, *94*, 8-17.

Kirmayer, L.J., Robbins, J.M., & Paris, J. (1994). Somatoform disorders: Personality and social matrix of somatic distress. *Journal of Abnormal Psychology, 103,* 125-136.

Kirmayer, L.J., Rousseau, C., Jarvis, G.E., & Guzder, J. (2003). The cultural context of clinical assessment. In A. Tasman, J. Kay, & J.A. Lieberman (Eds.), *Psychiatry, Second Edition, Vol. 2* (pp. 19-29). Chichester, West Sussex, England: Wiley.

Kirmayer, L.J., Rousseau, C., & Santhanam, R. (2003). Models of diagnosis and treatment planning in multicultural mental health. In A. Rummens, M. Beiser, & S. Noh (Eds.), *Immigration, health, and ethnicity*. Toronto: University of Toronto Press.

Kirmayer, L.J., & Young, A. (1998). Culture and somatization: Clinical, epidemiological, and ethnographic perspectives. *Psychosomatic Medicine, 60,* 420-430.

Kirschbaum, C., Prussner, J.C., & Stone, A.A. (1995). Persistent high cortisol responses to repeated psychological stress in a subpopulation of healthy men. *Psychosomatic Medicine, 57,* 468-474.

Kirsh, G.A., & Kuiper, N.A. (2003). Positive and negative aspects of sense of humor: Associations with the constructs of individualism and relatedness. *Humor: International Journal of Humor Research*, *16*, 33-62.

Kivlighan, D.M., & Mullison, D. (1988). Participants' perception of therapeutic factors in group counseling: The role of interpersonal style and stage of group development. *Small Group Development, 19,* 452-468.

Klein, B., & Richards, J.C. (2001). A brief Internet-based treatment of panic disorder. *Behavioral and Cognitive Psychotherapy*, *29*, 113-118.

Klein, D. (1992, April 1). The empty pot. *Los Angeles Times*, pp. A3, A14.

Klein, D.F. (1993). False suffocation alarms, spontaneous panics, and related conditions: An integrative hypothesis. *Archives of General Psychiatry, 50,* 306-317.

Klein, D.F. (1996). Preventing hung juries about therapy studies. *Journal of Consulting and Clinical Psychology, 64,* 81-87.

Klein, D.F., & Ross, D.C. (1993). Reanalysis of the National Institute of Mental Health Treatment of Depression Collaborative Research Program general effectiveness report. *Neuropsychopharmacology, 8,* 241-251.

Klein, D.N., Taylor, E.B., Dickstein, S., & Harding, K. (1988). Primary early-onset dysthymia: Comparison with primary nonbipolar nonchronic major depression on demographic, clinical, familial, personality, and socioenvironmental characteristics and short-term outcome. *Journal of Abnormal Psychology, 97,* 387-398.

Klein, R.M., Doane, B.K., & Curtis, J. (1994). Introduction: Demystifying dissociative phenomena. In R. M. Klein & B. K. Doane (Eds.), *Psychological concepts and dissociative disorders* (pp. 1-6). Hillsdale, NJ: Erlbaum.

Klerman, G.L. (1983). Problems in the definition and diagnosis of depression in the elderly. In M. Hauge & L. Breslau (Eds.), *Depression in the elderly: Causes, care, consequences*. New York: Springer.

Klerman, G.L. (1988a). Depression and related disorders of mood (affective disorders). In A.M. Nicholi, Jr. (Ed.), *The new Harvard guide to psychiatry*. Cambridge, MA: Harvard University Press.

Klerman, G.L. (1988b). The current age of youthful melancholia. *British Journal of Psychiatry, 152,* 4-14.

Klerman, G.L., & Weissman, M.M. (Eds.), (1993). *New applications of interpersonal psychotherapy*. Washington, DC: American Psychiatric Press.

Klerman, G.L., Weissman, M.M., Markowitz, J.C., Glick, I., Wilner, P.J., Mason, B., & Shear, M.K. (1994). Medication and psychotherapy. In A.E. Bergin & S.L. Garfield (Eds.), *Handbook of psychotherapy and behavior change*. Fourth edition (pp. 734-782). New York: Wiley.

Klerman, G.L., Weissman, M.M., Rounsaville, B.J., & Chevron, E.S. (1984). *Interpersonal psychotherapy of depression*. New York: Basic Books.

Klosko, J.S., Barlow, D.H., Tassinari, R., & Cerny, J.A. (1990). A comparison of alprazolam and behavior therapy in treatment of panic disorder. *Journal of Consulting and Clinical Psychology, 58,* 77-84.

Kluft, R.P. (1984a). An introduction to multiple personality disorder. *Psychiatric Annals, 7,* 19-24.

Kluft, R.P. (1984b). Multiple personality in childhood. *Psychiatric Clinics of North America, 7,* 121-134.

Kluft, R.P. (1984c). Treatment of multiple personality disorder: A study of 33 cases. *Psychiatric Clinics of North America, 7,* 929.

Kluft, R.P. (1988). The dissociative disorders. In R.E. Hales & S.C. Yudofsky (Eds.), *Textbook of psychiatry*. (pp. 557-585). Washington, DC: American Psychiatric Press.

Kluft, R.P. (1994). Treatment trajectories in multiple personality disorder. *Dissociation, 7,* 63-75.

Knapp, M.J., Knopman, D.S., Solomon, P.R., et al. (1994). A 30-week randomized controlled trial of high-dose tacrine in patients with Alzheimer's disease. *JAMA, 271,* 985-989.

Knapp, S., & Vandecreek, L. (1982). Tarasoff: Five years later. *Professional Psychology, 13,* 511-516.

Knehnle, K. (1998). Child sexual abuse allegations: The scientist-practioner model. *Behavioral Science and the Law, 16,* 5-20.

Knight, B. (1983). An evaluation of a mobile geriatric team. In M.A. Smyer & M. Gatz (Eds.), *Mental health and aging: Programs and evaluations*. Beverly Hills, CA: Sage.

Knight, B.G., Lutzky, S.M., & Olshevski, J.L. (1992). *A randomized comparison of stress reduction training to problem solving training for dementia caregivers: Processes and outcomes.* Unpublished manuscript, University of Southern California, Los Angeles.

Knockwood, I. (1992). *Out of the depths: The experiences of Mi'kmaw children at the Indian residential school at Shubenaacadie, Nova Scotia*. Lockeport, Nova Scotia: Roseway Publishing.

Knopman, D.S. (2000). Management of cognition and function: New results from the clinical trials programme of Aricept (donepezil HCI). *The International Journal of Neuropsychopharmacology, 3*, 13-20.

Knopp, E.H. (1984). *Retraining adult sex offenders*. New York: Safer Society Press.

Kobak, K.A., Rock, A.L., & Greist, J.H. (1995). Group behavior therapy for obsessive-compulsive disorder. *Journal for Specialists in Group Work, 20,* 26-32.

Koegel, R.L., Bimbela, A., & Schreibman, L. (1996). Collateral effects of parent training on family interactions. *Journal of Autism and Developmental Disorders, 26,* 347-359.

Koegel, R.L., Schreibman, L., Britten, K.R., Burkey, J.C., & O'Neill, R.E. (1982). A comparison of parent training to direct child treatment. In R.L. Koegel, A. Rincover, & A.L. Egel (Eds.), *Educating and understanding autistic children*. San Diego, CA: College-Hill.

Koenig, H.G., & Blazer, D.G. (1992). Mood disorders and suicide. In J.E. Birren, R.B. Sloane, & G.D. Cohen (Eds.), *Handbook of mental health and aging* (pp. 379-407). San Diego: Academic Press.

Koenig, K., & Masters, J. (1965). Experimental treatment of habitual smoking. *Behaviour Research and Therapy, 3,* 235-243.

Koenigsberg, H.W., & Handley, R. (1986). Expressed emotion: From predictive index to clinical construct. *American Journal of Psychiatry, 143,* 1361-1373.

Kohen, D.E., Brooks-Gunn, J., Leventhal, T., & Hertzman, C. (2002). Neighborhood income and physical and social disorder in Canada: Associations with young children's competencies. *Child Development, 73,* 1844-1860.

Kohn, M.L. (1968). Social class and schizophrenia: A critical review. In D. Rosenthal & S.S. Kety (Eds.), *The transmission of schizophrenia*. Elmsford, NY: Pergamon.

Kohn, P.M., Lafreniere, K., & Gurevich, M. (1990). The Inventory of College Students' Recent Life Experiences: A decontaminated hassles scale for a special population. *Journal of Behavioral Medicine, 13*, 619-630.

Kohn, P.M., & Milrose, J.A. (1993). The Inventory of High-School Students Recent Life Experiences: A decontaminated measure of adolescents' hassles. *Journal of Youth and Adolescence, 22*, 43-55.

Kohut, H. (1971). *The analysis of the self.* New York: International Universities Press.

Kohut, H. (1977). *The restoration of the self.* New York: International Universities Press.

Kohut, H., & Wolf, E.S. (1978). The disorders of the self and their treatment: An outline. *International Journal of Psychoanalysis, 59,* 413-425.

Kolden, G.G. (1991). The generic model of psychotherapy: An empirical investigation of patterns of process and outcome relationships. *Psychotherapy Research, 1,* 62-73.

Kolko, D.J., Brent, D.A., Baugher, M., Bridge, J., & Birmaher, B. (2000). Cognitive and family therapies for adolescent depression: Treatment specificity, mediation, and moderation. *Journal of Consulting and Clinical Psychology, 68*, 603-614.

Kolmen, B.K., Feldman, H.E., Handen, B.L., & Janosky, J.E. (1995). Naltrexone in young autistic children: A double-blind, placebo-controlled crossover study. *Journal of the American Academy of Child and Adolescent Psychiatry, 34,* 223-231.

Koltek, M., Wilkes, T.C.R., & Atkinson, M. (1998). Prevalence of posttraumatic stress disorder in an adolescent inpatient unit. *Canadian Journal of Psychiatry, 43*, 64-67.

Kolvin I., McKeith, R.C., & Meadows, S.R. (1973). *Bladder control and enuresis*. Philadelphia: Lippincott.

Komahashi, T., Ganesan, S., Ohmori, K., & Nakano, T. (1997). Expression of depressed mood: A comparative study among Japanese and Canadian aged people. *Canadian Journal of Psychiatry, 42*, 852-857.

Konstantareas, M.M. (2001). How shall a thing be called: The overlap and differences between Asperger's disorder and high functioning autism. *Canadian Psychology, 42*, 146 (Abstract).

Kopelowicz, A., & Liberman, R.P. (1998) Psychosocial treatments for schizophrenia. In P.E. Nathan, & J.M. Gorman (Eds.), *A guide to treatments that work* (pp. 190-211). New York: Oxford.

Korchin, S.J. (1976). *Modern clinical psychology*. New York: Basic Books.

Korn, D. (2000). Expansion of gambling in Canada: Implications for health and social policy. *Canadian Medical Association Journal, 163,* 61-64.

Kornetsky, C. (1976). Hyporesponsivity of chronic schizophrenic patients to dextroamphetamine. *Archives of General Psychiatry, 33,* 1425-1428.

Koski-Jannes, A., & Cunningham, J. (2001). Interest in different forms of self-help in a general population sample of drinkers. *Addictive Behaviors, 26*, 91-99.

Koss, M.P. (1985). The hidden rape victim: Personality, attitudinal, and situational characteristics. *Psychology of Women Quarterly, 9,* 193-212.

Koss, M.P., & Butcher, J.N. (1986). Research on brief psychotherapy. In S.L. Garfield & A.E. Bergin (Eds.), *Handbook of psychotherapy and behavior change* (3rd ed.). New York: Wiley.

Koss, M.P., & Shiang, J. (1994). Research of brief psychotherapy. In A.E. Bergin & S.L. Garfield (Eds.), *Handbook of psychotherapy and behavior change*. Fourth edition (pp. 664-700). New York: Wiley.

Kosten, T.R., Mason, J.W., Giller, E.L., Ostroff, R., & Harkness, I. (1987). Sustained urinary norepinephrine and epinephrine elevation in posttraumatic stress disorder. *Psychoneuroendocrinology, 12,* 13-20.

Kosten, T.R., Morgan, C.M., Falcione, J., & Schottenfeld, R.S. (1992). Pharmacotherapy for cocaine-abusing methadone-maintained patients using amantadine or desipramine. *Archives of General Psychiatry, 49,* 894-898.

Kosteniuk, J.G., & Dickinson, H.D. (2003). Tracing the social gradient in the health of Canadians: Primary and secondary determinants. *Social Science and Medicine, 57*, 263-276.

Koston, T.R., & Ziedonis, D.M. (1997). Substance abuse and schizophrenia: Editors' introduction. *Schizophrenia Bulletin, 23,* 181-186.

Kovacs, M. (1990). Comorbid anxiety disorders in childhood-onset depressions. In J.D. Maser & C.R. Cloninger (Eds.), *Comorbidity of mood and anxiety disorders* (pp. 272-281). Washington, DC: American Psychiatric Press.

Kovacs, M., Rush, A.J., Beck, A.T., & Hollon, S.D. (1981). Depressed outpatients treated with cognitive therapy or pharmacotherapy: A one-year follow-up. *Archives of General Psychiatry, 38,* 33-39.

Kovess, V., Murphy, H.B.M., & Tousignant, M. (1987). Urban-rural comparison of depressive disorders in French Canada. *Journal of Nervous and Mental Disease, 175*, 457-466.

Kowalik, D.L., & Gotlib, I.H. (1987). Depression and marital interation: Concordance between intent and perception of communication. *Journal of Abnormal Psychology, 96,* 127-134.

Kowall, N.K., & Beal, M.F. (1988). Cortical somatostatin, neuropeptide Y, and NADPH diphorase neurons: Normal anatomy and alterations in Alzheimer's disease. *Annals of Neurology, 23,* 105-113.

Kozel, N.J., & Adams, E.H. (1986). Epidemiology of drug abuse: An overview. *Science, 234,* 970-974.

Kozel, N.J., Crider, R.A., & Adams, E.H. (1982). National surveillance of cocaine use and related health consequences. *Morbidity and Mortality Weekly Report 31,* 20, 265-273.

Kozol, H., Boucher, R., & Garofalo, R. (1972). The diagnosis and treatment of dangerousness. *Crime and Delinquency, 18,* 37-92.

Kraepelin, E. (1981). *Clinical psychiatry*. (A.R. Diefendorf, Trans.). Delmar, NY: Scholars' Facsimiles and Reprints. (Original work published 1883)

Kral, M., Arnakaq, M., Ekho, N., Konuk, O., Ootoova, E., Papatse, M., & Taparti, L. (1998). In A. A. Leenaars, S. Wenckstern, I. Sakinofsky, R. J. Dyck, M. J. Kral, & R. C. Bland (Eds.), *Suicide in Canada* (pp. 179-188). Toronto: University of Toronto Press.

Kramer, E.F. (1995). Controversial litigation issue may be shifting our focus away from a more serious problem. *Res Gestae, 12,* 10-22.

Krantz, S., & Hammen, C.L. (1979). Assessment of cognitive bias in depression. *Journal of Abnormal Psychology, 88,* 611-619.

Kranzler, H.R., Burleson, J.A., Del Boca, F.K., Babor, T.F., Korner, P., et al. (1994). Busipirone treatment of anxious alcoholics: A controlled trial. *Archives of General Psychiatry, 51,* 720-731.

Kravitz, S. (2004, April 13). Child psychiatrist Dr. Dan Offord helped thousands: Doctor founded Offord Centre for Child studies, Died at home in Ottawa after battling cancer. *The Toronto Star, B3.*

Kreuger, R.B., & Kaplan, M.S. (1997). Frotteurism: Assessment and treatment. In D.R. Laws & W. O'Donohue (Eds.), *Sexual deviance*. (pp. 131-151). NY: Guilford Press.

Kring, A.M., & Neale, J.M. (1996). Do schizophrenics show a disjunctive relationship among expressive, experiential and physiological components of emotion? *Journal of Abnormal Psychology, 105,* 249-257.

Kringlen, E. (1970). Natural history of obsessional neurosis. *Seminars in Psychiatry, 2,* 403-419.

Kristiansen, C.M., Gareau, C., Mittleholt, J., DeCourville, N.H., & Hovdestad, W.E. (1999). The sociopolitical context of the delayed memory debate. In L.M. Williams & V.L. Banyard (Eds.), *Trauma and recovery* (pp. 331-347). Thousand Oaks, CA: Sage Publications.

Kronig, M.H., Apter, J., Asnis, G., Bystritsky, A., Curtis, G., et al. (1999). Placebo-controlled, multicenter study of sertraline treatment for obsessive-compulsive diosorder. *Journal of Clinical Psychopharmacology, 19,* 172-176.

Kruger, S., & Kennedy, S.H. (2000). Psychopharmacology of anorexia nervosa, bulimia nervosa and binge-eating disorder. *Journal of Psychiatry and Neuroscience, 25,* 497-508.

Kruger, S., McVey, G., & Kennedy, S.H. (1998). The changing profile of anorexia nervosa at the Toronto Programmeme for Eating Disorders. *Journal of Psychosomatic Research, 45,* 533-547.

Krystal, J.H., Karper, L.P., Seibyl, J.P., Freeman, G.K., Delaney, R., et al. (1995). Subanesthetic effects of the non-competitive NMDA antagonist, ketamine, in humans: Psychotomimetic, perceptual, cognitive, and neuroendocrine effects. *Archives of General Psychiatry, 51,* 199-214.

Krystal, J.H., Kosten, T.R., Southwick, S., Mason, J.W., Perry, B.D., & Giller, E.L. (1989). Neurobiological aspects of PTSD: Review of clinical and preclinical studies. *Behavior Therapy, 20,* 177-198.

Kuch, K., & Cox, B.J. (1992). Symptoms of PTSD in 124 survivors of the Holocaust. *American Journal of Psychiatry, 149,* 337-340.

Kuhn, T.S. (1962). *The structure of scientific revolutions.* Chicago: University of Chicago Press.

Kuhn, T.S. (1970). *The structure of scientific revolutions.* Chicago: University of Chicago Press.

Kuiper, N.A., & MacDonald, M.R. (1983). Schematic processing in depression: The self-based consensus bias. *Cognitive Theory and Research, 7,* 469-484.

Kuiper, N.A., Martin, R.A., & Olinger, L.J. (1993). Coping, humour, stress, and cognitive appraisals. *Canadian Journal of Behavioural Science, 25,* 81-96.

Kuiper, N.A., Martin, R.A., Olinger, L.J., Kazarian, S.S., & Jette, J.L. (1998). Sense of humor, self-concept, and psychological well-being in psychiatric patients. *Humor: International Journal of Humor Research, 11,* 357-381.

Kundera, M. (1991). *Immortality.* New York: Grove Press.

Kung, H.-C., Liu, X., & Joun, H.-S. (1998). Risk factors for suicide in Caucasians and African-Americans: A matched case-control study. *Social Psychiatry, 33,* 155-161.

Kunst-Wilson, W.R., & Zajonc, R.B. (1980). Affective discrimination of stimuli that cannot be recognized. *Science, 207,* 557-558.

Kuo, M., Adlaf, E.M., Lee, H., Gliksman, L., Demers, A., & Wechsler, H. (2002). More Canadian students drink but American students drink more: Comparing college alcohol use in two countries. *Addiction, 97,* 1583-1592.

Kuriansky, J.B., Deming, W.E., & Gurland, B.J. (1974). On trends in the diagnosis of schizophrenia. *American Journal of Psychiatry, 131,* 402-407.

Kutcher, S., et al. (2004). International consensus statement on attention-deficit/hyperactivity disorder (ADHD) and disruptive behavior disorders (DBDs): Clinical implications and treatment practice suggestions. *European Neuropsychopharmacology, 14,* 11-28.

Kutchinsky, B. (1970). *Studies on pornography and sex crimes in Denmark.* Copenhagen: New Social Science Monographs.

Labelle, R., Lachance, L., & Morval, M. (1996). Validation of a French-Canadian version of the Reasons For Living Inventory. *Science et Comportement, 24,* 237-248.

Laberge, M., Dugas, M.J., & Ladouceur, R. (2000). Modification of beliefs relative to worries following treatment for generalized anxiety disorder. *Canadian Journal of Behavioural Science, 32,* 91-96.

Lacey, J.I. (1967). Somatic response patterning and stress: Some revisions of activation theory. In M.H. Appley & R. Trumball (Eds.), *Psychological stress.* New York: McGraw-Hill.

Ladd, G.W. (1981). Effectiveness of a social learning method for enhancing children's social interaction and peer acceptance. *Child Development, 52,* 171-178.

Ladouceur, R., Dube, D., & Bujold, A. (1994). Prevalence of pathological gambling and related problems among college students in the Quebec metropolitan area. *Canadian Journal of Psychiatry, 39,* 289-293.

Ladouceur, R., Gosselin, P., & Dugas, M.J. (2000). Experimental manipulation of intolerance of uncertainty: A study of a theoretical model of worry. *Behaviour Research and Therapy, 38,* 933-941.

Ladouceur, R., Freeston, M.H., Gagnon, F., Thibodeau, N., & Dumont, J. (1995). Cognitive-behavioral treatment of obsessions. *Behavior Modification, 19,* 247-257.

Ladouceur, R., Rheaume, J., & Aublet, F. (1997). Excessive responsibility in obsessional concerns: A fine grained experimental analysis. *Behaviour Research and Therapy, 35,* 423-437.

Ladouceur, R., Sylvain, C., Letarte, H., Giroux, I., & Jacques, C. (1998). Cognitive treatment of pathological gamblers. *Behaviour Research and Therapy, 36,* 1111-1119.

Ladouceur, R., Sylvain, C., Letarte, H., Giroux, I., & Jacques, C. (1998). Cognitive treatment of pathological gamblers. *Behaviour Research and Therapy, 36,* 1111-1119.

Ladouceur, R., & Walker, M. (1998). **Cognitive approach to understanding and treating pathological gambling.** In A. S. Bellack & M. Hersen (Eds.), *Comprehensive clinical psychology,* vol. 6, pp. 587-601. Oxford, England: Elsevier Science.

La Greca, A. M., Silverman, W.K., Vernberg, E.M., & Prinstein, M.J. (1996). Symptoms of posttraumatic stress in children after Hurricane Andrew: A prospective study. *Journal of Consulting and Clinical Psychology, 64,* 712-723.

La Greca, A.M., Silverman, W.K., & Wasserstein, S.B. (1998). Children's predisaster functioning as a predictor of posttraumatic stress following Hurricane Andrew. *Journal of Consulting and Clinical Psychology, 66,* 883-892.

Lahey, B.B., Loeber, R., Hart, E.L., Frick, P.J., Applegate, B., Zhang, Q., Green, S.M., & Russo, M.F. (1995). Four-year longitudinal study of conduct disorder in boys: Patterns and predictors of persistence. *Journal of Abnormal Psychology, 104,* 83-93.

LaGreca, A. M., Silverman, W. K., Vernberg, E. M., & Prinstein, M. J. (1996). Symptoms of posttraumatic stress in children after Hurricane Andrew: A prospective study. *Journal of Consulting and Clinical psychology, 64,* 712-723.

LaGreca, A. M., Silverman, W. K., & Wasserstein, S. B. (1998). Children's predisaster functioning as a predictor of posttraumatic stress following Hurricane Andrew. *Journal of Consulting and Clinical psychology, 66,* 883-892.

Lahey, B.B., Piacentini, J.C., McBurnett, K., Stone, P., Hartdagen, S., & Hynd, G. (1988). Psychopathology in the parents of children with conduct disorder and hyperactivity. *Journal of the American Academy of Child and Adolescent Psychiatry, 27,* 163-170.

Lai, D.W.L. (2000). Depression among the elderly Chinese in Canada. *Canadian Journal on Aging, 19,* 409-429.

Lai, M.C., & Yue, K.M. (1990). The Chinese. In N. Waxler-Morrison, J.. Anderson, & E. Richardson, (Eds.), *Cross-cultural caring: A handbook for health professionals in western Canada.* (pp. 68-90). Vancouver: University of British Columbia Press.

LaJeunesse, R. (2002). *Political asylums.* Edmonton: University of Alberta Press.

Lalinec-Michaud, M., Subak, M.E., Ghadirian, A.M., & Kovess, V. (1991). Substance misuse among native and rural high school students in Quebec. *International Journal of the Addictions, 26,* 1003-1012.

Lalonde, J.K., Hudson, J.I., Gigante, R.A., & Pope, H.G. (2001). Canadian and American psychiatrists' attitudes toward dissociative disorders diagnoses. *Canadian Journal of Psychiatry, 46,* 407-412.

Lalumiere, M.L., & Quinsey, V.L. (1998). Pavlovian conditioning of sexual interests in human males. *Archives of Sexual Behavior, 27, 241-252.*

Lam, R.W. (1994). Morning light therapy for winter depression: Predictors of response. *Acta Psychiatrica Scandinavica, 89,* 97-101.

Lam, R.W., & Levitan, R.D. (2000). Pathophysiology of seasonal affective disorder: A review. *Journal of Psychiatry and Neuroscience, 25,* 469-480.

Lam, R.W., & Levitt, A.J. (1999). *Canadian consensus guidelines for the treatment of seasonal affective disorder.* Vancouver: Clinical and Academic

Publishing.

Lam, R.W., Tam, E.M., Shiah, I.S., Yatham, L.N., & Zis, A.P. (2000). Effects of light therapy on suicidal ideation in patients with winter depression. *Journal of Clinical Psychiatry, 61*, 30-32.

Lam, R.W., Zis, A.P., Grewal, A., Delgado, P.L., Charney, D.S., & Krystal, J.H. (1996). Effects of rapid tryptophan depletion in patients with seasonal affective disorder in remission after light therapy. *Archives of General Psychiatry, 53,* 41-46.

Lambe, E.K., Katzman, D.K., Mikulis, D.J., Kennedy, S.H., & Zipursky, R.B. (1997). Cerebral gray matter volume deficits after weight recovery from anorexia nervosa. *Archives of General Psychiatry, 54,* 537-542.

Lamberg, L. (1998). New drug for erectile dysfunction boon for many, "Viagravation" for some. *JAMA, 280,* 867-869.

Lambert, M.J., & Bergin, A.E. (1994). The effectiveness of psychotherapy. In A.E. Bergin & S.L. Garfield (Eds.), *Handbook of psychotherapy and behavior change*. Fourth edition (pp. 143-189). New York: Wiley.

Lambert, M.J., Bergin, A.E., & Collins, J.L. (1977). Therapist-induced deterioration in psychotherapy. In A.S. Gurman & A.M. Razin (Eds.), *Effective psychotherapy: A handbook of research*. Elmsford, New York: Pergamon.

Lambert, M.J., Shapiro, D.A., & Bergin, A.E. (1986). The effectiveness of psychotherapy. In S.L. Garfield & A.E. Bergin (Eds.), *Handbook of psychotherapy and behavior change* (3rd ed.). New York: Wiley.

Lamerson, C. D., & Kelloway, E. K. (1996). Towards a model of peacekeeping stress: Traumatic and contextual influences. *Canadian Psychology, 37*, 195-204.

Lando, H.A. (1977). Successful treatment of smokers with a broad-spectrum behavioral approach. *Journal of Consulting and Clinical Psychology, 45,* 361-366.

Landreville, P., & Cappeliez, P. (1992). Social support and depressive symptoms in the elderly. *Canadian Journal on Aging, 11*, 322-346.

Landreville, P., Landry, J., Baillargeon, L., Gurette, A., & Matteau, E. (2001). Older adults' acceptance of psychological and pharmacological treatments for depression. *Journal of Gerontology: Psychological Sciences, 56*, P285-P291.

Lane, E.A., & Albee, G.W. (1965). Childhood intellectual differences between schizophrenic adults and their siblings. *American Journal of Orthopsychiatry, 35,* 747-753.

Lang, A.R., Goeckner, D.J., Adessor, V.J., & Marlatt, G.A. (1975). Effects of alcohol on aggression in male social drinkers. *Journal of Abnormal Psychology, 84,* 508-518.

Lang, P.J., & Lazovik, A.D. (1963). Experimental desensitization of a phobia. *Journal of Abnormal and Social Psychology, 66,* 519-525.

Lang, P.J., & Melamed, B.G. (1969). Case report: Avoidance conditioning therapy of an infant with chronic ruminative vomiting. *Journal of Abnormal Psychology, 74,* 1-8.

Langeluddeke, A. (1963). *Castration of sexual criminals*. Berlin: de Gruyter.

Langenbucher, J.W., & Chung, T. (1995). Onset and staging of DSM-IV alcohol dependence using mean age and survival hazard methods. *Journal of Abnormal Psychology, 104,* 346-354.

Langer, E.J. (1981). Old age: An artifact? In J. McGaugh & S. Kiesler (Eds.), *Aging: Biology and behavior*. New York: Academic Press.

Langer, E.J. (1989). *Mindfulness*. Reading, MA: Addison-Wesley.

Langer, E.J., & Rodin, J. (1976). The effects of choice and enhanced personal responsibility for the aged. *Journal of Personality and Social Psychology, 34,* 191-198.

Langille, D.B., Joffres, M.R., MacPherson, K.M., Andreou, P., Kirkland, S.A., & MacLean, D.R. (1999). Prevalence of risk factors for cardiovascular disease in Canadians 55 to 74 years of age: Results from the Canadian Heart Health Surveys, 1986-1992. *Canadian Medical Association Journal, 161 (8, Supplement)*, S3-S9.

Lannin, D.R., Mathews, H.F., Mitchell, J., Swanson, M.S., et al. (1998). Influence of socioeconomic and racial diferences in late-stage presentation of breast cancer. *JAMA, 279,* 1801-1807.

Lantz, P.M., House, J.S., Lepkowski, J.M., Williams, D.R., et al. (1998). Socioeconomic factors, health behaviors, and mortality. *JAMA, 279,* 1703-1708.

Laplante, D.P., Barr, R.G., Brunet, A., Galbaud du Fort, G., Meaney, M., Saucier, J-F., Zelazo, P.R., and King, S. (in press). Stress during pregnancy affects general intellectual and language functioning in human toddlers. *Pediatric Research.*

Laposa, J.M., & Alden, L.E. (2003). Posttraumatic stress disorder in the emergency room: Exploration of a cognitive model. *Behaviour Research and Therapy, 41*, 49-65.

***Lara, M.E., & Klein, D.N.** (in press). Processes underlying chronicity in depression.

Larstone, R.M., Jang, K.L., Livesley, W.J., Vernon, P.A., & Wolf, K. (2002). The relationship between Eysenck's P-E-N model of personality, the five-factor model of personality, and traits delineating personality dysfunction. *Personality and Individual Differences, 33*, 25-37.

LaRue, A., Dessonville, C., & Jarvik, L.F. (1985). Aging and mental disorders. In J.E. Birren & K.W. Schaie (Eds.), *Handbook of psychology of aging* (2nd ed.). New York: Van Nostrand-Reinhold.

Lassano, D., del Buono, G., & Latapano, P. (1993). The relationship between obsessive-compulsive personality and obsessive-compulsive disorder: Data obtained by the personality disorder examination. *European Psychiatry, 8,* 219-221.

Last, C.G., & Strauss, C.C. (1990). School refusal in anxiety-disordered children and adolescents. *Journal of the American Academy of Child and Adolescent Psychiatry, 29,* 31-35.

Laub, J.H., & Sampson, R.J. (1995). The long term effects of punitive discipline. In J. McCord (Ed.), *Coercion and punishment in long-term perspective* (pp. 247-258). Cambridge, MA: Cambridge University Press.

Laumann, E.O., Gagnon, J.H., Michael, R.T., & Michaels, S. (1994). *The social organization of sexuality*. Chicago: University of Chicago Press.

Lautenschlager, N.T., Cupples, L.A., Rao, V.S., Auerbach, S.A., Becker, R., & Burke J. (1996). Risk of dementia among relatives of Alzheimer's disease patients in the MIRAGE study: What is in store for the oldest old? *Neurology, 46*, 641-650.

Lavelle, T.L., Metalsky, G.I., & Coyne, J.C. (1979). Learned helplessness, test anxiety, and acknowledgment of contingencies. *Journal of Abnormal Psychology, 88,* 381-387.

Law, M., & Tang, J.L. (1995). An analysis of the effectiveness of interventions intended to help people stop smoking. *Archives of Internal Medicine, 155,* 1933-1941.

Laws, D.R., Hanson, K.R., Osborn, C.A., & Greenbaum, P.E. (2000). Classification of child molesters by plethysmographic assessment of sexual arousal and a self-report measure of sexual preference. *Journal of Interpersonal Violence, 15*, 1297-1312.

Lawton, V. (2001, June 22). Chretien will ask Romanow to study medicare user fees: Private meeting with Swedish leader sparks interest in examining health-care concept. *The Toronto Star,* p. A6.

Lawton, V. (2001, August 11). A fragile truce: The government wants to reform the Indian Act. Can it be trusted to do the job properly at last? *The Toronto Star,* p. H1, H4.

Layne, C. (1986). Painful truths about depressives' cognitions. *Journal of Clinical Psychology, 39,* 848-853.

Lazar, I. (1979). Social services in Head Start. In E. Zigler & J. Valentine (Eds.), *Project Head Start*. New York: Free Press.

Lazarus, A.A. (1961). Group therapy of phobic disorders by systematic desensitization. *Journal of Abnormal and Social Psychology, 63,* 504-510.

Lazarus, A.A. (1965). Behavior therapy, incomplete treatment, and symptom substitution. *Journal of Nervous and Mental Disease, 140,* 80-86.

Lazarus, A.A. (1968a). Behavior therapy in groups. In G.M. Gazda (Ed.), *Basic approaches to group psychotherapy and counseling*. Springfield, IL: Charles C. Thomas.

Lazarus, A.A. (1968b). Learning theory and the treatment of depression. *Behavior Research and Therapy, 6,* 83-89.

Lazarus, A.A. (1973). Multimodal behavior therapy: Treating the basic ID. *Journal of Nervous and Mental Disease, 156,* 404-411.

Lazarus, A.A. (1989). *The practice of multimodal therapy*. Baltimore: Johns Hopkins University Press.

Lazarus, A.A. (1997). *Brief but comprehensive psychotherapy: The multimodal way*. New York: Springer.

Lazarus, A.A., & Davison, G.C. (1971). Clinical innovation in research and practice. In A.E. Bergin & S.L. Garfield (Eds.), *Handbook of psychotherapy and behavior change: An empirical analysis*. New York: Wiley.

Lazarus, A.A., Davison, G.C., & Polefka, D. (1965). Classical and operant factors in the treatment of school phobia. *Journal of Abnormal Psychology, 70,*

225-229.

Lazarus, A.A., & Messer, S.B. (1991). Does chaos prevail? An exchange on technical eclecticism and assimilative integration. *Journal of Psychotherapy Integration, 1,* 143-158.

Lazarus, R.S. (1966). *Psychological stress and the coping process*. New York: McGraw-Hill.

Lazarus, R.S., & Folkman, S. (1984). *Stress, appraisal, and coping*. New York: Springer.

Lazo, J. (1995). True or false: Expert testimony on repressed memory. *Loyola of Los Angeles Law Review, 28,* 1345-1413.

Leach, S., & Roy, S.S. (1986). Adverse drug reactions: An investigation on an acute geriatric ward. *Age and Ageing, 15,* 241-246.

Leblond, J., Ladouceur, R., & Blaszczynski, A. (2003). Which pathological gamblers will complete treatment? *British Journal of Clinical Psychology, 42,* 205-209.

Lebow, J.L., & Gurman, A.S. (1995). Research assessing couple and family therapy. *Annual Review of Psychology, 46,* 27-57.

Le Couteur, A., Bailey, A., Goode, S., Pickles, A., Robertson, S., Gottesman, I., & Rutter, M. (1996). A broader phenotype of autism: The clinical spectrum in twins. *Journal of Child Psychology and Psychiatry and Allied Disciplines, 37,* 785-801.

Lecrubier, Y., & Weiller, E. (1997). Comorbidities in social phobia. *Interntational Clinical Psychopharmacology, 12,* International s17-s21.

Ledgerwood, D.M., & Downey, K.K. (2002). Relationship between problem gambling and substance use in a methadone maintenance population. *Addictive Behaviors, 27,* 483-491.

Lee, D., DeQuattro, V., Cox, T., Pyter, L., Foti, A., Allen, J., Barndt, R., Azen, S., & Davison, G.C. (1987). Neurohormonal mechanisms and left ventricular hypertrophy: Effects of hygienic therapy. *Journal of Human Hypertension, 1,* 147-151.

Lee, S. (1994). The Diagnostic Interview Schedule and anorexia nervosa in Hong Kong. *Archives of General Psychiatry, 51,* 251-252.

Lee, V.E., Brooks-Gunn, J., & Schnur, E. (1988). Does Head Start work? A 1-year follow-up comparison of disadvantaged children attending Head Start, no preschool, and other preschool programs. *Developmental Psychology, 24,* 210-222.

Leenaars, A.A. (2000). Suicide prevention in Canada: A history of the community approach. *Canadian Journal of Community Mental Health, 19,* 57-73.

Leenaars, A.A., & Lester, D. (1995). Impact of suicide prevention centers on suicide in Canada. *Crisis, 16,* 39.

Leenaars, A. A., & Lester, D. (1996). Gender and the impact of gun control on suicide and homicide. *Archives of Suicide Research, 2,* 223-234.

Leenaars, A.A., Wenckstern, S., Sakinofsky, I., Dyck, R., Kral, M., & Bland, R. (1998). *Suicide in Canada*. Toronto: University of Toronto Press.

Leeper, P. (1988). Having a place to live is vital to good health. *News Report, 38,* 5-8.

Lefcourt, H.M., Davidson, K., Prkachin, K.M., & Mills, D.E. (1997). Humor as a stress moderator in the prediction of blood pressure obtained during five stressful tasks. *Journal of Research in Personality, 31,* 523-542.

Lefcourt, H.M., & Thomas, S. (1998). Humor and stress revisited. In W. Ruch (Ed.), *The sense of humor: Explorations of a personality characteristic. Humor Research 3* (pp. 179-202). Berlin, Germany: Walter de Gruyter and Company.

Lefcourt, H.M., & Thomas, S. (1998). Humor and stress revisited. In W. Ruch (Ed.), *The sense of humor: Explorations of a personality characteristic* (pp. 179-202). Berlin, Germany: Walter de Gruyter.

Lefrancois, R., Leclerc, G., Hamel, S., & Gaulin, P. (2000). Stressful life events and psychological distress of the very old: Does social support have a moderating effect? *Archives of Gerontology and Geriatrics, 31,* 243-255.

Legido, A., Tonyes, L., Carter, D., Schoemaker, A., DiGeorge, A., & Grover, W.D. (1993). Treatment variables and intellectual outcome in children with classic phenylketonuria: A single-center-based study. *Clinical Pediatrics, 32,* 417-425.

Lehman, A.F., Steinwachs, D.M., & the survey co-investigators from the Schizophrenia Patient Outcomes Research Team (PORT) client survey. (1998). Patterns of usual care for schizophrenia: Initial results from the Schizophrenia Patient Outcomes Research Team (PORT) client survey. *Schizophrenia Bulletin, 24,* 11-20.

Lehrer, P.M., & Woolfolk, R.L. (1993) *Principles and practice of stress management* (2nd ed.). New York: Guilford.

Leibel, R.I., Rosenbaum, M., & Hirsch, J. (1995). Changes in energy expenditure resulting from altered body weight. *The New England Journal of Medicine, 332,* 621-628.

Leibenluft, E. (1996). Women with bipolar illness: Clinical and research issues. *American Journal of Psychiatry, 153,* 163-173.

Leiblum, S.R. (1997). Sexual pain disorders. In G.O. Gabbard & S.D. Atkinson (Eds.), *Synopsis of treatments of psychiatric disorders*. Second edition. (pp. 805-810). Washington,DC: American Psychiatric Press.

Leiblum, S.R., & Rosen, R.C. (Eds.). (1988). *Sexual desire disorders*. New York: Guilford.

Leichner, P., Arnett, J., Rallo, J.S., Srilcamesuaran, S., & Vulcano, B. (1986). An epidemiological study of maladaptive eating attitudes in a Canadian school-aged population. *International Journal of Eating Disorders, 5,* 969-982.

Leichsenring, F. (2001). Comparative effects of short-term psychodynamic psychotherapy and cognitive-behavioral therapy in depression: A meta-analytic approach. *Clinical Psychology Review, 21,* 401-419.

Leighton, A. H. (1959). *My name is legion: The Stirling County study of psychiatric disorder and social environment* (Vol. 1). New York: Basic Books.

Leitenberg, H., Gross, H., Peterson, H., & Rosen, J.C. (1984). Analysis of an anxiety model in the process of change during exposure plus response prevention treatment of bulimia nervosa. *Behavior Therapy, 15,* 3-20.

Lemonick, M. D., & Park, A. (2001,May 14). The nun study: How one scientist and 678 sisters are helping unlock the secrets of Alzheimer's. *Time: Canadian Edition,* p. 40-48.

Lenane, M.C., Swedo, S.F., Leonard, H., Pauls, D.L., Sceery, W., et al. (1990). Psychiatric disorders in first degree relatives of children and adolescents with obsessive compulsive disorder. *Journal of the American Academy of Child and Adolescent Psychiatry, 29,* 407-412.

Lenzenwenger, M.F., Dworkin, R.H., & Wethington, E. (1991). Examining the underlying structure of schizophrenic phenomenology: Evidence for a 3-process model. *Schizophrenia Bulletin, 17,* 515-524.

Leon, G.R., Fulkerson, J.A., Perry, C.L., & Early-Zald, M.B. (1995). Prospective analysis of personality and behavioral vulnerabilities and gender influences in the later development of disordered eating. *Journal of Abnormal Psychology, 104,* 140-149.

Leonard, K.E., & Eiden, R.D. (1999). Husband's and wife's drinking: Unilateral or bilateral influences among newlyweds in a general population sample. *Journal of Studies on Alcohol, 60* (Supplement 13), 130-138.

Leonard, S., Steiger, H., & Kao, A. (2003). Childhood and adulthood abuse in bulimic and nonbulimic women: Prevalences and psychological correlates. *International Journal of Eating Disorders, 33,* 397-405.

Leong, F. T. L. (1994). Asian-Americans differential patterns of utilization of inpatient and outpatient public mental health services in Hawaii. *Journal of Community Psychology, 22,* 82-96.

Lepage, C., Ladouceur, R., & Jacques, C. (2000). Prevalence of problem gambling among community service users. *Community Mental Health Journal, 36,* 597-601.

Lerman, C., & Glanz, K. (1997). Stress, coping, and health behavior. In K. Glanz, F. Lewis, & B. Rimer (Eds.), *Health behavior and health education: Theory, research and practice.* San Francisco: Jossey-Bass.

Lerman, C., Caporaso, N.E., Audrain, J., Main, D., Bowman, E.D., et al. (1999). Evidence suggesting the role of specific genetic factors in cigarette smoking. *Health Psychology, 18,* 14-20.

Lerman, C., Schwartz, M.D., Lin, T.H., Narod, S., & Lynch, H.T. (1997). The influence of psychological distress on use of genetic testing for cancer risk. *Journal of Consulting and Clinical Psychology, 65,* 414-420.

Lerman, C., Schwartz, M.D., Miller, S.M., Daly, M., Sands, C., & Rimer, B.K. (1996). A randomized trial of breast cancer risk counseling: Interacting effects of counseling, educational level, and coping style. *Health Psychology, 15,* 75-83.

Lerner, H.P. (1983). Contemporary psychoanalytic perpectives on gorge-vomiting: A case illustration. *International Journal of Eating Disorders, 3,* 47-63.

Lesage, A., & Lamontagne, Y. (1985). Paradoxical intention and exposure in vivo in the treatment of psychogenic nausea: Report of two cases. *Behavioral Psychotherapy, 13,* 69-75.

Lesage, A.D., Boyer, R., Grunberg, R., Vanier, C., Morrisette, R., Menard-Buteau, C., & Loyer, M. (1994). Suicide and mental disorders: A case-control study of young men. *American Journal of Psychiatry, 151,* 1063-1068.

Lesage, A. D., & Morrissette, R. (1993). Residential and palliative needs of persons with severe mental illness who are subject to long-term hospitalization. *Canada's Mental Health, 41,* 12-17.

LeSage, A.D., Morissette, R., Fortier, L., Reinharz, D., & Contandriopoulos, A.P. (2000). I. Downsizing psychiatric hospitals: Needs for care and services of current and discharged long-stay patients. *Canadian Journal of Psychiatry, 45,* 526-532.

Leschied, A.W., Cunningham, A., & Hawkins, L. (2000). *Clinical trials of multisytemic therapy in Ontario, 1997 to 2001: Evaluation update report.* Ottawa: National Crime Prevention Centre.

Lesieur, H. R., & Blume, S. B. (1993). Revising the South Oaks Gambling Screen in different settings, *Journal of Gambling Studies, 9,* 213-219.

Lessard, J.C., & Moretti, M.M. (1998). Suicidal ideation in an adolescent clinical sample: Attachment patterns and clinical implications. *Journal of Adolescence, 21,* 383-395.

Lester, D. (1991). Do suicide prevention centers prevent suicide? *Homeostasis in Health and Disease, 33,* 190-194.

Leung, F., Schwartzman, A., & Steiger, H. (1996). Testing a dual-process family model in understanding the development of eating pathology: A structural equation modeling analysis. *International Journal of Eating Disorders, 20,* 367-375.

Leung, P.W., Luk, S.L., Ho, T.P., Taylor, E., Mak, F.L., & Bacon-Shone, J. (1996). The diagnosis and prevalence of hyperactivity in Chinese schoolboys. *British Journal of Psychiatry, 168,* 486-496.

Levav, I., Kohn, R., Golding, J.M., & Weissman, M.M. (1997). Vulnerability of Jews to major depression. *American Journal of Psychiatry, 154,* 941-947.

Levenson, M. (1972). *Cognitive and perceptual factors in suicidal individuals.* Unpublished doctoral dissertation, University of Kansas, Lawrence.

Leventhal, B.L., Cook, E.H., Morford, M., Ravitz, A.J., Heller, W., & Freedman, D.X. (1993). Clinical and neurochemical effects of fenfluramine in children with autism. *The Journal of Neuropsychiatry and Clinical Neurosciences, 5,* 307-315.

Levin, R.L. (1992). The mechanisms of human female sexual arousal. *Annual Review of Sex Research, 3,* 1-48.

Levine, S.B., & Yost, M.A. (1976). Frequency of sexual dysfunction in a general gynecological clinic: An epidemiological approach. *Archives of Sexual Behavior, 5,* 229-238.

Levitan, R.D., Kaplan, A.S., Joffe, R.T., Levitt, A.J., & Brown, G.M. (1997). Hormonal and subjective responses to intravenous metachlorophenylpiperazine in bulimia nervosa. *Archives of General Psychiatry, 54,* 521-528.

Levitan, R.D., Parikh, S.V., Lesage, A.D., Hegadoren, K.M., Adams, M., Kennedy, S.H., & Goering, P.N. (1998). Major depression in individuals with a history of childhood physical or sexual abuse: Relationship to neurovegatative features, mania, and gender. *American Journal of Psychiatry, 155,* 1746-1752.

Levitsky, A., & Perls, F.S. (1970). The rules and games of Gestalt therapy. In J. Fagan & I.L. Shepherd (Eds.), *Gestalt therapy now: Theory, techniques, applications.* Palo Alto, CA: Science & Behavior Books.

Levitt, A. J., Boyle, M. H., Joffe, R. T., & Baumal, Z. (2000). Estimated prevalence of the seasonal subtype of major depression in a Canadian community sample. *Canadian Journal of Psychiatry, 45,* 650-654

Levitt, A.J., Lam, R.W., & Levitan, R. (2002). A comparison of open treatment of seasonal major and minor depression with light therapy. *Journal of Affective Disorders, 71,* 243-248.

Levitt, H., Korman, Y., & Angus, L. (2000). A metaphor analysis in treatments of depression: Metaphor as a marker for change. *Counseling Psychology Quarterly, 13,* 23-35.

Levy, F., Hay, D.A., McStephen, M., Wood, C., & Waldman, I. (1997). Attention-deficit hyperactivity disorder: A category or a continuum? Genetic analysis of a large-scale twin study. *Journal of the American Academy of Child and Adolescent Psychiatry, 36,* 737-744.

Levy, M.L., Miller, B.L., Cummings, J.L., Fairbanks, L.A., & Craig, A. (1996). Alzheimer disease and frontotemporal dementias. *Archives of Neurology, 53,* 687-690.

Levy, S., & Fletcher, E. (1998). Kamatsiaqtut, Baffin Crisis Line: Community ownership of support in a small town. In A. A. Leenaars, S. Wenckstern, I. Sakinofsky, R. J. Dyck, M. J. Kral, & R. C. Bland (Eds.), *Suicide in Canada* (pp. 351-366). Toronto: University of Toronto Press.

Levy, S.M., Herberman, R.B., Whiteside, T., Sanzo, K., Lee, J., & Kirkwood, J. (1990). Perceived social support and tumor estrogen/progesterone receptor status as predictors of natural killer cell activity in breast cancer patients. *Psychosomatic Medicine, 52,* 73-85.

Levy-Lehad, E., & Bird, T.D. (1996). Genetic factors in Alzheimer's disease: A review of the recent evidence. *Annals of Neurology, 40,* 829-840.

Lewinsohn, P.M. (1974). A behavioral approach to depression. In R.J. Friedman and M.M. Katz (Eds.), *The psychology of depression: Contemporary theory and research.* Washington, DC: Winston-Wiley.

Lewinsohn, P.M., & Clarke, G.N. (1999). Psychosocial treatments for adolescent depression. *Clinical Psychology Review, 19,* 329-342.

Lewinsohn, P.M., Clarke, G.N., Hops, H., & Andrews, J. (1990). Cognitive-behavioral treatment for depressed adolescents. *Behavior Therapy, 21,* 385-401.

Lewinsohn, P.M., & Gotlib, I.H. (1995). Behavioral and cognitive treatment of depression. In E.E. Becker & W.R. Leber (Eds.), *Handbook of depression.* (pp. 352-375). NY: Guilford Press.

Lewinsohn, P.M., Hops, H., Roberts, R.E., Seeley, J.R., & Andrews, J.A. (1993). Adolescent psychopathology: 1. prevalence and incidence of depression and other DSM-III disorders in high school students. *Journal of Abnormal Psychology, 102,* 133-144.

Lewinsohn, P.M., Mischef, W., Chapion, W., & Barton, R. (1980). Social competence and depression: The role of illusory self-perceptions. *Journal of Abnormal Psychology, 89,* 203-212.

Lewinsohn, P.M., Roberts, R.E., Seeley, J.R., Rohde, P., Gotlib, I.H., & Hops, H. (1994). Adolescent psychopathology: 2. Psychosocial risk factors for depression. *Journal of Abnormal Psychology, 103,* 302-315.

Lewinsohn, P.M., Rohde, P., Fischer, S.A., & Seeley, J.R. (1991). Age and depression: Unique and shared effects. *Psychology and Aging, 6,* 247-260.

Lewinsohn, P.M., Steimetz, J.L., Larsen, D.W., & Franklin, J. (1981). Depression related cognitions: Antecedent or consequences? *Journal of Abnormal Psychology, 90,* 213-219.

Lewinsohn, P.M., Weinstein, M., & Alper, T. (1970). A behavioral approach to the group treatment of depressed persons: A methodological contribution. *Journal of Clinical Psychology, 26,* 525-532.

Lewis, D.O., Yeager, C.A., Swica, Y., Pincus, J.H., & Lewis, M. (1997). Objective documentation of child abuse and dissociation on 12 murderers with dissociative identity disorder. *American Journal of Psychiatry, 154,* 1703-1710.

Ley, R. (1987). Panic disorder: A hyperventilation interpretation. In L. Michelson & L.M. Asher (Eds.), *Anxiety and stress disorders.* New York: Guilford.

Li, H. Z., & Browne, A. (2000). Defining mental illness and accessing mental health services: Perspectives of Asian Canadians. *Canadian Journal of Community Mental Health, 19,* 143-149.

Li, T-K., Lumeng, L., McBride, W.J., & Waller, M.B. (1981). Indiana selection studies on alcohol related behaviors. In R.A. McClearn, R.A. Deitrich, & V.G. Erwin (Eds.), *Development of animal models as pharmacogenetic tools.* Washington, DC: U.S. Government Printing Office.

Lian, J.Z., & Mathews, D.R. (1999). Does the vertical mosaic still exist? Ethnicity and income in Canada, 1991. *Canadian Review of Sociology and Anthropology, 35,* 461-481.

Liashko, V., & Manassis, K. (2003). Medicated anxious children: Characteristics and cognitive-behavioural treatment response. *Canadian Journal of Psychiatry, 48,* 741-748.

Liberman, R.P. (1972). Reinforcement of social interaction in a group of chronic mental patients. In R. Rubin et al., *Advances in behavior therapy.* New York: Academic Press.

Liberman, R.P. (1994). Psychosocial treatments for schizophrenia. *Psychiatry: Interpersonal and Biological Processes, 57,* 104-114.

Liberman, R.P. (Ed). (1992). *Handbook of psychiatric rehabilitation.* New

York: Macmillan.

Liberman, R.P., DeRisi, W.J., & Mueser, K.T. (1989). *Social skills training for psychiatric patients*. Elmsford, NY: Pergamon.

Liberman, R.P., Wallace, C.J., Blackwell, G., Kopelowicz, J.V., et al. (1998). Skills training versus psychosocial occupational therapy for persons with persistent schizophrenia. *American Journal of Psychiatry, 155,* 1087-1091.

Liberto, J.G., Oslin, D.W., & Ruskin, P.E. (1996). Alcoholism in the older population. In L.L. Carstensen, B.A. Edelstein, & L. Dornbrand (Eds.), *The practical handbook of clinical gerontology* (pp. 324-348). Thousand Oaks, CA: Sage.

Libman, E., Rothenberg, I., Fichten, C.S., & Amsel, R. (1985). The SSES-E—A measure of sexual self-efficacy in erectile functioning. *Journal of Sex and Marital Therapy, 11,* 233-247.

Lichstein, K.L., & Morin, C.M. (2000). *Treatment of late-life insomnia.* Thousand Oaks, CA: Sage.

Liddle, P.F. (2000). Cognitive impairment in schizophrenia: Its impact on social functioning. *Acta Psychiatrica Scandinavica, 400 (Supplement),* 11-16.

Lieberman, M.A., Yalom, J.D., & Miles, M.B. (1973). *Encounter groups: First facts.* New York: Basic Books.

Liebson, I. (1967). Conversion reaction: A teaming theory approach. *Behaviour Research and Therapy, 7,* 217-218.

Lief, H.I., & Hubschman, L. (1993). Orgasm in the postoperative transsexual. *Archives of Sexual Behavior, 22,* 145-155.

Light, E., & Lebowitz, B.D. (Eds). (1991). *The elderly with chronic mental illness.* New York: Springer.

Light, K.C., Dolan, C.A., Davis, M.R., & Sherwood, A. (1992). Cardiovascular responses to an active coping challenge as predictors of blood pressure patterns 10 to 15 years later. *Psychosomatic Medicine, 54,* 217-230.

Light, L.L. (1990). Interactions between memory and language in old age. In J.E. Birren & K.W. Schaie (Eds.), *Handbook of the psychology of aging* (pp. 275-290). San Diego: Academic Press.

Lilienfeld, L.R., Kaye, W.H., Greeno, C.G., Merikangas, K.R., Plotnicov, K., et al. (1998). A controlled family study of anorexia nervosa and bulimia nervosa: Psychiatric disorders in first-degree relatives and effects of proband comorbidity. *Archives of General Psychiatry, 55,* 603-610.

Lilienfeld, L.R.R., Stein, D., Bulik, C.M., Strober, M., Plotnicov, K., Pollice, C., Rao, R., Merikangas, K.R., Nagy, L., & Kaye, W.H. (2000). Personality traits among currently eating disordered, recovered, and never ill first-degree female relatives of bulimic and control women. *Psychological Medicine, 30,* 1399-1410.

Lilienfeld, S.O., Lynn, S.J., Kirsch, I., Chaves, J.F., et al. (1999). Dissociative identity disorder and the sociogenic model: Recalling lessons from the past. *Psychological Bulletin, 125,* 507-523.

Lin, E., Goering, P. Offord, D. R., Campbell, D., & Boyle, M. H. (1996). The use of mental health services in Ontario: Epidemiologic findings. *Canadian Journal of Psychiatry, 41,* 572-577.

Lindemann, E. (1944). Symptomatology and management of acute grief. *American Journal of Psychiatry, 101,* American 141-148.

Linden, W. (2003). Cardiac conditions. In S. Llewelyn & P. Kennedy (Eds.), *Handbook of clinical health psychology* (pp. 81-101). Chichester, West Sussex, England: Wiley.

Linden, W., Chambers, L., Maurice, J., & Lenz, J.W. (1993). Sex differences in social support, self-deception, hostility, and ambulatory cardiovascular activity. *Health Psychology, 12,* 376-380.

Linden, W., & Lamensdorf, A.M. (1990). Hostile affect and casual blood pressure. *Psychology and Health, 4,* 343-349.

Linehan, M.M. (1985). The reasons for living inventory. In P. Keller & L. Ritt (Eds.), *Innovations in clinical practice: A sourcebook* (pp. 321-330). Sarasota, FL: Professional Resource Exchange.

Linehan, M.M. (1987). Dialectical behavior therapy for borderline personality disorder. *Bulletin of the Menninger Clinic, 51,* 261-276.

Linehan, M.M. (1993a). *Behavioral skills training manual for treating borderline personality disorder.* New York: Guilford Press.

Linehan, M.M. (1993b). *Cognitive behavioral treatment of borderline personality disorder: The dialectics of effective treatment.* New York: Guilford.

Linehan, M.M. (1997). Behavioral treatments of suicidal behaviors: Definitional obfuscation and treatment outcomes. In D.M. Stoff & J.J. Mann (Eds.), *Neurobiology of suicide.* (pp. 302-327). New York: Annals of the New York Academy of Sciences.

Linehan, M.M., Armstrong, H.E., Suarez, A., Allmon, D., & Heard, H.L. (1991). Cognitive-behavioral treatment of chronically parasuicidal borderline patients. *Archives of General Psychiatry, 48,* 1060-1064.

Linehan, M.M., Camper, P., Chiles, J.A., Strosahl, K., & Shearin, E.N. (1987). Interpersonal problem-solving and parasuicide. *Cognitive Therapy and Research, 11,* 1-12.

Linehan, M.M., Goodstein, J.L., Nielsen, S.L., & Chiles, J.A. (1983). Reasons for staying alive when you are thinking of killing yourself. *Journal of Consulting and Clinical Psychology, 51,* 276-286.

Linehan, M.M., Heard, H.L., & Armstrong, H.E. (1993). Naturalistic follow-up of a behavioral treatment for chronically parasuicidal borderline patients. *Archives of General Psychiatry, 50,* 971-974.

Linehan, M.M., Heard, H.L., & Armstrong, H.E. (1994). Naturalistic follow-up of a behavioral treatment for chronically parasuicidal borderline patients. *Archives of General Psychiatry, 51,* 422-434.

Linehan, M.M., Schmidt, H., Dimeff, L.A., Craft, J.C., Kanter, J., & Comtois, K.A. (1999). Dialectical behavior therapy for patients with borderline personality disorder and drug dependence. *American Journal on Addiction, 8,* 279-292.

Linehan, M.M., & Shearin, E.N. (1988). Lethal stress: A social-behavioral model of suicidal behavior. In S. Fisher & J. Reason (Eds.), *Handbook of life stress, cognition, and health.* New York: Wiley.

Link, B., Cullen, F., Frank, J., & Wozniak, J. (1987). The social rejection of former mental patients: Understanding why labels matter. *American Journal of Sociology, 92,* 1401-1500.

Links, P.S., Gould, B., & Ratnayake, R. (2003). Assessing suicidal youth with antisocial, borderline, or narcissistic personality disorder. *Canadian Journal of Psychiatry, 48,* 301-310.

Links, P.S., Heslegrave, R., & van Reekum, R. (1998). Prospective follow-up of borderline personality disorder: Prognosis, prediction outcome, and Axis II comorbidity. *Canadian Journal of Psychiatry, 43,* 265-270.

Links, P.S., Heslegrave, R., & van Reekum, R. (1999). Impulsivity: Core aspect of borderline personality disorder. *Journal of Personality Disorders, 13,* 1-9.

Links, P.S., & van Reekum, R. (1993). Childhood sexual abuse, parental impairment, and the development of borderline personality disorder. *Canadian Journal of Psychiatry, 38,* 472-474.

Linn, R.T., Wolf, P.A., Bachman, D.L., Knoefel, J.E., Cobb, J., et al. (1999). The "preclinical phase" of probable Alzheimer's disease: A 13-year prospective study of the Framingham cohort. *Archives of Neurology, 52,* 485-490.

Linney, J.A. (1989). Optimizing research strategies in the schools. In L.A. Bond & B.E. Compas (Eds.), *Primary prevention and promotion in the schools* (pp. 50-76). Newbury Park, CA: Sage.

Liotti, G. (1992). Disorganized disoriented attachment in the etiology of dissociative disorders. *Dissociation, 4,* 196-204.

Lipowski, C.J. (1990). *Acute confusional states.* New York: Oxford University Press.

Lipowski, P., Kerkhofs, M., VanOnderbergen, A., Hubain, P., Copinschi, G., et al. (1994). The 24 hour profiles of cortisol, prolactin, and growth hormone secretion in mania. *Archives of General Psychiatry, 51,* 616-624.

Lipowski, Z.J. (1980). *Delirium: Acute brain failure in man.* Springfield, IL: Charles C. Thomas.

Lipowski, Z.J. (1983). Transient cognitive disorders (delirium and acute confusional states) in the elderly. *American Journal of Psychiatry, 140,* 1426-1436.

Liskow, B. (1982). Substance induced and substance use disorders: Barbiturates and similarly acting sedative hypnotics. In J.H. Greist, J.W. Jefferson, & R.L. Spitzer (Eds.), *Treatment of mental disorders.* New York: Oxford University Press.

Liston, E.H. (1982). Delirium in the aged. In L.E. Jarvik & G.W. Small (Eds.), *Psychiatric clinics of North America.* Philadelphia: Saunders.

Litwack, T.R. (1985). The prediction of violence. *The Clinical Psychologist, 38,* 87-90.

Litwack, T. R. (2001). Actuarial versus clinical assessments of dangerousness. *Psychology, Public Policy, and Law, 7,* 409-443.

Livesley, W.J. (1998). Suggestions for a framework for an empirically based classification of personality disorders. *Canadian Journal of Psychiatry, 43,* 137-147.

Livesley, W.J., & Jackson, D.N. (2002). *Manual for the Dimensional Assessment of Personality Problems-Basic Questionnaire*. Port Huron, MI: Sigma.

Livesley, W.J., & Jang, K.L. (2000). Toward an empirically based classification of personality disorder. *Journal of Personality Disorders, 14*, 137-151.

Livesley, W.J., Jang, K.L., & Vernon, P.A. (1998). Phenotypic and genetic structure of traits in delineating personality disorder. *Archives of General Psychiatry, 55,* 941-948.

Livesley, W.J., Schroeder, M.L., Jackson, D.N., & Jung, K.L. (1994). Categorical distinctions in the study of personality disorder: Implications for classification. *Journal of Abnormal Psychology, 103,* 6-17.

Livingston, J.D., Wilson, D., Tien, G., & Bond, L. (2003). A follow-up study of persons found not criminally responsible on account of mental disorder in British Columbia. *Canadian Journal of Psychiatry, 48*, 408-415.

Lobel, T.E., Gilat, I., & Endler, N.S. (1993). The Gulf War: Distressful reactions to SCUD missile attacks. *Anxiety, Stress and Coping, 6*, 9-23.

Lobitz, W.C., & Post, R.D. (1979). Parameters of self-reinforcement and depression. *Journal of Abnormal Psychology, 88,* 33-41.

Lodge, J., Tripp, G., & Harte, D. K. (2000). Think-aloud, thought-listing, and video-mediated recall procedures in the assessment of children's self-talk. *Cognitive Therapy and Research, 24*, 399-418.

Loeber, R., & Keenan, K. (1994). Interaction between conduct disorder and its comorbid conditions: Effects of age and gender. *Clinical Psychology Review, 14,* 497-523.

Loeber, R., Keenan, K., Lahey, B.B., Green, S.M., & Thomas, C. (1993). Evidence for developmentally based diagnoses of oppositional defiant disorder and conduct disorder. *Journal of Abnormal Child Psychology, 21,* 377-410.

Loeber, R., Lahey, B., & Thomas, C. (1991). Diagnostic conundrum of oppositional defiant disorder and conduct disorder. *Journal of Abnormal Psychology, 100,* 379-390.

Loeber, R., Stouthamer-Loeber, M., Van Kammen, W., & Farrington, D.P. (1989). Development of a new measure of self-reported antisocial behavior for young children: Prevalence and reliability. In M. Klein (Ed.), *Cross-national research in self-reported crime and delinquency* (pp. 203-226). Boston: Kluwer-Nijhoff.

Loewenstein, R.J. (1991). Psychogenic amnesia and psychogenic fugue: A comprehensive review. In A. Tasman & S.M. Goldfinger (Eds.), *American Psychiatric Press Review of Psychiatry*. (pp. 189-222). Washington, DC: American Psychiatric Press.

Loffin, R.B., & Kenny, P.J. (1998). Training the Hubble space telescope flight team. *IEEE Computer Graphics and Applications,* 31-37.

Loftus, E.F. (1993). The reality of repressed memories. *American Psychologist, 48,* 518-537.

Loftus, E.F. (1997). Memory for a past that never was. *Current Directions in Psychological Science, 6,* 60-62.

Lomas, J. (1997).

Lomas, J., Woods, J., & Veenstra, G. (1997). Devolving authority for health care in Canada's provinces: 1. An introduction to the issues. *Canadian Medical Association Journal, 156,* 371-377.

London, P. (1964). *The modes and morals of psychotherapy*. New York: Holt, Rinehart & Winston.

London, P. (1986). *The modes and morals of psychotherapy* (2nd ed.). New York: Hemisphere.

Loney, J., Langhorne, J.E., Jr., & Paternite, C.E. (1978). An empirical basis for subgrouping the hyperkinetic-minimal brain dysfunction syndrome. *Journal of Abnormal Psychology, 87,* 431-441.

Long, W.R. (1995, November 24). A changing world proves deadly to Brazil Indians. *Los Angeles Times*, pp. A1, A47, A48.

Looman, J. (1995). Sexual fantasies of child molesters. *Canadian Journal of Behavioural Science, 27,* 321-332.

Looper, K.J., & Paris, J. (2000). What dimensions underlie Cluster B personality disorders? *Comprehensive Psychiatry, 41*, 432-437.

Loos, C., & Bowd, A. (1997). Caregivers of persons with Alzheimer's disease: Some neglected implications of the experience of personal loss and grief. *Death Studies, 21*, 501-514.

Lopez, S.R. (1994). Latinos and the expression of psychopathology: A call for direct assessment of cultural influences. In C. Telles & M. Karno (Eds.), *Latino mental health: Current research and policy perspectives*. Los Angeles: UCLA.

Lopez, S.R. (1996). Testing ethnic minority children. In B.B. Wolman (Ed.), *The encyclopedia of psychology, psychiatry, and psychoanalysis*. New York: Henry Holt.

Lopez, S.R., & Guarnaccia, P.J. (2000). Cultural psychopathology: Uncovering the social world of mental illness. *Annual Review of Psychology, 51,* 571-598.

Lopez, S.R., & Hernandez, P. (1986). How culture is considered in evaluations of psychopathology. *Journal of Nervous and Mental Disease, 176,* 598-606.

Lopez, S.R., Nelson, K.A., Snyder, K.S., & Mintz, J. (1999). Attributions and affective reactions of family members and course of schizophrenia. *Journal of Abnormal Psychology, 108,* 307-314.

LoPiccolo, J. (1991). Counseling and therapy for sexual problems in the elderly. *Clinics in Geriatric Medicine, 7,* 161-179.

LoPiccolo, J. (1992a). Post-modern sex therapy for erectile failure. In R.C. Rosen & S.R. Leiblum (Eds.), *Erectile failure: Assessment and treatment*. New York: Guilford.

LoPiccolo, J. (1992b). Psychological evaluation of erectile failure. In R. Kirby, C. Carson, & G. Webster (Eds.), *Diagnosis and management of male erectile failure dysfunction*. Oxford: Butterworth-Heinemann.

LoPiccolo, J. (2002). Postmodern sex therapy. In F. W. Kaslow & J. L. Lebow (Eds.), *Comprehensive handbook of psychotherapy, Volume 4, Integrative/eclectic* (pp. 411-435). London: Wiley.

LoPiccolo, J., & Friedman, J. (1988). Broad-spectrum treatment of low sexual desire: Integration of cognitive, behavioral, and systemic therapy. In S. Leiblum & R.C. Rosen (Eds.), *Sexual desire disorders*. New York: Guilford.

LoPiccolo, J., & Friedman, J.M. (1985). Sex therapy: An integrated model. In S.J. Lynn & J.P. Garskee (Eds.), *Contemporary psychotherapies: Models and methods*. New York: Merrill.

LoPiccolo, J., & Hogan, D.R. (1979). Multidimensional treatment of sexual dysfunction. In O.F. Pomerleau & J.P. Brady (Eds.), *Behavioral medicine: Theory and practice*. Baltimore: Williams & Wilkins.

LoPiccolo, J., & Lobitz, W.C. (1972). The role of masturbaton in the treatment of orgasmic dysfunction. *Archives of Sexual Behavior, 2,* 163-171.

LoPiccolo, J., & Stock, W.E. (1987). Sexual function, dysfunction, and counseling in gynecological practice. In Z. Rosenwaks, F. Benjamin, & M.L. Stone (Eds.), *Gynecology*. New York: Macmillan.

Loranger, A.W. (1988). *Personality Disorder Examination (PDE) Manual*. Yonkers: DV Communications.

Loranger, A.W., Oldham, J., Russakoff, L.M. & Susman, V. (1987). Structured interviews and borderline personality disorder. *Archives of General Psychiatry, 41,* 565-568.

Loranger, A.W., Sartorius, N., Andreoli, A., Berger, P., Buchleim, P., et al. (1994). The International Personality Disorders Examination: The World Health Organization/Alcohol, Drug Abuse and Mental Health Administration international pilot study of personality disorders. *Archives of General Psychiatry, 51,* 215-223.

Loranger, A.W., Susamn, V.L., Oldham, J.M., & Russakoff, L.M. (1987). The Personality Disorder Examination: A preliminary report. *Journal of Personality Disorders, 1*, 1-13.

Lord, J., & Pedlar, A. (1991). Life in the community: Four years after the closure of an institution. *Mental Retardation, 29*, 213-221.

Lorenz, J., Kunze, K., & Bromm, B. (1998). Differentiation of conversive sensory loss and malingering by P300 in a modified oddball task. *NeuroReport, 9,* 187-191.

Lotter, V. (1978). Follow-up studies. In M. Rutter & E. Schopler (Eds.), *Autism: A reappraisal of concepts and treatment*. New York: Plenum.

Lovaas, O.I. (1987). Behavioral treatment and normal educational and intellectual functioning in young autistic children. *Journal of Consulting and Clinical Psychology, 55,* 3-9.

Lovaas, O.I., Berberich, J.P., Perloff, B.F., & Schaeffer, B. (1966). Acquisition of imitative speech by schizophrenic children. *Science, 151,* 705-707.

Lovaas, O.I., Freitag, G., Gold, V.J., & Kassoria, I.C. (1965). Experimental studies in childhood schizophrenia: Analysis of self-destructive behavior. *Journal of Applied Behavior Analysis, 6,* 131-166.

Lovaas, O.I., Newsom, C., & Hickman, C. (1987). Self-stimulatory behavior and perceptual reinforcement. *Journal of Applied Behavior Analysis, 20,* 45-68.

Lovallo, W.R., & Al'Absi, M. (1998). Hemodynamics during rest and behavioral stress in normotensive men at high risk for hypertension. *Psychophysiology, 35,* 47-53.

Lovass, O.I., Schreibman, L., Koegel, R., & Rehm, R. (1971). Selective responding by autistic children to multiple sensory input. *Journal of Abnormal Psychology, 77,* 221-222.

Lubin, B. (1983). Group therapy. In I.B. Weiner (Ed.), *Clinical methods in psychology* (2nd ed.). New York: Wiley.

Luborsky, L., Rosenthal, R., Diguer, L., Andrusyna, T.P., Berman, J.S., Levitt, J.T., Seligman, D.A., & Krause, E.D. (2002). The Dodo bird verdict is alive and well—mostly. *Clinical Psychology: Science and Practice, 9,* 1-12.

Luborsky, L., & Spence, D.P. (1978). Quantitative research on psychoanalytic therapy. In S.L. Garfield & A.E. Bergin (Eds.), *Handbook of psychotherapy and behavior change: An empirical analysis* (2nd ed.). New York: Wiley.

Luecken, L.J., Suarez, E.C., Kuhn, C.M., Barefoot, J.C., Blumenthal, J.A., et al. (1997). Stress in employed women: Impact of marital status and children in the home on neurohormone output and home strain. *Psychosomatic Medicine, 59,* 352-359.

Luepnitz, R.R., Randolph, D.L., & Gutsch, K.U. (1982). Race and socioeconomic status as confounding variables in the accurate diagnosis of alcoholism. *Journal of Clinical Psychology, 38,* 665-669.

Lykken, D.T. (1957). A study of anxiety in the sociopathic personality. *Journal of Abnormal and Social Psychology, 55,* 6-10.

Lymburner, J.A., & Roesch, R. (1999). The insanity defense: Five years of research (1993-1997). *International Journal of Law and Psychiatry, 22,* 213-240.

Lynam, D.R. (1996). Early identification of chronic offenders: Who is the fledgling psychopath? *Psychological Bulletin, 120,* 209-234.

Lynam, D.R. (1997). Pursuing the psychopath: Capturing the fledgling psychopath in a nomological net. *Journal of Abnormal Psychology, 106,* 425-438.

Lynch, J., Kaplan, G.A., Salonen, R., & Salonen, J.T. (1997). Workplace demands, economic reward, and the progression of atherosclerosis. *Circulation, 96,* 302-307.

Lynch, J., Krause, N., Kaplan, G.A., Tuomilehto, J., & Salonen, J.T. (1997). Workplace conditions, socioeconomic status, and the risk of mortality and acute myocardial infarction. *American Journal of Public Health, 87,* 617-622.

Lynch, J.W., Kaplan, G.A., Cohen, R.D., Tuomilehto, J., & Salonen, J.T. (1996). Do cardiovascular risk factors explain the relation between socioeconomic status, risk of all-cause mortality, cardiovascular mortality, and acute myocardial infarction? *American Journal of Epidemiology, 144,* 934-942.

Lynch, T.R., Compton, J.S., Mendelson, T., Robins, C.J., & Krishnan, K.R.R. (2000). Anxious depression among the elderly: Clinical and phenomenological correlates. *Aging and Mental Health, 4,* 268-274.

Lyon, D.R., Hart, S.D., & Webster, C.D. (2001). Violence and risk assessment. In R.A. Schuller & J.R. Ogloff (Eds.), *Introduction to psychology and law: Canadian perspectives* (pp. 314-350). Toronto: University of Toronto Press.

Lyon, G.R., & Moats, L.C. (1988). Critical issues in the instruction of the learning disabled. *Journal of Consulting and Clinical Psychology, 56,* 830-835.

Lyon, H.M., Startup, M., & Bentall, R.P. (1999). Social cognition and the manic defense: Attribution, selective attention, and self-schema in bipolar affective disorder. *Journal of Abnormal Psychology, 108,* 273-282.

Lyons, M.J., True, W.S., Eisen, A., Goldberg, J., Meyer, J.M., et al. (1995). Differential heritability of adult and juvenile antisocial traits. *Archives of General Psychiatry, 52,* 906-915.

Lystad, M.M. (1957). Social mobility among selected groups of schizophrenics. *American Sociological Review, 22,* 288-292.

MacCharles, T. (2001, February 6). Liberal bill to reform Young Offenders Act: Alliance, Tories say it's not tough enough on crime. *The Toronto Star,* A6.

Maccoby, N., & Altman, D.G. (1988). Disease prevention in communities: The Stanford Heart Disease Prevention Program. In R.H. Price, E.L. Cowen, R.P. Lorion, & J. Ramos-McKay (Eds.), *14 ounces of prevention: A casebook for practitioners* (pp. 165-174). Washington, DC: American Psychological Association.

MacDonald, H.A., Colotla, V., Flamer, S., & Karlinsky, H. (2003). Post-traumatic stress disorder (PTSD) in the workplace: A descriptive study of workers experiencing PTSD resulting from work injury. *Journal of Occupational Rehabilitation, 13,* 63-82.

MacDonald, M.R., & Kuiper, N.A. (1984). Self-schema decision consistency in clinical depression. *Journal of Social and Clinical Psychology, 2,* 264-272.

Macdonald, S., Wells, S., Giesbrecht, N., & Cherpitel, C.J. (1999). Demographic and substance use factors related to violent and accidental injuries: Results from an emergency room study. *Drug and Alcohol Dependence, 55,* 53-61.

Mackenzie, C.S., Gekoski, W.L., & Knox, J.V. (1999). Do family physicians treat older patients with mental disorders differently from younger patients? *Canadian Family Physician, 45,* 1219-1224.

MacLatchy-Gaudet, H.A., & Stewart, S.H. (2001). The context-specific positive alcohol outcome expectancies of university women. *Addictive Behaviors, 26,* 31-49.

Mace, C.J., & Trimble, M.R. (1996). Ten-year prognosis of conversion disorder. *British Journal of Psychiatry, 169,* 282-288.

MacGregor, M.W. (1996). Multiple personality disorder: Etiology, treatment, and techniques from a psychodynamic perspective. *Psychoanalytic Psychology, 13,* 389-402.

Machon, R.A., Mednick, S.A., & Huttunen, M.O. (1997). Adult major affective disorder after prenatal exposure to an influenza epidemic. *Archives of General Psychiatry, 54,* 322-328.

Macklin, M.L., Metzger, L.J., Litz, B.T., McNally, R.J., Lasko, N.B., et al. (1998). Lower precombat intelligence is a risk factor for posttraumatic stress disorder. *Journal of Consulting and Clinical Psychology, 66,* 323-326.

MacLean, D.R. (1999). Cardiovascular disease: Risk factors in older Canadians. *Canadian Medical Association Journal, 161 (8, Supplement),* S1-S2.

MacLeod, A.K., Haynes, C., & Sensky, T. (1998). Attributions about common bodily sensations: Their associations with hyponchondriasis and anxiety. *Psychological Medicine, 28,* 225-228.

MacLeod, C., & Hemsley, D.R. (1985). Visual feedback of vocal intensity in the treatment of hysterical aphonia. *Journal of Behaviour Therapy and Experimental Psychiatry, 4,* 347-353.

MacLeod, C., Mathews, A., & Tata, P. (1986). Attentional bias in emotional disorders. *Journal of Abnormal Psychology, 95,* 15-20.

MacMillan, H.L., Fleming, J.E., Trocme, N., Boyle, M.H., Wong, M., Racine, Y. A. et al. (1997). Prevalence of child physical and sexual abuse in the community—results from the Ontario Health Supplement. *Journal of the American Medical Association, 278,* 131-135.

MacMillan, H.L., Boyle, M. H., Wong, M. Y-Y., Duku, E. K., Fleming, J. E., & Walsh, C. A. (1999). Slapping and spanking in childhood and its association with lifetime prevalence of psychiatric disorders in a general population. *Canadian Medical Association Journal, 161,* 805-809.

MacNamara, M. (1993). Fade away: The rise and fall of the repressed memory theory in the courtroom. *California Lawyer, 15,* 36-41.

Macrodimitris, S.D., & Endler, N.S. (in press). Coping, control, and adjustment in Type II diabetes. *Health Psychology.*

Maddux, J.E., Roberts, M.C., Sledden, E.A., & Wright, L. (1986). Developmental issues in child health psychology. *American Psychologist, 41,* 25-34.

Madonna, P.G., Van Scoyk, S., & Jones, D.B. (1991). Family interactions within incest and nonincest families. *American Journal of Psychiatry, 148,* 46-49.

Maffei, C., Fossati, A., Agostini, I., Barraco, A., et al. (1997). Interrater relaibility and internal consistency of the Structured Clinical Interview for Axis II Personality Disorders (SCID-II), Version 2.0. *Journal of Personality Disorders, 11,* 279-284.

Magee, W.J., Eaton, W.W., Wittchern, H.U., McGonagle, K.A., & Kessler, R.C. (1996). Agoraphobia, simple phobia and social phobia in the National Comorbidity Survey. *Archives of General Psychiatry, 53,* 159-168.

Magnusson, A., & Axelsson, J. (1993). The prevalence of seasonal affective disorder is low among descendants of Icelandic emigrants in Canada. *Archives of General Psychiatry, 50,* 947-951.

Maher, B.A. (1966). *Principles of psychopathology: An experimental approach.* New York: McGraw-Hill.

Mahoney, L.J. (1977). Early diagnosis of breast cancer: The breast self-examination problem. *Progress in Clinical and Biological Research, 12,* 203-206.

Mahoney, M.J. (1974). Cognition and behavior modification. Cambridge, MA: Ballinger.

Mahoney, M.J. (1982). Psychotherapy and human change processes. In *Psychotherapy research and behavior change* (Vol. 1). Washington, DC: American Psychological Association.

Mahoney, M.J. (1989) Scientific psychology and radical behaviorism: Important distinctions based in scientism and objectivism. *American Psychologist, 44,* 1372-1377.

Mahoney, M.J. (1993). Theoretical developments in the cognitive psychotherapies. *Journal of Consulting and Clinical Psychology, 7,* 138-157.

Mahoney, M.J., & Moes, A.J. (1997). Complexity and psychotherapy: Promising dialogues and practical issues. In F. Masterpasque & A. Perna (Eds.), *The psychological meaning of chaos: Self-organization in human development and psychotherapy*. Washington, DC: American Psychological Association.

Mai, F.M. (1995). Psychiatrists' attitudes to multiple personality disorder: A questionnaire study. *Canadian Journal of Psychiatry*, *40*, 154-157.

Maj, M., Pirozzi, R., Magliono, L., & Bartoli, L. (1998). Long-term outcome of lithium prophylaxis in bipolar disorder: A 5-year prospective study of 402 patients at a lithium clinic. *American Journal of Psychiatry, 155,* 30-35.

Makela, K., Rooms, R., Single, E., Sulkunen, P., Walsh, B., et al. (1981). John. *Alcohol, society, and the state: A comparative study of alcohol control*. Toronto: Addiction Research Foundation.

Makomaski-Illing, E.M., & Kaiserman, M.J. (1999). Mortality attributable to tobacco use in Canada and its regions, 1994 and 1996. *Chronic Diseases in Canada*, *20*, 111-117.

Maladonado, J.R., Butler, L.D., & Spiegel, D. (1998). Treatments for dissociative disorders. In P.E. Nathan & J.M. Gorman (Eds.), *A guide to treatments that work*, (pp. 423-447). NY: Oxford.

Malamuth, N.M., & Brown, L.M. (1994). Sexually aggresive men's perceptions of women's communications: Testing three explanations. *Journal of Personality and Social Psychology, 67,* 699-712.

Malamuth, N.M., & Check, J.V.P. (1983). Sexual arousal to rape depictions: Individual differences. *Journal of Abnormal Psychology, 92,* 55-67.

Malatesta, C.Z., & Izard, C.E. (1984). The facial expression of emotion: Young, middle-aged, and older adult expressions. In C.Z. Malatesta & C.E. Izard (Eds.), *Emotion in adult development* (pp. 253-273). Beverly Hills, CA: Sage.

Malchy, B., Enns, M.W., Young, T.K., & Cox, B.J. (1997). Suicide among Manitoba's aboriginal people, 1988 to 1994. *Canadian Medical Association Journal*, *156*, 1133-1138.

Maldonado, J.R., Butler, L.D., & Spiegel, D. (1998). Treatments for dissociative disorders. In P.E. Nathan & J.M. Gorman (Eds.), *A guide to treatments that work*. (pp. 423-446). New York: Oxford University Press.

Maletzky, B.M. (1991). *Treating the sexual offender*. Newbury Park, CA: Sage.

Maletzky, B.M. (1997). Exhibitionism: Assessment and treatment. In D.R. Laws & W. O'Donohue (Eds.), *Sexual deviance*. (pp. 40-74). NY: Guilford Press.

Malizia, A.L., Cunningham, V.J., Bell, C.J., Liddle, P.F., et al. (1998). Decreased brain GABAa-benzodiazepine receptor binding in panic disorder: Preliminary results from a quantitative study. *Archives of General Psychiatry, 55,* 715-720.

Malkoff-Schwartz, S., Frank, E., Anderson, B., Sherrill, J.T., Siegel, L., et al. (1998). Stressful life events and social rhythm disruption in the onset of manic and depressive bipolar episodes: A preliminary investigation. *Archives of General Psychiatry, 55,* 702-707.

Malla, A.K. (1988). Characteristics of patients who receive electroconvulsive therapy. *Canadian Journal of Psychiatry*, *33*, 696-701.

Malla, A.K., Mittal, C., Lee, M., Scholten, D.J., Assis, L., & Norman, R.M.G. (2002). Computed tomography of the brain morphology of patients with first-episode schizophrenic psychosis. *Journal of Psychiatry and Neuroscience*, *27*, 350-358.

Malla, A.K., Norman, R.M.G., Manchanda, R., Ahmed, M.R., Scholten, D., Harricharan, R., Cortese, L., & Takhar, J. (2002). One year outcome in first episode psychosis: Influence of DUP and other predictors. *Schizophrenia Research*, *54*, 231-242.

Malla, A.K., Norman, R.M.G., Scholten, D.J., Zirul, S., & Kotteda, V. (2001). A comparison of long-term outcome in first episode schizophrenia following treatment with risperidone or a typical antipsychotic. *Journal of Clinical Psychiatry, 62,* 179-184.

Manassis, K., Avery, D., Butalia, S., & Mendlowitz, S. (2004). Cognitive-behavioral therapy with childhood anxiety disorders: Functioning in adolescence. *Depression and Anxiety*, *19*, 209-216.

Manassis, K., & Menna, R. (1999). Depression in anxious children: Possible factors in comorbidity. *Depression and Anxiety*, *10*, 18-24.

Manassis, K., & Monga, S. (2001). A therapeutic approach to children and adolescents with anxiety disorders and associated comorbid conditions. *Journal of the American Academy of Child and Adolecent Psychiatry*, *40*, 115-117.

Mancini, C., van Ameringen, M., Szatmair, P., Fugere, C., & Boyle, M. (1996). A high-risk pilot study of the children of adults with social phobia. *Journal of the American Academy of Child and Adolescent Psychiatry*, *35*, 1511-1517.

Mandler, G. (1966). Anxiety. In D.L. Sills (Ed.), *International encyclopedia of the social sciences*. New York: Macmillan.

Mangalmurti, V.S. (1994). Psychotherapists' fear of Tarasoff: All in the mind? *Journal of Psychiatry and Law, 22,* 379-409.

Manji, H.K., Chen, G., Shimon, H., Hsiao, J.K., Potter, W.Z., & Belmaker, R.H. (1995). Guanine nucleotide-binding proteins in bipolar affective disorder: Effects of long-term lithium treatment. *Archives of General Psychiatry, 52,* 135-144.

Mann, V.A., & Brady, S. (1988). Reading disability: The role of language deficiencies. *Journal of Consulting and Clinical Psychology, 56,* 811-816.

Manne, S., Jacobsen, P.B., & Redd, W.H. (1992). Assessment of acute pediatric pain: Do child self-report, parent ratings, and nurse ratings measure the same phenomenon? *Pain, 48,* 45-52.

Manne, S.L., Bakeman, R., & Jacobsen, P.B. (1994). An analysis of behavioral intervention for children undergoing venipuncture. *Health Psychology, 13,* 556-566.

Mannuzza, S., Schneier, F.R., Chapman, T.F., Leibowitz, M.R., Klein, D.F., & Fyer, A.J. (1995). Generalized social phobia: Reliability and validity. *Archives of General Psychiatry, 52,* 230-237.

Manos, N., Vasilopoulou, E., & Sotiriou, M. (1987). DSM-III diagnoses of borderline disorder and depression. *Journal of Personality Disorders, 1,* 263-268.

Mansdorf, I. J., Calapai, P., Caselli, L., & Burstein, Y. (1999). Reducing psychotropic medication usage in nursing home residents: The effects of behaviorally oriented psychotherapy. *the Behavior Therapist, 22,* 21-39.

Manton, K.G., Blazer, D.G., & Woodbury, M.A. (1987). Suicide in middle age and later life: Sex and race specific life table and cohort analyses. *Journal of Gerontology, 42,* 219-227.

Manuck, S.B., Kamarck, T.M., Kasprowicz, A.S., & Waldstein, S., R. (1993). Stability and patterning of behaviorally evoked cardiovascular activity. In J. Blascovich & E.S. Katkin (Eds.), *Cardiovascular reactivity*. (pp. 111-134). Washington, DC: American Psychological Association.

Manuck, S.B., Kaplan, J.R., Adams, M.R., & Clarkson, T.B. (1989). Behaviorally elicited heart rate reactivity and atherosclerosis in female cynomolgus monkeys (Macaca fascicularis). *Psychosomatic Medicine, 51,* 306-318.

Manuck, S.B., Kaplan, J.R., & Clarkson, T.B. (1983). Behaviorally induced heart rate reactivity and atherosclerosis in cynomolgus monkeys. *Psychosomatic Medicine, 49,* 95-108.

Manuel, D.G., Leung, M., Nguyen, K., Tanuseputro, P., & Johansen, H. (2003). Burden of cardiovascular disease in Canada. *Canadian Journal of Cardiology*, *19*, 997-1004.

Manuzza, S., Gittelman-Klein, R., Bessler, A., Malloy, P., & LaPadula, M. (1993). Adult outcome of hyperactive boys: Educational achievement, occupational rank, and psychiatric status. *Archives of General Psychiatry, 50,* 565-576.

March, J.S. (1995). Cognitive-behavioral psychotherapy for children and adolescents with OCD: A review and recommendations for treatment. *Journal of the American Academy of Child and Adolescent Psychiatry, 34,* 7-18.

Marchand, Y., D'Arcy, R.C., & Connolly, J.F. (2002). Linking neurophysiological and neuropsychological measures for aphasia assessment. *Clinical Neurophysiology*, *113*, 1165-1166.

Marco, C.A., Schwartz, J.E., Neale, J.M., Shiffman, S., Catley, D., & Stone, A.A. (2000). Impact of gender and having children in the household on ambulatory blood pressure in work and nonwork settings: A partial replication and new findings. *Annals of Behavioral Medicine*, *22*, 110-115.

Marcos, L.R. (1979). Effects of interpreters on the evaluation of psychopathology in non-English-speaking patients. *American Journal of Psychiatry, 136,* 171-174.

Marcus, J., Hans, S.L., Nagier, S., Auerbach, J.G., Mirsky, A.F., & Aubrey, A. (1987). Review of the NIMH Israeli Kibbutz-City and the Jerusalem infant development study. *Schizophrenia Bulletin, 13,* 425-438.

Marder, S.R., & Meibach, R.C. (1994). Risperidone in the treatment of schizophrenia. *American Journal of Psychiatry, 151,* 825-836.

Marder, S.R., Wirshing, W.C., Mintz, J., McKenzie, J., Johnston, K., et al. (1996). Two-year outcome of social-skills training and group psychotherapy for outpatients with schizophrenia. *American Journal of Psychiatry, 153,* 1585-1592.

Marengo, J., & Westermeyer, J.F. (1996). Schizophrenia and delusional disorder. In L.L. Carstensen, B.A. Edelstein, & L. Dornbrand (Eds.), *The practical handbook of clinical gerontology* (pp. 255-273). Thousand Oaks, CA: Sage.

Margolin, G. (1981). Behavior exchange in happy and unhappy marriages: A family cycle perspective. *Behavior Therapy, 12,* 329-343.

Margolin, G. (1982). Ethical and legal considerations in marital and family therapy. *American Psychologist, 37,* 788-801.

Margolin, G., & Burman, B. (1993). Wife abuse vs. marital violence: Different terminologies, explanations, and solutions. *Clinical Psychology Review, 13,* 59-73.

Margolin, G., & Fernandez, V. (1985). Marital dysfunction. In M. Hersen & A.S. Bellack (Eds.), *Handbook of clinical behavior therapy with adults.* New York: Plenum.

Margolin, G., & Wampold, B.F. (1981). Sequential analysis of conflict and accord in distressed and non-distressed marital partners. *Journal of Consulting and Clinical Psychology, 49,* 554-567.

Marijuana research findings. (1980). Washington, DC: U.S. Government Printing Office.

Maris, R.W., Berman, A.L., Maltsberger, J.T., & Yufit, R.I. (1992). *Assessment and prediction of suicide.* New York: Guilford.

Margraf, J., Ehlers, A., & Roth, W.T. (1986). Sodium lactate infusions and panic attacks: A review and critique. *Psychosomatic Medicine, 48,* 23-51.

Markman, H.J., Floyd, F.J., Stanley, S.M., & Storaasli, R.D. (1989). Prevention of marital distress: A longitudinal investigation. *Journal of Consulting and Clinical Psychology, 56,* 210-217.

Markman, H.J., Silvern, L., Clements, M., & Kraft-Hanak, S. (1993). Men and women dealing with conflict in heterosexual relationships. *Journal of Social Issues, 49,* 107-125.

Markovitz, J.H., Matthews, K.A., Kiss, J., & Smitherman, T.C. (1996). Effects of hostility on platelet reactivity to stress in coronary heart disease patients and in healthy controls. *Psychosomatic Medicine, 58,* 143-149.

Markovitz, J.H., Tucker, D., Sanders, P.W., & Warnock, D.G. (1998). Inverse relationship between urinary cyclic GMP to blood pressure reactivity in the CARDIA study: Vasodilatory regulation of sympathetic vasoconstriction. *Psychosomatic Medicine, 60,* 319-326.

Markowitz, J.C., Rabkin, J., & Perry, S. (1994). Treating depression in HIV-positive patients. *AIDS, 8,* 403-412.

Marks, I., Lovell, K., Noshirvani, H., Livanou, M., & Thrasher, S. (1998). Treatment of posttraumatic stress disorder by exposure and/or cognitive restructuring. *Acrhives of General Psychiatry, 55,* 317-325.

Marks, I.M. (1969). *Fears and phobias.* New York: Academic Press.

Marks, I.M. (1995). Advances in behavioral-cognitive therapy of social phobia. *Journal of Clinical Psychiatry, 56,* 25-31.

Marks, I.M., Stern, R.S., Mawson, D., Cobb, J., & Markson, E. W. (1995). Issues affecting older women. In L. A. Bond & S. J. Cutter (Eds.), *Promoting successful and productive aging* (pp. 261-278). Thousand Oaks, CA: Sage Publications.

Marlatt, G.A. (1983). The controlled drinking controversy: A commentary. *American Psychologist, 38,* 1097-1110.

Marlatt, G.A. (1985). Relapse prevention: Theoretical rationale and overview of the model. In G.A. Marlatt & J. Gordon (Eds.), *Relapse prevention: Maintenance strategies in addictive behavior change.* New York: Guilford.

Marlatt, G.A. (1999). From hindsight to foresight: A commentary on Project MATCH. In J. A. Tucker, D. M. Donovan, & G. A. Marlatt (Eds.), *Changing addictive behavior: Bridging clinical and public health strategies* (pp. 45-66). New York: Guilford.

Marlatt, G.A., Baer, J.S., Kivlahan, D.R., Dimeff, L.A., Larimer, M.E., Quigley, L.A., Somers, J.M., & Williams, E. (1998). Screening and brief intervention for high-risk college student drinkers: Results from a 2-year follow-up assessment. *Journal of Consulting and Clinical Psychology, 66,* 604-615.

Marlatt, G.A., Baer, J.S., & Larimer, M. (1995). Preventing alcohol abuse in college students: A harm-reduction approach. In G. M. Boyd, J. Howard, & R. A. Zucker (Eds.), *Alcohol problems among adolescents: Current directions in prevention research* (pp. 147-172). Hillsdale, NJ: Erlbaum.

Marlatt, G.A., Blume, A.W., & Parks, G.A. (2001). Integrating harm reduction therapy and traditional substance abuse treatment. *Journal of Psychoactive Drugs, 33,* 13-21.

Marlatt, G.A., & Gordon, J.R. (1985). (Eds.), *Relapse prevention: Maintenance strategies in the treatment of addictive behaviors.* New York: Guilford.

Marlatt, G.A., & Witkiewitz, K. (2002). Harm reduction approaches to alcohol use: Health promotion, prevention, and treatment. *Addictive Behaviors, 27,* 867-886.

Marmar, C., & Horowitz, M.J. (1988). Diagnosis and phase-oriented treatment of post-traumatic stress disorders. In J. Wilson (Ed.), *Human adaptation to extreme stress: From the Holocaust to Vietnam.* New York: Brunner/Mazel.

Marmor, J. (1962). Psychoanalytic therapy as an educational process: Common denominators in the therapeutic approaches of different psychoanalytic schools. In J.H. Masserman (Ed.), *Science and psychoanalysis: Vol. 5. Psychoanalytic education.* New York: Grune & Stratton.

Marmot, M.G., Bosma, H., Hemingway, H., Brunner, E., & Stansfeld, S. (1997). Contribution of job control and other risk factors to social variations in coronary heart disease incidence. *The Lancet, 350,* 235-239.

Marrazzi, M.A., & Luby, E.D. (1986). An auto-addiction model of chronic anorexia nervosa. *International Journal of Eating Disorders, 5,* 191-208.

Marsh, B. (1996, July 7). Meth at work: In virtually every industry, use among employees is on the rise [editorial]. *Los Angeles Times,* pp. D1, D4.

Marshall, J. (1982). *Madness: An indictment of the mental health care system in Ontario.* Toronto: Ontario Public Services Employee Union.

Marshall, K. (1998). The gambling industry: Raising the stakes. *Perspectives on Labour Income, 10 (4),* 7-11.

Marshall, R.D., Printz, D., Cardenas, D., Abbate, I., & Liebowitz, M.R. (1995). Adverse events in PTSD patients taking fluoxetine. *American Journal of Psychiatry, 152,* 1238-1239.

Marshall, W. L. (1996). Assessment, treatment, and theorizing about sex offenders: Developments during the past twenty years and future directions. *Criminal Justice and Behavior, 23,* 162-199.

Marshall, W.L. (1997). Pedophilia: Psychopathology and theory. In D.R. Laws & W. O'Donohue (Eds.), *Sexual deviance.* (pp. 152-174). NY: Guilford Press.

Marshall, W.L. (1999). Current status of North American assessment and treatment programs for sexual offenders. *Journal of Interpersonal Violence, 14,* 221-239.

Marshall, W.L., Anderson, D., & Fernandez, Y. (1999). *Cognitive behavioural treatment of sexual offenders.* Toronto: Wiley.

Marshall, W. L., & Barbaree, H. E. (1990). Outcome of comprehensive cognitive-behavioral treatment programs. In W. L. Marshall & D. R. Laws (Eds.), *Handbook of sexual assault: Issues, theories, and treatment of the offender* (pp. 363-385). New York: Plenum Press.

Marshall, W. L., Barbaree, H., & Christophe, D. (1986). Sexual offenders against female children: Sexual preferences for age of victims and type of behaviour. *Canadian Journal of Behavioural Sciences, 18,* 424-439.

Marshall, W.L., Champagne, F., Brown, C., & Miller, S. (1997). Empathy, intimacy, loneliness, and self-esteem in non-familial child molesters: A brief report. *Journal of Child Sexual Abuse, 6,* 87-98.

Marshall, W.L., Cripps, E., Anderson, D., & Cortoni, F.A. (1999). Self-esteem and coping strategies in child molesters. *Journal of Interpersonal Violence, 14,* 955-962.

Marshall, W.L., & Fernandez, Y.M. (2000). Phallometric testing with sexual offenders: Limits to its value. *Clinical Psychology Review, 20,* 807-822.

Marshall, W.L., Hamilton, K., & Fernandez, Y. (2001). Empathy deficits and cognitive distortions in child molesters. *Sexual Abuse: A Journal of Research and Treatment, 13,* 123-130.

Marshall, W.L., Jones, R., Ward, T., Johnston, P., & Barbaree, H.E. (1991). Treatment outcomes with sex offenders. *Clinical Psychology Review, 11,* 465-485.

Marshall, W.L., & McGuire, J. (2003). Effect sizes in the treatment of sexual offenders. *International Journal of Offender Therapy and Comparative Criminology*, *47*, 653-663.

Marshall, W.L., & Moulden, H. (2001). Hostility toward women and victim empathy in rapists. *Sexual Abuse*, *13*, 249-255.

Marshall, W.L., & Serin, R. (1997). Personality disorder. In S. M. Turner & M. Hersen (Eds.), *Adult psychopathology and diagnosis, Vol. 3 (pp. 508-543)*. New York: Wiley.

Marshall, W.L., Thornton, D., Marshall, L.E., Fernandez, Y.M., & Mann, R. (2001). Treatment of sexual offenders who are in categorical denial: A pilot project. *Sexual Abuse: A Journal of Research and Treatment*, *13*, 205-215.

Martin, B.A. (2000). The Clarke Institute experience with completed suicide: 1966 to 1997. *Canadian Journal of Psychiatry*, *45*, 630-638.

Martin, J.E., Dubbert, P.M., & Cushman, W.C. (1991). Controlled trial of aerobic exercise in hypertension. *Circulation, 81,* 1560-1567.

Martin, J. K., Pscosolido, B. A., Tuch, S. A. (2000). Of fear and loathing: The role of "disturbing behavior, " labels, and causal attributions in shaping public attitudes toward people with mental illness. *Journal of Health and Social Behavior, 41, (June),* 208-223.

Martin, P.A., & Bird, H.W. (1953). An approach to the psychotherapy of marriage partners: The stereoscopic technique. *Psychiatry, 16,* 123-127.

Martin, R.A. (1996). The Situational Humor Response Questionnaire and Coping Humor Scale (CHS): A decade of research findings. *Humor: International Journal of Humor Research*, *9*, 251-272.

Martin, R.A. (2001). Humor, laughter, and physical health: Methodological issues and findings. *Psychological Bulletin*, *127*, 504-519.

Martin, R.A., & Kuiper, N.A. (1999). Daily occurrence of laughter: Relationships with age, gender, and Type A personality. *Humor: International Journal of Humor Research*, *12*, 355-384.

Martin, R.A., & Lefcourt, H.M. (1983). Sense of humor as a moderator of the relation between stressors and mood. *Journal of Personality and Social Psychology*, *45*, 1313-1324.

Martin, R.A., & Lefcourt, H.M. (1984). The Situational Humor Response Questionnaire: A quantitative measure of the sense of humor. *Journal of Personality and Social Psychology*, *47*, 145-155.

Maruish, M.E., Sawicki, R.F., Franzen, M.D., & Golden, C.J. (1984). Alpha coefficient reliabilities for the Luria-Nebraska Neuropsychological Battery summary and localization scales by diagnostic category. *The International Journal of Clinical Neuropsychology, 7,* 10-12.

Marziali, E. (1984). Prediction of outcome of brief psychotherapy from therapist interpretive interventions. *Archives of General Psychiatry, 41,* 301-304.

Masellis, M., Rector, N.A., & Richter, M.A. (2003). Quality of life in OCD: Differential impact of obsessions, compulsions, and depression comorbidity. *Canadian Journal of Psychiatry*, *48*, 72-77.

Masling, J. (1960). The influences of situational and interpersonal variables in projective testing. *Psychological Bulletin, 57,* 65-85.

Maslow, A.H. (1968). *Toward a psychology of being*. New York: Van Nostrand-Reinhold.

Mason, F.L. (1997). Fetishism: Psychopathology and theory. In D.R. Laws & W. O'Donohue (Eds.), *Sexual deviance*. (pp. 75-91). NY: Guilford Press.

Masse, L.C., & Tremblay, R.E. (1997). Behavior of boys in kindergarten and the course of substance use during adolescence. *Archives of General Psychiatry, 54,* 62-68.

Masson, J.M. (1984). *The assault on truth: Freud's suppression of the seduction theory*. New York: Farrar, Strauss, Giroux.

Masters, W.H., & Johnson, V.E. (1966). *Human sexual response*. Boston: Little, Brown.

Masters, W.H., & Johnson, V.E. (1970). *Human sexual inadequacy*. Boston: Little, Brown.

Masters, W.H., Johnson, V.E., & Kolodny, R.C. (1988). *Human sexuality* (3rd ed.). Boston: Little Brown.

Mathews, A., & MacLeod, C. (1994). Cognitive approaches to emotion and emotional disorders. In L.W. Porter & M.R. Rosenzweig (Eds.), *Annual Review of Psychology* (pp. 25-50). Stanford, CA: Stanford University Press.

Mathews, F. (1996). *The invisible boy: Revisioning the victimization of male children & their teens*. Ottawa, ON: The National Clearinghouse on Family Violence and Health Canada.

Mathews, H.F., Lannin, D.R., & Mitchell, J.P. (1994). Coming to terms with advanced breast cancer: Black women's narratives from eastern North Carolina. *Social Science and Medicine, 38,* 789-800.

Matthews, K.A. (1982). Psychological perspectives on the type A behavior pattern. *Psychological Bulletin, 91,* 293-323.

Matthews, K.A., Glass, D.C., Rosenman, R.H., & Bonner, R.W. (1977). Competitive drive, pattern A, and coronary heart disease: A further analysis of some data from the Western Collaborative Group Study. *Journal of Chronic Diseases, 30,* 489-498.

Matthews, K.A., Meilan, E., Kuller, L.M., Kelsey, S.F., Caggiula, A., et al. (1989). Menopause and risk factors in coronary heart disease. *New England Journal of Medicine, 321,* 641-646.

Matthews, K.A., Owens, J.F., Allen, M.T., & Stoney, C.M. (1992). Do cardiovascular responses to laboratory stress relate to ambulatory blood pressure levels?: Yes, in some of the people, some of the time. *Psychosomatic Medicine, 54,* 686-697.

Matthews, K.A., & Rakaczky, C.J. (1987). Familial aspects of type A behavior and physiologic reactivity to stress. In T. Dembroski & T. Schmidt (Eds.), *Behavioral factors in coronary heart disease*. Heidelberg: Springer-Verlag.

Matthews, K.A., Shumaker, S.A., Bowen, D.J., Langer, R.D., Hunt, J.R., et al. (1997). Women's health initiative: Why now? What is it? What's new? *American Psychologist, 52,* 101-116.

Matthews, K.A., Woodall, K.L., Jacob, T., & Kenyon, K. (1995). Negative family environment as a predictor of boy's future status on measures of hostile attitudes, interview behavior, and anger expression. *Health Psychology, 15,* 30-37.

Mattick, R.P., & Andrews, G. (1994). Social phobia. In M. Hersen & R.T. Ammerman (Eds.), *Handbook of prescriptive treatments for adults* (pp. 157-177). New York: Plenum.

Mattson, M.E., Allen, J.P., Longabaugh, R., Nickless, C.J., Connors, G.J., & Kadden, R.M. (1994). A chronological review of empirical studies matching alcoholic clients to treatment. *Journal of Studies on Alcohol, 55,* 16-29.

Mavissikalian, M., Hammen, M.S., & Jones, B. (1990). DSM-III personality disorders in obsessive-compulsive disorder. *Comprehensive Psychiatry, 31,* 432-437.

Mayhew, D.R., Beirness, D.J., & Simpson, H.M. (2000). Trends in drinking-driving fatalities in Canada – progress continues. In *Alcohol, Drugs, and Traffic Safety –T2000*. Stockholm, Sweden: Swedish National Road Safety.

Mayor's Homelessness Action Task Force. (1999). *Taking responsibility for homelessness: An action plan for Toronto: Report of the Mayor's Homelessness Action Task Force*. City of Toronto: Author.

Mays, D.T., & Franks, C.M. (1980). Getting worse: Psychotherapy or no treatment: The jury should still be out. *Professional Psychology, 11,* 78-92.

McArthur, D.S., & Roberts, G.E. (1982). *Roberts Apperception Test for Children Manual*. Los Angeles: Western Psychological Services.

McBride, P.A., Anderson, G.M., & Shapiro, T. (1996). Autism research: Bringing together approaches to pull apart the disorder. *Archives of General Psychiatry, 53,* 980-983.

McCabe, R.E. (1999). Implicit and explicit memory for threat words in high- and low-anxiety-sensitive participants. *Cognitive Therapy and Research*, *23*, 21-38.

McCabe, R.E., & Blankstein, K.R. (2000, November). *The experience of panic in college students: A comparison of cognitive-personality vulnerabilities, life stress, coping, attachment, and panic beliefs in panic disorder, panic attack, and non-panic groups*. Poster presented at the Association for the Advancement of Behavior Therapy (AABT) annual convention, New Orleans, Louisiana.

McCabe, R.E., McFarlane, T.D., Blankstein, K.R., & Olmsted, M.P. (2000, May). *Dimensions of perfectionism in individuals with eating disorders, dieters, and non-dieters*. Paper presented at the Academy for Eating Disorders Ninth International Conference on Eating Disorders, New York.

McCabe, S.B., & Gotlib, I.H. (1995). Selective attention and clinical depression: Performance on a deployment-of-attention task. *Journal of Abnormal Psychology*, *104*, 241-245.

McCabe, S.B., Gotlib, I.H., & Martin, R. (2000). Cognitive vulnerability for depression: Deployment of attention as a function of history of depression and current mood state. *Cognitive Therapy and Research*, *24*, 427-444.

McCabe, S.B., & Tonan, P.E. (2000). Stimulus exposure duration in a deployment-of-attention task: Effects on dysphoric, recently dysphoric, and nondysphoric individuals. *Cognition and Emotion, 14*, 125-142.

McCain, M., & Mustard, F. (1999). *Reversing the real brain drain: Final report of the early year study.* Toronto: Canadian Institute for Advanced Research.

McCarthy, B.W. (1986). A cognitive-behavioral approach to understanding and treating sexual trauma. *Journal of Sex and Marital Therapy, 12,* 322-329.

McCollum, V.J.C. (1997). Evolution of the African American family personality: Considerations for family therapy. *Journal of Multicultural Counseling and Development, 25,* 219-229.

McConaghy, N. (1990). Sexual deviation. In A.S. Bellack, M. Hersen, & A.E. Kazdin (Eds.), *International handbook of behavior modification and therapy* (2nd ed., pp. 565-580). New York: Plenum.

McConaghy, N. (1993). *Sexual behavior: Problems and management.* NY: Plenum.

McConaghy, N. (1994). Paraphilias and gender identity disorders. In M. Hersen & R.T. Ammerman (Eds.), *Handbook of prescriptive treatments for adults* (pp. 317-346). New York: Plenum.

McConaghy, N. (1997). Sexual and gender identity disorders. In S.M. Turner & M. Hersen (Eds.), *Adult psychopathology and diagnosis.* (pp. 409-464). NY: Wiley.

McConaghy, N. (1998). *Sexual behavior: Problems and management.* 2nd edition. NY: Plenum.

McConaghy, N., Blaszczynski, A., & Kidson, W. (1988). Treatment of sex offenders with imaginal desensitization and/or medroxyprogesterone. *Acta Psychiatrica Scandinavica, 77,* 199-206.

McCord, W., & McCord, J. (1964). *The psychopath: An essay on the criminal mind.* New York: Van Nostrand-Reinhold.

McCormick, N.B. (1999). When pleasure causes pain: Living with interstitial cystitis. *Sexuality and Disability, 17,* 7-18.

McCrady, B.S. (1985). Alcoholism. In D.H. Barlow (Ed.), *Clinical handbook of psychological disorders.* New York: Guilford.

McCrady, B.S., & Epstein, E.E. (1998). Directions for research on alcoholic relationships: Marital- and individual-based models of heterogeneity. *Psychology of Addictive Behaviors, 9,* 157-166.

McCrady, B.S., Noel, N.E., Abrams, D.B., Stout, R.L., Nelson, H.F., & Hay, W.M. (1986). Comparative effectiveness of three types of spouse involvement in outpatient behavioral alcoholism treatment. *Journal of Studies on Alcohol, 47,* 459-467.

McCrady, B.S., Stout, R., Noel, N., Abrams, D., & Nelson, H.F. (1991). Effectiveness of three types of spouse-involved behavioral alcoholism treatment. *British Journal of the Addictions, 86,* 1415-1424.

McCrady, B.S., Stout, R.L., Noel, N.E., Abrams, D.B., & Nelson, H.F. (in press). Comparative effectiveness of three types of spouse involved behavioral alcoholism treatment: Outcomes 18 months after treatment. *British Journal of Addictions.*

McCrae, R.R., & Costa, P.T., Jr. (1990). *Personality in adulthood.* New York: Guilford.

McCreary Centre Society. (1999). *Adolescent health survey II: Province of British Columbia.* Vancouver: The McCreary Centre Society.

McCreary, D.R., Newcomb, M.D., & Sadava, S.W. (1999). The male role, alcohol use, and alcohol problems: A structural modeling examination in adult women and men. *Journal of Counseling Psychology, 46*, 109-124.

McCreary, D.R., & Sadava, S.W. (1998). Stress, drinking, and the adverse consequences of drinking in two samples of young adults. *Psychology of Addictive Behaviors, 12*, 247-261.

McCusker, J., Boulenger, J-P., Boyer, R., Bellavance, F., & Miller, J-M. (1997). Use of health services for anxiety disorders: A multisite study in Quebec. *Canadian Journal of Psychiatry, 42*, 730-736.

McCusker, J., Cole, M., Abrahamowicz, M., Primeau, F., & Belzile, E. (2002). Delirium predicts 12-month mortality. *Archives of Internal Medicine, 162*, 457-463.

McCusker, J., Cole, M., Dendukuri, N., Belzile, E., & Primeau, F. (2001). Delirium in older medical inpatients and subsequent cognitive and functional status: A prospective study. *Canadian Medical Association Journal, 165*, 575-583.

McDowell, I., et al. (2002). Patterns and health effects of caring for people with dementia: The impact of changing cognitive and residential status. *Gerontologist, 42*, 643-652.

McEvoy, M., & Daniluk, J. (1995). Wounds to the soul: The experiences of aboriginal women survivors of sexual abuse. *Canadian Psychology, 36,* 221-235.

McNally, R.J., Kaspi, S.P., Riemann, B.C., & Zeitlin, S.B. (1990). Selective processing of threat cues in panic disorder. *Behaviour Research and Therapy, 28*, 407-412.

McDonald, R. (1980). Clomimpramine and exposure for obsessive-compulsive rituals — I. *British Journal of Psychiatry, 136,* 1-25.

McDougle, C.J., Goodman, W.K., Leckman, J.F., Lee, N.C., Heninger, G.R., & Price, L.H. (1994). Haloperidal addition in fluvoxamine-refractory obsessive-compulsive disorder: A double-blind, placebo controlled study in patients with and without tics. *Archives of General Psychiatry, 51,* 302-308.

McDougle, C.J., Naylor, S.T., Volkmar, F.R., Heninger, G.R., & Price, L.H. (1996). A double-blind placebo-controlled study of fluvoxamine in adults with autistic disorder. *Archives* of General Psychiatry, 53, 1001-1008.

McEachin, J.J., Smith, T., & Lovaas, O.I. (1993). Long-term outcome for children with autism who received early intensive behavioral treatment. *American Journal on Mental Retardation, 97,* 359-372.

McEvoy, M., & Daniluk, J. (1995). Wounds to the soul: The experiences of aboriginal women survivors of sexual abuse. *Canadian Psychology, 36,* 221-235.

McEwen, B.S. (1998). Protective and damaging effects of stress mediators. *New England Journal of Medicine, 338,* 171-179.

McFall, R.M., & Hammen, C.L. (1971). Motivation, structure, and self-monitoring: Role of nonspecific factors in smoking reduction. *Journal of Consulting and Clinical Psychology, 37,* 80-86.

McFall, R.M., & Lillesand, D.B. (1971). Behavior rehearsal with modeling and coaching in assertion training. *Journal of Abnormal Psychology, 77,* 313-323.

McFarlane, T., Polivy, J., & Herman, C.P. (1998). Effects of false weight feedback on mood, self-evaluation, and food intake in restrained and unrestrained eaters. *Journal of Abnormal Psychology, 107,* 312-318.

McFarlane, T., Polivy, J., & McCabe, R.E. (1999). Help, not harm: Psychological foundation for a nondieting approach toward health. *Journal of Social Issues, 55*, 261-276.

McGee, R., & Feehan, M. (1991). Are girls with problems of attention underrecognized? *Journal of Psychopathology and Behavioral Assessment, 13,* 187-198.

McGhie, A., & Chapman, I.S. (1961). Disorders of attention and perception in early schizophrenia. *British Journal of Medical Psychology, 34,* 103-116.

McGlashan, T. H., Zipursky, R.B., Perkins, D., Addington, J., Miller, T.J. et al. (2003). The PRIME North America randomized double-blind clinical trial of olanzapine versus placebo in patients at risk of being prodromally symptomatic for psychosis: I. Study rationale and design. *Schizophrenia Research, 61*, 7-18.

McGlynn, F.D. (1994). Simple phobia. In M. Hersen & R.T. Ammerman (Eds.), *Handbook of prescriptive treatments for adults* (pp. 179-196). New York: Plenum.

McGlynn, F.D., Karg, S., & Lawyer, S.R. (2003). Fear responses to mock magnetic resonance imaging among college students: Toward a prototype experiment. *Journal of Anxiety Disorders, 17*, 335-347.

McGrady, A.V., & Bernal, G.A.A. (1986). Relaxation-based treatment of stress induced syncope. *Journal of Behavior Therapy and Experimental Psychiatry, 17,* 23-27.

McGregor, M.J., Wiebe, E., Marion, S.A., & Livingstone, C. (2000). Why don't more women report sexual assault to the police? *Canadian Medical Association Journal, 162*, 659-660.

McGue, M., Pickens, R.W., & Svikis, D.S. (1992). Sex and age effects on the inheritance of alcohol problems: A twin study. *Journal of Abnormal Psychology, 101,* 3-17.

McGuiness, D. (1981). Auditory and motor aspects of language development in males and females. In A. Ansara (Ed.), *Sex differences in dyslexia.* Towson, MD: The Orton Dyslexia Society.

McGuire, J., Nieri, D., Abbott, D., Sheridan, K., et al. (1995). Do Tarasoff principles apply in AIDS-related psychotherapy? Ethical decision making and the role of therapist homophobia and perceived client dangerousness. *Professional Psychology: Research and Practice, 26,* 608-611.

McGuire, R.J., Carlisle, J.M., & Young, B.G. (1965). Sexual deviations as conditioned behaviour: A hypothesis. *Behaviour Research and Therapy, 2,* 185-190.

McIntosh, J.L. (1995). Suicide prevention in the elderly (65-99). In M.M. Silverman & R.W. Maris (Eds.), *Suicide prevention toward the year 2000* (pp. 180-192). New York: Guilford.

McIntosh, J.L., Santos, J.F., Hubbard, R.W., & Overholser, J.C. (1994). *Elder suicide: Research, theory, and treatment*. Washington, DC: American Psychological Association.

McIntyre-Kingsolver, K., Lichtenstein, E., & Mermelstein, R.J. (1986). Spouse training in a multicomponent smoking-cessation program. *Behavior Therapy, 17,* 67-74.

McKay, D., Nezeroglu, F., & Yaryura-Tobias, J.A. (1997). Comparison of clinical characteristics in obsessive-compulsive disorder and body dysmorphic disorder. *Journal of Anxiety Disorders, 11,* 447-454.

McKee, S.A., Hinson, R.E., Wall, A-M., & Spriel, P. (1998). Alcohol outcome expectancies and coping styles as predictors of alcohol use in young adults. *Addictive Behaviors, 23,* 17-22.

McKeon, P., & Murray, R. (1987). Familial aspects of obsessive-compulsive neurosis. *British Journal of Psychiatry, 151,* 528-534.

McKibben, A., Proulx, J., & Lusignan, R. (1994). Relationships between conflict, affect, and deviant sexual behaviors in rapists and pedophiles. *Behaviour Research and Therapy, 32,* 571-575.

McKim, W.A. (1991). *Drugs and behavior: An introduction to behavioral pharmacology*. Englewood Cliffs, NJ: Prentice-Hall.

McLarnon, L.D., & Kaloupek, D.G. (1988). Psychological investigation of genital herpes recurrence: Prospective assessment and cognitive-behavioral intervention for a chronic physical disorder. *Health Psychology, 7,* 231-249.

McLean, L.K., Brady, N.C., & McLean, J.E. (1996). Reported communication abilities of individuals with severe mental retardation. *American Journal on Mental Retardation, 100,* 580-591.

McMain, S., Korman, L.M., & Dimeff, L. (2001). Dialectical behavior therapy and the treatment of emotion dysregulation. *Journal of Clinical Psychology, 57,* 183-196.

McMullen, L.M. (1999). Metaphors in the talk of "depressed" women in psychotherapy. *Canadian Psychology, 40,* 102-111.

McMullen, S., & Rosen, R.C. (1979). Self-administered masturbation training in the treatment of primary orgasmic dysfunction. *Journal of Consulting and Clinical Psychology, 47,* 912-918.

McNally, R.J. (1994). *Panic disorder: A critical analysis*. New York: Guilford.

McNally, R.J. (1997). Atypical phobias. In G.C.L. Davey (Ed.), *Phobias: A handbook of theory, research and treatment*. (pp. 183-199). Chichester,UK: Wiley.

McNally, R.J., Caspi, S.P., Riemann, B.C., & Zeitlin, S.B. (1990). Selective processing of threat cues in posttraumatic stress disorder. *Journal of Abnormal Psychology, 99,* 398-406.

McNeal, E.T., & Cimbolic, P. (1986). Antidepressants and biochemical theories of depression. *Psychological Bulletin, 99,* 361-374.

McNeil, E. (1967). *The quiet furies*. Englewood Cliffs, NJ: Prentice-Hall.

McNulty, J.L., Graham, J.R., Ben-Porath, Y.S., & Stein, L.A.R. (1997). Comparative validity of MMPI-II scales of African-American and Caucasian mental health center clients. *Psychological Assessment, 9,* 464-470.

McVey, G.L., & Davis, R. (2002). A program to promote positive body image: A 1-year follow-up evaluation. *Journal of Early Adolescence, 22,* 96-108.

McVey, G.L., Lieberman, M., Voorberg, N., Wardrope, D., & Blackmore, E. (2003). School-based peer support groups: A new approach to the prevention of disordered eating. *Eating Disorders, 11,* 169-186.

McVey, G.L., Lieberman, M., Voorberg, N., Wardrope, D., Blackmore, E., & Tweed, S. (2003). Replication of a peer support program designed to prevent disordered eating: Is a life skills approach sufficient for all middle school students? *Eating Disorders, 11,* 187-195.

McVey, G.L., Tweed, S., & Blackmore, E. (2004). Dieting among preadolescent and young adolescent females. *Canadian Medical Associaton Journal, 170,* 1559-1561.

Meador, D.M. & Ellis, N.R. (1987). Automatic and effortful processing by mentally retarded and nonretarded persons. *American Journal of Mental Deficiency, 91,* 613-619.

Meana, M., Binik, I., Khalife, S., & Cohen, D. (1998). Affect and marital adjustment in women's ratings of dyspareunic pain. *Canadian Journal of Psychiatry, 43,* 381-385.

Meana, M., Binik, Y.M., Khalife, S., & Cohen, D. (1997). Dyspareunia: Sexual dysfunction or pain syndrome? *Journal of Nervous and Mental Disease, 185,* 561-569.

Medical Research Council of Canada (1987). Guidelines on Research Involving Human Subjects. Ottawa: Medical Research Council of Canada.

Mednick, S.A., Gabrielli, W.F., & Hutchings, B. (1984). Genetic influences in criminal convictions: Evidence from an adoption cohort. *Science, 224,* 891-894.

Mednick, S.A., Huttonen, M.O., & Machon, R.A. (1994). Prenatal influenza infections and adult schizophrenia. *Schizophrenia Bulletin, 20,* 263-268.

Mednick, S.A., Machon, R., Hottunen, M.O., & Bonett, D. (1988). Fetal viral infection and adult schizophrenia. *Archives of General Psychiatry, 45,* 189-192.

Mednick, S.A., & Schulsinger, F. (1968). Some premorbid characteristics related to breakdown in children with schizophrenic mothers. In D. Rosenthal & S.S. Kety (Eds.), *The transmission of schizophrenia*. Elmsford, NY: Pergamon.

Medvedev, Z. (1972). *A question of madness*. New York: Knopf.

Meehl, P.E. (1962). Schizotaxia, schizotypy, schizophrenia. *American Psychologist, 17,* 827-838.

Meehl, P.E. (1986). Diagnostic taxa as open concepts: Methodological and statistical questions about reliability and construct validity in the grand strategy of nosological revision. In T. Millon & G.L. Klerman (Eds.), *Contemporary directions in psychopathology*. New York: Wiley.

Meichenbaum, D.H. (1969). The effects of instructions and reinforcement on thinking and language behaviours of schizophrenics. *Behaviour Research and Therapy, 7,* 101-114.

Meichenbaum, D.H. (1971). Examination of model characteristics in reducing avoidance behavior. *Journal of Personality and Social Psychology, 17,* 298-307.

Meichenbaum, D.H. (1973). Cognitive factors in behavior modification: Modifying what clients say to themselves. In C. M. Franks & G. T. Wilson (Eds.), *Annual review of behavior therapy: Theory and practice* (pp. 416-432). New York: Brunner/Mazel.

Meichenbaum, D.H. (1977). *Cognitive-behavior modification.* New York : Plenum Press.

Meichenbaum, D. H. (1985). *Stress-inoculation training: A clinical guidebook.* New York: Pergamon Press.

Meichenbaum, D. H. (1993). Stress-inoculation training: A twenty-year update. In R.L. Woolfolk & P. M. Lehrer (Eds.), *Principles and practice of stress management* (2nd ed. pp. 152-174). New York: Guilford Press.

Meichenbaum, D. H. (1994). *A clinical handbook/practical therapist manual for assessing and treating adults with posttraumatic stress disorder.* Waterloo, Ontario, Canada: Institute Press. (Republished as: Meichenbaum, D. H. (1997). *Treating post-traumatic stress disorder: A handbook and practice manual for therapy.* Chichester : John Wiley & Sons.)

Meichenbaum, D. (1995). Cognitive behavioral therapy in historical perspective. In B. Bongar & L. Beutler (Eds.), *Comprehensive textbook of psychotherapy* (pp. 141-158). New York: Oxford University Press.

Meichenbaum, D. (2003). Every parent's worst nightmare. In J. A. Kottler & J. Carlson (Eds.), *The mummy at the dining room table: Eminent therapists reveal their most unusual cases* (pp. 299-304). San Francisco: Jossey-Bass.

Meichenbaum, D.H., & Asarnow, J. (1979). Cognitive-behavioral modification and metacognitive development: Implications for the classroom. In P.C. Kendall & S.D. Hollon (Eds.), *Cognitive-behavioral interventions: Theory, research, and procedures.* New York: Academic Press.

Meichenbaum, D.H., & Butler, (1980). Cognitive ethology : Assessing the streams of cognition and emotion. In K.R., Blankstein, P.Pliner, & J. Polivy (Eds.) (1980). *Advances in the study of communication and affect, Vol.6: Assessment and modification of emotional behavior* (pp. 139-163). New York and London: Plenum.

Meichenbaum, D.H., & Cameron, R. (1981). Issues in cognitive assessment: An overview. In T. Merluzzi, C. R. Glass, & M. Genest (Eds.), *Cognitive assessment* (pp. 3-15). New York: Guilford Press.

Meichenbaum, D. H., & Deffenbacher, J. L. (1988). Stress inoculation training. *Counseling Psychologist, 16,* 69-90.

Meichenbaum, D. H., & Jaremko, M. (1983). *Stress management and prevention: A cognitive-behavioral perspective.* New York: Plenum Press.

Meichenbaum, D. H., & Turk, D. (1976). The cognitive-behavioral management of anxiety, angerr, and pain. In P. O. Davidson (Ed.), *The behavioral management of anxiety, depression, and pain* (pp. 1-34). New York: Brunner/Mazel.

Meichenbaum, D. H., Turk, D., & Burstein, S. (1975). The nature of coping with stress. In I. G. Sarason & C. D. Spielberger (Eds.), *Stress and anxiety* (Vol. 2, pp. 337-360). New York: Wiley.

Meissner, D. (2000). Montreux Clinic for eating disorders was under investigation when license surrendered. *The Canadian Press*, August 29.

Melamed, B.G., Hawes, R.R., Heiby, E., & Glick, J. (1975). Use of filmed modeling to reduce uncooperative behavior of children during dental treatment. *Journal of Dental Research, 54,* 797-801.

Melamed, B.G., & Siegel, L.J. (1975). Reduction of anxiety in children facing hospitalization and surgery by use of filmed modeling. *Journal of Consulting and Clinical Psychology, 43,* 511-521.

Mellinger, G.D., Balter, M.B., & Uhlenhuth, E.H. (1985). Insomnia and its treatment. *Archives of General Psychiatry, 42,* 225-232.

Mello, N.K., & Mendelson, J.H. (1970). Experimentally induced intoxication in alcoholics: A comparison between programmed and spontaneous drinking. *Journal of Pharmacology and Experimental Therapy, 173,* 101.

Mellor, C.S. (1970). First rank symptoms of schizophrenia. *British Journal of Psychiatry, 117,* 15-23.

Melman, A., & Rossman, B. (1989). *Penile vein ligation for corporal incompetence: An evaluation of short and long term results.* Paper presented at the 15th Annual Meeting of the International Academy of Sex Research, Princeton. As cited in Wincze & Carey (1991).

Melnick, S.M. & Hinshaw, S.P. (1996). What they want and what they get: The social goals of boys with ADHD and comparison boys. *Journal of Abnormal Child Psychology, 24,* 169-185.

Meltzer, H.Y., Alps, L., Green, A.I., Altamura, C., Anand, R., Bertoldi, A., Bourgeois, M., Chouinard, G., et al. (2003). Clozapine treatment for suicidality in schizophrenia: International Suicide Prevention Trial (InterSept). *Archives of General Psychiatry, 60,* 82-91.

Melzack, R. (1998). Pain and stress: Clues toward understanding chronic pain. In M. Sabourin & F. I. M. Craik (Eds.), *Advances in psychological science, Vol. 2: Biological and cognitive aspects* (pp. 63-85). Hove, England: Psychology Press/Erlbaum (UK) Taylor and Francis.

Melzack, R. (1999). From the gate to the neuromatrix. *Pain, Supplement 6,* S121-S126.

Melzack, R., & Wall, P.D. (1965). Pain mechanisms: A new theory. *Science, 150,* 971-979.

Melzack, R., & Wall, P.D. (1982). *The challenge of pain.* New York: Basic Books.

Meltzer, H.Y. (1998). Suicide in schizophrenia: Risk factors and clozapine treatment. *Journal of Clinical Psychiatry, 59,* 15-20.

Mendels, J. (1970). Concepts of depression. New York: Wiley.

Mendels, J., Stinnett, J.L., Burns, D., & Frazer, A. (1975). Amine precursors and depression. *Archives of General Psychiatry, 32,* 22-30.

Menditto, A.A., Valdes, L.A., & Beck, N.C. (1994). Implementing a comprehensive social-learning program within the forensic psychiatric service of Fulton State Hospital. In P.W. Corrigan & R.P. Liberman (Eds.), *Behavior therapy in psychiatric hospitals.* (pp. 61-78). New York: Springer.

Mendlewicz, J., & Rainer, J.D. (1977). Adoption study supporting genetic transmission in manic-depressive illness. *Nature, 268,* 327-329.

Mendlowicz, M.V., & Stein, M.B. (2000). Quality of life in individuals with anxiety disorders. *American Journal of Psychiatry, 157,* 669-682.

Mendlowitz, S.L., et al. (1999). Cognitive-behavioral group treatments in childhood anxiety disorders: The role of parental involvement. *Journal of the American Academy of Child and Adolescent Psychiatry, 38,* 1223-1229.

Mendonca, J.D., Velamoor, V.R., & Sauve, D. (1996). Key features of maltreatment of the infirm elderly in home settings. *Canadian Journal of Psychiatry, 41,* 107-113.

Menzies, R., & Webster, C.D. (1995). Construction and validation of risk assessments in a six-year follow-up of forensic patients: A tridimensional analysis. *Journal of Consulting and Clinical Psychology, 63,* 766-778.

Merali, N. (1999). Resolution of value conflicts in multicultural counseling. *Canadian Journal of Counselling, 33,* 28-36.

Mercado, A.C., Carroll, L.J., Cassidy, J.D., & Cote, P. (2000). Coping with neck and low back pain in the general population. *Health Psychology, 19,* 333-338.

Merckelbach, H., de Ruiter, C., van den Hout, M.A., & Hoekstra, R. (1989). Conditioning experiences and phobias. *Behaviour Research and Therapy, 27,* 657-662.

Merikangas, K.R., Mehta, R.L., Molnar, B.E., Walters, E.E., Swendsen, J.D., Aguilar-Gaziola, J.J., DeWit, D.J., Kolody, B., Vega, W.A., Wittchen, H-U., & Kessler, K. (1998). Comorbidity of substance use disorders with mood and anxiety disorders: Results of the International Consortium in Psychiatric Epidemiology. *Addictive Behaviors, 23,* 893-907.

Merikangas, K.R., Stolar, M., Stevens, D.E., Goulet, J., Preisig, M.A., et al. (1998). Familial transmission of substance use disorders. *Archives of General Psychiatry, 55,* 973-981.

Merrill, E.C. & McCauley, C. (1988). Phasic alertness and differences in picture encoding speed. *American Journal of Mental Retardation, 93,* 245-249.

Merrill, E.C. & O'Dekirk, J.M. (1994). Visual selective attention and mental retardation. *Cognitive neuropsychology, 11,* 117-132.

Merzenich, M.M., Jenkins, W.M., Johnson, P., Schreiner, C., Miller, S.L., & Tallal, P. (1996). Temporal processing deficits of language-learning impaired children ameliorated by training. *Science, 271,* 77-81.

Meshefedjian, G., McCusker, J., Bellavance, F., & Baumgarten, M. (1998). Factors associated with symptoms of depression among informal caregivers of demented elders in the community. *Gerontologist, 38,* 247-253.

Messer, S.B., Sass, L.A., & Woolfolk, R.L. (Eds.). *Hermeneutics and psychological theory: Integrative perspectives on personality, psychotherapy and psychopathology.* New Brunswick, NJ: Rutgers University Press.

Meston, C.M., & Gorzalka, B.B. (1996). Differential effects of sympathetic activation on sexual arousal in sexually dysfunctional and functional women. *Journal of Abnormal Psychology, 105,* 582-591.

Metalsky, G.I., Halberstadt, L.J., & Abramson, L.Y. (1987). Vulnerability and invulnerability to depressive mood reactions: Toward a more powerful test of the diathesis-stress and causal mediation components of the reformulated theory of depression. *Journa! of Personality and Social Psychology, 52,* 386-393.

Metalsky, G.I., Joiner, T.E., Hardin, T.S., & Abramson, L.Y. (1993). Depressive reactions to failure in a natural setting: A test of the hopelessness and self-esteem theories of depression. *Journal of Abnormal Psychology, 102,* 101-109.

Metalsky, G.I., Joiner, T.E., Wonderlich, S.A., Beatty, W.W., Staton, R.D., et al. (1997). When will bulimics be depressed and when not? The moderating role of attributional style. *Cognitive Therapy and Research, 21,* 61-72.

Metz, M.E., Pryor, J.L., Nesvacil, L.J., Abuzzahab, F., et al. (1997). Premature ejaculation: A psychophysiological review. *Journal of Sex and Marital Therapy, 23,* 3-23.

Meyer, G.J. (1997). Thinking clearly about reliability: More critical corrections regarding the Rorschach Comprehensive System. *Psychological Assessment, 9,* 495-498.

Meyer, I. (1995). Minority stress and mental health in gay men. *Journal of Health Sciences and Social Behavior, 36,* 38-56.

Meyer, J.J., & Reter, D.J. (1979). Sex reassignment follow-up. *Archives of General Psychiatry, 36,* 1010-1015.

Meyer, J.K. (1995). Paraphilias. In H.I. Kaplan & B.J. Sadock (Eds.), *Comprehensive textbook of psychiatry* (pp. 1334-1347). Baltimore: Williams & Wilkins.

Meyer, V. (1966). Modification of expectations in cases with obsessional rituals. *Behaviour Research and Therapy, 4,* 273-280.

Meyer, V., & Chesser, E.S. (1970). *Behavior therapy in clinical psychiatry.* Baltimore: Penguin.

Meyerowitz, B.E., & Chaiken, S. (1987). The effect of message framing on breast self-examination attitudes, intentions, and behavior. *Journal of Personality and Social Psychology, 52,* 500-510.

Meyerowitz, B.E., Richardson, J., Hudson, S., & Leedham, B. (1998). Ethnicity and cancer outcomes: Behavioral and psychosocial considerations. *Psychological Bulletin, 123,* 47-70.

Mezzich, A.C., Moss, H., Tarter, R.E., Wolfenstein, M., et al. (1994). Gender differences in the pattern and progression of substance use in conduct disordered adolescents. *American Journal on Addiction, 3* , 289-295.

Mhatre, S.L., & Deber, R.B. (1992). From equal access to health care to equitable access to health: A review of Canadian provincial health commissions and reports. *International Journal of Health Services, 22,* 645-668.

Michelson, L., Mavissakalian, M., & Marchione, K. (1985). Cognitive and behavioral treatments of agoraphobia: Clinical, behavioral, and psychophysiological treatments of agoraphobia. *Journal of Consulting and Clinical Psychology, 53,* 913-925.

Michelson, L., Sugai, D.P., Wood, R.P., & Kazdin, A.E. (1983). *Social skills as-*

sessment and training with children: An empirically based handbook. New York: Plenum.

Mikulincer, M., & Solomon, Z. (1988). Attributional style and post-traumatic stress disorder. *Journal of Abnormal Psychology, 97*, 308-313.

Miklowitz, D.J. (1985). *Family interaction and illness outcome in bipolar and schizophrenic patients*. Unpublished Ph.D. thesis, University of California at Los Angeles.

Miklowitz, D.J., Simoneau, T.L., Sachs-Ericsson, N., Warner, R., & Suddath, R. (1996). Family risk indicators in the course of bipolar affective disorder. In E. Mundt et al. (Eds.), *Interpersonal factors in the origin and course of affective disorders* . (pp. 204-217). London: Gaskell Press.

Mikulincer, M., & Solomon, Z. (1988). Attributional style and posttraumatic stress disorder. *Journal of Abnormal Psychology, 97*, 308-313.

Milberger, S. (1997, October). *Impact of adversity on functioning and comorbidity of girls with ADHD*. Paper presented at the American Academy of Child and Adolescent Psychiatry, Toronto, Canada.

Milberger, S., Biederman, J., Faraone, S. V., & Chen, L. (1996) Is maternal smoking during pregnancy a risk factor for attention deficit hyperactivity disorder in children? *American Journal of Psychiatry, 153*, 1138-1142.

Miles, L.E., & Dement, W.C. (1980). Sleep and aging. *Sleep, 3*, 119-220.

Milin, R., Walker, S., & Chow, J. (2003). Major depressive disorder in adolescence: A brief review of the recent treatment literature. *Canadian Journal of Psychiatry, 48*, 600-606.

Miller, A., Lee, S.K., Raina, P., Klassen, A., Zupancic, J., & Olsen, L. (1998). *A review of therapies for attention-deficit hyperactivity disorder*. Ottawa: Canadian Coordinating Office For Health Technology Assessment.

Miller, A.C., Rathus, J.H., Linehan, M.M., Wetzler, S., & Leigh, E. (1997). Dialectical behavior therapy adapted for suicidal adolescents. *Journal of Practice Psychology and Behavioral Health*, 78-86.

Miller, H.R. (1981). Psychiatric morbidity in elderly surgical patients. *British Journal of Psychiatry, 128*, 17-20.

Miller, J. R. (1996). Shingwauk's vision: A history of native residential schools. Toronto: University of Toronto Press.

Miller, M.A., & Rahe, R.H. (1997). Life changes scaling for the 1990s. *Journal of Psychosomatic Research, 43*, 279-292.

Miller, N.E. (1948). Studies of fear as an acquirable drive: I. Fear as motivation and fear-reduction as reinforcement in the learning of new responses. *Journal of Experimental Psychology, 38*, 89-101.

Miller, N.E. (1959). Liberalization of basic S-R concepts: Extensions to conflict behavior, motivation, and social learning. In S. Koch (Ed.), *Psychology: A study of a science* (Vol. 2). New York: McGraw-Hill.

Miller, N.S. (1995). History and review of contemporary addiction treatment. *Alcoholism Treatment Quarterly, 12*, 1-22.

Miller, S.B. (1994). Parasympathetic nervous system control of heart rate responses to stress in offspring of hypertensives. *Psychophysiology, 31*, 11-16.

Miller, S.O. (1989). Optical differences in cases of multiple personality disorder. *Journal of Nervous and Mental Disease, 177*, 480-487.

Miller, T.Q., & Volk, R.J. (1996). Weekly marijuana use as a risk factor for initial cocaine use.: Results from a six wave national survey. *Journal of Chld and Adolescent Substance Abuse, 5*, 55-78.

Miller, W.R., & Hester, R.K. (1986). Inpatient alcoholism treatment: Who benefits? *American Psychologist, 41*, 794-805.

Miller, W.R., & Rollnick, S.(Eds). (1991). *Motivational interviewing: Preparing people to change addictive behavior*. New York: Guilford.

Miller, W.R., Zweben, A., DiClemente, C.C., & Rychtarik, R.G. (1992). Motivational Enhancement Therapy manual: A clinical research guide for therapists treating individuals with alcohol abuse and dependence. *NIAA Project MATCH Monograph, Vol. 2*, DHHS Publication No. (ADM) 92-1894.

Millon, T.H. (1994). *Manual for the Millon Clinical Multiaxial Inventory-III (MCMI-III) (3rd ed.)*. Minneapolis: National Computer Systems.

Millon, T. H. (1996). *Disorders of personality: DSM-IV and beyond*. (2nd ed.). New York: Wiley.

Mills, J.S., Polivy, J., Herman, C.P., & Tiggemann, M. (2002). Effects of exposure to thin media images: Evidence of self-enhancement among restrained eaters. *Personality and Social Psychology Bulletin, 28*, 1687-1699.

Millsaps, C.L., Azrin, R.L., & Mittenberg, W. (1994). Neuropsychological effects of chronic cannabis use on the memory and intelligence of adolescents. *Journal of Child and Adolescent Substance Abuse, 3*, 47-55.

Milton, F., & Hafner, J. (1979). The outcome of behavior therapy for agoraphobia in relation to marital adjustment. *Archives of General Psychiatry, 36*, 807-811.

Minde, K., Eakin, L., Hechtman, L., Ochs, E., Bouffard, R., Greenfield, B., & Looper, K. (2003). The psychosocial functioning of children and spouses of adults with ADHD. *Journal of Child Psychology and Psychiatry and Allied Disciplines, 44*, 637-646.

Mineka, S. (1992). Evolutionary memories, emotional processing, and the emotional disorders. In D. Medin (Ed.), *The psychology of learning and motivation* (Vol. 28). New York: Academic Press.

Mineka, S., & Zinbarg, R. (1996). *Perspectives on anxiety, panic, and fear. In Nebraska symposium on motivation*. (pp. 135-210). Lincoln: University of Nebraska Press.

Mintz, A.R., Dobson, K.S., & Romney, D.M. (2003). Insight in schizophrenia: A meta-analysis. *Schizophrenia Research, 61*, 75-88.

Mintz, E. (1967). Time-extended marathon groups. *Psychotherapy, 4*, 65-70.

Mintz, M. (1991). Tobacco roads: Delivering death to the third world. *Progressive, 55*, 24-29.

Mintz, R.S. (1968). Psychotherapy of the suicidal patient. In H.L.P. Resnik (Ed.), *Suicidal behaviors*. Boston: Little, Brown.

Minuchin, S., Baker, L., Rosman, B.L., Lieberman, R., Milman, L., & Todd, T.C. (1975). A conceptual model of psychosomatic illness in children. *Archives of General Psychiatry, 32*, 1031-1038.

Miranda, J., Gross, J.J., Persons, J.B., & Hahn, J. (1998). Mood matters: Negative mood induction activates dysfunctional attitudes in women vulnerable to depression. *Cognitive Therapy and Research, 22*, 363-376.

Miranda, J., & Persons, J.B. (1988). Dysfunctional thoughts are mood-state dependent. *Journal of Abnormal Psychology, 97*, 237-241.

Mireault, M., & deMan, A.F. (1996). Suicidal ideation among the elderly: Personality variables, stress and social support. *Social Behavior and Personality, 24*, 385-392.

Mirenda, P.L., Donnellan, A.M., & Yoder, D.E. (1983). Gaze behavior: A new look at an old problem. *Journal of Autism and Developmental Disorders, 13*, 397-409.

Mirsky, A.F., Bieliauskas, L.A., French, L.M., Van Kammen, D.P., Jonsson, E., & Sedvall, G. (2000). A 39-year followup of the Genain quadruplets. *Schizophrenia Bulletin, 26*, 699-708.

Mirsky, A. F. & Quinn, O. W. (1988). The Genain quadruplets. *Schizophrenia Bulletin, 14*, 595-612.

Mischel, W. (1968). *Personality and assessment*. New York: Wiley.

Mischel, W. (1977). On the future of personality assessment. *American Psychologist, 32*, 246-254.

Mishara, B.L. (1999). Suicide in the Montreal subway system: Characteristics of the victims, antecedents, and implications for prevention. *Canadian Journal of Psychiatry, 44*, 690-696.

Mishkind, M.E., Rodin, J., Silberstein, L.R., & Striegel-Moore, R.H. (1986). The embodiment of masculinity: Cultural, psychological, and behavioral dimensions. *American Behavioral Scientist, 29*, 545-562.

Mitchell, B. (2004, April 23). Teen killer gets life sentence: Decision ends landmark case. *The Toronto Star*, B1.

Mitchell, J., McCauley, E., Burke, P.M., & Moss, S.J. (1988). Phenomenology of depression in children and adolescents. *Journal of the American Academy of Child and Adolescent Psychiatry, 27*, 12-20.

Mitchell, J.E. (1992). Subtyping of bulimia nervosa. *International Journal of Eating Disorders, 11*, 327-332.

Mitchell, J.E., & Pyle, R.L. (1985). Characteristics of bulimia. In J.E. Mitchell (Ed.), *Anorexia nervosa and bulimia: Diagnosis and treatment*. Minneapolis: University of Minnesota Press.

Mitchell, T.L., Griffin, K., Stewart, S.H., & Loba, P. (2004). "We will never ever forget": The Swissair flight 111 disaster and its impact on volunteers and communities. *Journal of Health Psychology, 9*, 245-262.

Mittleman, M.A., Maclure, M., Sherwood, J.B., Murly, R.P., Tofler, G.A., et al., (1997). Triggering of acute myocardial infarction onset by episodes of anger. *Circulation, 92*, 1720-1725.

Modestin, J. (1987). Quality of interpersonal relationships: The most characteristic DSM-III BPD characteristic. *Comprehensive Psychiatry, 28*, 397-

402.

Moen, P. (1996). Gender, age, and the life course. In R. H. Binstock & L. K. George (Eds.), *Handbook of aging and the social sciences* (4th ed.) (pp. 171-187). San Diego, CA: Academic Press.

Moffatt, M.E.K., Kato, C., & Pless, I.B. (1987). Improvements in self-concept after treatment of nocturnal enuresis: Randomized controlled trial. *The Journal of Pediatrics, 110,* 647-652.

Moffitt, T.E. (1990). Juvenile delinquency and attention deficit disorder: Boys' developmental trajectories from age 13 to 15. *Child Development, 61,* 893-910.

Moffitt, T.E. (1993). Adolescence-limited and life-course-persistent antisocial behavior: A developmental taxonomy. *Psychological Review, 100,* 674-701.

Moffitt, T.E., Lynam, D., & Silva, P.A. (1994). Neuropsychological tests predict persistent male delinquency. *Criminology, 32,* 101-124.

Mohr, D.C., & Beutler, L.E. (1990). Erectile dysfunction: A review of diagnostic and treatment procedures. *Clinical Psychology Review, 10,* 123-150.

Mohr, J.W., Turner, R.E., & Jerry, M.B. (1964). *Pedophilia and exhibitionism.* Toronto: University of Toronto Press.

Monahan, J. (1973). The psychiatrization of criminal behavior. *Hospital and Community Psychiatry, 24,* 105-107.

Monahan, J. (1976). The prevention of violence. In J. Monahan (Ed.), *Community mental health and the criminal justice system.* Elmsford, NY: Pergamon.

Monahan, J. (1978). Prediction research and the emergency commitment of dangerous mentally ill persons: A reconsideration. *American Journal of Psychiatry, 135,* 198-201.

Monahan, J. (1984). The prediction of violent behavior: Toward a second generation of theory and policy. *American Journal of Psychiatry, 141,* 10-15.

Monahan, J. (1992). Mental disorder and violent behavior: Perceptions and evidence. *American Psychologist, 47,* 511-521.

Monahan, J. (1993). Limiting therapist exposure to Tarasoff liability: Guidelines for risk containment. *American Psychologist, 48,* 242-250.

Monahan, J., & Shah, S. (1989). Dangerousness and commitment of the mentally disordered in the United States. *Schizophrenia Bulletin, 15,* 541-553.

Monahan, J., & Steadman, H. (1994). Toward a rejuvenation of risk assessment research. In J. Monahan & H. Steadman (Eds.), *Violence and mental disorder: Developments in risk assessment.* Chicago: University of Chicago Press.

Moncton Times and Transcript. (1998, October 22). *New Brunswick Youth Centre*, A8.

Mongrain, M., Vetesse, L.C., Shuster, B., & Kendal, N. (1998). Perceptual biases, affect, and behavior in the relationships of dependents and self-critics. *Journal of Personality and Social Psychology*, *75*, 230-241.

Mongrain, M., & Zuroff, D.C. (1994). Ambivalence over emotional expression and negative life events: Mediators for depression in dependent and self-critical individuals. *Personality and Individual Differences*, *16*, 447-458.

Moniz, E. (1936). *Tentatives operatoires dans le traitement de ceretaines psychoses.* Paris: Mason.

Monroe, S.M., & Simons, A.D. (1991). Diathesis-stress theories in the context of life stress research: Implications for the depressive disorders. *Psychological Bulletin, 110,* 406-425.

Monson, R., & Smith, C.R. (1983). Current concepts in psychiatry: Somatization disorder in primary care. *New England Journal of Medicine, 308,* 1464-1465.

Morain, D. 1998. New state TV ads link smoking to impotence in men. *Los Angeles Times*, A3-A18.

Moran, C.C., & Massam, M.M. (1999). Differential influences of coping humor and humor bias on mood. *Behavioral Medicine*, *25*, 36-42.

Moran, M. (1991). Psychological factors affecting pulmonary and rheumatological diseases: A review. *Psychosomatics, 32,* 14-23.

Moreau, D., Mufson, L., Weissman, M.M., & Klerman, G.L. (1992). Interpersonal psychotherapy for adolescent depression: Description of modification and preliminary application. *Journal of the Academy of Child and Adolescent Psychiatry, 30,* 642-651.

Morenz, B., & Becker, J.V. (1995). The treatment of youthful sexual offenders. *Applied and Preventive Psychology, 4,* 247-256.

Moretti, M.M., Emmrys, C., Grizenko, N., Holland, R., Moore, K., Shamsie, J., & Hamilton, H. (1997). The treatment of conduct disorder: Perspectives across Canada. *Canadian Journal of Psychiatry*, *42*, 637-648.

Moretti, M.M., Rein, A.S, & Wiebe, V.J. (1998). Relational self-regulation: Gender differences in risk for dysphoria. *Canadian Journal of Behavioural Science*, *30*, 243-252.

Moretti, M.M., Segal, Z.V., McCann, C.D., Shaw, B.F., Miller, D.T., & Vella, D. (1996). Self-referent versus other-referent information processing in dysphoric, clinically depressed, and remitted depressed subjects. *Personality and Social Psychology Bulletin*, *22*, 68-80.

Morey, L.C. (1988). Personality disorders in DSM-III and DSM-IIIR: Convergence, coverage, and internal consistency. *American Journal of Psychiatry, 145,* 573-577.

Morey, L.C., Waugh, M.H., & Blashfield, R.K. (1985). MMPI scales for DSM-III personality disorders: Their derivation and correlates. *Journal of Personality Assessment, 49,* 245-251.

Morgan, C.A., Grillon, C., Lubin, H., & Southwick, S.M. (1997). Startle reflex abnormalities in women with sexual assault-related posttraumatic stress disorder. *American Journal of Psychiatry, 154,* 1076-1080.

Morgan, C.A., Grillon, C., Southwick, S.M., Davis, M., & Charney, D.S. (1996). Exaggerated acoustic startle reflex in Gulf War veterans with posttraumatic stress disorder. *American Journal of Psychiatry, 153,* 64-68.

Morgan, K. (1992). Sleep, insomnia, and mental health. *Reviews in Clinical Gerontology, 2,* 246-253.

Morgernstern, J., Langenbucher, J., Labouvie, E., & Miller, K.J. (1997). The comorbidity of alcoholism and personality disorders in a clinical population; Prevalence rates and relation to alcohol typology variables. *Journal of Abnormal Psychology, 106,* 74-84.

Mori, D., Pliner, P., & Chaiken, S. (1987). Eating lightly and the self-presentation of femininity. *Journal of Personality and Social Psychology*, *53*, 693-702.

Moriarty, D., Shore, R., & Maxim, N. (1990). Evaluation of an eating disorders curriculum. *Evaluation and Programme Planning*, *13*, 407-413.

Morin, C.M., & Azrin, N.H. (1988). Behavioral and cognitive treatments of geriatric insomnia. *Journal of Consulting and Clinical Psychology, 56,* 748-753.

Morin, C.M., Bastien, C.H., Brink, D., & Brown, T.R. (2003). Adverse effects of temazepam in older adults with chronic insomnia. *Human Psychopharmacology*, *18*, 75-82.

Morin, C.M., Bastien, C., Guay, B., Radouco-Thomas, M., Leblanc, J., & Vallieres, A. (2004). Randomized clinical trial of supervised tapering and cognitive behavior therapy to facilitate benzodiazepine discontinuation in older adults with chronic insomnia. *American Journal of Psychiatry*, *161*, 332-342.

Morin, C.M., Blais, F., & Savard, J. (2002). Are changes in beliefs and attitudes about sleep related to sleep improvements in the treatment of insomnia? *Behaviour Research and Therapy*, *40*, 741-752.

Morin, C.M., Colecchi, C., Stone, J., Sood, R., & Brink, D. (1999). Behavioral and pharmacological therapies for late-life insomnia: A randomized controlled trial. *Journal of the American Medical Association, 281,* 991-999.

Morin, C.M., & Gramling, S.E. (1989). Sleep patterns and aging: Comparisons of older adults with and without insomnia complaints. *Psychology and Aging*, *4*, 290-294.

Morley, S. (1997). Pain management. In A. Baum, S. Newman, J. Weinman, R. West, & C. McManus (Eds.), *Cambridge handbook of psychology, health and medicine*. (pp. 234-237). Cambridge, UK: Cambridge University Press.

Morokoff, P.J., & Gilliland, R. (1993). Stress, sexual functioning, and marital satisfaction. *Journal of Sex Research, 30,* 43-53.

Moroney, J.T., Tang, M-X., Berglund, L., Small, S., Merchant, C., et al. (1999). Low-density lipoprotein cholesterol and the risk of dementia with stroke. *JAMA, 282,* 254-260.

Morris, A.A. (1968). Criminal insanity. *Washington Review, 43,* 583-622.

Morris, N. (1966). Impediments to legal reform. *University of Chicago Law Review, 33,* 627-656.

Morris, N. (1968). Psychiatry and the dangerous criminal. *Southern California Law Review, 41,* 514-547.

Morrow, G.R., Leirer, V., & Sheikh, J. (1988). Adherence and medication instructions: Review and recommendations. *Journal of the American Geriatrics Society, 36,* 1147-1160.

Morse, R.M. (1988). Substance abuse among the elderly. *Bulletin of the Menninger Clinic, 52,* 259-268.

Morse, S.J. (1982a, June 23). In defense of the insanity defense. *Los Angeles Times.*

Morse, S.J. (1982b). Failed explanation and criminal responsibility: Experts and the unconscious. *Virginia Law Review, 678,* 971-1084.

Morse, S.J. (1982c). A preference for liberty: The case against involuntary commitment of the mentally disordered. *California Law Review, 70,* 54-106.

Morse, S.J. (1992). The "guilty mind": Mens rea. In D.K. Kagehiro & W.S. Laufer (Eds.), *Handbook of psychology and law* (pp. 207-229). New York: Springer-Verlag.

Morse, S.J. (1996). Blame and danger: An essay on preventive detention. *Boston University Law Review, 76,* 113-155.

Moscicki, E.K. (1995). Epidemiology of suicidal behavior. In M.M. Silverman & R.W. Maris (Eds.), *Suicide prevention: Toward the year 2000* (pp. 22-35). New York: Guilford.

Moser, C., & Levitt, E.E. (1987). An exploratory-descriptive study of a sado-masochistically oriented sample. *The Journal of Sex Research, 23,* 322-337.

Moser, P.W. (1989, January). Double vision: Why do we never match up to our mind's ideal? *Self Magazine*, pp. 51-52.

Moses, J.A. (1983). Luria-Nebraska Neuropsychological Battery performance of brain dysfunctional patients with positive or negative findings on current neurological examination. *International Journal of Neuroscience, 22,* 135-146.

Moses, J.A., & Purisch, A.D. (1997). The evolution of the Luria-Nebraska Battery. In G. Goldstein & T. Incagnoli (Eds.), *Contemporary approaches to neuropsychological assessment.* (pp. 131-170). New York: PLenum.

Moses, J.A., & Schefft, B.K. (1984). Interrater reliability analyses of the Luria-Nebraska Neuropsychological Battery. *The International Journal of Clinical Neuropsychology, 7,* 31-38.

Moses, J.A., Schefft, B.A., Wong, J.L., & Berg, R.A. (1992). Interrater reliability analyses of the Luria-Nebraska neuropsychological battery, form II. *Archives of Clinical Neurology, 7,* 251-269.

Mosher, L.R., & Burti, L. (1989). *Community mental health: Principles and practice.* New York: Norton.

Mosher, L.R., Kresky-Wolff, M., Mathews, S., & Menn, A. (1986). Milieu therapy in the 1980s: A comparison of two residential alternatives to hospitalization. *Bulletin of the Menninger Clinic, 50,* 257-268.

Moss, H.B. (1990). Pharmacotherapy. In A.S. Bellack & M. Hersen (Eds.), *Handbook of comparative treatments for adult disorders* (pp. 506-520). New York: Wiley.

Mothers Against Drunk Driving. (2001). Canadian impaired driving statistics and facts. (http://www.madd.ca/library/statfact.htm; accessed on April 7, 2001)

Motto, J.A. (1976). Suicide prevention for high-risk persons who refuse treatment. *Suicide: A Quarterly Journal of Life-Threatening Behavior, 6,* 223-230.

Mowrer, O.H. (1939). A stimulus-response analysis of anxiety and its role as a reinforcing agent. *Psychological Review, 46,* 553-565.

Mowrer, O.H. (1947). On the dual nature of learning: A reinterpretation of "conditioning" and "problem-solving." *Harvard Educational Review, 17,* 102-148.

Mowrer, O.H. (1950). *Learning theory and personality dynamics.* New York: Ronald Press.

Mowrer, O.H., & Mowrer, W.M. (1938). Enuresis: A method for its study and treatment. *American Journal of Orthopsychiatry, 8,* 436-459.

Mrazek, P.J., & Haggerty, R.J. (1994). *Reducing risks for mental disorders: Frontiers for preventive intervention research.* Washington, DC: National Academy Press.

Mueser, K., Bellack, A.S., & Blanchard, J.J. (1992). Co-morbidity of schizophrenia and substance abuse: Implications for treatment. *Journal of Consulting and Clinical Psychology, 60,* 845-856.

Mueser, K.T., Bond, G.R., Drake, R.E., & Resnick, S.G. (1998). Models of community care for severe mental illness: A review of research on case management. *Schizophrenia Bulletin, 24,* 37-74.

Mueser, K.T., & Glynn, S.M. (1995). *Behavioral family therapy for psychiatric disorders.* Boston: Allyn & Bacon.

Mueser, K.T., & Liberman, R.P. (1995). Behavior therapy in practice. In B. Bongar & L.E. Beutler (Eds.), *Comprehensive textbook of psychotherapy: Theory and practice* (pp. 84-110). New York: Oxford University Press.

Muller, R.T., Endler, N.S., & Parker, J.D.A. (1990). The interaction model of anxiety in two different public speaking situations. *Personality and Individual Differences, 11,* 371-377.

Muller, R.T., Goh, H.H., Lemieux, K.E., & Fish, S. (2000). The social supports of high-risk, formerly maltreated adults. *Canadian Journal of Behavioural Science, 32,* 1-5.

Muller, R.T., Sicoli, L.A., & Lemieux, K.E. (2000). Relationship between attachment style and posttraumatic stress symptomatology among adults who report the experience of childhood abuse. *Journal of Traumatic Stress, 13,* 321-332.

Mulligan, T., Retchin, S.M., Chinchilli, V.M., & Bettinger, C.B. (1988). The role of aging and chronic disease in sexual dysfunction. *Journal of the American Geriatrics Society, 36,* 520-524.

Mulvey, E.P. (1994). Assessing the evidence of a link between mental illness and violence. *Hospital and Community Psychiatry, 45,* 663-668.

Mumford, D.B., Whitehouse, A.M., & Choudry, I.Y. (1992). Survey of eating disorders in English-medium schools in Lahore, Pakistan. *International Journal of Eating Disorders, 11,* 173-184.

Munjack, D.J. (1984). The onset of driving phobias. *Journal of Behavior Therapy and Experimental Psychiatry, 15,* 305-308.

Murdoch, D., Pihl, R.O., & Ross, D. (1990). Alcohol and crimes of violence: Present issues. *International Journal of Addiction, 25,* 1059-1075.

Murphy, J.K., Stoney, C.M., Alpert, B.S., & Walker, S.S. (1995). Gender and ethnicity in children's cardiovascular reactivity: 7 years of study. *Health Psychology, 14,* 48-55.

Murphy, J.M., Laird, N.M., Monson, R.R., Sobol, A.M., & Leighton, A.H. (2000). A 40-year perspective on the prevalence of depression: The Stirling County study. *Archives of General Psychiatry, 57,* 209-215.

Murphy, W.D. (1997). Exhibitionism: Psychopathology and theory. In D.R. Laws & W. O'Donohue (Eds.), *Sexual deviance.* (pp. 22-39). NY: Guilford Press.

Murray, M. (2000, February 5). Mentally ill Portuguese face language barrier. *The Toronto Star.*

Muscettola, G., Potter, W.Z., Pickar, D., & Goodwin, F.K. (1984). Urinary 3-methoxy-4-hydroxyphenyl glycol and major affective disorders. *Archives of General Psychiatry, 41,* 337-342.

Muse, M. (1986). Stress-related, posttraumatic chronic pain syndrome: Behavioral treatment approach. *Pain, 25,* 389-394.

Musetti, L., Perugi, G., Soriani, A., Rossi, V.M., Cassano, G.B., & Akiskal, H.S. (1989). Depression before and after age 65: A re-examination. *British Journal of Psychiatry, 155,* 330-336.

Musselman, D.L., Evans, D.L., & Nemeroff, C.B. (1998). The relationship of depression to cardiovascular disease: Epidemiology, biology, and treatment. *Archives of General Psychiatry, 55,* 580-592.

Myers, J.K., Weissman, M.M., Tischler, G.L., Holzer, C.E., Leaf, P.J., Orvaschel, H.A., Anthony, J.C., Boyd, J.H., Burke, J.E., Kramer, M., & Stoltzman, R. (1984). Six-month prevalence of psychiatric disorders in three communities: 1980-1982. *Archives of General Psychiatry, 41,* 959-967.

Myers, M.G., Stewart, D.G., & Brown, S.A. (1998). Progression from conduct disorder to antisocial personality disorder. *American Journal of Psychiatry, 155,* 479-485.

Nagin, D.S., & Tremblay, R.E. (2001). Parental and early childhood predictors of persistent physical aggression in boys from kindergarten to high school. *Archives of General Psychiatry, 58,* 389-394.

Nahas, G.G., & Manger, W.M. (1995). Marijuana as medicine: In reply. *Journal of the American Medical Association, 274,* 1837-1838.

Naidoo, J. C. (1992). The mental health of visible ethnic minorities in Canada. *Psychology and Developing Societies, 4,* 165-187.

Nakao, M., Yano, E., Nomura, S., & Kuboki, T. (2003). Blood pressure lowering effects of biofeedback treatment in hypertension: A meta-analysis of randomized controlled trials. *Hypertension Research, 26,* 37-46.

Narduzzi, K. J., & Jackson, T. (2000). Personality differences between eating-disordered women and a nonclinical comparison sample: A discriminant classification analysis. *Journal of Clinical Psychology, 56,* 699-710.

Nathan, P.E., & Langenbucher, J. W. (1999). Psychopathology: Description and classification. *Annual Review of Psychology, 50, 79-107.*

Nathan, P.E., Stuart, S.P., & Dolan, S.L. (2000). Research on psychotherapy efficacy and effectiveness: Between Scylla and Charbydis? *Psychological Bulletin, 126,* 964-981.

National Cancer Institute. (1977). *The smoking digest: Progress report on a nation kicking the habit*. Washington, DC: U.S. Department of Health, Education and Welfare.

National Center for Child Abuse and Neglect. (1988). *Study of national incidence and prevalence of child abuse and neglect*, 1988. Washington, DC: U.S. Department of Health and Human Services.

National Center for Health Statistics (1989). *National nursing home survey* (DHHS Publication No. PHS 89-1758, Series 13, No. 97). Washington, DC: U.S. Government Printing Office.

National Center for Health Statistics. (1988). *Advance report of final mortality statistics*, 1986. NCHS Monthly Vital Statistics Report, 37 (Suppl. 6).

National Center for Health Statistics. (1994). *Advance report of final mortality statistics*, 1991. Monthly Vital Statistics Report, 42.

National Heart, Lung and Blood Institute. (1998). *Behavioral research in cardiovascular, lung, and blood health and disease*. Washington,DC: U.S. Department of Health and Human Services.

National Institute on Drug Abuse. (1982). *National Survey on Drug Abuse*. Washington, DC: Author.

National Institute on Drug Abuse. (1983a). *National Survey on Drug Abuse: Main Findings 1982* (DHHS Publication No. ADM 83-1263). Washington, DC: U.S. Government Printing Office.

National Institute on Drug Abuse. (1983b). *Population projections, based on the National Survey on Drug Abuse, 1982*. Rockville, MD: Author.

National Institute on Drug Abuse. (1988). *National household survey on drug abuse: Main findings 1985*. Washington, DC: Department of Health and Human Services.

National Institute on Drug Abuse. (1995). *National survey results on drug use from the Monitoring the Future study, 1975-1994*. Washington: U.S. Department of Health and Human Services.

National Institute on Drug Abuse. (1996). *National household survey on drug abuse: Population estimates 1995*. Washington: Department of Health and Human Services.

Nauss, D.W. (1996, March 9). Kevorkian found not guilty of aiding two suicides. *Los Angeles Times*, pp. A1, A15.

Nawas, M.M., Fishman, S.T., & Pucel, J.C. (1970). The standardized densensitization program applicable to group and individual treatment. *Behaviour Research and Therapy, 6,* 63-68.

Neale, J.M., & Liebert, R.M. (1986). *Science and behavior: An introduction to methods of research* (3rd ed.). Englewood Cliffs, NJ: Prentice-Hall.

Neale, J.M., & Oltmanns, T. (1980). *Schizophrenia*. NY: Wiley.

Nechi Institute, The Four Winds Development Project, The Native Training Institute and New Direction Training—Alkali Lake. (1988). *Healing is possible: A joint statement on the healing of sexual abuse in native communities*. Edmonton, Alta: Nechi Institute.

Neimeyer, R. A., & Raskin, J. D. (2001). Varieties of constructivism in psychotherapy. In K. S. Dobson (Ed.), *Handbook of cognitive-behavioral therapies, 2nd edition* (pp. 393-430). NY: Guilford.

Neisser, U. (1976). *Cognition and reality*. San Francisco: Freeman.

Neisser, U., & Harsch, N. (1991). Phantom flashbulbs: False recognitions of hearing the news about Challenger. In E. Winograd & U. Neisser (Eds.), *Affect and accuracy of recall: Studies of "flashbulb" memories*. New York: Cambridge University Press.

Nelson, G., Prilleltensky, I., Laurendeau, M.C., & Powell, B. (1996). The prevention of mental health problems in Canada; A survey of provincial policies, structures, and programs. *Canadian Psychology*, *37*, 161-172.

Nelson, J.C., & Davis, J.M. (1997). DST studies in psychotic depression: A meta-analysis. *American Journal of Psychiatry, 154,* 1497-1503.

Nelson, R.E., & Craighead, W.E. (1977). Selective recall of positive and negative feedback, self-control behaviors, and depression. *Journal of Abnormal Psychology, 86,* 379-388.

Nelson, R.O., Lipinski, D.P., & Black, J.L. (1976). The reactivity of adult retardates' self-monitoring: A comparison among behaviors of different valences, and a comparison with token reinforcement. *Psychological Record, 26,* 189-201.

Nemeroff, C.B., & Schatzberg, A.F. (1998). Pharmacological treatment of unipolar depression. In P.E. Nathan & J.M. Gorman (Eds.), *A guide to treatments that work*. (pp. 212-225). New York: Oxford University Press.

Nemeroff, C.F., Stein, R.I., Diehl, N.S., & Smilack, K.M. (1994). From the Cleavers to the Clintons: Role choices and body orientation as reflected in magazine article content. *International Journal of Eating Disorders, 16,* 167-176.

Nemeroff, C.J., & Karoly, P. (1991). Operant methods. In F.H. Kanfer & A.P. Goldstein (Eds.), *Helping people change: A textbook of methods* (4th ed.) Elmsford, NY: Pergamon.

Nemetz, G.H., Craig, K.D., & Reith, G. (1978). Treatment of female sexual dysfunction through symbolic modeling. *Journal of Consulting and Clinical Psychology, 46,* 62-73.

Neron, S., Lacroix, D., & Chaput, Y. (1995). Group vs. individual cognitive behaviour therapy in panic disorder: An open clinical trial with a six month follow-up. *Canadian Journal of Behavioural Science, 27,* 379-392.

Nestadt, G., Romanoski, A., Chahal, R., Merchant, A., et al. (1990). An epidemiological study of histrionic personality disorder. *Psychological Medicine, 20,* 413-422.

Nettelbeck, T. (1985). Inspection time and mild mental retardation. In N.R. Ellis & N.W. Bray (Eds.), *International review of research in mental retardation* (Vol. 13). New York: Academic Press.

Neufeld, R.W.J. (1999). Dynamic differentials of stress and coping. *Psychological Review*, *106*, 385-397.

Neugarten, B.L. (1977). Personality and aging. In J.E. Birren & K.W. Schaie (Eds.), *Handbook of the psychology of aging* (pp. 626-649). New York: Van Nostrand.

Neugebauer, R. (1979). Mediaeval and early modern theories of mental illness. *Archives of General Psychiatry, 36,* 477-484.

Neuringer, C. (1964). Rigid thinking in suicidal individuals. *Journal of Consulting Psychology, 28,* 54-58.

Newlin, D.B., & Thomson, J.B. (1990). Alcohol challenge with sons of alcoholics: A critical review and analysis. *Psychological Bulletin, 108,* 383-402.

Newman, D.L., Moffitt, T.E., Caspi, A., & Silva, P.A. (1998). Comorbid mental disorders: Implications for treatment and sample selection. *Journal of Abnormal Psychology, 107,* 305-311.

Newman, J.P., Patterson, C.M., & Kosson, D.S. (1987). Response perseveration in psychopaths. *Journal of Abnormal Psychology, 96,* 145-149.

Newman, J.P., Schmitt, W.A., & Voss, W.D. (1997). The impact of motivationally neutral cues on psychopathic individuals: Assessing the generality of the response modulation hypothesis. *Journal of Abnormal Psychology, 196,* 563-575.

Newman, M.G. (2000). Recommendatins for a cost-offset model of psychotherapy allocation using generalized anxiety disorder as an example. *Journal of Consulting and Clinical Psychology, 68,* 549-555.

Newman, S.C. (1999). The prevalence of depression in Alzheimer's disease and vascular dementia in a population sample. *Journal of Affective Disorders*, *52*, 169-176.

Newman, S.C., Bland, R.C., & Orn, H.T. (1998). The prevalence of mental disorders in the elderly in Edmonton: A community survey using GMS-AGECAT. *Canadian Journal of Psychiatry*, *43*, 910-914.

Newman, S.C., Sheldon, C.T., & Bland, R.C. (1998). Prevalence of depression in an elderly community sample: A comparison of GMS-AGECAT and DSM-IV criteria. *Psychological Medicine*, *28*, 1339-1345.

Newman, S.C., & Thompson, A.H. (2003). A population-based study of the association between pathological gambling and attempted suicide. *Suicide and Life-Threatening Behavior*, *33*, 80-87.

Newton-Taylor, B., DeWit, D., & Gliksman, L. (1998). Prevalence and factors associated with physical and sexual assault of female university students in Ontario. *Health Care For Women International*, *19*, 155-164.

Nezu, A.A., Nezu, C.M., Friedman, S.H., Houts, P.S., & Faddis, S. (1997). Project Genesis: Application of problem-solving therapy to individuals with cancer. *the Behavior Therapist, 20,* 155-158.

Nezu, A.M. (1986). Efficacy of a social problem-solving therapy approach for unipolar depression. *Journal of Consulting and Clinical Psychology, 54,* 196-202.

Nezu, A.M., Nezu, C.M., D'Zurilla, T.J., & Rothenberg, J.L. (1996). Problem-solving therapy. In J.S. Kantor (Ed.), *Clinical depression during addiction recovery* (pp. 187-219). New York: Marcel Dekker.

Nezu, A.M., & Perri, M.G. (1989). Social problem-solving therapy for unipolar depression: An initial dismantling investigation. *Journal of Consulting and Clinical Psychology, 57,* 408-413.

Nguyet, N.M., Beland, F., & Otis, J. (1998). Is the intention to quit smoking influenced by other heart-healthy lifestyle habits in 30- to 60-year-old men? *Addictive Behaviors*, *23*, 23-30.

NIAA. (1997). Youth drinking: Risk factors and consequences. Alcohol Alert, 1-7.

Nicholaichuk, T., Gordon, A., Gu, D., & Wong, S. (2000). Outcome of an institutional sexual offender treatment program: A comparison between treated and matched untreated offenders. *Sexual Abuse: A Journal of Treatment and Research*, *12*, 139-153.

Nichols, M. (with S. Doyle Driedger & D. Ballon) (1995, January 30). Schizophrenia: Hidden torment. *Maclean's*. [On-line]. Available: http://www.mentalhealth.com/mag1/p51-sc01.html

Nicholson, I.R., & Neufeld, R.W.J. (1993). Classification of the schizophrenias according to symptomatology: A two-factor model. *Journal of Abnormal Psychology*, *102*, 259-270.

Nicholson, R.A., & Berman, J.S. (1983). Is follow-up necessary in evaluating psychotherapy? *Psychological Bulletin, 93,* 261-278.

Nicolson, R., & Szatmari, P. (2003). Genetic and neurodevelopmental influences in autistic disorder. *Canadian Journal of Psychiatry*, *48, 526-537.*

NIDA. (1998a). *The economic costs of alcohol and drug abuse in the United States*. Rockville, MD: National Clearinghouse for Drug and Alcohol Information.

NIDA. (1998b). *Director's report to the National Advisory Council on Drug Abuse*. Rockville, MD: Author.

Niedhammer, I., Goldberg, M., Leclerc, A., David, S., et al. (1998). Psychosocial work environment and cardiovascular risk factors in an occupational cohort in France. *Journal of Epidemiology and Community Health, 52,* 93-100.

Nielsen, G. H., Nordhus, I. H., & Kvale, G. (1998). Insomnia in older adults. In I.H. Nordhus, G.R. VandenBos, S. Berg, & P. Fromholt, (Eds.), *Clinical geropsychology* (pp. 167-175). Washington, D.C.: American Psychological Association.

Nigg, J.T., & Goldsmith, H.H. (1994). Genetics of personality disorders: Perspectives from personality and psychopathology research. *Psychological Bulletin, 115,* 346-380.

Nihira, K., Foster, R., Shenhaas, M., & Leland, H. (1975). *AAMD-Adaptive Behavior Scale*. Washington, DC: American Association on Mental Deficiency.

Nimgaonkar, V.L., Fujiwara, T.M., Dutta, M., Wood, J., Gentry, K., Maendel, S. et al. (2000). Low prevalence of psychoses among the Hutterites, an isolated religious community. *American Journal of Psychiatry*, *157*, 1065-1070.

Nisbett, R.E., & Wilson, T.D. (1977). Telling more than we can know: Verbal reports on mental processes. *Psychological Review, 84,* 231-259.

Nobler, M.S., Sackeim, H.A., Prohovnik, I., Moeller, J.R., Mukherjee, S., et al. (1994). Regional cerebral blood flow in mood disorders, 3. Treatment and clinical response. *Archives of General Psychiatry, 51,* 884-896.

Nocks, B.C., Learner, R.M., Blackman, D., & Brown, T.E. (1986). The effects of a community-based long term care project on nursing home utilization. *The Gerontologist, 26,* 150-157.

Noh, S., Beiser, M., Kaspar, V., Hou, F., & Rummens, J. (1999). Perceived racial discrimination, depression, and coping: A study of Southeast Asian refugees in Canada. *Journal of Health and Social Behaviour, 40,* 193-207.

Noh, S., Speechley, M., Kaspar, V., & Wu, A., (1992). Depression in Korean immigrants in Canada: Method of the study and prevalence. *Journal of Nervous and Mental Disease, 180,* 573-582.

Nolen-Hoeksema, S., & Girgus, J.S. (1994). The emergence of gender differences in depression during adolescence. *Psychological Bulletin, 115,* 424-443.

Nolen-Hoeksema, S., Larson, J., & Grayson, C. (1999). Explaining the gender difference in depressive symptoms. *Journal of Personality and Social Psychology*, *77*, 1061-1072.

Noorsdy, D.L., Drake, R.E., & Teague, G.B. (1991). Subjective experiences related to alcohol use among schizophrenics. *Journal of Nervous and Mental Disease, 79,* 410-414.

Norgaard, J.P. (1989a). Urodynamics in enuretics: 1. Reservoir function. *Neurourology and Urodynamics, 8,* 199-211.

Norgaard, J.P. (1989b). Urodynamics in enuretics: 2. A pressure/flow study. *Neurourology and Urodynamics, 8,* 213-217.

Norman, R.M.G., & Malla, A.K. (2001). Duration of untreated psychosis: A critical examination of the concept and its importance. *Psychological Medicine*, *31*, 381-400.

Norman, R.M.G., Malla, A.K., McLean, T.S., McIntosh, E.M., Neufeld, R.W.J., Voruganti, L.P., & Cortese, L. (2002). An evaluation of a stress management program for individuals with schizophrenia. *Schizophrenia Research*, *58*, 293-303.

Norman, R.M.G., & Townsend, L.A. (1999). Cognitive-behavioral therapy for psychosis: A status report. *Canadian Journal of Psychiatry*, *44*, 245-252.

North, A.F. (1979). Health services in Head Start. In E. Zigler & J. Valentine (Eds.), *Project Head Start*. New York: Free Press.

Norton, G.R., Dorward, J., & Cox, B.J. (1986). Factors associated with panic attacks in nonclinical subjects. *Behavior Therapy*, *17*, 239-252.

Norton, G.R., McLeod, L., Guertin, J., Hewitt, P.L., Walker, J.R., & Stein, M.B. (1996). Panic disorder or social phobia: Which is worse? *Behaviour Research and Therapy*, *34*, 273-276.

Norton, J.P. (1982). *Expressed emotion, affective style, voice tone and communication deviance as predictors of offspring schizophrenia spectrum disorders*. Unpublished doctoral dissertation, University of California at Los Angeles.

Noshirvani, H.F., Homa, F., Kasvikis, Y., Marks, I.M., Tsakiris, F., et al. (1991). Gender-divergent factors in obsessive-compulsive disorder. *British Journal of Psychiatry, 158,* 260-263.

Nottelmann, E.D., & Jensen, P.S. (1995). Comorbidity of disorders in children and adolescents: Developmental perspectives. *Advances in Clinical Child Psychology, 17,* 109-155.

Nowlan, R., & Cohen, S. (1977). Tolerance to marijuana: Heart rate and subjective "high." *Clinical Pharmacology Therapeutics, 22,* 550-556.

Noyes, R., Holt, C.S., Happel, R.L., Kathol, R.G., & Yagla, S.J. (1997). A family study of hypochondriasis. *Journal of Nervous and Mental Disease, 185,* 223-232.

Noyes, R., Kathol, R.G., Fisher, M.M., Phillips, S.B., & Suezer, M.T. (1994). Psychiatric comorbidity among patients with hypochondriasis. *General Hospital Psychiatry, 16,* 78-87.

Noyes, R., Woodman, C., Garvey, M.J., Cook, B.C., Suezer, M., et al. (1992). Generalized anxiety disorder versus panic disorder: Distinguishing characteristics and patterns of comorbidity. *Journal of Nervous and Mental Disease, 180,* 369-379.

Nuechterlein, K.H., Dawson, M.E., Ventura, J., Gitlin, M., Subotnik, K.L., Snyder, K.S., Mintz, J., & Bartzokis, G. (1994). The vulnerability/stress model of schizophrenic relapse. *Acta Psychiatrica Scandinavica, 89,* 58-64.

Nunes, E.V., Quitkin, F.M., Donovan, S.J., Deliyannides, D., et al. (1998). Imipramine treatment of opiate-dependent patients with depressive disorders: A placebo-controlled trial. *Archives of General Psychiatry, 55,* 153-160.

Nunes, J., & Simmie, S. (2002). *Beyond crazy: Journeys through mental illness*. Toronto: McClelland and Stewart.

Nunn, R.G., Newton, K.S., & Faucher, P. (1992). 2.5 year follow-up of weight and body mass index values in the weight control for life program. *Addictive Behaviors, 17,* 579-585.

O'Brien, W.H., & Haynes, S.N. (1995). Behavioral assessment. In L.A. Heiden & M. Hersen (Eds.), *Introduction to clinical psychology*. (pp. 103-139). New York: Plenum.

O'Conner, M.C. (1989). Aspects of differential performance by minorities on standardized tests: Linguistic and sociocultural factors. In B.R. Gifford (Ed.), *Test policy and test performance: Education, language, and culture* (pp. 129-181). Boston: Kluwer Academic Publishers.

O'Connor, B.P. (2002). The search for dimensional structure differences between normality and abnormality: A statistical review of published data on personality and psychopathology. *Journal of Personality and Social Psychology*, *83*, 962-982.

O'Connor, B.P., & Dyce, J.A. (1998). A test of models of personality disorder configuration. *Journal of Abnormal Psychlogy, 107,* 3-16.

O'Connor, B.P., & Dyce, J.A. (2001). Rigid and extreme: A geometric representation of personality disorders in five-factor model space. *Journal of Personality and Social Psychology*, *81*, 1119-1130.

O'Connor, D.W., Pollitt, P.A., Roth, M., Brook, P.B., & Reiss, B.B. (1990). Memory complaints and impairment in normal, depressed, and demented elderly persons identified in a community survey. *Archives of General Psy-*

chiatry, 47, 224-227.

O'Connor, K., & Robillard, S. (1995). Inference processes in obsessive-compulsive disorder: Some clinical observations. *Behaviour Research and Therapy, 33,* 887-896.

O'Connor, K., & Robillard, S. (2000). A cognitive approach to the treatment of primary inferences in obsessive-compulsive disorder. *Journal of Cognitive Psychotherapy: An International Quarterly, 13,* 359-375.

O'Connor, R.D. (1969). Modification of social withdrawal through symbolic modeling. *Journal of Applied Behavior Analysis, 2,* 15-22.

O'Connor, T.G., & Jenkins, J.M. (2000). *Marital transitions and children's adjustment: Understanding why families differ from one another and why children in the same family show different patterns of adjustment.* Ottawa: Government of Canada.

O'Donnell, P., & Grace, A.A. (1998). Dysfunctions in multiple interrelated systems as the neurobiological bases of schizophrenic symptom clusters. *Schizophrenia Bulletin, 24,* 267-283.

O'Donohoe, W. (1993). The spell of Kuhn on psychology: An exegetical elixir. *Philosophical Psychology, 6,* 267-287.

O'Donohue, W., Dopke, C.A., & Swingen, D.N. (1997). Psychotherapy for female sexual dysfunction: A review. *Clinical Psychology Review, 17,* 537-566.

O'Donohue, W., & Plaud, J.J. (1994). The conditioning of human sexual arousal. *Archives of Sexual Behavior, 23,* 321-344.

O'Farrell, T.J. (1993). A behavioral marital therapy couples group program for alcoholics and their spouses. In T.J. O'Farrell (Ed.), *Treating alcohol problems: Marital and family interventions.* (pp. 170-209). New York: Guilford Press.

O'Leary, K.D., & Beach, S.R.H. (1990). Marital therapy: A viable treatment for depression and marital discord. *American Journal of Psychiatry, 147,* 183-186.

O'Leary, K.D., Pelham, W.E., Rosenbaum, A., & Price, G.H. (1976). Behavioral treatment of hyperkinetic children: An experimental evaluation of its usefulness. *Clinical Pediatrics, 15,* 510-515.

O'Leary, K.D., & Wilson, G.T. (1987). *Behavior therapy: Application and outcome.* Englewood Cliffs, NJ: Prentice-Hall.

O'Malley, S.S., Jaffe, A.J., Chang, G., Rode, S., Schottenfeld, R., et al. (1996). Six month follow-up of naltrexone and psychotherapy for alcohol dependence. *Archives of General Psychiatry, 53,* 217-224.

O'Neal, J.M. (1984). First person account: Finding myself and loving it. *Schizophrenia Bulletin, 10,* 109-110.

O'Neill, M.E., & Douglas, V.I. (1996). Rehearsal strategies and recall performance in boys with and without attention deficit hyperactivity disorder. *Journal of Pediatric Psychology, 21,* 73-88.

O'Neil, P.M., & Jarrell, M.P. (1992). Psychological aspects of obesity and dieting. In T.A. Wadden & T.B. VanItallie (Eds.), *Treatment of the seriously obese patient* (pp. 231-251). New York: Guilford.

Obrist, P.A., Gaebelein, C.J., Teller, E.S., Langer, A.W., Grignolo, A., Light, K.C., & McCubbin, J.A. (1978). The relationship among heart rate, carotid dP/dt, and blood pressure in humans as a function of the type of stress. *Psychophysiology, 15,* 102-115.

Ochitil, H. (1982). Conversion disorder. In J.H. Greist, J.W. Jefferson, & R.L. Spitzer (Eds.), *Treatment of mental disorders.* New York: Oxford University Press.

Office of the Chief Coroner of British Columbia (1994). *Report of the Task Force Into Illicit Narcotic Overdose Deaths in British Columbia.* British Columbia: Ministry of the Attorney General.

Offord, D. R., Boyle, M. H., Campbell, D., Goering, P., Lin, E., Wong, M., & Racine, Y. A. (1996). One-year prevalence of psychiatric disorders in Ontarians 15 to 64 years of age. *Canadian Journal of Psychiatry, 41,* 559-563.

Offord, D.R., Boyle, M.H., & Racine, Y. (1989). Ontario Child Health Study: Correlates of disorder. *Journal of the American Academy of Child and Adolescent Psychiatry, 35,* 1078-1085.

Offord, D.R., Boyle, M.H., Szatmari, P., Rae-Grant, N.I., Links, P.S., Cadman, D.T., Byles, J.A., Crawford, J.W., Blum, H.M., Byrne, C., Thomas, H., & Woodward, C.A. (1987). Ontario Child Health Study: 2. Six-month prevalence of disorder and rates of service utilization. *Archives of General Psychiatry, 44,* 832-836.

Ogborne, A.C., & DeWit, D.J. (1999). Lifetime use of professional and community services for help with drinking: Results from a Canadian population survey. *Journal of Studies in Alcohol, 60,* 867-872.

Ogborne, A.C., Smart, R.G., & Adlaf, E.M. (2000). Self-reported medical use of marijuana: A survey of the general population. *Canadian Medical Association Journal, 162,* 1685-1686.

Ogborne, A.C., Wild, T.C., Braun, K., & Newton-Taylor, B. (1998). Measuring treatment process beliefs among staff of specialized addiction treatment services. *Journal of Substance Abuse Treatment, 15,* 301-312.

Ogilvie, D.M., Stone, P.J., & Shneidman, E.S. (1983). A computer analysis of suicide notes. In E.S. Shneidman, N. Farberow, & R. Litman (Eds.), *The psychology of suicide* (pp. 249-256). New York: Jason Aronson.

Ogloff, J.R.P. (1999). Ethical and legal contours of forensic psychology. In R. Roesch & S.D. Hart (Eds.), *Psychology and law: The state of the discipline* (pp. 401-435). New York: Plenum.

Ogloff, J.R.P., & Whittemore, K.E. (2001). Fitness to stand trial and criminal responsibility in Canada. In R. A. Schuller & J. R. Ogloff (Eds.), *Introduction to psychology and law: Canadian perspectives* (pp. 283-313). Toronto: University of Toronto Press.

Ogloff, J.R., & Wong, S. (1990). Electrodermal and cardiovascular evidence of a coping response in psychopaths. *Criminal Justice and Behavior, 17,* 231-245.

Ogloff, J.R., Wong, S., & Greenwood, A. (1990). Treating criminal psychopaths in a therapeutic community program. *Behavioral Sciences and the Law, 8,* 181-190.

Ogrodniczuk, J.S., Piper, W.E., Joyce, A.S., & McCallum, M. (1999). Transference interpretations in short-term dynamic psychotherapy. *Journal of Nervous and Mental Disease, 187,* 571-578.

Oh, S. (1999, July 19). The hidden horror: Many elderly are abused by the people they trust the most—their own kids. *Maclean's,* pp. 48-49.

Öhman, A., & Soares, J.J.F. (1994). "Unconscious anxiety": Phobic responses to masked stimuli. *Journal of Abnormal Psychology, 103,* 231-240.

Olds, D.L. (1984). *Final report: Prenatal/early infancy project.* Washington, DC: Maternal and Child Health Research, National Institute of Health.

Olivardia, R., Pope, H.G., Mangweth, B., & Hudson, J.I. (1995). Eating disorders in college men. *American Journal of Psychiatry, 152,* 1279-1284.

Olson, D., Portner, J., and Lavee, Y. (1985). *FACES III.* St. Paul: University of Minnesota, Department of Family Social Service.

Olson, D.H., Sprenkle, D., & Russell, C. (1979). Circumplex models of marital and family systems, I. *Family Process, 18,* 3-28.

Oltmanns, T.F., Broderick, J.E., & O'Leary, K.D. (1976). *Marital adjustment and the efficacy of behavior therapy with children.* Paper presented at the Association for the Advancement of Behavior Therapy, New York.

Oltmanns, T.F., Neale, J.M., & Davison, G.C. (1995). *Case studies in abnormal psychology.* Fourth edition. New York: Wiley.

Ondersma, S.J. & Walker, C.E. (1998). Elimination disorders. In T.H. Ollendick & M. Hersen (Eds.), *Handbook of Child Psychopathology,* 3rd Ed. New York: Plenum Press.

Ono, Y., Yoshimura, K., Sueoka, R., Yaumachi, K., et al. (1996). Avoidant personality disorder and taijin kyoufu: Sociocultural implications of the WHO/ADAMHA International Study of Personality Disorders in Japan. *Acta Psychiatrica Scandanavica, 93,* 172-176.

Ontario Ministry of Health (1994). *Ontario Health Survey: Mental health supplement.* Catalogue No. 2224153. Toronto, ON. Queen's Printer for Ontario.

O'Reilly, R.L., Keegan, D.L., & Elias, J.W. (2000). A survey of the use of community treatment orders by psychiatrists in Saskatchewan. *Canadian Journal of Psychiatry, 45,* 79-81.

Organista, K.C., & Munoz, R.F. (1996). Cognitive behavioral therapy with Latinos. *Cognitive and Behavioral Practice, 3,* 255-270.

Orleans, C.T., Schoenbach, V.J., Wagner, E.H., Quade, D., Salmon, M.A., Pearson, D.C., Fiedler, J., Porter, C.Q., & Kaplan, B.H. (1991). Self-help quit smoking interventions: Effects of self-help materials, social support instructions, and telephone counseling. *Journal of Consulting and Clinical Psychology, 59,* 439-448.

Orne, M.T., Dinges, D.F., & Orne, E.C. (1984). The differential diagnosis of multiple personality in the forensic court. *International Journal of Clinical and Experimental Hypnosis, 32,* 118-169.

Ornitz, E.M. (1973). Childhood autism: A review of the clinical and experimental literature. *California Medicine, 118,* 21-47.

Ornitz, E.M. (1989). Autism at the interface between sensory and information processing. In G. Dawson (Ed.), *Autism: Nature, diagnosis, and treatment* (pp. 174-207). New York: Guilford.

O'Rourke, N., & Hadjistavropoulos, T. (1997). The relative efficacy of psychotherapy in the treatment of geriatric depression. *Aging and Mental Health, 1*, 305-310.

O'Rourke, N., Tuokko, H., Hayden, S., & Beattie, B.L. (1997). Early identification of dementia: Predictive validity of the Clock Test. *Archives of Clinical Neuropsychology, 12*, 257-267.

Orr, S.P., Lasko, N.B., Shalev, A.Y., & Pitman, R.K. (1995). Physiological responses to loud tones in Vietnam veterans with post-traumatic stress disorder. *Journal of Abnormal Psychology, 104,* 75-82.

Orth-Gomer, K., & Unden, A.L. (1990). Type A behavior, social support, and coronary risk: Interaction and significance for mortality in cardiac patients. *Psychosomatic Medicine, 52,* 59-72.

Orvaschel, H., Walsh-Allis, G., & Ye, W. (1988). Psychopathology in children of parents with recurrent depression. *Journal of Abnormal Child Psychology, 16,* 17-28.

Orwen, P. (2001, July 15). Spanking law divides town and country: Friends become foes after police remove children. *The Toronto Star*, A1, A10.

Ost, L-G. (1987a). Age of onset in different phobias. *Journal of Abnormal Psychology, 96,* 223-229.

Ost, L-G. (1987b). Applied relaxation: Description of a coping technique and review of controlled studies. *Behaviour Research and Therapy, 25,* 397-409.

Ost, L-G. (1992). Blood and injection phobia: Background and cognitive, physiological, and behavioral correlates. *Journal of Abnormal Psychology, 101,* 68-74.

Ostbye, T., Steenhuis, R., Walton, R., & Cairney, J. (2000). Correlates of dysphoria in Canadian seniors: The Canadian study of health and aging. *Canadian Journal of Public Health, 91*, 313-317.

Otto, M.W., Pollack, M.H., & Maki, K.M. (2000). Empirically supported treatments for panic disorder: Costs, benefits, and stepped care. *Journal of Consulting and Clinical Psychology, 68,* 556-563.

Ouimette, P.C., Finney, J.W., & Moos, R.H. (1997). Twelve-step and cognitive-behavioral treatment for substance abuse: A comparison of treatment effectiveness. *Journal of Consulting and Clinical Psychology, 65,* 230-240.

Ouimette, P.C., Moos, R.H., & Finney, J.W. (2003). PTSD treatment and 5-year remission among patients with substance use and posttraumatic stress disorders. *Journal of Consulting and Clinical Psychology, 71*, 410-414.

Overholser, J.C., & Beck, S. (1986). Multimethod assessment of rapists, child molesters, and three control groups on behavioral and psychological measures. *Journal of Consulting and Clinical Psychology, 54,* 682-687.

Owen, P.R., & Laurel-Seller, E. (2000). Weight and shape ideals: Thin is dangerously in. *Journal of Applied Social Psychology, 30*, 979-990.

Owens, E.B., et al. (2003). Which treatment for whom for ADHD? Moderators of treatment response in the MTA. *Journal of Consulting and Clinical Psychology, 71*, 540-552.

Page, A.C. (1994). Blood-injection phobia. *Clinical Psychology Review, 14,* 443-461.

Page, S., & Day, D. (1990). Acceptance of the "mentally ill" in Canadian society: Reality and illusion. *Canadian Journal of Community Mental Health, 9*, 51-61.

Paglia, A., & Room, R. (1999). Expectancies about the effects of alcohol on the self and others as determinants of alcohol policy attitudes. *Journal of Applied Social Psychology, 29*, 2632-2651.

Pahkala, K. (1990). Social and environmental factors and atypical depression in old age. *International Journal of Geriatric Psychiatry, 5,* 99-113.

Paivio, S.C., & Bahr, L.M. (1998). Interpersonal problems, working alliance, and outcomes in short-term experiential therapy. *Psychotherapy Research, 8*, 392-407.

Palmer, K., Montgomery, R., & Harland, A. (2003). Emergency telemental health: Canada's first. *Telemedicine Journal and e-Health, 9* (Supplement 1), S63.

Palmer, T. (1984). Treatment and the role of classification: Review of basics. *Crime and Delinquency, 30,* 245-267.

Parent, K., & Anderson, M. (2001). *Home care by default, not by design: CARP's report card on home care in Canada 2001.* (from: www.50plus.com).

Parent, K., Anderson, M., Neuwelt, B., & Elliott, L. (2002). *Seniors' mental health and home care: A report prepared for: The Canadian Mental Health Association (CMHA).* Ottawa: Canadian Mental Health Association.

Paris, J. (2002). Chronic suicidality among patients with borderline personality disorder. *Psychiatric Services, 53*, 738-742.

Paris, J., & Zweig-Frank, H. (2001). A 27-year follow-up of patients with borderline personality disorder. *Comprehensive Psychiatry, 42*, 482-487.

Paris, J., Zweig, F.M., & Guzder, J. (1994). Psychological risk factors for borderline personality disorder in female patients. *Comprehensive Psychiatry, 35,* 301-305.

Park, D.C., & Radford, J.P. (1998). From the case files: Reconstructing a history of involuntary sterilization. *Disability and Society, 13*, 317-342.

Parker J.D.A., Taylor, G.J., & Bagby R.M. (2001). The relationship between emotional intelligence and alexithymia. *Personality and Individual Differences, 30*, 107-115.

Parker, K.C.H., Hanson, R.K., & Hunsley, J. (1988). MMPI, Rorschach, and WAIS: A meta-analytic comparison of reliability, stability, and validity. *Psychological Bulletin, 103,* 367-373.

Parker, G., Gladstone, G., & Chee, K.T. (2001). Depression in the planet's largest ethnic group: The Chinese. *American Journal of Psychiatry, 158*, 857-864.

Parker, G., Tupling, H., & Brown, L.B. (1979). A parental bonding instrument. *British Journal of Medical Psychology, 52*, 1-10.

Parkinson, L., & Rachman, S. (1981). Intrusive thoughts: The effects of an uncontrived stress. *Advances in Behavior Research and Therapy, 3,* 111-118.

Parks, C.V., Jr., & Hollon, S.D. (1988). Cognitive assessment. In A.S. Bellack & M. Hersen (Eds.), *Behavioral assessment* (3rd ed.). Elmsford, NY: Pergamon.

Patel, C., Marmot, M.G., Terry, D.J., Carruthers, M., Hunt, B., & Patel, M. (1985). Trial of relaxation in reducing coronary risk: Four year follow-up. *British Medical Journal, 290,* 1103-1106.

Pato, M.T., Zohar-Kadouch, R., Zohar, J., & Murphy, D.L. (1988). Return of symptoms after discontinuation of clomipramine and patients with obsessive-compulsive disorder. *American Journal of Psychiatry, 145,* 1521-1525.

Paton, A. (1995). *Education in the virtual factory*. Paper presented at The Spring VR WORLD '95 Conference, San Jose, CA.

Patten, S.B. (2000). Major depression prevalence in Calgary. *Canadian Journal of Psychiatry, 45*, 923-925.

Patten, S.B. (2002). Progress against major depression in Canada. *Canadian Journal of Psychiatry, 47*, 775-780.

Patten, S.B., Stuart, H.L., Russell, M.L., Maxwell, C.J., & Arboleda-Florez, J. (2003). Epidemiology of major depression in a predominantly rural health region. *Social Psychiatry and Psychiatric Epidemiology, 38*, 360-365.

Patterson, C.J.S., Gauthier, S., Bergman, H., Cohen, C. A., Feightner, J.W., Feldman, H., & Hogan, D.B. (1999). The recognition, assessment and management of dementing disorders: Conclusions from the Canadian Consensus Conference on Dementia. *Canadian Medical Association Journal, 160 (Supplement)*, S1-S12.

Patterson, C.M., & Newman, J.P. (1993). Reflectivity and learning from aversive events: Toward a psychological mechanism for the syndromes of disinhibition. *Psychological Review, 100,* 716-736.

Patterson, G.R. (1974). A basis for identifying stimuli which control behaviors in natural settings. *Child Development, 45,* 900-911.

Patterson, G. R. (1982). Coercive family process. Eugene, OR: Castilia.

Patterson, G.R., Crosby, L., & Vuchinich, S. (1992). Predicting risk for early police arrest. *Journal of Quantitative Criminology, 8,* 335-355.

Patterson, G.R., Ray, R.S., Shaw, D.A., & Cobb, J.A. (1969). *Manual for coding of family interactions*. New York: ASIS/NAPS, Microfiche Publications.

Paul, G.L. (1966). *Insight vs. desensitization in psychotherapy*. Stanford, CA: Stanford University Press.

Paul, G.L. (1969). Chronic mental patient: Current status-future directions. *Psychological Bulletin, 71,* 81-94.

Paul, G.L., & Lentz, R.J. (1977). *Psychosocial treatment of chronic mental patients: Milieu versus social learning programs*. Cambridge, MA: Harvard University Press.

Paul, G.L., & Menditto, A.A. (1992). Effectiveness of inpatient treatment programs for mentally ill adults in public psychiatric facilities. *Applied and Preventive Psychology: Current Scientific Perspectives, 1,* 41-63.

Paul, G.L., & Shannon, D.T. (1966). Treatment of anxiety through systematic desensitization in therapy groups. *Journal of Abnormal Psychology, 71,* 124-135.

Paul, G.L., Stuve, P., & Cross, J.V. (in press). Real-world inpatient programs: Shedding some light. *Applied and Preventive Psychology.*

Paul, G.L., Stuve, P., & Menditto, A.A. (in press). Social-learning program (with token economy) for adult psychiatric inpatients. *The Clinical Psychologist.*

Paul, R. (1987). Communication. In D.J. Cohen, A.M. Donnellan, & R. Paul (Eds.), *Handbook of autism and pervasive developmental disorders* (pp. 61-84). New York: Wiley.

Pauls, D.L., Alsobrook, J.P., Goodman, W., Rasmussen, S., & Leckman, J.F. (1995). A family study of obsessive-compulsive disorder. *American Journal of Psychiatry, 152,* 76-84.

Paxton, S.J., Schutz, H.K., Wertheim, E.H., & Muir, S.L. (1999). Friendship clique and peer influences on body image concerns, dietary restraint, extreme weight-loss behaviors,. and binge eating in adolescent girls. *Journal of Abnormal Psychology, 108,* 255-264.

Payne, A., & Blanchard, E.B. (1995). A controlled comparison of cognitive therapy and self-help support groups in the treatment of irritable bowel syndrome. *Journal of Consulting and Clinical Psychology, 63,* 779-786.

Peacock, E.J., & Wong, P.T.P. (1996). Anticipatory stress: The relation of locus of control, optimism, and control appraisals to coping. *Journal of Research in Personality, 30,* 204-222.

Peacock, E.J., Wong, P.T.P., & Reker, G.T. (1993). Relations between appraisals and coping schemas: Support for the congruence model. *Canadian Journal of Behavioural Science, 25,* 64-80.

Pearlson, G.D., & Rabins, P.V. (1988). The late-onset psychoses: Possible risk factors. *Psychiatric Clinics of North America, 11,* 15-32.

Pearlson, G.D., Wong, D.F., Tune, L.E., Ross, C.A., Chase, G.A., et al. (1995). In vivo D2 dopamine receptor density in psychotic and non-psychotic patients with bipolar disorder. *Archives of General Psychiatry, 52,* 471-477.

Pearson, C., & Gatz, M. (1982). Health and mental health in older adults: First steps in the study of a pedestrian complaint. *Rehabilitation Psychology, 27,* 37-50.

Pearson, J.L., & Brown, G.K. (2000). Suicide prevention in late life: Directions for science and practice. *Clinical Psychology Review, 20,* 685-705.

Pedersen, S.S., & Denollet, J. (2003). Type D personality, cardiac events, and impaired quality of life: A review. *Journai of Cardiovascular Risk, 10,* 241-248.

Pedro-Carroll, J.L., & Cowen, E.L. (1985). The children of divorce intervention program: An investigation of the efficacy of a school-based prevention program. *Journal of Consulting and Clinical Psychology, 53,* 603-611.

Pedro-Carroll, J.L., Cowen, E.L., Hightower, A.D., & Guare, J.C. (1986). Preventive intervention with latency-aged children of divorce: A replication study. *American Journal of Community Psychology, 14,* 277-290.

Peeples, F. & Loeber, R. (1994). Do individual factors and neighborhood context explain ethnic differences in juvenile delinquency? *Journal of Quantitative Criminology, 10,* 141-157.

Peet, M., & Harvey, N.S. (1991). Lithium maintenance: I. A standard education programme for patients. *British Journal of Psychiatry, 158,* 197-200.

Pelham, W.E., Carlson, C., Sams, S.E., Vallano, G., Dixon, M.J., & Hoza, B. (1993). Separate and combined effects of methylphenidate and behavior modification on boys with attention deficit/hyperactivity disorder in the classroom. *Journal of Consulting and Clinical Psychology, 61,* 506-515.

Pelham, W.E., McBurnett, K., Harper, G.W., Milich, R., Murphy, D.A., Clinton, J., & Thiele, C. (1990). Methylphenidate and baseball playing in ADHD children: Who's on first? *Journal of Consulting and Clinical Psychology, 58,* 130-133.

Penn, D.L., & Mueser, K.T. (1996). Research update on the psychosocial treatment of schizophrenia. *American Journal of Psychiatry, 153,* 607-617.

Pennebaker, J., Kiecolt-Glaser, J.K., & Glaser, R. (1988). Disclosure of traumas and immune function: Health implications for psychotherapy. *Journal of Consulting and Clinical Psychology, 56,* 239-245.

Pennebaker, J.W. (1990). *Opening up: The healing power of confiding in others.* New York: William Morrow & Co.

Pennington, B.F. (1995). Genetics of learning disabilities. *Journal of Child Neurology, 10,* S69-S77.

Pentoney, P. (1966). Value change in psychotherapy. *Human Relations, 19,* 39-46.

Pepler, D.J., and Sedighdeilami, F. (1998). *Aggressive girls in Canada* (No. W-98-30E). Ottawa: Human Resources Development Canada.

Perez, M.A., Meyerowitz, B.E., Lieskovsky, G., Skinner, D.G., Reynolds, B., & Skinner, E.C. (1997). Quality of life and sexuality following radical prostatectomy in patients with prostate cancer who use or do not use erectile aids. *Urology, 50,* 740-746.

Perley, M.J., & Guze, S.B. (1962). Hysteria: The stability and usefulness of clinical criteria. *New England Journal of Medicine, 266,* 421-426.

Perlin, M. L. (1994). *Law and mental disability.* Charlottesville, The Michie Company.

Perls, F.S. (1947). *Ego, hunger, and aggression.* New York: Vintage.

Perls, F.S. (1969). *Gestalt therapy verbatim.* Moab, UT: Real People Press.

Perls, F.S. (1970). Four lectures. In J. Fagan & I.L. Shepherd (Eds.), *Gestalt therapy now: Therapy, techniques, applications.* Palo Alto, CA: Science & Behavior Books.

Perls, F.S., Hefferline, R.F., & Goodman, P. (1951). *Gestalt therapy: Excitement and growth in the human personality.* New York: Julian Press.

Perr, I.N. (1992). The trial of Louis Riel: A study in Canadian psychiatry. *Journal of Forensic Sciences, 37,* 845-852.

Perr, I.N., & Federoff, J.P. (1992). Misunderstanding of self and the Riel phenomenon. *Journal of Forensic Sciences, 37,* 839-844.

Perris, C., Arrindell, W. A., & Eisemann, M. (Eds.) (1994). *Parenting and psychopathology.* Chichester: Wiley.

Perris, C., Jacobsson, L., Lindstrom, H., Von Knorring, L., & Perris, H. (1980). Development of a new inventory for assessing memories of parental rearing behaviour. *Acta Psychiatrica Scandinavica, 61,* 265-274.

Perry, J.C., Hoglend, P., Shear, K., Vaillant, G.E., Horowitz, M., et al. (1998). Field trial of a diagnostic axis for defense mechanisms for DSM-IV. *Journal of Personality Disorders, 12,* 56-68.

Perry, R., Campbell, M., Adams, P., Lynch, N., Spencer, E.K., Curren, E.L., & Overall, J.E. (1989). Long-term efficacy of haloperidol in autistic children: Continuous versus discontinuous administration. *Journal of the American Academy of Child and Adolescent Psychiatry, 28,* 87-92.

Persons, J. (1989). *Cognitive therapy in practice: A case formulation approach.* New York: Norton.

Persons, J.B., & Davidson, J. (2001). Cognitive-behavioral case formulation. In K.S. Dobson (Ed.), *Handbook of psychotherapy case formulation* (pp. 314-339). New York: Guilford Press.

Persons, J.B., & Miranda, J. (1992). Cognitive theories of vulnerability to depression: Reconciling negative evidence. *Cognitive Therapy and Research, 16,* 185-202.

Perugi, G., Akiskal, H.S., Giannotti, D., Frare, F., et al. (1997). Gender-related differences in body dysmorphic disorder. *Journal of Nervous and Mental Disease, 185,* 578-582.

Peters, M. (1977). Hypertension and the nature of stress. *Science, 198,* 80.

Peters, R. deV. (1994). Better beginnings, better futures: A community-based approach to primary prevention. *Canadian Journal of Community Mental Health, 13,* 183-188.

Peters, R. deV., Peters, J.E., Laurendeau, M.C., Chamberland, C., & Peirson, L. (1999). Social policies for promoting the well-being of Canadian children and families. In I. Prilleltensky, G. Nelson, & L. Peirson (Eds.), *Promoting family wellness and preventing child maltreatment: Fundamentals for thinking and action,* Final report for Social Development Partnerships, Human Resources Development Canada, Waterloo, Ontario.

Peters, R. deV., Petrunka, K., & Arnold, R. (2003). The Better Beginnings, Better Futures Project: A universal, comprehensive, community-based prevention approach for primary school children and their families. *Journal of Clinical Child and Adolescent Psychology, 32,* 215-227.

Peterson, C., & Seligman, M.E.P. (1984). Causal explanations as a risk factor for depression: Theory and evidence. *Psychological Review, 91,* 347-374.

Peterson, D. (1995). The reflective educator. *American Psychologist, 50,* 975-984.

Pfefferman, A., Sullivan, E.V., Rosenbloom, M.J., Mathalon, D.H., & Lim, K.O. (1998). A controlled study of cortical grey matter and ventricular changes in alcoholic men over a 5-year interval. *Archives of General Psychiatry, 55,* 905-912.

Pfeiffer, E. (1977). Psychopathology and social pathology. In J.E. Birren & K.W. Schaie (Eds.), *Handbook of psychology and aging.* New York: Van Nostrand- Reinhold.

Phares, E.J., & Trull, T.J. (1997). *Clinical psychology*. Pacific Grove, CA: Brooks/Cole.

Phares, V. (2003). *Understanding abnormal child psychology*. Hoboken, NJ: Wiley.

Phelan, J. C., Link, B. G., Stueve, A., & Pescsolido, B. A. (2000). Public conceptions of mental illness in 1950 and 1996: What is mental illness and is it to be feared? *Journal of Health and Social Behavior, 41, (June),* 188-207.

Phillip, M., & Fickinger, M. (1993). Psychotropic drugs in the management of chronic pain syndromes. *Pharmacopsychiatry, 26,* 221-234.

Phillips, D.P. (1974). The influence of suggestion on suicide: Substantive and theoretical implications of the Werther effect. *American Sociological Review, 39,* 340-354.

Phillips, D.P. (1977). Motor vehicle fatalities increase just after publicized suicide stories. *Science, 196,* 1464-1465.

Phillips, D.P. (1985). The found experiment: A new technique for assessing impact of mass media violence on real-world aggressive behavior. In G. Comstock (Ed)., *Public communication and behavior* (Vol. 1). New York: Academic Press.

Phillips, K.A., McElroy, S.L., Keck, P.E., Pope, H.G., & Hudson, J.L. (1993). Body dysmorphic disorder: 30 cases of imagined ugliness. *American Journal of Psychiatry, 150,* 302-308.

Phipps, S. (1999). *An international comparison of policies and outcomes for young children.* CPRN Study No. F\05. Ottawa: Canadian Policy Research Networks, Inc.

Pierce, J.P., Choi, W.S., Gilpin, E.A., Farkas, A.J., & Berry, C.C. (1998). Tobacco ads, promotional items linked with teen smoking. *JAMA, 279,* 511-515.

Pierce, W.D., & Epling, F.W. (1996). Theoretical developments in activity anorexia. In W. F. Epling & W. D. Pierce (Eds.), *Activity anorexia: Theory, research, and treatment* (pp. 23-41). Mahwah, NJ: Erlbaum.

Pigott, T.A., Pato, M.T., Bernstein, S.E., Grover, G.N., Hill, J.L., et al. (1990). Controlled comparison of clomipramine and fluoxetine in the treatment of obsessive-compulsive disorder. *Archives of General Psychiatry, 47,* 926-932.

Pike, K. M., & Rodin, J. (1991). Mothers, daughters, and disordered eating. *Journal of Abnormal Psychology*, *100*, 198-204.

Pilowsky, I. (1970). Primary and secondary hypochondriasis. *Acta Psychiatrica Scandinavica, 46,* 273-285.

Pinel, J.P.J., Assanand, S., & Lehman, D.R. (2000). Hunger, eating, and ill health. *American Psychologist*, *55*, 1105-1116.

Pinel, P. (1962). *A treatise on insanity, 1801.* English (D.D. Davis, Trans.). New York: Hafner.

Pinhas, L., Toner, B. B., Ali, A., Garfinkel, P. E., & Stuckless, N. (1999). The effects of the ideal of female beauty on mood and satisfaction. *International Journal of Eating Disorders*, *25*, 223-226.

Pinkston, E., & Linsk, N. (1984). Behavioral family intervention with the impaired elderly. *The Gerontologist, 24,* 576-583.

Piper, W.E., Azim, F.A., Joyce, S.A., McCallum, M., Nixon, G., & Segal, P.S. (1991). Quality of object relations vs. interpersonal functioning as predictors of alliance and outcome. *Archives of General Psychiatry, 48,* 946-953.

Piper, W.E., Ogrodniczuk, J.S., Joyce, A.S., McCallum, M., Rosie, J. S., O'Kelly, J.G., & Steinberg, P.I. (1999). Prediction of dropping out in time-limited interpretive individual psychotherapy. *Psychotherapy*, *36*, 114-122.

Piran, N. (1999). Eating disorders: A trial of prevention in a high risk school setting. *Journal of Primary Prevention*, *20*, 75-90.

Piran, N., Kennedy, S., Garfinkel, P.E., & Owens, M. (1985). Affective disturbance in eating disorders. *Journal of Nervous and Mental Disease, 173,* 395-400.

Pirsig, R.M. (1974). *Zen and the art of motorcycle maintenance: An inquiry into values*. New York: Morrow.

Pisterman, S., Firestone, P., McGrath, P., & Goodman, J.T. (1992). The role of parent training in treatment of preschoolers with ADHD. *American Journal of Orthopsychiatry, 62,* 397-408.

Pitman, R.K., Orr, S.P., Forgue, D.F., Altman, B., deJong, J.B., et al. (1990). Psychophysiologic responses to combat imagery of Vietnam veterans with post-traumatic stress disorder vs. other anxiety disorders. *Journal of Abnormal Psychology, 99,* 49-54.

Pliner, P., & Chaiken, S. (1990). Eating, social motives, and self-presentation in women and men. *Journal of Experimental Social Psychology*, *26*, 693-702.

Pliner, P., Chaiken, S., & Flett, G.L. (1990). Gender differences in concern with body-weight and physical appearance over the life-span. *Personality and Social Psychology Bulletin*, *16*, 263-273.

Pliner, P., & Haddock, G. (1996). Perfectionism in weight-concerned and unconcerned women: An experimental approach. *International Journal of Eating Disorders, 19,* 381-389.

Plotkin, D.A., Mintz, J., & Jarvik, L.F. (1985). Subjective memory complaints in geriatric depression. *American Journal of Psychiatry, 142,* 1103-1105.

Podneiks, E., & Pillemar, K. (1990). *National Survey on Abuse of the Elderly in Canada.* Ryerson Polytechnic Institute, Toronto, ON.

Pokorny, A.D. (1968). Myths about suicide. In H.L.P. Resnik (Ed.), *Suicidal behaviors*. Boston: Little, Brown.

Polich, J.M., Armor, D.J., & Braiker, H.B. (1980). Patterns of alcoholism over four years. *Journal of Studies on Alcohol, 41,* 397-415.

Polivy, J. (1976). Perception of calories and regulation of intake in restrained and unrestrained eaters. *Addictive Behaviors, 1,* 237-244.

Polivy, J. (2001). The false hope syndrome: Unrealistic expectations of self-change. *International Journal of Obesity*, *25*, S80-S84 (Supplement).

Polivy, J., Heatherton, T.F., & Herman, C.P. (1988). Self-esteem, restraint and eating behavior. *Journal of Abnormal Psychology, 97,* 354-356.

Polivy, J., & Herman, C.P. (1985). Dieting and binging: A causal analysis. *American Psychologist, 40,* 193-201.

Polivy, J., & Herman, C.P. (1999). The effects of resolving to diet on restrained and unrestrained eaters: The "false hope syndrome." *International Journal of Eating Disorders*, *26*, 434-447.

Polivy, J., & Herman, C.P. (2002). If at first you don't succeed: False hopes of self-change. *American Psychologist*, *57*, 677-689.

Polivy, J., Herman, C.P., & Howard, K. (1980). The Restraint Scale. In A. Stunkard (Ed.), *Obesity*. Philadelphia: Saunders.

Polivy, J., Herman, C.P., & McFarlane, T. (1994). Effects of anxiety on eating: Does palatability moderate distress-induced overeating in dieters? *Journal of Abnormal Psychology, 103,* 505-510.

Pollak, M.H. (1994). Heart rate reactivity to laboratory tests and in two daily life settings. *Psychosomatic Medicine, 56,* 271-276.

Pollak, R. (1997). *The creation of Dr. B.* New York: Simon & Schuster.

Pollard, C.A., Pollard, H.J., & Corn, K.J. (1989). Panic onset and major events in the lives of agoraphobics: A test of contiguity. *Journal of Abnormal Psychology, 98,* 318-321.

Polusny, M.A., & Follette, V.M. (1995). Long-term correlates of child sexual abuse: Theory and review of the empirical literature. *Applied and Preventive Psychology, 4,* 143-166.

Pope, H.G., & Hudson, J.I. (1988). Is bulimia a heterogeneous disorder? Lessons from the history of medicine. *International Journal of Eating Disorders, 7,* 155-166.

Pope, H.G., Oliva, P.S., Hudson, J.I., Bodkin, J.A., & Gruber, A.J. (1999). Attitudes toward DSM-IV dissociative disorders among board-certified American psychiatrists. *American Journal of Psychiatry, 156,* 321-323.

Pope, K.S. (1995). What psychologists better know about recovered memories, research, lawsuits, and the pivotal experiment: A review of "The Myth of Repressed Memory: False Memories and Allegations of Sexual Abuse," by Elizabeth Loftus and Katherine Ketcham. *Clinical Psychology: Science and Practice, 2,* 304-315.

Porter, S., Woodworth, M., Earle, J., Drugge, J., & Boer, D. (2003). Characteristics of sexual homicides committed by psychopathic and nonpsychopathic offenders. *Law and Human Behavior, 27*, 459-470.

Pos, A.E., Greenberg, L.S., Goldman, R.N., & Korman, L.M. (2003). Emotional processing during experiential treatment of depression. *Journal of Consulting and Clinical Psychology*, *71*, 1007-1016.

Posner, M.I. (1992). Attention as a cognitive and neural system. *Current Directions in Psychological Science, 1,* 11-14.

Post, F. (1987). Paranoid and schizophrenic disorders among the aging. In L.L. Carstensen & B.A. Edelstein (Eds.), *Handbook of clinical gerontology*. New York: Pergamon.

Post, R.M. (1992). Transduction of psychosocial stress into the neurobiology of recurrent affective disorder. *American Journal of Psychiatry, 149,* 999-1010.

Post, R.M., & Weiss, S.R.B. (1995). The neurobiology of treatment-resistent mood disorders. In F. E. Bloom & D. J. Kupfer, (Eds.), *Psychopharmacology: The fourth generation of progress* (pp. 1155-1170). New York: Raven Press.

Poster, D.S., Penta, J.S., Bruno, S., & Macdonald, J.S. (1981). Delta 9-tetrahydrocannabinol in clinical oncology. *Journal of the American Medical Association, 245,* 2047-2051.

Potter, M. (2001, June 9). How home care became latest health crisis: Frail, elderly and disabled suffer in silence. *The Toronto Star,* pp. A1, A26.

Poulin, C. (2000). Problem gambling among adolescent students in the Atlantic provinces of Canada. *Journal of Gambling Studies, 16,* 53-77.

Poulin, C., Fralick, P., Whynot, E.M., El-Guebaly, N., Kennedy, D., Bernstein, J., Boivin, D., & Rinehart, J. (1998). The epidemiology of cocaine and opiate abuse in urban Canada. *Canadian Journal of Public Health, 89,* 234-238.

Poulin, C., Van Til, L., Wilbur, B., Clarke, B., MacDonald, C.A., Barcelo, A., & Lethbridge, L. (1999). Alcohol and other drug use among adolescent students in the Atlantic provinces. *Canadian Journal of Public Health, 90,* 27-29.

Poundmaker's Lodge.(January 21, 2001). Poundmaker's Lodge: Mission, philosophy and facilities. [On-line]. Available: http://poundmaker.org

Powell, L.H., Friedman, M., Thoresen, C.E., Gill, J.J., & Ulmer, D.K. (1984). Can the type A behavior pattern be altered after myocardial infarction? A second year report from the Recurrent Coronary Prevention Project. *Psychosomatic Medicine, 46,* 293-313.

Power, K.G., Simpson, R.J., Swanson, V., Wallace, I.A., Feistner, A.T.C., & Sharp, D. (1990). A controlled comparison of cognitive-behaviour therapy, diazepam, and placebo, alone and in combination, for the treatment of generalized anxiety disorder. *Journal of Anxiety Disorders, 4,* 267-292.

Praderas, K., & MacDonald, M.L. (1986). Telephone conversational skills training with socially isolated impaired nursing home residents. *Journal of Applied Behavior Analysis, 19,* 337-348.

Premack, D. (1959). Toward empirical behavior laws: 1. Positive reinforcement. *Psychological Review, 66,* 219-233.

Prescott, C.A., & Kendler, K.S. (1999). Genetic and environmental contributions to alcohol abuse and dependence in a population-based sample of male twins. *American Journal of Psychiatry, 156,* 34-40.

Pressman, B., & Sheps, A. (1994). Treating wife abuse: An integrated model. *International Journal of Group Psychotherapy, 44,* 477-498.

Prete, C. (2000). Criminally insane. *Hamilton Spectator*, May 15, A12.

Price, R.A., Cadoret, R.J., Stunkard, A.J., & Troughton, E. (1987). Genetic contributions to human fatness: An adoption study. *American Journal of Psychiatry, 144,* 1003-1008.

Prien, R.F., & Potter, W.Z. (1993). Maintenance treatment for mood disorders. In D.L. Dunner (Ed.), *Current psychiatric therapy.* Philadelphia: Saunders.

Prieto, S.L., Cole D.A., & Tageson, C.W. (1992). Depressive self-schemas in clinic and nonclinic children. *Cognitive Therapy and Research, 16,* 521-534.

Prilleltensky, I., & Nelson, G. (2000). Promoting child and family wellness: Priorities for psychological and social interventions. *Journal of Community and Applied Social Psychology*, *10*, 85-105.

Prinz, P., & Raskind, M. (1978). Aging and sleep disorders. In R. Williams & R. Karacan (Eds.), *Sleep disorders: Diagnosis and treatment.* New York: Wiley.

Prizant, B. M. (1983). Language acquisition and communicative behavior in autism: Toward an understanding of the "whole" of it. *Journal of Speech and Hearing Disorders, 48,* 296-307.

Prochaska, J.O. (1984). *Systems of psychotherapy* (2nd ed.). Homewood, IL: Dorsey Press.

Project Match Research Group. (1997). Matching alcoholism treatments to client heterogeneity: Project MATCH posttreatment drinking outcomes. *Journal of Studies on Alcohol, 58,* 7-29.

Prout, P.I., & Dobson, K.S. (1998). Recovered memories of childhood sexual abuse: Searching for the middle ground in clinical practice. *Canadian Psychology*, *39*, 257-265.

Provencher, H.L., & Fincham, F.D. (2000). Attributions of causality, responsibility and blame for positive and negative symptom behaviours in caregivers of persons with schizophrenia. *Psychological Medicine*, *30*, 899-910.

Provencher, H.L., Perreault, M., St-Onge, M., & Rousseau, M. (2003). Predictors of psychological distress in family caregivers of persons with psychiatric disabilities. *Journal of Psychiatric and Mental Health Nursing, 10,* 592-607.

Pryor, T., Wiederman, M.W., & McGilley, B. (1996). Clinical correlates of anorexia subtypes. *International Journal of Eating Disorders, 19,* 371-379.

Pu, T., Mohamed, E., Imam, K., & El-Roey, A.M. (1986). One hundred cases of hysteria in eastern Libya. *British Journal of Psychiatry, 148,* 606-609.

Pugh, G.M., & Boer, D.P. (1989). An examination of culturally appropriate items for the WAIS-R Information subtest with Canadian subjects. *Journal of Psychoeducational Assessment, 7,* 131-140.

Puig-Antich, J., Goetz, D., Davies, M., Kaplan, T., Davies, S., Ostrow, L., Asnis, L., Twomey, J., Iyengar, S., & Ryan, N.D. (1989). A controlled family history study of prepubertal major depressive disorder. *Archives of General Psychiatry, 46,* 406-418.

Puig-Antich, J., Kaufman, J., Ryan, N.D., Williamson, D.E., Dahl, R.E., Lukens, E., Todak, G., Ambrosini, P., Rabinovich, H., & Nelson, B. (1993). The psychosocial functioning and family environment of depressed adolescents. *American Academy of Child and Adolescent Psychiatry, 32,* 244-253.

Puig-Antich, J., Lukens, E., Davies, M., Goetz, D., Brennan-Quattrock, J., & Todak, G. (1985). Psychosocial functioning in prepubertal major depressive disorders: 1. Interpersonal relationships during the depressive period. *Archives of General Psychiatry, 42,* 500-507.

Puig-Antich, J., Perel, J.M., Lupatkin, W., Chambers, W.J., Tabrizi, M.A., King, J., Goetz, R., Davies, M., & Stiller, R.L. (1987). Imipramine in prepubertal major depressive disorders. *Archives of General Psychiatry, 44,* 81-89.

Purdie, F.R., Honigman, T.B., & Rosen, P. (1981). Acute organic brain syndrome: A view of 100 cases. *Annals of Emergency Medicine, 10,* 455-461.

Purdon, C. (1999). Thought suppression and psychopathology. *Behaviour Research and Therapy*, *37*, 1029-1054.

Purdon, C., & Clark, D.A. (1994). Perceived control and appraisal of obsessional intrusive thoughts: A replication and extension. *Behavioural and Cognitive Psychotherapy*, *22*, 269-285.

Putnam, F.W. (1993). Dissociative disorders in children: Behavioral profiles and problems. *Child Abuse and Neglect, 17,* 39-45.

Putnam, F.W. (1996). A brief history of multiple personality disorder. *Child and Adolescent Psychiatric Clinics of North America, 5,* 263-271.

Putnam, F.W., Guroff, J.J., Silberman, E.K., Barban, L., & Post, R.M. (1986). The clinical phenomenology of multiple personality disorder: Review of 100 recent cases. *Journal of Clinical Psychiatry, 47,* 285-293.

Putnam, F.W., Post, R.M., & Guroff, J.J. (1983). *100 cases of multiple personality disorder.* Paper presented at the annual meeting of the American Psychiatric Association, New York.

Putnam, F.W., Zahn, T.P., & Post, R.M. (1990). Differential autonomic nervous system activity in multiple personality disorder. *Psychiatry Research, 31,* 251-260.

Pyle, A. (1999, May 28). Seeking a remedy for nursing homes' ills. *Los Angeles Times*, A1-A30.

Qizilbash, N., Whitehead, A., Higgins, J., Wilcock, G., Schneider, L., et al. (1998). Cholinesterase inhibition for Alzheimer disease: A meta-analysis of Tacrine trials. *JAMA, 280,* 1777-1782.

Quan, H., Arboleda-Florez, J., Fick, G.H., Stuart, H.L., & Love, E.J. (2002). Association between physical illness and suicide among the elderly. *Social Psychiatry and Psychiatric Epidemiology*, *37*, 190-197.

Quay, H.C. (1979). Classification. In H.C. Quay & J.S. Werry (Eds.), *Psychopathological disorders of childhood* (2nd ed.). New York: Wiley.

Quay, H.C., & Parskeuopoulos, I.N. (1972, August). *Dimensions of problem behavior in elementary school children in Greece, Iran, and Finland.* Paper presented at the 20th International Congress of Psychology, Tokyo.

Quinsey, V.L., Khanna, A., & Malcolm, P.B. (1998). A retrospective evaluation of the Regional Treatment Centre Sex Offender Treatment Program. *Journal of Interpersonal Violence*, *13*, 621-644.

Quinsey, V.L., Harris, G.T., Rice, M.E., & Cormier, C.A. (1998). *Violent offenders: Appraising and managing risk.* Washington: American Psychological Association.

Rabavilas, A., & Boulougouris, J. (1974). Physiological accompaniments of ruminations, flooding and thought-stopping in obsessional patients. *Behaviour Research and Therapy, 12,* 239-244.

Rabins, P.V., & Folstein, M.F. (1982). Delirium and dementia: Diagnostic criteria and fatality rates. *British Journal of Psychiatry, 140,* 149-153.

Rabkin, J.G. (1974). Public attitudes toward mental illness: A review of the literature. *Schizophrenia Bulletin*, 9-33.

Raboch, J., & Faltus, F. (1991). Sexuality of women with anorexia nervosa. *Acta Psychiatrica Scandinavica, 84,* 9-11.

Rachman, S. & deSilva, P. (1978). Abnormal and normal obsessions. *Behaviour Research and Therapy, 16,* 233-248.

Rachman, S.J. (1966). Sexual fetishism: An experimental analogue. *Psychological Record, 16,* 293-296.

Rachman, S. (1998). A cognitive theory of obsessions. In E. Sanavio (Ed.), *Behaviour and cognitive therapy today: Essays in honour of Hans J. Eysenck* (pp. 209-222). Oxford, England: Elsevier Science Limited.

Rachman, S. (2002). A cognitive theory of compulsive checking. *Behaviour Research and Therapy*, *40*, 625-639.

Rachman, S. (2003a). Compulsive checking. In R. G. Menzie & P. de Silva (Eds.)., *Obsessive-compulsive disorder: Theory, research, and treatment* (pp. 139-162). Chichester, West Sussex, England: Wiley.

Rachman, S. (2003b). Primary obsessional slowness. In R. G. Menzie & P. de Silva (Eds.)., *Obsessive-compulsive disorder: Theory, research, and treatment* (pp. 181-194). Chichester, West Sussex, England: Wiley.

Rachman, S., Gruter-Andrew, J., & Shafran, R. (2000). Post-event processing in social anxiety. *Behaviour Research and Therapy*, *38*, 611-617.

Rachman, S.J., & Hodgson, R.J. (1980). *Obsessions and compulsions*. Englewood Cliffs, NJ: Prentice-Hall.

Rachman, S., & Shafran, R. (1998). Cognitive and behavioural features of obsessive-compulsive disorder. In R. P. Swinson, M. M. Antony, S. Rachman, & M. A. Richter (Eds.), *Obsessive-compulsive disorder: Theory, research, and treatment* (pp. 51-78). NY: Guilford.

Rachman, S.J., & Wilson, G.T. (1980). *The effects of psychological therapy* (2nd ed.). Elmsford, NY: Pergamon.

Rahe, R.H., & Lind, E. (1971). Psychosocial factors and sudden cardiac death: A pilot study. *Journal of Psychosomatic Research, 15,* 19-24.

Raikkonen, K., Matthews, K.A., Flory, J.D., & Owens, J.F. (1999). Effects of hostility on ambulatory blood pressure and mood during daily living. *Health Psychology, 18,* 44-53.

Raj, B.A., Corvea, M.H., & Dagon, E.M. (1993). The clinical characteristics of panic disorder in the elderly: A retrospective study. *Journal of Clinical Psychiatry, 54,* 150-155.

Rajkowska, G., Selemon, L.D., & Goldman-Rakic, P.S. (1998). Neuronal and glial soma size in the prefrontal cortex: A postmortem morphometric study of schizophrenia and Huntington disease. *Archives of General Psychiatry, 55,* 215-224.

Ralph, J.A., & Mineka, S. (1998). Attributional style and self-esteem: The prediction of emotional distress following a midterm exam. *Journal of Abnormal Psychology, 107,* 203-215.

Ramsey, J.M., Andreason, P., Zametkin, A.J., Aquino, T., King, A.C., Hamburger, S.D., Pikus, A., Rapoport, J.L., & Cohen, R.M. (1992). Failure to activate the left tempoparietal cortex in dyslexia: An oxygen 15 positron emission tomographic study. *Archives of Neurology, 49,* 527-534.

Ramsey, J.M., Zametkin, A.J., Andreason, P., Hanahan, A.P., Hamburger, S.D., Aquino, T., King, A.C., Pikus, A., & Cohen, R.M. (1994). Normal activation of frontotemporal language cortex in dyslexia, as measured with oxygen 15 positron emission tomography. *Archives of Neurology, 51,* 27-38.

Rankin, J., Pron, N., & Duncanson, J. (1995, August 16). "I didn't kill these girls." But Bernardo admits kidnapping, rape. *The Toronto Star,* pp. A1, A12-A13.

Rapaport, D. (1951). *The organization and pathology of thought.* New York: Columbia University Press.

Rapee, R.M., & Heimberg, R.G. (1997). A cognitive-behavioral model of anxiety in social phobia. *Behaviour Research and Therapy*, *35*, 741-756.

Rapp, S.R., Parisi, S.A., Walsh, D.A., & Wallace, C.E. (1988). Detecting depression in elderly medical impatients. *Journal of Consulting and Clinical Psychology, 56,* 509-513.

Rappaport, J. (1977). *Community psychology: Values, research, and action.* New York: Holt, Rinehart & Winston.

Rappaport, J., & Chinsky, J.M. (1974). Models for delivery of service from a historical and conceptual perspective. *Professional Psychology, 5,* 42-50.

Rasmussen, B., & Angus, L. (1996). Metaphor in psychodynamic psychotherapy with borderline and non-borderline clients: A qualitative analysis. *Psychotherapy, 33,* 521-530.

Rasmussen, D.X., Brandt, J., Martin, D.B., & Folstein, M.F. (1995). Head injury as a risk factor in Alzheimer's disease. *Brain Injury, 9,* 213-219.

Rauch, S.L., & Jenike, M.A. (1993). Neurobiological models of obsessive-compulsive disorder. *Psychosomatics, 34,* 20-30.

Rauch, S.L., Jenike, M.A., Alpert, N.M., Baer, L., Breiter, H.C.R., et al. (1994). Regional cerebral blood flow measured during symptom provocation in obsessive-compulsive disorder using oxygen-15 labeled carbon dioxide and positron emission tomography. *Archives of General Psychiatry, 51,* 62-70.

Raymond, N.C., Coleman, E., Ohlerking, F., Christenson, G.A., & Miner, M. (1999). Psychiatric comorbidity in pedophilic sex offenders. *American Journal of Psychiatry, 156,* 786-788.

Rechlin, T., Loew, T.H., & Joraschky, P. (1997). Pseudoseizure "status.". *Journal of Psychosomatic Research, 42,* 495-498.

Rector, N.A., Bagby, R.M., Segal, Z.V., Joffe, R., & Levitt, A. (2000). Self-criticism and dependency in depressed patients treated with cognitive therapy or pharmacotherapy. *Cognitive Therapy and Research*, *24*, 571-584.

Rector, N.A., & Beck, A.T. (2001). Cognitive behavioral therapy for schizophrenia: An empirical review. *Journal of Nervous and Mental Disease*, *189*, 278-287.

Rector, N.A., & Beck, A.T. (2002). Cognitive therapy for schizophrenia: From conceptualization to intervention. *Canadian Journal of Psychiatry*, *47*, 39-48.

Rector, N.A., Seeman, M.V., & Segal, Z.V. (2003). Cognitive therapy for schizophrenia: A preliminary randomized controlled trial. *Schizophrenia Research*, *63*, 1-11.

Rector, N.A., Segal, Z.V., & Gemar, M. (1998). Schema research in depression: A Canadian perspective. *Canadian Journal of Behavioural Science*, *30*, 213-224.

Rector, N.A., Zuroff, D.C., & Segal, Z.V. (1999). Cognitive change and the therapeutic alliance: The role of technical and nontechnical factors in cognitive therapy. *Psychotherapy*, *36*, 320-327.

Red Horse, Y. (1982). A cultural network model: Perspectives for adolescent services and paraprofessional training. In S. Manson (Ed.), *New directions in prevention among American Indians and Alaskan Native communities.* Portland: Oregon Health Sciences University.

Redmond, D.E. (1977). Alterations in the function of the nucleus locus coeruleus. In I. Hanin & E. Usdin (Eds.), *Animal models in psychiatry and neurology*. New York: Pergamon.

Reed, J.C., & Reed, H.B.C. (1997). The Halstead-Reitan Neuropsychological Battery. In G. Goldstein & T. Incagnoli (Eds.), *Contemporary approaches to neuropsychological assessment.* (pp. 93-130). New York: Plenum.

Reed, S.D., Katkin, E.S., & Goldband, S. (1986). Biofeedback and behavioral medicine. In F.H. Kanfer & A.P. Goldstein (Eds.), *Helping people change: A textbook of methods* (3rd ed.). Elmsford, NY: Pergamon.

Regehr, C., Cadell, S., & Jansen, K. (1999). Perceptions of control and long-term recovery from rape. *American Journal of Orthopsychiatry*, *69*, 110-115.

Regehr, C., Goldberg, G., Glancy, G.D., & Knott, T. (2002). Posttraumatic symptoms and disability in paramedics. *Canadian Journal of Psychiatry*, *47*, 953-958.

Regehr, C., Regehr, G., & Bradford, J. (1998). A model for predicting depression in victims of rape. *Journal of the American Academy of Psychiatry and Law*, *26*, 595-605.

Regier, R. (1998). *Manufacturing MPD: The case of Sybil.* Unpublished manuscript.

Reich, J. (1990). Comparison of males and females with DSM-III dependent personality disorder. *Psychiatry Research, 33,* 207-214.

Reid, D.H., Wilson, P.G., & Faw, G.D. (1991). Teaching self-help skills. In J.L. Matson & J.A. Mulick (Eds.), *Handbook of Mental Retardation*, New York: Pergamon Press.

Reifler, B.V. (1994). Depression: Diagnosis and comorbidity. In L.S. Schneider, C.F.

Reynolds, III, B.D. Lebowitz, & A.J. Friedhoff (Eds.), *Diagnosis and treatment of depression in late life* (pp. 55-59). Washington, DC: American Psychiatric Press.

Reinecke, M.A., Ryan, N.E., & Dubois, D.L. (1998). Cognitive-behavioral therapy of depression and depressive symptoms during adolescence: A review and meta-analysis. *Journal of the American Academy of Child and Adolescent Psychiatry, 37*, 26-34.

Reiss, D., Heatherington, E.M., Plomin, R., Howe, G.W., Simmens, S.J., et al. (1995). Genetic questions for environmental studies: Differential parenting and psychopathology in adolescence. *Archives of General Psychiatry, 52*, 925-936.

Reiss, I.L., & Leik, R.K. (1989). Evaluating strategies to avoid AIDS: Number of partners vs. use of condoms. *The Journal of Sex Research, 26*, 411-433.

Reissing, E.D., Binik, Y.M., & Khalife, S. (1999). Does vaginismus exist? A critical review of the literature. *Journal of Nervous and Mental Disease, 187*, 261-274.

Reker, G.T. (1997). Personal meaning, optimism, and choice: Existential predictors of depression in community and institutional elderly. *Gerontologist, 37*, 709-716.

Reker, G.T., Peacock, E., & Wong, P.T.P. (1987). Meaning and purpose in life and well-being: A life-span perspective. *Journal of Gerontology, 42*, 44-49.

Rekers, G.A., & Lovaas, O.I. (1974). Behavioral treatment of deviant sex role behaviors in a male child. *Journal of Applied Behavioral Analysis, 7*, 173-190.

Remington, G., Sloman, L., Konstantareas, M., Parker, K., & Gow, R. (2001). Clomipramine versus haloperidol in the treatment of autistic disorder: A double-blind, placebo-controlled, crossover study. *Journal of Clinical Psychopharmacology, 21*, 440-444.

Renneberg, B., Goldstein, A.J., Phillips, D., & Chambless, D.L. (1990). Intensive behavioral group treatment of avoidant personality disorder. *Behavior Therapy, 21*, 363-377.

Rennie, D.L. (1998). *Person-centred counseling: An experiential approach.* London, England: Sage.

Renshaw, D.C. (1988). Profile of 2376 patients treated at Loyola Sex Clinic between 1972 and 1987. *Sexual and Marital Therapy, 3*, 111-117.

Renvoize, E.B., & Beveridge, A.W. (1989). Mental illness and the late Victorians: A study of patients admitted to three asylums in York, 1880-1884. *Psychological Medicine, 19*, 19-28.

Reppucci, N.D., & Haugaard, J.J. (1989). Prevention of child sexual abuse: Myth or reality. *American Psychologist, 44*, 1266-1275.

Reppucci, N.D., Jones, L.M., & Cook, S.L. (1994). Involving parents in child sexual abuse prevention programs. *Journal of Child and Family Studies, 3*, 137-142.

Rescorla, R.A. (1988). Pavlovian conditioning: It's not what you think it is. *American Psychologist, 43*, 151-160.

Resick, P.A. (1992). Cognitive treatment of crime-related post-traumatic stress disorder. In R. Peters, R. McMahon, & V. Quinsey (Eds.), *Aggression and violence throughout the life span.* (pp. 171-191). Newbury Park, CA: Sage.

Resick, P.A. (1993). The psychological impact of rape. *Journal of Interpersonal Violence, 8*, 223-255.

Resick, P.A., & Schnicke, M.K. (1992). Cognitive processing therapy for sexual assault victims. *Journal of Consulting and Clinical Psychology, 60*, 748-756.

Reuters (1999, October 27). Pontiff says he continues to enjoy life despite aging. *The Toronto Star.*

Reynolds, C.R., Chastain, R.L., Kaufman, A.S., & McLean, J.E. (1997). Demographic characteristics and IQ among adults: Analysis of the WAIS-R standardization sample as a function of the stratification variables. *Journal of School Psychology, 25*, 323-342.

Rhodes, A.E., Goering, P.N., To, T., & Williams, J.I. (2002). Gender and outpatient mental health service use. *Social Science and Medicine, 54*, 1-10.

Rhynard, J., Krebs, M., & Glover, J. (1997). Sexual assault in dating relationships. *Journal of School Health, 67*, 89-93.

Rice, M.E., & Harris, G.T. (2002). Men who molest their sexually immature daughters: Is a special explanation required? *Journal of Abnormal Psychology, 111*, 329-339.

Rice, M.E., & Quinsey, V.L. (1986). Contributions of Canadian applied psychological research to correctional and psychiatric institutions. *Canadian Psychology, 27*, 1-21.

Rice, M.E. (1997). Violent offender research and implications for the criminal justice system. *American Psychologist, 52*, 414-423.

Rice, M.E., & Harris, G.T. (1993). Ontario's maximum security hospital at Penetanguishene: Past, present, and future. *International Journal of Law and Psychiatry, 16*, 195-215.

Rice, M.E., & Harris, G.T. (1995). Violent recidivism: Assessing predictive validity. *Journal of Consulting and Clinical Psychology, 63*, 737-748.

Rice, M.E., & Harris, G.T. (1997). The treatment of mentally disordered offenders. *Psychology, Public Policy, and the Law, 3*, 126-183.

Rice, M.E., Harris, G.T., & Quinsey, V.L. (2002). The appraisal of violence risk. *Current Opinion in Psychiatry, 15*, 589-593.

Rice, M.E., & Quincey, V. L. (1986). Contributions of Canadian applied psychological research to correctional and psychiatric institutions. *Canadian Psychology, 27*, 1-21.

Ricca, V., Mannucci, E., Zucchi, T., Rotella, C.M., & Favarelli, C. (2000). Cognitive-behavioral therapy for bulimia nervosa and binge eating disorder: A review. *Psychotherapy and Psychosomatics, 69*, 287-295.

Riccardo, N., & Leeds, J. (1997, February 24). Megan's law calling up old, minor offenses. *Los Angeles Times*, pp. A1, A16.

Richardson, J.L., Dwyer, K.M., McGuigan, K., Hansen, W.B., Dent, C.W., Johnson, C.A., Sussman, S.Y., Brannon, B., & Flay, B. (1989). Substance use among eighth grade students who
take care of themselves after school. *Pediatrics, 84*, 556-566.

Richman, D.D. (1996). HIV therapeutics. *Science, 272*, 1886-1888.

Richters, J.E., Arnold, L.E., Jensen, P.S., Abikoff, H. (1995). NIMH collaborative multisite multimodal treatment study of children with ADHD: I. Background and rationale. *Journal of the American Academy of Child and Adolescent Psychiatry, 34*, 987-1000.

Ricks, D.M. (1972). *The beginning of vocal communication in infants and autistic children.* Unpublished doctoral dissertation, University of London.

Rieder, R.O., Mann, L.S., Weinberger, D.R., van Kammen, D.P., & Post, R.M. (1983). Computer tomographic scans in patients with schizophrenia, schizoaffective, and bipolar affective disorder. *Archives of General Psychiatry, 40*, 735-739.

Rief, W., Hiller, W., & Margraf, J. (1998). Cognitive aspects of hypochondriasis and somatization syndrome. *Journal of Abnormal Psychology, 107*, 587-596.

Rief, W., Shaw, R., & Fichter, M.M. (1998). Elevated levels of psychophysiological arousal and cortisol in patients with somatization syndrome. *Psychosomatic Medicine, 60*, 198-203.

Riesmann, F. (1990). Restructuring help: A human services paradigm for the 1990s. *American Journal of Community Psychology, 18*, 221-231.

Riggs, D. et al. (1991). *Post-traumatic stress disorder following rape and nonsexual assault: A predictive model.* Unpublished manuscript.

Rind, B., Tromovitch, P., & Bauserman, R. (1998). A meta-analytic examination of assumed properties of child sexual abuse using college students. *Psychological Bulletin, 124*, 22-53.

Ringwalt, C., Ennett, S.T., & Holt, K.D. (1991). An outcome evaluation of Project DARE (Drug Abuse Resistance Education). *Health Education Research, 6*, 327-337.

Ritchie, P.L.-J., & Edwards, H.P. (1998). The evolution of Canada's health-care system and its implications for the practice of psychology as a health profession. In A. S. Bellack & M. Hersen, Eds., *Comprehensive clinical psychology,* vol. 2 *(Arthur N. Wiens, vol. Ed.: Professional issues)* (pp. 377-391*).* Oxford, England: Elsevier Science.

Ritter, B. (1968). The group treatment of children's snake phobias, using vicarious and contact desensitization procedures. *Behaviour Research and Therapy, 6*, 1-6.

Rittig, S., Knudsen, U.B., Norgaard, J.P., Pedersen, E.B., & Djurhuus, J.C. (1989). Abnormal diurnal rhythm of plasma vasopressin and urinary output in patients with enuresis. *American Journal of Physiology, 256*, 664-671.

Rizzo, A.A., Buckwalter, J.G., Neumann, U., Kesselman, C., & Thiebaux, M. (1998). Basic issues in the application of virtual reality for the assessment and rehabilitation of cognitive impairments and functional disabilities. *CyberPsychology and Behavior, 1*, 59-78.

Roberts, J. Browne, G., Gafni, A., Varieur, M., Loney, P. & de Ruijter, M. (2000). Specialized continuing care models for persons with dementia: A systematic review of the research literature. *Canadian Journal on Aging, 19*, 106-126.

Roberts, J.E., & Kassel, J.D. (1997). Labile self-esteem, life stress, and depressive symptoms: Prospective data and a model of vulnerability. *Cognitive Therapy and Research, 21*, 569-589.

Roberts, M.C., Wurtele, S.K., Boone, R.R., Ginther, L.J., & Elkins, P.D. (1981). Reduction of medical fears by use of modeling: A preventive application in a general population of children. *Journal of Pediatric Psychology, 6,* 293-300.

Roberts, N., & Crockford, D. (1997). Psychiatric admissions of Asian Canadians to an adolescent inpatient unit. *Canadian Journal of Psychiatry, 42,* 847-851.

Robertson, H.A., Kutcher, S.P., Bird, D., & Grasswick, L. (2001). Impact of early onset bipolar disorder on family functioning: Adolescents' perceptions of family dynamics, communication, and problems. *Journal of Affective Disorder, 66,* 25-37.

Robin, R.W., Chester, B., Rasmussen, J.K., Jaranson, J.M., & Goldman, D. (1997). Prevalence and characteristics of trauma and posttraumatic stress disorder in a Southwestern American indian community. *American Journal of Psychiatry, 154,* 1582-1588.

Robins, L.N. (1966). *Deviant children grown up.* Baltimore: Williams & Wilkins.

Robins, L.N. (1978). Sturdy childhood predictors of adult antisocial behavior: Replications from longitudinal studies. *Psychological Medicine, 8,* 611-622.

Robins, L.N., Helzer, J.E., Przybec, T.R., & Regier, D.A. (1988). Alcohol disorders in the community: A report from the Epidemiologic Catchment Area. In R.M. Rose & J.E. Barrett (Eds.), *Alcoholism: Origins and outcome.* NY: Raven.

Robins, L.N., & Regier, D. (1991). *Psychiatric disorders in America.* NY: Free Press.

Robinson, D., Woerner, M.G., Alvir, J., Bilder, R., Goldman, R., et al. (1999). Predictors of relapse following response from a first episode of schizophrenia or schizaffective disorder. *Archives of General Psychiatry, 56,* 241-247.

Robinson, L.A., Klesges, R.C., Zbikowski, S.M., & Glaser, R. (1997). Predictors of risk for different stages of adolescent smoking in a biracial sample. *Journal of Consulting and Clinical Psychology, 65,* 653-662.

Robinson, N.M., & Robinson, H.B. (1976). *The mentally retarded child* (2nd ed.). New York: McGraw-Hill.

Robinson, N.S., Garber, J., & Hillsman, R. (1995). Cognitions and stress: Direct and moderating effects on depression versus externalizing symptoms during the junior high school transition. *Journal of Abnormal Psychology, 104,* 453-463.

Robson, L.S., Single, E., Xie, X., & Rehm, J. (1998). The cost of alcohol-attributable injuries and poisonings in Canada, 1992. *Contemporary Drug Problems,* 25-421-433.

Rockwood, K., Cosway, S., Carver, D., Jarrett. P., Stadnyk, K., & Fisk J. (1999). The risk of dementia and death after delirium. *Age And Ageing, 28,* 551-556.

Rodin, J. (1980). Managing the stress of aging: The control of control and coping. In H. Ursin & S. Levine (Eds.), *Coping and health.* New York: Academic Press.

Rodin, J. (1983). Behavioral medicine: Beneficial effects of self-control training in aging. *International Review of Applied Psychology, 32,* 153-181.

Rodin, J. (1986). Aging and health: Effects of the sense of control. *Science, 233,* 1271-1276.

Rodin, J., & Ickovics, J.R. (1990). Women's health: Review and research agenda as we approach the 21st century. *American Psychologist, 45,* 1018-1034.

Rodin, J., & Langer, E.J. (1977). Long-term effects of a control-relevant intervention with the institutionalized aged. *Journal of Personality and Social Psychology, 35,* 897-902.

Rodin, J., McAvay, G., & Timko, C. (1988). A longitudinal study of depressed mood and sleep disturbances in elderly adults. *Journal of Gerontology: Psychological Sciences, 43,* 45-53.

Roesch, R., & Golding, S.L. (1980). *Competency to stand trial.* Urbana: University of Illinois Press.

Roesch, R., Zapf, P., Webster, C.D., & Eaves, D. (1994). *The Fitness Interview Test.* Simon Fraser University: Mental Health Law and Policy Institute.

Roffman, R.A., Stephens, R.S., Curtin, L., Gordon, J.R., Craver, J.N., Stern, M., Beadnell, B., & Downey, L. (1998). Relapse prevention as an intervention model for HIV risk reduction in gay and bisexual men. *AIDS Education and Prevention, 10,* 1-18.

Rogers, C.R. (1942). Counseling and psychotherapy: New concepts in practice. Boston: Houghton Mifflin.

Rogers, C.R. (1951). *Client-centered therapy.* Boston: Houghton Mifflin.

Rogers, C.R. (1961). *On becoming a person: A therapist's view of psychotherapy.* Boston: Houghton Mifflin.

Rogers, C.R. (1970). *Carl Rogers on encounter groups.* New York: Harper & Row.

Rogers, R. (2000). The uncritical acceptance of risk assessment in forensic practice. *Law and Human Behavior, 24,* 595-605.

Rogers, S.L., Doody, R.S., Mohs, R.C., Friedhoff, L.T., & the Donepezil Study Group. (1998). Donepezil improves cognition and global function in Alzheimer disease. *Archives of Internal Medicine, 158,* 1021-1031.

Rogler, L.H., & Hollingshead, A.B. (1985). *Trapped: Families and schizophrenia* (3rd ed.). Maplewood, NJ: Waterfront Press.

Rokeach, M. (1973). *The nature of human values.* New York: Free Press.

Roland, C.G. (1990). *Clarence Hincks: Mental health crusader.* Toronto: Hannah Institute, Dundurn Press.

Romanczyk, R.G., Diament, C., Goren, E.R., Trundeff, G., & Harris, S.L. (1975). Increasing isolate and social play in severely disturbed children: Intervention and postintervention effectiveness. *Journal of Autism and Childhood Schizophrenia, 43,* 730-739.

Romano, E., Tremblay, R. E., Vitaro, F., Zoccolillo, M., & Pagani, L. (2001). Prevalence of psychiatric diagnoses and the role of perceived impairment: Findings from an adolescent community sample. *Journal of ChildPsychology and Psychiatry, 42,* 451-461.

Romanow, R.J., & Marchildon, G.P. (2003). Psychological services and the future of health care in Canada. *Canadian Psychology, 44,* 283-295.

Romero, D. (1992, March 7). Two drugs crash the party scene. *Los Angeles Times,* pp. A1, A22-23.

Ronningstam, E., & Gunderson, J.G. (1990). Identifying criteria for narcissistic personality disorder. *American Journal of Psychiatry, 147,* 918-922.

Room, R., Turner, N. E., & Ialomiteanu. (1999). Community effects of the opening of the Niagara casino. *Addiction, 94,* 1449-1466.

Root, M.P. (1990). Disordered eating in women of color. *Sex Roles, 22,* 525-536.

Rooth, F.G. (1973). Exhibitionism, sexual violence, and pedophilia. *British Journal of Psychiatry, 122,* 705-710.

Rorsman, B., Hagnell, O., & Lanke, J. (1986). Prevalence and incidence of senile and multi-infarct dementia in the Lundby Study: A comparison between time periods 1947-1957 and 1957-1972. *Neuropsychobiology, 15,* 122-129.

Rorty, M., Yager, J., & Rossotto, E. (1994). Childhood sexual, physical, and psychological abuse in bulimia nervosa. *American Journal of Psychiatry, 151,* 1122-1126.

Rosch, P.J. (1998). Reminiscences of Hans Selye and the birth of "stress". *Stress Medicine, 14,* 1-6.

Rose, D.T., Abramson, L.Y., Hodulik, C.J., Halberstadt, L., & Gaye, L. (1994). Heterogeneity of cognitive style among depressed inpatients. *Journal of Abnormal Psychology, 103,* 419-429.

Rose, J. (1996). Anger management: A group treatment program for people with mental retardation. *Journal of Developmental and Physical Disabilities, 8,* 133-149.

Rose, S.D. (1986). Group methods. In F.H. Kanfer & A.P. Goldstein (Eds.), *Helping people change: A textbook of methods* (3rd ed.). Elmsford, NY: Pergamon.

Rosen, G.M. (1999). Treatment fidelity and research on Eye Movement Desensitization and Reprocessing (EMDR). *Journal of Anxiety Disorders, 13,* 173-184.

Rosen, R.C. (1991). Alcohol and drug effects on sexual response: Human experimental and clinical studies. *Annual Review of Sex Research, 2,* 119-180.

Rosen, R.C., & Beck, J.G. (1988). *Patterns of sexual arousal: Psychophysiological processes and clinical applications.* New York: Guilford.

Rosen, R.C., & Leiblum, S.R. (1995). Treatment of sexual disorders in the 1990s: An integrated approach. *Journal of Consulting and Clinical Psychology, 63,* 877-890.

Rosen, R.C., Leiblum, S.R., & Spector, I. (1994). Psychologically based treatment for male erectile disorder: A cognitive-interpersonal model. *Journal of Sex and Marital Therapy, 20,* 67-85.

Rosen, R.C., & Rosen, L. (1981). *Human sexuality.* New York: Knopf.

Rosenbaum, M. (1980). The role of the term schizophrenia in the decline of diagnoses of multiple personality. *Archives of General Psychiatry, 37,* 1383-1385.

Rosenberg, D.R., Keshavan, M.S., O'Hearn, K.M., Seymour, A.B., Birmaher, B., et al. (1997). Frontostriatal measurement in treatment-naive children with obsessive-compulsive disorder. *Archives of General Psychiatry, 54,* 824-830.

Rosenberg, M.S., & Reppucci, N.D. (1985). Primary prevention of child abuse. *Journal of Consulting and Clinical Psychology, 53,* 576-585.

Rosenblatt, R.A. (1998, October 27). Alzhimer's focus shifts to delay, not cure. *Los Angeles Times*, A1-A16.

Rosenfarb, I.S., Goldstein, M.J., Mintz, J., & Neuchterlein, K.H. (1994). Expressed emotion and subclinical psychopathology observable within transactions between schizophrenics and their family members. *Journal of Abnormal Psychology, 104,* 259-267.

Rosenman, R.H., Brand, R.J., Jenkins, C.D., Friedman, M., Straus, R., & Wurm, M. (1975). Coronary heart disease in the Western Collaborative Group Study: Final follow-up experience of 8 years. *Journal of the American Medical Association, 233,* 872-877.

Rosenthal, N.E., Carpenter, C.J., James, S.P., Parry, B.L., Rogers, S.L.B., & Wehr, T.A. (1986). Seasonal affective disorder in children and adolescents. *American Journal of Psychiatry, 143,* 356-358.

Rosenthal, R. (1966). *Experimenter bias in behavioral research.* New York: Appleton-Century-Crofts.

Rosenthal, R. (1995). Critiquing Pygmalion: A 25 year perspective. *Current Directions in Psychological Science, 4,* 171-172.

Rosenthal, T.L., & Bandura, A. (1978). Psychological modeling: Theory and practice. In S.L. Garfield & A.E. Bergin (Eds.), *Handbook of psychotherapy and behavior change: An empirical analysis* (2nd ed.). New York: Wiley.

Rosenzweig, S. (1936). Some implicit common factors in diverse methods of psychotherapy. *American Journal of Orthopsychiatry*, *6*, 412-415.

Roser, K. & Buchholz, E.S. (1996). Autism from an intersubjective perspective. *Psychoanalytic Review, 83,* 305-323.

Rosman, B.L., Minuchin, S., & Liebman, R. (1975). Family lunch session: An introduction to family therapy in anorexia nervosa. *American Journal of Orthopsychiatry, 45,* 846-852.

Rosman, B.L., Minuchin, S., & Liebman, R. (1976). Input and outcome of family therapy of anorexia nervosa. In J.L. Claghorn (Ed.), *Successful psychotherapy*. New York: Brunner/Mazel.

Ross, C.A. (1989). *Multiple personality disorder: Diagnosis, clinical features, and treatment.* New York: Wiley.

Ross, C.A. (1991). Epidemiology of multiple personality disorder and dissociation. *Psychiatric Clinics of North America, 14,* 503-517.

Ross, C. A. (1997). *Dissociative Identity Disorder: Diagnosis, Clinical Features, and Treatment of Multiple Personality*, pp. 107-108. Toronto: John Wiley & Sons, Inc.,.

Ross, C.A. (1997, April 13). *Mind control series: Ryerson CKLN Radio in Toronto: Producer Wayne Morris interviews Dr. Colin Ross.* Toronto: Ryerson CKLN Radio.

Ross, C. A., Joshi, S., & Currie, R. P. (1991). Dissociative experiences in the general population: A factor analysis. *Hospital and Community Psychiatry, 42,* 297-301.

Ross, C.A., Miller, S.D., Reagor, P., Bjornson, L., Fraser, G.A., & Anderson, G. (1990). Structured interview data on 102 cases of multiple personality disorder from four centers. *American Journal of Psychiatry*, *147*, 596-601.

Ross, D.M., & Ross, S.A. (1982). *Hyperactivity: Research, theory, and action.* New York: Wiley.

Ross, D.M., & Ross, S.A. (1984). Childhood pain: The school-aged child's view. *Pain, 20,* 179-191.

Ross, R.S., Bush, J.P., & Crummette, B.D. (1991). Factors affecting nurses' decisions to administer PRN analgesia medication to children after surgery: An analogue investigation. *Journal of Pediatric Psychology, 16,* 151-167.

Rossiter, E.M., & Agras, W.S. (1990). An empirical test of the DSM-IIIR definition of binge. *International Journal of Eating Disorders, 9,* 513-518.

Rost, K., Kashner, T.M., & Smith, G.R. (1994). Effectiveness of psychiatic intervention with somatization disorder patients: Improved outcomes at reduced costs. *General Hospital Psychiatry, 16,* 381-387.

Roth, D., Antony, M.M.,& Swinson, R.P. (2001). Interpretations of anxiety symptoms in social phobia. *Behaviour Research and Therapy*, *39*, 129-138.

Roth, D., & Rehm, L.P. (1980). Relationships among self-monitoring processes, memory, and depression. *Cognitive Therapy and Research, 4,* 149-157.

Roth, M., & Kay, D.W.K. (1956). Affective disorder arising in the senium: 2. Physical disability as an etiological factor. *Journal of Mental Science, 102,* 141-150.

Rothbaum, B.O., & Foa, E.B. (1992). Exposure therapy for rape victims with post-traumatic stress disorder. *the Behavior Therapist, 15,* 219-222.

Rothbaum, B.O., Foa, E.B., Murdock, T., Riggs, D.S., & Walsh, W. (1992). A prospective examination of post-traumatic stress disorder in rape victims. *Journal of Traumatic Stress, 5,* 455-475.

Rothbaum, B.O., Hodges, L.F., Kooper, R., Opdyke, D., Williford, J.S., & North, M. (1995a). The efficacy of virtual reality graded exposure in the treatment of acrophobia. *American Journal of Psychiatry, 152,* 626-628.

Rothbaum, B.O., Hodges, L.F., Kooper, R., Opdyke, D., Williford, J.S., & North, M. (1995b). Virtual reality graded exposure in the treatment of acrophobia. A case report. *Behavior Therapy, 26,* 547-554.

Rothbaum, B.O., Hodges, L., Watson, B.A., Kessler, G.D., et al. (1996). Virtual reality exposure therapy in the treatment of fear of flying: A case report. *Behaviour Research and Therapy, 34,* 477-481.

Rothman, A.J., & Salovey, P. (1997). Shaping perceptions to motivate healthy behavior: The role of message framing. *Psychological Bulletin, 121,* 3-19.

Rothman, K.J., & Michels, K.B. (1994). The continuing unethical use of placebo controls. *New England Journal of Medicine, 331,* 394-397.

Rounsaville, B.J., Chevron, E.S., & Weissman, M.M. (1984). Specification of techniques in interpersonal psychotherapy. In J.B.W. Williams & R.L. Spitzer (Eds.), *Psychotherapy research: Where are we and where should we go*? New York: Guilford.

Rourke, B.P. (2000). Neuropsychological and psychosocial subtyping: A review of investigations within the University of Windsor laboratory. *Canadian Psychology, 41,* 34-50.

Roussy, S., & Toupin, J. (2000). Behavioral inhibition deficits in juvenile psychopaths. *Aggressive Behavior, 26*, 413-424.

Rovner, B.W., Kafonek, S., Filipp, L., Lucas, M.J., & Folstein, M.F. (1986). Prevalence of mental illness in a community nursing home. *American Journal of Psychiatry, 143,* 1446-1449.

Rowa, K., Antony, M.M., Brar, S., Summerfeldt, L.J., & Swinson, R.P. (2000). Treatment histories of patients with three anxiety disorders. *Depression and Anxiety*, *12*, 92-98.

Rowa, K., & Purdon, C. (2003). Why are certain intrusive thoughts more upsetting than others? *Behavioural and Cognitive Psychotherapy*, *31*, 1-11.

Rowland, D.L., Cooper, S.E., & Slob, A.K. (1996). Genital and psychoaffective responses to erotic stimulation in sexually functional and dysfunctional men. *Journal of Abnormal Psychology, 105,* 194-203.

Rowston, W.M., & Lacey, H.J. (1992). Stealing in bulimia nervosa. *International Journal of Social Psychiatry, 38,* 309-313.

Roy, A. (1982). Suicide in chronic schizophrenia. *British Journal of Psychiatry, 141,* 171-180.

Roy, A. (1994). Recent biologic studies on suicide. *Suicide and Life Threatening Behaviors, 24,* 10-24.

Roy, A. (1995). Suicide. In H.I. Kaplan & B.J. Sadock (Eds.), *Comprehensive textbook of psychiatry* (pp. 1739-1752). Baltimore: Williams & Wilkins.

Roy, A., Segal, N., Centerwall, B., & Robinette, D. (1991). Suicide in twins. *Archives of General Psychiatry, 48,* 29-36.

Royal Commission on Aboriginal Peoples (RCAP). Residential Schools. In *Report of the Royal Commission on aboriginal peoples* (pp. 333-385). Ottawa: Canada Communication Group

Roy-Byrne, P.P., & Cowley, D.S. (1998). Pharmacological treatment of panic, generalized anxiety, and phobic disorders. In P.E. Nathan & J.M. Gorman (Eds.), *A guide to treatments that work.* (pp. 319-338). New York: Oxford University Press.

Ruberman, W., Weinblatt, E., Goldberg, J.D., & Chaudhary, B.S. (1984). Psychosocial influences on mortality after myocardial infarction. *New England Journal of Medicine, 311,* 552-559.

Rubia, K., Overmeyer, S., Taylor, E., Brammer, M., Williams, S.C.R., et al. (1999). Hypofrontality in attention deficit hyperactivity disorder during higher-order motor control: A study with functional MRI. *American Journal of Psychiatry, 156,* 891-896.

Rubin, A.J. (1998a, August 15). Court rules FDA cannot regulate tobacco as a drug. *Los Angeles Times*, A1-A10.

Rubin, A.J. (1998b, September 15). Fight ensues to block undoing of doctor-assisted suicide law. *Los Angeles Times*, A5

Rubin, P., Holm, S., Madsen, R.L., Friberg, L., et al. (1993). Regional cerebral blood flow in newly diagnosed schizophrenic and schizophreniform disorders. *Psychiatry Research, 53,* 57-75.

Rubin, R.T., Phillips, J.J., Sadow, T.F., & McCracken, J.T. (1995). Adrenal gland volume in major depression: Increase during the depressive episode and decrease with successful treatment. *Archives of General Psychiatry, 52,* 213-218.

Ruch, L.O., & Leon, J.J. (1983). Sexual assault trauma and trauma change. *Women and Health, 8,* 5-21.

Rucklidge, J.J., & Kaplan, B.J. (1997). Psychological functioning in women identified in adulthood with attention-deficit/hyperactivity disorder. *Journal of Attention Disorders*, *2*, 167-176.

Rucklidge, J.J., & Tannock, R. (2001). Psychiatric, psychosocial, and cognitive functioning of female adolescents with ADHD. *Journal of the American Academy of Child and Adolescent Psychiatry*, *40*, 530-540.

Rumstein-McKean, O., & Hunsley, J. (2001). Interpersonal and family functioning of female survivors of childhood sexual abuse. *Clinical Psychology Review*, *21*, 471-490.

Rush, A.J., Beck, A.T., Kovacs, M., Weissenberger, J., & Hollon, S.D. (1982). Comparison of the effects of cognitive therapy on hopelessness and self-concept. *American Journal of Psychiatry, 139,* 862-866.

Russell, M.A.H., Feyerabend, C., & Cole, P.V. (1976). Plasma nicotine levels after cigarette smoking and chewing nicotine gum. *British Medical Journal, 290,* 1043-1046.

Russo, D.C., & Varni, J.W. (1982). Behavioral pediatrics. In D.C. Russo & J.W. Varni (Eds.), *Behavioral pediatrics: Research and practice*. New York: Plenum.

Rutherford, J., & Noegel, R. (1993). Genetic influences on eating attitudes in a normal female twin population. *Psychological Medicine, 23,* 425-436.

Rutherford, M.J., Cacciola, J.S., & Alterman, A.I. (1999). Antisocial personality disorder and psychopathy in cocaine-dependent women. *American Journal of Psychiatry, 156,* 849-856.

Rutter, M. (1967). Psychotic disorders in early childhood. In A.J. Cooper (Ed.), Recent developments in schizophrenia [Special publication]. *British Journal of Psychiatry*.

Rutter, M. (1971). Parent-child separation: Psychological effects on the children. *Journal of Child Psychology and Psychiatry, 12,* 233-260.

Rutter, M. (1988). Stress, coping, and development: Some issues and some questions. In N. Garmezy, R. Norman, & M. Rutter (Eds.) *Stress, coping, and development in children* (pp. 1-41). Baltimore, MD: Johns Hopkins University Press.

Rutter, M. (1996). Stress research: Accomplishments and tasks ahead. In R. J. Haggerty, & Sherrod, L. R. (Eds.), *Stress, risk, and resilience in children and adolescents: Processes, mechanisms, and interventions* (pp. 354-385). New York: Cambridge University Press.

Rutter, M., & Schopler, E. (1987). Autism and pervasive developmental disorders: Concepts and diagnostic issues. *Journal of Autism and Developmental Disorders, 17,* 159-186.

Ryall, R. (1974). Delinquency: The problem for treatment. *Social Work Today, 15,* 98-104.

Ryan, W. (1971). *Blaming the victim*. New York: Random House.

Rybstein-Blinchik, E. (1979). Effects of different cognitive strategies on chronic pain experience. *Journal of Behavioral Medicine, 2,* 93-101.

Ryder, A.G., & Bagby, R.M. (1999). Diagnostic viability of depressive personality disorder: Theoretical and conceptual issues. *Journal of Personality Disorders*, *13*, 99-117.

Sabin, J.E. (1975). Translating despair. *American Journal of Psychiatry, 132,* 197-199.

Sabol, S.Z., Nelson, M.L., Fisher, C., Gunzerath, L., Brody, C.L., et al. (1999). A genetic association for cigarette smoking behavior. *Health Psychology, 18,* 7-13.

Sacco, R.L., Elkind, M., Boden-Albala, B., Lin, I., Kargman, D.E., et al. (1999). The protective effect of moderate alcohol consumption on ischemic stroke. *JAMA, 281,* 53-60.

Sachs, J.S. (1983). Negative factors in brief psychotherapy: An empirical assessment. *Journal of Consulting and Clinical Psychology, 51,* 557-564.

Sackeim, H.A., Haskett, R.F., Mulsant, B.H., Thase, M.E., Mann, J.J., Pettinati, H.M. et al. (2001). Continuation pharmacotherapy in the prevention of relapse following electroconvulsive therapy: A randomized controlled trial. *Journal of the American Medical Association, 285*, 1299-1307.

Sackeim, H.A., Nordlie, J.W., & Gur, R.C. (1979). A model of hysterical and hypnotic blindness: Cognition, motivation and awareness. *Journal of Abnormal Psychology, 88,* 474-489.

Sadava, S.W., & Pak, A. W. (1993). Stress-related problem drinking and alcohol problems: A longitudinal study and extension of Marlatt's model. *Canadian Journal of Behavioural Science*, *25*, 446-464.

Sadler, J. (in press). Democratic values in the construction of psychiatric nosology. In J. Sadler (Ed.,), *Values and psychiatric classification.* Baltimore: Johns Hopkins University Press.

Safer, D.J., & Krager, J.M. (1988). A survey of medication treatment for hyperactive/inattentive students. *Journal of the American Medical Association, 260,* 2256-2258.

Saffer, H. (1991). Alcohol advertising bans and alcohol abuse: An international perspective. *Journal of Health Economics, 10,* 65-79.

Safran, J.D., Vallis, T.M., Segal, Z.V., & Shaw, B.F. (1986). Assessment of core cognitive processes in cognitive therapy. *Cognitive Therapy and Research, 10,* 509-526.

Sager, C.J. (1990). Foreword. In I.L. Kutash & A. Wolf (Eds.), *The group psychotherapist's handbook: Contemporary theory and technique*. New York: Columbia University Press.

Sahay, S., Piran, N., & Maddocks, S. (2000). Sexual victimization and clinical challenges in women receiving hospital treatment for depression. *Canadian Journal of Community Mental Health*, *19*, 161-174.

Sakel, M. (1938). The pharmacological shock treatment of schizophrenia. *Nervous and Mental Disease Monograph, 62*.

Sakinofsky, I. (1998). The epidemiology of suicide in Canada. In A. A. Leenaars, S. Wenckstern, I. Sakinofsky, R. J. Dyck, M. J. Kral, & R. C. Bland (Eds.), *Suicide in Canada* (pp. 37-66). Toronto: University of Toronto Press.

Sakinofsky, I. (2003). Suicide: The persisting challenge . *Canadian Journal of Psychiatry*, *48*, 289-291.

Saks, E.R. (1997). *Jekyll on trial: Multiple personality disorder and criminal law*. New York: New York University Press.

Saklofske, D.H., Austin, E.J., & Minski, P.S. (2003). Factor structure and validity of a trait emotional intelligence measure. *Personality and Individual Differences*, *34*, 707-721.

Saklofske, D.H., & Hildebrand, D.K. (1999). The Wechsler Adult Intelligence Scale-Third Edition: The Canadian Standardization Study. *Canadian Clinical Psychologist, 9*, 11-12.

Saklofske, D.H., Hildebrand, D.K., & Gorsuch, R.L. (2000). Replication of the factor structure of the Wechsler Adult Intelligence Scale-Third Edition with a Canadian sample. *Psychological Assessment*, *12*, 436-439.

Salan, S.E., Zinberg, N.E., & Frei, E. (1975). Antiemetic effect of delta-9-THC in patients receiving cancer chemotherapy. *New England Journal of Medicine, 293,* 795-797.

Salekin, R.T., Rogers, R., & Sewell, K.W. (1997). Construct validity of psychopathy in a female offender sample: A multitrait-multimethid evaluation. *Journal of Abnormal Psychology, 106,* 576-585.

Salkovskis, P.M. (1985). Obsessional-compulsive problems: A cognitive-behavioural analysis. *Behaviour Research and Therapy*, *27*, 677-682.

Salkovskis, P.M. (1989). Cognitive-behavioural factors and the persistence of intrusive thoughts in obsessional problems. *Behaviour Research and Therapy*, *27*, 677-682.

Salkovskis, P.M. (1996). Cognitive-behavioral approaches to the understanding of obsessional problems. In R. M. Rapee (Eds.), *Current controversies in the anxiety disorders* (pp. 103-133). New York: Guilford Press.

Salkovskis, P.M. (1998). Psychological approaches to the understanding of obsessional problems. In R. P. Swinson, M. M. Antony, S. Rachman, & M. A. Richter (Eds.), *Obsessive-compulsive disorder: Theory, research, and treatment* (pp. 33-50). New York: Guilford Press.

Salkovskis, P.M., & Clark, D.M. (1991). Cognitive therapy for panic disorder. *Journal of Cognitive Psychotherapy, 5,* 215-226.

Salkovskis, P.M., & Warwick, H.M.C. (1986). Morbid preoccupations, health anxiety, and reassurance: A cognitive-behavioural approach to hypochondriasis. *Behaviour Research and Therapy, 24,* 597-602.

Salkovskis, P.M., & Warwick, H.M.C. (2001). Making sense of hypochondriasis: A cognitive theory of health anxiety. In G.J.G. Asmundson, S. Taylor, & B.J. Cox (Eds.), *Health anxiety: Clinical and research perspectives on hypochondriasis and related conditions* (pp. 46-64). Toronto: Wiley.

Salovey, P., & Singer, J.A. (1991). Cognitive behavior modification. In F.H. Kanfer & A.P. Goldstein (Eds.), *Helping people change: A textbook of methods* (4th ed.). Elmsford, NY: Pergamon.

Salter, A. (1949). *Conditioned reflex therapy*. New York: Farrar, Straus.

Salzman, L. (1980). *Psychotherapy of the obsessive personality*. New York: Jason Aronson.

Salzman, L. (1985). Psychotherapeutic management of obsessive-compulsive patients. *American Journal of Psychotherapy, 39,* 323-330.

Sanday, P.R. (1981). The socio-cultural context of rape: A cross-cultural study. *The Journal of Social Issues, 37,* 5-27.

Sanders, G.L. (1996). Recovering from paraphilia: An adolescent's journey from despair to hope. *Journal of Child and Youth Care, 11*, 43-54.

Sanderson, W.C., DiNardo, P.A., Rapee, R.M., & Barlow, D.H. (1990). Syndrome comorbidity in patients diagnosed with a DSM-IIIR anxiety disorder. *Journal of Abnormal Psychology, 99,* 308-312.

Sanderson, W.C., Rapee, R.M., & Barlow, D.H. (1989). The influence of an illusion of control on panic attacks induced via inhalation of 5.5% carbon dioxide-enriched air. *Archives of General Psychiatry, 46,* 157-162.

Sanderson, W. C., & Rego, S. A. (2000). Empirically supported treatment for panic disorder: Research, theory, and application of cognitive behavioral therapy. *Journal of Cognitive Psychotherapy*, *14*, 219-244.

Sanford, K., Bingham, C.R., & Zucker, R.A. (1999). Validity issues with the Family Environment Scale: Psychometric resolution and research applications. *Psychological Assessment*, *11*, 315-327.

Sanger, T.M., Lieberman, J.A., Tohen, M., Grundy, S., et al. (1999). Olanzapine versus haloperidol in first-episode psychosis. *American Journal of Psychhiatry, 156,* 79-87.

Sano, M., Ernesto, C., Thomas, R. G., Klauber, M. R., Schafer, K., Grundman, M., Woodbury, P., Growdon, J., Cotman, C. W., Pfeiffer, E., Schneider, L. S., Thai, L. J., for the Members of the Alzheimer's Disease Cooperative Study. (1997). A controlled trial of selegiline, alpha-tocopherol, or both as treatment for Alzheimer's disease. *New England Journal of Medicine, 336,* 1216-1222.

Santonastaso, P., Ferrara, S., & Favaro, A. (1999). Differences between binge eating disorder and nonpurging bulimia nervosa. *International Journal of Eating Disorders, 25,* 215-218.

Santor, D.A., & Zuroff, D.C. (1994). Effects of negative affectivity and failing to accept the past. *Journal of Personality Assessment*, *63*, 294-312.

Santor, D.A., Zuroff, D.C., Mongrain, M., & Fielding, A. (1997). Validity of the McGill revision of the Depressive Experiences Questionnaire. *Journal of Personality Assessment*, *69*, 164-182.

Sartorius, N., Shapiro, R., & Jablonsky, A. (1974). The international pilot study of schizophrenia. *Schizophrenia Bulletin, 2,* 21-35.

Sarwer, D.B., & Sayers, S.L. (1998). Behavioral interviewing. In A.S. Bellack & M. Hersen (Eds.), *Behavioral assessment: A practical handbook*. (pp. 63-103). Boston: Allyn and Bacon.

Satava, R.M. (1996). Medical virtual reality: The current status of the future. In S.J. Weghorst, H.B. Sieburg, & K.S. Morgan (Eds.), *Proceedings of the Medical Meets Virtual Reality Conference*. (pp. 100-106). Amsterdam: IOS Press.

Sato, T., & McCann, D. (1998). Sociotropy-autonomy and the Beck Depression Inventory. *European Journal of Psychological Assessment*, *16*, 66-76.

Saucier, A. (1992). Le portait des personnes ayant des incapacites au Quebec en 1986. *Direction de l'evaluation.* Ministere de la Sante et des Services Sociaux. Quebec, Canada.

Savage, D.G. (1996, December 11). High court debates sexual predator law. *Los Angeles Times*, p. A26.

Savage, D.G., & Dolan, M. (1996, December 12). Sex predator law faces high court challenge. *Los Angeles Times*, pp. A1, A22.

Sayette, M.A., & Wilson, G.T. (1991). Intoxication and exposure to stress: Effects of temporal patterning. *Journal of Abnormal Psychology, 100,* 56-62.

Saylor, C. F., Powell, P., & Swenson, C. (1992). Hurricane Hugo blows down the broccoli: Preschoolers' post-traumatic play and adjustment. *Child Psychiatry and Human Development, 22,* 139-149.

Scarborough, H.S. (1990). Very early language deficits in dyslexic children. *Child Development, 61,* 128-174.

Scarlett, W. (1980). Social isolation from age-mates among nursery school children. *Journal of Child Psychology and Psychiatry, 21,* 231-240.

Schaefer, L.C., Wheeler, C.C., & Futterweit, W. (1997). Gender identity disorders (transsexualism). In G.O. Gabbard & S.D. Atkinson (Eds.), *Synopsis of treatments of psychiatric disorders, second edition*. (pp. 843-858). Washington, DC: American Psychiatric Press.

Schaie, K.W., & Hertzog, C. (1982). Longitudinal methods. In B.B. Wolman (Ed.), *Handbook of developmental psychology*. Englewood Cliffs, NJ: Prentice- Hall.

Schall, P.L., Landsbergis, P.A., & Baker, D. (1994). Job strain and cardiovascular disease. *Annual Review of Public Health, 15,* 381-411.

Scharff, J.S. (1995). Psychoanalytic marital therapy. In N.S. Jacobson & A.S. Gurman (Eds.), *Clinical handbook of couple therapy*. New York: Guilford.

Schatzberg, A.F. (1991). Overview of anxiety disorders: Prevalence, biology, course, and treatment. *Journal of Clinical Psychiatry, 52,* 5-9.

Schecter, N.L., Allen, D.A., & Hanson, K. (1986). Status of pediatric pain control: A comparison of hospital analgesic usage in children and adults. *Pediatrics, 77,* 11-15.

Schiavi, R.C. (1997). Male erectile disorder. In G.O. Gabbard & S.D. Atkinson (Eds.), *Synopsis of treatments of psychiatric disorders , second edition*. (pp. 781-788). Washington,DC: American Psychiatric Press.

Schizophrenia Society of Canada (2002). *Schizophrenia: Youth's greatest disabler—A report on psychiatrist and patient attitudes and opinions towards schizophrenia*. Ottawa: Schizophrenia Society of Canada.

Schlundt, D.G., & Johnson, W.G. (1990). *Eating disorders: Assessment and treatment*. Needham Heights, MA: Allyn & Bacon.

Schmitt, B.D. (1982). Nocturnal enuresis: An update on treatment. *Pediatric Clinics of North America, 29,* 21-37.

Schmitt, W.A., & Newman, J.P. (1999). Are all psychopathic individuals low-anxious? *Journal of Abnormal Psychology, 108,* 353-358.

Schnall, P.L., Landsbergis, P.A., & Baker, D. (1994). Job strain and cardiovascular disease. *Annual Review of Public Health, 15,* 381-411.

Schneider, J. (1996). Geriatric psychopharmacology. In L.L. Carstensen, B.A. Edelstein, & L. Dornbrand (Eds.), *The practical handbook of clinical gerontology* (pp. 481-542). Thousand Oaks, CA: Sage.

Schneider, J.A., O'Leary, A., & Agras, W.S. (1987). The role of perceived self-efficacy in recovery from bulimia: A preliminary examination. *Behaviour Research and Therapy, 25,* 429-432.

Schneider, K. (1959). *Clinical psychopathology*. New York: Grune & Stratton.

Schneider, N.G. (1987). Nicotine gum in smoking cessation: Rationale, efficacy, and proper use. *Comprehensive Therapy, 13,* 32-37.

Schneider, R. D. (2000). *Statistical Survey of Provincial and Territorial Review Boards*. Ottawa: Federal Department of Justice.

Schneider, R. (2001, July). *Fitness to stand trial: Obligation of the court to inquire?* Paper presented in a symposium chaired by R. Cooper entitled "Adjudicating mental illness: Dilemmas in the courtroom and in practice," 26th International Congress on Law and Mental Health, Montreal, Quebec.

Schneider, R.A., Staggers, F., Alexander, C.N., Sheppard, W., Rainforth, M., Kondwani, K., Smith, S., & King, C.G. (1995). A randomized controlled trial of stress reduction for hypertension in older African Americans. *Hypertension, 26,* 820-827.

Schneider, R.D., Glancy, G.D., Bradford, J.M., et al. (2000). Canadian landmark case, Winko v. British Columbia: Revisiting the conundrum of the mentally disordered accused. *Journal of the American Academy of Psychiatry and the Law*, *28*, 206-212.

Schnittker, J. (2000). Gender and reactions to psychological problems: An examination of social tolerance and perceived dangerousness. *Journal of Health and Social Behavior, 44, (June),* 224-240.

Schoenbach, V., Kaplan, B.H., Fredman, L., & Kleinaum, D.G. (1986). Social ties and mortality in Evans County, Georgia. *American Journal of Epidemiology, 123,* 577-591.

Schoeneman, T.J. (1977). The role of mental illness in the European witch-hunts of the sixteenth and seventeenth centuries: An assessment. *Journal of the History of the Behavioral Sciences, 13,* 337-351.

Schofield, W. (1964). *Psychotherapy: The purchase of friendship*. Englewood Cliffs, NJ: Prentice-Hall.

Schooler, C., Flora, J.A., & Farquhar, J.W. (1993). Moving toward synergy:

Media supplementation in the Stanford Five-City Project. *Communication Research, 26,* 587-610.

Schooler, N.R., Keith, S.J., Severe, J.B., Matthews, S.M., Bellack, A.S., et al. (1997). Relapse and rehospitalization during maintenance treatment of schizophrenia: The effects of dose reduction and family treatment. *Archives of General Psychiatry, 54,* 453-464.

Schopler, E., Short, B., & Mesibov, G.B. (1989). Comments. *Journal of Consulting and Clinical Psychology, 157,* 162-167.

Schover, L. R. (1981). Unpublished research. As cited in Spector & Carey (1990).

Schreiber, F.L. (1973). *Sybil.* Chigaco: Regnery.

Schuckit, M.A. (1983). The genetics of alcoholism. In B. Tabakoff, P.B. Sulker, & C.L. Randall (Eds.), *Medical and social aspects of alcohol use.* New York: Plenum.

Schuckit, M.A. (1994). Low level of response to alcohol as a predictor of future alcoholism. *American Journal of Psychiatry, 151,* 184-189.

Schuckit, M.A., Daeppen, J.-B., Danko, G.P., Tripp, M.L., Smith, T.L., & et al. (1999). Clinical implications for four drugs of the DSM-IV distinction between substance with and without a physiological component. *American Journal of Psychiatry, 156,* 41-49.

Schuckit, M.A., & Smith, T.L. (1996). An 8-year follow-up of 450 sons of alcoholic and control subjects. *Archives of General Psychiatry, 53,* 202-210.

Schuckit, M.A., Smith, T.L., Daeppen, J.-B., Eng, M., Li, T.-K., et al. (1998). Clinical relevance of the distinction between alcohol dependence with and without a physiological component. *American Journal of Psychiatry, 155,* 733-740.

Schultz, J. (1991). Smoking-attributable mortality and years of potential life lost: U.S., 1988. *Morbidity and Mortality Weekly Report, 40,* 63-71.

Schultz, R., & Brenner, G. (1977). Relocation of the aged: A review and theoretical analysis. *Journal of Gerontology, 32,* 323-333.

Schulz, R. (1982). Emotionality and aging: A theoretical and empirical analysis. *Journal of Gerontology, 37,* 42-51.

Schulz, R., & Williamson, G.M. (1991). A 2-year longitudinal study of depression among Alzheimer's caregivers. *Psychology and Aging, 6,* 569-578.

Schultz, S. K. (2000). Editorial: Dementia in the twenty-first century. *American Journal of Psychiatry, 157,* 666-668.

Schuster, M.A. et al.(2001). A national survey of stress reactions after the September 11, 2001 terrorist attacks. *New England Journal of Medicine, 345,* 1507-1512.

Schwartz, J. M. (1998). Neuroanatomical aspects of cognitive-behavior therapy response in obsessive-compulsive disorder. *British Journal of Psychiatry, 173,* 38-44.

Schwartz, G.E. (1973). Biofeedback as therapy: Some theoretical and practical issues. *American Psychologist, 28,* 666-673.

Schwartz, G.E., & Weiss, S. (1977). What is behavioral medicine? *Psychosomatic Medicine, 36,* 377-381.

Schwartz, M.S. (1946). *The economic and spatial mobility of paranoid schizophrenics.* Unpublished master's thesis, University of Chicago.

Schwartz, P.J., Murphy, D.L., Wehr, T.A., Garcia-Borreguero, D., Oren, D.A., et al. (1997). Effects of Meta-chlorphenylpiperazine infusions in patients with seasonal affective disorder and healthy control subjects. *Archives of General Psychiatry, 54,* 375-385.

Schwartz, R., & Schwartz, L.J. (1980). *Becoming a couple.* Englewood Cliffs, NJ: Prentice-Hall.

Schwartz, R.M., & Gottman, J.M. (1976). Toward a task analysis of assertive behavior. *Journal of Consulting and Clinical Psychology, 44,* 910-920.

Schwartz, S.H., & Inbar-Saban, N. (1988). Value self-confrontation as a method to aid in weight loss. *Journal of Personality and Social Psychology, 54,* 396-404.

Schwarz, J.R. (1981). *The Hillside Strangler: A murderer's mind.* New York: New American Library.

Schweizer, E., Rickels, K., Case, G., & Greenblatt, D.J. (1990). Long-term therapeutic use of benzodiazapines: Effects of gradual taper. *Archives of General Psychiatry, 47,* 908-915.

Schwitzgebel, R.L., & Schwitzgebel, R.K. (1980). *Law and psychological practice.* New York: Wiley.

Scientific perspectives on cocaine abuse. (1987). *Pharmacologist, 29,* 20-27.

Scogin, F. (1998). Anxiety in old age. In I.H. Nordhus, G.R. VandenBos, S. Berg, & P. Fromholt, (Eds.), *Clinical geropsychology* (pp. 205-209). Washington, D.C.: American Psychological Association.

Scoggin, F., & McElreath, L. (1994). Efficacy of psychosocial treatments for geriatric depression: A quantitative review. *Journal of Consulting and Clinical Psychology, 62,* 69-74.

Scroppo, J.C., Drob, S.L., Weinberger, J.L., & Eagle, P. (1998). Identifying dissociative identity disorder: A self-report and projective study. *Journal of Abnormal Psychology, 107,* 272-284.

Searight, H.R., & Pound, P. (1994). The HIV-positive psychiatric patient and the duty to protect: Ethical and legal issues. *International Journal of Psychiatry in Medicine, 24,* 259-270.

Seeman, P., & Nizik, H.B. (1990). Dopamine receptors and transporters in Parkinson's disease and schizophrenia. *Federation of Associated Society of Experimental Biology, 4,* 2737-2744.

Seeman, T.E., & Syme, S.L. (1987). Social networks and coronary artery disease: A comparison of the structure and function of social relations as predictors of disease. *Psychosomatic Medicine, 49,* 381-406.

Segal, Z.V., & Gemar, M. (1997). Changes in cognitive organization for negative self-relevant material following cognitive behaviour therapy for depression: A primed Stroop study. *Cognition and Emotion, 11,* 501-516.

Segal, Z.V., Gemar, M., Truchon, C., Guirguis, M., & Horowitz, L.M. (1995). A priming methodology for studying self-representation in major depressive disorder. *Journal of Abnormal Psychology, 104,* 205-213.

Segal, Z.V., Gemar, M., & Williams, S. (1999). Differential cognitive response to a mood challenge following successful cognitive therapy or pharmacotherapy for unipolar depression. *Journal of Abnormal Psychology, 108,* 3-10.

Segal, Z.V., & Shaw, B.F. (1988). Cognitive assessment: Issues and methods. In K.S. Dobson (Ed.), *Handbook of cognitive behavioral therapies* (pp. 39-81). New York: Guilford.

Segal, Z.V., Shaw, B.F., Vella, D.D., & Katz, R. (1992). Cognitive and life stress predictors of relapse in remitted unipolar depressed patients: Tests of the congruency hypothesis. *Journal of Abnormal Psychology, 101,* 26-36.

Segal, Z.V., Teasdale, J.D., Williams, J.M., & Gemar, M.C. (2002). The Mindfulness-Based Cognitive Therapy Adherence Scale: Inter-rater reliability, adherence to protocol, and treatment distinctiveness. *Clinical Psychology and Psychotherapy, 9,* 131-138.

Segal, Z.V., Vincent, P., & Levitt, A. (2002). Efficacy of combined, sequential, and crossover psychotherapy and pharmacotherapy in improving outcomes in depression. *Journal of Psychiatry and Neuroscience, 27,* 281-290.

Segraves, K.B., & Segraves, R.T. (1991). Hypoactive sexual desire disorder: Prevalence and comorbidity in 906 subjects. *Journal of Sex and Marital Therapy, 17,* 55-58.

Segraves, R.T. (1990). Theoretical orientations in the treatment of marital discord. In F.D. Fincham & T.N. Bradbury (Eds.), *The psychology of marriage: Basic issues and applications* (pp. 281-298). New York: Guilford.

Segraves, R.T., & Althof, S. (1998). Psychotherapy and pharmacotherapy of sexual dysfunctions. In P.E. Nathan & J.M. Gorman (Eds.), *A guide to treatments that work.* NY: Oxford.

Seguin, L., Potvin, L., St-Denis, M., & Loiselle, J. (1999). Socio-environmental factors and postnatal depressive symptomatology: A longitudinal study. *Women and Health, 29,* 57-72.

Seidman, L.J., & Bruder, G.E. (2003). Neuropsychological testing and neurophysiological assessment. In A. Tasman, J. Kay, & J.A. Lieberman (Eds.), *Psychiatry, 2nd ed., Vol. 1* (pp. 560-572). Chichester, West Sussex, England: Wiley.

Selemon, L.D., Rajkowska, G., & Goldman-Rakic, P.S. (1995). Abnormally high neuronal density in the schizophrenic cortex: A morphometric analysis of prefrontal area 9 and occipital area 17. *Archives of General Psychiatry, 52,* 805-818.

Seligman, L. (1990). *Selecting effective treatments: A comprehensive, systematic guide to treating adult mental disorders.* San Francisco: Jossey-Bass.

Seligman, M.E.P. (1971). Phobias and preparedness. *Behavior Therapy, 2,* 307-320.

Seligman, M.E.P. (1974). Depression and learned helplessness. In R.J. Friedman & M.M. Katz (Eds.), *The psychology of depression: Contemporary theory and research.* Washington, DC: Winston-Wiley.

Seligman, M.E.P. (1995). The effectiveness of psychotherapy: The Consumer

Reports study. *American Psychologist, 50,* 965-974.

Seligman, M.E.P. (1996). Science as an ally of practice. *American Psychologist, 51,* 1072-1079.

Seligman, M.E.P., Abramson, L.V., Semmel, A., & Von Baeyer, C. (1979). Depressive attributional style. *Journal of Abnormal Psychology, 88,* 242-247.

Seligman, M.E.P., & Binik, U. (1977). The safety signal hypothesis. In H. Davis & H. Horowitz (Eds.), *Operant-Pavlovian interaction*. Hillsdale, NJ: Erlbaum.

Selling, L.S. (1940). *Men against madness*. New York: Greenberg.

Seltzer, L.F. (1986). *Paradoxical strategies in psychotherapy: A comprehensive overview and guidebook*. New York: Wiley.

Selye, H. (1950). *The physiology and pathology of exposure to stress*. Montreal: Acta.

Selye, H. (1974). *Stress without distress*. Philadelphia: J. B. Lippincott Company.

Senior, K. (2000). Bigger and better tobacco warning labels. *Lancet, 356,* 139.

Serdula, M.K., Mokdad, A.H., Williamson, D.F., Galuska, D.A., et al. (1999). Prevalence of attempting weight loss and strategies for controlling weight. *JAMA, 282,* 1353-1358.

Serin, R.C. (1996). Violent recidivism in criminal psychopaths. *Law and Human Behavior, 20,* 207-217.

Serin, R.C., & Amos, N.L. (1995). The role of psychopathy in the assessment of dangerousness. *International Journal of Law and Psychiatry, 18,* 231-238.

Serin, R.C., & Brown, S.L. (2000). The clinical use of the Hare Psychopathy Checklist-Revised in contemporary risk assessment. In C. B. Gacono (Ed.), *The clinical and forensic assessment of psychopathy: A practitioner's guide. The LEA series in personality and clinical psychology* (pp. 251-268). Mahwah, NJ: Erlbaum.

Serin, R.C., Mailloux, D.L., & Malcolm, P.B. (2001). Psychopathy, deviant sexual arousal, and recidivism among sexual offenders. *Journal of Interpersonal Violence, 16,* 234-246.

Serran, G., Fernandez, W.L., & Mann, R.E. (2003). Process issues in treatment: Application to sexual offender programs. *Professional Psychology: Research and Practice, 34,* 368-374.

Seto, M.C., & Barbaree, H.E. (1999). Psychopathy, treatment behavior, and sex offender recidivism. *Journal of Interpersonal Violence, 14,* 1235-1248.

Seto, M.C., & Lalumiere, M.L. (2001). A brief screening scale to identify pedophilic interests among child molesters. *Sexual Abuse: A Journal of Research and Treatment, 13,* 15-25.

Seto, M.C., Lalumiere, M.L., & Blanchard, R. (2000). The discriminative validity of a phallometric test for pedophilic interests among adolescent sex offenders against children. *Psychological Assessment, 12,* 319-327.

Seto, M.C., Lalumiere, M.L., & Kuban, M. (1999). The sexual preferences of incest offenders. *Journal of Abnormal Psychology, 108,* 267-272.

Seto, M.C., Maric, A., & Barbaree, H.E. (2001). The role of pornography in the etiology of sexual aggression. *Aggression and Violent Behavior, 6,* 35-53.

Settin, J.M. (1982). Clinical judgment in geropsychology practice. *Psychotherapy: Theory, Research and Practice, 19,* 397-404.

Seyfort, B., Spreen, O., & Lahmer, V. (1980). A critical look at the WISC-R with Native Indian children. *Alberta Journal of Educational Research, 26,* 14-24.

Shachnow, J., Clarkin, J., DiPalma, C.-S., Thurston, F., et al. (1997). Biparental psychopathology and borderline personality disorder. *Psychiatry—Interpersonal and Biological Processes, 60,* 171-181.

Shader, R.I., & DiMascio, A. (1970). *Psychotropic drug side-effects: Clinical and theoretical perspectives*. Baltimore: Williams & Wilkins.

Shaffer, H. J., Hall, M. H., & Vander Bilt, J. (1997). *Estimating the prevalence of disordered gambling behavior in the United States and Canada: A meta-analysis.* Boston: Presidents and Fellows of Harvard College.

Shafran, R., Thordarson, D. S., & Rachman, S. (1996). Thought-disorder fusion in obsessive-compulsive disorder. *Journal of Anxiety Disorders, 10,* 379-391.

Shahar, G., Blatt, S.J., Zuroff, D.C., & Pilkonis, P.A. (2003). Role of perfectionism and personality disorder features in response to brief treatment for depression. *Journal of Consulting and Clinical Psychology, 71,* 629-633.

Shalev, A.Y., Peri, T., Canetti, L., & Schreiber, S. (1996). Predictors of posttraumatic stress disorder in injured trauma survivors: A prospective study. *American Journal of Psychiatry, 153,* 219-225.

Shalev, A.Y., Sahar, T., Freedman, S., Peri, T., Glick, N., Brandes, D., et al. (1998). A prospective study of heart rate response following trauma and the subsequent development of posttraumatic stress disorder. *Archives of General Psychiatry, 55,* 553-560.

Sham, P.C., Jones, P., Russell, A., Gilvarry, K., Bebbington, P., et al. (1994). Age of onset, sex and familial psychiatric morbidity in schizophrenia. *British Journal of Psychiatry, 165,* 466-473.

Shaper, A.G. (1990). Alcohol and mortality: A review of prospective studies. *British Journal of Addiction, 85,* 837-847.

Shapiro, D., Goldstein, I.B., & Jamner, L.D. (1995). Effects of anger and hostility, defensiveness, gender and family history of hypertension on cardiovascular reactivity. *Psychophysiology, 32,* 425-435.

Shapiro, D., Jamner, L.D., & Goldstein, I.B. (1993). Ambulatory stress psychophysiology: The study of "compensatory and defensive counterforces" and conflict in a natural setting. *Psychosomatic Medicine, 55,* 309-323.

Shapiro, D., Tursky, B., & Schwartz, G.E. (1970). Control of blood pressure in man by operant conditioning. *Circulation Research, 26,* 127-132.

Shapiro, F. (1999). Eye Movement Desensitization and Reprocessing (EMDR) and the anxiety disorders: Clinical and research implications of an integrated psychotherapy treatment. *Journal of Anxiety Disorders, 13,* 35-67.

Shaw, B.F. (1984). Specification of the training and evaluation of cognitive therapists for outcome studies. In J.B.W. Williams & R.L. Spitzer (Eds.), *Psychotherapy research: Where are we and where should we go*? New York: Guilford.

Shaw, B.F. (1999). How to use the allegiance effect to maximize competence and therapeutic outcomes. *Clinical Psychology: Science and Practice, 6,* 131-132.

Shaw, B.F., Elkin, I., Yamaguchi, J., Olmsted, M., Vallis, T.M., Dobson, K.S., Lowery, A., Sotsky, S.M., Watkins, J.T., & Imber, S.D. (1999). Therapist competence ratings in relation to clinical outcome in cognitive therapy of depression. *Journal of Consulting and Clinical Psychology, 67,* 837-846.

Shaywitz, S.E., Shaywitz, B.A., Fletcher, J.M., & Escobar, M.D. (1990). Prevalence of reading disability in boys and girls. *Journal of the American Medical Association, 264,* 998-1002.

Shea, M.T., Elkin, I., Imber, S.D., Sotsky, S.M., Watkins, J.T., Collins, J.F., Beckham, E., Glass, D.R., Dolan, R.T., & Parloff, M.B. (1992). Course of depressive symptoms over follow-up: Findings from the National Institute of Mental Health Treatment of Depression Collaborative Research Program. *Archives of General Psychiatry, 49,* 782-787.

Shea, M.T., Pilkonis, P.A., Beckham, E., Collins, J.F., Elkin, I., Sotsky, S.M., & Docherty, J.P. (1990). Personality disorders and treatment outcome in the NIMH Treatment of Depression Collaborative Research Program. *American Journal of Psychiatry, 147,* 711-718.

Shekelle, R.B., Honey, S.B., Neaton, J., Billings, J., Borlani, N., Gerace, T., Jacobs, D., Lasser, N., & Stander, J. (1983). Type A behavior pattern and coronary death in MRFIT. *American Heart Association Cardiovascular Disease Newsletter*, 33, 34.

Shenal, B.V., Harrison, D.W., & Demaree, H.A. (2003). The neuropsychology of depression: A literature review and preliminary model. *Neuropsychology Review, 13,* 33-42.

Sheppard, D.M., Bradshaw, J.L., Purcell, R., & Pantelis, C. (1999). Tourette's and comorbid syndromes: Obsessive-compulsive and attention deficit hyperactivity disorder. A common etiology? *Clinical Psychology Review, 19,* 531-552.

Sher, K.J., Bartholow, B.D., & Wood, M.D. (2000). Personality and substance use disorders: A prospective study. *Journal of Consulting and Clinical Psychology, 68,* 818-829.

Sher, K.J., & Levenson, R.W. (1982). Risk for alcoholism and individual differences in the stress-response-dampening effects of alcohol. *Journal of Abnormal Psychology, 91,* 350-367.

Sher, K.J., Martin, E.D., Wood, P.K., & Rutledge, P.C., . (1997). Alcohol use disorders and neuropsychological functioning in first year undergraduates. *Experimental and Clinical Psychopharmacology, 5,* 304-315.

Sher, K.J., & Otto, R. (1983). Cognitive deficits in compulsive checkers: An exploratory study. *Behaviour Research and Therapy, 21,* 357-363.

Sher, K.J., Walitzer, K.S., Wood, P.K., & Brent, E.F. (1991). Characteristics of children of alcoholics: Putative risk factors, substance use and abuse, and psychopathology. *Journal of Abnormal Psychology, 100,* 427-448.

Sherwood, G. C., & Gray, J. E. (1974). Two "classic behaviour modification patients": A decade later. *Canadian Journal of Behavioural Science, 6,* 420-427.

Shiffman, S., Fischer, L.A., Paty, J.A., Gnys, M., et al. (1994). Drinking and smoking: A field study of their association. *Annals of Behavioral Medicine, 16,* 203-209.

Shneidman, E.S. (1973). *Suicide.* In Encyclopedia Britannica. Chicago: Encyclopedia Britannica.

Shneidman, E.S. (1976). A psychological theory of suicide. *Psychiatric Annals, 6,* 51-66.

Shneidman, E.S. (1985). *Definition of suicide.* New York: Wiley.

Shneidman, E.S. (1987). A psychological approach to suicide. In G.R. VandenBos & B.K. Bryant (Eds.), *Cataclysms, crises, and catastrophes: Psychology in action.* Washington, DC: American Psychological Association.

Shneidman, E.S., & Farberow, N.L. (1970). A psychological approach to the study of suicide notes. In E.S. Shneidman, N.L. Farberow, & R.E. Litman (Eds.), *The psychology of suicide.* New York: Jason Aronson.

Shneidman, E.S., Farberow, N.L., & Litman, R.E. (Eds.). (1970). *The psychology of suicide.* New York: Jason Aronson.

Shobe, K.K., & Kihlstrom, J.F. (1997). Is traumatic memory special? *Current Directions in Psychological Science,* 6, 70-74.

Shoda, Y., Mischel, W., & Wright, J.C. (1994). Intraindividual stability in the organization and patterning of behavior: Incorporating psychological situations into the idiographic analysis of personality. *Journal of Personality and Social Psychology, 67,* 674-687.

Shogren, E. (1994, August 18). Treatment against their will. *Los Angeles Times*, pp. A1, A16.

Shoham,V., Bootzin, R.R., Rohrbaugh, M., & Urry, H. (1995). Paradoxical versus relaxation treatment for insomnia: The moderating role of practice. *Sleep Research, 25a,* 365.

Shoham, V., Rohrbaugh, M., & Patterson, J. (1995). Problem- and solution-focused couple therapies: The MRI and Milwaukee models. In N.S. Jacobson & A.S. Gurman (Eds.), *Clinical handbook of couple therapy* (pp. 142-163). New York: Guilford.

Shoham-Salomon, V., & Rosenthal, R. (1987). Paradoxical interventions: A meta-analysis. *Journal of Consulting and Clinical Psychology, 55,* 22-27.

Shoham-Salomon, V., Avner, R., & Neeman, R. (1989). You're changed if you do and changed if you don't: Mechanisms underlying paradoxical interventions. *Journal of Consulting and Clinical Psychology, 57,* 590-598.

Shontz, F.C., & Green, P. (1992). Trends in research on the Rorschach: Review and recommendations. *Applied and Preventive Psychology, 1,* 149-156.

Shopsin, B., Friedman, E., & Gershon, S. (1976). Parachlorophenylalanine reversal of tranylcypromine effects in depressed patients. *Archives of General Psychiatry, 33,* 811-819.

Shorter, E. (1996). *TPH: History and memories of the Toronto Psychiatric Hospital, 1925-1966.* Toronto: Wall & Emerson.

Shulman, K.I. (1993). Mania in the elderly. *International Review of Psychiatry, 5,* 445-453.

Shulman, K. I., & Herrmann, N. (1999). The nature and management of mania in old age. *Psychiatric Clinics of North America, 22,* 649-???.

Shulman, K. I., Tohen, M., Satlin, A., Mallya, G., & Kalunian, D. (1992). Mania compared with unipolar depression in old age. *American Journal of Psychiatry, 149,* 341-345.

Shure, M., & Spivack, G. (1988). Interpersonal cognitive problem-solving. In R. Price, E. Cowen, R. Lorion, & X. Ramos-McKay (Eds.), *14 ounces of prevention* (pp. 111-122). Washington, DC: American Psychological Association.

Sicoli, L.A., & Hallberg, E.T. (1998). An analysis of client performance in the two-chair method. *Canadian Journal of Counselling, 32,* 151-161.

Sieg, K.G., Gaffney, G.R., Preston, D.F., & Hellings, J.A. (1995). SPECT brain imaging abnormalities in attention deficit hyperactivity disorder. *Clinical Nuclear Medicine, 20,* 55-60.

Siegel, J.M., Sorenson, S.B., Golding, J.M., Burnam, M.A., & Stein, J.A. (1987). The prevalence of childhood sexual assault: The Los Angeles Epidemiological Catchment Area Project. *American Journal of Epidemiology, 126,* 1141-1153.

Siegel, R.K. (1982). Cocaine smoking. *Journal of Psychoactive Drugs, 14,* 277-359.

Siegel, S. (1975). Evidence from rats that morphine tolerance is a learned response. *Journal of Comparative and Physiological Psychology, 89,* 498-506.

Siegel, S. (1991). Feedforward processes in drug tolerance and dependence. In R. G. Lister & H. J. Weingartner (Eds.), *Perspectives on cognitive neuroscience* (pp. 405-416). New York: Oxford University Press.

Siegel, S. (1999). Drug anticipation and drug addiction. The 1998 H. David Archibald lecture. *Addiction, 94,* 1113-1124.

Siegel, S., Krank, M.D., & Hinson, R.E. (1987). Anticipation of pharmacological and nonpharmacological events: Classical conditioning and addictive behavior. *Journal of Drug Issues, 17,* 83-110.

Siegel, S., Baptista, M.A.S., Kim, J.A., McDonald, R.V., & Weise-Kelly, L. (2000). Pavlovian psychpharmacology: The associative basis of tolerance. *Experimental and Clinical Psychopharmacology, 8,* 276-293.

Siever, L.J., Rotter, M., Losonczy, M., Guo, S.-L., et al. (1997). Lateral ventricular enlargement in schizotypal personality disorder. *Psychiatry Research, 57,* 109-118.

Sifton, D.W. (1988). *PDR drug interactions and side effects index.* Oradell, NJ: Medical Economics.

Sigman, M. (1994). What are the core deficits in autism? In S.H. Broman, & J. Grafman (Eds.), *Atypical cognitive deficits in developmental disorders: Implications for brain function.* (pp. 139-157). Hillsdale, NJ: Lawrence Erlbaum Associates.

Sigman, M., Ungerer, J.A., Mundy, P., & Sherman, T. (1987). Cognition in autistic children. In D.J. Cohen, A.M. Donnellan, & R. Paul (Eds.), *Handbook of autism and pervasive developmental disorders* (pp. 103-120). New York: Wiley.

Silberg, J., Rutter, M., Meyer, J., Maes, H., Hewitt, J., Simonoff, E., Pickles, A., Loeber, R., & Eaves, L. (1996). Genetic and environmental influences on the covariation between hyperactivity and conduct disturbance in juvenile twins. *Journal of Child Psychology and Psychiatry, 37,* 803-816.

Silverman, J.M., Li, G., Zaccario, M.L., Smith, C., Schmeidler, J., et al. (1994). Patterns of risk in first-degree relatives with Alzheimer's disease. *Archives of General Psychiatry, 51,* 568-576.

Silverman, K., Evans, S.M., Strain, E.C., & Griffiths, R.R. (1992). Withdrawal syndrome after the double-blind cessation of caffeine consumption. *New England Journal of Medicine, 327,* 1109-1114.

Silverman, K., Higgins, S.T., Brooner, R.K., Montoya, I.D., Cone, E.J., Schuster, C.R., & Preston, K.I. (1996). Sustained cocaine abstinence in methadone maintenance patients through voucher-based reinforcement therapy. *Archives of General Psychiatry, 53,* 409-413.

Silverstein, B., Feld, S., & Kozlowski, L.T. (1980). The availability of low-nicotine cigarettes as a cause of cigarette smoking among teenage females. *Journal of Health and Social Behavior, 21,* 383-388.

Silverstein, C. (1972). *Behavior modification and the gay community.* Paper presented at the annual convention of the Association for Advancement of Behavior Therapy, New York.

Simeon, D., Gross, S., Guralnik, O., Stein, D.J., Schmeidler, J., & Hollander, E. (1997). Feeling unreal: 30 cases of DSM-III-R depersonalization disorder. *American Journal of Psychiatry, 154,* 1107-1112.

Simeons, A.T.W. (1961). *Man's presumptuous brain: An evolutionary interpretation of psychosomatic disease.* New York: Dutton.

Simmie, S., (1998, October 3-10). Atkinson Fellowship investigation into mental health: Out of Mind (Series). *The Toronto Star.*

Simmie, S. (1998). True reform is up to all of us. *Toronto Star*, October 10, 1998.

Simmie, S., & Nunes, J. (2001). *The last taboo: A survival guide to mental health care in Canada.* Toronto: McLelland and Stewart.

Simmons, H.G. (1987). Psychosurgery and the abuse of psychiatric authority in Ontario. *Journal of Health Politics, 12,* 537-550.

Simon, G.E. (1998). Management of somatoform and factitious disorders. In P.E. Nathan & J.M. Gorman (Eds.), *A guide to treatments that work.* (pp. 408-422). New York: Oxford University Press.

Simon, G.E., & Gureje, O. (1999). Stability of somatization disorder and somatization symptoms among primary care patients. *Archives of General Psychiatry, 56,* 90-95.

Simon, G.E., VonKorff, M., Piccinelli, M., Fullerton, C., & Ormel, J. (1999). An international study of the relation between somatic symptoms and depression. *New England Journal of Medicine, 341,* 1329-1335.

Simon, R.J., & Aaronson, D.E. (1988). *The insanity defense: A critical assessment of law and policy in the post-Hinckley era.* New York: Praeger.

Simons, A.D., Garfield, S.L., & Murphy, G.E. (1984). The process of change in cognitive therapy and pharmacotherapy for depression: Changes in mood and cognition. *Archives of General Psychiatry, 41,* 45-51.

Simpson, J., Doze, S., Urness, D., Hailey, D., & Jacobs, P. (2001a). Evaluation of a routine telepsychiatry service. *Journal of Telemedicine and Telecare, 7,* 90-98.

Simpson, J., Doze, S., Urness, D., Hailey, D., & Jacobs, P. (2001b). Telepsychiatry as a routine service—The perspective of the patient. *Journal of Telemedicine and Telecare, 7,* 155-160.

Sinclair, C. (1993). Codes of ethics and standards of practice. In K. G. Dobson & D. J. G. Dobson (Eds.), *Professional psychology in Canada* (pp. 167-199). Toronto: Hogrefe and Huber.

Sinclair, C., Poizner, S., Gilmour-Barrett, K., & Randall, D. (1987). The development of a code of ethics for Canadian psychologists. *Canadian Psychology, 28,* 1-8.

Sinclair, J.J., Larzelere, R.E., Paine, M., Jones, P., et al. (1995). Outcome of group treatment for sexually abused adolescent females living in a group home setting: Preliminary findings. *Journal of Interpersonal Violence, 10,* 533-542.

Singer, J.L. (1984). The private personality. *Personality and Social Psychology Bulletin, 10,* 7-30.

Single, E., Brewster, J.M., MacNeil, P., Hatcher, J., & Trainor, C. (1995). The 1993 General Social Survey I: Alcohol use in Canada. *Canadian Journal of Public Health, 86,* 397-401.

Single, E., MacLennan, A., & MacNeil. (1994). *Horizons 1994: Alcohol and other drug use in Canada.* Ottawa, ON: Health Canada, Health Promotion Directorate.

Single, E., Rehm, J., Robson, L., & Van Truong, M. (2000). The relative risks and etiologic fractions of different causes of death and disease attributable to alcohol, tobacco, and illicit drug use in Canada. *Canadian Medical Association Journal, 162,* 1669-1175.

Sinha, B.K., & Watson, D.C. (2001). Personality disorder in university students: A multitrait-multimethod matrix study. *Journal of Personality Disorders, 15,* 235-244.

Sinnott, J.D. (1986). *Sex roles and aging: Theory and research from a systems perspective.* Basel, Switzerland: Karger.

Sintchak, G.H., & Geer, J.H. (1975). A vaginal plethysmograph system. *Psychophysiology, 12,* 113-115.

Siris, S.G., Bermanzohn, P.C., Mason, S.E., & Shuwall, M.A. (1994). Maintenance imipramine therapy for secondary depression in schizophrenia: A controlled trial. *Archives of General Psychiatry, 51,* 109-115.

Sisson, R.W., & Azrin, N.H. (1989). The community-reinforcement approach. In R.K. Hester & W.R. Miller (Eds.), *Handbook of alcoholism treatment approaches: Effective alternatives* (pp. 242-258). New York: Pergamon.

Sizemore, C.C., & Pittillo, E.S. (1977). *I'm Eve.* Garden City, NY: Doubleday.

Sizemore, J.P. (1995). Alabama's confidentiality quagmire: Psychotherapists, AIDS, mandatory reporting, and Tarasoff. *Law and Psychology Review, 19,* 241-257.

Skarborn, M., & Nicki, R. (1996). Worry among Canadian seniors. *International Journal of Aging and Human Development, 43,* 169-178.

Skilling, T.A., Harris, G.T., Rice, M.E., & Quinsey, V.L. (2002). Identifying persistently antisocial offenders using the Hare Psychopathy Checklist and DSM antisocial personality disorder criteria. *Psychological Assessment, 14,* 27-38.

Skinner, H., Steinhauer, P.D., & Santa-Barbera, J. (1983). The Family Assessment Measure. *Canadian Journal of Community Mental Health, 2,* 91-105.

Skinner, H., Steinhauer, P., & Sitarenios, G. (2000). Family Assessment Measure (FAM), and the process model of family functioning. *Journal of Family Therapy, 22,* 190-210.

Skinner, B.F. (1953). Science and human behavior. New York: Macmillan.

Sklar, L.A., & Anisman, H. (1979). Stress and coping factors influence tumor growth. *Science, 205,* 513-515.

Skodol, A.E., Gallaher, P.E., & Oldham, J.M. (1997). Excessive dependency and depression: Is the relationship specific? *Journal of Nervous and Mental Disease, 184,* 165-171.

Skodol, A.E., Oldham, J.M., & Gallaher, P.E. (1999). Axis II comorbidity of substance use disorders among parients referred for treatment of personality disorders. *American Journal of Psychiatry, 156,* 733-738.

Skolnick, A.S. (1998). Guidelines for treating erectile dysfunction issued. *JAMA, 277,* 24-26.

Skoog, G., & Skoog, I. (1999). A 40-year follow-up of patients with obsessive-compulsive disorder. *Archives of General Psychiatry, 56,* 121-130.

Slater, E. (1961). The thirty-fifth Maudsley lecture: Hysteria 311. *Journal of Mental Science, 107,* 358-381.

Slater, E., & Glithero, E. (1965). A follow-up of patients diagnosed as suffering from hysteria. *Journal of Psychosomatic Research, 9,* 9-13.

Slavson, S.R. (1950). *Analytic group psychotherapy with children, adolescents and adults.* New York: Columbia University Press.

Sloane, R.B. (1980). Organic brain syndrome. In J.E. Birren & R.B. Sloane (Eds.), *Handbook of mental health and aging.* Englewood Cliffs, NJ: Prentice-Hall.

Slutske, W.S., Heath, A.C., Dinwiddie, S.H., Madden, P.A.F., Bucholz, K.K., Dunne, M.P., Stathan, D.J., & Martin, N.G. (1997). Modeling genetic and environmental influences in the etiology of conduct disorder: A study of 2,682 adult twin pairs. *Journal of Abnormal Psychology, 106,* 266-279.

Small, G.W., & Jarvik, L.F. (1982). The dementia syndrome. *Lancet,* 1443-1446.

Small, G.W., Komanduri, R., Gitlin, M., & Jarvik, L.F. (1986). The influence of age on guilt expression in major depression. *International Journal of Geriatric Psychiatry, 1,* 121-126.

Small, J.C., Klapper, M.H., Milstein, V., Kellans, J.J., Miller, M.J., et al. (1991). Carbamazapine compared with lithium in the treatment of mania. *Archives of General Psychiatry, 48,* 915-921.

Smart, R.G., & Ogborne, A.C. (2000). Drug use and drinking among students in 36 countries. *Addictive Behaviors, 25,* 455-460.

Smith, D.W., Bierman, E.L., & Robinson, N.M. (1978). *The biologic ages of man: From conception through old age.* Philadelphia: Saunders.

Smith, F.A., Fenton, F.R., Benoit, C., & Barzell, E. (1976). Home-care treatment of acutely ill psychiatric patients: A review of 78 cases. *Canadian Psychiatric Association Journal, 21,* 269-274.

Smith, G.T., Goldman, M.S., Greenbaum, P.E., & Christiansen, B.A. (1995). Expectancy for social facilitation from drinking: The divergent paths of high expectancy and low expectancy adolescents. *Journal of Abnormal Psychology, 104,* 32-40.

Smith, J., Frawley, P.J., & Polissar, L. (1991). Six- and twelve-month abstinence rates in inpatient alcoholics treated with aversion therapy compared with matched inpatients from a treatment registry. *Alcoholism: Clinical and Experimental Research, 15,* 862-870.

Smith, J., & Prior, M. (1995). Temperament and stress resilience in school-age children: A within-families study. *Journal of the American Academy of Child and Adolescent Psychiatry, 34,* 168-179.

Smith, K.A., Fairburn, C.G., & Cowen, P.J. (1999). Symptomatic relapse in bulimia nervosa following acute tryptophan depletion. *Archives of General Psychiatry, 56,* 171-176.

Smith, K.F., & Bengston, V.L. (1979). Positive consequences of institutionalization: Solidarity between elderly parents and their middle aged children. *The Gerontologist, 5,* 438-447.

Smith, P.B. (1975). Controlled studies of the outcome of sensitivity training. *Psychological Bulletin, 82,* 597-622.

Smith, S.S., & Newman, J.P. (1990). Alcohol and drug dependence in psychopathic and nonpsychopathic criminal offenders. *Journal of Abnormal Psychology, 99,* 430-439.

Smith, T., Snyder, C.R., & Perkins, S.C. (1983). Self-serving function of hypochondriacal complaints: Physical symptoms as self-handicapping strategies. *Journal of Personality and Social Psychology, 44,* 787-797.

Smith, T.W. (1983). Change in irrational beliefs and the outcome of rational-emotive psychotherapy. *Journal of Consulting and Clinical Psychology, 51,* 156-157.

Smolowe, J. (1996, Fall). Older, longer. *Time, 148* (Special Issue), 76-80.

Smyer, M.A., & Gatz, M. (1995). The public policy context of mental health care for older adults. *The Clinical Psychologist, 48,* 31-36.

Smyth, C., Kalsi, G., Brynjofsson, J., O'Neill, J., Curtis, D., et al. (1996). Further tests for linkage of bipolar affective disorder to the tyrosine hydroxylase gene of chromosome 11p15 in a new series of multiplex British affective disorder pedigrees. *American Journal of Psychiatry, 153,* 271-274.

Snow, W.G. (1987). Standardization of test administration and scoring criteria: Some shortcomings of current practice with the Halstead-Reitan test battery. *The Clinical Neurologist, 1,* 250-262.

Snowdon, D.A., Kemper, S.J., Mortimer, J.A., Greiner, L.H., et al. (1996). Linguistic ability in early life and cognitive function and Alzheimer's disease in late life: Findings from the nun study. *JAMA, 275,* 528-534.

Snyder, A.G., & Stanley, M.A. (2001). Hypochondriasis and health anxiety in the elderly. In G.J.G. Asmundson, S. Taylor, & B.J. Cox, *Health anxiety: Clinical and research perspectives on hypochondriasis and related conditions* (pp. 246-274). Chichester, West Sussex, England: Wiley.

Snyder, D.K., & Wills, R.M. (1989). Behavioral versus insight-oriented marital therapy: Effects of individual and interspousal functioning. *Journal of Consulting and Clinical Psychology, 57,* 39-46.

Snyder, D.K., Wills, R.M., & Grady-Fletcher, A. (1991). Long-term effectiveness of behavioral versus insight-oriented marital therapy: A 4-year follow-up study. *Journal of Consulting and Clinical Psychology, 59,* 138-141.

Snyder, M., & White, E. (1982). Moods and memories: Elation, depression, and remembering the events of one's life. *Journal of Personality, 50,* 149-167.

Snyder, S.H. (1974). Madness and the brain. New York: McGraw-Hill.

Sobell, L.C., Cunningham, J.A., Sobell, M.B., Agrawal, S., Gavin, D.R., Leo, G.I., & Singh, K.N. (1996). Fostering self-change among problem drinkers: A protective community intervention. *Addictive Behaviors, 21,* 817-833.

Sobell, M.B., & Sobell, L.C. (1976). Second-year treatment outcome of alcoholics treated by individualized behavior therapy: Results. *Behaviour Research and Therapy, 14,* 195-215.

Sobell, M.B., & Sobell, L.C. (1993). *Problem drinkers: Guided self-change treatment.* New York: Guilford.

Sobell, M.B., & Sobell, L.C. (1998).

Sobell, M.B., & Sobell, L.C. (2000). Stepped care as a heuristic approach to the treatment of alcohol problems. *Journal of Consulting and Clinical Psychology, 68,* 573-579.

Sobell, M.B., Sobell, L.C., & Leo, (2000).

Society of Behavioral Medicine. (1989). *Bylaws of the Society of Behavioral Medicine.* Washington, DC: Author.

Solomon, Z., Mikulincer, M., & Flum, H. (1988). Negative life events, coping response, and combat-related psychopathology: A prospective study. *Journal of Abnormal Psychology, 97,* 302-307.

Sorenson, S.B., & Brown, V.B. (1990). Interpersonal violence and crisis intervention on the college campus. *New Directions for Student Services, 49,* 57-66.

Soueif, M.I. (1976). Some determinants of psychological deficits associated with chronic cannabis consumption. *Bulletin of Narcotics, 28,* 25-42.

Southwick, S.M., Krystal, J.H., Morgan, C.A., Johnson, D., Nagy, L.M., et al. (1993). Abnormal noradrenergic function in posttraumatic stress disorder. *Archives of General Psychiatry, 50,* 266-274.

Spacapan, S., & Oskamp, S. (1989). Introduction to the social psychology of aging. In S. Spacapan & S. Oskamp (Eds.), *The social psychology of aging* (pp. 9-24). Newbury Park, CA: Sage.

Spanos, N.P. (1994). Multiple identity enactments and multiple personality disorder: A sociocognitive perspective. *Psychological Bulletin, 116,* 143-165.

Spanos, N.P., Burgess, C.A., Burgess, M.F., Samuels, C., & Blois, W.O. (1999). Creating false memories of infancy with hypnotic and non-hypnotic procedures. *Applied Cognitive Psychology, 13,* 210-218.

Spanos, N. P., Cross, P. A., Dickson, K., & DeBreuil, S. C. (1993). Close encounters: An examination of UFO experiences. *Journal of Abnormal Psychology, 102,* 624-632.

Spanos, N.P., Weekes, J.R., & Bertrand, L.D. (1985). Multiple personality: A social psychological perspective. *Journal of Abnormal Psychology, 94,* 362-376.

Sparks, B.F., et al. (2002). Brain structural abnormalities in children and adults with autism. *Neurology, 59,* 184-192.

Sparrow, S.S., Ballo, D.A., & Cicchetti, D.V. (1984). *Vineland Adaptive Behavior Scales.* Circle Pines, MI: American Guidance Service.

Spector, I.P., & Carey, M.P. (1990). Incidence and prevalence of the sexual dysfunctions: A critical review of the empirical literature. *Archives of Sexual Behavior, 19,* 389-408.

Spence, J.D., Barnett, P.A., Linden, W., Ramsden, V., & Taenzer, P. (1999). Recommendations on stress management. *Canadian Medical Association Journal, 160,* S46-S50.

Spencer, C. (1996). *Diminishing returns: An examination of financial responsibility, decision-making, and financial abuse among older adults in British Columbia.* Vancouver: Gerontology Research Centre, Simon Fraser University.

Spencer, G. (1989). *Projections of the population of the United States, by age, sex, and race: 1988 to 2080.* Washington, DC: U.S. Department of Commerce.

Spencer, T., Biederman, J., Wilens, T., Harding, M., O'Donnell, D., & Griffin, S. (1996). Pharmacotherapy of attention-deficit hyperactivity disorder across the life cycle. *Journal of the American Academy of Child and Adolescent Psychiatry, 35,* 409-432.

Spengler, A. (1977). Manifest sadomasochism of males: Results of an empirical study. *Archives of Sexual Behavior, 6,* 441-456.

Spiegel, D. (1990). Can psychotherapy prolong cancer survival? *Psychosomatics, 31,* 361-366.

Spiegel, D., Bloom, J.R., Kraemer, H.C., & Gottheil, E. (1989). Effect of psychosocial treatment on survival of patients with metastatic breast cancer. *Lancet, 2,* 888-891.

Spiegel, D., Bloom, J.R., & Yalom, I. (1981). Group support for patients with metastatic cancer: A randomized prospective outcome study. *Archives of General Psychiatry, 38,* 527-534.

Spiers, P.A. (1982). The Luria-Nebraska Neuropsychological Battery revisited: A theory in practice or just practicing? *Journal of Consulting and Clinical Psychology, 50,* 301-306.

Spiess, W.F.J., Geer, J.H., & O'Donohue, W.T. (1984). Premature ejaculation: Investigation of factors in ejaculatory latency. *Journal of Abnormal Psychology, 93,* 242-245.

Spinetta, J.J. (1980). Disease-related communication: How to tell. In J. Kellerman (Ed.), *Psychological aspects of childhood cancer.* Springfield, IL: Charles C. Thomas.

Spitzer, B.L., Henderson, K.A., & Zivian, M.T. (1999). Gender differences in population versus media body sizes: A comparison over four decades. *Sex Roles, 40,* 545-565.

Spitzer, C., Spelsberg, B., Grabe, H.-J., Mundt, B., & Freyberger, H.J. (1999). Dissociative experiences and psychopathology in conversion disorders. *Journal of Psychosomatic Research, 46,* 291-294.

Spitzer, R.L., Endicott, J., & Gibbon, M. (1979). Crossing the border into borderline personality and borderline schizophrenia. *Archives of General Psychiatry, 36,* 17-24.

Spitzer, R.L., Gibbon, M., & Williams, J.B.W. (1986). *Structured clinical interview of DSM-IV Axis I disorders.* New York: N.Y. State Psychiatric Institute, Biometrics Research Department.

Spitzer, R.M., Stunkard, A., Yanovski, S., Marcus, M.D., Wadden, T., et al. (1993). Binge eating disorders should be included in DSM-IV. *International Journal of Eating Disorders, 13,* 161-169.

Sprague, R.L., & Gadow, K.D. (1976). The role of the teacher in drug treatment. *School Review, 85,* 109-140.

Spreen, O., & Strauss, E. (1998). *A compendium of neuropsychological tests* (2nd ed.). New York: Oxford University Press.

Spunt, B., Goldstein, P., Brownstein, H., & Fendrich, M. (1994). The role of marijuana in homicide. *International Journal of the Addictions, 29,* 195-213.

Squires-Wheeler, E., Skodal, A., Agamo, O.M., Bassett, A.S., et al. (1993). Personality features and disorder in the subjects in the New York High-Risk Project. *Journal of Psychiatric Research, 27,* 379-393.

Srinivasagam, N. M., Kaye, W. H., Plotnicov, K. H., Greeno, C., Weltzin, T. E., & Rao, R. (1995). Persistent perfectionism, symmetry, and exactness after long-term recovery from anorexia nervosa. *American Journal of Psychiatry, 152,* 1630-1634.

St. Lawrence, J., Jefferson, K.W., Banks, P.G., Cline, T.R., et al. (1994). Cognitive-behavioral group intervention to assist substance-dependent adolescents in lowering HIV infection. *AIDS Education and Prevention, 6,* 425-435.

St. Lawrence, J.S., & Madakasira, S. (1992). Evaluation and treatment of premature ejaculation: A critical review. *International Journal of Psychiatry in Medicine, 22,* 77-97.

Staats, A.W., & Staats, C.K. (1963). *Complex human behavior.* New York: Holt, Rinehart & Winston.

Stacy, A.W., Newcomb, M.D., & Bentler, P.M. (1991). Cognitive motivation and drug use: A 9-year longitudinal study. *Journal of Abnormal Psychology, 100,* 502-515.

Stacy, A.W., Sussman, S., Dent, C.W., Burton, D., & Flay, B.R. (1992). Moderators of peer social influence in adolescent smoking. *Personality and Social Psychology Bulletin, 18,* 163-172.

Stader, S.R., & Hokanson, J.E. (1998). Psychosocial antecendents of depressive symptoms: An evaluation using daily experiences methodology. *Journal of Abnormal Psychology, 107,* 17-26.

Stall, R.D., McKusick, L., Wiley, J., Coates, T., & Ostrow, D. (1986). Alcohol and drug use during sexual activity and compliance with safe sex guidelines for AIDS: The AIDS Behavioral Research Project. *Health Education Quarterly, 13,* 359-371.

Stampfer, M.J., Colditz, G.A., Willett, W.C., Speizer, F.E., & Hennekens, C.H. (1988). A prospective study of moderate alcohol consumption and risk of coronary disease and stroke in women. *New England Journal of Medicine, 319,* 267-273.

Stanford, J.L., & Greenberg, R.S. (1989). Breast cancer incidence in young women by estrogen receptor status and race. *American Journal of Public Health, 79,* 71-73.

Stanley, M.A., & Turner, S.M. (1995). Current status of pharmacological and behavioral treatment of obsessive-compulsive disorder. *Behavior Therapy, 26,* 163-186.

Stanley, M.A., Beck, J.G., & Glassco, J.D. (1997). Treatment of generalized anxiety disorder in older adults: A preliminary comparison of cognitive-behavioral and supportive approaches. *Behavior Therapy, 27,* 565-581.

Stanley, M.A., et al. (2003). Cognitive-behavioral treatment of late-life generalized anxiety disorder. *Journal of Consulting and Clinical Psychology, 71,* 309-319.

Stanley, M.A., & Novy, D.M. (2000). Cognitive-behavior therapy for generalized anxiety in late life: An evaluative overview. *Journal of Anxiety Disorders, 14,* 191-207.

Stansfield, J.M. (1973). Enuresis and urinary tract infection. In I. Kolvin, R.C. MacKeith, & S.R. Meadow (Eds.), *Bladder control and enuresis* (pp. 102-103). London: William Heinemann.

Stanton, A.L., Danoff-Burg, S., & Huggins, M.E. (2002). The first year after breast cancer diagnoss: Hope and coping strategies as predictors of adjustment. *Psychooncology, 11,* 93-102.

Stanton, A.L., Kirk, S.B., Cameron, C.L., & Danoff-Burg, S. (2000). Coping through emotional approach: Scale construction and validation. *Journal of Personality and Social Psychology, 78,* 1150-1169.

Stanton, A.L., & Snider, P. (1993). Coping with breast cancer diagnosis: A prospective study. *Health Psychology, 12,* 16-23.

Stanton, M.D., & Bardoni, A. (1972). Drug flashbacks: Reported frequency in a military population. *American Journal of Psychiatry, 129,* 751-755.

Starfield, B. (1972). Enuresis: Its pathogenesis and management. *Clinical Pediatrics, 11,* 343-350.

Stark, K.D., Kaslow, N.J., & Reynolds, W.M. (1987). A comparison of the relative efficacy of self-control therapy and a behavioral problem-solving therapy for depression in children. *Journal of Abnormal Child Psychology, 15,* 91-113.

Stark, K.D., Linn, J.D., MacGuire, M., & Kaslow, N.J. (in press). The social functioning of depressed and anxious children: Social skills, social knowledge, automatic thoughts, and physical arousal. *Journal of Clinical Child Psychology.*

Stark, K.D., Napolitano, S., Swearer, S., Schmidt, K., Jaramillo, D., & Hoyle, J. (1996). Issues in the treatment of depressed children. *Applied and Preventive Psychology, 5,* 59-83.

Stark, K.D., Schmidt, K., Joiner, T.E., & Lux, M.G. (1996). Cognitive triad: Relationship to depressive symptoms, parents' cognitive triad, and perceived parental messages. *Journal of Abnormal Child Psychology, 24,* 615-631.

Stark, K.D., Swearer, S., Sommer, D., Hickey, B.B., Napolitano, S., Kurowski, C., & Dempsey, M. (1998). School-based group treatment for depressive disorders in children. In T.R. Kratochwill & K.C. Stoiber (Eds.), *Handbook of group intervention for children and families.* (pp. 68-99). Boston: Allyn & Bacon.

Startup, M. (1999). Confirmatory factor analysis of the Level of Expressed Emotion (LEE) Scale. *British Journal of Medical Psychology, 72,* 421-424.

Statistics Canada. (1978-1979). *Mental health statistics, Volume III, Institutional Facilities, Services, and Finances (83-205).* Ottawa: Author.

Statistics Canada (1995). *National Population Health Survey Overview.* Catalogue No. 82-567. Ottawa: Author.

Statistics Canada (1996). *Ethnocultural and social characteristics of the Canadian population* (CD-ROM 94F0004xCB, (ethno.1.ivt)). Ottawa, ON: Statistics Canada.

Statistics Canada (1999). Sex offenders, 1997. (available from htpp://www.stanca.ca)

Statistics Canada (2003). Canadian Community Health Survey: Mental health and well-being, 2002 (82-617-XIE, free) (available from htpp://www.stanca.ca; for a summary see The Daily, September 3, 2003).

Statistics Canada (2004). *Health report: Use of cannabis and other illicit drugs* (available from http://www.statca.ca; for a summary see *The Daily,* July 21, 2004).

Statistics Canada (2004). *Youth smoking survey.* Ottawa: Statistics Canada.

Statistics Canada and Heart and Stroke Foundation of Canada (1997). *Heart disease and stroke in Canada.* Ottawa, Canada: Statistics Canada.

Steadman, H.J. (1979). *Beating a rap: Defendants found incompetent to stand trial.* Chicago: University of Chicago Press.

Steadman, H.J., McGreevy, M.A., Morrissey, J.P., Callahan, L.A., Robbins, P.C., & Cirincione, C. (1993). *Before and after Hinckley: Evaluating insanity defense reform.* New York: Guilford.

Steadman, H.J., Mulvey, E.P., Monahan, J., Robbins, P.C., Appelbaum, P.S., Grisso, T., Roth, L.H., & Silver, E. (1998). Violence by people discharged from acute psychiatric inpatient facilities and by others in the same neighborhoods. *Archives of General Psychiatry, 55,* 393-401.

Steenhuis, R.E., & Ostbye, T. (1995). Neuropsychological test performance of specific diagnostic groups in the Canadian Study of Health and Aging (CSHA). *Journal of Clinical and Experimental Neuropsychology, 17,* 773-785.

Steffy, R. A., Hart, J., Craw, M., Torney, D., & Marlett, N. (1969). Operant behaviour modification techniques applied to a ward of severely regressed and aggressive patients. *Canadian Psychiatric Association Journal, 14,* 59-67.

Steiger, H., Gauvin, L., Jabalpurwala, S., Seguin, J.R., & Stotland, S. (1999). Hypersensitivity to social interactions in bulimia syndromes: Relationship to binge eating. *Journal of Consulting and Clinical Psychology, 67,* 765-775.

Steiger, H., & Israel, M. (1999). A psychodynamically informed, integrated psychotherapy for anorexia nervosa. *Journal of Clinical Psychology, 55,* 741-753.

Steiger, H., Israel, M., Gauvin, L., Kin, Y.K., & Young, S.N. (2003). Implications of compulsive and impulsive traits for serotonin status in women with bulimia nervosa. *Psychiatry Research, 120,* 219-229.

Steiger, H., Stotland, S., Trottier, J., & Ghadirian, A.M. (1996). Familial eating concerns and psychopathological traits: Causal implications of transgenerational effects. *International Journal of Eating Disorders, 19,* 147-157.

Steiger, H., et al. (2001). Implications of impulsive and affective symptoms for serotonin function in bulimia nervosa. *Psychological Medicine, 31,* 85-95.

Steiger, H., & Zanko, M. (1990). Sexual traumata in eating-disordered, psychiatric and normal female groups: Comparison of prevalences and defense styles. *Journal of Interpersonal Violence, 5,* 74-86.

Stein, E.A., Pankiewicz, J., Harsch, H.H., Cho, J.-K., Fuller, S.A., et al. (1998). Nicotine-induced limbic cortical activation in the human brain: A functional MRI study. *American Journal of Psychiatry, 155,* 1009-1015.

Stein, L.I., & Test, M.A. (1980). Alternative to mental hospital treatment: I. Conceptual model, treatment program, and clinical evaluation. *Archives of General Psychiatry, 37,* 392-397.

Stein, M.B., Chartier, M.J., Hazen, A.L., Kozak, M.V., Tancer, M.E., et al. (1998). A direct-interview family study of generalized social phobia. *American Journal of Psychiatry, 155,* 90-97.

Stein, M.B., Forde, D.R., Anderson, G., & Walker, J.R. (1997). Obsessive-compulsive disorder in the community: An epidemiologic survey with clinical reappraisal. *American Journal of Psychiatry, 154,* 1120-1126.

Stein, M.B., Fyer, A.J., Davidson, J.R.T., Pollack, M.H., & Wiita, B. (1999). Fluvoxamine treatment of social phobia (social anxiety disorder): A double-blind, placebo-controlled study. *American Journal of Psychiatry, 156,* 756-760.

Stein, M.B., Jang, K.L., & Livesley, W.J. (1999). Heritability of anxiety sensitivity: A twin study. *American Journal of Psychiatry, 156,* 246-251.

Stein, M.B., Jang, K.L., Taylor, S., Vernon, P.A., & Livesley, W.J. (2002). Genetic and environmental influences on trauma exposure and posttraumatic stress disorder symptoms: A twin study. *American Journal of Psychiatry, 159,* 1675-1681.

Stein, M.B., & Kean, Y.M. (2000). Disability and quality of life in social phobia: Epidemiologic findings. *American Journal of Psychiatry, 157,* 1606-1613.

Stein, M.B., Liebowitz, M.R., Lydiard, R.B., Pitts, C.D., et al. (1998). Paroxetine treatment of generalized social phobia (social anxiety disorder). *JAMA, 280,* 708-713.

Stein, M.B., Torgrud, L.J., & Walker, J.R. (2000). Social phobia symptoms, subtypes, and severity. *Archives of General Psychiatry, 57,* 1046-1052.

Stein, M.B., Walker, J.R., & Forde, D.R. (1996). Public-speaking fears in a community sample: Prevalence, impact on functioning, and diagnostic classification. *Archives of General Psychiatry, 53,* 169-174.

Stein, M.B., Walker, J.R., & Forde, D.R. (2000). Gender differences in susceptibility to posttraumatic stress disorder. *Behaviour Research and Therapy, 38,* 619-628.

Stein, M.B., Walker, J.R., Hazen, A.L., & Forde, D.R. (1997). Full and partial posttraumatic stress disorder: Findings from a community survey. *American Journal of Psychiatry, 154,* 1114-1119.

Steiner, M. (1997). Premenstrual syndromes. *Annual Review of Medicine, 48,* 447-455.

Stephens, B.J. (1985). Suicidal women and their relationships with husbands, boyfriends, and lovers. *Suicide and Life-Threatening Behavior, 15,* 77-89.

Stephens, J.H., & Kamp, M. (1962). On some aspects of hysteria: A clinical study. *Journal of Nervous and Mental Disease, 134,* 305-315.

Stephens, R.S., Roffman, R.A., & Simpson, E.E. (1993). Adult marijuana users seeking treatment. *Journal of Consulting and Clinical Psycology, 61,* 1100-1104.

Stephens, T. (1994). *Smoking among Aboriginal people in Canada, 1991.* Ottawa: Ministry of Supply and Services.

Stephens, T., Dulberg, C., & Joubert, N. (1999). Mental health of the Canadian population: A comprehensive analysis. *Chronic Diseases in Canada,* [On-line], *20, (3).* Available: (http://www.hc-sc.gc.ca/hpb/lcdc/publicat/cdic/cdic221/cd221d_e.html; accessed September 22, 2001).

Stephens, T., & Joubert, N. (2001). The economic burden of mental health problems in Canada. *Chronic Diseases in Canada,* [On-line], *22, (1).* Available: (http://www.hc-sc.gc.ca/hpb/lcdc/publicat/cdic/cdic221/cd221d_e.html; accessed September 22, 2001).

Stephens, T., Kaiserman, M.J., McCall, D.J., & Sutherland-Brown, C. (2000). School-based smoking prevention: Economic costs versus benefits. *Chronic Diseases in Canada, 21,* 62-67.

Stephenson, R., Marchand, A., & Lavallee, M.-C. (1997). Validation de l'Inventaire de Mobilite pour l'Agoraphobie aupres de la population quebecoise francophone [Validation of the Mobility Inventory for Agoraphobia in the Quebec francophone population.]. *Science et Comportement, 26,* 35-38.

Stephenson, R., Marchand, A., & Lavallee, M.-C. (1998). Traduction et validation Canadienne-francaise du Questionnaire des Pensees Phobiques [French Canadian translation and validation of the Agoraphobic Cognitions Questionnaire.]. *Encephale, 24,* 415-425.

Stephenson, R., Marchand, A., & Lavallee, M.-C. (1999). A French Canadian adaptation of the Agoraphobic Cognitions Questionnaire: Cross-cultural validation and gender differences. *Scandinavian Journal of Behaviour Therapy, 28,* 1-12.

Stephensoncino, P., Steiner, M., Krames, L., Ryan, E. B., & Huxley, G. (1992). Depression in elderly persons and its correlates in family practice: A Canadian study. *Psychological Reports, 70,* 359-368.

Steptoe, A. (1997). Stress management. In A. Baum, S. Newman, J. Weinman, R. West, & C. McManus (Eds.), *Cambridge encyclopedia of psychology, health and medicine.* (pp. 262-264). Cambridge, UK: Cambridge University Press.

Stermac, L., Du Mont, J., & Dunn, S. (1998). Violence in known-assailant sexual assaults. *Journal of Interpersonal Violence, 13,* 398-412.

Stermac, L., Du Mont, J., & Kalemba, V. (1995). Comparison of sexual assaults by strangers and known assailants in an urban population of women. *Canadian Medical Association Journal, 153,* 1089-1095.

Stern, R.S., & Cobb, J.P. (1978). Phenomenology of obsessive-compulsive neurosis. *British Journal of Psychiatry, 132,* 233-234.

Sternberger, R.T., Turner, S.M., Beidel, D.C., & Calhoun, K.S. (1995). Social phobia: An analysis of possible developmental pathways. *Journal of Abnormal Psychology, 104,* 526-531.

Stets, J.E., & Straus, M.A. (1989). The marriage license as a hitting license: A comparison of assaults in dating, cohabiting, and married couples. *Journal of Family Violence, 4,* 161-180.

Stevenson, J., & Jones, I.H. (1972). Behavior therapy technique for exhibitionism: A preliminary report. *Archives of General Psychiatry, 27,* 839-841.

Stevenson, J.S., & Topp, R. (1990). Effects of moderate and low intensity long-term exercise by older adults. *Research in Nursing and Health, 13,* 209-213.

Stewart, B.D., Hughes, C., Frank, E., Anderson, B., Kendall, K., & West, D. (1987). Profiles of immediate and delayed treatment seekers. *Journal of Nervous and Mental Disease, 175,* 90-94.

Stewart, J.W., Quitkin, F.M., McGrath, P.J., Amsterdam, J., Fava, M., et al. (1998). Use of pattern analysis to predict differential relapse of remitted patients with major depression during 1 year of treatment with flouxetine or placebo. *Archives of General Psychiatry, 55,* 334-345.

Stewart, S., Boase, P., & Lamble, R.W. (2000). Criminal profiles of drinking drivers in Ontario. In *Alcohol, Drugs, and Traffic Safety –T2000.* Stockholm, Sweden: Swedish National Road Safety.

Stewart, S.H., Conrod, P.J., Gignac, M.L., & Pihl, R.O. (1998). Selective processing biases in anxiety-sensitive men and women. *Cognition and Emotion, 12,* 105-33.

Stewart, S.H., Conrod, P.J., Pihl, R.O., & Dongier, M. (1999). Relations between posttraumatic stress symptom dimensions and substance dependence in a community-recruited sample of substance-abusing women. *Psychology of Addictive Behaviors, 13,* 78-88.

Stewart, S.H., & Devine, H. (2000). Relations between personality domains and drinking motives in young adults. *Personality and Individual Differences, 29,* 495-511.

Stewart, S.H., Loughlin, H.L., & Rhyno, E. (2001). Internal drinking motives mediate personality domain-drinking relations in young adults. *Personality and Individual Differences, 30,* 271-286.

Stewart, S.H., Peterson, J.B., & Pihl, R.O. (1995). Anxiety sensitivity and self-reported alcohol consumption rates in university women. *Journal of Anxiety Disorders, 9,* 283-292.

Stewart, S.H., & Watt, M.C. (2001). Assessment of health anxiety. In G.J.G. Asmundson, S. Taylor, & B.J. Cox (Eds.), *Health anxiety: Clinical and research perspectives on hypochondriasis and related conditions* (pp. 95-131). Toronto: Wiley.

Stewart, W.F., Kawas, C., Corrada, M., & Metter, J.E. (1997). Risk of Alzheimer's disease and duration of NSAID use. *Neurology, 48,* 626-632.

Stice, E. (1998). Relations of restraint and negative affect to bulimic pathology: A longitudinal test of three competing models. *International Journal of Eating Disorders, 23,* 243-260.

Stice, E., Barrera, M., & Chasin, L. (1998). Prospective differential prediction of adolescent alcohol use and problem use: Examining the mechanisms of effect. *Journal of Abnormal Psychology, 107,* 616-628.

Stice, E., Killen, J.D., Hayward, C., & Taylor, C.B. (1998). Age of onset for binge eating and purging during late adolescence: A 4-year survival analysis. *Journal of Abnormal Psychology, 107,* 671-675.

Stinson, F.S., & DeBakey, S.F. (1992). Alcohol-related mortality in the United States 1979-1988. *British Journal of Addiction, 87,* 777-783.

Stip, E., Caron, J. & Lane, C.J. (2001). Schizophrenia: People's perceptions in Quebec. *Canadian Medical Association Journal, 164,* 1299-1300.

Stirman, S.W., DeRubesis, R.J., Crits-Cristoph, P., & Brody, P.E. (2003). Are samples in randomized controlled studies of psychotherapy representative of community outpatients? A new methodology and initial findings. *Journal of Consulting and Clinical Psychology, 71,* 963-972.

St. John, J., Krichev, A., & Bauman, E. (1976). Northwestern Ontario Indian children and the WISC. *Psychology in the Schools, 13,* 407-411.

St. John, P., & Montgomery, P. (2002). Are cognitively intact seniors with subjective memory loss more likely to develop dementia? *International Journal of Geriatric Psychiatry, 17,* 814-820.

St. John, P., Montgomery, P. R., Kristjansson, B., & McDowell, I. (2002). Cognitive scores, even within the normal range, predict death and institutionalization. *Age and Ageing, 31*, 373-378.

Stokes, J., & Lindsay, J. (1996). Major causes of death and hospitalization in Canadian seniors. *Chronic Diseases in Canada, 17*, 63-72

Stolberg, A.L., & Garrison, K.M. (1985). Evaluating a primary prevention program for children of divorce. *American Journal of Community Psychology, 13*, 111-124.

Stolberg, S. (1996a, August 24). Clinton imposes wide crackdown on tobacco firms. *Los Angeles Times*, pp. A1, A10.

Stolberg, S. (1996b, October 1). Ending life on their own terms. *Los Angeles Times*, pp. A1, A14.

Stoller, E.P., & Gibson, R.C. (1994). *Worlds of difference: Inequality in the aging experience*. Thousand Oaks, CA: Pine Forge Press.

Stoller, F.H. (1968). Accelerated interaction: A time-limited approach based on the brief intensive group. *International Journal of Group Psychotherapy, 18*, 220-235.

Stom, M., French, S.A., Resnick, M.D., & Blum, R.W. (1995). Ethnic/racial and socioeconomic differences in dieting behaviors and body image perceptions in adolescents. *International Journal of Eating Disorders, 18*, 173-179.

Stone, A.A. (1975). *Mental health and law: A system in transition*. Rockville, MD: National Institute of Mental Health.

Stone, A.A., Bovbjerg, D.H., Neale, J.M., Napoli, A., Valdimarsdottir, H., et al. (1992). Development of common cold symptoms following experimental rhinovirus infection is related to prior stressful life events. *Behavioral Medicine, 18*, 115-120.

Stone, A.A., Cox, D.S., Valdimarsdottir, H., Jandorf, L., & Neale, J.M. (1987). Evidence that secretory IgA antibody is associated with daily mood. *Journal of Personality and Social Psychology, 52*, 988-993.

Stone, A.A., & Neale, J.M. (1982). Development of a methodology for assessing daily experiences. In A. Baum and J. Singer (Eds.), *Environment and health. Hillsdale*, NJ: Erlbaum.

Stone, A.A., & Neale, J.M. (1984). The effects of "severe" daily events on mood. *Journal of Personality and Social Psychology, 46*, 137-144.

Stone, A.A., Reed, B.R., & Neale, J.M. (1987). Changes in daily event frequency precede episodes of physical symptoms. *Journal of Human Stress, 13*, 70-74.

Stone, A.A., Schwartz, J., Neale, J.M., Shiffman, S., Marco, C.A., et al. (1998). A comparison of coping assessed by Ecological Momentary Assessment and retrospective recall. *Journal of Personality and Social Psychology, 74*, 1670-1680.

Stone, A.A., & Shiffman, S. (1994). Ecological momentary assessment (EMA) in behavioral medicnie. *Annals of Behavioral Medicine, 16*, 199-202.

Stone, G. (1982). Health Psychology, a new journal for a new field. *Health Psychology, 1*, 1-6.

Stone, M.H. (1986). Exploratory psychotherapy in schizophrenia-spectrum patients: A reevaluation in the light of long-term follow-up of schizophrenic and borderline patients. *Bulletin of the Menninger Clinic, 50*, 287-306.

Stone, M.H. (1987). Psychotherapy of borderline patients in light of long-term follow-up. *Bulletin of the Menninger Clinic, 51*, 231-247.

Stone, M.H. (1993). *Abnormalities of personality. Within and beyond the realm of treatment*. New York: Norton.

Stone, S.V., & Costa, P.T. (1990). Disease-prone personality or distress-prone personality? The role of neuroticism in coronary heart disease. In H.S. Friedman (Ed.), *Personality and Disease*. New York: Wiley.

Stoppard, J.M. (2000). *Understanding depression: Feminist social constructionist approaches*. Florence, KY: Taylor and Francis/Routledge.

Stoppard, J.M. (1999). Why new perspectives are needed for understanding depression in women. *Canadian Psychology, 40*, 79-90.

Stormer, S.M., & Thompson, J.K. (1996). Explanations of body image disturbance: A test of maturational status, negative verbal commentary, and sociological hypotheses. *International Journal of Eating Disorders, 19*, 193-202.

Story, M., French, S.A., Resnick, M.D., & Blum, R.W. (1995). Ethnic/racial and socioeconomic differences in dieting behaviors and body image perceptions in adolescents. *International Journal of Eating Disorders, 18*, 173-179.

Strain, E.C., Bigelow, G.E., Liebson, I.A., & Stitzer, M.L. (1999). Moderate-vs low-dose methadone in the treatment of opioid dependence. *JAMA, 281*, 1000-1005.

Strassberg, D.S., de Gouveia Brazao, C.A., Rowland, D.L., Tan, P., & Slob, A.K. (1999). Clomipramine in the treatment of rapid (premature) ejaculation. *Journal of Sex and Marital Therapy, 25*, 89-101.

Strauss, J.S., Carpenter, W.T., & Bartko, J.J. (1974). The diagnosis and understanding of schizophrenia: Part 3. Speculations on the processes that underlie schizophrenic signs and symptoms. *Schizophrenia Bulletin, 1*, 61-69.

Strauss, M.E., & Ogrocki, P.K. (1996). Confirmation of an association between family history of affective disorder and the depressive syndrome in Alzheimer's disease. *American Journal of Psychiatry, 153*, 1340-1342.

Stravynski, A., Arbel, N., Bounader, J., Gaudette, G., Lachance, L., Borgeat, F., Fabian, J., Lamontagne, Y., Sidoun, P., & Todorov, C. (2000). Social phobia treated as a problem in social functioning: A controlled comparison of two behavioural group approaches. *Acta Psychiatrica Scandinavica, 102*, 188-198.

Stravynski, A., & Boyer, R. (2001). Loneliness in relation to suicide ideation and parasuicide: A population-wide study. *Suicide and Life-Threatening Behavior, 31*, 32-40.

Stretch, R.H. (1990). Post-traumatic stress disorder and the Canadian Vietnam veteran. *Journal of Traumatic Stress, 3*, 239-254.

Stretch, R.H. (1991). Psychosocial readjustment of Canadian Vietnam veterans. *Journal of Consulting and Clinical Psychology, 59*, 188-189.

Streigel-Moore, R.H., Silberstein, L.R., & Rodin, J. (1993). The social self in bulimia nervosa: Public self-consciousness, social anxiety, and perceived fradulence. *Journal of Abnormal Psychology, 102*, 297-303.

Striegel-Moore, R.H., Wilson, G.T., Wilfley, D.E., Elder, K.A., & Brownell, K.D. (1998). Binge eating in an obese community sample. *International Journal of Eating Disorders, 23*, 27-36.

Strickland, C.J. (1997). Suicide among American Indian, Alaskan native, and Canadian aboriginal youth: Advancing the research agenda. *International Journal of Mental Health, 25*, 11-32.

Stringer, A.Y., & Josef, N.C. (1983). Methylphenidate in the treatment of aggression in two patients with antisocial personality disorder. *American Journal of Psychiatry, 140*, 1365-1366.

Strober, M., Freeman, R., & Morrell, W. (1997). The long-term course of severe anorexia nervosa in adolescents: Survival analysis of recovery, relapse, and outcome predictors over 10-15 years in a prospective study. *International Journal of Eating Disorders, 22*, 339-360.

Strober, M., Lampert, C., Morrell, W., Burroughs, J., & Jacobs, C. (1990). A controlled family study of anorexia nervosa: Evidence of family aggregation and lack of shared transmission with affective disorders. *International Journal of Eating Disorders, 9*, 239-253.

Strober, M., Morrell, B., Burroughs, J., Salkin, B., & Jacobs, C. (1985). A controlled family study of anorexia nervosa. *Journal of Psychiatric Research, 19*, 239-246.

Strober, M., Salkin, B., Burroughs, J., & Morrell, W. (1982). Validity of the bulimia-restrictor distinction in anorexia nervosa. *Journal of Nervous and Mental Disease, 170*, 345-351.

Stroebe, M., van Son, M., Stroebe, W., Kleber, M., Schut, H., & van den Bout, J. (2000). On the classification and diagnosis of pathological grief. *Clinical Psychology Review, 20*, 57-75.

Strong, R., Huang, J.S., Huang, S.S., Chung, H.D., Hale, C., et al. (1991). Degeneration of the cholinergic innervation of the locus ceruleus in Alzheimer's disease. *Brain Research, 542*, 23-28.

Strongman, K.T., & Russell, P.N. (1986). Salience of emotion in recall. *Bulletin of the Psychonomic Society, 24*, 25-27.

Strupp, H.H. (1989). Psychotherapy: Can the practitioner learn from the researcher? *American Psychologist, 44*, 717-724.

Strupp, H.H., Hadley, S.W., & Gomes-Schwartz, B. (1977). *Psychotherapy for better or worse: An analysis of the problem of negative effects*. New York: Jason Aronson.

Stuart, H. (2000). Access to physician treatment for a mental disorder: A regional analysis. *Social Psychiatry and Psychiatric Epidemiology, 35*, 61-70.

Stuart, H. (2003). Stigma and the daily news: Evaluation of a newspaper intervention. *Canadian Journal of Psychiatry, 48*, 651-666.

Stuart, H. L. & Arboleda-Florez, J. (2000). Homeless shelter users in the postdeinstitutionalization era. *Canadian Journal of Psychiatry, 45*, 55-62.

Stuart, H. L. & Arboleda-Florez, J. (2001). Community attitudes toward people with schizophrenia. *Canadian Journal of Psychiatry, 46,* 245-251.

Stuart, H.L., Arboleda-Florez, J., & Crisanti, A.J. (2001). Impact of legal reforms on length of forensic assessments in Alberta, Canada. *International Journal of Law and Psychiatry, 24,* 527-538.

Stuart, F.M., Hammond, D.C., & Pett, M.A. (1987). Inhibited sexual desire in women. *Archives of Sexual Behavior, 16,* 91-106.

Stuart, I.R., & Greer, J.G. (Eds.). (1984). *Victims of sexual aggression: Treatment of children, women and men.* New York: Van Nostrand-Reinhold.

Stuart, R.B. (1976). An operant interpersonal program for couples. In D.H.L. Olson (Ed.), *Treating relationships.* Lake Mills, IA: Graphic Publishing.

Stuart, R.B. (1978). Protection of the right to informed consent to participate in research. *Behavior Therapy, 9,* 73-82.

Studer, L. H., Clelland, S. R., Aylwin, A. S., Reddon, J. R., & Monro, A. (2000). Rethinking risk assessment for incest offenders. *International Journal of Law and Psychiatry, 23,* 15-22.

Sturgis, E.T., & Adams, H.E. (1978). The right to treatment: Issues in the treatment of homosexuality. *Journal of Consulting and Clinical Psychology, 46,* 165-169.

Stuss, D.T., & Benson, D.F. (1983). Emotional concomitants of psychosurgery. In K. M. Heilman & P. Satz (Eds.), *Advances in Neuropsychology and behavioural neurology: Vol. 1. Neuropsychology of human emotion* (pp. 111-140). New York: The Guilford Press.

Substance Abuse and Mental Health Services Administration (1998). *Substance abuse among older adults.* Treatment Improvement Protocol (TIP) Series #26. Rockville, MD: U.S. Department of Health and Human Services.

Suddath, R.L., Christison, G.W., Torrey, E.F., Cassonova, M.F., Weinberger, D.R. et al. (1990). Anatomical abnormalities in the brains of monozygotic twins discordant for schizophrenia. *New England Journal of Medicine, 322,* 789-793.

Sue, D.W., & Sue, D. (1992). *Counseling the culturally different.* New York: Wiley.

Sue, D.W., & Sue, D. (1999). *Counseling the culturally different.* Second edition. NY: Wiley.

Sue, S. (1998). In search of cultural competence in psychotherapy and counseling. *American Psychologist, 53,* 440-448.

Sue, S., Zane, N., & Young, K. (1994). Research on psychotherapy with culturally diverse populations. In A.E. Bergin & S.L. Garfield (Eds.), *Handbook of psychotherapy and behavior change.* Fourth edition (pp. 783-820). New York: Wiley.

Sugarman, P., Dumughn, C., Saad, K., Hinder, S., & Bluglass, S. (1994). Dangerousness in exhibitionists. *Journal of Forensic Psychiatry, 5,* 287-296.

Suinn, R.M., & Richardson, R. (1971). Anxiety management training: A nonspecific behavior therapy program for anxiety control. *Behavior Therapy, 2,* 498-510.

Sukhai, R.N., Mol, J., & Harris, A.S. (1989). Combined therapy of enuresis alarm and desmopressin in the treatment of nocturnal enuresis. *European Journal of Pediatrics, 148,* 465-467.

Sullivan, H.S. (1953). *The interpersonal theory of psychiatry.* New York: Norton.

Sullivan, P.F. (1995). Mortality in anorexia nervosa. *American Journal of Psychiatry, 152,* 1073-1075.

Suls, J., & Fletcher, B. (1985). The relative efficacy of avoidant and nonavoidant coping strategies: A meta-analysis. *Health Psychology, 4,* 249-288.

Sultenfuss, J., & Geczy, B., Jr. (1996). Group therapy on state hospital chronic wards: Some guidelines. *International Journal of Group Psychotherapy, 46,* 163-176.

Sumi, C. (1998, February 18). Halton PACT should benefit the mentally ill. *The Hamilton Spectator.*

Summerfeldt, L.J., & Endler, N.S. (1998). Examining the evidence for anxiety-related cognitive biases in obsessive-compulsive disorder. *Journal of Anxiety Disorders, 12,* 579-598.

Sundin, O., Ohman, A., Palm, T., & Strom, G. (1995). Cardiovascular reactivity, Type A behavior, and coronary heart disease: Comparisions between myocardial infarction patients and controls during laboratory-induced stress. *Psychophysiology, 32,* 28-35.

Suppes, T., Baldessarini, R.J., Faedda, G.L., & Tohen, M. (1991). Risk of recurrence following discontinuation of lithium treatment in bipolar disorder. *Archives of General Psychiatry, 48,* 1082-1087.

Surles, R.C., Blanch, A.K., Shern, D.L., & Donahue, S.A. (1992). Case management as a strategy for systems change. *Health Affairs, 11,* 151-163.

Susser, E., Neugebauer, R., Hoek, H.W., Brown, A.S., Lin, S., et al. (1996). Schizophrenia after prenatal famine: Further evidence. *Archives of General Psychiatry, 53,* 25-31.

Susser, E., & Wanderling, J. (1994). Epidemiology of nonaffective acute remitting psychosis versus schizophrenia: Sex and sociocultural setting. *Archives of General Psychiatry, 51,* 294-301.

Sussman, S. (1996). Development of a school-based drug abuse prevention curriculum for high-risk youth. *Journal of Psychoactive Drugs, 28,* 169-182.

Sussman, S. (1998). The first asylums in Canada: A response to neglectful community care and current trends. *Canadian Journal of Psychiatry, 43,* 260-264.

Sussman, S., Dent, C.W., Burton, D., Stacy, A.W., & Flay, B.R. (1995). *Developing school-based tobacco use prevention and cessation programs.* Thousand Oaks, CA: Sage.

Sussman, S., Dent, C.W., McAdams, L., Stacy, A.W., Burton, D., & Flay, B.R. (1994). Group self-identification and adolescent cigarette smoking: A 1-year prospective study. *Journal of Abnormal Psychology, 103,* 576-580.

Sussman, S., Dent, C.W., Simon, T.R., Stacy, A.W., Galaif, E.R., Moss, M.A., Craig, S., & Johnson, C.A. (1995). Immediate impact of social influence-oriented substance abuse prevention curricula in traditional and continuation high schools. *Drugs and Society, 8,* 65-81.

Sussman, S., Dent, C.W., Stacy, A.W., Burciage, C., Raynor, A., et al. (1990). Peer-group association and adolescent tobacco use. *Journal of Abnormal Psychology, 99,* 349-352.

Sussman, S., Stacy, A.W., Dent, C.W., Simon, T.R., & Johnson, C.A. (1996). Marijuana use: Current issues and new research directions. *The Journal of Drug Issues, 26,* 695-733.

Sutcliffe, J.P., & Jones, J. (1962). Personal identity, multiple personality, and hypnosis. *International Journal of Clinical and Experimental Hypnosis, 10,* 231-269.

Sutherland, S. (1999). Eating-disorder clinic risked lives of patients: Health authorities. *The Chronic Herald-Metropolitan,* December 2, A23.

Sutker, P.B., Davis, J.M., Uddo, M., & Ditta, A. (1995). Warzone stress, personal resources, and post-traumatic stress disorder in Persian Gulf War returnees. *Journal of Abnormal Psychology, 104,* 444-453.

Svartberg, M., & Stiles, T.C. (1991). Comparative effects of short-term psychodynamic psychotherapy: A meta-analysis. *Journal of Consulting and Clinical Psychology, 59,* 704-714.

Swain, A., & Suls, J. (1996). Reproducibility of blood pressure and heart rate reactivity: A meta-analysis. *Psychophysiology, 33,* 162-174.

Swan, N. (1994). Marijuana, other drug use among teens continues to rise. *NIDA Notes, 10,* 8-9.

Swann, W.B., Jr. (1996). *Self-traps: The elusive quest for higher self-esteem.* New York: W.H. Freeman.

Swanson, J., McBurnett, K., Christian, D.L., & Wigal, T. (1995). Stimulant medications and the treatment of children with ADHD. In T.H. Ollendick & R.J. Prinz (Eds.), *Advances in clinical child psychology,* (vol 17, pp. 265-322). New York: Plenum.

Swanson, J.W., Borum, R., Swartz, M.S., Hiday, V.A., Wagner, H.R., & Burns, B. J. (2001). Can involuntary outpatient commitment reduce arrests among persons with severe mental disorder? *Criminal Justice and Behavior, 28,* 156-189.

Swanson, J.W., Holzer, C.E., Ganju, V.K., & Jono, R.T. (1990). Violence and psychiatric disorder in the community: Evidence from the Epidemiological Catchment Area surveys. *Hospital and Community Psychiatry, 41,* 761-770.

Swanson, M.C., Bland, R.C., & Newman, S.C. (1994). Epidemiology of psychiatric disorders in Edmonton: Antisocial personality disorders. *Acta Psychiatrica Scandinavica, 376 (Supplement),* 63-70.

Swartz, M., Blazer, D., George, L., & Landerman, R. (1986). Somatization disorder in a community population. *American Journal of Psychiatry, 143,* 1403-1408.

Swartz, M., Blazer, D., George, L., & Winfield, I. (1990). Estimating the prevalence of borderline personality in the community. *Journal of Personality Disorders, 4,* 257-272.

Sweet, J.J., Carr , M.A., Rossini, E., & Kasper, C. (1986). Relationship between the Luria-Nebraska Neuropsychological Battery and the WISC-R: Further examination using Kaufman's factors. *International Journal of*

Clinical Neuropsychology, 8, 177-180.

Sweet, L., Savoie, J.A., & Lemyre, L. (1999). Appraisals, coping, and stress in breast cancer screening: A longitudinal investigation of causal structure. *Canadian Journal of Behavioural Science, 31,* 240-253.

Sweet, R.A., Mulsant, B.H., Gupta, B., Rifai, A.H., Pasternak, R.E., et al. (1995). Duration of neuroleptic treatment and prevalence of tardive dyskinesia in late life. *Archives of General Psychiatry, 52,* 478-486.

Sweeting, H.W. (1995). Family life and health in adolescence. *Social Science and Medicine, 40,* 163-175.

Swinson, R.P., Antony, M.M., Rachman, S., & Richter, M.A. (Eds.) (1998). *Obsessive compulsive disorder: Theory, research, and treatment.* New York, NY: Guilford Publications.

Swinson, R.P., Cox, B.J., Kerr, S.A., Kuch, K., & Fergus, K. (1992). A survey of anxiety disorder clinics in Canadian hospitals. *Canadian Journal of Psychiatry, 37,* 188-191.

Swinson, R.P., Fergus, K.D., Cox, B. J., & Wiskwire, K. (1995). Efficacy of telephone-administered behavioral therapy for panic disorder with agoraphobia. *Behaviour Research and Therapy, 33,* 464-469.

Swinson, R.P., Soulios, C., Cox, B.J., & Kuch, K. (1992). Brief treatment of emergency room patients with panic attacks. *American Journal of Psychiatry, 149,* 944-946.

Syndulko, K. (1978). Electrocortical investigations of sociopathy. In R.D. Hare & D. Schalling (Eds.), *Psychopathic behaviour: Approaches to research.* New York: Wiley.

Szasz, T.S. (1963). *Law, liberty, and psychiatry.* New York: Macmillan.

Szasz, T.S. (Ed.). (1974). *The age of madness: The history of involuntary hospitalization.* New York: Jason Aronson.

Szasz, T.S. (1986). The case against suicide prevention. *American Psychologist, 41,* 806-812.

Szasz, T.S. (1999). *Fatal freedom: The ethics and politics of suicide.* Westport, CT: Praeger.

Szatmari, P. (2003). The causes of autism spectrum disorders: Multiple factors have been identified, but a unifying cascade of events is still elusive. *British Medical Journal, 326,* 173-174.

Szatmari, P., Bryson, S.E., Boyle, M.H., Streiner, D.L., & Duku, E. (2003). Predictors of outcome among high functioning children with autism and Asberger syndrome. *Journal of Child Psychology and Psychiatry and Allied Disciplines, 44,* 520-528.

Szatmari, P., Offord, D.R., & Boyle, M.H. (1989a). Correlates, associated impairments and patterns of service utilization of children with attention deficit disorder: Findings from the Ontario Child Health Study. *Journal of Child Psychology and Psychiatry, 30,* 205-217.

Szatmari, P., Offord, D.R., & Boyle, M.H. (1989b). Ontario Child Health Study: Prevalence of attention deficit disorder with hyperactivity. *Journal of Child Psychology and Psychiatry, 30,* 219-230.

Szymanski, M.L., & Cash, T.F. (1995). Body-image disturbances and self-discrepancy theory: Expansion of the Body-Images Ideals Questionnaire. *Journal of Social and Clinical Psychology, 14,* 134-146.

Taft, C.T., Stern, A.S., King, L.A., & King, D.W. (1999). Modeling physical health and functional health status: The role of combat exposure, posttraumatic stress disorder, and personal resource attributes. *Journal of Traumatic Stress, 12,* 3-23.

Takata, T. (1983). *Nikkei Legacy: The story of Japanese Canadians from settlement to today.* Toronto: NC Press Limited.

Tallal, P., Miller, S.L., Bedi, G., Byma, G., Wang, X., Nagarajan, S.S., Schreiner, C., Jenkins, W.M., & Merzenich, M.M. (1996). Language comprehension in language-learning impaired children improved with acoustically modified speech. *Science, 271,* 81-84.

Tallis, F., Pratt, P., & Jamani, N. (1999). Obsessive compulsive disorder, checking, and non-verbal memory: A neuropsychological investigation. *Behaviour Research and Therapy, 37,* 161-166.

Tannock, R. (1998). Attention deficit hyperactivity disorder: Advances in cognitive, neurobiological, and genetic research. *Journal of Child Psychology and Psychiatry, 39,* 65-100.

Tannock, R., Purvis, K.L., & Schachar, R. (1993). Narrative ability in children with Attention Deficit Hyperactivity Disorder and normal peers. *Journal of Abnormal Child Psychology, 21,* 103-117.

*Tarrier, (1998). Randomised control trial of intensive cognitive behaviour therapy for patients with chronic schizophrenia. *British Medical Journal, 317,* 303-307.

Task Force on Promotion and Dissemination of Psychological Procedures. (1995). Training in and dissemination of empirically-validated psychological treatments: Report and recommendations. *The Clinical Psychologist, 48,* 3-23.

Tate, B.G., & Baroff, G.S. (1966). Aversive control of self-injurious behavior in a psychotic boy. *Behaviour Research and Therapy, 4,* 281-287.

Taylor, C.B. (1983). DSM-III and behavioral assessment. *Behavioral Assessment, 5,* 5-14.

Taylor, C.B., Hayward, C., King, R., et al. (1990). Cardiovascular and symptomatic reduction effects of alprazolam and imipramine in patients with panic disorder: Results of a double-blind, placebo-controlled trial. *Journal of Clinical Psychopharmacology, 10,* 112-118.

Taylor, C.B., Ironson, G., & Burnett, K. (1990). Adult medical disorders. In A.S. Bellak, M. Hersen, & A.E. Kazdin (Eds.), *International handbook of behavior modification and therapy.* New York: Plenum.

Taylor, J., Loney, B.R., Bobadilla, L., Iacono, W.G., & McGue, M. (2003). Genetic and environmental influences on psychopathy trait dimensions in a community sample of male twins. *Journal of Abnormal Child Psychology, 31,* 633-645.

Taylor, S. (1999). *Anxiety sensitivity: Theory, research, and treatment of the fear of anxiety.* Mahwah, NJ: Erlbaum.

Taylor, S. (1995). Anxiety sensitivity: Theoretical perspectives and recent findings. *Behaviour Research and Therapy, 33,* 243-258.

Taylor, S., & Cox, B.J. (1998a). An expanded Anxiety Sensitivity Index: Evidence for a hierarchic structure in a clinical sample. *Journal of Anxiety Disorders, 12,* 463-483.

Taylor, S., & Cox, B.J. (1998b). Anxiety sensitivity: Multiple dimensions and hierarchic structure. *Behaviour Research and Therapy, 36,* 37-51.

Taylor, S., Koch, W.J., McNally, R.J., & Crockett, D.J. (1992). Conceptualizations of anxiety sensitivity. *Psychological Assessment, 4,* 245-250.

Taylor, S., Thordarson, D.S., Maxfield, L., Federoff, I.C., Lovell, K., & Ogrodniczuk, J. (2003). Comparative efficacy, speed, and adverse effects of three PTSD treatments: Exposure therapy, EMDR, and relaxation training. *Journal of Consulting and Clinical Psychology, 71,* 330-338.

Taylor, S.E., Kemeny, M.E., Aspinwall, L.G., Schneider, S.G., Rodriguez, R., & Herbert, M. (1992). Optimism, coping, psychological distress, and high-risk sexual behavior among men at risk for acquired immunodeficiency syndrome (AIDS). *Journal of Personality and Social Psychology, 63,* 460-473.

Teachman, B.A., & Woody, S.R. (2003). Automatic processing in spider phobia: Implicit fear association over the course of treatment. *Journal of Abnormal Psychology, 112,* 100-109.

Teasdale, J.D., Fennell, M.J.V., Hibbert, G.A., & Amies, P.L. (1984). Cognitive therapy for major depressive disorder in primary care. *British Journal of Psychiatry, 44,* 400-406.

Teasdale, J.D., Moore, R.G., Hayhurst, H., Pope, M., Williams, S., & Segal, Z.V. (2002). Metacognitive awareness and prevention of relapse in depression: Empirical evidence. *Journal of Consulting and Clinical Psychology, 70,* 275-287.

Teasdale, J.D., Segal, Z.V., & Williams, J.M.G. (2003). Mindfulness training and problem formulation. *Clinical Psychology: Science and Practice, 10,* 157-160.

Teasdale, J.D., Segal, Z.V., Williams, J.M.G., Ridgeway, V.A., Soulsby, J.M., & Lau, M.A. (2000). Prevention of relapse/recurrence in major depression by mindfulness-based cognitive therapy. *Journal of Consulting and Clinical Psychology, 68,* 615-623.

Telch, C.F., & Telch, M.J. (1986). Group coping skills instruction and supportive group therapy for cancer patients: A comparison of strategies. *Journal of Consulting and Clinical Psychology, 54,* 802-808.

*Telch, M.J., & Harrington, P.J. (in press). Anxiety sensitivity and expectedness of arousal in mediating affective response to 35% carbon dioxide inhalation.

Teplin, L.A. (1984). Criminalizing mental disorder: The comparative arrest rate of the mentally ill. *American Psychologist, 29,* 794-803.

Teri, L., & Lewinsohn, P.M. (1986). Individual and group treatment of unipolar depression: Comparison of treatment outcome and identification of predictors of successful treatment outcome. *Behavior Therapy, 17,* 215-228.

Teri, L., & Logsdon, R.G. (1992). The future of psychotherapy with older adults. *Psychotherapy, 29,* 81-87.

Terman, L.M. (1995). *Genetic studies of genius*. Stanford, CA: Stanford University Press.

Terman, M., Terman, J.S., & Ross, D.C. (1998). A controlled trial of timed bright light and negative air ionization for treatment of winter depression. *Archives of General Psychiatry, 55,* 875-882.

Terr, L. (1995). Childhood traumas: An outline and overview. In G. S. Everly & J. M. Lating (Eds.), *Psychotraumatology* (pp. 301-320). New York: Plenum.

Terry, D.J., & Hynes, G.J. (1998). Adjustment to a low-control situation: Reexamining the role of coping responses. *Journal of Personality and Social Psychology, 74,* 1078-1092.

Terry, D.J., Mayocchi, L., & Hynes, G.J. (1996). Depressive symptomatology in new mothers: A stress and coping perspective. *Journal of Abnormal Psychology*, *105*, 220-231.

Test, M.A. (1992). Training in community living. In R.P. Liberman (Ed.), *Handbook of psychiatric rehabilitation*. (pp. 153-170). New York: Macmillan.

Tester, F. J. & Kulchyski, P. (1994). *Tammarmiit (mistakes): Inuit relocation in the eastern arctic 1939-63*. Vancouver: University of British Columbia Press.

The MTA Cooperative Group (1999). A 14-month randomized clinical trial of treatment strategies for attention-deficit/hyperactivity disorder. *Archives of General Psychiatry, 56,* 1073-1086.

The United Way of Greater Toronto. (1997). *Beyond survival: Homelessness in Metro Toronto: Discussion paper.* Toronto: Author.

Theodor, L.H., & Mandelcorn, M.S. (1973). Hysterical blindness: A case report using a psychophysical technique. *Journal of Abnormal Psychology, 82,* 552-553.

Thibaut, J.W., & Kelley, H.H. (1959). *The social psychology of groups*. New York: Wiley.

Thigpen, C.H., & Cleckley, H. (1954). *The three faces of Eve*. Kingsport, TN: Kingsport Press.

Thiruchelvam, D., Charach, A., & Schachar, R.J. (2001). Moderators and mediators of long-term adherence to stimulant treatment in children with ADHD. *Journal of the American Academy of Child and Adolescent Psychiatry*, *40*, 922-928.

Thomas, S., Gilliam, A., & Iwrey, C. (1989). Knowledge about AIDS and reported risk behaviors among black college students. *Journal of American College Health, 31,* 61-66.

Thomas, V.S., & Rockwood, K.J. (2001). Alcohol abuse, cognitive impairment, and mortality among older people. *Journal of the American Geriatric Society*, *49*, 415-420.

Thompson, A.H., et al. (2002). Attitudes about schizophrenia from the pilot site of the WPA worldwide campaign against the stigma of schizophrenia. *Social Psychiatry and Psychiatric Epidemiology*, *37*, 475-482.

Thompson, L.W., Gallagher, D., & Breckenridge, J.S. (1987). Comparative effectiveness of psychotherapies for depressed elders. *Journal of Consulting and Clinical Psychology, 55,* 385-390.

Thoresen, C.E., Friedman, M., Powell, L.H., Gill, J.J., & Ulmer, D.K. (1985). Altering the type A behavior pattern in postinfarction patients. *Journal of Cardiopulmonary Rehabilitation, 5,* 258-266.

Thorne, S. (2000, February 17). Military will treat stress as a disability: Posttraumatic disorders eligible for compensation. *The Toronto Star*, A7.

Thorpe, L. (1997). The treatment of psychotic disorders in late life. *Canadian Journal of Psychiatry*, *42*, S19-S27.

Thorpe, L., & Groulx, B. (2001). Depressive syndromes in dementia. *Canadian Journal of Neurological Sciences*, *28*, S83-S95.

Thyer, B.A., & Curtis, G.C. (1984). The effects of ethanol on phobic anxiety. *Behaviour Research and Therapy, 22,* 599-610.

Tidmarsh, L., & Volkmar, F.R. (2003). Diagnosis and epidemiology of autism spectrum disorders. *Canadian Journal of Psychiatry*, *48*, 517-525.

Tiefer, L., Pedersen, B., & Melman, A. (1988). Psychosocial follow-up of penile prosthesis implant with patients and partners. *Journal of Sex and Marital Therapy, 14,* 184-201.

Tienari, P. (1991). Interaction between genetic vulnerability and family environment: The Finnish adoptive family study of schizophrenia. *Acta Psychiatrica Scandinavica, 84,* 460-465.

Tienari, P., et al. (2004). Genotype-environment interaction in schizophrenia-spectrum disorder : Long-term follow-up study of Finnish adoptees. *British Journal of Psychiatry*, *184*, 216-222.

Tillich, P. (1952). *The courage to be*. New Haven, CT: Yale University Press.

Time/CNN Poll (2001, November). *National poll shows American concerns over bio-terrorism prevail as Thanksgiving nears*. (retrieved from www.time.com)

Tobin, D.L., Griffing, A., & Griffing, S. (1997). An examination of subtype criteria for bulimia nervosa. *International Journal of Eating Disorders, 22,* 179-186.

Tollefson, D.J. (1972). *The relationship between the occurrence of fractures and life crisis events*. Unpublished Master of Nursing thesis, University of Washington, Seattle.

Tollefson, G.D., Beasley, C.M., Tamura, R.N., Tran, P.V., & Potvin, J.H. (1997). Blind, controlled, long-term study of the comparative incidence of treatment-emergent tardive dyskinesia with olanzapine or haloperidol. *American Journal of Psychiatry, 154,* 1248-1254.

Tollefson, G.D., Rampey, A.H., Jr., Potvin, J.H., Jenike, M.A., Rush, A.J., et al. (1994). A multicenter investigation of fixed-dose fluoxetine in the treatment of obsessive-compulsive disorder. *Archives of General Psychiatry, 51,* 552-558.

Tollefson, G.D., Sanger, T., Lu, L., & Thieme, M.E. (1998). Depressive signs and symptoms in schizophrenia: A prospective trial of olanzapine and haloperidol. *Archives of General Psychiatry, 55,* 250-258.

Tolomiczenko, G.S., & Goering, P.N. (2000). The process and politics of community-based research with people currently homeless. *Psychiatric Rehabilitation Journal*, *24*, 46-51.

Tomasson, K., Kent, D., & Coryell, W. (1991). Somatization and conversion disorders: Comorbidity and demographics at presentation. *Acta Psychiatrica Scandinavica, 84,* 288-293.

Tondo, L., Baldessarini, R.J., Hennen, J., & Floris, G. (1998). Lithium maintainance treatment of depression and mania in bipolar I disorders. *American Journal of Psychiatry, 155,* 647-652.

Toneatto, T., Ferguson, D., & Brennan, J. (2003). Effect of a new casino on problem gambling in treatment-seeking substance abusers. *Canadian Journal of Psychiatry*, *48*, 40-44.

Toneatto, T., Skinner, W., & Dragonetti, R. (2002). Patterns of substance use in treatment-seeking problem gamblers. *Journal of Clinical Psychology*, *58*, 853-859.

Torgersen, S. (1986). Genetics of somatoform disorder. *Archives of General Psychiatry, 43,* 502-505.

Torgersen, S., Kringlen, E., & Cramer, V. (2001). The prevalence of personality disorders in a community sample. *Archives of General Psychiatry*, *58*, 590-596.

Torrey, E.F. (1995). Prevalence of psychosis among the Hutterites: A reanalysis of the 1950-53 study. *Schizophrenia Research*, *16*, 167-170.

Torrey, E.F. (1996). *Out of the shadows: Confronting America's mental health crisis*. New York: Wiley.

Torrey, E.F., Taylor, E., Bowler, A., & Gottesman, I. (1994). *Schizophrenia and manic depressive disorder. The biological roots of mental illness as revealed by the landmark study of identical twins*. New York: Basic Books.

Toupin, J., Dery, M., Pauze, R., Mercier, H., & Fortin, L. (2000). Cognitive and familial contributions to conduct disorder in children. *Journal of Child Psychology and Psychiatry*, *41*, 333-344.

Tousignant, M., Bastien, M.F., & Hamel, S. (1993). Suicidal attempts and ideations among adolescents and young adults: The contributions of the father's and mother's care and of parental separation. *Social Psychiatry and Psychiatric Epidemiology*, *28*, 256-261.

Tramontana, J., & Stimbert, V. (1970). Some techniques of behavior modification with an autistic child. *Psychological Reports, 27,* 498-515.

Tran, G.Q., Haaga, D.A.F., & Chambless, D.L. (1997). Expecting that alcohol will reduce social anxiety moderates the relation between social anxiety and alcohol consumption. *Cognitive Therapy and Research, 21,* 535-553.

Treffert, D.A., McAndrew, J.B., & Dreifuerst, P. (1973). An inpatient treatment program and outcome for 57 autistic and schizophrenic children. *Journal of Autism and Childhood Schizophrenia, 3,* 138-153.

Tremblay, C., Hebert, M., & Piche, C. (2000). Type I and Type II posttraumatic stress disorder in sexually abused children. *Journal of Child Sexual Abuse*, *9*, 65-90.

Tremblay, R.E., Masse, B., Perron, D., Leblanc, M., Schwartzman, A.E., & Ledingham, J.E. (1992). Early disruptive behavior, poor school achievement, delinquent behavior, and delinquent personality: Longitudinal analyses. *Journal of Consulting and Clinical Psychology, 60*, 64-72.

Tremblay, R.E., Vitaro, F., Bertrand, L., LeBlanc, M., Beauchesne, H., Boileau, H., & David, L. (1992). Parent and child training to prevent early onset of delinquence: The Montreal Longitudinal-Experimental Study. In J. McCord & R. E. Tremblay (Eds.), *Preventing antisocial behavior: Interventions from birth through adolescence* (pp. 117-138). New York: Guilford.

Trevitt, C. & Gallagher, E. (1996). Elder abuse in Canada and Australia: Implications for nurses. *International Journal of Nursing Studies, 33,* 651-699.

Treynor, W., Gonzalez, R., & Nolen-Hoeksema, S. (2003). Rumination reconsidered: A psychometric analysis. *Cognitive Therapy and Research, 27,* 247-259.

Triandis, H.C. (1994). Culture and social behavior. In W.J. Lonner & R.S. Malpass (Eds.), *Psychology and culture* (pp. 169-174). Boston: Allyn & Bacon.

Trickett, P.K., & Putnam, F.W. (1993). Impact of child sexual abuse on females: Toward a developmental, psychobiological integration. *Psychological Science, 4,* 81-87.

Tri-Council Working Group on Ethics (1997). *Code of ethical conduct for research involving humans [final report].* Ottawa: The Medical Research Council of Canada.

True, W.R., Rice, J., Eisen, S.A., Heath, A.C., Goldberg, J., et al. (1993). A twin study of genetic and environmental contributions to liability for post-traumatic stress disorder. *Archives of General Psychiatry, 50,* 257-264.

True, W.R., Xiam, H., Scherrer, J.F., Madden, P., Bucholz, K.K., et al. (1999). Common genetic vulnerability for nicotine and alcohol dependence in men. *Archives of General Psychiatry, 56,* 655-662.

Trull, T.J. (2001). Relationships of borderline features to parental mental illness, childhood abuse, Axis I disorder, and current functioning. *Journal of Personality Disorders, 15,* 19-32.

Trull, T.J., Useda, J.D., Costa, P.T., Jr., & McCrae, R.R. (1995). Comparsion of the MMPI-2 personality psychopathology five (PSY-5), the NEO-PI, and the NEO-PI-R. *Psychological Assessment, 7,* 508-516.

Trull, T.J., Widiger, T.A., & Frances, A. (1987). Covariation of criteria for avoidant, schizoid, and dependent personality disorders. *American Journal of Psychiatry, 144,* 767-771.

Tsai, G., Parssani, L.A., Slusher, B.S., Carter, R., Baer, L., et al. (1995). Abnormal excitatory neurotransmitter metabolism in schizophrenic brains. *Archives of General Psychiatry, 52,* 829-836.

Tsoi, W.F. (1990). Developmental profile of 200 male and 100 female transsexuals in Singapore. *Archives of Sexual Behavior, 19,* 595-605.

Tsuang, M.T., & Faraone, S.V. (1990). *The genetics of mood disorders.* Baltimore: Johns Hopkins University Press.

Tsuang, M.T., Lyons, M.J., Meyer, J.M., Doyle, T., Eisen, S.A., et al. (1998). Co-occurrence of abuse of different drugs in men: The role of drug-specific and shared vulnerabilities. *Archives of General Psychiatry, 55,* 967-972.

Tucker, J.A., Vuchinich, R.E., & Downey, K.K. (1992). Substance abuse. In S.M. Turner, K.S. Calhoun, & H.E. Adams (Eds.), *Handbook of clinical behavior therapy* (pp. 203-223). New York: Wiley.

Tugrul, C., & Kabacki, E. (1997). Vaginismus and its correlates. *Sexual and Marital Therapy, 12,* 23-34.

Tuokko, H., et al. (2003). Five-year follow-up of cognitive impairment with no dementia. *Archives of Neurology, 60,* 577-582.

Tuokko, H., Frerichs, R., Halpern, S., & Eisner, M. (1999). Delusional symptomatology as seen by a community mental health outreach team. *Aging and Mental Health, 3,* 136-142.

Tuokko, H., Hadjistavropoulos, T., Miller, J.A., & Beattie, B.L. (1992). The Clock Test: A sensitive measure to differentiate normal elderly from those with Alzheimers disease. *Journal of the American Geriatrics Society, 40,* 579-584.

Tuokko, H., Hadjistavropoulos, T., Rae, S., & O'Rourke, N. (2000). A comparison of alternative approaches to the scoring of clock drawing. *Archives of Clinical Neuropsychology, 15,* 137-148.

Tuokko, H., Kristjansson, E., & Miller, J. (1995). Neuropsychological detection of dementia: An overview of the neuropsychological component of the Canadian Study of Health and Aging. *Journal of Clinical and Experimental Neuropsychology, 17,* 352-373.

Tuokko, H., MacCourt, P., & Heath, Y. (1999). Home alone with dementia. *Aging and Mental Health, 3,* 21-27.

Tuomilehto, J., Geboers, J., Salonen, J.T., Nissinen, A., Kuulasman, K., & Puska, P. (1986). Decline in cardiovascular mortality in North Karelia and other parts of Finland. *British Medical Journal, 293,* 1068-1071.

Tuomisto, M.T. (1997). Intra-arterial blood pressure and heart rate reactivity to behavioral stress in normotensive, borderline, and mild hypertensive men. *Health Psychology, 16,* 554-565.

Turecki, G., Briere, R., Dewar, K., Antonetti, T., Seguin, M., et al. (1999). Prediction of level of serotonin 2A receptor binding by serotonin receptor 2A genetic variation in postmortem brain sample from subjects who did or did not commit suicide. *American Journal of Psychiatry, 156,* 1456-1458.

Turk, D.C. (1996). Cognitive factors in chronic pain and disability. In K.S. Dobson & K.D. Craig (Eds.), *Advances in cognitive-behavioral therapy* (pp. 83-115). Thousand Oaks, CA: Sage.

Turk, D.C., Meichenbaum, D.H., & Genest, M. (1983). *Pain and behavioral medicine: A cognitive behavioral perspective.* New York: Guilford.

Turk, D.C., & Monarch, E.S. (2003). Chronic pain. In S. Llewelyn & P. Kennedy (Eds.), *Handbook of clinical health psychology* (pp. 81-101). Chichester, West Sussex, England: Wiley.

Turk, D.C., Wack, J.T., & Kerns, R.D. (1985). An empirical examination of the "pain behavior" construct. *Journal of Behavioral Medicine, 8,* 119-130.

Turk-Charles, S., Rose, T., & Gatz, M. (1996). The significance of gender in the treatment of older adults. In L.L. Carstensen, B.A. Edelstein, & L. Dornbrand (Eds.), *The practical handbook of clinical gerontology* (pp. 107-128). Thousand Oaks, CA: Sage.

Turkewitz, H., & O'Leary, K.D. (1977). *A comparison of communication and behavioral marital therapy.* Paper presented at the Eleventh Annual Convention of the Association for Advancement of Behavior Therapy, Atlanta.

Turkheimer, E. (1998). Heritability and biological explanation. *Psychological Review, 105,* 782-791.

Turkheimer, E., & Parry, C.D. (1992). Why the gap? Practice and policy in civil commitment hearings. *American Psychologist, 47,* 646-655.

Turner, C.F., Ku, S.M., Rogers, L.D., Lindberg, J.H., & Pleck, F.L. (1998). Adolescent sexual behavior, drug use, and violence: Increased reporting with computer survey technology. *Science, 280,* 867-873.

Turner, J.A., Deyo, R.A., Loeser, J.D., Von Korff, M., & Fordyce, W.E. (1994). The importance of placebo effects in pain treatment and research. *JAMA, 271,* 1609-1614.

Turner, L.A., Althof, S.E., Levine, S.B., Risen, C.B., Bodner, D.R., Kursh, E.D., & Resnick, M.I. (1989). Self-injection of papaverine and phentolamine in the treatment of psychogenic impotence. *Journal of Sex and Marital Therapy, 15,* 163-176.

Turner, R.J., & Wagonfeld, M.O. (1967). Occupational mobility and schizophrenia. *American Sociological Review, 32,* 104-113.

Turner, R.M. (1993). Dynamic-cognitive-behavior therapy. In T. Giles (Ed.), *Handbook of effective psychotherapy* (pp. 437-454). New York: Plenum.

Turner, R.M. (1994). Borderline, narcissistic, and histrionic personality disorders. In M. Hersen & R.T. Ammerman (Eds.), *Handbook of prescriptive treatments for adults* (pp. 393-420). New York: Plenum.

Turner, S.M., Beidel, D.C., & Cooley-Quille, M.R. (1995). Two-year follow-up of social phobics treated with Social Effectiveness Therapy. *Behaviour Research and Therapy, 33,* 553-555.

Turner, S.M., Beidel, D.C., & Townsley, R.M. (1992). Behavioral treatment of social phobia. In S.M. Turner, K.S. Calhoun, & H.E. Adams (Eds.), *Handbook of clinical behavior therapy* (2nd ed., pp. 13-37). New York: Wiley.

Turvey, C L., Carney, C., Arndt, S., Wallace, R.B., & Herzog, R. (1999). Conjugal loss and syndromal depression in a sample of elders aged 70 years or older. *American Journal of Psychiatry, 156,* 1596-1601.

Tuschen, B., & Bent, H. (1995). Intensive brief inpatient treatment of bulimia nervosa. In K.D. Brownell & C.G. Fairburn (Eds.), *Eating disorders and obesity: A comprehensive handbook.* New York: Guilford.

Tustin, F. (1990). *Autistic states in children: Revised edition.* London and New York: Tavistock/Routledge.

Tustin, F. (1994). Autistic children who are assessed as not brain-damaged. *Association of Child Psychotherapists, 20,* 103-131.

Tustin, F. (1995). *Autism and childhood psychosis.* London: Karnac Books.

Tweed, R.G., & Dutton, D.G. (1998). A comparison of impulsive and instrumental subgroups of batterers. *Violence and Victims, 13,* 217-230.

Twentyman, C.T., & McFall, R.M. (1975). Behavioral training of social skills in shy males. *Journal of Consulting and Clinical Psychology, 43,* 384-395.

Tye, J. (1991). *Stop teenage addiction to tobacco.* Springfield, MA: Stop Teenage Addiction to Tobacco.

Tykra, A.R., Cannon, T.D., Haslam, N., Mednick, S.A, Schulsinger, F., et al. (1995). The latent structure of schizotypy. I. Premorbid indicators of a taxon of individuals at risk for schizophrenia spectrum disorders. *Journal of Abnormal Psychology, 104,* 173-184.

Tyler, T. (2001, January 23). Patients drugged in experiments at psychiatric facility, suit claims. *The Toronto Star,* A18.

Urbszat, D., Herman, C.P., & Polivy, J. (2002). Eat, drink, and be merry, for tomorrow we diet: Effects of anticipated deprivation on food intake in restrained and unrestrained eaters. *Journal of Abnormal Psychology, 111,* 396-401.

U. S. Bureau of the Census (1999). *Current population reports, special studies.* Washington, DC: U.S. Government Printing Office.

U.S. Department of Health and Human Services. (1982). Prevention in adulthood: Self-motivated quitting. In *Cancer: The health consequences of smoking, a report of the Surgeon General.* Washington, DC: U.S. Government Printing Office.

U.S. Department of Health and Human Services. (1989). *Reducing the health consequences of smoking: 25 years of progress. A report of the Surgeon General, Executive summary* (DHHS Publication No. CDC 89-8411). Washington, DC: U.S. Government Printing Office.

U.S. Department of Health and Human Services, National Center for Health Statistics. (1990a, August 30). *Monthly vital statistics.*

U.S. Department of Health and Human Services. (1990b). *The health benefits of smoking cessation: A report of the surgeon general.* Alexandria, VA: Author.

U. S. Department of Health and Human Services (1991). *Health United States: 1990.* Washington, DC. U.S. Government Printing Office.

U.S. Department of Health and Human Services. (1993). *Eighth special report to the U.S. Congress on alcohol and health.* Alexandria, VA: Author.

U.S. Department of Health and Human Services. (1994). *National survey results on drug use from the Monitoring the Future Study, 1975-1993.* Rockville, MD: National Institute on Drug Abuse.

U.S. Department of Health and Human Services. (1997). *Alcohol and health.* Washington, DC: NIH.

Ullmann, L., & Krasner, L. (1975). *A psychological approach to abnormal behavior* (2nd ed.). Englewood Cliffs, NJ: Prentice-Hall.

Upper, D., & Ross, S.M. (Eds.). (1980). *Behavioral group therapy 1980: An annual review.* Champaign, IL: Research Press.

Usman, M.A. (1997). Frontotemporal dementias. In P.D. Nussbaum (Ed.), *Handbook of neuropsychology and aging.* (pp. 159-176). NY: Plenum.

Vaillant, G.E. (1979). Natural history of male psychologic health: Effects of mental health on physical health. *New England Journal of Medicine, 301,* 1249-1254.

Vaillant, G.E. (1996). A long-term follow-up of male alcohol abuse. *Archives of General Psychiatry, 53,* 243-250.

Valdes, M., Garcia, L., Treserra, J., et al. (1989). Psychogenic pain and depressive disorders: An empirical study. *Journal of Affective Disorders, 16,* 21-25.

van den Broucke, S., Vandereycken, W., & Vertommen, H. (1995). Marital communication in eating disorders: A controlled observational study. *International Journal of Eating Disorders, 17,* 1-23.

Vallis, T.M., Howes, J.L., & Standage, K. (2000). Is cognitive therapy suitable for treating individuals with personality dysfunction? *Cognitive Therapy and Research, 24,* 595-606.

Van Den Kerkhof, E.G., Hopman, W.M., Towheed, T.E., Anastassiades, T.P., & Goldstein, D.H. (2003). The impact of sampling and measurement on the prevalence of self-reported pain in Canada. *Pain Research and Management, 8,* 157-163.

Van den Oord, E.J., Boomsma, D.I., & Verhulst, F.C. (1994). A study of problem behaviors in 10- to 15-year-old biologically related and unrelated international adoptees. *Behavior Genetics, 24,* 193-205.

van Egeren, L.F., & Madarasmi, S. (1987). A computerized diary for ambulatory blood pressure monitoring. In N. Schneiderman (Ed.), *Handbook on methods and measurements in cardiovascular behavioral medicine.* New York: Plenum.

van Praag, H., Plutchik, R., & Apter, A. (Eds.), (1990). *Violence and suicidality.* New York: Brunner/Mazel.

van Reekum, R., Conway, C.A., Gansler, D., & White, R. (1993). Neurobehavioral study of borderline personality disorder. *Journal of Psychiatry and Neuroscience, 18,* 121-129.

van Reekum, R., Simard, M., Clarke, D., Binns, M.A., & Conn, D. (1999). Late-life depression as a possible predictor of dementia: Cross-sectional and short-term follow-up results. *American Journal of Geriatric Psychiatry, 7,* 151-159.

vanKammen, D.P., Bunney, W.E., Docherty, J.P., Jimerson, D.C., Post, R.M., Sivis, S., Ebart, M., & Gillin, J.C. (1977). Amphetamine-induced catecholamine activation in schizophrenia and depression. *Advances in Biochemical Psychopharmacology, 16,* 655-659.

vanKammen, D.P., Hommer, D.W., & Malas, K.L. (1987). Effects of pimozide on positive and negative symptoms in schizophrenic patients: Are negative symptoms state dependent? *Neuropsychobiology, 18,* 113-117.

vanKammen, W.B., Loeber, R., & Stouthamer-Loeber, M. (1991). Substance use and its relationship to conduct problems and delinquency in young boys. *Journal of Youth and Adolescence, 20,* 399-413.

Van Zelst, W.H., de Beurs, E., Beckman, A.T., Deej, D.T., & van Dyck, R. (2003). Prevalence and risk factors of posttraumatic stress disorder in older adults. *Psychotherapy and Psychosomatics, 72,* 333-342.

van Vliet, I.M., den Boer, J.A., & Westernberg, H. (1994). Psychopharmacological treatment of social phobia: A double-blind placebo-controlled study with fluvoxamine. *Psychopharmacology, 115,* 128-134.

Vanzi, M. (1996, August 31). Drug castration bill passes, goes to Gov. Wilson. *Los Angeles Times,* pp. A1, A26.

Vardaris, R.M., Weisz, D.J., Fazel, A., & Rawitch, A.B. (1976). Chronic administration of delta-9-tetrahydrocannabinol to pregnant rats: Studies of pup behavior and placental transfer. *Pharmacology and Biochemistry of Behavior, 4,* 249-254.

Varner, R.V., & Gaitz, C.M. (1982). Schizophrenic and paranoid disorders in the aged. In L.F. Jarvik & G.W. Small (Eds.), *Psychiatric Clinics of North America.* Philadelphia: Saunders.

Varni, J.M., Katz, E.R., Colegrove, R., & Dolgin, M. (1993). The impact of social skills training on the adjustment of children with newly diagnosed cancer. *Journal of Pediatric Psychology, 18,* 751-767.

Varni, J.W. (1981). Self-regulation techniques in the management of chronic arthritic pain in hemophilia. *Behavior Therapy, 12,* 185-194.

Varni, J.W., & Bernstein, B.H. (1991). Evaluation and management of pain in children with rheumatoid diseases. *Pediatric Rheumatology, 17,* 985-1000.

Varni, J.W., Blount, R.L., Waldron, S.A., & Smith, A.J. (1997). Management of pain and distress. In M.C. Roberts (Ed.), *Handbook of pediatric psychology.* New York: Guilford..

Varni, J.W., & Dietrich, S.L. (1981). Behavioral pediatrics: Towards a reconceptualization. *Behavioral Medicine Update, 3,* 5-7.

Varni, J.W., & Wallander, J.L. (1984). Adherence to health-related regimens in pediatric chronic disorders. *Clinical Psychology Review, 4,* 585-596.

Vatcher, C.A., & Bogo, M. (2001). The feminist/emotionally focused therapy practice model: An integrated approach for couple therapy. *Journal of Marital and Family Therapy, 27,* 69-83.

Veale, D., Boocook, A., Gournay, K., & Dryden, W. (1996). Body dysmorphic disorder: A survey of fifty cases. *British Journal of Psychiatry, 169,* 196-201.

Vega, W.A., et al. (2002). Prevalence and age of onset for drug use in seven international sites: Results from the international consortium of psyciatric epidemiology. *Drug and Alcohol Dependence, 68,* 285-297.

Velakoulis, D., Pantelis, C., McGorry, P.D., Dudgeon, P., Brewer, W., et al. (1999). Hippocampal volume in first-epiode psychoses and chronic schizophrnnia: A high-resolution magnetic resonance imaging study. *Archives of General Psychiatry, 56,* 133-141.

Verdoux, H., Geddes, J.R., Takei, N., Lawrie, S.M., Bovet, P., et al. (1997). Obstetric complications and age at onset in schizophrenia: An international collaborative meta-analysis of individual patient data. *American Journal of Psychiatry, 154,* 1220-1227.

Verdun-Jones, S.N. (2000). Forensic psychiatry, ethics, and protective sentencing: What are the limits of psychiatric participation in the criminal justice system? *Acta Psychiatrica Scandinavica, 101,* 77-82.

Verlaan, P., & Schwartzman, A.E. (2002). Mother's and father's parental adjustment : Links to externalising behaviour problems in sons and daughters. *International Journal of Behavioral Development*, *26*, 214-224.

Vernberg, E.M., LaGreca, A.M., Silverman, W.K., & Prinstein, M.J. (1996). Prediction of post-traumatic stress symptoms in children after hurricane Andrew. *Journal of Abnormal Psychology, 105,* 237-249.

Vernon, P. (1977). Final report on modification of the WISC-R for Canadian use. *Canadian Psychological Association Bulletin, 7,* 5-7.

Vettese, L.C., & Mongrain, M. (2000). Communication about the self and partner in the relationships of dependents and self-critics. *Cognitive Therapy and Research*, *24*, 609-626.

Vezina, J., & Bourque, P. (1984). The relationship between cognitive structure and symptoms of depression in the elderly. *Cognitive Therapy and Research*, *8*, 29-36.

Vida, S., Monks, S., & Des Rosiers, P. (2002). Prevalence and correlates of elder abuse and neglect in a geriatric psychiatry service. *Canadian Journal of Psychiatry*, *47*, 459-467.

Vienneau, D. (1998, January 10). Give Alzheimer's patients right to die, doctor says. *The Toronto Star,* p. L8.

Viglione, D.J. (1999). A review of recent research addesssing the utility of the Rorschach. *Psychological Assessment, 11,* 251-265.

Viljoen, J.L., Roesch, R., Ogloff, J.R.P., & Zapf, P.A. (2003). The role of Canadian psychologists in conducting fitness and criminal responsibility evaluations. *Canadian Psychology*, *44*, 369-381.

Viljoen, J.L., Roesch, R., & Zapf, P.A. (2002). An examination of the relationship between competency to stand trial, competency to waive interrogation rights, and psychopathology. *Law and Human Behavior*, *26*, 481-506.

Vincent, D., Boyle, T. (1998, January 10-17). Madness: How we're failing the mentally ill. *The Toronto Star.*

Vinkers, D.J., et al. (2004). The 15-item Geriatric Depression Scale (GDS-15) detects changes in depressive symptoms after a major negative life event: The Leiden 85-plus study. *International Journal of Geriatric Psychiatry*, *19*, 80-84.

Vinogradov, S., & Yalom, I. (1989). *Group therapy*. Washington, DC: American Psychiatric Press.

Visser, S., & Bouman, T.K. (1992). Cognitive-behavioural approaches to the treatment of hypochondriasis: Six single-case crossover studies. *Behaviour Research and Therapy, 30,* 301-306.

Vitousek, K., & Manke, F. (1994). Personality variables and disorders in anorexia nervosa and bulimia nervosa. *Journal of Abnormal Psychology, 103,* 137-147.

Vogel, V.G., Graves, D.S., Vernon, S.W., Lord, J.A., Winn, R.J., & Peters, G.N. (1990). Mammographic screening of women with increased risk of breast cancer. *Cancer, 66,* 1613-1620.

Vogel-Sprott, M., Kartechner, W., & McDonnell, D. (1989). Consequences of behavior influence the effect of alcohol. *Journal of Substance Abuse*, *1*, 369-379.

Voglmaier, M.M., Seidman, L.J., Salisbury, D., & McCarley, R.W. (1997). Neuropsychological dysfunction in schizotypal personality disorder: A profile analysis. *Biological Psychiatry, 41,* 530-540.

Vogt, T.M., Mullooly, J.P., Ernst, D., Pope, C.R., & Hollis, J.F. (1992). Social networks as predictors of ischemic heart disease, stroke, and hypertension. *Journal of Clinical Epidemiology, 45,* 659-666.

Vohs, K.D., Bardone, A.M., Joiner, T.E., Jr., Abramson, L.Y., & Heatherton, T.F. (1999). Perfectionism, perceived weight status, and self-esteem interact to predict bulimic symptoms: A model of bulimic symptom development. *Journal of Abnormal Psychology*, *108*, 695-700.

Vohs, K.D., et al. (2001). Perfectionism, body dissatisfaction, and self-esteem: An interactive model of bulimic symptom development. *Journal of Social and Clinical Psychology*, *20*, 476-497.

Volkow, N.D., Wang, G.J., Fischman, M.W., & Foltin, R.W. (1997). Relationship between subjective effects of cocaine and dopamine transporter occupancy. *Nature, 386,* 827-830.

Volpicelli, J.R., Rhines, K.C., Rhines, J.S., Volpicelli, L.A., et al. (1997). Naltrexone and alcohol dependence: Role of subject compliance. *Archives of General Psychiatry, 54,* 737-743.

Volpicelli, J.R., Watson, N.T., King, A.C., Shermen, C.E., & O'Brien, C.P. (1995). Effects of naltrexone on alcohol "high" in alcoholics. *American Journal of Psychiatry, 152,* 613-617.

Von Knorring, A.L. & Hagglof, B. (1993). Autism in northern Sweden: A population-based follow-up study: Psychopathology. *European Child and Adolescent Psychiatry, 2,* 91-97.

von Krafft-Ebing, R. (1902). *Psychopathia sexualis*. Brooklyn, NY: Physicians and Surgeons Books.

von Ranson, K.M., Iaconon, W.G., & McGue, M. (2002). Disordered eating and substance use in an epidemiological sample: I. Associations within individuals. *International Journal of Eating Disorders, 31*, 389-403.

von Strauss, E., Viitanen, M., De Ronchi, D., Winblad, B., & Fratiglioni, L. (1999). Aging and the occurrence of dementia: Findings from a population-based cohort with a large sample of nonagenarians. *Archives of Neurology, 56,* 587-592.

Vontress, C.E., & Epp, L.R. (1997). Historical hostility in the African American client: Implications for counseling. *Journal of Multicultural Counseling and Development, 25,* 170-184.

Voyer, M., & Cappeliez, P. (2002). Congruency between depressogenic schemas and life events for the prediction of depressive relapse in remitted older patients. *Behavioural and Cognitive Psychotherapy*, *30*, 165-177.

Vrana, S.R., Roodham, A., & Beckham, J.C. (1995). Selective processing of trauma-relevant words in posttraumatic stress disorder. *Journal of Anxiety Disorders, 9,* 515-530.

Vredenburg, K., Flett, G.L., & Krames, L. (1993). Analogue versus clinical depression: A critical re-appraisal. *Psychological Bulletin, 113,* 327-344.

Vygotsky, L.S. (1978). *Mind in society: The development of higher psyhological processes* (M. Cole, V. John-Steiner, S. Scribner, & E. Souberman, Eds. and Trans.). Cambridge, MA: Harvard University Press.

Vygotsky, L. (1988). *Thought and language*. Cambridge, MA: MIT Press.

Wachtel, E.F., & Wachtel, P.L. (1986). *Family dynamics in individual psychotherapy: A guide to clinical strategies*. New York: Guilford.

Wachtel, P.L. (1977). *Psychoanalysis and behavior therapy: Toward an integration*. New York: Basic Books.

Wachtel, P.L. (1997). *Psychoanalysis, behavior therapy and the relational world*. Washington, DC: American Psychological Association.

Wachtel, P.L. (2002). Termination of therapy: An effort at integration. *Journal of Psychotherapy Integration*, *12*, 373-383.

Waddell, C., Lipman, E., & Offord, D. (1999). Conduct disorder: Practice parameters for assessment, treatment, and prevention. *Canadian Journal of Psychiatry*, *44 (Supplement 2)*, 35S-40S.

Waddell, C., Offord, D.R., Shepherd, C.A., Hua, J.M., & McEwan, K. (2002). Child psychiatric epidemiology and Canadian public policy-making: The state of the science and the art of the possible. *Canadian Journal of Psychiatry*, *47*, 825-832.

Wade, T.J., Cairney, J., & Pevalin, D.J. (2002). Emergence of gender differences in depression during adolescence: National panel results from three countries. *Journal of the American Academy of Child and Adolescent Psychiatry, 41*, 190-198.

Wade, T.J., Pevalin, D.J., & Brannigan, A. (1999). The clustering of severe behavioural, health, and educational deficits in Canadian children: Preliminary evidence from the National Longitudinal Survey of Children and Youth. *Canadian Journal of Public Health*, *90*, 253-259.

Wagner, A.W., & Linehan, M.M. (1997). The relationship between childhood sexual abuse and suicidal behaviors in borderline patients. In M. Zanarini (Ed.), *The role of sexual abuse in the etiology of borderline personality disorder*. Washington,DC: American Psychiatric Association.

Wahl, O.F. & Harrman, C.R. (1989). Family views of stigma. *Schizophrenia Bulletin, 15,* 131-139.

Wahlbeck, K., Cheine, M., Essali, A., & Adams, C. (1999). Evidence of clozapine's effectiveness in schizophrenia: A systemic review and meta-analysis of randomized trials. *American Journal of Psychiatry, 156,* 990-999.

Wakefield, H., & Underwager, R. (1994). *Return of the furies: An investigation into recovered memory therapy*. Chicago: Open Court Publishing.

Wakefield, J. (1992). Disorder as dysfunction: A conceptual critique of DSM-III-R's definition of mental disorder. *Psychological Review, 99,* 232-247.

Wakeman, S. (2002). Working with the center: Psychiatric rehabilitation with people who dissociate. *Psychiatric Rehabilitation Journal*, *26*, 115-122.

Walco, G.A., Varni, J.W., & Ilowite, N.T. (1992). Cognitive-behavioral pain management in children with juvenile rheumatoid arthritis. *Pediatrics, 89,* 1075-1079.

Waldenger, R.J., & Frank, A.E. (1989). Clinicians' experiences in combining medication and psychotherapy in the treatment of borderline patients. *Hospital and Community Psychiatry, 40,* 712-718.

Waldron, I. (1976). Why do women live longer than men? *Journal of Human Stress, 2,* 1-13.

Walen, S., Hauserman, N.M., & Lavin, P.J. (1977). *Clinical guide to behavior therapy*. Baltimore: Williams & Wilkins.

Walitzer, K.S., & Connors, G.J. (1994). Psychoactive substance use disorders. In M. Hersen & R.T. Ammerman (Eds.), *Handbook of prescriptive treatments for adults* (pp. 53-71). New York: Plenum.

Walker, C.E. (1995). Elimination disorders: Enuresis and encopresis. In P. Magrab (Ed.), *Psychological management of pediatric problems* (Vol 1, pp. 129-189). Baltimore, MD: University Park Press.

Walker, C.E., Milling, L.S., & Bonner, B.L. (1988). Incontinence disorders: Enuresis and encopresis. In D.K. Routh (Ed.), *Handbook of pediatric psychology* (pp. 363-397). New York: Guilford Press.

Walker, E.F., Davis, D.M., & Savoie, T.D. (1994). Neuromotor precursors of schizophrenia. *Schizophrenia Bulletin, 20,* 441-451.

Walker, E., Kestler, L., Bollini, A., & Hochman, K.M. (2004). Schizophrenia: Etiology and course. *Annual Review of Psychology, 55,* 401-430.

Walker, E.F., & DiForio, D. (1997). Schizophrenia: A neural diathesis-stress model. *Psychological Review, 104,* 667-685.

Walker, E.F., Grimes, K.E., Davis, D.M., & Adina, J. (1993). Childhood precursors of schizophrenia: Facial expressions of emotion. *American Journal of Psychiatry, 150,* 1654-1660.

Walker, J.L., Lahey, B.B., Russo, M.F., Frick, P.J., Christ, M.A.G., McBurnett, K., Loeber, R., Stouthamer-Loeber, M., & Green, S.M. (1991). Anxiety, inhibition, and conduct disorder in children: 1. Relations to social impairment. *Journal of the American Academy of Child and Adolescent Psychiatry, 30,* 187-191.

Walkom, T. (2003, September 20). Now, medical waiting lists include healthcare reform: Proposed changes collecting dust, Ottawa, provinces blamed for delay. *Toronto Star,* B4.

Wall, A-M., McKee, S.A., & Hinson, R.E. (2000). Assessing variation in alcohol outcome expectancies across environmental context: An examination of the situational-specificity hypothesis. *Psychology of Addictive Behaviors, 14,* 367-375.

Wall, A.-M., Wekerle, C., & Bissonette, M. (2000). Childhood maltreatment, parental alcoholism, and beliefs about alcohol: Sub-group variation among alcohol-dependent adults. *Alcoholism Treatment Quarterly, 18,* 49-60.

Wallace, C.J., Boone, S.E., Donahoe, C.P., & Foy, D.W. (1985). The chronically mentally disabled: Independent living skills training. In D.H. Barlow (Ed.), *Clinical handbook of psychological disorders*. New York: Guilford.

Wallace, C.J., & Liberman, R.P. (1985). Social skills training for patients with schizophrenia: A controlled clinical trial. *Psychiatric Research, 15,* 239-247.

Wallace, S.T., & Alden, L.E. (1997). Social phobia and positive social events: The price of success. *Journal of Abnormal Psychology, 106,* 416-424.

Waller, D.A., Kiser, S., Hardy, B.W., Fuchs, I., & Feigenbaum, L.P. (1986). Eating behavior and plasma beta-endorphin in bulimia. *American Journal of Clinical Nutrition, 4,* 20-23.

Waller, G., & Kennerly, H. (2003). Cognitive-behavioral treatments. In J. Treasure, U. Schmidt, & van Furth, E, *Handbook of eating disorders* (2nd edition, pp. 233-252). Chichester, West Sussex: Wiley.

Wallerstein, R.S. (1986). *Forty-two lives in treatment: A study of psychoanalysis and psychotherapy*. New York: Guilford.

Wallerstein, R.S. (1989). The Psychotherapy Research Project of the Menninger Foundation: An overview. *Journal of Consulting and Clinical Psychology, 57,* 195-205.

Walling, M., Anderson, B.L., & Johnson, S.R. (1990). Hormonal replacement therapy for postmenopausal women: A review of sexual outcomes and related gynecologic effects. *Archives of Sexual Behavior, 19,* 119-137.

Walsh, B.T., Wilson, G.T., Loeb, K.L., Devin, M.J., et al. (1997). Medication and psychotherapy in the treatment of bulimia nervosa. *American Journal of Psychiatry, 154,* 523-531.

Walsh, D.C., Hingson, R.W., et al. (1991). A randomized trial of treatment options for alcohol abusing workers. *New England Journal of Medicine, 325,* 775-782.

Walsh-Bowers, R. (1998). Community psychology in the Canadian psychological family. *Canadian Psychology, 39,* 280-287.

Walters, D. (1995). Mandatory reporting of child abuse: Legal, ethical, and clinical implications within a Canadian context. *Canadian Psychology, 36,* 163-182.

Walters, E., & Kendler, K.S. (1994). Anorexia nervosa and anorexia-like symptoms in a population based twin sample. *American Journal of Psychiatry, 152,* 62-71.

Walters, E.E., Neale, M.C., Eaves, L.J., Lindon, J., & Heath, A.C. (1992). Bulimia nervosa and major depression: A study of common genetic and environmental factors. *Psychological Medicine, 22,* 617-622.

Wang, M.Q., Fitzhugh, E.C., Eddy, J.M., Fu, Q., et al. (1997). Social influences on adolescents' smoking progress: A longitudinal analysis. *American Journal of Health Behavior, 21,* 111-117.

Wannamethee, S.G., Shaper, A.G., & Walker, M. (1998). Changes in physical activity, mortality, and incidence of coronary heart disease in older men. *The Lancet, 351,* 1603-1608.

Ward, C.H., Beck, A.T., Mendelson, M., Mock, E., & Erbaugh, J.K. (1962). The psychiatric nomenclature: Reasons for diagnostic disagreement. *Archives of General Psychiatry, 7,* 198-205.

Warner, R.E. (1991). A survey of theoretical orientations of Canadian clinical psychologists. *Canadian Psychology, 32,* 525-528.

Warren, C.A.B. (1982). *The court as last resort: Mental illness and the law*. Chicago: University of Chicago Press.

Warren, J. (1998, May 27). Officials suggest ways to distribute medical marijuana. *Los Angeles Times*, pp. A3-A22.

Warren, S. L., Huston, L., Egeland, B., & Sroufe, L. A. (1997). Child and adolescent anxiety disorders and early attachment. *Journal of the American Academy of Child and Adolescent Psychiatry, 36,* 637-644.

Warsh, C. K. (1989). *Moments of unreason: The practice of Canadian psychiatry and the Homewood Retreat, 1883-1923.* Montreal: McGill-Queen's University Press.

Wartenberg, A.A., Nirenberg, T.D., Liepman, M.R., Silvia, L.Y., Begin, A.M., & Monti, P.M. (1990). Detoxification of alcoholics: Improving care by symptom-triggered sedation. *Alcoholism: Clinical and Experimental Research, 14,* 71-75.

Waschbusch, D.A., Kipp, H.L., & Pelham, W.E. (1998). Generalization of behavioral and psychostimulant treatment of attention-deficit/hyperactivity disorder (ADHD): Discussion and examples. *Behaviour Research and Therapy, 36,* 675-694.

Waserman, J., & Criollo, M. (2000). Subjective experiences of clozapine treatment by patients with chronic schizophrenia. *Psychiatric Services, 51,* 666-668.

Waskow, I.E. (1984). Specification of the technique variable in the NIMH Treatment of Depression Collaborative Research Program. In J.B.W. Williams & R.L. Spitzer (Eds.), *Psychotherapy research: Where are we and where should we go?* New York: Guilford.

Watson, D., & Pennebaker, J.W. (1989). Health complaints, stress, and distress: Exploring the central role of negative affectivity. *Psychological Review, 96,* 234-254.

Watson, J.C., Gordon, L.B., Stermac, L., Kalogerakos, F., & Steckley, P. (2003). Comparing the effectiveness of process-experiential with cognitive-behavioral psychotherapy in the treatment of depression. *Journal of Consulting and Clinical Psychology, 71,* 773-781.

Watson, J.B. (1913). Psychology as the behaviorist views it. *Psychological Review, 20,* 158-177.

Watson, J.B., & Rayner, R. (1920). Conditioned emotional reactions. *Journal of Experimental Psychology, 3,* 1-14.

Watt, L.M., & Cappeliez, P. (2000). Integrative and instrumental reminiscence therapies for depression in older adults: Intervention strategies and treatment effectiveness. *Aging and Mental Health, 4,* 166-177.

Watt, M.C., Stewart, S.H., & Cox, B.J. (1998). A retrospective study of the learning history origins of anxiety sensitivity. *Behaviour Research and Therapy, 36,* 505-525.

Watt, N.F. (1974). Childhood and adolescent roots of schizophrenia. In D. Ricks, A. Thomas, & M. Roll (Eds.), *Life history research in psychopathology* (Vol. 3). Minneapolis: University of Minnesota Press.

Watt, N.F., Stolorow, R.D., Lubensky, A.W., & McClelland, D.C. (1970). School adjustment and behavior of children hospitalized for schizophrenia as adults. *American Journal of Orthopsychiatry, 40,* 637-657.

Wattis, J.P. (1990). Diagnostic issues in depression in old age. *International*

Clinical Psychopharmacology, 5, 1-6.

Watzlawick, P., Beavin, J., & Jackson, D.D. (1967). *Pragmatics of human communication: A study of interactional patterns, pathologies, and paradoxes.* New York: Norton.

Waxer, P. (1990). Cantonese versus Canadian evaluation of directive and non-directive therapy. *Canadian Journal of Counseling, 23,* 263-272.

Weaver, T.L., & Clum, G.A. (1993). Early family environments and traumatic experiences associated with borderline personality disorder. *Journal of Consulting and Clinical Psychology, 61,* 1068-1075.

Webb, W.B., & Campbell, S.S. (1980). Awakenings and the return to sleep in an older population. *Sleep, 3,* 41-66.

Weber, T. (1996, December 2). Tarnishing the golden years with addiction. *Los Angeles Times*, pp. A1, A37.

Webster, C.D., Douglas, K.S., Eaves, D., & Hart, S.D. (1997). Assessing risk of violence to others. In C.D. Webster & M.A. Jackson (Eds.), *Impulsivity: Theory, assessment, and treatment* (pp. 251-277). New York: Guilford.

Wechsler, H., Davenport, A., Dowdell, G., Moeykens, B., & Castillo, S. (1994). Health and behavioral consequences of binge drinking in college: A national survey of students at 140 campuses. *Journal of the American Medical Association, 272,* 1672-1677.

Wechsler *Intelligence Scale for Children*. Third Edition. (1991). San Antonio: The Psychological Corporation.

Wegner, D.M., Schneider, D.J., Carter, S.R., & White, T.L. (1987). Paradoxical effects of thought suppression. *Journal of Personality and Social Psychology, 53,* 5-13.

Wegner, D.M., Schneider, D.J., Knutson, B., & McMahon, S.R. (1991). Polluting the stream of consciousness: The effect of thought suppression on the mind's environment. *Cognitive Therapy and Research, 15,* 141-152.

Weidner, G., & Collins, R.L. (1993). Gender, coping, and health. In H.W. Krohne (Ed.), *Attention and avoidance*. New York: Springer-Verlag.

Weidner, G., Connor, S.L., Hollis, J.F., & Connor, W.E. (1992). Improvements in hostility and depression in relation to dietary change and cholesterol lowering. *Annals of Internal Medicine, 117,* 820-823.

Weidner, G., Friend, R., Ficarroto, T.J., & Mendell, N.R. (1989). Hostility and cardiovascular reactivity to stress in women and men. *Psychosomatic Medicine, 51,* 36-45.

Weidner, G., & Griffin, K.W. (1995). Psychological aspects of cholesterol-lowering. *Cardiovascular Risk Factors, 5,* 1-7.

Weidner, G., Sexton, G., McLellarn, R., Connor, S.L., & Matarazzo, J.D. (1987). The role of Type A behavior and hostility in the elevation of plasma lipids in adult women and men. *Psychosomatic Medicine, 49,* 136-146.

Weikel, D. (1996, April 7). Meth labs: How young lives are put in peril. *Los Angeles Times*, pp. A1, A18.

Weinberger, D.R. (1987). Implications of normal brain development for the pathogenesis of schizophrenia. *Archives of General Psychiatry, 44,* 660-669.

Weinberger, D.R., Berman, K.F., & Illowsky, B.P. (1988). Physiological dysfunction of dorsolateral prefrontal cortex in schizophrenia: 3. A new cohort and evidence for a monoaminergic mechanism. *Archives of General Psychiatry, 45,* 609-615.

Weinberger, D.R., Cannon-Spoor, H.E., Potkin, S.G., & Wyatt, R.J. (1980). Poor premorbid adjustment and CT scan abnormalities in chronic schizophrenia. *American Journal of Psychiatry, 137,* 1410-1413.

Weinberger, D.R., Wagner, R.L., & Wyatt, R.J. (1983). Neuropathological studies of schizophrenia: A selective review. *Schizophrenia Bulletin, 9,* 193-212.

Weiner, B. (1986). *An attributional theory of motivation and emotion*. Unpublished manuscript, University of California at Los Angeles.

Weiner, B., Frieze, L., Kukla, A., Reed, L., Rest, S., & Rosenbaum, R.M. (1971). *Perceiving the causes of success and failure*. New York: General Learning Press.

Weiner, H. (1977). *Psychobiology and human disease*. New York: Elsevier.

Weinstein, H. (1996, March 7). Assisted deaths ruled legal: 9th Circuit lifts ban of doctor-aided suicide. *Los Angeles Times*, pp. A1, A16.

Weinstein, H. (1998, May 8). Big tobacco settles Minnesota lawsuit for $6.6 billion. *Los Angeles Times*, pp. A1-A12.

Weinstein, H. M. (1990). *Psychiatry and the CIA: Victims of mind control.* Washington, DC: American Psychiatric Press.

Weinstein, H., & Groves, M. (1996, March 14). Tobacco firm agrees to settle a health suit. *Los Angeles Times*, pp. A1, A12.

Weintraub, S., Liebert, D.E., & Neale, J.M. (1975). Teacher ratings of children vulnerable to psychopathology. *American Journal of Orthopsychiatry, 45,* 838-845.

Weintraub, S., Prinz, R., & Neale, J.M. (1978). Peer evaluations of the competence of children vulnerable to psychopathology. *Journal of Abnormal Child Psychology, 6,* 461-473.

Weintraub, S., Winters, K.C., & Neale, J.M. (1986). Competence and vulnerability in children with an affectively disordered parent. In M. Rutter, C.E. Izard, & P.B. Read (Eds.), *Depression in young people: Development and clinical perspectives.* New York: Guilford.

Weisman, A.G., Nuechterlein, K.H., Goldstein, M.J., & Snyder, K.S. (1998). Expressed emotion, attributions, and schizophrenia symptom dimensions. *Journal of Abnormal Psychology, 107,* 355-359.

Weisman, R. (1995). Reflections on the Oak Ridge experiment with mentally disordered offenders, 1965-1968. *International Journal of Law and Psychiatry, 18,* 265-290.

Weiss, B., Weisz, J.R., & Bromfield, R. (1986). Performance of retarded and nonretarded persons on information-processing tasks: Further tests of the similar structure hypothesis. *Psychological Bulletin, 100,* 157-175.

Weiss, G. (1983). Long-term outcome: Findings, concepts, and practical implications. In M. Rutter (Ed.), *Developmental neuropsychiatry*. New York: Guilford.

Weiss, G., & Hechtman, L. (1986). *Hyperactive children grown up*. New York: Guilford.

Weiss, G., & Hechtman, L. (1993). *Hyperactive children grown up* (2nd ed.). New York: Guilford Press.

Weiss, R.L., & Cerreto, M.C. (1980). The Marital Status Inventory: Development of a measure of dissolution potential. *American Journal of Family Therapy, 8,* 80-85.

Weissberg, R.P., Caplan, M., & Harwood, R.L. (1991). Promoting competent young people in competence-enhancing environments: A systems-based perspective on primary prevention. *Journal of Consulting and Clinical Psychology, 59,* 830-841.

Weissberg, R .P., Caplan, M. Z., & Sivo, P. J. (1989). A new conceptual framework for establishing school-based social competence promotion programs. In L. A. Bond, & B. E. Compas (Eds.), *Primary prevention and promotion in the schools*. Vol. 12 (pp. 255-296). Newbury Park, CA: Sage Publications.

Weissberg, R.P., Gesten, E.L., Rapkin, B.D., Cowen, E.L., Davidson, E., deApodaca, R.F., & McKim, B.J. (1981). Evaluation of a social-problem-solving training program for suburban and inner-city third-grade children. *Journal of Consulting and Clinical Psychology, 49,* 251-261.

Weissman, A.N., & Beck, A.T. (1978). *Development and validation of the Dysfunctional Attitude Scale: A preliminary investigation.* Paper presented at the annual meeting of the American Educational Research Association, Toronto.

Weissman, M.M. (1993). The epidemiology of personality disorders: A 1990 update. *Journal of Personality Disorders, 7,* 44-61.

Weissman, M.M. (1995). *Mastering depression: A patient's guide to interpersonal psychotherapy*. New York: Graywind.

Weissman, M.M., Bland, R.C., Canino, G.J., Faravelli, C., Greenwald, S., et al. (1996). Cross-national epidemiology of major depression and bipolar disorder. *JAMA, 276,* 293-299.

Weissman, M.M., Bland, R.C., Canino, G.J., Faravelli, C., Greenwald, S., et al. (1997). The cross-national epidemiology of panic disorder. *Archives of General Psychiatry, 54,* 305-312.

Weissman, M.M., Bland, R.C., Canino, G.J., Greenwald, S., et al. (1994). The cross-national epidemiology of obsessive compulsive disorder: The Cross National Collaborative Group. *Journal of Clinical Psychiatry*, *55 (Supplement)*, 5-10.

Weissman, M.M., Bland, R.C., Canino, G.J., Greenwald, S., Hwu, H.-G., Joyce, P.R., Karam, E.G., Lee, C.-K., Lellouch, J., Lepine, J.-P., Newman, S. ., Rubio-Stipec, M., Wells, J. E., Wickramaratne, P.J., Wittchen, H.-U., & Yeh, E.-K. (1999). Prevalence of suicide ideation and suicide attempts in nine countries. *Psychological Medicine*, *29*, 9-17.

Weissman, M.M., Klerman, G.L., & Paykel, E.S. (1971). Clinical evaluation of hostility in depression. *American Journal of Psychiatry, 128,* 261-266.

Weissman, M.M., & Markowitz, J.C. (1994). Interpersonal psychotherapy: Current status. *Archives of General Psychiatry, 51,* 599-605.

Weissman, M.M., Prusoff, B.A., DiMascio, A., New, C., Goklaney, M., & Klerman, G.L. (1979). The efficacy of drugs and psychotherapy in the treatment of acute depressive episodes. *American Journal of Psychiatry, 36,* 555-558.

Weisz, J.R., Sigman, M., Weiss, B., & Mosk, J. (1993). Parent reports of behavioral and emotional problems among children in Kenya, Thailand and the United States. *Child Development, 64,* 98-109.

Weisz, J. R., Suwanlert, S. C., Wanchai, W., & Bernadette, R. (1987). Over- and undercontrolled referral problems among children and adolescents from Thailand and the United States: The wat and wai of cultural differences. *Journal of Consulting and Clinical Psychology, 55,* 719-726.

Weisz, J.R., & Weiss, B. (1991). Studying the "referability" of child clinical problems. *Journal of Consulting and Clinical Psychology, 59,* 266-273.

Weisz, J.R., & Yeates, K.D. (1981). Cognitive development in retarded and nonretarded persons: Piagetian tests of the similar structure hypothesis. *Psychological Bulletin, 90,* 153-178.

Weizmann, F., Wiener, N. I., Wiesenthal, D. L., & Ziegler, M. (1991). Eggs, eggplants and eggheads: A rejoinder to Rushton. *Canadian Psychology, 32,* 43-50.

Wekerle, C., & Wall, A.-M.(2002). *The violence and addiction equation: Theoretical and clinical issues in substance abuse and relationship violence.* Philadelphia, PA: Brunner/Mazel.

Wekerle, C., & Wolfe, D.A. (1998). The role of child maltreatment and attachment style in adolescent relationship violence. *Development and Psychopathology, 10,* 571-586.

Welch, S.L., & Fairburn, C.G. (1994). Sexual abuse and bulimia nervosa: Three integrated case-control comparisons. *American Journal of Psychiatry, 151,* 402-407.

Welder, A.N. (2000). Sexual abuse victimization and the child witness in Canada: Legal, ethical, and professional issues for psychologists. *Canadian Psychology, 41,* 160-173.

Wells, C.E., & Duncan, G.W. (1980). *Neurology for psychiatrists.* Philadelphia: F.A. Davis.

Wells, S., Graham, K., & West, P. (2000). Alcohol-related aggression in the general population. *Journal of Studies on Alcohol, 61,* 626-632.

Welsh, R., Burcham, B., DeMoss, K., Martin, C., & Milich, R. (1997). *Attention deficit hyperactivity disorder diagnosis and management: A training program for teachers.* Franfurt: Kentucky Department of Education.

Wente, M. (2000, December 14). Who gets to be a woman? *The Globe and Mail.*

Wente, M. (2003, June 10). The case of the crazy professor. *Globe and Mail,* A17.

Wenzlaff, R.M., Wegner, D.M., & Klein, S.B. (1991). The role of thought suppression in the bonding of thought and affect. *Journal of Personality and Social Psychology, 60,* 500-508.

West, D.J. (1977). *Homosexuality re-rexamined.* Minneapolis: University of Minnesota Press.

West, M., Adams, K., Spreng, S., & Rose, S. (2001). Attachment disorganization and dissociative symptoms in clinically treated adolescents. *Canadian Journal of Psychiatry, 46,* 627-631.

Westen, D., Novotny, C.M., & Thompson-Brenner, H. (2004). The empirical status of empirically supported psychotherapies: Assumptions, findings, and reporting in controlled clinical trials. *Psychological Bulletin, 130,* 631-663.

Wester, P., Eriksson, S., Forsell, A., Puu, G., & Adolfsson, R. (1988). Monoamine metabolite concentrations and cholinesterase activities in cerebrospinal fluid of progressive dementia patents: Relation to clinical parameters. *Acta Neurologica Scandinavica, 77,* 12-21.

Wetherell, J.L. (in press). *Treatment of anxiety in older adults. Psychotherapy.*

Wetherell, J.L., Gatz, M., & Craske, M.G. (2003). Treatment of generalized anxiety disorder in older adults. *Journal of Consulting and Clinical Psychology, 71,* 31-40.

Whalen, C.K. (1983). Hyperactivity, learning problems, and the attention deficit disorders. In T.H. Ollendick & M. Hersen (Eds.), *Handbook of child psychopathology.* New York: Plenum.

Whalen, C.K., & Henker, B. (1991). Therapies for hyperactive children: Comparisons, combinations, and compromises. *Journal of Consulting and Clinical Psychology, 59,* 126-137.

Whalen, C.K. & Henker, B. (1992). The social profile of attention-deficit hyperactivity disorder: Five fundamental facts. *Child and Adolescent Psychiatric Clinics of North America, 1,* 395-409.

Whalen, C.K., Henker, B., Hinshaw, S.P., Heller, T., & Huber-Dressler, A. (1991). Messages of medication: Effects of actual versus informed medication status on hyperactive boys' expectancies and self-evaluations. *Journal of Consulting and Clinical Psychology, 59,* 602-606.

Wheaton, B. (1997). The nature of chronic stress. In B. H. Gottlieb (Ed.), *Coping with chronic stress* (pp. 43-73). New York: Plenum.

Whelton, P.K., Appel, L.J., Espeland, M.A., Applegate, W.B., Ettinger, W.H., Kostis, J.B., Kumanyika, S., Lacy, C.R., Johnson, K.C., Folmar, S., Cutler, J.A. for the TONE Collaborative Research Group. (1998). Sodium reduction and weight loss in the treatment of hypertension in older persons: A randomized controlled trial of nonpharmacologic interventions in the elderly (TONE). *Journal of the American Medical Association, 279,* 839-846.

Whiffen, V. (1992). Is postpartum depression a distinct diagnosis? *Clinical Psychology Review, 12,* 485-508.

Whiffen, V.E., & Aube, J.A. (1999). Personality, interpersonal context and depression in couples. *Journal of Social and Personal Relationships, 16,* 369-383.

Whiffen, V.E., & Clark, S.E. (1997). Does victimization account for sex differences in depressive symptoms? *British Journal of Clinical Psychology, 36,* 185-193.

Whiffen, V., & Gotlib, I.H. (1991). Infants of postpartum depressed mothers: Temperament and cognitive status. *Journal of Abnormal Psychology, 98,* 274-279.

Whiffen, V., & Gotlib, I.H. (1993). Comparison of postpartum and nonpostpartum depression: Clinical presentation, psychiatric history, and psychosocial functioning. *Journal of Consulting and Clinical Psychology, 61,* 485-494.

Whiffen, V.E., & Johnson, S.M. (1998). An attachment theory framework for the treatment of childbearing depression. *Clinical Psychology: Science and Practice, 5,* 478-493.

Whisman, M.A. (1993). Mediators and moderators of change in cognitive therapy of depression. *Psychological Bulletin, 114,* 248-265.

Whisman, M.A., Sheldon, C.T., & Goering, P. (2000). Psychiatric disorders and dissatisfaction with social relationships: Does type of relationship matter? *Journal of Abnormal Psychology, 109,* 803-808.

White, J., Davison, G.C., Haaga, D.A.F., & White, K. (1992). Articulated thoughts and cognitive distortion in depressed and nondepressed psychiatric patients. *Journal of Nervous and Mental Disease, 180,* 77-81.

White, J., Dyck, R.J., Harrington, G., Auburn, F., & Meurin, S. (1993). *Suicide prevention in Alberta: Working toward results.* Edmonton, AB: Alberta Health.

White, K., & Cole, J.O. (1990). Pharmacotherapy. In A.S. Bellack & M. Hersen (Eds.), *Handbook of comparative treatments for adult disorders* (pp. 266-284). New York: Wiley.

White, P.F. (1986). Patient-controlled analgesia: A new approach to the management of postoperative pain. *Seminars in Anesthesia, 4,* 255-266.

Whitehead, W.E., Burgio, K.L., & Engel, B.T. (1985). Biofeedback treatment of fecal incontinence in geriatric patients. *Journal of the American Geriatrics Society, 33,* 320-324.

Whitehouse, P.J. (1997). Genesis of Alzheimer's disease. *Neurology, 48,* Supplement 7, s2-s6.

Whitford, R., & Parr, V. (1995). Use of rational emotive behavior therapy with juvenile sex offenders. *Journal of Rational-Emotive and Cognitive Behavior Therapy, 13,* 273-282.

Whitman, T.L. (1990). Self-regulation and mental retardation. *American Journal on Mental Retardation, 94,* 347-362.

Whittal, M.L., Agras, S.W., & Gould, R.A. (1999). Bulimia nervosa: A meta-analysis of psychosocial anf pharmacological treatments. *Behavior Therapy, 30,* 117-135.

Whittemore, A., Wu-Williams, A., Lee, M., Zheng, S., Gallagher, R., Jiao, D.A., Zhou, L., Wang, X., Chen, K., Jung, D., Teh, C.Z., Ling, C., Xu, J.Y., Paffenberger, R., & Henderson, B.E. (1990). Diet, physical activity and colorectal cancer among Chinese in North America and the People's Republic of China. *Journal of the National Cancer Institute, 82,* 915-926.

Whyte, S., Bayreuther, K., & Masters, C.L. (1994). Rational therapeutic strategies for Alzheimer's disease. In D.B. Calne (Ed.), *Neurodegenerative diseases*. Philadelphia: Saunders.

Wicks-Nelson, R., & Israel, A.C. (1997). *Behavior disorders of childhood* (3rd Ed.). Upper Saddle River, NJ: Prentice-Hall.

Wicks-Nelson, R., & Israel, A.C. (2000). *Behavior disorders of childhood* (4th Ed.). Upper Saddle River, NJ: Prentice-Hall.

Widiger, T.A., & Clark, L. A. (2000). Toward DSM-V and the classification of psychopathology. *Psychological Bulletin, 126,* 946-963.

Widiger, T.A., & Costa, P.T., Jr. (1994). Personality and personality disorders. *Journal of Abnormal Psychology, 95,* 43-51.

Widiger, T.A., Frances, A., Spitzer, R.L., & Williams, J.B.W. (1988). The DSM-III personality disorders: An overview. *American Journal of Psychiatry, 145,* 786-795.

Widiger, T.A., Frances, A., & Trull, T.J. (1987). A psychometric analysis of the social-interpersonal and cognitive-perceptual items for schizotypal personality disorder. *Archives of General Psychiatry, 44,* 741-745.

Widiger, T.A., Verheul, R., & van den Brink, W. (1999). Personality and psychopathology. In L. A. Pervin & O. P. John (Eds.), *Handbook of personality; Theory and research, 2nd edition* (pp. 347-366). NY: Guilford.

Wiebe, J., & Cox, B. J. (2001). A profile of Canadian adults seeking treatment for gambling problems and comparisons with adults entering an alcohol treatment program. *Canadian Journal of Psychiatry, 46,* 418-421.

Wiederhold, B.K., & Wiederhold, M.D. (1998). A review of virtual reality as a psychotherapeutic tool. *CyberPsychology and Behavior, 1,* 45-52.

Wielgosz, A.T., & Nolan, R.P. (2000). Biobehavioral factors in the context of ischemic cardiovascular diseases. *Journal of Psychosomatic Research, 48,* 339-345.

Wig, N.N., & Varma, V.K. (1977). Patterns of long-term heavy cannabis use in North India and its effects on cognitive functions. A preliminary report. *Drug and Alcohol Dependence, 2,* 211-219.

Wigdor, B., & Morris, G. (1977). A comparison of twenty-year medical histories of individuals with depressive and paranoid states. *Journal of Gerontology, 32,* 160-163.

Wikler, A. (1980). *Opioid dependence: Mechanisms and treatment.* NY: Plenum.

Wild, T.C., & Cunningham, J. (2001). Psychosocial determinants of perceived vulnerability to harm among adult drinkers. *Journal of Studies in Alcohol, 62,* 105-113.

Wildes, J.E., Harkness, K.L., & Simons, A.D. (2002). Life events, number of social relationships, and twelve-month naturalistic course of major depression in a community sample of women. *Depression and Anxiety, 16,* 104-113.

Wilfley, D., Stein, R., & Welch, R. (2003). Interpersonal psychotherapy. In J. Treasure, U. Schmidt, & van Furth, E, *Handbook of eating disorders* (2nd edition, pp. 253-270). Chichester, West Sussex: Wiley.

Wilgosh, L., Mulcahy, R., & Watters, B. (1986). Assessing intellectual performance of culturally different, Inuit children with the WISC-R. *Canadian Journal of Behavioural Science, 18,* 270-277.

Wilkie, C., Macdonald, S., & Hildahl, K. (1998). Community case study: Suicide cluster in a small Manitoba community. *Canadian Journal of Psychiatry, 43,* 823-828.

Willemsen-Swinkels, S.H.N., Buitelaar, J.K., & van Engeland, H. (1996). The effects of chronic naltrexone treatment in young autistic children: A double-blind placebo-controlled crossover study. *Biological Psychiatry, 39,* 1023-1031.

Willemsen-Swinkels, S.H.N., Buitelaar, J.K., Weijnen, F.G., & van Engeland, H. (1995). Placebo-controlled acute dosage naltrexone study in young autistic children. *Psychiatry Research, 58,* 203-215.

Willi, J., & Grossman, S. (1983). Epidemiology of anorexia nervosa in a defined region of Switzerland. *American Journal of Psychiatry, 140,* 564-567.

Williams, C.J. (1999, May 27). In Kosovo, rape seen as awful as death. *Los Angeles Times*, pp. A1, A18.

Williams, J.B.W., Gibbon, M., First, M.B., Spitzer, R.L., Davies, M., et al. (1992). The Structured Clinical Interview for DSM-III-R (SCID): 2. Multisite test-retest reliability. *Archives of General Psychiatry, 49,* 630-636.

Williams, J.M.G., Teasdale, J.D., Segal, Z.V., & Soulsby, J. (2000). Mindfulness-based cognitive therapy reduces overgeneral autobiographical memory in formerly depressed patients. *Journal of Abnormal Psychology, 109,* 150-155.

Williams, L.M. (1994). Recall of childhood trauma: A prospective study of women's memories of child sexual abuse. *Journal of Consulting and Clinical Psychology, 62,* 1167-1176.

Williams, M.E., Davison, G.C., Nezami, E., & DeQuattro, V. (1992). Cognitions of type A and type B individuals in response to social criticism. *Cognitive Therapy and Research, 16,* 19-30.

Williams, R.B. (1987). Psychological factors in coronary artery disease: Epidemiological evidence. *Circulation, 76,* 117-123.

Williams, R.J., McDermitt, D.R., Bertrand, L.D., & Davis, R.M. (2003). Parental awareness of adolescent substance abuse. *Addictive Behaviors, 28,* 803-809.

Williamson, D.A., Goreczny, A.J., Davis, C.J., Ruggiero, L., & MacKenzie, S.L. (1988). Psychophysiological analysis of the anxiety model of bulimia nervosa. *Behavior Therapy, 19,* 1-9.

Wills, T.A., & Cleary, S.D. (1999). Peer and adolescent substance use among 6th-9th graders: Latent growth analysis of influence versus selection mechanisms. *Health Psychology, 18,* 453-463.

Wills, T.A., DuHamel, K., & Vaccaro, D. (1995). Activity and mood temperament as predictors of adolescent substance use: Test of a self-regulation model. *Journal of Personality and Social Psychology, 68,* 901-916.

Wilsnak, S.C. (1984). *Drinking, sexuality, and sexual dysfunction in women.* In S.C.

Wilsnak & L.J. Beckman (Eds.), *Alcohol problems in women: Antecedents, consequences, and intervention* (pp. 189-227). New York: Guilford.

Wilson, G.T. (in press). *Manual-based treatment and clinical practice.* Clinical Psychology: Science and Practice.

Wilson, G.T. (1991). Chemical aversion conditioning in the treatment of alcoholism: Further comments. *Behaviour Research and Therapy, 29,* 405-420.

Wilson, G.T. (1995). Empirically validated treatments as a basis for clinical practice: Problems and prospects. In S.C. Hayes, V.M. Follette, R.M. Dawes, & K.E. Grady (Eds.), *Scientific standards of psychological practice: Issues and recommendations.* Reno, NV: Context Press.

Wilson, G.T. (1996). Manual-based treatments: The clinical application of research findings. *Behaviour Research and Therapy, 34,* 295-314.

Wilson, G.T., & Davison, G.C. (1971). Processes of fear reduction in systematic desensitization. Animal studies. *Psychological Bulletin, 76,* 1-14.

Wilson, G.T., Eldredge, K.L., Smith, D., & Niles, B. (1991). Cognitive-behavioural treatment with and without response prevention for bulimia. *Behaviour Research and Therapy, 29,* 575-583.

Wilson, G.T., & Lawson, D.M. (1976). The effects of alcohol on sexual arousal in women. *Journal of Abnormal Psychology, 85,* 489-497.

Wilson, G.T., Vitousek, K., & Loeb, K.L. (2000). Stepped care treatment for eating disorders. *Journal of Consulting and Clinical Psychology, 68,* 564-572.

Wilson, K.G., Sandler, L.S., & Asmundson, G.J.G. (1993). Fearful and nonfearful panic attacks in a student population. *Behaviour Research and Therapy, 31,* 407-411.

Wilson, K.G., Sandler, L.S., Asmundson, G.J.G., Ediger, J.M., Larsen, D.K., & Walker, J.R. (1992). Panic attacks in the nonclinical population: An empirical approach to case identification. *Journal of Abnormal Psychology, 101,* 460-468.

Wilson, K.G., Sandler, L.S., Asmundson, G.J.G., Larsen, D.K., & Ediger, J.M. (1991). Effects of instructional set on self-reports of panic attacks. *Journal of Anxiety Disorders, 5,* 43-63.

Wilson, T.D., Goldin, J.C., & Charbonneau-Powis, M. (1983). Comparative efficacy of behavioral and cognitive treatments of depression. *Cognitive Therapy and Research, 7,* 111-124.

Winchester, E., & Collier, D. (2003). Genetic aetiology of eating disorders and obesity. In J. Treasure, U. Schmidt, & van Furth, E, *Handbook of eating disorders* (2nd edition, pp. 35-62). Chichester, West Sussex: Wiley.

Wincze, J.P., & Carey, M.P. (1991). *Sexual dysfunction: A guide for assessment and treatment.* New York: Guilford.

Winett, R.A., & Winkler, R.C. (1972). Current behavior modification in the classroom: Be still, be quiet, be docile. *Journal of Applied Behavior Analysis, 5,* 499-504.

Wing, L. (1976). Diagnosis, clinical description, and prognosis. In L. Wing (Ed.), *Early childhood autism: Clinical, educational, and social aspects.* New York: Pergamon.

Wing, L., & Attwood, A. (1987). Syndromes of autism and atypical development. In D.J. Cohen, A.M. Donnellan, & R. Paul (Eds.), *Handbook of autism and pervasive developmental disorders* (pp. 3-19). New York: Wiley.

Winick, B.J. (1993). Psychotropic medication in the criminal trial process: The constitutional and therapeutic implications of Riggins v. Nevada. *New York Law School Journal of Human Rights, 10,* 637-709.

Winick, B.J. (1994). The right to refuse mental health treatment: A therapeutic jurisprudence analysis. *International Journal of Law and Psychiatry, 17,* 99-117.

Winick, B.J. (1996a). Advance directive instruments for those with mental illnesses. *University of Miami Law Review, 51,* 57-78.

Winick, B.J. (1996b). The MacArthur Treatment Competence Study: Legal and therapeutic implications. *Psychology, Public Policy, and Law, 2,* 137-166.

Winick, B.J. (1997) *The right to refuse mental health treatment.* Washington, DC: American Psychological Association.

Winick, C. (1962). Maturing out of narcotic addiction. *Bulletin on Narcotics, 14,* 1-7.

Winkleby, M.A., Kraemer, H.C., Ahn, D.K., & Varady, A.N. (1998). Ethnic and socioeconomic differences in cardiovascular disease risk factors. *JAMA, 280,* 356-362.

Winkleby, M.A., Robinson, T.N., Sundquist, J., & Kraemer, H.C. (1999). Ethnic variation in cardiovascular disease risk factors among children and young adults. *JAMA, 281,* 1006-1013.

Winko v. British Columbia (1999). 2 S. C. R., 625, File No. 25856.

Winters, K.C., & Neale, J.M. (1985). Mania and low self-esteem. *Journal of Abnormal Psychology, 94,* 282-290.

Wintre, M.G., Sugar, L.A., Yaffe, M., & Costin, D. (2000). Generational status: A Canadian response to the Editors' Consortium statement with regard to race/ethnicity. *Canadian Psychology, 41,* 230-243.

Wischik, C. (1994). Molecular neuropathology of Alzheimer's disease. In C.L.A. Katona (Ed.), *Dementia disorders: Advances and prospects.* London: Chapman and Hall.

Wise, T. (1978). Where the public peril begins: A survey of psychotherapists to determine the effects of Tarasoff. *Stanford Law Review, 31,* 165-190.

Wiseman, C.V., Gray, J.J., Mosimann, J.E., & Arhens, A.H. (1992). Cultural expectations of thinness in women: An update. *International Journal of Eating Disorders, 11,* 85-89.

Wittchen, H.-U. (1994). Reliability and validity studies of the WHO-composite international diagnostic interview (CIDI): A critical review. *Journal of Psychiatric Research, 28,* 57-84.

Wittchen, H.-U., Stein, M.B., & Kessler, R.C. (1999). Social fears and social phobia in a community sample of adolescents and young adults: Prevalence, risk factors, and co-morbidity. *Psychological Medicine, 29,* 309-323.

Wittchen, H.U., Zhao, S., Kessler, R.C., & Eaton, W.W. (1994). DSM-III-R generalized anxiety disorder in the national comorbidity survey. *Archives of General Psychiatry, 51,* 355-364.

Whittington, (2001).

Wold, D.A. (1968). *The adjustment of siblings to childhood leukemia.* Unpublished medical thesis, University of Washington, Seattle.

Wolf, A. (1949). The psychoanalysis of group. *American Journal of Psychotherapy, 3,* 16-50.

Wolf, A., & Kutash, I.L. (1990). Psychoanalysis in groups. In I.L. Kutash & A. Wolf (Eds.), *The group psychotherapist's handbook: Contemporary theory and technique.* New York: Columbia University Press.

Wolf, M., Bally, H., & Morris, R. (1986). Automaticity, retrieval processes, and reading: A longitudinal study in average and impaired readers. *Child Development, 57,* 988-1000.

Wolfe, D.A., Reppucci, N.D., & Hart, S. (1995). Child abuse prevention: Knowledge and priorities. *Journal of Clinical Child Psychology, 24,* 5-22.

Wolfe, J.L. (1995). Rational emotive behavior therapy women's groups: A twenty year retrospective. *Journal of Rational-Emotive and Cognitive Behavior Therapy, 13,* 153-170.

Wolfe, R., Morrow, J., & Frederickson, B.L. (1996). Mood disorders in older adults. In L.L. Carstensen, B.A. Edelstein, & L. Dornbrand (Eds.), *The practical handbook of clinical gerontology* (pp. 274-303). Thousand Oaks, CA: Sage.

Wolfe, V.V. (1990). Sexual abuse of children. In A.S. Bellack, M. Hersen, & A.E. Kazdin (Eds.), *International handbook of behavior modification and therapy* (2nd ed., pp. 707-729). New York: Plenum.

Wolfe, V.V. (1999). Child sexual abuse. In E. Mash & R. Barkley (Eds.), *Treatment for childhood disorders* (pp. 545-597). New York: Guilford.

Wolfe, V.V., & Gentile, C. (1992). Psychological assessment of sexually abused children. In W. O'Donohue & J. H. Geer (Eds.), *The sexual abuse of children: Clinical issues* (pp. 143-187). Mahwah, NJ: Erlbaum

Wolff, P. H., & Melngailis, I. (1996). Reversing letters and reading transformed text in dyslexia: A reassessment. *Reading and Writing, 8,* 341-355.

Wolf-Maier, K., et al. (2003). Hypertension prevalence and blood pressure levels in 6 European countries, Canada, and the United States. *Journal of the American Medical Association, 289,* 2363-2369.

Wolfson, C., Wolfson, D.B., Asgharian, M., M'Lan, C.E., Ostbye, T., Rockwood, K., et al. (2001). A reevaluation of the duration of survival after the onset of dementia. *The New England Journal of Medicine, 344,* 1160-1161.

Wolin, S.J. (1980). *Introduction: Psychosocial consequences. In Alcoholism and alcohol abuse among women: Research issues.* Rockville, MD: National Institute on Alcohol Abuse and Alcoholism.

Wolitzky, D. (1995). Traditional psychoanalytic psychotherapy. In A.S. Gurman & S.B. Messer (Eds.), *Essential psychotherapies: Theory and practice.* New York: Guilford.

Wolitzky, D.L., & Eagle, M.N. (1990). Psychotherapy. In A.S. Bellack & M. Hersen (Eds.), *Handbook of comparative treatments for adult disorders* (pp. 123-143). New York: Wiley.

Wolpe, J. (1958). *Psychotherapy by reciprocal inhibition.* Stanford, CA: Stanford University Press.

Wolraich, M., Milich, R., Stumbo, P., & Schultz, F. (1985). The effects of sucrose ingestion on the behavior of hyperactive boys. *Pediatrics, 106,* 675-682.

Wolraich, M.L., Wilson, D.B., & White, J.W. (1995). The effect of sugar on behavior or cognition in children: A meta-analysis. *Journal of the American Medical Association, 274,* 1617-1621.

Wong, A.H.C., Smith, M., & Boon, H.S. (1998). Herbal remedies in psychiatric practice. *Archives of General Psychiatry, 55,* 1033-1044.

Wong, N. (1995). Group psychotherapy, combined individual and group psychotherapy, and psychodrama. In H.I. Kaplan & B.J. Sadock (Eds.), *Comprehensive textbook of psychiatry* (pp. 1821-1838). Baltimore: Williams & Wilkins.

Wong, P.T.P. (1993). Effective management of life stress: The resource-congruence model. *Stress Medicine, 9,* 51-60.

Wood, J.M., Nezworski, M.T., & Stejskal, W.J. (1996). The Comprehensive System for the Rorschach: A critical examination. *Psychological Science, 7,* 3-10.

Wood, J.M., Nezworski, M.T., & Stejskal, W.J. (1997). The reliability of the Comprehensive System for the Rorschach: A comment on Meyer (1997). *Psychological Assessment, 9,* 490-494.

Wood, L.F., & Jacobson, N.S. (1985). Marital distress. In D.H. Barlow (Ed.), *Clinical handbook of psychological disorders.* New York: Guilford.

Woodill, G. (1992). Controlling the sexuality of developmentally disabled persons: Historical perspectives. *Journal of Developmental Disabilities, 1,* 1-14

Woodman, C.L., Noyes, R., Black, D.W., Schlosser, S., & Yagla, S.J. (1999). A 5-year follow-up study of generalized anxiety disorder and panic disorder. *Journal of Nervous and Mental Disease, 187,* 3-9.

Woodmansee, M.A. (1996). The guilty but mentally ill verdict: Political expediency at the expense of moral principle. *Notre Dame Journal of Law, Ethics and Public Policy, 10,* 341-387.

Woodside, D.B., Lackstrom, J., Shekter-Wolfson, L., & Heinmaa, M. (1996). Long-term follow-up of patient-reported family functioning in eating disorders after intensive hospital day treatment. *Journal of Psychosomatic Research, 41,* 269-277.

Woodside, D.B., Shekter-Wolfson, L.F., Garfinkel, P.E., & Olmsted, M.P. (1995). Family interactions in bulimia nervosa: Study design, comparisons to established population norms and changes over the course of an intensive day hospital treatment program. *International Journal of Eating Disorders, 17,* 105-115.

Woodword, C.A., Abelson, J., Tedford, S., & Hutchison, B. (2004). What is important to continuity in home care? Perspectives of key stakeholders. *Social Science and Medicine, 58,* 177-192.

Woodworth, M., & Porter, S. (2002). In cold blood: Characteristics of criminal homicides as a function of psychopathology. *Journal of Abnormal Psy-*

chology, 111, 436-445.

Woody, G.E., Luborsky, L., McLellan, A.T., & O'Brien, C.P. (1990). Corrections and revised analyses for psychotherapy in methadone maintenance programs. *Archives of General Psychiatry, 47,* 788-789.

Woody, G.M., McLellan, T., Luborsky, L., & O'Brien, C.P. (1995). Psychotherapy in community methadone programs: A validation study. *American Journal of Psychiatry, 152,* 1302-1308.

Woody, S., Detweiler-Bedell, J., Teachman, B.A., & O'Hearn, T. (2003). *Treatment planning in psychotherapy: Taking the guesswork out of clinical care.* London: Guilford.

Woody, S., & Rodriguez, B.F. (2000). Self-focused attention and social anxiety in social phobics and normal controls. *Cognitive Therapy and Research, 24*, 473-488.

Woogh, C. (2001). Is schizophrenia on the decline in Canada? *Canadian Journal of Psychiatry, 46*, 61-66.

World Health Organization. (1948). *Manual of the international statistical classification of diseases, injuries, and causes of death.* Geneva: Author.

World Health Organization (1990).

World Health Organization. (1993). *1992 world health statistics annual.* Geneva: Author.

World Health Organization (2000). *Multisite intervention study on suicidal behaviours—SUPRE-MISS: Components and instruments.* Geneva, Switzerland: World Health Organization, Department of Mental Health and Substance Dependence.

World Health Organization. (2002). *Reducing stigma and discrimination against older people with mental disorders: A technical consensus statement.* Geneva, Switzerland: World Health Organization.

World Health Organization International Consortium in Psychiatric Epidemiology. (2000). Cross-national comparisons of the prevalence and correlates of mental disorders. *Bulletin of the World Health Organization, 78 (4),* 413-426.

Worling, J.R. (1995). Sexual abuse histories of adolescent male sex offenders: Differences on the basis of the age and gender of their victims. *Journal of Abnormal Psychology, 104,* 610-613.

Worling, J.R. (2001). Personality-based typology of adolescent male sexual offenders: Differences in recidivism rates, victim-selection characteristics, and personal victimization histories. *Sexual Abuse: A Journal of Research and Treatment, 13*, 149-166.

Wortman, C.B., & Brehm, J.W. (1975). Responses to uncontrollable outcomes: An integration of the reactance theory and the learned helplessness model. In L. Berkowitz (Ed.), *Advances in social psychology*. New York: Academic Press.

Wouda, J.C., Hartman, P.M., Bakker, R.M., Bakker, J.O., et al. (1998). Vaginal plethysmography in women with dyspareunia. *Journal of Sex Research, 35,* 141-147.

Wright, M.J. (1991). Identifying child sexual abuse using the Personality Inventory for Children. *Dissertation Abstracts International, 52,* 1744.

Wulsin, L., Bachop, M., & Hoffman, D. (1988). Group therapy in manic-depressive illness. *American Journal of Psychotherapy, 2,* 263-271.

Wurtele, S.K., & Miller-Perrin, C.L. (1987). An evaluation of side-effects associated with participation in a child sexual abuse prevention program. *Journal of School Health, 57,* 228-231.

Wylie, K.R. (1997). Treatment outcome of brief couple therapy in psychogenic male erectile disorder. Archives of Sexual Behavior, 26, 527-545.

Wynne, L.C., & Singer, M.T. (1963). Thought disorder and family relations in schizophrenia. 2: A classification of forms of thinking. *Archives of General Psychiatry, 9,* 199-206.

Yalom, I.D. (1985). *The theory and practice of group psychotherapy* (3rd ed.). New York: Basic Books.

Yalom, I.D., Green, R., & Fisk, N. (1973). Prenatal exposure to female hormones: Effect on psychosexual development in boys. *Archives of General Psychiatry, 28,* 554-561.

Yates, A. (1989). Current perspectives on the eating disorders. *Journal of the American Academy of Child and Adolescent Psychiatry, 28,* 813-828.

***Yelaja** (2000, December 13). Mentally ill struggle to get home care: Study: Lack of services force some into homelessness, others to jail, hospital. *The Toronto Star,*

Yesavage, J.A., Brink, T.L., Rose, T.L., Lum, O., Huang, V., Adey, M., & Leirer, V.O. (1983). Development and validation of a geriatric screening scale: A preliminary report. *Journal of Psychiatric Research, 17*, 37-49.

Yetman, N.R. (1994). Race and ethnic inequality. In C. Calhoun & G. Ritzer (Eds.), *Social problems*. New York: McGraw-Hill.

Yirmiya, N., & Sigman, M. (1991). High functioning individuals with autism: Diagnosis, empirical findings, and theoretical issues. *Clinical Psychology Review, 11,* 669-683.

Yoshioka, R.B., Tashima, N., Chew, M., & Murase, K. (1981). *Mental health services for Pacific/Asian Americans*. San Francisco: Pacific American Mental Health Project.

Young, D.A., Zakzanis, K.K., Bailey, C., Davila, R., Griese, J., Sartory, G., & Thom, A. (1998). Further parameters of insight and neuropsychological deficit in schizophrenia and other chronic mental disease. *Journal of Nervous and Mental Disease, 186,* 44-50.

Young, D.A., Zakzanis, K.K., Campbell, Z., Freyslinger, M.G., & Meichenbaum, D.H. (2002). Scaffolded instruction remediates Wisconsin Card Sorting Test deficits in schizophrenia: A comparison to other techniques. *Neuropsychological Rehabilitation, 12*, 257-287.

Young, G.C. (1965). The aetiology of enuresis in terms of learning theory. *Medical Officer, 113,* 19-22.

Young, S. (1998). Risk in research: From the Nuremberg Code to the Tri-Council Code: Implications for clinical trials of psychotropic drugs. *Journal of Psychiatry and Neuroscience, 23*, 149-155.

Yurgelon-Todd, D., Waternaux, C.M., Cohen, B.N., Gruber, S.A., English, C.D., & Renshaw, P.F. (1996). Functional magnetic resonance imagery of schizophrenia patients and comparison subjects during word production. *American Journal of Psychiatry, 153,* 200-206.

Zack, M., Toneatto, T., & MacLeod, C.M. (1999). Implicit activation of alcohol concepts by negative affective cues distinguishes between problem drinkers with high and low psychiatric distress. *Journal of Abnormal Psychology, 108*, 518-531.

Zakowski, S., Hall, M.H., & Baum, A. (1992). Stress, stress management, and the immune system. *Applied and Preventive Psychology, 1,* 1-13.

Zakzanis, K.K., Graham, S.J., & Campbell, Z. (2003). A meta-analysis of structural and functional brain imaging in dementia of Alzheimer's type: A neuroimaging profile. *Neuropsychology Review, 13*, 1-19.

Zakzanis, K.K., & Heinrichs, R.W. (1999). Schizophrenia and the frontal brain: A quantitative review. *Journal of the International Neuropsychological Society, 5*, 556-566.

Zakzanis, K.K., Leach, L., & Kaplan, E. (1999). *Neuropsychological differential diagnosis.* Swets and Zeitlinger, Publishers.

Zakzanis, K.K., Leach, L., & Kaplan, E. (1999). Temporal, clinical, and demographic correlates of neuropsychological function in patients with Alzheimer's disease. *Archives of Clinical Neuropsychology, 14*, 617-618.

Zakzanis, K.K., Poulin, P., Hansen, K.T., & Jolic, D. (2000). Searching the schizophrenic brain for temporal lobe deficits: A systematic review and meta-analysis. *Psychological Medicine, 30*, 491-504.

Zakzanis, K.K., Troyer, A.K., Rich, J.B., & Heinrichs, W. (2000). Component analysis of verbal fluency in patients with schizophrenia. *Neuropsychiatry, Neuropsychology, and Behavioral Neurology, 13*, 239-245.

Zanarini, M.C., Frankenberg, F.R., Dubo, E.D., Sickel, A.E., Trikha, A., et al. (1998). Axis I comorbidity of borderline personality disorder. *American Journal of Psychiatry, 155,* 1733-1739.

Zanarini, M.C., Frankenberg, F.R., Dubo, E.D., Sickel, A.E., Tricka, A., & et al. (1998). Axis II comorbidity of borderline personality disorder. *Comprehensive Psychiatry, 39,* 296-302.

Zanarani, M. C., Skodol, A. E., Bender, D. et al. (2000). The Collaborative Longitudinal Personality Disorders Study: Reliability of axes I and II diagnoses. *Journal of Personality Disorders, 14,* 291-299.

Zanarini, M.C., Williams, A.A., Lewis, R.E., Reich, R.B., Vera, S.C., et al. (1997). Reported pathological childhood experiences associated with the development of borderline personality disorder. *American Journal of Psychiaty, 154,* 1101-1106.

Zane, M.D. (1984). Psychoanalysis and contextual analysis of phobias. *Journal of the American Academy of Psychoanalysis, 12,* 553-568.

Zapf, P.A., & Roesch, R. (1997). Assessing fitness to stand trial: A comparison of institution-based evaluations and a brief screening interview. *Canadian Journal of Community Mental Health, 16*, 53-66.

Zapf, P.A., Roesch, R., & Hart, S. D. (1996). An examination of the relationship of homelessness to mental disorder, criminal behaviour, and health care in a pretrial jail population. *Canadian Journal of Psychiatry*, *41*, 435-440.

Zarit, S.H. (1980). *Aging and mental disorders: Psychological approaches to assessment and treatment.* New York: Free Press.

Zarit, S. H., Dolan, M. M., & Leitsch, S. A. (1998). Interventions in nursing homes and other alternative living settings. In I.H. Nordhus, G.R. VandenBos, S. Berg, & P. Fromholt, (Eds.), *Clinical geropsychology* (pp. 329-343). Washington, D.C.: American Psychological Association.

Zarit, S.H., Eiler, J., & Hassinger, M. (1985). Clinical assessment. In J.E. Birren & K.W. Schaie (Eds.), *Handbook of psychology of aging* (2nd ed.). New York: Van Nostrand-Reinhold.

Zarit, S. H., & Zarit, J. M. (1998). *Mental disorders in older adults: Fundamentals of assessment and treatment.* New York: Guilford Press.

Zatzick, D.F., Marmer, C.R., Weiss, D.S., Browner, W.S., Metzler, T.J., et al. (1997). Posttraumatic stress disorder and functioning and quality of life in a nationally representative sample of male Vietnam veterans. *American Journal of Psychiatry, 154,* 1690-1695.

Zaza, C., Stolee, P., & Prkachin, K. (1999). The application of goal attainment scaling in chronic pain settings. *Journal of Pain and Symptom Management*, *17*, 55-64.

Zeaman, D., & Hanley, P. (1983). Stimulus preferences as structural features. In T.J. Tighe & B.E. Shepp (Eds.), *Perception, cognition, and development.* Hillsdale, NJ: Erlbaum.

Zeiss, A.M., & Steffen, A.M. (1996). Interdisciplinary health care teams: The basic unit of geriatric care. In L.L. Carstensen, B.A. Edelstein, & L. Dornbrand (Eds.), *The practical handbook of clinical gerontology* (pp. 423-450). Thousand Oaks, CA: Sage.

Zelkowitz, P., & Milet, T.H. (1995). Screening for postpartum depression in a community sample. *Canadian Journal of Psychiatry*, *40*, 80-86.

Zelkowitz, P., & Milet, T.H. (1996). Postpartum psychiatric disorders: Their relationship to psychological adjustment and marital satisfaction in the spouses. *Journal of Abnormal Psychology*, *105*, 281-285.

Zelkowitz, P., & Milet, T.H. (1997). Stress and support as related to postpartum paternal mental health and perceptions of the infant. *Infant Mental Health Journal*, *18*, 424-435.

Zelkowitz, P., & Milet, T.H. (2001). The course of postpartum psychiatric disorders in women and their partners. *Journal of Nervous and Mental Disease*, *189*, 575-582.

Zellner, D.A., Harner, D.E., & Adler, R.L. (1989). Effects of eating abnormalities and gender on perceptions of desirable body shape. *Journal of Abnormal Psychology, 98,* 93-96.

Ziegler, F.J., Imboden, J.B., & Meyer, E. (1960). Contemporary conversion reactions: A clinical study. *American Journal of Psychiatry, 116,* 901-910.

Zigler, E. (1967). Familial mental retardation: A continuing dilemma. *Science, 155,* 292-298.

Zigler, E., Hodapp, R.M., & Edison, M.R. (1990). From theory to practice in the care and education of mentally retarded individuals. *American Journal on Mental Retardation, 95,* 1-12.

Zilboorg, G., & Henry, G.W. (1941). *A history of medical psychology.* New York: Norton.

Zimbardo, P.G., Andersen, S.M., & Kabat, L.G. (1981). Paranoia and deafness: An experimental investigation. *Science, 212,* 1529-1531.

Zimbardo, P.G., LaBerge, S., & Butler, L.D. (1993). Psychophysiological consequences of unexplained arousal: A post-hypnotic suggestion paradigm. *Journal of Abnormal Psychology, 102,* 466-473.

Zimmer, L., & Morgan, J.P. (1995). *Exposing marijuana myths: A review of the scientific evidence.* New York: The Lindemith Center.

Zimmerman, M. (1994). Diagnosing personality disorders: A review of issues and research methods. *Archives of General Psychiatry, 51,* 225-245.

Zimmerman, M., & Coryell, W. (1989). DSM-III personality disorder diagnoses in a nonpatient sample. *Archives of General Psychiatry, 46,* 682-689.

Zimmerman, M., Coryell, W., Pfohl, B., & Staid, D. (1986). The validity of four types of endogenous depression. *Archives of General Psychiatry, 43,* 234-245.

Zinatelli, M., & Vogel-Sprott, M. (1993). Behavioral tolerance to alcohol in humans is enhanced by prior drug-free treatment. *Experimental and Clinical Psychpharmacology*, *1*, 194-199.

Zipursky, R.B., Seeman, M.V., Bury, A., Langevin, R., Wortzman, G., & Katz, R. (1997). Deficits in gray matter volume are present in schizophrenia but not bipolar disorder. *Schizophrenia Research*, *26*, 85-92.

Zivian, M.T., Gekoski, W., Knox, V.J., Larsen, W., & Hatchette, V. (1994). Psychotherapy for the elderly: Public opinion. *Psychotherapy*, *31*, 492-502.

Zoccolillo, M., Pickles, A., Quinton, D., & Rutter, M. (1992). The outcome of childhood conduct disorder: Implications for defining antisocial personality disorder and conduct disorder. *Psychological Medicine, 22,* 971-986.

Zoccolillo, M., & Rogers, K. (1991). Characteristics and outcome of hospitalized adolescent girls with conduct disorder. *Journal of the American Academy of Child and Adolescent Psychiatry, 30,* 973-981.

Zoccolillo, M., Vitaro, F., & Tremblay, R.E. (1999). Problem drug use and alcohol use in a community sample of adolescents. *Journal of the American Academy of Child and Adolescent Psychiatry*, *38*, 900-907.

Zucker, K.J. (2000). Gender identity disorder. In A.J. Sameroff, M. Lewis, & M. Miller (Eds.), *Handbook of developmental psychopathology* (2nd ed., pp. 671-686). New York: Kluwer Academic/Plenum.

Zucker, K.J., & Blanchard, R. (1997). Transvestic fetishism: Psychopathology and theory. In D.R. Laws & W. O'Donohue (Eds.), *Sexual deviance.* (pp. 280-296). NY: Guilford Press.

Zucker, K.J., Bradley, S.J., Kuksis, M., Pecore, K., Birkenfeld-Adams, A., Doering, R.W., Mitchell, J.N., & Wild, J. (1999). Gender constancy judgments in children with gender identity disorder: Evidence for a developmental lag. *Archives of Sexual Behavior*, *28*, 475-502.

Zucker, K.J., Bradley, S.J., & Sanikhana, M. (1997). Sex difference in referral rates of children with gender identity disorder: Some hypotheses. *Journal of Abnormal Child Psychology, 25,* 217-227.

Zucker, K.J., Finegan, J.K., Deering, R.W., & Bradley, S.J. (1984). Two subgroups of gender-problem children. *Archives of Sexual Behavior, 13,* 27-39.

Zucker, K.J., Green, R., Garofano, C., Bradley, S.J., et al. (1994). Prenatal gender preference of mothers of feminine and masculine boys: Relation to sibling sex composition and birth order. *Journal of Abnormal Child Psychology, 22,* 1-13.

Zucker, K.J., Wild, J., Bradley, S.J., & Stern, A. (1993). Physical attractiveness of boys with gender identiy disorder. *Archives of Sexual Behavior, 22,* 23-36.

Zuckerman, M. (1994). *Behavioral expressions and biosocial bases of sensation seeking.* New York: Cambridge University Press.

Zunzunegui, M.V., Llacer-Centro, A., & Beland, F. (2002). The role of social and psychological resources in the evolution of depression in caregivers. *Canadian Journal on Aging*, *21*, 357-369.

Zuroff, D.C., Blatt, S.J., Sotsky, S.M., Krupnick, J.L., Martin, D.J., Sanislow, C.A., & Simmens, S. (2000). Relation of therapeutic alliance and perfectionism to outcome in brief outpatient treatment of depression. *Journal of Consulting and Clinical Psychology*, *68*, 114-124.

Zuroff, D.C., & Mongrain, M. (1987). Dependency and self-criticism: Vulnerability factors for depressiveaffective states. *Journal of Abnormal Psychology*, *96*, 14-22.

Zvolensky, M.J., Arrindell, W.A., Taylor, S., Bouvard, M., Cox, B.J., Stewart, S.H., Sandin, B., Cardenas, S.J., & Eifert, G.H. (2003). Anxiety sensitivity in six countries. *Behaviour Research and Therapy*, *41*, 841-859.

Zweig-Frank, H., & Paris, J. (2002). Predictors of outcome in a 27-year follow-up of patients with borderline personality disorder. *Comprehensive Psychiatry*, *43*, 103-107.

Photo Credits

Chapter 1 1: Photo by Carlo Catenazzi/AGO. 4: CP Image Archive/Mike Ridewood. 5: (left) Bill Aron/Photo Researchers. 7: The Auger Photo Archive. 8: (left) Topham/The Image Works; (right) Granger Collection. 9: Culver Pictures Inc. 10: (left) CORBIS; (right) Historical Picture Services. 11: CORBIS. 14: Metro Toronto Library Board. 16: (top) Jean Loup Charmet/Photo Researchers; (bottom) CORBIS. 23: Archives of the Centre for Addiction and Mental Health. 29: CP Image Archive/Fred Chartrand.

Chapter 2 32: Photo by Carlo Catenazzi/AGO. 34: Courtesy of Kerry Jang. 41: National Library of Medicine/Science Photo Library/Photo Researchers. 42: Ken Cavanagh/Photo Researchers. 45: UPI/CORBIS. 47: Michael Rougier/Life Magazine/ © Time Inc. 49: Courtesy Gestalt Institute of Cleveland. 52: Culver Pictures Inc. 53. (left) Rick Friedman/Black Star; (right) Ken Cavanagh/Photo Researchers. 54: Courtesy Frank Pajares/Albert Bandura. 56: (right) Courtesy Public Relations Department, Temple University-Health Sciences Centre; (left) The Palma Collection/PhotoDisc/Getty Images. 59: Dan Miller/New York Times Pictures. 61: Courtesy Donald Meichenbaum. 63. CALM 65: (left) TV Ontario; (right) Kirk Blankstein. 71: National Archives of Canada/Department of Interior 69: Jonathan Hayward/CP Picture Archive.

Chapter 3 78: Photo by Carlos Catenazzi/AGO. 82: SUPERSTOCK. 84: Donovan Rose. 88: Will & Deni McIntyre/Science Source/Photo Researchers. 91: Ken Cavanagh/ Photo Researchers. 97: Richard Nowitz/Photo Researchers.

Chapter 4 100: Photo by Bill Wilson/AGO. 101: Philippe Landreville. ©Supreme Court of Canada 108: Courtesy Dr. Henri R. Ellenberger. 109: Courtesy Archives of the History of American Psychology/The University of Akron. 112: Jeff Isaac Greenberg/Photo Researchers. 113: CP Image Archive/Kevin Frayer. 114: Renata Hiller/Monkmeyer Press Photo. 120: (left) Dan McCoy/Rainbow; (right) Courtesy D. Yurgelun-Todd, McLean Hospital. 121: (top) Dan McCoy/Rainbow; (bottom) Richard Nowitz/Photo Researchers. 123: Doug Plummer/Photo Researchers. 126: Jacques Jangoux/Photo Researchers. 128: Health Canada.

Chapter 5 133: Photo by Sean Weaver/AGO. 137: Geral Martineau/The Washington Post. 148: Richard Lucas/The Image Works. 149: Martin Rogers/Woodfin Camp & Associates.

Chapter 6 156: Photo by Carlos Catenazzi/AGO. 158: (left) Harvey Stein; (right) CP Image Archive/Adrian Wyld. 159: (left) Bill Gallery/Stock Boston/Picture Network International; (right) Richard Nowitz/Photo Researchers. 160: Courtesy Professor Benjamin Harris, University of Wisconsin, Parkside. 161: Brett Froomer/The Image Bank/Picture Network International. 164: (left) Sheila Terry/Science Photo Library/Photo Researchers; (right) Mimi Forsyth/Monkmeyer Press Photo. 166: (top left) Aaron Harris/CP Picture Archive; (bottom left) B. & C. Alexander/Photo Researchers; (right) Rich Iwasaki/Picture Network International. 176: (left) Courtesy New York Public Library, Astor, Lenox & Tilden Foundations; (right) Sun Media Corporation. 181: Courtesy Dr. Martin Antony. 184: Paul Chiasson/CP Picture Archive. 185: Jonathan Hayward/Toronto Star. 189: Andrew Vaughan/CP Picture Archive.

Chapter 7 194: Courtesy of Sperone Westwater, N.Y. 196: Cp Image Archive/Extrapress. 199: Courtesy Sun-Sentinel. 207: (left) Springer/CORBIS; (right) CP Image Archive/Andrew Vaughan. 210: Courtesy Jerry Ohlinger's. 211: Comstock Inc. 212: Courtesy Nicholas P. Spanos. 213: AP/Wide World Photos.

Chapter 8 220: Photo by Carlos Catenazzi/AGO. 223: © Canada Post Corporation, 1999, Reproduced with Permission. 224: (left) Bruce Ayres/Tony Stone Images; (right) Borrfdon/Explorer/Photo Researchers. 236: Cindy Karp/Black Star. 227: Herve Donezan/Photo Researchers. 228: Courtesy Norman Endler/York University. 229: Michael J. Gadomski/Science Source/Photo Researchers. 232: Benelux/Photo Researchers. 235: Thomas S. England/Photo Researchers. 239: Bruce Ayres/Tony Stone Images. 241: Claudia Kunin/Tony Stone Images. 249: Bernie/Harry Mayerovitch. 253: Courtesy of Victoria Pain Clinic.

Chapter 9 255: Courtesy of the AGO. 256: AP/Wide World Photos. 259: (left) Susan Rosenberg/Photo Researchers; (right) Sun Media Corporation. 262: (left) CORBIS; (centre) Eve Arnold/Magnum Photos, Inc.; (right) Maria C. Valentino/Sygma. 264: Cp Image Archive/Alexander Zemlianichenko. 265: Femmes de Tahiti (Sur la Plage), by Paul Gaugain/Musee d'Orsay, Paris/Lauris-Giraudon, Paris/SUPERSTOCK. 268: Penny Tweedie/Tony Stone Images. 271: (top) Jill Greenberg © 1996 The Walt Disney Company, reprinted with permission of Discover magazine. 273: Dr. Peter Berndt/Custom Medical Stock Photo. 278: Mark O'Neill/Sun Media Corporation.

Chapter 10 281: Photo by Carlos Catenazzi/AGO. 284: CP Picture Archive. 285: CP Image Archive/Kevin Frayer. 286: (left) Self Portrait in Caricature, by Paul Gaugain/National Gallery of Art, Washington D.C./SUPERSTOCK; (right) Archive/Photo Researchers. 289: Griffin/The Image Works. 290: Richard Hutchings/Photo Researchers. 303: Courtesy of Zindel Segal. 306: Will & Deni McIntyre/Photo Researchers. 307: CP Image Archive. 308: Jonathan Hayward/Sun Media Corporation. 309: Murray & Associates/Tony Stone Images. 311: CORBIS. 312: Kevin Estrada/Retna. 313: CP Image Archive/Per Lochen. 317: Archives of the Centre for Addiction and Mental Health. 318: Courtesy of Paul Links. 319: Blake Discher/Sygma.

Chapter 11 322: Courtesy of the AGO. 325: Courtesy Heidi Schneider. 327: From Sander L. Gilman, "Seeing the Insane", 1996, University of Nebraska Press. 328: (top) Radio Times/Hulton Picture Library; (bottom) CORBIS. 335: (bottom) Courtesy Dr. William Iacono, University of Minnesota. 339: Weinberger, Berman and Illossky, 1988. 340. Courtesy of Seaton House. 344: Courtesy Sarnoff Mednick. 346: Photofest. 347: Archives of the Centre for Addiction and Mental Health. 355: CP Image Archive/John Ulan. 358: Andrew Stawicki/Toronto Star.

Chapter 12 363: Photo by Carlos Catenazzi/AGO. 365: Hal L. Harder. 366: Timothy Shonnard/Tony Stone Images. 368: CP Image Archive. 369: CP Image Archive/Jerome Delay. 370: Courtesy Dr. James A. Hanson, University of Iowa. 371: CP Image Archive/Ryan Remiorz. 372: (left) Ben Wicks; (right) Courtesy California Department of Health Services. 374: CP Image Archive/Tobin Grimshaw. 375: Culver Photos Inc. 376: (left) CP Picture Archive/Frank Gunn. 377: (right) Dr. Jeremy Burgess/Science Photo Library/Photo Researchers; (right) National Library of Medicine/Photo Researchers. 378: CP Image Archive/John E. Lightfoot Jr. 380: Dr. Morley Reed/Science Photo Library/Photo Researchers. 381: Russell Einhon/Gamma Liaison. 382: CORBIS. 385: CP Image Archive/ Chuck Stoody. 390: Hank Morgan/Photo Researchers.392: Poundmaker's Lodge. 396: Courtesy G. Alan Marlatt. 399: John Giordano/Picture Group. 400: David M. Grossman/Photo Researchers. 401: Monkmeyer/Rogers. 402: Jim Selby/Photo Researchers. 403: Edmonton Journal/Greg Southam.

Chapter 13 407: Courtesy of the AGO. 413: CP Image Archive/Fred Prouse. 416: Culver Pictures Inc. 417: Courtesy Susan Kohut. 419: Gamma Liaison. 421: CP Image Archive/Bryan Schlosser. 423: Ken Cavanagh/Photo Researchers. 427: Courtesy Otto Kernberg. 428: Courtesy Marsha M. Linehan, Dept. of Psychology, University of Washington. 432: Oak Ridge Division of the Penetanguishene Mental Health Centre.

Chapter 14 435: Photo by Larry Ostrom/AGO. 437: Antonello Nusca/Gamma Liaison. 439: Courtesy of Ken Zucker. 440: (left) CORBIS; (right) Robin Laurence/New York Times Pictures. 442: Nick Didlick. 443: Frank Fournier/Contact Press Images Inc. 444: CP Image Archive/Tammy Hoy. 445: CP Image Archive/Robert Wilson. 448: CP Picture Archive/Amy Sancetta. 452: Jeff Greenberg/Photo Researchers. 458: (left) Norm Betts/Sun Media Corporation; (right) Ottawa Rape Crisis Centre. 462: Ira Wyman/Sygma. 465: Corbis Sygma. 470: CP Picture Archive/Ryan Remiorz.

Chapter 15 473: Photo by Larry Ostrom/AGO. 476: Tourette Syndrome Foundation of Canada. 479: Courtesy of Virginia Douglas. 484: Lew Merrin/Monkmeyer Press Photo. 486: Ken Lax/Photo Researchers. 488: CP Image Archive/Tom Hanson. 492: Courtesy of Richard Tremblay. 493: TV Ontario. 494: Hattie Young/Photo Researchers. 497: Gene Peach/Gamma Liaison. 499: (left) Kunkel/Phototake; (right) Terry McKoy/The Picture Cube. 500: James Keyser/©Time, Inc. 504: Will & Deni McIntyre/Photo Researchers. 508: Nancy Pierce/Photo Researchers. 509: Courtesy of Eric Courchesne/Laboratory for Research on the Neuroscience of Autism, Children's Hospital Research Centre, San Diego, CA. 510: CP Image Archive/Greg Anew. 511: Photo by Susan Oliver Young, courtesy of Ivar Lovaas. 515: Health Canada.

Chapter 16 526: Photo by Carlos Catenazzi/AGO. 528: Mike Cassese/Sun Media Corporation. 529: Hulton Getty/Liaison Agency, Inc. 531: (top) Martin Rotker/Phototake; (bottom) Alfred Pasieka/Science Photo Library/Photo Researchers. 535: CP Image Archive/Joe Marquette. 542: PhotoDisc, Inc. 546: © Gary A. Connor/Index Stock. 548: Dion Ogust/The Image Works. 551: PhotoDisc, Inc. 553: © Benelux Press/Index Stock. 558: Courtesy of Elizabeth Podnieks. 559: Lori Adamski Peck/Tony Stone Images. 560: © Rob Gage/FPG International.

Chapter 17 565: Photo by Carlo Catenazzi/AGO. 567: Courtesy Martin M. Antony Ph.D. & Richard P. Swinson, M.D. 568: Jeff Isaac Greenberg/Photo Researchers. 572: Richard Nowitz/Photo Researchers. 576: Zigy Kaluzny/Tony Stone Images. 577: Peter Byron/Monkmeyer Press Photo. 583: Bernie, Harry Mayerovitch. 587: Michael Newman/PhotoEdit/Picture Network International. 589: Courtesy of Susan Johnson.

Chapter 18 603: Photo by Carlos Catenazzi/AGO. 608: Sygma. 610: Courtesy Jerry Ohrlinger's. 615: Trent Maracle. 619: (both) AP/Wide World Photos. 621: CP Image Archive/ Toronto Star. 625: The Toronto Star. 627: Liaison Agency, Inc. 631: (top) Bill Bachmann/The Image Works; (bottom) Larry Kolvoord/The Image Works. 632: M. McDowall/The Everett Collection.

Name Index

Subject Index

DSM-IV-TR Multiaxial Classification System

Axis I	Axis II	Axis III
Clinical syndromes: Disorders Usually First Diagnosed in Infancy, Childhood, or Adolescence Delirium, Dementia, Amnestic and other Cognitive Disorders Substance-related Disorders Schizophrenia and Other Psychotic Disorders Mood Disorders Anxiety Disorders Somatoform Disorders Factitious Disorder Dissociative Disorders Sexual and Gender Identity Disorders Eating Disorders Sleep Disorders Impulse Control Disorders Not Elsewhere Classified Adjustment Disorders	Mental Retardation Personality Disorders	General Medical Conditions

Axis IV

Psychosocial and Environmental Problems

Check:

_____ Problems with primary support group. Specify:

_____ Problems related to the social environment. Specify:

_____ Educational problem. Specify:

_____ Occupational problem. Specify:

_____ Housing problem. Specify:

_____ Economic problem. Specify:

_____ Problems with access to health care services. Specify:

_____ Problems related to interaction with the legal system/crime. Specify:

_____ Other psychosocial and environmental problems. Specify: